ذلك الكتب لا ريب فيه

THE HOLY QUR'ÂN

COLOUR CODED TAJWEED RULES

Transliteration in Roman Script with Arabic Text and English Translation

English Translation By

Abdullah Yusuf Ali

Transliteration By

M. Abdul Haleem Eliyasee

Islamic Book Service

القرآن الكريم

THE HOLY QUR'ÂN

COLOUR CODED TAJWEED RULES

Transliteration in Roman Script with Arabic Text and English Translation

English Translation By
Abdullah Yusuf Ali

Transliteration By
M. Abdul Haleem Eliyasee

ISBN 81-7231-780-8

1st Edition: 2007
2nd Edition: 2009

Published by *Abdul Naeem* for

Islamic Book Service
2872-74, Kucha Chelan, Darya Ganj,
New Delhi 110 002 (INDIA)
Ph.: 011-23253514, 23286551, 23244556
Fax: 011-23277913, 23247899
E-mail: islamic@eth.net / ibsdelhi@del2.vsnl.net.in
Website: www.islamicindia.co.in / www.islamicindia.in

Our Associates:

- **Al-Munna Book Shop Ltd., (U.A.E.)**
  (Sharjah) ***Tel.:*** 06-561-5483, 06-561-4650 **(Dubai)** ***Tel.:*** 04-352-9294
- **Azhar Academy Ltd., London (United Kingdom)**
  Tel.: 020 8911 9797
- **Lautan Lestari (Lestari Books), Jakarta (Indonesia)**
  Tel.: 0062-21-35-23456
- **Husami Book Depot, Hyderabad (India)**
  Tel.: 040-6680-6285

Printed in India

Contents

		Page No.
1.	Copyrights	*iv*
2.	Certificate of Authenticity	*v*
3.	Introduction	*vi*
4.	Colour Coded Tajweed Rules	*vii*
5.	Important Disclosure	*viii*
6.	Transliteration Key of Arabic Letters	*xii*
7.	Arabic Words Explained	*xiv*
8.	List of Prostration Places in The Qur'ân	*xv*
9.	The Holy Qur'ân	2- 679
10.	Symbols Denoting Pauses	680
11.	Index	681- 704
12.	Prophets and Others Mentioned in The Qur'ân	705-706
13.	Index of Sûras – Chapters	707-710
14.	Tajweed	711

Government of India
Copyright Office
Extracts from Register of Copyrights

Dated: 05/05/2005

1.	Registration No:	L-23171/2005
2.	Name,address and nationality of the applicant:	ABDUL NAEEM, M/S ISLAMIC BOOK SERVICE 2241, KUCHE CHELAN, DARYAGANJ, NEW DELHI - 110002 INDIAN
3.	Nature of applicant's interest in the copyright of the work	OWNER
4.	Class and description of the work	LITERARY
5.	Title of the work:	THE HOLY QURAN COLOUR CODED TAJWEED RULES
6.	Language of the work:	ENGLISH/ARABIC
7.	Name, address and nationality of the author and if the author is deceased, date of his decease:	SAME AS IN COL. 2 ABOVE INDIAN
8.	Whether the work is published or unpublished:	PUBLISHED
9.	Year and country of the first publication and name, address and nationality of the publisher:	2002 INDIA SAME AS IN COL. 2 ABOVE INDIAN
10.	Years and countries of subsequent publications, if any, and names, addresses and nationalities of the publishers:	NIL
11.	Names, addresses and nationalities of the owners of various rights comprising the copyright in the work and the extent of rights held by each, together with particulars of assignments and licences, if any:	SAME AS IN COL. 2 ABOVE INDIAN
12.	Names, addresses and nationalities of other persons, if any, authorised to assign of licence of rights comprising the copyright:	SAME AS IN COL. 11 ABOVE INDIAN
13.	If the work is an Artistic work, the location of the original work, including name, address and nationality of the person in possession of it. (In the case of an architectural work, the year of completion of the work should also be shown)	N.A.
14.	Remarks:	
	Diary No.	827/2004-CO/L
	Date of Application:	14/06/2004
	Date of Receipt:	13/07/2004

DEPUTY REGISTRAR OF COPYRIGHTS

PH: 0131- 2442408

Maulana Mohammad Imran Qasmi

مولانا محمد عمران قاسمی بِگیانوی

FAZIL DARUL ULOOM DEOBAND - M.A. (ALIG.)
EX-ARABIC LECTURER
JAMIA TIBBIYA, G.T. ROAD. DEOBAND-247554

فاضل دارالعلوم دیوبند۔ایم اے، مسلم یونیورسٹی علی گڑھ
سابق استاذ عربی جامعہ طبیہ دیوبند ضلع سہارنپور یوپی

RESI: 79, MOHALLA MAHMOOD NAGAR, GALI NO. 6 MUZAFFAR NAGAR (U.P) 251001

بسم اللہ الرحمن الرحیم

Date: 01/01/2004

Certificate of Authenticity

All Glory is for Allah. This humble servant has had the opportunity to go through al-Qur'ân al-Kareem (Colour Coded Tajweed Rules) published by the Islamic Book Service and have read it with utmost devotion and attention so that to mistake in Arabic words and spelling remains in its text.

I certify that inspite of my best efforts to mistake was discovered in words or spellings, or in the text.

Yet inspite of all my strivings it may be possible that some minor mistakes may not have caught my critical eye. Therefore, it is my request that if any well-informed person detects any error in the text, the same may be please reported to the publisher so that it can be corrected subsequently.

Maulana Mohammad Imran Qasmi Bigyanvi
Darul Uloom, Deoband
(M.A. Arabic, Muslim University Aligarh)

Introduction

THE HOLY QUR'ÂN

COLOUR CODED TAJWEED RULES

It is a great pleasure for **Islamic Book Service, New Delhi** to introduce this project in India for the first time. This humble effort is an attempt to facilitate the Tilaawah of the Qur'ân with Tajweed.

Seven different colour shades have been used and each colour represents a Tajweed Rule.

The colour coding system has been introduced to highlight the Rules of Tajweed found in the Qur'ânic text. Having a colour block on the Tajweed Rule allows the reciter to emphasise the accent, phonetics, rhythm and temper of the Qur'ânic recitation.

It is imperative for the reciter to have a working knowledge of the Rules of Tajweed in order to know how to pronounce the letters on which emphasis has to be laid.

We shall appreciate feedback, if any, on this colour coded concept for the benefit of the reciter.

ISLAMIC BOOK SERVICE
New Delhi - India

COLOUR CODED TAJWEED RULES

Ikhfa

If any one of these letters

ت ث ج د ذ ز س ش ص ض ط ظ ف ق ك

appear after a نْ or ـًـٍـٌ it will be pronounced with a light nasal sound.

Ikhfa Meem Saakin

When the letter ب appears after a مْ it will be pronounced with a light sound in the nose.

Qalqala

The five letters of Qalqala are ق ط ب ج د. When any of these letters in a word has a Sukoon on it or if deciding on pausing on any of these letters which appear at the end of a sentence it will appear to have an echoing or jerking sound.

Qalb

If after a نْ or ـًـٍـٌ the letter ب appears then the Noon Saakin or Tanween will be incorporated into the letter م and will be recited with Ghunna.

Idghaam

If after a نْ or ـًـٍـٌ there appear any of these letters (ي ن م و) it will become assimilated into the letter and will be read with Ghunna.

Idghaam Meem Saakin

If after a مْ there appear another مّ the two meems will become incorporated and will be read with Ghunna.

Ghunna

The sound emanates from the nose and is observed on the نّ & مّ.

بسم الله الرحمن الرحيم

Important Disclosure

Praise be to Allah, the Cherisher and Sustainer of the worlds, Who has said in His Noble Book:

There has come to you from Allah
Light and a Perspicuous Book. (1)

And may peace and blessings be upon the Seal of the Prophets, Mohammad, who has said that:

The best among you is he who learned
The Qur'ân and then taught it. (2)

May the peace and blessings of Allah be upon him, his family and all his Companions.

The Glorious Qur'ân is the Book of Allah, the Wise and Worthy of all Praise, Who has promised to safeguard it from any violations in its purity. It becomes incumbent upon each and every person who seeks the dignity of this world and the bliss of the Hereafter to regulate his life according to it, to implement its commandments and to pay homage to the magnificence of the One Who revealed it. This can be an easy task for those favoured with guidance from Allah, especially those blessed by a understanding of Arabic, the language of the divine communication. But for those not acquainted with Arabic, their ignorance is a barrier between them and this source of guidance and illumination. A translation of the message of Allah is thus a task not to be taken lightly or performed superficially.

Before the reader begins to study the Qur'ân he must realise that unlike all other writings, this is a unique book with a supreme author, an eternal message and a universal relevance. Its contents are not confined to a particular theme or style, but contain the foundations for an entire system of life, covering a whole spectrum of issues, which range from specific articles of faith and commandments to general moral teachings, rights and obligations, crime and punishment, personal and public law, and a host of other private and social concerns. These issues are discussed in a variety of ways, such as direct stipulations, reminders of Allah's favours of His creation, admonitions and rebukes. Stories of past communities are narrated, followed by the lessons to be learned from their actions and subsequent fates.

The Qur'ân enjoys a number of characteristics unique to it alone, some of which are as follows:

1. It is the actual Word of Allah; not created but revealed for the benefit of all mankind.

   Blessed is He Who sent down the Criterion
   To His servant, that it may be
   An admonition to all creatures. (3)

2. It is complete and comprehensive. The Almighty says:

   Nothing have We omitted from the Book. (4)

   In another place we read,

   And We have sent down to thee
   The Book explaining all things. (5)

3. It is a theoretical and a practical Book, not only moralising but also defining specifically the permissible and the forbidden. The importance of understanding the message of the

(1) Sûrat al-Mâ'idah: 15. (2) Narrated by the six ones except Muslim. (3) Sûrat al-Furqân: 1.
(4) Sūrat al-An'âm: 38. (5) Surat an-Naḥl: 89.

Qur'ân is undeniable, but simply reciting it with the intention of seeking Allah's pleasure and reward is also an act of worship and meritorious in itself. Allah Almighty says:

So take what the Prophet gives you
And refrain from what he prohibits you. (6)

4. Allah has perfected His religion for all mankind with the revelation of this Book. He say:

This day have I perfected your religion for you,
Completed my favour upon you and have chosen
For you Islam as your religion. (7)

5. It is Allah's eternal miracle revealed to the Prophet Muhammad for all succeeding generations. In response to those who doubt the authorship of the Qur'ân, Allah Almighty has challenged the most articulate Arabs to produce a whole book, ten chapters or even one solitary chapter which can be remotely comparable to the Qur'ân. But to this day, no one has succeeded in meeting the challenge of the Almighty. The critics of the Qur'ân have been struck dumb by its ineffable eloquence and surpassing beauty.

Say, if the whole of mankind and jinns
Were to gather together to produce the
Like of this Qur'ân, they could not
Produce the like thereof; even if they
Backed up each other with help and support. (8)

The Almighty also says:

Or they may say: he forged it.
Say: Bring ye then ten chapters
Forged, like unto it and call
(To your aid) whomsoever ye can
Other than Allah, if ye speak
The truth. (9)

And again:

Or do they say: he forged it?
Say: Bring then a chapter like
Unto it and call (to your aid)
Anyone ye can besides Allah,
If it be ye speak the truth. (10)

6. It has been revealed to re-establish the sincere worship of Allah alone, without association of any partners with Him.

This is a Book with verses basic or
Fundamental (of established meaning),
Further explained in detail,-
From One who is Wise and Well-Aware.
(It teaches) that you should worship
None but Allah. (11)
And they have been commanded no more
Than this: to worship Allah,
Offering Him sincere devotion, being true

---

(6) Sûrat al-Ḥashr: 7. (7) Sûrat al-Mâ'idah: 3. (8) Sûrat Banî Isrâ'îl: 88.
(9) Sûrat Hûd: 13 (10) Sûrat Yûnus: 38 (11) Sûrat Hûd: 1-2.

In faith, to establish regular prayer
And to give Zakat, and that is
The religion Right and Straight. (12)

7. It contains a complete code which provides for all areas of life, whether spiritual, intellectual, political, social or economic. It is a code which has no boundaries of time, place or nation.

   Verily this Qur'ân doth guide
   To that which is most right. (13)

8. Allah Almighty has taken upon Himself the duty of preserving the Qur'ân for ever in its entirety, as He says:

   We have without doubt sent down
   The Message, and We will assuredly
   Guard it (from corruption). (14)

So well has it been preserved, both in memory and in writing, that the Arabic text we have today is identical to the text as it was revealed to the Prophet. Not even a single letter has yielded for corruption during the passage of the centuries. And so it will remain for ever, by the consent of Allah.

Given the depth as well as the sublimity of the Qur'ânic text, a faithful translation of it into another language is virtually impossible. The various translations that exist today, however accurate they may be, cannot be designated as the Qur'ân, since they can never hope to imitate the diction or the style of the Book of Allah. But as translation is one of the few ways to export the message of the Qur'ân to allow those lacking in knowledge of Arabic to share this priceless gift, it becomes a duty for those in a position to fulfil this task.

A number of individuals have in the past ventured to translate the Qur'ân, but their works have generally been private attempts, greatly influenced by their own prejudices. In order to produce a reliable translation free from personal bias, a Royal decree (No. 19888, dated 16/8/1400 AH) was issued by the Custodian of the Two Holy Mosques, King Fahd ibn Abdul Aziz, at that time the deputy prime minister, authorising the General Presidency of the Departments of Islamic Researches, Ifta, Call and Guidance to undertake the responsibility of revising and correcting a particular translation which would be selected for this purpose and made publicly available later.

To accomplish this enormous task, a number of committees were formed, comprising scholars well-qualified both in Islamic Shari'a and the English language. Some of these scholars were associated with the General Presidency of the Departments of Islamic Researches, Ifta, Call and Guidance.

The first committee was given the task of examining the existing translations and choosing the most suitable one from among them. The committee discovered that there was no translation free from defects and so there were two options open for consideration: the first was to select the best translation available and then adopt it as a base for further works as well as a source of reference, with the objective of revising its contents and correcting any faults in view of the objections raised against it; the second was to prepare a fresh and independent translation, starting from scratch.

It became obvious from studying these translations that the second option demanded much time and efforts, neither of which were available at the time.

---

(12) Sûrat al-Bayyinah: 5. (13) Sûrat Banî Isrâ'îl: 9. (14) Sûrat al-Ḥijr: 9.

The first option was therefore considered to be more practical, since it met the existing urgent requirements and helped to achieve the desired goal in a comparatively short period of time. The translation by the late Ustadh ABDULLAH YUSUF ALI was consequently chosen for its distinguishing characteristics, such as highly elegant style, a choice of words close to the meaning of the original text, accompanied by scholarly notes and commentaries.

The committee began revising and correcting this translation with the aid of other translations available, by comparing and then adopting best expressions as well as by introducing fresh expressions where necessary. The committee was fully aware of all the criticisms that had been directed against this translation and which had been carefully brought to the notice of the presidency by a number of academic bodies and other involved parties. In the second stage, the entire work of this committee was referred to a number of individuals and organizations who then augmented any deficiencies in the work of the committee.

A third committee was set up to collate all their suggestions. It then compared all such views regarding specific issues, selected the appropriate one (s) and arrived at a text as authentic and defect-free as was humanly possible.

Finally, a fourth committee was formed to look into the findings of the second and third committees and to implement the recommendations made by them. Furthermore, this committee had to finalise the text by adopting the most accurate expression where needed, besides checking the notes vigilantly so as to clear any misconceptions regarding the articles of faith, varying juristic opinions and thoughts not in conformity with the sound Islamic point of view.

According to the Royal decree (No.12412, dated 27/10/1405 AH), this translation is printed at King Fahd Holy Qur'ân Printing Complex in Al-Madinah Al-Munawarah and also with coordination of the General Presidency of the Departments of Islamic Researches, Ifta, Call and Guidance.

To implement the directions of the Custodian of the Two Holy Mosques (May Allah preserve him) concerning the Propagation of the Book of Allah, its distribution and translation into every language spoken by Muslims the worldwide, and due to the cooperation between the General Secretariat of King Fahd Holy Qur'ân Printing Complex and the Presidency of Islamic Researches, Ifta, Call and Guidance regarding a faithful, specific and scholarly translation of the meanings of the Holy Qur'ân, we are pleased to present to all Muslims and those seeking spiritual light among English-speaking people this translation which comes as one of the Series of the translations of the meanings of the Holy Qur'ân into various languages printed by the Complex in Al-Madinah Al-Munawarah.

May Allah reward bounteously those who were behind this blessed work.

Transliteration Key of Arabic Letters

The following table shows the system which I have followed in transliterating the letters of the Arabic alphabet:

1. Alphabet

No.	Name of Arabic Letters	Arabic Letters	Latin Characters	Pronunciation
1	Hamzah	ء	’	Pronounced as *a*, *i*, *u* preceded by a very slight aspiration.
2	Bâ’	ب	b	In English like the ‘big’.
3	Tâ’	ت	t	A soft dental, as in Italian *t*.
4	Thâ’	ث	s̱	A nearly sound between *th* and *s*.
5	Jîm	ج	j	In English like the ‘judge’.
6	Ḥâ’	ح	ḥ	A strong and sustained expulsion of breath.
7	Khâ’	خ	kh	Guttural, as similar to the German ‘ach’.
8	Dâl	د	d	A soft dental, as in English ‘the’.
9	Dhâl	ذ	ẕ	A sound between *ḍ* and *z*.
10	Râ’	ر	r	In English like the ‘roll’.
11	Zâ’	ز	z	In English like the ‘zone’.
12	Sîn	س	s	In English like the ‘sea’.
13	Shîn	ش	sh	In English like the ‘sheet’.
14	Ṣâd	ص	ṣ	A strongly articulated *sw*, as in English ‘swallow’.
15	Ḍâd	ض	ḍ	A strong sound between *d* and *z*, articulated as letter ‘Ṣâd’.
16	Ṭâ’	ط	ṭ	A strongly articulated palatal *t*.
17	Ẓâ’	ظ	ẓ	A strongly articulated *z*.
18	‘Ayn	ع	‘	A guttural an, the pronunciation must be learnt by an Arabic teacher.
19	Ghayn	غ	gh	A strong guttural *gh*.
20	Fâ’	ف	f	In English like the ‘foot’.
21	Qâf	ق	q	A strongly articulated semi guttural *k*.
22	Kâf	ك	k	In English like the ‘king’.
23	Lâm	ل	l	In English like the ‘love’.
24	Mîm	م	m	In English like the ‘mat’.

25	Nûn	ن	n	In English like the 'never'.
26	Hâ'	ه	h	In English like the 'happy'.
27	Wâw	و	w	In English like the 'work'.
28	Yâ'	ی	y	In English like the 'yet'.

2. Short Vowels

ـَ	Fatḥa	a	كَتَبَ	kataba
ـِ	Kasra	i	سُئِلَ	su'ila
ـُ	Ḍamma	u	يَذْهَبُ	yaẕhabu

3. Long Vowels

اَ	aa	قَالَ	qaala
اِیْ	ee	قِيْلَ	qeela
اُوْ	oo	يَقُوْلُ	yaqoolu

4. Diphthong

اَیْ	ay	كَيْفَ	kayfa
اَوْ	aw	حَوْلَ	ḥawla

5. Points to Remember

- Alif (ا) is not be confused with Hamza (ء). If it has diacritical marks (as ـَ , ـِ , ـُ) it is hamza. Alif is always followed by another letter as بَ = ba بَا = baa.
- Alif Jaazim (اْ) = å . It gives a glottal stop while reading the letter 'Alif' above which it is placed, *e.g.*, تَاْتِيَهُمْ = taåtiyahum.
- Gunna = ñ (nasal sound), as *n* is pronounced in 'uncle'.
- When silent نْ = n or Tanween (nunation) were followed by ب = b. They are pronounced like م = m with a gunna, *e.g.*, اَنْبَا = 'ambaa / خَبِيْرٌ بِمَا = khabeerum bimaa.
- Shaddah (ّ) (double letter). It is pronounced with a sustained emphasis on that letter, *e.g.*, دَلَّ = dalla.
- For Madd (~) (elongation of vowels) three symbols have been introduced: *a, i, u,* as in بَ = ba بَا = baa بَآ = baaa, بِ = bi بِیْ = bee بِیٓ = beee, بُ = bu بُوْ = boo بُوٓ = booo.
- There is only 'Mâ'roof' (known) sound in the Qur'ân as بِ = bi, بُ = bu. There is no 'Majhool' (unknown) sound in the Qur'ân except in one word: مَجْرٖىهَا 'Majrayhaa' (as in English 'ray') (P. 12, S. 11:41).

Arabic Words Explained

A comprehensive list of names, places and topics appears as an index at the end of the book. Here some oft-repeated Arabic words occurring in the translation are given with brief explanation.

ALLAH:	The proper name of God in Arabic.
HAJJ:	The pilgrimage to Makkah which takes place in the last month of the Islamic calendar.
IBLÎS:	Satan.
ISLÂM:	Literally, to submit. The Religion of all the Prophets of Allah confirmed finally by the mission of the Prophet Muhammad ﷺ.
JINN:	Invisible beings constituting a whole race like mankind.
MUHAJIR:	Literally, the emigrant. One who leaves the home town to join a Muslim community.
MUSLIM:	One who professes the faith of Islam or born to a Muslim family.
QIBLA:	The Ka'ba. The direction for the daily prayers of a Muslim.
QUR'ÂN:	Literally, the recital. The final revelation given to the Prophet Muhammad ﷺ in Arabic.
RAMADAN:	The ninth month of the Islamic calendar during which the Muslims fast.
SÛRAH:	A chapter of the Qur'ân.
ṬAGUT:	Literally, a tyrant, oppresser, false god, temper to error. Tagut is applied to any object which is worshipped besides Allah.
UMRAH:	A minor form of pilgrimage to Makkah.
UMMAH:	Literally, a nation but is usually applied to the Muslim Brotherhood.
YATHRIB:	The name by which Madinah was known before the Prophet's migration to that city.
ZAKAT:	Literally, to grow, to purify. The third pillar of Islam. It is a definite portion of wealth which is given to needy at the turn of the year.

List of Prostration Places in The Qur'ân

It is a good practice to prostrate at the following places while reciting the Qur'ân.

No.	Part No.	Name of Sûrah	Sûrah No.	Verse No.
1	9	Al-A'râf	7	206
2.	13	Ar-Ra'd	13	15
3.	14	An-Naḥl	16	50
4.	15	Banî Isrâ'îl	17	109
5.	16	Maryam	19	58
6.	17	Al-Ḥajj	22	18
7.	17	Al-Ḥajj	22	77*
8.	19	Al-Furqân	25	60
9.	19	An-Naml	27	26
10.	21	As-Sajdah	32	15
11.	23	Ṣâd	38	24
12.	24	Ḥâ-Mîm Sajdah	41	38
13.	27	An-Najm	53	62
14.	30	Al-Inshiqâq	84	21
15.	30	Al-'Alaq	96	19

* In all, fourteen places of prostration are agreed upon by all Muslim religious scholars and '*Ulama*, while Imâm Shâf'i (R.A) suggests prostration at this place also.

The following invocation is usually recited during the prostration:

﴿سَجَدَ وَجْهِيَ لِلَّذِي خَلَقَهُ وَصَوَّرَهُ وَشَقَّ سَمْعَهُ وَبَصَرَهُ تَبَارَكَ اللّٰهُ أَحْسَنُ الْخَالِقِينَ﴾

Sajada wajhiya lillazee khalaqahoo wa ṣawwarahoo, wa shaqqa sam'ahoo wa baṣarahoo, tabaarak-Allaahu Aḥsanul-Khaaliqeen.

[*Sahih Muslim,* Vol.4, *Hadîth* No.201].

بسم الله الرحمن الرحيم

ذَٰلِكَ الْكِتَابُ لَا رَيْبَ فِيهِ

القرآن الكريم

أَحْكَامُ التَّجْوِيدِ الْمُدَوَّنِ بِالْأَلْوَان

وَتَرْجَمَةُ مَعَانِيهِ مَعَ الْحُرُوفِ الْمَنْقُولَةِ إِلَى اللُّغَةِ الْإِنْجِلِيزِيَّة

الترجمة
عبد اللّٰه يوسف علي

اسلامك بك سروس

(١) سُوْرَةُ الْفَاتِحَةِ مَكِّيَّةٌ (٥)

بِسْمِ اللّٰهِ الرَّحْمٰنِ الرَّحِيْمِ ۝

اَلْحَمْدُ لِلّٰهِ رَبِّ الْعٰلَمِيْنَ ۙ﴿۱﴾ الرَّحْمٰنِ

الرَّحِيْمِ ۙ﴿۲﴾ مٰلِكِ يَوْمِ الدِّيْنِ ؕ﴿۳﴾

اِيَّاكَ نَعْبُدُ وَاِيَّاكَ نَسْتَعِيْنُ ؕ﴿۴﴾

اِهْدِنَا الصِّرَاطَ الْمُسْتَقِيْمَ ۙ﴿۵﴾ صِرَاطَ

الَّذِيْنَ اَنْعَمْتَ عَلَيْهِمْ ۙ۬ غَيْرِ

الْمَغْضُوْبِ عَلَيْهِمْ وَلَا الضَّآلِّيْنَ ﴿۷﴾ ع

Revealed at Makkah

Sûrat al-Fâtiḥa–1
1. The Opening

Bismillaahir Raḥmaanir Raḥeem
In the name of Allah, Most Gracious, Most Merciful.

1. Praise be to Allah, the Cherisher and Sustainer of the Worlds;

1. Alḥamdu lillaahi Rabbil-'aalameen;

2. Most Gracious, Most Merciful;

2. Ar-Raḥmaanir-Raḥeem;

3. Master of the Day of Judgment.

3. Maaliki Yawmid-Deen.

4. You do we worship, and Your aid do we seek.

4. Iyyaaka na'budu wa Iyyaaka nasta'een.

5. Show us the straight way,

5. Ihdinaṣ-Ṣiraaṭal-Mustaqeem,

6. The way of those on whom You have bestowed Your Grace, those whose (portion) is not wrath, and who do not go astray. **(Section 1)**

6. Ṣiraaṭal-lazeena an'amta 'alayhim ghayril-maghḍoobi 'alayhim wa laḍ-ḍaaalleen.

English	Transliteration	Arabic
2. The Cow **In the name of Allah, Most Gracious, Most Merciful.**	**Sûrat al-Baqarah–2** (Revealed at Madinah) **Bismillaahir Raḥmaanir Raḥeem**	(٢) سُوْرَةُ الْبَقَرَةِ مَدَنِيَّةٌ (٨٧) بِسْمِ اللّٰهِ الرَّحْمٰنِ الرَّحِيْمِ
1. *Alif-Lam-Mim.*	1. Alif-Laaam-Meeem.	الٓمٓ ۝١
2. This is the Book; in it is guidance sure, without doubt, to those who fear God;	2. Zaalikal-Kitaabu laa rayba feeh; hudal-lilmuttaqeen.	ذٰلِكَ الْكِتٰبُ لَا رَيْبَ ۛ فِيْهِ ۛ هُدًى لِّلْمُتَّقِيْنَ ۝٢
3. Who believe in the Unseen, are steadfast in prayer, and spend out of what We have provided for them;	3. Allazeena yu'minoona bilghaybi wa yuqeemoonaṣ-Ṣalaata wa mimmaa razaqnaahum yunfiqoon.	الَّذِيْنَ يُؤْمِنُوْنَ بِالْغَيْبِ وَيُقِيْمُوْنَ الصَّلٰوةَ وَمِمَّا رَزَقْنٰهُمْ يُنْفِقُوْنَ ۝٣
4. And who believe in the Revelation sent to you, and sent before thy time, and (in their hearts) have the assurance of the Hereafter.	4. Wallazeena yu'minoona bimaaa unzila ilayka wa maaa unzila min qablika wa bil-Aakhirati hum yooqinoon.	وَالَّذِيْنَ يُؤْمِنُوْنَ بِمَآ اُنْزِلَ اِلَيْكَ وَمَآ اُنْزِلَ مِنْ قَبْلِكَ ۚ وَبِالْاٰخِرَةِ هُمْ يُوْقِنُوْنَ ۝٤
5. They are on (true) guidance, from their Lord, and it is these who will prosper.	5. Ulaaa'ika 'alaa hudam-mir-Rabbihim wa ulaaa'ika humul-mufliḥoon.	اُولٰٓئِكَ عَلٰى هُدًى مِّنْ رَّبِّهِمْ ۗ وَاُولٰٓئِكَ هُمُ الْمُفْلِحُوْنَ ۝٥
6. As to those who reject Faith, it is the same to them whether you warn them or do not warn them; they will not believe.	6. Innal-lazeena kafaroo sawaaa'un 'alayhim 'a-anzar-tahum am lam tunzirhum laa yu'minoon.	اِنَّ الَّذِيْنَ كَفَرُوْا سَوَآءٌ عَلَيْهِمْ ءَاَنْذَرْتَهُمْ اَمْ لَمْ تُنْذِرْهُمْ لَا يُؤْمِنُوْنَ ۝٦
7. God hath set a seal on their hearts and on their hearing, and on their eyes is a veil; great is the penalty they (incur).	7. Khatamal-laahu 'alaa quloobihim wa 'alaa sam'i-him wa 'alaaa abṣaarihim ghishaa-watuñw-wa lahum 'azaabun 'azeem. **(Section 1)**	خَتَمَ اللّٰهُ عَلٰى قُلُوْبِهِمْ وَعَلٰى سَمْعِهِمْ ۗ وَعَلٰٓى اَبْصَارِهِمْ غِشَاوَةٌ ۫ وَّلَهُمْ عَذَابٌ عَظِيْمٌ ۝٧ ع
8. Of the people there are some who say: "We believe in God and the Last Day;" but they do not (really) believe.	8. Wa minan-naasi mañy-yaqoolu aamannaa billaahi wa bil-Yawmil-Aakhiri wa maa hum bimu'mineen.	وَمِنَ النَّاسِ مَنْ يَّقُوْلُ اٰمَنَّا بِاللّٰهِ وَبِالْيَوْمِ الْاٰخِرِ وَمَا هُمْ بِمُؤْمِنِيْنَ ۝٨
9. Fain would they deceive Allah and those who believe, but they only deceive themselves, and realise (it) not!	9. Yukhaadi'oonal-laaha wallazeena aamanoo wa maa yakhda'oona illaaa anfusahum wa maa yash'uroon.	يُخٰدِعُوْنَ اللّٰهَ وَالَّذِيْنَ اٰمَنُوْا ۚ وَمَا يَخْدَعُوْنَ اِلَّآ اَنْفُسَهُمْ وَمَا يَشْعُرُوْنَ ۝٩
10. In their hearts is a disease; and Allah has increased their disease: And grievous is the penaltey they (incur), because they are false (to themselves).	10. Fee quloobihim mara-ḍun fazaadahumul-laahu maraḍan wa lahum 'azaabun aleemum bimaa kaanoo yakziboon.	فِيْ قُلُوْبِهِمْ مَّرَضٌ ۙ فَزَادَهُمُ اللّٰهُ مَرَضًا ۚ وَلَهُمْ عَذَابٌ اَلِيْمٌ ۢ بِمَا كَانُوْا يَكْذِبُوْنَ ۝١٠
11. When it is said to them: "Make not mischief on the earth," they say: "Why, we only want to make peace!"	11. Wa izaa qeela lahum laa tufsidoo fil-arḍi qaalooo innamaa naḥnu muṣliḥoon.	وَاِذَا قِيْلَ لَهُمْ لَا تُفْسِدُوْا فِي الْاَرْضِ ۙ قَالُوْٓا اِنَّمَا نَحْنُ مُصْلِحُوْنَ ۝١١

(١) معانقة عند المتاخرين ١٢

ع ١

وقف لازم

Ikhfa اخفاء · Ghunna غُنّة · Ikhfa Meem Saakin اخفاء میم ساکن · Idghaam ادغام · Qalqala قلقلہ · Qalb قلب · Idghaam Meem Saakin ادغام میم ساکن

12. Of a surety, they are the ones who make mischief, but they realise (it) not.

12. Alaaa innahum humul-mufsidoona wa laakil-laa yash'uroon.

أَلَآ إِنَّهُمْ هُمُ الْمُفْسِدُونَ وَلٰكِن لَّا
يَشْعُرُونَ ﴿١٢﴾

13. When it is said to them: "Believe as the others believe:" They say: "Shall we believe as the fools believe?" No, of a surety they are the fools, but they do not know.

13. Wa iz̲aa qeela lahum aaminoo kamaaa aamanan-naasu qaalooo anu'minu kamaaa aamanas-sufahaaa'; alaaa innahum humus-sufahaaa'u wa laakil-laa ya'lamoon.

وَإِذَا قِيلَ لَهُمْ ءَامِنُوا كَمَآ ءَامَنَ النَّاسُ
قَالُوٓا أَنُؤْمِنُ كَمَآ ءَامَنَ السُّفَهَآءُ ۗ
أَلَآ إِنَّهُمْ هُمُ السُّفَهَآءُ وَلٰكِن لَّا
يَعْلَمُونَ ﴿١٣﴾

14. When they meet those who believe, they say: "We believe;" but when they are alone with their evil ones, they say: "We are really with you: We (were) only jesting."

14. Wa iz̲aa laqul-laz̲eena aamanoo qaalooo aamannaa wa iz̲aa khalaw ilaa shayaaṭeenihim qaalooo innaa ma'akum innamaa naḥnu mustahzi'oon.

وَإِذَا لَقُوا الَّذِينَ ءَامَنُوا قَالُوٓا ءَامَنَّا ۚ
وَإِذَا خَلَوْا إِلَىٰ شَيَٰطِينِهِمْ قَالُوٓا إِنَّا
مَعَكُمْ إِنَّمَا نَحْنُ مُسْتَهْزِءُونَ ﴿١٤﴾

15. Allah will throw back their mockery on them, and give them rope in their wrong-doing; so they will wander like blind ones (to and fro).

15. Allaahu yastahzi'u bihim wa yamudduhum fee ṭughyaanihim ya'mahoon.

اللَّهُ يَسْتَهْزِئُ بِهِمْ وَيَمُدُّهُمْ فِى
طُغْيَٰنِهِمْ يَعْمَهُونَ ﴿١٥﴾

16. These are they who have bartered guidance for error: But their traffic is profitless, and they have lost true direction.

16. Ulaaa'ikal-laz̲eenash-tarawuḍ-ḍalaalata bilhudaa famaa rabiḥat-tijaaratuhum wa maa kaanoo muhtadeen.

أُولَٰٓئِكَ الَّذِينَ اشْتَرَوُا الضَّلَٰلَةَ
بِالْهُدَىٰ فَمَا رَبِحَت تِّجَٰرَتُهُمْ
وَمَا كَانُوا مُهْتَدِينَ ﴿١٦﴾

17. Their similitude is that of a man who kindled a fire; when it lighted all around him, Allah took away their light and left them in utter darkness. So they could not see.

17. Mas̲aluhum kamas̲alillaz̲is-tawqada naaran falammaaa aḍaaa'at maa ḥawlahoo z̲ahabal-laahu binoorihim wa tarakahum fee ẓulumaatil-laa yubṣiroon.

مَثَلُهُمْ كَمَثَلِ الَّذِى اسْتَوْقَدَ نَارًا ۚ
فَلَمَّآ أَضَآءَتْ مَا حَوْلَهُۥ ذَهَبَ اللَّهُ
بِنُورِهِمْ وَتَرَكَهُمْ فِى ظُلُمَٰتٍ
لَّا يُبْصِرُونَ ﴿١٧﴾

18. Deaf, dumb, and blind, they hwill not return (to the path).

18. Ṣummum bukmun 'umyun fahum laa yarji'oon.

صُمٌّۢ بُكْمٌ عُمْىٌ فَهُمْ لَا يَرْجِعُونَ ﴿١٨﴾

19. Or (another similitude) is that of a rain-laden cloud from the sky: In it are zones of darkness, and thunder and lightning: They press their fingers in their ears to keep out the stunning thunder-clap, the while they are in terror of death. But Allah is ever round the rejecters of Faith!

19. Aw kaṣayyibim-minas-samaaa'i feehi ẓulumaatuñw-wa ra'duñw-wa barq, yaj'aloona aṣaabi'ahum feee aaz̲aanihim minaṣ-ṣawaa'iqi ḥaz̲aral-mawt; wallaahu muḥeeṭum bilkaafireen.

أَوْ كَصَيِّبٍ مِّنَ السَّمَآءِ فِيهِ ظُلُمَٰتٌ
وَرَعْدٌ وَبَرْقٌ يَجْعَلُونَ أَصَٰبِعَهُمْ
فِىٓ ءَاذَانِهِم مِّنَ الصَّوَٰعِقِ حَذَرَ
الْمَوْتِ ۚ وَاللَّهُ مُحِيطٌۢ بِالْكَٰفِرِينَ ﴿١٩﴾

20. The lightning all but snatches away their sight; every time the light (helps) them, they walk therein, and when the darkness grows on them, they stand still. And if Allah willed,

20. Yakaadul-barqu yakhṭafu abṣaarahum kullamaaa aḍaaa'a lahum mashaw feehi wa iz̲aaa aẓlama 'alayhim qaamoo; wa law shaaa'al-laahu

يَكَادُ الْبَرْقُ يَخْطَفُ أَبْصَٰرَهُمْ ۖ
كُلَّمَآ أَضَآءَ لَهُم مَّشَوْا فِيهِ وَإِذَآ
أَظْلَمَ عَلَيْهِمْ قَامُوا ۚ وَلَوْ شَآءَ اللَّهُ

Ikhfa اخفاء | Ghunna غُنّہ | Ikhfa Meem Saakin اخفاء میم ساکن | Idghaam ادغام | Qalqala قلقلہ | Qalb قلب | Idghaam Meem Saakin ادغام میم ساکن

He could take away their faculty of hearing and seeing; for Allah has power over all things.

lazahaba bisam'ihim wa abṣaarihim; innal-laaha 'alaa kulli shay'in Qadeer. **(Section 2)**

لَذَهَبَ بِسَمْعِهِمْ وَأَبْصَارِهِمْ ط
إِنَّ اللّٰهَ عَلٰى كُلِّ شَيْءٍ قَدِيرٌ ﴿٢٠﴾

21. O you people! Adore your Guardian-Lord, who created you and those who came before you, that you may have the chance to learn righteousness;

21. Yaaa ayyuhan-naasu'budoo Rabbakumul-lazee khalaqakum wallazeena min qablikum la'allakum tattaqoon.

يٰٓأَيُّهَا النَّاسُ اعْبُدُوا رَبَّكُمُ الَّذِي
خَلَقَكُمْ وَالَّذِينَ مِنْ قَبْلِكُمْ
لَعَلَّكُمْ تَتَّقُونَ ﴿٢١﴾

22. Who has made the earth your couch, and the heavens your canopy; and sent down rain from the heavens; and brought forth therewith Fruits for your sustenance; then set not up rivals unto Allah when you know (the truth).

22. Allazee ja'ala lakumul-arḍa firaashañw-wassamaaa'a binaaa-'añw-wa anzala minassamaaa'i maaa'an fa-akhraja bihee minas-samaraati rizqal-lakum falaa taj'aloo lillaahi andaadañw-wa antum ta'lamoon.

الَّذِي جَعَلَ لَكُمُ الْأَرْضَ فِرَاشًا
وَّالسَّمَآءَ بِنَآءً وَّأَنْزَلَ مِنَ السَّمَآءِ
مَآءً فَأَخْرَجَ بِهٖ مِنَ الثَّمَرٰتِ
رِزْقًا لَّكُمْ ۚ فَلَا تَجْعَلُوا لِلّٰهِ أَنْدَادًا وَّ
أَنْتُمْ تَعْلَمُونَ ﴿٢٢﴾

23. And if you are in doubt as to what We have revealed from time to time to Our servant, then produce a Sura like thereof; and call your witnesses or helpers (if there are any) besides Allah, if your (doubts) are true.

23. Wa in kuntum fee raybim-mimmaa nazzalnaa 'alaa 'abdinaa fa-too bi-Sooratim-mim-mislihee wad'oo shu-hadaaa'akum min doonil-laahi in kuntum ṣaadiqeen.

وَإِنْ كُنْتُمْ فِي رَيْبٍ مِّمَّا نَزَّلْنَا عَلٰى
عَبْدِنَا فَأْتُوا بِسُورَةٍ مِّنْ مِّثْلِهٖ ص
وَادْعُوا شُهَدَآءَكُمْ مِّنْ دُونِ اللّٰهِ
إِنْ كُنْتُمْ صٰدِقِينَ ﴿٢٣﴾

24. But if you cannot- and of a surety you cannot- then fear the Fire whose fuel is men and stones,- which is prepared for those who reject Faith.

24. Fail-lam taf'aloo wa lan taf'aloo fattaqun-Naaral-latee waqooduhan-naasu walḥijaaratu u'iddat lilkaafireen.

فَإِنْ لَّمْ تَفْعَلُوا وَلَنْ تَفْعَلُوا فَاتَّقُوا
النَّارَ الَّتِي وَقُودُهَا النَّاسُ وَ
الْحِجَارَةُ ۚ أُعِدَّتْ لِلْكٰفِرِينَ ﴿٢٤﴾

25. But give glad tidings to those who believe and work righteousness, that their portion is Gardens beneath which rivers flow. Every time they are fed with fruits therefrom, they say: "Why, this is what we were fed with before," for they are given things in similitude; and they have therein companions pure (and holy); and they abide therein (for ever).

25. Wa bashshiril-lazeena aamanoo wa 'amiluṣ-ṣaaliḥaati anna lahum Jannaatin tajree min taḥtihal-anhaaru kullamaa ruziqoo minhaa min samaratir-rizqan qaaloo haazal-lazee ruziqnaa min qablu wa utoo bihee mutashaabihaa, wa lahum feehaaa azwaajum-muṭahhara-tuñw-wa hum feehaa khaalidoon.

وَبَشِّرِ الَّذِينَ آمَنُوا وَعَمِلُوا الصّٰلِحٰتِ
أَنَّ لَهُمْ جَنّٰتٍ تَجْرِي مِنْ تَحْتِهَا
الْأَنْهٰرُ ۖ كُلَّمَا رُزِقُوا مِنْهَا مِنْ
ثَمَرَةٍ رِّزْقًا ۙ قَالُوا هٰذَا الَّذِي
رُزِقْنَا مِنْ قَبْلُ وَأُتُوا بِهٖ مُتَشَابِهًا ط
وَلَهُمْ فِيهَا أَزْوَاجٌ مُّطَهَّرَةٌ ۙ وَّهُمْ
فِيهَا خٰلِدُونَ ﴿٢٥﴾

26. Allah disdains not to use the similitude of things, lowest as well as highest. Those who

26. Innal-laaha laa yastaḥyeee añy-yaḍriba masalam-maa ba'ooḍatan famaa fawqahaa; fa-ammal-lazeena

إِنَّ اللّٰهَ لَا يَسْتَحْيِي أَنْ يَّضْرِبَ مَثَلًا
مَّا بَعُوضَةً فَمَا فَوْقَهَا ۚ فَأَمَّا الَّذِينَ

believe know that it is truth from their Lord; but those who reject Faith say: "What means Allah by this similitude?" By it He causes many to stray, and many He leads into the right path; but He causes not to stray, except those who forsake (the path),-

aamanoo faya'lamoona anna-hul-ḥaqqu mir-Rabbihim wa ammal-lazeena kafaroo faya-qooloona maazaaa araadal-laahu bihaazaa masalaa; yuḍillu bihee kaseerañw-wa yahdee bihee kaseeraa; wa maa yuḍillu biheee illal-faasiqeen.

اٰمَنُوْا فَيَعْلَمُوْنَ اَنَّهُ الْحَقُّ مِنْ رَّبِّهِمْ
وَاَمَّا الَّذِيْنَ كَفَرُوْا فَيَقُوْلُوْنَ مَاذَآ
اَرَادَ اللّٰهُ بِهٰذَا مَثَلًا ۘ يُضِلُّ بِهٖ
كَثِيْرًا ۙ وَّيَهْدِيْ بِهٖ كَثِيْرًا ۭ وَمَا يُضِلُّ
بِهٖٓ اِلَّا الْفٰسِقِيْنَ ۙ ﴿٢٦﴾

وقف لازم

27. Those who break Allah's Covenant after it is ratified, and who sunder what Allah Has ordered to be joined, and do mischief on earth: there cause loss (only) to themselves.

27. Allazeena yanquḍoona 'Ahdal-laahi mim ba'di meesaaqihee wa yaqṭa'oona maaa amaral-laahu biheee añy-yooṣala wa yufsidoona fil-arḍ; ulaaa'ika humul-khaasiroon.

الَّذِيْنَ يَنْقُضُوْنَ عَهْدَ اللّٰهِ مِنْۢ بَعْدِ
مِيْثَاقِهٖ ۠ وَيَقْطَعُوْنَ مَآ اَمَرَ اللّٰهُ بِهٖٓ
اَنْ يُّوْصَلَ وَيُفْسِدُوْنَ فِي الْاَرْضِ ۭ
اُولٰۗىِٕكَ هُمُ الْخٰسِرُوْنَ ﴿٢٧﴾

28. How can you reject the faith in Allah?- seeing that you were without life, and He gave you life; then will He cause you to die, and will again bring you to life; and again to Him will you return.

28. Kayfa takfuroona billaahi wa kuntum amwaatan fa-aḥyaakum summa yumeetukum summa yuḥyeekum summa ilayhi turja'oon.

كَيْفَ تَكْفُرُوْنَ بِاللّٰهِ وَكُنْتُمْ اَمْوَاتًا
فَاَحْيَاكُمْ ۚ ثُمَّ يُمِيْتُكُمْ ثُمَّ يُحْيِيْكُمْ
ثُمَّ اِلَيْهِ تُرْجَعُوْنَ ﴿٢٨﴾

29. It is He Who has created for you all things that are on earth; moreover His design comprehended the heavens, for He gave order and perfection to the seven firmaments; and of all things He has perfect knowledge.

29. Huwal-lazee khalaqa lakum-maa fil-arḍi jamee'an summas-tawaaa ilas-samaaa'i fasaw-waahunna sab'a samaa-waat; wa Huwa bikulli shay'in 'Aleem.

(Section 3)

هُوَ الَّذِيْ خَلَقَ لَكُمْ مَّا فِي الْاَرْضِ
جَمِيْعًا ۤ ثُمَّ اسْتَوٰٓى اِلَى السَّمَاۗءِ فَسَوّٰىهُنَّ
سَبْعَ سَمٰوٰتٍ ۭ وَھُوَ بِكُلِّ شَيْءٍ عَلِيْمٌ ﴿٢٩﴾ ع

ع ٣

30. Behold, your Lord said to the angels: "I will create a vicegerent on earth." They said: "Will you place therein one who will make mischief therein and shed blood?- while we do celebrate your praises and glorify your holy (name)?" He said: "I know what you know not."

30. Wa iz qaala Rabbuka lil-malaaa'ikati innee jaa'ilun fil-arḍi khaleefatan qaalooo ataj'alu feehaa mañy-yufsidu feehaa wa yasfikud-dimaaa'a wa naḥnu nusabbiḥu biḥamdika wa nuqaddisu laka qaala inneee a'lamu maa laa ta'lamoon.

وَاِذْ قَالَ رَبُّكَ لِلْمَلٰۗىِٕكَةِ اِنِّىْ جَاعِلٌ
فِي الْاَرْضِ خَلِيْفَةً ۭ قَالُوْٓا اَتَجْعَلُ
فِيْهَا مَنْ يُّفْسِدُ فِيْهَا وَيَسْفِكُ الدِّمَاۗءَ ۚ
وَنَحْنُ نُسَبِّحُ بِحَمْدِكَ وَنُقَدِّسُ لَكَ ۭ
قَالَ اِنِّىْٓ اَعْلَمُ مَا لَا تَعْلَمُوْنَ ﴿٣٠﴾

31. And He taught Adam the nature of all things; then He placed them before the angels, and said: "Tell me the nature of these if you are right."

31. Wa 'allama Aadamal-asmaaa'a kullahaa summa 'araḍahum 'alal-malaaa'ikati faqaala ambi'oonee bias-maaa'i haaa'ulaaa'i in kuntum ṣaadi-qeen.

وَعَلَّمَ اٰدَمَ الْاَسْمَاۗءَ كُلَّهَا ثُمَّ عَرَضَهُمْ
عَلَي الْمَلٰۗىِٕكَةِ ۙ فَقَالَ اَنْۢبِــُٔوْنِيْ بِاَسْمَاۗءِ
هٰٓؤُلَاۗءِ اِنْ كُنْتُمْ صٰدِقِيْنَ ﴿٣١﴾

32. They said: "Glory to You, of knowledge we have none, save what You have taught us: in truth it is You Who are perfect in knowledge and wisdom."

32. Qaaloo subḥaanaka laa 'ilma lanaaa illaa maa 'allamtanaaa innaka Antal-'Aleemul-Ḥakeem.

قَالُوْا سُبْحٰنَكَ لَا عِلْمَ لَنَآ اِلَّا مَا عَلَّمْتَنَا ۭ
اِنَّكَ اَنْتَ الْعَلِيْمُ الْحَكِيْمُ ﴿٣٢﴾

33. He said: "O Adam! tell them their natures." When

33. Qaala yaaa Aadamu ambi'-hum biasmaaa'ihim falammaaa

قَالَ يٰٓاٰدَمُ اَنْۢبِئْهُمْ بِاَسْمَاۗىِٕهِمْ ۚ فَلَمَّآ

Ikhfa اخفاء | Ghunna غُنّہ | Ikhfa Meem Saakin اخفاء میم ساکن | Idghaam ادغام | Qalqala قلقلہ | Qalb قلب | Idghaam Meem Saakin ادغام میم ساکن

he had told them, Allah said: "Did I not tell you that I know the secrets of heaven and earth, and I know what you reveal and what you conceal?"

amba-ahum bi-asmaaa'ihim qaala alam aqul lakum inneee a'lamu ghaybas-samaawaati wal-arḍi wa a'lamu maa tubdoona wa maa kuntum taktumoon.

أَنْبَأَهُمْ بِأَسْمَآئِهِمْ قَالَ اَلَمْ اَقُلْ
لَّكُمْ اِنِّيْٓ اَعْلَمُ غَيْبَ السَّمٰوٰتِ وَالْاَرْضِ ۙ
وَاَعْلَمُ مَا تُبْدُوْنَ وَمَا كُنْتُمْ تَكْتُمُوْنَ ﴿٣٣﴾

34. And behold, We said to the angels: "Bow down to Adam" and they bowed down: not so Iblis: he refused and was haughty: he was of those who reject Faith.

34. Wa iz qulnaa lilmalaaa'i-katis-judoo li-Aadama fasaja-dooo illaaa Ibleesa abaa wastak-bara wa kaana minal-kaafireen.

وَاِذْ قُلْنَا لِلْمَلٰٓئِكَةِ اسْجُدُوْا لِاٰدَمَ
فَسَجَدُوْٓا اِلَّآ اِبْلِيْسَ ۭ اَبٰى وَاسْتَكْبَرَ ۤ
وَكَانَ مِنَ الْكٰفِرِيْنَ ﴿٣٤﴾

35. We said: "O Adam! dwell you and your wife in the Garden; and eat of the bountiful things therein as (where and when) you will; but approach not this tree, or you run into harm and transgression."

35. Wa qulnaa yaaa Aadamus-kun anta wa zawjukal-Jannata wa kulaa minhaa raghadan ḥaysu shi'tumaa wa laa taqrabaa haazihish-shajarata fatakoonaa minaẓ-ẓaalimeen.

وَقُلْنَا يٰٓاٰدَمُ اسْكُنْ اَنْتَ وَزَوْجُكَ
الْجَنَّةَ وَكُلَا مِنْهَا رَغَدًا حَيْثُ شِئْتُمَا ۠
وَلَا تَقْرَبَا هٰذِهِ الشَّجَرَةَ فَتَكُوْنَا
مِنَ الظّٰلِمِيْنَ ﴿٣٥﴾

36. Then did Satan make them slip from the (Garden), and get them out of the state (of felicity) in which they had been. We said: "Get you down, all (you people), with enmity between yourselves. On earth will be your dwelling-place and your means of livelihood for a time."

36. Fa-azallahumash-Shay-ṭaanu 'anhaa fa-akhrajahumaa mimmaa kaanaa feehi wa qulnah-biṭoo ba'ḍukum liba'ḍin 'aduwwuñw-wa lakum fil-arḍi mustaqarruñw-wa mataa'un ilaa ḥeen.

فَاَزَلَّهُمَا الشَّيْطٰنُ عَنْهَا فَاَخْرَجَهُمَا
مِمَّا كَانَا فِيْهِ ۠ وَقُلْنَا اهْبِطُوْا بَعْضُكُمْ
لِبَعْضٍ عَدُوٌّ ۚ وَلَكُمْ فِي الْاَرْضِ
مُسْتَقَرٌّ وَّمَتَاعٌ اِلٰى حِيْنٍ ﴿٣٦﴾

37. Then learnt Adam from his Lord words (of repentance), and his Lord turned towards him; for He is Oft-Returning, Most Merciful.

37. Fatalaqqaaa Aadamu mir-Rabbihee Kalimaatin fataaba 'alayh; innahoo Huwat-Taw-waabur-Raḥeem.

فَتَلَقّٰٓى اٰدَمُ مِنْ رَّبِّهٖ كَلِمٰتٍ فَتَابَ
عَلَيْهِ ۭ اِنَّهٗ هُوَ التَّوَّابُ الرَّحِيْمُ ﴿٣٧﴾

38. We said: "Get you down all from here; and if, as is sure, there comes to you guidance from Me, whosoever follows My guidance, on them shall be no fear, nor shall they grieve.

38. Qulnah-biṭoo minhaa jamee-'an fa-immaa yaåtiyannakum minnee hudan faman tabi'a hudaaya falaa khawfun 'alayhim wa laa hum yaḥza-noon.

قُلْنَا اهْبِطُوْا مِنْهَا جَمِيْعًا ۚ فَاِمَّا
يَاْتِيَنَّكُمْ مِّنِّىْ هُدًى فَمَنْ تَبِعَ هُدَاىَ
فَلَا خَوْفٌ عَلَيْهِمْ وَلَا هُمْ يَحْزَنُوْنَ ﴿٣٨﴾

39. "But those who reject Faith and belie Our Signs, they shall be Companions of the Fire; they shall abide therein."

39. Wallazeena kafaroo wa kaz zaboo bi-Aayaatinaaa ulaaa'ika Aṣḥaabun-Naari hum feehaa khaalidoon. **(Section 4)**

وَالَّذِيْنَ كَفَرُوْا وَكَذَّبُوْا بِاٰيٰتِنَآ
اُولٰۗئِكَ اَصْحٰبُ النَّارِ ۚ هُمْ فِيْهَا
خٰلِدُوْنَ ﴿٣٩﴾ ع

ع ٤

40. O Children of Israel! call to mind the (special) favour which I bestowed upon you, and fulfil your covenant with Me as I fulfil My Covenant with you, and fear none but Me.

40. Yaa Baneee Israaa'eelaz kuroo ni'matiyal-latee an'amtu 'alaykum wa awfoo bi-'Ahdeee oofi bi'ahdikum wa iyyaaya farhaboon.

يٰبَنِىْٓ اِسْرَاۗءِيْلَ اذْكُرُوْا نِعْمَتِىَ الَّتِىْٓ
اَنْعَمْتُ عَلَيْكُمْ وَاَوْفُوْا بِعَهْدِىْٓ
اُوْفِ بِعَهْدِكُمْ ۚ وَاِيَّاىَ فَارْهَبُوْنِ ﴿٤٠﴾

41. And believe in what I reveal, confirming the revelation which is

41. Wa aaminoo bimaaa anzaltu muṣaddiqal-limaa

وَاٰمِنُوْا بِمَآ اَنْزَلْتُ مُصَدِّقًا لِّمَا

Ikhfa اخفاء · Ghunna غُنّہ · Ikhfa Meem Saakin اخفاء میم ساکن · Idghaam ادغام · Qalqala قلقلہ · Qalb قلب · Idghaam Meem Saakin ادغام میم ساکن

with you, and be not the first to reject Faith therein, nor sell My Signs for a small price; and fear Me, and Me alone.

ma'akum wa laa takoonooo awwala kaafirim bihee wa laa tashtaroo bi-Aayaatee samanan qaleelañw- wa iyyaaya fattaqoon.

مَعَكُمْ وَلَا تَكُونُوٓا أَوَّلَ كَافِرٍۭ بِهِۦ
وَلَا تَشْتَرُوا بِـَٔايَٰتِى ثَمَنًا قَلِيلًا
وَإِيَّٰىَ فَٱتَّقُونِ ﴿٤١﴾

42. And cover not Truth with falsehood, nor conceal the Truth when you know (what it is).

42. Wa laa talbisul-ḥaqqa bilbaaṭili wa taktumul-ḥaqqa wa antum ta'lamoon.

وَلَا تَلْبِسُوا ٱلْحَقَّ بِٱلْبَٰطِلِ
وَتَكْتُمُوا ٱلْحَقَّ وَأَنتُمْ تَعْلَمُونَ ﴿٤٢﴾

43. And be steadfast in prayer; practise regular charity; and bow down your heads with those who bow down (in worship).

43. Wa aqeemuṣ-Ṣalaata wa aatuz-Zakaata warka'oo ma'ar-raaki'een.

وَأَقِيمُوا ٱلصَّلَوٰةَ وَءَاتُوا ٱلزَّكَوٰةَ
وَٱرْكَعُوا مَعَ ٱلرَّٰكِعِينَ ﴿٤٣﴾

44. Do you enjoin right conduct on the people, and forget (to practise it) yourselves, and yet you study the Scripture? Will you not understand?

44. Ataåmuroonan-naasa bilbirri wa tansawna anfusakum wa antum tatloonal-Kitaab; afalaa ta'qiloon.

أَتَأْمُرُونَ ٱلنَّاسَ بِٱلْبِرِّ وَتَنسَوْنَ
أَنفُسَكُمْ وَأَنتُمْ تَتْلُونَ ٱلْكِتَٰبَ ۚ
أَفَلَا تَعْقِلُونَ ﴿٤٤﴾

45. Nay, seek (Allah's) help with patient perseverance and prayer: it is indeed hard, except to those who bring a lowly spirit,-

45. Wasta'eenoo biṣṣabri waṣ-Ṣalaah; wa innahaa lakabee-ratun illaa alal-khaashi'een.

وَٱسْتَعِينُوا بِٱلصَّبْرِ وَٱلصَّلَوٰةِ ۚ
وَإِنَّهَا لَكَبِيرَةٌ إِلَّا عَلَى ٱلْخَٰشِعِينَ ﴿٤٥﴾

46. Who bear in mind the certainty that they are to meet their Lord, and that they are to return to Him.

46. Allazeena yazunnoona annahum mulaaqoo Rabbihim wa annahum ilayhi raaji'oon.

(Section 5)

ٱلَّذِينَ يَظُنُّونَ أَنَّهُم مُّلَٰقُوا رَبِّهِمْ
وَأَنَّهُمْ إِلَيْهِ رَٰجِعُونَ ﴿٤٦﴾ ع

الربع

47. O,Children of Israel! call to mind the (special) favour which I bestowed upon you, and that I preferred you to all others (for My Message).

47. Yaa Baneee Israaa'eelaz-kuroo ni'matiyal-lateee an'amtu 'alaykum wa annee faḍḍaltukum 'alal-'aalameen.

يَٰبَنِىٓ إِسْرَٰٓءِيلَ ٱذْكُرُوا نِعْمَتِىَ
ٱلَّتِىٓ أَنْعَمْتُ عَلَيْكُمْ وَأَنِّى فَضَّلْتُكُمْ
عَلَى ٱلْعَٰلَمِينَ ﴿٤٧﴾

48. Then guard yourselves against a day when one soul shall not avail another nor shall intercession be accepted for her, nor shall compensation be taken from her, nor shall anyone be helped (from outside).

48. Wattaqoo Yawmal-laa tajzee nafsun 'an nafsin shay'añw-wa laa yuqbalu minhaa shafaa'atuñw-wa laa yu'khazu minhaa 'adluñw-wa laa hum yunṣaroon.

وَٱتَّقُوا يَوْمًا لَّا تَجْزِى نَفْسٌ عَن
نَّفْسٍ شَيْـًٔا وَلَا يُقْبَلُ مِنْهَا شَفَٰعَةٌ
وَلَا يُؤْخَذُ مِنْهَا عَدْلٌ وَلَا هُمْ
يُنصَرُونَ ﴿٤٨﴾

49. And remember, We delivered you from the people of Pharaoh: they set you hard tasks and punishments, slaughtered your sons and let your women-folk live; therein was a tremendous trial from your Lord.

49. Wa iz najjaynaakum min Aali Fir'awna yasoomoonakum sooo'al-'azaabi yuzabbiḥoona abnaaa'akum wa yastaḥyoona nisaaa'akum; wa fee zaalikum balaaa'um mir-Rabbikum 'aẓeem.

وَإِذْ نَجَّيْنَٰكُم مِّنْ ءَالِ فِرْعَوْنَ
يَسُومُونَكُمْ سُوٓءَ ٱلْعَذَابِ
يُذَبِّحُونَ أَبْنَآءَكُمْ وَيَسْتَحْيُونَ
نِسَآءَكُمْ ۚ وَفِى ذَٰلِكُم بَلَآءٌ مِّن
رَّبِّكُمْ عَظِيمٌ ﴿٤٩﴾

Ikhfa	Ghunna	Ikhfa Meem Saakin	Idghaam	Qalqala	Qalb	Idghaam Meem Saakin
اخفاء	غنّہ	اخفاء میم ساکن	ادغام	قلقلہ	قلب	ادغام میم ساکن

50. And remember, We divided the sea for you and saved you and drowned Pharaoh's people within your very sight.

50. Wa iẕ faraqnaa bikumul-baḥra fa-anjaynaakum wa-aghraqnaaa Aala Fir‘awna wa antum tanẓuroon.

وَإِذْ فَرَقْنَا بِكُمُ الْبَحْرَ فَأَنْجَيْنٰكُمْ
وَأَغْرَقْنَآ اٰلَ فِرْعَوْنَ وَأَنْتُمْ تَنْظُرُوْنَ ﴿٥٠﴾

51. And remember We appointed forty nights for Moses, and in his absence, you took the calf (for worship), and you did grievous wrong.

51. Wa iẕ waa‘adnaa Moosaaa arba‘eena laylatan s̱ummat-takhaẕtumul-‘ijla mim ba‘dihee wa antum ẓaalimoon.

وَإِذْ وٰعَدْنَا مُوْسٰىٓ أَرْبَعِيْنَ لَيْلَةً
ثُمَّ اتَّخَذْتُمُ الْعِجْلَ مِنْۢ بَعْدِهٖ
وَأَنْتُمْ ظٰلِمُوْنَ ﴿٥١﴾

52. Even then We did forgive you; there was a chance for you to be grateful.

52. S̱umma ‘afawnaa ‘ankum mim ba‘di ẕaalika la‘allakum tashkuroon.

ثُمَّ عَفَوْنَا عَنْكُمْ مِّنْۢ بَعْدِ ذٰلِكَ
لَعَلَّكُمْ تَشْكُرُوْنَ ﴿٥٢﴾

53. And remember We gave Moses the Scripture and the Criterion (between right and wrong): there was a chance for you to be guided aright.

53. Wa iẕ aataynaa Moosal Kitaaba wal-Furqaana la‘allakum tahtadoon.

وَإِذْ اٰتَيْنَا مُوْسَى الْكِتٰبَ وَ
الْفُرْقَانَ لَعَلَّكُمْ تَهْتَدُوْنَ ﴿٥٣﴾

54. And remember, Moses said to his people: "O my people! you have indeed wronged yourselves by your worship of the calf: So turn (in repentance) to your Maker, and slay yourselves (the wrong-doers); that will be better for you in the sight of your Maker." Then He turned towards you (in forgiveness): for He is Oft- Returning, Most Merciful.

54. Wa iẕ qaala Moosaa liqawmihee yaa qawmi innakum ẓalamtum anfusakum bittikhaaẕikumul-‘ijla fatooboo ilaa Baari'ikum faqtulooo anfusakum ẕaalikum khayrul-lakum ‘inda Baari'ikum fataaba ‘alaykum; innahoo Huwat-Tawwaabur-Raḥeem.

وَإِذْ قَالَ مُوْسٰى لِقَوْمِهٖ يٰقَوْمِ
إِنَّكُمْ ظَلَمْتُمْ أَنْفُسَكُمْ بِاتِّخَاذِكُمُ
الْعِجْلَ فَتُوْبُوْٓا إِلٰى بَارِئِكُمْ فَاقْتُلُوْٓا
أَنْفُسَكُمْ ۭ ذٰلِكُمْ خَيْرٌ لَّكُمْ عِنْدَ
بَارِئِكُمْ ۭ فَتَابَ عَلَيْكُمْ ۭ إِنَّهٗ هُوَ
التَّوَّابُ الرَّحِيْمُ ﴿٥٤﴾

55. And remember, you said: "O Moses! we shall never believe in you until we see Allah manifestly," but you were dazed with thunder and lightning even as you looked on.

55. Wa iẕ qultum yaa Moosaa lan nu'mina laka ḥattaa naral-laaha jahratan fa-akhaẕat-kumuṣ-ṣaa‘iqatu wa antum tanẓuroon.

وَإِذْ قُلْتُمْ يٰمُوْسٰى لَنْ نُّؤْمِنَ لَكَ
حَتّٰى نَرَى اللّٰهَ جَهْرَةً فَأَخَذَتْكُمُ
الصّٰعِقَةُ وَأَنْتُمْ تَنْظُرُوْنَ ﴿٥٥﴾

56. Then We raised you up after your death: you had the chance to be grateful.

56. S̱umma ba‘as̱naakum mim ba‘di mawtikum la‘allakum tashkuroon.

ثُمَّ بَعَثْنٰكُمْ مِّنْۢ بَعْدِ مَوْتِكُمْ
لَعَلَّكُمْ تَشْكُرُوْنَ ﴿٥٦﴾

57. And We gave you the shade of clouds and sent down to you manna and quails, saying: "Eat of the good things We have provided for you:" (But they rebelled); to us they did not harm, but they harmed their own souls.

57. Wa ẓallalnaa ‘alaykumul-ghamaama wa anzalnaa ‘alaykumul-Manna was-Salwaa kuloo min ṭayyibaati maa razaqnaakum wa maa ẓalamoonaa wa laakin kaanooo anfusahum yaẓlimoon.

وَظَلَّلْنَا عَلَيْكُمُ الْغَمَامَ وَأَنْزَلْنَا
عَلَيْكُمُ الْمَنَّ وَالسَّلْوٰى ۭ كُلُوْا مِنْ
طَيِّبٰتِ مَا رَزَقْنٰكُمْ ۭ وَمَا ظَلَمُوْنَا
وَلٰكِنْ كَانُوْٓا أَنْفُسَهُمْ يَظْلِمُوْنَ ﴿٥٧﴾

58. And remember, We said: "Enter this town, and eat of the plenty therein as you wish;

58 Wa iẕ qulnad-khuloo haaẕihil-qaryata fakuloo minhaa hays̱u shi'tum raghadañw-

وَإِذْ قُلْنَا ادْخُلُوْا هٰذِهِ الْقَرْيَةَ
فَكُلُوْا مِنْهَا حَيْثُ شِئْتُمْ رَغَدًا

Ikhfa اخفاء | Ghunna غُنّہ | Ikhfa Meem Saakin اخفاء میم ساکن | Idghaam ادغام | Qalqala قلقلہ | Qalb قلب | Idghaam Meem Saakin ادغام میم ساکن

but enter the gate with humility, in posture and in words, and We shall forgive you your faults and increase (the portion of) those who do good."

wadkhulul-baaba sujjadañw-wa qooloo ḥiṭṭatun naghfir lakum khaṭaayaakum; wa sanazeedul-muḥsineen.

وَّادْخُلُوا الْبَابَ سُجَّدًا وَّقُوْلُوْا
حِطَّةٌ نَّغْفِرْ لَكُمْ خَطٰيٰكُمْ ۚ وَسَنَزِيْدُ
الْمُحْسِنِيْنَ ﴿٥٨﴾

59. But the transgressors changed the word from that which had been given them; so We sent on the transgressors a plague from heaven, for that they infringed (Our command) repeatedly.

59. Fabaddalal-lazeena ẓalamoo qawlan ghayral-lazee qeela lahum fa-anzalnaa 'alal-lazeena ẓalamoo rijzam-minas-samaaa'i bimaa kaanoo yafsuqoon. **(Section 6)**

فَبَدَّلَ الَّذِيْنَ ظَلَمُوْا قَوْلًا غَيْرَ
الَّذِيْ قِيْلَ لَهُمْ فَاَنْزَلْنَا عَلَى الَّذِيْنَ
ظَلَمُوْا رِجْزًا مِّنَ السَّمَآءِ بِمَا
كَانُوْا يَفْسُقُوْنَ ﴿٥٩﴾ ع

60. And remember, Moses prayed for water for his people; We said: "Strike the rock with your staff." Then gushed forth therefrom twelve springs. Each group knew its own place for water. So eat and drink of the sustenance provided by Allah, and do no evil nor mischief on the (face of the) earth.

60. Wa izis-tasqaa Moosaa liqawmihee faqulnaḍ-rib bi'aṣaakal-ḥajara fanfajarat minhusnataa 'ashrata 'aynan qad 'alima kullu unaasim-mash-rabahum kuloo washraboo mir-rizqil-laahi wa laa ta'saw fil-arḍi mufsideen.

وَاِذِ اسْتَسْقٰى مُوْسٰى لِقَوْمِهٖ
فَقُلْنَا اضْرِبْ بِّعَصَاكَ الْحَجَرَ ۚ
فَانْفَجَرَتْ مِنْهُ اثْنَتَا عَشْرَةَ عَيْنًا ۚ
قَدْ عَلِمَ كُلُّ اُنَاسٍ مَّشْرَبَهُمْ ۚ كُلُوْا
وَاشْرَبُوْا مِنْ رِّزْقِ اللّٰهِ وَلَا تَعْثَوْا
فِى الْاَرْضِ مُفْسِدِيْنَ ﴿٦٠﴾

61. And remember, you said: "O Moses! we cannot endure one kind of food (always); so beseech your Lord for us to produce for us of what the earth grows, - its pot-herbs, and cucumbers, its garlic, lentils, and onions." He said: "Will you exchange the better for the worse? You go down to any town, and you shall find what you want!" They were covered with humiliation and misery; they drew on themselves the wrath of Allah. This because they went on rejecting the Signs of Allah and slaying His Messengers without just cause. This because they rebelled and went on transgressing.

61. Wa iz qultum yaa Moosaa lan naṣbira 'alaa ṭa'aamiñw-waaḥidin fad'u lanaa Rabbaka yukhrij lanaa mimmaa tumbitul-arḍu mimbaqlihaa wa qissaaa'ihaa wa foomihaa wa 'adasihaa wa baṣalihaa qaala atastabdiloonal-lazee huwa adnaa billazee huwa khayr; ihbiṭoo miṣran fa-inna lakum maa sa-altum; wa ḍuribat 'alayhimuz-zillatu walmaskanatu wa baaa'oo bighaḍabim-minal-laah; zaalika bi-annahum kaanoo yakfuroona bi-Aayaatil-laahi wa yaqtuloonan-Nabiy-yeena bighayril-haqq; zaalika bimaa 'aṣaw wa kaanoo ya'tadoon. **(Section 7)**

وَاِذْ قُلْتُمْ يٰمُوْسٰى لَنْ نَّصْبِرَ عَلٰى
طَعَامٍ وَّاحِدٍ فَادْعُ لَنَا رَبَّكَ يُخْرِجْ
لَنَا مِمَّا تُنْۢبِتُ الْاَرْضُ مِنْۢ بَقْلِهَا
وَقِثَّآئِهَا وَفُوْمِهَا وَعَدَسِهَا وَبَصَلِهَا ۚ
قَالَ اَتَسْتَبْدِلُوْنَ الَّذِيْ هُوَ اَدْنٰى
بِالَّذِيْ هُوَ خَيْرٌ ۚ اِهْبِطُوْا مِصْرًا فَاِنَّ
لَكُمْ مَّا سَاَلْتُمْ ۚ وَضُرِبَتْ عَلَيْهِمُ
الذِّلَّةُ وَالْمَسْكَنَةُ ۚ وَبَآءُوْ بِغَضَبٍ
مِّنَ اللّٰهِ ۚ ذٰلِكَ بِاَنَّهُمْ كَانُوْا يَكْفُرُوْنَ
بِاٰيٰتِ اللّٰهِ وَيَقْتُلُوْنَ النَّبِيّٖنَ بِغَيْرِ
الْحَقِّ ۚ ذٰلِكَ بِمَا عَصَوْا وَّكَانُوْا
يَعْتَدُوْنَ ﴿٦١﴾ ع

62. Those who believe (in the Qur'an), and those who follow the Jewish (scriptures),

62. Innal-lazeena aamanoo wallazeena haadoo

اِنَّ الَّذِيْنَ اٰمَنُوْا وَالَّذِيْنَ هَادُوْا

Ikhfa اخفاء | Ghunna غنّہ | Ikhfa Meem Saakin اخفاء میم ساکن | Idghaam ادغام | Qalqala قلقلہ | Qalb قلب | Idghaam Meem Saakin ادغام میم ساکن

and the Christians and the Sabians, - and who believe in Allah and the Last Day, and work righteousness, shall have their reward with their Lord; on them shall be no fear, nor shall they grieve.

wan-Naṣaaraa waṣ-Ṣaabi'eena man aamana billaahi wal-Yawmil-Aakhiri wa 'amila ṣaaliḥan falahum ajruhum 'inda Rabbihim wa laa khawfun 'alayhim wa laa hum yahzanoon.

وَالنَّصٰرٰى وَالصّٰبِـِٕيْنَ مَنْ اٰمَنَ
بِاللّٰهِ وَالْيَوْمِ الْاٰخِرِ وَعَمِلَ صَالِحًا
فَلَهُمْ اَجْرُهُمْ عِنْدَ رَبِّهِمْ وَلَا
خَوْفٌ عَلَيْهِمْ وَلَا هُمْ يَحْزَنُوْنَ ﴿٦٢﴾

63. And remember, We took your covenant and We raised above you (the towering height) of Mount (Sinai): (saying): "Hold firmly to what We have given you and bring (ever) to remembrance what is therein: perchance you may fear Allah."

63. Wa iz akhaznaa meesaaqakum wa rafa'naa fawqakumuṭ-Ṭoora khuzoo maaa aataynaakum biquwwatiñw-wazkuroo maa feehi la'allakum tattaqoon.

وَاِذْ اَخَذْنَا مِيْثَاقَكُمْ وَرَفَعْنَا فَوْقَكُمُ
الطُّوْرَ خُذُوْا مَا اٰتَيْنٰكُمْ بِقُوَّةٍ وَّ
اذْكُرُوْا مَا فِيْهِ لَعَلَّكُمْ تَتَّقُوْنَ ﴿٦٣﴾

64. But you turned back thereafter: had it not been for the Grace and Mercy of Allah to you, you had surely been among the lost.

64. Summa tawallaytum mim ba'di zaalika falawlaa faḍlul-laahi 'alaykum wa raḥmatuhoo lakuntum minal-khaasireen.

ثُمَّ تَوَلَّيْتُمْ مِّنْ بَعْدِ ذٰلِكَ ۚ فَلَوْلَا
فَضْلُ اللّٰهِ عَلَيْكُمْ وَرَحْمَتُهٗ لَكُنْتُمْ
مِّنَ الْخٰسِرِيْنَ ﴿٦٤﴾

65. And well you knew those amongst you who transgressed in the matter of the Sabbath: We said to them: "Be you apes, despised and rejected."

65. Wa laqad 'alimtumul-lazeena'-tadaw minkum fis-Sabti faqulnaa lahum koonoo qiradatan khaasi'een.

وَلَقَدْ عَلِمْتُمُ الَّذِيْنَ اعْتَدَوْا
مِنْكُمْ فِي السَّبْتِ فَقُلْنَا لَهُمْ كُوْنُوْا
قِرَدَةً خٰسِـِٕيْنَ ﴿٦٥﴾

66. So We made it an example to their own time and to their posterity, and a lesson to those who fear Allah.

66. Faja'alnaahaa nakaalal-limaa bayna yadayhaa wa maa khalfahaa wa maw'izatal-lilmuttaqeen.

فَجَعَلْنٰهَا نَكَالًا لِّمَا بَيْنَ يَدَيْهَا وَمَا
خَلْفَهَا وَمَوْعِظَةً لِّلْمُتَّقِيْنَ ﴿٦٦﴾

67. And remember, Moses said to his people: "Allah commands that you sacrifice a heifer". They said: "Makes you a laughing-stock of us?" He said: "Allah save me from being an ignorant (fool)!"

67. Wa iz qaala Moosaa liqawmiheee innal-laaha yaámurukum an tazbaḥoo baqaratan qaalooo atattakhizunaa huzuwan qaala a'oozu billaahi an akoona minal-jaahileen.

وَاِذْ قَالَ مُوْسٰى لِقَوْمِهٖٓ اِنَّ اللّٰهَ
يَاْمُرُكُمْ اَنْ تَذْبَحُوْا بَقَرَةً ؕ قَالُوْٓا
اَتَتَّخِذُنَا هُزُوًا ؕ قَالَ اَعُوْذُ بِاللّٰهِ
اَنْ اَكُوْنَ مِنَ الْجٰهِلِيْنَ ﴿٦٧﴾

68. They said: "Beseech on our behalf your Lord to make plain to us what (heifer) it is!" He said; "He says: the heifer should be neither too old nor too young, but of middling age: now do what you are commanded!"

68. Qaalud-'u lanaa Rabbaka yubayyil-lanaa maa hee; qaala innahoo yaqoolu innahaa baqaratul-laa faariḍuñw-wa laa bikrun 'awaanum bayna zaalika faf'aloo maa tu'maroon.

قَالُوا ادْعُ لَنَا رَبَّكَ يُبَيِّنْ لَّنَا مَا هِيَ ؕ
قَالَ اِنَّهٗ يَقُوْلُ اِنَّهَا بَقَرَةٌ لَّا
فَارِضٌ وَّلَا بِكْرٌ ؕ عَوَانٌۢ بَيْنَ ذٰلِكَ ؕ
فَافْعَلُوْا مَا تُؤْمَرُوْنَ ﴿٦٨﴾

69. They said: "Beseech on our behalf your Lord to make plain to us her colour." He said: "He says: a fawn-coloured heifer, pure and rich in tone, the admiration of beholders!"

69. Qaalud-'u lanaa Rabbaka yubayyil-lanaa maa lawnuhaa; qaala innahoo yaqoolu innahaa baqaratun ṣafraaa'u faaqi'ul-lawnuhaa tasurrunnaazireen.

قَالُوا ادْعُ لَنَا رَبَّكَ يُبَيِّنْ لَّنَا مَا
لَوْنُهَا ؕ قَالَ اِنَّهٗ يَقُوْلُ اِنَّهَا بَقَرَةٌ
صَفْرَآءُ ۙ فَاقِعٌ لَّوْنُهَا تَسُرُّ النّٰظِرِيْنَ ﴿٦٩﴾

Ikhfa اخفاء | Ghunna غُنّہ | Ikhfa Meem Saakin اخفاءمیم ساکن | Idghaam ادغام | Qalqala قلقلہ | Qalb قلب | Idghaam Meem Saakin ادغام میم ساکن

70. They said: "Beseech on our behalf your Lord to make plain to us what she is: to us all heifers are alike: we wish indeed for guidance, if Allah wills."

70. Qaalud-'u lanaa Rabbaka yubayyil-lanaa maa hiya innal-baqara tashaabaha 'alaynaa wa innaaa in-shaaa'al-laahu lamuhtadoon.

قَالُوا ادْعُ لَنَا رَبَّكَ يُبَيِّن لَّنَا مَا هِيَ
إِنَّ الْبَقَرَ تَشَٰبَهَ عَلَيْنَا وَإِنَّآ إِن
شَآءَ اللَّهُ لَمُهْتَدُونَ ٧٠

71. He said: "He says: a heifer not trained to till the soil or water the fields; sound and without blemish". They said: "Now you has brought the truth." Then they offered her in sacrifice, but not with good-will.

71. Qaala innahoo yaqoolu innahaa baqaratul-laa z̲aloolun tuseerul-arḍa wa laa tasqil-ḥars̲a musallamatullaa shiyata feehaa; qaalul 'aana ji'ta bilhaqq; faz̲abaḥoohaa wa maa kaadoo yaf'aloon. **(Section 8)**

قَالَ إِنَّهُ يَقُولُ إِنَّهَا بَقَرَةٌ لَّا ذَلُولٌ
تُثِيرُ الْأَرْضَ وَلَا تَسْقِي الْحَرْثَ
مُسَلَّمَةٌ لَّا شِيَةَ فِيهَا قَالُوا
الْـَٰٔنَ جِئْتَ بِالْحَقِّ فَذَبَحُوهَا
وَمَا كَادُوا يَفْعَلُونَ ٧١ ع ٨

72. Remember, you slew a man and fell into a dispute among yourselves as to the crime: but Allah was to bring forth what you did hide.

72. Wa iz̲ qataltum nafsan faddaara'tum feehaa wallaahu mukhrijum-maa kuntum taktumoon.

وَإِذْ قَتَلْتُمْ نَفْسًا فَادَّٰرَءْتُمْ فِيهَا
وَاللَّهُ مُخْرِجٌ مَّا كُنتُمْ تَكْتُمُونَ ٧٢

73. So We said: "Strike the (body) with a piece of the (heifer)." Thus Allah brings the dead to life and shows you His Signs: perchance you may understand.

73. Faqulnaḍ-riboohu biba'ḍihaa; kaz̲aalika yuḥyil-laahul-mawtaa wa yureekum Aayaatihee la'allakum ta'qiloon.

فَقُلْنَا اضْرِبُوهُ بِبَعْضِهَا كَذَٰلِكَ
يُحْيِ اللَّهُ الْمَوْتَىٰ وَيُرِيكُمْ ءَايَٰتِهِ
لَعَلَّكُمْ تَعْقِلُونَ ٧٣

74. Thenceforth your hearts were hardened: they became like a rock and even worse in hardness. For among rocks there are some from which rivers gush forth; others there are which when split asunder send forth water; and others which sink for fear of Allah. And Allah is not unmindful of what you do.

74. Summa qasat quloobukum mim ba'di z̲aalika fahiya kalḥijaarati aw-ashaddu qaswah; wa inna minal-ḥijaarati lamaa yatafajjaru minhul-anhaar; wa-inna minhaa lamaa yash-shaqqaqu fayakhruju minhul-maaa'; wa inna minhaa lamaa yahbiṭu min khashyatil-laah; wa mal-laahu bighaafilin 'ammaa ta'maloon.

ثُمَّ قَسَتْ قُلُوبُكُم مِّن بَعْدِ ذَٰلِكَ
فَهِيَ كَالْحِجَارَةِ أَوْ أَشَدُّ قَسْوَةً
وَإِنَّ مِنَ الْحِجَارَةِ لَمَا يَتَفَجَّرُ مِنْهُ
الْأَنْهَٰرُ وَإِنَّ مِنْهَا لَمَا يَشَّقَّقُ
فَيَخْرُجُ مِنْهُ الْمَآءُ وَإِنَّ مِنْهَا لَمَا
يَهْبِطُ مِنْ خَشْيَةِ اللَّهِ وَمَا اللَّهُ
بِغَٰفِلٍ عَمَّا تَعْمَلُونَ ٧٤

75. Can you (O you men of Faith) entertain the hope that they will believe in you?- seeing that a party of them heard the Word of Allah, and perverted it knowingly after they understood it.

75. Afataṭma'oona any-yu'minoo lakum wa qad kaana fareequm-minhum yasma'oona Kalaamal-laahi summa yuḥarrifoonahoo mim ba'di maa 'aqaloohu wa hum ya'lamoon.

أَفَتَطْمَعُونَ أَن يُؤْمِنُوا لَكُمْ
وَقَدْ كَانَ فَرِيقٌ مِّنْهُمْ يَسْمَعُونَ
كَلَٰمَ اللَّهِ ثُمَّ يُحَرِّفُونَهُ مِن بَعْدِ
مَا عَقَلُوهُ وَهُمْ يَعْلَمُونَ ٧٥

76. Behold! when they meet the men of Faith, they say: "We believe": but when they meet each other in private,

76. Wa iz̲aa laqul-laz̲eena aamanoo qaalooo aamannaa wa iz̲aa khalaa ba'ḍuhum ilaa ba'ḍin

وَإِذَا لَقُوا الَّذِينَ ءَامَنُوا قَالُوٓا
ءَامَنَّا وَإِذَا خَلَا بَعْضُهُمْ إِلَىٰ بَعْضٍ

Ikhfa اخفاء | Ghunna غنّہ | Ikhfa Meem Saakin اخفاء میم ساکن | Idghaam ادغام | Qalqala قلقلہ | Qalb قلب | Idghaam Meem Saakin ادغام میم ساکن

they say: "Shall you tell them what Allah has revealed to you, that they may engage you in argument about it before your Lord?"- do you not understand (their aim)?

qaalooo atuḥaddiṡoonahum bimaa fataḥal-laahu 'alaykum liyuḥaajjookum bihee 'inda Rabbikum; afalaa ta'qiloon.

قَالُوْٓا اَتُحَدِّثُوْنَهُمْ بِمَا فَتَحَ اللّٰهُ
عَلَيْكُمْ لِيُحَآجُّوْكُمْ بِهٖ عِنْدَ
رَبِّكُمْ ؕ اَفَلَا تَعْقِلُوْنَ ۝

77. Do they not know that Allah knows what they conceal and what they reveal?

77. Awalaa ya'lamoona annal-laaha ya'lamu maa yusirroona wa maa yu'linoon.

اَوَلَا يَعْلَمُوْنَ اَنَّ اللّٰهَ يَعْلَمُ
مَا يُسِرُّوْنَ وَمَا يُعْلِنُوْنَ ۝

78. And there are among them illiterates, who know not the Book, but (see therein their own) desires, and they do nothing but conjecture.

78. Wa minhum ummiyyoona laa ya'lamoonal-Kitaaba illaaa amaaniyya wa in hum illaa yaẓunnoon.

وَمِنْهُمْ اُمِّيُّوْنَ لَا يَعْلَمُوْنَ الْكِتٰبَ
اِلَّآ اَمَانِيَّ وَاِنْ هُمْ اِلَّا يَظُنُّوْنَ ۝ النّصف

79. Then woe to those who write the Book with their own hands, and then say:"This is from Allah," to traffic with it for miserable price!- Woe to them for what their hands do write, and for the gain they make thereby.

79. Fawaylul-lillaẕeena yaktuboonal-kitaaba bi-aydeehim ṡumma yaqooloona haaẕaa min 'indil-laahi liyashtaroo bihee ṡamanan qaleelan fawaylul-lahum mimmaa katabat aydeehim wa waylul-lahum mimmaa yaksiboon.

فَوَيْلٌ لِّلَّذِيْنَ يَكْتُبُوْنَ الْكِتٰبَ
بِاَيْدِيْهِمْ ۗ ثُمَّ يَقُوْلُوْنَ هٰذَا مِنْ
عِنْدِ اللّٰهِ لِيَشْتَرُوْا بِهٖ ثَمَنًا قَلِيْلًا ؕ
فَوَيْلٌ لَّهُمْ مِّمَّا كَتَبَتْ اَيْدِيْهِمْ
وَوَيْلٌ لَّهُمْ مِّمَّا يَكْسِبُوْنَ ۝

80. And they say: "The Fire shall not touch us but for a few numbered days:" Say: "Have you taken a promise from Allah, for He never breaks His promise? or is it that you say of Allah what you do not know?"

80. Wa qaaloo lan tamassanan-Naaru illaaa ayyaamam-ma'doodah; qul attakhaẕtum 'indal-laahi 'ahdan falañy-yukhlifal-laahu 'ahdahooo am taqooloona 'alal-laahi maa laa ta'lamoon.

وَقَالُوْا لَنْ تَمَسَّنَا النَّارُ اِلَّآ اَيَّامًا
مَّعْدُوْدَةً ؕ قُلْ اَتَّخَذْتُمْ عِنْدَ اللّٰهِ
عَهْدًا فَلَنْ يُّخْلِفَ اللّٰهُ عَهْدَهٗٓ اَمْ
تَقُوْلُوْنَ عَلَى اللّٰهِ مَا لَا تَعْلَمُوْنَ ۝

81. No, those who seek gain in evil, and are girt round by their sins,- they are companions of the Fire: therein shall they abide (Forever).

81. Balaa man kasaba sayyi'atañw-wa aḥaaṭat bihee khateee'atuhoo fa-ulaaa'ika Aṣḥaabun-Naari hum feehaa khaalidoon.

بَلٰى مَنْ كَسَبَ سَيِّئَةً وَّاَحَاطَتْ
بِهٖ خَطِيْٓئَتُهٗ فَاُولٰٓئِكَ اَصْحٰبُ النَّارِ ۚ
هُمْ فِيْهَا خٰلِدُوْنَ ۝

82. But those who have faith and work righteousness, they are companions of the Garden: therein shall they abide (Forever).

82. Wallaẕeena aamanoo wa 'amiluṣ-ṣaaliḥaati ulaaa'ika Aṣḥaabul-Jannati hum feehaa khaalidoon. **(Section 9)**

وَالَّذِيْنَ اٰمَنُوْا وَعَمِلُوا الصّٰلِحٰتِ
اُولٰٓئِكَ اَصْحٰبُ الْجَنَّةِ ۚ هُمْ فِيْهَا
خٰلِدُوْنَ ۝ ع ١١/٩

83. And remember, We took a covenant from the Children of Israel (to this effect): worship none but Allah; treat with kindness your parents and kindred, and orphans and those in need; speak fair to the people;

83. Wa iẕ akhaẕnaa meeṡaaqa Baneee Israaa'eela laa ta'budoona illal-laaha wa bil-waalidayni iḥsaanañw-wa ẕil-qurbaa walyataamaa walmasaakeeni wa qooloo linnaasi ḥusnañw-

وَاِذْ اَخَذْنَا مِيْثَاقَ بَنِيْٓ اِسْرَآءِيْلَ
لَا تَعْبُدُوْنَ اِلَّا اللّٰهَ ۟ وَبِالْوَالِدَيْنِ
اِحْسَانًا وَّذِي الْقُرْبٰى وَالْيَتٰمٰى
وَالْمَسٰكِيْنِ وَقُوْلُوْا لِلنَّاسِ حُسْنًا

Ikhfa اخفاء · Ghunna غُنّہ · Ikhfa Meem Saakin اخفاء میم ساکن · Idghaam ادغام · Qalqala قلقلہ · Qalb قلب · Idghaam Meem Saakin ادغام میم ساکن

be steadfast in prayer; and practise regular charity. Then you turned back, except a few among you, and you backslide (even now).

wa aqeemuṣ-Ṣalaata wa aatuz-Zakaata summa tawallaytum illaa qaleelam-minkum wa antum mu'riḍoon.

وَّاَقِيْمُوا الصَّلٰوةَ وَاٰتُوا الزَّكٰوةَ ط
ثُمَّ تَوَلَّيْتُمْ اِلَّا قَلِيْلًا مِّنْكُمْ
وَاَنْتُمْ مُّعْرِضُوْنَ ﴿٨٣﴾

84. And remember We took your Covenant (to this effect): shed no blood amongst you, nor turn out your own people from your homes: and this you solemnly ratified, and to this you can bear witness.

84. Wa iz akhaznaa meesaa-qakum laa tasfikoona dimaa-a'akum wa laa tukhrijoona anfusakum min diyaarikum summa aqrartum wa antum tashhadoon.

وَاِذْ اَخَذْنَا مِيْثَاقَكُمْ لَا تَسْفِكُوْنَ
دِمَآءَكُمْ وَلَا تُخْرِجُوْنَ اَنْفُسَكُمْ
مِّنْ دِيَارِكُمْ ثُمَّ اَقْرَرْتُمْ وَاَنْتُمْ
تَشْهَدُوْنَ ﴿٨٤﴾

85. After this it is you, the same people, who slay among yourselves, and banish a party of you from their homes; assist (their enemies) against them, in guilt and rancour; and if they come to you as captives, you ransom them, though it was not lawful for you to banish them. Then is it only a part of the Book that you believe in, and do you reject the rest? But what is the reward for those among you who behave like this but disgrace in this life?- and on the Day of Judgment they shall be consigned to the most grievous Chastisement. For Allah is not unmindful of what you do.

85. Summa antum haaa'ulaaa'i taqtuloona anfusakum wa tukhrijoona fareeqam-minkum min diyaarihim taẓaaharoona 'alayhim bil-ismi wal'udwaani wa iñy-yaåtookum usaaraa tufaa-doohum wahuwa muḥarramun 'alaykum ikhraajuhum; afatu'-mi-noona biba'ḍil-Kitaabi wa takfuroona biba'ḍ; famaa jazaaa'u mañy-yaf'alu zaalika minkum illaa khizyun fil-ḥayaatid-dunyaa wa Yawmal-Qiyaamati yuraddoona ilaaa ashaddil-'azaab; wa mal-laahu bighaafilin 'ammaa ta'maloon.

ثُمَّ اَنْتُمْ هٰٓؤُلَآءِ تَقْتُلُوْنَ اَنْفُسَكُمْ
وَتُخْرِجُوْنَ فَرِيْقًا مِّنْكُمْ مِّنْ دِيَارِهِمْ
تَظٰهَرُوْنَ عَلَيْهِمْ بِالْاِثْمِ وَالْعُدْوَانِ ط
وَاِنْ يَّاْتُوْكُمْ اُسٰرٰى تُفٰدُوْهُمْ
وَهُوَ مُحَرَّمٌ عَلَيْكُمْ اِخْرَاجُهُمْ ط
اَفَتُؤْمِنُوْنَ بِبَعْضِ الْكِتٰبِ وَتَكْفُرُوْنَ
بِبَعْضٍ فَمَا جَزَآءُ مَنْ يَّفْعَلُ ذٰلِكَ
مِنْكُمْ اِلَّا خِزْيٌ فِى الْحَيٰوةِ الدُّنْيَا ج
وَيَوْمَ الْقِيٰمَةِ يُرَدُّوْنَ اِلٰٓى اَشَدِّ
الْعَذَابِ ط وَمَا اللّٰهُ بِغَافِلٍ عَمَّا
تَعْمَلُوْنَ ﴿٨٥﴾

86. These are the people who buy the life of this world at the price of the Hereafter: their Chastisement shall not be lightened nor shall they be helped.

86. Ulaaa'ikal-lazeenash-tarawul ḥayaatad-dunyaa bil-Aakhirati falaa yukhaffafu 'anhumul-'azaabu wa laa hum yunṣaroon. **(Section 10)**

اُولٰٓئِكَ الَّذِيْنَ اشْتَرَوُا الْحَيٰوةَ
الدُّنْيَا بِالْاٰخِرَةِ فَلَا يُخَفَّفُ عَنْهُمُ
الْعَذَابُ وَلَا هُمْ يُنْصَرُوْنَ ﴿٨٦﴾ ع ركوع

87. We gave Moses the Book and followed him up with a succession of Apostles; We gave Jesus the son of Mary, clear (Signs) and strengthened him with the holy spirit. Is it that whenever there comes to you an Apostle with what you yourselves desire not, you are puffed hup with pride?-

87. Wa laqad aataynaa Moosal-Kitaaba wa qaffaynaa mim ba'dihee bir-Rusuli wa aataynaa 'Eesab-na-Maryamal-bayyinaati wa ayyadnaahu bi-Rooḥil Qudus; afakullamaa jaaa'akum Rasoolum bimaa laa tahwaaa anfusukumus-takbartum

وَلَقَدْ اٰتَيْنَا مُوْسَى الْكِتٰبَ وَقَفَّيْنَا
مِنْۢ بَعْدِهٖ بِالرُّسُلِ وَاٰتَيْنَا عِيْسَى
ابْنَ مَرْيَمَ الْبَيِّنٰتِ وَاَيَّدْنٰهُ بِرُوْحِ
الْقُدُسِ ط اَفَكُلَّمَا جَآءَكُمْ رَسُوْلٌۢ
بِمَا لَا تَهْوٰٓى اَنْفُسُكُمُ اسْتَكْبَرْتُمْ

Ikhfa اخفاء · Ghunna غنّہ · Ikhfa Meem Saakin اخفاءمیم ساکن · Idghaam ادغام · Qalqala قلقلہ · Qalb قلب · Idghaam Meem Saakin ادغام میم ساکن

some you called impostors, and others you slay!

88. They say, "Our hearts are the wrappings (which preserve Allah's Word: we need no more)." Nay, Allah's curse is on them for their blasphemy: little is it they believe.

89. And when there comes to them a Book from Allah, confirming what is with them,- although from of old they had prayed for victory against those without Faith,- when there comes to them that which they (should) have recognised, they refuse to believe in it but the curse of Allah is on those without Faith.

90. Miserable is the price for which they have sold their souls, in that they deny (the revelation) which Allah has sent down, in insolent envy that Allah of His Grace should send it to any of His servants He pleases: thus they have drawn on themselves Wrath upon Wrath. And humiliating is the punishment of those who reject Faith.

91. When it is said to them, "Believe in what Allah has sent down," they say, "We believe in what was sent down to us:" yet they reject all besides, even if it be Truth confirming what is with them. Say: "Why then have you slain the prophets of Allah in times gone by, if you did indeed believe?"

92. There came to you Moses with clear (Signs); yet you worshipped the Calf (even) after that, and you did behave wrongfully.

93. And remember, We took your Covenant and We raised above you (the towering height) of Mount (Sinai): (saying): "Hold firmly to what We have given you and hear ken (to the Law)": they said: "We hear, and we disobey:" and they had to drink into their hearts (of the taint) of the Calf

fafareeqan kazzabtum wa fareeqan taqtuloon.

88. Wa qaaloo quloobunaa ghulf; bal la'anahumul-laahu bikufrihim faqaleelam-maa yu'minoon.

89. Wa lammaa jaaa'ahum Kitaabum-min 'indil-laahi muṣaddiqul-limaa ma'ahum wa kaanoo min qablu yastaftiḥoona 'alal-lazeena kafaroo falammaa jaaa'ahum maa 'arafoo kafaroo bih; fala'natul-laahi 'alal-kaafireen.

90. Bi'samash-taraw biheee anfusahum añy-yakfuroo bimaaa anzalal-laahu baghyan añy-yunazzilal-laahu min faḍlihee 'alaa mañy-yashaaa'u min 'ibaadihee fabaaa'oo bighaḍabin 'alaa ghaḍab; wa lilkaafireena 'azaabum-muheen.

91. Wa izaa qeela lahum aaminoo bimaaa anzalal-laahu qaaloo nu'minu bimaaa unzila 'alaynaa wa yakfuroona bimaa waraaa'ahoo wa huwal-ḥaqqu muṣaddiqal-limaa ma'ahum; qul falima taqtuloona Ambiyaaa'al-laahi min qablu in kuntum mu'mineen.

92. Wa laqad jaaa'akum Moosaa bilbayyinaati summat-takhaztumul-'ijla mim ba'dihee wa antum ẓaalimoon.

93. Wa iz akhaznaa meesaa-qakum wa rafa'naa fawqa-kumuṭ-Ṭoora khuzoo maaa aataynaakum biquwwatiñw-wasma'oo qaaloo sami'naa wa 'aṣaynaa wa ushriboo fee quloobihimul 'ijla

ففريقا كذبتم وفريقا تقتلون ﴿٨٧﴾
وقالوا قلوبنا غلف بل لعنهم
الله بكفرهم فقليلا ما يؤمنون ﴿٨٨﴾
ولما جاءهم كتب من عند الله
مصدق لما معهم وكانوا من
قبل يستفتحون على الذين كفروا
فلما جاءهم ما عرفوا كفروا به
فلعنة الله على الكفرين ﴿٨٩﴾
بئسما اشتروا به انفسهم ان
يكفروا بما انزل الله بغيا ان ينزل
الله من فضله على من يشاء من
عباده فباءو بغضب على غضب
وللكفرين عذاب مهين ﴿٩٠﴾
واذا قيل لهم امنوا بما انزل الله
قالوا نؤمن بما انزل علينا
ويكفرون بما وراءه وهو الحق
مصدقا لما معهم قل فلم تقتلون
انبياء الله من قبل ان كنتم
مؤمنين ﴿٩١﴾
ولقد جاءكم موسى بالبينت ثم
اتخذتم العجل من بعده وانتم
ظلمون ﴿٩٢﴾
واذ اخذنا ميثاقكم ورفعنا
فوقكم الطور خذوا ما اتينكم
بقوة واسمعوا قالوا سمعنا
وعصينا واشربوا في قلوبهم العجل

because of their Faithlessness. Say: "Vile indeed are the behests of your Faith if you have any faith!"

94. Say: "If the last Home, with Allah, be for you specially, and not for anyone else, then seek you for death, if you are sincere."

95. But they will never seek for death, on account of the (sins) which their hands have sent on before them. And Allah is well-acquainted with the wrong-doers.

96. You will indeed find them, of all people, most greedy of life,- even more than the idolators: each one of them wishes he could be given a life of a thousand years: but the grant of such life will not save him from (due) punishment. For Allah sees well all that they do.

97. Say: Whoever is an enemy to Gabriel - he has brought down the (revelation) to your heart by Allah's will, a confirmation of what went before, and guidance and glad tidings for those who believe,

98. Whoever is an enemy to Allah and His Angels and Apostles, to Gabriel and Michael,- certainly Allah is an enemy to those who reject Faith.

99. We have sent down to you Manifest Signs (ayaat); and none reject them but those who are perverse.

100. Is it not (the case) that every time they make Covenant, some party among them throw it aside?- Nay, most of them are faithless.

101. And when there came to them an Apostle from Allah, confirming what was with them, a party of the People of the Book threw away the Book of Allah

bikufrihim; qul bi'samaa yaåmurukum biheee eemaanukum in kuntum mu'mineen.

94. Qul in kaanat lakumud-Daarul-Aakhiratu 'indal-laahi khaaliṣatam-min doonin-naasi fatamannawul-mawta in kuntum ṣaadiqeen.

95. Wa lañy-yatamannawhu abadam bimaa qaddamat aydeehim; wallaahu 'aleemum bizzaalimeen.

96. Wa latajidannahum aḥraṣan-naasi 'alaa ḥayaatiñw wa minal-lazeena ashrakoo; yawaddu aḥaduhum law yu'ammaru alfa sanatiñw wa maa huwa bi muzaḥziḥihee minal-'azaabi añy-yu'ammar; wallaahu baṣeerum bimaa ya'maloon.

(Section 11)

97. Qul man kaana 'aduwwal-li-Jibreela fainnahoo nazzalahoo 'alaa qalbika bi-iznil-laahi muṣaddiqal-limaa bayna yadayhi wa hudañw-wa bushraa lilmu'mineen.

98. Man kaana 'aduwwal-lillaahi wa malaaa'ikatihee wa Rusulihee wa Jibreela wa Meekaala fa-innal-laaha 'aduw-wul-lilkaafireen.

99. Wa laqad anzalnaaa ilayka Aayaatim bayyinaatiñw wa maa yakfuru bihaaa illalfaasiqoon.

100. Awa kullamaa 'aahadoo 'ahdan nabazahoo fareequm-minhum; bal aksaruhum laa yu'minoon.

101. Wa lammaa jaaa'ahum Rasoolum min 'indil-laahi muṣaddiqul-limaa ma'ahum nabaza fareequm-minal-lazeena ootul-Kitaaba Kitaabal-laahi

بِكُفْرِهِمْ ۚ قُلْ بِئْسَمَا يَأْمُرُكُم بِهِۦٓ إِيمَٰنُكُمْ
إِن كُنتُم مُّؤْمِنِينَ ﴿٩٣﴾
قُلْ إِن كَانَتْ لَكُمُ ٱلدَّارُ ٱلْءَاخِرَةُ
عِندَ ٱللَّهِ خَالِصَةً مِّن دُونِ ٱلنَّاسِ
فَتَمَنَّوُا۟ ٱلْمَوْتَ إِن كُنتُمْ صَٰدِقِينَ ﴿٩٤﴾
وَلَن يَتَمَنَّوْهُ أَبَدًۢا بِمَا قَدَّمَتْ أَيْدِيهِمْ ۗ
وَٱللَّهُ عَلِيمٌۢ بِٱلظَّٰلِمِينَ ﴿٩٥﴾
وَلَتَجِدَنَّهُمْ أَحْرَصَ ٱلنَّاسِ عَلَىٰ
حَيَوٰةٍ وَمِنَ ٱلَّذِينَ أَشْرَكُوا۟ ۚ يَوَدُّ
أَحَدُهُمْ لَوْ يُعَمَّرُ أَلْفَ سَنَةٍ وَمَا
هُوَ بِمُزَحْزِحِهِۦ مِنَ ٱلْعَذَابِ أَن
يُعَمَّرَ ۗ وَٱللَّهُ بَصِيرٌۢ بِمَا يَعْمَلُونَ ﴿٩٦﴾
قُلْ مَن كَانَ عَدُوًّا لِّجِبْرِيلَ فَإِنَّهُۥ
نَزَّلَهُۥ عَلَىٰ قَلْبِكَ بِإِذْنِ ٱللَّهِ مُصَدِّقًا
لِّمَا بَيْنَ يَدَيْهِ وَهُدًى وَبُشْرَىٰ
لِلْمُؤْمِنِينَ ﴿٩٧﴾
مَن كَانَ عَدُوًّا لِّلَّهِ وَمَلَٰٓئِكَتِهِۦ
وَرُسُلِهِۦ وَجِبْرِيلَ وَمِيكَىٰلَ فَإِنَّ
ٱللَّهَ عَدُوٌّ لِّلْكَٰفِرِينَ ﴿٩٨﴾
وَلَقَدْ أَنزَلْنَآ إِلَيْكَ ءَايَٰتٍۭ بَيِّنَٰتٍ ۖ
وَمَا يَكْفُرُ بِهَآ إِلَّا ٱلْفَٰسِقُونَ ﴿٩٩﴾
أَوَكُلَّمَا عَٰهَدُوا۟ عَهْدًا نَّبَذَهُۥ فَرِيقٌ
مِّنْهُم ۚ بَلْ أَكْثَرُهُمْ لَا يُؤْمِنُونَ ﴿١٠٠﴾
وَلَمَّا جَآءَهُمْ رَسُولٌ مِّنْ عِندِ ٱللَّهِ
مُصَدِّقٌ لِّمَا مَعَهُمْ نَبَذَ فَرِيقٌ
مِّنَ ٱلَّذِينَ أُوتُوا۟ ٱلْكِتَٰبَ كِتَٰبَ ٱللَّهِ

Ikhfa اخفاء | Ghunna غنّہ | Ikhfa Meem Saakin اخفاء میم ساکن | Idghaam ادغام | Qalqala قلقلہ | Qalb قلب | Idghaam Meem Saakin ادغام میم ساکن

behind their backs, as if (it had been something) they did not know!

102. They followed what the evil ones gave out (falsely) against the power of Solomon: the blasphemers were, and not Solomon, but the evil ones, teaching men magic, and such things as came down at Babylon to the angels Harut and Marut. But neither of these taught anyone (such things) without saying: "We are only for trial; so do not blaspheme." They learned from them the means to sow discord between man and wife. But they could not thus harm anyone except by Allah's permission. And they learned what harmed them, not what profited them. And they knew that the buyers of (magic) would have no share in the happiness of the Hereafter. And vile was the price for which they did sell their souls, if they but knew!

waraaa'a ẓuhoorihim kaannahum laa ya'lamoon.

102. Wattaba'oo maa tatlush-Shayaaṭeenu 'alaa mulki Sulaymaana wa maa kafara Sulaymaanu wa laakinnash-Shayaaṭeena kafaroo yu'allimoonan-naasas-siḥra wa maaa unzila 'alal-malakayni bi-Baabila Haaroota wa Maaroot; wa maa yu'allimaani min aḥadin ḥattaa yaqoolaaa innamaa naḥnu fitnatun falaa takfur fayata'allamoona minhumaa maa yufarriqoona bihee baynal-mar'i wa zawjih; wa maa hum biḍaaarreena bihee min aḥadin illaa bi-iẕnillaah; wa yata'allamoona maa yaḍurruhum wa laa yanfa'uhum; wa laqad 'alimoo lamanish-taraahu maa lahoo fil-Aakhirati min khalaaq; wa labi'sa maa sharaw biheee anfusahum; law kaanoo ya'lamoon.

وَرَآءَ ظُهُورِهِمْ كَأَنَّهُمْ لَا يَعْلَمُونَ ۝١٠١
وَاتَّبَعُوا مَا تَتْلُوا الشَّيٰطِينُ عَلٰى
مُلْكِ سُلَيْمٰنَ ۚ وَمَا كَفَرَ سُلَيْمٰنُ
وَلٰكِنَّ الشَّيٰطِينَ كَفَرُوا يُعَلِّمُونَ
النَّاسَ السِّحْرَ ۚ وَمَا أُنْزِلَ عَلَى
الْمَلَكَيْنِ بِبَابِلَ هٰرُوتَ وَمٰرُوتَ ۚ
وَمَا يُعَلِّمٰنِ مِنْ أَحَدٍ حَتّٰى يَقُولَا
إِنَّمَا نَحْنُ فِتْنَةٌ فَلَا تَكْفُرْ ۖ فَيَتَعَلَّمُونَ
مِنْهُمَا مَا يُفَرِّقُونَ بِهِ بَيْنَ الْمَرْءِ
وَزَوْجِهِ ۚ وَمَا هُمْ بِضَآرِّينَ بِهِ
مِنْ أَحَدٍ إِلَّا بِإِذْنِ اللّٰهِ ۚ وَيَتَعَلَّمُونَ
مَا يَضُرُّهُمْ وَلَا يَنْفَعُهُمْ ۚ وَلَقَدْ
عَلِمُوا لَمَنِ اشْتَرٰىهُ مَا لَهُ فِي الْاٰخِرَةِ
مِنْ خَلٰقٍ ۚ وَلَبِئْسَ مَا شَرَوْا بِهِ
أَنْفُسَهُمْ ۚ لَوْ كَانُوا يَعْلَمُونَ ۝١٠٢

103. If they had kept their Faith and guarded themselves from evil, far better had been the reward from their Lord, if they but knew!

103. Wa law annahum aamanoo wattaqaw lamaṯoobatum-min 'indillaahi khayrun law kaanoo ya'lamoon. **(Section 12)**

وَلَوْ أَنَّهُمْ اٰمَنُوا وَاتَّقَوْا لَمَثُوبَةٌ
مِنْ عِنْدِ اللّٰهِ خَيْرٌ ۚ لَوْ كَانُوا
يَعْلَمُونَ ۝١٠٣ ع ١٢

104. O you who believe! say not (to the Apostle) words of ambiguous import, but words of respect; and listen (to him): to those without Faith is a grievous punishment.

104. Yaaa ayyuhal-laẕeena aamanoo laa taqooloo raa'inaa wa qoolun-ẕurnaa wasma'oo; wa lilkaafireena 'aẕaabun aleem.

يٰأَيُّهَا الَّذِينَ اٰمَنُوا لَا تَقُولُوا
رٰعِنَا وَقُولُوا انْظُرْنَا وَاسْمَعُوا ۗ
وَلِلْكٰفِرِينَ عَذَابٌ أَلِيمٌ ۝١٠٤

105. It is never the wish of those without Faith among the People of the Book, nor of the Pagans, that anything good should come down to you from your Lord. But Allah will choose for His special Mercy whom He will - for Allah is Lord of grace abounding.

105. Maa yawaddul-laẕeena kafaroo min Ahlil-Kitaabi wa lal-mushrikeena añy-yunazzala 'alaykum min khayrim-mir-Rabbikum; wallaahu yakhtaṣṣu biraḥmatihee mañy-yashaaa'; wallaahu ẕul-faḍlil'aẓeem.

مَا يَوَدُّ الَّذِينَ كَفَرُوا مِنْ أَهْلِ
الْكِتٰبِ وَلَا الْمُشْرِكِينَ أَنْ يُنَزَّلَ
عَلَيْكُمْ مِنْ خَيْرٍ مِنْ رَبِّكُمْ ۗ وَاللّٰهُ
يَخْتَصُّ بِرَحْمَتِهِ مَنْ يَشَآءُ ۗ وَاللّٰهُ
ذُو الْفَضْلِ الْعَظِيمِ ۝١٠٥

Ikhfa اخفاء | Ghunna غنّہ | Ikhfa Meem Saakin اخفاء میم ساکن | Idghaam ادغام | Qalqala قلقلہ | Qalb قلب | Idghaam Meem Saakin ادغام میم ساکن

106. None of Our revelations do We abrogate or cause to be forgotten, but We substitute something better or similar: do you not know that Allah has power over all things?

106. Maa nansakh min Aayatin aw nunsihaa na-ti bikhayrim-minhaaa aw mislihaaa; alam ta'lam annal-laaha 'alaa kulli shay'in Qadeer.

مَا نَنْسَخْ مِنْ اٰيَةٍ اَوْ نُنْسِهَا نَاْتِ
بِخَيْرٍ مِّنْهَآ اَوْ مِثْلِهَا ؕ اَلَمْ تَعْلَمْ
اَنَّ اللّٰهَ عَلٰى كُلِّ شَیْءٍ قَدِیْرٌ ﴿۱۰۶﴾

107. Do you not know that to Allah belongs the dominion of the heavens and the earth? And besides Him you have neither patron nor helper.

107. Alam ta'lam annallaaha lahoo mulkus-samaawaati wal-arḍ; wa maa lakum min doonil-laahi miñw-waliyyiñw-wa laa naṣeer.

اَلَمْ تَعْلَمْ اَنَّ اللّٰهَ لَهٗ مُلْكُ السَّمٰوٰتِ
وَالْاَرْضِ ؕ وَمَا لَكُمْ مِّنْ دُوْنِ اللّٰهِ
مِنْ وَّلِیٍّ وَّلَا نَصِیْرٍ ﴿۱۰۷﴾

108. Would you question your Apostle as Moses was questioned of old? But whoever changes from Faith to Unbelief, has strayed without doubt from the even way.

108. Am tureedoona an tas'aloo Rasoolakum kamaa su'ila Moosaa min qabl; wa mañy-yatabaddalil-kufra bil-eemaani faqad ḍalla sawaaa'as-Sabeel.

اَمْ تُرِیْدُوْنَ اَنْ تَسْـَٔلُوْا رَسُوْلَكُمْ
كَمَا سُئِلَ مُوْسٰى مِنْ قَبْلُ ؕ وَمَنْ
یَّتَبَدَّلِ الْكُفْرَ بِالْاِیْمَانِ فَقَدْ
ضَلَّ سَوَآءَ السَّبِیْلِ ﴿۱۰۸﴾

109. Quite a number of the People of the Book wish they could turn you (people) back to infidelity after you have believed, from selfish envy, after the Truth has become Manifest to them: but forgive and overlook, till Allah accomplish His purpose; for Allah has power over all things.

109. Wadda kaseerum-min Ahlil-Kitaabi law yaruddoo-nakum mim-ba'di eemaanikum kuffaaran ḥasadam-min 'indi anfusihim mim ba'di maa tabayyana lahumul-ḥaqqu fa'foo waṣfaḥoo ḥattaa yaâ-tiyallaahu bi-amrih; innal-laaha 'alaa kulli shay'in Qadeer.

وَدَّ كَثِیْرٌ مِّنْ اَهْلِ الْكِتٰبِ لَوْ یَرُدُّوْنَكُمْ
مِّنْۢ بَعْدِ اِیْمَانِكُمْ كُفَّارًا ۚۖ حَسَدًا
مِّنْ عِنْدِ اَنْفُسِهِمْ مِّنْۢ بَعْدِ مَا
تَبَیَّنَ لَهُمُ الْحَقُّ ۚ فَاعْفُوْا وَاصْفَحُوْا
حَتّٰى یَاْتِیَ اللّٰهُ بِاَمْرِهٖ ؕ اِنَّ اللّٰهَ عَلٰى
كُلِّ شَیْءٍ قَدِیْرٌ ﴿۱۰۹﴾

الثلثة

110. And be steadfast in prayer and regular in charity: and whatever good you send forth for your souls before you, you shall find it with Allah: for Allah sees well all that you do.

110. Wa aqeemuṣ-Ṣalaata wa aatuz-Zakaah; wa maa tuqad-dimoo li-anfusikum min khayrin tajidoohu 'indal-laah; innal-laaha bimaa ta'maloona Baṣeer.

وَاَقِیْمُوا الصَّلٰوةَ وَاٰتُوا الزَّكٰوةَ ؕ
وَمَا تُقَدِّمُوْا لِاَنْفُسِكُمْ مِّنْ خَیْرٍ
تَجِدُوْهُ عِنْدَ اللّٰهِ ؕ اِنَّ اللّٰهَ بِمَا
تَعْمَلُوْنَ بَصِیْرٌ ﴿۱۱۰﴾

111. And they say: "None shall enter Paradise unless he be a Jew or a Christian." Those are their (vain) desires. Say: "Produce your proof if you are truthful."

111. Wa qaaloo lañy-yadkhulal-Jannata illaa man kaana Hoodan aw Naṣaaraa; tilka amaaniy-yuhum; qul haatoo burhaa-nakum in kuntum ṣaadiqeen.

وَقَالُوْا لَنْ یَّدْخُلَ الْجَنَّةَ اِلَّا مَنْ
كَانَ هُوْدًا اَوْ نَصٰرٰى ؕ تِلْكَ
اَمَانِیُّهُمْ ؕ قُلْ هَاتُوْا بُرْهَانَكُمْ اِنْ
كُنْتُمْ صٰدِقِیْنَ ﴿۱۱۱﴾

112. Nay,- whoever submits his whole self to Allah and is a doer of good,- he will get his reward with his Lord;

112. Balaa man aslama wajhahoo lillaahi wa huwa muḥsinun falahooo ajruhoo 'inda Rabbihee wa laa

بَلٰى ۚ مَنْ اَسْلَمَ وَجْهَهٗ لِلّٰهِ وَهُوَ
مُحْسِنٌ فَلَهٗۤ اَجْرُهٗ عِنْدَ رَبِّهٖ ۪ وَلَا

Ikhfa اخفاء | Ghunna غُنّہ | Ikhfa Meem Saakin اخفاء میم ساکن | Idghaam ادغام | Qalqala قلقلہ | Qalb قلب | Idghaam Meem Saakin ادغام میم ساکن

on such shall be no fear, nor shall they grieve.

khawfun 'alayhim wa laa hum yaḥzanoon. **(Section 13)**

خَوْفٌ عَلَيْهِمْ وَلَا هُمْ يَحْزَنُوْنَ ﴿١١٢﴾ ع

113. The Jews say: "The Christians have nothing (to stand) upon"; and the Christians say: "The Jews have nothing (to stand) upon." Yet they (profess to) study the (same) Book. Like unto their word is what those say who know not; but Allah will judge between them in their dispute on the Day of Judgment.

113. Wa qaalatil-Yahoodu laysatin-Naṣaaraa 'alaa shay' iñw-wa qaalatin-Naṣ aaraa laysatil-Yahoodu 'alaa shay-'iñw-wa hum yatloonal-Kitaab; kazaalika qaalal-lazeena laa ya'lamoona misla qawlihim; fallaahu yaḥkumu baynahum Yawmal-Qiyaamati feemaa kaanoo feehi yakhtalifoon.

وَقَالَتِ الْيَهُوْدُ لَيْسَتِ النَّصٰرٰى
عَلٰى شَيْءٍ ۖ وَّقَالَتِ النَّصٰرٰى لَيْسَتِ
الْيَهُوْدُ عَلٰى شَيْءٍ ۙ وَّهُمْ يَتْلُوْنَ الْكِتٰبَ ۗ
كَذٰلِكَ قَالَ الَّذِيْنَ لَا يَعْلَمُوْنَ
مِثْلَ قَوْلِهِمْ ۚ فَاللّٰهُ يَحْكُمُ بَيْنَهُمْ يَوْمَ
الْقِيٰمَةِ فِيْمَا كَانُوْا فِيْهِ يَخْتَلِفُوْنَ ﴿١١٣﴾

114. And who is more unjust than he who forbids that in places for the worship of Allah, Allah's name should be celebrated?-whose zeal is (in fact) to ruin them? It was not fitting that such should themselves enter them except in fear. For them there is nothing but disgrace in this world, and in the world to come, an exceeding torment.

114. Wa man-aẓlamu mimmam-mana'a masaajidal-laahi añy-yuzkara feehas-muhoo wa sa'aa fee kharaabihaaa; ulaaa'ika maa kaana lahum añy- yadkhuloohaaa illaa khaaa'ifeen; lahum fid-dunyaa khizyuñw-wa lahum fil-Aakhirati 'azaabun 'aẓeem.

وَمَنْ اَظْلَمُ مِمَّنْ مَّنَعَ مَسٰجِدَ اللّٰهِ
اَنْ يُّذْكَرَ فِيْهَا اسْمُهٗ وَسَعٰى فِيْ
خَرَابِهَا ۭ اُولٰۗىِٕكَ مَا كَانَ لَهُمْ اَنْ
يَّدْخُلُوْهَآ اِلَّا خَاۗىِٕفِيْنَ ۥ لَهُمْ فِي
الدُّنْيَا خِزْيٌ وَّلَهُمْ فِي الْاٰخِرَةِ
عَذَابٌ عَظِيْمٌ ﴿١١٤﴾

115. To Allah belong the East and the West: whithersoever you turn, there is the presence of Allah. For Allah is All-Pervading, All-Knowing.

115. Wa lillaahil - mashriqu walmaghrib; fa-aynamaa tuwalloo fasamma Wajhullaah; innal-laaha Waasi'un 'Aleem.

وَلِلّٰهِ الْمَشْرِقُ وَالْمَغْرِبُ ۤ فَاَيْنَمَا
تُوَلُّوْا فَثَمَّ وَجْهُ اللّٰهِ ۭ اِنَّ اللّٰهَ
وَاسِعٌ عَلِيْمٌ ﴿١١٥﴾

116. They say: "Allah has begotten a son": glory be to Him.-Nay, to Him belongs all that is in the heavens and on earth: everything renders worship to Him.

116. Wa qaalut-takhazal-laahu waladan Subḥaanahoo bal lahoo maa fis-samaawaati wal-arḍi kullul-lahoo qaanitoon.

وَقَالُوا اتَّخَذَ اللّٰهُ وَلَدًا ۙ سُبْحٰنَهٗ ۭ
بَلْ لَّهٗ مَا فِي السَّمٰوٰتِ وَالْاَرْضِ ۭ
كُلٌّ لَّهٗ قٰنِتُوْنَ ﴿١١٦﴾

117. To Him is due the primal origin of the heavens and the earth: when He decrees a matter, He says to it: "Be," and it is.

117. Badee'us-samaawaati wal-arḍi wa izaa qaḍaaa amran fa-innamaa yaqoolu lahoo kun fayakoon.

بَدِيْعُ السَّمٰوٰتِ وَالْاَرْضِ ۭ وَاِذَا قَضٰٓى
اَمْرًا فَاِنَّمَا يَقُوْلُ لَهٗ كُنْ فَيَكُوْنُ ﴿١١٧﴾

118. Those without knowledge say: "Why does not Allah speak to us? Or why does a Sign not come to us?" So said the people before them words of similar import. Their hearts are alike. We have indeed made clear the Signs for any people who hold firmly to Faith (in their hearts).

118. Wa qaalal-lazeena laa ya'lamoona law laa yukalli-munal-laahu aw taåteenaaa Aayah; kazaalika qaalal-lazeena min qablihim misla qawlihim; tashaabahat quloobuhum; qad bayyannal-Aayaati liqawmiñy-yooqinoon.

وَقَالَ الَّذِيْنَ لَا يَعْلَمُوْنَ لَوْلَا
يُكَلِّمُنَا اللّٰهُ اَوْ تَاْتِيْنَآ اٰيَةٌ ۭ كَذٰلِكَ
قَالَ الَّذِيْنَ مِنْ قَبْلِهِمْ مِّثْلَ قَوْلِهِمْ ۭ
تَشَابَهَتْ قُلُوْبُهُمْ ۭ قَدْ بَيَّنَّا الْاٰيٰتِ
لِقَوْمٍ يُّوْقِنُوْنَ ﴿١١٨﴾

Ikhfa اخفاء | Ghunna غُنّہ | Ikhfa Meem Saakin اخفاء میم ساکن | Idghaam ادغام | Qalqala قلقلہ | Qalb قلب | Idghaam Meem Saakin ادغام میم ساکن

119. Surely We have sent you in truth as a bearer of glad tidings and a warner: but of you no question shall be asked of the Companions of the Blazing Fire.

119. Innaaa arsalnaaka bilḥaqqi basheerañw-wa nazeerañw-wa laa tus'alu 'an Aṣḥaabil-Jaḥeem.

اِنَّآ اَرْسَلْنٰكَ بِالْحَقِّ بَشِيْرًا وَّنَذِيْرًا ۙ
وَّلَا تُسْـَٔلُ عَنْ اَصْحٰبِ الْجَحِيْمِ ﴿١١٩﴾

120. Never will the Jews or the Christians be satisfied with you unless you follow their form of religion. Say: "The Guidance of Allah,- that is the (only) Guidance." If you were to follow their desires after the knowledge which has reached you, then would you find neither Protector nor Helper against Allah.

120. Wa lan tarḍaa 'ankal-Yahoodu wa lan-Naṣaaraa ḥattaa tattabi'a millatahum; qul inna hudal-laahi huwalhudaa; wa la'init-taba'ta ahwaaa'ahum ba'dal-lazee jaaa'aka minal-'ilmi maa laka minal-laahi miñw-waliyyiñw-wa laa naṣeer.

وَلَنْ تَرْضٰى عَنْكَ الْيَهُوْدُ وَلَا
النَّصٰرٰى حَتّٰى تَتَّبِعَ مِلَّتَهُمْ ؕ قُلْ
اِنَّ هُدَى اللّٰهِ هُوَ الْهُدٰى ؕ وَلَئِنِ
اتَّبَعْتَ اَهْوَآءَهُمْ بَعْدَ الَّذِىْ
جَآءَكَ مِنَ الْعِلْمِ ۙ مَا لَكَ مِنَ
اللّٰهِ مِنْ وَّلِىٍّ وَّلَا نَصِيْرٍ ﴿١٢٠﴾ وقف منزل

121. Those to whom We have sent the Book study it as it should be studied: they are the ones that believe therein: those who reject faith therein, - the loss is their own.

121. Allazeena aataynaahumul-Kitaaba yatloonahoo ḥaqqa tilaawatiheee ulaaa'ika yu'mi-noona bih; wa mañy-yakfur bihee fa-ulaaa'ika humul-khaasiroon.

(Section 14)

اَلَّذِيْنَ اٰتَيْنٰهُمُ الْكِتٰبَ يَتْلُوْنَهٗ حَقَّ
تِلَاوَتِهٖ ؕ اُولٰٓئِكَ يُؤْمِنُوْنَ بِهٖ ؕ وَمَنْ
يَّكْفُرْ بِهٖ فَاُولٰٓئِكَ هُمُ الْخٰسِرُوْنَ ﴿١٢١﴾ ع

122. O Children of Israel! call to mind the special favour which I bestowed upon you, and that I preferred you to all others (for My Message).

122. Yaa Baneee-Israaa'eelaz-kuroo ni'matiyal-lateee an'amtu 'alaykum wa annee faḍḍaltukum 'alal-'aalameen.

يٰبَنِىْٓ اِسْرَآءِيْلَ اذْكُرُوْا نِعْمَتِىَ
الَّتِىْٓ اَنْعَمْتُ عَلَيْكُمْ وَاَنِّىْ فَضَّلْتُكُمْ
عَلَى الْعٰلَمِيْنَ ﴿١٢٢﴾

123. Then guard yourselves against a Day when one soul shall not avail another, nor shall compensation be accepted from her nor shall intercession profit her nor shall anyone be helped (from outside).

123. Wattaqoo Yawmal-laa tajzee nafsun 'an nafsin shay-'añw-wa laa yuqbalu minhaa 'adluñw-wa laa tanfa'uhaa shafaa'atuñw-wa laa hum yunṣaroon.

وَاتَّقُوْا يَوْمًا لَّا تَجْزِىْ نَفْسٌ
عَنْ نَّفْسٍ شَيْـًٔا وَّلَا يُقْبَلُ مِنْهَا
عَدْلٌ وَّلَا تَنْفَعُهَا شَفَاعَةٌ وَّلَا
هُمْ يُنْصَرُوْنَ ﴿١٢٣﴾

124. And remember that Abraham was tried by his Lord with certain commands, which he fulfilled: He said: "I will make you an Imam to the Nations." He pleaded: "And also (Imams) from my offspring!" He answered: "But My Promise is not within the reach of evil-doers."

124. Wa izib-talaaa Ibraaheema Rabbuhoo bi-Kalimaatin fa-atammahunna qaala Innee jaa'iluka linnaasi Imaaman qaala wa min zurriyyatee qaala laa yanaalu 'Ahdiz-zaalimeen.

وَاِذِ ابْتَلٰٓى اِبْرٰهٖمَ رَبُّهٗ بِكَلِمٰتٍ
فَاَتَمَّهُنَّ ؕ قَالَ اِنِّىْ جَاعِلُكَ لِلنَّاسِ
اِمَامًا ؕ قَالَ وَمِنْ ذُرِّيَّتِىْ ؕ قَالَ
لَا يَنَالُ عَهْدِى الظّٰلِمِيْنَ ﴿١٢٤﴾

125. And remember, We made the House a place of assembly for men and a place of safety; and take you the station of Abraham as a place of prayer; and We covenanted with Abraham and Isma'il, that they should sanctify My House for those who compass it round,

125. Wa iz ja'alnal-Bayta maṣaabatal-linnaasi wa amnañw wattakhizoo mim-Maqaami Ibraaheema muṣallaa; wa 'ahidnaaa ilaaa Ibraaheema wa Ismaa'eela an ṭahhiraa Baytiya liṭṭaaa'ifeena

وَاِذْ جَعَلْنَا الْبَيْتَ مَثَابَةً لِّلنَّاسِ
وَاَمْنًا ؕ وَاتَّخِذُوْا مِنْ مَّقَامِ
اِبْرٰهٖمَ مُصَلًّى ؕ وَعَهِدْنَآ اِلٰٓى اِبْرٰهٖمَ وَ
اِسْمٰعِيْلَ اَنْ طَهِّرَا بَيْتِىَ لِلطَّآئِفِيْنَ

Ikhfa اخفاء | Ghunna غنّہ | Ikhfa Meem Saakin اخفاء میم ساکن | Idghaam ادغام | Qalqala قلقلہ | Qalb قلب | Idghaam Meem Saakin ادغام میم ساکن

or use it as a retreat, or bow, or prostrate themselves (therein in prayer).

126. And remember, Abraham said: "My Lord, make this a City of Peace, and feed its people with fruits,- such of them as believe in Allah and the Last Day." He said: "(Yes), and such as reject Faith,- for a while will I grant them their pleasure, but will soon drive them to the torment of Fire, - an evil destination (indeed)!"

127. And remember, Abraham and Isma'il raised the foundations of the House (with this prayer): "Our Lord! accept (this service) from us: for You are the All-Hearing, the All-Knowing.

128. "Our Lord! make of us Muslims, bowing to Your (Will), and of our progeny a people Muslim, bowing to Your (Will); and show us our place for the celebration of (due) rites; and turn unto us (in Mercy); for You are the Oft-Returning, Most Merciful.

129. "Our Lord! send among them an Apostle of their own, who shall rehearse Your Signs to them and instruct them in scripture and wisdom, and sanctify them: for You are the Exalted in Might, the Wise."

130. And who turns away from the religion of Abraham but such as debase their souls with folly? Him We chose and rendered pure in this world: and he will be in the Hereafter in the ranks of the Righteous.

131. Behold! his Lord said to him: "Bow (your will to Me):" he said: "I bow (my will) to the Lord and Cherisher of the Universe."

132. And this was the legacy that Abraham left to his sons, and so did Jacob; "Oh my sons! Allah has chosen the Faith for you;

wal'aakifeena warrukka'is-sujood.

126. Wa iz qaala Ibraaheemu Rabbij-'al haazaa baladan aaminañw-warzuq ahlahoo minas-samaraati man aamana minhum billaahi wal-Yawmil Aakhiri qaala wa man kafara fa-umatti'uhoo qaleelan summa adtarruhooo ilaa 'azaabin-Naari wa bi'salmaseer.

127. Wa iz yarfa'u Ibraaheemul-qawaa'ida minal-Bayti wa Ismaa'eelu Rabbanaa taqabbal minnaa innaka Antas-Samee'ul-'Aleem.

128. Rabbanaa waj'alnaa muslimayni laka wa min zurriyyatinaaa ummatam-muslimatal-laka wa arinaa manaasikanaa wa tub 'alaynaa innaka Antat-Tawwaabur-Raheem.

129. Rabbanaa wab'as feehim Rasoolam-minhum yatloo 'alayhim Aayaatika wa yu'allimuhumul-Kitaaba wal-Hikmata wa yuzakkeehim; innaka Antal-'Azeezul-Hakeem. **(Section 15)**

130. Wa mañy-yarghabu 'am-Millati Ibraaheema illaa man safiha nafsah; wa laqadiṣ-ṭafaynaahu fid-dunyaa wa innahoo fil-Aakhirati laminaṣ-ṣaaliḥeen.

131. Iz qaala lahoo Rabbuhooo aslim qaala aslamtu li-Rabbil-'aalameen.

132. Wa waṣṣaa bihaaa Ibraaheemu baneehi wa Ya'qoob, yaa baniyya innal laahaṣ-ṭafaa lakumud-deena

وَالْعٰكِفِيْنَ وَالرُّكَّعِ السُّجُوْدِ ﴿١٢٥﴾
وَاِذْ قَالَ اِبْرٰهٖمُ رَبِّ اجْعَلْ هٰذَا بَلَدًا
اٰمِنًا وَّارْزُقْ اَهْلَهٗ مِنَ الثَّمَرٰتِ مَنْ
اٰمَنَ مِنْهُمْ بِاللّٰهِ وَالْيَوْمِ الْاٰخِرِ ؕ
قَالَ وَمَنْ كَفَرَ فَاُمَتِّعُهٗ قَلِيْلًا
ثُمَّ اَضْطَرُّهٗۤ اِلٰى عَذَابِ النَّارِ ؕ وَ
بِئْسَ الْمَصِيْرُ ﴿١٢٦﴾
وَاِذْ يَرْفَعُ اِبْرٰهٖمُ الْقَوَاعِدَ مِنَ
الْبَيْتِ وَاِسْمٰعِيْلُ ؕ رَبَّنَا تَقَبَّلْ مِنَّا ؕ
اِنَّكَ اَنْتَ السَّمِيْعُ الْعَلِيْمُ ﴿١٢٧﴾
رَبَّنَا وَاجْعَلْنَا مُسْلِمَيْنِ لَكَ وَمِنْ
ذُرِّيَّتِنَآ اُمَّةً مُّسْلِمَةً لَّكَ ۪ وَاَرِنَا
مَنَاسِكَنَا وَتُبْ عَلَيْنَا ۚ اِنَّكَ اَنْتَ
التَّوَّابُ الرَّحِيْمُ ﴿١٢٨﴾
رَبَّنَا وَابْعَثْ فِيْهِمْ رَسُوْلًا مِّنْهُمْ
يَتْلُوْا عَلَيْهِمْ اٰيٰتِكَ وَيُعَلِّمُهُمُ
الْكِتٰبَ وَالْحِكْمَةَ وَيُزَكِّيْهِمْ ؕ اِنَّكَ
اَنْتَ الْعَزِيْزُ الْحَكِيْمُ ﴿١٢٩﴾ ع ١٥
وَمَنْ يَّرْغَبُ عَنْ مِّلَّةِ اِبْرٰهٖمَ اِلَّا
مَنْ سَفِهَ نَفْسَهٗ ؕ وَلَقَدِ اصْطَفَيْنٰهُ
فِى الدُّنْيَا ۚ وَاِنَّهٗ فِى الْاٰخِرَةِ
لَمِنَ الصّٰلِحِيْنَ ﴿١٣٠﴾
اِذْ قَالَ لَهٗ رَبُّهٗۤ اَسْلِمْ ۙ قَالَ
اَسْلَمْتُ لِرَبِّ الْعٰلَمِيْنَ ﴿١٣١﴾
وَوَصّٰى بِهَآ اِبْرٰهٖمُ بَنِيْهِ وَيَعْقُوْبُ ؕ
يٰبَنِىَّ اِنَّ اللّٰهَ اصْطَفٰى لَكُمُ الدِّيْنَ

Ikhfa اخفاء | Ghunna غُنّہ | Ikhfa Meem Saakin اخفاء میم ساکن | Idghaam ادغام | Qalqala قلقلہ | Qalb قلب | Idghaam Meem Saakin ادغام میم ساکن

then die not except in the Faith of Islam."

133. Were you witnesses when Death appeared before Jacob? Be-hold, he said to his sons: "What will you worship after me?" They said: "We shall worship your God (Allah) and the God (Allah) of your fathers, of Abraham, Isma'il and Isaac, - the One (True) God (Allah): to Him we bow (in Islam)."

134. That was a people that has passed away. They shall reap the fruit of what they did, and you of what you do! Of their merits there is no question in your case!

135. They say: "Become Jews or Christians if any would be guided (to salvation)." You say: "Nay! (I would rather) the Religion of Abraham the True, and he joined not gods with Allah."

136. You say: "We believe in Allah, and the revelation given to us, and to Abraham, Isma'il, Isaac, Jacob, and the Tribes, and that given to Moses and Jesus, and that given to (all) prophets from their Lord: we make no difference between one and another of them: and we bow to Allah (in Islam)."

137. So if they believe as you believe, they are indeed on the right path; but if they turn back, it is they who are in schism; but Allah will suffice you as against them, and He is the All-Hearing, the All-Knowing.

138. (Our religion is) the Baptism of Allah: and who can beptize better than Allah? And it is He Whom we worship.

139. Say: Will you dispute with us about Allah, seeing that He is our Lord and your Lord; that we are responsible for our doings and you for

falaa tamootunna illaa wa antum muslimoon.

133. Am kuntum shuhadaaa'a iz̲ ḥaḍara Ya'qoobal-mawtu iz̲ qaala libaneehi maa ta'budoona mim ba'dee qaaloo na'budu ilaahaka wa ilaaha aabaaa'ika Ibraaheema wa Ismaa'eela wa Isḥaaqa Ilaahañw-waaḥidañw-wa naḥnu lahoo muslimoon.

134. Tilka ummatun qad khalat lahaa maa kasabat wa lakum maa kasabtum wa laa tus'aloona 'ammaa kaanoo ya'maloon.

135. Wa qaaloo koonoo Hoodan aw Naṣaaraa tahtadoo; qul bal Millata Ibraaheema Ḥaneefañw-wa maa kaana minal mush-rikeen.

136. Qoolooo aamannaa bil-laahi wa maaa unzila ilaynaa wa maaa unzila ilaaa Ibraaheema wa Ismaa'eela wa Isḥaaqa wa Ya'qooba wal-Asbaaṭi wa maaa ootiya Moosaa wa 'Eesaa wa maaa ootiyan Nabiyyoona mir-Rabbihim laa nufarriqu bayna aḥadim-minhum wa naḥnu lahoo muslimoon.

137. Fa-in aamanoo bimis̲li maaa aamantum bihee faqadih-tadaw wa-in tawallaw fa-innamaa hum fee shiqaaq; fasayakfeekahumul-laah; wa Huwas-Samee'ul-'Aleem.

138. Ṣibghatal-laahi wa man aḥsanu minal-laahi ṣibghatañw-wa naḥnu lahoo 'aabidoon.

139. Qul atuḥaaajjoonanaa fil-laahi wa Huwa Rabbunaa wa Rabbukum wa lanaaa a'maa-lunaa wa lakum

فَلَا تَمُوتُنَّ إِلَّا وَأَنتُم مُّسْلِمُونَ ﴿١٣٢﴾
أَمْ كُنتُمْ شُهَدَآءَ إِذْ حَضَرَ يَعْقُوبَ
الْمَوْتُ إِذْ قَالَ لِبَنِيهِ مَا تَعْبُدُونَ
مِنۢ بَعْدِى قَالُوا نَعْبُدُ إِلَٰهَكَ وَإِلَٰهَ
ءَابَآئِكَ إِبْرَٰهِيمَ وَإِسْمَٰعِيلَ وَإِسْحَٰقَ
إِلَٰهًا وَٰحِدًا وَنَحْنُ لَهُۥ مُسْلِمُونَ ﴿١٣٣﴾
تِلْكَ أُمَّةٌ قَدْ خَلَتْ لَهَا مَا كَسَبَتْ
وَلَكُم مَّا كَسَبْتُمْ وَلَا تُسْـَٔلُونَ
عَمَّا كَانُوا يَعْمَلُونَ ﴿١٣٤﴾
وَقَالُوا كُونُوا هُودًا أَوْ نَصَٰرَىٰ تَهْتَدُوا
قُلْ بَلْ مِلَّةَ إِبْرَٰهِيمَ حَنِيفًا وَمَا
كَانَ مِنَ الْمُشْرِكِينَ ﴿١٣٥﴾
قُولُوٓا ءَامَنَّا بِاللَّهِ وَمَآ أُنزِلَ إِلَيْنَا
وَمَآ أُنزِلَ إِلَىٰٓ إِبْرَٰهِيمَ وَإِسْمَٰعِيلَ
وَإِسْحَٰقَ وَيَعْقُوبَ وَالْأَسْبَاطِ وَمَآ
أُوتِىَ مُوسَىٰ وَعِيسَىٰ وَمَآ أُوتِىَ
النَّبِيُّونَ مِن رَّبِّهِمْ لَا نُفَرِّقُ بَيْنَ
أَحَدٍ مِّنْهُمْ وَنَحْنُ لَهُۥ مُسْلِمُونَ ﴿١٣٦﴾
فَإِنْ ءَامَنُوا بِمِثْلِ مَآ ءَامَنتُم بِهِۦ فَقَدِ
اهْتَدَوا وَّإِن تَوَلَّوْا فَإِنَّمَا هُمْ فِى
شِقَاقٍ فَسَيَكْفِيكَهُمُ اللَّهُ
وَهُوَ السَّمِيعُ الْعَلِيمُ ﴿١٣٧﴾
صِبْغَةَ اللَّهِ وَمَنْ أَحْسَنُ مِنَ اللَّهِ
صِبْغَةً وَنَحْنُ لَهُۥ عَٰبِدُونَ ﴿١٣٨﴾
قُلْ أَتُحَآجُّونَنَا فِى اللَّهِ وَهُوَ رَبُّنَا
وَرَبُّكُمْ وَلَنَآ أَعْمَٰلُنَا وَلَكُمْ

Ikhfa اخفاء | Ghunna غُنّہ | Ikhfa Meem Saakin اخفاء میم ساکن | Idghaam ادغام | Qalqala قلقلہ | Qalb قلب | Idghaam Meem Saakin ادغام میم ساکن

yours; and that we are sincere (in our faith) in Him?

a'maalukum wa naḥnu lahoo mukhliṣoon.

اَعْمَالُكُمْ ۚ وَنَحْنُ لَهٗ مُخْلِصُوْنَ ﴿١٣٩﴾

140. Or do you say that Abraham, Isma'il, Isaac, Jacob and the Tribes were Jews or Christians? Say: Do you know better than Allah? Ah! who is more unjust than those who conceal the testimony they have from Allah? But Allah is not unmindful of what you do!

140. Am taqooloona-inna Ibraaheema wa Ismaa'eela wa Isḥaaqa wa Ya'qooba wal Asbaaṭa kaanoo Hoodan aw Naṣaaraa; qul 'a-antum a'lamu amil-laah; wa man aẓlamu mimman katama shahaadatan 'indahoo minallaah; wa mal-laahu bighaafilin 'ammaa ta'maloon.

اَمْ تَقُوْلُوْنَ اِنَّ اِبْرٰهٖمَ وَاِسْمٰعِيْلَ
وَاِسْحٰقَ وَيَعْقُوْبَ وَالْاَسْبَاطَ
كَانُوْا هُوْدًا اَوْ نَصٰرٰى ؕ قُلْ ءَاَنْتُمْ
اَعْلَمُ اَمِ اللّٰهُ ؕ وَمَنْ اَظْلَمُ مِمَّنْ
كَتَمَ شَهَادَةً عِنْدَهٗ مِنَ اللّٰهِ ؕ وَمَا
اللّٰهُ بِغَافِلٍ عَمَّا تَعْمَلُوْنَ ﴿١٤٠﴾

141. That was a people that have passed away. They shall reap the fruit of what they did, and you of what you do! Of their merits there is no question in your case:

141. Tilka ummatun qad khalat lahaa maa kasabat wa lakum maa kasabtum wa laa tus'aloona 'ammaa kaanoo ya'maloon.

(Section 16)

تِلْكَ اُمَّةٌ قَدْ خَلَتْ ۚ لَهَا مَا كَسَبَتْ
وَلَكُمْ مَّا كَسَبْتُمْ ۚ وَلَا تُسْئَلُوْنَ عَمَّا
كَانُوْا يَعْمَلُوْنَ ﴿١٤١﴾ ع

الجزء الثاني (٢) ع ١

142. The fools among the people will say: "What has turned them from the Qibla to which they were used?" Say: To Allah belong both East and West: He guides whom He will to a Way that is straight.

142. Sayaqoolus-sufahaaa'u minan-naasi maa wallaahum 'an Qiblatihimul-latee kaanoo 'alayhaa; qul lillaahil mashriqu walmaghrib; yahdee mañy-yashaaa'u ilaa Ṣiraaṭim-Mustaqeem.

سَيَقُوْلُ السُّفَهَآءُ مِنَ النَّاسِ
مَا وَلّٰىهُمْ عَنْ قِبْلَتِهِمُ الَّتِیْ
كَانُوْا عَلَيْهَا ؕ قُلْ لِّلّٰهِ الْمَشْرِقُ وَ
الْمَغْرِبُ ؕ يَهْدِیْ مَنْ يَّشَآءُ اِلٰى
صِرَاطٍ مُّسْتَقِيْمٍ ﴿١٤٢﴾

143. Thus, have We made of you an Ummat justly balanced, that you might be witnesses over the nations, and the Apostle a witness over yourselves; and We appointed the Qibla to which you were used, only to test those who followed the Apostle from those who would turn on their heels (from the Faith). Indeed it was (a change) momentous, except to those guided by Allah. And never would Allah make your faith of no effect. For Allah is to all people most surely full of kindness, Most Merciful.

143. Wa kaẕaalika ja'alnaakum ummatañw-wasaṭal-litakoonoo shuhadaaa'a 'alan-naasi wa yakoonar-Rasoolu 'alaykum shaheedaa; wa maa ja'alnal-Qiblatal-latee kunta 'alayhaaa illaa lina'lama mañy-yattabi'ur-Rasoola mimmañy-yanqalibu 'alaa 'aqibayh; wa in kaanat lakabeeratan illaa 'alal-laẕeena hadal-laah; wa maa kaanal-laahu liyuḍee'a eemaanakum; innal-laaha binnaasi la-Ra'oofur-Raḥeem.

وَكَذٰلِكَ جَعَلْنٰكُمْ اُمَّةً وَّسَطًا
لِّتَكُوْنُوْا شُهَدَآءَ عَلَى النَّاسِ
وَيَكُوْنَ الرَّسُوْلُ عَلَيْكُمْ شَهِيْدًا ؕ
وَمَا جَعَلْنَا الْقِبْلَةَ الَّتِیْ كُنْتَ عَلَيْهَاۤ
اِلَّا لِنَعْلَمَ مَنْ يَّتَّبِعُ الرَّسُوْلَ مِمَّنْ
يَّنْقَلِبُ عَلٰى عَقِبَيْهِ ؕ وَاِنْ كَانَتْ
لَكَبِيْرَةً اِلَّا عَلَى الَّذِيْنَ هَدَى اللّٰهُ ؕ
وَمَا كَانَ اللّٰهُ لِيُضِيْعَ اِيْمَانَكُمْ ؕ اِنَّ
اللّٰهَ بِالنَّاسِ لَرَءُوْفٌ رَّحِيْمٌ ﴿١٤٣﴾

144. We see the turning of your face (for guidance) to the heavens: now shall We turn you to a Qibla that shall please you. Turn then

144. Qad naraa taqalluba wajhika fis-samaaa'i falanuwalliyannaka Qiblatan tarḍaahaa; fawalli

قَدْ نَرٰى تَقَلُّبَ وَجْهِكَ فِى السَّمَآءِ ۚ
فَلَنُوَلِّيَنَّكَ قِبْلَةً تَرْضٰهَا ۪ فَوَلِّ

Ikhfa اخفاء | Ghunna غُنَّہ | Ikhfa Meem Saakin اخفاء میم ساکن | Idghaam ادغام | Qalqala قلقلہ | Qalb قلب | Idghaam Meem Saakin ادغام میم ساکن

your face in the direction of the sacred Mosque: wherever you are, turn your faces in that direction. The people of the Book know well that that is the truth from their Lord. Nor is Allah unmindful of what they do.

wajhaka shatral-Masjidil-Ḥaraam; wa ḥaysu maa kuntum fawalloo wujoohakum shatrah; wa innal-lazeena ootul-Kitaaba laya'lamoona annahul-ḥaqqu mir-Rabbihim; wa mal-laahu bighaafilin 'ammaa ya'maloon.

وَجْهَكَ شَطْرَ الْمَسْجِدِ الْحَرَامِ ۚ وَحَيْثُ
مَا كُنْتُمْ فَوَلُّوا وُجُوهَكُمْ شَطْرَهُ ۗ
وَإِنَّ الَّذِينَ أُوتُوا الْكِتَابَ لَيَعْلَمُونَ
أَنَّهُ الْحَقُّ مِنْ رَبِّهِمْ ۗ وَمَا اللَّهُ
بِغَافِلٍ عَمَّا يَعْمَلُونَ ﴿١٤٤﴾

145. Even if you were to bring to the people of the Book all the Signs (together), they would not follow your Qibla; nor are you going to follow their Qibla; nor indeed will they follow each other's Qibla. If you after the knowledge has reached you were to follow their (vain) desires,- then you were indeed (clearly) in the wrong.

145. Wa la'in ataytal-lazeena ootul-Kitaaba bikulli Aayatim-maa tabi'oo Qiblatak; wa maaa anta bitaabi'in-Qiblatahum; wa maa ba'ḍuhum bitaabi'in Qiblata ba'ḍ; wa la'init-taba'ta ahwaaa'ahum mim ba'di maa jaaa'aka minal-'ilmi innaka izal-laminaz-zaalimeen.

وَلَئِنْ أَتَيْتَ الَّذِينَ أُوتُوا الْكِتَابَ
بِكُلِّ آيَةٍ مَا تَبِعُوا قِبْلَتَكَ ۚ وَمَا
أَنْتَ بِتَابِعٍ قِبْلَتَهُمْ ۚ وَمَا بَعْضُهُمْ
بِتَابِعٍ قِبْلَةَ بَعْضٍ ۚ وَلَئِنِ اتَّبَعْتَ
أَهْوَاءَهُمْ مِنْ بَعْدِ مَا جَاءَكَ مِنَ
الْعِلْمِ ۙ إِنَّكَ إِذًا لَمِنَ الظَّالِمِينَ ﴿١٤٥﴾ وقف لازم

146. The people of the Book know this as they know their own sons; but some of them conceal the truth which they themselves know.

146. Allazeena-aataynaahumul Kitaaba ya'rifoonahoo kamaa ya'rifoona abnaaa'ahum wa inna fareeqam-minhum layaktumoonal-ḥaqqa wa hum ya'lamoon.

الَّذِينَ آتَيْنَاهُمُ الْكِتَابَ يَعْرِفُونَهُ
كَمَا يَعْرِفُونَ أَبْنَاءَهُمْ ۖ وَإِنَّ فَرِيقًا
مِنْهُمْ لَيَكْتُمُونَ الْحَقَّ وَهُمْ يَعْلَمُونَ ﴿١٤٦﴾ وقف منزل ١٢

147. The Truth is from your Lord; so be not at all in doubt.

147. Alḥaqqu mir-Rabbika falaa takoonanna minal-mumtareen. **(Section 17)**

الْحَقُّ مِنْ رَبِّكَ ۖ فَلَا تَكُونَنَّ مِنَ
الْمُمْتَرِينَ ﴿١٤٧﴾ ع

148. To each is a goal to which Allah turns him; then strive together (as in a race) toward all that is good. Wheresoever you are, Allah will bring you together. For Allah has power over all things.

148. Wa likulliñw-wijhatun huwa muwalleehaa fastabiqul-khayraat; ayna maa takoonoo yaâti bikumullaahu jamee'aa; innal-laaha 'alaa kulli shay'in Qadeer.

وَلِكُلٍّ وِجْهَةٌ هُوَ مُوَلِّيهَا ۖ فَاسْتَبِقُوا
الْخَيْرَاتِ ۚ أَيْنَ مَا تَكُونُوا يَأْتِ بِكُمُ
اللَّهُ جَمِيعًا ۚ إِنَّ اللَّهَ عَلَىٰ كُلِّ شَيْءٍ
قَدِيرٌ ﴿١٤٨﴾

149. From wheresoever you start forth, turn your face in the direction of the Sacred Mosque; that is indeed the truth from the Lord. And Allah is not unmindful of what you do.

149. Wa min ḥaysu kharajta fawalli wajhaka shatral-Masjidil-Ḥaraami wa innahoo lalḥaqqu mir-Rabbik; wa mallaahu bighaafilin 'ammaa ta'maloon.

وَمِنْ حَيْثُ خَرَجْتَ فَوَلِّ وَجْهَكَ
شَطْرَ الْمَسْجِدِ الْحَرَامِ ۖ وَإِنَّهُ لَلْحَقُّ
مِنْ رَبِّكَ ۗ وَمَا اللَّهُ بِغَافِلٍ عَمَّا
تَعْمَلُونَ ﴿١٤٩﴾

150. So from wheresoever you start forth, turn your face in the direction of the Sacred Mosque; and wheresoever

150. Wa min ḥaysu kharajta fawalli wajhaka shatral-Masjidil-Ḥaraam; wa ḥaysu maa

وَمِنْ حَيْثُ خَرَجْتَ فَوَلِّ وَجْهَكَ
شَطْرَ الْمَسْجِدِ الْحَرَامِ ۚ وَحَيْثُ مَا

وقف النبي صلى الله عليه وآله وسلم ١٢

Ikhfa اخفاء | Ghunna غُنّہ | Ikhfa Meem Saakin اخفاء میم ساکن | Idghaam ادغام | Qalqala قلقلہ | Qalb قلب | Idghaam Meem Saakin ادغام میم ساکن

you are, turn your face to it: that there be no ground of dispute against you among the people, except those of them that are bent on wickedness; so fear them not, but fear Me; and that I may complete My favours on you, and you May (consent to) be guided;

kuntum fawalloo wujoohakum shaṭrahoo li'allaa yakoona linnaasi 'alaykum ḥujjatun illal-lazeena ẓalamoo minhum falaa takhshawhum wakhshawnee wa liutimma ni'matee 'alaykum wa la'allakum tahtadoon.

كُنتُمْ فَوَلُّوا وُجُوهَكُمْ شَطْرَهُ لِئَلَّا
يَكُونَ لِلنَّاسِ عَلَيْكُمْ حُجَّةٌ
إِلَّا الَّذِينَ ظَلَمُوا مِنْهُمْ فَلَا
تَخْشَوْهُمْ وَاخْشَوْنِي وَلِأُتِمَّ نِعْمَتِي
عَلَيْكُمْ وَلَعَلَّكُمْ تَهْتَدُونَ ١٥٠

151. A similar (favour have you already received) in that We have sent among you an Apostle of your own, rehearsing to you Our Signs, and sanctifying you, and instructing you in Scripture and Wisdom, and in new Knowledge.

151. Kamaaa arsalnaa feekum Rasoolam-minkum yatloo 'alaykum Aayaatinaa wa yuzakkeekum wa yu'allimukumul-Kitaaba wal-Ḥikmata wa yu'allimukum maa lam takoonoo ta'lamoon.

كَمَا أَرْسَلْنَا فِيكُمْ رَسُولًا مِّنكُمْ
يَتْلُوا عَلَيْكُمْ آيَاتِنَا وَيُزَكِّيكُمْ
وَيُعَلِّمُكُمُ الْكِتَابَ وَالْحِكْمَةَ
وَيُعَلِّمُكُم مَّا لَمْ تَكُونُوا تَعْلَمُونَ ١٥١

152. Then you remember Me; I will remember you. Be grateful to Me, and reject not Faith.

152. Fazkurooneee azkurkum washkuroo lee wa laa takfuroon. **(Section 18)**

فَاذْكُرُونِي أَذْكُرْكُمْ وَاشْكُرُوا لِي
وَلَا تَكْفُرُونِ ١٥٢

153. O you who believe! seek help with patient perseverance and prayer; for Allah is with those who patiently persevere.

153. Yaaa ayyuhal-lazeena aamanus-ta'eenoo biṣṣabri waṣ-Ṣalaah; innal-laaha ma'aṣ-ṣaabireen.

يَا أَيُّهَا الَّذِينَ آمَنُوا اسْتَعِينُوا بِالصَّبْرِ
وَالصَّلَاةِ إِنَّ اللَّهَ مَعَ الصَّابِرِينَ ١٥٣

154. And say not of those who are slain in the way of Allah: "They are dead." Nay, they are living, though you perceive (it) not.

154. Wa laa taqooloo limañy-yuqtalu fee sabeelil-laahi amwaat; bal aḥyaaa'uñw-wa laakil-laa tash'uroon.

وَلَا تَقُولُوا لِمَن يُقْتَلُ فِي سَبِيلِ اللَّهِ
أَمْوَاتٌ بَلْ أَحْيَاءٌ وَلَٰكِن لَّا تَشْعُرُونَ ١٥٤

155. Be sure We shall test you with something of fear and hunger, some loss in goods or lives or the fruits (of your toil), but give glad tidings to those who patiently persevere,

155. Wa lanablu-wannakum bishay'im-minal-khawfi waljoo'i wa naqṣim-minal-amwaali wal-anfusi was samaraat; wa bashshiriṣ-ṣaabireen.

وَلَنَبْلُوَنَّكُم بِشَيْءٍ مِّنَ الْخَوْفِ وَالْجُوعِ
وَنَقْصٍ مِّنَ الْأَمْوَالِ وَالْأَنفُسِ
وَالثَّمَرَاتِ وَبَشِّرِ الصَّابِرِينَ ١٥٥

156. Who say, when afflicted with calamity: "To Allah we belong, and to Him is our return":-

156. Allazeena izaaa aṣaabat-hum muṣeebatun qaalooo innaa lillaahi wa innaaa ilayhi raaji'oon.

الَّذِينَ إِذَا أَصَابَتْهُم مُّصِيبَةٌ
قَالُوا إِنَّا لِلَّهِ وَإِنَّا إِلَيْهِ رَاجِعُونَ ١٥٦

157. They are those on whom (descend) blessings from Allah, and Mercy, and they are the ones that receive guidance.

157. Ulaaa'ika 'alayhim ṣalawaatum-mir-Rabbihim wa raḥmah; wa ulaaa'ika humul-muhtadoon.

أُولَٰئِكَ عَلَيْهِمْ صَلَوَاتٌ مِّن رَّبِّهِمْ وَ
رَحْمَةٌ وَأُولَٰئِكَ هُمُ الْمُهْتَدُونَ ١٥٧

158. Behold! Safa and Marwa are among the Symbols of Allah. So if those who visit the House in the Season or at other times, should compass them round, it is no sin in them. And if any one obeys his own impulse to Good,- be sure that Allah is He Who recognises and knows.

158. Innaṣ-Ṣafaa wal-Marwata min sha'aaa'iril-laahi faman ḥajjal-Bayta awi'-tamara falaa junaaḥa 'alayhi añy-yaṭṭawwafa bihimaa; wa man taṭawwa'a khayran fa-innal-laaha Shaakirun 'Aleem.

إِنَّ الصَّفَا وَالْمَرْوَةَ مِن شَعَائِرِ
اللَّهِ فَمَنْ حَجَّ الْبَيْتَ أَوِ اعْتَمَرَ فَلَا
جُنَاحَ عَلَيْهِ أَن يَطَّوَّفَ بِهِمَا وَمَن
تَطَوَّعَ خَيْرًا فَإِنَّ اللَّهَ شَاكِرٌ عَلِيمٌ ١٥٨

معانقة ٣ عند المتأخرين ١٢

Ikhfa اخفاء | Ghunna غنّہ | Ikhfa Meem Saakin اخفاء میم ساکن | Idghaam ادغام | Qalqala قلقلہ | Qalb قلب | Idghaam Meem Saakin ادغام میم ساکن

159. Those who conceal the clear (Signs) We have sent down, and the Guidance, after We have made it clear for the People in the Book,- on them shall be Allah's curse, and the curse of those entitled to curse,-

159. Innal-lazeena yaktumoona maaa anzalnaa minal-bayyinaati walhudaa mim ba'di maa bayyannaahu linnaasi fil-Kitaabi ulaaa'ika yal'anuhumul-laahu wa yal'anuhumul-laa'inoon.

إِنَّ الَّذِينَ يَكْتُمُونَ مَآ أَنزَلْنَا
مِنَ الْبَيِّنَٰتِ وَالْهُدَىٰ مِنۢ بَعْدِ
مَا بَيَّنَّٰهُ لِلنَّاسِ فِى الْكِتَٰبِ ۙ أُولَٰٓئِكَ
يَلْعَنُهُمُ اللَّهُ وَيَلْعَنُهُمُ اللَّٰعِنُونَ ﴿١٥٩﴾

160. Except those who repent and make amends and openly declare (the Truth): to them I turn; for I am Oft-returning, Most Merciful.

160. Illal-lazeena taaboo wa aslaḥoo wa bayyanoo fa-ulaaa'ika atoobu 'alayhim; wa Anat-Tawwaabur-Raḥeem.

إِلَّا الَّذِينَ تَابُوا وَأَصْلَحُوا وَبَيَّنُوا
فَأُولَٰٓئِكَ أَتُوبُ عَلَيْهِمْ ۚ وَأَنَا
التَّوَّابُ الرَّحِيمُ ﴿١٦٠﴾

161. Those who reject Faith, and die rejecting,- on them is Allah's curse, and the curse of angels, and of all mankind.

161. Innal-lazeena kafaroo wamaa-too wa hum kuffaarun ulaaa'ika 'alayhim la'natul-laahi walmalaaa'ikati wannaasi ajma'een.

إِنَّ الَّذِينَ كَفَرُوا وَمَاتُوا وَهُمْ
كُفَّارٌ أُولَٰٓئِكَ عَلَيْهِمْ لَعْنَةُ اللَّهِ
وَالْمَلَٰٓئِكَةِ وَالنَّاسِ أَجْمَعِينَ ﴿١٦١﴾

162. They will abide therein: their Chastisement will not be lightened, nor will respite be their (lot).

162. Khaalideena feehaa laa yukhaffafu 'anhumul-'azaabu wa laa hum yunzaroon.

خَٰلِدِينَ فِيهَا ۖ لَا يُخَفَّفُ عَنْهُمُ
الْعَذَابُ وَلَا هُمْ يُنظَرُونَ ﴿١٦٢﴾

163. And your God (Allah) is One God (Allah): There is no god but He, Most Gracious, Most Merciful.

163. Wa ilaahukum Ilaahuñw-waaḥid, laaa ilaaha illaa Huwar-Raḥmaanur-Raḥeem. **(Section 19)**

وَإِلَٰهُكُمْ إِلَٰهٌ وَٰحِدٌ ۖ لَّآ إِلَٰهَ إِلَّا
هُوَ الرَّحْمَٰنُ الرَّحِيمُ ﴿١٦٣﴾ ع ١٩

164. Behold! in the creation of the heavens and the earth; in the alternation of the night and the day; in the sailing of the ships through the ocean for the profit of mankind; in the rain which Allah sends down from the skies, and the life which He gives therewith to an earth that is dead; in the beasts of all kinds that He scatters through the earth; in the change of the winds, and the clouds which trail like their slaves between the sky and the earth;- (here) indeed are Signs for a people that are wise.

164. Inna fee khalqis-samaa-waati wal-arḍi wakhtilaafil-layli wannahaari walfulkil-latee tajree fil-baḥri bimaa yanfa'un-naasa wa maaa anzalal-laahu minas-samaaa'i mim-maaa'in fa-aḥyaa bihil-arḍa ba'da mawtihaa wa bas sa feehaa min kulli daaabbatiñw-wa taṣreefir-riyaaḥi wassaḥaabil-musakh-khari baynas-samaaa'i wal-arḍi la-Aayaatil-liqawmiñy-ya'qiloon.

إِنَّ فِى خَلْقِ السَّمَٰوَٰتِ وَالْأَرْضِ وَ
اخْتِلَٰفِ الَّيْلِ وَالنَّهَارِ وَالْفُلْكِ
الَّتِى تَجْرِى فِى الْبَحْرِ بِمَا يَنفَعُ
النَّاسَ وَمَآ أَنزَلَ اللَّهُ مِنَ السَّمَآءِ
مِن مَّآءٍ فَأَحْيَا بِهِ الْأَرْضَ بَعْدَ
مَوْتِهَا وَبَثَّ فِيهَا مِن كُلِّ دَآبَّةٍ
وَتَصْرِيفِ الرِّيَٰحِ وَالسَّحَابِ
الْمُسَخَّرِ بَيْنَ السَّمَآءِ وَالْأَرْضِ
لَآيَٰتٍ لِّقَوْمٍ يَعْقِلُونَ ﴿١٦٤﴾

165. Yet there are men who take (for worship) others besides Allah, as equal (with Allah): they love them as they should love Allah. But those of Faith are overflowing in their love for Allah. If

165. Wa minan-naasi mañy-yattakhizu min doonil-laahi andaadañy-yuḥibboonahum kaḥubbil-laahi wallazeena aamanooo ashaddu ḥubbal-lillaah; wa law yaral-

وَمِنَ النَّاسِ مَن يَتَّخِذُ مِن دُونِ
اللَّهِ أَندَادًا يُحِبُّونَهُمْ كَحُبِّ اللَّهِ ۖ
وَالَّذِينَ آمَنُوٓا أَشَدُّ حُبًّا لِّلَّهِ ۗ وَلَوْ يَرَى

Ikhfa	Ghunna	Ikhfa Meem Saakin	Idghaam	Qalqala	Qalb	Idghaam Meem Saakin
اخفاء	غُنّہ	اخفاء میم ساکن	ادغام	قلقلہ	قلب	ادغام میم ساکن

only the unrighteous could see, behold, they would see the Chastisement: that to Allah belongs all power, and Allah will strongly enforce the Chastisement.

laz̲eena z̲alamooo iz̲ yarawnal 'az̲aaba annal-quwwata lillaahi jamee'añw-wa annallaaha shadeedul-'az̲aab.

الَّذِينَ ظَلَمُوٓا إِذْ يَرَوْنَ الْعَذَابَ
أَنَّ الْقُوَّةَ لِلَّهِ جَمِيعًا وَّأَنَّ اللَّهَ
شَدِيدُ الْعَذَابِ ﴿١٦٥﴾

166. Then would those who are followed clear themselves of those who follow (them): they would see the Chastisement, and all relations between them would be cut off.

166. Iz̲ tabarra-al-laz̲eenat-tubi'oo minal-laz̲eenattaba'oo wa ra-awul-'az̲aaba wa taqatta'at bihimul asbaab.

إِذْ تَبَرَّأَ الَّذِينَ اتُّبِعُوا مِنَ الَّذِينَ
اتَّبَعُوا وَرَأَوُا الْعَذَابَ وَتَقَطَّعَتْ
بِهِمُ الْأَسْبَابُ ﴿١٦٦﴾

167. And those who followed would say: "If only we had one more chance, we would clear ourselves of them, as they have cleared themselves of us." Thus will Allah show them (the fruits of) their deeds as (nothing but) regrets. Nor will there be a way for them out of the Fire.

167. Wa qaalal-laz̲eenat-taba'oo law anna lanaa karratan fanatabarra-a minhum kamaa tabarra'oo minnaa; kaz̲aalika yureehimullaahu a'maalahum ḥasaraatin 'alayhim wa maa hum bikhaarijeena minan-Naar.

(Section 20)

وَقَالَ الَّذِينَ اتَّبَعُوا لَوْ أَنَّ لَنَا
كَرَّةً فَنَتَبَرَّأَ مِنْهُمْ كَمَا تَبَرَّءُوا مِنَّا
كَذَٰلِكَ يُرِيهِمُ اللَّهُ أَعْمَالَهُمْ
حَسَرَاتٍ عَلَيْهِمْ وَمَا هُمْ بِخَارِجِينَ
مِنَ النَّارِ ﴿١٦٧﴾ ع ٢٠

168. O you people! Eat of what is on earth, lawful and good; and do not follow the footsteps of the Satan, for he is to you an avowed enemy.

168. Yaaa ayyuhan-naasu kuloo mimmaa fil-arḍi ḥalaalan ṭayyibañw-wa laa tattabi'oo khuṭu-waatish-Shayṭaan; innahoo lakum 'aduwwum-mubeen.

يَا أَيُّهَا النَّاسُ كُلُوا مِمَّا فِي الْأَرْضِ
حَلَالًا طَيِّبًا وَلَا تَتَّبِعُوا خُطُوَاتِ
الشَّيْطَانِ إِنَّهُ لَكُمْ عَدُوٌّ مُبِينٌ ﴿١٦٨﴾

169. For he commands you what is evil and shameful, and that you should say of Allah that of which you have no knowledge.

169. Innamaa yaâmurukum bissooo'i walfaḥshaaa'i wa an taqooloo 'alal-laahi maa laa ta'lamoon.

إِنَّمَا يَأْمُرُكُمْ بِالسُّوءِ وَالْفَحْشَاءِ
وَأَنْ تَقُولُوا عَلَى اللَّهِ مَا لَا تَعْلَمُونَ ﴿١٦٩﴾

170. When it is said to them: "Follow what Allah has revealed:" they say: "Nay! we shall follow the ways of our fathers." What! even though their fathers were void of wisdom and guidance?

170. Wa iz̲aa qeela lahumut-tabi'oo maaa-anzalal-laahu qaaloo bal nattabi'u maaa alfaynaa 'alayhi aabaaa'anaaa; awalaw kaana aabaaa'uhum laa ya'qiloona shay'añw-wa laa yahtadoon.

وَإِذَا قِيلَ لَهُمُ اتَّبِعُوا مَا أَنْزَلَ
اللَّهُ قَالُوا بَلْ نَتَّبِعُ مَا أَلْفَيْنَا
عَلَيْهِ آبَاءَنَا أَوَلَوْ كَانَ آبَاؤُهُمْ
لَا يَعْقِلُونَ شَيْئًا وَلَا يَهْتَدُونَ ﴿١٧٠﴾

171. The parable of those who reject Faith is as if one were to shout like a goat- herd, to things that listen to nothing but calls and cries: deaf, dumb, and blind, they are void of wisdom.

171. Wa mas̲alul-laz̲eena kafaroo kamas̲alil-laz̲ee yan'iqu bimaa laa yasma'u illaa du'aaa'añw-wa nidaaa'aa; summum-bukmun 'umyun fahum laa ya'qiloon.

وَمَثَلُ الَّذِينَ كَفَرُوا كَمَثَلِ
الَّذِي يَنْعِقُ بِمَا لَا يَسْمَعُ إِلَّا
دُعَاءً وَنِدَاءً صُمٌّ بُكْمٌ عُمْيٌ
فَهُمْ لَا يَعْقِلُونَ ﴿١٧١﴾

172. O you who believe! Eat of the good things that We have provided for you and be grateful

172. Yaaa ayyuhal-laz̲eena aamanoo kuloo min ṭayyibaati maa razaqnaakum washkuroo

يَا أَيُّهَا الَّذِينَ آمَنُوا كُلُوا مِنْ
طَيِّبَاتِ مَا رَزَقْنَاكُمْ وَاشْكُرُوا

Ikhfa اخفاء | Ghunna غنّہ | Ikhfa Meem Saakin اخفاء میم ساکن | Idghaam ادغام | Qalqala قلقلہ | Qalb قلب | Idghaam Meem Saakin ادغام میم ساکن

to allah, if it is Him you worship.

lillaahi in kuntum iyyaahu ta'budoon.

لِلّٰهِ اِنۡ كُنۡتُمۡ اِيَّاهُ تَعۡبُدُوۡنَ ﴿۱۷۲﴾

173. He has only forbidden you dead meat, and blood, and the flesh of swine, and that on which any other name has been invoked besides that of Allah. But if one is forced by necessity, without wilful disobedience, nor transgressing due limits,- then is he guiltless, for Allah is Oft-Forgiving, Most Merciful.

173. Innamaa ḥarrama 'alaykumul-maytata waddama wa laḥmal-khinzeeri wa maaa uhilla bihee lighayril-laahi famaniḍ-ṭurra ghayra baaghiñw-wa laa 'aadin falaaa isma 'alayh; innal-laaha Ghafoorur-Raḥeem.

اِنَّمَا حَرَّمَ عَلَيۡكُمُ الۡمَيۡتَةَ وَالدَّمَ
وَلَحۡمَ الۡخِنۡزِيۡرِ وَمَاۤ اُهِلَّ بِهٖ لِغَيۡرِ
اللّٰهِ ۚ فَمَنِ اضۡطُرَّ غَيۡرَ بَاغٍ وَّلَا
عَادٍ فَلَاۤ اِثۡمَ عَلَيۡهِ ؕ اِنَّ اللّٰهَ
غَفُوۡرٌ رَّحِيۡمٌ ﴿۱۷۳﴾

174. Those who conceal Allah's revelations in the Book, and purchase for them a miserable profit,- they swallow into themselves nothing but Fire; Allah will not address them on the Day of Resurrection, nor purify them: grievous will be their Chastisement.

174. Innal-lazeena yaktumoona maaa anzalal laahu minal-Kitaabi wa yashtaroona bihee samanan qaleelan ulaaa'ika maa yaåkuloona fee buṭoonihim illan-Naara wa laa yukallimu-humul-laahu Yawmal Qiyaamati wa laa yuzakkeehim wa lahum 'azaabun aleem.

اِنَّ الَّذِيۡنَ يَكۡتُمُوۡنَ مَاۤ اَنۡزَلَ اللّٰهُ
مِنَ الۡكِتٰبِ وَيَشۡتَرُوۡنَ بِهٖ ثَمَنًا
قَلِيۡلًا ۙ اُولٰٓـئِكَ مَا يَاۡكُلُوۡنَ فِىۡ
بُطُوۡنِهِمۡ اِلَّا النَّارَ وَلَا يُكَلِّمُهُمُ
اللّٰهُ يَوۡمَ الۡقِيٰمَةِ وَلَا يُزَكِّيۡهِمۡ ۖۚ
وَلَهُمۡ عَذَابٌ اَلِيۡمٌ ﴿۱۷۴﴾

175. They are the ones who buy Error in place of Guidance and Torment in place of Forgiveness. Ah! what boldness (they show) for the Fire!

175. Ulaaa'ikal-lazeenash-tarawuḍ-ḍalaalata bilhudaa wal'azaaba bilmaghfirah; famaaa asbarahum 'alan-Naar.

اُولٰٓـئِكَ الَّذِيۡنَ اشۡتَرَوُا الضَّلٰلَةَ
بِالۡهُدٰى وَالۡعَذَابَ بِالۡمَغۡفِرَةِ ۚ
فَمَاۤ اَصۡبَرَهُمۡ عَلَى النَّارِ ﴿۱۷۵﴾

176. (Their doom is) because Allah sent down the Book in truth but those who seek causes of dispute in the Book are in a schism far (from the purpose).

176. Zaalika bi-annal-laaha nazzalal-Kitaaba bilḥaqq; wa innal-lazeenakh-talafoo fil-Kitaabi lafee shiqaaqim ba'eed.

(Section 21)

ذٰلِكَ بِاَنَّ اللّٰهَ نَزَّلَ الۡكِتٰبَ بِالۡحَقِّ ؕ
وَاِنَّ الَّذِيۡنَ اخۡتَلَفُوۡا فِى الۡكِتٰبِ
لَفِىۡ شِقَاقٍۢ بَعِيۡدٍ ﴿۱۷۶﴾ ع

177. It is not righteousness that you turn your faces toward East or West; but it is righteousness - to believe in Allah and the Last Day, and the Angels, and the Book, and the Messengers; to spend of your substance, out of love for Him, for your kin, for orphans, for the needy, for the wayfarer, for those who ask, and for the ransom of slaves; to be steadfast in prayer, and practice regular charity; to fulfil the

177. Laysal-birra an tuwalloo wujoohakum qibalal-mashriqi walmaghribi wa laakinnal birra man aamana billaahi wal-Yawmil-Aakhiri walmalaaa-'ikati wal-Kitaabi wan-Nabiyyeena wa aatalmaala 'alaa ḥubbihee zawilqurbaa walyataamaa walmasaakeena wabnas-sabeeli wassaaa'ileena wa firriqaabi wa aqaamaṣ-Ṣalaata wa aataz-Zakaata walmoofoona

لَيۡسَ الۡبِرَّ اَنۡ تُوَلُّوۡا وُجُوۡهَكُمۡ
قِبَلَ الۡمَشۡرِقِ وَالۡمَغۡرِبِ وَلٰكِنَّ
الۡبِرَّ مَنۡ اٰمَنَ بِاللّٰهِ وَالۡيَوۡمِ الۡاٰخِرِ
وَالۡمَلٰٓـئِكَةِ وَالۡكِتٰبِ وَالنَّبِيّٖنَ ۚ
وَاٰتَى الۡمَالَ عَلٰى حُبِّهٖ ذَوِى الۡقُرۡبٰى
وَالۡيَتٰمٰى وَالۡمَسٰكِيۡنَ وَابۡنَ السَّبِيۡلِ ۙ
وَالسَّآئِلِيۡنَ وَفِى الرِّقَابِ ۚ وَاَقَامَ
الصَّلٰوةَ وَاٰتَى الزَّكٰوةَ ۚ وَالۡمُوۡفُوۡنَ

Ikhfa اخفاء | Ghunna غنّہ | Ikhfa Meem Saakin اخفاء میم ساکن | Idghaam ادغام | Qalqala قلقلہ | Qalb قلب | Idghaam Meem Saakin ادغام میم ساکن

contracts which you have made; and to be firm and patient, in pain (or suffering) and adversity, and throughout all periods of panic. Such are the people of truth, those who fear Allah.

bi'ahdihim izaa 'aahadoo waṣṣaabireena fil-baåsaaa'i waḍḍarraaa'i wa ḥeenal-baås; ulaaa'ikal-lazeena ṣadaqoo wa ulaaa'ika humul-muttaqoon.

بِعَهْدِهِمْ إِذَا عَٰهَدُوا ۖ وَالصَّٰبِرِينَ
فِي الْبَأْسَاءِ وَالضَّرَّاءِ وَحِينَ الْبَأْسِ ۗ
أُولَٰئِكَ الَّذِينَ صَدَقُوا ۖ وَأُولَٰئِكَ
هُمُ الْمُتَّقُونَ ﴿١٧٧﴾

178. O you who believe! The law of equality is prescribed to you in cases of murder: the free for the free, the slave for the slave, the woman for the woman. But if any remission is made by the brother of the slain, then grant any reasonable demand, and compensate him with handsome gratitude, this is a concession and a Mercy from your Lord. After this whoever exceeds the limits shall be in grave Chastisement.

178. Yaaa ayyuhal-lazeena aamanoo kutiba 'alaykumul-qiṣaaṣu fil-qatlaa alḥurru bilḥurri wal'abdu bil'abdi wal-unsaa bil-unsaa; faman 'ufiya lahoo min akheehi shay'un fattibaa'um-bilma'roofi wa adaaa'un ilayhi bi-ihsaan; zaalika takhfeefum-mir-Rabbikum wa-raḥmah; famani'-tadaa ba'da zaalika falahoo 'azaabun aleem.

يَٰأَيُّهَا الَّذِينَ ءَامَنُوا كُتِبَ عَلَيْكُمُ
الْقِصَاصُ فِي الْقَتْلَى ۖ الْحُرُّ بِالْحُرِّ
وَالْعَبْدُ بِالْعَبْدِ وَالْأُنثَىٰ بِالْأُنثَىٰ ۚ
فَمَنْ عُفِيَ لَهُ مِنْ أَخِيهِ شَيْءٌ
فَاتِّبَاعٌ بِالْمَعْرُوفِ وَأَدَاءٌ إِلَيْهِ
بِإِحْسَٰنٍ ۗ ذَٰلِكَ تَخْفِيفٌ مِّن
رَّبِّكُمْ وَرَحْمَةٌ ۗ فَمَنِ اعْتَدَىٰ
بَعْدَ ذَٰلِكَ فَلَهُ عَذَابٌ أَلِيمٌ ﴿١٧٨﴾

179. In the Law of Equality there is (saving of) Life to you, O you men of understanding; that you may restrain yourselves.

179. Wa lakum fil-qiṣaaṣi ḥayaatuñy-yaaa-ulil-albaabi la-'allakum tattaqoon.

وَلَكُمْ فِي الْقِصَاصِ حَيَوٰةٌ يَٰأُولِي
الْأَلْبَٰبِ لَعَلَّكُمْ تَتَّقُونَ ﴿١٧٩﴾

180. It is prescribed, when death approaches any of you, if he leave any goods that he make a bequest to parents and next of kin, according to reasonable usage; this is due from those who fear Allah.

180. Kutiba 'alaykum izaa ḥaḍara aḥadakumul-mawtu in taraka khayranil-waṣiyyatu lilwaalidayni wal-aqrabeena bilma'roofi ḥaqqan 'alalmut-taqeen.

كُتِبَ عَلَيْكُمْ إِذَا حَضَرَ أَحَدَكُمُ
الْمَوْتُ إِن تَرَكَ خَيْرًا ۚ الْوَصِيَّةُ
لِلْوَٰلِدَيْنِ وَالْأَقْرَبِينَ بِالْمَعْرُوفِ ۖ
حَقًّا عَلَى الْمُتَّقِينَ ﴿١٨٠﴾

181. If anyone changes the bequest after hearing it, the guilt shall be on those who make the change. For Allah hears and knows (all things).

181. Famam-baddalahoo ba'da maa sami'ahoo fa-innamaaa ismuhoo 'alallazeena yubaddi-loonah; innallaaha Samee'un 'Aleem.

فَمَنۢ بَدَّلَهُ بَعْدَ مَا سَمِعَهُ فَإِنَّمَا
إِثْمُهُ عَلَى الَّذِينَ يُبَدِّلُونَهُ ۚ إِنَّ
اللَّهَ سَمِيعٌ عَلِيمٌ ﴿١٨١﴾

182. But if anyone fears partiality or wrong-doing on the part of the testator, and makes peace between (the parties concerned), there is no wrong in him: for Allah is Oft-Forgiving, Most Merciful.

182. Faman khaafa mim-mooṣin janafan aw isman fa-aṣlaḥa baynahum falaaa isma 'alayh; innal-laaha Ghafoorur-Raḥeem. **(Section 22)**

فَمَنْ خَافَ مِن مُّوصٍ جَنَفًا أَوْ
إِثْمًا فَأَصْلَحَ بَيْنَهُمْ فَلَا إِثْمَ
عَلَيْهِ ۚ إِنَّ اللَّهَ غَفُورٌ رَّحِيمٌ ﴿١٨٢﴾ ع

183. O you who believe! Fasting is prescribed to you as it was prescribed to those

183. Yaaa ayyuhal-lazeena aamanoo kutiba 'alaykumuṣ-Ṣiyaamu kamaa kutiba 'alal lazeena

يَٰأَيُّهَا الَّذِينَ ءَامَنُوا كُتِبَ عَلَيْكُمُ
الصِّيَامُ كَمَا كُتِبَ عَلَى الَّذِينَ

Ikhfa اخفاء | Ghunna غنّہ | Ikhfa Meem Saakin اخفاء میم ساکن | Idghaam ادغام | Qalqala قلقلہ | Qalb قلب | Idghaam Meem Saakin ادغام میم ساکن

before you, that you may (learn) self-restraint,-

184. (Fasting is) for a fixed number of days; but if any of you is ill, or on a journey, the prescribed number (should be made up) from days later. For those who can do it (with hardship), is a ransom, the feeding of one that is indigent. But he that will give more, of his own free will,- it is better for him. And it is better for you that you fast, if you only knew.

185. Ramadhan is the (month) in which was sent down the Qur'an, as a guide to mankind, also clear (Signs) for guidance and judgment (between right and wrong). So every one of you who is present (at his home) during that month should spend it in fasting, but if any one is ill, or on a journey, the prescribed period (should be made up) by days later. Allah intends every facility for you; He does not want to put you to difficulties. (He wants you) to complete the prescribed period, and to glorify Him in that He has guided you; and perchance you shall be grateful.

186. When My servants ask you concerning Me, I am indeed close (to them): I listen to the prayer of every suppliant when he calls on Me: let them also, with a will, listen to My call, and believe in Me: that they may walk in the right way.

187. Permitted to you, on the night of the fasts, is the approach to your wives. They are your garments and you are their garments. Allah knows what you used to do secretly among yourselves; but He turned to you and forgave you; so now associate with them, and seek what Allah has ordained

min qablikum la-'allakum tattaqoon.

184. Ayyaamam-ma'doodaat; faman kaana minkum mareedan aw 'alaa safarin fa'iddatum-min ayyaamin ukhar; wa 'alal-lazeena yuteeqoonahoo fidyatun ta'aamu miskeenin faman tatawwa'a khayran fahuwa khayrul-lahoo wa an tasoomoo khayrul-lakum in kuntum ta'lamoon.

185. Shahru Ramadaanallazeee unzila feehil-Qur'aanu hudal-linnaasi wa bayyinaatim-minal-hudaa wal-furqaan; faman shahida minkumush-shahra falyasumhu wa man kaana mareedan aw 'alaa safarin fa'iddatum-min ayyaamin ukhar; yureedul-laahu bikumul-yusra wa laa yureedu bikumul-'usra wa litukmilul'iddata wa litukabbirul-laaha 'alaa maa hadaakum wa la'allakum tashkuroon.

186 Wa izaa sa-alaka 'ibaadee 'annee fa-innee qareebun ujeebu da'wataddaa'i izaa da'aani falyastajeeboo lee walyu'minoo bee la'allahum yarshudoon.

187. Uhilla lakum laylatas Siyaamir-rafasu ilaa nisaaa'i-kum; hunna libaasullakum wa antum libaasullahunn; 'alimal-laahu annakum kuntum takhtaanoona anfusakum fataaba 'alaykum wa 'afaa 'ankum fal'aana baashiroo-hunna wabtaghoo maa katabal-laahoo

مِنْ قَبْلِكُمْ لَعَلَّكُمْ تَتَّقُونَ ﴿١٨٣﴾
أَيَّامًا مَّعْدُودٰتٍ ۚ فَمَنْ كَانَ مِنْكُمْ
مَّرِيضًا أَوْ عَلٰى سَفَرٍ فَعِدَّةٌ مِّنْ
أَيَّامٍ أُخَرَ ۚ وَعَلَى الَّذِيْنَ يُطِيْقُوْنَهٗ
فِدْيَةٌ طَعَامُ مِسْكِيْنٍ ۚ فَمَنْ تَطَوَّعَ
خَيْرًا فَهُوَ خَيْرٌ لَّهٗ ۚ وَأَنْ تَصُوْمُوْا
خَيْرٌ لَّكُمْ إِنْ كُنْتُمْ تَعْلَمُوْنَ ﴿١٨٤﴾
شَهْرُ رَمَضَانَ الَّذِيْٓ أُنْزِلَ فِيْهِ
الْقُرْاٰنُ هُدًى لِّلنَّاسِ وَبَيِّنٰتٍ
مِّنَ الْهُدٰى وَالْفُرْقَانِ ۚ فَمَنْ شَهِدَ
مِنْكُمُ الشَّهْرَ فَلْيَصُمْهُ ۚ وَمَنْ كَانَ
مَرِيْضًا أَوْ عَلٰى سَفَرٍ فَعِدَّةٌ مِّنْ
أَيَّامٍ أُخَرَ ۚ يُرِيْدُ اللّٰهُ بِكُمُ الْيُسْرَ
وَلَا يُرِيْدُ بِكُمُ الْعُسْرَ ۫ وَلِتُكْمِلُوا
الْعِدَّةَ وَلِتُكَبِّرُوا اللّٰهَ عَلٰى مَا هَدٰىكُمْ
وَلَعَلَّكُمْ تَشْكُرُوْنَ ﴿١٨٥﴾
وَإِذَا سَأَلَكَ عِبَادِيْ عَنِّيْ فَإِنِّيْ
قَرِيْبٌ ۚ أُجِيْبُ دَعْوَةَ الدَّاعِ إِذَا
دَعَانِ ۙ فَلْيَسْتَجِيْبُوْا لِيْ وَلْيُؤْمِنُوْا بِيْ
لَعَلَّهُمْ يَرْشُدُوْنَ ﴿١٨٦﴾
أُحِلَّ لَكُمْ لَيْلَةَ الصِّيَامِ الرَّفَثُ
إِلٰى نِسَآئِكُمْ ۚ هُنَّ لِبَاسٌ لَّكُمْ
وَأَنْتُمْ لِبَاسٌ لَّهُنَّ ۚ عَلِمَ اللّٰهُ
أَنَّكُمْ كُنْتُمْ تَخْتَانُوْنَ أَنْفُسَكُمْ
فَتَابَ عَلَيْكُمْ وَعَفَا عَنْكُمْ ۚ فَالْـٰٔنَ
بَاشِرُوْهُنَّ وَابْتَغُوْا مَا كَتَبَ اللّٰهُ

Ikhfa اخفاء | Ghunna غنّہ | Ikhfa Meem Saakin اخفاء میم ساکن | Idghaam ادغام | Qalqala قلقلہ | Qalb قلب | Idghaam Meem Saakin ادغام میم ساکن

for you, and eat and drink, until the white thread of dawn appear to you distinct from its black thread; then complete your fast till the night appears; but do not associate with your wives while you are in retreat in the mosques. Those are limits (set by) Allah: do not go near to those. Thus Allah makes clear His Signs to men: that they may learn self-restraint.

lakum; wa kuloo washraboo ḥattaa yatabayyana lakumul-khayṭul abyaḍu minal-khayṭil-aswadi minal-fajri summa atimmuṣ-Ṣiyaama ilal-layl; wa laa tubaashiroo-hunna wa antum ʻaakifoona fil-masaajid; tilka ḥudoodul-laahi falaa taqraboo-haa; kazaalika yubayyinul-laahu Aayaatihee linnaasi laʻallahum yattaqoon.

لَكُمْ وَكُلُوْا وَاشْرَبُوْا حَتّٰى يَتَبَيَّنَ
لَكُمُ الْخَيْطُ الْاَبْيَضُ مِنَ الْخَيْطِ
الْاَسْوَدِ مِنَ الْفَجْرِ ثُمَّ اَتِمُّوا
الصِّيَامَ اِلَى الَّيْلِ وَلَا تُبَاشِرُوْهُنَّ
وَاَنْتُمْ عٰكِفُوْنَ فِي الْمَسٰجِدِ
تِلْكَ حُدُوْدُ اللّٰهِ فَلَا تَقْرَبُوْهَا
كَذٰلِكَ يُبَيِّنُ اللّٰهُ اٰيٰتِهٖ لِلنَّاسِ
لَعَلَّهُمْ يَتَّقُوْنَ ﴿١٨٧﴾

188. And do not eat up your property among yourselves for vanities, nor use it as bait for the judges, with intent that you may eat up wrongfully and knowingly a little of (other) people's property.

188. Wa laa taàkulooo amwaa-lakum baynakum bilbaaṭili wa tudloo bihaaa ilal-ḥukkaami litaà-kuloo fareeqam min amwaalin-naasi bil-is̲mi wa antum taʻlamoon. **(Section 23)**

وَلَا تَاْكُلُوْٓا اَمْوَالَكُمْ بَيْنَكُمْ بِالْبَاطِلِ
وَتُدْلُوْا بِهَآ اِلَى الْحُكَّامِ لِتَاْكُلُوْا
فَرِيْقًا مِّنْ اَمْوَالِ النَّاسِ بِالْاِثْمِ
وَاَنْتُمْ تَعْلَمُوْنَ ﴿١٨٨﴾ ع

189. They ask you concerning the New Moons. Say: They are but signs to mark fixed periods of time in (the affairs of) men, and for Pilgrimage. It is no virtue if you enter your houses from the back: it is virtue if you fear Allah. Enter houses through the proper doors: and fear Allah: that you may achieve success.

189. Yas'aloonaka ʻanil-ahillati qul hiya mawaaqeetu linnaasi wal-Ḥajj; wa laysal-birru bi-an taàtul-buyoota min ẓuhoorihaa wa laakinnal-birra manit-taqaa; waàtul-buyoota min abwaa-bihaa; wattaqullaaha laʻallakum tufliḥoon.

يَسْـَٔلُوْنَكَ عَنِ الْاَهِلَّةِ قُلْ هِيَ
مَوَاقِيْتُ لِلنَّاسِ وَالْحَجِّ وَلَيْسَ
الْبِرُّ بِاَنْ تَاْتُوا الْبُيُوْتَ مِنْ ظُهُوْرِهَا
وَلٰكِنَّ الْبِرَّ مَنِ اتَّقٰى وَاْتُوا الْبُيُوْتَ
مِنْ اَبْوَابِهَا وَاتَّقُوا اللّٰهَ لَعَلَّكُمْ
تُفْلِحُوْنَ ﴿١٨٩﴾

190. Fight in the cause of Allah those who fight you, but do not transgress limits; for Allah love not transgressors.

190. Wa qaatiloo fee sabeelil-laahil-laz̲eena yuqaatiloonakum wa laa taʻtadooo; innal-laaha laa yuḥibbul-muʻtadeen.

وَقَاتِلُوْا فِيْ سَبِيْلِ اللّٰهِ الَّذِيْنَ
يُقَاتِلُوْنَكُمْ وَلَا تَعْتَدُوْا اِنَّ
اللّٰهَ لَا يُحِبُّ الْمُعْتَدِيْنَ ﴿١٩٠﴾

191. And slay them wherever you catch them, and turn them out from where they have turned you out; for tumult and oppression are worse than slaughter; but fight them not at the Sacred Mosque, unless they (first) fight you there; but if they fight you,

191. Waqtuloohum ḥays̲u s̲aqif-tumoohum wa akhrijoohum min ḥays̲u akhrajookum; walfitnatu ashaddu minal-qatl; wa laa tuqaatiloohum ʻindal-Masjidil-Ḥaraami ḥattaa yuqaatilookum feehi fa-in qaatalookum

وَاقْتُلُوْهُمْ حَيْثُ ثَقِفْتُمُوْهُمْ
وَاَخْرِجُوْهُمْ مِّنْ حَيْثُ اَخْرَجُوْكُمْ
وَالْفِتْنَةُ اَشَدُّ مِنَ الْقَتْلِ وَلَا
تُقٰتِلُوْهُمْ عِنْدَ الْمَسْجِدِ الْحَرَامِ
حَتّٰى يُقٰتِلُوْكُمْ فِيْهِ فَاِنْ قٰتَلُوْكُمْ

Ikhfa اخفاء — Ghunna غنّہ — Ikhfa Meem Saakin اخفاء میم ساکن — Idghaam ادغام — Qalqala قلقلہ — Qalb قلب — Idghaam Meem Saakin ادغام میم ساکن

slay them. Such is the reward of those who suppress faith.

192. But if they cease, Allah is Oft-Forgiving, Most Merciful.

193. And fight them on until there is no more tumult or oppression, and there prevail justice and faith in Allah; but if they cease, let there be no hostility except to those who practise oppression.

194. The prohibited month for the prohibited month,- and so for all things prohibited,- there is the law of equality. If then any one transgresses the prohibition against you, transgress you likewise against him. But fear Allah, and know that Allah is with those who restrain themselves.

195. And spend of your substance in the cause of Allah, and make not your own hands contribute to (your) destruction; but do good; for Allah loves those who do good.

196. And complete the Hajj or 'umra in the service of Allah. But if you are prevented (from completing it), send an offering for sacrifice, such as you may find, and do not shave your heads until the offering reaches the place of sacrifice. And if any of you is ill, or has an ailment in his scalp, (necessitating shaving), (he should) in compensation either fast, or feed the poor, or offer sacrifice; and when you are in peaceful conditions (again), if any one wishes to continue the 'Umra or the Hajj, he must make an offering, such as he can afford, but if he cannot afford it, he should fast three days during the Hajj and seven days on his return, making ten days in all. This is for those whose household is not in (the precincts of) the Sacred Mosque. And fear Allah,

faqtuloohum; kazaalika jazaaa'ul-kaafireen.

192. Fa-ini-ntahaw fa-innal-laaha Ghafoorur-Raḥeem.

193. Wa qaatiloohum ḥattaa laa takoona fitnatuñw-wa yakoonad-deenu lillaahi fa-inin-tahaw falaa 'udwaana illaa 'alaẓ-ẓaalimeen.

194. Ash-Shahrul-Ḥaraamu bish-Shahril-Ḥaraami wal-ḥurumaatu qiṣaaṣ; famani'tadaa 'alaykum fa'tadoo 'alayhi bimisli ma'-tadaa 'alaykum; wattaqul-laaha wa'lamooo annal-laaha ma'al-muttaqeen.

195. Wa anfiqoo fee sabeelil-laahi wa laa tulqoo bi-aydeekum ilat-tahlukati wa aḥsinoo; innal-laaha yuḥibbul-muḥsineen.

196. Wa atimmul-Ḥajja wal-'Umrata lillaah; fain uḥṣirtum famas-taysara minal-hadyi walaa taḥliqoo ru'oosakum ḥattaa yablughal-hadyu maḥil-lah; faman kaana minkum mareeḍan aw biheee azam-mir-raåsihee fafidyatum-min Ṣiyaamin aw ṣadaqatin aw nusuk; fa-izaaa amintum faman tamatta'a bil-'Umrati ilal-Ḥajji famastaysara minal-hady; famal-lam yajid fa-Ṣiyaamu salaasati ayyaamin fil-Ḥajji wa sab'atin izaa raja'tum; tilka 'asharatun kaamilah; zaalika limal-lam yakun ahluhoo ḥaaḍiril-Masjidil-Ḥaraam; wattaqul-laaha

فَاقْتُلُوهُمْ ۗ كَذَٰلِكَ جَزَاءُ الْكَافِرِينَ ﴿١٩١﴾
فَإِنِ انْتَهَوْا فَإِنَّ اللَّهَ غَفُورٌ رَحِيمٌ ﴿١٩٢﴾
وَقَاتِلُوهُمْ حَتَّىٰ لَا تَكُونَ فِتْنَةٌ
وَيَكُونَ الدِّينُ لِلَّهِ ۖ فَإِنِ انْتَهَوْا
فَلَا عُدْوَانَ إِلَّا عَلَى الظَّالِمِينَ ﴿١٩٣﴾
الشَّهْرُ الْحَرَامُ بِالشَّهْرِ الْحَرَامِ
وَالْحُرُمَاتُ قِصَاصٌ ۚ فَمَنِ اعْتَدَىٰ
عَلَيْكُمْ فَاعْتَدُوا عَلَيْهِ بِمِثْلِ
مَا اعْتَدَىٰ عَلَيْكُمْ ۚ وَاتَّقُوا اللَّهَ
وَاعْلَمُوا أَنَّ اللَّهَ مَعَ الْمُتَّقِينَ ﴿١٩٤﴾
وَأَنْفِقُوا فِي سَبِيلِ اللَّهِ وَلَا تُلْقُوا
بِأَيْدِيكُمْ إِلَى التَّهْلُكَةِ ۛ وَأَحْسِنُوا ۛ
إِنَّ اللَّهَ يُحِبُّ الْمُحْسِنِينَ ﴿١٩٥﴾
وَأَتِمُّوا الْحَجَّ وَالْعُمْرَةَ لِلَّهِ ۚ فَإِنْ
أُحْصِرْتُمْ فَمَا اسْتَيْسَرَ مِنَ الْهَدْيِ ۖ
وَلَا تَحْلِقُوا رُءُوسَكُمْ حَتَّىٰ يَبْلُغَ
الْهَدْيُ مَحِلَّهُ ۚ فَمَنْ كَانَ مِنْكُمْ
مَرِيضًا أَوْ بِهِ أَذًى مِنْ رَأْسِهِ
فَفِدْيَةٌ مِنْ صِيَامٍ أَوْ صَدَقَةٍ
أَوْ نُسُكٍ ۚ فَإِذَا أَمِنْتُمْ فَمَنْ تَمَتَّعَ
بِالْعُمْرَةِ إِلَى الْحَجِّ فَمَا اسْتَيْسَرَ
مِنَ الْهَدْيِ ۚ فَمَنْ لَمْ يَجِدْ فَصِيَامُ
ثَلَاثَةِ أَيَّامٍ فِي الْحَجِّ وَسَبْعَةٍ إِذَا
رَجَعْتُمْ ۗ تِلْكَ عَشَرَةٌ كَامِلَةٌ ۗ ذَٰلِكَ
لِمَنْ لَمْ يَكُنْ أَهْلُهُ حَاضِرِي
الْمَسْجِدِ الْحَرَامِ ۚ وَاتَّقُوا اللَّهَ

مع

Ikhfa اخفاء | Ghunna غنّہ | Ikhfa Meem Saakin اخفاء میم ساکن | Idghaam ادغام | Qalqala قلقلہ | Qalb قلب | Idghaam Meem Saakin ادغام میم ساکن

and know that Allah is strict in punishment.

197. For Hajj are the months well known. If any one undertakes that duty therein, let there be no obscenity, nor wickedness, nor wrangling in the Hajj. And whatever good you do, (be sure) Allah knows it. And take a provision (with you) for the journey, but the best of provisions is right conduct. So fear Me, O you that are wise.

198. It is no crime in you if you seek of the bounty of your Lord (during pilgrimage). Then when you pour down from (Mount) 'Arafat, celebrate the praises of Allah at the Sacred Monument, and celebrate His praises as He has directed you, even though, be fore this, you went astray.

199. Then pass on at a quick pace from the place whence it is usual for the multitude so to do, and ask for Allah's forgiveness. For Allah is Oft-Forgiving, Most Merciful.

200. So when you have accomplished your holy rites, celebrate the praises of Allah, as you used to celebrate the praises of your fathers,- yes, with far more heart and soul. There are men who say: "Our Lord! Give us (Your bounties) in this world!" but they will have no portion in the Hereafter.

201. And there are men who say: "Our Lord! Give us good in this world and good in the Hereafter, and save us from the torment of the Fire!"

202. To these will be allotted what they have earned; and Allah is quick in account.

203. Celebrate the praises of Allah during the Appointed Days.

wa'lamoo annal-laaha shadeedul-'iqaab. **(Section 24)**

197. Al-Ḥajju ashhurum ma'loomaat; faman faraḍa feehinnal-Ḥajja falaa rafasa wa laa fusooqa wa laa jidaala fil-Ḥajj; wa maa taf'aloo min khayriñy-ya'lamhul-laah; wa tazawwadoo fa-inna khayraz-zaadit-taqwaa; wattaqooni yaaa ulil-albaab.

198. Laysa 'alaykum junaaḥun an tabtaghoo faḍlam-mir-Rabbikum; fa-izaaa afaḍtum min 'Arafaatin fazkurul-laaha 'indal-Mash'aril-Ḥaraami wazkuroohu kamaa hadaakum wa in kuntum min qablihee laminaḍ-ḍaaalleen.

199. Summa afeeḍoo min ḥaysu afaaḍan-naasu wastagh-firul-laah; innal-laaha Ghafoo-rur-Raḥeem.

200. Fa-izaa qaḍaytum manaasikakum fazkurul-laaha kazikrikum aabaaa'akum aw ashadda zikraa; faminannaasi mañy-yaqoolu Rabbanaaa aatinaa fiddunyaa wa maa lahoo fil-Aakhirati min khalaaq.

201. Wa minhum mañy-yaqoolu Rabbanaaa aatinaa fid-dunyaa ḥasanatañw-wa fil-Aakhirati ḥasanatañw-wa qinaa 'azaaban-Naar.

202. Ulaaa'ika lahum naṣeebum-mimmaa kasaboo; wallaahu saree'ul-ḥisaab.

203. Wazkurul-laaha feee ayyaamim-ma'doodaat;

وَاعْلَمُوْٓا اَنَّ اللّٰهَ شَدِيْدُ الْعِقَابِ ﴿١٩٦﴾ ع ٢٤
اَلْحَجُّ اَشْهُرٌ مَّعْلُوْمٰتٌ ۚ فَمَنْ
فَرَضَ فِيْهِنَّ الْحَجَّ فَلَا رَفَثَ
وَلَا فُسُوْقَ ۙ وَلَا جِدَالَ فِي الْحَجِّ ؕ
وَمَا تَفْعَلُوْا مِنْ خَيْرٍ يَّعْلَمْهُ اللّٰهُ ؕ
وَتَزَوَّدُوْا فَاِنَّ خَيْرَ الزَّادِ التَّقْوٰى ۫ وقف النبي صلى الله عليه وآله وسلم ١٢
وَاتَّقُوْنِ يٰٓاُولِي الْاَلْبَابِ ﴿١٩٧﴾
لَيْسَ عَلَيْكُمْ جُنَاحٌ اَنْ تَبْتَغُوْا فَضْلًا
مِّنْ رَّبِّكُمْ ؕ فَاِذَآ اَفَضْتُمْ مِّنْ
عَرَفٰتٍ فَاذْكُرُوا اللّٰهَ عِنْدَ الْمَشْعَرِ
الْحَرَامِ ۪ وَاذْكُرُوْهُ كَمَا هَدٰىكُمْ ۚ
وَاِنْ كُنْتُمْ مِّنْ قَبْلِهٖ لَمِنَ الضَّآلِّيْنَ ﴿١٩٨﴾
ثُمَّ اَفِيْضُوْا مِنْ حَيْثُ اَفَاضَ
النَّاسُ وَاسْتَغْفِرُوا اللّٰهَ ؕ اِنَّ اللّٰهَ
غَفُوْرٌ رَّحِيْمٌ ﴿١٩٩﴾
فَاِذَا قَضَيْتُمْ مَّنَاسِكَكُمْ فَاذْكُرُوا
اللّٰهَ كَذِكْرِكُمْ اٰبَآءَكُمْ اَوْ اَشَدَّ
ذِكْرًا ؕ فَمِنَ النَّاسِ مَنْ يَّقُوْلُ
رَبَّنَآ اٰتِنَا فِي الدُّنْيَا وَمَا لَهٗ فِي
الْاٰخِرَةِ مِنْ خَلَاقٍ ﴿٢٠٠﴾
وَمِنْهُمْ مَّنْ يَّقُوْلُ رَبَّنَآ اٰتِنَا فِي
الدُّنْيَا حَسَنَةً وَّفِي الْاٰخِرَةِ حَسَنَةً
وَّقِنَا عَذَابَ النَّارِ ﴿٢٠١﴾ النصف
اُولٰٓئِكَ لَهُمْ نَصِيْبٌ مِّمَّا كَسَبُوْا ؕ
وَاللّٰهُ سَرِيْعُ الْحِسَابِ ﴿٢٠٢﴾
وَاذْكُرُوا اللّٰهَ فِيْٓ اَيَّامٍ مَّعْدُوْدٰتٍ ؕ

Ikhfa اخفاء · Ghunna غنّہ · Ikhfa Meem Saakin اخفاء میم ساکن · Idghaam ادغام · Qalqala قلقلہ · Qalb قلب · Idghaam Meem Saakin ادغام میم ساکن

But if any one hastens to leave in two days, there is no blame on him, and if any one stays on, there is no blame on him, if his aim is to do right. Then fear Allah, and know that you will surely be gathered unto Him.

faman ta'ajjala fee yawmayni falaaa isma 'alayhi wa man ta-akhkhara falaaa isma 'alayh; limanit-taqaa; wattaqul-laaha wa'lamooo annakum ilayhi tuhsharoon.

فَمَنْ تَعَجَّلَ فِيْ يَوْمَيْنِ فَلَآ اِثْمَ
عَلَيْهِ ۚ وَمَنْ تَاَخَّرَ فَلَآ اِثْمَ عَلَيْهِ ۙ
لِمَنِ اتَّقٰى ؕ وَاتَّقُوا اللّٰهَ وَاعْلَمُوْٓا
اَنَّكُمْ اِلَيْهِ تُحْشَرُوْنَ ﴿٢٠٣﴾

204. There is the type of man whose speech about this world's life may dazzle you, and he calls Allah to witness about what is in his heart; yet he is the most contentious of enemies.

204. Wa minan-naasi mañy-yu'jibuka qawluhoo fil hayaatid-dunyaa wa yushhidul-laaha 'alaa maa fee qalbihee wa huwa aladdulkhisaam.

وَمِنَ النَّاسِ مَنْ يُّعْجِبُكَ قَوْلُهٗ فِى
الْحَيٰوةِ الدُّنْيَا وَيُشْهِدُ اللّٰهَ عَلٰى
مَا فِىْ قَلْبِهٖ ۙ وَهُوَ اَلَدُّ الْخِصَامِ ﴿٢٠٤﴾

205. When he turns his back, his aim everywhere is to spread mischief through the earth and destroy crops and cattle. But Allah loves not mischief.

205. Wa izaa tawallaa sa'aa fil-ardi liyufsida feehaa wa yuhlikal-harsa wannasl; wallaahu laa yuhibbul-fasaad.

وَاِذَا تَوَلّٰى سَعٰى فِى الْاَرْضِ لِيُفْسِدَ
فِيْهَا وَيُهْلِكَ الْحَرْثَ وَالنَّسْلَ ؕ
وَاللّٰهُ لَا يُحِبُّ الْفَسَادَ ﴿٢٠٥﴾

206. When it is said to him, "Fear Allah", he is led by arrogance to (more) crime. Enough for him is Hell; - an evil bed indeed (to lie on)!

206. Wa izaa qeela lahuttaqil-laaha akhazathul-izzatu bil-ism; fahasbuhoo Jahannam; wa labi'sal-mihaad.

وَاِذَا قِيْلَ لَهُ اتَّقِ اللّٰهَ اَخَذَتْهُ
الْعِزَّةُ بِالْاِثْمِ فَحَسْبُهٗ جَهَنَّمُ ؕ
وَلَبِئْسَ الْمِهَادُ ﴿٢٠٦﴾

207. And there is the type of man who gives his life to earn the pleasure of Allah: and Allah is full of kindness to (His) devotees.

207. Wa minan-naasi mañy-yashree nafsahub-tighaaa'a mardaatil-laah; wallaahu ra'oofum-bil'ibaad.

وَمِنَ النَّاسِ مَنْ يَّشْرِىْ نَفْسَهُ
ابْتِغَآءَ مَرْضَاتِ اللّٰهِ ؕ وَاللّٰهُ رَءُوْفٌ
بِالْعِبَادِ ﴿٢٠٧﴾

208. O you who believe! Enter into Islam whole-heartedly; and follow not the footsteps of the Satan; for he is to you an avowed enemy.

208. Yaaa ayyuhal-lazeena aamanud-khuloo fis-silmi kaaaffatañw-wa laa tattabi'oo khutuwaatish-Shaytaan; innahoo lakum 'aduwwum-mubeen.

يٰٓاَيُّهَا الَّذِيْنَ اٰمَنُوا ادْخُلُوْا فِى السِّلْمِ
كَآفَّةً ۪ وَّلَا تَتَّبِعُوْا خُطُوٰتِ
الشَّيْطٰنِ ؕ اِنَّهٗ لَكُمْ عَدُوٌّ مُّبِيْنٌ ﴿٢٠٨﴾

209. If you backslide after the clear (Signs) have come to you, then know that Allah is Exalted in Power, Wise.

209. Fa-in zalaltum mimba'di maa jaaa'atkumul-bayyinaatu fa'lamoo annallaaha 'Azeezun-Hakeem.

فَاِنْ زَلَلْتُمْ مِّنْۢ بَعْدِ مَا جَآءَتْكُمُ
الْبَيِّنٰتُ فَاعْلَمُوْٓا اَنَّ اللّٰهَ عَزِيْزٌ حَكِيْمٌ ﴿٢٠٩﴾

210. Will they wait until Allah comes to them in canopies of clouds, with Angels (in His train) and the question is (thus) settled? but to Allah do all questions go back (for decision).

210. Hal yanzuroona illaaa añy-yaåtiyahumul-laahu fee zulalim-minal-ghamaami walmalaaa'ikatu wa qudiyal-amr; wa ilal-laahi turja'ul-umoor. **(Section 25)**

هَلْ يَنْظُرُوْنَ اِلَّآ اَنْ يَّاْتِيَهُمُ اللّٰهُ
فِىْ ظُلَلٍ مِّنَ الْغَمَامِ وَالْمَلٰٓئِكَةُ
وَقُضِىَ الْاَمْرُ ؕ وَاِلَى اللّٰهِ تُرْجَعُ الْاُمُوْرُ ﴿٢١٠﴾

211. Ask the Children of Israel how many clear (Signs) We have sent them. But if any one,

211. Sal Baneee Israaa'eela kam aataynaahum min Aayatim-bayyinah; wa mañy-yubaddil

سَلْ بَنِىْٓ اِسْرَآءِيْلَ كَمْ اٰتَيْنٰهُمْ
مِّنْ اٰيَةٍۢ بَيِّنَةٍ ؕ وَمَنْ يُّبَدِّلْ

after Allah's favour has come to him, substitutes (something else), Allah is strict in punishment.

212. The life of this world is alluring to those who reject faith, and they scoff at those who believe. But the righteous will be above them on the Day of Resurrection; for Allah bestows His abundance without measure on whom He will.

213. Mankind was one single nation, and Allah sent Messengers with glad tidings and warnings; and with them He sent the Book in truth, to judge between people in matters wherein they differed; but the People of the Book, after the clear signs came to them, did not differ among themselves, except through selfish contumacy. Allah by His Grace Guided the believers to the Truth, concerning that wherein they differed. For Allah guided whom He will to a path that is straight.

214. Or do you think that you shall enter the Garden (of Bliss) without such (trials) as came to those who passed away before you? They encountered suffering and adversity, and were so shaken in spirit that even the Apostle and those of faith who were with him cried: "When (will come) the help of Allah?" Ah! Verily, the help of Allah is (always) near!

215. They ask you what they should spend (in charity). Say: Whatever you spend that is good, is for parents and kindred and orphans and those in want and for wayfarers. And whatever you do that is

ni'matal-laahi mim ba'di maa jaaa'athu fa-innallaaha shadeedul-'iqaab.

212. Zuyyina lillazeena kafarul-ḥayaatud-dunyaa wa yaskharoona minal-lazeena aamanoo; wallazeenat-taqaw fawqahum YawmalQiyaamah; wallaahu yarzuqu mañy-yashaaa'u bighayri ḥisaab.

213. Kaanan-naasu ummatañw-waaḥidatan faba'aṡal-laahun-Nabiyyeena mubashshireena wa munzireena wa anzala ma'ahumul-Kitaaba bilḥaqqi liyaḥkuma baynan-naasi feemakh-talafoo feeh; wa makh-talafa feehi 'illallazeena ootoohu mim-ba'di maa jaaa'athumul-bayyinaatu baghyam baynahum fahadal-laahul-lazeena aamanoo limakh-talafoo feehi minal-ḥaqqi bi-iznih; wallaahu yahdee mañy-yashaaa'u ilaa Ṣiraaṭim-Mustaqeem.

214. Am ḥasibtum an tadkhulul-Jannata wa lammaa yaåtikum masalul-lazeena khalaw min qablikum massathumul-baåsaaa'u waḍḍarraaa'u wa zulziloo ḥattaa yaqoolar-Rasoolu wallazeena aamanoo ma'ahoo mataa naṣrul-laah; alaaa inna naṣral-laahiqareeb.

215. Yas'aloonaka maazaa yunfiqoona qul maaa anfaqtum min khayrin falilwaalidayni wal-aqrabeena walyataamaa walmasaakeeni wabnis-sabeel; wa maa taf'aloo min

نِعْمَةَ اللّٰهِ مِنْۢ بَعْدِ مَا جَآءَتْهُ
فَاِنَّ اللّٰهَ شَدِيْدُ الْعِقَابِ ﴿٢١١﴾
زُيِّنَ لِلَّذِيْنَ كَفَرُوا الْحَيٰوةُ الدُّنْيَا
وَيَسْخَرُوْنَ مِنَ الَّذِيْنَ اٰمَنُوْا ۘ
وَالَّذِيْنَ اتَّقَوْا فَوْقَهُمْ يَوْمَ الْقِيٰمَةِ ؕ
وَاللّٰهُ يَرْزُقُ مَنْ يَّشَآءُ بِغَيْرِ حِسَابٍ ﴿٢١٢﴾
كَانَ النَّاسُ اُمَّةً وَّاحِدَةً ۫ فَبَعَثَ
اللّٰهُ النَّبِيّٖنَ مُبَشِّرِيْنَ وَمُنْذِرِيْنَ ۪
وَاَنْزَلَ مَعَهُمُ الْكِتٰبَ بِالْحَقِّ لِيَحْكُمَ
بَيْنَ النَّاسِ فِيْمَا اخْتَلَفُوْا فِيْهِ ؕ
وَمَا اخْتَلَفَ فِيْهِ اِلَّا الَّذِيْنَ اُوْتُوْهُ
مِنْۢ بَعْدِ مَا جَآءَتْهُمُ الْبَيِّنٰتُ بَغْيًا
بَيْنَهُمْ ۚ فَهَدَى اللّٰهُ الَّذِيْنَ اٰمَنُوْا
لِمَا اخْتَلَفُوْا فِيْهِ مِنَ الْحَقِّ بِاِذْنِهٖ ؕ
وَاللّٰهُ يَهْدِيْ مَنْ يَّشَآءُ اِلٰى صِرَاطٍ
مُّسْتَقِيْمٍ ﴿٢١٣﴾
اَمْ حَسِبْتُمْ اَنْ تَدْخُلُوا الْجَنَّةَ وَلَمَّا
يَاْتِكُمْ مَّثَلُ الَّذِيْنَ خَلَوْا مِنْ
قَبْلِكُمْ ؕ مَسَّتْهُمُ الْبَاْسَآءُ وَالضَّرَّآءُ
وَزُلْزِلُوْا حَتّٰى يَقُوْلَ الرَّسُوْلُ
وَالَّذِيْنَ اٰمَنُوْا مَعَهٗ مَتٰى نَصْرُ اللّٰهِ ؕ
اَلَآ اِنَّ نَصْرَ اللّٰهِ قَرِيْبٌ ﴿٢١٤﴾
يَسْـَٔلُوْنَكَ مَاذَا يُنْفِقُوْنَ ؕ قُلْ مَآ
اَنْفَقْتُمْ مِّنْ خَيْرٍ فَلِلْوَالِدَيْنِ
وَالْاَقْرَبِيْنَ وَالْيَتٰمٰى وَالْمَسٰكِيْنِ
وَابْنِ السَّبِيْلِ ؕ وَمَا تَفْعَلُوْا مِنْ

وقف لازم

Ikhfa اخفاء · Ghunna غُنّہ · Ikhfa Meem Saakin اخفاء میم ساکن · Idghaam ادغام · Qalqala قلقلہ · Qalb قلب · Idghaam Meem Saakin ادغام میم ساکن

good, - Allah knows it well.

216. Fighting is prescribed for you, and you dislike it. But it is possible that you dislike a thing which is good for you, and that you love a thing which is bad for you. But Allah knows, and you know not.

217. They ask you concerning fighting in the Prohibited Month. Say: "Fighting therein is a grave (offence); but graver is still in the sight of Allah to prevent access to the path of Allah, to deny Him, to prevent access to the Sacred Mosque, and drive out its members." Tumult and oppression are worse than slaughter. Nor will they cease fighting you until they turn you back from your faith if they can. And if any of you turn back from their faith and die in unbelief, their works will bear no fruit in this life and in the Hereafter; they will be companions of the Fire and will abide therein.

218. Those who believed and those who suffered exile and fought (and strove and struggled) in the path of Allah,- they have the hope of the Mercy of Allah: and Allah is Oft-Forgiving, Most Merciful.

219. They ask you concerning wine and gambling. Say: "In them is great sin, and some profit, for men; but the sin is greater than the profit." They ask you how much they are to spend; Say: "What is beyond your needs." Thus does Allah make Clear to you

khayrin fa-innal-laaha bihee 'Aleem

216. Kutiba 'alaykumulqitaalu wa huwa kurhullakum wa 'asaaa an takrahoo shay'añw-wa huwa khayrullakum wa 'asaaa an tuḥibboo shay'añw-wa huwa sharrullakum; wallaahu ya'lamu wa-antum laa ta'lamoon.

(Section 26)

217. Yas'aloonaka 'anish-Shahril-Ḥaraami qitaalin feehi qul qitaalun feehi kabeeruñw-wa ṣaddun 'an sabeelil-laahi wa kufrum-bihee wal-Masjidil-Ḥaraami wa ikhraaju ahlihee minhu akbaru 'indal-laah; walfitnatu akbaru minal-qatl; wa laa yazaaloona yuqaati-loonakum ḥattaa yaruddookum 'an deenikum inis-taṭaa'oo; wa mañy-yartadid minkum 'an deenihee fayamut wahuwa kaafirun fa-ulaaa'ika ḥabiṭat a'maaluhum fid-dunyaa wal-Aakhirati wa ulaaa'ika Aṣhaabun-Naari hum feehaa khaalidoon.

218. Innal-lazeena aamanoo wallazeena haajaroo wa jaahadoo fee sabeelil-laahi ulaaa'ika yarjoona raḥmatal-laah; wallaahu Ghafoorur-Raḥeem.

219. Yas'aloonaka 'anilkhamri walmaysiri qul feehimaaa ismun kabeeruñw-wa manaafi'u linnaasi wa ismuhumaaa akbaru min naf'ihimaa; wa yas'aloonaka maazaa yunfiqoona qulil-'afw; kazaalika yubayyinul-laahu lakumul-

خَيْرٍ فَاِنَّ اللّٰهَ بِهٖ عَلِيْمٌ ﴿٢١٥﴾
كُتِبَ عَلَيْكُمُ الْقِتَالُ وَهُوَ كُرْهٌ لَّكُمْ ۚ
وَعَسٰٓى اَنْ تَكْرَهُوْا شَيْـًٔا وَّهُوَ
خَيْرٌ لَّكُمْ ۚ وَعَسٰٓى اَنْ تُحِبُّوْا شَيْـًٔا
وَّهُوَ شَرٌّ لَّكُمْ ۗ وَاللّٰهُ يَعْلَمُ
وَاَنْتُمْ لَا تَعْلَمُوْنَ ﴿٢١٦﴾ ع
يَسْـَٔلُوْنَكَ عَنِ الشَّهْرِ الْحَرَامِ قِتَالٍ
فِيْهِ ۗ قُلْ قِتَالٌ فِيْهِ كَبِيْرٌ ۗ وَصَدٌّ
عَنْ سَبِيْلِ اللّٰهِ وَكُفْرٌۢ بِهٖ وَالْمَسْجِدِ
الْحَرَامِ وَاِخْرَاجُ اَهْلِهٖ مِنْهُ اَكْبَرُ
عِنْدَ اللّٰهِ ۚ وَالْفِتْنَةُ اَكْبَرُ مِنَ
الْقَتْلِ ۗ وَلَا يَزَالُوْنَ يُقَاتِلُوْنَكُمْ
حَتّٰى يَرُدُّوْكُمْ عَنْ دِيْنِكُمْ اِنِ
اسْتَطَاعُوْا ۗ وَمَنْ يَّرْتَدِدْ مِنْكُمْ
عَنْ دِيْنِهٖ فَيَمُتْ وَهُوَ كَافِرٌ
فَاُولٰٓئِكَ حَبِطَتْ اَعْمَالُهُمْ فِى
الدُّنْيَا وَالْاٰخِرَةِ ۚ وَاُولٰٓئِكَ
اَصْحٰبُ النَّارِ ۚ هُمْ فِيْهَا خٰلِدُوْنَ ﴿٢١٧﴾
اِنَّ الَّذِيْنَ اٰمَنُوْا وَالَّذِيْنَ هَاجَرُوْا
وَجٰهَدُوْا فِىْ سَبِيْلِ اللّٰهِ ۙ اُولٰٓئِكَ
يَرْجُوْنَ رَحْمَتَ اللّٰهِ ۗ وَاللّٰهُ غَفُوْرٌ رَّحِيْمٌ ﴿٢١٨﴾
يَسْـَٔلُوْنَكَ عَنِ الْخَمْرِ وَالْمَيْسِرِ ۗ قُلْ
فِيْهِمَآ اِثْمٌ كَبِيْرٌ وَّمَنَافِعُ لِلنَّاسِ ۫
وَاِثْمُهُمَآ اَكْبَرُ مِنْ نَّفْعِهِمَا ۗ
وَيَسْـَٔلُوْنَكَ مَاذَا يُنْفِقُوْنَ ۥ قُلِ
الْعَفْوَ ۗ كَذٰلِكَ يُبَيِّنُ اللّٰهُ لَكُمُ

Ikhfa اخفاء | Ghunna غُنّہ | Ikhfa Meem Saakin اخفاء میم ساکن | Idghaam ادغام | Qalqala قلقلہ | Qalb قلب | Idghaam Meem Saakin ادغام میم ساکن

His Signs: in order that you may consider-

220. (Their bearings) on this life and the Hereafter. They ask you concerning orphans. Say: "The best thing to do is what is for their good; if you mix their affairs with yours, they are your brethren; but Allah knows the man who means mischief from the man who means good. And if Allah had wished, He could have put you into difficulties: He is indeed Exalted in Power, Wise."

221. Do not marry unbelieving women (idolators), until they believe: a slave woman who believes is better than an unbelieving woman, even though she allures you. Nor marry (your girls) to unbelievers until they believe: a man slave who believes is better than an unbeliever, even though he allures you. Unbelievers do (but) beckon you to the Fire. But Allah beckons by His Grace to the Garden (of Bliss) and forgiveness, and makes His Signs clear to mankind so that they may celebrate His praise.

222. They ask you concerning women's courses. Say: They are a hurt and a pollution: so keep away from women in their courses, and do not approach them until they are clean. But when they have purified themselves, you may approach them in any manner , time, or place ordained for you by Allah. For Allah loves those who turn to Him constantly and He loves those who keep themselves pure and clean.

223. Your wives are as a tilth unto you; so approach your tilth when or how you will; but do some good act for your souls beforehand; and fear Allah. And know that you are to meet Him (in the Hereafter), and give (these) good tidings to those who believe.

224. And make not Allah's (name) an excuse in your oaths

aayaati la'allakum tatafakkaroon.

220. Fid-dunyaa wal-Aakhirah; wa yas'aloonaka 'anil-yataamaa qul iṣlaaḥullahum khayr, wa in tukhaaliṭoohum fa-ikhwaanukum; wallaahu ya'lamul-mufsida minalmuṣliḥ; wa law shaaa'al-laahu la-a'natakum; innal-laaha 'Azeezun Ḥakeem.

221. Wa laa tankiḥul-mushrikaati ḥattaa yu'minn; wa la-amatum mu'minatun khayrum-mim-mushrikatiñw-wa law a'jabatkum; wa laa tunkiḥul-mushrikeena ḥattaa yu'minoo; wa la'abdummu'minun khayrum-mimmushrikiñw-wa law 'ajabakum; ulaaa'ika yad'oona ilan-Naari wallaahu yad'ooo ilal-Jannati walmaghfirati bi-iznihee wa yubayyinu Aayaatihee linnaasi la'allahum yatazakkaroon. **(Section 27)**

222. Wa yas'aloonaka 'anil maheeḍi qul huwa azan fa'tazilun-nisaaa'a fil-maḥeeḍi wa laa taqraboo-hunna ḥattaa yaṭhurna fa-izaa taṭahharna faåtoohunna min ḥaysu amarakumul-laah; innallaaha yuḥibbut-Tawwaabeena wa yuḥibbul-mutaṭahhireen.

223. Nisaaa'ukum ḥarsullakum faåtoo ḥarsakum annaa shi'tum wa qaddimoo li-anfusikum; wattaqul-laaha wa'lamooo annakum mulaaqooh;wa bash-shirilmu'mineen.

224. Wa laa taj'alul-laaha 'urḍatal-li-aymaanikum

الْاٰيٰتِ لَعَلَّكُمْ تَتَفَكَّرُوْنَ ﴿٢١٩﴾
فِي الدُّنْيَا وَالْاٰخِرَةِ ۭ وَيَسْـَٔلُوْنَكَ
عَنِ الْيَتٰمٰى ۭ قُلْ اِصْلَاحٌ لَّهُمْ خَيْرٌ ۭ
وَاِنْ تُخَالِطُوْهُمْ فَاِخْوَانُكُمْ ۭ وَاللّٰهُ
يَعْلَمُ الْمُفْسِدَ مِنَ الْمُصْلِحِ ۭ وَلَوْ شَاۗءَ
اللّٰهُ لَاَعْنَتَكُمْ ۭ اِنَّ اللّٰهَ عَزِيْزٌ حَكِيْمٌ ﴿٢٢٠﴾
وَلَا تَنْكِحُوا الْمُشْرِكٰتِ حَتّٰى يُؤْمِنَّ ۭ
وَلَاَمَةٌ مُّؤْمِنَةٌ خَيْرٌ مِّنْ مُّشْرِكَةٍ
وَّلَوْ اَعْجَبَتْكُمْ ۚ وَلَا تُنْكِحُوا الْمُشْرِكِيْنَ
حَتّٰى يُؤْمِنُوْا ۭ وَلَعَبْدٌ مُّؤْمِنٌ خَيْرٌ
مِّنْ مُّشْرِكٍ وَّلَوْ اَعْجَبَكُمْ ۭ اُولٰۗىِٕكَ
يَدْعُوْنَ اِلَى النَّارِ ښ وَاللّٰهُ يَدْعُوْٓا
اِلَى الْجَنَّةِ وَالْمَغْفِرَةِ بِاِذْنِهٖ ۚ
وَيُبَيِّنُ اٰيٰتِهٖ لِلنَّاسِ لَعَلَّهُمْ
يَتَذَكَّرُوْنَ ﴿٢٢١﴾ ع
وَيَسْـَٔلُوْنَكَ عَنِ الْمَحِيْضِ ۭ قُلْ
هُوَ اَذًى ۙ فَاعْتَزِلُوا النِّسَاۗءَ فِي
الْمَحِيْضِ ۙ وَلَا تَقْرَبُوْهُنَّ حَتّٰى
يَطْهُرْنَ ۚ فَاِذَا تَطَهَّرْنَ فَاْتُوْهُنَّ
مِنْ حَيْثُ اَمَرَكُمُ اللّٰهُ ۭ اِنَّ اللّٰهَ يُحِبُّ
التَّوَّابِيْنَ وَيُحِبُّ الْمُتَطَهِّرِيْنَ ﴿٢٢٢﴾
نِسَاۗؤُكُمْ حَرْثٌ لَّكُمْ ۠ فَاْتُوْا حَرْثَكُمْ
اَنّٰى شِئْتُمْ ۡ وَقَدِّمُوْا لِاَنْفُسِكُمْ ۭ
وَاتَّقُوا اللّٰهَ وَاعْلَمُوْٓا اَنَّكُمْ مُّلٰقُوْهُ ۭ
وَبَشِّرِ الْمُؤْمِنِيْنَ ﴿٢٢٣﴾
وَلَا تَجْعَلُوا اللّٰهَ عُرْضَةً لِّاَيْمَانِكُمْ

Ikhfa اخفاء | Ghunna غُنّہ | Ikhfa Meem Saakin اخفاء میم ساکن | Idghaam ادغام | Qalqala قلقلہ | Qalb قلب | Idghaam Meem Saakin ادغام میم ساکن

against doing good, or acting rightly, or making peace between persons; for Allah is One Who hears and knows all things.

an tabarroo wa tattaqoo wa tuṣliḥoo baynan-naas; wallaahu Samee'un-'Aleem.

أَن تَبَرُّوا وَتَتَّقُوا وَتُصْلِحُوا بَيْنَ
النَّاسِ ط وَاللَّهُ سَمِيعٌ عَلِيمٌ ﴿٢٢٤﴾

225. Allah will not call you to account for thoughtlessness in your oaths, but for the intention in your hearts; and He is Oft-Forgiving, Most Forbearing.

225. Laa yu'aakhi-zukumul-laahu billaghwi feee aymaa-nikum wa laakiñy-yu'aakhi-zukum bimaa kasabat quloo-bukum; wallaahu Ghafoorun Ḥaleem.

لَا يُؤَاخِذُكُمُ اللَّهُ بِاللَّغْوِ فِي أَيْمَانِكُمْ
وَلَٰكِن يُؤَاخِذُكُم بِمَا كَسَبَتْ
قُلُوبُكُمْ ط وَاللَّهُ غَفُورٌ حَلِيمٌ ﴿٢٢٥﴾

226. For those who take an oath for abstention from their wives, a waiting for four months is ordained; if then they return, Allah is Oft-Forgiving, Most Merciful.

226. Lillazeena yu'loona min nisaaa'ihim tarabbuṣu arba'ati ashhurin fain faaa'oo fa-innal-laaha Ghafoorur-Raḥeem.

لِّلَّذِينَ يُؤْلُونَ مِن نِّسَائِهِمْ
تَرَبُّصُ أَرْبَعَةِ أَشْهُرٍ ج فَإِن فَاءُو
فَإِنَّ اللَّهَ غَفُورٌ رَّحِيمٌ ﴿٢٢٦﴾

227. But if their intention is firm for divorce, Allah hears and knows all things.

227. Wa in 'azamuṭ-ṭalaaqa fa-innal-laaha Samee'un 'Aleem

وَإِنْ عَزَمُوا الطَّلَاقَ فَإِنَّ اللَّهَ
سَمِيعٌ عَلِيمٌ ﴿٢٢٧﴾

228. Divorced women shall wait concerning themselves for three monthly periods. Nor is it lawful for them to hide what Allah has created in their wombs, if they have faith in Allah and the Last Day. And their husbands have the better right to take them back in that period, if they wish for reconciliation. And women shall have rights similar to the rights against them, according to what is equitable; but men have a degree (of advantage) over them. And Allah is Exalted in Power, Wise.

228. Walmutallaqaatu yatarab-baṣna bi-anfusihinna salaasata qurooo'; wa laa yaḥillu lahunna añy-yaktumna maa khalaqal-laahu feee arḥaamihinna in kunna yu'minna billaahi wal-Yawmil-Aakhir; wa bu'oola-tuhunna aḥaqqu biraddihinna fee zaalika in araadooo iṣlaaḥaa; wa lahunna mislul-lazee 'alayhinna bilma'roof; wa lirrijaali 'alayhinna darajah; wallaahu 'Azeezun Ḥakeem.

(Section 28)

وَالْمُطَلَّقَاتُ يَتَرَبَّصْنَ بِأَنفُسِهِنَّ
ثَلَاثَةَ قُرُوءٍ ط وَلَا يَحِلُّ لَهُنَّ أَن
يَكْتُمْنَ مَا خَلَقَ اللَّهُ فِي أَرْحَامِهِنَّ
إِن كُنَّ يُؤْمِنَّ بِاللَّهِ وَالْيَوْمِ
الْآخِرِ ط وَبُعُولَتُهُنَّ أَحَقُّ بِرَدِّهِنَّ
فِي ذَٰلِكَ إِنْ أَرَادُوا إِصْلَاحًا ط وَ
لَهُنَّ مِثْلُ الَّذِي عَلَيْهِنَّ بِالْمَعْرُوفِ
وَلِلرِّجَالِ عَلَيْهِنَّ دَرَجَةٌ ط وَاللَّهُ
عَزِيزٌ حَكِيمٌ ﴿٢٢٨﴾ ٢٨ ع ١٢

229. A divorce is only permissible twice: after that, the parties should either hold together on equitable terms, or separate with kindness. It is not lawful for you, (men), to take back any of your gifts (from your wives), except when both parties fear that they would be unable to keep the limits ordained by Allah. If you (judges) do indeed fear that they would be unable to keep the limits ordained by Allah, there is no blame on either of them if she give something for her freedom. These are the limits ordained by Allah; so do not

229. Aṭṭalaaqu marrataani fa-imsaakum bima'roofin aw tasreeḥum bi-iḥsaan; wa laa yaḥillu lakum an taåkhuzoo mimmaaa aataytumoohunna shay'an illaaa añy-yakhaafaaa allaa yuqeemaa ḥudoodallaahi fa-in khiftum allaa yuqeemaa ḥudoodal-laahi falaa Junaaḥa 'Alaihimaa feemaf-tadat bihee tilka Ḥudoodul-laahi falaa

الطَّلَاقُ مَرَّتَانِ فَإِمْسَاكٌ بِمَعْرُوفٍ
أَوْ تَسْرِيحٌ بِإِحْسَانٍ ط وَلَا يَحِلُّ لَكُمْ
أَن تَأْخُذُوا مِمَّا آتَيْتُمُوهُنَّ شَيْئًا
إِلَّا أَن يَخَافَا أَلَّا يُقِيمَا حُدُودَ اللَّهِ ط
فَإِنْ خِفْتُمْ أَلَّا يُقِيمَا حُدُودَ
اللَّهِ لا فَلَا جُنَاحَ عَلَيْهِمَا فِيمَا
افْتَدَتْ بِهِ ط تِلْكَ حُدُودُ اللَّهِ فَلَا

Ikhfa اخفاء | Ghunna غُنّہ | Ikhfa Meem Saakin اخفاء میم ساکن | Idghaam ادغام | Qalqala قلقلہ | Qalb قلب | Idghaam Meem Saakin ادغام میم ساکن

transgress them, if any do transgress the limits ordained by Allah, such persons wrong (themselves as well as others).

ta'tadoohaa; wa mañy-yata'adda ḥudoodal-laahi fa-ulaaa'ika humuẓẓaa-limoon.

تَعْتَدُوهَا ۚ وَمَن يَتَعَدَّ حُدُودَ
اللَّهِ فَأُولَٰئِكَ هُمُ الظَّالِمُونَ ﴿٢٢٩﴾

230. So if a husband divorces his wife (irrevocably), he cannot, after that, re- marry her until after she has married another husband and he has divorced her. In that case there is no blame on either of them if they re-unite, provided they feel that they can keep the limits ordained by Allah. Such are the limits ordained by Allah, which He makes plain to those who understand.

230. Fa-in ṭallaqahaa falaa taḥillu lahoo mim ba'du ḥattaa tankiḥa zawjan ghayrah; fa-in ṭallaqahaa falaa junaaḥa 'alayhimaaa añy-yataraaja'aaa in ẓannaaa añy-yuqeemaa ḥudoodal-laah; wa tilka ḥudoodul-laahi yubayyinuhaa liqawmiñy-ya'lamoon.

فَإِن طَلَّقَهَا فَلَا تَحِلُّ لَهُ مِن بَعْدُ
حَتَّىٰ تَنكِحَ زَوْجًا غَيْرَهُ ۗ فَإِن
طَلَّقَهَا فَلَا جُنَاحَ عَلَيْهِمَا أَن
يَتَرَاجَعَا إِن ظَنَّا أَن يُقِيمَا حُدُودَ
اللَّهِ ۗ وَتِلْكَ حُدُودُ اللَّهِ يُبَيِّنُهَا
لِقَوْمٍ يَعْلَمُونَ ﴿٢٣٠﴾

231. When you divorce women, and they fulfil the term of their ('Iddat), either take them back on equitable terms or set them free on equitable terms; but do not take them back to injure them, (or) to take undue advantage; if any one does that; he wrongs his own soul. Do not treat Allah's Signs as a jest, but solemnly rehearse Allah's favours on you, and the fact that He sent down to you the Book and Wisdom, for your instruction. And fear Allah, and know that Allah is well acquainted with all things.

231. Wa izaa ṭallaqtumun-nisaaa'a fabalaghna ajala-hunna fa-amsikoohunna bima'roofin law sarriḥoo-hunna bima'roof; wa laa tumsikoo-hunna ḍiraa-rallita'tadoo; wa mañy-yaf'al zaalika faqad ẓalama nafsah; wa laa tattakhizooo Aayaatillaahi huzuwaa; wazkuroo ni'matal-laahi 'alaykum wa maaa anzala 'alaykum minal-Kitaabi wal-Ḥikmati ya'iẓukum bih; wattaqul-laaha wa'lamooo annal-laaha bikulli shay'i 'Aleem. **(Section 29)**

وَإِذَا طَلَّقْتُمُ النِّسَاءَ فَبَلَغْنَ
أَجَلَهُنَّ فَأَمْسِكُوهُنَّ بِمَعْرُوفٍ
أَوْ سَرِّحُوهُنَّ بِمَعْرُوفٍ ۚ وَلَا
تُمْسِكُوهُنَّ ضِرَارًا لِّتَعْتَدُوا ۚ وَمَن
يَفْعَلْ ذَٰلِكَ فَقَدْ ظَلَمَ نَفْسَهُ ۚ
وَلَا تَتَّخِذُوا آيَاتِ اللَّهِ هُزُوًا ۚ
وَاذْكُرُوا نِعْمَتَ اللَّهِ عَلَيْكُمْ
وَمَا أَنزَلَ عَلَيْكُم مِّنَ الْكِتَابِ
وَالْحِكْمَةِ يَعِظُكُم بِهِ ۚ وَاتَّقُوا اللَّهَ
وَاعْلَمُوا أَنَّ اللَّهَ بِكُلِّ شَيْءٍ عَلِيمٌ ﴿٢٣١﴾ الربع

232. When you divorce women, and they fulfil the term of their ('Iddat), do not prevent them from marrying their (former) husbands, if they mutually agree on equitable terms. This instruction is for all among you, who believe in Allah and the Last Day. That is (the course making for) most virtue and purity among you and Allah knows, and you know not.

232. Wa izaa ṭallaqtumun-nisaaa'a fabalaghna ajalahunna falaa ta'ḍuloo-hunna añy-yankiḥna azwaaja-hunna izaa taraaḍaw baynahum bilma'-roof; zaalika yoo'azu bihee man kaana minkum yu'minu billaahi walYawmil-Aakhir; zaalikum azkaa lakum wa aṭhar; wallaahu ya'lamu wa antum laa ta'lamoon.

وَإِذَا طَلَّقْتُمُ النِّسَاءَ فَبَلَغْنَ
أَجَلَهُنَّ فَلَا تَعْضُلُوهُنَّ أَن يَنكِحْنَ
أَزْوَاجَهُنَّ إِذَا تَرَاضَوْا بَيْنَهُم
بِالْمَعْرُوفِ ۗ ذَٰلِكَ يُوعَظُ بِهِ مَن
كَانَ مِنكُمْ يُؤْمِنُ بِاللَّهِ وَالْيَوْمِ
الْآخِرِ ۗ ذَٰلِكُمْ أَزْكَىٰ لَكُمْ وَأَطْهَرُ ۚ
وَاللَّهُ يَعْلَمُ وَأَنتُمْ لَا تَعْلَمُونَ ﴿٢٣٢﴾

233. The mothers shall give suck to their offspring

233. Walwaalidaatu yurḍi'na awlaadahunna

وَالْوَالِدَاتُ يُرْضِعْنَ أَوْلَادَهُنَّ

Ikhfa	Ghunna	Ikhfa Meem Saakin	Idghaam	Qalqala	Qalb	Idghaam Meem Saakin
اخفاء	غُنّہ	اخفاء میم ساکن	ادغام	قلقلہ	قلب	ادغام میم ساکن

for two whole years, if the father desires to complete the term. But he shall bear the cost of their food and clothing on equitable terms. No soul shall have a burden laid on it greater than it can bear. No mother shall be treated unfairly on account of her child. Nor father on account of his child, an heir shall be chargeable in the same way. If they both decide on weaning, by mutual consent, and after due consultation, there is no blame on them. If you decide on a foster-mother for your offspring, there is no blame on you, provided you pay (the mother) what you offered, on equitable terms. But fear Allah and know that Allah sees well what you do.

ḥawlayni kaamilayni liman araada añy-yutimmar-raḍaa'ah; wa 'alalmawloodi lahoo rizquhunna wa kiswatuhunna bilma'roof; laa tukallafu nafsun illaa wus'ahaa; laa tuḍaaarra waalidatum-biwaladihaa wa laa mawloodul-lahoo biwaladih;Wa 'alal-waarisi mislu zaalik; fa-in araadaa Fiṣaalan 'an taraaḍim-minhumaa wa tashaawurin falaa junaaḥa 'alayhimaa; wa in arattum an tastarḍi'ooo awlaadakum falaa junaaḥa 'alaykum izaa sallamtum maaa aataytum bilma'roof; wattaqul-laaha wa'lamooo annal-laaha bimaa ta'maloona Baṣeer.

حَوْلَيْنِ كَامِلَيْنِ لِمَنْ أَرَادَ أَنْ
يُتِمَّ الرَّضَاعَةَ ۚ وَعَلَى الْمَوْلُودِ لَهُ
رِزْقُهُنَّ وَكِسْوَتُهُنَّ بِالْمَعْرُوفِ ۚ
لَا تُكَلَّفُ نَفْسٌ إِلَّا وُسْعَهَا ۚ
لَا تُضَارَّ وَالِدَةٌ بِوَلَدِهَا وَلَا
مَوْلُودٌ لَهُ بِوَلَدِهِ ۚ وَعَلَى الْوَارِثِ
مِثْلُ ذَٰلِكَ ۗ فَإِنْ أَرَادَا فِصَالًا عَنْ
تَرَاضٍ مِنْهُمَا وَتَشَاوُرٍ فَلَا جُنَاحَ
عَلَيْهِمَا ۗ وَإِنْ أَرَدْتُمْ أَنْ تَسْتَرْضِعُوا
أَوْلَادَكُمْ فَلَا جُنَاحَ عَلَيْكُمْ إِذَا
سَلَّمْتُمْ مَا آتَيْتُمْ بِالْمَعْرُوفِ ۗ
وَاتَّقُوا اللَّهَ وَاعْلَمُوا أَنَّ اللَّهَ بِمَا
تَعْمَلُونَ بَصِيرٌ ﴿٢٣٣﴾

234. If any of you die and leave widows behind, they shall wait concerning themselves four months and ten days: when they have fulfilled their term, there is no blame on you if they dispose of themselves in a just and reasonable manner. And Allah is well acquainted with what you do.

234. Wallazeena yutawaffawna minkum wa yazaroona azwaajañy-yatarabbaṣna bi-anfusihinna arba'ata ashhuriñw-wa 'ashran fa-izaa balaghna ajalahunna falaa junaaḥa 'alaykum feemaa fa'alna feee anfusihinna bilma'roof; wallaahu bimaa ta'maloona Khabeer.

وَالَّذِينَ يُتَوَفَّوْنَ مِنْكُمْ وَيَذَرُونَ
أَزْوَاجًا يَتَرَبَّصْنَ بِأَنْفُسِهِنَّ
أَرْبَعَةَ أَشْهُرٍ وَعَشْرًا ۖ فَإِذَا بَلَغْنَ
أَجَلَهُنَّ فَلَا جُنَاحَ عَلَيْكُمْ فِيمَا
فَعَلْنَ فِي أَنْفُسِهِنَّ بِالْمَعْرُوفِ ۗ
وَاللَّهُ بِمَا تَعْمَلُونَ خَبِيرٌ ﴿٢٣٤﴾

235. There is no blame on you if you make an offer of betrothal or hold it in your hearts. Allah knows that you cherish them in your hearts: but do not make a secret contract with them except in terms honourable, nor resolve on the tie of marriage till the term prescribed is fulfilled. And know that Allah Knows what is

235. Wa laa junaaḥa 'alaykum feemaa 'arraḍtum bihee min khiṭbatin-nisaaa'i aw aknantum feee anfusikum; 'alimal-laahu annakum satazkuroonahunna wa laakil-laa tuwaa'idoohunna sirran illaaa an taqooloo qawlamma'roofaa; wa laa ta'zimoo 'uqdatan-nikaaḥi ḥattaa yablughal-kitaabu ajalah; wa'lamooo annal-laaha ya'lamu maa

وَلَا جُنَاحَ عَلَيْكُمْ فِيمَا عَرَّضْتُمْ بِهِ
مِنْ خِطْبَةِ النِّسَاءِ أَوْ أَكْنَنْتُمْ فِي
أَنْفُسِكُمْ ۚ عَلِمَ اللَّهُ أَنَّكُمْ سَتَذْكُرُونَهُنَّ
وَلَٰكِنْ لَا تُوَاعِدُوهُنَّ سِرًّا إِلَّا أَنْ
تَقُولُوا قَوْلًا مَعْرُوفًا ۚ وَلَا تَعْزِمُوا
عُقْدَةَ النِّكَاحِ حَتَّىٰ يَبْلُغَ الْكِتَابُ
أَجَلَهُ ۚ وَاعْلَمُوا أَنَّ اللَّهَ يَعْلَمُ مَا

Ikhfa اخفاء | Ghunna غنّة | Ikhfa Meem Saakin اخفاء میم ساکن | Idghaam ادغام | Qalqala قلقلہ | Qalb قلب | Idghaam Meem Saakin ادغام میم ساکن

in your hearts, and take heed of Him; and know that Allah is Oft-Forgiving, Most Forbearing.

feee anfusikum faḥzarooh; wa'lamooo annallaaha Ghafoorun Ḥaleem **(Section 30)**

فِيٓ أَنفُسِكُمْ فَٱحْذَرُوهُ ۚ وَٱعْلَمُوٓا۟
أَنَّ ٱللَّهَ غَفُورٌ حَلِيمٌ ﴿٢٣٥﴾

236. There is no blame on you if you divorce women before consummation or the fixation of their dower; but bestow on them (a suitable gift), the wealthy according to his means, and the poor according to his means;- a gift of a reasonable amount is due from those who wish to do the right thing.

236. Laa junaaḥa 'alaykum in ṭallaqtumun-nisaaa'a maa lam tamassoohunna aw tafriḍoo lahunna fareeḍah; wa matti'oohunna 'alal-moosi'i qadaruhoo wa 'alal-muqtiri qadaruhoo mattaa'am-bilma'roofi ḥaqqan 'alalmuḥsineen.

لَّا جُنَاحَ عَلَيْكُمْ إِن طَلَّقْتُمُ ٱلنِّسَآءَ
مَا لَمْ تَمَسُّوهُنَّ أَوْ تَفْرِضُوا۟ لَهُنَّ
فَرِيضَةً ۚ وَمَتِّعُوهُنَّ عَلَى
ٱلْمُوسِعِ قَدَرُهُۥ وَعَلَى ٱلْمُقْتِرِ قَدَرُهُۥ
مَتَٰعًۢا بِٱلْمَعْرُوفِ ۖ حَقًّا عَلَى
ٱلْمُحْسِنِينَ ﴿٢٣٦﴾

237. And if you divorce them before consummation, but after the fixation of a dower for them, then the half of the dower (is due to them), unless they remit it or (the man's half) is remitted by him in whose hands is the marriage tie; and the remission (of the man's half) is the nearest to righteousness. And do not forget liberality between yourselves. For Allah sees well all that you do.

237. Wa in tallaqtumoohunna min qabli an tamassoohunna wa qad faraḍtum lahunna fareeḍatan faniṣfu maa faraḍtum illaaa añy-ya'foona aw ya'fuwallazee biyadihee 'uqdatunnikaaḥ; wa an ta'fooo aqrabu littaqwaa; wa laa tansawulfaḍla baynakum; innal-laaha bimaa ta'maloona Baṣeer.

وَإِن طَلَّقْتُمُوهُنَّ مِن قَبْلِ أَن
تَمَسُّوهُنَّ وَقَدْ فَرَضْتُمْ لَهُنَّ
فَرِيضَةً فَنِصْفُ مَا فَرَضْتُمْ
إِلَّآ أَن يَعْفُونَ أَوْ يَعْفُوَا۟ ٱلَّذِى
بِيَدِهِۦ عُقْدَةُ ٱلنِّكَاحِ ۚ وَأَن
تَعْفُوٓا۟ أَقْرَبُ لِلتَّقْوَىٰ ۚ وَلَا تَنسَوُا۟
ٱلْفَضْلَ بَيْنَكُمْ ۚ إِنَّ ٱللَّهَ بِمَا
تَعْمَلُونَ بَصِيرٌ ﴿٢٣٧﴾

238. Guard strictly your (habit of) prayers, especially the Middle Prayer; and stand before Allah in a devout (frame of mind).

238. Ḥaafizoo 'alaṣ-Ṣalawaati waṣ-Ṣalaatil-Wusṭaa wa qoomoo lillaahi qaaniteen.

حَٰفِظُوا۟ عَلَى ٱلصَّلَوَٰتِ وَٱلصَّلَوٰةِ
ٱلْوُسْطَىٰ وَقُومُوا۟ لِلَّهِ قَٰنِتِينَ ﴿٢٣٨﴾

239. If you fear (an enemy), pray on foot, or riding, (as may be most convenient), but when you are in security, celebrate Allah's praises in the manner He has taught you, which you knew not (before).

239. Fa-in khiftum farijaalan aw rukbaanan fa-izaaa amintum fazkurul-laaha kamaa 'allamakum maa lam takoonoo ta'lamoon.

فَإِنْ خِفْتُمْ فَرِجَالًا أَوْ رُكْبَانًا ۖ
فَإِذَآ أَمِنتُمْ فَٱذْكُرُوا۟ ٱللَّهَ كَمَا
عَلَّمَكُم مَّا لَمْ تَكُونُوا۟ تَعْلَمُونَ ﴿٢٣٩﴾

240. Those of you who die and leave widows should bequeath for their widows a year's maintenance and residence; but if they leave (the residence), there is no blame on you for what they do with themselves, provided it is

240. Wallazeena yutawaffawna minkum wa yazaroona azwaajañw-waṣiyyatal-liazwaajihim mataa'an ilal-ḥawli ghayra ikhraaj; fa-in kharajna falaa junaaḥa 'alaykum fee maa fa'alna feee anfusihinna mim

وَٱلَّذِينَ يُتَوَفَّوْنَ مِنكُمْ وَيَذَرُونَ
أَزْوَٰجًا وَصِيَّةً لِّأَزْوَٰجِهِم
مَّتَٰعًا إِلَى ٱلْحَوْلِ غَيْرَ إِخْرَاجٍ ۚ
فَإِنْ خَرَجْنَ فَلَا جُنَاحَ عَلَيْكُمْ فِى
مَا فَعَلْنَ فِىٓ أَنفُسِهِنَّ مِن

Ikhfa إخفاء | Ghunna غُنّہ | Ikhfa Meem Saakin اخفاء میم ساکن | Idghaam ادغام | Qalqala قلقلہ | Qalb قلب | Idghaam Meem Saakin ادغام میم ساکن

reasonable. And Allah is Exalted in Power, Wise.	ma'roof; wallaahu 'Azeezun Ḥakeem.	مَعْرُوفٍ ۗ وَاللّٰهُ عَزِيزٌ حَكِيمٌ (٢٤٠)
241. For divorced women Maintenance (should be provided) on a reasonable (scale). This is a duty on the righteous.	241. Wa lilmuṭallaqaati mataa-'um-bilma'roofi ḥaqqan 'alal-muttaqeen.	وَلِلْمُطَلَّقٰتِ مَتَاعٌ بِالْمَعْرُوفِ ۖ حَقًّا عَلَى الْمُتَّقِينَ (٢٤١)
242. Thus Allah Makes clear His Signs to you: in order that you may understand.	242. Kaẕaalika yubayyinul-laahu lakum Aayaatihee la'allakum ta'qiloon. **(Section 31)**	كَذٰلِكَ يُبَيِّنُ اللّٰهُ لَكُمْ اٰيٰتِهٖ لَعَلَّكُمْ تَعْقِلُونَ (٢٤٢) ع ربع ١٥
243. Did you not Turn by vision to those who abandoned their homes, though they were thousands (in number), for fear of death? Allah said to them: "Die"! Then He restored them to life. For Allah is full of bounty to mankind, but Most of them are ungrateful.	243. Alam tara ilal-laẕeena kharajoo min diyaarihim wa hum uloofun ḥaẕaral-mawti faqaala lahumul-laahu mootoo s̱umma aḥyaahum; innal-laaha laẕoo faḍlin 'alannaasi wa laakinna aks̱arannaasi laa yashkuroon	اَلَمْ تَرَ اِلَى الَّذِينَ خَرَجُوا مِنْ دِيَارِهِمْ وَهُمْ اُلُوفٌ حَذَرَ الْمَوْتِ فَقَالَ لَهُمُ اللّٰهُ مُوتُوا ثُمَّ اَحْيَاهُمْ ۗ اِنَّ اللّٰهَ لَذُو فَضْلٍ عَلَى النَّاسِ وَلٰكِنَّ اَكْثَرَ النَّاسِ لَا يَشْكُرُونَ (٢٤٣)
244. Then fight in the cause of Allah, and know that Allah hears and knows all things.	244. Wa qaatiloo fee sabeelil-laahi wa'lamooo annal-laaha Samee'un 'Aleem.	وَقَاتِلُوا فِي سَبِيلِ اللّٰهِ وَاعْلَمُوا اَنَّ اللّٰهَ سَمِيعٌ عَلِيمٌ (٢٤٤)
245. Who is he that will loan to Allah a beautiful loan, which Allah will double unto his credit and multiply many times? It is Allah that gives (you) Want or Plenty, and to Him shall be your return.	245. Man ẕal-laẕee yuqriḍul-laaha qarḍan ḥasanan fayuḍaa-'ifahoo lahooo aḍ'aafan kas̱ee-rah; wallaahu yaqbiḍu wa yabsuṭ(u) wa ilayhi turja'oon.	مَنْ ذَا الَّذِي يُقْرِضُ اللّٰهَ قَرْضًا حَسَنًا فَيُضٰعِفَهُ لَهٗ اَضْعَافًا كَثِيرَةً ۗ وَاللّٰهُ يَقْبِضُ وَيَبْصُۜطُ وَاِلَيْهِ تُرْجَعُونَ (٢٤٥)
246. Have you not turned you vision to the Chiefs of the Children of Israel after (the time of) Moses? They said to a prophet (that was) among them: "Appoint for us a king, that we may fight in the cause of Allah." He said: "Is it not possible, if you were commanded to fight, that you will not fight?" They said: "How could we refuse to fight in the cause of Allah, seeing that we were turned out of our homes and our families?" But when they were commanded to fight, they turned back, except a small band among them. But Allah has full knowledge of those who do wrong.	246. Alam tara ilal-malai mim-Baneee Israaa'eela mim ba'di Moosaaa iẕ qaaloo li-Nabiyyil-lahumub-'as̱ lanaa malikan nuqaatil fee sabeelillaahi qaala hal 'asaytum in kutiba 'alaykumul-qitaalu allaa tuqaatiloo qaaloo wa maa lanaaa allaa nuqaatila fee sabeelil-laahi wa qad ukhrijnaa min diyaarinaa wa abnaaa'inaa falammaa kutiba 'alayhimul-qitaalu tawallaw illaa qaleelam-minhum; wallaahu 'aleemum-bizẓaalimeen.	اَلَمْ تَرَ اِلَى الْمَلَاِ مِنْ بَنِيٓ اِسْرَآءِيلَ مِنْ بَعْدِ مُوسٰى ۘ اِذْ قَالُوا لِنَبِيٍّ لَّهُمُ ابْعَثْ لَنَا مَلِكًا نُّقَاتِلْ فِي سَبِيلِ اللّٰهِ ۖ قَالَ هَلْ عَسَيْتُمْ اِنْ كُتِبَ عَلَيْكُمُ الْقِتَالُ اَلَّا تُقَاتِلُوا ۖ قَالُوا وَمَا لَنَآ اَلَّا نُقَاتِلَ فِي سَبِيلِ اللّٰهِ وَقَدْ اُخْرِجْنَا مِنْ دِيَارِنَا وَاَبْنَآئِنَا ۖ فَلَمَّا كُتِبَ عَلَيْهِمُ الْقِتَالُ تَوَلَّوْا اِلَّا قَلِيلًا مِّنْهُمْ ۗ وَاللّٰهُ عَلِيمٌ بِالظّٰلِمِينَ (٢٤٦) وقف لازم

Ikhfa اخفاء · Ghunna غنّہ · Ikhfa Meem Saakin اخفاء میم ساکن · Idghaam ادغام · Qalqala قلقلہ · Qalb قلب · Idghaam Meem Saakin ادغام میم ساکن

247. Their Prophet said to them: "Allah has appointed Talut as king over you." They said: "How can he exercise authority over us when we are better fitted than he to exercise authority, and he is not even gifted, with wealth in abundance?" He said: "Allah has chosen him above you, and has gifted him abundantly with knowledge and bodily prowess: Allah grants His authority to whom He pleases. Allah cares for all, and He knows all things."

247. Wa qaala lahum Nabiy-yuhum innal-laaha qad ba'asa lakum Ṭaalootа malikaa; qaalooo annaa yakoonu lahul-mulku 'alaynaa wa naḥnu aḥaqqu bilmulki minhu wa lam yu'ta sa'atammminal-maal; qaala innallaahaṣ-ṭafaahu 'alaykum wa zaadahoo basṭatan fil-'ilmi waljismi wallaahu yu'tee mulkahoo mañy-yashaaa'; wallaahu Waasi'un 'Aleem.

وَقَالَ لَهُمْ نَبِيُّهُمْ إِنَّ اللّٰهَ قَدْ بَعَثَ
لَكُمْ طَالُوتَ مَلِكًا ۚ قَالُوٓا أَنّٰى يَكُونُ
لَهُ الْمُلْكُ عَلَيْنَا وَنَحْنُ أَحَقُّ بِالْمُلْكِ
مِنْهُ وَلَمْ يُؤْتَ سَعَةً مِّنَ الْمَالِ ۚ
قَالَ إِنَّ اللّٰهَ اصْطَفٰهُ عَلَيْكُمْ وَزَادَهُ
بَسْطَةً فِي الْعِلْمِ وَالْجِسْمِ ۚ وَاللّٰهُ
يُؤْتِي مُلْكَهُ مَنْ يَّشَآءُ ۚ وَاللّٰهُ
وَاسِعٌ عَلِيمٌ ﴿٢٤٧﴾

248. And (further) their Prophet said to them: "A Sign of his authority is that there shall come to you the Ark of the Covenant, with (an assurance) therein of security from your Lord, and the relics left by the family of Moses and the family of Aaron, carried by Angels. In this is a symbol for you if you indeed have faith."

248. Wa qaala lahum Nabiy-yuhum inna Aayata mulkiheee añy-yaåtiyakumut-Taabootu feehi sakeenatummir-Rabbi-kum wa baqiyyatummimmaa taraka Aalu Moosaa wa Aalu Haaroona taḥmiluhul-malaaa'ikah; inna fee zaalika la-Aayatal-lakum in kuntum mu'mineen. **(Section 32)**

وَقَالَ لَهُمْ نَبِيُّهُمْ إِنَّ اٰيَةَ مُلْكِهٖٓ
أَنْ يَّأْتِيَكُمُ التَّابُوتُ فِيهِ
سَكِينَةٌ مِّنْ رَّبِّكُمْ وَبَقِيَّةٌ مِّمَّا
تَرَكَ اٰلُ مُوسٰى وَاٰلُ هٰرُونَ تَحْمِلُهُ
الْمَلٰٓئِكَةُ ۚ إِنَّ فِي ذٰلِكَ لَاٰيَةً لَّكُمْ
إِنْ كُنْتُمْ مُّؤْمِنِينَ ﴿٢٤٨﴾ ع ٣٢ ١٦

249. When Talut set forth with the armies, he said: "Allah will test you at the stream: if any drinks of its water, he goes not with my army: only those who taste not of it go with me: a mere sip out of the hand is excused." But they all drank of it, except a few. When they crossed the river,- He and the faithful ones with him,- they said: "This day We cannot cope with Goliath and his forces." But those who were convinced that they must meet Allah, said: "How oft, by Allah's will, has a small force vanquished a big one? Allah is with those who steadfastly persevere."

249. Falammaa faṣala Ṭaalootu biljunoodi qaala innal-laaha mubtaleekum binaharin faman shariba minhu falaysa minnee wa mallam yaṭ'amhu fa-innahoo minneee illaa manigh-tarafa ghurfatam biyadih; fashariboo minhu illaa qaleelamminhum; falammaa jaawazahoo huwa wallazeena aamanoo ma'ahoo qaaloo laa ṭaaqata lanal-yawma bi-Jaaloota wa junoodih; qaalallazeena yaẓunnoona annahum mulaaqul-laahi kam min fi'atin qaleelatin ghalabat fi'atan kaseeratam bi-iznil-laah; wallaahu ma'as-ṣaabireen.

فَلَمَّا فَصَلَ طَالُوتُ بِالْجُنُودِ ۙ
قَالَ إِنَّ اللّٰهَ مُبْتَلِيكُمْ بِنَهَرٍ ۚ
فَمَنْ شَرِبَ مِنْهُ فَلَيْسَ مِنِّي ۚ
وَمَنْ لَّمْ يَطْعَمْهُ فَإِنَّهُ مِنِّيٓ إِلَّا
مَنِ اغْتَرَفَ غُرْفَةًۢ بِيَدِهٖ ۚ فَشَرِبُوا
مِنْهُ إِلَّا قَلِيلًا مِّنْهُمْ ۚ فَلَمَّا جَاوَزَهُ
هُوَ وَالَّذِينَ اٰمَنُوا مَعَهُ ۙ قَالُوا
لَا طَاقَةَ لَنَا الْيَوْمَ بِجَالُوتَ وَجُنُودِهٖ ۚ
قَالَ الَّذِينَ يَظُنُّونَ أَنَّهُمْ مُّلٰقُوا
اللّٰهِ ۙ كَمْ مِّنْ فِئَةٍ قَلِيلَةٍ غَلَبَتْ
فِئَةً كَثِيرَةًۢ بِإِذْنِ اللّٰهِ ۚ وَاللّٰهُ
مَعَ الصّٰبِرِينَ ﴿٢٤٩﴾

Ikhfa اخفاء | Ghunna غُنّہ | Ikhfa Meem Saakin اخفاء میم ساکن | Idghaam ادغام | Qalqala قلقلہ | Qalb قلب | Idghaam Meem Saakin ادغام میم ساکن

250. When they advanced to meet Goliath and his forces, they prayed: "Our Lord! Pour out constancy on us and make our steps firm: Help us against those that reject faith."

250. Wa lammaa barazoo liJaaloota wa junoodihee qaaloo Rabbanaaa afrigh 'alaynaa ṣabrañw-wa sabbit aqdaamanaa wanṣurnaa 'alal-qawmil-kaafireen.

وَلَمَّا بَرَزُوا۟ لِجَالُوتَ وَجُنُودِهِۦ
قَالُوا۟ رَبَّنَآ أَفْرِغْ عَلَيْنَا صَبْرًا وَثَبِّتْ
أَقْدَامَنَا وَٱنصُرْنَا عَلَى ٱلْقَوْمِ
ٱلْكَٰفِرِينَ ﴿٢٥٠﴾

251. By Allah's will they routed them; and David slew Goliath; and Allah gave him power and wisdom and taught him whatever (else) He willed. And had not Allah checked one set of people by means of another, the earth would indeed be full of mischief: But Allah is full of bounty to all the worlds.

251. Fahazamoohum bi-iznillaahi wa qatala Daawoodu Jaaloota wa aataahul-laahulmulka wal-Ḥikmata wa 'allamahoo mimmaa yashaaa'; wa law laa daf'ullaahin-naasa ba'ḍahum biba'ḍil-lafasadatil-arḍu wa laakinnal-laaha zoo faḍlin 'alal-'aalameen.

فَهَزَمُوهُم بِإِذْنِ ٱللَّهِ وَقَتَلَ
دَاوُۥدُ جَالُوتَ وَءَاتَىٰهُ ٱللَّهُ ٱلْمُلْكَ
وَٱلْحِكْمَةَ وَعَلَّمَهُۥ مِمَّا يَشَآءُ ۗ
وَلَوْلَا دَفْعُ ٱللَّهِ ٱلنَّاسَ بَعْضَهُم
بِبَعْضٍ لَّفَسَدَتِ ٱلْأَرْضُ وَلَٰكِنَّ
ٱللَّهَ ذُو فَضْلٍ عَلَى ٱلْعَٰلَمِينَ ﴿٢٥١﴾

252. These are the Signs of Allah: we rehearse them to you in truth: verily you are one of the apostles.

252. Tilka Aayaatul-laahi natloohaa 'alayka bilḥaqq; wa innaka laminal-mursaleen.

تِلْكَ ءَايَٰتُ ٱللَّهِ نَتْلُوهَا عَلَيْكَ
بِٱلْحَقِّ ۚ وَإِنَّكَ لَمِنَ ٱلْمُرْسَلِينَ ﴿٢٥٢﴾ وقف لازم ٱلْجُزْءُ ٱلثَّالِثُ (٣)

253. Those Messengers We endowed with gifts, some above others: to one of them Allah spoke; others He raised to degrees (of honour); to Jesus the son of Mary We gave Clear (Signs), and strengthened him with the holy spirit. If Allah had so willed, succeeding generations would not have fought among each other, after Clear (Signs) had come to them, but they (chose) to wrangle, some believing and others rejecting. If Allah had so willed, they would not have fought each other; but Allah fulfills His plan.

253. Tilkar-Rusulu faḍḍalnaa ba'ḍahum 'alaa ba'ḍ; minhum man kallamal-laahu wa rafa'a ba'ḍahum darajaat; wa aataynaa 'Eesab-na Maryamal-bayyinaati wa ayyadnaahu bi-Rooḥil-Qudus; wa law shaaa'al-laahu maqtatalal-lazeena mim-ba'dihim mim ba'di maa jaaa'athumul-bayyinaatu wa laakinikh-talafoo faminhum man aamana wa minhum man kafar; wa law shaaa'al-laahu maq-tataloo wa laakinnallaaha yaf'alu maa yureed. **(Section 33)**

تِلْكَ ٱلرُّسُلُ فَضَّلْنَا بَعْضَهُمْ
عَلَىٰ بَعْضٍ ۘ مِّنْهُم مَّن كَلَّمَ ٱللَّهُ
وَرَفَعَ بَعْضَهُمْ دَرَجَٰتٍ ۚ وَءَاتَيْنَا
عِيسَى ٱبْنَ مَرْيَمَ ٱلْبَيِّنَٰتِ وَأَيَّدْنَٰهُ
بِرُوحِ ٱلْقُدُسِ ۗ وَلَوْ شَآءَ ٱللَّهُ مَا
ٱقْتَتَلَ ٱلَّذِينَ مِنۢ بَعْدِهِم مِّنۢ
بَعْدِ مَا جَآءَتْهُمُ ٱلْبَيِّنَٰتُ وَلَٰكِنِ
ٱخْتَلَفُوا۟ فَمِنْهُم مَّنْ ءَامَنَ وَمِنْهُم
مَّن كَفَرَ ۚ وَلَوْ شَآءَ ٱللَّهُ مَا ٱقْتَتَلُوا۟
وَلَٰكِنَّ ٱللَّهَ يَفْعَلُ مَا يُرِيدُ ﴿٢٥٣﴾ ع ٥ ٤

254. O you who believe! Spend out of (the bounties) We have provided for you, before the Day comes when no bargaining (will avail), nor friendship nor intercession. Those who reject Faith- they are the wrong-doers.

254. Yaaa ayyuhal-lazeena aamanooo anfiqoo mimmaa razaqnaakum min qabli añy-yaåtiya Yawmul-laa bay'un feehi wa laa khullatuñw-wa laa shafaa'ah; walkaafiroona humuẓ-ẓaalimoon.

يَٰٓأَيُّهَا ٱلَّذِينَ ءَامَنُوٓا۟ أَنفِقُوا۟ مِمَّا
رَزَقْنَٰكُم مِّن قَبْلِ أَن يَأْتِىَ يَوْمٌ
لَّا بَيْعٌ فِيهِ وَلَا خُلَّةٌ وَلَا شَفَٰعَةٌ ۗ
وَٱلْكَٰفِرُونَ هُمُ ٱلظَّٰلِمُونَ ﴿٢٥٤﴾

Ikhfa اخفاء | Ghunna غنّہ | Ikhfa Meem Saakin اخفاء میم ساکن | Idghaam ادغام | Qalqala قلقلہ | Qalb قلب | Idghaam Meem Saakin ادغام میم ساکن

255. Allah! There is no god but He,-the Living, the Self-subsisting, Eternal. No slumber can seize Him nor sleep. His are all things in the heavens and on earth. Who is there can intercede in His presence except as He permits? He knows what (appears to His creatures as) Before or After or Behind them. Nor shall they compass of His knowledge except as He wills. His Throne does extend over the heavens and the earth, and He feels no fatigue in guarding and preserving them for He is the Most High, the Supreme (in glory).

255. Allaahu laaa ilaaha illaa Huwal-Ḥayyul-Qay-yoom; laa taåkhuzuhoo sinatuñw-wa laa nawm; lahoo maa fissamaa-waati wa maa fil-arḍ; man zal-lazee yashfa'u 'indahooo illaa bi-iznih; ya'lamu maa bayna aydeehim wa maa khalfahum wa laa yuḥeeṭoona bishay'im-min 'ilmihee illaa bimaa shaaa'; wasi'a Kursiyyuhus-samaa-waati wal-arḍa wa laa ya'oo-duhoo ḥifẓuhumaa; wa Huwal-Aliyyul-'Aẓeem.

اَللّٰهُ لَآ اِلٰهَ اِلَّا هُوَ ۚ اَلْحَیُّ الْقَیُّوْمُ ۚ
لَا تَاْخُذُهٗ سِنَةٌ وَّلَا نَوْمٌ ؕ
لَهٗ مَا فِی السَّمٰوٰتِ وَمَا فِی الْاَرْضِ ؕ
مَنْ ذَا الَّذِیْ یَشْفَعُ عِنْدَهٗۤ اِلَّا
بِاِذْنِهٖ ؕ یَعْلَمُ مَا بَیْنَ اَیْدِیْهِمْ وَمَا
خَلْفَهُمْ ۚ وَلَا یُحِیْطُوْنَ بِشَیْءٍ مِّنْ
عِلْمِهٖۤ اِلَّا بِمَا شَآءَ ۚ وَسِعَ كُرْسِیُّهُ
السَّمٰوٰتِ وَالْاَرْضَ ۚ وَلَا یَئُوْدُهٗ
حِفْظُهُمَا ۚ وَهُوَ الْعَلِیُّ الْعَظِیْمُ ﴿۲۵۵﴾

256. Let there be no compulsion in religion: Truth stands out clear from Error: whoever rejects evil and believes in Allah has grasped the most trustworthy hand-hold, that never breaks. And Allah hears and knows all things.

256. Laaa ikraaha fid-deeni qat-tabayyanar-rushdu minal-ghayy; famañy-yakfur biṭ-Ṭaaghooti wa yu'mim-billaahi faqadis-tamsaka bil'urwatil-wusqaa lan-fiṣaama lahaa; wallaahu Samee'un-'Aleem.

لَآ اِكْرَاهَ فِی الدِّیْنِ ۙ قَدْ تَّبَیَّنَ الرُّشْدُ
مِنَ الْغَیِّ ۚ فَمَنْ یَّكْفُرْ بِالطَّاغُوْتِ
وَیُؤْمِنْۢ بِاللّٰهِ فَقَدِ اسْتَمْسَكَ بِالْعُرْوَةِ
الْوُثْقٰی ۗ لَا انْفِصَامَ لَهَا ؕ وَاللّٰهُ
سَمِیْعٌ عَلِیْمٌ ﴿۲۵۶﴾

257. Allah is the Protector of those who have faith: from the depths of darkness He will lead them forth into light. Of those who reject faith the patrons are the Evil Ones: from light they will lead them forth into the depths of darkness. They will be companions of the fire, to dwell therein (For ever).

257. Allaahu waliyyul-lazeena aamanoo yukhrijuhum-minaẓ-ẓulumaati ilan-noori walla-zeena kafarooo awli-yaaa'uhumuṭ-Ṭaaghootu yukhrijoonahum-minan-noori ilaẓ-ẓulumaat; ulaaa'ika Aṣḥaabun-Naari hum feehaa khaalidoon. **(Section 34)**

اَللّٰهُ وَلِیُّ الَّذِیْنَ اٰمَنُوْا ۙ یُخْرِجُهُمْ
مِّنَ الظُّلُمٰتِ اِلَی النُّوْرِ ؕ۬ وَالَّذِیْنَ
كَفَرُوْٓا اَوْلِیٰٓـُٔهُمُ الطَّاغُوْتُ ۙ
یُخْرِجُوْنَهُمْ مِّنَ النُّوْرِ اِلَی
الظُّلُمٰتِ ؕ اُولٰٓئِكَ اَصْحٰبُ النَّارِ ۚ
هُمْ فِیْهَا خٰلِدُوْنَ ﴿۲۵۷﴾ ع ٣٤ ٤

258. Have you not turned your vision to one who disputed with Abraham about his Lord, because Allah had granted him power? Abraham said: "My Lord is He Who gives life and death."He said: "I give life and death". Said Abraham: "But it is Allah that causes the sun to rise from the east: Do you then cause him to rise from the West."

258. Alam tara ilal-lazee Ḥaaajja Ibraaheema fee Rabbiheee an aataahullaahul-mulka iz qaala Ibraaheemu Rabbiyal-lazee yuḥyee wa yumeetu qaala ana uḥyee wa umeetu qaala-Ibraaheemu fa-innal-laaha yaåtee bishshamsi minal-mashriqi faåti bihaa minal-maghribi

اَلَمْ تَرَ اِلَی الَّذِیْ حَآجَّ اِبْرٰهٖمَ
فِیْ رَبِّهٖۤ اَنْ اٰتٰىهُ اللّٰهُ الْمُلْكَ ۘ وقف لازم
اِذْ قَالَ اِبْرٰهٖمُ رَبِّیَ الَّذِیْ یُحْیٖ
وَیُمِیْتُ ۙ قَالَ اَنَا اُحْیٖ وَاُمِیْتُ ؕ
قَالَ اِبْرٰهٖمُ فَاِنَّ اللّٰهَ یَاْتِیْ بِالشَّمْسِ
مِنَ الْمَشْرِقِ فَاْتِ بِهَا مِنَ الْمَغْرِبِ

Ikhfa اخفاء | Ghunna غُنّہ | Ikhfa Meem Saakin اخفاء میم ساکن | Idghaam ادغام | Qalqala قلقلہ | Qalb قلب | Idghaam Meem Saakin ادغام میم ساکن

Thus was he confounded who (in arrogance) rejected faith. Nor does Allah Give guidance to a people unjust.

fabuhital-lazee kafar; wallaahu laa yahdil-qawmaz-zaalimeen.

فَبُهِتَ الَّذِىْ كَفَرَ ؕ وَاللّٰهُ لَا يَهْدِى
الْقَوْمَ الظّٰلِمِيْنَ ۚ﴿۲۵۸﴾

259. Or (take) the similitude of one who passed by a hamlet, all in ruins to its roofs. He said: "Oh! how shall Allah bring it (ever) to life, after (this) its death?" but Allah caused him to die for a hundred years, then raised him up (again). He said: "How long did you tarry (thus)?" He said: (Perhaps) a day or part of a day." He said: "No you hast tarried thus a hundred years; but look at your food and your drink; they show no signs of age; and look at your donkey: And that We may make of you a sign for the people, Look further at the bones, how We bring them together and clothe them with flesh." When this was shown clearly to him, he said: "I know that Allah has power over all things."

259. Aw kallazee marra 'alaa qaryatiñw-wa hiya khaawiyatun 'alaa 'urooshihaa qaala annaa yuhyee haazihil-laahu ba'da mawtihaa fa-amaatahul-laahu mi'ata 'aamin summa ba'asahoo qaala kam labista qaala labistu yawman aw ba'da yawmin qaala bal labista mi'ata 'aamin fanzur ilaa ta'aamika wa sharaabika lam yatasannah wanzur ilaa himaarika wa linaj'alaka Aayatal-linnaasi wanzur ilal'izaami kayfa nunshizuhaa summa naksoohaa lahmaa; falammaa tabayyana lahoo qaala a'lamu annal-laaha 'alaa kulli shay'in Qadeer.

اَوْ كَالَّذِىْ مَرَّ عَلٰى قَرْيَةٍ وَّهِىَ خَاوِيَةٌ
عَلٰى عُرُوْشِهَا ۚ قَالَ اَنّٰى يُحْىٖ هٰذِهِ
اللّٰهُ بَعْدَ مَوْتِهَا ۚ فَاَمَاتَهُ اللّٰهُ
مِائَةَ عَامٍ ثُمَّ بَعَثَهٗ ؕ قَالَ كَمْ لَبِثْتَ ؕ
قَالَ لَبِثْتُ يَوْمًا اَوْ بَعْضَ يَوْمٍ ؕ
قَالَ بَلْ لَّبِثْتَ مِائَةَ عَامٍ
فَانْظُرْ اِلٰى طَعَامِكَ وَشَرَابِكَ لَمْ
يَتَسَنَّهْ ۚ وَانْظُرْ اِلٰى حِمَارِكَ ۟ وَلِنَجْعَلَكَ
اٰيَةً لِّلنَّاسِ وَانْظُرْ اِلَى الْعِظَامِ
كَيْفَ نُنْشِزُهَا ثُمَّ نَكْسُوْهَا
لَحْمًا ؕ فَلَمَّا تَبَيَّنَ لَهٗ ۙ قَالَ اَعْلَمُ
اَنَّ اللّٰهَ عَلٰى كُلِّ شَىْءٍ قَدِيْرٌ ﴿۲۵۹﴾

260. Behold! Abraham said: "My Lord! Show me how You give life to the dead." He said: "Do you not then believe?" He said: "Yes! but to satisfy my own understanding." He said: "Take four birds; Tame them to turn to you; put a portion of them on every hill and call to them: They will come to you (Flying) with speed. Then know that Allah is Exalted in Power, Wise."

260. Wa iz qaala Ibraaheemu Rabbi arinee kayfa tuhyil-mawtaa qaala-awa lam tu'min qaala balaa wa laakil-liyatma'inna qalbee qaala fakhuz arba'atam-minat-tayri fasurhunna ilayka summaj-'al 'alaa kulli jabalim-minhunna juz'an summad-'uhunna yaâ-teenaka sa'yaa; wa'lam annal-laaha 'Azeezun Hakeem.

(Section 35)

وَاِذْ قَالَ اِبْرٰهٖمُ رَبِّ اَرِنِىْ كَيْفَ
تُحْىِ الْمَوْتٰى ؕ قَالَ اَوَلَمْ تُؤْمِنْ ؕ
قَالَ بَلٰى وَلٰكِنْ لِّيَطْمَئِنَّ قَلْبِىْ ؕ
قَالَ فَخُذْ اَرْبَعَةً مِّنَ الطَّيْرِ
فَصُرْهُنَّ اِلَيْكَ ثُمَّ اجْعَلْ عَلٰى
كُلِّ جَبَلٍ مِّنْهُنَّ جُزْءًا ثُمَّ
ادْعُهُنَّ يَاْتِيْنَكَ سَعْيًا ؕ وَاعْلَمْ
اَنَّ اللّٰهَ عَزِيْزٌ حَكِيْمٌ ﴿۲۶۰﴾ ع ٣٥ ٣

261. The parable of those who spend their substance in the way of Allah is that of a grain of corn: it grows seven ears, and each ear has a hundred grains. Allah gives manifold increase to whom He pleases:

261. Masalul-lazeena yunfi-qoona amwaalahum fee sabeelil-laahi kamasali habbatin ambatat sab'a sanaabila fee kulli sumbulatim-mi'atu habbah; wallaahu yudaa'ifu limañy-yashaaa';

مَثَلُ الَّذِيْنَ يُنْفِقُوْنَ اَمْوَالَهُمْ
فِىْ سَبِيْلِ اللّٰهِ كَمَثَلِ حَبَّةٍ اَنْبَتَتْ
سَبْعَ سَنَابِلَ فِىْ كُلِّ سُنْبُلَةٍ مِّائَةُ
حَبَّةٍ ؕ وَاللّٰهُ يُضٰعِفُ لِمَنْ يَّشَآءُ ؕ

Ikhfa اخفاء | Ghunna غُنّہ | Ikhfa Meem Saakin اخفاء میم ساکن | Idghaam ادغام | Qalqala قلقلہ | Qalb قلب | Idghaam Meem Saakin ادغام میم ساکن

and Allah cares for all and He knows all things.

wallaahu Waasi'un-'Aleem.

وَاللّٰهُ وَاسِعٌ عَلِيْمٌ ﴿٢٦١﴾

262. Those who spend their substance in the cause of Allah, and follow not up their gifts with reminders of their generosity or with injury,-for them their reward is with their Lord: on them shall be no fear, nor shall they grieve.

262. Alla<u>z</u>eena yunfiqoona amwaalahum fee sabeelillaahi summa laa yutbi'oona maaa anfaqoo mannañw-wa laaa a<u>z</u>al-lahum ajruhum 'inda Rabbihim; wa laa khawfun 'alayhim wa laa hum yaḥzanoon.

اَلَّذِيْنَ يُنْفِقُوْنَ اَمْوَالَهُمْ فِيْ سَبِيْلِ
اللّٰهِ ثُمَّ لَا يُتْبِعُوْنَ مَآ اَنْفَقُوْا مَنًّا وَّلَآ
اَذًى لَّهُمْ اَجْرُهُمْ عِنْدَ رَبِّهِمْ ج
وَلَا خَوْفٌ عَلَيْهِمْ وَلَا هُمْ يَحْزَنُوْنَ ﴿٢٦٢﴾

263. Kind words and the covering of faults are better than charity followed by injury. Allah is free of all wants, and He is Most Forbearing.

263. Qawlum-ma'roofuñw-wa maghfiratun khayrum-min sadaqatiñy-yatba'uhaaa a<u>z</u>aa; wallaahu Ghaniyyun Ḥaleem.

قَوْلٌ مَّعْرُوْفٌ وَّمَغْفِرَةٌ خَيْرٌ مِّنْ
صَدَقَةٍ يَّتْبَعُهَآ اَذًى ط وَاللّٰهُ غَنِيٌّ
حَلِيْمٌ ﴿٢٦٣﴾

264. O you who believe! waste not your charity by reminders of your generosity or by injury,-like those who spend their substance to be seen of men, but believe neither in Allah nor in the Last Day. They are in parable like a hard, barren rock, on which is a little soil: on it falls heavy rain, which leaves it (Just) a bare stone. They will be able to do nothing with anything they have earned. And Allah does not guide those who reject faith.

264. Yaaa ayyuhal-la<u>z</u>eena aamanoo laa tubṭiloo ṣadaqaatikum bilmanni wal-a<u>z</u>aa kalla<u>z</u>ee yunfiqu maalahoo ri'aaa'an-naasi wa laa yu'minu billaahi wal-Yawmil-Aakhiri fama<u>s</u>aluhoo kama<u>s</u>ali ṣafwaanin 'alayhi turaabun fa-aṣaabahoo waabilun fatara-kahoo ṣaldaa: laa yaqdiroona 'alaa shay'im mimmaa kasaboo; wallaahu laa yahdil-qawmal-kaafireen.

يٰٓاَيُّهَا الَّذِيْنَ اٰمَنُوْا لَا تُبْطِلُوْا
صَدَقٰتِكُمْ بِالْمَنِّ وَالْاَذٰى لا
كَالَّذِيْ يُنْفِقُ مَالَهٗ رِئَآءَ النَّاسِ
وَلَا يُؤْمِنُ بِاللّٰهِ وَالْيَوْمِ الْاٰخِرِ ط
فَمَثَلُهٗ كَمَثَلِ صَفْوَانٍ عَلَيْهِ
تُرَابٌ فَاَصَابَهٗ وَابِلٌ فَتَرَكَهٗ
صَلْدًا ط لَا يَقْدِرُوْنَ عَلٰى شَيْءٍ مِّمَّا
كَسَبُوْا ط وَاللّٰهُ لَا يَهْدِي الْقَوْمَ
الْكٰفِرِيْنَ ﴿٢٦٤﴾

265. And the likeness of those who spend their substance, seeking to please Allah and to strengthen their souls, is as a garden, high and fertile: heavy rain falls on it but makes it yield a double increase of harvest, and if it does not receives heavy rain, light moisture suffice it. Allah sees well whatever you do.

265. Wa ma<u>s</u>alul-la<u>z</u>eena yunfiqoona amwaalahumub-ti ghaaa'a marḍaatil-laahi wa ta<u>s</u>beetam-min anfusihim kama<u>s</u>ali jannatim birabwatin aṣaabahaa waabilun fa-aatat ukulahaa ḍi'fayni fa-il-lam yuṣibhaa waabilun faṭall; wallaahu bimaa ta'maloona Baṣeer.

وَمَثَلُ الَّذِيْنَ يُنْفِقُوْنَ اَمْوَالَهُمُ ابْتِغَآءَ
مَرْضَاتِ اللّٰهِ وَتَثْبِيْتًا مِّنْ اَنْفُسِهِمْ
كَمَثَلِ جَنَّةٍ بِرَبْوَةٍ اَصَابَهَا وَابِلٌ
فَاٰتَتْ اُكُلَهَا ضِعْفَيْنِ ج فَاِنْ لَّمْ
يُصِبْهَا وَابِلٌ فَطَلٌّ ط وَاللّٰهُ بِمَا
تَعْمَلُوْنَ بَصِيْرٌ ﴿٢٦٥﴾

266. Does any of you wish that he should have a garden with date-palms and vines and streams flowing underneath, and

266. Ayawaddu aḥadukum an takoona lahoo jannatum-min nakheeliñw-wa a'naabin tajree min taḥtihal-anhaaru lahoo feehaa min

اَيَوَدُّ اَحَدُكُمْ اَنْ تَكُوْنَ لَهٗ جَنَّةٌ
مِّنْ نَّخِيْلٍ وَّاَعْنَابٍ تَجْرِيْ مِنْ
تَحْتِهَا الْاَنْهٰرُ لا لَهٗ فِيْهَا مِنْ

Ikhfa اخفاء | Ghunna غُنّہ | Ikhfa Meem Saakin اخفاء میم ساکن | Idghaam ادغام | Qalqala قلقلہ | Qalb قلب | Idghaam Meem Saakin ادغام میم ساکن

all kinds of fruit, while he is stricken with old age, and his children are not strong (enough to look after themselves)- that it should be caught in a whirlwind, with fire therein, and be burnt up? Thus does Allah make clear to you (His) Signs; that you may consider.

kulliṡ-ṡamaraati wa aṣaabahul-kibaru wa lahoo zurriyyatun ḍu'afaaa'u fa-aṣaabahaaa i'ṣaa-run feehi naarun faḥtaraqat; kazaalika yubayyinul-laahu lakumul-Aayaati la'allakum tatafakkaroon. **(Section 36)**

كُلِّ الثَّمَرٰتِۙ وَاَصَابَهُ الْكِبَرُ وَلَهٗ
ذُرِّيَّةٌ ضُعَفَآءُ ۖۚ فَاَصَابَهَآ اِعْصَارٌ
فِيْهِ نَارٌ فَاحْتَرَقَتْ ؕ كَذٰلِكَ يُبَيِّنُ
اللّٰهُ لَكُمُ الْاٰيٰتِ لَعَلَّكُمْ تَتَفَكَّرُوْنَ ٢٦٦

267. O you who believe! Give of the good things which you have (honourably) earned, and of the fruits of the earth which We have produced for you, and do not ever aim at getting anything which is bad, in order that out of it you may give away something, when you yourselves would not receive it except with closed eyes. And know that Allah is Free of all wants, and Worthy of all praise.

267. Yaaa 'ayyuhal-lazeena aamanooo anfiqoo min ṭayyi-baati maa kasabtum wa mimmaaa akhrajnaa lakum minal-arḍi wa laa tayammamul-khabeesa minhu tunfiqoona wa lastum bi-aakhizeehi illaaa an tughmiḍoo feeh; wa'lamooo annal-laaha Ghaniyyun Ḥameed.

يٰٓاَيُّهَا الَّذِيْنَ اٰمَنُوْٓا اَنْفِقُوْا مِنْ
طَيِّبٰتِ مَا كَسَبْتُمْ وَمِمَّآ اَخْرَجْنَا
لَكُمْ مِّنَ الْاَرْضِ ۖ وَلَا تَيَمَّمُوا
الْخَبِيْثَ مِنْهُ تُنْفِقُوْنَ وَلَسْتُمْ
بِاٰخِذِيْهِ اِلَّآ اَنْ تُغْمِضُوْا فِيْهِ ؕ
وَاعْلَمُوْٓا اَنَّ اللّٰهَ غَنِيٌّ حَمِيْدٌ ٢٦٧

268. Satan threatens you with poverty and bids you to conduct unseemly. Allah promises you His forgiveness and bounties. And Allah cares for all and He knows all things.

268. Ash-Shayṭaanu ya'idu-kumul-faqra wa yaämurukum bilfaḥshaaa'i wallaahu ya'idu-kum maghfiratam-minhu wa faḍlaa; wallaahu Waasi'un 'Aleem.

اَلشَّيْطٰنُ يَعِدُكُمُ الْفَقْرَ وَيَاْمُرُكُمْ
بِالْفَحْشَآءِ ۚ وَاللّٰهُ يَعِدُكُمْ مَّغْفِرَةً
مِّنْهُ وَفَضْلًا ؕ وَاللّٰهُ وَاسِعٌ عَلِيْمٌ ۖۙ ٢٦٨

269. He grants wisdom to whom He pleases; and he to whom wisdom is granted receives indeed a benefit overflowing; but none will grasp the Message but men of understanding.

269. Yu'til-Ḥikmata mañy-yashaaa'; wa mañy-yu'tal-Ḥikmata faqad ootiya khayran kaseeraa; wa maa yazzakkaru illaaa ulul-albaab.

يُّؤْتِي الْحِكْمَةَ مَنْ يَّشَآءُ ۚ وَمَنْ يُّؤْتَ
الْحِكْمَةَ فَقَدْ اُوْتِيَ خَيْرًا كَثِيْرًا ؕ
وَمَا يَذَّكَّرُ اِلَّآ اُولُوا الْاَلْبَابِ ٢٦٩

270. And whatever you spend in charity or devotion, be sure Allah knows it all. But the wrong-doers have no helpers.

270. Wa maaa anfaqtum min nafaqatin aw nazartum min nazrin fa-innal-laaha ya'lamuh; wa maa liẓẓaalimeena min anṣaar.

وَمَآ اَنْفَقْتُمْ مِّنْ نَّفَقَةٍ اَوْ
نَذَرْتُمْ مِّنْ نَّذْرٍ فَاِنَّ اللّٰهَ
يَعْلَمُهٗ ؕ وَمَا لِلظّٰلِمِيْنَ مِنْ اَنْصَارٍ ٢٧٠

271. If you disclose (acts of) charity, even so it is well, but if you conceal them, and make them reach those (really) in need, that is best for you: It will remove from you some of your (stains of) evil. And Allah is well acquainted with what you do.

271. In tubduṣ-ṣadaqaati fani-'immaa hiya wa in tukhfoohaa wa tu'toohal-fuqaraaa'a fahuwa khayrul-lakum; wa yukaffiru 'ankum min sayyi-aatikum; wallaahu bimaa ta'maloona Khabeer.

اِنْ تُبْدُوا الصَّدَقٰتِ فَنِعِمَّا هِيَ ۚ
وَاِنْ تُخْفُوْهَا وَتُؤْتُوْهَا الْفُقَرَآءَ
فَهُوَ خَيْرٌ لَّكُمْ ؕ وَيُكَفِّرُ عَنْكُمْ
مِّنْ سَيِّاٰتِكُمْ ؕ وَاللّٰهُ بِمَا تَعْمَلُوْنَ
خَبِيْرٌ ٢٧١

272. It is not required of you (O Apostle), to set them on the right path, but Allah sets on the right path whom He pleases. Whatever of

272. Laysa 'alayka hudaahum wa laakinnal-laaha yahdee mañy-yashaaa'; wa maa tunfiqoo

لَيْسَ عَلَيْكَ هُدٰىهُمْ وَلٰكِنَّ اللّٰهَ
يَهْدِيْ مَنْ يَّشَآءُ ؕ وَمَا تُنْفِقُوْا

Ikhfa اخفاء | Ghunna غُنّہ | Ikhfa Meem Saakin اخفاء میم ساکن | Idghaam ادغام | Qalqala قلقلہ | Qalb قلب | Idghaam Meem Saakin ادغام میم ساکن

good you give benefits your own souls, and you shall only do so seeking the "Face" of Allah. Whatever good you give, shall be rendered back to you, and you shall not be dealt with unjustly.

min khayrin fali-anfusikum; wa maa tunfiqoona illab-tighaaa'a Wajhil-laah; wa maa tunfiqoo min khayriñy-yuwaffa ilaykum wa antum laa tuẓlamoon.

مِنْ خَيْرٍ فَلِأَنْفُسِكُمْ ۚ وَمَا تُنْفِقُونَ
إِلَّا ابْتِغَاءَ وَجْهِ اللَّهِ ۚ وَمَا تُنْفِقُوا
مِنْ خَيْرٍ يُوَفَّ إِلَيْكُمْ وَأَنْتُمْ
لَا تُظْلَمُونَ ﴿٢٧٢﴾

273. (Charity is) for those in need, who, in Allah's cause are restricted (from travel), and cannot move about in the land, seeking (For trade or work): the ignorant man thinks, because of their modesty, that they are free from want. You shall know them by their (Unfailing) mark: They beg not importunately from all the sundry. And whatever of good you give, be assured Allah knows it well.

273. Lilfuqaraaa'il-laz̲eena uḥṣiroo fee sabeelil-laahi laa yastaṭee'oona ḍarban fil-arḍi yaḥsabuhumul-jaahilu aghniyaaa'a minat-ta'affufi ta'rifuhum biseemaahum laa yas'aloonan-naasa ilḥaafaa; wa maa tunfiqoo min khayrin fa-innal-laaha bihee 'Aleem.

(Section 37)

لِلْفُقَرَاءِ الَّذِينَ أُحْصِرُوا فِي سَبِيلِ
اللَّهِ لَا يَسْتَطِيعُونَ ضَرْبًا فِي الْأَرْضِ
يَحْسَبُهُمُ الْجَاهِلُ أَغْنِيَاءَ مِنَ
التَّعَفُّفِ تَعْرِفُهُمْ بِسِيمَاهُمْ لَا يَسْأَلُونَ
النَّاسَ إِلْحَافًا ۗ وَمَا تُنْفِقُوا مِنْ
خَيْرٍ فَإِنَّ اللَّهَ بِهِ عَلِيمٌ ﴿٢٧٣﴾ ع

الربع

274. Those who (in charity) spend of their goods by night and by day, in secret and in public, have their reward with their Lord: on them shall be no fear, nor shall they grieve.

274. Allaz̲eena yunfiqoona amwaalahum billayli wan-nahaari sirrañw-wa 'alaaniyatan falahum ajruhum 'inda Rabbihim wa laa khawfun 'alayhim wa laa hum yaḥzanoon.

الَّذِينَ يُنْفِقُونَ أَمْوَالَهُمْ بِاللَّيْلِ
وَالنَّهَارِ سِرًّا وَعَلَانِيَةً فَلَهُمْ
أَجْرُهُمْ عِنْدَ رَبِّهِمْ وَلَا خَوْفٌ
عَلَيْهِمْ وَلَا هُمْ يَحْزَنُونَ ﴿٢٧٤﴾

وقف منزل

275. Those who devour interest will not stand except as stand one whom the Satan one by his touch has driven to madness. That is because they say: "Trade is like interest," but Allah has permitted trade and forbidden interest. Those who after receiving direction from their Lord, desist, shall be pardoned for the past; their case is for Allah (to judge); but those who repeat (the offence) are companions of the Fire: They will abide therein (for ever).

275. Allaz̲eena yaåkuloonar-ribaa laa yaqoomoona illaa kamaa yaqoomul-laz̲ee yatakhabbaṭuhush-Shayṭaanu minal-mass; z̲aalika bi-annahum qaalooo innamal-bay'u mis̲lur-ribaa; wa aḥallal-laahul-bay'a wa ḥarramar-ribaa; faman jaaa'ahoo maw'iz̲atum-mir-Rabbihee fantahaa falahoo maa salafa wa amruhooo ilal-laahi wa man 'aada fa-ulaaa'ika Aṣḥaabun-Naari hum feehaa khaalidoon.

الَّذِينَ يَأْكُلُونَ الرِّبَا لَا يَقُومُونَ
إِلَّا كَمَا يَقُومُ الَّذِي يَتَخَبَّطُهُ
الشَّيْطَانُ مِنَ الْمَسِّ ۚ ذَٰلِكَ بِأَنَّهُمْ
قَالُوا إِنَّمَا الْبَيْعُ مِثْلُ الرِّبَا ۘ
وَأَحَلَّ اللَّهُ الْبَيْعَ وَحَرَّمَ الرِّبَا ۚ
فَمَنْ جَاءَهُ مَوْعِظَةٌ مِنْ رَبِّهِ
فَانْتَهَىٰ فَلَهُ مَا سَلَفَ وَأَمْرُهُ
إِلَى اللَّهِ ۖ وَمَنْ عَادَ فَأُولَٰئِكَ
أَصْحَابُ النَّارِ ۖ هُمْ فِيهَا خَالِدُونَ ﴿٢٧٥﴾

وقف لازم

276. Allah will deprive usury of all blessing, but will give increase for deeds of charity: for He does not love ungrateful and wicked creatures.

276. Yamḥaqul-laahur-ribaa wa yurbiṣ-ṣadaqaat; wallaahu laa yuḥibbu kulla kaffaarin as̲eem.

يَمْحَقُ اللَّهُ الرِّبَا وَيُرْبِي الصَّدَقَاتِ ۗ
وَاللَّهُ لَا يُحِبُّ كُلَّ كَفَّارٍ أَثِيمٍ ﴿٢٧٦﴾

277. Those who believe, and do deeds of righteousness,

277. Innal-laz̲eena aamanoo wa 'amiluṣ-ṣaalihaati

إِنَّ الَّذِينَ آمَنُوا وَعَمِلُوا الصَّالِحَاتِ

Ikhfa اخفاء | Ghunna غُنّہ | Ikhfa Meem Saakin اخفاء میم ساکن | Idghaam ادغام | Qalqala قلقلہ | Qalb قلب | Idghaam Meem Saakin ادغام میم ساکن

وَأَقَامُوا الصَّلَوٰةَ وَآتَوُا الزَّكَوٰةَ
لَهُمْ أَجْرُهُمْ عِندَ رَبِّهِمْ ۚ وَلَا خَوْفٌ
عَلَيْهِمْ وَلَا هُمْ يَحْزَنُونَ ﴿٢٧٧﴾

wa aqaamuṣ-Ṣalaata wa aatawuz-Zakaata lahum ajruhum 'inda Rabbihim wa laa khawfun 'alayhim wa laa hum yaḥzanoon.

and establish regular prayers and regular charity, will have their reward with their Lord: on them shall be no fear, nor shall they grieve.

يَا أَيُّهَا الَّذِينَ آمَنُوا اتَّقُوا اللَّهَ
وَذَرُوا مَا بَقِيَ مِنَ الرِّبَوٰا إِن
كُنتُم مُّؤْمِنِينَ ﴿٢٧٨﴾

278. Yaaa ayyhual-lazeena aamanut-taqul-laaha wa zaroo maa baqiya minar-ribaaa in kuntum mu'mineen.

278. O you who believe! Fear Allah, and give up what remains of your demand for usury, if you are indeed believers.

فَإِن لَّمْ تَفْعَلُوا فَأْذَنُوا بِحَرْبٍ
مِّنَ اللَّهِ وَرَسُولِهِ ۖ وَإِن تُبْتُمْ فَلَكُمْ
رُءُوسُ أَمْوَالِكُمْ ۖ لَا تَظْلِمُونَ
وَلَا تُظْلَمُونَ ﴿٢٧٩﴾

279. Fail-lam taf'aloo faâzanoo biḥarbim-minal-laahi wa Rasoolihee wa in tubtum falakum ru'oosu amwaalikum laa taẓlimoona wa laa tuẓlamoon.

279. If you do it not, take notice of war from Allah and His Apostle: But if you turn back, you shall have your capital sums: deal not unjustly, and you shall not be dealt with unjustly.

وَإِن كَانَ ذُو عُسْرَةٍ فَنَظِرَةٌ إِلَىٰ
مَيْسَرَةٍ ۚ وَأَن تَصَدَّقُوا خَيْرٌ
لَّكُمْ ۖ إِن كُنتُمْ تَعْلَمُونَ ﴿٢٨٠﴾

280. Wa in kaana zoo 'usratin fanaẓiratun ilaa maysarah; wa an taṣaddaqoo khayrul-lakum in kuntum ta'lamoon.

280. If the debtor is in a difficulty, grant him time till it is easy for him to repay. But if you remit it by way of charity, that is best for you if you only knew.

وَاتَّقُوا يَوْمًا تُرْجَعُونَ فِيهِ إِلَى
اللَّهِ ۖ ثُمَّ تُوَفَّىٰ كُلُّ نَفْسٍ مَّا كَسَبَتْ
وَهُمْ لَا يُظْلَمُونَ ﴿٢٨١﴾ ٤٨٢

281. Wattaqoo Yawman turja'oona feehi ilal-laahi summa tuwaffaa kullu nafsim-maa kasabat wa hum laa yuẓlamoon. **(Section 38)**

281. And fear the Day when you shall be brought back to Allah. Then shall every soul be paid what it earned, and none shall be dealt with unjustly.

يَا أَيُّهَا الَّذِينَ آمَنُوا إِذَا تَدَايَنتُم
بِدَيْنٍ إِلَىٰ أَجَلٍ مُّسَمًّى فَاكْتُبُوهُ ۚ
وَلْيَكْتُب بَّيْنَكُمْ كَاتِبٌ بِالْعَدْلِ ۚ
وَلَا يَأْبَ كَاتِبٌ أَن يَكْتُبَ كَمَا عَلَّمَهُ
اللَّهُ ۚ فَلْيَكْتُبْ وَلْيُمْلِلِ الَّذِي عَلَيْهِ
الْحَقُّ وَلْيَتَّقِ اللَّهَ رَبَّهُ وَلَا يَبْخَسْ
مِنْهُ شَيْئًا ۚ فَإِن كَانَ الَّذِي عَلَيْهِ
الْحَقُّ سَفِيهًا أَوْ ضَعِيفًا أَوْ لَا
يَسْتَطِيعُ أَن يُمِلَّ هُوَ فَلْيُمْلِلْ
وَلِيُّهُ بِالْعَدْلِ ۚ وَاسْتَشْهِدُوا

282. Yaaa ayyuhal-lazeena aamanooo izaa tadaayantum bidaynin ilaaa ajalimmusamman faktubooh; walyaktub baynakum kaatibum bil'adl; wa laa yaâba kaatibun añy-yaktuba kamaa 'allamahul-laah; falyaktub walyumlilil-lazee 'alayhil-ḥaqqu walyattaqil-laaha rabbahoo wa laa yabkhas minhu shay'aa; fa-in kaanal-lazee 'alayhil-ḥaqqu safeehan aw ḍa'eefan aw laa yastaṭee'u añy-yumilla huwa falyumlil waliyyuhoo bil'adl; wastash-hidoo

282. O you who believe! When you deal with each other, in transactions involving future obligations in a fixed period of time, reduce them to writing. Let a scribe write down faithfully as between the parties: let not the scribe refuse to write: as Allah has taught him, so let him write. Let him who incurs the liability dictate, but let him fear His Lord Allah, and not diminish anything of what he owes. If the party liable is mentally deficient, or weak, or unable himself to dictate, Let his guardian dictate faithfully, and get

Ikhfa اخفاء | Ghunna غنّہ | Ikhfa Meem Saakin اخفاء میم ساکن | Idghaam ادغام | Qalqala قلقلہ | Qalb قلب | Idghaam Meem Saakin ادغام میم ساکن

two witnesses, out of your own men, and if there are not two men, then a man and two women, such as you choose, for witnesses, so that if one of them errs, the other can remind her. The witnesses should not refuse when they are called on (for evidence). Disdain not to reduce to writing (your contract) for a future period, whether it be small or big: it is juster in the sight of Allah, more suitable as evidence, and more convenient to prevent doubts among yourselves but if it be a transaction which you carry out on the spot among your-selves, there is no blame on you if you reduce it not to writing. But take witness whenever you make a commercial contract; and let neither scribe nor witness suffer harm. If you do (such harm), it would be wickedness in you. So fear Allah; for it is Allah that teaches you. And Allah is well acquainted with all things.

shaheedayni mir-rijaalikum fa-il-lam yakoonaa rajulayni farajuluñw-wamra-ataani mimman tarḍawna minash-shuhadaaa'i an taḍilla iḥdaahumaa fatuzakkira iḥdaahumal-ukhraa; wa laa yaå-bash-shuhadaaa'u izaa maa du'oo; wa laa tas'amooo an taktuboohu ṣagheeran aw kabeeran ilaaa ajalih; zaalikum aqsaṭu 'indal-laahi wa aqwamu lishshahaadati wa adnaaa allaa tartaabooo illaaa an takoona tijaaratan ḥaaḍiratan-tudeeroonahaa baynakum falaysa 'alaykum junaaḥun allaa taktuboohaa; wa ashhidooo izaa tabaaya'tum; wa laa yuḍaarra kaatibuñw-wa laa shaheed; wa in taf'aloo fa-innahoo fusooqum-bikum; wattaqul-laaha wa yu'allimu-kumul-laah; wallaahu bikulli shay'in 'Aleem.

شَهِيْدَيْنِ مِنْ رِّجَالِكُمْ ۚ فَاِنْ لَّمْ
يَكُوْنَا رَجُلَيْنِ فَرَجُلٌ وَّامْرَاَتٰنِ
مِمَّنْ تَرْضَوْنَ مِنَ الشُّهَدَآءِ اَنْ
تَضِلَّ اِحْدٰىهُمَا فَتُذَكِّرَ اِحْدٰىهُمَا
الْاُخْرٰى ؕ وَلَا يَاْبَ الشُّهَدَآءُ اِذَا
مَا دُعُوْا ؕ وَلَا تَسْـَٔمُوْٓا اَنْ تَكْتُبُوْهُ
صَغِيْرًا اَوْ كَبِيْرًا اِلٰٓى اَجَلِهٖ ؕ ذٰلِكُمْ
اَقْسَطُ عِنْدَ اللّٰهِ وَاَقْوَمُ لِلشَّهَادَةِ
وَاَدْنٰٓى اَلَّا تَرْتَابُوْٓا اِلَّآ اَنْ تَكُوْنَ
تِجَارَةً حَاضِرَةً تُدِيْرُوْنَهَا
بَيْنَكُمْ فَلَيْسَ عَلَيْكُمْ جُنَاحٌ اَلَّا
تَكْتُبُوْهَا ؕ وَاَشْهِدُوْٓا اِذَا تَبَايَعْتُمْ ۪
وَلَا يُضَآرَّ كَاتِبٌ وَّلَا شَهِيْدٌ ؕ۬
وَاِنْ تَفْعَلُوْا فَاِنَّهٗ فُسُوْقٌۢ بِكُمْ ؕ
وَاتَّقُوا اللّٰهَ ؕ وَيُعَلِّمُكُمُ اللّٰهُ ؕ
وَاللّٰهُ بِكُلِّ شَیْءٍ عَلِيْمٌ ﴿۲۸۲﴾

283. If you are on a journey, and cannot find a scribe, a pledge with possession (may serve the purpose). And if one of you deposits a thing on trust with another, Let the trustee (faithfully) discharge His trust, and let him fear his Lord. Conceal not evidence; for whoever conceals it,- his heart is tainted with sin. And Allah knows all that you do.

283. Wa in kuntum 'alaa safa-riñw-wa lam tajidoo kaatiban farihaanum-maqbooḍatun fa-in amina ba'ḍukum ba'ḍan falyu'addil-lazi'-tumina amaa-natahoo walyattaqil-laaha Rabbah; wa laa taktumush-shahaadah; wa mañy-yaktumhaa fa-innahooo aasimun qalbuh; wallaahu bimaa ta'maloona 'Aleem. **(Section 39)**

وَاِنْ كُنْتُمْ عَلٰى سَفَرٍ وَّلَمْ تَجِدُوْا
كَاتِبًا فَرِهٰنٌ مَّقْبُوْضَةٌ ؕ فَاِنْ
اَمِنَ بَعْضُكُمْ بَعْضًا فَلْيُؤَدِّ الَّذِی
اؤْتُمِنَ اَمَانَتَهٗ وَلْيَتَّقِ اللّٰهَ
رَبَّهٗ ؕ وَلَا تَكْتُمُوا الشَّهَادَةَ ؕ وَمَنْ
يَّكْتُمْهَا فَاِنَّهٗٓ اٰثِمٌ قَلْبُهٗ ؕ وَاللّٰهُ
بِمَا تَعْمَلُوْنَ عَلِيْمٌ ﴿۲۸۳﴾ ع ٣٩ ٢ ٧

284. To Allah belongs all that is in the heavens and on earth. Whether you show what is in your minds or conceal it, Allah calls you to account for it.

284. Lillaahi maa fissamaa-waati wa maa fil-arḍ; wa in tubdoo maa feee anfusikum aw tukhfoohu yuḥaasibkum bihil-laahu

لِلّٰهِ مَا فِی السَّمٰوٰتِ وَمَا فِی الْاَرْضِ ؕ
وَاِنْ تُبْدُوْا مَا فِیْٓ اَنْفُسِكُمْ
اَوْ تُخْفُوْهُ يُحَاسِبْكُمْ بِهِ اللّٰهُ ؕ

Ikhfa اخفاء | Ghunna غُنّہ | Ikhfa Meem Saakin اخفاء میم ساکن | Idghaam ادغام | Qalqala قلقلہ | Qalb قلب | Idghaam Meem Saakin ادغام میم ساکن

He forgives whom He pleases, and punishes whom He pleases, for Allah has power over all things.

285. The Apostle believes in what has been revealed to him from his Lord, as do the men of faith. Each one (of them) believes in Allah, His Angels, His Books, and His Apostles. “We make no distinction (they say) between one and another of His Apostles.” And they say: “We hear, and we obey: (We seek) your forgive-ness, our Lord, and to you is the end of all journeys.”

286. On no soul Allah places a burden greater than it can bear. It gets every good that it earns, and it suffers every ill that it earns. (Pray:) “Our Lord! condemn us not if we forget or fall into error; Our Lord! lay not on us a burden like that which you did lay on those before us; Our Lord! lay not on us a burden greater than we have strength to bear. Blot out our sins, and grant us forgiveness. Have mercy on us. You are our Protector; help us against those who stand against Faith.

fayaghfiru limañy-yashaaa’u wa yu‘azzibu mañy-yashaaa’; wallaahu ‘alaa kulli shay’in Qadeer.

285. Aamanar-Rasoolu bimaaa unzila ilayhi mir-Rabbihee walmu’minoon; kullun aamana billaahi wa Malaaa’ikatihee wa Kutubihee wa Rusulihee laa nufarriqu bayna aḥadim-mir-Rusulih; wa qaaloo sami‘naa wa aṭa‘naa ghufraanaka Rabbanaa wa ilaykal-maṣeer.

286. Laa yukalliful-laahu nafsan illaa wus‘ahaa; lahaa maa kasabat wa ‘alayhaa maktasabat; Rabbanaa laa tu’aakhiznaaa in naseenaaa aw akhṭaånaa; Rabbanaa wa laa taḥmil-‘alaynaaa iṣran kamaa ḥamaltahoo ‘alal-lazeena min qablinaa; Rabbanaa wa laa tuḥammilnaa maa laa ṭaaqata lanaa bihee wa‘fu ‘annaa waghfir lanaa warḥamnaa; Anta mawlaanaa fanṣurnaa ‘alal-qawmil-kaafireen. **(Section 40)**

فَيَغْفِرُ لِمَنْ يَّشَآءُ وَيُعَذِّبُ مَنْ
يَّشَآءُ ۗ وَاللّٰهُ عَلٰى كُلِّ شَيْءٍ قَدِيْرٌ ﴿٢٨٤﴾
اٰمَنَ الرَّسُوْلُ بِمَآ اُنْزِلَ اِلَيْهِ
مِنْ رَّبِّهٖ وَالْمُؤْمِنُوْنَ ۗ كُلٌّ اٰمَنَ
بِاللّٰهِ وَمَلٰٓئِكَتِهٖ وَكُتُبِهٖ وَرُسُلِهٖ ۣ
لَا نُفَرِّقُ بَيْنَ اَحَدٍ مِّنْ رُّسُلِهٖ ۣ
وَقَالُوْا سَمِعْنَا وَاَطَعْنَا ۗ غُفْرَانَكَ
رَبَّنَا وَاِلَيْكَ الْمَصِيْرُ ﴿٢٨٥﴾
لَا يُكَلِّفُ اللّٰهُ نَفْسًا اِلَّا وُسْعَهَا ۭ لَهَا
مَا كَسَبَتْ وَعَلَيْهَا مَا اكْتَسَبَتْ ۭ
رَبَّنَا لَا تُؤَاخِذْنَآ اِنْ نَّسِيْنَآ اَوْ
اَخْطَاْنَا ۚ رَبَّنَا وَلَا تَحْمِلْ عَلَيْنَآ
اِصْرًا كَمَا حَمَلْتَهٗ عَلَى الَّذِيْنَ
مِنْ قَبْلِنَا ۚ رَبَّنَا وَلَا تُحَمِّلْنَا مَا
لَا طَاقَةَ لَنَا بِهٖ ۚ وَاعْفُ عَنَّا ۣ
وَاغْفِرْ لَنَا ۣ وَارْحَمْنَا ۣ اَنْتَ مَوْلٰىنَا
فَانْصُرْنَا عَلَى الْقَوْمِ الْكٰفِرِيْنَ ﴿٢٨٦﴾ ع ٨

3. The Family of ‘Imran

In the name of Allah, Most Gracious, Most Merciful.

Sûrat Âl ‘Imrân–3

(Revealed at Madinah)

Bismillaahir Raḥmaanir Raḥeem

(٣) سُوْرَةُ اٰلِ عِمْرٰنَ مَدَنِيَّةٌ (٨٩)

بِسْمِ اللّٰهِ الرَّحْمٰنِ الرَّحِيْمِ

1. *Alif-Lam-Mim*

2. Allah! There is no Allah but He,-the Living, the Self-Subsisting, Eternal.

3. It is He Who sent down to you (step by step), in truth, the Book, confirming what went before it; and He sent down the Law (of Moses) and the Gospel (of Jesus) before this, as a guide to mankind, and He sent down the criterion (of judgment between right and wrong).

4. Then those who reject Faith in the Signs of

1. Alif-Laaam-Meeem.

2. Allaahu laaa ilaaha illaa Huwal-Ḥayyul-Qayyoom.

3. Nazzala ‘alaykal-Kitaaba bilhaqqi muṣaddiqal-limaa bayna yadayhi wa anzalat-Tawraata wal-Injeel.

4. Min qablu hudal-linnaasi wa anzalal-Furqaan; innallazeena kafaroo bi-Aayaatil-

الٓمّٓ ﴿١﴾
اللّٰهُ لَآ اِلٰهَ اِلَّا هُوَ ۙ الْحَيُّ الْقَيُّوْمُ ﴿٢﴾
نَزَّلَ عَلَيْكَ الْكِتٰبَ بِالْحَقِّ
مُصَدِّقًا لِّمَا بَيْنَ يَدَيْهِ وَاَنْزَلَ
التَّوْرٰىةَ وَالْاِنْجِيْلَ ﴿٣﴾
مِنْ قَبْلُ هُدًى لِّلنَّاسِ وَاَنْزَلَ
الْفُرْقَانَ ۥ اِنَّ الَّذِيْنَ كَفَرُوْا بِاٰيٰتِ

Ikhfa اخفاء | Ghunna غنّہ | Ikhfa Meem Saakin اخفاء میم ساکن | Idghaam ادغام | Qalqala قلقلہ | Qalb قلب | Idghaam Meem Saakin ادغام میم ساکن

Translation	Transliteration	Arabic
Allah will suffer the severest chastisement, and Allah is Exalted in Might, Lord of Retribution.	laahi lahum 'azaabun shadeed; wallaahu 'Azeezun zun-tiqaam.	اللّٰهِ لَهُمْ عَذَابٌ شَدِيْدٌ ؕ وَاللّٰهُ عَزِيْزٌ ذُو انْتِقَامٍ ۝
5. From Allah, verily nothing is hidden on earth or in the heavens.	5. Innal-laaha laa yakhfaa 'alayhi shay'un fil-arḍi wa laa fis-samaaa'.	اِنَّ اللّٰهَ لَا يَخْفٰى عَلَيْهِ شَيْءٌ فِي الْاَرْضِ وَلَا فِي السَّمَآءِ ۝٥
6. He it is Who shapes you in the wombs as He pleases. There is no Allah but He, the Exalted in Might, the Wise.	6. Huwal-lazee yuṣawwiru-kum fil-arḥaami kayfa yashaaa'; laaa ilaaha illaa Huwal-'Azeezul-Ḥakeem.	هُوَ الَّذِيْ يُصَوِّرُكُمْ فِي الْاَرْحَامِ كَيْفَ يَشَآءُ ؕ لَآ اِلٰهَ اِلَّا هُوَ الْعَزِيْزُ الْحَكِيْمُ ۝٦
7. He it is Who has sent down to you the Book: In it are verses basic or fundamental (of established meaning); they are the foundation of the Book: others are allegorical. But those in whose hearts is perversity follow the part thereof that is allegorical, seeking discord, and searching for its hidden meanings, but no one knows its hidden meanings except Allah. And those who are firmly grounded in knowledge say: "We believe in the Book; the whole of it is from our Lord:" and none will grasp the Message except men of understanding.	7. Huwal-lazeee anzala 'alaykal-Kitaaba minhu Aayaatum-Muḥkamaatun hunna Ummul-Kitaabi wa ukharu Mutashaabihaatun fa-ammal-lazeena fee quloobihim zayghun fa-yattabi'oona maa tashaabaha minhubtighaaa'al-fitnati wabtighaaa'a taåweelih; wa maa ya'lamu taåweelahooo illal-laah; warraasikhoona fil-'ilmi yaqooloona aamannaa bihee kullum-min 'indi Rabbinaa; wa maa yazzakkaru illaaa ulul-albaab.	هُوَ الَّذِيْٓ اَنْزَلَ عَلَيْكَ الْكِتٰبَ مِنْهُ اٰيٰتٌ مُّحْكَمٰتٌ هُنَّ اُمُّ الْكِتٰبِ وَاُخَرُ مُتَشٰبِهٰتٌ ؕ فَاَمَّا الَّذِيْنَ فِيْ قُلُوْبِهِمْ زَيْغٌ فَيَتَّبِعُوْنَ مَا تَشَابَهَ مِنْهُ ابْتِغَآءَ الْفِتْنَةِ وَابْتِغَآءَ تَاْوِيْلِهٖ ۚ وَمَا يَعْلَمُ تَاْوِيْلَهٗٓ اِلَّا اللّٰهُ ۘ وَالرّٰسِخُوْنَ فِي الْعِلْمِ يَقُوْلُوْنَ اٰمَنَّا بِهٖ ۙ كُلٌّ مِّنْ عِنْدِ رَبِّنَا ۚ وَمَا يَذَّكَّرُ اِلَّآ اُولُوا الْاَلْبَابِ ۝٧
8. "Our Lord!" (they say), "Let not our hearts deviate now after You have guided us, but grant us mercy from Your own Presence; for You are the Grantor of bounties without measure.	8. Rabbanaa laa tuzigh quloobanaa ba'da iz hadaytanaa wa hab lanaa mil-ladunka raḥmah; innaka Antal-Wahhaab.	رَبَّنَا لَا تُزِغْ قُلُوْبَنَا بَعْدَ اِذْ هَدَيْتَنَا وَهَبْ لَنَا مِنْ لَّدُنْكَ رَحْمَةً ۚ اِنَّكَ اَنْتَ الْوَهَّابُ ۝٨
9. "Our Lord! You are He that will gather mankind together against a day about which there is no doubt; for Allah never fails in His promise."	9. Rabbanaaa innaka jaami-'un-naasi li-Yawmil-laa rayba feeh; innal-laaha laa yukhliful-mee'aad. **(Section 1)**	رَبَّنَآ اِنَّكَ جَامِعُ النَّاسِ لِيَوْمٍ لَّا رَيْبَ فِيْهِ ؕ اِنَّ اللّٰهَ لَا يُخْلِفُ الْمِيْعَادَ ۝٩ ع
10. Those who reject Faith,- neither their possessions nor their (numerous) progeny will avail them nothing against Allah: They are themselves but fuel for the Fire.	10. Innal-lazeena kafaroo lan tughniya 'anhum amwaaluhum wa laaa awlaaduhum minal-laahi shay'añw-wa ulaaa'ika hum waqoodun-Naar.	اِنَّ الَّذِيْنَ كَفَرُوْا لَنْ تُغْنِيَ عَنْهُمْ اَمْوَالُهُمْ وَلَآ اَوْلَادُهُمْ مِّنَ اللّٰهِ شَيْئًا ؕ وَاُولٰٓئِكَ هُمْ وَقُوْدُ النَّارِ ۝١٠

Ikhfa اخفاء · Ghunna غُنّہ · Ikhfa Meem Saakin اخفاء میم ساکن · Idghaam ادغام · Qalqala قلقلہ · Qalb قلب · Idghaam Meem Saakin ادغام میم ساکن

11. (Their plight will be) no better than that of the people of Pharaoh, and their predecessors: They denied our Signs, and Allah called them to account for their sins. For Allah is strict in punishment.

11. Kadaåbi Aali Fir'awna wallaz̲eena min qablihim; kaz̲z̲aboo bi-Aayaatinaa fa-akhaz̲ahumul-laahu biz̲unoobihim; wallaahu shadeedul-'iqaab.

كَدَأْبِ اٰلِ فِرْعَوْنَ ۙ وَالَّذِيْنَ
مِنْ قَبْلِهِمْ ؕ كَذَّبُوْا بِاٰيٰتِنَا ۚ
فَاَخَذَهُمُ اللّٰهُ بِذُنُوْبِهِمْ ؕ وَاللّٰهُ
شَدِيْدُ الْعِقَابِ ﴿۱۱﴾

12. Say to those who reject Faith: "Soon will you be vanquished and gathered together to Hell,-an evil bed indeed (to lie on)!

12. Qul lillaz̲eena kafaroo satughlaboona wa tuḥsharoona ilaa Jahannam; wa bi'sal-mihaad.

قُلْ لِّلَّذِيْنَ كَفَرُوْا سَتُغْلَبُوْنَ
وَتُحْشَرُوْنَ اِلٰى جَهَنَّمَ ؕ وَبِئْسَ
الْمِهَادُ ﴿۱۲﴾

13. "There has already been for you a Sign in the two armies that met (in combat): One was fighting in the cause of Allah, the other resisting Allah; these saw with their own eyes twice their number. But Allah does support with His aid whom He pleases. In this is a warning for such as have eyes to see."

13. Qad kaana lakum Aayatun fee fi'ataynil-taqataa fi'atun tuqaatilu fee sabeelil-laahi wa ukhraa kaafiratuñy-yarawnahum mis̲layhim raåyal-'ayn; wallaahu yu'ayyidu bi-naṣrihee mañy-yashaaa'; inna fee z̲aalika la-'ibratal-li-ulil-abṣaar.

قَدْ كَانَ لَكُمْ اٰيَةٌ فِىْ فِئَتَيْنِ
الْتَقَتَا ؕ فِئَةٌ تُقَاتِلُ فِىْ سَبِيْلِ
اللّٰهِ وَاُخْرٰى كَافِرَةٌ يَّرَوْنَهُمْ
مِّثْلَيْهِمْ رَاْىَ الْعَيْنِ ؕ وَاللّٰهُ يُؤَيِّدُ
بِنَصْرِهٖ مَنْ يَّشَآءُ ؕ اِنَّ فِىْ ذٰلِكَ
لَعِبْرَةً لِّاُولِى الْاَبْصَارِ ﴿۱۳﴾

14. Fair in the eyes of men is the love of things they covet: Women and sons; heaped-up hoards of gold and silver; horses branded (for breed and excellence); and (wealth of) cattle and well-tilled land. Such are the possessions of this world's life; but in nearness to Allah is the best of the goals (to return to).

14. Zuyyina linnaasi ḥubbush-shahawaati minannisaaa'i wal-baneena walqanaaṭeeril-muqanṭarati minaz̲-z̲ahabi walfiḍḍati walkhaylil-musawwamati wal-an'aami walḥars̲; z̲aalika mataa'ul-ḥayaatid-dunyaa wallaahu 'indahoo ḥusnul-ma-aab.

زُيِّنَ لِلنَّاسِ حُبُّ الشَّهَوٰتِ مِنَ
النِّسَآءِ وَالْبَنِيْنَ وَالْقَنَاطِيْرِ الْمُقَنْطَرَةِ
مِنَ الذَّهَبِ وَالْفِضَّةِ وَالْخَيْلِ
الْمُسَوَّمَةِ وَالْاَنْعَامِ وَالْحَرْثِ ؕ
ذٰلِكَ مَتَاعُ الْحَيٰوةِ الدُّنْيَا ۚ
وَاللّٰهُ عِنْدَهٗ حُسْنُ الْمَاٰبِ ﴿۱۴﴾

15. Say: Shall I give you glad tidings of things for better than those? For the righteous are Gardens in nearness to their Lord, with rivers flowing beneath; therein is their eternal home; with companions pure (and holy); and the good pleasure of Allah. For in Allah's sight are (all) His servants,-

15. Qul a'unabbi'ukum bikhayrim-min z̲aalikum; lillaz̲eenat-taqaw 'inda Rabbihim Jannaatun tajree min taḥtihal-anhaaru khaalideena feehaa wa azwaajum-muṭahharatuñw-wa riḍwaanum-minal-laah; wallaahu baṣeerum bil-'ibaad.

قُلْ اَؤُنَبِّئُكُمْ بِخَيْرٍ مِّنْ ذٰلِكُمْ ؕ
لِلَّذِيْنَ اتَّقَوْا عِنْدَ رَبِّهِمْ جَنّٰتٌ
تَجْرِىْ مِنْ تَحْتِهَا الْاَنْهٰرُ خٰلِدِيْنَ
فِيْهَا وَاَزْوَاجٌ مُّطَهَّرَةٌ وَّرِضْوَانٌ
مِّنَ اللّٰهِ ؕ وَاللّٰهُ بَصِيْرٌ ۢ بِالْعِبَادِ ﴿۱۵﴾

16. (Namely), those who say: "Our Lord! we have indeed believed: forgive us, then, our sins, and save us from the agony of the Fire;"-

16. Allaz̲eena yaqooloona Rabbanaaa innanaaa aamannaa faghfir lanaa z̲unoobanaa wa qinaa 'az̲aaban-Naar.

اَلَّذِيْنَ يَقُوْلُوْنَ رَبَّنَآ اِنَّنَآ اٰمَنَّا
فَاغْفِرْ لَنَا ذُنُوْبَنَا وَقِنَا عَذَابَ النَّارِ ﴿۱۶﴾

Ikhfa اخفاء | Ghunna غُنّہ | Ikhfa Meem Saakin اخفاءمیم ساکن | Idghaam ادغام | Qalqala قلقلہ | Qalb قلب | Idghaam Meem Saakin ادغام میم ساکن

اَلصّٰبِرِيْنَ وَالصّٰدِقِيْنَ وَالْقٰنِتِيْنَ
وَالْمُنْفِقِيْنَ وَالْمُسْتَغْفِرِيْنَ بِالْاَسْحَارِ ﴿١٧﴾
شَهِدَ اللّٰهُ اَنَّهٗ لَآ اِلٰهَ اِلَّا هُوَ ۙ وَ
الْمَلٰٓئِكَةُ وَاُولُوا الْعِلْمِ قَآئِمًاۢ بِالْقِسْطِ ؕ
لَآ اِلٰهَ اِلَّا هُوَ الْعَزِيْزُ الْحَكِيْمُ ﴿١٨﴾ النّصف
اِنَّ الدِّيْنَ عِنْدَ اللّٰهِ الْاِسْلَامُ ۟
وَمَا اخْتَلَفَ الَّذِيْنَ اُوْتُوا الْكِتٰبَ
اِلَّا مِنْۢ بَعْدِ مَا جَآءَهُمُ الْعِلْمُ
بَغْيًاۢ بَيْنَهُمْ ؕ وَمَنْ يَّكْفُرْ بِاٰيٰتِ
اللّٰهِ فَاِنَّ اللّٰهَ سَرِيْعُ الْحِسَابِ ﴿١٩﴾
فَاِنْ حَآجُّوْكَ فَقُلْ اَسْلَمْتُ وَجْهِىَ
لِلّٰهِ وَمَنِ اتَّبَعَنِ ؕ وَقُلْ لِّلَّذِيْنَ
اُوْتُوا الْكِتٰبَ وَالْاُمِّيّٖنَ ءَاَسْلَمْتُمْ ؕ
فَاِنْ اَسْلَمُوْا فَقَدِ اهْتَدَوْا ۚ وَاِنْ
تَوَلَّوْا فَاِنَّمَا عَلَيْكَ الْبَلٰغُ ؕ
وَاللّٰهُ بَصِيْرٌۢ بِالْعِبَادِ ﴿٢٠﴾ ع ٢
اِنَّ الَّذِيْنَ يَكْفُرُوْنَ بِاٰيٰتِ اللّٰهِ
وَيَقْتُلُوْنَ النَّبِيّٖنَ بِغَيْرِ حَقٍّ ۙ
وَّيَقْتُلُوْنَ الَّذِيْنَ يَاْمُرُوْنَ بِالْقِسْطِ
مِنَ النَّاسِ ۙ فَبَشِّرْهُمْ بِعَذَابٍ اَلِيْمٍ ﴿٢١﴾
اُولٰٓئِكَ الَّذِيْنَ حَبِطَتْ اَعْمَالُهُمْ فِى
الدُّنْيَا وَالْاٰخِرَةِ ۫ وَمَا لَهُمْ مِّنْ نّٰصِرِيْنَ ﴿٢٢﴾
اَلَمْ تَرَ اِلَى الَّذِيْنَ اُوْتُوْا نَصِيْبًا
مِّنَ الْكِتٰبِ يُدْعَوْنَ اِلٰى كِتٰبِ اللّٰهِ
لِيَحْكُمَ بَيْنَهُمْ ثُمَّ يَتَوَلّٰى فَرِيْقٌ
مِّنْهُمْ وَهُمْ مُّعْرِضُوْنَ ﴿٢٣﴾

17. Aṣṣaabireena waṣṣaadiqeena walqaaniteena walmunfiqeena walmustaghfireena bil-asḥaar.

18. Shahidal-laahu annahoo laaa ilaaha illaa Huwa walmalaaa'ikatu wa ulul-'ilmi qaaa'imam bilqisṭ; laaa ilaaha illaa Huwal-'Azeezul-Ḥakeem.

19. Innad-deena 'indal-laahil-Islaam; wa makhtalafal-lazeena ootul-Kitaaba illaa mim ba'di maa jaaa'ahumul-'ilmu baghyam baynahum; wa mañy-yakfur bi-Aayaatil-laahi fa-innal-laaha saree'ul-ḥisaab.

20. Fa-in ḥaaajjooka faqul aslamtu wajhiya lillaahi wa manit-taba'an; wa qul lillazeena ootul-Kitaaba wal-ummiyyeena 'a-aslamtum; fa-in aslamoo faqadih-tadaw wa in tawallaw fa-innamaa 'alaykal-balaagh; wallaahu baṣeerum bil-'ibaad.

(Section 2)

21. Innal-lazeena yakfuroona bi-Aayaatil-laahi wa yaqtuloonan-Nabiyyeena bighayri ḥaqqiñw-wa yaqtuloonal-lazeena yaåmuroona bilqisṭi minannaasi fabashshirhum bi'azaabin aleem.

22. Ulaaa'ikal-lazeena ḥabiṭat a'maaluhum fid-dunyaa wal-Aakhirati wa maa lahum min naaṣireen.

23. Alam tara ilal-lazeena ootoo naṣeebam-minal-Kitaabi yud'awna ilaa Kitaabil-laahi liyaḥkuma baynahum summa yatawallaa fareequm-minhum wa hum mu'riḍoon.

17. Those who show patience, firmness and self-control; who are true (in word and deed); who worship devoutly; who spend (in the way of Allah); and who pray for forgiveness in the early hours of the morning.

18. There is no Allah but He: that is the witness of Allah, His angels, and those endued with knowledge, standing firm on justice. There is no Allah but He, the Exalted in Power, the Wise.

19. The Religion before Allah is Islam (submission to His Will): nor did the People of the Book dissent therefrom except through envy of each other, after knowledge had come to them. But if any deny the Signs of Allah, Allah is swift in calling to account.

20. So if they dispute with you, say: "I have submitted my whole self to Allah and so have those who follow me." And say to the People of the Book and to those who are unlearned: "Do you (also) submit yourselves?" If they do, they are in right guidance, but if they turn back, your duty is to convey the Message; and in Allah's sight are (all) His servants.

21. As to those who deny the Signs of Allah and in defiance of right, slay the prophets, and slay those who teach just dealing with mankind, announce to them a grievous chastisement.

22. They are those whose works will bear no fruit in this world and in the Hereafter nor will they have anyone to help.

23. Has you not turned your vision to those who have been given a portion of the Book? They are invited to the Book of Allah, to settle their dispute, but a party of them turn back and decline (The arbitration).

Ikhfa اخفاء | Ghunna غُنّہ | Ikhfa Meem Saakin اخفاء میم ساکن | Idghaam ادغام | Qalqala قلقلہ | Qalb قلب | Idghaam Meem Saakin ادغام میم ساکن

24. This because they say: "The Fire shall not touch us but for a few numbered days": their forgeries deceive them as to their own religion.

24. Z̲aalika bi-annahum qaaloo lan tamassanan-Naaru illaaa ayyaamam ma'doodaatiñw-wa gharrahum fee deenihim maa kaanoo yaftaroon.

ذٰلِكَ بِاَنَّهُمْ قَالُوْا لَنْ تَمَسَّنَا النَّارُ
اِلَّآ اَيَّامًا مَّعْدُوْدٰتٍ ص وَّغَرَّهُمْ
فِيْ دِيْنِهِمْ مَّا كَانُوْا يَفْتَرُوْنَ ﴿٢٤﴾

25. But how (will they fare) when we gather them together against a day about which there is no doubt, and each soul will be paid out just what it has earned, without (favour or) injustice?

25. Fakayfa iz̲aa jama'naahum li-Yawmil-laa rayba feehi wa wuffiyat kullu nafsim-maa kasabat wa hum laa yuẓlamoon.

فَكَيْفَ اِذَا جَمَعْنٰهُمْ لِيَوْمٍ لَّا رَيْبَ
فِيْهِ قف وَوُفِّيَتْ كُلُّ نَفْسٍ مَّا
كَسَبَتْ وَهُمْ لَا يُظْلَمُوْنَ ﴿٢٥﴾

26. Say: "O Allah! Lord of Power (And Rule), You give power to whom You please, and You strip off power from whom You please: You endow with honour whom You please, and you bring low whom You please: In Your hand is all good. Verily, over all things You have power.

26. Qulil-laahumma Maalikal-Mulki tu'til-mulka man tashaaa'u wa tanzi'ul-mulka mimman tashaaa'u wa tu'izzu man tashaaa'u wa tuz̲illu man tashaaa'u biyadikal-khayru innaka 'alaa kulli shay'in Qadeer.

قُلِ اللّٰهُمَّ مٰلِكَ الْمُلْكِ تُؤْتِي الْمُلْكَ
مَنْ تَشَآءُ وَتَنْزِعُ الْمُلْكَ مِمَّنْ
تَشَآءُ ز وَتُعِزُّ مَنْ تَشَآءُ وَتُذِلُّ
مَنْ تَشَآءُ ط بِيَدِكَ الْخَيْرُ ط اِنَّكَ
عَلٰى كُلِّ شَيْءٍ قَدِيْرٌ ﴿٢٦﴾

27. "You cause the Night to gain on the Day, and You cause the Day to gain on the night; You bring the living out of the Dead, and You bring the Dead out of the Living; and You give sustenance to whom You please, without measure."

27. Toolijul-layla fin-nahaari wa toolijun-nahaara fil-layli wa tukhrijul-hayya minalmayyiti wa tukhrijul-mayyita minal-ḥayyi wa tarzuqu man tashaaa'u bighayri ḥisaab.

تُوْلِجُ الَّيْلَ فِي النَّهَارِ ز وَتُوْلِجُ
النَّهَارَ فِي الَّيْلِ ز وَتُخْرِجُ الْحَيَّ مِنَ
الْمَيِّتِ وَتُخْرِجُ الْمَيِّتَ مِنَ الْحَيِّ ز
وَتَرْزُقُ مَنْ تَشَآءُ بِغَيْرِ حِسَابٍ ﴿٢٧﴾

28. Let not the believers take for friends or helpers Unbelievers rather than believers: if any do that, in nothing will there be help from Allah: except by way of precaution, that you may guard yourselves from them. But Allah cautions you (to remember) Himself; for the final goal is to Allah.

28. Laa yattakhiz̲il-mu'mi-noonal-kaafireena awliyaaa'a min doonil-mu'mineena wa mañy-yaf'al z̲aalika falaysa minal-laahi fee shay'in illaaa an tattaqoo minhum tuqaah; wa yuḥaz̲z̲irukumul-laahu nafsah; wa ilal-laahil-maṣeer.

لَا يَتَّخِذِ الْمُؤْمِنُوْنَ الْكٰفِرِيْنَ
اَوْلِيَآءَ مِنْ دُوْنِ الْمُؤْمِنِيْنَ ج وَ
مَنْ يَّفْعَلْ ذٰلِكَ فَلَيْسَ مِنَ اللّٰهِ
فِيْ شَيْءٍ اِلَّآ اَنْ تَتَّقُوْا مِنْهُمْ
تُقٰىةً ط وَيُحَذِّرُكُمُ اللّٰهُ نَفْسَهٗ ط
وَاِلَى اللّٰهِ الْمَصِيْرُ ﴿٢٨﴾

29. Say: "Whether you hide what is in your hearts or reveal it, Allah knows it all: He knows what is in the heavens, and what is on earth. And Allah has power over all things.

29. Qul in tukhfoo maa fee ṣudoorikum aw tubdoohu ya'lamhul-laah; wa ya'lamu maa fis-samaawaati wa maa fil-arḍ; wallaahu 'alaa kulli shay'in Qadeer.

قُلْ اِنْ تُخْفُوْا مَا فِيْ صُدُوْرِكُمْ اَوْ
تُبْدُوْهُ يَعْلَمْهُ اللّٰهُ ط وَيَعْلَمُ مَا
فِي السَّمٰوٰتِ وَمَا فِي الْاَرْضِ ط
وَاللّٰهُ عَلٰى كُلِّ شَيْءٍ قَدِيْرٌ ﴿٢٩﴾

30. "On the Day when every soul will be confronted with all

30. Yawma tajidu kullu nafsim-maa 'amilat min

يَوْمَ تَجِدُ كُلُّ نَفْسٍ مَّا عَمِلَتْ مِنْ

Ikhfa اخفاء | Ghunna غُنّہ | Ikhfa Meem Saakin اخفاء میم ساکن | Idghaam ادغام | Qalqala قلقلہ | Qalb قلب | Idghaam Meem Saakin ادغام میم ساکن

the good it has done, and all the evil it has done, it will wish there were a great distance between it and its evil. But Allah cautions you (to remember) Himself. And Allah is full of kindness to those that serve Him."

31. Say: "If you do love Allah, Follow me: Allah will love you and forgive you your sins: For Allah is Oft-Forgiving, Most Merciful."

32. Say: "Obey Allah and His Apostle": But if they turn back, Allah loves not those who reject Faith.

33. Allah did choose Adam and Noah, the family of Abraham, and the family of 'Imran above all people,-

34. Offspring, one of the other: And Allah hears and knows all things.

35. Behold! a woman of 'Imran said: "O my Lord! I do dedicate unto You what is in my womb for your special service: So accept this of me: For You hears and knows all things."

36. When she delivered (the baby girl) she said: "O my Lord! Behold! I am delivered of a female child!"- and Allah knew best what she brought forth- "And no wise is the male like the female. I have named her Mary, and I commend her and her offspring to Your protection from Satan, the Rejected."

37. Right graciously did her Lord accept her: He made her grow in purity and beauty: To the care of Zakariya was she assigned. Every time that he entered (Her) chamber to see her, He found her supplied with sustenance. He said:

khayrim muḥḍarañw-wa maa 'amilat min sooo'in tawaddu law anna baynahaa wa baynahooo amadam ba'eedaa; wa yuḥazzirukumul-laahu nafsah; wallaahu ra'oofum bil'ibaad. **(Section 3)**

31. Qul in kuntum tuḥibboonal-laaha fattabi'oonee yuḥbibkumul-laahu wa yaghfir lakum zunoobakum; wallaahu Ghafoorur-Raḥeem.

32. Qul aṭee'ul-laaha war-Rasoola fa-in tawallaw fa-innal-laaha laa yuḥibbul-kaafireen.

33. Innal-laahaṣ-ṭafaaa Aadama wa Nooḥañw-wa Aala Ibraaheema wa Aala 'Imraana 'alal-'aalameen.

34 Zurriyyatam ba'ḍuhaa mim-ba'ḍ, wallaahu Samee'un 'Aleem.

35. Iz qaalatim-ra-atu 'Imraana Rabbi innee nazartu laka maa fee baṭnee muḥarraran fataqabbal minnee innaka Antas-Samee'ul-'Aleem.

36. Falammaa waḍa'athaa qaalat Rabbi innee waḍa'tuhaaa unsaa wallaahu a'lamu bimaa waḍa'at wa laysaz-zakaru kal-unsaa wa innee sammaytuhaa Maryama wa inneee u'eezuhaa bika wa zurriyyatahaa minash-Shayṭaanir-Rajeem.

37. Fataqabbalahaa Rabbuhaa biqaboolin ḥasaniñw-wa ambatahaa nabaatan ḥasanañw-wa kaffalahaa Zakariyyaa kullamaa dakhala 'alayhaa Zakariyyal-Miḥraaba wajada 'indahaa rizqan qaala

خَيْرٍ مُّحْضَرًا ۛ وَّمَا عَمِلَتْ مِنْ سُوْٓءٍ ۛ
تَوَدُّ لَوْ اَنَّ بَيْنَهَا وَبَيْنَهٗٓ اَمَدًۢا بَعِيْدًا ؕ
وَيُحَذِّرُكُمُ اللّٰهُ نَفْسَهٗ ؕ وَاللّٰهُ رَءُوْفٌۢ
بِالْعِبَادِ ۝٣٠
قُلْ اِنْ كُنْتُمْ تُحِبُّوْنَ اللّٰهَ فَاتَّبِعُوْنِيْ
يُحْبِبْكُمُ اللّٰهُ وَيَغْفِرْ لَكُمْ ذُنُوْبَكُمْ ؕ
وَاللّٰهُ غَفُوْرٌ رَّحِيْمٌ ۝٣١
قُلْ اَطِيْعُوا اللّٰهَ وَالرَّسُوْلَ ۚ فَاِنْ تَوَلَّوْا
فَاِنَّ اللّٰهَ لَا يُحِبُّ الْكٰفِرِيْنَ ۝٣٢
اِنَّ اللّٰهَ اصْطَفٰٓى اٰدَمَ وَنُوْحًا وَّاٰلَ
اِبْرٰهِيْمَ وَاٰلَ عِمْرٰنَ عَلَى الْعٰلَمِيْنَ ۝٣٣
ذُرِّيَّةًۢ بَعْضُهَا مِنْۢ بَعْضٍ ؕ وَاللّٰهُ
سَمِيْعٌ عَلِيْمٌ ۝٣٤
اِذْ قَالَتِ امْرَاَتُ عِمْرٰنَ رَبِّ اِنِّيْ
نَذَرْتُ لَكَ مَا فِيْ بَطْنِيْ مُحَرَّرًا
فَتَقَبَّلْ مِنِّيْ ۚ اِنَّكَ اَنْتَ السَّمِيْعُ
الْعَلِيْمُ ۝٣٥
فَلَمَّا وَضَعَتْهَا قَالَتْ رَبِّ اِنِّيْ
وَضَعْتُهَآ اُنْثٰى ؕ وَاللّٰهُ اَعْلَمُ بِمَا
وَضَعَتْ ؕ وَلَيْسَ الذَّكَرُ كَالْاُنْثٰى ۚ
وَاِنِّيْ سَمَّيْتُهَا مَرْيَمَ وَاِنِّيْٓ اُعِيْذُهَا
بِكَ وَذُرِّيَّتَهَا مِنَ الشَّيْطٰنِ الرَّجِيْمِ ۝٣٦
فَتَقَبَّلَهَا رَبُّهَا بِقَبُوْلٍ حَسَنٍ
وَّاَنْۢبَتَهَا نَبَاتًا حَسَنًا ۙ وَّكَفَّلَهَا
زَكَرِيَّا ۚ كُلَّمَا دَخَلَ عَلَيْهَا زَكَرِيَّا
الْمِحْرَابَ ۙ وَجَدَ عِنْدَهَا رِزْقًا ۚ قَالَ

Ikhfa اخفاء | Ghunna غنّہ | Ikhfa Meem Saakin اخفاء میم ساکن | Idghaam ادغام | Qalqala قلقلہ | Qalb قلب | Idghaam Meem Saakin ادغام میم ساکن

"O Mary! Wherefrom (comes) this to you?" She said: "From Allah: for Allah provides sustenance to whom He pleases without measure."

yaa Maryamu annaa laki haa<u>z</u>aa qaalat huwa min 'indil-laahi innal-laaha yarzuqu mañy-yashaaa'u bighayri ḥisaab.

يٰمَرۡيَمُ اَنّٰى لَكِ هٰذَا ؕ قَالَتۡ هُوَ
مِنۡ عِنۡدِ اللّٰهِ ؕ اِنَّ اللّٰهَ يَرۡزُقُ مَنۡ
يَّشَآءُ بِغَيۡرِ حِسَابٍ ﴿۳۷﴾

38. Zakariya prayed there to his Lord, saying: "O my Lord! Grant for me from You a progeny that is pure: for You are He that hears prayer!

38. Hunaaalika da'aa Zakariyyaa Rabbahoo qaala Rabbi hab lee mil-ladunka <u>z</u>urriyyatan ṭayyibatan innaka samee'ud-du'aaa'.

هُنَالِكَ دَعَا زَكَرِيَّا رَبَّهٗ ۚ قَالَ
رَبِّ هَبۡ لِىۡ مِنۡ لَّدُنۡكَ ذُرِّيَّةً
طَيِّبَةً ۚ اِنَّكَ سَمِيۡعُ الدُّعَآءِ ﴿۳۸﴾

39. While he was standing in prayer in the chamber, the angels called to him: "Allah does give you glad tidings of Yahya, confirming the truth of a Word from Allah, and be (besides) noble, chaste, and a prophet,- of the (goodly) company of the righteous."

39. Fanaadat-hul-malaaa'ikatu wa huwa qaaa'imuñy-yuṣallee fil-Miḥraabi annal-laaha yubashshiruka bi-Yaḥyaa muṣaddiqam bi-Kalimatim-minal-laahi wa sayyidañw-wa ḥaṣooorañw-wa Nabiyyam minaṣ-ṣaaliḥeen.

فَنَادَتۡهُ الۡمَلٰٓـئِكَةُ وَهُوَ قَآئِمٌ يُّصَلِّىۡ
فِى الۡمِحۡرَابِ ۙ اَنَّ اللّٰهَ يُبَشِّرُكَ
بِيَحۡيٰى مُصَدِّقًاۢ بِكَلِمَةٍ مِّنَ اللّٰهِ
وَسَيِّدًا وَّحَصُوۡرًا وَّنَبِيًّا مِّنَ
الصّٰلِحِيۡنَ ﴿۳۹﴾

40. He said: "O my Lord! How shall I have son, seeing I am very old, and my wife is barren?" "Thus," was the answer, "Does Allah accomplish what He wills."

40. Qaala Rabbi annaa yakoonu lee ghulaamuñw-wa qad balaghaniyal-kibaru wamraatee 'aaqirun qaala ka<u>z</u>aalikal-laahu yaf'alu maa yashaaa'.

قَالَ رَبِّ اَنّٰى يَكُوۡنُ لِىۡ غُلٰمٌ وَّقَدۡ
بَلَغَنِىَ الۡكِبَرُ وَامۡرَاَتِىۡ عَاقِرٌ ؕ قَالَ
كَذٰلِكَ اللّٰهُ يَفۡعَلُ مَا يَشَآءُ ﴿۴۰﴾

41. He said: "O my Lord! Give me a Sign!" "Your Sign," was the answer, "Shall be that you shall speak to no man for three days but with signals. Then celebrate the praises of your Lord again and again, and glorify Him in the evening and in the morning."

41. Qaala Rabbij-'al-leee Aayatan qaala Aayatuka allaa tukalliman-naasa <u>s</u>alaa<u>s</u>ata ayyaamin illaa ramzaa; wa<u>z</u>kur Rabbaka ka<u>s</u>eerañw-wa sabbiḥ bil'ashiyyi wal-ibkaar.

(Section 4)

قَالَ رَبِّ اجۡعَلۡ لِّىۡۤ اٰيَةً ؕ قَالَ
اٰيَتُكَ اَلَّا تُكَلِّمَ النَّاسَ ثَلٰثَةَ
اَيَّامٍ اِلَّا رَمۡزًا ؕ وَاذۡكُرۡ رَّبَّكَ كَثِيۡرًا
وَّسَبِّحۡ بِالۡعَشِىِّ وَالۡاِبۡكَارِ ﴿۴۱﴾

42. Behold! the angels said: "O Mary! Allah has chosen you and purified you- chosen you above the women of all nations.

42. Wa i<u>z</u> qaalatil-malaaa'ikatu yaa Maryamu innal-laahaṣ-ṭafaaki wa ṭahharaki waṣṭafaaki 'alaa nisaaa'il-'aalameen.

وَاِذۡ قَالَتِ الۡمَلٰٓـئِكَةُ يٰمَرۡيَمُ اِنَّ اللّٰهَ
اصۡطَفٰٮكِ وَطَهَّرَكِ وَاصۡطَفٰٮكِ
عَلٰى نِسَآءِ الۡعٰلَمِيۡنَ ﴿۴۲﴾

43. "O Mary! Worship your Lord devoutly: Prostrate yourself and bow down (in prayer) with those who bow down."

43. Yaa Maryamuq-nutee li-Rabbiki wasjudee warka'ee ma'ar-raaki'een.

يٰمَرۡيَمُ اقۡنُتِىۡ لِرَبِّكِ وَاسۡجُدِىۡ
وَارۡكَعِىۡ مَعَ الرّٰكِعِيۡنَ ﴿۴۳﴾

44. This is part of the tidings of the things unseen, which We reveal unto you (O Apostle!) by inspiration: You were not with them when they cast lots with arrows, as to which of them should be charged with the care of Marry;

44. <u>Z</u>aalika min ambaaa'il-ghaybi nooḥeehi ilayk; wa maa kunta ladayhim i<u>z</u> yulqoona aqlaamahum ayyuhum yakfulu Maryama

ذٰلِكَ مِنۡ اَنۡۢبَآءِ الۡغَيۡبِ نُوۡحِيۡهِ
اِلَيۡكَ ؕ وَمَا كُنۡتَ لَدَيۡهِمۡ اِذۡ
يُلۡقُوۡنَ اَقۡلَامَهُمۡ اَيُّهُمۡ يَكۡفُلُ مَرۡيَمَ

Ikhfa اخفاء | Ghunna غُنّہ | Ikhfa Meem Saakin اخفاء میم ساکن | Idghaam ادغام | Qalqala قلقلہ | Qalb قلب | Idghaam Meem Saakin ادغام میم ساکن

nor were you with them when they disputed (the point).

wa maa kunta ladayhim iz yakhtaṣimoon.

وَمَا كُنْتَ لَدَيْهِمْ إِذْ يَخْتَصِمُونَ ﴿٤٤﴾

45. Behold! the angels said: "O Mary! Allah gives you glad tidings of a Word from Him: his name will be Christ Jesus, the son of Mary, held in honour in this world and the Hereafter and of (the company of) those nearest to Allah;

45. Iz qaalatil-malaaa'ikatu yaa Maryamu innal-laaha yubashshiruki bi-Kalimatim-minhus-muhul-Maseeḥu 'Eesab-nu-Maryama wajeehan fid-dunyaa wal-Aakhirati wa minal-muqarrabeen.

إِذْ قَالَتِ الْمَلٰٓئِكَةُ يٰمَرْيَمُ إِنَّ
اللّٰهَ يُبَشِّرُكِ بِكَلِمَةٍ مِّنْهُ ۖ اسْمُهُ
الْمَسِيحُ عِيسَى ابْنُ مَرْيَمَ وَجِيهًا
فِي الدُّنْيَا وَالْآخِرَةِ وَمِنَ
الْمُقَرَّبِينَ ﴿٤٥﴾

46. "He shall speak to the people in infancy and in maturity. And he shall be (of the company) of the righteous."

46. Wa yukallimun-naasa filmahdi wa kahlañw-wa minaṣṣaaliḥeen

وَيُكَلِّمُ النَّاسَ فِي الْمَهْدِ وَكَهْلًا
وَّمِنَ الصّٰلِحِينَ ﴿٤٦﴾

47. She said: "O my Lord! how shall I have a son when no man has touched me?" He said: "Even so: Allah creates what He wills: When He has decreed a Plan, He but says to it, 'Be,' and it is!

47. Qaalat Rabbi annaa yakoonu lee waladuñw-wa lam yamsasnee basharun qaala kazaalikil-laahu yakhluqu maa yashaaa'; izaa qaḍaaa amran fa-innamaa yaqoolu lahoo kun fa-yakoon.

قَالَتْ رَبِّ أَنّٰى يَكُونُ لِي وَلَدٌ وَّلَمْ
يَمْسَسْنِي بَشَرٌ ۖ قَالَ كَذٰلِكِ اللّٰهُ
يَخْلُقُ مَا يَشَاءُ ۚ إِذَا قَضٰى أَمْرًا
فَإِنَّمَا يَقُولُ لَهُ كُنْ فَيَكُونُ ﴿٤٧﴾

48. "And Allah will teach him the Book and Wisdom, the Torah and the Gospel,?

48. Wa yu'allimuhul-Kitaaba wal-Ḥikmata wat-Tawraata wal-Injeel.

وَيُعَلِّمُهُ الْكِتٰبَ وَالْحِكْمَةَ وَالتَّوْرٰىةَ
وَالْإِنْجِيلَ ﴿٤٨﴾

49. "And (appoint him) an apostle to the Children of Israel, (with this message): "'I have come to you, with a Sign from your Lord, in that I make for you out of clay, as it were, the figure of a bird, and breathe into it, and it becomes a bird by Allah's leave: And I heal those born blind, and the lepers, and I quicken the dead, by Allah's leave; and I declare to you what you eat, and what you store in your houses. Surely therein is a Sign for you if you did believe;

49. Wa Rasoolan-ilaa Baneee Israaa'eela annee qad ji'tukum bi-Aayatim-mir-Rabbikum anneee akhluqu lakum minaṭ-ṭeeni kahay'atiṭṭayri fa-anfukhu feehi fayakoonu ṭayram bi-iznil-laahi wa ubri'ul-akmaha wal-abraṣa wa-uḥyil-mawtaa bi-iznil-laahi wa unabbi'ukum bimaa taåkuloona wa maa taddakhiroona fee buyootikum; inna fee zaalika la-Aayatal-lakum in kuntum mu'mineen.

وَرَسُولًا إِلٰى بَنِيٓ إِسْرَآئِيلَ ۙ أَنِّي
قَدْ جِئْتُكُمْ بِآيَةٍ مِّنْ رَّبِّكُمْ ۙ
أَنِّيٓ أَخْلُقُ لَكُمْ مِّنَ الطِّينِ كَهَيْئَةِ
الطَّيْرِ فَأَنْفُخُ فِيهِ فَيَكُونُ طَيْرًا
بِإِذْنِ اللّٰهِ ۖ وَأُبْرِئُ الْأَكْمَهَ وَالْأَبْرَصَ
وَأُحْيِ الْمَوْتٰى بِإِذْنِ اللّٰهِ ۖ وَأُنَبِّئُكُمْ
بِمَا تَأْكُلُونَ وَمَا تَدَّخِرُونَ ۙ
فِي بُيُوتِكُمْ ۚ إِنَّ فِي ذٰلِكَ لَآيَةً
لَّكُمْ إِنْ كُنْتُمْ مُّؤْمِنِينَ ﴿٤٩﴾

50. "'(I have come to you), to attest the Torah which was before me. And to make lawful to you part of what was (Before) forbidden to you; I have come to you with a Sign from

50. Wa muṣaddiqal-limaa bayna yadayya minat-Tawraati wa li-uḥilla lakum ba'ḍal-lazee ḥurrima 'alaykum; wa ji'tukum bi-Aayatim-mir-

وَمُصَدِّقًا لِّمَا بَيْنَ يَدَيَّ مِنَ
التَّوْرٰىةِ وَلِأُحِلَّ لَكُمْ بَعْضَ الَّذِي
حُرِّمَ عَلَيْكُمْ وَجِئْتُكُمْ بِآيَةٍ مِّنْ

Ikhfa	Ghunna	Ikhfa Meem Saakin	Idghaam	Qalqala	Qalb	Idghaam Meem Saakin
اخفاء	غُنّہ	اخفاء میم ساکن	ادغام	قلقلہ	قلب	ادغام میم ساکن

your Lord. So fear Allah, and obey me.

Rabbikum fattaqul-laaha wa aṭee'oon.

رَبِّكُمْ فَاتَّقُوا اللّٰهَ وَاَطِيْعُوْنِ ۝٥٠

51. "'It is Allah Who is my Lord and your Lord; then worship Him. This is a Way that is straight.'"

51. Innal-laaha Rabbee wa Rabbukum fa'budooh; haaẕaa Ṣiraaṭum-Mustaqeem.

اِنَّ اللّٰهَ رَبِّيْ وَرَبُّكُمْ فَاعْبُدُوْهُ ۭ
هٰذَا صِرَاطٌ مُّسْتَقِيْمٌ ۝٥١

52. When Jesus found unbelief on their part He said: "Who will be My helpers to (the work of) Allah?" Said the disciples: "We are Allah's helpers: We believe in Allah, and you bear witness that we are Muslims.

52. Falammaaa aḥassa 'Eesaa minhumul-kufra qaala man anṣaareee ilal-laahi qaalal-Ḥawaariyyoona naḥnu anṣaarul-laahi aamannaa billaahi washhad bi-annaa muslimoon.

فَلَمَّآ اَحَسَّ عِيْسٰى مِنْهُمُ الْكُفْرَ
قَالَ مَنْ اَنْصَارِيْٓ اِلَى اللّٰهِ ۭ قَالَ
الْحَوَارِيُّوْنَ نَحْنُ اَنْصَارُ اللّٰهِ ۚ اٰمَنَّا
بِاللّٰهِ ۚ وَاشْهَدْ بِاَنَّا مُسْلِمُوْنَ ۝٥٢

53. "Our Lord! we believe in what You have revealed, and we follow the Apostle; then write us down among those who bear witness."

53. Rabbanaaa aamannaa bimaaa anzalta wattaba'nar-Rasoola faktubnaa ma'ash-shaahideen.

رَبَّنَآ اٰمَنَّا بِمَآ اَنْزَلْتَ وَاتَّبَعْنَا
الرَّسُوْلَ فَاكْتُبْنَا مَعَ الشّٰهِدِيْنَ ۝٥٣

54. And (the unbelievers) plotted and planned, and Allah too planned, and the best of planners is Allah.

54. Wa makaroo wa makaral-laahu wallaahu khayrul-maakireen. **(Section 5)**

وَمَكَرُوْا وَمَكَرَ اللّٰهُ ۭ وَاللّٰهُ خَيْرُ
الْمٰكِرِيْنَ ۝٥٤ ع

النصف

55. Behold! Allah said: "O Jesus! I will take you and raise you to Myself and clear you (of the falsehoods) of those who blaspheme; I will make those who follow you superior to those who reject faith, to the Day of Resurrection: then shall you all return unto me, and I will judge between you of the matters wherein you dispute.

55. Iẕ qaalal-laahu yaa 'Eesaaa innee mutawaffeeka wa raafi'uka ilayya wa muṭahhiruka minal-laẕeena kafaroo wa jaa'ilul-laẕeenattaba'ooka fawqal-laẕeena kafarooo ilaa Yawmil-Qiyaamati summa ilayya marji'ukum fa-aḥkumu baynakum feemaa kuntum feehi takhtalifoon.

اِذْ قَالَ اللّٰهُ يٰعِيْسٰٓى اِنِّىْ مُتَوَفِّيْكَ
وَرَافِعُكَ اِلَيَّ وَمُطَهِّرُكَ مِنَ
الَّذِيْنَ كَفَرُوْا وَجَاعِلُ الَّذِيْنَ
اتَّبَعُوْكَ فَوْقَ الَّذِيْنَ كَفَرُوْٓا اِلٰى
يَوْمِ الْقِيٰمَةِ ۚ ثُمَّ اِلَيَّ مَرْجِعُكُمْ
فَاَحْكُمُ بَيْنَكُمْ فِيْمَا كُنْتُمْ
فِيْهِ تَخْتَلِفُوْنَ ۝٥٥

56. "As to those who reject faith, I will punish them with terrible agony in this world and in the Hereafter, nor will they have anyone to help."

56. Fa-ammal-laẕeena kafaroo fa-u'aẕ ẕibuhum 'aẕaaban shadeedan fiddunyaa wal-Aakhirati wa maa lahum min naaṣireen.

فَاَمَّا الَّذِيْنَ كَفَرُوْا فَاُعَذِّبُهُمْ
عَذَابًا شَدِيْدًا فِي الدُّنْيَا وَالْاٰخِرَةِ ۡ
وَمَا لَهُمْ مِّنْ نّٰصِرِيْنَ ۝٥٦

57. "As to those who believe and work righteousness, Allah will pay them (in full) their reward; but Allah loves not those who do wrong."

57. Wa ammal-laẕeena aamanoo wa 'amiluṣ-ṣaaliḥaati fa-yuwaffeehim ujoorahum; wallaahu laa yuḥibbuẓ-ẓaalimeen

وَاَمَّا الَّذِيْنَ اٰمَنُوْا وَعَمِلُوا الصّٰلِحٰتِ
فَيُوَفِّيْهِمْ اُجُوْرَهُمْ ۭ وَاللّٰهُ لَا يُحِبُّ
الظّٰلِمِيْنَ ۝٥٧

58. "This is what we rehearse unto you of the Signs and the Message of Wisdom."

58. Ẕaalika natloohu 'alayka minal-Aayaati waẕ-Ẕikril-Ḥakeem.

ذٰلِكَ نَتْلُوْهُ عَلَيْكَ مِنَ الْاٰيٰتِ
وَالذِّكْرِ الْحَكِيْمِ ۝٥٨

Ikhfa اخفاء	Ghunna غُنّہ	Ikhfa Meem Saakin اخفاء میم ساکن	Idghaam ادغام	Qalqala قلقلہ	Qalb قلب	Idghaam Meem Saakin ادغام میم ساکن

59. The similitude of Jesus before Allah is as that of Adam; He created him from dust, then said to him: "Be". And he was.

59. Inna ma<u>s</u>ala ʻEesaa ʻindal-laahi kama<u>s</u>ali Aadama khalaqahoo min turaabin <u>s</u>umma qaala lahoo kun fa-yakoon.

إِنَّ مَثَلَ عِيسَىٰ عِندَ اللَّهِ كَمَثَلِ
آدَمَ ۖ خَلَقَهُ مِن تُرَابٍ ثُمَّ قَالَ
لَهُ كُن فَيَكُونُ ﴿٥٩﴾

60. The Truth (comes) from Allah alone; so be not of those who doubt.

60. Alḥaqqu mir-Rabbika falaa takum-minal-mumtareen.

الْحَقُّ مِن رَّبِّكَ فَلَا تَكُن مِّنَ
الْمُمْتَرِينَ ﴿٦٠﴾

61. If any one disputes in this matter with you, now after (full) knowledge has come to you, say: "Come! let us gather together,- our sons and your sons, our women and your women, ourselves and yourselves: Then let us earnestly pray, and invoke the curse of Allah on those who lie!"

61. Faman ḥaaajjaka feehi mim baʻdi maa jaaa'aka minal-ʻilmi faqul taʻaalaw nadʻu abnaaa'anaa wa abnaaa'akum wa nisaaa'anaa wa nisaaa'akum wa anfusanaa wa anfusakum <u>s</u>umma nabtahil fanajʻal laʻnatal-laahi ʻalal-kaa<u>z</u>ibeen.

فَمَنْ حَاجَّكَ فِيهِ مِن بَعْدِ مَا
جَاءَكَ مِنَ الْعِلْمِ فَقُلْ تَعَالَوْا
نَدْعُ أَبْنَاءَنَا وَأَبْنَاءَكُمْ وَنِسَاءَنَا
وَنِسَاءَكُمْ وَأَنفُسَنَا وَأَنفُسَكُمْ قف
ثُمَّ نَبْتَهِلْ فَنَجْعَل لَّعْنَتَ اللَّهِ
عَلَى الْكَاذِبِينَ ﴿٦١﴾

62. This is the true account: there is no god except Allah; and Allah-He is indeed the Exalted in Power, the Wise.

62. Inna haa<u>z</u>aa lahuwal-qaṣaṣul-ḥaqq; wa maa min ilaahin illal-laah; wa innal-laaha la-Huwal-ʻAzeezul-Ḥakeem.

إِنَّ هَٰذَا لَهُوَ الْقَصَصُ الْحَقُّ ۚ وَمَا
مِنْ إِلَٰهٍ إِلَّا اللَّهُ ۚ وَإِنَّ اللَّهَ لَهُوَ
الْعَزِيزُ الْحَكِيمُ ﴿٦٢﴾

63. But if they turn back, Allah has full knowledge of those who do mischief.

63. Fa-in tawallaw fa-innal-laaha ʻaleemum bil-mufsideen.

(Section 6)

فَإِن تَوَلَّوْا فَإِنَّ اللَّهَ عَلِيمٌ
بِالْمُفْسِدِينَ ﴿٦٣﴾

64. Say: "O People of the Book! come to common terms as between us and you: That we worship none but Allah; that we associate no partners with him; that we erect not, from among ourselves, Lords and patrons other than Allah." If then they turn back, say you: "Bear witness that we (at least) are Muslims (bowing to Allah's Will).

64. Qul yaaa Ahlal-Kitaabi taʻaalaw ilaa Kalimatin sawaaa'im baynanaa wa baynakum allaa naʻbuda illal-laaha wa laa nushrika bihee shay'añw-wa laa yattakhi<u>z</u>a baʻḍunaa baʻḍan arbaabam-min doonil-laah; fa-in tawallaw faqoolush-hadoo bi-annaa muslimoon.

قُلْ يَا أَهْلَ الْكِتَابِ تَعَالَوْا إِلَىٰ
كَلِمَةٍ سَوَاءٍ بَيْنَنَا وَبَيْنَكُمْ أَلَّا
نَعْبُدَ إِلَّا اللَّهَ وَلَا نُشْرِكَ بِهِ شَيْئًا
وَلَا يَتَّخِذَ بَعْضُنَا بَعْضًا أَرْبَابًا
مِّن دُونِ اللَّهِ ۚ فَإِن تَوَلَّوْا فَقُولُوا
اشْهَدُوا بِأَنَّا مُسْلِمُونَ ﴿٦٤﴾

65. You People of the Book! Why dispute you about Abraham, when the Torah and the Gospel Were not revealed till after him? Have you no understanding?

65. Yaaa Ahlal-Kitaabi lima tuhaaajjoona feee Ibraaheema wa maaa unzilatit-Tawraatu wal-Injeelu illaa mim baʻdih; afalaa taʻqiloon.

يَا أَهْلَ الْكِتَابِ لِمَ تُحَاجُّونَ فِي
إِبْرَاهِيمَ وَمَا أُنزِلَتِ التَّوْرَاةُ
وَالْإِنجِيلُ إِلَّا مِن بَعْدِهِ ۚ
أَفَلَا تَعْقِلُونَ ﴿٦٥﴾

Ikhfa اخفاء | Ghunna غنّہ | Ikhfa Meem Saakin اخفاء میم ساکن | Idghaam ادغام | Qalqala قلقلہ | Qalb قلب | Idghaam Meem Saakin ادغام میم ساکن

66. Ah! You are those who fell to disputing (Even) in matters of which you had some knowledge! but why dispute you in matters of which you have no knowledge? It is Allah Who knows, and you who know not!

66. Haaa-antum haaa'ulaaa'i ḥaajajtum feemaa lakum bihee 'ilmun falima tuḥaaajjoona feemaa laysa lakum bihee 'ilm; wallaahu ya'lamu wa antum laa ta'lamoon.

هَٰٓأَنتُمْ هَٰٓؤُلَآءِ حَٰجَجْتُمْ فِيمَا لَكُم
بِهِۦ عِلْمٌ فَلِمَ تُحَآجُّونَ فِيمَا لَيْسَ
لَكُم بِهِۦ عِلْمٌ ۚ وَٱللَّهُ يَعْلَمُ وَأَنتُمْ
لَا تَعْلَمُونَ ﴿٦٦﴾

67. Abraham was not a Jew nor yet a Christian; but he was true in Faith, and bowed his will to Allah's (Which is Islam), and he joined not gods with Allah.

67. Maa kaana Ibraaheemu Yahoodiyyañw-wa laa Naṣraaniyyañw-wa laakin kaana Ḥaneefam-Muslimañw wa maa kaana minal-mushrikeen.

مَا كَانَ إِبْرَٰهِيمُ يَهُودِيًّا وَلَا
نَصْرَانِيًّا وَلَٰكِن كَانَ حَنِيفًا
مُّسْلِمًا وَمَا كَانَ مِنَ ٱلْمُشْرِكِينَ ﴿٦٧﴾

68. Without doubt, among men, the nearest of kin to Abraham, are those who follow him, as are also this Apostle and those who believe: And Allah is the Protector of those who have Faith.

68. Inna awlan-naasi bi-Ibraaheema lallaẕeenat-taba-'oohu wa haaẕan-Nabiyyu wallaẕeena aamanoo; wallaahu waliyyul-mu'mineen.

إِنَّ أَوْلَى ٱلنَّاسِ بِإِبْرَٰهِيمَ لَلَّذِينَ
ٱتَّبَعُوهُ وَهَٰذَا ٱلنَّبِىُّ وَٱلَّذِينَ
ءَامَنُوا۟ ۗ وَٱللَّهُ وَلِىُّ ٱلْمُؤْمِنِينَ ﴿٦٨﴾

69. It is the wish of a section of the People of the Book to lead you astray. But they shall lead astray (not you), but themselves, and they do not perceive!

69. Waddaṭ-ṭaaa'ifatum-min Ahlil-Kitaabi law yuḍilloonakum wa maa yuḍilloona illaaa anfusahum wa maa yash'uroon.

وَدَّت طَّآئِفَةٌ مِّنْ أَهْلِ ٱلْكِتَٰبِ
لَوْ يُضِلُّونَكُمْ وَمَا يُضِلُّونَ إِلَّآ
أَنفُسَهُمْ وَمَا يَشْعُرُونَ ﴿٦٩﴾

70. You People of the Book! Why do you reject the Signs of Allah, of which you are (Yourselves) witnesses?

70. Yaaa Ahlal-Kitaabi lima takfuroona bi-Aayaatil-laahi wa antum tashhadoon.

يَٰٓأَهْلَ ٱلْكِتَٰبِ لِمَ تَكْفُرُونَ
بِـَٔايَٰتِ ٱللَّهِ وَأَنتُمْ تَشْهَدُونَ ﴿٧٠﴾

71. You People of the Book! Why do you clothe Truth with falsehood, and conceal the Truth, while you have knowledge?

71. Yaaa Ahlal-Kitaabi lima talbisoonal-ḥaqqa bilbaaṭili wa taktumoonal-ḥaqqa wa antum ta'lamoon. **(Section 7)**

يَٰٓأَهْلَ ٱلْكِتَٰبِ لِمَ تَلْبِسُونَ ٱلْحَقَّ
بِٱلْبَٰطِلِ وَتَكْتُمُونَ ٱلْحَقَّ وَأَنتُمْ
تَعْلَمُونَ ﴿٧١﴾ ع ٧ ١٥

72. A section of the People of the Book say: "Believe in the morning what is revealed to the believers, but reject it at the end of the day; perchance they may (themselves) turn back;

72. Wa qaalaṭ-ṭaaa'ifatum-min Ahlil-Kitaabi aaminoo billaẕeee unzila 'alal-laẕeena aamanoo wajhan-nahaari wakfurooo aakhirahoo la'allahum yarji'oon.

وَقَالَت طَّآئِفَةٌ مِّنْ أَهْلِ ٱلْكِتَٰبِ
ءَامِنُوا۟ بِٱلَّذِىٓ أُنزِلَ عَلَى ٱلَّذِينَ ءَامَنُوا۟
وَجْهَ ٱلنَّهَارِ وَٱكْفُرُوٓا۟ ءَاخِرَهُۥ لَعَلَّهُمْ
يَرْجِعُونَ ﴿٧٢﴾

73. "And believe no one unless he follows your religion." Say: "True guidance is the Guidance of Allah: (Fear you) lest a revelation be sent to someone (else) Like that which was sent unto you? or that those (receiving such revelation) should engage you in argument before your Lord?"

73. Wa laa tu'minooo illaa liman tabi'a deenakum qul innal-hudaa hudal-laahi añy-yu'taaa aḥadum-misla maaa ooteetum aw yuḥaaajjookum 'inda Rabbikum, qul innal-

وَلَا تُؤْمِنُوٓا۟ إِلَّا لِمَن تَبِعَ دِينَكُمْ
قُلْ إِنَّ ٱلْهُدَىٰ هُدَى ٱللَّهِ أَن
يُؤْتَىٰٓ أَحَدٌ مِّثْلَ مَآ أُوتِيتُمْ أَوْ
يُحَآجُّوكُمْ عِندَ رَبِّكُمْ ۗ قُلْ إِنَّ

Ikhfa اخفاء | Ghunna غُنّہ | Ikhfa Meem Saakin اخفاء میم ساکن | Idghaam ادغام | Qalqala قلقلہ | Qalb قلب | Idghaam Meem Saakin ادغام میم ساکن

Say: "All bounties are in the hand of Allah: He grants them to whom He pleases: And Allah cares for all, and He knows all things."

faḍla biyadil-laah; yu'teehi mañy-yashaaa'; wallaahu Waasi'un 'Aleem.

الْفَضْلَ بِيَدِ اللّٰهِ ۚ يُؤْتِيْهِ مَنْ
يَّشَآءُ ؕ وَاللّٰهُ وَاسِعٌ عَلِيْمٌ ﴿٧٣﴾

74. For His Mercy He specially chooses whom He pleases; for Allah is the Lord of bounties unbounded.

74. Yakhtaṣṣu biraḥmatihee mañy-yashaaa'; wallaahu zulfaḍlil-'aẓeem.

يَّخْتَصُّ بِرَحْمَتِهٖ مَنْ يَّشَآءُ ؕ
وَاللّٰهُ ذُو الْفَضْلِ الْعَظِيْمِ ﴿٧٤﴾

75. Among the People of the Book are some who, if entrusted with a hoard of gold, will (readily) pay it back; others, who, if entrusted with a single silver coin, will not repay it unless you constantly stood demanding, because, they say, "there is no call on us (to keep faith) with these ignorant (Pagans)." But they tell a lie against Allah, and (well) they know it.

75. Wa min Ahlil-Kitaabi man in taåmanhu biqinṭaariñy-yu'addiheee ilayka wa minhum man in taåmanhu bideenaaril-laa yu'addiheee ilayka illaa maa dumta 'alayhi qaaa'imaa; zaalika biannahum qaaloo laysa 'alaynaa fil-ummiyyeena sabeeluñw wa yaqooloona 'alal-laahil-kaziba wa hum ya'lamoon.

وَمِنْ اَهْلِ الْكِتٰبِ مَنْ اِنْ تَاْمَنْهُ
بِقِنْطَارٍ يُّؤَدِّهٖٓ اِلَيْكَ ۚ وَمِنْهُمْ مَّنْ
اِنْ تَاْمَنْهُ بِدِيْنَارٍ لَّا يُؤَدِّهٖٓ اِلَيْكَ
اِلَّا مَا دُمْتَ عَلَيْهِ قَآئِمًا ؕ ذٰلِكَ
بِاَنَّهُمْ قَالُوْا لَيْسَ عَلَيْنَا فِي الْاُمِّيّٖنَ
سَبِيْلٌ ۚ وَيَقُوْلُوْنَ عَلَى اللّٰهِ الْكَذِبَ
وَهُمْ يَعْلَمُوْنَ ﴿٧٥﴾

76. Nay, those that keep their plighted faith and act aright, verily Allah loves those who act aright.

76. Balaa man awfaa bi'ahdihee wattaqaa fainnal-laaha yuḥibbul-muttaqeen.

بَلٰى مَنْ اَوْفٰى بِعَهْدِهٖ وَاتَّقٰى فَاِنَّ
اللّٰهَ يُحِبُّ الْمُتَّقِيْنَ ﴿٧٦﴾

77. As for those who sell the faith they owe to Allah and their own plighted word for a small price, they shall have no portion in the Hereafter: nor will Allah speak to them or look at them on the Day of Judgment, nor will He cleans them (of sin): They shall have a grievous Chastisement.

77. Innal-lazeena yashtaroona bi-'Ahdil-laahi wa aymaanihim samanan qaleelan ulaaa'ika laa khalaaqa lahum fil-Aakhirati wa laa yukallimuhumul-laahu wa laa yanẓuru ilayhim Yawmal-Qiyaamati wa laa yuẓakkeehim wa lahum 'azaabun 'aleem.

اِنَّ الَّذِيْنَ يَشْتَرُوْنَ بِعَهْدِ اللّٰهِ
وَاَيْمَانِهِمْ ثَمَنًا قَلِيْلًا اُولٰٓئِكَ
لَا خَلَاقَ لَهُمْ فِي الْاٰخِرَةِ وَلَا
يُكَلِّمُهُمُ اللّٰهُ وَلَا يَنْظُرُ اِلَيْهِمْ
يَوْمَ الْقِيٰمَةِ وَلَا يُزَكِّيْهِمْ ۪ وَلَهُمْ
عَذَابٌ اَلِيْمٌ ﴿٧٧﴾

78. There is among them a section who distort the Book with their tongues: (As they read) you would think it is a part of the Book, but it is no part of the Book; and they say, "That is from Allah," but it is not from Allah: It is they who tell a lie against Allah, and (well) they know it!

78. Wa inna minhum lafareeqañy-yalwoona alsinatahum bil-Kitaabi litaḥsaboohu minal-Kitaab, wa maa huwa minal-Kitaabi wa yaqooloona huwa min 'indillaahi wa maa huwa min 'indillaahi wa yaqooloona 'alal-laahil-kaziba wa hum ya'lamoon.

وَاِنَّ مِنْهُمْ لَفَرِيْقًا يَّلْوٗنَ اَلْسِنَتَهُمْ
بِالْكِتٰبِ لِتَحْسَبُوْهُ مِنَ الْكِتٰبِ وَمَا
هُوَ مِنَ الْكِتٰبِ ۚ وَيَقُوْلُوْنَ هُوَ مِنْ
عِنْدِ اللّٰهِ وَمَا هُوَ مِنْ عِنْدِ اللّٰهِ ۚ
وَيَقُوْلُوْنَ عَلَى اللّٰهِ الْكَذِبَ وَهُمْ
يَعْلَمُوْنَ ﴿٧٨﴾

79. It is not (possible) that a man, to whom is given

79. Maa kaana libasharin añy-yu'tiyahul-laahul-

مَا كَانَ لِبَشَرٍ اَنْ يُّؤْتِيَهُ اللّٰهُ

Ikhfa اخفاء | Ghunna غُنّہ | Ikhfa Meem Saakin اخفاء میم ساکن | Idghaam ادغام | Qalqala قلقلہ | Qalb قلب | Idghaam Meem Saakin ادغام میم ساکن

the Book, and Wisdom, and the prophetic office, should say to people: "Be you my worshippers rather than Allah's": on the contrary (He would say) "Be you worshippers of Him Who is truly the Cherisher of all: for you had been taught by the Book, and as you read it still."

80. Nor would he instruct you to take angels and prophets for Lords and patrons. What! would he bid you to unbelief after you have bowed your will (to Allah in Islam)?

81. Behold! Allah took the Covenant of the Prophets, saying: "I give you a Book and Wisdom; then comes to you an Apostle, confirming what is with you; do you believe in him and render him help." Allah said: "Do you agree, and take this my Covenant as binding on you?" They said: "We agree." He said: "Then bear witness, and I am with you among the witnesses."

82. If any turn back after this, they are perverted transgressors.

83. Do they seek for other than the Religion of Allah?- While all creatures in the heavens and on the earth have, willingly or unwillingly, bowed to His Will (accepted Islam), and to Him shall they all be brought back.

84. Say: "We believe in Allah, and in what has been revealed to us and what was revealed to Abraham, Isma'il, Isaac, Jacob, and the Tribes, and in (the Books) given to Moses, Jesus, and the Prophets, from their Lord: we make no distinction between one and another among them, and to Allah do we bow our will (in Islam)."

Kitaaba walḥukma wan-Nubuwwata summa yaqoola linnaasi koonoo 'ibaadal-lee min doonil-laahi wa laakin koonoo rabbaaniy-yeena bimaa kuntum tu'allimoonal-Kitaaba wa bimaa kuntum tadrusoon.

80. Wa laa yaâmurakum an tattakhizul-malaaa'ikata wan-Nabiyyeena arbaabaa; a-yaâmurukum bilkufri ba'da iz antum muslimoon. **(Section 8)**

81. Wa iz akhazal-laahu meesaaqan-Nabiyyeena lamaaa aataytukum min Kitaabiñw-wa Ḥikmatin summa jaaa'akum Rasoolum-muṣaddiqul-limaa ma'akum latu'minunna bihee wa latanṣurunnah; qaala 'a-aqrartum wa akhaztum alaa zaalikum iṣree qaalooo aqrarnaa; qaala fashhadoo wa ana ma'akum minaṣ h-shaahideen.

82. Faman tawallaa ba'da zaalika fa ulaaa'ika humul-faasiqoon.

83. Afaghayra deenil-laahi yabghoona wa lahooo aslama man fis-samaawaati wal-arḍi ṭaw'añw-wa karhañw-wa ilayhi yurja'oon.

84. Qul aamannaa billaahi wa maaa unzila 'alaynaa wa maaa unzila 'alaaa Ibraaheema wa Ismaa'eela wa Iṣhaaqa wa Ya'qooba wal-Asbaaṭi wa maaa ootiya Moosaa wa 'Eesaa wan-Nabiyyoona mir-Rabbihim laa nufarriqu bayna aḥadim-minhum wa naḥnu lahoo muslimoon.

الْكِتٰبَ وَالْحُكْمَ وَالنُّبُوَّةَ ثُمَّ يَقُولَ
لِلنَّاسِ كُونُوا عِبَادًا لِّي مِن دُونِ
اللّٰهِ وَلٰكِن كُونُوا رَبّٰنِيّٖنَ بِمَا
كُنتُمْ تُعَلِّمُونَ الْكِتٰبَ وَبِمَا كُنتُمْ
تَدْرُسُونَ ﴿٧٩﴾
وَلَا يَأْمُرَكُمْ أَن تَتَّخِذُوا الْمَلٰٓئِكَةَ
وَالنَّبِيّٖنَ أَرْبَابًا ۗ أَيَأْمُرُكُم بِالْكُفْرِ
بَعْدَ إِذْ أَنتُم مُّسْلِمُونَ ﴿٨٠﴾
وَإِذْ أَخَذَ اللّٰهُ مِيثَاقَ النَّبِيّٖنَ لَمَآ
ءَاتَيْتُكُم مِّن كِتٰبٍ وَحِكْمَةٍ ثُمَّ
جَآءَكُمْ رَسُولٌ مُّصَدِّقٌ لِّمَا مَعَكُمْ
لَتُؤْمِنُنَّ بِهِۦ وَلَتَنصُرُنَّهُۥ ۚ قَالَ ءَأَقْرَرْتُمْ
وَأَخَذْتُمْ عَلٰى ذٰلِكُمْ إِصْرِي ۖ قَالُوٓا
أَقْرَرْنَا ۚ قَالَ فَاشْهَدُوا وَأَنَا
مَعَكُم مِّنَ الشّٰهِدِينَ ﴿٨١﴾
فَمَن تَوَلّٰى بَعْدَ ذٰلِكَ فَأُولٰٓئِكَ
هُمُ الْفٰسِقُونَ ﴿٨٢﴾
أَفَغَيْرَ دِينِ اللّٰهِ يَبْغُونَ وَلَهُۥٓ
أَسْلَمَ مَن فِي السَّمٰوٰتِ وَالْأَرْضِ
طَوْعًا وَكَرْهًا وَإِلَيْهِ يُرْجَعُونَ ﴿٨٣﴾
قُلْ ءَامَنَّا بِاللّٰهِ وَمَآ أُنزِلَ عَلَيْنَا
وَمَآ أُنزِلَ عَلٰىٓ إِبْرٰهِيمَ وَإِسْمٰعِيلَ
وَإِسْحٰقَ وَيَعْقُوبَ وَالْأَسْبَاطِ وَمَآ
أُوتِيَ مُوسٰى وَعِيسٰى وَالنَّبِيُّونَ
مِن رَّبِّهِمْ لَا نُفَرِّقُ بَيْنَ أَحَدٍ
مِّنْهُمْ وَنَحْنُ لَهُۥ مُسْلِمُونَ ﴿٨٤﴾

Ikhfa اخفاء | Ghunna غنّہ | Ikhfa Meem Saakin اخفاء میم ساکن | Idghaam ادغام | Qalqala قلقلہ | Qalb قلب | Idghaam Meem Saakin ادغام میم ساکن

85. If anyone desires a religion other than Islam (submission to Allah), never will it be accepted of him; and in the Hereafter he will be in the ranks of those who have lost (All spiritual good).

86. How shall Allah guide those who reject Faith after they accepted it and bore witness that the Apostle was true and that Clear Signs had come unto them? But Allah guides not a people unjust.

87. Of such the reward is that on them (rests) the curse of Allah, of His angels, and of all mankind;-

88. In that will they dwell; nor will their Chastisement be lightened, nor respite be (their lot);-

89. Except for those that repent (even) after that, and make amends; for verily Allah is Oft-Forgiving, Most Merciful.

90. But those who reject Faith after they accepted it, and then go on adding to their defiance of Faith, - never will their repentance be accepted; for they are those who have (of set purpose) gone astray.

91. As to those who reject Faith, and die rejecting, - never would be accepted from any such as much gold as the earth contains, though they should offer it for ransom. For such is (in store) a Chastisement grievous, and they will find no helpers.

92. By no means shall you attain righteousness unless you give (freely) of that which you love; and whatever you give, of a truth Allah knows it well.

93. All food was lawful to the Children of Israel, except what Israel made unlawful for itself,

85. Wa mañy-yabtaghi ghayral-Islaami deenan falañy-yuqbala minhu wa huwa fil-Aakhirati minal-khaasireen.

86. Kayfa yahdil-laahu qawman kafaroo ba'da eemaanihim wa shahidooo annar-Rasoola ḥaqquñw-wa jaaa'ahumul-bayyinaat; wallaahu laa yahdil-qawmaẓ-ẓaalimeen.

87. Ulaaa'ika jazaaa'uhum anna 'alayhim la'natal-laahi walmalaaa'ikati wannaasi ajma'een.

88. Khaalideena feehaa laa yukhaffafu 'anhumul-'azaabu wa laa hum yunẓaroon.

89. Illal-lazeena taaboo mim ba'di zaalika wa aṣlaḥoo fa-innal-laaha Ghafoorur-Raḥeem.

90. Innal-lazeena kafaroo ba'da eemaanihim summaz-daadoo kufral-lan tuqbala tawbatuhum wa ulaaa'ika humuḍ-ḍaaalloon.

91. Innal-lazeena kafaroo wa maatoo wa hum kuffaarun falañy-yuqbala min aḥadihim mil'ul-arḍi zahabañw-wa lawiftadaa bih; ulaaa'ika lahum 'azaabun aleemuñw-wa maa lahum min naaṣireen. **(Section 9)**

92. Lan tanaalul-birra ḥattaa tunfiqoo mimmaa tuḥibboon; wa maa tunfiqoo min shay'in fa-innal-laaha bihee 'Aleem.

93. Kulluṭ-ṭa'aami kaana ḥillal-li-Baneee Israaa'eela illaa maa ḥarrama Israaa'eelu 'alaa nafsihee min

وَمَن يَبْتَغِ غَيْرَ الْإِسْلَامِ دِينًا
فَلَن يُقْبَلَ مِنْهُ وَهُوَ فِي الْآخِرَةِ
مِنَ الْخَاسِرِينَ ﴿٨٥﴾
كَيْفَ يَهْدِي اللَّهُ قَوْمًا كَفَرُوا بَعْدَ
إِيمَانِهِمْ وَشَهِدُوا أَنَّ الرَّسُولَ
حَقٌّ وَجَاءَهُمُ الْبَيِّنَاتُ ۚ وَاللَّهُ لَا
يَهْدِي الْقَوْمَ الظَّالِمِينَ ﴿٨٦﴾
أُولَٰئِكَ جَزَاؤُهُمْ أَنَّ عَلَيْهِمْ لَعْنَةَ
اللَّهِ وَالْمَلَائِكَةِ وَالنَّاسِ أَجْمَعِينَ ﴿٨٧﴾
خَالِدِينَ فِيهَا لَا يُخَفَّفُ عَنْهُمُ
الْعَذَابُ وَلَا هُمْ يُنظَرُونَ ﴿٨٨﴾
إِلَّا الَّذِينَ تَابُوا مِن بَعْدِ ذَٰلِكَ
وَأَصْلَحُوا فَإِنَّ اللَّهَ غَفُورٌ رَّحِيمٌ ﴿٨٩﴾
إِنَّ الَّذِينَ كَفَرُوا بَعْدَ إِيمَانِهِمْ ثُمَّ
ازْدَادُوا كُفْرًا لَّن تُقْبَلَ تَوْبَتُهُمْ
وَأُولَٰئِكَ هُمُ الضَّالُّونَ ﴿٩٠﴾
إِنَّ الَّذِينَ كَفَرُوا وَمَاتُوا وَهُمْ
كُفَّارٌ فَلَن يُقْبَلَ مِنْ أَحَدِهِم
مِّلْءُ الْأَرْضِ ذَهَبًا وَلَوِ افْتَدَىٰ
بِهِ ۗ أُولَٰئِكَ لَهُمْ عَذَابٌ أَلِيمٌ
وَمَا لَهُم مِّن نَّاصِرِينَ ﴿٩١﴾
لَن تَنَالُوا الْبِرَّ حَتَّىٰ تُنفِقُوا
مِمَّا تُحِبُّونَ ۚ وَمَا تُنفِقُوا مِن
شَيْءٍ فَإِنَّ اللَّهَ بِهِ عَلِيمٌ ﴿٩٢﴾
كُلُّ الطَّعَامِ كَانَ حِلًّا لِّبَنِي إِسْرَائِيلَ
إِلَّا مَا حَرَّمَ إِسْرَائِيلُ عَلَىٰ نَفْسِهِ مِن

Ikhfa اخفاء | Ghunna غنّہ | Ikhfa Meem Saakin اخفاء میم ساکن | Idghaam ادغام | Qalqala قلقلہ | Qalb قلب | Idghaam Meem Saakin ادغام میم ساکن

before the Law (of Moses) was revealed. Say: "Bring you the Law and study it, if you be men of truth."

94. If any, after this, invent a lie and attribute it to Allah, they are indeed unjust wrong-doers.

95. Say: "Allah speaks the Truth: follow the religion of Abraham, the sane in faith; he was not of the Pagans."

96. The first House (of worship) appointed for men was that at Bakka (Makkah); full of blessing and of guidance for all kinds of beings:

97. In it are Signs manifest; (for example), the Station of Abraham; whoever enters it attains security; pilgrimage thereto is a duty men owe to Allah,- those who can afford the journey; but if any deny faith, Allah stands not in need of any of His creatures.

98. Say: "O People of the Book! Why do you reject the Signs of Allah, when Allah is Himself witness to all you do?"

99. Say: "O you People of the Book! Why do you obstruct those who believe, from the path of Allah, seeking to make it crooked, while you were yourselves witnesses (to Allah's Covenant)? But Allah is not unmindful of all that you do."

100. O you who believe! If you listen to a faction among the People of the Book, they would (indeed) render you apostates after you have believed!

101. And how would you deny Faith while unto you are rehearsed the Signs of Allah, and among you lives the Apostle? Whoever holds firmly to Allah will be shown

qabli an tunazzalat-Tawraah; qul faåtoo bit-Tawraati fatloo-haaa in kuntum ṣaadiqeen.

94. Famanif-taraa 'alal-laahilkaẕiba mim ba'di ẕaalika fa-ulaaa'ika humuẓ-ẓaalimoon.

95. Qul ṣadaqal-laah; fattabi'oo Millata Ibraaheema Ḥaneefañw wa maa kaana minal-mush-rikeen.

96. Inna awwala Baytiñw-wuḍi'a linnaasi lallaẕee bi-Bakkata mubaarakañw-wa hudal-lil-'aalameen.

97. Feehi Aayaatum-bayyinaa-tum-Maqaamu Ibraaheema wa man dakhalahoo kaana aaminaa; wa lillaahi 'alan-naasi Hijjul-Bayti manis-taṭaa'a ilayhi sabeelaa; wa man kafara fa-innal-laaha ghaniyyun 'anil-'aalameen.

98. Qul yaaa Ahlal-Kitaabi lima takfuroona bi-Aayaatillaahi wallaahu shaheedun 'alaa maa ta'maloon.

99. Qul yaaa Ahlal-Kitaabi lima taṣuddoona 'an sabeelil-laahi man aamana tabghoonahaa 'iwajañw-wa antum shuhadaaa'; wa mallaahu bighaafilin 'ammaa ta'maloon.

100. Yaaa-ayyuhal-laẕeena aamanooo in tuṭee'oo faree-qam-minal-laẕeena ootul-Kitaaba yaruddookum ba'da eemaanikum kaafireen.

101. Wa kayfa takfuroona wa antum tutlaa 'alaykum Aayaatul-laahi wa feekum Rasooluh; wa mañy-ya'taṣim billaahi faqad hudiya

قَبْلِ أَنْ تُنَزَّلَ التَّوْرٰىةُ قُلْ فَأْتُوا
بِالتَّوْرٰىةِ فَاتْلُوهَا إِنْ كُنْتُمْ صٰدِقِينَ ﴿٩٣﴾
فَمَنِ افْتَرٰى عَلَى اللّٰهِ الْكَذِبَ مِنْ
بَعْدِ ذٰلِكَ فَأُولٰٓئِكَ هُمُ الظّٰلِمُونَ ﴿٩٤﴾
قُلْ صَدَقَ اللّٰهُ فَاتَّبِعُوا مِلَّةَ
إِبْرٰهِيمَ حَنِيفًا وَمَا كَانَ مِنَ
الْمُشْرِكِينَ ﴿٩٥﴾
إِنَّ أَوَّلَ بَيْتٍ وُضِعَ لِلنَّاسِ لَلَّذِي
بِبَكَّةَ مُبٰرَكًا وَهُدًى لِلْعٰلَمِينَ ﴿٩٦﴾
فِيهِ ءَايٰتٌ بَيِّنٰتٌ مَقَامُ إِبْرٰهِيمَ
وَمَنْ دَخَلَهُ كَانَ ءَامِنًا وَلِلّٰهِ عَلَى
النَّاسِ حِجُّ الْبَيْتِ مَنِ اسْتَطَاعَ
إِلَيْهِ سَبِيلًا وَمَنْ كَفَرَ فَإِنَّ اللّٰهَ
غَنِيٌّ عَنِ الْعٰلَمِينَ ﴿٩٧﴾
قُلْ يٰٓأَهْلَ الْكِتٰبِ لِمَ تَكْفُرُونَ بِـَٔايٰتِ
اللّٰهِ وَاللّٰهُ شَهِيدٌ عَلٰى مَا تَعْمَلُونَ ﴿٩٨﴾
قُلْ يٰٓأَهْلَ الْكِتٰبِ لِمَ تَصُدُّونَ
عَنْ سَبِيلِ اللّٰهِ مَنْ ءَامَنَ تَبْغُونَهَا
عِوَجًا وَأَنْتُمْ شُهَدَآءُ وَمَا اللّٰهُ
بِغٰفِلٍ عَمَّا تَعْمَلُونَ ﴿٩٩﴾
يٰٓأَيُّهَا الَّذِينَ ءَامَنُوٓا إِنْ تُطِيعُوا فَرِيقًا
مِنَ الَّذِينَ أُوتُوا الْكِتٰبَ يَرُدُّوكُمْ بَعْدَ
إِيمٰنِكُمْ كٰفِرِينَ ﴿١٠٠﴾
وَكَيْفَ تَكْفُرُونَ وَأَنْتُمْ تُتْلٰى
عَلَيْكُمْ ءَايٰتُ اللّٰهِ وَفِيكُمْ رَسُولُهُ
وَمَنْ يَعْتَصِمْ بِاللّٰهِ فَقَدْ هُدِىَ

وقف جبريل عليه السلام

Ikhfa اخفاء · Ghunna غنّہ · Ikhfa Meem Saakin اخفاء میم ساکن · Idghaam ادغام · Qalqala قلقلہ · Qalb قلب · Idghaam Meem Saakin ادغام میم ساکن

English	Transliteration	Arabic
a Way that is straight.	ilaa Ṣiraaṭim-Mustaqeem. **(Section 10)**	إِلَىٰ صِرَاطٍ مُّسْتَقِيمٍ ﴿١٠١﴾ ع
102. O you who believe! Fear Allah as He should be feared, and die not except in a state of Islam.	102. Yaaa ayyuhal-lazeena aamanut-taqul-laaha ḥaqqa tuqaatihee wa laa tamootunna illaa wa antum muslimoon.	يَٰٓأَيُّهَا ٱلَّذِينَ ءَامَنُوا ٱتَّقُوا ٱللَّهَ حَقَّ تُقَاتِهِۦ وَلَا تَمُوتُنَّ إِلَّا وَأَنتُم مُّسْلِمُونَ ﴿١٠٢﴾
103. And hold fast, all together, by the rope which Allah (stretches out for you), and be not divided among yourselves; and remember with gratitude Allah's favour on you; for you were enemies and He joined your hearts in love, so that by His Grace, you became brethren; and you were on the brink of the Pit of Fire, and He saved you from it. Thus Allah makes His Signs clear to you: that you may be guided.	103. Wa‘taṣimoo bi-Ḥablil-laahi jamee‘añw-wa laa tafarraqoo; wazkuroo ni‘matal-laahi ‘alaykum iz kuntum a‘daaa’an fa-allafa bayna quloobikum fa-aṣbaḥtum bini‘matiheee ikhwaanañw wa kuntum ‘alaa shafaa ḥufratim-minan-Naari fa-anqazakum minhaa; kazaalika yubayyinul-laahu lakum Aayaatihee la‘allakum tahtadoon.	وَٱعْتَصِمُوا بِحَبْلِ ٱللَّهِ جَمِيعًا وَلَا تَفَرَّقُوا ۚ وَٱذْكُرُوا نِعْمَتَ ٱللَّهِ عَلَيْكُمْ إِذْ كُنتُمْ أَعْدَآءً فَأَلَّفَ بَيْنَ قُلُوبِكُمْ فَأَصْبَحْتُم بِنِعْمَتِهِۦٓ إِخْوَٰنًا ج وَكُنتُمْ عَلَىٰ شَفَا حُفْرَةٍ مِّنَ ٱلنَّارِ فَأَنقَذَكُم مِّنْهَا ۗ كَذَٰلِكَ يُبَيِّنُ ٱللَّهُ لَكُمْ ءَايَٰتِهِۦ لَعَلَّكُمْ تَهْتَدُونَ ﴿١٠٣﴾
104. Let there arise out of you a band of people inviting to all that is good, enjoining what is right, and forbidding what is wrong: they are the ones to attain felicity.	104. Waltakum-minkum ummatuñy-yad‘oona ilal-khayri wa yaåmuroona bilma‘roofi wa yanhawna ‘anil-munkar; wa ulaaa’ika humul-mufliḥoon.	وَلْتَكُن مِّنكُمْ أُمَّةٌ يَدْعُونَ إِلَى ٱلْخَيْرِ وَيَأْمُرُونَ بِٱلْمَعْرُوفِ وَيَنْهَوْنَ عَنِ ٱلْمُنكَرِ ۚ وَأُولَٰٓئِكَ هُمُ ٱلْمُفْلِحُونَ ﴿١٠٤﴾
105. Be not like those who are divided amongst themselves and fall into disputations after receiving Clear Signs: for them is a dreadful Chastisement,-	105. Wa laa takoonoo kalla-zeena tafarraqoo wakhtalafoo mim ba‘di maa jaaa’ahumul-bayyinaat; wa ulaaa’ika lahum ‘azaabun ‘aẓeem.	وَلَا تَكُونُوا كَٱلَّذِينَ تَفَرَّقُوا وَٱخْتَلَفُوا مِنۢ بَعْدِ مَا جَآءَهُمُ ٱلْبَيِّنَٰتُ ۚ وَأُولَٰٓئِكَ لَهُمْ عَذَابٌ عَظِيمٌ ﴿١٠٥﴾
106. On the Day when some faces will be (lit up with) white, and some faces will be (in the gloom of) black: to those whose faces will be black, (will be said): "Did you reject Faith after accepting it? Taste then the Chastisement for rejecting Faith."	106. Yawma tabyaḍḍu wujoo-huñw-wa taswaddu wujooh; fa-ammal-lazeenas-waddat wujoohuhum akafartum ba‘da eemaanikum fazooqul-‘azaaba bimaa kuntum takfuroon.	يَوْمَ تَبْيَضُّ وُجُوهٌ وَتَسْوَدُّ وُجُوهٌ ج فَأَمَّا ٱلَّذِينَ ٱسْوَدَّتْ وُجُوهُهُمْ أَكَفَرْتُم بَعْدَ إِيمَٰنِكُمْ فَذُوقُوا ٱلْعَذَابَ بِمَا كُنتُمْ تَكْفُرُونَ ﴿١٠٦﴾
107. But those whose faces will be (lit with) white,- they will be in (the light of) Allah's mercy: therein to dwell (for ever).	107. Wa ammal-lazeenabyaḍ-ḍat wujoohuhum fafee raḥmatil-laahi hum feehaa khaalidoon.	وَأَمَّا ٱلَّذِينَ ٱبْيَضَّتْ وُجُوهُهُمْ فَفِى رَحْمَةِ ٱللَّهِ ۖ هُمْ فِيهَا خَٰلِدُونَ ﴿١٠٧﴾
108. These are the Signs of Allah: We rehearse them to you in Truth: And Allah means no injustice to any of His creatures.	108. Tilka Aayaatul-laahi natloohaa ‘alayka bilḥaqq; wa mal-laahu yureedu ẓulmallil-‘aalameen.	تِلْكَ ءَايَٰتُ ٱللَّهِ نَتْلُوهَا عَلَيْكَ بِٱلْحَقِّ ۗ وَمَا ٱللَّهُ يُرِيدُ ظُلْمًا لِّلْعَٰلَمِينَ ﴿١٠٨﴾
109. To Allah belongs all that is in the heavens and on earth: to Him do all questions go back (for decision).	109. Wa lillaahi maa fissamaa-waati wa maa fil-arḍ; wa ilal-laahi turja‘ul-umoor. **(Section 11)**	وَلِلَّهِ مَا فِى ٱلسَّمَٰوَٰتِ وَمَا فِى ٱلْأَرْضِ ۚ وَإِلَى ٱللَّهِ تُرْجَعُ ٱلْأُمُورُ ﴿١٠٩﴾ ع

Ikhfa اخفاء · Ghunna غُنّہ · Ikhfa Meem Saakin اخفاء میم ساکن · Idghaam ادغام · Qalqala قلقلہ · Qalb قلب · Idghaam Meem Saakin ادغام میم ساکن

110. You are the best of peoples, evolved for mankind, enjoining what is right, forbidding what is wrong, and believing in Allah. If only the People of the Book had faith, it were best for them: among them are some who have faith, but most of them are perverted transgressors.

110. Kuntum khayra ummatin ukhrijat linnaasi taåmuroona bilma'roofi wa tanhawna 'anil-munkari wa tu'minoona billaah; wa law aamana Ahlul-Kitaabi lakaana khayral-lahum; minhumul-mu'minoona wa akṣaruhumul-faasiqoon.

كُنْتُمْ خَيْرَ أُمَّةٍ أُخْرِجَتْ لِلنَّاسِ
تَأْمُرُونَ بِالْمَعْرُوفِ وَتَنْهَوْنَ عَنِ
الْمُنْكَرِ وَتُؤْمِنُونَ بِاللّٰهِ ۗ وَلَوْ اٰمَنَ
أَهْلُ الْكِتٰبِ لَكَانَ خَيْرًا لَّهُمْ ۚ مِنْهُمُ
الْمُؤْمِنُونَ وَأَكْثَرُهُمُ الْفٰسِقُونَ ﴿١١٠﴾

111. They will do you no harm, barring a trifling annoyance; if they come out to fight you, they will show you their backs, and no help shall they get.

111. Lañy-yaḍurrookum 'illaaa azañw wa iñy-yuqaatilookum yuwallookumul-adbaara summa laa yunṣaroon.

لَنْ يَّضُرُّوْكُمْ إِلَّآ أَذًى ۖ وَإِنْ
يُّقٰتِلُوْكُمْ يُوَلُّوْكُمُ الْأَدْبَارَ
ثُمَّ لَا يُنْصَرُوْنَ ﴿١١١﴾

112. Shame is pitched over them (like a tent) wherever they are found, except when under a covenant (of protection) from Allah and from men; they draw on themselves wrath from Allah, and pitched over them is (the tent of) destitution. This because they rejected the Signs of Allah, and slew the Prophets in defiance of right; this because they rebelled and transgressed beyond bounds.

112. Ḍuribat 'alayhimuz̲z̲illatu ayna maa s̲uqifooo illaa biḥablim-minal-laahi wa ḥablim-minan-naasi wa baaa'oo bighaḍabim-minallaahi wa ḍuribat 'alayhimul-maskanah; z̲aalika bi-annahum kaanoo yakfuroona bi-Aayaatil-laahi wa yaqtuloonal-Ambiyaaa'a bighayri ḥaqq; z̲aalika bimaa 'aṣaw wa kaanoo ya'tadoon.

ضُرِبَتْ عَلَيْهِمُ الذِّلَّةُ أَيْنَ مَا
ثُقِفُوْٓا إِلَّا بِحَبْلٍ مِّنَ اللّٰهِ وَحَبْلٍ
مِّنَ النَّاسِ وَبَآءُوْ بِغَضَبٍ مِّنَ اللّٰهِ
وَضُرِبَتْ عَلَيْهِمُ الْمَسْكَنَةُ ۚ ذٰلِكَ
بِأَنَّهُمْ كَانُوْا يَكْفُرُوْنَ بِاٰيٰتِ اللّٰهِ
وَيَقْتُلُوْنَ الْأَنْبِيَآءَ بِغَيْرِ حَقٍّ ۚ ذٰلِكَ
بِمَا عَصَوْا وَّكَانُوْا يَعْتَدُوْنَ ﴿١١٢﴾

113. Not all of them are alike: of the People of the Book are a portion that stand (for the right): they rehearse the Signs of Allah all night long, and they prostrate themselves in adoration.

113. Laysoo sawaaa'a; min Ahlil-Kitaabi ummatun qaaa'imatuñy-yatloona Aayaatil-laahi aanaaa'al-layli wa hum yasjudoon.

لَيْسُوْا سَوَآءً ۗ مِنْ أَهْلِ الْكِتٰبِ أُمَّةٌ
قَآئِمَةٌ يَّتْلُوْنَ اٰيٰتِ اللّٰهِ اٰنَآءَ الَّيْلِ
وَهُمْ يَسْجُدُوْنَ ﴿١١٣﴾

114. They believe in Allah and the Last Day; they enjoin what is right, and forbid what is wrong; and they hasten (in emulation) in (all) good works: they are in the ranks of the righteous.

114. Yu'minoona billaahi wal-Yawmil-Aakhiri wa yaåmuroona bilma'roofi wa yanhawna 'anil-munkari wa yusaari'oona fil-khayraati wa ulaaa'ika minaṣ-ṣaaliheen.

يُؤْمِنُوْنَ بِاللّٰهِ وَالْيَوْمِ الْاٰخِرِ
وَيَأْمُرُوْنَ بِالْمَعْرُوْفِ وَيَنْهَوْنَ
عَنِ الْمُنْكَرِ وَيُسَارِعُوْنَ فِي الْخَيْرٰتِ
وَأُولٰٓئِكَ مِنَ الصّٰلِحِيْنَ ﴿١١٤﴾

115. Of the good that they do, nothing will be rejected of them; for Allah knows well those that do right.

115. Wa maa yaf'aloo min khayrin falañy-yukfarooh; wallaahu 'aleemum bilmuttaqeen.

وَمَا يَفْعَلُوْا مِنْ خَيْرٍ فَلَنْ يُّكْفَرُوْهُ ۗ
وَاللّٰهُ عَلِيْمٌ بِالْمُتَّقِيْنَ ﴿١١٥﴾

116. Those who reject Faith,- neither their possessions nor their (numerous) progeny will avail them anything against Allah:

116. Innal-laz̲eena kafaroo lan tughniya 'anhum amwaaluhum wa laaa awlaaduhum minal-laahi

إِنَّ الَّذِيْنَ كَفَرُوْا لَنْ تُغْنِيَ عَنْهُمْ
أَمْوَالُهُمْ وَلَآ أَوْلَادُهُمْ مِّنَ اللّٰهِ

Ikhfa اخفاء | Ghunna غُنّہ | Ikhfa Meem Saakin اخفاء میم ساکن | Idghaam ادغام | Qalqala قلقلہ | Qalb قلب | Idghaam Meem Saakin ادغام میم ساکن

they will be companions of the Fire,- dwelling therein (for ever).

117. What they spend in the life of this (material) world may be likened to a wind which brings a nipping frost: it strikes and destroys the harvest of men who have wronged their own souls:it is not Allah that has wronged them, but they wrong themselves.

118. O you who believe! take not into your intimacy those outside your ranks: they will not fail to corrupt you. They only desire your ruin: rank hatred has already appeared from their mouths: what their hearts conceal is far worse. We have made plain to you the Signs, if you have wisdom.

119. Ah! you are those who love them, but they love you not,- though you believe in the whole of the Book. When they meet you, they say, "We believe": but when they are alone, they bite off the very tips of their fingers at you in their rage. Say: "Perish in you rage; Allah knows well all the secrets of the heart."

120. If anything that is good befalls you, it grieves them; but if some misfortune overtakes you, they rejoice at it. But if you are constant and do right, not the least harm will their cunning do to you; for Allah compasses round about all that they do.

121. Remember that morning you left your household (early) to post the faithful at their stations for battle: and Allah hears and knows all things:

shay'añw wa ulaaa'ika Aşhaabun-Naar; hum feehaa khaalidoon.

117. Masalu maa yunfiqoona fee haazihil-ḥayaatid-dunyaa kamasali reeḥin feehaa şirrun aşaabat ḥarsa qawmin zalamooo anfusahum fa-ahlakath; wa maa zalamahumullaahu wa laakin anfusahum yazlimoon.

118. Yaaa ayyuhal-lazeena aamanoo laa tattakhizoo bitaanatam-min doonikum laa yaảloonakum khabaalañw waddoo maa 'anittum qad badatil-baghḍaaa'u min afwaahihim; wa maa tukhfee şudooruhum akbar; qad bayyannaa lakumul-Aayaati in kuntum ta'qiloon.

119. Haaa-antum ulaaa'i tuḥibboonahum wa laa yuḥibboonakum wa tu'minoona bil-Kitaabi kullihee wa izaa laqookum qaalooo aamannaa wa izaa khalaw 'aḍḍoo 'alaykumul-anaamila minal-ghayẓ,; qul mootoo bighayẓikum; innal-laaha 'aleemum bizaatiş-şudoor.

120. In tamsaskum ḥasanatun tasu'hum wa in tuşibkum sayyi'atuñy-yafraḥoo bihaa wa in taşbiroo wa tattaqoo laa yaḍurrukum kayduhum shay'aa; innal-laaha bimaa ya'maloona muḥeet. **(Section 12)**

121. Wa iz ghadawta min ahlika tubawwi'ul-mu'mineena maqaa'ida lilqitaal; wallaahu Samee'un 'Aleem.

شيئا ط واولئك اصحب النار ج هم
فيها خلدون ﴿١١٦﴾
مثل ما ينفقون في هذه الحيوة
الدنيا كمثل ريح فيها صر اصابت
حرث قوم ظلموا انفسهم فاهلكته ط
وما ظلمهم الله ولكن انفسهم
يظلمون ﴿١١٧﴾
يايها الذين امنوا لا تتخذوا بطانة
من دونكم لا يالونكم خبالا ط ودوا
ما عنتم ج قد بدت البغضاء من
افواههم صلے وما تخفي صدورهم
اكبر ط قد بينا لكم الايت ان
كنتم تعقلون ﴿١١٨﴾
هانتم اولاء تحبونهم ولا
يحبونكم وتؤمنون بالكتب
كله ج واذا لقوكم قالوا امنا صلے ج واذا
خلوا عضوا عليكم الانامل من
الغيظ ط قل موتوا بغيظكم ط ان الله
عليم بذات الصدور ﴿١١٩﴾
ان تمسسكم حسنة تسؤهم ز وان
تصبكم سيئة يفرحوا بها ط وان
تصبروا وتتقوا لا يضركم كيدهم
شيئا ط ان الله بما يعملون محيط ﴿١٢٠﴾
واذ غدوت من اهلك تبوئ
المؤمنين مقاعد للقتال ط
والله سميع عليم ﴿١٢١﴾

Ikhfa اخفاء · Ghunna غنّہ · Ikhfa Meem Saakin اخفاء میم ساکن · Idghaam ادغام · Qalqala قلقلہ · Qalb قلب · Idghaam Meem Saakin ادغام میم ساکن

122. Remember two of your parties meditated cowardice; but Allah was their Protector, and in Allah the faithful should (ever) put their trust.

122. Iz hammaṭ-ṭaaa'ifataani minkum an tafshalaa wallaahu waliyyuhumaa; wa ʻalal-laahi falyatawakkalil-mu'minoon.

إِذْ هَمَّت طَّآئِفَتَانِ مِنكُمْ أَن تَفْشَلَا
وَاللَّهُ وَلِيُّهُمَا ۗ وَعَلَى اللَّهِ فَلْيَتَوَكَّلِ
الْمُؤْمِنُونَ ﴿١٢٢﴾

123. Allah had helped you at Badr, when you were a insignificant little force; then fear Allah; thus you may show your gratitude.

123. Wa laqad naṣarakumul-laahu bi-Badriñw-wa antum azillatun fattaqul-laaha laʻallakum tashkuroon.

وَلَقَدْ نَصَرَكُمُ اللَّهُ بِبَدْرٍ وَّ
أَنتُمْ أَذِلَّةٌ ۖ فَاتَّقُوا اللَّهَ لَعَلَّكُمْ
تَشْكُرُونَ ﴿١٢٣﴾

124. Remember you said to the Faithful: "Is it not enough for you that Allah should help you with three thousand angels (Specially) sent down?

124. Iz taqoolu lilmu'mineena alañy-yakfiyakum añy-yumiddakum Rabbukum bisalaasati aalaafim-minal-malaaa'ikati munzaleen.

إِذْ تَقُولُ لِلْمُؤْمِنِينَ أَلَن يَكْفِيَكُمْ
أَن يُمِدَّكُمْ رَبُّكُم بِثَلَاثَةِ آلَافٍ
مِّنَ الْمَلَآئِكَةِ مُنزَلِينَ ﴿١٢٤﴾

125. "Yes, - if you remain firm, and act aright, even if the enemy should rush here on you in hot haste, your Lord would help you with five thousand angels making a terrific onslaught.

125. Balaaa; in taṣbiroo wa tattaqoo wa yaåtookum min fawrihim haazaa yumdidkum Rabbukum bikhamsati aalaafim-minal-malaaa'ikati musawwimeen.

بَلَىٰ ۚ إِن تَصْبِرُوا وَتَتَّقُوا وَيَأْتُوكُم
مِّن فَوْرِهِمْ هَٰذَا يُمْدِدْكُمْ
رَبُّكُم بِخَمْسَةِ آلَافٍ مِّنَ الْمَلَآئِكَةِ
مُسَوِّمِينَ ﴿١٢٥﴾ الربع

126. Allah made it but a message of hope for you, and an assurance to your hearts: (in any case) there is no help except from Allah, the Exalted, the Wise:

126. Wa maa jaʻalahul-laahu illaa bushraa lakum wa litaṭma'inna quloobukum bih; wa man-naṣru illaa min ʻindil-laahil-ʻAzeezil-Ḥakeem.

وَمَا جَعَلَهُ اللَّهُ إِلَّا بُشْرَىٰ لَكُمْ
وَلِتَطْمَئِنَّ قُلُوبُكُم بِهِ ۗ وَمَا النَّصْرُ
إِلَّا مِنْ عِندِ اللَّهِ الْعَزِيزِ الْحَكِيمِ ﴿١٢٦﴾

127. That He might cut off a fringe of the Unbelievers or expose them to infamy, and they should then be turned back, frustrated of their purpose.

127. Liyaqṭaʻa ṭarafam-minal-lazeena kafarooo aw yakbitahum fayanqaliboo khaaa'ibeen.

لِيَقْطَعَ طَرَفًا مِّنَ الَّذِينَ كَفَرُوا
أَوْ يَكْبِتَهُمْ فَيَنقَلِبُوا خَآئِبِينَ ﴿١٢٧﴾

128. Not for you, (but for Allah), is the decision: whether He turn in mercy to them, or punish them; for they are indeed wrong-doers.

128. Laysa laka minal-amri shay'un aw yatooba ʻalayhim aw yuʻaz-zi-bahum fa innahum ẓaalimoon.

لَيْسَ لَكَ مِنَ الْأَمْرِ شَيْءٌ أَوْ يَتُوبَ
عَلَيْهِمْ أَوْ يُعَذِّبَهُمْ فَإِنَّهُمْ ظَالِمُونَ ﴿١٢٨﴾

129. To Allah belonges all that is in the heavens and on earth. He forgives whom He pleases and punishes whom He pleases; but Allah is Oft-Forgiving, Most Merciful.

129. Wa lillaahi maa fissamaawaati wa maa fil-arḍ; yaghfiru limañy-yashaaa'u wa yuʻazzibu mañy-yashaaa'; wallaahu Ghafoorur-Raḥeem. **(Section 13)**

وَلِلَّهِ مَا فِي السَّمَاوَاتِ وَمَا فِي الْأَرْضِ ۚ
يَغْفِرُ لِمَن يَشَآءُ وَيُعَذِّبُ مَن
يَشَآءُ ۚ وَاللَّهُ غَفُورٌ رَّحِيمٌ ﴿١٢٩﴾ ع ١٣

130. O you who believe! Devour not interest, doubled and multiplied; but fear Allah; that you may (really) prosper.

130. Yaaa ayyuhal-lazeena aamanoo laa taåkulur-ribaaa aḍʻaafam-muḍaaʻafatañw wattaqul-laaha laʻallakum tufliḥoon.

يَا أَيُّهَا الَّذِينَ آمَنُوا لَا تَأْكُلُوا
الرِّبَا أَضْعَافًا مُّضَاعَفَةً ۖ وَاتَّقُوا
اللَّهَ لَعَلَّكُمْ تُفْلِحُونَ ﴿١٣٠﴾

Ikhfa اخفاء | Ghunna غنّہ | Ikhfa Meem Saakin اخفاء میم ساکن | Idghaam ادغام | Qalqala قلقلہ | Qalb قلب | Idghaam Meem Saakin ادغام میم ساکن

131. Fear the Fire, which is prepared for those who reject Faith:
132. And obey Allah and the Apostle; that you may obtain mercy.

131. Wattaqun-Naaral-lateee u'iddat lilkaafireen.
132. Wa atee'ul-laaha war-Rasoola la'allakum turhamoon.

وَاتَّقُوا النَّارَ الَّتِيٓ اُعِدَّتْ لِلْكٰفِرِيْنَ ﴿١٣١﴾
وَاَطِيْعُوا اللّٰهَ وَالرَّسُوْلَ لَعَلَّكُمْ
تُرْحَمُوْنَ ﴿١٣٢﴾

133. Be quick in the race for seeking forgiveness from your Lord, and for a Garden whose width is that (of the whole) of the heavens and of the earth, prepared for the righteous,-

133. Wa saari'ooo ilaa maghfiratim-mir-Rabbikum wa-Jannatin arduhassamaawaatu wal-ardu u'iddat lilmuttaqeen.

وَسَارِعُوْٓا اِلٰى مَغْفِرَةٍ مِّنْ رَّبِّكُمْ
وَجَنَّةٍ عَرْضُهَا السَّمٰوٰتُ وَالْاَرْضُ
اُعِدَّتْ لِلْمُتَّقِيْنَ ﴿١٣٣﴾

134. Those who spend (freely), whether in prosperity, or in adversity; who restrain anger, and pardon (all) men; - for Allah loves those who do good,-

134. Allazeena yunfiqoona fis-sarraaa'i waddarraaa'i wal-kaazimeenal-ghayza wal-aafeena 'anin-naas; wallaahu yuhibbul-muhsineen.

الَّذِيْنَ يُنْفِقُوْنَ فِي السَّرَّآءِ وَ
الضَّرَّآءِ وَالْكٰظِمِيْنَ الْغَيْظَ
وَالْعَافِيْنَ عَنِ النَّاسِ ؕ وَاللّٰهُ
يُحِبُّ الْمُحْسِنِيْنَ ﴿١٣٤﴾

135. And those who, having done something to be ashamed of, or wronged their own souls, earnestly bring Allah to mind, and ask for forgiveness for their sins, - and who can forgive sins except Allah? - and are never obstinate in persisting knowingly in (the wrong) they have done.

135. Wallazeena izaa fa'aloo faahishatan aw zalamooo anfusahum zakarul-laaha fastaghfaroo lizunoobihim; wa mañy-yaghfiruz-zunooba illal-laahu wa lam yusirroo 'alaa maa fa'aloo wa hum ya'lamoon.

وَالَّذِيْنَ اِذَا فَعَلُوْا فَاحِشَةً اَوْ
ظَلَمُوْٓا اَنْفُسَهُمْ ذَكَرُوا اللّٰهَ
فَاسْتَغْفَرُوْا لِذُنُوْبِهِمْ وَمَنْ يَّغْفِرُ
الذُّنُوْبَ اِلَّا اللّٰهُ ۟ وَلَمْ يُصِرُّوْا
عَلٰى مَا فَعَلُوْا وَهُمْ يَعْلَمُوْنَ ﴿١٣٥﴾

136. For such the reward is forgiveness from their Lord, and Gardens with rivers flowing underneath,- an eternal dwelling: how excellent a recompense for those who work (and strive)!

136. Ulaaa'ika jazaaa'uhum maghfiratum-mir-Rabbihim wa Jannaatun tajree min tahtihal-anhaaru khaalideena feehaa; wa ni'ma ajrul-'aamileen.

اُولٰٓئِكَ جَزَآؤُهُمْ مَّغْفِرَةٌ مِّنْ
رَّبِّهِمْ وَجَنّٰتٌ تَجْرِيْ مِنْ تَحْتِهَا
الْاَنْهٰرُ خٰلِدِيْنَ فِيْهَا ؕ وَنِعْمَ
اَجْرُ الْعٰمِلِيْنَ ﴿١٣٦﴾

137. Many were the Ways of Life that have passed away before you: travel through the earth, and see what was the end of those who rejected Truth.

137. Qad khalat min qablikum sunanun faseeroo fil-ardi fanzuroo kayfa kaana 'aaqibatul-mukazzibeen

قَدْ خَلَتْ مِنْ قَبْلِكُمْ سُنَنٌ ۙ
فَسِيْرُوْا فِي الْاَرْضِ فَانْظُرُوْا
كَيْفَ كَانَ عَاقِبَةُ الْمُكَذِّبِيْنَ ﴿١٣٧﴾

138. Here is a plain statement to men, a guidance and instruction to those who fear Allah.

138. Haazaa bayaanul-linnaasi wa hudañw-wa maw'izatul-lilmuttaqeen.

هٰذَا بَيَانٌ لِّلنَّاسِ وَهُدًى
وَّمَوْعِظَةٌ لِّلْمُتَّقِيْنَ ﴿١٣٨﴾

139. So lose not heart, nor fall into despair: for you must gain mastery if you are true in Faith.

139. Wa laa tahinoo wa laa tahzanoo wa antumul-a'lawna in kuntum mu'mineen.

وَلَا تَهِنُوْا وَلَا تَحْزَنُوْا وَاَنْتُمُ
الْاَعْلَوْنَ اِنْ كُنْتُمْ مُّؤْمِنِيْنَ ﴿١٣٩﴾

Ikhfa اخفاء | Ghunna غُنّہ | Ikhfa Meem Saakin اخفاء میم ساکن | Idghaam ادغام | Qalqala قلقلہ | Qalb قلب | Idghaam Meem Saakin ادغام میم ساکن

140. If a wound has touched you, be sure a similar wound has touched the others. Such days (of varying fortunes) We give to men and men by turns: that Allah may know those that believe, and that He may take to Himself from your ranks Martyr-witnesses (to Truth). And Allah loves not those that do wrong.

140. Iñy-yamsaskum qarḥun faqad massal-qawma qarḥum mis̲luh; wa tilkal-ayyaamu nudaawiluhaa baynan-naasi wa liya'lamal-laahul-laz̲eena aamanoo wa yattakhiz̲a minkum shuhadaaa'; wallaahu laa yuḥibbuẓ-ẓaalimeen.

إِن يَمۡسَسۡكُمۡ قَرۡحٞ فَقَدۡ مَسَّ
ٱلۡقَوۡمَ قَرۡحٞ مِّثۡلُهُۥۚ وَتِلۡكَ ٱلۡأَيَّامُ
نُدَاوِلُهَا بَيۡنَ ٱلنَّاسِ وَلِيَعۡلَمَ
ٱللَّهُ ٱلَّذِينَ ءَامَنُواْ وَيَتَّخِذَ مِنكُمۡ
شُهَدَآءَۗ وَٱللَّهُ لَا يُحِبُّ ٱلظَّٰلِمِينَ ١٤٠

141. Allah's object also is to purge those that are true in Faith and to deprive of blessing those that resist Faith.

141. Wa liyumaḥḥiṣal-laahul-laz̲eena aamanoo wa yamḥaqal-kaafireen.

وَلِيُمَحِّصَ ٱللَّهُ ٱلَّذِينَ ءَامَنُواْ
وَيَمۡحَقَ ٱلۡكَٰفِرِينَ ١٤١

142. Did you think that you would enter Heaven without Allah testing those of you who fought hard (in His Cause) and remained steadfast?

142. Am ḥasibtum an tadkhulul-Jannata wa lammaa ya'lamil-laahul-laz̲eena jaahadoo minkum wa ya'lamaṣ-ṣaabireen.

أَمۡ حَسِبۡتُمۡ أَن تَدۡخُلُواْ ٱلۡجَنَّةَ وَلَمَّا
يَعۡلَمِ ٱللَّهُ ٱلَّذِينَ جَٰهَدُواْ مِنكُمۡ
وَيَعۡلَمَ ٱلصَّٰبِرِينَ ١٤٢

143. You did indeed wish for death before you met him: now you have seen him with your own eyes, (and you flinch!)

143. Wa laqad kuntum tamannawnal-mawta min qabli an talqawhu faqad ra-aytumoohu wa antum tanẓuroon. **(Section 14)**

وَلَقَدۡ كُنتُمۡ تَمَنَّوۡنَ ٱلۡمَوۡتَ مِن
قَبۡلِ أَن تَلۡقَوۡهُ فَقَدۡ رَأَيۡتُمُوهُ
وَأَنتُمۡ تَنظُرُونَ ١٤٣ ع

144. Muhammad is no more than an Apostle: many were the Apostles that passed away before him. If he died or were slain, will you then turn back on your heels? If any did turn back on his heels, not the least harm will he do to Allah; but Allah (on the other hand) will swiftly reward those who (serve Him) with gratitude.

144. Wa maa Muḥammadun illaa Rasoolun qad khalat min qablihir-Rusul; afa'im-maata aw qutilan-qalabtum 'alaaa a'qaabikum; wa mañy-yanqalib 'alaa-aqibayhi falañy-yaḍurral-laaha shay'aa; wa sayajzil-laahush-shaakireen.

وَمَا مُحَمَّدٌ إِلَّا رَسُولٞ قَدۡ خَلَتۡ
مِن قَبۡلِهِ ٱلرُّسُلُۚ أَفَإِيْن مَّاتَ
أَوۡ قُتِلَ ٱنقَلَبۡتُمۡ عَلَىٰٓ أَعۡقَٰبِكُمۡۚ
وَمَن يَنقَلِبۡ عَلَىٰ عَقِبَيۡهِ فَلَن
يَضُرَّ ٱللَّهَ شَيۡـٔٗاۗ وَسَيَجۡزِي ٱللَّهُ
ٱلشَّٰكِرِينَ ١٤٤

145. Nor can a soul die except by Allah's leave, the term being fixed as by writing. If any do desire a reward in this life, We shall give it to him; and if any do desire a reward in the Hereafter, We shall give it to him. And swiftly shall We reward those that (serve Us with) gratitude.

145. Wa maa kaana linafsin an tamoota illaa bi-iz̲nillaahi kitaabam-mu'ajjalaa; wa mañy-yurid s̲awaabad-dunyaa nu'tihee minhaa wa mañy-yurid s̲awaabal-Aakhirati nu'tihee minhaa; wa sanajzish-shaakireen.

وَمَا كَانَ لِنَفۡسٍ أَن تَمُوتَ إِلَّا
بِإِذۡنِ ٱللَّهِ كِتَٰبٗا مُّؤَجَّلٗاۗ وَمَن
يُرِدۡ ثَوَابَ ٱلدُّنۡيَا نُؤۡتِهِۦ مِنۡهَا
وَمَن يُرِدۡ ثَوَابَ ٱلۡأٓخِرَةِ نُؤۡتِهِۦ
مِنۡهَاۚ وَسَنَجۡزِي ٱلشَّٰكِرِينَ ١٤٥

146. How many of the prophets fought (in Allah's way), and with them (fought) large bands of godly men? But they never lost heart if they

146. Wa ka-ayyim-min Nabiyyin qaatala ma'ahoo ribbiyyoona kas̲eerun famaa wahanoo limaaa

وَكَأَيِّن مِّن نَّبِيّٖ قَٰتَلَ مَعَهُۥ
رِبِّيُّونَ كَثِيرٞ فَمَا وَهَنُواْ لِمَا

Ikhfa اخفاء | Ghunna غنّہ | Ikhfa Meem Saakin اخفاء میم ساکن | Idghaam ادغام | Qalqala قلقلہ | Qalb قلب | Idghaam Meem Saakin ادغام میم ساکن

met with disaster in Allah's way, nor did they weaken (in will) nor give in. And Allah loves those who are firm and steadfast.

Aṣaabahum fee sabeelil-laahi wa maa ḍa'ufoo wa mastakaanoo; wallaahu yuḥibbuṣ-ṣaabireen.

اصابهم في سبيل الله وما
ضعفوا وما استكانوا ۗ والله
يحب الصبرين ﴿١٤٦﴾

147. All that they said was: "Our Lord! forgive us our sins and anything we may have done that transgressed our duty: establish our feet firmly, and help us against those that resist Faith."

147. Wa maa kaana qawlahum illaaa an qaaloo Rabbanagh-fir lanaa zunoobanaa wa israafanaa feee amrinaa wa sabbit aqdaamanaa wanṣurnaa 'alal-qawmil-kaafireen.

وما كان قولهم الا ان قالوا
ربنا اغفر لنا ذنوبنا واسرافنا
في امرنا وثبت اقدامنا
وانصرنا على القوم الكفرين ﴿١٤٧﴾

148. And Allah gave them a reward in this world, and the excellent reward of the Hereafter. For Allah loves those who do good.

148. Fa-aataahumul-laahu sawaabad-dunyaa wa ḥusna sawaabil-Aakhirah; wallaahu yuḥibbul-muḥsineen. **(Section 15)**

فاتىهم الله ثواب الدنيا و
حسن ثواب الاخرة ۗ والله
يحب المحسنين ﴿١٤٨﴾ ع ١٥

149. O you who believe! If you obey the Unbelievers, they will drive you back on your heels, and you will turn back (from Faith) to your own loss.

149. Yaaa ayyuhal-lazeena aamanooo in tuṭee'ullazeena kafaroo yaruddookum 'alaaa a'qaabikum fatanqaliboo khaasireen.

يايها الذين امنوا ان تطيعوا
الذين كفروا يردوكم على
اعقابكم فتنقلبوا خسرين ﴿١٤٩﴾

150. No, Allah is your protector, and He is the best of helpers.

150. Balil-laahu mawlaakum wa Huwa khayrun-naaṣireen.

بل الله مولىكم ۚ وهو خير
النصرين ﴿١٥٠﴾

151. Soon shall We cast terror into the hearts of the Unbelievers, for that they joined companions with Allah, for which He had sent no authority: their abode will be the Fire: and evil is the home of the wrong-doers!

151. Sanulqee fee quloobil-lazeena kafarur-ru'ba bimaaa ashrakoo billaahi maa lam yunazzil bihee sulṭaana(ñw)wa maåwaahumun-Naar; wa bi'sa masw az-ẓaalimeen.

سنلقي في قلوب الذين كفروا
الرعب بما اشركوا بالله ما لم
ينزل به سلطنا ۚ ومأوىهم
النار ۚ وبئس مثوى الظلمين ﴿١٥١﴾

152. Allah did indeed fulfil His promise to you when you with His permission were about to annihilate your enemy, - until you flinched and fell to disputing about the order, and disobeyed it after He brought you in sight (of the booty) which you covet. Among you are some that hanker after this world and some that desire the Hereafter. Then He diverted you from your foes in order to test you. But

152. Wa laqad ṣadaqakumul-laahu wa'dahooo iz taḥussoonahum bi-iznihee ḥattaaa-izaa fashiltum wa tanaaza'tum fil-amri wa 'aṣaytum mim ba'di maaa araakum maa tuḥibboon; minkum mañy-yureedud-dunyaa wa minkum mañy-yureedul-Aakhirah; summa ṣarafakum 'anhum liyabtaliyakum wa laqad

ولقد صدقكم الله وعده اذ
تحسونهم باذنه ۚ حتى اذا فشلتم
وتنازعتم في الامر وعصيتم
من بعد ما اركم ما تحبون ۚ
منكم من يريد الدنيا و
منكم من يريد الاخرة ۚ ثم
صرفكم عنهم ليبتليكم ۚ ولقد

He forgave you: for Allah is full of grace to those who believe.

'afaa 'ankum; wallaahu zoo faḍlin 'alal-mu'mineen.

عَفَا عَنْكُمْ ۗ وَاللّٰهُ ذُوْ فَضْلٍ
عَلَى الْمُؤْمِنِيْنَ ﴿١٥٢﴾

153. Behold! you were climbing up the high ground, without even casting a side glance at any one, and the Apostle in your rear was calling you back. There did Allah give you one distress after another by way of requital, to teach you not to grieve for (the booty) that had escaped you and for (the ill) that had befallen you. For Allah is well aware of all that you do.

153. Iz tuṣ'idoona wa laa talwoona 'alaaa aḥadiñw-war-Rasoolu yad'ookum feee ukhraakum fa-asaabakum ghammam bighammil-likaylaa taḥzanoo 'alaa maa faatakum wa laa maaa aṣaabakum; wallaahu khabeerum bimaa ta'maloon.

إِذْ تُصْعِدُوْنَ وَلَا تَلْوٗنَ عَلٰٓى أَحَدٍ
وَّالرَّسُوْلُ يَدْعُوْكُمْ فِيْٓ أُخْرٰىكُمْ
فَأَثَابَكُمْ غَمًّا بِغَمٍّ لِّكَيْلَا تَحْزَنُوْا
عَلٰى مَا فَاتَكُمْ وَلَا مَآ أَصَابَكُمْ ۗ
وَاللّٰهُ خَبِيْرٌ بِمَا تَعْمَلُوْنَ ﴿١٥٣﴾

154. After (the excitement) of the distress, He sent down calm on a band of you overcome with slumber, while another band was stirred to anxiety by their own feelings, moved by wrong suspicions of Allah-suspicions due to ignorance. They said: "What affair is this of ours?" Say you: "Indeed, this affair is wholly Allah's." They hide in their minds what they dare not reveal to you. They say (to themselves): "If we had had anything to do with this affair, We should not have been in the slaughter here ." Say: "Even if you had remained in your homes, those for whom death was decreed would certainly have gone forth to the place of their death"; but (all this was) that Allah might test what is in your breasts and purge what is in your hearts. For Allah knows well the secrets of your hearts.

154. Summa anzala 'alaykum mim ba'dil-ghammi-amanatan nu'aasañy-yaghshaa ṭaaa'ifatam-minkum wa ṭaaa'ifatun qad ahammathum anfusuhum yaẓunnoona billaahi ghayral-ḥaqqi ẓannal-Jaahiliyyati yaqooloona hal lanaa minal-amri min shay'; qul-innal-amra kullahoo lillaah; yukhfoona feee anfusihim-maa laa yubdoona laka yaqooloona law kaana lanaa minal-amri shay'ummaa qutilnaa haahunaa; qul law kuntum fee buyootikum labarazal-lazeena kutiba 'alayhimul-qatlu ilaa maḍaaji'ihim wa liyabtaliyal-laahu maa fee ṣudoorikum wa liyumaḥḥiṣa maa fee quloobikum; wallaahu 'aleemum bizaatiṣ-ṣudoor.

ثُمَّ أَنْزَلَ عَلَيْكُمْ مِّنْ بَعْدِ الْغَمِّ
أَمَنَةً نُّعَاسًا يَّغْشٰى طَآئِفَةً
مِّنْكُمْ ۙ وَطَآئِفَةٌ قَدْ أَهَمَّتْهُمْ
أَنْفُسُهُمْ يَظُنُّوْنَ بِاللّٰهِ غَيْرَ الْحَقِّ
ظَنَّ الْجَاهِلِيَّةِ ۗ يَقُوْلُوْنَ هَلْ
لَّنَا مِنَ الْأَمْرِ مِنْ شَيْءٍ ۗ قُلْ إِنَّ
الْأَمْرَ كُلَّهٗ لِلّٰهِ ۗ يُخْفُوْنَ فِيْٓ
أَنْفُسِهِمْ مَّا لَا يُبْدُوْنَ لَكَ ۗ
يَقُوْلُوْنَ لَوْ كَانَ لَنَا مِنَ الْأَمْرِ
شَيْءٌ مَّا قُتِلْنَا هٰهُنَا ۗ قُلْ لَّوْ
كُنْتُمْ فِيْ بُيُوْتِكُمْ لَبَرَزَ الَّذِيْنَ كُتِبَ
عَلَيْهِمُ الْقَتْلُ إِلٰى مَضَاجِعِهِمْ ۚ
وَلِيَبْتَلِيَ اللّٰهُ مَا فِيْ صُدُوْرِكُمْ
وَلِيُمَحِّصَ مَا فِيْ قُلُوْبِكُمْ ۗ
وَاللّٰهُ عَلِيْمٌ بِذَاتِ الصُّدُوْرِ ﴿١٥٤﴾

155. Those of you who turned back on the day the two hosts met - it was Satan who caused them to fail, because of some (evil) they had done. But Allah has blotted out (their fault): for Allah is

155. Innal-lazeena tawallaw minkum yawmal-taqal jam'aani innamas tazallahumush-Shayṭaanu biba'ḍi maa kasaboo wa laqad 'afal-laahu 'anhum; innal-laaha

إِنَّ الَّذِيْنَ تَوَلَّوْا مِنْكُمْ يَوْمَ
الْتَقَى الْجَمْعٰنِ ۙ إِنَّمَا اسْتَزَلَّهُمُ
الشَّيْطٰنُ بِبَعْضِ مَا كَسَبُوْا ۚ
وَلَقَدْ عَفَا اللّٰهُ عَنْهُمْ ۗ إِنَّ اللّٰهَ

Ikhfa اخفاء | Ghunna غُنّہ | Ikhfa Meem Saakin اخفاء میم ساکن | Idghaam ادغام | Qalqala قلقلہ | Qalb قلب | Idghaam Meem Saakin ادغام میم ساکن

ع ١٦

Oft-Forgiving, Most Forbearing.

Ghafoorun Ḥaleem. **(Section 16)**

غَفُورٌ حَلِيمٌ ﴿١٥٥﴾ ع

156. O you who believe! Be not like the Unbelievers, who say of their brethren, when they are travelling through the Earth or engaged in fighting: "If they had stayed with us, they would not have died, or been slain." This that Allah may make it a cause of sighs and regrets in their hearts. It is Allah that gives Life and Death, and Allah sees well all that you do.

156. Yaaa-ayyuhal-lazeena aamanoo laa takoonoo kallazeena kafaroo wa qaaloo li-ikhwaanihim-izaa ḍaraboo fil-arḍi aw kaanoo ghuzzal-law kaanoo 'indanaa maa maatoo wa maa qutiloo liyaj'alal-laahu zaalika ḥasratan fee quloobihim; wallaahu yuḥyee wa yumeet; wallaahu bimaa ta'maloona Baṣeer.

يَٰٓأَيُّهَا ٱلَّذِينَ ءَامَنُوا۟ لَا تَكُونُوا۟
كَٱلَّذِينَ كَفَرُوا۟ وَقَالُوا۟ لِإِخْوَٰنِهِمْ
إِذَا ضَرَبُوا۟ فِى ٱلْأَرْضِ أَوْ كَانُوا۟
غُزًّى لَّوْ كَانُوا۟ عِندَنَا مَا مَاتُوا۟
وَمَا قُتِلُوا۟ لِيَجْعَلَ ٱللَّهُ ذَٰلِكَ
حَسْرَةً فِى قُلُوبِهِمْ ۗ وَٱللَّهُ يُحْىِۦ
وَيُمِيتُ ۗ وَٱللَّهُ بِمَا تَعْمَلُونَ بَصِيرٌ ﴿١٥٦﴾

157. And if you are slain, or die, in the way of Allah, forgiveness and mercy from Allah are far better than all they could amass.

157. Wa la'in qutiltum fee sabeelil-laahi aw muttum lamaghfiratum-minal-laahi wa raḥmatun khayrum-mimmaa yajma'oon.

وَلَئِن قُتِلْتُمْ فِى سَبِيلِ ٱللَّهِ أَوْ مُتُّمْ
لَمَغْفِرَةٌ مِّنَ ٱللَّهِ وَرَحْمَةٌ خَيْرٌ
مِّمَّا يَجْمَعُونَ ﴿١٥٧﴾

158. And if you die, or are slain, Lo! it is unto Allah that you are brought together.

158. Wa la'im-muttum 'aw qutiltumla-ilal-laahi tuḥsharoon.

وَلَئِن مُّتُّمْ أَوْ قُتِلْتُمْ لَإِلَى ٱللَّهِ
تُحْشَرُونَ ﴿١٥٨﴾

159. It is part of the Mercy of Allah that you deal gently with them. If you were severe or harsh-hearted, they would have broken away from about you: so pass over (their faults), and ask for (Allah's) forgiveness for them; and consult them in affairs (of moment). Then, when you has taken a decision put your trust in Allah. For Allah loves those who put their trust (in Him).

159. Fabimaa raḥmatim minal-laahi linta lahum wa law kunta faẓẓan ghaleeẓal-qalbi lanfaḍḍoo min ḥawlika fa'fu 'anhum wastaghfir lahum wa shaawirhum fil-amri fa-izaa 'azamta fatawakkal 'alal-laah; innallaaha yuḥibbul-mutawakkileen.

فَبِمَا رَحْمَةٍ مِّنَ ٱللَّهِ لِنتَ لَهُمْ ۖ
وَلَوْ كُنتَ فَظًّا غَلِيظَ ٱلْقَلْبِ
لَٱنفَضُّوا۟ مِنْ حَوْلِكَ ۖ فَٱعْفُ
عَنْهُمْ وَٱسْتَغْفِرْ لَهُمْ وَشَاوِرْهُمْ
فِى ٱلْأَمْرِ ۖ فَإِذَا عَزَمْتَ فَتَوَكَّلْ عَلَى
ٱللَّهِ ۚ إِنَّ ٱللَّهَ يُحِبُّ ٱلْمُتَوَكِّلِينَ ﴿١٥٩﴾

160. If Allah helps you, none can overcome you: If He forsakes you, who is there, after that, that can help you? In Allah, then, let Believers put their trust.

160. Iñy-yanṣurkumul-laahu falaa ghaaliba lakum wa iñy-yakhzulkum faman zal-lazee yanṣurukum mim ba'dih; wa 'alal-laahi falyatawakkalil-mu'minoon.

إِن يَنصُرْكُمُ ٱللَّهُ فَلَا غَالِبَ لَكُمْ ۖ
وَإِن يَخْذُلْكُمْ فَمَن ذَا ٱلَّذِى
يَنصُرُكُم مِّنۢ بَعْدِهِۦ ۗ وَعَلَى ٱللَّهِ
فَلْيَتَوَكَّلِ ٱلْمُؤْمِنُونَ ﴿١٦٠﴾

161. No prophet could (ever) be false to his trust. If any person is so false, he shall, on the Day of Judgment, restore what he misappropriated; then shall every soul receive its due, whatever it earned,-

161. Wa maa kaana li-Nabiyyin añy-yaghull; wa mañy-yaghlul yaâti bimaa ghalla Yawmal-Qiyaamah; summa tuwaffaa kullu nafsim-maa kasabat

وَمَا كَانَ لِنَبِىٍّ أَن يَغُلَّ ۚ وَمَن
يَغْلُلْ يَأْتِ بِمَا غَلَّ يَوْمَ ٱلْقِيَٰمَةِ ۚ
ثُمَّ تُوَفَّىٰ كُلُّ نَفْسٍ مَّا كَسَبَتْ

Ikhfa اخفاء | Ghunna غُنّہ | Ikhfa Meem Saakin اخفاء میم ساکن | Idghaam ادغام | Qalqala قلقلہ | Qalb قلب | Idghaam Meem Saakin ادغام میم ساکن

and none shall be dealt with unjustly.

162. Is the man who follows the good pleasure of Allah like the man who draws on himself the wrath of Allah, and whose abode is in Hell?- A woeful refuge!

163. They are in varying grades in the sight of Allah, and Allah sees well all that they do.

164. Allah did confer a great favour on the believers when He sent among them an Apostle from among themselves, rehearsing unto them the Signs of Allah, sanctifying them, and instructing them in Scripture and Wisdom, while, before that, they had been in manifest error.

165. What! When a single disaster smites you, although you smote (your enemies) with one twice as great, do you say?- "Wherefrom is this?" Say (to them): "It is from yourselves: for Allah has power over all things."

166. What you suffered on the day the two armies met, was with the leave of Allah, in order that He might test the Believers,

167. And the Hypocrites also. These were told: "Come, fight in the way of Allah, or (at least) drive (the foe from your city)." They said: "Had we known there would be a fight, we should certainly have followed you." They were that day nearer to Unbelief than to Faith, saying with their lips what was not in their hearts. But Allah has full knowledge of all they conceal.

168. (They are) the ones that say, (of their brethren slain), while they themselves sit (at ease): "If only they had listened to us they would not have been slain." Say: "Avert

wa hum laa yuẓlamoon.

162. Afamanit-taba'a Riḍwaa-nal-laahi kamam baaa'a bisakhaṭim-minal-laahi wa maå-waahu Jahannam; wa bi'sal-maṣeer.

63. Hum darajaatun 'indal-laah; wallaahu baṣeerum bimaa ya'maloon.

164. Laqad mannal-laahu 'alal-mu'mineena iz ba'asa feehim Rasoolam-min anfusihim yatloo 'alayhim Aayaatihee wa yuzakkeehim wa yu'allimu-humul-Kitaaba walḤikmata wa in kaanoo min qablu lafee ḍalaalim mubeen.

165. Awa lammaaa aṣaabat-kum muṣeebatun qad aṣabtum mislayhaa qultum annaa haazaa qul huwa min 'indi anfusikum; innal-laaha 'alaa kulli shay'in Qadeer.

166. Wa maaa aṣaabakum yawmal-taqal-jam'aani fabi-iznil-laahi wa liya'lamal-mu'mineen.

167. Wa liya'lamal-lazeena naafaqoo; wa qeela lahum ta'aalaw qaatiloo fee sabeelil-laahi awid-fa'oo qaaloo law na'lamu qitaalallat-taba'naa-kum; hum lilkufri yawma'izin aqrabu minhum lil-eemaan; yaqooloona bi-afwaahihim maa laysa fee quloobihim; wallaahu a'lamu bimaa yaktumoon.

168. Allazeena qaaloo li-ikhwaanihim wa qa'adoo law aṭaa'oonaa maa qutiloo; qul fadra'oo 'an

وَهُمْ لَا يُظْلَمُونَ ١٦١
أَفَمَنِ اتَّبَعَ رِضْوَانَ اللَّهِ كَمَنْ بَاءَ
بِسَخَطٍ مِّنَ اللَّهِ وَمَأْوَاهُ جَهَنَّمُ ۚ
وَبِئْسَ الْمَصِيرُ ١٦٢
هُمْ دَرَجَاتٌ عِندَ اللَّهِ ۗ وَاللَّهُ بَصِيرٌ
بِمَا يَعْمَلُونَ ١٦٣
لَقَدْ مَنَّ اللَّهُ عَلَى الْمُؤْمِنِينَ
إِذْ بَعَثَ فِيهِمْ رَسُولًا مِّنْ أَنفُسِهِمْ
يَتْلُو عَلَيْهِمْ آيَاتِهِ وَيُزَكِّيهِمْ
وَيُعَلِّمُهُمُ الْكِتَابَ وَالْحِكْمَةَ وَإِن
كَانُوا مِن قَبْلُ لَفِي ضَلَالٍ مُّبِينٍ ١٦٤ النصف
أَوَلَمَّا أَصَابَتْكُم مُّصِيبَةٌ قَدْ أَصَبْتُم
مِّثْلَيْهَا قُلْتُمْ أَنَّىٰ هَٰذَا ۖ قُلْ هُوَ
مِنْ عِندِ أَنفُسِكُمْ ۗ إِنَّ اللَّهَ عَلَىٰ
كُلِّ شَيْءٍ قَدِيرٌ ١٦٥
وَمَا أَصَابَكُمْ يَوْمَ الْتَقَى الْجَمْعَانِ
فَبِإِذْنِ اللَّهِ وَلِيَعْلَمَ الْمُؤْمِنِينَ ١٦٦
وَلِيَعْلَمَ الَّذِينَ نَافَقُوا ۚ وَقِيلَ
لَهُمْ تَعَالَوْا قَاتِلُوا فِي سَبِيلِ اللَّهِ
أَوِ ادْفَعُوا ۖ قَالُوا لَوْ نَعْلَمُ قِتَالًا لَّا
تَّبَعْنَاكُمْ ۗ هُمْ لِلْكُفْرِ يَوْمَئِذٍ أَقْرَبُ
مِنْهُمْ لِلْإِيمَانِ ۚ يَقُولُونَ بِأَفْوَاهِهِم
مَّا لَيْسَ فِي قُلُوبِهِمْ ۗ وَاللَّهُ أَعْلَمُ
بِمَا يَكْتُمُونَ ١٦٧
الَّذِينَ قَالُوا لِإِخْوَانِهِمْ وَقَعَدُوا لَوْ
أَطَاعُونَا مَا قُتِلُوا ۗ قُلْ فَادْرَءُوا عَنْ

Ikhfa اخفاء | Ghunna غنّہ | Ikhfa Meem Saakin اخفاء میم ساکن | Idghaam ادغام | Qalqala قلقلہ | Qalb قلب | Idghaam Meem Saakin ادغام میم ساکن

Translation	Transliteration	Arabic
death from your own selves, if you speak the truth."	anfusikumul-mawta in kuntum ṣaadiqeen.	أَنفُسِكُمُ الْمَوْتَ إِن كُنتُمْ صَادِقِينَ ﴿١٦٨﴾
169. Think not of those who are slain in Allah's way as dead. Nay, they live, finding their sustenance in the presence of their Lord;	169. Wa laa taḥsabannal-lazeena qutiloo fee sabeelillaahi amwaataa; bal aḥyaa'un 'inda Rabbihim yurzaqoon.	وَلَا تَحْسَبَنَّ الَّذِينَ قُتِلُوا فِي سَبِيلِ اللَّهِ أَمْوَاتًا ۚ بَلْ أَحْيَاءٌ عِندَ رَبِّهِمْ يُرْزَقُونَ ﴿١٦٩﴾
170. They rejoice in the bounty provided by Allah: and with regard to those left behind, who have not yet joined them (in their bliss), the (martyrs) glory in the fact that on them is no fear, nor have they (cause to) grieve.	170. Fariḥeena bimaaa aataahumul-laahu min faḍlihee wa yastabshiroona billazeena lam yalḥaqoo bihim min khalfihim allaa khawfun 'alay-him wa laa hum yaḥzanoon.	فَرِحِينَ بِمَا آتَاهُمُ اللَّهُ مِن فَضْلِهِ وَيَسْتَبْشِرُونَ بِالَّذِينَ لَمْ يَلْحَقُوا بِهِم مِّنْ خَلْفِهِمْ أَلَّا خَوْفٌ عَلَيْهِمْ وَلَا هُمْ يَحْزَنُونَ ﴿١٧٠﴾
171. They glory in the Grace and the bounty from Allah, and in the fact that Allah lets not the reward of the Faithful to be lost (in the least).	171. Yastabshiroona bini-'matim-minal-laahi wa faḍ liñw-wa annal-laaha laa yuḍee'u ajral-mu'mineen. **(Section 17)**	يَسْتَبْشِرُونَ بِنِعْمَةٍ مِّنَ اللَّهِ وَفَضْلٍ وَأَنَّ اللَّهَ لَا يُضِيعُ أَجْرَ الْمُؤْمِنِينَ ﴿١٧١﴾
172. Of those who answered the call of Allah and the Apostle, even after being wounded, those who do right and refrain from wrong have a great reward;-	172. Allazeenas-tajaaboo lil-laahi war-Rasooli mim ba'di maaa aṣaabahumulqarḥ; lillazeena aḥsanoo minhum wattaqaw ajrun 'aẓeem.	الَّذِينَ اسْتَجَابُوا لِلَّهِ وَالرَّسُولِ مِن بَعْدِ مَا أَصَابَهُمُ الْقَرْحُ ۚ لِلَّذِينَ أَحْسَنُوا مِنْهُمْ وَاتَّقَوْا أَجْرٌ عَظِيمٌ ﴿١٧٢﴾
173. Men said to them: "A great army is gathering against you": and frightened them: but it (only) increased their Faith: they said: "For us Allah sufficient, and He is the best Disposer of affairs."	173. Allazeena qaala lahumun-naasu innan-naasa qad jama'oo lakum fakhshawhum fazaadahum eemaanañw-wa qaaloo ḥasbunal-laahu wa ni'mal-wakeel.	الَّذِينَ قَالَ لَهُمُ النَّاسُ إِنَّ النَّاسَ قَدْ جَمَعُوا لَكُمْ فَاخْشَوْهُمْ فَزَادَهُمْ إِيمَانًا وَقَالُوا حَسْبُنَا اللَّهُ وَنِعْمَ الْوَكِيلُ ﴿١٧٣﴾
174. And they returned with Grace and Bounty from Allah: no harm ever touched them: for they followed the good pleasure of Allah: and Allah is the Lord of bounties unbounded.	174. Fanqalaboo bini'matim-minal-laahi wa faḍlil-lam yam-sashum sooo'uñw-wattaba'oo riḍwaanal-laah; wallaahu zoo faḍlin 'aẓeem.	فَانقَلَبُوا بِنِعْمَةٍ مِّنَ اللَّهِ وَفَضْلٍ لَّمْ يَمْسَسْهُمْ سُوءٌ وَاتَّبَعُوا رِضْوَانَ اللَّهِ ۗ وَاللَّهُ ذُو فَضْلٍ عَظِيمٍ ﴿١٧٤﴾
175. It is only the Satan that suggests to you the fear of his votaries: be you not afraid of them, but fear Me, if you have Faith.	175. Innamaa zaalikumush-Shayṭaanu yukhawwifu awli-yaaa'ahoo falaa takhaafoohum wa khaafooni in kuntum mu'mineen.	إِنَّمَا ذَٰلِكُمُ الشَّيْطَانُ يُخَوِّفُ أَوْلِيَاءَهُ فَلَا تَخَافُوهُمْ وَخَافُونِ إِن كُنتُم مُّؤْمِنِينَ ﴿١٧٥﴾
176. Let not those grieve you who rush headlong into	176. Wa laa yaḥzunkal-lazeena yusaari'oona fil-	وَلَا يَحْزُنكَ الَّذِينَ يُسَارِعُونَ فِي

Ikhfa اخفاء | Ghunna غُنّہ | Ikhfa Meem Saakin اخفاء میم ساکن | Idghaam ادغام | Qalqala قلقلہ | Qalb قلب | Idghaam Meem Saakin ادغام میم ساکن

Unbelief: not the least harm will they do to Allah: Allah's plan is that He will give them no portion in the Hereafter, but a severe punishment.

Kufr; innahum lañy-yaḍurrul-laaha shay'aa; yureedul-laahu allaa yaj'ala lahum ḥazzan fil-Aakhirati wa lahum 'azaabun 'azeem.

الْكُفْرِ ۚ إِنَّهُمْ لَنْ يَضُرُّوا اللَّهَ شَيْئًا ۗ
يُرِيدُ اللَّهُ أَلَّا يَجْعَلَ لَهُمْ حَظًّا فِي
الْآخِرَةِ ۖ وَلَهُمْ عَذَابٌ عَظِيمٌ ﴿١٧٦﴾

177. Those who purchase Unbelief at the price of faith,- not the least harm will they do to Allah, but they will have a grievous punishment.

177. Innal-lazeenash-tarawul-kufra bil-eemaani lañy-yaḍurrul-laaha shay'añw-wa lahum-'azdaabun aleem.

إِنَّ الَّذِينَ اشْتَرَوُا الْكُفْرَ بِالْإِيمَانِ
لَنْ يَضُرُّوا اللَّهَ شَيْئًا ۖ وَلَهُمْ
عَذَابٌ أَلِيمٌ ﴿١٧٧﴾

178. Let not the Unbelievers think that our respite to them is good for themselves: We grant them respite that they may grow in their iniquity: but they will have a shameful punishment.

178. Wa laa yaḥsabannal-lazeena kafarooo annamaa numlee lahum khayrulli-anfusihim; innamaa numlee lahum liyazdaadooo ismaa wa lahum 'azaabum-muheen.

وَلَا يَحْسَبَنَّ الَّذِينَ كَفَرُوا أَنَّمَا
نُمْلِي لَهُمْ خَيْرٌ لِأَنْفُسِهِمْ ۚ إِنَّمَا
نُمْلِي لَهُمْ لِيَزْدَادُوا إِثْمًا ۚ وَلَهُمْ
عَذَابٌ مُهِينٌ ﴿١٧٨﴾

179. Allah will not leave the Believers in the state in which you are now, until He separates what is evil from what is good. Nor will He disclose to you the secrets of the Unseen, but He chooses of His Apostles (for the purpose) whom He pleases. So believe in Allah and His Apostles: and if you believe and do right, you have a reward without measure.

179. Maa kaanal-laahu liyazar-al-mu'mineena 'alaa maaa antum 'alayhi ḥattaa yameezal-khabeesa minat-ṭayyib; wa maa kaanal-laahu liyuṭli'akum 'alal-ghaybi wa laakinnal-laaha yajtabee mir-Rusulihee mañy-yashaaa'u fa-aaminoo billaahi wa Rusulih; wa in tu'minoo wa tattaqoo falakum ajrun 'aẓeem.

مَا كَانَ اللَّهُ لِيَذَرَ الْمُؤْمِنِينَ عَلَىٰ
مَا أَنْتُمْ عَلَيْهِ حَتَّىٰ يَمِيزَ الْخَبِيثَ
مِنَ الطَّيِّبِ ۗ وَمَا كَانَ اللَّهُ لِيُطْلِعَكُمْ
عَلَى الْغَيْبِ وَلَٰكِنَّ اللَّهَ يَجْتَبِي مِنْ
رُسُلِهِ مَنْ يَشَاءُ ۖ فَآمِنُوا بِاللَّهِ
وَرُسُلِهِ ۚ وَإِنْ تُؤْمِنُوا وَتَتَّقُوا
فَلَكُمْ أَجْرٌ عَظِيمٌ ﴿١٧٩﴾

180. And let not those who covetously withhold of the gifts which Allah has given them of His Grace, think that it is good for them: Nay, it will be the worse for them: soon shall the things which they covetously withheld be tied to their necks like a twisted collar, on the Day of Judgment. To Allah belongs the heritage of the heavens and the earth; and Allah is well-acquainted with all that you do.

180. Wa laa yaḥsabannal-lazeena yabkhaloona bimaaa aataahumul-laahu min faḍlihee huwa khayral-lahum bal huwa sharrul-lahum sayuṭaw-waqoona maa bakhiloo bihee Yawmal-Qiyaamah; wa lillaahi meeraasus-samaawaati wal-arḍ; wallaahu bimaa ta'maloona Khabeer. **(Section 18)**

وَلَا يَحْسَبَنَّ الَّذِينَ يَبْخَلُونَ بِمَا
آتَاهُمُ اللَّهُ مِنْ فَضْلِهِ هُوَ خَيْرًا
لَهُمْ ۖ بَلْ هُوَ شَرٌّ لَهُمْ ۖ سَيُطَوَّقُونَ
مَا بَخِلُوا بِهِ يَوْمَ الْقِيَامَةِ ۗ وَلِلَّهِ
مِيرَاثُ السَّمَاوَاتِ وَالْأَرْضِ ۗ وَاللَّهُ
بِمَا تَعْمَلُونَ خَبِيرٌ ﴿١٨٠﴾ ع١٨

181. Allah has heard the taunt of those who say: "Truly, Allah is indigent and we are rich!"-We shall certainly record their word and (their act) of slaying the Prophets

181. Laqad sami'al-laahu qawlal-lazeena qaalooo innal-laaha faqeeruñw-wa nahnu aghniyaaa'; sanaktubu maa qaaloo wa qatlahumul-Ambiyaa'a

لَقَدْ سَمِعَ اللَّهُ قَوْلَ الَّذِينَ قَالُوا
إِنَّ اللَّهَ فَقِيرٌ وَنَحْنُ أَغْنِيَاءُ ۘ وقف لازم
سَنَكْتُبُ مَا قَالُوا وَقَتْلَهُمُ الْأَنْبِيَاءَ

Ikhfa اخفاء | Ghunna غنّہ | Ikhfa Meem Saakin اخفاء میم ساکن | Idghaam ادغام | Qalqala قلقلہ | Qalb قلب | Idghaam Meem Saakin ادغام میم ساکن

in defiance of right, and We shall say: "Taste the Chastisement of the Scorching Fire!

182. "This is because of the (unrighteous deeds) which your hands sent on before you: for Allah never harms those who serve Him."

183. They (also) said: "Allah took our promise not to believe in an Apostle unless he showed us a sacrifice consumed by fire (from heaven)." Say: "There came to you Apostles before me, with Clear Signs and even with what you ask for: why then did you slay them, if you speak the truth?"

184. Then if they reject you, so were rejected Apostles before you, who came with Clear Signs, Books of dark prophecies, and the Book of Enlightenment.

185. Every soul shall have a taste of death: and only on the Day of Judgment shall you be paid your full recompense. Only he who is saved far from the Fire and admitted to the Garden will have attained the object (of Life): for the life of this world is but goods and chattels of deception.

186. You shall certainly be tried and tested in your possessions and in your personal selves; and you shall certainly hear much that will grieve you, from those who received the Book before you and from those who worship many gods. But if you persevere patiently, and guard against evil,- then that will be a determining factor in all affairs.

187. And remember Allah took a Covenant from the People of the Book, to make it known and clear to mankind, and not to hide it; but they threw it away behind their backs,

bighayri ḥaqqiñw-wa naqoolu zooqoo 'azaaba-lḥareeq.

182. Zaalika bimaa qaddamat aydeekum wa annal-laaha laysa biẓallaamil-lil'abeed.

183. Allazeena qaalooo innal-laaha 'ahida ilaynaaa allaa nu'mina li-Rasoolin ḥattaa yaåtiyanaa biqurbaanin taåkuluhun-naar; qul qad jaaa'akum Rusulum-min qablee bilbayyinaati wa billazee qultum falima qataltumoohum in kuntum ṣaadiqeen.

184. Fa-in kaz-zabooka faqad kuz ziba Rusulum-min qablika jaaa'oo bilbayyinaati waz-Zuburi wal-Kitaabil-Muneer.

185 Kullu nafsin zaaa'iqatul-mawt; wa innamaa tuwaffawna ujoorakum Yawmal-Qiyaamati faman zuḥziḥa 'anin-Naari waudkhilal-Jannata faqad faaz; wa mal-ḥayaatud-dunyaaa illaa mataa'ul-ghuroor.

186. Latublawunna feee amwaalikum wa anfusikum wa latasma'unna minal-lazeena ootul-Kitaaba min qablikum wa minal-lazeena ashrakooo azan kaseeraa; wa in taṣbiroo wa tattaqoo fa-inna zaalika min 'azmil-umoor.

187. Wa-iz-akhazal-laahu meesaaqal -lazeena ootul-Kitaaba latubayyinunnahoo linnaasi wa laa taktumoona-hoo fanabazoohu waraaa'a ẓuhoorihim

بِغَيْرِ حَقٍّ وَّنَقُولُ ذُوقُوا
عَذَابَ الْحَرِيقِ ﴿١٨١﴾
ذٰلِكَ بِمَا قَدَّمَتْ أَيْدِيكُمْ وَأَنَّ
اللّٰهَ لَيْسَ بِظَلَّامٍ لِّلْعَبِيدِ ﴿١٨٢﴾
الَّذِينَ قَالُوا إِنَّ اللّٰهَ عَهِدَ إِلَيْنَا
أَلَّا نُؤْمِنَ لِرَسُولٍ حَتّٰى يَأْتِيَنَا
بِقُرْبَانٍ تَأْكُلُهُ النَّارُ قُلْ قَدْ جَاءَكُمْ
رُسُلٌ مِّنْ قَبْلِي بِالْبَيِّنٰتِ وَبِالَّذِي
قُلْتُمْ فَلِمَ قَتَلْتُمُوهُمْ إِنْ
كُنْتُمْ صٰدِقِينَ ﴿١٨٣﴾
فَإِنْ كَذَّبُوكَ فَقَدْ كُذِّبَ رُسُلٌ
مِّنْ قَبْلِكَ جَاءُوا بِالْبَيِّنٰتِ وَالزُّبُرِ
وَالْكِتٰبِ الْمُنِيرِ ﴿١٨٤﴾
كُلُّ نَفْسٍ ذَائِقَةُ الْمَوْتِ وَإِنَّمَا
تُوَفَّوْنَ أُجُورَكُمْ يَوْمَ الْقِيٰمَةِ فَمَنْ
زُحْزِحَ عَنِ النَّارِ وَأُدْخِلَ الْجَنَّةَ
فَقَدْ فَازَ وَمَا الْحَيٰوةُ الدُّنْيَا إِلَّا
مَتَاعُ الْغُرُورِ ﴿١٨٥﴾
لَتُبْلَوُنَّ فِي أَمْوَالِكُمْ وَأَنْفُسِكُمْ
وَلَتَسْمَعُنَّ مِنَ الَّذِينَ أُوتُوا الْكِتٰبَ
مِنْ قَبْلِكُمْ وَمِنَ الَّذِينَ أَشْرَكُوا
أَذًى كَثِيرًا وَإِنْ تَصْبِرُوا وَتَتَّقُوا
فَإِنَّ ذٰلِكَ مِنْ عَزْمِ الْأُمُورِ ﴿١٨٦﴾
وَإِذْ أَخَذَ اللّٰهُ مِيثَاقَ الَّذِينَ
أُوتُوا الْكِتٰبَ لَتُبَيِّنُنَّهُ لِلنَّاسِ
وَلَا تَكْتُمُونَهُ فَنَبَذُوهُ وَرَاءَ ظُهُورِهِمْ

Ikhfa اخفاء | Ghunna غنّہ | Ikhfa Meem Saakin اخفاء میم ساکن | Idghaam ادغام | Qalqala قلقلہ | Qalb قلب | Idghaam Meem Saakin ادغام میم ساکن

and purchased with it some miserable gain! and vile was the bargain they made!

washtaraw bihee samanan qaleelan fabi'sa maa yashtaroon.

وَاشْتَرَوْا بِهٖ ثَمَنًا قَلِيْلًاؕ فَبِئْسَ
مَا يَشْتَرُوْنَ ﴿۱۸۷﴾

188. Think not that those who exult in what they have brought about, and love to be praised for what they have not done,- think not that they can escape the Chastisement. For them is a Chastisement grievous indeed.

188. Laa taḥsabannal-lazeena yafraḥoona bimaaa ataw wa yuḥibboona añy-yuḥmadoo bimaa lam yaf'aloo falaa taḥsabannahum bimafaazatim-minal-'azaabi wa lahum 'azaabun aleem.

لَا تَحْسَبَنَّ الَّذِيْنَ يَفْرَحُوْنَ بِمَاۤ اَتَوْا
وَّيُحِبُّوْنَ اَنْ يُّحْمَدُوْا بِمَا لَمْ يَفْعَلُوْا
فَلَا تَحْسَبَنَّهُمْ بِمَفَازَةٍ مِّنَ الْعَذَابِۚ
وَلَهُمْ عَذَابٌ اَلِيْمٌ ﴿۱۸۸﴾

189. To Allah belongeth the dominion of the heavens and the earth; and Allah has power over all things.

189. Wa lillaahi mulkus-samaawaati wal-arḍ; wallaahu 'alaa kulli shay'in Qadeer.

(Section 19)

وَلِلّٰهِ مُلْكُ السَّمٰوٰتِ وَالْاَرْضِؕ
وَاللّٰهُ عَلٰى كُلِّ شَیْءٍ قَدِيْرٌ ﴿۱۸۹﴾ ع

190. Behold! In the creation of the heavens and the earth, and the alternation of Night and Day,- there are indeed Signs for men of understanding,-

190. Inna fee khalqis-samaawaati wal-arḍi wakhtilaafil-layli wannahaari la-Aayaatil-li-ulil-albaab.

اِنَّ فِیْ خَلْقِ السَّمٰوٰتِ وَالْاَرْضِ
وَاخْتِلَافِ الَّيْلِ وَالنَّهَارِ لَاٰيٰتٍ
لِّاُولِی الْاَلْبَابِ ﴿۱۹۰﴾

191. Men who celebrate the praises of Allah, standing, sitting, and lying down on their sides, and contemplate the (wonders of) creation in the heavens and the earth, (with the thought): "Our Lord! You have created (all) this not for nothing! Glory to You! Give us salvation from the Chastisement of the Fire.

191. Allazeena yazkuroonal-laaha qiyaamañw-wa qu'oodañ w-wa 'alaa juno-obihim wa yatafakkaroona fee khalqis-samaawaati wal-arḍi Rabbanaa maa khalaqta haazaa baaṭilan Subḥaanaka-faqinaa 'azaaban-Naar.

الَّذِيْنَ يَذْكُرُوْنَ اللّٰهَ قِيٰمًا وَّ
قُعُوْدًا وَّعَلٰى جُنُوْبِهِمْ وَيَتَفَكَّرُوْنَ
فِیْ خَلْقِ السَّمٰوٰتِ وَالْاَرْضِۚ رَبَّنَا
مَا خَلَقْتَ هٰذَا بَاطِلًاۚ سُبْحٰنَكَ
فَقِنَا عَذَابَ النَّارِ ﴿۱۹۱﴾

192. "Our Lord! any whom You admit to the Fire, Truly You have covered with shame, and never will wrong-doers find any helpers!

192. Rabbanaaa innaka man tudkhilin-Naara faqad akhzaytahoo wa maa lizzaalimeena min anṣaar.

رَبَّنَاۤ اِنَّكَ مَنْ تُدْخِلِ النَّارَ فَقَدْ
اَخْزَيْتَهٗؕ وَمَا لِلظّٰلِمِيْنَ مِنْ اَنْصَارٍ ﴿۱۹۲﴾

193. "Our Lord! we have heard the call of one calling (us) to Faith, 'Believe you in the Lord,' and we have believed. Our Lord! Forgive us our sins, blot out from us our iniquities, and take to yourself our souls in the company of the righteous.

193. Rabbanaaa innanaa sami'naa munaadiyañy-yunaadee lil-eemaani an aaminoo bi-Rabbikum fa-aamannaa; Rab-banaa faghfir lanaa zunoobanaa wa kaffir 'annaa sayyi-aatinaa wa tawaffanaa ma'al-abraar.

رَبَّنَاۤ اِنَّنَا سَمِعْنَا مُنَادِيًا يُّنَادِیْ
لِلْاِيْمَانِ اَنْ اٰمِنُوْا بِرَبِّكُمْ فَاٰمَنَّاۖ
رَبَّنَا فَاغْفِرْ لَنَا ذُنُوْبَنَا وَكَفِّرْ عَنَّا
سَيِّاٰتِنَا وَتَوَفَّنَا مَعَ الْاَبْرَارِۚ ﴿۱۹۳﴾

194. "Our Lord! Grant us what you promised unto us through Your Apostles, and save us from shame on the Day of Judgment: for You never break Your promise."

194. Rabbanaa wa aatinaa maa wa'attanaa 'alaa Rusulika wa laa tukhzinaa Yawmal-Qiyaamah; innaka laa tukhliful-mee'aad.

رَبَّنَا وَاٰتِنَا مَا وَعَدْتَّنَا عَلٰى رُسُلِكَ
وَلَا تُخْزِنَا يَوْمَ الْقِيٰمَةِؕ اِنَّكَ
لَا تُخْلِفُ الْمِيْعَادَ ﴿۱۹۴﴾

195. And their Lord has accepted of them, and answered them: "Never will I

195. Fastajaaba lahum Rabbuhum annee laaa

فَاسْتَجَابَ لَهُمْ رَبُّهُمْ اَنِّیْ لَاۤ

Ikhfa اخفاء | Ghunna غُنّہ | Ikhfa Meem Saakin اخفاء میم ساکن | Idghaam ادغام | Qalqala قلقلہ | Qalb قلب | Idghaam Meem Saakin ادغام میم ساکن

suffer to be lost the work of any of you, be he male or female: you are members, one of another: those who have left their homes, or been driven out therefrom, or suffered harm in My Cause, or fought or been slain,- verily, I will blot out from them their iniquities, and admit them into Gardens with rivers flowing beneath; - A reward from the Presence of Allah, and from His Presence is the best of rewards."

Uḍee'u 'amala 'aamilim-minkum min zakarin aw unsaa ba'ḍukum mim-ba'ḍin fal-lazeena haajaroo wa ukhrijoo min diyaarihim wa oozoo fee sabeelee wa qaataloo wa qutiloo la-ukaffiranna 'anhum sayyi-aatihim wa la-udkhilanna-hum Jannaatin tajree min taḥtihal-anhaaru sawaabam-min 'indil-laah; wallaahu 'indahoo ḥusnus-sawaab.

أُضِيعُ عَمَلَ عَامِلٍ مِّنكُم مِّن
ذَكَرٍ أَوْ أُنثَىٰ ۖ بَعْضُكُم مِّنۢ
بَعْضٍ ۖ فَالَّذِينَ هَاجَرُوا وَأُخْرِجُوا
مِن دِيَارِهِمْ وَأُوذُوا فِي سَبِيلِي
وَقَاتَلُوا وَقُتِلُوا لَأُكَفِّرَنَّ عَنْهُمْ
سَيِّئَاتِهِمْ وَلَأُدْخِلَنَّهُمْ جَنَّاتٍ
تَجْرِي مِن تَحْتِهَا الْأَنْهَارُ ثَوَابًا
مِّنْ عِندِ اللَّهِ ۗ وَاللَّهُ عِندَهُ
حُسْنُ الثَّوَابِ ﴿١٩٥﴾

196. Let not the strutting about of the Unbelievers through the land deceive you:

196. Laa yaghurrannaka taqal-lubul-lazeena kafaroo fil-bilaad.

لَا يَغُرَّنَّكَ تَقَلُّبُ الَّذِينَ كَفَرُوا
فِي الْبِلَادِ ﴿١٩٦﴾

197. Little is it for enjoyment: their ultimate abode is Hell: what an evil bed (to lie on)!

197. Mataa'un qaleelun summa maåwaahum Jahannam; wa bi'sal-mihaad.

مَتَاعٌ قَلِيلٌ ثُمَّ مَأْوَاهُمْ جَهَنَّمُ ۚ
وَبِئْسَ الْمِهَادُ ﴿١٩٧﴾

198. On the other hand, for those who fear their Lord, are Gardens, with rivers flowing beneath; therein are they to dwell (for ever),- a gift from the presence of Allah; and that which is in the Presence of Allah is the best (bliss) for the righteous.

198. Laakinil-lazeenat-taqaw Rabbahum lahum Jannaatun tajree min taḥtihal-anhaaru khaalideena feehaa nuzulam-min 'indil-laah; wa maa 'indal-laahi khayrul-lil-abraar.

لَٰكِنِ الَّذِينَ اتَّقَوْا رَبَّهُمْ لَهُمْ جَنَّاتٌ
تَجْرِي مِن تَحْتِهَا الْأَنْهَارُ خَالِدِينَ
فِيهَا نُزُلًا مِّنْ عِندِ اللَّهِ ۗ وَمَا
عِندَ اللَّهِ خَيْرٌ لِّلْأَبْرَارِ ﴿١٩٨﴾ الثلثة

199. And there are, certainly, among the People of the Book, those who believe in Allah, in the revelation to you, and in the revelation to them, bowing in humility to Allah: they will not sell the Signs of Allah for a miserable gain! for them is a reward with their Lord, and Allah is swift in account.

199. Wa inna min Ahlil-Kitaabi lamañy-yu'minu billaahi wa maaa unzila ilaykum wa maaa unzila ilayhim khaashi'eena lillaahi laa yashtaroona bi-Aayaatil-laahi samanan qaleelaa; ulaaa'ika lahum ajruhum 'inda Rabbihim; innal-laaha saree'ul-ḥisaab.

وَإِنَّ مِنْ أَهْلِ الْكِتَابِ لَمَن يُؤْمِنُ
بِاللَّهِ وَمَا أُنزِلَ إِلَيْكُمْ وَمَا أُنزِلَ
إِلَيْهِمْ خَاشِعِينَ لِلَّهِ لَا يَشْتَرُونَ
بِآيَاتِ اللَّهِ ثَمَنًا قَلِيلًا ۗ أُولَٰئِكَ
لَهُمْ أَجْرُهُمْ عِندَ رَبِّهِمْ ۗ إِنَّ اللَّهَ
سَرِيعُ الْحِسَابِ ﴿١٩٩﴾

200. O you who believe! Persevere in patience and constancy; vie in such perseverance; strengthen each other; and fear Allah; that you may prosper.

200. Yaaa ayyuhal-lazeena aamanuṣ-biroo wa ṣaabiroo wa raabiṭoo wattaqul-laaha la'allakum tufliḥoon. **(Section 20)**

يَا أَيُّهَا الَّذِينَ آمَنُوا اصْبِرُوا
وَصَابِرُوا وَرَابِطُوا وَاتَّقُوا اللَّهَ
لَعَلَّكُمْ تُفْلِحُونَ ﴿٢٠٠﴾ ع ٢٠

Ikhfa اخفاء · Ghunna غُنّہ · Ikhfa Meem Saakin اخفاء میم ساکن · Idghaam ادغام · Qalqala قلقلہ · Qalb قلب · Idghaam Meem Saakin ادغام میم ساکن

4. The Women

In the name of Allah, Most Gracious, Most Merciful.

1. O mankind! reverence your Guardian-Lord, Who created you from a single Person, created, of like nature, his mate, and from them twain scattered (like seeds) countless men and women;- reverence Allah, through Whom you demand your mutual (rights), and (reverence) the wombs (that bore you): for Allah ever watches over you.

2. To orphans restore their property (when they reach their age), nor substitute (your) worthless things for (their) good ones; and devour not their substance (by mixing it up) with your own. For this is indeed a great sin.

3. If you fear that you shall not be able to deal justly with the orphans, marry women of your choice, two or three or four; but if you fear that you shall not be able to deal justly (with them), then only one, or (a captive) that your right hands possess, that will be more suitable, to prevent you from doing injustice.

4. And give the women (on marriage) their dower as a free gift; but if they, of their own good pleasure, remit any part of it to you, take it and enjoy it with right good cheer.

5. To those weak of understanding make not over your property, which Allah has made a means of support for you, but feed and clothe them therewith, and speak to them words of kindness and justice.

6. Make trial of orphans until they reach the age of marriage; if then you find sound judgment in them, release

Sûrat an-Nisâ'–4

(Revealed at Madinah)

Bismillaahir Raḥmaanir Raḥeem

1. Yaaa ayyuhan-naasut-taqoo Rabbakumul-laz̲ee khalaqakum min nafsiñw-waaḥidatiñw-wa khalaqa minhaa zawjahaa wa bas̲-s̲a minhumaa rijaalan kas̲eerañw-wa nisaaa'aa; wattaqul-laahallaz̲ee tasaaa-'aloona bihee wal-arḥaam; innal-laaha kaana 'alaykum Raqeebaa.

2. Wa aatul-yataamaaa amwaalahum wa laa tatabad-dalul-khabees̲a biṭṭayyibi wa laa taåkulooo amwaalahum ilaaa amwaalikum; innahoo kaana ḥooban kabeeraa.

3. Wa-in khiftum allaa tuqsiṭoo fil-yataamaa fankiḥoo maa ṭaaba lakum minan-nisaaa'i mas̲naa wa s̲ulaas̲a wa rubaa'a fa-in khiftum allaa ta'diloo fawaaḥidatan aw maa malakat aymaanukum; z̲aalika adnaaa allaa ta'ooloo.

4. Wa aatun-nisaaa'a ṣadu-qaatihinna niḥlah; fa-in ṭibna lakum 'an shay'im minhu nafsan fakuloohu haneee'am-mareee'aa.

5. Wa laa tu'tus-sufahaaa'a amwaalakumul-latee ja'alal,-laahu lakum qiyaamañw-warzuqoohum feehaa waksoohum wa qooloo lahum qawlam-ma'roofaa.

6. Wabtalul-yataamaa ḥattaaa iz̲aa balaghun-nikaaḥa fa-in aanastum minhum rushdan fad-fa'ooo

(٤) سُوْرَةُ النِّسَآءِ مَدَنِيَّةٌ (٩٢)

بِسْمِ اللّٰهِ الرَّحْمٰنِ الرَّحِيْمِ

يٰٓاَيُّهَا النَّاسُ اتَّقُوْا رَبَّكُمُ الَّذِيْ
خَلَقَكُمْ مِّنْ نَّفْسٍ وَّاحِدَةٍ وَّ
خَلَقَ مِنْهَا زَوْجَهَا وَبَثَّ مِنْهُمَا
رِجَالًا كَثِيْرًا وَّنِسَآءً ۚ وَاتَّقُوا اللّٰهَ
الَّذِيْ تَسَآءَلُوْنَ بِهٖ وَالْاَرْحَامَ ۗ
اِنَّ اللّٰهَ كَانَ عَلَيْكُمْ رَقِيْبًا ﴿١﴾
وَاٰتُوا الْيَتٰمٰٓى اَمْوَالَهُمْ وَلَا تَتَبَدَّلُوا
الْخَبِيْثَ بِالطَّيِّبِ ۠ وَلَا تَاْكُلُوْٓا
اَمْوَالَهُمْ اِلٰٓى اَمْوَالِكُمْ ۗ اِنَّهٗ كَانَ
حُوْبًا كَبِيْرًا ﴿٢﴾
وَاِنْ خِفْتُمْ اَلَّا تُقْسِطُوْا فِي الْيَتٰمٰى
فَانْكِحُوْا مَا طَابَ لَكُمْ مِّنَ النِّسَآءِ
مَثْنٰى وَثُلٰثَ وَرُبٰعَ ۚ فَاِنْ خِفْتُمْ
اَلَّا تَعْدِلُوْا فَوَاحِدَةً اَوْ مَا مَلَكَتْ
اَيْمَانُكُمْ ۗ ذٰلِكَ اَدْنٰٓى اَلَّا تَعُوْلُوْا ﴿٣﴾ۭ
وَاٰتُوا النِّسَآءَ صَدُقٰتِهِنَّ نِحْلَةً ۗ
فَاِنْ طِبْنَ لَكُمْ عَنْ شَيْءٍ مِّنْهُ
نَفْسًا فَكُلُوْهُ هَنِيْٓــًٔا مَّرِيْٓــًٔا ﴿٤﴾
وَلَا تُؤْتُوا السُّفَهَآءَ اَمْوَالَكُمُ الَّتِيْ
جَعَلَ اللّٰهُ لَكُمْ قِيٰمًا وَّارْزُقُوْهُمْ
فِيْهَا وَاكْسُوْهُمْ وَقُوْلُوْا لَهُمْ قَوْلًا
مَّعْرُوْفًا ﴿٥﴾
وَابْتَلُوا الْيَتٰمٰى حَتّٰٓى اِذَا بَلَغُوا النِّكَاحَ ۚ
فَاِنْ اٰنَسْتُمْ مِّنْهُمْ رُشْدًا فَادْفَعُوْٓا

Ikhfa اخفاء | Ghunna غنّہ | Ikhfa Meem Saakin اخفاء میم ساکن | Idghaam ادغام | Qalqala قلقلہ | Qalb قلب | Idghaam Meem Saakin ادغام میم ساکن

their property to but consume it not wastefully, nor in haste against their growing up. If the guardian is well-off, let him claim no remuneration, but if he is poor, let him have for himself what is just and reasonable. When you release their property to them, take witnesses in their presence: but all-sufficient is Allah in taking account.

7. From what is left by parents and those nearest related there is a share for men and a share for women, whether the property be small or large,- a determinate share.

8. But if at the time of division other relatives, or orphans or poor, are present, feed them out of the (property), and speak to them words of kindness and justice.

9. Let those (disposing of an estate) have the same fear in their minds as they would have for their own if they had left a helpless family behind: let them fear Allah, and speak words of appropriate (comfort).

10. Those who unjustly eat up the property of orphans, eat up a Fire into their own bodies: they will soon be enduring a blazing Fire!

11. Allah (thus) directs you as regards your Children's (inheritance): to the male, a portion equal to that of two females: if only daughters, two or more, their share is two-thirds of the inheritance; if only one, her share is a half. For parents, a sixth share of the inheritance to each, if the deceased left children; if no children, and the parents are the (only) heirs, the mother has a third;

ilayhim amwaalahum wa laa taåkuloohaaa israafañw-wa bidaaran añy-yakbaroo; wa man kaana ghaniyyan falyasta'fif wa man kaana faqeeran falyaåkul bilma'roof; fa-izaa dafa'tum ilayhim amwaalahum fa-ashhidoo 'alayhim; wa kafaa billaahi Ḥaseebaa.

7. Lirrijaali naṣeebum-mimmaa tarakal-waalidaani wal-aqraboona wa lin-nisaaa'i naṣeebum-mimmaa tarakal-waalidaani wal-aqraboona mimmaa qalla minhu aw kasur; naṣeebam-mafrooḍaa.

8. Wa izaa ḥaḍaral-qismata ulul-qurbaa walyataamaa walmasaakeenu farzuqoohum minhu wa qooloo lahum qawlam-ma'roofaa.

9. Walyakhshal-lazeena law tarakoo min khalfihim zurriyyatan ḍi'aafan khaafoo 'alayhim falyattaqul-laaha walyaqooloo qawlan sadeedaa.

10. Innal-lazeena yaåkuloona amwaalal-yataamaa ẓulman innamaa yaåkuloona fee buṭoonihim Naarañw-wa sayaṣlawna sa'eeraa. **(Section 1)**

11. Yooṣeekumul-laahu feee awlaadikum liz-zakari mislu ḥazzil-unsayayn; fa-in kunna nisaaa'an fawqas-natayni falahunna sulusaa maa taraka wa in kaanat waaḥidatan falahan-niṣf; wa li-abawayhi likulli waaḥidim-minhumas-sudusu mimmaa taraka in kaana lahoo walad; fa-il-lam yakul-lahowaladuñw-wa warisahooo abawaahu fali-ummihis-sulus;

إِلَيْهِمْ أَمْوَالَهُمْ ۚ وَلَا تَأْكُلُوهَا إِسْرَافًا
وَبِدَارًا أَن يَكْبَرُوا ۚ وَمَن كَانَ غَنِيًّا
فَلْيَسْتَعْفِفْ ۖ وَمَن كَانَ فَقِيرًا فَلْيَأْكُلْ
بِالْمَعْرُوفِ ۚ فَإِذَا دَفَعْتُمْ إِلَيْهِمْ
أَمْوَالَهُمْ فَأَشْهِدُوا عَلَيْهِمْ ۚ
وَكَفَىٰ بِاللَّهِ حَسِيبًا ﴿٦﴾
لِّلرِّجَالِ نَصِيبٌ مِّمَّا تَرَكَ الْوَالِدَانِ
وَالْأَقْرَبُونَ وَلِلنِّسَاءِ نَصِيبٌ مِّمَّا
تَرَكَ الْوَالِدَانِ وَالْأَقْرَبُونَ مِمَّا قَلَّ
مِنْهُ أَوْ كَثُرَ ۚ نَصِيبًا مَّفْرُوضًا ﴿٧﴾
وَإِذَا حَضَرَ الْقِسْمَةَ أُولُو الْقُرْبَىٰ
وَالْيَتَامَىٰ وَالْمَسَاكِينُ فَارْزُقُوهُم مِّنْهُ
وَقُولُوا لَهُمْ قَوْلًا مَّعْرُوفًا ﴿٨﴾
وَلْيَخْشَ الَّذِينَ لَوْ تَرَكُوا مِنْ خَلْفِهِمْ
ذُرِّيَّةً ضِعَافًا خَافُوا عَلَيْهِمْ فَلْيَتَّقُوا
اللَّهَ وَلْيَقُولُوا قَوْلًا سَدِيدًا ﴿٩﴾
إِنَّ الَّذِينَ يَأْكُلُونَ أَمْوَالَ الْيَتَامَىٰ
ظُلْمًا إِنَّمَا يَأْكُلُونَ فِي بُطُونِهِمْ
نَارًا ۖ وَسَيَصْلَوْنَ سَعِيرًا ﴿١٠﴾
يُوصِيكُمُ اللَّهُ فِي أَوْلَادِكُمْ ۖ لِلذَّكَرِ
مِثْلُ حَظِّ الْأُنثَيَيْنِ ۚ فَإِن كُنَّ نِسَاءً
فَوْقَ اثْنَتَيْنِ فَلَهُنَّ ثُلُثَا مَا تَرَكَ ۖ
وَإِن كَانَتْ وَاحِدَةً فَلَهَا النِّصْفُ ۚ
وَلِأَبَوَيْهِ لِكُلِّ وَاحِدٍ مِّنْهُمَا السُّدُسُ
مِمَّا تَرَكَ إِن كَانَ لَهُ وَلَدٌ ۚ فَإِن لَّمْ يَكُن
لَّهُ وَلَدٌ وَوَرِثَهُ أَبَوَاهُ فَلِأُمِّهِ الثُّلُثُ ۚ

Ikhfa اخفاء | Ghunna غُنّہ | Ikhfa Meem Saakin اخفاء میم ساکن | Idghaam ادغام | Qalqala قلقلہ | Qalb قلب | Idghaam Meem Saakin ادغام میم ساکن

if the deceased left brothers (or sister) the mother has a sixth. (The distribution in all cases is) after the payment of legacies and debts. You know not whether your parents or your children are nearest to you in benefit. These are settled portions ordained by Allah; and Allah is All-knowing, All-wise.

fa-in kaana lahooo ikhwatun fali-ummihis-sudus; mim ba'di waṣiyyatiñy-yooṣee bihaaa aw dayn; aabaaa'ukum wa abnaaa'ukum laa tadroona ayyuhum aqrabu lakum naf'aa; fareeḍatam-minallaah; innal-laaha kaana 'Aleeman Ḥakeemaa.

فَإِن كَانَ لَهُۥٓ إِخْوَةٌ فَلِأُمِّهِ ٱلسُّدُسُ
مِنۢ بَعْدِ وَصِيَّةٍ يُوصِى بِهَآ أَوْ دَيْنٍ ۗ
ءَابَآؤُكُمْ وَأَبْنَآؤُكُمْ لَا تَدْرُونَ أَيُّهُمْ أَقْرَبُ
لَكُمْ نَفْعًا ۚ فَرِيضَةً مِّنَ ٱللَّهِ ۗ إِنَّ
ٱللَّهَ كَانَ عَلِيمًا حَكِيمًا ﴿١١﴾

12. In what your wives leave, your share is a half, if they leave no child; but if they leave a child, you get a fourth; after payment of legacies and debts. In what you leave, their share is a fourth, if you leave no child; but if you leave a child, they get one eighth; after payment of legacies and debts. If the man or woman whose inheritance is in question, has left neither ascendants nor descendants, but has left a brother or a sister, each one of the two gets a sixth; but if more than two, they share in a third; after payment of legacies and debts; so that no loss is caused (to any one). Thus is it ordained by Allah; and Allah is All-knowing, Most Forbearing.

12. Wa lakum niṣfu maa taraka azwaajukum il-lam yakul-lahunna walad; fa-in kaana lahunna waladun falakumur-rubu'u mimmaa tarakna mim ba'di waṣiyyatiñy-yooṣeena bihaaa aw dayn; wa lahunnar-rubu'u mimmaa taraktum il-lam yakul-lakum walad; fa-in kaana lakum waladun falahunnas-sumunu mimmaa taraktum; mim ba'di waṣiyyatin tooṣoona bihaaa aw dayn; wa in kaana rajuluñy-yoorasu kalaalatan awim-ra-atuñw-wa lahooo akhun aw ukhtun falikulli waaḥidim-minhumas-sudus; fa-in kaanooo aksara min zaalika fahum shurakaaa'u fis-sulusi mim ba'di waṣiyyatiñy-yooṣaa bihaaa aw daynin ghayra muḍaaarr; waṣiyyatam-minal-laah; wallaahu 'Aleemun Ḥaleem.

۞ وَلَكُمْ نِصْفُ مَا تَرَكَ أَزْوَٰجُكُمْ إِن
لَّمْ يَكُن لَّهُنَّ وَلَدٌ ۚ فَإِن كَانَ
لَهُنَّ وَلَدٌ فَلَكُمُ ٱلرُّبُعُ مِمَّا تَرَكْنَ ۚ
مِنۢ بَعْدِ وَصِيَّةٍ يُوصِينَ بِهَآ
أَوْ دَيْنٍ ۚ وَلَهُنَّ ٱلرُّبُعُ مِمَّا تَرَكْتُمْ
إِن لَّمْ يَكُن لَّكُمْ وَلَدٌ ۚ فَإِن كَانَ
لَكُمْ وَلَدٌ فَلَهُنَّ ٱلثُّمُنُ مِمَّا
تَرَكْتُم ۚ مِّنۢ بَعْدِ وَصِيَّةٍ تُوصُونَ
بِهَآ أَوْ دَيْنٍ ۗ وَإِن كَانَ رَجُلٌ يُورَثُ
كَلَٰلَةً أَوِ ٱمْرَأَةٌ وَلَهُۥٓ أَخٌ أَوْ أُخْتٌ
فَلِكُلِّ وَٰحِدٍ مِّنْهُمَا ٱلسُّدُسُ ۚ فَإِن
كَانُوٓا۟ أَكْثَرَ مِن ذَٰلِكَ فَهُمْ شُرَكَآءُ
فِى ٱلثُّلُثِ ۚ مِنۢ بَعْدِ وَصِيَّةٍ يُوصَىٰ
بِهَآ أَوْ دَيْنٍ غَيْرَ مُضَآرٍّ ۚ وَصِيَّةً
مِّنَ ٱللَّهِ ۗ وَٱللَّهُ عَلِيمٌ حَلِيمٌ ﴿١٢﴾

13. Those are limits set by Allah: those who obey Allah and His Apostle will be admitted to Gardens with rivers flowing beneath, to abide therein (for ever) and that will be the supreme achievement.

13. Tilka ḥudoodul-laah; wa mañy-yuṭi'il-laaha wa Rasoo-lahoo yudkhilhu Jannaatin tajree min taḥtihal-anhaaru khaalideena feehaa; wa zaalikal-fawzul-'aẓeem.

تِلْكَ حُدُودُ ٱللَّهِ ۚ وَمَن يُطِعِ ٱللَّهَ
وَرَسُولَهُۥ يُدْخِلْهُ جَنَّٰتٍ تَجْرِى مِن
تَحْتِهَا ٱلْأَنْهَٰرُ خَٰلِدِينَ فِيهَا ۚ وَذَٰلِكَ
ٱلْفَوْزُ ٱلْعَظِيمُ ﴿١٣﴾

14. But those who disobey Allah and His Apostle and transgress His limits will be admitted to a Fire, to abide therein:

14. Wa mañy-ya'ṣil-laaha wa Rasoolahoo wa yata'adda ḥudoodahoo yudkhilhu Naaran khaalidan feehaa

وَمَن يَعْصِ ٱللَّهَ وَرَسُولَهُۥ وَيَتَعَدَّ
حُدُودَهُۥ يُدْخِلْهُ نَارًا خَٰلِدًا فِيهَا

Ikhfa اخفاء | Ghunna غنّہ | Ikhfa Meem Saakin اخفاء میم ساکن | Idghaam ادغام | Qalqala قلقلہ | Qalb قلب | Idghaam Meem Saakin ادغام میم ساکن

ع ٢ / ١٣

وَلَهُۥ عَذَابٌ مُّهِينٌ ﴿١٤﴾

wa lahoo 'az̲aabum-muheen.

(Section 2)

and they shall have a humiliating punishment.

وَٱلَّٰتِى يَأْتِينَ ٱلْفَٰحِشَةَ مِن نِّسَآئِكُمْ
فَٱسْتَشْهِدُوا۟ عَلَيْهِنَّ أَرْبَعَةً مِّنكُمْ ۖ
فَإِن شَهِدُوا۟ فَأَمْسِكُوهُنَّ فِى ٱلْبُيُوتِ
حَتَّىٰ يَتَوَفَّىٰهُنَّ ٱلْمَوْتُ أَوْ يَجْعَلَ ٱللَّهُ
لَهُنَّ سَبِيلًا ﴿١٥﴾

15. Wallaatee yaåteenal-faaḥishata min nisaaa'ikum fastashhidoo 'alayhinna arba'atam-minkum fa-in shahidoo fa-amsikoohunna fil-buyooti ḥattaa yatawaffaa-hunnal-mawtu aw yaj'alal-laahu lahunna sabeelaa.

15. If any of your women are guilty of lewdness, take the evidence of four (reliable) witnesses from amongst you against them; and if they testify, confine them to houses until death do claim them, or Allah ordain for them some (other) way.

وَٱلَّذَانِ يَأْتِيَٰنِهَا مِنكُمْ فَـَٔاذُوهُمَا ۖ
فَإِن تَابَا وَأَصْلَحَا فَأَعْرِضُوا۟ عَنْهُمَآ ۗ
إِنَّ ٱللَّهَ كَانَ تَوَّابًا رَّحِيمًا ﴿١٦﴾

16. Wallaz̲aani yaåtiyaanihaa minkum fa-aaz̲oohumaa fa-in taabaa wa aṣlaḥaa fa-a'riḍoo 'anhumaaa; innal-laaha kaana Tawwaabar-Raḥeemaa.

16. If two men among you are guilty of lewdness, punish them both. If they repent and amend, leave them alone; for Allah is Oft-returning, Most Merciful.

إِنَّمَا ٱلتَّوْبَةُ عَلَى ٱللَّهِ لِلَّذِينَ
يَعْمَلُونَ ٱلسُّوٓءَ بِجَهَٰلَةٍ ثُمَّ
يَتُوبُونَ مِن قَرِيبٍ فَأُو۟لَٰٓئِكَ يَتُوبُ
ٱللَّهُ عَلَيْهِمْ ۗ وَكَانَ ٱللَّهُ
عَلِيمًا حَكِيمًا ﴿١٧﴾

17. Innamat-tawbatu 'alallaahi lillaz̲eena ya'maloonas-sooo'a bijahaalatin s̲umma yatooboona min qareebin faulaaa'ika yatoobul-laahu 'alayhim; wa kaanal-laahu 'Aleeman Ḥakeemaa.

17. Allah accepts the repentance of those who do evil in ignorance and repent soon afterwards; to them will Allah turn in mercy: for Allah is full of knowledge and wisdom.

وَلَيْسَتِ ٱلتَّوْبَةُ لِلَّذِينَ يَعْمَلُونَ
ٱلسَّيِّـَٔاتِ حَتَّىٰٓ إِذَا حَضَرَ أَحَدَهُمُ
ٱلْمَوْتُ قَالَ إِنِّى تُبْتُ ٱلْـَٰٔنَ وَلَا
ٱلَّذِينَ يَمُوتُونَ وَهُمْ كُفَّارٌ ۚ
أُو۟لَٰٓئِكَ أَعْتَدْنَا لَهُمْ عَذَابًا أَلِيمًا ﴿١٨﴾

18. Wa laysatit-tawbatu lillaz̲eena ya'maloonas-sayyi-aati ḥattaaa iz̲aa ḥaḍara aḥadahumul-mawtu qaala innee tubtul-'aana wa lallaz̲eena yamootoona wa hum kuffaar; ulaaa'ika a'tadnaa lahum 'az̲aaban aleemaa.

18. Of no effect is the repentance of those who continue to do evil, until death faces one of them, and he says, "Now have I repented indeed;" nor of those who die rejecting Faith: for them have We prepared a punishment most grievous.

يَٰٓأَيُّهَا ٱلَّذِينَ ءَامَنُوا۟ لَا يَحِلُّ
لَكُمْ أَن تَرِثُوا۟ ٱلنِّسَآءَ كَرْهًا ۖ
وَلَا تَعْضُلُوهُنَّ لِتَذْهَبُوا۟ بِبَعْضِ
مَآ ءَاتَيْتُمُوهُنَّ إِلَّآ أَن يَأْتِينَ
بِفَٰحِشَةٍ مُّبَيِّنَةٍ ۚ وَعَاشِرُوهُنَّ
بِٱلْمَعْرُوفِ ۚ فَإِن كَرِهْتُمُوهُنَّ
فَعَسَىٰٓ أَن تَكْرَهُوا۟ شَيْـًٔا وَيَجْعَلَ

19. Yaaa ayyuhal-laz̲eena aamanoo laa yaḥillu lakum an tarisun-nisaaa'a karhan wa laa ta'ḍuloohunna litaz̲haboo biba'ḍi maaa aataytumoohunna illaaa añy-yaåteena bifaaḥishatim-mubayyinah; wa 'aashiroo-hunna bilma'roof; fa-in karihtumoohunna fa'asaaa an takrahoo shay'añ w-wa yaj'alal-

19. O you who believe! you are forbidden to inherit women against their will. Nor should you treat them with harshness, that you may take away part of the dower you have given them,- except where they have been guilty of open lewdness; on the contrary live with them on a footing of kindness and equity. If you take a dislike to them it may be that you dislike a thing, and

Allah brings about through it a great deal of good.

laahu feehi khayran kas̲eeraa.

اللّٰهُ فِيْهِ خَيْرًا كَثِيْرًا ﴿١٩﴾

20. But if you decide to take one wife in place of another, even if you had given the latter a whole treasure for dower, Take not the least bit of it back: will you take it by slander and manifest wrong?

20. Wa in arattumustib-daala zawjim-makaana zawjin wa aataytum iḥdaahunna qinṭaaran falaa taåkhuz̲oo minhu shay'aa; ataåkhuz̲oonahoo buhtaanañw-wa is̲mam-mubeenaa.

وَاِنْ اَرَدْتُّمُ اسْتِبْدَالَ زَوْجٍ مَّكَانَ
زَوْجٍ ۙ وَّاٰتَيْتُمْ اِحْدٰىهُنَّ قِنْطَارًا فَلَا
تَاْخُذُوْا مِنْهُ شَيْـًٔا ؕ اَتَاْخُذُوْنَهٗ
بُهْتَانًا وَّاِثْمًا مُّبِيْنًا ﴿٢٠﴾

21. And how could you take it when you have gone in to each other, and they have taken from you a solemn covenant?

21. Wa kayfa taåkhuz̲oonahoo wa qad afḍaa ba'ḍukum ilaa ba'ḍiñw-wa akhaz̲na minkum mees̲aaqan ghaleeẓaa.

وَكَيْفَ تَاْخُذُوْنَهٗ وَقَدْ اَفْضٰى
بَعْضُكُمْ اِلٰى بَعْضٍ وَّاَخَذْنَ
مِنْكُمْ مِّيْثَاقًا غَلِيْظًا ﴿٢١﴾

22. And marry not women whom your fathers married,- except what is past: it was shameful and odious,- an abominable custom indeed.

22. Wa laa tankihoo maa nakaḥa aabaaa'ukum minan-nisaaa'i illaa maa qad salaf; innahoo kaana faaḥishatañw-wa maqtañw wa saaa'a sabeelaa. **(Section 3)**

وَلَا تَنْكِحُوْا مَا نَكَحَ اٰبَآؤُكُمْ مِّنَ
النِّسَآءِ اِلَّا مَا قَدْ سَلَفَ ؕ اِنَّهٗ كَانَ
فَاحِشَةً وَّمَقْتًا ؕ وَسَآءَ سَبِيْلًا ﴿٢٢﴾ ع

23. Prohibited to you (for marriage) are:- your mothers, daughters, sisters; father's sisters, mother's sisters; brother's daughters, sister's daughters; foster-mothers (who gave you suck), foster-sisters; your wives' mothers; your step-daughters under your guardian-ship, born of your wives to whom you have gone in, - no prohibition if you have not gone in; - (those who have been) wives of your sons proceeding from your loins; and two sisters in wedlock at one and the same time, except for what is past; for Allah is Oft-Forgiving, Most Merciful;-

23. Ḥurrimat 'alaykum ummahaatukum wa banaatukum wa akhawaatukum wa 'ammaatukum wa khaalaatukum wa banaatul-akhi wa banaatul-ukhti wa ummahaatu-kumul-laateee arḍa'nakum wa akhawaatu-kum-minarraḍaa'ati wa ummahaatu nisaaa'ikum wa rabaaa'ibukumul-laatee fee ḥujoorikum min nisaaa'ikumul-laatee dakhaltum-bihinna Fa-il-lam takoonoo dakhaltum bihinna falaa junaaḥa 'alaykum wa halaaa'ilu abnaaa'ikumul-laz̲eena min aṣlaabikum wa an tajma'oo baynal-ukhtayni illaa maa qad salaf; innallaaha kaana Ghafoorar-Raḥeemaa.

حُرِّمَتْ عَلَيْكُمْ اُمَّهٰتُكُمْ وَبَنٰتُكُمْ
وَاَخَوٰتُكُمْ وَعَمّٰتُكُمْ وَخٰلٰتُكُمْ
وَبَنٰتُ الْاَخِ وَبَنٰتُ الْاُخْتِ وَ
اُمَّهٰتُكُمُ الّٰتِيْٓ اَرْضَعْنَكُمْ وَاَخَوٰتُكُمْ
مِّنَ الرَّضَاعَةِ وَاُمَّهٰتُ نِسَآئِكُمْ
وَرَبَآئِبُكُمُ الّٰتِيْ فِيْ حُجُوْرِكُمْ
مِّنْ نِّسَآئِكُمُ الّٰتِيْ دَخَلْتُمْ بِهِنَّ ۫
فَاِنْ لَّمْ تَكُوْنُوْا دَخَلْتُمْ بِهِنَّ فَلَا
جُنَاحَ عَلَيْكُمْ ۫ وَحَلَآئِلُ اَبْنَآئِكُمُ
الَّذِيْنَ مِنْ اَصْلَابِكُمْ ۙ وَاَنْ تَجْمَعُوْا
بَيْنَ الْاُخْتَيْنِ اِلَّا مَا قَدْ سَلَفَ ؕ
اِنَّ اللّٰهَ كَانَ غَفُوْرًا رَّحِيْمًا ﴿٢٣﴾

24. Also (prohibited are) women already married, except those whom your right hands possess: thus has Allah ordained (prohi-bitions) against you: except for these, all others are lawful,

24. Walmuḥṣanaatu minan-nisaaa'i illaa maa malakat aymaanukum kitaabal-laahi 'alaykum; wa uḥilla lakum maa waraaa'a z̲aalikum

وَّالْمُحْصَنٰتُ مِنَ النِّسَآءِ اِلَّا مَا
مَلَكَتْ اَيْمَانُكُمْ ۚ كِتٰبَ اللّٰهِ
عَلَيْكُمْ ۚ وَاُحِلَّ لَكُمْ مَّا وَرَآءَ ذٰلِكُمْ

الجزء الخامس (٥)

Ikhfa اخفاء | Ghunna غنّہ | Ikhfa Meem Saakin اخفاءمیم ساکن | Idghaam ادغام | Qalqala قلقلہ | Qalb قلب | Idghaam Meem Saakin ادغام میم ساکن

provided you seek (them in marriage) with gifts from your property,- desiring chastity, not lust, seeing that you derive benefit from them, give them their dowers (at least) as prescribed; but if, after a dower is prescribed, agree mutually (to vary it), there is no blame on you, and Allah is All-knowing, All-wise.

an tabtaghoo bi-amwaali-kum muḥṣineena ghayra musaafiḥeen; famastamta'tum bihee minhunna fa-aatoohunna ujoorahunna fareeḍah; wa laa junaaḥa 'alaykum feemaa taraaḍaytum bihee mim-ba'dil-fareeḍah; innal-laaha kaana 'Aleeman Ḥakeemaa.

أَن تَبْتَغُوا بِأَمْوَالِكُم مُّحْصِنِينَ
غَيْرَ مُسَافِحِينَ ۚ فَمَا اسْتَمْتَعْتُم بِهِ
مِنْهُنَّ فَآتُوهُنَّ أُجُورَهُنَّ
فَرِيضَةً ۚ وَلَا جُنَاحَ عَلَيْكُمْ فِيمَا
تَرَاضَيْتُم بِهِ مِن بَعْدِ الْفَرِيضَةِ ۚ
إِنَّ اللَّهَ كَانَ عَلِيمًا حَكِيمًا ﴿٢٤﴾

25. If any of you have not the means wherewith to wed free believing women, they may wed believing girls from among those whom your right hands possess: and Allah has full knowledge about your faith. You are one from another: wed them with the leave of their owners, and give them their dowers, according to what is reasonable: they should be chaste, not lustful, nor taking paramours: when they are taken in wedlock, if they fall into shame, their punishment is half that for free women. This (permission) is for those among you who fear sin; but it is better for you that you practise self-restraint. And Allah is Oft-forgiving, Most Merciful.

25. Wa mal-lam yastaṭi' minkum ṭawlan añy-yankiḥal-muḥṣanaatil-mu'minaati famim-maa malakat aymaanukum min fatayaatikumul-mu'minaat; wallaahu a'lamu bi-eemaanikum; ba'ḍukum mim ba'ḍ; fankiḥoohunna bi-izni ahlihinna wa aatoohunna ujoorahunna bilma'roofi muḥṣanaatin ghayra musaa-fiḥ aatiñw-wa laa muttakhizaati akhdaan; fa-izaaa uḥṣinna fa-in atayna bifaaḥishatin fa-'alayhinna niṣfu maa 'alal-muḥṣanaati minal-'azaab; zaalika liman khashiyal-'anata minkum; wa an taṣbiroo khayrul-lakum; wallaahu Ghafoorur-Raḥeem. **(Section 4)**

وَمَن لَّمْ يَسْتَطِعْ مِنكُمْ طَوْلًا أَن
يَنكِحَ الْمُحْصَنَاتِ الْمُؤْمِنَاتِ فَمِن
مَّا مَلَكَتْ أَيْمَانُكُم مِّن فَتَيَاتِكُمُ
الْمُؤْمِنَاتِ ۚ وَاللَّهُ أَعْلَمُ بِإِيمَانِكُم ۚ
بَعْضُكُم مِّن بَعْضٍ ۚ فَانكِحُوهُنَّ
بِإِذْنِ أَهْلِهِنَّ وَآتُوهُنَّ أُجُورَهُنَّ
بِالْمَعْرُوفِ مُحْصَنَاتٍ غَيْرَ مُسَافِحَاتٍ
وَلَا مُتَّخِذَاتِ أَخْدَانٍ ۚ فَإِذَا أُحْصِنَّ
فَإِنْ أَتَيْنَ بِفَاحِشَةٍ فَعَلَيْهِنَّ
نِصْفُ مَا عَلَى الْمُحْصَنَاتِ مِنَ
الْعَذَابِ ۚ ذَٰلِكَ لِمَنْ خَشِيَ الْعَنَتَ
مِنكُمْ ۚ وَأَن تَصْبِرُوا خَيْرٌ لَّكُمْ ۗ
وَاللَّهُ غَفُورٌ رَّحِيمٌ ﴿٢٥﴾ ع

26. Allah wishes to make clear to you and to show you the ordinances of those before you; and (He does wish to) turn to you (in Mercy): and Allah is All-knowing, All-wise.

26. Yureedul-laahu liyubayyina lakum wa yahdiyakum sunanal-lazeena min qablikum wa yatooba 'alaykum; wallaahu 'Aleemun Ḥakeem.

يُرِيدُ اللَّهُ لِيُبَيِّنَ لَكُمْ وَيَهْدِيَكُمْ
سُنَنَ الَّذِينَ مِن قَبْلِكُمْ وَيَتُوبَ
عَلَيْكُمْ ۗ وَاللَّهُ عَلِيمٌ حَكِيمٌ ﴿٢٦﴾

27. Allah wishes to turn to you, but the wish of those who follow their lusts is that you should turn away (from Him),- far, far away.

27. Wallaahu yureedu añy-yatooba 'alaykum wa yureedul-lazeena yattabi'oonash-shahawaati an tameeloo maylan 'azeemaa.

وَاللَّهُ يُرِيدُ أَن يَتُوبَ عَلَيْكُمْ
وَيُرِيدُ الَّذِينَ يَتَّبِعُونَ الشَّهَوَاتِ
أَن تَمِيلُوا مَيْلًا عَظِيمًا ﴿٢٧﴾

28. Allah wishes to lighten your (difficulties):

28. Yureedul-laahu añy-yukhaffifa 'ankum;

يُرِيدُ اللَّهُ أَن يُخَفِّفَ عَنكُمْ ۚ

Ikhfa اخفاء | Ghunna غُنّہ | Ikhfa Meem Saakin اخفاء میم ساکن | Idghaam ادغام | Qalqala قلقلہ | Qalb قلب | Idghaam Meem Saakin ادغام میم ساکن

وَخُلِقَ الْإِنْسَانُ ضَعِيفًا ﴿٢٨﴾

wa khuliqal-insaanu ḍa‘eefaa.

for man was created weak (in flesh).

يَا أَيُّهَا الَّذِينَ آمَنُوا لَا تَأْكُلُوا
أَمْوَالَكُمْ بَيْنَكُمْ بِالْبَاطِلِ إِلَّا
أَنْ تَكُونَ تِجَارَةً عَنْ تَرَاضٍ مِنْكُمْ ۚ
وَلَا تَقْتُلُوا أَنْفُسَكُمْ ۚ إِنَّ اللَّهَ كَانَ
بِكُمْ رَحِيمًا ﴿٢٩﴾

29. Yaaa ayyuhal-lazeena aamanoo laa taåkulooo amwaalakum baynakum bilbaaṭili 'illaaa an takoona tijaaratan ‘an taraaḍim minkum; wa laa taqtulooo anfusakum; innal-laaha kaana bikum Raḥeemaa.

29. O you who believe! Eat not up your property among yourselves in vanities: but let there be among you traffic and trade by mutual good-will: nor kill (or destroy) yourselves: for verily Allah has been to you Most Merciful!

وَمَنْ يَفْعَلْ ذَٰلِكَ عُدْوَانًا وَظُلْمًا
فَسَوْفَ نُصْلِيهِ نَارًا ۚ وَكَانَ ذَٰلِكَ
عَلَى اللَّهِ يَسِيرًا ﴿٣٠﴾

30. Wa mañy-yaf‘al zaalika ‘udwaanañw-wa ẓulman fasawfa nuṣleehi Naaraa; wa kaana zaalika ‘alal-laahi yaseeraa.

30. If any do that in rancour and injustice,- soon shall We cast them into the Fire: and easy it is for Allah.

إِنْ تَجْتَنِبُوا كَبَائِرَ مَا تُنْهَوْنَ عَنْهُ
نُكَفِّرْ عَنْكُمْ سَيِّئَاتِكُمْ وَنُدْخِلْكُمْ
مُدْخَلًا كَرِيمًا ﴿٣١﴾

31. In tajtaniboo kabaaa'ira maa tunhawna ‘anhu nukaffir ‘ankum sayyi-aatikum wa nudkhilkum mudkhalan kareemaa.

31. If you (but) eschew the most heinous of the things which you are forbidden to do, We shall expel out of you all the evil in you, and admit you to a gate of great honour.

وَلَا تَتَمَنَّوْا مَا فَضَّلَ اللَّهُ بِهِ بَعْضَكُمْ
عَلَىٰ بَعْضٍ ۚ لِلرِّجَالِ نَصِيبٌ مِمَّا
اكْتَسَبُوا ۖ وَلِلنِّسَاءِ نَصِيبٌ مِمَّا
اكْتَسَبْنَ ۚ وَاسْأَلُوا اللَّهَ مِنْ فَضْلِهِ ۗ
إِنَّ اللَّهَ كَانَ بِكُلِّ شَيْءٍ عَلِيمًا ﴿٣٢﴾

32. Wa laa tatamannaw maa faḍḍalal-laahu bihee ba‘ḍakum ‘alaa ba‘ḍ; lirrijaali naṣeebum-mimmak-tasaboo wa linnisaaa'i naṣeebum-mimmak-tasabna; was'alullaaha min faḍlih; innal-laaha kaana bikulli shay'in ‘Aleemaa.

32. And in no wise covet those things in which Allah has bestowed His gifts more freely on some of you than on others: to men is allotted what they earn, and to women what they earn: but ask Allah of His bounty. For Allah has full knowledge of all things.

وَلِكُلٍّ جَعَلْنَا مَوَالِيَ مِمَّا تَرَكَ الْوَالِدَانِ
وَالْأَقْرَبُونَ ۚ وَالَّذِينَ عَقَدَتْ
أَيْمَانُكُمْ فَآتُوهُمْ نَصِيبَهُمْ ۚ إِنَّ
اللَّهَ كَانَ عَلَىٰ كُلِّ شَيْءٍ شَهِيدًا ﴿٣٣﴾

33. Wa likullin ja‘alnaa mawaaliya mimmaa tarakal-waalidaani wal-aqraboon; wallazeena ‘aqadat aymaanukum fa-aatoohum naṣeebahum; innal-laaha kaana ‘alaa kulli shay'in Shaheedaa. **(Section 5)**

33. To (benefit) every one, We have appointed shares and heirs to property left by parents and relatives. To those, also, to whom your right hand was pledged, give their due portion. For truly Allah is witness to all things.

الرِّجَالُ قَوَّامُونَ عَلَى النِّسَاءِ بِمَا
فَضَّلَ اللَّهُ بَعْضَهُمْ عَلَىٰ بَعْضٍ وَبِمَا
أَنْفَقُوا مِنْ أَمْوَالِهِمْ ۚ فَالصَّالِحَاتُ
قَانِتَاتٌ حَافِظَاتٌ لِلْغَيْبِ بِمَا حَفِظَ
اللَّهُ ۚ وَاللَّاتِي تَخَافُونَ نُشُوزَهُنَّ

34. Arrijaalu qawwaamoona ‘alan-nisaaa'i bimaa faḍḍalallaahu ba‘ḍahum ‘alaa ba‘ḍiñw-wa bimaaa-anfaqoo min amwaalihim; faṣṣaaliḥaatu qaanitaatun ḥaafiẓaatul-lilghaybi bimaa ḥafiẓal-laah; wallaatee takhaafoona nushoozahunna

34. Men are the protectors and maintainers of women, because Allah has given the one more (strength) than the other, and because they support them from their means. Therefore, the righteous women are devoutly obedient, and guard in (the husband's) absence what Allah would have them guard. As to those women on whose part you fear disloyalty and ill-conduct,

Ikhfa اخفاء | Ghunna غنّہ | Ikhfa Meem Saakin اخفاء میم ساکن | Idghaam ادغام | Qalqala قلقلہ | Qalb قلب | Idghaam Meem Saakin ادغام میم ساکن

admonish them (first), (next), refuse to share their beds, (and last) beat them (lightly); but if they return to obedience, seek not against them means (of annoyance): for Allah is Most High, Great (above you all).

fa-'izoohunna wahjuroohunna fil-maḍaaji'i waḍriboohunna fa-in aṭa'nakum falaa tabghoo 'alayhinna sabeelaa; innallaaha kaana 'Aliyyan Kabeeraa.

فَعِظُوهُنَّ وَاهْجُرُوهُنَّ فِي الْمَضَاجِعِ
وَاضْرِبُوهُنَّ ۚ فَإِنْ أَطَعْنَكُمْ فَلَا
تَبْغُوا عَلَيْهِنَّ سَبِيلًا ۗ إِنَّ اللَّهَ
كَانَ عَلِيًّا كَبِيرًا ﴿٣٤﴾

35. If you fear a breach between them twain, appoint (two) arbiters, one from his family, and the other from hers; if they wish for peace, Allah will cause their reconciliation: for Allah has full knowledge, and is acquainted with all things.

35. Wa in khiftum shiqaaqa bayni-himaa fab'asoo ḥakamam-min ahlihee wa ḥakamam-min ahlihaa; iñy-yureedaaa iṣlaaḥañy-yuwaffiqil-laahu baynahumaa; innal-laaha kaana 'Aleeman Khabeeraa.

وَإِنْ خِفْتُمْ شِقَاقَ بَيْنِهِمَا فَابْعَثُوا
حَكَمًا مِّنْ أَهْلِهِ وَحَكَمًا مِّنْ
أَهْلِهَا ۚ إِنْ يُرِيدَا إِصْلَاحًا
يُوَفِّقِ اللَّهُ بَيْنَهُمَا ۗ إِنَّ اللَّهَ كَانَ
عَلِيمًا خَبِيرًا ﴿٣٥﴾

36. Serve Allah, and join not any partners with Him; and do good - to parents, kinsfolk, orphans, those in need, neighbours who are near, neighbours who are strangers, the companion by your side, the way-farer (you meet), and what your right hands possess: for Allah loves not the arrogant, the vainglorious.

36. Wa'budul-laaha wa laa tushrikoo bihee shay'añw-wa bilwaalidayni iḥsaanañw-wa bizil-qurbaa walyataamaa walmasaakeeni waljaari zilqurbaa waljaaril-junubi waṣṣaaḥibi biljambi wabnis-sabeeli wa maa malakat aymaanukum; innal-laaha laa yuḥibbu man kaana mukhtaalan fakhooraa.

وَاعْبُدُوا اللَّهَ وَلَا تُشْرِكُوا بِهِ
شَيْئًا وَّبِالْوَالِدَيْنِ إِحْسَانًا وَّبِذِي
الْقُرْبَىٰ وَالْيَتَامَىٰ وَالْمَسَاكِينِ وَ
الْجَارِ ذِي الْقُرْبَىٰ وَالْجَارِ الْجُنُبِ
وَالصَّاحِبِ بِالْجَنْبِ وَابْنِ السَّبِيلِ
وَمَا مَلَكَتْ أَيْمَانُكُمْ ۗ إِنَّ اللَّهَ
لَا يُحِبُّ مَنْ كَانَ مُخْتَالًا فَخُورًا ﴿٣٦﴾

37. (Nor) those who are niggardly or enjoin niggardliness on others, or hide the bounties which Allah has bestowed on them; for We have prepared, for those who resist Faith, a punishment that steeps them in contempt;-

37. Allazeena yabkhaloona wa yaâmuroonan-naasa bilbukhli wa yaktumoona maaa aataahumullaahu min faḍlih; wa-a'tadnaa lilkaafireena 'azaabam-muheenaa.

الَّذِينَ يَبْخَلُونَ وَيَأْمُرُونَ
النَّاسَ بِالْبُخْلِ وَيَكْتُمُونَ مَا
آتَاهُمُ اللَّهُ مِنْ فَضْلِهِ ۗ وَأَعْتَدْنَا
لِلْكَافِرِينَ عَذَابًا مُّهِينًا ﴿٣٧﴾

38. Nor those who spend of their substance, to be seen of men, but have no faith in Allah and the Last Day: If any take the Satan for their intimate, what a dreadful intimate he is!

38. Wallazeena yunfiqoona amwaalahum ri'aaa'an-naasi wa laa yu'minoona billaahi wa laa bil-Yawmil-Aakhir; wa mañy-yakunish-Shayṭaanu lahoo qareenan fasaaa'a qareenaa.

وَالَّذِينَ يُنْفِقُونَ أَمْوَالَهُمْ رِئَاءَ
النَّاسِ وَلَا يُؤْمِنُونَ بِاللَّهِ وَلَا
بِالْيَوْمِ الْآخِرِ ۗ وَمَنْ يَكُنِ الشَّيْطَانُ
لَهُ قَرِينًا فَسَاءَ قَرِينًا ﴿٣٨﴾

39. And what burden were it on them if they had faith in Allah and in the Last Day, and they spent out of what Allah has given them for sustenance?

39. Wa maazaa 'alayhim law aamanoo billaahi wal-Yawmil-Aakhiri wa anfaqoo mimmaa razaqahumul-

وَمَاذَا عَلَيْهِمْ لَوْ آمَنُوا بِاللَّهِ وَ
الْيَوْمِ الْآخِرِ وَأَنْفَقُوا مِمَّا رَزَقَهُمُ

Ikhfa اخفاء | Ghunna غُنّہ | Ikhfa Meem Saakin اخفاء میم ساکن | Idghaam ادغام | Qalqala قلقلہ | Qalb قلب | Idghaam Meem Saakin ادغام میم ساکن

For Allah has full knowledge of them.

laah; wa kaanallaahu bihim 'Aleemaa.

اللّٰهُ ۚ وَكَانَ اللّٰهُ بِهِمْ عَلِيمًا ﴿٣٩﴾

40. Allah is never unjust in the least degree: if there is any good (done), He doubles it, and gives from His Own Presence a great reward.

40. Innal-laaha laa yaẓlimu misqaala zarratiñw wa in taku ḥasanatañy-yuḍaa'ifhaa wa yu'ti mil-ladunhu ajran 'aẓeemaa.

إِنَّ اللّٰهَ لَا يَظْلِمُ مِثْقَالَ ذَرَّةٍ ۚ وَإِن
تَكُ حَسَنَةً يُضٰعِفْهَا وَيُؤْتِ مِن
لَّدُنْهُ أَجْرًا عَظِيمًا ﴿٤٠﴾

41. How then if We brought from each People a witness, and We brought you as a witness against these People!

41. Fakayfa izaa ji'naa min kulli ummatim bishaheediñw-wa ji'naa bika 'alaa haaa'ulaaa'i Shaheedaa.

فَكَيْفَ إِذَا جِئْنَا مِن كُلِّ أُمَّةٍ
بِشَهِيدٍ وَجِئْنَا بِكَ عَلٰى هٰٓؤُلَآءِ
شَهِيدًا ﴿٤١﴾

42. On that day those who reject Faith and disobey the Apostle will wish that the earth were made one with them: but never will they hide a single fact from Allah!

42. Yawma'iziñy-yawad-dullazeena kafaroo wa 'aṣawur-Rasoola law tusawwaa bihimul-arḍu wa laa yaktumoonal-laaha ḥadeesaa. **(Section 6)**

يَوْمَئِذٍ يَوَدُّ الَّذِينَ كَفَرُوا وَعَصَوُا
الرَّسُولَ لَوْ تُسَوّٰى بِهِمُ الْأَرْضُ ۗ
وَلَا يَكْتُمُونَ اللّٰهَ حَدِيثًا ﴿٤٢﴾

43. O you who believe! Approach not prayers with a mind befogged, until you can understand all that you say,- nor in a state of ceremonial impurity (except when travelling on the road), until after washing your whole body. If you are ill, or on a journey, or one of you comes from offices of nature, or you have been in contact with women, and you find no water, then take for yourselves clean sand or earth, and rub there with your faces and hands. For Allah does blot out sins and forgive again and again.

43. Yaaa ayyuhal-lazeena aamanoo laa taqrabuṣ-Ṣalaata wa antum sukaaraa ḥattaa ta'lamoo maa taqooloona wa laa junuban illaa 'aabiree sabeelin ḥattaa taghtasiloo; wa in kuntum marḍaaa aw 'alaa safarin aw jaaa'a aḥadum-minkum minal-ghaaa'iṭi aw laamastumun-nisaaa'a falam tajidoo maaa'an fatayam-mamoo ṣa'eedan ṭayyiban famsaḥoo biwujoohikum wa aydeekum; innal-laaha kaana 'Afuwwan Ghafooraa.

يٰٓأَيُّهَا الَّذِينَ ءَامَنُوا لَا تَقْرَبُوا
الصَّلٰوةَ وَأَنتُمْ سُكٰرٰى حَتّٰى تَعْلَمُوا
مَا تَقُولُونَ وَلَا جُنُبًا إِلَّا عَابِرِى
سَبِيلٍ حَتّٰى تَغْتَسِلُوا ۚ وَإِن كُنتُم
مَّرْضٰٓى أَوْ عَلٰى سَفَرٍ أَوْ جَآءَ أَحَدٌ
مِّنكُم مِّنَ الْغَآئِطِ أَوْ لٰمَسْتُمُ
النِّسَآءَ فَلَمْ تَجِدُوا مَآءً فَتَيَمَّمُوا
صَعِيدًا طَيِّبًا فَامْسَحُوا بِوُجُوهِكُمْ
وَأَيْدِيكُمْ ۗ إِنَّ اللّٰهَ كَانَ عَفُوًّا
غَفُورًا ﴿٤٣﴾

44. Have you not turned your vision to those who were given a portion of the Book? They traffic in error, and wish that you should lose the right path.

44. Alam tara ilal-lazeena ootoo naṣeebam-minal-Kitaabi yashtaroonaḍ-ḍalaalata wa yureedoona an taḍillus-sabeel.

أَلَمْ تَرَ إِلَى الَّذِينَ أُوتُوا نَصِيبًا
مِّنَ الْكِتٰبِ يَشْتَرُونَ الضَّلٰلَةَ
وَيُرِيدُونَ أَن تَضِلُّوا السَّبِيلَ ﴿٤٤﴾

45. But Allah has full knowledge of your enemies: Allah is enough for a Protector, and Allah is enough for a Helper.

45. Wallaahu a'lamu bi-a'daaa'i-kum; wa kafaa billaahi waliyyañw-wa kafaa billaahi naṣeeraa.

وَاللّٰهُ أَعْلَمُ بِأَعْدَآئِكُمْ ۚ وَكَفٰى بِاللّٰهِ
وَلِيًّا ۙ وَكَفٰى بِاللّٰهِ نَصِيرًا ﴿٤٥﴾

46. Of the Jews there are those who displace

46. Minal-lazeena haadoo yuḥarrifoonal-

مِّنَ الَّذِينَ هَادُوا يُحَرِّفُونَ

Ikhfa اخفاء | Ghunna غنّہ | Ikhfa Meem Saakin اخفاء میم ساکن | Idghaam ادغام | Qalqala قلقلہ | Qalb قلب | Idghaam Meem Saakin ادغام میم ساکن

words from their (right) places, and say: "We hear and we disobey"; and "Hear what is not heard"; and "Ra'ina"; with a twist of their tongues and a slander to Faith. If only they had said: "We hear and we obey"; and "Do hear"; and "Do look at us"; it would have been better for them, and more proper; but Allah has cursed them for their Unbelief; and but few of them will believe.

Kalima-'am-mawaaḍi'ihee wa yaqooloona sami'naa wa 'aṣaynaa wasma' ghayra musma'iñw-wa raa'inaa layyam bi-alsinatihim wa ṭa'nan fid-deen; wa law annahum qaaloo sami'naa wa aṭa'naa wasma' wanẓurnaa lakaana khayral-lahum wa aqwama wa laakil-la-'anahumul-laahu bikufrihim falaa yu'minoona illaa qaleela

الْكَلِمَ عَن مَّوَاضِعِهِ وَيَقُولُونَ
سَمِعْنَا وَعَصَيْنَا وَاسْمَعْ غَيْرَ مُسْمَعٍ
وَرَاعِنَا لَيًّا بِأَلْسِنَتِهِمْ وَطَعْنًا فِي
الدِّينِ ۚ وَلَوْ أَنَّهُمْ قَالُوا سَمِعْنَا
وَأَطَعْنَا وَاسْمَعْ وَانظُرْنَا لَكَانَ
خَيْرًا لَّهُمْ وَأَقْوَمَ وَلَٰكِن لَّعَنَهُمُ اللَّهُ
بِكُفْرِهِمْ فَلَا يُؤْمِنُونَ إِلَّا قَلِيلًا ﴿٤٦﴾

47. O you People of the Book! believe in what We have (now) revealed, confirming what was (already) with you, before We change the face and fame of some (of you) beyond all recognition, and turn them hindwards, or curse them as We cursed the Sabbath-breakers, for the decision of Allah must be carried out.

47. Yaaa-ayyuhal-lazeena ootul-Kitaaba aaminoo bimaa nazzalnaa muṣaddiqallimaa ma'akum min qabli an naṭmisa wujoohan fanaruddahaa 'alaaa adbaarihaaa aw nal'anahum kamaa la'annaaa Aṣḥaabas-Sabt; wa kaana amrul-laahi maf'oolaa.

يَا أَيُّهَا الَّذِينَ أُوتُوا الْكِتَابَ آمِنُوا
بِمَا نَزَّلْنَا مُصَدِّقًا لِّمَا مَعَكُم
مِّن قَبْلِ أَن نَّطْمِسَ وُجُوهًا
فَنَرُدَّهَا عَلَىٰ أَدْبَارِهَا أَوْ نَلْعَنَهُمْ
كَمَا لَعَنَّا أَصْحَابَ السَّبْتِ ۚ وَكَانَ
أَمْرُ اللَّهِ مَفْعُولًا ﴿٤٧﴾

48. Allah forgives not that partners should be set up with Him; but He forgives anything else, to whom He pleases; to set up partners with Allah is to devise a sin most heinous indeed.

48. Innal-laaha laa yaghfiru añy-yushraka bihee wa yaghfiru maa doona zaalika limañy-yashaaa'; wa mañy-yushrik billaahi faqadif-taraaa isman 'aẓeemaa.

إِنَّ اللَّهَ لَا يَغْفِرُ أَن يُشْرَكَ بِهِ
وَيَغْفِرُ مَا دُونَ ذَٰلِكَ لِمَن يَشَاءُ ۚ
وَمَن يُشْرِكْ بِاللَّهِ فَقَدِ افْتَرَىٰ
إِثْمًا عَظِيمًا ﴿٤٨﴾

49. Have you not turned your vision to those who claim sanctity for themselves? Nay- but Allah does sanctify whom He pleases. But never will they fail to receive justice in the least little thing.

49. Alam tara ilal-lazeena yuzakkoona anfusahum; balil-laahu yuzakkee mañy-yashaaa'u wa laa yuẓlamoona fateelaa.

أَلَمْ تَرَ إِلَى الَّذِينَ يُزَكُّونَ أَنفُسَهُم ۚ
بَلِ اللَّهُ يُزَكِّي مَن يَشَاءُ وَلَا
يُظْلَمُونَ فَتِيلًا ﴿٤٩﴾

50. See! how they invent a lie against Allah! but that by itself is a manifest sin!

50. Unẓur kayfa yaftaroona 'alal-laahil-kazib, wa kafaa biheee ismam-mubeenaa.
(Section 7)

انظُرْ كَيْفَ يَفْتَرُونَ عَلَى اللَّهِ
الْكَذِبَ ۖ وَكَفَىٰ بِهِ إِثْمًا مُّبِينًا ﴿٥٠﴾ ع ٨

51. Have you not turned your vision to those who were given a portion of the Book? They believe in sorcery and evil, and say to the Unbelievers that they are better guided in the (right) way than the Believers!

51. Alam tara-ilal-lazeena 'ootoo naṣeebam-minal-Kitaabi yu'minoona bil-Jibti waṭ-Ṭaaghooti wa yaqooloona lillazeena kafaroo haaa-ulaaa'i ahdaa minal-lazeena aamanoo sabeelaa.

أَلَمْ تَرَ إِلَى الَّذِينَ أُوتُوا نَصِيبًا مِّنَ
الْكِتَابِ يُؤْمِنُونَ بِالْجِبْتِ وَالطَّاغُوتِ
وَيَقُولُونَ لِلَّذِينَ كَفَرُوا هَٰؤُلَاءِ أَهْدَىٰ
مِنَ الَّذِينَ آمَنُوا سَبِيلًا ﴿٥١﴾

Ikhfa اخفاء | Ghunna غُنّہ | Ikhfa Meem Saakin اخفاء میم ساکن | Idghaam ادغام | Qalqala قلقلہ | Qalb قلب | Idghaam Meem Saakin ادغام میم ساکن

52. They are (men) whom Allah has cursed: and those whom Allah has cursed, you will find, have no one to help.

52. Ulaaa'ikal-lazeena la'anahumul-laahu wa mañy-yal'anil-
laahu falan tajida lahoo
naṣeeraa.

اُولٰٓئِكَ الَّذِيْنَ لَعَنَهُمُ اللّٰهُ ؕ وَمَنْ
يَّلْعَنِ اللّٰهُ فَلَنْ تَجِدَ لَهٗ نَصِيْرًا ؕ ﴿٥٢﴾

53. Have they a share in dominion or power? Behold, they give not a farthing to their fellow-men.

53. Am lahum naṣeebum-
minal-mulki fa-izal-laa yu'too-
nan-naasa naqeeraa.

اَمْ لَهُمْ نَصِيْبٌ مِّنَ الْمُلْكِ فَاِذًا
لَّا يُؤْتُوْنَ النَّاسَ نَقِيْرًا ۙ ﴿٥٣﴾

54. Or do they envy mankind for what Allah has given them of his bounty? But We had already given the people of Abraham the Book and wisdom, and conferred upon them a great kingdom.

54. Am yaḥsudoonan-naasa
'alaa maaa aataahumul-laahu
min faḍlihee faqad aataynaaa
Aala Ibraaheemal-Kitaaba wal-
Ḥikmata wa aataynaahum
mulkan 'aẓeemaa.

اَمْ يَحْسُدُوْنَ النَّاسَ عَلٰى مَآ
اٰتٰىهُمُ اللّٰهُ مِنْ فَضْلِهٖ ۚ فَقَدْ
اٰتَيْنَآ اٰلَ اِبْرٰهِيْمَ الْكِتٰبَ وَالْحِكْمَةَ
وَاٰتَيْنٰهُمْ مُّلْكًا عَظِيْمًا ﴿٥٤﴾

55. Some of them believed, and some of them averted their faces from him: and enough is Hell for a burning fire.

55. Faminhum man aamana
bihee wa minhum man ṣadda
'anh; wa kafaa bi-Jahannama
sa'eeraa.

فَمِنْهُمْ مَّنْ اٰمَنَ بِهٖ وَمِنْهُمْ مَّنْ
صَدَّ عَنْهُ ؕ وَكَفٰى بِجَهَنَّمَ سَعِيْرًا ﴿٥٥﴾

56. Those who reject Our Signs, We shall soon cast (them) into the Fire: as often as their skins are roasted through, We shall change them for fresh skins, that they may taste the Chastisement: for Allah is Exalted in Power, Wise.

56. Innal-lazeena kafaroo bi-
Aayaatinaa sawfa nuṣleehim
Naaran kullamaa naḍijat
julooduhum baddalnaahum
juloodan ghayrahaa liyazooqul-
'azaab; innallaaha kaana
'Azeezan Ḥakeemaa.

اِنَّ الَّذِيْنَ كَفَرُوْا بِاٰيٰتِنَا سَوْفَ
نُصْلِيْهِمْ نَارًا ؕ كُلَّمَا نَضِجَتْ
جُلُوْدُهُمْ بَدَّلْنٰهُمْ جُلُوْدًا غَيْرَهَا
لِيَذُوْقُوا الْعَذَابَ ؕ اِنَّ اللّٰهَ كَانَ
عَزِيْزًا حَكِيْمًا ﴿٥٦﴾

الربع

57. But those who believe and do deeds of righteousness, We shall soon admit (them) to Gardens, with rivers flowing beneath, - their eternal home: therein shall they have Companions pure and holy: We shall admit them to shades, cool and ever deepening.

57. Wallazeena aamanoo wa
'amiluṣ-ṣaaliḥaati sanud-
khiluhum Jannaatin tajree min
taḥtihal-anhaaru khaalideena
feehaaa abadaa, lahum feehaaa
azwaajum-muṭahharatuñw-wa
nudkhiluhum ẓillan ẓaleelaa.

وَالَّذِيْنَ اٰمَنُوْا وَعَمِلُوا الصّٰلِحٰتِ
سَنُدْخِلُهُمْ جَنّٰتٍ تَجْرِيْ مِنْ تَحْتِهَا
الْاَنْهٰرُ خٰلِدِيْنَ فِيْهَآ اَبَدًا ؕ
لَهُمْ فِيْهَآ اَزْوَاجٌ مُّطَهَّرَةٌ ۫ وَّ
نُدْخِلُهُمْ ظِلًّا ظَلِيْلًا ﴿٥٧﴾

58. Allah does command you to render back your trusts to those to whom they are due; and when you judge between man and man, that you judge with justice: verily how excellent is the teaching which He gives you! for Allah is He Who hears and sees all things.

58. Innal-laaha yaåmurukum
an tu'addul-amaanaati ilaaa
ahlihaa wa izaa ḥakamtum
baynan-naasi an taḥkumoo bil-
'adl; innal-laaha ni'immaa
ya'izukum bih; innal-laaha
kaana Samee'am Baṣeeraa.

اِنَّ اللّٰهَ يَاْمُرُكُمْ اَنْ تُؤَدُّوا الْاَمٰنٰتِ
اِلٰٓى اَهْلِهَا ۙ وَاِذَا حَكَمْتُمْ بَيْنَ
النَّاسِ اَنْ تَحْكُمُوْا بِالْعَدْلِ ؕ
اِنَّ اللّٰهَ نِعِمَّا يَعِظُكُمْ بِهٖ ؕ اِنَّ
اللّٰهَ كَانَ سَمِيْعًۢا بَصِيْرًا ﴿٥٨﴾

59. O you who believe! obey Allah,

59. Yaaa-ayyuhal-lazeena
aamanooo aṭee'ul-laaha

يٰٓاَيُّهَا الَّذِيْنَ اٰمَنُوْٓا اَطِيْعُوا اللّٰهَ

Ikhfa اخفاء | Ghunna غنّہ | Ikhfa Meem Saakin اخفاء میم ساکن | Idghaam ادغام | Qalqala قلقلہ | Qalb قلب | Idghaam Meem Saakin ادغام میم ساکن

and obey the Apostle, and those charged with authority among you. If you differ in anything among yourselves, refer it to Allah and His Apostle, if you do believe in Allah and the Last Day: that is best, and most suitable for final determination.

wa aṭee'ur-Rasoola wa ulil-amri minkum fa-in tanaaza'tum fee shay'in faruddoohu ilal-laahi war-Rasooli in kuntum tu'minoona billaahi wal-Yawmil-Aakhir; z̲aalika khayruñw-wa aḥsanu taåweelaa.

(Section 8)

وَأَطِيعُوا الرَّسُولَ وَأُولِي الْأَمْرِ مِنكُمْ ۖ فَإِن تَنَازَعْتُمْ فِي شَيْءٍ فَرُدُّوهُ إِلَى اللَّهِ وَالرَّسُولِ إِن كُنتُمْ تُؤْمِنُونَ بِاللَّهِ وَالْيَوْمِ الْآخِرِ ۚ ذَٰلِكَ خَيْرٌ وَأَحْسَنُ تَأْوِيلًا ﴿٥٩﴾

60. Have you not turned your vision to those who declare that they believe in the revelations that have come to you and to those before you? Their (real) wish is to resort together for judgment (in their disputes) to the Satan, though they were ordered to reject him. But Satan's wish is to lead them astray far away (from the right).

60. Alam tara ilal-laz̲eena yaz'umoona annahum aamanoo bimaa unzila ilayka wa maaa unzila min qablika yureedoona añy-yataḥaakamooo ilaṭ-Ṭaaghooti wa qad umirooo añy-yakfuroo bih, wa yureedush-Shayṭaanu añy-yuḍillahum ḍalaalam-ba'eedaa.

أَلَمْ تَرَ إِلَى الَّذِينَ يَزْعُمُونَ أَنَّهُمْ آمَنُوا بِمَا أُنزِلَ إِلَيْكَ وَمَا أُنزِلَ مِن قَبْلِكَ يُرِيدُونَ أَن يَتَحَاكَمُوا إِلَى الطَّاغُوتِ وَقَدْ أُمِرُوا أَن يَكْفُرُوا بِهِ وَيُرِيدُ الشَّيْطَانُ أَن يُضِلَّهُمْ ضَلَالًا بَعِيدًا ﴿٦٠﴾

61. When it is said to them: "Come to what Allah has revealed, and to the Apostle": you sees the Hypocrites avert their faces from you in disgust.

61. Wa iz̲aa qeela lahum ta'aalaw ilaa maaa anzalallaahu wa ilar-Rasooli ra-aytal-munaafiqeena yaṣuddoona 'anka ṣudoodaa.

وَإِذَا قِيلَ لَهُمْ تَعَالَوْا إِلَىٰ مَا أَنزَلَ اللَّهُ وَإِلَى الرَّسُولِ رَأَيْتَ الْمُنَافِقِينَ يَصُدُّونَ عَنكَ صُدُودًا ﴿٦١﴾

62. How then, when they are seized by misfortune, because of the deeds which their hands have sent forth? Then they come to you, swearing by Allah: "We meant no more than good-will and conciliation!"

62. Fakayfa iz̲aaa aṣaabat-hum muṣeebatum bimaa qaddamat aydeehim s̲umma jaaa'ooka yaḥlifoona billaahi in aradnaaa illaaa iḥsaanañw-wa tawfeeqaa.

فَكَيْفَ إِذَا أَصَابَتْهُم مُّصِيبَةٌ بِمَا قَدَّمَتْ أَيْدِيهِمْ ثُمَّ جَاءُوكَ يَحْلِفُونَ بِاللَّهِ إِنْ أَرَدْنَا إِلَّا إِحْسَانًا وَتَوْفِيقًا ﴿٦٢﴾

63. Those men, Allah knows what is in their hearts; so keep clear of them, but admonish them, and speak to them a word to reach their very souls.

63. Ulaaa'ikal-laz̲eena ya'lamullaahu maa fee quloobihim fa-a'riḍ 'anhum wa 'iẓhum wa qul lahum feee anfusihim qawlam-baleeghaa.

أُولَٰئِكَ الَّذِينَ يَعْلَمُ اللَّهُ مَا فِي قُلُوبِهِمْ فَأَعْرِضْ عَنْهُمْ وَعِظْهُمْ وَقُل لَّهُمْ فِي أَنفُسِهِمْ قَوْلًا بَلِيغًا ﴿٦٣﴾

64. We sent not an Apostle, but to be obeyed, in accordance with the Will of Allah. If they had only, when they were unjust to themselves, come to you and asked Allah's forgiveness, and the Apostle had asked forgiveness for them, they would have found Allah indeed Oft-returning, Most Merciful.

64. Wa maaa arsalnaa mir-Rasoolin illaa liyuṭaa'a bi-iz̲nil-laah; wa law annahum 'iz̲ ẓalamooo anfusahum jaaa'ooka fastaghfarul-laaha wastaghfara lahumur-Rasoolu la-wajadul-laaha Tawwaabar-Raḥeemaa.

وَمَا أَرْسَلْنَا مِن رَّسُولٍ إِلَّا لِيُطَاعَ بِإِذْنِ اللَّهِ ۚ وَلَوْ أَنَّهُمْ إِذ ظَّلَمُوا أَنفُسَهُمْ جَاءُوكَ فَاسْتَغْفَرُوا اللَّهَ وَاسْتَغْفَرَ لَهُمُ الرَّسُولُ لَوَجَدُوا اللَّهَ تَوَّابًا رَّحِيمًا ﴿٦٤﴾

Ikhfa اخفاء | Ghunna غُنّہ | Ikhfa Meem Saakin اخفاء میم ساکن | Idghaam ادغام | Qalqala قلقلہ | Qalb قلب | Idghaam Meem Saakin ادغام میم ساکن

65. But no, by your Lord, they can have no (real) Faith, until they make you judge in all disputes between them, and find in their souls no resistance against your decisions, but accept them with the fullest conviction.

65. Falaa wa Rabbika laa yu'minoona ḥattaa yuḥakkimooka fe-emaa shajara baynahum summa laa yajidoo feee anfusihim ḥarajam-mimmaa qaḍayta wa yusallimoo tasleemaa.

فَلَا وَرَبِّكَ لَا يُؤْمِنُونَ حَتَّىٰ
يُحَكِّمُوكَ فِيمَا شَجَرَ بَيْنَهُمْ ثُمَّ لَا
يَجِدُوا فِي أَنفُسِهِمْ حَرَجًا مِّمَّا
قَضَيْتَ وَيُسَلِّمُوا تَسْلِيمًا ﴿٦٥﴾

66. If We had ordered them to sacrifice their lives or to leave their homes, very few of them would have done it: but if they had done what they were (actually) told, it would have been best for them, and would have gone farthest to strengthen their (faith);

66. Wa law annaa katabnaa 'alayhim aniq-tulooo anfusakum awikh-rujoo min diyaarikum maa fa'aloohu illaa qaleelum-minhum wa law annahum fa'aloo maa yoo'aẓoona bihee lakaana khayral-lahum wa ashadda tasbeetaa.

وَلَوْ أَنَّا كَتَبْنَا عَلَيْهِمْ أَنِ اقْتُلُوا
أَنفُسَكُمْ أَوِ اخْرُجُوا مِن دِيَارِكُم
مَّا فَعَلُوهُ إِلَّا قَلِيلٌ مِّنْهُمْ ۖ وَلَوْ
أَنَّهُمْ فَعَلُوا مَا يُوعَظُونَ بِهِ لَكَانَ
خَيْرًا لَّهُمْ وَأَشَدَّ تَثْبِيتًا ﴿٦٦﴾

67. And We would then have given them from Our Presence a great reward;

67. Wa-izal-la-aataynaahum mil-ladunnaa-ajran 'aẓeemaa.

وَإِذًا لَّآتَيْنَاهُم مِّن لَّدُنَّا أَجْرًا
عَظِيمًا ﴿٦٧﴾

68. And We would have shown them the Straight Way.

68. Wa lahadaynaahum Ṣiraaṭam-Mustaqeemaa.

وَلَهَدَيْنَاهُمْ صِرَاطًا مُّسْتَقِيمًا ﴿٦٨﴾

69. All who obey Allah and the Apostle are in the company of those on whom is the Grace of Allah, - of the Prophets (who teach), the Sincere (lovers of Truth), the Witnesses (who testify), and the Righteous (who do good): ah! what a beautiful Fellowship!

69. Wa mañy-yuṭi'il-laaha war-Rasoola fa-ulaaa'ika ma'al-lazeena an'amal-laahu 'alayhim minan-Nabiyyeena waṣṣiddeeqeena washshuhadaaa'i waṣṣaaliḥeen; wa ḥasuna ulaaa'ika rafeeqaa.

وَمَن يُطِعِ اللَّهَ وَالرَّسُولَ فَأُولَٰئِكَ
مَعَ الَّذِينَ أَنْعَمَ اللَّهُ عَلَيْهِم مِّنَ
النَّبِيِّينَ وَالصِّدِّيقِينَ وَالشُّهَدَاءِ
وَالصَّالِحِينَ ۚ وَحَسُنَ أُولَٰئِكَ رَفِيقًا ﴿٦٩﴾

70. Such is the bounty from Allah: and sufficient is it that Allah knows all.

70. Zaalikal-faḍlu minal-laah; wa kafaa billaahi 'Aleemaa.

(Section 9)

ذَٰلِكَ الْفَضْلُ مِنَ اللَّهِ ۚ وَكَفَىٰ
بِاللَّهِ عَلِيمًا ﴿٧٠﴾

71. O you who believe! take your precautions, and either go forth in parties or go forth all together.

71. Yaaa-ayyuhal-lazeena aamanoo khuzoo ḥizrakum fanfiroo subaatin awin-firoo jamee'aa.

يَا أَيُّهَا الَّذِينَ آمَنُوا خُذُوا حِذْرَكُمْ
فَانفِرُوا ثُبَاتٍ أَوِ انفِرُوا جَمِيعًا ﴿٧١﴾

72. There are certainly among you men who would tarry behind: if a misfortune befalls you, they say: "Allah did favour us in that we were not present among them."

72. Wa inna minkum lamal-layubaṭṭi'anna fa-in aṣaabatkum muṣeebatun qaala qad an'amal-laahu 'alayya iz lam akum-ma'ahum shaheedaa.

وَإِنَّ مِنكُمْ لَمَن لَّيُبَطِّئَنَّ فَإِنْ
أَصَابَتْكُم مُّصِيبَةٌ قَالَ قَدْ أَنْعَمَ اللَّهُ
عَلَيَّ إِذْ لَمْ أَكُن مَّعَهُمْ شَهِيدًا ﴿٧٢﴾

73. But if good fortune comes to you from Allah, they would be sure to say - as if there had never been ties of affection between you and them - "Oh! I wish I had been with them; a fine thing should I then have made of it!"

73. Wa la'in aṣaabakum faḍlum-minal-laahi la-yaqoolanna ka-al-lam takum-baynakum wa baynahoo mawaddatuñy-yaa laytanee kuntu ma'ahum fa-afooza fawzan 'aẓeemaa.

وَلَئِنْ أَصَابَكُمْ فَضْلٌ مِّنَ اللَّهِ لَيَقُولَنَّ
كَأَن لَّمْ تَكُن بَيْنَكُمْ وَبَيْنَهُ مَوَدَّةٌ
يَا لَيْتَنِي كُنتُ مَعَهُمْ فَأَفُوزَ فَوْزًا عَظِيمًا ﴿٧٣﴾

Ikhfa اخفاء | Ghunna غُنّہ | Ikhfa Meem Saakin اخفاء میم ساکن | Idghaam ادغام | Qalqala قلقلہ | Qalb قلب | Idghaam Meem Saakin ادغام میم ساکن

74. Let those fight in the cause of Allah Who sell the life of this world for the Hereafter. To him who fights in the cause of Allah,- whether he is slain or gets victory - soon shall We give him a reward of great (value).

75. And why should you not fight in the cause of Allah and of those who, being weak, are ill-treated (and oppressed)?- men, women, and children, whose cry is: "Our Lord! Rescue us from this town, whose people are oppressors; and raise for us from You one who will protect; and raise for us from You one who will help!"

76. Those who believe fight in the cause of Allah, and those who reject Faith fight in the cause of Evil: so fight you against the friends of Satan: feeble indeed is the cunning of Satan.

77. Have you not turned your vision to those who were told to hold back their hands (from fight) but establish regular prayers and spend in regular charity? When (at length) the order for fighting was issued to them, behold! a section of them feared men as - or even more than - they should have feared Allah: they said: "Our Lord! Why have You ordered us to fight? Would You not Grant us respite to our (natural) term, near (enough)?" Say: "Short is the enjoyment of this world: the Hereafter is the best for those who do right: never will you be dealt with unjustly in the very least!

78. "Wherever you are, death will find you out, even if you are in towers built up strong and high!" If some good befalls them, they say, "This is from

74. Falyuqaatil fee sabeelil-laahil-lazeena yashroonal-ḥayaatad-dunyaa bil-Aakhirah; wa mañy-yuqaatil fee sabeelil-laahi fa-yuqtal aw yaghlib fasawfa nu'teehi ajran 'azeemaa.

75. Wa maa lakum laa tuqaatiloona fee sabeelil-laahi walmustaḍ'afeena minar-rijaali wannisaaa'i walwildaanil-lazeena yaqooloona Rabbanaaa akhrijnaa min haazihil-qarya-tiẓ-ẓaalimi ahluhaa waj'al-lanaa mil-ladunka waliyyañw-waj'al-lanaa mil-ladunka naṣeeraa.

76. Allazeena aamanoo yuqaatiloona fee sabeelil-laahi wallazeena kafaroo yuqaati-loona fee sabeeliṭ-Ṭaaghoot faqaatilooo awliyaaa'ash-Shayṭaan; inna kaydash-Shay-ṭaani kaana ḍa'eefaa. **(Section 10)**

77. Alam tara ilal-lazeena qeela lahum kuffooo aydiyakum wa aqeemuṣ-Ṣalaata wa aatuz-Zakaata falammaa kutiba-'alayhimul-qitaalu izaa faree-qum-minhum yakhshawnan-naasa kakhashyatil-laahi aw ashadda khashyah; wa qaaloo Rabbanaa lima katabta 'alaynal-qitaala law laaa akhkhartanaaa ilaaa ajalin qareeb; qul mataa'ud-dunyaa qaleeluñw wal-Aakhiratu khayrul-limanit-taqaa wa laa tuzlamoona fateelaa.

78. Aynamaa takoonoo yudrikkumul-mawtu wa law kuntum fee buroojim-mushay-yadah; wa in tusibhum ḥasa-natuñy-yaqooloo haazihee min

فَلْيُقَاتِلْ فِي سَبِيلِ اللّٰهِ الَّذِينَ
يَشْرُونَ الْحَيٰوةَ الدُّنْيَا بِالْاٰخِرَةِ ؕ
وَمَنْ يُّقَاتِلْ فِي سَبِيلِ اللّٰهِ فَيُقْتَلْ
اَوْ يَغْلِبْ فَسَوْفَ نُؤْتِيهِ اَجْرًا عَظِيمًا ﴿٧٤﴾
وَمَا لَكُمْ لَا تُقَاتِلُونَ فِي سَبِيلِ
اللّٰهِ وَالْمُسْتَضْعَفِينَ مِنَ الرِّجَالِ
وَالنِّسَاءِ وَالْوِلْدَانِ الَّذِينَ يَقُولُونَ
رَبَّنَا اَخْرِجْنَا مِنْ هٰذِهِ الْقَرْيَةِ الظَّالِمِ
اَهْلُهَا ۚ وَاجْعَلْ لَنَا مِنْ لَّدُنْكَ وَلِيًّا ۚ
وَّاجْعَلْ لَنَا مِنْ لَّدُنْكَ نَصِيرًا ﴿٧٥﴾
اَلَّذِينَ اٰمَنُوا يُقَاتِلُونَ فِي سَبِيلِ اللّٰهِ ۚ
وَالَّذِينَ كَفَرُوا يُقَاتِلُونَ فِي سَبِيلِ
الطَّاغُوتِ فَقَاتِلُوا اَوْلِيَاءَ الشَّيْطٰنِ ۚ
اِنَّ كَيْدَ الشَّيْطٰنِ كَانَ ضَعِيفًا ﴿٧٦﴾ ع
اَلَمْ تَرَ اِلَى الَّذِينَ قِيلَ لَهُمْ كُفُّوا
اَيْدِيَكُمْ وَاَقِيمُوا الصَّلٰوةَ وَاٰتُوا
الزَّكٰوةَ ۚ فَلَمَّا كُتِبَ عَلَيْهِمُ الْقِتَالُ
اِذَا فَرِيقٌ مِّنْهُمْ يَخْشَوْنَ النَّاسَ
كَخَشْيَةِ اللّٰهِ اَوْ اَشَدَّ خَشْيَةً ۚ وَ
قَالُوا رَبَّنَا لِمَ كَتَبْتَ عَلَيْنَا الْقِتَالَ ۚ
لَوْلَا اَخَّرْتَنَا اِلٰى اَجَلٍ قَرِيبٍ ؕ قُلْ
مَتَاعُ الدُّنْيَا قَلِيلٌ ۚ وَالْاٰخِرَةُ خَيْرٌ
لِّمَنِ اتَّقٰى ۟ وَلَا تُظْلَمُونَ فَتِيلًا ﴿٧٧﴾
اَيْنَ مَا تَكُونُوا يُدْرِكْكُّمُ الْمَوْتُ
وَلَوْ كُنْتُمْ فِي بُرُوجٍ مُّشَيَّدَةٍ ؕ وَاِنْ
تُصِبْهُمْ حَسَنَةٌ يَّقُولُوا هٰذِهٖ مِنْ

Ikhfa اخفاء | Ghunna غُنّہ | Ikhfa Meem Saakin اخفاء میم ساکن | Idghaam ادغام | Qalqala قلقلہ | Qalb قلب | Idghaam Meem Saakin ادغام میم ساکن

Allah"; but if evil, they say, "This is from you" (O Prophet). Say: "All things are from Allah." But what have come to these people, that they fail to understand a single fact?

'indil-laahi wa in tuṣibhum sayyi'atuñy-yaqooloo haazihee min 'indik; qul kullum-min 'indillaahi famaa lihaaa-'ulaaa'il-qawmi laa yakaadoona yafqahoona ḥadeesaa.

عِندِ اللّٰهِ ۚ وَإِن تُصِبْهُمْ سَيِّئَةٌ
يَقُولُوا هٰذِهِۦ مِنْ عِندِكَ ۚ قُلْ كُلٌّ
مِّنْ عِندِ اللّٰهِ ۖ فَمَالِ هٰٓؤُلَآءِ الْقَوْمِ
لَا يَكَادُونَ يَفْقَهُونَ حَدِيثًا ﴿٧٨﴾

79. Whatever good, (O man!) happens to you is from Allah; but whatever evil happens to you, is from your (own) soul. and We have sent you as an Apostle to (instruct) mankind. And enough is Allah for a Witness.

79. Maaa aṣaabaka min ḥasanatin faminal-laahi wa maaa aṣaaabaka min sayyi'atin famin-nafsik; wa arsalnaaka linnaasi Rasoolaa; wa kafaa billaahi Shaheedaa.

مَّآ أَصَابَكَ مِنْ حَسَنَةٍ فَمِنَ اللّٰهِ ۖ
وَمَآ أَصَابَكَ مِن سَيِّئَةٍ فَمِن نَّفْسِكَ ۚ
وَأَرْسَلْنٰكَ لِلنَّاسِ رَسُولًا ۚ وَكَفٰى
بِاللّٰهِ شَهِيدًا ﴿٧٩﴾

80. He who obeys the Apostle, obeys Allah: but if any turn away, We have not sent you to watch over their (evil deeds).

80. Man yuṭi'ir-Rasoola faqad aṭaa'al-laaha wa man tawallaa famaaa arsalnaaka 'alayhim ḥafeezaa.

مَّن يُطِعِ الرَّسُولَ فَقَدْ أَطَاعَ اللّٰهَ ۖ
وَمَن تَوَلّٰى فَمَآ أَرْسَلْنٰكَ عَلَيْهِمْ
حَفِيظًا ﴿٨٠﴾

81. They have "Obedience" on their lips; but when they leave you, a section of them meditate all night on things very different from what you tell them. But Allah records their nightly (plots): so keep clear of them, and put your trust in Allah, and enough is Allah as a disposer of affairs.

81. Wa yaqooloona ṭaa'atun fa-izaa barazoo min 'indika bayyata ṭaaa'ifatum-minhum ghayral-lazee taqoolu wallaahu yaktubu maa yubayyitoona fa-a'riḍ 'anhum wa tawakkal 'alal-laah; wa kafaa billaahi Wakeelaa.

وَيَقُولُونَ طَاعَةٌ فَإِذَا بَرَزُوا مِنْ
عِندِكَ بَيَّتَ طَآئِفَةٌ مِّنْهُمْ غَيْرَ
الَّذِى تَقُولُ ۖ وَاللّٰهُ يَكْتُبُ مَا يُبَيِّتُونَ ۖ
فَأَعْرِضْ عَنْهُمْ وَتَوَكَّلْ عَلَى اللّٰهِ ۚ
وَكَفٰى بِاللّٰهِ وَكِيلًا ﴿٨١﴾

82. Do they not consider the Qur'an (with care)? Had it been from other than Allah, they would surely have found therein much discrepancy.

82. Afalaa yatadabbaroonal-Qur'aan; wa law kaana min 'indi ghayril-laahi la-wajadoo fee-hikh-tilaafan kaseeraa.

أَفَلَا يَتَدَبَّرُونَ الْقُرْءَانَ ۚ وَلَوْ كَانَ
مِنْ عِندِ غَيْرِ اللّٰهِ لَوَجَدُوا فِيهِ
اخْتِلٰفًا كَثِيرًا ﴿٨٢﴾

83. When there comes to them some matter touching (public) safety or fear, they divulge it. If they had only referred it to the Apostle, or to those charged with authority among them, the proper investigators would have tested it from them (direct). Were it not for the Grace and Mercy of Allah unto you, all but a few of you would have fallen into the clutches of Satan.

83. Wa izaa jaaa'ahum amrum-minal-amni awil-khawfi azaa'oo bihee wa law raddoohu ilar-Rasooli wa ilaaa ulil-amri minhum la'alimahul-lazeena yastambiṭoonahoo minhum; wa law laa faḍlul-laahi 'alaykum wa raḥmatuhoo lattaba'tu-mush-Shayṭaana illaa qaleelaa.

وَإِذَا جَآءَهُمْ أَمْرٌ مِّنَ الْأَمْنِ
أَوِ الْخَوْفِ أَذَاعُوا بِهِۦ ۖ وَلَوْ رَدُّوهُ
إِلَى الرَّسُولِ وَإِلٰىٓ أُولِى الْأَمْرِ مِنْهُمْ
لَعَلِمَهُ الَّذِينَ يَسْتَنۢبِطُونَهُۥ مِنْهُمْ ۗ
وَلَوْلَا فَضْلُ اللّٰهِ عَلَيْكُمْ وَرَحْمَتُهُۥ
لَاتَّبَعْتُمُ الشَّيْطٰنَ إِلَّا قَلِيلًا ﴿٨٣﴾

84. Then fight in Allah's cause - you are held responsible only

84. Faqaatil fee sabeelil-laahi laa tukallafu illaa

فَقٰتِلْ فِى سَبِيلِ اللّٰهِ لَا تُكَلَّفُ إِلَّا

Ikhfa اخفاء | Ghunna غُنّہ | Ikhfa Meem Saakin اخفاء میم ساکن | Idghaam ادغام | Qalqala قلقلہ | Qalb قلب | Idghaam Meem Saakin ادغام میم ساکن

for yourself - and motivate the Believers. It may be that Allah will restrain the fury of the Unbelievers; for Allah is the strongest in might and in punishment.

nafsaka wa ḥarriḍil-mu'mineena 'asallaahu añy-yakuffa baåsallazeena kafaroo; wallaahu ashaddu baåsañw-wa ashaddu tankeelaa.

نفسك وحرض المؤمنين ج عسى
الله ان يكف باس الذين كفروا ط
والله اشد باسا واشد تنكيلا ﴿٨٤﴾

85. Whoever recommends and helps a good cause becomes a partner therein: and whoever recommends and helps an evil cause, shares in its burden: and Allah has power over all things.

85. Mañy-yashfa' shafaa'atan ḥasanatañy-yakul-lahoo naṣeebum-minhaa wa mañy-yashfa' shafaa'atan sayyi'atañy-yakul-lahoo kiflum-minhaa; wa kaanal-laahu 'alaa kulli shay'im-Muqeetaa.

من يشفع شفاعة حسنة يكن له
نصيب منها ج ومن يشفع شفاعة
سيئة يكن له كفل منها ط وكان
الله على كل شيء مقيتا ﴿٨٥﴾

86. When a (courteous) greeting is offered you, meet it with a greeting still more courteous, or (at least) of equal courtesy. Allah takes careful account of all things.

86. Wa izaa ḥuyyeetum bitaḥiyyatin faḥayyoo bi-aḥsana minhaaa aw ruddoohaa; innal-laaha kaana 'alaa kulli shay'in Ḥaseebaa.

واذا حييتم بتحية فحيوا باحسن
منها او ردوها ط ان الله كان على
كل شيء حسيبا ﴿٨٦﴾ النصف

87. Allah! There is no god but He: of a surety He will gather you together against the Day of Judgment, about which there is no doubt. And whose word can be truer than Allah's?

87. Allaahu laaa ilaaha illaa huwa la-yajma'annakum ilaa Yawmil-Qiyaamati laa rayba feeh; wa man aṣdaqu minallaahi ḥadeesaa. **(Section 11)**

الله لا اله الا هو ط ليجمعنكم الى
يوم القيمة لا ريب فيه ط ومن
اصدق من الله حديثا ﴿٨٧﴾ ع ٨

88. Why should you be divided into two parties about the Hypocrites? Allah has upset them for their (evil) deeds. Would you guide those whom Allah has thrown out of the Way? For those whom Allah has thrown out of the Way, never shall you find the Way.

88. Famaa lakum filmunaafiqeena fi'atayni wallaahu arkasahum bimaa kasaboo; atureedoona an tahdoo man aḍallal-laahu wa mañy-yuḍlilil-laahu falan tajida lahoo sabeelaa.

فما لكم في المنفقين فئتين
والله اركسهم بما كسبوا ط اتريدون
ان تهدوا من اضل الله ط ومن
يضلل الله فلن تجد له سبيلا ﴿٨٨﴾

89. They but wish that you should reject Faith, as they do, and thus be on the same footing (as they): but take not friends from their ranks until they flee in the way of Allah (from what is forbidden). But if they turn renegades, seize them and slay them wherever you find them; and (in any case) take no friends or helpers from their ranks;-

89. Wadoo law takfuroona kamaa kafaroo fatakoonoona sawaaa'an falaa tattakhizoo minhum awliyaaa'a ḥattaa yuhaajiroo fee sabeelil-laah; fa-in tawallaw fa-khuzoohum waqtuloohum ḥaysu wajattumoohum wa laa tattakhizoo minhum waliyyañw wa laa naṣeeraa.

ودوا لو تكفرون كما كفروا
فتكونون سواء فلا تتخذوا منهم
اولياء حتى يهاجروا في سبيل
الله ط فان تولوا فخذوهم واقتلوهم
حيث وجدتموهم ص ولا تتخذوا
منهم وليا ولا نصيرا ﴿٨٩﴾ لا

90. Except those who join a group between whom and you there is a treaty (of peace), or those who approach you with hearts restraining them from fighting

90. Illal-lazeena yaṣiloona ilaa qawmim-baynakum wa baynahum meesaaqun aw jaaa'ookum ḥaṣirat ṣudooruhum añy-yuqaatilookum

الا الذين يصلون الى قوم
بينكم وبينهم ميثاق او جاءوكم
حصرت صدورهم ان يقاتلوكم

Ikhfa اخفاء	Ghunna غنّہ	Ikhfa Meem Saakin اخفاء میم ساکن	Idghaam ادغام	Qalqala قلقلہ	Qalb قلب	Idghaam Meem Saakin ادغام میم ساکن

you as well as fighting their own people. If Allah had pleased, He could have given them power over you, and they would have fought you: therefore if they withdraw from you but fight you not, and (instead) send you (guarantees of) peace, then Allah has opened no way for you (to war against them).

91. Others you will find that wish to gain your confidence as well as that of their people: every time they are sent back to temptation, they succumb thereto: if they withdraw not from you nor give you (guarantees) of peace besides restraining their hands, seize them and slay them wherever you get them: in their case We have provided you with a clear argument against them.

92. Never should a believer kill a believer; but (if it so happens) by mistake, (compensation is due): if one (so) kills a believer, it is ordained that he should free a believing slave, and pay compensation to the deceased's family, unless they remit it freely. If the deceased belonged to a people at war with you, and he was a believer, the freeing of a believing slave (is enough). If he belonged to a people with whom you have treaty of mutual alliance, compensation should be paid to his family, and a believing slave be freed. For those who find this beyond their means, (is prescribed) a fast for two months running: by way of repentance to Allah: for Allah has all knowledge and all wisdom.

93. If a man kills a Believer intentionally, his recompense is

aw yuqaatiloo qawmahum, wa law shaaa'al-laahu lasallaṭahum 'alaykum falaqaatalookum; fa-ini'-tazalookum falam yuqaatilookum wa alqaw ilaykumus-salama famaa ja'alal-laahu lakum 'alayhim sabeelaa.

91. Satajidoona aakhareena yureedoona añy-yaåmanookum wa yaåmanoo qawmahum kullamaa ruddooo ilal-fitnati urkisoo feehaa; fa-il-lam ya'tazilookum wa yulqooo ilay-kumus-salama wa yakuffooo aydiyahum fakhuzoohum waqtuloohum ḥaysu saqif-tumoohum; wa ulaaa'ikum ja'alnaa lakum 'alayhim sulṭaanam-mubeenaa.

(Section 12)

92. Wa maa kaana limu'minin añy-yaqtula mu'minan illaa khaṭa'aa; waman qatala mu'minan khaṭa'an fataḥreeru raqabatim-mu'minatiñw-wa diyatum-musallamatun ilaaa ahliheee illaaa añy-yaṣṣad-daqoo; fa-in kaana min qawmin 'aduwwil-lakum wa huwa mu'minun fataḥreeru raqa-batim mu'minah; wa in kaana min qawmim baynakum wa baynahum meesaaqun fadiyatum-musallamatun ilaaa ahlihee wa taḥreeru raqabatim-mu'minatin famal-lam yajid fa-Ṣiyaamu shahrayni muta-taabi'ayni tawbatam-minal-laah; wa kaanal-laahu 'Aleeman Ḥakeemaa.

93. Wa mañy-yaqtul mu'minam-muta'ammidan fajazaaa'uhoo

أَوْ يُقَاتِلُوا قَوْمَهُمْ ۚ وَلَوْ شَاءَ اللَّهُ
لَسَلَّطَهُمْ عَلَيْكُمْ فَلَقَاتَلُوكُمْ ۚ فَإِنِ
اعْتَزَلُوكُمْ فَلَمْ يُقَاتِلُوكُمْ وَأَلْقَوْا
إِلَيْكُمُ السَّلَمَ فَمَا جَعَلَ اللَّهُ
لَكُمْ عَلَيْهِمْ سَبِيلًا ﴿٩٠﴾
سَتَجِدُونَ آخَرِينَ يُرِيدُونَ
أَنْ يَأْمَنُوكُمْ وَيَأْمَنُوا قَوْمَهُمْ
كُلَّمَا رُدُّوا إِلَى الْفِتْنَةِ أُرْكِسُوا
فِيهَا ۚ فَإِنْ لَمْ يَعْتَزِلُوكُمْ وَيُلْقُوا
إِلَيْكُمُ السَّلَمَ وَيَكُفُّوا أَيْدِيَهُمْ
فَخُذُوهُمْ وَاقْتُلُوهُمْ حَيْثُ
ثَقِفْتُمُوهُمْ ۚ وَأُولَٰئِكُمْ جَعَلْنَا لَكُمْ
عَلَيْهِمْ سُلْطَانًا مُبِينًا ﴿٩١﴾ ع
وَمَا كَانَ لِمُؤْمِنٍ أَنْ يَقْتُلَ مُؤْمِنًا
إِلَّا خَطَأً ۚ وَمَنْ قَتَلَ مُؤْمِنًا خَطَأً
فَتَحْرِيرُ رَقَبَةٍ مُؤْمِنَةٍ وَدِيَةٌ
مُسَلَّمَةٌ إِلَىٰ أَهْلِهِ إِلَّا أَنْ يَصَّدَّقُوا
فَإِنْ كَانَ مِنْ قَوْمٍ عَدُوٍّ لَكُمْ وَهُوَ
مُؤْمِنٌ فَتَحْرِيرُ رَقَبَةٍ مُؤْمِنَةٍ ۖ
وَإِنْ كَانَ مِنْ قَوْمٍ بَيْنَكُمْ وَبَيْنَهُمْ
مِيثَاقٌ فَدِيَةٌ مُسَلَّمَةٌ إِلَىٰ
أَهْلِهِ وَتَحْرِيرُ رَقَبَةٍ مُؤْمِنَةٍ ۖ
فَمَنْ لَمْ يَجِدْ فَصِيَامُ شَهْرَيْنِ
مُتَتَابِعَيْنِ تَوْبَةً مِنَ اللَّهِ ۗ وَكَانَ
اللَّهُ عَلِيمًا حَكِيمًا ﴿٩٢﴾
وَمَنْ يَقْتُلْ مُؤْمِنًا مُتَعَمِّدًا فَجَزَاؤُهُ

Hell, to abide therein (for ever): and the wrath and the curse of Allah are upon him, and a dreadful Chastisement is prepared for him.

Jahannamu khaalidan feehaa wa ghaḍibal-laahu ʻalayhi wa laʻanahoo wa aʻadda lahoo ʻaẕaaban ʻaẓeemaa.

جَهَنَّمُ خٰلِدًا فِيْهَا وَغَضِبَ اللّٰهُ عَلَيْهِ
وَلَعَنَهٗ وَاَعَدَّ لَهٗ عَذَابًا عَظِيْمًا ﴿٩٣﴾

94. O you who believe! When you go abroad in the cause of Allah, investigate carefully, and say not to any one who offers you a salutation: "you are not a Believer!" coveting the perishable goods of this life: with Allah are profits and spoils abundant. Even thus were you yourselves before, till Allah conferred on you His favours: therefore carefully investigate. For Allah is well aware of all that you do.

94. Yaaa-ayyuhal-laẕeena aamanooo iẕaa ḍarabtum fee sabeelil-laahi fatabayyanoo wa laa taqooloo liman alqaaa ilaykumus-salaama lasta mu'minan tabtaghoona ʻaraḍal-ḥayaatid-dunyaa faʻindal-laahi maghaanimu kaṯeerah; kaẕaalika kuntum min qablu famannal-laahu ʻalaykum fatabayyanoo; innallaaha kaana bimaa taʻmaloona Khabeeraa.

يٰٓاَيُّهَا الَّذِيْنَ اٰمَنُوْٓا اِذَا ضَرَبْتُمْ
فِيْ سَبِيْلِ اللّٰهِ فَتَبَيَّنُوْا وَلَا تَقُوْلُوْا
لِمَنْ اَلْقٰٓى اِلَيْكُمُ السَّلٰمَ لَسْتَ مُؤْمِنًا ۚ
تَبْتَغُوْنَ عَرَضَ الْحَيٰوةِ الدُّنْيَا ۡ
فَعِنْدَ اللّٰهِ مَغَانِمُ كَثِيْرَةٌ ۭ كَذٰلِكَ
كُنْتُمْ مِّنْ قَبْلُ فَمَنَّ اللّٰهُ عَلَيْكُمْ
فَتَبَيَّنُوْا ۭ اِنَّ اللّٰهَ كَانَ بِمَا
تَعْمَلُوْنَ خَبِيْرًا ﴿٩٤﴾

95. Not equal are those believers who sit (at home) and receive no hurt, and those who strive and fight in the cause of Allah with their goods and their persons. Allah has granted a grade higher to those who strive and fight with their goods and persons than to those who sit (at home). Unto all (in Faith) has Allah promised good: but those who strive and fight He has distinguished above those who sit (at home) by a special reward,-

95. Laa yastawil-qaaʻidoona Minal-mu'mineena ghayru uliḍ-ḍarari walmujaahidoona fee sabeelil-laahi bi-amwaalihim wa anfusihim; faḍḍalal-laahul-mujaahideena bi-amwaalihim wa anfusihim ʻalal-qaaʻideena darajah; wa kullañw waʻadal-laahul-ḥusnaa; wa faḍḍalal-laahul-mujaahideena ʻalal-qaaʻideena ajran ʻaẓeemaa.

لَا يَسْتَوِي الْقٰعِدُوْنَ مِنَ الْمُؤْمِنِيْنَ
غَيْرُ اُولِي الضَّرَرِ وَالْمُجٰهِدُوْنَ فِيْ
سَبِيْلِ اللّٰهِ بِاَمْوَالِهِمْ وَاَنْفُسِهِمْ ۭ
فَضَّلَ اللّٰهُ الْمُجٰهِدِيْنَ بِاَمْوَالِهِمْ
وَاَنْفُسِهِمْ عَلَى الْقٰعِدِيْنَ دَرَجَةً ۭ
وَكُلًّا وَّعَدَ اللّٰهُ الْحُسْنٰى ۭ وَفَضَّلَ
اللّٰهُ الْمُجٰهِدِيْنَ عَلَى الْقٰعِدِيْنَ
اَجْرًا عَظِيْمًا ﴿٩٥﴾

96. Ranks specially bestowed by Him, and Forgiveness and Mercy. For Allah is Oft-forgiving, Most Merciful.

96. Darajaatim-minhu wa maghfiratañw-wa raḥmah; wa kaanal-laahu Ghafoorar-Raḥeemaa. **(Section 13)**

دَرَجٰتٍ مِّنْهُ وَمَغْفِرَةً وَّرَحْمَةً ۭ
وَكَانَ اللّٰهُ غَفُوْرًا رَّحِيْمًا ﴿٩٦﴾

97. When angels take the souls of those who die in sin against their souls, they say: "In what (plight) were you?" They reply: "Weak and oppressed were we in the earth." They say: "Was not the earth of Allah spacious enough for you to move yourselves away (from evil)?" Such men will find their abode in Hell, - What an evil refuge! -

97. Innal-laẕeena tawaffaahumul-malaaa'ikatu ẕaalimeee-anfusihim qaaloo feema kuntum qaaloo kunnaa mustaḍʻafeena fil-arḍ; qaalooo alam takun arḍul-laahi waasiʻatan fatuhaajiroo feehaa; fa-ulaaa'ika maåwaahum Jahannamu wa saaa'at maṣeeraa.

اِنَّ الَّذِيْنَ تَوَفّٰىهُمُ الْمَلٰۗىِٕكَةُ
ظَالِمِيْٓ اَنْفُسِهِمْ قَالُوْا فِيْمَ كُنْتُمْ ۭ
قَالُوْا كُنَّا مُسْتَضْعَفِيْنَ فِي الْاَرْضِ ۭ
قَالُوْٓا اَلَمْ تَكُنْ اَرْضُ اللّٰهِ وَاسِعَةً
فَتُهَاجِرُوْا فِيْهَا ۭ فَاُولٰۗىِٕكَ مَاْوٰىهُمْ
جَهَنَّمُ ۭ وَسَاۗءَتْ مَصِيْرًا ﴿٩٧﴾

Ikhfa اخفاء	Ghunna غُنّہ	Ikhfa Meem Saakin اخفاءمیم ساکن	Idghaam ادغام	Qalqala قلقلہ	Qalb قلب	Idghaam Meem Saakin ادغام میم ساکن

98. Except those who are (really) weak and oppressed - men, women, and children - who have no means in their power, nor (a guide-post) to their way.

98. Illal-mustaḍ'afeena minar-rijaali wannisaaa'i walwildaani laa yastatee'oona heelatañw-wa laa yahtadoona sabeelaa.

إِلَّا الْمُسْتَضْعَفِينَ مِنَ الرِّجَالِ
وَالنِّسَآءِ وَالْوِلْدَانِ لَا يَسْتَطِيعُونَ
حِيلَةً وَّلَا يَهْتَدُونَ سَبِيلًا ﴿٩٨﴾

99. For these, there is hope that Allah will forgive: for Allah blots out (sins) and forgive again and again.

99. Fa-ulaaa'ika 'asal-laahu añy-ya'fuwa 'anhum; wa kaanal-laahu 'Afuwwan Ghafooraa.

فَأُولَٰٓئِكَ عَسَى اللَّهُ أَن يَعْفُوَ عَنْهُمْ
وَكَانَ اللَّهُ عَفُوًّا غَفُورًا ﴿٩٩﴾

100. He who forsakes his home in the cause of Allah, finds in the earth many a refuge, wide and spacious: should he die as a refugee from home for Allah and His Apostle, His reward becomes due and sure with Allah: And Allah is Oft-forgiving, Most Merciful.

100. Wa mañy-yuhaajir fee sabeelil-laahi yajid fil-arḍi muraaghaman kaseerañw-wa sa'ah; wa mañy-yakhruj mim-baytihee muhaajiran ilal-laahi wa Rasoolihee summa yudrik-hul-mawtu faqad waqa'a ajruhoo 'alal-laah; wa kaanal-laahu Ghafoorar-Raḥeemaa.

وَمَن يُهَاجِرْ فِي سَبِيلِ اللَّهِ يَجِدْ
فِي الْأَرْضِ مُرَاغَمًا كَثِيرًا وَسَعَةً
وَمَن يَخْرُجْ مِن بَيْتِهِ مُهَاجِرًا
إِلَى اللَّهِ وَرَسُولِهِ ثُمَّ يُدْرِكْهُ الْمَوْتُ
فَقَدْ وَقَعَ أَجْرُهُ عَلَى اللَّهِ وَكَانَ
اللَّهُ غَفُورًا رَّحِيمًا ﴿١٠٠﴾ ع ١٤

(Section 14)

101. When you travel through the earth, there is no blame on you if you shorten your prayers, for fear the Unbelievers may attack you: for the Unbelievers are open enemies to you.

101. Wa izaa ḍarabtum fil-arḍi falaysa 'alaykum junaaḥun an taqṣuroo minaṣ-Ṣalaati in khiftum añy-yaftinakumul-lazeena kafarooo; innal-kaafireena kaanoo lakum aduwwam-mubeenaa.

وَإِذَا ضَرَبْتُمْ فِي الْأَرْضِ فَلَيْسَ
عَلَيْكُمْ جُنَاحٌ أَن تَقْصُرُوا مِنَ
الصَّلَوٰةِ إِنْ خِفْتُمْ أَن يَفْتِنَكُمُ
الَّذِينَ كَفَرُوا إِنَّ الْكَافِرِينَ كَانُوا
لَكُمْ عَدُوًّا مُّبِينًا ﴿١٠١﴾

102. When you (O Apostle) are with them, and stand to lead them in prayer, let one party of them stand up (in prayer) with you, taking their arms with them: when they finish their prostrations, let them take their position in the rear. And let the other party come up which has not yet prayed - and let them pray with you, taking all precaution, and bearing arms: the Unbelievers wish, if you were negligent of your arms and your baggage, to assault you in a single rush. But there is no blame

102. Wa izaa kunta feehim fa-aqamta lahumuṣ-Ṣalaata faltaqum ṭaaa'ifatum-minhum ma'aka walyaåkhuzooo asliḥatahum fa-izaa sajadoo fal-yakoonoo miñw-waraaa'ikum waltaåti ṭaaa'ifatun ukhraa lam yuṣalloo falyuṣalloo ma'aka walyaåkhuzoo ḥizrahum wa asliḥatahum; waddal-lazeena kafaroo law taghfuloona 'an asliḥatikum wa amti'atikum fa-yameeloona 'alaykum maylatañw-waaḥidah; wa laa junaaḥa

وَإِذَا كُنتَ فِيهِمْ فَأَقَمْتَ لَهُمُ
الصَّلَوٰةَ فَلْتَقُمْ طَآئِفَةٌ مِّنْهُم مَّعَكَ
وَلْيَأْخُذُوا أَسْلِحَتَهُمْ فَإِذَا سَجَدُوا
فَلْيَكُونُوا مِن وَرَآئِكُمْ وَلْتَأْتِ
طَآئِفَةٌ أُخْرَىٰ لَمْ يُصَلُّوا فَلْيُصَلُّوا
مَعَكَ وَلْيَأْخُذُوا حِذْرَهُمْ
وَأَسْلِحَتَهُمْ وَدَّ الَّذِينَ كَفَرُوا
لَوْ تَغْفُلُونَ عَنْ أَسْلِحَتِكُمْ وَ
أَمْتِعَتِكُمْ فَيَمِيلُونَ عَلَيْكُم
مَّيْلَةً وَاحِدَةً وَلَا جُنَاحَ

Ikhfa اخفاء | Ghunna غنّہ | Ikhfa Meem Saakin اخفاء میم ساکن | Idghaam ادغام | Qalqala قلقلہ | Qalb قلب | Idghaam Meem Saakin ادغام میم ساکن

on you if you put away your arms because of the inconvenience of rain or because you are ill; but take (every) precaution for your-selves. For the Unbelievers Allah has prepared a humiliating punishment.

'alaykum in kaana bikum azam-mimmaṭarin aw kuntum marḍaaa an taḍa'ooo asliḥatakum wa khuzoo ḥizrakum; innal-laaha a'adda lilkaafireena 'azaabam-muheenaa.

عَلَيْكُمْ اِنْ كَانَ بِكُمْ اَذًى مِّنْ
مَّطَرٍ اَوْ كُنْتُمْ مَّرْضٰٓى اَنْ تَضَعُوْٓا
اَسْلِحَتَكُمْ ۚ وَخُذُوْا حِذْرَكُمْ ۗ اِنَّ اللّٰهَ
اَعَدَّ لِلْكٰفِرِيْنَ عَذَابًا مُّهِيْنًا ﴿١٠٢﴾

103. When you pass (congregational) prayers, celebrate Allah's praises, standing, sitting down, or lying down on your sides; but when you are free from danger, set up regular Prayers: for such prayers are enjoined on Believers at stated times.

103. Fa-izaa qaḍaytumuṣ-Ṣalaata fazkurul-laaha qiyaamañw-wa qu'oodañw-wa 'alaa junoobikum; fa-izaṭ-maånantum fa-aqeemuṣ-Ṣalaah; innaṣ-Ṣalaata kaanat 'alal-mu'mineena kitaabam-mawqootaa.

فَاِذَا قَضَيْتُمُ الصَّلٰوةَ فَاذْكُرُوا
اللّٰهَ قِيٰمًا وَّقُعُوْدًا وَّعَلٰى جُنُوْبِكُمْ ۚ
فَاِذَا اطْمَاْنَنْتُمْ فَاَقِيْمُوا الصَّلٰوةَ ۚ
اِنَّ الصَّلٰوةَ كَانَتْ عَلَى الْمُؤْمِنِيْنَ
كِتٰبًا مَّوْقُوْتًا ﴿١٠٣﴾

104. And slacken not in following up the enemy: if you are suffering hardships, they are suffering similar hardships; but you have hope from Allah, while they have none. And Allah is full of knowledge and wisdom.

104. Wa laa tahinoo fibtighaaa'il-qawmi in takoonoo taålamoona fa-innahum yaålamoona kamaa taålamoona wa tarjoona minal-laahi maa laa yarjoon; wa kaanal-laahu 'Aleeman Ḥakeemaa. **(Sec. 15)**

وَلَا تَهِنُوْا فِي ابْتِغَآءِ الْقَوْمِ ۗ اِنْ
تَكُوْنُوْا تَاْلَمُوْنَ فَاِنَّهُمْ يَاْلَمُوْنَ
كَمَا تَاْلَمُوْنَ ۚ وَتَرْجُوْنَ مِنَ اللّٰهِ
مَا لَا يَرْجُوْنَ ۗ وَكَانَ اللّٰهُ
عَلِيْمًا حَكِيْمًا ﴿١٠٤﴾ ع

ع ١٥ ٤ ١٢

105. We have sent down to you the Book in truth, that you might judge between men, as guided by Allah: so be not (used) as an advocate by those who betray their trust;

105. Innaaa anzalnaaa ilaykal-Kitaaba bilḥaqqi litaḥkuma baynan-naasi bimaaa araakal-laah; wa laa takul-lilkhaaa'ineena khaṣeemaa.

اِنَّآ اَنْزَلْنَآ اِلَيْكَ الْكِتٰبَ بِالْحَقِّ
لِتَحْكُمَ بَيْنَ النَّاسِ بِمَآ اَرٰىكَ اللّٰهُ ۗ
وَلَا تَكُنْ لِّلْخَآئِنِيْنَ خَصِيْمًا ﴿١٠٥﴾

106. But seek the forgiveness of Allah; for Allah is Oft-forgiving, Most Merciful.

106. Wastaghfiril-laaha innal-laaha kaana Ghafoorar-Raḥeemaa.

وَّاسْتَغْفِرِ اللّٰهَ ۗ اِنَّ اللّٰهَ كَانَ
غَفُوْرًا رَّحِيْمًا ﴿١٠٦﴾ ۚ

107. Contend not on behalf of such as betray their own souls; for Allah loves not one given to perfidy and crime:

107. Wa laa tujaadil 'anil-lazeena yakhtaanoona anfusahum; innal-laaha laa yuḥibbu man kaana khawwaanan aseemaa.

وَلَا تُجَادِلْ عَنِ الَّذِيْنَ يَخْتَانُوْنَ
اَنْفُسَهُمْ ۗ اِنَّ اللّٰهَ لَا يُحِبُّ مَنْ
كَانَ خَوَّانًا اَثِيْمًا ﴿١٠٧﴾ ۙ

108. They may hide (their crimes) from men, but they cannot hide (them) from Allah, seeing that He is in their midst when they plot by night, in words that He cannot approve: And Allah does compass round all that they do.

108. Yastakhfoona minannaasi wa laa yastakh-foona minal-laahi wa huwa ma'ahum iz yubayyitoona maa laa yarḍaa minal-qawl; wa kaanal-laahu bimaa ya'maloona muḥeeṭaa.

يَّسْتَخْفُوْنَ مِنَ النَّاسِ وَلَا يَسْتَخْفُوْنَ
مِنَ اللّٰهِ وَهُوَ مَعَهُمْ اِذْ يُبَيِّتُوْنَ
مَا لَا يَرْضٰى مِنَ الْقَوْلِ ۗ وَكَانَ
اللّٰهُ بِمَا يَعْمَلُوْنَ مُحِيْطًا ﴿١٠٨﴾

Ikhfa اخفاء — Ghunna غُنّہ — Ikhfa Meem Saakin اخفاء میم ساکن — Idghaam ادغام — Qalqala قلقلہ — Qalb قلب — Idghaam Meem Saakin ادغام میم ساکن

109. Ah! These are the sort of men on whose behalf you may contend in this world; but who will contend with Allah on their behalf on the Day of Judgment, or who will carry their affairs through?

109. Haaa-antum haaa'ulaaa'i jaadaltum 'anhum fil-ḥayaatid-dunyaa famañy-yujaadilul-laaha 'anhum Yawmal-Qiyaamati am mañy-yakoonu 'alayhim wakeelaa.

هٰٓأَنتُمْ هٰٓؤُلَآءِ جٰدَلْتُمْ عَنْهُمْ فِى
الْحَيٰوةِ الدُّنْيَا فَمَن يُجٰدِلُ
اللّٰهَ عَنْهُمْ يَوْمَ الْقِيٰمَةِ أَم مَّن
يَكُونُ عَلَيْهِمْ وَكِيلًا ﴿١٠٩﴾

110. If any one does evil or wrongs his own soul but afterwards seeks Allah's forgiveness, he will find Allah Oft-forgiving, Most Merciful.

110. Wa mañy-ya'mal sooo'an aw yaẓlim nafsahoo summa yastaghfiril-laaha yajidil-laaha Ghafoorar-Raḥeemaa.

وَمَن يَعْمَلْ سُوٓءًا أَوْ يَظْلِمْ
نَفْسَهُۥ ثُمَّ يَسْتَغْفِرِ اللّٰهَ يَجِدِ اللّٰهَ
غَفُورًا رَّحِيمًا ﴿١١٠﴾

111. And if any one earns sin. he earns it against his own soul: for Allah is full of knowledge and wisdom.

111. Wa mañy-yaksib ismam fa-innamaa yaksibuhoo 'alaa nafsih; wa kaanal-laahu 'Aleeman Ḥakeemaa.

وَمَن يَكْسِبْ إِثْمًا فَإِنَّمَا يَكْسِبُهُۥ
عَلٰى نَفْسِهِۦ ۚ وَكَانَ اللّٰهُ
عَلِيمًا حَكِيمًا ﴿١١١﴾

112. But if any one earns a fault or a sin and throws it on to one that is innocent, he carries (on himself) (both) a falsehood and a flagrant sin.

112. Wa mañy-yaksib kha-ṭeee'atan aw isman summa yarmi bihee bareee'an faqadiḥ-tamala buhtaanañw-wa ismam-mubeenaa. **(Section 16)**

وَمَن يَكْسِبْ خَطِيٓـَٔةً أَوْ إِثْمًا ثُمَّ
يَرْمِ بِهِۦ بَرِيٓـًٔا فَقَدِ احْتَمَلَ بُهْتٰنًا
وَإِثْمًا مُّبِينًا ﴿١١٢﴾ ع ١٦

113. But for the Grace of Allah to you and His Mercy, a party of them would certainly have plotted to lead you astray. But (in fact) they will only lead their own souls astray, and to you they can do no harm in the least. For Allah has sent down to you the Book and wisdom and taught you what you knew not (before): and great is the Grace of Allah unto you.

113. Wa law laa faḍlul-laahi 'alayka wa raḥmatuhoo lahammaṭ-ṭaaa'ifatum minhum añy-yuḍillooka wa maa yuḍilloona illaaa anfusahum wa maa yaḍurroonaka min shay'; wa anzalal-laahu 'alaykal-Kitaaba wal-Ḥikmata wa 'allamaka maa lam takun ta'lam; wa kaana faḍlul-laahi 'alayka 'aẓeemaa.

وَلَوْلَا فَضْلُ اللّٰهِ عَلَيْكَ وَرَحْمَتُهُۥ
لَهَمَّت طَّآئِفَةٌ مِّنْهُمْ أَن يُضِلُّوكَ
وَمَا يُضِلُّونَ إِلَّآ أَنفُسَهُمْ وَمَا
يَضُرُّونَكَ مِن شَىْءٍ ۚ وَأَنزَلَ اللّٰهُ
عَلَيْكَ الْكِتٰبَ وَالْحِكْمَةَ وَعَلَّمَكَ
مَا لَمْ تَكُن تَعْلَمُ ۚ وَكَانَ
فَضْلُ اللّٰهِ عَلَيْكَ عَظِيمًا ﴿١١٣﴾ الثلثة

114. In most of their secret talks there is no good: but if one exhorts to a deed of charity or justice or conciliation between men, (secrecy is permissible): to him who does this, seeking the good pleasure of Allah, We shall soon give a reward of the highest (value).

114. Laa khayra fee kaseerim-min najwaahum illaa man amara biṣadaqatin aw ma'roo-fin aw iṣlaaḥim-baynan-naas; wa mañy-yaf'al zaalikab-tighaaa'a marḍaatil-laahi fa-sawfa nu'teehi ajran 'aẓeemaa.

لَّا خَيْرَ فِى كَثِيرٍ مِّن نَّجْوٰىهُمْ إِلَّا
مَنْ أَمَرَ بِصَدَقَةٍ أَوْ مَعْرُوفٍ
أَوْ إِصْلٰحٍۭ بَيْنَ النَّاسِ ۚ وَمَن
يَفْعَلْ ذٰلِكَ ابْتِغَآءَ مَرْضَاتِ اللّٰهِ
فَسَوْفَ نُؤْتِيهِ أَجْرًا عَظِيمًا ﴿١١٤﴾

115. If anyone contends with the Apostle even after

115. Wa mañy-yushaaqiqir-Rasoola mim-ba'di

وَمَن يُشَاقِقِ الرَّسُولَ مِنۢ بَعْدِ

Ikhfa اخفاء | Ghunna غنّة | Ikhfa Meem Saakin اخفاء میم ساکن | Idghaam ادغام | Qalqala قلقلہ | Qalb قلب | Idghaam Meem Saakin ادغام میم ساکن

guidance has been plainly conveyed to him, and follows a path other than that becoming to men of Faith, We shall leave him in the path he has chosen, and land him in Hell, - what an evil refuge!

116. Allah forgives not (the sin of) joining other gods with Him; but He forgives whom He pleases other sins than this: one who joins other gods with Allah has strayed far, far away (from the Right).

117. (The Pagans), leaving Him, call but upon female deities: they call but upon Satan the persistent rebel!

118. Allah did curse him, but he said: "I will take of Your servants a portion marked off;

119. "I will mislead them, and I will create in them false desires; I will order them to slit the ears of cattle, and to deface the (fair) nature created by Allah." Whoever, forsaking Allah, takes Satan for a friend, has of a surety suffered a loss that is manifest.

120. Satan makes them promises, and creates in them false desires; but Satan's promises are nothing but deception.

121. They (his dupes) will have their dwelling in Hell, and from it they will find no way of escape.

122. But those who believe and do deeds of righteousness, - We shall soon admit them to Gardens, with rivers flowing beneath, - to dwell therein for ever. Allah's promise is the truth, and whose word can be truer than Allah's?

123. Not your desires, nor those of the People of

maa tabayyana lahul-hudaa wa yattabi' ghayra sabeelil-mu'mineena nuwallihee maa tawallaa wa nuṣlihee Jahannama wa saaa'at maṣeeraa.

(Section 17)

116. Innal-laaha laa yaghfiru añy-yushraka bihee wayaghfiru maa doona zaalika limañy yashaaa'; wa mañy-yushrik billaahi faqad ḍalla ḍalaalamba'eedaa.

117. Iñy-yad'oona min dooniheee illaaa inaasañw wa iñy-yad'oona illaa Shayṭaanam-mareedaa.

118. La'anahul-laah; wa qaala la-attakhizanna min 'ibaadika naṣeebam-mafrooḍaa.

119. Wa la-uḍillannahum wa la-umanni yannahum wa la-aamurannahum fala-yubattikunna aazaanal-an'aami wa la-aamurannahum fala-yughayyirunna khalqal-laah; wa mañy-yattakhizish-Shayṭaana waliyyam-min doonil-laahi faqad khasira khusraanam-mubeenaa.

120. Ya'iduhum wa yumanneehim wa maa ya'iduhumush-Shayṭaanu illaa ghurooraa.

121. Ulaaa'ika maåwaahum Jahannamu wa laa yajidoona 'anhaa maḥeeṣaa.

122. Wallazeena aamanoo wa 'amiluṣ-ṣaaliḥaati sanudkhiluhum Jannaatin tajree min taḥtihal-anhaaru khaalideena feehaaa abadaa; wa'dal-laahi ḥaqqaa; wa man aṣdaqu minallaahi qeelaa.

123. Laysa bi-amaaniyyikum wa laaa amaaniyyi Ahlil-

مَا تَبَيَّنَ لَهُ الْهُدٰى وَيَتَّبِعْ
غَيْرَ سَبِيْلِ الْمُؤْمِنِيْنَ نُوَلِّهٖ مَا تَوَلّٰى
وَنُصْلِهٖ جَهَنَّمَ ؕ وَسَآءَتْ مَصِيْرًا ﴿۱۱۵﴾ ع
اِنَّ اللّٰهَ لَا يَغْفِرُ اَنْ يُّشْرَكَ بِهٖ
وَيَغْفِرُ مَا دُوْنَ ذٰلِكَ لِمَنْ يَّشَآءُ ؕ
وَمَنْ يُّشْرِكْ بِاللّٰهِ فَقَدْ ضَلَّ
ضَلٰلًا بَعِيْدًا ﴿۱۱۶﴾
اِنْ يَّدْعُوْنَ مِنْ دُوْنِهٖٓ اِلَّآ اِنٰثًا ۚ
وَاِنْ يَّدْعُوْنَ اِلَّا شَيْطٰنًا مَّرِيْدًا ﴿۱۱۷﴾ ۙ
لَّعَنَهُ اللّٰهُ ۘ وَقَالَ لَاَتَّخِذَنَّ مِنْ وقف لازم
عِبَادِكَ نَصِيْبًا مَّفْرُوْضًا ﴿۱۱۸﴾ ۙ
وَّلَاُضِلَّنَّهُمْ وَلَاُمَنِّيَنَّهُمْ وَلَاٰمُرَنَّهُمْ
فَلَيُبَتِّكُنَّ اٰذَانَ الْاَنْعَامِ وَلَاٰمُرَنَّهُمْ
فَلَيُغَيِّرُنَّ خَلْقَ اللّٰهِ ؕ وَمَنْ يَّتَّخِذِ
الشَّيْطٰنَ وَلِيًّا مِّنْ دُوْنِ اللّٰهِ فَقَدْ
خَسِرَ خُسْرَانًا مُّبِيْنًا ﴿۱۱۹﴾ ؕ
يَعِدُهُمْ وَيُمَنِّيْهِمْ ؕ وَمَا يَعِدُهُمُ
الشَّيْطٰنُ اِلَّا غُرُوْرًا ﴿۱۲۰﴾
اُولٰٓئِكَ مَاْوٰىهُمْ جَهَنَّمُ ز وَلَا
يَجِدُوْنَ عَنْهَا مَحِيْصًا ﴿۱۲۱﴾
وَالَّذِيْنَ اٰمَنُوْا وَعَمِلُوا الصّٰلِحٰتِ
سَنُدْخِلُهُمْ جَنّٰتٍ تَجْرِيْ مِنْ
تَحْتِهَا الْاَنْهٰرُ خٰلِدِيْنَ فِيْهَآ اَبَدًا ؕ
وَعْدَ اللّٰهِ حَقًّا ؕ وَمَنْ اَصْدَقُ
مِنَ اللّٰهِ قِيْلًا ﴿۱۲۲﴾
لَيْسَ بِاَمَانِيِّكُمْ وَلَآ اَمَانِيِّ اَهْلِ

Ikhfa اخفاء | Ghunna غُنّہ | Ikhfa Meem Saakin اخفاء میم ساکن | Idghaam ادغام | Qalqala قلقلہ | Qalb قلب | Idghaam Meem Saakin ادغام میم ساکن

the Book (can prevail): whoever works evil, will be requited accordingly. Nor will he find, besides Allah any protector or helper.

Kitaab; mañy-ya'mal sooo'añy-yujza bihee wa laa yajid lahoo min doonil-laahi waliyyañw-wa laa naṣeeraa.

الْكِتٰبِ ؕ مَنْ يَّعْمَلْ سُوْٓءًا يُّجْزَ بِهٖ ۙ
وَلَا يَجِدْ لَهٗ مِنْ دُوْنِ اللّٰهِ وَلِيًّا
وَّلَا نَصِيْرًا ﴿١٢٣﴾

124. If any do deeds of righteousness,- be they male or female - and have faith, they will enter Heaven, and not the least injustice will be done to them.

124. Wa mañy-ya'mal minaṣ-ṣaaliḥaati min zakarin aw unsaa wa huwa mu'minun fa-ulaaa'ika yadkhuloonal-Jannata wa laa yuẓlamoona naqeeraa.

وَمَنْ يَّعْمَلْ مِنَ الصّٰلِحٰتِ مِنْ
ذَكَرٍ اَوْ اُنْثٰى وَهُوَ مُؤْمِنٌ
فَاُولٰٓئِكَ يَدْخُلُوْنَ الْجَنَّةَ وَلَا
يُظْلَمُوْنَ نَقِيْرًا ﴿١٢٤﴾

125. Who can be better in religion than one who submits his whole self to Allah, does good, and follows the way of Abraham the true in faith? For Allah did take Abraham for a friend.

125. Wa man aḥsanu deenam-mimman aslama wajhahoo lillaahi wa huwa muḥsinuñw-wattaba'a Millata Ibraaheema Ḥaneefaa; wattakhazal-laahu Ibraaheema khaleelaa.

وَمَنْ اَحْسَنُ دِيْنًا مِّمَّنْ اَسْلَمَ
وَجْهَهٗ لِلّٰهِ وَهُوَ مُحْسِنٌ وَّاتَّبَعَ
مِلَّةَ اِبْرٰهِيْمَ حَنِيْفًا ؕ وَاتَّخَذَ
اللّٰهُ اِبْرٰهِيْمَ خَلِيْلًا ﴿١٢٥﴾

126. But to Allah belong all things in the heavens and on earth: and He it is that encompasses all things.

126. Wa lillaahi maa fis-samaawaati wa maa fil-arḍ; wa kaanal-laahu bikulli shay'im-muḥeeṭaa.

(Section 18)

وَلِلّٰهِ مَا فِي السَّمٰوٰتِ وَمَا فِي الْاَرْضِ ؕ
وَكَانَ اللّٰهُ بِكُلِّ شَيْءٍ مُّحِيْطًا ﴿١٢٦﴾ ع ١٨ ١٥

127. They ask your instruction concerning the Women. Say: Allah does instruct you about them: and (remember) what has been rehearsed unto you in the Book, concerning the orphans of women to whom you give not the portions prescribed, and yet whom you desire to marry, as also concerning the children who are weak and oppressed: that you stand firm for justice to orphans. There is not a good deed which you do, but Allah is well-acquainted therewith.

127. Wa yastaftoonaka finnisaaa'i qulil-laahu yufteekum feehinna wa maa yutlaa 'alaykum fil-Kitaabi fee yataaman-nisaaa'il-laatee laa tu'toonahunna maa kutiba lahunna wa targhaboona an tankiḥoohunna wal-mustaḍ'afeena minal-wildaani wa an taqoomoo lilyataamaa bilqisṭ; wa maa taf'aloo min khayrin fa-innal-laaha kaana bihee 'Aleemaa.

وَيَسْتَفْتُوْنَكَ فِي النِّسَآءِ ؕ قُلِ اللّٰهُ
يُفْتِيْكُمْ فِيْهِنَّ ۙ وَمَا يُتْلٰى عَلَيْكُمْ
فِي الْكِتٰبِ فِيْ يَتٰمَى النِّسَآءِ الّٰتِيْ
لَا تُؤْتُوْنَهُنَّ مَا كُتِبَ لَهُنَّ
وَتَرْغَبُوْنَ اَنْ تَنْكِحُوْهُنَّ وَ
الْمُسْتَضْعَفِيْنَ مِنَ الْوِلْدَانِ ۙ وَاَنْ
تَقُوْمُوْا لِلْيَتٰمٰى بِالْقِسْطِ ؕ وَمَا
تَفْعَلُوْا مِنْ خَيْرٍ فَاِنَّ اللّٰهَ كَانَ
بِهٖ عَلِيْمًا ﴿١٢٧﴾

128. If a wife fears cruelty or desertion on her husband's part, there is no blame on them if they arrange an amicable settlement between themselves; and such settlement is best; even though men's souls are

128. Wa inimra-atun khaafat mim ba'lihaa nushoozan aw i'raaḍan falaa junaaḥa 'alayhimaaa añy-yuṣliḥaa baynahumaa ṣulḥaa; waṣṣulḥu khayr; wa uḥḍiratil-anfusush-

وَاِنِ امْرَاَةٌ خَافَتْ مِنْۢ بَعْلِهَا
نُشُوْزًا اَوْ اِعْرَاضًا فَلَا جُنَاحَ
عَلَيْهِمَآ اَنْ يُّصْلِحَا بَيْنَهُمَا صُلْحًا ؕ
وَالصُّلْحُ خَيْرٌ ؕ وَاُحْضِرَتِ الْاَنْفُسُ

Ikhfa اخفاء | Ghunna غُنّہ | Ikhfa Meem Saakin اخفاء میم ساکن | Idghaam ادغام | Qalqala قلقلہ | Qalb قلب | Idghaam Meem Saakin ادغام میم ساکن

swayed by greed. But if you do good and practise self-restraint, Allah is well-acquainted with all that you do.

129. You are never able to be fair and just as between women, even if it is your ardent desire: but turn not away (from a woman) altogether, so as to leave her (as it were) hanging (in the air). If you come to a friendly understanding, and practise self-restraint, Allah is Oft-forgiving, Most Merciful.

130. But if they disagree (and must part), Allah will provide abundance for all from His all-reaching bounty: for Allah is He that cares for all and is Wise.

131. To Allah belong all things in the heavens and on earth. Verily We have directed the People of the Book before you, and you (O Muslims) to fear Allah. But if you deny Him, lo! to Allah belong all things in the heavens and on earth, and Allah is free of all wants, worthy of all praise.

132. Yes, to Allah belong all things in the heavens and on earth, and enough is Allah to carry through all affairs.

133. If it were His Will, He could destroy you, O mankind, and create another race; for Allah has power to do this.

134. If any one desires a reward in this life, in Allah's (gift) is the reward (both) of this life and of the hereafter: for Allah is He that hears and sees (all things).

135. O you who believe! stand out firmly for justice, as witnesses to Allah, even as against yourselves, or your parents, or your kin,

shuḥḥ; wa in tuḥsinoo wa tattaqoo fa-innal-laaha kaana bimaa ta'maloona Khabeeraa.

129. Wa lan tastaṭee'ooo an ta'diloo baynan-nisaaa'i wa law ḥaraṣtum falaa tameeloo kullal-mayli fataẓaroohaa kalmu'al-laqah; wa in tuṣliḥoo wa tattaqoo fa-innal-laaha kaana Ghafoorar-Raḥeemaa.

130. Wa iñy-yatafarraqaa yugh-nil-laahu kullam-min sa'atih; wa kaanal-laahu Waasi'an Ḥakeemaa.

131. Wa lillaahi maafis-sa-maawaati wa maa fil-arḍ; wa laqad waṣṣaynal-lazeena ootul-Kitaaba min qablikum wa iyyaakum anit-taqul-laah; wa in takfuroo fa-inna lillaahi maa fis-samaawaati wa maa fil-arḍ; wa kaanal-laahu Ghaniyyan Ḥameedaa.

132. Wa lillaahi maa fis-sa-maawaati wa maa fil-arḍ; wa kafaa billaahi Wakeelaa.

133. Iñy-yashaå yuẕhibkum ayyuhan-naasu wa yaåti bi-aakhareen; wa kaanal-laahu 'alaa ẕaalika Qadeeraa.

134. Man kaana yureedu ṯawaabad-dunyaa fa'indallaahi ṯawaabud-dunyaa wal-Aakhi-rah; wa kaanal-laahu Samee-'am-Baṣeeraa. **(Section 19)**

135. Yaaa-ayyuhal-lazeena aamanoo koonoo qawwa-ameena bilqisṭi shuhadaaa'a lillaahi wa law 'alaaa anfusikum awil-waalidayni wal-aqrabeen;

الشُّحَّ ۚ وَإِنْ تُحْسِنُوا وَتَتَّقُوا فَإِنَّ
اللّٰهَ كَانَ بِمَا تَعْمَلُونَ خَبِيرًا ﴿١٢٨﴾
وَلَنْ تَسْتَطِيعُوا أَنْ تَعْدِلُوا بَيْنَ
النِّسَاءِ وَلَوْ حَرَصْتُمْ فَلَا تَمِيلُوا كُلَّ
الْمَيْلِ فَتَذَرُوهَا كَالْمُعَلَّقَةِ ۚ
وَإِنْ تُصْلِحُوا وَتَتَّقُوا فَإِنَّ اللّٰهَ
كَانَ غَفُورًا رَّحِيمًا ﴿١٢٩﴾
وَإِنْ يَتَفَرَّقَا يُغْنِ اللّٰهُ كُلًّا مِّنْ
سَعَتِهِ ۚ وَكَانَ اللّٰهُ وَاسِعًا حَكِيمًا ﴿١٣٠﴾
وَلِلّٰهِ مَا فِي السَّمٰوٰتِ وَمَا فِي الْأَرْضِ ۗ
وَلَقَدْ وَصَّيْنَا الَّذِينَ أُوتُوا الْكِتٰبَ
مِنْ قَبْلِكُمْ وَإِيَّاكُمْ أَنِ اتَّقُوا اللّٰهَ ۚ
وَإِنْ تَكْفُرُوا فَإِنَّ لِلّٰهِ مَا فِي
السَّمٰوٰتِ وَمَا فِي الْأَرْضِ ۚ وَكَانَ اللّٰهُ
غَنِيًّا حَمِيدًا ﴿١٣١﴾
وَلِلّٰهِ مَا فِي السَّمٰوٰتِ وَمَا فِي
الْأَرْضِ ۚ وَكَفٰى بِاللّٰهِ وَكِيلًا ﴿١٣٢﴾
إِنْ يَشَأْ يُذْهِبْكُمْ أَيُّهَا النَّاسُ
وَيَأْتِ بِآخَرِينَ ۚ وَكَانَ اللّٰهُ
عَلٰى ذٰلِكَ قَدِيرًا ﴿١٣٣﴾
مَنْ كَانَ يُرِيدُ ثَوَابَ الدُّنْيَا فَعِنْدَ
اللّٰهِ ثَوَابُ الدُّنْيَا وَالْآخِرَةِ ۚ وَكَانَ
اللّٰهُ سَمِيعًا بَصِيرًا ﴿١٣٤﴾ ع ١٩ ١٦
يٰأَيُّهَا الَّذِينَ آمَنُوا كُونُوا قَوَّامِينَ
بِالْقِسْطِ شُهَدَاءَ لِلّٰهِ وَلَوْ عَلٰى
أَنْفُسِكُمْ أَوِ الْوَالِدَيْنِ وَالْأَقْرَبِينَ ۚ

Ikhfa اخفاء | Ghunna غُنّہ | Ikhfa Meem Saakin اخفاء میم ساکن | Idghaam ادغام | Qalqala قلقلہ | Qalb قلب | Idghaam Meem Saakin ادغام میم ساکن

and whether it be (against) rich or poor: for Allah can best protect both. Follow not the lusts (of your hearts), lest you swerve, and if you distort (justice) or decline to do justice, verily Allah is well- acquainted with all that you do.

136. O you who believe! Believe in Allah and His Apostle, and the scripture which He has sent to His Apostle and the scripture which He sent to those before (him). Any who denies Allah, His Angels, His Books, His Apostles, and the Day of Judgment, has gone far, far astray.

137. Those who believe, then reject faith, then believe (again) and (again) reject faith, and go on increasing in unbelief, - Allah will not forgive them nor guide them on the Way.

138. To the Hypocrites give the glad tidings that there is for them (but) a grievous Chastisement.

139. Yes, to those who take for friends Unbelievers rather than Believers: is it honour they seek among them? No,- all honour is with Allah.

140. Already has He sent you Word in the Book, that when you hear the signs of Allah held in defiance and ridicule, you are not to sit with them unless they turn to a different theme: if you did, you would be like them. For Allah will collect the hypocrites and those who defy Faith - all in Hell:-

141. (These are) the ones who wait and watch about you: if

iñy-yakun ghaniyyan aw faqeeran fallaahu awlaa bihimaa falaaa tattabi'ul hawaaa an ta'diloo; wa in talwooo aw tu'riḍoo fa-innal-laaha kaana bimaa ta'maloona Khabeeraa.

136. Yaaa-ayyuhal-lazeena aamanooo aaminoo billaahi wa Rasoolihee wal-Kitaabil-lazee nazzala 'alaa Rasoolihee wal-Kitaabil-lazeee anzala min qabl; wa mañy-yakfur billaahi wa Malaaa'ikatihee wa Kutubihee wa Rusulihee wal-Yawmil-Aakhiri faqad ḍalla ḍalaalam-ba'eedaa.

137. Innal-lazeena aamanoo summa kafaroo summa aamanoo summa kafaroo summaz-daadoo kufral-lam yakunil-laahu liyaghfira lahum wa laa liyahdiyahum sabeelaa.

138. Bashshiril-munaafiqeena bi-anna lahum 'azaaban aleemaa.

139. Allazeena yattakhizoo-nal-kaafireena awliyaaa'a min doonil-mu'mineen; a-yabta-ghoona 'indahumul-'izzata fa-innal-'izzata lillaahi jamee'aa.

140. Wa qad nazzala 'alaykum fil-Kitaabi an izaa sami'tum Aayaatil-laahi yukfaru bihaa wa yustahza-u bihaa falaa taq'udoo ma'ahum ḥattaa yakhooḍoo fee ḥadeesin ghayrih; innakum izam-misluhum; innal-laaha jaami'ul-munaafiqeena wal-kaafireena fee Jahannama jamee'aa.

141. Allazeena yatarab-baṣoona bikum fa-in kaana

إِن يَكُنْ غَنِيًّا أَوْ فَقِيرًا فَاللَّهُ أَوْلَىٰ
بِهِمَا ۖ فَلَا تَتَّبِعُوا الْهَوَىٰ أَن
تَعْدِلُوا ۚ وَإِن تَلْوُوا أَوْ تُعْرِضُوا فَإِنَّ
اللَّهَ كَانَ بِمَا تَعْمَلُونَ خَبِيرًا ﴿١٣٥﴾
يَا أَيُّهَا الَّذِينَ آمَنُوا آمِنُوا بِاللَّهِ
وَرَسُولِهِ وَالْكِتَابِ الَّذِي نَزَّلَ عَلَىٰ
رَسُولِهِ وَالْكِتَابِ الَّذِي أَنزَلَ مِن
قَبْلُ ۚ وَمَن يَكْفُرْ بِاللَّهِ وَمَلَائِكَتِهِ
وَكُتُبِهِ وَرُسُلِهِ وَالْيَوْمِ الْآخِرِ
فَقَدْ ضَلَّ ضَلَالًا بَعِيدًا ﴿١٣٦﴾
إِنَّ الَّذِينَ آمَنُوا ثُمَّ كَفَرُوا ثُمَّ
آمَنُوا ثُمَّ كَفَرُوا ثُمَّ ازْدَادُوا كُفْرًا
لَّمْ يَكُنِ اللَّهُ لِيَغْفِرَ لَهُمْ وَلَا
لِيَهْدِيَهُمْ سَبِيلًا ﴿١٣٧﴾
بَشِّرِ الْمُنَافِقِينَ بِأَنَّ لَهُمْ عَذَابًا أَلِيمًا ﴿١٣٨﴾
الَّذِينَ يَتَّخِذُونَ الْكَافِرِينَ أَوْلِيَاءَ
مِن دُونِ الْمُؤْمِنِينَ ۚ أَيَبْتَغُونَ
عِندَهُمُ الْعِزَّةَ فَإِنَّ الْعِزَّةَ لِلَّهِ
جَمِيعًا ﴿١٣٩﴾
وَقَدْ نَزَّلَ عَلَيْكُمْ فِي الْكِتَابِ أَنْ إِذَا
سَمِعْتُمْ آيَاتِ اللَّهِ يُكْفَرُ بِهَا وَيُسْتَهْزَأُ
بِهَا فَلَا تَقْعُدُوا مَعَهُمْ حَتَّىٰ يَخُوضُوا
فِي حَدِيثٍ غَيْرِهِ ۚ إِنَّكُمْ إِذًا مِّثْلُهُمْ ۗ
إِنَّ اللَّهَ جَامِعُ الْمُنَافِقِينَ وَالْكَافِرِينَ
فِي جَهَنَّمَ جَمِيعًا ﴿١٤٠﴾
الَّذِينَ يَتَرَبَّصُونَ بِكُمْ فَإِن كَانَ

Ikhfa اخفاء | Ghunna غُنّہ | Ikhfa Meem Saakin اخفاء میم ساکن | Idghaam ادغام | Qalqala قلقلہ | Qalb قلب | Idghaam Meem Saakin ادغام میم ساکن

you do gain a victory from Allah, they say: "Were we not with you?"- but if the Unbelievers gain a success, they say (to them): "Did we not gain an advantage over you, and did we not guard you from the Believers?" But Allah will judge between you on the Day of Judgment. And never will Allah grant to the Unbelievers a way (to triumphs) over the Believers.

142. The Hypocrites - they think they are over-reaching Allah, but He will over- reach them: when they stand up to prayer, they stand without earnestness, to be seen of men, but little do they hold Allah in remembrance;

143. (They are) distracted in mind even in the midst of it,- being (sincerely) for neither one group nor for another. Whom Allah leaves straying,- never will you find for him the Way.

144. O you who believe! Take not for friends Unbelievers rather than Believers: do you wish to offer Allah an open proof against yourselves?

145. The Hypocrites will be in the lowest depths of the Fire: no helper will you find for them;-

146. Except for those who repent, mend (their lives) hold fast to Allah, and purify their religion as in Allah's sight: if so they will be (numbered) with the believers. And soon will Allah grant to the believers a reward of immense value.

147. What can Allah gain by your punishment, if you are grateful and you believe? No, it is Allah that recogniseth (all good), and knows all things.

148. Allah does not love that evil should be noised

lakum fatḥum-minal-laahi qaalooo alam nakum ma'akum wa in kaana lilkaafireena naṣeebun qaalooo alam nastaḥwiz̲ 'alaykum wa namna'kum minal-mu'mineen; fallaahu yaḥkumu baynakum Yawmal-Qiyaamah; wa lañy-yaj'alal-laahu lilkaafireena 'alal-mu'mineena sabeelaa.

(Section 20)

142. Innal-munaafiqeena yukhaadi'oonal-laaha wa huwa khaadi'uhum wa iz̲aa qaamooo ilaṣ-Ṣalaati qaamoo kusaalaa yuraaa'oonan-naasa wa laa yaz̲kuroonal-laaha illaa qaleelaa.

143. Muz̲abz̲abeena bayna z̲aalika laaa ilaa haaa'ulaaa'i wa laaa ilaa haaa'ulaaa'; wa mañy-yuḍlilil-laahu falan tajida lahoo sabeelaa.

144. Yaaa-ayyuhal-laz̲eena aamanoo laa tattakhiz̲ul-kaafireena awliyaaa'a min doonil-mu'mineen; atureedoona an taj'aloo lillaahi 'alaykum sulṭaanam-mubeenaa.

145. Innal-munaafiqeena fid-darkil-asfali minan-Naari wa lan tajida lahum naṣeeraa.

146. Illal-laz̲eena taaboo wa aṣlaḥoo wa'taṣamoo billaahi wa akhlaṣoo deenahum lillaahi faulaaa'ika ma'al-mu'mineena wa sawfa yu'til-laahul-mu'mineena ajran 'aẓeemaa.

147. Maa yafa'lul-laahu bi-'az̲aabikum in shakartum wa aamantum; wa kaanal-laahu Shaakiran 'Aleemaa.

148. Laa yuhibbullaahul-jahra bis-sooo'i

لَكُمْ فَتْحٌ مِّنَ اللّٰهِ قَالُوْٓا اَلَمْ نَكُنْ
مَّعَكُمْ ۖ وَاِنْ كَانَ لِلْكٰفِرِيْنَ نَصِيْبٌ ۙ
قَالُوْٓا اَلَمْ نَسْتَحْوِذْ عَلَيْكُمْ وَنَمْنَعْكُمْ
مِّنَ الْمُؤْمِنِيْنَ ؕ فَاللّٰهُ يَحْكُمُ بَيْنَكُمْ
يَوْمَ الْقِيٰمَةِ ؕ وَلَنْ يَّجْعَلَ اللّٰهُ لِلْكٰفِرِيْنَ
عَلَى الْمُؤْمِنِيْنَ سَبِيْلًا ﴿١٤١﴾ ربع
اِنَّ الْمُنٰفِقِيْنَ يُخٰدِعُوْنَ اللّٰهَ وَهُوَ
خَادِعُهُمْ ۚ وَاِذَا قَامُوْٓا اِلَى الصَّلٰوةِ
قَامُوْا كُسَالٰى ۙ يُرَآءُوْنَ النَّاسَ وَلَا
يَذْكُرُوْنَ اللّٰهَ اِلَّا قَلِيْلًا ۙ ﴿١٤٢﴾
مُّذَبْذَبِيْنَ بَيْنَ ذٰلِكَ ۖ لَآ اِلٰى
هٰٓؤُلَآءِ وَلَآ اِلٰى هٰٓؤُلَآءِ ؕ وَمَنْ يُّضْلِلِ
اللّٰهُ فَلَنْ تَجِدَ لَهٗ سَبِيْلًا ﴿١٤٣﴾
يٰٓاَيُّهَا الَّذِيْنَ اٰمَنُوْا لَا تَتَّخِذُوا
الْكٰفِرِيْنَ اَوْلِيَآءَ مِنْ دُوْنِ الْمُؤْمِنِيْنَ ؕ
اَتُرِيْدُوْنَ اَنْ تَجْعَلُوْا لِلّٰهِ عَلَيْكُمْ
سُلْطٰنًا مُّبِيْنًا ﴿١٤٤﴾
اِنَّ الْمُنٰفِقِيْنَ فِى الدَّرْكِ الْاَسْفَلِ
مِنَ النَّارِ ۚ وَلَنْ تَجِدَ لَهُمْ نَصِيْرًا ۙ ﴿١٤٥﴾
اِلَّا الَّذِيْنَ تَابُوْا وَاَصْلَحُوْا وَاعْتَصَمُوْا
بِاللّٰهِ وَاَخْلَصُوْا دِيْنَهُمْ لِلّٰهِ فَاُولٰٓئِكَ
مَعَ الْمُؤْمِنِيْنَ ؕ وَسَوْفَ يُؤْتِ اللّٰهُ
الْمُؤْمِنِيْنَ اَجْرًا عَظِيْمًا ﴿١٤٦﴾
مَا يَفْعَلُ اللّٰهُ بِعَذَابِكُمْ اِنْ شَكَرْتُمْ
وَاٰمَنْتُمْ ؕ وَكَانَ اللّٰهُ شَاكِرًا عَلِيْمًا ﴿١٤٧﴾ الجزء السادس (٦)
لَا يُحِبُّ اللّٰهُ الْجَهْرَ بِالسُّوْٓءِ

Ikhfa اخفاء | Ghunna غُنّہ | Ikhfa Meem Saakin اخفاء میم ساکن | Idghaam ادغام | Qalqala قلقلہ | Qalb قلب | Idghaam Meem Saakin ادغام میم ساکن

abroad in public speech, except where injustice has been done; for Allah is He who hears and knows all things.	minal-qawli illaa man ẓulim; wa kaanallaahu Samee'an 'Aleemaa.	مِنَ الْقَوْلِ إِلَّا مَن ظُلِمَ ۚ وَكَانَ اللَّهُ سَمِيعًا عَلِيمًا ﴿١٤٨﴾
149. Whether you publish a good deed or conceal it or cover evil with pardon, verily Allah blots out (sins) and has power (in the judgment of values).	149. In tubdoo khayran aw tukhfoohu aw ta'foo 'an sooo'in fa-innal-laaha kaana 'Afuwwan Qadeeraa.	إِن تُبْدُوا خَيْرًا أَوْ تُخْفُوهُ أَوْ تَعْفُوا عَن سُوٓءٍ فَإِنَّ اللَّهَ كَانَ عَفُوًّا قَدِيرًا ﴿١٤٩﴾
150. Those who deny Allah and His apostles, and (those who) wish to separate Allah from His apostles, saying: "We believe in some but reject others": And (those who) wish to take a course midway,-	150. Innal-lazeena yakfuroona billaahi wa Rusulihee wa yureedoona añy-yufarriqoo baynal-laahi wa Rusulihee wa yaqooloona nu'minu biba'ḍiñw-wa nakfuru biba'ḍiñw-wa yureedoona añy-yattakhizoo bayna zaalika sabeelaa.	إِنَّ الَّذِينَ يَكْفُرُونَ بِاللَّهِ وَرُسُلِهِ وَيُرِيدُونَ أَن يُفَرِّقُوا بَيْنَ اللَّهِ وَرُسُلِهِ وَيَقُولُونَ نُؤْمِنُ بِبَعْضٍ وَنَكْفُرُ بِبَعْضٍ وَيُرِيدُونَ أَن يَتَّخِذُوا بَيْنَ ذَٰلِكَ سَبِيلًا ﴿١٥٠﴾
151. They are in truth (equally) unbelievers; and we have prepared for Unbelievers a humiliating punishment.	151. Ulaaa'ika humul-kaafiroona ḥaqqaa; wa a'tadnaa lilkaafireena 'azaabam-muheenaa.	أُولَٰٓئِكَ هُمُ الْكَٰفِرُونَ حَقًّا ۚ وَأَعْتَدْنَا لِلْكَٰفِرِينَ عَذَابًا مُّهِينًا ﴿١٥١﴾
152. To those who believe in Allah and His apostles and make no distinction between any of the apostles, we shall soon give their (due) rewards: for Allah is Oft- forgiving, Most Merciful.	152. Wallazeena aamanoo billaahi wa Rusulihee wa lam yufarriqoo bayna aḥadim-minhum ulaaa'ika sawfa yu'teehim ujoorahum; wa kaanal-laahu Ghafoorar-Raḥeemaa. **(Section 21)**	وَالَّذِينَ ءَامَنُوا بِاللَّهِ وَرُسُلِهِ وَلَمْ يُفَرِّقُوا بَيْنَ أَحَدٍ مِّنْهُمْ أُولَٰٓئِكَ سَوْفَ يُؤْتِيهِمْ أُجُورَهُمْ ۗ وَكَانَ اللَّهُ غَفُورًا رَّحِيمًا ﴿١٥٢﴾ ع ١١
153. The people of the Book ask you to cause a book to descend to them from heaven: Indeed they asked Moses for an even greater (miracle), for they said: "Show us Allah in public," but they were dazed for their presumption, with thunder and lightning. Yet they worshipped the calf even after clear signs had come to them; even so we forgave them; and gave Moses manifest proofs of authority.	153. Yas'aluka Ahlul-Kitaabi an tunazzila 'alayhim Kitaabam-minas-samaaa'i faqad sa-aloo Moosaaa-akbara min zaalika faqaalooo arinal-laaha jahratan fa-akhazat-humuṣ-ṣaa'iqatu biẓulmihim; summat-takhazul-'ijla mim ba'di maa jaa'at-humul-bayyinaatu fa'afawnaa 'an zaalik; wa aataynaa Moosaa sulṭaanam-mubeenaa.	يَسْـَٔلُكَ أَهْلُ الْكِتَٰبِ أَن تُنَزِّلَ عَلَيْهِمْ كِتَٰبًا مِّنَ السَّمَآءِ ۚ فَقَدْ سَأَلُوا مُوسَىٰٓ أَكْبَرَ مِن ذَٰلِكَ فَقَالُوٓا أَرِنَا اللَّهَ جَهْرَةً فَأَخَذَتْهُمُ الصَّٰعِقَةُ بِظُلْمِهِمْ ۚ ثُمَّ اتَّخَذُوا الْعِجْلَ مِنۢ بَعْدِ مَا جَآءَتْهُمُ الْبَيِّنَٰتُ فَعَفَوْنَا عَن ذَٰلِكَ ۚ وَءَاتَيْنَا مُوسَىٰ سُلْطَٰنًا مُّبِينًا ﴿١٥٣﴾
154. And for their Covenant we raised over them (the towering height) of Mount (Sinai); and (on another occasion) we said: "Enter the gate with humility"; and (once again) we commanded them: "Transgress not in the matter of the Sabbath."	154. Wa rafa'naa fawqahumuṭ-Ṭoora bimeesaaqihim wa qulnaa lahumud-khulul-baaba sujjadañw-wa qulnaa lahum laa ta'doo fis-Sabti	وَرَفَعْنَا فَوْقَهُمُ الطُّورَ بِمِيثَٰقِهِمْ وَقُلْنَا لَهُمُ ادْخُلُوا الْبَابَ سُجَّدًا وَقُلْنَا لَهُمْ لَا تَعْدُوا فِى السَّبْتِ

Ikhfa اخفاء | Ghunna غُنّہ | Ikhfa Meem Saakin اخفاء میم ساکن | Idghaam ادغام | Qalqala قلقلہ | Qalb قلب | Idghaam Meem Saakin ادغام میم ساکن

And We took from them a solemn Covenant.

wa akhaznaa minhum meesaaqan ghaleezaa.

وَأَخَذْنَا مِنْهُم مِّيثَاقًا غَلِيظًا ﴿١٥٤﴾

155. (They have incurred divine displeasure): In that they broke their Covenant; that they rejected the signs of Allah; that they slew the Messengers in defiance of right; that they said, "Our hearts are the wrappings (which preserve Allah's Word; We need no more)";- No, Allah has set the seal on their hearts for their blasphemy, and little is it they believe;-

155. Fabimaa naqdihim meesaaqahum wa kufrihim bi-Aayaatil-laahi wa qatlihimul-Ambiyaaa'a bighayri ḥaqqiñw-wa qawlihim quloobunaa ghulf; bal ṭaba'al-laahu 'alayhaa bikufrihim falaa yu'minoona illaa qaleelaa.

فَبِمَا نَقْضِهِم مِّيثَاقَهُمْ وَكُفْرِهِم
بِآيَاتِ اللَّهِ وَقَتْلِهِمُ الْأَنبِيَاءَ بِغَيْرِ
حَقٍّ وَقَوْلِهِمْ قُلُوبُنَا غُلْفٌ ۚ بَلْ طَبَعَ
اللَّهُ عَلَيْهَا بِكُفْرِهِمْ فَلَا يُؤْمِنُونَ
إِلَّا قَلِيلًا ﴿١٥٥﴾

156. That they rejected Faith; that they uttered against Mary a grave false charge;

156. Wa bikufrihim wa qawlihim 'alaa Maryama buh-taanan 'azeemaa.

وَبِكُفْرِهِمْ وَقَوْلِهِمْ عَلَىٰ مَرْيَمَ
بُهْتَانًا عَظِيمًا ﴿١٥٦﴾

157. That they said (in boast), "We killed Christ Jesus the son of Mary, the Apostle of Allah";- but they killed him not, nor crucified him, but so it was made to appear to them, and those who differ therein are full of doubts, with no (certain) knowledge, but only conjecture to follow, for of a surety they killed him not:-

157. Wa qawlihim innaa qatal-nal-Maseeḥa 'Eesab-na-Maryama Rasoolal-laahi wa maa qataloohu wa maa ṣalaboohu wa laakin shubbiha lahum; wa innal-lazeenakh-talafoo feehi lafee shakkim-minh; maa lahum bihee min 'ilmin illat-tibaa'az-zann; wa maa qataloohu yaqeenaa.

وَقَوْلِهِمْ إِنَّا قَتَلْنَا الْمَسِيحَ عِيسَى
ابْنَ مَرْيَمَ رَسُولَ اللَّهِ وَمَا قَتَلُوهُ
وَمَا صَلَبُوهُ وَلَٰكِن شُبِّهَ لَهُمْ ۚ
وَإِنَّ الَّذِينَ اخْتَلَفُوا فِيهِ لَفِي شَكٍّ
مِّنْهُ ۚ مَا لَهُم بِهِ مِنْ عِلْمٍ إِلَّا
اتِّبَاعَ الظَّنِّ ۚ وَمَا قَتَلُوهُ يَقِينًا ﴿١٥٧﴾

158. No, Allah raised him up unto Himself; and Allah is Exalted in Power, Wise;-

158. Bar-rafa'ahul-laahu ilayh; wa kaanal-laahu 'Azee-zan Hakeemaa.

بَل رَّفَعَهُ اللَّهُ إِلَيْهِ ۚ وَكَانَ اللَّهُ
عَزِيزًا حَكِيمًا ﴿١٥٨﴾

159. And there is none of the People of the Book but must believe in him before his death; and on the Day of Judgment he will be a witness against them;-

159. Wa im-min Ahlil-Kitaabi illaa layu'minanna bihee qabla mawtihee wa Yawmal-Qiyaamati yakoonu 'alayhim shaheedaa.

وَإِن مِّنْ أَهْلِ الْكِتَابِ إِلَّا لَيُؤْمِنَنَّ
بِهِ قَبْلَ مَوْتِهِ ۖ وَيَوْمَ الْقِيَامَةِ
يَكُونُ عَلَيْهِمْ شَهِيدًا ﴿١٥٩﴾

160. For the iniquity of the Jews We made unlawful for them certain (foods) good and wholesome which had been lawful for them;- in that they hindered many from Allah's Way;-

160. Fabiẓulmim-minal-lazeena haadoo ḥarramnaa 'alayhim ṭayyibaatin uḥillat lahum wa biṣaddihim 'an sabeelil-laahi kaseeraa.

فَبِظُلْمٍ مِّنَ الَّذِينَ هَادُوا حَرَّمْنَا
عَلَيْهِمْ طَيِّبَاتٍ أُحِلَّتْ لَهُمْ وَبِصَدِّهِمْ
عَن سَبِيلِ اللَّهِ كَثِيرًا ﴿١٦٠﴾

161. That they took interest, though they were forbidden; and that they devoured men's substance wrongfully;- we have prepared for those among them who reject Faith a grievous punishment.

161. Wa akhzihimur-ribaa wa qad nuhoo 'anhu wa aklihim amwaalan-naasi bilbaaṭil; wa a'tadnaa lilkaafireena minhum 'azaaban aleemaa.

وَأَخْذِهِمُ الرِّبَا وَقَدْ نُهُوا عَنْهُ
وَأَكْلِهِمْ أَمْوَالَ النَّاسِ بِالْبَاطِلِ ۚ
وَأَعْتَدْنَا لِلْكَافِرِينَ مِنْهُمْ عَذَابًا
أَلِيمًا ﴿١٦١﴾

Ikhfa اخفاء | Ghunna غُنّہ | Ikhfa Meem Saakin اخفاء میم ساکن | Idghaam ادغام | Qalqala قلقلہ | Qalb قلب | Idghaam Meem Saakin ادغام میم ساکن

162. But those among them who are well-grounded in knowledge, and the believers, believe in what has been revealed to you and what was revealed before you: And (especially) those who establish regular prayer and practise regular charity and believe in Allah and in the Last Day: To them shall We soon give a great reward.

162. Laakinir-raasikhoona fil'ilmi minhum walmu'minoona yu'minoona bimaaa unzila ilayka wa maaa unzila min qablika walmuqeemeenaṣ-Ṣalaata walmu'toonaz-Zakaata walmu'minoona billaahi wal-Yawmil-Aakhir; ulaaa'ika sanu'teehim ajran 'aẓeemaa.

(Section 22)

لَٰكِنِ الرَّٰسِخُونَ فِي الْعِلْمِ مِنْهُمْ
وَالْمُؤْمِنُونَ يُؤْمِنُونَ بِمَآ أُنزِلَ
إِلَيْكَ وَمَآ أُنزِلَ مِن قَبْلِكَ وَ
الْمُقِيمِينَ الصَّلَوٰةَ وَالْمُؤْتُونَ الزَّكَوٰةَ
وَالْمُؤْمِنُونَ بِاللَّهِ وَالْيَوْمِ الْآخِرِ ط
أُولَٰٓئِكَ سَنُؤْتِيهِمْ أَجْرًا عَظِيمًا ﴿١٦٢﴾

ع

163. We have sent you inspiration, as We sent it to Noah and the Messengers after him: we sent inspiration to Abraham, Isma'il, Isaac, Jacob and the Tribes, to Jesus, Job, Jonah, Aaron, and solomon, and to David We gave the Psalms.

163. Innaaa awḥaynaaa ilayka kamaaa awḥaynaaa ilaa Nooḥiñw-wan-Nabiyyeena mim ba'dih; wa awḥaynaaa ilaaa Ibraaheema wa Ismaa'eela wa Isḥaaqa wa Ya'qooba wal-Asbaaṭi wa 'Eesaa wa Ayyooba wa Yoonusa wa Haaroona wa Sulaymaan; wa aataynaa Daawooda Zabooraa.

إِنَّآ أَوْحَيْنَآ إِلَيْكَ كَمَآ أَوْحَيْنَآ
إِلَىٰ نُوحٍ وَالنَّبِيِّۦنَ مِنۢ بَعْدِهِۦ ج
وَأَوْحَيْنَآ إِلَىٰٓ إِبْرَٰهِيمَ وَإِسْمَٰعِيلَ
وَإِسْحَٰقَ وَيَعْقُوبَ وَالْأَسْبَاطِ وَعِيسَىٰ
وَأَيُّوبَ وَيُونُسَ وَهَٰرُونَ وَسُلَيْمَٰنَ ج
وَءَاتَيْنَا دَاوُۥدَ زَبُورًا ﴿١٦٣﴾

164. Of some apostles We have already told you the story; of others We have not;- and to Moses Allah spoke direct;-

164. Wa Rusulan qad qaṣaṣ-naahum 'alayka min qablu wa Rusulal-lam naqṣuṣhum 'alayk; wa kallamallaahu Moosaa takleemaa.

وَرُسُلًا قَدْ قَصَصْنَٰهُمْ عَلَيْكَ
مِن قَبْلُ وَرُسُلًا لَّمْ نَقْصُصْهُمْ
عَلَيْكَ ط وَكَلَّمَ اللَّهُ مُوسَىٰ تَكْلِيمًا ﴿١٦٤﴾

165. Apostles who gave good news as well as warning, that mankind, after (the coming) of the Apostles, should have no plea against Allah: For Allah is Exalted in Power, Wise.

165. Rusulam-mubashshireena wa munzireena li'allaa yakoona linnaasi 'alal-laahi ḥujjatum ba'dar-Rusul; wa kaanallaahu 'Azeezan Ḥakeemaa.

رُّسُلًا مُّبَشِّرِينَ وَمُنذِرِينَ لِئَلَّا
يَكُونَ لِلنَّاسِ عَلَى اللَّهِ حُجَّةٌۢ بَعْدَ
الرُّسُلِ ط وَكَانَ اللَّهُ عَزِيزًا حَكِيمًا ﴿١٦٥﴾

166. But Allah hears witness that what He has sent unto you He has sent from His (own) knowledge, and the Angels bear witness: But enough is Allah for a witness.

166. Laakinil-laahu yashhadu bimaaa anzala ilayka anzalahoo bi'ilmihee wal-malaaa'ikatu yashhadoon; wa kafaa billaahi Shaheedaa.

لَّٰكِنِ اللَّهُ يَشْهَدُ بِمَآ أَنزَلَ إِلَيْكَ
أَنزَلَهُۥ بِعِلْمِهِۦ ج وَالْمَلَٰٓئِكَةُ
يَشْهَدُونَ ط وَكَفَىٰ بِاللَّهِ شَهِيدًا ﴿١٦٦﴾

167. Those who reject Faith and keep off (men) from the way of Allah, have verily strayed far, far away from the Path.

167. Innal-lazeena kafaroo wa ṣaddoo 'an sabeelil-laahi qad ḍalloo ḍalaalam-ba'eedaa.

إِنَّ الَّذِينَ كَفَرُوا وَصَدُّوا عَن
سَبِيلِ اللَّهِ قَدْ ضَلُّوا ضَلَٰلًۢا بَعِيدًا ﴿١٦٧﴾

168. Those who reject Faith and do wrong,- Allah will not forgive them nor guide them to any way-

168. Innal-lazeena kafaroo wa ẓalamoo lam yakunillaahu liyaghfira lahum wa laa liyahdiyahum ṭareeqaa.

إِنَّ الَّذِينَ كَفَرُوا وَظَلَمُوا لَمْ يَكُنِ
اللَّهُ لِيَغْفِرَ لَهُمْ وَلَا لِيَهْدِيَهُمْ
طَرِيقًا ﴿١٦٨﴾

Ikhfa اخفاء | Ghunna غنّہ | Ikhfa Meem Saakin اخفاء میم ساکن | Idghaam ادغام | Qalqala قلقلہ | Qalb قلب | Idghaam Meem Saakin ادغام میم ساکن

169. Except the way of Hell, to dwell therein for ever. And this to Allah is easy.

169. Illaa ṭareeqa Jahannama khaalideena feehaaa abadaa; wa kaana zaalika 'alal-laahi yaseeraa.

اِلَّا طَرِيْقَ جَهَنَّمَ خٰلِدِيْنَ فِيْهَآ اَبَدًا ؕ وَكَانَ ذٰلِكَ عَلَى اللّٰهِ يَسِيْرًا ﴿١٦٩﴾

170. O mankind! The Apostle has come to you in truth from Allah: believe in him: It is best for you. But if you reject Faith, to Allah belong all things in the heavens and on earth: And Allah is All-knowing, All-wise.

170. Yaaa ayyuhan-naasu qad jaaa'akumur-Rasoolu bilḥaqqi mir-Rabbikum fa-aaminoo khayral-lakum; wa in takfuroo fainna lillaahi maa fis-samaawaati wal-arḍ; wa kaanal-laahu 'Aleeman Ḥakeemaa.

يٰۤاَيُّهَا النَّاسُ قَدْ جَآءَكُمُ الرَّسُوْلُ بِالْحَقِّ مِنْ رَّبِّكُمْ فَاٰمِنُوْا خَيْرًا لَّكُمْ ؕ وَاِنْ تَكْفُرُوْا فَاِنَّ لِلّٰهِ مَا فِى السَّمٰوٰتِ وَالْاَرْضِ ؕ وَكَانَ اللّٰهُ عَلِيْمًا حَكِيْمًا ﴿١٧٠﴾

171. O People of the Book! commit no excesses in your religion: Nor say of Allah anything but the truth. Christ Jesus the son of Mary was (no more than) an Apostle of Allah, and His Word, which He bestowed on Mary, and a spirit proceeding from Him: so believe in Allah and His Apostles. Say not "Trinity" desist: it will be better for you: for Allah is one Allah: Glory be to Him: (far exalted is He) above having a son. To Him belong all things in the heavens and on earth. And enough is Allah as a Disposer of affairs.

171. Yaaa Ahlal-Kitaabi laa taghloo fee deenikum wa laa taqooloo 'alal-laahi illalḥaqq; innamal-Maseeḥu 'Eesab-nu-Maryama Rasoolul-laahi wa Kalimatuhooo alqaahaaa ilaa Maryama wa rooḥum-minhu fa-aaminoo billaahi wa Rusulihee wa laa taqooloo salaasah; intahoo khayrallakum; innamal-laahu Ilaahuñw-Waaḥid, Subḥaanahooo añy-yakoona lahoo walad; lahoo maa fis-samaawaati wa maa fil-arḍ; wa kafaa billaahi Wakeelaa.

(Section 23)

يٰۤاَهْلَ الْكِتٰبِ لَا تَغْلُوْا فِىْ دِيْنِكُمْ وَلَا تَقُوْلُوْا عَلَى اللّٰهِ اِلَّا الْحَقَّ ؕ اِنَّمَا الْمَسِيْحُ عِيْسَى ابْنُ مَرْيَمَ رَسُوْلُ اللّٰهِ وَكَلِمَتُهٗ ۚ اَلْقٰهَاۤ اِلٰى مَرْيَمَ وَرُوْحٌ مِّنْهُ ز فَاٰمِنُوْا بِاللّٰهِ وَرُسُلِهٖ ۚ قف وَلَا تَقُوْلُوْا ثَلٰثَةٌ ؕ اِنْتَهُوْا خَيْرًا لَّكُمْ ؕ اِنَّمَا اللّٰهُ اِلٰهٌ وَّاحِدٌ ؕ سُبْحٰنَهٗۤ اَنْ يَّكُوْنَ لَهٗ وَلَدٌ ۘ لَهٗ مَا فِى السَّمٰوٰتِ وَمَا فِى الْاَرْضِ ؕ وَكَفٰى بِاللّٰهِ وَكِيْلًا ﴿١٧١﴾ ع

وقف لازم ع ٢٣

172. Christ does not disdain to serve and worship Allah, nor do the angels, those nearest (to Allah): those who disdain His worship and are arrogant,-He will gather them all together unto Himself to (answer).

172. Lañy-yastankifal-Maseeḥu añy-yakoona 'abdal-lillaahi wa lal-malaaa'ikatul-muqarraboon; wa mañy-yastankif 'an 'ibaadatihee wa yastakbir fasa-yaḥshuruhum ilayhi jamee'aa.

لَنْ يَّسْتَنْكِفَ الْمَسِيْحُ اَنْ يَّكُوْنَ عَبْدًا لِّلّٰهِ وَلَا الْمَلٰۤئِكَةُ الْمُقَرَّبُوْنَ ؕ وَمَنْ يَّسْتَنْكِفْ عَنْ عِبَادَتِهٖ وَيَسْتَكْبِرْ فَسَيَحْشُرُهُمْ اِلَيْهِ جَمِيْعًا ﴿١٧٢﴾

173. But to those who believe and do deeds of righteousness, He will give their (due) rewards,- and more, out of His bounty: But those who are disdainful and arrogant, He will punish with a grievous Chastisement; Nor will they find, besides Allah, any to protect or help them.

173. Fa-ammal-lazeena aamanoo wa 'amiluṣ-ṣaaliḥaati fa-yuwaffeehim ujoorahum wa yazeeduhum-min faḍlihee wa ammal-lazeenas-tankafoo wastakbaroo fa-yu'azzibuhum 'azaaban aleemañw-wa laa yajidoona lahum min doonil-laahi waliyyañw-wa laa naṣeeraa.

فَاَمَّا الَّذِيْنَ اٰمَنُوْا وَعَمِلُوا الصّٰلِحٰتِ فَيُوَفِّيْهِمْ اُجُوْرَهُمْ وَيَزِيْدُهُمْ مِّنْ فَضْلِهٖ ۚ وَاَمَّا الَّذِيْنَ اسْتَنْكَفُوْا وَاسْتَكْبَرُوْا فَيُعَذِّبُهُمْ عَذَابًا اَلِيْمًا ۙ لا وَّلَا يَجِدُوْنَ لَهُمْ مِّنْ دُوْنِ اللّٰهِ وَلِيًّا وَّلَا نَصِيْرًا ﴿١٧٣﴾

Ikhfa اخفاء | Ghunna غنّہ | Ikhfa Meem Saakin اخفاء میم ساکن | Idghaam ادغام | Qalqala قلقلہ | Qalb قلب | Idghaam Meem Saakin ادغام میم ساکن

174. O mankind! verily there has come to you a convincing proof from your Lord: For We have sent unto you a light (that is) manifest.

174. Yaaa-ayyuhan-naasu qad jaaa'akum burhaanum-mir-Rabbikum wa anzalnaaa ilaykum Nooram-Mubeenaa.

يٰاَيُّهَا النَّاسُ قَدْ جَآءَكُمْ بُرْهَانٌ مِّنْ رَّبِّكُمْ وَاَنْزَلْنَآ اِلَيْكُمْ نُوْرًا مُّبِيْنًا ﴿١٧٤﴾

175. Then those who believe in Allah, and hold fast to Him,- soon will He admit them to mercy and grace from Himself, and guide them to Himself by a straight way.

175. Fa-ammal-lazeena aamanoo billaahi wa'taṣamoo bihee fasa-yudkhiluhum fee raḥmatim-minhu wa faḍliñw-wa yahdeehim ilayhi Ṣiraaṭam-Mustaqeema.

فَاَمَّا الَّذِيْنَ اٰمَنُوْا بِاللّٰهِ وَاعْتَصَمُوْا بِهٖ فَسَيُدْخِلُهُمْ فِيْ رَحْمَةٍ مِّنْهُ وَفَضْلٍ ۙ وَّيَهْدِيْهِمْ اِلَيْهِ صِرَاطًا مُّسْتَقِيْمًا ﴿١٧٥﴾ ؕ

176. They ask you for a legal decision. Say: Allah directs (thus) about those who leave no descendants or ascendants as heirs. If it is a man that dies, leaving a sister but no child, she shall have half the inheritance: If (such a deceased was) a woman, who left no child, Her brother takes her inheritance: If there are two sisters, they shall have two-thirds of the inheritance (between them): if there are brothers and sisters, (they share), the male having twice the share of the female. Thus does Allah make clear to you (His law), lest you err. And Allah has knowledge of all things.

176. Yastaftoonaka qulillaahu yufteekum fil-kalaalah; inim-ru'un halaka laysa lahoo waladuñw-wa lahooo ukhtun falahaa niṣfu maa tarak; wa huwa yariṡuhaaa il-lam yakul-lahaa walad; fa-in kaanataṡ-natayni falahumaṡ-ṡuluṡaani mimmaa tarak; wa in kaanooo ikhwatar-rijaalañw-wa nisaaa'an faliẕ-ẕakari miṡlu ḥaẕẕil-unṡayayn; yubayyinullaahu lakum an taḍilloo; wallaahu bikulli shay'in 'Aleem.

(Section 24)

يَسْتَفْتُوْنَكَ ؕ قُلِ اللّٰهُ يُفْتِيْكُمْ فِى الْكَلٰلَةِ ؕ اِنِ امْرُؤٌا هَلَكَ لَيْسَ لَهٗ وَلَدٌ وَّلَهٗۤ اُخْتٌ فَلَهَا نِصْفُ مَا تَرَكَ ۚ وَهُوَ يَرِثُهَاۤ اِنْ لَّمْ يَكُنْ لَّهَا وَلَدٌ ؕ فَاِنْ كَانَتَا اثْنَتَيْنِ فَلَهُمَا الثُّلُثٰنِ مِمَّا تَرَكَ ؕ وَاِنْ كَانُوْۤا اِخْوَةً رِّجَالًا وَّنِسَآءً فَلِلذَّكَرِ مِثْلُ حَظِّ الْاُنْثَيَيْنِ ؕ يُبَيِّنُ اللّٰهُ لَكُمْ اَنْ تَضِلُّوْا ؕ وَاللّٰهُ بِكُلِّ شَىْءٍ عَلِيْمٌ ﴿١٧٦﴾ ع ٢٤

5. The Table Spread

In the name of Allah, Most Gracious, Most Merciful.

Sûrat al-Mâ'idah–5

(Revealed at Madinah)

Bismillaahir Raḥmaanir Raḥeem

(٥) سُوْرَةُ الْمَآئِدَةِ مَدَنِيَّةٌ (١١٢)

بِسْمِ اللّٰهِ الرَّحْمٰنِ الرَّحِيْمِ

1. O you who believe! fulfil (all) obligations. Lawful to you (for food) are all four-footed animals, with the exceptions named: But animals of the chase are forbidden while you are in the sacred precincts or in pilgrim garb: for Allah does command according to His will and plan.

1. Yaaa-ayyuhal-lazeena aamanooo awfoo bil'uqood; uḥillat lakum baheematul-an'aami illaa maa yutlaa 'alaykum ghayra muḥilliṣ-ṣaydi wa antum ḥurum; innal-laaha yaḥkumu maa yureed.

يٰۤاَيُّهَا الَّذِيْنَ اٰمَنُوْۤا اَوْفُوْا بِالْعُقُوْدِ ؕ اُحِلَّتْ لَكُمْ بَهِيْمَةُ الْاَنْعَامِ اِلَّا مَا يُتْلٰى عَلَيْكُمْ غَيْرَ مُحِلِّى الصَّيْدِ وَاَنْتُمْ حُرُمٌ ؕ اِنَّ اللّٰهَ يَحْكُمُ مَا يُرِيْدُ ﴿١﴾

2. O you who believe! violate not the sanctity of the symbols of Allah, nor of the Sacred Month, nor of the animals brought for sacrifice, nor the Garlands that mark out such animals, nor the people resorting to the Sacred House, seeking of the bounty and good pleasure of their Lord.

2. Yaaa ayyuhal-lazeena aamanoo laa tuḥilloo sha'aa-'iral-laahi wa lash-Shahral-Ḥaraama wa lal-hadya wa lal-qalaaa'ida wa laaa aaammee-nal-Baytal-Ḥaraama yabta-ghoona faḍlam-mir-Rabbihim wa riḍwaanaa;

يٰۤاَيُّهَا الَّذِيْنَ اٰمَنُوْا لَا تُحِلُّوْا شَعَآئِرَ اللّٰهِ وَلَا الشَّهْرَ الْحَرَامَ وَلَا الْهَدْىَ وَلَا الْقَلَآئِدَ وَلَاۤ اٰمِّيْنَ الْبَيْتَ الْحَرَامَ يَبْتَغُوْنَ فَضْلًا مِّنْ رَّبِّهِمْ وَرِضْوَانًا ؕ

اَلْمَنْزِلُ الثَّانِىْ (٢)

Ikhfa اخفاء · Ghunna غُنّہ · Ikhfa Meem Saakin اخفاء میم ساکن · Idghaam ادغام · Qalqala قلقلہ · Qalb قلب · Idghaam Meem Saakin ادغام میم ساکن

But when you are clear of the Sacred precincts and of pilgrim garb, you may hunt and let not the hatred of some people in (once) shutting you out of the Sacred Mosque lead you to transgression (and hostility on your part). Help you one another in righteousness and piety, but help you not one another in sin and rancour: fear Allah: for Allah is strict in punishment.

3. Forbidden to you (for food) are: dead meat, blood, the flesh of swine, and that on which has been invoked the name of other than Allah; that which has been killed by strangling, or by a violent blow, or by a headlong fall, or by being gored to death; that which has been (partly) eaten by a wild animal; unless you are able to slaughter it (in due form); that which is sacrificed on stone (altars); (forbidden) also is the division (of meat) by raffling with arrows: that is impiety. This day have those who reject faith given up all hopes of your religion: yet fear them not but fear Me. This day have I perfected your religion for you, completed My favour upon you, and have chosen for you Islam as your religion. But if any is forced by hunger, with no inclination to transgression, Allah is indeed Oft-forgiving, Most Merciful.

4. They ask you what is lawful to them (as food). Say: lawful unto you are (all) things good and pure: and what you have taught your trained hunting animals (to catch) in the manner directed to you by Allah: eat what they catch for you, but pronounce the name of Allah over it: and fear Allah; for Allah is swift in taking account.

5. This day are (all) things good and pure made lawful for you. The food of the People of the Book is lawful for you and

wa izaa halaltum fastaadoo; wa laa yajrimannakum shana-aanu qawmin an saddookum 'anil-Masjidil-Haraami an ta'tadoo; wa ta'aawanoo 'alalbirri wattaqwaa; wa laa ta'aawanoo 'alal-ismi wal'udwaan; wattaqul-laah; innal-laaha shadeedul-'iqaab.

3 Hurrimat 'alaykumul-maytatu waddamu wa lahmul-khinzeeri wa maaa uhilla lighayril-laahi bihee walmun-khani-qatu walmawqoozatu walmutarad-diyatu wanna-teehatu wa maaa akalas-sabu'u illaa maa zakkaytum wa maa zubiha 'alan-nusubi wa an tastaqsimoo bil-azlaam; zaalikum fisq; alyawma ya'isal-lazeena kafaroo min deenikum falaa takhshawhum wakh-shawn; alyawma akmaltu lakum deenakum wa atmamtu 'alaykum ni'matee wa radeetu lakumul-Islaama deenaa; famanidturra fee makhmasatin ghayra mutajaanifil-li-ismin fa-innallaaha Ghafoorur Raheem.

4. Yas'aloonaka maazaaa uhilla lahum; qul uhilla lakumut-tayyibaatu wa maa 'allamtum minal-jawaarihi mukallibeena tu'allimoonahunna mimmaa 'allamakumul-laahu fakuloo mimmaaa amsakna 'alaykum wazkurus-mal-laahi 'alayh; wattaqul-laah; innal-laaha saree'ul-hisaab.

5. Alyawma uhilla lakumut-tayyibaatu wa ta'aamul-lazeena ootul-Kitaaba hillul-lakum wa

وَإِذَا حَلَلْتُمْ فَاصْطَادُوا وَلَا يَجْرِمَنَّكُمْ
شَنَآنُ قَوْمٍ أَنْ صَدُّوكُمْ عَنِ الْمَسْجِدِ
الْحَرَامِ أَنْ تَعْتَدُوا وَتَعَاوَنُوا عَلَى الْبِرِّ
وَالتَّقْوَىٰ وَلَا تَعَاوَنُوا عَلَى الْإِثْمِ
وَالْعُدْوَانِ وَاتَّقُوا اللَّهَ إِنَّ اللَّهَ
شَدِيدُ الْعِقَابِ ۝ ٢
حُرِّمَتْ عَلَيْكُمُ الْمَيْتَةُ وَالدَّمُ وَلَحْمُ
الْخِنْزِيرِ وَمَا أُهِلَّ لِغَيْرِ اللَّهِ بِهِ
وَالْمُنْخَنِقَةُ وَالْمَوْقُوذَةُ وَالْمُتَرَدِّيَةُ
وَالنَّطِيحَةُ وَمَا أَكَلَ السَّبُعُ إِلَّا مَا
ذَكَّيْتُمْ وَمَا ذُبِحَ عَلَى النُّصُبِ وَأَنْ
تَسْتَقْسِمُوا بِالْأَزْلَامِ ذَٰلِكُمْ فِسْقٌ
الْيَوْمَ يَئِسَ الَّذِينَ كَفَرُوا مِنْ دِينِكُمْ
فَلَا تَخْشَوْهُمْ وَاخْشَوْنِ الْيَوْمَ أَكْمَلْتُ
لَكُمْ دِينَكُمْ وَأَتْمَمْتُ عَلَيْكُمْ
نِعْمَتِي وَرَضِيتُ لَكُمُ الْإِسْلَامَ دِينًا
فَمَنِ اضْطُرَّ فِي مَخْمَصَةٍ غَيْرَ مُتَجَانِفٍ
لِإِثْمٍ فَإِنَّ اللَّهَ غَفُورٌ رَحِيمٌ ۝ ٣
يَسْأَلُونَكَ مَاذَا أُحِلَّ لَهُمْ قُلْ أُحِلَّ
لَكُمُ الطَّيِّبَاتُ وَمَا عَلَّمْتُمْ مِنَ الْجَوَارِحِ
مُكَلِّبِينَ تُعَلِّمُونَهُنَّ مِمَّا عَلَّمَكُمُ اللَّهُ
فَكُلُوا مِمَّا أَمْسَكْنَ عَلَيْكُمْ وَاذْكُرُوا
اسْمَ اللَّهِ عَلَيْهِ وَاتَّقُوا اللَّهَ إِنَّ اللَّهَ
سَرِيعُ الْحِسَابِ ۝ ٤
الْيَوْمَ أُحِلَّ لَكُمُ الطَّيِّبَاتُ وَطَعَامُ
الَّذِينَ أُوتُوا الْكِتَابَ حِلٌّ لَكُمْ وَ

وقف لازم

الربع

Ikhfa اخفاء | Ghunna غنّة | Ikhfa Meem Saakin اخفاء ميم ساكن | Idghaam ادغام | Qalqala قلقله | Qalb قلب | Idghaam Meem Saakin ادغام ميم ساكن

yours is lawful to them. (Lawful to you in marriage) are (not only) chaste women who are believers, but chaste women among the People of the Book, revealed before your time,- when you give them their due dowers, and desire chastity, not lewdness, nor secret intrigues if any one rejects faith, fruitless is his work, and in the Hereafter he will be in the ranks of those who have lost (all spiritual good).

ṭa'aamukum ḥillul-lahum wal-muḥṣanaatu minal-mu'minaati walmuḥṣanaatu minal-lazeena ootul-Kitaaba min qablikum izaaa aataytumoohunna ujoorahunna muḥṣineena ghayra musaafiḥeena wa laa muttakhizeee akhdaan; wa mañy-yakfur bil-eemaani faqad ḥabiṭa 'amaluhoo wa huwa fil-Aakhirati minal-khaasireen.

(Section 1)

طَعَامُكُمْ حِلٌّ لَّهُمْ ۖ وَالْمُحْصَنٰتُ مِنَ
الْمُؤْمِنٰتِ وَالْمُحْصَنٰتُ مِنَ الَّذِيْنَ
اُوْتُوا الْكِتٰبَ مِنْ قَبْلِكُمْ اِذَآ اٰتَيْتُمُوْهُنَّ
اُجُوْرَهُنَّ مُحْصِنِيْنَ غَيْرَ مُسٰفِحِيْنَ
وَلَا مُتَّخِذِيْٓ اَخْدَانٍ ۗ وَمَنْ يَّكْفُرْ
بِالْاِيْمَانِ فَقَدْ حَبِطَ عَمَلُهٗ ۡ وَهُوَ فِي
الْاٰخِرَةِ مِنَ الْخٰسِرِيْنَ ۝٥ ع ١

6. O you who believe! when you prepare for prayer, wash your faces, and your hands (and arms) to the elbows; rub your heads (with water); and (wash) your feet to the ankles. If you are in a state of ceremonial impurity, bathe your whole body. But if you are ill, or on a journey, or one of you comes from offices of nature, or you have been in contact with women, and you find no water, then take for yourselves clean sand or earth, and rub therewith your faces and hands, Allah does not wish to place you in a difficulty, but to make you clean, and to complete his favour to you, that you may be grateful.

6. Yaaa-ayyuhal-lazeena aamanooo izaa qumtum-ilaṣ-Ṣalaati faghsiloo wujoohakum wa Aydiyakum ilal maraafiqi wamsaḥoo biru'oosikum wa arjulakum ilal-ka'bayn; wa in kuntum junuban faṭṭahharoo; wain kuntum marḍaaa aw 'alaa safarin aw jaaa'a aḥadum-minkum minal-ghaaa'iṭi aw laamastumunnisaaa'a falam tajidoo maaa'an fatayammamoo ṣa'eedan ṭayyiban famsaḥoo biwujoohikum wa aydeekum-minh; maa yureedul-laahu liyaj'ala 'alaykum min ḥarajiñw-wa laakiñy-yureedu liyuṭahhirakum wa liyutimma ni'matahoo 'alaykum la'allakum tashkuroon.

يٰٓاَيُّهَا الَّذِيْنَ اٰمَنُوْٓا اِذَا قُمْتُمْ اِلَى
الصَّلٰوةِ فَاغْسِلُوْا وُجُوْهَكُمْ وَاَيْدِيَكُمْ
اِلَى الْمَرَافِقِ وَامْسَحُوْا بِرُءُوْسِكُمْ وَ
اَرْجُلَكُمْ اِلَى الْكَعْبَيْنِ ۗ وَاِنْ كُنْتُمْ
جُنُبًا فَاطَّهَّرُوْا ۗ وَاِنْ كُنْتُمْ مَّرْضٰٓى
اَوْ عَلٰى سَفَرٍ اَوْ جَآءَ اَحَدٌ مِّنْكُمْ مِّنَ
الْغَآئِطِ اَوْ لٰمَسْتُمُ النِّسَآءَ فَلَمْ تَجِدُوْا
مَآءً فَتَيَمَّمُوْا صَعِيْدًا طَيِّبًا فَامْسَحُوْا
بِوُجُوْهِكُمْ وَاَيْدِيْكُمْ مِّنْهُ ۗ مَا يُرِيْدُ
اللّٰهُ لِيَجْعَلَ عَلَيْكُمْ مِّنْ حَرَجٍ وَّلٰكِنْ
يُّرِيْدُ لِيُطَهِّرَكُمْ وَلِيُتِمَّ نِعْمَتَهٗ عَلَيْكُمْ
لَعَلَّكُمْ تَشْكُرُوْنَ ۝٦

7. And call in remembrance the favour of Allah to you, and His Covenant, which He ratified with you, when you said: "We hear and we obey": And fear Allah, for Allah knows well the secrets of your hearts.

7. Wazkuroo ni'matal-laahi 'alaykum wa meesaaqahul-lazee waasaqakum biheee iz qultum sami'naa wa aṭa'naa wattaqul-laah; innal-laaha 'aleemum-bizaatiṣ-ṣudoor.

وَاذْكُرُوْا نِعْمَةَ اللّٰهِ عَلَيْكُمْ وَمِيْثَاقَهُ
الَّذِيْ وَاثَقَكُمْ بِهٖٓ ۙ اِذْ قُلْتُمْ سَمِعْنَا
وَاَطَعْنَا ۡ وَاتَّقُوا اللّٰهَ ۗ اِنَّ اللّٰهَ
عَلِيْمٌۢ بِذَاتِ الصُّدُوْرِ ۝٧

8. O you who believe! stand out firmly for Allah, as witnesses to fair dealing, and let not the hatred of others to you make you swerve to wrong and depart from justice. Be just:

8. Yaaa ayyuhal-lazeena aamanoo koonoo qawwaameena lillaahi shuhadaaa'a bilqist, wa laa yajrimannakum shana-aanu qawmin 'alaaa allaa ta'diloo; i'diloo;

يٰٓاَيُّهَا الَّذِيْنَ اٰمَنُوْا كُوْنُوْا قَوّٰمِيْنَ
لِلّٰهِ شُهَدَآءَ بِالْقِسْطِ ۡ وَلَا يَجْرِمَنَّكُمْ
شَنَاٰنُ قَوْمٍ عَلٰٓى اَلَّا تَعْدِلُوْا ۗ اِعْدِلُوْا

Ikhfa اخفاء | Ghunna غُنّہ | Ikhfa Meem Saakin اخفاءمیم ساکن | Idghaam ادغام | Qalqala قلقلہ | Qalb قلب | Idghaam Meem Saakin ادغام میم ساکن

that is next to piety: and fear Allah. For Allah is well-acquainted with all that you do.

9. To those who believe and do deeds of righteousness has Allah promised forgiveness and a great reward.

10. Those who reject faith and deny our signs will be companions of Hell-fire.

11. O you who believe! call in remembrance the favour of Allah unto you when certain men formed the design to stretch out their hands against you, but (Allah) held back their hands from you: so fear Allah. And on Allah let Believers put (all) their trust.

12. Allah did (aforetime) take a Covenant from the Children of Israel, and we appointed twelve captains among them. And Allah said: "I am with you: if you (but) establish regular prayers, practise regular charity, believe in my Apostles, honour and assist them, and loan to Allah a beautiful loan, verily I will wipe out from you your evils, and admit you to gardens with rivers flowing beneath; but if any of you, after this, resists faith, he has truly wandered from the path of rectitude."

13. But because of their breach of their Covenant, We cursed them, and made their hearts grow hard; they change the words from their (right) places and forget a good part of the message that was sent them, nor will you cease to find them- barring a few - ever bent on (new) deceits:

huwa aqrabu littaqwaa wattaqul-laah; innal-laaha khabeerum-bimaa ta'maloon.

9. Wa'adal-laahul-lazeena aamanoo wa 'amiluṣ-ṣaaliḥaati lahum maghfiratuñw-wa ajrun 'aẓeem.

10. Wallazeena kafaroo wa kazzaboo bi-Aayaatinaaa ulaaa'ika Aṣḥaabul-Jaḥeem.

11. Yaaa ayyuhal-lazeena aamanuz-kuroo ni'matallaahi 'alaykum iz hamma qawmun añy-yabsuṭooo ilaykum aydiyahum fakaffa aydiyahum 'ankum wattaqullaah; wa 'alal-laahi fal-yatawakkalil-mu'minoon. **(Section 2)**

12. Wa laqad akhazal-laahu meesaaqa Baneee Israaa'eela wa ba'asnaa minhumus-nay 'ashara naqeebañw wa qaalal-laahu innee ma'akum la'in aqamtumuṣ-Ṣalaata wa aataytumuz-Zakaata wa aamantum bi-Rusulee wa 'azzartumoohum wa aqraḍtumul-laaha qarḍan ḥasanal-la-ukaffiranna 'ankum sayyi-aatikum wa la-udkhilannakum Jannaatin tajree min taḥtihal-anhaar; faman kafara ba'da zaalika minkum faqad ḍalla sawaaa'as-Sabeel.

13. Fabimaa naqḍihim meesaaqahum la'annaahum wa ja'alnaa quloobahum qaasiyatañy yuḥarrifoonal-kalima 'ammawaaḍi'ihee wa nasoo ḥazzam-mimmaa zukkiroo bih; wa laa tazaalu taṭṭali'u 'alaa khaaa'inatim-minhum illaa qaleelam-minhum

هُوَ أَقْرَبُ لِلتَّقْوَىٰ وَاتَّقُوا اللَّهَ
إِنَّ اللَّهَ خَبِيرٌ بِمَا تَعْمَلُونَ ٨
وَعَدَ اللَّهُ الَّذِينَ آمَنُوا وَعَمِلُوا
الصَّالِحَاتِ لَهُمْ مَغْفِرَةٌ وَأَجْرٌ
عَظِيمٌ ٩
وَالَّذِينَ كَفَرُوا وَكَذَّبُوا بِآيَاتِنَا
أُولَٰئِكَ أَصْحَابُ الْجَحِيمِ ١٠
يَا أَيُّهَا الَّذِينَ آمَنُوا اذْكُرُوا
نِعْمَتَ اللَّهِ عَلَيْكُمْ إِذْ هَمَّ قَوْمٌ
أَنْ يَبْسُطُوا إِلَيْكُمْ أَيْدِيَهُمْ فَكَفَّ
أَيْدِيَهُمْ عَنْكُمْ وَاتَّقُوا اللَّهَ وَ
عَلَى اللَّهِ فَلْيَتَوَكَّلِ الْمُؤْمِنُونَ ١١
وَلَقَدْ أَخَذَ اللَّهُ مِيثَاقَ بَنِي إِسْرَائِيلَ
وَبَعَثْنَا مِنْهُمُ اثْنَيْ عَشَرَ نَقِيبًا
وَقَالَ اللَّهُ إِنِّي مَعَكُمْ لَئِنْ أَقَمْتُمُ
الصَّلَاةَ وَآتَيْتُمُ الزَّكَاةَ وَآمَنْتُمْ
بِرُسُلِي وَعَزَّرْتُمُوهُمْ وَأَقْرَضْتُمُ اللَّهَ
قَرْضًا حَسَنًا لَأُكَفِّرَنَّ عَنْكُمْ سَيِّئَاتِكُمْ
وَلَأُدْخِلَنَّكُمْ جَنَّاتٍ تَجْرِي مِنْ
تَحْتِهَا الْأَنْهَارُ فَمَنْ كَفَرَ بَعْدَ ذَٰلِكَ
مِنْكُمْ فَقَدْ ضَلَّ سَوَاءَ السَّبِيلِ ١٢
فَبِمَا نَقْضِهِمْ مِيثَاقَهُمْ لَعَنَّاهُمْ
وَجَعَلْنَا قُلُوبَهُمْ قَاسِيَةً يُحَرِّفُونَ
الْكَلِمَ عَنْ مَوَاضِعِهِ وَنَسُوا حَظًّا
مِمَّا ذُكِّرُوا بِهِ وَلَا تَزَالُ تَطَّلِعُ عَلَىٰ
خَائِنَةٍ مِنْهُمْ إِلَّا قَلِيلًا مِنْهُمْ

Ikhfa اخفاء | Ghunna غنّہ | Ikhfa Meem Saakin اخفاء میم ساکن | Idghaam ادغام | Qalqala قلقلہ | Qalb قلب | Idghaam Meem Saakin ادغام میم ساکن

but forgive them, and overlook (their misdeeds): for Allah loves those who are kind.

fa'fu 'anhum waṣfaḥ; innal-laaha yuḥibbul-muḥsineen.

فَاعْفُ عَنْهُمْ وَاصْفَحْ ۚ إِنَّ اللّٰهَ
يُحِبُّ الْمُحْسِنِينَ ﴿١٣﴾

14. From those, too, who call themselves Christians, We did take a Covenant, but they forgot a good part of the message that was sent them: so we estranged them, with enmity and hatred between the one and the other, to the Day of judgment. And soon will Allah show them what it is they have done.

14. Wa minal-lazeena qaalooo innaa Naṣaaraaa akhaznaa meesaaqahum fanasoo hazzam-mimmaa zukkiroo bihee fa-aghraynaa baynahumul-'adaawata walbaghḍaaa'a ilaa Yawmil-Qiyaamah; wa sawfa yunabbi'uhumul-laahu bimaa kaanoo yaṣna'oon.

وَمِنَ الَّذِينَ قَالُوا إِنَّا نَصٰرٰى أَخَذْنَا
مِيثَاقَهُمْ فَنَسُوا حَظًّا مِّمَّا ذُكِّرُوا بِهٖ ص
فَأَغْرَيْنَا بَيْنَهُمُ الْعَدَاوَةَ وَالْبَغْضَاءَ
إِلٰى يَوْمِ الْقِيٰمَةِ ۚ وَسَوْفَ يُنَبِّئُهُمُ اللّٰهُ
بِمَا كَانُوا يَصْنَعُونَ ﴿١٤﴾

15. O people of the Book! there has come to you our Apostle, revealing to you much that you used to hide in the Book, and passing over much (that is now unnecessary). There has come to you from Allah a (new) light and a perspicuous Book,

15. Yaaa Ahlal-Kitaabi qad jaaa'akum Rasoolunaa yubay-yinu lakum kaseeram-mimmaa kuntum tukhfoona minal-Kitaabi wa ya'foo 'an kaseer; qad jaaa'akum minal-laahi nooruñw-wa Kitaabum-Mubeen.

يٰأَهْلَ الْكِتٰبِ قَدْ جَاءَكُمْ رَسُولُنَا
يُبَيِّنُ لَكُمْ كَثِيرًا مِّمَّا كُنْتُمْ تُخْفُونَ
مِنَ الْكِتٰبِ وَيَعْفُوا عَنْ كَثِيرٍ ۚ قَدْ
جَاءَكُمْ مِّنَ اللّٰهِ نُورٌ وَّكِتٰبٌ مُّبِينٌ ﴿١٥﴾

16. Wherewith Allah guides all who seek His good pleasure to ways of peace and safety, and leads them out of darkness, by His will, unto the light,- guides them to a path that is straight.

16. Yahdee bihil-laahu manit-taba'a riḍwaanahoo subulas-salaami wa yukhrijuhum minaẓ-ẓulumaati ilan-noori bi-iznihee wa yahdeehim ilaa Ṣiraaṭim-Mustaqeem.

يَّهْدِي بِهِ اللّٰهُ مَنِ اتَّبَعَ رِضْوَانَهٗ
سُبُلَ السَّلٰمِ وَيُخْرِجُهُمْ مِّنَ
الظُّلُمٰتِ إِلَى النُّورِ بِإِذْنِهٖ وَيَهْدِيهِمْ
إِلٰى صِرَاطٍ مُّسْتَقِيمٍ ﴿١٦﴾

17. In blasphemy indeed are those that say that Allah is Christ the son of Mary. Say: "Who then has the least power against Allah, if His will were to destroy Christ the son of Mary, his mother, and all every - one that is on the earth? For to Allah belonges the dominion of the heavens and the earth, and all that is between. He creates what He pleases. For Allah has power over all things."

17. Laqad kafaral-lazeena qaalooo innal-laaha Huwal-Maseeḥub-nu-Maryam; qul famañy-yamliku minal-laahi shay'an in araada añy-yuhlikal Maseeḥab-na-Maryama wa ummahoo wa man fil-arḍi jamee'aa; wa lillaahi mulkus-samaawaati wal-arḍi wa maa baynahumaa; yakhluqu maa-Yashaaa'; wallaahu 'alaa kulli shay'in Qadeer.

لَقَدْ كَفَرَ الَّذِينَ قَالُوا إِنَّ اللّٰهَ هُوَ
الْمَسِيحُ ابْنُ مَرْيَمَ ۚ قُلْ فَمَنْ يَّمْلِكُ
مِنَ اللّٰهِ شَيْـًٔا إِنْ أَرَادَ أَنْ يُّهْلِكَ
الْمَسِيحَ ابْنَ مَرْيَمَ وَأُمَّهٗ وَمَنْ فِي
الْأَرْضِ جَمِيعًا ۚ وَلِلّٰهِ مُلْكُ السَّمٰوٰتِ
وَالْأَرْضِ وَمَا بَيْنَهُمَا ۚ يَخْلُقُ
مَا يَشَاءُ ۚ وَاللّٰهُ عَلٰى كُلِّ شَيْءٍ قَدِيرٌ ﴿١٧﴾

18. (Both) the Jews and the Christians say: "We are sons of Allah, and His beloved." Say: "Why then does He punish you for your sins? Nay, you are but men,- of the men he has created: He forgives whom He pleases, and He punishes

18. Wa qaalatil-Yahoodu wan-Naṣaaraa naḥnu abnaaa'ul-laahi wa aḥibbaaa'uh; qul falima yu'azzibukum bizunoobikum bal antum basharum-mimman khalaq; yaghfiru limañy-yashaaa'u wa yu'azzibu

وَقَالَتِ الْيَهُودُ وَالنَّصٰرٰى نَحْنُ أَبْنٰٓؤُا
اللّٰهِ وَأَحِبَّٰٓؤُهٗ ۚ قُلْ فَلِمَ يُعَذِّبُكُمْ
بِذُنُوبِكُمْ ۚ بَلْ أَنْتُمْ بَشَرٌ مِّمَّنْ
خَلَقَ ۚ يَغْفِرُ لِمَنْ يَّشَاءُ وَيُعَذِّبُ

Ikhfa اخفاء | Ghunna غُنّہ | Ikhfa Meem Saakin اخفاء میم ساکن | Idghaam ادغام | Qalqala قلقلہ | Qalb قلب | Idghaam Meem Saakin ادغام میم ساکن

whom He pleases: and to Allah belongs the dominion of the heavens and the earth, and all that is between: and unto Him is the final goal (of all)".

19. O People of the Book! now has come to you, making (things) clear to you, Our Apostle, after the break in (the series of) Our apostles, lest you should say: "There came unto us no bringer of glad tidings and no warner (from evil)": But now has come unto you a bringer of glad tidings and a warner (from evil). And Allah has power over all things.

20. Remember Moses said to his people: "O my people! call in remembrance the favour of Allah to you, when He produced prophets among you, made you kings, and gave you what He had not given to any other among the people.

21. "O my people! Enter the holy land which Allah has assigned unto you, and turn not back ignominiously, for then will you be overthrown, to your own ruin."

22. They said: "O Moses! In this land are a people of exceeding strength: Never shall we enter it until they leave it: if (once) they leave, then shall we enter."

23. (But) among (their) Allah-fearing men were two on whom Allah had bestowed His grace: They said: "Assault them at the (proper) gate: when once you are in, victory will be yours; But on Allah put your trust if you have faith."

24. They said: "O Moses! while they remain there, never shall we be able to enter, to the end of time. Go you,

mañy-yashaaa'; wa lillaahi mulkus-samaawaati wal-arḍi wa maa baynahumaa wa ilayhil-maṣeer.

19. Yaaa Ahlal-Kitaabi qad jaaa'akum Rasoolunaa yubayyinu lakum 'alaa fatra-tim-minar-Rusuli an taqooloo maa jaaa'anaa mim basheeriñw-wa laa naẕeerin faqad jaaa'akum basheeruñw-wa naẕeer; wallaahu 'alaa kulli shay'in Qadeer. **(Section 3)**

20. Wa iẕ qaala Moosaa liqawmihee yaa-qawmiẕ-kuroo ni'matal-laahi 'alaykum iẕ ja'ala feekum ambiyaaa'a wa ja'alakum mulookañw-wa aataakum maa lam yu'ti aḥadam-minal-'aalameen.

21. Yaa qawmid-khulul-Arḍal-Muqaddasatal-latee katabal-laahu lakum wa laa tartaddoo 'alaaa adbaarikum fatanqaliboo khaasireen.

22. Qaaloo yaa Moosaaa inna feehaa qawman jabbaareena wa innaa lan nadkhulahaa ḥattaa yakhrujoo minhaa fa-iñy-yakhrujoo minhaa fa-innaa daakhiloon.

23. Qaala rajulaani minal-laẕeena yakhaafoona an'amal-laahu 'alayhimad-khuloo 'alayhimul-baab, fa-iẕaa dakhaltumoohu fa-innakum ghaaliboon; wa 'alal-laahi fatawakkalooo in kuntum mu'mineen.

24. Qaaloo yaa Moosaaa innaa lan nadkhulahaaa abadam-maa daamoo feehaa faẕhab anta

مَنْ يَّشَآءُ ۭ وَلِلّٰهِ مُلْكُ السَّمٰوٰتِ
وَالْاَرْضِ وَمَا بَيْنَهُمَا ۡ وَاِلَيْهِ
الْمَصِيْرُ ﴿۱۸﴾
يٰۤاَهْلَ الْكِتٰبِ قَدْ جَآءَكُمْ رَسُوْلُنَا
يُبَيِّنُ لَكُمْ عَلٰى فَتْرَةٍ مِّنَ الرُّسُلِ
اَنْ تَقُوْلُوْا مَا جَآءَنَا مِنْۢ بَشِيْرٍ
وَّلَا نَذِيْرٍ ۡ فَقَدْ جَآءَكُمْ بَشِيْرٌ
وَّنَذِيْرٌ ۭ وَاللّٰهُ عَلٰى كُلِّ شَيْءٍ قَدِيْرٌ ﴿۱۹﴾ ع
وَاِذْ قَالَ مُوْسٰى لِقَوْمِهٖ يٰقَوْمِ
اذْكُرُوْا نِعْمَةَ اللّٰهِ عَلَيْكُمْ اِذْ جَعَلَ
فِيْكُمْ اَنْۢبِيَآءَ وَجَعَلَكُمْ مُّلُوْكًا ۖۗ
وَّاٰتٰىكُمْ مَّا لَمْ يُؤْتِ اَحَدًا مِّنَ
الْعٰلَمِيْنَ ﴿۲۰﴾
يٰقَوْمِ ادْخُلُوا الْاَرْضَ الْمُقَدَّسَةَ
الَّتِيْ كَتَبَ اللّٰهُ لَكُمْ وَلَا تَرْتَدُّوْا
عَلٰۤى اَدْبَارِكُمْ فَتَنْقَلِبُوْا خٰسِرِيْنَ ﴿۲۱﴾
قَالُوْا يٰمُوْسٰۤى اِنَّ فِيْهَا قَوْمًا جَبَّارِيْنَ ۖۗ
وَاِنَّا لَنْ نَّدْخُلَهَا حَتّٰى يَخْرُجُوْا مِنْهَا ۚ
فَاِنْ يَّخْرُجُوْا مِنْهَا فَاِنَّا دٰخِلُوْنَ ﴿۲۲﴾
قَالَ رَجُلٰنِ مِنَ الَّذِيْنَ يَخَافُوْنَ
اَنْعَمَ اللّٰهُ عَلَيْهِمَا ادْخُلُوْا عَلَيْهِمُ
الْبَابَ ۚ فَاِذَا دَخَلْتُمُوْهُ فَاِنَّكُمْ
غٰلِبُوْنَ ۚ۬ وَعَلَى اللّٰهِ فَتَوَكَّلُوْۤا اِنْ
كُنْتُمْ مُّؤْمِنِيْنَ ﴿۲۳﴾
قَالُوْا يٰمُوْسٰۤى اِنَّا لَنْ نَّدْخُلَهَاۤ
اَبَدًا مَّا دَامُوْا فِيْهَا فَاذْهَبْ اَنْتَ

Ikhfa اخفاء | Ghunna غُنّہ | Ikhfa Meem Saakin اخفاء میم ساکن | Idghaam ادغام | Qalqala قلقلہ | Qalb قلب | Idghaam Meem Saakin ادغام میم ساکن

and your Lord, and fight you two, while we sit here (and watch)."

25. He said: "O my Lord! I have power only over myself and my brother: so separate us from this rebellious people!"

26. Allah said: "Therefore the land will be out of their reach for forty years: In distraction they will wander through the land: But you dont grieve over these rebellious people.

27. Recite to them the truth of the story of the two sons of Adam. Behold! they each presented a sacrifice (to Allah): It was accepted from one, but not from the other. Said the latter: "Be sure I will slay you." "Surely," said the former, "Allah accepts of the sacrifice of those who are righteous.

28. "If you do stretch your hand against me, to slay me, it is not for me to stretch my hand against you to slay you: for I do fear Allah, the Cherisher of the worlds.

29. "For me, I intend to let you draw on yourself my sin as well as yours, for you will be among the companions of the fire, and that is the reward of those who do wrong."

30. The (selfish) soul of the other led him to the murder of his brother: he murdered him, and became (himself) one of the lost ones.

31. Then Allah sent a raven, who scratched the ground, to show him how to hide the shame of his brother. "Woe is me!" said he; "Was I not even able to be as this raven, and to hide the shame of my brother?" then he became full of regrets-

32. On that account: We ordained for the Children of

Wa Rabbuka faqaatilaaa innaa haahunaa qaa'idoon.

25. Qaala Rabbi innee laaa amliku illaa nafsee wa akhee fafruq baynanaa wa baynal-qawmil-faasiqeen.

26. Qaala fa-innahaa muḥar-ramatun 'alayhim arba'eena sanah; yateehoona fil-arḍ; falaa taåsa 'alal-qawmil-faasiqeen.

(Section 4)

27. Watlu 'alayhim naba-abnay Aadama bilḥaqq; iz qarrabaa qurbaanan fatuqubbila min aḥadihimaa wa lam yutaqabbal minal-aakhari qaala la-aqtulannaka qaala innamaa yataqabbalul-laahu minal-muttaqeen.

28. La'im basatta ilayya yadaka litaqtulanee maaa ana bibaasiṭiñy-yadiya ilayka li-aqtulaka inneee akhaaful-laaha Rabbal-'aalameen.

29. Ineee ureedu an tabooo'a bi-ismee wa ismika fatakoona min Aṣḥaabin-Naar; wa zaalika jazaaa'uẓ-ẓaalimeen.

30. Faṭawwa'at lahoo nafsu-hoo qatla akheehi faqatalahoo fa-aṣbaḥa minal-khaasireen.

31. Faba'asal-laahu ghu-raabañy-yabḥasu fil-arḍi liyuri-yahoo kayfa yuwaaree sawata akheeh; qaala yaa waylataaa a'ajaztu an akoona misla haazal-ghuraabi fa-uwaariya saw-ata akhee fa-aṣbaḥa minan-naadimeen.

32. Min ajli zaalika katabnaa 'alaa Baneee

وَرَبُّكَ فَقَٰتِلَآ إِنَّا هَٰهُنَا قَٰعِدُونَ ﴿٢٤﴾
قَالَ رَبِّ إِنِّي لَآ أَمْلِكُ إِلَّا نَفْسِي
وَأَخِي فَٱفْرُقْ بَيْنَنَا وَبَيْنَ ٱلْقَوْمِ
ٱلْفَٰسِقِينَ ﴿٢٥﴾
قَالَ فَإِنَّهَا مُحَرَّمَةٌ عَلَيْهِمْ أَرْبَعِينَ
سَنَةً ۛ يَتِيهُونَ فِي ٱلْأَرْضِ ۚ فَلَا
تَأْسَ عَلَى ٱلْقَوْمِ ٱلْفَٰسِقِينَ ﴿٢٦﴾ ع
وَٱتْلُ عَلَيْهِمْ نَبَأَ ٱبْنَيْ ءَادَمَ بِٱلْحَقِّ ۘ
إِذْ قَرَّبَا قُرْبَانًا فَتُقُبِّلَ مِنْ أَحَدِهِمَا
وَلَمْ يُتَقَبَّلْ مِنَ ٱلْءَاخَرِ ط قَالَ
لَأَقْتُلَنَّكَ ط قَالَ إِنَّمَا يَتَقَبَّلُ
ٱللَّهُ مِنَ ٱلْمُتَّقِينَ ﴿٢٧﴾
لَئِنۢ بَسَطتَ إِلَيَّ يَدَكَ لِتَقْتُلَنِي
مَآ أَنَا۠ بِبَاسِطٍ يَدِيَ إِلَيْكَ لِأَقْتُلَكَ ۚ
إِنِّيٓ أَخَافُ ٱللَّهَ رَبَّ ٱلْعَٰلَمِينَ ﴿٢٨﴾
إِنِّيٓ أُرِيدُ أَن تَبُوٓأَ بِإِثْمِي وَإِثْمِكَ
فَتَكُونَ مِنْ أَصْحَٰبِ ٱلنَّارِ ۚ وَذَٰلِكَ
جَزَٰٓؤُا۟ ٱلظَّٰلِمِينَ ﴿٢٩﴾ ج
فَطَوَّعَتْ لَهُۥ نَفْسُهُۥ قَتْلَ أَخِيهِ
فَقَتَلَهُۥ فَأَصْبَحَ مِنَ ٱلْخَٰسِرِينَ ﴿٣٠﴾
فَبَعَثَ ٱللَّهُ غُرَابًا يَبْحَثُ فِي ٱلْأَرْضِ
لِيُرِيَهُۥ كَيْفَ يُوَٰرِى سَوْءَةَ أَخِيهِ ط
قَالَ يَٰوَيْلَتَىٰٓ أَعَجَزْتُ أَنْ أَكُونَ
مِثْلَ هَٰذَا ٱلْغُرَابِ فَأُوَٰرِيَ سَوْءَةَ
أَخِي ج فَأَصْبَحَ مِنَ ٱلنَّٰدِمِينَ ﴿٣١﴾
مِنْ أَجْلِ ذَٰلِكَ ۛ كَتَبْنَا عَلَىٰ بَنِيٓ

الربع - وقف لازم

النصف

Ikhfa اخفاء | Ghunna غنّہ | Ikhfa Meem Saakin اخفاءمیم ساکن | Idghaam ادغام | Qalqala قلقلہ | Qalb قلب | Idghaam Meem Saakin ادغام میم ساکن

Israel that if any one slew a person - unless it be for murder or for spreading mischief in the land - it would be as if he slew the whole people: and if any one saved a life, it would be as if he saved the life of the whole people. Then although there came to them our apostles with clear signs, yet, even after that, many of them continued to commit excesses in the land.

Israaa'eela annahoo man qatala nafsam bighayri nafsin aw fasaadin fil-arḍi faka-annamaa qatalan-naasa jamee'añw wa man aḥyaahaa faka-annamaaa aḥyan-naasa jamee'aa; wa laqad jaaa'at-hum Rusulunaa bilbayyinaati summa inna kaseeram-minhum ba'da zaalika fil-arḍi lamusrifoon.

إِسۡرَآءِيلَ أَنَّهُۥ مَن قَتَلَ نَفۡسَۢا
بِغَيۡرِ نَفۡسٍ أَوۡ فَسَادٖ فِي ٱلۡأَرۡضِ
فَكَأَنَّمَا قَتَلَ ٱلنَّاسَ جَمِيعٗا وَمَنۡ
أَحۡيَاهَا فَكَأَنَّمَآ أَحۡيَا ٱلنَّاسَ
جَمِيعٗاۚ وَلَقَدۡ جَآءَتۡهُمۡ رُسُلُنَا
بِٱلۡبَيِّنَٰتِ ثُمَّ إِنَّ كَثِيرٗا مِّنۡهُم
بَعۡدَ ذَٰلِكَ فِي ٱلۡأَرۡضِ لَمُسۡرِفُونَ ٣٢

33. The punishment of those who wage war against Allah and His Apostle, and strive with might and main for mischief through the land is: execution, or crucifixion, or the cutting off of hands and feet from opposite sides, or exile from the land: that is their disgrace in this world, and a heavy punishment is theirs in the Hereafter;

33. Innamaa jazaaa'ul-lazeena yuḥaariboonal-laaha wa Rasoolahoo wa yas'awna fil-arḍi fasaadan añy-yuqattalooo aw yuṣallabooo aw tuqaṭṭa'a aydeehim wa arjuluhum min khilaafin aw yunfaw minalarḍ; zaalika lahum khizyun fid-dunyaa wa lahum fil-Aakhirati 'azaabun 'aẓeem.

إِنَّمَا جَزَٰٓؤُاْ ٱلَّذِينَ يُحَارِبُونَ ٱللَّهَ
وَرَسُولَهُۥ وَيَسۡعَوۡنَ فِي ٱلۡأَرۡضِ فَسَادًا
أَن يُقَتَّلُوٓاْ أَوۡ يُصَلَّبُوٓاْ أَوۡ تُقَطَّعَ
أَيۡدِيهِمۡ وَأَرۡجُلُهُم مِّنۡ خِلَٰفٍ
أَوۡ يُنفَوۡاْ مِنَ ٱلۡأَرۡضِۚ ذَٰلِكَ
لَهُمۡ خِزۡيٞ فِي ٱلدُّنۡيَاۖ وَلَهُمۡ فِي
ٱلۡأٓخِرَةِ عَذَابٌ عَظِيمٌ ٣٣

34. Except for those who repent before they fall into your power: in that case, know that Allah is Oft-forgiving, Most Merciful.

34. Illal-lazeena taaboo min qabli an taqdiroo 'alayhim fa'lamooo annal-laaha Ghafoorur-Raḥeem. **(Section 5)**

إِلَّا ٱلَّذِينَ تَابُواْ مِن قَبۡلِ أَن
تَقۡدِرُواْ عَلَيۡهِمۡۖ فَٱعۡلَمُوٓاْ أَنَّ
ٱللَّهَ غَفُورٞ رَّحِيمٞ ٣٤

35. O you who believe! Do your duty to Allah, seek the means of approach unto Him, and strive with might and main in his cause: that you may prosper.

35. Yaaa ayyuhal-lazeena aamanut-taqul-laaha wabtaghooo ilayhil-waseelata wa jaahidoo fee sabeelihee la'allakum tufliḥoon.

يَٰٓأَيُّهَا ٱلَّذِينَ ءَامَنُواْ ٱتَّقُواْ ٱللَّهَ
وَٱبۡتَغُوٓاْ إِلَيۡهِ ٱلۡوَسِيلَةَ وَجَٰهِدُواْ
فِي سَبِيلِهِۦ لَعَلَّكُمۡ تُفۡلِحُونَ ٣٥

36. As to those who reject Faith,- if they had everything on earth, and twice repeated, to give as ransom for the Chastisement of the Day of Judgment, it would never be accepted of them, theirs would be a grievous Chastisement.

36. Innal-lazeena kafaroo law anna lahum maa fil-arḍi jamee'añw-wa mislahoo ma'ahoo liyaftadoo bihee min 'azaabi Yawmil-Qiyaamati maa tuqubbila minhum wa lahum 'azaabun aleem.

إِنَّ ٱلَّذِينَ كَفَرُواْ لَوۡ أَنَّ لَهُم مَّا
فِي ٱلۡأَرۡضِ جَمِيعٗا وَمِثۡلَهُۥ مَعَهُۥ
لِيَفۡتَدُواْ بِهِۦ مِنۡ عَذَابِ يَوۡمِ ٱلۡقِيَٰمَةِ
مَا تُقُبِّلَ مِنۡهُمۡۖ وَلَهُمۡ عَذَابٌ أَلِيمٞ ٣٦

37. Their wish will be to get out of the Fire, but never will they get out therefrom: their

37. Yureedoona añy-yakhrujoo minan-Naari wa maa hum bikhaarijeena minhaa wa lahum

يُرِيدُونَ أَن يَخۡرُجُواْ مِنَ ٱلنَّارِ
وَمَا هُم بِخَٰرِجِينَ مِنۡهَاۖ وَلَهُمۡ

Ikhfa اخفاء | Ghunna غُنّہ | Ikhfa Meem Saakin اخفاء میم ساکن | Idghaam ادغام | Qalqala قلقلہ | Qalb قلب | Idghaam Meem Saakin ادغام میم ساکن

Chastisement will be one that endures.

38. As to the thief, male or female, cut off his or her hands: a punishment by way of example, from Allah, for their crime: and Allah is Exalted in power.

39. But if the thief repents after his crime, and amends his conduct, Allah turns to him in forgiveness; for Allah is Oft-forgiving, Most Merciful.

40. Do you not know that to Allah (alone) belongs the dominion of the heavens and the earth? He punishes whom He pleases, and He forgives whom He pleases: and Allah has power over all things.

41. O Apostle! let not those grieve you, who race each other into unbelief: (whether it be) among those who say "We believe" with their lips but whose hearts have no faith; or it be among the Jews,- men who will listen to any lie,- will listen even to others who have never so much as come to you. They change the words from their (right) times and places: they say, "If you are given this, take it, but if not, beware!" If any one's trial is intended by Allah you have no authority in the least for him against Allah. For such - it is not Allah's will to purify their hearts. For them there is disgrace in this world, and in the Hereafter a heavy punishment.

42. (They are fond of) listening to falsehood, of devouring anything forbidden.

'azaabum-muqeem.

38. Wassaariqu wassaariqatu faqṭa'ooo aydiyahumaa jazaaa-'am-bimaa kasabaa nakaalam-minal-laah; wallaahu 'Azeezun Ḥakeem.

39. Faman taaba mim ba'di ẓulmihee wa aṣlaḥa fa-innal-laaha yatoobu 'alayh; innal-laaha Ghafoorur-Raḥeem.

40. Alam ta'lam annal-laaha lahoo mulkus-samaawaati wal-arḍi yu'az-zibu mañy-yashaa'u wa yaghfiru limañy-yashaaa'; wallaahu 'alaa kulli shay'in Qadeer.

41. Yaaa-ayyuhar-Rasoolu laa yaḥzunkal-lazeena yusaa-ri'oona fil-kufri minal-lazeena qaalooo aamannaa bi-afwaahi-him wa lam tu'min quloobu-hum; wa minal-lazeena haadoo sammaa'oona lilkazibi sam-maa'oona liqawmin aakhareena lam yaâtooka yuḥarrifoonal-kalima mim ba'di mawaaḍi'i-hee yaqooloona in ooteetum haazaa fakhuzoohu wa il-lam tu'tawhu faḥzaroo; wa mañy-yuridil-laahu fitnatahoo falan tamlika lahoo minal-laahi shay'aa; ulaaa'ikal-lazeena lam yuridil-laahu añy-yuṭahhira quloobahum; lahum fid-dunyaa khizyuñw-wa lahum fil-Aakhirati 'azaabun 'aẓeem.

42. Sammaa'oona lilkazibi akkaaloona lissuḥt;

عَذَابٌ مُّقِيمٌ ﴿٣٧﴾
وَالسَّارِقُ وَالسَّارِقَةُ فَاقْطَعُوٓا
أَيْدِيَهُمَا جَزَآءًۢ بِمَا كَسَبَا نَكَالًا
مِّنَ اللّٰهِ ۗ وَاللّٰهُ عَزِيزٌ حَكِيمٌ ﴿٣٨﴾
فَمَن تَابَ مِنۢ بَعْدِ ظُلْمِهٖ وَأَصْلَحَ
فَإِنَّ اللّٰهَ يَتُوبُ عَلَيْهِ ۗ إِنَّ اللّٰهَ
غَفُورٌ رَّحِيمٌ ﴿٣٩﴾
أَلَمْ تَعْلَمْ أَنَّ اللّٰهَ لَهٗ مُلْكُ
السَّمٰوٰتِ وَالْأَرْضِ ۗ يُعَذِّبُ مَن
يَشَآءُ وَيَغْفِرُ لِمَن يَشَآءُ ۗ وَاللّٰهُ
عَلٰى كُلِّ شَيْءٍ قَدِيرٌ ﴿٤٠﴾
يَٰٓأَيُّهَا الرَّسُولُ لَا يَحْزُنكَ الَّذِينَ
يُسَارِعُونَ فِى الْكُفْرِ مِنَ الَّذِينَ
قَالُوٓا اٰمَنَّا بِأَفْوَاهِهِمْ وَلَمْ تُؤْمِن
قُلُوبُهُمْ ۛ وَمِنَ الَّذِينَ هَادُوا ۛ
سَمّٰعُونَ لِلْكَذِبِ سَمّٰعُونَ لِقَوْمٍ
اٰخَرِينَ ۙ لَمْ يَأْتُوكَ ۗ يُحَرِّفُونَ
الْكَلِمَ مِنۢ بَعْدِ مَوَاضِعِهٖ ۚ يَقُولُونَ
إِنْ أُوتِيتُمْ هٰذَا فَخُذُوهُ وَإِن
لَّمْ تُؤْتَوْهُ فَاحْذَرُوا ۗ وَمَن يُرِدِ
اللّٰهُ فِتْنَتَهٗ فَلَن تَمْلِكَ لَهٗ مِنَ
اللّٰهِ شَيْـًٔا ۗ أُولٰٓئِكَ الَّذِينَ لَمْ يُرِدِ
اللّٰهُ أَن يُطَهِّرَ قُلُوبَهُمْ ۗ لَهُمْ فِى
الدُّنْيَا خِزْيٌ ۚ وَلَهُمْ فِى الْاٰخِرَةِ
عَذَابٌ عَظِيمٌ ﴿٤١﴾
سَمّٰعُونَ لِلْكَذِبِ أَكّٰلُونَ لِلسُّحْتِ ۗ

مع عند المتقدمين الوقف على الاول اجوز ١٢

Ikhfa اخفاء | Ghunna غنّہ | Ikhfa Meem Saakin اخفاء میم ساکن | Idghaam ادغام | Qalqala قلقلہ | Qalb قلب | Idghaam Meem Saakin ادغام میم ساکن

If they do come to you, either judge between them, or decline to interfere. If you decline, they cannot hurt you in the least. If you judge, judge in equity between them. For Allah loves those who judge in equity.

Fa-in jaaa'ooka faḥkum baynahum aw a'riḍ 'anhum wa in tu'riḍ 'anhum falañy-yaḍurrooka shay'añw wa in ḥakamta faḥkum baynahum bilqisṭ; innal-laaha yuḥibbul-muqsiṭeen.

فَإِنْ جَاءُوكَ فَاحْكُمْ بَيْنَهُمْ أَوْ
أَعْرِضْ عَنْهُمْ ۚ وَإِنْ تُعْرِضْ عَنْهُمْ
فَلَنْ يَضُرُّوكَ شَيْئًا ۖ وَإِنْ حَكَمْتَ
فَاحْكُمْ بَيْنَهُمْ بِالْقِسْطِ ۚ إِنَّ اللَّهَ
يُحِبُّ الْمُقْسِطِينَ ﴿٤٢﴾

43. But why do they come to you for decision, when they have (their own) law before them?- therein is the (plain) command of Allah; yet even after that, they would turn away. For they are not (really) People of Faith.

43. Wa kayfa yuḥakkimoonaka wa 'indahumut-Tawraatu feehaa hukmul-laahi summa yatawallawna mim ba'di zaalik; wa maaa ulaaa'ika bilmu'mineen. **(Section 6)**

وَكَيْفَ يُحَكِّمُونَكَ وَعِنْدَهُمُ
التَّوْرَاةُ فِيهَا حُكْمُ اللَّهِ ثُمَّ
يَتَوَلَّوْنَ مِنْ بَعْدِ ذَٰلِكَ ۚ وَمَا أُولَٰئِكَ
بِالْمُؤْمِنِينَ ﴿٤٣﴾ ع

44. It was We who revealed the law (to Moses): therein was guidance and light. By its standard have been judged the Jews, by the prophets who bowed (as in Islam) to Allah's will, by the rabbis and the doctors of law: for to them was entrusted the protection of Allah's book, and they were witnesses there to: therefore fear not men, but fear me, and sell not my signs for a miserable price. If any do fail to judge by (the light of) what Allah has revealed, they are (no better than) Unbelievers.

44. Innaaa anzalnat Tawraata feehaa hudañw-wa noor; yaḥkumu bihan-Nabiyyoonal-lazeena aslamoo lillazeena haadoo war-rabbaaniyyoona wal-aḥbaaru bimas-tuḥfiẓoo min Kitaabil-laahi wa kaanoo 'alayhi shuhadaaa'; falaa takhshawun-naasa wakhshawni wa laa tashtaroo bi-Aayaatee samanan qaleelaa; wa mal-lam yaḥkum bimaaa anzalal-laahu fa-ulaaa'ika humul-kaafiroon.

إِنَّا أَنْزَلْنَا التَّوْرَاةَ فِيهَا هُدًى
وَنُورٌ ۚ يَحْكُمُ بِهَا النَّبِيُّونَ
الَّذِينَ أَسْلَمُوا لِلَّذِينَ هَادُوا
وَالرَّبَّانِيُّونَ وَالْأَحْبَارُ بِمَا
اسْتُحْفِظُوا مِنْ كِتَابِ اللَّهِ وَكَانُوا
عَلَيْهِ شُهَدَاءَ ۚ فَلَا تَخْشَوُا النَّاسَ
وَاخْشَوْنِ وَلَا تَشْتَرُوا بِآيَاتِي ثَمَنًا
قَلِيلًا ۚ وَمَنْ لَمْ يَحْكُمْ بِمَا أَنْزَلَ
اللَّهُ فَأُولَٰئِكَ هُمُ الْكَافِرُونَ ﴿٤٤﴾

45. We ordained therein for them: "Life for life, eye for eye, nose for nose, ear for ear, tooth for tooth, and wounds equal for equal." But if any one remits the retaliation by way of charity, it is an act of atonement for himself. And if any fail to judge by (the light of) what Allah has revealed, they are (no better than) wrong-doers.

45. Wa katabnaa 'alayhim feehaaa annan-nafsa binnafsi wal'ayna bil'ayni wal-anfa bilanfi wal-uzuna bil-uzuni wassinna bissinni waljurooḥa qiṣaaṣ; faman taṣaddaqa bihee fahuwa kaffaaratul-lah; wa mal-lam yaḥkum bimaaa anzalal-laahu fa-ulaaa'ika humuẓ-ẓalimoon.

وَكَتَبْنَا عَلَيْهِمْ فِيهَا أَنَّ النَّفْسَ
بِالنَّفْسِ وَالْعَيْنَ بِالْعَيْنِ وَالْأَنْفَ
بِالْأَنْفِ وَالْأُذُنَ بِالْأُذُنِ وَالسِّنَّ
بِالسِّنِّ وَالْجُرُوحَ قِصَاصٌ ۚ فَمَنْ
تَصَدَّقَ بِهِ فَهُوَ كَفَّارَةٌ لَهُ ۚ
وَمَنْ لَمْ يَحْكُمْ بِمَا أَنْزَلَ اللَّهُ
فَأُولَٰئِكَ هُمُ الظَّالِمُونَ ﴿٤٥﴾

46. And in their footsteps We sent Jesus the son of

46. Wa qaffaynaa 'alaaa aasaarihim bi-'Eesab-ni-

وَقَفَّيْنَا عَلَىٰ آثَارِهِمْ بِعِيسَى ابْنِ

Ikhfa اخفاء | Ghunna غنّہ | Ikhfa Meem Saakin اخفاء میم ساکن | Idghaam ادغام | Qalqala قلقلہ | Qalb قلب | Idghaam Meem Saakin ادغام میم ساکن

Mary, confirming the Law that had come before him: We sent him the Gospel: therein was guidance and light, and confirmation of the Law that had come before him: a guidance and an admonition to those who fear Allah.

Maryama muṣaddiqal-limaa bayna yadayhi minat-Tawraati wa aataynaahul-Injeela feehi hudañw-wa nooruñw-wa muṣaddiqal-limaa bayna yadayhi minat-Tawraati wa hudañw-wa maw'iẓatal-lilmuttaqeen.

مَرْيَمَ مُصَدِّقًا لِّمَا بَيْنَ يَدَيْهِ مِنَ
التَّوْرٰىةِ وَاٰتَيْنٰهُ الْاِنْجِيْلَ فِيْهِ
هُدًى وَّنُوْرٌ ۙ وَّمُصَدِّقًا لِّمَا بَيْنَ
يَدَيْهِ مِنَ التَّوْرٰىةِ وَهُدًى وَّ
مَوْعِظَةً لِّلْمُتَّقِيْنَ ﴿٤٦﴾

47. Let the people of the Gospel judge by what Allah has revealed therein. If any do fail to judge by (the light of) what Allah has revealed, they are (no better than) those who rebel.

47. Walyaḥkum Ahlul-Injeeli bimaaa anzalal-laahu feeh; wa mal-lam yaḥkum bimaaa anzalal-laahu fa-ulaaa'ika humul-faasiqoon.

وَلْيَحْكُمْ اَهْلُ الْاِنْجِيْلِ بِمَآ اَنْزَلَ
اللّٰهُ فِيْهِ ۗ وَمَنْ لَّمْ يَحْكُمْ بِمَآ اَنْزَلَ
اللّٰهُ فَاُولٰٓئِكَ هُمُ الْفٰسِقُوْنَ ﴿٤٧﴾

48. To you We sent the Scripture in truth, confirming the scripture that came before it, and guarding it in safety: so judge between them by what Allah has revealed, and follow not their vain desires, diverging from the Truth that has come to you. To each among you we have prescribed a law and an open way. If Allah had so willed, He would have made you a single people, but (His plan is) to test you in what He have given you: so strive as in a race in all virtues. The goal of you all is to Allah; it is He that will show you the truth of the matters in which you dispute;

48. Wa anzalnaaa ilaykal-Kitaaba bilḥaqqi muṣad-diqallimaa bayna yadayhi minal-Kitaabi wa muhayminan 'alayhi faḥkum baynahum bimaaa anzalal-laahu wa laa tattabi' ahwaaa'ahum 'ammaa jaaa'aka minal-ḥaqq; likullin ja'alnaa minkum shir'atañw-wa minhaajaa; wa law shaaa'al-laahu laja'alakum ummatañw-waaḥidatañw-wa laakil-liyablu-wakum fee maaa aataakum fastabiqul-khayraat; ilal-laahi marji'ukum jamee'an fayunab-bi'ukum bimaa kuntum feehi takhtalifoon.

وَاَنْزَلْنَآ اِلَيْكَ الْكِتٰبَ بِالْحَقِّ
مُصَدِّقًا لِّمَا بَيْنَ يَدَيْهِ مِنَ
الْكِتٰبِ وَمُهَيْمِنًا عَلَيْهِ فَاحْكُمْ
بَيْنَهُمْ بِمَآ اَنْزَلَ اللّٰهُ وَلَا تَتَّبِعْ
اَهْوَآءَهُمْ عَمَّا جَآءَكَ مِنَ الْحَقِّ ۗ
لِكُلٍّ جَعَلْنَا مِنْكُمْ شِرْعَةً وَّمِنْهَاجًا ۗ
وَلَوْ شَآءَ اللّٰهُ لَجَعَلَكُمْ اُمَّةً وَّاحِدَةً
وَّلٰكِنْ لِّيَبْلُوَكُمْ فِيْ مَآ اٰتٰىكُمْ
فَاسْتَبِقُوا الْخَيْرٰتِ ۗ اِلَى اللّٰهِ مَرْجِعُكُمْ
جَمِيْعًا فَيُنَبِّئُكُمْ بِمَا كُنْتُمْ فِيْهِ
تَخْتَلِفُوْنَ ۙ﴿٤٨﴾

49. And this (He commands): Judge you between them by what Allah has revealed, and follow not their vain desires, but beware of them lest they beguile you from any of that (teaching) which Allah has sent down to you. And if they turn away, be assured that for some of their crime it is Allah's purpose to punish them. And truly most men are rebellious.

49. Wa aniḥ-kum baynahum bimaaa anzalal-laahu wa laa tattabi' ahwaaa'ahum waḥzar-hum añy-yaftinooka 'am ba'ḍi maaa anzalal-laahu ilayka fa-in tawallaw fa'lam annamaa yureedul-laahu añy-yuṣeebahum biba'ḍi ẕunoobihim; wa inna kaseeram-minan-naasi lafaa-siqoon.

وَاَنِ احْكُمْ بَيْنَهُمْ بِمَآ اَنْزَلَ
اللّٰهُ وَلَا تَتَّبِعْ اَهْوَآءَهُمْ وَاحْذَرْهُمْ
اَنْ يَّفْتِنُوْكَ عَنْ بَعْضِ مَآ اَنْزَلَ
اللّٰهُ اِلَيْكَ ۗ فَاِنْ تَوَلَّوْا فَاعْلَمْ اَنَّمَا
يُرِيْدُ اللّٰهُ اَنْ يُّصِيْبَهُمْ بِبَعْضِ
ذُنُوْبِهِمْ ۗ وَاِنَّ كَثِيْرًا مِّنَ
النَّاسِ لَفٰسِقُوْنَ ﴿٤٩﴾

Ikhfa اخفاء | Ghunna غُنّہ | Ikhfa Meem Saakin اخفاء میم ساکن | Idghaam ادغام | Qalqala قلقلہ | Qalb قلب | Idghaam Meem Saakin ادغام میم ساکن

50. Do they then seek after a judgment of (the days of) ignorance? But who, for a people whose faith is assured, can give better judgment than Allah?

50. Afaḥukmal-Jaahiliyyati yabghoon; wa man aḥsanu minal-laahi ḥukmal-liqawmiñy-yooqinoon. **(Section 7)**

اَفَحُكْمَ الْجَاهِلِيَّةِ يَبْغُوْنَ ؕ
وَمَنْ اَحْسَنُ مِنَ اللّٰهِ حُكْمًا
لِّقَوْمٍ يُّوْقِنُوْنَ ؏ ﴿٥٠﴾

ع ٧ ٢٠

51. O you who believe! take not the Jews and the Christians for your friends and protectors: they are but friends and protectors to each other. And he amongst you that turns to them (for friendship) is of them. Verily Allah guides not a people unjust.

51. Yaaa-ayyuhal-lazeena aamanoo laa tattakhizul-Yahooda wan-Naṣaaraaa awliyaaa'; ba'ḍuhum-awliyaaa'u ba'ḍ; wa mañy-yatawallahum minkum fa-innahoo minhum; innal-laaha laa yahdil-qawmaẓ-ẓaalimeen.

يٰۤاَيُّهَا الَّذِيْنَ اٰمَنُوْا لَا تَتَّخِذُوا
الْيَهُوْدَ وَالنَّصٰرٰۤى اَوْلِيَآءَ ؔ بَعْضُهُمْ
اَوْلِيَآءُ بَعْضٍ ؕ وَمَنْ يَّتَوَلَّهُمْ
مِّنْكُمْ فَاِنَّهٗ مِنْهُمْ ؕ اِنَّ اللّٰهَ
لَا يَهْدِى الْقَوْمَ الظّٰلِمِيْنَ ﴿٥١﴾

معانقة وقف غفران ١٢ وقف منزل عند البعض ١٢

52. Those in whose hearts is a disease - you see how eagerly they run about amongst them, saying: "We do fear lest a change of fortune bring us disaster." Ah! perhaps Allah will give (thee) victory, or a decision according to His will. Then will they repent of the thoughts which they secretly harboured in their hearts.

52. Fataral-lazeena fee quloobihim maraḍuñy-yusaari'oona feehim yaqooloona nakhshaaa-an tuṣeebanaa daaa'irah; fa'asallaahu-añy-yaåtiya bilfatḥi aw amrim-min 'indihee fa-yuṣbiḥoo 'alaa maaa asarroo feee anfusihim naadimeen.

فَتَرَى الَّذِيْنَ فِىْ قُلُوْبِهِمْ مَّرَضٌ
يُّسَارِعُوْنَ فِيْهِمْ يَقُوْلُوْنَ نَخْشٰٓى
اَنْ تُصِيْبَنَا دَآئِرَةٌ ؕ فَعَسَى اللّٰهُ
اَنْ يَّاْتِىَ بِالْفَتْحِ اَوْ اَمْرٍ مِّنْ
عِنْدِهٖ فَيُصْبِحُوْا عَلٰى مَاۤ اَسَرُّوْا فِىۤ
اَنْفُسِهِمْ نٰدِمِيْنَ ؕ ﴿٥٢﴾

53. And those who believe will say: "Are these the men who swore their strongest oaths by Allah, that they were with you?" All that they do will be in vain, and they will fall into (nothing but) ruin.

53. Wa yaqoolul-lazeena aamanooo ahaaa'ulaaa'il-lazeena aqsamoo billaahi jahda aymaanihim innahum lama-'akum; ḥabiṭat a'maaluhum fa-aṣbaḥoo khaasireen.

وَيَقُوْلُ الَّذِيْنَ اٰمَنُوْۤا اَهٰۤؤُلَآءِ
الَّذِيْنَ اَقْسَمُوْا بِاللّٰهِ جَهْدَ اَيْمَانِهِمْ ۙ
اِنَّهُمْ لَمَعَكُمْ ؕ حَبِطَتْ اَعْمَالُهُمْ
فَاَصْبَحُوْا خٰسِرِيْنَ ﴿٥٣﴾

الثلثة

54. O you who believe! if any from among you turn back from his Faith, soon will Allah produce a people whom He will love as they will love Him,- lowly with the believers, mighty against the rejecters, fighting in the way of Allah, and never afraid of the reproaches of such as find fault. That is the grace of Allah, which He will bestow on whom He pleases. And Allah encompasses all, and He knows all things.

54. Yaaa ayyuhal-lazeena aamanoo mañy-yartadda minkum 'an deenihee fasawfa yaåtil-laahu biqawmiñy-yuḥibbuhum wa yuḥibboonahooo azillatin 'alal-mu'mineena a'izzatin 'alal-kaafireena yujaahidoona fee sabeelil-laahi wa laa yakhaafoona lawmata laaa'im; zaalika faḍlul-laahi yu'teehi mañy-yashaaa'; wallaahu Waasi'un 'Aleem.

يٰۤاَيُّهَا الَّذِيْنَ اٰمَنُوْا مَنْ يَّرْتَدَّ
مِنْكُمْ عَنْ دِيْنِهٖ فَسَوْفَ يَاْتِى اللّٰهُ
بِقَوْمٍ يُّحِبُّهُمْ وَيُحِبُّوْنَهٗۤ ۙ اَذِلَّةٍ
عَلَى الْمُؤْمِنِيْنَ اَعِزَّةٍ عَلَى الْكٰفِرِيْنَ ز
يُجَاهِدُوْنَ فِىْ سَبِيْلِ اللّٰهِ وَلَا
يَخَافُوْنَ لَوْمَةَ لَآئِمٍ ؕ ذٰلِكَ
فَضْلُ اللّٰهِ يُؤْتِيْهِ مَنْ يَّشَآءُ ؕ
وَاللّٰهُ وَاسِعٌ عَلِيْمٌ ﴿٥٤﴾

Ikhfa اخفاء | Ghunna غنّہ | Ikhfa Meem Saakin اخفاءمیم ساکن | Idghaam ادغام | Qalqala قلقلہ | Qalb قلب | Idghaam Meem Saakin ادغام میم ساکن

55. Your (real) friends are (no less than) Allah, His Apostle, and the (fellowship of) Believers,- those who establish regular prayers and regular charity, and they bow down humbly (in worship).

55. Innamaa waliyyukumul-laahu wa Rasooluhoo wal-lazeena aamanul-lazeena yu-qeemoonaṣ-Ṣalaata wa yu'too-naz-Zakaata wa hum raaki'oon.

56. As to those who turn (for friendship) to Allah, His Apostle, and the (fellowship of) Believers,- it is the fellowship of Allah that must certainly triumph.

56. Wa mañy-yatawallal-laaha wa Rasoolahoo wallazeena aamanoo fa-inna ḥizbal-laahi humul-ghaaliboon. **(Section 8)**

57. O you who believe! take not for friends and protectors those who take your religion for a mockery or sport,- whether among those who received the Scripture before you, or among those who reject Faith; but fear you Allah, if you have Faith (indeed).

57. Yaaa ayyuhal-lazeena aamanoo laa tattakhizul-lazeenat-takhazoo deenakum huzuwañw-wa la'ibam-minal-lazeena ootul-Kitaaba min qablikum walkuffaara awliyaaa'; wattaqul-laaha in kuntum mu'mineen.

58. When you proclaim your call to prayer, they take it (but) as mockery and sport; that is because they are a people without understanding.

58. Wa izaa naadaytum ilaṣ-Ṣalaatit-takhazoohaa huzu-wañw-wa la'ibaa; zaalika bi-annahum qawmul-laa ya'qiloon.

59. Say: "O people of the Book! Do you disapprove of us for no other reason than that we believe in Allah, and the revelation that has come to us and that which came before (us), and (perhaps) that most of you are rebellious and disobedient?"

59. Qul yaaa Ahlal-Kitaabi hal tanqimoona minnaaa illaaa an aamannaa billaahi wa maaa unzila ilaynaa wa maaa unzila min qablu wa anna aksarakum faasiqoon.

60. Say: "Shall I point out to you something much worse than this, (as judged) by the treatment it received from Allah? those who incurred the curse of Allah and His wrath, those of whom some He transformed into apes and swine, those who worshipped evil;- these are (many times) worse in rank, and far more astray from the even path!"

60. Qul hal unabbi'ukum bisharrim-min zaalika masoo-batan 'indal-laah; malla'ana-hul-laahu wa ghaḍiba 'alayhi wa ja'ala minhumul-qiradata wal-khanaazeera wa 'abadaṭ-Ṭaaghoot; ulaaa'ika sharrum-makaanañw-wa aḍallu 'an Sawaaa'is-Sabeel.

61. When they come to you, they say: "We believe": but in fact they enter with a mind against Faith, and they go out with the same. But Allah knows fully all that they hide.

61. Wa-izaa jaaa'ookum qaalooo aamannaa wa qad dakhaloo bilkufri wa hum qad kharajoo bih; wallaahu a'lamu bimaa kaanoo yaktumoon.

إِنَّمَا وَلِيُّكُمُ اللّٰهُ وَرَسُوْلُهٗ وَالَّذِيْنَ
اٰمَنُوا الَّذِيْنَ يُقِيْمُوْنَ الصَّلٰوةَ
وَيُؤْتُوْنَ الزَّكٰوةَ وَهُمْ رٰكِعُوْنَ ﴿٥٥﴾
وَمَنْ يَّتَوَلَّ اللّٰهَ وَرَسُوْلَهٗ وَالَّذِيْنَ
اٰمَنُوْا فَاِنَّ حِزْبَ اللّٰهِ هُمُ الْغٰلِبُوْنَ ﴿٥٦﴾ ع ٨ ١٢
يٰۤاَيُّهَا الَّذِيْنَ اٰمَنُوْا لَا تَتَّخِذُوا
الَّذِيْنَ اتَّخَذُوْا دِيْنَكُمْ هُزُوًا وَّ
لَعِبًا مِّنَ الَّذِيْنَ اُوْتُوا الْكِتٰبَ مِنْ
قَبْلِكُمْ وَالْكُفَّارَ اَوْلِيَآءَ ۚ وَاتَّقُوا
اللّٰهَ اِنْ كُنْتُمْ مُّؤْمِنِيْنَ ﴿٥٧﴾
وَاِذَا نَادَيْتُمْ اِلَى الصَّلٰوةِ اتَّخَذُوْهَا
هُزُوًا وَّلَعِبًا ؕ ذٰلِكَ بِاَنَّهُمْ قَوْمٌ
لَّا يَعْقِلُوْنَ ﴿٥٨﴾
قُلْ يٰۤاَهْلَ الْكِتٰبِ هَلْ تَنْقِمُوْنَ
مِنَّاۤ اِلَّاۤ اَنْ اٰمَنَّا بِاللّٰهِ وَمَاۤ اُنْزِلَ
اِلَيْنَا وَمَاۤ اُنْزِلَ مِنْ قَبْلُ ۙ
وَاَنَّ اَكْثَرَكُمْ فٰسِقُوْنَ ﴿٥٩﴾
قُلْ هَلْ اُنَبِّئُكُمْ بِشَرٍّ مِّنْ ذٰلِكَ
مَثُوْبَةً عِنْدَ اللّٰهِ ؕ مَنْ لَّعَنَهُ اللّٰهُ
وَغَضِبَ عَلَيْهِ وَجَعَلَ مِنْهُمُ الْقِرَدَةَ
وَالْخَنَازِيْرَ وَعَبَدَ الطَّاغُوْتَ ؕ
اُولٰٓئِكَ شَرٌّ مَّكَانًا وَّاَضَلُّ عَنْ
سَوَآءِ السَّبِيْلِ ﴿٦٠﴾
وَاِذَا جَآءُوْكُمْ قَالُوْۤا اٰمَنَّا وَقَدْ
دَّخَلُوْا بِالْكُفْرِ وَهُمْ قَدْ خَرَجُوْا بِهٖ ؕ
وَاللّٰهُ اَعْلَمُ بِمَا كَانُوْا يَكْتُمُوْنَ ﴿٦١﴾

Ikhfa اخفاء | Ghunna غُنّہ | Ikhfa Meem Saakin اخفاء میم ساکن | Idghaam ادغام | Qalqala قلقلہ | Qalb قلب | Idghaam Meem Saakin ادغام میم ساکن

62. You see many of them, racing each other in sin and rancour, and their eating of things forbidden. Evil indeed are the things that they do.

63. Why do not the rabbis and the doctors of Law forbid them from their (habit of) uttering sinful words and eating things forbidden? Evil indeed are their works.

64. The Jews say: "Allah's hand is tied up." Be their hands tied up and be they accursed for the (blasphemy) they utter. No, both His hands are widely outstretched: He gives and spends (of His bounty) as He pleases. But the revelation that comes to you from Allah increases in most of them their obstinate rebellion and blasphemy. Amongst them we have placed enmity and hatred till the Day of Judgment. Every time they kindle the fire of war, Allah does extinguish it; but they (ever) strive to do mischief on earth. And Allah loves not those who do mischief.

65. If only the People of the Book had believed and been righteous, We should indeed have blotted out their iniquities and admitted them to gardens of bliss.

66. If only they had stood fast by the Law, the Gospel, and all the revelation that was sent to them from their Lord, they would have enjoyed happiness from every side. There is from among them a party on the right course: but many of them follow a course that is evil.

67. O Apostle! proclaim the (message) which has been sent to you from your Lord. If you did not, you would not have fulfilled and proclaimed

62. Wa taraa kaseeram-minhum yusaari'oona fil-ismi wal-'udwaani wa aklihimus-suht; labi'sa maa kaanoo ya'maloon.

63. Law laa yanhaahumur-rabbaaniyyoona wal-ahbaaru 'an qawlihimul-isma wa aklihimus-suht; labi'sa maa kaanoo yasna'oon.

64. Wa qaalatil-Yahoodu Yadullaahi maghloolah; ghullat aydeehim wa lu'inoo bimaa qaaloo; bal Yadaahu mabsootataani yunfiqu kayfa yashaaa'; wa la-yazeedanna kaseeram-minhum-maaa unzila ilayka mir-Rabbika tughyaanañw-wa kufraa; wa alqaynaa baynahumul-'adaawata wal-baghdaaa-a' ilaa Yawmil-Qiyaamah; kullamaaa awqadoo naaral-lilharbi atfa-ahal-laah; wa yas'awna fil-ardi fasaadaa; wal-laahu laa yuhibbul-mufsideen.

65. Wa law anna Ahlal-Kitaabi aamanoo wattaqaw lakaffarnaa 'anhum sayyi-aatihim wa la-adkhalnaahum Jannaatin-Na'eem.

66. Wa law annahum aqaamut-Tawraata wal-Injeela wa maaa unzila ilayhim-mir-Rabbihim la-akaloo min fawqihim wa min tahti arjulihim; minhum ummatum-muqtasidatuñw wa kaseerum-minhum saaa'a maa ya'maloon.

(Section 9)

67. Yaaa ayyuhar-Rasoolu balligh maaa unzila ilayka mir-Rabbika wa il-lam taf'al famaa ballaghta

وَتَرٰى كَثِيْرًا مِّنْهُمْ يُسَارِعُوْنَ فِي
الْاِثْمِ وَالْعُدْوَانِ وَاَكْلِهِمُ السُّحْتَ ط
لَبِئْسَ مَا كَانُوْا يَعْمَلُوْنَ ﴿٦٢﴾
لَوْلَا يَنْهٰىهُمُ الرَّبّٰنِيُّوْنَ وَالْاَحْبَارُ
عَنْ قَوْلِهِمُ الْاِثْمَ وَاَكْلِهِمُ السُّحْتَ ط
لَبِئْسَ مَا كَانُوْا يَصْنَعُوْنَ ﴿٦٣﴾
وَقَالَتِ الْيَهُوْدُ يَدُ اللّٰهِ مَغْلُوْلَةٌ ط
غُلَّتْ اَيْدِيْهِمْ وَلُعِنُوْا بِمَا قَالُوْا م بَلْ
يَدٰهُ مَبْسُوْطَتٰنِ لا يُنْفِقُ كَيْفَ يَشَآءُ ط
وَلَيَزِيْدَنَّ كَثِيْرًا مِّنْهُمْ مَّآ اُنْزِلَ
اِلَيْكَ مِنْ رَّبِّكَ طُغْيَانًا وَّكُفْرًا ط
وَاَلْقَيْنَا بَيْنَهُمُ الْعَدَاوَةَ وَالْبَغْضَآءَ
اِلٰى يَوْمِ الْقِيٰمَةِ ط كُلَّمَآ اَوْقَدُوْا نَارًا
لِّلْحَرْبِ اَطْفَاَهَا اللّٰهُ لا وَيَسْعَوْنَ
فِي الْاَرْضِ فَسَادًا ط وَاللّٰهُ لَا يُحِبُّ
الْمُفْسِدِيْنَ ﴿٦٤﴾
وَلَوْ اَنَّ اَهْلَ الْكِتٰبِ اٰمَنُوْا وَاتَّقَوْا
لَكَفَّرْنَا عَنْهُمْ سَيِّاٰتِهِمْ وَلَاَدْخَلْنٰهُمْ
جَنّٰتِ النَّعِيْمِ ﴿٦٥﴾
وَلَوْ اَنَّهُمْ اَقَامُوا التَّوْرٰىةَ وَالْاِنْجِيْلَ
وَمَآ اُنْزِلَ اِلَيْهِمْ مِّنْ رَّبِّهِمْ لَاَكَلُوْا
مِنْ فَوْقِهِمْ وَمِنْ تَحْتِ اَرْجُلِهِمْ ط
مِنْهُمْ اُمَّةٌ مُّقْتَصِدَةٌ ط وَكَثِيْرٌ
مِّنْهُمْ سَآءَ مَا يَعْمَلُوْنَ ﴿٦٦﴾
يٰٓاَيُّهَا الرَّسُوْلُ بَلِّغْ مَآ اُنْزِلَ اِلَيْكَ
مِنْ رَّبِّكَ ط وَاِنْ لَّمْ تَفْعَلْ فَمَا بَلَّغْتَ

وقف لازم

ع

Ikhfa اخفاء | Ghunna غنّہ | Ikhfa Meem Saakin اخفاء میم ساکن | Idghaam ادغام | Qalqala قلقلہ | Qalb قلب | Idghaam Meem Saakin ادغام میم ساکن

His mission. And Allah will defend you from men (who mean mischief). For Allah guides not those who reject Faith.

68. Say: "O People of the Book! you have no ground to stand upon unless you stand fast by the Law, the Gospel, and all the revelation that has come to you from your Lord." It is the revelation that comes to you from your Lord, that increases in most of them their obstinate rebellion and blasphemy. But you do not grieve over (these) people without Faith.

69. Those who believe (in the Qur'an), those who follow the Jewish (scriptures), and the Sabians and the Christians,- any who believe in Allah and the Last Day, and work righteousness,- on them shall be no fear, nor shall they grieve.

70. We took the Covenant of the Children of Israel and sent them Apostles, every time, there came to them an Apostle with what they themselves desired not - some (of these) they called impostors, and some they (go so far as to) slay.

71. They thought there would be no trial (or punishment); so they became blind and deaf; yet Allah (in mercy) turned to them; yet again many of them became blind and deaf. But Allah sees well all that they do.

72. They do blaspheme who say: "Allah is Christ the son of Mary." But Christ said: "O Children of Israel! worship Allah, my Lord and your Lord." Whoever joins other gods with Allah,- Allah will forbid

Risaalatah; wallaahu ya'ṣimuka minan-naas; innal-laaha laa yahdil-qawmal-kaafireen.

68. Qul yaaa Ahlal-Kitaabi lastum 'alaa shay'in ḥattaa tuqeemut-Tawraata wal-Injeela wa maaa unzila ilaykum-mir-Rabbikum; wa layazeedanna kas̲eeram-minhum-maaa unzila ilayka mir-Rabbika ṭugh-yaanañw-wa kufran falaa taåsa 'alal-qawmil-kaafireen.

69. Innal-laz̲eena aamanoo wallaz̲eena haadoo waṣ-Ṣaabi'oona wan-Naṣaaraa man aamana billaahi wal-Yawmil-Aakhiri wa 'amila ṣaaliḥan falaa khawfun 'alayhim wa laa hum yaḥzanoon.

70. Laqad akhaz̲naa meesaaqa Baneee Israaa'eela wa arsal-naaa ilayhim Rusulan kullamaa jaaa'ahum Rasoolum-bimaa laa tahwaaa anfusuhum fareeqan kaz̲z̲aboo wa fareeqañy-yaqtuloon.

71. Wa ḥasibooo allaa takoona fitnatun fa'amoo wa ṣammoo summa taabal-laahu 'alayhim summa 'amoo wa ṣammoo kas̲eerum-minhum; wallaahu baṣeerum-bimaa ya'maloon.

72. Laqad kafaral-laz̲eena qaalooo innal-laaha Huwal-Maseeḥub-nu-Maryama wa qaalal-Maseeḥu yaa Baneee Israaa'eela'-budul-laaha Rabbee wa Rabbakum innahoo mañy-yushrik billaahi faqad ḥarramal-laahu

رِسَالَتَهٗ ؕ وَاللّٰهُ يَعۡصِمُكَ مِنَ النَّاسِ ؕ
اِنَّ اللّٰهَ لَا يَهۡدِى الۡقَوۡمَ الۡكٰفِرِيۡنَ ﴿۶۷﴾
قُلۡ يٰۤاَهۡلَ الۡكِتٰبِ لَسۡتُمۡ عَلٰى شَىۡءٍ
حَتّٰى تُقِيۡمُوا التَّوۡرٰٮةَ وَالۡاِنۡجِيۡلَ وَمَاۤ
اُنۡزِلَ اِلَيۡكُمۡ مِّنۡ رَّبِّكُمۡ ؕ وَلَيَزِيۡدَنَّ
كَثِيۡرًا مِّنۡهُمۡ مَّاۤ اُنۡزِلَ اِلَيۡكَ مِنۡ
رَّبِّكَ طُغۡيَانًا وَّكُفۡرًا ۚ فَلَا تَاۡسَ
عَلَى الۡقَوۡمِ الۡكٰفِرِيۡنَ ﴿۶۸﴾
اِنَّ الَّذِيۡنَ اٰمَنُوۡا وَالَّذِيۡنَ هَادُوۡا
وَالصّٰبِـُٔوۡنَ وَالنَّصٰرٰى مَنۡ اٰمَنَ
بِاللّٰهِ وَالۡيَوۡمِ الۡاٰخِرِ وَعَمِلَ
صَالِحًـا فَلَا خَوۡفٌ عَلَيۡهِمۡ وَلَا
هُمۡ يَحۡزَنُوۡنَ ﴿۶۹﴾
لَـقَدۡ اَخَذۡنَا مِيۡثَاقَ بَنِىۡۤ اِسۡرَاۤءِيۡلَ
وَاَرۡسَلۡنَاۤ اِلَيۡهِمۡ رُسُلًا ؕ كُلَّمَا
جَآءَهُمۡ رَسُوۡلٌۢ بِمَا لَا تَهۡوٰٓى اَنۡفُسُهُمۡ ۙ
فَرِيۡقًا كَذَّبُوۡا وَفَرِيۡقًا يَّقۡتُلُوۡنَ ﴿۷۰﴾
وَحَسِبُوۡۤا اَلَّا تَكُوۡنَ فِتۡنَةٌ فَعَمُوۡا
وَصَمُّوۡا ثُمَّ تَابَ اللّٰهُ عَلَيۡهِمۡ ثُمَّ
عَمُوۡا وَصَمُّوۡا كَثِيۡرٌ مِّنۡهُمۡ ؕ وَاللّٰهُ
بَصِيۡرٌۢ بِمَا يَعۡمَلُوۡنَ ﴿۷۱﴾
لَـقَدۡ كَفَرَ الَّذِيۡنَ قَالُوۡۤا اِنَّ اللّٰهَ
هُوَ الۡمَسِيۡحُ ابۡنُ مَرۡيَمَ ؕ وَقَالَ
الۡمَسِيۡحُ يٰبَنِىۡۤ اِسۡرَاۤءِيۡلَ اعۡبُدُوا
اللّٰهَ رَبِّىۡ وَرَبَّكُمۡ ؕ اِنَّهٗ مَنۡ
يُّشۡرِكۡ بِاللّٰهِ فَقَدۡ حَرَّمَ اللّٰهُ

Ikhfa اخفاء | Ghunna غنّہ | Ikhfa Meem Saakin اخفاءمیم ساکن | Idghaam ادغام | Qalqala قلقلہ | Qalb قلب | Idghaam Meem Saakin ادغام میم ساکن

him the Garden, and the Fire will be his abode. There will for the wrong-doers be no one to help.

73. They do blaspheme who say: Allah is one of three in a Trinity; for there is no Allah except One Allah. If they desist not from their word (of blasphemy), verily a grievous Chastisement will befall the blasphemers among them.

74. Why turn they not to Allah, and seek His forgiveness? For Allah is Oft-forgiving, Most Merciful.

75. Christ the son of Mary was no more than an Apostle; many were the Apostles that passed away before him. His mother was a woman of truth. They had both to eat their (daily) food. See how Allah does make His signs clear to them; yet see in what ways they are deluded away from the truth!

76. Say: "Will you worship, besides Allah, something which has no power either to harm or benefit you? But Allah,- He it is that hears and knows all things."

77. Say: "O people of the Book! exceed not in your religion the bounds (of what is proper), trespassing beyond the truth, nor follow the vain desires of people who went wrong in times gone by,- who misled many, and strayed (themselves) from the even way.

78. Curses were pronounced on those among the Children of Israel who rejected Faith, by the tongue of David and of Jesus the son of Mary: because they disobeyed and persisted in excesses.

79. Nor did they (usually) forbid one another the iniquities

'alayhil-Jannata wa maå-waahun-Naaru wa maa lizzaalimeena min anṣaar.

73. Laqad kafaral-lazeena qaalooo innal-laaha saalisu salaasah; wa maa min ilaahin illaaa Ilaahuñw-Waaḥid; wa il-lam yantahoo 'ammaa yaqoo-loona layamas-sannal-lazeena kafaroo minhum 'azaabun aleem.

74. Afalaa-yatooboona ilal-laahi wa yastaghfiroonah; wallaahu Ghafoorur- Raḥeem.

75. Mal-Maseeḥub-nu-Maryama illaa Rasoolun qad khalat min qablihir-Rusulu wa ummu-hoo ṣiddeeqatun kaanaa yaå-kulaaniṭ-ṭa'aam; unẓur kayfa nubayyinu lahumul-Aayaati summan-ẓur annaa yu'fakoon.

76. Qul ata'budoona min doonil-laahi maa laa yamliku lakum ḍarrañw-wa laa naf'aa; wallaahu Huwas-Samee'ul 'Aleem.

77. Qul yaaa Ahlal-Kitaabi laa taghloo fee deenikum ghayral-ḥaqqi wa laa tattabi-'ooo ahwaaa'a qawmin qad ḍalloo min qablu wa aḍalloo kaseerañw-wa ḍalloo 'an Sawaaa'is-Sabeel. **(Section 10)**

78. Lu'inal-lazeena kafaroo mim Baneee Israaa'eela 'alaa lisaani Daawooda wa 'Eesab-ni-Maryam; zaalika bimaa 'aṣaw wa kaanoo ya'tadoon.

79. Kaanoo laa yatanaahawna 'am-munkarin

عَلَيْهِ الْجَنَّةَ وَمَاْوٰىهُ النَّارُ ؕ وَمَا
لِلظّٰلِمِيْنَ مِنْ اَنْصَارٍ ﴿۷۲﴾
لَقَدْ كَفَرَ الَّذِيْنَ قَالُوْۤا اِنَّ
اللّٰهَ ثَالِثُ ثَلٰثَةٍ ۘ وَمَا مِنْ اِلٰهٍ
اِلَّاۤ اِلٰهٌ وَّاحِدٌ ؕ وَاِنْ لَّمْ يَنْتَهُوْا
عَمَّا يَقُوْلُوْنَ لَيَمَسَّنَّ الَّذِيْنَ
كَفَرُوْا مِنْهُمْ عَذَابٌ اَلِيْمٌ ﴿۷۳﴾
اَفَلَا يَتُوْبُوْنَ اِلَى اللّٰهِ وَيَسْتَغْفِرُوْنَهٗ ؕ
وَاللّٰهُ غَفُوْرٌ رَّحِيْمٌ ﴿۷۴﴾
مَا الْمَسِيْحُ ابْنُ مَرْيَمَ اِلَّا رَسُوْلٌ ۚ
قَدْ خَلَتْ مِنْ قَبْلِهِ الرُّسُلُ ؕ
وَاُمُّهٗ صِدِّيْقَةٌ ؕ كَانَا يَاْكُلٰنِ
الطَّعَامَ ؕ اُنْظُرْ كَيْفَ نُبَيِّنُ لَهُمُ
الْاٰيٰتِ ثُمَّ انْظُرْ اَنّٰى يُؤْفَكُوْنَ ﴿۷۵﴾
قُلْ اَتَعْبُدُوْنَ مِنْ دُوْنِ اللّٰهِ
مَا لَا يَمْلِكُ لَكُمْ ضَرًّا وَّلَا نَفْعًا ؕ
وَاللّٰهُ هُوَ السَّمِيْعُ الْعَلِيْمُ ﴿۷۶﴾
قُلْ يٰۤاَهْلَ الْكِتٰبِ لَا تَغْلُوْا فِيْ
دِيْنِكُمْ غَيْرَ الْحَقِّ وَلَا تَتَّبِعُوْۤا
اَهْوَآءَ قَوْمٍ قَدْ ضَلُّوْا مِنْ
قَبْلُ وَاَضَلُّوْا كَثِيْرًا وَّضَلُّوْا
عَنْ سَوَآءِ السَّبِيْلِ ﴿۷۷﴾ ع
لُعِنَ الَّذِيْنَ كَفَرُوْا مِنْۢ بَنِيْۤ اِسْرَآءِيْلَ
عَلٰى لِسَانِ دَاوٗدَ وَعِيْسَى ابْنِ مَرْيَمَ ؕ
ذٰلِكَ بِمَا عَصَوْا وَّكَانُوْا يَعْتَدُوْنَ ﴿۷۸﴾
كَانُوْا لَا يَتَنَاهَوْنَ عَنْ مُّنْكَرٍ

وقف لازم

Ikhfa اخفاء | Ghunna غُنّہ | Ikhfa Meem Saakin اخفاء میم ساکن | Idghaam ادغام | Qalqala قلقلہ | Qalb قلب | Idghaam Meem Saakin ادغام میم ساکن

which they committed: Evil indeed were the deeds which theydid.

fa'aluhoo; labi'sa maa kaanoo yafa'loon.

فَعَلُوْهُ ؕ لَبِئْسَ مَا كَانُوْا يَفْعَلُوْنَ ٧٩

80. You see many of them turning in friendship to the Unbelievers. Evil indeed are (the works) which their souls have sent forward before them (with the result), that Allah's wrath is on them, and in torment will they abide.

80. Taraa kas̱eeram-minhum yatawallawnal-laẕeena kafaroo; labi'sa maa qaddamat lahum anfusuhum an sakhiṭal-laahu 'alayhim wa fil-'aẕaabi hum khaalidoon.

تَرٰى كَثِيْرًا مِّنْهُمْ يَتَوَلَّوْنَ الَّذِيْنَ
كَفَرُوْا ؕ لَبِئْسَ مَا قَدَّمَتْ لَهُمْ
اَنْفُسُهُمْ اَنْ سَخِطَ اللّٰهُ عَلَيْهِمْ وَفِى
الْعَذَابِ هُمْ خٰلِدُوْنَ ٨٠

81. If only they had believed in Allah, in the Apostle, and in what has been revealed to him, never would they have taken them for friends and protectors, but most of them are rebellious wrong-doers.

81. Wa law kaanoo yu'minoona billaahi wan-Nabiyyi wa maaa unzila ilayhi mattakhaẕoohum awliyaaa'a wa laakinna kas̱eeram-minhum faasiqoon.

وَلَوْ كَانُوْا يُؤْمِنُوْنَ بِاللّٰهِ وَالنَّبِىِّ
وَمَآ اُنْزِلَ اِلَيْهِ مَا اتَّخَذُوْهُمْ
اَوْلِيَآءَ وَلٰكِنَّ كَثِيْرًا مِّنْهُمْ فٰسِقُوْنَ ٨١

82. Strongest among men in enmity to the believers will you find the Jews and Pagans; and nearest among them in love to the believers will you find those who say, "We are Christians": because among these are men devoted to learning and men who have renounced the world, and they are not arrogant.

82. Latajidanna ashad-dannaasi 'adaawatal-lillaẕeena aamanul-Yahooda wallaẕeena ashrakoo wa latajidanna aqrabahum-mawaddatal-lillaẕeena aamanul-laẕeena qaalooo innaa Naṣaaraa; ẕaalika bi-anna minhum qisseeseena wa ruhbaanañw-wa annahum laa yastakbiroon.

لَتَجِدَنَّ اَشَدَّ النَّاسِ عَدَاوَةً
لِّلَّذِيْنَ اٰمَنُوا الْيَهُوْدَ وَالَّذِيْنَ
اَشْرَكُوْا ۚ وَلَتَجِدَنَّ اَقْرَبَهُمْ
مَّوَدَّةً لِّلَّذِيْنَ اٰمَنُوا الَّذِيْنَ
قَالُوْٓا اِنَّا نَصٰرٰى ؕ ذٰلِكَ بِاَنَّ
مِنْهُمْ قِسِّيْسِيْنَ وَرُهْبَانًا وَّ
اَنَّهُمْ لَا يَسْتَكْبِرُوْنَ ٨٢

83. And when they listen to the revelation received by the Apostle, you will see their eyes overflowing with tears, for they recognise the truth: they pray: "Our Lord! we believe; write us down among the witnesses.

83. Wa iẕaa sami'oo maaa unzila ilar-Rasooli taraaa a'yunahum tafeeḍu minad-dam'i mimmaa 'arafoo minalḥaqq; yaqooloona Rabbanaaa aamannaa faktubnaa ma'ash-shaahideen.

وَاِذَا سَمِعُوْا مَآ اُنْزِلَ اِلَى الرَّسُوْلِ
تَرٰٓى اَعْيُنَهُمْ تَفِيْضُ مِنَ الدَّمْعِ
مِمَّا عَرَفُوْا مِنَ الْحَقِّ ۚ يَقُوْلُوْنَ رَبَّنَآ
اٰمَنَّا فَاكْتُبْنَا مَعَ الشّٰهِدِيْنَ ٨٣

84. "What cause can we have not to believe in Allah and the truth which has come to us, seeing that we long for our Lord to admit us to the company of the righteous?"

84. Wa maa lanaa laa nu'minu billaahi wa maa jaaa'anaa minal-ḥaqqi wa naṭma'u añy-yudkhilanaa Rabbunaa ma'al-qawmiṣ-ṣaaliḥeen.

وَمَا لَنَا لَا نُؤْمِنُ بِاللّٰهِ وَمَا جَآءَنَا
مِنَ الْحَقِّ ۙ وَنَطْمَعُ اَنْ يُّدْخِلَنَا رَبُّنَا
مَعَ الْقَوْمِ الصّٰلِحِيْنَ ٨٤

85. And for this their prayer has Allah rewarded them with gardens, with rivers flowing underneath,- their eternal home. Such is the recompense of those who do good.

85. Fa-as̱aabahumul-laahu bimaa qaaloo Jannaatin tajree min taḥtihal-anhaaru khaalideena feehaa; wa ẕaalika jazaaa'ul-muḥsineen.

فَاَثَابَهُمُ اللّٰهُ بِمَا قَالُوْا جَنّٰتٍ تَجْرِىْ
مِنْ تَحْتِهَا الْاَنْهٰرُ خٰلِدِيْنَ فِيْهَا ؕ
وَذٰلِكَ جَزَآءُ الْمُحْسِنِيْنَ ٨٥

86. But those who reject Faith and belie our Signs,-

86. Wallaẕeena kafaroo wa kaẕ-ẕaboo bi-Aayaatinaaa

وَالَّذِيْنَ كَفَرُوْا وَكَذَّبُوْا بِاٰيٰتِنَآ

اَلْجُزْءُ السَّابِعُ (٧)

Ikhfa اخفاء | Ghunna غُنّہ | Ikhfa Meem Saakin اخفاء میم ساکن | Idghaam ادغام | Qalqala قلقلہ | Qalb قلب | Idghaam Meem Saakin ادغام میم ساکن

they shall be Companions of Hell-fire.

ulaaa'ika Aṣḥaabul-Jaḥeem.

(Section 11)

أُولَٰٓئِكَ أَصْحَٰبُ ٱلْجَحِيمِ ٨٦ ع

87. O you who believe! make not unlawful the good things which Allah has made lawful for you, but commit no excess: for Allah loves not those given to excess.

87. Yaaa ayyuhal-lazeena aamanoo laa tuḥarrimoo ṭayyibaati maaa aḥallal-laahu lakum wa laa ta'tadooo; innal-laaha laa yuḥibbul-mu'tadeen.

يَٰٓأَيُّهَا ٱلَّذِينَ ءَامَنُوا۟ لَا تُحَرِّمُوا۟ طَيِّبَٰتِ
مَآ أَحَلَّ ٱللَّهُ لَكُمْ وَلَا تَعْتَدُوٓا۟ ۚ
إِنَّ ٱللَّهَ لَا يُحِبُّ ٱلْمُعْتَدِينَ ٨٧

88. Eat of the things which Allah has provided for you, lawful and good; but fear Allah, in Whom you believe.

88. Wa kuloo mimmaa razaqakumul-laahu ḥalaalan ṭayyibaa; wattaqul-laahallazeee antum bihee mu'minoon.

وَكُلُوا۟ مِمَّا رَزَقَكُمُ ٱللَّهُ حَلَٰلًا طَيِّبًا ۚ
وَٱتَّقُوا۟ ٱللَّهَ ٱلَّذِىٓ أَنتُم بِهِۦ مُؤْمِنُونَ ٨٨

89. Allah will not call you to account for what is futile in your oaths, but He will call you to account for your deliberate oaths: for expiation, feed ten indigent persons, on a scale of the average for the food of your families; or clothe them; or give a slave his freedom. If that is beyond your means, fast for three days. That is the expiation for the oaths you have sworn. But keep to your oaths. Thus Allah makes clear to you His Signs, that you may be grateful.

89. Laa yu'aakhizukumul-laahu billaghwi feee aymaanikum wa laakiñy-yu'aakhizukum bimaa 'aqqattumul-aymaana fakaf-faaratuhooo iṭ'aamu 'asharati masaakeena min awsaṭi maa tuṭ'imoona ahleekum aw kiswatuhum aw taḥreeru raqabatin famallam yajid fa-Ṣiyaamu salaasati ayyaam; zaalika kaffaaratu aymaanikum izaa ḥalaftum; waḥfaẓooo ay-maanakum; kazaalika yubayyi-nul-laahu lakum Aayaatihee la'allakum tashkuroon.

لَا يُؤَاخِذُكُمُ ٱللَّهُ بِٱللَّغْوِ فِىٓ أَيْمَٰنِكُمْ
وَلَٰكِن يُؤَاخِذُكُم بِمَا عَقَّدتُّمُ
ٱلْأَيْمَٰنَ ۖ فَكَفَّٰرَتُهُۥٓ إِطْعَامُ عَشَرَةِ
مَسَٰكِينَ مِنْ أَوْسَطِ مَا تُطْعِمُونَ
أَهْلِيكُمْ أَوْ كِسْوَتُهُمْ أَوْ تَحْرِيرُ رَقَبَةٍ ۖ
فَمَن لَّمْ يَجِدْ فَصِيَامُ ثَلَٰثَةِ أَيَّامٍ ۚ
ذَٰلِكَ كَفَّٰرَةُ أَيْمَٰنِكُمْ إِذَا حَلَفْتُمْ ۚ
وَٱحْفَظُوٓا۟ أَيْمَٰنَكُمْ ۚ كَذَٰلِكَ يُبَيِّنُ
ٱللَّهُ لَكُمْ ءَايَٰتِهِۦ لَعَلَّكُمْ تَشْكُرُونَ ٨٩

90. O you who believe! Intoxicants and gambling, (dedication of) stones, and (divination by) arrows, are an abomination,- of Satan's handwork: eschew such (abomination), that you may prosper.

90. Yaaa ayyuhal-lazeena aamanooo innamal-khamru walmaysiru wal-anṣaabu wal-azlaamu rijsum-min 'amalish-shayṭaani fajtaniboohu la'al-lakum tufliḥoon.

يَٰٓأَيُّهَا ٱلَّذِينَ ءَامَنُوٓا۟ إِنَّمَا ٱلْخَمْرُ
وَٱلْمَيْسِرُ وَٱلْأَنصَابُ وَٱلْأَزْلَٰمُ رِجْسٌ
مِّنْ عَمَلِ ٱلشَّيْطَٰنِ فَٱجْتَنِبُوهُ
لَعَلَّكُمْ تُفْلِحُونَ ٩٠

91. Satan's plan is (but) to excite enmity and hatred between you, with intoxicants and gambling, and hinder you from the remembrance of Allah, and from prayer: will you not then abstain?

91. Innamaa yureedush-Shay-ṭaanu añy-yooqi'a baynakumul-'adaawata wal-baghḍaaa'a fil-khamri walmaysiri wa yaṣud-dakum 'an zikril-laahi wa 'aniṣ-Ṣalaati fahal antum muntahoon.

إِنَّمَا يُرِيدُ ٱلشَّيْطَٰنُ أَن يُوقِعَ بَيْنَكُمُ
ٱلْعَدَٰوَةَ وَٱلْبَغْضَآءَ فِى ٱلْخَمْرِ وَٱلْمَيْسِرِ
وَيَصُدَّكُمْ عَن ذِكْرِ ٱللَّهِ وَعَنِ ٱلصَّلَوٰةِ ۖ
فَهَلْ أَنتُم مُّنتَهُونَ ٩١

92. Obey Allah, and obey the Apostle, and beware (of evil): if you do turn back, you should know that it is Our Apostle's duty to proclaim (the message) in the clearest manner.

92. Wa aṭee'ul-laaha wa aṭee'ur-Rasoola waḥzaroo; fa-in tawal-laytum fa'lamooo annamaa 'alaa Rasoolinal-balaaghul-mubeen.

وَأَطِيعُوا۟ ٱللَّهَ وَأَطِيعُوا۟ ٱلرَّسُولَ
وَٱحْذَرُوا۟ ۚ فَإِن تَوَلَّيْتُمْ فَٱعْلَمُوٓا۟
أَنَّمَا عَلَىٰ رَسُولِنَا ٱلْبَلَٰغُ ٱلْمُبِينُ ٩٢

Ikhfa اخفاء · Ghunna غنّہ · Ikhfa Meem Saakin اخفاءمیم ساکن · Idghaam ادغام · Qalqala قلقلہ · Qalb قلب · Idghaam Meem Saakin ادغام میم ساکن

93. On those who believe and do deeds of righteousness there is no blame for what they ate (in the past), when they guard themselves from evil, and believe, and do deeds of righteousness,- (or) again, guard themselves from evil and believe,- (or) again, guard them-selves from evil and do good. For Allah loves those who do good.

94. O you who believe! Allah makes a trial of you in a little matter of game well within reach of your hands and your lances, that He may test who fears Him unseen: and who transgress thereafter, will have a grievous Chastisement.

95. O you who believe! Don't kill game while in the Sacred precincts or in pilgrim garb. If any of you does so intentionally, the compensation is an offering, brought to the Ka'ba, of a domestic animal equivalent to the one he killed, as adjudged by two just men among you; or by way of atonement, the feeding of the indigent; or its equivalent in fasts: that he may taste of the Chastisement of his deed. Allah forgives what is past: for repetition Allah will exact from him the Chastisement. For Allah is Exalted, and Lord of Retribution.

96. Lawful to you is the pursuit of water-game and its use for food,- for the benefit of yourselves and those who travel; but forbidden is the pursuit of land-game;- as long as you are in the Sacred Precincts or in pilgrim garb. And fear Allah, to Whom you shall be gathered back.

97. Allah made the Ka'ba, the Sacred House, an asylum of security for men, as also the Sacred Months, the animals for offerings, and the garlands that mark them: that you may know that Allah

93. Laysa 'alal-lazeena aamanoo wa 'amiluṣ-ṣaaliḥaati junaaḥun feemaa ṭa'imooo izaa mat-taqaw wa aamanoo wa 'amiluṣ-ṣaalihaati summat-taqaw wa aamanoo summat-taqaw wa aḥsanoo; wallaahu yuḥibbul-muḥsineen.

94. Yaaa ayyuhal-lazeena aamanoo la-yabluwannakumul-laahu bishay'im-minaṣ-ṣaydi tanaaluhooo aydeekum wa rimaaḥukum liya'lamal-laahu mañy-yakhaafuhoo bilghayb; famani'-tadaa ba'da zaalika falahoo 'azaabun aleem.

(Section 12)

95. Yaaa ayyuhal-lazeena aamanoo laa taqtuluṣ-ṣayda wa antum ḥurum; wa man qatalahoo minkum muta'ammidan fajazaaa'um mislu maa qatala minanna'ami yaḥkumu bihee zawaa 'adlim-minkum hadyam baalighal-Ka'bati aw kaffaaratun ṭa'aamu masaakeena aw 'adlu zaalika Ṣiyaamal-liyazooqa wabaala amrih; 'afal-laahu 'ammaa salaf; wa man 'aada fayantaqimul-laahu minh; wallaahu 'azeezun zuntiqaam.

96. Uḥilla lakum ṣaydul-baḥri wa ṭa'aamuhoo mataa'al-lakum wa lissayyaarati wa ḥurrima 'alaykum ṣaydul-barri maa dumtum ḥurumaa; wattaqul-laahal-lazeee ilayhi tuḥsharoon.

97. Ja'alal-laahul-Ka'batal-Baytal-Ḥaraama qiyaamal-linnaasi wash-Shahral-Ḥaraama walhadya walqalaaa'id; zaalika lita'lamooo annal-laaha

لَيْسَ عَلَى الَّذِينَ آمَنُوا وَعَمِلُوا الصَّالِحَاتِ
جُنَاحٌ فِيمَا طَعِمُوا إِذَا مَا اتَّقَوا
وَّآمَنُوا وَعَمِلُوا الصَّالِحَاتِ ثُمَّ اتَّقَوا
وَّآمَنُوا ثُمَّ اتَّقَوا وَّأَحْسَنُوا ۗ وَاللَّهُ
يُحِبُّ الْمُحْسِنِينَ ﴿٩٣﴾
يَا أَيُّهَا الَّذِينَ آمَنُوا لَيَبْلُوَنَّكُمُ اللَّهُ
بِشَيْءٍ مِّنَ الصَّيْدِ تَنَالُهُ أَيْدِيكُمْ
وَرِمَاحُكُمْ لِيَعْلَمَ اللَّهُ مَن يَخَافُهُ
بِالْغَيْبِ ۚ فَمَنِ اعْتَدَىٰ بَعْدَ ذَٰلِكَ
فَلَهُ عَذَابٌ أَلِيمٌ ﴿٩٤﴾ ع
يَا أَيُّهَا الَّذِينَ آمَنُوا لَا تَقْتُلُوا الصَّيْدَ
وَأَنتُمْ حُرُمٌ ۚ وَمَن قَتَلَهُ مِنكُم
مُّتَعَمِّدًا فَجَزَاءٌ مِّثْلُ مَا قَتَلَ مِنَ
النَّعَمِ يَحْكُمُ بِهِ ذَوَا عَدْلٍ مِّنكُمْ هَدْيًا
بَالِغَ الْكَعْبَةِ أَوْ كَفَّارَةٌ طَعَامُ مَسَاكِينَ
أَوْ عَدْلُ ذَٰلِكَ صِيَامًا لِّيَذُوقَ وَبَالَ
أَمْرِهِ ۗ عَفَا اللَّهُ عَمَّا سَلَفَ ۚ وَمَنْ
عَادَ فَيَنتَقِمُ اللَّهُ مِنْهُ ۗ وَاللَّهُ
عَزِيزٌ ذُو انتِقَامٍ ﴿٩٥﴾
أُحِلَّ لَكُمْ صَيْدُ الْبَحْرِ وَطَعَامُهُ
مَتَاعًا لَّكُمْ وَلِلسَّيَّارَةِ ۖ وَحُرِّمَ عَلَيْكُمْ
صَيْدُ الْبَرِّ مَا دُمْتُمْ حُرُمًا ۗ وَاتَّقُوا
اللَّهَ الَّذِي إِلَيْهِ تُحْشَرُونَ ﴿٩٦﴾
جَعَلَ اللَّهُ الْكَعْبَةَ الْبَيْتَ الْحَرَامَ
قِيَامًا لِّلنَّاسِ وَالشَّهْرَ الْحَرَامَ وَالْهَدْيَ
وَالْقَلَائِدَ ۚ ذَٰلِكَ لِتَعْلَمُوا أَنَّ اللَّهَ

Ikhfa اخفاء | Ghunna غُنّہ | Ikhfa Meem Saakin اخفاء میم ساکن | Idghaam ادغام | Qalqala قلقلہ | Qalb قلب | Idghaam Meem Saakin ادغام میم ساکن

has knowledge of what is in the heavens and on earth and that Allah is well acquainted with all things.

98. You should know that Allah is strict in punishment and that Allah is Oft-forgiving, Most Merciful.

99. The Apostle's duty is but to proclaim (the message). But Allah knows all that you reveal and all that you conceal.

100. Say: "Not equal are things that are bad and things that are good, even though the abundance of the bad may dazzle you; so fear Allah, O you that understand; that (so) you may prosper."

101. O you who believe! do not ask questions about things which, if made plain to you, may cause you trouble. But if you ask about things when the Qur'an is being revealed, they will be made plain to you, Allah will forgive those: for Allah is Oft-forgiving, Most Forbearing.

102. Some people before you did ask such questions, and on that account lost their faith.

103. It was not Allah who instituted (superstitions like those of) a slit-ear she- camel, or a she-camel let loose for free pasture, or idol sacrifices for twin-births in animals, or stallion-camels freed from work: It is blasphemers who invent a lie against Allah; but most of them lack wisdom.

104. When it is said to them: "Come to what Allah has revealed; come to the Apostle": they say: "Enough for us are the ways we found our fathers following." what! even though their fathers were void of knowledge and guidance?

105. O you who believe! Guard your own souls:

ya'lamu maa fis-samaawaati wa maa fil-arḍi wa annal-laaha bikulli shay'in 'Aleem.

98. I'lamooo annal-laaha shadeedul-'iqaabi wa annal-laaha Ghafoorur-Raḥeem.

99. Maa 'alar-Rasooli illal-balaagh; wallaahu ya'lamu maa tubdoona wa maa taktumoon.

100. Qul laa yastawil-khabeesu waṭṭayyibu wa law a'jabaka kasratul-khabees; fattaqul-laaha yaaa-ulil-albaabi la'allakum tufliḥoon. **(Section 13)**

101. Yaaa ayyuhal-lazeena aamanoo laa tas'aloo 'an ashyaaa'a in tubda lakum tasu'kum; wa in tas'aloo 'anhaa ḥeena yunazzalul-Qur'aanu tubda lakum; 'afallaahu 'anhaa; wallaahu Ghafoorun Ḥaleem.

102. Qad sa-alahaa qawmum min qablikum summa aṣbaḥoo bihaa kaafireen.

103. Maa ja'alal-laahu mim baḥeeratiñw-wa laa saaa'ibatiñw-wa laa waṣeelatiñw-wa laa ḥaamiñw wa laakinnal-lazeena kafaroo yaftaroona 'alallaahil-kazib; wa aksaruhum laa ya'qiloon.

104. Wa izaa qeela lahum ta'aalaw ilaa maaa anzalallaahu wa ilar-Rasooli qaaloo hasbunaa maa wajadnaa 'alayhi aabaaa'anaa; awa law kaana aabaaa'uhum laa ya'lamoona shay'añw-wa laa yahtadoon.

105. Yaaa ayyuhal-lazeena aamanoo 'alaykum anfusakum

يَعْلَمُ مَا فِي السَّمٰوٰتِ وَمَا فِي الْأَرْضِ
وَأَنَّ اللّٰهَ بِكُلِّ شَيْءٍ عَلِيْمٌ ﴿٩٧﴾
اِعْلَمُوْٓا أَنَّ اللّٰهَ شَدِيْدُ الْعِقَابِ
وَأَنَّ اللّٰهَ غَفُوْرٌ رَّحِيْمٌ ﴿٩٨﴾
مَا عَلَى الرَّسُوْلِ إِلَّا الْبَلٰغُ ۗ وَاللّٰهُ
يَعْلَمُ مَا تُبْدُوْنَ وَمَا تَكْتُمُوْنَ ﴿٩٩﴾
قُلْ لَّا يَسْتَوِي الْخَبِيْثُ وَالطَّيِّبُ وَلَوْ
أَعْجَبَكَ كَثْرَةُ الْخَبِيْثِ ۚ فَاتَّقُوا اللّٰهَ
يٰٓأُولِي الْأَلْبَابِ لَعَلَّكُمْ تُفْلِحُوْنَ ﴿١٠٠﴾ ربع
يٰٓأَيُّهَا الَّذِيْنَ اٰمَنُوْا لَا تَسْـَٔلُوْا عَنْ
أَشْيَآءَ إِنْ تُبْدَ لَكُمْ تَسُؤْكُمْ ۚ
وَإِنْ تَسْـَٔلُوْا عَنْهَا حِيْنَ يُنَزَّلُ
الْقُرْاٰنُ تُبْدَ لَكُمْ ۗ عَفَا اللّٰهُ عَنْهَا ۗ
وَاللّٰهُ غَفُوْرٌ حَلِيْمٌ ﴿١٠١﴾
قَدْ سَأَلَهَا قَوْمٌ مِّنْ قَبْلِكُمْ ثُمَّ
أَصْبَحُوْا بِهَا كٰفِرِيْنَ ﴿١٠٢﴾
مَا جَعَلَ اللّٰهُ مِنْ بَحِيْرَةٍ وَّلَا سَآئِبَةٍ
وَّلَا وَصِيْلَةٍ وَّلَا حَامٍ ۙ وَّلٰكِنَّ الَّذِيْنَ
كَفَرُوْا يَفْتَرُوْنَ عَلَى اللّٰهِ الْكَذِبَ ۗ
وَأَكْثَرُهُمْ لَا يَعْقِلُوْنَ ﴿١٠٣﴾
وَإِذَا قِيْلَ لَهُمْ تَعَالَوْا إِلٰى مَآ
أَنْزَلَ اللّٰهُ وَإِلَى الرَّسُوْلِ قَالُوْا
حَسْبُنَا مَا وَجَدْنَا عَلَيْهِ اٰبَآءَنَا ۗ
أَوَلَوْ كَانَ اٰبَآؤُهُمْ لَا يَعْلَمُوْنَ شَيْـًٔا
وَّلَا يَهْتَدُوْنَ ﴿١٠٤﴾
يٰٓأَيُّهَا الَّذِيْنَ اٰمَنُوْا عَلَيْكُمْ أَنْفُسَكُمْ ۚ

Ikhfa اخفاء · Ghunna غنّہ · Ikhfa Meem Saakin اخفاء میم ساکن · Idghaam ادغام · Qalqala قلقلہ · Qalb قلب · Idghaam Meem Saakin ادغام میم ساکن

if you follow (right) guidance, no hurt can come to you from those who stray. The goal of you all is to Allah: it is He that will show you the truth of all that you do.

laa yaḍurrukum man ḍalla izahtadaytum; ilal-laahi marji'ukum jamee'an fayunabbi'ukum bimaa kuntum ta'maloon.

لَا يَضُرُّكُم مَّن ضَلَّ إِذَا اهْتَدَيْتُمْ ۚ
إِلَى اللَّهِ مَرْجِعُكُمْ جَمِيعًا فَيُنَبِّئُكُم
بِمَا كُنتُمْ تَعْمَلُونَ ﴿١٠٥﴾

106. O you who believe! When death approaches any of you, (take) witnesses among yourselves when making bequests,- two just men of your own (brotherhood) or others from outside if you are jour-neying through the earth, and the chance of death befalls you (thus). If you doubt (their truth), detain them both after prayer, and let them both swear by Allah: "We wish not in this for any worldly gain, even though the (beneficiary) be our near relation: we shall hide not the evidence before Allah: if we do, then behold! the sin be upon us!"

106. Yaaa ayyuhal-lazeena aamanoo shahaadatu baynikum izaa ḥaḍara aḥadakumul-mawtu ḥeenal-waṣiyyatis-naani zawaa 'adlim-minkum aw aakharaani min ghayrikum in antum ḍarabtum fil-arḍi fa-aṣaabatkum-muṣeebatul-mawt; taḥbisoonahumaa mim-ba'diṣ-Ṣalaati fa-yuqsimaani billaahi inirtabtum laa nashtaree bihee samanañw-wa law kaana zaa qurbaa wa laa naktumu shahaadatal-laahi innaaa izallaminal-aasimeen.

يَا أَيُّهَا الَّذِينَ آمَنُوا شَهَادَةُ بَيْنِكُمْ
إِذَا حَضَرَ أَحَدَكُمُ الْمَوْتُ حِينَ
الْوَصِيَّةِ اثْنَانِ ذَوَا عَدْلٍ مِّنكُمْ أَوْ
آخَرَانِ مِنْ غَيْرِكُمْ إِنْ أَنتُمْ ضَرَبْتُمْ
فِي الْأَرْضِ فَأَصَابَتْكُم مُّصِيبَةُ
الْمَوْتِ ۚ تَحْبِسُونَهُمَا مِن بَعْدِ الصَّلَاةِ
فَيُقْسِمَانِ بِاللَّهِ إِنِ ارْتَبْتُمْ لَا نَشْتَرِي
بِهِ ثَمَنًا وَلَوْ كَانَ ذَا قُرْبَىٰ ۙ وَلَا نَكْتُمُ
شَهَادَةَ اللَّهِ إِنَّا إِذًا لَّمِنَ الْآثِمِينَ ﴿١٠٦﴾

107. But if it gets known that these two were guilty of the sin (of perjury), let two others stand forth in their places,- nearest in kin from among those who claim a lawful right: let them swear by Allah: "We affirm that our witness is truer than that of those two, and that we have not trespassed (beyond the truth): if we did, behold! the wrong be upon us!"

107. Fa-in 'usira 'alaaa annahumas-taḥaqqaaa isman fa-aakharaani yaqoomaani maqaamahumaa minal-lazeenas-taḥaqqa 'alayhimul-awlayaani fa-yuqsimaani billaahi lashahaadatunaaa aḥaqqu min shahaadatihimaa wa ma'tadaynaaa innaaa izal-laminaẓ-ẓaalimeen.

فَإِنْ عُثِرَ عَلَىٰ أَنَّهُمَا اسْتَحَقَّا إِثْمًا
فَآخَرَانِ يَقُومَانِ مَقَامَهُمَا مِنَ الَّذِينَ
اسْتَحَقَّ عَلَيْهِمُ الْأَوْلَيَانِ فَيُقْسِمَانِ بِاللَّهِ
لَشَهَادَتُنَا أَحَقُّ مِن شَهَادَتِهِمَا وَمَا
اعْتَدَيْنَا إِنَّا إِذًا لَّمِنَ الظَّالِمِينَ ﴿١٠٧﴾

108. That is most suitable: that they may give the evidence in its true nature and shape, or else they would fear that other oaths would be taken after their oaths. But fear Allah, and listen (to His counsel): for Allah guides not a rebellious people:

108. Zaalika adnaaa añy-yaåtoo bishshahaadati 'alaa wajhihaaa aw yakhaafooo an turadda aymaanum ba'da aymaanihim; wattaqul-laaha wasma'oo; wallaahu laa yahdil-qawmal-faasiqeen. **(Section 14)**

ذَٰلِكَ أَدْنَىٰ أَن يَأْتُوا بِالشَّهَادَةِ عَلَىٰ
وَجْهِهَا أَوْ يَخَافُوا أَن تُرَدَّ أَيْمَانٌ بَعْدَ
أَيْمَانِهِمْ ۗ وَاتَّقُوا اللَّهَ وَاسْمَعُوا ۗ
وَاللَّهُ لَا يَهْدِي الْقَوْمَ الْفَاسِقِينَ ﴿١٠٨﴾ ع ١٤

109. One day will Allah gather the apostles together, and ask: "What was the response you received (from men to your teaching)?" They will say: "We have no knowledge: it is you Who knows in full all that is hidden."

109. Yawma yajma'ul-laahur-Rusula fa-yaqoolu maazaaa ujibtum qaaloo laa 'ilma lanaa innaka Anta 'Allaamul-Ghuyoob.

يَوْمَ يَجْمَعُ اللَّهُ الرُّسُلَ فَيَقُولُ
مَاذَا أُجِبْتُمْ ۖ قَالُوا لَا عِلْمَ لَنَا ۖ
إِنَّكَ أَنتَ عَلَّامُ الْغُيُوبِ ﴿١٠٩﴾

110. Then will Allah say: "O Jesus the son of Mary! recount My favour to you and to your mother.

110. Iz qaalal-laahu yaa 'Eesab-na-Maryamaz-kur ni'matee 'alayka wa 'alaa waalidatik;

إِذْ قَالَ اللَّهُ يَا عِيسَى ابْنَ مَرْيَمَ
اذْكُرْ نِعْمَتِي عَلَيْكَ وَعَلَىٰ وَالِدَتِكَ وقف لازم

Ikhfa اخفاء | Ghunna غنّہ | Ikhfa Meem Saakin اخفاء میم ساکن | Idghaam ادغام | Qalqala قلقلہ | Qalb قلب | Idghaam Meem Saakin ادغام میم ساکن

Behold! I strengthened you with the holy spirit, so that you did speak to the people in childhood and in maturity. Behold! I taught you the Book and Wisdom, the Law and the Gospel and behold! you made out of clay, as it were, the figure of a bird, by My leave, and you breathed into it and it became a bird by My leave, and you healed those born blind, and the lepers, by My leave. And behold ! you brought forth the dead by My leave. And behold! I did restrain the Children of Israel from (violence to) you when you showed them the Clear Signs, and the unbelievers among them said: 'This is nothing but evident magic.'

111. "And behold! I inspired the Disciples to have faith in Me and Mine Apostle: they said, 'We have faith, and You bear witness that we bow to Allah as Muslims'".

112. Behold! the disciples, said: "O Jesus the son of Mary! can your Lord send down to us a table set (with viands) from heaven?" Said Jesus: "Fear Allah, if you have faith."

113. They said: "We only wish to eat thereof and satisfy our hearts, and to know that you have indeed told us the truth; and that we ourselves may be witnesses to the miracle."

114. Jesus the son of Mary said: "O Allah our Lord! send us from heaven a table set (with viands), that there may be for us - for the first and the last of us - a solemn festival and a sign from You; and provide for our sustenance, for You are the best Sustainer (of our needs)."

115. Allah said: "I will send it down unto you: But if any

iz ayyattuka bi-Rooḥil-Qudusi tukallimun-naasa fil-mahdi wa kahlañw wa iz 'allamtukal-Kitaaba wal-Ḥikmata wat-Tawraata wal-Injeela wa iz Takhluqu minaṭ-ṭeeni kahay'atiṭ-ṭayri bi-iznee fatanfukhu feehaa fatakoonu ṭayram-bi-iznee wa tubri'ul-akmaha wal-abraṣa bi-iznee wa iz tukhrijul-mawtaa bi-iznee wa iz kafaftu Baneee Israaa'eela 'anka iz ji'tahum bil-bayyinaati fa-qaalal-lazeena kafaroo minhum in haazaaa illaa siḥrum-mubeen.

111. Wa iz awḥaytu ilal-Ḥawaariyyeena an aaminoo bee wa bi-Rasoolee qaalooo aamannaa washhad bi-annanaa muslimoon.

112. Iz qaalal-Ḥawaariyyoona yaa 'Eesab-na-Maryama hal yastaṭee'u Rabbuka añy-yunaz-zila 'alaynaa maaa'idatam-minas-samaaa'i qaalat-taqul-laaha in kuntum mu'mineen.

113. Qaaloo nureedu an naåkula minhaa wa taṭma'inna quloo-bunaa wa na'lama an qad ṣadaqtanaa wa nakoona 'alayhaa minash-shaahideen.

114. Qaala 'Eesab-nu-Marya-mal-laahumma Rabbanaaa anzil 'alaynaa maaa'idatam-minas-samaaa'i takoonu lanaa 'eedal-li-awwalinaa wa aakhi-rinaa wa Aayatam-minka warzuqnaa wa Anta khayrur-raaziqeen.

115. Qaalal-laahu innee munaz-ziluhaa 'alaykum faman

إِذْ أَيَّدتُّكَ بِرُوحِ الْقُدُسِ
تُكَلِّمُ النَّاسَ فِي الْمَهْدِ وَكَهْلًا ۖ وَإِذْ
عَلَّمْتُكَ الْكِتَابَ وَالْحِكْمَةَ وَالتَّوْرَاةَ
وَالْإِنجِيلَ ۖ وَإِذْ تَخْلُقُ مِنَ الطِّينِ
كَهَيْئَةِ الطَّيْرِ بِإِذْنِي فَتَنفُخُ فِيهَا
فَتَكُونُ طَيْرًا بِإِذْنِي ۖ وَتُبْرِئُ الْأَكْمَهَ
وَالْأَبْرَصَ بِإِذْنِي ۖ وَإِذْ تُخْرِجُ الْمَوْتَىٰ
بِإِذْنِي ۖ وَإِذْ كَفَفْتُ بَنِي إِسْرَائِيلَ
عَنكَ إِذْ جِئْتَهُم بِالْبَيِّنَاتِ فَقَالَ
الَّذِينَ كَفَرُوا مِنْهُمْ إِنْ هَٰذَا إِلَّا
سِحْرٌ مُّبِينٌ ﴿١١٠﴾
وَإِذْ أَوْحَيْتُ إِلَى الْحَوَارِيِّينَ أَنْ آمِنُوا
بِي وَبِرَسُولِي قَالُوا آمَنَّا وَاشْهَدْ
بِأَنَّنَا مُسْلِمُونَ ﴿١١١﴾
إِذْ قَالَ الْحَوَارِيُّونَ يَا عِيسَى ابْنَ
مَرْيَمَ هَلْ يَسْتَطِيعُ رَبُّكَ أَن يُنَزِّلَ
عَلَيْنَا مَائِدَةً مِّنَ السَّمَاءِ ۖ قَالَ اتَّقُوا
اللَّهَ إِن كُنتُم مُّؤْمِنِينَ ﴿١١٢﴾
قَالُوا نُرِيدُ أَن نَّأْكُلَ مِنْهَا وَتَطْمَئِنَّ
قُلُوبُنَا وَنَعْلَمَ أَن قَدْ صَدَقْتَنَا وَ
نَكُونَ عَلَيْهَا مِنَ الشَّاهِدِينَ ﴿١١٣﴾ الربع
قَالَ عِيسَى ابْنُ مَرْيَمَ اللَّهُمَّ رَبَّنَا
أَنزِلْ عَلَيْنَا مَائِدَةً مِّنَ السَّمَاءِ تَكُونُ
لَنَا عِيدًا لِّأَوَّلِنَا وَآخِرِنَا وَآيَةً مِّنكَ
وَارْزُقْنَا وَأَنتَ خَيْرُ الرَّازِقِينَ ﴿١١٤﴾
قَالَ اللَّهُ إِنِّي مُنَزِّلُهَا عَلَيْكُمْ ۖ فَمَن

Ikhfa اخفاء | Ghunna غنّہ | Ikhfa Meem Saakin اخفاء میم ساکن | Idghaam ادغام | Qalqala قلقلہ | Qalb قلب | Idghaam Meem Saakin ادغام میم ساکن

of you after that resists faith, I will punish him with a Chastisement such as I have not inflicted on any one among all the peoples."

116. And behold! Allah will say: "O Jesus the son of Mary! Did you say to men, worship me and my mother as gods in derogation of Allah'?" He will say: "Glory to You! never could I say what I had no right (to say). Had I said such a thing, you would indeed have known it. You know what is in my heart, though I dont know what is in Yours. For You know in full all that is hidden.

117. "Never said I to them anything except what You commanded me to say, to wit, 'Worship Allah, my Lord and your Lord'; and I was a witness over them while I dwelt amongst them; when You took me up, You were the Watcher over them, and You are a Witness to all things.

118. "If You punish them, they are Your servant: If You forgive them, You are the Exalted in power, the Wise."

119. Allah will say: "This is a day on which the truthful will profit from their truth: theirs are Gardens, with rivers flowing beneath,- their eternal home: Allah well-pleased with them, and they with Allah: that is the great salvation, (the fulfilment of all desires).

120. To Allah belongs the dominion of the heavens and the earth, and all that is therein, and it is He Who has power over all things.

6. The Cattle

In the name of Allah, Most Gracious, Most Merciful

1. Praise be to Allah, Who created the heavens and

---

yakfur ba'du minkum fa-inneee u'azzibuhoo 'azaabal-laaa u'azzibuhooo ahadam-minal-'aalameen. **(Section 15)**

116. Wa iz qaalal-laahu yaa 'Eesab-na-Maryama 'a-anta qulta linnaasit-takhizoonee wa ummiya ilaahayni min doonil-laahi qaala Subhaanaka maa yakoonu leee an aqoola maa laysa lee bihaqq; in kuntu qultuhoo faqad 'alimtah; ta'lamu maa fee nafsee wa laaa a'lamu maa fee nafsik; innaka Anta 'Allaamul-Ghuyoob.

117. Maa qultu lahum illaa maaa amartanee bihee ani'budul-laaha Rabbeee wa Rabbakum; wa kuntu 'alayhim shaheedam-maa dumtu feehim falammaa tawaffaytanee kunta Antar-Raqeeba 'alayhim; wa Anta 'alaa kulli shay'in Shaheed.

118. In tu'azzibhum fa-innahum 'ibaaduka wa in taghfir lahum fa-innaka Antal-'Azeezul-Hakeem.

119. Qaalal-laahu haazaa Yawmu yanfa'uṣ-ṣaadiqeena ṣidquhum; lahum Jannaatun tajree min taḥtihal-anhaaru khaalideena feehaaa abadaa; raḍiyal-laahu 'anhum wa raḍoo 'anh; zaalikal-fawzul-'azeem.

120. Lillaahi mulkus-samaawaati wal-arḍi wa maa feehinn; wa Huwa 'alaa kulli shay'in Qadeer. **(Section 16)**

Sûrat al-An'âm–6

(Revealed at Makkah)

Bismillaahir Rahmaanir Raheem

1. Alhamdu lillaahil-lazee khalaqas-samaawaati wal-

يَكْفُرْ بَعْدُ مِنْكُمْ فَإِنِّىٓ أُعَذِّبُهُۥ عَذَابًا
لَّآ أُعَذِّبُهُۥٓ أَحَدًا مِّنَ الْعٰلَمِينَ ﴿١١٥﴾
وَإِذْ قَالَ اللّٰهُ يٰعِيسَى ابْنَ مَرْيَمَ
ءَأَنتَ قُلْتَ لِلنَّاسِ اتَّخِذُونِى وَأُمِّىَ
إِلٰهَيْنِ مِن دُونِ اللّٰهِ ۖ قَالَ سُبْحٰنَكَ
مَا يَكُونُ لِىٓ أَنْ أَقُولَ مَا لَيْسَ لِى
بِحَقٍّ ۚ إِن كُنتُ قُلْتُهُۥ فَقَدْ عَلِمْتَهُۥ ۚ
تَعْلَمُ مَا فِى نَفْسِى وَلَآ أَعْلَمُ مَا فِى
نَفْسِكَ ۚ إِنَّكَ أَنتَ عَلّٰمُ الْغُيُوبِ ﴿١١٦﴾
مَا قُلْتُ لَهُمْ إِلَّا مَآ أَمَرْتَنِى بِهِۦٓ
أَنِ اعْبُدُوا اللّٰهَ رَبِّى وَرَبَّكُمْ ۚ وَكُنتُ
عَلَيْهِمْ شَهِيدًا مَّا دُمْتُ فِيهِمْ ۖ فَلَمَّا
تَوَفَّيْتَنِى كُنتَ أَنتَ الرَّقِيبَ عَلَيْهِمْ ۚ
وَأَنتَ عَلٰى كُلِّ شَىْءٍ شَهِيدٌ ﴿١١٧﴾
إِن تُعَذِّبْهُمْ فَإِنَّهُمْ عِبَادُكَ ۖ وَإِن
تَغْفِرْ لَهُمْ فَإِنَّكَ أَنتَ الْعَزِيزُ الْحَكِيمُ ﴿١١٨﴾
قَالَ اللّٰهُ هٰذَا يَوْمُ يَنفَعُ
الصّٰدِقِينَ صِدْقُهُمْ ۚ لَهُمْ جَنّٰتٌ
تَجْرِى مِن تَحْتِهَا الْأَنْهٰرُ خٰلِدِينَ
فِيهَآ أَبَدًا ۚ رَّضِىَ اللّٰهُ عَنْهُمْ وَرَضُوا
عَنْهُ ۚ ذٰلِكَ الْفَوْزُ الْعَظِيمُ ﴿١١٩﴾
لِلّٰهِ مُلْكُ السَّمٰوٰتِ وَالْأَرْضِ وَمَا
فِيهِنَّ ۚ وَهُوَ عَلٰى كُلِّ شَىْءٍ قَدِيرٌ ﴿١٢٠﴾

(٦) سُورَةُ الْأَنْعَامِ مَكِّيَّةٌ (٥٥)

بِسْمِ اللّٰهِ الرَّحْمٰنِ الرَّحِيمِ

الْحَمْدُ لِلّٰهِ الَّذِى خَلَقَ السَّمٰوٰتِ وَ

Ikhfa اخفاء | Ghunna غنّة | Ikhfa Meem Saakin اخفاء ميم ساكن | Idghaam ادغام | Qalqala قلقله | Qalb قلب | Idghaam Meem Saakin ادغام ميم ساكن

the earth, and made the darkness and the light. Yet those who reject Faith hold (others) as equal, with their Guardian-Lord.	arḍa wa ja'alaẓ-ẓulumaati wannoor; ṯummal-laẕeena kafaroo bi-Rabbihim ya'diloon.	الْاَرْضَ وَجَعَلَ الظُّلُمٰتِ وَالنُّوْرَ ۬ؕ ثُمَّ الَّذِيْنَ كَفَرُوْا بِرَبِّهِمْ يَعْدِلُوْنَ ١
2. He it is who created you from clay, and then decreed a stated term (for you). And there is in His presence another determined term; yet you doubt within yourselves!	2. Huwal-laẕee khalaqakum min ṭeenin ṯumma qaḍaaa ajalañw wa ajalum musamman 'indahoo ṯumma antum tamtaroon.	هُوَ الَّذِيْ خَلَقَكُمْ مِّنْ طِيْنٍ ثُمَّ قَضٰٓى اَجَلًا ؕ وَاَجَلٌ مُّسَمًّى عِنْدَهٗ ثُمَّ اَنْتُمْ تَمْتَرُوْنَ ٢
3. And He is Allah in the heavens and on earth. He knows what you hide, and what you reveal, and He knows the (recompense) which you earn (by your deeds).	3. Wa Huwal-laahu fissamaa-waati wa fil-arḍi ya'lamu sirrakum wa jahrakum wa ya'lamu maa taksiboon.	وَهُوَ اللّٰهُ فِي السَّمٰوٰتِ وَفِي الْاَرْضِ ؕ يَعْلَمُ سِرَّكُمْ وَجَهْرَكُمْ وَيَعْلَمُ مَا تَكْسِبُوْنَ ٣
4. But never did a single one of the Signs of their Lord reach them, but they turned away therefrom.	4. Wa maa taåteehim min Aaya-tim-min Aayaati Rabbihim illaa kaanoo 'anhaa mu'riḍeen.	وَمَا تَاْتِيْهِمْ مِّنْ اٰيَةٍ مِّنْ اٰيٰتِ رَبِّهِمْ اِلَّا كَانُوْا عَنْهَا مُعْرِضِيْنَ ٤
5. And now they reject the truth when it reaches them: but soon shall they learn the reality of what they used to mock at.	5. Faqad kaẕẕaboo bilḥaqqi lammaa jaaa'ahum fasawfa yaåteehim ambaaa'u maa kaanoo bihee yastahzi'oon.	فَقَدْ كَذَّبُوْا بِالْحَقِّ لَمَّا جَآءَهُمْ ؕ فَسَوْفَ يَاْتِيْهِمْ اَنْۢبٰٓؤُا مَا كَانُوْا بِهٖ يَسْتَهْزِءُوْنَ ٥
6. Don't they see how many of those before them We destroyed?- generations We had established on the earth, in strength such as We have not given to you - for whom We poured out rain from the skies in abundance, and gave (fertile) streams flowing beneath their (feet): yet for their sins We destroyed them, and raised in their wake fresh generations (to succeed them).	6. Alam yaraw kam ahlaknaa min qablihim min qarnim-makkannaahum fil-arḍi maa lam numakkil-lakum wa arsalnas-samaaa'a 'alayhim midraarañw-wa ja'alnal-anhaara tajree min taḥtihim fa-ahlak-naahum biẕunoobihim wa anshaånaa mim-ba'dihim qarnan aakhareen.	اَلَمْ يَرَوْا كَمْ اَهْلَكْنَا مِنْ قَبْلِهِمْ مِّنْ قَرْنٍ مَّكَّنّٰهُمْ فِي الْاَرْضِ مَا لَمْ نُمَكِّنْ لَّكُمْ وَاَرْسَلْنَا السَّمَآءَ عَلَيْهِمْ مِّدْرَارًا ۪ وَّجَعَلْنَا الْاَنْهٰرَ تَجْرِيْ مِنْ تَحْتِهِمْ فَاَهْلَكْنٰهُمْ بِذُنُوْبِهِمْ وَاَنْشَاْنَا مِنْۢ بَعْدِهِمْ قَرْنًا اٰخَرِيْنَ ٦
7. If We had sent to you a written (message) on parch-ment, so that they could touch it with their hands, the Unbelie-vers would have been sure to say: "This is nothing but ob-vious magic!"	7. Wa law nazzalnaa 'alayka Kitaaban fee qirṭaasin falamasoohu bi-aydeehim laqaalal-laẕeena kafarooo in haaẕaaa illaa siḥrum-mubeen.	وَلَوْ نَزَّلْنَا عَلَيْكَ كِتٰبًا فِيْ قِرْطَاسٍ فَلَمَسُوْهُ بِاَيْدِيْهِمْ لَقَالَ الَّذِيْنَ كَفَرُوْٓا اِنْ هٰذَآ اِلَّا سِحْرٌ مُّبِيْنٌ ٧
8. They say: "Why is not an angel sent down to him?" If we sent down an angel, the matter would be settled at once, and no respite would be granted them.	8. Wa qaaloo law laaa unzila 'alayhi malakuñw wa law anzalna malakal-laquḍiyal-amru ṯumma laa yunẓaroon.	وَقَالُوْا لَوْلَآ اُنْزِلَ عَلَيْهِ مَلَكٌ ؕ وَلَوْ اَنْزَلْنَا مَلَكًا لَّقُضِيَ الْاَمْرُ ثُمَّ لَا يُنْظَرُوْنَ ٨

Ikhfa اخفاء | Ghunna غُنّہ | Ikhfa Meem Saakin اخفاءمیم ساکن | Idghaam ادغام | Qalqala قلقلہ | Qalb قلب | Idghaam Meem Saakin ادغام میم ساکن

9. If We had made it an angel, We should have sent him as a man, and We should certainly have caused them confusion in a matter which they have already covered with confusion.
10. Mocked were (many) Apostles before you; but their scoffers were hemmed in by the thing that they mocked.
11. Say: "Travel through the earth and see what was the end of those who rejected Truth."
12. Say: "To whom belongs all that is in the heavens and on earth?" Say: "To Allah. He has inscribed for Himself (the rule of) Mercy. That He will gather you together for the Day of Judgment, there is no doubt whatever. It is they who have lost their own souls, that will not believe.
13. To him belongs all that dwells (or lurks) in the Night and the Day. For He is the One Who hears and knows all things."
14. Say: "Shall I take for my protector any other than Allah, the Maker of the heavens and the earth? And He it is that feeds but is not fed." Say: "Nay! but I am commanded to be the first of those who bow to Allah (in Islam), and be not of the company of those who join gods with Allah."
15. Say: "I would, if I disobeyed my Lord, indeed have fear of the Chastisement of a Mighty Day.
16. "On that day, if the Chastisement is averted from any, it is due to Allah's mercy; And that would be (Salvation), the obvious fulfilment of all desire.
17. "If Allah touch you with affliction, none can remove it but He; if He touch you with happiness, He has power over all things.

9. Wa law ja'alnaahu malakal-laja'alnaahu rajulañw-wa lalabasnaa 'alayhim maa yalbisoon.

10. Wa laqadis-tuhzi'a bi-Rusulim-min qablika fahaaqa billaz̲eena sakhiroo minhum maa kaanoo bihee yastahzi'oon.
(Section 1)

11. Qul seeroo fil-arḍi summan-ẓuroo kayfa kaana 'aaqibatul-mukaz̲z̲ibeen.

12. Qul limam-maa fis-samaawaati wal-arḍi qul lillaah; kataba 'alaa nafsihir-raḥmah; la-yajma'annakum ilaa Yawmil-Qiyaamati laa rayba feeh; allaz̲eena khasirooo anfusahum fahum laa yu'minoon.

13. Wa lahoo maa sakana fillayli wannahaar; wa Huwas-Samee'ul-'Aleem.

14. Qul aghayral-laahi attakhiz̲u waliyyan faaṭiris-samaawaati wal-arḍi wa Huwa yuṭ'imu wa laa yuṭ'am; qul inneee umirtu an akoona awwala man aslama wa laa takoonanna minal-mushrikeen.

15. Qul inneee akhaafu in 'aṣaytu Rabbee 'az̲aaba Yawmin 'Aẓeem.

16. Mañy-yuṣraf 'anhu Yawma'iz̲in faqad raḥimah; wa z̲aalikal-fawzul-mubeen.

17. Wa iñy-yamsaskal-laahu biḍurrin falaaa kaashifa lahooo illaa Huwa wa iñy-yamsaska bikhayrin fa-Huwa 'alaa kulli shay'in Qadeer.

وَلَوْ جَعَلْنٰهُ مَلَكًا لَّجَعَلْنٰهُ رَجُلًا وَّ
لَلَبَسْنَا عَلَيْهِمْ مَّا يَلْبِسُوْنَ ﴿٩﴾
وَلَقَدِ اسْتُهْزِئَ بِرُسُلٍ مِّنْ قَبْلِكَ
فَحَاقَ بِالَّذِيْنَ سَخِرُوْا مِنْهُمْ
مَّا كَانُوْا بِهٖ يَسْتَهْزِءُوْنَ ﴿١٠﴾ ع
قُلْ سِيْرُوْا فِي الْاَرْضِ ثُمَّ انْظُرُوْا
كَيْفَ كَانَ عَاقِبَةُ الْمُكَذِّبِيْنَ ﴿١١﴾
قُلْ لِّمَنْ مَّا فِي السَّمٰوٰتِ وَالْاَرْضِ ؕ
قُلْ لِّلّٰهِ ؕ كَتَبَ عَلٰى نَفْسِهِ الرَّحْمَةَ ؕ
لَيَجْمَعَنَّكُمْ اِلٰى يَوْمِ الْقِيٰمَةِ لَا رَيْبَ
فِيْهِ ؕ اَلَّذِيْنَ خَسِرُوْٓا اَنْفُسَهُمْ فَهُمْ
لَا يُؤْمِنُوْنَ ﴿١٢﴾
وَلَهٗ مَا سَكَنَ فِي الَّيْلِ وَالنَّهَارِ ؕ
وَهُوَ السَّمِيْعُ الْعَلِيْمُ ﴿١٣﴾
قُلْ اَغَيْرَ اللّٰهِ اَتَّخِذُ وَلِيًّا فَاطِرِ
السَّمٰوٰتِ وَالْاَرْضِ وَهُوَ يُطْعِمُ وَلَا
يُطْعَمُ ؕ قُلْ اِنِّيْٓ اُمِرْتُ اَنْ اَكُوْنَ
اَوَّلَ مَنْ اَسْلَمَ وَلَا تَكُوْنَنَّ مِنَ
الْمُشْرِكِيْنَ ﴿١٤﴾
قُلْ اِنِّيْٓ اَخَافُ اِنْ عَصَيْتُ رَبِّيْ
عَذَابَ يَوْمٍ عَظِيْمٍ ﴿١٥﴾
مَنْ يُّصْرَفْ عَنْهُ يَوْمَئِذٍ فَقَدْ
رَحِمَهٗ ؕ وَذٰلِكَ الْفَوْزُ الْمُبِيْنُ ﴿١٦﴾
وَاِنْ يَّمْسَسْكَ اللّٰهُ بِضُرٍّ فَلَا كَاشِفَ
لَهٗٓ اِلَّا هُوَ ؕ وَاِنْ يَّمْسَسْكَ بِخَيْرٍ فَهُوَ
عَلٰى كُلِّ شَيْءٍ قَدِيْرٌ ﴿١٧﴾

Ikhfa اخفاء | Ghunna غنّہ | Ikhfa Meem Saakin اخفاء میم ساکن | Idghaam ادغام | Qalqala قلقلہ | Qalb قلب | Idghaam Meem Saakin ادغام میم ساکن

18. "He is the irresistible, (watching) from above over His worshippers; and He is the Wise, acquainted with all things."

19. Say: "What thing is most weighty in evidence?" Say: "Allah is witness between me and you; This Qur'an has been revealed to me by inspiration, that I may warn you and all whom it reaches. Can you possibly bear witness that besides Allah there is another God?" Say: "Nay! I cannot bear witness!" Say: "But in truth He is the one Allah, and I truly am innocent of (your blasphemy of) joining others with Him."

20. Those to whom We have given the Book know this as they know their own sons. Those who have lost their own souls refuse therefore to believe.

21. Who does more wrong than he who invents a lie against Allah or rejects His signs? But verily the wrong-doers never shall prosper.

22. One day We shall gather them all together: We shall say to those who ascribed partners (to Us): "Where are the partners whom you (invented and) talked about?"

23. There will then be (left) no subterfuge for them but to say: "By Allah, our Lord, we were not those who joined gods with Allah."

24. Behold! how they lie against their own souls! But the (lie) which they invented will leave them in the lurch.

25. Of them there are some who (pretend to) listen to you; but We have thrown veils on their hearts, So they do not understand it, and deafness in their ears; if they saw every one of the signs, they will not believe in them; in so much that when they come to you,

18. Wa Huwal-qaahiru fawqa 'ibaadih; wa Huwal-Ḥakeemul-Khabeer.

19. Qul ayyu shay'in akbaru shahaadatan qulil-laahu shaheedum baynee wa baynakum; wa ooḥiya ilayya haaẕal-Qur'aanu li-unẕirakum bihee wa mam-balagh; a'innakum latashhadoona anna ma'al-laahi aalihatan ukhraa; qul laaa ashhad; qul innamaa Huwa Ilaahuñw-Waaḥiduñw-wa innanee bareee'um-mimmaa tushrikoon.

20. Allaẕeena aataynaahumul-Kitaaba ya'rifoonahoo kamaa ya'rifoona abnaaa'ahum; allaẕeena khasirooo anfusahum fahum laa yu'minoon. **(Section 2)**

21. Wa man aẓlamu mimmanif-taraa 'alal-laahi kaẕiban aw kaẕẕaba bi-Aayaatih; innahoo laa yufliḥuẓ-ẓaalimoon.

22. Wa Yawma naḥshuruhum jamee'an summa naqoolu lillaẕeena ashrakooo ayna shurakaaa'ukumul-laẕeena kuntum taz'umoon.

23. Summa lam takun fitnatuhum illaaa an qaaloo wallaahi Rabbinaa maa kunnaa mushrikeen.

24. Unẓur kayfa kaẕaboo 'alaaa anfusihim, wa ḍalla 'anhum maa kaanoo yaftaroon.

25. Wa minhum mañy-yastami'u ilayka wa ja'alnaa 'alaa quloobihim akinnatan añy-yafqahoohu wa feee aaẕaanihim waqraa; wa iñy-yaraw kulla Aayatil-laa yu'minoo bihaa; ḥattaaa iẕaa jaaa'ooka

وَهُوَ الْقَاهِرُ فَوْقَ عِبَادِهِ ۚ وَهُوَ
الْحَكِيمُ الْخَبِيرُ ﴿١٨﴾
قُلْ أَيُّ شَيْءٍ أَكْبَرُ شَهَادَةً ۖ قُلِ
اللَّهُ ۖ شَهِيدٌ بَيْنِي وَبَيْنَكُمْ ۚ
وَأُوحِيَ إِلَيَّ هَٰذَا الْقُرْآنُ لِأُنْذِرَكُمْ
بِهِ وَمَنْ بَلَغَ ۚ أَئِنَّكُمْ لَتَشْهَدُونَ
أَنَّ مَعَ اللَّهِ آلِهَةً أُخْرَىٰ ۚ قُلْ
لَا أَشْهَدُ ۚ قُلْ إِنَّمَا هُوَ إِلَٰهٌ وَاحِدٌ
وَإِنَّنِي بَرِيءٌ مِمَّا تُشْرِكُونَ ﴿١٩﴾
الَّذِينَ آتَيْنَاهُمُ الْكِتَابَ يَعْرِفُونَهُ كَمَا
يَعْرِفُونَ أَبْنَاءَهُمُ ۘ الَّذِينَ خَسِرُوا
أَنْفُسَهُمْ فَهُمْ لَا يُؤْمِنُونَ ﴿٢٠﴾
وَمَنْ أَظْلَمُ مِمَّنِ افْتَرَىٰ عَلَى اللَّهِ
كَذِبًا أَوْ كَذَّبَ بِآيَاتِهِ ۗ إِنَّهُ
لَا يُفْلِحُ الظَّالِمُونَ ﴿٢١﴾
وَيَوْمَ نَحْشُرُهُمْ جَمِيعًا ثُمَّ نَقُولُ
لِلَّذِينَ أَشْرَكُوا أَيْنَ شُرَكَاؤُكُمُ
الَّذِينَ كُنْتُمْ تَزْعُمُونَ ﴿٢٢﴾
ثُمَّ لَمْ تَكُنْ فِتْنَتُهُمْ إِلَّا أَنْ قَالُوا
وَاللَّهِ رَبِّنَا مَا كُنَّا مُشْرِكِينَ ﴿٢٣﴾
انْظُرْ كَيْفَ كَذَبُوا عَلَىٰ أَنْفُسِهِمْ ۚ
وَضَلَّ عَنْهُمْ مَا كَانُوا يَفْتَرُونَ ﴿٢٤﴾
وَمِنْهُمْ مَنْ يَسْتَمِعُ إِلَيْكَ ۖ وَجَعَلْنَا
عَلَىٰ قُلُوبِهِمْ أَكِنَّةً أَنْ يَفْقَهُوهُ وَفِي
آذَانِهِمْ وَقْرًا ۚ وَإِنْ يَرَوْا كُلَّ آيَةٍ
لَا يُؤْمِنُوا بِهَا ۚ حَتَّىٰ إِذَا جَاءُوكَ

وقف لازم باختلاف

وقف لازم

Ikhfa اخفاء | Ghunna غُنّہ | Ikhfa Meem Saakin اخفاء میم ساکن | Idghaam ادغام | Qalqala قلقلہ | Qalb قلب | Idghaam Meem Saakin ادغام میم ساکن

they (but) dispute with you; the Unbelievers say: "These are nothing but tales of the ancients."

26. Others they keep away from it, and themselves they keep away; but they only destroy their own souls, and they do not perceive it.

27. If you could but see when they are confronted with the Fire! They will say: "Would that we were but sent back! Then would we not reject the signs of our Lord, but would be amongst those who believe!"

28. Yes, in their own (eyes) will become manifest what before they concealed. But if they were returned, they would certainly relapse to the things they were forbidden, for they are indeed liars.

29. And they (sometimes) say: "There is nothing except our life on this earth, and never shall we be raised up again."

30. If you could but see when they are confronted with their Lord! He will say: "Is not this the truth?" They will say: "Yes, by our Lord!" He will say: "You then test the Chastisement, because you rejected Faith."

31. Lost indeed are they who treat it as a falsehood that they must meet Allah,- until on a sudden the hour is on them, and they say: "Ah! woe unto us that we took no thought of it"; for they bear their burdens on their backs, and evil indeed are the burdens that they bear?

32. What is the life of this world but play and amusement? But best is the Home in the Hereafter, for those who are righteous. Will you not then understand?

33. We know indeed the grief which

yujaadiloonaka yaqoolul-lazeena kafarooo in haazaaa illaaa asaateerul-awwaleen.

26. Wa hum yanhawna 'anhu wa yan'awna 'anhu wa iñy-yuhlikoona illaaa anfusahum wa maa yash'uroon.

27. Wa law taraaa iz wuqifoo 'alan-Naari faqaaloo yaa laytanaa nuraddu wa laa nukaz-ziba bi-Aayaati Rabbinaa wa nakoona minal-mu'mineen.

28. Bal badaa lahum maa kaanoo yukhfoona min qablu wa law ruddoo la'aadoo limaa nuhoo 'anhu wa innahum lakaaziboon.

29. Wa qaalooo in hiya illaa hayaatunad-dunyaa wa maa nahnu bimab'ooseen.

30. Wa law taraaa iz wuqifoo 'alaa Rabbihim; qaala alaysa haazaa bilhaqq; qaaloo balaa wa Rabbinaa; qaala fazooqul-'azaaba bimaa kuntum takfuroon. **(Section 3)**

31. Qad khasiral-lazeena kaz-zaboo biliqaaa'il-laahi hattaaa izaa jaaa'at-humus-Saa'atu baghtatan qaaloo yaa hasra-tanaa 'alaa maa farratnaa feehaa wa hum yahmiloona awzaarahum 'alaa zuhoorihim; alaa saaa'a maa yaziroon.

32. Wa mal-hayaatud-dun-yaaa illaa la'ibuñw-wa lahwuñw wa lad-Daarul-Aakhiratu kahyrul-lillazeena yattaqoon; afalaa ta'qiloon.

33. Qad na'lamu innahoo layahzunukal-lazee

يُجَادِلُونَكَ يَقُولُ الَّذِينَ كَفَرُوٓا
اِنْ هٰذَآ اِلَّآ اَسَاطِيْرُ الْاَوَّلِيْنَ ۝٢٥
وَهُمْ يَنْهَوْنَ عَنْهُ وَيَنْـَٔوْنَ عَنْهُ ۚ
وَاِنْ يُّهْلِكُوْنَ اِلَّآ اَنْفُسَهُمْ وَمَا
يَشْعُرُوْنَ ۝٢٦
وَلَوْ تَرٰٓى اِذْ وُقِفُوْا عَلَى النَّارِ فَقَالُوْا
يٰلَيْتَنَا نُرَدُّ وَلَا نُكَذِّبَ بِاٰيٰتِ رَبِّنَا
وَنَكُوْنَ مِنَ الْمُؤْمِنِيْنَ ۝٢٧
بَلْ بَدَا لَهُمْ مَّا كَانُوْا يُخْفُوْنَ مِنْ
قَبْلُ ۭ وَلَوْ رُدُّوْا لَعَادُوْا لِمَا نُهُوْا
عَنْهُ وَاِنَّهُمْ لَكٰذِبُوْنَ ۝٢٨
وَقَالُوْٓا اِنْ هِيَ اِلَّا حَيَاتُنَا الدُّنْيَا
وَمَا نَحْنُ بِمَبْعُوْثِيْنَ ۝٢٩
وَلَوْ تَرٰٓى اِذْ وُقِفُوْا عَلٰى رَبِّهِمْ ۭ قَالَ
اَلَيْسَ هٰذَا بِالْحَقِّ ۭ قَالُوْا بَلٰى وَرَبِّنَا ۭ
قَالَ فَذُوْقُوا الْعَذَابَ بِمَا كُنْتُمْ
تَكْفُرُوْنَ ۝٣٠
قَدْ خَسِرَ الَّذِيْنَ كَذَّبُوْا بِلِقَاۗءِ اللّٰهِ ۭ
حَتّٰٓى اِذَا جَاۗءَتْهُمُ السَّاعَةُ بَغْتَةً
قَالُوْا يٰحَسْرَتَنَا عَلٰي مَا فَرَّطْنَا فِيْهَا ۙ
وَهُمْ يَحْمِلُوْنَ اَوْزَارَهُمْ عَلٰي ظُهُوْرِهِمْ ۭ
اَلَا سَاۗءَ مَا يَزِرُوْنَ ۝٣١
وَمَا الْحَيٰوةُ الدُّنْيَآ اِلَّا لَعِبٌ وَّلَهْوٌ ۭ
وَلَلدَّارُ الْاٰخِرَةُ خَيْرٌ لِّلَّذِيْنَ
يَتَّقُوْنَ ۭ اَفَلَا تَعْقِلُوْنَ ۝٣٢
قَدْ نَعْلَمُ اِنَّهٗ لَيَحْزُنُكَ الَّذِيْ

Ikhfa اخفاء | Ghunna غنّہ | Ikhfa Meem Saakin اخفاء میم ساکن | Idghaam ادغام | Qalqala قلقلہ | Qalb قلب | Idghaam Meem Saakin ادغام میم ساکن

their words do cause you: It is not you they reject: it is the Signs of Allah, which the wicked disdain.

34. Rejected were the Apostles before you: with patience and constancy they bore their rejection and their wrongs, until Our aid reached them: there is none that can alter the words (and decrees) of Allah. Already you have received some account of those apostles.

35. If their spurning is hard on your mind, yet if you were able to seek a tunnel in the ground or a ladder to the skies and bring them a Sign,- (what good?). If it were Allah's will, He could gather them together unto true guidance: so you be not amongst those who are swayed by ignorance (and impatience)!

36. Those who listen (in truth), be sure, will accept: as to the dead, Allah will raise them up; then will they be turned unto Him.

37. They say: "Why is not a Sign sent down to him from his Lord?" Say: "Allah has certainly power to send down a Sign: but most of them do not understand.

38. There is not an animal (that lives) on the earth, nor a being that flies on its wings, but (forms part of) communities like you. Nothing have we omitted from the Book, and they (all) shall be gathered to their Lord in the end.

39. Those who reject Our Signs are deaf and dumb,- in the midst of darkness profound: whom Allah wills, He leaves to wander: whom He wills, He places on the Way that is Straight.

40. Say: "You think to yourselves, if there come upon you the wrath of Allah, or the Hour (that you dread), would you then call upon other than Allah?-

yaqooloona fa-innahum laa yukazziboonaka wa laakinnaẓ-ẓaalimeena bi-Aayaatil-laahi yajḥadoon.

34. Wa laqad kuzzibat Rusulum-min qablika faṣabaroo 'alaa maa kuzziboo wa oozoo ḥattaaa ataahum naṣrunaa; wa laa mubaddila li-Kalimaatil-laah; wa laqad jaaa'aka min naba'il-mursaleen.

35. Wa in kaana kabura 'alayka i'raaḍuhum fa-inistaṭa'ta an tabtaghiya nafaqan fil-arḍi aw sullaman fis-samaaa'i fataåtiyahum bi-Aayah; wa law shaaa'al-laahu lajama'ahum 'alal-hudaa; falaa takoonanna minal-jaahileen.

36. Innamaa yastajeebul-lazeena yasma'oon; walmawtaa yab'asuhumul-laahu summa ilayhi yurja'oon.

37. Wa qaaloo law laa nuzzila 'alayhi Aayatum-mir-Rabbih; qul innal-laaha qaadirun 'alaaa añy-yunazzila 'Aayatañw-wa laakinna aksarahum laa ya'lamoon.

38. Wa maa min daaabbatin fil-arḍi wa laa ṭaa'iriñy-yaṭeeru bijanaaḥayhi illaaa umamun amsaalukum; maa farraṭnaa fil-Kitaabi min shay'in summa ilaa Rabbihim yuḥsharoon.

39. Wallazeena kazzaboo bi-Aayaatinaa ṣummuñw-wa bukmun fiẓ-ẓulumaat; mañy-yasha-il-laahu yuḍlilh; wa mañy-yashaå yaj'alhu 'alaa Ṣiraaṭim-Mustaqeem.

40. Qul ara'aytakum in ataakum 'azaabul-laahi aw atatkumus-Saa'atu a-ghayral-laahi tad'oona

يَقُولُونَ فَإِنَّهُمْ لَا يُكَذِّبُونَكَ وَلَٰكِنَّ
ٱلظَّٰلِمِينَ بِـَٔايَٰتِ ٱللَّهِ يَجْحَدُونَ ٣٣
وَلَقَدْ كُذِّبَتْ رُسُلٌ مِّن قَبْلِكَ
فَصَبَرُوا۟ عَلَىٰ مَا كُذِّبُوا۟ وَأُوذُوا۟ حَتَّىٰٓ
أَتَىٰهُمْ نَصْرُنَا ۚ وَلَا مُبَدِّلَ لِكَلِمَٰتِ ٱللَّهِ ۚ
وَلَقَدْ جَآءَكَ مِن نَّبَإِى۟ ٱلْمُرْسَلِينَ ٣٤
وَإِن كَانَ كَبُرَ عَلَيْكَ إِعْرَاضُهُمْ فَإِنِ
ٱسْتَطَعْتَ أَن تَبْتَغِىَ نَفَقًا فِى ٱلْأَرْضِ
أَوْ سُلَّمًا فِى ٱلسَّمَآءِ فَتَأْتِيَهُم بِـَٔايَةٍ ۚ
وَلَوْ شَآءَ ٱللَّهُ لَجَمَعَهُمْ عَلَى ٱلْهُدَىٰ ۚ
فَلَا تَكُونَنَّ مِنَ ٱلْجَٰهِلِينَ ٣٥
إِنَّمَا يَسْتَجِيبُ ٱلَّذِينَ يَسْمَعُونَ ۘ
وَٱلْمَوْتَىٰ يَبْعَثُهُمُ ٱللَّهُ ثُمَّ إِلَيْهِ
يُرْجَعُونَ ٣٦
وَقَالُوا۟ لَوْلَا نُزِّلَ عَلَيْهِ ءَايَةٌ مِّن رَّبِّهِۦ ۚ
قُلْ إِنَّ ٱللَّهَ قَادِرٌ عَلَىٰٓ أَن يُنَزِّلَ
ءَايَةً وَلَٰكِنَّ أَكْثَرَهُمْ لَا يَعْلَمُونَ ٣٧
وَمَا مِن دَآبَّةٍ فِى ٱلْأَرْضِ وَلَا طَٰٓئِرٍ
يَطِيرُ بِجَنَاحَيْهِ إِلَّآ أُمَمٌ أَمْثَالُكُم ۚ
مَّا فَرَّطْنَا فِى ٱلْكِتَٰبِ مِن شَىْءٍ ۚ ثُمَّ
إِلَىٰ رَبِّهِمْ يُحْشَرُونَ ٣٨
وَٱلَّذِينَ كَذَّبُوا۟ بِـَٔايَٰتِنَا صُمٌّ وَبُكْمٌ فِى
ٱلظُّلُمَٰتِ ۗ مَن يَشَإِ ٱللَّهُ يُضْلِلْهُ وَمَن
يَشَأْ يَجْعَلْهُ عَلَىٰ صِرَٰطٍ مُّسْتَقِيمٍ ٣٩
قُلْ أَرَءَيْتَكُمْ إِنْ أَتَىٰكُمْ عَذَابُ ٱللَّهِ
أَوْ أَتَتْكُمُ ٱلسَّاعَةُ أَغَيْرَ ٱللَّهِ تَدْعُونَ

النّصف وقف غفران ١٢
وقف منزل عند البعض علٰى يسمعون ١٣

Ikhfa اخفاء | Ghunna غنّہ | Ikhfa Meem Saakin اخفاء میم ساکن | Idghaam ادغام | Qalqala قلقلہ | Qalb قلب | Idghaam Meem Saakin ادغام میم ساکن

(reply) if you are truthful!

in kuntum ṣaadiqeen.

إِن كُنتُمْ صَٰدِقِينَ ٤٠

41. "Nay,- On Him would you call, and if it be His will, He would remove (the distress) which occasioned your call upon Him, and you would forget (the false gods) which you join with Him!"

41. Bal iyyaahu tad'oona fa-yakshifu maa tad'oona ilayhi in shaaa'a wa tansawna maa tushrikoon. **(Section 4)**

بَلْ إِيَّاهُ تَدْعُونَ فَيَكْشِفُ مَا
تَدْعُونَ إِلَيْهِ إِن شَآءَ وَتَنسَوْنَ
مَا تُشْرِكُونَ ٤١

42. Before you We sent (Apostles) to many nations, and We afflicted the nations with suffering and adversity, that they might learn humility.

42. Wa laqad arsalnaaa ilaaa umamim min qablika fa-akhaẕnaahum bilbaåsaaa'i waḍḍarraaa'i la'allahum yata-ḍarra'oon.

وَلَقَدْ أَرْسَلْنَآ إِلَىٰٓ أُمَمٍ مِّن قَبْلِكَ
فَأَخَذْنَٰهُم بِٱلْبَأْسَآءِ وَٱلضَّرَّآءِ
لَعَلَّهُمْ يَتَضَرَّعُونَ ٤٢

43. When the suffering reached them from Us, why then did they not learn humility? On the contrary their hearts became hardened, and Satan made their (sinful) acts seem alluring to them.

43. Falaw laaa iẕ jaaa'ahum baåsunaa taḍarra'oo wa laakin qasat quloobuhum wa zayyana lahumush-Shayṭaanu maa kaanoo ya'maloon.

فَلَوْلَآ إِذْ جَآءَهُم بَأْسُنَا تَضَرَّعُوا
وَلَٰكِن قَسَتْ قُلُوبُهُمْ وَزَيَّنَ لَهُمُ
ٱلشَّيْطَٰنُ مَا كَانُوا يَعْمَلُونَ ٤٣

44. But when they forgot the warning they had received, We opened to them the gates of all (good) things, until, in the midst of their enjoyment of Our gifts, on a sudden, We called them to account, when lo! they were plunged in despair!

44. Falammaa nasoo maa ẕukkiroo bihee fataḥnaa 'alayhim abwaaba kulli shay'in ḥattaaa iẕaa fariḥoo bimaaa ootooo akhaẕnaahum baghtatan fa-iẕaa hum mublisoon.

فَلَمَّا نَسُوا مَا ذُكِّرُوا بِهِۦ فَتَحْنَا عَلَيْهِمْ
أَبْوَٰبَ كُلِّ شَىْءٍ حَتَّىٰٓ إِذَا فَرِحُوا
بِمَآ أُوتُوٓا أَخَذْنَٰهُم بَغْتَةً فَإِذَا هُم
مُّبْلِسُونَ ٤٤

45. Of the wrong-doers the last remnant was cut off. Praise be to Allah, the Cherisher of the worlds.

45. Faquṭi'a daabirul-qawmil-laẕeena ẓalamoo; walḥamdu lillaahi Rabbil-'aalameen.

فَقُطِعَ دَابِرُ ٱلْقَوْمِ ٱلَّذِينَ ظَلَمُوا ۚ
وَٱلْحَمْدُ لِلَّهِ رَبِّ ٱلْعَٰلَمِينَ ٤٥

46. Say: "Do you think, if Allah took away your hearing and your sight, and sealed up your hearts, who - a god other than Allah - could restore them to you?" See how We explain the Signs by various (symbols); yet they turn aside.

46. Qul ara'aytum in akhaẕal-laahu sam'akum wa abṣaara-kum wa khatama 'alaa quloobikum man ilaahun ghay-rul-laahi yaåteekum bih; unẓur kayfa nuṣarriful-Aayaati ṯumma hum yaṣdifoon.

قُلْ أَرَءَيْتُمْ إِنْ أَخَذَ ٱللَّهُ سَمْعَكُمْ
وَأَبْصَٰرَكُمْ وَخَتَمَ عَلَىٰ قُلُوبِكُم مَّنْ
إِلَٰهٌ غَيْرُ ٱللَّهِ يَأْتِيكُم بِهِ ۗ ٱنظُرْ كَيْفَ
نُصَرِّفُ ٱلْءَايَٰتِ ثُمَّ هُمْ يَصْدِفُونَ ٤٦

47. Say: "Do you think, if the punishment of Allah comes to you, whether suddenly or openly, will any be destroyed except those who do wrong?

47. Qul ara'aytakum in ataakum 'aẕaabul-laahi baghtatan aw jahratan hal yuhlaku illal-qawmuẓ-ẓaalimoon.

قُلْ أَرَءَيْتَكُمْ إِنْ أَتَىٰكُمْ عَذَابُ
ٱللَّهِ بَغْتَةً أَوْ جَهْرَةً هَلْ يُهْلَكُ
إِلَّا ٱلْقَوْمُ ٱلظَّٰلِمُونَ ٤٧

48. We send the Apostles only to give good news and to warn: so those who believe and mend (their lives),- upon them shall be no fear, nor shall they grieve.

48. Wa maa nursilul-mursaleena illaa mubashshireena wa munẕireena faman aamana wa aṣlaḥa falaa khawfun 'alayhim wa laa hum yaḥzanoon.

وَمَا نُرْسِلُ ٱلْمُرْسَلِينَ إِلَّا مُبَشِّرِينَ
وَمُنذِرِينَ ۖ فَمَنْ ءَامَنَ وَأَصْلَحَ فَلَا
خَوْفٌ عَلَيْهِمْ وَلَا هُمْ يَحْزَنُونَ ٤٨

Ikhfa إخفاء | Ghunna غنّة | Ikhfa Meem Saakin اخفاء میم ساکن | Idghaam ادغام | Qalqala قلقلة | Qalb قلب | Idghaam Meem Saakin ادغام میم ساکن

49. But those who reject our Signs,- punishment shall touch them, for that they ceased not from transgressing.

49. Wallazeena kazzaboo bi-Aayaatinaa yamassuhumul-'azaabu bimaa kaanoo yafsuqoon..

وَالَّذِيْنَ كَذَّبُوْا بِاٰيٰتِنَا يَمَسُّهُمُ الْعَذَابُ
بِمَا كَانُوْا يَفْسُقُوْنَ ﴿٤٩﴾

50. Say: "I tell you not that with me are the treasures of Allah, nor do I know what is hidden, nor do I tell you I am an angel. I but follow what is revealed to me." Say: "can the blind be held equal to the seeing?" Will you then not consider?

50. Qul laaa aqoolu lakum 'indee khazaaa'inul-laahi wa laaa a'lamul-ghayba wa laaa aqoolu lakum innee malakun in attabi'u illaa maa yooḥaaa ilayy; qul hal yastawil-a'maa walbaṣeer; afalaa tatafakkaroon. **(Section 5)**

قُلْ لَّآ اَقُوْلُ لَكُمْ عِنْدِيْ خَزَآئِنُ
اللّٰهِ وَلَآ اَعْلَمُ الْغَيْبَ وَلَآ اَقُوْلُ
لَكُمْ اِنِّيْ مَلَكٌ ۚ اِنْ اَتَّبِعُ اِلَّا مَا يُوْحٰٓى
اِلَيَّ ۗ قُلْ هَلْ يَسْتَوِي الْاَعْمٰى
وَالْبَصِيْرُ ۗ اَفَلَا تَتَفَكَّرُوْنَ ﴿٥٠﴾

51. Give this warning to those in whose (hearts) is the fear that they will be brought (to judgment) before their Lord: except for Him they will have no protector nor intercessor: that they may guard (against evil).

51. Wa anzir bihil-lazeena yakhaafoona añy-yuḥsharooo ilaa Rabbihim laysa lahum min doonihee waliyyuñw-wa laa shafee'ul-la'allahum yattaqoon.

وَاَنْذِرْ بِهِ الَّذِيْنَ يَخَافُوْنَ اَنْ يُّحْشَرُوْٓا
اِلٰى رَبِّهِمْ لَيْسَ لَهُمْ مِّنْ دُوْنِهٖ
وَلِيٌّ وَّلَا شَفِيْعٌ لَّعَلَّهُمْ يَتَّقُوْنَ ﴿٥١﴾

52. Do not send away those who call on their Lord morning and evening, seeking His Face. In nothing are you accountable for them, and in nothing are they accountable for you, that you should turn them away, and thus be (one) of the unjust.

52. Wa laa taṭrudil-lazeena yad'oona Rabbahum bilghadaati wal'ashiyyi yureedoona Wajhahoo maa 'alayka min ḥisaabihim min shay'iñw-wa maa min ḥisaabika 'alayhim min shay'in fataṭrudahum fatakoona minaẓ-ẓaalimeen.

وَلَا تَطْرُدِ الَّذِيْنَ يَدْعُوْنَ رَبَّهُمْ
بِالْغَدٰوةِ وَالْعَشِيِّ يُرِيْدُوْنَ
وَجْهَهٗ ۗ مَا عَلَيْكَ مِنْ حِسَابِهِمْ
مِّنْ شَيْءٍ وَّمَا مِنْ حِسَابِكَ
عَلَيْهِمْ مِّنْ شَيْءٍ فَتَطْرُدَهُمْ فَتَكُوْنَ
مِنَ الظّٰلِمِيْنَ ﴿٥٢﴾

53. Thus did We try some of them by comparison with others that they should say: "Is it these then that Allah has favoured from amongst us?" Does not Allah know best those who are grateful?

53. Wa kazaalika fatannaa ba'ḍahum biba'ḍil-liyaqoolooo ahaaa'ulaaa'i mannal-laahu 'alayhim mim bayninaa; alaysal-laahu bi-a'lama bishshaakireen.

وَكَذٰلِكَ فَتَنَّا بَعْضَهُمْ بِبَعْضٍ
لِّيَقُوْلُوْٓا اَهٰٓؤُلَآءِ مَنَّ اللّٰهُ عَلَيْهِمْ
مِّنْۢ بَيْنِنَا ۗ اَلَيْسَ اللّٰهُ بِاَعْلَمَ
بِالشّٰكِرِيْنَ ﴿٥٣﴾

54. When those come to you who believe in Our Signs, Say: "Peace be on you: Your Lord has inscribed for Himself (the rule of) mercy: verily, if any of you did evil in ignorance, and thereafter repented, and amended (his conduct), lo! He is Oft-forgiving, Most Merciful.

54. Wa izaa jaaa'akal-lazeena yu'minoona bi-Aayaatinaa faqul salaamun 'alaykum kataba Rabbukum 'alaa nafsihir-raḥmata annahoo man 'amila minkum sooo'am bijahaalatin summa taaba mim ba'dihee wa aṣlaḥa fa-annahoo Ghafoorur-Raḥeem.

وَاِذَا جَآءَكَ الَّذِيْنَ يُؤْمِنُوْنَ بِاٰيٰتِنَا
فَقُلْ سَلٰمٌ عَلَيْكُمْ كَتَبَ رَبُّكُمْ عَلٰى
نَفْسِهِ الرَّحْمَةَ ۙ اَنَّهٗ مَنْ عَمِلَ مِنْكُمْ
سُوْٓءًۢا بِجَهَالَةٍ ثُمَّ تَابَ مِنْۢ بَعْدِهٖ
وَاَصْلَحَ فَاَنَّهٗ غَفُوْرٌ رَّحِيْمٌ ﴿٥٤﴾

55. Thus do We explain the Signs in detail: so that

55. Wa kazaalika nufaṣṣilul-Aayaati wa litastabeena

وَكَذٰلِكَ نُفَصِّلُ الْاٰيٰتِ وَلِتَسْتَبِيْنَ

Ikhfa اخفاء | Ghunna غُنّہ | Ikhfa Meem Saakin اخفاء میم ساکن | Idghaam ادغام | Qalqala قلقلہ | Qalb قلب | Idghaam Meem Saakin ادغام میم ساکن

the way of the sinners may be shown up.

56. Say: "I am forbidden to worship those - other than Allah- whom you call upon." Say: "I will not follow your vain desires: If I did, I would stray from the path, and be not of the company of those who receive guidance."

57. Say: "For me, I (work) on a clear Sign from my Lord, but you reject Him. What you wish to see hastened, is not in my power. The Command rests with none but Allah: He declares the Truth, and He is the best of judges."

58. Say: "If what you would see hastened were in my power, the matter would be settled at once between you and me. But Allah knows best those who do wrong."

59. With Him are the keys of the Unseen, the treasures that none knows but He. He knows whatever there is on the earth and in the sea. Not a leaf falls but with His knowledge: there is not a grain in the darkness (or depths) of the earth, nor anything fresh or dry (green or withered), but is (inscribed) in a Record clear (to those who can read).

60. It is He who takes your souls by night, and has knowledge of all that you have done by day: by day He raises you up again; that a term appointed be fulfilled; In the end unto Him will be your return; then will He show you the truth of all that you did.

61. He is the irresistible, (watching) from above over His worshippers, and He sets guardians over you. At length, when death approaches one of you, Our angels take his soul,

sabeelul-mujrimeen. **(Section 6)**

56. Qul innee nuheetu an a'budal-lazeena tad'oona min doonil-laah; qul laaa attabi'u ahwaaa'akum qad ḍalaltu izañw-wa maaa ana minal-muhtadeen.

57. Qul innee 'alaa bayyinatim-mir-Rabbee wa kazzabtum bih; maa 'indee maa tasta'jiloona bih; inil-ḥukmu illaa lillaahi yaquṣṣul-ḥaqqa wa Huwa khayrul-faaṣileen.

58. Qul law anna 'indee maa tasta'jiloona bihee laquḍiyal-amru baynee wa baynakum; wallaahu a'lamu bizzaalimeen.

59. Wa 'indahoo mafaatiḥul-ghaybi laa ya'lamuhaaa illaa Hoo; wa ya'lamu maa fil-barri walbaḥr; wa maa tasquṭu miñw-waraqatin illaa ya'lamuhaa wa laa ḥabbatin fee ẓulumaatil-arḍi wa laa raṭbiñw-wa laa yaabisin illaa fee Kitaabim-Mubeen.

60. Wa Huwal-lazee yatawaffaakum billayli wa ya'lamu maa jaraḥtum binnahaari summa yab'asukum feehi liyuqḍaaa ajalum-musamman summa ilayhi marji'ukum summa yunabbi'ukum bimaa kuntum ta'maloon. **(Section 7)**

61. Wa Huwal-qaahiru fawqa 'ibaadihee wa yursilu 'alaykum ḥafaẓatan ḥattaaa izaa jaaa'a aḥadakumul-mawtu tawaffat-hu rusulunaa

سَبِيلُ الْمُجْرِمِينَ ﴿٥٥﴾ ع
قُلْ إِنِّي نُهِيتُ أَنْ أَعْبُدَ الَّذِينَ
تَدْعُونَ مِنْ دُونِ اللَّهِ ۚ قُلْ لَا
أَتَّبِعُ أَهْوَاءَكُمْ ۙ قَدْ ضَلَلْتُ إِذًا
وَمَا أَنَا مِنَ الْمُهْتَدِينَ ﴿٥٦﴾
قُلْ إِنِّي عَلَىٰ بَيِّنَةٍ مِنْ رَبِّي وَكَذَّبْتُمْ
بِهِ ۚ مَا عِنْدِي مَا تَسْتَعْجِلُونَ بِهِ ۚ
إِنِ الْحُكْمُ إِلَّا لِلَّهِ ۖ يَقُصُّ الْحَقَّ
وَهُوَ خَيْرُ الْفَاصِلِينَ ﴿٥٧﴾
قُلْ لَوْ أَنَّ عِنْدِي مَا تَسْتَعْجِلُونَ
بِهِ لَقُضِيَ الْأَمْرُ بَيْنِي وَبَيْنَكُمْ ۗ
وَاللَّهُ أَعْلَمُ بِالظَّالِمِينَ ﴿٥٨﴾
وَعِنْدَهُ مَفَاتِحُ الْغَيْبِ لَا يَعْلَمُهَا
إِلَّا هُوَ ۚ وَيَعْلَمُ مَا فِي الْبَرِّ وَالْبَحْرِ ۚ
وَمَا تَسْقُطُ مِنْ وَرَقَةٍ إِلَّا يَعْلَمُهَا
وَلَا حَبَّةٍ فِي ظُلُمَاتِ الْأَرْضِ وَلَا
رَطْبٍ وَلَا يَابِسٍ إِلَّا فِي كِتَابٍ
مُبِينٍ ﴿٥٩﴾
وَهُوَ الَّذِي يَتَوَفَّاكُمْ بِاللَّيْلِ وَ
يَعْلَمُ مَا جَرَحْتُمْ بِالنَّهَارِ ثُمَّ
يَبْعَثُكُمْ فِيهِ لِيُقْضَىٰ أَجَلٌ
مُسَمًّى ۖ ثُمَّ إِلَيْهِ مَرْجِعُكُمْ ثُمَّ
يُنَبِّئُكُمْ بِمَا كُنْتُمْ تَعْمَلُونَ ﴿٦٠﴾ ع
وَهُوَ الْقَاهِرُ فَوْقَ عِبَادِهِ ۖ وَيُرْسِلُ
عَلَيْكُمْ حَفَظَةً حَتَّىٰ إِذَا جَاءَ
أَحَدَكُمُ الْمَوْتُ تَوَفَّتْهُ رُسُلُنَا

Ikhfa اخفاء | Ghunna غنّہ | Ikhfa Meem Saakin اخفاء میم ساکن | Idghaam ادغام | Qalqala قلقلہ | Qalb قلب | Idghaam Meem Saakin ادغام میم ساکن

and they never fail in their duty.

62. Then men are returned unto Allah, their protector, the (only) reality: Is not His the command? and He is the swiftest in taking account.

63. Say: "Who is it that deliveres you from the dark recesses of land and sea, when you call upon Him in humility and silent terror: 'If He only delivers us from these (dangers), (we vow) we shall truly show our gratitude'.?"

64. Say "It is Allah that delivers you from these and all (other) distresses: and yet you worship false gods!"

65. Say: "He has power to send calamities on you, from above and below, or to cover you with confusion in party strife, giving you a taste of mutual vengeance- each from the other." See how We explain the Signs by various (symbols); that they may understand.

66. But your people reject this, though it is the truth. Say: "Not mine is the responsibility for arranging your affairs;

67. For every Message is a limit of time, and soon shall you know it."

68. When you see men engaged in vain discourse about Our Signs, turn away from them unless they turn to a different theme. If Satan ever makes you forget, then after recollection, do not sit in the company of those who do wrong.

69. On their account no responsibility falls on the righteous, but (their duty) is to remind them, that they may (learn to) fear Allah.

70. Leave alone those who take their religion to be mere play

wa hum laa yufarriṭoon.

62. S̲umma ruddooo ilallaahi mawlaahumul-ḥaqq; alaa lahul-ḥukmu wa Huwa asra'ul-ḥaasibeen.

63. Qul mañy-yunajjeekum min z̲ulumaatil-barri walbaḥri tad'oonahoo taḍarru'añw-wa khufyatan la'in anjaanaa min haaz̲ihee lanakoonanna minash-shaakireen.

64. Qulil-laahu yunajjeekum minhaa wa min kulli karbin s̲umma antum tushrikoon.

65. Qul Huwal-Qaadiru 'alaaa añy-yab'as̲a 'alaykum 'az̲aa-bam-min fawqikum aw min taḥti arjulikum aw yalbisakum shiya'añw-wa yuz̲eeqa ba'ḍa-kum baåsa ba'ḍ; unẓur kayfa nuṣarriful-Aayaati la'allahum yafqahoon.

66. Wa kaz̲-z̲aba bihee qawmuka wa huwal-ḥaqq; qul lastu 'alaykum biwakeel.

67. Likulli naba-im-mustaqar-ruñw-wa sawfa ta'lamoon.

68. Wa iz̲aa ra-aytal-laz̲eena yakhooḍoona feee Aayaatinaa fa-a'riḍ 'anhum ḥattaa yakhoo-ḍoo fee ḥadees̲in ghayrih; wa immaa yunsiyannakash-Shayṭaanu falaa taq'ud ba'daz̲-z̲ikraa ma'al-qawmiẓ-ẓaali-meen.

69. Wa maa 'alal-laz̲eena yattaqoona min ḥisaabihim min shay'iñw-wa laakin z̲ikraa la'allahum yattaqoon.

70. Wa z̲aril-laz̲eenat-takhaz̲oo deenahum la'ibañw-

وَهُمْ لَا يُفَرِّطُونَ ٦١

ثُمَّ رُدُّوٓا إِلَى ٱللَّهِ مَوْلَىٰهُمُ ٱلْحَقِّ

أَلَا لَهُ ٱلْحُكْمُ وَهُوَ أَسْرَعُ ٱلْحَـٰسِبِينَ ٦٢

قُلْ مَن يُنَجِّيكُم مِّن ظُلُمَـٰتِ ٱلْبَرِّ

وَٱلْبَحْرِ تَدْعُونَهُۥ تَضَرُّعًا وَخُفْيَةً

لَّئِنْ أَنجَىٰنَا مِنْ هَـٰذِهِۦ لَنَكُونَنَّ

مِنَ ٱلشَّـٰكِرِينَ ٦٣

قُلِ ٱللَّهُ يُنَجِّيكُم مِّنْهَا وَمِن كُلِّ

كَرْبٍ ثُمَّ أَنتُمْ تُشْرِكُونَ ٦٤

قُلْ هُوَ ٱلْقَادِرُ عَلَىٰٓ أَن يَبْعَثَ عَلَيْكُمْ

عَذَابًا مِّن فَوْقِكُمْ أَوْ مِن تَحْتِ

أَرْجُلِكُمْ أَوْ يَلْبِسَكُمْ شِيَعًا وَيُذِيقَ

بَعْضَكُم بَأْسَ بَعْضٍ ۗ ٱنظُرْ كَيْفَ

نُصَرِّفُ ٱلْـَٔايَـٰتِ لَعَلَّهُمْ يَفْقَهُونَ ٦٥

وَكَذَّبَ بِهِۦ قَوْمُكَ وَهُوَ ٱلْحَقُّ

قُل لَّسْتُ عَلَيْكُم بِوَكِيلٍ ٦٦

لِّكُلِّ نَبَإٍ مُّسْتَقَرٌّ ۚ وَسَوْفَ تَعْلَمُونَ ٦٧

وَإِذَا رَأَيْتَ ٱلَّذِينَ يَخُوضُونَ فِىٓ

ءَايَـٰتِنَا فَأَعْرِضْ عَنْهُمْ حَتَّىٰ يَخُوضُوا۟

فِى حَدِيثٍ غَيْرِهِۦ ۚ وَإِمَّا يُنسِيَنَّكَ

ٱلشَّيْطَـٰنُ فَلَا تَقْعُدْ بَعْدَ ٱلذِّكْرَىٰ

مَعَ ٱلْقَوْمِ ٱلظَّـٰلِمِينَ ٦٨

وَمَا عَلَى ٱلَّذِينَ يَتَّقُونَ مِنْ حِسَابِهِم

مِّن شَىْءٍ وَلَـٰكِن ذِكْرَىٰ لَعَلَّهُمْ

يَتَّقُونَ ٦٩

وَذَرِ ٱلَّذِينَ ٱتَّخَذُوا۟ دِينَهُمْ لَعِبًا

Ikhfa اخفاء · Ghunna غُنّہ · Ikhfa Meem Saakin اخفاءمیم ساکن · Idghaam ادغام · Qalqala قلقلہ · Qalb قلب · Idghaam Meem Saakin ادغام میم ساکن

and amusement, and are deceived by the life of this world. But proclaim (to them) this (truth): that every soul delivers itself to ruin by its own acts: it will find for itself no protector or intercessor except Allah: if it offered every ransom, (or reparation), none will be accepted: such is (the end of) those who deliver themselves to ruin by their own acts: they will have for drink (only) boiling water, and for punishment, one most grievous: for they persisted in rejecting Allah.

71. Say: "Shall we indeed call on others besides Allah,- things that can do us neither good nor harm,- and turn on our heels after receiving guidance from Allah? - like one whom the evil ones have made into a fool, wandering bewildered through the earth, his friends calling, 'Come to us', (vainly) guiding him to the path." Say: "Allah's guidance is the (only) guidance, and we have been directed to submit ourselves to the Lord of the worlds;-

72. "To establish regular prayers and to fear Allah for it is to Him that we shall be gathered together."

73. It is He who created the heavens and the earth in true (proportions): the day He says, "Be," Behold! it is. His word is the Truth. His will be the dominion the day the trumpet will be blown. He knows the Unseen as well as that which is open. For He is the Wise, well acquainted (with all things).

74. Lo! Abraham said to his father Azar: "Do you take idols for gods? For I see you and your people in manifest error."

75. So also did We show Abraham the power and the laws of

wa lahwañw-wa gharrat-humul-ḥa-yaatud-dunyaa; wa z̲akkir biheee an tubsala nafsum bimaa kasabat laysa lahaa min doonil-laahi waliyyuñw-wa laa shafee'uñw wa in ta'dil kulla 'adlil-laa yu'khaz̲ minhaa; ulaaa'ikal-laz̲eena ubsiloo bimaa kasaboo lahum sharaa-bum-min ḥameemiñw-wa 'az̲aabun aleemum bimaa kaanoo yakfuroon. **(Section 8)**

71. Qul anad'oo min doonil-laahi maa laa yanfa'unaa wa laa yaḍurrunaa wa nuraddu 'alaaa a'qaabinaa ba'da iz̲ hadaanal-laahu kallaz̲is-tahwat-hush-Shayaaṭeenu fil-arḍi ḥayraana lahooo asḥaabuñy-yad'oo-nahooo ilal-huda'-tinaa; qul inna hudal-laahi huwal-hudaa wa umirnaa linuslima li-Rabbil-'aalameen.

72. Wa an aqeemuṣ-Ṣalaata wattaqooh; wa Huwal-laz̲eee ilayhi tuḥsharoon.

73. Wa Huwal-laz̲ee khala-qas-samaawaati wal-arḍa bilḥaqq; wa Yawma yaqoolu kun fa-yakoon; Qawluhul-ḥaqq; wa lahul-mulku Yawma yunfakhu fiṣ-Ṣoor; 'Aalimul-Ghaybi wash-shahaadah; wa Huwal-Ḥakeemul-Khabeer.

74. Wa iz̲ qaala Ibraaheemu li-abeehi Aazara a-tattakhiz̲u aṣnaaman aalihatan inneee araaka wa qawmaka fee ḍalaalim-mubeen.

75. Wa kaz̲aalika nureee Ibraaheema malakootas-

وَّلَهْوًا وَّغَرَّتْهُمُ الْحَيٰوةُ الدُّنْيَا
وَذَكِّرْ بِهٖٓ اَنْ تُبْسَلَ نَفْسٌ بِمَا
كَسَبَتْ ۖ لَيْسَ لَهَا مِنْ دُوْنِ اللّٰهِ
وَلِيٌّ وَّلَا شَفِيْعٌ ۚ وَاِنْ تَعْدِلْ كُلَّ
عَدْلٍ لَّا يُؤْخَذْ مِنْهَا ؕ اُولٰٓئِكَ
الَّذِيْنَ اُبْسِلُوْا بِمَا كَسَبُوْا ۚ لَهُمْ شَرَابٌ
مِّنْ حَمِيْمٍ وَّعَذَابٌ اَلِيْمٌۢ بِمَا كَانُوْا
يَكْفُرُوْنَ ۝ ع
قُلْ اَنَدْعُوْا مِنْ دُوْنِ اللّٰهِ مَا لَا يَنْفَعُنَا
وَلَا يَضُرُّنَا وَنُرَدُّ عَلٰٓى اَعْقَابِنَا
بَعْدَ اِذْ هَدٰىنَا اللّٰهُ كَالَّذِى اسْتَهْوَتْهُ
الشَّيٰطِيْنُ فِى الْاَرْضِ حَيْرَانَ ۪ لَهٗٓ
اَصْحٰبٌ يَّدْعُوْنَهٗٓ اِلَى الْهُدَى
ائْتِنَا ؕ قُلْ اِنَّ هُدَى اللّٰهِ هُوَ الْهُدٰى ؕ
وَاُمِرْنَا لِنُسْلِمَ لِرَبِّ الْعٰلَمِيْنَ ۝
وَاَنْ اَقِيْمُوا الصَّلٰوةَ وَاتَّقُوْهُ ؕ
وَهُوَ الَّذِيْٓ اِلَيْهِ تُحْشَرُوْنَ ۝
وَهُوَ الَّذِيْ خَلَقَ السَّمٰوٰتِ وَالْاَرْضَ
بِالْحَقِّ ؕ وَيَوْمَ يَقُوْلُ كُنْ فَيَكُوْنُ ؕ الثلثة
قَوْلُهُ الْحَقُّ ؕ وَلَهُ الْمُلْكُ يَوْمَ
يُنْفَخُ فِى الصُّوْرِ ؕ عٰلِمُ الْغَيْبِ
وَالشَّهَادَةِ ؕ وَهُوَ الْحَكِيْمُ الْخَبِيْرُ ۝
وَاِذْ قَالَ اِبْرٰهِيْمُ لِاَبِيْهِ اٰزَرَ اَتَتَّخِذُ
اَصْنَامًا اٰلِهَةً ۚ اِنِّيْٓ اَرٰىكَ وَقَوْمَكَ
فِيْ ضَلٰلٍ مُّبِيْنٍ ۝
وَكَذٰلِكَ نُرِيْٓ اِبْرٰهِيْمَ مَلَكُوْتَ

Ikhfa اخفاء · Ghunna غنّہ · Ikhfa Meem Saakin اخفاء میم ساکن · Idghaam ادغام · Qalqala قلقلہ · Qalb قلب · Idghaam Meem Saakin ادغام میم ساکن

the heavens and the earth, that he might (with understanding) have certitude.

samaawaati wal-arḍi wa liyakoona minal-mooqineen.

السَّمٰوٰتِ وَالْاَرْضِ وَلِيَكُوْنَ
مِنَ الْمُوْقِنِيْنَ ۝٧٥

76. When the night covered him over, He saw a star: He said: "This is my Lord." But when it set, He said: "I love not those that set."

76. Falammaa janna 'alayhil-laylu ra-aa kawkaban qaala haaz̲aa Rabbee falammaaa afala qaala laaa uḥibbul-aafileen.

فَلَمَّا جَنَّ عَلَيْهِ الَّيْلُ رَاٰ كَوْكَبًا ۚ
قَالَ هٰذَا رَبِّيْ ۚ فَلَمَّآ اَفَلَ قَالَ
لَآ اُحِبُّ الْاٰفِلِيْنَ ۝٧٦

77. When he saw the moon rising in splendour, he said: "This is my Lord." But when the moon set, He said: "unless my Lord guide me, I shall surely be among those who go astray."

77. Falammaa ra-al-qamara baazighan qaala haaz̲aa Rabbee falammaaa afala qaala la'il-lam yahdinee Rabbee la-akoonanna minal-qawmiḍ-ḍaaalleen.

فَلَمَّا رَاَ الْقَمَرَ بَازِغًا قَالَ هٰذَا رَبِّيْ ۚ
فَلَمَّآ اَفَلَ قَالَ لَئِنْ لَّمْ يَهْدِنِيْ
رَبِّيْ لَاَكُوْنَنَّ مِنَ الْقَوْمِ الضَّآلِّيْنَ ۝٧٧

78. When he saw the sun rising in splendour, he said: "This is my Lord; this is the greatest (of all)." But when the sun set, he said: "O my people! I am indeed free from your (guilt) of giving partners to Allah.

78. Falammaa ra-ash-shamsa baazighatan qaala haaz̲aa Rabbee haaz̲aaa akbaru falammaaa afalat qaala yaa qawmi innee bareee'um-mimmaa tushrikoon.

فَلَمَّا رَاَ الشَّمْسَ بَازِغَةً قَالَ هٰذَا
رَبِّيْ هٰذَآ اَكْبَرُ ۚ فَلَمَّآ اَفَلَتْ قَالَ
يٰقَوْمِ اِنِّيْ بَرِيْٓءٌ مِّمَّا تُشْرِكُوْنَ ۝٧٨

79. "For me, I have set my face, firmly and truly, towards Him Who created the heavens and the earth, and never shall I give partners to Allah."

79. Innee wajjahtu wajhiya lillaz̲ee faṭaras-samaawaati wal-arḍa Ḥaneefañw-wa maaa ana minal-mushrikeen.

اِنِّيْ وَجَّهْتُ وَجْهِيَ لِلَّذِيْ فَطَرَ
السَّمٰوٰتِ وَالْاَرْضَ حَنِيْفًا وَّمَآ اَنَا
مِنَ الْمُشْرِكِيْنَ ۝٧٩

80. His people disputed with him. He said: "Do you (come) to dispute with me, about Allah, when He (Himself) has guided me? I fear not (the beings) you associate with Allah: Unless my Lord wills, (nothing can happen). My Lord comprehends in His knowledge all things. Will you not (yourselves) be admonished?

80. Wa ḥaaajjahoo qawmuh; qaala a-tuḥaaajjooonnee fillaahi wa qad hadaan; wa laaa akhaafu maa tushrikoona biheee illaaa añy-yashaaa'a Rabbee shay'añw wasi'a Rabbee kulla shay'in 'ilman afalaa tataz̲akkaroon.

وَحَآجَّهٗ قَوْمُهٗ ۭ قَالَ اَتُحَآجُّوْٓنِّيْ
فِي اللّٰهِ وَقَدْ هَدٰىنِ ۭ وَلَآ اَخَافُ
مَا تُشْرِكُوْنَ بِهٖٓ اِلَّآ اَنْ يَّشَاۗءَ
رَبِّيْ شَيْـًٔا ۭ وَسِعَ رَبِّيْ كُلَّ شَيْءٍ
عِلْمًا ۭ اَفَلَا تَتَذَكَّرُوْنَ ۝٨٠

81. "How should I fear (the beings) you associate with Allah, when you fear not to give partners to Allah without any warrant having been given to you? Which of (us) two parties has more right to security? (Tell me) if you know.

81. Wa kayfa akhaafu maaa ashraktum wa laa takhaafoona annakum ashraktum billaahi maa lam yunazzil bihee 'alaykum sulṭaanaa; fa-ayyul-fareeqayni aḥaqqu bil-amni in kuntum ta'lamoon.

وَكَيْفَ اَخَافُ مَآ اَشْرَكْتُمْ وَلَا
تَخَافُوْنَ اَنَّكُمْ اَشْرَكْتُمْ بِاللّٰهِ
مَا لَمْ يُنَزِّلْ بِهٖ عَلَيْكُمْ سُلْطٰنًا ۭ
فَاَيُّ الْفَرِيْقَيْنِ اَحَقُّ بِالْاَمْنِ ۚ
اِنْ كُنْتُمْ تَعْلَمُوْنَ ۝٨١ وقف لازم

82. "It is those who believe and confuse not their beliefs with wrong - that are (truly) in security, for they are

82. Allaz̲eena aamanoo wa lam yalbisooo eemaanahum biẓulmin ulaaa'ika lahumul-amnu wa hum

اَلَّذِيْنَ اٰمَنُوْا وَلَمْ يَلْبِسُوْٓا اِيْمَانَهُمْ
بِظُلْمٍ اُولٰۗىِٕكَ لَهُمُ الْاَمْنُ وَهُمْ

Ikhfa اخفاء | Ghunna غنّہ | Ikhfa Meem Saakin اخفاء میم ساکن | Idghaam ادغام | Qalqala قلقلہ | Qalb قلب | Idghaam Meem Saakin ادغام میم ساکن

on (right) guidance."

83. That was the reasoning about Us, which We gave to Abraham (to use) against his people: We raise whom We will, degree after degree: for your Lord is full of wisdom and knowledge.

84. We gave him Isaac and Jacob: all (three) guided: and before him, We guided Noah, and among his progeny, David, Solomon, Job, Joseph, Moses, and Aaron: thus do We reward those who do good:

85. And Zakariya and John, and Jesus and Elias: all in the ranks of the righteous:

86. And Isma'il and Elisha, and Jonas, and Lot: and to all We gave favour above the nations:

87. (To them) and to their fathers, and progeny and brethren: We chose them, and we guided them to a straight way.

88. This is the guidance of Allah: He gives that guidance to whom He pleases, of His worshippers. If they were to join other Allah's with Him, all that they did would be vain for them.

89. These were the men to whom We gave the Book, and authority, and prophethood: if these (their descendants) reject them, Behold! We shall entrust their charge to a new people who reject them not.

90. Those were the (prophets) who received Allah's guidance: follow the guidance they received; Say: "No reward for this do I ask of you: This is no less than a message for the nations."

muhtadoon. **(Section 9)**

83. Wa tilka ḥujjatunaaa aataynaahaaa Ibraaheema 'alaa qawmih; narfa'u darajaatim-man nashaaa'; inna Rabbaka Ḥakeemun 'Aleem.

84. Wa wahabnaa lahooo Isḥaaqa wa ya'qoob; kullan hadaynaa; wa Nooḥan hadaynaa min qablu wa min zurriyyatihee Daawooda wa Sulaymaana wa Ayyooba wa Yoosufa wa Moosaa wa Haaroon; wa kazaalika najzil-muḥsineen.

85. Wa Zakariyyaa wa Yaḥyaa wa 'Eesaa wa Ilyaasa kullum-minaṣ-ṣaaliḥeen.

86. Wa Ismaa'eela wal-Yasa'a wa Yoonusa wa Looṭaa; wa kullan faḍḍalnaa 'alal-'aalameen.

87. Wa min aabaaa'ihim wa zurriyyaatihim wa ikhwaanihim wajtabaynaahum wa hadaynaa-hum ilaa Ṣiraaṭim-Mustaqeem.

88. Zaalika hudal-laahi yahdee bihee mañy-yashaaa'u min 'ibaadih; wa law ashrakoo laḥabiṭa 'anhum maa kaanoo ya'maloon.

89. Ulaaa'ikal-lazeena aataynaahumul-Kitaaba wal-ḥukma wan-Nubuwwah; fa-iny-yakfur bihaa haaa'ulaaa'i faqad wakkalnaa bihaa qawmal-laysoo bihaa bikaafireen.

90. Ulaaa'ikal-lazeena hadal-laahu fabihudaahumuq-tadih; qul laaa as'alukum 'alayhi ajran in huwa illaa zikraa lil-'aalameen. **(Section 10)**

مُّهْتَدُوْنَ ﴿٨٢﴾ ع ١٢ ١٥
وَتِلْكَ حُجَّتُنَآ اٰتَيْنٰهَآ اِبْرٰهِيْمَ
عَلٰى قَوْمِهٖ ؕ نَرْفَعُ دَرَجٰتٍ مَّنْ نَّشَآءُ ؕ
اِنَّ رَبَّكَ حَكِيْمٌ عَلِيْمٌ ﴿٨٣﴾
وَوَهَبْنَا لَهٗۤ اِسْحٰقَ وَيَعْقُوْبَ ؕ كُلًّا
هَدَيْنَا ۚ وَنُوْحًا هَدَيْنَا مِنْ قَبْلُ
وَمِنْ ذُرِّيَّتِهٖ دَاوٗدَ وَسُلَيْمٰنَ وَاَيُّوْبَ
وَيُوْسُفَ وَمُوْسٰى وَهٰرُوْنَ ؕ وَكَذٰلِكَ
نَجْزِى الْمُحْسِنِيْنَ ﴿٨٤﴾
وَزَكَرِيَّا وَيَحْيٰى وَعِيْسٰى وَاِلْيَاسَ ؕ
كُلٌّ مِّنَ الصّٰلِحِيْنَ ﴿٨٥﴾
وَاِسْمٰعِيْلَ وَالْيَسَعَ وَيُوْنُسَ وَلُوْطًا ؕ
وَكُلًّا فَضَّلْنَا عَلَى الْعٰلَمِيْنَ ﴿٨٦﴾
وَمِنْ اٰبَآئِهِمْ وَذُرِّيّٰتِهِمْ وَاِخْوَانِهِمْ ۚ
وَاجْتَبَيْنٰهُمْ وَهَدَيْنٰهُمْ اِلٰى صِرَاطٍ
مُّسْتَقِيْمٍ ﴿٨٧﴾
ذٰلِكَ هُدَى اللّٰهِ يَهْدِىْ بِهٖ مَنْ
يَّشَآءُ مِنْ عِبَادِهٖ ؕ وَلَوْ اَشْرَكُوْا لَحَبِطَ
عَنْهُمْ مَّا كَانُوْا يَعْمَلُوْنَ ﴿٨٨﴾
اُولٰٓئِكَ الَّذِيْنَ اٰتَيْنٰهُمُ الْكِتٰبَ
وَالْحُكْمَ وَالنُّبُوَّةَ ۚ فَاِنْ يَّكْفُرْ بِهَا
هٰٓؤُلَآءِ فَقَدْ وَكَّلْنَا بِهَا قَوْمًا لَّيْسُوْا
بِهَا بِكٰفِرِيْنَ ﴿٨٩﴾
اُولٰٓئِكَ الَّذِيْنَ هَدَى اللّٰهُ فَبِهُدٰىهُمُ
اقْتَدِهْ ؕ قُلْ لَّآ اَسْئَلُكُمْ عَلَيْهِ اَجْرًا ؕ
اِنْ هُوَ اِلَّا ذِكْرٰى لِلْعٰلَمِيْنَ ﴿٩٠﴾ ع ٨ ١٦

Ikhfa اخفاء | Ghunna غنّہ | Ikhfa Meem Saakin اخفاء میم ساکن | Idghaam ادغام | Qalqala قلقلہ | Qalb قلب | Idghaam Meem Saakin ادغام میم ساکن

91. No just estimate of Allah do they make when they say: "Nothing does Allah send down to man (by way of revelation)" Say: "Who then sent down the Book which Moses brought?- a light and guidance to man: but you make it into (separate) sheets for show, while you conceal much (of its contents): therein were you taught that which you knew not- neither you nor your fathers." Say: "Allah (sent it down)": then leave them to plunge in vain discourse and trifling.

92. And this is a Book which We have sent down, bringing blessings, and confirming (the revelations) which came before it: that you may warn the mother of cities and all around her. Those who believe in the Hereafter believe in this (Book), and they are constant in guarding their prayers.

93. Who can be more wicked than one who invents a lie against Allah, or says, "I have received inspiration," when he has received none, or (again) who says, "I can reveal the like of what Allah has revealed"? If you could but see how the wicked (do fare) in the flood of confusion at death! - the angels stretch forth their hands, (saying),"Yield up your souls: this day shall you receive your reward,- a Chastisement of shame, for that you used to tell lies against Allah, and scornfully to reject of His Signs!"

94. "And behold! you come to us bare and alone as We created you for the first time: you have left behind you all (the favours) which We bestowed on you: We see not with you your intercessors whom you thought to be partners in your affairs: so now all relations between you have been cut off, and your (pet) fancies have left you in the lurch!"

91. Wa maa qadarul-laaha ḥaqqa qadriheee iz̲ qaaloo maaa anzalal-laahu 'alaa basharim-min shay'; qul man anzalal-Kitaabal-laz̲ee jaaa'a bihee Moosaa nooranw-wa hudal-linnaasi taj'aloonahoo qaraaṭeesa tubdoonahaa wa tukhfoona kas̲eeranw wa 'ullimtum maa lam ta'lamooo antum wa laaa aabaaa'ukum qulil-laahu summa z̲arhum fee khawḍihim yal'aboon

92. Wa haaz̲aa Kitaabun anzalnaahu Mubaarakum-muṣaddiqul-laz̲ee bayna yadayhi wa litunz̲ira Ummal-Quraa wa man ḥawlahaa; wallaz̲eena yu'minoona bil-Aakhirati yu'minoona bihee wa hum 'alaa Ṣalaatihim yuḥaafiẓoon.

93. Wa man aẓlamu mimmanif-taraa 'alal-laahi kaz̲iban aw qaala ooḥiya ilayya wa lam yooḥa ilayhi shay'unw-wa man qaala sa-unzilu mis̲la maaa anzalal-laah; wa law taraaa iẓiẓ-ẓaalimoona fee ghamaraatil-mawti walmalaaa'ikatu baasiṭooo aydeehim akhrijooo anfusakum; al-yawma tujzawna 'az̲aabal-hooni bimaa kuntum taqooloona 'alal-laahi ghayral-ḥaqqi wa kuntum 'an Aayaatihee tastakbiroon.

94. Wa laqad ji'tumoonaa furaadaa kamaa khalaqnaakum awwala marratinw-wa taraktum maa khawwalnaakum waraaa'a ẓuhoorikum wa maa naraa ma'akum shufa'aa'akumul-laz̲eena za-'amtum annahum feekum shurakaaa'; laqattaqaṭṭa'a baynakum wa ḍalla 'ankum maa kuntum taz'umoon.

(Section 11)

وَمَا قَدَرُوا اللّٰهَ حَقَّ قَدْرِهٖٓ اِذْ قَالُوْا
مَآ اَنْزَلَ اللّٰهُ عَلٰى بَشَرٍ مِّنْ شَيْءٍ ؕ
قُلْ مَنْ اَنْزَلَ الْكِتٰبَ الَّذِيْ جَآءَ بِهٖ
مُوْسٰى نُوْرًا وَّهُدًى لِّلنَّاسِ تَجْعَلُوْنَهٗ
قَرَاطِيْسَ تُبْدُوْنَهَا وَتُخْفُوْنَ كَثِيْرًا ۚ
وَعُلِّمْتُمْ مَّا لَمْ تَعْلَمُوْٓا اَنْتُمْ وَلَآ اٰبَآؤُكُمْ ؕ
قُلِ اللّٰهُ ۙ ثُمَّ ذَرْهُمْ فِيْ خَوْضِهِمْ يَلْعَبُوْنَ ﴿٩١﴾
وَهٰذَا كِتٰبٌ اَنْزَلْنٰهُ مُبٰرَكٌ مُّصَدِّقُ
الَّذِيْ بَيْنَ يَدَيْهِ وَلِتُنْذِرَ اُمَّ الْقُرٰى
وَمَنْ حَوْلَهَا ؕ وَالَّذِيْنَ يُؤْمِنُوْنَ
بِالْاٰخِرَةِ يُؤْمِنُوْنَ بِهٖ وَهُمْ عَلٰى
صَلَاتِهِمْ يُحَافِظُوْنَ ﴿٩٢﴾
وَمَنْ اَظْلَمُ مِمَّنِ افْتَرٰى عَلَى اللّٰهِ كَذِبًا
اَوْ قَالَ اُوْحِيَ اِلَيَّ وَلَمْ يُوْحَ اِلَيْهِ شَيْءٌ
وَّمَنْ قَالَ سَاُنْزِلُ مِثْلَ مَآ اَنْزَلَ اللّٰهُ ؕ
وَلَوْ تَرٰٓى اِذِ الظّٰلِمُوْنَ فِيْ غَمَرٰتِ الْمَوْتِ
وَالْمَلٰٓئِكَةُ بَاسِطُوْٓا اَيْدِيْهِمْ ۚ اَخْرِجُوْٓا
اَنْفُسَكُمْ ؕ اَلْيَوْمَ تُجْزَوْنَ عَذَابَ الْهُوْنِ
بِمَا كُنْتُمْ تَقُوْلُوْنَ عَلَى اللّٰهِ غَيْرَ الْحَقِّ
وَكُنْتُمْ عَنْ اٰيٰتِهٖ تَسْتَكْبِرُوْنَ ﴿٩٣﴾
وَلَقَدْ جِئْتُمُوْنَا فُرَادٰى كَمَا خَلَقْنٰكُمْ
اَوَّلَ مَرَّةٍ وَّتَرَكْتُمْ مَّا خَوَّلْنٰكُمْ وَرَآءَ
ظُهُوْرِكُمْ ۚ وَمَا نَرٰى مَعَكُمْ شُفَعَآءَكُمُ
الَّذِيْنَ زَعَمْتُمْ اَنَّهُمْ فِيْكُمْ شُرَكٰٓؤُا ؕ
لَقَدْ تَّقَطَّعَ بَيْنَكُمْ وَضَلَّ عَنْكُمْ مَّا
كُنْتُمْ تَزْعُمُوْنَ ﴿٩٤﴾ ع

Ikhfa اخفاء | Ghunna غنّہ | Ikhfa Meem Saakin اخفاء میم ساکن | Idghaam ادغام | Qalqala قلقلہ | Qalb قلب | Idghaam Meem Saakin ادغام میم ساکن

95. It is Allah Who causes the seed-grain and the date-stone to split and sprout. He causes the living to issue from the dead, and He is the one to cause the dead to issue from the living. That is Allah: then how are you deluded away from the truth?

96. He it is that cleaves the day-break (from the dark): He makes the night for rest and tranquillity, and the sun and moon for the reckoning (of time): Such is the judgment and ordering of (Him), the Exalted in Power, the Omniscient.

97. It is He Who makes the stars (as beacons) for you, that you may guide yourselves, with their help, through the dark spaces of land and sea: We detail Our Signs for people who know.

98. It is He Who has produced you from a single person: here is a place of sojourn and a place of departure: We detail Our Signs for people who understand.

99. It is He Who sends down rain from the skies: with it We produce vegetation of all kinds: from some We produce green (crops), out of which We produce grain, heaped up (at harvest); out of the date-palm and its sheaths (or spathes) (come) clusters of dates hanging low and near: and (then there are) gardens of grapes, and olives, and pomegranates, each similar (in kind) yet different (in variety): when they begin to bear fruit, feast your eyes with the fruit and the ripeness thereof. Behold! in these things there are signs for people who believe.

100. Yet they make the Jinns equals with Allah, though Allah did create the Jinns; and they falsely, having no knowledge, attribute to Him sons and daughters. Praise and glory be to Him! (for He is) above what they attribute to Him!

101. To Him is due the primal origin of the heavens and the earth: how can He have a son when He has no consort? He created all things, and He has full knowledge of all things.

95. Innal-laaha faaliqul-ḥabbi wannawaa yukhrijul-ḥayya minal-mayyiti wa mukhrijul-mayyiti minal-ḥayy; zaalikumul-laahu fa-annaa tu'fakoon.

96. Faaliqul-iṣbaaḥi wa ja-'alal-layla sakanañw-washshamsa walqamara ḥusbaanaa; zaalika taqdeerul-'Azeezil-'Aleem.

97. Wa Huwal-lazee ja'ala lakumun-nujooma litahtadoo bihaa fee ẓulumaatil-barri walbaḥr; qad faṣṣalnal-Aayaati liqawmiñy-ya'lamoon.

98. Wa Huwal-lazeee anshaakum min nafsiñw-waaḥidatin famustaqarruñw-wa mustawda'; qad faṣṣalnal-Aayaati liqawmiñy-yafqahoon.

99. Wa Huwal-lazeee anzala minas-samaaa'i maaa'an fa-akhrajnaa bihee nabaata kulli shay'in fa-akhrajnaa minhu khaḍiran-nukhriju minhu ḥabbam-mutaraakibañw wa minan-nakhli min ṭal'ihaa qinwaanun daaniyatuñw-wa jannaatim-min a'naabiñw-wazzaytoona warrummaana mushtabihañw-wa ghayra mutashaabih; unẓurooo ilaa samariheee izaaa asmara wa yan'ih; inna fee zaalikum la-Aayaatil-liqawmiñy-yu'minoon.

100. Wa ja'aloo lillaahi shurakaaa'al-jinna wa khalaqa hum wa kharaqoo lahoo baneena wa banaatim bighayri 'ilm; Subḥaanahoo wa Ta'aalaa 'ammaa yaṣifoon. **(Section 12)**

101. Badee'us-samaawaati wal-arḍi annaa yakoonu lahoo waladuñw-wa lam takul-lahoo ṣaahibatuñw wa khalaqa kulla shay'iñw wa Huwa bikulli shay'in 'Aleem.

إِنَّ اللّٰهَ فَالِقُ الْحَبِّ وَالنَّوٰى ؕ يُخْرِجُ
الْحَيَّ مِنَ الْمَيِّتِ وَمُخْرِجُ الْمَيِّتِ مِنَ
الْحَيِّ ؕ ذٰلِكُمُ اللّٰهُ فَاَنّٰى تُؤْفَكُوْنَ ﴿٩٥﴾
فَالِقُ الْاِصْبَاحِ ۚ وَجَعَلَ الَّيْلَ سَكَنًا
وَّالشَّمْسَ وَالْقَمَرَ حُسْبَانًا ؕ ذٰلِكَ
تَقْدِيْرُ الْعَزِيْزِ الْعَلِيْمِ ﴿٩٦﴾
وَهُوَ الَّذِيْ جَعَلَ لَكُمُ النُّجُوْمَ لِتَهْتَدُوْا
بِهَا فِيْ ظُلُمٰتِ الْبَرِّ وَالْبَحْرِ ؕ قَدْ فَصَّلْنَا
الْاٰيٰتِ لِقَوْمٍ يَّعْلَمُوْنَ ﴿٩٧﴾
وَهُوَ الَّذِيْٓ اَنْشَاَكُمْ مِّنْ نَّفْسٍ
وَّاحِدَةٍ فَمُسْتَقَرٌّ وَّمُسْتَوْدَعٌ ؕ قَدْ
فَصَّلْنَا الْاٰيٰتِ لِقَوْمٍ يَّفْقَهُوْنَ ﴿٩٨﴾
وَهُوَ الَّذِيْٓ اَنْزَلَ مِنَ السَّمَآءِ مَآءً ۚ
فَاَخْرَجْنَا بِهٖ نَبَاتَ كُلِّ شَيْءٍ فَاَخْرَجْنَا
مِنْهُ خَضِرًا نُّخْرِجُ مِنْهُ حَبًّا مُّتَرَاكِبًا ۚ
وَمِنَ النَّخْلِ مِنْ طَلْعِهَا قِنْوَانٌ دَانِيَةٌ
وَّجَنّٰتٍ مِّنْ اَعْنَابٍ وَّالزَّيْتُوْنَ
وَالرُّمَّانَ مُشْتَبِهًا وَّغَيْرَ مُتَشَابِهٍ ؕ
اُنْظُرُوْٓا اِلٰى ثَمَرِهٖٓ اِذَآ اَثْمَرَ وَيَنْعِهٖ ؕ
اِنَّ فِيْ ذٰلِكُمْ لَاٰيٰتٍ لِّقَوْمٍ يُّؤْمِنُوْنَ ﴿٩٩﴾
وَجَعَلُوْا لِلّٰهِ شُرَكَآءَ الْجِنَّ وَخَلَقَهُمْ
وَخَرَقُوْا لَهٗ بَنِيْنَ وَبَنٰتٍۢ بِغَيْرِ عِلْمٍ ؕ
سُبْحٰنَهٗ وَتَعٰلٰى عَمَّا يَصِفُوْنَ ﴿١٠٠﴾ ع ١٨
بَدِيْعُ السَّمٰوٰتِ وَالْاَرْضِ ؕ اَنّٰى يَكُوْنُ لَهٗ
وَلَدٌ وَّلَمْ تَكُنْ لَّهٗ صَاحِبَةٌ ؕ وَخَلَقَ
كُلَّ شَيْءٍ ۚ وَهُوَ بِكُلِّ شَيْءٍ عَلِيْمٌ ﴿١٠١﴾

Ikhfa اخفاء | Ghunna غنّہ | Ikhfa Meem Saakin اخفاء میم ساکن | Idghaam ادغام | Qalqala قلقلہ | Qalb قلب | Idghaam Meem Saakin ادغام میم ساکن

102. That is Allah, your Lord! there is no Allah but He, the Creator of all things: then worship Him: and He has power to dispose of all affairs.

103. No vision can grasp Him, but His grasp is over all vision: He is above all comprehension, yet is acquainted with all things.

104. "Now have come to you, from your Lord, proofs (to open your eyes): if any will see, it will be for (the good of) his own soul; if any will be blind, it will be to his own (harm): I am not (here) to watch over your doings."

105. Thus do we explain the signs by various (symbols): that they may say, "You have taught (us) diligently," and that We may make the matter clear to those who know.

106. Follow what you are taught by inspiration from your Lord: there is no god but He: and turn aside from those who join gods with Allah.

107. If it had been Allah's plan, they would not have taken false Allah's: but We made you not one to watch over their doings, nor are you set over them to dispose of their affairs.

108. Revile not those whom they call upon besides Allah, lest they out of spite revile Allah in their ignorance. Thus have We made alluring to each people its own doings. In the end will they return to their Lord, and We shall then tell them the truth of all that they did.

109. They swear their strongest oaths by Allah, that if a (special) sign came to them, by it they would believe. Say: "Certainly (all) Signs are in the power of Allah: but what he wishes you (Muslims) realise that (even) if (special) signs came, they will not believe."?

110. We (too) shall turn to (confusion) their hearts and their eyes, even as they refused to believe in this in the first instance: We shall leave them

102. Zaalikumul-laahu Rabbukum laaa ilaaha illaa Huwa khaaliqu kulli shay'in fa'budooh; wa Huwa 'alaa kulli shay'iñw-Wakeel.

103. Laa tudrikuhul-abṣaaru wa Huwa yudrikul-abṣaara wa Huwal-Laṭeeful-Khabeer.

104. Qad jaaa'akum baṣaaa'iru mir-Rabbikum faman abṣara falinafsihee wa man 'amiya fa'alayhaa; wa maaa ana 'alaykum biḥafeeẓ.

105. Wa kazaalika nuṣarriful-Aayaati wa liyaqooloo darasta wa linubayyinahoo liqawmiñy-ya'lamoon.

106. Ittabi' maaa ooḥiya ilayka mir-Rabbika laaa ilaaha illaa Huwa wa a'riḍ 'anil-mush-rikeen.

107. Wa law shaaa'al-laahu maaa ashrakoo; wa maa ja'alnaaka 'alayhim ḥafeeẓañw wa maaa anta 'alayhim biwakeel.

108. Wa laa tasubbul-lazeena yad'oona min doonil-laahi fa-yasubbul-laaha 'adwam bighayri 'ilm; kazaalika zayyannaa likulli ummatin 'amalahum summa ilaa Rabbihim marji'uhum fa-yunabbi'uhum bimaa kaanoo ya'maloon.

109. Wa aqsamoo billaahi jahda aymaanihim la'in jaaa'at-hum Aayatul-la-yu'minunna bihaa; qul innamal-Aayaatu 'indal-laahi wa maa yush'irukum annahaaa izaa jaaa'at laa yu'minoon.

110. Wa nuqallibu af'idatahum wa abṣaarahum kamaa lam yu'minoo biheee awwala marratiñwa-wa naẓaruhum fee

ذَٰلِكُمُ ٱللَّهُ رَبُّكُمْ ۖ لَآ إِلَٰهَ إِلَّا هُوَ ۖ خَٰلِقُ
كُلِّ شَىْءٍ فَٱعْبُدُوهُ ۚ وَهُوَ عَلَىٰ كُلِّ
شَىْءٍ وَكِيلٌ ﴿١٠٢﴾
لَّا تُدْرِكُهُ ٱلْأَبْصَٰرُ وَهُوَ يُدْرِكُ ٱلْأَبْصَٰرَ ۖ
وَهُوَ ٱللَّطِيفُ ٱلْخَبِيرُ ﴿١٠٣﴾
قَدْ جَآءَكُم بَصَآئِرُ مِن رَّبِّكُمْ ۖ فَمَنْ
أَبْصَرَ فَلِنَفْسِهِۦ ۖ وَمَنْ عَمِىَ فَعَلَيْهَا ۚ
وَمَآ أَنَا۠ عَلَيْكُم بِحَفِيظٍ ﴿١٠٤﴾
وَكَذَٰلِكَ نُصَرِّفُ ٱلْءَايَٰتِ وَلِيَقُولُوا۟
دَرَسْتَ وَلِنُبَيِّنَهُۥ لِقَوْمٍ يَعْلَمُونَ ﴿١٠٥﴾
ٱتَّبِعْ مَآ أُوحِىَ إِلَيْكَ مِن رَّبِّكَ ۖ لَآ إِلَٰهَ
إِلَّا هُوَ ۖ وَأَعْرِضْ عَنِ ٱلْمُشْرِكِينَ ﴿١٠٦﴾
وَلَوْ شَآءَ ٱللَّهُ مَآ أَشْرَكُوا۟ ۗ وَمَا
جَعَلْنَٰكَ عَلَيْهِمْ حَفِيظًا ۖ وَمَآ أَنتَ
عَلَيْهِم بِوَكِيلٍ ﴿١٠٧﴾
وَلَا تَسُبُّوا۟ ٱلَّذِينَ يَدْعُونَ مِن دُونِ
ٱللَّهِ فَيَسُبُّوا۟ ٱللَّهَ عَدْوًۢا بِغَيْرِ عِلْمٍ ۗ
كَذَٰلِكَ زَيَّنَّا لِكُلِّ أُمَّةٍ عَمَلَهُمْ
ثُمَّ إِلَىٰ رَبِّهِم مَّرْجِعُهُمْ فَيُنَبِّئُهُم
بِمَا كَانُوا۟ يَعْمَلُونَ ﴿١٠٨﴾
وَأَقْسَمُوا۟ بِٱللَّهِ جَهْدَ أَيْمَٰنِهِمْ لَئِن
جَآءَتْهُمْ ءَايَةٌ لَّيُؤْمِنُنَّ بِهَا ۚ قُلْ
إِنَّمَا ٱلْءَايَٰتُ عِندَ ٱللَّهِ ۖ وَمَا يُشْعِرُكُمْ
أَنَّهَآ إِذَا جَآءَتْ لَا يُؤْمِنُونَ ﴿١٠٩﴾
وَنُقَلِّبُ أَفْـِٔدَتَهُمْ وَأَبْصَٰرَهُمْ كَمَا لَمْ
يُؤْمِنُوا۟ بِهِۦٓ أَوَّلَ مَرَّةٍ وَنَذَرُهُمْ فِى

Ikhfa اخفاء · Ghunna غنّہ · Ikhfa Meem Saakin اخفاء میم ساکن · Idghaam ادغام · Qalqala قلقلہ · Qalb قلب · Idghaam Meem Saakin ادغام میم ساکن

English	Transliteration	Arabic
in their trespasses, to wander in distraction.	ṭughyaanihim ya'mahoon. **(Section 13)**	طُغْيَانِهِمْ يَعْمَهُونَ ١١٠ ع
111. Even if We sent angels to them, and the dead spoke to them, and We gathered together all things before their very eyes, they are not the ones to believe, unless it is in Allah's plan. But most of them ignore (the truth).	111. Wa law annanaa nazzalnaaa ilayhimul-malaaa'ikata wa kallamahumul-mawtaa wa ḥasharnaa 'alayhim kulla shay'in qubulam-maa kaanoo liyu'minooo illaaa añy-yashaaa'al-laahu wa laakinna aks̲arahum yajhaloon.	وَلَوْ أَنَّنَا نَزَّلْنَا إِلَيْهِمُ الْمَلَٰٓئِكَةَ وَكَلَّمَهُمُ الْمَوْتَىٰ وَحَشَرْنَا عَلَيْهِمْ كُلَّ شَيْءٍ قُبُلًا مَّا كَانُوا لِيُؤْمِنُوٓا إِلَّآ أَن يَشَآءَ اللَّهُ وَلَٰكِنَّ أَكْثَرَهُمْ يَجْهَلُونَ ١١١
112. Likewise, We made for every Messenger an enemy, Satan among men and jinns, inspiring each other with flowery discourses by way of deception. If your Lord had so planned,they would not have done it: so leave them and their inventions alone.	112. Wa kaẕaalika ja'alnaa likulli Nabiyyin 'aduwwan Shayaaṭeenal-insi waljinni yooḥee ba'ḍuhum ilaa ba'ḍin zukhrufal-qawli ghurooraa; wa law shaaa'a Rabbuka maa fa'aloohu faẕarhum wa maa yaftaroon.	وَكَذَٰلِكَ جَعَلْنَا لِكُلِّ نَبِيٍّ عَدُوًّا شَيَٰطِينَ الْإِنسِ وَالْجِنِّ يُوحِي بَعْضُهُمْ إِلَىٰ بَعْضٍ زُخْرُفَ الْقَوْلِ غُرُورًا ۚ وَلَوْ شَآءَ رَبُّكَ مَا فَعَلُوهُ فَذَرْهُمْ وَمَا يَفْتَرُونَ ١١٢
113. To such (deceit) let the hearts of those incline, who have no faith in the Hereafter: let them delight in it, and let them earn from it what they may.	113. Wa litaṣghaaa ilayhi af'idatul-laẕeena laa yu'minoona bil-Aakhirati wa liyarḍawhu wa liyaqtarifoo maa hum muqtarifoon.	وَلِتَصْغَىٰٓ إِلَيْهِ أَفْـِٔدَةُ الَّذِينَ لَا يُؤْمِنُونَ بِالْآخِرَةِ وَلِيَرْضَوْهُ وَلِيَقْتَرِفُوا مَا هُم مُّقْتَرِفُونَ ١١٣
114. Say: "Shall I seek for judge other than Allah? - when He it is Who has sent unto you the Book, explained in detail." They know full well, to whom We have given the Book, that it has been sent down from your Lord in truth. Never be then of those who doubt.	114. Afaghayral-laahi abtaghee ḥakamañw-wa Huwal-laẕee anzala ilaykumul-Kitaaba mufaṣṣalaa; wallaẕeena aataynaahumul-Kitaaba ya'lamoona annahoo munazzalum-mir-Rabbika bilḥaqqi falaa takoonanna minal-mumtareen.	أَفَغَيْرَ اللَّهِ أَبْتَغِي حَكَمًا وَهُوَ الَّذِيٓ أَنزَلَ إِلَيْكُمُ الْكِتَٰبَ مُفَصَّلًا ۚ وَالَّذِينَ آتَيْنَٰهُمُ الْكِتَٰبَ يَعْلَمُونَ أَنَّهُ مُنَزَّلٌ مِّن رَّبِّكَ بِالْحَقِّ فَلَا تَكُونَنَّ مِنَ الْمُمْتَرِينَ ١١٤
115. The Word of your Lord finds its fulfilment in truth and in justice: None can change His Words: for He is the one who hears and knows all.	115. Wa tammat Kalimatu Rabbika ṣidqañw-wa 'adlaa; laa mubaddila li-Kalimaatih; wa Huwas-Samee'ul-'Aleem.	وَتَمَّتْ كَلِمَتُ رَبِّكَ صِدْقًا وَّ عَدْلًا ۚ لَّا مُبَدِّلَ لِكَلِمَٰتِهِ ۚ وَهُوَ السَّمِيعُ الْعَلِيمُ ١١٥
116. Were you to follow the common run of those on earth, they will lead you away from the Way of Allah. They follow nothing but conjecture: they do nothing but lie.	116. Wa in tuṭi' aks̲ara man fil-arḍi yuḍillooka 'an sabeelil-laah; iñy-yattabi'oona illaẓ-ẓanna wa in hum illaa yakhruṣoon.	وَإِن تُطِعْ أَكْثَرَ مَن فِي الْأَرْضِ يُضِلُّوكَ عَن سَبِيلِ اللَّهِ ۚ إِن يَتَّبِعُونَ إِلَّا الظَّنَّ وَإِنْ هُمْ إِلَّا يَخْرُصُونَ ١١٦
117. Your Lord knows best who strays	117. Inna Rabbaka Huwa a'lamu mañy-yaḍillu	إِنَّ رَبَّكَ هُوَ أَعْلَمُ مَن يَضِلُّ

Ikhfa اخفاء · Ghunna غنّہ · Ikhfa Meem Saakin اخفاء میم ساکن · Idghaam ادغام · Qalqala قلقلہ · Qalb قلب · Idghaam Meem Saakin ادغام میم ساکن

from His Way: He knows best who they are that receive His guidance.

118. So eat of (meats) on which Allah's name has been pronounced, if you have faith in His Signs.

119. Why should you not eat of (meats) on which Allah's name has been pronounced, when He has explained to you in detail what is forbidden to you - except under compulsion of necessity? But many do mislead (men) by their appetites unchecked by knowledge. Your Lord knows best those who transgress.

120. Eschew all sin, open or secret: those who earn sin will get due recompense for their "earnings."

121. Do not eat of (meats) on which Allah's name has not been pronounced: that would be impiety. But the evil ones ever inspire their friends to contend with you if you were to obey them, you would indeed be Pagans.

122. Can he who was dead, to whom We gave life, and a light whereby he can walk amongst men, be like him who is in the depths of darkness, from which he can never come out? Thus to those without Faith their own deeds seem pleasing.

123. Thus have We placed leaders in every town, its wicked men, to plot (and burrow) therein: but they only plot against their own souls, and they do not perceive it.

124. When there comes to them a Sign (from Allah), they say: "We shall not believe until we receive one (exactly) like those received by Allah's apostles."

'an sabeelihee wa Huwa a'lamu bilmuhtadeen.

118. Fakuloo mimmaa zukirasmul-laahi 'alayhi in kuntum bi-Aayaatihee mu'mineen.

119. Wa maa lakum allaa taåkuloo mimmaa zukirasmul-laahi 'alayhi wa qad faṣṣala lakum maa ḥarrama 'alaykum illaa maḍ-ṭurirtum ilayh; wa inna kaseeral-la-yuḍilloona bi-ahwaaa'ihim bighayri 'ilm; inna Rabbaka Huwa a'lamu bilmu'tadeen.

120. Wa zaroo zaahiral-ismi wa baaṭinah; innal-lazeena yaksiboonal-isma sa-yujzawna bimaa kaanoo yaqtarifoon.

121. Wa laa taåkuloo mimmaa lam yuzkaris-mullaahi 'alayhi wa innahoo lafisq; wa innash-Shayaaṭeena la-yooḥoona ilaaa awliyaaa'ihim liyujaadilookum wa in aṭa'tumoohum innakum lamushrikoon. **(Section 14)**

122. Awa man kaana maytan fa-aḥyaynaahu wa ja'alnaa lahoo nooraňy-yamshee bihee fin-naasi kamam-masaluhoo fiz-zulumaati laysa bikhaarijim-minhaa; kazaalika zuyyina lilkaafireena maa kaanoo ya'maloon.

123. Wa kazaalika ja'alnaa fee kulli qaryatin akaabira mujrimeehaa liyamkuroo feehaa wa maa yamkuroona illaa bi-anfusihim wa maa yash'uroon.

124. Wa izaa jaaa'athum Aayatun qaaloo lan nu'mina ḥattaa nu'taa misla maaa ootiya Rusulul-laah;

عَن سَبِيلِهِۦ ۖ وَهُوَ أَعْلَمُ بِٱلْمُهْتَدِينَ ﴿١١٧﴾
فَكُلُوا۟ مِمَّا ذُكِرَ ٱسْمُ ٱللَّهِ عَلَيْهِ إِن
كُنتُم بِـَٔايَٰتِهِۦ مُؤْمِنِينَ ﴿١١٨﴾
وَمَا لَكُمْ أَلَّا تَأْكُلُوا۟ مِمَّا ذُكِرَ ٱسْمُ
ٱللَّهِ عَلَيْهِ وَقَدْ فَصَّلَ لَكُم مَّا حَرَّمَ
عَلَيْكُمْ إِلَّا مَا ٱضْطُرِرْتُمْ إِلَيْهِ ۗ
وَإِنَّ كَثِيرًا لَّيُضِلُّونَ بِأَهْوَآئِهِم
بِغَيْرِ عِلْمٍ ۗ إِنَّ رَبَّكَ هُوَ أَعْلَمُ
بِٱلْمُعْتَدِينَ ﴿١١٩﴾
وَذَرُوا۟ ظَٰهِرَ ٱلْإِثْمِ وَبَاطِنَهُۥٓ ۚ إِنَّ
ٱلَّذِينَ يَكْسِبُونَ ٱلْإِثْمَ سَيُجْزَوْنَ
بِمَا كَانُوا۟ يَقْتَرِفُونَ ﴿١٢٠﴾
وَلَا تَأْكُلُوا۟ مِمَّا لَمْ يُذْكَرِ ٱسْمُ ٱللَّهِ
عَلَيْهِ وَإِنَّهُۥ لَفِسْقٌ ۗ وَإِنَّ ٱلشَّيَٰطِينَ
لَيُوحُونَ إِلَىٰٓ أَوْلِيَآئِهِمْ لِيُجَٰدِلُوكُمْ ۖ
وَإِنْ أَطَعْتُمُوهُمْ إِنَّكُمْ لَمُشْرِكُونَ ﴿١٢١﴾ ع ١٤
أَوَمَن كَانَ مَيْتًا فَأَحْيَيْنَٰهُ وَجَعَلْنَا
لَهُۥ نُورًا يَمْشِى بِهِۦ فِى ٱلنَّاسِ كَمَن
مَّثَلُهُۥ فِى ٱلظُّلُمَٰتِ لَيْسَ بِخَارِجٍ
مِّنْهَا ۚ كَذَٰلِكَ زُيِّنَ لِلْكَٰفِرِينَ مَا
كَانُوا۟ يَعْمَلُونَ ﴿١٢٢﴾
وَكَذَٰلِكَ جَعَلْنَا فِى كُلِّ قَرْيَةٍ أَكَٰبِرَ
مُجْرِمِيهَا لِيَمْكُرُوا۟ فِيهَا ۖ وَمَا
يَمْكُرُونَ إِلَّا بِأَنفُسِهِمْ وَمَا يَشْعُرُونَ ﴿١٢٣﴾
وَإِذَا جَآءَتْهُمْ ءَايَةٌ قَالُوا۟ لَن نُّؤْمِنَ
حَتَّىٰ نُؤْتَىٰ مِثْلَ مَآ أُوتِىَ رُسُلُ ٱللَّهِ ۘ وقف لازم وقف منزل

Ikhfa اخفاء | Ghunna غُنّہ | Ikhfa Meem Saakin اخفاء میم ساکن | Idghaam ادغام | Qalqala قلقلہ | Qalb قلب | Idghaam Meem Saakin ادغام میم ساکن

Allah knows best where (and how) to carry out His mission. Soon will the wicked be overtaken by humiliation before Allah, and a severe punishment, for all their plots.

Allaahu a'lamu ḥaysu yaj'alu Risaalatah; sa-yuṣeebul-lazeena ajramoo ṣaghaarun 'indal-laahi wa 'azaabun shadeedum bimaa kaanoo yamkuroon.

ٱللَّهُ أَعْلَمُ حَيْثُ يَجْعَلُ رِسَالَتَهُۥ سَيُصِيبُ ٱلَّذِينَ أَجْرَمُوا۟ صَغَارٌ عِندَ ٱللَّهِ وَعَذَابٌ شَدِيدٌۢ بِمَا كَانُوا۟ يَمْكُرُونَ ﴿١٢٤﴾

125. Those whom Allah (in His Plan) wills to guide,- He opens their breast to Islam; those whom He wills to leave straying,- He makes their breast close and constricted, as if they had to climb up to the skies: thus Allah (heaps) the Chastisement on those who refuse to believe.

125. Famañy-yuridil-laahu añy-yahdiyahoo yashraḥ ṣadrahoo lil-Islaami wa mañy-yurid añy-yuḍillahoo yaj'al ṣadrahoo ḍayyiqan ḥarajan ka-annamaa yaṣṣa'-'adu fis-samaaa'; kazaalika yaj'alul-laahur-rijsa 'alal-lazeena laa yu'minoon.

فَمَن يُرِدِ ٱللَّهُ أَن يَهْدِيَهُۥ يَشْرَحْ صَدْرَهُۥ لِلْإِسْلَـٰمِ ۖ وَمَن يُرِدْ أَن يُضِلَّهُۥ يَجْعَلْ صَدْرَهُۥ ضَيِّقًا حَرَجًا كَأَنَّمَا يَصَّعَّدُ فِى ٱلسَّمَآءِ ۚ كَذَٰلِكَ يَجْعَلُ ٱللَّهُ ٱلرِّجْسَ عَلَى ٱلَّذِينَ لَا يُؤْمِنُونَ ﴿١٢٥﴾

126. This is the Way of your Lord, leading straight: We have detailed the Signs for those who receive admonition.

126. Wa haazaa Ṣiraaṭu Rabbika Mustaqeemaa; qad faṣṣalnal-Aayaati liqawmiñy-yazzakkaroon.

وَهَـٰذَا صِرَٰطُ رَبِّكَ مُسْتَقِيمًا ۗ قَدْ فَصَّلْنَا ٱلْـَٔايَـٰتِ لِقَوْمٍ يَذَّكَّرُونَ ﴿١٢٦﴾

127. For them will be a Home of peace in the presence of their Lord: He will be their friend, because they practised (righteousness).

127. Lahum daarus-salaami 'inda Rabbihim wa Huwa waliyyuhum bimaa kaanoo ya'maloon.

۞ لَهُمْ دَارُ ٱلسَّلَـٰمِ عِندَ رَبِّهِمْ ۖ وَهُوَ وَلِيُّهُم بِمَا كَانُوا۟ يَعْمَلُونَ ﴿١٢٧﴾

128. One day He will gather them all together, (and say): "O you assembly of Jinns! much (toll) did you take of men." Their friends amongst men will say: "Our Lord! we made profit from each other: but (alas!) we reached our term - which you appointed for us." He will say: "The Fire be your dwelling-place: you will dwell therein for ever, except as Allah wills." for your Lord is full of wisdom and knowledge.

128. Wa Yamwa yaḥshuruhum jamee'añy yaa ma'sharal-jinni qadistaksartum minal-insi wa qaala awliyaaa'uhum minal-insi Rabbanas-tamta'a ba'ḍunaa biba'ḍiñw-wa balaghnaaa ajalanal-lazeee ajjalta lanaa; qaalan-Naaru maswaakum khaalideena feehaaa illaa maa shaaa'allaah; inna Rabbaka Ḥakeemun 'Aleem.

وَيَوْمَ يَحْشُرُهُمْ جَمِيعًا يَـٰمَعْشَرَ ٱلْجِنِّ قَدِ ٱسْتَكْثَرْتُم مِّنَ ٱلْإِنسِ ۖ وَقَالَ أَوْلِيَآؤُهُم مِّنَ ٱلْإِنسِ رَبَّنَا ٱسْتَمْتَعَ بَعْضُنَا بِبَعْضٍ وَبَلَغْنَآ أَجَلَنَا ٱلَّذِىٓ أَجَّلْتَ لَنَا ۚ قَالَ ٱلنَّارُ مَثْوَىٰكُمْ خَـٰلِدِينَ فِيهَآ إِلَّا مَا شَآءَ ٱللَّهُ ۗ إِنَّ رَبَّكَ حَكِيمٌ عَلِيمٌ ﴿١٢٨﴾

129. Thus do we make the wrong-doers turn to each other, because of what they earn.

129. Wa kazaalika nuwallee ba'ḍaẓ-ẓaalimeena ba'ḍam bimaa kaanoo yaksiboon.

(Section 15)

وَكَذَٰلِكَ نُوَلِّى بَعْضَ ٱلظَّـٰلِمِينَ بَعْضًۢا بِمَا كَانُوا۟ يَكْسِبُونَ ﴿١٢٩﴾ ١٥ ع ٨ ٢

130. "O you assembly of Jinns and men! did not the Messengers come to you from amongst you, setting forth unto you My Signs, and warning you of the meeting of this Day of yours?"

130. Yaa ma'sharal-jinni wal-insi alam yaåtikum Rusulum-minkum yaqussoona 'alaykum Aayaatee wa yunziroonakum liqaaa'a Yawmikum

يَـٰمَعْشَرَ ٱلْجِنِّ وَٱلْإِنسِ أَلَمْ يَأْتِكُمْ رُسُلٌ مِّنكُمْ يَقُصُّونَ عَلَيْكُمْ ءَايَـٰتِى وَيُنذِرُونَكُمْ لِقَآءَ يَوْمِكُمْ

Ikhfa اخفاء | Ghunna غنّہ | Ikhfa Meem Saakin اخفاء میم ساکن | Idghaam ادغام | Qalqala قلقلہ | Qalb قلب | Idghaam Meem Saakin ادغام میم ساکن

They will say: "We bear witness against ourselves." It was the life of this world that deceived them. So against themselves will they bear witness that they rejected Faith.

131. (The apostles were sent) thus, for your Lord would not destroy for their wrong-doing men's habitations whilst their occupants were unwarned.

132. To all are degrees (or ranks) according to their deeds: for your Lord is not unmindful of anything that they do.

133. Your Lord is Self-sufficient, full of Mercy: if it were His will, He could destroy you, and in your place appoint whom He will as your successors, even as He raised you up from the posterity of other people.

134. All that has been promised unto you will come to pass: nor can you frustrate it (in the least bit).

135. Say: "O my people! Do whatever you can: I will do (my part): soon will you know who it is whose end will be (best) in the Hereafter: certain it is that the wrong- doers will not prosper."

136. Out of what Allah has produced in abundance in tilth and in cattle, they assigned Him a share: they say, according to their fancies: "This is for Allah, and this" - for our "partners"! but the share of their "partners" does not reach Allah, whilst the share of Allah reaches their "partners" ! evil (and unjust) is their assignment!

137. Even so, in the eyes of most of the pagans, their "partners" made alluring the slaughter of their children, in order to lead them to their own destruction, and cause confusion in their religion. If Allah had willed,

haaẕaa; qaaloo shahidnaa 'alaaa anfusinaa wa gharrat-humul-ḥayaatud-dunyaa wa shahidoo 'alaaa anfusihim annahum kaanoo kaafireen.

131. Ẕaalika al-lam yakur-Rabbuka muhlikal-quraa biẓulmiñw-wa ahluhaa ghaa-filoon.

132. Wa likullin darajaatum-mimmaa 'amiloo; wa maa Rabbuka bighaafilin 'ammaa ya'maloon.

133. Wa Rabbukal-ghaniyyu zur-raḥmah; iñy-yashaå yuẕ-hibkum wa yastakhlif mim ba'dikum maa yashaaa'u kamaaa ansha-akum min ẕurriyyati qawmin aakhareen.

134. Inna maa too'adoona la-aatiñw-wa maaa antum bimu'jizeen.

135. Qul yaa qawmi'-maloo 'alaa makaanatikum innee 'aamilun fasawfa ta'lamoona man takoonu lahoo 'aaqibatud-daar; innahoo laa yufliḥuẓ-ẓaalimoon.

136. Wa ja'aloo lillaahi mimmaa ẕara-a minal-ḥarsi walan'aami naṣeeban faqaaloo haaẕaa lillaahi biza'mihim wa haaẕaa lishurakaaa'inaa famaa kaana lishurakaaa'ihim falaa yaṣilu ilal-laahi wa maa kaana lillaahi fahuwa yaṣilu ilaa shurakaaa'ihim; saaa'a maa yaḥkumoon.

137. Wa kaẕaalika zayyana likaṡeerim-minal-mushrikeena qatla awlaadihim shura-kaaa'uhum liyurdoohum wa liyalbisoo 'alayhim deenahum wa law shaaa-'al-

هٰذَا ؕ قَالُوْا شَهِدْنَا عَلٰٓى اَنْفُسِنَا
وَغَرَّتْهُمُ الْحَيٰوةُ الدُّنْيَا وَشَهِدُوْا
عَلٰٓى اَنْفُسِهِمْ اَنَّهُمْ كَانُوْا كٰفِرِيْنَ ﴿١٣٠﴾
ذٰلِكَ اَنْ لَّمْ يَكُنْ رَّبُّكَ مُهْلِكَ الْقُرٰى
بِظُلْمٍ وَّاَهْلُهَا غٰفِلُوْنَ ﴿١٣١﴾
وَلِكُلٍّ دَرَجٰتٌ مِّمَّا عَمِلُوْا ؕ وَمَا
رَبُّكَ بِغَافِلٍ عَمَّا يَعْمَلُوْنَ ﴿١٣٢﴾
وَرَبُّكَ الْغَنِيُّ ذُو الرَّحْمَةِ ؕ اِنْ يَّشَاْ
يُذْهِبْكُمْ وَيَسْتَخْلِفْ مِنْ بَعْدِكُمْ
مَّا يَشَآءُ كَمَآ اَنْشَاَكُمْ مِّنْ ذُرِّيَّةِ
قَوْمٍ اٰخَرِيْنَ ﴿١٣٣﴾
اِنَّ مَا تُوْعَدُوْنَ لَاٰتٍ ۙ وَّمَآ اَنْتُمْ
بِمُعْجِزِيْنَ ﴿١٣٤﴾
قُلْ يٰقَوْمِ اعْمَلُوْا عَلٰى مَكَانَتِكُمْ
اِنِّيْ عَامِلٌ ۚ فَسَوْفَ تَعْلَمُوْنَ ۙ مَنْ
تَكُوْنُ لَهٗ عَاقِبَةُ الدَّارِ ؕ اِنَّهٗ
لَا يُفْلِحُ الظّٰلِمُوْنَ ﴿١٣٥﴾
وَجَعَلُوْا لِلّٰهِ مِمَّا ذَرَاَ مِنَ الْحَرْثِ
وَالْاَنْعَامِ نَصِيْبًا فَقَالُوْا هٰذَا
لِلّٰهِ بِزَعْمِهِمْ وَهٰذَا لِشُرَكَآئِنَا ۚ فَمَا
كَانَ لِشُرَكَآئِهِمْ فَلَا يَصِلُ اِلَى
اللّٰهِ ۚ وَمَا كَانَ لِلّٰهِ فَهُوَ يَصِلُ اِلٰى
شُرَكَآئِهِمْ ؕ سَآءَ مَا يَحْكُمُوْنَ ﴿١٣٦﴾
وَكَذٰلِكَ زَيَّنَ لِكَثِيْرٍ مِّنَ الْمُشْرِكِيْنَ
قَتْلَ اَوْلَادِهِمْ شُرَكَآؤُهُمْ لِيُرْدُوْهُمْ
وَلِيَلْبِسُوْا عَلَيْهِمْ دِيْنَهُمْ ؕ وَلَوْ شَآءَ

they would not have done so: But leave them and their inventions alone.

138. And they say that such and such cattle and crops are taboo, and none should eat of them except those whom - so they say - We wish; further, there are cattle forbidden to yoke or burden, and cattle on which, (at slaughter), the name of Allah is not pronounced; - inventions against Allah's name: soon will He requite them for their inventions.

139. They say: "What is in the wombs of such and such cattle is specially reserved (for food) for our men, and forbidden to our women; but if it is still-born, then all have shares therein. For their (false) attribution (of superstitions to Allah), He will soon punish them: for He is full of wisdom and knowledge.

140. Lost are those who slay their children, from folly, without knowledge, and forbid food which Allah has provided for them, inventing (lies) against Allah. They have indeed gone astray and heeded no guidance.

141. It is He Who produces gardens, with trellises and without, and dates, and tilth with produce of all kinds, and olives and pomegranates, similar (in kind) and different (in variety): eat of their fruit in their season, but render the dues that are proper on the day that the harvest is gathered. But waste not by excess: for Allah does not loves the wasters.

142. Of the cattle are some for burden and some for meat: eat what Allah has provided for you, and follow not the footsteps of Satan: for he is to you an avowed enemy.

143. (Take) eight (head of cattle) in (four) pairs: of sheep a pair, and of goats a pair; say, has He forbidden the two males,

laahu maa fa'aloohu fazarhum wa maa yaftaroon.

138. Wa qaaloo haaziheee an'aamuñw-wa ḥarsun ḥijrun laa yaṭ'amuhaaa illaa man nashaaa'u biza'mihim wa an'aamun ḥurrimat ẓuhooruhaa wa an'aamul-laa yazkuroonas-mal-laahi 'alayhaf-tiraaa'an 'alayh; sa-yajzeehim bimaa kaanoo yaftaroon.

139. Wa qaaloo maa fee buṭooni haazihil-an'aami khaaliṣatul-lizukoorinaa wa muḥarramun 'alaaa azwaajinaa wa iñy-yakum maytatan fahum feehi shurakaaa'; sa-yajzeehim waṣfahum; innahoo Ḥakeemun 'Aleem.

140. Qad khasiral-lazeena qatalooo awlaadahum safaham bighayri 'ilmiñw-wa ḥarramoo maa razaqahumul-laahuf-tiraaa'an 'alal-laah; qad ḍalloo wa maa kaanoo muhtadeen.

(Section 16)

141. Wa Huwal-lazeee ansha-a jannaatim-ma'rooshaatiñw-wa ghayra ma'rooshaatiñw-wan-nakhla wazzar'a mukhtalifan ukuluhoo wazzaytoona warrum-maana mutashaabihañw-wa ghayra mutashaabih; kuloo min samariheee izaaa asmara wa aatoo ḥaqqahoo yawma ḥaṣaa-dihee wa laa tusrifoo; innahoo laa yuḥibbul-musrifeen.

142. Wa minal-an'aami ḥamoolatañw-wa farshaa; kuloo mimmaa razaqakumul-laahu wa laa tattabi'oo khuṭuwaatish-Shayṭaan; innahoo lakum 'aduwwum-mubeen.

143. Samaaniyata azwaaj(im) minaḍ-ḍaånis-nayni wa minal-ma'zis-nayn; qul 'aaazzaka-rayni

اللّٰهُ مَا فَعَلُوْهُ فَذَرْهُمْ وَمَا يَفْتَرُوْنَ ﴿١٣٧﴾
وَقَالُوْا هٰذِهٖٓ اَنْعَامٌ وَّحَرْثٌ حِجْرٌ ۖ
لَّا يَطْعَمُهَآ اِلَّا مَنْ نَّشَآءُ بِزَعْمِهِمْ
وَاَنْعَامٌ حُرِّمَتْ ظُهُوْرُهَا وَاَنْعَامٌ
لَّا يَذْكُرُوْنَ اسْمَ اللّٰهِ عَلَيْهَا افْتِرَآءً
عَلَيْهِ ۚ سَيَجْزِيْهِمْ بِمَا كَانُوْا يَفْتَرُوْنَ ﴿١٣٨﴾
وَقَالُوْا مَا فِيْ بُطُوْنِ هٰذِهِ الْاَنْعَامِ
خَالِصَةٌ لِّذُكُوْرِنَا وَمُحَرَّمٌ عَلٰٓى
اَزْوَاجِنَا ۚ وَاِنْ يَّكُنْ مَّيْتَةً فَهُمْ
فِيْهِ شُرَكَآءُ ۚ سَيَجْزِيْهِمْ وَصْفَهُمْ ۚ
اِنَّهٗ حَكِيْمٌ عَلِيْمٌ ﴿١٣٩﴾
قَدْ خَسِرَ الَّذِيْنَ قَتَلُوْٓا اَوْلَادَهُمْ
سَفَهًاۢ بِغَيْرِ عِلْمٍ وَّحَرَّمُوْا مَا
رَزَقَهُمُ اللّٰهُ افْتِرَآءً عَلَى اللّٰهِ ۚ قَدْ
ضَلُّوْا وَمَا كَانُوْا مُهْتَدِيْنَ ﴿١٤٠﴾ ع
وَهُوَ الَّذِيْٓ اَنْشَاَ جَنّٰتٍ مَّعْرُوْشٰتٍ وَّغَيْرَ
مَعْرُوْشٰتٍ وَّالنَّخْلَ وَالزَّرْعَ مُخْتَلِفًا
اُكُلُهٗ وَالزَّيْتُوْنَ وَالرُّمَّانَ مُتَشَابِهًا
وَّغَيْرَ مُتَشَابِهٍ ۚ كُلُوْا مِنْ ثَمَرِهٖٓ اِذَآ
اَثْمَرَ وَاٰتُوْا حَقَّهٗ يَوْمَ حَصَادِهٖ ۖ وَلَا
تُسْرِفُوْا ۚ اِنَّهٗ لَا يُحِبُّ الْمُسْرِفِيْنَ ﴿١٤١﴾
وَمِنَ الْاَنْعَامِ حَمُوْلَةً وَّفَرْشًا ۚ كُلُوْا
مِمَّا رَزَقَكُمُ اللّٰهُ وَلَا تَتَّبِعُوْا خُطُوٰتِ
الشَّيْطٰنِ ۚ اِنَّهٗ لَكُمْ عَدُوٌّ مُّبِيْنٌ ﴿١٤٢﴾
ثَمٰنِيَةَ اَزْوَاجٍ ۚ مِنَ الضَّاْنِ اثْنَيْنِ
وَمِنَ الْمَعْزِ اثْنَيْنِ ۚ قُلْ آٰلذَّكَرَيْنِ

الربع

حَرَّمَ أَمِ الْأُنثَيَيْنِ أَمَّا اشْتَمَلَتْ
عَلَيْهِ أَرْحَامُ الْأُنثَيَيْنِ ۖ نَبِّئُونِي
بِعِلْمٍ إِن كُنتُمْ صَادِقِينَ ﴿١٤٣﴾

ḥarrama amil-unsayayni ammash-tamalat 'alayhi arḥaamul-unsayayni nabbi-'oonee bi'ilmin in kuntum ṣaadiqeen.

or the two females, or (the young) which the wombs of the two females enclose? Tell me with knowledge if you are truthful:

وَمِنَ الْإِبِلِ اثْنَيْنِ وَمِنَ الْبَقَرِ
اثْنَيْنِ ۗ قُلْ آلذَّكَرَيْنِ حَرَّمَ أَمِ
الْأُنثَيَيْنِ أَمَّا اشْتَمَلَتْ عَلَيْهِ
أَرْحَامُ الْأُنثَيَيْنِ ۖ أَمْ كُنتُمْ شُهَدَاءَ
إِذْ وَصَّاكُمُ اللَّهُ بِهَٰذَا ۚ فَمَنْ أَظْلَمُ
مِمَّنِ افْتَرَىٰ عَلَى اللَّهِ كَذِبًا لِّيُضِلَّ
النَّاسَ بِغَيْرِ عِلْمٍ ۗ إِنَّ اللَّهَ لَا
يَهْدِي الْقَوْمَ الظَّالِمِينَ ﴿١٤٤﴾ ع

144. Wa minal-ibilis-nayni wa minal-baqaris-nayn; qul 'aazzakarayni ḥarrama amil-unsayayni ammash-tamalat 'alayhi arḥaamul-unsayayni am kuntum shuhadaaa'a iz waṣṣaakumul-laahu bihaazaa; faman aẓlamu mimmanif-taraa 'alal-laahi kazibal-liyuḍillan-naasa bighayri 'ilm; innal-laaha laa yahdil-qawmaẓ-ẓaalimeen.

(Section 17)

144. Of camels a pair, and oxen a pair; say, has He forbidden the two males, or the two females, or (the young) which the wombs of the two females enclose? - Were you present when Allah ordered you such a thing? But who does more wrong than one who invents a lie against Allah, to lead astray men without knowledge? For Allah guides not people who do wrong.

قُل لَّا أَجِدُ فِي مَا أُوحِيَ إِلَيَّ مُحَرَّمًا
عَلَىٰ طَاعِمٍ يَطْعَمُهُ إِلَّا أَن يَكُونَ
مَيْتَةً أَوْ دَمًا مَّسْفُوحًا أَوْ لَحْمَ
خِنزِيرٍ فَإِنَّهُ رِجْسٌ أَوْ فِسْقًا أُهِلَّ
لِغَيْرِ اللَّهِ بِهِ ۚ فَمَنِ اضْطُرَّ غَيْرَ بَاغٍ
وَلَا عَادٍ فَإِنَّ رَبَّكَ غَفُورٌ رَّحِيمٌ ﴿١٤٥﴾

145. Qul laaa ajidu fee maaa ooḥiya ilayya muḥarraman 'alaa ṭaa'imiñy-yaṭ'amuhooo illaaa añy-yakoona maytatan aw damam-masfooḥan aw laḥma khinzeerin fa-innahoo rijsun aw fisqan uhilla lighayril-laahi bih; famaniḍ-ṭurra ghayra baa-ghiñw-wa laa 'aadin fa-inna Rabbaka Ghafoorur-Raḥeem.

145. Say: "I do not find in the Message received by me by inspiration any (meat) forbidden to be eaten by one who wishes to eat it, unless it be dead meat, or blood poured forth, or the flesh of swine,- for it is an abomination - or, what is impious, (meat) on which a name has been invoked, other than Allah's". But (even so), if a person is forced by necessity, without wilful disobedience, nor transgressing due limits,- your Lord is Oft-forgiving, Most Merciful.

وَعَلَى الَّذِينَ هَادُوا حَرَّمْنَا كُلَّ
ذِي ظُفُرٍ ۖ وَمِنَ الْبَقَرِ وَالْغَنَمِ حَرَّمْنَا
عَلَيْهِمْ شُحُومَهُمَا إِلَّا مَا حَمَلَتْ
ظُهُورُهُمَا أَوِ الْحَوَايَا أَوْ مَا اخْتَلَطَ
بِعَظْمٍ ۚ ذَٰلِكَ جَزَيْنَاهُم بِبَغْيِهِمْ ۖ وَإِنَّا
لَصَادِقُونَ ﴿١٤٦﴾

146. Wa 'alal-lazeena haadoo ḥarramnaa kulla zee ẓufuriñw wa minal-baqari walghanami ḥarramnaa 'alayhim shuḥoomahumaaa illaa maa ḥamalat ẓuhooruhumaaa awil-ḥawaayaaa aw makhtalaṭa bi'aẓm; zaalika jazaynaahum bibaghyihim wa innaa laṣaadiqoon.

146. For those who followed the Jewish Law, We forbade every (animal) with undivided hoof, and We forbade them that fat of the ox and the sheep, except what adheres to their backs or their entrails, or is mixed up with a bone: this in recompense for their wilful disobedience: for We are true (in Our ordinances).

فَإِن كَذَّبُوكَ فَقُل رَّبُّكُمْ ذُو رَحْمَةٍ
وَاسِعَةٍ وَلَا يُرَدُّ بَأْسُهُ عَنِ
الْقَوْمِ الْمُجْرِمِينَ ﴿١٤٧﴾

147. Fa-in kazzabooka faqur-Rabbukum zoo raḥmatiñw-waasi'atiñw wa laa yuraddu baåsuhoo 'anil-qawmil-mujrimeen.

147. If they accuse you of falsehood, say: "Your Lord is full of mercy all- embracing; but from people in guilt never will His wrath be turned back.

Ikhfa اخفاء | Ghunna غُنّہ | Ikhfa Meem Saakin اخفاء میم ساکن | Idghaam ادغام | Qalqala قلقلہ | Qalb قلب | Idghaam Meem Saakin ادغام میم ساکن

148. Those who give partners (to Allah) will say: "If Allah had wished, we should not have given partners to Him nor would our fathers; nor should we have had any taboos." So did their ancestors argue falsely, until they tasted of Our wrath. Say: "Have you any (certain) knowledge? If so, produce it before us. You follow nothing but conjecture: you do nothing but lie."

148. Sayaqoolul-lazeena ashrakoo law shaaa'al-laahu maaa ashraknaa wa laaa aabaaa'unaa wa laa ḥarramnaa min shay'; kazaalika kazzabal-lazeena min qablihim ḥattaa zaaqoo baåsanaa; qul hal 'indakum min 'ilmin fatukh-rijoohu lanaa in tattabi'oona illaz-zanna wa in antum illaa takhruṣoon.

سَيَقُولُ الَّذِينَ أَشْرَكُوا لَوْ شَاءَ اللَّهُ مَا أَشْرَكْنَا وَلَا آبَاؤُنَا وَلَا حَرَّمْنَا مِنْ شَيْءٍ ۚ كَذَٰلِكَ كَذَّبَ الَّذِينَ مِنْ قَبْلِهِمْ حَتَّىٰ ذَاقُوا بَأْسَنَا ۗ قُلْ هَلْ عِنْدَكُمْ مِنْ عِلْمٍ فَتُخْرِجُوهُ لَنَا ۖ إِنْ تَتَّبِعُونَ إِلَّا الظَّنَّ وَإِنْ أَنْتُمْ إِلَّا تَخْرُصُونَ ﴿١٤٨﴾

149. Say: "With Allah is the argument that reaches home: if it had been His will, He could indeed have guided you all."

149. Qul falillaahil-ḥujjatul-baalighatu falaw shaaa'a lahadaakum ajma'een.

قُلْ فَلِلَّهِ الْحُجَّةُ الْبَالِغَةُ ۖ فَلَوْ شَاءَ لَهَدَاكُمْ أَجْمَعِينَ ﴿١٤٩﴾

150. Say: "Bring forward your witnesses to prove that Allah forbade you so and so." If they bring such witnesses, you should not be amongst them: nor you should follow the vain desires of such as treat our Signs as falsehoods, and such as do not believe in the Hereafter: for they hold others as equal with their Guardian-Lord.

150. Qul halumma shuha-daaa'akumul-lazeena yash-hadoona annal-laaha ḥarrama haazaa fa-in shahidoo falaa tashhad ma'ahum; wa laa tattabi' ahwaaa'al-lazeena kazzaboo bi-Aayaatinaa wallazeena laa yu'minoona bil-Aakhirati wa hum bi-Rabbihim ya'diloon. **(Section 18)**

قُلْ هَلُمَّ شُهَدَاءَكُمُ الَّذِينَ يَشْهَدُونَ أَنَّ اللَّهَ حَرَّمَ هَٰذَا ۖ فَإِنْ شَهِدُوا فَلَا تَشْهَدْ مَعَهُمْ ۚ وَلَا تَتَّبِعْ أَهْوَاءَ الَّذِينَ كَذَّبُوا بِآيَاتِنَا وَالَّذِينَ لَا يُؤْمِنُونَ بِالْآخِرَةِ وَهُمْ بِرَبِّهِمْ يَعْدِلُونَ ﴿١٥٠﴾ ع

151. Say: "Come, I will rehearse what Allah has (really) prohibited you from": Join not anything as equal with Him; be good to your parents; kill not your children on a plea of want;- We provide sustenance for you and for them;- do not come near to shameful deeds. Whether open or secret; take not life, which Allah has made sacred, except by way of justice and law: thus does He command you, that you may learn wisdom.

151. Qul ta'aalaw atlu maa ḥarrama Rabbukum 'alaykum allaa tushrikoo bihee shay'añw-wa bilwaalidayni iḥsaanañw wa laa taqtulooo awlaadakum min imlaaq; naḥnu narzuqukum wa iyyaahum wa laa taqrabul-fawaaḥisha maa zahara minhaa wa maa baṭana wa laa taqtulun-nafsal-latee ḥarramal-laahu illaa bilḥaqq; zaalikum waṣṣaakum bihee la'allakum ta'qiloon.

قُلْ تَعَالَوْا أَتْلُ مَا حَرَّمَ رَبُّكُمْ عَلَيْكُمْ ۖ أَلَّا تُشْرِكُوا بِهِ شَيْئًا ۖ وَبِالْوَالِدَيْنِ إِحْسَانًا ۖ وَلَا تَقْتُلُوا أَوْلَادَكُمْ مِنْ إِمْلَاقٍ ۖ نَحْنُ نَرْزُقُكُمْ وَإِيَّاهُمْ ۖ وَلَا تَقْرَبُوا الْفَوَاحِشَ مَا ظَهَرَ مِنْهَا وَمَا بَطَنَ ۖ وَلَا تَقْتُلُوا النَّفْسَ الَّتِي حَرَّمَ اللَّهُ إِلَّا بِالْحَقِّ ۚ ذَٰلِكُمْ وَصَّاكُمْ بِهِ لَعَلَّكُمْ تَعْقِلُونَ ﴿١٥١﴾

152. And come not near to the orphan's property, except to improve it, until he attain the age of full strength; give measure and weight with (full) justice;-

152. Wa laa taqraboo maalal-yateemi illaa billatee hiya aḥsanu ḥattaa yablugha ashuddahoo wa awful-kayla walmeezaana bilqisṭi

وَلَا تَقْرَبُوا مَالَ الْيَتِيمِ إِلَّا بِالَّتِي هِيَ أَحْسَنُ حَتَّىٰ يَبْلُغَ أَشُدَّهُ ۖ وَأَوْفُوا الْكَيْلَ وَالْمِيزَانَ بِالْقِسْطِ ۖ

Ikhfa اخفاء | Ghunna غنّہ | Ikhfa Meem Saakin اخفاء میم ساکن | Idghaam ادغام | Qalqala قلقلہ | Qalb قلب | Idghaam Meem Saakin ادغام میم ساکن

no burden do We place on any soul, but that which it can bear;- whenever you speak, speak justly, even if a near relative is concerned; and fulfil the Covenant of Allah: thus He commands you, that you may remember.

laa nukallifu nafsan illaa wus'ahaa wa izaa qultum fa'diloo wa law kaana zaa qurbaa wa bi-'Ahdil-laahi awfoo; zaalikum waṣṣaakum bihee la'allakum tazakkaroon.

لَا نُكَلِّفُ نَفْسًا إِلَّا وُسْعَهَا ۖ وَإِذَا
قُلْتُمْ فَاعْدِلُوا وَلَوْ كَانَ ذَا قُرْبَىٰ ۖ
وَبِعَهْدِ اللَّهِ أَوْفُوا ۚ ذَٰلِكُمْ وَصَّاكُمْ
بِهِ لَعَلَّكُمْ تَذَكَّرُونَ ﴿١٥٢﴾

153. Verily, this is My Way, leading straight: follow it: do not follow (other) paths: they will scatter you about from His (great) path: thus He commands you that you may be righteous.

153. Wa anna haazaa Ṣiraaṭee Mustaqeeman fattabi'oohu wa laa tattabi'us-subula fatafarraqa bikum 'an sabeelih; zaalikum waṣṣaakum bihee la'allakum tattaqoon.

وَأَنَّ هَٰذَا صِرَاطِي مُسْتَقِيمًا
فَاتَّبِعُوهُ ۖ وَلَا تَتَّبِعُوا السُّبُلَ
فَتَفَرَّقَ بِكُمْ عَنْ سَبِيلِهِ ۚ ذَٰلِكُمْ
وَصَّاكُمْ بِهِ لَعَلَّكُمْ تَتَّقُونَ ﴿١٥٣﴾

154. Moreover, We gave Moses the Book, completing (Our favour) to those who would do right, and explained all things in detail,- and a guide and a mercy, that they might believe in the meeting with their Lord.

154. Summa aataynaa Moosal-Kitaaba tamaaman 'alal-lazeee aḥsana wa tafṣeelal-likulli shay'iñw-wa hudañw-wa raḥmatal-la'allahum biliqaaa'i Rabbihim yu'minoon.

(Section 19)

ثُمَّ آتَيْنَا مُوسَى الْكِتَابَ تَمَامًا
عَلَى الَّذِي أَحْسَنَ وَتَفْصِيلًا لِكُلِّ
شَيْءٍ وَهُدًى وَرَحْمَةً لَعَلَّهُمْ بِلِقَاءِ
رَبِّهِمْ يُؤْمِنُونَ ﴿١٥٤﴾

155. And this is a Book which We have revealed as a blessing: so follow it and be righteous, that you may receive mercy:

155. Wa haazaa Kitaabun anzalnaahu Mubaarakun fattabi'oohu wattaqoo la'allakum turḥamoon.

وَهَٰذَا كِتَابٌ أَنْزَلْنَاهُ مُبَارَكٌ
فَاتَّبِعُوهُ وَاتَّقُوا لَعَلَّكُمْ تُرْحَمُونَ ﴿١٥٥﴾

156. Lest you should say: "The Book was sent down to two Peoples before us, and for our part, we remained unacquainted with all that they learned by assiduous study:"

156. An taqoolooo innamaaa unzilal-Kitaabu 'alaa ṭaaa'ifatayni min qablinaa wa in kunnaa 'an diraasatihim laghaafileen.

أَنْ تَقُولُوا إِنَّمَا أُنْزِلَ الْكِتَابُ عَلَىٰ
طَائِفَتَيْنِ مِنْ قَبْلِنَا وَإِنْ كُنَّا
عَنْ دِرَاسَتِهِمْ لَغَافِلِينَ ﴿١٥٦﴾

157. Or lest you should say: "If the Book had only been sent down to us, we should have followed its guidance better than they." Now then has come unto you a Clear (Sign) from your Lord,- and a guide and a mercy: then who could do more wrong than one who rejects Allah's Signs, and turns away therefrom? In good time shall We requite those who turn away from Our Signs, with a dreadful Chastisement, for their turning away.

157. Aw taqooloo law annaaa unzila 'alaynal-Kitaabu lakunnaaa ahdaa minhum; faqad jaaa'akum bayyinatum-mir-Rabbikum wa hudañw-wa raḥmah; faman azlamu mimman kazzaba bi-Aayaatil-laahi wa ṣadafa 'anhaa; sanajzil-lazeena yaṣdifoona 'an Aayaatinaa sooo'al-'azaabi bimaa kaanoo yaṣdifoon.

أَوْ تَقُولُوا لَوْ أَنَّا أُنْزِلَ عَلَيْنَا الْكِتَابُ
لَكُنَّا أَهْدَىٰ مِنْهُمْ ۚ فَقَدْ جَاءَكُمْ
بَيِّنَةٌ مِنْ رَبِّكُمْ وَهُدًى وَرَحْمَةٌ ۚ
فَمَنْ أَظْلَمُ مِمَّنْ كَذَّبَ بِآيَاتِ
اللَّهِ وَصَدَفَ عَنْهَا ۗ سَنَجْزِي الَّذِينَ
يَصْدِفُونَ عَنْ آيَاتِنَا سُوءَ الْعَذَابِ
بِمَا كَانُوا يَصْدِفُونَ ﴿١٥٧﴾

158. Are they waiting to see if the angels come to them, or your Lord (Himself), or

158. Hal yanzuroona illaaa an taåtiyahumul-malaaa'ikatu aw yaåtiya Rabbuka aw yaåtiya

هَلْ يَنْظُرُونَ إِلَّا أَنْ تَأْتِيَهُمُ
الْمَلَائِكَةُ أَوْ يَأْتِيَ رَبُّكَ أَوْ يَأْتِيَ

Ikhfa اخفاء | Ghunna غنّہ | Ikhfa Meem Saakin اخفاءمیم ساکن | Idghaam ادغام | Qalqala قلقلہ | Qalb قلب | Idghaam Meem Saakin ادغام میم ساکن

certain of the Signs of your Lord! the day that certain of the Signs of your Lord do come, no good will it do to a soul to believe in them then, if it believed not before nor earned righteousness through its faith. Say: "Wait you: we too are waiting."

159. As for those who divide their religion and break up into sects, you have no part in them in the least: their affair is with Allah: He will in the end tell them the truth of all that they did.

160. He that does good shall have ten times as much to his credit: He that does evil shall only be recompensed according to his evil: no wrong shall be done to (any of) them.

161. Say: "Verily, my Lord has guided me to a way that is straight,- a religion of right,- the path (trod) by Abraham, the true in faith, and he (certainly) did not join gods with Allah."

162. Say: "Truly, my prayer and my service of sacrifice, my life and my death, are (all) for Allah, the Cherisher of the Worlds:

163. No partner has He: this I am commanded, and I am the first of those who bow to His Will.

164. Say: "Shall I seek for (my) Cherisher other than Allah, when He is the Cherisher of all things (that exist)? Every soul draws the meed of its acts on none but itself: no bearer of burdens can bear the burden of another. Your goal in the end is towards Allah: He will tell you the truth of the things wherein you disputed."

165. It is He Who has made you (His) agents, inheritors of the earth: He has raised you in ranks, some above others:

ba‘ḍu Aayaati Rabbik; Yawma yaåtee ba‘ḍu Aayaati Rabbika laa yanfa‘u nafsan eemaanuhaa lam takun aamanat min qablu aw kasabat feee eemaanihaa khayraa; qulin-taẓirooo innaa muntaẓiroon.

159. Innal-lazeena farraqoo deenahum wa kaanoo shiya‘allasta minhum fee shay'; innamaaa amruhum ilallaahi summa yunabbi'uhum bimaa kaanoo yaf‘aloon.

160. Man jaaa'a bilḥasanati falahoo ‘ashru amsaalihaa wa man jaaa'a bissayyi'ati falaa yujzaaa illaa mislahaa wa hum laa yuẓlamoon.

161. Qul innanee hadaanee Rabbeee ilaa Ṣiraaṭim-Mustaqeemin deenan qiyamam-Millata Ibraaheema Ḥaneefaa; wa maa kaana minal-mushrikeen.

162. Qul inna Ṣalaatee wa nusukee wa maḥyaaya wa mamaatee lillaahi Rabbil ‘aalameen.

163. Laa shareeka lahoo wa bizaalika umirtu wa ana awwalul-muslimeen.

164. Qul aghayral-laahi abghee Rabbañw-wa Huwa Rabbu kulli shay'; wa laa taksibu kullu nafsin illaa ‘alayhaa; wa laa taziru waaziratuñw-wizra ukhraa; summa ilaa Rabbikum marji‘ukum fa-yunabbi'ukum bimaa kuntum feehi takhtalifoon.

165. Wa Huwal-lazee ja‘alakum khalaaa'ifal-arḍi wa rafa‘a ba‘ḍakum fawqa ba‘ḍin darajaatil-

بَعْضُ اٰيٰتِ رَبِّكَ ؕ يَوْمَ يَاْتِيْ بَعْضُ
اٰيٰتِ رَبِّكَ لَا يَنْفَعُ نَفْسًا اِيْمَانُهَا
لَمْ تَكُنْ اٰمَنَتْ مِنْ قَبْلُ اَوْ كَسَبَتْ
فِيْۤ اِيْمَانِهَا خَيْرًا ؕ قُلِ انْتَظِرُوْۤا
اِنَّا مُنْتَظِرُوْنَ ﴿۱۵۸﴾
اِنَّ الَّذِيْنَ فَرَّقُوْا دِيْنَهُمْ وَكَانُوْا
شِيَعًا لَّسْتَ مِنْهُمْ فِيْ شَيْءٍ ؕ اِنَّمَاۤ
اَمْرُهُمْ اِلَى اللّٰهِ ثُمَّ يُنَبِّئُهُمْ بِمَا
كَانُوْا يَفْعَلُوْنَ ﴿۱۵۹﴾
مَنْ جَآءَ بِالْحَسَنَةِ فَلَهٗ عَشْرُ
اَمْثَالِهَا ۚ وَمَنْ جَآءَ بِالسَّيِّئَةِ فَلَا
يُجْزٰۤى اِلَّا مِثْلَهَا وَهُمْ لَا يُظْلَمُوْنَ ﴿۱۶۰﴾
قُلْ اِنَّنِيْ هَدٰىنِيْ رَبِّيْۤ اِلٰى صِرَاطٍ
مُّسْتَقِيْمٍ ۚ دِيْنًا قِيَمًا مِّلَّةَ اِبْرٰهِيْمَ
حَنِيْفًا ۚ وَمَا كَانَ مِنَ الْمُشْرِكِيْنَ ﴿۱۶۱﴾
قُلْ اِنَّ صَلَاتِيْ وَنُسُكِيْ وَمَحْيَايَ
وَمَمَاتِيْ لِلّٰهِ رَبِّ الْعٰلَمِيْنَ ﴿۱۶۲﴾
لَا شَرِيْكَ لَهٗ ۚ وَبِذٰلِكَ اُمِرْتُ
وَاَنَا اَوَّلُ الْمُسْلِمِيْنَ ﴿۱۶۳﴾
قُلْ اَغَيْرَ اللّٰهِ اَبْغِيْ رَبًّا وَّهُوَ رَبُّ
كُلِّ شَيْءٍ ؕ وَلَا تَكْسِبُ كُلُّ
نَفْسٍ اِلَّا عَلَيْهَا ۚ وَلَا تَزِرُ وَازِرَةٌ
وِّزْرَ اُخْرٰى ۚ ثُمَّ اِلٰى رَبِّكُمْ مَّرْجِعُكُمْ
فَيُنَبِّئُكُمْ بِمَا كُنْتُمْ فِيْهِ تَخْتَلِفُوْنَ ﴿۱۶۴﴾
وَهُوَ الَّذِيْ جَعَلَكُمْ خَلٰٓئِفَ الْاَرْضِ
وَرَفَعَ بَعْضَكُمْ فَوْقَ بَعْضٍ دَرَجٰتٍ

Ikhfa اخفاء | Ghunna غنّہ | Ikhfa Meem Saakin اخفاء میم ساکن | Idghaam ادغام | Qalqala قلقلہ | Qalb قلب | Idghaam Meem Saakin ادغام میم ساکن

that He may try you in the gifts He has given you: for your Lord is quick in punishment: He is indeed Oft-forgiving, Most Merciful.

liyabluwakum fee maaa aataakum; inna Rabbaka saree'ul-'iqaab; wa innahoo la-Ghafoorur-Raḥeem. **(Section 20)**

لِّيَبْلُوَكُمْ فِي مَآ ءَاتَىٰكُمْ ۗ إِنَّ رَبَّكَ
سَرِيعُ ٱلْعِقَابِ وَإِنَّهُۥ لَغَفُورٌ
رَّحِيمٌۢ ﴿١٦٥﴾

ٱلنِّصْف

7. The Heights

In the name of Allah, Most Gracious, Most Merciful.

Sûrat al-A'râf–7

(Revealed at Makkah)

Bismillaahir Raḥmaanir Raḥeem

(٧) سُورَةُ ٱلْأَعْرَافِ مَكِّيَّةٌ (٣٩)

بِسْمِ ٱللَّهِ ٱلرَّحْمَٰنِ ٱلرَّحِيمِ

1. *Alif-Lam-Mim-Sad.*

1. Alif-Laaam-Meeem-Ṣaad.

الٓمٓصٓ ﴿١﴾

2. A Book revealed unto you,- So let your heart be oppressed no more by any difficulty on that account,- that with it you might warn (the erring) and teach the Believers).

2. Kitaabun unzila ilayka falaa yakun fee ṣadrika ḥarajum-minhu litunzira bihee wa zikraa lilmu'mineen.

كِتَٰبٌ أُنزِلَ إِلَيْكَ فَلَا يَكُن فِي
صَدْرِكَ حَرَجٌ مِّنْهُ لِتُنذِرَ بِهِۦ
وَذِكْرَىٰ لِلْمُؤْمِنِينَ ﴿٢﴾

3. Follow (O men!) the revelation given unto you from your Lord, and follow not, as friends or protectors, other than Him. Little it is you remember of admonition.

3. Ittabi'oo maaa unzila 'ilaykum mir-Rabbikum wa laa tattabi'oo min dooniheee awliyaaa'; qaleelam-maa tazakkaroon.

ٱتَّبِعُوا۟ مَآ أُنزِلَ إِلَيْكُم مِّن رَّبِّكُمْ
وَلَا تَتَّبِعُوا۟ مِن دُونِهِۦٓ أَوْلِيَآءَ ۗ
قَلِيلًا مَّا تَذَكَّرُونَ ﴿٣﴾

4. How many towns have We destroyed (for their sins)? Our punishment took them on a sudden by night or while they slept for their afternoon rest.

4. Wa kam min qaryatin ahlaknaahaa fajaaa'ahaa baåsunaa bayaatan aw hum qaaa'iloon.

وَكَم مِّن قَرْيَةٍ أَهْلَكْنَٰهَا فَجَآءَهَا
بَأْسُنَا بَيَٰتًا أَوْ هُمْ قَآئِلُونَ ﴿٤﴾

5. When (thus) Our punishment took them, no cry did they utter but this: "Indeed we did wrong."

5. Famaa kaana da'waahum iz jaaa'ahum baåsunaaa illaaa an qaalooo innaa kunnaa ẓaalimeen.

فَمَا كَانَ دَعْوَىٰهُمْ إِذْ جَآءَهُم بَأْسُنَآ
إِلَّآ أَن قَالُوٓا۟ إِنَّا كُنَّا ظَٰلِمِينَ ﴿٥﴾

6. Then shall we question those to whom Our message was sent and those by whom We sent it.

6. Falanas'alannal-lazeena ursila ilayhim wa lanas'alannal-mursaleen.

فَلَنَسْـَٔلَنَّ ٱلَّذِينَ أُرْسِلَ إِلَيْهِمْ
وَلَنَسْـَٔلَنَّ ٱلْمُرْسَلِينَ ﴿٦﴾

7. And verily, We shall recount their whole story with knowledge, for We were never absent (at any time or place).

7. Falanaquṣṣanna 'alayhim bi'ilmiñw-wa maa kunnaa ghaaa'ibeen.

فَلَنَقُصَّنَّ عَلَيْهِم بِعِلْمٍ ۖ وَمَا كُنَّا
غَآئِبِينَ ﴿٧﴾

8. The balance that day will be true (to a nicety): those whose scale (of good) will be heavy, will prosper:

8. Walwaznu Yawma'izinil-ḥaqq; faman saqulat mawaazeenuhoo fa-ulaaa'ika humul-mufliḥoon.

وَٱلْوَزْنُ يَوْمَئِذٍ ٱلْحَقُّ ۚ فَمَن ثَقُلَتْ
مَوَٰزِينُهُۥ فَأُو۟لَٰٓئِكَ هُمُ ٱلْمُفْلِحُونَ ﴿٨﴾

9. Those whose scale will be light, will find their souls in perdition, for that they wrongfully treated Our Signs.

9. Wa man khaffat mawaazeenuhoo fa-ulaaa'ikal-lazeena khasirooo anfusahum bimaa kaanoo bi-Aayaatinaa yaẓlimoon.

وَمَنْ خَفَّتْ مَوَٰزِينُهُۥ فَأُو۟لَٰٓئِكَ
ٱلَّذِينَ خَسِرُوٓا۟ أَنفُسَهُم بِمَا كَانُوا۟
بِـَٔايَٰتِنَا يَظْلِمُونَ ﴿٩﴾

10. It is We Who have placed you with authority on earth, and

10. Wa laqad makkannaakum fil-arḍi wa

وَلَقَدْ مَكَّنَّٰكُمْ فِي ٱلْأَرْضِ وَ

Ikhfa اخفاء | Ghunna غُنّہ | Ikhfa Meem Saakin اخفاء میم ساکن | Idghaam ادغام | Qalqala قلقلہ | Qalb قلب | Idghaam Meem Saakin ادغام میم ساکن

provided you therein with means for the fulfilment of your life: small are the thanks that you give!

11. It is We Who created you and gave you shape; then We said the angels bow down to Adam, and they bowed down; not so Iblis; He refused to be of those who bow down.

12. (Allah) said: "What prevented you from bowing down when I commanded you?" He said: "I am better than he: you created me from fire, and him from clay."

13. (Allah) said: "Get you down from here: it is not for you to be arrogant here: get out, for you are of the meanest(of creatures)."

14. He said: "Give me respite till the day they are raised up."

15. (Allah) said: "Be you among those who have respite."

16. He said: "Because You have thrown me out of the way, I will lie in wait for them on Your Straight Way:

17. "Then I will assault them from before them and behind them, from their right and their left: Nor will You find, in most of them, gratitude (for Your mercies)."

18. (Allah) said: "Get out from this, disgraced and expelled. If any of them follow you,- I will fill Hell with you all.

19. "O Adam! You and your wife dwell in the Garden, and enjoy (its good things) as you wish: but do not approach this tree, or you run into harm and transgression."

20. Then began Satan to whisper suggestions to them, in order to reveal to them

ja'alnaa lakum feehaa ma'aayish; qaleelam maa tashkuroon. **(Section 1)**

11. Wa laqad khalaqnaakum summa ṣawwarnaakum summa qulnaa lilmalaaa'ikatis-judoo li-Aadama fa-sajadooo illaaa Ibleesa lam yakum-minas-saajideen.

12. Qaala maa mana'aka allaa tasjuda iz amartuka qaala ana khayrum-minhu khalaqtanee min naariñw-wa khalaqtahoo min ṭeen.

13. Qaala fahbiṭ minhaa famaa yakoonu laka an tatakabbara feehaa fakhruj innaka minaṣ-ṣaaghireen.

14. Qaala anẓirneee ilaa Yawmi yub'asoon.

15. Qaala innaka minal-munẓareen.

16. Qaala fabimaaa aghway-tanee la-aq'udanna lahum Ṣiraaṭakal-Mustaqeem

17. Summa la-aatiyannahum mim bayni aydeehim wa min khalfihim wa 'an aymaanihim wa 'an shamaaa'ilihim wa laa tajidu aksarahum shaakireen.

18. Qaalakh-ruj minhaa maz'oomam-madḥooraa; laman tabi'aka minhum la-amla'anna Jahannama minkum ajma'een.

19. Wa yaaa Aadamus-kun anta wa zawjukal-Jannata fakulaa min ḥaysu shi'tumaa wa laa taqrabaa haazihish-shajarata fatakoonaa minaẓ-ẓaalimeen.

20. Fawaswasa lahumash-Shayṭaanu liyubdiya lahumaa

جَعَلْنَا لَكُمْ فِيهَا مَعَايِشَ ۗ قَلِيلًا
مَّا تَشْكُرُونَ ﴿١٠﴾
ع ١ ٨
وَلَقَدْ خَلَقْنَٰكُمْ ثُمَّ صَوَّرْنَٰكُمْ ثُمَّ قُلْنَا
لِلْمَلَٰٓئِكَةِ اسْجُدُوا لِآدَمَ ۖ فَسَجَدُوٓا
إِلَّآ إِبْلِيسَ لَمْ يَكُن مِّنَ السَّٰجِدِينَ ﴿١١﴾
قَالَ مَا مَنَعَكَ أَلَّا تَسْجُدَ إِذْ أَمَرْتُكَ ۖ
قَالَ أَنَا خَيْرٌ مِّنْهُ خَلَقْتَنِي مِن نَّارٍ
وَخَلَقْتَهُۥ مِن طِينٍ ﴿١٢﴾
قَالَ فَاهْبِطْ مِنْهَا فَمَا يَكُونُ لَكَ
أَن تَتَكَبَّرَ فِيهَا فَاخْرُجْ إِنَّكَ
مِنَ الصَّٰغِرِينَ ﴿١٣﴾
قَالَ أَنظِرْنِيٓ إِلَىٰ يَوْمِ يُبْعَثُونَ ﴿١٤﴾
قَالَ إِنَّكَ مِنَ الْمُنظَرِينَ ﴿١٥﴾
قَالَ فَبِمَآ أَغْوَيْتَنِي لَأَقْعُدَنَّ
لَهُمْ صِرَٰطَكَ الْمُسْتَقِيمَ ﴿١٦﴾
ثُمَّ لَآتِيَنَّهُم مِّنۢ بَيْنِ أَيْدِيهِمْ
وَمِنْ خَلْفِهِمْ وَعَنْ أَيْمَٰنِهِمْ وَ
عَن شَمَآئِلِهِمْ ۖ وَلَا تَجِدُ أَكْثَرَهُمْ
شَٰكِرِينَ ﴿١٧﴾
قَالَ اخْرُجْ مِنْهَا مَذْءُومًا
مَّدْحُورًا ۖ لَّمَن تَبِعَكَ مِنْهُمْ
لَأَمْلَأَنَّ جَهَنَّمَ مِنكُمْ أَجْمَعِينَ ﴿١٨﴾
وَيَٰٓآدَمُ اسْكُنْ أَنتَ وَزَوْجُكَ الْجَنَّةَ
فَكُلَا مِنْ حَيْثُ شِئْتُمَا وَلَا تَقْرَبَا هَٰذِهِ
الشَّجَرَةَ فَتَكُونَا مِنَ الظَّٰلِمِينَ ﴿١٩﴾
فَوَسْوَسَ لَهُمَا الشَّيْطَٰنُ لِيُبْدِيَ لَهُمَا

Ikhfa اخفاء | Ghunna غُنّہ | Ikhfa Meem Saakin اخفاء میم ساکن | Idghaam ادغام | Qalqala قلقلہ | Qalb قلب | Idghaam Meem Saakin ادغام میم ساکن

their shame that was hidden from them (before): he said: "Your Lord only forbade you this tree, lest you should become angels or such beings as live for ever."

21. And he swore to them both, that he was their sincere adviser.

22. So by deceit he brought about their fall: when they tasted of the tree, their shame became manifest to them, and they began to sew together the leaves of the Garden over their bodies. And their Lord called unto them: "Did I not forbid you that tree, and tell you that Satan was an avowed enemy to you?"

23. They said: "Our Lord! We have wronged our own souls: If You do not forgive us and bestow not upon us Your Mercy, we shall certainly be lost."

24. (Allah) said: "Get you down. With enmity between yourselves. On earth will be your dwelling-place and your means of livelihood,- for a time."

25. He said: "Therein you shall live, and therein you shall die; but from it you shall be taken out (at last)."

26. O you Children of Adam! We have bestowed raiment upon you to cover your shame, as well as to be an adornment to you. But the raiment of righteousness,- that is the best. Such are among the Signs of Allah, that they may receive admonition!

27. O you Children of Adam! Let not Satan seduce you, in the same manner as He got your parents out of the Garden, stripping them of their raiment, to expose their shame:

maa wooriya 'anhumaa min saw-aatihimaa wa qaala maa nahaakumaa Rabbukumaa 'an haazihish-shajarati illaaa an takoonaa malakayni aw takoonaa minal-khaalideen.

21. Wa qaasamahumaaa innee lakumaa laminan-naasiheen.

22. Fadallaahumaa bighuroor; falammaa zaaqash-shajarata badat lahumaa saw-aatuhumaa wa tafiqaa yakhsifaani 'alayhimaa miñw-waraqil-jannati wa naadaahumaa Rabbuhumaaa alam anhakumaa 'an tilkumash-shajarati wa aqul lakumaaa innash-Shaytaana lakumaa 'aduwwum-mubeen.

23. Qaalaa Rabbanaa zalamnaaa anfusanaa wa illam taghfir lanaa wa tarhamnaa lanakoonanna minal-khaasireen.

24. Qaalah-bitoo ba'dukum liba'din 'aduwwuñw-wa lakum fil-ardi mustaqarruñw-wa mataa'un ilaa heen.

25. Qaala feehaa tahyawna wa feehaa tamootoona wa minhaa tukhrajoon. **(Section 2)**

26. Yaa Baneee Aadama qad anzalnaa 'alaykum libaasañy-yuwaaree saw-aatikum wa reeshañw wa libaasut-taqwaa zaalika khayr; zaalika min Aayaatil-laahi la'allahum yazzakkaroon.

27. Yaa Baneee Aadama laa yaftinannakumush-Shaytaanu kamaaa akhraja abawaykum minal-Jannati yanzi'u 'anhumaa libaasahumaa liyuriyahumaa saw-aatihimaaa;

مَا وُرِيَ عَنْهُمَا مِنْ سَوْاٰتِهِمَا وَ
قَالَ مَا نَهٰكُمَا رَبُّكُمَا عَنْ هٰذِهِ
الشَّجَرَةِ اِلَّآ اَنْ تَكُوْنَا مَلَكَيْنِ
اَوْ تَكُوْنَا مِنَ الْخٰلِدِيْنَ ﴿٢٠﴾
وَقَاسَمَهُمَآ اِنِّيْ لَكُمَا لَمِنَ النّٰصِحِيْنَ ﴿٢١﴾
فَدَلّٰىهُمَا بِغُرُوْرٍ ۚ فَلَمَّا ذَاقَا الشَّجَرَةَ
بَدَتْ لَهُمَا سَوْاٰتُهُمَا وَطَفِقَا يَخْصِفٰنِ
عَلَيْهِمَا مِنْ وَّرَقِ الْجَنَّةِ ؕ وَنَادٰىهُمَا
رَبُّهُمَآ اَلَمْ اَنْهَكُمَا عَنْ تِلْكُمَا
الشَّجَرَةِ وَاَقُلْ لَّكُمَآ اِنَّ الشَّيْطٰنَ
لَكُمَا عَدُوٌّ مُّبِيْنٌ ﴿٢٢﴾
قَالَا رَبَّنَا ظَلَمْنَآ اَنْفُسَنَا ٚ وَ
اِنْ لَّمْ تَغْفِرْ لَنَا وَتَرْحَمْنَا لَنَكُوْنَنَّ
مِنَ الْخٰسِرِيْنَ ﴿٢٣﴾
قَالَ اهْبِطُوْا بَعْضُكُمْ لِبَعْضٍ عَدُوٌّ ۚ
وَلَكُمْ فِي الْاَرْضِ مُسْتَقَرٌّ وَّمَتَاعٌ
اِلٰى حِيْنٍ ﴿٢٤﴾
قَالَ فِيْهَا تَحْيَوْنَ وَفِيْهَا تَمُوْتُوْنَ
وَمِنْهَا تُخْرَجُوْنَ ﴿٢٥﴾ ع
يٰبَنِيْٓ اٰدَمَ قَدْ اَنْزَلْنَا عَلَيْكُمْ لِبَاسًا
يُّوَارِيْ سَوْاٰتِكُمْ وَرِيْشًا ؕ وَلِبَاسُ
التَّقْوٰى ۙ ذٰلِكَ خَيْرٌ ؕ ذٰلِكَ مِنْ
اٰيٰتِ اللّٰهِ لَعَلَّهُمْ يَذَّكَّرُوْنَ ﴿٢٦﴾
يٰبَنِيْٓ اٰدَمَ لَا يَفْتِنَنَّكُمُ الشَّيْطٰنُ كَمَآ
اَخْرَجَ اَبَوَيْكُمْ مِّنَ الْجَنَّةِ يَنْزِعُ
عَنْهُمَا لِبَاسَهُمَا لِيُرِيَهُمَا سَوْاٰتِهِمَا

Ikhfa اخفاء | Ghunna غنّہ | Ikhfa Meem Saakin اخفاء میم ساکن | Idghaam ادغام | Qalqala قلقلہ | Qalb قلب | Idghaam Meem Saakin ادغام میم ساکن

for he and his tribe watch you from a position where you cannot see them: We made the Satan friends (only) to those without Faith.

innahoo yaraakum huwa wa qabeeluhoo min ḥayṣu laa tarawnahum; innaa ja'alnash-Shayaaṭeena awliyaaa'a lillazeena laa yu'minoon.

إِنَّهُۥ يَرَىٰكُمْ هُوَ وَقَبِيلُهُۥ مِنْ حَيْثُ
لَا تَرَوْنَهُمْ ۗ إِنَّا جَعَلْنَا ٱلشَّيَٰطِينَ
أَوْلِيَآءَ لِلَّذِينَ لَا يُؤْمِنُونَ ﴿٢٧﴾

28. When they do anything that is shameful, they say: "We found our fathers doing so"; and "Allah commanded us thus": Say: "Nay, Allah never commands what is shameful: do you say of Allah what you do not know?"

28. Wa izaa fa'aloo faaḥishatan qaaloo wajadnaa 'alayhaaa aabaaa'anaa wallaahu amaranaa bihaa; qul innal-laaha laa yaâmuru bilfaḥshaaa'i a-taqooloona 'alal-laahi maa laa ta'lamoon.

وَإِذَا فَعَلُوا۟ فَٰحِشَةً قَالُوا۟ وَجَدْنَا
عَلَيْهَآ ءَابَآءَنَا وَٱللَّهُ أَمَرَنَا بِهَا ۗ
قُلْ إِنَّ ٱللَّهَ لَا يَأْمُرُ بِٱلْفَحْشَآءِ ۖ
أَتَقُولُونَ عَلَى ٱللَّهِ مَا لَا تَعْلَمُونَ ﴿٢٨﴾

29. Say: "My Lord has commanded justice; and that you set your whole selves (to Him) at every time and place of prayer, and call upon Him, making your devotion sincere as in His sight: such as He created you in the beginning, so shall you return."

29. Qul amara Rabbee bilqisti wa aqeemoo wujoohakum 'inda kulli masjidiñw-wad'oohu mukhliṣeena lahud-deen; kamaa bada-akum ta'oodoon.

قُلْ أَمَرَ رَبِّى بِٱلْقِسْطِ ۖ وَأَقِيمُوا۟
وُجُوهَكُمْ عِندَ كُلِّ مَسْجِدٍ وَٱدْعُوهُ
مُخْلِصِينَ لَهُ ٱلدِّينَ ۚ كَمَا بَدَأَكُمْ
تَعُودُونَ ﴿٢٩﴾

30. Some He has guided: Others have (by their choice) deserved the loss of their way; in that they took the Satan, in preference to Allah, for their friends and protectors, and think that they receive guidance.

30. Fareeqan hadaa wa fareeqan ḥaqqa 'alayhimuḍ-ḍalaalah; innahumut-takhazush-Shayaaṭeena awliyaaa'a min doonil-laahi wa yaḥsaboona annahum muhtadoon.

فَرِيقًا هَدَىٰ وَفَرِيقًا حَقَّ عَلَيْهِمُ
ٱلضَّلَٰلَةُ ۗ إِنَّهُمُ ٱتَّخَذُوا۟ ٱلشَّيَٰطِينَ
أَوْلِيَآءَ مِن دُونِ ٱللَّهِ وَيَحْسَبُونَ
أَنَّهُم مُّهْتَدُونَ ﴿٣٠﴾

31. O Children of Adam! wear your beautiful apparel at every time and place of prayer: eat and drink: but do not waste by excess, for Allah does not loves the wasters.

31. Yaa Baneee Adama khuzoo zeenatakum 'inda kulli masjidiñw-wa kuloo washraboo wa laa tusrifoo; innahoo laa yuḥibbul-musrifeen. **(Section 3)**

يَٰبَنِىٓ ءَادَمَ خُذُوا۟ زِينَتَكُمْ عِندَ
كُلِّ مَسْجِدٍ وَكُلُوا۟ وَٱشْرَبُوا۟ وَلَا
تُسْرِفُوٓا۟ ۚ إِنَّهُۥ لَا يُحِبُّ ٱلْمُسْرِفِينَ ﴿٣١﴾

32. Say: Who has forbidden the beautiful (gifts) of Allah, which He has produced for His servants, and the things, clean and pure, which (He has provided) for sustenance? Say: They are, in the life of this world, for those who believe, (and) purely for them on the Day of Judgment. Thus do We explain the Signs in detail for those who understand.

32. Qul man ḥarrama zeenatal-laahil-lateee akhraja li'ibaadihee waṭṭayyibaati minar-rizq; qul hiya lillazeena aamanoo fil-ḥayaatid-dunyaa khaaliṣatañy-Yawmal Qiyaamah; kazaalika nufaṣṣilul-Aayaati liqawmiñy-ya'lamoon.

قُلْ مَنْ حَرَّمَ زِينَةَ ٱللَّهِ ٱلَّتِىٓ أَخْرَجَ
لِعِبَادِهِۦ وَٱلطَّيِّبَٰتِ مِنَ ٱلرِّزْقِ ۚ قُلْ
هِىَ لِلَّذِينَ ءَامَنُوا۟ فِى ٱلْحَيَوٰةِ ٱلدُّنْيَا
خَالِصَةً يَوْمَ ٱلْقِيَٰمَةِ ۗ كَذَٰلِكَ
نُفَصِّلُ ٱلْءَايَٰتِ لِقَوْمٍ يَعْلَمُونَ ﴿٣٢﴾

33. Say: The things that my Lord has indeed forbidden are: shameful deeds, whether open or secret; sins and trespasses against truth or reason; assigning of partners to Allah,

33. Qul innamaa ḥarrama Rabbiyal-fawaaḥisha maa ẓahara minhaa wa maa baṭana wal-isma walbaghya bighayril-ḥaqqi wa an tushrikoo billaahi maa lam

قُلْ إِنَّمَا حَرَّمَ رَبِّىَ ٱلْفَوَٰحِشَ مَا
ظَهَرَ مِنْهَا وَمَا بَطَنَ وَٱلْإِثْمَ وَٱلْبَغْىَ
بِغَيْرِ ٱلْحَقِّ وَأَن تُشْرِكُوا۟ بِٱللَّهِ مَا لَمْ

Ikhfa اخفاء · Ghunna غنّہ · Ikhfa Meem Saakin اخفاءمیم ساکن · Idghaam ادغام · Qalqala قلقلہ · Qalb قلب · Idghaam Meem Saakin ادغام میم ساکن

for which He has given no authority; and saying things about Allah of which you have no knowledge.

34. To every people is a term appointed: when their term is reached, not an hour can they cause delay, nor (an hour) can they advance (it in anticipation).

35. O you Children of Adam! whenever there come to you Apostles from amongst you, rehearsing My Signs to you,- those who are righteous and mend (their lives),- on them shall be no fear nor shall they grieve.

36. But those who reject Our Signs and treat them with arrogance,- they are Companions of the Fire, to dwell therein (for ever).

37. Who is more unjust than one who invents a lie against Allah or rejects His Signs? For such, their portion appointed must reach them from the Book (of decrees): until, when our messengers (of death) arrive and take their souls, they say: "Where are the things that you used to invoke besides Allah?" They will reply, "They have left us in the lurch," and they will bear witness against themselves, that they had rejected Allah.

38. He will say: "You enter in the company of the peoples who passed away before you - men and jinns, - into the Fire." Every time a new people enters, it curses its sister-people (that went before), until they follow each other, all into the Fire. Says the last about the first: "Our Lord! it is these that misled us: so give them a double Chastisement in the Fire." He will say: "Doubled for all" : but

yunazzil bihee sulṭaanañw-wa an taqooloo 'alal-laahi maa laa ta'lamoon.

34. Wa likulli ummatin ajalun fa-izaa jaaa'a ajaluhum laa yastaåkhiroona saa'atañw-wa laa yastaqdimoon.

35. Yaa Baneee Aadama immaa yaåtiyannakum Rusulum-minkum yaquṣṣoona 'alaykum Aayaatee famanit-taqaa wa aṣlaḥa falaa khawfun 'alayhim wa laa hum yaḥzanoon.

36. Wallazeena kazzaboo bi-Aayaatinaa wastakbaroo 'anhaaa ulaaa'ika Aṣḥaabun Naari hum feehaa khaalidoon.

37. Faman azlamu mimmanif-taraa 'alal-laahi kaziban aw kazzaba bi-Aayaatih; ulaaa'ika yanaaluhum naṣeebuhum minal-Kitaab; ḥattaaa izaa jaaa'at-hum rusulunaa yatawaffawnahum qaalooo ayna maa kuntum tad'oona min doonil-laahi qaaloo ḍalloo 'annaa wa shahidoo 'alaaa anfusihim annahum kaanoo kaafireen.

38. Qaalad-khuloo feee umamin qad khalat min qablikum minal-jinni wal-insi fin-Naari kullamaa dakhalat ummatul-la'anat ukhtahaa ḥattaaa izad-daarakoo feehaa jamee'an qaalat ukhraahum li-oolaahum Rabbanaa haaa'u-laaa'i aḍalloonaa fa-aatihim 'azaaban ḍi'fam-minan-Naari qaala likullin ḍi'fuñw-wa laakil

يُنَزِّلْ بِهٖ سُلْطٰنًا وَّ اَنْ تَقُوْلُوْا عَلَى
اللّٰهِ مَا لَا تَعْلَمُوْنَ ﴿٣٣﴾
وَلِكُلِّ اُمَّةٍ اَجَلٌ ۚ فَاِذَا جَآءَ
اَجَلُهُمْ لَا يَسْتَاْخِرُوْنَ سَاعَةً
وَّلَا يَسْتَقْدِمُوْنَ ﴿٣٤﴾
يٰبَنِيْٓ اٰدَمَ اِمَّا يَاْتِيَنَّكُمْ رُسُلٌ
مِّنْكُمْ يَقُصُّوْنَ عَلَيْكُمْ اٰيٰتِيْ ۙ فَمَنِ
اتَّقٰى وَاَصْلَحَ فَلَا خَوْفٌ عَلَيْهِمْ وَلَا
هُمْ يَحْزَنُوْنَ ﴿٣٥﴾
وَالَّذِيْنَ كَذَّبُوْا بِاٰيٰتِنَا وَاسْتَكْبَرُوْا
عَنْهَآ اُولٰٓئِكَ اَصْحٰبُ النَّارِ ۚ هُمْ
فِيْهَا خٰلِدُوْنَ ﴿٣٦﴾
فَمَنْ اَظْلَمُ مِمَّنِ افْتَرٰى عَلَى اللّٰهِ
كَذِبًا اَوْ كَذَّبَ بِاٰيٰتِهٖ ۗ اُولٰٓئِكَ
يَنَالُهُمْ نَصِيْبُهُمْ مِّنَ الْكِتٰبِ ۗ حَتّٰٓى
اِذَا جَآءَتْهُمْ رُسُلُنَا يَتَوَفَّوْنَهُمْ ۙ
قَالُوْٓا اَيْنَ مَا كُنْتُمْ تَدْعُوْنَ مِنْ
دُوْنِ اللّٰهِ ۗ قَالُوْا ضَلُّوْا عَنَّا وَشَهِدُوْا
عَلٰٓى اَنْفُسِهِمْ اَنَّهُمْ كَانُوْا كٰفِرِيْنَ ﴿٣٧﴾
قَالَ ادْخُلُوْا فِيْٓ اُمَمٍ قَدْ خَلَتْ مِنْ
قَبْلِكُمْ مِّنَ الْجِنِّ وَالْاِنْسِ فِي النَّارِ ۗ
كُلَّمَا دَخَلَتْ اُمَّةٌ لَّعَنَتْ اُخْتَهَا ۗ
حَتّٰٓى اِذَا ادَّارَكُوْا فِيْهَا جَمِيْعًا ۙ
قَالَتْ اُخْرٰىهُمْ لِاُوْلٰىهُمْ رَبَّنَا هٰٓؤُلَآءِ
اَضَلُّوْنَا فَاٰتِهِمْ عَذَابًا ضِعْفًا مِّنَ
النَّارِ ۗ قَالَ لِكُلٍّ ضِعْفٌ وَّلٰكِنْ

Ikhfa اخفاء | Ghunna غُنّہ | Ikhfa Meem Saakin اخفاء میم ساکن | Idghaam ادغام | Qalqala قلقلہ | Qalb قلب | Idghaam Meem Saakin ادغام میم ساکن

this you do not understand.

39. Then the first will say to the last: "See then! You do not have any advantage over us; so you taste of the Chastisement for all that you did."

40. To those who reject Our Signs and treat them with arrogance, no opening will there be of the gates of heaven, nor will they enter the Garden, until the camel can pass through the eye of the needle: such is Our reward for those in sin.

41. For them there is Hell, as a couch (below) and folds of covering above: such is Our requital of those who do wrong.

42. But those who believe and work righteousness,- no burden do We place on any soul, but that which it can bear,-they will be Companions of the Garden, therein to dwell (for ever).

43. And We shall remove from their hearts any lurking sense of injury;- beneath them will be rivers flowing;- and they shall say: "Praise be to Allah, who has guided us to this (felicity): never could we have found guidance, had it not been for the guidance of Allah: indeed it was the truth, that the Apostles of our Lord brought to us." And they shall hear the cry: "Behold! the Garden before you! You have been made its inheritors, for your deeds (of righteousness)."

44. The Companions of the Garden will call out to the Companions of the Fire: "We have indeed found the promises of our Lord to us true: Have you also found Your Lord's promises true?" They shall say, "Yes"; But a

laa ta'lamoon.

39. Wa qaalat oolaahum li-ukhraahum famaa kaana lakum 'alaynaa min faḍlin fazooqul-azaaba bimaa kuntum taksiboon. **(Section 4)**

40. Innal-lazeena kazzaboo bi-Aayaatinaa wastakbaroo 'anhaa laa tufattaḥu lahum abwaabus-samaaa'i wa laa yadkhuloonal-jannata ḥattaa yalijal-jamalu fee sammil-khiyaaṭ; wa kazaalika najzil-mujrimeen.

41. Lahum min jahannama mihaaduñw-wa min fawqihim ghawaash; wa kazaalika najziẓ-ẓaalimeen.

42.Wallazeena aamanoo wa 'amiluṣ-ṣaaliḥaati laa nukallifu nafsan illaa wus'ahaaa ulaaa'ika Aṣḥaabul-jannati hum feehaa khaalidoon.

43. Wa naza'naa maa fee ṣudoorihim min ghillin tajree min taḥtihimul-anhaaru wa qaalul-ḥamdu lillaahil-lazee hadaanaa lihaazaa wa maa kunnaa linahtadiya law laaa an hadaanal-laahu laqad jaaa'at Rusulu Rabbinaa bilḥaqq; wa noodooo an tilkumul-jannatu ooristumoohaa bimaa kuntum ta'maloon.

44. Wa naadaaa Aṣḥaabul-jannati Aṣḥaaban-Naari an qad wajadnaa maa wa'adanaa Rabbunaa ḥaqqan fahal wajattum maa wa'ada Rabbukum ḥaqqan qaaloo na'am; fa-azzana

لَا تَعْلَمُونَ ﴿٣٨﴾
وَقَالَتْ أُولٰىهُمْ لِأُخْرٰىهُمْ فَمَا كَانَ
لَكُمْ عَلَيْنَا مِنْ فَضْلٍ فَذُوقُوا
الْعَذَابَ بِمَا كُنْتُمْ تَكْسِبُونَ ﴿٣٩﴾ ع
إِنَّ الَّذِينَ كَذَّبُوا بِاٰيٰتِنَا وَاسْتَكْبَرُوا
عَنْهَا لَا تُفَتَّحُ لَهُمْ أَبْوَابُ السَّمَاءِ
وَلَا يَدْخُلُونَ الْجَنَّةَ حَتّٰى يَلِجَ
الْجَمَلُ فِي سَمِّ الْخِيَاطِ ط وَكَذٰلِكَ
نَجْزِي الْمُجْرِمِينَ ﴿٤٠﴾
لَهُمْ مِنْ جَهَنَّمَ مِهَادٌ وَمِنْ فَوْقِهِمْ
غَوَاشٍ ط وَكَذٰلِكَ نَجْزِي الظّٰلِمِينَ ﴿٤١﴾
وَالَّذِينَ اٰمَنُوا وَعَمِلُوا الصّٰلِحٰتِ
لَا نُكَلِّفُ نَفْسًا إِلَّا وُسْعَهَا ز
أُولٰٓئِكَ أَصْحٰبُ الْجَنَّةِ ج هُمْ فِيهَا
خٰلِدُونَ ﴿٤٢﴾
وَنَزَعْنَا مَا فِي صُدُورِهِمْ مِنْ غِلٍّ
تَجْرِي مِنْ تَحْتِهِمُ الْأَنْهٰرُ ج وَقَالُوا
الْحَمْدُ لِلّٰهِ الَّذِي هَدٰىنَا لِهٰذَا قف وَمَا
كُنَّا لِنَهْتَدِيَ لَوْلَا أَنْ هَدٰىنَا اللّٰهُ ج
لَقَدْ جَاءَتْ رُسُلُ رَبِّنَا بِالْحَقِّ ط
وَنُودُوا أَنْ تِلْكُمُ الْجَنَّةُ أُورِثْتُمُوهَا
بِمَا كُنْتُمْ تَعْمَلُونَ ﴿٤٣﴾
وَنَادٰى أَصْحٰبُ الْجَنَّةِ أَصْحٰبَ
النَّارِ أَنْ قَدْ وَجَدْنَا مَا وَعَدَنَا
رَبُّنَا حَقًّا فَهَلْ وَجَدْتُمْ مَا وَعَدَ
رَبُّكُمْ حَقًّا ط قَالُوا نَعَمْ ج فَأَذَّنَ

Ikhfa اخفاء | Ghunna غنّة | Ikhfa Meem Saakin اخفاء ميم ساكن | Idghaam ادغام | Qalqala قلقله | Qalb قلب | Idghaam Meem Saakin ادغام ميم ساكن

crier shall proclaim between them: "The curse of Allah is on the wrong-doers;-

mu'azzinum baynahum al-la'natul-laahi 'alaz-zaalimeen.

مُؤَذِّنٌۢ بَيْنَهُمْ اَنْ لَّعْنَةُ اللّٰهِ
عَلَى الظّٰلِمِيْنَ ﴿٤٤﴾

45. "Those who would hinder (men) from the path of Allah and would seek in it something crooked: they were those who denied the Hereafter."

45. Allazeena yaṣuddoona 'an sabeelil-laahi wa yabghoo-nahaa 'iwajañw wa hum bil-Aakhirati kaafiroon.

الَّذِيْنَ يَصُدُّوْنَ عَنْ سَبِيْلِ
اللّٰهِ وَيَبْغُوْنَهَا عِوَجًا ۚ وَهُمْ
بِالْاٰخِرَةِ كٰفِرُوْنَ ﴿٤٥﴾ وقف لازم

46. Between them shall be a veil, and on the Heights will be men who would know every one by his marks: they will call out to the Companions of the Garden, "peace on you": they will not have entered, but they will have an assurance (thereof).

46. Wa baynahumaa ḥijaab; wa 'alal-A'raafi rijaaluñy-ya'ri-foona kullam biseemaahum; wa naadaw Aṣḥaabal-Jannati an salaamun 'alaykum; lam yadkhuloohaa wa hum yaṭma'oon.

وَبَيْنَهُمَا حِجَابٌ ۚ وَعَلَى الْاَعْرَافِ
رِجَالٌ يَّعْرِفُوْنَ كُلًّاۢ بِسِيْمٰىهُمْ ۚ
وَنَادَوْا اَصْحٰبَ الْجَنَّةِ اَنْ سَلٰمٌ
عَلَيْكُمْ ۣ لَمْ يَدْخُلُوْهَا وَهُمْ
يَطْمَعُوْنَ ﴿٤٦﴾

47. When their eyes shall be turned towards the Companions of the Fire, they will say: "Our Lord! do not send us to the company of the wrong-doers."

47. Wa izaa ṣurifat abṣaaru-hum tilqaaa'a Aṣḥaabin-Naari qaalo Rabbanaa laa taj'alnaa ma'al-qawmiz-zaalimeen.

(Section 5)

وَاِذَا صُرِفَتْ اَبْصَارُهُمْ تِلْقَآءَ
اَصْحٰبِ النَّارِ ۙ قَالُوْا رَبَّنَا لَا تَجْعَلْنَا
مَعَ الْقَوْمِ الظّٰلِمِيْنَ ﴿٤٧﴾ ع ٥

48. The men on the Heights will call to certain men whom they will know from their marks, saying: "Of what profit to you were your hoards and your arrogant ways?

48. Wa naadaaa Aṣḥaabul-A'raafi rijaalañy-ya'rifoona-hum biseemaahum qaaloo maaa aghnaa 'ankum jam'ukum wa maa kuntum tastakbiroon.

وَنَادٰۤى اَصْحٰبُ الْاَعْرَافِ رِجَالًا
يَّعْرِفُوْنَهُمْ بِسِيْمٰىهُمْ قَالُوْا مَآ
اَغْنٰى عَنْكُمْ جَمْعُكُمْ وَمَا كُنْتُمْ
تَسْتَكْبِرُوْنَ ﴿٤٨﴾

49. "Behold! are these not the men whom you swore that Allah would never bless? with His Mercy you enter the Garden: no fear shall be on you, nor shall you grieve."

49. A-haaa'ulaaa'il-lazeena aqsamtum laa yanaaluhumul-laahu biraḥmah; udkhulul-Jannata laa khawfun 'alaykum wa laaa antum taḥzanoon.

اَهٰٓؤُلَآءِ الَّذِيْنَ اَقْسَمْتُمْ لَا يَنَالُهُمُ
اللّٰهُ بِرَحْمَةٍ ۭ اُدْخُلُوا الْجَنَّةَ لَا
خَوْفٌ عَلَيْكُمْ وَلَآ اَنْتُمْ تَحْزَنُوْنَ ﴿٤٩﴾

50. The Companions of the Fire will call to the Companions of the Garden: "Pour down to us water or anything that Allah provides for your sustenance." They will say: "Allah has forbidden Both these things to those who rejected Him."

50. Wa naadaaa Aṣḥaabun-Naari Aṣḥaabal-Jannati an afeeḍoo 'alaynaa minal-maaa'i aw mimmaa razaqakumul-laah; qaalooo innal-laaha ḥarrama-humaa 'alal-kaafireen.

وَنَادٰۤى اَصْحٰبُ النَّارِ اَصْحٰبَ الْجَنَّةِ
اَنْ اَفِيْضُوْا عَلَيْنَا مِنَ الْمَآءِ اَوْ مِمَّا
رَزَقَكُمُ اللّٰهُ ۭ قَالُوْٓا اِنَّ اللّٰهَ
حَرَّمَهُمَا عَلَى الْكٰفِرِيْنَ ﴿٥٠﴾

51. "Such as took their religion to be mere amusement and play, and were deceived by the life of the world." That day

51. Allazeenat-takhazoo deenahum lahwañw-wa la'i-bañw-wa gharrat-humul-ḥayaa-tud-dunyaa; fal-Yawma

الَّذِيْنَ اتَّخَذُوْا دِيْنَهُمْ لَهْوًا وَّلَعِبًا
وَّغَرَّتْهُمُ الْحَيٰوةُ الدُّنْيَا ۚ فَالْيَوْمَ

Ikhfa اخفاء | Ghunna غُنّہ | Ikhfa Meem Saakin اخفاء میم ساکن | Idghaam ادغام | Qalqala قلقلہ | Qalb قلب | Idghaam Meem Saakin ادغام میم ساکن

We shall forget them as they forgot the meeting of this day of theirs, and as they were wont to reject Our Signs.

nansaahum kamaa nasoo liqaaa'a Yawmihim haazaa wa maa kaanoo bi-Aayaatinaa yajhadoon.

نَنْسٰهُمْ كَمَا نَسُوْا لِقَآءَ يَوْمِهِمْ هٰذَا ۙ وَمَا كَانُوْا بِاٰيٰتِنَا يَجْحَدُوْنَ ﴿٥١﴾

52. For We had certainly sent to them a Book, based on knowledge, which We explained in detail,- a guide and a mercy to all who believe.

52. Wa laqad ji'naahum bi-Kitaabin fassalnaahu 'alaa 'ilmin hudañw-wa rahmatal-liqawmiñy-yu'minoon.

وَلَقَدْ جِئْنٰهُمْ بِكِتٰبٍ فَصَّلْنٰهُ عَلٰى عِلْمٍ هُدًى وَّرَحْمَةً لِّقَوْمٍ يُّؤْمِنُوْنَ ﴿٥٢﴾

53. Do they just wait for the final fulfilment of the event? On the day the event is finally fulfilled, those who disregarded it before will say: "The Apostles of our Lord did indeed bring true (tidings). Have we no intercessors now to intercede on our behalf? Or could we be sent back? Then should we behave differently from our behaviour in the past." In fact they will have lost their souls, and the things they invented will leave them in the lurch.

53. Hal yanzuroona illaa taå-weelah; Yawma yaåtee taå-weeluhoo yaqoolul-lazeena nasoohu min qablu qad jaaa'at Rusulu Rabbinaa bilhaqq; fahal lanaa min shufa'aaa'a fa-yashfa'oo lanaaa aw nuraddu fana'mala ghayral-lazee kunnaa na'mal; qad khasirooo anfusahum wa dalla 'anhum maa kaanoo yaftaroon.

(Section 6)

هَلْ يَنْظُرُوْنَ اِلَّا تَاْوِيْلَهٗ ؕ يَوْمَ يَاْتِيْ تَاْوِيْلُهٗ يَقُوْلُ الَّذِيْنَ نَسُوْهُ مِنْ قَبْلُ قَدْ جَآءَتْ رُسُلُ رَبِّنَا بِالْحَقِّ ۚ فَهَلْ لَّنَا مِنْ شُفَعَآءَ فَيَشْفَعُوْا لَنَآ اَوْ نُرَدُّ فَنَعْمَلَ غَيْرَ الَّذِيْ كُنَّا نَعْمَلُ ؕ قَدْ خَسِرُوْٓا اَنْفُسَهُمْ وَضَلَّ عَنْهُمْ مَّا كَانُوْا يَفْتَرُوْنَ ﴿٥٣﴾ ع

54. Your Guardian-Lord is Allah, Who created the heavens and the earth in six Days, and is firmly established on the Throne (of authority): He draws the night as a veil over the day, each seeking the other in rapid succession: He created the sun, the moon, and the stars, (all) governed by laws under His Command. Is it not His to create and to govern? Blessed be Allah, the Cherisher and Sustainer of the Worlds.

54. Inna Rabbakumul-laahul-lazee khalaqas-samaawaati walarda fee sittati ayyaamin summas-tawaa 'alal-'arshi yughshil-laylan-nahaara yatlu-buhoo haseesañw-washshamsa walqamara wannujooma musakhkharaatim bi-amrih; alaa lahul-khalqu wal-amr; tabaarakal-laahu Rabbul-'aala-meen.

اِنَّ رَبَّكُمُ اللّٰهُ الَّذِيْ خَلَقَ السَّمٰوٰتِ وَالْاَرْضَ فِيْ سِتَّةِ اَيَّامٍ ثُمَّ اسْتَوٰى عَلَى الْعَرْشِ ۫ يُغْشِي الَّيْلَ النَّهَارَ يَطْلُبُهٗ حَثِيْثًا ۙ وَّالشَّمْسَ وَالْقَمَرَ وَالنُّجُوْمَ مُسَخَّرٰتٍ ۭ بِاَمْرِهٖ ؕ اَلَا لَهُ الْخَلْقُ وَالْاَمْرُ ؕ تَبٰرَكَ اللّٰهُ رَبُّ الْعٰلَمِيْنَ ﴿٥٤﴾

55. Call on your Lord with humility and in private: for Allah does not loves those who trespass beyond bounds.

55. Ud'oo Rabbakum tadar-ru'añw-wa khufyah; innahoo laa yuhibbul-mu'tadeen.

اُدْعُوْا رَبَّكُمْ تَضَرُّعًا وَّخُفْيَةً ؕ اِنَّهٗ لَا يُحِبُّ الْمُعْتَدِيْنَ ﴿٥٥﴾

56. Do no mischief on the earth, after it has been set in order, but call on Him with fear and longing (in your hearts): for the Mercy of Allah is (always) near to those who do good.

56. Wa laa tufsidoo fil-ardi ba'da islaahihaa wad'oohu khawfañw-wa tama'aa; inna rahmatal-laahi qareebum-minal-muhsineen.

وَلَا تُفْسِدُوْا فِي الْاَرْضِ بَعْدَ اِصْلَاحِهَا وَادْعُوْهُ خَوْفًا وَّطَمَعًا ؕ اِنَّ رَحْمَتَ اللّٰهِ قَرِيْبٌ مِّنَ الْمُحْسِنِيْنَ ﴿٥٦﴾

57. It is He Who sends the winds like heralds of glad tidings, going before His mercy: when

57. Wa Huwal-lazee yursilur-riyaaha bushram bayna yaday rahmatihee hattaaa izaaa

وَهُوَ الَّذِيْ يُرْسِلُ الرِّيٰحَ بُشْرًاۢ بَيْنَ يَدَيْ رَحْمَتِهٖ ؕ حَتّٰٓى اِذَآ

Ikhfa اخفاء · Ghunna غُنّہ · Ikhfa Meem Saakin اخفاء میم ساکن · Idghaam ادغام · Qalqala قلقلہ · Qalb قلب · Idghaam Meem Saakin ادغام میم ساکن

اَقَلَّتْ سَحَابًا ثِقَالًا سُقْنٰهُ لِبَلَدٍ
مَّيِّتٍ فَاَنْزَلْنَا بِهِ الْمَآءَ فَاَخْرَجْنَا
بِهٖ مِنْ كُلِّ الثَّمَرٰتِ ؕ كَذٰلِكَ نُخْرِجُ
الْمَوْتٰى لَعَلَّكُمْ تَذَكَّرُوْنَ ﴿٥٧﴾

aqallat saḥaaban siqaalan suqnaahu libaladim-mayyitin fa-anzalnaa bihil-maaa'a fa-akhrajnaa bihee min kullis-samaraat; kazaalika nukhrijul-mawtaa la'allakum tazakkaroon.

they have carried the heavy-laden clouds, We drive them to a land that is dead, make rain to descend thereon, and produce every kind of harvest therewith: thus shall We raise up the dead: perchance you may remember.

وَالْبَلَدُ الطَّيِّبُ يَخْرُجُ نَبَاتُهٗ
بِاِذْنِ رَبِّهٖ ۚ وَالَّذِیْ خَبُثَ لَا يَخْرُجُ
اِلَّا نَكِدًا ؕ كَذٰلِكَ نُصَرِّفُ الْاٰيٰتِ
لِقَوْمٍ يَّشْكُرُوْنَ ﴿٥٨﴾ ع ٧ ٥ ١٤

58. Walbaladuṭ-ṭayyibu yakhruju nabaatuhoo bi-izni Rabbihee wallazee khabusa laa yakhruju illaa nakidaa; kazaalika nuṣarriful-Aayaati liqawmiñy-yashkuroon.

(Section 7)

58. From the land that is clean and good, by the will of its Cherisher, springs up produce, (rich) after its kind: but from the land that is bad, springs up nothing but that which is niggardly: thus do we explain the Signs by various (symbols) to those who are grateful.

لَقَدْ اَرْسَلْنَا نُوْحًا اِلٰى قَوْمِهٖ
فَقَالَ يٰقَوْمِ اعْبُدُوا اللّٰهَ مَا لَكُمْ
مِّنْ اِلٰهٍ غَيْرُهٗ ؕ اِنِّیْۤ اَخَافُ
عَلَيْكُمْ عَذَابَ يَوْمٍ عَظِيْمٍ ﴿٥٩﴾

59. Laqad arsalnaa Nooḥan ilaa qawmihee faqaala yaa qawmi'-budul-laaha maa lakum min ilaahin ghayruhoo inneee akhaafu 'alaykum 'azaaba Yawmin 'Aẓeem.

59. We sent Noah to his people. He said: "O my people! worship Allah! you have no other god but Him. I fear for you the punishment of a dreadful Day!

قَالَ الْمَلَاُ مِنْ قَوْمِهٖۤ اِنَّا لَنَرٰىكَ
فِیْ ضَلٰلٍ مُّبِيْنٍ ﴿٦٠﴾

60. Qaalal-mala-u min qawmiheee innaa lanaraaka fee ḍalaalim-mubeen.

60. The leaders of his people said: "Ah! we see you evidently wandering (in mind)."

قَالَ يٰقَوْمِ لَيْسَ بِیْ ضَلٰلَةٌ وَّلٰكِنِّیْ
رَسُوْلٌ مِّنْ رَّبِّ الْعٰلَمِيْنَ ﴿٦١﴾

61. Qaala yaa qawmi laysa bee ḍalaalatuñw-wa laakinnee Rasoolum-mir-Rabbil-'aalameen.

61. He said: "O my people! no wandering is there in my (mind): on the contrary I am an apostle from the Lord and Cherisher of the Worlds!

اُبَلِّغُكُمْ رِسٰلٰتِ رَبِّیْ وَاَنْصَحُ لَكُمْ
وَاَعْلَمُ مِنَ اللّٰهِ مَا لَا تَعْلَمُوْنَ ﴿٦٢﴾

62. Uballighukum Risaalaati Rabbee wa anṣaḥu lakum wa a'lamu minal-laahi maa laa ta'lamoon.

62. "I but fulfil towards you the duties of my Lord's mission: sincere is my advice to you, and I know from Allah something that you do not know.

اَوَعَجِبْتُمْ اَنْ جَآءَكُمْ ذِكْرٌ مِّنْ
رَّبِّكُمْ عَلٰى رَجُلٍ مِّنْكُمْ لِيُنْذِرَكُمْ
وَلِتَتَّقُوْا وَلَعَلَّكُمْ تُرْحَمُوْنَ ﴿٦٣﴾

63. Awa 'ajibtum an jaaa'akum zikrum-mir-Rabbikum 'alaa rajulim-minkum liyunzirakum wa litattaqoo wa la'allakum turḥamoon.

63. "Do you wonder that there has come to you a message from your Lord, through a man of your own people, to warn you,- so that you may fear Allah and haply receive His Mercy?"

فَكَذَّبُوْهُ فَاَنْجَيْنٰهُ وَالَّذِيْنَ
مَعَهٗ فِی الْفُلْكِ وَاَغْرَقْنَا
الَّذِيْنَ كَذَّبُوْا بِاٰيٰتِنَا ؕ اِنَّهُمْ
كَانُوْا قَوْمًا عَمِيْنَ ﴿٦٤﴾ ع ٨ ٦ ١٥

64. Fakazzaboohu fa-anjaynaahu wallazeena ma'ahoo fil-fulki wa aghraqnal-lazeena kazzaboo bi-Aayaatinaa; innahum kaanoo qawman 'ameen.

(Section 8)

64. But they rejected him, and We delivered him, and those with him, in the Ark: but We overwhelmed in the Flood those who rejected Our Signs. They were indeed a blind people!

وَاِلٰى عَادٍ اَخَاهُمْ هُوْدًا ؕ قَالَ

65. Wa ilaa 'Aadin akhaahum Hoodaa; qaala

65. To the 'Ad people, (We sent) Hud, one of their (own) brethren: He said:

Ikhfa اخفاء | Ghunna غنّہ | Ikhfa Meem Saakin اخفاء میم ساکن | Idghaam ادغام | Qalqala قلقلہ | Qalb قلب | Idghaam Meem Saakin ادغام میم ساکن

O my people! worship Allah! you have no other god but Him, will you not fear (Allah)?"

yaa qawmi'-budul-laaha maa lakum min ilaahin ghayruh; afalaa tattaqoon.

يٰقَوْمِ اعْبُدُوا اللّٰهَ مَا لَكُمْ مِّنْ
اِلٰهٍ غَيْرُهٗ ؕ اَفَلَا تَتَّقُوْنَ ﴿٦٥﴾

66. The leaders of the Unbelievers among his people said: "Ah! we see you are an imbecile!" and "We think you are a liar!"

66. Qaalal-mala-ul-lazeena kafaroo min qawmiheee innaa lanaraaka fee safaahatiñw-wa innaa lanazunnuka minal-kaazibeen.

قَالَ الْمَلَاُ الَّذِيْنَ كَفَرُوْا مِنْ
قَوْمِهٖۤ اِنَّا لَنَرٰىكَ فِيْ سَفَاهَةٍ وَّ
اِنَّا لَنَظُنُّكَ مِنَ الْكٰذِبِيْنَ ﴿٦٦﴾

67. He said: "O my people! I am no imbecile, but (I am) an Apostle from the Lord and Cherisher of the worlds!

67. Qaala yaa qawmi laysa bee safaahatuñw-wa laakinnee Rasoolum-mir-Rabbil-'aala-meen.

قَالَ يٰقَوْمِ لَيْسَ بِيْ سَفَاهَةٌ وَّ
لٰكِنِّيْ رَسُوْلٌ مِّنْ رَّبِّ الْعٰلَمِيْنَ ﴿٦٧﴾

68. "I but fulfil towards you the duties of my Lord's mission: I am to you a sincere and trustworthy adviser.

68. Uballighukum Risaalaati Rabbee wa ana lakum naaṣiḥun ameen.

اُبَلِّغُكُمْ رِسٰلٰتِ رَبِّيْ وَاَنَا لَكُمْ
نَاصِحٌ اَمِيْنٌ ﴿٦٨﴾

69. "Do you wonder that there has come to you a message from your Lord through a man of your own people, to warn you? Call in remembrance that He made you inheritors after the people of Noah, and gave you a stature tall among the nations. Call in remembrance the benefits (you have received) from Allah: that so you may prosper."

69. Awa 'ajibtum an jaaa'akum zikrum-mir-Rabbikum 'alaa rajulim-minkum liyunzirakum; wazkurooo iz ja'alakum khulafaaa'a mim ba'di qawmi Nooḥiñw-wa zaadakum filkhal-qi basṭatan fazkurooo aalaaa'al-laahi la'allakum tufliḥoon.

اَوَعَجِبْتُمْ اَنْ جَآءَكُمْ ذِكْرٌ مِّنْ
رَّبِّكُمْ عَلٰى رَجُلٍ مِّنْكُمْ لِيُنْذِرَكُمْ
وَاذْكُرُوْۤا اِذْ جَعَلَكُمْ خُلَفَآءَ
مِنْۢ بَعْدِ قَوْمِ نُوْحٍ وَّزَادَكُمْ فِي
الْخَلْقِ بَصْۜطَةً ۚ فَاذْكُرُوْۤا
اٰلَآءَ اللّٰهِ لَعَلَّكُمْ تُفْلِحُوْنَ ﴿٦٩﴾

70. They said: "Do you come to us saying, that we may worship Allah alone, and give up the cult of our fathers? Bring us what you threaten us with, if so be that you tell the truth!"

70. Qaalooo aji'tanaa lina'bu-dal-laaha waḥdahoo wa nazara maa kaana ya'budu aabaaa'u-naa faâtinaa bimaa ta'idunaaa in kunta minaṣ-ṣaadiqeen.

قَالُوْۤا اَجِئْتَنَا لِنَعْبُدَ اللّٰهَ وَحْدَهٗ
وَنَذَرَ مَا كَانَ يَعْبُدُ اٰبَآؤُنَا ۚ
فَاْتِنَا بِمَا تَعِدُنَاۤ اِنْ كُنْتَ
مِنَ الصّٰدِقِيْنَ ﴿٧٠﴾

71. He said: "Punishment and wrath have already come upon you from your Lord: do you dispute with me over names which you have devised - you and your fathers,- without authority from Allah? Then wait: I am amongst you, also waiting."

71. Qaala qad waqa'a alaykum-mir-Rabbikum rijsuñw-wa ghaḍab, atujaadiloonanee feee asmaaa'in sammaytumoohaaa antum wa aabaaa'ukum maa nazzalal-laahu bihaa min sulṭaan; fantazirooo innee ma'akum minal-muntazireen.

قَالَ قَدْ وَقَعَ عَلَيْكُمْ مِّنْ رَّبِّكُمْ
رِجْسٌ وَّغَضَبٌ ؕ اَتُجَادِلُوْنَنِيْ
فِيْۤ اَسْمَآءٍ سَمَّيْتُمُوْهَاۤ اَنْتُمْ وَ
اٰبَآؤُكُمْ مَّا نَزَّلَ اللّٰهُ بِهَا مِنْ
سُلْطٰنٍ ؕ فَانْتَظِرُوْۤا اِنِّيْ مَعَكُمْ
مِّنَ الْمُنْتَظِرِيْنَ ﴿٧١﴾

72. We saved him and those who adhered to him,

72. Fa-anjaynaahu wallazeena ma'ahoo biraḥmatim-

فَاَنْجَيْنٰهُ وَالَّذِيْنَ مَعَهٗ بِرَحْمَةٍ

Ikhfa اخفاء · Ghunna غنّہ · Ikhfa Meem Saakin اخفاءمیم ساکن · Idghaam ادغام · Qalqala قلقلہ · Qalb قلب · Idghaam Meem Saakin ادغام میم ساکن

by Our Mercy, and We cut off the roots of those who rejected Our Signs and did not believe.

minnaa wa qaṭa'naa daabiral-lazeena kazzaboo bi-Aayaati-naa wa maa kaanoo mu'mineen. **(Section 9)**

مِّنَّا وَقَطَعْنَا دَابِرَ الَّذِينَ كَذَّبُوا
بِآيَاتِنَا وَمَا كَانُوا مُؤْمِنِينَ ﴿٧٢﴾

ع ٩ وقف لازم

73. To the Thamud people (We sent) Salih, one of their own brethren: He said: "O my people! worship Allah: you have no other god but Him. Now has come to you a clear (Sign) from your Lord! This she-camel of Allah is a Sign for you: So leave her to graze in Allah's earth, and let her come to no harm, or you shall be seized with a grievous punishment.

73. Wa ilaa Samooda akhaahum Ṣaaliḥaa; qaala yaa qawmi'-budul-laaha maa lakum min ilaahin ghayruhoo qad jaaa'atkum bayyinatum-mir-Rabbikum haazihee naaqatul-laahi lakum Aayatan fazaroohaa taåkul feee arḍil-laahi wa laa tamassoohaa bisooo'in fa-yaåkhuzakum 'azaabun aleem.

وَإِلَىٰ ثَمُودَ أَخَاهُمْ صَالِحًا ۗ قَالَ
يَا قَوْمِ اعْبُدُوا اللَّهَ مَا لَكُم مِّنْ
إِلَٰهٍ غَيْرُهُ ۖ قَدْ جَاءَتْكُم بَيِّنَةٌ
مِّن رَّبِّكُمْ ۖ هَٰذِهِ نَاقَةُ اللَّهِ لَكُمْ
آيَةً ۖ فَذَرُوهَا تَأْكُلْ فِي أَرْضِ
اللَّهِ ۖ وَلَا تَمَسُّوهَا بِسُوءٍ فَيَأْخُذَكُمْ
عَذَابٌ أَلِيمٌ ﴿٧٣﴾

74. "And remember how He made you inheritors after the 'Ad people and gave you habitations in the land: you build for yourselves palaces and castles in (open) plains, and carve out homes in the mountains; so bring to remembrance the benefits (you have received) from Allah, and refrain from evil and mischief on the earth."

74. Wazkurooo iz ja'alakum khulafaaa'a mim ba'di 'Aadiñw-wa bawwa-akum fil-arḍi tattakhizoona min suhoolihaa quṣooraññw-wa tanḥitoonal-jibaala buyootan fazkurooo aalaaa'al-laahi wa laa ta'saw fil-arḍi mufsideen.

وَاذْكُرُوا إِذْ جَعَلَكُمْ خُلَفَاءَ مِن
بَعْدِ عَادٍ وَبَوَّأَكُمْ فِي الْأَرْضِ
تَتَّخِذُونَ مِن سُهُولِهَا قُصُورًا
وَتَنْحِتُونَ الْجِبَالَ بُيُوتًا ۖ فَاذْكُرُوا
آلَاءَ اللَّهِ وَلَا تَعْثَوْا فِي الْأَرْضِ
مُفْسِدِينَ ﴿٧٤﴾

75. The leaders of the arrogant party among his people said to those who were reckoned powerless - those among them who believed: "Do you know indeed that Salih is an Apostle from his Lord?" They said: "We do indeed believe in the revelation which has been sent through him."

75. Qaalal-mala-ul-lazeenas-takbaroo min qawmihee lillazeenas-tuḍ'ifoo liman aamana minhum ata'lamoona anna Ṣaaliḥam-mursalum-mir-Rabbih; qaalooo innaa bimaaa ursila bihee mu'minoon.

قَالَ الْمَلَأُ الَّذِينَ اسْتَكْبَرُوا مِن
قَوْمِهِ لِلَّذِينَ اسْتُضْعِفُوا لِمَنْ
آمَنَ مِنْهُمْ أَتَعْلَمُونَ أَنَّ صَالِحًا
مُّرْسَلٌ مِّن رَّبِّهِ ۚ قَالُوا إِنَّا بِمَا
أُرْسِلَ بِهِ مُؤْمِنُونَ ﴿٧٥﴾

76. The Arrogant party said: "For our part, we reject what you believe in."

76.Qaalal-lazeenas-takbarooo innaa billazeee aamantum bihee kaafiroon.

قَالَ الَّذِينَ اسْتَكْبَرُوا إِنَّا بِالَّذِي
آمَنتُم بِهِ كَافِرُونَ ﴿٧٦﴾

77. Then they ham-strung the she-camel, and insolently defied the order of their Lord, saying: "O Salih! bring about your threats, if you are an Apostle (of Allah)!"

77. Fa'aqarun-naaqata wa 'ataw 'an amri Rabbihim wa qaaloo yaa Ṣaaliḥu'-tinaa bimaa ta'idunaaa in kunta minal-mursaleen.

فَعَقَرُوا النَّاقَةَ وَعَتَوْا عَنْ أَمْرِ
رَبِّهِمْ وَقَالُوا يَا صَالِحُ ائْتِنَا بِمَا
تَعِدُنَا إِن كُنتَ مِنَ الْمُرْسَلِينَ ﴿٧٧﴾

78. So the earthquake took them unawares, and they lay

78. Fa-akhazat-humur-rajfatu fa-aṣbaḥoo fee

فَأَخَذَتْهُمُ الرَّجْفَةُ فَأَصْبَحُوا فِي

Ikhfa اخفاء · Ghunna غُنّہ · Ikhfa Meem Saakin اخفاء میم ساکن · Idghaam ادغام · Qalqala قلقلہ · Qalb قلب · Idghaam Meem Saakin ادغام میم ساکن

prostrate in their homes in the morning!

79. So Salih left them, saying: "O my people! I did indeed convey to you the message for which I was sent by my Lord: I gave you good counsel, but you do not love good counsellors!"

80. We also (sent) Lut: He said to his people: "Do you commit lewdness such as no people in creation (ever) committed before you?

81. "For you practise your lusts on men in preference to women : you are indeed a people transgressing beyond bounds."

82. And his people gave no answer but this: they said, "Drive them out of your city: these are indeed men who want to be clean and pure!"

83. But we saved him and his family, except his wife: she was of those who lagged behind.

84. And we rained down on them a shower (of brimstone): then see what was the end of those who indulged in sin and crime!

85. To the Madyan people We sent Shu'aib, one of their own brethren: he said: "O my people! worship Allah; You have no other god but Him. Now has come unto you a clear (Sign) from your Lord! so give just measure and weight, nor withhold from the people the things that are their due; and do no mischief on the earth after it has been set in order: that will be best for you, if you have Faith.

86. "And do not squat on every road, breathing threats, hindering from the path of Allah those who believe in Him, and seeking in it something crooked;

daarihim jaasimeen.

79. Fa-tawallaa 'anhum wa qaala yaa qawmi laqad ablaghtukum Risaalata Rabbee wa naṣaḥtu lakum wa laakil-laa tuḥibboonan-naaṣiḥeen.

80. Wa Looṭan iz qaala liqawmiheee ataåtoonal-faaḥishata maa sabaqakum bihaa min aḥadim-minal-'aalameen.

81. Innakum lataåtoonar-rijaala shahwatam-min doonin-nisaaa'; bal antum qawmum-musrifoon.

82. Wa maa kaana jawaaba qawmiheee illaa an qaalooo akhrijoohum min qaryatikum innahum unaasuñy-yataṭah-haroon.

83. Fa-anjaynaahu wa ahla-hooo illam-ra-atahoo kaanat minal-ghaabireen.

84. Wa 'amṭarnaa 'alayhim maṭaran fanẓur kayfa kaana aaqibatul-mujrimeen.

(Section 10)

85. Wa ilaa Madyana akhaa-hum Shu'aybaa; qaala yaa qawmi'-budul-laaha maa lakum min ilaahin ghayruhoo qad jaaa'atkum bayyinatum-mir-Rabbikum fa-awful-kayla walmeezaana wa laa tabkhasun-naasa ashyaaa'ahum wa laa tufsidoo fil-arḍi ba'da iṣlaaḥi-haa; zaalikum khayrul-lakum in kuntum mu'mineen.

86. Wa laa taq'udoo bikulli ṣiraaṭin too'idoona wa taṣud-doona 'an sabeelil-laahi man aamana bihee wa tabghoonahaa 'iwajaa; waz-

دَارِهِمْ جٰثِمِيْنَ ﴿٧٨﴾

فَتَوَلّٰى عَنْهُمْ وَقَالَ يٰقَوْمِ لَقَدْ

اَبْلَغْتُكُمْ رِسَالَةَ رَبِّيْ وَنَصَحْتُ

لَكُمْ وَلٰكِنْ لَّا تُحِبُّوْنَ النّٰصِحِيْنَ ﴿٧٩﴾

وَلُوْطًا اِذْ قَالَ لِقَوْمِهٖٓ اَتَاْتُوْنَ

الْفَاحِشَةَ مَا سَبَقَكُمْ بِهَا مِنْ

اَحَدٍ مِّنَ الْعٰلَمِيْنَ ﴿٨٠﴾

اِنَّكُمْ لَتَاْتُوْنَ الرِّجَالَ شَهْوَةً مِّنْ

دُوْنِ النِّسَآءِ ؕ بَلْ اَنْتُمْ قَوْمٌ مُّسْرِفُوْنَ ﴿٨١﴾

وَمَا كَانَ جَوَابَ قَوْمِهٖٓ اِلَّآ اَنْ

قَالُوْٓا اَخْرِجُوْهُمْ مِّنْ قَرْيَتِكُمْ ۚ اِنَّهُمْ

اُنَاسٌ يَّتَطَهَّرُوْنَ ﴿٨٢﴾

فَاَنْجَيْنٰهُ وَاَهْلَهٗٓ اِلَّا امْرَاَتَهٗ ۖ

كَانَتْ مِنَ الْغٰبِرِيْنَ ﴿٨٣﴾

وَاَمْطَرْنَا عَلَيْهِمْ مَّطَرًا ؕ فَانْظُرْ

كَيْفَ كَانَ عَاقِبَةُ الْمُجْرِمِيْنَ ﴿٨٤﴾ ع ١٠ ١٢ ١٧

وَاِلٰى مَدْيَنَ اَخَاهُمْ شُعَيْبًا ؕ قَالَ

يٰقَوْمِ اعْبُدُوا اللّٰهَ مَا لَكُمْ مِّنْ اِلٰهٍ

غَيْرُهٗ ؕ قَدْ جَآءَتْكُمْ بَيِّنَةٌ مِّنْ رَّبِّكُمْ

فَاَوْفُوا الْكَيْلَ وَالْمِيْزَانَ وَلَا تَبْخَسُوا

النَّاسَ اَشْيَآءَهُمْ وَلَا تُفْسِدُوْا فِي

الْاَرْضِ بَعْدَ اِصْلَاحِهَا ؕ ذٰلِكُمْ خَيْرٌ

لَّكُمْ اِنْ كُنْتُمْ مُّؤْمِنِيْنَ ﴿٨٥﴾ ۚ

وَلَا تَقْعُدُوْا بِكُلِّ صِرَاطٍ تُوْعِدُوْنَ

وَتَصُدُّوْنَ عَنْ سَبِيْلِ اللّٰهِ مَنْ

اٰمَنَ بِهٖ وَتَبْغُوْنَهَا عِوَجًا ۚ وَ

Ikhfa اخفاء | Ghunna غُنّہ | Ikhfa Meem Saakin اخفاء میم ساکن | Idghaam ادغام | Qalqala قلقلہ | Qalb قلب | Idghaam Meem Saakin ادغام میم ساکن

But remember how you were small in numbers, and He gave you increase. And hold in your mind's eye what was the end of those who did mischief.

87. "And if there is a party among you who believes in the message with which I have been sent, and a party which does not believe, hold yourselves in patience until Allah decides between us: for He is the best to decide.

88. The leaders, the arrogant party among his people, said: "O Shu'aib! we shall certainly drive you out of our city - (you) and those who believe with you; or else you (and they) shall have to return to our ways and religion." He said: "What! even though we do detest (them)?

89. "We should indeed invent a lie against Allah, if we returned to your ways after Allah has rescued us therefrom; nor could we by any manner of means return thereto unless it be as in the will and plan of Allah, Our Lord. Our Lord can reach out to the utmost recesses of things by His knowledge. In Allah is our trust. Our Lord! You decide between us and our people in truth, for you are the best to decide."

90. The leaders, the unbelievers among his people, said: "If you follow Shu'aib, be sure then you are ruined!"

91. But the earthquake took them unawares, and they lay prostrate in their homes before the morning!

92. The men who rejected Shu'aib became as if they had never been in the homes where they had flourished: the men who rejected Shu'aib - it was they who were ruined!

93. So Shu'aib left them, saying: "O my people! I did indeed

kurooo iz kuntum qaleelan fakassarakum wanzuroo kayfa kaana 'aaqibatul-mufsideen.

87. Wa in kaana ṭaaa'ifatum-minkum aamanoo billazeee ursiltu bihee wa ṭaaa'ifatul-lam yu'minoo faṣbiroo ḥattaa yaḥkumal-laahu baynanaa; wa Huwa khayrul-ḥaakimeen.

88. Qaalal-mala-ul-lazeenas-takbaroo min qawmihee lanukhrijannaka yaa Shu'aybu wallazeena aamanoo ma'aka min qaryatinaaa aw lata'oodunna fee millatinaa; qaala awa law kunnaa kaariheen.

89. Qadif-taraynaa 'alal-laahi kaziban in 'udnaa fee millatikum ba'da iz najjaanal-laahu minhaa; wa maa yakoonu lanaaa an na'ooda feehaaa illaaa añy-yashaaa'al-laahu Rabbunaa; wasi'a Rabbunaa kulla shay'in 'ilmaa; 'alal-laahi tawakkalnaa; Rabbanaf-taḥ baynanaa wa bayna qawminaa bilḥaqqi wa Anta khayrul-faatiḥeen.

90. Wa qaalal-mala-ul-lazeena kafaroo min qawmihee la'init-taba'tum Shu'ayban innakum izal-lakhaasiroon.

91. Fa-akhazat-humur-rajfatu fa-aṣbaḥoo fee daarihim jaasimeen.

92. Allazeena kazzaboo Shu'ayban ka-al-lam yaghnaw feehaa; allazeena kazzaboo Shu'ayban kaanoo humul-khaasireen.

93. Fatawallaa 'anhum wa qaala yaa qawmi laqad

اذْكُرُوٓا إِذْ كُنتُمْ قَلِيلًا
فَكَثَّرَكُمْ ۖ وَانظُرُوا كَيْفَ كَانَ
عَاقِبَةُ الْمُفْسِدِينَ ﴿٨٦﴾
وَإِن كَانَ طَآئِفَةٌ مِّنكُمْ ءَامَنُوا
بِالَّذِىٓ أُرْسِلْتُ بِهِۦ وَطَآئِفَةٌ لَّمْ
يُؤْمِنُوا فَاصْبِرُوا حَتَّىٰ يَحْكُمَ اللَّهُ
بَيْنَنَا ۚ وَهُوَ خَيْرُ الْحَٰكِمِينَ ﴿٨٧﴾
قَالَ الْمَلَأُ الَّذِينَ اسْتَكْبَرُوا مِن
قَوْمِهِۦ لَنُخْرِجَنَّكَ يَٰشُعَيْبُ وَالَّذِينَ
ءَامَنُوا مَعَكَ مِن قَرْيَتِنَآ أَوْ لَتَعُودُنَّ
فِى مِلَّتِنَا ۚ قَالَ أَوَلَوْ كُنَّا كَٰرِهِينَ ﴿٨٨﴾
قَدِ افْتَرَيْنَا عَلَى اللَّهِ كَذِبًا إِنْ عُدْنَا
فِى مِلَّتِكُم بَعْدَ إِذْ نَجَّىٰنَا اللَّهُ مِنْهَا ۚ
وَمَا يَكُونُ لَنَآ أَن نَّعُودَ فِيهَآ إِلَّآ
أَن يَشَآءَ اللَّهُ رَبُّنَا ۚ وَسِعَ رَبُّنَا
كُلَّ شَىْءٍ عِلْمًا ۚ عَلَى اللَّهِ تَوَكَّلْنَا ۚ
رَبَّنَا افْتَحْ بَيْنَنَا وَبَيْنَ قَوْمِنَا بِالْحَقِّ
وَأَنتَ خَيْرُ الْفَٰتِحِينَ ﴿٨٩﴾
وَقَالَ الْمَلَأُ الَّذِينَ كَفَرُوا مِن قَوْمِهِۦ
لَئِنِ اتَّبَعْتُمْ شُعَيْبًا إِنَّكُمْ إِذًا لَّخَٰسِرُونَ ﴿٩٠﴾
فَأَخَذَتْهُمُ الرَّجْفَةُ فَأَصْبَحُوا فِى
دَارِهِمْ جَٰثِمِينَ ﴿٩١﴾
الَّذِينَ كَذَّبُوا شُعَيْبًا كَأَن لَّمْ
يَغْنَوْا فِيهَا ۚ الَّذِينَ كَذَّبُوا شُعَيْبًا
كَانُوا هُمُ الْخَٰسِرِينَ ﴿٩٢﴾
فَتَوَلَّىٰ عَنْهُمْ وَقَالَ يَٰقَوْمِ لَقَدْ

الجزء التاسع (٩)

مع عند المتقدمين ١٢

Ikhfa	Ghunna	Ikhfa Meem Saakin	Idghaam	Qalqala	Qalb	Idghaam Meem Saakin
اخفاء	غنّة	اخفاء میم ساکن	ادغام	قلقله	قلب	ادغام میم ساکن

convey to you the Messages for which I was sent by my Lord: I gave you good counsel, but how shall I lament over a people who refuse to believe!"

94. Whenever We sent a prophet to a town, We took up its people in suffering and adversity, in order that they might learn humility.

95. Then We changed their suffering into prosperity, until they grew and multiplied, and began to say: "Our fathers (too) were touched by suffering and affluence" ... Behold! We called them to account of a sudden, while they did not realised (their peril).

96. If the people of the towns had but believed and feared Allah, We should indeed have opened out to them (All kinds of) blessings from heaven and earth; but they rejected (the truth), and We brought them to book for their misdeeds.

97. Did the people of the towns feel secure against the coming of Our wrath by night while they were asleep?

98. Or else did they feel secure against its coming in broad daylight while they played about (care-free)?

99. Did they then feel secure against the Plan of Allah?- but no one can feel secure from the Plan of Allah, except those (doomed) to ruin!

100. To those who inherit the earth in succession to its (previous) possessors, is it not a guiding, (lesson) that, if We so willed, We could punish them (too) for their sins, and seal up their hearts so that they could not hear?

101. Such were the towns whose story We (thus) relate unto you: there came indeed to them their Apostles with clear (Signs): But they would not believe what

---

ablaghtukum Risaalaati Rabbee wa naṣaḥtu lakum fakayfa aasaa 'alaa qawmin kaafireen.

(Section 11)

94. Wa maaa arsalnaa fee qaryatim-min-Nabiyyin illaaa akhaznaaa ahlahaa bil-baåsaaa'i waḍḍarraaa'i la'allahum yaḍḍarra'oon.

95. Summa baddalnaa makaa-nas-sayyi'atil-ḥasanata ḥattaa 'afaw wa qaaloo qad massa aabaaa'anaḍ-ḍarraaa'u wassar-raaa'u fa-akhaznaahum baghta-tañw-wa hum laa yash'uroon.

96. Wa law anna ahlal-quraaa aamanoo wattaqaw lafataḥnaa 'alayhim barakaatim-minas-samaaa'i wal-arḍi wa laakin kazzaboo fa-akhaznaahum bimaa kaanoo yaksiboon.

97. Afa-amina ahlul-quraaa añy-yaåtiyahum baåsunaa bayaatañw-wa hum naaa'imoon.

98. Awa amina ahlul-quraaa añy-yaåtiyahum baåsunaa ḍuḥañw-wa hum yal'aboon.

99. Afa-aminoo makral-laah; falaa yaåmanu makral-laahi illal-qawmul-khaasiroon.

(Section 12)

100. Awa lam yahdi lillazeena yarisoonal-arḍa mim ba'di ahlihaaa al-law nashaaa'u aṣabnaahum bizunoobihim; wa natba'u 'alaa quloobihim fahum laa yasma'oon.

101. Tilkal-quraa naquṣṣu 'alayka min ambaaa'ihaa; wa laqad jaaa'at-hum Rusuluhum bilbayyinaati famaa kaanoo liyu'minoo bimaa

---

أَبْلِغُكُمْ رِسٰلٰتِ رَبِّي وَنَصَحْتُ لَكُمْ ۚ
فَكَيْفَ آسٰى عَلٰى قَوْمٍ كٰفِرِينَ ﴿٩٣﴾ ع ١١ ٩
وَمَآ أَرْسَلْنَا فِي قَرْيَةٍ مِّن نَّبِيٍّ إِلَّآ
أَخَذْنَآ أَهْلَهَا بِالْبَأْسَآءِ وَالضَّرَّآءِ
لَعَلَّهُمْ يَضَّرَّعُونَ ﴿٩٤﴾
ثُمَّ بَدَّلْنَا مَكَانَ السَّيِّئَةِ الْحَسَنَةَ
حَتّٰى عَفَوا وَّقَالُوا قَدْ مَسَّ آبَآءَنَا
الضَّرَّآءُ وَالسَّرَّآءُ فَأَخَذْنٰهُم بَغْتَةً
وَّهُمْ لَا يَشْعُرُونَ ﴿٩٥﴾
وَلَوْ أَنَّ أَهْلَ الْقُرٰىٓ آمَنُوا وَاتَّقَوْا
لَفَتَحْنَا عَلَيْهِم بَرَكٰتٍ مِّنَ السَّمَآءِ
وَالْأَرْضِ وَلٰكِن كَذَّبُوا فَأَخَذْنٰهُم
بِمَا كَانُوا يَكْسِبُونَ ﴿٩٦﴾
أَفَأَمِنَ أَهْلُ الْقُرٰىٓ أَن يَأْتِيَهُم
بَأْسُنَا بَيٰتًا وَّهُمْ نَآئِمُونَ ﴿٩٧﴾
أَوَأَمِنَ أَهْلُ الْقُرٰىٓ أَن يَأْتِيَهُم
بَأْسُنَا ضُحًى وَّهُمْ يَلْعَبُونَ ﴿٩٨﴾
أَفَأَمِنُوا مَكْرَ اللّٰهِ ۚ فَلَا يَأْمَنُ
مَكْرَ اللّٰهِ إِلَّا الْقَوْمُ الْخٰسِرُونَ ﴿٩٩﴾ ع ١٢ ٢
أَوَلَمْ يَهْدِ لِلَّذِينَ يَرِثُونَ الْأَرْضَ
مِن بَعْدِ أَهْلِهَآ أَن لَّوْ نَشَآءُ أَصَبْنٰهُم
بِذُنُوبِهِمْ ۚ وَنَطْبَعُ عَلٰى قُلُوبِهِمْ
فَهُمْ لَا يَسْمَعُونَ ﴿١٠٠﴾
تِلْكَ الْقُرٰى نَقُصُّ عَلَيْكَ مِنْ
أَنۢبَآئِهَا ۚ وَلَقَدْ جَآءَتْهُمْ رُسُلُهُم
بِالْبَيِّنٰتِ ۚ فَمَا كَانُوا لِيُؤْمِنُوا بِمَا

Ikhfa اخفاء | Ghunna غنّہ | Ikhfa Meem Saakin اخفاءمیم ساکن | Idghaam ادغام | Qalqala قلقلہ | Qalb قلب | Idghaam Meem Saakin ادغام میم ساکن

English	Transliteration	Arabic
they had rejected before. Thus does Allah seal up the hearts of those who reject faith.	kazzaboo min qabl; kazaalika yatba'ul-laahu 'alaa quloobil-kaafireen.	كَذَّبُوا مِنْ قَبْلُ ۚ كَذَٰلِكَ يَطْبَعُ اللَّهُ عَلَىٰ قُلُوبِ الْكَافِرِينَ ﴿١٠١﴾
102. Most of the men We did not find (true) to their covenant: but most of them We found rebellious and disobedient.	102. Wa maa wajadnaa li-aksarihim min 'ahd; wa iñw-wajadnaaa aksarahum lafaasiqeen.	وَمَا وَجَدْنَا لِأَكْثَرِهِمْ مِنْ عَهْدٍ ۖ وَإِنْ وَجَدْنَا أَكْثَرَهُمْ لَفَاسِقِينَ ﴿١٠٢﴾
103. Then after them We sent Moses with Our Signs to Pharaoh and his chiefs, but they wrongfully rejected them: So see what was the end of those who made mischief.	103. Summa ba'asnaa mim ba'dihim Moosaa bi-Aayaatinaaa ilaa Fir'awna wa mala'ihee fazalamoo bihaa fanzur kayfa kaana 'aaqibatul-mufsideen.	ثُمَّ بَعَثْنَا مِنْ بَعْدِهِمْ مُوسَىٰ بِآيَاتِنَا إِلَىٰ فِرْعَوْنَ وَمَلَئِهِ فَظَلَمُوا بِهَا ۖ فَانْظُرْ كَيْفَ كَانَ عَاقِبَةُ الْمُفْسِدِينَ ﴿١٠٣﴾
104. Moses said: "O Pharaoh! I am an Apostle from the Lord of the worlds,-	104. Wa qaala Moosaa yaa Fir'awnu innee Rasoolum-mir-Rabbil-'aalameen.	وَقَالَ مُوسَىٰ يَا فِرْعَوْنُ إِنِّي رَسُولٌ مِنْ رَبِّ الْعَالَمِينَ ﴿١٠٤﴾
105. One for whom it is right to say nothing but truth about Allah. Now I have come to you (people), from your Lord, with a clear (Sign): So let the Children of Israel depart along with me."	105. Haqeequn 'alaaa al-laaa aqoola 'alal-laahi illal-haqq; qad ji'tukum bibayyinatim-mir-Rabbikum fa-arsil ma'iya Baneee Israaa'eel.	حَقِيقٌ عَلَىٰ أَنْ لَا أَقُولَ عَلَى اللَّهِ إِلَّا الْحَقَّ ۚ قَدْ جِئْتُكُمْ بِبَيِّنَةٍ مِنْ رَبِّكُمْ فَأَرْسِلْ مَعِيَ بَنِي إِسْرَائِيلَ ﴿١٠٥﴾
106. (Pharaoh) said: "If indeed you have come with a Sign, show it forth,- if you are telling the truth."	106. Qaala in kunta ji'ta bi-Aayatin faåti bihaaa in kunta minas-saadiqeen.	قَالَ إِنْ كُنْتَ جِئْتَ بِآيَةٍ فَأْتِ بِهَا إِنْ كُنْتَ مِنَ الصَّادِقِينَ ﴿١٠٦﴾
107. Then (Moses) threw his rod, and behold! it was a serpent, plain (for all to see)!	107. Fa-alqaa 'asaahu fa-izaa hiya su'baanum-mubeen.	فَأَلْقَىٰ عَصَاهُ فَإِذَا هِيَ ثُعْبَانٌ مُبِينٌ ﴿١٠٧﴾
108. And he drew out his hand, and behold! it was white to all beholders!	108. Wa naza'a yadahoo fa-izaa hiya baydaaa'u linnaazireen. **(Section 13)**	وَنَزَعَ يَدَهُ فَإِذَا هِيَ بَيْضَاءُ لِلنَّاظِرِينَ ﴿١٠٨﴾
109. Said the Chiefs of the people of Pharaoh: "This is indeed a sorcerer well- versed.	109. Qaalal-mala-u min qawmi Fir'awna inna haazaa lasaahirun 'aleem.	قَالَ الْمَلَأُ مِنْ قَوْمِ فِرْعَوْنَ إِنَّ هَٰذَا لَسَاحِرٌ عَلِيمٌ ﴿١٠٩﴾
110. "His plan is to get you out of your land: then what is it you counsel?"	110. Yureedu añy-yukhrijakum min ardikum famaazaa taåmuroon.	يُرِيدُ أَنْ يُخْرِجَكُمْ مِنْ أَرْضِكُمْ ۖ فَمَاذَا تَأْمُرُونَ ﴿١١٠﴾
111. They said: "Keep him and his brother in suspense (for a while); and send to the cities men to collect-	111. Qaalooo arjih wa akhaahu wa arsil filmadaaa'ini haashireen.	قَالُوا أَرْجِهْ وَأَخَاهُ وَأَرْسِلْ فِي الْمَدَائِنِ حَاشِرِينَ ﴿١١١﴾
112. And bring up to you all (our) sorcerers well-versed."	112. Yaåtooka bikulli saahirin 'aleem.	يَأْتُوكَ بِكُلِّ سَاحِرٍ عَلِيمٍ ﴿١١٢﴾
113. So there came the sorcerers to Pharaoh: They said, "of course we shall have a (suitable) reward if we win!"	113. Wa jaaa'as-saharatu Fir-'awna qaaloo inna lanaa la-ajran in kunnaa nahnul-ghaalibeen.	وَجَاءَ السَّحَرَةُ فِرْعَوْنَ قَالُوا إِنَّ لَنَا لَأَجْرًا إِنْ كُنَّا نَحْنُ الْغَالِبِينَ ﴿١١٣﴾
114. He said: "Yes, (and more),- for you shall in that case be (raised to posts) nearest (to my person)."	114. Qaala na'am wa innakum laminal-muqarrabeen.	قَالَ نَعَمْ وَإِنَّكُمْ لَمِنَ الْمُقَرَّبِينَ ﴿١١٤﴾

Ikhfa اخفاء · Ghunna غنّہ · Ikhfa Meem Saakin اخفاء میم ساکن · Idghaam ادغام · Qalqala قلقلہ · Qalb قلب · Idghaam Meem Saakin ادغام میم ساکن

115. They said: "O Moses! will you throw (first), or shall we have the (first) throw?"

116. Said Moses: "You throw (first)." So when they threw, they bewitched the eyes of the people, and struck terror into them: for they showed a great (feat of) magic.

117. We put it into Moses's mind by inspiration: "Throw (now) your rod":and behold! it swallows up straight away all the falsehoods which they fake!

118. Thus truth was confirmed, and all that they did was made of no effect.

119. So the (great ones) were vanquished there and then, and were made to look small.

120. But the sorcerers fell down prostrate in adoration.

121. Saying: "We believe in the Lord of the Worlds,-

122. "The Lord of Moses and Aaron."

123. Said Pharaoh: "Do you believe in Him before I give you permission? Surely this is a trick which you have planned in the city to drive out its people: but soon you shall know (the consequences).

124. "Be sure I will cut off your hands and your feet on opposite sides, and I will cause you all to die on the cross."

125. They said: "For us, We are but sent back to our Lord:

126. "But you wreak your vengeance on us simply because we believed in the Signs of our Lord when they reached us! Our Lord! pour out on us patience and constancy, and take our souls unto You as Muslims (who bow to Your Will)!

127. Said the chiefs of Pharaoh's people:" Will you leave Moses and his people, to spread mischief in the land, and to abandon you and your gods?" He said:

115. Qaaloo yaa Moosaaa immaaa an tulqiya wa immaaa an nakoona naḥnul-mulqeen.

116. Qaala alqoo falam-maaa alqaw saḥarooo a'yunannaasi wastarhaboohum wa jaaa'oo bisiḥrin 'aẓeem.

117. Wa awḥaynaaa ilaa Moosaaa an alqi 'aṣaaka fa-izaa hiya talqafu maa yaåfikoon.

118. Fawaqa'al-ḥaqqu wa baṭala maa kaanoo ya'maloon.

119. Faghuliboo hunaalika wanqalaboo ṣaaghireen.

120. Wa ulqiyas-saḥaratu saajideen.

121. Qaalooo aamannaa bi-Rabbil-'aalameen.

122. Rabbi Moosaa wa Haaroon.

123. Qaala Fir'awnu aamantum bihee qabla an aazana lakum; inna haazaa lamakrum-makartumoohu filmadeenati litukhrijoo minhaaa ahlahaa fasawfa ta'lamoon.

124. La-uqaṭṭi'anna aydiyakum wa arjulakum min khilaafin summa la-uṣallibannakum ajma'een.

125. Qaalooo innaaa ilaa Rabbinaa munqaliboon.

126. Wa maa tanqimu minnaaa illaaa an aamannaa bi-Aayaati Rabbinaa lammaa jaaa'atnaa; Rabbanaaa afrigh 'alaynaa ṣabrañw-wa tawaffanaa muslimeen. **(Section 14)**

127. Wa qaalal-mala-u min qawmi Fir'awna atazaru Moosaa wa qawmahoo liyufsidoo fil-arḍi wa yazaraka wa aalihatak; qaala

قَالُوا يٰمُوسٰى إِمَّا أَن تُلْقِيَ وَإِمَّا
أَن نَّكُونَ نَحْنُ الْمُلْقِينَ ﴿١١٥﴾
قَالَ أَلْقُوا ۚ فَلَمَّا أَلْقَوْا سَحَرُوا
أَعْيُنَ النَّاسِ وَاسْتَرْهَبُوهُمْ وَجَاءُو
بِسِحْرٍ عَظِيمٍ ﴿١١٦﴾
وَأَوْحَيْنَا إِلَىٰ مُوسَىٰ أَنْ أَلْقِ عَصَاكَ
فَإِذَا هِيَ تَلْقَفُ مَا يَأْفِكُونَ ﴿١١٧﴾
فَوَقَعَ الْحَقُّ وَبَطَلَ مَا كَانُوا
يَعْمَلُونَ ﴿١١٨﴾
فَغُلِبُوا هُنَالِكَ وَانقَلَبُوا صٰغِرِينَ ﴿١١٩﴾
وَأُلْقِيَ السَّحَرَةُ سٰجِدِينَ ﴿١٢٠﴾
قَالُوا آمَنَّا بِرَبِّ الْعٰلَمِينَ ﴿١٢١﴾
رَبِّ مُوسَىٰ وَهٰرُونَ ﴿١٢٢﴾
قَالَ فِرْعَوْنُ آمَنتُم بِهِ قَبْلَ أَنْ آذَنَ
لَكُمْ ۖ إِنَّ هٰذَا لَمَكْرٌ مَّكَرْتُمُوهُ
فِي الْمَدِينَةِ لِتُخْرِجُوا مِنْهَا
أَهْلَهَا ۖ فَسَوْفَ تَعْلَمُونَ ﴿١٢٣﴾
لَأُقَطِّعَنَّ أَيْدِيَكُمْ وَأَرْجُلَكُم مِّنْ
خِلٰفٍ ثُمَّ لَأُصَلِّبَنَّكُمْ أَجْمَعِينَ ﴿١٢٤﴾
قَالُوا إِنَّا إِلَىٰ رَبِّنَا مُنقَلِبُونَ ﴿١٢٥﴾
وَمَا تَنقِمُ مِنَّا إِلَّا أَنْ آمَنَّا بِآيٰتِ
رَبِّنَا لَمَّا جَاءَتْنَا ۚ رَبَّنَا أَفْرِغْ عَلَيْنَا
صَبْرًا وَتَوَفَّنَا مُسْلِمِينَ ﴿١٢٦﴾ ع ١٤
وَقَالَ الْمَلَأُ مِن قَوْمِ فِرْعَوْنَ
أَتَذَرُ مُوسَىٰ وَقَوْمَهُ لِيُفْسِدُوا
فِي الْأَرْضِ وَيَذَرَكَ وَآلِهَتَكَ ۚ قَالَ

Ikhfa اخفاء | Ghunna غنّہ | Ikhfa Meem Saakin اخفاءمیم ساکن | Idghaam ادغام | Qalqala قلقلہ | Qalb قلب | Idghaam Meem Saakin ادغام میم ساکن

"We will slay their male children; we will save alive (only) their females; and we have irresistible power over them."

sanuqattilu abnaaa'ahum wa nastaḥyee nisaaa'ahum wa innaa fawqahum qaahiroon.

سَنُقَتِّلُ اَبْنَآءَهُمْ وَنَسْتَحْيٖ نِسَآءَهُمْ
وَاِنَّا فَوْقَهُمْ قٰهِرُوْنَ ﴿١٢٧﴾

128. Moses said to his people: "Pray for help from Allah, and (wait) in patience and constancy: for the earth is Allah's, to give as a heritage to such of His servants as He pleases; and the end is (best) for the righteous.

128. Qaala Moosaa liqawmihis-ta‘eenoo billaahi waṣbiroo innal-arḍa lillaahi yoori<u>s</u>uhaa mañy-yashaaa'u min 'ibaadihee wal‘aaqibatu lilmuttaqeen.

قَالَ مُوْسٰى لِقَوْمِهِ اسْتَعِيْنُوْا
بِاللّٰهِ وَاصْبِرُوْا ۚ اِنَّ الْاَرْضَ لِلّٰهِ ۙ قف
يُوْرِثُهَا مَنْ يَّشَآءُ مِنْ عِبَادِهٖ ؕ
وَالْعَاقِبَةُ لِلْمُتَّقِيْنَ ﴿١٢٨﴾

129. They said: "We have had (nothing but) trouble, both before and after you came to us." He said: "It may be that your Lord will destroy your enemy and make you inheritors in the earth; that so He may try you by your deeds."

129. Qaalooo oo<u>z</u>eenaa min qabli an taåtiyanaa wa mim ba‘di maa ji'tanaa; qaala 'asaa Rabbukum añy-yuhlika 'aduwwakum wa yastakhlifakum fil-arḍi fayanẓura kayfa ta‘maloon. **(Section 15)**

قَالُوْٓا اُوْذِيْنَا مِنْ قَبْلِ اَنْ تَاْتِيَنَا وَ
مِنْۢ بَعْدِ مَا جِئْتَنَا ؕ قَالَ عَسٰى رَبُّكُمْ
اَنْ يُّهْلِكَ عَدُوَّكُمْ وَيَسْتَخْلِفَكُمْ
فِي الْاَرْضِ فَيَنْظُرَ كَيْفَ تَعْمَلُوْنَ ﴿١٢٩﴾ ع ١٥

130. We punished the people of Pharaoh with years (of droughts) and shortness of crops; that they might receive admonition.

130. Wa laqad akha<u>z</u>naaa Aala Fir‘awna bis-sineena wa naqṣ im-minas-<u>s</u>amaraati la‘allahum ya<u>zz</u>akkaroon.

وَلَقَدْ اَخَذْنَآ اٰلَ فِرْعَوْنَ
بِالسِّنِيْنَ وَنَقْصٍ مِّنَ الثَّمَرٰتِ
لَعَلَّهُمْ يَذَّكَّرُوْنَ ﴿١٣٠﴾

131. But when good (times) came, they said, "This is due to us;" when gripped by calamity, they ascribed it to evil omens connected with Moses and those with him! Behold! in truth the omens of evil are theirs in Allah's sight, but most of them do not understand!

131. Fa-i<u>z</u>aa jaaa'at-humulḥasanatu qaaloo lanaa haa<u>z</u>ihee wa in tuṣibhum sayyi'atuñy-yaṭṭayyaroo bi Moosaa wa mam-ma‘ah; alaaa innamaa ṭaaa'iruhum 'indal-laahi wa laakinna ak<u>s</u>arahum laa ya‘lamoon.

فَاِذَا جَآءَتْهُمُ الْحَسَنَةُ قَالُوْا
لَنَا هٰذِهٖ ۚ وَاِنْ تُصِبْهُمْ سَيِّئَةٌ
يَّطَّيَّرُوْا بِمُوْسٰى وَمَنْ مَّعَهٗ ؕ اَلَآ
اِنَّمَا طٰٓئِرُهُمْ عِنْدَ اللّٰهِ وَلٰكِنَّ
اَكْثَرَهُمْ لَا يَعْلَمُوْنَ ﴿١٣١﴾

132. They said (to Moses): "Whatever be the Signs you bring, to work therewith your sorcery on us, we shall never believe in you.

132. Wa qaaloo mahmaa taåtinaa bihee min Aayatil-litasḥaranaa bihaa famaa naḥnu laka bimu'mineen.

وَقَالُوْا مَهْمَا تَاْتِنَا بِهٖ مِنْ اٰيَةٍ
لِّتَسْحَرَنَا بِهَا ۙ فَمَا نَحْنُ لَكَ
بِمُؤْمِنِيْنَ ﴿١٣٢﴾

133. So We sent (plagues) on them: wholesale Death, Locusts, Lice, Frogs, and Blood: Signs openly self-explained: but they were steeped in arrogance,- a people given to sin.

133. Fa-arsalnaa 'alayhimuṭ-ṭoofaana waljaraada walqummala waḍḍafaadi‘a waddama Aayaatim-mufaṣṣalaatin fastakbaroo wa kaanoo qawmam-mujrimeen.

فَاَرْسَلْنَا عَلَيْهِمُ الطُّوْفَانَ وَالْجَرَادَ
وَالْقُمَّلَ وَالضَّفَادِعَ وَالدَّمَ
اٰيٰتٍ مُّفَصَّلٰتٍ ۫ فَاسْتَكْبَرُوْا وَ
كَانُوْا قَوْمًا مُّجْرِمِيْنَ ﴿١٣٣﴾

134. Every time the Chastisement fell on them, they said: "O Moses!

134. Wa lammaa waqa‘a 'alayhimur-rijzu qaaloo yaa Moosad-

وَلَمَّا وَقَعَ عَلَيْهِمُ الرِّجْزُ قَالُوْا يٰمُوْسَى

Ikhfa اخفاء | Ghunna غنّہ | Ikhfa Meem Saakin اخفاء میم ساکن | Idghaam ادغام | Qalqala قلقلہ | Qalb قلب | Idghaam Meem Saakin ادغام میم ساکن

ادْعُ لَنَا رَبَّكَ بِمَا عَهِدَ عِنْدَكَ ۚ لَئِنْ
كَشَفْتَ عَنَّا الرِّجْزَ لَنُؤْمِنَنَّ لَكَ
وَلَنُرْسِلَنَّ مَعَكَ بَنِيٓ اِسْرَآءِيْلَ ۚ ﴿١٣٤﴾

'u lanaa rabbaka bimaa 'ahida 'indaka la'in kashafta 'annar-rijza lanu'minanna laka wa lanursilanna ma'aka Baneee Israaa'eel.

on our behalf call on your Lord in virtue of his promise to you: If you will remove the Chastisement from us, we shall truly believe in you, and we shall send away the Children of Israel with you."

فَلَمَّا كَشَفْنَا عَنْهُمُ الرِّجْزَ اِلٰٓى اَجَلٍ
هُمْ بٰلِغُوْهُ اِذَا هُمْ يَنْكُثُوْنَ ﴿١٣٥﴾

135. Falammaa kashafnaa 'anhumur-rijza ilaaa ajalin hum baalighoohu izaa hum yankusoon.

135. But every time We removed the plague from them according to a fixed term which they had to fulfil,- Behold! they broke their word!

فَانْتَقَمْنَا مِنْهُمْ فَاَغْرَقْنٰهُمْ فِى الْيَمِّ
بِاَنَّهُمْ كَذَّبُوْا بِاٰيٰتِنَا وَكَانُوْا
عَنْهَا غٰفِلِيْنَ ﴿١٣٦﴾

136. Fantaqamnaa minhum fa-aghraqnaahum fil-yammi bi-annahum kazzaboo bi-Aayaatinaa wa kaanoo 'anhaa ghaafileen.

136. So We exacted retribution from them: We drowned them in the sea, because they rejected Our Signs and failed to take warning from them.

وَاَوْرَثْنَا الْقَوْمَ الَّذِيْنَ كَانُوْا
يُسْتَضْعَفُوْنَ مَشَارِقَ الْاَرْضِ وَ
مَغَارِبَهَا الَّتِيْ بٰرَكْنَا فِيْهَا ۗ
وَتَمَّتْ كَلِمَتُ رَبِّكَ الْحُسْنٰى عَلٰى
بَنِيٓ اِسْرَآءِيْلَ ۙ۬ بِمَا صَبَرُوْا ۗ وَ
دَمَّرْنَا مَا كَانَ يَصْنَعُ فِرْعَوْنُ
وَقَوْمُهٗ وَمَا كَانُوْا يَعْرِشُوْنَ ﴿١٣٧﴾ الربع

137. Wa awrasnal-qawmallazeena kaanoo yustaḍ'afoona mashaariqal-arḍi wa maghaaribahal-latee baaraknaa feehaa wa tammat Kalimatu Rabbikal-ḥusnaa 'alaa Baneee Israaa'eela bimaa ṣabaroo wa dammarnaa maa kaana yaṣna'u Fir'awnu wa qawmuhoo wa maa kaanoo ya'rishoon.

137. And We made a people, considered weak (and of no account), inheritors of lands in both East and West, - lands whereon We sent down Our blessings. The fair promise of your Lord was fulfilled for the Children of Israel, because they had patience and constancy, and We levelled to the ground the great works and fine buildings which Pharaoh and his people erected (with such pride).

وَجٰوَزْنَا بِبَنِيٓ اِسْرَآءِيْلَ الْبَحْرَ
فَاَتَوْا عَلٰى قَوْمٍ يَّعْكُفُوْنَ عَلٰٓى
اَصْنَامٍ لَّهُمْ ۚ قَالُوْا يٰمُوْسَى اجْعَلْ
لَّنَآ اِلٰهًا كَمَا لَهُمْ اٰلِهَةٌ ۗ قَالَ
اِنَّكُمْ قَوْمٌ تَجْهَلُوْنَ ﴿١٣٨﴾

138. Wa jaawaznaa bi-Baneee Israaa'eelal-baḥra fa-ataw 'alaa qawmiñy-ya'kufoona 'alaaa aṣnaamil-lahum; qaaloo yaa Moosaj'al-lanaaa ilaahan kamaa lahum aalihah; qaala innakum qawmun tajhaloon.

138. We took the Children of Israel (with safety) across the sea. They came upon a people devoted entirely to some idols they had. They said: "O Moses! fashion for us a god like the gods they have." He said: "Surely you are a people without knowledge.

اِنَّ هٰٓؤُلَآءِ مُتَبَّرٌ مَّا هُمْ فِيْهِ وَ
بٰطِلٌ مَّا كَانُوْا يَعْمَلُوْنَ ﴿١٣٩﴾

139. Inna haaa'ulaaa'i mutabbarum-maa hum feehi wa baaṭilum-maa kaanoo ya'maloon.

139. "As to these folks,- the cult they are in is (but) a fragment of a ruin, and vain is the (worship) which they practise."

قَالَ اَغَيْرَ اللّٰهِ اَبْغِيْكُمْ اِلٰهًا وَّ
هُوَ فَضَّلَكُمْ عَلَى الْعٰلَمِيْنَ ﴿١٤٠﴾

140. Qaala a-ghayral-laahi abgheekum ilaahañw-wa Huwa faḍḍalakum 'alal-'aalameen.

140. He said: "Shall I seek for you a god other than the (true) God, when it is Allah who has endowed you with gifts above the nations?"

وَاِذْ اَنْجَيْنٰكُمْ مِّنْ اٰلِ فِرْعَوْنَ
يَسُوْمُوْنَكُمْ سُوْٓءَ الْعَذَابِ ۚ يُقَتِّلُوْنَ

141. Wa iz anjaynaakum min Aali Fir'awna yasoomoonakum sooo'al-'azaab, yuqattiloona

141. And remember We rescued you from Pharaoh's people, who afflicted you with the worst of penalties, Who slew

Ikhfa اخفاء | Ghunna غُنّہ | Ikhfa Meem Saakin اخفاءمیم ساکن | Idghaam ادغام | Qalqala قلقلہ | Qalb قلب | Idghaam Meem Saakin ادغام میم ساکن

your male children and saved alive your females: in that was a momentous trial from your Lord.

142. We appointed for Moses thirty nights, and completed (the period) with ten (more): thus was completed the term (of communion) with his Lord, forty nights. And Moses had charged his brother Aaron (before he went up): "Act for me amongst my people: do right, and follow not the way of those who do mischief."

143. When Moses came to the place appointed by Us, and his Lord addressed him, He said: "O my Lord! show (Yourself) to me, that I may look upon You." Allah said: "By no means can you see Me (direct); But look upon the mount; if it abide in its place, then shall you see Me." When his Lord manifested His glory on the Mount, He made it as dust, and Moses fell down in a swoon. When he recovered his senses he said: "Glory be to You! to You I turn in repentance, and I am the first to believe."

144. (Allah) said: "O Moses! I have chosen you above (other) men, by the mission I (have given you) and the words I (have spoken to you): take then the (revelation) which I give you, and be of those who give thanks."

145. And We ordained laws for him in the tablets in all matters, both commanding and explaining all things, (and said): "Take and hold these with firmness, and enjoin your people to hold fast by the best in the precepts: soon shall I show you the homes of the wicked,- (How they lie desolate)."

146. Those who behave arrogantly on the earth in defiance of right - I will turn them away from My Signs: Even if they see all the Signs, they will not believe in them;

abnaaa'akum wa yastaḥyoona nisaaa'akum; wa fee zaalikum balaaa'um-mir-Rabbikum 'azeem. **(Section 16)**

142. Wa waa'adnaa Moosaa salaaseena laylatañw-wa atmamnaahaa bi'ashrin fatamma meeqaatu Rabbiheee arba'eena laylah; wa qaala Moosaa liakheehi Haaroonakh-lufnee fee qawmee wa aṣliḥ wa laa tattabi' sabeelal-mufsideen.

143. Wa lammaa jaaa'a Moosaa limeeqaatinaa wa kallamahoo Rabbuhoo qaala Rabbi arineee anẓur ilayk; qaala lan taraanee wa laakininẓur ilal-jabali fainistaqarra makaanahoo fasawfa taraanee; falammaa tajallaa Rabbuhoo liljabali ja'alahoo dakkañw-wa kharra Moosaa ṣa'iqaa; falammaaa afaaqa qaala Subḥaanaka tubtu ilayka wa ana awwalulmu'mineen.

144. Qaala yaa Moosaaa inniṣṭafaytuka 'alan-naasi bi-Risaalaatee wa bi-Kalaamee fakhuz maaa aataytuka wa kum-minash-shaakireen.

145. Wa katabnaa lahoo filalwaaḥi min kulli shay'im-maw'iẓatañw-wa tafṣeelal-likulli shay'in fakhuzhaa biquwwatiñw-waåmur qawmaka yaåkhuzoo bi-aḥsanihaa; saureekum daaral-faasiqeen.

146.Sa-aṣrifu 'an Aayaatiyal-lazeena yatakabbaroona fil-arḍi bighayril-ḥaqq; wa iñy-yaraw kulla Aayatil-laa yu'minoo bihaa

اَبْنَآءَكُمْ وَيَسْتَحْيُوْنَ نِسَآءَكُمْ ط وَ
فِيْ ذٰلِكُمْ بَلَآءٌ مِّنْ رَّبِّكُمْ عَظِيْمٌ ﴿١٤١﴾
وَوٰعَدْنَا مُوْسٰى ثَلٰثِيْنَ لَيْلَةً وَّ
اَتْمَمْنٰهَا بِعَشْرٍ فَتَمَّ مِيْقَاتُ رَبِّهٖٓ
اَرْبَعِيْنَ لَيْلَةً ج وَقَالَ مُوْسٰى لِاَخِيْهِ
هٰرُوْنَ اخْلُفْنِيْ فِيْ قَوْمِيْ وَاَصْلِحْ
وَلَا تَتَّبِعْ سَبِيْلَ الْمُفْسِدِيْنَ ﴿١٤٢﴾
وَلَمَّا جَآءَ مُوْسٰى لِمِيْقَاتِنَا وَ
كَلَّمَهٗ رَبُّهٗ لا قَالَ رَبِّ اَرِنِيْٓ اَنْظُرْ
اِلَيْكَ ط قَالَ لَنْ تَرٰىنِيْ وَلٰكِنِ انْظُرْ
اِلَى الْجَبَلِ فَاِنِ اسْتَقَرَّ مَكَانَهٗ
فَسَوْفَ تَرٰىنِيْ ج فَلَمَّا تَجَلّٰى رَبُّهٗ لِلْجَبَلِ
جَعَلَهٗ دَكًّا وَّخَرَّ مُوْسٰى صَعِقًا ج
فَلَمَّآ اَفَاقَ قَالَ سُبْحٰنَكَ تُبْتُ
اِلَيْكَ وَاَنَا اَوَّلُ الْمُؤْمِنِيْنَ ﴿١٤٣﴾
قَالَ يٰمُوْسٰٓى اِنِّى اصْطَفَيْتُكَ عَلَى
النَّاسِ بِرِسٰلٰتِيْ وَبِكَلَامِيْ صلے فَخُذْ
مَآ اٰتَيْتُكَ وَكُنْ مِّنَ الشّٰكِرِيْنَ ﴿١٤٤﴾
وَكَتَبْنَا لَهٗ فِي الْاَلْوَاحِ مِنْ كُلِّ
شَيْءٍ مَّوْعِظَةً وَّتَفْصِيْلًا لِّكُلِّ
شَيْءٍ ج فَخُذْهَا بِقُوَّةٍ وَّاْمُرْ قَوْمَكَ
يَاْخُذُوْا بِاَحْسَنِهَا ط سَاُورِيْكُمْ
دَارَ الْفٰسِقِيْنَ ﴿١٤٥﴾
سَاَصْرِفُ عَنْ اٰيٰتِيَ الَّذِيْنَ
يَتَكَبَّرُوْنَ فِي الْاَرْضِ بِغَيْرِ الْحَقِّ ط
وَاِنْ يَّرَوْا كُلَّ اٰيَةٍ لَّا يُؤْمِنُوْا بِهَا ج

Ikhfa اخفاء | Ghunna غُنّہ | Ikhfa Meem Saakin اخفاء میم ساکن | Idghaam ادغام | Qalqala قلقلہ | Qalb قلب | Idghaam Meem Saakin ادغام میم ساکن

and if they see the way of right conduct, they will not adopt it as the way; but if they see the way of error, that is the way they will adopt. For they have rejected Our Signs, and failed to take warning from them.

147. Those who reject Our Signs and the Meeting in the Hereafter,- vain are their deeds: can they expect to be rewarded except as they have wrought?

148. The people of Moses made, in his absence, out of their ornaments, the image of a calf, (for worship) having lowing sound. Did they not see that it could neither speak to them, nor show them the way? They took it for worship and they did wrong.

149. When they repented, and saw that they had erred, they said: "If our Lord have not mercy upon us and forgive us, we shall indeed be of those who perish."

150. When Moses came back to his people, angry and grieved, he said: "Evil it is that you have done in my place in my absence: did you make haste to bring on the judgment of your Lord?" He put down the Tablets, seized his brother by (the hair of) his head, and dragged him to him. Aaron said: "Son of my mother! The people did indeed reckon me as nothing, and went near to slaying me! Make not the enemies rejoice over my misfortune, nor count you me amongst the people of sin."

151. Moses prayed: "O my Lord! forgive me and my brother! Admit us to Your mercy! for You are the Most Merciful of those who show mercy!"

152. Those who took the calf (for worship) will indeed be

wa iñy-yaraw sabeelar-rushdi laa yattakhizoohu sabeelañw wa iñy-yaraw sabeelal-ghayyi yattakhizoohu sabeelaa; zaalika bi-annahum kazzaboo bi-Aayaatinaa wa kaanoo 'anhaa ghaafileen.

147. Wallazeena kazzaboo bi-Aayaatinaa wa liqaaa'il-Aakhirati ḥabiṭat 'amaaluhum; hal yujzawna illaa maa kaanoo ya'maloon. **(Section 17)**

148. Wattakhaza qawmu Moosaa mim ba'dihee min ḥuliyyihim 'ijlan jasadal-lahoo khuwaar; alam yaraw annahoo laa yukallimuhum wa laa yahdeehim sabeelaa; ittakhazoohu wa kaanoo ẓaalimeen.

149. Wa lammaa suqiṭa feee aydeehim wa ra-aw annahum qad ḍalloo qaaloo la'il-lam yarḥamnaa Rabbunaa wa yaghfir lanaa lanakoonanna minal-khaasireen.

150. Wa lammaa raja'a Moosaaa ilaa qawmihee ghaḍbaana asifan qaala bi'samaa khalaftumoonee mim ba'dee a-'ajiltum amra Rabbikum wa alqal-alwaaḥa wa akhaza biraåsi akheehi yajurruhooo ilayh; qaalab-na-umma innal-qawmas taḍ'afoonee wa kaadoo yaqtuloonanee; falaa tushmit biyal-a'daaa'a wa laa taj'alnee ma'al-qawmiẓ-ẓaalimeen.

151. Qaala Rabbigh-fir lee wa li-akhee wa adkhilnaa fee raḥmatika wa Anta arḥamur-raaḥimeen. **(Section 18)**

152 Innal-lazeenat-takhazul-'ijla sa-yanaaluhum

وَاِنْ يَّرَوْا سَبِيْلَ الرُّشْدِ لَا يَتَّخِذُوْهُ
سَبِيْلًا ۚ وَاِنْ يَّرَوْا سَبِيْلَ الْغَيِّ
يَتَّخِذُوْهُ سَبِيْلًا ؕ ذٰلِكَ بِاَنَّهُمْ كَذَّبُوْا
بِاٰيٰتِنَا وَكَانُوْا عَنْهَا غٰفِلِيْنَ ﴿١٤٦﴾
وَالَّذِيْنَ كَذَّبُوْا بِاٰيٰتِنَا وَلِقَآءِ
الْاٰخِرَةِ حَبِطَتْ اَعْمَالُهُمْ ؕ هَلْ
يُجْزَوْنَ اِلَّا مَا كَانُوْا يَعْمَلُوْنَ ﴿١٤٧﴾ ع ١٧
وَاتَّخَذَ قَوْمُ مُوْسٰى مِنْۢ بَعْدِهٖ مِنْ
حُلِيِّهِمْ عِجْلًا جَسَدًا لَّهٗ خُوَارٌ ؕ اَلَمْ
يَرَوْا اَنَّهٗ لَا يُكَلِّمُهُمْ وَلَا يَهْدِيْهِمْ
سَبِيْلًا ۘ اِتَّخَذُوْهُ وَكَانُوْا ظٰلِمِيْنَ ﴿١٤٨﴾ وقف لازم
وَلَمَّا سُقِطَ فِيْٓ اَيْدِيْهِمْ وَرَاَوْا اَنَّهُمْ
قَدْ ضَلُّوْا ۙ قَالُوْا لَئِنْ لَّمْ يَرْحَمْنَا رَبُّنَا
وَيَغْفِرْ لَنَا لَنَكُوْنَنَّ مِنَ الْخٰسِرِيْنَ ﴿١٤٩﴾
وَلَمَّا رَجَعَ مُوْسٰٓى اِلٰى قَوْمِهٖ غَضْبَانَ
اَسِفًا ۙ قَالَ بِئْسَمَا خَلَفْتُمُوْنِيْ مِنْۢ
بَعْدِيْ ۚ اَعَجِلْتُمْ اَمْرَ رَبِّكُمْ ۚ وَاَلْقَى
الْاَلْوَاحَ وَاَخَذَ بِرَاْسِ اَخِيْهِ يَجُرُّهٗٓ
اِلَيْهِ ؕ قَالَ ابْنَ اُمَّ اِنَّ الْقَوْمَ
اسْتَضْعَفُوْنِيْ وَكَادُوْا يَقْتُلُوْنَنِيْ ۫ۖ
فَلَا تُشْمِتْ بِيَ الْاَعْدَآءَ وَلَا تَجْعَلْنِيْ
مَعَ الْقَوْمِ الظّٰلِمِيْنَ ﴿١٥٠﴾
قَالَ رَبِّ اغْفِرْ لِيْ وَلِاَخِيْ وَاَدْخِلْنَا
فِيْ رَحْمَتِكَ ۫ۖ وَاَنْتَ اَرْحَمُ
الرّٰحِمِيْنَ ﴿١٥١﴾ ع ١٨
اِنَّ الَّذِيْنَ اتَّخَذُوا الْعِجْلَ سَيَنَالُهُمْ

Ikhfa اخفاء | Ghunna غُنّہ | Ikhfa Meem Saakin اخفاء میم ساکن | Idghaam ادغام | Qalqala قلقلہ | Qalb قلب | Idghaam Meem Saakin ادغام میم ساکن

overwhelmed with wrath from their Lord, and with shame in this life: thus do We recompense those who invent (falsehoods).

ghaḍabum-mir-Rabbihim wa zillatun fil-ḥayaatid-dunyaa; wa kazaalika najzil-muftareen.

غَضَبٌ مِّنْ رَّبِّهِمْ وَذِلَّةٌ فِي
الْحَيٰوةِ الدُّنْيَا ؕ وَكَذٰلِكَ نَجْزِي
الْمُفْتَرِيْنَ ﴿١٥٢﴾

153. But those who do wrong but repent thereafter and (truly) believe,- verily your Lord is thereafter Oft-Forgiving, Most Merciful.

153. Wallazeena 'amilus-sayyi-aati summa taaboo mim ba'dihaa wa aamanooo inna Rabbaka mim ba'dihaa la-Ghafoorur-Raḥeem.

وَالَّذِيْنَ عَمِلُوا السَّيِّاٰتِ ثُمَّ تَابُوْا مِنْ
بَعْدِهَا وَاٰمَنُوْٓا ز اِنَّ رَبَّكَ مِنْ
بَعْدِهَا لَغَفُوْرٌ رَّحِيْمٌ ﴿١٥٣﴾

154. When the anger of Moses was appeased, he took up the Tablets: in the writing thereon was Guidance and Mercy for such as fear their Lord.

154. Wa lammaa sakata 'am-Moosal-ghaḍabu akhazal-al-waaḥa wa fee nuskhatihaa hudañw-wa raḥmatul-lillazeena hum li-Rabbihim yarhaboon.

وَلَمَّا سَكَتَ عَنْ مُّوْسَى الْغَضَبُ
اَخَذَ الْاَلْوَاحَ ۚ وَفِيْ نُسْخَتِهَا
هُدًى وَّرَحْمَةٌ لِّلَّذِيْنَ هُمْ لِرَبِّهِمْ
يَرْهَبُوْنَ ﴿١٥٤﴾

155. And Moses chose seventy of his people for Our place of meeting: when they were seized with violent quaking, he prayed: "O my Lord! if it had been Your will You could have destroyed, long before, both them and me: would You destroy us for the deeds of the foolish ones among us? this is no more than trial from You by it. You cause whom You will to stray, and You lead whom You will into the right path. You are our Protector: so forgive us and give us Your mercy; for You are the best of those who forgive.

155. Wakhtaara Moosaa qawmahoo sab'eena rajulal-limeeqaatinaa falammaaa akha-zat-humur-rajfatu qaala Rabbi law shi'ta ahlaktahum min qablu wa iyyaaya atuhlikunaa bimaa fa'alas-sufahaaa'u minnaa in hiya illaa fitnatuka tuḍillu bihaa man tashaaa'u wa tahdee man tashaaa'u Anta waliyyunaa faghfir lanaa warḥamnaa wa Anta khayrul-ghaafireen.

وَاخْتَارَ مُوْسٰى قَوْمَهٗ سَبْعِيْنَ رَجُلًا
لِّمِيْقَاتِنَا ۚ فَلَمَّآ اَخَذَتْهُمُ الرَّجْفَةُ
قَالَ رَبِّ لَوْ شِئْتَ اَهْلَكْتَهُمْ
مِّنْ قَبْلُ وَاِيَّايَ ؕ اَتُهْلِكُنَا بِمَا
فَعَلَ السُّفَهَآءُ مِنَّا ۚ اِنْ هِيَ اِلَّا
فِتْنَتُكَ ؕ تُضِلُّ بِهَا مَنْ تَشَآءُ
وَتَهْدِيْ مَنْ تَشَآءُ ؕ اَنْتَ وَلِيُّنَا
فَاغْفِرْ لَنَا وَارْحَمْنَا وَاَنْتَ خَيْرُ
الْغٰفِرِيْنَ ﴿١٥٥﴾

156. "And ordain for us that which is good, in this life and in the Hereafter: for we have turned unto You." He said: "With My punishment I visit whom I will; but My mercy extends to all things. That (mercy) I shall ordain for those who do right, and pay Zakat, and those who believe in Our Signs;-

156. Waktub lanaa fee haazi-hid-dunyaa ḥasanatañw-wa fil-Aakhirati innaa hudnaa ilayk; qaala 'azaabeee uṣeebu bihee man ashaaa'u wa raḥmatee wasi'at kulla shay'; fasa-aktubuhaa lillazeena yatta-qoona wa yu'toonaz-Zakaata wallazeena hum bi-Aayaatinaa yu'minoon.

وَاكْتُبْ لَنَا فِيْ هٰذِهِ الدُّنْيَا حَسَنَةً
وَّفِي الْاٰخِرَةِ اِنَّا هُدْنَآ اِلَيْكَ ؕ قَالَ
عَذَابِيْٓ اُصِيْبُ بِهٖ مَنْ اَشَآءُ ۚ وَرَحْمَتِيْ
وَسِعَتْ كُلَّ شَيْءٍ ؕ فَسَاَكْتُبُهَا
لِلَّذِيْنَ يَتَّقُوْنَ وَيُؤْتُوْنَ الزَّكٰوةَ
وَالَّذِيْنَ هُمْ بِاٰيٰتِنَا يُؤْمِنُوْنَ ﴿١٥٦﴾ ۚ

157. "Those who follow the Apostle, the unlettered Prophet,

157. Allazeena yattabi'oonar-Rasoolan-Nabiyyal-

اَلَّذِيْنَ يَتَّبِعُوْنَ الرَّسُوْلَ النَّبِيَّ

Ikhfa اخفاء | Ghunna غُنّہ | Ikhfa Meem Saakin اخفاء میم ساکن | Idghaam ادغام | Qalqala قلقلہ | Qalb قلب | Idghaam Meem Saakin ادغام میم ساکن

whom they find mentioned in their own (scriptures),- in the Torah and the Gospel;- for he commands them what is just and forbids them what is evil; he allows them as lawful what is good (and pure) and prohibits them from what is bad (and impure); He releases them from their heavy burdens and from the yokes that are upon them. So it is those who believe in him, honour him, help him, and follow the light which is sent down with him,- it is they who will prosper."

ummiyyal-lazee yajidoonahoo maktooban 'indahum fit-Tawraati wal-Injeeli yaå-muruhum bilma'roofi wa yanhaahum 'anil-munkari wa yuḥillu lahumuṭ-ṭayyibaati wa yuḥarrimu 'alayhimul-khabaaa'iṣa wa yaḍa'u 'anhum iṣrahum wal-aghlaalal-latee kaanat 'alayhim; fallazeena aamanoo bihee wa 'azzaroohu wa naṣaroohu wattaba'un-nooral-lazeee unzila ma'ahooo ulaaa'ika humul-mufliḥoon.

(Section 19)

الْاُمِّيَّ الَّذِيْ يَجِدُوْنَهٗ مَكْتُوْبًا
عِنْدَهُمْ فِي التَّوْرٰىةِ وَالْاِنْجِيْلِ
يَاْمُرُهُمْ بِالْمَعْرُوْفِ وَيَنْهٰىهُمْ عَنِ
الْمُنْكَرِ وَيُحِلُّ لَهُمُ الطَّيِّبٰتِ وَيُحَرِّمُ
عَلَيْهِمُ الْخَبٰٓئِثَ وَيَضَعُ عَنْهُمْ
اِصْرَهُمْ وَالْاَغْلٰلَ الَّتِيْ كَانَتْ عَلَيْهِمْ
فَالَّذِيْنَ اٰمَنُوْا بِهٖ وَعَزَّرُوْهُ
وَنَصَرُوْهُ وَاتَّبَعُوا النُّوْرَ الَّذِيْٓ
اُنْزِلَ مَعَهٗٓ اُولٰٓئِكَ هُمُ الْمُفْلِحُوْنَ ١٥٧ ربع

158. Say: "O men! I am sent unto you all, as the Apostle of Allah, to Whom belongs the dominion of the heavens and the earth: there is no god but He: it is He that gives both life and death. So believe in Allah and His Apostle, the unlettered Prophet, who believes in Allah and His Words: follow him that (so) you may be guided."

158. Qul yaaa ayyuhan-naasu innee Rasoolul-laahi ilaykum jamee'anil-lazee lahoo mulkus-samaawaati wal-arḍi laaa ilaaha illaa Huwa yuḥyee wa yumeetu fa-aaminoo billaahi wa Rasoolihin-Nabiyyil-ummiy-yil-lazee yu'minu billaahi wa Kalimaatihee wattabi'oohu la'allakum tahtadoon.

قُلْ يٰٓاَيُّهَا النَّاسُ اِنِّيْ رَسُوْلُ اللّٰهِ
اِلَيْكُمْ جَمِيْعَا الَّذِيْ لَهٗ مُلْكُ
السَّمٰوٰتِ وَالْاَرْضِ لَآ اِلٰهَ اِلَّا
هُوَ يُحْيٖ وَيُمِيْتُ فَاٰمِنُوْا بِاللّٰهِ
وَرَسُوْلِهِ النَّبِيِّ الْاُمِّيِّ الَّذِيْ يُؤْمِنُ
بِاللّٰهِ وَكَلِمٰتِهٖ وَاتَّبِعُوْهُ لَعَلَّكُمْ
تَهْتَدُوْنَ ١٥٨

159. Of the people of Moses there is a section who guide and do justice in the light of truth.

159. Wa min qawmi Moosaaa ummatuñy-yahdoona bilḥaqqi wa bihee ya'diloon.

وَمِنْ قَوْمِ مُوْسٰٓى اُمَّةٌ يَّهْدُوْنَ
بِالْحَقِّ وَبِهٖ يَعْدِلُوْنَ ١٥٩

160. We divided them into twelve tribes or nations. We directed Moses by inspiration, when his (thirsty) people asked him for water: "Strike the rock with your staff": out of it there gushed forth twelve springs: each group knew its own place for water. We gave them the shade of clouds, and sent down to them manna and quails, (saying): "Eat of the good things We have provided for you": (but they rebelled); to Us they did no harm,

160. Wa qaṭṭa'naahumus-natay 'ashrata asbaaṭan umamaa; wa awḥaynaaa ilaa Moosaaa izis-tasqaahu qawmuhooo aniḍ-rib bi'aṣaakal-ḥajara fambajasat minhus-nataa 'ashrata 'aynan qad 'alima kullu unaasim-mashrabahum; wa ẓallalnaa 'alayhimul-ghamaama wa anzalnaa 'alayhimul-Manna was-Salwaa kuloo min ṭayyi-baati maa razaqnaakum; wa maa ẓalamoonaa

وَقَطَّعْنٰهُمُ اثْنَتَيْ عَشْرَةَ اَسْبَاطًا اُمَمًا
وَاَوْحَيْنَآ اِلٰى مُوْسٰٓى اِذِ اسْتَسْقٰىهُ
قَوْمُهٗٓ اَنِ اضْرِبْ بِّعَصَاكَ الْحَجَرَ
فَانْۢبَجَسَتْ مِنْهُ اثْنَتَا عَشْرَةَ
عَيْنًا قَدْ عَلِمَ كُلُّ اُنَاسٍ مَّشْرَبَهُمْ
وَظَلَّلْنَا عَلَيْهِمُ الْغَمَامَ وَاَنْزَلْنَا
عَلَيْهِمُ الْمَنَّ وَالسَّلْوٰى كُلُوْا مِنْ
طَيِّبٰتِ مَا رَزَقْنٰكُمْ وَمَا ظَلَمُوْنَا

but they harmed their own souls.

161. And remember it was said to them: "Dwell in this town and eat therein as you wish, but say the word of humility and enter the gate in a posture of humility: We shall forgive you your faults; We shall increase (the portion of) those who do good."

162. But the transgressors among them changed the word from that which had been given them so We sent on them a plague from heaven. For that they repeatedly transgressed.

163. Ask them concerning the town standing close by the sea. Behold! they transgressed in the matter of the Sabbath. For on the day of their Sabbath their fish did come to them, openly holding up their heads, but on the day they had no Sabbath, they came not: thus did We make a trial of them, for they were given to transgression.

164. When some of them said: "Why do you preach to a people whom Allah will destroy or visit with a terrible punishment?"- said the preachers:" To discharge our duty to your Lord, and perchance they may fear Him."

165. When they disregarded the warnings that had been given them, We rescued those who forbade Evil; but We visited the wrong-doers with a grievous punishment because they were given to transgression.

166. When in their insolence they transgressed (all) prohibitions, We said to them: "Be you apes, despised and rejected."

167. Behold! Your Lord did declare that He would send against them, to the Day of Judgment, those who would afflict them with

wa laakin kaanooo anfusahum yaẓlimoon.

161. Wa iz qeela lahumuskunoo haazihil-qaryata wa kuloo minhaa ḥaysu shi'tum wa qooloo ḥiṭṭatuñw-wadkhulul-baaba sujjadan naghfir lakum khaṭeee'aatikum; sanazeedul-muḥsineen.

162. Fabaddalal-lazeena ẓalamoo minhum qawlan ghayral-lazee qeela lahum fa-arsalnaa 'alayhim rijzam-minas-samaaa'i bimaa kaanoo yaẓlimoon. **(Section 20)**

163. Was'alhum 'anil-qaryatil-latee kaanat ḥaaḍiratal-baḥri iz ya'doona fis-Sabti iz taâteehim ḥeetaanuhum yawma Sabtihim shurra'añw-wa yawma laa yasbitoona laa taâteehim; kazaalika nabloohum bimaa kaanoo yafsuqoon.

164. Wa iz qaalat ummatum-minhum lima ta'iẓoona qaw-manil-laahu muhlikuhum aw mu'azzibuhum 'azaaban shadeedan qaaloo ma'ziratan ilaa Rabbikum wa la'allahum yattaqoon.

165. Falammaa nasoo maa zukkiroo biheee anjaynal-lazeena yanhawna 'anis-sooo'i wa akhaznal-lazeena ẓalamoo bi'azaabim ba'eesim bimaa kaanoo yafsuqoon.

166. Falammaa 'ataw 'ammaa nuhoo 'anhu qulnaa lahum koonoo qiradatan khaasi'een.

167. Wa iz ta-azzana Rabbuka la-yab'asanna 'alayhim ilaa Yawmil-Qiyaamati mañy-yasoomuhum

وَلٰكِنْ كَانُوْٓا اَنْفُسَهُمْ يَظْلِمُوْنَ ١٦٠
وَاِذْ قِيْلَ لَهُمُ اسْكُنُوْا هٰذِهِ الْقَرْيَةَ
وَكُلُوْا مِنْهَا حَيْثُ شِئْتُمْ وَقُوْلُوْا
حِطَّةٌ وَّادْخُلُوا الْبَابَ سُجَّدًا نَّغْفِرْ لَكُمْ
خَطِيْٓئٰتِكُمْ ؕ سَنَزِيْدُ الْمُحْسِنِيْنَ ١٦١
فَبَدَّلَ الَّذِيْنَ ظَلَمُوْا مِنْهُمْ قَوْلًا غَيْرَ
الَّذِيْ قِيْلَ لَهُمْ فَاَرْسَلْنَا عَلَيْهِمْ رِجْزًا
مِّنَ السَّمَآءِ بِمَا كَانُوْا يَظْلِمُوْنَ ١٦٢ ع
وَسْئَلْهُمْ عَنِ الْقَرْيَةِ الَّتِيْ كَانَتْ
حَاضِرَةَ الْبَحْرِ ۘ اِذْ يَعْدُوْنَ فِي
السَّبْتِ اِذْ تَاْتِيْهِمْ حِيْتَانُهُمْ يَوْمَ
سَبْتِهِمْ شُرَّعًا وَّيَوْمَ لَا يَسْبِتُوْنَ ۙ
لَا تَاْتِيْهِمْ ۛ كَذٰلِكَ ۛ نَبْلُوْهُمْ
بِمَا كَانُوْا يَفْسُقُوْنَ ١٦٣
وَاِذْ قَالَتْ اُمَّةٌ مِّنْهُمْ لِمَ تَعِظُوْنَ
قَوْمَا ۙ اللّٰهُ مُهْلِكُهُمْ اَوْ مُعَذِّبُهُمْ
عَذَابًا شَدِيْدًا ؕ قَالُوْا مَعْذِرَةً اِلٰى
رَبِّكُمْ وَلَعَلَّهُمْ يَتَّقُوْنَ ١٦٤
فَلَمَّا نَسُوْا مَا ذُكِّرُوْا بِهٖٓ اَنْجَيْنَا
الَّذِيْنَ يَنْهَوْنَ عَنِ السُّوْٓءِ وَاَخَذْنَا
الَّذِيْنَ ظَلَمُوْا بِعَذَابٍۭ بَئِيْسٍۭ
بِمَا كَانُوْا يَفْسُقُوْنَ ١٦٥
فَلَمَّا عَتَوْا عَنْ مَّا نُهُوْا عَنْهُ قُلْنَا
لَهُمْ كُوْنُوْا قِرَدَةً خٰسِئِيْنَ ١٦٦
وَاِذْ تَاَذَّنَ رَبُّكَ لَيَبْعَثَنَّ عَلَيْهِمْ
اِلٰى يَوْمِ الْقِيٰمَةِ مَنْ يَّسُوْمُهُمْ

ع ٢٠ وقف لازم معانقة النصف

Ikhfa اخفاء | Ghunna غُنّہ | Ikhfa Meem Saakin اخفاء میم ساکن | Idghaam ادغام | Qalqala قلقلہ | Qalb قلب | Idghaam Meem Saakin ادغام میم ساکن

grievous chastisement. Your Lord is quick in retribution, but He is also Oft-forgiving, Most Merciful.

168. We broke them up into sections on this earth. There are among them some that are the righteous, and some that are the opposite. We have tried them with both prosperity and adversity: in order that they might turn (to us).

169. After them succeeded an (evil) generation: they inherited the Book, but they chose (for themselves) the vanities of this world, saying (for excuse): "(Everything) will be forgiven us." (Even so), if similar vanities came their way, they would (again) seize them. Was not the covenant of the Book taken from them, that they would not ascribe to Allah anything but the truth? And they study what is in the Book. But best for the righteous is the home in the Hereafter. Will you not understand?

170. As to those who hold fast by the Book and establish regular prayer,- never shall We suffer the reward of the righteous to perish.

171. When We raised the Mount over them, as if it had been a canopy, and they thought it was going to fall on them (We said): "Hold firmly to what We have given you, and bring (ever) to remembrance what is therein; perchance you may fear Allah."

172. When your Lord drew forth from the Children of Adam- from their loins - their descendants, and made them testify concerning themselves, (saying): "Am I not your Lord (who cherishes and sustains you)?"- They said: "Yes! We do testify!" (This), lest you should say on the Day of Judgment: "Of this we were never mindful":

sooo'al-'azaab; inna Rabbaka lasaree'ul-'iqaab, wa innahoo la-Ghafoorur-Raheem.

168. Wa qatta'naahum fil-ardi umamam minhumus-saalihoona wa minhum doona zaalika wa balawnaahum bilhasanaati wassayyi-aati la'allahum yarji'oon.

169. Fakhalafa mim ba'dihim khalfuñw-warisul-Kitaaba yaåkhuzoona 'arada haazal-adnaa wa yaqooloona sayughfaru lanaa wa iñy-yaåtihim 'aradum-misluhoo yaåkhuzooh; alam yu'khaz 'alayhim meesaaqul-Kitaabi al-laa yaqooloo 'alal-laahi illal-haqqa wa darasoo maa feeh; wad-Daarul-Aakhiratu khayrul-lillazeena yattaqoon; afalaa ta'qiloon.

170. Wallazeena yumassikoona bil-Kitaabi wa aqaamus-Salaata innaa laa nudee'u ajral-musliheen.

171. Wa iz nataqnal-jabala fawqahum ka-annahoo zullatuñw-wa zannooo annahoo waaqi'um bihim khuzoo maaa aataynaakum biquwwatiñw-wazkuroo maa feehi la'allakum tattaqoon. **(Section 21)**

172. Wa iz akhaza Rabbuka mim Baneee Aadama min zuhoorihim zurriyyatahum wa ash-hadahum 'alaaa anfusihim alastu bi-Rabbikum qaaloo balaa shahidnaaa; an taqooloo Yawmal-Qiyaamati innaa kunnaa 'an haazaa ghaafileen.

سُوْٓءَ الْعَذَابِ ۭ اِنَّ رَبَّكَ لَسَرِيْعُ
الْعِقَابِ ښ وَاِنَّهٗ لَغَفُوْرٌ رَّحِيْمٌ ١٦٧
وَقَطَّعْنٰهُمْ فِي الْاَرْضِ اُمَمًا ۚ مِنْهُمُ
الصّٰلِحُوْنَ وَمِنْهُمْ دُوْنَ ذٰلِكَ ۡ
وَبَلَوْنٰهُمْ بِالْحَسَنٰتِ وَالسَّيِّاٰتِ
لَعَلَّهُمْ يَرْجِعُوْنَ ١٦٨
فَخَلَفَ مِنْۢ بَعْدِهِمْ خَلْفٌ وَّرِثُوا
الْكِتٰبَ يَاْخُذُوْنَ عَرَضَ هٰذَا
الْاَدْنٰى وَيَقُوْلُوْنَ سَيُغْفَرُ لَنَا ۚ وَاِنْ
يَّاْتِهِمْ عَرَضٌ مِّثْلُهٗ يَاْخُذُوْهُ ۭ اَلَمْ
يُؤْخَذْ عَلَيْهِمْ مِّيْثَاقُ الْكِتٰبِ اَنْ
لَّا يَقُوْلُوْا عَلَى اللّٰهِ اِلَّا الْحَقَّ وَدَرَسُوْا
مَا فِيْهِ ۭ وَالدَّارُ الْاٰخِرَةُ خَيْرٌ
لِّلَّذِيْنَ يَتَّقُوْنَ ۭ اَفَلَا تَعْقِلُوْنَ ١٦٩
وَالَّذِيْنَ يُمَسِّكُوْنَ بِالْكِتٰبِ وَاَقَامُوا
الصَّلٰوةَ ۭ اِنَّا لَا نُضِيْعُ اَجْرَ
الْمُصْلِحِيْنَ ١٧٠
وَاِذْ نَتَقْنَا الْجَبَلَ فَوْقَهُمْ كَاَنَّهٗ
ظُلَّةٌ وَّظَنُّوْٓا اَنَّهٗ وَاقِعٌۢ بِهِمْ ۚ
خُذُوْا مَآ اٰتَيْنٰكُمْ بِقُوَّةٍ وَّاذْكُرُوْا
مَا فِيْهِ لَعَلَّكُمْ تَتَّقُوْنَ ١٧١ ع
وَاِذْ اَخَذَ رَبُّكَ مِنْۢ بَنِيْٓ اٰدَمَ
مِنْ ظُهُوْرِهِمْ ذُرِّيَّتَهُمْ وَاَشْهَدَهُمْ
عَلٰٓي اَنْفُسِهِمْ ۚ اَلَسْتُ بِرَبِّكُمْ ۭ قَالُوْا
بَلٰي ڔ شَهِدْنَا ڔ اَنْ تَقُوْلُوْا يَوْمَ
الْقِيٰمَةِ اِنَّا كُنَّا عَنْ هٰذَا غٰفِلِيْنَ ١٧٢ ۙ

معانقة عند المتاخرين ١٢

Ikhfa اخفاء · Ghunna غنّہ · Ikhfa Meem Saakin اخفاء میم ساکن · Idghaam ادغام · Qalqala قلقلہ · Qalb قلب · Idghaam Meem Saakin ادغام میم ساکن

173. Or lest you should say: "Our fathers before us may have taken false Allah's, but we are (their) descendants after them: will you then destroy us because of the deeds of men who followed falsehood?"

173. Aw taqoolooo innamaaa ashraka aabaaa'unaa min qablu wa kunnaa zurriyyatam-mim ba'dihim afatuhlikunaa bimaa fa'alal-mubṭiloon.

أَوْ تَقُولُوٓا إِنَّمَآ أَشْرَكَ ءَابَآؤُنَا مِن
قَبْلُ وَكُنَّا ذُرِّيَّةً مِّنۢ بَعْدِهِمْ ۖ
أَفَتُهْلِكُنَا بِمَا فَعَلَ ٱلْمُبْطِلُونَ ﴿١٧٣﴾

174. Thus do We explain the signs in detail; and perchance they may turn (unto Us).

174. Wa kazaalika nufaṣṣilul-Aayaati wa la'allahum yarji'oon.

وَكَذَٰلِكَ نُفَصِّلُ ٱلْءَايَٰتِ وَلَعَلَّهُمْ
يَرْجِعُونَ ﴿١٧٤﴾

175. Relate to them the story of the man to whom We sent Our signs, but he passed them by: so Satan followed him up, and he went astray.

175. Watlu 'alayhim naba-al-lazeee aataynaahu Aayaatinaa fansalakha minhaa fa-atba'a-hush-Shayṭaanu fakaana minal-ghaaween.

وَٱتْلُ عَلَيْهِمْ نَبَأَ ٱلَّذِىٓ ءَاتَيْنَٰهُ
ءَايَٰتِنَا فَٱنسَلَخَ مِنْهَا فَأَتْبَعَهُ
ٱلشَّيْطَٰنُ فَكَانَ مِنَ ٱلْغَاوِينَ ﴿١٧٥﴾

176. If it had been Our will, We should have elevated him with Our signs; but he inclined to the earth, and followed his own vain desires. His similitude is that of a dog: if you attack him, he lolls out his tongue, or if you leave him alone, he (still) lolls out his tongue. That is the similitude of those who reject Our signs; so relate the story; perchance they may reflect.

176. Wa law shi'naa lara-fa'naahu bihaa wa laakin-nahooo akhlada ilal-arḍi watta-ba'a hawaah; famasaluhoo kamasalil-kalb; in taḥmil 'alayhi yalhas aw tatruk-hu yalhas; zaalika masalul-qawmil-lazeena kazzaboo bi-Aayaatinaa; faqṣuṣil-qaṣaṣa la'allahum yatafakkaroon.

وَلَوْ شِئْنَا لَرَفَعْنَٰهُ بِهَا وَلَٰكِنَّهُۥٓ
أَخْلَدَ إِلَى ٱلْأَرْضِ وَٱتَّبَعَ هَوَىٰهُ ۚ
فَمَثَلُهُۥ كَمَثَلِ ٱلْكَلْبِ إِن تَحْمِلْ
عَلَيْهِ يَلْهَثْ أَوْ تَتْرُكْهُ يَلْهَث ۚ
ذَّٰلِكَ مَثَلُ ٱلْقَوْمِ ٱلَّذِينَ كَذَّبُوا
بِـَٔايَٰتِنَا ۚ فَٱقْصُصِ ٱلْقَصَصَ
لَعَلَّهُمْ يَتَفَكَّرُونَ ﴿١٧٦﴾

177. Evil as an example are people who reject Our signs and wrong their own souls.

177. Saaa'a masalanil-qaw-mul-lazeena kazzaboo bi-Aayaatinaa wa anfusahum kaanoo yazlimoon.

سَآءَ مَثَلًا ٱلْقَوْمُ ٱلَّذِينَ كَذَّبُوا
بِـَٔايَٰتِنَا وَأَنفُسَهُمْ كَانُوا يَظْلِمُونَ ﴿١٧٧﴾

178. Whom Allah does guide,- he is on the right path: whom He rejects from His guidance,- such are the persons who perish.

178. Mañy-yahdil-laahu fa-huwal-muhtadee wa mañy-yuḍlil fa-ulaaa'ika humul-khaasiroon.

مَن يَهْدِ ٱللَّهُ فَهُوَ ٱلْمُهْتَدِى ۖ وَمَن
يُضْلِلْ فَأُو۟لَٰٓئِكَ هُمُ ٱلْخَٰسِرُونَ ﴿١٧٨﴾

179. Many are the Jinns and men we have made for Hell: they have hearts wherewith they do not understand, eyes wherewith they do not see, and ears wherewith they do not hear. They are like cattle,- nay more misguided: for they are heedless (of warning).

179. Wa laqad zaraånaa li-Jahannama kaseeram-minal-jinni wal-insi lahum quloobul-laa yafqahoona bihaa wa lahum a'yunul-laa yubṣiroona bihaa wa lahum aazaanul-laa yasma'oona bihaa; ulaaa'ika kal-an'aami bal hum aḍall; ulaaa'ika humul-ghaafiloon.

وَلَقَدْ ذَرَأْنَا لِجَهَنَّمَ كَثِيرًا مِّنَ
ٱلْجِنِّ وَٱلْإِنسِ ۖ لَهُمْ قُلُوبٌ لَّا
يَفْقَهُونَ بِهَا وَلَهُمْ أَعْيُنٌ
لَّا يُبْصِرُونَ بِهَا وَلَهُمْ ءَاذَانٌ
لَّا يَسْمَعُونَ بِهَآ ۚ أُو۟لَٰٓئِكَ كَٱلْأَنْعَٰمِ
بَلْ هُمْ أَضَلُّ ۚ أُو۟لَٰٓئِكَ هُمُ
ٱلْغَٰفِلُونَ ﴿١٧٩﴾

Ikhfa اخفاء | Ghunna غُنّہ | Ikhfa Meem Saakin اخفاءمیم ساکن | Idghaam ادغام | Qalqala قلقلہ | Qalb قلب | Idghaam Meem Saakin ادغام میم ساکن

180. The most beautiful names belong to Allah: so call on Him by them; but shun such men as use profanity in His names: for what they do, they will soon be requited.

180. Wa lillaahil-Asmaaa'ul-Ḥusnaa fad'oohu bihaa wa zarul-lazeena yulḥidoona feee Asmaaa'ih; sa-yujzawna maa kaanoo ya'maloon.

وَلِلّٰهِ الْاَسْمَآءُ الْحُسْنٰى فَادْعُوْهُ
بِهَا ۪ وَذَرُوا الَّذِيْنَ يُلْحِدُوْنَ
فِيْٓ اَسْمَآئِهٖ ؕ سَيُجْزَوْنَ مَا
كَانُوْا يَعْمَلُوْنَ ﴿١٨٠﴾

181. Of those We have created are people who direct (others) with truth. And dispense justice therewith.

181. Wa mimman khalaqnaaa ummatuñy-yahdoona bilḥaqqi wa bihee ya'diloon. **(Section 22)**

وَمِمَّنْ خَلَقْنَآ اُمَّةٌ يَّهْدُوْنَ
بِالْحَقِّ وَبِهٖ يَعْدِلُوْنَ ﴿١٨١﴾ ع

182. Those who reject Our Signs, We will lead them step by step to rain while they know not;

182. Wallazeena kazzaboo bi-Aayaatinaa sanastadrijuhum min ḥaysu laa ya'lamoon.

وَالَّذِيْنَ كَذَّبُوْا بِاٰيٰتِنَا سَنَسْتَدْرِجُهُمْ
مِّنْ حَيْثُ لَا يَعْلَمُوْنَ ﴿١٨٢﴾

183. Respite will I grant unto them: for My scheme is strong (and unfailing).

183. Wa umlee lahum; inna kaydee mateen.

وَاُمْلِيْ لَهُمْ ۚ اِنَّ كَيْدِيْ مَتِيْنٌ ﴿١٨٣﴾

184. Do they not reflect? Their companion is not seized with madness: he is but a perspicuous warner.

184. Awalam yatafakkaroo maa biṣaaḥibihim min jinnah; in huwa illaa nazeerum-mubeen.

اَوَلَمْ يَتَفَكَّرُوْا ٜ مَا بِصَاحِبِهِمْ
مِّنْ جِنَّةٍ ؕ اِنْ هُوَ اِلَّا نَذِيْرٌ مُّبِيْنٌ ﴿١٨٤﴾

185. Do they see nothing in the kingdom of the heavens and the earth and all that Allah has created? (Do they not see) that it may well be that their terms is drawing to an end? In what message after this will they then believe?

185. Awalam yanẓuroo fee malakootis-samaawaati wal-arḍi wa maa khalaqal-laahu min shay'iñw-wa an 'asaaa añy-yakoona qadiqtaraba ajaluhum fabi-ayyi ḥadeesim ba'dahoo yu'minoon.

اَوَلَمْ يَنْظُرُوْا فِيْ مَلَكُوْتِ السَّمٰوٰتِ
وَالْاَرْضِ وَمَا خَلَقَ اللّٰهُ مِنْ
شَيْءٍ ۙ وَّاَنْ عَسٰٓى اَنْ يَّكُوْنَ قَدِ
اقْتَرَبَ اَجَلُهُمْ ۚ فَبِاَيِّ حَدِيْثٍۭ
بَعْدَهٗ يُؤْمِنُوْنَ ﴿١٨٥﴾

186. To such as Allah rejects from His guidance, there can be no guide: He will leave them in their trespasses, wandering in distraction.

186. Mañy-yuḍlilil-laahu falaa haadiya lah; wa yazaruhum fee ṭughyaanihim ya'mahoon.

مَنْ يُّضْلِلِ اللّٰهُ فَلَا هَادِيَ لَهٗ ؕ
وَيَذَرُهُمْ فِيْ طُغْيَانِهِمْ يَعْمَهُوْنَ ﴿١٨٦﴾

187. They ask you about the (final) Hour - when will be its appointed time? Say: "The knowledge thereof is with my Lord (alone): none but He can reveal as to when it will occur. Heavy were its burden through the heavens and the earth. Only, all of a sudden will it come to you." They ask you as if you were eager in search thereof: say: "The knowledge thereof is with Allah (alone), but most men know not."

187. Yas'aloonaka 'anis-Saa'ati ayyaana mursaahaa qul innamaa 'ilmuhaa 'inda Rabbee laa yujalleehaa liwaqtihaaa illaa Hoo; saqulat fis-samaawaati wal-arḍ; laa taâteekum illaa baghtah; yas'aloonaka ka-annaka ḥafiyyun 'anhaa qul innamaa 'ilmuhaa 'indal-laahi wa laakinna aksaran-naasi laa ya'lamoon.

يَسْــَٔلُوْنَكَ عَنِ السَّاعَةِ اَيَّانَ
مُرْسٰىهَا ؕ قُلْ اِنَّمَا عِلْمُهَا عِنْدَ
رَبِّيْ ۚ لَا يُجَلِّيْهَا لِوَقْتِهَآ اِلَّا هُوَ ؔۘ
ثَقُلَتْ فِي السَّمٰوٰتِ وَالْاَرْضِ ؕ لَا
تَاْتِيْكُمْ اِلَّا بَغْتَةً ؕ يَسْــَٔلُوْنَكَ كَاَنَّكَ
حَفِيٌّ عَنْهَا ؕ قُلْ اِنَّمَا عِلْمُهَا عِنْدَ
اللّٰهِ وَلٰكِنَّ اَكْثَرَ النَّاسِ لَا يَعْلَمُوْنَ ﴿١٨٧﴾

188. Say: "I have no power over any good or harm to myself

188. Qul laaa amliku linafsee naf'añw-wa laa ḍarran

قُلْ لَّآ اَمْلِكُ لِنَفْسِيْ نَفْعًا وَّلَا ضَرًّا

Ikhfa اخفاء | Ghunna غنّہ | Ikhfa Meem Saakin اخفاء میم ساکن | Idghaam ادغام | Qalqala قلقلہ | Qalb قلب | Idghaam Meem Saakin ادغام میم ساکن

except as Allah wills. If I had knowledge of the unseen, I should have multiplied all good, and no evil should have touched me: I am but a warner, and a bringer of glad tidings to those who have faith."

illaa maa shaaaa'al-laah; wa law kuntu a'lamul-ghayba lastaksartu minal-khayri wa maa massaniyas-soo'; in ana illaa nazeeruñw-wa basheerul-liqawmiñy-yu'minoon.

(Section 23)

إِلَّا مَا شَاءَ اللَّهُ ۚ وَلَوْ كُنتُ أَعْلَمُ
الْغَيْبَ لَاسْتَكْثَرْتُ مِنَ الْخَيْرِ
وَمَا مَسَّنِيَ السُّوءُ ۚ إِنْ أَنَا إِلَّا
نَذِيرٌ وَبَشِيرٌ لِّقَوْمٍ يُؤْمِنُونَ ﴿١٨٨﴾

معانقة ٨ عند المتأخرين ١٢ — ع ٢٣

189. It is He Who created you from a single person, and made his mate of like nature, in order that he might dwell with her (in love). When they are united, she bears a light burden and carries it about (unnoticed). When she grows heavy, they both pray to Allah their Lord, (saying): "If you give us a goodly child, we vow we shall (ever) be grateful."

189. Huwal-lazee khalaqakum min nafsiñw-waaḥidatiñw-wa ja'ala minhaa zawjahaa liyaskuna ilayhaa falammaa taghashshaahaa ḥamalat ḥamlan khafeefan famarrat bihee falammaaa asqalad-da'awal-laaha Rabbahumaa la'in aataytanaa ṣaaliḥal-lanakoonanna minash-shaakireen.

هُوَ الَّذِي خَلَقَكُم مِّن نَّفْسٍ
وَاحِدَةٍ وَجَعَلَ مِنْهَا زَوْجَهَا
لِيَسْكُنَ إِلَيْهَا ۖ فَلَمَّا تَغَشَّاهَا
حَمَلَتْ حَمْلًا خَفِيفًا فَمَرَّتْ بِهِ ۖ
فَلَمَّا أَثْقَلَت دَّعَوَا اللَّهَ رَبَّهُمَا لَئِنْ
آتَيْتَنَا صَالِحًا لَّنَكُونَنَّ مِنَ
الشَّاكِرِينَ ﴿١٨٩﴾

190. But when He gives them a goodly child, they ascribe to others a share in the gift they have received: but Allah is exalted high above the partners they ascribe to Him.

190. Falammaaa aataahumaa ṣaaliḥan ja'alaa lahoo shurakaaa'a feemaaa aataahumaa; fata'aalal-laahu 'ammaa yushrikoon.

فَلَمَّا آتَاهُمَا صَالِحًا جَعَلَا لَهُ
شُرَكَاءَ فِيمَا آتَاهُمَا ۚ فَتَعَالَى
اللَّهُ عَمَّا يُشْرِكُونَ ﴿١٩٠﴾

191. Do they indeed ascribe to Him as partners things that can create nothing, but are themselves created?

191. A yushrikoona maa laa yakhluqu shay'añw-wa hum yukhlaqoon.

أَيُشْرِكُونَ مَا لَا يَخْلُقُ شَيْئًا
وَهُمْ يُخْلَقُونَ ﴿١٩١﴾

192. No aid can they give them, nor can they aid themselves!

192. Wa laa yastaṭee'oona lahum naṣrañw-wa laaa anfusahum yanṣuroon

وَلَا يَسْتَطِيعُونَ لَهُمْ نَصْرًا وَلَا
أَنفُسَهُمْ يَنصُرُونَ ﴿١٩٢﴾

193. If you call them to guidance, they will not obey: For you it is the same whether you call them or you hold your peace!

193. Wa in tad'oohum ilalhudaa laa yattabi'ookum; sawaaa'un 'alaykum a-da'awtumoohum am antum ṣaamitoon.

وَإِن تَدْعُوهُمْ إِلَى الْهُدَىٰ لَا
يَتَّبِعُوكُمْ ۚ سَوَاءٌ عَلَيْكُمْ أَدَعَوْتُمُوهُمْ
أَمْ أَنتُمْ صَامِتُونَ ﴿١٩٣﴾

194. Verily those whom you call upon besides Allah are servants like unto you: call upon them, and let them listen to your prayer, if you are (indeed) truthful!

194. Innal-lazeena tad'oona min doonil-laahi 'ibaadun amsaalukum fad'oohum falyastajeeboo lakum in kuntum ṣaadiqeen.

إِنَّ الَّذِينَ تَدْعُونَ مِن دُونِ
اللَّهِ عِبَادٌ أَمْثَالُكُمْ ۖ فَادْعُوهُمْ
فَلْيَسْتَجِيبُوا لَكُمْ إِن كُنتُمْ
صَادِقِينَ ﴿١٩٤﴾

195. Have they feet to walk with? Or

195. A-lahum arjuluñy-yamshoona bihaaa am lahum

أَلَهُمْ أَرْجُلٌ يَمْشُونَ بِهَا ۖ أَمْ لَهُمْ

Ikhfa اخفاء | Ghunna غنّہ | Ikhfa Meem Saakin اخفاء میم ساکن | Idghaam ادغام | Qalqala قلقلہ | Qalb قلب | Idghaam Meem Saakin ادغام میم ساکن

hands to lay hold with? Or eyes to see with? Or ears to hear with? Say: "Call your 'Allah-partners', scheme (your worst) against me, and give me no respite!

aydiñy-yabṭishoona bihaaa am lahum a'yunuñy-yubṣiroona bihaaa am lahum aazaanuñy-yasma'oona bihaa; qulid-'oo shurakaaa'akum summa keedooni falaa tunẓiroon.

اَيْدٍ يَّبْطِشُوْنَ بِهَا ۡ اَمْ لَهُمْ اَعْيُنٌ
يُّبْصِرُوْنَ بِهَا ۡ اَمْ لَهُمْ اٰذَانٌ
يَّسْمَعُوْنَ بِهَا ؕ قُلِ ادْعُوْا شُرَكَآءَكُمْ
ثُمَّ كِيْدُوْنِ فَلَا تُنْظِرُوْنِ ﴿١٩٥﴾

196. "For my Protector is Allah, Who revealed the Book (from time to time), and He will choose and befriend the righteous.

196. Inna waliyyiyal-laahul-lazee nazzalal-Kitaaba wa Huwa yatawallaṣ-ṣaaliḥeen.

اِنَّ وَلِيِّ ـۧ اللّٰهُ الَّذِيْ نَزَّلَ
الْكِتٰبَ ۖۗ وَهُوَ يَتَوَلَّى الصّٰلِحِيْنَ ﴿١٩٦﴾

197. "But those you call upon besides Him, are unable to help you, and indeed to help themselves."

197. Wallazeena tad'oona min doonihee laa yastaṭee'oona naṣrakum wa laaa anfusahum yanṣuroon.

وَالَّذِيْنَ تَدْعُوْنَ مِنْ دُوْنِهٖ لَا
يَسْتَطِيْعُوْنَ نَصْرَكُمْ وَلَآ اَنْفُسَهُمْ
يَنْصُرُوْنَ ﴿١٩٧﴾

198. If you call them to guidance, they do not hear. You will see them looking at you, but they do not see.

198. Wa in tad'oohum ilal-hudaa laa yasma'oo wa taraahum yanẓuroona ilayka wa hum laa yubṣiroon.

وَاِنْ تَدْعُوْهُمْ اِلَى الْهُدٰى لَا
يَسْمَعُوْا ؕ وَتَرٰىهُمْ يَنْظُرُوْنَ اِلَيْكَ
وَهُمْ لَا يُبْصِرُوْنَ ﴿١٩٨﴾

199. Hold to forgiveness; command what is right; but turn away from the ignorant.

199. Khuzil-'afwa waåmur bil'urfi wa a'riḍ 'anil-jaahileen.

خُذِ الْعَفْوَ وَاْمُرْ بِالْعُرْفِ وَاَعْرِضْ
عَنِ الْجٰهِلِيْنَ ﴿١٩٩﴾

200. If a suggestion from Satan assail your (mind), seek refuge with Allah; for He hears and knows (all things).

200. Wa immaa yanzaghannaka minash-Shayṭaani nazghun fasta'iz billaah; innahoo Samee'un 'Aleem.

وَاِمَّا يَنْزَغَنَّكَ مِنَ الشَّيْطٰنِ نَزْغٌ
فَاسْتَعِذْ بِاللّٰهِ ؕ اِنَّهٗ سَمِيْعٌ عَلِيْمٌ ﴿٢٠٠﴾

201. Those who fear Allah, when a thought of evil from Satan assaults them, bring Allah to remembrance, when lo! they see (aright)!

201. Innal-lazeenat-taqaw izaa massahum ṭaaa'ifum minash-Shayṭaani tazakkaroo fa-izaa hum mubṣiroon.

اِنَّ الَّذِيْنَ اتَّقَوْا اِذَا مَسَّهُمْ طٰٓئِفٌ
مِّنَ الشَّيْطٰنِ تَذَكَّرُوْا فَاِذَا هُمْ
مُّبْصِرُوْنَ ﴿٢٠١﴾ ج

202. But their brethren (the evil ones) plunge them deeper into error, and never relax (their efforts).

202. Wa ikhwaanuhum yamud-doonahum fil-ghayyi summa laa yuqṣiroon.

وَاِخْوَانُهُمْ يَمُدُّوْنَهُمْ فِي الْغَيِّ ثُمَّ
لَا يُقْصِرُوْنَ ﴿٢٠٢﴾

203. If you bring them not a revelation, they say: "Why have you not got it together?" Say: "I but follow what is revealed to me from my Lord: this is (nothing but) lights from your Lord, and Guidance, and Mercy, for any who have faith."

203. Wa izaa lam taåtihim bi-Aayatin qaaloo law lajtabay-tahaa; qul innamaaa attabi'u maa yooḥaaa ilayya mir-Rabbee; haazaa baṣaaa'iru mir-Rabbikum wa hudañw-wa raḥmatul-liqawmiñy-yu'mi-noon.

وَاِذَا لَمْ تَاْتِهِمْ بِاٰيَةٍ قَالُوْا لَوْلَا
اجْتَبَيْتَهَا ؕ قُلْ اِنَّمَآ اَتَّبِعُ مَا
يُوْحٰٓى اِلَيَّ مِنْ رَّبِّيْ ۚ هٰذَا بَصَآئِرُ
مِنْ رَّبِّكُمْ وَهُدًى وَّرَحْمَةٌ
لِّقَوْمٍ يُّؤْمِنُوْنَ ﴿٢٠٣﴾

Ikhfa اخفاء | Ghunna غُنّہ | Ikhfa Meem Saakin اخفاء میم ساکن | Idghaam ادغام | Qalqala قلقلہ | Qalb قلب | Idghaam Meem Saakin ادغام میم ساکن

204. When the Qur'an is read, listen to it with attention, and hold your peace: that you may receive Mercy.

204. Wa izaa quri'al-Qur-aanu fastami'oo lahoo wa anṣitoo la'allakum turḥamoon.

وَإِذَا قُرِئَ الْقُرْاٰنُ فَاسْتَمِعُوْا لَهٗ وَاَنْصِتُوْا لَعَلَّكُمْ تُرْحَمُوْنَ ﴿٢٠٤﴾

205. And you (O reader!) bring your Lord to remembrance in your (very) soul, with humility and in reverence, without loudness in words, in the mornings and evenings; and be not you of those who are unheedful.

205. Wazkur Rabbaka fee nafsika taḍarru'añw-wa khee-fatañw-wa doonal-jahri minal-qawli bilghuduwwi wal-aaṣaali wa laa takum minal-ghaafileen.

وَاذْكُرْ رَّبَّكَ فِيْ نَفْسِكَ تَضَرُّعًا وَّخِيْفَةً وَّدُوْنَ الْجَهْرِ مِنَ الْقَوْلِ بِالْغُدُوِّ وَالْاٰصَالِ وَلَا تَكُنْ مِّنَ الْغٰفِلِيْنَ ﴿٢٠٥﴾

(Bow Down)

206. Those who are near to your Lord, disdain not to do Him worship: they celebrate His praises, and bow down before Him.

206. Innal-lazeena 'inda Rabbika laa yastakbiroona 'an 'ibaadatihee wa yusab-biḥoonahoo wa lahoo yasju-doon. **(Section 24)**

اِنَّ الَّذِيْنَ عِنْدَ رَبِّكَ لَا يَسْتَكْبِرُوْنَ عَنْ عِبَادَتِهٖ وَيُسَبِّحُوْنَهٗ وَلَهٗ يَسْجُدُوْنَ ﴿٢٠٦﴾ السجدة

السجدة (١) ع ٢٤ / ٨ الثلاث

8. The Spoil of War

In the name of Allah, Most Gracious, Most Merciful.

Sûrat al-Anfâl–8

(Revealed at Madinah)

Bismillaahir Raḥmaanir Raḥeem

(٨) سُوْرَةُ الْاَنْفَالِ مَدَنِيَّةٌ (٨٨)

بِسْمِ اللّٰهِ الرَّحْمٰنِ الرَّحِيْمِ

1. They ask you concerning (things taken as) spoils of war. Say: "(Such) spoils are at the disposal of Allah and the Apostle: so fear Allah, and keep straight the relations between yourselves: obey Allah and His Apostle, if you do believe."

1. Yas'aloonaka 'anil-anfaali qulil-anfaalu lillaahi war-Rasooli fattaqul-laaha wa aṣliḥoo zaata baynikum wa aṭee'ul-laaha wa Rasoolahooo in kuntum mu'mineen.

يَسْـَٔلُوْنَكَ عَنِ الْاَنْفَالِ ؕ قُلِ الْاَنْفَالُ لِلّٰهِ وَالرَّسُوْلِ ۚ فَاتَّقُوا اللّٰهَ وَاَصْلِحُوْا ذَاتَ بَيْنِكُمْ ۪ وَاَطِيْعُوا اللّٰهَ وَرَسُوْلَهٗۤ اِنْ كُنْتُمْ مُّؤْمِنِيْنَ ﴿١﴾

2. For, Believers are those who, when Allah is mentioned, feel a tremor in their hearts, and when they hear His Signs rehearsed, find their faith strengthened, and put (all) their trust in their Lord;

2. Innamal-mu'minoonal-lazeena izaa zukiral-laahu wajilat quloobuhum wa izaa tuliyat 'alayhim Aayaatuhoo zaadat-hum eemaanañw-wa 'alaa Rabbihim yatawakkaloon.

اِنَّمَا الْمُؤْمِنُوْنَ الَّذِيْنَ اِذَا ذُكِرَ اللّٰهُ وَجِلَتْ قُلُوْبُهُمْ وَاِذَا تُلِيَتْ عَلَيْهِمْ اٰيٰتُهٗ زَادَتْهُمْ اِيْمَانًا وَّعَلٰى رَبِّهِمْ يَتَوَكَّلُوْنَ ﴿٢﴾

3. Who establish regular prayers and spend (freely) out of the gifts We have given them for sustenance:

3. Allazeena yuqeemoonaṣ-Ṣalaata wa mimmaa razaq-naahum yunfiqoon.

الَّذِيْنَ يُقِيْمُوْنَ الصَّلٰوةَ وَمِمَّا رَزَقْنٰهُمْ يُنْفِقُوْنَ ﴿٣﴾

4. Such in truth are the Believers: they have grades of dignity with their Lord, and forgiveness, and generous sustenance:

4. Ulaaa'ika humul-mu'mi-noona ḥaqqaa; lahum darajaa-tun 'inda Rabbihim wa magh-firatuñw-wa rizqun kareem.

اُولٰٓئِكَ هُمُ الْمُؤْمِنُوْنَ حَقًّا ؕ لَهُمْ دَرَجٰتٌ عِنْدَ رَبِّهِمْ وَمَغْفِرَةٌ وَّرِزْقٌ كَرِيْمٌ ﴿٤﴾

5. Just as your Lord ordered you out of your house in truth, even though a party among the Believers

5. Kamaaa akhrajaka Rabbuka mim baytika bilḥaqq, wa inna fareeqam-minal-mu'mineena

كَمَاۤ اَخْرَجَكَ رَبُّكَ مِنْۢ بَيْتِكَ بِالْحَقِّ ۪ وَاِنَّ فَرِيْقًا مِّنَ الْمُؤْمِنِيْنَ

Ikhfa اخفاء | Ghunna غنّہ | Ikhfa Meem Saakin اخفاء میم ساکن | Idghaam ادغام | Qalqala قلقلہ | Qalb قلب | Idghaam Meem Saakin ادغام میم ساکن

disliked it.

6. Disputing with you concerning the truth after it was made manifest, as if they were being driven to death and they (actually) saw it.

7. Behold! Allah promised you one of the two (enemy) parties, that it should be yours: you wished that the one unarmed should be yours, but Allah willed to justify the Truth according to His words and to cut off the roots of the Unbelievers;-

8. That He might justify Truth and prove Falsehood false, distasteful though it be to those in guilt.

9. Remember you implored the assistance of your Lord, and He answered you: "I will assist you with a thousand of the angels, ranks on ranks."

10. Allah made it but a message of hope, and an assurance to your hearts: (in any case) there is no help except from Allah: and Allah is Exalted in Power, Wise.

11. Remember He covered you with a sort of drowsiness, to give you calm as from Himself, and He caused rain to descend on you from heaven, to clean you therewith, to remove from you the stain of Satan, to strengthen your hearts, and to plant your feet firmly therewith.

12. Remember your Lord inspired the angels (with the message): "I am with you: give firmness to the Believers: I will instil terror into the hearts of the Unbelievers: smite you above their necks

lakaarihoon.

6. Yujaadiloonaka fil-ḥaqqi ba'da maa tabayyana ka-annamaa yusaaqoona ilal-mawti wa hum yanẓuroon.

7. Wa iẕ ya'idukumul-laahu iḥdaṭ-ṭaaa'ifatayni annahaa lakum wa tawaddoona anna ghayra ẕaatish-shawkati takoonu lakum wa yureedul-laahu añy-yuḥiqqal-ḥaqqa bikalimaatihee wa yaqṭa'a daabiral-kaafireen.

8. Liyuḥiqqal-ḥaqqa wa yubṭilal-baaṭila wa law karihal-mujrimoon.

9. Iẕ tastagheesoona Rabba-kum fastajaaba lakum annee mumiddukum bi-alfim-minal-malaaa'ikati murdifeen.

10. Wa maa ja'alahul-laahu illaa bushraa wa litaṭma'inna bihee quloobukum; wa man-naṣru-illaa min 'indil-laah; innal-laaha Azeezun Ḥakeem.

(Section 1)

11. Iẕ yughashsheekumun-nu'aasa amanatam-minhu wa yunazzilu 'alaykum minas-samaaa'i maaa'al-liyuṭah-hirakum bihee wa yuẕhiba 'ankum rijzash-Shayṭaani wa liyarbiṭa 'ala quloobikum wa yusabbita bihil-aqdaam.

12. Iẕ yooḥee Rabbuka ilal-malaaa'ikati annee ma'akum fasabbitul-laẕeena aamanoo; sa-ulqee fee quloobil-laẕeena kafarur-ru'ba faḍriboo fawqal-a'naaqi

لَكٰرِهُوْنَ ۝٥

يُجَادِلُوْنَكَ فِي الْحَقِّ بَعْدَ مَا
تَبَيَّنَ كَاَنَّمَا يُسَاقُوْنَ اِلَى الْمَوْتِ
وَهُمْ يَنْظُرُوْنَ ۝٦

وَاِذْ يَعِدُكُمُ اللّٰهُ اِحْدَى
الطَّآئِفَتَيْنِ اَنَّهَا لَكُمْ وَتَوَدُّوْنَ اَنَّ
غَيْرَ ذَاتِ الشَّوْكَةِ تَكُوْنُ لَكُمْ
وَيُرِيْدُ اللّٰهُ اَنْ يُّحِقَّ الْحَقَّ بِكَلِمٰتِهٖ
وَيَقْطَعَ دَابِرَ الْكٰفِرِيْنَ ۝٧

لِيُحِقَّ الْحَقَّ وَيُبْطِلَ الْبَاطِلَ وَ
لَوْ كَرِهَ الْمُجْرِمُوْنَ ۝٨

اِذْ تَسْتَغِيْثُوْنَ رَبَّكُمْ فَاسْتَجَابَ
لَكُمْ اَنِّيْ مُمِدُّكُمْ بِاَلْفٍ مِّنَ
الْمَلٰٓئِكَةِ مُرْدِفِيْنَ ۝٩

وَمَا جَعَلَهُ اللّٰهُ اِلَّا بُشْرٰى وَلِتَطْمَئِنَّ
بِهٖ قُلُوْبُكُمْ ۚ وَمَا النَّصْرُ اِلَّا مِنْ
عِنْدِ اللّٰهِ ؕ اِنَّ اللّٰهَ عَزِيْزٌ حَكِيْمٌ ۝١٠ ع ١٥

اِذْ يُغَشِّيْكُمُ النُّعَاسَ اَمَنَةً مِّنْهُ
وَيُنَزِّلُ عَلَيْكُمْ مِّنَ السَّمَآءِ مَآءً
لِّيُطَهِّرَكُمْ بِهٖ وَيُذْهِبَ عَنْكُمْ
رِجْزَ الشَّيْطٰنِ وَلِيَرْبِطَ عَلٰى
قُلُوْبِكُمْ وَيُثَبِّتَ بِهِ الْاَقْدَامَ ۝١١

اِذْ يُوْحِيْ رَبُّكَ اِلَى الْمَلٰٓئِكَةِ
اَنِّيْ مَعَكُمْ فَثَبِّتُوا الَّذِيْنَ اٰمَنُوْا ؕ
سَاُلْقِيْ فِيْ قُلُوْبِ الَّذِيْنَ كَفَرُوا
الرُّعْبَ فَاضْرِبُوْا فَوْقَ الْاَعْنَاقِ

Ikhfa اخفاء | Ghunna غُنّہ | Ikhfa Meem Saakin اخفاء میم ساکن | Idghaam ادغام | Qalqala قلقلہ | Qalb قلب | Idghaam Meem Saakin ادغام میم ساکن

and smite all their finger-tips off them."	waḍriboo minhum kulla banaan.	وَاضْرِبُوْا مِنْهُمْ كُلَّ بَنَانٍ ﴿١٢﴾
13. This because they contended against Allah and His Apostle: if any contend against Allah and His Apostle, Allah is strict in punishment.	13. Zaalika bi-annahum shaaaqqul-laaha wa Rasoolah; wa mañy-yushaqiqil-laaha wa Rasoolahoo fa-innal-laaha shadeedul-'iqaab.	ذٰلِكَ بِاَنَّهُمْ شَآقُّوا اللّٰهَ وَرَسُوْلَهٗ ۚ وَمَنْ يُّشَاقِقِ اللّٰهَ وَرَسُوْلَهٗ فَاِنَّ اللّٰهَ شَدِيْدُ الْعِقَابِ ﴿١٣﴾
14. Thus (will it be said): "You taste then of the (punishment): for those who resist Allah, is the Chastisement of the Fire."	14. Zaalikum fazooqoohu wa anna lilkaafireena 'azaaban-Naar.	ذٰلِكُمْ فَذُوْقُوْهُ وَاَنَّ لِلْكٰفِرِيْنَ عَذَابَ النَّارِ ﴿١٤﴾
15. O you who believe! when you meet the Unbelievers in hostile array, never turn your backs to them.	15. Yaaa ayyuhal-lazeena aamanooo izaa laqeetumul-lazeena kafaroo zaḥfan falaa tuwalloohumul-adbaar.	يٰۤاَيُّهَا الَّذِيْنَ اٰمَنُوْۤا اِذَا لَقِيْتُمُ الَّذِيْنَ كَفَرُوْا زَحْفًا فَلَا تُوَلُّوْهُمُ الْاَدْبَارَ ﴿١٥﴾
16. If any do turn his back to them on such a day - unless it be in a stratagem of war, or to retreat to a troop (of his own) - he draws on himself the wrath of Allah, and his abode is Hell,- an evil refuge (indeed)!	16. Wa mañy-yuwallihim yawma'izin duburahooo illaa mutaḥarrifal-liqitaalin aw mutaḥayyizan ilaa fi'atin faqad baaa'a bighaḍabim-minal-laahi wa maåwaahu Jahannamu wa bi'sal-maṣeer.	وَمَنْ يُّوَلِّهِمْ يَوْمَئِذٍ دُبُرَهٗۤ اِلَّا مُتَحَرِّفًا لِّقِتَالٍ اَوْ مُتَحَيِّزًا اِلٰى فِئَةٍ فَقَدْ بَآءَ بِغَضَبٍ مِّنَ اللّٰهِ وَمَاْوٰىهُ جَهَنَّمُ ۗ وَبِئْسَ الْمَصِيْرُ ﴿١٦﴾
17. It is not you who slew them; it was Allah: when you threwest (a handful of dust), it was not your act, but Allah's: in order that He might test the Believers by a gracious trial from Himself: for Allah is He Who heareth and knoweth (all things).	17. Falam taqtuloohum wa laakinnal-laaha qatalahum; wa maa ramayta iz ramayta wa laakinnal-laaha ramaa; wa liyubliyal-mu'mineena minhu balaaa'an ḥasanaa; innal-laaha Samee'un 'Aleem.	فَلَمْ تَقْتُلُوْهُمْ وَلٰكِنَّ اللّٰهَ قَتَلَهُمْ ۪ وَمَا رَمَيْتَ اِذْ رَمَيْتَ وَلٰكِنَّ اللّٰهَ رَمٰى ۚ وَلِيُبْلِيَ الْمُؤْمِنِيْنَ مِنْهُ بَلَآءً حَسَنًا ۗ اِنَّ اللّٰهَ سَمِيْعٌ عَلِيْمٌ ﴿١٧﴾
18. That, and also because Allah is He Who makes feeble the plans and stratagem of the Unbelievers.	18. Zaalikum wa annal-laaha moohinu kaydil-kaafireen.	ذٰلِكُمْ وَاَنَّ اللّٰهَ مُوْهِنُ كَيْدِ الْكٰفِرِيْنَ ﴿١٨﴾
19. (O Unbelievers!) if you prayed for victory and judgment, now has the judgment come to you: if you desist (from wrong), it will be best for you: if you return (to the attack), so shall We. Not the least good will your forces be to you even if they were multiplied: for verily Allah is with those who believe!	19. In tastaftiḥoo faqad jaaa'akumul-fatḥu wa in tantahoo fahuwa khayrul-lakum wa in ta'oodoo na'ud wa lan tughniya 'ankum fi'atukum shay'añw-wa law kasurat wa annal-laaha ma'al-mu'mineen. **(Section 2)**	اِنْ تَسْتَفْتِحُوْا فَقَدْ جَآءَكُمُ الْفَتْحُ ۚ وَاِنْ تَنْتَهُوْا فَهُوَ خَيْرٌ لَّكُمْ ۚ وَاِنْ تَعُوْدُوْا نَعُدْ ۚ وَلَنْ تُغْنِيَ عَنْكُمْ فِئَتُكُمْ شَيْئًا وَّلَوْ كَثُرَتْ ۙ وَ اَنَّ اللّٰهَ مَعَ الْمُؤْمِنِيْنَ ﴿١٩﴾ ع ٢ ١٦
20. O you who believe! Obey Allah and His Apostle, and do not turn away from him when you	20. Yaaa ayyuhal-lazeena aṭee'ul-laaha wa Rasoolahoo wa laa tawallaw 'anhu wa antum	يٰۤاَيُّهَا الَّذِيْنَ اٰمَنُوْۤا اَطِيْعُوا اللّٰهَ وَرَسُوْلَهٗ وَلَا تَوَلَّوْا عَنْهُ وَاَنْتُمْ

Ikhfa اخفاء · Ghunna غنّہ · Ikhfa Meem Saakin اخفاء میم ساکن · Idghaam ادغام · Qalqala قلقلہ · Qalb قلب · Idghaam Meem Saakin ادغام میم ساکن

hear (him speak).	tasma'oon.	تَسْمَعُونَ ۝٢٠
21. Nor be like those who say, "We hear," but listen not.	21. Wa laa takoonoo kal-la<u>z</u>eena qaaloo sami'naa wa hum laa yasma'oon.	وَلَا تَكُونُوا كَالَّذِينَ قَالُوا سَمِعْنَا وَهُمْ لَا يَسْمَعُونَ ۝٢١
22. For the worst of beasts in the sight of Allah are the deaf and the dumb,- those who do not understand.	22. Inna sharrad-dawaaabbi 'indal-laahiṣ-ṣummul-bukmul-la<u>z</u>eena laa ya'qiloon.	إِنَّ شَرَّ الدَّوَابِّ عِنْدَ اللَّهِ الصُّمُّ الْبُكْمُ الَّذِينَ لَا يَعْقِلُونَ ۝٢٢
23. If Allah had found in them any good, He would indeed have made them listen: (As it is), if He had made them listen, they would but have turned back and declined (Faith).	23. Wa law 'alimal-laahu feehim khayral-la-asma'ahum; wa law asma'ahum latawallaw wa hum mu'riḍoon.	وَلَوْ عَلِمَ اللَّهُ فِيهِمْ خَيْرًا لَأَسْمَعَهُمْ وَلَوْ أَسْمَعَهُمْ لَتَوَلَّوْا وَهُمْ مُعْرِضُونَ ۝٢٣
24. O you who believe! give your response to Allah and His Apostle, when He calls you to that which will give you life; and know that Allah comes in between a man and his heart, and that it is He to Whom you shall (all) be gathered.	24. Yaaa ayyuhal-la<u>z</u>eena aamanus-tajeeboo lillaahi wa lir-Rasooli i<u>z</u>aa da'aakum limaa yuḥyeekum wa'lamooo annal-laaha yaḥoolu baynal-mar'i wa qalbihee wa annahooo ilayhi tuḥsharoon.	يَا أَيُّهَا الَّذِينَ آمَنُوا اسْتَجِيبُوا لِلَّهِ وَلِلرَّسُولِ إِذَا دَعَاكُمْ لِمَا يُحْيِيكُمْ وَاعْلَمُوا أَنَّ اللَّهَ يَحُولُ بَيْنَ الْمَرْءِ وَقَلْبِهِ وَأَنَّهُ إِلَيْهِ تُحْشَرُونَ ۝٢٤
25. And fear tumult or oppression, which affects not in particular (only) those of you who do wrong: and know that Allah is strict in punishment.	25. Wattaqoo fitnatal-laa tuṣeebannal-la<u>z</u>eena ẓalamoo minkum khaaaṣṣatañw wa'la-mooo annal-laaha shadeedul-'iqaab.	وَاتَّقُوا فِتْنَةً لَا تُصِيبَنَّ الَّذِينَ ظَلَمُوا مِنْكُمْ خَاصَّةً وَاعْلَمُوا أَنَّ اللَّهَ شَدِيدُ الْعِقَابِ ۝٢٥
26. Call to mind when you were a small (band), deemed weak through the land, and afraid that men might despoil and kidnap you; but He provided a safe asylum for you, strengthened you with His aid, and gave you good things for sustenance: that you might be grateful.	26. Wa<u>z</u>kurooo i<u>z</u> antum qaleelum-mustaḍ'afoona fil-arḍi takhaafoona añy-yatakhaṭ-ṭafakumun-naasu fa-aawaakum wa ayyadakum binaṣrihee wa razaqakum minaṭ-ṭayyibaati la'allakum tashkuroon.	وَاذْكُرُوا إِذْ أَنْتُمْ قَلِيلٌ مُسْتَضْعَفُونَ فِي الْأَرْضِ تَخَافُونَ أَنْ يَتَخَطَّفَكُمُ النَّاسُ فَآوَاكُمْ وَأَيَّدَكُمْ بِنَصْرِهِ وَ رَزَقَكُمْ مِنَ الطَّيِّبَاتِ لَعَلَّكُمْ تَشْكُرُونَ ۝٢٦
27. O you that believe! do not betray the trust of Allah and the Apostle, nor misappropriate knowingly things entrusted to you.	27. Yaaa ayyuhal-la<u>z</u>eena aamanoo laa takhoonul-laaha war-Rasoola wa takhoonooo amaanaatikum wa antum ta'lamoon.	يَا أَيُّهَا الَّذِينَ آمَنُوا لَا تَخُونُوا اللَّهَ وَالرَّسُولَ وَتَخُونُوا أَمَانَاتِكُمْ وَأَنْتُمْ تَعْلَمُونَ ۝٢٧
28. And know you that your possessions and your progeny are but a trial; and that it is Allah with Whom lies your highest reward.	28. Wa'lamooo annamaaa amwaalukum wa awlaadukum fitnatuñw-wa annal-laaha 'indahooo ajrun aẓeem. **(Sec. 3)**	وَاعْلَمُوا أَنَّمَا أَمْوَالُكُمْ وَأَوْلَادُكُمْ فِتْنَةٌ وَأَنَّ اللَّهَ عِنْدَهُ أَجْرٌ عَظِيمٌ ۝٢٨ ع
29. O you who believe! if you fear Allah, He will grant you a Criterion (to judge between right and wrong), remove from you (all) evil (that may afflict) you, and forgive you: for Allah	29. Yaaa ayyuhal-la<u>z</u>eena aamanooo in tattaqul-laaha yaj'al lakum furqaanañw-wa yukaffir 'ankum sayyi-aatikum wa yaghfir lakum; wallaahu	يَا أَيُّهَا الَّذِينَ آمَنُوا إِنْ تَتَّقُوا اللَّهَ يَجْعَلْ لَكُمْ فُرْقَانًا وَيُكَفِّرْ عَنْكُمْ سَيِّئَاتِكُمْ وَيَغْفِرْ لَكُمْ وَاللَّهُ

Ikhfa اخفاء | Ghunna غنّہ | Ikhfa Meem Saakin اخفاء میم ساکن | Idghaam ادغام | Qalqala قلقلہ | Qalb قلب | Idghaam Meem Saakin ادغام میم ساکن

is the Lord of grace unbounded.

30. Remember how the Unbelievers plotted against you, to keep you in bonds, or slay you, or get you out (of your home). They plot and plan, and Allah too plans, but the best of planners is Allah.

31. When Our Signs are rehearsed to them, they say: "We have heard this (before): if we wished, we could say (words) like these: these are nothing but tales of the ancients."

32. Remember how they said: "O Allah if this is indeed the Truth from You, rain down on us a shower of stones form the sky, or send us a grievous Chastisement."

33. But Allah was not going to send them a Chastisement whilst you were amongst them; nor was He going to send it whilst they could ask for pardon.

34. But what plea have they that Allah should not punish them, when they keep out (men) from the Sacred Mosque - and they are not its guardians? No men can be its guardians except the righteous; but most of them do not understand.

35. Their prayer at the House (of Allah) is nothing but whistling and clapping of hands: (its only answer can be), "You taste the Chastisement because you blasphemed."

36. The Unbelievers spend their wealth to hinder (man) from the path of Allah, and so will they continue to spend; but in the end they will have (only) regrets and sighs; at length they will be overcome: and the

z̲ul-faḍlil-'aẓeem.

30. Wa iz̲ yamkuru bikal-laz̲eena kafaroo liyus̲bitooka aw yaqtulooka aw yukhrijook; wa yamkuroona wa yamkurul-laahu wallaahu khayrul-maakireen.

31. Wa iz̲aa tutlaa 'alayhim Aayaatunaa qaaloo qad sami'-naa law nashaaa'u laqulnaa mis̲la haaz̲aaa in haaz̲aaa illaaa asaaṭeerul-awwaleen.

32. Wa iz̲ qaalul-laahumma in kaana haaz̲aa huwal-ḥaqqa min 'indika fa-amṭir 'alaynaa ḥijaaratam-minas-samaaa'i awi'-tinaa bi'az̲aabin aleem.

33. Wa maa kanal-laahu liyu'az̲-z̲ibahum wa anta feehim; wa maa kaanal-laahu mu'az̲-z̲ibahum wa hum yastagh-firoon.

34. Wa maa lahum allaa yu'az̲-z̲ibahumul-laahu wa hum yaṣuddoona 'anil-Masjidil-Ḥaraami wa maa kaanooo awliyaaa'ah; in awliyaaa'uhooo illal-muttaqoona wa laakinna aks̲arahum laa ya'lamoon.

.35. Wa maa kaana Ṣalaatuhum 'indal-Bayti illaa mukaaa'añw-wa taṣdiyah; faz̲ooqul-'az̲aaba bimaa kuntum takfuroon.

36. Innal-laz̲eena kafaroo yunfiqoona amwaalahum liyaṣuddoo 'an sabeelil-laah; fasayunfiqoonahaa summa takoonu 'alayhim ḥasratan summa yughlaboon; wal-laz̲eena

ذُوالْفَضْلِ الْعَظِيمِ ﴿٢٩﴾
وَإِذْ يَمْكُرُ بِكَ الَّذِينَ كَفَرُوا
لِيُثْبِتُوكَ أَوْ يَقْتُلُوكَ أَوْ يُخْرِجُوكَ ۚ
وَيَمْكُرُونَ وَيَمْكُرُ اللَّهُ ۖ وَاللَّهُ
خَيْرُ الْمَاكِرِينَ ﴿٣٠﴾
وَإِذَا تُتْلَىٰ عَلَيْهِمْ آيَاتُنَا قَالُوا قَدْ
سَمِعْنَا لَوْ نَشَاءُ لَقُلْنَا مِثْلَ هَٰذَا ۙ
إِنْ هَٰذَا إِلَّا أَسَاطِيرُ الْأَوَّلِينَ ﴿٣١﴾
وَإِذْ قَالُوا اللَّهُمَّ إِنْ كَانَ
هَٰذَا هُوَ الْحَقَّ مِنْ عِنْدِكَ فَأَمْطِرْ
عَلَيْنَا حِجَارَةً مِنَ السَّمَاءِ أَوِ ائْتِنَا
بِعَذَابٍ أَلِيمٍ ﴿٣٢﴾
وَمَا كَانَ اللَّهُ لِيُعَذِّبَهُمْ وَأَنْتَ
فِيهِمْ ۚ وَمَا كَانَ اللَّهُ مُعَذِّبَهُمْ
وَهُمْ يَسْتَغْفِرُونَ ﴿٣٣﴾
وَمَا لَهُمْ أَلَّا يُعَذِّبَهُمُ اللَّهُ وَهُمْ
يَصُدُّونَ عَنِ الْمَسْجِدِ الْحَرَامِ وَمَا
كَانُوا أَوْلِيَاءَهُ ۚ إِنْ أَوْلِيَاؤُهُ إِلَّا
الْمُتَّقُونَ وَلَٰكِنَّ أَكْثَرَهُمْ لَا يَعْلَمُونَ ﴿٣٤﴾
وَمَا كَانَ صَلَاتُهُمْ عِنْدَ الْبَيْتِ
إِلَّا مُكَاءً وَتَصْدِيَةً ۚ فَذُوقُوا
الْعَذَابَ بِمَا كُنْتُمْ تَكْفُرُونَ ﴿٣٥﴾
إِنَّ الَّذِينَ كَفَرُوا يُنْفِقُونَ
أَمْوَالَهُمْ لِيَصُدُّوا عَنْ سَبِيلِ اللَّهِ ۚ
فَسَيُنْفِقُونَهَا ثُمَّ تَكُونُ عَلَيْهِمْ
حَسْرَةً ثُمَّ يُغْلَبُونَ ۗ وَالَّذِينَ

Ikhfa اخفاء · Ghunna غنّہ · Ikhfa Meem Saakin اخفاء میم ساکن · Idghaam ادغام · Qalqala قلقلہ · Qalb قلب · Idghaam Meem Saakin ادغام میم ساکن

Unbelievers will be gathered together to Hell;

37. In order that Allah may separate the impure from the pure, put the impure, one on another, heap them together, and cast them into Hell. They will be the ones to have lost.

38. Say to the Unbelievers, if (now) they desist (from Unbelief), their past would be forgiven them; but if they persist, the punishment of those before them is already (a matter of warning for them).

39. And fight them on until there is no more tumult or oppression, and religion becomes Allah's in its entirety, but if they cease, surely Allah sees all that they do.

40. If they refuse, be sure that Allah is your Protector - the Best to protect and the best to help.

41. And know that out of all the booty that you may acquire (in war), a fifth share is assigned to Allah,- and to the Apostle, and to near relatives, orphans, the needy, and the wayfarer,- if you do believe in Allah and in the revelation We sent down to Our Servant on the Day of discrimination,- the Day of the meeting of the two forces. For Allah has power over all things.

42. Remember you were on the hither side of the valley, and they on the farther side, and the caravan on lower ground than you. Even if you had made a mutual appointment to meet, you would certainly have failed in the appointment: but (thus you met), that Allah might accomplish a matter already decided; that those who died might die after a clear Sign (had been given), and those who lived might live after

kafarooo ilaa Jahannama yuḥsharoona.

37. Liyameezal-laahul khabeesa minaṭ-ṭayyibi wa yaj'alal-khabeesa ba'ḍahoo 'ala ba'din fayarkumahoo jamee'an fayaj'alahoo fee Jahannam; ulaaa'ika humul-khaasiroon.

(Section 4)

38. Qul-lillazeena kafarooo iñy-yantahoo yughfar lahum maa qad salafa wa iñy-ya'oodoo faqad maḍat sunnatul-awwaleen.

39. Wa qaatiloohum ḥattaa laa takoona fitnatuñw-wa yakoonaddeenu kulluhoo lillaah; fa-inin-tahaw fa-innallaaha bimaa ya'maloona Baṣeer.

40. Wa in tawallaw fa'lamooo annal-laaha mawlaakum; ni'mal-mawlaa wa ni'man-naṣeer.

41. Wa'lamooo annamaa ghanimtum min shay'in fa-anna lillaahi khumusahoo wa lir-Rasooli wa lizil-qurbaa walyataamaa walmasaakeeni wabnis-sabeeli in kuntum aamantum billaahi wa maaa anzalnaa 'ala 'abdinaa yawmal-Furqaani yawmaltaqal-jam'aan; wallaahu 'alaa kulli shay'in Qadeer.

42. Iz antum bil'udwatid-dunyaa wa hum bil'udwatil-quṣwaa warrakbu asfala minkum; wa law tawaa'attum lakhtalaftum fil-mee'aadi wa laakil-liyaqḍiyal-laahu amran kaana maf'oolal liyahlika man halaka 'am bayyinatiñw-wa yaḥyaa man ḥayya 'am

كَفَرُوٓا إِلَىٰ جَهَنَّمَ يُحْشَرُونَ ٣٦
لِيَمِيزَ ٱللَّهُ ٱلْخَبِيثَ مِنَ ٱلطَّيِّبِ
وَيَجْعَلَ ٱلْخَبِيثَ بَعْضَهُۥ عَلَىٰ
بَعْضٍ فَيَرْكُمَهُۥ جَمِيعًا فَيَجْعَلَهُۥ
فِى جَهَنَّمَ ۚ أُو۟لَٰٓئِكَ هُمُ ٱلْخَٰسِرُونَ ٣٧ ع ١٨
قُل لِّلَّذِينَ كَفَرُوٓا إِن يَنتَهُوا يُغْفَرْ
لَهُم مَّا قَدْ سَلَفَ وَإِن يَعُودُوا
فَقَدْ مَضَتْ سُنَّتُ ٱلْأَوَّلِينَ ٣٨
وَقَٰتِلُوهُمْ حَتَّىٰ لَا تَكُونَ فِتْنَةٌ وَ
يَكُونَ ٱلدِّينُ كُلُّهُۥ لِلَّهِ ۚ فَإِنِ ٱنتَهَوْا
فَإِنَّ ٱللَّهَ بِمَا يَعْمَلُونَ بَصِيرٌ ٣٩
وَإِن تَوَلَّوْا فَٱعْلَمُوٓا أَنَّ ٱللَّهَ مَوْلَىٰكُمْ
نِعْمَ ٱلْمَوْلَىٰ وَنِعْمَ ٱلنَّصِيرُ ٤٠
وَٱعْلَمُوٓا أَنَّمَا غَنِمْتُم مِّن شَىْءٍ
فَأَنَّ لِلَّهِ خُمُسَهُۥ وَلِلرَّسُولِ وَلِذِى
ٱلْقُرْبَىٰ وَٱلْيَتَٰمَىٰ وَٱلْمَسَٰكِينِ وَٱبْنِ
ٱلسَّبِيلِ إِن كُنتُمْ ءَامَنتُم بِٱللَّهِ وَمَآ
أَنزَلْنَا عَلَىٰ عَبْدِنَا يَوْمَ ٱلْفُرْقَانِ
يَوْمَ ٱلْتَقَى ٱلْجَمْعَانِ ۗ وَٱللَّهُ عَلَىٰ
كُلِّ شَىْءٍ قَدِيرٌ ٤١
إِذْ أَنتُم بِٱلْعُدْوَةِ ٱلدُّنْيَا وَهُم
بِٱلْعُدْوَةِ ٱلْقُصْوَىٰ وَٱلرَّكْبُ أَسْفَلَ
مِنكُمْ ۚ وَلَوْ تَوَاعَدتُّمْ لَٱخْتَلَفْتُمْ
فِى ٱلْمِيعَٰدِ ۙ وَلَٰكِن لِّيَقْضِىَ ٱللَّهُ أَمْرًا
كَانَ مَفْعُولًا لِّيَهْلِكَ مَنْ هَلَكَ
عَنۢ بَيِّنَةٍ وَيَحْيَىٰ مَنْ حَىَّ عَنۢ

Ikhfa اخفاء | Ghunna غنّہ | Ikhfa Meem Saakin اخفاء میم ساکن | Idghaam ادغام | Qalqala قلقلہ | Qalb قلب | Idghaam Meem Saakin ادغام میم ساکن

a Clear Sign (had been given). And verily Allah is He Who hears and knows (all things).

43. Remember in your dream Allah showed them to you as few: if He had shown them to you as many, you would surely have been discouraged, and you would surely have disputed in (your) decision; but Allah saved (you): for He knows well the (secrets) of (all) hearts.

44. And remember when you met, He showed them to you as few in your eyes, and He made you appear as contemptible in their eyes: that Allah might accomplish a matter already decided. For to Allah do all questions go back (for decision).

45. O you who believe! When you meet a force, be firm, and call Allah in remembrance much (and often); that you may prosper:

46. And obey Allah and His Apostle; and fall into no disputes, lest you lose heart and your power depart; and be patient and persevering: for Allah is with those who patiently persevere:

47. And be not like those who started from their homes insolently and to be seen of men, and to hinder (men) from the path of Allah: for Allah compasses round about all that they do.

48. Remember Satan made their (sinful) acts seem alluring to them, and said: "No one among men can overcome you this day, while I am near to you": But when the two forces came in sight of each other, he turned on his heels, and said: "Lo! I am clear of you; Lo! I see what you see not; Lo! I fear Allah: for Allah is strict in punishment."

bayyinah; wa innal-laaha la-Samee'un 'Aleem.

43. Iz yureekahumul-laahu fee manaamika qaleela(ñw-) wa law araakahum kaseeral-lafashil-tum wa latanaaza'tum fil-amri wa laakinnal-laaha sallam; innahoo 'aleemum bizaatiṣ-ṣudoor.

44. Wa iz yureekumoohum izil-taqaytum feee a'yunikum qaleelañw-wa yuqallilukum feee a'yunihim liyaqḍiyal-laahu amran kaana maf'oolaa; wa ilal-laahi turja'ul-umoor. **(Section 5)**

45. Yaaa ayyuhal-lazeena aamanooo izaa laqeetum fi'atan fasbutoo wazkurul-laaha kaseeral-la'allakum tufliḥoon.

46. Wa aṭee'ul-laaha wa Rasoolahoo wa laa tanaaza'oo fatafshaloo wa tazhaba reeḥu-kum waṣbiroo; innal-laaha ma'aṣ-ṣaabireen.

47. Wa laa takoonoo kallazeena kharajoo min diyaarihim baṭarañw-wa ri'aaa'an-naasi wa yaṣuddoona 'an sabeelil-laah; wallaahu bimaa ya'maloona muḥeet.

48. Wa iz-zayyana lahumush-Shayṭaanu a'ma-alahum wa qaala laa ghaaliba lakumul yawma minan-naasi wa innee jaarul-lakum falammaa taraaa'atil-fi'ataani nakaṣa 'alaa aqibayhi wa qaala innee bareee'um-minkum innee araa maa laa tarawna inneee akhaaful-laah; wallaahu sha-deedul-'iqaab. **(Section 6)**

بَيِّنَةٍ ۗ وَإِنَّ اللَّهَ لَسَمِيعٌ عَلِيمٌ ﴿٤٢﴾
إِذْ يُرِيكَهُمُ اللَّهُ فِي مَنَامِكَ قَلِيلًا ۖ وَلَوْ
أَرَاكَهُمْ كَثِيرًا لَّفَشِلْتُمْ وَلَتَنَازَعْتُمْ
فِي الْأَمْرِ وَلَٰكِنَّ اللَّهَ سَلَّمَ ۗ إِنَّهُ
عَلِيمٌ بِذَاتِ الصُّدُورِ ﴿٤٣﴾
وَإِذْ يُرِيكُمُوهُمْ إِذِ الْتَقَيْتُمْ فِي
أَعْيُنِكُمْ قَلِيلًا وَيُقَلِّلُكُمْ فِي أَعْيُنِهِمْ
لِيَقْضِيَ اللَّهُ أَمْرًا كَانَ مَفْعُولًا ۗ
وَإِلَى اللَّهِ تُرْجَعُ الْأُمُورُ ﴿٤٤﴾ ع
يَا أَيُّهَا الَّذِينَ آمَنُوا إِذَا لَقِيتُمْ
فِئَةً فَاثْبُتُوا وَاذْكُرُوا اللَّهَ كَثِيرًا
لَّعَلَّكُمْ تُفْلِحُونَ ﴿٤٥﴾
وَأَطِيعُوا اللَّهَ وَرَسُولَهُ وَلَا تَنَازَعُوا
فَتَفْشَلُوا وَتَذْهَبَ رِيحُكُمْ ۖ وَاصْبِرُوا ۚ
إِنَّ اللَّهَ مَعَ الصَّابِرِينَ ﴿٤٦﴾
وَلَا تَكُونُوا كَالَّذِينَ خَرَجُوا
مِن دِيَارِهِم بَطَرًا وَرِئَاءَ النَّاسِ
وَيَصُدُّونَ عَن سَبِيلِ اللَّهِ ۚ
وَاللَّهُ بِمَا يَعْمَلُونَ مُحِيطٌ ﴿٤٧﴾
وَإِذْ زَيَّنَ لَهُمُ الشَّيْطَانُ أَعْمَالَهُمْ
وَقَالَ لَا غَالِبَ لَكُمُ الْيَوْمَ مِنَ
النَّاسِ وَإِنِّي جَارٌ لَّكُمْ ۖ فَلَمَّا تَرَاءَتِ
الْفِئَتَانِ نَكَصَ عَلَىٰ عَقِبَيْهِ وَقَالَ
إِنِّي بَرِيءٌ مِّنكُمْ إِنِّي أَرَىٰ
مَا لَا تَرَوْنَ إِنِّي أَخَافُ اللَّهَ ۚ
وَاللَّهُ شَدِيدُ الْعِقَابِ ﴿٤٨﴾ ع

Ikhfa اخفاء · Ghunna غنّہ · Ikhfa Meem Saakin اخفاء میم ساکن · Idghaam ادغام · Qalqala قلقلہ · Qalb قلب · Idghaam Meem Saakin ادغام میم ساکن

49. Lo! the hypocrites say, and those in whose hearts is a disease: "These people,- their religion has misled them." But if any trust in Allah, behold! Allah is Exalted in might, Wise.

49. Iz yaqoolul-munaafiqoona wallazeena fee quloobihim maradun gharra haaa'ulaaa'i deenuhum; wa mañy-yatawakkal 'alal-laahi fa-innal-laaha 'Azee-zun Ḥakeem.

إِذْ يَقُولُ الْمُنٰفِقُونَ وَالَّذِينَ
فِي قُلُوبِهِم مَّرَضٌ غَرَّ هٰٓؤُلَآءِ
دِينُهُمْ ۗ وَمَن يَتَوَكَّلْ عَلَى اللّٰهِ
فَإِنَّ اللّٰهَ عَزِيزٌ حَكِيمٌ ﴿٤٩﴾

50. If you could see, when the angels take the souls of the Unbelievers (at death), (How) they smite their faces and their backs, (saying): "Taste the Chastisement of the blazing Fire-

50. Wa law taraaa iz yatawaffal-lazeena kafarul malaaa'ikatu yaḍriboona wujoohahum wa adbaarahum wa zooqoo 'azaabal-ḥareeq.

وَلَوْ تَرٰىٓ إِذْ يَتَوَفَّى الَّذِينَ
كَفَرُوا ۙ الْمَلٰٓئِكَةُ يَضْرِبُونَ
وُجُوهَهُمْ وَأَدْبٰرَهُمْ ۚ وَذُوقُوا
عَذَابَ الْحَرِيقِ ﴿٥٠﴾

51. "Because of (the deeds) which your (own) hands sent forth; for Allah is never unjust to His servants:

51. Zaalika bimaa qaddamat aydeekum wa annal-laaha laysa biẓallaamil-lil'abeed.

ذٰلِكَ بِمَا قَدَّمَتْ أَيْدِيكُمْ وَ
أَنَّ اللّٰهَ لَيْسَ بِظَلّٰمٍ لِّلْعَبِيدِ ﴿٥١﴾

52. "(Deeds) after the manner of the people of Pharaoh and of those before them: they rejected the Signs of Allah, and Allah punished them for their crimes: for Allah is Strong, and Strict in punishment:

52. Kadaåbi Aali Fir'awna wallazeena min qablihim; kafaroo bi-Aayaatil-laahi fa-akhazahumul-laahu bizunoobihim; innallaaha qawiyyun shadeedul-'iqaab.

كَدَأْبِ اٰلِ فِرْعَوْنَ ۙ وَالَّذِينَ
مِن قَبْلِهِمْ ۚ كَفَرُوا بِاٰيٰتِ اللّٰهِ
فَأَخَذَهُمُ اللّٰهُ بِذُنُوبِهِمْ ۗ إِنَّ اللّٰهَ
قَوِيٌّ شَدِيدُ الْعِقَابِ ﴿٥٢﴾

53. "Because Allah will never change the grace which He has bestowed on a people until they change what is in their (own) souls, and surely Allah is He Who hears and knows (all things)."

53. Zaalika bi-annal-laaha lam yaku mughayyiran-ni'matan an'amahaa 'alaa qawmin ḥattaa yughayyiroo maa bianfusihim wa annallaaha Samee'un 'Aleem.

ذٰلِكَ بِأَنَّ اللّٰهَ لَمْ يَكُ مُغَيِّرًا
نِّعْمَةً أَنْعَمَهَا عَلٰى قَوْمٍ حَتّٰى
يُغَيِّرُوا مَا بِأَنفُسِهِمْ ۙ وَأَنَّ اللّٰهَ
سَمِيعٌ عَلِيمٌ ﴿٥٣﴾

54. "(Deeds) after the manner of the people of Pharaoh and those before them": they treated as false the Signs of their Lord, so We destroyed them for their crimes, and We drowned the people of Pharaoh: for they were all oppressors and wrong-doers.

54. Kadaåbi Aali Fir'awna wallazeena min qablihim; kazzaboo bi-Aayaati Rabbihim fa-ahlaknaahum bizunoobihim wa aghraqnaaa Aala Fir'awn; wa kullun kaanoo ẓaalimeen.

كَدَأْبِ اٰلِ فِرْعَوْنَ ۙ وَالَّذِينَ
مِن قَبْلِهِمْ ۚ كَذَّبُوا بِاٰيٰتِ
رَبِّهِمْ فَأَهْلَكْنٰهُم بِذُنُوبِهِمْ
وَأَغْرَقْنَآ اٰلَ فِرْعَوْنَ ۚ وَكُلٌّ
كَانُوا ظٰلِمِينَ ﴿٥٤﴾

55. For the worst of beasts in the sight of Allah are those who reject Him: they will not believe.

55. Inna sharrad-dawaaabbi 'indal-laahil-lazeena kafaroo fahum laa yu'minoon.

إِنَّ شَرَّ الدَّوَآبِّ عِندَ اللّٰهِ الَّذِينَ
كَفَرُوا فَهُمْ لَا يُؤْمِنُونَ ﴿٥٥﴾

56. They are those with whom you made a covenant, but

56. Allazeena 'aahatta minhum summa

الَّذِينَ عٰهَدتَّ مِنْهُمْ ثُمَّ

Ikhfa اخفاء | Ghunna غُنّہ | Ikhfa Meem Saakin اخفاء میم ساکن | Idghaam ادغام | Qalqala قلقلہ | Qalb قلب | Idghaam Meem Saakin ادغام میم ساکن

they break their covenant every time, and they do not have the fear (of Allah).

yanquḍoona 'ahdahum fee kulli marratiñw-wa hum laa yattaqoon.

يَنْقُضُوْنَ عَهْدَهُمْ فِيْ كُلِّ
مَرَّةٍ وَّهُمْ لَا يَتَّقُوْنَ ﴿٥٦﴾

57. If you encounter them in a battle deal severely with them so as to put terror in those who follow them, that they may remember.

57. Fa-immaa tasqafannahum fil-ḥarbi fasharrid bihim man khalfahum la'allahum yazzakkaroon.

فَاِمَّا تَثْقَفَنَّهُمْ فِي الْحَرْبِ فَشَرِّدْ بِهِمْ
مَّنْ خَلْفَهُمْ لَعَلَّهُمْ يَذَّكَّرُوْنَ ﴿٥٧﴾

58. If you fear treachery from any group, throw back (their covenant) to them, (so as to be) on equal terms: for Allah does not love the treacherous.

58. Wa immaa takhaafanna min qawmin khiyaanatan fambiz ilayhim 'alaa sawaaa'; innallaaha laa yuḥibbul-khaaa'ineen.

(Section 7)

وَاِمَّا تَخَافَنَّ مِنْ قَوْمٍ خِيَانَةً
فَانْۢبِذْ اِلَيْهِمْ عَلٰى سَوَآءٍ ؕ اِنَّ
اللّٰهَ لَا يُحِبُّ الْخَآئِنِيْنَ ﴿٥٨﴾ ع ٧ ١٠ ٣

59. Let not the Unbelievers think that they can get the better (of the godly): they will never frustrate (them).

59. Wa laa yaḥsabannal-lazeena kafaroo sabaqooo; innahum laa yu'jizoon.

وَلَا يَحْسَبَنَّ الَّذِيْنَ كَفَرُوْا سَبَقُوْا ؕ
اِنَّهُمْ لَا يُعْجِزُوْنَ ﴿٥٩﴾

60. Against them make ready your strength to the utmost of your power, including steeds of war, to strike terror into (the hearts of) the enemies, of Allah and your enemies, and others besides, whom you may not know, but whom Allah knows. Whatever you shall spend in the Cause of Allah, shall be repaid to you, and you shall not be treated unjustly.

60. Wa a'iddoo lahum mastaṭa'tum min quwwatiñw-wa mirribaaṭil-khayli turhiboona bihee 'aduwwal-laahi wa 'aduwwakum wa-aakhareena min doonihim laa ta'lamoonahum Allaahu ya'lamuhum; wa maa tunfiqoo min shay'in fee sabeelil-laahi yuwaf-fa-ilaykum wa antum laa tuẓlamoon.

وَاَعِدُّوْا لَهُمْ مَّا اسْتَطَعْتُمْ مِّنْ
قُوَّةٍ وَّمِنْ رِّبَاطِ الْخَيْلِ تُرْهِبُوْنَ
بِهٖ عَدُوَّ اللّٰهِ وَعَدُوَّكُمْ وَاٰخَرِيْنَ
مِنْ دُوْنِهِمْ ۚ لَا تَعْلَمُوْنَهُمْ ۚ
اَللّٰهُ يَعْلَمُهُمْ ؕ وَمَا تُنْفِقُوْا مِنْ
شَيْءٍ فِيْ سَبِيْلِ اللّٰهِ يُوَفَّ اِلَيْكُمْ
وَاَنْتُمْ لَا تُظْلَمُوْنَ ﴿٦٠﴾

61. But if the enemy incline towards peace, do you (also) incline towards peace, and trust in Allah: for He is One that hears and knows (all things).

61. Wa in janaḥoo lissalmi fajnaḥ lahaa wa tawakkal 'alallaah; innahoo Huwas-Samee-'ul-'Aleem.

وَاِنْ جَنَحُوْا لِلسَّلْمِ فَاجْنَحْ
لَهَا وَتَوَكَّلْ عَلَى اللّٰهِ ؕ اِنَّهٗ هُوَ
السَّمِيْعُ الْعَلِيْمُ ﴿٦١﴾

62. Should they intend to deceive you,- verily Allah suffices you: He it is That has strengthened you with His aid and with (the company of) the Believers;

62. Wa iñy-yureedooo añy-yakhda'ooka fainna ḥasbakallaah; Huwal-lazeee ayyadaka binaṣrihee wa bilmu'mineen.

وَاِنْ يُّرِيْدُوْا اَنْ يَّخْدَعُوْكَ فَاِنَّ
حَسْبَكَ اللّٰهُ ؕ هُوَ الَّذِيْۤ اَيَّدَكَ
بِنَصْرِهٖ وَبِالْمُؤْمِنِيْنَ ﴿٦٢﴾

63. And (moreover) He has put affection between their hearts: not if you had spent all that is in the earth, could you have produced that affection, but Allah has done it: for He is Exalted in might, Wise.

63. Wa allafa bayna quloobihim; law-anfaqta maa fil-arḍi jamee'am-maaa-allafta bayna quloobihim wa laakinnallaaha allafa baynahum; innahoo 'Azeezun Ḥakeem.

وَاَلَّفَ بَيْنَ قُلُوْبِهِمْ ؕ لَوْ اَنْفَقْتَ
مَا فِي الْاَرْضِ جَمِيْعًا مَّاۤ اَلَّفْتَ
بَيْنَ قُلُوْبِهِمْ وَلٰكِنَّ اللّٰهَ اَلَّفَ
بَيْنَهُمْ ؕ اِنَّهٗ عَزِيْزٌ حَكِيْمٌ ﴿٦٣﴾

Ikhfa اخفاء | Ghunna غُنّہ | Ikhfa Meem Saakin اخفاء میم ساکن | Idghaam ادغام | Qalqala قلقلہ | Qalb قلب | Idghaam Meem Saakin ادغام میم ساکن

64. O Apostle! sufficient to you is Allah,- (to you) and to those who follow you among the Believers.

65. O Apostle! rouse the Believers to the fight. If there are twenty amongst you, patient and persevering, they will vanquish two hundred: if a hundred, they will vanquish a thousand of the Unbelievers: for these are a people without understanding.

66. For the present, Allah has lightened your (task), for He knows that there is a weak spot in you: but (even so), if there are a hundred of you, patient and persevering, they will vanquish two hundred, and if a thousand, they will vanquish two thousand, with the leave of Allah: for Allah is with those who patiently persevere.

67. It is not fitting for an Apostle that he should have prisoners of war until he has thoroughly subdued the land. You look for the temporal goods of this world; but Allah looks to the Hereafter: and Allah is Exalted in might, Wise.

68. Had it not been for a previous ordainment from Allah, a severe penalty would have reached you for the (ransom) that you took.

69. But (now) enjoy what you took in war, lawful and good: but fear Allah: for Allah is Oft-forgiving, Most Merciful.

70. O Apostle! say to those who are captives in your hands: "If Allah finds any good in your hearts, He will give you something better than what has been taken from you, and He will forgive you: for Allah is Oft-forgiving, Most Merciful."

64. Yaaa ayyuhan-Nabiyyu ḥasbukal-laahu wa manittaba'aka minal-mu'mineen.

(Section 8)

65. Yaaa ayyuhan-Nabiyyu ḥarriḍil-mu'mineena 'alalqitaal; iñy-yakum-minkum 'ishroona ṣaabiroona yaghliboo mi'atayn; wa iñy-yakum-minkum mi'atuñy-yaghlibooo alfam-minal-lazeena kafaroo bi-annahum qawmul-laa yafqahoon.

66. Al'aana khaffafal-laahu 'ankum wa 'alima anna feekum ḍa'faa; fa-iñy-yakum-minkum mi'atun ṣaabiratuñy-yaghliboo mi'atayn; wa iñy-yakum-minkum alfuñy-yaghlibooo alfayni bi-iznil-laah; wallaahu ma'aṣ-ṣaabireen.

67. Maa kaana li-Nabiyyin añy-yakoona lahooo asraa ḥattaa yuskhina fil-arḍ; tureedoona araḍad-dunyaa wallaahu yureedul-Aakhirah; wallaahu 'Azeezun Ḥakeem.

68. Law laa Kitaabum-minal-laahi sabaqa lamassakum feemaaa akhaztum 'azaabun 'azeem.

69. Fakuloo mimmaa ghanimtum ḥalaalan ṭayyibaa; wattaqullaah; innal-laaha Ghafoorur-Raḥeem.

(Section 9)

70. Yaaa ayyuhan-Nabiyyu qul liman feee aydeekum minal-asraaa iñy-ya'lamillaahu fee quloobikum khayrañy-yu'tikum khayram-mimmaaa ukhiza minkum wa yaghfir lakum; wallaahu Ghafoorur-Raḥeem.

يَٰٓاَيُّهَا النَّبِيُّ حَسْبُكَ اللّٰهُ وَمَنِ
اتَّبَعَكَ مِنَ الْمُؤْمِنِيْنَ ۝٦٤ ع
يَٰٓاَيُّهَا النَّبِيُّ حَرِّضِ الْمُؤْمِنِيْنَ عَلَى
الْقِتَالِ ط اِنْ يَّكُنْ مِّنْكُمْ عِشْرُوْنَ
صٰبِرُوْنَ يَغْلِبُوْا مِائَتَيْنِ ج وَاِنْ
يَّكُنْ مِّنْكُمْ مِّائَةٌ يَّغْلِبُوْٓا
اَلْفًا مِّنَ الَّذِيْنَ كَفَرُوْا بِاَنَّهُمْ
قَوْمٌ لَّا يَفْقَهُوْنَ ۝٦٥
اَلْـٰٔنَ خَفَّفَ اللّٰهُ عَنْكُمْ وَعَلِمَ اَنَّ
فِيْكُمْ ضَعْفًا ط فَاِنْ يَّكُنْ مِّنْكُمْ مِّائَةٌ
صَابِرَةٌ يَّغْلِبُوْا مِائَتَيْنِ ج وَاِنْ
يَّكُنْ مِّنْكُمْ اَلْفٌ يَّغْلِبُوْٓا اَلْفَيْنِ
بِاِذْنِ اللّٰهِ ط وَاللّٰهُ مَعَ الصّٰبِرِيْنَ ۝٦٦
مَا كَانَ لِنَبِيٍّ اَنْ يَّكُوْنَ لَهٗٓ اَسْرٰى
حَتّٰى يُثْخِنَ فِي الْاَرْضِ ط تُرِيْدُوْنَ
عَرَضَ الدُّنْيَا ۖ وَاللّٰهُ يُرِيْدُ
الْاٰخِرَةَ ط وَاللّٰهُ عَزِيْزٌ حَكِيْمٌ ۝٦٧
لَوْلَا كِتٰبٌ مِّنَ اللّٰهِ سَبَقَ لَمَسَّكُمْ
فِيْمَآ اَخَذْتُمْ عَذَابٌ عَظِيْمٌ ۝٦٨
فَكُلُوْا مِمَّا غَنِمْتُمْ حَلٰلًا طَيِّبًا ۖ وَّ
اتَّقُوا اللّٰهَ ط اِنَّ اللّٰهَ غَفُوْرٌ رَّحِيْمٌ ۝٦٩ ع
يَٰٓاَيُّهَا النَّبِيُّ قُلْ لِّمَنْ فِيْٓ اَيْدِيْكُمْ
مِّنَ الْاَسْرٰٓى لا اِنْ يَّعْلَمِ اللّٰهُ فِيْ
قُلُوْبِكُمْ خَيْرًا يُّؤْتِكُمْ خَيْرًا
مِّمَّآ اُخِذَ مِنْكُمْ وَيَغْفِرْ لَكُمْ ط
وَاللّٰهُ غَفُوْرٌ رَّحِيْمٌ ۝٧٠

Ikhfa اخفاء | Ghunna غُنّہ | Ikhfa Meem Saakin اخفاء میم ساکن | Idghaam ادغام | Qalqala قلقلہ | Qalb قلب | Idghaam Meem Saakin ادغام میم ساکن

71. But if they have treacherous designs against you,(O Apostle!), they have already been in treason against Allah, and so has He given (you) power over them. And Allah is He Who has (full) knowledge and wisdom.

72. Those who believed, and adopted exile, and fought for the Faith, with their property and their persons, in the cause of Allah, as well as those who gave (them) asylum and aid,- these are (all) friends and protectors, one of another. As to those who believed but came not into exile, you owe no duty of protection to them until they come into exile; but if they seek your aid in religion, it is your duty to help them, except against a people with whom you have a treaty of mutual alliance. And (remember) Allah sees all that you do.

73. The Unbelievers are protectors, one of another: unless you do this, (protect each other), there would be tumult and oppression on earth, and great mischief.

74. Those who believe, and adopt exile, and fight for the Faith, in the cause of Allah as well as those who give (them) asylum and aid,- these are (all) in very truth the Believers: for them is the forgiveness of sins and a provision most generous.

75. And those who accept Faith subsequently, and adopt exile, and fight for the Faith in your company,- they are of you. But kindred by blood have prior rights against each other in the Book of Allah. Verily Allah is well-acquainted with all things.

71. Wa iñy-yureedoo khiyaanataka faqad khaanullaaha min qablu fa-amkana minhum; wallaahu ʻAleemun Ḥakeem.

72. Innal-lazeena aamanoo wa haajaroo wa jaahadoo bi-amwaalihim wa anfusihim fee sabeelil-laahi wallazeena aawaw wa naṣarooo ulaaa'ika baʻḍuhum awliyaaa'u baʻḍ; wallazeena aamanoo wa lam yuhaajiroo maa lakum miñw-walaayatihim min shay'in ḥattaa yuhaajiroo; wa instanṣarookum fid-deeni faʻalaykumunnaṣru illaa ʻalaa qawmim baynakum wa baynahum meeṣaaq; wallaahu bimaa taʻmaloona Baṣeer.

73. Wallazeena kafaroo baʻḍuhum awliyaaa'u baʻḍ; illaa tafʻaloohu takun fitnatun fil-arḍi wa fasaadun kabeer.

74. Wallazeena aamanoo wa haajaroo wa jaahadoo fee sabeelil-laahi wallazeena aawaw wa naṣarooo ulaaa'ika humul-mu'minoona ḥaqqaa; lahum maghfiratuñw-wa rizqun kareem.

75. Wallazeena aamanoo mim baʻdu wa haajaroo wa jaahadoo maʻakum faulaaa'ika minkum; wa ulul-arḥaami baḍuhum awlaa bibaʻḍin fee Kitaabil-laah; innal-laaha bikulli shay'in ʻAleem. **(Section 10)**

وَإِن يُرِيدُوا خِيَانَتَكَ فَقَدْ
خَانُوا اللَّهَ مِن قَبْلُ فَأَمْكَنَ
مِنْهُمْ ۗ وَاللَّهُ عَلِيمٌ حَكِيمٌ ﴿٧١﴾
إِنَّ الَّذِينَ آمَنُوا وَهَاجَرُوا وَ
جَاهَدُوا بِأَمْوَالِهِمْ وَأَنفُسِهِمْ
فِي سَبِيلِ اللَّهِ وَالَّذِينَ آوَوا وَّ
نَصَرُوا أُولَٰئِكَ بَعْضُهُمْ أَوْلِيَاءُ
بَعْضٍ ۚ وَالَّذِينَ آمَنُوا وَلَمْ
يُهَاجِرُوا مَا لَكُم مِّن وَلَايَتِهِم
مِّن شَيْءٍ حَتَّىٰ يُهَاجِرُوا ۚ وَإِنِ
اسْتَنصَرُوكُمْ فِي الدِّينِ فَعَلَيْكُمُ
النَّصْرُ إِلَّا عَلَىٰ قَوْمٍ بَيْنَكُمْ وَبَيْنَهُم
مِّيثَاقٌ ۗ وَاللَّهُ بِمَا تَعْمَلُونَ بَصِيرٌ ﴿٧٢﴾
وَالَّذِينَ كَفَرُوا بَعْضُهُمْ أَوْلِيَاءُ
بَعْضٍ ۚ إِلَّا تَفْعَلُوهُ تَكُن فِتْنَةٌ
فِي الْأَرْضِ وَفَسَادٌ كَبِيرٌ ﴿٧٣﴾
وَالَّذِينَ آمَنُوا وَهَاجَرُوا وَ
جَاهَدُوا فِي سَبِيلِ اللَّهِ وَالَّذِينَ
آوَوا وَّنَصَرُوا أُولَٰئِكَ هُمُ
الْمُؤْمِنُونَ حَقًّا ۚ لَّهُم مَّغْفِرَةٌ
وَرِزْقٌ كَرِيمٌ ﴿٧٤﴾
وَالَّذِينَ آمَنُوا مِن بَعْدُ وَهَاجَرُوا
وَجَاهَدُوا مَعَكُمْ فَأُولَٰئِكَ مِنكُمْ ۚ
وَأُولُو الْأَرْحَامِ بَعْضُهُمْ أَوْلَىٰ
بِبَعْضٍ فِي كِتَابِ اللَّهِ ۗ إِنَّ اللَّهَ
بِكُلِّ شَيْءٍ عَلِيمٌ ﴿٧٥﴾

Ikhfa اخفاء | Ghunna غنّہ | Ikhfa Meem Saakin اخفاء میم ساکن | Idghaam ادغام | Qalqala قلقلہ | Qalb قلب | Idghaam Meem Saakin ادغام میم ساکن

9. Repentance or Immunity

1. A (declaration) of immunity from Allah and His Apostle, to those of the Pagans with whom you have contracted mutual alliances:-

2. You go, then, for four months, backwards and forwards, (as you will), throughout the land, but know that you cannot frustrate Allah (by your falsehood) but that Allah will cover with shame those who reject Him.

3. And an announcement from Allah and His Apostle, to the people (assembled) on the day of the Great Pilgrimage,- that Allah and His Apostle dissolve (treaty) obligations with the Pagans. If then, you repent, it were best for you; but if you turn away, you (should) know that you cannot frustrate Allah. And proclaim a grievous Chastisement to those who reject Faith.

4. (But the treaties are) not dissolved with those Pagans with whom you have entered into alliance and who have not subsequently failed you in any thing, nor aided any one against you. So fulfil your agreements with them to the end of their term: for Allah loves the righteous.

5. But when the forbidden months are past, then fight and slay the Pagans wherever you find them, and seize them, beleaguer them, and lie in wait for them in every strategem (of war); but if they repent, and establish regular prayers and practise regular charity, then open the way for them: for Allah is Oft-forgiving, Most Merciful.

6. If one amongst the Pagans ask you for asylum, grant it to him, so that he may hear the Word of Allah; and then escort him to where he can be secure. This is because they are

Sûrat al-Taubah/Barâ'at –9

(Revealed at Madinah)

1. Baraaa'atum-minal-laahi wa Rasooliheee ilal-la<u>z</u>eena 'aahattum-minal-mushrikeen.

2. Faseeḥoo fil-arḍi arba'ata ashhuriñw-wa'lamooo annakum ghayru mu'jizil-laahi wa annal-laaha mukhzil-kaafireen.

3. Wa a<u>z</u>aanum-minal-laahi wa Rasooliheee ilan-naasi yawmal-Hajjil-Akbari annal-laaha bareee'um-minal-mushrikeena wa Rasooluh; fa-in tubtum fahuwa khayrullakum wa in tawallaytum fa'lamooo annakum ghayru mu'jizil-laah; wa bashshiril-la<u>z</u>eena kafaroo bia<u>z</u>aabin aleem.

4. Illal-la<u>z</u>eena 'aahattum minal-mushrikeena <u>s</u>umma lam yanquṣookum shay'añw-wa lam yuẓaahiroo 'alaykum aḥadan fa-atimmooo ilayhim 'ahdahum ilaa muddatihim; innal-laaha yuḥibbul-muttaqeen.

5. Fa-i<u>z</u>ansalakhal Ash-hurul Ḥurumu faqtulul-mushrikeena ḥay<u>s</u>u wajattumoohum wa khu<u>z</u>oohum waḥṣuroohum waq'udoo lahum kulla marṣad; fa-in taaboo wa aqaamuṣ-Ṣalaata wa aatawuz-Zakaata fakhalloo sabeelahum; innal-laaha Ghafoorur-Raḥeem.

6. Wa in aḥadum-minal-mushrikeenas-tajaaraka fa-ajirhu ḥattaa yasma'a Kalaamal-laahi <u>s</u>umma ablighhu maâmanah; <u>z</u>aalika bi-annahum

(٩) سُورَةُ التَّوْبَةِ مَدَنِيَّةٌ (١١٣)

بَرَآءَةٌ مِّنَ اللّٰهِ وَرَسُولِهٖۤ اِلَى الَّذِينَ
عٰهَدْتُّمْ مِّنَ الْمُشْرِكِينَ ١
فَسِيحُوا فِي الْاَرْضِ اَرْبَعَةَ اَشْهُرٍ
وَّاعْلَمُوٓا اَنَّكُمْ غَيْرُ مُعْجِزِي اللّٰهِ
وَاَنَّ اللّٰهَ مُخْزِي الْكٰفِرِينَ ٢
وَاَذَانٌ مِّنَ اللّٰهِ وَرَسُولِهٖۤ اِلَى النَّاسِ
يَوْمَ الْحَجِّ الْاَكْبَرِ اَنَّ اللّٰهَ بَرِيٓءٌ
مِّنَ الْمُشْرِكِينَ ۙ وَرَسُولُهٗ ۚ فَاِنْ
تُبْتُمْ فَهُوَ خَيْرٌ لَّكُمْ ۚ وَاِنْ تَوَلَّيْتُمْ
فَاعْلَمُوٓا اَنَّكُمْ غَيْرُ مُعْجِزِي اللّٰهِ ۗ
وَبَشِّرِ الَّذِينَ كَفَرُوا بِعَذَابٍ اَلِيمٍ ٣
اِلَّا الَّذِينَ عٰهَدْتُّمْ مِّنَ الْمُشْرِكِينَ
ثُمَّ لَمْ يَنْقُصُوكُمْ شَيْـًٔا وَّلَمْ
يُظَاهِرُوا عَلَيْكُمْ اَحَدًا فَاَتِمُّوٓا اِلَيْهِمْ
عَهْدَهُمْ اِلٰى مُدَّتِهِمْ ۗ اِنَّ اللّٰهَ
يُحِبُّ الْمُتَّقِينَ ٤
فَاِذَا انْسَلَخَ الْاَشْهُرُ الْحُرُمُ فَاقْتُلُوا
الْمُشْرِكِينَ حَيْثُ وَجَدْتُّمُوهُمْ
وَخُذُوهُمْ وَاحْصُرُوهُمْ وَاقْعُدُوا لَهُمْ
كُلَّ مَرْصَدٍ ۚ فَاِنْ تَابُوا وَاَقَامُوا
الصَّلٰوةَ وَاٰتَوُا الزَّكٰوةَ فَخَلُّوا
سَبِيلَهُمْ ۗ اِنَّ اللّٰهَ غَفُورٌ رَّحِيمٌ ٥
وَاِنْ اَحَدٌ مِّنَ الْمُشْرِكِينَ اسْتَجَارَكَ
فَاَجِرْهُ حَتّٰى يَسْمَعَ كَلٰمَ اللّٰهِ ثُمَّ
اَبْلِغْهُ مَاْمَنَهٗ ۗ ذٰلِكَ بِاَنَّهُمْ

Ikhfa اخفاء | Ghunna غُنّہ | Ikhfa Meem Saakin اخفاء میم ساکن | Idghaam ادغام | Qalqala قلقلہ | Qalb قلب | Idghaam Meem Saakin ادغام میم ساکن

men without knowledge.

qawmul-laa ya'lamoon.

قَوْمٌ لَّا يَعْلَمُوْنَ ۝٦ ع

(Section 1)

7. How can there be a league, before Allah and His Apostle, with the Pagans, except those with whom you made a treaty near the Sacred Mosque? As long as these stand true to you, you stand true to them: for Allah loves the righteous.

7. Kayfa yakoonu lilmushrikeena 'ahdun 'indallaahi wa 'inda Rasooliheee illal-lazeena 'aahattum 'indal-Masjidil-Haraami famas-taqaamoo lakum fastaqeemoo lahum; innallaaha yuhibbul-muttaqeen.

كَيْفَ يَكُوْنُ لِلْمُشْرِكِيْنَ عَهْدٌ عِنْدَ
اللّٰهِ وَعِنْدَ رَسُوْلِهٖٓ اِلَّا الَّذِيْنَ
عٰهَدْتُّمْ عِنْدَ الْمَسْجِدِ الْحَرَامِ ۚ فَمَا
اسْتَقَامُوْا لَكُمْ فَاسْتَقِيْمُوْا لَهُمْ ؕ
اِنَّ اللّٰهَ يُحِبُّ الْمُتَّقِيْنَ ۝٧

8. How (can there be such a league), seeing that if they get an advantage over you, they do not respect in you the ties either of kinship or of covenant? With (fair words from) their mouths they please you, but their hearts are averse from you; and most of them are rebellious and wicked.

8. Kayfa wa iñy-yazharoo 'alaykum laa yarquboo feekum illañw-wa laa zimmah; yurdoonakum biafwaahihim wa taåbaa quloobuhum wa aksaruhum faasiqoon.

كَيْفَ وَاِنْ يَّظْهَرُوْا عَلَيْكُمْ
لَا يَرْقُبُوْا فِيْكُمْ اِلًّا وَّلَا ذِمَّةً ؕ
يُرْضُوْنَكُمْ بِاَفْوَاهِهِمْ وَتَاْبٰى
قُلُوْبُهُمْ ۚ وَاَكْثَرُهُمْ فٰسِقُوْنَ ۝٨ ج

9. The Signs of Allah have they sold for a miserable price, and (many) have they hindered from His Way: evil indeed are the deeds they have done.

9. Ishtaraw bi-Aayaatil-laahi samanan qaleelan fasaddoo'an sabeelih; innahum saaa'a maa kaanoo ya'maloon.

اِشْتَرَوْا بِاٰيٰتِ اللّٰهِ ثَمَنًا قَلِيْلًا
فَصَدُّوْا عَنْ سَبِيْلِهٖ ؕ اِنَّهُمْ
سَآءَ مَا كَانُوْا يَعْمَلُوْنَ ۝٩

10. In a Believer they do not respect the ties either of kinship or of covenant! It is they who have transgressed all bounds.

10. Laa yarquboona fee mu'-minin illañw-wa laa zimmah; wa ulaaa'ika humulmu'ta-doon.

لَا يَرْقُبُوْنَ فِيْ مُؤْمِنٍ اِلًّا وَّلَا ذِمَّةً ؕ
وَاُولٰٓئِكَ هُمُ الْمُعْتَدُوْنَ ۝١٠

11. But (even so), if they repent, establish regular prayers, and practise regular charity,- then they are your brethren in Faith: (thus) do We explain the Signs in detail, for those who understand.

11. Fa-in taaboo wa aqaamus-Salaata wa aatawuz-Zakaata fa-ikhwaanukum fid-deen; wa nufassilul-Aayaati liqawmiñy-ya'lamoon.

فَاِنْ تَابُوْا وَاَقَامُوا الصَّلٰوةَ وَاٰتَوُا
الزَّكٰوةَ فَاِخْوَانُكُمْ فِي الدِّيْنِ ؕ
وَنُفَصِّلُ الْاٰيٰتِ لِقَوْمٍ يَّعْلَمُوْنَ ۝١١

12. But if they violate their oaths after their covenant, and taunt you for your Faith,- you fight the chiefs of Unfaith: for their oaths are nothing to them: that thus they may be restrained.

12. Wa in nakasooo aymaana-hum mim ba'di-'ahdihim wa ta'anoo fee deenikum faqaati-looo a'immatal-kufri innahum laaa aymaana lahum la'allahum yantahoon.

وَاِنْ نَّكَثُوْٓا اَيْمَانَهُمْ مِّنْۢ بَعْدِ
عَهْدِهِمْ وَطَعَنُوْا فِيْ دِيْنِكُمْ
فَقَاتِلُوْٓا اَئِمَّةَ الْكُفْرِ ۙ اِنَّهُمْ لَآ
اَيْمَانَ لَهُمْ لَعَلَّهُمْ يَنْتَهُوْنَ ۝١٢

13. Will you not fight people who violated their oaths, plotted to expel the Apostle, and took the aggressive by being the first (to assault) you? Do you fear them? Nay, it is Allah Whom you should more justly fear, if you

13. Alaa tuqaatiloona qaw-man nakasooo aymaanahum wa hammoo bi-ikhraajir-Rasooli wa hum bada'ookum awwala marrah; atakhshawnahum; fallaahu ahaqqu an takhshawhu in kuntum

اَلَا تُقَاتِلُوْنَ قَوْمًا نَّكَثُوْٓا اَيْمَانَهُمْ
وَهَمُّوْا بِاِخْرَاجِ الرَّسُوْلِ وَهُمْ
بَدَءُوْكُمْ اَوَّلَ مَرَّةٍ ؕ اَتَخْشَوْنَهُمْ ۚ
فَاللّٰهُ اَحَقُّ اَنْ تَخْشَوْهُ اِنْ كُنْتُمْ

Ikhfa اخفاء | Ghunna غنّہ | Ikhfa Meem Saakin اخفاء میم ساکن | Idghaam ادغام | Qalqala قلقلہ | Qalb قلب | Idghaam Meem Saakin ادغام میم ساکن

believe!

14. Fight them, and Allah will punish them by your hands, cover them with shame, help you (to victory) over them, heal the breasts of Believers,

15. And still the indignation of their hearts. For Allah will turn (in mercy) to whom He will; and Allah is All-Knowing, All-Wise.

16. On do you think that you shall be abandoned, as though Allah did not know those among you who strive with might and main, and take none for friends and protectors except Allah, His Apostle, and the (community of) Believers? But Allah is well-acquainted with (all) that you do.

17. It is not for such as join gods with Allah, to visit or maintain the mosques of Allah while they witness against their own souls to infidelity. The works of such bear no fruit: In Fire shall they dwell.

18. The mosques of Allah shall be visited and maintained by such as believe in Allah and the Last Day, establish regular prayers, and practise regular charity, and fear none (at all) except Allah. It is they who are expected to be on true guidance.

19. Do you make the giving of drink to pilgrims, or the maintenance of the Sacred Mosque, equal to (the pious service of) those who believe in Allah and the Last Day, and strive with might and main in the cause of Allah? They are not comparable in the sight of Allah: and Allah does not guides those who do wrong.

mu'mineen.

14. Qaatiloohum yu'az-zib-humul-laahu bi-aydeekum wa yukhzihim wa yanṣurkum 'alayhim wa yashfi ṣudoora qawmim mu'mineen.

15. Wa yuzhib ghayẓa quloo-bihim; wa yatoobullaahu 'alaa mañy-yashaaa'; wallaahu 'Aleemun Ḥakeem.

16. Am ḥasibtum an tutrakoo wa lammaa ya'lamil-laahul-lazeena jaahadoo minkum wa lam yattakhizoo min doonil-laahi wa laa Rasoolihee wa lalmu'mineena waleejah; wallaahu-khabeerum bimaa ta'maloon. **(Section 2)**

17. Maa kaana lilmushrikeena añy-ya'muroo masaajidal-laahi shaahideena 'alaaa anfusihim bilkufr; ulaaa'ika ḥabiṭat a'maaluhum wa fin-Naari hum khaalidoon.

18. Innamaa ya'muru masaa-jidal-laahi man aamana billaahi wal-Yawmil-Aakhiri wa aqaa-maṣ-Ṣalaata wa aataz-Zakaata wa lam yakhsha illal-laaha fa'asaaa ulaaa'ika añy-yakoo-noo minal-muhtadeen.

19. Aja'altum siqaayatal-ḥaaajji wa 'imaaratal-Masjidil-Ḥaraami kaman aamana billaahi wal-Yawmil-Aakhiri wa jaahada fee sabeelil-laah; laa yastawoona 'indal-laah; wallaahu laa yahdil-qawmaẓ-ẓaalimeen.

مُّؤْمِنِينَ ﴿١٣﴾
قَاتِلُوهُمْ يُعَذِّبْهُمُ اللَّهُ بِأَيْدِيكُمْ
وَيُخْزِهِمْ وَيَنصُرْكُمْ عَلَيْهِمْ
وَيَشْفِ صُدُورَ قَوْمٍ مُّؤْمِنِينَ ﴿١٤﴾
وَيُذْهِبْ غَيْظَ قُلُوبِهِمْ ۗ وَيَتُوبُ
اللَّهُ عَلَىٰ مَن يَشَاءُ ۗ وَاللَّهُ
عَلِيمٌ حَكِيمٌ ﴿١٥﴾
أَمْ حَسِبْتُمْ أَن تُتْرَكُوا وَلَمَّا
يَعْلَمِ اللَّهُ الَّذِينَ جَاهَدُوا مِنكُمْ
وَلَمْ يَتَّخِذُوا مِن دُونِ اللَّهِ وَلَا
رَسُولِهِ وَلَا الْمُؤْمِنِينَ وَلِيجَةً ۚ
وَاللَّهُ خَبِيرٌ بِمَا تَعْمَلُونَ ﴿١٦﴾ ع ٨
مَا كَانَ لِلْمُشْرِكِينَ أَن يَعْمُرُوا
مَسَاجِدَ اللَّهِ شَاهِدِينَ عَلَىٰ أَنفُسِهِم
بِالْكُفْرِ ۚ أُولَٰئِكَ حَبِطَتْ أَعْمَالُهُمْ
وَفِي النَّارِ هُمْ خَالِدُونَ ﴿١٧﴾
إِنَّمَا يَعْمُرُ مَسَاجِدَ اللَّهِ مَنْ آمَنَ
بِاللَّهِ وَالْيَوْمِ الْآخِرِ وَأَقَامَ الصَّلَاةَ
وَآتَى الزَّكَاةَ وَلَمْ يَخْشَ إِلَّا
اللَّهَ ۖ فَعَسَىٰ أُولَٰئِكَ أَن يَكُونُوا
مِنَ الْمُهْتَدِينَ ﴿١٨﴾
أَجَعَلْتُمْ سِقَايَةَ الْحَاجِّ وَعِمَارَةَ
الْمَسْجِدِ الْحَرَامِ كَمَنْ آمَنَ بِاللَّهِ
وَالْيَوْمِ الْآخِرِ وَجَاهَدَ فِي سَبِيلِ
اللَّهِ ۚ لَا يَسْتَوُونَ عِندَ اللَّهِ ۗ وَاللَّهُ
لَا يَهْدِي الْقَوْمَ الظَّالِمِينَ ﴿١٩﴾ وقف لازم

Ikhfa	Ghunna	Ikhfa Meem Saakin	Idghaam	Qalqala	Qalb	Idghaam Meem Saakin
اخفاء	غنّہ	اخفاء میم ساکن	ادغام	قلقلہ	قلب	ادغام میم ساکن

20. Those who believe, and suffer exile and strive with might and main, in Allah's cause, with their goods and their persons, have the highest rank in the sight of Allah: they are the people who will achieve (salvation).

20. Allazeena aamanoo wa haajaroo wa jaahadoo fee sabeelil-laahi bi-amwaalihim wa anfusihim a'ẓamu darajatan 'indal-laah; wa ulaaa'ika humul-faaa'izoon.

اَلَّذِيْنَ اٰمَنُوْا وَهَاجَرُوْا وَجٰهَدُوْا
فِيْ سَبِيْلِ اللّٰهِ بِاَمْوَالِهِمْ وَاَنْفُسِهِمْ ۙ
اَعْظَمُ دَرَجَةً عِنْدَ اللّٰهِ ؕ وَاُولٰٓئِكَ
هُمُ الْفَآئِزُوْنَ ۝٢٠

21. Their Lord gives them glad tidings of a Mercy from Himself, of His good pleasure, and of gardens for them, wherein are delights that endure:

21. Yubashshiruhum Rabbuhum birahmatim-minhu wa riḍwaaniñw-wa Jannaatil-lahum feehaa na'eemum-muqeem.

يُبَشِّرُهُمْ رَبُّهُمْ بِرَحْمَةٍ مِّنْهُ
وَرِضْوَانٍ وَّجَنّٰتٍ لَّهُمْ فِيْهَا
نَعِيْمٌ مُّقِيْمٌ ۝٢١ ۙ

22. They will dwell therein for ever. Verily in Allah's presence is a reward, the greatest (of all).

22. Khaalideena feehaaa abadaa; innal-laaha 'indahooo ajrun 'aẓeem.

خٰلِدِيْنَ فِيْهَآ اَبَدًا ؕ اِنَّ اللّٰهَ
عِنْدَهٗٓ اَجْرٌ عَظِيْمٌ ۝٢٢

23. O you who believe! Do not take for protectors your fathers and your brothers if they love infidelity above Faith: if any of you do so, they do wrong.

23. Yaaa ayyuhal-lazeena aamanoo laa tattakhizooo aabaaa'akum wa ikhwaanakum awliyaaa'a inis-taḥabbul-kufra 'alal-eemaan; wa mañy-yatawal-lahum minkum fa-ulaaa'ika humuẓ-ẓaalimoon.

يٰٓاَيُّهَا الَّذِيْنَ اٰمَنُوْا لَا تَتَّخِذُوْٓا
اٰبَآءَكُمْ وَاِخْوَانَكُمْ اَوْلِيَآءَ اِنِ
اسْتَحَبُّوا الْكُفْرَ عَلَى الْاِيْمَانِ ؕ
وَمَنْ يَّتَوَلَّهُمْ مِّنْكُمْ فَاُولٰٓئِكَ
هُمُ الظّٰلِمُوْنَ ۝٢٣

24. Say: If it be that your fathers, your sons, your brothers, your mates, or your kindred; the wealth that you have gained; the commerce in which you fear a decline: or the dwellings in which you delight - are dearer to you than Allah, or His Apostle, or the striving in His cause;- then wait until Allah brings about His Decision: and Allah does not guides the rebellious.

24. Qul in kaana aabaa'ukum wa abnaaa'ukum wa ikhwaanukum wa azwaajukum wa 'asheeratukum wa amwaaluniq-taraftumoohaa wa tijaaratun takhshawna kasaadahaa wa masaakinu tarḍawnahaaa aḥabba ilaykum minal-laahi wa Rasoolihee wa Jihaadin fee Sabeelihee fatarabbaṣoo ḥattaa yaåtiyallaahu bi-amrih; wallaahu laa yahdil-qawmal-faasiqeen.

(Section 3)

قُلْ اِنْ كَانَ اٰبَآؤُكُمْ وَاَبْنَآؤُكُمْ
وَاِخْوَانُكُمْ وَاَزْوَاجُكُمْ وَعَشِيْرَتُكُمْ
وَاَمْوَالُ ۨ اقْتَرَفْتُمُوْهَا وَتِجَارَةٌ
تَخْشَوْنَ كَسَادَهَا وَمَسٰكِنُ
تَرْضَوْنَهَآ اَحَبَّ اِلَيْكُمْ مِّنَ اللّٰهِ وَ
رَسُوْلِهٖ وَجِهَادٍ فِيْ سَبِيْلِهٖ فَتَرَبَّصُوْا
حَتّٰى يَاْتِيَ اللّٰهُ بِاَمْرِهٖ ؕ وَاللّٰهُ
لَا يَهْدِي الْقَوْمَ الْفٰسِقِيْنَ ۝٢٤ ٣ ع ٨ ٩

25. Assuredly Allah did help you in many battle-fields and on the day of Hunain: Behold! your great numbers elated you, but they availed you nothing: the land, for all that it is wide,

25. Laqad naṣarakumul-laahu fee mawaaṭina kaseeratiñw-wa yawma Ḥunaynin iz a'jabatkum kasratukum falam tughni 'ankum shay'añw-wa ḍaaqat 'alaykumul-arḍu bimaa

لَقَدْ نَصَرَكُمُ اللّٰهُ فِيْ مَوَاطِنَ
كَثِيْرَةٍ ۙ وَّيَوْمَ حُنَيْنٍ ۙ اِذْ اَعْجَبَتْكُمْ
كَثْرَتُكُمْ فَلَمْ تُغْنِ عَنْكُمْ شَيْئًا
وَّضَاقَتْ عَلَيْكُمُ الْاَرْضُ بِمَا

Ikhfa اخفاء | Ghunna غنّہ | Ikhfa Meem Saakin اخفاء میم ساکن | Idghaam ادغام | Qalqala قلقلہ | Qalb قلب | Idghaam Meem Saakin ادغام میم ساکن

did constrain you, and you turned back in retreat.

26. But Allah poured His calm on the Apostle and on the Believers, and sent down forces which you did not see: He punished the Unbelievers; thus does He reward those without Faith.

27. Again will Allah, after this, turn (in mercy) to whom He will: for Allah is Oft- forgiving, Most Merciful.

28. O you who believe! Truly the Pagans are unclean; so let them not, after this year of theirs, approach the Sacred Mosque. And if you fear poverty, soon will Allah enrich you, if He wills, out of His bounty, for Allah is All-Knowing, All-Wise.

29. Fight those who did not believe in Allah nor the Last Day, nor hold that forbidden which has been forbidden by Allah and His Apostle, nor acknowledge the Religion of Truth, (even if they are) of the People of the Book, until they pay the Jizya with willing submission, and feel themselves subdued.

30. The Jews call 'Uzair a son of Allah, and the Christians call Christ the son of Allah. That is a saying from their mouth;(in this) they but imitate what the Unbelievers of old used to say. Allah's curse be on them: how they are deluded away from the Truth!

31. They take their priests and their anchorites to be their lords in derogation of Allah, and (they take as their Lord) Christ the son of

raḥubat summa wallaytum mudbireen.

26. Summa anzalal-laahu sakeenatahoo 'alaa Rasoolihee wa 'alalmu'mineena wa anzala junoodal-lam tarawhaa wa azzabal-lazeena kafaroo; wa zaalika jazaaa'ul-kaafireen.

27. Summa yatoobul-laahu mim ba'di zaalika 'alaa mañy-yashaaa'; wallaahu Ghafoorur-Raḥeem.

28. Yaaa ayyuhal-lazeena aamanooo innamal-mushrikoona najasun falaa yaqrabul-Masjidal-Ḥaraama ba'da 'aamihim haazaa; wa in khiftum 'aylatan fasawfa yughneekumul-laahu min faḍliheee in shaaa'; innallaaha 'Aleemun Ḥakeem.

29. Qaatilul-lazeena laa yu'minoona billaahi wa laa bil-Yawmil-Aakhiri wa laa yuḥarrimoona maa ḥarramal-laahu wa Rasooluhoo wa laa yadeenoona deenal-ḥaqqi minal-lazeena ootul-Kitaaba ḥattaa yu'ṭul-jizyata 'añy-yadiñw-wa hum ṣaaghiroon. **(Section 4)**

30. Wa qaalatil-Yahoodu 'Uzayrunib-nul-laahi wa qaalatin-Naṣaaral-Maseeḥub-nul-laahi zaalika qawluhum bi-afwaahihim yuḍaahi'oona qawlal-lazeena kafaroo min qabl; qatalahumul-laah; annaa yu'fakoon.

31. Ittakhazooo aḥbaarahum wa ruhbaanahum arbaabammin doonil-laahi wal-Maseeḥab-na-

رَحُبَتْ ثُمَّ وَلَّيْتُم مُّدْبِرِينَ ﴿٢٥﴾
ثُمَّ أَنزَلَ اللَّهُ سَكِينَتَهُ عَلَىٰ رَسُولِهِ
وَعَلَى الْمُؤْمِنِينَ وَأَنزَلَ جُنُودًا
لَّمْ تَرَوْهَا وَعَذَّبَ الَّذِينَ كَفَرُوا ۚ
وَذَٰلِكَ جَزَاءُ الْكَافِرِينَ ﴿٢٦﴾
ثُمَّ يَتُوبُ اللَّهُ مِن بَعْدِ ذَٰلِكَ عَلَىٰ
مَن يَشَاءُ ۗ وَاللَّهُ غَفُورٌ رَّحِيمٌ ﴿٢٧﴾
يَا أَيُّهَا الَّذِينَ آمَنُوا إِنَّمَا الْمُشْرِكُونَ
نَجَسٌ فَلَا يَقْرَبُوا الْمَسْجِدَ الْحَرَامَ
بَعْدَ عَامِهِمْ هَٰذَا ۚ وَإِنْ خِفْتُمْ
عَيْلَةً فَسَوْفَ يُغْنِيكُمُ اللَّهُ مِن
فَضْلِهِ إِن شَاءَ ۚ إِنَّ اللَّهَ
عَلِيمٌ حَكِيمٌ ﴿٢٨﴾
قَاتِلُوا الَّذِينَ لَا يُؤْمِنُونَ بِاللَّهِ
وَلَا بِالْيَوْمِ الْآخِرِ وَلَا يُحَرِّمُونَ
مَا حَرَّمَ اللَّهُ وَرَسُولُهُ وَلَا يَدِينُونَ
دِينَ الْحَقِّ مِنَ الَّذِينَ أُوتُوا الْكِتَابَ
حَتَّىٰ يُعْطُوا الْجِزْيَةَ عَن يَدٍ وَ
هُمْ صَاغِرُونَ ﴿٢٩﴾ ع
وَقَالَتِ الْيَهُودُ عُزَيْرٌ ابْنُ اللَّهِ
وَقَالَتِ النَّصَارَى الْمَسِيحُ ابْنُ اللَّهِ ۖ
ذَٰلِكَ قَوْلُهُم بِأَفْوَاهِهِمْ ۖ يُضَاهِئُونَ
قَوْلَ الَّذِينَ كَفَرُوا مِن قَبْلُ ۚ
قَاتَلَهُمُ اللَّهُ ۚ أَنَّىٰ يُؤْفَكُونَ ﴿٣٠﴾
اتَّخَذُوا أَحْبَارَهُمْ وَرُهْبَانَهُمْ
أَرْبَابًا مِّن دُونِ اللَّهِ وَالْمَسِيحَ ابْنَ

Ikhfa اخفاء | Ghunna غنّہ | Ikhfa Meem Saakin اخفاء میم ساکن | Idghaam ادغام | Qalqala قلقلہ | Qalb قلب | Idghaam Meem Saakin ادغام میم ساکن

Mary; yet they were commanded to worship but One God (Allah): there is no god but He. Praise and glory to Him: (Far is He) from having the partners they associate (with Him).

32. Fain would they extinguish Allah's light with their mouths, but Allah will not allow but that His Light should be perfected, even though the Unbelievers may detest (it).

33. It is He Who has sent His Apostle with guidance and the Religion of Truth, to proclaim it over all religion, even though the Pagans may detest (it).

34. O you who believe! there are indeed many among the priests and anchorites, who in falsehood devour the substance of men and hinder (them) from the Way of Allah. And there are those who bury gold and silver and do not spend it in the Way of Allah: announce to them a most grievous Chastisement-

35. On the Day when heat will be produced out of that (wealth) in the fire of Hell, and with it will be branded their foreheads, their flanks, and their backs- "This is the (treasure) which you buried for yourselves: you then taste, the (treasures) you buried!"

36. The number of months in the sight of Allah is twelve (in a year)- so ordained by Him the day He created the heavens and the earth; of them four are sacred: that is the straight usage. So do not wrong yourselves therein,

Maryama wa maaa umirooo illaa liya'budooo Ilaahañw-Waa-ḥidan laaa ilaaha illaa Hoo; Subḥaanahoo 'ammaa yushrikoon.

32. Yureedoona añy-yuṭfi'oo nooral-laahi bi-afwaahihim wa yaåballaahu illaaa añy- yutimma noorahoo wa law karihal-kaafiroon.

33. Huwal-laẕeee ar-sala Rasoolahoo bilhudaa wa deenil-ḥaqqi liyuẓhirahoo 'alad-deeni kullihee wa law karihal-mushrikoon.

34. Yaaa ayyuhal-laẕeena aamanooo inna kaseeramminal-aḥbaari warruhbaani la-yaå-kuloona amwaalan-naasi bil-baaṭili wa yaṣuddoona 'an sabeelil-laah; wallaẕeena yak-nizoonaẕ-ẕahaba walfiḍḍata wa laayunfiqoonahaa fee sabeelil-laahi fabashshirhum bi'aẕaabin aleem.

35. Yawma yuḥmaa 'alayhaa fee Naari Jahannama fatukwaa bihaa jibaahuhum wa junoo-buhum wa ẓuhooruhum haaẕaa maa kanaztum li-anfusikum faẕooqoo maa kuntum takni-zoon.

36. Inna 'iddatash-shuhoori 'indal-laahis-naa 'ashara shah-ran fee Kitaabil-laahi yawma khalaqas-samaawaati wal-arḍa minhaaa arba'atun ḥurum; ẕaalikad-deenul-qayyim; falaa taẓlimoo feehinna anfusakum;

مَرْيَمَ ۚ وَمَآ أُمِرُوٓا إِلَّا لِيَعْبُدُوٓا
إِلَٰهًا وَٰحِدًا ۖ لَّآ إِلَٰهَ إِلَّا هُوَ ۚ
سُبْحَٰنَهُۥ عَمَّا يُشْرِكُونَ ﴿٣١﴾
يُرِيدُونَ أَن يُطْفِـُٔوا نُورَ ٱللَّهِ
بِأَفْوَٰهِهِمْ وَيَأْبَى ٱللَّهُ إِلَّآ أَن
يُتِمَّ نُورَهُۥ وَلَوْ كَرِهَ ٱلْكَٰفِرُونَ ﴿٣٢﴾
هُوَ ٱلَّذِىٓ أَرْسَلَ رَسُولَهُۥ بِٱلْهُدَىٰ
وَدِينِ ٱلْحَقِّ لِيُظْهِرَهُۥ عَلَى ٱلدِّينِ
كُلِّهِۦ وَلَوْ كَرِهَ ٱلْمُشْرِكُونَ ﴿٣٣﴾
يَٰٓأَيُّهَا ٱلَّذِينَ ءَامَنُوٓا إِنَّ كَثِيرًا
مِّنَ ٱلْأَحْبَارِ وَٱلرُّهْبَانِ لَيَأْكُلُونَ
أَمْوَٰلَ ٱلنَّاسِ بِٱلْبَٰطِلِ وَيَصُدُّونَ
عَن سَبِيلِ ٱللَّهِ ۗ وَٱلَّذِينَ يَكْنِزُونَ
ٱلذَّهَبَ وَٱلْفِضَّةَ وَلَا يُنفِقُونَهَا
فِى سَبِيلِ ٱللَّهِ فَبَشِّرْهُم
بِعَذَابٍ أَلِيمٍ ﴿٣٤﴾
يَوْمَ يُحْمَىٰ عَلَيْهَا فِى نَارِ جَهَنَّمَ
فَتُكْوَىٰ بِهَا جِبَاهُهُمْ وَجُنُوبُهُمْ
وَظُهُورُهُمْ ۖ هَٰذَا مَا كَنَزْتُمْ
لِأَنفُسِكُمْ فَذُوقُوا مَا كُنتُمْ
تَكْنِزُونَ ﴿٣٥﴾
إِنَّ عِدَّةَ ٱلشُّهُورِ عِندَ ٱللَّهِ ٱثْنَا
عَشَرَ شَهْرًا فِى كِتَٰبِ ٱللَّهِ يَوْمَ
خَلَقَ ٱلسَّمَٰوَٰتِ وَٱلْأَرْضَ مِنْهَآ
أَرْبَعَةٌ حُرُمٌ ۚ ذَٰلِكَ ٱلدِّينُ ٱلْقَيِّمُ ۚ
فَلَا تَظْلِمُوا فِيهِنَّ أَنفُسَكُمْ

النّصف

Ikhfa اخفاء | Ghunna غُنّہ | Ikhfa Meem Saakin اخفاء میم ساکن | Idghaam ادغام | Qalqala قلقلہ | Qalb قلب | Idghaam Meem Saakin ادغام میم ساکن

and fight the Pagans all together as they fight you all together. But know that Allah is with those who restrain themselves.

37. Verily the transposing (of a prohibited month) is an addition to Unbelief: the Unbelievers are led to wrong thereby: for they make it lawful one year, and forbidden another year, in order to adjust the number of months forbidden by Allah and make such forbidden ones lawful. The evil of their course seems pleasing to them. But Allah does not guides those who reject Faith.

38. O you who believe! what is the matter with you, that, when you are asked to go forth in the Cause of Allah, you cling heavily to the earth? Do you prefer the life of this world to the Hereafter? But little is the comfort of this life, as compared with the Hereafter.

39. Unless you go forth, He will punish you with a grievous Chastisement, and put others in your place; but Him you would not harm in the least. For Allah has power over all things.

40. If you help not (your leader), (it is no matter): for Allah did indeed help him, when the Unbelievers drove him out: he had no more than one companion; they two were in the Cave, and he said to his companion, "Have no fear, for Allah is with us": then Allah sent down His peace upon him, and strengthened him with forces which you did not see, and humbled to the depths the word of the Unbelievers. But the word of Allah is exalted to the heights: for Allah is Exalted in might, Wise.

wa qaatilul-mushrikeena kaaaf-fatan kamaa yuqaati-loonakum kaaaffah; wa'lamooo annal-laaha ma'al-muttaqeen.

37. Innaman-naseee'u ziyaa-datun filkufri yuḍallu bihil-lazeena kafaroo yuḥil-loonahoo 'aamañw-wa yuḥar-rimoonahoo 'aamalliyu-waaṭi'oo 'iddata maa ḥarramal-laahu fayuḥilloo maa ḥarramal-laah; zuyyina lahum sooo'u a'maalihim; wallaahu laa yahdil-qawmal-kaafireen **(Section 5)**

38. Yaaa ayyuhal-lazeena aamanoo maa lakum izaa qeela lakumun-firoo fee sabeelil-laahis-saaqaltum ilal-arḍ; ara-ḍeetum bilḥayaatid-dunyaa minal-Aakhirah; famaa ma-taa'ul-ḥayaatiddunyaa fil-Aakhirati illaa qaleel.

39. Illaa tanfiroo yu'az-zib-kum 'azaaban aleemañw-wa yastabdil qawman ghayrakum wa laa taḍurroohu shay'aa; wal-laahu 'alaa kulli shay'in Qadeer.

40. Illaa tanṣuroohu faqad naṣarahul-laahu iz akhrajahul-lazeena kafaroo saaniyasnayni iz humaa filghaari iz yaqoolu liṣaaḥibihee laa taḥzan innal-laaha ma'anaa fa-anzalallaahu sakeenatahoo 'alayhi wa ayyadahoo bijunoodil-lam ta-rawhaa wa ja'ala kalimatal-lazeena kafarus-suflaa; wa Kalimatul-laahi hiyal-'ulyaa; wallaahu 'Azeezun Ḥakeem.

وَقَاتِلُوا الْمُشْرِكِينَ كَافَّةً كَمَا
يُقَاتِلُونَكُمْ كَافَّةً ۚ وَاعْلَمُوا أَنَّ
اللَّهَ مَعَ الْمُتَّقِينَ ﴿٣٦﴾
إِنَّمَا النَّسِيءُ زِيَادَةٌ فِي الْكُفْرِ
يُضَلُّ بِهِ الَّذِينَ كَفَرُوا يُحِلُّونَهُ
عَامًا وَيُحَرِّمُونَهُ عَامًا لِيُوَاطِئُوا
عِدَّةَ مَا حَرَّمَ اللَّهُ فَيُحِلُّوا مَا حَرَّمَ
اللَّهُ ۚ زُيِّنَ لَهُمْ سُوءُ أَعْمَالِهِمْ ۗ
وَاللَّهُ لَا يَهْدِي الْقَوْمَ الْكَافِرِينَ ﴿٣٧﴾ ع
يَا أَيُّهَا الَّذِينَ آمَنُوا مَا لَكُمْ إِذَا
قِيلَ لَكُمُ انْفِرُوا فِي سَبِيلِ اللَّهِ
اثَّاقَلْتُمْ إِلَى الْأَرْضِ ۚ أَرَضِيتُمْ
بِالْحَيَاةِ الدُّنْيَا مِنَ الْآخِرَةِ ۚ فَمَا
مَتَاعُ الْحَيَاةِ الدُّنْيَا فِي الْآخِرَةِ
إِلَّا قَلِيلٌ ﴿٣٨﴾
إِلَّا تَنْفِرُوا يُعَذِّبْكُمْ عَذَابًا أَلِيمًا
وَيَسْتَبْدِلْ قَوْمًا غَيْرَكُمْ وَلَا تَضُرُّوهُ
شَيْئًا ۗ وَاللَّهُ عَلَىٰ كُلِّ شَيْءٍ قَدِيرٌ ﴿٣٩﴾
إِلَّا تَنْصُرُوهُ فَقَدْ نَصَرَهُ اللَّهُ إِذْ
أَخْرَجَهُ الَّذِينَ كَفَرُوا ثَانِيَ اثْنَيْنِ
إِذْ هُمَا فِي الْغَارِ إِذْ يَقُولُ
لِصَاحِبِهِ لَا تَحْزَنْ إِنَّ اللَّهَ مَعَنَا ۖ
فَأَنْزَلَ اللَّهُ سَكِينَتَهُ عَلَيْهِ وَأَيَّدَهُ
بِجُنُودٍ لَمْ تَرَوْهَا وَجَعَلَ كَلِمَةَ
الَّذِينَ كَفَرُوا السُّفْلَىٰ ۗ وَكَلِمَةُ اللَّهِ
هِيَ الْعُلْيَا ۗ وَاللَّهُ عَزِيزٌ حَكِيمٌ ﴿٤٠﴾

Ikhfa اخفاء | Ghunna غنّہ | Ikhfa Meem Saakin اخفاء میم ساکن | Idghaam ادغام | Qalqala قلقلہ | Qalb قلب | Idghaam Meem Saakin ادغام میم ساکن

41. You go forth, (whether equipped) lightly or heavily, and strive and struggle, with your goods and your persons, in the Cause of Allah. That is best for you, if you (but) knew.

41. Infiroo khifaafañw-wa siqaalañw-wa jaahidoo bi-amwaalikum wa anfusikum fee sabeelil-laah; zaalikum khay-rul-lakum in kuntum ta'lamoon.

اِنْفِرُوْا خِفَافًا وَّ ثِقَالًا وَّ جَاهِدُوْا
بِاَمْوَالِكُمْ وَ اَنْفُسِكُمْ فِيْ سَبِيْلِ
اللّٰهِ ؕ ذٰلِكُمْ خَيْرٌ لَّكُمْ اِنْ
كُنْتُمْ تَعْلَمُوْنَ ﴿٤١﴾

42. If there had been immediate gain (in sight), and the journey easy, they would (all) without doubt have followed you, but the distance was long, (and weighed) on them. They would indeed swear by Allah, "If we only could, we should certainly have come out with you": they would destroy their own souls; for Allah knows that they are certainly lying.

42. Law kaana 'araḍan qareebañw-wa safaran qaasiḍal-lattaba'ooka wa laakim ba'udat 'alayhimush-shuqqah; wa sayaḥlifoona billaahi lawis-taṭa'naa lakharajnaa ma'akum; yuhlikoona anfusahum wal-laahu ya'lamu innahum lakaa-ziboon. **(Section 6)**

لَوْ كَانَ عَرَضًا قَرِيْبًا وَّ سَفَرًا
قَاصِدًا لَّاتَّبَعُوْكَ وَلٰكِنْ بَعُدَتْ
عَلَيْهِمُ الشُّقَّةُ ؕ وَ سَيَحْلِفُوْنَ
بِاللّٰهِ لَوِ اسْتَطَعْنَا لَخَرَجْنَا مَعَكُمْ ۚ
يُهْلِكُوْنَ اَنْفُسَهُمْ ۚ وَاللّٰهُ يَعْلَمُ
اِنَّهُمْ لَكٰذِبُوْنَ ﴿٤٢﴾ ع

43. Allah gave you grace! why did you grant them exemption until those who told the truth were seen by you in a clear light, and you had proved the liars?

43. 'Afal-laahu 'anka lima azinta lahum ḥattaa yatabay-yana lakal-lazeena ṣadaqoo wa ta'lamal-kaazibeen.

عَفَا اللّٰهُ عَنْكَ ۚ لِمَ اَذِنْتَ لَهُمْ
حَتّٰى يَتَبَيَّنَ لَكَ الَّذِيْنَ صَدَقُوْا
وَ تَعْلَمَ الْكٰذِبِيْنَ ﴿٤٣﴾

44. Those who believe in Allah and the Last Day ask you for no exemption from fighting with their goods and persons. And Allah knows well those who do their duty.

44. Laa yastaåzinukal-lazeena yu'minoona billaahi wal-Yawmil-Aakhiri añy-yujaa-hidoo bi-amwaalihim wa anfusihim; wallaahu 'aleemum bilmut-taqeen.

لَا يَسْتَاْذِنُكَ الَّذِيْنَ يُؤْمِنُوْنَ بِاللّٰهِ
وَالْيَوْمِ الْاٰخِرِ اَنْ يُّجَاهِدُوْا
بِاَمْوَالِهِمْ وَ اَنْفُسِهِمْ ؕ وَاللّٰهُ
عَلِيْمٌ بِالْمُتَّقِيْنَ ﴿٤٤﴾

45. Only those ask you for exemption who do not believe in Allah and the Last Day, and whose hearts are in doubt, so that they are tossed in their doubts to and fro.

45. Innamaa yastaåzinukal-lazeena laa yu'minoona billaahi wal-Yawmil-Aakhiri wartaabat quloobuhum fahum fee raybi-him yataraddadoon.

اِنَّمَا يَسْتَاْذِنُكَ الَّذِيْنَ لَا يُؤْمِنُوْنَ
بِاللّٰهِ وَالْيَوْمِ الْاٰخِرِ وَارْتَابَتْ
قُلُوْبُهُمْ فَهُمْ فِيْ رَيْبِهِمْ
يَتَرَدَّدُوْنَ ﴿٤٥﴾

46. If they had intended to come out, they would certainly have made some preparation therefor; but Allah was averse to their being sent forth; so He made them lag behind, and they were told, "You sit among those who sit (inactive)."

46. Wa law araadul-khurooja la-a'addoo lahoo 'uddatañw-wa laakin karihal-laahum-bi'aa-sahum fasabbaṭahum wa qeelaq-'udoo ma'al-qaa'ideen.

وَلَوْ اَرَادُوا الْخُرُوْجَ لَاَعَدُّوْا لَهٗ
عُدَّةً وَّلٰكِنْ كَرِهَ اللّٰهُ انْۢبِعَاثَهُمْ
فَثَبَّطَهُمْ وَقِيْلَ اقْعُدُوْا مَعَ
الْقٰعِدِيْنَ ﴿٤٦﴾

47. If they had come out with you, they would not have added to your (strength) but

47. Law kharajoo feekum maa zaadookum illaa

لَوْ خَرَجُوْا فِيْكُمْ مَّا زَادُوْكُمْ اِلَّا

Ikhfa اخفاء | Ghunna غنّہ | Ikhfa Meem Saakin اخفاء میم ساکن | Idghaam ادغام | Qalqala قلقلہ | Qalb قلب | Idghaam Meem Saakin ادغام میم ساکن

only (made for) disorder, hurrying here and there in your midst and sowing sedition among you, and there would have been some among you who would have listened to them . But Allah knows well those who do wrong.

Khabaalañw-wa la-awḍa‘oo khilaalakum yabghoona-kumul-fitnata wa feekum sam-maa‘oona lahum; wallaahu ‘aleemum biẓ-ẓaalimeen.

خَبَالًا وَّلَاۡاَوۡضَعُوۡا خِلٰلَكُمۡ
يَبۡغُوۡنَكُمُ الۡفِتۡنَةَ ۚ وَفِيۡكُمۡ
سَمّٰعُوۡنَ لَهُمۡ ؕ وَاللّٰهُ عَلِيۡمٌۢ
بِالظّٰلِمِيۡنَ ﴿۴۷﴾

48. Indeed they had plotted sedition before, and upset matters for you, until,- the Truth arrived, and the Decree of Allah became manifest, much to their disgust.

48. Laqadib-taghawul-fitnata min qablu wa qallaboo lakal-umoora ḥattaa jaaa’al-ḥaqqu wa ẓahara amrul-laahi wa hum kaarihoon.

لَقَدِ ابۡتَغَوُا الۡفِتۡنَةَ مِنۡ قَبۡلُ
وَقَلَّبُوۡا لَكَ الۡاُمُوۡرَ حَتّٰى جَآءَ الۡحَقُّ
وَظَهَرَ اَمۡرُ اللّٰهِ وَهُمۡ كٰرِهُوۡنَ ﴿۴۸﴾

49. Among them is (many) a man who says: “Grant me exemption and do not draw me into trial.” Have they not fallen into trial already? and indeed Hell surrounds the Unbelievers (on all sides).

49. Wa minhum mañy-yaqoo-lu’-ẕal-lee wa laa taftinneee; alaa fil-fitnati saqaṭoo; wa inna Jahannama lamuḥeeṭatum bil-kaafireen.

وَمِنۡهُمۡ مَّنۡ يَّقُوۡلُ ائۡذَنۡ لِّىۡ وَلَا
تَفۡتِنِّىۡ ؕ اَلَا فِى الۡفِتۡنَةِ سَقَطُوۡا ؕ
وَاِنَّ جَهَنَّمَ لَمُحِيۡطَةٌ ۢ بِالۡكٰفِرِيۡنَ ﴿۴۹﴾

50. If good befalls you, it grieves them; but if a misfortune befalls you, they say, “We took indeed our precautions beforehand,” and they turn away rejoicing.

50. In tuṣibka ḥasanatun tasu’hum; wa in tuṣibka muṣeebatuñy-yaqooloo qad akhaẕnaaa amranaa min qablu wa yatawallaw wa hum fariḥoon.

اِنۡ تُصِبۡكَ حَسَنَةٌ تَسُؤۡهُمۡ ۚ وَاِنۡ
تُصِبۡكَ مُصِيۡبَةٌ يَّقُوۡلُوۡا قَدۡ
اَخَذۡنَاۤ اَمۡرَنَا مِنۡ قَبۡلُ وَيَتَوَلَّوۡا
وَّهُمۡ فَرِحُوۡنَ ﴿۵۰﴾

51. Say: “Nothing will happen to us except what Allah has decreed for us: He is our Protector”: and on Allah let the Believers put their trust.

51. Qul lañy-yuṣeebanaaa illaa maa katabal-laahu lanaa Huwa mawlaanaa; wa ‘alal-laahi falyatawak-kalilmu’minoon.

قُلۡ لَّنۡ يُّصِيۡبَنَاۤ اِلَّا مَا كَتَبَ
اللّٰهُ لَنَا ۚ هُوَ مَوۡلٰٮنَا ۚ وَعَلَى اللّٰهِ
فَلۡيَتَوَكَّلِ الۡمُؤۡمِنُوۡنَ ﴿۵۱﴾

52. Say: “Can you expect for us (any fate) other than one of two glorious things- (Martyrdom or victory)? But we can expect for you either that Allah will send His punishment from Himself, or by our hands. So wait (expectant); we too will wait with you.”

52. Qul hal tarabbaṣoona binaaa illaaa iḥdal-ḥusnayayni wa naḥnu natarabbaṣu bikum añy-yuṣ eebakumul-laahu bi‘aẕaa-bim-min ‘indiheee aw biaydee-naa fatarabbaṣooo innaa ma‘akum mutarabbiṣoon.

قُلۡ هَلۡ تَرَبَّصُوۡنَ بِنَاۤ اِلَّاۤ اِحۡدَى
الۡحُسۡنَيَيۡنِ ؕ وَنَحۡنُ نَتَرَبَّصُ بِكُمۡ
اَنۡ يُّصِيۡبَكُمُ اللّٰهُ بِعَذَابٍ مِّنۡ
عِنۡدِهٖۤ اَوۡ بِاَيۡدِيۡنَا ۖ فَتَرَبَّصُوۡۤا
اِنَّا مَعَكُمۡ مُّتَرَبِّصُوۡنَ ﴿۵۲﴾

53. Say: “Spend (for the Cause) willingly or unwillingly: from you it will not be accepted: for you are indeed a people rebellious and wicked.”

53. Qul anfiqoo ṭaw‘an aw karhal-lañy-yutaqabbala min-kum innakum kuntum qawman faasiqeen.

قُلۡ اَنۡفِقُوۡا طَوۡعًا اَوۡ كَرۡهًا لَّنۡ
يُّتَقَبَّلَ مِنۡكُمۡ ؕ اِنَّكُمۡ كُنۡتُمۡ
قَوۡمًا فٰسِقِيۡنَ ﴿۵۳﴾

54. The only reasons why their contributions are not

54. Wa maa mana‘ahum an tuqbala minhum

وَمَا مَنَعَهُمۡ اَنۡ تُقۡبَلَ مِنۡهُمۡ

Ikhfa اخفاء | Ghunna غُنّہ | Ikhfa Meem Saakin اخفاء میم ساکن | Idghaam ادغام | Qalqala قلقلہ | Qalb قلب | Idghaam Meem Saakin ادغام میم ساکن

accepted are: that they reject Allah and His Apostle; that they come to prayer without reluctantly and that they offer contributions unwillingly.

nafaqaatuhum illaaa annahum kafaroo billaahi wa bi-Rasoolihee wa laa yaåtoonaṣ-Ṣalaata illaa wa hum kusaalaa wa laa yunfiqoona illaa wa hum kaarihoon.

نَفَقٰتُهُمْ اِلَّآ اَنَّهُمْ كَفَرُوْا بِاللّٰهِ
وَبِرَسُوْلِهٖ وَلَا يَاْتُوْنَ الصَّلٰوةَ
اِلَّا وَهُمْ كُسَالٰى وَلَا يُنْفِقُوْنَ اِلَّا
وَهُمْ كٰرِهُوْنَ ﴿۵۴﴾

55. Let not their wealth nor their (following in) sons dazzle you: in reality Allah's plan is to punish them with these things in this life, and that their souls may perish in their (very) denial of Allah.

55. Falaa tu'jibka amwaaluhum wa laaa awlaaduhum; innamaa yureedul-laahu liyu'az-zibahum bihaa fil-ḥayaatid-dunyaa wa tazhaqa anfusuhum wa hum kaafiroon.

فَلَا تُعْجِبْكَ اَمْوَالُهُمْ وَلَآ اَوْلَادُهُمْ ط
اِنَّمَا يُرِيْدُ اللّٰهُ لِيُعَذِّبَهُمْ بِهَا فِي
الْحَيٰوةِ الدُّنْيَا وَتَزْهَقَ اَنْفُسُهُمْ
وَهُمْ كٰفِرُوْنَ ﴿۵۵﴾

56. They swear by Allah that they are indeed of you; but they are not of you: yet they are afraid (to appear in their true colours).

56. Wa yaḥlifoona billaahi innahum laminkum wa maa hum minkum wa laakinnahum qawmuñy-yafraqoon.

وَيَحْلِفُوْنَ بِاللّٰهِ اِنَّهُمْ لَمِنْكُمْ ط
وَمَا هُمْ مِّنْكُمْ وَلٰكِنَّهُمْ قَوْمٌ
يَّفْرَقُوْنَ ﴿۵۶﴾

57. If they could find a place to flee to, or caves, or a place of concealment, they would turn straightaway thereto, with an obstinate rush.

57. Law yajidoona malja'an aw maghaaraatin aw mudda-khalal-lawallaw ilayhi wa hum yajmaḥoon.

لَوْ يَجِدُوْنَ مَلْجَاً اَوْ مَغٰرٰتٍ اَوْ
مُدَّخَلًا لَّوَلَّوْا اِلَيْهِ وَهُمْ يَجْمَحُوْنَ ﴿۵۷﴾

58. And among them are men who slander you in the matter of (the distribution of) the alms: if they are given part thereof, they are pleased, but if not, behold! they are indignant!

58. Wa minhum mañy-yalmizuka fiṣ-ṣadaqaati Fa-in u'ṭoo minhaa raḍoo wa illam yu'ṭaw minhaaa izaa hum yaskhaṭoon.

وَمِنْهُمْ مَّنْ يَّلْمِزُكَ فِي الصَّدَقٰتِ ج
فَاِنْ اُعْطُوْا مِنْهَا رَضُوْا وَاِنْ لَّمْ
يُعْطَوْا مِنْهَآ اِذَا هُمْ يَسْخَطُوْنَ ﴿۵۸﴾

59. If only they had been content with what Allah and His Apostle gave them, and had said, "Sufficient unto us is Allah! Allah and His Apostle will soon give us of His bounty: to Allah do we turn our hopes!" (that would have been the right course).

59. Wa law annahum raḍoo maaa aataahumul-laahu wa Rasooluhoo wa qaaloo ḥasbunal-laahu sayu'teenallaahu min faḍlihee wa Rasooluhooo innaaa ilallaahi raaghiboon.

(Section 7)

وَلَوْ اَنَّهُمْ رَضُوْا مَآ اٰتٰىهُمُ اللّٰهُ
وَرَسُوْلُهٗ لا وَقَالُوْا حَسْبُنَا اللّٰهُ
سَيُؤْتِيْنَا اللّٰهُ مِنْ فَضْلِهٖ وَرَسُوْلُهٗٓ لا
اِنَّآ اِلَى اللّٰهِ رٰغِبُوْنَ ﴿۵۹﴾ ع

60. Alms are for the poor and the needy, and those employed to administer the (funds); for those whose hearts have been (recently) reconciled (to Truth); for those in bondage and in debt; in the cause of Allah; and for the wayfarer: (thus is it) ordained by Allah, and Allah is full of knowledge and wisdom.

60. Innamaṣ-ṣadaqaatu lilfuqaraaa'i walmasaakeeni wal-'aamileena 'alayhaa walmu'al-lafati quloobuhum wa fir-riqaabi-walghaarimeena wa fee sabeelil-laahi wabnis-sabeeli fareeḍatam-minal-laah; wal-laahu 'Aleemun Ḥakeem.

اِنَّمَا الصَّدَقٰتُ لِلْفُقَرَآءِ وَ
الْمَسٰكِيْنِ وَالْعٰمِلِيْنَ عَلَيْهَا وَ
الْمُؤَلَّفَةِ قُلُوْبُهُمْ وَفِي الرِّقَابِ
وَالْغٰرِمِيْنَ وَفِيْ سَبِيْلِ اللّٰهِ
وَابْنِ السَّبِيْلِ ط فَرِيْضَةً مِّنَ
اللّٰهِ ط وَاللّٰهُ عَلِيْمٌ حَكِيْمٌ ﴿۶۰﴾

Ikhfa اخفاء | Ghunna غنّہ | Ikhfa Meem Saakin اخفاء میم ساکن | Idghaam ادغام | Qalqala قلقلہ | Qalb قلب | Idghaam Meem Saakin ادغام میم ساکن

61. Among them are men who slander the Prophet and say, "He is (all) ear." Say, "He listens to what is best for you: he believes in Allah, has faith in the Believers, and is a Mercy to those of you who believe." But those who slander the Apostle will have a grievous Chastisement.

61. Wa minhumul-lazeena yu'zoonan-Nabiyya wa yaqooloona huwa -uzun; qul uzunu khayril-lakum yu'minu billaahi wa yu'minu lilmu'mi-neena wa raḥmatul-lillazeena aamanoo minkum; wallazeena yu'zoona Rasoolal-laahi lahum 'azaabun aleem.

وَمِنْهُمُ الَّذِينَ يُؤْذُونَ النَّبِيَّ وَيَقُولُونَ هُوَ أُذُنٌ ۚ قُلْ أُذُنُ خَيْرٍ لَّكُمْ يُؤْمِنُ بِاللَّهِ وَيُؤْمِنُ لِلْمُؤْمِنِينَ وَرَحْمَةٌ لِّلَّذِينَ آمَنُوا مِنكُمْ ۚ وَالَّذِينَ يُؤْذُونَ رَسُولَ اللَّهِ لَهُمْ عَذَابٌ أَلِيمٌ ﴿٦١﴾

62. To you they swear by Allah, In order to please you: But it is more fitting that they should please Allah and His Apostle, if they are Believers.

62. Yaḥlifoona billaahi lakum liyurḍookum wallaahu wa Rasooluhooo aḥaqqu añy-yurḍoohu in kaanoo mu'mineen.

يَحْلِفُونَ بِاللَّهِ لَكُمْ لِيُرْضُوكُمْ وَاللَّهُ وَرَسُولُهُ أَحَقُّ أَن يُرْضُوهُ إِن كَانُوا مُؤْمِنِينَ ﴿٦٢﴾

الثلثة

63. Do they not know that for those who oppose Allah and His Apostle, is the Fire of Hell?- wherein they shall dwell. That is the supreme disgrace.

63. Alam ya'lamooo annahoo mañy-yuḥaadidillaaha wa Rasoolahoo faanna lahoo Naara Jahannama khaalidan feehaa; zaalikal-khizyul-'aẓeem.

أَلَمْ يَعْلَمُوا أَنَّهُ مَن يُحَادِدِ اللَّهَ وَرَسُولَهُ فَأَنَّ لَهُ نَارَ جَهَنَّمَ خَالِدًا فِيهَا ۚ ذَٰلِكَ الْخِزْيُ الْعَظِيمُ ﴿٦٣﴾

64. The Hypocrites are afraid lest a Sura should be sent down about them, showing them what is (really passing) in their hearts. Say: "Mock you! But verily Allah will bring to light all that you fear (should be revealed).

64. Yaḥzarul-munaafiqoona an tunaz-zala 'alayhim Sooratun tunabbi'uhum bimaa fee quloobihim; qulistahzi'oo innal-laaha mukhrijum-maa taḥzaroon.

يَحْذَرُ الْمُنَافِقُونَ أَن تُنَزَّلَ عَلَيْهِمْ سُورَةٌ تُنَبِّئُهُم بِمَا فِي قُلُوبِهِمْ ۚ قُلِ اسْتَهْزِئُوا إِنَّ اللَّهَ مُخْرِجٌ مَّا تَحْذَرُونَ ﴿٦٤﴾

65. If you question them, they declare (with emphasis): "We were only talking idly and in play." Say: "Was it at Allah, and His Signs, and His Apostle, that you were mocking?"

65. Wala'in sa-altahum-layaqoolunna innamaa kunnaa nakhooḍu wa nal'ab; qul abillaahi wa 'Aayaatihee wa Rasoolihee kuntum tastahzi'oon.

وَلَئِن سَأَلْتَهُمْ لَيَقُولُنَّ إِنَّمَا كُنَّا نَخُوضُ وَنَلْعَبُ ۚ قُلْ أَبِاللَّهِ وَآيَاتِهِ وَرَسُولِهِ كُنتُمْ تَسْتَهْزِئُونَ ﴿٦٥﴾

66. You do not make any excuses: you have rejected Faith after you had accepted it. If We pardon some of you, We will punish others amongst you, for that they are in sin.

66. Laa ta'taziroo qad kafartum ba'da eemaanikum; in na'fu 'an ṭaaa'ifatim-minkum nu'az-zib ṭaaa'ifatam bi-annahum kaanoo mujrimeen.

(Section 8)

لَا تَعْتَذِرُوا قَدْ كَفَرْتُم بَعْدَ إِيمَانِكُمْ ۚ إِن نَّعْفُ عَن طَائِفَةٍ مِّنكُمْ نُعَذِّبْ طَائِفَةً بِأَنَّهُمْ كَانُوا مُجْرِمِينَ ﴿٦٦﴾

ع ٧

67. The Hypocrites, men and women, (have an understanding) with each other: They enjoin evil, and forbid what is just, and are close

67. Almunaafiqoona walmunaafiqaatu ba'ḍuhum mim ba'ḍ; yaåmuroona bilmunkari wa yanhawna 'anil-ma'roofi wa yaqbiḍoona

الْمُنَافِقُونَ وَالْمُنَافِقَاتُ بَعْضُهُم مِّن بَعْضٍ ۚ يَأْمُرُونَ بِالْمُنكَرِ وَيَنْهَوْنَ عَنِ الْمَعْرُوفِ وَيَقْبِضُونَ

وقف لازم

Ikhfa اخفاء | Ghunna غنّہ | Ikhfa Meem Saakin اخفاء میم ساکن | Idghaam ادغام | Qalqala قلقلہ | Qalb قلب | Idghaam Meem Saakin ادغام میم ساکن

with their hands. They have forgotten Allah; so He has forgotten them. Verily the Hypocrites are rebellious and perverse.

68. Allah has promised the Hypocrites men and women, and the rejecters, of Faith, the fire of Hell: therein shall they dwell: Sufficient is it for them: for them is the curse of Allah, and an enduring punishment,-

69. As in the case of those before you: they were mightier than you in power, and more flourishing in wealth and children. They had their enjoyment of their portion: and you have of yours, as did those before you; and you indulge in idle talk as they did. They!- their works are fruitless in this world and in the Hereafter, and they will lose (all spiritual good).

70. Has not the story reached them of those before them?- the People of Noah, and 'Ad, and Thamud; the People of Abraham, the men of Midian, and the cities overthrown. To them came their Apostles with Clear Signs. It is not Allah Who wrongs them, but they wrong their own souls.

71. The Believers, men and women, are protectors, one of another: they enjoin what is just, and forbid what is evil: they observe regular prayers, practise regular charity, and obey Allah and His Apostle. On them will Allah pour His mercy: for Allah is Exalted in power,

aydiyahum; nasul-laaha fanasiyahum; innal- munaafiqeena humul-faasi-qoon.

68. Wa'adal-laahul-munaafiqeena wal-munaafiqaati walkuffaara Naara Jahannama khaalideena feehaa; hiya ḥasbuhum; wa la'anahumul-laahu wa lahum 'azaabum-muqeem.

69. Kallazeena min qablikum kaanooo ashadda minkum quwwatañw-wa aksara amwaalañw-wa awlaadan fastamta'oo bikhalaaqihim fastamta'tum bikhalaaqikum kamas-tamta'allazeena min qablikum bikhalaaqihim wa khuḍtum kallazee khaaḍooo; ulaaa'ika ḥabiṭat a'maaluhum fid-dunyaa wal-Aakhirati wa ulaaa'ika humul-khaasiroon.

70. Alam yaåtihim naba-ul-lazeena min qablihim qawmi Nooḥiñw-wa 'Aadiñw-wa Samooda wa qawmi Ibraaheema wa asḥaabi Madyana walmu'tafikaat; atathum Rusuluhum bilbayyinaati famaa kaanal-laahu liyaẓlimahum wa laakin kaanooo anfusahum yaẓlimoon.

71. Walmu'minoona walmu'minaatu ba'ḍuhum awliyaaa'u ba'ḍ; yaåmuroona bilma'roofi wa yanhawna 'anil-munkari wa yuqeemoonaṣ-Ṣalaata wa yu'toonaz-Zakaata wa yuṭee'oonal-laaha wa Rasoolah; ulaaa'ika sayarḥamuhumul-laah; innallaaha 'Azeezun

أيديهم نسوا الله فنسيهم إن
المنفقين هم الفسقون ﴿٦٧﴾
وعد الله المنفقين والمنفقت
والكفار نار جهنم خلدين
فيها هي حسبهم ولعنهم
الله ولهم عذاب مقيم ﴿٦٨﴾
كالذين من قبلكم كانوا
أشد منكم قوة وأكثر أموالا
وأولادا فاستمتعوا بخلاقهم
فاستمتعتم بخلاقكم كما استمتع
الذين من قبلكم بخلاقهم
وخضتم كالذي خاضوا أولئك
حبطت أعملهم في الدنيا
والآخرة وأولئك هم الخسرون ﴿٦٩﴾
ألم يأتهم نبأ الذين من قبلهم
قوم نوح وعاد وثمود و
قوم إبرهيم وأصحب مدين
والمؤتفكت أتتهم رسلهم
بالبينت فما كان الله ليظلمهم
ولكن كانوا أنفسهم يظلمون ﴿٧٠﴾
والمؤمنون والمؤمنت بعضهم
أولياء بعض يأمرون بالمعروف
وينهون عن المنكر ويقيمون
الصلوة ويؤتون الزكوة و
يطيعون الله ورسوله أولئك
سيرحمهم الله إن الله عزيز

وقف لازم

Ikhfa اخفاء | Ghunna غنة | Ikhfa Meem Saakin اخفاء ميم ساكن | Idghaam ادغام | Qalqala قلقله | Qalb قلب | Idghaam Meem Saakin ادغام ميم ساكن

Wise.

72. Allah has promised to Believers, men and women, Gardens under which rivers flow, to dwell therein, and beautiful mansions in Gardens of everlasting bliss. But the greatest bliss is the Good pleasure of Allah: that is the supreme felicity.

73. O Prophet! strive hard against the unbelievers and the Hypocrites, and be firm against them, their abode is Hell,- an evil refuge indeed.

74. They swear by Allah that they said nothing (evil), but indeed they uttered blasphemy, and they did it after accepting Islam; and they meditated a plot which they were unable to carry out: this revenge of theirs was (their) only return for the bounty with which Allah and His Apostle had enriched them! If they repent, it will be best for them; but if they turn back (to their evil ways), Allah will punish them with a grievous Chastisement in this life and in the Hereafter: they shall have none on earth to protect or help them.

75. Amongst them are men who made a Covenant with Allah, that if He bestowed on them of His bounty, they would give (largely) in charity, and be truly amongst those who are righteous.

76. But when He did bestow of His bounty, they became covetous, and turned back (from their Covenant), averse (from its fulfilment).

77. So He has put as a consequence Hypocrisy into their hearts, (to last) till the Day, whereon they shall meet Him: because they broke their

Ḥakeem.

72. Wa‘adal-laahulmu’mineena walmu’minaati Jannaatin tajree min taḥtihal anhaaru khaali-deena feehaa wa masaakina ṭayyibatan fee Jannaati ‘Adn; wa riḍwaanum-minal-laahi akbar; zaalika huwal-fawzul-‘aẓeem. **(Section 9)**

73. Yaaa-ayyuhan-Nabiyyu jaahidil-kuffaara walmunaafi-qeena waghluẓ ‘alayhim; wa maåwaahum Jahannamu wa bi’sal-maṣeer.

74. Yaḥlifoona billaahi maa qaaloo wa laqad qaaloo kalimatal-kufri wa kafaroo ba‘da Islaamihim wa hammoo bimaa lam yanaaloo; wa maa naqamooo illaaa an aghnaa-humullaahu wa Rasooluhoo min faḍlih; faiñy yatooboo yaku khayral-lahum wa iñy-yatawal-law yu‘az-zibhumullaahu ‘azaaban aleeman fiddunyaa wal-Aakhirah; wamaa lahum fil-arḍi miñw-waliyyiñw-wa laa naṣeer.

75. Wa minhum man ‘aaha-dal-laaha la’in aataanaa min faḍlihee lanaṣ-ṣaddaqanna wa lanakoonanna minaṣṣaaliḥeen.

76. Falammaaa aataahum min faḍlihee bakhiloo bihee wa tawallaw wa hum mu‘riḍoon.

77. Fa-a‘qabahum nifaaqan fee quloobihim ilaa Yawmi yalqaw-nahoo bimaaa akhlaful-laaha maa

حَكِيمٌ ٧١
وَعَدَ اللّٰهُ الْمُؤْمِنِينَ وَالْمُؤْمِنٰتِ
جَنّٰتٍ تَجْرِي مِنْ تَحْتِهَا الْأَنْهٰرُ
خٰلِدِينَ فِيهَا وَمَسٰكِنَ طَيِّبَةً
فِي جَنّٰتِ عَدْنٍ ۚ وَرِضْوٰنٌ مِّنَ
اللّٰهِ أَكْبَرُ ۚ ذٰلِكَ هُوَ الْفَوْزُ الْعَظِيمُ ٧٢ ع ١٥
يٰٓأَيُّهَا النَّبِيُّ جٰهِدِ الْكُفَّارَ
وَالْمُنٰفِقِينَ وَاغْلُظْ عَلَيْهِمْ ۚ وَ
مَأْوٰىهُمْ جَهَنَّمُ ۖ وَبِئْسَ الْمَصِيرُ ٧٣
يَحْلِفُونَ بِاللّٰهِ مَا قَالُوا ۖ وَ
لَقَدْ قَالُوا كَلِمَةَ الْكُفْرِ وَ
كَفَرُوا بَعْدَ إِسْلٰمِهِمْ وَهَمُّوا
بِمَا لَمْ يَنَالُوا ۚ وَمَا نَقَمُوٓا إِلَّآ
أَنْ أَغْنٰىهُمُ اللّٰهُ وَرَسُولُهُ مِنْ
فَضْلِهِ ۚ فَإِنْ يَتُوبُوا يَكُ خَيْرًا
لَّهُمْ ۖ وَإِنْ يَتَوَلَّوْا يُعَذِّبْهُمُ
اللّٰهُ عَذَابًا أَلِيمًا فِي الدُّنْيَا وَ
الْاٰخِرَةِ ۚ وَمَا لَهُمْ فِي الْأَرْضِ
مِنْ وَّلِيٍّ وَّلَا نَصِيرٍ ٧٤
وَمِنْهُمْ مَّنْ عٰهَدَ اللّٰهَ لَئِنْ
اٰتٰىنَا مِنْ فَضْلِهِ لَنَصَّدَّقَنَّ
وَلَنَكُونَنَّ مِنَ الصّٰلِحِينَ ٧٥
فَلَمَّآ اٰتٰىهُمْ مِّنْ فَضْلِهِ بَخِلُوا
بِهِ وَتَوَلَّوْا وَّهُمْ مُّعْرِضُونَ ٧٦
فَأَعْقَبَهُمْ نِفَاقًا فِي قُلُوبِهِمْ إِلٰى
يَوْمِ يَلْقَوْنَهُ بِمَآ أَخْلَفُوا اللّٰهَ مَا

Ikhfa اخفاء | Ghunna غنّہ | Ikhfa Meem Saakin اخفاء میم ساکن | Idghaam ادغام | Qalqala قلقلہ | Qalb قلب | Idghaam Meem Saakin ادغام میم ساکن

Covenant with Allah, and because they lied (again and again).

78. Do they not know that Allah knows their secret (thoughts) and their secret counsels, and that Allah knows well all things unseen?

79. Those who slander such of the Believers as give themselves freely to (deeds of) charity, as well as such as can find nothing to give except the fruits of their labour,- and throw ridicule on them,- Allah will throw back their ridicule on them: and they shall have a grievous Chastisement.

80. Whether you ask for their forgiveness, or not, (their sin is unforgivable): if you ask seventy times for their forgiveness, Allah will not forgive them: because they have rejected Allah and His Apostle: and Allah does not guides those who are perversely rebellious.

81. Those who were left behind (in the Tabuk expedition) rejoiced in their inaction behind the back of the Apostle of Allah: they hated to strive and fight, with their goods and their persons, in the Cause of Allah: they said, "Do not go forth in the heat." Say, "The fire of Hell is fiercer in heat." If only they could understand!

82. Let them laugh a little: much will they weep: a recompense for the (evil) that they do.

83. If, then, Allah brings you back to any of them, and they ask your permission to come out (with you), say: "Never shall you come out with me, nor fight an enemy with me: for you preferred to sit inactive on the first occasion: then you sit (now) with those who lag behind."

84. Nor do you ever pray for any of them that dies,

wa'adoohu wa bimaa kaanoo yakziboon.

78. Alam ya'lamooo annal-laaha ya'lamu sirrahum wa najwaahum wa annal-laaha 'Allaamul-Ghuyoob.

79. Allazeena yalmizoonal-muṭ-ṭawwi'eena minalmu'mineena fiṣ-ṣadaqaati wallazeena laa yajidoona illaa juhdahum fayaskharoona minhum sakhiral-laahu minhum wa lahum azaabun aleem.

80. Istaghfir lahum aw laa tastaghfir lahum in tastaghfir lahum sab'eena marratan falañy-yaghfiral-laahu lahum; zaalika bi-annahum kafaroo billaahi wa Rasoolih; wallaahu laa yahdil-qawmal-faasiqeen.

(Section 10)

81. Fariḥal-mukhallafoona bimaq'adihim khilaafa Rasoolil-laahi wa karihooo añy-yujaahidoo bi-amwaalihim wa anfusihim fee sabeelil-laahi wa qaaloo laa tanfiroo fil-harr; qul Naaru Jahannama ashaddu harraa; law kaanoo yafqahoon.

82. Falyaḍḥakoo qaleelañw-walyabkoo kaseeran jazaaa'am bimaa kaanoo yaksiboon.

83. Fa-ir-raja'akal-laahu ilaa ṭaaa'ifatim-minhum fastaåzanooka lilkhurooji faqul-lan takhrujoo ma'iya abadañw-wa lan tuqaatiloo ma'iya 'aduwwan innakum raḍeetum-bilqu'oodi awwala marratin faq'udoo ma'al-khaalifeen.

84. Wa laa tuṣalli 'alaaa aḥadim-minhum maata

وَعَدُوهُ وَبِمَا كَانُوا يَكْذِبُونَ ﴿٧٧﴾
أَلَمْ يَعْلَمُوا أَنَّ اللَّهَ يَعْلَمُ سِرَّهُمْ وَ
نَجْوَاهُمْ وَأَنَّ اللَّهَ عَلَّامُ الْغُيُوبِ ﴿٧٨﴾
الَّذِينَ يَلْمِزُونَ الْمُطَّوِّعِينَ مِنَ
الْمُؤْمِنِينَ فِي الصَّدَقَاتِ وَالَّذِينَ لَا
يَجِدُونَ إِلَّا جُهْدَهُمْ فَيَسْخَرُونَ
مِنْهُمْ ۙ سَخِرَ اللَّهُ مِنْهُمْ ۡ وَلَهُمْ
عَذَابٌ أَلِيمٌ ﴿٧٩﴾
اسْتَغْفِرْ لَهُمْ أَوْ لَا تَسْتَغْفِرْ لَهُمْ
إِنْ تَسْتَغْفِرْ لَهُمْ سَبْعِينَ مَرَّةً
فَلَنْ يَغْفِرَ اللَّهُ لَهُمْ ۚ ذَٰلِكَ بِأَنَّهُمْ
كَفَرُوا بِاللَّهِ وَرَسُولِهِ ۗ وَاللَّهُ لَا
يَهْدِي الْقَوْمَ الْفَاسِقِينَ ﴿٨٠﴾
فَرِحَ الْمُخَلَّفُونَ بِمَقْعَدِهِمْ خِلَافَ
رَسُولِ اللَّهِ وَكَرِهُوا أَنْ يُجَاهِدُوا
بِأَمْوَالِهِمْ وَأَنْفُسِهِمْ فِي سَبِيلِ اللَّهِ
وَقَالُوا لَا تَنْفِرُوا فِي الْحَرِّ ۗ قُلْ نَارُ
جَهَنَّمَ أَشَدُّ حَرًّا ۚ لَوْ كَانُوا يَفْقَهُونَ ﴿٨١﴾
فَلْيَضْحَكُوا قَلِيلًا وَلْيَبْكُوا كَثِيرًا
جَزَاءً بِمَا كَانُوا يَكْسِبُونَ ﴿٨٢﴾
فَإِنْ رَجَعَكَ اللَّهُ إِلَىٰ طَائِفَةٍ مِنْهُمْ
فَاسْتَأْذَنُوكَ لِلْخُرُوجِ فَقُلْ لَنْ
تَخْرُجُوا مَعِيَ أَبَدًا وَلَنْ تُقَاتِلُوا مَعِيَ
عَدُوًّا ۖ إِنَّكُمْ رَضِيتُمْ بِالْقُعُودِ أَوَّلَ
مَرَّةٍ فَاقْعُدُوا مَعَ الْخَالِفِينَ ﴿٨٣﴾
وَلَا تُصَلِّ عَلَىٰ أَحَدٍ مِنْهُمْ مَاتَ

Ikhfa اخفاء | Ghunna غُنّہ | Ikhfa Meem Saakin اخفاء میم ساکن | Idghaam ادغام | Qalqala قلقلہ | Qalb قلب | Idghaam Meem Saakin ادغام میم ساکن

nor stand at his grave; for they rejected Allah and His Apostle, and died in a state of perverse rebellion.

abadañw-wa laa taqum 'alaa qabriheee innahum kafaroo billaahi wa Rasoolihee wa maatoo wa hum faasiqoon.

ابدا ولا تقم على قبره ط انهم
كفروا بالله ورسوله وماتوا
وهم فسقون ﴿٨٤﴾

85. Nor let their wealth nor their children dazzle you: Allah's plan is to punish them with these things in this world, and that their souls may perish in their (very) denial of Allah.

85. Wa laa tu'jibka amwaaluhum wa awlaaduhum; innamaa yureedul-laahu añy-yu'a<u>z</u>-<u>z</u>ibahum bihaa fid-dunyaa wa tazhaqa anfusuhum wa hum kaafiroon.

ولا تعجبك اموالهم واولادهم ط انما
يريد الله ان يعذبهم بها في الدنيا
وتزهق انفسهم وهم كفرون ﴿٨٥﴾

86. When a Sura comes down, enjoining them to believe in Allah and to strive and fight along with His Apostle, those with wealth and influence among them ask you for exemption, and say: "Leave us (behind): we would be with those who sit (at home)."

86. Wa i<u>z</u>aaa unzilat Sooratun an aaminoo billaahi wa jaahidoo ma'a Rasoolihis-taå<u>z</u>anaka uluṭṭawli minhum wa qaaloo <u>z</u>arnaa nakum-ma'alqaa'ideen.

واذا انزلت سورة ان امنوا بالله
وجاهدوا مع رسوله استاذنك
اولوا الطول منهم وقالوا ذرنا
نكن مع القعدين ﴿٨٦﴾

87. They prefer to be with (the women), who remain behind (at home): their hearts are sealed and so they do not understand.

87. Raḍoo bi-añy-yakoonoo ma'al-khawaalifi wa ṭubi'a 'alaa quloobihim fahum laa yafqahoon.

رضوا بان يكونوا مع الخوالف وطبع
على قلوبهم فهم لا يفقهون ﴿٨٧﴾

88. But the Apostle, and those who believe with him, strive and fight with their wealth and their persons: for them are (all) good things: and it is they who will prosper.

88. Laakinir-Rasoolu wal-la<u>z</u>eena aamanoo ma'ahoo jaahadoo bi-amwaalihim wa anfusihim; wa ulaaa'ika lahumul-khayraatu wa ulaaa'i-ka humul-mufliḥoon.

لكن الرسول والذين امنوا معه
جهدوا باموالهم وانفسهم ط و
اولئك لهم الخيرت ز واولئك
هم المفلحون ﴿٨٨﴾

89. Allah has prepared for them Gardens under which rivers flow, to dwell therein: that is the supreme felicity.

89. A'addal-laahu lahum Jannaatin tajree min taḥtihal-anhaaru khaalideena feehaa; <u>z</u>aalikal-fawzul 'aẓeem.

(Section 11)

اعد الله لهم جنت تجري من
تحتها الانهر خلدين فيها ط
ذلك الفوز العظيم ع ﴿٨٩﴾ ع ١١ ٩ ١٧

90. And there were, among the desert Arabs (also), men who made excuses and came to claim exemption; and those who were false to Allah and His Apostle (merely) sat inactive. Soon will a grievous Chastisement seize the Unbelievers among them.

90. Wa jaaa'al-mu'a<u>z</u>-<u>z</u>iroona minal-A'raabi liyu'<u>z</u>ana lahum wa qa'adal-la<u>z</u>eena ka<u>z</u>abul-laaha wa Rasoolah; sayuṣeebul-la<u>z</u>eena kafaroo minhum 'a<u>z</u>aabun aleem.

وجاء المعذرون من الاعراب
ليؤذن لهم وقعد الذين كذبوا
الله ورسوله ط سيصيب الذين
كفروا منهم عذاب اليم ﴿٩٠﴾

91. There is no blame on those who are infirm, or ill, or who find no resources to spend (on the Cause), if they are sincere (in duty) to Allah and

91. Laysa 'alaḍ-ḍu'afaaa'i wa laa 'alal-marḍaa wa laa 'alal-la<u>z</u>eena laa yajidoona maa yunfiqoona ḥarajun i<u>z</u>aa naṣaḥoo lillaahi wa

ليس على الضعفاء ولا على المرضى
ولا على الذين لا يجدون ما
ينفقون حرج اذا نصحوا لله و

Ikhfa اخفاء | Ghunna غنّہ | Ikhfa Meem Saakin اخفاء میم ساکن | Idghaam ادغام | Qalqala قلقلہ | Qalb قلب | Idghaam Meem Saakin ادغام میم ساکن

His Apostle: no ground (of complaint) can there be against such as do right: and Allah is Oft-forgiving, Most Merciful.

Rasoolih; maa 'alal-muḥsineena min sabeel; wallaahu Ghafoorur-Raḥeem.

رَسُوْلِهٖ ؕ مَا عَلَى الْمُحْسِنِيْنَ مِنْ
سَبِيْلٍ ؕ وَاللّٰهُ غَفُوْرٌ رَّحِيْمٌ ۙ ﴿٩١﴾

92. Nor (is there blame) on those who came to you to be provided with mounts, and when you said, "I can not find any mounts for you," they turned back, their eyes streaming with tears of grief that they had no resources wherewith to provide the expenses.

92. Wa laa 'alal-lazeena izaa maaa atawka litaḥmilahum qulta laaa ajidu maaa aḥmilukum 'alayhi tawallaw wa a'yunuhum tafeeḍu minad-dam'i ḥazanan allaa yajidoo maa yunfiqoon.

وَّلَا عَلَى الَّذِيْنَ اِذَا مَاۤ اَتَوْكَ
لِتَحْمِلَهُمْ قُلْتَ لَاۤ اَجِدُ مَاۤ
اَحْمِلُكُمْ عَلَيْهِ ۪ تَوَلَّوْا وَّاَعْيُنُهُمْ
تَفِيْضُ مِنَ الدَّمْعِ حَزَنًا اَلَّا
يَجِدُوْا مَا يُنْفِقُوْنَ ؕ ﴿٩٢﴾

93. The ground (of complaint) is against such as claim exemption while they are rich. They prefer to stay with the (women) who remain behind: Allah has sealed their hearts; so they do not know (what they miss).

93. Innamas-sabeelu 'alal-lazeena yastaåzinoonaka wa hum aghniyaaa'; raḍoo biañy-yakoonoo ma'al-khawaalifi wa ṭaba'al-laahu 'alaa quloobihim fahum laa ya'lamoon.

اِنَّمَا السَّبِيْلُ عَلَى الَّذِيْنَ
يَسْتَاْذِنُوْنَكَ وَهُمْ اَغْنِيَآءُ ۚ
رَضُوْا بِاَنْ يَّكُوْنُوْا مَعَ الْخَوَالِفِ ۙ
وَطَبَعَ اللّٰهُ عَلٰى قُلُوْبِهِمْ فَهُمْ لَا
يَعْلَمُوْنَ ﴿٩٣﴾

94. They will present their excuses to you when you return to them. You say: "Present no excuses: we shall not believe you: Allah has already informed us of the true state of matters concerning you: It is your actions that Allah and His Apostle will observe: in the end you will be brought back to Him Who knows what is hidden and what is open: then He will show you the truth of all that you did."

94. Ya'taziroona ilaykum izaa raja'tum ilayhim; qul-laa ta'taziroo lan-nu'mina lakum qad nabba-anal-laahu min akhbaarikum; wa sa-yaral-laahu 'amalakum wa Rasooluhoo summa turaddoona ilaa 'Aalimil-Ghaybi washshahaadati fa-yunabbi'ukum bimaa kuntum ta'maloon.

يَعْتَذِرُوْنَ اِلَيْكُمْ اِذَا رَجَعْتُمْ
اِلَيْهِمْ ؕ قُلْ لَّا تَعْتَذِرُوْا لَنْ نُّؤْمِنَ
لَكُمْ قَدْ نَبَّاَنَا اللّٰهُ مِنْ اَخْبَارِكُمْ ؕ
وَسَيَرَى اللّٰهُ عَمَلَكُمْ وَرَسُوْلُهٗ ثُمَّ
تُرَدُّوْنَ اِلٰى عٰلِمِ الْغَيْبِ وَالشَّهَادَةِ
فَيُنَبِّئُكُمْ بِمَا كُنْتُمْ تَعْمَلُوْنَ ﴿٩٤﴾

95. They will swear to you by Allah, when you return to them, that you may leave them alone. So leave them alone: For they are an abomination, and Hell is their dwelling-place,-a fitting recompense for the (evil) that they did.

95. Sa-yaḥlifoona billaahi lakum izanqalabtum ilayhim litu'riḍoo 'anhum fa-a'riḍoo 'anhum innahum rijsuñw-wa maåwaahum Jahannamu jazaaa-'am bimaa kaanoo yaksiboon.

سَيَحْلِفُوْنَ بِاللّٰهِ لَكُمْ اِذَا انْقَلَبْتُمْ
اِلَيْهِمْ لِتُعْرِضُوْا عَنْهُمْ ؕ فَاَعْرِضُوْا
عَنْهُمْ ؕ اِنَّهُمْ رِجْسٌ ۫ وَّمَاْوٰىهُمْ
جَهَنَّمُ ۚ جَزَآءًۢ بِمَا كَانُوْا يَكْسِبُوْنَ ﴿٩٥﴾

96. They will swear unto you, that you may be pleased with them but if you are pleased with them, Allah is not pleased with those who disobey.

96. Yaḥlifoona lakum litar-ḍaw 'anhum fa-in tarḍaw 'anhum fa-innal-laaha laa yar-ḍaa 'anil-qawmil-faasiqeen.

يَحْلِفُوْنَ لَكُمْ لِتَرْضَوْا عَنْهُمْ ۚ فَاِنْ
تَرْضَوْا عَنْهُمْ فَاِنَّ اللّٰهَ لَا يَرْضٰى
عَنِ الْقَوْمِ الْفٰسِقِيْنَ ﴿٩٦﴾

97. The Arabs of the desert are the worst in Unbelief and hypocrisy, and most fitted

97. Al-A'raabu ashaddu kuf-rañw-wa nifaaqañw-wa ajdaru

اَلْاَعْرَابُ اَشَدُّ كُفْرًا وَّنِفَاقًا وَّاَجْدَرُ

Ikhfa	Ghunna	Ikhfa Meem Saakin	Idghaam	Qalqala	Qalb	Idghaam Meem Saakin
اخفاء	غنّہ	اخفاء میم ساکن	ادغام	قلقلہ	قلب	ادغام میم ساکن

to be in ignorance of the command which Allah has sent down to His Apostle: But Allah is All-knowing, All-Wise.

allaa ya'lamoo ḥudooda maaa anzalal-laahu 'alaa Rasoolih; wallaahu 'Aleemun Ḥakeem.

اَلَّا يَعْلَمُوْا حُدُوْدَ مَآ اَنْزَلَ اللّٰهُ عَلٰى
رَسُوْلِهٖ ؕ وَاللّٰهُ عَلِيْمٌ حَكِيْمٌ ﴿٩٧﴾

98. Some of the desert Arabs look upon their payments as a fine, and watch for disasters for you: on them be the disaster of evil: for Allah is He that hears and knows (all things).

98. Wa minal-A'raabi mañy-yattakhizu maa yunfiqu maghramañw-wa yatarabbaṣu bikumud-dawaaa'ir; 'alayhim daaa'iratus-saw'; wallaahu Samee'un 'Aleem.

وَمِنَ الْاَعْرَابِ مَنْ يَّتَّخِذُ مَا
يُنْفِقُ مَغْرَمًا وَّيَتَرَبَّصُ بِكُمُ
الدَّوَآئِرَ ؕ عَلَيْهِمْ دَآئِرَةُ السَّوْءِ ؕ
وَاللّٰهُ سَمِيْعٌ عَلِيْمٌ ﴿٩٨﴾

99. But some of the desert Arabs believe in Allah and the Last Day, and look on their payments as pious gifts bringing them nearer to Allah and obtaining the prayers of the Apostle. Yes, indeed they bring them nearer (to Him): soon will Allah admit them to His Mercy: for Allah is Oft-forgiving, Most Merciful.

99. Wa minal-A'raabi mañy-yu'minu billaahi wal-Yawmil Aakhiri wa yattakhizu maa yunfiqu qurubaatin 'indal-laahi wa ṣalawaatir-Rasool; alaaa innahaa qurbatul-lahum; sa-yudkhiluhumul-laahu fee raḥmatih; innal-laaha Ghafoo-rur-Raḥeem. **(Section 12)**

وَمِنَ الْاَعْرَابِ مَنْ يُّؤْمِنُ بِاللّٰهِ
وَالْيَوْمِ الْاٰخِرِ وَيَتَّخِذُ مَا يُنْفِقُ
قُرُبٰتٍ عِنْدَ اللّٰهِ وَصَلَوٰتِ الرَّسُوْلِ ؕ
اَلَآ اِنَّهَا قُرْبَةٌ لَّهُمْ ؕ سَيُدْخِلُهُمُ اللّٰهُ
فِىْ رَحْمَتِهٖ ؕ اِنَّ اللّٰهَ غَفُوْرٌ رَّحِيْمٌ ﴿٩٩﴾ ع

100. The vanguard (of Islam)- the first of those who forsook (their homes) and of those who gave them aid, and (also) those who follow them in (all) good deeds,- well- pleased is Allah with them, as are they with Him: for them He has prepared Gardens under which rivers flow, to dwell therein for ever: that is the supreme felicity.

100. Was-saabiqoonal awwaloona minal-Muhaajireena wal-Anṣaari wallazeenat-taba'oo-hum bi-iḥsaanir-raḍiyal-laahu 'anhum wa raḍoo 'anhu wa a'adda lahum Jannaatin tajree taḥtahal-anhaaru khaalideena feehaaa abadaa; zaalikal-fawzul-'aẓeem.

وَالسّٰبِقُوْنَ الْاَوَّلُوْنَ مِنَ الْمُهٰجِرِيْنَ
وَالْاَنْصَارِ وَالَّذِيْنَ اتَّبَعُوْهُمْ
بِاِحْسَانٍ ۙ رَّضِىَ اللّٰهُ عَنْهُمْ وَ
رَضُوْا عَنْهُ وَاَعَدَّ لَهُمْ جَنّٰتٍ
تَجْرِىْ تَحْتَهَا الْاَنْهٰرُ خٰلِدِيْنَ
فِيْهَآ اَبَدًا ؕ ذٰلِكَ الْفَوْزُ الْعَظِيْمُ ﴿١٠٠﴾

101. Certain of the desert Arabs round about you are Hypocrites, as well as (desert Arabs) among the Medina folk: they are obstinate in hypocrisy: you do not know them: We know them: twice shall We punish them: and in addition they shall be sent to a grievous Chastisement.

101. Wa mimman ḥawlakum minal-A'raabi munaafiqoona wa min ahlil-Madeenati maradoo 'alan-nifaaq, laa ta'lamuhum naḥnu na'lamu-hum; sanu'azzibuhum marra-tayni summa yuraddoona ilaa 'azaabin 'aẓeem.

وَمِمَّنْ حَوْلَكُمْ مِّنَ الْاَعْرَابِ
مُنٰفِقُوْنَ ۛؕ وَمِنْ اَهْلِ الْمَدِيْنَةِ ۛ
مَرَدُوْا عَلَى النِّفَاقِ لَا تَعْلَمُهُمْ ؕ
نَحْنُ نَعْلَمُهُمْ ؕ سَنُعَذِّبُهُمْ مَّرَّتَيْنِ
ثُمَّ يُرَدُّوْنَ اِلٰى عَذَابٍ عَظِيْمٍ ﴿١٠١﴾

102. Others (there are who) have acknowledged their wrong-doings: they have mixed an act that was good with another that was evil. Perhaps Allah will turn to them (in Mercy): for Allah is Oft-Forgiving, Most Merciful.

102. Wa aakharoona'-tarafoo bizunoobihim khalaṭoo 'amalan ṣaaliḥañw-wa aakhara sayyi'an 'asal-laahu añy-yatooba 'alayhim; innal-laaha Ghafoo-rur-Raḥeem.

وَاٰخَرُوْنَ اعْتَرَفُوْا بِذُنُوْبِهِمْ
خَلَطُوْا عَمَلًا صَالِحًا وَّاٰخَرَ سَيِّئًا ؕ
عَسَى اللّٰهُ اَنْ يَّتُوْبَ عَلَيْهِمْ ؕ اِنَّ
اللّٰهَ غَفُوْرٌ رَّحِيْمٌ ﴿١٠٢﴾

Ikhfa اخفاء | Ghunna غنّہ | Ikhfa Meem Saakin اخفاء میم ساکن | Idghaam ادغام | Qalqala قلقلہ | Qalb قلب | Idghaam Meem Saakin ادغام میم ساکن

103. Of their goods, take alms, that so you might purify and sanctify them; and pray on their behalf. Verily your prayers are a source of security for them: and Allah is One Who hears and knows.

103. Khuz̲ min amwaalihim ṣadaqtan tuṭahhiruhum wa tuzakkeehim bihaa wa ṣalli ‘alayhim inna ṣalaataka sakanul-lahum; wallaahu Samee‘un ‘Aleem.

خُذْ مِنْ اَمْوَالِهِمْ صَدَقَةً تُطَهِّرُهُمْ
وَتُزَكِّيْهِمْ بِهَا وَصَلِّ عَلَيْهِمْ ؕ
اِنَّ صَلٰوتَكَ سَكَنٌ لَّهُمْ ؕ وَاللّٰهُ
سَمِيْعٌ عَلِيْمٌ ﴿۱۰۳﴾

104. Do they not know that Allah accepts repentance from His votaries and receives their gifts of charity, and that Allah is verily He, the Oft-Returning, Most Merciful.

104. Alam ya‘lamooo annal-laaha Huwa yaqbalut-tawbata ‘an ‘ibaadihee wa yaåkhuz̲uṣ-ṣadaqaati wa annal-laaha Huwat-Tawwaabur-Raḥeem.

اَلَمْ يَعْلَمُوْٓا اَنَّ اللّٰهَ هُوَ يَقْبَلُ التَّوْبَةَ
عَنْ عِبَادِهٖ وَيَاْخُذُ الصَّدَقٰتِ وَاَنَّ
اللّٰهَ هُوَ التَّوَّابُ الرَّحِيْمُ ﴿۱۰۴﴾

105. And say: "Work (righteousness): soon will Allah observe your work, and His Apostle, and the Believers: soon will you be brought back to the Knower of what is hidden and what is open: then will He show you the truth of all that you did."

105. Wa quli‘-maloo fasayaral-laahu ‘amalakum wa Rasooluhoo walmu’minoona wa saturaddoona ilaa ‘Aalimil-Ghaybi washshahaadati fayunabbi’ukum bimaa kuntum ta‘maloon.

وَقُلِ اعْمَلُوْا فَسَيَرَى اللّٰهُ عَمَلَكُمْ وَ
رَسُوْلُهٗ وَالْمُؤْمِنُوْنَ ؕ وَسَتُرَدُّوْنَ
اِلٰى عٰلِمِ الْغَيْبِ وَالشَّهَادَةِ فَيُنَبِّئُكُمْ
بِمَا كُنْتُمْ تَعْمَلُوْنَ ﴿۱۰۵﴾ ج

106. There are (yet) others, held in suspense for the command of Allah, whether He will punish them, or turn in mercy to them: and Allah is All-Knowing, Wise.

106. Wa aakharoona murjawna li-amril-laahi immaa yu‘az̲zibuhum wa immaa yatoobu ‘alayhim; wallaahu ‘Aleemun Ḥakeem.

وَاٰخَرُوْنَ مُرْجَوْنَ لِاَمْرِ اللّٰهِ
اِمَّا يُعَذِّبُهُمْ وَاِمَّا يَتُوْبُ عَلَيْهِمْ ؕ
وَاللّٰهُ عَلِيْمٌ حَكِيْمٌ ﴿۱۰۶﴾

107. And there are those who put up a mosque by way of mischief and infidelity - to disunite the Believers - and in preparation for one who warred against Allah and His Apostle afore time. They will indeed swear that their intention is nothing but good ; but Allah declares that they are certainly liars.

107. Wallaz̲eenat-takhaz̲oo masjidan ḍiraarañw-wa kufrañw-wa tafreeqam baynal-mu’mineena wa irṣaadal-liman ḥaarabal-laaha wa Rasoolahoo min qabl; wa la-yaḥlifunna in aradnaaa illal-ḥusnaa wallaahu yash-hadu innahum lakaaz̲iboon.

وَالَّذِيْنَ اتَّخَذُوْا مَسْجِدًا ضِرَارًا
وَّكُفْرًا وَّتَفْرِيْقًا بَيْنَ الْمُؤْمِنِيْنَ
وَاِرْصَادًا لِّمَنْ حَارَبَ اللّٰهَ وَ
رَسُوْلَهٗ مِنْ قَبْلُ ؕ وَلَيَحْلِفُنَّ
اِنْ اَرَدْنَآ اِلَّا الْحُسْنٰى ؕ وَاللّٰهُ
يَشْهَدُ اِنَّهُمْ لَكٰذِبُوْنَ ﴿۱۰۷﴾

108. You never stand forth therein. There is a mosque whose foundation was laid from the first day on piety; it is more worthy of the standing forth (for prayer) therein. In it are men who love to be purified; and Allah loves those who make themselves pure.

108. Laa taqum feehi abadaa; lamasjidun ussisa ‘alat-taqwaa min awwali yawmin aḥaqqu an taqooma feeh; feehi rijaaluñy-yuḥibboona añy-yataṭahharoo, wallaahu yuḥibbul-muṭṭahhireen.

لَا تَقُمْ فِيْهِ اَبَدًا ؕ لَمَسْجِدٌ اُسِّسَ عَلَى
التَّقْوٰى مِنْ اَوَّلِ يَوْمٍ اَحَقُّ اَنْ تَقُوْمَ
فِيْهِ ؕ فِيْهِ رِجَالٌ يُّحِبُّوْنَ اَنْ يَّتَطَهَّرُوْا ؕ
وَاللّٰهُ يُحِبُّ الْمُطَّهِّرِيْنَ ﴿۱۰۸﴾

109. Which then is best? - he that lays his foundation on piety to Allah and His Good Pleasure? - or he

109. Afaman assasa bunyaanahoo ‘alaa taqwaa minal-laahi wa riḍwaanin khayrun am-man

اَفَمَنْ اَسَّسَ بُنْيَانَهٗ عَلٰى تَقْوٰى
مِنَ اللّٰهِ وَرِضْوَانٍ خَيْرٌ اَمْ مَّنْ

that lays his foundation on an undermined sand-cliff ready to crumble to pieces? And it crumbles to pieces with him, into the fire of Hell. And Allah does not guides people that do wrong.

assasa bunyaanahoo 'alaa shafaa jurufin haarin fanhaara bihee fee Naari Jahannam; wallaahu laa yahdil-qawmaẓ-ẓaalimeen.

أَسَّسَ بُنْيَانَهُ عَلَىٰ شَفَا جُرُفٍ هَارٍ فَانْهَارَ بِهِ فِي نَارِ جَهَنَّمَ ۗ وَاللَّهُ لَا يَهْدِي الْقَوْمَ الظَّالِمِينَ ﴿١٠٩﴾

110. The foundation of those who so build is never free from suspicion and shakiness in their hearts, until their hearts are cut to pieces. And Allah is All-Knowing, Wise.

110. Laa yazaalu bunyaanu-humul-lazee banaw reebatan fee quloobihim illaaa an taqaṭṭa'a quloobuhum; wal-laahu 'Aleemun Ḥakeem.

لَا يَزَالُ بُنْيَانُهُمُ الَّذِي بَنَوْا رِيبَةً فِي قُلُوبِهِمْ إِلَّا أَنْ تَقَطَّعَ قُلُوبُهُمْ ۗ وَاللَّهُ عَلِيمٌ حَكِيمٌ ﴿١١٠﴾

(Section 13)

111. Allah has purchased of the Believers their persons and their goods; for theirs (in return) is the Garden (of Paradise): they fight in His Cause, and slay and are slain: a promise binding on Him in Truth, through the Torah, the Gospel, and the Qur 'an: and who is more faithful to his Covenant than Allah? Then rejoice in the bargain which you have concluded: that is the supreme achievement.

111. Innal-laahash-taraa minal-mu'mineena anfusahum wa amwaalahum bi-anna lahumul-jannah; yuqaatiloona fee sabeelil-laahi fa-yaqtuloona wa yuqtaloona wa'dan 'alayhi ḥaqqan fit-Tawraati wal-Injeeli wal-Qur-aan; wa man awfaa bi'ahdihee minal-laah; fastab-shiroo bibay'ikumul-lazee baaya'tum bih; wa zaalika huwal-fawzul-'aẓeem.

إِنَّ اللَّهَ اشْتَرَىٰ مِنَ الْمُؤْمِنِينَ أَنْفُسَهُمْ وَأَمْوَالَهُمْ بِأَنَّ لَهُمُ الْجَنَّةَ ۚ يُقَاتِلُونَ فِي سَبِيلِ اللَّهِ فَيَقْتُلُونَ وَيُقْتَلُونَ ۖ وَعْدًا عَلَيْهِ حَقًّا فِي التَّوْرَاةِ وَالْإِنْجِيلِ وَالْقُرْآنِ ۚ وَمَنْ أَوْفَىٰ بِعَهْدِهِ مِنَ اللَّهِ ۚ فَاسْتَبْشِرُوا بِبَيْعِكُمُ الَّذِي بَايَعْتُمْ بِهِ ۚ وَذَٰلِكَ هُوَ الْفَوْزُ الْعَظِيمُ ﴿١١١﴾

112. Those that turn (to Allah) in repentance; that serve Him, and praise Him; that wander in devotion to the Cause of Allah,: that bow down and prostrate themselves in prayer; that enjoin good and forbid evil; and observe the limits set by Allah;- (these do rejoice). So proclaim the glad tidings to the Believers.

112. At-taaa'iboonal-'aabidoo-nal-ḥaamidoonas-saaa'iḥoo-nar-raaki'oonas-saajidoonal-aamiroona bilma'roofi wannaa-hoona 'anil-munkari walḥaafi-ẓoona liḥudoodil-laah; wa bashshiril-mu'mineen.

التَّائِبُونَ الْعَابِدُونَ الْحَامِدُونَ السَّائِحُونَ الرَّاكِعُونَ السَّاجِدُونَ الْآمِرُونَ بِالْمَعْرُوفِ وَالنَّاهُونَ عَنِ الْمُنْكَرِ وَالْحَافِظُونَ لِحُدُودِ اللَّهِ ۗ وَبَشِّرِ الْمُؤْمِنِينَ ﴿١١٢﴾

113. It is not fitting, for the Prophet and those who believe, that they should pray for forgiveness for Pagans, even though they be of kin, after it is clear to them that they are companions of the Fire.

113. Maa kaana lin-Nabiyyi wallazeena aamanooo añy-yastaghfiroo lilmushrikeena wa law kaanooo ulee qurbaa mim ba'di maa tabayyana lahum annahum Aṣḥaabul-jaḥeem.

مَا كَانَ لِلنَّبِيِّ وَالَّذِينَ آمَنُوا أَنْ يَسْتَغْفِرُوا لِلْمُشْرِكِينَ وَلَوْ كَانُوا أُولِي قُرْبَىٰ مِنْ بَعْدِ مَا تَبَيَّنَ لَهُمْ أَنَّهُمْ أَصْحَابُ الْجَحِيمِ ﴿١١٣﴾

114. And Abraham prayed for his father's forgiveness only because of a promise he had made to him. But when it became clear to him that he was an enemy to Allah, he dissociated himself from him:

114. Wa maa kaanas-tighfaaru Ibraaheema li-abeehi illaa 'am-maw'idatiñw-wa'adahaaa iyyaahu falammaa tabayyana lahooo annahoo 'aduwwul-lillaahi tabarra-a minh;

وَمَا كَانَ اسْتِغْفَارُ إِبْرَاهِيمَ لِأَبِيهِ إِلَّا عَنْ مَوْعِدَةٍ وَعَدَهَا إِيَّاهُ فَلَمَّا تَبَيَّنَ لَهُ أَنَّهُ عَدُوٌّ لِلَّهِ تَبَرَّأَ مِنْهُ ۚ

Ikhfa اخفاء | Ghunna غنّہ | Ikhfa Meem Saakin اخفاء میم ساکن | Idghaam ادغام | Qalqala قلقلہ | Qalb قلب | Idghaam Meem Saakin ادغام میم ساکن

for Abraham was most tender-hearted, forbearing.

115. And Allah will not mislead a people after He has guided them, in order that He may make clear to them what to fear (and avoid)- for Allah has knowledge of all things.

116. To Allah belongs the dominion of the heavens and the earth. He gives life and He takes it. Except for Him you have no protector nor helper.

117. Allah turned with favour to the Prophet, the Muhajirs, and the Ansar,- who followed him in a time of distress, after that the hearts of a part of them had nearly swerved (from duty); but He turned to them (also): for He is to them Most Kind, Most Merciful.

118. (He turned in mercy also) to the three who were left behind; (they felt guilty) to such a degree that the earth seemed constrained to them, for all its spaciousness, and their (very) souls seemed straitened to them,- and they perceived that there is no fleeing from Allah (and no refuge) but to Himself. Then He turned to them, that they might repent: for Allah is Oft-Returning, Most Merciful.

119. O you who believe! Fear Allah and be with those who are true (in word and deed).

120. It was not fitting for the people of Medina and the Bedouin Arabs of the neighbourhood, to refuse to follow Allah's Apostle, nor to prefer their own lives to his: because nothing could they suffer or do, but was reckoned to their credit as a deed of righteousness, whether they suffered thirst, or fatigue, or hunger, in the Cause of Allah, or trod paths to raise the ire of

inna Ibraaheema la-awwaahun ḥaleem.

115. Wa maa kaanal-laahu liyuḍilla qawmam ba'da iz hadaahum ḥattaa yubayyina lahum-maa yattaqoon; innal-laaha bikulli shay'in 'Aleem.

116. Innal-laaha lahoo mulkus-samaawaati walarḍi yuḥyee wa yumeet; wa maa lakum-min doonil-laahi miñw-waliyyiñw-wa laa naṣeer.

117. Laqat-taabal-laahu 'alan-Nabiyyi wal-Muhaajireena wal-Anṣaaril-lazeenat-taba'oohu fee saa'atil-'usrati mim ba'di maa kaada yazeeghu quloobu fareeqim-minhum summa taaba 'alayhim; innahoo bihim Ra'oofur-Raḥeem.

118. Wa 'alas-salaasatil-lazee-na khullifoo ḥattaaa izaa ḍaaqat 'alayhimul-arḍu bimaa raḥubat wa ḍaaqat 'alayhim anfusuhum wa ẓannooo al-laa malja-a minal-laahi illaaa ilayhi summa taaba 'alayhim liyatooboo; innal-laaha Huwat-Tawwaabur-Raḥeem. **(Section 14)**

119. Yaaa ayyuhal-lazeena aamanut-taqul-laaha wa koonoo ma'aṣ-ṣaadiqeen.

120. Maa kaana li-ahlil-Madeenati wa man ḥawlahum-minal-A'raabi añy-yatakhal-lafoo 'ar-Rasoolil-laahi wa laa yarghaboo bi-anfusihim 'an nafsih; zaalika bi-annahum laa yuṣeebuhum ẓama-uñw-wa laa naṣabuñw-wa laa makhmaṣatun fee sabeelil-laahi wa laa yata-'oona mawṭi'añy- yagheeẓul-

إِنَّ إِبْرٰهِيْمَ لَأَوَّاهٌ حَلِيْمٌ ﴿١١٤﴾
وَمَا كَانَ اللّٰهُ لِيُضِلَّ قَوْمًا بَعْدَ إِذْ
هَدٰىهُمْ حَتّٰى يُبَيِّنَ لَهُمْ مَّا يَتَّقُوْنَ ط
إِنَّ اللّٰهَ بِكُلِّ شَيْءٍ عَلِيْمٌ ﴿١١٥﴾
إِنَّ اللّٰهَ لَهٗ مُلْكُ السَّمٰوٰتِ وَالْأَرْضِ ط
يُحْيٖ وَيُمِيْتُ ط وَمَا لَكُمْ مِّنْ دُوْنِ
اللّٰهِ مِنْ وَّلِيٍّ وَّلَا نَصِيْرٍ ﴿١١٦﴾
لَقَدْ تَّابَ اللّٰهُ عَلَى النَّبِيِّ وَالْمُهٰجِرِيْنَ
وَالْأَنْصَارِ الَّذِيْنَ اتَّبَعُوْهُ فِيْ سَاعَةِ
الْعُسْرَةِ مِنْ بَعْدِ مَا كَادَ يَزِيْغُ
قُلُوْبُ فَرِيْقٍ مِّنْهُمْ ثُمَّ تَابَ عَلَيْهِمْ ط
إِنَّهٗ بِهِمْ رَءُوْفٌ رَّحِيْمٌ ﴿١١٧﴾
وَّعَلَى الثَّلٰثَةِ الَّذِيْنَ خُلِّفُوْا ط
حَتّٰى إِذَا ضَاقَتْ عَلَيْهِمُ الْأَرْضُ
بِمَا رَحُبَتْ وَضَاقَتْ عَلَيْهِمْ أَنْفُسُهُمْ
وَظَنُّوْا أَنْ لَّا مَلْجَأَ مِنَ اللّٰهِ إِلَّا
إِلَيْهِ ط ثُمَّ تَابَ عَلَيْهِمْ لِيَتُوْبُوْا ط
إِنَّ اللّٰهَ هُوَ التَّوَّابُ الرَّحِيْمُ ﴿١١٨﴾
يٰٓأَيُّهَا الَّذِيْنَ اٰمَنُوا اتَّقُوا اللّٰهَ وَ
كُوْنُوْا مَعَ الصّٰدِقِيْنَ ﴿١١٩﴾
مَا كَانَ لِأَهْلِ الْمَدِيْنَةِ وَمَنْ
حَوْلَهُمْ مِّنَ الْأَعْرَابِ أَنْ يَّتَخَلَّفُوْا
عَنْ رَّسُوْلِ اللّٰهِ وَلَا يَرْغَبُوْا بِأَنْفُسِهِمْ
عَنْ نَّفْسِهٖ ط ذٰلِكَ بِأَنَّهُمْ لَا يُصِيْبُهُمْ
ظَمَأٌ وَّلَا نَصَبٌ وَّلَا مَخْمَصَةٌ فِيْ
سَبِيْلِ اللّٰهِ وَلَا يَطَئُوْنَ مَوْطِئًا يَّغِيْظُ

Ikhfa اخفاء | Ghunna غنّہ | Ikhfa Meem Saakin اخفاء میم ساکن | Idghaam ادغام | Qalqala قلقلہ | Qalb قلب | Idghaam Meem Saakin ادغام میم ساکن

the Unbelievers, or received any injury whatever from an enemy: for Allah does not suffer the reward to be lost of those who do good;-

kuffaara wa laa yanaaloona min 'aduwwin naylan illaa kutiba lahum bihee 'amalun ṣaaliḥ; innal-laaha laa yuḍee'u ajral-muḥsineen.

الْكُفَّارَ وَلَا يَنَالُونَ مِنْ عَدُوٍّ نَّيْلًا
إِلَّا كُتِبَ لَهُم بِهِ عَمَلٌ صَالِحٌ ۚ إِنَّ
اللَّهَ لَا يُضِيعُ أَجْرَ الْمُحْسِنِينَ ﴿١٢٠﴾

121. Nor could they spend anything (for the Cause) - small or great- nor cut across a valley, but the deed is inscribed to their credit: that Allah may requite their deed with the best (possible reward).

121. Wa laa yunfiqoona nafaqatan ṣagheeratañw-wa laa kabeeratañw-wa laa yaqṭa'oona waadiyan illaa kutiba lahum liyajziyahumul-laahu aḥsana maa kaanoo ya'maloon.

وَلَا يُنفِقُونَ نَفَقَةً صَغِيرَةً وَلَا
كَبِيرَةً وَلَا يَقْطَعُونَ وَادِيًا إِلَّا
كُتِبَ لَهُمْ لِيَجْزِيَهُمُ اللَّهُ أَحْسَنَ مَا
كَانُوا يَعْمَلُونَ ﴿١٢١﴾

122. Nor should the Believers all go forth together: if a contingent from every expedition remained behind, they could devote themselves to studies in religion, and admonish the people when they return to them,- that thus they (may learn) to guard themselves (against evil).

122. Wa maa kaanal-mu'minoona liyanfiroo kaaaffah; falaw laa nafara min kulli firqatim-minhum ṭaaa'ifatul-liyatafaqqahoo fiddeeni wa liyunziroo qawmahum izaa raja'ooo ilayhim la'allahum yaḥẕaroon. **(Section 15)**

وَمَا كَانَ الْمُؤْمِنُونَ لِيَنفِرُوا كَافَّةً ۚ
فَلَوْلَا نَفَرَ مِن كُلِّ فِرْقَةٍ مِّنْهُمْ
طَائِفَةٌ لِّيَتَفَقَّهُوا فِي الدِّينِ
وَلِيُنذِرُوا قَوْمَهُمْ إِذَا رَجَعُوا
إِلَيْهِمْ لَعَلَّهُمْ يَحْذَرُونَ ﴿١٢٢﴾ ع

123. O you who believe! Fight the Unbelievers who gird you about, and let them find firmness in you: and know that Allah is with those who fear Him.

123. Yaaa ayyuhal-lazeena aamanoo qaatilul-lazeena yaloonakum minal-kuffaari walyajidoo feekum ghilẓah; wa'lamooo annal-laaha ma'al-muttaqeen.

يَا أَيُّهَا الَّذِينَ آمَنُوا قَاتِلُوا
الَّذِينَ يَلُونَكُم مِّنَ الْكُفَّارِ وَلْيَجِدُوا
فِيكُمْ غِلْظَةً ۚ وَاعْلَمُوا أَنَّ اللَّهَ
مَعَ الْمُتَّقِينَ ﴿١٢٣﴾ الربع

124. Whenever there comes down a Sura, some of them say: "Which of you has had his faith increased by it?" Yes, those who believe,- their faith is increased and they do rejoice.

124. Wa izaa maaa unzilat Sooratun faminhum mañy-yaqoolu ayyukum zaadat-hu haaziheee eemaanaa; fa-ammal-lazeena aamanoo fazaadat-hum eemaanañw-wa hum yastabshiroon.

وَإِذَا مَا أُنزِلَتْ سُورَةٌ فَمِنْهُم مَّن
يَقُولُ أَيُّكُمْ زَادَتْهُ هَٰذِهِ إِيمَانًا ۚ
فَأَمَّا الَّذِينَ آمَنُوا فَزَادَتْهُمْ إِيمَانًا
وَهُمْ يَسْتَبْشِرُونَ ﴿١٢٤﴾

125. But those in whose hearts is a disease,- it will add doubt to their doubt, and they will die in a state of Unbelief.

125. Wa ammal-lazeena fee quloobihim maraḍun fazaadat-hum rijsan ilaa rijsihim wa maatoo wa hum kaafiroon.

وَأَمَّا الَّذِينَ فِي قُلُوبِهِم مَّرَضٌ
فَزَادَتْهُمْ رِجْسًا إِلَىٰ رِجْسِهِمْ وَمَاتُوا
وَهُمْ كَافِرُونَ ﴿١٢٥﴾

126. Don't they see that they are tried every year once or twice? Yet they do not turn in repentance, and they take no heed.

126. Awalaa yarawna annahum yuftanoona fee kulli 'aamim marratan aw marratayni summa laa yatooboona wa laa hum yazzakkaroon.

أَوَلَا يَرَوْنَ أَنَّهُمْ يُفْتَنُونَ فِي كُلِّ
عَامٍ مَّرَّةً أَوْ مَرَّتَيْنِ ثُمَّ لَا يَتُوبُونَ
وَلَا هُمْ يَذَّكَّرُونَ ﴿١٢٦﴾

Ikhfa	Ghunna	Ikhfa Meem Saakin	Idghaam	Qalqala	Qalb	Idghaam Meem Saakin
اخفاء	غنّہ	اخفاء میم ساکن	ادغام	قلقلہ	قلب	ادغام میم ساکن

127. Whenever there comes down a Sura, they look at each other, (saying), "Does anyone see you?" Then they turn aside: Allah has turned their hearts (from the light); for they are a people that do not understand.

128. Now has come to you an Apostle from amongst yourselves: it grieves him that you should perish: he is ardently anxious over you: to the Believers he is most kind and merciful.

129. But if they turn away, say: "Allah is sufficient for me: there is no god but He: On Him is my trust,- He the Lord of the Throne (of Glory) Supreme!"

127. Wa izaa maaa unzilat Sooratun nazara ba'duhum ilaa ba'din hal yaraakum min ahadin summan-sarafoo; sarafal-laahu quloobahum bi-annahum qawmul-laa yafqahoon.

128. Laqad jaaa'akum Rasoolum-min anfusikum 'azeezun 'alayhi maa 'anittum hareesun 'alaykum bilmu'mineena ra'oofur-raheem.

129. Fa-in tawallaw faqul hasbiyal-laahu laaa ilaaha illaa Huwa 'alayhi tawakkaltu wa Huwa Rabbul-'Arshil-'Azeem.

(Section 16)

وَإِذَا مَا أُنزِلَتْ سُورَةٌ نَّظَرَ بَعْضُهُمْ
إِلَىٰ بَعْضٍ هَلْ يَرَاكُم مِّنْ أَحَدٍ
ثُمَّ انصَرَفُوا صَرَفَ اللَّهُ قُلُوبَهُم
بِأَنَّهُمْ قَوْمٌ لَّا يَفْقَهُونَ ١٢٧
لَقَدْ جَاءَكُمْ رَسُولٌ مِّنْ أَنفُسِكُمْ
عَزِيزٌ عَلَيْهِ مَا عَنِتُّمْ حَرِيصٌ عَلَيْكُم
بِالْمُؤْمِنِينَ رَءُوفٌ رَّحِيمٌ ١٢٨
فَإِن تَوَلَّوْا فَقُلْ حَسْبِيَ اللَّهُ
لَا إِلَٰهَ إِلَّا هُوَ عَلَيْهِ تَوَكَّلْتُ
وَهُوَ رَبُّ الْعَرْشِ الْعَظِيمِ ١٢٩ ع

ع ١٦ ٧

10. Yunus, or Jonah

In the name of Allah, Most Gracious, Most Merciful.

Sûrat Yûnus–10

(Revealed at Makkah)

Bismillaahir Rahmaanir Raheem

(١٠) سُورَةُ يُونُسَ مَكِّيَّةٌ (٥١)

بِسْمِ اللَّهِ الرَّحْمَٰنِ الرَّحِيمِ

1. *Alif-Lam-Ra.* These are the *ayats* of the Book of Wisdom.

2. Is it a matter of wonderment to men that We have sent Our inspiration to a man from among themselves?- that he should warn mankind (of their danger), and give the good news to the Believers that they have before their Lord, the lofty rank of Truth. (But) the Unbelievers say: "This is indeed an evident sorcerer!"

3. Verily your Lord is Allah, who created the heavens and the earth in six days, and is firmly established on the throne (of authority), regulating and governing all things. No intercessor (can plead with Him) except after His leave (has been obtained). This is Allah your Lord; you therefore serve Him: will you not receive admonition?

4. To Him will be your return- of all of you. The promise of Allah is true and sure. It is He Who begins the process of creation, and repeats it, that He may reward with justice those who believe and work righteousness;

1. Alif-Laaam-Raa; tilka Aayaatul-Kitaabil-Hakeem.

2. A kaana linnaasi 'ajaban an awhaynaaa ilaa rajulim-minhum an anzirin-naasa wa bashshiril-lazeena aamanooo anna lahum qadama sidqin 'inda Rabbihim; qaalal-kaafiroona inna haazaa lasaahirum-mubeen.

3. Inna Rabbakumul-laahul-lazee khalaqas-samaawaati wal-arda fee sittati ayyaamin-summas-tawaa 'alal-'Arshi yudabbirul-amra maa min shafee'in illaa mim ba'di iznih; zalikumul-laahu Rabbukum fa'budooh; afalaa tazakkaroon.

4. Ilayhi marji'ukum jamee-'añw wa'dal-laahi haqqaa; innahoo yabda'ul-khalqa summa yu'eeduhoo liyajziyal-lazeena aamanoo wa 'amilus-saalihaati

الٓر تِلْكَ آيَاتُ الْكِتَابِ الْحَكِيمِ ١
أَكَانَ لِلنَّاسِ عَجَبًا أَنْ أَوْحَيْنَا
إِلَىٰ رَجُلٍ مِّنْهُمْ أَنْ أَنذِرِ النَّاسَ
وَبَشِّرِ الَّذِينَ آمَنُوا أَنَّ لَهُمْ قَدَمَ
صِدْقٍ عِندَ رَبِّهِمْ قَالَ الْكَافِرُونَ
إِنَّ هَٰذَا لَسَاحِرٌ مُّبِينٌ ٢
إِنَّ رَبَّكُمُ اللَّهُ الَّذِي خَلَقَ السَّمَاوَاتِ
وَالْأَرْضَ فِي سِتَّةِ أَيَّامٍ ثُمَّ اسْتَوَىٰ
عَلَى الْعَرْشِ يُدَبِّرُ الْأَمْرَ مَا مِن
شَفِيعٍ إِلَّا مِن بَعْدِ إِذْنِهِ ذَٰلِكُمُ
اللَّهُ رَبُّكُمْ فَاعْبُدُوهُ أَفَلَا تَذَكَّرُونَ ٣
إِلَيْهِ مَرْجِعُكُمْ جَمِيعًا وَعْدَ اللَّهِ حَقًّا
إِنَّهُ يَبْدَأُ الْخَلْقَ ثُمَّ يُعِيدُهُ لِيَجْزِيَ
الَّذِينَ آمَنُوا وَعَمِلُوا الصَّالِحَاتِ

المنزل الثالث (٣)

وقف النبي صلى الله عليه وآله وسلم ١٢

Ikhfa اخفاء | Ghunna غنّہ | Ikhfa Meem Saakin اخفاء میم ساکن | Idghaam ادغام | Qalqala قلقلہ | Qalb قلب | Idghaam Meem Saakin ادغام میم ساکن

but those who reject Him will have draughts of boiling fluids, and a Chastisement grievous, because they did reject Him.

bilqist; wallazeena kafaroo lahum sharaabum-min hameemiñw-wa 'azaabun aleemum bimaa kaanoo yakfuroon.

بِالْقِسْطِ ۚ وَالَّذِينَ كَفَرُوا لَهُمْ
شَرَابٌ مِّنْ حَمِيمٍ وَعَذَابٌ أَلِيمٌ بِمَا
كَانُوا يَكْفُرُونَ ﴿٤﴾

5. It is He Who made the sun to be a shining glory and the moon to be a light (of beauty), and measured out stages for it, that you might know the number of years and the count (of time). Nowise did Allah create this but in truth and righteousness. (Thus) He explains His Signs in detail, for those who understand.

5. Huwal-lazee ja'alash-shamsa diyaaa'añw-walqamara noorañw-wa qaddarahoo manaazila lita'lamoo 'adadas-sineena walhisaab; maa khalaqal-laahu zaalika illaa bilhaqq; yufassilul-Aayaati liqawmiñy-ya'lamoon.

هُوَ الَّذِي جَعَلَ الشَّمْسَ ضِيَاءً
وَالْقَمَرَ نُورًا وَقَدَّرَهُ مَنَازِلَ
لِتَعْلَمُوا عَدَدَ السِّنِينَ وَالْحِسَابَ ۚ
مَا خَلَقَ اللَّهُ ذَٰلِكَ إِلَّا بِالْحَقِّ ۚ
يُفَصِّلُ الْآيَاتِ لِقَوْمٍ يَعْلَمُونَ ﴿٥﴾

6. Verily, in the alternation of the night and the day, and in all that Allah has created, in the heavens and the earth, are Signs for those who fear Him.

6. Inna fikh-tilaafil-layli wannahaari wa maa khalaqal-laahu fis-samaawaati wal-ardi la-Aayaatil-liqawmiñy-yattaqoon.

إِنَّ فِي اخْتِلَافِ اللَّيْلِ وَالنَّهَارِ
وَمَا خَلَقَ اللَّهُ فِي السَّمَاوَاتِ وَالْأَرْضِ
لَآيَاتٍ لِّقَوْمٍ يَتَّقُونَ ﴿٦﴾

7. Those who do not rest their hope on their meeting with Us, but are pleased and satisfied with the life of the present, and those who do not heed Our Signs,-

7. Innal-lazeena laa yarjoona liqaaa'anaa wa radoo bilhayaatid-dunyaa watma-annoo bihaa wallazeena hum 'an Aayaatinaa ghaafiloon.

إِنَّ الَّذِينَ لَا يَرْجُونَ لِقَاءَنَا وَرَضُوا
بِالْحَيَاةِ الدُّنْيَا وَاطْمَأَنُّوا بِهَا وَالَّذِينَ
هُمْ عَنْ آيَاتِنَا غَافِلُونَ ﴿٧﴾

8. Their abode is the Fire, because of the (evil) they earned.

8. Ulaaa'ika maåwaahumun Naaru bimaa kaanoo yaksiboon.

أُولَٰئِكَ مَأْوَاهُمُ النَّارُ بِمَا كَانُوا
يَكْسِبُونَ ﴿٨﴾

9. Those who believe, and work righteousness,- their Lord will guide them because of their faith: beneath them will flow rivers in Gardens of Bliss.

9. Innal-lazeena aamanoo wa 'amilus-saalihaati yahdeehim Rabbuhum bi-eemaanihim tajree min tahtihimul-anhaaru fee Jannaatin-Na'eem.

إِنَّ الَّذِينَ آمَنُوا وَعَمِلُوا الصَّالِحَاتِ
يَهْدِيهِمْ رَبُّهُم بِإِيمَانِهِمْ ۖ تَجْرِي مِن
تَحْتِهِمُ الْأَنْهَارُ فِي جَنَّاتِ النَّعِيمِ ﴿٩﴾

10. (This will be) their cry therein: "Glory to You, O Allah!" And "Peace" will be their greeting therein! and the close of their cry will be: "Praise be to Allah, the Cherisher and Sus-tainer of the Worlds!"

10. Da'waahum feehaa Subhaanakal-laahumma wa tahiyyatuhum feehaa salaam; wa aakhiru da'waahum anil-hamdu lillaahi Rabbil-'aalameen.

(Section 1)

دَعْوَاهُمْ فِيهَا سُبْحَانَكَ اللَّهُمَّ وَ
تَحِيَّتُهُمْ فِيهَا سَلَامٌ ۚ وَآخِرُ دَعْوَاهُمْ
أَنِ الْحَمْدُ لِلَّهِ رَبِّ الْعَالَمِينَ ﴿١٠﴾

11. If Allah were to hasten for men the ill (they have earned) as they would fain hasten on the good,- then would their respite be settled at once. But We leave those who do not rest their hope on their meeting with Us, in their trespasses, wandering in distraction to and fro.

11. Wa law yu'ajjilul-laahu linnaasish-sharras-ti'jaalahum bilkhayri laqudiya ilayhim ajaluhum fanazarul-lazeena laa yarjoona liqaaa'anaa fee tughyaanihim ya'mahoon.

وَلَوْ يُعَجِّلُ اللَّهُ لِلنَّاسِ الشَّرَّ
اسْتِعْجَالَهُم بِالْخَيْرِ لَقُضِيَ إِلَيْهِمْ
أَجَلُهُمْ ۖ فَنَذَرُ الَّذِينَ لَا يَرْجُونَ
لِقَاءَنَا فِي طُغْيَانِهِمْ يَعْمَهُونَ ﴿١١﴾

Ikhfa اخفاء | Ghunna غُنّہ | Ikhfa Meem Saakin اخفاء میم ساکن | Idghaam ادغام | Qalqala قلقلہ | Qalb قلب | Idghaam Meem Saakin ادغام میم ساکن

12. When trouble touches a man, He cries unto Us (in all postures)- lying down on his side, or sitting, or standing. But when We have solved his trouble, he passes on his way as if he had never cried to us for a trouble that touched him! Thus do the deeds of transgressors seem fair in their eyes!

12. Wa izaa massal-insaanaḍ-ḍurru da'aanaa lijambiheee aw qaa'idan aw qaaa'iman falammaa kashafnaa 'anhu ḍurrahoo marra ka-al-lam yad'unaaa ilaa ḍurrim-massah; kazaalika zuyyina lilmusrifeena maa kaanoo ya'maloon.

وَإِذَا مَسَّ الْإِنسَانَ الضُّرُّ دَعَانَا
لِجَنۢبِهِۦٓ أَوْ قَاعِدًا أَوْ قَآئِمًا فَلَمَّا
كَشَفْنَا عَنْهُ ضُرَّهُۥ مَرَّ كَأَن لَّمْ
يَدْعُنَآ إِلَىٰ ضُرٍّ مَّسَّهُۥ ۚ كَذَٰلِكَ زُيِّنَ
لِلْمُسْرِفِينَ مَا كَانُوا۟ يَعْمَلُونَ ﴿١٢﴾

13. We destroyed generations before you when they did wrong: their Apostles came to them with Clear-Signs, but they would not believe! Thus do We requite those who sin!

13. Wa laqad ahlaknal-quroona min qablikum lammaa ẓalamoo wa jaaa'at-hum Rusuluhum bil-bayyinaati wa maa kaanoo liyu'minoo; kazaalika najzil-qawmal-mujrimeen.

وَلَقَدْ أَهْلَكْنَا الْقُرُونَ مِن قَبْلِكُمْ
لَمَّا ظَلَمُوا۟ ۙ وَجَآءَتْهُمْ رُسُلُهُم
بِالْبَيِّنَٰتِ وَمَا كَانُوا۟ لِيُؤْمِنُوا۟ ۚ
كَذَٰلِكَ نَجْزِى الْقَوْمَ الْمُجْرِمِينَ ﴿١٣﴾

14. Then We made you heirs in the land after them, to see how you would behave!

14. Summa ja'alnaakum khalaaa'ifa fil-arḍi mim ba'dihim linanẓura kayfa ta'maloon.

ثُمَّ جَعَلْنَٰكُمْ خَلَٰٓئِفَ فِى الْأَرْضِ مِنۢ
بَعْدِهِمْ لِنَنظُرَ كَيْفَ تَعْمَلُونَ ﴿١٤﴾

15. But when Our Clear Signs are rehearsed to them, those who do not rest their hope on their meeting with Us, Say: "Bring us a Qur'an other than this, or change this," Say: "It is not for me, of my own accord, to change it: I follow nothing but what is revealed unto me: if I were to disobey my Lord, I should myself fear the Chastisement of a Great Day (to come)."

15. Wa izaa tutlaa 'alayhim Aayaatunaa bayyinaatin qaalal-lazeena laa yarjoona liqaaa-'ana'-ti bi-Qur-aanin ghayri haazaaa aw baddilh; qul maa yakoonu leee an ubaddilahoo min tilqaaa'i nafsee in attabi'u illaa maa yooḥaaa ilayya inneee akhaafu in 'aṣaytu Rabbee 'azaaba Yawmin 'Aẓeem.

وَإِذَا تُتْلَىٰ عَلَيْهِمْ ءَايَاتُنَا بَيِّنَٰتٍ ۙ
قَالَ الَّذِينَ لَا يَرْجُونَ لِقَآءَنَا ائْتِ
بِقُرْءَانٍ غَيْرِ هَٰذَآ أَوْ بَدِّلْهُ ۚ قُلْ مَا
يَكُونُ لِىٓ أَنْ أُبَدِّلَهُۥ مِن تِلْقَآئِ
نَفْسِىٓ ۖ إِنْ أَتَّبِعُ إِلَّا مَا يُوحَىٰٓ إِلَىَّ ۖ
إِنِّىٓ أَخَافُ إِنْ عَصَيْتُ رَبِّى عَذَابَ
يَوْمٍ عَظِيمٍ ﴿١٥﴾

16. Say: "If Allah had so willed, I should not have rehearsed it to you, nor would He have made it known to you. A whole life-time before this I have tarried amongst you: will you not then understand?"

16. Qul law shaaa'al-laahu maa talawtuhoo 'alaykum wa laaa adraakum bihee faqad labistu feekum 'umuram-min qablih; afalaa ta'qiloon.

قُل لَّوْ شَآءَ اللَّهُ مَا تَلَوْتُهُۥ عَلَيْكُمْ
وَلَآ أَدْرَىٰكُم بِهِۦ ۖ فَقَدْ لَبِثْتُ فِيكُمْ
عُمُرًا مِّن قَبْلِهِۦٓ ۚ أَفَلَا تَعْقِلُونَ ﴿١٦﴾

17. Who does more wrong than such as forge a lie against Allah, or deny His Signs? But never will prosper those who sin.

17. Faman aẓlamu mimmanif-taraa 'alal-laahi kaziban aw kazzaba bi-Aayaatih; innahoo laa yufliḥul-mujrimoon.

فَمَنْ أَظْلَمُ مِمَّنِ افْتَرَىٰ عَلَى اللَّهِ
كَذِبًا أَوْ كَذَّبَ بِـَٔايَٰتِهِۦٓ ۚ إِنَّهُۥ لَا
يُفْلِحُ الْمُجْرِمُونَ ﴿١٧﴾

18. They serve, besides Allah, things that do not hurt them nor profit them, and they say:

18. Wa ya'budoona min doonil-laahi maa laa yaḍurruhum wa laa yanfa'uhum wa yaqooloona

وَيَعْبُدُونَ مِن دُونِ اللَّهِ مَا لَا
يَضُرُّهُمْ وَلَا يَنفَعُهُمْ وَيَقُولُونَ

Ikhfa اخفاء | Ghunna غُنّہ | Ikhfa Meem Saakin اخفاء میم ساکن | Idghaam ادغام | Qalqala قلقلہ | Qalb قلب | Idghaam Meem Saakin ادغام میم ساکن

"These are our intercessors with Allah." Say: "Do you indeed inform Allah of something He knows not, in the heavens or on earth?- Glory to Him! and far is He above the partners they ascribe (to Him)!"

haaa'ulaaa'i shufa'aaa'unaa 'indal-laah; qul atunabbi'oonal-laaha bimaa laa ya'lamu fis-samaawaati wa laa fil-arḍ; Subḥaanahoo wa Ta'aalaa 'ammaa yushrikoon.

هٰٓؤُلَآءِ شُفَعَآؤُنَا عِنْدَ اللّٰهِ ۗ قُلْ
اَتُنَبِّـُٔوْنَ اللّٰهَ بِمَا لَا يَعْلَمُ فِى
السَّمٰوٰتِ وَلَا فِى الْاَرْضِ ۗ سُبْحٰنَهٗ
وَتَعٰلٰى عَمَّا يُشْرِكُوْنَ ﴿١٨﴾

19. Mankind was but one nation, but differed (later). Had it not been for a word that went forth before from your Lord, their differences would have been settled between them.

19. Wa maa kaanan-naasu illaaa ummatañw-waaḥidatan fakhtalafoo; wa law laa kalimatun sabaqat mir-Rabbika laquḍiya baynahum feemaa feehi yakhtalifoon.

وَمَا كَانَ النَّاسُ اِلَّآ اُمَّةً وَّاحِدَةً
فَاخْتَلَفُوْا ۗ وَلَوْلَا كَلِمَةٌ سَبَقَتْ
مِنْ رَّبِّكَ لَقُضِىَ بَيْنَهُمْ فِيْمَا
فِيْهِ يَخْتَلِفُوْنَ ﴿١٩﴾

20. They say: "Why is not a Sign sent down to him from his Lord?" Say: "The Unseen is only for Allah (to know), Then wait you: I too will wait with you."

20. Wa yaqooloona law laaa unzila 'alayhi Aayatum-mir-Rabbihee faqul innamal-ghaybu lillaahi fantaẓiroo innee ma'akum minal-muntaẓireen.

(Section 2)

وَيَقُوْلُوْنَ لَوْلَآ اُنْزِلَ عَلَيْهِ اٰيَةٌ مِّنْ
رَّبِّهٖ ۚ فَقُلْ اِنَّمَا الْغَيْبُ لِلّٰهِ فَانْتَظِرُوْا ۚ
اِنِّىْ مَعَكُمْ مِّنَ الْمُنْتَظِرِيْنَ ﴿٢٠﴾ ع ٢ ١٠ ٧

21. When We make mankind taste of some mercy after adversity has touched them, behold! they take to plotting against Our Signs! Say: "Swifter to plan is Allah!" Verily, Our angels record all the plots that you make.

21. Wa izaaa azaqnan-naasa raḥmatam-mim ba'di ḍarraaa'a massat-hum izaa lahum makrun feee Aayaatinaa; qulil-laahu asra'u makraa; inna rusulanaa yaktuboona maa tamkuroon.

وَاِذَآ اَذَقْنَا النَّاسَ رَحْمَةً مِّنْۢ
بَعْدِ ضَرَّآءَ مَسَّتْهُمْ اِذَا لَهُمْ مَّكْرٌ فِىْٓ
اٰيَاتِنَا ۗ قُلِ اللّٰهُ اَسْرَعُ مَكْرًا ۗ
اِنَّ رُسُلَنَا يَكْتُبُوْنَ مَا تَمْكُرُوْنَ ﴿٢١﴾

22. He it is Who enables you to traverse through land and sea; so that you even board ships;- they sail with them with a favourable wind, and they rejoice thereat; then comes a stormy wind and the waves come to them from all sides, and they think they are being overwhelmed: they cry to Allah, sincerely offering (their) duty to Him saying, "If You deliver us from this, we shall truly show our gratitude!"

22. Huwal-lazee yusayyirukum fil-barri walbaḥri ḥattaaa izaa kuntum fil-fulki wa jarayna bihim bireeḥin ṭayyibatiñw-wa fariḥoo bihaa jaaa'at-haa reeḥun 'aaṣifuñw-wa jaaa'ahumul-mawju min kulli makaaniñw-wa ẓannooo annahum uḥeeṭa bihim da'awul-laaha mukhliṣeena lahud-deena la'in anjaytanaa min haazihee lanakoonanna minash-shaakireen.

هُوَ الَّذِىْ يُسَيِّرُكُمْ فِى الْبَرِّ وَ
الْبَحْرِ ۗ حَتّٰٓى اِذَا كُنْتُمْ فِى الْفُلْكِ ۚ
وَجَرَيْنَ بِهِمْ بِرِيْحٍ طَيِّبَةٍ وَّ
فَرِحُوْا بِهَا جَآءَتْهَا رِيْحٌ عَاصِفٌ
وَّجَآءَهُمُ الْمَوْجُ مِنْ كُلِّ مَكَانٍ
وَّظَنُّوْٓا اَنَّهُمْ اُحِيْطَ بِهِمْ ۙ دَعَوُا اللّٰهَ
مُخْلِصِيْنَ لَهُ الدِّيْنَ ۚ لَئِنْ اَنْجَيْتَنَا
مِنْ هٰذِهٖ لَنَكُوْنَنَّ مِنَ الشّٰكِرِيْنَ ﴿٢٢﴾

23. But when He delivers them, behold! they transgress insolently through the earth in defiance of right! O mankind! your insolence is against your own souls,- an enjoyment of the life of the present:

23. Falammaaa anjaahum izaa hum yabghoona fil-arḍi bighayril-ḥaqq; yaaa ayyuhan-naasu innamaa bagh-yukum 'alaaa anfusikum-mataa'al-ḥayaatid-dunyaa

فَلَمَّآ اَنْجٰىهُمْ اِذَا هُمْ يَبْغُوْنَ فِى الْاَرْضِ
بِغَيْرِ الْحَقِّ ۗ يٰٓاَيُّهَا النَّاسُ اِنَّمَا بَغْيُكُمْ
عَلٰٓى اَنْفُسِكُمْ ۙ مَّتَاعَ الْحَيٰوةِ الدُّنْيَا ۫

Ikhfa اخفاء | Ghunna غنّہ | Ikhfa Meem Saakin اخفاء میم ساکن | Idghaam ادغام | Qalqala قلقلہ | Qalb قلب | Idghaam Meem Saakin ادغام میم ساکن

in the end, to Us is your return, and We shall show you the truth of all that you did.

summa ilaynaa marji'ukum fanunabbi'ukum bimaa kuntum ta'maloon.

ثُمَّ إِلَيْنَا مَرْجِعُكُمْ فَنُنَبِّئُكُم بِمَا
كُنتُمْ تَعْمَلُونَ ﴿٢٣﴾

24. The likeness of the life of the Present is as the rain which We send down from the skies: by its mingling arises the produce of the earth- which provides food for men and animals: (It grows) till the earth is clad with its golden ornaments and is decked out (in beauty): the people to whom it belongs think they have all powers of disposal over it: there reaches it Our command by night or by day, and We make it like a harvest clean-mown, as if it had not flourished only the day before! Thus do We explain the Signs in detail for those who reflect.

24. Innamaa ma<u>s</u>alul-ḥayaatid-dunyaa kamaaa'in anzalnaahu minas-samaaa'i fakhtalaṭa bihee nabaatul-arḍi mimmaa yaåkulun-naasu wal-an'aam; ḥattaaa i<u>z</u>aaa akha<u>z</u>atil-arḍu zukhrufahaa wazzayyanat wa ẓanna ahluhaaa annahum qaadiroona 'alayhaaa ataahaaa amrunaa laylan aw nahaaran faja'alnaahaa ḥaṣeedan ka-al-lam taghna bil-ams; ka<u>z</u>aalika nufaṣṣilul-Aayaati liqawmiñy-yatafakkaroon.

إِنَّمَا مَثَلُ الْحَيٰوةِ الدُّنْيَا كَمَآءٍ
أَنزَلْنٰهُ مِنَ السَّمَآءِ فَاخْتَلَطَ بِهِ
نَبَاتُ الْأَرْضِ مِمَّا يَأْكُلُ النَّاسُ وَ
الْأَنْعَامُ ۖ حَتّٰىٓ إِذَآ أَخَذَتِ الْأَرْضُ
زُخْرُفَهَا وَازَّيَّنَتْ وَظَنَّ أَهْلُهَآ
أَنَّهُمْ قٰدِرُونَ عَلَيْهَآ ۙ أَتٰىهَآ أَمْرُنَا
لَيْلًا أَوْ نَهَارًا فَجَعَلْنٰهَا حَصِيدًا
كَأَن لَّمْ تَغْنَ بِالْأَمْسِ ۚ كَذٰلِكَ
نُفَصِّلُ الْاٰيٰتِ لِقَوْمٍ يَتَفَكَّرُونَ ﴿٢٤﴾

25. But Allah calls to the Home of Peace: He guides those whom He pleases to a Way that is straight.

25. Wallaahu yad'ooo ilaa daaris-salaami wa yahdee mañy-yashaaa'u ilaa Ṣiraaṭim-Mustaqeem.

وَاللّٰهُ يَدْعُوٓا إِلٰى دَارِ السَّلٰمِ ۖ وَيَهْدِي
مَن يَشَآءُ إِلٰى صِرٰطٍ مُّسْتَقِيمٍ ﴿٢٥﴾

26. To those who do right is a goodly (reward)- Yes, more (than in measure)! No darkness nor shame shall cover their faces! They are companions of the Garden; they will abide therein (for ever).

26. Lillazeena aḥsanul-ḥusnaa wa ziyaadahtuñw wa laa yarhaqu wujoohahum qataruñw-wa laa <u>z</u>illah; ulaaa'ika Aṣḥaabul-jannati hum feehaa khaalidoon.

لِلَّذِينَ أَحْسَنُوا الْحُسْنٰى وَزِيَادَةٌ ۖ وَلَا
يَرْهَقُ وُجُوهَهُمْ قَتَرٌ وَلَا ذِلَّةٌ ۚ أُولٰٓئِكَ
أَصْحٰبُ الْجَنَّةِ ۖ هُمْ فِيهَا خٰلِدُونَ ﴿٢٦﴾

27. But those who have earned evil will have a reward of like evil: ignominy will cover their (faces): no defender will they have from (the wrath of) Allah: their faces will be covered, as it were, with pieces from the depths of the darkness of Night : they are Companions of the Fire: they will abide therein (for ever)!

27. Walla<u>z</u>eena kasabus-sayyi-aati jazaaa'u sayyi'atim bimi<u>s</u>lihaa wa tarhaquhum <u>z</u>illah; maa lahum minal-laahi min 'aaṣimin ka-annamaa ughshiyat wujoohuhum qiṭa-'am-minal-layli muẓlimaa; ulaaa'ika Aṣḥaabun-Naari hum feeha khaalidoon.

وَالَّذِينَ كَسَبُوا السَّيِّـَٔاتِ جَزَآءُ
سَيِّئَةٍۭ بِمِثْلِهَا وَتَرْهَقُهُمْ ذِلَّةٌ ۖ
مَّا لَهُم مِّنَ اللّٰهِ مِنْ عَاصِمٍ ۖ كَأَنَّمَآ
أُغْشِيَتْ وُجُوهُهُمْ قِطَعًا مِّنَ الَّيْلِ
مُظْلِمًا ۚ أُولٰٓئِكَ أَصْحٰبُ النَّارِ ۖ
هُمْ فِيهَا خٰلِدُونَ ﴿٢٧﴾

28. One Day We shall gather them all together. Then We shall say to those who joined gods (with Us): "To your place! you and those you joined as 'partners' We shall separate them, and their "Partners" shall say: "It was not us that you worshipped!

28. Wa Yawma naḥshuruhum jamee'an summa naqoolu lilla<u>z</u>eena ashrakoo makaanakum antum wa shurakaaa'ukum; fazayyalnaa baynahum wa qaala shurakaaa'uhum maa kuntum iyyaanaa ta'budoon.

وَيَوْمَ نَحْشُرُهُمْ جَمِيعًا ثُمَّ نَقُولُ
لِلَّذِينَ أَشْرَكُوا مَكَانَكُمْ أَنتُمْ وَ
شُرَكَآؤُكُمْ ۚ فَزَيَّلْنَا بَيْنَهُمْ ۖ وَقَالَ
شُرَكَآؤُهُم مَّا كُنتُمْ إِيَّانَا تَعْبُدُونَ ﴿٢٨﴾

Ikhfa اخفاء | Ghunna غُنّہ | Ikhfa Meem Saakin اخفاء میم ساکن | Idghaam ادغام | Qalqala قلقلہ | Qalb قلب | Idghaam Meem Saakin ادغام میم ساکن

29. "Enough is Allah for a witness between us and you: we certainly knew nothing of your worship of us!"

29. Fakafaa billaahi shaheedam-baynanaa wa baynakum in kunnaa 'an 'ibaadatikum laghaafileen.

فَكَفٰى بِاللّٰهِ شَهِيْدًا ۢ بَيْنَنَا وَبَيْنَكُمْ
اِنْ كُنَّا عَنْ عِبَادَتِكُمْ لَغٰفِلِيْنَ ﴿٢٩﴾

30. There will every soul prove (the fruits of) the deeds it sent before: they will be brought back to Allah their rightful Lord, and their invented falsehoods will leave them in the lurch.

30. Hunaalika tabloo kullu nafsim-maaa aslafat; wa ruddooo ilal-laahi mawlaahumul-ḥaqqi wa ḍalla 'anhum maa kaanoo yaftaroon. **(Section 3)**

هُنَالِكَ تَبْلُوْا كُلُّ نَفْسٍ مَّآ اَسْلَفَتْ
وَرُدُّوْٓا اِلَى اللّٰهِ مَوْلٰىهُمُ الْحَقِّ وَضَلَّ
عَنْهُمْ مَّا كَانُوْا يَفْتَرُوْنَ ﴿٣٠﴾ ع

النصف

31. Say: "Who is it that sustains you (in life) from the sky and from the earth? Or who is it that has power over hearing and sight? And who is it that brings out the living from the dead and the dead from the living? And who is it that rules and regulates all affairs?" They will soon say, "Allah". Say, "Will you not then show piety (to Him)?"

31. Qul mañy-yarzuqukum minas-samaaa'i wal-arḍi ammañy-yamlikus-sam'a wal-abṣaara wa mañy-yukhrijul-ḥayya minal-mayyiti wa yukhrijul-mayyita minal-ḥayyi wa mañy-yudabbirul-amr; fasayaqooloonal-laah; faqul afalaa tattaqoon.

قُلْ مَنْ يَّرْزُقُكُمْ مِّنَ السَّمَآءِ وَ
الْاَرْضِ اَمَّنْ يَّمْلِكُ السَّمْعَ
وَالْاَبْصَارَ وَمَنْ يُّخْرِجُ الْحَيَّ
مِنَ الْمَيِّتِ وَيُخْرِجُ الْمَيِّتَ مِنَ
الْحَيِّ وَمَنْ يُّدَبِّرُ الْاَمْرَ ؕ فَسَيَقُوْلُوْنَ
اللّٰهُ ۚ فَقُلْ اَفَلَا تَتَّقُوْنَ ﴿٣١﴾

32. Such is Allah, your real cherisher and sustainer; apart from Truth, what (remains) but error? How then are you turned away?

32. Fazaalikumul-laahu Rabbukumul-ḥaqq; famaazaa ba'dal-ḥaqqi illaḍ-ḍalaalu fa-annaa tuṣrafoon.

فَذٰلِكُمُ اللّٰهُ رَبُّكُمُ الْحَقُّ ۚ فَمَاذَا بَعْدَ
الْحَقِّ اِلَّا الضَّلٰلُ ۚۖ فَاَنّٰى تُصْرَفُوْنَ ﴿٣٢﴾

33. Thus is the Word of your Lord proved true against those who rebel: verily they will not believe.

33. Kazaalika ḥaqqat Kalimatu Rabbika 'alal-lazeena fasaqooo annahum laa yu'minoon.

كَذٰلِكَ حَقَّتْ كَلِمَتُ رَبِّكَ عَلَى
الَّذِيْنَ فَسَقُوْٓا اَنَّهُمْ لَا يُؤْمِنُوْنَ ﴿٣٣﴾

34. Say: "Of your 'partners', can any originate creation and repeat it?" Say: "It is Allah Who originates creation and repeats it: then how are you deluded away (from the truth)?"

34. Qul hal min shurakaaa'ikum mañy-yabda'ul-khalqa summa yu'eeduh; qulil-laahu yabda'ul-khalqa summa yu'eeduhoo fa-annaa tu'fakoon.

قُلْ هَلْ مِنْ شُرَكَآئِكُمْ مَّنْ يَّبْدَؤُا
الْخَلْقَ ثُمَّ يُعِيْدُهٗ ؕ قُلِ اللّٰهُ
يَبْدَؤُا الْخَلْقَ ثُمَّ يُعِيْدُهٗ فَاَنّٰى
تُؤْفَكُوْنَ ﴿٣٤﴾

35. Say: "Of your 'partners' is there any that can give any guidance towards Truth?" Say: "It is Allah Who gives guidance towards Truth. Is then He Who gives guidance to truth more worthy to be followed, or he who finds not guidance (himself) unless he is guided? what then is the matter with you? How do you judge.

35. Qul hal min shurakaaa'ikum mañy-yahdeee ilal-ḥaqq; qulil-laahu yahdee lilḥaqq; afamañy-yahdeee ilal-ḥaqqi aḥaqqu añy-yuttaba'a ammal-laa yahiddeee illaaa añy-yuhdaa famaa lakum kayfa taḥkumoon.

قُلْ هَلْ مِنْ شُرَكَآئِكُمْ مَّنْ يَّهْدِيْٓ
اِلَى الْحَقِّ ؕ قُلِ اللّٰهُ يَهْدِيْ لِلْحَقِّ ؕ
اَفَمَنْ يَّهْدِيْٓ اِلَى الْحَقِّ اَحَقُّ اَنْ
يُّتَّبَعَ اَمَّنْ لَّا يَهِدِّيْٓ اِلَّآ اَنْ
يُّهْدٰى ۚ فَمَا لَكُمْ ۟ كَيْفَ تَحْكُمُوْنَ ﴿٣٥﴾

36. But most of them follow nothing but conjecture: truly conjecture can be of no avail against Truth.

36. Wa maa yattabi'u aksaruhum illaa ẓannaa; innaẓ-ẓanna laa yughnee minal-ḥaqqi shay'aa;

وَمَا يَتَّبِعُ اَكْثَرُهُمْ اِلَّا ظَنًّا ؕ اِنَّ
الظَّنَّ لَا يُغْنِيْ مِنَ الْحَقِّ شَيْـًٔا ؕ

Ikhfa اخفاء | Ghunna غنّہ | Ikhfa Meem Saakin اخفاء میم ساکن | Idghaam ادغام | Qalqala قلقلہ | Qalb قلب | Idghaam Meem Saakin ادغام میم ساکن

Verily Allah is well aware of all that they do.

innal-laaha 'Aleemum bimaa yaf'aloon.

اِنَّ اللّٰهَ عَلِيْمٌۢ بِمَا يَفْعَلُوْنَ ﴿٣٦﴾

37. This Qur'an is not such as can be produced by other than Allah; on the contrary it is a confirmation of (revelations) that went before it, and a fuller explanation of the Book - wherein there is no doubt - from the Lord of the Worlds.

37. Wa maa kaana haazal-Quraanu añy-yuftaraa min doonil-laahi wa laakin taṣdeeqal-lazee bayna yadayhi wa tafṣeelal-Kitaabi laa rayba feehi mir-Rabbil-'aalameen.

وَمَا كَانَ هٰذَا الْقُرْاٰنُ اَنْ يُّفْتَرٰى
مِنْ دُوْنِ اللّٰهِ وَلٰكِنْ تَصْدِيْقَ
الَّذِيْ بَيْنَ يَدَيْهِ وَتَفْصِيْلَ
الْكِتٰبِ لَا رَيْبَ فِيْهِ مِنْ رَّبِّ
الْعٰلَمِيْنَ ﴿٣٧﴾

38. Or do they say, "He forged it"? Say: "Bring then a Sura like it, and call (to your aid) anyone you can, besides Allah, if it be you speak the truth!"

38. Am yaqooloonaf-taraahu qul faåtoo bisooratim-mislihee wad'oo manis-taṭa'tum-min doonil-laahi in kuntum ṣaadiqeen.

اَمْ يَقُوْلُوْنَ افْتَرٰىهُ ؕ قُلْ فَاْتُوْا
بِسُوْرَةٍ مِّثْلِهٖ وَادْعُوْا مَنِ اسْتَطَعْتُمْ
مِّنْ دُوْنِ اللّٰهِ اِنْ كُنْتُمْ صٰدِقِيْنَ ﴿٣٨﴾

39. Nay, they charge with falsehood that whose knowledge they cannot compass, even before the elucidation thereof has reached them: thus did those before them make charges of falsehood: but see what was the end of those who did wrong!

39. Bal kazzaboo bimaa lam yuḥeeṭoo bi'ilmihee wa lammaa yaåtihim taåweeluh; kazaalika kazzabal-lazeena min qablihim fanẓur kayfa kaana 'aaqibatuẓ-ẓaalimeen.

بَلْ كَذَّبُوْا بِمَا لَمْ يُحِيْطُوْا بِعِلْمِهٖ
وَلَمَّا يَاْتِهِمْ تَاْوِيْلُهٗ ؕ كَذٰلِكَ كَذَّبَ
الَّذِيْنَ مِنْ قَبْلِهِمْ فَانْظُرْ كَيْفَ
كَانَ عَاقِبَةُ الظّٰلِمِيْنَ ﴿٣٩﴾

40. Of them there are some who believe therein, and some who do not: and your Lord knows best those who are out for mischief.

40. Wa minhum-mañy-yu'minu bihee wa minhum-mal-laa yu'minu bih; wa Rabbuka a'lamu bilmufsideen. **(Section 4)**

وَمِنْهُمْ مَّنْ يُّؤْمِنُ بِهٖ وَمِنْهُمْ
مَّنْ لَّا يُؤْمِنُ بِهٖ ؕ وَرَبُّكَ اَعْلَمُ
بِالْمُفْسِدِيْنَ ﴿٤٠﴾ ع

41. If they charge you with falsehood, say: "My work to me, and yours to you! you are free from responsibility for what I do, and I for what you do!"

41. Wa in kazzabooka faqul lee 'amalee wa lakum 'amalukum antum bareee'oona mimmaa a'malu wa ana bareee'um-mimmaa ta'maloon.

وَاِنْ كَذَّبُوْكَ فَقُلْ لِّيْ عَمَلِيْ وَلَكُمْ
عَمَلُكُمْ ۚ اَنْتُمْ بَرِيْٓـُٔوْنَ مِمَّاۤ اَعْمَلُ
وَاَنَا بَرِيْٓءٌ مِّمَّا تَعْمَلُوْنَ ﴿٤١﴾

42. Among them are some who (pretend to) listen to you: but can you make the deaf to hear,- even though they are without understanding?

42. Wa minhum-mañy-yastami-'oona ilayk; afa-anta tusmi'uṣ-ṣumma wa law kaanoo laa ya'qiloon.

وَمِنْهُمْ مَّنْ يَّسْتَمِعُوْنَ اِلَيْكَ ؕ
اَفَاَنْتَ تُسْمِعُ الصُّمَّ وَلَوْ كَانُوْا
لَا يَعْقِلُوْنَ ﴿٤٢﴾

43. And among them are some who look at you: but can you guide the blind,- even though they will not see?

43. Wa minhum mañy-yanẓuru ilayk; afa-anta tahdil-'umya wa law kaanoo laa yubṣiroon.

وَمِنْهُمْ مَّنْ يَّنْظُرُ اِلَيْكَ ؕ
اَفَاَنْتَ تَهْدِي الْعُمْيَ وَلَوْ كَانُوْا
لَا يُبْصِرُوْنَ ﴿٤٣﴾

44. Verily Allah will not deal unjustly with man in anything:

44. Innal-laaha laa yaẓlimun-naasa shay'añw-

اِنَّ اللّٰهَ لَا يَظْلِمُ النَّاسَ شَيْـًٔا

Ikhfa اخفاء | Ghunna غُنّہ | Ikhfa Meem Saakin اخفاء میم ساکن | Idghaam ادغام | Qalqala قلقلہ | Qalb قلب | Idghaam Meem Saakin ادغام میم ساکن

It is man that wrongs his own soul.

45. One day He will gather them together: (It will be) as if they had tarried but an hour of a day: they will recognise each other: assuredly those will be lost who denied the meeting with Allah and refused to receive true guidance.

46. Whether We show you (realized in your life-time) some part of what We promise them,- or We take your soul (to Our Mercy) (before that),- in any case, to Us is their return: ultimately Allah is Witness to all that they do.

47. To every people (was sent) an Apostle: when their Apostle comes (before them), the matter will be judged between them with justice, and they will not be wronged.

48. They say: "When will this promise come to pass,- if you speak the truth?"

49. Say: "I have no power over any harm or profit to myself except as Allah wills. To every people is a term appointed: when their term is reached, not an hour can they cause delay, nor (an hour) can they advance (it in antici-pation)."

50. Say: "Do you see,- if His punishment should come to you by night or by day,- what portion of it would the Sinners wish to hasten?

51. "Would you then believe in it at last, when it actually comes to pass? (It will then be said): 'Ah! now? and you wanted (aforetime) to hasten it on!'

52. "At length will be said to the wrong-doers: 'you taste the enduring punishment! You get but the recompense of what you earned!'"

wa laakin-nannaasa anfusahum yaẕlimoon.

45. Wa Yawma yaḥshuruhum ka-al-lam yalbasooo illaa saa'atam-minan-nahaari yata'aarafoona baynahum; qad khasiral-lazeena kazzaboo biliqaaa'il-laahi wa maa kaanoo muhtadeen.

46. Wa imma nuriyannaka ba'ḍal-lazee na'iduhum aw natawaffayannaka fa-ilaynaa marji'uhum summal-laahu shaheedun 'alaa maa yaf'aloon.

47. Wa likulli ummatir-Rasoolun fa-izaa jaaa'a Rasooluhum quḍiya baynahum bilqisṭi wa hum laa yuẕlamoon.

48. Wa yaqooloona mataa haazal-wa'du in kuntum ṣaadiqeen.

49. Qul laaa amliku linafsee ḍarrañw-wa laa naf'an illaa maa shaaa'al-laah; likulli ummatin ajalun izaa jaaa'a ajaluhum falaaa yastaåkhiroona saa'atañw-wa laa yastaqdimoon.

50. Qul ara'aytum in ataakum 'azaabuhoo bayaatan aw nahaaram-maazaa yasta'jilu minhul-mujrimoon.

51. Asumma izaa maa waqa'a aamantum bih; aal'aana wa qad kuntum bihee tasta'jiloon.

52. Summa qeela lillazeena ẕalamoo zooqoo 'azaabal-khuld, hal tujzawna illaa bimaa kuntum taksiboon.

وَلٰكِنَّ النَّاسَ اَنْفُسَهُمْ يَظْلِمُوْنَ ﴿٤٤﴾
وَيَوْمَ يَحْشُرُهُمْ كَاَنْ لَّمْ يَلْبَثُوْٓا
اِلَّا سَاعَةً مِّنَ النَّهَارِ يَتَعَارَفُوْنَ
بَيْنَهُمْ ؕ قَدْ خَسِرَ الَّذِيْنَ كَذَّبُوْا
بِلِقَآءِ اللّٰهِ وَمَا كَانُوْا مُهْتَدِيْنَ ﴿٤٥﴾
وَاِمَّا نُرِيَنَّكَ بَعْضَ الَّذِيْ نَعِدُهُمْ
اَوْ نَتَوَفَّيَنَّكَ فَاِلَيْنَا مَرْجِعُهُمْ ثُمَّ
اللّٰهُ شَهِيْدٌ عَلٰى مَا يَفْعَلُوْنَ ﴿٤٦﴾
وَلِكُلِّ اُمَّةٍ رَّسُوْلٌ ۚ فَاِذَا جَآءَ
رَسُوْلُهُمْ قُضِيَ بَيْنَهُمْ بِالْقِسْطِ
وَهُمْ لَا يُظْلَمُوْنَ ﴿٤٧﴾
وَيَقُوْلُوْنَ مَتٰى هٰذَا الْوَعْدُ اِنْ
كُنْتُمْ صٰدِقِيْنَ ﴿٤٨﴾
قُلْ لَّآ اَمْلِكُ لِنَفْسِيْ ضَرًّا
وَّلَا نَفْعًا اِلَّا مَا شَآءَ اللّٰهُ ؕ لِكُلِّ
اُمَّةٍ اَجَلٌ ؕ اِذَا جَآءَ اَجَلُهُمْ
فَلَا يَسْتَاْخِرُوْنَ سَاعَةً وَّلَا
يَسْتَقْدِمُوْنَ ﴿٤٩﴾
قُلْ اَرَءَيْتُمْ اِنْ اَتٰىكُمْ عَذَابُهٗ
بَيَاتًا اَوْ نَهَارًا مَّاذَا يَسْتَعْجِلُ
مِنْهُ الْمُجْرِمُوْنَ ﴿٥٠﴾
اَثُمَّ اِذَا مَا وَقَعَ اٰمَنْتُمْ بِهٖ ؕ آٰلْـٰٔنَ
وَقَدْ كُنْتُمْ بِهٖ تَسْتَعْجِلُوْنَ ﴿٥١﴾
ثُمَّ قِيْلَ لِلَّذِيْنَ ظَلَمُوْا ذُوْقُوْا
عَذَابَ الْخُلْدِ ۚ هَلْ تُجْزَوْنَ اِلَّا
بِمَا كُنْتُمْ تَكْسِبُوْنَ ﴿٥٢﴾

Ikhfa اخفاء | Ghunna غُنّہ | Ikhfa Meem Saakin اخفاء میم ساکن | Idghaam ادغام | Qalqala قلقلہ | Qalb قلب | Idghaam Meem Saakin ادغام میم ساکن

English	Transliteration	Arabic
53. They seek to be informed by you: "Is that true?" Say: "Yes, by my Lord! it is the very truth and you cannot frustrat it!"	53. Wa yastambi'oonaka aḥaqqun huwa qul ee wa Rabbeee innahoo laḥaqq; wa maaa antum bimu'jizeen. **(Section 5)**	وَيَسْتَنْۢبِـُٔوْنَكَ اَحَقٌّ هُوَ ۭ قُلْ اِيْ وَرَبِّيْٓ اِنَّهٗ لَحَقٌّ ۚ وَمَآ اَنْتُمْ بِمُعْجِزِيْنَ ۝٥٣
54. Every soul that has sinned, if it possessed all that is on earth, would fain give it in ransom: they would declare (their) repentance when they see the Chastisement: but the judgment between them will be with justice, and no wrong will be done to them.	54. Wa law anna likulli nafsin ẓalamat maa fil-arḍi laftadat bih; wa asarrun-nadaamata lammaa ra-awul-'azaab, wa quḍiya baynahum bilqisṭ; wa hum laa yuẓlamoon.	وَلَوْ اَنَّ لِكُلِّ نَفْسٍ ظَلَمَتْ مَا فِي الْاَرْضِ لَافْتَدَتْ بِهٖ ۭ وَاَسَرُّوا النَّدَامَةَ لَمَّا رَاَوُا الْعَذَابَ ۚ وَقُضِيَ بَيْنَهُمْ بِالْقِسْطِ وَهُمْ لَا يُظْلَمُوْنَ ۝٥٤
55. Is it not (the case) that to Allah belongs whatever is in the heavens and on earth? Is it not (the case) that Allah's promise is assuredly true? Yet most of them understand do not.	55. Alaaa inna lillaahi maa fis-samaawaati wal-arḍ; alaaa inna wa'dal-laahi ḥaqquñw-wa laakinna aksarahum laa ya'lamoon.	اَلَآ اِنَّ لِلّٰهِ مَا فِي السَّمٰوٰتِ وَالْاَرْضِ ۭ اَلَآ اِنَّ وَعْدَ اللّٰهِ حَقٌّ وَّلٰكِنَّ اَكْثَرَهُمْ لَا يَعْلَمُوْنَ ۝٥٥
56. It is He Who gives life and who takes it, and to Him shall you all be brought back.	56. Huwa yuḥyee wa yumeetu wa ilayhi turja'oon.	هُوَ يُحْيٖ وَيُمِيْتُ وَاِلَيْهِ تُرْجَعُوْنَ ۝٥٦
57. O mankind! there has come to you a direction from your Lord and a healing for the (diseases) in your hearts,- and for those who believe, a Guidance and a Mercy.	57. Yaaa ayyuhan-naasu qad jaaa'atkum-maw'iẓatum-mir-Rabbikum wa shifaaa'ul-limaa fiṣ-ṣudoori wa hudañw-wa raḥmatul-lilmu'mineen.	يٰٓاَيُّهَا النَّاسُ قَدْ جَاۗءَتْكُمْ مَّوْعِظَةٌ مِّنْ رَّبِّكُمْ وَشِفَاۗءٌ لِّمَا فِي الصُّدُوْرِ ۥ وَهُدًى وَّرَحْمَةٌ لِّلْمُؤْمِنِيْنَ ۝٥٧
58. Say: "In the Bounty of Allah, and in His Mercy,- in that let them rejoice": that is better than the (wealth) they hoard.	58. Qul bifaḍlil-laahi wa biraḥmatihee fabizaalika falyafraḥoo huwa khayrum-mimmaa yajma'oon.	قُلْ بِفَضْلِ اللّٰهِ وَبِرَحْمَتِهٖ فَبِذٰلِكَ فَلْيَفْرَحُوْا ۭ هُوَ خَيْرٌ مِّمَّا يَجْمَعُوْنَ ۝٥٨
59. Say: "Do you see what things Allah has sent down to you for sustenance? Yet you hold forbidden some things thereof and (some things) lawful." Say: "Has Allah indeed permitted you, or do you invent (things) to attribute to Allah?"	59. Qul ara'aytum-maaa anzalal-laahu lakum-mir-rizqin faja'altum-minhu ḥaraamañw-wa ḥalaalan qul aaallaahu azina lakum am 'alal-laahi taftaroon.	قُلْ اَرَءَيْتُمْ مَّآ اَنْزَلَ اللّٰهُ لَكُمْ مِّنْ رِّزْقٍ فَجَعَلْتُمْ مِّنْهُ حَرَامًا وَّحَلٰلًا ۭ قُلْ اٰۗللّٰهُ اَذِنَ لَكُمْ اَمْ عَلَي اللّٰهِ تَفْتَرُوْنَ ۝٥٩
60. And what do those think who invent lies against Allah, of the Day of Judgment? Verily Allah is full of Bounty to mankind, but most of them are ungrateful.	60. Wa maa ẓannul-lazeena yaftaroona 'alal-laahil-kaziba Yawmal-Qiyaamah; innal-laaha lazoo faḍlin 'alan-naasi wa laakinna aksarahum laa yashkuroon. **(Section 6)**	وَمَا ظَنُّ الَّذِيْنَ يَفْتَرُوْنَ عَلَي اللّٰهِ الْكَذِبَ يَوْمَ الْقِيٰمَةِ ۭ اِنَّ اللّٰهَ لَذُوْ فَضْلٍ عَلَي النَّاسِ وَلٰكِنَّ اَكْثَرَهُمْ لَا يَشْكُرُوْنَ ۝٦٠
61. In whatever business you may be, and whatever portion you may be reciting	61. Wa maa takoonu fee shaaniñw-wa maa tatloo	وَمَا تَكُوْنُ فِيْ شَاْنٍ وَّمَا تَتْلُوْا

Ikhfa اخفاء · Ghunna غُنّہ · Ikhfa Meem Saakin اخفاء میم ساکن · Idghaam ادغام · Qalqala قلقلہ · Qalb قلب · Idghaam Meem Saakin ادغام میم ساکن

from the Qur'an,- and whatever deed you (mankind) may be doing,- We are Witnesses thereof when you are deeply engrossed therein. Nor is hidden from your Lord (so much as) the weight of an atom on the earth or in heaven. And not the least and not the greatest of these things but are recorded in a clear Record.

62. Behold! verily on the friends of Allah there is no fear, nor shall they grieve;

63. Those who believe and (constantly) guard against evil;-

64. For them are Glad Tidings, in the life of the Present and in the Hereafter; no change can there be in the Words of Allah. This is indeed the supreme felicity.

65. Let not their speech grieve you: for all power and honour belong to Allah: It is He Who hears and knows (all things).

66. Behold! verily to Allah belong all creatures, in the heavens and on earth. What do they follow who worship as His "partners" other than Allah? They follow nothing but fancy, and they do nothing but lie.

67. He it is that has made for you the Night that you may rest therein, and the Day to make things visible (to you). Verily in this are Signs for those who listen (to His Message).

68. They say: "God (Alalh) has begotten a son!" - Glory be to Him! He is self- sufficient! His are all things in the heavens and on earth! No warrant have you

minhu min Qur-aaniñw-wa laa ta'maloona min 'amalin illaa kunnaa 'alaykum shuhoodan iz̲ tufeeḍoona feeh; wa maa ya'zubu 'ar-Rabbika mim-mis̲-qaali z̲arratin fil-arḍi wa laa fis-samaaa'i wa laaa aṣghara min z̲aalika wa laaa akbara illaa fee Kitaabim-Mubeen.

62. Alaaa inna awliyaaa'al-laahi laa khawfun 'alayhim wa laa hum yaḥzanoon.

63. Allaz̲eena aamanoo wa kaanoo yattaqoon.

64. Lahumul-bushraa filḥa-yaatid-dunyaa wa fil Aakhirah; laa tabdeela likalimaatil-laah; z̲aalika huwal-fawzul-'aẓeem.

65. Wa laa yaḥzunka qawlu-hum; innal-'izzata lillaahi jamee'aa; Huwas-Samee'ul-'Aleem.

66. Alaaa inna lillaahi man fis-samaawaati wa man fil-arḍ; wa maa yattabi'ul-laz̲eena yad'oona min doonil-laahi shurakaaa'; iñy-yattabi'oona illaẓ-ẓanna wa in hum illaa yakhruṣoon.

67. Huwal-laz̲ee ja'ala laku-mul-layla litaskunoo feehi wannahaara mubṣiraa; inna fee z̲aalika la-Aayaatil-liqawmiñy-yasma'oon.

68. Qaalut-takhaz̲al-laahu waladan Subḥaanahoo Huwal-Ghaniyyu lahoo maa fis-samaawaati wa maa fil-arḍ; in 'indakum-min

مِنْهُ مِنْ قُرْاٰنٍ وَّلَا تَعْمَلُوْنَ مِنْ
عَمَلٍ اِلَّا كُنَّا عَلَيْكُمْ شُهُوْدًا
اِذْ تُفِيْضُوْنَ فِيْهِ ؕ وَمَا يَعْزُبُ
عَنْ رَّبِّكَ مِنْ مِّثْقَالِ ذَرَّةٍ فِي
الْاَرْضِ وَلَا فِي السَّمَآءِ وَلَآ اَصْغَرَ
مِنْ ذٰلِكَ وَلَآ اَكْبَرَ اِلَّا فِيْ
كِتٰبٍ مُّبِيْنٍ ﴿٦١﴾
اَلَآ اِنَّ اَوْلِيَآءَ اللّٰهِ لَا خَوْفٌ
عَلَيْهِمْ وَلَا هُمْ يَحْزَنُوْنَ ﴿٦٢﴾
اَلَّذِيْنَ اٰمَنُوْا وَكَانُوْا يَتَّقُوْنَ ﴿٦٣﴾
لَهُمُ الْبُشْرٰى فِي الْحَيٰوةِ الدُّنْيَا
وَفِي الْاٰخِرَةِ ؕ لَا تَبْدِيْلَ لِكَلِمٰتِ
اللّٰهِ ؕ ذٰلِكَ هُوَ الْفَوْزُ الْعَظِيْمُ ﴿٦٤﴾
وَلَا يَحْزُنْكَ قَوْلُهُمْ ۘ اِنَّ الْعِزَّةَ وقف لازم
لِلّٰهِ جَمِيْعًا ؕ هُوَ السَّمِيْعُ الْعَلِيْمُ ﴿٦٥﴾
اَلَآ اِنَّ لِلّٰهِ مَنْ فِي السَّمٰوٰتِ وَمَنْ
فِي الْاَرْضِ ؕ وَمَا يَتَّبِعُ الَّذِيْنَ
يَدْعُوْنَ مِنْ دُوْنِ اللّٰهِ شُرَكَآءَ ؕ
اِنْ يَّتَّبِعُوْنَ اِلَّا الظَّنَّ وَاِنْ هُمْ
اِلَّا يَخْرُصُوْنَ ﴿٦٦﴾
هُوَ الَّذِيْ جَعَلَ لَكُمُ الَّيْلَ لِتَسْكُنُوْا
فِيْهِ وَالنَّهَارَ مُبْصِرًا ؕ اِنَّ
فِيْ ذٰلِكَ لَاٰيٰتٍ لِّقَوْمٍ يَّسْمَعُوْنَ ﴿٦٧﴾
قَالُوا اتَّخَذَ اللّٰهُ وَلَدًا سُبْحٰنَهٗ ؕ
هُوَ الْغَنِيُّ ؕ لَهٗ مَا فِي السَّمٰوٰتِ
وَمَا فِي الْاَرْضِ ؕ اِنْ عِنْدَكُمْ مِّنْ

Ikhfa اخفاء | Ghunna غُنّہ | Ikhfa Meem Saakin اخفاء میم ساکن | Idghaam ادغام | Qalqala قلقلہ | Qalb قلب | Idghaam Meem Saakin ادغام میم ساکن

for this! Do you say about Allah what you do you know?

sulṭaanim bihaaẕaaa; ataqoo-loona 'alal-laahi maa laa ta'lamoon.

سُلْطٰنٍۢ بِهٰذَا ؕ اَتَقُوْلُوْنَ عَلَى
اللّٰهِ مَا لَا تَعْلَمُوْنَ ﴿٦٨﴾

69. Say: "Those who invent a lie against Allah will never prosper."

69. Qul innal-laẕeena yafta-roona 'alal-laahil-kaẕiba laa yufliḥoon.

قُلْ اِنَّ الَّذِيْنَ يَفْتَرُوْنَ عَلَى
اللّٰهِ الْكَذِبَ لَا يُفْلِحُوْنَ ﴿٦٩﴾ؕ

70. A little enjoyment in this world!- and then, to Us will be their return, then shall We make them taste the severest Chastisement for their blasphemies.

70. Mataa'un fid-dunyaa summa ilaynaa marji'uhum summa nuẕeequhumul-'aẕaabash-shadeeda bimaa kaanoo yakfuroon. **(Section 7)**

مَتَاعٌ فِى الدُّنْيَا ثُمَّ اِلَيْنَا مَرْجِعُهُمْ
ثُمَّ نُذِيْقُهُمُ الْعَذَابَ الشَّدِيْدَ بِمَا
كَانُوْا يَكْفُرُوْنَ ﴿٧٠﴾

وقف لازم

71. Relate to them the story of Noah. Behold! he said to his people: "O my people, if it be hard on your (mind) that I should stay (with you) and commemorate the Signs of Allah,- yet I put my trust in Allah. You then get an agreement about your plan and among your partners, so your plan be not to you dark and dubious. Then pass your sentence on me, and give me no respite.

71. Watlu 'alayhim naba-a Nooḥin iẕ qaala liqawmihee yaa qawmi in kaana kabura 'alaykum-maqaamee wa taẕkeeree bi-Aayaatil-laahi fa'alal-laahi tawakkaltu fa-ajmi'ooo amrakum wa shura-kaaa'akum summa laa yakun amrukum 'alaykum ghumma-tan summaq-ḍooo ilayya wa laa tunẕiroon.

وَاتْلُ عَلَيْهِمْ نَبَاَ نُوْحٍ ۘ اِذْ قَالَ
لِقَوْمِهٖ يٰقَوْمِ اِنْ كَانَ كَبُرَ عَلَيْكُمْ
مَّقَامِىْ وَتَذْكِيْرِىْ بِاٰيٰتِ اللّٰهِ
فَعَلَى اللّٰهِ تَوَكَّلْتُ فَاَجْمِعُوْٓا اَمْرَكُمْ
وَشُرَكَآءَكُمْ ثُمَّ لَا يَكُنْ اَمْرُكُمْ
عَلَيْكُمْ غُمَّةً ثُمَّ اقْضُوْٓا اِلَىَّ
وَلَا تُنْظِرُوْنِ ﴿٧١﴾

72. "But if you turn back, (consider): no reward have I asked of you: my reward is only due from Allah, and I have been commanded to be of those who submit to Allah's Will (in Islam)."

72. Fa-in tawallaytum famaa sa-altukum-min ajrin in ajriya illaa 'alal-laahi wa umirtu an akoona minal-muslimeen.

فَاِنْ تَوَلَّيْتُمْ فَمَا سَاَلْتُكُمْ مِّنْ
اَجْرٍ ؕ اِنْ اَجْرِىَ اِلَّا عَلَى اللّٰهِ ۙ
وَاُمِرْتُ اَنْ اَكُوْنَ مِنَ الْمُسْلِمِيْنَ ﴿٧٢﴾

73. They rejected him, but We delivered him, and those with him, in the Ark, and We made them inherit (the earth), while We overwhelmed in the flood those who rejected Our Signs. Then see what was the end of those who were warned (but heeded not)!

73. Fakaẕẕaboohu fanaj-jaynaahu wa mamma'ahoo fil-fulki wa ja'alnaahum kha-laaa'ifa wa aghraqnal-laẕeena kaẕẕaboo bi-Aayaatinaa fan-ẕur kayfa kaana 'aaqibatul-munẕareen.

فَكَذَّبُوْهُ فَنَجَّيْنٰهُ وَمَنْ مَّعَهٗ فِى
الْفُلْكِ وَجَعَلْنٰهُمْ خَلٰٓئِفَ وَاَغْرَقْنَا
الَّذِيْنَ كَذَّبُوْا بِاٰيٰتِنَا ۚ فَانْظُرْ كَيْفَ
كَانَ عَاقِبَةُ الْمُنْذَرِيْنَ ﴿٧٣﴾

74. Then after him We sent (many) Apostles to their peoples: they brought them Clear Signs, but they would not believe what they had already rejected beforehand. Thus do We seal the hearts of the transgressors.

74. Summa ba'asnaa mim ba'dihee Rusulan ilaa qawmi-him fajaaa'oohum bilbayyi-naati famaa kaanoo liyu'minoo bimaa kaẕẕaboo bihee min qabl; kaẕaalika natba'u 'alaa quloobil-mu'tadeen.

ثُمَّ بَعَثْنَا مِنْ بَعْدِهٖ رُسُلًا اِلٰى
قَوْمِهِمْ فَجَآءُوْهُمْ بِالْبَيِّنٰتِ فَمَا
كَانُوْا لِيُؤْمِنُوْا بِمَا كَذَّبُوْا بِهٖ مِنْ
قَبْلُ ؕ كَذٰلِكَ نَطْبَعُ عَلٰى قُلُوْبِ
الْمُعْتَدِيْنَ ﴿٧٤﴾

Ikhfa اخفاء | Ghunna غنّہ | Ikhfa Meem Saakin اخفاء میم ساکن | Idghaam ادغام | Qalqala قلقلہ | Qalb قلب | Idghaam Meem Saakin ادغام میم ساکن

75. Then after them sent We Moses and Aaron to Pharaoh and his chiefs with Our Signs. But they were arrogant: they were a people in sin.

75. Summa ba‘as̱naa mim ba‘dihim-Moosaa wa Haaroona ilaa Fir‘awna wa mala'ihee bi-Aayaatinaa fastakbaroo wa kaanoo qawmam-mujrimeen.

ثُمَّ بَعَثْنَا مِنۢ بَعْدِهِم مُّوسَىٰ وَهَٰرُونَ
إِلَىٰ فِرْعَوْنَ وَمَلَإِيْهِۦ بِـَٔايَٰتِنَا
فَٱسْتَكْبَرُوا۟ وَكَانُوا۟ قَوْمًا مُّجْرِمِينَ ﴿٧٥﴾

76. When the Truth did come to them from Us, they said: "This is indeed evident sorcery!"

76. Falammaa jaaa'ahumul-ḥaqqu min ‘indinaa qaalooo inna haaẕaa lasiḥrum-mubeen.

فَلَمَّا جَآءَهُمُ ٱلْحَقُّ مِنْ عِندِنَا قَالُوٓا۟
إِنَّ هَٰذَا لَسِحْرٌ مُّبِينٌ ﴿٧٦﴾

77. Moses said: "Did you say (this) about the Truth when it has (actually) reached you? Is sorcery (like) this? But sorcerers will not prosper."

77. Qaala Moosaaa ataqooloona lilḥaqqi lammaa jaaa'akum asiḥrun haaẕaa wa laa yufliḥus-saaḥiroon.

قَالَ مُوسَىٰٓ أَتَقُولُونَ لِلْحَقِّ لَمَّا
جَآءَكُمْ ۖ أَسِحْرٌ هَٰذَا وَلَا يُفْلِحُ
ٱلسَّٰحِرُونَ ﴿٧٧﴾

78. They said: "Have you come to us to turn us away from the ways we found our fathers following,- in order that you and your brother may have greatness in the land? But we shall not believe in you!"

78. Qaalooo aji'tanaa litalfitanaa ‘ammaa wajadnaa ‘alayhi aabaaa'anaa wa takoona lakumal-kibriyaaa'u fil-arḍi wa maa naḥnu lakumaa bimu'mineen.

قَالُوٓا۟ أَجِئْتَنَا لِتَلْفِتَنَا عَمَّا
وَجَدْنَا عَلَيْهِ ءَابَآءَنَا وَتَكُونَ
لَكُمَا ٱلْكِبْرِيَآءُ فِى ٱلْأَرْضِ وَمَا
نَحْنُ لَكُمَا بِمُؤْمِنِينَ ﴿٧٨﴾

79. Pharaoh said: "Bring me every sorcerer well versed."

79. Wa qaala Fir‘awnu'-toonee bikulli saaḥirin ‘aleem.

وَقَالَ فِرْعَوْنُ ٱئْتُونِى بِكُلِّ
سَٰحِرٍ عَلِيمٍ ﴿٧٩﴾

80. When the sorcerers came, Moses said to them: "You throw what you (wish) to throw!"

80. Falammaa jaaa'assa-ḥaratu qaala lahum-Moosaaa alqoo maaa antum-mulqoon.

فَلَمَّا جَآءَ ٱلسَّحَرَةُ قَالَ لَهُم
مُّوسَىٰٓ أَلْقُوا۟ مَآ أَنتُم مُّلْقُونَ ﴿٨٠﴾

81. When they had had their throw, Moses said: "What you have brought is sorcery: Allah will surely make it of no effect: for Allah does not prosper the work of those who make mischief.

81. Falammaaa alqaw qaala Moosaa maa ji'tum bihis-siḥru innal-laaha sa-yubṭiluhoo innal-laaha laa yuṣliḥu ‘amalal-mufsideen.

فَلَمَّآ أَلْقَوْا۟ قَالَ مُوسَىٰ مَا جِئْتُم بِهِ
ٱلسِّحْرُ ۖ إِنَّ ٱللَّهَ سَيُبْطِلُهُۥٓ ۖ إِنَّ
ٱللَّهَ لَا يُصْلِحُ عَمَلَ ٱلْمُفْسِدِينَ ﴿٨١﴾

82. "And Allah by His Words proves and establishes His Truth, however much the Sinners may hate it!"

82. Wa yuḥiqqul-laahul-ḥaqqa bi-Kalimaatihee wa law karihal-mujrimoon. **(Section 8)**

وَيُحِقُّ ٱللَّهُ ٱلْحَقَّ بِكَلِمَٰتِهِۦ وَلَوْ كَرِهَ
ٱلْمُجْرِمُونَ ﴿٨٢﴾

83. But none believed in Moses except some children of his people, because of the fear of Pharaoh and his chiefs, lest they should persecute them; and certainly Pharaoh was mighty on the earth and one who transgressed all bounds.

83. Famaaa aamana li-Moosaa illaa ẕurriyyatum-min qawmihee ‘alaa khawfim-min Fir‘awna wa mala'ihim añy-yaftinahum; wa inna Fir‘awna la‘aalin fil-arḍi wa innahoo laminal-musrifeen.

فَمَآ ءَامَنَ لِمُوسَىٰٓ إِلَّا ذُرِّيَّةٌ مِّن
قَوْمِهِۦ عَلَىٰ خَوْفٍ مِّن فِرْعَوْنَ
وَمَلَإِيْهِمْ أَن يَفْتِنَهُمْ ۚ وَإِنَّ
فِرْعَوْنَ لَعَالٍ فِى ٱلْأَرْضِ ۖ وَإِنَّهُۥ
لَمِنَ ٱلْمُسْرِفِينَ ﴿٨٣﴾

84. Moses said: "O my people! If you do (really) believe in Allah, then in Him put your trust if you submit (your will to His)."

84. Wa qaala Moosaa yaa qawmi in kuntum aamantum billaahi fa'alayhi tawakkalooo in kuntum-muslimeen.

وَقَالَ مُوْسٰى يٰقَوْمِ اِنْ كُنْتُمْ
اٰمَنْتُمْ بِاللّٰهِ فَعَلَيْهِ تَوَكَّلُوْٓا اِنْ
كُنْتُمْ مُّسْلِمِيْنَ ﴿٨٤﴾

85. They said: "In Allah do we put our trust. Our Lord! do not make us a trial for those who practise oppression;

86. "And deliver us by Your Mercy from those who reject (You)."

85. Faqaaloo 'alal-laahi tawakkalnaa Rabbanaa laa taj'alnaa fitnatal-lilqawmiẓ-ẓaalimeen.

86. Wa najjinaa biraḥmatika minal-qawmil-kaafireen.

فَقَالُوْا عَلَى اللّٰهِ تَوَكَّلْنَا ۚ رَبَّنَا لَا
تَجْعَلْنَا فِتْنَةً لِّلْقَوْمِ الظّٰلِمِيْنَ ﴿٨٥﴾
وَنَجِّنَا بِرَحْمَتِكَ مِنَ الْقَوْمِ
الْكٰفِرِيْنَ ﴿٨٦﴾

87. We inspired Moses and his brother with this Message: "Provide dwellings for your people in Egypt, make your dwellings into places of worship, and establish regular prayers: and give Glad Tidings to those who believe!"

87. Wa awḥaynaaa ilaa Moosaa wa akheehi an tabaw-wa-aa liqawmikumaa bi-Miṣra bu-yootañw-waj'aloo bu-yoota-kum qiblatañw-wa aqeemuṣ-Ṣa-laah; wa bashshiril-mu'mineen.

وَاَوْحَيْنَآ اِلٰى مُوْسٰى وَاَخِيْهِ
اَنْ تَبَوَّاٰ لِقَوْمِكُمَا بِمِصْرَ بُيُوْتًا
وَّاجْعَلُوْا بُيُوْتَكُمْ قِبْلَةً وَّاَقِيْمُوا
الصَّلٰوةَ ۗ وَبَشِّرِ الْمُؤْمِنِيْنَ ﴿٨٧﴾

88. Moses prayed: "Our Lord! You have indeed bestowed on Pharaoh and his Chiefs splendour and wealth in the life of the Present, and so, our Lord, they mislead (men) from Your Path. Our Lord deface, the features of their wealth, and send hardness to their hearts, so they will not believe until they see the grievous Chastisement."

88. Wa qaala Moosaa Rabba-naaa innaka aatayta Fir'awna wa mala-ahoo zeenatañw-wa amwaalan fil-ḥayaatid-dunyaa Rabbanaa liyuḍilloo 'an sabeelika Rabbanaṭ-mis 'alaaa amwaalihim washdud 'alaa quloobihim falaa yu'minoo ḥattaa yarawul-'aẕaabal-aleem.

وَقَالَ مُوْسٰى رَبَّنَآ اِنَّكَ اٰتَيْتَ
فِرْعَوْنَ وَمَلَاَهٗ زِيْنَةً وَّاَمْوَالًا
فِي الْحَيٰوةِ الدُّنْيَا ۙ رَبَّنَا لِيُضِلُّوْا
عَنْ سَبِيْلِكَ ۚ رَبَّنَا اطْمِسْ عَلٰٓى
اَمْوَالِهِمْ وَاشْدُدْ عَلٰى قُلُوْبِهِمْ فَلَا
يُؤْمِنُوْا حَتّٰى يَرَوُا الْعَذَابَ الْاَلِيْمَ ﴿٨٨﴾

89. Allah said: "Accepted is your prayer (O Moses and Aaron)! So you stand straight, and do not follow the path of those who do not know."

89. Qaala qad ujeebad-da'wa-tukumaa fastaqeemaa wa laa tattabi'aaanni sabeelal-laẕeena laa ya'lamoon.

قَالَ قَدْ اُجِيْبَتْ دَّعْوَتُكُمَا
فَاسْتَقِيْمَا وَلَا تَتَّبِعٰٓنِّ سَبِيْلَ
الَّذِيْنَ لَا يَعْلَمُوْنَ ﴿٨٩﴾

90. We took the Children of Israel across the sea: Pharaoh and his hosts followed them in insolence and spite. At length, when overwhelmed with the flood, he said: "I believe that there is no god except Him Whom the Children of Israel believe in: I am of those who submit (to Allah in Islam)."

90. Wa jaawaznaa bi-Baneee Israaa'eelal-baḥra fa-atba'a-hum Fir'awnu wa junooduhoo baghyañw-wa 'adwan ḥattaaa iẕaaa adrakahul-gharaqu qaala aamantu annahoo laaa ilaaha illal-laẕeee aamanat bihee Banooo Israaa'eela wa ana minal-muslimeen.

وَجٰوَزْنَا بِبَنِيْٓ اِسْرَآءِيْلَ الْبَحْرَ
فَاَتْبَعَهُمْ فِرْعَوْنُ وَجُنُوْدُهٗ بَغْيًا
وَّعَدْوًا ۭ حَتّٰٓى اِذَآ اَدْرَكَهُ الْغَرَقُ ۙ
قَالَ اٰمَنْتُ اَنَّهٗ لَآ اِلٰهَ اِلَّا الَّذِيْٓ
اٰمَنَتْ بِهٖ بَنُوْٓا اِسْرَآءِيْلَ وَاَنَا
مِنَ الْمُسْلِمِيْنَ ﴿٩٠﴾

Ikhfa اخفاء | Ghunna غُنّہ | Ikhfa Meem Saakin اخفاء میم ساکن | Idghaam ادغام | Qalqala قلقلہ | Qalb قلب | Idghaam Meem Saakin ادغام میم ساکن

91. (It was said to him): "Ah now!- But a little while before, you were in rebellion!- and you did mischief (and violence)!

92. "This day shall We save you in the body, that you may be a Sign to those who come after you! but verily, many among mankind are heedless of Our Signs!"

93. We settled the Children of Israel in a beautiful dwelling-place, and provided for them sustenance of the best: it was after knowledge had been granted to them, that they fell into schisms. Verily Allah will judge between them as to the schisms amongst them, on the Day of Judgment.

94. If you were in doubt as to what We have revealed to you, then ask those who have been reading the Book from before you: the Truth has indeed come to you from your Lord: so be in no wise of those in doubt.

95. Nor be of those who reject the Signs of Allah, or you shall be of those who perish.

96. Those against whom the word of your Lord has been verified would not believe-

97. Even if every Sign was brought to them,- until they see (for themselves) the Chastisement grievous.

98. Why was there not a single township (among those We warned), which believed,- so its faith should have profited it,- except the people of Jonah? When they believed, We removed from them the Chastisement of ignominy in the life of the present, and permitted them to enjoy (their life) for a while.

91. Aaal'aana wa qad 'aṣayta qablu wa kunta minal-mufsideen.

92. Falyawma nunajjeeka bibadanika litakoona liman khalfaka Aayah; wa inna kaseeram-minan-naasi 'an Aayaatinaa laghaafiloon.

(Section 9)

93. Wa laqad bawwaånaa Baneee Israaa'eela mubawwa-a ṣidqiñw-wa razaqnaahum-minaṭ-ṭayyibaati famakh-talafoo ḥattaa jaaa'ahumul-'ilm; inna Rabbaka yaqḍee baynahum Yawmal-Qiyaamati feemaa kaanoo feehi yakhtalifoon.

94. Fa-in kunta fee shakkim-mimmaaa anzalnaaa ilayka fas'alil-lazeena yaqra'oonal-Kitaaba min qablik; laqad jaaa'akal-ḥaqqu mir-Rabbika falaa takoonanna minal-mumtareen.

95. Wa laa takoonanna minal-lazeena kazzaboo bi-Aayaatil-laahi fatakoona minal-khaasireen.

96. Innal-lazeena ḥaqqat 'alayhim Kalimatu Rabbika laa yu'minoon.

97. Wa law jaaa'at-hum kullu Aayatin ḥattaa yarawul-'azaabal-aleem.

98. Falaw laa kaanat qaryatun aamanat fanafa'ahaaa eemaanuhaaa illaa qawma Yoonusa lammaaa aamanoo kashafnaa 'anhum 'azaabal-khizyi fil-ḥayaatid-dunyaa wa matta'naahum ilaa ḥeen.

آلْـَٔـٰنَ وَقَدْ عَصَيْتَ قَبْلُ وَكُنتَ
مِنَ ٱلْمُفْسِدِينَ ﴿٩١﴾
فَٱلْيَوْمَ نُنَجِّيكَ بِبَدَنِكَ لِتَكُونَ
لِمَنْ خَلْفَكَ ءَايَةً ۚ وَإِنَّ كَثِيرًا
مِّنَ ٱلنَّاسِ عَنْ ءَايَـٰتِنَا لَغَـٰفِلُونَ ﴿٩٢﴾ ع
وَلَقَدْ بَوَّأْنَا بَنِىٓ إِسْرَٰٓءِيلَ مُبَوَّأَ
صِدْقٍ وَرَزَقْنَـٰهُم مِّنَ ٱلطَّيِّبَـٰتِ
فَمَا ٱخْتَلَفُوا۟ حَتَّىٰ جَآءَهُمُ ٱلْعِلْمُ ۚ
إِنَّ رَبَّكَ يَقْضِى بَيْنَهُمْ يَوْمَ ٱلْقِيَـٰمَةِ
فِيمَا كَانُوا۟ فِيهِ يَخْتَلِفُونَ ﴿٩٣﴾
فَإِن كُنتَ فِى شَكٍّ مِّمَّآ أَنزَلْنَآ
إِلَيْكَ فَسْـَٔلِ ٱلَّذِينَ يَقْرَءُونَ
ٱلْكِتَـٰبَ مِن قَبْلِكَ ۚ لَقَدْ جَآءَكَ
ٱلْحَقُّ مِن رَّبِّكَ فَلَا تَكُونَنَّ مِنَ
ٱلْمُمْتَرِينَ ﴿٩٤﴾
وَلَا تَكُونَنَّ مِنَ ٱلَّذِينَ كَذَّبُوا۟
بِـَٔايَـٰتِ ٱللَّهِ فَتَكُونَ مِنَ ٱلْخَـٰسِرِينَ ﴿٩٥﴾
إِنَّ ٱلَّذِينَ حَقَّتْ عَلَيْهِمْ كَلِمَتُ
رَبِّكَ لَا يُؤْمِنُونَ ﴿٩٦﴾
وَلَوْ جَآءَتْهُمْ كُلُّ ءَايَةٍ حَتَّىٰ يَرَوُا۟
ٱلْعَذَابَ ٱلْأَلِيمَ ﴿٩٧﴾
فَلَوْلَا كَانَتْ قَرْيَةٌ ءَامَنَتْ فَنَفَعَهَآ
إِيمَـٰنُهَآ إِلَّا قَوْمَ يُونُسَ لَمَّآ ءَامَنُوا۟
كَشَفْنَا عَنْهُمْ عَذَابَ ٱلْخِزْىِ
فِى ٱلْحَيَوٰةِ ٱلدُّنْيَا وَمَتَّعْنَـٰهُمْ
إِلَىٰ حِينٍ ﴿٩٨﴾

Ikhfa اخفاء | Ghunna غنّہ | Ikhfa Meem Saakin اخفاء میم ساکن | Idghaam ادغام | Qalqala قلقلہ | Qalb قلب | Idghaam Meem Saakin ادغام میم ساکن

99. If it had been your Lord's will, they would all have believed,- all who are on earth! Will you then compel mankind, against their will, to believe!

99. Wa law shaaa'a Rabbuka la-aamana man fil-arḍi kullu-hum jamee'aa; afa-anta tukri-hun-naasa ḥattaa yakoonoo mu'mineen.

وَلَوْ شَاءَ رَبُّكَ لَآمَنَ مَنْ فِي
الْأَرْضِ كُلُّهُمْ جَمِيعًا ۚ أَفَأَنْتَ تُكْرِهُ
النَّاسَ حَتَّىٰ يَكُونُوا مُؤْمِنِينَ ﴿٩٩﴾

100. No soul can believe, except by the Will of Allah, and He will place Doubt (or obscurity) on those who will not understand.

100. Wa maa kaana linafsin an tu'mina illaa bi-iznil-laah; wa yaj'alur-rijsa 'alal-lazeena laa ya'qiloon.

وَمَا كَانَ لِنَفْسٍ أَنْ تُؤْمِنَ إِلَّا
بِإِذْنِ اللَّهِ ۚ وَيَجْعَلُ الرِّجْسَ
عَلَى الَّذِينَ لَا يَعْقِلُونَ ﴿١٠٠﴾

101. Say: "Behold all that is in the heavens and on earth"; but neither Signs nor Warners profit those who do not believe.

101. Qulin-ẓuroo maazaa fis-samaawaati wal-arḍ; wa maa tughnil-Aayaatu wannuzuru 'an qawmil-laa yu'minoon.

قُلِ انْظُرُوا مَاذَا فِي السَّمَاوَاتِ
وَالْأَرْضِ ۚ وَمَا تُغْنِي الْآيَاتُ
وَالنُّذُرُ عَنْ قَوْمٍ لَا يُؤْمِنُونَ ﴿١٠١﴾

102. Do they then expect (any thing) but (what happened in) the days of the men who passed away before them? Say: "You wait then: for I, too, will wait with you."

102. Fahal yantaẓiroona illaa misla ayyaamil-lazeena khalaw min qablihim; qul fantaẓirooo innee ma'akum minal-muntaẓireen.

فَهَلْ يَنْتَظِرُونَ إِلَّا مِثْلَ أَيَّامِ
الَّذِينَ خَلَوْا مِنْ قَبْلِهِمْ ۚ قُلْ
فَانْتَظِرُوا إِنِّي مَعَكُمْ مِنَ
الْمُنْتَظِرِينَ ﴿١٠٢﴾

103. In the end We deliver Our Apostles and those who believe: thus is it fitting on Our part that We should deliver those who believe!

103. Summa nunajjee Rus-lanaa wallazeena aamanoo; kazaalika ḥaqqan 'alaynaa nunjil-mu'mineen. **(Section 10)**

ثُمَّ نُنَجِّي رُسُلَنَا وَالَّذِينَ آمَنُوا
كَذَٰلِكَ حَقًّا عَلَيْنَا نُنْجِ الْمُؤْمِنِينَ ﴿١٠٣﴾ ع ١٥

104. Say: "O you men! If you are in doubt as to my religion, (behold!) I do not worship what you worship, other than Allah! But I worship Allah - Who will take your souls (at death): I am commanded to be (in the ranks) of the Believers,

104. Qul yaaa ayyuhan-naasu in kuntum fee shakkim-min deenee falaaa a'budul-lazeena ta'budoona min doonil-laahi wa laakin a'budul-laahal-lazee yatawaffaakum wa umirtu an akoona minal-mu'mineen.

قُلْ يَا أَيُّهَا النَّاسُ إِنْ كُنْتُمْ فِي
شَكٍّ مِنْ دِينِي فَلَا أَعْبُدُ الَّذِينَ
تَعْبُدُونَ مِنْ دُونِ اللَّهِ وَلَٰكِنْ
أَعْبُدُ اللَّهَ الَّذِي يَتَوَفَّاكُمْ ۖ وَأُمِرْتُ
أَنْ أَكُونَ مِنَ الْمُؤْمِنِينَ ﴿١٠٤﴾

105. "And further (thus): 'set your face towards religion with true piety, and never in any wise be of the Unbelievers;

105. Wa an aqim wajhaka liddeeni Ḥaneefañw wa laa takoonanna minal-mushrikeen.

وَأَنْ أَقِمْ وَجْهَكَ لِلدِّينِ حَنِيفًا
وَلَا تَكُونَنَّ مِنَ الْمُشْرِكِينَ ﴿١٠٥﴾

106. "'Nor call on any, other than Allah;- Such will neither profit you nor hurt you: if you do so, behold! you shall certainly be of those who do wrong.'"

106. Wa laa tad'u min doonil-laahi maa laa yanfa'uka wa laa yaḍurruka fa-in fa'alta fa-innaka izam-minaẓ-ẓaalimeen.

وَلَا تَدْعُ مِنْ دُونِ اللَّهِ مَا لَا
يَنْفَعُكَ وَلَا يَضُرُّكَ ۖ فَإِنْ فَعَلْتَ
فَإِنَّكَ إِذًا مِنَ الظَّالِمِينَ ﴿١٠٦﴾

107. If Allah touches you with hurt, there is none

107. Wa iñy-yamsaskal-laahu biḍurrin falaa

وَإِنْ يَمْسَسْكَ اللَّهُ بِضُرٍّ فَلَا

Ikhfa إخفاء | Ghunna غُنّہ | Ikhfa Meem Saakin اخفاءميم ساكن | Idghaam ادغام | Qalqala قلقلہ | Qalb قلب | Idghaam Meem Saakin ادغام ميم ساكن

can remove it but He: if He do design some benefit for you, there is none can keep back His favour: He causes it to reach whomsoever of His servants He pleases. And He is the Oft-Forgiving, Most Merciful.

kaashifa lahooo illaa Huwa wa iñy-yuridka bikhayrin falaa raaadda lifaḍlih; yuṣeebu bihee mañ-yashaaa'u min 'ibaadih; wa huwal-Ghafoorur-Raḥeem.

كَاشِفَ لَهٗٓ اِلَّا هُوَ ۚ وَاِنْ يُّرِدْكَ
بِخَيْرٍ فَلَا رَآدَّ لِفَضْلِهٖ ۗ يُصِيْبُ
بِهٖ مَنْ يَّشَآءُ مِنْ عِبَادِهٖ ۗ وَهُوَ
الْغَفُوْرُ الرَّحِيْمُ ﴿١٠٧﴾

108. Say: "O you men! Now Truth has reached you from your Lord! those who receive guidance, do so for the good of their own souls; those who stray, do so to their own loss: and I am not (set) over you to arrange your affairs."

108. Qul yaaa ayyuhan-naasu qad jaaa'akumul-ḥaqqu mir-Rabbikum famanih-tadaa fa-innamaa yahtadee linafsihee wa man ḍalla fa-innamaa yaḍillu 'alayhaa wa maaa ana 'alaykum biwakeel.

قُلْ يٰٓاَيُّهَا النَّاسُ قَدْ جَآءَكُمُ
الْحَقُّ مِنْ رَّبِّكُمْ ۚ فَمَنِ اهْتَدٰى
فَاِنَّمَا يَهْتَدِيْ لِنَفْسِهٖ ۚ وَمَنْ ضَلَّ
فَاِنَّمَا يَضِلُّ عَلَيْهَا ۚ وَمَآ اَنَا
عَلَيْكُمْ بِوَكِيْلٍ ۗ ﴿١٠٨﴾

109. You follow the inspiration sent to you, and be patient and constant, till Allah do decide: for He is the Best to decide.

109. Wattabi' maa yooḥaaa ilayka waṣbir ḥattaa yaḥkumal-laah; wa Huwa khayrul-ḥaakimeen. **(Section 11)**

وَاتَّبِعْ مَا يُوْحٰٓى اِلَيْكَ وَاصْبِرْ حَتّٰى
يَحْكُمَ اللّٰهُ ۚۖ وَهُوَ خَيْرُ الْحٰكِمِيْنَ ﴿١٠٩﴾ ع ١١ ١٠ ١٢

11. Hud (The Prophet Hud)

In the name of Allah, Most Gracious, Most Merciful.

Sûrat Hûd–11

(Revealed at Makkah)

Bismillaahir Raḥmaanir Raḥeem

(١١) سُوْرَةُ هُوْدٍ مَكِّيَّةٌ (٥٢)

بِسْمِ اللّٰهِ الرَّحْمٰنِ الرَّحِيْمِ

1. *Alif-Lam-Ra*. (This is) a Book, with verses basic or fundamental (of established meaning), further explained in detail,- from One Who is Wise and Well-acquainted (with all things):

1. Alif-Laaam-Raa; Kitaabun uḥkimat Aayaatuhoo summa fuṣṣilat mil-ladun Ḥakeemin Khabeer.

الٓرٰ ۟ قف كِتٰبٌ اُحْكِمَتْ اٰيٰتُهٗ ثُمَّ
فُصِّلَتْ مِنْ لَّدُنْ حَكِيْمٍ خَبِيْرٍ ۙ ﴿١﴾

2. (It teaches) that you should worship none but Allah. (Say): "Verily I am (sent) to you from Him to warn and to bring glad tidings:

2. Allaa ta'budooo illal-laah; innanee lakum minhu nazeeruñw-wa basheer.

اَلَّا تَعْبُدُوْٓا اِلَّا اللّٰهَ ۗ اِنَّنِيْ لَكُمْ
مِّنْهُ نَذِيْرٌ وَّبَشِيْرٌ ۙ ﴿٢﴾

3. "(And to preach thus), 'You seek the forgiveness of your Lord, and turn to Him in repentance; that He may grant you enjoyment, good (and true), for a term appointed, and bestow His abounding grace on all who abound in merit! But if you turn away , then I fear for you the Chastisement of a Great Day:

3. Wa anis-taghfiroo Rabbakum summa toobooo ilayhi yumatti'kum mataa'an ḥasanan ilaaa ajalim-musammañw-wa yu'ti kulla zee faḍlin faḍlahoo wa in tawallaw fa-inneee akhaafu 'alaykum 'azaaba Yawmin Kabeer.

وَّاَنِ اسْتَغْفِرُوْا رَبَّكُمْ ثُمَّ تُوْبُوْٓا
اِلَيْهِ يُمَتِّعْكُمْ مَّتَاعًا حَسَنًا اِلٰٓى
اَجَلٍ مُّسَمًّى وَّيُؤْتِ كُلَّ ذِيْ
فَضْلٍ فَضْلَهٗ ۗ وَاِنْ تَوَلَّوْا فَاِنِّيْٓ
اَخَافُ عَلَيْكُمْ عَذَابَ يَوْمٍ كَبِيْرٍ ﴿٣﴾

4. 'To Allah is your return, and He has power over all things."

4. Ilal-laahi marji'ukum wa Huwa 'alaa kulli shay'in Qadeer.

اِلَى اللّٰهِ مَرْجِعُكُمْ ۚ وَهُوَ عَلٰى كُلِّ
شَيْءٍ قَدِيْرٌ ﴿٤﴾

5. Behold! they fold up their hearts, that they may lie hid from Him! Ah! even when

5. Alaaa innahum yasnoona ṣudoorahum liyastakhfoo minh; alaa ḥeena

اَلَآ اِنَّهُمْ يَثْنُوْنَ صُدُوْرَهُمْ
لِيَسْتَخْفُوْا مِنْهُ ۗ اَلَا حِيْنَ

Ikhfa اخفاء | Ghunna غُنَّة | Ikhfa Meem Saakin اخفاء میم ساکن | Idghaam ادغام | Qalqala قلقله | Qalb قلب | Idghaam Meem Saakin ادغام میم ساکن

يَسْتَغْشُوْنَ ثِيَابَهُمْ ۙ يَعْلَمُ مَا
يُسِرُّوْنَ وَمَا يُعْلِنُوْنَ ۚ اِنَّهٗ
عَلِيْمٌۢ بِذَاتِ الصُّدُوْرِ ۝٥
وَمَا مِنْ دَآبَّةٍ فِي الْاَرْضِ اِلَّا عَلَى
اللّٰهِ رِزْقُهَا وَيَعْلَمُ مُسْتَقَرَّهَا وَ
مُسْتَوْدَعَهَا ۭ كُلٌّ فِيْ كِتٰبٍ مُّبِيْنٍ ۝٦
وَهُوَ الَّذِيْ خَلَقَ السَّمٰوٰتِ وَالْاَرْضَ
فِيْ سِتَّةِ اَيَّامٍ وَّكَانَ عَرْشُهٗ عَلَى
الْمَاۗءِ لِيَبْلُوَكُمْ اَيُّكُمْ اَحْسَنُ عَمَلًا ۭ
وَلَىِٕنْ قُلْتَ اِنَّكُمْ مَّبْعُوْثُوْنَ مِنْۢ
بَعْدِ الْمَوْتِ لَيَقُوْلَنَّ الَّذِيْنَ كَفَرُوْٓا
اِنْ هٰذَآ اِلَّا سِحْرٌ مُّبِيْنٌ ۝٧
وَلَىِٕنْ اَخَّرْنَا عَنْهُمُ الْعَذَابَ اِلٰٓى
اُمَّةٍ مَّعْدُوْدَةٍ لَّيَقُوْلُنَّ مَا يَحْبِسُهٗ ۭ
اَلَا يَوْمَ يَاْتِيْهِمْ لَيْسَ مَصْرُوْفًا عَنْهُمْ
وَحَاقَ بِهِمْ مَّا كَانُوْا بِهٖ يَسْتَهْزِءُوْنَ ۝٨
وَلَىِٕنْ اَذَقْنَا الْاِنْسَانَ مِنَّا رَحْمَةً
ثُمَّ نَزَعْنٰهَا مِنْهُ ۚ اِنَّهٗ لَيَـُٔوْسٌ
كَفُوْرٌ ۝٩
وَلَىِٕنْ اَذَقْنٰهُ نَعْمَاۗءَ بَعْدَ ضَرَّاۗءَ
مَسَّتْهُ لَيَقُوْلَنَّ ذَهَبَ السَّيِّاٰتُ
عَنِّيْ ۭ اِنَّهٗ لَفَرِحٌ فَخُوْرٌ ۝١٠
اِلَّا الَّذِيْنَ صَبَرُوْا وَعَمِلُوا الصّٰلِحٰتِ ۭ
اُولٰۗىِٕكَ لَهُمْ مَّغْفِرَةٌ وَّاَجْرٌ كَبِيْرٌ ۝١١
فَلَعَلَّكَ تَارِكٌۢ بَعْضَ مَا يُوْحٰٓى
اِلَيْكَ وَضَاۗىِٕقٌۢ بِهٖ صَدْرُكَ اَنْ

اَلْجُزْءُ الثَّانِيْ عَشَرَ (١٢)

ع ١

yastaghshoona siyaabahum ya'lamu maa yusirroona wa maa yu'linoon; innahoo 'aleemum bizaatiṣ-ṣudoor.

6. Wa maa min daaabbatin fil-arḍi illaa 'alal-laahi rizquhaa wa ya'lamu mustaqarrahaa wa mustawda'ahaa; kullun fee Kitaabim-Mubeen.

7. Wa Huwal-lazee khalaqas-samaawaati wal-arḍa fee sittati ayyaamiñw-wa kaana-'Arshuhoo alal-maaa'i liyabluwakum ayyukum aḥsanu 'amalaa; wa la'in qulta innakum mab'oosoona mim ba'dil-mawti la-yaqoolannal-lazeena kafarooo in haazaaa illaa siḥrum-mubeen.

8. Wala'in akhkharnaa 'anhumul-'azaaba ilaaa ummatim-ma'doodatil-la-yaqoolunna maa yaḥbisuh; alaa yawma yaåteehim laysa maṣroofan 'anhum wa ḥaaqa bihim-maa kaanoo bihee yastahzi'oon. **(Section 1)**

9. Wa la'in azaqnal-insaana minnaa raḥmatan summa naza'naahaa minhu, innahoo laya'oosun kafoor.

10. Wala'in azaqnaahu na'-maaa'a ba'da ḍarraaa'a massat-hu la-yaqoolanna zahabas-sayyi-aatu 'anneee; innahoo lafariḥun fakhoor.

11. Illal-lazeena ṣabaroo wa 'amiluṣ-ṣaaliḥaati ulaaa'ika lahum-maghfiratuñw-wa ajrun kabeer.

12. Fala'allaka taarikum ba'ḍa maa yooḥaaa ilayka wa ḍaaa'iqum-bihee ṣadruka añy-

they cover themselves with their garments, He knows what they conceal, and what they reveal: for He knows well the (inmost secrets) of the hearts.

6. There is no moving creature on earth but its sustenance depends on Allah: He knows the time and place of its definite abode and its temporary deposit: all is in a clear Record.

7. He it is Who created the heavens and the earth in six Days - and His Throne was over the waters - that He might try you, which of you is best in conduct. But if you were to say to them, "You shall indeed be raised up after death", the Unbelievers would be sure to say, "This is nothing but obvious sorcery!"

8. If We delay the Chastisement for them for a definite term, they are sure to say, "What keeps it back?" Ah! On the day it (actually) reaches them, nothing will turn it away from them, and they will be completely encircled by that which they used to mock at!

9. If We give man a taste of Mercy from Ourselves, and then withdraw it from him, behold! he is in despair and (falls into) blasphemy.

10. But if We give him a taste of (Our) favours after adversity has touched him, he is sure to say, "All evil has departed from me:" behold! he falls into exultation and pride.

11. Not so do those who show patience and constancy, and work righteousness; for them is forgiveness (of sins) and a great reward.

12. Perchance you may (feel the inclination) to give up a part of what is revealed to you, and your heart feels straitened lest

Ikhfa اخفاء | Ghunna غنّہ | Ikhfa Meem Saakin اخفاء میم ساکن | Idghaam ادغام | Qalqala قلقلہ | Qalb قلب | Idghaam Meem Saakin ادغام میم ساکن

they say, "Why is not a treasure sent down to him, or why does not an angel come down with him?" But you are there only to warn! It is Allah that arranges all affairs!

13. Or they may say, "He forged it," Say, "You then bring ten Suras forged, like unto it, and call (to your aid) whomsoever you can, other than Allah!- If you speak the truth!

14. "If then they (your false gods) do not answer your (call), you (should) know that this Revelation is sent down (replete) with the knowledge of Allah, and that there is no god but He! Will you even then not submit (to Islam)?"

15. Those who desire the life of the present and its glitter,- to them We shall pay (the price of) their deeds therein,- without diminution.

16. They are those for whom there is nothing in the Hereafter but the Fire: vain are the designs they frame therein, and of no effect and the deeds that they do!

17. Can they be (like) those who accept a Clear (Sign) from their Lord, and whom a witness from Himself teaches, as did the Book of Moses before it,- a guide and a mercy? They believe therein; but those of the Sects that reject it,- the Fire will be their promised meeting-place. Be not then in doubt thereon: for it is the Truth from your Lord: yet many among men do not believe!

18. Who does more wrong than those who invent a lie against Allah? They will be turned back to the presence of their Lord, and the witnesses will say, "These are the ones

yaqooloo law laaa unzila 'alayhi kanzun aw jaaa'a ma'ahoo malak; innamaaa anta nazeer; wallaahu 'alaa kulli shay'iñw-wakeel.

13. Am yaqooloonaf-taraahu qul faåtoo bi'ashri Suwarim-mislihee muftarayaatiñw-wad'oo manis-taṭa'tum min doonil-laahi in kuntum ṣaadiqeen.

14. Fa-il-lam yastajeeboo lakum fa'lamooo annamaaa unzila bi'ilmil-laahi wa al-laaa ilaaha illaa Huwa fahal antum muslimoon.

15. Man kaana yureedul-ḥayaatad-dunyaa wa zeenatahaa nuwaffi ilayhim a'maalahum feehaa wa hum feehaa laa yubkhasoon.

16. Ulaaa'ikal-lazeena laysa lahum fil-Aakhirati illan-Naaru wa ḥabiṭa maa ṣana'oo feehaa wa baaṭilum-maa kaanoo ya'maloon.

17. Afaman kaana 'alas bayyinatim-mir-Rabbihee wa yatloohu shaahidum-minhu wa min qablihee Kitaabu Moosaaa imaamañw-wa raḥmah; ulaaa-'ika yu'minoona bih; wa mañy-yakfur bihee minal-Aḥzaabi fan-Naaru maw'iduh; falaa taku fee miryatim-minh; innahul-ḥaqqu mir-Rabbika wa laakinna aksaran-naasi laa yu'minoon.

18. Wa man aẓlamu mimmanif-taraa 'alal-laahi kazibaa; ulaaa'ika yu'raḍoona 'alaa Rabbihim wa yaqoolul-ashhaadu haaa'ulaaa'il-lazeena

يَقُولُوا لَوْلَآ أُنزِلَ عَلَيْهِ كَنزٌ أَوْ
جَآءَ مَعَهُۥ مَلَكٌ ۚ إِنَّمَآ أَنتَ نَذِيرٌ ۚ
وَٱللَّهُ عَلَىٰ كُلِّ شَىْءٍ وَكِيلٌ ١٢
أَمْ يَقُولُونَ ٱفْتَرَىٰهُ ۖ قُلْ فَأْتُوا۟ بِعَشْرِ
سُوَرٍ مِّثْلِهِۦ مُفْتَرَيَٰتٍ وَٱدْعُوا۟ مَنِ
ٱسْتَطَعْتُم مِّن دُونِ ٱللَّهِ إِن كُنتُمْ
صَٰدِقِينَ ١٣
فَإِلَّمْ يَسْتَجِيبُوا۟ لَكُمْ فَٱعْلَمُوٓا۟
أَنَّمَآ أُنزِلَ بِعِلْمِ ٱللَّهِ وَأَن لَّآ إِلَٰهَ
إِلَّا هُوَ ۖ فَهَلْ أَنتُم مُّسْلِمُونَ ١٤
مَن كَانَ يُرِيدُ ٱلْحَيَوٰةَ ٱلدُّنْيَا وَ
زِينَتَهَا نُوَفِّ إِلَيْهِمْ أَعْمَٰلَهُمْ
فِيهَا وَهُمْ فِيهَا لَا يُبْخَسُونَ ١٥
أُو۟لَٰٓئِكَ ٱلَّذِينَ لَيْسَ لَهُمْ فِى ٱلْءَاخِرَةِ
إِلَّا ٱلنَّارُ ۖ وَحَبِطَ مَا صَنَعُوا۟ فِيهَا وَ
بَٰطِلٌ مَّا كَانُوا۟ يَعْمَلُونَ ١٦
أَفَمَن كَانَ عَلَىٰ بَيِّنَةٍ مِّن رَّبِّهِۦ وَ
يَتْلُوهُ شَاهِدٌ مِّنْهُ وَمِن قَبْلِهِۦ
كِتَٰبُ مُوسَىٰٓ إِمَامًا وَرَحْمَةً ۚ أُو۟لَٰٓئِكَ
يُؤْمِنُونَ بِهِۦ ۚ وَمَن يَكْفُرْ بِهِۦ مِنَ
ٱلْأَحْزَابِ فَٱلنَّارُ مَوْعِدُهُۥ ۚ فَلَا تَكُ
فِى مِرْيَةٍ مِّنْهُ ۚ إِنَّهُ ٱلْحَقُّ مِن رَّبِّكَ
وَلَٰكِنَّ أَكْثَرَ ٱلنَّاسِ لَا يُؤْمِنُونَ ١٧
وَمَنْ أَظْلَمُ مِمَّنِ ٱفْتَرَىٰ عَلَى ٱللَّهِ
كَذِبًا ۚ أُو۟لَٰٓئِكَ يُعْرَضُونَ عَلَىٰ رَبِّهِمْ
وَيَقُولُ ٱلْأَشْهَٰدُ هَٰٓؤُلَآءِ ٱلَّذِينَ

Ikhfa اخفاء | Ghunna غُنّہ | Ikhfa Meem Saakin اخفاء میم ساکن | Idghaam ادغام | Qalqala قلقلہ | Qalb قلب | Idghaam Meem Saakin ادغام میم ساکن

who lied against their Lord! Behold! the Curse of Allah is on those who do wrong!-

kazaboo 'alaa Rabbihim; alaa la'natul-laahi 'alaz-zaalimeen.

كَذَبُوا عَلَىٰ رَبِّهِمْ ۚ أَلَا لَعْنَةُ اللَّهِ
عَلَى الظَّالِمِينَ ⑱

19. "Those who would hinder (men) from the path of Allah and would seek in it something crooked: these were they who denied the Hereafter!"

19. Allazeena yaşuddoona 'an sabeelil-laahi wa yabghoonahaa 'iwajañw wa hum bil-Aakhirati hum kaafiroon.

الَّذِينَ يَصُدُّونَ عَنْ سَبِيلِ اللَّهِ
وَيَبْغُونَهَا عِوَجًا وَهُمْ بِالْآخِرَةِ
هُمْ كَافِرُونَ ⑲

20. They will in no wise frustrate (His design) on earth, nor have they protectors besides Allah! Their Chastisement will be doubled! They lost the power to hear, and they did not see!

20. Ulaaa'ika lam yakoonoo mu'jizeena fil-arḍi wa maa kaana lahum-min doonil-laahi min awliyaaa'; yuḍaa'afu lahumul-'azaab; maa kaanoo yastaṭee'oonas-sam'a wa maa kaanoo yubşiroon.

أُولَٰئِكَ لَمْ يَكُونُوا مُعْجِزِينَ فِي
الْأَرْضِ وَمَا كَانَ لَهُمْ مِنْ دُونِ
اللَّهِ مِنْ أَوْلِيَاءَ ۘ يُضَاعَفُ لَهُمُ وقف لازم
الْعَذَابُ ۚ مَا كَانُوا يَسْتَطِيعُونَ
السَّمْعَ وَمَا كَانُوا يُبْصِرُونَ ⑳

21. They are the ones who have lost their own souls: and the (fancies) they invented have left them in the lurch!

21. Ulaaa'ikal-lazeena khasirooo anfusahum wa ḍalla 'anhum maa kaanoo yaftaroon.

أُولَٰئِكَ الَّذِينَ خَسِرُوا أَنْفُسَهُمْ وَ
ضَلَّ عَنْهُمْ مَا كَانُوا يَفْتَرُونَ ㉑

22. Without a doubt, these are the very ones who will lose most in the Hereafter!

22. Laa jarama annahum fil-Aakhirati humul-akhsaroon.

لَا جَرَمَ أَنَّهُمْ فِي الْآخِرَةِ هُمُ
الْأَخْسَرُونَ ㉒

23. But those who believe and work righteousness, and humble themselves before their Lord,- they will be Companions of the Garden, to dwell therein for ever!

23. Innal-lazeena aamanoo wa 'amiluş-şaaliḥaati wa akhbatooo ilaa Rabbihim ulaaa'ika Aşḥaabul-Jannati hum feehaa khaalidoon.

إِنَّ الَّذِينَ آمَنُوا وَعَمِلُوا الصَّالِحَاتِ
وَأَخْبَتُوا إِلَىٰ رَبِّهِمْ أُولَٰئِكَ أَصْحَابُ
الْجَنَّةِ ۖ هُمْ فِيهَا خَالِدُونَ ㉓

24. These two kinds (of men) may be compared to the blind and deaf, and those who can see and hear well. Are they equal when compared? Will you not then take heed?

24. Masalul-fareeqayni kal-a'maa wal-aşammi walbaşeeri wassamee'; hal yastawiyaani masalaa; afalaa tazakkaroon.

(Section 2)

مَثَلُ الْفَرِيقَيْنِ كَالْأَعْمَىٰ وَالْأَصَمِّ
وَالْبَصِيرِ وَالسَّمِيعِ ۚ هَلْ يَسْتَوِيَانِ
مَثَلًا ۚ أَفَلَا تَذَكَّرُونَ ㉔ ع

25. We sent Noah to his people (with a mission): "I have come to you with a Clear Warning:

25. Wa laqad arsalnaa Nooḥan ilaa qawmihee innee lakum nazeerum-mubeen.

وَلَقَدْ أَرْسَلْنَا نُوحًا إِلَىٰ قَوْمِهِ
إِنِّي لَكُمْ نَذِيرٌ مُبِينٌ ㉕

26. "That you serve none but Allah: Verily I do fear for you the Chastisement of a Grievous Day."

26. Al-laa ta'budooo illal-laaha inneee akhaafu 'alaykum 'azaaba Yawmin aleem.

أَنْ لَا تَعْبُدُوا إِلَّا اللَّهَ ۖ إِنِّي أَخَافُ
عَلَيْكُمْ عَذَابَ يَوْمٍ أَلِيمٍ ㉖

27. But the chiefs of the Unbelievers among his people said: "We see (in) you nothing but a man like ourselves:

27. Faqaalal-mala-ul-lazeena kafaroo min qawmihee maa naraaka illaa basharam-mislanaa

فَقَالَ الْمَلَأُ الَّذِينَ كَفَرُوا مِنْ
قَوْمِهِ مَا نَرَاكَ إِلَّا بَشَرًا مِثْلَنَا

Ikhfa اخفاء | Ghunna غُنّہ | Ikhfa Meem Saakin اخفاءمیم ساکن | Idghaam ادغام | Qalqala قلقلہ | Qalb قلب | Idghaam Meem Saakin ادغام میم ساکن

nor do we see that any follow you but the meanest among us, in judgment immature: nor do we see in you (all) any merit above us: in fact we think you are liars!"

wa maa naraakat-taba'aka illal-lazeena hum araazilunaa baadiyar-raåyi wa maa naraa lakum 'alaynaa min faḍlim-bal naẓunnukum kaazibeen.

وَمَا نَرٰىكَ اتَّبَعَكَ اِلَّا الَّذِيْنَ
هُمْ اَرَاذِلُنَا بَادِيَ الرَّاْيِ ۚ وَمَا
نَرٰى لَكُمْ عَلَيْنَا مِنْ فَضْلٍۭ بَلْ
نَظُنُّكُمْ كٰذِبِيْنَ ﴿٢٧﴾

28. He said: "O my people! do you see if (it be that) I have a Clear Sign from my Lord, and that He has sent Mercy to me from His Own Presence, but that the Mercy has been obscured from your sight? Shall we compel you to accept it when you are averse to it?

28. Qaala yaa qawmi ara'ay-tum in kuntu 'alaa bayyinatim-mir-Rabbee wa aataanee raḥmatam-min 'indihee fa'um-miyat 'alaykum anulzimuku-moohaa wa antum lahaa kaarihoon.

قَالَ يٰقَوْمِ اَرَءَيْتُمْ اِنْ كُنْتُ عَلٰى
بَيِّنَةٍ مِّنْ رَّبِّيْ وَاٰتٰىنِيْ رَحْمَةً مِّنْ
عِنْدِهٖ فَعُمِّيَتْ عَلَيْكُمْ ؕ اَنُلْزِمُكُمُوْهَا
وَاَنْتُمْ لَهَا كٰرِهُوْنَ ﴿٢٨﴾

29. "And O my people! I ask you for no wealth in return: my reward is from none but Allah: but I will not drive away (in contempt) those who believe: for verily they are to meet their Lord, and you, I see are the ignorant ones!

29. Wa yaa qawmi laaa as'alukum 'alayhi maalan in ajriya illaa 'alal-laah; wa maaa ana biṭaaridil-lazeena aama-noo; innahum mulaaqoo Rabbihim wa laakinneee araakum qawman tajhaloon.

وَيٰقَوْمِ لَاۤ اَسْـَٔلُكُمْ عَلَيْهِ مَالًا ؕ اِنْ
اَجْرِيَ اِلَّا عَلَى اللّٰهِ وَمَاۤ اَنَا بِطَارِدِ
الَّذِيْنَ اٰمَنُوْا ؕ اِنَّهُمْ مُّلٰقُوْا رَبِّهِمْ
وَلٰكِنِّيْۤ اَرٰىكُمْ قَوْمًا تَجْهَلُوْنَ ﴿٢٩﴾

30. "And O my people! who would help me against Allah if I drove them away? Will you not then take heed?

30. Wa yaa qawmi mañy-yanṣurunee minal-laahi in ṭarattuhum; afalaa tazak-karoon.

وَيٰقَوْمِ مَنْ يَّنْصُرُنِيْ مِنَ اللّٰهِ اِنْ
طَرَدْتُّهُمْ ؕ اَفَلَا تَذَكَّرُوْنَ ﴿٣٠﴾

31. "I do not tell you that with me are the Treasures of Allah, nor do I know what is hidden, nor I claim to be an angel. Nor yet do I say, of those whom your eyes do despise that Allah will not grant them (all) that is good: Allah knows best what is in their souls: I should, if I did, indeed be a wrong-doer."

31. Wa laaa aqoolu lakum 'indee khazaa'inul-laahi wa laaa a'lamul-ghayba wa laaa aqoolu innee malakuñw-wa laaa aqoolu lillazeena tazdareee a'yunukum lañy-yu'tiyahumul-laahu khayran Allaahu a'lamu bimaa feee anfusihim inneee izal-laminaẓ-ẓaalimeen.

وَلَاۤ اَقُوْلُ لَكُمْ عِنْدِيْ خَزَآئِنُ اللّٰهِ
وَلَاۤ اَعْلَمُ الْغَيْبَ وَلَاۤ اَقُوْلُ اِنِّيْ
مَلَكٌ وَّلَاۤ اَقُوْلُ لِلَّذِيْنَ تَزْدَرِيْۤ
اَعْيُنُكُمْ لَنْ يُّؤْتِيَهُمُ اللّٰهُ خَيْرًا ؕ
اَللّٰهُ اَعْلَمُ بِمَا فِيْۤ اَنْفُسِهِمْ ۚۖ اِنِّيْۤ
اِذًا لَّمِنَ الظّٰلِمِيْنَ ﴿٣١﴾

32. They said: "O Noah! You have disputed with us, and much have you prolonged the dispute with us: now bring upon us what you threaten us with, if you speak the truth!?"

32. Qaaloo yaa Nooḥu qad jaadaltanaa fa-aksarta jidaa-lanaa faåtinaa bimaa ta'idunaaa in kunta minaṣ-ṣaadiqeen.

قَالُوْا يٰنُوْحُ قَدْ جٰدَلْتَنَا فَاَكْثَرْتَ
جِدَالَنَا فَاْتِنَا بِمَا تَعِدُنَاۤ اِنْ كُنْتَ
مِنَ الصّٰدِقِيْنَ ﴿٣٢﴾

33. He said: "Truly, Allah will bring it on you if He wills,- and then, you will not be able to frustrate it!

33. Qaala innamaa yaåteekum bihil-laahu in shaaa'a wa maaa antum bimu'jizeen.

قَالَ اِنَّمَا يَاْتِيْكُمْ بِهِ اللّٰهُ اِنْ شَآءَ
وَمَاۤ اَنْتُمْ بِمُعْجِزِيْنَ ﴿٣٣﴾

34. "Of no profit will be my counsel to you, much as I desire

34. Wa laa yanfa'ukum nuṣḥeee in arattu

وَلَا يَنْفَعُكُمْ نُصْحِيْۤ اِنْ اَرَدْتُّ

to give you (good) counsel, if it be that Allah wills to leave you astray: He is your Lord! and to Him will you return!"

an anṣaḥa lakum in kaanal-laahu yureedu añy-yughwi-yakum; Huwa Rabbukum wa ilayhi turja'oon.

أَنْ أَنصَحَ لَكُمْ إِن كَانَ ٱللَّهُ
يُرِيدُ أَن يُغْوِيَكُمْ ۚ هُوَ رَبُّكُمْ قف
وَإِلَيْهِ تُرْجَعُونَ ﴿٣٤﴾

35. Or do they say, "He has forged it"? Say: "If I had forged it, on me were my sin! and I am free of the sins of which you are guilty!

35. Am yaqooloonaf-taraahu qul inif-taraytuhoo fa'alayya ijraamee wa ana bareee'um-mimmaa tujrimoon. **(Section 3)**

أَمْ يَقُولُونَ ٱفْتَرَىٰهُ ۖ قُلْ إِنِ
ٱفْتَرَيْتُهُۥ فَعَلَيَّ إِجْرَامِى وَأَنَا۠
بَرِىٓءٌ مِّمَّا تُجْرِمُونَ ﴿٣٥﴾ ع

36. It was revealed to Noah: "None of your people will believe except those who have believed already! So grieve no longer over their (evil) deeds.

36. Wa ooḥiya ilaa Nooḥin annahoo lañy-yu'mina min qawmika illaa man qad aamana falaa tabta'is bimaa kaanoo yaf'aloon.

وَأُوحِىَ إِلَىٰ نُوحٍ أَنَّهُۥ لَن يُؤْمِنَ
مِن قَوْمِكَ إِلَّا مَن قَدْ ءَامَنَ فَلَا
تَبْتَئِسْ بِمَا كَانُوا۟ يَفْعَلُونَ ﴿٣٦﴾

37. "But construct an Ark under Our eyes and Our inspiration, and address Me no (further) on behalf of those who are in sin: for they are about to be overwhelmed (in the Flood)."

37. Waṣna'il-fulka bi-a'yuninaa wa waḥyinaa wa laa tukhaa-ṭibnee fil-lazeena ẓalamoo; innahum-mughraqoon.

وَٱصْنَعِ ٱلْفُلْكَ بِأَعْيُنِنَا وَوَحْيِنَا
وَلَا تُخَـٰطِبْنِى فِى ٱلَّذِينَ ظَلَمُوٓا۟ ۚ
إِنَّهُم مُّغْرَقُونَ ﴿٣٧﴾

38. Forthwith he (starts) constructing the Ark: every time that the Chiefs of his people passed by him, they threw ridicule on him. He said: "If you ridicule us now, we (in our turn) can look down on you with ridicule likewise!

38. Wa yaṣna'ul-fulka wa kullamaa marra 'alayhi mala-um-min qawmihee sakhiroo minh; qaala in taskharoo minnaa fa-innaa naskharu minkum kamaa taskharoon.

وَيَصْنَعُ ٱلْفُلْكَ قف وَكُلَّمَا مَرَّ عَلَيْهِ
مَلَأٌ مِّن قَوْمِهِۦ سَخِرُوا۟ مِنْهُ ۚ قَالَ
إِن تَسْخَرُوا۟ مِنَّا فَإِنَّا نَسْخَرُ
مِنكُمْ كَمَا تَسْخَرُونَ ﴿٣٨﴾

39. "But soon you will know who it is on whom will descend a Chastisement that will cover them with shame,- on whom will be unloosed a lasting Chastisement:"

39. Fasawfa ta'lamoona mañy-yaâteehi 'azaabuñy-yukhzeehi wa yaḥillu 'alayhi 'azaabum-muqeem.

فَسَوْفَ تَعْلَمُونَ مَن يَأْتِيهِ عَذَابٌ
يُخْزِيهِ وَيَحِلُّ عَلَيْهِ عَذَابٌ مُّقِيمٌ ﴿٣٩﴾

40. At length, behold! there came Our Command, and the fountains of the earth gushed forth! We said: "Embark therein, of each kind two, male and female, and your family - except those against whom the Word has already gone forth,- and the Believers." But only a few believed with him.

40. Ḥattaaa izaa jaaa'a amrunaa wa faarat-tannooru qulnaḥ-mil feehaa min kullin zawjaynis-nayni wa ahlaka illaa man sabaqa 'alayhil-qawlu wa man aaman; wa maaa aamana ma'ahooo illaa qaleel.

حَتَّىٰٓ إِذَا جَآءَ أَمْرُنَا وَفَارَ ٱلتَّنُّورُ
قُلْنَا ٱحْمِلْ فِيهَا مِن كُلٍّ زَوْجَيْنِ
ٱثْنَيْنِ وَأَهْلَكَ إِلَّا مَن سَبَقَ عَلَيْهِ
ٱلْقَوْلُ وَمَنْ ءَامَنَ ۚ وَمَآ ءَامَنَ مَعَهُۥٓ
إِلَّا قَلِيلٌ ﴿٤٠﴾

41. So he said: "You embark on the Ark, In the name of Allah, whether it move or be at rest! For my Lord is, be sure, Oft-Forgiving, Most Merciful!"

41. Wa qaalar-kaboo feehaa bismil-laahi majrayhaa wa mursaahaa; inna Rabbee la-Ghafoorur-Raḥeem.

وَقَالَ ٱرْكَبُوا۟ فِيهَا بِسْمِ ٱللَّهِ مَجْر۪ىٰهَا
وَمُرْسَىٰهَآ ۚ إِنَّ رَبِّى لَغَفُورٌ رَّحِيمٌ ﴿٤١﴾

42. So the Ark floated with them on the waves (towering) like mountains,

42. Wa hiya tajree bihim fee mawjin kaljibaali

وَهِىَ تَجْرِى بِهِمْ فِى مَوْجٍ كَٱلْجِبَالِ قف

قرأ حفص بفتح الميم وامالة الراء ١٢

Ikhfa	Ghunna	Ikhfa Meem Saakin	Idghaam	Qalqala	Qalb	Idghaam Meem Saakin
اخفاء	غنّہ	اخفاء میم ساکن	ادغام	قلقلہ	قلب	ادغام میم ساکن

and Noah called out to his son, who had separated himself (from the rest): "O my son! embark with us, and be not with the Unbelievers!"	wa naadaa Nooḥunib-nahoo wa kaana fee ma'ziliñy-yaa bunayyarkam-ma'anaa wa laa takum ma'al-kaafireen.	وَنَادَىٰ نُوحٌ ٱبْنَهُۥ وَكَانَ فِى مَعْزِلٍ يَٰبُنَىَّ ٱرْكَب مَّعَنَا وَلَا تَكُن مَّعَ ٱلْكَٰفِرِينَ ٤٢
43. The son replied: "I will betake myself to some mountain: it will save me from the water." Noah said: "This day nothing can save, from the Command of Allah, any but those on whom He has mercy! "And the waves came between them, and the son was among those overwhelmed in the Flood.	43. Qaala sa-aaweee ilaa jabaliñy-ya'ṣimunee minal-maaa'; qaala laa 'aaṣimal-yawma min amril-laahi illaa marraḥim; wa ḥaala baynahumal-mawju fakaana minal-mughraqeen.	قَالَ سَـَٔاوِىٓ إِلَىٰ جَبَلٍ يَعْصِمُنِى مِنَ ٱلْمَآءِ ۚ قَالَ لَا عَاصِمَ ٱلْيَوْمَ مِنْ أَمْرِ ٱللَّهِ إِلَّا مَن رَّحِمَ ۚ وَحَالَ بَيْنَهُمَا ٱلْمَوْجُ فَكَانَ مِنَ ٱلْمُغْرَقِينَ ٤٣
44. Then the word went forth: "O earth! swallow up your water, and O sky! withhold (your rain)!" And the water abated, and the matter was ended. The Ark rested on Mount Judi, and the word went forth: "Away with those who do wrong!"	44. Wa qeela yaaa arḍubla'ee maaa'aki wa yaa samaaa'u aqli'ee wa gheeḍal-maaa'u wa quḍiyal-amru wastawat 'alal-joodiyyi wa qeela bu'dal-lilqawmiẓ-ẓaalimeen.	وَقِيلَ يَٰٓأَرْضُ ٱبْلَعِى مَآءَكِ وَيَٰسَمَآءُ أَقْلِعِى وَغِيضَ ٱلْمَآءُ وَقُضِىَ ٱلْأَمْرُ وَٱسْتَوَتْ عَلَى ٱلْجُودِىِّ ۖ وَقِيلَ بُعْدًا لِّلْقَوْمِ ٱلظَّٰلِمِينَ ٤٤ الربع
45. And Noah called upon his Lord, and said: "O my Lord! surely my son is of my family! And Your promise is true, and You are the justest of Judges!"	45. Wa naadaa Nooḥur-Rabbahoo faqaala Rabbi innab-nee min ahlee wa inna wa'dakal-ḥaqqu wa Anta aḥkamul-ḥaakimeen.	وَنَادَىٰ نُوحٌ رَّبَّهُۥ فَقَالَ رَبِّ إِنَّ ٱبْنِى مِنْ أَهْلِى وَإِنَّ وَعْدَكَ ٱلْحَقُّ وَأَنتَ أَحْكَمُ ٱلْحَٰكِمِينَ ٤٥
46. He said: "O Noah! He is not of your family: for his conduct is unrighteous. So do not ask of Me that of which you have no knowledge! I give you counsel, lest you act like the ignorant!"	46. Qaala yaa Nooḥu innahoo laysa min ahlika innahoo 'amalun ghayru ṣaaliḥin falaa tas'alni maa laysa laka bihee 'ilmun inneee a'iẓuka an takoona minal-jaahileen.	قَالَ يَٰنُوحُ إِنَّهُۥ لَيْسَ مِنْ أَهْلِكَ ۖ إِنَّهُۥ عَمَلٌ غَيْرُ صَٰلِحٍ ۖ فَلَا تَسْـَٔلْنِ مَا لَيْسَ لَكَ بِهِۦ عِلْمٌ ۖ إِنِّىٓ أَعِظُكَ أَن تَكُونَ مِنَ ٱلْجَٰهِلِينَ ٤٦
47. Noah said: "O my Lord! I do seek refuge with You, lest I ask You for that of which I have no knowledge. And unless You forgive me and have Mercy on me, I should indeed be lost!"	47. Qaala Rabbi inneee a'oozu bika an as'alaka maa laysa lee bihee 'ilmuñw wa illaa taghfir lee wa tarḥamneee akum-minal-khaasireen.	قَالَ رَبِّ إِنِّىٓ أَعُوذُ بِكَ أَنْ أَسْـَٔلَكَ مَا لَيْسَ لِى بِهِۦ عِلْمٌ ۖ وَإِلَّا تَغْفِرْ لِى وَتَرْحَمْنِىٓ أَكُن مِّنَ ٱلْخَٰسِرِينَ ٤٧
48. The word came: "O Noah! come down (from the Ark) with peace from Us, and Blessing on you and on some of the peoples (who will spring) from those with you: but (there will be other) peoples to whom We shall grant their pleasures (for a time), but in the end a grievous Chastisement will reach them from Us."	48. Qeela yaa Nooḥuh-biṭ bisalaamim-minnaa wa barakaatin 'alayka wa 'alaaa umamim-mimmam-ma'ak; wa umamun sanumatti'uhum summa yamassuhum-minnaa 'azaabun aleem.	قِيلَ يَٰنُوحُ ٱهْبِطْ بِسَلَٰمٍ مِّنَّا وَبَرَكَٰتٍ عَلَيْكَ وَعَلَىٰٓ أُمَمٍ مِّمَّن مَّعَكَ ۚ وَأُمَمٌ سَنُمَتِّعُهُمْ ثُمَّ يَمَسُّهُم مِّنَّا عَذَابٌ أَلِيمٌ ٤٨
49. Such are some of the stories of the Unseen, which We have revealed	49. Tilka min ambaaa'il ghaybi nooḥeehaaa	تِلْكَ مِنْ أَنۢبَآءِ ٱلْغَيْبِ نُوحِيهَآ

Ikhfa اخفاء	Ghunna غنّہ	Ikhfa Meem Saakin اخفاء میم ساکن	Idghaam ادغام	Qalqala قلقلہ	Qalb قلب	Idghaam Meem Saakin ادغام میم ساکن

to you: before this, neither you nor your people knew them. So persevere patiently: for the End is for those who are righteous.

50. To the 'Ad People (We sent) Hud, one of their own brethren. He said: "O my people! worship Allah! you have no other god but Him. (Your other gods) you do nothing but invent!

51. "O my people! I ask of you no reward for this (Message). My reward is from none but Him who created me: will you not then understand?

52. "And O my people! Ask forgiveness of your Lord, and turn to Him (in repentance): He will send you the skies pouring abundant rain, and add strength to your strength: so you do not turn back in sin!"

53. They said: "O Hud! You have brought us no Clear (Sign), and we are not the ones to desert our gods on your word! Nor shall we believe in you!

54. "We say nothing but that (perhaps) some of our gods may have seized you with imbecility." He said: "I call Allah to witness, and you do bear witness, that I am free from the sin of ascribing, to Him,

55. "Other gods as partners! So scheme (your worst) against me, all of you, and give me no respite.

56. "I put my trust in Allah, my Lord and your Lord! There is not a moving creature, but He has grasp of its fore-lock. Verily, it is my Lord that is on a straight Path.

57. "If you turn away,- I (at least) have conveyed the Message with which I was sent to you. My Lord will make another

ilayka maa kunta ta'lamuhaaa anta wa laa qawmuka min qabli haazaa faṣbir innal-'aaqibata lilmuttaqeen. **(Section 4)**

50. Wa ilaa 'Aadin akhaahum Hoodaa; qaala yaa qawmi'-budul-laaha maa lakum min ilaahin ghayruhooo in antum illaa muftaroon.

51. Yaa qawmi laaa as'alukum 'alayhi ajran in ajriya illaa 'alal-lazee faṭaranee; afalaa ta'qiloon.

52. Wa yaa qawmis-taghfiroo Rabbakum summa toobooo ilayhi yursilis-samaaa'a 'alay-kum-midraarañw-wa yazidkum quwwatan ilaa quwwatikum wa laa tatawallaw mujrimeen.

53. Qaaloo yaa Hoodu maa ji'tanaa bibayyinatiñw-wa maa naḥnu bitaarikeee aalihatinaa 'an qawlika wa maa naḥnu laka bimu'mineen.

54. In naqoolu illa'-taraaka ba'ḍu aalihatinaa bisooo'; qaala inneee ushhidul-laaha wash-hadooo annee bareee'um-mimmaa tushrikoon.

55. Min doonihee fakeedoonee jamee'an summa laa tunziroon.

56. Innee tawakkaltu 'alallaahi Rabbee wa Rabbikum; maa min daaabbatin illaa Huwa aakhi-zum binaaṣiyatihaa; inna Rabbee 'alaa Ṣiraaṭim-Musta-qeem.

57. Fa-in tawallaw faqad ablaghtukum-maaa ursiltu biheee ilaykum; wa yastakhlifu Rabbee qawman

إِلَيْكَ مَا كُنْتَ تَعْلَمُهَآ أَنْتَ وَلَا
قَوْمُكَ مِنْ قَبْلِ هٰذَا ۛ فَاصْبِرْ ۛ
إِنَّ الْعَاقِبَةَ لِلْمُتَّقِينَ ﴿٤٩﴾
وَإِلَىٰ عَادٍ أَخَاهُمْ هُودًا ۚ قَالَ
يٰقَوْمِ اعْبُدُوا اللّٰهَ مَا لَكُمْ مِّنْ
إِلٰهٍ غَيْرُهُ ۖ إِنْ أَنْتُمْ إِلَّا مُفْتَرُونَ ﴿٥٠﴾
يٰقَوْمِ لَآ أَسْأَلُكُمْ عَلَيْهِ أَجْرًا ۖ إِنْ
أَجْرِيَ إِلَّا عَلَى الَّذِي فَطَرَنِي ۚ
أَفَلَا تَعْقِلُونَ ﴿٥١﴾
وَيٰقَوْمِ اسْتَغْفِرُوا رَبَّكُمْ ثُمَّ تُوبُوٓا
إِلَيْهِ يُرْسِلِ السَّمَآءَ عَلَيْكُمْ مِّدْرَارًا
وَّيَزِدْكُمْ قُوَّةً إِلَىٰ قُوَّتِكُمْ وَلَا
تَتَوَلَّوْا مُجْرِمِينَ ﴿٥٢﴾
قَالُوا يٰهُودُ مَا جِئْتَنَا بِبَيِّنَةٍ وَّمَا
نَحْنُ بِتَارِكِيٓ اٰلِهَتِنَا عَنْ قَوْلِكَ وَمَا
نَحْنُ لَكَ بِمُؤْمِنِينَ ﴿٥٣﴾
إِنْ نَّقُولُ إِلَّا اعْتَرَاكَ بَعْضُ اٰلِهَتِنَا
بِسُوٓءٍ ۗ قَالَ إِنِّيٓ أُشْهِدُ اللّٰهَ وَاشْهَدُوٓا
أَنِّي بَرِيٓءٌ مِّمَّا تُشْرِكُونَ ﴿٥٤﴾
مِنْ دُونِهٖ فَكِيدُونِي جَمِيعًا ثُمَّ
لَا تُنْظِرُونِ ﴿٥٥﴾
إِنِّي تَوَكَّلْتُ عَلَى اللّٰهِ رَبِّي وَرَبِّكُمْ ۚ
مَا مِنْ دَآبَّةٍ إِلَّا هُوَ اٰخِذٌۢ بِنَاصِيَتِهَا ۚ
إِنَّ رَبِّي عَلَىٰ صِرَاطٍ مُّسْتَقِيمٍ ﴿٥٦﴾
فَإِنْ تَوَلَّوْا فَقَدْ أَبْلَغْتُكُمْ مَّآ أُرْسِلْتُ
بِهٖٓ إِلَيْكُمْ ۚ وَيَسْتَخْلِفُ رَبِّي قَوْمًا

Ikhfa اخفاء | Ghunna غُنّہ | Ikhfa Meem Saakin اخفاء میم ساکن | Idghaam ادغام | Qalqala قلقلہ | Qalb قلب | Idghaam Meem Saakin ادغام میم ساکن

غَيْرَكُمْ ۚ وَلَا تَضُرُّونَهُ شَيْئًا ۚ إِنَّ
رَبِّي عَلَىٰ كُلِّ شَيْءٍ حَفِيظٌ ﴿٥٧﴾

ghayrakum wa laa taḏurroonahoo shay'aa; inna Rabbee 'alaa kulli shay'in Ḥafeez.

another people to succeed you, and you will not harm Him in the least. For my Lord has care and watch over all things."

وَلَمَّا جَاءَ أَمْرُنَا نَجَّيْنَا هُودًا وَ
الَّذِينَ آمَنُوا مَعَهُ بِرَحْمَةٍ مِّنَّا
وَنَجَّيْنَاهُم مِّنْ عَذَابٍ غَلِيظٍ ﴿٥٨﴾

58. Wa lammaa jaaa'a amrunaa najjaynaa Hoodañw-wallazeena aamanoo ma'ahoo birahmatim-minnaa wa najjaynaahum-min 'azaabin ghaleez.

58. So when Our decree issued, We saved Hud and those who believed with him, by (special) Grace from Ourselves: We saved them from a severe Chastisement.

وَتِلْكَ عَادٌ ۖ جَحَدُوا بِآيَاتِ رَبِّهِمْ
وَعَصَوْا رُسُلَهُ وَاتَّبَعُوا أَمْرَ كُلِّ
جَبَّارٍ عَنِيدٍ ﴿٥٩﴾

59. Wa tilka 'Aad, jaḥadoo bi-Aayaati Rabbihim wa 'aṣaw Rusulahoo wattaba'ooo amra kulli jabbaarin 'aneed.

59. Such were the 'Ad People: they rejected the Signs of their Lord and Cherisher; disobeyed His Apostles; and followed the command of every powerful, obstinate transgressor.

وَأُتْبِعُوا فِي هَٰذِهِ الدُّنْيَا لَعْنَةً وَ
يَوْمَ الْقِيَامَةِ ۗ أَلَا إِنَّ عَادًا كَفَرُوا
رَبَّهُمْ ۗ أَلَا بُعْدًا لِّعَادٍ قَوْمِ هُودٍ ﴿٦٠﴾ ع ٥ وقف لازم

60. Wa utbi'oo fee haazihid-dunyaa la'natañw-wa Yawmal-Qiyaamah; alaaa inna 'Aadan kafaroo Rabbahum; alaa bu'dal-li-'Aadin qawmi Hood.

(Section 5)

60. And they were pursued by a Curse in this life,- and on the Day of Judgment. Ah! Behold! For the 'Ad rejected their Lord and Cherisher! Ah! Behold! Removed (from sight) were 'Ad, the people of Hud!

وَإِلَىٰ ثَمُودَ أَخَاهُمْ صَالِحًا ۚ قَالَ
يَا قَوْمِ اعْبُدُوا اللَّهَ مَا لَكُم مِّنْ
إِلَٰهٍ غَيْرُهُ ۖ هُوَ أَنشَأَكُم مِّنَ
الْأَرْضِ وَاسْتَعْمَرَكُمْ فِيهَا
فَاسْتَغْفِرُوهُ ثُمَّ تُوبُوا إِلَيْهِ ۚ إِنَّ
رَبِّي قَرِيبٌ مُّجِيبٌ ﴿٦١﴾

61. Wa ilaa Samooda akhaahum Ṣaaliḥaa; qaala yaa qawmi'-budul-laaha maa lakum min ilaahin ghayruhoo Huwa ansha-akum-minal-arḍi wasta'marakum feehaa fastaghfiroohu summa toobooo ilayh; inna Rabbee Qareebum-Mujeeb.

61. To the Thamud People (We sent) Salih, one of their own brethren. He said: "O my people! Worship Allah: you have no other god but Him. It is He Who has produced you from the earth and settled you therein: then ask forgiveness of Him, and turn to Him (in repentance): for my Lord is (always) near, ready to answer."

قَالُوا يَا صَالِحُ قَدْ كُنتَ فِينَا مَرْجُوًّا
قَبْلَ هَٰذَا ۖ أَتَنْهَانَا أَن نَّعْبُدَ مَا
يَعْبُدُ آبَاؤُنَا وَإِنَّنَا لَفِي شَكٍّ
مِّمَّا تَدْعُونَا إِلَيْهِ مُرِيبٍ ﴿٦٢﴾

62. Qaaloo yaa Ṣaaliḥu qad kunta feenaa marjuwwan qabla haazaaa atanhaanaaa an na'buda maa ya'budu aabaaa'unaa wa innanaa lafee shakkim-mimmaa tad'oonaaa ilayhi mureeb.

62. They said: "O Salih! you have been of us!- a centre of our hopes hitherto! Do you (now) forbid us the worship of what our fathers worshipped? But we are really in suspicious (disquieting) doubt as to that to which you invite us."

قَالَ يَا قَوْمِ أَرَأَيْتُمْ إِن كُنتُ عَلَىٰ
بَيِّنَةٍ مِّن رَّبِّي وَآتَانِي مِنْهُ رَحْمَةً
فَمَن يَنصُرُنِي مِنَ اللَّهِ إِنْ عَصَيْتُهُ ۖ
فَمَا تَزِيدُونَنِي غَيْرَ تَخْسِيرٍ ﴿٦٣﴾

63. Qaala yaa qawmi ara'aytum in kuntu 'alaa bayyinatim-mir-Rabbee wa aataanee minhu raḥmatan famañy-yanṣurunee minal-laahi in 'aṣaytuhoo famaa tazeedoonanee ghayra takhseer.

63. He said: "O my people! Do you see? if I have a Clear (Sign) from my Lord and He has sent Mercy to me from Himself,- who then can help me against Allah if I were to disobey Him? What then would you add to my (portion) but perdition?

وَيَا قَوْمِ هَٰذِهِ نَاقَةُ اللَّهِ لَكُمْ

64. Wa yaa qawmi haazihee naaqatul-laahi lakum

64. "And O my people! this she-camel of Allah is a symbol to

ءَايَةً فَذَرُوهَا تَأْكُلْ فِىٓ أَرْضِ
ٱللَّهِ وَلَا تَمَسُّوهَا بِسُوٓءٍ فَيَأْخُذَكُمْ
عَذَابٌ قَرِيبٌ ﴿٦٤﴾

Aayatan fazaroohaa taåkul feee ardil-laahi wa laa tamassoohaa bisooo'in fa-yaåkhuzakum azaabun qareeb.

you: leave her to feed on Allah's (free) earth, and inflict no harm on her, or a swift Chastisement will seize you!"

فَعَقَرُوهَا فَقَالَ تَمَتَّعُوا۟ فِى دَارِكُمْ
ثَلَـٰثَةَ أَيَّامٍ ۖ ذَٰلِكَ وَعْدٌ غَيْرُ
مَكْذُوبٍ ﴿٦٥﴾

65. Fa'aqaroohaa faqaala tamatta'oo fee daarikum salaasata ayyaamin zaalika wa'dun ghayru makzoob.

65. But they hamstrung her. So he said: "Enjoy yourselves in your homes for three days: (then will be your ruin): (behold) there is a promise not to be belied!"

فَلَمَّا جَآءَ أَمْرُنَا نَجَّيْنَا صَـٰلِحًا
وَٱلَّذِينَ ءَامَنُوا۟ مَعَهُۥ بِرَحْمَةٍ مِّنَّا
وَمِنْ خِزْىِ يَوْمِئِذٍ ۗ إِنَّ رَبَّكَ
هُوَ ٱلْقَوِىُّ ٱلْعَزِيزُ ﴿٦٦﴾

66. Falammaa jaaa'a amrunaa najjaynaa Ṣaaliḥañw-wal-lazeena aamanoo ma'ahoo biraḥmatim-minnaa wa min khizyi Yawmi'iz, inna Rabbaka Huwal-Qawiyyul-'Azeez.

66. When Our Decree issued, We saved Salih and those who believed with him, by (special) Grace from Ourselves - and from the Ignominy of that Day. For your Lord - He is the Strong One, and Able to enforce His Will.

وَأَخَذَ ٱلَّذِينَ ظَلَمُوا۟ ٱلصَّيْحَةُ
فَأَصْبَحُوا۟ فِى دِيَـٰرِهِمْ جَـٰثِمِينَ ﴿٦٧﴾

67. Wa akhazal-lazeena ẓalamuṣ-ṣayḥatu fa-aṣbaḥoo fee diyaarihim jaasimeena.

67. The (mighty) Blast overtook the wrong-doers, and they lay prostrate in their homes before the morning,-

كَأَن لَّمْ يَغْنَوْا۟ فِيهَآ ۗ أَلَآ إِنَّ ثَمُودَا۟
كَفَرُوا۟ رَبَّهُمْ ۗ أَلَا بُعْدًا لِّثَمُودَ ﴿٦٨﴾ ع

68. Ka-al-lam yaghnaw fee-haaa; alaaa inna Samooda kafaroo Rabbahum; alaa bu'dal-li-Samood. **(Section 6)**

68. As if they had never dwelt and flourished there. Ah! Behold! For the Thamud rejected their Lord and Cherisher! Ah! Behold! Removed (from sight) were the Thamud!

وَلَقَدْ جَآءَتْ رُسُلُنَآ إِبْرَٰهِيمَ
بِٱلْبُشْرَىٰ قَالُوا۟ سَلَـٰمًا ۖ قَالَ سَلَـٰمٌ
فَمَا لَبِثَ أَن جَآءَ بِعِجْلٍ حَنِيذٍ ﴿٦٩﴾

69. Wa laqad jaaa'at Rusulunaaa Ibraaheema bilbushraa qaaloo salaaman qaala salaamun famaa labisa an jaaa'a bi'ijlin ḥaneez.

69. There came Our Messengers to Abraham with glad tidings. They said, "Peace!" He answered, "Peace!" and hastened to entertain them with a roasted calf.

فَلَمَّا رَءَآ أَيْدِيَهُمْ لَا تَصِلُ إِلَيْهِ نَكِرَهُمْ
وَأَوْجَسَ مِنْهُمْ خِيفَةً ۚ قَالُوا۟ لَا
تَخَفْ إِنَّآ أُرْسِلْنَآ إِلَىٰ قَوْمِ لُوطٍ ﴿٧٠﴾

70. Falammaa ra-aaa aydiya-hum laa taṣilu ilayhi nakirahum wa awjasa minhum kheefah; qaaloo laa takhaf innaaa ursilnaaa ilaa qawmi Looṭ.

70. But when he saw their hands did not go towards the (meal), he felt some mistrust of them, and conceived a fear of them. They said: "Fear not: we have been sent against the people of Lut."

وَٱمْرَأَتُهُۥ قَآئِمَةٌ فَضَحِكَتْ فَبَشَّرْنَـٰهَا
بِإِسْحَـٰقَ وَمِن وَرَآءِ إِسْحَـٰقَ يَعْقُوبَ ﴿٧١﴾

71. Wamra-atuhoo qaaa'imatun faḍaḥikat fabashsharnaahaa bi-Isḥaaqa wa miñw-waraaa'i Isḥaaqa Ya'qoob.

71. And his wife was standing (there), and she laughed: but We gave her glad tidings of Isaac, and after him, of Jacob.

قَالَتْ يَـٰوَيْلَتَىٰٓ ءَأَلِدُ وَأَنَا۠ عَجُوزٌ
وَهَـٰذَا بَعْلِى شَيْخًا ۖ إِنَّ هَـٰذَا
لَشَىْءٌ عَجِيبٌ ﴿٧٢﴾

72. Qaalat yaa waylataaa 'a-alidu wa ana 'ajoozuñw-wa haazaa ba'lee shaykhan inna haazaa lashay'un 'ajeeb.

72. She said: "Alas for me! shall I bear a child, seeing I am an old woman, and my husband here is an old man? That would indeed be a wonderful thing!"

قَالُوٓا۟ أَتَعْجَبِينَ مِنْ أَمْرِ ٱللَّهِ ۖ رَحْمَتُ

73. Qaalooo ata'jabeena min amril-laahi raḥmatul-

73. They said: "Do you wonder at Allah's decree? The Grace

Ikhfa اخفاء | Ghunna غنّہ | Ikhfa Meem Saakin اخفاء میم ساکن | Idghaam ادغام | Qalqala قلقلہ | Qalb قلب | Idghaam Meem Saakin ادغام میم ساکن

of Allah and His blessings on you, O you people of the house! for He is indeed worthy of all praise, full of all glory!"

74. When fear had passed from (the mind of) Abraham and the glad tidings had reached him, he began to plead with us for Lut's people.

75. For Abraham was, without doubt, forbearing (of faults), compassionate, and given to look to Allah.

76. O Abraham! Do not seek this. The decree of your Lord has gone forth: for them there comes a Chastisement that cannot be turned back!

77. When Our Messengers came to Lut, he was grieved on their account and felt himself powerless (to protect) them. He said: "This is a distressful day."

78. And his people came rushing towards him, and they had been long in the habit of practising abominations. He said: "O my people! Here are my daughters: they are purer for you (if you marry)! Now fear Allah, and do not cover me with shame about my guests! Isn't there among you a single right-minded man?"

79. They said: "You know well we have no need of your daughters: indeed you know quite well what we want!"

80. He said: "Would that I had power to suppress you or that I could betake myself to some powerful support."

81. (The Messengers) said: "O Lut! We are Messengers from your Lord! By no means they shall reach you! Now travel with your family while yet a part of the night remains, and let not any of you look back: but your wife (will remain behind): to her will happen what happens to the people. Morning is their appointed time:

laahi wa barakaatuhoo 'alaykum Ahlal-Bayt; innahoo Ḥameedum-Majeed.

74. Falammaa zahaba an Ibraaheemar-raw'u wa jaaa'athul-bushraa yujaadilunaa fee qawmi Looṭ.

75. Inna Ibraaheema laḥaleemun awwaahum-muneeb.

76. Yaaa Ibraaheemu a'riḍ 'an haazaaa innahoo qad jaaa'a amru Rabbika wa innahum aateehim 'azaabun ghayru mardood.

77. Wa lammaa jaaa'at Rusulunaa Looṭan seee'a bihim wa ḍaaqa bihim zar'añw-wa qaala haazaa yawmun 'aṣeeb.

78. Wa jaaa'ahoo qawmuhoo yuhra'oona ilayhi wa min qablu kaanoo ya'maloonas-sayyi-aat; qaala yaa qawmi haaa'ulaaa'i banaatee hunna aṭharu lakum fattaqul-laaha wa laa tukhzooni fee ḍayfee alaysa minkum rajulur-rasheed.

79. Qaaloo laqad 'alimta maa lanaa fee banaatika min ḥaqq, wa innaka lata'lamu maa nureed.

80. Qaala law anna lee bikum quwwatan aw aaweee ilaa ruknin shadeed.

81. Qaaloo yaa Looṭu innaa Rusulu Rabbika lañy-yaṣilooo ilayka fa-asri bi-ahlika biqiṭ'im-minal-layli wa laa yaltafit minkum aḥadun illamra-ataka innahoo muṣeebuhaa maaa aṣaabahum; inna maw'idahumuṣ-ṣubḥ;

اللّٰهِ وَبَرَكٰتُهٗ عَلَيْكُمْ اَهْلَ الْبَيْتِ ؕ
اِنَّهٗ حَمِيْدٌ مَّجِيْدٌ ﴿۷۳﴾
فَلَمَّا ذَهَبَ عَنْ اِبْرٰهِيْمَ الرَّوْعُ
وَجَآءَتْهُ الْبُشْرٰى يُجَادِلُنَا
فِىْ قَوْمِ لُوْطٍ ﴿۷۴﴾
اِنَّ اِبْرٰهِيْمَ لَحَلِيْمٌ اَوَّاهٌ مُّنِيْبٌ ﴿۷۵﴾
يٰۤاِبْرٰهِيْمُ اَعْرِضْ عَنْ هٰذَا ۚ اِنَّهٗ
قَدْ جَآءَ اَمْرُ رَبِّكَ ۚ وَاِنَّهُمْ اٰتِيْهِمْ
عَذَابٌ غَيْرُ مَرْدُوْدٍ ﴿۷۶﴾
وَلَمَّا جَآءَتْ رُسُلُنَا لُوْطًا سِیْٓءَ
بِهِمْ وَضَاقَ بِهِمْ ذَرْعًا وَّقَالَ
هٰذَا يَوْمٌ عَصِيْبٌ ﴿۷۷﴾
وَجَآءَهٗ قَوْمُهٗ يُهْرَعُوْنَ اِلَيْهِ ؕ
وَمِنْ قَبْلُ كَانُوْا يَعْمَلُوْنَ السَّيِّاٰتِ ؕ
قَالَ يٰقَوْمِ هٰۤؤُلَآءِ بَنَاتِىْ هُنَّ اَطْهَرُ
لَكُمْ فَاتَّقُوا اللّٰهَ وَلَا تُخْزُوْنِ فِىْ
ضَيْفِىْ ؕ اَلَيْسَ مِنْكُمْ رَجُلٌ رَّشِيْدٌ ﴿۷۸﴾
قَالُوْا لَقَدْ عَلِمْتَ مَا لَنَا فِىْ بَنٰتِكَ
مِنْ حَقٍّ ۚ وَاِنَّكَ لَتَعْلَمُ مَا نُرِيْدُ ﴿۷۹﴾
قَالَ لَوْ اَنَّ لِىْ بِكُمْ قُوَّةً اَوْ اٰوِىْۤ
اِلٰى رُكْنٍ شَدِيْدٍ ﴿۸۰﴾
قَالُوْا يٰلُوْطُ اِنَّا رُسُلُ رَبِّكَ لَنْ
يَّصِلُوْۤا اِلَيْكَ فَاَسْرِ بِاَهْلِكَ بِقِطْعٍ
مِّنَ الَّيْلِ وَلَا يَلْتَفِتْ مِنْكُمْ اَحَدٌ
اِلَّا امْرَاَتَكَ ؕ اِنَّهٗ مُصِيْبُهَا مَآ
اَصَابَهُمْ ؕ اِنَّ مَوْعِدَهُمُ الصُّبْحُ ؕ

Ikhfa اخفاء | Ghunna غُنّہ | Ikhfa Meem Saakin اخفاء میم ساکن | Idghaam ادغام | Qalqala قلقلہ | Qalb قلب | Idghaam Meem Saakin ادغام میم ساکن

is not the morning near?"

82. When Our decree issued, We turned (the cities) upside down, and rained down on them brimstones hard as baked clay, spread, layer on layer,-

83. Marked as from your Lord: nor are they ever far from those who do wrong!

84. To the Madyan People (We sent) Shu'aib, one of their own brethren: he said: "O my people! worship Allah: You have no other god but Him. And do not give short measure or weight: I see you in prosperity, but I fear for you the Chastisement of a Day that will compass (you) all round.

85. "And O my people! give just measure and weight, nor withhold from the people the things that are their due: do not commit evil in the land with intent to do mischief.

86. "That which is left you by Allah is best for you, if you (but) believed! but I am not set over you to keep watch!"

87. They said: "O Shu'aib! Does your (religion of) prayer command you that we leave off the worship which our fathers practised, or that we leave off doing what we like with our property? truly, you are the one that forbears with faults and is right-minded!"

88. He said: "O my people! Do you see whether I have a Clear (Sign) from my Lord, and He has given me sustenance (pure and) good as from Himself? I do not wish, in opposition to you, to do that which I forbid you to do. I only desire (your) betterment to the best of my power; and my success (in my task) can only come from Allah. In Him I trust,

alaysaṣ-ṣubḥu biqareeb.

82. Falammaa jaaa'a amrunaa ja'alnaa 'aaliyahaa saafilahaa wa amṭarnaa 'alayhaa ḥijaaratam-min sijjeelim-manḍood.

83. Musawwamatan 'inda Rabbik; wa maa hiya minaẓ-ẓaalimeena biba'eed. **(Section 7)**

84. Wa ilaa Madyana akhaahum Shu'aybaa; qaala yaa qawmi'-budul-laaha maa lakum min ilaahin ghayruhoo wa laa tanquṣul-mikyaala walmeezaan; inneee araakum bikhayriñw-wa inneee akhaafu 'alaykum 'azaaba Yawmim-muḥeeṭ.

85. Wa yaa qawmi awful-mikyaala walmeezaana bilqisṭi wa laa tabkhasun-naasa ashyaaa'ahum wa laa ta'saw fil-arḍi mufsideen.

86. Baqiyyatul-laahi khayrul-lakum in kuntum-mu'mineen; wa maa ana 'alaykum biḥafeeẓ.

87. Qaaloo yaa Shu'aybu aṣalaatuka taâmuruka an natruka maa ya'budu aabaaa'unaaa aw an naf'ala feee amwaalinaa maa nashaaa'oo innaka la-antal ḥaleemur-rasheed.

88. Qaala yaa qawmi ara'aytum in kuntu 'alaa bayyinatim-mir-Rabbee wa razaqanee minhu rizqan ḥasanaa; wa maaa ureedu an ukhaalifakum ilaa maaa anhaakum 'anh; in ureedu illal-iṣlaaḥa mastaṭa't; wa maa tawfeeqeee illaa billaah; 'alayhi tawakkaltu

اَلَيْسَ الصُّبْحُ بِقَرِيْبٍ ﴿٨١﴾
فَلَمَّا جَآءَ اَمْرُنَا جَعَلْنَا عَالِيَهَا
سَافِلَهَا وَاَمْطَرْنَا عَلَيْهَا حِجَارَةً
مِّنْ سِجِّيْلٍ ۙ مَّنْضُوْدٍ ﴿٨٢﴾
مُّسَوَّمَةً عِنْدَ رَبِّكَ ؕ وَمَا هِيَ
مِنَ الظّٰلِمِيْنَ بِبَعِيْدٍ ﴿٨٣﴾
وَاِلٰى مَدْيَنَ اَخَاهُمْ شُعَيْبًا ؕ قَالَ
يٰقَوْمِ اعْبُدُوا اللّٰهَ مَا لَكُمْ مِّنْ
اِلٰهٍ غَيْرُهٗ ؕ وَلَا تَنْقُصُوا الْمِكْيَالَ
وَالْمِيْزَانَ اِنِّيْٓ اَرٰىكُمْ بِخَيْرٍ وَّاِنِّيْٓ اَخَافُ
عَلَيْكُمْ عَذَابَ يَوْمٍ مُّحِيْطٍ ﴿٨٤﴾
وَيٰقَوْمِ اَوْفُوا الْمِكْيَالَ وَالْمِيْزَانَ
بِالْقِسْطِ وَلَا تَبْخَسُوا النَّاسَ اَشْيَآءَهُمْ
وَلَا تَعْثَوْا فِى الْاَرْضِ مُفْسِدِيْنَ ﴿٨٥﴾
بَقِيَّتُ اللّٰهِ خَيْرٌ لَّكُمْ اِنْ كُنْتُمْ
مُّؤْمِنِيْنَ ۚ وَمَآ اَنَا عَلَيْكُمْ بِحَفِيْظٍ ﴿٨٦﴾
قَالُوْا يٰشُعَيْبُ اَصَلٰوتُكَ تَاْمُرُكَ اَنْ
نَّتْرُكَ مَا يَعْبُدُ اٰبَآؤُنَآ اَوْ اَنْ
نَّفْعَلَ فِيْٓ اَمْوَالِنَا مَا نَشٰٓؤُا ؕ اِنَّكَ
لَاَنْتَ الْحَلِيْمُ الرَّشِيْدُ ﴿٨٧﴾
قَالَ يٰقَوْمِ اَرَءَيْتُمْ اِنْ كُنْتُ عَلٰى
بَيِّنَةٍ مِّنْ رَّبِّيْ وَرَزَقَنِيْ مِنْهُ
رِزْقًا حَسَنًا ؕ وَمَآ اُرِيْدُ اَنْ اُخَالِفَكُمْ
اِلٰى مَآ اَنْهٰىكُمْ عَنْهُ ؕ اِنْ اُرِيْدُ اِلَّا
الْاِصْلَاحَ مَا اسْتَطَعْتُ ؕ وَمَا
تَوْفِيْقِيْٓ اِلَّا بِاللّٰهِ ؕ عَلَيْهِ تَوَكَّلْتُ

النّصف

Ikhfa اخفاء | Ghunna غنّہ | Ikhfa Meem Saakin اخفاءمیم ساکن | Idghaam ادغام | Qalqala قلقلہ | Qalb قلب | Idghaam Meem Saakin ادغام میم ساکن

and to Him I turn.

wa ilayhi uneeb.

وَإِلَيْهِ أُنِيبُ ۝٨٨

89. "And O my people! let not my dissent (from you) cause you to sin, lest you suffer a fate similar to that of the people of Noah or of Hud or of Salih, nor are the people of Lut far off from you!

89. Wa yaa qawmi laa yajrimannakum shiqaaqeee añy-yuṣeebakum-mislu maaa aṣaaba qawma Nooḥin aw qawma Hoodin aw qawma Ṣaaliḥ; wa maa qawmu Looṭim-minkum biba'eed.

وَيٰقَوْمِ لَا يَجْرِمَنَّكُمْ شِقَاقِيْٓ أَنْ
يُّصِيبَكُمْ مِّثْلُ مَآ أَصَابَ قَوْمَ نُوحٍ
أَوْ قَوْمَ هُودٍ أَوْ قَوْمَ صٰلِحٍ ۚ وَمَا
قَوْمُ لُوطٍ مِّنْكُمْ بِبَعِيدٍ ۝٨٩

90. "But ask forgiveness of your Lord, and turn to Him (in repentance): for my Lord is indeed full of mercy and loving-kindness."

90. Wastaghfiroo Rabbakum summa toobooo ilayh; inna Rabbee Raḥeemuñw-Wadood.

وَاسْتَغْفِرُوا رَبَّكُمْ ثُمَّ تُوبُوٓا إِلَيْهِ ۚ
إِنَّ رَبِّي رَحِيمٌ وَّدُودٌ ۝٩٠

91. They said: "O Shu'aib! much of what you say we do not understand! In fact among us we see that you have no strength! Were it not for your family, we should certainly have stoned you! For you have among us no great position!"

91. Qaaloo yaa Shu'aybu maa nafqahu kaseeram-mimmaa taqoolu wa innaa lanaraaka feenaa ḍa'eefañw wa law laa rahṭuka larajamnaaka wa maaa anta 'alaynaa bi'azeez.

قَالُوا يٰشُعَيْبُ مَا نَفْقَهُ كَثِيرًا مِّمَّا
تَقُولُ وَإِنَّا لَنَرٰىكَ فِينَا ضَعِيفًا ۚ
وَلَوْلَا رَهْطُكَ لَرَجَمْنٰكَ ۖ وَمَآ أَنْتَ
عَلَيْنَا بِعَزِيزٍ ۝٩١

92. He said: "O my people! is then my family of more consideration with you than Allah? For you cast Him away behind your backs (with contempt). But verily my Lord encompasses on all sides all that you do!

92. Qaala yaa qawmi arahṭeee a'azzu 'alaykum-minal-laahi wattakhaztumoohu waraaa'akum ẓihriyyan inna Rabbee bimaa ta'maloona muḥeet.

قَالَ يٰقَوْمِ أَرَهْطِيْٓ أَعَزُّ عَلَيْكُمْ مِّنَ
اللّٰهِ ۖ وَاتَّخَذْتُمُوهُ وَرَآءَكُمْ ظِهْرِيًّا ۚ
إِنَّ رَبِّي بِمَا تَعْمَلُونَ مُحِيطٌ ۝٩٢

93. "And O my people! do whatever you can: I will do (my part): soon will you know who it is on whom descends the Chastisement of ignominy; and who is a liar! and watch you! for I too am watching with you!"

93. Wa yaa qawmi'-maloo 'alaa makaanatikum innee 'aamilun sawfa ta'lamoona mañy-yaåteehi 'azaabuñy-yukhzeehi wa man huwa kaazib; wartaqibooo innee ma'akum raqeeb.

وَيٰقَوْمِ اعْمَلُوا عَلٰى مَكَانَتِكُمْ إِنِّي
عَامِلٌ ۖ سَوْفَ تَعْلَمُونَ ۙ مَنْ يَّأْتِيهِ
عَذَابٌ يُّخْزِيهِ وَمَنْ هُوَ كَاذِبٌ ۚ
وَارْتَقِبُوٓا إِنِّي مَعَكُمْ رَقِيبٌ ۝٩٣

94. When Our decree issued, We saved Shu'aib and those who believed with him, by (special) Mercy from Our selves: but the (mighty) Blast seized the wrong-doers, and they lay prostrate in their homes by the morning,-

94. Wa lammaa jaaa'a amrunaa najjaynaa Shu'aybañw-wallazeena aamanoo ma'ahoo biraḥmatim-minnaa wa akhazatil-lazeena ẓalamuṣ-ṣayḥatu fa-aṣbaḥoo fee diyaarihim jaasimeen.

وَلَمَّا جَآءَ أَمْرُنَا نَجَّيْنَا شُعَيْبًا وَّ
الَّذِينَ اٰمَنُوا مَعَهٗ بِرَحْمَةٍ مِّنَّا ۚ
وَأَخَذَتِ الَّذِينَ ظَلَمُوا الصَّيْحَةُ
فَأَصْبَحُوا فِي دِيَارِهِمْ جٰثِمِينَ ۝٩٤

95. As if they had never dwelt and flourished there! Ah! Behold! How the Madyan were removed (from sight) as were removed the Thamud.

95. Ka-al-lam yaghnaw feehaa; alaa bu'dal-li-Madyana kamaa ba'idat Samood.

كَأَنْ لَّمْ يَغْنَوْا فِيهَا ۗ أَلَا بُعْدًا
لِّمَدْيَنَ كَمَا بَعِدَتْ ثَمُودُ ۝٩٥ ع ٨

(Section 8)

96. And we sent Moses, with Our Clear (Signs) and an authority manifest,

96. Wa laqad arsalnaa Moosaa bi-Aayaatinaa wa sulṭaanim-mubeen.

وَلَقَدْ أَرْسَلْنَا مُوسٰى بِاٰيٰتِنَا
وَسُلْطٰنٍ مُّبِينٍ ۝٩٦

Ikhfa اخفاء | Ghunna غنّہ | Ikhfa Meem Saakin اخفاء میم ساکن | Idghaam ادغام | Qalqala قلقلہ | Qalb قلب | Idghaam Meem Saakin ادغام میم ساکن

97. Unto Pharaoh and his Chiefs: but they followed the command of Pharaoh and the command of Pharaoh was no right (guide).

98. He will go before his people on the Day of Judgment, and lead them into the Fire (as cattle are led to water): but woeful indeed will be the place to which they are led!

99. And they are followed by a curse in this (life) and on the Day of Judgment: and woeful is the gift which shall be given (to them)!

100. These are some of the stories of communities which We relate to you: of them some are standing, and some have been mown down (by the sickle of time).

101. It was not We that wronged them: they wronged their own souls: the deities, other than Allah, whom they invoked, profited them no whit when there issued the decree of your Lord: nor did they add anything (to their lot) but perdition!

102. Such is the chastisement of your Lord when He chastises communities in the midst of their wrong: grievous, indeed, and severe is His chastisement.

103. In that is a Sign for those who fear the Chastisement of the Hereafter: that is a Day for which mankind will be gathered together: that will be a Day of Testimony.

104. Nor shall We delay it but for a term appointed.

105. The day it arrives, no soul shall speak except by His leave: of those (gathered) some will be wretched and some will be blessed.

106. Those who are wretched shall be in the Fire: there will be for them therein (nothing but) the heaving of sighs and sobs:

107. They will dwell therein for all the time that the heavens and the earth endure, except as your Lord wills: for

97. Ilaa Fir'awna wa mala'ihee fattaba'ooo amra Fir'awna wa maaa amru Fir'awna birasheed.

98. Yaqdumu qawmahoo Yawmal-Qiyaamati fa-awradahumun-Naara wa bi'sal-wirdul-mawrood.

99. Wa utbi'oo fee haazihee la'natañw-wa Yawmal-Qiyaamah; bi'sar- rifdul-marfood.

100. Zaalika min ambaaa'il-quraa naquṣṣuhoo 'alayka minhaa qaaa'imuñw-wa ḥaṣeed.

101. Wa maa ẓalamnaahum wa laakin ẓalamooo anfusahum famaaa aghnat 'anhum aalihatuhumul-latee yad'oona min doonil-laahi min shay'il-lammaa jaaa'a amru Rabbika wa maa zaadoohum ghayra tatbeeb.

102. Wa kazaalika akhzu Rabbika izaaa akhazal-quraa wa hiya ẓaalimah; inna akhzahooo aleemun shadeed.

103. Inna fee zaalika la-Aayatal-liman khaafa 'azaabal-Aakhirah; zaalika Yawmum-majmoo'ul-lahun-naasu wa zaalika Yawmum-mashhood.

104. Wa maa nu'akhkhiruhooo illaa li-ajalim-ma'dood.

105. Yawma yaåti laa takallamu nafsun illaa bi-iznih; faminhum shaqiyyuñw-wa sa'eed.

106. Fa-ammal-lazeena shaqoo fafin-Naari lahum feehaa zafeeruñw-wa shaheeq.

107. Khaalideena feehaa maa daamatis-samaawaatu wal-arḍu illaa maa shaaa'a Rabbuk; inna

إِلَىٰ فِرْعَوْنَ وَمَلَإِيْهِ فَاتَّبَعُوٓا أَمْرَ
فِرْعَوْنَ ۖ وَمَآ أَمْرُ فِرْعَوْنَ بِرَشِيدٍ ﴿٩٧﴾
يَقْدُمُ قَوْمَهُۥ يَوْمَ ٱلْقِيَٰمَةِ فَأَوْرَدَهُمُ
ٱلنَّارَ ۖ وَبِئْسَ ٱلْوِرْدُ ٱلْمَوْرُودُ ﴿٩٨﴾
وَأُتْبِعُوا فِى هَٰذِهِۦ لَعْنَةً وَيَوْمَ
ٱلْقِيَٰمَةِ ۚ بِئْسَ ٱلرِّفْدُ ٱلْمَرْفُودُ ﴿٩٩﴾
ذَٰلِكَ مِنْ أَنۢبَآءِ ٱلْقُرَىٰ نَقُصُّهُۥ
عَلَيْكَ ۖ مِنْهَا قَآئِمٌ وَحَصِيدٌ ﴿١٠٠﴾
وَمَا ظَلَمْنَٰهُمْ وَلَٰكِن ظَلَمُوٓا أَنفُسَهُمْ
فَمَآ أَغْنَتْ عَنْهُمْ ءَالِهَتُهُمُ ٱلَّتِى
يَدْعُونَ مِن دُونِ ٱللَّهِ مِن شَىْءٍ
لَّمَّا جَآءَ أَمْرُ رَبِّكَ ۖ وَمَا زَادُوهُمْ
غَيْرَ تَتْبِيبٍ ﴿١٠١﴾
وَكَذَٰلِكَ أَخْذُ رَبِّكَ إِذَآ أَخَذَ
ٱلْقُرَىٰ وَهِىَ ظَٰلِمَةٌ ۚ إِنَّ أَخْذَهُۥٓ
أَلِيمٌ شَدِيدٌ ﴿١٠٢﴾
إِنَّ فِى ذَٰلِكَ لَءَايَةً لِّمَنْ خَافَ
عَذَابَ ٱلْءَاخِرَةِ ۚ ذَٰلِكَ يَوْمٌ مَّجْمُوعٌ
لَّهُ ٱلنَّاسُ وَذَٰلِكَ يَوْمٌ مَّشْهُودٌ ﴿١٠٣﴾
وَمَا نُؤَخِّرُهُۥٓ إِلَّا لِأَجَلٍ مَّعْدُودٍ ﴿١٠٤﴾
يَوْمَ يَأْتِ لَا تَكَلَّمُ نَفْسٌ إِلَّا بِإِذْنِهِۦ
فَمِنْهُمْ شَقِىٌّ وَسَعِيدٌ ﴿١٠٥﴾
فَأَمَّا ٱلَّذِينَ شَقُوا فَفِى ٱلنَّارِ
لَهُمْ فِيهَا زَفِيرٌ وَشَهِيقٌ ﴿١٠٦﴾
خَٰلِدِينَ فِيهَا مَا دَامَتِ ٱلسَّمَٰوَٰتُ
وَٱلْأَرْضُ إِلَّا مَا شَآءَ رَبُّكَ ۚ إِنَّ

Ikhfa اخفاء | Ghunna غُنّہ | Ikhfa Meem Saakin اخفاء میم ساکن | Idghaam ادغام | Qalqala قلقلہ | Qalb قلب | Idghaam Meem Saakin ادغام میم ساکن

your Lord is the (sure) Accomplisher of what He plans.

Rabbaka fa'-'aalul-limaa yureed.

رَبَّكَ فَعَّالٌ لِّمَا يُرِيدُ ﴿١٠٧﴾

108. And those who are blessed shall be in the Garden: they will dwell therein for all the time that the heavens and the earth endure, except as your Lord willeth: a gift without break.

108. Wa ammal-lazeena su'i-doo fafil-Jannati khaalideena feehaa maa daamatis-samaawaatu wal-arḍu illaa maa shaaa'a Rabbuk; 'aṭaaa'an ghayra majzooz.

وَأَمَّا الَّذِينَ سُعِدُوا فَفِي الْجَنَّةِ خٰلِدِينَ فِيهَا مَا دَامَتِ السَّمٰوٰتُ وَالْأَرْضُ إِلَّا مَا شَاءَ رَبُّكَ ۖ عَطَاءً غَيْرَ مَجْذُوذٍ ﴿١٠٨﴾

109. Be not then in doubt as to what these men worship. They worship nothing but what their fathers worshipped before (them): but verily We shall pay them back (in full) their portion without (the least) abatement.

109. Falaa taku fee miryatim-mimmaa ya'budu haaa'ulaaa'; maa ya'budoona illaa kamaa ya'budu aabaaa'uhum-min qabl; wa innaa lamuwaf-foohum naṣeebahum ghayra manqooṣ. **(Section 9)**

فَلَا تَكُ فِي مِرْيَةٍ مِّمَّا يَعْبُدُ هٰؤُلَاءِ ۚ مَا يَعْبُدُونَ إِلَّا كَمَا يَعْبُدُ آبَاؤُهُم مِّن قَبْلُ ۚ وَإِنَّا لَمُوَفُّوهُمْ نَصِيبَهُمْ غَيْرَ مَنقُوصٍ ﴿١٠٩﴾ ع

110. We certainly gave the Book to Moses, but differences arose therein: had it not been that a Word had gone forth before from your Lord, the matter would have been decided between them, but they are in suspicious doubt concerning it.

110. Wa laqad aataynaa Moo-sal-Kitaaba fakhtulifa feeh; wa law laa Kalimatun sabaqat mir-Rabbika laquḍiya baynahum; wa innahum lafee shakkim-minhu mureeb.

وَلَقَدْ آتَيْنَا مُوسَى الْكِتٰبَ فَاخْتُلِفَ فِيهِ ۚ وَلَوْلَا كَلِمَةٌ سَبَقَتْ مِن رَّبِّكَ لَقُضِيَ بَيْنَهُمْ ۚ وَإِنَّهُمْ لَفِي شَكٍّ مِّنْهُ مُرِيبٍ ﴿١١٠﴾

111. And, of a surety, to all will your Lord pay back (in full the recompense) of their deeds: for He knows well all that they do.

111. Wa inna kullal-lammaa la-yuwaffiyannahum Rabbuka a'maalahum; innahoo bimaa ya'maloona Khabeer.

وَإِنَّ كُلًّا لَّمَّا لَيُوَفِّيَنَّهُمْ رَبُّكَ أَعْمَالَهُمْ ۚ إِنَّهُ بِمَا يَعْمَلُونَ خَبِيرٌ ﴿١١١﴾

112. Therefore stand firm (in the straight Path) as you are commanded,- you and those who with you turn (unto Allah); and do not transgress (from the Path): for He sees well all that you do.

112. Fastaqim kamaaa umirta wa man taaba ma'aka wa laa taṭghaw; innahoo bimaa ta'maloona Baṣeer.

فَاسْتَقِمْ كَمَا أُمِرْتَ وَمَن تَابَ مَعَكَ وَلَا تَطْغَوْا ۚ إِنَّهُ بِمَا تَعْمَلُونَ بَصِيرٌ ﴿١١٢﴾

113. And incline not to those who do wrong, or the Fire will seize you; and you have no protectors other than Allah, nor shall you be helped.

113. Wa laa tarkanooo ilal-lazeena ẓalamoo fatamassa-kumun-Naaru wa maa lakum-min doonil-laahi min awli-yaaa'a summa laa tunṣaroon.

وَلَا تَرْكَنُوا إِلَى الَّذِينَ ظَلَمُوا فَتَمَسَّكُمُ النَّارُ وَمَا لَكُم مِّن دُونِ اللّٰهِ مِنْ أَوْلِيَاءَ ثُمَّ لَا تُنصَرُونَ ﴿١١٣﴾

114. And establish regular prayers at the two ends of the day and at the approaches of the night: for those things, that are good remove those that are evil: be that the word of remembrance to those who remember (their Lord):

114. Wa aqimiṣ-Ṣalaata ṭara-fayin-nahaari wa zulafam-minal-layl; innal-ḥasanaati yuzhibnas-sayyi-aat; zaalika zikraa liz zaakireen.

وَأَقِمِ الصَّلٰوةَ طَرَفَيِ النَّهَارِ وَزُلَفًا مِّنَ اللَّيْلِ ۚ إِنَّ الْحَسَنٰتِ يُذْهِبْنَ السَّيِّئَاتِ ۚ ذٰلِكَ ذِكْرَىٰ لِلذّٰكِرِينَ ﴿١١٤﴾

115. And be steadfast in patience; for verily Allah will not suffer the reward of the righteous to perish.

115. Waṣbir fa-innal-laaha laa yuḍee'u ajral-muḥsineen.

وَاصْبِرْ فَإِنَّ اللّٰهَ لَا يُضِيعُ أَجْرَ الْمُحْسِنِينَ ﴿١١٥﴾

Ikhfa اخفاء | Ghunna غنّہ | Ikhfa Meem Saakin اخفاء میم ساکن | Idghaam ادغام | Qalqala قلقلہ | Qalb قلب | Idghaam Meem Saakin ادغام میم ساکن

116. Why were there not, among the generations before you, persons possessed of balanced good sense, prohibiting (men) from mischief in the earth - except a few among them whom We saved (from harm)? But the wrong-doers pursued the enjoyment of the good things of life which were given them, and persisted in sin.

116. Falaw laa kaana minal-qurooni min qablikum uloo baqiyyatiñy-yanhawna 'anil-fasaadi fil-arḍi illaa qaleelam-mimman anjaynaa minhum; wattaba'al-lazeena ẓalamoo maaa utrifoo feehi wa kaanoo mujrimeen.

فَلَوْلَا كَانَ مِنَ الْقُرُوْنِ مِنْ
قَبْلِكُمْ اُولُوْا بَقِيَّةٍ يَّنْهَوْنَ عَنِ
الْفَسَادِ فِي الْاَرْضِ اِلَّا قَلِيْلًا مِّمَّنْ
اَنْجَيْنَا مِنْهُمْ ۚ وَاتَّبَعَ الَّذِيْنَ ظَلَمُوْا
مَآ اُتْرِفُوْا فِيْهِ وَكَانُوْا مُجْرِمِيْنَ ﴿١١٦﴾

117. Nor would your Lord be the One to destroy communities for a single wrong- doing, if its members were likely to mend.

117. Wa maa kaana Rabbuka liyuhlikal-quraa bizulmiñw-wa ahluhaa muṣliḥoon.

وَمَا كَانَ رَبُّكَ لِيُهْلِكَ الْقُرٰى
بِظُلْمٍ وَّ اَهْلُهَا مُصْلِحُوْنَ ﴿١١٧﴾

118. If your Lord had so willed, He could have made mankind one people: but they will not cease to dispute.

118. Wa law shaaa'a Rabbuka laja'alannaasa ummatañw-waa-ḥidatañw-wa laa yazaaloona mukhtalifeen.

وَلَوْ شَآءَ رَبُّكَ لَجَعَلَ النَّاسَ اُمَّةً
وَّاحِدَةً وَّلَا يَزَالُوْنَ مُخْتَلِفِيْنَ ۙ﴿١١٨﴾

119. Except those on whom your Lord has bestowed His Mercy: and for this He created them: and the Word of your Lord shall be fulfilled: "I will fill Hell with (disobedient) jinns and men all together."

119. Illaa mar-raḥima Rabbuk; wa lizaalika khalaqahum; wa tammat Kalimatu Rabbika la-amla'anna Jahannama minal-jinnati wannaasi ajma'een.

اِلَّا مَنْ رَّحِمَ رَبُّكَ ۭ وَلِذٰلِكَ خَلَقَهُمْ ۭ
وَتَمَّتْ كَلِمَةُ رَبِّكَ لَاَمْلَئَنَّ جَهَنَّمَ
مِنَ الْجِنَّةِ وَالنَّاسِ اَجْمَعِيْنَ ﴿١١٩﴾

120. All that we relate to you of the stories of the Apostles,- with it We make firm your heart: in them there comes to you the Truth, as well as an exhortation and a message of remembrance to those who believe.

120. Wa kullan-naquṣṣu 'alay-ka min ambaaa'ir-Rusuli maa nusabbitu bihee fu'aadak; wa jaaa'aka fee haazihil-ḥaqqu wa maw'iẓatuñw-wa zikraa lilmu'-mineen.

وَكُلًّا نَّقُصُّ عَلَيْكَ مِنْ اَنْۢبَآءِ
الرُّسُلِ مَا نُثَبِّتُ بِهٖ فُؤَادَكَ ۚ
وَجَآءَكَ فِيْ هٰذِهِ الْحَقُّ وَمَوْعِظَةٌ
وَّذِكْرٰى لِلْمُؤْمِنِيْنَ ﴿١٢٠﴾

121. Say to those who do not believe: "Do whatever you can: we shall do our part;

121. Wa qul lillazeena laa yu'minoona'-maloo 'alaa ma-kaanatikum innaa 'aamiloon.

وَقُلْ لِّلَّذِيْنَ لَا يُؤْمِنُوْنَ اعْمَلُوْا
عَلٰى مَكَانَتِكُمْ ۭ اِنَّا عٰمِلُوْنَ ۙ﴿١٢١﴾

122. "And you wait! we too shall wait."

122. Wantaẓiroo innaa mun-taẓiroon.

وَانْتَظِرُوْا ۚ اِنَّا مُنْتَظِرُوْنَ ﴿١٢٢﴾

123. To Allah do belong the unseen (secrets) of the heavens and the earth, and to Him goes back every affair (for decision): then worship Him, and put your trust in Him: and your Lord is not unmindful of anything that you do.

123. Wa lillaahi ghaybus-samaawaati wal-arḍi wa ilayhi yurja'ul-amru kulluhoo fa'bu-dhu wa tawakkal 'alayh; wa maa Rabbuka bighaafilin 'ammaa ta'maloon. **(Section 10)**

وَلِلّٰهِ غَيْبُ السَّمٰوٰتِ وَالْاَرْضِ
وَاِلَيْهِ يُرْجَعُ الْاَمْرُ كُلُّهٗ فَاعْبُدْهُ
وَتَوَكَّلْ عَلَيْهِ ۭ وَمَا رَبُّكَ بِغَافِلٍ
عَمَّا تَعْمَلُوْنَ ﴿١٢٣﴾

ع

12. Yusuf or Joseph

In the name of Allah, Most Gracious, Most Merciful.

Sûrat Yûsuf–12

(Revealed at Makkah)

Bismillaahir Raḥmaanir Raḥeem

(١٢) سُوْرَةُ يُوْسُفَ مَكِّيَّةٌ (٥٣)

بِسْمِ اللّٰهِ الرَّحْمٰنِ الرَّحِيْمِ

1. *Alif-Lam-Ra*. These are the symbols (or Verses) of the Perspicuous Book.

1. Alif-Laaam-Raa; tilka Aayaatul-Kitaabil-Mubeen.

الٓرٰ ۣ تِلْكَ اٰيٰتُ الْكِتٰبِ الْمُبِيْنِ ۣ﴿١﴾

Ikhfa اخفاء	Ghunna غُنّہ	Ikhfa Meem Saakin اخفاءمیم ساکن	Idghaam ادغام	Qalqala قلقلہ	Qalb قلب	Idghaam Meem Saakin ادغام میم ساکن

2. We have sent it down as an Arabic Qur'an, in order that you may learn wisdom.	2. Innaaa anzalnaahu Qur-aa-nan 'Arabiyyal-la'allakum ta'qiloon.	إِنَّآ أَنزَلْنَٰهُ قُرْءَٰنًا عَرَبِيًّا لَّعَلَّكُمْ تَعْقِلُونَ ٢
3. We do relate to you the most beautiful of stories, in that We reveal to you this (portion of the) Qur'an: before this, you too was among those who did not know it.	3. Naḥnu naquṣṣu 'alayka aḥsanal-qaṣaṣi bimaaa awḥay-naaa ilayka haaẕal-Qur-aana wa in kunta min qablihee laminal-ghaafileen.	نَحْنُ نَقُصُّ عَلَيْكَ أَحْسَنَ ٱلْقَصَصِ بِمَآ أَوْحَيْنَآ إِلَيْكَ هَٰذَا ٱلْقُرْءَانَ وَإِن كُنتَ مِن قَبْلِهِۦ لَمِنَ ٱلْغَٰفِلِينَ ٣
4. Behold! Joseph said to his father: "O my father! I saw eleven stars and the sun and the moon: I saw them prostrate themselves to me!"	4. Iẕ qaala Yoosufu li-abeehi yaaa abati innee ra-aytu aḥada 'ashara kawkabañw-wash-shamsa walqamara ra-aytuhum lee saajideen.	إِذْ قَالَ يُوسُفُ لِأَبِيهِ يَٰٓأَبَتِ إِنِّى رَأَيْتُ أَحَدَ عَشَرَ كَوْكَبًا وَٱلشَّمْسَ وَٱلْقَمَرَ رَأَيْتُهُمْ لِى سَٰجِدِينَ ٤
5. Said (the father): "My (dear) little son! do not relate your vision to your brothers, lest they concoct a plot against you: for Satan is to man an avowed enemy!	5. Qaala yaa bunayya laa taqṣuṣ ru'yaaka 'alaaa ikhwatika fa-yakeedoo laka kaydaa; innash-Shayṭaana lil-insaani 'aduw-wum-mubeen.	قَالَ يَٰبُنَىَّ لَا تَقْصُصْ رُءْيَاكَ عَلَىٰٓ إِخْوَتِكَ فَيَكِيدُوا۟ لَكَ كَيْدًا ۖ إِنَّ ٱلشَّيْطَٰنَ لِلْإِنسَٰنِ عَدُوٌّ مُّبِينٌ ٥
6. "Thus will your Lord choose you and teach you the interpretation of stories (and events) and perfect His favour to you and to the posterity of Jacob - even as He perfected it to your fathers Abraham and Isaac aforetime! for Allah is full of knowledge and wisdom."	6. Wa kaẕaalika yajtabeeka Rabbuka wa yu'allimuka min taåweelil-aḥaadeesi wa yutim-mu ni'matahoo 'alayka wa 'alaaa Aali Ya'qooba kamaaa atammahaa 'alaaa abawayka min qablu Ibraaheema wa Isḥaaq; inna Rabbaka 'Aleemun Ḥakeem. **(Section 1)**	وَكَذَٰلِكَ يَجْتَبِيكَ رَبُّكَ وَيُعَلِّمُكَ مِن تَأْوِيلِ ٱلْأَحَادِيثِ وَيُتِمُّ نِعْمَتَهُۥ عَلَيْكَ وَعَلَىٰٓ ءَالِ يَعْقُوبَ كَمَآ أَتَمَّهَا عَلَىٰٓ أَبَوَيْكَ مِن قَبْلُ إِبْرَٰهِيمَ وَإِسْحَٰقَ ۚ إِنَّ رَبَّكَ عَلِيمٌ حَكِيمٌ ٦
7. Verily in Joseph and his brethren are signs (or Symbols) for Seekers (after Truth).	7. Laqad kaana fee Yoosufa wa ikhwatiheee Aayaatul-lissaaa'i-leen.	لَّقَدْ كَانَ فِى يُوسُفَ وَإِخْوَتِهِۦٓ ءَايَٰتٌ لِّلسَّآئِلِينَ ٧
8. They said: "Truly Joseph and his brother are loved more by our father than we: but we are a goodly body! really our father is obviously wandering (in his mind)!	8. Iẕ qaaloo la-Yoosufu wa akhoohu aḥabbu ilaaa Abeenaa minnaa wa naḥnu 'uṣbah; inna abaanaa lafee ḍalaalim-mubeen.	إِذْ قَالُوا۟ لَيُوسُفُ وَأَخُوهُ أَحَبُّ إِلَىٰٓ أَبِينَا مِنَّا وَنَحْنُ عُصْبَةٌ إِنَّ أَبَانَا لَفِى ضَلَٰلٍ مُّبِينٍ ٨
9. "You slay Joseph or cast him out to some (unknown) land, that so the favour of your father may be given to you alone: (there will be time enough) for you to be righteous after that!"	9. Uqtuloo Yoosufa awiṭra-ḥoohu arḍañy-yakhlu lakum wajhu abeekum wa takoonoo mim ba'dihee qawman ṣaali-ḥeen.	ٱقْتُلُوا۟ يُوسُفَ أَوِ ٱطْرَحُوهُ أَرْضًا يَخْلُ لَكُمْ وَجْهُ أَبِيكُمْ وَتَكُونُوا۟ مِنۢ بَعْدِهِۦ قَوْمًا صَٰلِحِينَ ٩
10. Said one of them: "do not slay Joseph, but if you must do	10. Qaala qaaa'ilum-minhum laa taqtuloo Yoosufa	قَالَ قَآئِلٌ مِّنْهُمْ لَا تَقْتُلُوا۟ يُوسُفَ

something, throw him down to the bottom of the well: he will be picked up by some caravan of travellers."

11. They said: "O our father! why do you not trust us with Joseph,- seeing we are indeed his sincere well-wishers?

12. "Send him with us tomorrow to enjoy himself and play, and we shall take every care of him."

13. (Jacob) said: "Really it saddens me that you should take him away: I fear lest the wolf should devour him while you do not attend to him."

14. They said: "If the wolf were to devour him while we are (so large) a party, then should we indeed (first) have perished ourselves!"

15. So they took him away, and they all agreed to throw him down to the bottom of the well: and We put into his heart (this Message): 'Of a surety you shall (one day) tell them the truth of this their affair while they do not know (you)'

16. Then they came to their father in the early part of the night, weeping.

17. They said: "O our father! We went racing with one another, and left Joseph with our things; and the wolf devoured him.... But you will never believe us even though we tell the truth."

18. They stained his shirt with false blood. He said: "Nay, but your minds have made up a tale (that may pass) with you. (For me) patience is most fitting: against that which you assert, it is Allah (alone) Whose help can be sought"..

19. Then there came a caravan of travellers: they sent their water-carrier (for water), and he let down his bucket (into the well)...He said: "Ah there! Good news! Here is

wa alqoohu fee ghayaabatil-jubbi yaltaqitḥu baḍus-sayyaarati in kuntum faa'ileen.

11. Qaaloo yaaa abaanaa maa laka laa taåmannaa 'alaa Yoosufa wa innaa lahoo lanaa-ṣiḥoon.

12. Arsilhu ma'anaa ghadañy-yarta' wa yal'ab wa innaa lahoo lahaafiẓoon.

13. Qaala innee la-yaḥzunuuneee an taẕhaboo bihee wa akhaafu añy-yaåkulahuz-zi'bu wa antum 'anhu ghaafiloon.

14. Qaaloo la-in akalahuz-zi'bu wa naḥnu 'uṣbatun innaaa izal-lakhaasiroon.

15. Falammaa ẕahaboo bihee wa ajma'ooo añy-yaj'aloohu fee ghayaabatil-jubb; wa awḥaynaaa ilayhi latunabbi-'annahum bi-amrihim haaẕaa wa hum laa yash'uroon.

16. Wa jaaa'ooo abaahum 'ishaaa'añy-yabkoon.

17. Qaaloo yaaa abaanaaa innaa ẕahabnaa nastabiqu wa taraknaa Yoosufa 'inda mataa'inaa fa-akalahuz-zi'b, wa maaa anta bimu'minil-lanaa wa law kunnaa ṣaadiqeen.

18. Wa jaaa'oo 'alaa qameeṣihee bidamin kaẕib; qaala bal sawwalat lakum anfusukum amraa; faṣabrun jameel; wallaahul-musta'aanu 'alaa maa taṣifoon.

19. Wa jaaa'at sayyaaratun fa-arsaloo waaridahum fa-adlaa dalwah; qaala yaa bushraa haaẕaa

وَاَلْقُوْهُ فِيْ غَيٰبَتِ الْجُبِّ يَلْتَقِطْهُ
بَعْضُ السَّيَّارَةِ اِنْ كُنْتُمْ فٰعِلِيْنَ ۝١٠
قَالُوْا يٰٓاَبَانَا مَالَكَ لَا تَاْمَنَّا عَلٰى
يُوْسُفَ وَاِنَّا لَهٗ لَنٰصِحُوْنَ ۝١١
اَرْسِلْهُ مَعَنَا غَدًا يَّرْتَعْ وَيَلْعَبْ
وَاِنَّا لَهٗ لَحٰفِظُوْنَ ۝١٢
قَالَ اِنِّيْ لَيَحْزُنُنِيْٓ اَنْ تَذْهَبُوْا
بِهٖ وَاَخَافُ اَنْ يَّاْكُلَهُ الذِّئْبُ
وَاَنْتُمْ عَنْهُ غٰفِلُوْنَ ۝١٣
قَالُوْا لَىِٕنْ اَكَلَهُ الذِّئْبُ وَنَحْنُ
عُصْبَةٌ اِنَّآ اِذًا لَّخٰسِرُوْنَ ۝١٤
فَلَمَّا ذَهَبُوْا بِهٖ وَاَجْمَعُوْٓا اَنْ يَّجْعَلُوْهُ
فِيْ غَيٰبَتِ الْجُبِّ ۚ وَاَوْحَيْنَآ اِلَيْهِ
لَتُنَبِّئَنَّهُمْ بِاَمْرِهِمْ هٰذَا وَهُمْ
لَا يَشْعُرُوْنَ ۝١٥
وَجَآءُوْٓ اَبَاهُمْ عِشَآءً يَّبْكُوْنَ ۝١٦
قَالُوْا يٰٓاَبَانَآ اِنَّا ذَهَبْنَا نَسْتَبِقُ
وَتَرَكْنَا يُوْسُفَ عِنْدَ مَتَاعِنَا فَاَكَلَهُ
الذِّئْبُ ۚ وَمَآ اَنْتَ بِمُؤْمِنٍ لَّنَا
وَلَوْ كُنَّا صٰدِقِيْنَ ۝١٧
وَجَآءُوْ عَلٰى قَمِيْصِهٖ بِدَمٍ كَذِبٍ ؕ
قَالَ بَلْ سَوَّلَتْ لَكُمْ اَنْفُسُكُمْ اَمْرًا ؕ
فَصَبْرٌ جَمِيْلٌ ؕ وَاللّٰهُ الْمُسْتَعَانُ
عَلٰى مَا تَصِفُوْنَ ۝١٨
وَجَآءَتْ سَيَّارَةٌ فَاَرْسَلُوْا وَارِدَهُمْ
فَاَدْلٰى دَلْوَهٗ ۚ قَالَ يٰبُشْرٰى هٰذَا

الثلثة

Ikhfa اخفاء | Ghunna غنّہ | Ikhfa Meem Saakin اخفاء میم ساکن | Idghaam ادغام | Qalqala قلقلہ | Qalb قلب | Idghaam Meem Saakin ادغام میم ساکن

a (fine) young man!" So they concealed him as a treasure! But Allah knows well all that they do!

ghulaam; wa asarroohu bi-ḍaa'ah; wallaahu 'aleemum bimaa ya'maloon.

غُلٰمٌ ؕ وَاَسَرُّوْهُ بِضَاعَةً ؕ وَاللّٰهُ
عَلِيْمٌ ۢبِمَا يَعْمَلُوْنَ ﴿١٩﴾

20. The (Brethren) sold him for a miserable price, for a few dirhams counted out: in such low estimation did they hold him!

20. Wa sharawhu bisamanim bakhsin daraahima ma'doo-datiñw wa kaanoo feehi minaz-zaahideen. **(Section 2)**

وَشَرَوْهُ بِثَمَنٍۢ بَخْسٍ دَرَاهِمَ مَعْدُوْدَةٍ ۚ
وَكَانُوْا فِيْهِ مِنَ الزَّاهِدِيْنَ ﴿٢٠﴾

21. The man in Egypt who bought him, said to his wife: "Make his stay (among us) honourable: may be he will bring us much good, or we shall adopt him as a son." Thus We established Joseph in the land, that We might teach him the interpretation of stories (and events). And Allah has full power and control over His affairs; but most among mankind do not know it.

21. Wa qaalal-lazish-taraahu mim-Miṣra limra-atiheee akrimee maswaahu 'asaaa añy-yanfa'anaaa aw nattakhizahoo waladaa; wa kazaalika mak-kannaa li-Yoosufa fil-arḍi wa linu'allimahoo min taåweelil-aḥaadees; wallaahu ghaalibun 'alaaa amrihee wa laakinna aksaran-naasi laa ya'lamoon.

وَقَالَ الَّذِى اشْتَرٰىهُ مِنْ مِّصْرَ
لِامْرَاَتِهٖۤ اَكْرِمِىْ مَثْوٰىهُ عَسٰٓى اَنْ
يَّنْفَعَنَاۤ اَوْ نَتَّخِذَهٗ وَلَدًا ؕ وَكَذٰلِكَ
مَكَّنَّا لِيُوْسُفَ فِى الْاَرْضِ وَلِنُعَلِّمَهٗ
مِنْ تَاْوِيْلِ الْاَحَادِيْثِ ؕ وَاللّٰهُ
غَالِبٌ عَلٰۤى اَمْرِهٖ وَلٰكِنَّ اَكْثَرَ النَّاسِ
لَا يَعْلَمُوْنَ ﴿٢١﴾

22. When Joseph attained his full manhood, We gave him power and knowledge: thus do We reward those who do right.

22. Wa lammaa balagha ashuddahooo aataynaahu ḥukmañw-wa 'ilmaa; wa kazaa-lika najzil-muḥsineen.

وَلَمَّا بَلَغَ اَشُدَّهٗۤ اٰتَيْنٰهُ حُكْمًا
وَّعِلْمًا ؕ وَكَذٰلِكَ نَجْزِى الْمُحْسِنِيْنَ ﴿٢٢﴾

23. But she in whose house he was, sought to seduce him from his (true) self: she fastened the doors, and said: "Now come, you (dear one)!" He said: "Allah forbid! truly (your husband) is my lord! he made my sojourn agreeable! truly to no good come those who do wrong!"

23. Wa raawadat-hul-latee huwa fee baytihaa 'an-nafsihee wa ghallaqatil-abwaaba wa qaalat hayta lak; qaala ma'aazal-laahi innahoo rabbeee aḥsana maswaay; innahoo laa yufliḥuẓ-ẓaalimoon.

وَرَاوَدَتْهُ الَّتِىْ هُوَ فِىْ بَيْتِهَا عَنْ
نَّفْسِهٖ وَغَلَّقَتِ الْاَبْوَابَ وَقَالَتْ
هَيْتَ لَكَ ؕ قَالَ مَعَاذَ اللّٰهِ اِنَّهٗ
رَبِّىْۤ اَحْسَنَ مَثْوَاىَ ؕ اِنَّهٗ لَا يُفْلِحُ
الظّٰلِمُوْنَ ﴿٢٣﴾

24. And (with passion) she desired him, and he would have desired her, but that he saw the evidence of his Lord: thus (did We order) that We might turn away from him (all) evil and shameful deeds: for he was one of Our servants, sincere and purified.

24. Wa laqad hammat bihee wa hamma bihaa law laaa ar-ra-aa burhaana Rabbih; kazaalika linaṣrifa 'anhus-sooo'a walfa-ḥshaaa'; innahoo min 'ibaadi-nal-mukhlaṣeen.

وَلَقَدْ هَمَّتْ بِهٖ ۚ وَهَمَّ بِهَا لَوْلَاۤ
اَنْ رَّاٰ بُرْهَانَ رَبِّهٖ ؕ كَذٰلِكَ لِنَصْرِفَ
عَنْهُ السُّوْٓءَ وَالْفَحْشَآءَ ؕ اِنَّهٗ مِنْ
عِبَادِنَا الْمُخْلَصِيْنَ ﴿٢٤﴾

25. So they both raced each other to the door, and she tore his shirt from the back: they both found her lord near the door. She said: "What is the (fitting) punishment for one who formed an evil design against your wife, but prison or

25. Wastabaqal-baaba wa qaddat qameeṣahoo min dubu-riñw-wa alfayaa sayyidahaa ladal-baab; qaalat maa jazaaa'u man araada bi-ahlika sooo'an illaaa añy-yusjana aw

وَاسْتَبَقَا الْبَابَ وَقَدَّتْ قَمِيْصَهٗ
مِنْ دُبُرٍ وَّاَلْفَيَا سَيِّدَهَا لَدَا
الْبَابِ ؕ قَالَتْ مَا جَزَآءُ مَنْ اَرَادَ
بِاَهْلِكَ سُوْٓءًا اِلَّاۤ اَنْ يُّسْجَنَ اَوْ

Ikhfa اخفاء | Ghunna غُنّہ | Ikhfa Meem Saakin اخفاء میم ساکن | Idghaam ادغام | Qalqala قلقلہ | Qalb قلب | Idghaam Meem Saakin ادغام میم ساکن

a grievous chastisement?"

'azaabun aleem.

عَذَابٌ اَلِيْمٌ ﴿٢٥﴾

26. He said: "It was she that sought to seduce me - from my (true) self." And one of her household saw (this) and bore witness, (thus):- "If it be that his shirt is rent from the front, then is her tale true, and he is a liar!

26. Qaala hiya raawadatnee 'an nafsee wa shahida shaahidum-min ahlihaa in kaana qameeṣuhoo qudda min qubulin faṣadaqat wa huwa minal-kaazibeen.

قَالَ هِيَ رَاوَدَتْنِيْ عَنْ نَّفْسِيْ وَشَهِدَ
شَاهِدٌ مِّنْ اَهْلِهَا ۚ اِنْ كَانَ
قَمِيْصُهٗ قُدَّ مِنْ قُبُلٍ فَصَدَقَتْ
وَهُوَ مِنَ الْكٰذِبِيْنَ ﴿٢٦﴾

27. "But if it be that his shirt is torn from the back, then is she the liar, and he is telling the truth!"

27. Wa in kaana qameeṣuhoo qudda min duburin fakazabat wa huwa minaṣ-ṣaadiqeen.

وَاِنْ كَانَ قَمِيْصُهٗ قُدَّ مِنْ دُبُرٍ
فَكَذَبَتْ وَهُوَ مِنَ الصّٰدِقِيْنَ ﴿٢٧﴾

28. So when he saw his shirt,- that it was torn at the back,- (her husband) said: "Behold! It is a snare of you women! truly, mighty is your snare!

28. Falammaa ra-aa qameeṣahoo qudda min duburin qaala innahoo min kaydikunna inna kaydakunna 'aẓeem.

فَلَمَّا رَاٰ قَمِيْصَهٗ قُدَّ مِنْ دُبُرٍ قَالَ
اِنَّهٗ مِنْ كَيْدِكُنَّ ؕ اِنَّ كَيْدَكُنَّ
عَظِيْمٌ ﴿٢٨﴾

29. "O Joseph, pass this over! (O wife), ask forgiveness for your sin, for truly you have been at fault!"

29. Yoosufu a'riḍ 'an haazaa wastaghfiree lizambiki innaki kunti minal-khaaṭi'een.

(Section 3)

يُوْسُفُ اَعْرِضْ عَنْ هٰذَا ٚ
وَاسْتَغْفِرِيْ لِذَنْۢبِكِ ۖۚ اِنَّكِ كُنْتِ
مِنَ الْخٰطِـِٕيْنَ ﴿٢٩﴾ ع

30. Ladies said in the City: "The wife of the (great) 'Aziz is seeking to seduce her slave from his (true) self: Truly has he inspired her with violent love: we see she is evidently going astray."

30. Wa qaala niswatun filmadeenatim-ra-atul-'Azeezi turaawidu fataahaa 'an-nafsihee qad shaghafahaa ḥubbaa; innaa lanaraahaa fee ḍalaalim-mubeen.

وَقَالَ نِسْوَةٌ فِى الْمَدِيْنَةِ امْرَاَتُ
الْعَزِيْزِ تُرَاوِدُ فَتٰىهَا عَنْ نَّفْسِهٖ ۚ
قَدْ شَغَفَهَا حُبًّا ؕ اِنَّا لَنَرٰىهَا فِيْ
ضَلٰلٍ مُّبِيْنٍ ﴿٣٠﴾

31. When she heard of their malicious talk, she sent for them and prepared a banquet for them: she gave each of them a knife: and she said (to Joseph), "Come out before them." When they saw him, they extolled him, and (in their amazement) cut their hands: they said, "Allah preserve us! no mortal is this! this is none other than a noble angel!"

31. Falammaa sami'at bimakrihinna arsalat ilayhinna wa a'tadat lahunna muttaka-añw-wa aatat kulla waaḥidatim-minhunna sikkeenañw-wa qaalatikh-ruj 'alayhinna falammaa ra-aynahooo akbarnahoo wa qaṭṭa'na aydiyahunna wa qulna ḥaasha lillaahi maa haazaa basharaa; in haazaaa illaa malakun kareem.

فَلَمَّا سَمِعَتْ بِمَكْرِهِنَّ اَرْسَلَتْ
اِلَيْهِنَّ وَاَعْتَدَتْ لَهُنَّ مُتَّكَاً وَّ
اٰتَتْ كُلَّ وَاحِدَةٍ مِّنْهُنَّ سِكِّيْنًا
وَّقَالَتِ اخْرُجْ عَلَيْهِنَّ ۚ فَلَمَّا رَاَيْنَهٗۤ
اَكْبَرْنَهٗ وَقَطَّعْنَ اَيْدِيَهُنَّ وَقُلْنَ
حَاشَ لِلّٰهِ مَا هٰذَا بَشَرًا ؕ اِنْ هٰذَاۤ
اِلَّا مَلَكٌ كَرِيْمٌ ﴿٣١﴾

32. She said: "There before you is the man about whom you blamed me! I sought to seduce him from his (true) self but he firmly saved himself guiltless!....

32. Qaalat fazaalikunnal-lazee lumtunnanee feeh; wa laqad raawattuhoo 'an-nafsihee fasta'ṣam;

قَالَتْ فَذٰلِكُنَّ الَّذِيْ لُمْتُنَّنِيْ فِيْهِ ؕ
وَلَقَدْ رَاوَدْتُّهٗ عَنْ نَّفْسِهٖ فَاسْتَعْصَمَ ؕ

Ikhfa اخفاء | Ghunna غنّہ | Ikhfa Meem Saakin اخفاء میم ساکن | Idghaam ادغام | Qalqala قلقلہ | Qalb قلب | Idghaam Meem Saakin ادغام میم ساکن

and now, if he do not my bidding, he shall certainly be cast into prison, and (what is more) be of the company of the vilest!"

33. He said: "O my Lord! the prison is more to my liking than that to which they invite me: unless You turn away their snare from me, I should (in my youthful folly) feel inclined toward them and join the ranks of the ignorant."

34. So his Lord hearkened to him (in his prayer), and turned away from him their snare: verily He hears and knows (all things).

35. Then it occurred to the men, after they had seen the Signs, (that it was best) to imprison him for a time.

36. Now with him there came into the prison two young men, said one of them: "I see myself (in a dream) pressing wine." Said the other: "I see myself (in a dream) carrying bread on my head, and birds are eating, thereof." "Tell us" (they said) "the truth and meaning thereof: for we see you are one that does good (to all)."

37. He said: "Before any food comes (in due course) to feed either of you, I will surely reveal to you the truth and meaning of this are it befall you: that is part of the (duty) which my Lord has taught me. I have (I assure you) abandoned the ways of a people that believe not in Allah and that (even) deny the Hereafter.

38. "And I follow the ways of my fathers,- Abraham, Isaac, and Jacob; and never could we attribute any partners whatever to Allah: that (comes) of the grace of Allah to us and to mankind: yet most men are not grateful.

39. "O my two companions of the prison! (I ask you): are many lords differing among Themselves

wa la'il-lam yaf'al maaa aamuruhoo la-yusjananna wa la-yakoonam-minaṣ-ṣaaghireen.

33. Qaala Rabbis-sijnu aḥabbu ilayya mimmaa yad'oonaneee ilayhi wa illaa taṣrif 'annee kaydahunna aṣbu ilayhinna wa akum-minal-jaahileen.

34. Fastajaaba lahoo Rabbuhoo faṣarafa 'anhu kaydahunn; innahoo Huwas-Samee'ul-'Aleem.

35. Summa badaa lahum-mim ba'di maa ra-awul-Aayaati layasjununnahoo ḥattaa ḥeen.

(Section 4)

36. Wa dakhala ma'ahussijna fata-yaan; qaala aḥaduhumaaa inneee araaneee a'ṣiru khamrañw wa qaalal-aakharu inneee araaneee aḥmilu fawqa raåsee khubzan taåkuluṭ-ṭayru minh; nabbi'naa bitaåweelihee innaa naraaka minal-muḥsineen.

37. Qaala laa yaåteekumaa ṭa'aamun turzaqaaniheee illaa nabbaåtukumaa bitaåweelihee qabla añy-yaåtiyakumaa; ẕaalikumaa mimmaa 'allamanee Rabbee; innee taraktu millata qawmil-laa yu'minoona billaahi wahum bil-Aakhirati hum kaafiroon.

38. Wattaba'tu Millata aabaaa'eee Ibraaheema wa Isḥaaqa wa Ya'qoob; maa kaana lanaaa an-nushrika billaahi min shay'; ẕaalikamin faḍlil-laahi 'alaynaa wa 'alan-naasi wa laakinna akṡaran-naasi laa yashkuroon.

39. Yaa ṣaaḥibayis-sijni 'a-arbaabum-mutafarriqoona

وَلَئِنْ لَّمْ يَفْعَلْ مَآ اٰمُرُهٗ لَيُسْجَنَنَّ
وَلَيَكُوْنًا مِّنَ الصّٰغِرِيْنَ ﴿۳۲﴾
قَالَ رَبِّ السِّجْنُ اَحَبُّ اِلَیَّ مِمَّا
يَدْعُوْنَنِیْٓ اِلَيْهِ ۚ وَاِلَّا تَصْرِفْ
عَنِّیْ كَيْدَهُنَّ اَصْبُ اِلَيْهِنَّ وَاَكُنْ
مِّنَ الْجٰهِلِيْنَ ﴿۳۳﴾
فَاسْتَجَابَ لَهٗ رَبُّهٗ فَصَرَفَ عَنْهُ
كَيْدَهُنَّ ؕ اِنَّهٗ هُوَ السَّمِيْعُ الْعَلِيْمُ ﴿۳۴﴾
ثُمَّ بَدَا لَهُمْ مِّنْۢ بَعْدِ مَا رَاَوُا الْاٰيٰتِ
لَيَسْجُنُنَّهٗ حَتّٰى حِيْنٍ ﴿۳۵﴾ ع ۴
وَدَخَلَ مَعَهُ السِّجْنَ فَتَيٰنِ ؕ قَالَ
اَحَدُهُمَآ اِنِّیْٓ اَرٰىنِیْٓ اَعْصِرُ خَمْرًا ۚ
وَقَالَ الْاٰخَرُ اِنِّیْٓ اَرٰىنِیْٓ اَحْمِلُ فَوْقَ
رَاْسِیْ خُبْزًا تَاْكُلُ الطَّيْرُ مِنْهُ ؕ نَبِّئْنَا
بِتَاْوِيْلِهٖ ۚ اِنَّا نَرٰىكَ مِنَ الْمُحْسِنِيْنَ ﴿۳۶﴾
قَالَ لَا يَاْتِيْكُمَا طَعَامٌ تُرْزَقٰنِهٖٓ اِلَّا
نَبَّاْتُكُمَا بِتَاْوِيْلِهٖ قَبْلَ اَنْ يَّاْتِيَكُمَا ؕ
ذٰلِكُمَا مِمَّا عَلَّمَنِیْ رَبِّیْ ؕ اِنِّیْ تَرَكْتُ
مِلَّةَ قَوْمٍ لَّا يُؤْمِنُوْنَ بِاللّٰهِ وَهُمْ
بِالْاٰخِرَةِ هُمْ كٰفِرُوْنَ ﴿۳۷﴾
وَاتَّبَعْتُ مِلَّةَ اٰبَآءِیْٓ اِبْرٰهِيْمَ
وَاِسْحٰقَ وَيَعْقُوْبَ ؕ مَا كَانَ لَنَآ
اَنْ نُّشْرِكَ بِاللّٰهِ مِنْ شَیْءٍ ؕ ذٰلِكَ
مِنْ فَضْلِ اللّٰهِ عَلَيْنَا وَعَلَى النَّاسِ
وَلٰكِنَّ اَكْثَرَ النَّاسِ لَا يَشْكُرُوْنَ ﴿۳۸﴾
يٰصَاحِبَیِ السِّجْنِ ءَاَرْبَابٌ مُّتَفَرِّقُوْنَ

Ikhfa اخفاء | Ghunna غُنّہ | Ikhfa Meem Saakin اخفاء میم ساکن | Idghaam ادغام | Qalqala قلقلہ | Qalb قلب | Idghaam Meem Saakin ادغام میم ساکن

better, or the One god (Allah), Supreme and Irresistible?

khayrun amil-laahul-Waaḥi-dul-Qahhaar.

خَيْرٌ اَمِ اللّٰهُ الْوَاحِدُ الْقَهَّارُ ﴿٣٩﴾

40. "If not Him, you worship nothing but names which you have named,- you and your fathers,- for which Allah has sent down no authority: the Command is for none but Allah: He has commanded that you worship none but Him: that is the right religion, but most men do not understand.

40. Maa ta'budoona min doo-niheee illaaa asmaaa'an sam-maytumoohaaa antum wa aabaaa'ukum-maaa anzalal laahu bihaa min sulṭaan; inil-ḥukmu illaa lillaah; amara allaa ta'budooo illaaa iyyaah; zaali-kad-deenul-qayyimu wa laakin-na aksaran-naasi laa ya'lamoon.

مَا تَعْبُدُوْنَ مِنْ دُوْنِهٖٓ اِلَّآ اَسْمَآءً
سَمَّيْتُمُوْهَآ اَنْتُمْ وَاٰبَآؤُكُمْ مَّآ اَنْزَلَ
اللّٰهُ بِهَا مِنْ سُلْطٰنٍ ؕ اِنِ الْحُكْمُ اِلَّا
لِلّٰهِ ؕ اَمَرَ اَلَّا تَعْبُدُوْٓا اِلَّآ اِيَّاهُ ؕ
ذٰلِكَ الدِّيْنُ الْقَيِّمُ وَلٰكِنَّ اَكْثَرَ
النَّاسِ لَا يَعْلَمُوْنَ ﴿٤٠﴾

41. "O my two companions of the prison! As to one of you, he will pour out the wine for his lord to drink: as for the other, he will hang from the cross, and the birds will eat from off his head. (So) has been decreed that matter whereof you twain do enquire"...

41. Yaa ṣaaḥibayis-sijni am-maaa aḥadukumaa fa-yasqee rabbahoo khamrañw wa ammal-aakharu fa-yuṣlabu fataåkuluṭ-ṭayru mir-raåsih; quḍiyal-amrul-lazee feehi tastaftiyaan.

يٰصَاحِبَيِ السِّجْنِ اَمَّآ اَحَدُكُمَا
فَيَسْقِيْ رَبَّهٗ خَمْرًا ۚ وَاَمَّا الْاٰخَرُ
فَيُصْلَبُ فَتَاْكُلُ الطَّيْرُ مِنْ رَّاْسِهٖ ؕ
قُضِيَ الْاَمْرُ الَّذِيْ فِيْهِ تَسْتَفْتِيٰنِ ﴿٤١﴾

42. And of the two, to that one whom he consider about to be saved, he said: "Mention me to your lord." But Satan made him forget to mention him to his lord: and (Joseph) lingered in prison a few (more) years.

42. Wa qaala lillazee ẓanna annahoo naajim-minhumaz-kurnee 'inda rabbika fa-ansaahush-Shayṭaanu zikra Rabbihee falabisa fis-sijni biḍ'a sineen. **(Section 5)**

وَقَالَ لِلَّذِيْ ظَنَّ اَنَّهٗ نَاجٍ مِّنْهُمَا
اذْكُرْنِيْ عِنْدَ رَبِّكَ ۫ فَاَنْسٰىهُ
الشَّيْطٰنُ ذِكْرَ رَبِّهٖ فَلَبِثَ فِي السِّجْنِ
بِضْعَ سِنِيْنَ ؕ ﴿٤٢﴾

43. The king (of Egypt) said: "I do see (in a vision) seven fat kine, whom seven lean ones devour,- and seven green ears of corn, and seven (others) withered. O you chiefs! Expound to me my vision if it be that you can interpret visions."

43. Wa qaalal-maliku inneee araa sab'a baqaraatin simaaniñy-yaåkuluhunna sab'un 'ijaafuñw-wa sab'a sumbulaatin khuḍriñw-wa ukhara yaabisaat; yaaa-ayyuhal-mala-u aftoonee fee ru'yaaya in kuntum lirru'yaa ta'buroon.

وَقَالَ الْمَلِكُ اِنِّيْٓ اَرٰى سَبْعَ
بَقَرٰتٍ سِمَانٍ يَّاْكُلُهُنَّ سَبْعٌ عِجَافٌ
وَّسَبْعَ سُنْۢبُلٰتٍ خُضْرٍ وَّاُخَرَ
يٰبِسٰتٍ ؕ يٰٓاَيُّهَا الْمَلَاُ اَفْتُوْنِيْ فِيْ
رُءْيَايَ اِنْ كُنْتُمْ لِلرُّءْيَا تَعْبُرُوْنَ ﴿٤٣﴾

44. They said: "A confused medley of dreams: and we are not skilled in the interpretation of dreams."

44. Qaalooo aḍghaasu aḥlaa-miñw wa maa naḥnu bitaåweelil-aḥlaami bi'aalimeen.

قَالُوْٓا اَضْغَاثُ اَحْلَامٍ ۚ وَمَا نَحْنُ
بِتَاْوِيْلِ الْاَحْلَامِ بِعٰلِمِيْنَ ﴿٤٤﴾

45. But the man who had been released, one of the two (who had been in prison) and who now remembered him after (so long) a space of time, said: "I will tell you the truth of its interpretation: you send me (therefore)."

45. Wa qaalal-lazee najaa minhumaa waddakara ba'da ummatin ana unabbi'ukum bitaåweelihee fa-arsiloon.

وَقَالَ الَّذِيْ نَجَا مِنْهُمَا وَادَّكَرَ
بَعْدَ اُمَّةٍ اَنَا اُنَبِّئُكُمْ بِتَاْوِيْلِهٖ
فَاَرْسِلُوْنِ ﴿٤٥﴾

46. "O Joseph!" (he said) "O man of truth! Expound to us

46. Yoosufu ayyuhaṣ-ṣiddee-qu aftinaa fee

يُوْسُفُ اَيُّهَا الصِّدِّيْقُ اَفْتِنَا فِيْ

Ikhfa اخفاء | Ghunna غُنّہ | Ikhfa Meem Saakin اخفاء میم ساکن | Idghaam ادغام | Qalqala قلقلہ | Qalb قلب | Idghaam Meem Saakin ادغام میم ساکن

(the dream) of seven fat kine whom seven lean ones devour, and of seven green ears of corn and (seven) others withered: that I may return to the people, and that they may understand."

47. (Joseph) said: "For seven years you shall diligently sow as is your wont: and the harvests that you reap, you shall leave them in the ear,- except a little, of which you shall eat.

48. "Then will come after that (period) seven dreadful (years), which will devour what you shall have laid by in advance for them,- (all) except a little which you shall have (specially) guarded.

49. "Then will come after that (period) a year in which the people will have abundant water, and in which they will press (wine and oil)."

50. So the king said: "You bring him to me." But when the messenger came to him, (Joseph) said: "You go back to your lord, and ask him, 'What is the state of mind of the ladies who cut their hands'? For my Lord is certainly well aware of their snare."

51. (The king) said (to the ladies): "What was your affair when you sought to seduce Joseph from his (true) self?" The ladies said: "Allah preserve us! We do not know any evil against him!" Said the 'Aziz's wife: "Now is the truth manifest (to all): it was I who sought to seduce him from his (true) self: he is indeed of those who are (ever) true (and virtuous).

52. "This (I say), in order that he may know that I have never been false to him in his absence, and that Allah will never guide the snare of the false ones.

53. "Nor do I absolve my own self (of blame): the (human) soul is certainly prone to evil, unless my Lord do bestow His Mercy: but surely my Lord is Oft-Forgiving, Most Merciful."

sab'i baqaraatin simaaniñy-yaåkuluhunna sab'un 'ijaafuñw-wa sab'i sumbulaatin khuḍriñw-wa ukhara yaabisaatil-la'alleee arji'u ilan-naasi la'allahum ya'lamoon.

47. Qaala tazra'oona sab'a sineena da-aban famaa ḥaṣattum fazaroohu fee sumbuliheee illaa qaleelam-mimmaa taåkuloon.

48. Summa yaåtee mim-ba'di zaalika sab'un shidaaduñy-yaåkulna maa qaddamtum lahunna illaa qaleelam-mimmaa tuḥṣinoon.

49. Summa yaåtee mim ba'di zaalika 'aamun feehi yughaasun-naasu wa feehi ya'ṣiroon.

(Section 6)

50. Wa qaalal-maliku'-toonee bihee falammaa jaaa'ahur-rasoolu qaalar-ji' ilaa rabbika fas'alhu maa baalun-niswatil-laatee qaṭṭa'na aydiyahunn; inna Rabbee bikaydihinna 'Aleem.

51. Qaala maa khaṭbukunna iz raawattunna Yoosufa 'an-nafsih; qulna ḥaasha lillaahi maa 'alimnaa 'alayhi min sooo'; qaalatim-ra-atul-'Azeezil-'aana ḥaṣḥaṣal-ḥaqq, ana raawattuhoo 'an-nafsihee wa innahoo laminaṣ-ṣaadiqeen.

52. Zaalika liya'lama annee lam akhunhu bilghaybi wa annal-laaha laa yahdee kaydal-khaaa'ineen.

53. Wa maaa ubarri'u nafsee; innan-nafsa la-ammaaratum bissooo'i illaa maa raḥima Rabbee; inna Rabbee Ghafoorur-Raḥeem.

سَبْعِ بَقَرٰتٍ سِمَانٍ يَّاْكُلُهُنَّ سَبْعٌ
عِجَافٌ وَّسَبْعِ سُنْۢبُلٰتٍ خُضْرٍ وَّ
اُخَرَ يٰبِسٰتٍ لَّعَلِّيْٓ اَرْجِعُ اِلَى النَّاسِ
لَعَلَّهُمْ يَعْلَمُوْنَ ﴿٤٦﴾
قَالَ تَزْرَعُوْنَ سَبْعَ سِنِيْنَ دَاَبًا ۚ
فَمَا حَصَدْتُّمْ فَذَرُوْهُ فِيْ سُنْۢبُلِهٖٓ
اِلَّا قَلِيْلًا مِّمَّا تَاْكُلُوْنَ ﴿٤٧﴾
ثُمَّ يَاْتِيْ مِنْۢ بَعْدِ ذٰلِكَ سَبْعٌ شِدَادٌ
يَّاْكُلْنَ مَا قَدَّمْتُمْ لَهُنَّ اِلَّا قَلِيْلًا
مِّمَّا تُحْصِنُوْنَ ﴿٤٨﴾
ثُمَّ يَاْتِيْ مِنْۢ بَعْدِ ذٰلِكَ عَامٌ فِيْهِ
يُغَاثُ النَّاسُ وَفِيْهِ يَعْصِرُوْنَ ﴿٤٩﴾ ع
وَقَالَ الْمَلِكُ ائْتُوْنِيْ بِهٖ ۚ فَلَمَّا
جَآءَهُ الرَّسُوْلُ قَالَ ارْجِعْ اِلٰى رَبِّكَ
فَسْئَلْهُ مَا بَالُ النِّسْوَةِ الّٰتِيْ قَطَّعْنَ
اَيْدِيَهُنَّ ؕ اِنَّ رَبِّيْ بِكَيْدِهِنَّ عَلِيْمٌ ﴿٥٠﴾
قَالَ مَا خَطْبُكُنَّ اِذْ رَاوَدْتُّنَّ يُوْسُفَ
عَنْ نَّفْسِهٖ ؕ قُلْنَ حَاشَ لِلّٰهِ مَا عَلِمْنَا
عَلَيْهِ مِنْ سُوْٓءٍ ؕ قَالَتِ امْرَاَتُ الْعَزِيْزِ
الْـٰٔنَ حَصْحَصَ الْحَقُّ اَنَا رَاوَدْتُّهٗ عَنْ
نَّفْسِهٖ وَاِنَّهٗ لَمِنَ الصّٰدِقِيْنَ ﴿٥١﴾
ذٰلِكَ لِيَعْلَمَ اَنِّيْ لَمْ اَخُنْهُ بِالْغَيْبِ
وَاَنَّ اللّٰهَ لَا يَهْدِيْ كَيْدَ الْخَآئِنِيْنَ ﴿٥٢﴾
وَمَآ اُبَرِّئُ نَفْسِيْ ۚ اِنَّ النَّفْسَ
لَاَمَّارَةٌۢ بِالسُّوْٓءِ اِلَّا مَا رَحِمَ
رَبِّيْ ؕ اِنَّ رَبِّيْ غَفُوْرٌ رَّحِيْمٌ ﴿٥٣﴾

الجزء الثالث عشر (١٣)

Ikhfa اخفاء | Ghunna غُنّہ | Ikhfa Meem Saakin اخفاء میم ساکن | Idghaam ادغام | Qalqala قلقلہ | Qalb قلب | Idghaam Meem Saakin ادغام میم ساکن

54. So the king said: "Bring him to me; I will take him specially to serve about my own person." Therefore when he had spoken to him, he said: "Be assured this day, you are, before our own pre-sence, with rank firmly established, and fidelity fully proved!"

55. (Joseph) said: "Set me over the store-houses of the land: I will indeed guard them, as one that knows (their importance)."

56. Thus We gave established power to Joseph in the land, to take possession therein as, when, or where he pleased. We bestow of Our Mercy on whom We please, and We suffer not, to be lost, the reward of those who do good.

57. But verily the reward of the Hereafter is the best, for those who believe, and are constant in righteousness.

58. Then came Joseph's brethren: they entered his presence, and he knew them, but they did not know him.

59. And when he had furnished them forth with provisions (suitable) for them, he said: "Bring to me a brother you have, of the same father as yourselves, (but a different mother): do you not see that I pay out full measure, and that I do provide the best hospitality?

60. "Now if you do not bring him to me, you shall have no measure (of corn) from me, nor you shall (even) come near me."

61. They said: "We shall certainly seek to get our wish about him from his father: indeed we shall do it."

62. And (Joseph) told his servants to put their stock-in-trade (with which they had bartered) into their saddle-bags, so they should know it only when they returned to their people, in order that they might come back.

63. Now when they returned to their father, they said: "O our father! No more measure of grain shall we get (unless we take our brother): so send

54. Wa qaalal-maliku'-toonee biheee astakhliṣhu linafsee falammaa kallamahoo qaala innakal-yawma ladaynaa makeenun ameen.

55. Qaalaj-'alnee 'alaa khazaaa'inil-arḍi innee ḥafeeẓun 'aleem.

56. Wa kazaalika makkannaa li-Yoosufa fil-arḍi yatabawwa-u minhaa ḥaysu yashaaa'; nuṣeebu biraḥmatinaa man-nashaaa'u wa laa nuḍee'u ajral muḥsineen.

57. Wa la-ajrul-Aakhirati khayrul-lillazeena aamanoo wa kaanoo yattaqoon. **(Section 7)**

58. Wa jaaa'a ikhwatu Yoosufa fadakhaloo 'alayhi fa'arafahum wa hum lahoo munkiroon.

59. Wa lammaa jahhazahum bijahaazihim qaala'-toonee biakhil-lakum-min abeekum; alaa tarawna anneee oofil-kayla wa ana khayrul-munzileen.

60. Fa-il-lam taåtoonee bihee falaa kayla lakum 'indee wa laa taqraboon.

61. Qaaloo sanuraawidu 'anhu abaahu wa innaa lafaa'iloon.

62. Wa qaala lifityaanihij-'aloo biḍaa'atahum fee riḥaalihim la'allahum ya'rifoonahaaa izan-qalabooo ilaaa ahlihim la'allahum yarji'oon.

63. Falammaa raja'ooo ilaaa abeehim qaaloo yaaa abaanaa muni'a minnal-kaylu fa-arsil

وَقَالَ الْمَلِكُ ائْتُونِي بِهٖٓ اَسْتَخْلِصْهُ
لِنَفْسِيْ ۚ فَلَمَّا كَلَّمَهٗ قَالَ اِنَّكَ
الْيَوْمَ لَدَيْنَا مَكِيْنٌ اَمِيْنٌ ﴿٥٤﴾
قَالَ اجْعَلْنِيْ عَلٰى خَزَآئِنِ الْاَرْضِ ۚ
اِنِّيْ حَفِيْظٌ عَلِيْمٌ ﴿٥٥﴾
وَكَذٰلِكَ مَكَّنَّا لِيُوْسُفَ فِي الْاَرْضِ ۚ
يَتَبَوَّاُ مِنْهَا حَيْثُ يَشَآءُ ۭ نُصِيْبُ
بِرَحْمَتِنَا مَنْ نَّشَآءُ وَلَا نُضِيْعُ
اَجْرَ الْمُحْسِنِيْنَ ﴿٥٦﴾
وَلَاَجْرُ الْاٰخِرَةِ خَيْرٌ لِّلَّذِيْنَ
اٰمَنُوْا وَكَانُوْا يَتَّقُوْنَ ﴿٥٧﴾
وَجَآءَ اِخْوَةُ يُوْسُفَ فَدَخَلُوْا
عَلَيْهِ فَعَرَفَهُمْ وَهُمْ لَهٗ مُنْكِرُوْنَ ﴿٥٨﴾
وَلَمَّا جَهَّزَهُمْ بِجَهَازِهِمْ قَالَ
ائْتُوْنِيْ بِاَخٍ لَّكُمْ مِّنْ اَبِيْكُمْ ۚ
اَلَا تَرَوْنَ اَنِّيْٓ اُوْفِي الْكَيْلَ وَاَنَا
خَيْرُ الْمُنْزِلِيْنَ ﴿٥٩﴾
فَاِنْ لَّمْ تَاْتُوْنِيْ بِهٖ فَلَا كَيْلَ لَكُمْ
عِنْدِيْ وَلَا تَقْرَبُوْنِ ﴿٦٠﴾
قَالُوْا سَنُرَاوِدُ عَنْهُ اَبَاهُ وَاِنَّا
لَفٰعِلُوْنَ ﴿٦١﴾
وَقَالَ لِفِتْيٰنِهِ اجْعَلُوْا بِضَاعَتَهُمْ فِيْ
رِحَالِهِمْ لَعَلَّهُمْ يَعْرِفُوْنَهَآ اِذَا انْقَلَبُوْٓا
اِلٰٓى اَهْلِهِمْ لَعَلَّهُمْ يَرْجِعُوْنَ ﴿٦٢﴾
فَلَمَّا رَجَعُوْٓا اِلٰٓى اَبِيْهِمْ قَالُوْا
يٰٓاَبَانَا مُنِعَ مِنَّا الْكَيْلُ فَاَرْسِلْ

Ikhfa اخفاء | Ghunna غُنّہ | Ikhfa Meem Saakin اخفاءمیم ساکن | Idghaam ادغام | Qalqala قلقلہ | Qalb قلب | Idghaam Meem Saakin ادغام میم ساکن

مَعَنَآ اَخَانَا نَكْتَلْ وَاِنَّا لَهٗ لَحٰفِظُوْنَ ﴿٦٣﴾
قَالَ هَلْ اٰمَنُكُمْ عَلَيْهِ اِلَّا كَمَآ
اَمِنْتُكُمْ عَلٰٓى اَخِيْهِ مِنْ قَبْلُ ؕ فَاللّٰهُ
خَيْرٌ حٰفِظًا ۪ وَّهُوَ اَرْحَمُ الرّٰحِمِيْنَ ﴿٦٤﴾

ma'anaaa akhaanaa naktal wa innaa lahoo laḥaafiẓoon
64. Qaala hal aamanukum 'alayhi illaa kamaaa amintukum 'alaaa akheehimin qabl; fal-laahu khayrun ḥaafiẓañw-wa Huwa arḥamur-Raaḥimeen.

our brother with us, that we may get our measure; and we will indeed take every care of him."
64. He said: "Shall I trust you with him with any result other than when I trusted you with his brother aforetime? But Allah is the best to take care (of him), and He is the Most Merciful of those who show mercy!"

وَلَمَّا فَتَحُوْا مَتَاعَهُمْ وَجَدُوْا
بِضَاعَتَهُمْ رُدَّتْ اِلَيْهِمْ ؕ قَالُوْا
يٰٓاَبَانَا مَا نَبْغِيْ ؕ هٰذِهٖ بِضَاعَتُنَا
رُدَّتْ اِلَيْنَا ۚ وَنَمِيْرُ اَهْلَنَا وَنَحْفَظُ
اَخَانَا وَنَزْدَادُ كَيْلَ بَعِيْرٍ ؕ ذٰلِكَ
كَيْلٌ يَّسِيْرٌ ﴿٦٥﴾

65. Wa lammaa fataḥoo mataa-'ahum wajadoo biḍaa'atahum ruddat ilayhim qaaloo yaaa abaanaa maa nabghee; haaz̲i-hee biḍaa'atunaa ruddat ilaynaa wa nameeru ahlanaa wa naḥfaẓu akhaanaa wa nazdaadu kayla ba'eer; z̲aalika kayluñy-yaseer.

65. Then when they opened their baggage, they found their stock-in-trade had been returned to them. They said: "O our father! What (more) can we desire? this our stock-in-trade has been returned to us: we shall get (more) food for our family; we shall take care of our brother; and add (at the same time) a full camel's load (of grain to our provisions). This is but a small quantity.

قَالَ لَنْ اُرْسِلَهٗ مَعَكُمْ حَتّٰى تُؤْتُوْنِ
مَوْثِقًا مِّنَ اللّٰهِ لَتَاْتُنَّنِيْ بِهٖٓ اِلَّآ
اَنْ يُّحَاطَ بِكُمْ ۚ فَلَمَّآ اٰتَوْهُ مَوْثِقَهُمْ
قَالَ اللّٰهُ عَلٰى مَا نَقُوْلُ وَكِيْلٌ ﴿٦٦﴾

66. Qaala lan ursilahoo ma'akum ḥattaa tu'tooni mawsiqam-minal-laahis lataå-tunnanee biheee illaaa añy-yuḥaaṭa bikum falammaaa aatawhu mawsiqahum qaalal-laahu 'alaa maa naqoolu Wakeel.

66. (Jacob) said: "Never will I send him with you until you swear a solemn oath to me, in Allah's name, that you will be sure to bring him back to me unless you are yourselves hemmed in (and made powerless). And when they had sworn their solemn oath, he said: "Over all that we say, be Allah the Witness and Guardian!"

وَقَالَ يٰبَنِيَّ لَا تَدْخُلُوْا مِنْۢ
بَابٍ وَّاحِدٍ وَّادْخُلُوْا مِنْ اَبْوَابٍ
مُّتَفَرِّقَةٍ ؕ وَمَآ اُغْنِيْ عَنْكُمْ مِّنَ
اللّٰهِ مِنْ شَيْءٍ ؕ اِنِ الْحُكْمُ اِلَّا لِلّٰهِ ؕ
عَلَيْهِ تَوَكَّلْتُ ۚ وَعَلَيْهِ فَلْيَتَوَكَّلِ
الْمُتَوَكِّلُوْنَ ﴿٦٧﴾

67. Wa qaala yaa baniyya laa tadkhuloo mim baabiñw-waa-ḥidiñw-wadkhuloo min abwaa-bim-mutafarriqah; wa maaa ughnee 'ankum-minal-laahi min shay'i; inil-ḥukmu illaa lillaahi 'alayhi tawakkaltu wa 'alayhi fal-yatawakkalil-Mutawakki-loon.

67. Further he said: "O my sons! enter not all by one gate: you enter by different gates. Not that I can profit you anything against Allah (with my advice): none can command except Allah: on Him do I put my trust: and let all that trust put their trust on Him."

وَلَمَّا دَخَلُوْا مِنْ حَيْثُ اَمَرَهُمْ
اَبُوْهُمْ ؕ مَا كَانَ يُغْنِيْ عَنْهُمْ مِّنَ
اللّٰهِ مِنْ شَيْءٍ اِلَّا حَاجَةً فِيْ نَفْسِ
يَعْقُوْبَ قَضٰىهَا ؕ وَاِنَّهٗ لَذُوْ عِلْمٍ
لِّمَا عَلَّمْنٰهُ وَلٰكِنَّ اَكْثَرَ النَّاسِ
لَا يَعْلَمُوْنَ ﴿٦٨﴾ ع ٨ / ١١ / ٢

68. Wa lammaa dakhaloo min ḥaysu amarahum aboohum-maa kaana yughnee 'anhum-minal-laahi min shay'in illaa ḥaajatan fee nafsi Ya'qooba qaḍaahaa; wa innahoo laz̲oo 'ilmil-limaa 'allamnaahu wa laakinna aksaran-naasi laa ya'lamoon.
(Section 8)

68. And when they entered in the manner their father had enjoined, it did not profit them in the least against (the plan of) Allah: it was but a necessity of Jacob's soul, which he discharged. For he was, by Our instruction, full of knowledge (and experience): but most men do not know.

Ikhfa اخفاء | Ghunna غنّہ | Ikhfa Meem Saakin اخفاء میم ساکن | Idghaam ادغام | Qalqala قلقلہ | Qalb قلب | Idghaam Meem Saakin ادغام میم ساکن

69. Now when they came into Joseph's presence, he received his (full) brother to stay with him. He said (to him): "Behold! I am your (own) brother; so grieve not at aught of their doings."

70. At length when he had furnished them forth with provisions (suitable) for them, he put the drinking cup into his brother's saddle-bag. Then shouted out a Crier:"O you (in) the caravan! behold! you are thieves, without doubt!"

71. They said, turning toward them: "What is it that you miss?"

72. They said: "We miss the great beaker of the King; for him who produces it, is (the reward of) a camel load; I will be bound by it."

73. (The brothers) said: "By Allah! you know well that we did not come to make mischief in the land, and we are no thieves!"

74. (The Egyptians) said: "What then shall be the penalty of this, if you are (proved) to have lied?"

75. They said: "The penalty should be that he in whose saddle-bag it is found, should be held (as bondman) to atone for the (crime). Thus it is we punish the wrong- doers!"

76. So he began (the search) with their baggage, before (he came to) the baggage of his brother: at length he brought it out of his brother's baggage. Thus did We plan for Joseph. He could not take his brother by the law of the king except that Allah willed it (so). We raise to degrees (of wisdom) whom We please: but over all endued with knowledge is One, the All-Knowing.

77. They said: "If he steals, there was a brother of his who stole before (him)." But these things Joseph kept locked in his heart, revealing not the secrets to them. He (simply) said (to himself): "You are the worse situated; and Allah knows best the truth of what you assert!"

69. Wa lammaa dakhaloo 'alaa Yoosufa aawaaa ilayhi akhaahu qaala inneee ana akhooka falaa tabta'is bimaa kaanoo ya'maloon.

70. Falammaa jahhazahum bijahaazihim ja'alas-siqaayata fee raḥli akheehi summa azzana mu'azzinun ayyatuhal-'eeru innakum lasaariqoon.

71. Qaaloo wa aqbaloo 'alayhim-maazaa tafqidoon.

72. Qaaloo nafqidu ṣuwaa'al-maliki wa liman jaaa'a bihee ḥimlu ba'eeriñw-wa ana bihee za'eem.

73. Qaaloo tallaahi laqad 'alimtum-maa ji'naa linufsida fil-arḍi wa maa kunnaa saariqeen.

74. Qaaloo famaa jazaaa'uhooo in kuntum kaazibeen.

75. Qaaloo jazaaa'uhoo mañw-wujida fee raḥlihee fahuwa jazaaa'uh; kazaalika najziẓ-ẓaalimeen.

76. Fabada-a bi-aw'iyatihim qabla wi'aaa'i akheehi summas-takhrajahaa miñw-wi'aaa'i akheeh; kazaalika kidnaa li-Yoosuf; maa kaana liyaåkhuza akhaahu fee deenil-maliki illaaa añy-yashaaa'al-laah; narfa'u darajaatim-man-nashaaa'; wa fawqa kulli zee 'ilmin 'Aleem.

77. Qaalooo iñy-yasriq faqad saraqa akhul-lahoo min qabl; fa-asarrahaa Yoosufu fee nafsihee wa lam yubdihaa lahum; qaala antum sharrum-makaanañw wallaahu a'lamu bimaa taṣifoon.

وَلَمَّا دَخَلُوا عَلٰى يُوسُفَ اٰوٰى
اِلَيْهِ اَخَاهُ قَالَ اِنِّىْۤ اَنَا اَخُوكَ
فَلَا تَبْتَئِسْ بِمَا كَانُوا يَعْمَلُونَ ﴿٦٩﴾
فَلَمَّا جَهَّزَهُمْ بِجَهَازِهِمْ جَعَلَ
السِّقَايَةَ فِىْ رَحْلِ اَخِيهِ ثُمَّ اَذَّنَ
مُؤَذِّنٌ اَيَّتُهَا الْعِيرُ اِنَّكُمْ لَسٰرِقُونَ ﴿٧٠﴾
قَالُوا وَاَقْبَلُوا عَلَيْهِمْ مَّاذَا تَفْقِدُونَ ﴿٧١﴾
قَالُوا نَفْقِدُ صُوَاعَ الْمَلِكِ وَلِمَنْ
جَآءَ بِهٖ حِمْلُ بَعِيرٍ وَّاَنَا بِهٖ زَعِيمٌ ﴿٧٢﴾
قَالُوا تَاللّٰهِ لَقَدْ عَلِمْتُمْ مَّا جِئْنَا لِنُفْسِدَ
فِى الْاَرْضِ وَمَا كُنَّا سٰرِقِينَ ﴿٧٣﴾
قَالُوا فَمَا جَزَآؤُهٗۤ اِنْ كُنْتُمْ كٰذِبِينَ ﴿٧٤﴾
قَالُوا جَزَآؤُهٗ مَنْ وُّجِدَ فِىْ رَحْلِهٖ
فَهُوَ جَزَآؤُهٗ ۚ كَذٰلِكَ نَجْزِى
الظّٰلِمِينَ ﴿٧٥﴾
فَبَدَاَ بِاَوْعِيَتِهِمْ قَبْلَ وِعَآءِ اَخِيهِ
ثُمَّ اسْتَخْرَجَهَا مِنْ وِّعَآءِ اَخِيهِ ۚ
كَذٰلِكَ كِدْنَا لِيُوسُفَ ۚ مَا كَانَ
لِيَاْخُذَ اَخَاهُ فِىْ دِينِ الْمَلِكِ اِلَّاۤ
اَنْ يَّشَآءَ اللّٰهُ ۚ نَرْفَعُ دَرَجٰتٍ مَّنْ
نَّشَآءُ ۚ وَفَوْقَ كُلِّ ذِىْ عِلْمٍ عَلِيمٌ ﴿٧٦﴾
قَالُوۤا اِنْ يَّسْرِقْ فَقَدْ سَرَقَ اَخٌ لَّهٗ
مِنْ قَبْلُ ۚ فَاَسَرَّهَا يُوسُفُ فِىْ
نَفْسِهٖ وَلَمْ يُبْدِهَا لَهُمْ ۚ قَالَ
اَنْتُمْ شَرٌّ مَّكَانًا ۚ وَاللّٰهُ اَعْلَمُ
بِمَا تَصِفُونَ ﴿٧٧﴾

Ikhfa اخفاء | Ghunna غُنّہ | Ikhfa Meem Saakin اخفاء میم ساکن | Idghaam ادغام | Qalqala قلقلہ | Qalb قلب | Idghaam Meem Saakin ادغام میم ساکن

78. They said: "O exalted one! Behold! he has a father, aged and venerable, (who will grieve for him); so take one of us in his place; for we see that you are (gracious) in doing good."

78. Qaaloo yaaa ayyuhal-'Azeezu inna lahooo aban shaykhan kabeeran fakhuẕ aḥadanaa makaanahoo innaa naraaka minal-muḥsineen.

قَالُوْا يٰٓاَيُّهَا الْعَزِيْزُ اِنَّ لَهٗٓ اَبًا
شَيْخًا كَبِيْرًا فَخُذْ اَحَدَنَا مَكَانَهٗ ۚ
اِنَّا نَرٰىكَ مِنَ الْمُحْسِنِيْنَ ﴿٧٨﴾

79. He said: "Allah forbid that we take other than him with whom we found our property: indeed (if we did so), we should be acting wrongfully.

79. Qaala ma'aaẕal-laahi an naåkhuẕa illaa mañw-wajadnaa mataa'anaa 'indahooo innaaa iẕal-laẕaalimoon. **(Section 9)**

قَالَ مَعَاذَ اللّٰهِ اَنْ نَّاْخُذَ اِلَّا
مَنْ وَّجَدْنَا مَتَاعَنَا عِنْدَهٗٓ ۙ
اِنَّآ اِذًا لَّظٰلِمُوْنَ ﴿٧٩﴾

80. Now when they saw no hope of his (yielding), they held a conference in private. The leader among them said: "Don't you know that your father did took an oath from you in Allah's name, and how, before this, you failed in your duty with Joseph? Therefore I will not leave this land until my father permits me, or Allah commands me; and He is the best to command.

80. Falammas-tay'asoo minhu khalaṣoo najiyyan qaala kabeeruhum alam ta'lamooo anna abaakum qad akhaẕa 'alaykum mawṯiqam-minal-laahi wa min qablu maa farraṭṭum fee Yoosufa falan abraḥal-arḍa ḥattaa yaåẕana leee abeee aw yaḥkumal-laahu lee wa huwa khayrul-ḥaakimeen.

فَلَمَّا اسْتَيْئَسُوْا مِنْهُ خَلَصُوْا
نَجِيًّا ۗ قَالَ كَبِيْرُهُمْ اَلَمْ تَعْلَمُوْٓا
اَنَّ اَبَاكُمْ قَدْ اَخَذَ عَلَيْكُمْ
مَّوْثِقًا مِّنَ اللّٰهِ وَمِنْ قَبْلُ مَا
فَرَّطْتُّمْ فِيْ يُوْسُفَ ۚ فَلَنْ اَبْرَحَ
الْاَرْضَ حَتّٰى يَاْذَنَ لِيْٓ اَبِيْٓ اَوْ
يَحْكُمَ اللّٰهُ لِيْ ۚ وَهُوَ خَيْرُ الْحٰكِمِيْنَ ﴿٨٠﴾

81. "You turn back to your father, and say, 'O our father! Behold! your son committed theft! we bear witness only to what we know, and we could not well guard against the unseen!

81. Irji'ooo ilaaa abeekum faqooloo yaaa abaanaaa innabnaka saraq; wa maa shahidnaaa illaa bimaa 'alimnaa wa maa kunnaa lilghaybi ḥaafiẕeen.

اِرْجِعُوْٓا اِلٰٓى اَبِيْكُمْ فَقُوْلُوْا
يٰٓاَبَانَآ اِنَّ ابْنَكَ سَرَقَ ۚ وَمَا
شَهِدْنَآ اِلَّا بِمَا عَلِمْنَا وَمَا كُنَّا
لِلْغَيْبِ حٰفِظِيْنَ ﴿٨١﴾

82. "'Ask at the town where we have been and the caravan in which we returned, and (you will find) we are indeed telling the truth.'"

82. Was'alil-qaryatal-latee kunnaa feehaa wal'eeral-lateee aqbalnaa feehaa wa innaa laṣaadiqoon.

وَسْئَلِ الْقَرْيَةَ الَّتِيْ كُنَّا فِيْهَا
وَالْعِيْرَ الَّتِيْٓ اَقْبَلْنَا فِيْهَا ۗ وَاِنَّا
لَصٰدِقُوْنَ ﴿٨٢﴾

83. Jacob said: "Nay, but you have yourselves contrived a story (good enough) for you. So patience is most fitting (for me). May be Allah will bring them (back) all to me (in the end). For He is indeed full of knowledge and wisdom."

83. Qaala bal sawwalat lakum anfusukum amran faṣabrun jameelun 'asal-laahu añy-yaåtiyanee bihim jamee'aa; innahoo Huwal-'Aleemul-Ḥakeem.

قَالَ بَلْ سَوَّلَتْ لَكُمْ اَنْفُسُكُمْ اَمْرًا ۗ
فَصَبْرٌ جَمِيْلٌ ۗ عَسَى اللّٰهُ اَنْ
يَّاْتِيَنِيْ بِهِمْ جَمِيْعًا ۗ اِنَّهٗ هُوَ
الْعَلِيْمُ الْحَكِيْمُ ﴿٨٣﴾

84. And he turned away from them, and said: "How great is my grief for Joseph!" And his eyes became white with

84. Wa tawallaa 'anhum wa qaala yaaa asafaa 'alaa Yoosufa wabyaḍḍat 'aynaahu minal-

وَتَوَلّٰى عَنْهُمْ وَقَالَ يٰٓاَسَفٰى
عَلٰى يُوْسُفَ وَابْيَضَّتْ عَيْنٰهُ مِنَ

Ikhfa اخفاء | Ghunna غُنّہ | Ikhfa Meem Saakin اخفاء میم ساکن | Idghaam ادغام | Qalqala قلقلہ | Qalb قلب | Idghaam Meem Saakin ادغام میم ساکن

sorrow, and he fell into silent melancholy.

85. They said: "By Allah! (Never) will you cease to remember Joseph until you reach the last extremity of illness, or until you die!"

86. He said: "I only complain of my distraction and anguish to Allah, and I know from Allah that which you do not know.

87. "O my sons! you go and enquire about Joseph and his brother, and never give up hope of Allah's Soothing Mercy: truly no one despairs of Allah's Soothing Mercy, except those who have no faith."

88. Then, when they came (back) into (Joseph's) presence they said: "O exalted one! distress has seized us and our family: we have (now) brought but scanty capital: so pay us full measure, (we pray you), and treat it as charity to us: for Allah rewards the charitable."

89. He said: "Do you know how you dealt with Joseph and his brother, not knowing (what you were doing)?"

90. They said: "Are you indeed Joseph?" He said, "I am Joseph, and this is my brother: Allah has indeed been gracious to us (all): behold, he that is righteous and patient,- never will Allah suffer the reward to be lost, of those who do right."

91. They said: "By Allah! indeed Allah has preferred you above us, and we certainly have been guilty of sin!"

92. He said: "This day let no reproach be (cast) on you: Allah will forgive you, and He is the Most Merciful of those who show mercy!

93. "Go with this my shirt, and cast it

ḥuzni fahuwa kaẓeem.

85. Qaaloo tallaahi tafta'u tazkuru Yoosufa ḥattaa takoona ḥaraḍan aw takoona minal-haalikeen.

86. Qaala innamaaa ashkoo bassee wa ḥuzneee ilal-laahi wa a'lamu minal-laahi maa laa ta'lamoon.

87. Yaa baniyyaz-haboo fataḥassasoo miñy-Yoosufa wa akheehi wa laa tay'asoo mir-rawḥil-laahi innahoo laa yay'asu mir-rawḥil-laahi illal-qawmul-kaafiroon.

88. Falammaa dakhaloo 'alayhi qaaloo yaaa ayyuhal-'Azeezu massanaa wa ahlanaḍ-ḍurru wa ji'naa bibiḍaa'atim-muzjaatin fa-awfi lanal-kayla wa taṣaddaq 'alaynaa innal-laaha yajzil-mutaṣaddiqeen.

89. Qaala hal 'alimtum maa fa'altum bi-Yoosufa wa akhee-hi iz antum jaahiloon.

90. Qaalooo 'a-innaka la-anta Yoosufu qaala ana Yoosufu wa haazaaa akhee qad mannal-laahu 'alaynaa innahoo mañy-yattaqi wa yaṣbir fa-innal-laaha laa yuḍee'u ajral-muḥsineen.

91. Qaaloo tallaahi laqad aasarakal-laahu 'alaynaa wa in kunnaa lakhaaṭi'een.

92. Qaala laa tasreeba 'alay-kumul-yawma yaghfirul-laahu lakum wa Huwa arḥamur-raaḥimeen.

93. Izhaboo biqameeṣee haa-zaa fa-alqoohu

الْحُزْنِ فَهُوَ كَظِيمٌ ﴿٨٤﴾
قَالُوا تَاللَّهِ تَفْتَؤُا تَذْكُرُ يُوسُفَ
حَتَّىٰ تَكُونَ حَرَضًا أَوْ تَكُونَ
مِنَ الْهَالِكِينَ ﴿٨٥﴾
قَالَ إِنَّمَا أَشْكُو بَثِّي وَحُزْنِي إِلَى
اللَّهِ وَأَعْلَمُ مِنَ اللَّهِ مَا لَا تَعْلَمُونَ ﴿٨٦﴾
يَا بَنِيَّ اذْهَبُوا فَتَحَسَّسُوا مِنْ يُوسُفَ
وَأَخِيهِ وَلَا تَيْأَسُوا مِنْ رَوْحِ اللَّهِ
إِنَّهُ لَا يَيْأَسُ مِنْ رَوْحِ اللَّهِ إِلَّا
الْقَوْمُ الْكَافِرُونَ ﴿٨٧﴾
فَلَمَّا دَخَلُوا عَلَيْهِ قَالُوا يَا أَيُّهَا
الْعَزِيزُ مَسَّنَا وَأَهْلَنَا الضُّرُّ وَجِئْنَا
بِبِضَاعَةٍ مُزْجَاةٍ فَأَوْفِ لَنَا الْكَيْلَ
وَتَصَدَّقْ عَلَيْنَا إِنَّ اللَّهَ يَجْزِي
الْمُتَصَدِّقِينَ ﴿٨٨﴾
قَالَ هَلْ عَلِمْتُمْ مَا فَعَلْتُمْ بِيُوسُفَ
وَأَخِيهِ إِذْ أَنْتُمْ جَاهِلُونَ ﴿٨٩﴾
قَالُوا أَإِنَّكَ لَأَنْتَ يُوسُفُ قَالَ
أَنَا يُوسُفُ وَهَٰذَا أَخِي قَدْ مَنَّ
اللَّهُ عَلَيْنَا إِنَّهُ مَنْ يَتَّقِ وَيَصْبِرْ
فَإِنَّ اللَّهَ لَا يُضِيعُ أَجْرَ الْمُحْسِنِينَ ﴿٩٠﴾
قَالُوا تَاللَّهِ لَقَدْ آثَرَكَ اللَّهُ عَلَيْنَا
وَإِنْ كُنَّا لَخَاطِئِينَ ﴿٩١﴾
قَالَ لَا تَثْرِيبَ عَلَيْكُمُ الْيَوْمَ يَغْفِرُ
اللَّهُ لَكُمْ وَهُوَ أَرْحَمُ الرَّاحِمِينَ ﴿٩٢﴾
اذْهَبُوا بِقَمِيصِي هَٰذَا فَأَلْقُوهُ

Ikhfa اخفاء | Ghunna غُنّہ | Ikhfa Meem Saakin اخفاء میم ساکن | Idghaam ادغام | Qalqala قلقلہ | Qalb قلب | Idghaam Meem Saakin ادغام میم ساکن

over the face of my father: he will come to see (clearly). Then you come (here) to me together with all your family."

94. When the Caravan left (Egypt), their father said: "I do indeed scent the presence of Joseph: Nay, think me not a dotard."

95. They said: "By Allah! truly you are in your old wandering mind."

96. Then when the bearer of the good news came, He cast (the shirt) over his face, and he forthwith regained clear sight. He said: "Did I not say to you, 'I know from Allah that which you do not know?'"

97. They said: "O our father! ask for us forgiveness for our sins, for we were truly at fault."

98. He said: "Soon will I ask my Lord for forgiveness for you: for he is indeed Oft-Forgiving, Most Merciful."

99. Then when they entered the presence of Joseph, he provided a home for his parents with himself, and said: "you enter Egypt (all) in safety if it please Allah."

100. And he raised his parents high on the throne (of dignity), and they fell down in prostration, (all) before him. He said: "O my father! this is the fulfilment of my vision of old! Allah has made it come true! He was indeed good to me when He took me out of prison and brought you (all here) out of the desert, (even) after Satan had sown enmity between me and my brothers. Verily my Lord understands best the mysteries of all that He plans to do. For verily He is full of knowledge and wisdom.

'alaa wajhi abee yaâti baṣeerañw waâtoonee bi-ahlikum ajma-'een. **(Section 10)**

94. Wa lammaa faṣalatil-'eeru qaala aboohum innee la-ajidu reeḥa Yoosufa law laaa an tufannidoon.

95. Qaaloo tallaahi innaka lafee ḍalaalikal-qadeem.

96. Falammaaa an jaaa'al-basheeru alqaahu 'alaa wajhihee fartadda baṣeeran qaala alam aqul lakum inneee a'lamu minal-laahi maa laa ta'lamoon.

97. Qaaloo yaaa abaanas-taghfir lanaa ẕunoobanaaa innaa kunnaa khaaṭi'een.

98. Qaala sawfa astaghfiru lakum Rabbeee innahoo Huwal-Ghafoorur-Raḥeem.

99. Falammaa dakhaloo 'alaa Yoosufa aawaaa ilayhi abawayhi wa qaalad-khuloo Miṣra in shaaa'al-laahu aamineen.

100. Wa rafa'a abawayhi 'alal-'arshi wa kharroo lahoo sujjadaa; wa qaala yaaa abati haaẕaa taâweelu ru'yaaya min qablu qad ja'alahaa Rabbee ḥaqqaa; wa qad aḥsana beee iẕ akhrajanee minas-sijni wa jaaa'a bikum-minal-badwi mim ba'di an nazaghash-Shayṭaanu baynee wa bayna ikhwatee; inna Rabbee laṭeeful-limaa yashaaa'; innahoo Huwal-'Aleemul-Ḥakeem.

عَلٰى وَجْهِ اَبِىْ يَاْتِ بَصِيْرًا ۚ وَاْتُوْنِىْ
بِاَهْلِكُمْ اَجْمَعِيْنَ ﴿٩٣﴾ ع
وَلَمَّا فَصَلَتِ الْعِيْرُ قَالَ اَبُوْهُمْ
اِنِّىْ لَاَجِدُ رِيْحَ يُوْسُفَ لَوْلَاۤ
اَنْ تُفَنِّدُوْنِ ﴿٩٤﴾
قَالُوْا تَاللّٰهِ اِنَّكَ لَفِىْ ضَلٰلِكَ الْقَدِيْمِ ﴿٩٥﴾ الربع
فَلَمَّاۤ اَنْ جَاۤءَ الْبَشِيْرُ اَلْقٰىهُ عَلٰى
وَجْهِهٖ فَارْتَدَّ بَصِيْرًا ۚ قَالَ اَلَمْ
اَقُلْ لَّكُمْ ۚ اِنِّىْۤ اَعْلَمُ مِنَ اللّٰهِ
مَا لَا تَعْلَمُوْنَ ﴿٩٦﴾
قَالُوْا يٰۤاَبَانَا اسْتَغْفِرْ لَنَا ذُنُوْبَنَاۤ
اِنَّا كُنَّا خٰطِـِٕيْنَ ﴿٩٧﴾
قَالَ سَوْفَ اَسْتَغْفِرُ لَكُمْ رَبِّىْ ۗ اِنَّهٗ
هُوَ الْغَفُوْرُ الرَّحِيْمُ ﴿٩٨﴾
فَلَمَّا دَخَلُوْا عَلٰى يُوْسُفَ اٰوٰۤى
اِلَيْهِ اَبَوَيْهِ وَقَالَ ادْخُلُوْا مِصْرَ
اِنْ شَاۤءَ اللّٰهُ اٰمِنِيْنَ ﴿٩٩﴾
وَرَفَعَ اَبَوَيْهِ عَلَى الْعَرْشِ وَخَرُّوْا
لَهٗ سُجَّدًا ۚ وَقَالَ يٰۤاَبَتِ هٰذَا
تَاْوِيْلُ رُءْيَاىَ مِنْ قَبْلُ ۫ قَدْ
جَعَلَهَا رَبِّىْ حَقًّا ۗ وَقَدْ اَحْسَنَ
بِىْۤ اِذْ اَخْرَجَنِىْ مِنَ السِّجْنِ وَجَاۤءَ
بِكُمْ مِّنَ الْبَدْوِ مِنْۢ بَعْدِ اَنْ نَّزَغَ
الشَّيْطٰنُ بَيْنِىْ وَبَيْنَ اِخْوَتِىْ ۗ
اِنَّ رَبِّىْ لَطِيْفٌ لِّمَا يَشَاۤءُ ۗ اِنَّهٗ
هُوَ الْعَلِيْمُ الْحَكِيْمُ ﴿١٠٠﴾

Ikhfa	Ghunna	Ikhfa Meem Saakin	Idghaam	Qalqala	Qalb	Idghaam Meem Saakin
اخفاء	غُنّہ	اخفاءمیم ساکن	ادغام	قلقلہ	قلب	ادغام میم ساکن

101. "O my Lord! You have indeed bestowed on me some power, and taught me something of the interpretation of dreams and events,- O you Creator of the heavens and the earth! You are my Protector in this world and in the Hereafter. You take my soul (at death) as one submitting to Your Will (as a Muslim), and unite me with the righteous."

102. Such is one of the stories of what happened unseen, which We reveal by inspiration unto you; nor were you (present) with them when they concerted their plans together in the process of weaving their plots.

103. Yet no faith will the greater part of mankind have, however ardently you do desire it.

104. And no reward do you ask of them for this: it is no less than a message for all creatures.

105. And how many Signs in the heavens and the earth do they pass by? Yet they turn (their faces) away from them!

106. And most of them do not believe in Allah without associating (others as partners) with Him!

107. Do they then feel secure from the coming against them of the covering veil of the wrath of Allah,- or of the coming against them of the (final) Hour all of a sudden while they perceive not?

108. Say you: "This is my way: I do invite to Allah,- on evidence clear as the seeing with one's eyes,- I and whoever follows me. Glory to Allah! and never will I join gods with Allah!"

109. Nor did We send before you (as Messenger) any but men, whom we inspired,- (men) living in human habitations. Do they not travel through the earth, and see what

101. Rabbi qad aataytanee minal-mulki wa 'allamtanee min taåweelil-aḥaadee<u>s</u>; faaṭi-ras-samaawaati wal-arḍi Anta waliyyee fid-dunyaa wal-Aa-khirati tawaffanee muslimañw-wa alḥiqnee biṣṣaaliḥeen.

102. <u>Z</u>aalika min ambaaa'il-ghaybi nooḥeehi ilayka wa maa kunta ladayhim i<u>z</u> ajma'ooo amrahum wa hum yamkuroon.

103. Wa maaa ak<u>s</u>arun-naasi wa law ḥaraṣta bimu'mineen.

104. Wa maa tas'aluhum 'alayhi min ajr; in huwa illaa <u>z</u>ikrul-lil'aalameen. **(Section 11)**

105. Wa ka-ayyim-min Aayatin fis-samaawaati wal-arḍi yamur-roona 'alayhaa wa hum 'anhaa mu'riḍoon.

106. Wa maa yu'minu ak<u>s</u>aru-hum billaahi illaa wa hum mushrikoon.

107. Afa-aminooo an taåtiya-hum ghaashiyatum-min 'a<u>z</u>aa-bil-laahi aw taåtiyahumus-Saa'atu baghtatañw-wa hum laa yash'uroon.

108. Qul haa<u>z</u>ihee sabeeleee ad'ooo ilal-laah; 'alaa baṣeera-tin ana wa manit-taba'anee wa Subḥaanal-laahi wa maaa ana minal-mushrikeen.

109. Wa maaa arsalnaa min qablika illaa rijaalan nooḥeee ilayhim min ahlil-quraa; afalam yaseeroo fil-arḍi fa-yanẓuroo kayfa

رَبِّ قَدْ اٰتَيْتَنِيْ مِنَ الْمُلْكِ وَ
عَلَّمْتَنِيْ مِنْ تَاْوِيْلِ الْاَحَادِيْثِ ۚ
فَاطِرَ السَّمٰوٰتِ وَالْاَرْضِ ۣ اَنْتَ
وَلِيّٖ فِي الدُّنْيَا وَالْاٰخِرَةِ ۚ تَوَفَّنِيْ
مُسْلِمًا وَّاَلْحِقْنِيْ بِالصّٰلِحِيْنَ ﴿١٠١﴾
ذٰلِكَ مِنْ اَنْۢبَآءِ الْغَيْبِ نُوْحِيْهِ
اِلَيْكَ ۚ وَمَا كُنْتَ لَدَيْهِمْ اِذْ اَجْمَعُوْٓا
اَمْرَهُمْ وَهُمْ يَمْكُرُوْنَ ﴿١٠٢﴾
وَمَآ اَكْثَرُ النَّاسِ وَلَوْ حَرَصْتَ
بِمُؤْمِنِيْنَ ﴿١٠٣﴾
وَمَا تَسْـَٔلُهُمْ عَلَيْهِ مِنْ اَجْرٍ ۭ اِنْ
هُوَ اِلَّا ذِكْرٌ لِّلْعٰلَمِيْنَ ﴿١٠٤﴾ ع ١١
وَكَاَيِّنْ مِّنْ اٰيَةٍ فِي السَّمٰوٰتِ
وَالْاَرْضِ يَمُرُّوْنَ عَلَيْهَا وَهُمْ
عَنْهَا مُعْرِضُوْنَ ﴿١٠٥﴾
وَمَا يُؤْمِنُ اَكْثَرُهُمْ بِاللّٰهِ اِلَّا
وَهُمْ مُّشْرِكُوْنَ ﴿١٠٦﴾
اَفَاَمِنُوْٓا اَنْ تَاْتِيَهُمْ غَاشِيَةٌ مِّنْ
عَذَابِ اللّٰهِ اَوْ تَاْتِيَهُمُ السَّاعَةُ
بَغْتَةً وَّهُمْ لَا يَشْعُرُوْنَ ﴿١٠٧﴾
قُلْ هٰذِهٖ سَبِيْلِيْٓ اَدْعُوْٓا اِلَى اللّٰهِ ۣ
عَلٰى بَصِيْرَةٍ اَنَا وَمَنِ اتَّبَعَنِيْ ۭ
وَسُبْحٰنَ اللّٰهِ وَمَآ اَنَا مِنَ الْمُشْرِكِيْنَ ﴿١٠٨﴾
وَمَآ اَرْسَلْنَا مِنْ قَبْلِكَ اِلَّا رِجَالًا
نُّوْحِيْٓ اِلَيْهِمْ مِّنْ اَهْلِ الْقُرٰى ۭ اَفَلَمْ
يَسِيْرُوْا فِي الْاَرْضِ فَيَنْظُرُوْا كَيْفَ

Ikhfa اخفاء | Ghunna غُنّہ | Ikhfa Meem Saakin اخفاء میم ساکن | Idghaam ادغام | Qalqala قلقلہ | Qalb قلب | Idghaam Meem Saakin ادغام میم ساکن

was the end of those before them? But the home of the Hereafter is best, for those who do right. Will you not then understand?

kaana ‘aaqibatul-laz̲eena min qablihim; wa la-Daarul-Aakhirati khayrul-lillaz̲eenat-taqaw; afalaa ta‘qiloon.

كَانَ عَاقِبَةُ الَّذِينَ مِن قَبْلِهِمْ ۗ
وَلَدَارُ الْآخِرَةِ خَيْرٌ لِّلَّذِينَ اتَّقَوْا ۗ
أَفَلَا تَعْقِلُونَ ﴿١٠٩﴾

110. (Respite will be granted) until, when the messengers give up hope (of their people) and (come to) think that they were treated as liars, there reaches them Our help, and those whom We will are delivered into safety. But never will be warded off Our punishment from those who are in sin.

110. Ḥattaaa iz̲as-tay’asar-Rusulu wa z̲annooo annahum qad kuz̲iboo jaaa’ahum naṣrunaa fanujjiya man naṣhaaa’u wa laa yuraddu baåsunaa ‘anil-qawmil-mujrimeen.

حَتَّىٰ إِذَا اسْتَيْأَسَ الرُّسُلُ وَ
ظَنُّوا أَنَّهُمْ قَدْ كُذِبُوا جَاءَهُمْ
نَصْرُنَا فَنُجِّيَ مَن نَّشَاءُ ۖ وَلَا
يُرَدُّ بَأْسُنَا عَنِ الْقَوْمِ الْمُجْرِمِينَ ﴿١١٠﴾

111. There is, in their stories, instruction for men endued with understanding. It is not a tale invented, but a confirmation of what went before it,- a detailed exposition of all things, and a Guide and a Mercy to any such as believe.

111. Laqad kaana fee qaṣaṣihim ‘ibratul-li-ulil-albaab; maa kaana ḥadees̲añy-yuftaraa wa laakin taṣdeeqal-laz̲ee bayna yadayhi wa tafṣeela kulli shay’iñw-wa hudañw-wa raḥmatal-liqawmiñy-yu’minoon.

(Section 12)

لَقَدْ كَانَ فِي قَصَصِهِمْ عِبْرَةٌ
لِّأُولِي الْأَلْبَابِ ۗ مَا كَانَ حَدِيثًا
يُفْتَرَىٰ وَلَٰكِن تَصْدِيقَ الَّذِي
بَيْنَ يَدَيْهِ وَتَفْصِيلَ كُلِّ شَيْءٍ
وَهُدًى وَرَحْمَةً لِّقَوْمٍ يُؤْمِنُونَ ﴿١١١﴾ ع

13. Thunder

In the name of Allah, Most Gracious, Most Merciful.

Sûrat ar-Ra‘d–13

(Revealed at Makkah)

Bismillaahir Raḥmaanir Raḥeem

(١٣) سُورَةُ الرَّعْدِ مَكِّيَّةٌ (٩٦)

بِسْمِ اللَّهِ الرَّحْمَٰنِ الرَّحِيمِ

1. *Alif-Lam-Mim-Ra.* These are the Signs (or Verses) of the Book: that which has been revealed to you from your Lord is the Truth; but most men do not believe.

1. Alif-Laam-Meeem-Raa; tilka Aayaaul-Kitaab; wallaz̲eee unzila ilayka mir-Rabbikal-ḥaqqu wa laakinna aks̲aran-naasi laa yu’minoon.

الٓمٓرٰ ۚ تِلْكَ آيَاتُ الْكِتَابِ ۗ وَالَّذِي
أُنزِلَ إِلَيْكَ مِن رَّبِّكَ الْحَقُّ
وَلَٰكِنَّ أَكْثَرَ النَّاسِ لَا يُؤْمِنُونَ ﴿١﴾

2. Allah is He Who raised the heavens without any pillars that you can see; is firmly established on the throne (of authority); He has subjected the sun and the moon (to His Law)! Each one runs (its course) for a term appointed. He regulates all affairs, explaining the Signs in detail, that you may believe with certainty in the meeting with your Lord.

2. Allaahul-laz̲ee rafa‘as-samaawaati bighayri ‘amadin tarawnahaa s̲ummas-tawaa ‘alal-‘Arshi wa sakhkharash-shamsa walqamara kulluñy-yajree li-ajalim-musammaa; yudabbirul-amra yufaṣṣilul-Aayaati la‘allakum biliqaaa’i Rabbikum tooqinoon.

اللَّهُ الَّذِي رَفَعَ السَّمَاوَاتِ بِغَيْرِ
عَمَدٍ تَرَوْنَهَا ۖ ثُمَّ اسْتَوَىٰ عَلَى الْعَرْشِ ۖ
وَسَخَّرَ الشَّمْسَ وَالْقَمَرَ ۖ كُلٌّ
يَجْرِي لِأَجَلٍ مُّسَمًّى ۚ يُدَبِّرُ الْأَمْرَ
يُفَصِّلُ الْآيَاتِ لَعَلَّكُم بِلِقَاءِ
رَبِّكُمْ تُوقِنُونَ ﴿٢﴾

3. And it is He Who spread out the earth, and set thereon mountains standing firm and (flowing) rivers: and fruit of every kind He made in pairs, two and two:

3. Wa Huwal-laz̲ee maddal-arḍa wa ja‘ala feehaa rawaasiya wa anhaaraa; wa min kullis̲-s̲amaraati ja‘ala feehaa zawjaynis̲-nayni

وَهُوَ الَّذِي مَدَّ الْأَرْضَ وَجَعَلَ
فِيهَا رَوَاسِيَ وَأَنْهَارًا ۖ وَمِن كُلِّ
الثَّمَرَاتِ جَعَلَ فِيهَا زَوْجَيْنِ اثْنَيْنِ

Ikhfa اخفاء | Ghunna غُنّہ | Ikhfa Meem Saakin اخفاء میم ساکن | Idghaam ادغام | Qalqala قلقلہ | Qalb قلب | Idghaam Meem Saakin ادغام میم ساکن

He draws the night as a veil over the day. Behold, verily in these things there are signs for those who consider!

4. And in the earth are tracts (diverse though) neighboring, and gardens of vines and fields sown with corn, and palm-trees growing out of single roots or otherwise: watered with the same water, yet some of them We make more excellent than others to eat. Behold, verily in these things there are signs for those who understand!

5. If you do marvel (at their want of faith), strange is their saying: "When we are (actually) dust, shall we indeed then be in a renewed creation?" They are those who deny their Lord! They are those round whose necks will be yokes (of servitude): they will be Companions of the Fire, to dwell therein (for ever)!

6. They ask you to hasten on the evil in preference to the good: yet before them, have come to pass, (many) exemplary punishments! But verily your Lord is full of forgiveness for mankind for their wrong-doing. And verily your Lord is (also) strict in punishment.

7. And the Unbelievers say: "Why is not a Sign sent down to him from his Lord?" But you are truly a warner, and to every people a guide.

8. Allah knows what every female (womb) bears, by how much the wombs fall short (of their time or number) or do exceed. Every single thing is before His sight, in (due) proportion.

9. He knows the unseen and that which is open:

yughshil-laylan-nahaar; inna fee zaalika la-Aayaatil-liqawmiñy-yatafakkaroon.

4. Wa fil-arḍi qiṭa‘um-mutajaawiraatuñw-wa jannaatum-min a‘naabiñw-wa zar‘uñw-wa nakheelun ṣinwaanuñw-wa ghayru ṣinwaaniñy-yusqaa bimaaa’iñw-waaḥid; wa nufaḍḍilu ba‘ḍahaa ‘alaa ba‘ḍin fil-ukul; inna fee zaalika la-Aayaatil-liqawmiñy-ya‘qiloon.

5. Wa in ta‘jab fa‘ajabun qawluhum ’a-izaa kunnaa turaaban ’a-innaa lafee khalqin jadeed; ulaaa’ikal-lazeena kafaroo bi-Rabbihim wa ulaaa’ikal-aghlaalu feee a‘naaqihim wa ulaaa’ika Aṣḥaabun-Naari hum feehaa khaalidoon.

6. Wa yasta‘jiloonaka bis-sayyi’ati qablal-ḥasanati wa qad khalat min qablihimul-masulaat; wa inna Rabbaka lazoo maghfiratil-linnaasi ‘alaa ẓulmihim wa inna Rabbaka lashadeedul-‘iqaab.

7. Wa yaqoolul-lazeena kafaroo law laaa unzila ‘alayhi Aayatum-mir-Rabbih; innamaaa anta munziruñw-wa likulli qawmin haad. **(Section 1)**

8. Allaahu ya‘lamu maa taḥmilu kullu unsaa wa maa tagheeḍul-arḥaamu wa maa tazdaad, wa kullu shay’in ‘indahoo bimiqdaar.

9. ‘Aalimul-Ghaybi wash-shahaadatil-

يُغْشِى الَّيْلَ النَّهَارَ ؕ اِنَّ فِىْ ذٰلِكَ
لَاٰيٰتٍ لِّقَوْمٍ يَّتَفَكَّرُوْنَ ۝٣
وَفِى الْاَرْضِ قِطَعٌ مُّتَجٰوِرٰتٌ وَّجَنّٰتٌ
مِّنْ اَعْنَابٍ وَّزَرْعٌ وَّنَخِيْلٌ صِنْوَانٌ
وَّغَيْرُ صِنْوَانٍ يُّسْقٰى بِمَآءٍ وَّاحِدٍ ۟ قف
وَنُفَضِّلُ بَعْضَهَا عَلٰى بَعْضٍ فِى
الْاُكُلِ ؕ اِنَّ فِىْ ذٰلِكَ لَاٰيٰتٍ
لِّقَوْمٍ يَّعْقِلُوْنَ ۝٤
وَاِنْ تَعْجَبْ فَعَجَبٌ قَوْلُهُمْ ءَاِذَا
كُنَّا تُرٰبًا ءَاِنَّا لَفِىْ خَلْقٍ جَدِيْدٍ ۬ؕ
اُولٰٓئِكَ الَّذِيْنَ كَفَرُوْا بِرَبِّهِمْ ۚ
وَاُولٰٓئِكَ الْاَغْلٰلُ فِىْٓ اَعْنَاقِهِمْ ۚ
وَاُولٰٓئِكَ اَصْحٰبُ النَّارِ ۚ هُمْ
فِيْهَا خٰلِدُوْنَ ۝٥
وَيَسْتَعْجِلُوْنَكَ بِالسَّيِّئَةِ قَبْلَ
الْحَسَنَةِ وَقَدْ خَلَتْ مِنْ قَبْلِهِمُ
الْمَثُلٰتُ ؕ وَاِنَّ رَبَّكَ لَذُوْ مَغْفِرَةٍ
لِّلنَّاسِ عَلٰى ظُلْمِهِمْ ۚ وَاِنَّ رَبَّكَ
لَشَدِيْدُ الْعِقَابِ ۝٦
وَيَقُوْلُ الَّذِيْنَ كَفَرُوْا لَوْلَآ اُنْزِلَ
عَلَيْهِ اٰيَةٌ مِّنْ رَّبِّهٖ ؕ اِنَّمَآ اَنْتَ
مُنْذِرٌ وَّلِكُلِّ قَوْمٍ هَادٍ ۝٧ ع
اَللّٰهُ يَعْلَمُ مَا تَحْمِلُ كُلُّ اُنْثٰى
وَمَا تَغِيْضُ الْاَرْحَامُ وَمَا تَزْدَادُ ؕ
وَكُلُّ شَىْءٍ عِنْدَهٗ بِمِقْدَارٍ ۝٨
عٰلِمُ الْغَيْبِ وَالشَّهَادَةِ

Ikhfa اخفاء | Ghunna غُنّہ | Ikhfa Meem Saakin اخفاء میم ساکن | Idghaam ادغام | Qalqala قلقلہ | Qalb قلب | Idghaam Meem Saakin ادغام میم ساکن

He is the Great, the Most High.

10. It is the same (to Him) whether any of you conceal his speech or declare it openly; whether he lie hid by night or walk forth freely by day.

11. For each (such person) there are (angels) in succession, before and behind him: they guard him by command of Allah. Verily never will Allah change the condition of a people until they change it themselves (with their own souls). But when (once) Allah wills a people's punishment, there can be no turning it back, nor will they find, besides Him, any to protect.

12. It is He Who shows you the lightning, by way both of fear and of hope: it is He Who raises up the clouds, heavy with (fertilising) rain!

13. Nay, thunder repeats His praises, and so do the angels, with awe: He flings the loud-voiced thunder-bolts, and therewith He strikes whomsoever He will..Yet these (are the men) who (dare to) dispute about Allah, with the strength of His power (supreme)!

14. For Him (alone) is prayer in Truth: any others that they call upon besides Him hear them no more than if they were to stretch forth their hands for water to reach their mouths but it reaches them not: for the prayer of those without Faith is nothing but (futile) wandering (in the mind).

15. Whatever beings there are in the heavens and the earth do prostrate themselves to Allah (Acknowledging subjection),- with good-will or in spite of themselves: so do their shadows in the mornings and evenings.

16. Say: "Who is the Lord and Sustainer of the heavens and the earth?"

(Bow Down)

Kabeerul-Muta'aal.

10. Sawaaa'um-minkum man asarral-qawla wa man jahara bihee wa man huwa mustakhfim-billayli wa saaribum binnahaar.

11. Lahoo mu'aqqibaatum-mim bayni yadayhi wa min khalfihee yaḥfaẓoonahoo min amril-laah; innal-laaha laa yughayyiru maa biqawmin ḥattaa yughayyiroo maa bi-anfusihim; wa izaaa araadal-laahu biqawmin sooo'an falaa maradda lah; wa maa lahum min dooniheemiñw-waal.

12. Huwal-lazee yureekumul-barqa khawfañw-wa ṭama'añw-wa yunshi'us-saḥaabas-siqaal.

13. Wa yusabbiḥur-ra'du biḥamdihee walmalaaa'ikatu min kheefatihee wa yursiluṣ-ṣawaa'iqa fa-yuṣeebu bihaa mañy-yashaaa'u wa hum yujaadiloona fil-laahi wa Huwa shadeedul-miḥaal.

14. Lahoo da'watul-ḥaqq; wallazeena yad'oona min doonihee laa yastajeeboona lahum bishay'in illaa kabaasiṭi kaffayhi ilal-maaa'i liyablugha faahu wa maa huwa bibaalighih; wa maa du'aaa'ul-kaafireena illaa fee ḍalaal.

15. Wa lillaahi yasjudu man fis-samaawaati wal-arḍi ṭaw-'añw-wa karhañw-wa ẓilaaluhum bilghuduwwi wal-aaṣaal.

16. Qul mar-Rabbus-samaawaati wal-arḍ;

الْكَبِيرُ الْمُتَعَالِ ﴿٩﴾
سَوَآءٌ مِّنكُم مَّنْ أَسَرَّ الْقَوْلَ وَمَن
جَهَرَ بِهِۦ وَمَنْ هُوَ مُسْتَخْفٍۢ بِالَّيْلِ
وَسَارِبٌۢ بِالنَّهَارِ ﴿١٠﴾
لَهُۥ مُعَقِّبَٰتٌ مِّنۢ بَيْنِ يَدَيْهِ وَ
مِنْ خَلْفِهِۦ يَحْفَظُونَهُۥ مِنْ أَمْرِ
اللَّهِ ۗ إِنَّ اللَّهَ لَا يُغَيِّرُ مَا بِقَوْمٍ
حَتَّىٰ يُغَيِّرُوا۟ مَا بِأَنفُسِهِمْ ۗ وَإِذَآ
أَرَادَ اللَّهُ بِقَوْمٍ سُوٓءًا فَلَا مَرَدَّ لَهُۥ ۚ
وَمَا لَهُم مِّن دُونِهِۦ مِن وَالٍ ﴿١١﴾
هُوَ الَّذِى يُرِيكُمُ الْبَرْقَ خَوْفًا وَ
طَمَعًا وَيُنشِئُ السَّحَابَ الثِّقَالَ ﴿١٢﴾
وَيُسَبِّحُ الرَّعْدُ بِحَمْدِهِۦ وَالْمَلَٰٓئِكَةُ
مِنْ خِيفَتِهِۦ وَيُرْسِلُ الصَّوَٰعِقَ
فَيُصِيبُ بِهَا مَن يَشَآءُ وَهُمْ
يُجَٰدِلُونَ فِى اللَّهِ ج وَهُوَ
شَدِيدُ الْمِحَالِ ﴿١٣﴾
لَهُۥ دَعْوَةُ الْحَقِّ ۖ وَالَّذِينَ يَدْعُونَ
مِن دُونِهِۦ لَا يَسْتَجِيبُونَ لَهُم
بِشَىْءٍ إِلَّا كَبَٰسِطِ كَفَّيْهِ إِلَى الْمَآءِ
لِيَبْلُغَ فَاهُ وَمَا هُوَ بِبَٰلِغِهِۦ ۚ وَمَا
دُعَآءُ الْكَٰفِرِينَ إِلَّا فِى ضَلَٰلٍ ﴿١٤﴾
وَلِلَّهِ يَسْجُدُ مَن فِى السَّمَٰوَٰتِ
وَالْأَرْضِ طَوْعًا وَكَرْهًا وَظِلَٰلُهُم
بِالْغُدُوِّ وَالْآصَالِ ﴿١٥﴾ السجدة
قُلْ مَن رَّبُّ السَّمَٰوَٰتِ وَالْأَرْضِ ۗ

السجدة (٢)

Ikhfa اخفاء | Ghunna غُنّہ | Ikhfa Meem Saakin اخفاءمیم ساکن | Idghaam ادغام | Qalqala قلقلہ | Qalb قلب | Idghaam Meem Saakin ادغام میم ساکن

Say: "(It is) Allah." Say: "Do you then take (for worship) protectors other than Him, such as have no power either for good or for harm to themselves?" Say: "Are the blind equal with those who see? Or the depths of darkness equal with light?" Or do they assign to Allah partners who have created (anything) as He has created, so that the creation seemed to them similar? Say: "Allah is the Creator of all things: He is the One, the Supreme and Irresistible."

qulillaah; qul afattakhaz̲tum min dooniheee awliyaaa'a laa yamlikoona li-anfusihim naf-'añw-wa laa ḍarraa; qul hal yastawil-a'maa wal-baṣeeru am hal tastawiẓ-ẓulumaatu wannoor; am ja'aloo lillaahi shurakaaa'a khalaqoo kakhalqihee fatashaabahal-khalqu 'alayhim; qulillaahu Khaaliqu kulli shay'iñw-wa Huwal-Waaḥidul-Qahhaar.

قُلِ اللّٰهُ ۭ قُلْ اَفَاتَّخَذْتُمْ مِّنْ
دُوْنِهٖٓ اَوْلِيَاۗءَ لَا يَمْلِكُوْنَ لِاَنْفُسِهِمْ
نَفْعًا وَّلَا ضَرًّا ۭ قُلْ هَلْ يَسْتَوِي
الْاَعْمٰى وَالْبَصِيْرُ ڏ اَمْ هَلْ تَسْتَوِي
الظُّلُمٰتُ وَالنُّوْرُ ڬ اَمْ جَعَلُوْا لِلّٰهِ
شُرَكَاۗءَ خَلَقُوْا كَخَلْقِهٖ فَتَشَابَهَ
الْخَلْقُ عَلَيْهِمْ ۭ قُلِ اللّٰهُ خَالِقُ
كُلِّ شَيْءٍ وَّهُوَ الْوَاحِدُ الْقَهَّارُ ﴿١٦﴾

17. He sends down water from the skies, and the channels flow, each according to its measure: But the torrent bears away to foam that mounts up to the surface. Even so, from that (ore) which they heat in the fire, to make ornaments or utensils therewith, there is a scum likewise. Thus does Allah (by parables) show forth Truth and Vanity. For the scum disappears like forth cast out; while that which is for the good of mankind remains on the earth. Thus Allah sets forth parables.

17. Anzala minas-samaaa'i maaa'an fasaalat awdiyatum biqadarihaa faḥtamalas-saylu-zabadar-raabiyaa; wa mimmaa yooqidoona 'alayhi fin-naaribtighaaa'a ḥilyatin aw mataa'in zabadum-mis̲luh; kaz̲aalika yaḍribul-laahul-ḥaqqa wal-baaṭil; fa-ammaz-zabadu fa-yaz̲habu jufaaa'aa; wa ammaa maa yanfa'un-naasa fa-yamkus̲u fil-arḍ; kaz̲aalika yaḍribul-laahul-ams̲aal.

اَنْزَلَ مِنَ السَّمَاۗءِ مَاۗءً فَسَالَتْ اَوْدِيَةٌۢ
بِقَدَرِهَا فَاحْتَمَلَ السَّيْلُ زَبَدًا
رَّابِيًا ۭ وَمِمَّا يُوْقِدُوْنَ عَلَيْهِ
فِي النَّارِ ابْتِغَاۗءَ حِلْيَةٍ اَوْ مَتَاعٍ
زَبَدٌ مِّثْلُهٗ ۭ كَذٰلِكَ يَضْرِبُ اللّٰهُ
الْحَقَّ وَالْبَاطِلَ ڛ فَاَمَّا الزَّبَدُ
فَيَذْهَبُ جُفَاۗءً ۚ وَاَمَّا مَا يَنْفَعُ
النَّاسَ فَيَمْكُثُ فِي الْاَرْضِ ۭ كَذٰلِكَ
يَضْرِبُ اللّٰهُ الْاَمْثَالَ ﴿١٧﴾

18. For those who respond to their Lord, are (all) good things. But those who do not respond to Him,- even if they had all that is in the heavens and on earth, and as much more, (in vain) would they offer it for ransom. For them will the reckoning be terrible: their abode will be Hell,- what a bed of misery!

18. Lillaz̲eenas-tajaaboo li-rabbihimul-ḥusnaa; wallaz̲eena lam yastajeeboo lahoo law anna lahum maa fil-arḍi jamee'añw-wa mis̲lahoo ma'ahoo laftadaw bih; ulaaa'ika lahum sooo'ul-ḥisaab; wa maåwaahum Jahannamu wa bi'sal-mihaad.

(Section 2)

لِلَّذِيْنَ اسْتَجَابُوْا لِرَبِّهِمُ الْحُسْنٰى ڼ
وَالَّذِيْنَ لَمْ يَسْتَجِيْبُوْا لَهٗ لَوْ اَنَّ
لَهُمْ مَّا فِي الْاَرْضِ جَمِيْعًا وَّمِثْلَهٗ
مَعَهٗ لَافْتَدَوْا بِهٖ ۭ اُولٰۗىِٕكَ لَهُمْ
سُوْۗءُ الْحِسَابِ ڏ وَمَاْوٰىهُمْ جَهَنَّمُ ۭ
وَبِئْسَ الْمِهَادُ ﴿١٨﴾ ع

وقف النبي صلى الله عليه وآله وسلم

النصف

19. Is then one who knows that that which has been revealed to you from your Lord is the Truth, like one who is blind? It is those who are endued with understanding that receive admonition;-

19. Afamañy-ya'lamu annamaaa unzila ilayka mir-Rabbikal-ḥaqqu kaman huwa a'maa; innamaa yataz̲akkaru ulul-albaab.

اَفَمَنْ يَّعْلَمُ اَنَّمَآ اُنْزِلَ اِلَيْكَ
مِنْ رَّبِّكَ الْحَقُّ كَمَنْ هُوَ اَعْمٰى ۭ
اِنَّمَا يَتَذَكَّرُ اُولُوا الْاَلْبَابِ ﴿١٩﴾ لا

Ikhfa اخفاء | Ghunna غُنّہ | Ikhfa Meem Saakin اخفاء میم ساکن | Idghaam ادغام | Qalqala قلقلہ | Qalb قلب | Idghaam Meem Saakin ادغام میم ساکن

20. Those who fulfil the covenant of Allah and do not fail in their plighted word;

20. Allazeena yoofoona bi‘ahdil-laahi wa laa yanquḍoonal-meesaaq.

الَّذِينَ يُوفُونَ بِعَهْدِ اللّٰهِ وَلَا
يَنقُضُونَ الْمِيثَاقَ ۝٢٠

21. Those who join together those things which Allah has commanded to be joined, hold their Lord in awe, and fear the terrible reckoning;

21. Wallazeena yaṣiloona maaa amaral-laahu biheee an yooṣala wa yakhshawna Rabbahum wa yakhaafoona sooo’al-ḥisaab.

وَالَّذِينَ يَصِلُونَ مَا أَمَرَ اللّٰهُ
بِهِ أَن يُوصَلَ وَيَخْشَوْنَ رَبَّهُمْ
وَيَخَافُونَ سُوءَ الْحِسَابِ ۝٢١

22. Those who patiently persevere, seeking the countenance of their Lord; establish regular prayers; spend, out of (the gifts) We have bestowed for their sustenance, secretly and openly; and turn off Evil with good: for such there is the final attainment of the (Eternal) Home,-

22. Wallazeena ṣabarub-tighaa’a Wajhi Rabbihim wa aqaamuṣ-Ṣalaata wa anfaqoo mimmaa razaqnaahum sirrañw-wa‘alaaniyatañw-wa yad-ra’oona bilḥasanatis-sayyi’ata ulaaa’ika lahum ‘uqbad-daar.

وَالَّذِينَ صَبَرُوا ابْتِغَاءَ وَجْهِ رَبِّهِمْ
وَأَقَامُوا الصَّلٰوةَ وَأَنفَقُوا مِمَّا رَزَقْنٰهُمْ
سِرًّا وَعَلَانِيَةً وَيَدْرَءُونَ بِالْحَسَنَةِ
السَّيِّئَةَ أُولٰئِكَ لَهُمْ عُقْبَى الدَّارِ ۝٢٢

23. Gardens of perpetual bliss: they shall enter there, as well as the righteous among their fathers, their spouses, and their offspring: and angels shall enter unto them from every gate (with the salutation):

23. Jannaatu ‘Adniñy-yadkhu-loonahaa wa man ṣalaḥa min aabaaa’ihim wa azwaajihim wa zurriyyaatihim walmalaaa’i-katu yadkhuloona ‘alayhim min kulli baab.

جَنّٰتُ عَدْنٍ يَدْخُلُونَهَا وَمَن
صَلَحَ مِنْ آبَائِهِمْ وَأَزْوَاجِهِمْ
وَذُرِّيّٰتِهِمْ وَالْمَلٰئِكَةُ يَدْخُلُونَ
عَلَيْهِم مِّن كُلِّ بَابٍ ۝٢٣

24. “Peace unto you for that you persevered in patience! Now how excellent is the final home!”

24. Salaamun ‘alaykum bimaa ṣabartum; fani‘ma ‘uqbad-daar.

سَلٰمٌ عَلَيْكُم بِمَا صَبَرْتُمْ فَنِعْمَ
عُقْبَى الدَّارِ ۝٢٤

25. But those who break the Covenant of Allah, after having plighted their word thereto, and cut asunder those things which Allah has commanded to be joined, and work mischief in the land;- on them is the Curse; for them is the terrible Home!

25. Wallazeena yanquḍoona ‘Ahdal-laahi mim ba‘di mee-saaqihee wa yaqṭa‘oona maaa amaral-laahu biheee añy-yooṣala wa yufsidoona fil-arḍi ulaaa’ika lahumul-la‘natu wa lahum sooo’ud-daar.

وَالَّذِينَ يَنقُضُونَ عَهْدَ اللّٰهِ مِن
بَعْدِ مِيثَاقِهِ وَيَقْطَعُونَ مَا أَمَرَ
اللّٰهُ بِهِ أَن يُوصَلَ وَيُفْسِدُونَ
فِي الْأَرْضِ أُولٰئِكَ لَهُمُ اللَّعْنَةُ
وَلَهُمْ سُوءُ الدَّارِ ۝٢٥

26. Allah enlarges, or grants by (strict) measure, the sustenance (which He gives) to whomso He pleases. (The wordly) rejoice in the life of this world: But the life of this world is but little comfort in the Hereafter.

26. Allaahu yabsuṭur-rizqa limañy-yashaaa’u wa yaqdir; wa fariḥoo bilḥayaatid-dunyaa wa mal-ḥayaatud-dunyaa fil-Aakhirati illaa mataa‘.

(Section 3)

اللّٰهُ يَبْسُطُ الرِّزْقَ لِمَن يَشَاءُ وَ
يَقْدِرُ وَفَرِحُوا بِالْحَيٰوةِ الدُّنْيَا وَمَا
الْحَيٰوةُ الدُّنْيَا فِي الْآخِرَةِ إِلَّا مَتَاعٌ ۝٢٦ ع

27. The Unbelievers say: “Why is not a sign sent down to him from his Lord?” Say: “Truly Allah leave to stray, whom He will; But He guides

27. Wa yaqoolul-lazeena ka-faroo law laaa unzila ‘alayhi Aayatum-mir-Rabbih; qul innal-laaha yuḍillu mañy-yashaa’u wa yahdeee

وَيَقُولُ الَّذِينَ كَفَرُوا لَوْلَا أُنزِلَ
عَلَيْهِ آيَةٌ مِّن رَّبِّهِ ۚ قُلْ إِنَّ
اللّٰهَ يُضِلُّ مَن يَشَاءُ وَيَهْدِي

Ikhfa اخفاء | Ghunna غنّہ | Ikhfa Meem Saakin اخفاءمیم ساکن | Idghaam ادغام | Qalqala قلقلہ | Qalb قلب | Idghaam Meem Saakin ادغام میم ساکن

to Himself those who turn to Him in penitence;

28. "Those who believe, and whose hearts find satisfaction in the remembrance of Allah: for without doubt in the remembrance of Allah do hearts find satisfaction.

29. "For those who believe and work righteousness, is (every) blessedness, and a beautiful place of (final) return."

30. Thus have we sent you amongst a People before whom (long since) have (other) Peoples (gone and) passed away; in order that you might rehearse unto them what We send down unto you by inspiration; yet they reject (Him), the Most Gracious! Say: "He is my Lord! There is no god but He! On Him is my trust, and to Him do I turn!"

31. If there were a Qur'an with which mountains were moved, or the earth were cloven asunder, or the dead were made to speak, (this would be the one!) but, truly, the command is with Allah in all things! Do not the Believers know, that, had Allah (so) willed, He could have guided all mankind (to the right)? But the Unbelievers,- never will disaster cease to seize them for their (ill) deeds, or to settle close to their homes, until the promise of Allah come to pass, for, verily, Allah will not fail in His promise.

32. Mocked were (many) Messengers before you: but I granted respite to the Unbelievers, and finally I punished them: then how (terrible) was My requital!

33. Is then He who stands over every soul (and knows) all that it does, (like any others)? And yet they ascribe partners to Allah. Say:

ilayhi man anaab.

28. Allazeena aamanoo wa taṭma'innu quloobuhum bizikril-laah; alaa bizikril-laahi taṭma'innul-quloob.

29. Allazeena aamanoo wa 'amiluṣ-ṣaaliḥaati ṭoobaa lahum wa ḥusnu ma-aab.

30. Kazaalika arsalnaaka feee ummatin qad khalat min qablihaaa umamul-litatluwa 'alayhimul-lazeee awḥaynaaa ilayka wa hum yakfuroona bir-Raḥmaan; qul Huwa Rabbee laaa ilaaha illaa Huwa 'alayhi-tawakkaltu wa ilayhi mataab.

31. Wa law anna Qur-aanan suyyirat bihil-jibaalu aw quṭ-ṭi'at bihil-arḍu aw kullima bihil-mawtaa; bal lillaahil-amru jamee'aa; afalam yay'asil-lazee-na aamanooo al-law yashaaa-'ullaahu lahadan-naasa jamee-'aa; wa laa yazaalul-lazeena kafaroo tuṣeebuhum bimaa ṣana'oo qaari'atun aw taḥullu qareebam-min daarihim ḥattaa yaåtiya wa'dul-laah; innal-laaha laa yukhliful-mee'aad.

(Section 4)

32. Wa laqadis-tuhzi'a bi-Rusulim-min qablika fa-amlay-tu lillazeena kafaroo summa akhaztuhum fakayfa kaana 'iqaab.

33. Afaman Huwa qaaa'imun 'alaa kulli nafsim bimaa kasabat; wa ja'aloo lillaahi shurakaaa'a qul

إِلَيْهِ مَنْ أَنَابَ ﴿٢٧﴾
الَّذِينَ آمَنُوا وَتَطْمَئِنُّ قُلُوبُهُم
بِذِكْرِ اللَّهِ ۗ أَلَا بِذِكْرِ اللَّهِ
تَطْمَئِنُّ الْقُلُوبُ ﴿٢٨﴾
الَّذِينَ آمَنُوا وَعَمِلُوا الصَّالِحَاتِ
طُوبَىٰ لَهُمْ وَحُسْنُ مَآبٍ ﴿٢٩﴾
كَذَٰلِكَ أَرْسَلْنَاكَ فِي أُمَّةٍ قَدْ
خَلَتْ مِن قَبْلِهَا أُمَمٌ لِّتَتْلُوَ
عَلَيْهِمُ الَّذِي أَوْحَيْنَا إِلَيْكَ وَهُمْ
يَكْفُرُونَ بِالرَّحْمَٰنِ ۚ قُلْ هُوَ رَبِّي
لَا إِلَٰهَ إِلَّا هُوَ عَلَيْهِ تَوَكَّلْتُ
وَإِلَيْهِ مَتَابِ ﴿٣٠﴾
وَلَوْ أَنَّ قُرْآنًا سُيِّرَتْ بِهِ الْجِبَالُ
أَوْ قُطِّعَتْ بِهِ الْأَرْضُ أَوْ كُلِّمَ بِهِ
الْمَوْتَىٰ ۗ بَل لِّلَّهِ الْأَمْرُ جَمِيعًا ۗ
أَفَلَمْ يَيْأَسِ الَّذِينَ آمَنُوا أَن لَّوْ
يَشَاءُ اللَّهُ لَهَدَى النَّاسَ جَمِيعًا ۗ
وَلَا يَزَالُ الَّذِينَ كَفَرُوا تُصِيبُهُم
بِمَا صَنَعُوا قَارِعَةٌ أَوْ تَحُلُّ قَرِيبًا
مِّن دَارِهِمْ حَتَّىٰ يَأْتِيَ وَعْدُ اللَّهِ ۚ
إِنَّ اللَّهَ لَا يُخْلِفُ الْمِيعَادَ ﴿٣١﴾
وَلَقَدِ اسْتُهْزِئَ بِرُسُلٍ مِّن قَبْلِكَ
فَأَمْلَيْتُ لِلَّذِينَ كَفَرُوا ثُمَّ أَخَذْتُهُمْ ۖ
فَكَيْفَ كَانَ عِقَابِ ﴿٣٢﴾
أَفَمَنْ هُوَ قَائِمٌ عَلَىٰ كُلِّ نَفْسٍ بِمَا
كَسَبَتْ ۗ وَجَعَلُوا لِلَّهِ شُرَكَاءَ قُلْ

Ikhfa اخفاء | Ghunna غنّہ | Ikhfa Meem Saakin اخفاء میم ساکن | Idghaam ادغام | Qalqala قلقلہ | Qalb قلب | Idghaam Meem Saakin ادغام میم ساکن

"But name them! Is it that you will inform Him of something He does not know on earth, or is it (just) a show of words?" Nay! to those who believe not, their pretence seems pleasing, but they are kept back (thereby) from the Path. And those whom Allah leaves to stray, no one can guide.

sammoohum; am tunabbi'oonahoo bimaa laa ya‘lamu fil-arḍi; am biẓaahirim-minal-qawl; bal zuyyina lillazeena kafaroo makruhum wa ṣuddoo ‘anis-sabeel; wa mañy-yuḍlilil-laahu famaa lahoo min haad.

سَمُّوهُمْ ۚ أَمْ تُنَبِّئُونَهُ بِمَا لَا يَعْلَمُ
فِي الْأَرْضِ أَمْ بِظَاهِرٍ مِّنَ الْقَوْلِ ۗ
بَلْ زُيِّنَ لِلَّذِينَ كَفَرُوا مَكْرُهُمْ
وَصُدُّوا عَنِ السَّبِيلِ ۗ وَمَن يُضْلِلِ
اللَّهُ فَمَا لَهُ مِنْ هَادٍ ﴿٣٣﴾

34. For them is a Panalty in the life of this world, but harder, truly, is the Penalty of the Hereafter: and they do not have any defender against Allah.

34. Lahum ‘azaabun fil-ḥayaatid-dunyaa wa la‘azaabul-Aakhirati ashaqq, wa maa lahum minal-laahi miñw-waaq.

لَّهُمْ عَذَابٌ فِي الْحَيَاةِ الدُّنْيَا
وَلَعَذَابُ الْآخِرَةِ أَشَقُّ ۖ وَمَا لَهُم
مِّنَ اللَّهِ مِن وَاقٍ ﴿٣٤﴾

35. The parable of the Garden which the righteous are promised!- beneath it flow rivers: perpetual is the enjoyment thereof and the shade therein: such is the End of the Righteous; and the End of Unbelievers in the Fire.

35. Masalul-Jannatil-latee wu‘idal-muttaqoona tajree min taḥtihal-anhaaru ukuluhaa daaa'imuñw-wa ẓilluhaa; tilka uqbal-lazeenat-taqaw wa ‘uqbal-kafireenan-Naar.

مَّثَلُ الْجَنَّةِ الَّتِي وُعِدَ الْمُتَّقُونَ ۖ
تَجْرِي مِن تَحْتِهَا الْأَنْهَارُ ۖ أُكُلُهَا
دَائِمٌ وَظِلُّهَا ۚ تِلْكَ عُقْبَى الَّذِينَ
اتَّقَوا ۖ وَّعُقْبَى الْكَافِرِينَ النَّارُ ﴿٣٥﴾

36. Those to whom We have given the Book rejoice at what has been revealed unto you: but there are among the clans those who reject a part thereof. Say: "I am commanded to worship Allah, and not to join partners with Him. To Him I call, and to Him is my return."

36. Wallazeena aataynaahumul-Kitaaba yafraḥoona bimaaa unzila ilayka wa minal-Aḥzaabi mañy-yunkiru ba‘ḍah; qul innamaaa umirtu an a‘budal-laaha wa laaa ushrika bih; ilayhi ad‘oo wa ilayhi maaab.

وَالَّذِينَ آتَيْنَاهُمُ الْكِتَابَ يَفْرَحُونَ
بِمَا أُنزِلَ إِلَيْكَ ۖ وَمِنَ الْأَحْزَابِ
مَن يُنكِرُ بَعْضَهُ ۚ قُلْ إِنَّمَا أُمِرْتُ
أَنْ أَعْبُدَ اللَّهَ وَلَا أُشْرِكَ بِهِ ۚ
إِلَيْهِ أَدْعُو وَإِلَيْهِ مَآبِ ﴿٣٦﴾

37. Thus have We revealed it to be a judgment of authority in Arabic. Were you to follow their (vain) desires after the knowledge which has reached you, then you would find neither protector nor defender against Allah.

37. Wa kazaalika anzalnaahu ḥukman ‘Arabiyyaa; wa la'inittaba‘ta ahwaaa'ahum ba‘da maa jaaa'aka minal-‘ilmi maa laka minal-laahi miñw-waliyyiñw-wa laa waaq. **(Section 5)**

وَكَذَٰلِكَ أَنزَلْنَاهُ حُكْمًا عَرَبِيًّا ۚ
وَلَئِنِ اتَّبَعْتَ أَهْوَاءَهُم بَعْدَ مَا
جَاءَكَ مِنَ الْعِلْمِ مَا لَكَ مِنَ اللَّهِ
مِن وَلِيٍّ وَلَا وَاقٍ ﴿٣٧﴾ ع

38. We sent Messenger before you, and appointed for them wives and children: and it was never the part of a Messenger to bring a Sign except as Allah permitted (or commanded). For each period is a Book (revealed).

38. Wa laqad arsalnaa Rusulam-min qablika wa ja‘alnaa lahum azwaajañw-wa zurriyyah; wa maa kaana lirasoolin añy-yaåtiya bi-aayatin illaa bi-iznil-laah; likulli ajalin kitaab.

وَلَقَدْ أَرْسَلْنَا رُسُلًا مِّن قَبْلِكَ
وَجَعَلْنَا لَهُمْ أَزْوَاجًا وَذُرِّيَّةً ۚ
وَمَا كَانَ لِرَسُولٍ أَن يَأْتِيَ بِآيَةٍ إِلَّا
بِإِذْنِ اللَّهِ ۗ لِكُلِّ أَجَلٍ كِتَابٌ ﴿٣٨﴾

39. Allah blots out or confirms what He pleases:

39. Yamḥul-laahu maa yashaaa'u wa yusbitu

يَمْحُو اللَّهُ مَا يَشَاءُ وَيُثْبِتُ ۖ

with Him is the Mother of the Book.

wa 'indahooo Ummul-Kitaab.

وَعِنْدَهٗٓ اُمُّ الْكِتٰبِ ﴿٣٩﴾

40. Whether We shall show you (within your life-time) part of what we promised them or take to Ourselves your soul (before it is all accomplished),- your duty is to make (the Message) reach them: it is Our part to call them to account.

40. Wa im-maa nuriyannaka ba'ḍal-lazee na'iduhum aw nata-waffayannaka fa-innamaa 'alaykal-balaaghu wa 'alaynal-ḥisaab.

وَاِنْ مَّا نُرِيَنَّكَ بَعْضَ الَّذِيْ نَعِدُهُمْ
اَوْ نَتَوَفَّيَنَّكَ فَاِنَّمَا عَلَيْكَ الْبَلٰغُ
وَعَلَيْنَا الْحِسَابُ ﴿٤٠﴾

41. Don't they see that We gradually reduce the land (in their control) from its outlying borders? (Where) Allah commands, there is none to put back His command: and He is swift in calling to account.

41. Awalam yaraw annaa naâtil-arḍa nanquṣuhaa min aṭraafihaa; wallaahu yaḥkumu laa mu'aqqiba liḥukmih; wa Huwa saree'ul-ḥisaab.

اَوَلَمْ يَرَوْا اَنَّا نَاْتِي الْاَرْضَ نَنْقُصُهَا
مِنْ اَطْرَافِهَا ؕ وَاللّٰهُ يَحْكُمُ لَا
مُعَقِّبَ لِحُكْمِهٖ ؕ وَهُوَ سَرِيْعُ
الْحِسَابِ ﴿٤١﴾

42. Those before them (also) devised plots; but in all things the master- planning is Allah's, He knows the doings of every soul: and soon will the Unbelievers know who gets home in the end.

42. Wa qad makaral-lazeena min qablihim falillaahil-makru jamee'aa; ya'lamu maa taksibu kullu nafs; wa sa-ya'lamul-kuffaaru liman 'uqbad-daar.

وَقَدْ مَكَرَ الَّذِيْنَ مِنْ قَبْلِهِمْ فَلِلّٰهِ
الْمَكْرُ جَمِيْعًا ؕ يَعْلَمُ مَا تَكْسِبُ
كُلُّ نَفْسٍ ؕ وَسَيَعْلَمُ الْكُفّٰرُ لِمَنْ
عُقْبَى الدَّارِ ﴿٤٢﴾

43. The Unbelievers say: "No Messenger are you." Say: "Enough for a witness between me and you is Allah, and such as have knowledge of the Book."

43. Wa yaqoolul-lazeena kafaroo lasta mursalaa; qul kafaa billaahi shaheedam baynee wa baynakum wa man 'indahoo 'ilmul-Kitaab. **(Sec. 6)**

وَيَقُوْلُ الَّذِيْنَ كَفَرُوْا لَسْتَ مُرْسَلًا ؕ
قُلْ كَفٰى بِاللّٰهِ شَهِيْدًاۢ بَيْنِيْ وَبَيْنَكُمْ ۙ
وَمَنْ عِنْدَهٗ عِلْمُ الْكِتٰبِ ﴿٤٣﴾ ع

14. Abraham

In the name of Allah, Most Gracious, Most Merciful.

Sûrat Ibrâhîm–14

(Revealed at Makkah)

Bismillaahir Raḥmaanir Raḥeem

(١٤) سُوْرَةُ اِبْرٰهِيْمَ مَكِّيَّةٌ (٧٢)

بِسْمِ اللّٰهِ الرَّحْمٰنِ الرَّحِيْمِ

1. *Alif-Lam-Ra.* A Book which We have revealed to you, in order that you might lead mankind out of the depths of darkness into light - by the leave of their Lord - to the Way of (Him) the Exalted in Power, worthy of all Praise!-

1. Alif-Laaam-Raa; Kitaabun anzalnaahu ilayka litukhrijan-naasa minaẓ-ẓulumaati ilan-noori bi-izni Rabbihim ilaa ṣiraaṭil-'Azeezil-Ḥameed.

الٓرٰ ۫ كِتٰبٌ اَنْزَلْنٰهُ اِلَيْكَ لِتُخْرِجَ
النَّاسَ مِنَ الظُّلُمٰتِ اِلَى النُّوْرِ ۙ۬
بِاِذْنِ رَبِّهِمْ اِلٰى صِرَاطِ الْعَزِيْزِ
الْحَمِيْدِ ۙ ﴿١﴾

2. Of Allah, to Whom do belong all things in the heavens and on earth! But alas for the Unbelievers for a terrible Penalty (their Unfaith will bring them)!-

2. Allaahil-lazee lahoo maa fis-samaawaati wa maa fill arḍ; wa waylul-lilkaafireena min 'azaabin shadeed.

اللّٰهِ الَّذِيْ لَهٗ مَا فِي السَّمٰوٰتِ وَمَا
فِي الْاَرْضِ ؕ وَوَيْلٌ لِّلْكٰفِرِيْنَ
مِنْ عَذَابٍ شَدِيْدِ ۙ ﴿٢﴾

3. Those who love the life of this world more than the Hereafter, who hinder (men) from the Path

3. Allazeena yastaḥibboonal-ḥayaatad-dunyaa 'alal Aakhirati wa yaṣuddoona 'an sabeelil-

الَّذِيْنَ يَسْتَحِبُّوْنَ الْحَيٰوةَ الدُّنْيَا
عَلَى الْاٰخِرَةِ وَيَصُدُّوْنَ عَنْ سَبِيْلِ

seek therein something crooked: they are astray by a long distance.

4. We did not send a Messenger except (to teach) in the language of his (own) people, in order to make (things) clear to them. Now Allah leaves straying those whom He pleases and guides whom He pleases: and He is Exalted in Power, full of Wisdom.

5. We sent Moses with Our Signs (and the command). "Bring out your people from the depths of darkness into light, and teach them to remember the Days of Allah." Verily in this there are Signs for such as are firmly patient and constant,-grateful and appreciative.

6. Remember! Moses said to his people: "Call to mind the favor of Allah to you when He delivered you from the people of Pharaoh: they set you hard tasks and punishments, slaughtered your sons, and let your women-folk live: therein was a tremendous trial from your Lord."

7. And remember! your Lord caused to be declared (publicly): "If you are grateful, I will add more (favors) to you; But if you show ingratitude, truly My punishment is terrible indeed."

8. And Moses said: "If you show ingratitude, you and all on earth together, yet is Allah free of all wants, worthy of all praise.

9. Has not the story reached you, (O people!), of those who (went) before you? - of the people of Noah, and 'Ad, and Thamud? - And of those who (came) after them? None knows them but Allah. To them came Messengers with Clear (Signs);

laahi wa yabghoonahaa 'iwajaa; ulaaa'ika fee ḍalaalim ba'eed.

4. Wa maaa arsalnaa mir-Rasoolin illaa bilisaani qawmihee liyubayyina lahum fayuḍillul-laahu mañy-yashaaa'u wa yahdee mañy-yashaaa'; wa Huwal-'Azeezul-Ḥakeem

5. Wa laqad arsalnaa Moosaa bi-Aayaatinaaa an akhrij qawmaka minaẓ-ẓulumaati ilan-noori wa zakkirhum bi-ayyaamil-laah; inna fee zaalika la-Aayaatil-likulli ṣabbaarin shakoor.

6. Wa iz qaala Moosaa liqawmihiz-kuroo ni'matal-laahi 'alaykum iz anjaakum-min Aali-Fir'awna yasoomoonakum sooo'al-'azaabi wa yuzabbiḥoona abnaaa'akum wa yastaḥyoona nisaaa'akum; wa fee zaalikum balaaa'um-mir-Rabbikum 'aẓeem. **(Section 1)**

7. Wa iz ta-azzana Rabbukum la'in shakartum la-azeedannakum wa la'in kafartum inna 'azaabee lashadeed.

8. Wa qaala Moosaaa in takfurooo antum wa man filarḍi jamee'an fa-innal-laaha la-Ghaniyyun Ḥameed.

9. Alam yaåtikum naba'ul-lazeena min qablikum qawmi Nooḥiñw-wa 'Aadiñw-wa Samood, wallazeena mim ba'dihim; laa ya'lamuhum illallaah; jaaa'at-hum Rusuluhum bilbayyinaati

اللّٰهِ وَيَبْغُوْنَهَا عِوَجًا ۭ اُولٰۗىِٕكَ فِيْ
ضَلٰلٍۢ بَعِيْدٍ ③
وَمَآ اَرْسَلْنَا مِنْ رَّسُوْلٍ اِلَّا بِلِسَانِ
قَوْمِهٖ لِيُبَيِّنَ لَهُمْ ۭ فَيُضِلُّ اللّٰهُ مَنْ
يَّشَاۗءُ وَيَهْدِيْ مَنْ يَّشَاۗءُ ۭ وَهُوَ
الْعَزِيْزُ الْحَكِيْمُ ④
وَلَقَدْ اَرْسَلْنَا مُوْسٰى بِاٰيٰتِنَآ اَنْ
اَخْرِجْ قَوْمَكَ مِنَ الظُّلُمٰتِ اِلَى النُّوْرِ ڏ
وَذَكِّرْهُمْ بِاَيّٰىمِ اللّٰهِ ۭ اِنَّ فِيْ ذٰلِكَ
لَاٰيٰتٍ لِّكُلِّ صَبَّارٍ شَكُوْرٍ ⑤
وَاِذْ قَالَ مُوْسٰى لِقَوْمِهِ اذْكُرُوْا
نِعْمَةَ اللّٰهِ عَلَيْكُمْ اِذْ اَنْجٰىكُمْ
مِّنْ اٰلِ فِرْعَوْنَ يَسُوْمُوْنَكُمْ سُوْۗءَ
الْعَذَابِ وَيُذَبِّحُوْنَ اَبْنَاۗءَكُمْ
وَيَسْتَحْيُوْنَ نِسَاۗءَكُمْ ۭ وَفِيْ ذٰلِكُمْ
بَلَاۗءٌ مِّنْ رَّبِّكُمْ عَظِيْمٌ ⑥ ع
وَاِذْ تَاَذَّنَ رَبُّكُمْ لَىِٕنْ شَكَرْتُمْ
لَاَزِيْدَنَّكُمْ وَلَىِٕنْ كَفَرْتُمْ اِنَّ عَذَابِيْ
لَشَدِيْدٌ ⑦
وَقَالَ مُوْسٰٓى اِنْ تَكْفُرُوْٓا اَنْتُمْ
وَمَنْ فِي الْاَرْضِ جَمِيْعًا ۙ فَاِنَّ
اللّٰهَ لَغَنِيٌّ حَمِيْدٌ ⑧
اَلَمْ يَاْتِكُمْ نَبَؤُا الَّذِيْنَ مِنْ قَبْلِكُمْ
قَوْمِ نُوْحٍ وَّعَادٍ وَّثَمُوْدَ ڛ وَالَّذِيْنَ
مِنْۢ بَعْدِهِمْ ڜ لَا يَعْلَمُهُمْ اِلَّا
اللّٰهُ ۭ جَاۗءَتْهُمْ رُسُلُهُمْ بِالْبَيِّنٰتِ

Ikhfa اخفاء | Ghunna غنّہ | Ikhfa Meem Saakin اخفاء میم ساکن | Idghaam ادغام | Qalqala قلقلہ | Qalb قلب | Idghaam Meem Saakin ادغام میم ساکن

but they put their hands up to their mouths, and said: "We do deny (the mission) on which you have been sent, and we are really in suspicious (disquieting) doubt as to that to which you invite us."

faraddooo aydiyahum feee afwaahihim wa qaalooo innaa kafarnaa bimaaa ursiltum bihee wa innaa lafee shakkim-mimmaa tad'oonanaaa ilayhi mureeb.

فَرَدُّوْٓا اَيْدِيَهُمْ فِيْٓ اَفْوَاهِهِمْ
وَقَالُوْٓا اِنَّا كَفَرْنَا بِمَآ اُرْسِلْتُمْ بِهٖ
وَاِنَّا لَفِيْ شَكٍّ مِّمَّا تَدْعُوْنَنَآ
اِلَيْهِ مُرِيْبٍ (9)

الثلثة

10. Their Messengers said: "Is there a doubt about Allah, the Creator of the heavens and the earth? It is He Who invites you, in order that He may forgive you your sins and give you respite for a term appointed!" They said: "Ah! you are no more than human, like ourselves! You wish to turn us away from the (gods) our fathers used to worship: then bring us some clear authority."

10. Qaalat Rusuluhum afillaahi shakkun faatiris-samaawaati wal-ardi yad'ookum liyaghfira lakum-min zunoobikum wa yu'akhkhirakum ilaaa ajalim-musam-maa; qaaloo in antum illaa basharum-mislunaa tureedoona an tasuddoonaa 'ammaa kaana ya'budu aabaaa'unaa faåtoonaa bisultaanim-mubeen.

قَالَتْ رُسُلُهُمْ اَفِي اللّٰهِ شَكٌّ فَاطِرِ
السَّمٰوٰتِ وَالْاَرْضِ ؕ يَدْعُوْكُمْ
لِيَغْفِرَ لَكُمْ مِّنْ ذُنُوْبِكُمْ وَيُؤَخِّرَكُمْ
اِلٰٓى اَجَلٍ مُّسَمًّى ؕ قَالُوْٓا اِنْ اَنْتُمْ
اِلَّا بَشَرٌ مِّثْلُنَا ؕ تُرِيْدُوْنَ اَنْ
تَصُدُّوْنَا عَمَّا كَانَ يَعْبُدُ اٰبَآؤُنَا
فَاْتُوْنَا بِسُلْطٰنٍ مُّبِيْنٍ (10)

11. Their Messengers said to them: "True, we are human like yourselves, but Allah grants His grace to such of his servants as He pleases. It is not for us to bring you an authority except as Allah permits. And on Allah let all men of faith put their trust.

11. Qaalat lahum Rusuluhum in nahnu illaa basharum-mislukum wa laakinnal-laaha yamunnu 'alaa mañy-yashaaa'u min 'ibaadihee wa maa kaana lanaaa an naåtiyakum bisultaanin illaa bi-iznil-laah; wa 'alal-laahi falyatawakkalil-mu'minoon.

قَالَتْ لَهُمْ رُسُلُهُمْ اِنْ نَّحْنُ اِلَّا
بَشَرٌ مِّثْلُكُمْ وَلٰكِنَّ اللّٰهَ يَمُنُّ عَلٰى مَنْ
يَّشَآءُ مِنْ عِبَادِهٖ ؕ وَمَا كَانَ لَنَآ
اَنْ نَّاْتِيَكُمْ بِسُلْطٰنٍ اِلَّا بِاِذْنِ اللّٰهِ ؕ
وَعَلَى اللّٰهِ فَلْيَتَوَكَّلِ الْمُؤْمِنُوْنَ (11)

12. "We do not have any reason why we should not put our trust on Allah. Indeed He Has guided us to the Ways we (follow). We shall certainly bear with patience all the hurt you may cause us. For those who put their trust should put their trust on Allah."

12. Wa maa lanaaa allaa natawakkala 'alal-laahi wa qad hadaanaa subulanaa; wa lanasbiranna 'alaa maaa aazaytumoonaa; wa 'alal-laahi falyatawakkalil-mutawakkiloon.

(Section 2)

وَمَا لَنَآ اَلَّا نَتَوَكَّلَ عَلَى اللّٰهِ وَقَدْ
هَدٰىنَا سُبُلَنَا ؕ وَلَنَصْبِرَنَّ عَلٰى مَآ
اٰذَيْتُمُوْنَا ؕ وَعَلَى اللّٰهِ فَلْيَتَوَكَّلِ
الْمُتَوَكِّلُوْنَ (12) ع

ع

13. And the Unbelievers said to their Messengers: "Be sure we shall drive you out of our land, or you shall return to our religion." But their Lord inspired (this Message) to them: "Verily We shall cause the wrong-doers to perish!

13. Wa qaalal-lazeena kafaroo li-Rusulihim lanukhrijannakum min ardinaaa aw lata'oodunna fee millatinaa fa-awhaaa ilayhim Rabbuhum lanuhlikannaz-zalimeen.

وَقَالَ الَّذِيْنَ كَفَرُوْا لِرُسُلِهِمْ
لَنُخْرِجَنَّكُمْ مِّنْ اَرْضِنَآ اَوْ لَتَعُوْدُنَّ
فِيْ مِلَّتِنَا ؕ فَاَوْحٰٓى اِلَيْهِمْ رَبُّهُمْ
لَنُهْلِكَنَّ الظّٰلِمِيْنَ (13)

14. "And verily We shall cause you to abide in the land, and succeed them. This for such as fear the Time when they shall stand before My tribunal,- Such as fear

14. Wa lanuskinan-nakumul-arda mim ba'dihim; zaalika liman khaafa maqaamee wa khaafa

وَلَنُسْكِنَنَّكُمُ الْاَرْضَ مِنْۢ بَعْدِهِمْ ؕ
ذٰلِكَ لِمَنْ خَافَ مَقَامِيْ وَخَافَ

Ikhfa اخفاء | Ghunna غُنّہ | Ikhfa Meem Saakin اخفاء میم ساکن | Idghaam ادغام | Qalqala قلقلہ | Qalb قلب | Idghaam Meem Saakin ادغام میم ساکن

the punishment denounced."

15. But they sought victory and decision (there and then), and frustration was the lot of every powerful obstinate transgressor.

16. In front of such a one is Hell, and he is given, for drink, boiling fetid water.

17. In gulps will he sip it, but never will he be near swallowing it down his throat: death will come to him from every quarter, yet he will not die: and in front of him will be a chastisement unrelenting.

18. The parable of those who reject their Lord is that their works are as ashes, on which the wind blows furiously on a tempestuous day: no power have they over anything that they have earned: that is the straying far, far (from the goal).

19. Don't you see that Allah created the heavens and the earth in Truth? If He so will, He can remove you and put (in your place) a new Creation?

20. Nor is that for Allah any great matter.

21. They will all be marshalled before Allah together: then will the weak say to those who were arrogant, "For us, we but followed you; can you then avail us to all against the Wrath of Allah?" They will reply, "If we had received the Guidance of Allah, we should have given it to you: to us it makes no difference (now) whether we rage, or bear (these torments) with patience: for ourselves there is no way of escape."

22. And Satan will say when the matter is decided:

wa'eed.

15. Wastaftaḥoo wa khaaba kullu jabbaarin 'aneed.

16. Miñw-waraaa'ihee Jahannamu wa yusqaa mim-maaa'in ṣadeed.

17. Yatajarra'uhoo wa laa yakaadu yuseeghuhoo wa yaåteehil-mawtu min kulli makaaniñw-wa maa huwa bimayyitiñw wa miñw-waraaa'ihee 'azaabun ghaleeẓ.

18. Masalul-lazeena kafaroo bi-Rabbihim a'maaluhum karamaadinish-taddat bihir-reeḥu fee yawmin 'aaṣif; laa yaqdiroona mimmaa kasaboo 'alaa shay'; zaalika huwaḍ-ḍalaalul-ba'eed.

19. Alam tara annal-laaha khalaqas-samaawaati wal arḍa bilḥaqq; iñy-yashaå yuzhibkum wa yaåti bikhalqin jadeed.

20. Wa maa zaalika 'alal-laahi bi'azeez.

21. Wa barazoo lillaahi jamee'an faqaalaḍ-ḍu'afaaa'u lillazeenas-takbarooo innaa kunnaa lakum taba'an fahal antum mughnoona 'annaa min 'azaabil-laahi min shay'; qaaloo law hadaanal-laahu lahadaynaakum sawaaa'un 'alaynaa ajazi'naa am ṣabarnaa maa lanaa mim-maḥeeṣ. **(Section 3)**

22. Wa qaalash-Shayṭaanu lammaa quḍiyal-amru

وَعِيْدِ ﴿١٤﴾
وَاسْتَفْتَحُوْا وَخَابَ كُلُّ جَبَّارٍ
عَنِيْدٍ ﴿١٥﴾
مِّنْ وَّرَآىِٕهٖ جَهَنَّمُ وَيُسْقٰى مِنْ
مَّآءٍ صَدِيْدٍ ﴿١٦﴾
يَّتَجَرَّعُهٗ وَلَا يَكَادُ يُسِيْغُهٗ وَيَاْتِيْهِ
الْمَوْتُ مِنْ كُلِّ مَكَانٍ وَّمَا هُوَ
بِمَيِّتٍ ؕ وَمِنْ وَّرَآىِٕهٖ عَذَابٌ
غَلِيْظٌ ﴿١٧﴾
مَثَلُ الَّذِيْنَ كَفَرُوْا بِرَبِّهِمْ اَعْمَالُهُمْ
كَرَمَادِ ِۨاشْتَدَّتْ بِهِ الرِّيْحُ فِيْ
يَوْمٍ عَاصِفٍ ؕ لَا يَقْدِرُوْنَ مِمَّا
كَسَبُوْا عَلٰى شَيْءٍ ؕ ذٰلِكَ هُوَ
الضَّلٰلُ الْبَعِيْدُ ﴿١٨﴾
اَلَمْ تَرَ اَنَّ اللّٰهَ خَلَقَ السَّمٰوٰتِ وَ
الْاَرْضَ بِالْحَقِّ ؕ اِنْ يَّشَاْ يُذْهِبْكُمْ
وَيَاْتِ بِخَلْقٍ جَدِيْدٍ ﴿١٩﴾
وَّمَا ذٰلِكَ عَلَى اللّٰهِ بِعَزِيْزٍ ﴿٢٠﴾
وَبَرَزُوْا لِلّٰهِ جَمِيْعًا فَقَالَ الضُّعَفٰٓؤُا
لِلَّذِيْنَ اسْتَكْبَرُوْٓا اِنَّا كُنَّا لَكُمْ
تَبَعًا فَهَلْ اَنْتُمْ مُّغْنُوْنَ عَنَّا مِنْ
عَذَابِ اللّٰهِ مِنْ شَيْءٍ ؕ قَالُوْا لَوْ
هَدٰىنَا اللّٰهُ لَهَدَيْنٰكُمْ ؕ سَوَآءٌ عَلَيْنَآ
اَجَزِعْنَآ اَمْ صَبَرْنَا مَا لَنَا
مِنْ مَّحِيْصٍ ﴿٢١﴾ ع ١٥ ٣
وَقَالَ الشَّيْطٰنُ لَمَّا قُضِيَ الْاَمْرُ

Ikhfa اخفاء | Ghunna غُنّہ | Ikhfa Meem Saakin اخفاء میم ساکن | Idghaam ادغام | Qalqala قلقلہ | Qalb قلب | Idghaam Meem Saakin ادغام میم ساکن

"It was Allah Who gave you a promise of Truth: I too promised, but I failed in my promise to you. I had no authority over you except to call you but you listened to me: then reproach not me, but reproach your own souls. I cannot listen to your cries, nor can you listen to mine. I reject your former act in associating me with Allah. For wrong-doers there must be a grievous Penalty."

innal-laaha wa'adakum wa'dal-ḥaqqi wa wa'attukum fa-akhlaftukum wa maa kaana liya 'alaykum-min sulṭaanin illaaa an da'awtukum fastajabtum lee falaa taloomoonee wa loomooo anfusakum maaa ana bimuṣ-rikhikum wa maaa antum bimuṣrikhiyya innee kafartu bimaaa ashraktumooni min qabl; innaẓ-ẓaalimeena lahum aẕaabun aleem.

إِنَّ اللّٰهَ وَعَدَكُمْ وَعْدَ الْحَقِّ وَ
وَعَدْتُّكُمْ فَأَخْلَفْتُكُمْ ۖ وَمَا كَانَ
لِيَ عَلَيْكُمْ مِّنْ سُلْطٰنٍ إِلَّآ أَنْ
دَعَوْتُكُمْ فَاسْتَجَبْتُمْ لِيْ ۚ فَلَا تَلُوْمُوْنِيْ
وَلُوْمُوْٓا أَنْفُسَكُمْ ۖ مَآ أَنَا بِمُصْرِخِكُمْ
وَمَآ أَنْتُمْ بِمُصْرِخِيَّ ۖ إِنِّيْ كَفَرْتُ بِمَآ
أَشْرَكْتُمُوْنِ مِنْ قَبْلُ ۗ إِنَّ الظّٰلِمِيْنَ
لَهُمْ عَذَابٌ أَلِيْمٌ ﴿٢٢﴾

23. But those who believe and work righteousness will be admitted to gardens beneath which rivers flow,- to dwell therein for ever with the leave of their Lord. Their greeting therein will be: "Peace!"

23. Wa udkhilal-laẕeena aamanoo wa 'amiluṣ-ṣaaliḥaati Jannaatin tajree min taḥtihal-anhaaru khaalideena feehaa bi-iẕni Rabbihim taḥiyyatuhum feehaa salaam.

وَأُدْخِلَ الَّذِيْنَ اٰمَنُوْا وَعَمِلُوا
الصّٰلِحٰتِ جَنّٰتٍ تَجْرِيْ مِنْ تَحْتِهَا
الْأَنْهٰرُ خٰلِدِيْنَ فِيْهَا بِإِذْنِ رَبِّهِمْ ۖ
تَحِيَّتُهُمْ فِيْهَا سَلٰمٌ ﴿٢٣﴾

24. Do you not see how Allah sets forth a parable? - A goodly word like a goodly tree, whose root is firmly fixed, and its branches (reach) to the heavens.

24. Alam tara kayfa ḍarabal-laahu maṯalan kalimatan ṭayyibatan kashajaratin ṭayyi-batin aṣluhaa ṯaabituñw-wa far'uhaa fis-samaaa'.

أَلَمْ تَرَ كَيْفَ ضَرَبَ اللّٰهُ مَثَلًا
كَلِمَةً طَيِّبَةً كَشَجَرَةٍ طَيِّبَةٍ
أَصْلُهَا ثَابِتٌ وَّفَرْعُهَا فِي السَّمَآءِ ﴿٢٤﴾

25. It brings forth its fruit at all times, by the leave of its Lord. So Allah sets forth parables for men, in order that they may receive admonition.

25. Tu'teee ukulahaa kulla ḥeenim bi-iẕni Rabbihaa; wa yaḍribul-laahul-amṯaala lin-naasi la'allahum yataẕak-karoon.

تُؤْتِيْٓ أُكُلَهَا كُلَّ حِيْنٍۭ بِإِذْنِ رَبِّهَا ۗ
وَيَضْرِبُ اللّٰهُ الْأَمْثَالَ لِلنَّاسِ
لَعَلَّهُمْ يَتَذَكَّرُوْنَ ﴿٢٥﴾

26. And the parable of an evil word is that of an evil tree: It is torn up by the root from the surface of the earth: it has no stability.

26. Wa maṯalu kalimatin kha-beeṯatin kashajaratin khabee-ṯatinij-tuṯṯat min fawqil-arḍi maa lahaa min qaraar.

وَمَثَلُ كَلِمَةٍ خَبِيْثَةٍ كَشَجَرَةٍ
خَبِيْثَةِ ۨاجْتُثَّتْ مِنْ فَوْقِ
الْأَرْضِ مَا لَهَا مِنْ قَرَارٍ ﴿٢٦﴾

27. Allah will establish in strength those who believe, with the word that stands firm, in this world and in the Hereafter; but Allah will leave, to stray, those who do wrong: Allah does what He wills.

27. Yuṯabbitul-laahul-laẕeena aamanoo bilqawliṯ-ṯaabiti fil-ḥayaatid-dunyaa wa fil-Aakhirati wa yuḍillul-laahuẓ-ẓaalimeen; wa yaf'alul-laahu maa yashaaa'. **(Section 4)**

يُثَبِّتُ اللّٰهُ الَّذِيْنَ اٰمَنُوْا بِالْقَوْلِ
الثَّابِتِ فِي الْحَيٰوةِ الدُّنْيَا وَفِي
الْاٰخِرَةِ ۚ وَيُضِلُّ اللّٰهُ الظّٰلِمِيْنَ ۙ
وَيَفْعَلُ اللّٰهُ مَا يَشَآءُ ﴿٢٧﴾ ع

28. Have you not turned your vision to those who have exchanged the favor of Allah

28. Alam tara ilal-laẕeena baddaloo ni'matal-laahi

أَلَمْ تَرَ إِلَى الَّذِيْنَ بَدَّلُوْا نِعْمَتَ اللّٰهِ

Ikhfa اخفاء | Ghunna غنّہ | Ikhfa Meem Saakin اخفاء میم ساکن | Idghaam ادغام | Qalqala قلقلہ | Qalb قلب | Idghaam Meem Saakin ادغام میم ساکن

into blasphemy and caused their People to descend to the House of Perdition?-

29. Into Hell? They will burn therein,- an evil place to stay in!

30. And they set up (idols) as equal to Allah, to mislead (men) from the Path! Say: "Enjoy (your brief power)! But verily you are making straight way for Hell!"

31. Speak to my servants who have believed, that they may establish regular prayers, and spend (in charity) out of the sustenance we have given them, secretly and openly, before the coming of a Day in which there will be neither mutual bargaining nor befriending.

32. It is Allah Who has created the heavens and the earth and sendeth down rain from the skies, and with it bringeth out fruits wherewith to feed you; it is He Who have made the ships subject to you, that they may sail through the sea by His command; and the rivers (also) have He made subject to you.

33. And He has made subject to you the sun and the moon, both diligently pursuing their courses; and he has (also) made the Night and the Day subject to you.

34. And He gives you of all that you ask for. But if you count the favours of Allah, never will you be able to number them. Verily, man is given up to injustice and ingratitude.

35. Remember Abraham said: "O my Lord! make this city one of peace and security: and preserve me and my sons from worshipping idols.

36. "O my Lord! they have indeed led astray many among mankind; He then who follows my (ways) is of me, and he that disobeys me,- but you are indeed Oft-Forgiving, Most Merciful.

37. "O our Lord! I have made some of my offspring to dwell

kufrañw-wa aḥalloo qawmahum daaral-bawaar.

29. Jahannama yaṣlawnahaa wa bi'sal-qaraar.

30. Wa ja'aloo lillaahi andaadal-liyuḍilloo 'an sabeelih; qul tamatta'oo fa-inna maṣeerakum ilan-Naar.

31. Qul li'ibaadiyal-lazeena aamanoo yuqeemuṣ-Ṣalaata wa yunfiqoo mimmaa razaqnaahum sirrañw-wa 'alaaniyatam-min qabli añy-yaåtiya Yawmul-laa bay'un feehi wa laa khilaal.

32. Allaahul-lazee khalaqas-samaawaati wal-arḍa wa anzala minas-samaaa'i maaa'an fa-akhraja bihee minas-samaraati rizqal-lakum wa sakhkhara lakumul-fulka litajriya fil-baḥri bi-amrihee wa sakhkhara lakumul-anhaar.

33. Wa sakhkhara lakumush-shamsa walqamara daaa'ibayni wa sakhkhara lakumul-layla wannahaar.

34. Wa aataakum min kulli maa sa-altumooh; wa in ta'uddoo ni'matal-laahi laa tuḥṣoohaa; innal-insaana laẓaloomun kaffaar. **(Section 5)**

35. Wa iz qaala Ibraaheemu Rabbij-'al haazal-balada aaminañw-wajnubnee wa baniyya an na'budal-aṣnaam.

36. Rabbi innahunna aḍlalna kaseeram-minan-naasi faman tabi'anee fa-innahoo minnee wa man 'aṣaanee fa-innaka Ghafoorur-Raḥeem.

37. Rabbanaaa inneee askantu min zurriyyatee

كُفْرًا وَّاَحَلُّوْا قَوْمَهُمْ دَارَ الْبَوَارِ ﴿٢٨﴾
جَهَنَّمَ ۚ يَصْلَوْنَهَا ۗ وَبِئْسَ الْقَرَارُ ﴿٢٩﴾
وَجَعَلُوْا لِلّٰهِ اَنْدَادًا لِّيُضِلُّوْا عَنْ
سَبِيْلِهٖ ۗ قُلْ تَمَتَّعُوْا فَاِنَّ مَصِيْرَكُمْ
اِلَى النَّارِ ﴿٣٠﴾
قُلْ لِّعِبَادِيَ الَّذِيْنَ اٰمَنُوْا يُقِيْمُوا
الصَّلٰوةَ وَيُنْفِقُوْا مِمَّا رَزَقْنٰهُمْ
سِرًّا وَّعَلَانِيَةً مِّنْ قَبْلِ اَنْ يَّاْتِيَ
يَوْمٌ لَّا بَيْعٌ فِيْهِ وَلَا خِلٰلٌ ﴿٣١﴾
اَللّٰهُ الَّذِيْ خَلَقَ السَّمٰوٰتِ وَالْاَرْضَ
وَاَنْزَلَ مِنَ السَّمَآءِ مَآءً فَاَخْرَجَ بِهٖ
مِنَ الثَّمَرٰتِ رِزْقًا لَّكُمْ ۚ وَسَخَّرَ لَكُمُ
الْفُلْكَ لِتَجْرِيَ فِي الْبَحْرِ بِاَمْرِهٖ ۚ
وَسَخَّرَ لَكُمُ الْاَنْهٰرَ ﴿٣٢﴾
وَسَخَّرَ لَكُمُ الشَّمْسَ وَالْقَمَرَ دَآئِبَيْنِ ۚ
وَسَخَّرَ لَكُمُ الَّيْلَ وَالنَّهَارَ ﴿٣٣﴾
وَاٰتٰىكُمْ مِّنْ كُلِّ مَا سَاَلْتُمُوْهُ ۗ وَاِنْ
تَعُدُّوْا نِعْمَتَ اللّٰهِ لَا تُحْصُوْهَا ۗ اِنَّ
الْاِنْسَانَ لَظَلُوْمٌ كَفَّارٌ ﴿٣٤﴾ الربع
وَاِذْ قَالَ اِبْرٰهِيْمُ رَبِّ اجْعَلْ هٰذَا
الْبَلَدَ اٰمِنًا وَّاجْنُبْنِيْ وَبَنِيَّ اَنْ
نَّعْبُدَ الْاَصْنَامَ ﴿٣٥﴾
رَبِّ اِنَّهُنَّ اَضْلَلْنَ كَثِيْرًا مِّنَ
النَّاسِ ۚ فَمَنْ تَبِعَنِيْ فَاِنَّهٗ مِنِّيْ ۚ
وَمَنْ عَصَانِيْ فَاِنَّكَ غَفُوْرٌ رَّحِيْمٌ ﴿٣٦﴾
رَبَّنَآ اِنِّيْٓ اَسْكَنْتُ مِنْ ذُرِّيَّتِيْ

Ikhfa اخفاء | Ghunna غُنّہ | Ikhfa Meem Saakin اخفاء میم ساکن | Idghaam ادغام | Qalqala قلقلہ | Qalb قلب | Idghaam Meem Saakin ادغام میم ساکن

in a valley without cultivation, by your Sacred House; in order, O our Lord, that they may establish regular Prayer: so fill the hearts of some among men with love toward them, and feed them with fruits: so that they may give thanks.

38. "O our Lord! truly You do know what we conceal and what we reveal: for nothing whatever is hidden from Allah, whether on earth or in heaven.

39. "Praise be to Allah, Who has granted unto me in old age Isma'il and Isaac: for truly my Lord is He, the Hearer of Prayer!

40. O my Lord! make me one who establishes regular Prayer, and also (raise such) among my offspring O our Lord! and you accept my Prayer.

41. "O our Lord! cover (us) with Your Forgiveness - me, my parents, and (all) Believers, on the Day that the Reckoning will be established!

42. Think not that Allah does not heed the deeds of those who do wrong. He but gives them respite against a Day when the eyes will fixedly stare in horror,-

43. They running forward with necks outstretched, their heads uplifted, their gaze returning not toward them, and their hearts a (gaping) void!

44. So warn mankind of the Day when the Wrath will reach them: then will the wrong-doers say: "Our Lord! respite us (if only) for a short Term: we will answer Your Call, and follow the Messengers!" "What! were you not wont to swear aforetime that you should suffer no

biwaadin ghayri zee zar'in 'inda Baytikal-Muḥarrami Rabbanaa liyuqeemuṣ-Ṣalaata faj'al af'idatam-minan-naasi tahweee ilayhim warzuqhum-minas-samaraati la'allahum yashkuroon.

38. Rabbanaaa innaka ta'lamu maa nukhfee wa maa nu'lin; wa maa yakhfaa 'alal-laahi min shay'in fil-arḍi wa laa fis-samaaa'.

39. Alḥamdu lillaahil-lazee wahaba lee 'alal-kibari Ismaa-'eela wa Isḥaaq; inna Rabbee lasamee'ud-du'aaa'.

40. Rabbij-'alnee muqeemaṣ-Ṣalaati wa min zurriyyatee; Rabbanaa wa taqabbal du'aaa'.

41. Rabbanagh-fir lee wa liwaalidayya wa lilmu'mineena Yawma yaqoomul-ḥisaab.

(Section 6)

42. Wa laa taḥsabannal-laaha ghaafilan 'ammaa ya'maluẓ-ẓaalimoon; innamaa yu'akh-khiruhum li-Yawmin tashkhaṣu feehil-abṣaar.

43. Muhṭi'eena muqni'ee ru'oosihim laa yartaddu ilayhim ṭarfuhum wa af-'idatuhum hawaaa'.

44. Wa anzirin-naasa Yawma yaàteehimul-'azaabu fa-yaqoo-lul-lazeena ẓalamoo Rabbanaaa akhkhirnaaa ilaaa ajalin qaree-bin-nujib da'wataka wa nattabi-'ir-Rusul; awalam takoonooo aqsamtum min qablu maa lakum

بِوَادٍ غَيْرِ ذِي زَرْعٍ عِندَ بَيْتِكَ
الْمُحَرَّمِ رَبَّنَا لِيُقِيمُوا الصَّلَوٰةَ
فَاجْعَلْ أَفْئِدَةً مِّنَ النَّاسِ تَهْوِيٓ
إِلَيْهِمْ وَارْزُقْهُم مِّنَ الثَّمَرَٰتِ
لَعَلَّهُمْ يَشْكُرُونَ ٣٧
رَبَّنَآ إِنَّكَ تَعْلَمُ مَا نُخْفِي وَمَا نُعْلِنُ
وَمَا يَخْفَىٰ عَلَى اللَّهِ مِن شَيْءٍ فِي
الْأَرْضِ وَلَا فِي السَّمَآءِ ٣٨
الْحَمْدُ لِلَّهِ الَّذِي وَهَبَ لِي عَلَى
الْكِبَرِ إِسْمَٰعِيلَ وَإِسْحَٰقَ إِنَّ رَبِّي
لَسَمِيعُ الدُّعَآءِ ٣٩
رَبِّ اجْعَلْنِي مُقِيمَ الصَّلَوٰةِ وَمِن
ذُرِّيَّتِي رَبَّنَا وَتَقَبَّلْ دُعَآءِ ٤٠
رَبَّنَا اغْفِرْ لِي وَلِوَٰلِدَيَّ وَ
لِلْمُؤْمِنِينَ يَوْمَ يَقُومُ الْحِسَابُ ٤١ ع ١٨/٦
وَلَا تَحْسَبَنَّ اللَّهَ غَٰفِلًا عَمَّا يَعْمَلُ
الظَّٰلِمُونَ إِنَّمَا يُؤَخِّرُهُمْ لِيَوْمٍ
تَشْخَصُ فِيهِ الْأَبْصَٰرُ ٤٢
مُهْطِعِينَ مُقْنِعِي رُءُوسِهِمْ لَا
يَرْتَدُّ إِلَيْهِمْ طَرْفُهُمْ وَ
أَفْـِٔدَتُهُمْ هَوَآءٌ ٤٣
وَأَنذِرِ النَّاسَ يَوْمَ يَأْتِيهِمُ
الْعَذَابُ فَيَقُولُ الَّذِينَ ظَلَمُوا رَبَّنَآ
أَخِّرْنَآ إِلَىٰ أَجَلٍ قَرِيبٍ نُّجِبْ
دَعْوَتَكَ وَنَتَّبِعِ الرُّسُلَ أَوَلَمْ
تَكُونُوٓا أَقْسَمْتُم مِّن قَبْلُ مَا لَكُم

Ikhfa اخفاء | Ghunna غنّہ | Ikhfa Meem Saakin اخفاء میم ساکن | Idghaam ادغام | Qalqala قلقلہ | Qalb قلب | Idghaam Meem Saakin ادغام میم ساکن

decline?

45. "And you dwelt in the dwellings of men who wronged their own souls; you were clearly shown how We dealt with them; and We put forth (many) Parables in your behoof!"

46. Mighty indeed were the plots which they made, but their plots were (well) within the sight of Allah, even though they were such as to shake the hills!

47. Never think that Allah would fail His Messengers in His promise: for Allah is Exalted in Power, - the Lord of Retribution.

48. One day the earth will be changed to a different Earth, and so will be the Heavens, and (men) will be marshalled forth, before Allah, the One, the Irresistible;

49. And you will see the Sinners that day bound together in fetters;-

50. Their garments of liquid pitch, and their faces covered with Fire;

51. That Allah may requite each soul according to its deserts; and verily Allah is swift in calling to account.

52. Here is a Message for mankind: let them take warning therefrom, and let them know that He is (no other than) One God (Allah): let men of under-standing take heed.

15. The Rocky Tract

In the name of Allah, Most Gracious, Most Merciful.

1. *Alif-Lam-Ra.* These are the *Ayats* of Revelation,- of a Qur'an that makes things clear.

2. Again and again will those who disbelieve, wish that

min zawaal.

45. Wa sakantum fee masaakinil-lazeena ẓalamooo anfusahum wa tabayyana lakum kayfa fa'alnaa bihim wa ḍarabnaa lakumul-amsaal.

46. Wa qad makaroo makrahum wa 'indal-laahi makruhum wa in kaana makruhum litazoola minhul-jibaal.

47. Falaa taḥsabannal-laaha mukhlifa wa'dihee Rusulah; innal-laaha 'azeezun zuntiqaam.

48. Yawma tubaddalul-arḍu ghayral-arḍi wassamaawaatu wa barazoo lillaahil-Waaḥidil-Qahhaar.

49. Wa taral-mujrimeena Yawma'izim-muqarraneena fil-aṣfaad.

50. Saraabeeluhum min qaṭiraaniñw-wa taghshaa wujoohahumun-Naar.

51. Liyajziyal-laahu kulla nafsim-maa kasabat; innal-laaha saree'ul-ḥisaab.

52. Haazaa balaaghul-linnaasi wa liyunzaroo bihee wa liya'lamooo annamaa Huwa Ilaahuñw-Waaḥiduñw-wa liyazzakkara ulul-albaab. **(Section 7)**

Sûrat al-Ḥijr–15

(Revealed at Makkah)

Bismillaahir Raḥmaanir Raḥeem

1. Alif-Laaam-Raa; tilka Aayaatul-Kitaabi wa Qur-aanim-Mubeen.

2. Rubamaa yawaddul-lazeena kafaroo law

مِّن زَوَالٍ ﴿٤٤﴾
وَسَكَنتُمْ فِي مَسَٰكِنِ الَّذِينَ ظَلَمُوٓا۟
أَنفُسَهُمْ وَتَبَيَّنَ لَكُمْ كَيْفَ فَعَلْنَا
بِهِمْ وَضَرَبْنَا لَكُمُ الْأَمْثَالَ ﴿٤٥﴾
وَقَدْ مَكَرُوا مَكْرَهُمْ وَعِندَ اللَّهِ
مَكْرُهُمْ ۚ وَإِن كَانَ مَكْرُهُمْ
لِتَزُولَ مِنْهُ الْجِبَالُ ﴿٤٦﴾
فَلَا تَحْسَبَنَّ اللَّهَ مُخْلِفَ وَعْدِهِۦ
رُسُلَهُۥٓ ۗ إِنَّ اللَّهَ عَزِيزٌ ذُو انتِقَامٍ ﴿٤٧﴾
يَوْمَ تُبَدَّلُ الْأَرْضُ غَيْرَ الْأَرْضِ
وَالسَّمَٰوَٰتُ ۖ وَبَرَزُوا لِلَّهِ الْوَٰحِدِ
الْقَهَّارِ ﴿٤٨﴾
وَتَرَى الْمُجْرِمِينَ يَوْمَئِذٍ
مُّقَرَّنِينَ فِي الْأَصْفَادِ ﴿٤٩﴾
سَرَابِيلُهُم مِّن قَطِرَانٍ وَتَغْشَىٰ
وُجُوهَهُمُ النَّارُ ﴿٥٠﴾
لِيَجْزِيَ اللَّهُ كُلَّ نَفْسٍ مَّا كَسَبَتْ ۚ
إِنَّ اللَّهَ سَرِيعُ الْحِسَابِ ﴿٥١﴾
هَٰذَا بَلَٰغٌ لِّلنَّاسِ وَلِيُنذَرُوا بِهِۦ
وَلِيَعْلَمُوٓا أَنَّمَا هُوَ إِلَٰهٌ وَٰحِدٌ
وَلِيَذَّكَّرَ أُولُوا الْأَلْبَٰبِ ﴿٥٢﴾ ع

(١٥) سُورَةُ الْحِجْرِ مَكِّيَّةٌ (٥٤)
بِسْمِ اللَّهِ الرَّحْمَٰنِ الرَّحِيمِ
الٓر ۚ تِلْكَ ءَايَٰتُ الْكِتَٰبِ وَقُرْءَانٍ
مُّبِينٍ ﴿١﴾
رُّبَمَا يَوَدُّ الَّذِينَ كَفَرُوا لَوْ

الجزء الرابع عشر (١٤)

Ikhfa اخفاء | Ghunna غنّہ | Ikhfa Meem Saakin اخفاء میم ساکن | Idghaam ادغام | Qalqala قلقلہ | Qalb قلب | Idghaam Meem Saakin ادغام میم ساکن

they had bowed (to Allah's will) in Islam.	kaanoo muslimeen.	كَانُوا مُسْلِمِينَ ﴿٢﴾
3. Leave them alone, to enjoy (the good things of this life) and to please themselves: let (false) hope amuse them: soon will knowledge (undeceive them).	3. Zarhum yaåkuloo wa yatamatta'oo wa yulhihimul-amalu fasawfa ya'lamoon.	ذَرْهُمْ يَأْكُلُوا وَيَتَمَتَّعُوا وَيُلْهِهِمُ الْأَمَلُ فَسَوْفَ يَعْلَمُونَ ﴿٣﴾
4. We never destroyed a population that had not a term decreed and assigned beforehand.	4. Wa maaa ahlaknaa min qaryatin illaa wa lahaa kitaa-bum-ma'loom.	وَمَا أَهْلَكْنَا مِنْ قَرْيَةٍ إِلَّا وَلَهَا كِتَابٌ مَعْلُومٌ ﴿٤﴾
5. Neither can a people anticipate its Term, nor delay it.	5. Maa tasbiqu min ummatin ajalahaa wa maa yastaåkhiroon.	مَا تَسْبِقُ مِنْ أُمَّةٍ أَجَلَهَا وَمَا يَسْتَأْخِرُونَ ﴿٥﴾
6. They say: "O you to whom the Message is being revealed! truly you are mad (or possessed)!	6. Wa qaaloo yaaa ayyuhal-lazee nuzzila 'alayhiz-Zikru innaka lamajnoon.	وَقَالُوا يَا أَيُّهَا الَّذِي نُزِّلَ عَلَيْهِ الذِّكْرُ إِنَّكَ لَمَجْنُونٌ ﴿٦﴾
7. "Why don't you bring not angels to us if it be that you have the Truth?"	7. Law maa taåteenaa bil-malaaa'ikati in kunta minaṣ-ṣaadiqeen.	لَوْ مَا تَأْتِينَا بِالْمَلَائِكَةِ إِنْ كُنْتَ مِنَ الصَّادِقِينَ ﴿٧﴾
8. We don't send not the angels down except for just cause: if they came (to the ungodly), behold! no respite would they have!	8. Maa nunazzilul-malaaa'ikata illaa bilḥaqqi wa maa kaanooo izam-munẓareen.	مَا نُنَزِّلُ الْمَلَائِكَةَ إِلَّا بِالْحَقِّ وَمَا كَانُوا إِذًا مُنْظَرِينَ ﴿٨﴾
9. We have, without doubt, sent down the Message; and We will assuredly guard it (from corruption).	9. Innaa Naḥnu nazalnaz-Zikra wa Innaa lahoo laḥaa-fiẓoon.	إِنَّا نَحْنُ نَزَّلْنَا الذِّكْرَ وَإِنَّا لَهُ لَحَافِظُونَ ﴿٩﴾
10. We sent Messengers before you amongst the religious sects of old:	10. Wa laqad arsalnaa min qablika fee shiya'il-awwaleen.	وَلَقَدْ أَرْسَلْنَا مِنْ قَبْلِكَ فِي شِيَعِ الْأَوَّلِينَ ﴿١٠﴾
11. But never came a Messenger to them but they mocked him.	11. Wa maa yaåteehim-mir-Rasoolin illaa kaanoo bihee yastahzi'oon.	وَمَا يَأْتِيهِمْ مِنْ رَسُولٍ إِلَّا كَانُوا بِهِ يَسْتَهْزِئُونَ ﴿١١﴾
12. Even so do We let it creep into the hearts of the sinners.	12. Kazaalika naslukuhoo fee quloobil-mujrimeen.	كَذَٰلِكَ نَسْلُكُهُ فِي قُلُوبِ الْمُجْرِمِينَ ﴿١٢﴾
13. That they should not believe in the (Message); but the ways of the ancients have passed away.	13. Laa yu'minoona bihee wa qad khalat sunnatul-awwaleen.	لَا يُؤْمِنُونَ بِهِ وَقَدْ خَلَتْ سُنَّةُ الْأَوَّلِينَ ﴿١٣﴾
14. Even if We opened out to them a gate from heaven, and they were to continue (all day) ascending therein,	14. Wa law fataḥnaa 'alayhim baabam-minas-samaaa'i faẓal-loo feehi ya'rujoon.	وَلَوْ فَتَحْنَا عَلَيْهِمْ بَابًا مِنَ السَّمَاءِ فَظَلُّوا فِيهِ يَعْرُجُونَ ﴿١٤﴾
15. They would only say: "Our eyes have been intoxicated: No, we have been bewitched by sorcery."	15. Laqaalooo innamaa sukki-rat abṣaarunaa bal naḥnu qawmum-masḥooroon. **(Section 1)**	لَقَالُوا إِنَّمَا سُكِّرَتْ أَبْصَارُنَا بَلْ نَحْنُ قَوْمٌ مَسْحُورُونَ ﴿١٥﴾ ع ١٥

Ikhfa اخفاء · Ghunna غنّہ · Ikhfa Meem Saakin اخفاءميم ساكن · Idghaam ادغام · Qalqala قلقلہ · Qalb قلب · Idghaam Meem Saakin ادغام ميم ساكن

16. It is We Who have set out the zodiacal signs in the heavens, and made them fair-seeming to (all) beholders;

16. Wa laqad ja'alnaa fis-samaaa'i buroojañw-wa zayyannaahaa linnaaẓireen.

وَلَقَدْ جَعَلْنَا فِي السَّمَاءِ بُرُوجًا
وَزَيَّنَّاهَا لِلنّٰظِرِينَ ⑯

17. And (moreover) We have guarded them from every evil spirit accursed:

17. Wa ḥafiẓnaahaa min kulli Shayṭaanir-rajeem.

وَحَفِظْنٰهَا مِنْ كُلِّ شَيْطٰنٍ رَّجِيمٍ ⑰

18. But any that gains a hearing by stealth, is pursued by a flaming fire, bright (to see).

18. Illaa manis-taraqas-sam'a fa-atba'ahoo shihaabum-mubeen.

إِلَّا مَنِ اسْتَرَقَ السَّمْعَ فَأَتْبَعَهُ
شِهَابٌ مُّبِينٌ ⑱

19. And the earth We have spread out (like a carpet); set thereon mountains firm and immovable; and produced therein all kinds of things in due balance.

19. Wal-arḍa madadnaahaa wa alqaynaa feehaa rawaasiya wa ambatnaa feehaa min kulli shay'im-mawzoon.

وَالْأَرْضَ مَدَدْنٰهَا وَأَلْقَيْنَا فِيهَا
رَوَاسِيَ وَأَنْبَتْنَا فِيهَا مِنْ كُلِّ شَيْءٍ
مَّوْزُونٍ ⑲

20. And We have provided therein means of subsistence,- for you and for those for whose sustenance you are not responsible.

20. Wa ja'alnaa lakum feehaa ma'aayisha wa mal-lastum lahoo biraaziqeen.

وَجَعَلْنَا لَكُمْ فِيهَا مَعَايِشَ وَمَنْ
لَّسْتُمْ لَهُ بِرٰزِقِينَ ⑳

21. And there is not a thing but its (sources and) treasures (inexhaustible) are with Us; but We only send down thereof in due and ascertainable measures.

21. Wa im-min shay'in illaa 'indanaa khazaaa'inuhoo wa maa nunazziluhooo illaa biqadarim-ma'loom.

وَإِنْ مِّنْ شَيْءٍ إِلَّا عِنْدَنَا
خَزَائِنُهُ وَمَا نُنَزِّلُهُ إِلَّا بِقَدَرٍ
مَّعْلُومٍ ㉑

22. And We send the fecundating winds, then cause the rain to descend from the sky, therewith providing you with water (in abundance), though you are not the guardians of its stores.

22. Wa arsalnar-riyaaḥa la-waaqiḥa fa-anzalnaa minas-samaaa'i maaa'an fa-asqaynaakumoohu wa maaa antum lahoo bikhaazineen.

وَأَرْسَلْنَا الرِّيٰحَ لَوَاقِحَ فَأَنْزَلْنَا
مِنَ السَّمَاءِ مَاءً فَأَسْقَيْنٰكُمُوهُ وَمَا
أَنْتُمْ لَهُ بِخٰزِنِينَ ㉒

23. And verily, it is We Who give life, and Who give death: it is We Who remain inheritors (after all else passes away).

23. Wa innaa la-naḥnu nuḥyee wa numeetu wa naḥnul-waaris̲oon.

وَإِنَّا لَنَحْنُ نُحْيِي وَنُمِيتُ وَنَحْنُ
الْوٰرِثُونَ ㉓

24. To Us are known those of you who hasten forward, and those who lag behind.

24. Wa la-qad 'alimnal-mustaqdimeena minkum wa laqad 'alimnal-mustaåkhireen.

وَلَقَدْ عَلِمْنَا الْمُسْتَقْدِمِينَ مِنْكُمْ
وَلَقَدْ عَلِمْنَا الْمُسْتَأْخِرِينَ ㉔

25. Assuredly it is your Lord Who will gather them together: for He is perfect in Wisdom and Knowledge.

25. Wa inna Rabbaka Huwa yaḥshuruhum; innahoo Ḥakeemun 'Aleem. **(Section 2)**

وَإِنَّ رَبَّكَ هُوَ يَحْشُرُهُمْ إِنَّهُ
حَكِيمٌ عَلِيمٌ ㉕

26. We created man from sounding clay, from mud moulded into shape;

26. Wa laqad khalaqnal insaana min ṣalṣaalim-min ḥama-im-masnoon.

وَلَقَدْ خَلَقْنَا الْإِنْسَانَ مِنْ صَلْصَالٍ
مِّنْ حَمَإٍ مَّسْنُونٍ ㉖

27. And the Jinn race, We had created before, from the fire of a scorching wind.

27. Waljaaanna khalaqnaahu min qablu min naaris-samoom.

وَالْجَانَّ خَلَقْنٰهُ مِنْ قَبْلُ مِنْ
نَّارِ السَّمُومِ ㉗

Ikhfa اخفاء | Ghunna غُنّہ | Ikhfa Meem Saakin اخفاءمیم ساکن | Idghaam ادغام | Qalqala قلقلہ | Qalb قلب | Idghaam Meem Saakin ادغام میم ساکن

28. Behold! your Lord said to the angels: "I am about to create man, from sounding clay from mud moulded into shape;	28. Wa iz̲ qaala Rabbuka lilmalaaa'ikati innee khaaliqum basharam-min ṣalṣaalim-min ḥama-im-masnoon.	وَإِذْ قَالَ رَبُّكَ لِلْمَلَٰٓئِكَةِ إِنِّي خَٰلِقٌۢ بَشَرًا مِّن صَلْصَٰلٍ مِّنْ حَمَإٍ مَّسْنُونٍ ﴿٢٨﴾
29. "When I have fashioned him (in due proportion) and breathed into him of My spirit, you fall down in obeisance to him."	29. Fa-iz̲aa sawwaytuhoo wa nafakhtu feehi mir-rooḥee faqa'oo lahoo saajideen.	فَإِذَا سَوَّيْتُهُۥ وَنَفَخْتُ فِيهِ مِن رُّوحِي فَقَعُوا۟ لَهُۥ سَٰجِدِينَ ﴿٢٩﴾
30. So the angels prostrated themselves, all of them together:	30. Fasajadal-malaaa'ikatu kulluhum ajma'oon.	فَسَجَدَ ٱلْمَلَٰٓئِكَةُ كُلُّهُمْ أَجْمَعُونَ ﴿٣٠﴾
31. Not so Iblis: he refused to be among those who prostrated themselves.	31. Illaaa Ibleesa abaaa añy-yakoona ma'as-saajideen.	إِلَّآ إِبْلِيسَ أَبَىٰٓ أَن يَكُونَ مَعَ ٱلسَّٰجِدِينَ ﴿٣١﴾
32. (Allah) said: "O Iblis! what is your reason for not being among those who prostrated themselves?"	32. Qaala yaaa Ibleesu maa laka allaa takoona ma'as-saajideen.	قَالَ يَٰٓإِبْلِيسُ مَا لَكَ أَلَّا تَكُونَ مَعَ ٱلسَّٰجِدِينَ ﴿٣٢﴾
33. (Iblis) said: "I am not one to prostrate myself to man, whom you created from sounding clay, from mud moulded into shape."	33. Qaala lam akul-li-asjuda libasharin khalaqtahoo min ṣalṣaalim-min ḥama-im-masnoon.	قَالَ لَمْ أَكُن لِّأَسْجُدَ لِبَشَرٍ خَلَقْتَهُۥ مِن صَلْصَٰلٍ مِّنْ حَمَإٍ مَّسْنُونٍ ﴿٣٣﴾
34. (Allah) said: "Then get out from here; for you are rejected, accursed.	34. Qaala fakhruj minhaa fa-innaka rajeem.	قَالَ فَٱخْرُجْ مِنْهَا فَإِنَّكَ رَجِيمٌ ﴿٣٤﴾
35. "And the curse shall be on you till the day of Judgment."	35. Wa inna 'alaykal-la'nata ilaa Yawmid-Deen.	وَإِنَّ عَلَيْكَ ٱللَّعْنَةَ إِلَىٰ يَوْمِ ٱلدِّينِ ﴿٣٥﴾
36. (Iblis) said: "O my Lord! give me then respite till the Day the (dead) are raised."	36. Qaala Rabbi fa-anẓirneee ilaa Yawmi yub'as̲oon.	قَالَ رَبِّ فَأَنظِرْنِيٓ إِلَىٰ يَوْمِ يُبْعَثُونَ ﴿٣٦﴾
37. (Allah) said: "Respite is granted to you,	37. Qaala fa-innaka minal-munẓareen.	قَالَ فَإِنَّكَ مِنَ ٱلْمُنظَرِينَ ﴿٣٧﴾
38. "Till the Day of the Time Appointed."	38. Ilaa Yawmil-waqtil-ma'loom.	إِلَىٰ يَوْمِ ٱلْوَقْتِ ٱلْمَعْلُومِ ﴿٣٨﴾
39. (Iblis) said: "O my Lord! because You have put me in the wrong, I will make (wrong) fair-seeming to them on the earth, and I will put them all in the wrong,-	39. Qaala Rabbi bimaaa aghwaytanee la-uzayyinanna lahum fil-arḍi wa la-ughwiyannahum ajma'een.	قَالَ رَبِّ بِمَآ أَغْوَيْتَنِي لَأُزَيِّنَنَّ لَهُمْ فِي ٱلْأَرْضِ وَلَأُغْوِيَنَّهُمْ أَجْمَعِينَ ﴿٣٩﴾
40. "Except your servants among them, sincere and purified (by your Grace)."	40. Illaa 'ibaadaka minhumul-mukhlaṣeen.	إِلَّا عِبَادَكَ مِنْهُمُ ٱلْمُخْلَصِينَ ﴿٤٠﴾
41. (Allah) said: "This (way of My sincere servants) is indeed a Way that leads straight to Me.	41. Qaala haaz̲aa Ṣiraaṭun 'alayya Mustaqeem.	قَالَ هَٰذَا صِرَٰطٌ عَلَيَّ مُسْتَقِيمٌ ﴿٤١﴾
42. "For over My servants no authority shall you have, except such as put themselves	42. Inna 'ibaadee laysa laka 'alayhim sulṭaanun illaa manit-taba'aka minal-	إِنَّ عِبَادِي لَيْسَ لَكَ عَلَيْهِمْ سُلْطَٰنٌ إِلَّا مَنِ ٱتَّبَعَكَ مِنَ

Ikhfa اخفاء | Ghunna غنّہ | Ikhfa Meem Saakin اخفاء میم ساکن | Idghaam ادغام | Qalqala قلقلہ | Qalb قلب | Idghaam Meem Saakin ادغام میم ساکن

in the wrong and follow you."	ghaaween.	الْغَاوِينَ ﴿٤٢﴾
43. And verily, Hell is the promised abode for them all!	43. Wa inna Jahannama lamaw'iduhum ajma'een.	وَإِنَّ جَهَنَّمَ لَمَوْعِدُهُمْ أَجْمَعِينَ ﴿٤٣﴾
44. To it are seven gates: for each of those gates is a (special) class (of sinners) assigned.	44. Lahaa sab'atu abwaab; likulli baabim-minhum juz'um-maqsoom. **(Section 3)**	لَهَا سَبْعَةُ أَبْوَابٍ لِّكُلِّ بَابٍ مِّنْهُمْ جُزْءٌ مَّقْسُومٌ ﴿٤٤﴾
45. The righteous (will be) amid Gardens and fountains (of clear-flowing water).	45. Innal-muttaqeena fee Jannaatiñw-wa 'uyoon.	إِنَّ الْمُتَّقِينَ فِي جَنَّاتٍ وَعُيُونٍ ﴿٤٥﴾
46. (Their greeting will be): "You enter here in peace and security."	46. Udkhuloohaa bisalaamin aamineen.	ادْخُلُوهَا بِسَلَامٍ آمِنِينَ ﴿٤٦﴾
47. And We shall remove from their hearts any lurking sense of injury: (they will be) brothers (joyfully) facing each other on thrones (of dignity).	47. Wa naza'naa maa fee sudoorihim-min ghillin ikhwaanan 'alaa sururim-mutaqaabileen.	وَنَزَعْنَا مَا فِي صُدُورِهِم مِّنْ غِلٍّ إِخْوَانًا عَلَىٰ سُرُرٍ مُّتَقَابِلِينَ ﴿٤٧﴾
48. There no sense of fatigue shall touch them, nor shall they (ever) be asked to leave.	48. Laa yamas-suhum feehaa naṣabuñw-wa maa hum-minhaa bimukhrajeen.	لَا يَمَسُّهُمْ فِيهَا نَصَبٌ وَمَا هُم مِّنْهَا بِمُخْرَجِينَ ﴿٤٨﴾
49. Tell My servants that I am indeed the Oft-forgiving, Most Merciful;	49. Nabbi' 'ibaadeee anneee anal-Ghafoorur-Raḥeem.	نَبِّئْ عِبَادِي أَنِّي أَنَا الْغَفُورُ الرَّحِيمُ ﴿٤٩﴾
50. And that My Penalty will be indeed the most grievous Penalty.	50. Wa anna 'azaabee huwal-'azaabul-aleem.	وَأَنَّ عَذَابِي هُوَ الْعَذَابُ الْأَلِيمُ ﴿٥٠﴾
51. Tell them about the guests of Abraham.	51. Wa nabbi'hum 'an ḍayfi Ibraaheem.	وَنَبِّئْهُمْ عَن ضَيْفِ إِبْرَاهِيمَ ﴿٥١﴾
52. When they entered his presence and said, "Peace!" He said, "We feel afraid of you!"	52. Iz dakhaloo 'alayhi faqaaloo salaaman qaala innaa minkum wajiloon.	إِذْ دَخَلُوا عَلَيْهِ فَقَالُوا سَلَامًا قَالَ إِنَّا مِنكُمْ وَجِلُونَ ﴿٥٢﴾
53. They said: "Fear not! We give you glad tidings of a son endowed with wisdom."	53. Qaaloo laa tawjal innaa nubashshiruka bighulaamin 'aleem.	قَالُوا لَا تَوْجَلْ إِنَّا نُبَشِّرُكَ بِغُلَامٍ عَلِيمٍ ﴿٥٣﴾
54. He said: "Do you give me glad tidings that old age has seized me? Of what, then, is your good news?"	54. Qaala abashshartumoonee 'alaaa am-massaniyal-kibaru fabima tubashshiroon.	قَالَ أَبَشَّرْتُمُونِي عَلَىٰ أَن مَّسَّنِيَ الْكِبَرُ فَبِمَ تُبَشِّرُونَ ﴿٥٤﴾
55. They said: "We give you glad tidings in truth: be not then in despair!"	55. Qaaloo bashsharnaaka bilḥaqqi falaa takum-minal-qaaniṭeen.	قَالُوا بَشَّرْنَاكَ بِالْحَقِّ فَلَا تَكُن مِّنَ الْقَانِطِينَ ﴿٥٥﴾
56. He said: "And who despairs of the mercy of his Lord, but such as go astray?"	56. Qaala wa mañy-yaqnaṭu mir-raḥmati Rabbiheee illaḍ-ḍaaalloon.	قَالَ وَمَن يَقْنَطُ مِن رَّحْمَةِ رَبِّهِ إِلَّا الضَّالُّونَ ﴿٥٦﴾
57. Abraham said: "What then is the business on which you (have come), O you messengers (of Allah)?"	57. Qaala famaa khaṭbukum ayyuhal-mursaloon.	قَالَ فَمَا خَطْبُكُمْ أَيُّهَا الْمُرْسَلُونَ ﴿٥٧﴾
58. They said: "We have been sent to a people (deep) in sin,	58. Qaalooo innaaa ursilnaaa ilaa qawmim-mujrimeen.	قَالُوا إِنَّا أُرْسِلْنَا إِلَىٰ قَوْمٍ مُّجْرِمِينَ ﴿٥٨﴾

ع ٣

وقف لازم

Ikhfa اخفاء · Ghunna غُنّہ · Ikhfa Meem Saakin اخفاء میم ساکن · Idghaam ادغام · Qalqala قلقلہ · Qalb قلب · Idghaam Meem Saakin ادغام میم ساکن

59. "Excepting the adherents of Lut: We are certainly (charged) to save them (from harm),- all -

59. Illaaa Aala Looṭ; innaa lamunajjoohum ajma'een.

إِلَّآ ءَالَ لُوطٍ ۖ إِنَّا لَمُنَجُّوهُمْ أَجْمَعِينَ ۝٥٩

60. "Except his wife, who, We have ascertained, will be among those who will lag behind."

60. Illam-ra-atahoo qaddarnaaa innahaa laminal-ghaabireen. **(Section 4)**

إِلَّا ٱمْرَأَتَهُۥ قَدَّرْنَآ ۙ إِنَّهَا لَمِنَ ٱلْغَٰبِرِينَ ۝٦٠

61. At length when the messengers arrived among the adherents of Lut,

61. Falammaa jaaa'a Aala Looṭinil-mursaloon.

فَلَمَّا جَآءَ ءَالَ لُوطٍ ٱلْمُرْسَلُونَ ۝٦١

62. He said: "You appear to be uncommon folk."

62. Qaala innakum qawmum-munkaroon.

قَالَ إِنَّكُمْ قَوْمٌ مُّنكَرُونَ ۝٦٢

63. They said: "Yes, we have come to you to accomplish that of which they doubt.

63. Qaaloo bal ji'naaka bimaa kaanoo feehi yamtaroon.

قَالُوا۟ بَلْ جِئْنَٰكَ بِمَا كَانُوا۟ فِيهِ يَمْتَرُونَ ۝٦٣

64. "We have brought to you that which is inevitably due, and assuredly we tell the truth.

64. Wa ataynaaka bilḥaqqi wa innaa laṣaadiqoon.

وَأَتَيْنَٰكَ بِٱلْحَقِّ وَإِنَّا لَصَٰدِقُونَ ۝٦٤

65. "Then travel by night with your household, when a portion of the night (yet remains), and do you bring up the rear: let no one amongst you look back, but pass on whither you are ordered."

65. Fa-asri bi-ahlika biqiṭ'im-minal-layli wattabi' adbaarahum wa laa yaltafit minkum aḥaduñw-wamḍoo ḥaysu tu'maroon.

فَأَسْرِ بِأَهْلِكَ بِقِطْعٍ مِّنَ ٱلَّيْلِ وَٱتَّبِعْ أَدْبَٰرَهُمْ وَلَا يَلْتَفِتْ مِنكُمْ أَحَدٌ وَٱمْضُوا۟ حَيْثُ تُؤْمَرُونَ ۝٦٥

66. And We made known this decree to him, that the last remnants of those (sinners) should be cut off by the morning.

66. Wa qaḍaynaaa ilayhi zaalikal-amra anna daabira haaa'ulaaa'i maqṭoo'um-muṣbiḥeen.

وَقَضَيْنَآ إِلَيْهِ ذَٰلِكَ ٱلْأَمْرَ أَنَّ دَابِرَ هَٰٓؤُلَآءِ مَقْطُوعٌ مُّصْبِحِينَ ۝٦٦

67. The inhabitants of the city came in (mad) joy (at news of the young men).

67. Wa jaaa'a ahlul-madeenati yastabshiroon.

وَجَآءَ أَهْلُ ٱلْمَدِينَةِ يَسْتَبْشِرُونَ ۝٦٧

68. Lut said: "These are my guests: do not me disgrace:

68. Qaala inna haaa'ulaaa'i ḍayfee falaa tafḍaḥoon.

قَالَ إِنَّ هَٰٓؤُلَآءِ ضَيْفِى فَلَا تَفْضَحُونِ ۝٦٨

69. "But fear Allah, and shame me not."

69. Wattaqul-laaha wa laa tukhzoon.

وَٱتَّقُوا۟ ٱللَّهَ وَلَا تُخْزُونِ ۝٦٩

70. They said: "Did we not forbid you (to speak) for all and sundry?"

70. Qaalooo awalam nanhaka 'anil-'aalameen.

قَالُوٓا۟ أَوَلَمْ نَنْهَكَ عَنِ ٱلْعَٰلَمِينَ ۝٧٠

71. He said: "There are my daughters (to marry), if you must act (so)."

71. Qaala haaa'ulaaa'i banaateee in kuntum faa'ileen.

قَالَ هَٰٓؤُلَآءِ بَنَاتِىٓ إِن كُنتُمْ فَٰعِلِينَ ۝٧١

72. Verily, by your life (O Prophet), in their wild intoxication, they wander in distraction, to and fro.

72. La'amruka innahum lafee sakratihim ya'mahoon.

لَعَمْرُكَ إِنَّهُمْ لَفِى سَكْرَتِهِمْ يَعْمَهُونَ ۝٧٢

73. But the (mighty) Blast overtook them before morning,

73. Fa-akhazat-humuṣ-ṣayḥatu mushriqeen.

فَأَخَذَتْهُمُ ٱلصَّيْحَةُ مُشْرِقِينَ ۝٧٣

74. And We turned (the cities) upside down, and rained down on them brimstones hard as baked clay.

74. Faja'alnaa 'aaliyahaa saafilahaa wa amṭarnaa 'alayhim ḥijaaratam-min sijjeel.

فَجَعَلْنَا عَٰلِيَهَا سَافِلَهَا وَأَمْطَرْنَا عَلَيْهِمْ حِجَارَةً مِّن سِجِّيلٍ ۝٧٤

75. Behold! in this are Signs for those who by tokens do understand.

75. Inna fee zaalika la-Aayaatil-lilmutawassimeen.

إِنَّ فِى ذَٰلِكَ لَءَايَٰتٍ لِّلْمُتَوَسِّمِينَ ۝٧٥

Ikhfa اخفاء | Ghunna غنّہ | Ikhfa Meem Saakin اخفاء میم ساکن | Idghaam ادغام | Qalqala قلقلہ | Qalb قلب | Idghaam Meem Saakin ادغام میم ساکن

76. And the (cities were) right on the high-road.	76. Wa innahaa labi-sabeelim-muqeem.	وَإِنَّهَا لَبِسَبِيلٍ مُّقِيمٍ ﴿٧٦﴾
77. Behold! in this is a Sign for those who believe!	77. Inna fee ẕaalika la-Aayatal-lilmu'mineen.	إِنَّ فِي ذَٰلِكَ لَآيَةً لِّلْمُؤْمِنِينَ ﴿٧٧﴾
78. And the Companions of the Wood were also wrong-doers;	78. Wa in kaana Aṣḥaabul-Aykati lazaalimeen.	وَإِن كَانَ أَصْحَابُ الْأَيْكَةِ لَظَالِمِينَ ﴿٧٨﴾
79. So We exacted retribution from them. They were both on an open highway, plain to see.	79. Fantaqamnaa minhum wa innahumaa labi-imaamim-mubeen. **(Section 5)**	فَانتَقَمْنَا مِنْهُمْ وَإِنَّهُمَا لَبِإِمَامٍ مُّبِينٍ ﴿٧٩﴾
80. The Companions of the Rocky Tract also rejected the Messengers:	80. Wa laqad kaẕẕaba Aṣḥaabul-Ḥijril-mursaleen.	وَلَقَدْ كَذَّبَ أَصْحَابُ الْحِجْرِ الْمُرْسَلِينَ ﴿٨٠﴾
81. We sent them Our Sings, but they persisted in turning away from them.	81. Wa aataynaahum Aayaatinaa fakaanoo 'anhaa mu'riḍeen.	وَآتَيْنَاهُمْ آيَاتِنَا فَكَانُوا عَنْهَا مُعْرِضِينَ ﴿٨١﴾
82. Out of the mountains did they hew (their) edifices, (feeling themselves) secure.	82. Wa kaanoo yanḥitoona minal-jibaali buyootan aamineen.	وَكَانُوا يَنْحِتُونَ مِنَ الْجِبَالِ بُيُوتًا آمِنِينَ ﴿٨٢﴾
83. But the (mighty) Blast seized them of a morning,	83. Fa-akhaẕat-humuṣ-ṣayḥatu muṣbiḥeen.	فَأَخَذَتْهُمُ الصَّيْحَةُ مُصْبِحِينَ ﴿٨٣﴾
84. And of no avail to them was all that they did (with such art and care)!	84. Famaaa aghnaa 'anhum maa kaanoo yaksiboon.	فَمَا أَغْنَىٰ عَنْهُم مَّا كَانُوا يَكْسِبُونَ ﴿٨٤﴾
85. We did not create the heavens, the earth, and all between them, but for just ends. And the Hour is surely coming (when this will be manifest). So overlook (any human faults) with gracious forgiveness.	85. Wa maa khalaqnas-samaawaati wal-arḍa wa maa baynahumaaa illaa bilḥaqq; wa innas-Saa'ata la-aatiyatun faṣfaḥiṣ-ṣafḥal-jameel.	وَمَا خَلَقْنَا السَّمَاوَاتِ وَالْأَرْضَ وَمَا بَيْنَهُمَا إِلَّا بِالْحَقِّ ۗ وَإِنَّ السَّاعَةَ لَآتِيَةٌ ۖ فَاصْفَحِ الصَّفْحَ الْجَمِيلَ ﴿٨٥﴾
86. For verily it is your Lord Who is the Master-Creator, knowing all things.	86. Inna Rabbaka Huwal-khallaaqul-'aleem.	إِنَّ رَبَّكَ هُوَ الْخَلَّاقُ الْعَلِيمُ ﴿٨٦﴾
87. And We have bestowed upon you the Seven Oft-repeated (verses) and the Grand Qur'an.	87. Wa laqad aataynaaka sab'am-minal-masaanee wal-Qur-aanal-'Aẓeem.	وَلَقَدْ آتَيْنَاكَ سَبْعًا مِّنَ الْمَثَانِي وَالْقُرْآنَ الْعَظِيمَ ﴿٨٧﴾
88. Do not strain your eyes (wistfully) at what We have bestowed on certain classes of them, nor grieve over them: but lower your wing (in gentleness) to the believers.	88. Laa tamuddanna 'aynayka ilaa maa matta'naa biheee azwaajam-minhum wa laa taḥzan 'alayhim wakhfiḍ janaaḥaka lilmu'mineen.	لَا تَمُدَّنَّ عَيْنَيْكَ إِلَىٰ مَا مَتَّعْنَا بِهِ أَزْوَاجًا مِّنْهُمْ وَلَا تَحْزَنْ عَلَيْهِمْ وَاخْفِضْ جَنَاحَكَ لِلْمُؤْمِنِينَ ﴿٨٨﴾
89. And say: "I am indeed he that warns openly and without ambiguity,"-	89. Wa qul inneee ananna-ẕeerul-mubeen.	وَقُلْ إِنِّي أَنَا النَّذِيرُ الْمُبِينُ ﴿٨٩﴾
90. (Of just such wrath) as We sent down on those who divided (Scripture into arbitrary parts),-	90. Kamaaa anzalnaa 'alal-muqtasimeen.	كَمَا أَنزَلْنَا عَلَى الْمُقْتَسِمِينَ ﴿٩٠﴾
91. (So also on such) as have made Qur'an into shreds (as they please).	91. Allaẕeena ja'alul-Qur-aana 'iḍeen.	الَّذِينَ جَعَلُوا الْقُرْآنَ عِضِينَ ﴿٩١﴾
92. Therefore, by the Lord, We will, of a surety, call them to account,	92. Fawa Rabbika lanas'alannahum ajma'eena.	فَوَرَبِّكَ لَنَسْأَلَنَّهُمْ أَجْمَعِينَ ﴿٩٢﴾

وقف لازم

Ikhfa اخفاء · Ghunna غنّہ · Ikhfa Meem Saakin اخفاء میم ساکن · Idghaam ادغام · Qalqala قلقلہ · Qalb قلب · Idghaam Meem Saakin ادغام میم ساکن

الربع

93. For all their deeds.

93. **'Ammaa** kaanoo ya'ma-loon.

عَمَّا كَانُوا يَعْمَلُونَ ٩٣

94. Therefore expound openly what you are commanded, and turn away from those who join false gods with Allah.

94. Faṣda' bimaa tu'maru wa a'riḍ 'anil-mushrikeen.

فَاصْدَعْ بِمَا تُؤْمَرُ وَأَعْرِضْ عَنِ الْمُشْرِكِينَ ٩٤

95. For sufficient are We to you against those who scoff,

95. Innaa kafaynaakal-mustahzi'een.

إِنَّا كَفَيْنَاكَ الْمُسْتَهْزِءِينَ ٩٥

96. Those who adopt, with Allah, another god: but soon will they come to know.

96. Allaẕeena yaj'aloona ma'al-laahi ilaahan aakhar; fasawfa ya'lamoon.

الَّذِينَ يَجْعَلُونَ مَعَ اللَّهِ إِلَٰهًا آخَرَ فَسَوْفَ يَعْلَمُونَ ٩٦

97. We do indeed know how your heart is distressed at what they say.

97. Wa laqad na'lamu annaka yaḍeequ ṣadruka bimaa yaqooloon.

وَلَقَدْ نَعْلَمُ أَنَّكَ يَضِيقُ صَدْرُكَ بِمَا يَقُولُونَ ٩٧

98. But celebrate the praises of your Lord, and be of those who prostrate themselves in adoration.

98. Fasabbiḥ biḥamdi Rabbika wa kum-minas-saajideen.

فَسَبِّحْ بِحَمْدِ رَبِّكَ وَكُنْ مِنَ السَّاجِدِينَ ٩٨

99. And serve your Lord until there come unto you the Hour that is Certain.

99. Wa'bud Rabbaka ḥattaa yaåtiyakal-yaqeen. **(Section 6)**

وَاعْبُدْ رَبَّكَ حَتَّىٰ يَأْتِيَكَ الْيَقِينُ ٩٩

16. The Bee

In the name of Allah, Most Gracious, Most Merciful.

Sûrat an-Naḥl–16

(Revealed at Makkah)

Bismillaahir Raḥmaanir Raḥeem

(١٦) سُورَةُ النَّحْلِ مَكِّيَّةٌ (٧٠)

بِسْمِ اللَّهِ الرَّحْمَٰنِ الرَّحِيمِ

1. (Inevitable) comes (to pass) the Command of Allah: seek you not then to hasten it: glory to Him, and far is He above having the partners they ascribe to Him!

1. Ataaa amrul-laahi falaa tasta'jilooh; Subḥaanahoo wa Ta'aalaa 'ammaa yushrikoon.

أَتَىٰ أَمْرُ اللَّهِ فَلَا تَسْتَعْجِلُوهُ سُبْحَانَهُ وَتَعَالَىٰ عَمَّا يُشْرِكُونَ ١

2. He sends down His angels with inspiration of His Command, to such of His servants as He pleases, (saying): "Warn (Man) that there is no god but I: so do your duty unto Me."

2. Yunazzilul-malaaa'ikata birrooḥi min amrihee 'alaa mañy-yashaaa'u min 'ibaadiheee an anzirooo annahoo laaa ilaaha illaaa ana fattaqoon.

يُنَزِّلُ الْمَلَائِكَةَ بِالرُّوحِ مِنْ أَمْرِهِ عَلَىٰ مَنْ يَشَاءُ مِنْ عِبَادِهِ أَنْ أَنْذِرُوا أَنَّهُ لَا إِلَٰهَ إِلَّا أَنَا فَاتَّقُونِ ٢

3. He has created the heavens and the earth for just ends: far is He above having the partners they ascribe to Him!

3. Khalaqas-samaawaati wal-arḍa bilḥaqq; Ta'aalaa 'ammaa yushrikoon.

خَلَقَ السَّمَاوَاتِ وَالْأَرْضَ بِالْحَقِّ تَعَالَىٰ عَمَّا يُشْرِكُونَ ٣

4. He has created man from a sperm-drop; and behold this same (man) becomes an open disputer!

4. Khalaqal-insaana min nuṭfatin fa-izaa huwa khaṣeemum-mubeen.

خَلَقَ الْإِنْسَانَ مِنْ نُطْفَةٍ فَإِذَا هُوَ خَصِيمٌ مُبِينٌ ٤

5. And He has created cattle for you (men): from them you derive warmth, and numerous benefits, and of their (meat) you eat.

5. Wal-an'aama khalaqahaa; lakum feehaa dif'uñw-wa manaafi'u wa minhaa taåkuloon.

وَالْأَنْعَامَ خَلَقَهَا لَكُمْ فِيهَا دِفْءٌ وَمَنَافِعُ وَمِنْهَا تَأْكُلُونَ ٥

Ikhfa اخفاء | Ghunna غنّہ | Ikhfa Meem Saakin اخفاء میم ساکن | Idghaam ادغام | Qalqala قلقلہ | Qalb قلب | Idghaam Meem Saakin ادغام میم ساکن

6. And you have a sense of pride and beauty in them as you drive them home in the evening, and as you lead them forth to pasture in the morning.

6. Wa lakum feehaa jamaa-lun ḥeena tureeḥoona wa ḥeena tasraḥoon.

وَلَكُمْ فِيهَا جَمَالٌ حِينَ تُرِيحُونَ
وَحِينَ تَسْرَحُونَ ﴿٦﴾

7. And they carry your heavy loads to lands that you could not (otherwise) reach except with souls distressed: for your Lord is indeed Most Kind, Most Merciful,

7. Wa taḥmilu as̱qaalakum ilaa baladil-lam takoonoo baaligheehi illaa bishiqqil anfus; inna Rabbakum la-Ra'oofur-Raḥeem.

وَتَحْمِلُ أَثْقَالَكُمْ إِلَىٰ بَلَدٍ لَّمْ
تَكُونُوا بَالِغِيهِ إِلَّا بِشِقِّ الْأَنفُسِ ۚ
إِنَّ رَبَّكُمْ لَرَءُوفٌ رَّحِيمٌ ﴿٧﴾

8. And (He has created) horses, mules, and donkeys, for you to ride and use for show; and He has created (other) things of which you have no knowledge.

8. Walkhayla wal-bighaala wal-ḥameera litarkaboohaa wa zeenah; wa yakhluqu maa laa ta'lamoon.

وَالْخَيْلَ وَالْبِغَالَ وَالْحَمِيرَ
لِتَرْكَبُوهَا وَزِينَةً ۚ وَيَخْلُقُ مَا
لَا تَعْلَمُونَ ﴿٨﴾

9. And to Allah leads straight the Way, but there are ways that turn aside: if Allah had willed, He could have guided all of you.

9. Wa 'alal-laahi qaṣdus-sabeeli wa minhaa jaaa'ir; wa law shaaa'a lahadaakum ajma'een. **(Section 1)**

وَعَلَى اللَّهِ قَصْدُ السَّبِيلِ وَمِنْهَا
جَائِرٌ ۚ وَلَوْ شَاءَ لَهَدَاكُمْ
أَجْمَعِينَ ﴿٩﴾

10. It is He who sends down rain from the sky: from it you drink, and out of it (grows) the vegetation on which you feed your cattle.

10. Huwal-lazeee anzala minas-samaaa'i maaa'al-lakum minhu sharaabuñw-wa minhu shajarun feehi tuseemoon.

هُوَ الَّذِي أَنزَلَ مِنَ السَّمَاءِ
مَاءً لَّكُم مِّنْهُ شَرَابٌ وَمِنْهُ شَجَرٌ
فِيهِ تُسِيمُونَ ﴿١٠﴾

11. With it He produces for you corn, olives, date-palms, grapes and every kind of fruit: verily in this is a Sign for those who give thought.

11. Yumbitu lakum bihiz-zar'a wazzaytoona wanna-kheela wal-a'naaba wa min kullis̱-s̱amaraat; inna fee zaalika la-Aayatal-liqawmiñy-yatafakkaroon.

يُنبِتُ لَكُم بِهِ الزَّرْعَ وَالزَّيْتُونَ
وَالنَّخِيلَ وَالْأَعْنَابَ وَمِن كُلِّ
الثَّمَرَاتِ ۗ إِنَّ فِي ذَٰلِكَ لَآيَةً
لِّقَوْمٍ يَتَفَكَّرُونَ ﴿١١﴾

12. He has made subject to you the Night and the Day; the Sun and the Moon; and the Stars are in subjection by His Command: verily in this are Signs for men who are wise.

12. Wa sakhkhara lakumul-layla wannahaara wash-shamsa walqamara wannujoomu musakhkharaatum-bi-amrih; inna fee zaalika la-Aayaatil-liqawmiñy-ya'qiloon.

وَسَخَّرَ لَكُمُ اللَّيْلَ وَالنَّهَارَ وَ
الشَّمْسَ وَالْقَمَرَ ۖ وَالنُّجُومُ مُسَخَّرَاتٌ
بِأَمْرِهِ ۗ إِنَّ فِي ذَٰلِكَ لَآيَاتٍ
لِّقَوْمٍ يَعْقِلُونَ ﴿١٢﴾

13. And the things on this earth which He has multiplied in varying colours (and qualities): verily in this is a sign for men who celebrate the praises of Allah (in gratitude).

13. Wa maa zara-a lakum fil-arḍi mukhtalifan alwaanuh; inna fee zaalika la-Aayatal-liqawmiñy-yazzakkaroon.

وَمَا ذَرَأَ لَكُمْ فِي الْأَرْضِ مُخْتَلِفًا
أَلْوَانُهُ ۗ إِنَّ فِي ذَٰلِكَ لَآيَةً
لِّقَوْمٍ يَذَّكَّرُونَ ﴿١٣﴾

14. It is He Who has made the sea subject,

14. Wa Huwal-lazee sakh-kharal-baḥra

وَهُوَ الَّذِي سَخَّرَ الْبَحْرَ

Ikhfa اخفاء | Ghunna غُنّہ | Ikhfa Meem Saakin اخفاءمایم ساکن | Idghaam ادغام | Qalqala قلقلہ | Qalb قلب | Idghaam Meem Saakin ادغام مایم ساکن

that you may eat thereof flesh that is fresh and tender, and that you may extract therefrom ornaments to wear; and you see the ships therein that plough the waves, that you may seek (thus) of the bounty of Allah and that you may be grateful.

litaåkuloo minhu laḥman ṭariyyañw-wa tastakhrijoo minhu ḥilyatan talbasoonahaa wa taral-fulka mawaakhira feehi wa litabtaghoo min faḍlihee wa la'allakum tashkuroon.

لِتَأْكُلُوا مِنْهُ لَحْمًا طَرِيًّا
وَّتَسْتَخْرِجُوا مِنْهُ حِلْيَةً
تَلْبَسُونَهَا ۚ وَتَرَى الْفُلْكَ مَوَاخِرَ
فِيهِ وَلِتَبْتَغُوا مِنْ فَضْلِهِ
وَلَعَلَّكُمْ تَشْكُرُونَ ﴿١٤﴾

15. And He has set up on the earth mountains standing firm, lest it should shake with you; and rivers and roads; that you may guide yourselves;

15. Wa alqaa fil-arḍi rawaasiya an tameeda bikum wa anhaarañw-wa subulal-la'allakum tahtadoon.

وَأَلْقَىٰ فِي الْأَرْضِ رَوَاسِيَ أَنْ
تَمِيدَ بِكُمْ وَأَنْهَارًا وَّسُبُلًا لَّعَلَّكُمْ
تَهْتَدُونَ ﴿١٥﴾

16. And marks and sign-posts; and by the stars (men) guide themselves.

16. Wa 'alaamaat; wa bin-najmi hum yahtadoon.

وَعَلٰمٰتٍ ۚ وَبِالنَّجْمِ هُمْ يَهْتَدُونَ ﴿١٦﴾

17. Is then He Who creates like one that creates not? Will you not receive admonition?

17. Afamañy-yakhluqu kamal-laa yakhluq; afalaa tazakkaroon.

أَفَمَنْ يَّخْلُقُ كَمَنْ لَّا يَخْلُقُ ۗ
أَفَلَا تَذَكَّرُونَ ﴿١٧﴾

18. If you would count up the favours of Allah, never would you be able to number them: for Allah is Oft-Forgiving, Most Merciful.

18. Wa in ta'uddoo ni'matal-laahi laa tuḥsoohaa; innal-laaha la-Ghafoorur-Raḥeem.

وَإِنْ تَعُدُّوا نِعْمَةَ اللهِ لَا تُحْصُوهَا ۗ
إِنَّ اللهَ لَغَفُورٌ رَّحِيمٌ ﴿١٨﴾

19. And Allah knows what you conceal, and what you reveal.

19. Wallaahu ya'lamu maa tusirroona wa maa tu'linoon.

وَاللهُ يَعْلَمُ مَا تُسِرُّونَ وَمَا
تُعْلِنُونَ ﴿١٩﴾

20. Those whom they invoke besides Allah create nothing and are themselves created.

20. Wallazeena yad'oona min doonil-laahi laa yakhluqoona shay'añw-wa hum yukhlaqoon.

وَالَّذِينَ يَدْعُونَ مِنْ دُونِ اللهِ
لَا يَخْلُقُونَ شَيْئًا وَّهُمْ يُخْلَقُونَ ﴿٢٠﴾

21. (They are things) dead, lifeless: nor do they know when they will be raised up.

21. Amwaatun ghayru aḥyaaa'iñw-wa maa yash'uroona ayyaana yub'asoon. **(Section 2)**

أَمْوَاتٌ غَيْرُ أَحْيَاءٍ ۚ وَمَا يَشْعُرُونَ
أَيَّانَ يُبْعَثُونَ ﴿٢١﴾

22. Your God (Allah) is One God (Allah): as to those who do not believe in the Hereafter, their hearts refuse to know, and they are arrogant.

22. Ilaahukum Ilaahuñw-Waaḥid; fallazeena laa yu'minoona bil-Aakhirati quloobuhum-munkiratuñw-wa hum-mustakbiroon.

إِلٰهُكُمْ إِلٰهٌ وَّاحِدٌ ۚ فَالَّذِينَ لَا
يُؤْمِنُونَ بِالْآخِرَةِ قُلُوبُهُمْ
مُّنْكِرَةٌ وَّهُمْ مُّسْتَكْبِرُونَ ﴿٢٢﴾

23. Undoubtedly Allah knows what they conceal, and what they reveal: verily He loves not the arrogant.

23. Laa jarama annal-laaha ya'lamu maa yusirroona wa maa yu'linoon; innahoo laa yuḥibbul-mustakbireen.

لَا جَرَمَ أَنَّ اللهَ يَعْلَمُ مَا يُسِرُّونَ
وَمَا يُعْلِنُونَ ۚ إِنَّهُ لَا يُحِبُّ
الْمُسْتَكْبِرِينَ ﴿٢٣﴾

24. When it is said to them, "What is it that your Lord has

24. Wa izaa qeela lahum-maazaaa anzala

وَإِذَا قِيلَ لَهُمْ مَّاذَا أَنْزَلَ

Ikhfa اخفاء | Ghunna غنّہ | Ikhfa Meem Saakin اخفاء میم ساکن | Idghaam ادغام | Qalqala قلقلہ | Qalb قلب | Idghaam Meem Saakin ادغام میم ساکن

Translation	Transliteration	Arabic
revealed?" they say, "Tales of the ancients!"	Rabbukum qaalooo asaaṭeerul-awwaleen.	رَبُّكُمْ ۙ قَالُوْٓا اَسَاطِيْرُ الْاَوَّلِيْنَ ﴿٢٤﴾
25. Let them bear, on the Day of Judgment, their own burdens in full, and also (something) of the burdens of those without knowledge, whom they misled. Alas, how grievous the burdens they will bear!	25. Liyaḥmilooo awzaarahum kaamilatañy-Yawmal-Qiyaamati wa min awzaaril-lazeena yuḍilloonahum bighayri 'ilm; alaa saaa'a maa yaziroon. **(Section 3)**	لِيَحْمِلُوْٓا اَوْزَارَهُمْ كَامِلَةً يَّوْمَ الْقِيٰمَةِ ۙ وَمِنْ اَوْزَارِ الَّذِيْنَ يُضِلُّوْنَهُمْ بِغَيْرِ عِلْمٍ ؕ اَلَا سَآءَ مَا يَزِرُوْنَ ﴿٢٥﴾ ع
26. Those before them did also plot (against Allah's Way): but Allah took their structures from their foundations, and the roof fell down on them from above; and the Wrath seized them from directions they did not perceive.	26. Qad makaral-lazeena min qablihim fa-atal-laahu bunyaanahum-minal-qawaa'idi fakharra 'alayhimus-saqfu min fawqihim wa ataahumul-'azaabu min ḥaysu laa yash'uroon.	قَدْ مَكَرَ الَّذِيْنَ مِنْ قَبْلِهِمْ فَاَتَى اللّٰهُ بُنْيَانَهُمْ مِّنَ الْقَوَاعِدِ فَخَرَّ عَلَيْهِمُ السَّقْفُ مِنْ فَوْقِهِمْ وَاَتٰىهُمُ الْعَذَابُ مِنْ حَيْثُ لَا يَشْعُرُوْنَ ﴿٢٦﴾
27. Then, on the Day of Judgment, He will cover them with shame, and say: "Where are My 'partners' concerning whom you used to dispute (with the godly)?" Those endued with knowledge will say: "This Day, indeed, are the Unbelievers covered with Shame and Misery,-	27. Summa Yawmal-Qiyaamati yukhzeehim wa yaqoolu ayna shurakaaa'iyal-lazeena kuntum tushaaaqqoona feehim; qaalal-lazeena ootul-'ilma innal-khizyal-Yawma wassooo'a 'alal-kaafireen.	ثُمَّ يَوْمَ الْقِيٰمَةِ يُخْزِيْهِمْ وَيَقُوْلُ اَيْنَ شُرَكَآءِيَ الَّذِيْنَ كُنْتُمْ تُشَآقُّوْنَ فِيْهِمْ ؕ قَالَ الَّذِيْنَ اُوْتُوا الْعِلْمَ اِنَّ الْخِزْيَ الْيَوْمَ وَالسُّوْٓءَ عَلَى الْكٰفِرِيْنَ ﴿٢٧﴾
28. "(Namely) those whose lives the angels take in a state of wrong-doing to their own souls." Then would they offer submission (with the pretence), "We did no evil (knowingly)." (The angels will reply), "Nay, but verily Allah knows all that you did;	28. Allazeena tatawaf-faahumul-malaaa'ikatu ẓaalimeee anfusihim fa-alqawus-salama maa kunnaa na'malu min sooo'; balaaa innal-laaha 'aleemum bimaa kuntum ta'maloon.	الَّذِيْنَ تَتَوَفّٰىهُمُ الْمَلٰٓئِكَةُ ظَالِمِيْٓ اَنْفُسِهِمْ ۪ فَاَلْقَوُا السَّلَمَ مَا كُنَّا نَعْمَلُ مِنْ سُوْٓءٍ ؕ بَلٰٓى اِنَّ اللّٰهَ عَلِيْمٌ بِمَا كُنْتُمْ تَعْمَلُوْنَ ﴿٢٨﴾
29. "So enter the gates of Hell, to dwell therein. Thus evil indeed is the abode of the arrogant."	29. Fadkhulooo abwaaba Jahannama khaalideena feehaa falabi'sa maswal-mutakabbireen.	فَادْخُلُوْٓا اَبْوَابَ جَهَنَّمَ خٰلِدِيْنَ فِيْهَا ؕ فَلَبِئْسَ مَثْوَى الْمُتَكَبِّرِيْنَ ﴿٢٩﴾
30. To the righteous (when) it is said, "What is it that your Lord has revealed?" they say, "All that is good." To those who do good, there is good in this world, and the Home of the Hereafter is even better and excellent indeed is the Home of the righteous,-	30. Wa qeela lillazeenattaqaw maazaaa anzala Rabbukum; qaaloo khayraa; lillazeena aḥsanoo fee haazihid-dunyaa ḥasanah; wa la-Daarul-Aakhirati khayr; wa lani'ma daarul-muttaqeen.	وَقِيْلَ لِلَّذِيْنَ اتَّقَوْا مَاذَآ اَنْزَلَ رَبُّكُمْ ؕ قَالُوْا خَيْرًا ؕ لِلَّذِيْنَ اَحْسَنُوْا فِيْ هٰذِهِ الدُّنْيَا حَسَنَةٌ ؕ وَلَدَارُ الْاٰخِرَةِ خَيْرٌ ؕ وَلَنِعْمَ دَارُ الْمُتَّقِيْنَ ﴿٣٠﴾
31. Gardens of Eternity which they will enter: beneath them	31. Jannaatu 'Adniñy-yadkhuloonahaa tajree	جَنّٰتُ عَدْنٍ يَّدْخُلُوْنَهَا تَجْرِيْ

Ikhfa اخفاء | Ghunna غُنّہ | Ikhfa Meem Saakin اخفاء میم ساکن | Idghaam ادغام | Qalqala قلقلہ | Qalb قلب | Idghaam Meem Saakin ادغام میم ساکن

flow (pleasant) rivers: they will have therein all that they wish: thus Allah rewards the righteous,-

min taḥtihal-anhaaru lahum feehaa maa yashaaa'oon; kaẕaalika yajzil-laahul-muttaqeen.

مِنْ تَحْتِهَا الْاَنْهٰرُ لَهُمْ فِيْهَا مَا
يَشَآءُوْنَ ؕ كَذٰلِكَ يَجْزِى اللّٰهُ
الْمُتَّقِيْنَ ۙ ﴿٣١﴾

32. (Namely) those whose lives the angels take in a state of purity, saying (to them), "Peace be on you; you enter the Garden, because of (the good) which you did (in the world)."

32. Allaẕeena tatawaf-faahumul-malaaa'ikatu ṭayyibeena yaqooloona salaamun 'alaykumud-khulul-Jannata bimaa kuntum ta'maloon.

الَّذِيْنَ تَتَوَفّٰىهُمُ الْمَلٰٓئِكَةُ طَيِّبِيْنَ ۙ
يَقُوْلُوْنَ سَلٰمٌ عَلَيْكُمُ ۙ ادْخُلُوا
الْجَنَّةَ بِمَا كُنْتُمْ تَعْمَلُوْنَ ﴿٣٢﴾

33. Do the (ungodly) wait until the angels come to them, or there comes the Command of your Lord (for their doom)? So did those who went before them. But Allah did not wrong them: nay, they wronged their own souls.

33. Hal yanẓuroona illaaa an taåtiyahumul-malaaa'ikatu aw yaåtiya amru Rabbik; kaẕaalika fa'alal-laẕeena min qablihim; wa maa ẓalamahumul-laahu wa laakin kaanooo anfusahum yaẓlimoon.

هَلْ يَنْظُرُوْنَ اِلَّآ اَنْ تَاْتِيَهُمُ
الْمَلٰٓئِكَةُ اَوْ يَاْتِىَ اَمْرُ رَبِّكَ ؕ
كَذٰلِكَ فَعَلَ الَّذِيْنَ مِنْ قَبْلِهِمْ ؕ
وَمَا ظَلَمَهُمُ اللّٰهُ وَلٰكِنْ كَانُوْٓا
اَنْفُسَهُمْ يَظْلِمُوْنَ ﴿٣٣﴾

34. But the evil results of their deeds overtook them, and that very (Wrath) at which they had scoffed hemmed them in.

34. Fa-aṣaabahum sayyi-aatu maa 'amiloo wa ḥaaqa bihim maa kaanoo bihee yastahzi'oon.

(Section 4)

فَاَصَابَهُمْ سَيِّاٰتُ مَا عَمِلُوْا وَحَاقَ
بِهِمْ مَّا كَانُوْا بِهٖ يَسْتَهْزِءُوْنَ ﴿٣٤﴾ ع

35. The worshippers of false gods say: "If Allah had so willed, we should not have worshipped aught but Him - neither we nor our fathers,- nor should we have prescribed prohibitions other than His." So did those who went before them. But what is the mission of Messengers but to preach the Clear Message?

35. Wa qaalal-laẕeena ashrakoo law shaaa'al-laahu maa 'abadnaa min doonihee min shay'in-naḥnu wa laaa aabaaa'unaa wa laa ḥarramnaa min doonihee min shay'; kaẕaalika fa'alal-laẕeena min qablihim fahal 'alar-Rusuli illal-balaaghul-mubeen.

وَقَالَ الَّذِيْنَ اَشْرَكُوْا لَوْ شَآءَ اللّٰهُ
مَا عَبَدْنَا مِنْ دُوْنِهٖ مِنْ شَىْءٍ نَّحْنُ
وَلَآ اٰبَآؤُنَا وَلَا حَرَّمْنَا مِنْ دُوْنِهٖ
مِنْ شَىْءٍ ؕ كَذٰلِكَ فَعَلَ الَّذِيْنَ مِنْ
قَبْلِهِمْ ۚ فَهَلْ عَلَى الرُّسُلِ اِلَّا
الْبَلٰغُ الْمُبِيْنُ ﴿٣٥﴾

36. For We assuredly sent amongst every People a Messenger, (with the Command), "Serve Allah, and eschew Evil": of the People were some whom Allah guided, and some on whom error became inevitably (established). So travel through the earth, and see what was the end of those who denied (the Truth).

36. Wa laqad ba'asnaa fee kulli ummatir-Rasoolan ani'budul-laaha wajtanibuṭ-Ṭaaghoota faminhum man hadal-laahu wa minhum-man ḥaqqat 'alayhiḍ-ḍalaalah; faseeroo fil-arḍi fanẓuroo kayfa kaana 'aaqibatul-mukaẕẕibeen.

وَلَقَدْ بَعَثْنَا فِىْ كُلِّ اُمَّةٍ رَّسُوْلًا
اَنِ اعْبُدُوا اللّٰهَ وَاجْتَنِبُوا الطَّاغُوْتَ ۚ
فَمِنْهُمْ مَّنْ هَدَى اللّٰهُ وَمِنْهُمْ
مَّنْ حَقَّتْ عَلَيْهِ الضَّلٰلَةُ ؕ فَسِيْرُوْا
فِى الْاَرْضِ فَانْظُرُوْا كَيْفَ كَانَ
عَاقِبَةُ الْمُكَذِّبِيْنَ ﴿٣٦﴾

37. If you are anxious for their guidance, yet Allah

37. In taḥriṣ 'alaa hudaahum fa-innal-laaha

اِنْ تَحْرِصْ عَلٰى هُدٰىهُمْ فَاِنَّ اللّٰهَ

Ikhfa اخفاء | Ghunna غُنّہ | Ikhfa Meem Saakin اخفاء میم ساکن | Idghaam ادغام | Qalqala قلقلہ | Qalb قلب | Idghaam Meem Saakin ادغام میم ساکن

does not guid (any) such as He leaves to stray, and there is none to help them.

38. They swear their strongest oaths by Allah, that Allah will not raise up those who die: nay, but it is a promise (binding) on Him in truth: but most among mankind do not realise it not.

39. (They must be raised up), in order that He may manifest to them the truth of that wherein they differ, and that the rejecters of Truth may realise that they had indeed (surrendered to) Falsehood.

40. For to anything which We have willed, We but say the Word, "Be", and it is.

41. To those who leave their homes in the cause of Allah, after suffering oppression,- We will assuredly give a goodly home in this world; but truly the reward of the Hereafter will be greater. If they only realised (this)!

42. (They are) those who persevere in patience, and put their trust on their Lord.

43. And before you also the Messengers We sent were but men, to whom We granted inspiration: if you do not realise this, ask of those who possess the Message.

44. (We sent them) with Clear Signs and Books of dark prophesies; and We have sent down to you (also) the Message; that you may explain clearly to men what is sent for them, and that they may give thought.

45. Do then those who devise evil (plots) feel secure that Allah will not cause the earth to swallow them up, or that the Wrath will not seize them from directions they little perceive?-

laa yahdee mañy-yuḍillu wa maa lahum-min-naaṣireen.

38. Wa aqsamoo billaahi jahda aymaanihim laa yab'aṣul-laahu mañy-yamoot; balaa wa'dan 'alayhi ḥaqqañw-wa laakinna akṣaran-naasi laa ya'lamoon.

39. Liyubayyina lahumul-lazee yakhtalifoona feehi wa liya'lamal-lazeena kafarooo annahum kaanoo kaazibeen.

40. Innamaa qawlunaa lishay'in izaaa aradnaahu an-naqoola lahoo kun fa-yakoon. **(Section 5)**

41. Wallazeena haajaroo fil-laahi mim-ba'di maa ẓulimoo lanubawwi'annahum fid-dunyaa ḥasanatañw wa la-ajrul-Aakhirati akbar; law kaanoo ya'lamoon.

42. Allazeena ṣabaroo wa 'alaa Rabbihim yatawak-kaloon.

43. Wa maaa arsalnaa min qablika illaa rijaalan-nooḥeee ilayhim; fas'alooo ahlaz-zikri in kuntum laa ta'lamoon.

44. Bilbayyinaati waz-Zubur; wa anzalnaaa ilaykaz-Zikra litubayyina linnaasi maa nuzzila ilayhim wa la'allahum yatafakkaroon.

45. Afa-aminal-lazeena makarus-sayyi-aati añy-yakhsifal-laahu bihimul-arḍa aw yaå-tiyahumul-'azaabu min ḥaysu laa yash'uroon.

لَا يَهْدِىْ مَنْ يُّضِلُّ وَمَا لَهُمْ
مِّنْ نّٰصِرِيْنَ ۝٣٧
وَاَقْسَمُوْا بِاللّٰهِ جَهْدَ اَيْمَانِهِمْ ۙ
لَا يَبْعَثُ اللّٰهُ مَنْ يَّمُوْتُ ۭ بَلٰى
وَعْدًا عَلَيْهِ حَقًّا وَّلٰكِنَّ اَكْثَرَ
النَّاسِ لَا يَعْلَمُوْنَ ۝٣٨
لِيُبَيِّنَ لَهُمُ الَّذِىْ يَخْتَلِفُوْنَ
فِيْهِ وَلِيَعْلَمَ الَّذِيْنَ كَفَرُوْٓا اَنَّهُمْ
كَانُوْا كٰذِبِيْنَ ۝٣٩
اِنَّمَا قَوْلُنَا لِشَىْءٍ اِذَآ اَرَدْنٰهُ اَنْ
نَّقُوْلَ لَهٗ كُنْ فَيَكُوْنُ ۝٤٠ ع ٥/١٥
وَالَّذِيْنَ هَاجَرُوْا فِى اللّٰهِ مِنْۢ
بَعْدِ مَا ظُلِمُوْا لَنُبَوِّئَنَّهُمْ فِى
الدُّنْيَا حَسَنَةً ۭ وَلَاَجْرُ الْاٰخِرَةِ
اَكْبَرُ ۘ لَوْ كَانُوْا يَعْلَمُوْنَ ۝٤١ وقف لازم
الَّذِيْنَ صَبَرُوْا وَعَلٰى رَبِّهِمْ يَتَوَكَّلُوْنَ ۝٤٢
وَمَآ اَرْسَلْنَا مِنْ قَبْلِكَ اِلَّا رِجَالًا
نُّوْحِىْٓ اِلَيْهِمْ فَسْئَلُوْٓا اَهْلَ الذِّكْرِ
اِنْ كُنْتُمْ لَا تَعْلَمُوْنَ ۝٤٣
بِالْبَيِّنٰتِ وَالزُّبُرِ ۭ وَاَنْزَلْنَآ اِلَيْكَ
الذِّكْرَ لِتُبَيِّنَ لِلنَّاسِ مَا نُزِّلَ
اِلَيْهِمْ وَلَعَلَّهُمْ يَتَفَكَّرُوْنَ ۝٤٤ النّصف
اَفَاَمِنَ الَّذِيْنَ مَكَرُوا السَّيِّاٰتِ
اَنْ يَّخْسِفَ اللّٰهُ بِهِمُ الْاَرْضَ اَوْ
يَاْتِيَهُمُ الْعَذَابُ مِنْ حَيْثُ لَا
يَشْعُرُوْنَ ۝٤٥

Ikhfa اخفاء | Ghunna غُنّہ | Ikhfa Meem Saakin اخفاء میم ساکن | Idghaam ادغام | Qalqala قلقلہ | Qalb قلب | Idghaam Meem Saakin ادغام میم ساکن

46. Or that He may not call them to account in the midst of their goings to and fro, without a chance of their frustrating Him?

46. Aw yaâkhuzahum fee taqallubihim famaa hum bi-mu'jizeen.

أَوْ يَأْخُذَهُمْ فِي تَقَلُّبِهِمْ فَمَا هُم
بِمُعْجِزِينَ ﴿٤٦﴾

47. Or that He may not call them to account by a process of slow wastage - for your Lord is indeed full of kindness and mercy.

47. Aw yaâkhuzahum 'alaa takhawwuf; fa-inna Rabba-kum la-Ra'oofur-Raḥeem.

أَوْ يَأْخُذَهُمْ عَلَىٰ تَخَوُّفٍ فَإِنَّ
رَبَّكُمْ لَرَءُوفٌ رَّحِيمٌ ﴿٤٧﴾

48. Do they not look at Allah's creation, (even) among (inanimate) things,- how their (very) shadows turn round, from the right and the left, prostrating themselves to Allah, and that in the humblest manner?

48. Awa lam yaraw ilaa maa khalaqal-laahu min shay'iñy-yatafayya'u ẓilaaluhoo 'anil-yameeni washshamaaa'ili sujjadal-lillaahi wa hum daa-khiroon.

أَوَلَمْ يَرَوْا إِلَىٰ مَا خَلَقَ اللَّهُ مِن
شَيْءٍ يَتَفَيَّأُ ظِلَالُهُ عَنِ الْيَمِينِ
وَالشَّمَائِلِ سُجَّدًا لِّلَّهِ وَهُمْ دَاخِرُونَ ﴿٤٨﴾

49. And to Allah does obeisance all that is in the heavens and on earth, whether moving (living) creatures or the angels: for none are arrogant (before their Lord).

49. Wa lillaahi yasjudu maa fis-samaawaati wa maa fil-arḍi min daabbatiñw-walma-laaa'ikatu wa hum laa yastak-biroon.

وَلِلَّهِ يَسْجُدُ مَا فِي السَّمَاوَاتِ وَمَا
فِي الْأَرْضِ مِن دَابَّةٍ وَالْمَلَائِكَةُ
وَهُمْ لَا يَسْتَكْبِرُونَ ﴿٤٩﴾

50. They all revere their Lord, high above them, and they do all that they are commanded.

50. Yakhaafoona Rabbahum min fawqihim wa yaf'aloona maa yu'maroon. **(Section 6)**

يَخَافُونَ رَبَّهُم مِّن فَوْقِهِمْ وَيَفْعَلُونَ
مَا يُؤْمَرُونَ ﴿٥٠﴾

(Bow Down)

السجدة ٢

51. Allah has said: "Take not (for worship) two gods: for He is just One God (Allah): then fear Me (and Me alone)."

51. Wa qaalal-laahu laa tatta-khizooo ilaahaynis-nayni innamaa Huwa Ilaahuñw-Waa-ḥid; fa-iyyaaya farhaboon.

وَقَالَ اللَّهُ لَا تَتَّخِذُوا إِلَٰهَيْنِ اثْنَيْنِ
إِنَّمَا هُوَ إِلَٰهٌ وَاحِدٌ فَإِيَّايَ
فَارْهَبُونِ ﴿٥١﴾

52. To Him belongs whatever is in the heavens and on earth, and to Him is duty due always: then will you fear other than Allah?

52. Wa lahoo maa fis-samaa-waati wal-arḍi wa lahud-deenu waaṣibaa; afaghayral-laahi tattaqoon.

وَلَهُ مَا فِي السَّمَاوَاتِ وَالْأَرْضِ وَلَهُ
الدِّينُ وَاصِبًا أَفَغَيْرَ اللَّهِ تَتَّقُونَ ﴿٥٢﴾

53. And you have no good thing but is from Allah: and moreover, when you are touched by distress, to Him you cry with groans;

53. Wa maa bikum-min ni'matin faminal-laahi summa izaa massakumuḍ-ḍurru fa-ilayhi taj'aroon.

وَمَا بِكُم مِّن نِّعْمَةٍ فَمِنَ اللَّهِ ثُمَّ إِذَا
مَسَّكُمُ الضُّرُّ فَإِلَيْهِ تَجْأَرُونَ ﴿٥٣﴾

54. Yet, when He removes the distress from you, behold! some of you turn to other gods to join with their Lord-

54. Summa izaa kashafaḍ-ḍurra 'ankum izaa fareequm-minkum bi-Rabbihim yushri-koon.

ثُمَّ إِذَا كَشَفَ الضُّرَّ عَنكُمْ إِذَا
فَرِيقٌ مِّنكُم بِرَبِّهِمْ يُشْرِكُونَ ﴿٥٤﴾

55. (As if) to show their ingratitude for the favours we have bestowed on them! then enjoy (your brief day): but soon will you know (your folly)!

55. Liyakfuroo bimaa aatay-naahum; fatamatta'oo, fasawfa ta'lamoon.

لِيَكْفُرُوا بِمَا آتَيْنَاهُمْ فَتَمَتَّعُوا
فَسَوْفَ تَعْلَمُونَ ﴿٥٥﴾

56. And they (even) assign, to things they do not know, a portion out of that which We have bestowed for their sustenance! By Allah, you shall certainly be called to account for your false inventions.

56. Wa yaj'aloona limaa laa ya'lamoona naṣeebam-mimmaa razaqnaahum; tallaahi latus'alunna 'ammaa kuntum taftaroon.

وَيَجْعَلُونَ لِمَا لَا يَعْلَمُونَ نَصِيبًا
مِّمَّا رَزَقْنَاهُمْ تَاللَّهِ لَتُسْأَلُنَّ عَمَّا
كُنتُمْ تَفْتَرُونَ ﴿٥٦﴾

Ikhfa اخفاء | Ghunna غنّہ | Ikhfa Meem Saakin اخفاء میم ساکن | Idghaam ادغام | Qalqala قلقلہ | Qalb قلب | Idghaam Meem Saakin ادغام میم ساکن

57. And they assign daughters for Allah! - Glory be to Him! - and for themselves (sons,- the issue) they desire!

57. Wa yaj'aloona lillaahil-banaati Subhaanahoo wa lahum maa yashtahoon.

وَيَجْعَلُوْنَ لِلّٰهِ الْبَنٰتِ سُبْحٰنَهٗ ۙ وَلَهُمْ مَّا يَشْتَهُوْنَ ﴿٥٧﴾

58. When news is brought to one of them, of (the birth of) a female (child), his face darkens, and he is filled with inward grief!

58. Wa izaa bushshira ahaduhum bil-unsaa zalla wajhuhoo muswaddañw-wa huwa kazeem.

وَاِذَا بُشِّرَ اَحَدُهُمْ بِالْاُنْثٰى ظَلَّ وَجْهُهٗ مُسْوَدًّا وَّهُوَ كَظِيْمٌ ۚ ﴿٥٨﴾

59. With shame he hides himself from his people, because of the bad news he has had! Shall he retain it on (sufferance and) contempt, or bury it in the dust? Ah! what an evil (choice) they decide on?

59. Yatawaaraa minal-qawmi min sooo'i maa bushshira bih; a-yumsikuhoo 'alaa hoonin am yadussuhoo fit-turaab; alaa saaa'a maa yahkumoon.

يَتَوَارٰى مِنَ الْقَوْمِ مِنْ سُوْٓءِ مَا بُشِّرَ بِهٖ ؕ اَيُمْسِكُهٗ عَلٰى هُوْنٍ اَمْ يَدُسُّهٗ فِى التُّرَابِ ؕ اَلَا سَآءَ مَا يَحْكُمُوْنَ ﴿٥٩﴾

60. To those who believe not in the Hereafter, applies the similitude of evil: to Allah applies the highest similitude: for He is the Exalted in Power, full of Wisdom.

60. Lillazeena laa yu'minoona bil-Aakhirati masalus-saw'i wa lillaahil-masalul-a'laa; wa Huwal-'Azeezul-Hakeem. **(Section 7)**

لِلَّذِيْنَ لَا يُؤْمِنُوْنَ بِالْاٰخِرَةِ مَثَلُ السَّوْءِ ۚ وَلِلّٰهِ الْمَثَلُ الْاَعْلٰى ؕ وَهُوَ الْعَزِيْزُ الْحَكِيْمُ ﴿٦٠﴾ ع ١٤

61. If Allah were to punish men for their wrong-doing, He would not leave, on the (earth), a single living creature: but He gives them respite for a stated Term: when their Term expires, they would not be able to delay (the punishment) for a single hour, just as they would not be able to advance it (for a single hour).

61. Wa law yu'aakhizul-laahun-naasa bizulmihim-maa taraka 'alayhaa min daaabbatiñw-wa laakiñy-yu'akhkhiruhum ilaaa ajalim-musamman fa-izaa jaaa'a ajaluhum laa yastaåkhiroona saa'atañw-wa laa yastaqdimoon.

وَلَوْ يُؤَاخِذُ اللّٰهُ النَّاسَ بِظُلْمِهِمْ مَّا تَرَكَ عَلَيْهَا مِنْ دَآبَّةٍ وَّلٰكِنْ يُّؤَخِّرُهُمْ اِلٰٓى اَجَلٍ مُّسَمًّى ۚ فَاِذَا جَآءَ اَجَلُهُمْ لَا يَسْتَاْخِرُوْنَ سَاعَةً وَّلَا يَسْتَقْدِمُوْنَ ﴿٦١﴾

62. They attribute to Allah what they hate (for themselves), and their tongues assert the falsehood that all good things are for themselves: without doubt for them is the Fire, and they will be the first to be hastened on into it!

62. Wa yaj'aloona lillaahi maa yakrahoona wa tasifu alsinatuhumul-kaziba anna lahumul-husnaa laa jarama anna lahumun-Naara wa annahum-mufratoon.

وَيَجْعَلُوْنَ لِلّٰهِ مَا يَكْرَهُوْنَ وَتَصِفُ اَلْسِنَتُهُمُ الْكَذِبَ اَنَّ لَهُمُ الْحُسْنٰى ؕ لَا جَرَمَ اَنَّ لَهُمُ النَّارَ وَاَنَّهُمْ مُّفْرَطُوْنَ ﴿٦٢﴾

63. By Allah, We (also) sent (Our Messengers) to Peoples before you but Satan made, (to the wicked), their own acts seem alluring: He is also their patron today, but they shall have a most grievous Penalty.

63. Tallaahi laqad arsalnaaa ilaaa umamim-min qablika fazayyana lahumush-Shaytaanu a'maalahum fahuwa waliyyuhumul-yawma wa lahum 'azaabun aleem.

تَاللّٰهِ لَقَدْ اَرْسَلْنَآ اِلٰٓى اُمَمٍ مِّنْ قَبْلِكَ فَزَيَّنَ لَهُمُ الشَّيْطٰنُ اَعْمَالَهُمْ فَهُوَ وَلِيُّهُمُ الْيَوْمَ وَلَهُمْ عَذَابٌ اَلِيْمٌ ﴿٦٣﴾

64. And We sent down the Book to you for the express purpose, that you should make clear to them those things in which they differ,

64. Wa maaa anzalnaa 'alaykal-Kitaaba illaa litubayyina lahumul-lazikh-talafoo feehi

وَمَآ اَنْزَلْنَا عَلَيْكَ الْكِتٰبَ اِلَّا لِتُبَيِّنَ لَهُمُ الَّذِى اخْتَلَفُوْا فِيْهِ ۙ

Ikhfa اخفاء | Ghunna غُنّہ | Ikhfa Meem Saakin اخفاء میم ساکن | Idghaam ادغام | Qalqala قلقلہ | Qalb قلب | Idghaam Meem Saakin ادغام میم ساکن

English	Transliteration	Arabic
and that it should be a guide and a mercy to those who believe.	wa hudañw-wa raḥmatal-liqawmiñy-yu'minoon.	وَهُدًى وَّرَحْمَةً لِّقَوْمٍ يُّؤْمِنُوْنَ ﴿٦٤﴾
65. And Allah sends down rain from the skies, and gives therewith life to the earth after its death: verily in this is a Sign for those who listen.	65. Wallaahu anzala minas-samaaa'i maaa'an fa-aḥyaa bihil-arḍa ba'da mawtihaa; inna fee zaalika la-Aayatal-liqaw-miñy-yasma'oon. **(Section 8)**	وَاللّٰهُ اَنْزَلَ مِنَ السَّمَآءِ مَآءً فَاَحْيَا بِهِ الْاَرْضَ بَعْدَ مَوْتِهَا ۗ اِنَّ فِيْ ذٰلِكَ لَاٰيَةً لِّقَوْمٍ يَّسْمَعُوْنَ ﴿٦٥﴾ ع ٨ ١٤
66. And verily in cattle (too) will you find an instructive sign. From what is within their bodies between excretions and blood, We produce, for your drink, milk, pure and agreeable to those who drink it.	66. Wa inna lakum fil-an'aami la'ibrah; nusqeekum mimmaa fee buṭoonihee mim bayni farsiñw-wa damil-labanan khaaliṣan saaa'ighal-lish-shaaribeen.	وَاِنَّ لَكُمْ فِي الْاَنْعَامِ لَعِبْرَةً ۗ نُسْقِيْكُمْ مِّمَّا فِيْ بُطُوْنِهٖ مِنْۢ بَيْنِ فَرْثٍ وَّدَمٍ لَّبَنًا خَالِصًا سَآئِغًا لِّلشّٰرِبِيْنَ ﴿٦٦﴾
67. And from the fruit of the date-palm and the vine, you get out wholesome drink and food; behold, in this also is a Sign for those who are wise.	67. Wa min samaraatin-nakheeli wal-a'naabi tattakhi-zoona minhu sakarañw-wa riz-qan ḥasanaa; inna fee zaalika la-Aayatal-liqawmiñy-ya'qiloon.	وَمِنْ ثَمَرٰتِ النَّخِيْلِ وَالْاَعْنَابِ تَتَّخِذُوْنَ مِنْهُ سَكَرًا وَّرِزْقًا حَسَنًا ۗ اِنَّ فِيْ ذٰلِكَ لَاٰيَةً لِّقَوْمٍ يَّعْقِلُوْنَ ﴿٦٧﴾
68. And your Lord taught the Bee to build its cells in hills, on trees, and in (men's) habitations;	68. Wa awḥaa Rabbuka ilannaḥli anit-takhizee minal-jibaali buyootañw-wa minash-shajari wa mimmaa ya'rishoon.	وَاَوْحٰى رَبُّكَ اِلَى النَّحْلِ اَنِ اتَّخِذِيْ مِنَ الْجِبَالِ بُيُوْتًا وَّمِنَ الشَّجَرِ وَمِمَّا يَعْرِشُوْنَ ﴿٦٨﴾
69. Then to eat of all the produce (of the earth), and find with skill the spacious paths of its Lord: there issues from within their bodies a drink of varying colors, wherein is healing for men: verily in this is a Sign for those who give thought.	69. Summa kulee min kullis-samaraati faslukee subula Rabbiki zululaa; yakhruju mim buṭoonihaa sharaabum-mukh-talifun alwaanuhoo feehi shifaaa'ul-linnaas, inna fee zaalika la-Aayatal-liqawmiñy-yatafakkaroon.	ثُمَّ كُلِيْ مِنْ كُلِّ الثَّمَرٰتِ فَاسْلُكِيْ سُبُلَ رَبِّكِ ذُلُلًا ۗ يَخْرُجُ مِنْۢ بُطُوْنِهَا شَرَابٌ مُّخْتَلِفٌ اَلْوَانُهٗ فِيْهِ شِفَآءٌ لِّلنَّاسِ ۗ اِنَّ فِيْ ذٰلِكَ لَاٰيَةً لِّقَوْمٍ يَّتَفَكَّرُوْنَ ﴿٦٩﴾
70. It is Allah who creates you and takes your souls at death; and of you there are some who are sent back to a feeble age, so that they know nothing after having known (much): for Allah is All-Knowing, All-Powerful.	70. Wallaahu khalaqakum summa yatawaffaakum; wa minkum mañy-yuraddu ilaaa arzalil-'umuri likay laa ya'lama ba'da 'ilmin shay'aa; innal-laaha 'Aleemun Qadeer. **(Section 9)**	وَاللّٰهُ خَلَقَكُمْ ثُمَّ يَتَوَفّٰىكُمْ ۗ وَمِنْكُمْ مَّنْ يُّرَدُّ اِلٰٓى اَرْذَلِ الْعُمُرِ لِكَيْ لَا يَعْلَمَ بَعْدَ عِلْمٍ شَيْئًا ۗ اِنَّ اللّٰهَ عَلِيْمٌ قَدِيْرٌ ﴿٧٠﴾ ع ٩ ١٥
71. Allah has bestowed His gifts of sustenance more freely	71. Wallaahu faḍḍala ba'ḍa-kum 'alaa ba'ḍin	وَاللّٰهُ فَضَّلَ بَعْضَكُمْ عَلٰى بَعْضٍ

on some of you than on others: those more favored are not going to throw back their gifts to those whom their right hands possess, so as to be equal in that respect. Will they then deny the favors of Allah?

fir-rizq; famal-lazeena fuḍḍiloo biraaaddee rizqihim 'alaa maa malakat aymaanuhum fahum feehi sawaaa'; afabini'matil-laahi yajḥadoon.

فِي الرِّزْقِ ۚ فَمَا الَّذِينَ فُضِّلُوا
بِرَآدِّي رِزْقِهِمْ عَلَىٰ مَا مَلَكَتْ
أَيْمَانُهُمْ فَهُمْ فِيهِ سَوَآءٌ ؕ
أَفَبِنِعْمَةِ اللَّهِ يَجْحَدُونَ ﴿٧١﴾

72. And Allah has made for you mates (and companions) of your own nature, and made for you, out of them, sons and daughters and grandchildren, and provided for you sustenance of the best: will they then believe in vain things, and be ungrateful for Allah's favors?-

72. Wallaahu ja'ala lakum min anfusikum azwaajañw-wa ja'ala lakum min azwaajikum baneena wa ḥafadatañw-wa razaqakum minaṭ-ṭayyibaat; afabil-baaṭili yu'minoona wa bini'matil-laahi hum yakfuroon.

وَاللَّهُ جَعَلَ لَكُمْ مِنْ أَنْفُسِكُمْ
أَزْوَاجًا وَجَعَلَ لَكُمْ مِنْ أَزْوَاجِكُمْ
بَنِينَ وَحَفَدَةً وَرَزَقَكُمْ مِنَ
الطَّيِّبَاتِ ؕ أَفَبِالْبَاطِلِ يُؤْمِنُونَ
وَبِنِعْمَتِ اللَّهِ هُمْ يَكْفُرُونَ ﴿٧٢﴾ لا

73. And worship others than Allah,- such as have no power of providing them, for sustenance, with anything in heavens or earth, and cannot possibly have such power?

73. Wa ya'budoona min doonil-laahi maa laa yamliku lahum rizqam-minas-samaawaati wal-arḍi shay'añw-wa laa yastaṭee'oon.

وَيَعْبُدُونَ مِنْ دُونِ اللَّهِ مَا لَا
يَمْلِكُ لَهُمْ رِزْقًا مِنَ السَّمَاوَاتِ
وَالْأَرْضِ شَيْئًا وَلَا يَسْتَطِيعُونَ ﴿٧٣﴾ ج

74. Do not invent similitudes for Allah: for Allah knows, and you do not know.

74. Falaa taḍriboo lillaahil-amsaal; innal-laaha ya'lamu wa antum laa ta'lamoon.

فَلَا تَضْرِبُوا لِلَّهِ الْأَمْثَالَ ؕ إِنَّ
اللَّهَ يَعْلَمُ وَأَنْتُمْ لَا تَعْلَمُونَ ﴿٧٤﴾

75. Allah sets forth the Parable (of two men: one) a slave under the dominion of another; he has no power of any sort; and (the other) a man on whom We have bestowed goodly favors from Ourselves, and he spends thereof (freely), privately and publicly: are the two equal? (By no means;) praise be to Allah. But most of them understand not.

75. Ḍarabal-laahu masalan 'abdam-mamlookal-laa yaqdiru 'alaa shay'iñw-wa marrazaqnaahu minnaa rizqan ḥasanan fahuwa yunfiqu minhu sirrañw-wa jahra; hal yasta-woon; alḥamdu lillaah; bal aksaruhum laa ya'lamoon.

ضَرَبَ اللَّهُ مَثَلًا عَبْدًا مَمْلُوكًا
لَا يَقْدِرُ عَلَىٰ شَيْءٍ وَمَنْ رَزَقْنَاهُ
مِنَّا رِزْقًا حَسَنًا فَهُوَ يُنْفِقُ مِنْهُ
سِرًّا وَجَهْرًا ؕ هَلْ يَسْتَوُونَ ؕ الْحَمْدُ
لِلَّهِ ؕ بَلْ أَكْثَرُهُمْ لَا يَعْلَمُونَ ﴿٧٥﴾

76. Allah sets forth (another) Parable of two men: one of them dumb, with no power of any sort; a wearisome burden is he to his master; whichever way he directs him, he brings no good: is such a man equal with one who commands Justice, and is on a Straight Way?

76. Wa ḍarabal-laahu masalar-rajulayni aḥaduhumaaa abkamu laa yaqdiru 'alaa shay'iñw-wa huwa kallun 'alaa mawlaahu aynamaa yuwajjihhu laa yaåti bikhayrin hal yastawee huwa wa mañy-yaåmuru bil-'adli wa huwa 'alaa Ṣiraaṭim-Mustaqeem. **(Section 10)**

وَضَرَبَ اللَّهُ مَثَلًا رَجُلَيْنِ
أَحَدُهُمَا أَبْكَمُ لَا يَقْدِرُ عَلَىٰ شَيْءٍ
وَهُوَ كَلٌّ عَلَىٰ مَوْلَاهُ ۙ أَيْنَمَا
يُوَجِّهْهُ لَا يَأْتِ بِخَيْرٍ ؕ هَلْ
يَسْتَوِي هُوَ ۙ وَمَنْ يَأْمُرُ بِالْعَدْلِ ۙ
وَهُوَ عَلَىٰ صِرَاطٍ مُسْتَقِيمٍ ﴿٧٦﴾ ع

ع ١٢

77. To Allah belongs the Mystery of the heavens and the Earth.

77. Wa lillaahi ghaybus-samaawaati wal-arḍ;

وَلِلَّهِ غَيْبُ السَّمَاوَاتِ وَالْأَرْضِ ؕ

Ikhfa اخفاء | Ghunna غُنّہ | Ikhfa Meem Saakin اخفاء میم ساکن | Idghaam ادغام | Qalqala قلقلہ | Qalb قلب | Idghaam Meem Saakin ادغام میم ساکن

And the Decision of the Hour (of Judgment) is as the twinkling of an eye, or even quicker: for Allah has power over all things.

wa maaa amrus-Saa'ati illaa kalamḥil-baṣari aw huwa aqrab; innal-laaha 'alaa kulli shay'in Qadeer.

وَمَآ أَمْرُ السَّاعَةِ إِلَّا كَلَمْحِ الْبَصَرِ
أَوْ هُوَ أَقْرَبُ ۚ إِنَّ اللَّهَ عَلَىٰ كُلِّ
شَيْءٍ قَدِيرٌ ٧٧

78. It is He Who brought you forth from the wombs of your mothers when you knew nothing; and He gave you hearing and sight and intelligence and affections: that you may give thanks (to Allah).

78. Wallaahu akhrajakum mim buṭooni ummahaatikum laa ta'lamoona shay'añw-wa ja'ala lakumus-sam'a wal-abṣaara wal-af'idata la'allakum tashkuroon.

وَاللَّهُ أَخْرَجَكُم مِّنۢ بُطُونِ أُمَّهَٰتِكُمْ
لَا تَعْلَمُونَ شَيْـًٔا ۙ وَجَعَلَ لَكُمُ
السَّمْعَ وَالْأَبْصَٰرَ وَالْأَفْـِٔدَةَ ۙ
لَعَلَّكُمْ تَشْكُرُونَ ٧٨

79. Do they not look at the birds, held poised in the midst of (the air and) the sky? Nothing holds them up but (the power of) Allah. Verily in this are signs for those who believe.

79. Alam yaraw ilaṭ-ṭayri musakhkharaatin fee jawwis-samaaa'i maa yumsikuhunna illal-laah; inna fee zaalika la-Aayaatil-liqawmiñy-yu'minoon.

أَلَمْ يَرَوْا إِلَى الطَّيْرِ مُسَخَّرَٰتٍ
فِي جَوِّ السَّمَآءِ ۖ مَا يُمْسِكُهُنَّ إِلَّا
اللَّهُ ۗ إِنَّ فِي ذَٰلِكَ لَءَايَٰتٍ لِّقَوْمٍ
يُؤْمِنُونَ ٧٩

80. It is Allah Who made your habitations homes of rest and quiet for you; and made for you, out of the skins of animals, (tents for) dwellings, which you find so light (and handy) when you travel and when you stop (in your travels); and out of their wool, and their soft fibres (between wool and hair),and their hair, rich stuff and articles of convenience (to serve you) for a time.

80. Wallaahu ja'ala lakum mim buyootikum sakanañw-wa ja'ala lakum min juloodil an'aami buyootan tastakhif-foonahaa yawma ẓa'nikum wa yawma iqaamatikum wa min aṣwaafihaa wa awbaarihaa wa ash'aarihaaa asaasañw-wa mataa'an ilaa ḥeen.

وَاللَّهُ جَعَلَ لَكُم مِّنۢ بُيُوتِكُمْ
سَكَنًا وَجَعَلَ لَكُم مِّن جُلُودِ
الْأَنْعَٰمِ بُيُوتًا تَسْتَخِفُّونَهَا يَوْمَ
ظَعْنِكُمْ وَيَوْمَ إِقَامَتِكُمْ ۙ وَمِنْ
أَصْوَافِهَا وَأَوْبَارِهَا وَأَشْعَارِهَآ
أَثَٰثًا وَمَتَٰعًا إِلَىٰ حِينٍ ٨٠

81. It is Allah Who made out of the things He created, some things to give you shade; of the hills He made some for your shelter; He made you garments to protect you from heat, and coats of mail to protect you from your (mutual) violence. Thus He completes His favours on you, that you may bow to His Will (in Islam).

81. Wallaahu ja'ala lakum mimmaa khalaqa ẓilaalañw-wa ja'ala lakum-minal-jibaali aknaanañw-wa ja'ala lakum saraabeela taqeekumul-ḥarra wa saraabeela taqeekum baå-sakum; kazaalika yutimmu ni'matahoo 'alaykum la'allakum tuslimoon.

وَاللَّهُ جَعَلَ لَكُم مِّمَّا خَلَقَ ظِلَٰلًا
وَجَعَلَ لَكُم مِّنَ الْجِبَالِ أَكْنَٰنًا
وَجَعَلَ لَكُمْ سَرَٰبِيلَ تَقِيكُمُ
الْحَرَّ وَسَرَٰبِيلَ تَقِيكُم بَأْسَكُمْ ۚ
كَذَٰلِكَ يُتِمُّ نِعْمَتَهُۥ عَلَيْكُمْ
لَعَلَّكُمْ تُسْلِمُونَ ٨١

82. But if they turn away, your duty is only to preach the clear Message.

82. Fa-in tawallaw fa-innamaa 'alaykal-balaaghul-mubeen.

فَإِن تَوَلَّوْا فَإِنَّمَا عَلَيْكَ الْبَلَٰغُ
الْمُبِينُ ٨٢

83. They recognise the favours of Allah; then they deny them;

83. Ya'rifoona ni'matal-laahi summa yunkiroonahaa

يَعْرِفُونَ نِعْمَتَ اللَّهِ ثُمَّ يُنكِرُونَهَا

Ikhfa اخفاء | Ghunna غنّہ | Ikhfa Meem Saakin اخفاء میم ساکن | Idghaam ادغام | Qalqala قلقلہ | Qalb قلب | Idghaam Meem Saakin ادغام میم ساکن

and most of them are (creatures) ungrateful.

84. One Day We shall raise from all Peoples a Witness: then will no excuse be accepted from Unbelievers, nor will they receive any favors.

85. When the wrong-doers (actually) see the Penalty, then will it in no way be mitigated, nor will they then receive respite.

86. When those who gave partners to Allah will see their "partners", they will say: "Our Lord! these are our 'partners,' those whom we used to invoke besides you." But they will throw back their word at them (and say): "Indeed you are liars!"

87. That Day they shall (openly) show (their) submission to Allah; and all their inventions shall leave them in the lurch.

88. Those who reject Allah and hinder (men) from the Path of Allah - for them will We add Penalty to Penalty; for that they used to spread mischief.

89. One day We shall raise from all Peoples a witness against them, from amongst themselves: and We shall bring you as a witness against these (your people): and We have sent down to you the Book explaining all things, a Guide, a Mercy, and Glad Tidings to Muslims.

90. Allah commands justice, the doing of good, and liberality to kith and kin, and He forbids all shameful deeds, and injustice and rebellion: He instructs you, that you may receive admonition.

91. Fulfil the Covenant of Allah when you have entered into

wa aks̲aruhumul-kaafiroon.

(Section 11)

84. Wa yawma nab'as̲u min kulli ummatin shaheedan s̲umma laa yu'z̲anu lillaz̲eena kafaroo wa laa hum yusta'taboon.

85. Wa iz̲aa ra-al-laz̲eena ẓalamul-'az̲aaba falaa yukhaffafu 'anhum wa laa hum yunẓaroon.

86. Wa iz̲aa ra-al-laz̲eena ashrakoo shurakaaa'ahum qaaloo Rabbanaa haaa'ulaaa'i shurakaaa'unal-laz̲eena kunnaa nad'oo min doonika fa-alqaw ilayhimul-qawla innakum lakaaz̲iboon.

87. Wa alqaw ilal-laahi yawma'iz̲inis-salama wa ḍalla 'anhum-maa kaanoo yaftaroon.

88. Allaz̲eena kafaroo wa ṣaddoo 'an sabeelil-laahi zidnaahum 'az̲aaban fawqal-'az̲aabi bimaa kaanoo yufsidoon.

89. Wa yawma nab'as̲u fee kulli ummatin shaheedan 'alayhim-min anfusihim wa ji'naa bika shaheedan 'alaa haaa'ulaaa'; wa nazzalnaa 'alaykal-Kitaaba tibyaanal-likulli shay'iñw-wa hudañw-wa raḥmatañw-wa bushraa lilmuslimeen.

(Section 12)

90. Innal-laaha yaâmuru bil-'adli wal-iḥsaani wa eetaaa'i z̲il-qurbaa wa yanhaa 'anil-faḥshaaa'i walmunkari walbagh-y; ya'iẓukum la'allakum taz̲akkaroon.

91. Wa awfoo bi-Ahdil-laahi iz̲aa 'aahattum wa laa

وَأَكْثَرُهُمُ الْكٰفِرُونَ ﴿٨٣﴾
وَيَوْمَ نَبْعَثُ مِنْ كُلِّ أُمَّةٍ شَهِيدًا
ثُمَّ لَا يُؤْذَنُ لِلَّذِينَ كَفَرُوا وَلَا هُمْ
يُسْتَعْتَبُونَ ﴿٨٤﴾
وَإِذَا رَأَى الَّذِينَ ظَلَمُوا الْعَذَابَ فَلَا
يُخَفَّفُ عَنْهُمْ وَلَا هُمْ يُنْظَرُونَ ﴿٨٥﴾
وَإِذَا رَأَى الَّذِينَ أَشْرَكُوا شُرَكَاءَهُمْ
قَالُوا رَبَّنَا هٰؤُلَاءِ شُرَكَاؤُنَا الَّذِينَ
كُنَّا نَدْعُوا مِنْ دُونِكَ ۚ فَأَلْقَوْا
إِلَيْهِمُ الْقَوْلَ إِنَّكُمْ لَكٰذِبُونَ ﴿٨٦﴾
وَأَلْقَوْا إِلَى اللّٰهِ يَوْمَئِذٍ السَّلَمَ
وَضَلَّ عَنْهُمْ مَا كَانُوا يَفْتَرُونَ ﴿٨٧﴾
الَّذِينَ كَفَرُوا وَصَدُّوا عَنْ سَبِيلِ
اللّٰهِ زِدْنٰهُمْ عَذَابًا فَوْقَ الْعَذَابِ
بِمَا كَانُوا يُفْسِدُونَ ﴿٨٨﴾
وَيَوْمَ نَبْعَثُ فِي كُلِّ أُمَّةٍ شَهِيدًا
عَلَيْهِمْ مِنْ أَنْفُسِهِمْ وَجِئْنَا بِكَ
شَهِيدًا عَلٰى هٰؤُلَاءِ ۚ وَنَزَّلْنَا
عَلَيْكَ الْكِتٰبَ تِبْيَانًا لِكُلِّ
شَيْءٍ وَهُدًى وَرَحْمَةً وَبُشْرٰى
لِلْمُسْلِمِينَ ﴿٨٩﴾
إِنَّ اللّٰهَ يَأْمُرُ بِالْعَدْلِ وَالْإِحْسَانِ
وَإِيتَاءِ ذِي الْقُرْبٰى وَيَنْهٰى عَنِ
الْفَحْشَاءِ وَالْمُنْكَرِ وَالْبَغْيِ ۚ يَعِظُكُمْ
لَعَلَّكُمْ تَذَكَّرُونَ ﴿٩٠﴾
وَأَوْفُوا بِعَهْدِ اللّٰهِ إِذَا عٰهَدْتُّمْ وَلَا

Ikhfa اخفاء | Ghunna غنّہ | Ikhfa Meem Saakin اخفاء میم ساکن | Idghaam ادغام | Qalqala قلقلہ | Qalb قلب | Idghaam Meem Saakin ادغام میم ساکن

it, and break not your oaths after you have confirmed them; indeed you have made Allah your surety; for Allah knows all that you do.

tanquḍul-aymaana ba'da tawkeedihaa wa qad ja'altumul-laaha 'alaykum kafeelaa; innal-laaha ya'lamu maa taf'aloon.

تَنقُضُوا الْأَيْمَانَ بَعْدَ تَوْكِيدِهَا
وَقَدْ جَعَلْتُمُ اللَّهَ عَلَيْكُمْ كَفِيلًا ۚ
إِنَّ اللَّهَ يَعْلَمُ مَا تَفْعَلُونَ ﴿٩١﴾

92. And be not like a woman who breaks into untwisted strands the yarn which she has spun, after it has become strong. Nor take your oaths to practise deception between yourselves, lest one party should be more numerous than another: for Allah will test you by this; and on the Day of Judgment He will certainly make clear to you (the truth of) that wherein you disagree.

92. Wa laa takoonoo kallatee naqaḍat ghazlahaa mim ba'di quwwatin ankaasaa; tattakhi-zoona aymaanakum dakhalam baynakum an takoona ummatun hiya arbaa min ummah; innamaa yablookumul-laahu bih; wa la-yubayyinanna lakum Yawmal-Qiyaamati maa kuntum feehi takhtalifoon.

وَلَا تَكُونُوا كَالَّتِي نَقَضَتْ غَزْلَهَا
مِن بَعْدِ قُوَّةٍ أَنكَاثًا تَتَّخِذُونَ
أَيْمَانَكُمْ دَخَلًا بَيْنَكُمْ أَن تَكُونَ
أُمَّةٌ هِيَ أَرْبَىٰ مِنْ أُمَّةٍ ۚ إِنَّمَا
يَبْلُوكُمُ اللَّهُ بِهِ ۚ وَلَيُبَيِّنَنَّ لَكُمْ يَوْمَ
الْقِيَامَةِ مَا كُنتُمْ فِيهِ تَخْتَلِفُونَ ﴿٩٢﴾

93. If Allah so willed, He could make you all one People: but He leaves straying whom He pleases, and He guides whom He pleases: but you shall certainly be called to account for all your actions.

93. Wa law shaaa'al-laahu laja'alakum ummatañw-waaḥi-datañw-wa laakiñy-yuḍillu mañy-yashaaa'u wa yahdee mañy-yashaaa'; wa latus'alunna 'ammaa kuntum ta'maloon.

وَلَوْ شَاءَ اللَّهُ لَجَعَلَكُمْ أُمَّةً وَاحِدَةً
وَلَٰكِن يُضِلُّ مَن يَشَاءُ وَيَهْدِي
مَن يَشَاءُ ۚ وَلَتُسْأَلُنَّ عَمَّا كُنتُمْ
تَعْمَلُونَ ﴿٩٣﴾

94. And do not take your oaths, to practise deception between yourselves, with the result that someone's foot may slip after it was firmly planted, and you may have to taste the evil (consequences) of having hindered (men) from the Path of Allah, and a mighty Wrath descend on you.

94. Wa laa tattakhizooo aymaanakum dakhalam-bayna-kum fatazilla qadamum-ba'da subootihaa wa tazooqus-sooo'a bimaa ṣadattum 'an sabeelil-laahi wa lakum 'azaabun 'aẓeem.

وَلَا تَتَّخِذُوا أَيْمَانَكُمْ دَخَلًا بَيْنَكُمْ
فَتَزِلَّ قَدَمٌ بَعْدَ ثُبُوتِهَا وَتَذُوقُوا
السُّوءَ بِمَا صَدَدتُّمْ عَن سَبِيلِ
اللَّهِ ۖ وَلَكُمْ عَذَابٌ عَظِيمٌ ﴿٩٤﴾

95. Nor sell the Covenant of Allah for a miserable price: for with Allah is (a prize) far better for you, if you only knew.

95. Wa laa tashtaroo bi-'Ahdil-laahi samanan qaleelaa; innamaa 'indal-laahi huwa khayrul-lakum in kuntum ta'lamoon.

وَلَا تَشْتَرُوا بِعَهْدِ اللَّهِ ثَمَنًا قَلِيلًا ۚ
إِنَّمَا عِندَ اللَّهِ هُوَ خَيْرٌ لَّكُمْ إِن
كُنتُمْ تَعْلَمُونَ ﴿٩٥﴾

96. What is with you must vanish: what is with Allah will endure. And We will certainly bestow, on those who patiently persevere, their reward according to the best of their actions.

96. Maa 'indakum yanfadu wa maa 'indal-laahi baaq; wa lanajziyannal-lazeena ṣabarooo ajrahum bi-aḥsani maa kaanoo ya'maloon.

مَا عِندَكُمْ يَنفَدُ ۖ وَمَا عِندَ اللَّهِ
بَاقٍ ۗ وَلَنَجْزِيَنَّ الَّذِينَ صَبَرُوا
أَجْرَهُم بِأَحْسَنِ مَا كَانُوا يَعْمَلُونَ ﴿٩٦﴾

97. Whoever works righteousness, man or woman, and has Faith, verily, to him will We give a new Life, a life that is good and pure and We will bestow on such

97. Man 'amila saaliḥam-min zakarin aw unsaa wa huwa mu'minun falanuḥyiyannahoo ḥayaatan ṭayyibatañw wa lanajzi-yannahum

مَنْ عَمِلَ صَالِحًا مِّن ذَكَرٍ أَوْ
أُنثَىٰ وَهُوَ مُؤْمِنٌ فَلَنُحْيِيَنَّهُ
حَيَاةً طَيِّبَةً ۖ وَلَنَجْزِيَنَّهُمْ

Ikhfa اخفاء | Ghunna غُنّہ | Ikhfa Meem Saakin اخفاء میم ساکن | Idghaam ادغام | Qalqala قلقلہ | Qalb قلب | Idghaam Meem Saakin ادغام میم ساکن

their reward according to the best of their actions.

ajrahum bi-aḥsani maa kaanoo ya'maloon.

أَجْرَهُم بِأَحْسَنِ مَا كَانُوا يَعْمَلُونَ ٩٧

98. When you read the Qur'an, seek Allah's protection from Satan the rejected one.

98. Fa-iz̲aa qara-tal-Qur-aana fasta'iz̲ billaahi minash-Shayṭaanir-rajeem.

فَإِذَا قَرَأْتَ الْقُرْآنَ فَاسْتَعِذْ بِاللَّهِ
مِنَ الشَّيْطَانِ الرَّجِيمِ ٩٨

99. No authority has he over those who believe and put their trust in their Lord.

99. Innahoo laysa lahoo sulṭaanun 'alal-laz̲eena aamanoo wa 'alaa Rabbihim yatawakkaloon.

إِنَّهُ لَيْسَ لَهُ سُلْطَانٌ عَلَى الَّذِينَ
آمَنُوا وَعَلَىٰ رَبِّهِمْ يَتَوَكَّلُونَ ٩٩

100. His authority is over those only, who take him as patron and who join partners with Allah.

100. Innamaa sulṭaanuhoo 'alal-laz̲eena yatawallawnahoo wallaz̲eena hum bihee mushrikoon. **(Section 13)**

إِنَّمَا سُلْطَانُهُ عَلَى الَّذِينَ يَتَوَلَّوْنَهُ
وَالَّذِينَ هُم بِهِ مُشْرِكُونَ ١٠٠ ع ١٩

101. When We substitute one revelation for another,- and Allah knows best what He reveals (in stages),- they say, "You are but a forger": but most of them do not understand not.

101. Wa iz̲aa baddalnaaa Aayatam-makaana Aayatiñw-wallaahu a'lamu bimaa yunazzilu qaalooo innamaaa anta muftar; bal aks̲aruhum laa ya'lamoon.

وَإِذَا بَدَّلْنَا آيَةً مَّكَانَ آيَةٍ
وَاللَّهُ أَعْلَمُ بِمَا يُنَزِّلُ قَالُوا إِنَّمَا
أَنتَ مُفْتَرٍ ۚ بَلْ أَكْثَرُهُمْ
لَا يَعْلَمُونَ ١٠١

102. Say, the Holy Spirit has brought the revelation from your Lord in Truth, in order to strengthen those who believe, and as a Guide and Glad Tidings to Muslims.

102. Qul nazzalahoo Rooḥul-Qudusi mir-Rabbika bilḥaqqi liyus̲abbital-laz̲eena aamanoo wa hudañw-wa bushraa lilmuslimeen.

قُلْ نَزَّلَهُ رُوحُ الْقُدُسِ مِن
رَّبِّكَ بِالْحَقِّ لِيُثَبِّتَ الَّذِينَ آمَنُوا
وَهُدًى وَبُشْرَىٰ لِلْمُسْلِمِينَ ١٠٢

103. We know indeed that they say, "It is a man that teaches him." The tongue of him they wickedly point to is notably foreign, while this is Arabic, pure and clear.

103. Wa laqad na'lamu annahum yaqooloona innamaa yu'allimuhoo bashar; lisaanul-laz̲ee yulḥidoona ilayhi a'jamiyyuñw-wa haaz̲aa lisaanun 'Arabiyyum-mubeen.

وَلَقَدْ نَعْلَمُ أَنَّهُمْ يَقُولُونَ إِنَّمَا
يُعَلِّمُهُ بَشَرٌ ۗ لِّسَانُ الَّذِي
يُلْحِدُونَ إِلَيْهِ أَعْجَمِيٌّ وَهَٰذَا
لِسَانٌ عَرَبِيٌّ مُّبِينٌ ١٠٣

104. Those who do not believe in the Signs of Allah,- Allah will not guide them, and theirs will be a grievous Penalty.

104. Innal-laz̲eena laa yu'minoona bi-Aayaatil-laahi laa yahdeehimul-laahu wa lahum 'az̲aabun aleem.

إِنَّ الَّذِينَ لَا يُؤْمِنُونَ بِآيَاتِ
اللَّهِ لَا يَهْدِيهِمُ اللَّهُ وَلَهُمْ
عَذَابٌ أَلِيمٌ ١٠٤

105. It is those who do not believe in the Signs of Allah, that forge falsehood: it is they who lie!

105. Innamaa yaftaril-kaz̲ibal-laz̲eena laa yu'minoona bi-Aayaatil-laahi wa ulaaa'ika humul-kaaz̲iboon.

إِنَّمَا يَفْتَرِي الْكَذِبَ الَّذِينَ
لَا يُؤْمِنُونَ بِآيَاتِ اللَّهِ ۖ وَأُولَٰئِكَ
هُمُ الْكَاذِبُونَ ١٠٥

106. Any one who, after accepting faith in Allah, utters Unbelief,- except under compulsion, his heart remaining firm

106. Man kafara billaahi mim ba'di eemaaniheee illaa man ukriha wa qalbuhoo muṭ-ma'innum-

مَن كَفَرَ بِاللَّهِ مِن بَعْدِ إِيمَانِهِ
إِلَّا مَنْ أُكْرِهَ وَقَلْبُهُ مُطْمَئِنٌّ

Ikhfa اخفاء	Ghunna غنّہ	Ikhfa Meem Saakin اخفاء میم ساکن	Idghaam ادغام	Qalqala قلقلہ	Qalb قلب	Idghaam Meem Saakin ادغام میم ساکن

بِالْإِيمَانِ وَلَٰكِن مَّن شَرَحَ
بِالْكُفْرِ صَدْرًا فَعَلَيْهِمْ غَضَبٌ مِّنَ
اللَّهِ وَلَهُمْ عَذَابٌ عَظِيمٌ ﴿١٠٦﴾

bil-eemaani wa laakim-man sharaḥa bilkufri ṣadran fa'alayhim ghaḍabum-minal-laahi wa lahum 'azaabun 'aẓeem.

in Faith - but such as open their breast to Unbelief, on them is Wrath from Allah, and for them will be a dreadful Penalty.

ذَٰلِكَ بِأَنَّهُمُ اسْتَحَبُّوا الْحَيَاةَ
الدُّنْيَا عَلَى الْآخِرَةِ وَأَنَّ اللَّهَ
لَا يَهْدِي الْقَوْمَ الْكَافِرِينَ ﴿١٠٧﴾

107. Zaalika bi-annahumus-taḥabbul-ḥayaatad-dunyaa 'alal-Aakhirati wa annal-laaha laa yahdil-qawmal-kaafireen.

107. This because they love the life of this world better than the Hereafter: and Allah will not guide those who reject Faith.

أُولَٰئِكَ الَّذِينَ طَبَعَ اللَّهُ عَلَىٰ
قُلُوبِهِمْ وَسَمْعِهِمْ وَأَبْصَارِهِمْ ۖ
وَأُولَٰئِكَ هُمُ الْغَافِلُونَ ﴿١٠٨﴾

108. Ulaaa'ikal-lazeena ṭaba'al-laahu 'alaa quloobihim wa sam'ihim wa abṣaarihim wa ulaaa'ika humul-ghaafiloon.

108. Those are they whose hearts, ears, and eyes Allah has sealed up, and they take no heed.

لَا جَرَمَ أَنَّهُمْ فِي الْآخِرَةِ
هُمُ الْخَاسِرُونَ ﴿١٠٩﴾

109. Laa jarama annahum fil-Aakhirati humul-khaasiroon.

109. Without doubt, in the Hereafter they will perish.

ثُمَّ إِنَّ رَبَّكَ لِلَّذِينَ هَاجَرُوا مِن
بَعْدِ مَا فُتِنُوا ثُمَّ جَاهَدُوا وَصَبَرُوا
إِنَّ رَبَّكَ مِن بَعْدِهَا لَغَفُورٌ
رَّحِيمٌ ﴿١١٠﴾ ع

110. Summa inna Rabbaka lillazeena haajaroo mim ba'di maa futinoo summa jaahadoo wa ṣabarooo inna Rabbaka mim ba'dihaa la-Ghafoorur-Raḥeem.

(Section 14)

110. But verily your Lord,- to those who leave their homes after trials and persecutions,- and who thereafter strive and fight for the faith and patiently persevere,- your Lord, after all this is Oft-Forgiving, Most Merciful.

يَوْمَ تَأْتِي كُلُّ نَفْسٍ تُجَادِلُ
عَن نَّفْسِهَا وَتُوَفَّىٰ كُلُّ نَفْسٍ
مَّا عَمِلَتْ وَهُمْ لَا يُظْلَمُونَ ﴿١١١﴾

111. Yawma taåtee kullu nafsin tujaadilu 'an-nafsihaa wa tuwaffaa kullu nafsim-maa 'amilat wa hum laa yuẓlamoon.

111. One Day every soul will come up struggling for itself, and every soul will be recompensed (fully) for all its actions, and none will be unjustly dealt with.

وَضَرَبَ اللَّهُ مَثَلًا قَرْيَةً كَانَتْ
آمِنَةً مُّطْمَئِنَّةً يَأْتِيهَا رِزْقُهَا
رَغَدًا مِّن كُلِّ مَكَانٍ فَكَفَرَتْ بِأَنْعُمِ
اللَّهِ فَأَذَاقَهَا اللَّهُ لِبَاسَ الْجُوعِ
وَالْخَوْفِ بِمَا كَانُوا يَصْنَعُونَ ﴿١١٢﴾

112. Wa ḍarabal-laahu masalan qaryatan kaanat aaminatam-muṭma'innatañy-yaåteehaa rizquhaa raghadam-min kulli makaanin fakafarat bi-an'umil-laahi fa-azaaqahal-laahu libaasal-joo'i walkhawfi bimaa kaanoo yaṣna'oon.

112. Allah sets forth a Parable: a city enjoying security and quiet, abundantly supplied with sustenance from every place: Yet was it ungrateful for the favors of Allah: so Allah made it taste of hunger and terror (in extremes) (closing in on it) like a garment (from every side), because of the (evil) which (its people) wrought.

وَلَقَدْ جَاءَهُمْ رَسُولٌ مِّنْهُمْ
فَكَذَّبُوهُ فَأَخَذَهُمُ الْعَذَابُ
وَهُمْ ظَالِمُونَ ﴿١١٣﴾

113. Wa laqad jaaa'ahum Rasoolum-minhum fakaz-zaboohu fa-akhazahumul-'azaabu wa hum ẓaalimoon.

113. And there came to them a Messenger from among themselves, but they falsely rejected him; so the Wrath seized them even in the midst of their iniquities.

Ikhfa اخفاء | Ghunna غُنّہ | Ikhfa Meem Saakin اخفاء میم ساکن | Idghaam ادغام | Qalqala قلقلہ | Qalb قلب | Idghaam Meem Saakin ادغام میم ساکن

114. So eat of the sustenance which Allah has provided for you, lawful and good; and be grateful for the favors of Allah, if it is He Whom you serve.

114. Fakuloo mimmaa razaqa-kumul-laahu ḥalaalan ṭayyi-bañw-washkuroo ni'matal-laahi in kuntum iyyaahu ta'budoon.

فَكُلُوْا مِمَّا رَزَقَكُمُ اللّٰهُ حَلٰلًا
طَيِّبًا ۖ وَّاشْكُرُوْا نِعْمَتَ اللّٰهِ
اِنْ كُنْتُمْ اِيَّاهُ تَعْبُدُوْنَ ﴿١١٤﴾

115. He has only forbidden you dead meat, and blood, and the flesh of swine, and any (food) over which the name of other than Allah has been invoked. But if one is forced by necessity, without wilful disobedience, nor transgressing due limits,- then Allah is Oft-Forgiving, Most Merciful.

115. Innamaa ḥarrma 'alay-kumul-maytata waddama wa laḥmal-khinzeeri wa maaa uhilla lighayril-laahi bihee famaniḍ-ṭurra ghayra baaghiñw-wa laa 'aadin fa-innal-laaha-Ghafoo-rur-Raḥeem.

اِنَّمَا حَرَّمَ عَلَيْكُمُ الْمَيْتَةَ وَالدَّمَ
وَلَحْمَ الْخِنْزِيْرِ وَمَآ اُهِلَّ لِغَيْرِ
اللّٰهِ بِهٖ ۚ فَمَنِ اضْطُرَّ غَيْرَ بَاغٍ وَّلَا
عَادٍ فَاِنَّ اللّٰهَ غَفُوْرٌ رَّحِيْمٌ ﴿١١٥﴾

116. But say not - for any false thing that your tongues may put forth,- "This is lawful, and this is forbidden," so as to ascribe false things to Allah. For those who ascribe false things to Allah, will never prosper.

116. Wa laa taqooloo limaa taṣifu alsinatukumul-kaẕiba haaẕaa ḥalaaluñw-wa haaẕaa ḥaraamul-litaftaroo 'alal-laahil-kaẕib; innal-laẕeena yaftaroona 'alal-laahil-kaẕiba laa yufli-ḥoon.

وَلَا تَقُوْلُوْا لِمَا تَصِفُ اَلْسِنَتُكُمُ
الْكَذِبَ هٰذَا حَلٰلٌ وَّهٰذَا حَرَامٌ
لِّتَفْتَرُوْا عَلَى اللّٰهِ الْكَذِبَ ۗ
اِنَّ الَّذِيْنَ يَفْتَرُوْنَ عَلَى اللّٰهِ
الْكَذِبَ لَا يُفْلِحُوْنَ ۗ ﴿١١٦﴾

117. (In such falsehood) is but a paltry profit; but they will have a most grievous Penalty.

117. Mataa'un qaleeluñw-wa lahum 'aẕaabun aleem.

مَتَاعٌ قَلِيْلٌ ۖ وَّلَهُمْ عَذَابٌ
اَلِيْمٌ ﴿١١٧﴾

118. To the Jews We prohibited such things as We have mentioned to you before: We did them no wrong, but they were used to doing wrong to themselves.

118. Wa 'alal-laẕeena ḥaadoo ḥarramnaa maa qaṣaṣnaa 'alayka min qablu wa maa ẓalamnaahum wa laakin kaanooo anfusahum yaẓlimoon.

وَعَلَى الَّذِيْنَ هَادُوْا حَرَّمْنَا مَا
قَصَصْنَا عَلَيْكَ مِنْ قَبْلُ ۚ وَمَا
ظَلَمْنٰهُمْ وَلٰكِنْ كَانُوْٓا اَنْفُسَهُمْ
يَظْلِمُوْنَ ﴿١١٨﴾

119. But verily your Lord,- to those who do wrong in ignorance, but who thereafter repent and make amends,- your Lord, after all this, is Oft-Forgiving, Most Merciful.

119. S̲umma inna Rabbaka lillaẕeena 'amilus-sooo'a bijahaalatin summa taaboo mim ba'di ẕaalika wa aṣlaḥooo inna Rabbaka mim ba'dihaa la-Ghafoorur-Raḥeem. **(Section 15)**

ثُمَّ اِنَّ رَبَّكَ لِلَّذِيْنَ عَمِلُوا
السُّوْٓءَ بِجَهَالَةٍ ثُمَّ تَابُوْا مِنْ
بَعْدِ ذٰلِكَ وَاَصْلَحُوْٓا ۙ اِنَّ رَبَّكَ
مِنْ بَعْدِهَا لَغَفُوْرٌ رَّحِيْمٌ ﴿١١٩﴾

120. Abraham was indeed a model, devoutly obedient to Allah, (and) true in Faith, and he joined not gods with Allah:

120. Inna Ibraaheema kaana ummatan qaanital-lillaahi Ḥaneefañw-wa lam yaku minal-mushrikeen.

اِنَّ اِبْرٰهِيْمَ كَانَ اُمَّةً قَانِتًا
لِّلّٰهِ حَنِيْفًا ۗ وَلَمْ يَكُ مِنَ
الْمُشْرِكِيْنَ ﴿١٢٠﴾

121. He showed his gratitude for the favors of Allah, who chose him, and guided him

121. Shaakiral-li-an'umih; ijtabaahu wa hadaahu

شَاكِرًا لِّاَنْعُمِهٖ ۭ اِجْتَبٰىهُ وَهَدٰىهُ

Ikhfa اخفاء | Ghunna غُنّہ | Ikhfa Meem Saakin اخفاء میم ساکن | Idghaam ادغام | Qalqala قلقلہ | Qalb قلب | Idghaam Meem Saakin ادغام میم ساکن

to a Straight Way.

ilaa Ṣiraaṭim-Mustaqeem.

اِلٰى صِرَاطٍ مُّسْتَقِيْمٍ ﴿١٢١﴾

122. And We gave him Good in this world, and he will be, in the Hereafter, in the ranks of the Righteous.

122. Wa aataynaahu fid-dunyaa ḥasanah; wa innahoo fil-Aakhirati laminaṣ-ṣaaliḥeen.

وَاٰتَيْنٰهُ فِى الدُّنْيَا حَسَنَةً ۭ وَاِنَّهٗ
فِى الْاٰخِرَةِ لَمِنَ الصّٰلِحِيْنَ ﴿١٢٢﴾ۭ

123. So We have taught you the inspired (message), "Follow the ways of Abraham the True in Faith, and he joined not gods with Allah."

123. Summa awḥaynaaa ilayka anit-tabi' Millata Ibraaheema Ḥaneefaa; wa maa kaana minal-mushrikeen.

ثُمَّ اَوْحَيْنَآ اِلَيْكَ اَنِ اتَّبِعْ
مِلَّةَ اِبْرٰهِيْمَ حَنِيْفًا ۭ وَمَا كَانَ
مِنَ الْمُشْرِكِيْنَ ﴿١٢٣﴾

124. The Sabbath was only made (strict) for those who disagreed (as to its observance); But Allah will judge between them on the Day of Judgment, as to their differences.

124. Innamaa ju'ilas-Sabtu 'alal-lazeenakhtalafoo feeh; wa inna Rabbaka la-yaḥkumu baynahum Yawmal-Qiyaamati feemaa kaanoo feehi yakhta-lifoon.

اِنَّمَا جُعِلَ السَّبْتُ عَلَى الَّذِيْنَ
اخْتَلَفُوْا فِيْهِ ۭ وَاِنَّ رَبَّكَ لَيَحْكُمُ
بَيْنَهُمْ يَوْمَ الْقِيٰمَةِ فِيْمَا كَانُوْا
فِيْهِ يَخْتَلِفُوْنَ ﴿١٢٤﴾

125. Invite (all) to the Way of your Lord with wisdom and beautiful preaching; and argue with them in ways that are best and most gracious: for your Lord knows best, who have strayed from His Path, and who receive guidance.

125. Ud'u ilaa sabeeli Rabbika bilḥikmati walmaw'iẓatil-ḥasanati wa jaadilhum billatee hiya aḥsan; inna Rabbaka Huwa a'lamu biman ḍalla 'an sabeelihee wa Huwa a'lamu bilmuhtadeen.

اُدْعُ اِلٰى سَبِيْلِ رَبِّكَ بِالْحِكْمَةِ
وَالْمَوْعِظَةِ الْحَسَنَةِ وَجَادِلْهُمْ
بِالَّتِيْ هِيَ اَحْسَنُ ۭ اِنَّ رَبَّكَ هُوَ
اَعْلَمُ بِمَنْ ضَلَّ عَنْ سَبِيْلِهٖ
وَهُوَ اَعْلَمُ بِالْمُهْتَدِيْنَ ﴿١٢٥﴾

126. And if you do catch them out, catch them out no worse than they catch you out: but if you show patience, that is indeed the best (course) for those who are patient.

126. Wa in 'aaqabtum fa'aaqi-boo bimisli maa 'ooqibtum bihee wa la'in ṣabartum lahuwa khayrul-liṣṣaabireen.

وَاِنْ عَاقَبْتُمْ فَعَاقِبُوْا بِمِثْلِ
مَا عُوْقِبْتُمْ بِهٖ ۭ وَلَىِٕنْ صَبَرْتُمْ
لَهُوَ خَيْرٌ لِّلصّٰبِرِيْنَ ﴿١٢٦﴾

127. And you be patient, for your patience is with the help from Allah; nor grieve over them: and do not distress yourself because of their plots.

127. Waṣbir wa maa ṣabruka illaa billaah; wa laa taḥzan 'alayhim wa laa taku fee ḍayqim-mimmaa yamkuroon.

وَاصْبِرْ وَمَا صَبْرُكَ اِلَّا بِاللّٰهِ
وَلَا تَحْزَنْ عَلَيْهِمْ وَلَا تَكُ فِيْ
ضَيْقٍ مِّمَّا يَمْكُرُوْنَ ﴿١٢٧﴾

128. For Allah is with those who restrain themselves, and those who do good.

128. Innal-laaha ma'al-lazee-nat-taqaw wal-lazeena hum-muḥsinoon. **(Section 16)**

اِنَّ اللّٰهَ مَعَ الَّذِيْنَ اتَّقَوْا
وَّالَّذِيْنَ هُمْ مُّحْسِنُوْنَ ﴿١٢٨﴾ ع

ركوع ١٦

17. The Children of Israel

In the name of Allah, Most Gracious, Most Merciful.

Sûrat Banî Isrâ'îl–17

(Revealed at Makkah)

Bismillaahir Raḥmaanir Raḥeem

(١٧) سُوْرَةُ بَنِيْٓ اِسْرَآءِيْلَ مَكِّيَّةٌ (٥٠)

بِسْمِ اللّٰهِ الرَّحْمٰنِ الرَّحِيْمِ

1. Glory to (Allah) Who took His servant for a Journey by night

1. Subḥaanal-lazeee asraa bi'abdihee laylam-minal-

سُبْحٰنَ الَّذِيْٓ اَسْرٰى بِعَبْدِهٖ لَيْلًا مِّنَ

الجزء الخامس عشر (١٥) المنزل الرابع (٤)

Ikhfa اخفاء | Ghunna غُنّہ | Ikhfa Meem Saakin اخفاء میم ساکن | Idghaam ادغام | Qalqala قلقلہ | Qalb قلب | Idghaam Meem Saakin ادغام میم ساکن

from the Sacred Mosque to the Farthest Mosque, whose precincts We did bless,- in order that We might show him some of Our Signs: for He is the One Who hears and sees (all things).

2. We gave Moses the Book, and made it a Guide to the Children of Israel, (commanding): "Do not take other than Me as Disposer of (your) affairs."

3. O you that are sprung from those whom We carried (in the Ark) with Noah! Verily he was a devotee most grateful.

4. And We gave (clear) warning to the Children of Israel in the Book, that twice would they do mischief on the earth and be elated with mighty arrogance (and twice would they be punished)!

5. When the first of the warnings came to pass, We sent against you Our servants given to terrible warfare: They entered the very inmost parts of your homes; and it was a warning (comp-letely) fulfilled.

6. Then We granted you the Return as against them: We gave you increase in resources and sons, and made you the more numerous in man-power.

7. If you did well, you did well for yourselves; if you did evil, (you did it) against yourselves. So when the second of the warnings came to pass, (We permitted your enemies) to disfigure your faces, and to enter your Temple as they had entered it before, and to visit with destruction all that fell into their power.

8. It may be that your Lord may (yet) show Mercy to you; but if you revert (to your sins), We shall revert (to Our punishments): And we have made Hell a prison for those who reject (all Faith).

9. Verily this Qur'an guides to that which is

Masjidil-Ḥaraami ilal-Masjidil-Aqṣal-lazee baaraknaa ḥawlahoo linuriyahoo min Aayaatinaa; innahoo Huwas-Samee'ul-Baṣeer.

2. Wa aataynaa Moosal-Kitaaba wa ja'alnaahu hudal-li-Baneee Israaa'eela allaa tattakhizoo min doonee wakeelaa.

3. Zurriyyata man ḥamalnaa ma'a Nooḥ; innahoo kaana 'abdan shakooraa.

4. Wa qaḍaynaaa ilaa Baneee Israaa'eela fil-Kitaabi-latufsidunna fil-arḍi marratayni wa lata'lunna'uluwwan kabeeraa.

5. Fa-izaa jaaa'a wa'duoolaahumaa ba'asnaaa 'alykum 'ibaadal-lanaaa ulee baåsin shadeedin fajaasoo khilaaladdiyaar; wa kaana wa'dam-maf'oolaa.

6. Summa radadnaa lakumulkarrata 'alayhim wa amdadnaakum-bi-amwaaliñw-wa baneena wa ja'alnaakum aksara nafeeraa.

7. In aḥsantum aḥsantum li-anfusikum wa in asaåtum falahaa; fa-izaa jaaa'a wa'dulaakhirati liyasooo'oo wujoohakum wa liyadkhulul-masjida kamaa dakhaloohu awwala marratiñw-wa liyutabbiroo maa 'alaw tatbeeraa.

8. 'Asaa Rabbukum añyyarḥamakum; wa in 'uttum 'udnaa; wa ja'alnaa Jahannama lilkaafireena ḥaṣeeraa.

9. Inna haazal-Qur-aana yahdee lillatee hiya

الْمَسْجِدِ الْحَرَامِ إِلَى الْمَسْجِدِ الْأَقْصَا
الَّذِي بَارَكْنَا حَوْلَهُ لِنُرِيَهُ مِنْ
آيَاتِنَا ۚ إِنَّهُ هُوَ السَّمِيعُ الْبَصِيرُ ①
وَآتَيْنَا مُوسَى الْكِتَابَ وَجَعَلْنَاهُ
هُدًى لِبَنِي إِسْرَائِيلَ أَلَّا تَتَّخِذُوا
مِنْ دُونِي وَكِيلًا ②
ذُرِّيَّةَ مَنْ حَمَلْنَا مَعَ نُوحٍ ۚ إِنَّهُ
كَانَ عَبْدًا شَكُورًا ③
وَقَضَيْنَا إِلَىٰ بَنِي إِسْرَائِيلَ فِي
الْكِتَابِ لَتُفْسِدُنَّ فِي الْأَرْضِ مَرَّتَيْنِ
وَلَتَعْلُنَّ عُلُوًّا كَبِيرًا ④
فَإِذَا جَاءَ وَعْدُ أُولَاهُمَا بَعَثْنَا عَلَيْكُمْ
عِبَادًا لَنَا أُولِي بَأْسٍ شَدِيدٍ فَجَاسُوا
خِلَالَ الدِّيَارِ ۚ وَكَانَ وَعْدًا مَفْعُولًا ⑤
ثُمَّ رَدَدْنَا لَكُمُ الْكَرَّةَ عَلَيْهِمْ وَ
أَمْدَدْنَاكُمْ بِأَمْوَالٍ وَبَنِينَ وَجَعَلْنَاكُمْ
أَكْثَرَ نَفِيرًا ⑥
إِنْ أَحْسَنْتُمْ أَحْسَنْتُمْ لِأَنْفُسِكُمْ ۖ
وَإِنْ أَسَأْتُمْ فَلَهَا ۚ فَإِذَا جَاءَ وَعْدُ
الْآخِرَةِ لِيَسُوءُوا وُجُوهَكُمْ وَلِيَدْخُلُوا
الْمَسْجِدَ كَمَا دَخَلُوهُ أَوَّلَ مَرَّةٍ وَ
لِيُتَبِّرُوا مَا عَلَوْا تَتْبِيرًا ⑦
عَسَىٰ رَبُّكُمْ أَنْ يَرْحَمَكُمْ ۚ وَإِنْ
عُدْتُمْ عُدْنَا ۘ وَجَعَلْنَا جَهَنَّمَ لِلْكَافِرِينَ وقف لازم
حَصِيرًا ⑧
إِنَّ هَٰذَا الْقُرْآنَ يَهْدِي لِلَّتِي هِيَ

Ikhfa اخفاء | Ghunna غنّہ | Ikhfa Meem Saakin اخفاء میم ساکن | Idghaam ادغام | Qalqala قلقلہ | Qalb قلب | Idghaam Meem Saakin ادغام میم ساکن

most right (or stable), and gives the Glad Tidings to the Believers who work deeds of righteousness, that they shall have a magnificent reward;

10. And to those who do not believe in the Hereafter, (it Announces) that We have prepared for them a Penalty Grievous (indeed).

11. The prayer that man should make for good, he makes for evil; for man is given to hasty (deeds).

12. We have made the Night and the Day as two (of Our) Signs: the Sign of the Night have We made dark, while the Sign of the Day We have made to enlighten you; that you may seek bounty from your Lord, and that you may know the number and count of the years: all things have We explained in detail.

13. Every man's fate We have fastened on his own neck: On the Day of Judgment We shall bring out for him a scroll, which he will see spread open.

14. (It will be said to him:) "Read your (own) record: Sufficient is your soul this day to make out an account against you."

15. Who receives guidance, receives it for his own benefit: who goes astray does so to his own loss: no bearer of burdens can bear the burden of another: nor would We visit with Our Wrath until We had sent a Messenger (to give warning).

16. When We decide to destroy a population, We (first) send a definite order to those among them who are given the good things of this life and yet transgress; so that the word is proved true against them: then (it is) We destroy them utterly.

17. How many generations have We destroyed after Noah? And enough is your Lord to note

aqwamu wa yubashshirul-mu'mineenal-lazeena ya'maloonaṣ-ṣaaliḥaati anna lahum ajran kabeeraa.

10. Wa annal-lazeena laa yu'minoona bil-Aakhirati a'tadnaa lahum 'azaaban aleemaa. **(Section 1)**

11. Wa yad'ul-insaanu bish-sharri du'aa'ahoo bilkhayr; wa kaanal-insaanu 'ajoolaa.

12. Wa ja'alnal-layla wannahaara Aayatayni famaḥawnaaa Aayatal-layli wa ja'alnaaa Aayatan-nahaari mubṣiratal-litabtaghoo faḍlam-mir-Rabbikum wa lita'lamoo 'adadas-sineena walḥisaab; wa kulla shay'in faṣṣalnaahu tafṣeelaa.

13. Wa kulla insaanin alzamnaahu ṭaaa'irahoo fee 'unuqihee wa nukhriju lahoo Yawmal-Qiyaamati kitaabañy-yalqaahu manshooraa.

14. Iqra kitaabak kafaa binafsikal-Yawma 'alayka ḥaseebaa.

15. Manihtadaa fa-innamaa yahtadee linafsihee wa man ḍalla fa-innamaa yaḍillu 'alayhaa; wa laa taziru waaziratuñw-wizra ukhraa; wa maa kunnaa mu'azzibeena ḥattaa nab'asa Rasoolaa.

16. Wa izaaa aradnaaa an nuhlika qaryatan amarnaa mutrafeehaa fafasaqoo feehaa faḥaqqa 'alayhal-qawlu fadammarnaahaa tadmeeraa.

17. Wa kam ahlaknaa minal-qurooni mim ba'di Nooḥ; wa kafaa bi-Rabbika bizunoobi

أَقْوَمُ وَيُبَشِّرُ الْمُؤْمِنِينَ الَّذِينَ
يَعْمَلُونَ الصَّٰلِحَٰتِ أَنَّ لَهُمْ أَجْرًا
كَبِيرًا ٩
وَأَنَّ الَّذِينَ لَا يُؤْمِنُونَ بِالْآخِرَةِ
أَعْتَدْنَا لَهُمْ عَذَابًا أَلِيمًا ١٠ ع
وَيَدْعُ الْإِنسَٰنُ بِالشَّرِّ دُعَآءَهُۥ
بِالْخَيْرِ ۖ وَكَانَ الْإِنسَٰنُ عَجُولًا ١١
وَجَعَلْنَا الَّيْلَ وَالنَّهَارَ ءَايَتَيْنِ ۖ فَمَحَوْنَآ
ءَايَةَ الَّيْلِ وَجَعَلْنَآ ءَايَةَ النَّهَارِ
مُبْصِرَةً لِّتَبْتَغُوا فَضْلًا مِّن رَّبِّكُمْ
وَلِتَعْلَمُوا عَدَدَ السِّنِينَ وَالْحِسَابَ ۚ
وَكُلَّ شَيْءٍ فَصَّلْنَٰهُ تَفْصِيلًا ١٢
وَكُلَّ إِنسَٰنٍ أَلْزَمْنَٰهُ طَٰٓئِرَهُۥ
فِي عُنُقِهِۦ ۖ وَنُخْرِجُ لَهُۥ يَوْمَ الْقِيَٰمَةِ
كِتَٰبًا يَلْقَىٰهُ مَنشُورًا ١٣
اقْرَأْ كِتَٰبَكَ كَفَىٰ بِنَفْسِكَ الْيَوْمَ
عَلَيْكَ حَسِيبًا ١٤
مَّنِ اهْتَدَىٰ فَإِنَّمَا يَهْتَدِي لِنَفْسِهِۦ ۖ
وَمَن ضَلَّ فَإِنَّمَا يَضِلُّ عَلَيْهَا ۚ وَلَا
تَزِرُ وَازِرَةٌ وِزْرَ أُخْرَىٰ ۗ وَمَا كُنَّا
مُعَذِّبِينَ حَتَّىٰ نَبْعَثَ رَسُولًا ١٥
وَإِذَآ أَرَدْنَآ أَن نُّهْلِكَ قَرْيَةً أَمَرْنَا
مُتْرَفِيهَا فَفَسَقُوا فِيهَا فَحَقَّ عَلَيْهَا
الْقَوْلُ فَدَمَّرْنَٰهَا تَدْمِيرًا ١٦
وَكَمْ أَهْلَكْنَا مِنَ الْقُرُونِ مِنۢ
بَعْدِ نُوحٍ ۗ وَكَفَىٰ بِرَبِّكَ بِذُنُوبِ

Ikhfa اخفاء | Ghunna غنّہ | Ikhfa Meem Saakin اخفاء میم ساکن | Idghaam ادغام | Qalqala قلقلہ | Qalb قلب | Idghaam Meem Saakin ادغام میم ساکن

and see the sins of His servants.

'ibaadihee Khabeeram-Baṣeeraa.

عِبَادِهٖ خَبِيْرًاۢ بَصِيْرًا ﴿١٧﴾

18. If any do wish for the transitory things (of this life), We readily grant them - such things as We will, to such person as We will: in the end have We provided Hell for them: they will burn therein, disgraced and rejected.

18. Man kaana yureedul-
'aajilata 'ajjalnaa lahoo feehaa
maa nashaaa'u liman-nureedu
summa ja'alnaa lahoo Jahannama yaṣlaahaa mazmoomam-
mad-ḥooraa.

مَنْ كَانَ يُرِيْدُ الْعَاجِلَةَ عَجَّلْنَا
لَهٗ فِيْهَا مَا نَشَآءُ لِمَنْ نُّرِيْدُ
ثُمَّ جَعَلْنَا لَهٗ جَهَنَّمَ ۚ يَصْلٰىهَا
مَذْمُوْمًا مَّدْحُوْرًا ﴿١٨﴾

19. Those who do wish for the (things of) the Hereafter, and strive therefor with all due striving, and have Faith,- they are the ones whose striving is acceptable (to Allah).

19. Wa man araadal Aakhirata
wa sa'aa lahaa sa'yahaa wa
huwa mu'minun fa-ulaaa'ika
kaana sa'yuhum-mashkooraa.

وَمَنْ اَرَادَ الْاٰخِرَةَ وَسَعٰى لَهَا
سَعْيَهَا وَهُوَ مُؤْمِنٌ فَاُولٰٓئِكَ كَانَ
سَعْيُهُمْ مَّشْكُوْرًا ﴿١٩﴾

20. Of the bounties of your Lord We bestow freely on all-these as well as those: the bounties of your Lord are not closed (to anyone).

20. Kullan-numiddu haaa-
'ulaaa'i wa haaa'ulaaa'i min
'aṭaaa'i Rabbik; wa maa kaana
'aṭaaa'u Rabbika maḥẓooraa.

كُلًّا نُّمِدُّ هٰٓؤُلَآءِ وَهٰٓؤُلَآءِ مِنْ عَطَآءِ رَبِّكَ ؕ
وَمَا كَانَ عَطَآءُ رَبِّكَ مَحْظُوْرًا ﴿٢٠﴾

21. See how We have bestowed more on some than on others; but verily the Hereafter is more in rank and gradation and more in excellence.

21. Unẓur kayfa faḍḍalnaa
ba'ḍahum 'alaa ba'ḍ; wa lal-
Aakhiratu akbaru darajaatiñw-
wa akbaru tafḍeelaa.

اُنْظُرْ كَيْفَ فَضَّلْنَا بَعْضَهُمْ عَلٰى بَعْضٍ ؕ
وَلَلْاٰخِرَةُ اَكْبَرُ دَرَجٰتٍ وَّاَكْبَرُ تَفْضِيْلًا ﴿٢١﴾

22. Take not with Allah another object of worship; or you (O man!) will sit in disgrace and destitution.

22. Laa taj'al ma'al-laahi
ilaahan aakhara fataq'uda
mazmoomam-makhzoolaa.

(Section 2)

لَا تَجْعَلْ مَعَ اللّٰهِ اِلٰهًا اٰخَرَ فَتَقْعُدَ
مَذْمُوْمًا مَّخْذُوْلًا ﴿٢٢﴾ ع

23. Your Lord has decreed that you worship none but Him, and that you be kind to parents. Whether one or both of them attain old age in your life, say not to them a word of contempt, nor repel them, but address them in terms of honor.

23. Wa qaḍaa Rabbuka allaa
ta'budooo illaaa iyyaahu wa
bilwaalidayni iḥsaanaa; immaa
yablughanna 'indakal-kibara
aḥaduhumaaa aw kilaahumaa
falaa taqul-lahumaaa uffiñw-
wa laa tanharhumaa wa qul-
lahumaa qawlan kareemaa.

وَقَضٰى رَبُّكَ اَلَّا تَعْبُدُوْٓا اِلَّآ اِيَّاهُ وَ
بِالْوَالِدَيْنِ اِحْسَانًا ؕ اِمَّا يَبْلُغَنَّ
عِنْدَكَ الْكِبَرَ اَحَدُهُمَآ اَوْ كِلٰهُمَا فَلَا
تَقُلْ لَّهُمَآ اُفٍّ وَّلَا تَنْهَرْهُمَا وَقُلْ
لَّهُمَا قَوْلًا كَرِيْمًا ﴿٢٣﴾

24. And, out of kindness, lower to them the wing of humility, and say: "My Lord! bestow on them Your Mercy even as they cherished me in childhood."

24. Wakhfiḍ lahumaa janaa-
haz-zulli minar-raḥmati wa qur-
Rabbir-ḥamhumaa kamaa
rabbayaanee ṣagheeraa.

وَاخْفِضْ لَهُمَا جَنَاحَ الذُّلِّ مِنَ
الرَّحْمَةِ وَقُلْ رَّبِّ ارْحَمْهُمَا كَمَا
رَبَّيٰنِيْ صَغِيْرًا ﴿٢٤﴾ ط

25. Your Lord knows best what is in your hearts: If you do deeds of righteousness, verily He is Most Forgiving to those who turn to Him again and again (in true penitence).

25. Rabbukum a'lamu bimaa
fee nufoosikum; in takoonoo
ṣaaliḥeena fa-innahoo kaana lil-
awwaabeena Ghafoooraa.

رَبُّكُمْ اَعْلَمُ بِمَا فِيْ نُفُوْسِكُمْ ؕ
اِنْ تَكُوْنُوْا صٰلِحِيْنَ فَاِنَّهٗ كَانَ
لِلْاَوَّابِيْنَ غَفُوْرًا ﴿٢٥﴾

26. And render to the kindred their due rights, as (also) to those in want,

26. Wa aati zal-qurbaa
ḥaqqahoo walmiskeena

وَاٰتِ ذَا الْقُرْبٰى حَقَّهٗ وَالْمِسْكِيْنَ

Ikhfa اخفاء | Ghunna غُنّہ | Ikhfa Meem Saakin اخفاء میم ساکن | Idghaam ادغام | Qalqala قلقلہ | Qalb قلب | Idghaam Meem Saakin ادغام میم ساکن

وَابْنَ السَّبِيْلِ وَلَا تُبَذِّرْ تَبْذِيْرًا ﴿٢٦﴾

wabnas-sabeeli wa laa tubazzir tabzeeraa.

and to the wayfarer: but squander not (your wealth) in the manner of a spendthrift.

اِنَّ الْمُبَذِّرِيْنَ كَانُوْٓا اِخْوَانَ الشَّيٰطِيْنِؕ
وَكَانَ الشَّيْطٰنُ لِرَبِّهٖ كَفُوْرًا ﴿٢٧﴾

27. Innal-mubazzireena kaanooo ikhwaanash-shayaaṭeeni wa kaanash-Shayṭaanu li-Rabbihee kafooraa.

27. Verily spendthrifts are brothers of the Evil Ones; and the Evil One is to his Lord (himself) ungrateful.

وَاِمَّا تُعْرِضَنَّ عَنْهُمُ ابْتِغَآءَ رَحْمَةٍ
مِّنْ رَّبِّكَ تَرْجُوْهَا فَقُلْ لَّهُمْ
قَوْلًا مَّيْسُوْرًا ﴿٢٨﴾

28. Wa immaa tu'riḍanna 'anhumub-tighaaa'a raḥmatim-mir-Rabbika tarjoohaa faqul-lahum qawlam-maysooraa.

28. And even if you have to turn away from them in pursuit of the Mercy from your Lord which you do expect, yet speak to them a word of easy kindness.

وَلَا تَجْعَلْ يَدَكَ مَغْلُوْلَةً اِلٰى
عُنُقِكَ وَلَا تَبْسُطْهَا كُلَّ الْبَسْطِ
فَتَقْعُدَ مَلُوْمًا مَّحْسُوْرًا ﴿٢٩﴾

29. Wa laa taj'al yadaka maghloolatan ilaa 'unuqika wa laa tabsuṭ-haa kullal-basṭi fataq'uda maloomam-maḥsooraa.

29. Make not your hand tied (like a miser's) to your neck, nor stretch it forth to its utmost reach, so that you become blameworthy and destitute.

اِنَّ رَبَّكَ يَبْسُطُ الرِّزْقَ لِمَنْ يَّشَآءُ
وَيَقْدِرُؕ اِنَّهٗ كَانَ بِعِبَادِهٖ خَبِيْرًاۢ
بَصِيْرًا ﴿٣٠﴾ ع ٣ ٨ ٣

30. Inna Rabbaka yabsuṭur-rizqa limañy-yashaaa'u wa yaqdir; innahoo kaana bi'ibaadihee Khabeeram-Baṣeeraa.

(Section 3)

30. Verily your Lord provides sustenance in abundance for whom He pleases, and He provides in a just measure. For He knows and regards all His servants.

وَلَا تَقْتُلُوْٓا اَوْلَادَكُمْ خَشْيَةَ اِمْلَاقٍؕ
نَحْنُ نَرْزُقُهُمْ وَاِيَّاكُمْؕ اِنَّ قَتْلَهُمْ
كَانَ خِطْاً كَبِيْرًا ﴿٣١﴾

31. Wa laa taqtulooo awlaadakum khashyata imlaaq; naḥnu narzuquhum wa iyyaakum; inna qatlahum kaana khiṭ-an kabeeraa.

31. Kill not your children for fear of want: We shall provide sustenance for them as well as for you. Verily the killing of them is a great sin.

وَلَا تَقْرَبُوا الزِّنٰٓى اِنَّهٗ كَانَ فَاحِشَةًؕ
وَسَآءَ سَبِيْلًا ﴿٣٢﴾

32. Wa laa taqrabuz-zinaaa innahoo kaana faaḥishatañw wa saaa'a sabeelaa.

32. Nor come near to adultery: for it is a shameful (deed) and an evil, opening the road (to other evils).

وَلَا تَقْتُلُوا النَّفْسَ الَّتِيْ حَرَّمَ اللّٰهُ
اِلَّا بِالْحَقِّؕ وَمَنْ قُتِلَ مَظْلُوْمًا فَقَدْ
جَعَلْنَا لِوَلِيِّهٖ سُلْطٰنًا فَلَا يُسْرِفْ
فِّي الْقَتْلِؕ اِنَّهٗ كَانَ مَنْصُوْرًا ﴿٣٣﴾

33. Wa laa taqtulun-nafsal-latee ḥarramal-laahu illaa bil-ḥaqq; wa man qutila maẓlooman faqad ja'alnaa liwaliyyihee sulṭaanan falaa yusrif-fil-qatli innahoo kaana manṣooraa.

33. Nor take life - which Allah has made sacred - except for just cause. And if anyone is slain wrongfully, we have given his heir authority (to demand Qisas or to forgive): but let him nor exceed bounds in the matter of taking life; for he is helped (by the Law).

وَلَا تَقْرَبُوْا مَالَ الْيَتِيْمِ اِلَّا بِالَّتِيْ
هِيَ اَحْسَنُ حَتّٰى يَبْلُغَ اَشُدَّهٗ
وَاَوْفُوْا بِالْعَهْدِۚ اِنَّ الْعَهْدَ
كَانَ مَسْـُٔوْلًا ﴿٣٤﴾

34. Wa laa taqraboo maalal-yateemi illaa billatee hiya aḥsanu ḥattaa yablugha ashuddah; wa awfoo bil'ahd, innal-'ahda kaana mas'oolaa.

34. Come not near to the orphan's property except to improve it, until he attains the age of full strength; and fulfil (every) engagement, for (every) engagement will be enquired into (on the Day of Reckoning).

وَاَوْفُوا الْكَيْلَ اِذَا كِلْتُمْ وَزِنُوْا

35. Wa awful-kayla izaa kiltum wa zinoo

35. Give full measure when you measure, and weigh

Ikhfa اخفاء | Ghunna غُنّہ | Ikhfa Meem Saakin اخفاءمیم ساکن | Idghaam ادغام | Qalqala قلقلہ | Qalb قلب | Idghaam Meem Saakin ادغام میم ساکن

with a balance that is straight: that is the most fitting and the most advantageous in the final determination.

bilqisṭaasil-mustaqeem; zaalika khayruñw-wa aḥsanu taâweelaa.

بِالْقِسْطَاسِ الْمُسْتَقِيمِ ۚ ذَٰلِكَ
خَيْرٌ وَأَحْسَنُ تَأْوِيلًا ﴿٣٥﴾

36. And do not pursue that of which you have no knowledge; for every act of hearing, or of seeing or of (feeling in) the heart will be enquired into (on the Day of Reckoning).

36. Wa laa taqfu maa laysa laka bihee ‘ilm; innas-sam‘a walbaṣara walfu’aada kullu ulaaa’ika kaana ‘anhu mas-’oolaa.

وَلَا تَقْفُ مَا لَيْسَ لَكَ بِهِ عِلْمٌ ۚ
إِنَّ السَّمْعَ وَالْبَصَرَ وَالْفُؤَادَ كُلُّ
أُولَٰئِكَ كَانَ عَنْهُ مَسْئُولًا ﴿٣٦﴾

37. Nor walk on the earth with insolence: for you can not rend the earth asunder, nor reach the mountains in height.

37. Wa laa tamshi fil-arḍi maraḥan innaka lan takhriqal-arḍa wa lan tablughal-jibaala ṭoolaa.

وَلَا تَمْشِ فِي الْأَرْضِ مَرَحًا ۖ
إِنَّكَ لَنْ تَخْرِقَ الْأَرْضَ وَلَنْ تَبْلُغَ
الْجِبَالَ طُولًا ﴿٣٧﴾

38. Of all such things the evil is hateful in the sight of your Lord.

38. Kullu zaalika kaana sayyi’uhoo ‘inda Rabbika makroohaa.

كُلُّ ذَٰلِكَ كَانَ سَيِّئُهُ عِنْدَ رَبِّكَ
مَكْرُوهًا ﴿٣٨﴾

39. These are among the (precepts of) wisdom, which your Lord has revealed to you. Do not take, with Allah, another object of worship, lest you should be thrown into Hell, blameworthy and rejected.

39. Zaalika mimmaaa awḥaaa ilayka Rabbuka minal-ḥikmah; wa laa taj‘al-ma‘allaahi ilaahan aakhara fatulqaa fee Jahannama maloomam-mad-ḥooraa.

ذَٰلِكَ مِمَّا أَوْحَىٰ إِلَيْكَ رَبُّكَ مِنَ
الْحِكْمَةِ ۗ وَلَا تَجْعَلْ مَعَ اللَّهِ إِلَٰهًا
آخَرَ فَتُلْقَىٰ فِي جَهَنَّمَ مَلُومًا
مَدْحُورًا ﴿٣٩﴾

40. Has then your Lord (O Pagans!) preferred for you sons, and taken for Himself daughters among the angels? Truly you utter a most dreadful saying!

40. Afa-aṣfaakum Rabbukum bilbaneena wattakhaza minal-malaaa’ikati inaasaa; innakum lataqooloona qawlan ‘aẓeemaa.
(Section 4)

أَفَأَصْفَاكُمْ رَبُّكُمْ بِالْبَنِينَ وَاتَّخَذَ
مِنَ الْمَلَائِكَةِ إِنَاثًا ۚ إِنَّكُمْ لَتَقُولُونَ
قَوْلًا عَظِيمًا ﴿٤٠﴾ ع

41. We have explained (things) in various (ways) in this Qur’an, in order that they may receive admonition, but it only increases their flight (from the Truth)!

41. Wa laqad ṣarrafnaa fee haazal-Qur-aani liyazzakkaroo wa maa yazeeduhum illaa nufooraa.

وَلَقَدْ صَرَّفْنَا فِي هَٰذَا الْقُرْآنِ
لِيَذَّكَّرُوا وَمَا يَزِيدُهُمْ إِلَّا نُفُورًا ﴿٤١﴾

42. Say: If there had been (other) gods with Him, as they say,- behold, they would certainly have sought out a way to the Lord of the Throne!

42. Qul-law kaana ma‘ahooo aalihatun kamaa yaqooloona izal-labtaghaw ilaa zil-‘Arshi Sabeelaa.

قُلْ لَوْ كَانَ مَعَهُ آلِهَةٌ كَمَا
يَقُولُونَ إِذًا لَابْتَغَوْا إِلَىٰ ذِي
الْعَرْشِ سَبِيلًا ﴿٤٢﴾

43. Glory to Him! He is high above all that they say!- Exalted and Great (beyond measure)!

43. Subḥaanahoo wa Ta‘aalaa ‘ammaa yaqooloona ‘uluwwan kabeeraa.

سُبْحَانَهُ وَتَعَالَىٰ عَمَّا يَقُولُونَ
عُلُوًّا كَبِيرًا ﴿٤٣﴾

44. The seven heavens and the earth, and all beings therein, declare His glory: there is not a thing but celebrates

44. Tusabbiḥu lahus-samaa-waatus-sab‘u wal-arḍu wa man feehinn; wa im-min shay‘in illaa yusabbiḥu

تُسَبِّحُ لَهُ السَّمَاوَاتُ السَّبْعُ وَالْأَرْضُ
وَمَنْ فِيهِنَّ ۚ وَإِنْ مِنْ شَيْءٍ إِلَّا يُسَبِّحُ

Ikhfa اخفاء | Ghunna غنّہ | Ikhfa Meem Saakin اخفاء میم ساکن | Idghaam ادغام | Qalqala قلقلہ | Qalb قلب | Idghaam Meem Saakin ادغام میم ساکن

His praise; And yet you do not understand how they declare His glory! Verily He is Oft-Forbearing, Most Forgiving!

biḥamdihee wa laakil-laa tafqahoona tasbeeḥahum; innahoo kaana Ḥaleeman Ghafooraa.

بِحَمْدِهٖ وَلٰكِنْ لَّا تَفْقَهُوْنَ تَسْبِيْحَهُمْ
اِنَّهٗ كَانَ حَلِيْمًا غَفُوْرًا ﴿٤٤﴾

45. When you recite the Qur'an, We put, between you and those who do not believe in the Hereafter, an invisible veil:

45. Wa izaa qaraåtal-Qur-aana ja'alnaa baynaka wa baynal-lazeena laa yu'minoona bil-Aakhirati ḥijaabam-mastooraa.

وَاِذَا قَرَاْتَ الْقُرْاٰنَ جَعَلْنَا بَيْنَكَ
وَبَيْنَ الَّذِيْنَ لَا يُؤْمِنُوْنَ بِالْاٰخِرَةِ
حِجَابًا مَّسْتُوْرًا ﴿٤٥﴾

46. And We put coverings over their hearts (and minds) lest they should understand the Qur'an, and deafness into their ears: when you comme-morate your Lord and Him alone in the Qur'an, they turn on their backs, fleeing (from the Truth).

46. Wa ja'alnaa 'alaa quloo-bihim akinnatan añy-yafqa-hoohu wa feee aazaanihim waqraa; wa izaa zakarta Rabbaka fil-Qur-aani waḥda-hoo wallaw 'alaaa adbaarihim nufooraa.

وَّجَعَلْنَا عَلٰى قُلُوْبِهِمْ اَكِنَّةً اَنْ
يَّفْقَهُوْهُ وَفِيْۤ اٰذَانِهِمْ وَقْرًا ؕ وَاِذَا
ذَكَرْتَ رَبَّكَ فِي الْقُرْاٰنِ وَحْدَهٗ وَلَّوْا
عَلٰۤى اَدْبَارِهِمْ نُفُوْرًا ﴿٤٦﴾

47. We know best why it is they listen, when they listen to you: and when they meet in private conference, behold, the wicked say, "You follow none other than a man bewitched!"

47. Naḥnu a'lamu bimaa yastami'oona biheee iz yas-tami'oona ilayka wa iz hum najwaaa iz yaqooluẓ-ẓaali-moona in tattabi'oona illaa rajulam-mas-ḥooraa.

نَحْنُ اَعْلَمُ بِمَا يَسْتَمِعُوْنَ بِهٖۤ اِذْ
يَسْتَمِعُوْنَ اِلَيْكَ وَاِذْ هُمْ نَجْوٰۤى
اِذْ يَقُوْلُ الظّٰلِمُوْنَ اِنْ تَتَّبِعُوْنَ
اِلَّا رَجُلًا مَّسْحُوْرًا ﴿٤٧﴾

48. See what similes they strike for you: but they have gone astray, and never can they find a way.

48. Unẓur kayfa ḍaraboo lakal-amsaala faḍalloo falaa yastaṭee'oona sabeelaa.

اُنْظُرْ كَيْفَ ضَرَبُوْا لَكَ الْاَمْثَالَ
فَضَلُّوْا فَلَا يَسْتَطِيْعُوْنَ سَبِيْلًا ﴿٤٨﴾ الربع

49. They say: "What! when we are reduced to bones and dust, should we really be raised up (to be) a new creation?"

49. Wa qaalooo 'a-izaa kunnaa 'iẓaamañw-wa rufaatan 'a-innaa lamab'oosoona khalqan jadee-daa.

وَقَالُوْۤا ءَاِذَا كُنَّا عِظَامًا وَّرُفَاتًا
ءَاِنَّا لَمَبْعُوْثُوْنَ خَلْقًا جَدِيْدًا ﴿٤٩﴾

50. Say: "(Nay!) be you stones or iron.

50. Qul koonoo ḥijaaratan aw ḥadeedaa.

قُلْ كُوْنُوْا حِجَارَةً اَوْ حَدِيْدًا ﴿٥٠﴾

51. "Or any created matter which, in your minds, is hardest (to be raised up),- (Yet shall you be raised up)!" Then will they say: "Who will cause us to return?" Say: "He who created you first!" Then they will wag their heads toward you, and say, "When will that be?" Say, "May be it will be quite soon!

51. Aw khalqam-mimmaa yakburu fee ṣudoorikum; fasa-yaqooloona mañy-yu'eedunaa qulil-lazee faṭarakum awwala marrah; fasa-yunghiḍoona ilayka ru'oosahum wa yaqoo-loona mataa huwa qul 'asaaa añy-yakoona qareebaa.

اَوْ خَلْقًا مِّمَّا يَكْبُرُ فِيْ صُدُوْرِكُمْ ۚ
فَسَيَقُوْلُوْنَ مَنْ يُّعِيْدُنَا ؕ قُلِ الَّذِيْ
فَطَرَكُمْ اَوَّلَ مَرَّةٍ ۚ فَسَيُنْغِضُوْنَ
اِلَيْكَ رُءُوْسَهُمْ وَيَقُوْلُوْنَ مَتٰى
هُوَ ؕ قُلْ عَسٰۤى اَنْ يَّكُوْنَ قَرِيْبًا ﴿٥١﴾

52. "It will be on a Day when He will call you, and you will answer (His call) with (words of) His praise, and you will think that you tarried but a little while!"

52. Yawma yad'ookum fatas-tajeeboona biḥamdihee wa taẓunnoona il-labistum illaa qaleelaa. **(Section 5)**

يَوْمَ يَدْعُوْكُمْ فَتَسْتَجِيْبُوْنَ بِحَمْدِهٖ
وَتَظُنُّوْنَ اِنْ لَّبِثْتُمْ اِلَّا قَلِيْلًا ﴿٥٢﴾ ع ٥

53. Say to My servants that they should (only) say those things that are

53. Wa qul-li'ibaadee yaqoo-lul-latee hiya

وَقُلْ لِّعِبَادِيْ يَقُوْلُوا الَّتِيْ هِيَ

Ikhfa اخفاء | Ghunna غُنّہ | Ikhfa Meem Saakin اخفاء میم ساکن | Idghaam ادغام | Qalqala قلقلہ | Qalb قلب | Idghaam Meem Saakin ادغام میم ساکن

best: for Satan does sow dissensions among them: For Satan is to man an avowed enemy.

54. It is your Lord that knows you best: If He please, He grants you mercy, or if He please, punishment: We have not sent you to be a disposer of their affairs for them.

55. And it is your Lord that knows best all beings that are in the heavens and on earth: We bestowed on some prophets more (and other) gifts than on others: and We gave to David (the gift of) the Psalms.

56. Say: "Call on those - besides Him - whom you fancy: they have neither the power to remove your troubles from you nor to change them."

57. Those whom they call upon do desire (for themselves) means of access to their Lord, - even those who are nearest: they hope for His Mercy and fear His Wrath: for the Wrath of your Lord is something to take heed of.

58. There is not a population but We shall destroy it before the Day of Judgment or punish it with a dreadful Penalty: that is written in the (eternal) Record.

59. And We refrain from sending the signs, only because the men of former generations treated them as false: We sent the she-camel to the Thamud to open their eyes, but they treated her wrongfully: We only send the Signs by way of terror (and warning from evil).

60. Behold! We told you that your Lord encompasses mankind round about: We granted the vision which We showed you, but as a trial for men,- as also the Cursed Tree

aḥsan; innash-Shayṭaana yanzaghu baynahum; innash-Shayṭaana kaana lil-insaani 'aduwwam-mubeenaa.

54. Rabbukum a'lamu bikum iñy-yashaå yarḥamkum aw iñy-yashaå yu'azzibkum; wa maaa arsalnaaka 'alayhim wakeelaa.

55. Wa Rabbuka a'lamu-biman fis-samaawaati wal-arḍ; wa laqad faḍḍalnaa ba'ḍan-Nabiyyeena 'alaa ba'ḍiñw-wa aataynaa Daawooda Zabooraa.

56. Qulid-'ul-lazeena za'am-tum min doonihee falaa yamlikoona kashfaḍ-ḍurri 'ankum wa laa taḥweelaa.

57. Ulaaa'ikal-lazeena yad-'oona yabtaghoona ilaa Rabbi-himul-waseelata ayyuhum aqrabu wa yarjoona raḥmatahoo wa yakhaafoona 'azaabah; inna 'azaaba Rabbika kaana maḥzooraa.

58. Wa im-min qaryatin illaa Naḥnu muhlikoohaa qabla Yawmil-Qiyaamati aw mu'az-ziboohaa 'azaaban shadeedaa; kaana zaalika fil-Kitaabi mas-ṭooraa.

59. Wa maa mana'anaaa an nursila bil-Aayaati illaaa an kazzaba bihal-awwaloon; wa aataynaa Samoodan-naaqata mubṣiratan faẓalamoo bihaa; wa maa nursilu bil-Aayaati illaa takhweefaa.

60. Wa iz qulnaa laka inna Rabbaka aḥaaṭa binnaas; wa maa ja'alnar-ru'yal-lateee araynaaka illaa fitnatal-linnaasi washshajaratal-mal'oonata

أَحْسَنُ ۚ إِنَّ الشَّيْطَٰنَ يَنزَغُ بَيْنَهُمْ ۚ إِنَّ
الشَّيْطَٰنَ كَانَ لِلْإِنسَٰنِ عَدُوًّا مُّبِينًا ﴿٥٣﴾
رَّبُّكُمْ أَعْلَمُ بِكُمْ ۖ إِن يَشَأْ يَرْحَمْكُمْ
أَوْ إِن يَشَأْ يُعَذِّبْكُمْ ۚ وَمَآ أَرْسَلْنَٰكَ
عَلَيْهِمْ وَكِيلًا ﴿٥٤﴾
وَرَبُّكَ أَعْلَمُ بِمَن فِي السَّمَٰوَٰتِ وَ
الْأَرْضِ ۗ وَلَقَدْ فَضَّلْنَا بَعْضَ النَّبِيِّـۧنَ
عَلَىٰ بَعْضٍ ۖ وَءَاتَيْنَا دَاوُۥدَ زَبُورًا ﴿٥٥﴾
قُلِ ادْعُوا الَّذِينَ زَعَمْتُم مِّن
دُونِهِۦ فَلَا يَمْلِكُونَ كَشْفَ الضُّرِّ
عَنكُمْ وَلَا تَحْوِيلًا ﴿٥٦﴾
أُولَٰٓئِكَ الَّذِينَ يَدْعُونَ يَبْتَغُونَ
إِلَىٰ رَبِّهِمُ الْوَسِيلَةَ أَيُّهُمْ أَقْرَبُ
وَيَرْجُونَ رَحْمَتَهُۥ وَيَخَافُونَ عَذَابَهُۥٓ ۚ
إِنَّ عَذَابَ رَبِّكَ كَانَ مَحْذُورًا ﴿٥٧﴾
وَإِن مِّن قَرْيَةٍ إِلَّا نَحْنُ مُهْلِكُوهَا
قَبْلَ يَوْمِ الْقِيَٰمَةِ أَوْ مُعَذِّبُوهَا عَذَابًا
شَدِيدًا ۚ كَانَ ذَٰلِكَ فِي الْكِتَٰبِ
مَسْطُورًا ﴿٥٨﴾
وَمَا مَنَعَنَآ أَن نُّرْسِلَ بِالْءَايَٰتِ إِلَّآ
أَن كَذَّبَ بِهَا الْأَوَّلُونَ ۚ وَءَاتَيْنَا
ثَمُودَ النَّاقَةَ مُبْصِرَةً فَظَلَمُوا بِهَا ۚ
وَمَا نُرْسِلُ بِالْءَايَٰتِ إِلَّا تَخْوِيفًا ﴿٥٩﴾
وَإِذْ قُلْنَا لَكَ إِنَّ رَبَّكَ أَحَاطَ بِالنَّاسِ ۚ
وَمَا جَعَلْنَا الرُّءْيَا الَّتِيٓ أَرَيْنَٰكَ إِلَّا
فِتْنَةً لِّلنَّاسِ وَالشَّجَرَةَ الْمَلْعُونَةَ

Ikhfa اخفاء · Ghunna غُنّہ · Ikhfa Meem Saakin اخفاء میم ساکن · Idghaam ادغام · Qalqala قلقلہ · Qalb قلب · Idghaam Meem Saakin ادغام میم ساکن

(mentioned) in the Qur'an: We put terror (and warning) into them, but it only increases their inordinate transgression!

61. Behold! We said to the angels: "Bow down to Adam": They bowed down except Iblis: he said, "Shall I bow down to one whom You did create from clay?"

62. He said: "Do you see? this is the one whom You have honoured above me! If You will but respite me to the Day of Judgment, I will surely bring his descendants under my sway - all but a few!"

63. (Allah) said: "Go you away; if any of them follow you, verily Hell will be the recompense of you (all)- an ample recompense.

64. "Lead to destruction those whom you can among them, with your (seductive) voice; make assaults on them with your cavalry and your infantry; mutually share with them wealth and children; and make promises to them." But Satan promises them nothing but deceit.

65. "As for My servants, no authority shall you have over them:" Enough is your Lord for a Disposer of affairs.

66. Your Lord is He That makes the Ship go smoothly for you through the sea, in order that you may seek of His Bounty. For He is unto you most Merciful.

67. When distress seizes you at sea, those that you call upon - besides Himself - leave you in the lurch! but when He brings you back safe to land, you turn away (from Him). Most ungrateful is man!

68. Do you then feel secure that He will not cause you to be swallowed up beneath the earth when you are on land, or that He will not send against you a violent tornado (with showers of stones) so that you shall find no protector?

69. Or do you feel secure that He will not send you back a

fil-Qur-aan; wa nukhawwifuhum famaa yazeeduhum illaa tughyaanan kabeeraa.

(Section 6)

61. Wa iz̲ qulnaa lilmalaaa'ikatis-judoo li-Aadama fasajadooo illaaa Ibleesa qaala 'a-asjudu liman khalaqta ṭeenaa.

62. Qaala ara'aytaka haaz̲allaz̲ee karramta 'alayya la'in akhkhartani ilaa Yawmil-Qiyaamati la-aḥtanikanna z̲urriyyatahooo illaa qaleelaa.

63. Qaalaz̲-hab faman tabi'aka minhum fa-inna Jahannama jazaaa'ukum jazaaa'ammawfooraa.

64. Wastafziz manis-taṭa'ta minhum biṣawtika wa ajlib 'alayhim bikhaylika wa rajilika wa shaarik-hum fil-amwaali wal-awlaadi wa 'idhum; wa maa ya'iduhumush-Shayṭaanu illaa ghurooraa.

65. Inna 'ibaadee laysa laka 'alayhim sulṭaan; wa kafaa bi-Rabbika Wakeelaa.

66. Rabbukumul-laz̲ee yuzjee lakumul-fulka fil-baḥri litabtaghoo min faḍlih; innahoo kaana bikum Raḥeemaa.

67. Wa iz̲aa massakumuḍ-ḍurru fil-baḥri ḍalla man tad'oona illaaa iyyaahu falammaa najjaakum ilal-barri a'raḍtum; wa kaanal-insaanu kafooraa.

68. Afa-amintum añy-yakhsifa bikum jaanibal-barri aw yursila 'alaykum ḥaaṣiban s̲umma laa tajidoo lakum wakeelaa.

69. Am amintum añy-yu'eedakum feehi taaratan

فِي الْقُرْاٰنِ ؕ وَنُخَوِّفُهُمْ ۙ فَمَا يَزِيدُهُمْ
اِلَّا طُغْيَانًا كَبِيرًا ﴿٦٠﴾
وَاِذْ قُلْنَا لِلْمَلٰٓئِكَةِ اسْجُدُوا لِاٰدَمَ
فَسَجَدُوٓا اِلَّآ اِبْلِيسَ ؕ قَالَ ءَاَسْجُدُ
لِمَنْ خَلَقْتَ طِينًا ﴿٦١﴾
قَالَ اَرَءَيْتَكَ هٰذَا الَّذِي كَرَّمْتَ عَلَيَّ ؗ
لَئِنْ اَخَّرْتَنِ اِلٰى يَوْمِ الْقِيٰمَةِ لَاَحْتَنِكَنَّ
ذُرِّيَّتَهٗٓ اِلَّا قَلِيلًا ﴿٦٢﴾
قَالَ اذْهَبْ فَمَنْ تَبِعَكَ مِنْهُمْ فَاِنَّ
جَهَنَّمَ جَزَآؤُكُمْ جَزَآءً مَّوْفُورًا ﴿٦٣﴾
وَاسْتَفْزِزْ مَنِ اسْتَطَعْتَ مِنْهُمْ بِصَوْتِكَ
وَاَجْلِبْ عَلَيْهِمْ بِخَيْلِكَ وَرَجِلِكَ وَ
شَارِكْهُمْ فِي الْاَمْوَالِ وَالْاَوْلَادِ وَعِدْهُمْ ؕ
وَمَا يَعِدُهُمُ الشَّيْطٰنُ اِلَّا غُرُورًا ﴿٦٤﴾
اِنَّ عِبَادِي لَيْسَ لَكَ عَلَيْهِمْ
سُلْطٰنٌ ؕ وَكَفٰى بِرَبِّكَ وَكِيلًا ﴿٦٥﴾
رَبُّكُمُ الَّذِي يُزْجِي لَكُمُ الْفُلْكَ فِي
الْبَحْرِ لِتَبْتَغُوا مِنْ فَضْلِهٖ ؕ اِنَّهٗ
كَانَ بِكُمْ رَحِيمًا ﴿٦٦﴾
وَاِذَا مَسَّكُمُ الضُّرُّ فِي الْبَحْرِ ضَلَّ مَنْ
تَدْعُونَ اِلَّآ اِيَّاهُ ۚ فَلَمَّا نَجّٰىكُمْ اِلَى الْبَرِّ
اَعْرَضْتُمْ ؕ وَكَانَ الْاِنْسَانُ كَفُورًا ﴿٦٧﴾
اَفَاَمِنْتُمْ اَنْ يَّخْسِفَ بِكُمْ جَانِبَ الْبَرِّ
اَوْ يُرْسِلَ عَلَيْكُمْ حَاصِبًا ثُمَّ لَا تَجِدُوا
لَكُمْ وَكِيلًا ﴿٦٨﴾
اَمْ اَمِنْتُمْ اَنْ يُّعِيدَكُمْ فِيهِ تَارَةً

Ikhfa اخفاء | Ghunna غنّہ | Ikhfa Meem Saakin اخفاء میم ساکن | Idghaam ادغام | Qalqala قلقلہ | Qalb قلب | Idghaam Meem Saakin ادغام میم ساکن

second time to sea and send against you a heavy gale to drown you because of your ingratitude, so that you find no helper therein against Us?

70. We have honoured the sons of Adam; provided them with transport on land and sea; given them for sustenance things good and pure; and conferred on them special favours, above a great part of our creation.

71. One day We shall call together all human beings with their (respective) Imams: those who are given their record in their right hand will read it (with pleasure), and they will not be dealt with unjustly in the least.

72. But those who were blind in this world, will be blind in the Hereafter, and most astray from the Path.

73. And their purpose was to tempt you away from that which We had revealed unto you, to substitute in Our name something quite different; (in that case), behold! they would certainly have made you (their) friend!

74. And had We not given you strength, you would nearly have inclined to them a little.

75. In that case We should have made you taste double portion (of punishment) in this life, and an equal portion in death: moreover you wouldst have found none to help you against Us!

76. Their purpose was to scare you off the land, in order to expel you; but in that case they would not have stayed (therein) after you, except for a little while.

77. (This was Our) way with the Messengers We sent before you: you will find no change in Our ways.

78. Establish regular prayers at the sun's decline till the darkness of the night, and the recital of the Qur'an in morning prayer, for the recital in the morning

ukhraa fa-yursila 'alaykum qaaṣifam-minar-reeḥi fa-yughriqakum bimaa kafartum summa laa tajidoo lakum 'alaynaa bihee tabee'aa.

70. Wa laqad karramnaa Baneee Aadama wa ḥamalnaahum fil-barri walbaḥri wa razaqnaahum minaṭ-ṭayyibaati wa faḍḍalnaahum 'alaa kaseerim-mimman khalaqnaa tafḍeelaa.

(Section 7)

71. Yawma nad'oo kulla unaasim bi-imaamihim faman ootiya kitaabahoo bi-yameenihee fa-ulaaa'ika yaqra'oona kitaabahum wa laa yuẓlamoona fateelaa.

72. Wa man kaana fee haaziheee a'maa fahuwa fil-Aakhirati a'maa wa aḍallu sabeelaa.

73. Wa in kaadoo la-yaftinoonaka 'anil-lazeee awḥaynaaa ilayka litaftariya 'alaynaa ghayrahoo wa izallat-takhazooka khaleelaa.

74. Wa law laaa an sabbatnaaka laqad kitta tarkanu ilayhim shay'an qaleelaa.

75. Izal-la-azaqnaaka ḍi'fal-ḥayaati wa ḍi'fal-mamaati summa laa tajidu laka 'alaynaa naṣeeraa.

76. Wa in kaadoo la-yastafizzoonaka minal-arḍi liyukhrijooka minhaa wa izal-laa yalbasoona khilaafaka illaa qaleelaa.

77. Sunnata man qad arsalnaa qablaka mir-Rusulinaa wa laa tajidu lisunnatinaa taḥweelaa.

78. Aqimiṣ-Ṣalaata liduloo-kish-shamsi ilaa ghasaqil-layli wa qur-aanal-Fajri inna qur-aanal-Fajri

اُخْرٰى فَيُرْسِلَ عَلَيْكُمْ قَاصِفًا مِّنَ
الرِّيْحِ فَيُغْرِقَكُمْ بِمَا كَفَرْتُمْ ۙ ثُمَّ لَا
تَجِدُوْا لَكُمْ عَلَيْنَا بِهٖ تَبِيْعًا ﴿٦٩﴾
وَلَقَدْ كَرَّمْنَا بَنِيْٓ اٰدَمَ وَحَمَلْنٰهُمْ
فِي الْبَرِّ وَالْبَحْرِ وَرَزَقْنٰهُمْ مِّنَ
الطَّيِّبٰتِ وَفَضَّلْنٰهُمْ عَلٰى كَثِيْرٍ
مِّمَّنْ خَلَقْنَا تَفْضِيْلًا ﴿٧٠﴾
يَوْمَ نَدْعُوْا كُلَّ اُنَاسٍۢ بِاِمَامِهِمْ ۚ فَمَنْ
اُوْتِيَ كِتٰبَهٗ بِيَمِيْنِهٖ فَاُولٰٓئِكَ يَقْرَءُوْنَ
كِتٰبَهُمْ وَلَا يُظْلَمُوْنَ فَتِيْلًا ﴿٧١﴾
وَمَنْ كَانَ فِيْ هٰذِهٖٓ اَعْمٰى فَهُوَ فِي
الْاٰخِرَةِ اَعْمٰى وَاَضَلُّ سَبِيْلًا ﴿٧٢﴾
وَاِنْ كَادُوْا لَيَفْتِنُوْنَكَ عَنِ الَّذِيْٓ
اَوْحَيْنَآ اِلَيْكَ لِتَفْتَرِيَ عَلَيْنَا غَيْرَهٗ ۖ
وَاِذًا لَّاتَّخَذُوْكَ خَلِيْلًا ﴿٧٣﴾
وَلَوْلَآ اَنْ ثَبَّتْنٰكَ لَقَدْ كِدْتَّ تَرْكَنُ
اِلَيْهِمْ شَيْـًٔا قَلِيْلًا ﴿٧٤﴾
اِذًا لَّاَذَقْنٰكَ ضِعْفَ الْحَيٰوةِ وَضِعْفَ
الْمَمَاتِ ثُمَّ لَا تَجِدُ لَكَ عَلَيْنَا نَصِيْرًا ﴿٧٥﴾
وَاِنْ كَادُوْا لَيَسْتَفِزُّوْنَكَ مِنَ الْاَرْضِ
لِيُخْرِجُوْكَ مِنْهَا وَاِذًا لَّا يَلْبَثُوْنَ
خِلٰفَكَ اِلَّا قَلِيْلًا ﴿٧٦﴾
سُنَّةَ مَنْ قَدْ اَرْسَلْنَا قَبْلَكَ مِنْ
رُّسُلِنَا وَلَا تَجِدُ لِسُنَّتِنَا تَحْوِيْلًا ﴿٧٧﴾
اَقِمِ الصَّلٰوةَ لِدُلُوْكِ الشَّمْسِ اِلٰى غَسَقِ
الَّيْلِ وَقُرْاٰنَ الْفَجْرِ ۭ اِنَّ قُرْاٰنَ الْفَجْرِ

Ikhfa اخفاء | Ghunna غُنّہ | Ikhfa Meem Saakin اخفاء میم ساکن | Idghaam ادغام | Qalqala قلقلہ | Qalb قلب | Idghaam Meem Saakin ادغام میم ساکن

carry (angels') testimony.

79. And as for the night keep awake a part of it as an additional prayer for you, soon will your Lord raise you to a Station of Praise and Glory!

80. Say: "O my Lord! Let my entry be by the Gate of Truth and Honour, and likewise my exit by the Gate of Truth and Honour; and grant me from Your Presence an authority to aid (me)."

81. And say: "Truth has (now) arrived, and Falsehood perished: for Falsehood is (by its nature) bound to perish."

82. We send down (stage by stage) in the Qur'an that which is a healing and a mercy to those who believe: to the unjust it causes nothing but loss after loss.

83. Yet when We bestow Our favors on man, he turns away and becomes remote on his side (instead of coming to Us), and when evil seizes him he gives himself up to despair.

84. Say: "Everyone acts according to his own disposition: but your Lord knows best who it is that is best guided on the Way."

85. They ask you concerning the Spirit (of inspiration). Say: "The Spirit (comes) by command of my Lord: of knowledge it is only a little that is communicated to you, (O men!)"

86. If it were Our Will, We could take away that which We have sent you by inspiration: then would you find none to plead your affair in that matter as against Us,-

87. Except for Mercy from your Lord: for His bounty is to you (indeed) great.

88. Say: "If the whole of mankind and Jinns were to gather

kaana mashhoodaa.

79. Wa minal-layli fatahajjad bihee naafilatal-laka 'asaaa añy-yab'asaka Rabbuka Maqaamam-Maḥmoodaa.

80. Wa qur-Rabbi adkhilnee mudkhala ṣidqiñw-wa akhrijnee mukhraja ṣidqiñw-waj'al lee milladunka sulṭaanan naṣeeraa.

81. Wa qul jaaa'al-ḥaqqu wa zahaqal-baaṭil; innal-baaṭila kaana zahooqaa.

82. Wa nunazzilu minal-Qur-aani maa huwa shifaaa'uñw-wa raḥmatul-lilmu'mineena wa laa yazeeduẓ-ẓaalimeena illaa khasaaraa.

83. Wa iżaaa an'amnaa 'alal-insaani a'raḍa wa na-aa bijaanibihee wa iżaa massahush-sharru kaana ya'oosaa.

84. Qul kulluñy-ya'malu 'alaa shaakilatihee fa-Rabbukum a'lamu biman huwa ahdaa sabeelaa. **(Section 9)**

85. Wa yas'aloonaka 'anir-rooḥ; qulir-rooḥu min amri Rabbee wa maaa ooteetum-minal-'ilmi illaa qaleelaa.

86. Wa la'in shi'naa lanażhabanna billażeee awḥaynaaa ilayka summa laa tajidu laka bihee 'alaynaa wakeelaa.

87. Illaa raḥmatam-mir-Rabbik; inna faḍlahoo kaana 'alayka kabeeraa.

88. Qul la'inij-tama'atil-insu waljinnu

كَانَ مَشْهُوْدًا ﴿٧٨﴾
وَمِنَ الَّيْلِ فَتَهَجَّدْ بِهٖ نَافِلَةً
لَّكَ ۖ عَسٰٓى اَنْ يَّبْعَثَكَ رَبُّكَ
مَقَامًا مَّحْمُوْدًا ﴿٧٩﴾
وَقُلْ رَّبِّ اَدْخِلْنِىْ مُدْخَلَ صِدْقٍ
وَّاَخْرِجْنِىْ مُخْرَجَ صِدْقٍ وَّاجْعَلْ
لِّىْ مِنْ لَّدُنْكَ سُلْطٰنًا نَّصِيْرًا ﴿٨٠﴾
وَقُلْ جَآءَ الْحَقُّ وَزَهَقَ الْبَاطِلُ ؕ
اِنَّ الْبَاطِلَ كَانَ زَهُوْقًا ﴿٨١﴾
وَنُنَزِّلُ مِنَ الْقُرْاٰنِ مَا هُوَ
شِفَآءٌ وَّرَحْمَةٌ لِّلْمُؤْمِنِيْنَ ۙ وَلَا
يَزِيْدُ الظّٰلِمِيْنَ اِلَّا خَسَارًا ﴿٨٢﴾
وَاِذَآ اَنْعَمْنَا عَلَى الْاِنْسَانِ اَعْرَضَ
وَنَاٰ بِجَانِبِهٖ ۚ وَاِذَا مَسَّهُ الشَّرُّ كَانَ
يَـُٔوْسًا ﴿٨٣﴾
قُلْ كُلٌّ يَّعْمَلُ عَلٰى شَاكِلَتِهٖ ؕ فَرَبُّكُمْ
اَعْلَمُ بِمَنْ هُوَ اَهْدٰى سَبِيْلًا ﴿٨٤﴾ ع
وَيَسْـَٔلُوْنَكَ عَنِ الرُّوْحِ ؕ قُلِ الرُّوْحُ
مِنْ اَمْرِ رَبِّىْ وَمَآ اُوْتِيْتُمْ مِّنَ الْعِلْمِ
اِلَّا قَلِيْلًا ﴿٨٥﴾
وَلَئِنْ شِئْنَا لَنَذْهَبَنَّ بِالَّذِىْٓ
اَوْحَيْنَآ اِلَيْكَ ثُمَّ لَا تَجِدُ لَكَ
بِهٖ عَلَيْنَا وَكِيْلًا ﴿٨٦﴾
اِلَّا رَحْمَةً مِّنْ رَّبِّكَ ؕ اِنَّ فَضْلَهٗ
كَانَ عَلَيْكَ كَبِيْرًا ﴿٨٧﴾
قُلْ لَّئِنِ اجْتَمَعَتِ الْاِنْسُ وَالْجِنُّ

Ikhfa اخفاء | Ghunna غُنّہ | Ikhfa Meem Saakin اخفاء میم ساکن | Idghaam ادغام | Qalqala قلقلہ | Qalb قلب | Idghaam Meem Saakin ادغام میم ساکن

together to produce the like of this Qur'an, they could not produce the like thereof, even if they backed up each other with help and support.

89. And We have explained to man, in this Qur'an, every kind of similitude: yet the greater part of men refuse (to receive it) except with ingratitude!

90. They say: "We shall not believe in you, until you cause a spring to gush forth for us from the earth,

91. "Or (until) thou have a garden of date trees and vines, and cause rivers to gush forth in their midst, carrying abundant water;

92. "Or you cause the sky to fall in pieces, as you say (will happen), against us; or you bring Allah and the angels before (us) face to face:

93. "Or you have a house adorned with gold, or you mount a ladder right into the skies. No, we shall not even believe in your mounting until you send down to us a book that we could read." Say: "Glory to my Lord! Am I not but a man,- a Messenger?"

94. What kept men back from belief when Guidance came to them, was nothing but this: they said, "Has Allah sent a man (like us) to be (His) Messenger?"

95. Say, "If there were settled, on earth, angels walking about in peace and quiet, We should certainly have sent them down from the heavens an angel for a Messenger."

96. Say: "Enough is Allah for a witness between me and you: for He is well acquainted with His servants, and He sees (all things).

97. It is he whom Allah guides, that is on true guidance; but he whom

'alaaa añy-yaåtoo bimis̲li haaz̲al-Qur-aani laa yaåtoona bimis̲lihee wa law kaana ba'ḍuhum liba'ḍin ẓaheeraa.

89. Wa laqad ṣarrafnaa linnaasi fee haaz̲al-Qur-aani min kulli mas̲alin fa-abaaa aks̲arun-naasi illaa kufooraa.

90. Wa qaaloo lan-nu'mina laka ḥattaa tafjura lanaa minal-arḍi yamboo'aa.

91. Aw takoona laka jannatum-min nakheeliñw-wa 'inabin fatufajjiral-anhaara khilaalahaa tafjeeraa.

92. Aw tusqiṭas-samaaa'a kamaa za'amta 'alaynaa kisafan aw taåtiya billaahi walmalaaa'ikati qabeelaa.

93. Aw yakoona laka baytum-min zukhrufin aw tarqaa fis-samaaa'i wa lan-nu'mina liruqiyyika ḥattaa tunazzila 'alaynaa kitaaban-naqra'uh; qul Subḥaana Rabbee hal kuntu illaa basharar-Rasoolaa.

(Section 10)

94. Wa maa mana'an-naasa añy-yu'minooo iz̲ jaaa'ahumul-hudaaa illaaa an qaalooo aba-'as̲al-laahu basharar-Rasoolaa.

95. Qul law kaana fil-arḍi malaaa'ikatuñy-yamshoona muṭma'inneena lanazzalnaa 'alayhim-minas-samaaa'i malakar-Rasoolaa.

96. Qul kafaa billaahi shaheedam baynee wa baynakum; innahoo kaana bi'ibaadihee Khabeeram Baṣeeraa.

97. Wa mañy-yahdil-laahu fahuwal-muhtad; wa mañy-

عَلٰٓى اَنْ يَّاْتُوْا بِمِثْلِ هٰذَا الْقُرْاٰنِ
لَا يَاْتُوْنَ بِمِثْلِهٖ وَلَوْ كَانَ بَعْضُهُمْ
لِبَعْضٍ ظَهِيْرًا ﴿٨٨﴾
وَلَقَدْ صَرَّفْنَا لِلنَّاسِ فِيْ هٰذَا
الْقُرْاٰنِ مِنْ كُلِّ مَثَلٍ ز فَاَبٰٓى
اَكْثَرُ النَّاسِ اِلَّا كُفُوْرًا ﴿٨٩﴾
وَقَالُوْا لَنْ نُّؤْمِنَ لَكَ حَتّٰى تَفْجُرَ
لَنَا مِنَ الْاَرْضِ يَنْۢبُوْعًا ﴿٩٠﴾
اَوْ تَكُوْنَ لَكَ جَنَّةٌ مِّنْ نَّخِيْلٍ وَّ
عِنَبٍ فَتُفَجِّرَ الْاَنْهٰرَ خِلٰلَهَا تَفْجِيْرًا ﴿٩١﴾
اَوْ تُسْقِطَ السَّمَآءَ كَمَا زَعَمْتَ عَلَيْنَا
كِسَفًا اَوْ تَاْتِيَ بِاللّٰهِ وَالْمَلٰٓئِكَةِ قَبِيْلًا ﴿٩٢﴾
اَوْ يَكُوْنَ لَكَ بَيْتٌ مِّنْ زُخْرُفٍ
اَوْ تَرْقٰى فِي السَّمَآءِ ؕ وَلَنْ نُّؤْمِنَ
لِرُقِيِّكَ حَتّٰى تُنَزِّلَ عَلَيْنَا كِتٰبًا
نَّقْرَؤُهٗ ؕ قُلْ سُبْحَانَ رَبِّيْ هَلْ كُنْتُ
اِلَّا بَشَرًا رَّسُوْلًا ﴿٩٣﴾ ع ١٠
وَمَا مَنَعَ النَّاسَ اَنْ يُّؤْمِنُوْٓا اِذْ
جَآءَهُمُ الْهُدٰٓى اِلَّآ اَنْ قَالُوْٓا اَبَعَثَ
اللّٰهُ بَشَرًا رَّسُوْلًا ﴿٩٤﴾
قُلْ لَّوْ كَانَ فِي الْاَرْضِ مَلٰٓئِكَةٌ
يَّمْشُوْنَ مُطْمَئِنِّيْنَ لَنَزَّلْنَا عَلَيْهِمْ
مِّنَ السَّمَآءِ مَلَكًا رَّسُوْلًا ﴿٩٥﴾
قُلْ كَفٰى بِاللّٰهِ شَهِيْدًاۢ بَيْنِيْ وَبَيْنَكُمْ ؕ
اِنَّهٗ كَانَ بِعِبَادِهٖ خَبِيْرًاۢ بَصِيْرًا ﴿٩٦﴾
وَمَنْ يَّهْدِ اللّٰهُ فَهُوَ الْمُهْتَدِ ۚ وَمَنْ

Ikhfa اخفاء | Ghunna غُنّہ | Ikhfa Meem Saakin اخفاء میم ساکن | Idghaam ادغام | Qalqala قلقلہ | Qalb قلب | Idghaam Meem Saakin ادغام میم ساکن

He leaves astray - for such will you find no protector besides Him. On the Day of Judgment We shall gather them together, prone on their faces, blind, dumb, and deaf: their abode will be Hell: every time it shows abatement, We shall increase from them the fierceness of the Fire.

98. That is their recompense, because they rejected Our Signs, and said, "When we are reduced to bones and broken dust, should we really be raised up (to be) a new Creation?"

99. Don't they see that Allah, Who created the heavens and the earth, has power to create the like of them (anew)? Only He has decreed a term appointed, of which there is no doubt. But the unjust refuse (to receive it) except with ingratitude.

100. Say: "If you had control of the Treasures of the Mercy of my Lord, behold, you would keep them back, for fear of spending them: for man is (ever) Miserly!"

101. To Moses We did give Nine Clear Sings: ask the Children of Israel: when he came to them, Pharaoh said to him: "O Moses! I consider you, indeed, to have been worked upon by sorcery!

102. Moses said, "You know well that these things have been sent down by none but the Lord of the heavens and the earth as eye-opening evidence: and I consider you indeed, O Pharaoh, to be one doomed to destruction!"

103. So he resolved to remove them from the face of the earth: but We drowned him and all who were with him.

104. And We said thereafter to the Children of Israel, "Dwell securely in the land (of promise)": but when the second of the warnings came to pass, We gathered you together in a mingled crowd.

yuḍlil falan tajida lahum awliyaaa'a min doonih; wa naḥshuruhum Yawmal-Qiyaamati 'alaa wujoohihim umyañw-wa bukmañw-wa ṣummaa; maåwaahum Jahannamu kullamaa khabat zidnaahum sa'eeraa.

98. Ẕaalika jazaaa'uhum bi-annahum kafaroo bi-Aayaatinaa wa qaalooo 'a-iẕaa kunnaa 'iẓaamañw-wa rufaatan 'a-innaa lamaboosoona khalqan jadeedaa.

99. Awalam yaraw annal-laahal-laẕee khalaqas-samaawaati wal-arḍa qaadirun 'alaaa añy-yakhluqa misṯlahum wa ja'ala lahum ajalal-laa rayba feeh; fa-abaẓ-ẓaalimoona illaa kufooraa.

100. Qul law antum tamlikoona khazaaa'ina raḥmati Rabbeee iẕal-la-amsaktum khash-yatal-infaaq; wa kaanal-insaanu qatooraa. **(Section 11)**

101. Wa laqad aataynaa Moosaa tis'a Aayaatim bayyinaatin fas'al Baneee Israaa'eela iẕ jaaa'ahum faqaala lahoo Fir-'awnu innee la-aẓunnuka yaa Moosaa mas-ḥooraa.

102. Qaala laqad 'alimta maaa anzala haaa'ulaaa'i illaa Rabbus-samaawaati wal-arḍi baṣaaa'ira wa innee la-aẓunnuka yaa Fir'awnu masṯbooraa.

103. Fa-araada añy-yastafizzahum-minal-arḍi fa-aghraqnaahu wa mam-ma'ahoo jamee'aa.

104. Wa qulnaa mim ba'dihee li-Baneee Israaa'eelas-kunul-arḍa fa-iẕaa jaaa'a wa'dul-aakhirati ji'naa bikum lafeefaa.

يُّضْلِلْ فَلَنْ تَجِدَ لَهُمْ اَوْلِيَآءَ مِنْ
دُوْنِهٖ ؕ وَنَحْشُرُهُمْ يَوْمَ الْقِيٰمَةِ عَلٰى
وُجُوْهِهِمْ عُمْيًا وَّبُكْمًا وَّصُمًّا ؕ مَاْوٰىهُمْ
جَهَنَّمُ ؕ كُلَّمَا خَبَتْ زِدْنٰهُمْ سَعِيْرًا ﴿٩٧﴾
ذٰلِكَ جَزَآؤُهُمْ بِاَنَّهُمْ كَفَرُوْا بِاٰيٰتِنَا
وَقَالُوْٓا ءَاِذَا كُنَّا عِظَامًا وَّرُفَاتًا
ءَاِنَّا لَمَبْعُوْثُوْنَ خَلْقًا جَدِيْدًا ﴿٩٨﴾
اَوَلَمْ يَرَوْا اَنَّ اللّٰهَ الَّذِيْ خَلَقَ
السَّمٰوٰتِ وَالْاَرْضَ قَادِرٌ عَلٰٓى اَنْ يَّخْلُقَ
مِثْلَهُمْ وَجَعَلَ لَهُمْ اَجَلًا لَّا رَيْبَ فِيْهِ ؕ
فَاَبَى الظّٰلِمُوْنَ اِلَّا كُفُوْرًا ﴿٩٩﴾
قُلْ لَّوْ اَنْتُمْ تَمْلِكُوْنَ خَزَآئِنَ رَحْمَةِ
رَبِّيْٓ اِذًا لَّاَمْسَكْتُمْ خَشْيَةَ الْاِنْفَاقِ ؕ
وَكَانَ الْاِنْسَانُ قَتُوْرًا ﴿١٠٠﴾ ع
وَلَقَدْ اٰتَيْنَا مُوْسٰى تِسْعَ اٰيٰتٍۭ بَيِّنٰتٍ
فَسْـَٔلْ بَنِيْٓ اِسْرَآءِيْلَ اِذْ جَآءَهُمْ فَقَالَ
لَهٗ فِرْعَوْنُ اِنِّيْ لَاَظُنُّكَ يٰمُوْسٰى
مَسْحُوْرًا ﴿١٠١﴾
قَالَ لَقَدْ عَلِمْتَ مَآ اَنْزَلَ هٰٓؤُلَآءِ اِلَّا
رَبُّ السَّمٰوٰتِ وَالْاَرْضِ بَصَآئِرَ ۚ وَ
اِنِّيْ لَاَظُنُّكَ يٰفِرْعَوْنُ مَثْبُوْرًا ﴿١٠٢﴾
فَاَرَادَ اَنْ يَّسْتَفِزَّهُمْ مِّنَ الْاَرْضِ
فَاَغْرَقْنٰهُ وَمَنْ مَّعَهٗ جَمِيْعًا ﴿١٠٣﴾
وَّقُلْنَا مِنْۢ بَعْدِهٖ لِبَنِيْٓ اِسْرَآءِيْلَ
اسْكُنُوا الْاَرْضَ فَاِذَا جَآءَ وَعْدُ الْاٰخِرَةِ
جِئْنَا بِكُمْ لَفِيْفًا ﴿١٠٤﴾

النّصف

ع ٧ / ١١

Ikhfa اخفاء | Ghunna غُنّہ | Ikhfa Meem Saakin اخفاء میم ساکن | Idghaam ادغام | Qalqala قلقلہ | Qalb قلب | Idghaam Meem Saakin ادغام میم ساکن

105. We sent down the (Qur'an) in Truth, and in Truth has it descended: and We sent you but to give Glad Tidings and to warn (sinners).

105. Wa bilḥaqqi anzalnaahu wa bilḥaqqi nazal; wa maaa arsalnaaka illaa mubash-shirañw- wa nazeeraa.

وَبِالْحَقِّ أَنْزَلْنٰهُ وَبِالْحَقِّ نَزَلَ ۗ وَمَآ
أَرْسَلْنٰكَ إِلَّا مُبَشِّرًا وَّنَذِيْرًا ﴿١٠٥﴾

106. (It is) a Qur'an which We have divided (into parts from time to time), in order that you might recite it to men at intervals: We have revealed it by stages.

106. Wa Qur-aanan faraqnaahu litaqra-ahoo 'alan-naasi 'alaa muksiñw-wa nazzalnaahu tan-zeelaa.

وَقُرْاٰنًا فَرَقْنٰهُ لِتَقْرَاَهٗ عَلَى النَّاسِ
عَلٰى مُكْثٍ وَّنَزَّلْنٰهُ تَنْزِيْلًا ﴿١٠٦﴾

107. Say: "Whether you believe in it or not, it is true that those who were given knowledge beforehand, when it is recited to them, fall down on their faces in humble prostration,

107. Qul aaminoo biheee aw laa tu'minoo; innal-lazeena ootul-'ilma min qabliheee izaa yutlaa 'alayhim yakhirroona lil-azqaani sujjadaa.

قُلْ اٰمِنُوْا بِهٖٓ اَوْ لَا تُؤْمِنُوْا ۗ اِنَّ الَّذِيْنَ
اُوْتُوا الْعِلْمَ مِنْ قَبْلِهٖٓ اِذَا يُتْلٰى عَلَيْهِمْ
يَخِرُّوْنَ لِلْاَذْقَانِ سُجَّدًا ﴿١٠٧﴾

108. "And they say: 'Glory to our Lord! Truly has the promise of our Lord been fulfilled!'"

108. Wa yaqooloona Subḥaana Rabbinaaa in kaana wa'du Rabbinaa lamaf'oolaa.

وَّيَقُوْلُوْنَ سُبْحٰنَ رَبِّنَآ اِنْ كَانَ وَعْدُ
رَبِّنَا لَمَفْعُوْلًا ﴿١٠٨﴾

(Bow Down)

109. They fall down on their faces in tears, and it increases their (earnest) humility.

109. Wa yakhirroona lil-azqaa-ni yabkoona wa yazeeduhum khushoo'aa. ۩

وَيَخِرُّوْنَ لِلْاَذْقَانِ يَبْكُوْنَ وَ
يَزِيْدُهُمْ خُشُوْعًا ﴿١٠٩﴾ السجدة

110. Say: "Call upon Allah, or call upon Rahman: by whatever name you call upon Him, (it is well): for to Him belong the Most Beautiful Names. Neither speak your Prayer aloud, nor speak it in a low tone, but seek a middle course between."

110. Qulid-'ul-laaha awid'ur-Raḥmaana ayyam-maa tad'oo falahul-Asmaaa'ul-Ḥusnaa; wa laa tajhar bi-Ṣalaatika wa laa tukhaafit bihaa wabtaghi bayna zaalika sabeelaa.

قُلِ ادْعُوا اللّٰهَ اَوِ ادْعُوا الرَّحْمٰنَ ۗ
اَيًّا مَّا تَدْعُوْا فَلَهُ الْاَسْمَآءُ الْحُسْنٰى ۚ
وَلَا تَجْهَرْ بِصَلَاتِكَ وَلَا تُخَافِتْ
بِهَا وَابْتَغِ بَيْنَ ذٰلِكَ سَبِيْلًا ﴿١١٠﴾

111. Say: "Praise be to Allah, Who begets no son, and has no partner in (His) dominion: nor (needs) He any to protect Him from humiliation: yes, magnify Him for His greatness and glory!

111. Wa qulil-ḥamdu lillaahil-lazee lam yattakhiz waladañw-wa lam yakul-lahoo shareekun fil-mulki wa lam yakul-lahoo waliyyum-minaz-zulli wa kab-birhu takbeeraa. **(Section 12)**

وَقُلِ الْحَمْدُ لِلّٰهِ الَّذِيْ لَمْ يَتَّخِذْ
وَلَدًا وَّلَمْ يَكُنْ لَّهٗ شَرِيْكٌ فِى
الْمُلْكِ وَلَمْ يَكُنْ لَّهٗ وَلِيٌّ مِّنَ
الذُّلِّ وَكَبِّرْهُ تَكْبِيْرًا ﴿١١١﴾

وقف لازم | السجدة (٤) | ع ١٢

18. The Cave

In the name of Allah, Most Gracious, Most Merciful.

Sûrat al-Kahf–18

(Revealed at Makkah)

Bismillaahir Raḥmaanir Raḥeem

(١٨) سُوْرَةُ الْكَهْفِ مَكِّيَّةٌ (٦٩)

بِسْمِ اللّٰهِ الرَّحْمٰنِ الرَّحِيْمِ

1. Praise be to Allah, Who has sent to His Servant the Book, and has allowed therein no crookedness:

1. Alḥamdu lillaahil lazeee anzala 'alaa 'abdihil-Kitaaba wa lam yaj'al-lahoo 'iwajaa.

الْحَمْدُ لِلّٰهِ الَّذِيْٓ اَنْزَلَ عَلٰى عَبْدِهِ
الْكِتٰبَ وَلَمْ يَجْعَلْ لَّهٗ عِوَجًا ﴿١﴾

2. (He has made it) Straight (and Clear) in order that He may warn (the godless) of a terrible Punishment from Him, and that He may give Glad Tidings to the Believers who work righteous Deeds, that they shall have

2. Qayyimal-liyunzira baå-san shadeedam-mil-ladunhu wa yubashshiral-mu'mineenal-lazeena ya'maloonaṣ-ṣaaliḥaati anna lahum

قَيِّمًا لِّيُنْذِرَ بَاْسًا شَدِيْدًا مِّنْ
لَّدُنْهُ وَيُبَشِّرَ الْمُؤْمِنِيْنَ الَّذِيْنَ
يَعْمَلُوْنَ الصّٰلِحٰتِ اَنَّ لَهُمْ

Ikhfa اخفاء | Ghunna غنّہ | Ikhfa Meem Saakin اخفاء میم ساکن | Idghaam ادغام | Qalqala قلقلہ | Qalb قلب | Idghaam Meem Saakin ادغام میم ساکن

English	Transliteration	Arabic
a goodly Reward,	ajran ḥasanaa.	أَجْرًا حَسَنًا ②
3. Wherein they shall remain for ever:	3. Maakiṯeena feehi abadaa.	مَّاكِثِينَ فِيهِ أَبَدًا ③
4. Further, that He may warn those (also) who say, "Allah has begotten a son":	4. Wa yunẕiral-laẕeena qaalut-takhaẕal-laahu waladaa.	وَيُنذِرَ الَّذِينَ قَالُوا اتَّخَذَ اللَّهُ وَلَدًا ④
5. They do not have any knowledge of such a thing, nor had their fathers. It is a grievous thing that issues from their mouths as a saying. What they say is nothing but falsehood!	5. Maa lahum bihee min 'ilmiñw-wa laa li-aabaaa'ihim; kaburat kalimatan takhruju min afwaahihim; iñy-yaqooloona illaa kaẕibaa.	مَّا لَهُم بِهِ مِنْ عِلْمٍ وَلَا لِآبَائِهِمْ كَبُرَتْ كَلِمَةً تَخْرُجُ مِنْ أَفْوَاهِهِمْ إِن يَقُولُونَ إِلَّا كَذِبًا ⑤
6. You would only, perchance, fret yourself to death, following after them, in grief, if they do not believe in this Message.	6. Fala'allaka baakhi'un nafsaka 'alaaa aaṯaarihim illam yu'minoo bihaaẕal-ḥadeeṯi asafaa.	فَلَعَلَّكَ بَاخِعٌ نَّفْسَكَ عَلَىٰ آثَارِهِمْ إِن لَّمْ يُؤْمِنُوا بِهَٰذَا الْحَدِيثِ أَسَفًا ⑥
7. That which is on earth we have made but as a glittering show for the earth, in order that We may test them - as to which of them are best in conduct.	7. Innaa ja'alnaa maa 'alal-arḍi zeenatal-lahaa linabluwahum ayyuhum aḥsanu 'amalaa.	إِنَّا جَعَلْنَا مَا عَلَى الْأَرْضِ زِينَةً لَّهَا لِنَبْلُوَهُمْ أَيُّهُمْ أَحْسَنُ عَمَلًا ⑦
8. Verily what is on earth we shall make but as dust and dry soil (without growth or herbage).	8. Wa innaa lajaa'iloona maa 'alayhaa ṣa'eedan juruzaa.	وَإِنَّا لَجَاعِلُونَ مَا عَلَيْهَا صَعِيدًا جُرُزًا ⑧
9. Or do you not reflect that the Companions of the Cave and of the Inscription were wonders among Our Signs?	9. Am ḥasibta anna Aṣḥaabal-Kahfi war-Raqeemi kaanoo min Aayaatinaa 'ajabaa.	أَمْ حَسِبْتَ أَنَّ أَصْحَابَ الْكَهْفِ وَالرَّقِيمِ كَانُوا مِنْ آيَاتِنَا عَجَبًا ⑨
10. Behold, the youths betook themselves to the Cave: they said, "Our Lord! bestow on us Mercy from Yourself, and dispose of our affair for us in the right way!"	10. Iẕ awal-fityatu ilal-Kahfi faqaaloo Rabbanaaa aatinaa mil-ladunka raḥmatañw-wa hayyi' lanaa min amrinaa rashadaa.	إِذْ أَوَى الْفِتْيَةُ إِلَى الْكَهْفِ فَقَالُوا رَبَّنَا آتِنَا مِن لَّدُنكَ رَحْمَةً وَهَيِّئْ لَنَا مِنْ أَمْرِنَا رَشَدًا ⑩
11. Then We draw (a veil) over their ears, for a number of years, in the Cave, (so that they did not hear):	11. Faḍarabnaa 'alaaa aaẕaanihim fil-Kahfi sineena 'adadaa.	فَضَرَبْنَا عَلَىٰ آذَانِهِمْ فِي الْكَهْفِ سِنِينَ عَدَدًا ⑪
12. Then We roused them, in order to test which of the two parties was best at calculating the term of years they had tarried!	12. Ṯumma ba'aṯnaahum lina'lama ayyul-ḥizbayni aḥṣaa limaa labiṯooo amadaa. **(Section 1)**	ثُمَّ بَعَثْنَاهُمْ لِنَعْلَمَ أَيُّ الْحِزْبَيْنِ أَحْصَىٰ لِمَا لَبِثُوا أَمَدًا ⑫
13. We relate to you their story in truth: they were youths who believed in their Lord, and We advanced them in guidance:	13. Naḥnu naquṣṣu 'alayka naba-ahum bilḥaqq; innahum fityatun aamanoo bi-Rabbihim wa zidnaahum hudaa.	نَحْنُ نَقُصُّ عَلَيْكَ نَبَأَهُم بِالْحَقِّ إِنَّهُمْ فِتْيَةٌ آمَنُوا بِرَبِّهِمْ وَزِدْنَاهُمْ هُدًى ⑬

Ikhfa اخفاء | Ghunna غُنّہ | Ikhfa Meem Saakin اخفاء میم ساکن | Idghaam ادغام | Qalqala قلقلہ | Qalb قلب | Idghaam Meem Saakin ادغام میم ساکن

14. We gave strength to their hearts: behold, they stood up and said: "Our Lord is the Lord of the heavens and of the earth: never shall we call upon any god other than Him: if we did, we should indeed have uttered an enormity!

14. Wa rabaṭnaa 'alaa quloobihim iz̲ qaamoo faqaaloo Rabbunaa Rabbus-samaawaati wal-arḍi lan-nad'uwa min dooniheee ilaahal-laqad qulnaaa iz̲an shaṭaṭaa.

وَّرَبَطْنَا عَلٰى قُلُوْبِهِمْ اِذْ قَامُوْا
فَقَالُوْا رَبُّنَا رَبُّ السَّمٰوٰتِ وَالْاَرْضِ
لَنْ نَّدْعُوَا مِنْ دُوْنِهٖٓ اِلٰهًا لَّقَدْ
قُلْنَآ اِذًا شَطَطًا ﴿١٤﴾

15. "These our people have taken for worship gods other than Him: why do they not bring forward an authority clear (and convincing) for what they do? Who does more wrong than such as invent a falsehood against Allah?

15. Haaa'ulaaa'i qawmunat-takhaz̲oo min dooniheee aalihatal-law laa yaåtoona 'alayhim bisulṭaanim bayyin; faman aẓlamu mimmaniftaraa 'alal-laahi kaz̲ibaa.

هٰٓؤُلَآءِ قَوْمُنَا اتَّخَذُوْا مِنْ دُوْنِهٖٓ
اٰلِهَةً ۭ لَوْلَا يَاْتُوْنَ عَلَيْهِمْ بِسُلْطٰنٍۢ
بَيِّنٍ ۭ فَمَنْ اَظْلَمُ مِمَّنِ افْتَرٰى
عَلَى اللّٰهِ كَذِبًا ۭ ﴿١٥﴾

16. "When you turn away from them and the things they worship other than Allah, betake yourselves to the Cave: your Lord will shower His mercies on you and disposes of your affair towards comfort and ease."

16. Wa iz̲i'tazal-tumoohum wa maa ya'budoona illal-laaha faåwooo ilal-kahfi yanshur lakum Rabbukum-mir-raḥmatihee wa yuhayyi' lakum-min amrikum-mirfaqaa.

وَاِذِ اعْتَزَلْتُمُوْهُمْ وَمَا يَعْبُدُوْنَ اِلَّا
اللّٰهَ فَاْوٗٓا اِلَى الْكَهْفِ يَنْشُرْ لَكُمْ
رَبُّكُمْ مِّنْ رَّحْمَتِهٖ وَيُهَيِّئْ لَكُمْ
مِّنْ اَمْرِكُمْ مِّرْفَقًا ﴿١٦﴾

17. You would have seen the sun, when it rose, declining to the right from their Cave, and when it set, turning away from them to the left, while they lay in the open space in the midst of the Cave. Such are among the Signs of Allah: He whom Allah, guides is rightly guided; but he whom Allah leaves to stray,- for him will you find no protector to lead him to the Right Way.

17. Wa tarash-shamsa iz̲aa ṭala'at-tazaawaru 'an kahfihim z̲aatal-yameeni wa iz̲aa gharabat taqriḍuhum z̲aatash-shimaali wa hum fee fajwatim-minh; z̲aalika min Aayaatil-laah; mañy-yahdil-laahu fahuwal-muhtad, wa mañy-yuḍlil falan tajida lahoo waliyyam-murshidaa. **(Section 2)**

وَتَرَى الشَّمْسَ اِذَا طَلَعَتْ تَّزٰوَرُ
عَنْ كَهْفِهِمْ ذَاتَ الْيَمِيْنِ وَاِذَا
غَرَبَتْ تَّقْرِضُهُمْ ذَاتَ الشِّمَالِ
وَهُمْ فِيْ فَجْوَةٍ مِّنْهُ ۭ ذٰلِكَ مِنْ
اٰيٰتِ اللّٰهِ ۭ مَنْ يَّهْدِ اللّٰهُ فَهُوَ
الْمُهْتَدِ ۚ وَمَنْ يُّضْلِلْ فَلَنْ تَجِدَ
لَهٗ وَلِيًّا مُّرْشِدًا ﴿١٧﴾ ع ٢

18. You would have deemed them awake, whilst they were asleep, and We turned them on their right and on their left sides: their dog stretching forth his two fore-legs on the threshold: if you had come up on to them, you would have certainly turned back from them in flight, and would certainly have been filled with terror of them.

18. Wa taḥsabuhum ayqaaẓañw-wa hum ruqood; wa nuqallibuhum z̲aatal-yameeni wa z̲aatash-shimaali wa kalbuhum baasiṭun z̲iraa'ayhi bilwaṣeed; lawiṭ-ṭala'ta 'alayhim la-wallayta minhum firaarañw-wa lamuli'ta minhum ru'baa.

وَتَحْسَبُهُمْ اَيْقَاظًا وَّهُمْ رُقُوْدٌ ڰ
وَّنُقَلِّبُهُمْ ذَاتَ الْيَمِيْنِ وَذَاتَ
الشِّمَالِ ڰ وَكَلْبُهُمْ بَاسِطٌ ذِرَاعَيْهِ
بِالْوَصِيْدِ ۭ لَوِ اطَّلَعْتَ عَلَيْهِمْ لَوَلَّيْتَ
مِنْهُمْ فِرَارًا وَّلَمُلِئْتَ مِنْهُمْ رُعْبًا ﴿١٨﴾

19. Such (being their state), we raised them up (from sleep), that they might question each other. Said one of them,

19. Wa kaz̲aalika ba'as̲naahum liyatasaaa'aloo baynahum; qaala qaaa'ilum-minhum kam

وَكَذٰلِكَ بَعَثْنٰهُمْ لِيَتَسَاۗءَلُوْا
بَيْنَهُمْ ۭ قَالَ قَاۗىِٕلٌ مِّنْهُمْ كَمْ

Ikhfa اخفاء | Ghunna غنّہ | Ikhfa Meem Saakin اخفاء میم ساکن | Idghaam ادغام | Qalqala قلقلہ | Qalb قلب | Idghaam Meem Saakin ادغام میم ساکن

"How long have you stayed (here)?" They said, "We have stayed (perhaps) a day, or part of a day." (At length) they (all) said, "Allah (alone) knows best how long you have stayed here.... Now you send one of you with this money of yours to the town: let him find out which is the best food (to be had) and bring some to you, that (you may) satisfy your hunger there-with: And let him behave with care and courtesy, and let him not inform anyone about you.

20. "For if they should come upon you, they would stone you or force you to return to their cult, and in that case you would never attain prosperity."

21. Thus We made their case known to the people, that they might know that the promise of Allah is true, and that there can be no doubt about the Hour of Judgment. Behold, they disputed among them-selves as to their affair. (Some) said, "Construct a building over them": Their Lord knows best about them: those who prevailed over their affair said, "Let us surely build a place of worship over them."

22. (Some) say they were three, the dog being the fourth among them; (others) say they were five, the dog being the sixth,- doubtfully guessing at the unknown; (yet others) say they were seven, the dog being the eighth. You say: "My Lord knows best their number; it is but few that know their (real case)." Do not enter, therefore, into controversies concerning them, except on a matter that is clear, nor consult any of them about (the affair of) the Sleepers.

23. Nor say of anything, "I shall be sure to do

labistum qaaloo labisnaa yawman aw ba'ḍa yawm; qaaloo Rabbukum a'lamu bimaa labistum fab'asooo aḥadakum biwariqikum haaziheee ilal-madeenati falyanẓur ayyuhaaa azkaa ṭa'aaman falyaåtikum birizqim-minhu walyatalaṭṭaf wa laa yush'iranna bikum aḥadaa.

20. Innahum iñy-yaẓharoo 'alaykum yarjumookum aw yu'eedookum fee millatihim wa lan tufliḥooo izan abadaa.

21. Wa kazaalika a'sarnaa 'alayhim liya'lamooo anna wa'dal-laahi ḥaqquñw-wa annas-Saa'ata laa rayba feehaa iz yatanaaza'oona baynahum amrahum faqaalub-noo 'alayhim bunyaanaa; Rabbuhum a'lamu bihim; qaalal-lazeena ghalaboo 'alaaa amrihim lanattakhizanna 'alayhim-masjidaa.

22. Sa-yaqooloona salaasaturraabi'uhum kalbuhum wa yaqooloona khamsatun saadisuhum kalbuhum rajmam bilghayb; wa yaqooloona sab'atuñw-wa saaminuhum kalbuhum; qur-Rabbeee a'lamu bi'iddatihim-maa ya'lamuhum illaa qaleel; falaa tumaari feehim illaa miraaa'an ẓaahirañw-wa laa tastafti feehim-minhum aḥadaa. **(Section 3)**

23. Wa laa taqoolanna lishay'in innee faa'ilun

لَبِثْتُمْ ۚ قَالُوا لَبِثْنَا يَوْمًا أَوْ بَعْضَ
يَوْمٍ ۚ قَالُوا رَبُّكُمْ أَعْلَمُ بِمَا
لَبِثْتُمْ فَابْعَثُوا أَحَدَكُمْ بِوَرِقِكُمْ
هَٰذِهِ إِلَى الْمَدِينَةِ فَلْيَنْظُرْ أَيُّهَا
أَزْكَىٰ طَعَامًا فَلْيَأْتِكُمْ بِرِزْقٍ مِنْهُ
وَلْيَتَلَطَّفْ وَلَا يُشْعِرَنَّ
بِكُمْ أَحَدًا ﴿١٩﴾
إِنَّهُمْ إِنْ يَظْهَرُوا عَلَيْكُمْ
يَرْجُمُوكُمْ أَوْ يُعِيدُوكُمْ فِي مِلَّتِهِمْ
وَلَنْ تُفْلِحُوا إِذًا أَبَدًا ﴿٢٠﴾
وَكَذَٰلِكَ أَعْثَرْنَا عَلَيْهِمْ لِيَعْلَمُوا
أَنَّ وَعْدَ اللَّهِ حَقٌّ وَأَنَّ السَّاعَةَ
لَا رَيْبَ فِيهَا إِذْ يَتَنَازَعُونَ بَيْنَهُمْ
أَمْرَهُمْ ۖ فَقَالُوا ابْنُوا عَلَيْهِمْ بُنْيَانًا ۖ
رَبُّهُمْ أَعْلَمُ بِهِمْ ۚ قَالَ الَّذِينَ غَلَبُوا
عَلَىٰ أَمْرِهِمْ لَنَتَّخِذَنَّ عَلَيْهِمْ
مَسْجِدًا ﴿٢١﴾
سَيَقُولُونَ ثَلَاثَةٌ رَابِعُهُمْ
كَلْبُهُمْ وَيَقُولُونَ خَمْسَةٌ
سَادِسُهُمْ كَلْبُهُمْ رَجْمًا بِالْغَيْبِ ۖ
وَيَقُولُونَ سَبْعَةٌ وَثَامِنُهُمْ كَلْبُهُمْ ۚ
قُلْ رَبِّي أَعْلَمُ بِعِدَّتِهِمْ مَا
يَعْلَمُهُمْ إِلَّا قَلِيلٌ ۗ فَلَا تُمَارِ فِيهِمْ
إِلَّا مِرَاءً ظَاهِرًا وَلَا تَسْتَفْتِ
فِيهِمْ مِنْهُمْ أَحَدًا ﴿٢٢﴾
وَلَا تَقُولَنَّ لِشَيْءٍ إِنِّي فَاعِلٌ

نصف القرآن باعتبار عدد الحروف بأن التاء بعد الياء من النصف الأول واللام الثانية من النصف الأخير ١٢

Ikhfa اخفاء | Ghunna غنّہ | Ikhfa Meem Saakin اخفاء میم ساکن | Idghaam ادغام | Qalqala قلقلہ | Qalb قلب | Idghaam Meem Saakin ادغام میم ساکن

so and so tomorrow"-

zaalika ghadaa.

ذٰلِكَ غَدًا ﴿٢٣﴾

24. Without adding, "If Allah so wills" and call your Lord to mind when you forget, and say, "I hope that my Lord will guide me ever closer (even) than this to the right road."

24. Illaaa añy-yashaaa'al-laah; wazkur-Rabbaka izaa naseeta wa qul 'asaaa añy-yahdiyani Rabbee li-aqraba min haazaa rashadaa.

اِلَّآ اَنْ يَّشَآءَ اللّٰهُ ز وَاذْكُرْ رَّبَّكَ
اِذَا نَسِيْتَ وَقُلْ عَسٰٓى اَنْ يَّهْدِيَنِ
رَبِّيْ لِاَقْرَبَ مِنْ هٰذَا رَشَدًا ﴿٢٤﴾

25. So they stayed in their Cave three hundred years, and (some) add nine (more).

25. Wa labisoo fee kahfihim salaasa mi'atin sineena wazdaadoo tis'aa.

وَلَبِثُوْا فِيْ كَهْفِهِمْ ثَلٰثَ مِائَةٍ
سِنِيْنَ وَازْدَادُوْا تِسْعًا ﴿٢٥﴾

26. Say: "Allah knows best how long they stayed: with Him is (the knowledge of) the secrets of the heavens and the earth: how clearly He sees, how finely He hears (everything)! They have no protector other than Him; nor does He share His Command with any person whatsoever.

26. Qulil-laahu a'lamu bimaa labisoo lahoo ghaybus-samaa-waati wal-ardi absir bihee wa-asmi'; maa lahum-min doonihee miñw-waliyyiñw-wa laa yushriku fee hukmiheee ahadaa.

قُلِ اللّٰهُ اَعْلَمُ بِمَا لَبِثُوْا ج لَهٗ غَيْبُ
السَّمٰوٰتِ وَالْاَرْضِ ط اَبْصِرْ بِهٖ وَ
اَسْمِعْ ط مَا لَهُمْ مِّنْ دُوْنِهٖ مِنْ
وَّلِيٍّ ز وَّلَا يُشْرِكُ فِيْ حُكْمِهٖٓ
اَحَدًا ﴿٢٦﴾

27. And recite (and teach) what has been revealed to you of the Book of your Lord: none can change His Words, and none will you find as a refuge other than Him.

27. Watlu maaa oohiya ilayka min Kitaabi Rabbika laa mubaddila li-Kalimaatihee wa lan tajida min doonihee multahadaa.

وَاتْلُ مَآ اُوْحِيَ اِلَيْكَ مِنْ
كِتَابِ رَبِّكَ ج لَا مُبَدِّلَ لِكَلِمٰتِهٖ قف
وَلَنْ تَجِدَ مِنْ دُوْنِهٖ مُلْتَحَدًا ﴿٢٧﴾

28. And keep your soul content with those who call on their Lord morning and evening, seeking His Face; and let not your eyes pass beyond them, seeking the pomp and glitter of this Life; nor obey any whose heart We have permitted to neglect the remembrance of Us, one who follows his own desires, whose case has gone beyond all bounds.

28. Wasbir nafsaka ma'al-lazeena yad'oona Rabbahum bilghadaati wal'ashiyyi yuree-doona Wajhahoo wa laa ta'du 'aynaaka 'anhum tureedu zeenatal-hayaatid-dunyaa wa laa tuti' man aghfalnaa qalbahoo 'an zikrinaa wattaba'a hawaahu wa kaana amruhoo furutaa.

وَاصْبِرْ نَفْسَكَ مَعَ الَّذِيْنَ
يَدْعُوْنَ رَبَّهُمْ بِالْغَدٰوةِ وَالْعَشِيِّ
يُرِيْدُوْنَ وَجْهَهٗ وَلَا تَعْدُ عَيْنٰكَ
عَنْهُمْ ج تُرِيْدُ زِيْنَةَ الْحَيٰوةِ الدُّنْيَا ج
وَلَا تُطِعْ مَنْ اَغْفَلْنَا قَلْبَهٗ عَنْ
ذِكْرِنَا وَاتَّبَعَ هَوٰىهُ وَكَانَ
اَمْرُهٗ فُرُطًا ﴿٢٨﴾ الثلثة

29. Say, "The Truth is from your Lord": Let him who will believe, and let him who will, reject (it): for the wrong-doers We have prepared a Fire whose (smoke and flames), like the walls and roof of a tent, will hem them in: if they implore relief they will be granted water-like melted brass, that will scald their faces.

29. Wa qulil-haqqu mir-Rabbikum faman shaaa'a falyu'miñw-wa man shaaa'a falyakfur; innaaa a'tadnaa liz-zaalimeena Naaran ahaata bihim suraadiquhaa; wa iñy-yastagheesoo yughaasoo bi-maaa'in kalmuhli yashwil-wujooh;

وَقُلِ الْحَقُّ مِنْ رَّبِّكُمْ قف فَمَنْ شَآءَ
فَلْيُؤْمِنْ وَّمَنْ شَآءَ فَلْيَكْفُرْ لا
اِنَّآ اَعْتَدْنَا لِلظّٰلِمِيْنَ نَارًا لا اَحَاطَ
بِهِمْ سُرَادِقُهَا ط وَاِنْ يَّسْتَغِيْثُوْا
يُغَاثُوْا بِمَآءٍ كَالْمُهْلِ يَشْوِي الْوُجُوْهَ ط

Ikhfa اخفاء | Ghunna غنّہ | Ikhfa Meem Saakin اخفاءمیم ساکن | Idghaam ادغام | Qalqala قلقلہ | Qalb قلب | Idghaam Meem Saakin ادغام میم ساکن

how dreadful the drink! How uncomfortable a couch to recline on!

bi'sash-sharaab; wa saaa'at murtafaqaa.

بِئْسَ الشَّرَابُ ؕ وَسَاءَتْ مُرْتَفَقًا (٢٩)

30. As to those who believe and work righteousness, verily We shall not suffer to perish the reward of any who do a (single) righteous deed.

30. Innal-lazeena aamanoo wa 'amiluṣ-ṣaaliḥaati innaa laa nuḍee'u ajra man aḥsana 'amalaa.

إِنَّ الَّذِينَ آمَنُوا وَعَمِلُوا الصَّالِحَاتِ إِنَّا لَا نُضِيعُ أَجْرَ مَنْ أَحْسَنَ عَمَلًا (٣٠)

31. For them will be Gardens of Eternity; beneath them rivers will flow; they will be adorned therein with bracelets of gold, and they will wear green garments of fine silk and heavy brocade: They will recline therein on raised thrones. How good the recompense! How beautiful a couch to recline on!

31. Ulaaa'ika lahum Jannaatu 'Adnin tajree min taḥtihimul-anhaaru yuḥallawna feehaa min asaawira min zahabiñw-wa yalbasoona siyaaban khuḍram-min sundusiñw-wa istabraqim-muttaki'eena feehaa 'alal-araaa'ik; ni'mas-sawaab; wa ḥasunat murtafaqaa. **(Section 4)**

أُولَٰئِكَ لَهُمْ جَنَّاتُ عَدْنٍ تَجْرِي مِنْ تَحْتِهِمُ الْأَنْهَارُ يُحَلَّوْنَ فِيهَا مِنْ أَسَاوِرَ مِنْ ذَهَبٍ وَيَلْبَسُونَ ثِيَابًا خُضْرًا مِنْ سُنْدُسٍ وَإِسْتَبْرَقٍ مُتَّكِئِينَ فِيهَا عَلَى الْأَرَائِكِ ۚ نِعْمَ الثَّوَابُ ۚ وَحَسُنَتْ مُرْتَفَقًا (٣١)

32. Set forth to them the parable of two men: for one of them We provided two gardens of grape-vines and surrounded them with date palms; in between the two We placed corn-fields.

32. Waḍrib lahum-masalar-rajulayni ja'alnaa li-aḥadihimaa jannatayni min a'naabiñw-wa ḥafafnaahumaa binakhliñw-wa ja'alnaa baynahumaa zar'aa.

وَاضْرِبْ لَهُمْ مَثَلًا رَجُلَيْنِ جَعَلْنَا لِأَحَدِهِمَا جَنَّتَيْنِ مِنْ أَعْنَابٍ وَحَفَفْنَاهُمَا بِنَخْلٍ وَجَعَلْنَا بَيْنَهُمَا زَرْعًا (٣٢)

33. Each of those gardens brought forth its produce, and did not fail in the least therein: in the midst of them We caused a river to flow.

33. Kiltal-jannatayni aatat ukulahaa wa lam taẓlim-minhu shay'añw-wa fajjarnaa khilaalahumaa naharaa.

كِلْتَا الْجَنَّتَيْنِ آتَتْ أُكُلَهَا وَلَمْ تَظْلِمْ مِنْهُ شَيْئًا ۚ وَفَجَّرْنَا خِلَالَهُمَا نَهَرًا (٣٣)

34. (Abundant) was the produce this man had : he said to his companion, in the course of a mutual argument: "more wealth have I than you, and more honor and power in (my following of) men."

34. Wa kaana lahoo samarun faqaala liṣaaḥibihee wa huwa yuḥaawiruhooo ana aksaru minka maalañw-wa a'azzu nafaraa.

وَكَانَ لَهُ ثَمَرٌ فَقَالَ لِصَاحِبِهِ وَهُوَ يُحَاوِرُهُ أَنَا أَكْثَرُ مِنْكَ مَالًا وَأَعَزُّ نَفَرًا (٣٤)

35. He went into his garden in a state (of mind) unjust to his soul: He said, "I deem not that this will ever perish,

35. Wa dakhala jannatahoo wa huwa ẓaalimul-linafsihee qaala maaa aẓunnu an tabeeda haaziheee abadaa.

وَدَخَلَ جَنَّتَهُ وَهُوَ ظَالِمٌ لِنَفْسِهِ قَالَ مَا أَظُنُّ أَنْ تَبِيدَ هَٰذِهِ أَبَدًا (٣٥)

36. "Nor do I deem that the Hour (of Judgment) will (ever) come: Even if I am brought back to my Lord, I shall surely find (there) something better in exchange."

36. Wa maaa aẓunnus-Saa'ata qaaa'imatañw-wa la'ir-ruditttu ilaa Rabbee la-ajidanna khayram-minhaa munqalabaa.

وَمَا أَظُنُّ السَّاعَةَ قَائِمَةً وَلَئِنْ رُدِدْتُ إِلَىٰ رَبِّي لَأَجِدَنَّ خَيْرًا مِنْهَا مُنْقَلَبًا (٣٦)

37. His companion said to him, in the course of the argument with him: "Do you deny Him Who created you out of

37. Qaala lahoo ṣaaḥibuhoo wa huwa yuḥaawiruhooo akafarta billazee khalaqaka min

قَالَ لَهُ صَاحِبُهُ وَهُوَ يُحَاوِرُهُ أَكَفَرْتَ بِالَّذِي خَلَقَكَ مِنْ

Ikhfa اخفاء	Ghunna غنّہ	Ikhfa Meem Saakin اخفاء میم ساکن	Idghaam ادغام	Qalqala قلقلہ	Qalb قلب	Idghaam Meem Saakin ادغام میم ساکن

dust, then out of a sperm-drop, then fashioned you into a man?

turaabin summa min nutfatin summa sawwaaka rajulaa.

تُرَابٍ ثُمَّ مِنْ نُّطْفَةٍ ثُمَّ
سَوّٰىكَ رَجُلًا ۝٣٧

38. "But (I think) for my part that He is Allah, My Lord, and none shall I associate with my Lord.

38. Laakinna Huwal-laahu Rabbee wa laaa ushriku bi-Rabbeee ahadaa.

لٰكِنَّا۠ هُوَ اللّٰهُ رَبِّيْ وَلَآ اُشْرِكُ
بِرَبِّيْٓ اَحَدًا ۝٣٨

39. "Why did you not, as you went into your garden, say: 'Allah's Will (be done)! There is no power but with Allah!' If you see me less than you in wealth and sons,

39. Wa law laaa iz dakhalta jannataka qulta maa shaaa'al-laahu laa quwwata illaa billaah; in tarani ana aqalla minka maalañw-wa waladaa.

وَلَوْلَآ اِذْ دَخَلْتَ جَنَّتَكَ قُلْتَ
مَا شَآءَ اللّٰهُ ۙ لَا قُوَّةَ اِلَّا بِاللّٰهِ ۚ
اِنْ تَرَنِ اَنَا اَقَلَّ مِنْكَ مَالًا
وَّوَلَدًا ۝٣٩

40. "It may be that my Lord will give me something better than your garden, and that He will send on your garden thunderbolts (by way of reckoning) from heaven, making it (but) slippery sand!-

40. Fa'asaa Rabeee añy-yu'tiyani khayram-min jannatika wa yursila 'alayhaa husbaanam-minas-samaaa'i fatusbiha sa'eedan zalaqaa.

فَعَسٰى رَبِّيْٓ اَنْ يُّؤْتِيَنِ خَيْرًا
مِّنْ جَنَّتِكَ وَيُرْسِلَ عَلَيْهَا
حُسْبَانًا مِّنَ السَّمَآءِ فَتُصْبِحَ
صَعِيْدًا زَلَقًا ۝٤٠

41. "Or the water of the garden will run off underground so that you will never be able to find it."

41. Aw yusbiha maaa'uhaa ghawran falan tastatee'a lahoo talabaa.

اَوْ يُصْبِحَ مَآؤُهَا غَوْرًا فَلَنْ
تَسْتَطِيْعَ لَهٗ طَلَبًا ۝٤١

42. So his fruits (and enjoyment) were encompassed (with ruin), and he remained twisting and turning his hands over what he had spent on his property, which had (now) tumbled to pieces to its very foundations, and he could only say, "Woe is me! Would I had never ascribed partners to my Lord and Cherisher!"

42. Wa uheeta bisamarihee fa-asbaha yuqallibu kaffayhi 'alaa maaa anfaqa feehaa wa hiya khaawiyatun 'alaa 'urooshihaa wa yaqoolu yaalaytanee lam ushrik bi-Rabbeee ahadaa.

وَاُحِيْطَ بِثَمَرِهٖ فَاَصْبَحَ يُقَلِّبُ
كَفَّيْهِ عَلٰى مَآ اَنْفَقَ فِيْهَا
وَهِيَ خَاوِيَةٌ عَلٰى عُرُوْشِهَا
وَيَقُوْلُ يٰلَيْتَنِيْ لَمْ اُشْرِكْ
بِرَبِّيْٓ اَحَدًا ۝٤٢

43. Nor had he numbers to help him against Allah, nor was he able to deliver himself.

43. Wa lam takul-lahoo fi'atuñy-yansuroonahoo min doonil-laahi wa maa kaana muntasiraa.

وَلَمْ تَكُنْ لَّهٗ فِئَةٌ يَّنْصُرُوْنَهٗ
مِنْ دُوْنِ اللّٰهِ وَمَا كَانَ
مُنْتَصِرًا ۝٤٣

44. There, the (only) protection comes from Allah, the True One. He is the Best to reward, and the Best to give success.

44. Hunaalikal walaayatu lillaahil-haqq; huwa khayrun sawaabañw-wa khayrun 'uqbaa.

(Section 5)

هُنَالِكَ الْوَلَايَةُ لِلّٰهِ الْحَقِّ ۭ هُوَ
خَيْرٌ ثَوَابًا وَّخَيْرٌ عُقْبًا ۝٤٤ ع ٥/١٧

45. Set forth to them the similitude of the life of this world: It is like the rain which we send down from the skies:

45. Wadrib lahum-masalal-hayaatid-dunyaa kamaaa'in anzalnaahu minas-samaaa'i

وَاضْرِبْ لَهُمْ مَّثَلَ الْحَيٰوةِ الدُّنْيَا
كَمَآءٍ اَنْزَلْنٰهُ مِنَ السَّمَآءِ

Ikhfa اخفاء · Ghunna غنّہ · Ikhfa Meem Saakin اخفاء میم ساکن · Idghaam ادغام · Qalqala قلقلہ · Qalb قلب · Idghaam Meem Saakin ادغام میم ساکن

The earth's vegetation absorbs it, but soon it becomes dry stubble, which the winds do scatter: it is (only) Allah who prevails over all things.

46. Wealth and sons are allurements of the life of this world: but the things that endure, Good Deeds, are best in the sight of your Lord, as rewards, and best as (the foundation for) hopes.

47. One Day We shall remove the mountains, and you will see the earth as a level stretch, and We shall gather them, all together, nor shall We leave out any one of them.

48. And they will be marshalled before your Lord in ranks, (with the announcement), "Now have you come to Us (bare) as We created you first instance; yes, you thought We shall not fulfil the appointment made to you to meet (Us)!":

49. And the Book (of Deeds) will be placed (before you); and you will see the sinful in great terror because of what is (recorded) therein; they will say, "Ah! woe to us! what a Book is this! It leaves out nothing small or great, but takes account thereof!" They will find all that they did, placed before them: And not one will your Lord treat with injustice.

50. Behold! We said to the angels, "Bow down to Adam": They bowed down except Iblis. He was one of the Jinns, and he broke the Command of his Lord. Will you then take him and his progeny as protectors rather than Me? And they are enemies to you! Evil would be the exchange for the wrong-doers!

51. I called them not to witness the creation of the heavens and the earth, nor (even) their own creation: nor

fakhtalaṭa bihee nabaatul-arḍi fa-aṣbaḥa hasheeman tazroohur-riyaaḥ; wa kaanal-laahu 'alaa kulli shay'im-muqtadiraa.

46. Almaalu walbanoona zeenatul-ḥayaatid-dunyaa walbaaqiyaatuṣ-ṣaaliḥaatu khayrun 'inda Rabbika sawaabañw-wa khayrun amalaa.

47. Wa Yawma nusayyirul-jibaala wa taral-arḍa baarizatañw-wa ḥasharnaahum falam nughaadir minhum aḥadaa.

48. Wa 'uriḍoo 'alaa Rabbika ṣaffaa, laqad ji'tumoonaa kamaa khalaqnaakum awwala marrah; bal za'amtum allannaj'ala lakum-maw'idaa.

49. Wa wuḍi'al-kitaabu fataral-mujrimeena mushfiqeena mimmaa feehi wa yaqooloona yaa waylatanaa maa lihaazal-kitaabi laa yughaadiru ṣagheeratañw-wa laa kabeeratan illaaa aḥṣaahaa; wa wajadoo maa 'amiloo ḥaaḍiraa; wa laa yazlimu Rabbuka aḥadaa.

(Section 6)

50. Wa iz qulnaa lilmalaaa'ikatis-judoo li Aadama fasajadooo illaaa Ibleesa kaana minal-jinni fafasaqa 'an amri Rabbih; afatattakhizoonahoo wa zurriyyatahooo awliyaaa'a min doonee wa hum lakum 'aduww; bi'sa lizzaalimeena badalaa.

51. Maaa ash-hattuhum khalqas-samaawaati wal-arḍi wa laa khalqa anfusihim wa maa

فَاخْتَلَطَ بِهٖ نَبَاتُ الْاَرْضِ فَاَصْبَحَ
هَشِيْمًا تَذْرُوْهُ الرِّيٰحُ ؕ وَكَانَ
اللّٰهُ عَلٰى كُلِّ شَیْءٍ مُّقْتَدِرًا ﴿٤٥﴾
اَلْمَالُ وَالْبَنُوْنَ زِيْنَةُ الْحَيٰوةِ
الدُّنْيَا ۚ وَالْبٰقِيٰتُ الصّٰلِحٰتُ خَيْرٌ
عِنْدَ رَبِّكَ ثَوَابًا وَّخَيْرٌ اَمَلًا ﴿٤٦﴾
وَيَوْمَ نُسَيِّرُ الْجِبَالَ وَتَرَى الْاَرْضَ
بَارِزَةً ۙ وَّحَشَرْنٰهُمْ فَلَمْ نُغَادِرْ
مِنْهُمْ اَحَدًا ۚ ﴿٤٧﴾
وَعُرِضُوْا عَلٰى رَبِّكَ صَفًّا ؕ لَقَدْ
جِئْتُمُوْنَا كَمَا خَلَقْنٰكُمْ اَوَّلَ مَرَّةٍ ۢ
بَلْ زَعَمْتُمْ اَلَّنْ نَّجْعَلَ لَكُمْ مَّوْعِدًا ﴿٤٨﴾
وَوُضِعَ الْكِتٰبُ فَتَرَى الْمُجْرِمِيْنَ
مُشْفِقِيْنَ مِمَّا فِيْهِ وَيَقُوْلُوْنَ
يٰوَيْلَتَنَا مَالِ هٰذَا الْكِتٰبِ
لَا يُغَادِرُ صَغِيْرَةً وَّلَا كَبِيْرَةً اِلَّآ
اَحْصٰىهَا ۚ وَوَجَدُوْا مَا عَمِلُوْا
حَاضِرًا ؕ وَلَا يَظْلِمُ رَبُّكَ اَحَدًا ﴿٤٩﴾ ع ٦ / ٥ / ١٨
وَاِذْ قُلْنَا لِلْمَلٰٓئِكَةِ اسْجُدُوْا
لِاٰدَمَ فَسَجَدُوْٓا اِلَّآ اِبْلِيْسَ ؕ كَانَ
مِنَ الْجِنِّ فَفَسَقَ عَنْ اَمْرِ رَبِّهٖ ؕ
اَفَتَتَّخِذُوْنَهٗ وَذُرِّيَّتَهٗٓ اَوْلِيَآءَ
مِنْ دُوْنِيْ وَهُمْ لَكُمْ عَدُوٌّ ؕ
بِئْسَ لِلظّٰلِمِيْنَ بَدَلًا ﴿٥٠﴾
مَآ اَشْهَدْتُّهُمْ خَلْقَ السَّمٰوٰتِ
وَالْاَرْضِ وَلَا خَلْقَ اَنْفُسِهِمْ ۪ وَمَا

Ikhfa اخفاء | Ghunna غنّہ | Ikhfa Meem Saakin اخفاء میم ساکن | Idghaam ادغام | Qalqala قلقلہ | Qalb قلب | Idghaam Meem Saakin ادغام میم ساکن

is it for helpers such as Me to take as lead (men) astray!

kuntu muttakhizal-muḍilleena ‘aḍudaa.

كُنتُ مُتَّخِذَ ٱلْمُضِلِّينَ عَضُدًا ﴿٥١﴾

52. One Day He will say, “Call on those whom you thought to be My partners,” and they will call on them, but they will not listen to them; and We shall make for them a place of common perdition.

52. Wa Yawma yaqoolu naadoo shurakaaa’i-yal-lazeena za‘amtum fada‘aw-hum falam yastajeeboo lahum wa ja‘alnaa baynahum-maw-biqaa.

وَيَوْمَ يَقُولُ نَادُوا۟ شُرَكَآءِىَ
ٱلَّذِينَ زَعَمْتُمْ فَدَعَوْهُمْ فَلَمْ
يَسْتَجِيبُوا۟ لَهُمْ وَجَعَلْنَا بَيْنَهُم
مَّوْبِقًا ﴿٥٢﴾

53. And the Sinful shall see the fire and apprehend that they have to fall therein: no means will they find to turn away therefrom.

53. Wa ra-al-mujrimoonan-Naara faẓannooo annahum-muwaaqi‘oohaa wa lam yajidoo ‘anhaa maṣrifaa. **(Section 7)**

وَرَءَا ٱلْمُجْرِمُونَ ٱلنَّارَ فَظَنُّوٓا۟ أَنَّهُم
مُّوَاقِعُوهَا وَلَمْ يَجِدُوا۟ عَنْهَا
مَصْرِفًا ﴿٥٣﴾ ع ١٩

54. We have explained in detail in this Qur’an, for the benefit of mankind, every kind of similitude: but man is, in most things, contentious.

54. Wa laqad ṣarrafnaa fee haazal-Qur-aani linnaasi min kulli masal; wa kaanal-insaanu aksara shay’in jadalaa.

وَلَقَدْ صَرَّفْنَا فِى هَٰذَا ٱلْقُرْءَانِ
لِلنَّاسِ مِن كُلِّ مَثَلٍ ۚ وَكَانَ
ٱلْإِنسَٰنُ أَكْثَرَ شَىْءٍ جَدَلًا ﴿٥٤﴾

55. And what is there to keep back men from believing, now that guidance has come to them, nor from praying for forgiveness from their Lord, but that (they ask that) the ways of the ancients be repeated with them, or the Wrath be brought to them face to face?

55. Wa maa mana‘an-naasa añy-yu’minooo iz jaaa’ahumul-hudaa wa yastaghfiroo Rab-bahum illaaa an taåtiyahum sunnatul-awwaleena aw yaå-tiyahumul-‘azaabu qubulaa.

وَمَا مَنَعَ ٱلنَّاسَ أَن يُؤْمِنُوٓا۟ إِذْ
جَآءَهُمُ ٱلْهُدَىٰ وَيَسْتَغْفِرُوا۟
رَبَّهُمْ إِلَّآ أَن تَأْتِيَهُمْ سُنَّةُ
ٱلْأَوَّلِينَ أَوْ يَأْتِيَهُمُ ٱلْعَذَابُ
قُبُلًا ﴿٥٥﴾

56. We only send the Messengers to give glad tidings and to give warnings; But the Unbelievers dispute with vain argument, in order therewith to weaken the Truth, and they treat My Signs as a jest as also the fact that they are warned.

56. Wa maa nursilul-mursaleena illaa mubashshi-reena wa munzireen; wa yujaadilul-lazeena kafaroo bilbaaṭili liyudḥiḍoo bihil-ḥaqqa wattakhazooo Aayaatee wa maaa unziroo huzuwaa.

وَمَا نُرْسِلُ ٱلْمُرْسَلِينَ إِلَّا مُبَشِّرِينَ
وَمُنذِرِينَ ۚ وَيُجَٰدِلُ ٱلَّذِينَ كَفَرُوا۟
بِٱلْبَٰطِلِ لِيُدْحِضُوا۟ بِهِ ٱلْحَقَّ ۖ
وَٱتَّخَذُوٓا۟ ءَايَٰتِى وَمَآ أُنذِرُوا۟ هُزُوًا ﴿٥٦﴾

57. And who does more wrong than one who is reminded of the Signs of his Lord, but turns away from them, forgetting the (deeds) which his hands have sent forth? Verily We have set veils over their hearts lest they should understand this, and over their ears, deafness, if you call them to guidance, even then will they never accept guidance.

57. Wa man aẓlamu mimman zukkira bi-Aayaati Rabbihee fa-a‘raḍa ‘anhaa wa nasiya maa qaddamat yadaah; innaa ja‘al-naa ‘alaa quloobihim akinnatan añy-yafqahoohu wa feee aazaanihim waqraa; wa in tad‘uhum ilal-hudaa falañy-yahtadooo izan abadaa.

وَمَنْ أَظْلَمُ مِمَّن ذُكِّرَ بِـَٔايَٰتِ رَبِّهِۦ
فَأَعْرَضَ عَنْهَا وَنَسِىَ مَا قَدَّمَتْ
يَدَاهُ ۚ إِنَّا جَعَلْنَا عَلَىٰ قُلُوبِهِمْ
أَكِنَّةً أَن يَفْقَهُوهُ وَفِىٓ ءَاذَانِهِمْ
وَقْرًا ۖ وَإِن تَدْعُهُمْ إِلَى ٱلْهُدَىٰ
فَلَن يَهْتَدُوٓا۟ إِذًا أَبَدًا ﴿٥٧﴾

Ikhfa اخفاء | Ghunna غُنّہ | Ikhfa Meem Saakin اخفاء میم ساکن | Idghaam ادغام | Qalqala قلقلہ | Qalb قلب | Idghaam Meem Saakin ادغام میم ساکن

58. But your Lord is Most forgiving, full of Mercy. If He were to call them (at once) to account for what they have earned, then surely He would have hastened their punishment: but they have their appointed time, beyond which they will find no refuge.

59. Such were the populations we destroyed when they committed iniquities; but we fixed an appointed time for their destruction.

60. Behold, Moses said to his attendant, "I will not give up until I reach the junction of the two seas or (until) I spend years and years in travel."

61. But when they reached the Junction, they forgot (about) their Fish, which took its course through the sea (straight) as in a tunnel.

62. When they had passed on (some distance), Moses said to his attendant: "Bring us our early meal; truly we have suffered much fatigue at this (stage of) our journey."

63. He replied: "Did you see (what happened) when we betook ourselves to the rock? I did indeed forget (about) the Fish: none but Satan made me forget to tell (you) about it: it took its course through the sea in a marvellous way!"

64. Moses said: "That was what we were seeking after:" so they went back on their footsteps, following (the path they had come).

65. So they found one of Our servants, on whom We had bestowed Mercy from Ourselves and whom We had taught knowledge from Our own Presence.

66. Moses said to him: "May I follow you, on the footing that you teach me something of the (Higher) Truth which you have been taught?"

58. Wa Rabbukal-Ghafooru zur-raḥmati law yu'aakhizuhum bimaa kasaboo la'ajjala lahumul-'azaab; bal lahum maw'idul-lañy-yajidoo min doonihee maw'ilaa.

59. Wa tikal-quraaa ahlaknaahum lammaa ẓalamoo wa ja'alnaa limahlikihim-maw'idaa. **(Section 8)**

60. Wa iz qaala Moosaa lifataahu laaa abraḥu ḥattaaa ablugha majma'al-baḥrayni aw amḍiya ḥuqubaa.

61. Falammaa balaghaa majma'a baynihimaa nasiyaa ḥootahumaa fattakhaza sabeelahoo fil-baḥri sarabaa.

62. Falammaa jaawazaa qaala lifataahu aatinaa ghadaaa'anaa laqad laqeenaa min safarinaa haazaa naṣabaa.

63. Qaala ara'ayta iz awaynaaa ilaṣ-ṣakhrati fa-innee naseetul-ḥoota wa maaa ansaaneehu illash-Shayṭaanu an azkurah; wattakhaza sabeelahoo fil-baḥri 'ajabaa.

64. Qaala zaalika maa kunnaa nabgh; fartaddaa 'alaaa aasaarihimaa qaṣaṣaa.

65. Fa-wajadaa 'abdam-min 'ibaadinaaa aataynaahu Raḥmatam-min 'indinaa wa 'allamnaahu mil-ladunnaa 'ilmaa.

66. Qaala lahoo Moosaa hal attabi'uka 'alaaa an tu'allimani mimmaa 'ullimta rushdaa.

وَرَبُّكَ الْغَفُورُ ذُو الرَّحْمَةِ ط
لَوْ يُؤَاخِذُهُم بِمَا كَسَبُوا لَعَجَّلَ
لَهُمُ الْعَذَابَ ۚ بَل لَّهُم مَّوْعِدٌ
لَّن يَجِدُوا مِن دُونِهِ مَوْئِلًا ۝٥٨
وَتِلْكَ الْقُرَىٰ أَهْلَكْنَاهُمْ لَمَّا
ظَلَمُوا وَجَعَلْنَا لِمَهْلِكِهِم
مَّوْعِدًا ۝٥٩
وَإِذْ قَالَ مُوسَىٰ لِفَتَاهُ لَا أَبْرَحُ حَتَّىٰ
أَبْلُغَ مَجْمَعَ الْبَحْرَيْنِ أَوْ أَمْضِيَ حُقُبًا ۝٦٠
فَلَمَّا بَلَغَا مَجْمَعَ بَيْنِهِمَا نَسِيَا
حُوتَهُمَا فَاتَّخَذَ سَبِيلَهُ فِي
الْبَحْرِ سَرَبًا ۝٦١
فَلَمَّا جَاوَزَا قَالَ لِفَتَاهُ آتِنَا
غَدَاءَنَا لَقَدْ لَقِينَا مِن سَفَرِنَا
هَٰذَا نَصَبًا ۝٦٢
قَالَ أَرَأَيْتَ إِذْ أَوَيْنَا إِلَى الصَّخْرَةِ
فَإِنِّي نَسِيتُ الْحُوتَ وَمَا أَنسَانِيهُ
إِلَّا الشَّيْطَانُ أَنْ أَذْكُرَهُ ۚ وَاتَّخَذَ
سَبِيلَهُ فِي الْبَحْرِ عَجَبًا ۝٦٣
قَالَ ذَٰلِكَ مَا كُنَّا نَبْغِ ۚ فَارْتَدَّا
عَلَىٰ آثَارِهِمَا قَصَصًا ۝٦٤
فَوَجَدَا عَبْدًا مِّنْ عِبَادِنَا آتَيْنَاهُ
رَحْمَةً مِّنْ عِندِنَا وَعَلَّمْنَاهُ مِن
لَّدُنَّا عِلْمًا ۝٦٥
قَالَ لَهُ مُوسَىٰ هَلْ أَتَّبِعُكَ عَلَىٰ
أَن تُعَلِّمَنِ مِمَّا عُلِّمْتَ رُشْدًا ۝٦٦

Ikhfa اخفاء | Ghunna غُنّہ | Ikhfa Meem Saakin اخفاء میم ساکن | Idghaam ادغام | Qalqala قلقلہ | Qalb قلب | Idghaam Meem Saakin ادغام میم ساکن

67. (The other) said: "Verily you will not be able to have patience with me!"

67. Qaala innaka lan tasta-ṭee'a ma'iya ṣabraa.

قَالَ اِنَّكَ لَنْ تَسْتَطِيْعَ مَعِيَ صَبْرًا ﴿٦٧﴾

68. "And how can you have patience about things about which your understanding is not complete?"

68. Wa kayfa taṣbiru 'alaa maa lam tuḥiṭ bihee khubraa.

وَكَيْفَ تَصْبِرُ عَلٰى مَا لَمْ تُحِطْ بِهٖ خُبْرًا ﴿٦٨﴾

69. Moses said: "You will find me, if Allah so will, (truly) patient: nor shall I disobey you in any matter."

69. Qaala satajiduneee in shaaa'al-laahu ṣaabirañw-wa laaa a'ṣee laka amraa.

قَالَ سَتَجِدُنِيْٓ اِنْ شَآءَ اللّٰهُ صَابِرًا وَّلَآ اَعْصِيْ لَكَ اَمْرًا ﴿٦٩﴾

70. The other said: "If then you would follow me, ask me no questions about anything until I myself speak to you concerning it."

70. Qaala fa-init-taba'tanee falaa tas'alnee 'an shay'in ḥattaaa uḥdisa laka minhu zikraa. **(Section 9)**

قَالَ فَاِنِ اتَّبَعْتَنِيْ فَلَا تَسْـَٔلْنِيْ عَنْ شَيْءٍ حَتّٰٓى اُحْدِثَ لَكَ مِنْهُ ذِكْرًا ﴿٧٠﴾ ع

71. So they both proceeded: until, when they were in the boat, he scuttled it. Said Moses: "Have you scuttled it in order to drown those in it? Truly a strange thing you have done!"

71. Fanṭalaqaa ḥattaaa izaa rakibaa fis-safeenati khara-qahaa qaala akharaqtahaa litughriqa ahlahaa laqad ji'ta shay'an imraa.

فَانْطَلَقَا ٝ حَتّٰٓى اِذَا رَكِبَا فِي السَّفِيْنَةِ خَرَقَهَا ۭ قَالَ اَخَرَقْتَهَا لِتُغْرِقَ اَهْلَهَا ۚ لَقَدْ جِئْتَ شَيْـًٔا اِمْرًا ﴿٧١﴾

72. He answered: "Did I not tell you that you can have no patience with me?"

72. Qaala alam aqul innaka lan tastaṭee'a ma'iya ṣabraa.

قَالَ اَلَمْ اَقُلْ اِنَّكَ لَنْ تَسْتَطِيْعَ مَعِيَ صَبْرًا ﴿٧٢﴾

73. Moses said: "Rebuke me not for forgetting, nor grieve me by raising difficulties in my case."

73. Qaala laa tu'aakhiznee bimaa naseetu wa laa turhiqnee min amree 'usraa.

قَالَ لَا تُؤَاخِذْنِيْ بِمَا نَسِيْتُ وَلَا تُرْهِقْنِيْ مِنْ اَمْرِيْ عُسْرًا ﴿٧٣﴾

74. Then they proceeded: until, when they met a young man, he slew him. Moses said: "Have you slain an innocent person who had slain none? Truly a foul (unheard of) thing have you done!"

74. Fanṭalaqaa ḥattaaa izaa laqiyaa ghulaaman faqatalahoo qaala aqatalta nafsan zakiy-yatam bighayri nafs; laqad ji'ta shay'an-nukraa.

فَانْطَلَقَا ٝ حَتّٰٓى اِذَا لَقِيَا غُلٰمًا فَقَتَلَهٗ ۙ قَالَ اَقَتَلْتَ نَفْسًا زَكِيَّةًۢ بِغَيْرِ نَفْسٍ ۭ لَقَدْ جِئْتَ شَيْـًٔا نُّكْرًا ﴿٧٤﴾

75. He answered: "Did I not tell you that you can have no patience with me?"

75. Qaala alam aqul laka innaka lan tastaṭee'a ma'iya ṣabraa.

قَالَ اَلَمْ اَقُلْ لَّكَ اِنَّكَ لَنْ تَسْتَطِيْعَ مَعِيَ صَبْرًا ﴿٧٥﴾

76. (Moses) said: "If ever I ask you about anything after this, keep me not in your company: then would you have received (full) excuse from my side."

76. Qaala in sa-altuka 'an shay'im ba'dahaa falaa tuṣaaḥibnee qad balaghta mil-ladunnee 'uzraa.

قَالَ اِنْ سَاَلْتُكَ عَنْ شَيْءٍۢ بَعْدَهَا فَلَا تُصٰحِبْنِيْ ۚ قَدْ بَلَغْتَ مِنْ لَّدُنِّيْ عُذْرًا ﴿٧٦﴾

77. Then they proceeded: until, when they came to the inhabitants of a town, they asked them for food, but they refused them hospitality. They found there a wall on the point of falling down, but he set it up straight. (Moses) said:

77. Fanṭalaqaa ḥattaaa izaaa atayaaa ahla qaryatinis-taṭ'amaaa ahlahaa fa-abaw añy-yuḍayyifoohumaa fawajadaa feehaa jidaarañy-yureedu añy-yanqaḍḍa fa-aqaamah; qaala

فَانْطَلَقَا ٝ حَتّٰٓى اِذَآ اَتَيَآ اَهْلَ قَرْيَةِۨ اسْتَطْعَمَآ اَهْلَهَا فَاَبَوْا اَنْ يُّضَيِّفُوْهُمَا فَوَجَدَا فِيْهَا جِدَارًا يُّرِيْدُ اَنْ يَّنْقَضَّ فَاَقَامَهٗ ۭ قَالَ

اَلْجُزْءُ السَّادِسَ عَشَرَ (١٦)

Ikhfa اخفاء | Ghunna غُنّہ | Ikhfa Meem Saakin اخفاء میم ساکن | Idghaam ادغام | Qalqala قلقلہ | Qalb قلب | Idghaam Meem Saakin ادغام میم ساکن

"If you had wished, surely you could have exacted some recompense for it!"

law shi'ta lattakhazta 'alayhi ajraa.

لَوْ شِئْتَ لَتَّخَذْتَ عَلَيْهِ أَجْرًا ﴿٧٧﴾

78. He answered: "This is the parting between me and you: now will I tell you the interpretation of (those things) over which you were unable to hold patience.

78. Qaala haazaa firaaqu baynee wa baynik; sa-unabbi-'uka bitaåweeli maa lam tastaṭi' 'alayhi ṣabraa.

قَالَ هَٰذَا فِرَاقُ بَيْنِي وَبَيْنِكَ ۚ
سَأُنَبِّئُكَ بِتَأْوِيلِ مَا لَمْ تَسْتَطِع
عَّلَيْهِ صَبْرًا ﴿٧٨﴾

79. "As for the boat, it belonged to certain men in dire want: they plied on the water: I but wished to render it unserviceable, for there was after them a certain king who seized on every boat by force.

79. Ammas-safeenatu fakaanat limasaakeena ya'maloona fil-baḥri fa-arattu an a'eebahaa wa kaana waraaa'ahum-malikuñy-yaåkhuzu kulla safeenatin ghaṣbaa.

أَمَّا السَّفِينَةُ فَكَانَتْ لِمَسَاكِينَ
يَعْمَلُونَ فِي الْبَحْرِ فَأَرَدتُّ أَنْ
أَعِيبَهَا وَكَانَ وَرَاءَهُم مَّلِكٌ يَأْخُذُ
كُلَّ سَفِينَةٍ غَصْبًا ﴿٧٩﴾

80. "As for the youth, his parents were people of Faith, and we feared that he would grieve them by obstinate rebellion and ingratitude (to Allah).

80. Wa aammal-ghulaamu fakaana abawaahu mu'minayni fakhasheenaaa añy-yurhiqahumaa ṭughyaanañw-wa kufraa.

وَأَمَّا الْغُلَامُ فَكَانَ أَبَوَاهُ مُؤْمِنَيْنِ
فَخَشِينَا أَن يُرْهِقَهُمَا طُغْيَانًا وَكُفْرًا ﴿٨٠﴾

81. "So we desired that their Lord would give them in exchange (a son) better in purity (of conduct) and closer in affection.

81. Fa-aradnaaa añy-yubdilahumaa Rabbuhumaa khayram-minhu zakaatañw-wa aqraba ruḥmaa.

فَأَرَدْنَا أَن يُبْدِلَهُمَا رَبُّهُمَا خَيْرًا مِّنْهُ
زَكَاةً وَأَقْرَبَ رُحْمًا ﴿٨١﴾

82. "As for the wall, it belonged to two youths, orphans, in the Town; there was, beneath it, a buried treasure, to which they were entitled: their father had been a righteous man: so your Lord desired that they should attain their age of full strength and get out their treasure - a mercy (and favor) from your Lord. I did it not of my own accord. Such is the interpretation of (those things) over which you were unable to hold patience."

82. Wa ammal-jidaaru fakaana lighulaamayni yateemayni fil-madeenati wa kaana taḥtahoo kanzul-lahumaa wa kaana aboohumaa ṣaaliḥan fa-araada Rabbuka añy-yablughaaa ashuddahumaa wa yastakhrijaa kanzahumaa raḥmatam-mir-Rabbik; wa maa fa'altuhoo 'an amree; zaalika taåweelu maa lam tasṭi' 'alayhi ṣabraa.

(Section 10)

وَأَمَّا الْجِدَارُ فَكَانَ لِغُلَامَيْنِ يَتِيمَيْنِ
فِي الْمَدِينَةِ وَكَانَ تَحْتَهُ كَنزٌ لَّهُمَا
وَكَانَ أَبُوهُمَا صَالِحًا فَأَرَادَ
رَبُّكَ أَن يَبْلُغَا أَشُدَّهُمَا وَيَسْتَخْرِجَا
كَنزَهُمَا رَحْمَةً مِّن رَّبِّكَ ۚ وَمَا
فَعَلْتُهُ عَنْ أَمْرِي ۚ ذَٰلِكَ تَأْوِيلُ
مَا لَمْ تَسْطِع عَّلَيْهِ صَبْرًا ﴿٨٢﴾ ع

83. They ask you concerning Zul-qarnain. Say, "I will rehearse to you something of his story."

83. Wa yas'aloonaka 'an Zil-Qarnayni qul sa-atloo 'alaykum- minhu zikraa.

وَيَسْأَلُونَكَ عَن ذِي الْقَرْنَيْنِ ۖ قُلْ
سَأَتْلُو عَلَيْكُم مِّنْهُ ذِكْرًا ﴿٨٣﴾

84. Verily We established his power on earth, and We gave him the ways and the means to all ends.

84. Innaa makkannaa lahoo fil-arḍi wa aataynaahu min kulli shay'in sababaa.

إِنَّا مَكَّنَّا لَهُ فِي الْأَرْضِ وَآتَيْنَاهُ
مِن كُلِّ شَيْءٍ سَبَبًا ﴿٨٤﴾

85. One (such) way he followed,

85. Fa-atba'a sababaa.

فَأَتْبَعَ سَبَبًا ﴿٨٥﴾

86. Until, when he reached the setting of the sun, he found it set in a spring of murky water: Near it he found

86. Ḥattaaa izaa balagha maghribash-shamsi wajadahaa taghrubu fee 'aynin ḥami'atiñw-wa wajada

حَتَّىٰ إِذَا بَلَغَ مَغْرِبَ الشَّمْسِ وَجَدَهَا
تَغْرُبُ فِي عَيْنٍ حَمِئَةٍ وَوَجَدَ

Ikhfa اخفاء | Ghunna غُنّہ | Ikhfa Meem Saakin اخفاء میم ساکن | Idghaam ادغام | Qalqala قلقلہ | Qalb قلب | Idghaam Meem Saakin ادغام میم ساکن

a People: We said: "O Zul-qarnain! (you have authority,) either to punish them, or to treat them with kindness."

'indahaa qawmaa; qulnaa yaa Zal-Qarnayni immaaa an tu'az-ziba wa immaaa an tattakhiza feehim ḥusnaa.

عِنْدَهَا قَوْمًا ۬ قُلْنَا يٰذَا الْقَرْنَيْنِ
اِمَّآ اَنْ تُعَذِّبَ وَاِمَّآ اَنْ تَتَّخِذَ
فِيْهِمْ حُسْنًا ﴿٨٦﴾

87. He said: "Whoever does wrong, him shall we punish; then shall he be sent back to his Lord; and He will punish him with a punishment unheard-of (before).

87. Qaala ammaa man ẓalama fasawfa nu'azzibuhoo summa yuraddu ilaa Rabbihee fa-yu'azzibuhoo 'azaaban-nukraa.

قَالَ اَمَّا مَنْ ظَلَمَ فَسَوْفَ نُعَذِّبُهٗ ثُمَّ
يُرَدُّ اِلٰى رَبِّهٖ فَيُعَذِّبُهٗ عَذَابًا نُّكْرًا ﴿٨٧﴾

88. "But whoever believes, and works righteousness,- he shall have a goodly reward, and easy will be his task as We order it by our command."

88. Wa ammaa man aamana wa 'amila ṣaaliḥan falahoo jazaaa'anil-ḥusnaa wa sanaqoolu lahoo min amrinaa yusraa.

وَاَمَّا مَنْ اٰمَنَ وَعَمِلَ صَالِحًا
فَلَهٗ جَزَآءَ ۨالْحُسْنٰى ۚ وَسَنَقُوْلُ لَهٗ
مِنْ اَمْرِنَا يُسْرًا ﴿٨٨﴾ ؕ

89. Then he followed (another) way,

89. Summa atba'a sababaa.

ثُمَّ اَتْبَعَ سَبَبًا ﴿٨٩﴾

90. Until, when he came to the rising of the sun, he found it rising on a people for whom We had provided no covering protection against the sun.

90. Ḥattaaa izaa balagha maṭli'ash-shamsi wajadahaa taṭlu'u 'alaa qawmil-lam naj'al-lahum-min doonihaa sitraa.

حَتّٰٓى اِذَا بَلَغَ مَطْلِعَ الشَّمْسِ
وَجَدَهَا تَطْلُعُ عَلٰى قَوْمٍ لَّمْ نَجْعَلْ
لَّهُمْ مِّنْ دُوْنِهَا سِتْرًا ﴿٩٠﴾ ۙ

91. (He left them) as they were: We completely understood what was before him.

91. Kazaalika wa qad aḥaṭnaa bimaa ladayhi khubraa.

كَذٰلِكَ ؕ وَقَدْ اَحَطْنَا بِمَا لَدَيْهِ خُبْرًا ﴿٩١﴾

92. Then he followed (another) way,

92. Summa atba'a sababaa.

ثُمَّ اَتْبَعَ سَبَبًا ﴿٩٢﴾

93. Until, when he reached (a tract) between two mountains, he found, beneath them, a people who scarcely understood a word.

93. Ḥattaaa izaa balagha baynas-saddayni wajada min doonihimaa qawmal-laa yakaadoona yafqahoona qawlaa.

حَتّٰٓى اِذَا بَلَغَ بَيْنَ السَّدَّيْنِ وَجَدَ
مِنْ دُوْنِهِمَا قَوْمًا ۙ لَّا يَكَادُوْنَ
يَفْقَهُوْنَ قَوْلًا ﴿٩٣﴾

94. They said: "O Zul-qarnain! the Gog and Magog (People) do great mischief on earth: shall we then render you tribute in order that you might erect a barrier between us and them?

94. Qaaloo yaa Zal-Qarnayni inna Yaåjooja wa Maåjooja-mufsidoona fil-arḍi fahal naj'alu laka kharjan 'alaaa an taj'ala baynanaa wa baynahum saddaa.

قَالُوْا يٰذَا الْقَرْنَيْنِ اِنَّ يَاْجُوْجَ وَ
مَاْجُوْجَ مُفْسِدُوْنَ فِى الْاَرْضِ
فَهَلْ نَجْعَلُ لَكَ خَرْجًا عَلٰٓى اَنْ
تَجْعَلَ بَيْنَنَا وَبَيْنَهُمْ سَدًّا ﴿٩٤﴾

95. He said: "(The power) in which my Lord has established me is better (than tribute): Help me therefore with strength (and labor): I will erect a strong barrier between you and them:

95. Qaala maa makkannee feehi Rabbee khayrun fa-a'eenoonee biquwwatin aj'al baynakum wa baynahum radmaa.

قَالَ مَا مَكَّنِّىْ فِيْهِ رَبِّىْ خَيْرٌ
فَاَعِيْنُوْنِىْ بِقُوَّةٍ اَجْعَلْ بَيْنَكُمْ
وَبَيْنَهُمْ رَدْمًا ﴿٩٥﴾ ۙ

96. "Bring me blocks of iron." At length, when he had filled up the space between the two steep mountain-sides, he said, "Blow (with your bellows)"

96. Aatoonee zubaral-ḥadeed, ḥattaaa izaa saawaa baynaṣ-ṣadafayni qaalan-fukhoo

اٰتُوْنِىْ زُبَرَ الْحَدِيْدِ ؕ حَتّٰٓى اِذَا سَاوٰى
بَيْنَ الصَّدَفَيْنِ قَالَ انْفُخُوْا ؕ

Ikhfa اخفاء | Ghunna غُنّہ | Ikhfa Meem Saakin اخفاء میم ساکن | Idghaam ادغام | Qalqala قلقلہ | Qalb قلب | Idghaam Meem Saakin ادغام میم ساکن

Then, when he had made it (red) as fire, he said: "Bring me, that I may pour over it, molten lead."

ḥattaaa izaa ja'alahoo naaran qaala aatooneee ufrigh 'alayhi qiṭraa.

حَتّٰىٓ اِذَا جَعَلَهٗ نَارًا ۙ قَالَ اٰتُوْنِيْٓ اُفْرِغْ عَلَيْهِ قِطْرًا ۝٩٦

97. Thus they were made powerless to scale it or to dig through it.

97. Famas-ṭaa'ooo añy-yaẓharoohu wa mastaṭaa'oo lahoo naqbaa.

فَمَا اسْطَاعُوْٓا اَنْ يَّظْهَرُوْهُ وَمَا اسْتَطَاعُوْا لَهٗ نَقْبًا ۝٩٧

98. He said: "This is a mercy from my Lord: but when the promise of my Lord comes to pass, He will make it into dust; and the promise of my Lord is true."

98. Qaala haazaa raḥmatum-mir-Rabbee fa-izaa jaaa'a wa'du Rabbee ja'alahoo dakkaaa'a; wa kaana; wa'du Rabbee ḥaqqaa.

قَالَ هٰذَا رَحْمَةٌ مِّنْ رَّبِّيْ ۚ فَاِذَا جَآءَ وَعْدُ رَبِّيْ جَعَلَهٗ دَكَّآءَ ۚ وَكَانَ وَعْدُ رَبِّيْ حَقًّا ۝٩٨

99. On that day We shall leave them to surge like waves on one another: the trumpet will be blown, and We shall collect them all together.

99. Wa taraknaa ba'ḍahum Yawma'iziñy-yamooju fee ba'ḍiñw-wa nufikha fiṣ-Ṣoori fajama'naahum jam'aa.

وَتَرَكْنَا بَعْضَهُمْ يَوْمَئِذٍ يَّمُوْجُ فِيْ بَعْضٍ وَّنُفِخَ فِي الصُّوْرِ فَجَمَعْنٰهُمْ جَمْعًا ۝٩٩

100. And We shall present Hell that day for Unbelievers to see, all spread out,-

100. Wa 'araḍnaa Jahannama Yawma'izil-lilkaafireena 'arḍaa.

وَّعَرَضْنَا جَهَنَّمَ يَوْمَئِذٍ لِّلْكٰفِرِيْنَ عَرْضًا ۝١٠٠

101. (Unbelievers) whose eyes had been under a veil from remembrance of Me, and who had been unable even to hear.

101. Allazeena kaanat a'yunuhum fee ghiṭaaa'in 'an-zikree wa kaanoo laa yastaṭee'oona sam'aa. **(Section 11)**

الَّذِيْنَ كَانَتْ اَعْيُنُهُمْ فِيْ غِطَآءٍ عَنْ ذِكْرِيْ وَكَانُوْا لَا يَسْتَطِيْعُوْنَ سَمْعًا ۝١٠١ ع ١١ ٢

102. Do the Unbelievers think that they can take My servants as protectors besides Me? Verily We have prepared Hell for the Unbelievers for (their) entertainment.

102. Afaḥasibal-lazeena kafarooo añy-yattakhizoo 'ibaadee min dooneee awliyaaa'; innaaa a'tadnaa Jahannama lilkaafireena nuzulaa.

اَفَحَسِبَ الَّذِيْنَ كَفَرُوْٓا اَنْ يَّتَّخِذُوْا عِبَادِيْ مِنْ دُوْنِيْٓ اَوْلِيَآءَ ۚ اِنَّآ اَعْتَدْنَا جَهَنَّمَ لِلْكٰفِرِيْنَ نُزُلًا ۝١٠٢

103. Say: "Shall we tell you of those who lose most in respect of their deeds?-

103. Qul hal nunabbi'ukum bilakhsareena a'maalaa.

قُلْ هَلْ نُنَبِّئُكُمْ بِالْاَخْسَرِيْنَ اَعْمَالًا ۝١٠٣

104. "Those whose efforts have been wasted in this life, while they thought that they were acquiring good by their works?"

104. Allazeena ḍalla sa'yuhum fil-ḥayaatid-dunyaa wa hum yaḥsaboona annahum yuḥsinoona ṣun'aa.

الَّذِيْنَ ضَلَّ سَعْيُهُمْ فِي الْحَيٰوةِ الدُّنْيَا وَهُمْ يَحْسَبُوْنَ اَنَّهُمْ يُحْسِنُوْنَ صُنْعًا ۝١٠٤

105. They are those who deny the Signs of their Lord and the fact of their having to meet Him (in the Hereafter): vain will be their works, nor shall We, on the Day of Judgment, give them any weight.

105. Ulaaa'ikal-lazeena kafaroo bi-Aayaati Rabbihim wa liqaaa'ihee faḥabiṭat a'maaluhum falaa nuqeemu lahum Yawmal-Qiyaamati waznaa.

اُولٰٓئِكَ الَّذِيْنَ كَفَرُوْا بِاٰيٰتِ رَبِّهِمْ وَلِقَآئِهٖ فَحَبِطَتْ اَعْمَالُهُمْ فَلَا نُقِيْمُ لَهُمْ يَوْمَ الْقِيٰمَةِ وَزْنًا ۝١٠٥

106. That is their reward, Hell, because they rejected Faith, and took My Signs and My Messengers by way of jest.

106. Zaalika jazaaa'uhum Jahannamu bimaa kafaroo wattakhazooo Aayaatee wa Rusulee huzuwaa.

ذٰلِكَ جَزَآؤُهُمْ جَهَنَّمُ بِمَا كَفَرُوْا وَاتَّخَذُوْٓا اٰيٰتِيْ وَرُسُلِيْ هُزُوًا ۝١٠٦

Ikhfa اخفاء | Ghunna غُنّہ | Ikhfa Meem Saakin اخفاء میم ساکن | Idghaam ادغام | Qalqala قلقلہ | Qalb قلب | Idghaam Meem Saakin ادغام میم ساکن

107. As to those who believe and work righteous deeds, they have, for their entertainment, the Gardens of Paradise,
108. Wherein they shall dwell (for ever), no change will they wish for from them.
109. Say: "If the ocean were ink (wherewith to write out) the words of my Lord, sooner would the ocean be exhausted than would the words of my Lord, even if we added another ocean like it, for its aid."
110. Say: "I am but a man like yourselves, (but) the inspiration has come to me, that your Allah is one Allah: whoever expects to meet his Lord, let him work righteousness, and, in the worship of his Lord, admit no one as partner.

19. Mary

In the name of Allah, Most Gracious, Most Merciful.

1. *Kaf-Ha-Ya-Ain-Sad.*
2. (This is) a recital of the Mercy of your Lord to His servant Zakariya.
3. Behold! he cried to his Lord in secret,
4. Praying: "O my Lord! infirm indeed are my bones, and the hair of my head glistens with grey: but never am I unblest, O my Lord, in my prayer to You!
5. "Now I fear (what) my relatives (and colleagues) (will do) after me: but my wife is barren: so give me an heir as from yourself,-
6. "(One that) will (truly) represent me, and represent the posterity of Jacob; and make him, O my Lord! one with whom You are well-pleased!"
7. (His prayer was answered): "O Zakariya! We give you good news of a son: His name shall be Yahya: on none by that name have We conferred distinction before."
8. He said: "O my Lord! How shall I have a son, when

107. Innal-lazeena aamanoo wa 'amiluṣ-ṣaaliḥaati kaanat lahum Jannaatul-Firdawsi nuzulaa.
108. Khaalideena feehaa laa yabghoona 'anhaa ḥiwalaa.
109. Qul law kaanal-baḥru midaadal-li-Kalimaati Rabbee lanafidal-baḥru qabla an tanfada Kalimaatu Rabbee wa law ji'naa bimislihee madadaa.
110. Qul innamaaa ana basha-rum-mislukum yooḥaa ilayya annamaaa ilaahukum Ilaahuñw-Waaḥid; faman kaana yarjoo liqaaa'a Rabbihee falya'mal 'a-malan ṣaaliḥañw-wa laa yushrik bi'ibaadati Rabbiheee aḥadaa.
(Sec. 12)

Sûrat Maryam–19

(Revealed at Makkah)

Bismillaahir Raḥmaanir Raḥeem

1. Kaaaf-Haa-Yaa-'Ayyyn-Ṣaaad.
2. Zikru raḥmati Rabbika 'abdahoo Zakariyyaa.
3. Iz naadaa Rabbahoo nidaaa'an khafiyyaa.
4. Qaala Rabbi innee wahanal-'aẓmu minnee washta'alar-raå-su shaybañw-wa lam akum bidu'aaa'ika Rabbi shaqiyyaa.
5. Wa innee khiftul-mawaa-liya miñw-waraaa'ee wa kaana-tim-ra-atee 'aaqiran fahab lee mil-ladunka waliyyaa.
6. Yariṣunee wa yariṣu min aali Ya'qoob, waj'alhu Rabbi raḍiyyaa.
7. Yaa Zakariyyaaa innaa nubashshiruka bighulaami-nismuhoo Yaḥyaa lam naj'al-lahoo min qablu samiyyaa.
8. Qaala Rabbi annaa yakoo-nu lee ghulaamuñw-wa

إِنَّ الَّذِينَ آمَنُوا وَعَمِلُوا الصَّٰلِحَٰتِ
كَانَتْ لَهُمْ جَنَّٰتُ الْفِرْدَوْسِ نُزُلًا ﴿١٠٧﴾
خَٰلِدِينَ فِيهَا لَا يَبْغُونَ عَنْهَا حِوَلًا ﴿١٠٨﴾
قُلْ لَوْ كَانَ الْبَحْرُ مِدَادًا لِكَلِمَٰتِ رَبِّي
لَنَفِدَ الْبَحْرُ قَبْلَ أَنْ تَنْفَدَ كَلِمَٰتُ
رَبِّي وَلَوْ جِئْنَا بِمِثْلِهِ مَدَدًا ﴿١٠٩﴾
قُلْ إِنَّمَا أَنَا بَشَرٌ مِثْلُكُمْ يُوحَىٰ إِلَيَّ
أَنَّمَا إِلَٰهُكُمْ إِلَٰهٌ وَاحِدٌ فَمَنْ كَانَ يَرْجُوا
لِقَاءَ رَبِّهِ فَلْيَعْمَلْ عَمَلًا صَٰلِحًا وَلَا
يُشْرِكْ بِعِبَادَةِ رَبِّهِ أَحَدًا ﴿١١٠﴾ ع

(١٩) سُورَةُ مَرْيَمَ مَكِّيَّةٌ (٤٤)

بِسْمِ اللَّهِ الرَّحْمَٰنِ الرَّحِيمِ

كٓهيعٓصٓ ﴿١﴾
ذِكْرُ رَحْمَتِ رَبِّكَ عَبْدَهُ زَكَرِيَّا ﴿٢﴾
إِذْ نَادَىٰ رَبَّهُ نِدَاءً خَفِيًّا ﴿٣﴾
قَالَ رَبِّ إِنِّي وَهَنَ الْعَظْمُ مِنِّي
وَاشْتَعَلَ الرَّأْسُ شَيْبًا وَلَمْ أَكُنْ
بِدُعَائِكَ رَبِّ شَقِيًّا ﴿٤﴾
وَإِنِّي خِفْتُ الْمَوَٰلِيَ مِنْ وَرَاءِي
وَكَانَتِ امْرَأَتِي عَاقِرًا فَهَبْ لِي
مِنْ لَدُنْكَ وَلِيًّا ﴿٥﴾
يَرِثُنِي وَيَرِثُ مِنْ آلِ يَعْقُوبَ
وَاجْعَلْهُ رَبِّ رَضِيًّا ﴿٦﴾
يَٰزَكَرِيَّا إِنَّا نُبَشِّرُكَ بِغُلَٰمٍ اسْمُهُ يَحْيَىٰ
لَمْ نَجْعَلْ لَهُ مِنْ قَبْلُ سَمِيًّا ﴿٧﴾
قَالَ رَبِّ أَنَّىٰ يَكُونُ لِي غُلَٰمٌ وَ

Ikhfa اخفاء | Ghunna غنّہ | Ikhfa Meem Saakin اخفاء میم ساکن | Idghaam ادغام | Qalqala قلقلہ | Qalb قلب | Idghaam Meem Saakin ادغام میم ساکن

my wife is barren and I have grown quite decrepit from old age?"

kaanatim-ra-atee aaqirañw-wa qad balaghtu minal-kibari 'itiyyaa.

كانت امراتي عاقرا وقد بلغت
من الكبر عتيا ۝٨

9. He said: "So (it will be) your Lord says, 'That is easy for Me: I did indeed create you before, when you had been nothing!'"

9. Qaala kazaalika qaala Rabbuka huwa 'alayya hayyinuñw-wa qad khalaqtuka min qablu wa lam taku shay'aa.

قال كذلك قال ربك هو علي
هين وقد خلقتك من قبل ولم
تك شيئا ۝٩

10. (Zakariya) said: "O my Lord! give me a Sign." "your Sign," was the answer, "Shall be that you shall speak to no man for three nights, although you are not dumb."

10. Qaala Rabbij-'al-leee Aayah; qaala Aayatuka allaa tukalliman-naasa salaasa layaalin sawiyyaa.

قال رب اجعل لي اية قال ايتك
الا تكلم الناس ثلث ليال سويا ۝١٠

11. So Zakariya came out to his people from his chamber: he told them by signs to celebrate Allah's praises in the morning and in the evening.

11. Fakharaja 'alaa qawmihee minal-miḥraabi fa-awḥaaa ilayhim an sabbiḥoo bukratañw- wa 'ashiyyaa.

فخرج على قومه من المحراب فاوحى
اليهم ان سبحوا بكرة وعشيا ۝١١

12. (To his son came the command): "O Yahya! take hold of the Book with might," and We gave him Wisdom even as a youth,

12. Yaa Yaḥyaa khuzil-Kitaaba biquwwatiñw-wa aataynaahul-ḥukma ṣabiyyaa.

ييحيى خذ الكتب بقوة واتينه
الحكم صبيا ۝١٢

13. And piety (for all creatures) as from Us, and purity: he was devout,

13. Wa ḥanaanam-mil-ladunnaa wa zakaatañw wa kaana taqiyyaa.

وحنانا من لدنا وزكوة وكان تقيا ۝١٣

14. And kind to his parents, and he was not overbearing or rebellious.

14. Wa barram biwaalidayhi wa lam yakun jabbaaran 'aṣiyyaa.

وبرا بوالديه ولم يكن جبارا عصيا ۝١٤

15. So Peace on him the day he was born, the day that he dies, and the day that he will be raised up to life (again)!

15. Wa salaamun 'alayhi yawma wulida wa yawma yamootu wa yawma yub'asu ḥayyaa.

وسلم عليه يوم ولد ويوم يموت
ويوم يبعث حيا ۝١٥

(Section 1)

ع ١٥ وقف لازم

16. Relate in the Book (the story of) Mary, when she withdrew from her family to a place in the East.

16. Wazkur fil-Kitaabi Maryam; izin-tabazat min ahlihaa makaanan sharqiyyaa.

واذكر في الكتب مريم اذ انتبذت
من اهلها مكانا شرقيا ۝١٦

17. She placed a screen (to screen herself) from them; then We sent her Our angel, and he appeared before her as a man in all respects.

17. Fattakhazat min doonihim ḥijaaban fa-arsalnaaa ilayhaa rooḥanaa fatamassala lahaa basharan sawiyyaa.

فاتخذت من دونهم حجابا
فارسلنا اليها روحنا فتمثل
لها بشرا سويا ۝١٧

18. She said: "I seek refuge from you to (Allah) Most Gracious: (come not near) if you fear Allah."

18. Qaalat inneee a'oozu bir-Raḥmaani minka in kunta taqiyyaa.

قالت اني اعوذ بالرحمن منك
ان كنت تقيا ۝١٨

19. He said: "No, I am only a messenger from your Lord, (to announce) to you the gift of a holy son.

19. Qaala innamaaa ana rasoolu Rabbiki li ahaba laki ghulaaman zakiyyaa.

قال انما انا رسول ربك لاهب
لك غلما زكيا ۝١٩

20. She said: "How shall I have a son, seeing that no man has touched me, and I am not unchaste?"

20. Qaalat annaa yakoonu lee ghulaamuñw-wa lam yamsasnee basharuñw-wa lam aku baghiyyaa.

قالت انى يكون لي غلم ولم يمسسني
بشر ولم اك بغيا ۝٢٠

الربع

Ikhfa اخفاء · Ghunna غنّہ · Ikhfa Meem Saakin اخفاء میم ساکن · Idghaam ادغام · Qalqala قلقلہ · Qalb قلب · Idghaam Meem Saakin ادغام میم ساکن

21. He said: "So (it will be): your Lord says 'That is easy for Me: and (We wish) to appoint him as a Sign unto men and a Mercy from Us':It is a matter (so) decreed."

22. So she conceived him, and she retired with him to a remote place.

23. And the pains of childbirth drove her to the trunk of a palm-tree: She cried (in her anguish): "Ah! would that I had died before this! would that I had been a thing forgotten and out of sight!"

24. But (a voice) cried to her from beneath the (palm-tree): "Do not Grieve! for your Lord has provided a rivulet beneath you;

25. "And shake toward yourself the trunk of the palm-tree: it will let fall fresh ripe dates upon you.

26. "So eat and drink and cool (your) eye. And if you see any man, say, 'I have vowed a fast to (Allah) Most Gracious, and this day I will not enter into talk with any human being"

27. At length she brought the (babe) to her people, carrying him (in her arms). They said: "O Mary! truly an amazing thing you have brought!

28. "O sister of Aaron! your father was not a man of evil, nor your mother an un-chaste woman!"

29. But she pointed to the babe. They said: "How can we talk to one who is a child in the cradle?"

30. He said: "I am indeed a servant of Allah: He has given me revelation and made me a prophet;

31. "And He has made me blessed wheresoever I be, and has enjoined on me Prayer and Charity as long as I live;

21. Qaala kazaaliki qaala Rabbuki huwa 'alayya hayyi-nuñw wa linaj'alahooo Aayatal-linnaasi wa raḥmatam-minnaa; wa kaana amram-maqdiyyaa.

22. Faḥamalat-hu fantabazat bihee makaanan qaṣiyyaa.

23. Fa-ajaaa'ahal-makhaaḍu ilaa jiz'in-nakhlati qaalat yaa laytanee mittu qabla haazaa wa kuntu nasyam-mansiyyaa.

24. Fanaadaahaa min taḥti-haaa allaa taḥzanee qad ja'ala Rabbuki taḥtaki sariyyaa.

25. Wa huzzeee ilayki bijiz-'in-nakhlati tusaaqiṭ 'alayki ruṭaban janiyyaa.

26. Fakulee washrabee wa qarree 'aynaa; fa-immaa tarayinna minal-bashari aḥadan faqooleee innee nazartu lir-Raḥmaani ṣawman falan ukallimal-yawma insiyyaa.

27. Fa-atat bihee qawmahaa taḥmiluhoo qaaloo yaa Mar-yamu laqad ji'ti shay'an fariyyaa.

28. Yaaa ukhta Haaroona maa kaana abookim-ra-a saw'iñw-wa maa kaanat ummuki baghiyyaa.

29. Fa-ashaarat ilayh; qaaloo kayfa nukallimu man kaana fil-mahdi ṣabiyyaa.

30. Qaala innee 'abdullaahi aataaniyal-Kitaaba wa ja'alanee Nabiyyaa.

31. Wa ja'alanee mubaarakan ayna maa kuntu wa awṣaanee biṣ-Ṣalaati waz-Zakaati maa dumtu ḥayyaa.

قَالَ كَذٰلِكِ ۚ قَالَ رَبُّكِ هُوَ عَلَيَّ

هَيِّنٌ ۚ وَلِنَجْعَلَهٗٓ اٰيَةً لِّلنَّاسِ وَرَحْمَةً

مِّنَّا ۚ وَكَانَ اَمْرًا مَّقْضِيًّا ﴿٢١﴾

فَحَمَلَتْهُ فَانْتَبَذَتْ بِهٖ مَكَانًا قَصِيًّا ﴿٢٢﴾

فَاَجَآءَهَا الْمَخَاضُ اِلٰى جِذْعِ النَّخْلَةِ ۚ

قَالَتْ يٰلَيْتَنِيْ مِتُّ قَبْلَ هٰذَا وَ

كُنْتُ نَسْيًا مَّنْسِيًّا ﴿٢٣﴾

فَنَادٰىهَا مِنْ تَحْتِهَآ اَلَّا تَحْزَنِيْ قَدْ

جَعَلَ رَبُّكِ تَحْتَكِ سَرِيًّا ﴿٢٤﴾

وَهُزِّيْٓ اِلَيْكِ بِجِذْعِ النَّخْلَةِ تُسٰقِطْ

عَلَيْكِ رُطَبًا جَنِيًّا ﴿٢٥﴾

فَكُلِيْ وَاشْرَبِيْ وَقَرِّيْ عَيْنًا ۚ فَاِمَّا

تَرَيِنَّ مِنَ الْبَشَرِ اَحَدًا ۙ فَقُوْلِيْٓ اِنِّيْ

نَذَرْتُ لِلرَّحْمٰنِ صَوْمًا فَلَنْ اُكَلِّمَ

الْيَوْمَ اِنْسِيًّا ﴿٢٦﴾ ۚ

فَاَتَتْ بِهٖ قَوْمَهَا تَحْمِلُهٗ ۭ قَالُوْا

يٰمَرْيَمُ لَقَدْ جِئْتِ شَيْـًٔا فَرِيًّا ﴿٢٧﴾

يٰٓاُخْتَ هٰرُوْنَ مَا كَانَ اَبُوْكِ امْرَاَ

سَوْءٍ وَّمَا كَانَتْ اُمُّكِ بَغِيًّا ﴿٢٨﴾ ۖ

فَاَشَارَتْ اِلَيْهِ ۭ قَالُوْا كَيْفَ نُكَلِّمُ

مَنْ كَانَ فِي الْمَهْدِ صَبِيًّا ﴿٢٩﴾

قَالَ اِنِّيْ عَبْدُ اللّٰهِ ۣ اٰتٰىنِيَ الْكِتٰبَ وَ

جَعَلَنِيْ نَبِيًّا ﴿٣٠﴾ ۙ

وَّجَعَلَنِيْ مُبٰرَكًا اَيْنَ مَا كُنْتُ ۠ وَ

اَوْصٰنِيْ بِالصَّلٰوةِ وَالزَّكٰوةِ مَا

دُمْتُ حَيًّا ﴿٣١﴾ ۖ

Ikhfa اخفاء | Ghunna غنّہ | Ikhfa Meem Saakin اخفاء میم ساکن | Idghaam ادغام | Qalqala قلقلہ | Qalb قلب | Idghaam Meem Saakin ادغام میم ساکن

32. "(He) has made me kind to my mother, and not overbearing or miserable;

32. Wa barram biwaalidatee wa lam yaj'alnee jabbaaran shaqiyyaa.

وَبَرًّا بِوَالِدَتِي وَلَمْ يَجْعَلْنِي جَبَّارًا
شَقِيًّا ﴿٣٢﴾

33. "So peace is on me the day I was born, the day that I die, and the day that I shall be raised up to life (again)"!

33. Wassalaamu 'alayya yawma wulittu wa yawma amootu wa yawma ub'asu ḥayyaa.

وَالسَّلَامُ عَلَيَّ يَوْمَ وُلِدْتُ وَيَوْمَ
أَمُوتُ وَيَوْمَ أُبْعَثُ حَيًّا ﴿٣٣﴾

34. Such (was) Jesus the son of Mary: (it is) a statement of truth, about which they (vainly) dispute.

34. Zaalika 'Eesab-nu Maryam; qawlal-ḥaqqil-lazee feehi yamtaroon.

ذَٰلِكَ عِيسَى ابْنُ مَرْيَمَ ۚ قَوْلَ الْحَقِّ
الَّذِي فِيهِ يَمْتَرُونَ ﴿٣٤﴾

35. It is not befitting to (the majesty of) Allah that He should beget a son. Glory be to Him! when He determines a matter, He only says to it, "Be", and it is.

35. Maa kaana lillaahi añy-yattakhiza miñw-waladin Subḥaanah; izaa qaḍaaa amran fa-innamaa yaqoolu lahoo kun fa-yakoon.

مَا كَانَ لِلَّهِ أَنْ يَتَّخِذَ مِنْ وَلَدٍ ۖ
سُبْحَانَهُ ۚ إِذَا قَضَىٰ أَمْرًا فَإِنَّمَا يَقُولُ
لَهُ كُنْ فَيَكُونُ ﴿٣٥﴾

36. Verily Allah is my Lord and your Lord: you, therefore serve Him: this is a Way that is straight.

36. Wa innal-laaha Rabbee wa Rabbukum fa'budooh; haazaa Ṣiraaṭum-Mustaqeem.

وَإِنَّ اللَّهَ رَبِّي وَرَبُّكُمْ فَاعْبُدُوهُ ۚ
هَٰذَا صِرَاطٌ مُسْتَقِيمٌ ﴿٣٦﴾

37. But the sects differ among themselves: and woe to the Unbelievers because of the (coming) Judgment of a momentous Day!

37. Fakhtalafal-aḥzaabu mim baynihim fawaylul-lillazeena kafaroo mim-mashhadi Yawmin 'aẓeem.

فَاخْتَلَفَ الْأَحْزَابُ مِنْ بَيْنِهِمْ ۖ فَوَيْلٌ
لِلَّذِينَ كَفَرُوا مِنْ مَشْهَدِ يَوْمٍ عَظِيمٍ ﴿٣٧﴾

38. How plainly will they see and hear, the Day that they will appear before Us! but the unjust today are in manifest error!

38. Asmi' bihim wa abṣir Yawma yaåtoonanaa laakiniẓ-ẓaalimoonal-yawma fee ḍalaalim-mubeen.

أَسْمِعْ بِهِمْ وَأَبْصِرْ يَوْمَ يَأْتُونَنَا ۖ لَٰكِنِ
الظَّالِمُونَ الْيَوْمَ فِي ضَلَالٍ مُبِينٍ ﴿٣٨﴾

39. But warn them of the Day of Distress, when the matter will be determined: for (behold,) they are negligent and they do not believe!

39. Wa anzirhum Yawmal-ḥasrati iz quḍiyal-amr; wa hum fee ghaflatiñw-wa hum laa yu'minoon.

وَأَنْذِرْهُمْ يَوْمَ الْحَسْرَةِ إِذْ قُضِيَ الْأَمْرُ وقف لازم
وَهُمْ فِي غَفْلَةٍ وَهُمْ لَا يُؤْمِنُونَ ﴿٣٩﴾

40. It is We Who will inherit the earth, and all beings thereon: to Us will they all be returned.

40. Innaa Naḥnu narisul-arḍa wa man 'alayhaa wa ilaynaa yurja'oon. **(Section 2)**

إِنَّا نَحْنُ نَرِثُ الْأَرْضَ وَمَنْ عَلَيْهَا
وَإِلَيْنَا يُرْجَعُونَ ﴿٤٠﴾

41. (Also mention in the Book (the story of) Abraham: He was a man of Truth, a prophet.

41. Wazkur fil-Kitaabi Ibraaheem; innahoo kaana ṣiddeeqan-Nabiyyaa.

وَاذْكُرْ فِي الْكِتَابِ إِبْرَاهِيمَ ۚ إِنَّهُ
كَانَ صِدِّيقًا نَبِيًّا ﴿٤١﴾

42. Behold, he said to his father: "O my father! why worship that which does not hear and does not see, and can profit you nothing?

42. Iz qaala li-abeehi yaaa abati lima ta'budu maa laa yasma'u wa laa yubṣiru wa laa yughnee 'anka shay'aa.

إِذْ قَالَ لِأَبِيهِ يَا أَبَتِ لِمَ تَعْبُدُ
مَا لَا يَسْمَعُ وَلَا يُبْصِرُ وَلَا يُغْنِي
عَنْكَ شَيْئًا ﴿٤٢﴾

43. "O my father! to me has come knowledge which has not reached you: so follow me: I will guide you to a Way that is even and straight.

43. Yaaa abati innee qad jaaa'anee minal-'ilmi maa lam yaåtika fattabi'neee ahdika Ṣiraaṭan Sawiyyaa.

يَا أَبَتِ إِنِّي قَدْ جَاءَنِي مِنَ الْعِلْمِ مَا لَمْ
يَأْتِكَ فَاتَّبِعْنِي أَهْدِكَ صِرَاطًا سَوِيًّا ﴿٤٣﴾

Ikhfa اخفاء | Ghunna غنّہ | Ikhfa Meem Saakin اخفاء میم ساکن | Idghaam ادغام | Qalqala قلقلہ | Qalb قلب | Idghaam Meem Saakin ادغام میم ساکن

44. "O my father! Do not serve Satan: for Satan is a rebel against (Allah) Most Gracious.

45. "O my father! I fear lest a Penalty afflict you from (Allah) Most Gracious, so that you become a friend to Satan."

46. (The father) replied: "Do you hate my gods, O Abraham? If you do not forbear, I will indeed stone you: now get away from me for a good long while!"

47. Abraham said: "Peace be on you: I will pray to my Lord for your forgiveness: for He is to me Most Gracious.

48. "And I will turn away from you (all) and from those whom you invoke besides Allah: I will call on my Lord: perhaps, by my prayer to my Lord, I shall be not unblessed."

49. When he had turned away from them and from those whom they worshipped besides Allah, We bestowed on him Isaac and Jacob, and each one of them We made a prophet.

50. And We bestowed of Our Mercy on them, and We granted them lofty honor on the tongue of truth.

51. Also mention in the Book (the story of) Moses: for he was specially chosen, and he was a Messenger (and) a prophet.

52. And we called him from the right side of Mount (Sinai), and made him draw near to Us, for mystic (converse).

53. And, out of Our Mercy, We gave him his brother Aaron, (also) a prophet.

54. Also mention in the Book (the story of) Isma'il: he was (strictly) true to what he promised, and he was a Messenger (and) a prophet.

55. He used to enjoin on his people Prayer and

44. Yaaa abati laa ta'budish-Shayṭaana innash-Shayṭaana kaana lir-Raḥmaani 'aṣiyyaa.

45. Yaaa abati inneee akhaafu añy-yamassaka 'aẕaabum-minar-Raḥmaani fatakoona lish-Shayṭaani waliyyaa.

46. Qaala araaghibun anta 'an aalihatee yaaa Ibraaheemu la'il-lam tantahi la-arjumannaka wahjurnee maliyyaa.

47. Qaala salaamun 'alayka sa-astaghfiru laka Rabbeee innahoo kaana bee ḥafiyyaa.

48. Wa a'tazilukum wa maa tad'oona min doonil-laahi wa ad'oo Rabbee 'asaaa allaaa akoona bidu'aa'i Rabbee shaqiyyaa.

49. Falamma'-tazalahum wa maa ya'budoona min doonil-laahi wahabnaa lahoo Is-ḥaaqa wa Ya'qoob, wa kullan ja'alnaa Nabiyyaa.

50. Wa wahabnaa lahum-mirraḥmatinaa wa ja'alnaa lahum lisaana ṣidqin 'aliyyaa.

(Section 3)

51. Wazkur fil-Kitaabi Moo-saaa; innahoo kaana mukhla-ṣañw-wa kaana Rasoolan-Nabiyyaa.

52. Wa naadaynaahu min jaanibiṭ-Ṭooril-aymani wa qarrabnaahu najiyyaa.

53. Wa wahabnaa lahoo mir-raḥmatinaaa akhaahu Haaroona Nabiyyaa.

54. Wazkur fil-Kitaabi Ismaa-'eel; innahoo kaana ṣaadiqal-wa'di wa kaana Rasoolan-Nabiyyaa.

55. Wa kaana yaȧmuru ahlahoo biṣ-Ṣalaati waz-

يٰۤاَبَتِ لَا تَعْبُدِ الشَّيْطٰنَ ۖ اِنَّ الشَّيْطٰنَ
كَانَ لِلرَّحْمٰنِ عَصِيًّا ﴿٤٤﴾
يٰۤاَبَتِ اِنِّيْۤ اَخَافُ اَنْ يَّمَسَّكَ عَذَابٌ
مِّنَ الرَّحْمٰنِ فَتَكُوْنَ لِلشَّيْطٰنِ وَلِيًّا ﴿٤٥﴾
قَالَ اَرَاغِبٌ اَنْتَ عَنْ اٰلِهَتِيْ
يٰۤاِبْرٰهِيْمُ ۚ لَئِنْ لَّمْ تَنْتَهِ لَاَرْجُمَنَّكَ
وَاهْجُرْنِيْ مَلِيًّا ﴿٤٦﴾
قَالَ سَلٰمٌ عَلَيْكَ ۚ سَاَسْتَغْفِرُ لَكَ رَبِّيْ ۗ
اِنَّهٗ كَانَ بِيْ حَفِيًّا ﴿٤٧﴾
وَاَعْتَزِلُكُمْ وَمَا تَدْعُوْنَ مِنْ دُوْنِ
اللّٰهِ وَاَدْعُوْا رَبِّيْ ۖ عَسٰۤى اَلَّاۤ اَكُوْنَ
بِدُعَآءِ رَبِّيْ شَقِيًّا ﴿٤٨﴾
فَلَمَّا اعْتَزَلَهُمْ وَمَا يَعْبُدُوْنَ مِنْ
دُوْنِ اللّٰهِ ۙ وَهَبْنَا لَهٗۤ اِسْحٰقَ وَ
يَعْقُوْبَ ۗ وَكُلًّا جَعَلْنَا نَبِيًّا ﴿٤٩﴾
وَوَهَبْنَا لَهُمْ مِّنْ رَّحْمَتِنَا وَجَعَلْنَا
لَهُمْ لِسَانَ صِدْقٍ عَلِيًّا ﴿٥٠﴾ ع
وَاذْكُرْ فِي الْكِتٰبِ مُوْسٰۤى ۫ اِنَّهٗ كَانَ
مُخْلَصًا وَّكَانَ رَسُوْلًا نَّبِيًّا ﴿٥١﴾
وَنَادَيْنٰهُ مِنْ جَانِبِ الطُّوْرِ الْاَيْمَنِ
وَقَرَّبْنٰهُ نَجِيًّا ﴿٥٢﴾
وَوَهَبْنَا لَهٗ مِنْ رَّحْمَتِنَاۤ اَخَاهُ
هٰرُوْنَ نَبِيًّا ﴿٥٣﴾
وَاذْكُرْ فِي الْكِتٰبِ اِسْمٰعِيْلَ ۫ اِنَّهٗ كَانَ
صَادِقَ الْوَعْدِ وَكَانَ رَسُوْلًا نَّبِيًّا ﴿٥٤﴾
وَكَانَ يَأْمُرُ اَهْلَهٗ بِالصَّلٰوةِ وَ

ركوع

Ikhfa اخفاء | Ghunna غُنّہ | Ikhfa Meem Saakin اخفاء میم ساکن | Idghaam ادغام | Qalqala قلقلہ | Qalb قلب | Idghaam Meem Saakin ادغام میم ساکن

Charity, and he was most acceptable in the sight of his Lord.

56. Also mention in the Book the case of Idris: he was a man of truth (and sincerity), (and) a prophet:

57. And We raised him to a lofty station.

58. Those were some of the prophets on whom Allah bestowed His Grace,- of the posterity of Adam, and of those who We carried (in the Ark) with Noah, and of the posterity of Abraham and Israel of those whom We guided and chose. Whenever the Signs of (Allah) Most Gracious were rehearsed to them, they would fall down in prostrate adoration and in tears.

(Bow Down)

59. But after them there followed a posterity who missed prayers and followed after lusts soon, then, will they face Destruction,-

60. Except those who repent and believe, and work righteousness: for these will enter the Garden and will not be wronged in the least,-

61. Gardens of Eternity, those which (Allah) Most Gracious has promised to His servants in the Unseen: for His promise must (necessarily) come to pass.

62. They will not hear any vain discourse there, but only salutations of Peace: and therein they will have their sustenance, morning and evening.

63. Such is the Garden which We give as an inheritance to those of Our servants who guard against evil.

64. (The angels say:) "We do not descend but by command of your Lord: to Him belongs what is before us and what is behind us, and what is between: and your Lord never forgets,-

65. "Lord of the heavens and of the earth, and of all that is between them;

zakaati wa kaana 'inda Rabbihee marḍiyyaa.

56. Wazkur fil-Kitaabi Idrees; innahoo kaana ṣiddeeqan-Nabiyyaa.

57. Wa rafa'naahu makaanan 'aliyyaa.

58. Ulaaa'ikal-lazeena an'amal-laahu 'alayhim-minan-Nabiyyeena min zurriyyati Aadama wa mimman ḥamalnaa ma'a Nooḥiñw-wa min zurriyyati Ibraaheema wa Israaa'eela wa mimman hadaynaa wajtabaynaaa; izaa tutlaa 'alayhim Aayaatur-Raḥmaani kharroo sujjadañw-wa bukiyyaa. ۩

59. Fakhalafa mim ba'dihim khalfun aḍaa'uṣ-Ṣalaata wattaba'ush-shahawaati fasawfa yalqawna ghayyaa.

60. Illaa man taaba wa aamana wa 'amila ṣaaliḥan fa-ulaaa'ika yadkhuloonal-jannata wa laa yuẓlamoona shay'aa.

61. jannaati 'Adninil-latee wa'adar-Raḥmaanu 'ibaadahoo bilghayb; innahoo kaana wa'duhoo maåtiyyaa.

62. Laa yasma'oona feehaa laghwan illaa salaamaa; wa lahum rizquhum feehaa bukratañw-wa 'ashiyyaa.

63. Tilkal-jannatul-latee noorisu min 'ibaadinaa man kaana taqiyyaa.

64. Wa maa natanazzalu illaa bi-amri Rabbika lahoo maa bayna aydeenaa wa maa khalfanaa wa maa bayna zaalik; wa maa kaana Rabbuka nasiyyaa.

65. Rabbus-samaawaati wal-arḍi wa maa baynahumaa

الزَّكٰوةِ وَكَانَ عِنْدَ رَبِّهٖ مَرْضِيًّا ﴿٥٥﴾
وَاذْكُرْ فِي الْكِتٰبِ اِدْرِيْسَ اِنَّهٗ
كَانَ صِدِّيْقًا نَّبِيًّا ﴿٥٦﴾
وَّرَفَعْنٰهُ مَكَانًا عَلِيًّا ﴿٥٧﴾
اُولٰٓئِكَ الَّذِيْنَ اَنْعَمَ اللّٰهُ عَلَيْهِمْ مِّنَ
النَّبِيّٖنَ مِنْ ذُرِّيَّةِ اٰدَمَ وَمِمَّنْ
حَمَلْنَا مَعَ نُوْحٍ وَّمِنْ ذُرِّيَّةِ
اِبْرٰهِيْمَ وَاِسْرَآءِيْلَ وَمِمَّنْ هَدَيْنَا
وَاجْتَبَيْنَا اِذَا تُتْلٰى عَلَيْهِمْ اٰيٰتُ
الرَّحْمٰنِ خَرُّوْا سُجَّدًا وَّبُكِيًّا ﴿٥٨﴾ السجدة
فَخَلَفَ مِنْ بَعْدِهِمْ خَلْفٌ اَضَاعُوا
الصَّلٰوةَ وَاتَّبَعُوا الشَّهَوٰتِ فَسَوْفَ
يَلْقَوْنَ غَيًّا ﴿٥٩﴾
اِلَّا مَنْ تَابَ وَاٰمَنَ وَعَمِلَ صَالِحًا
فَاُولٰٓئِكَ يَدْخُلُوْنَ الْجَنَّةَ وَلَا
يُظْلَمُوْنَ شَيْـًٔا ﴿٦٠﴾
جَنّٰتِ عَدْنِ الَّتِيْ وَعَدَ الرَّحْمٰنُ عِبَادَهٗ
بِالْغَيْبِ اِنَّهٗ كَانَ وَعْدُهٗ مَاْتِيًّا ﴿٦١﴾
لَا يَسْمَعُوْنَ فِيْهَا لَغْوًا اِلَّا سَلٰمًا
وَلَهُمْ رِزْقُهُمْ فِيْهَا بُكْرَةً وَّعَشِيًّا ﴿٦٢﴾
تِلْكَ الْجَنَّةُ الَّتِيْ نُوْرِثُ مِنْ عِبَادِنَا
مَنْ كَانَ تَقِيًّا ﴿٦٣﴾
وَمَا نَتَنَزَّلُ اِلَّا بِاَمْرِ رَبِّكَ لَهٗ مَا
بَيْنَ اَيْدِيْنَا وَمَا خَلْفَنَا وَمَا بَيْنَ
ذٰلِكَ وَمَا كَانَ رَبُّكَ نَسِيًّا ﴿٦٤﴾
رَبُّ السَّمٰوٰتِ وَالْاَرْضِ وَمَا بَيْنَهُمَا

السَّجْدَة (٥)

Ikhfa اخفاء | Ghunna غنّہ | Ikhfa Meem Saakin اخفاء میم ساکن | Idghaam ادغام | Qalqala قلقلہ | Qalb قلب | Idghaam Meem Saakin ادغام میم ساکن

so worship Him, and be constant and patient in His worship: do you know of any who is worthy of the same Name as He?"

fa'bud-hu waṣṭabir li'ibaadatih; hal ta'lamu lahoo samiyyaa.

(Section 4)

فَاعْبُدْهُ وَاصْطَبِرْ لِعِبَادَتِهٖ ط
هَلْ تَعْلَمُ لَهٗ سَمِيًّا ﴿٦٥﴾

66. Man says: "What! When I am dead, shall I then be raised up alive?"

66. Wa yaqoolul-insaanu 'a-izaa maa mittu lasawfa ukhraju ḥayyaa.

وَيَقُوْلُ الْاِنْسَانُ ءَاِذَا مَا مِتُّ لَسَوْفَ
اُخْرَجُ حَيًّا ﴿٦٦﴾

67. But does not man call to mind that We created him before, out of nothing?

67. Awalaa yazkurul-insaanu annaa khalaqnaahu min qablu wa lam yaku shay'aa.

اَوَلَا يَذْكُرُ الْاِنْسَانُ اَنَّا خَلَقْنٰهُ مِنْ
قَبْلُ وَلَمْ يَكُ شَيْئًا ﴿٦٧﴾

68. So, by your Lord, without doubt, We shall gather them together, and (also) the Evil Ones (with them); then shall We bring them forth on their knees round about Hell:

68. Fawa Rabbika lanaḥshurannahum wash-shayaaṭeena summa lanuḥḍirannahum ḥawla Jahannama jisiyyaa.

فَوَرَبِّكَ لَنَحْشُرَنَّهُمْ وَالشَّيٰطِيْنَ ثُمَّ
لَنُحْضِرَنَّهُمْ حَوْلَ جَهَنَّمَ جِثِيًّا ﴿٦٨﴾

69. Then We shall certainly drag out from every sect all those who were worst in obstinate rebellion against (Allah) Most Gracious.

69. Summa lananzi'anna min kulli shee'atin ayyuhum ashaddu 'alar-Raḥmaani 'itiyyaa.

ثُمَّ لَنَنْزِعَنَّ مِنْ كُلِّ شِيْعَةٍ اَيُّهُمْ
اَشَدُّ عَلَى الرَّحْمٰنِ عِتِيًّا ﴿٦٩﴾

70. And certainly We know best those who are most worthy of being burned therein.

70. Summa lanaḥnu a'lamu billazeena hum awlaa bihaa ṣiliyyaa.

ثُمَّ لَنَحْنُ اَعْلَمُ بِالَّذِيْنَ هُمْ اَوْلٰى
بِهَا صِلِيًّا ﴿٧٠﴾

71. Not one of you but will pass over it: this is, with your Lord, a Decree which must be accomplished.

71. Wa im-minkum illaa waariduhaa; kaana 'alaa Rabbika ḥatmam-maqḍiyyaa.

وَاِنْ مِّنْكُمْ اِلَّا وَارِدُهَا ج كَانَ عَلٰى
رَبِّكَ حَتْمًا مَّقْضِيًّا ﴿٧١﴾

72. But We shall save those who guarded against evil, and We shall leave the wrong-doers therein, (humbled) to their knees.

72. Summa nunajjil-lazeenat-taqaw wa nazaruẓ-ẓaalimeena feehaa jisiyyaa.

ثُمَّ نُنَجِّي الَّذِيْنَ اتَّقَوْا وَّنَذَرُ
الظّٰلِمِيْنَ فِيْهَا جِثِيًّا ﴿٧٢﴾

73. When Our Clear Signs are rehearsed to them, the Unbelievers say to those who believe, "Which of the two sides is best in point of position? Which makes the best show in Council?"

73. Wa izaa tutlaa 'alayhim Aayaatunaa bayyinaatin qaalal-lazeena kafaroo lillazeena aamanooo ayyul-fareeqayni khayrum-maqaamañw-wa aḥsanu nadiyyaa.

وَاِذَا تُتْلٰى عَلَيْهِمْ اٰيٰتُنَا بَيِّنٰتٍ
قَالَ الَّذِيْنَ كَفَرُوْا لِلَّذِيْنَ اٰمَنُوْآ
اَيُّ الْفَرِيْقَيْنِ خَيْرٌ مَّقَامًا وَّ
اَحْسَنُ نَدِيًّا ﴿٧٣﴾

74. But how many (countless) generations before them have we destroyed, who were even better in equipment and in glitter to the eye?

74. Wa kam ahlaknaa qablahum-min qarnin hum aḥsanu asaasañw-wa ri'yaa.

وَكَمْ اَهْلَكْنَا قَبْلَهُمْ مِّنْ قَرْنٍ هُمْ
اَحْسَنُ اَثَاثًا وَّرِءْيًا ﴿٧٤﴾

75. Say: "If any men go astray, (Allah) Most Gracious extends (the rope) to them, until, when they see the warning of Allah (being fulfilled) - either in punishment or in (the approach of) the Hour,- they will at length realise who is worst

75. Qul man kaana fiḍḍalaalati falyamdud lahur-Raḥmaanu maddaa; ḥattaa izaa raaw maa yoo'adoona immal-'azaaba wa immas-Saa'ata fasa-ya'lamoona man huwa sharrum-

قُلْ مَنْ كَانَ فِي الضَّلٰلَةِ فَلْيَمْدُدْ
لَهُ الرَّحْمٰنُ مَدًّا ج حَتّٰى اِذَا رَاَوْا
مَا يُوْعَدُوْنَ اِمَّا الْعَذَابَ وَاِمَّا
السَّاعَةَ ط فَسَيَعْلَمُوْنَ مَنْ هُوَ شَرٌّ

Ikhfa اخفاء | Ghunna غُنّہ | Ikhfa Meem Saakin اخفاء میم ساکن | Idghaam ادغام | Qalqala قلقلہ | Qalb قلب | Idghaam Meem Saakin ادغام میم ساکن

in position, and (who) weakest in forces!

76. "And Allah advances those in guidance who seek guidance: and the things that endure, Good Deeds, are best in the sight of your Lord, as rewards, and best in respect of (their) eventual return."

77. Have you then seen the (sort of) man who rejects Our Signs, yet says: "I shall certainly be given wealth and children?"

78. Has he penetrated to the Unseen, or has he taken a contract with (Allah) Most Gracious?

79. Nay! We shall record what he says, and We shall add and add to his punishment.

80. To Us shall return all that he talks of, and he shall appear before Us bare and alone.

81. And they have taken (for worship) gods other than Allah, to give them power and glory!

82. Instead, they shall reject their worship, and become adversaries against them.

83. Don't you see that We have set the Evil Ones on against the unbelievers, to incite them with fury?

84. So make no haste against them, for We but count out to them a (limited) number (of days).

85. The day We shall gather the righteous to (Allah) Most Gracious, like a band presented before a king for honors,

86. And We shall drive the sinners to Hell, like thirsty cattle driven down to water,-

87. None shall have the power of intercession but such a one as has received permission (or promise) from (Allah) Most Gracious.

88. They say: "(Allah) Most Gracious has begotten a son!"

89. Indeed you have put forth a thing most monstrous!

makaanañw-wa aḍ'afu jundaa.

76. Wa yazeedul-laahul-lazeenah-tadaw hudaa; wal-baaqiyaatuṣ-ṣaaliḥaatu khayrun 'inda Rabbika sawaabañw-wa khayrum-maraddaa.

77. Afara'aytal-lazee kafara bi-Aayaatinaa wa qaala la-ootayanna maalañw-wa waladaa.

78. Aṭṭala'al-ghayba amittakhaza 'indar-Raḥmaani 'ahdaa.

79. Kallaa; sanaktubu maa yaqoolu wa namuddu lahoo minal-'azaabi maddaa.

80. Wa narisuhoo maa yaqoolu wa yaâteenaa fardaa.

81. Wattakhazoo min doonil-laahi aalihatal-liyakoonoo lahum 'izzaa.

82. Kallaa; sa-yakfuroona bi'ibaadatihim wa yakoonoona 'alayhim ḍiddaa. **(Section 5)**

83. Alam tara annaaa arsal-nash-Shayaaṭeena 'alal-kaafireena ta'uzzuhum azzaa.

84. Falaa ta'jal 'alayhim innamaa na'uddu lahum 'addaa.

85. Yawma naḥshurul-muttaqeena ilar-Raḥmaani wafdaa.

86. Wa nasooqul-mujrimeena ilaa Jahannama wirdaa.

87. Laa yamlikoonash-shafaa'ata illaa manittakhaza 'indar-Raḥmaani 'ahdaa.

88. Wa qaalut-takhazar-Raḥmaanu waladaa.

89. Laqad ji'tum shay'an iddaa.

مَّكَانًا وَّأَضْعَفُ جُندًا ﴿٧٥﴾
وَيَزِيدُ اللَّهُ الَّذِينَ اهْتَدَوْا هُدًى ۗ
وَالْبَاقِيَاتُ الصَّالِحَاتُ خَيْرٌ عِندَ
رَبِّكَ ثَوَابًا وَخَيْرٌ مَّرَدًّا ﴿٧٦﴾
أَفَرَأَيْتَ الَّذِي كَفَرَ بِآيَاتِنَا وَقَالَ
لَأُوتَيَنَّ مَالًا وَوَلَدًا ﴿٧٧﴾
أَطَّلَعَ الْغَيْبَ أَمِ اتَّخَذَ عِندَ
الرَّحْمَٰنِ عَهْدًا ﴿٧٨﴾
كَلَّا ۚ سَنَكْتُبُ مَا يَقُولُ وَنَمُدُّ لَهُ
مِنَ الْعَذَابِ مَدًّا ﴿٧٩﴾
وَنَرِثُهُ مَا يَقُولُ وَيَأْتِينَا فَرْدًا ﴿٨٠﴾
وَاتَّخَذُوا مِن دُونِ اللَّهِ آلِهَةً لِّيَكُونُوا
لَهُمْ عِزًّا ﴿٨١﴾
كَلَّا ۚ سَيَكْفُرُونَ بِعِبَادَتِهِمْ وَ
يَكُونُونَ عَلَيْهِمْ ضِدًّا ﴿٨٢﴾ ع ٥
أَلَمْ تَرَ أَنَّا أَرْسَلْنَا الشَّيَاطِينَ
عَلَى الْكَافِرِينَ تَؤُزُّهُمْ أَزًّا ﴿٨٣﴾
فَلَا تَعْجَلْ عَلَيْهِمْ ۖ إِنَّمَا نَعُدُّ لَهُمْ
عَدًّا ﴿٨٤﴾
يَوْمَ نَحْشُرُ الْمُتَّقِينَ إِلَى الرَّحْمَٰنِ
وَفْدًا ﴿٨٥﴾ وقف لازم
وَنَسُوقُ الْمُجْرِمِينَ إِلَىٰ جَهَنَّمَ وِرْدًا ﴿٨٦﴾
لَّا يَمْلِكُونَ الشَّفَاعَةَ إِلَّا مَنِ اتَّخَذَ
عِندَ الرَّحْمَٰنِ عَهْدًا ﴿٨٧﴾ وقف لازم
وَقَالُوا اتَّخَذَ الرَّحْمَٰنُ وَلَدًا ﴿٨٨﴾
لَّقَدْ جِئْتُمْ شَيْئًا إِدًّا ﴿٨٩﴾

Ikhfa اخفاء | Ghunna غُنّہ | Ikhfa Meem Saakin اخفاء میم ساکن | Idghaam ادغام | Qalqala قلقلہ | Qalb قلب | Idghaam Meem Saakin ادغام میم ساکن

90. At it the skies are ready to burst, the earth to split asunder, and the mountains to fall down in utter ruin,

90. Takaadus-samaawaatu yatafaṭṭarna minhu wa tanshaqqul-arḍu wa takhirrul-jibaalu haddaa.

تَكَادُ السَّمٰوٰتُ يَتَفَطَّرْنَ مِنْهُ وَ
تَنْشَقُّ الْأَرْضُ وَتَخِرُّ الْجِبَالُ هَدًّا ﴿٩٠﴾

91. That they should invoke a son for (Allah) Most Gracious.

91. An da‘aw lir-Raḥmaani waladaa.

أَنْ دَعَوْا لِلرَّحْمٰنِ وَلَدًا ﴿٩١﴾

92. For it is not consonant with the majesty of (Allah) Most Gracious that He should beget a son.

92. Wa maa yambaghee lir-Raḥmaani añy-yattakhiza waladaa.

وَمَا يَنْبَغِي لِلرَّحْمٰنِ أَنْ يَتَّخِذَ وَلَدًا ﴿٩٢﴾

93. Not one of the beings in the heavens and the earth but must come to (Allah) Most Gracious as a servant.

93. In kullu man fis-samaawaati wal-arḍi illaaa aatir-Raḥmaani ‘abdaa.

إِنْ كُلُّ مَنْ فِي السَّمٰوٰتِ وَالْأَرْضِ
إِلَّا آتِي الرَّحْمٰنِ عَبْدًا ﴿٩٣﴾

94. He takes an account of them (all), and has numbered them (all) exactly.

94. Laqad aḥṣaahum wa ‘addahum ‘addaa.

لَقَدْ أَحْصٰهُمْ وَعَدَّهُمْ عَدًّا ﴿٩٤﴾

95. And everyone of them will come to Him singly on the Day of Judgment.

95. Wa kulluhum aateehi Yawmal-Qiyaamati fardaa.

وَكُلُّهُمْ آتِيهِ يَوْمَ الْقِيٰمَةِ فَرْدًا ﴿٩٥﴾

96. On those who believe and work deeds of righteousness, will (Allah) Most Gracious bestow Love.

96. Innal-lazeena aamanoo wa ‘amiluṣ-ṣaaliḥaati sa-yaj‘alu lahumur-Raḥmaanu wuddaa.

إِنَّ الَّذِينَ آمَنُوا وَعَمِلُوا الصّٰلِحٰتِ
سَيَجْعَلُ لَهُمُ الرَّحْمٰنُ وُدًّا ﴿٩٦﴾

97. So We have made the (Qur’an) easy in your own tongue, that with it you may give glad ti-dings to the righteous, and warni-ngs to people given to contention

97. Fa-innamaa yassarnaahu bilisaanika litubashshira bihil-muttaqeena wa tunzira bihee qawmal-luddaa.

فَإِنَّمَا يَسَّرْنٰهُ بِلِسَانِكَ لِتُبَشِّرَ بِهِ
الْمُتَّقِينَ وَتُنْذِرَ بِهِ قَوْمًا لُدًّا ﴿٩٧﴾

98. But how many (countless) generations before them We have destroyed? Can you find a single one of them (now) or hear (so much as) a whisper of them?

98. Wa kam ahlaknaa qablahum-min qarnin hal tuḥissu minhum-min aḥadin aw tasma‘u lahum rikzaa. **(Section 6)**

وَكَمْ أَهْلَكْنَا قَبْلَهُمْ مِنْ قَرْنٍ هَلْ
تُحِسُّ مِنْهُمْ مِنْ أَحَدٍ أَوْ تَسْمَعُ
لَهُمْ رِكْزًا ﴿٩٨﴾

ع النصف

20. Ta-Ha (Mystic Letters, T. H.)

In the name of Allah, Most Gracious, Most Merciful.

Sûrat Ṭâ-Hâ–20

(Revealed at Makkah)

Bismillaahir Raḥmaanir Raḥeem

(٢٠) سُورَةُ طٰهٰ مَكِّيَّةٌ (٤٥)

بِسْمِ اللّٰهِ الرَّحْمٰنِ الرَّحِيمِ

1. *Ta-Ha.*

1. Ṭaa-Haa.

طٰهٰ ﴿١﴾

2. We have not sent down the Qur’an to you to be (an occa-sion) for your distress,

2. Maaa anzalnaa ‘alaykal-Qur-aana litashqaaa.

مَا أَنْزَلْنَا عَلَيْكَ الْقُرْآنَ لِتَشْقٰى ﴿٢﴾

3. But only as an admonition to those who fear (Allah),-

3. Illaa tazkiratal-limañy-yakhshaa.

إِلَّا تَذْكِرَةً لِمَنْ يَخْشٰى ﴿٣﴾

4. A revelation from Him Who created the earth and the heavens on high.

4. Tanzeelam-mimman khalaqal-arḍa was-samaawaatil-‘ulaa.

تَنْزِيلًا مِمَّنْ خَلَقَ الْأَرْضَ وَالسَّمٰوٰتِ
الْعُلٰى ﴿٤﴾

5. (Allah) Most Gracious is firmly established on the throne (of authority).

5. Ar-Raḥmaanu ‘alal-‘Arshis-tawaa.

الرَّحْمٰنُ عَلَى الْعَرْشِ اسْتَوٰى ﴿٥﴾

6. To Him belongs what is in the heavens and on earth, and all between them, and all beneath the soil.

6. Lahoo maa fis-samaawaati wa maa fil-arḍi wa maa baynahumaa wa maa taḥtas-saraa.

لَهُ مَا فِي السَّمٰوٰتِ وَمَا فِي الْأَرْضِ وَمَا
بَيْنَهُمَا وَمَا تَحْتَ الثَّرٰى ﴿٦﴾

7. If you pronounce the word aloud, (it is no matter): for verily He knows what is secret

7. Wa in tajhar bilqawli fa-innahoo ya‘lamus-sirra

وَإِنْ تَجْهَرْ بِالْقَوْلِ فَإِنَّهُ يَعْلَمُ السِّرَّ

Ikhfa اخفاء	Ghunna غُنّہ	Ikhfa Meem Saakin اخفاء میم ساکن	Idghaam ادغام	Qalqala قلقلہ	Qalb قلب	Idghaam Meem Saakin ادغام میم ساکن

English	Transliteration	Arabic
and what is yet more hidden.	wa akhfaa.	وَاَخْفٰى ۝٧
8. Allah! there is no god but He! To Him belong the most Beautiful Names.	8. Allaahu laaa ilaaha illaa Huwa lahul-Asmaaa'ul-Ḥusnaa.	اَللّٰهُ لَآ اِلٰهَ اِلَّا هُوَ ۚ لَهُ الْاَسْمَآءُ الْحُسْنٰى ۝٨
9. Has the story of Moses reached you?	9. Wa hal ataaka ḥadeesu Moosaa.	وَهَلْ اَتٰىكَ حَدِيْثُ مُوْسٰى ۝٩
10. Behold, he saw a fire: so he said to his family, "you Tarry; I perceive a fire; perhaps I can bring you some burning brand therefrom, or find some guidance at the fire."	10. Iz ra-aa naaran faqaala li-ahlihim-kusooo inneee aanastu naaral-la'alleee aateekum minhaa biqabasin aw ajidu 'alan-naari hudaa.	اِذْ رَاٰ نَارًا فَقَالَ لِاَهْلِهِ امْكُثُوْٓا اِنِّيْٓ اٰنَسْتُ نَارًا لَّعَلِّيْٓ اٰتِيْكُمْ مِّنْهَا بِقَبَسٍ اَوْ اَجِدُ عَلَى النَّارِ هُدًى ۝١٠
11. But when he came to the fire, a voice was heard: "O Moses!	11. Falammaaa ataahaa noodiya yaa Moosaa.	فَلَمَّآ اَتٰىهَا نُوْدِيَ يٰمُوْسٰى ۝١١
12. "Verily I am your Lord! Therefore (in My presence) put off your shoes: you are in the sacred valley Tuwa.	12. Inneee Ana Rabbuka fakhla' na'layka innaka bilwaadil-muqaddasi Ṭuwaa.	اِنِّيْٓ اَنَا رَبُّكَ فَاخْلَعْ نَعْلَيْكَ ۚ اِنَّكَ بِالْوَادِ الْمُقَدَّسِ طُوًى ۝١٢
13. "I have chosen you: listen, then, to the inspiration (sent to you).	13. Wa anakhtartuka fastami' limaa yooḥaa.	وَاَنَا اخْتَرْتُكَ فَاسْتَمِعْ لِمَا يُوْحٰى ۝١٣
14. "Verily, I am Allah: There is no god but I: so you serve Me (only), and establish regular prayer for celebrating My praise.	14. Innaneee Anal-laahu laaa ilaaha illaaa Ana fa'budnee wa-aqimiṣ-Ṣalaata lizikree.	اِنَّنِيْٓ اَنَا اللّٰهُ لَآ اِلٰهَ اِلَّآ اَنَا فَاعْبُدْنِيْ ۙ وَاَقِمِ الصَّلٰوةَ لِذِكْرِيْ ۝١٤
15. "Verily the Hour is coming My design is to keep it hidden- for every soul to receive its reward by the measure of its Endeavor.	15. Innas-Saa'ata aatiyatun akaadu ukhfeehaa litujzaa kullu nafsim bimaa tas'aa.	اِنَّ السَّاعَةَ اٰتِيَةٌ اَكَادُ اُخْفِيْهَا لِتُجْزٰى كُلُّ نَفْسٍۢ بِمَا تَسْعٰى ۝١٥
16. "Therefore let not such as do not believe therein but follow their own lusts, divert you therefrom, lest you perish!".	16. Falaa yaṣuddannaka 'anhaa mal-laa yu'minu bihaa wattaba'a hawaahu fatardaa.	فَلَا يَصُدَّنَّكَ عَنْهَا مَنْ لَّا يُؤْمِنُ بِهَا وَاتَّبَعَ هَوٰىهُ فَتَرْدٰى ۝١٦
17. "And what is that in your right hand, O Moses?"	17. Wa maa tilka bi-yameenika yaa Moosaa.	وَمَا تِلْكَ بِيَمِيْنِكَ يٰمُوْسٰى ۝١٧
18. He said, "It is my rod: on it I lean; with it I beat down fodder for my flocks; and in it I find other uses."	18. Qaala hiya 'aṣaaya atawakka'u 'alayhaa wa ahushshu bihaa 'alaa ghanamee wa liya feehaa ma-aaribu ukhraa.	قَالَ هِيَ عَصَايَ ۚ اَتَوَكَّؤُا عَلَيْهَا وَ اَهُشُّ بِهَا عَلٰى غَنَمِيْ وَلِيَ فِيْهَا مَاٰرِبُ اُخْرٰى ۝١٨
19. (Allah) said, "Throw it, O Moses!"	19. Qaala alqihaa yaa Moosaa.	قَالَ اَلْقِهَا يٰمُوْسٰى ۝١٩
20. He threw it, and behold! it was a snake, active in motion.	20. Fa-alqaahaa fa-izaa hiya ḥayyatun tas'aa.	فَاَلْقٰىهَا فَاِذَا هِيَ حَيَّةٌ تَسْعٰى ۝٢٠
21. (Allah) said, "Seize it, and fear not: We shall return it at once to its former condition"..	21. Qaala khuzhaa wa laa takhaf sanu'eeduhaa seeratahal-oolaa.	قَالَ خُذْهَا وَلَا تَخَفْ ٚ سَنُعِيْدُهَا سِيْرَتَهَا الْاُوْلٰى ۝٢١
22. "Now draw your hand close to your side: it shall come forth white (and shining), without harm (or stain),- as another Sign,-	22. Waḍmum yadaka ilaa janaaḥika takhruj bayḍaaa'a min ghayri sooo'in Aayatan ukhraa.	وَاضْمُمْ يَدَكَ اِلٰى جَنَاحِكَ تَخْرُجْ بَيْضَآءَ مِنْ غَيْرِ سُوْٓءٍ اٰيَةً اُخْرٰى ۝٢٢

وقف لازم

Ikhfa اخفاء | Ghunna غُنّہ | Ikhfa Meem Saakin اخفاء میم ساکن | Idghaam ادغام | Qalqala قلقلہ | Qalb قلب | Idghaam Meem Saakin ادغام میم ساکن

English	Transliteration	Arabic
23. "In order that We may show you (two) of our Greater Signs.	23. Linuriyaka min Aayaatinal-Kubraa.	لِنُرِيَكَ مِنْ اٰيٰتِنَا الْكُبْرٰى ﴿٢٣﴾
24. "You go to Pharaoh, for he has indeed transgressed all bounds."	24. Izhab ilaa Fir'awna innahoo ṭaghaa. **(Section 1)**	اِذْهَبْ اِلٰى فِرْعَوْنَ اِنَّهٗ طَغٰى ﴿٢٤﴾ ع
25. (Moses) said: "O my Lord! expand me my breast;	25. Qaala Rabbish-raḥ lee ṣadree.	قَالَ رَبِّ اشْرَحْ لِىْ صَدْرِىْ ﴿٢٥﴾
26. "Ease my task for me;	26. Wa yassir leee amree.	وَيَسِّرْ لِىْٓ اَمْرِىْ ﴿٢٦﴾
27. "And remove the impediment from my speech,	27. Waḥlul 'uqdatam-millisaanee.	وَاحْلُلْ عُقْدَةً مِّنْ لِّسَانِىْ ﴿٢٧﴾
28. "So they may understand what I say:	28. Yafqahoo qawlee.	يَفْقَهُوْا قَوْلِىْ ﴿٢٨﴾
29. "And give me a Minister from my family,	29. Waj'al-lee wazeeram-min ahlee.	وَاجْعَلْ لِّىْ وَزِيْرًا مِّنْ اَهْلِىْ ﴿٢٩﴾
30. "Aaron, my brother;	30. Haaroona akhee.	هٰرُوْنَ اَخِى ﴿٣٠﴾
31. "Add to my strength through him,	31. Ushdud biheee azree.	اشْدُدْ بِهٖٓ اَزْرِىْ ﴿٣١﴾
32. "And make him share my task:	32. Wa ashrik-hu feee amree.	وَاَشْرِكْهُ فِىْٓ اَمْرِىْ ﴿٣٢﴾
33. "That we may celebrate Your praise without stint,	33. Kay nusabbiḥaka kaseeraa.	كَىْ نُسَبِّحَكَ كَثِيْرًا ﴿٣٣﴾
34. "And remember You without stint:	34. Wa nazkuraka kaseeraa.	وَّنَذْكُرَكَ كَثِيْرًا ﴿٣٤﴾
35. "For You are He that (ever) regards us."	35. Innaka kunta binaa baṣeeraa.	اِنَّكَ كُنْتَ بِنَا بَصِيْرًا ﴿٣٥﴾
36. (Allah) said: "Granted is your prayer, O Moses!"	36. Qaala qad ooteeta su'laka yaa Moosaa.	قَالَ قَدْ اُوْتِيْتَ سُؤْلَكَ يٰمُوْسٰى ﴿٣٦﴾
37. "And indeed We conferred a favor on you another time (before).	37. Wa laqad manannaa 'alayka marratan ukhraaa.	وَلَقَدْ مَنَنَّا عَلَيْكَ مَرَّةً اُخْرٰٓى ﴿٣٧﴾
38. "Behold! We sent to your mother, by inspiration, the message:	38. Iz awḥaynaaa ilaaa ummika maa yooḥaaa.	اِذْ اَوْحَيْنَآ اِلٰٓى اُمِّكَ مَا يُوْحٰٓى ﴿٣٨﴾
39. "'Throw (the child) into the chest, and throw (the chest) into the river: the river will cast him up on the bank, and he will be taken up by one who is an enemy to Me and an enemy to him': but I cast (the garment of) love over you from Me: and (this) in order that you may be reared under Mine eye.	39. Aniqzifeehi fit-Taabooti faqzifeehi fil-yammi fal-yulqihil-yammu bis-saaḥili yaåkhuzhu 'aduwwul-lee wa 'aduwwul-lah; wa alqaytu 'alayka maḥabbatam-minnee wa lituṣna'a 'alaa 'aynee.	اَنِ اقْذِفِيْهِ فِى التَّابُوْتِ فَاقْذِفِيْهِ فِى الْيَمِّ فَلْيُلْقِهِ الْيَمُّ بِالسَّاحِلِ يَاْخُذْهُ عَدُوٌّ لِّىْ وَعَدُوٌّ لَّهٗ ؕ وَاَلْقَيْتُ عَلَيْكَ مَحَبَّةً مِّنِّىْ ۚ وَلِتُصْنَعَ عَلٰى عَيْنِىْ ﴿٣٩﴾ وقف لازم
40. "Behold! your sister goes forth and says, 'shall I show you one who will nurse and rear the (child)?' So We brought you back to your mother, that her eye might be cooled and she should not grieve. Then you slew a man, but We saved you from trouble, and We tried you in various ways. Then you tarried a number of years with the people of Midian. Then you came hither as ordained, O Moses!	40. Iz tamsheee ukhtuka fataqoolu hal adullukum 'alaa mañy-yakfuluhoo faraja'naaka ilaaa ummika kay taqarra 'aynuhaa wa laa taḥzan; wa qatalta nafsan fanajjaynaaka minal-ghammi wa fatannaaka futoonaa; falabista sineena feee ahli Madyana summa ji'ta 'alaa qadariñy-yaa Moosaa.	اِذْ تَمْشِىْٓ اُخْتُكَ فَتَقُوْلُ هَلْ اَدُلُّكُمْ عَلٰى مَنْ يَّكْفُلُهٗ ؕ فَرَجَعْنٰكَ اِلٰٓى اُمِّكَ كَىْ تَقَرَّ عَيْنُهَا وَلَا تَحْزَنَ ؕ وَقَتَلْتَ نَفْسًا فَنَجَّيْنٰكَ مِنَ الْغَمِّ وَفَتَنّٰكَ فُتُوْنًا ۚ فَلَبِثْتَ سِنِيْنَ فِىْٓ اَهْلِ مَدْيَنَ ۙ ثُمَّ جِئْتَ عَلٰى قَدَرٍ يّٰمُوْسٰى ﴿٤٠﴾

Ikhfa اخفاء · Ghunna غنّہ · Ikhfa Meem Saakin اخفاء میم ساکن · Idghaam ادغام · Qalqala قلقلہ · Qalb قلب · Idghaam Meem Saakin ادغام میم ساکن

41. "And I have prepared you for Myself (for service)"..

42. "Go, you and your brother, with My Signs, and slacken not, either of you, in keeping Me in remembrance.

43. "Go, both of you, to Pharaoh, for he has indeed transgressed all bounds;

44. "But speak to him mildly; perchance he may take warning or fear (Allah)."

45. They (Moses and Aaron) said: "Our Lord! We fear lest he hasten with insolence against us, or lest he transgress all bounds."

46. He said: "Do not fear: for I am with you: I hear and see (everything).

47. "So you both go to him, and say, 'Verily we are Messengers sent by your Lord: send forth, therefore, the Children of Israel with us, and afflict them not: with a Sign, indeed, have we come from your Lord! and peace to all who follow guidance!

48. "'Verily it has been revealed to us that the Chastisement (awaits) those who reject and turn away.'"

49. (When this message was delivered), (Pharaoh) said: "Who, then, O Moses, is the Lord of you two?"

50. He said: "Our Lord is He Who gave to each (created) thing its form and nature, and further, gave (it) guidance."

51. (Pharaoh) said: "What then is the condition of previous generations?"

52. He replied: "The knowledge of that is with my Lord, duly recorded: my Lord never errs, nor forgets,-

53. "He Who has, made for you the earth like a carpet spread out; has enabled you to go about therein by roads (and channels); and has sent down water from the sky." With it have We produced diverse pairs of plants each separate from the others.

41. Waṣṭana'tuka linafsee.

42. Izhab anta wa akhooka bi-Aayaatee wa laa taniyaa fee zikree.

43. Izhabaaa ilaa Fir'awna innahoo ṭaghaa.

44. Faqoolaa lahoo qawlal-layyinal-la'allahoo yatazakkaru 'aw yakhshaa.

45. Qaalaa Rabbanaaa innanaa nakhaafu añy-yafruṭa 'alaynaaa aw añy-yaṭghaa.

46. Qaala laa takhaafaaa innanee ma'akumaaa asma'u wa araa.

47. Faåtiyaahu faqoolaaa innaa Rasoolaa Rabbika fa-arsil ma'anaa Baneee Israaa'eela wa laa tu'azzibhum qad ji'naaka bi-Aayatim-mir-Rabbika wassalaamu 'alaa manit-taba'al-hudaa.

48. Innaa qad ooḥiya ilaynaaa annal-'azaaba 'alaa man kazzaba wa tawallaa.

49. Qaala famar-Rabbukumaa yaa Moosaa.

50. Qaala Rabbunal-lazeee a'ṭaa kulla shay'in khalqahoo summa hadaa.

51. Qaala famaa baalul-qurooonil-oolaa.

52. Qaala 'ilmuhaa 'inda Rabbee fee kitaab, laa yaḍillu Rabbee wa laa yansaa.

53. Allazee ja'ala lakumul-arḍa mahdañw-wa salaka lakum feehaa subulañw-wa anzala minas-samaaa'i maaa'an fa-akhrajnaa biheee azwaajam-min-nabaatin shattaa.

وَاصْطَنَعْتُكَ لِنَفْسِيْ ٤١

اِذْهَبْ اَنْتَ وَاَخُوْكَ بِاٰيٰتِيْ وَلَا تَنِيَا فِيْ ذِكْرِيْ ٤٢

اِذْهَبَآ اِلٰى فِرْعَوْنَ اِنَّهٗ طَغٰى ٤٣

فَقُوْلَا لَهٗ قَوْلًا لَّيِّنًا لَّعَلَّهٗ يَتَذَكَّرُ اَوْ يَخْشٰى ٤٤

قَالَا رَبَّنَآ اِنَّنَا نَخَافُ اَنْ يَّفْرُطَ عَلَيْنَآ اَوْ اَنْ يَّطْغٰى ٤٥

قَالَ لَا تَخَافَآ اِنَّنِيْ مَعَكُمَآ اَسْمَعُ وَاَرٰى ٤٦

فَاْتِيٰهُ فَقُوْلَآ اِنَّا رَسُوْلَا رَبِّكَ فَاَرْسِلْ مَعَنَا بَنِيْٓ اِسْرَآءِيْلَ ۙ۬ وَلَا تُعَذِّبْهُمْ ؕ قَدْ جِئْنٰكَ بِاٰيَةٍ مِّنْ رَّبِّكَ ؕ وَالسَّلٰمُ عَلٰى مَنِ اتَّبَعَ الْهُدٰى ٤٧

اِنَّا قَدْ اُوْحِيَ اِلَيْنَآ اَنَّ الْعَذَابَ عَلٰى مَنْ كَذَّبَ وَتَوَلّٰى ٤٨

قَالَ فَمَنْ رَّبُّكُمَا يٰمُوْسٰى ٤٩

قَالَ رَبُّنَا الَّذِيْٓ اَعْطٰى كُلَّ شَيْءٍ خَلْقَهٗ ثُمَّ هَدٰى ٥٠

قَالَ فَمَا بَالُ الْقُرُوْنِ الْاُوْلٰى ٥١

قَالَ عِلْمُهَا عِنْدَ رَبِّيْ فِيْ كِتٰبٍ ۚ لَا يَضِلُّ رَبِّيْ وَلَا يَنْسَى ٥٢

الَّذِيْ جَعَلَ لَكُمُ الْاَرْضَ مَهْدًا وَّسَلَكَ لَكُمْ فِيْهَا سُبُلًا وَّاَنْزَلَ مِنَ السَّمَآءِ مَآءً ؕ فَاَخْرَجْنَا بِهٖٓ اَزْوَاجًا مِّنْ نَّبَاتٍ شَتّٰى ٥٣

Ikhfa اخفاء | Ghunna غُنَّہ | Ikhfa Meem Saakin اخفاءمیم ساکن | Idghaam ادغام | Qalqala قلقلہ | Qalb قلب | Idghaam Meem Saakin ادغام میم ساکن

54. Eat (for yourselves) and pasture your cattle: verily, in this are Signs for men endued with understanding.

54. Kuloo war‘aw an‘aamakum; inna fee z̲aalika la-Aayaatil-li-ulin-nuhaa.

كُلُوا وَارْعَوْا أَنْعَامَكُمْ ۗ إِنَّ فِي
ذَٰلِكَ لَآيَاتٍ لِأُولِي النُّهَىٰ ﴿٥٤﴾ ع

(Section 2)

55. From the (earth) We created you, and into it shall We return you, and from it shall We bring you out once again.

55. Minhaa khalaqnaakum wa feehaa nu‘eedukum wa minhaa nukhrijukum taaratan ukhraa.

مِنْهَا خَلَقْنَاكُمْ وَفِيهَا نُعِيدُكُمْ
وَمِنْهَا نُخْرِجُكُمْ تَارَةً أُخْرَىٰ ﴿٥٥﴾

56. And We showed Pharaoh all Our Signs, but he rejected and refused.

56. Wa laqad araynaahu Aayaatinaa kullahaa fakaz̲z̲aba wa abaa.

وَلَقَدْ أَرَيْنَاهُ آيَاتِنَا كُلَّهَا فَكَذَّبَ
وَأَبَىٰ ﴿٥٦﴾

57. He said: “Have you come to drive us out of our land with your magic, O Moses?

57. Qaala aji’tanaa litukhrijanaa min arḍinaa bisiḥrika yaa Moosaa.

قَالَ أَجِئْتَنَا لِتُخْرِجَنَا مِنْ أَرْضِنَا
بِسِحْرِكَ يَا مُوسَىٰ ﴿٥٧﴾

58. “But we can surely produce magic to match yours! So make a tryst between us and you, which we shall not fail to keep - neither we nor you - in a place where both shall have even chances.”

58. Falanaåtiyannaka bisiḥrim-mis̲lihee faj‘al baynanaa wa baynaka maw‘idal-laa nukhlifuhoo naḥnu wa laaa anta makaanan suwaa.

فَلَنَأْتِيَنَّكَ بِسِحْرٍ مِثْلِهِ فَاجْعَلْ
بَيْنَنَا وَبَيْنَكَ مَوْعِدًا لَا نُخْلِفُهُ
نَحْنُ وَلَا أَنْتَ مَكَانًا سُوًى ﴿٥٨﴾

59. Moses said: “Your tryst is the Day of the Festival, and let the people be assembled when the sun is well up.”

59. Qaala maw‘idukum yawmuz-zeenati wa añy-yuḥsharan-naasu ḍuḥaa.

قَالَ مَوْعِدُكُمْ يَوْمُ الزِّينَةِ وَأَنْ
يُحْشَرَ النَّاسُ ضُحًى ﴿٥٩﴾

60. So Pharaoh withdrew: he concerted his plan, and then came (back).

60. Fatawallaa Fir‘awnu fajama‘a kaydahoo summa ataa.

فَتَوَلَّىٰ فِرْعَوْنُ فَجَمَعَ كَيْدَهُ ثُمَّ أَتَىٰ ﴿٦٠﴾

61. Moses said to him: Woe to you! You do not forge a lie against Allah, lest He destroy you (at once) utterly by chastisement: the forger must suffer frustration!”

61. Qaala lahum-Moosaa waylakum laa taftaroo ‘alallaahi kaz̲iban fa-yus-ḥitakum bi ‘az̲aab, wa qad khaaba maniftaraa.

قَالَ لَهُمْ مُوسَىٰ وَيْلَكُمْ لَا تَفْتَرُوا
عَلَى اللَّهِ كَذِبًا فَيُسْحِتَكُمْ بِعَذَابٍ ۖ
وَقَدْ خَابَ مَنِ افْتَرَىٰ ﴿٦١﴾

62. So they disputed, one with another, over their affair, but they kept their talk secret.

62. Fatanaaza‘ooo amrahum baynahum wa asarrun-najwaa.

فَتَنَازَعُوا أَمْرَهُمْ بَيْنَهُمْ وَأَسَرُّوا
النَّجْوَىٰ ﴿٦٢﴾

63. They said: “These two are certainly (expert) magicians: their object is to drive you out from your land with their magic, and to do away with your most cherished institutions.

63. Qaalooo in haaz̲aani lasaaḥiraani yureedaani añy-yukhrijaakum min arḍikum bisiḥrihimaa wa yaz̲habaa biṭareeqatikumul-mus̲laa.

قَالُوا إِنْ هَٰذَانِ لَسَاحِرَانِ يُرِيدَانِ
أَنْ يُخْرِجَاكُمْ مِنْ أَرْضِكُمْ بِسِحْرِهِمَا
وَيَذْهَبَا بِطَرِيقَتِكُمُ الْمُثْلَىٰ ﴿٦٣﴾

64. “Therefore concert your plan, and then assemble in (serried) ranks: he wins (all along) today who gains the upper hand.”

64. Fa-ajmi‘oo kaydakum summa’-too ṣaffaa; wa qad aflaḥal-yawma manis-ta‘laa.

فَأَجْمِعُوا كَيْدَكُمْ ثُمَّ ائْتُوا صَفًّا ۚ
وَقَدْ أَفْلَحَ الْيَوْمَ مَنِ اسْتَعْلَىٰ ﴿٦٤﴾

65. They said: “O Moses! whether will you that you throw (first) or that we be the first to throw?”

65. Qaaloo yaa Moosaaa immaaa an tulqiya wa immaaa an-nakoona awwala man alqaa.

قَالُوا يَا مُوسَىٰ إِمَّا أَنْ تُلْقِيَ وَإِمَّا
أَنْ نَكُونَ أَوَّلَ مَنْ أَلْقَىٰ ﴿٦٥﴾

Ikhfa اخفاء | Ghunna غنّة | Ikhfa Meem Saakin اخفاء میم ساکن | Idghaam ادغام | Qalqala قلقلہ | Qalb قلب | Idghaam Meem Saakin ادغام میم ساکن

66. He said, "Nay, you throw first!" Then behold their ropes and their rods-so it seemed to him on account of their magic - began to be in lively motion!

66. Qaala bal alqoo fa-izaa ḥibaaluhum wa 'iṣiyyuhum yukhayyalu ilayhi min siḥrihim annahaa tas'aa.

قَالَ بَلْ اَلْقُوْا ۚ فَاِذَا حِبَالُهُمْ وَ
عِصِيُّهُمْ يُخَيَّلُ اِلَيْهِ مِنْ سِحْرِهِمْ
اَنَّهَا تَسْعٰى ﴿٦٦﴾

67. So Moses conceived in his mind a (sort of) fear.

67. Fa-awjasa fee nafsihee kheefatam-Moosaa.

فَاَوْجَسَ فِيْ نَفْسِهٖ خِيْفَةً مُّوْسٰى ﴿٦٧﴾

68. We said: "Do not fear! for you have indeed the upper hand:

68. Qulnaa laa takhaf innaka antal-a'laa.

قُلْنَا لَا تَخَفْ اِنَّكَ اَنْتَ الْاَعْلٰى ﴿٦٨﴾

69. "Throw that which is in your right hand: quickly will it swallow up that which they have faked; what they have faked is but a magician's trick: and the magician does not thrive, (no matter) where he goes."

69. Wa alqi maa fee yameenika talqaf maa ṣana'oo; innamaa ṣana'oo kaydu ṣaahir; wa laa yufliḥus-saaḥiru ḥaysu ataa.

وَاَلْقِ مَا فِيْ يَمِيْنِكَ تَلْقَفْ مَا
صَنَعُوْا ۭ اِنَّمَا صَنَعُوْا كَيْدُ سٰحِرٍ ۭ
وَلَا يُفْلِحُ السَّاحِرُ حَيْثُ اَتٰى ﴿٦٩﴾

70. So the magicians were thrown down to prostration: they said, "We believe in the Lord of Aaron and Moses".

70. Fa-ulqiyas-saḥaratu sujjadan qaalooo aamannaa bi-Rabbi Haaroona wa Moosaa.

فَاُلْقِيَ السَّحَرَةُ سُجَّدًا قَالُوْٓا اٰمَنَّا
بِرَبِّ هٰرُوْنَ وَمُوْسٰى ﴿٧٠﴾

71. (Pharaoh) said: "Do you believe in Him before I give you permission? Surely this must be your leader, who has taught you magic! Be sure I will cut off your hands and feet on opposite sides, and I will have you crucified on trunks of palm-trees: so shall you know for certain, which of us can give the more severe and the more lasting punishment!"

71. Qaala aamantum lahoo qabla an aazana lakum; innahoo lakabeerukumul-lazee 'allamakumus-siḥra fala-uqaṭṭi'anna aydiyakum wa arjulakum-min khilaafiñw-wa la-uṣallibannakum fee juzoo'in-nakhli wa lata'lamunna ayyunaaa ashaddu 'azaabañw-wa abqaa.

قَالَ اٰمَنْتُمْ لَهٗ قَبْلَ اَنْ اٰذَنَ لَكُمْ ۭ
اِنَّهٗ لَكَبِيْرُكُمُ الَّذِيْ عَلَّمَكُمُ السِّحْرَ ۚ
فَلَاُقَطِّعَنَّ اَيْدِيَكُمْ وَاَرْجُلَكُمْ مِّنْ
خِلَافٍ وَّلَاُصَلِّبَنَّكُمْ فِيْ جُذُوْعِ
النَّخْلِ ۡ وَلَتَعْلَمُنَّ اَيُّنَآ اَشَدُّ
عَذَابًا وَّاَبْقٰى ﴿٧١﴾

72. They said: "Never shall we regard you as more than the Clear Sings that have come to us, or than Him Who created us! so decree whatever you desire to decree: for you can only decree (touching) the life of this world.

72. Qaaloo lan nu'siraka 'alaa maa jaaa'anaa minal-bayyinaati wallazee faṭaranaa faqḍi maaa anta qaaḍ; innamaa taqḍee haazihil-ḥayaatad-dunyaa.

قَالُوْا لَنْ نُّؤْثِرَكَ عَلٰى مَا جَآءَنَا
مِنَ الْبَيِّنٰتِ وَالَّذِيْ فَطَرَنَا فَاقْضِ
مَآ اَنْتَ قَاضٍ ۭ اِنَّمَا تَقْضِيْ هٰذِهِ
الْحَيٰوةَ الدُّنْيَا ۭ ﴿٧٢﴾

73. "For us, we have believed in our Lord: may He forgive us our faults, and the magic to which you compelled us: for Allah is Best and Most Abiding."

73. Innaaa aamannaa bi-Rabbinaa liyaghfira lanaa khaṭaayaanaa wa maaa akrahtanaa 'alayhi minas-siḥr; wallaahu khayruñw-wa abqaa.

اِنَّآ اٰمَنَّا بِرَبِّنَا لِيَغْفِرَ لَنَا خَطٰيٰنَا
وَمَآ اَكْرَهْتَنَا عَلَيْهِ مِنَ السِّحْرِ ۭ
وَاللّٰهُ خَيْرٌ وَّاَبْقٰى ﴿٧٣﴾

الثلثة

74. Verily he who comes to his Lord as a sinner (at Judgment),- for him is Hell: therein shall he neither die nor live.

74. Innahoo mañy-yaâti Rabbahoo mujriman fa-inna lahoo Jahannama laa yamootu feehaa wa laa yaḥyaa.

اِنَّهٗ مَنْ يَّاْتِ رَبَّهٗ مُجْرِمًا فَاِنَّ لَهٗ
جَهَنَّمَ ۭ لَا يَمُوْتُ فِيْهَا وَلَا يَحْيٰى ﴿٧٤﴾

75. But such as come to Him as Believers who have worked righteous deeds,-

75. Wa mañy-yaâtihee mu'minan qad 'amilaṣ-ṣaaliḥaati

وَمَنْ يَّاْتِهٖ مُؤْمِنًا قَدْ عَمِلَ الصّٰلِحٰتِ

Ikhfa اخفاء | Ghunna غنّہ | Ikhfa Meem Saakin اخفاء میم ساکن | Idghaam ادغام | Qalqala قلقلہ | Qalb قلب | Idghaam Meem Saakin ادغام میم ساکن

for them are ranks exalted,-	fa-ulaaa'ika lahumud-dara-jaatul-'ulaa.	فَأُولَٰٓئِكَ لَهُمُ ٱلدَّرَجَٰتُ ٱلْعُلَىٰ ﴿٧٥﴾
76. Gardens of Eternity, beneath which flow rivers: they will dwell therein for ever: such is the reward of those who purify themselves (from evil).	76. Jannaatu 'Adnin tajree min taḥtihal-anhaaru khaali-deena feehaa; wa ẕaalika jazaaa'u man tazakkaa. **(Section 3)**	جَنَّٰتُ عَدْنٍ تَجْرِى مِن تَحْتِهَا ٱلْأَنْهَٰرُ خَٰلِدِينَ فِيهَا ۚ وَذَٰلِكَ جَزَآءُ مَن تَزَكَّىٰ ﴿٧٦﴾
77. We sent an inspiration to Moses: "Travel by night with My servants, and strike a dry path for them through the sea, without fear of being overtaken (by Pharaoh) and without (any other) fear."	77. Wa laqad awḥaynaaa ilaa Moosaaa an asri bi'ibaadee faḍrib lahum ṭareeqan fil-baḥri yabasal-laa takhaafu darakañw-wa laa takhshaa.	وَلَقَدْ أَوْحَيْنَآ إِلَىٰ مُوسَىٰٓ أَنْ أَسْرِ بِعِبَادِى فَٱضْرِبْ لَهُمْ طَرِيقًا فِى ٱلْبَحْرِ يَبَسًا لَّا تَخَٰفُ دَرَكًا وَلَا تَخْشَىٰ ﴿٧٧﴾
78. Then Pharaoh pursued them with his forces, but the waters completely overwhelmed them and covered them up.	78. Fa-atba'ahum Fir'awnu bijunoodihee faghashiyahum-minal-yammi maa ghashi-yahum.	فَأَتْبَعَهُمْ فِرْعَوْنُ بِجُنُودِهِۦ فَغَشِيَهُم مِّنَ ٱلْيَمِّ مَا غَشِيَهُمْ ﴿٧٨﴾
79. Pharaoh led his people astray instead of leading them aright.	79. Wa aḍalla Fir'awnu qaw-mahoo wa maa hadaa.	وَأَضَلَّ فِرْعَوْنُ قَوْمَهُۥ وَمَا هَدَىٰ ﴿٧٩﴾
80. O you Children of Israel! We delivered you from your enemy, and We made a Covenant with you on the right side of Mount (Sinai), and We sent down to you Manna and quails:	80. Yaa Baneee Israaa'eela qad anjaynaakum-min 'aduw-wikum wa waa'adnaakum jaanibaṭ-Ṭooril-aymana wa nazzalnaa 'alaykumul-Manna was-Salwaa.	يَٰبَنِىٓ إِسْرَٰٓءِيلَ قَدْ أَنجَيْنَٰكُم مِّنْ عَدُوِّكُمْ وَوَٰعَدْنَٰكُمْ جَانِبَ ٱلطُّورِ ٱلْأَيْمَنَ وَنَزَّلْنَا عَلَيْكُمُ ٱلْمَنَّ وَٱلسَّلْوَىٰ ﴿٨٠﴾
81. (Saying): "Eat of the good things We have provided for your sustenance, but commit no excess therein, lest My Wrath should justly descend on you: and those on whom descends My Wrath do perish indeed!	81. Kuloo min ṭayyibaati maa razaqnaakum wa laa taṭghaw feehi fa-yaḥilla 'alaykum ghaḍabee wa mañy-yaḥlil 'alayhi ghaḍabee faqad hawaa.	كُلُوا۟ مِن طَيِّبَٰتِ مَا رَزَقْنَٰكُمْ وَلَا تَطْغَوْا۟ فِيهِ فَيَحِلَّ عَلَيْكُمْ غَضَبِى ۖ وَمَن يَحْلِلْ عَلَيْهِ غَضَبِى فَقَدْ هَوَىٰ ﴿٨١﴾
82. "But, without doubt, I am (also) He that forgives again and again, to those who repent, believe, and do right,- who, in fine, are ready to receive true guidance."	82. Wa innee la-Ghaffaarul-liman taaba wa aamana wa 'amila ṣaaliḥan ṡummah-tadaa.	وَإِنِّى لَغَفَّارٌ لِّمَن تَابَ وَءَامَنَ وَعَمِلَ صَٰلِحًا ثُمَّ ٱهْتَدَىٰ ﴿٨٢﴾
83. (When Moses was up on the Mount, Allah said:) "What made you hasten in advance of your people, O Moses?"	83. Wa maaa a'jalaka 'an qawmika yaa Moosaa.	وَمَآ أَعْجَلَكَ عَن قَوْمِكَ يَٰمُوسَىٰ ﴿٨٣﴾
84. He replied: "Behold, they are close on my footsteps: I hastened to you, O my Lord, to please You."	84. Qaala hum ulaaa'i 'alaaa aṡaree wa 'ajiltu ilayka Rabbi litarḍaa.	قَالَ هُمْ أُو۟لَآءِ عَلَىٰٓ أَثَرِى وَعَجِلْتُ إِلَيْكَ رَبِّ لِتَرْضَىٰ ﴿٨٤﴾
85. (Allah) said: "We have tested your people in your absence: the Samiri has led them astray."	85. Qaala fa-innaa qad fa-tannaa qawmaka mim ba'dika wa aḍallahumus-Saamiriyy.	قَالَ فَإِنَّا قَدْ فَتَنَّا قَوْمَكَ مِنۢ بَعْدِكَ وَأَضَلَّهُمُ ٱلسَّامِرِىُّ ﴿٨٥﴾
86. So Moses returned to his people in a state of indignation	86. Faraja'a Moosaaa ilaa qawmihee ghaḍbaana	فَرَجَعَ مُوسَىٰٓ إِلَىٰ قَوْمِهِۦ غَضْبَٰنَ

Ikhfa اخفاء · Ghunna غنّہ · Ikhfa Meem Saakin اخفاء میم ساکن · Idghaam ادغام · Qalqala قلقلہ · Qalb قلب · Idghaam Meem Saakin ادغام میم ساکن

and sorrow. He said: "O my people! did not your Lord make a handsome promise to you? Did then the promise seem to you long (in coming)? Or did you desire that Wrath should descend from y our Lord on you, and so you broke your promise to me?"

asifaa; qaala yaa qawmi alam ya'idkum Rabbukum wa'dan ḥasanaa; afaṭaala 'alaykumul-'ahdu am arattum añy-yaḥilla 'alaykum ghaḍabum-mir-Rabbikum fa-akhlaftum-maw'idee.

اَسِفًا ۚ قَالَ يٰقَوْمِ اَلَمْ يَعِدْكُمْ
رَبُّكُمْ وَعْدًا حَسَنًا ۚ اَفَطَالَ
عَلَيْكُمُ الْعَهْدُ اَمْ اَرَدْتُّمْ اَنْ
يَّحِلَّ عَلَيْكُمْ غَضَبٌ مِّنْ رَّبِّكُمْ
فَاَخْلَفْتُمْ مَّوْعِدِيْ ﴿٨٦﴾

87. They said: "We did not break the promise to you, as far as lay in our power: but we were made to carry the weight of the ornaments of the (whole) people, and we threw them (into the fire), and that was what the Samiri suggested.

87. Qaaloo maaa akhlafnaa maw'idaka bimalkinaa wa laakinnaa ḥummilnaaa awzaa-ram-min zeenatil-qawmi faqaẕafnaahaa fakaẕaalika alqas-Saamiriyy.

قَالُوْا مَآ اَخْلَفْنَا مَوْعِدَكَ بِمَلْكِنَا
وَلٰكِنَّا حُمِّلْنَآ اَوْزَارًا مِّنْ
زِيْنَةِ الْقَوْمِ فَقَذَفْنٰهَا فَكَذٰلِكَ
اَلْقَى السَّامِرِيُّ ﴿٨٧﴾

88. "Then he brought out (of the fire) before the (people) the image of a calf: it seemed to low: so they said: This is your god, and the god of Moses, but (Moses) has forgotten!"

88. Fa-akhraja lahum 'ijlan jasadal-lahoo khuwaarun faqaaloo haaẕaaa ilaahukum wa ilaahu Moosaa fanasee.

فَاَخْرَجَ لَهُمْ عِجْلًا جَسَدًا لَّهٗ
خُوَارٌ فَقَالُوْا هٰذَآ اِلٰهُكُمْ وَاِلٰهُ
مُوْسٰى ۥ فَنَسِيَ ﴿٨٨﴾

89. Could they not see that it could not return them a word (for answer), and that it had no power either to harm them or to do them good?

89. Afalaa yarawna allaa yarji'u ilayhim qawlañw-wa laa yamliku lahum ḍarrañw-wa laa naf'aa. **(Section 4)**

اَفَلَا يَرَوْنَ اَلَّا يَرْجِعُ اِلَيْهِمْ قَوْلًا ۥ
وَّلَا يَمْلِكُ لَهُمْ ضَرًّا وَّلَا نَفْعًا ﴿٨٩﴾

90. Aaron had already, before this said to them: "O my people! you are being tested in this: for verily your Lord is (Allah) Most Gracious; so follow me and obey my command."

90. Wa laqad qaala lahum Haaroonu min qablu yaa qawmi innamaa futintum bihee wa inna Rabbakumur-Raḥmaanu fatta-bi'oonee wa aṭee'ooo amree.

وَلَقَدْ قَالَ لَهُمْ هٰرُوْنُ مِنْ قَبْلُ
يٰقَوْمِ اِنَّمَا فُتِنْتُمْ بِهٖ ۚ وَاِنَّ رَبَّكُمُ
الرَّحْمٰنُ فَاتَّبِعُوْنِيْ وَاَطِيْعُوْٓا اَمْرِيْ ﴿٩٠﴾

91. They had said: "We will not cease to worship it, but we will devote ourselves to it until Moses returns to us."

91. Qaaloo lan-nabraḥa 'alayhi 'aakifeena ḥattaa yarji'a ilaynaa Moosaa.

قَالُوْا لَنْ نَّبْرَحَ عَلَيْهِ عٰكِفِيْنَ حَتّٰى
يَرْجِعَ اِلَيْنَا مُوْسٰى ﴿٩١﴾

92. (Moses) said: "O Aaron! what kept you back, when you saw them going wrong,

92. Qaala yaa Haaroonu maa mana'aka iẕ ra-aytahum ḍallooo.

قَالَ يٰهٰرُوْنُ مَا مَنَعَكَ اِذْ رَاَيْتَهُمْ
ضَلُّوْٓا ۙ ﴿٩٢﴾

93. "From following me? Did you then disobey my order?"

93. Allaa tattabi'ani afa-'aṣayta amree.

اَلَّا تَتَّبِعَنِ ۭ اَفَعَصَيْتَ اَمْرِيْ ﴿٩٣﴾

94. (Aaron) replied: "O son of my mother! Do not seize (me) by my beard nor by (the hair of) my head! Truly I feared lest you should say, 'you has caused a division among the children of Israel, and you did not respect my word!'"

94. Qaala yabna'umma laa taåkhuẕ biliḥyatee wa laa biraå-see innee khasheetu an taqoola farraqta bayna Baneee Israaa-'eela wa lam tarqub qawlee.

قَالَ يَبْنَؤُمَّ لَا تَاْخُذْ بِلِحْيَتِيْ وَلَا
بِرَاْسِيْ ۚ اِنِّيْ خَشِيْتُ اَنْ تَقُوْلَ فَرَّقْتَ
بَيْنَ بَنِيْٓ اِسْرَاۗءِيْلَ وَلَمْ تَرْقُبْ قَوْلِيْ ﴿٩٤﴾

95. (Moses) said: "What then is your case, O Samiri?"

95. Qaala famaa khaṭbuka yaa Saamiriyy.

قَالَ فَمَا خَطْبُكَ يٰسَامِرِيُّ ﴿٩٥﴾

Ikhfa اخفاء | Ghunna غنّہ | Ikhfa Meem Saakin اخفاء میم ساکن | Idghaam ادغام | Qalqala قلقلہ | Qalb قلب | Idghaam Meem Saakin ادغام میم ساکن

96. He replied: "I saw what they did not see: so I took a handful (of dust) from the footprint of the Messenger, and threw it (into the calf): thus did my soul suggest to me."

96. Qaala baṣurtu bimaa lam yabṣuroo bihee faqabaḍtu qabḍatam-min aṡarir-Rasooli fanabaẕtuhaa wa kaẕaalika sawwalat lee nafsee.

قَالَ بَصُرْتُ بِمَا لَمْ يَبْصُرُوا بِهِ
فَقَبَضْتُ قَبْضَةً مِّنْ أَثَرِ الرَّسُولِ
فَنَبَذْتُهَا وَكَذَٰلِكَ سَوَّلَتْ لِي نَفْسِي ﴿٩٦﴾

97. (Moses) said: "Get you gone! But your (punishment) in this life will be that you will say, 'Touch me not'; and moreover (for a future Penalty) you have a promise that will not fail: now look at your god, of whom you have become a devoted worshipper: we will certainly (melt) it in a blazing fire and scatter it broadcast in the sea!"

97. Qaala faẕhab fa-inna laka fil-ḥayaati an taqoola laa misaasa wa inna laka maw'idal-lan tukhlafahoo wanẓur ilaaa ilaahikal-laẕee ẓalta 'alayhi 'aakifaa; lanuḥarriqannahoo ṡumma lanansifannahoo fil-yammi nasfaa.

قَالَ فَاذْهَبْ فَإِنَّ لَكَ فِي الْحَيَاةِ أَن
تَقُولَ لَا مِسَاسَ ۖ وَإِنَّ لَكَ مَوْعِدًا
لَّن تُخْلَفَهُ ۖ وَانظُرْ إِلَىٰ إِلَٰهِكَ
الَّذِي ظَلْتَ عَلَيْهِ عَاكِفًا ۖ لَّنُحَرِّقَنَّهُ
ثُمَّ لَنَنسِفَنَّهُ فِي الْيَمِّ نَسْفًا ﴿٩٧﴾

98. But the god of you all is the One Allah: there is no god but He: all things He comprehends in His knowledge.

98. Innamaaa ilaahukumul-laahul-laẕee laaa ilaaha illaa Hoo; wasi'a kulla shay'in 'ilmaa.

إِنَّمَا إِلَٰهُكُمُ اللَّهُ الَّذِي لَا إِلَٰهَ إِلَّا
هُوَ ۚ وَسِعَ كُلَّ شَيْءٍ عِلْمًا ﴿٩٨﴾

99. Thus do We relate to you some stories of what happened before: for We have sent you a Message from Our own Presence.

99. Kaẕaalika naquṣṣu 'alayka min ambaaa'i maa qad sabaq; wa qad aataynaaka mil-ladunnaa Ẕikraa.

كَذَٰلِكَ نَقُصُّ عَلَيْكَ مِنْ أَنبَاءِ
مَا قَدْ سَبَقَ ۚ وَقَدْ آتَيْنَاكَ مِن
لَّدُنَّا ذِكْرًا ﴿٩٩﴾

100. If any do turn away therefrom, verily they will bear a burden on the Day of judgment;

100. Man a'raḍa 'anhu fa-innahoo yaḥmilu Yawmal-Qiyaamati wizraa.

مَّنْ أَعْرَضَ عَنْهُ فَإِنَّهُ يَحْمِلُ يَوْمَ
الْقِيَامَةِ وِزْرًا ﴿١٠٠﴾

101. They will abide in this (state): and grievous will the burden be to them on that Day,-

101. Khaalideena feehi wa saaa'a lahum Yawmal-Qiyaamati ḥimlaa.

خَالِدِينَ فِيهِ ۖ وَسَاءَ لَهُمْ يَوْمَ
الْقِيَامَةِ حِمْلًا ﴿١٠١﴾

102. The Day when the Trumpet will be sounded: that Day, We shall gather the sinful, blear-eyed (with terror).

102. Yawma yunfakhu fiṣ-Ṣoori wa naḥshurul-mujrimeena Yawma'iẕin zurqaa.

يَوْمَ يُنفَخُ فِي الصُّورِ ۚ وَنَحْشُرُ
الْمُجْرِمِينَ يَوْمَئِذٍ زُرْقًا ﴿١٠٢﴾

103. In whispers will they consult each other: "You tarried not longer than ten (Days);"

103. Yatakhaafatoona baynahum il-labiṡtum illaa 'ashraa.

يَتَخَافَتُونَ بَيْنَهُمْ إِن لَّبِثْتُمْ إِلَّا
عَشْرًا ﴿١٠٣﴾

104. We know best what they will say, when their leader most eminent in conduct will say: "You did not tarry longer than a day!"

104. Naḥnu a'lamu bimaa yaqooloona iẕ yaqoolu amṡaluhum ṭareeqatan illabiṡtum illaa yawmaa. **(Section 5)**

نَّحْنُ أَعْلَمُ بِمَا يَقُولُونَ إِذْ يَقُولُ
أَمْثَلُهُمْ طَرِيقَةً إِن لَّبِثْتُمْ إِلَّا
يَوْمًا ﴿١٠٤﴾ ع

105. They ask you concerning the Mountains: say, "My Lord will uproot them and scatter them as dust;

105. Wa yas'aloonaka 'anil-jibaali faqul yansifuhaa Rabbee nasfaa.

وَيَسْأَلُونَكَ عَنِ الْجِبَالِ فَقُلْ
يَنسِفُهَا رَبِّي نَسْفًا ﴿١٠٥﴾

Ikhfa اخفاء | Ghunna غُنّہ | Ikhfa Meem Saakin اخفاء میم ساکن | Idghaam ادغام | Qalqala قلقلہ | Qalb قلب | Idghaam Meem Saakin ادغام میم ساکن

106. "He will leave them as plains smooth and level;

107. "Nothing crooked or curved will you see in their place."

108. On that Day will they follow the Caller (straight): no crookedness (can they show) him: all sounds shall humble themselves in the Presence of (Allah) Most Gracious: nothing shall you hear but the tramp of their feet (as they march).

109. On that Day no intercession shall avail except for those for whom permission has been granted by (Allah) Most Gracious and whose word is acceptable to Him.

110. He knows what (appears to His creatures as) before or after or behind them: but they shall not compass it with their knowledge.

111. (All) faces shall be humbled before (Him) - the Living, the Self-subsisting, Eternal: hopeless indeed will be the man that carries iniquity (on his back).

112. But he who works deeds of righteousness, and has faith, will have no fear of harm nor of any curtailment (of what is his due).

113. Thus have We sent this down - an Arabic Qur'an - and explained therein in detail some of the warnings, in order that they may fear Allah, or that it may cause their remembrance (of Him).

114. High above all is Allah, the King, the Truth! Be not in haste with the Qur'an before its revelation to you is completed, but say, "O my Lord! advance me in knowledge."

115. We had already, beforehand, taken the covenant of Adam, but he forgot: and We found on his part no firm resolve.

116. When We said to the angels, "Prostrate yourselves to Adam", they prostrated themselves, but not Iblis: he refused.

117. Then We said: "O Adam! verily, this is an enemy to you and your wife: so let him not get you both out of the Garden, so that you are landed in misery.

106. Fa-yaẕaruhaa qaa'an ṣafṣafaa.

107. Laa taraa feehaa 'iwajañw-wa laaa amtaa.

108. Yawma'iẕiñy-yattabi'oonad-daa'iya laa 'iwaja lahoo wa khasha'atil-aṣwaatu lir-Raḥmaani falaa tasma'u illaa hamsaa.

109. Yawma'iẕil-laa tanfa'ush shafaa'atu illaa man aẕina lahur-Raḥmaanu wa raḍiya lahoo qawlaa

110. Ya'lamu maa bayna aydeehim wa maa khalfahum wa laa yuḥeeṭoona bihee 'ilmaa.

111. Wa 'anatil-wujoohu lil-Ḥayyil-Qayyoomi wa qad khaaba man ḥamala ẓulmaa

112. Wa mañy-ya'mal minaṣ-ṣaaliḥaati wa huwa mu'minun falaa yakhaafu ẓulmañw-wa laa haḍmaa.

113. Wa kaẕaalika anzalnaahu Qur-aanan 'Arabiyyañw-wa ṣarrafnaa feehi minal-wa'eedi la'allahum yattaqoona aw yuḥdiṡu lahum ẕikraa.

114. Fata'aalal-laahul-Malikul-Ḥaqq; wa laa ta'jal bil-Qur-aani min qabli añy-yuqdaaa ilayka waḥyuhoo wa qur-Rabbi zidnee 'ilmaa.

115. Wa laqad 'ahidnaaa ilaaa Aadama min qablu fanasiya wa lam najid lahoo 'azmaa.

(Section 6)

116. Wa iẕ qulnaa lilmalaaa'ikatis-judoo li Aadama fasajadooo illaaa Iblees; abaa.

117. Faqulnaa yaaa Aadamu inna haaẕaa 'aduwwul-laka wa lizawjika falaa yukhrijannakumaa minal-Jannati fatashqaa.

فَيَذَرُهَا قَاعًا صَفْصَفًا ﴿١٠٦﴾

لَّا تَرَىٰ فِيهَا عِوَجًا وَّلَآ أَمْتًا ﴿١٠٧﴾

يَوْمَئِذٍ يَتَّبِعُونَ الدَّاعِيَ لَا عِوَجَ لَهُ ۚ

وَخَشَعَتِ الْأَصْوَاتُ لِلرَّحْمَٰنِ

فَلَا تَسْمَعُ إِلَّا هَمْسًا ﴿١٠٨﴾

يَوْمَئِذٍ لَّا تَنفَعُ الشَّفَاعَةُ إِلَّا مَنْ

أَذِنَ لَهُ الرَّحْمَٰنُ وَرَضِيَ لَهُ قَوْلًا ﴿١٠٩﴾

يَعْلَمُ مَا بَيْنَ أَيْدِيهِمْ وَمَا

خَلْفَهُمْ وَلَا يُحِيطُونَ بِهِ عِلْمًا ﴿١١٠﴾

وَعَنَتِ الْوُجُوهُ لِلْحَيِّ الْقَيُّومِ ۖ

وَقَدْ خَابَ مَنْ حَمَلَ ظُلْمًا ﴿١١١﴾

وَمَن يَعْمَلْ مِنَ الصَّالِحَاتِ وَهُوَ

مُؤْمِنٌ فَلَا يَخَافُ ظُلْمًا وَّلَا هَضْمًا ﴿١١٢﴾

وَكَذَٰلِكَ أَنزَلْنَاهُ قُرْآنًا عَرَبِيًّا وَّ

صَرَّفْنَا فِيهِ مِنَ الْوَعِيدِ لَعَلَّهُمْ

يَتَّقُونَ أَوْ يُحْدِثُ لَهُمْ ذِكْرًا ﴿١١٣﴾

فَتَعَالَى اللَّهُ الْمَلِكُ الْحَقُّ ۗ وَلَا تَعْجَلْ

بِالْقُرْآنِ مِن قَبْلِ أَن يُقْضَىٰ إِلَيْكَ

وَحْيُهُ ۖ وَقُل رَّبِّ زِدْنِي عِلْمًا ﴿١١٤﴾

وَلَقَدْ عَهِدْنَا إِلَىٰ آدَمَ مِن قَبْلُ

فَنَسِيَ وَلَمْ نَجِدْ لَهُ عَزْمًا ﴿١١٥﴾ ع ١٥

وَإِذْ قُلْنَا لِلْمَلَائِكَةِ اسْجُدُوا

لِآدَمَ فَسَجَدُوا إِلَّا إِبْلِيسَ أَبَىٰ ﴿١١٦﴾

فَقُلْنَا يَا آدَمُ إِنَّ هَٰذَا عَدُوٌّ لَّكَ

وَلِزَوْجِكَ فَلَا يُخْرِجَنَّكُمَا مِنَ

الْجَنَّةِ فَتَشْقَىٰ ﴿١١٧﴾

Ikhfa اخفاء | Ghunna غُنّہ | Ikhfa Meem Saakin اخفاء میم ساکن | Idghaam ادغام | Qalqala قلقلہ | Qalb قلب | Idghaam Meem Saakin ادغام میم ساکن

118. "There is therein (enough provision) for you not to go hungry nor to go naked,

118. Inna laka allaa tajoo'a feeha wa laa ta'raa.

إِنَّ لَكَ أَلَّا تَجُوعَ فِيهَا وَلَا تَعْرَىٰ ﴿١١٨﴾

119. "Nor to suffer from thirst, nor from the sun's heat."

119. Wa annaka laa taẓma'u feehaa wa laa taḍḥaa.

وَأَنَّكَ لَا تَظْمَؤُا فِيهَا وَلَا تَضْحَىٰ ﴿١١٩﴾

120. But Satan whispered evil to him: he said, "O Adam! shall I lead you to the Tree of Eternity and to a kingdom that never decays?"

120. Fa-waswasa ilayhish-Shayṭaanu qaala yaaa Aadamu hal adulluka 'alaa shajaratil-khuldi wa mulkil-laa yablaa.

فَوَسْوَسَ إِلَيْهِ الشَّيْطَٰنُ قَالَ يَٰٓـَٔادَمُ
هَلْ أَدُلُّكَ عَلَىٰ شَجَرَةِ الْخُلْدِ
وَمُلْكٍ لَّا يَبْلَىٰ ﴿١٢٠﴾

121. In the result, they both ate of the tree, and so their nakedness appeared to them: they began to sew together, for their covering, leaves from the Garden: thus Adam disobeyed his Lord, and allow himself to be seduced.

121. Fa-akalaa minhaa fabadat lahumaa saw-aatuhumaa wa ṭafiqaa yakhṣifaani 'alayhimaa miñw-waraqil-jannah; wa 'aṣaaa Aadamu Rabbahoo faghawaa.

فَأَكَلَا مِنْهَا فَبَدَتْ لَهُمَا
سَوْءَٰتُهُمَا وَطَفِقَا يَخْصِفَانِ
عَلَيْهِمَا مِن وَرَقِ الْجَنَّةِ ۚ
وَعَصَىٰٓ ءَادَمُ رَبَّهُۥ فَغَوَىٰ ﴿١٢١﴾

122. But his Lord chose him (for His Grace): He turned to him, and gave him guidance.

122. Summaj-tabaahu Rabbuhoo fataaba 'alayhi wa hadaa.

ثُمَّ اجْتَبَٰهُ رَبُّهُۥ فَتَابَ عَلَيْهِ
وَهَدَىٰ ﴿١٢٢﴾

123. He said: "Get you down, both of you,- all together, from the Garden, with enmity one to another: but if, as is sure, there comes to you guidance from Me, whosoever follows My guidance, will not lose his way, nor fall into misery.

123. Qaalah-biṭaa minhaa jamee'am ba'ḍukum liba'ḍin 'aduww; fa-immaa yaâtiyannakum-minnee hudan famanit-taba'a hudaaya falaa yaḍillu wa laa yashqaa.

قَالَ اهْبِطَا مِنْهَا جَمِيعًا بَعْضُكُمْ
لِبَعْضٍ عَدُوٌّ ۖ فَإِمَّا يَأْتِيَنَّكُم
مِّنِّي هُدًى فَمَنِ اتَّبَعَ هُدَايَ فَلَا
يَضِلُّ وَلَا يَشْقَىٰ ﴿١٢٣﴾

124. "But whosoever turns away from My Message, verily for him is a life narrowed down, and We shall raise him up blind on the Day of Judgment."

124. Wa man a'raḍa 'an Zikree fa-inna lahoo ma'eeshatan ḍankañw-wa naḥshuruhoo Yawmal-Qiyaamati a'maa.

وَمَنْ أَعْرَضَ عَن ذِكْرِي فَإِنَّ
لَهُۥ مَعِيشَةً ضَنكًا وَنَحْشُرُهُۥ
يَوْمَ الْقِيَٰمَةِ أَعْمَىٰ ﴿١٢٤﴾

125. He will say: "O my Lord! why have you raised me up blind, while I had sight (before)?"

125. Qaala Rabbi lima ḥashartaneee a'maa wa qad kuntu baṣeeraa.

قَالَ رَبِّ لِمَ حَشَرْتَنِيٓ أَعْمَىٰ وَقَدْ
كُنتُ بَصِيرًا ﴿١٢٥﴾

126. (Allah) will say: "Thus you, did when Our Signs came unto you, disregard them: so will you, this day, be disregarded."

126. Qaala kazaalika atatka Aayaatunaa fanaseetahaa wa kazaalikal-Yawma tunsaa.

قَالَ كَذَٰلِكَ أَتَتْكَ ءَايَٰتُنَا
فَنَسِيتَهَا ۖ وَكَذَٰلِكَ الْيَوْمَ تُنسَىٰ ﴿١٢٦﴾

127. And thus do We recompense him who transgresses beyond bounds and believes not in the Sings of his Lord: and the Chastisement of the Hereafter is far more grievous and more enduring.

127. Wa kazaalika najzee man asrafa wa lam yu'mim bi-Aayaati-Rabbih; wa la'azaabul-Aakhirati ashaddu wa abqaa.

وَكَذَٰلِكَ نَجْزِي مَنْ أَسْرَفَ وَلَمْ
يُؤْمِن بِـَٔايَٰتِ رَبِّهِۦ ۚ وَلَعَذَابُ
الْآخِرَةِ أَشَدُّ وَأَبْقَىٰ ﴿١٢٧﴾

128. Is it not a warning to such men (to call to mind) how

128. Afalam yahdi lahum kam ahlaknaa

أَفَلَمْ يَهْدِ لَهُمْ كَمْ أَهْلَكْنَا

Ikhfa اخفاء | Ghunna غُنّہ | Ikhfa Meem Saakin اخفاء میم ساکن | Idghaam ادغام | Qalqala قلقلہ | Qalb قلب | Idghaam Meem Saakin ادغام میم ساکن

many generations before them We destroyed, in whose haunts they (now) move? Verily, in this are Signs for men endued with understanding.

129. Had it not been for a Word that went forth before from your Lord, (their punishment) must necessarily have come; but there is a Term appointed (for respite).

130. Therefore be patient with what they say, and celebrate (constantly) the praises of your Lord, before the rising of the sun, and before its setting; yes, celebrate them for part of the hours of the night, and at the sides of the day: that you may have (spiritual) joy.

131. Nor strain your eyes in longing for the things We have given for enjoyment to parties of them, the splendor of the life of this world, through which We test them: but the provision of your Lord is better and more enduring.

132. Enjoin prayer on your people, and be constant therein. We ask you not to provide sustenance: We provide it for you. But the (fruit of) the Hereafter is for righteousness.

133. They say: "Why does he not bring us a sign from his Lord?" Has not a Clear Sign come to them of all that was in the former Books of revelation?

134. And if We had inflicted on them a penalty before this, they would have said: "Our Lord! If only You had sent us a Messenger, we should certainly have followed Your Signs before we were humbled and put to shame."

135. Say: "Each one (of us) is waiting: you wait, therefore, and soon shall you know who it is that is on the straight and even way, and who it is that has received guidance."

qablahum-minal-qurooni yamshoona fee masaakinihim; inna fee zaalika la-Aayaatil-li-ulinnuhaa. **(Section 7)**

129. Wa law laa Kalimatun sabaqat mir-Rabbika lakaana lizaamañw-wa ajalum-musammaa.

130. Faṣbir 'alaa maa yaqooloona wa sabbiḥ biḥamdi Rabbika qabla ṭuloo'ish-shamsi wa qabla ghuroobihaa wa min aanaaa'il-layli fasabbiḥ wa aṭraafan-nahaari la'allaka tarḍaa.

131. Wa laa tamuddanna 'aynayka ilaa maa matta'naa biheee azwaajam-minhum zahratal-ḥayaatid-dunyaa linaftinahum feeh; wa rizqu Rabbika khayruñw-wa abqaa.

132. Waâmur ahlaka biṣ-Ṣalaati waṣṭabir 'alayhaa laa nas'aluka rizqaa; Naḥnu narzuquk; wal-'aaqibatu littaqwaa.

133. Wa qaaloo law laa yaâteenaa bi-Aayatim-mir-Rabbih; awalam taâtihim bayyinatu maa fiṣ-ṣuḥufil-oolaa.

134. Wa law annaaa ahlaknaahum bi'azaabim-min qablihee laqaaloo Rabbanaa law laaa arsalta ilaynaa Rasoolan fanattabi'a Aayaatika min qabli an-nazilla wa nakhzaa.

135. Qul kullum-mutarabbiṣun fatarabbaṣoo fasata'lamoona man Aṣḥaabuṣ-Ṣiraaṭis-Sawiyyi wa manih-tadaa. **(Section 8)**

قَبْلَهُمْ مِّنَ الْقُرُوْنِ يَمْشُوْنَ فِيْ
مَسٰكِنِهِمْ ۭ اِنَّ فِيْ ذٰلِكَ لَاٰيٰتٍ
لِّاُولِي النُّهٰى ١٢٨
وَلَوْلَا كَلِمَةٌ سَبَقَتْ مِنْ رَّبِّكَ
لَكَانَ لِزَامًا وَّاَجَلٌ مُّسَمًّى ١٢٩
فَاصْبِرْ عَلٰى مَا يَقُوْلُوْنَ وَسَبِّحْ
بِحَمْدِ رَبِّكَ قَبْلَ طُلُوْعِ الشَّمْسِ وَ
قَبْلَ غُرُوْبِهَا ۚ وَمِنْ اٰنَاۗئِ الَّيْلِ
فَسَبِّحْ وَاَطْرَافَ النَّهَارِ لَعَلَّكَ تَرْضٰى ١٣٠
وَلَا تَمُدَّنَّ عَيْنَيْكَ اِلٰى مَا مَتَّعْنَا
بِهٖٓ اَزْوَاجًا مِّنْهُمْ زَهْرَةَ الْحَيٰوةِ
الدُّنْيَا ڏ لِنَفْتِنَهُمْ فِيْهِ ۭ وَرِزْقُ
رَبِّكَ خَيْرٌ وَّاَبْقٰى ١٣١
وَاْمُرْ اَهْلَكَ بِالصَّلٰوةِ وَاصْطَبِرْ
عَلَيْهَا ۭ لَا نَسْــَٔــلُكَ رِزْقًا ۭ نَحْنُ
نَرْزُقُكَ ۭ وَالْعَاقِبَةُ لِلتَّقْوٰى ١٣٢
وَقَالُوْا لَوْلَا يَاْتِيْنَا بِاٰيَةٍ مِّنْ
رَّبِّهٖ ۭ اَوَلَمْ تَاْتِهِمْ بَيِّنَةُ مَا فِي
الصُّحُفِ الْاُوْلٰى ١٣٣
وَلَوْ اَنَّآ اَهْلَكْنٰهُمْ بِعَذَابٍ مِّنْ
قَبْلِهٖ لَقَالُوْا رَبَّنَا لَوْلَآ اَرْسَلْتَ
اِلَيْنَا رَسُوْلًا فَنَتَّبِعَ اٰيٰتِكَ مِنْ
قَبْلِ اَنْ نَّذِلَّ وَنَخْزٰى ١٣٤
قُلْ كُلٌّ مُّتَرَبِّصٌ فَتَرَبَّصُوْا ۚ
فَسَتَعْلَمُوْنَ مَنْ اَصْحٰبُ الصِّرَاطِ
السَّوِيِّ وَمَنِ اهْتَدٰى ١٣٥

ع ٧ ١٣ ١٢

ع ٨ ٧ ١٧

Ikhfa اخفاء | Ghunna غُنّہ | Ikhfa Meem Saakin اخفاء میم ساکن | Idghaam ادغام | Qalqala قلقلہ | Qalb قلب | Idghaam Meem Saakin ادغام میم ساکن

21. The Prophets

In the name of Allah, Most Gracious, Most Merciful.

1. Closer and closer to mankind comes their Reckoning: yet they do not heed and they turn away.

2. Never comes (anything) to them of a renewed Message from their Lord, but they listen to it as in jest,-

3. Their hearts toying as with trifles. The wrong-doers conceal their private counsels, (saying), "Is this (one) more than a man like yourselves? Will you go to witchcraft with your eyes open?"

4. Say: "My Lord knows (every) word (spoken) in the heavens and on earth: He is the One that hears and knows (all things)."

5. "Nay," they say, "(these are) medleys of dreams! - Nay, he forged it! - Nay, he is (but) a poet! Let him then bring us a Sign like the ones that were sent to (Prophets) of old!"

6. (As to those) before them, not one of the populations which We destroyed believed: will these believe?

7. Before you, also, the Messengers We sent were but men, to whom We granted inspiration: if you do not realise this, ask of those who possess the Message.

8. Nor did We give them bodies that ate no food, nor were they exempt from death.

9. In the end We fulfilled to them Our Promise, and We saved them and those whom We pleased, but We destroyed those who transgressed beyond bounds.

10. We have revealed for you (O men!) a book in which is a Message for you: will you not then understand?

Sûrat al-Anbiyâ'–21

(Revealed at Makkah)

Bismillaahir Raḥmaanir Raḥeem

1. Iqtaraba linnaasi ḥisaabuhum wa hum fee ghaflatim-mu'riḍoon.

2. Maa yaåteehim-min zikrim-mir-Rabbihim-muḥdasin illas-tama'oohu wa hum yal'aboon.

3. Laahiyatan quloobuhum; wa asarrun-najwal-lazeena ẓalamoo hal-haazaaa illaa basharum-mislukum afataåtoonas-siḥra wa antum tubṣiroon.

4. Qaala Rabbee ya'lamul-qawla fis-samaaa'i wal-arḍi wa Huwas-Samee'ul-'Aleem.

5. Bal qaalooo aḍghaasu aḥlaamim balif-taraahu bal huwa shaa'irun falyaåtinaa bi-Aayatin kamaaa ursilal-awwaloon.

6. Maaa aamanat qablahum min qaryatin ahlaknaahaa afahum yu'minoon.

7. Wa maaa arsalnaa qablaka illaa rijaalan-nooḥeee ilayhim fas'alooo ahlaz-zikri in kuntum laa ta'lamoon.

8. Wa maa ja'alnaahum jasadal-laa yaåkuloonaṭ-ṭa'aama wa maa kaanoo khaalideen.

9. Summa ṣadaqnaahumul-wa'da fa-anjaynaahum wa man nashaaa'u wa ahlaknal-musrifeen.

10. Laqad anzalnaaa ilaykum Kitaaban feehi zikrukum afalaa ta'qiloon. **(Section 1)**

(٢١) سُوْرَةُ الْاَنْبِيَاۤءِ مَكِّيَّةٌ (٧٣)

بِسْمِ اللّٰهِ الرَّحْمٰنِ الرَّحِيْمِ

اِقْتَرَبَ لِلنَّاسِ حِسَابُهُمْ وَهُمْ فِيْ
غَفْلَةٍ مُّعْرِضُوْنَ ۚ ١
مَا يَاْتِيْهِمْ مِّنْ ذِكْرٍ مِّنْ رَّبِّهِمْ مُّحْدَثٍ
اِلَّا اسْتَمَعُوْهُ وَهُمْ يَلْعَبُوْنَ ٢
لَاهِيَةً قُلُوْبُهُمْ ۗ وَاَسَرُّوا النَّجْوَى ۖ
الَّذِيْنَ ظَلَمُوْا ۖ هَلْ هٰذَآ اِلَّا بَشَرٌ
مِّثْلُكُمْ ۚ اَفَتَاْتُوْنَ السِّحْرَ وَاَنْتُمْ
تُبْصِرُوْنَ ٣
قٰلَ رَبِّيْ يَعْلَمُ الْقَوْلَ فِي السَّمَآءِ
وَالْاَرْضِ ۡ وَهُوَ السَّمِيْعُ الْعَلِيْمُ ٤
بَلْ قَالُوْٓا اَضْغَاثُ اَحْلَامٍۢ بَلِ افْتَرٰىهُ
بَلْ هُوَ شَاعِرٌ ۚ فَلْيَاْتِنَا بِاٰيَةٍ
كَمَآ اُرْسِلَ الْاَوَّلُوْنَ ٥
مَآ اٰمَنَتْ قَبْلَهُمْ مِّنْ قَرْيَةٍ
اَهْلَكْنٰهَا ۚ اَفَهُمْ يُؤْمِنُوْنَ ٦
وَمَآ اَرْسَلْنَا قَبْلَكَ اِلَّا رِجَالًا
نُّوْحِيْٓ اِلَيْهِمْ فَسْــَٔلُوْٓا اَهْلَ
الذِّكْرِ اِنْ كُنْتُمْ لَا تَعْلَمُوْنَ ٧
وَمَا جَعَلْنٰهُمْ جَسَدًا لَّا يَاْكُلُوْنَ
الطَّعَامَ وَمَا كَانُوْا خٰلِدِيْنَ ٨
ثُمَّ صَدَقْنٰهُمُ الْوَعْدَ فَاَنْجَيْنٰهُمْ
وَمَنْ نَّشَآءُ وَاَهْلَكْنَا الْمُسْرِفِيْنَ ٩
لَقَدْ اَنْزَلْنَآ اِلَيْكُمْ كِتٰبًا فِيْهِ
ذِكْرُكُمْ ۗ اَفَلَا تَعْقِلُوْنَ ١٠

اَلْجُزْءُ السَّابِعَ عَشَرَ (١٧)

ع ١

Ikhfa اخفاء | Ghunna غنّہ | Ikhfa Meem Saakin اخفاء میم ساکن | Idghaam ادغام | Qalqala قلقلہ | Qalb قلب | Idghaam Meem Saakin ادغام میم ساکن

11. How many were the populations We utterly destroyed because of their iniquities, setting up in their places other peoples?

11. Wa kam qaṣamnaa min qaryatin kaanat ẓaalimatañw-wa anshaånaa ba'dahaa qawman aakhareen.

وَكَمْ قَصَمْنَا مِنْ قَرْيَةٍ كَانَتْ
ظَالِمَةً وَّاَنْشَاْنَا بَعْدَهَا قَوْمًا
اٰخَرِيْنَ ﴿١١﴾

12. Yet, when they felt Our Punishment (coming), behold, they (tried to) flee from it.

12. Falammaaa aḥassoo baå-sanaaa iz̲aa hum-minhaa yarkuḍoon.

فَلَمَّآ اَحَسُّوْا بَاْسَنَآ اِذَا هُمْ
مِّنْهَا يَرْكُضُوْنَ ﴿١٢﴾ ط

13. Flee not, but return to the good things of this life which were given you, and to your homes in order that you may be called to account.

13. Laa tarkuḍoo warji'ooo ilaa maaa utriftum feehi wa masaakinikum la'allakum tus'aloon.

لَا تَرْكُضُوْا وَارْجِعُوْٓا اِلٰى مَآ اُتْرِفْتُمْ
فِيْهِ وَمَسٰكِنِكُمْ لَعَلَّكُمْ تُسْـَٔلُوْنَ ﴿١٣﴾

14. They said: "Ah! woe to us! We were indeed wrong-doers!"

14. Qaaloo yaa waylanaaa innaa kunnaa ẓaalimeen.

قَالُوْا يٰوَيْلَنَآ اِنَّا كُنَّا ظٰلِمِيْنَ ﴿١٤﴾

15. And that cry of theirs did not cease, till We made them as a field that is mown, as ashes silent and quenched.

15. Famaa zaalat tilka da'waahum ḥattaa ja'alnaahum ḥaṣeedan khaamideen.

فَمَا زَالَتْ تِّلْكَ دَعْوٰىهُمْ حَتّٰى
جَعَلْنٰهُمْ حَصِيْدًا خٰمِدِيْنَ ﴿١٥﴾

16. Not for (idle) sport did We create the heavens and the earth and all that is between!

16. Wa maa khalaqnas-samaaa'a wal-arḍa wa maa baynahumaa laa'ibeen.

وَمَا خَلَقْنَا السَّمَآءَ وَالْاَرْضَ وَمَا
بَيْنَهُمَا لٰعِبِيْنَ ﴿١٦﴾

17. If it had been Our wish to take (just) a pastime, We should surely have taken it from the things nearest to Us, if We would do (such a thing)!

17. Law aradnaaa an-nattakhiz̲a lahwal-lat-takhaz̲naahu mil-ladunnaaa in kunnaa faa'ileen.

لَوْ اَرَدْنَآ اَنْ نَّتَّخِذَ لَهْوًا لَّاتَّخَذْنٰهُ
مِنْ لَّدُنَّآ ۖ اِنْ كُنَّا فٰعِلِيْنَ ﴿١٧﴾

18. Nay, We hurl the Truth against falsehood, and it knocks out its brain, and behold, falsehood perishes! Ah! woe be to you for the (false) things you ascribe (to Us).

18. Bal naqz̲ifu bilḥaqqi 'alal-baaṭili fa-yadmaghuhoo fa-iz̲aa huwa zaahiq; wa lakumul-waylu mimmaa taṣifoon.

بَلْ نَقْذِفُ بِالْحَقِّ عَلَى الْبَاطِلِ
فَيَدْمَغُهٗ فَاِذَا هُوَ زَاهِقٌ ط وَلَكُمُ
الْوَيْلُ مِمَّا تَصِفُوْنَ ﴿١٨﴾

19. To Him belong all (creatures) in the heavens and on earth: even those who are in His (very) Presence are not too proud to serve Him, nor are they (ever) weary (of His service):

19. Wa lahoo man fis-samaawaati wal-arḍ; wa man 'indahoo laa yastakbiroona 'an 'ibaadatihee wa laa yastaḥsiroon.

وَلَهٗ مَنْ فِى السَّمٰوٰتِ وَالْاَرْضِ ط
وَمَنْ عِنْدَهٗ لَا يَسْتَكْبِرُوْنَ عَنْ
عِبَادَتِهٖ وَلَا يَسْتَحْسِرُوْنَ ﴿١٩﴾ ج

20. They celebrate His praises night and day, nor do they ever flag or intermit.

20. Yusabbiḥoonal-layla wannahaara laa yafturoon.

يُسَبِّحُوْنَ الَّيْلَ وَالنَّهَارَ لَا يَفْتُرُوْنَ ﴿٢٠﴾

21. Or have they taken (for worship) gods from the earth who can raise (the dead)?

21. Amit-takhaz̲ooo aalihatam-minal-arḍi hum yunshiroon.

اَمِ اتَّخَذُوْٓا اٰلِهَةً مِّنَ الْاَرْضِ
هُمْ يُنْشِرُوْنَ ﴿٢١﴾

22. If there were, in the heavens and the earth, other gods besides Allah, there would have been confusion in both! But glory to Allah, the Lord of the Throne: (high is He) above what they attribute to Him!

22. Law kaana feehimaaa aalihatun illal-laahu lafasadataa; fa-Subḥaanal-laahi Rabbil-'Arshi 'ammaa yaṣifoon.

لَوْ كَانَ فِيْهِمَآ اٰلِهَةٌ اِلَّا اللّٰهُ
لَفَسَدَتَا ج فَسُبْحٰنَ اللّٰهِ رَبِّ
الْعَرْشِ عَمَّا يَصِفُوْنَ ﴿٢٢﴾

23. He cannot be questioned for His acts, but they will be questioned (for theirs).

23. Laa yus'alu 'ammaa yaf'alu wa hum yus'aloon.

لَا يُسْـَٔلُ عَمَّا يَفْعَلُ وَهُمْ يُسْـَٔلُوْنَ ﴿٢٣﴾

24. Or have they taken for worship (other) gods besides Him? Say, "Bring your convincing proof: this is the Message of those with me and the Message of those before me." But most of them do not know the Truth, and so turn away.

24. Amit-takhaz̲oo min dooniheee aalihatan qul haatoo burhaanakum haaz̲aa z̲ikru mam-ma'iya wa z̲ikru man qablee; bal aks̲aruhum laa ya'lamoonal-ḥaqqa fahum-mu'riḍoon.

اَمِ اتَّخَذُوْا مِنْ دُوْنِهٖۤ اٰلِهَةً ؕ قُلْ
هَاتُوْا بُرْهَانَكُمْ ۚ هٰذَا ذِكْرُ مَنْ
مَّعِىَ وَذِكْرُ مَنْ قَبْلِىْ ؕ بَلْ اَكْثَرُهُمْ
لَا يَعْلَمُوْنَ ۙ الْحَقَّ فَهُمْ مُّعْرِضُوْنَ ﴿٢٤﴾

25. Not a Messenger did We send before you without this inspiration sent by Us to him: that there is no god but I; therefore worship and serve Me.

25. Wa maaa arsalnaa min qablika mir-Rasoolin illaa nooḥeee ilayhi annahoo laaa ilaaha illaaa Ana fa'budoon.

وَمَاۤ اَرْسَلْنَا مِنْ قَبْلِكَ مِنْ رَّسُوْلٍ
اِلَّا نُوْحِىْۤ اِلَيْهِ اَنَّهٗ لَاۤ اِلٰهَ اِلَّاۤ
اَنَا فَاعْبُدُوْنِ ﴿٢٥﴾

26. And they say: "(Allah) Most Gracious has begotten offspring." Glory to Him! They are (but) servants raised to honor.

26. Wa qaalut-takhaz̲ar-Raḥmaanu waladan-Subḥaanah; bal 'ibaadum-mukramoon.

وَقَالُوا اتَّخَذَ الرَّحْمٰنُ وَلَدًا سُبْحٰنَهٗ ؕ
بَلْ عِبَادٌ مُّكْرَمُوْنَ ۙ ﴿٢٦﴾

27. They do not speak before He speaks, and they act (in all things) by His Command.

27. Laa yasbiqoonahoo bil-qawli wa hum bi-amrihee ya'maloon.

لَا يَسْبِقُوْنَهٗ بِالْقَوْلِ وَهُمْ بِاَمْرِهٖ
يَعْمَلُوْنَ ﴿٢٧﴾

28. He knows what is before them, and what is behind them, and they offer no intercession except for those who are acceptable, and they stand in awe and reverence of His (glory).

28. Ya'lamu maa bayna aydeehim wa maa khalfahum wa laa yashfa'oona illaa limanir-taḍaa wa hum-min khash-yatihee mushfiqoon.

يَعْلَمُ مَا بَيْنَ اَيْدِيْهِمْ وَمَا خَلْفَهُمْ
وَلَا يَشْفَعُوْنَ ۙ اِلَّا لِمَنِ ارْتَضٰى
وَهُمْ مِّنْ خَشْيَتِهٖ مُشْفِقُوْنَ ﴿٢٨﴾

29. If any of them should say, "I am a god besides Him", such a one We should reward with Hell: thus do We reward those who do wrong.

29. Wa mañy-yaqul minhum inneee ilaahum-min doonihee faz̲aalika najzeehi Jahannam; kaz̲aalika najziẓ-ẓaalimeen.

(Section 2)

وَمَنْ يَّقُلْ مِنْهُمْ اِنِّىْۤ اِلٰهٌ مِّنْ
دُوْنِهٖ فَذٰلِكَ نَجْزِيْهِ جَهَنَّمَ ؕ
كَذٰلِكَ نَجْزِى الظّٰلِمِيْنَ ﴿٢٩﴾ ع ١٩ ٢

30. Do not the Unbelievers see that the heavens and the earth were joined together (as one unit of creation), before we clove them asunder? We made from water every living thing. Will they not then believe?

30. Awalam yaral-laz̲eena kafarooo annas-samaawaati wal-arḍa kaanataa ratqan fafataqnaahumaa wa ja'alnaa minal-maaa'i kulla shay'in ḥayyin afalaa yu'minoon.

اَوَلَمْ يَرَ الَّذِيْنَ كَفَرُوْۤا اَنَّ
السَّمٰوٰتِ وَالْاَرْضَ كَانَتَا رَتْقًا
فَفَتَقْنٰهُمَا ؕ وَجَعَلْنَا مِنَ الْمَآءِ
كُلَّ شَىْءٍ حَىٍّ ؕ اَفَلَا يُؤْمِنُوْنَ ﴿٣٠﴾

31. And We have set on the earth mountains standing firm, lest it should shake with them, and We have made therein broad highways (between mountains) for them to pass through: that they may receive guidance.

31. Wa ja'alnaa fil-arḍi rawaasiya an tameeda bihim wa ja'alnaa feehaa fijaajan subulal-la'allahum yahtadoon.

وَجَعَلْنَا فِى الْاَرْضِ رَوَاسِىَ اَنْ
تَمِيْدَ بِهِمْ ۪ وَجَعَلْنَا فِيْهَا فِجَاجًا
سُبُلًا لَّعَلَّهُمْ يَهْتَدُوْنَ ﴿٣١﴾

32. And We have made the heavens as a canopy well guarded:

32. Wa ja'alnas-samaaa'a saqfam-maḥfooẓañw-

وَجَعَلْنَا السَّمَآءَ سَقْفًا مَّحْفُوْظًا ۚۖ

Ikhfa اخفاء | Ghunna غنّہ | Ikhfa Meem Saakin اخفاءميم ساكن | Idghaam ادغام | Qalqala قلقلہ | Qalb قلب | Idghaam Meem Saakin ادغام ميم ساكن

yet do they turn away from the Signs which these things (point to)!	wa hum 'an Aayaatihaa mu'riḍoon.	وَّهُمْ عَنْ اٰيٰتِهَا مُعْرِضُوْنَ ﴿٣٢﴾
33. It is He Who created the Night and the Day, and the sun and the moon: all (the celestial bodies) swim along, each in its rounded course.	33. Wa Huwal-lazee khalaqal-layla wannahaara washshamsa walqamara kullun fee falakiñy-yasbaḥoon.	وَهُوَ الَّذِيْ خَلَقَ الَّيْلَ وَالنَّهَارَ وَالشَّمْسَ وَالْقَمَرَ ؕ كُلٌّ فِيْ فَلَكٍ يَّسْبَحُوْنَ ﴿٣٣﴾
34. We did not grant to any man before you permanent life (here): if then you should die, would they live permanently?	34. Wa maa ja'alnaa libasharim-min qablikal-khuld; afa'im-mitta fahumul-khaalidoon.	وَمَا جَعَلْنَا لِبَشَرٍ مِّنْ قَبْلِكَ الْخُلْدَ ؕ اَفَا۟ئِنْ مِّتَّ فَهُمُ الْخٰلِدُوْنَ ﴿٣٤﴾
35. Every soul shall have a taste of death: and We test you by evil and by good by way of trial and to Us must you return.	35. Kullu nafsin zaaa'iqatul-mawt; wa nablookum bish-sharri walkhayri fitnatañw wa ilaynaa turja'oon.	كُلُّ نَفْسٍ ذَآئِقَةُ الْمَوْتِ ؕ وَنَبْلُوْكُمْ بِالشَّرِّ وَالْخَيْرِ فِتْنَةً ؕ وَاِلَيْنَا تُرْجَعُوْنَ ﴿٣٥﴾
36. When the Unbelievers see you, they treat you not except with ridicule. "Is this," (they say), "the one who talks of your gods?" and they blaspheme at the mention of (Allah) Most Gracious!	36. wa izaa ra-aakal-lazeena kafarooo iñy-yattakhizoonaka illa huzuwaa; ahaazal-lazee yazkuru aalihatakum wa hum bi-zikrir-Raḥmaani hum kaafiroon.	وَاِذَا رَاٰكَ الَّذِيْنَ كَفَرُوْٓا اِنْ يَّتَّخِذُوْنَكَ اِلَّا هُزُوًا ؕ اَهٰذَا الَّذِيْ يَذْكُرُ اٰلِهَتَكُمْ ۚ وَهُمْ بِذِكْرِ الرَّحْمٰنِ هُمْ كٰفِرُوْنَ ﴿٣٦﴾
37. Man is a creature of haste: soon (enough) will I show you My Signs; then you will not ask Me to hasten them!	37. Khuliqal-insaanu min 'ajal; sa-ureekum Aayaatee falaa tasta'jiloon.	خُلِقَ الْاِنْسَانُ مِنْ عَجَلٍ ؕ سَاُورِيْكُمْ اٰيٰتِيْ فَلَا تَسْتَعْجِلُوْنِ ﴿٣٧﴾
38. They say: "When will this promise come to pass, if you are telling the truth?"	38. Wa yaqooloona mataa haazal-wa'du in kuntum ṣaadiqeen.	وَيَقُوْلُوْنَ مَتٰى هٰذَا الْوَعْدُ اِنْ كُنْتُمْ صٰدِقِيْنَ ﴿٣٨﴾
39. If only the Unbelievers knew (the time) when they will not be able to ward off the fire from their faces, nor yet from their backs, and (when) no help can reach them!	39. Law ya'lamul-lazeena kafaroo ḥeena laa yakuffoona 'añw-wujoohihimun-Naara wa laa 'an ẓuhoorihim wa laa hum yunṣaroon.	لَوْ يَعْلَمُ الَّذِيْنَ كَفَرُوْا حِيْنَ لَا يَكُفُّوْنَ عَنْ وُّجُوْهِهِمُ النَّارَ وَلَا عَنْ ظُهُوْرِهِمْ وَلَا هُمْ يُنْصَرُوْنَ ﴿٣٩﴾
40. Nay, it may come to them all of a sudden and confound them: no power will they have then to avert it, nor will they (then) get respite.	40. Bal taâteehim baghtatan fatabhatuhum falaa yasta-ṭee'oona raddahaa wa laa hum yunẓaroon.	بَلْ تَاْتِيْهِمْ بَغْتَةً فَتَبْهَتُهُمْ فَلَا يَسْتَطِيْعُوْنَ رَدَّهَا وَلَا هُمْ يُنْظَرُوْنَ ﴿٤٠﴾
41. Mocked were (many) Messenger before you; but their scoffers were hemmed in by the thing that they mocked.	41. Wa laqadis-tuhzi'a bi-Rusulim-min qablika faḥaaqa billazeena sakhiroo minhum-maa kaanoo bihee yastahzi'oon. **(Section 3)**	وَلَقَدِ اسْتُهْزِئَ بِرُسُلٍ مِّنْ قَبْلِكَ فَحَاقَ بِالَّذِيْنَ سَخِرُوْا مِنْهُمْ مَّا كَانُوْا بِهٖ يَسْتَهْزِءُوْنَ ﴿٤١﴾ ع

ع ٣

Ikhfa اخفاء · Ghunna غُنّہ · Ikhfa Meem Saakin اخفاء میم ساکن · Idghaam ادغام · Qalqala قلقلہ · Qalb قلب · Idghaam Meem Saakin ادغام میم ساکن

42. Say: "Who can keep you safe by night and by day from (the Wrath of Allah) Most Gracious?" Yet they turn away from the mention of their Lord.

42. Qul mañy-yakla'ukum billayli wannahaari minar-Raḥmaan; bal hum 'an z̲ikri Rabbihim-mu'riḍoon.

قُلْ مَنْ يَّكْلَؤُكُمْ بِالَّيْلِ وَ
النَّهَارِ مِنَ الرَّحْمٰنِ ۭ بَلْ هُمْ عَنْ
ذِكْرِ رَبِّهِمْ مُّعْرِضُوْنَ ﴿٤٢﴾

43. Or have they gods that can guard them from Us? They have no power to aid themselves, nor can they be defended from Us.

43. Am lahum aalihatun tamna'uhum-min dooninaa; laa yastaṭee'oona naṣra anfusihim wa laa hum-minnaa yuṣ-ḥaboon.

اَمْ لَهُمْ اٰلِهَةٌ تَمْنَعُهُمْ مِّنْ دُوْنِنَا ۭ
لَا يَسْتَطِيْعُوْنَ نَصْرَ اَنْفُسِهِمْ وَلَا
هُمْ مِّنَّا يُصْحَبُوْنَ ﴿٤٣﴾

44. Nay, We gave the good things of this life to these men and their fathers until the period grew long for them; Do not they see that We gradually reduce the land (in their control) from its outlying borders? Is it then they who will win?

44. Bal matta'naa haaa'u-laaa'i wa aabaaa'ahum ḥattaa ṭaala 'alayhimul-'umur; afalaa yarawna annaa naåtil-arḍa nanquṣuhaa min aṭraafihaa; afahumul-ghaaliboon.

بَلْ مَتَّعْنَا هٰٓؤُلَاۗءِ وَاٰبَاۗءَهُمْ حَتّٰى
طَالَ عَلَيْهِمُ الْعُمُرُ ۭ اَفَلَا يَرَوْنَ اَنَّا
نَاْتِي الْاَرْضَ نَنْقُصُهَا مِنْ اَطْرَافِهَا ۭ
اَفَهُمُ الْغٰلِبُوْنَ ﴿٤٤﴾

45. Say, "I do but warn you according to revelation": but the deaf will not hear the call, (even) when they are warned!

45. Qul innamaaa unz̲irukum bilwaḥyi; wa laa yasma'uṣ-ṣummud-du'aaa'a iz̲aa maa yunz̲aroon

قُلْ اِنَّمَآ اُنْذِرُكُمْ بِالْوَحْيِ ڮ
وَلَا يَسْمَعُ الصُّمُّ الدُّعَاۗءَ اِذَا
مَا يُنْذَرُوْنَ ﴿٤٥﴾

46. If but a breath of the Wrath of your Lord do touch them, they will then say, "Woe to us! we did wrong indeed!"

46. Wa la'im-massat-hum nafḥatum-min 'az̲aabi Rabbika la-yaqoolunna yaawaylanaaa innaa kunnaa z̲aalimeen.

وَلَىِٕنْ مَّسَّتْهُمْ نَفْحَةٌ مِّنْ عَذَابِ
رَبِّكَ لَيَقُوْلُنَّ يٰوَيْلَنَآ اِنَّا
كُنَّا ظٰلِمِيْنَ ﴿٤٦﴾

47. We shall set up scales of justice for the Day of Judgment, so that not a soul will be dealt with unjustly in the least, and if there be (no more than) the weight of a mustard seed, We will bring it (to account): and enough are We to take account.

47. Wa naḍa'ul-mawaazeenal-qisṭa li-Yawmil-Qiyaamati falaa tuẓlamu nafsun shay'aa; wa in kaana mis̲qaala ḥabba-tim-min khardalin ataynaa bihaa; wa kafaa binaa ḥaasi-been.

وَنَضَعُ الْمَوَازِيْنَ الْقِسْطَ لِيَوْمِ
الْقِيٰمَةِ فَلَا تُظْلَمُ نَفْسٌ شَيْـــًٔا ۭ
وَاِنْ كَانَ مِثْقَالَ حَبَّةٍ مِّنْ خَرْدَلٍ
اَتَيْنَا بِهَا ۭ وَكَفٰى بِنَا حٰسِبِيْنَ ﴿٤٧﴾

48. In the past We granted to Moses and Aaron the criterion (for judgment), and a Light and a Message for those who would do right,-

48. Wa laqad aataynaa Moosaa wa Haaroonal-Furqaa-na wa ḍiyaa'añw-wa z̲ikral-lilmuttaqeen.

وَلَقَدْ اٰتَيْنَا مُوْسٰى وَهٰرُوْنَ
الْفُرْقَانَ وَضِيَاۗءً وَّذِكْرًا
لِّلْمُتَّقِيْنَ ﴿٤٨﴾ ۙ

49. Those who fear their Lord in their most secret thoughts, and who hold the Hour (of Judgment) in awe.

49. Allaz̲eena yakhshawna Rabbahum bilghaybi wa hum-minas-Saa'ati mushfiqoon.

الَّذِيْنَ يَخْشَوْنَ رَبَّهُمْ بِالْغَيْبِ
وَهُمْ مِّنَ السَّاعَةِ مُشْفِقُوْنَ ﴿٤٩﴾

50. And this is a blessed Message which We have sent down: will you then

50. Wa haaz̲aa Z̲ikrum-Mu-baarakun anzalnaah; afa-antum

وَهٰذَا ذِكْرٌ مُّبٰرَكٌ اَنْزَلْنٰهُ ۭ اَفَاَنْتُمْ

Ikhfa اخفاء | Ghunna غُنّہ | Ikhfa Meem Saakin اخفاء میم ساکن | Idghaam ادغام | Qalqala قلقلہ | Qalb قلب | Idghaam Meem Saakin ادغام میم ساکن

الربع

reject it?	lahoo munkiroon. **(Section 4)**	لَهُۥ مُنكِرُونَ ۝٥٠ ع
51. We bestowed aforetime on Abraham his rectitude of conduct, and well were We acquainted with him.	51. Wa laqad aataynaaa Ibraaheema rushdahoo min qablu wa kunnaa bihee 'aalimeen.	وَلَقَدْ ءَاتَيْنَآ إِبْرَٰهِيمَ رُشْدَهُۥ مِن قَبْلُ وَكُنَّا بِهِۦ عَٰلِمِينَ ۝٥١
52. Behold! he said to his father and his people, "What are these images, to which you are (so assiduously) devoted?"	52. Iz qaala li-abeehi wa qawmihee maa haazihit-tamaaseelul-lateee antum lahaa 'aakifoon.	إِذْ قَالَ لِأَبِيهِ وَقَوْمِهِۦ مَا هَٰذِهِ ٱلتَّمَاثِيلُ ٱلَّتِىٓ أَنتُمْ لَهَا عَٰكِفُونَ ۝٥٢
53. They said, "We found our fathers worshipping them."	53. Qaaloo wajadnaaa aabaaa'anaa lahaa 'aabideen.	قَالُوا۟ وَجَدْنَآ ءَابَآءَنَا لَهَا عَٰبِدِينَ ۝٥٣
54. He said, "Indeed you have been in manifest error - you and your fathers."	54. Qaala laqad kuntum antum wa aabaaa'ukum fee ḍalaalim-mubeen.	قَالَ لَقَدْ كُنتُمْ أَنتُمْ وَءَابَآؤُكُمْ فِى ضَلَٰلٍ مُّبِينٍ ۝٥٤
55. They said, "Have you brought us the Truth, or are you one of those who jest?"	55. Qaalooo aji'tanaa bil-ḥaqqi am anta minal-laa'ibeen.	قَالُوٓا۟ أَجِئْتَنَا بِٱلْحَقِّ أَمْ أَنتَ مِنَ ٱللَّٰعِبِينَ ۝٥٥
56. He said, "Nay, your Lord is the Lord of the heavens and the earth, He Who created them (from nothing): and I am a witness to this (truth).	56. Qaala bar-Rabbukum Rabbus-samaawaati wal-arḍil-lazee faṭarahunna wa ana 'alaa zaalikum-minash-shaahideen.	قَالَ بَل رَّبُّكُمْ رَبُّ ٱلسَّمَٰوَٰتِ وَٱلْأَرْضِ ٱلَّذِى فَطَرَهُنَّ وَأَنَا۠ عَلَىٰ ذَٰلِكُم مِّنَ ٱلشَّٰهِدِينَ ۝٥٦
57. "And by Allah, I have a plan for your idols - after you go away and turn your backs".	57. Wa tallaahi la-akeedanna aṣnaamakum ba'da an tuwalloo mudbireen.	وَتَٱللَّهِ لَأَكِيدَنَّ أَصْنَٰمَكُم بَعْدَ أَن تُوَلُّوا۟ مُدْبِرِينَ ۝٥٧
58. So he broke them to pieces, (all) but the biggest of them, that they might turn (and address themselves) to it.	58. Faja'alahum juzaazan illaa kabeeral-lahum la'allahum ilayhi yarji'oon.	فَجَعَلَهُمْ جُذَٰذًا إِلَّا كَبِيرًا لَّهُمْ لَعَلَّهُمْ إِلَيْهِ يَرْجِعُونَ ۝٥٨
59. They said, "Who has done this to our gods? He must indeed be some man of impiety!"	59. Qaaloo man fa'ala haazaa bi-aalihatinaaa innahoo lamin-naẓ-ẓaalimeen.	قَالُوا۟ مَن فَعَلَ هَٰذَا بِـَٔالِهَتِنَآ إِنَّهُۥ لَمِنَ ٱلظَّٰلِمِينَ ۝٥٩
60. They said, "We heard a youth talk of them: he is called Abraham."	60. Qaaloo sami'naa fatañy-yazkuruhum yuqaalu lahooo Ibraaheem.	قَالُوا۟ سَمِعْنَا فَتًى يَذْكُرُهُمْ يُقَالُ لَهُۥٓ إِبْرَٰهِيمُ ۝٦٠
61. They said, "Then bring him before the eyes of the people, that they may bear witness."	61. Qaaloo faåtoo bihee 'alaaa a'yunin-naasi la'allahum yash-hadoon.	قَالُوا۟ فَأْتُوا۟ بِهِۦ عَلَىٰٓ أَعْيُنِ ٱلنَّاسِ لَعَلَّهُمْ يَشْهَدُونَ ۝٦١
62. They said, "are you the one that did this with our gods, O Abraham?"	62. Qaalooo 'a-anta fa'alta haazaa bi-aalihatinaa yaaa Ibraaheem.	قَالُوٓا۟ ءَأَنتَ فَعَلْتَ هَٰذَا بِـَٔالِهَتِنَا يَٰٓإِبْرَٰهِيمُ ۝٦٢
63. He said: "Nay, this was done by - this is their biggest one!	63. Qaala bal fa'alahoo kabeeruhum haazaa	قَالَ بَلْ فَعَلَهُۥ كَبِيرُهُمْ هَٰذَا

Ikhfa اخفاء | Ghunna غُنّہ | Ikhfa Meem Saakin اخفاء میم ساکن | Idghaam ادغام | Qalqala قلقلہ | Qalb قلب | Idghaam Meem Saakin ادغام میم ساکن

ask them, if they can speak intelligently!"

64. So they turned to themselves and said, "Surely you are the ones in the wrong!"

65. Then they were confounded with shame: (they said), "you know full well that these (idols) do not speak!"

66. (Abraham) said, "Do you then worship, besides Allah, things that can neither be of any good to you nor do you harm?

67. "Fie upon you, and upon the things that you worship besides Allah! Have you no sense?".

68. They said, "Burn him and protect your gods, if you do (anything at all)!"

69. We said, "O Fire! be you cool, and (a means of) safety for Abraham!"

70. Then they planned against him: but We made them the ones that lost most!

71. But We delivered him and (his nephew) Lut (and directed them) to the land which We have blessed for the nations.

72. And We bestowed on him Isaac and, as an additional gift, (a grandson), Jacob, and We made righteous men of every one (of them).

73. And We made them leaders, guiding (men) by Our Command, and We sent them inspiration to do good deeds, to establish regular prayers, and to practise regular charity; and they constantly served Us (and Us only).

74. And to Lut, too, We gave Judgment and Knowledge, and We saved him from the town which practised abominations: truly they were

fas'aloohum in kaanoo yanṭiqoon.

64. Faraja'ooo ilaaa anfusihim faqaalooo innakum antumuẓ-ẓaalimoon.

65. Summa nukisoo 'alaa ru'oosihim laqad 'alimta maa haaa'ulaaa'i yanṭiqoon.

66. Qaala afata'budoona min doonil-laahi maa laa yanfa'ukum shay'añw-wa laa yaḍurrukum.

67. Uffil-lakum wa limaa ta'budoona min doonil-laah; afalaa ta'qiloon.

68. Qaaloo ḥarriqoohu wanṣurooo aalihatakum in kuntum faa'ileen.

69. Qulnaa yaa naaru koonee bardañw-wa salaaman 'alaaa Ibraaheem.

70. Wa araadoo bihee kaydan faja'alnaahumul-akhsareen.

71. Wa najjaynaahu wa Looṭan ilal-arḍil-latee baaraknaa feehaa lil-'aalameen.

72. Wa wahabnaa lahooo Isḥaaq; wa Ya'qooba naafilah; wa kullan ja'alnaa ṣaaliḥeen.

73. Wa ja'alnaahum a'immatañy-yahdoona bi-amrinaa wa awḥaynaaa ilayhim fi'lal-khayraati wa iqaamaṣ-Ṣalaati wa eetaaa'az-Zakaati wa kaanoo lanaa 'aabideen.

74. Wa Looṭan aataynaahu ḥukmañw-wa 'ilmañw-wa najjaynaahu minal-qaryatil-latee kaanat-ta'malul-khabaaa'iṣ; innahum kaanoo

فَسْـَٔلُوهُمْ إِن كَانُوا۟ يَنطِقُونَ ٦٣
فَرَجَعُوٓا۟ إِلَىٰٓ أَنفُسِهِمْ فَقَالُوٓا۟
إِنَّكُمْ أَنتُمُ ٱلظَّٰلِمُونَ ٦٤
ثُمَّ نُكِسُوا۟ عَلَىٰ رُءُوسِهِمْ لَقَدْ
عَلِمْتَ مَا هَٰٓؤُلَآءِ يَنطِقُونَ ٦٥
قَالَ أَفَتَعْبُدُونَ مِن دُونِ ٱللَّهِ
مَا لَا يَنفَعُكُمْ شَيْـًٔا وَلَا يَضُرُّكُمْ ٦٦
أُفٍّ لَّكُمْ وَلِمَا تَعْبُدُونَ مِن
دُونِ ٱللَّهِ ۖ أَفَلَا تَعْقِلُونَ ٦٧
قَالُوا۟ حَرِّقُوهُ وَٱنصُرُوٓا۟ ءَالِهَتَكُمْ
إِن كُنتُمْ فَٰعِلِينَ ٦٨
قُلْنَا يَٰنَارُ كُونِى بَرْدًا وَسَلَٰمًا
عَلَىٰٓ إِبْرَٰهِيمَ ٦٩
وَأَرَادُوا۟ بِهِۦ كَيْدًا فَجَعَلْنَٰهُمُ
ٱلْأَخْسَرِينَ ٧٠
وَنَجَّيْنَٰهُ وَلُوطًا إِلَى ٱلْأَرْضِ
ٱلَّتِى بَٰرَكْنَا فِيهَا لِلْعَٰلَمِينَ ٧١
وَوَهَبْنَا لَهُۥٓ إِسْحَٰقَ ۖ وَيَعْقُوبَ
نَافِلَةً ۖ وَكُلًّا جَعَلْنَا صَٰلِحِينَ ٧٢
وَجَعَلْنَٰهُمْ أَئِمَّةً يَهْدُونَ بِأَمْرِنَا
وَأَوْحَيْنَآ إِلَيْهِمْ فِعْلَ ٱلْخَيْرَٰتِ
وَإِقَامَ ٱلصَّلَوٰةِ وَإِيتَآءَ ٱلزَّكَوٰةِ ۖ
وَكَانُوا۟ لَنَا عَٰبِدِينَ ٧٣
وَلُوطًا ءَاتَيْنَٰهُ حُكْمًا وَعِلْمًا وَ
نَجَّيْنَٰهُ مِنَ ٱلْقَرْيَةِ ٱلَّتِى كَانَت
تَّعْمَلُ ٱلْخَبَٰٓئِثَ ۗ إِنَّهُمْ كَانُوا۟

Ikhfa اخفاء | Ghunna غُنّہ | Ikhfa Meem Saakin اخفاءميم ساكن | Idghaam ادغام | Qalqala قلقله | Qalb قلب | Idghaam Meem Saakin ادغام ميم ساكن

a people given to Evil, a rebellious people.

qawma saw'in faasiqeen.

قَوْمَ سَوْءٍ فٰسِقِيْنَ ﴿٧٤﴾

75. And We admitted him to Our Mercy: for he was one of the Righteous.

75. Wa adkhalnaahu fee raḥmatinaa innahoo minaṣ-ṣaaliḥeen. **(Section 5)**

وَاَدْخَلْنٰهُ فِيْ رَحْمَتِنَا ۭ اِنَّهٗ مِنَ
الصّٰلِحِيْنَ ﴿٧٥﴾

76. (Remember) Noah, when he cried (to Us) aforetime: We listened to his (prayer) and delivered him and his family from great distress.

76. Wa Nooḥan iz̲ naadaa min qablu fastajabnaa lahoo fanajjaynaahu wa ahlahoo minal-karbil-'aẓeem.

وَنُوْحًا اِذْ نَادٰى مِنْ قَبْلُ فَاسْتَجَبْنَا
لَهٗ فَنَجَّيْنٰهُ وَاَهْلَهٗ مِنَ الْكَرْبِ
الْعَظِيْمِ ﴿٧٦﴾

77. We helped him against people who rejected Our Signs: truly they were a people given to Evil: so We drowned them (in the Flood) all together.

77. Wa naṣarnaahu minal-qawmil-laz̲eena kaz̲z̲aboo bi Aayaatinaa; innahum kaanoo qawma saw'in fa-aghraqnaahum ajma'een.

وَنَصَرْنٰهُ مِنَ الْقَوْمِ الَّذِيْنَ
كَذَّبُوْا بِاٰيٰتِنَا ۭ اِنَّهُمْ كَانُوْا قَوْمَ
سَوْءٍ فَاَغْرَقْنٰهُمْ اَجْمَعِيْنَ ﴿٧٧﴾

78. And remember David and Solomon, when they gave judgment in the matter of the field into which the sheep of certain people had strayed by night: We witnessed their judgment.

78. Wa Daawooda wa Sulaymaana iz̲ yaḥkumaani fil-ḥars̲i iz̲ nafashat feehi ghanamul-qawmi wa kunnaa liḥukmihim shaahideen.

وَدَاوٗدَ وَسُلَيْمٰنَ اِذْ يَحْكُمٰنِ فِي
الْحَرْثِ اِذْ نَفَشَتْ فِيْهِ غَنَمُ
الْقَوْمِ ۚ وَكُنَّا لِحُكْمِهِمْ شٰهِدِيْنَ ﴿٧٨﴾

79. To Solomon We inspired the (right) understanding of the matter: to each (of them) We gave Judgment and Knowledge; it was Our power that made the hills and the birds celebrate Our praises, with David: it was We Who did (all these things).

79. Fafahhamnaahaa sulaymaan; wa kullan aataynaa ḥukmañw-wa 'ilmañw-wa sakhkharnaa ma'a Daawoodal-jibaala yusabbiḥna waṭṭayr; wa kunnaa faa'ileen.

فَفَهَّمْنٰهَا سُلَيْمٰنَ ۚ وَكُلًّا اٰتَيْنَا
حُكْمًا وَّعِلْمًا ۡ وَّسَخَّرْنَا مَعَ دَاوٗدَ
الْجِبَالَ يُسَبِّحْنَ وَالطَّيْرَ ۭ وَكُنَّا
فٰعِلِيْنَ ﴿٧٩﴾

80. It was We Who taught him the making of coats of mail for your benefit, to guard you from each other's violence: will you then be grateful?

80. Wa 'allamnaahu ṣan'ata laboosil-lakum lituḥṣinakum mim baåsikum fahal antum shaakiroon.

وَعَلَّمْنٰهُ صَنْعَةَ لَبُوْسٍ لَّكُمْ
لِتُحْصِنَكُمْ مِّنْۢ بَاْسِكُمْ ۚ فَهَلْ
اَنْتُمْ شٰكِرُوْنَ ﴿٨٠﴾

81. (It was Our power that made) the violent (unruly) wind flow (tamely) for Solomon, to his order, to the land which We had blessed: for We do know all things.

81. Wa li-Sulaymaanar-reeḥa 'aaṣifatan tajree bi-amriheee ilal-arḍil-latee baaraknaa feehaa; wa kunnaa bikulli shay'in 'aalimeen.

وَلِسُلَيْمٰنَ الرِّيْحَ عَاصِفَةً تَجْرِيْ
بِاَمْرِهٖٓ اِلَى الْاَرْضِ الَّتِيْ بٰرَكْنَا فِيْهَا ۭ
وَكُنَّا بِكُلِّ شَيْءٍ عٰلِمِيْنَ ﴿٨١﴾

82. And of the evil ones, were some who dived for him, and did other work besides; and it was We Who guarded them.

82. Wa minash-Shayaaṭeeni mañy-yaghooṣoona lahoo wa ya'maloona 'amalan doona z̲aalika wa kunnaa lahum ḥaafiẓeen.

وَمِنَ الشَّيٰطِيْنِ مَنْ يَّغُوْصُوْنَ لَهٗ
وَيَعْمَلُوْنَ عَمَلًا دُوْنَ ذٰلِكَ ۚ وَكُنَّا
لَهُمْ حٰفِظِيْنَ ﴿٨٢﴾

83. And (remember) Job, when He cried to his Lord, "Truly distress has seized me,

83. Wa Ayyooba iz̲ naadaa Rabbahooo annee massaniyaḍ-

وَاَيُّوْبَ اِذْ نَادٰى رَبَّهٗٓ اَنِّيْ مَسَّنِيَ

Ikhfa اخفاء | Ghunna غُنّہ | Ikhfa Meem Saakin اخفاء میم ساکن | Idghaam ادغام | Qalqala قلقلہ | Qalb قلب | Idghaam Meem Saakin ادغام میم ساکن

but you are the Most Merciful of those that are merciful."

ḍurru wa Anta arḥamur-raaḥimeen.

الضُّرُّ وَاَنْتَ اَرْحَمُ الرّٰحِمِيْنَ ۚ ﴿٨٣﴾

84. So We listened to him: We removed the distress that was on him, and We restored his people to him, and doubled their number,- as a Grace from Ourselves, and a thing for commemoration, for all who serve Us.

84. Fastajabnaa lahoo fakashafnaa maa bihee min ḍurriñw-wa-aataynaahu ahlahoo wa mis̲lahum-ma'ahum raḥmatam-min 'indinaa wa z̲ikraa lil'aabideen.

فَاسْتَجَبْنَا لَهٗ فَكَشَفْنَا مَا بِهٖ مِنْ
ضُرٍّ وَّاٰتَيْنٰهُ اَهْلَهٗ وَمِثْلَهُمْ مَّعَهُمْ
رَحْمَةً مِّنْ عِنْدِنَا وَذِكْرٰى
لِلْعٰبِدِيْنَ ﴿٨٤﴾

85. And (remember) Isma'il, Idris, and Zul-kifl, all (men) of constancy and patience;

85. Wa Ismaa'eela wa Idreesa wa Z̲al-Kifli kullum-minaṣ-ṣaabireen.

وَاِسْمٰعِيْلَ وَاِدْرِيْسَ وَذَا الْكِفْلِ ؕ
كُلٌّ مِّنَ الصّٰبِرِيْنَ ۚ ﴿٨٥﴾

86. We admitted them to Our Mercy: for they were of the righteous ones.

86. Wa adkhalnaahum fee raḥmatinaa innahum-minaṣ-ṣaaliḥeen.

وَاَدْخَلْنٰهُمْ فِيْ رَحْمَتِنَا ؕ اِنَّهُمْ
مِّنَ الصّٰلِحِيْنَ ﴿٨٦﴾

87. And remember Zun-nun, when he departed in wrath: he imagined that We had no power over him! but he cried through the depths of darkness, "There is no god but You: glory to You: I was indeed wrong!"

87. Wa Z̲an-Nooni iz̲ z̲ahaba mughaaḍiban faẓaanna al-lan naqdira 'alayhi fanaadaa fiẓ-ẓulumaati al-laaa ilaaha illaaa Anta Subḥaanaka innee kuntu minaẓ-ẓaalimeen.

وَذَا النُّوْنِ اِذْ ذَّهَبَ مُغَاضِبًا
فَظَنَّ اَنْ لَّنْ نَّقْدِرَ عَلَيْهِ فَنَادٰى
فِي الظُّلُمٰتِ اَنْ لَّآ اِلٰهَ اِلَّآ
اَنْتَ سُبْحٰنَكَ ۖ اِنِّيْ كُنْتُ مِنَ
الظّٰلِمِيْنَ ۚ ﴿٨٧﴾

88. So We listened to him: and delivered him from distress: and thus do We deliver those who have faith.

88. Fastajabnaa lahoo wa najjaynaahu minal-ghamm; wa kaz̲aalika nunjil-mu'mineen.

فَاسْتَجَبْنَا لَهٗ ۙ وَنَجَّيْنٰهُ مِنَ
الْغَمِّ ؕ وَكَذٰلِكَ نُـْجِي الْمُؤْمِنِيْنَ ﴿٨٨﴾

89. And (remember) Zakariya, when he cried to his Lord: "O my Lord! leave me not without offspring, though You are the best of inheritors."

89. Wa Zakariyyaaa iz̲ naadaa Rabbahoo Rabbi laa taz̲arnee fardañw-wa Anta khayrul-waaris̲een.

وَزَكَرِيَّآ اِذْ نَادٰى رَبَّهٗ رَبِّ
لَا تَذَرْنِيْ فَرْدًا وَّاَنْتَ خَيْرُ
الْوٰرِثِيْنَ ۚ ﴿٨٩﴾

90. So We listened to him: and We granted him Yahya: We cured his wife's (Barrenness) for him. These (three) were ever quick in emulation in good works; they used to call on Us with love and reverence, and humble themselves before Us.

90. Fastajabnaa lahoo wa wahabnaa lahoo Yaḥyaa wa aṣlaḥnaa lahoo zawjah; innahum kaanoo yusaari'oona fil-khayraati wa yad'oonanaa raghabañw-wa rahabaa; wa kaanoo lanaa khaashi'een.

فَاسْتَجَبْنَا لَهٗ ۫ وَوَهَبْنَا لَهٗ يَحْيٰى
وَاَصْلَحْنَا لَهٗ زَوْجَهٗ ؕ اِنَّهُمْ
كَانُوْا يُسٰرِعُوْنَ فِي الْخَيْرٰتِ وَ
يَدْعُوْنَنَا رَغَبًا وَّرَهَبًا ؕ وَكَانُوْا
لَنَا خٰشِعِيْنَ ﴿٩٠﴾

91. And (remember) her who guarded her chastity: We breathed into her of Our spirit, and We made her

91. Wallateee aḥsanat farjahaa fanafakhnaa feehaa mirrooḥinaa wa ja'alnaahaa

وَالَّتِيْٓ اَحْصَنَتْ فَرْجَهَا فَنَفَخْنَا
فِيْهَا مِنْ رُّوْحِنَا وَجَعَلْنٰهَا

Ikhfa اخفاء | Ghunna غُنّہ | Ikhfa Meem Saakin اخفاء میم ساکن | Idghaam ادغام | Qalqala قلقلہ | Qalb قلب | Idghaam Meem Saakin ادغام میم ساکن

and her son a Sign for all peoples.

wabnahaaa Aayatal-lil'aala-meen.

وَابْنَهَآ اٰيَةً لِّلْعٰلَمِيْنَ ﴿٩١﴾

92. Verily, this brotherhood of yours is a single brotherhood, and I am your Lord and Cherisher: therefore serve Me (and no other).

92. Inna haaziheee ummatukum ummatañw-waahidatañw-wa Ana Rabbukum fa'budoon.

اِنَّ هٰذِهٖٓ اُمَّتُكُمْ اُمَّةً وَّاحِدَةً ۖ
وَّاَنَا رَبُّكُمْ فَاعْبُدُوْنِ ﴿٩٢﴾

93. But (later generations) cut off their affair (of unity), one from another: (yet) will they all return to Us.

93. Wa taqatta'ooo amrahum baynahum kullun ilaynaa raaji'oon. **(Section 6)**

وَتَقَطَّعُوْٓا اَمْرَهُمْ بَيْنَهُمْ ۭ كُلٌّ
اِلَيْنَا رٰجِعُوْنَ ﴿٩٣﴾ ع

94. Whoever works any act of righteousness and has faith,- his endeavour will not be rejected: We shall record it in his favor.

94. Famañy-ya'mal minas-saalihaati wa huwa mu'minun falaa kufraana lisa'yihee wa-innaa lahoo kaatiboon.

فَمَنْ يَّعْمَلْ مِنَ الصّٰلِحٰتِ وَهُوَ
مُؤْمِنٌ فَلَا كُفْرَانَ لِسَعْيِهٖ ۚ وَاِنَّا
لَهٗ كٰتِبُوْنَ ﴿٩٤﴾

95. But there is a ban on any population which We have destroyed: that they shall not return,

95. Wa haraamun 'alaa qaryatin ahlaknaahaaa annahum laa yarji'oon.

وَحَرٰمٌ عَلٰى قَرْيَةٍ اَهْلَكْنٰهَآ
اَنَّهُمْ لَا يَرْجِعُوْنَ ﴿٩٥﴾

96. Until the Gog and Magog (people) are let through (their barrier), and they swiftly swarm from every hill.

96. Hattaaa izaa futihat Yaâjooju wa Maâjooju wa hum-min kulli hadabiñy-yansiloon.

حَتّٰٓى اِذَا فُتِحَتْ يَاْجُوْجُ وَمَاْجُوْجُ
وَهُمْ مِّنْ كُلِّ حَدَبٍ يَّنْسِلُوْنَ ﴿٩٦﴾

97. Then will the True Promise draw near (of fulfilment): then behold! the eyes of the Unbelievers will fixedly stare in horror: "Ah! woe to us! we were indeed heedless of this; nay, we truly did wrong!"

97. Waqtarabal-wa'dul-haqqu fa-izaa hiya shaakhisatun absaarul-lazeena kafaroo yaa waylanaa qad kunnaa fee ghaflatim-min haazaa bal kunnaa zaalimeen.

وَاقْتَرَبَ الْوَعْدُ الْحَقُّ فَاِذَا هِيَ
شَاخِصَةٌ اَبْصَارُ الَّذِيْنَ كَفَرُوْا ۭ
يٰوَيْلَنَا قَدْ كُنَّا فِيْ غَفْلَةٍ مِّنْ
هٰذَا بَلْ كُنَّا ظٰلِمِيْنَ ﴿٩٧﴾

98. Verily you, (unbelievers), and the (false) gods that you worship besides Allah, are (but) fuel for Hell! To it will you (surely) come!

98. Innakum wa maa ta'budoona min doonil-laahi hasabu Jahannama antum lahaa waaridoon.

اِنَّكُمْ وَمَا تَعْبُدُوْنَ مِنْ دُوْنِ
اللّٰهِ حَصَبُ جَهَنَّمَ ۭ اَنْتُمْ لَهَا
وٰرِدُوْنَ ﴿٩٨﴾

99. If these had been gods, they would not have got there! but each one will abide therein.

99. Law kaana haaa'ulaaa'i aalihatam-maa waradoohaa wa kullun feehaa khaalidoon.

لَوْ كَانَ هٰٓؤُلَاۗءِ اٰلِهَةً مَّا وَرَدُوْهَا ۭ
وَكُلٌّ فِيْهَا خٰلِدُوْنَ ﴿٩٩﴾

100. There, sobbing will be their lot, nor will they there hear anything else.

100. Lahum feehaa zafeeruñw-wa hum feehaa laa yasma'oon.

لَهُمْ فِيْهَا زَفِيْرٌ وَّهُمْ فِيْهَا
لَا يَسْمَعُوْنَ ﴿١٠٠﴾

101. Those for whom the good (record) from Us has gone before, will be removed far therefrom.

101. Innal-lazeena sabaqat lahum-minnal-husnaaa ulaaa'ika 'anhaa mub'adoon.

اِنَّ الَّذِيْنَ سَبَقَتْ لَهُمْ مِّنَّا الْحُسْنٰٓى ۙ
اُولٰۗىِٕكَ عَنْهَا مُبْعَدُوْنَ ﴿١٠١﴾

102. Not the slightest sound will they hear of Hell:

102. Laa yasma'oona haseesahaa wa hum fee

لَا يَسْمَعُوْنَ حَسِيْسَهَا ۚ وَهُمْ فِيْ

Ikhfa اخفاء | Ghunna غُنّہ | Ikhfa Meem Saakin اخفاء میم ساکن | Idghaam ادغام | Qalqala قلقلہ | Qalb قلب | Idghaam Meem Saakin ادغام میم ساکن

what their souls desired, in that they will dwell.

mash-tahat anfusuhum khaali-doon.

مَا اشْتَهَتْ اَنْفُسُهُمْ خٰلِدُوْنَ ﴿١٠٢﴾

103. The Great Terror will bring them no grief: but the angels will meet them (with mutual greetings): "This is your Day,- (the Day) that you were promised."

103. Laa yaḥzunuhumul-faza'ul-akbaru wa tatalaq-qaahumul-malaaa'ikatu haaẕaa Yawmukumul-laẕee kuntum too'adoon.

لَا يَحْزُنُهُمُ الْفَزَعُ الْاَكْبَرُ وَ
تَتَلَقّٰىهُمُ الْمَلٰٓئِكَةُ ؕ هٰذَا يَوْمُكُمُ
الَّذِيْ كُنْتُمْ تُوْعَدُوْنَ ﴿١٠٣﴾

104. The Day that We roll up the heavens like a scroll rolled up for books (completed),- even as We produced the first creation, so shall We produce a new one: a promise We have undertaken: truly shall We fulfil it.

104. Yawma naṭwis-samaaa'a kaṭayyis-sijilli lilkutub; kamaa badaånaaa awwala khalqin-nu'eeduh; wa'dan 'alaynaa; innaa kunnaa faa'ileen.

يَوْمَ نَطْوِي السَّمَآءَ كَطَيِّ السِّجِلِّ
لِلْكُتُبِ ؕ كَمَا بَدَاْنَآ اَوَّلَ خَلْقٍ
نُّعِيْدُهٗ ؕ وَعْدًا عَلَيْنَا ؕ اِنَّا
كُنَّا فٰعِلِيْنَ ﴿١٠٤﴾

105. Before this We wrote in the Psalms, after the Message (given to Moses): My servants, the righteous, shall inherit the earth."

105. Wa laqad katabnaa fiz-Zaboori mim ba'diz-zikri annal-arḍa yarisuhaa 'ibaadi-yaṣ-ṣaaliḥoon.

وَلَقَدْ كَتَبْنَا فِي الزَّبُوْرِ مِنْ
بَعْدِ الذِّكْرِ اَنَّ الْاَرْضَ يَرِثُهَا
عِبَادِيَ الصّٰلِحُوْنَ ﴿١٠٥﴾

106. Verily in this (Qur'an) is a Message for people who would (truly) worship Allah.

106. Inna fee haaẕaa labalaa-ghal-liqawmin 'aabideen.

اِنَّ فِيْ هٰذَا لَبَلٰغًا لِّقَوْمٍ
عٰبِدِيْنَ ؕ ﴿١٠٦﴾

107. We sent you not, but as a Mercy for all creatures.

107. Wa maaa arsalnaaka illaa raḥmatal-lil'aalameen.

وَمَآ اَرْسَلْنٰكَ اِلَّا رَحْمَةً لِّلْعٰلَمِيْنَ ﴿١٠٧﴾

108. Say: "What has come to me by inspiration is that your Allah is One Allah: will you therefore bow to His Will (in Islam)?"

108. Qul innamaa yooḥaaa ilayya annamaaa ilaahukum Ilaahuñw-Waahid, fahal antum muslimoon.

قُلْ اِنَّمَا يُوْحٰٓى اِلَيَّ اَنَّمَآ اِلٰهُكُمْ
اِلٰهٌ وَّاحِدٌ ۚ فَهَلْ اَنْتُمْ مُّسْلِمُوْنَ ﴿١٠٨﴾

109. But if they turn back, Say: "I have proclaimed the Message to you all alike and in truth; but I do not know whether that which you are promised is near or far.

109. Fa-in tawallaw faqul aazantukum 'alaa sawaaa'; wa in adreee aqareebun am ba'eedum-maa too' adoon.

فَاِنْ تَوَلَّوْا فَقُلْ اٰذَنْتُكُمْ عَلٰى
سَوَآءٍ ؕ وَاِنْ اَدْرِيْٓ اَقَرِيْبٌ اَمْ
بَعِيْدٌ مَّا تُوْعَدُوْنَ ﴿١٠٩﴾

110. "It is He Who knows what is open in speech and what you hide (in your hearts).

110. Innahoo ya'lamul-jahra minal-qawli wa ya'lamu maa taktumoon.

اِنَّهٗ يَعْلَمُ الْجَهْرَ مِنَ الْقَوْلِ
وَيَعْلَمُ مَا تَكْتُمُوْنَ ﴿١١٠﴾

111. "I do not know but that it may be a trial for you, and a grant of (worldly) livelihood (to you) for a time."

111. Wa in adree la'allahoo fitnatul-lakum wa mataa'un ilaa ḥeen.

وَاِنْ اَدْرِيْ لَعَلَّهٗ فِتْنَةٌ لَّكُمْ
وَمَتَاعٌ اِلٰى حِيْنٍ ﴿١١١﴾

112. Say: "O my Lord! judge you in truth!" "Our Lord Most Gracious is the One Whose assistance should be sought against the blasphemies you utter!

112. Qaala Rabbiḥ-kum bil-ḥaqq; wa Rabbunar-Raḥmaa-nul-musta'aanu 'alaa maa taṣifoon. **(Section 7)**

قٰلَ رَبِّ احْكُمْ بِالْحَقِّ ؕ وَرَبُّنَا
الرَّحْمٰنُ الْمُسْتَعَانُ عَلٰى مَا
تَصِفُوْنَ ﴿١١٢﴾ ع

النصف

Ikhfa اخفاء | Ghunna غُنّہ | Ikhfa Meem Saakin اخفاء میم ساکن | Idghaam ادغام | Qalqala قلقلہ | Qalb قلب | Idghaam Meem Saakin ادغام میم ساکن

22. The Pilgrimage

In the name of Allah, Most Gracious, Most Merciful.

1. O mankind! fear your Lord! for the convulsion of the Hour (of Judgment) will be a thing terrible!

2. The Day you shall see it, every mother giving suck shall forget her suckling-babe, and every pregnant female shall drop her load (unformed): you shall see mankind as in a drunken riot, yet not drunk: but dreadful will be the Chastisement of Allah.

3. And yet among men there are such as dispute about Allah, without knowledge, and follow every evil one obstinate in rebellion!

4. About the (Evil One) it is decreed that whoever turns to him for friendship, he will lead him astray, and he will guide him to the Penalty of the Fire.

5. O mankind! if you have a doubt about the Resurrection, (consider) that We created you out of dust, then out of sperm, then out of a leech-like clot, then out of a morsel of flesh, partly formed and partly unformed, in order that We may manifest (Our power) to you; and We cause whom We will to rest in the wombs for an appointed term, then do We bring you out as babes, then (foster you) that you may reach your age of full strength; and some of you are called to die, and some are sent back to the feeblest old age, so that they know nothing after having known (much), and (further), you see the earth

Sûrat al-Ḥajj–22

(Revealed at Madinah)

Bismillaahir Raḥmaanir Raḥeem

1. Yaaa ayyuhan-naasuttaqoo Rabbakum; inna zalzalatas-Saa'ati shay'un 'azeem.

2. Yawma tarawnahaa tazhalu kullu murḍi'atin 'ammaaa arḍa'at wa taḍa'u kullu Zaati ḥamlin ḥamlahaa wa tarannaasa sukaaraa wa maa hum bisukaaraa wa laakinna 'azaabal-laahi shadeed.

3. Wa minan-naasi mañy-yujaadilu fil-laahi bighayri 'ilmiñw-wa yattabi'u kullaa shayṭaanim-mareed.

4. Kutiba 'alayhi annahoo man tawallaahu fa-annahoo yuḍil-luhoo wa yahdeehi ilaa 'azaa-bis-sa'eer.

5. Yaaa-ayyuhan-naasu in kuntum fee raybim-minal-ba'si fa-innaa khalaqnaakum-min turaabin summa min nuṭfatin summa min 'alaqatin summa mim-muḍghatim-mukhal-laqatiñw-wa ghayri mukhalla-qatil-linubayyina lakum; wa nuqirru fil-arḥaami maa nashaaa'u ilaaa ajalim-musam-man summa nukhrijukum ṭiflan summa litablughooo ashud-dakum wa minkum-mañy-yutawaffaa wa minkum-mañy-yuraddu ilaaa arzalil-'umuri likaylaa ya'lama mim ba'di 'ilmin shay'aa; wa taral-arḍa

(٢٢) سُورَةُ الْحَجِّ مَدَنِيَّةٌ (١٠٣)

بِسْمِ اللَّهِ الرَّحْمَٰنِ الرَّحِيمِ

يَٰٓأَيُّهَا النَّاسُ اتَّقُوا رَبَّكُمْ ۚ إِنَّ
زَلْزَلَةَ السَّاعَةِ شَيْءٌ عَظِيمٌ ①
يَوْمَ تَرَوْنَهَا تَذْهَلُ كُلُّ مُرْضِعَةٍ
عَمَّآ أَرْضَعَتْ وَتَضَعُ كُلُّ ذَاتِ
حَمْلٍ حَمْلَهَا وَتَرَى النَّاسَ
سُكَٰرَىٰ وَمَا هُم بِسُكَٰرَىٰ وَلَٰكِنَّ
عَذَابَ اللَّهِ شَدِيدٌ ②
وَمِنَ النَّاسِ مَن يُجَٰدِلُ فِي اللَّهِ
بِغَيْرِ عِلْمٍ وَيَتَّبِعُ كُلَّ شَيْطَٰنٍ
مَّرِيدٍ ③
كُتِبَ عَلَيْهِ أَنَّهُ مَن تَوَلَّاهُ
فَأَنَّهُ يُضِلُّهُ وَيَهْدِيهِ إِلَىٰ
عَذَابِ السَّعِيرِ ④
يَٰٓأَيُّهَا النَّاسُ إِن كُنتُمْ فِي
رَيْبٍ مِّنَ الْبَعْثِ فَإِنَّا خَلَقْنَٰكُم
مِّن تُرَابٍ ثُمَّ مِن نُّطْفَةٍ ثُمَّ مِنْ
عَلَقَةٍ ثُمَّ مِن مُّضْغَةٍ مُّخَلَّقَةٍ
وَغَيْرِ مُخَلَّقَةٍ لِّنُبَيِّنَ لَكُمْ ۚ وَ
نُقِرُّ فِي الْأَرْحَامِ مَا نَشَآءُ إِلَىٰٓ أَجَلٍ
مُّسَمًّى ثُمَّ نُخْرِجُكُمْ طِفْلًا ثُمَّ
لِتَبْلُغُوٓا أَشُدَّكُمْ ۖ وَمِنكُم مَّن
يُتَوَفَّىٰ وَمِنكُم مَّن يُرَدُّ إِلَىٰٓ
أَرْذَلِ الْعُمُرِ لِكَيْلَا يَعْلَمَ مِنۢ
بَعْدِ عِلْمٍ شَيْـًٔا ۚ وَتَرَى الْأَرْضَ

Ikhfa اخفاء | Ghunna غُنّہ | Ikhfa Meem Saakin اخفاء میم ساکن | Idghaam ادغام | Qalqala قلقلہ | Qalb قلب | Idghaam Meem Saakin ادغام میم ساکن

barren and lifeless, but when We pour down rain on it, it is stirred (to life), it swells, and it puts forth every kind of beautiful growth (in pairs).

6. This is so, because Allah is the Reality: it is He Who gives life to the dead, and it is He Who has power over all things.

7. And verily the Hour will come: there can be no doubt about it, or about (the fact) that Allah will raise up all who are in the graves.

8. Yet there is among men such a one as disputes about Allah, without knowledge, without guidance, and without a Book of Enlightenment,-

9. (Disdainfully) bending his side, in order to lead (men) astray from the Path of Allah: for him there is disgrace in this life, and on the Day of Judgment We shall make him taste the Penalty of burning (Fire).

10. (It will be said): "This is because of the deeds which your hands sent forth, for verily Allah is not unjust to His servants.

11. There are among men some who serve Allah, as it were, on the verge: if good befalls them, they are, there-with, well content; but if a trial comes to them, they turn on their faces: they lose both this world and the Hereafter: that is loss for all to see!

12. They call on such deities, besides Allah, as can neither hurt nor profit them: that is straying far indeed (from the Way)!

13. (Perhaps) they call on one whose hurt is nearer than his profit: evil, indeed, is the patron, and evil the companion (or help)!

haamidatan fa-izaaa anzalnaa 'alayhal-maaa'ah-tazzat wa rabat wa ambatat min kulli zawjim baheej.

6. Zaalika bi-annal-laaha Huwal-ḥaqqu wa annahoo yuḥyil-mawtaa wa annahoo 'alaa kulli shay'in Qadeer.

7. Wa annas-Saa'ata aatiya-tul-laa rayba feehaa wa annal-laaha yab'asu man fil-quboor.

8. Wa minan-naasi mañy-yujaadilu fil-laahi bighayri 'ilmiñw-wa laa hudañw-wa laa Kitaabim-Muneer.

9. Saaniya 'itfihee liyuḍilla 'an sabeelil-laahi lahoo fiddun-yaa khizyuñw-wa nuzeequhoo Yawmal-Qiyaamati 'azaabal-ḥareeq.

10. Zaalika bimaa qaddamat yadaaka wa annal-laaha laysa biẓallaamil-lil'abeed. **(Section 1)**

11. Wa minan-naasi mañy-ya'budul-laaha 'alaa ḥarfin fa-in aṣaabahoo khayrunit-ma-anna bihee wa in aṣaabat-hu fitnatunin-qalaba 'alaa wajhi-hee khasirad-dunyaa wal-Aakhirah; zaalika huwal-khusraanul-mubeen.

12. Yad'oo min doonil-laahi maa laa yaḍurruhoo wa maa laa yanfa'uh; zaalika huwaḍ-ḍalaalul-ba'eed.

13. Yad'oo laman ḍarruhooo aqrabu min-naf'ih; labi'sal-mawlaa wa labi'sal-'asheer.

هَامِدَةً فَإِذَآ أَنزَلْنَا عَلَيْهَا
الْمَآءَ اهْتَزَّتْ وَرَبَتْ وَأَنۢبَتَتْ
مِن كُلِّ زَوْجٍۭ بَهِيجٍ ٥
ذَٰلِكَ بِأَنَّ اللَّهَ هُوَ الْحَقُّ وَأَنَّهُۥ
يُحْيِ الْمَوْتَىٰ وَأَنَّهُۥ عَلَىٰ كُلِّ شَيْءٍ
قَدِيرٌ ٦
وَأَنَّ السَّاعَةَ ءَاتِيَةٌ لَّا رَيْبَ فِيهَا
وَأَنَّ اللَّهَ يَبْعَثُ مَن فِي الْقُبُورِ ٧
وَمِنَ النَّاسِ مَن يُجَٰدِلُ فِي
اللَّهِ بِغَيْرِ عِلْمٍ وَلَا هُدًى وَلَا
كِتَٰبٍ مُّنِيرٍ ٨
ثَانِيَ عِطْفِهِۦ لِيُضِلَّ عَن سَبِيلِ اللَّهِ
لَهُۥ فِي الدُّنْيَا خِزْيٌ وَنُذِيقُهُۥ
يَوْمَ الْقِيَٰمَةِ عَذَابَ الْحَرِيقِ ٩
ذَٰلِكَ بِمَا قَدَّمَتْ يَدَاكَ وَأَنَّ اللَّهَ
لَيْسَ بِظَلَّٰمٍ لِّلْعَبِيدِ ١٠ ع ٨
وَمِنَ النَّاسِ مَن يَعْبُدُ اللَّهَ عَلَىٰ
حَرْفٍ فَإِنْ أَصَابَهُۥ خَيْرٌ اطْمَأَنَّ
بِهِۦ وَإِنْ أَصَابَتْهُ فِتْنَةٌ انقَلَبَ
عَلَىٰ وَجْهِهِۦ خَسِرَ الدُّنْيَا وَالْءَاخِرَةَ
ذَٰلِكَ هُوَ الْخُسْرَانُ الْمُبِينُ ١١
يَدْعُوا مِن دُونِ اللَّهِ مَا لَا يَضُرُّهُۥ
وَمَا لَا يَنفَعُهُۥ ذَٰلِكَ هُوَ الضَّلَٰلُ
الْبَعِيدُ ١٢
يَدْعُوا لَمَن ضَرُّهُۥٓ أَقْرَبُ مِن نَّفْعِهِۦ
لَبِئْسَ الْمَوْلَىٰ وَلَبِئْسَ الْعَشِيرُ ١٣

Ikhfa اخفاء | Ghunna غُنّہ | Ikhfa Meem Saakin اخفاء میم ساکن | Idghaam ادغام | Qalqala قلقلہ | Qalb قلب | Idghaam Meem Saakin ادغام میم ساکن

14. Verily Allah will admit those who believe and work righteous deeds, to Gardens, beneath which rivers flow: for Allah carries out all that He plans.

14. Innal-laaha yudkhilul-lazeena aamanoo wa 'amiluṣ-ṣaaliḥaati Jannaatin tajree min taḥtihal-anhaar; innal-laaha yaf'alu maa yureed.

إِنَّ اللَّهَ يُدْخِلُ الَّذِينَ آمَنُوا وَعَمِلُوا الصَّالِحَاتِ جَنَّاتٍ تَجْرِي مِن تَحْتِهَا الْأَنْهَارُ ۚ إِنَّ اللَّهَ يَفْعَلُ مَا يُرِيدُ ﴿١٤﴾

15. If any think that Allah will not help him (His Messenger) in this world and the Hereafter, let him stretch out a rope to the ceiling and cut (himself) off: then let him see whether his plan will remove that which enrages (him)!

15. Man kaana yaẓunnu allañy-yanṣurahul-laahu fid-dunyaa wal-Aakhirati fal-yamdud bisababin ilas-samaaa'i summal-yaqṭa' falyanẓur hal yuẓhibanna kayduhoo maa yagheeẓ.

مَن كَانَ يَظُنُّ أَن لَّن يَنصُرَهُ اللَّهُ فِي الدُّنْيَا وَالْآخِرَةِ فَلْيَمْدُدْ بِسَبَبٍ إِلَى السَّمَاءِ ثُمَّ لْيَقْطَعْ فَلْيَنظُرْ هَلْ يُذْهِبَنَّ كَيْدُهُ مَا يَغِيظُ ﴿١٥﴾

16. Thus have We sent down Clear Sings; and verily Allah does guide whom He will!

16. Wa kazaalika anzalnaahu Aayaatim bayyinaatiñw-wa annal-laaha yahdee mañy-yureed.

وَكَذَٰلِكَ أَنزَلْنَاهُ آيَاتٍ بَيِّنَاتٍ وَأَنَّ اللَّهَ يَهْدِي مَن يُرِيدُ ﴿١٦﴾

17. Those who believe (in the Qur'an), those who follow the Jewish (scriptures), and the Sabians, Christians, Magians, and Polytheists,- Allah will judge between them on the Day of Judgment: for Allah is Witness of all things.

17. Innal-lazeena aamanoo wallazeena haadoo waṣ-Ṣaabi'eena wan-Naṣaaraa wal-Majoosa wallazeena ashrakooo innal-laaha yafṣilu baynahum Yawmal-Qiyaamah; innal-laaha 'alaa kulli shay'in Shaheed.

إِنَّ الَّذِينَ آمَنُوا وَالَّذِينَ هَادُوا وَالصَّابِئِينَ وَالنَّصَارَىٰ وَالْمَجُوسَ وَالَّذِينَ أَشْرَكُوا إِنَّ اللَّهَ يَفْصِلُ بَيْنَهُمْ يَوْمَ الْقِيَامَةِ ۚ إِنَّ اللَّهَ عَلَىٰ كُلِّ شَيْءٍ شَهِيدٌ ﴿١٧﴾

18. Do you not see that to Allah bow down in worship all things that are in the heavens and on earth,- the sun, the moon, the stars; the hills, the trees, the animals; and a great number among mankind? But a great number are (also) such as are fit for Punishment: and such as Allah shall disgrace,- None can raise to honor: for Allah carries out all that He wills.

(Bow Down)

18. Alam tara annal-laaha yasjudu lahoo man fis-samaawaati wa man fil-arḍi wash-shamsu walqamaru wan-nujoomu wal-jibaalu wash-shajaru wad-dawaaabbu wa kaseerum-minan-naasi wa kaseerun ḥaqqa 'alayhil-'azaab; wa mañy-yuhinil-laahu famaa lahoo mim-mukrim; innallaaha yaf'alu maa yashaaa'. ۩

أَلَمْ تَرَ أَنَّ اللَّهَ يَسْجُدُ لَهُ مَن فِي السَّمَاوَاتِ وَمَن فِي الْأَرْضِ وَالشَّمْسُ وَالْقَمَرُ وَالنُّجُومُ وَالْجِبَالُ وَالشَّجَرُ وَالدَّوَابُّ وَكَثِيرٌ مِّنَ النَّاسِ ۖ وَكَثِيرٌ حَقَّ عَلَيْهِ الْعَذَابُ ۗ وَمَن يُهِنِ اللَّهُ فَمَا لَهُ مِن مُّكْرِمٍ ۚ إِنَّ اللَّهَ يَفْعَلُ مَا يَشَاءُ ۩ ﴿١٨﴾

السجدة (٦)

19. These two antagonists dispute with each other about their Lord: but those who deny (their Lord),- for them will be cut out a garment of Fire: over their heads will be poured out boiling water.

19. Haazaani khaṣmaanikh-taṣamoo fee Rabbihim fal-lazeena kafaroo quṭṭi'at lahum siyaabum-min-naar; yuṣabbu min fawqi ru'oosihimul-ḥameem.

هَٰذَانِ خَصْمَانِ اخْتَصَمُوا فِي رَبِّهِمْ ۖ فَالَّذِينَ كَفَرُوا قُطِّعَتْ لَهُمْ ثِيَابٌ مِّن نَّارٍ يُصَبُّ مِن فَوْقِ رُءُوسِهِمُ الْحَمِيمُ ﴿١٩﴾

Ikhfa اخفاء | Ghunna غُنّہ | Ikhfa Meem Saakin اخفاء میم ساکن | Idghaam ادغام | Qalqala قلقلہ | Qalb قلب | Idghaam Meem Saakin ادغام میم ساکن

20. With it will be scalded what is within their bodies, as well as (their) skins.

21. In addition there will be maces of iron (to punish) them.

22. Every time they wish to get away therefrom, from anguish, they will be forced back therein, and (it will be said), "You taste the Penalty of Burning!"

23. Allah will admit those who believe and work righteous deeds, to Gardens beneath which rivers flow: they shall be adorned therein with bracelets of gold and pearls; and their garments there will be of silk.

24. For they have been guided (in this life) to the purest of speeches; they have been guided to the Path of Him Who is Worthy of (all) Praise.

25. As to those who have rejected (Allah), and would keep back (men) from the Way of Allah, and from the Sacred Mosque, which We have made (open) to (all) men - equal is the dweller there and the visitor from the country - and any whose purpose therein is profanity or wrong-doing - them will We cause to taste of a most grievous Penalty.

26. Behold! We gave the site, to Abraham, of the (Sacred) House, (saying): "Do not associate anything (in worship) with Me; and sanctify My House for those who compass it round, or stand up, or bow, or prostrate them-selves (therein in prayer).

27. "And proclaim the Pilgrimage among men: they will come to you on foot and (mounted) on every kind of camel, lean on account of journeys through deep and distant mountain highways;

28. "That they may witness the benefits (provided) for them, and celebrate

20. Yuṣharu bihee maa fee buṭoonihim waljulood.

21. Wa lahum-maqaami'u min ḥadeed.

22. Kullamaaa araadooo añy-yakhrujoo minhaa min ghammin u'eedoo feehaa wa zooqoo 'azaabal-ḥareeq. **(Sec. 2)**

23. Innal-laaha yudkhilul-lazeena aamanoo wa 'amiluṣ-ṣaaliḥaati Jannaatin tajree min taḥtihal-anhaaru yuḥallawna feehaa min asaawira min zahabiñw-wa lu'lu'aa; wa libaasuhum feehaa ḥareer.

24. Wa hudooo ilaṭ-ṭayyibi minal-qawli wa hudooo ilaa ṣiraaṭil-ḥameed.

25. Innal-lazeena kafaroo wa yaṣuddoona 'an sabeelil-laahi wal-Masjidil-Ḥaraamil-lazee ja'alnaahu linnaasi sawaaa'a-nil-'aakifu feehi walbaad; wa mañy-yurid feehi bi-ilḥaadim bizulmin-nuziqhu min 'azaabin aleem. **(Section 3)**

26. Wa iz bawwaånaa li-Ibraaheema makaanal-Bayti al-laa tushrik bee shay'añw-wa ṭahhir Baytiya liṭṭaaa'ifeena walqaaa'imeena warrukka'is-sujood.

27. Wa azzin fin-naasi bil-Ḥajji yaåtooka rijaalañw-wa 'alaa kulli ḍaamiriñy-yaåteena min kulli fajjin 'ameeq.

28. Li-yashhadoo manaafi'a lahum wa yazkurus-

يُصْهَرُ بِهِ مَا فِي بُطُونِهِمْ وَالْجُلُودُ ﴿٢٠﴾
وَلَهُمْ مَّقَامِعُ مِنْ حَدِيدٍ ﴿٢١﴾
كُلَّمَآ أَرَادُوٓا أَن يَخْرُجُوا مِنْهَا
مِنْ غَمٍّ أُعِيدُوا فِيهَا وَذُوقُوا
عَذَابَ الْحَرِيقِ ﴿٢٢﴾
إِنَّ اللَّهَ يُدْخِلُ الَّذِينَ آمَنُوا وَ
عَمِلُوا الصَّٰلِحَٰتِ جَنَّٰتٍ تَجْرِي
مِن تَحْتِهَا الْأَنْهَٰرُ يُحَلَّوْنَ فِيهَا
مِنْ أَسَاوِرَ مِن ذَهَبٍ وَلُؤْلُؤًا
وَلِبَاسُهُمْ فِيهَا حَرِيرٌ ﴿٢٣﴾
وَهُدُوٓا إِلَى الطَّيِّبِ مِنَ الْقَوْلِ
وَهُدُوٓا إِلَىٰ صِرَٰطِ الْحَمِيدِ ﴿٢٤﴾
إِنَّ الَّذِينَ كَفَرُوا وَيَصُدُّونَ
عَن سَبِيلِ اللَّهِ وَالْمَسْجِدِ الْحَرَامِ
الَّذِي جَعَلْنَٰهُ لِلنَّاسِ سَوَآءً
الْعَٰكِفُ فِيهِ وَالْبَادِ وَمَن
يُرِدْ فِيهِ بِإِلْحَادٍ بِظُلْمٍ نُّذِقْهُ
مِنْ عَذَابٍ أَلِيمٍ ﴿٢٥﴾
وَإِذْ بَوَّأْنَا لِإِبْرَٰهِيمَ مَكَانَ الْبَيْتِ
أَن لَّا تُشْرِكْ بِي شَيْـًٔا وَطَهِّرْ
بَيْتِيَ لِلطَّآئِفِينَ وَالْقَآئِمِينَ
وَالرُّكَّعِ السُّجُودِ ﴿٢٦﴾
وَأَذِّن فِي النَّاسِ بِالْحَجِّ يَأْتُوكَ
رِجَالًا وَعَلَىٰ كُلِّ ضَامِرٍ يَأْتِينَ
مِن كُلِّ فَجٍّ عَمِيقٍ ﴿٢٧﴾
لِّيَشْهَدُوا مَنَٰفِعَ لَهُمْ وَيَذْكُرُوا

Ikhfa اخفاء | Ghunna غُنّہ | Ikhfa Meem Saakin اخفاء میم ساکن | Idghaam ادغام | Qalqala قلقلہ | Qalb قلب | Idghaam Meem Saakin ادغام میم ساکن

the name of Allah, through the Days appointed, over the cattle which He has provided for them (for sacrifice): then you eat thereof and feed the distressed ones in want.

mal-laahi feee ayyaamim-ma'loomaatin 'alaa maa razaqahum-mim baheematil-an'aami fakuloo minhaa wa aṭ'imul-baaa'isal-faqeer.

اسْمَ اللّٰهِ فِيْٓ اَيَّامٍ مَّعْلُوْمٰتٍ
عَلٰى مَا رَزَقَهُمْ مِّنْۢ بَهِيْمَةِ
الْاَنْعَامِ ۚ فَكُلُوْا مِنْهَا وَاَطْعِمُوا
الْبَآئِسَ الْفَقِيْرَ ﴿٢٨﴾

29. "Then let them complete the rites prescribed for them, perform their vows, and (again) circumambulate the Ancient House."

29. Summal-yaqḍoo tafasahum wal-yoofoo nuzoorahum wal-yaṭṭawwafoo bil-Baytil-'Ateeq.

ثُمَّ لْيَقْضُوْا تَفَثَهُمْ وَلْيُوْفُوْا نُذُوْرَهُمْ
وَلْيَطَّوَّفُوْا بِالْبَيْتِ الْعَتِيْقِ ﴿٢٩﴾

30. Such (is the Pilgrimage): whoever honors the sacred rites of Allah, for him it is good in the sight of his Lord. Lawful to you (for food in Pilgrimage) are cattle, except those men-tioned to you (as exception): but shun the abomination of idols, and shun the word that is false,-

30. Zaalika wa mañy-yu'azzim ḥurumaatil-laahi fahuwa khayrul-lahoo 'inda Rabbih; wa uḥillat lakumul-an'aamu illaa maa yutlaa 'alaykum fajtanibur-rijsa minal-awsaani wajtaniboo qawlaz-zoor.

ذٰلِكَ ۚ وَمَنْ يُّعَظِّمْ حُرُمٰتِ اللّٰهِ
فَهُوَ خَيْرٌ لَّهٗ عِنْدَ رَبِّهٖ ۗ وَاُحِلَّتْ
لَكُمُ الْاَنْعَامُ اِلَّا مَا يُتْلٰى عَلَيْكُمْ
فَاجْتَنِبُوا الرِّجْسَ مِنَ الْاَوْثَانِ
وَاجْتَنِبُوْا قَوْلَ الزُّوْرِ ﴿٣٠﴾

31. Being true in faith to Allah, and never assigning partners to Him: if anyone assigns partners to Allah, he is as if he had fallen from heaven and been snatched up by birds, or the wind had swooped (like a bird on its prey) and thrown him into a far- distant place.

31. Ḥunafaaa'a lillaahi ghayra mushrikeena bih; wa mañy-yushrik billaahi faka-annamaa-kharra minas-samaaa'i fatakhṭafuhuṭ-ṭayru aw tahwee bihir-reeḥu fee makaanin saḥeeq.

حُنَفَآءَ لِلّٰهِ غَيْرَ مُشْرِكِيْنَ بِهٖ ۗ
وَمَنْ يُّشْرِكْ بِاللّٰهِ فَكَاَنَّمَا خَرَّ مِنَ
السَّمَآءِ فَتَخْطَفُهُ الطَّيْرُ اَوْ تَهْوِيْ
بِهِ الرِّيْحُ فِيْ مَكَانٍ سَحِيْقٍ ﴿٣١﴾

32. Such (is his state): and whoever holds in honor the symbols of Allah, (in the sacrifice of animals), such (honor) should come truly from piety of heart.

32. Zaalika wa mañy- yu'azzim sha'aaa'iral-laahi fa-innahaa min taqwal-quloob.

ذٰلِكَ ۚ وَمَنْ يُّعَظِّمْ شَعَآئِرَ اللّٰهِ
فَاِنَّهَا مِنْ تَقْوَى الْقُلُوْبِ ﴿٣٢﴾

33. In them you have benefits for a term appointed: in the end their place of sacrifice is near the Ancient House.

33. Lakum feehaa manaafi'u ilaaa ajalim-musamman summa maḥilluhaaa ilal-Baytil-'Ateeq.

(Section 4)

لَكُمْ فِيْهَا مَنَافِعُ اِلٰٓى اَجَلٍ مُّسَمًّى
ثُمَّ مَحِلُّهَآ اِلَى الْبَيْتِ الْعَتِيْقِ ﴿٣٣﴾

34. To every people did We appoint rites (of sacrifice), that they might celebrate the name of Allah over the sustenance He gave them from animals (fit for food). But your God is One Allah: submit then your wills to Him (in Islam): and you give the good news to those who humble themselves,-

34. Wa likulli ummatin ja'alnaa mansakal-liyazkurus-mal-laahi 'alaa maa razaqahum mim baheematil-an'aam; fa-ilaahukum Ilaahuñw-Waaḥidun falahooo aslimoo; wa bash-shiril-mukhbiteen.

وَلِكُلِّ اُمَّةٍ جَعَلْنَا مَنْسَكًا لِّيَذْكُرُوا
اسْمَ اللّٰهِ عَلٰى مَا رَزَقَهُمْ مِّنْۢ بَهِيْمَةِ
الْاَنْعَامِ ۗ فَاِلٰهُكُمْ اِلٰهٌ وَّاحِدٌ فَلَهٗٓ
اَسْلِمُوْا ۗ وَبَشِّرِ الْمُخْبِتِيْنَ ﴿٣٤﴾

35. To those whose hearts, when Allah is mentioned, are filled with fear, who show patient perseverance over their afflictions, keep up regular prayer,

35. Allazeena izaa zukiral-laahu wajilat quloobuhum waṣṣaabireena 'alaa maaa aṣaabahum walmuqeemiṣ-Ṣalaati

الَّذِيْنَ اِذَا ذُكِرَ اللّٰهُ وَجِلَتْ
قُلُوْبُهُمْ وَالصّٰبِرِيْنَ عَلٰى مَا
اَصَابَهُمْ وَالْمُقِيْمِي الصَّلٰوةِ ۙ

Ikhfa اخفاء | Ghunna غُنّہ | Ikhfa Meem Saakin اخفاء میم ساکن | Idghaam ادغام | Qalqala قلقلہ | Qalb قلب | Idghaam Meem Saakin ادغام میم ساکن

and spend (in charity) out of what We have bestowed upon them.

36. The sacrificial camels We have made for you as among the symbols from Allah: in them is (much) good for you: then pronounce the name of Allah over them as they line up (for sacrifice): when they are down on their sides (after slaughter), you eat thereof, and feed such as (beg not but) live in contentment, and such as beg with due humility: thus have We made animals subject to you, that you may be grateful.

37. It is not their meat nor their blood, that reaches Allah: it is your piety that reaches Him: He has thus made them subject to you, that you may glorify Allah for His guidance to you and proclaim the good news to all who do right.

38. Verily Allah will defend (from ill) those who believe: verily, Allah loves not any that is a traitor to faith, or show ingratitude.

39. To those against whom war is made, permission is given (to fight), because they are wronged;- and verily, Allah is most powerful for their aid;-

40. (They are) those who have been expelled from their homes in defiance of right,- (for no cause) except that they say, "Our Lord is Allah". Did not Allah check one set of people by means of another, there would surely have been pulled down monasteries, churches, synagogues, and mosques, in which the name of Allah is commemorated in abundant measure. Allah will certainly aid those who aid His (cause);- for verily Allah is full of Strength, Exalted in Might, (able to enforce His Will).

41. (They are) those who, if We establish them in the land, establish regular prayer and give regular charity,

wa mimmaa razaqnaahum yunfiqoon.

36. Walbudna ja'alnaahaa lakum-min sha'aa'iril-laahi lakum feehaa khayrun faz̲kurusmal-laahi 'alayhaa ṣawaaff; fa-iz̲aa wajabat junoobuhaa fakuloo minhaa wa aṭ'imul-qaani'a walmu'tarr; kaz̲aalika sakhkharnaahaa lakum la'allakum tashkuroon.

37. Lañy-yanaalal-laaha luḥoomuhaa wa laa dimaaa'uhaa wa laakiñy-yanaaluhut-taqwaa minkum; kaz̲aalika sakhkharahaa lakum litukabbirul-laaha 'alaa maa hadaakum; wa bashshiril-muḥsineen.

38. Innal-laaha yudaafi'u 'anil-laz̲eena aamanoo; innal-laaha laa yuḥibbu kulla khawwaanin kafoor. **(Section 5)**

39. Uz̲ina lillaz̲eena yuqaataloona bi-annahum ẓulimoo; wa innal-laaha 'alaa naṣrihim la-Qadeer.

40. Allaz̲eena ukhrijoo min diyaarihim bighayri ḥaqqin illaaa añy-yaqooloo Rabbunal-laah; wa law laa daf'ul-laahin-naasa ba'ḍahum biba'ḍil-lahuddimat ṣawaami'u wa biya'uñw-wa ṣalawaatuñw-wa masaajidu yuz̲karu feehasmul-laahi kas̲eeraa; wa layanṣurannal-laahu mañy-yanṣuruh; innal-laaha la-Qawiyyun 'Azeez.

41. Allaz̲eena im-makkannaahum fil-arḍi aqaamuṣ-Ṣalaata wa-aatawuz-Zakaata

وَمِمَّا رَزَقْنٰهُمْ يُنْفِقُوْنَ ۝٣٥
وَالْبُدْنَ جَعَلْنٰهَا لَكُمْ مِّنْ شَعَآئِرِ
اللّٰهِ لَكُمْ فِيْهَا خَيْرٌ ۖ فَاذْكُرُوا اسْمَ
اللّٰهِ عَلَيْهَا صَوَآفَّ ۚ فَاِذَا وَجَبَتْ
جُنُوْبُهَا فَكُلُوْا مِنْهَا وَاَطْعِمُوا
الْقَانِعَ وَالْمُعْتَرَّ ؕ كَذٰلِكَ سَخَّرْنٰهَا
لَكُمْ لَعَلَّكُمْ تَشْكُرُوْنَ ۝٣٦
لَنْ يَّنَالَ اللّٰهَ لُحُوْمُهَا وَلَا
دِمَآؤُهَا وَلٰكِنْ يَّنَالُهُ التَّقْوٰى
مِنْكُمْ ؕ كَذٰلِكَ سَخَّرَهَا لَكُمْ
لِتُكَبِّرُوا اللّٰهَ عَلٰى مَا هَدٰىكُمْ ؕ
وَبَشِّرِ الْمُحْسِنِيْنَ ۝٣٧
اِنَّ اللّٰهَ يُدٰفِعُ عَنِ الَّذِيْنَ اٰمَنُوْا ؕ اِنَّ
اللّٰهَ لَا يُحِبُّ كُلَّ خَوَّانٍ كَفُوْرٍ ۝٣٨ ع
اُذِنَ لِلَّذِيْنَ يُقٰتَلُوْنَ بِاَنَّهُمْ ظُلِمُوْا ؕ
وَاِنَّ اللّٰهَ عَلٰى نَصْرِهِمْ لَقَدِيْرُ ۝٣٩
الَّذِيْنَ اُخْرِجُوْا مِنْ دِيَارِهِمْ بِغَيْرِ
حَقٍّ اِلَّآ اَنْ يَّقُوْلُوْا رَبُّنَا اللّٰهُ ؕ
وَلَوْلَا دَفْعُ اللّٰهِ النَّاسَ بَعْضَهُمْ
بِبَعْضٍ لَّهُدِّمَتْ صَوَامِعُ وَبِيَعٌ
وَّصَلَوٰتٌ وَّمَسٰجِدُ يُذْكَرُ فِيْهَا
اسْمُ اللّٰهِ كَثِيْرًا ؕ وَلَيَنْصُرَنَّ
اللّٰهُ مَنْ يَّنْصُرُهٗ ؕ اِنَّ اللّٰهَ
لَقَوِيٌّ عَزِيْزٌ ۝٤٠
اَلَّذِيْنَ اِنْ مَّكَّنّٰهُمْ فِي الْاَرْضِ
اَقَامُوا الصَّلٰوةَ وَاٰتَوُا الزَّكٰوةَ

enjoin the right and forbid wrong: with Allah rests the end (and decision) of (all) affairs.

wa amaroo bilma'roofi wa nahaw 'anil-munkar; wa lillaahi 'aaqibatul-umoor.

وَاَمَرُوْا بِالْمَعْرُوْفِ وَنَهَوْا عَنِ
الْمُنْكَرِ ؕ وَلِلّٰهِ عَاقِبَةُ الْاُمُوْرِ ﴿٤١﴾

42. If they treat your (mission) as false so did the peoples before them (with their prophets),- the People of Noah, and 'Ad and Thamud;

42. Wa iñy-yukazzibooka faqad kazzabat qablahum qawmu Nooḥiñw-wa 'Aaduñw-wa Samood.

وَاِنْ يُّكَذِّبُوْكَ فَقَدْ كَذَّبَتْ
قَبْلَهُمْ قَوْمُ نُوْحٍ وَّعَادٌ وَّثَمُوْدُ ﴿٤٢﴾

43. Those of Abraham and Lut;

43. Wa qawmu Ibraaheema wa qawmu Loot.

وَقَوْمُ اِبْرٰهِيْمَ وَقَوْمُ لُوْطٍ ﴿٤٣﴾

44. And the Companions of the Madyan People; and Moses was rejected (in the same way). But I granted respite to the Unbelievers, and (only) after that did I punish them: but how (terrible) was My rejection (of them)!

44. Wa aṣ-ḥaabu Madyana wa kuzziba Moosaa fa-amlaytu lilkaafireena summa akhaztu-hum fakayfa kaana nakeer.

وَّاَصْحٰبُ مَدْيَنَ ۚ وَكُذِّبَ مُوْسٰى
فَاَمْلَيْتُ لِلْكٰفِرِيْنَ ثُمَّ اَخَذْتُهُمْ ۚ
فَكَيْفَ كَانَ نَكِيْرِ ﴿٤٤﴾

45. How many populations have We destroyed, which were given to wrong-doing? They tumbled down on their roofs. And how many wells are lying idle and neglected, and castles lofty and well-built?

45. Faka-ayyim-min qaryatin ahlaknaahaa wa hiya ẓaali-matun fahiya khaawiyatun 'alaa 'urooshihaa wa bi'rim-mu'aṭ-ṭalatiñw-wa qaṣrim-masheed.

فَكَاَيِّنْ مِّنْ قَرْيَةٍ اَهْلَكْنٰهَا
وَهِيَ ظَالِمَةٌ فَهِيَ خَاوِيَةٌ
عَلٰى عُرُوْشِهَا وَبِئْرٍ مُّعَطَّلَةٍ وَّ
قَصْرٍ مَّشِيْدٍ ﴿٤٥﴾

46. Do they not travel through the land, so that their hearts (and minds) may thus learn wisdom and their ears may thus learn to hear? Truly it is not their eyes that are blind, but their hearts which are in their breasts.

46. Afalam yaseeroo fil-arḍi fatakoona lahum qulooobuñy-ya'qiloona bihaaa aw aazaa-nuñy-yasma'oona bihaa fa-innahaa laa ta'mal-abṣaaru wa laakin ta'mal-quloobul-latee fiṣ-ṣudoor.

اَفَلَمْ يَسِيْرُوْا فِى الْاَرْضِ فَتَكُوْنَ
لَهُمْ قُلُوْبٌ يَّعْقِلُوْنَ بِهَاۤ اَوْ اٰذَانٌ
يَّسْمَعُوْنَ بِهَا ۚ فَاِنَّهَا لَا تَعْمَى
الْاَبْصَارُ وَلٰكِنْ تَعْمَى الْقُلُوْبُ
الَّتِىْ فِى الصُّدُوْرِ ﴿٤٦﴾

47. Yet they ask you to hasten on the Punishment! But Allah will not fail in His Promise. Verily a Day in the sight of your Lord is like a thousand years of your reckoning.

47. Wa yasta'jiloonaka bil-'azaabi wa lañy-yukhlifal-laahu wa'dah; wa inna yawman 'inda-Rabbika ka-alfi sanatim-mimmaa ta'uddoon.

وَيَسْتَعْجِلُوْنَكَ بِالْعَذَابِ وَ
لَنْ يُّخْلِفَ اللّٰهُ وَعْدَهٗ ؕ وَاِنَّ
يَوْمًا عِنْدَ رَبِّكَ كَاَلْفِ سَنَةٍ
مِّمَّا تَعُدُّوْنَ ﴿٤٧﴾

48. And to how many populations did I give respite, which were given to wrong-doing? In the end I punished them. To me is the destination (of all).

48. Wa ka-ayyim-min qarya-tin amlaytu lahaa wa hiya ẓaalimatun summa akhaztuhaa wa ilayyal-maṣeer. **(Section 6)**

وَكَاَيِّنْ مِّنْ قَرْيَةٍ اَمْلَيْتُ لَهَا
وَهِيَ ظَالِمَةٌ ثُمَّ اَخَذْتُهَا ۚ
وَاِلَىَّ الْمَصِيْرُ ﴿٤٨﴾

49. Say: "O men! I am (sent) to you only to give a Clear Warning:

49. Qul yaaa ayyuhan-naasu innamaaa ana lakum nazeerum-mubeen.

قُلْ يٰۤاَيُّهَا النَّاسُ اِنَّمَاۤ اَنَا
لَكُمْ نَذِيْرٌ مُّبِيْنٌ ﴿٤٩﴾

50. "Those who believe and work righteousness, for them is forgiveness and a sustenance most generous.

50. Fallaẕeena aamanoo wa 'amiluṣ-ṣaaliḥaati lahum-maghfiratuñw-wa rizqun kareem.

فَالَّذِيْنَ اٰمَنُوْا وَعَمِلُوا الصّٰلِحٰتِ لَهُمْ مَّغْفِرَةٌ وَّرِزْقٌ كَرِيْمٌ ﴿٥٠﴾

51. "But those who strive against Our Signs, to frustrate them,- they will be Companions of the Fire."

51. Wallaẕeena sa'aw feee Aayaatinaa mu'aajizeena ulaaa'ika Aṣ-ḥaabul-jaḥeem.

وَالَّذِيْنَ سَعَوْا فِيْٓ اٰيٰتِنَا مُعٰجِزِيْنَ اُولٰٓئِكَ اَصْحٰبُ الْجَحِيْمِ ﴿٥١﴾

52. Never did We send a Messenger or a prophet before you, but, when he framed a desire, Satan threw some (vanity) into his desire: but Allah will cancel anything (vain) that Satan throws in, and Allah will confirm (and establish) His Signs: for Allah is full of Knowledge and Wisdom:

52. Wa maaa arsalnaa min qablika mir-Rasooliñw-wa laa Nabiyyin illaaa iẕaa tamannaaa alqash-Shayṭaanu feee umniyyatihee fa-yansakhul-laahu maa yulqish-Shayṭaanu summa yuḥkimul-laahu Aayaatih; wallaahu 'Aleemun Ḥakeem.

وَمَآ اَرْسَلْنَا مِنْ قَبْلِكَ مِنْ رَّسُوْلٍ وَّلَا نَبِيٍّ اِلَّآ اِذَا تَمَنّٰٓى اَلْقَى الشَّيْطٰنُ فِيْٓ اُمْنِيَّتِهٖ ۚ فَيَنْسَخُ اللّٰهُ مَا يُلْقِي الشَّيْطٰنُ ثُمَّ يُحْكِمُ اللّٰهُ اٰيٰتِهٖ ۗ وَاللّٰهُ عَلِيْمٌ حَكِيْمٌ ۙ﴿٥٢﴾

53. That He may make the suggestions thrown in by Satan, but a trial for those in whose hearts is a disease and who are hardened of heart: verily the wrong-doers are in a schism far (from the Truth):

53. Liyaj'ala maa yulqish-Shayṭaanu fitnatal-lillaẕeena fee quloobihim-maraḍuñw-walqaasiyati quloobuhum; wa innaẓ-ẓaalimeena lafee shiqaaqim-ba'eed.

لِّيَجْعَلَ مَا يُلْقِي الشَّيْطٰنُ فِتْنَةً لِّلَّذِيْنَ فِيْ قُلُوْبِهِمْ مَّرَضٌ وَّالْقَاسِيَةِ قُلُوْبُهُمْ ۗ وَاِنَّ الظّٰلِمِيْنَ لَفِيْ شِقَاقٍۢ بَعِيْدٍ ۙ﴿٥٣﴾

54. And that those on whom knowledge has been bestowed may learn that the (Qur'an) is the Truth from your Lord, and that they may believe therein, and their hearts may be made humbly (open) to it: for verily Allah is the Guide of those who believe, to the Straight Way.

54. Wa liya'lamal-laẕeena ootul-'ilma annahul-ḥaqqu mir-Rabbika fa-yu'minoo bihee fatukhbita lahoo quloobuhum; wa innal-laaha lahaadil-laẕeena aamanooo ilaa Ṣiraaṭim-Mustaqeem.

وَّلِيَعْلَمَ الَّذِيْنَ اُوْتُوا الْعِلْمَ اَنَّهُ الْحَقُّ مِنْ رَّبِّكَ فَيُؤْمِنُوْا بِهٖ فَتُخْبِتَ لَهٗ قُلُوْبُهُمْ ۗ وَاِنَّ اللّٰهَ لَهَادِ الَّذِيْنَ اٰمَنُوْٓا اِلٰى صِرَاطٍ مُّسْتَقِيْمٍ ﴿٥٤﴾

55. Those who reject Faith will not cease to be in doubt concerning (Revelation) until the Hour (of Judgment) comes suddenly upon them, or there comes to them the Penalty of a Day of Disaster.

55. Wa laa yazaalul-laẕeena kafaroo fee miryatim-minhu ḥattaa taâtiyahumus-Saa'atu baghtatan aw yaâtiyahum 'aẕaabu Yawmin 'aqeem.

وَلَا يَزَالُ الَّذِيْنَ كَفَرُوْا فِيْ مِرْيَةٍ مِّنْهُ حَتّٰى تَاْتِيَهُمُ السَّاعَةُ بَغْتَةً اَوْ يَاْتِيَهُمْ عَذَابُ يَوْمٍ عَقِيْمٍ ﴿٥٥﴾

56. On that Day the Dominion will be that of Allah: He will judge between them: so those who believe and work righteous deeds will be in Gardens of Delight.

56. Almulku Yawma'iẕil-lillaahi yaḥkumu baynahum; fallaẕeena aamanoo wa 'amiluṣ-ṣaaliḥaati fee Jannaatin-Na'eem.

اَلْمُلْكُ يَوْمَئِذٍ لِّلّٰهِ ۗ يَحْكُمُ بَيْنَهُمْ ۗ فَالَّذِيْنَ اٰمَنُوْا وَعَمِلُوا الصّٰلِحٰتِ فِيْ جَنّٰتِ النَّعِيْمِ ﴿٥٦﴾

57. And for those who reject Faith and deny our Signs,

57. Wallaẕeena kafaroo wa kaẕẕaboo bi-Aayaatinaa

وَالَّذِيْنَ كَفَرُوْا وَكَذَّبُوْا بِاٰيٰتِنَا

Ikhfa اخفاء | Ghunna غُنّہ | Ikhfa Meem Saakin اخفاء میم ساکن | Idghaam ادغام | Qalqala قلقلہ | Qalb قلب | Idghaam Meem Saakin ادغام میم ساکن

there will be a humiliating Punishment.

fa-ulaaa'ika lahum 'azaabum-muheen. **(Section 7)**

فَأُولَٰٓئِكَ لَهُمْ عَذَابٌ مُّهِينٌ ﴿٥٧﴾ ع ٩ / ١٤

58. Those who leave their homes in the cause of Allah, and are then slain or die,- On them will Allah bestow verily a goodly Provision: truly Allah is He Who bestows the best Provision.

58. Wallazeena haajaroo fee sabeelil-laahi summa qutilooo law maatoo la-yarzuqannahumul-laahu rizqan ḥasanaa; wa innal-laaha la-Huwa khayrur-raaziqeen.

وَالَّذِينَ هَاجَرُوا فِي سَبِيلِ اللَّهِ
ثُمَّ قُتِلُوٓا أَوْ مَاتُوا لَيَرْزُقَنَّهُمُ
اللَّهُ رِزْقًا حَسَنًا ۚ وَإِنَّ اللَّهَ لَهُوَ
خَيْرُ الرَّٰزِقِينَ ﴿٥٨﴾

59. Verily He will admit them to a place with which they shall be well pleased: for Allah is All-Knowing, Most Forbearing.

59. La-yudkhilan-nahum-mudkhalañy-yarḍawnah; wa innal-laaha la-'Aleemun Ḥaleem.

لَيُدْخِلَنَّهُم مُّدْخَلًا يَرْضَوْنَهُۥ ۗ
وَإِنَّ اللَّهَ لَعَلِيمٌ حَلِيمٌ ﴿٥٩﴾

60. That (is so). And if one has retaliated to no greater extent than the injury he received, and is again set upon inordinately, Allah will help him: for Allah is One that blots out (sins) and forgives (again and again).

60. Zaalika wa man 'aaqaba bimisli maa 'ooqiba bihee-summa bughiya 'alayhi la-yansurannahul-laah; innal-laaha la-'Afuwwun Ghafoor.

ذَٰلِكَ ۖ وَمَنْ عَاقَبَ بِمِثْلِ مَا
عُوقِبَ بِهِۦ ثُمَّ بُغِيَ عَلَيْهِ لَيَنصُرَنَّهُ
اللَّهُ ۗ إِنَّ اللَّهَ لَعَفُوٌّ غَفُورٌ ﴿٦٠﴾

61. That is because Allah merges night into day, and He merges day into night, and verily it is Allah Who hears and sees (all things).

61. Zaalika bi-annal-laaha yoolijul-layla fin-nahaari wa yoolijun-nahaara fil-layli wa annal-laaha Samee'um-Baṣeer.

ذَٰلِكَ بِأَنَّ اللَّهَ يُولِجُ الَّيْلَ فِي
النَّهَارِ وَيُولِجُ النَّهَارَ فِي الَّيْلِ
وَأَنَّ اللَّهَ سَمِيعٌۢ بَصِيرٌ ﴿٦١﴾

62. That is because Allah - He is the Reality; and those besides Him whom they invoke,- they are but vain Falsehood: verily Allah is He, Most High, Most Great.

62. Zaalika bi-annal-laaha Huwal-ḥaqqu wa anna maa yad'oona min doonihee huwal-baaṭilu wa annal-laaha Huwal-'Aliyyul-Kabeer.

ذَٰلِكَ بِأَنَّ اللَّهَ هُوَ الْحَقُّ وَأَنَّ مَا
يَدْعُونَ مِن دُونِهِۦ هُوَ الْبَٰطِلُ
وَأَنَّ اللَّهَ هُوَ الْعَلِيُّ الْكَبِيرُ ﴿٦٢﴾

63. Don't you see that Allah sends down rain from the sky, and forthwith the earth becomes clothed with green? for Allah is He Who understands the finest mysteries, and is well-acquainted (with them).

63. Alam tara annal-laaha anzala minas-samaaa'i maaa'an fatuṣbiḥul-arḍu mukhḍarrah; innal-laaha Laṭeefun Khabeer.

أَلَمْ تَرَ أَنَّ اللَّهَ أَنزَلَ مِنَ السَّمَآءِ
مَآءً فَتُصْبِحُ الْأَرْضُ مُخْضَرَّةً ۗ
إِنَّ اللَّهَ لَطِيفٌ خَبِيرٌ ﴿٦٣﴾

64. To Him belongs all that is in the heavens and on earth: for verily Allah,- He is free of all wants, Worthy of all Praise.

64. Lahoo maa fis-samaawaati wa maa fil-arḍ; wa innal-laaha la-Huwal-Ghaniyyul-Ḥameed. **(Section 8)**

لَهُۥ مَا فِي السَّمَٰوَٰتِ وَمَا فِي الْأَرْضِ ۗ
وَإِنَّ اللَّهَ لَهُوَ الْغَنِيُّ الْحَمِيدُ ﴿٦٤﴾ ع ١٠ / ١٥

65. Don't you see that Allah has made subject to you (men) all that is on the earth, and the ships that sail through the sea by His Command? He withholds the sky (rain) from failing on the earth except by His leave: for Allah is Most Kind and Most Merciful to man.

65. Alam tara-annal-laaha sakhkhara lakum-maa fil-arḍi walfulka tajree fil-baḥri bi-amrihee wa yumsikus-samaaa'a an taqa'a 'alal-arḍi illaa bi-iznih; innal-laaha binnaasi la-Ra'oofur-Raḥeem.

أَلَمْ تَرَ أَنَّ اللَّهَ سَخَّرَ لَكُم مَّا فِي
الْأَرْضِ وَالْفُلْكَ تَجْرِي فِي الْبَحْرِ
بِأَمْرِهِۦ وَيُمْسِكُ السَّمَآءَ أَن تَقَعَ
عَلَى الْأَرْضِ إِلَّا بِإِذْنِهِۦٓ ۗ إِنَّ
اللَّهَ بِالنَّاسِ لَرَءُوفٌ رَّحِيمٌ ﴿٦٥﴾

Ikhfa اخفاء | Ghunna غُنّہ | Ikhfa Meem Saakin اخفاء میم ساکن | Idghaam ادغام | Qalqala قلقلہ | Qalb قلب | Idghaam Meem Saakin ادغام میم ساکن

66. It is He Who gave you life, will cause you to die, and will again give you life: truly man is a most ungrateful creature!

66. Wa Huwal-laz̲eee aḥyaakum summa yumeetukum summa yuḥyeekum; innal-insaana lakafoor.

وَهُوَ الَّذِيٓ اَحْيَاكُمْ ۡ ثُمَّ
يُمِيْتُكُمْ ثُمَّ يُحْيِيْكُمْ ۭ اِنَّ
الْاِنْسَانَ لَكَفُوْرٌ ۝٦٦

67. To every people have We appointed rites and ceremonies which they must follow: let them not then dispute with you on the matter, but do you invite (them) to your Lord: for you are assuredly on the Right Way.

67. Likulli ummatin ja'alnaa mansakan hum naasikoohu falaa yunaazi'unnaka fil-amr; wad'u ilaa Rabbika innaka la'alaa hudam-mustaqeem.

لِكُلِّ اُمَّةٍ جَعَلْنَا مَنْسَكًا هُمْ
نَاسِكُوْهُ فَلَا يُنَازِعُنَّكَ فِي الْاَمْرِ
وَادْعُ اِلٰى رَبِّكَ ۭ اِنَّكَ لَعَلٰى
هُدًى مُّسْتَقِيْمٍ ۝٦٧

68. If they do wrangle with you, say, "Allah knows best what it is you are doing."

68. Wa in jaadalooka faqulil-laahu a'lamu bimaa ta'maloon.

وَاِنْ جٰدَلُوْكَ فَقُلِ اللّٰهُ اَعْلَمُ
بِمَا تَعْمَلُوْنَ ۝٦٨

69. "Allah will judge between you on the Day of Judgment concerning the matters in which you differ."

69. Allaahu yaḥkumu baynakum Yawmal-Qiyaamati feemaa kuntum feehi takhtalifoon.

اَللّٰهُ يَحْكُمُ بَيْنَكُمْ يَوْمَ الْقِيٰمَةِ فِيْمَا
كُنْتُمْ فِيْهِ تَخْتَلِفُوْنَ ۝٦٩

70. Don't you know that Allah knows all that is in heaven and on earth? Indeed it is all in a Record, and that is easy for Allah.

70. Alam ta'lam annal-laaha ya'lamu maa fis-samaaa'i wal-arḍ; inna z̲aalika fee kitaab; inna z̲aalika 'alal-laahi yaseer.

اَلَمْ تَعْلَمْ اَنَّ اللّٰهَ يَعْلَمُ مَا فِي
السَّمَاۗءِ وَالْاَرْضِ ۭ اِنَّ ذٰلِكَ فِيْ
كِتٰبٍ ۭ اِنَّ ذٰلِكَ عَلَى اللّٰهِ يَسِيْرٌ ۝٧٠

71. Yet they worship, besides Allah, things for which no authority has been sent down to them, and of which they have (really) no knowledge: for those that do wrong there is no helper.

71. Wa ya'budoona min doonil-laahi maa lam yunazzil bihee sulṭaanañw-wa maa laysa lahum bihee 'ilm; wa maa liz̲z̲aalimeena min-naṣeer.

وَيَعْبُدُوْنَ مِنْ دُوْنِ اللّٰهِ مَا لَمْ
يُنَزِّلْ بِهٖ سُلْطٰنًا وَّمَا لَيْسَ لَهُمْ
بِهٖ عِلْمٌ ۭ وَمَا لِلظّٰلِمِيْنَ مِنْ نَّصِيْرٍ ۝٧١

72. When Our Clear Signs are rehearsed to them, you will notice a denial on the faces of the Unbelievers! they nearly attack with violence those who rehearse Our Signs to them. Say, "Shall I tell you of something (far) worse than these Signs? It is the Fire (of Hell)! Allah has promised it to the Unbelievers! and evil is that destination!"

72. Wa iz̲aa tutlaa 'alayhim Aayaatunaa bayyinaatin ta'rifu fee wujoohil-laz̲eena kafarul-munkara yakaadoona yasṭoona bil-laz̲eena yatloona 'alayhim Aayaatinaa; qul afa-unabbi'ukum bisharrim-min z̲aalikum; an-Naaru wa'adahal-laahul-laz̲eena kafaroo wa bi'sal-maṣeer. **(Section 9)**

وَاِذَا تُتْلٰى عَلَيْهِمْ اٰيٰتُنَا بَيِّنٰتٍ
تَعْرِفُ فِيْ وُجُوْهِ الَّذِيْنَ كَفَرُوا
الْمُنْكَرَ ۭ يَكَادُوْنَ يَسْطُوْنَ بِالَّذِيْنَ
يَتْلُوْنَ عَلَيْهِمْ اٰيٰتِنَا ۭ قُلْ
اَفَاُنَبِّئُكُمْ بِشَرٍّ مِّنْ ذٰلِكُمْ ۭ اَلنَّارُ ۭ
وَعَدَهَا اللّٰهُ الَّذِيْنَ كَفَرُوْا ۭ
وَبِئْسَ الْمَصِيْرُ ۝٧٢ ع

73. O men! Here is a parable set forth! listen to it! Those on whom, besides Allah, you call,

73. Yaaa ayyuhan-naasu ḍuriba mas̲alun fastami'oo lah; innal-laz̲eena tad'oona

يٰٓاَيُّهَا النَّاسُ ضُرِبَ مَثَلٌ
فَاسْتَمِعُوْا لَهٗ ۭ اِنَّ الَّذِيْنَ تَدْعُوْنَ

Ikhfa اخفاء | Ghunna غنّہ | Ikhfa Meem Saakin اخفاء میم ساکن | Idghaam ادغام | Qalqala قلقلہ | Qalb قلب | Idghaam Meem Saakin ادغام میم ساکن

cannot create (even) a fly, if they all met together for the purpose! And if the fly should snatch away anything from them, they would have no power to release it from the fly. Feeble are those who petition and those whom they petition!

min doonil-laahi lañy-yakhluqoo zubaabañw-wa lawijtama'oo lahoo wa iñy-yaslubhumuz-zubaabu shay'al-laa yastan-qizoohu minh; ḍa'ufaṭ-ṭaalibu walmaṭloob.

مِن دُونِ اللَّهِ لَن يَخْلُقُوا ذُبَابًا
وَلَوِ اجْتَمَعُوا لَهُ ۖ وَإِن يَسْلُبْهُمُ
الذُّبَابُ شَيْئًا لَّا يَسْتَنقِذُوهُ مِنْهُ ۚ
ضَعُفَ الطَّالِبُ وَالْمَطْلُوبُ ﴿٧٣﴾

74. No just estimate have they made of Allah: for Allah is He Who is strong and able to Carry out His Will.

74. Maa qadarul-laaha ḥaqqa qadrih; innal-laaha la-Qawiyyun 'Azeez.

مَا قَدَرُوا اللَّهَ حَقَّ قَدْرِهِ ۗ إِنَّ
اللَّهَ لَقَوِيٌّ عَزِيزٌ ﴿٧٤﴾

75. Allah chooses messengers from angels and from men for Allah is He Who hears and sees (all things).

75. Allaahu yaṣṭafee minal-malaaa'ikati Rusulañw-wa minan-naas; innal-laaha Samee'um Baṣeer.

اللَّهُ يَصْطَفِي مِنَ الْمَلَائِكَةِ رُسُلًا
وَمِنَ النَّاسِ ۚ إِنَّ اللَّهَ سَمِيعٌ بَصِيرٌ ﴿٧٥﴾

76. He knows what is before them and what is behind them: and to Allah go back all questions (for decision).

76. Ya'lamu maa bayna aydeehim wa maa khalfahum; wa ilal-laahi turja'ul-umoor.

يَعْلَمُ مَا بَيْنَ أَيْدِيهِمْ وَمَا خَلْفَهُمْ ۗ
وَإِلَى اللَّهِ تُرْجَعُ الْأُمُورُ ﴿٧٦﴾

(Bow Down)

77. O you who believe! Bow down, prostrate yourselves, and adore your Lord; and do good; that you may prosper.

77. Yaaa ayyuhal-lazeena aamanur-ka'oo wasjudoo wa'budoo Rabbakum waf'alul-khayra la'allakum tufliḥoon. ۩

يَا أَيُّهَا الَّذِينَ آمَنُوا ارْكَعُوا وَاسْجُدُوا
وَاعْبُدُوا رَبَّكُمْ وَافْعَلُوا الْخَيْرَ
لَعَلَّكُمْ تُفْلِحُونَ ۩ ﴿٧٧﴾

السجدة عند الامام الشافعي رحمه الله تعالى ١٢

78. And strive in His cause as you ought to strive, (with sincerity and under discipline). He has chosen you, and has imposed no difficulties on you in religion; it is the cult of your father Abraham. It is He Who has named you Muslims, both before and in this (Revelation); that the Messenger may be a witness for you, and you be witnesses for mankind! So establish regular Prayer, give regular Charity, and hold fast to Allah! He is your Protector - the Best to protect and the Best to help!

78. Wa jaahidoo fil-laahi ḥaqqa jihaadih; Huwaj-tabaakum wa maa ja'ala 'alaykum fid-deeni min ḥaraj; Millata abeekum Ibraaheem; Huwa sammaakumul-muslimeena min qablu wa fee haazaa li-yakoonar-Rasoolu shaheedan 'alaykum wa takoonoo shuhadaaa'a 'alan-naas; fa-aqeemuṣ-Ṣalaata wa aatuz-Zakaata wa'taṣimoo billaahi Huwa mawlaakum fani'mal-mawlaa wa ni'man-naṣeer. **(Section 10)**

وَجَاهِدُوا فِي اللَّهِ حَقَّ جِهَادِهِ ۚ
هُوَ اجْتَبَاكُمْ وَمَا جَعَلَ عَلَيْكُمْ فِي
الدِّينِ مِنْ حَرَجٍ ۚ مِّلَّةَ أَبِيكُمْ
إِبْرَاهِيمَ ۚ هُوَ سَمَّاكُمُ الْمُسْلِمِينَ
مِن قَبْلُ وَفِي هَٰذَا لِيَكُونَ
الرَّسُولُ شَهِيدًا عَلَيْكُمْ وَ
تَكُونُوا شُهَدَاءَ عَلَى النَّاسِ ۚ
فَأَقِيمُوا الصَّلَاةَ وَآتُوا الزَّكَاةَ
وَاعْتَصِمُوا بِاللَّهِ هُوَ مَوْلَاكُمْ ۖ
فَنِعْمَ الْمَوْلَىٰ وَنِعْمَ النَّصِيرُ ﴿٧٨﴾

23. The Believers

In the name of Allah, Most Gracious, Most Merciful.

Sûrat al-Mu'minûn–23

(Revealed at Makkah)

Bismillaahir Raḥmaanir Raḥeem

(٢٣) سُورَةُ الْمُؤْمِنُونَ مَكِّيَّةٌ (٧٤)

بِسْمِ اللَّهِ الرَّحْمَٰنِ الرَّحِيمِ

1. The believers must (eventually) win through,-

1. Qad aflaḥal-mu'minoon.

قَدْ أَفْلَحَ الْمُؤْمِنُونَ ﴿١﴾

Ikhfa اخفاء | Ghunna غنّہ | Ikhfa Meem Saakin اخفاء میم ساکن | Idghaam ادغام | Qalqala قلقلہ | Qalb قلب | Idghaam Meem Saakin ادغام میم ساکن

2. Those who humble themselves in their prayers;	2. Allazeena hum fee Ṣalaatihim khaashi'oon.	الَّذِينَ هُمْ فِي صَلَاتِهِمْ خَاشِعُونَ ۝٢
3. Who avoid vain talk;	3. Wallazeena hum 'anillaghwi mu'riḍoon.	وَالَّذِينَ هُمْ عَنِ اللَّغْوِ مُعْرِضُونَ ۝٣
4. Who are active in deeds of charity;	4. Wallazeena hum liz-Zakaati faa'iloon.	وَالَّذِينَ هُمْ لِلزَّكَاةِ فَاعِلُونَ ۝٤
5. Who abstain from sex,	5. Wallazeena hum lifuroojihim ḥaafiẓoon.	وَالَّذِينَ هُمْ لِفُرُوجِهِمْ حَافِظُونَ ۝٥
6. Except with those joined to them in the marriage bond, or (the captives) whom their right hands possess,- for (in their case) they are free from blame,	6. Illaa 'alaaa azwaajihim aw maa malakat aymaanuhum fa-innahum ghayru maloomeen.	إِلَّا عَلَىٰ أَزْوَاجِهِمْ أَوْ مَا مَلَكَتْ أَيْمَانُهُمْ فَإِنَّهُمْ غَيْرُ مَلُومِينَ ۝٦
7. But those whose desires exceed those limits are transgressors;-	7. Famanib-taghaa waraaa'a zaalika fa-ulaaa'ika humul-'aadoon.	فَمَنِ ابْتَغَىٰ وَرَاءَ ذَٰلِكَ فَأُولَٰئِكَ هُمُ الْعَادُونَ ۝٧
8. Those who faithfully observe their trusts and their covenants;	8. Wallazeena hum li-amaanaatihim wa 'ahdihim raa'oon.	وَالَّذِينَ هُمْ لِأَمَانَاتِهِمْ وَعَهْدِهِمْ رَاعُونَ ۝٨
9. And who (strictly) guard their prayers;-	9. Wallazeena hum 'alaa Ṣalawaatihim yuḥaafiẓoon.	وَالَّذِينَ هُمْ عَلَىٰ صَلَوَاتِهِمْ يُحَافِظُونَ ۝٩ وقف لازم
10. These will be the heirs,	10. Ulaaa'ika humul-waarisoon.	أُولَٰئِكَ هُمُ الْوَارِثُونَ ۝١٠
11. Who will inherit Paradise: they will dwell therein (for ever).	11. Allazeena yarisoonal-Firdawsa hum feehaa khaalidoon.	الَّذِينَ يَرِثُونَ الْفِرْدَوْسَ هُمْ فِيهَا خَالِدُونَ ۝١١
12. We created man from a quintessence (of clay);	12. Wa laqad khalaqnal-insaana min sulaalatim-min ṭeen.	وَلَقَدْ خَلَقْنَا الْإِنْسَانَ مِنْ سُلَالَةٍ مِنْ طِينٍ ۝١٢
13. Then We placed him as (a drop of) sperm in a place of rest, firmly fixed;	13. Summa ja'alnaahu nuṭfatan fee qaraarim-makeen.	ثُمَّ جَعَلْنَاهُ نُطْفَةً فِي قَرَارٍ مَكِينٍ ۝١٣
14. Then We made the sperm into a clot of congealed blood; then of that clot We made a (foetus) lump; then We made out of that lump bones and clothed the bones with flesh; then We developed out of it another creature. So blessed be Allah, the best to create!	14. Summa khalaqnan-nuṭfata 'alaqatan fakhalaqnal-'alaqata muḍghatan fakhalaqnal-muḍghata 'iẓaaman fakasawnal-'iẓaama laḥman summa anshaånaahu khalqan aakhar; fatabaarakal-laahu aḥsanul-khaaliqeen.	ثُمَّ خَلَقْنَا النُّطْفَةَ عَلَقَةً فَخَلَقْنَا الْعَلَقَةَ مُضْغَةً فَخَلَقْنَا الْمُضْغَةَ عِظَامًا فَكَسَوْنَا الْعِظَامَ لَحْمًا ثُمَّ أَنْشَأْنَاهُ خَلْقًا آخَرَ ۚ فَتَبَارَكَ اللَّهُ أَحْسَنُ الْخَالِقِينَ ۝١٤
15. After that, at length you will die.	15. Summa innakum ba'da zaalika la-mayyitoon.	ثُمَّ إِنَّكُمْ بَعْدَ ذَٰلِكَ لَمَيِّتُونَ ۝١٥
16. Again, on the Day of Judgment, will you be raised up.	16. Summa innakum Yawmal-Qiyaamati tub'asoon.	ثُمَّ إِنَّكُمْ يَوْمَ الْقِيَامَةِ تُبْعَثُونَ ۝١٦

Ikhfa اخفاء · Ghunna غُنّہ · Ikhfa Meem Saakin اخفاء میم ساکن · Idghaam ادغام · Qalqala قلقلہ · Qalb قلب · Idghaam Meem Saakin ادغام میم ساکن

17. And We have made, above you, seven tracts; and We are never unmindful of (Our) Creation.

17. Wa laqad khalaqnaa fawqakum sab'a ṭaraaa'iqa wa maa kunnaa 'anil-khalqi ghaafileen.

وَلَقَدْ خَلَقْنَا فَوْقَكُمْ سَبْعَ طَرَآئِقَ ۖ وَمَا
كُنَّا عَنِ الْخَلْقِ غٰفِلِيْنَ ﴿١٧﴾

18. And We send down water from the sky according to (due) measure, and We cause it to soak in the soil; and We certainly are able to drain it off (with ease).

18. Wa anzalnaa minas-samaaa'i maaa'am biqadarin fa-askannaahu fil-arḍi wa innaa 'alaa zahaabim bihee laqaa-diroon

وَ اَنْزَلْنَا مِنَ السَّمَآءِ مَآءًۢ بِقَدَرٍ
فَاَسْكَنّٰهُ فِى الْاَرْضِ ۖ وَاِنَّا عَلٰى
ذَهَابٍۢ بِهٖ لَقٰدِرُوْنَ ۚ ﴿١٨﴾

19. With it We grow for you gardens of date-palms and vines: in them have you abundant fruits: and of them you eat (and have enjoyment),-

19. Fa-anshaånaa lakum bihee Jannaatim-min-nakheeliñw-wa a'naab; lakum feehaa fawaa-kihu kaseeratuñw-wa minhaa taåkuloon.

فَاَنْشَاْنَا لَكُمْ بِهٖ جَنّٰتٍ مِّنْ نَّخِيْلٍ
وَّاَعْنَابٍ ۘ لَكُمْ فِيْهَا فَوَاكِهُ كَثِيْرَةٌ
وَّمِنْهَا تَاْكُلُوْنَ ۙ ﴿١٩﴾ وقف لازم

20. Also a tree springing out of Mount Sinai, which produces oil, and relish for those who use it for food.

20. Wa shajaratan takhruju min Ṭoori Saynaaa'a tambutu bidduhni wa ṣibghil-lil-aakileen.

وَ شَجَرَةً تَخْرُجُ مِنْ طُوْرِ سَيْنَآءَ
تَنْۢبُتُ بِالدُّهْنِ وَصِبْغٍ لِّلْاٰكِلِيْنَ ﴿٢٠﴾

21. And in cattle (too) you have an instructive example: from within their bodies We produce (milk) for you to drink; there are, in them, (besides), numerous (other) benefits for you; and of their (meat) you eat;

21. Wa inna lakum fil-an'aami la'ibrah; nusqeekum-mimmaa fee buṭoonihaa wa lakum feehaa manaafi'u kaseeratuñw-wa minhaa taå-kuloon.

وَاِنَّ لَكُمْ فِى الْاَنْعَامِ لَعِبْرَةً ؕ نُسْقِيْكُمْ
مِّمَّا فِىْ بُطُوْنِهَا وَلَكُمْ فِيْهَا مَنَافِعُ
كَثِيْرَةٌ وَّمِنْهَا تَاْكُلُوْنَ ۙ ﴿٢١﴾

22. And on them, as well as in ships, you ride.

22. Wa 'alayhaa wa 'alal-fulki tuḥmaloon. **(Section 1)**

وَعَلَيْهَا وَعَلَى الْفُلْكِ تُحْمَلُوْنَ ﴿٢٢﴾ ع ٢٢

23. We sent Noah to his people: he said, "O my people; worship Allah, you have no other god but Him. Will you not fear (Him)?"

23. Wa laqad arsalnaa Nooḥan ilaa qawmihee faqaala yaa qawmi'budul-laaha maa lakum min ilaahin ghayruhoo afalaa tattaqoon.

وَلَقَدْ اَرْسَلْنَا نُوْحًا اِلٰى قَوْمِهٖ فَقَالَ
يٰقَوْمِ اعْبُدُوا اللّٰهَ مَا لَكُمْ مِّنْ اِلٰهٍ
غَيْرُهٗ ؕ اَفَلَا تَتَّقُوْنَ ﴿٢٣﴾

24. The chiefs of the Unbelievers among his people said: "He is no more than a man like yourselves: his wish is to assert his superiority over you. If Allah had wished (to send Messengers), He could have sent down angels; never did we hear such a thing (as he says), among our ancestors of old."

24. Faqaalal-mala'ul-lazeena kafaroo min qawmihee maa haazaaa illaa basharum-mislukum yureedu añy-yatafaḍḍala 'alaykum wa law shaaa'al-laahu la-anzala malaaa'ikatam-maa sami'naa bihaazaa feee aabaaa'inal-awwaleen.

فَقَالَ الْمَلَؤُا الَّذِيْنَ كَفَرُوْا مِنْ قَوْمِهٖ
مَا هٰذَآ اِلَّا بَشَرٌ مِّثْلُكُمْ ۙ يُرِيْدُ
اَنْ يَّتَفَضَّلَ عَلَيْكُمْ ؕ وَلَوْ شَآءَ اللّٰهُ
لَاَنْزَلَ مَلٰٓئِكَةً ۖۚ مَّا سَمِعْنَا بِهٰذَا فِىْٓ
اٰبَآئِنَا الْاَوَّلِيْنَ ۚ ﴿٢٤﴾

25. (And some said): "He is only a man possessed; wait (and have patience) with him for a time."

25. In huwa illaa rajulum bihee jinnatun fatarabbaṣoo bihee ḥattaa ḥeen.

اِنْ هُوَ اِلَّا رَجُلٌۢ بِهٖ جِنَّةٌ فَتَرَبَّصُوْا
بِهٖ حَتّٰى حِيْنٍ ﴿٢٥﴾

26. (Noah) said: "O my Lord! help me: for that they accuse me of falsehood!"

26. Qaala Rabbin-ṣurnee bimaa kazzaboon.

قَالَ رَبِّ انْصُرْنِىْ بِمَا كَذَّبُوْنِ ﴿٢٦﴾

27. So We inspired him (with this message): "Construct the Ark

27. Fa-awḥaynaaa ilayhi aniṣ-na'il-fulka

فَاَوْحَيْنَآ اِلَيْهِ اَنِ اصْنَعِ الْفُلْكَ

Ikhfa اخفاء	Ghunna غُنّہ	Ikhfa Meem Saakin اخفاء میم ساکن	Idghaam ادغام	Qalqala قلقلہ	Qalb قلب	Idghaam Meem Saakin ادغام میم ساکن

within Our sight and under Our guidance: then when comes Our command, and the fountains of the earth gush forth, you take on board pairs of every species, male and female, and your family- except those of them against whom the Word has already gone forth: and do not address Me in favor of the wrong-doers; for they shall be drowned (in the Flood).

28. And when you have embarked on the Ark - you and those with you,- say: "Praise be to Allah, Who has saved us from the people who do wrong."

29. And say: "O my Lord! enable me to disembark with your blessing: for You are the Best to enable (us) to disembark."

30. Verily in this there are Signs (for men to understand); (thus) do We try (men).

31. Then We raised after them another generation.

32. And We sent to them a Messenger from among themselves, (saying), "Worship Allah! you have no other god but Him. Will you not fear (Him)?"

33. And the chiefs of his people, who disbelieved and denied the Meeting in the Hereafter, and on whom We had bestowed the good things of this life, said: "He is no more than a man like yourselves: he eats of that of which you eat, and drinks of what you drink.

34. "If you obey a man like yourselves, behold, it is certain you will be lost.

35. "Does he promise that when you die and become dust and bones, you shall be brought forth (again)?

36. "Far, very far is that which you are promised!

bi-a'yuninaa wa waḥyinaa fa-izaa jaaa'a amrunaa wa faarat-tannooru fasluk feehaa min kullin zawjaynis-nayni wa ahlaka illaa man sabaqa 'alayhil-qawlu minhum wa laa tukhaaṭibnee fil-lazeena ẓalamooo innahum-mughra-qoon.

28. Fa-izas-tawayta anta wa mam-ma'aka 'alal-fulki faqulil-ḥamdu lillaahil-lazee najjaanaa minal-qawmiẓ-ẓalimeen.

29. Wa qur-Rabbi anzilnee munzalam-mubaarakañw-wa Anta khayrul-munzileen.

30. Inna fee zaalika la-Aayaatiñw-wa in kunnaa lamubtaleen.

31. Summa anshaånaa mim ba'dihim qarnan aakhareen.

32. Fa-arsalnaa feehim Rasoolam-minhum ani'budul-laaha maa lakum-min ilaahin ghayruhoo afalaa tattaqoon.

(Section 2)

33. Wa qaalal-mala-u min qawmihil-lazeena kafaroo wa kazzaboo bi-liqaaa'il-Aakhirati wa atrafnaahum fil-ḥayaatid-dunyaa maa haazaaa illaa basharum-mislukum yaåkulu mimmaa taåkuloona minhu wa yashrabu mimmaa tashraboon.

34. Wa la'in aṭ'atum basharam-mislakum innakum izal-lakhaasiroon.

35. A-ya'idukum annakum izaa mittum wa kuntum turaabañw-wa iẓaaman anna-kum-mukhrajoon.

36. Hayhaata hayhaata limaa too'adoon.

بِاَعْيُنِنَا وَوَحْيِنَا فَاِذَا جَآءَ اَمْرُنَا
وَفَارَ التَّنُّوْرُ ۙ فَاسْلُكْ فِيْهَا مِنْ كُلٍّ
زَوْجَيْنِ اثْنَيْنِ وَاَهْلَكَ اِلَّا مَنْ سَبَقَ
عَلَيْهِ الْقَوْلُ مِنْهُمْ ۚ وَلَا تُخَاطِبْنِيْ
فِي الَّذِيْنَ ظَلَمُوْا ۚ اِنَّهُمْ مُّغْرَقُوْنَ ﴿٢٧﴾
فَاِذَا اسْتَوَيْتَ اَنْتَ وَمَنْ مَّعَكَ
عَلَى الْفُلْكِ فَقُلِ الْحَمْدُ لِلّٰهِ الَّذِيْ
نَجّٰىنَا مِنَ الْقَوْمِ الظّٰلِمِيْنَ ﴿٢٨﴾
وَقُلْ رَّبِّ اَنْزِلْنِيْ مُنْزَلًا مُّبٰرَكًا وَّ
اَنْتَ خَيْرُ الْمُنْزِلِيْنَ ﴿٢٩﴾
اِنَّ فِيْ ذٰلِكَ لَاٰيٰتٍ وَّاِنْ كُنَّا
لَمُبْتَلِيْنَ ﴿٣٠﴾
ثُمَّ اَنْشَاْنَا مِنْ بَعْدِهِمْ قَرْنًا اٰخَرِيْنَ ﴿٣١﴾
فَاَرْسَلْنَا فِيْهِمْ رَسُوْلًا مِّنْهُمْ اَنِ
اعْبُدُوا اللّٰهَ مَا لَكُمْ مِّنْ اِلٰهٍ غَيْرُهٗ ؕ
اَفَلَا تَتَّقُوْنَ ﴿٣٢﴾ ع
وَقَالَ الْمَلَاُ مِنْ قَوْمِهِ الَّذِيْنَ كَفَرُوْا
وَكَذَّبُوْا بِلِقَآءِ الْاٰخِرَةِ وَاَتْرَفْنٰهُمْ
فِي الْحَيٰوةِ الدُّنْيَا ۙ مَا هٰذَآ اِلَّا بَشَرٌ
مِّثْلُكُمْ ۙ يَاْكُلُ مِمَّا تَاْكُلُوْنَ مِنْهُ
وَيَشْرَبُ مِمَّا تَشْرَبُوْنَ ﴿٣٣﴾
وَلَئِنْ اَطَعْتُمْ بَشَرًا مِّثْلَكُمْ اِنَّكُمْ
اِذًا لَّخٰسِرُوْنَ ﴿٣٤﴾
اَيَعِدُكُمْ اَنَّكُمْ اِذَا مِتُّمْ وَكُنْتُمْ تُرَابًا
وَّعِظَامًا اَنَّكُمْ مُّخْرَجُوْنَ ﴿٣٥﴾
هَيْهَاتَ هَيْهَاتَ لِمَا تُوْعَدُوْنَ ﴿٣٦﴾

Ikhfa اخفاء | Ghunna غنّہ | Ikhfa Meem Saakin اخفاء میم ساکن | Idghaam ادغام | Qalqala قلقلہ | Qalb قلب | Idghaam Meem Saakin ادغام میم ساکن

English	Transliteration	Arabic
37. "There is nothing but our life in this world! We shall die and we live! But we shall never be raised up again!	37. In hiya illaa ḥayaatunad-dunyaa namootu wa naḥyaa wa maa naḥnu bimab'ooseen.	إن هي إلا حياتنا الدنيا نموت و نحيا وما نحن بمبعوثين ﴿٣٧﴾
38. "He is only a man who invents a lie against Allah, but we are not the ones to believe in him!"	38. In huwa illaa rajulunif-taraa 'alal-laahi kazibañw-wa maa naḥnu lahoo bimu'mineen.	إن هو إلا رجل افترى على الله كذبا وما نحن له بمؤمنين ﴿٣٨﴾
39. (The prophet) said: "O my Lord! help me: for that they accuse me of falsehood."	39. Qaala Rabbin-ṣurnee bimaa kazzaboon.	قال رب انصرني بما كذبون ﴿٣٩﴾
40. (Alalh) said: "In but a little while, they are sure to be sorry!"	40. Qaala 'ammaa qaleelil-la-yuṣbiḥunna naadimeen.	قال عما قليل ليصبحن نادمين ﴿٤٠﴾
41. Then the Blast overtook them with justice, and We made them as rubbish of dead leaves (floating on the stream of Time)! So away with the people who do wrong!	41. Fa-akhazat-humuṣ-ṣay-ḥatu bilḥaqqi faja'alnaahum ghusaaa'aa; fabu'dal-lilqaw-miẓ-ẓaalimeen.	فأخذتهم الصيحة بالحق فجعلناهم غثاء ۚ فبعدا للقوم الظالمين ﴿٤١﴾
42. Then We raised after them other generations.	42. Summa anshaånaa mim ba'dihim quroonan aakhareen.	ثم أنشأنا من بعدهم قرونا آخرين ﴿٤٢﴾
43. No people can hasten their term, nor can they delay (it).	43. Maa tasbiqu min ummatin ajalahaa wa maa yastaåkhiroon.	ما تسبق من أمة أجلها وما يستأخرون ﴿٤٣﴾
44. Then we sent our Messengers in succession: every time there came to a people their Messenger, they accused him of falsehood: so We made them follow each other (in punishment): We made them as a tale (that is told): so away with a people that will not believe!	44. Summa arsalnaa Rusu-lanaa tatraa kulla maa jaaa'a ummatar-Rasooluhaa kaz-zabooh; fa-atba'naa ba'ḍahum ba'ḍañw-wa ja'alnaahum aḥaadees; fabu'dal-liqawmil-laa yu'minoon.	ثم أرسلنا رسلنا تترا ۖ كلما جاء أمة رسولها كذبوه ۚ فأتبعنا بعضهم بعضا وجعلناهم أحاديث ۚ فبعدا لقوم لا يؤمنون ﴿٤٤﴾
45. Then We sent Moses and his brother Aaron, with Our Signs and authority manifest,	45. Summa arsalnaa Moosaa wa akhaahu Haaroona bi Aayaatinaa wa sulṭaanim-mu-been.	ثم أرسلنا موسى وأخاه هارون ۙ بآياتنا وسلطان مبين ﴿٤٥﴾
46. To Pharaoh and his Chiefs: but these behaved insolently: they were an arrogant people.	46. Ilaa Fir'awna wa mala'i-hee fastakbaroo wa kaanoo qawman 'aaleen.	إلى فرعون وملئه فاستكبروا وكانوا قوما عالين ﴿٤٦﴾
47. They said: "Shall we believe in two men like our-selves? And their people are subject to us!"	47. Faqaalooo anu'minu libasharayni mislinaa wa qawmuhumaa lanaa 'aabidoon.	فقالوا أنؤمن لبشرين مثلنا وقومهما لنا عابدون ﴿٤٧﴾
48. So they (rejected) and accused them of falsehood, and they became of those who were destroyed.	48. Fakazzaboohumaa fa-kaanoo minal-muhlakeen.	فكذبوهما فكانوا من المهلكين ﴿٤٨﴾
49. And We gave Moses the Book, in order that they might receive guidance.	49. Wa laqad aataynaa Moosal-Kitaaba la'allahum yahtadoon.	ولقد آتينا موسى الكتاب لعلهم يهتدون ﴿٤٩﴾
50. And We made the son of Mary and his mother as a Sign:	50. Wa ja'alnab-na-Maryama wa ummahooo Aayatañw-wa	وجعلنا ابن مريم وأمه آية و

Ikhfa اخفاء · Ghunna غنّہ · Ikhfa Meem Saakin اخفاء میم ساکن · Idghaam ادغام · Qalqala قلقلہ · Qalb قلب · Idghaam Meem Saakin ادغام میم ساکن

We gave them both shelter on high ground, affording rest and security and furnished with springs.

aawaynaahumaaa ilaa rabwatin zaati qaraariñw-wa ma'een.

(Section 3)

اٰوَيْنٰهُمَآ اِلٰى رَبْوَةٍ ذَاتِ قَرَارٍ
وَّمَعِيْنٍ ﴿٥٠﴾

51. O you Messengers! enjoy (all) things good and pure, and work righteousness: for I am well-acquainted with (all) that you do.

51. Yaaa ayyuhar-Rusulu kuloo minaṭ-ṭayyibaati wa'maloo ṣaaliḥan innee bimaa ta'maloona 'Aleem.

يٰۤاَيُّهَا الرُّسُلُ كُلُوْا مِنَ الطَّيِّبٰتِ
وَاعْمَلُوْا صَالِحًا ؕ اِنِّىْ بِمَا تَعْمَلُوْنَ
عَلِيْمٌ ﴿٥١﴾

52. And verily this Brotherhood of yours is a single Brotherhood, and I am your Lord and Cherisher: therefore fear Me (and no other).

52. Wa inna haaziheee ummatukum ummatañw-waaḥidatañw-wa Ana Rabbukum fattaqoon.

وَاِنَّ هٰذِهٖۤ اُمَّتُكُمْ اُمَّةً وَّاحِدَةً
وَّاَنَا رَبُّكُمْ فَاتَّقُوْنِ ﴿٥٢﴾

53. But people have cut off their affair (of unity), between them, into sects: each party rejoices in that which is with itself

53. Fataqaṭṭa'ooo amrahum baynahum zuburaa; kullu ḥizbim bimaa ladayhim fariḥoon.

فَتَقَطَّعُوْۤا اَمْرَهُمْ بَيْنَهُمْ زُبُرًا ؕ كُلُّ
حِزْبٍۭ بِمَا لَدَيْهِمْ فَرِحُوْنَ ﴿٥٣﴾

54. But leave them in their confused ignorance for a time.

54. Fazarhum fee ghamratihim ḥattaa ḥeen.

فَذَرْهُمْ فِىْ غَمْرَتِهِمْ حَتّٰى حِيْنٍ ﴿٥٤﴾

55. Do they think that because We have granted them abundance of wealth and sons,

55. A-yaḥsaboona annamaa numidduhum bihee mimmaaliñw-wa baneen.

اَيَحْسَبُوْنَ اَنَّمَا نُمِدُّهُمْ بِهٖ مِنْ
مَّالٍ وَّبَنِيْنَ ﴿٥٥﴾

56. We would hasten them on in every good? Nay, they do not understand.

56. Nusaari'u lahum fil-khayraat; bal laa yash'uroon.

نُسَارِعُ لَهُمْ فِى الْخَيْرٰتِ ؕ بَلْ لَّا
يَشْعُرُوْنَ ﴿٥٦﴾

57. Verily those who live in awe for fear of their Lord;

57. Innal-lazeena hum-min khashyati Rabbihim-mushfiqoon.

اِنَّ الَّذِيْنَ هُمْ مِّنْ خَشْيَةِ رَبِّهِمْ
مُّشْفِقُوْنَ ﴿٥٧﴾

58. Those who believe in the Signs of their Lord;

58. Wallazeena hum bi-Aayaati Rabbihim yu'minoon.

وَالَّذِيْنَ هُمْ بِاٰيٰتِ رَبِّهِمْ يُؤْمِنُوْنَ ﴿٥٨﴾

59. Those who do not join (in worship) partners with their Lord;

59. Wallazeena hum bi-Rabbihim laa yushrikoon.

وَالَّذِيْنَ هُمْ بِرَبِّهِمْ لَا يُشْرِكُوْنَ ﴿٥٩﴾

60. And those who dispense their charity with their hearts full of fear, because they will return to their Lord;-

60. Wallazeena yu'toona maaa aataw-wa quloobuhum wajilatun annahum ilaa Rabbihim raaji'oon.

وَالَّذِيْنَ يُؤْتُوْنَ مَآ اٰتَوْا وَّقُلُوْبُهُمْ
وَجِلَةٌ اَنَّهُمْ اِلٰى رَبِّهِمْ رٰجِعُوْنَ ﴿٦٠﴾

61. It is these who hasten in every good work, and these who are foremost in them.

61. Ulaaa'ika yusaari'oona fil-khayraati wa hum lahaa saabiqoon.

اُولٰٓئِكَ يُسٰرِعُوْنَ فِى الْخَيْرٰتِ وَهُمْ
لَهَا سٰبِقُوْنَ ﴿٦١﴾

62. On no soul do We place a burden greater than it can bear: before Us is a record which clearly speaks the truth: they will never be wronged.

62. Wa laa nukallifu nafsan illaa wus'ahaa wa ladaynaa kitaabuñy-yanṭiqu bilḥaqqi wa hum la yuẓlamoon.

وَلَا نُكَلِّفُ نَفْسًا اِلَّا وُسْعَهَا وَ
لَدَيْنَا كِتٰبٌ يَّنْطِقُ بِالْحَقِّ وَهُمْ
لَا يُظْلَمُوْنَ ﴿٦٢﴾

63. But their hearts are in confused ignorance of this;

63. Bal quloobuhum fee ghamratim-min haazaa

بَلْ قُلُوْبُهُمْ فِىْ غَمْرَةٍ مِّنْ هٰذَا

Ikhfa اخفاء | Ghunna غُنّہ | Ikhfa Meem Saakin اخفاء میم ساکن | Idghaam ادغام | Qalqala قلقلہ | Qalb قلب | Idghaam Meem Saakin ادغام میم ساکن

and there are, besides that, deeds of theirs, which they will (continue) to do,-

wa lahum a'maalum-min dooni zaalika hum lahaa 'aamiloon.

وَلَهُمْ اَعْمَالٌ مِّنْ دُوْنِ ذٰلِكَ هُمْ
لَهَا عٰمِلُوْنَ ﴿٦٣﴾

64. Until, when We seize in Punishment those of them who received the good things of this world, behold, they will groan in supplication!

64. Ḥattaaa izaaa akhaznaa mutrafeehim bil'azaabi izaa hum yaj'aroon.

حَتّٰٓى اِذَآ اَخَذْنَا مُتْرَفِيْهِمْ بِالْعَذَابِ
اِذَا هُمْ يَجْـَٔرُوْنَ ﴿٦٤﴾

65. (It will be said): "Do not groan in supplication this day: for you shall certainly not be helped by Us.

65. Laa taj'arul-yawma innakum-minnaa laa tunṣaroon.

لَا تَجْـَٔرُوا الْيَوْمَ اِنَّكُمْ مِّنَّا لَا
تُنْصَرُوْنَ ﴿٦٥﴾

66. "My Signs used to be rehearsed to you, but you used to turn back on your heels-

66. Qad kaanat Aayaatee tutlaa 'alaykum fakuntum 'alaaa a'qaabikum tankiṣoon.

قَدْ كَانَتْ اٰيٰتِىْ تُتْلٰى عَلَيْكُمْ فَكُنْتُمْ
عَلٰٓى اَعْقَابِكُمْ تَنْكِصُوْنَ ﴿٦٦﴾

67. "In arrogance: talking nonsense about the (Qur'an), like one telling fables by night."

67. Mustakbireena bihee saamiran tahjuroon.

مُسْتَكْبِرِيْنَ بِهٖ سٰمِرًا تَهْجُرُوْنَ ﴿٦٧﴾

68. Do they not ponder over the Word (of Allah), or has anything (new) come to them that did not come to their fathers of old?

68. Afalam yaddabbarul-qawla am jaaa'ahum-maa lam yaâti aabaaa'ahumul-awwaleen.

اَفَلَمْ يَدَّبَّرُوا الْقَوْلَ اَمْ جَآءَهُمْ
مَّا لَمْ يَاْتِ اٰبَآءَهُمُ الْاَوَّلِيْنَ ﴿٦٨﴾

69. Or do they not recognise their Messenger, that they deny him?

69. Am lam ya'rifoo Rasoolahum fahum lahoo munkiroon.

اَمْ لَمْ يَعْرِفُوْا رَسُوْلَهُمْ فَهُمْ لَهٗ
مُنْكِرُوْنَ ﴿٦٩﴾

70. Or do they say, "He is possessed"? Nay, he has brought them the Truth, but most of them hate the Truth.

70. Am yaqooloona bihee jinnah; bal jaaa'ahum bilḥaqqi wa aksaruhum lil-ḥaqqi kaarihoon.

اَمْ يَقُوْلُوْنَ بِهٖ جِنَّةٌ ؕ بَلْ جَآءَهُمْ
بِالْحَقِّ وَاَكْثَرُهُمْ لِلْحَقِّ كٰرِهُوْنَ ﴿٧٠﴾

71. If the Truth had been in accord with their desires, truly the heavens and the earth, and all beings therein would have been in confusion and corruption! Nay, We have sent them their admonition, but they turn away from their admonition.

71. Wa lawit-taba'al-ḥaqqu ahwaaa'ahum lafasadatis-samaawaatu wal-arḍu wa man feehinn; bal ataynaahum bizikrihim fahum 'an zikrihim-mu'riḍoon.

وَلَوِ اتَّبَعَ الْحَقُّ اَهْوَآءَهُمْ لَفَسَدَتِ
السَّمٰوٰتُ وَالْاَرْضُ وَمَنْ فِيْهِنَّ ؕ بَلْ
اَتَيْنٰهُمْ بِذِكْرِهِمْ فَهُمْ عَنْ ذِكْرِهِمْ
مُّعْرِضُوْنَ ﴿٧١﴾

72. Or is it that you ask them for some recompense? But the recompense of your Lord is best: He is the Best of those who give sustenance.

72. Am tas'aluhum kharjan fakharaaju Rabbika khayruñw-wa Huwa khayrur-raaziqeen.

اَمْ تَسْـَٔلُهُمْ خَرْجًا فَخَرَاجُ رَبِّكَ
خَيْرٌ ۖ وَّهُوَ خَيْرُ الرّٰزِقِيْنَ ﴿٧٢﴾

73. But verily you call them to the Straight Way;

73. Wa innaka latad'oohum ilaa Ṣiraaṭim-Mustaqeem.

وَاِنَّكَ لَتَدْعُوْهُمْ اِلٰى صِرَاطٍ
مُّسْتَقِيْمٍ ﴿٧٣﴾ الربع

74. And verily those who do not believe in the Hereafter are deviating from that Way.

74. Wa innal-lazeena laa yu'minoona bil-Aakhirati 'aniṣ-ṣiraaṭi lanaakiboon.

وَاِنَّ الَّذِيْنَ لَا يُؤْمِنُوْنَ بِالْاٰخِرَةِ
عَنِ الصِّرَاطِ لَنٰكِبُوْنَ ﴿٧٤﴾

75. If We had mercy on them and removed the distress which is on them,

75. Wa law raḥimnaahum wa kashafnaa maa bihim-min ḍurril-

وَلَوْ رَحِمْنٰهُمْ وَكَشَفْنَا مَا بِهِمْ مِّنْ ضُرٍّ

Ikhfa اخفاء | Ghunna غُنّہ | Ikhfa Meem Saakin اخفاء میم ساکن | Idghaam ادغام | Qalqala قلقلہ | Qalb قلب | Idghaam Meem Saakin ادغام میم ساکن

English	Transliteration	Arabic
they would obstinately persist in their Transgression, wandering in distraction to and fro.	lalajjoo fee ṭughyaanihim ya'mahoon.	لَّلَجُّوا فِي طُغْيَانِهِمْ يَعْمَهُونَ ﴿٧٥﴾
76. We inflicted Punishment on them, but they did not humbled themselves to their Lord, nor do they submissively entreat (Him)!-	76. Wa laqad akhaznaahum bil'azaabi famastakaanoo li-Rabbihim wa maa yataḍarra'oon.	وَلَقَدْ أَخَذْنَاهُم بِالْعَذَابِ فَمَا اسْتَكَانُوا لِرَبِّهِمْ وَمَا يَتَضَرَّعُونَ ﴿٧٦﴾
77. Until We open on them a gate leading to a severe Punishment: then lo! they will be plunged in despair therein!	77. Ḥattaaa izaa fataḥnaa 'alayhim baaban zaa 'azaabin shadeedin izaa hum feehi mublisoon. **(Section 4)**	حَتَّىٰ إِذَا فَتَحْنَا عَلَيْهِم بَابًا ذَا عَذَابٍ شَدِيدٍ إِذَا هُمْ فِيهِ مُبْلِسُونَ ﴿٧٧﴾
78. It is He Who has created for you (the faculties of) hearing, sight, feeling and understanding: But little thanks it is you give!	78. Wa Huwal-lazeee ansha-a-lakumus-sam'a wal-abṣaara wal-af'idah; qaleelam-maa tashkuroon.	وَهُوَ الَّذِي أَنشَأَ لَكُمُ السَّمْعَ وَالْأَبْصَارَ وَالْأَفْئِدَةَ ۚ قَلِيلًا مَّا تَشْكُرُونَ ﴿٧٨﴾
79. And He has multiplied you through the earth, and to Him you shall be gathered back.	79. Wa Huwal-lazee zara-akum fil-arḍi wa ilayhi tuḥsharoon.	وَهُوَ الَّذِي ذَرَأَكُمْ فِي الْأَرْضِ وَإِلَيْهِ تُحْشَرُونَ ﴿٧٩﴾
80. It is He Who gives life and death, and to Him (is due) the alternation of Night and Day: will you not then understand?	80. Wa Huwal-lazee yuḥyee wa yumeetu wa lahukh-tilaaful-layli wannahaar; afalaa ta'qiloon.	وَهُوَ الَّذِي يُحْيِي وَيُمِيتُ وَلَهُ اخْتِلَافُ اللَّيْلِ وَالنَّهَارِ ۚ أَفَلَا تَعْقِلُونَ ﴿٨٠﴾
81. On the contrary they say things similar to what the ancients said.	81. Bal qaaloo misla maa qaalal-awwaloon.	بَلْ قَالُوا مِثْلَ مَا قَالَ الْأَوَّلُونَ ﴿٨١﴾
82. They say: "What! when we die and become dust and bones, could we really be raised up again?	82. Qaalooo 'a-izaa mitnaa wa kunnaa turaabañw-wa 'izaaman 'a-innaa lamab-'oosoon.	قَالُوا أَإِذَا مِتْنَا وَكُنَّا تُرَابًا وَعِظَامًا أَإِنَّا لَمَبْعُوثُونَ ﴿٨٢﴾
83. "Such things have been promised to us and to our fathers before! they are nothing but tales of the ancients!"	83. Laqad wu'idnaa naḥnu wa aabaaa'unaa haazaa min qablu in haazaaa illaaa asaaṭeerul-awwaleen.	لَقَدْ وُعِدْنَا نَحْنُ وَآبَاؤُنَا هَٰذَا مِن قَبْلُ إِنْ هَٰذَا إِلَّا أَسَاطِيرُ الْأَوَّلِينَ ﴿٨٣﴾
84. Say: "To whom belong the earth and all beings therein? (say) if you know!"	84. Qul limanil-arḍu wa man feehaaa in kuntum ta'lamoon.	قُل لِّمَنِ الْأَرْضُ وَمَن فِيهَا إِن كُنتُمْ تَعْلَمُونَ ﴿٨٤﴾
85. They will say, "To Allah!" say: "Yet will you not receive admonition?"	85. Sa-yaqooloona lillaah; qul afalaa tazakkaroon.	سَيَقُولُونَ لِلَّهِ ۚ قُلْ أَفَلَا تَذَكَّرُونَ ﴿٨٥﴾
86. Say: "Who is the Lord of the seven heavens, and the Lord of the Throne (of Glory) Supreme?"	86. Qul mar-Rabbus-samaawaatis-sab'i wa Rabbul-'Arshil-'Azeem.	قُلْ مَن رَّبُّ السَّمَاوَاتِ السَّبْعِ وَرَبُّ الْعَرْشِ الْعَظِيمِ ﴿٨٦﴾
87. They will say, "(They belong) to Allah." Say: "Will you not then fear?"	87. Sa-yaqooloona lillaah; qul afalaa tattaqoon.	سَيَقُولُونَ لِلَّهِ ۚ قُلْ أَفَلَا تَتَّقُونَ ﴿٨٧﴾
88. Say: "Who is it in whose hands is the governance of all things,- who protects (all), but is not protected (of any)?	88. Qul mam bi-yadihee malakootu kulli shay'iñw-wa Huwa yujeeru wa laa yujaaru 'alayhi in kuntum	قُلْ مَن بِيَدِهِ مَلَكُوتُ كُلِّ شَيْءٍ وَهُوَ يُجِيرُ وَلَا يُجَارُ عَلَيْهِ إِن كُنتُمْ

Ikhfa اخفاء · Ghunna غنّہ · Ikhfa Meem Saakin اخفاء میم ساکن · Idghaam ادغام · Qalqala قلقلہ · Qalb قلب · Idghaam Meem Saakin ادغام میم ساکن

(say) if you know."

ta'lamoon.

تَعۡلَمُونَ ﴿٨٨﴾

89. They will say, "(It belongs) to Allah." Say: "Then how are you deluded?"

89. Sa-yaqooloona lillaah; qul fa-annaa tus-ḥaroon.

سَيَقُولُونَ لِلَّهِ ۚ قُلۡ فَأَنَّىٰ تُسۡحَرُونَ ﴿٨٩﴾

90. We have sent them the Truth: but they indeed practise Falsehood!

90. Bal ataynaahum bil-ḥaqqi wa innahum lakaaẕiboon.

بَلۡ أَتَيۡنَٰهُم بِٱلۡحَقِّ وَإِنَّهُمۡ لَكَٰذِبُونَ ﴿٩٠﴾

91. No son did Allah beget, nor is there any god along with Him: (if there were many gods), behold, each god would have taken away what he had created, and some would have lorded it over others! Glory to Allah! (He is free) from the (sort of) things they attribute to Him!

91. Mat-takhaẕal-laahu miñw-waladiñw-wa maa kaana ma'ahoo min ilaah; iẕal-laẕahaba kullu ilaahim bimaa khalaqa wa la'alaa ba'ḍuhum 'alaa ba'ḍ; Subḥaanal-laahi 'ammaa yaṣifoon.

مَا ٱتَّخَذَ ٱللَّهُ مِن وَلَدٖ وَمَا كَانَ
مَعَهُۥ مِنۡ إِلَٰهٍۚ إِذٗا لَّذَهَبَ كُلُّ إِلَٰهِۭ
بِمَا خَلَقَ وَلَعَلَا بَعۡضُهُمۡ عَلَىٰ بَعۡضٖۚ
سُبۡحَٰنَ ٱللَّهِ عَمَّا يَصِفُونَ ﴿٩١﴾

92. He knows what is hidden and what is open: too high is He for the partners they attribute to Him!

92. 'Aalimil-Ghaybi wash-shahaadati fata'aalaa 'ammaa yushrikoon. **(Section 5)**

عَٰلِمِ ٱلۡغَيۡبِ وَٱلشَّهَٰدَةِ فَتَعَٰلَىٰ عَمَّا
يُشۡرِكُونَ ﴿٩٢﴾ ع ٥

93. Say: "O my Lord! if You will show me (in my lifetime) that which they are warned against,-

93. Qur-Rabbi immaa turiyannee maa yoo'adoon.

قُل رَّبِّ إِمَّا تُرِيَنِّي مَا يُوعَدُونَ ﴿٩٣﴾

94. "Then, O my Lord! put me not amongst the people who do wrong!"

94. Rabbi falaa taj'alnee fil-qawmiẓ-ẓaalimeen.

رَبِّ فَلَا تَجۡعَلۡنِي فِي ٱلۡقَوۡمِ ٱلظَّٰلِمِينَ ﴿٩٤﴾

95. And We are certainly able to show you (in fulfilment) that against which they are warned.

95. Wa innaa 'alaaa an-nuriyaka maa na'iduhum laqaadiroon.

وَإِنَّا عَلَىٰٓ أَن نُّرِيَكَ مَا نَعِدُهُمۡ
لَقَٰدِرُونَ ﴿٩٥﴾

96. Repel evil with that which is best: We are well acquainted with the things they say.

96. Idfa' billatee hiya aḥsanus-sayyi'ah; Naḥnu a'lamu bimaa yaṣifoon.

ٱدۡفَعۡ بِٱلَّتِي هِيَ أَحۡسَنُ ٱلسَّيِّئَةَۚ
نَحۡنُ أَعۡلَمُ بِمَا يَصِفُونَ ﴿٩٦﴾

97. And say "O my Lord! I seek refuge with you from the suggestions of the Evil Ones.

97. Wa qur-Rabbi a'ooẕu bika min hamazaatish-Shayaaṭeen.

وَقُل رَّبِّ أَعُوذُ بِكَ مِنۡ هَمَزَٰتِ
ٱلشَّيَٰطِينِ ﴿٩٧﴾

98. "And I seek refuge with you O my Lord! lest they should come near me."

98. Wa a'ooẕu bika Rabbi añy-yaḥḍuroon.

وَأَعُوذُ بِكَ رَبِّ أَن يَحۡضُرُونِ ﴿٩٨﴾

99. (In Falsehood will they be) until, when death comes to one of them, he says: "O my Lord! send me back (to life),-

99. Ḥattaaa iẕaa jaaa'a aḥadahumul-mawtu qaala Rabbirji'oon.

حَتَّىٰٓ إِذَا جَآءَ أَحَدَهُمُ ٱلۡمَوۡتُ قَالَ
رَبِّ ٱرۡجِعُونِ ﴿٩٩﴾

100. "In order that I may work righteousness in the things I neglected." - "By no means! It is but a word he says."- Before them is a Partition till the Day they are raised up.

100. La'alleee a'malu ṣaaliḥan feemaa taraktu kallaa; innahaa kalimatun huwa qaaa'iluhaa wa miñw-waraaa'ihim barzakhun ilaa Yawmi yub'asoon.

لَعَلِّيٓ أَعۡمَلُ صَٰلِحٗا فِيمَا تَرَكۡتُۚ
كَلَّآۚ إِنَّهَا كَلِمَةٌ هُوَ قَآئِلُهَاۖ
وَمِن وَرَآئِهِم بَرۡزَخٌ إِلَىٰ يَوۡمِ
يُبۡعَثُونَ ﴿١٠٠﴾

101. Then when the Trumpet is blown, there will be no more relationships between them that Day, nor will one ask after another!

101. Fa-iẕaa nufikha fiṣ-Ṣoori falaaa ansaaba baynahum Yawma'iẕiñw-wa laa yatasaaa'aloon.

فَإِذَا نُفِخَ فِي ٱلصُّورِ فَلَآ أَنسَابَ
بَيۡنَهُمۡ يَوۡمَئِذٖ وَلَا يَتَسَآءَلُونَ ﴿١٠١﴾

Ikhfa اخفاء | Ghunna غنّہ | Ikhfa Meem Saakin اخفاء میم ساکن | Idghaam ادغام | Qalqala قلقلہ | Qalb قلب | Idghaam Meem Saakin ادغام میم ساکن

102. Then those whose balance (of good deeds) is heavy,- they will attain salvation:

102. Faman saqulat mawaazeenuhoo fa-ulaaa'ika humul-muflihoon.

فَمَنْ ثَقُلَتْ مَوَازِيْنُهٗ فَاُولٰٓئِكَ هُمُ الْمُفْلِحُوْنَ ۝١٠٢

103. But those whose balance is light, will be those who have lost their souls, in Hell will they abide.

103. Wa man khaffat mawaazeenuhoo fa-ulaaa'ikal-lazeena khasirooo anfusahum fee Jahannama khaalidoon.

وَمَنْ خَفَّتْ مَوَازِيْنُهٗ فَاُولٰٓئِكَ الَّذِيْنَ خَسِرُوْٓا اَنْفُسَهُمْ فِيْ جَهَنَّمَ خٰلِدُوْنَ ۝١٠٣

104. The Fire will burn their faces, and they will therein grin, with their lips displaced.

104. Talfahu wujoohahumun-Naaru wa hum feehaa kaalihoon.

تَلْفَحُ وُجُوْهَهُمُ النَّارُ وَهُمْ فِيْهَا كٰلِحُوْنَ ۝١٠٤

105. "Were not My Signs rehearsed to you, and you but treated them as falsehoods?"

105. Alam takun Aayaatee tutlaa 'alaykum fakuntum bihaa tukazziboon.

اَلَمْ تَكُنْ اٰيٰتِيْ تُتْلٰى عَلَيْكُمْ فَكُنْتُمْ بِهَا تُكَذِّبُوْنَ ۝١٠٥

106. They will say: "Our Lord! our misfortune overwhelmed us, and we became a people astray!

106. Qaaloo Rabbanaa ghalabat 'alaynaa shiqwatunaa wa kunnaa qawman daaalleen.

قَالُوْا رَبَّنَا غَلَبَتْ عَلَيْنَا شِقْوَتُنَا وَكُنَّا قَوْمًا ضَآلِّيْنَ ۝١٠٦

107. "Our Lord! bring us out of this: if ever we return (to Evil), then shall we be wrong-doers indeed!"

107. Rabbanaaa akhrijnaa minhaa fa-in 'udnaa fa-innaa zaalimoon.

رَبَّنَآ اَخْرِجْنَا مِنْهَا فَاِنْ عُدْنَا فَاِنَّا ظٰلِمُوْنَ ۝١٠٧

108. He will say: "Be you driven into it (with ignominy)! And do not speak to Me!

108. Qaalakh-sa'oo feehaa wa laa tukallimoon.

قَالَ اخْسَـُٔوْا فِيْهَا وَلَا تُكَلِّمُوْنِ ۝١٠٨

109. "A part of My servants there was, who used to pray 'Our Lord! we believe; then you forgive us, and have mercy upon us: for you are the Best of those who show mercy!"

109. Innahoo kaana fareequm-min 'ibaadee yaqooloona Rabbanaaa aamannaa faghfir lanaa warhamnaa wa Anta khayrur-raahimeen.

اِنَّهٗ كَانَ فَرِيْقٌ مِّنْ عِبَادِيْ يَقُوْلُوْنَ رَبَّنَآ اٰمَنَّا فَاغْفِرْ لَنَا وَارْحَمْنَا وَاَنْتَ خَيْرُ الرّٰحِمِيْنَ ۝١٠٩

110. "But you treated them with ridicule, so much so that (ridicule of) them made you forget My Message while you were laughing at them!

110. Fattakhaztumoohum sikhriyyan hattaaa ansawkum zikree wa kuntum-minhum tadhakoon.

فَاتَّخَذْتُمُوْهُمْ سِخْرِيًّا حَتّٰٓى اَنْسَوْكُمْ ذِكْرِيْ وَكُنْتُمْ مِّنْهُمْ تَضْحَكُوْنَ ۝١١٠

111. "I have rewarded them this Day for their patience and constancy: they are indeed the ones that have achieved bliss..."

111. Innee jazaytuhumul-Yawma bimaa sabarooo annahum humul-faaa'izoon.

اِنِّيْ جَزَيْتُهُمُ الْيَوْمَ بِمَا صَبَرُوْٓا اَنَّهُمْ هُمُ الْفَآئِزُوْنَ ۝١١١

112. He will say: "What number of years did you stay on earth?"

112. Qaala kam labistum fil-ardi 'adada sineen.

قٰلَ كَمْ لَبِثْتُمْ فِي الْاَرْضِ عَدَدَ سِنِيْنَ ۝١١٢

113. They will say: "We stayed a day or part of a day: but ask those who keep account."

113. Qaaloo labisnaa yawman aw ba'da yawmin fas'alil-'aaaddeen.

قَالُوْا لَبِثْنَا يَوْمًا اَوْ بَعْضَ يَوْمٍ فَسْـَٔلِ الْعَآدِّيْنَ ۝١١٣

114. He will say: "You stayed not but a little,- if you had only known!

114. Qaala il-labistum illaa qaleelal-law annakum kuntum ta'lamoon.

قٰلَ اِنْ لَّبِثْتُمْ اِلَّا قَلِيْلًا لَّوْ اَنَّكُمْ كُنْتُمْ تَعْلَمُوْنَ ۝١١٤

Ikhfa اخفاء | Ghunna غُنّہ | Ikhfa Meem Saakin اخفاء میم ساکن | Idghaam ادغام | Qalqala قلقلہ | Qalb قلب | Idghaam Meem Saakin ادغام میم ساکن

115. "Did you then think that We had created you in jest, and that you would not be brought back to Us (for account)?"

116. Therefore exalted be Allah, the King, the Reality: there is no god but He, the Lord of the Throne of Honor!

117. If anyone invokes, besides Allah, Any other god, he has no authority therefor; and his reckoning will be only with his Lord! and verily the Unbelievers shall not Prosper!

118. So say: "O my Lord! Grant us forgiveness and mercy! for you are the Best of those who show mercy!"

24. The Light

In the name of Allah, Most Gracious, Most Merciful.

1. A Surah which We have sent down and which We have ordained: in it We have sent down Clear Signs, in order that you may receive admonition.

2. The woman and the man guilty of adultery or fornication,- flog each of them with a hundred stripes: let not compassion move you in their case, in a matter prescribed by Allah, if you believe in Allah and the Last Day: and let a party of the Believers witness their punishment.

3. Let no man guilty of adultery or fornication marry any but a woman similarly guilty, or an Unbeliever: nor let any but such a man or an Unbeliever marry such a woman: to the Believers such a thing is forbidden.

4. And those who launch a charge against chaste women, and produce not four witnesses (to support their allegations),- flog them with eighty stripes; and reject their evidence ever after: for such men are wicked transgressors;-

115. Afaḥasibtum annamaa khalaqnaakum 'abasañw-wa annakum ilaynaa laa turja'oon.

116. Fata'aalal-laahul-Malikul-Ḥaqq; laaa ilaaha illaa Huwa Rabbul-'Arshil-Kareem.

117. Wa mañy-yad'u ma'allaahi ilaahan aakhara laa burhaana lahoo bihee fa-innamaa ḥisaabuhoo 'inda Rabbih; innahoo laa yufliḥul-kaafiroon.

118. Wa qur-Rabbigh-fir warḥam wa Anta khayrur-raaḥimeen. **(Section 6)**

Sûrat an-Nûr–24

(Revealed at Madinah)

Bismillaahir Raḥmaanir Raḥeem

1. Sooratun anzalnaahaa wa faraḍnaahaa wa anzalnaa feehaaa Aayaatim-bayyinaatil-la'allakum tazakkaroon.

2. Azzaaniyatu wazzaanee fajlidoo kulla waaḥidim-minhumaa mi'ata jaldatiñw-wa laa taåkhuzkum bihimaa raåfatun fee deenil-laahi in kuntum tu'minoona billaahi wal-Yawmil-Aakhiri wal-yashhad 'azaabahumaa ṭaaa'ifatum-minal-mu'mineen.

3. Azzaanee laa yankiḥu illaa zaaniyatan aw mushrikatañw-wazzaaniyatu laa yankiḥuhaaa illaa zaanin aw mushrik; wa ḥurrima zaalika 'alal-mu'mineen.

4. Wallazeena yarmoonal-muḥṣanaati summa lam yaåtoo bi-arba'ati shuhadaaa'a fajlidoohum samaaneena jaldatañw-wa laa taqbaloo lahum shahaadatan abadaa; wa ulaaa'ika humul-faasiqoon.

أَفَحَسِبْتُمْ أَنَّمَا خَلَقْنَٰكُمْ عَبَثًا
وَأَنَّكُمْ إِلَيْنَا لَا تُرْجَعُونَ ﴿١١٥﴾
فَتَعَٰلَى ٱللَّهُ ٱلْمَلِكُ ٱلْحَقُّ لَآ إِلَٰهَ إِلَّا
هُوَ رَبُّ ٱلْعَرْشِ ٱلْكَرِيمِ ﴿١١٦﴾
وَمَن يَدْعُ مَعَ ٱللَّهِ إِلَٰهًا ءَاخَرَ لَا
بُرْهَٰنَ لَهُۥ بِهِۦ فَإِنَّمَا حِسَابُهُۥ عِندَ
رَبِّهِۦٓ إِنَّهُۥ لَا يُفْلِحُ ٱلْكَٰفِرُونَ ﴿١١٧﴾
وَقُل رَّبِّ ٱغْفِرْ وَٱرْحَمْ وَأَنتَ
خَيْرُ ٱلرَّٰحِمِينَ ﴿١١٨﴾

سُورَةُ ٱلنُّورِ مَدَنِيَّةٌ (٢٤) (١٠٢)

بِسْمِ ٱللَّهِ ٱلرَّحْمَٰنِ ٱلرَّحِيمِ

سُورَةٌ أَنزَلْنَٰهَا وَفَرَضْنَٰهَا وَأَنزَلْنَا
فِيهَآ ءَايَٰتٍۭ بَيِّنَٰتٍ لَّعَلَّكُمْ تَذَكَّرُونَ ﴿١﴾
ٱلزَّانِيَةُ وَٱلزَّانِى فَٱجْلِدُوا۟ كُلَّ وَٰحِدٍ
مِّنْهُمَا مِا۟ئَةَ جَلْدَةٍ وَلَا تَأْخُذْكُم
بِهِمَا رَأْفَةٌ فِى دِينِ ٱللَّهِ إِن كُنتُمْ
تُؤْمِنُونَ بِٱللَّهِ وَٱلْيَوْمِ ٱلْءَاخِرِ وَلْيَشْهَدْ
عَذَابَهُمَا طَآئِفَةٌ مِّنَ ٱلْمُؤْمِنِينَ ﴿٢﴾
ٱلزَّانِى لَا يَنكِحُ إِلَّا زَانِيَةً أَوْ مُشْرِكَةً
وَٱلزَّانِيَةُ لَا يَنكِحُهَآ إِلَّا زَانٍ
أَوْ مُشْرِكٌ وَحُرِّمَ ذَٰلِكَ عَلَى
ٱلْمُؤْمِنِينَ ﴿٣﴾
وَٱلَّذِينَ يَرْمُونَ ٱلْمُحْصَنَٰتِ ثُمَّ لَمْ
يَأْتُوا۟ بِأَرْبَعَةِ شُهَدَآءَ فَٱجْلِدُوهُمْ
ثَمَٰنِينَ جَلْدَةً وَلَا تَقْبَلُوا۟ لَهُمْ شَهَٰدَةً
أَبَدًا وَأُو۟لَٰٓئِكَ هُمُ ٱلْفَٰسِقُونَ ﴿٤﴾

Ikhfa اخفاء	Ghunna غنّہ	Ikhfa Meem Saakin اخفاء میم ساکن	Idghaam ادغام	Qalqala قلقلہ	Qalb قلب	Idghaam Meem Saakin ادغام میم ساکن

5. Unless they repent thereafter and mend (their conduct); for Allah is Oft-Forgiving, Most Merciful.

5. Illal-lazeena taaboo mim ba'di zaalika wa aṣlaḥoo fa-innal-laaha Ghafoorur Raḥeem.

إِلَّا الَّذِينَ تَابُوا مِنْ بَعْدِ ذٰلِكَ
وَأَصْلَحُوا فَإِنَّ اللّٰهَ غَفُورٌ رَّحِيمٌ ﴿٥﴾

6. And for those who launch a charge against their spouses,or (wives) and have (in support) no evidence but their own,- their solitary evidence (can be received) if they bear witness four times (with an oath) by Allah that they are solemnly telling the truth;

6. Wallazeena yarmoona azwaajahum wa lam yakul-lahum shuhadaaa'u illaaa anfusuhum fashahaadatu aḥadihim arba'u shahaadaatim billaahi innahoo laminaṣ-ṣaadiqeen.

وَالَّذِينَ يَرْمُونَ أَزْوَاجَهُمْ وَلَمْ
يَكُنْ لَّهُمْ شُهَدَاءُ إِلَّا أَنْفُسُهُمْ
فَشَهَادَةُ أَحَدِهِمْ أَرْبَعُ شَهٰدٰتٍ
بِاللّٰهِ إِنَّهُ لَمِنَ الصّٰدِقِينَ ﴿٦﴾

7. And the fifth (oath) (should be) that they solemnly invoke the curse of Allah on themselves if they tell a lie.

7. Wal-khaamisatu anna la'natal-laahi 'alayhi in kaana minal-kaazibeen.

وَالْخَامِسَةُ أَنَّ لَعْنَتَ اللّٰهِ عَلَيْهِ
إِنْ كَانَ مِنَ الْكٰذِبِينَ ﴿٧﴾

8. But it would avert the punishment from the wife, if she bears witness four times (with an oath) By Allah, that (her husband) is telling a lie;

8. Wa yadra'u anhal-'azaaba an tashhada arba'a shahaa-daatim billaahi innahoo laminal-kaazibeen.

وَيَدْرَؤُا عَنْهَا الْعَذَابَ أَنْ تَشْهَدَ
أَرْبَعَ شَهٰدٰتٍ بِاللّٰهِ إِنَّهُ لَمِنَ
الْكٰذِبِينَ ﴿٨﴾

9. And the fifth (oath) should be that she solemnly invokes the wrath of Allah on herself if (her accuser) is telling the truth.

9. Wal-khaamisata anna ghaḍabal-laahi 'alayhaaa in kaana minaṣ-ṣaadiqeen.

وَالْخَامِسَةَ أَنَّ غَضَبَ اللّٰهِ عَلَيْهَا
إِنْ كَانَ مِنَ الصّٰدِقِينَ ﴿٩﴾

10. If it were not for Allah's grace and mercy on you, and that Allah is Oft- Returning, full of Wisdom,- (You would be ruined indeed).

10. Wa law laa faḍlul-laahi 'alaykum wa raḥmatuhoo wa annal-laaha Tawwaabun Ḥakeem. **(Section 1)**

وَلَوْلَا فَضْلُ اللّٰهِ عَلَيْكُمْ وَرَحْمَتُهُ
وَأَنَّ اللّٰهَ تَوَّابٌ حَكِيمٌ ﴿١٠﴾

11. Those who brought forward the lie are a body among yourselves: think it not to be an evil to you; on the contrary it is good for you: to every man among them (will come the punishment) of the sin that he earned, and for him who took on himself the lead among them, will be a Penalty grievous.

11. Innal-lazeena jaaa'oo bil-ifki 'uṣbatum-minkum; laa taḥsaboohu sharral-lakum bal huwa khayrul-lakum; likul-limri'im-minhum-mak-tasaba minal-ism; wallazee tawallaa kibrahoo minhum lahoo 'azaabun 'aẓeem.

إِنَّ الَّذِينَ جَاءُو بِالْإِفْكِ عُصْبَةٌ
مِّنْكُمْ لَا تَحْسَبُوهُ شَرًّا لَّكُمْ بَلْ هُوَ
خَيْرٌ لَّكُمْ لِكُلِّ امْرِئٍ مِّنْهُمْ مَّا
اكْتَسَبَ مِنَ الْإِثْمِ وَالَّذِي تَوَلّٰى
كِبْرَهُ مِنْهُمْ لَهُ عَذَابٌ عَظِيمٌ ﴿١١﴾

12. Why did not the believers - men and women - when you heard of the affair,- thought well of their people and say, "This (charge) is an obvious lie"?

12. Law laaa iz sami'tumoohu ẓannal-mu'minoona walmu'-minaatu bi-anfusihim khay-rañw-wa qaaloo haazaaa ifkum-mubeen.

لَوْلَا إِذْ سَمِعْتُمُوهُ ظَنَّ الْمُؤْمِنُونَ
وَالْمُؤْمِنٰتُ بِأَنْفُسِهِمْ خَيْرًا وَّقَالُوا
هٰذَا إِفْكٌ مُّبِينٌ ﴿١٢﴾

13. Why did they not bring four witnesses to prove it? When they have not brought the witnesses, such men, in the sight of Allah, (stand forth) themselves as liars!

13. Law laa jaaa'oo 'alayhi bi-arba'ati shuhadaaa'; fa-iz lam yaåtoo bishshuhadaaa'i fa-ulaaa'ika 'indal-laahi humul-kaaziboon.

لَوْلَا جَاءُو عَلَيْهِ بِأَرْبَعَةِ شُهَدَاءَ
فَإِذْ لَمْ يَأْتُوا بِالشُّهَدَاءِ فَأُولٰئِكَ
عِنْدَ اللّٰهِ هُمُ الْكٰذِبُونَ ﴿١٣﴾

Ikhfa اخفاء | Ghunna غنّہ | Ikhfa Meem Saakin اخفاء میم ساکن | Idghaam ادغام | Qalqala قلقلہ | Qalb قلب | Idghaam Meem Saakin ادغام میم ساکن

14. Were it not for the grace and mercy of Allah on you, in this world and the Hereafter, a grievous Penalty would have seized you in that you rushed glibly into this affair.

14. Wa law laa faḍlul-laahi 'alaykum wa raḥmatuhoo fiddunyaa wal-Aakhirati lamassakum fee maaa afaḍtum feehi 'azaabun 'aẓeem.

وَلَوْلَا فَضْلُ اللّٰهِ عَلَيْكُمْ وَرَحْمَتُهٗ
فِي الدُّنْيَا وَالْاٰخِرَةِ لَمَسَّكُمْ فِيْ مَآ
اَفَضْتُمْ فِيْهِ عَذَابٌ عَظِيْمٌ ﴿١٤﴾

15. Behold, you received it on your tongues, and said out of your mouths things of which you had no knowledge; and you thought it to be a light matter, while it was most serious in the sight of Allah.

15. Iz talaqqawnahoo bi-alsinatikum wa taqooloona bi-afwaahikum-maa laysa lakum bihee 'ilmuñw-wa taḥsaboo-nahoo hayyinañw-wa huwa 'indal-laahi 'aẓeem.

اِذْ تَلَقَّوْنَهٗ بِاَلْسِنَتِكُمْ وَتَقُوْلُوْنَ
بِاَفْوَاهِكُمْ مَّا لَيْسَ لَكُمْ بِهٖ عِلْمٌ
وَّتَحْسَبُوْنَهٗ هَيِّنًا ۖ وَّهُوَ عِنْدَ
اللّٰهِ عَظِيْمٌ ﴿١٥﴾

16. And why did you not, when you heard it, say? - "It is not right of us to speak of this: Glory to Allah! this is a most serious slander!"

16. Wa law laaa iz sami'tu-moohu qultum-maa yakoonu lanaaa an-natakallama bihaazaa Subḥaanaka haazaa buhtaanun 'aẓeem.

وَلَوْلَآ اِذْ سَمِعْتُمُوْهُ قُلْتُمْ مَّا يَكُوْنُ
لَنَآ اَنْ نَّتَكَلَّمَ بِهٰذَا ۖ سُبْحٰنَكَ
هٰذَا بُهْتَانٌ عَظِيْمٌ ﴿١٦﴾

17. Allah admonishes you, that you may never repeat such (conduct), if you are (true) Believers.

17. Ya'iẓukumul-laahu an ta'oodoo limisliheee abadan in kuntum-mu'mineen.

يَعِظُكُمُ اللّٰهُ اَنْ تَعُوْدُوْا لِمِثْلِهٖٓ اَبَدًا
اِنْ كُنْتُمْ مُّؤْمِنِيْنَ ﴿١٧﴾

18. And Allah makes the Signs plain to you: for Allah is full of knowledge and wisdom.

18. Wa yubayyinul-laahu lakumul-Aayaat; wallaahu 'Aleemun Ḥakeem.

وَيُبَيِّنُ اللّٰهُ لَكُمُ الْاٰيٰتِ ؕ وَاللّٰهُ
عَلِيْمٌ حَكِيْمٌ ﴿١٨﴾

19. Those who love (to see) scandal published broadcast among the Believers, will have a grievous Penalty in this life and in the Hereafter: Allah knows, and you do not know.

19. Innal-lazeena yuḥibboona an tashee'al-faaḥishatu fil-lazeena aamanoo lahum 'azaabun aleemun fid-dunyaa wal-Aakhirah; wallaahu ya'la-mu wa antum laa ta'lamoon.

اِنَّ الَّذِيْنَ يُحِبُّوْنَ اَنْ تَشِيْعَ الْفَاحِشَةُ
فِي الَّذِيْنَ اٰمَنُوْا لَهُمْ عَذَابٌ اَلِيْمٌ ۙ
فِي الدُّنْيَا وَالْاٰخِرَةِ ؕ وَاللّٰهُ يَعْلَمُ
وَاَنْتُمْ لَا تَعْلَمُوْنَ ﴿١٩﴾

20. Were it not for the grace and mercy of Allah on you, and that Allah is full of kindness and mercy, (you would be ruined indeed).

20. Wa law laa faḍlul-laahi 'alaykum wa raḥmatuhoo wa annal-laaha Ra'oofur-Raḥeem.

(Section 2)

وَلَوْلَا فَضْلُ اللّٰهِ عَلَيْكُمْ وَرَحْمَتُهٗ
وَاَنَّ اللّٰهَ رَءُوْفٌ رَّحِيْمٌ ﴿٢٠﴾ ع

ع ٨ النصف

21. O you who believe! Do not follow Satan's footsteps: if any will follow the footsteps of Satan, he will (but) command what is shameful and wrong: and were it not for the grace and mercy of Allah on you, not one of you would ever have been pure: but Allah does purify whom He pleases:

21. Yaaa ayyuhal-lazeena aamanoo laa tattabi'oo khuṭuwaatish-Shayṭaan; wa mañy-yattabi' khuṭuwaatish-Shayṭaani fa-innahoo yaåmuru bilfaḥshaaa'i walmunkar; wa law laa faḍlul-laahi 'alaykum wa raḥmatuhoo maa zakaa minkum-min aḥadin abadañw-wa laakinnal-laaha yuzakkee mañy-yashaaa';

يٰٓاَيُّهَا الَّذِيْنَ اٰمَنُوْا لَا تَتَّبِعُوْا خُطُوٰتِ
الشَّيْطٰنِ ؕ وَمَنْ يَّتَّبِعْ خُطُوٰتِ
الشَّيْطٰنِ فَاِنَّهٗ يَاْمُرُ بِالْفَحْشَآءِ
وَالْمُنْكَرِ ؕ وَلَوْلَا فَضْلُ اللّٰهِ عَلَيْكُمْ
وَرَحْمَتُهٗ مَا زَكٰى مِنْكُمْ مِّنْ اَحَدٍ
اَبَدًا ۙ وَّلٰكِنَّ اللّٰهَ يُزَكِّيْ مَنْ يَّشَآءُ ؕ

Ikhfa اخفاء | Ghunna غُنَّہ | Ikhfa Meem Saakin اخفاء میم ساکن | Idghaam ادغام | Qalqala قلقلہ | Qalb قلب | Idghaam Meem Saakin ادغام میم ساکن

and Allah is one Who hears and knows (all things).

wallaahu Samee'un 'Aleem.

وَاللّٰهُ سَمِيۡعٌ عَلِيۡمٌ ﴿۲۱﴾

22. Let not those among you who are endued with grace and amplitude of means resolve by oath against helping their kinsmen, those in want, and those who have left their homes in Allah's cause: let them forgive and overlook, do you not wish that Allah should forgive you? For Allah is Oft-Forgiving, Most Merciful.

22. Wa laa yaåtali ulul-faḍli minkum wassa'ati añy-yu'tooo ulil-qurbaa walmasaakeena walmuhaajireena fee sabeelillaahi walya'foo walyaṣfaḥoo; alaa tuḥibboona añy-yaghfiral-laahu lakum; wallaahu Ghafoorur-Raḥeem.

وَلَا يَاۡتَلِ اُولُوا الۡفَضۡلِ مِنۡكُمۡ
وَالسَّعَةِ اَنۡ يُّؤۡتُوۡۤا اُولِى الۡقُرۡبٰى
وَالۡمَسٰكِيۡنَ وَالۡمُهٰجِرِيۡنَ فِىۡ سَبِيۡلِ
اللّٰهِ ۖ وَلۡيَعۡفُوۡا وَلۡيَصۡفَحُوۡا ؕ اَلَا
تُحِبُّوۡنَ اَنۡ يَّغۡفِرَ اللّٰهُ لَكُمۡ ؕ وَاللّٰهُ
غَفُوۡرٌ رَّحِيۡمٌ ﴿۲۲﴾

23. Those who slander chaste women, indiscreet but believing, are cursed in this life and in the Hereafter: for them is a grievous Penalty,-

23. Innal-lazeena yarmoonal-muḥṣanaatil-ghaafilaatil-mu'minaati lu'inoo fid-dunyaa wal-Aakhirati wa lahum 'azaabun 'azeem.

اِنَّ الَّذِيۡنَ يَرۡمُوۡنَ الۡمُحۡصَنٰتِ
الۡغٰفِلٰتِ الۡمُؤۡمِنٰتِ لُعِنُوۡا فِى الدُّنۡيَا
وَالۡاٰخِرَةِ وَلَهُمۡ عَذَابٌ عَظِيۡمٌ ﴿۲۳﴾

24. On the Day when their tongues, their hands, and their feet will bear witness against them as to their actions.

24. Yawma tashhadu 'alayhim alsinatuhum wa aydeehim wa arjuluhum bimaa kaanoo ya'maloon.

يَّوۡمَ تَشۡهَدُ عَلَيۡهِمۡ اَلۡسِنَتُهُمۡ
وَاَيۡدِيۡهِمۡ وَاَرۡجُلُهُمۡ بِمَا كَانُوۡا
يَعۡمَلُوۡنَ ﴿۲۴﴾

25. On that Day Allah will pay them back (all) their just dues, and they will realise that Allah is the (very) Truth, that makes all things manifest.

25. Yawma'iziñy-yuwaffeehimul-laahu deenahumul-ḥaqqa wa ya'lamoona annal-laaha Huwal-Ḥaqqul-Mubeen.

يَوۡمَئِذٍ يُّوَفِّيۡهِمُ اللّٰهُ دِيۡنَهُمُ الۡحَقَّ
وَيَعۡلَمُوۡنَ اَنَّ اللّٰهَ هُوَ الۡحَقُّ الۡمُبِيۡنُ ﴿۲۵﴾

26. Women impure are for men impure, and men impure for women impure and women of purity are for men of purity, and men of purity are for women of purity: these are not affected by what people say: for them there is forgiveness, and a provision honorable.

26. Alkhabeesaatu lilkhabeeseena walkhabeesoona lilkhabeesaati waṭṭayyibaatu liṭṭayyibeena waṭṭayyiboona liṭṭayyibaat; ulaaa'ika mubarra'oona mimmaa yaqooloona lahum-maghfiratuñw-wa rizqun kareem. **(Section 3)**

اَلۡخَبِيۡثٰتُ لِلۡخَبِيۡثِيۡنَ وَالۡخَبِيۡثُوۡنَ
لِلۡخَبِيۡثٰتِ ۚ وَالطَّيِّبٰتُ لِلطَّيِّبِيۡنَ
وَالطَّيِّبُوۡنَ لِلطَّيِّبٰتِ ۚ اُولٰٓئِكَ مُبَرَّءُوۡنَ
مِمَّا يَقُوۡلُوۡنَ ؕ لَهُمۡ مَّغۡفِرَةٌ وَّرِزۡقٌ
كَرِيۡمٌ ﴿۲۶﴾ ع

27. O you who believe! Do not enter houses other than your own, until you have asked permission and saluted those in them: that is best for you, in order that you may heed (what is seemly).

27. Yaaa ayyuhal-lazeena aamanoo laa tadkhuloo buyootan ghayra buyootikum ḥattaa tastaånisoo wa tusallimoo 'allaa ahlihaa; zaalikum khayrul-lakum la'allakum tazakkaroon.

يٰۤاَيُّهَا الَّذِيۡنَ اٰمَنُوۡا لَا تَدۡخُلُوۡا
بُيُوۡتًا غَيۡرَ بُيُوۡتِكُمۡ حَتّٰى تَسۡتَاۡنِسُوۡا
وَتُسَلِّمُوۡا عَلٰٓى اَهۡلِهَا ؕ ذٰلِكُمۡ خَيۡرٌ
لَّكُمۡ لَعَلَّكُمۡ تَذَكَّرُوۡنَ ﴿۲۷﴾

28. If you find no one in the house, do not enter until permission is given to you: if

28. Fa-il-lam tajidoo feehaaa aḥadan falaa tadkhuloohaa ḥattaa yu'zana lakum wa in

فَاِنۡ لَّمۡ تَجِدُوۡا فِيۡهَاۤ اَحَدًا فَلَا
تَدۡخُلُوۡهَا حَتّٰى يُؤۡذَنَ لَكُمۡ ۚ وَاِنۡ

Ikhfa اخفاء | Ghunna غنّہ | Ikhfa Meem Saakin اخفاء میم ساکن | Idghaam ادغام | Qalqala قلقلہ | Qalb قلب | Idghaam Meem Saakin ادغام میم ساکن

you are asked to go back, go back: that makes for greater purity for yourselves: and Allah knows well all that you do.

29. It is no fault on your part to enter houses not used for living in, which serve some (other) use for you: And Allah has knowledge of what you reveal and what you conceal.

30. Say to the believing men that they should lower their gaze and guard their modesty: that will make for greater purity for them: and Allah is well acquainted with all that they do.

31. And say to the believing women that they should lower their gaze and guard their modesty; that they should not display their beauty and ornaments except what (must ordinarily) appear thereof; that they should draw their veils over their bosoms and not display their beauty except to their husbands, their fathers, their husband's fathers, their sons, their husbands' sons, their brothers or their brothers' sons, or their sisters' sons, or their women, or the slaves whom their right hands possess, or male servants free of sexual urge, or small children who have no sense of the shame of sex; and that they should not strike their feet in order to draw attention to their hidden ornaments. And O you Believers! You turn all together towards Allah, that you may attain Bliss.

qeela lakumurji'oo farji'oo huwa azkaa lakum; wallaahu bimaa ta'maloona 'Aleem.

29. Laysa 'alaykum junaaḥun an tadkhuloo buyootan ghayra maskoonatin feehaa mataa'ul-lakum; wallaahu ya'lamu maa tubdoona wa maa taktumoon.

30. Qul lilmu'mineena yaghuḍḍoo min abṣaarihim wa yaḥfaẓoo furoojahum; ẕaalika azkaa lahum; innallaaha khabeerum bimaa yaṣna'oon.

31. Wa qul lilmu'minaati yaghḍuḍna min abṣaarihinna wa yaḥfaẓna furoojahunna wa laa yubdeena zeenatahunna illaa maa ẓahara minhaa walyaḍribna bikhumurihinna 'alaa juyoobihinna wa laa yubdeena zeenatahunna illaa libu'oolatihinna aw aabaaa'i-hinna aw aabaaa'i bu'oolati-hinna aw abnaaa'ihinaa aw abnaaa'i bu'oolatihinna aw ikhwaanihinna aw baneee ikhwaanihinna aw baneee akhawaatihinna aw nisaaa'i-hinna aw maa malakat aymaanuhunna awit-taabi'eena ghayri ulil-irbati minar-rijaali awiṭ-ṭiflillaẕeena lam yaẓharoo 'alaa 'awraatin-nisaaa'i wa laa yaḍribna bi-arjulihinna liyu'lama maa yukhfeena min zeenatihinn; wa toobooo ilallaahi jamee'an ayyuhal-mu'minoona la'allakum tufliḥoon.

قِيلَ لَكُمُ ارْجِعُوا فَارْجِعُوا هُوَ أَزْكَىٰ
لَكُمْ ۚ وَاللَّهُ بِمَا تَعْمَلُونَ عَلِيمٌ ٢٨
لَيْسَ عَلَيْكُمْ جُنَاحٌ أَنْ تَدْخُلُوا
بُيُوتًا غَيْرَ مَسْكُونَةٍ فِيهَا مَتَاعٌ
لَكُمْ ۚ وَاللَّهُ يَعْلَمُ مَا تُبْدُونَ وَمَا
تَكْتُمُونَ ٢٩
قُلْ لِلْمُؤْمِنِينَ يَغُضُّوا مِنْ أَبْصَارِهِمْ
وَيَحْفَظُوا فُرُوجَهُمْ ۚ ذَٰلِكَ أَزْكَىٰ
لَهُمْ ۗ إِنَّ اللَّهَ خَبِيرٌ بِمَا يَصْنَعُونَ ٣٠
وَقُلْ لِلْمُؤْمِنَاتِ يَغْضُضْنَ مِنْ
أَبْصَارِهِنَّ وَيَحْفَظْنَ فُرُوجَهُنَّ
وَلَا يُبْدِينَ زِينَتَهُنَّ إِلَّا مَا ظَهَرَ
مِنْهَا ۖ وَلْيَضْرِبْنَ بِخُمُرِهِنَّ عَلَىٰ
جُيُوبِهِنَّ ۖ وَلَا يُبْدِينَ زِينَتَهُنَّ
إِلَّا لِبُعُولَتِهِنَّ أَوْ آبَائِهِنَّ أَوْ
آبَاءِ بُعُولَتِهِنَّ أَوْ أَبْنَائِهِنَّ أَوْ أَبْنَاءِ
بُعُولَتِهِنَّ أَوْ إِخْوَانِهِنَّ أَوْ بَنِي
إِخْوَانِهِنَّ أَوْ بَنِي أَخَوَاتِهِنَّ أَوْ
نِسَائِهِنَّ أَوْ مَا مَلَكَتْ أَيْمَانُهُنَّ
أَوِ التَّابِعِينَ غَيْرِ أُولِي الْإِرْبَةِ
مِنَ الرِّجَالِ أَوِ الطِّفْلِ الَّذِينَ لَمْ
يَظْهَرُوا عَلَىٰ عَوْرَاتِ النِّسَاءِ ۖ وَلَا
يَضْرِبْنَ بِأَرْجُلِهِنَّ لِيُعْلَمَ مَا يُخْفِينَ
مِنْ زِينَتِهِنَّ ۚ وَتُوبُوا إِلَى اللَّهِ
جَمِيعًا أَيُّهَ الْمُؤْمِنُونَ لَعَلَّكُمْ
تُفْلِحُونَ ٣١

Ikhfa اخفاء | Ghunna غُنّہ | Ikhfa Meem Saakin اخفاء میم ساکن | Idghaam ادغام | Qalqala قلقلہ | Qalb قلب | Idghaam Meem Saakin ادغام میم ساکن

32. Marry those among you who are single, or the virtuous ones among yourselves, male or female: if they are in poverty, Allah will give them means out of His grace: for Allah encompasses all, and he knows all things.

32. Wa ankiḥul-ayaamaa minkum waṣ-ṣaaliḥeena min ʻibaadikum wa imaa'ikum; iñy-yakoonoo fuqaraaa'a yughnihimul-laahu min faḍlih; wallaahu Waasiʻun ʻAleem.

وَاَنْكِحُوا الْاَيَامٰى مِنْكُمْ وَالصّٰلِحِيْنَ
مِنْ عِبَادِكُمْ وَاِمَآئِكُمْ ۭ اِنْ يَّكُوْنُوْا
فُقَرَآءَ يُغْنِهِمُ اللّٰهُ مِنْ فَضْلِهٖ ۭ
وَاللّٰهُ وَاسِعٌ عَلِيْمٌ ﴿٣٢﴾

33. Let those who find not the wherewithal for marriage keep themselves chaste, until Allah gives them means out of His grace. And if any of your slaves ask for a deed in writing (to enable them to earn their freedom for a certain sum), give them such a deed if you know any good in them: yes, give them something yourselves out of the means which Allah has given to you. But force not your maids to prostitution when they desire chastity, in order that you may make a gain in the goods of this life. But if anyone compels them, yet, after such compulsion, is Allah, Oft-Forgiving, Most Merciful (to them),

33. Wal-yastaʻfifil-lazeena laa yajidoona nikaaḥan ḥattaa yughniyahumul-laahu min faḍlih; wallazeena yabtaghoonal-kitaaba mimmaa malakat aymaanukum fakaatiboohum in ʻalimtum feehim khayrañw-wa aatoohum-mim-maalil-laahil-lazeee aataakum; wa laa tukrihoo fatayaatikum ʻalal-bighaaa'i in aradna taḥaṣṣunal-litabtaghoo ʻaraḍal-ḥayaatid-dunyaa; wa mañy-yukrihhunna fa-innal-laaha mim baʻdi ikraahihinna Ghafoorur-Raḥeem.

وَلْيَسْتَعْفِفِ الَّذِيْنَ لَا يَجِدُوْنَ
نِكَاحًا حَتّٰى يُغْنِيَهُمُ اللّٰهُ مِنْ
فَضْلِهٖ ۭ وَالَّذِيْنَ يَبْتَغُوْنَ الْكِتٰبَ
مِمَّا مَلَكَتْ اَيْمَانُكُمْ فَكَاتِبُوْهُمْ اِنْ
عَلِمْتُمْ فِيْهِمْ خَيْرًا ڰ وَّاٰتُوْهُمْ مِّنْ
مَّالِ اللّٰهِ الَّذِيْٓ اٰتٰىكُمْ ۭ وَلَا تُكْرِهُوْا
فَتَيٰتِكُمْ عَلَى الْبِغَاۗءِ اِنْ اَرَدْنَ تَحَصُّنًا
لِّتَبْتَغُوْا عَرَضَ الْحَيٰوةِ الدُّنْيَا ۭ وَمَنْ
يُّكْرِهْهُّنَّ فَاِنَّ اللّٰهَ مِنْ بَعْدِ
اِكْرَاهِهِنَّ غَفُوْرٌ رَّحِيْمٌ ﴿٣٣﴾

34. We have already sent down to you verses making things clear, an illustration from (the story of) people who passed away before you, and an admonition for those who fear (Allah).

34. Wa laqad anzalnaaa ilaykum Aayaatim-mubayyinaatiñw-wa masalam-minal-lazeena khalaw min qablikum wa mawʻiẓatal-lilmuttaqeen.

(Section 4)

وَلَقَدْ اَنْزَلْنَآ اِلَيْكُمْ اٰيٰتٍ مُّبَيِّنٰتٍ
وَّمَثَلًا مِّنَ الَّذِيْنَ خَلَوْا مِنْ
قَبْلِكُمْ وَمَوْعِظَةً لِّلْمُتَّقِيْنَ ﴿٣٤﴾ ع

35. Allah is the Light of the heavens and the earth. The parable of His Light is as if there were a Niche and within it a Lamp: the Lamp enclosed in Glass: the glass as it were a brilliant star: lit from a blessed Tree, an Olive, neither of the east nor of the west, whose oil is well-nigh Luminous, though fire scarce touched it: Light upon Light! Allah guides whom He will to His Light: Allah sets forth Parables for men: and Allah.

35. Allaahu noorus-samaawaati wal-arḍ; masalu noorihee kamishkaatin feehaa miṣbaaḥ; almiṣbaaḥu fee zujaajatin azzujaajatu ka-annahaa kawkabun durriyyuñy-yooqadu min shajaratim-mubaarakatin zaytoonatil-laa sharqiyyatiñw-wa laa gharbiyyatiñy-yakaadu zaytuhaa yuḍeee'u wa law lam tamsashu naar; noorun ʻalaa noor; yahdil-laahu linoorihee mañy-yashaaa'; wa yaḍribul-laahul-amsaala linnaas; wallaahu bikulli

اَللّٰهُ نُوْرُ السَّمٰوٰتِ وَالْاَرْضِ ۭ مَثَلُ
نُوْرِهٖ كَمِشْكٰوةٍ فِيْهَا مِصْبَاحٌ ۭ
اَلْمِصْبَاحُ فِيْ زُجَاجَةٍ ۭ اَلزُّجَاجَةُ
كَاَنَّهَا كَوْكَبٌ دُرِّيٌّ يُّوْقَدُ مِنْ شَجَرَةٍ
مُّبٰرَكَةٍ زَيْتُوْنَةٍ لَّا شَرْقِيَّةٍ وَّلَا
غَرْبِيَّةٍ ۙ يَّكَادُ زَيْتُهَا يُضِيْۗءُ وَلَوْ لَمْ
تَمْسَسْهُ نَارٌ ۭ نُوْرٌ عَلٰي نُوْرٍ ۭ يَهْدِي
اللّٰهُ لِنُوْرِهٖ مَنْ يَّشَاۗءُ ۭ وَيَضْرِبُ
اللّٰهُ الْاَمْثَالَ لِلنَّاسِ ۭ وَاللّٰهُ بِكُلِّ

Ikhfa اخفاء | Ghunna غُنّہ | Ikhfa Meem Saakin اخفاء میم ساکن | Idghaam ادغام | Qalqala قلقلہ | Qalb قلب | Idghaam Meem Saakin ادغام میم ساکن

knows all things.

shay'in 'Aleem.

شَيْءٍ عَلِيمٌ ٣٥

36. (Lit is such a Light) in houses, which Allah has permitted to be raised to honor; for the celebration, in them, of His name: in them is He glorified in the mornings and in the evenings, (again and again),-

36. Fee buyootin azinal-laahu an turfa'a wa yuzkara feehasmuhoo yusabbiḥu lahoo feehaa bilghuduwwi wal-aaṣaal.

فِي بُيُوتٍ أَذِنَ اللَّهُ أَنْ تُرْفَعَ وَيُذْكَرَ
فِيهَا اسْمُهُ يُسَبِّحُ لَهُ فِيهَا
بِالْغُدُوِّ وَالْآصَالِ ٣٦

37. By men whom neither traffic nor merchandise can divert from the remembrance of Allah, nor from regular Prayer, nor from paying Zakat; their (only) fear is for the Day when hearts and eyes will be turned about,-

37. Rijaalul-laa tulheehim tijaaratuñw-wa laa bay'un 'an zikril-laahi wa iqaamiṣ-Ṣalaati wa eetaaa'iz-Zakaati yakhaafoona Yawman tataqallabu feehil-quloobu wal-abṣaar.

رِجَالٌ لَا تُلْهِيهِمْ تِجَارَةٌ وَلَا بَيْعٌ
عَنْ ذِكْرِ اللَّهِ وَإِقَامِ الصَّلَاةِ وَإِيتَاءِ
الزَّكَاةِ يَخَافُونَ يَوْمًا تَتَقَلَّبُ فِيهِ
الْقُلُوبُ وَالْأَبْصَارُ ٣٧

38. That Allah may reward them according to the best of their deeds, and add even more for them out of His Grace: for Allah provides for those whom He will, without measure.

38. Liyajziyahumul-laahu aḥsana maa 'amiloo wa yazeedahum-min faḍlih; wal-laahu yarzuqu mañy-yashaaa'u bighayri ḥisaab.

لِيَجْزِيَهُمُ اللَّهُ أَحْسَنَ مَا عَمِلُوا
وَيَزِيدَهُمْ مِنْ فَضْلِهِ وَاللَّهُ
يَرْزُقُ مَنْ يَشَاءُ بِغَيْرِ حِسَابٍ ٣٨

39. But the Unbelievers,- their deeds are like a mirage in sandy deserts, which the man parched with thirst mistakes for water; until when he comes up to it, he finds it to be nothing: but he finds Allah (ever) with him, and Allah will pay him his account: and Allah is swift in taking account.

39. Wallazeena kafarooo a'maaluhum kasaraabim biqee'atiñy-yaḥsabuhuẓ-ẓamaanu maaa'an ḥattaaa izaa jaaa'ahoo lam yajid-hu shay-'añw-wa wajadal-laaha 'indahoo fa-waffaahu ḥisaabah; wallaahu saree'ul-ḥisaab.

وَالَّذِينَ كَفَرُوا أَعْمَالُهُمْ كَسَرَابٍ
بِقِيعَةٍ يَحْسَبُهُ الظَّمْآنُ مَاءً حَتَّى
إِذَا جَاءَهُ لَمْ يَجِدْهُ شَيْئًا وَوَجَدَ
اللَّهَ عِنْدَهُ فَوَفَّاهُ حِسَابَهُ وَاللَّهُ
سَرِيعُ الْحِسَابِ ٣٩

40. Or (the Unbelievers' state) is like the depths of darkness in a vast deep ocean, overwhelmed with billow topped by billow, topped by (dark) clouds: depths of darkness, one above another: if a man stretches out his hands, he can hardly see it! for any to whom Allah does not give light, there is no light!

40. Aw kaẓulumaatin fee baḥril-lujjiyyiñy-yaghshaahu mawjum-min fawqihee mawjum-min fawqihee saḥaab; ẓulumaatum ba'ḍuhaa fawqa ba'ḍin izaa akhraja yadahoo lam yakad yaraahaa wa mal-lam yaj'alil-laahu lahoo nooran famaa lahoo min-noor.

(Section 5)

أَوْ كَظُلُمَاتٍ فِي بَحْرٍ لُجِّيٍّ يَغْشَاهُ
مَوْجٌ مِنْ فَوْقِهِ مَوْجٌ مِنْ فَوْقِهِ
سَحَابٌ ظُلُمَاتٌ بَعْضُهَا فَوْقَ
بَعْضٍ إِذَا أَخْرَجَ يَدَهُ لَمْ
يَكَدْ يَرَاهَا وَمَنْ لَمْ يَجْعَلِ اللَّهُ لَهُ
نُورًا فَمَا لَهُ مِنْ نُورٍ ٤٠ ٥ ع ١١

41. Do not you see that it is Allah Whose praises all beings in the heavens and on earth do celebrate, and the birds (of the air) with wings outspread? Each one knows its own (mode of) prayer and praise. And Allah knows well all that they do.

41. Alam tara annal-laaha yusabbiḥu lahoo man fissamaawaati wal-arḍi waṭ-ṭayru ṣaaaffaatin kullun qad 'alima Ṣalaatahoo wa tasbeeḥah; wallaahu 'aleemum bimaa yaf'aloon.

أَلَمْ تَرَ أَنَّ اللَّهَ يُسَبِّحُ لَهُ مَنْ فِي
السَّمَاوَاتِ وَالْأَرْضِ وَالطَّيْرُ صَافَّاتٍ
كُلٌّ قَدْ عَلِمَ صَلَاتَهُ وَتَسْبِيحَهُ
وَاللَّهُ عَلِيمٌ بِمَا يَفْعَلُونَ ٤١

Ikhfa اخفاء | Ghunna غنّة | Ikhfa Meem Saakin اخفاء میم ساکن | Idghaam ادغام | Qalqala قلقلہ | Qalb قلب | Idghaam Meem Saakin ادغام میم ساکن

42. Yes, to Allah belongs the dominion of the heavens and the earth; and to Allah is the final goal (of all).

42. Wa lillaahi mulkus-samaawaati wal-arḍi wa ilal-laahil-maṣeer.

وَلِلّٰهِ مُلْكُ السَّمٰوٰتِ وَالْاَرْضِ ۚ
وَاِلَى اللّٰهِ الْمَصِيْرُ ﴿٤٢﴾

43. Don't you see that Allah makes the clouds move gently, then joins them together, then makes them into a heap? - then will you see rain issue forth from their midst. And He sends down from the sky mountain masses (of clouds) wherein is hail: He strikes therewith whom He pleases and He turns it away from whom He pleases, the vivid flash of His lightning well-nigh blinds the sight.

43. Alam tara annal-laaha yuzjee saḥaaban summa yu'allifu baynahoo summa yaj'aluhoo rukaaman fataral-wadqa yakhruju min khilaalihee wa yunazzilu minas-samaaa'i min jibaalin feehaa mim baradin fa-yuṣeebu bihee mañy-yashaaa'u wa yaṣrifuhoo 'am-mañy-yaṣhaaa'u yakaadu sanaa barqihee yaẕhabu bil-abṣaar.

اَلَمْ تَرَ اَنَّ اللّٰهَ يُزْجِيْ سَحَابًا ثُمَّ
يُؤَلِّفُ بَيْنَهٗ ثُمَّ يَجْعَلُهٗ رُكَامًا فَتَرَى
الْوَدْقَ يَخْرُجُ مِنْ خِلٰلِهٖ ۚ وَيُنَزِّلُ
مِنَ السَّمَآءِ مِنْ جِبَالٍ فِيْهَا مِنْۢ
بَرَدٍ فَيُصِيْبُ بِهٖ مَنْ يَّشَآءُ وَيَصْرِفُهٗ
عَنْ مَّنْ يَّشَآءُ ۗ يَكَادُ سَنَا بَرْقِهٖ
يَذْهَبُ بِالْاَبْصَارِ ﴿٤٣﴾

44. It is Allah Who alternates the Night and the Day: verily in these things is an instructive example for those who have vision!

44. Yuqallibul-laahul-layla wannahaar; inna fee ẕaalika la'ibratal-li-ulil-abṣaar.

يُقَلِّبُ اللّٰهُ الَّيْلَ وَالنَّهَارَ ۗ اِنَّ
فِيْ ذٰلِكَ لَعِبْرَةً لِّاُولِي الْاَبْصَارِ ﴿٤٤﴾

45. And Allah has created every animal from water: of them there are some that creep on their bellies; some that walk on two legs; and some that walk on four. Allah creates what He wills; for verily Allah has power over all things.

45. Wallaahu khalaqa kulla daaabbatim-mim-maaa'in faminhum-mañy-yamshee 'alaa baṭnihee wa minhum-mañy-yamshee 'alaa rijlayni wa minhum-mañy-yamshee 'alaaa arba'; yakhluqul-laahu maa yashaaa'; innal-laaha 'alaa kulli shay'in Qadeer.

وَاللّٰهُ خَلَقَ كُلَّ دَآبَّةٍ مِّنْ مَّآءٍ ۚ
فَمِنْهُمْ مَّنْ يَّمْشِيْ عَلٰى بَطْنِهٖ ۚ
وَمِنْهُمْ مَّنْ يَّمْشِيْ عَلٰى رِجْلَيْنِ ۚ
وَمِنْهُمْ مَّنْ يَّمْشِيْ عَلٰٓى اَرْبَعٍ ۗ يَخْلُقُ
اللّٰهُ مَا يَشَآءُ ۗ اِنَّ اللّٰهَ عَلٰى كُلِّ
شَيْءٍ قَدِيْرٌ ﴿٤٥﴾

46. We have indeed sent down signs that make things manifest: and Allah guides whom He wills to a way that is straight.

46. Laqad anzalnaaa Aayaatim-mubayyinaat; wallaahu yahdee mañy-yashaaa'u ilaa Ṣiraaṭim-Mustaqeem.

لَقَدْ اَنْزَلْنَآ اٰيٰتٍ مُّبَيِّنٰتٍ ۗ وَاللّٰهُ
يَهْدِيْ مَنْ يَّشَآءُ اِلٰى صِرَاطٍ
مُّسْتَقِيْمٍ ﴿٤٦﴾

47. They say, "We believe in Allah and in the Messenger, and we obey": but even after that, some of them turn away: they are not (really) Believers.

47. Wa yaqooloona aamannaa billaahi wa bir-Rasooli wa aṭa'naa summa yatawallaa fareequm-minhum-mim ba'di ẕaalik; wa maaa ulaaa'ika bilmu'mineen.

وَيَقُوْلُوْنَ اٰمَنَّا بِاللّٰهِ وَبِالرَّسُوْلِ
وَاَطَعْنَا ثُمَّ يَتَوَلّٰى فَرِيْقٌ مِّنْهُمْ
مِّنْۢ بَعْدِ ذٰلِكَ ۗ وَمَآ اُولٰٓئِكَ
بِالْمُؤْمِنِيْنَ ﴿٤٧﴾

48. When they are summoned to Allah and His Messenger, in order that He may judge between them, behold some of them decline (to come).

48. Wa iẕaa du'ooo ilal-laahi wa Rasoolihee li-yaḥkuma baynahum iẕaa fareequm-minhum-mu'riḍoon.

وَاِذَا دُعُوْٓا اِلَى اللّٰهِ وَرَسُوْلِهٖ لِيَحْكُمَ
بَيْنَهُمْ اِذَا فَرِيْقٌ مِّنْهُمْ مُّعْرِضُوْنَ ﴿٤٨﴾

Ikhfa	Ghunna	Ikhfa Meem Saakin	Idghaam	Qalqala	Qalb	Idghaam Meem Saakin
اخفاء	غُنّہ	اخفاء میم ساکن	ادغام	قلقلہ	قلب	ادغام میم ساکن

Translation	Transliteration	Arabic
49. But if the right is on their side, they come to him with all submission.	49. Wa iñy-yakul-lahumul-ḥaqqu yaåtooo ilayhi muẕ-ʻineen.	وَإِن يَكُن لَّهُمُ الْحَقُّ يَأْتُوا إِلَيْهِ مُذْعِنِينَ ﴿٤٩﴾
50. Is it that there is a disease in their hearts? or do they doubt, or are they in fear, that Allah and His Messenger will deal unjustly with them? Nay, it is they themselves who do wrong.	50. Afee quloobihim-maraḍun amirtaabooo am yakhaafoona añy-yaḥeefallaahu ʻalayhim wa Rasooluh; bal ulaaa'ika humuẓ-ẓaalimoon. **(Section 6)**	أَفِي قُلُوبِهِم مَّرَضٌ أَمِ ارْتَابُوا أَمْ يَخَافُونَ أَن يَحِيفَ اللَّهُ عَلَيْهِمْ وَرَسُولُهُ بَلْ أُولَٰئِكَ هُمُ الظَّالِمُونَ ﴿٥٠﴾
51. The answer of the Believers, when summoned to Allah and His Messenger, in order that he may judge between them, is no other than this: they say, "We hear and we obey": it is such as these that will attain felicity.	51. Innamaa kaana qawlal-mu'mineena iẕaa duʻooo ilal-laahi wa Rasoolihee li-yaḥkuma baynahum añy-yaqooloo samiʻnaa wa aṭaʻnaa; wa ulaaa'ika humul-mufliḥoon.	إِنَّمَا كَانَ قَوْلَ الْمُؤْمِنِينَ إِذَا دُعُوا إِلَى اللَّهِ وَرَسُولِهِ لِيَحْكُمَ بَيْنَهُمْ أَن يَقُولُوا سَمِعْنَا وَأَطَعْنَا وَأُولَٰئِكَ هُمُ الْمُفْلِحُونَ ﴿٥١﴾
52. It is such as obey Allah and His Messenger, and fear Allah and do right, that will win (in the end),	52. Wa mañy-yuṭiʻil-laaha wa Rasoolahoo wa yakhshal-laaha wa yattaqhi fa-ulaaa'ika humul-faaa'izoon.	وَمَن يُطِعِ اللَّهَ وَرَسُولَهُ وَيَخْشَ اللَّهَ وَيَتَّقْهِ فَأُولَٰئِكَ هُمُ الْفَائِزُونَ ﴿٥٢﴾
53. They swear their strongest oaths by Allah that, if only you would command them, they would leave (their homes). Say: "Do not swear obedience is (more) reasonable; verily, Allah is well acquainted with all that you do."	53. Wa aqsamoo billaahi jahda aymaanihim la-'in amartahum la-yakhrujunna qul laa tuqsimoo ṭaaʻatum-maʻroofah innal-laaha khabee-rum bimaa taʻmaloon.	وَأَقْسَمُوا بِاللَّهِ جَهْدَ أَيْمَانِهِمْ لَئِنْ أَمَرْتَهُمْ لَيَخْرُجُنَّ قُل لَّا تُقْسِمُوا طَاعَةٌ مَّعْرُوفَةٌ إِنَّ اللَّهَ خَبِيرٌ بِمَا تَعْمَلُونَ ﴿٥٣﴾
54. Say: "Obey Allah, and obey the Messenger: but if you turn away, he is only responsible for the duty placed on him and you for that placed on you. If you obey him, you shall be on right guidance. The Messenger's duty is only to preach the clear (Message).	54. Qul aṭeeʻul-laaha wa aṭeeʻur-Rasoola fa-in tawallaw fa-innamaa ʻalayhi maa ḥummila wa ʻalaykum-maa ḥummiltum wa in tuṭeeʻoohu tahtadoo; wa maa ʻalar-Rasooli illal-balaaghul-mubeen.	قُلْ أَطِيعُوا اللَّهَ وَأَطِيعُوا الرَّسُولَ فَإِن تَوَلَّوْا فَإِنَّمَا عَلَيْهِ مَا حُمِّلَ وَعَلَيْكُم مَّا حُمِّلْتُمْ وَإِن تُطِيعُوهُ تَهْتَدُوا وَمَا عَلَى الرَّسُولِ إِلَّا الْبَلَاغُ الْمُبِينُ ﴿٥٤﴾
55. Allah has promised, to those among you who believe and work righteous deeds, that He will, of a surety, grant them in the land, inheritance (of power), as He granted it to those before them; that He will establish in authority their religion - the one which He has chosen for them; and that He will change (their state), after the fear in which they (lived), to one of security and peace: 'They will worship Me (alone)	55. Waʻadal-laahul-laẕeena aamanoo minkum wa ʻamiluṣ-ṣaaliḥaati la-yastakhlifannahum fil-arḍi kamastakh-lafal-laẕeena min qablihim wa la-yumakkinanna lahum deenahumul-laẕir taḍaa lahum wa la-yubaddilannahum-mim baʻdi khawfihim amnaa; yaʻbudoonanee laa	وَعَدَ اللَّهُ الَّذِينَ آمَنُوا مِنكُمْ وَعَمِلُوا الصَّالِحَاتِ لَيَسْتَخْلِفَنَّهُم فِي الْأَرْضِ كَمَا اسْتَخْلَفَ الَّذِينَ مِن قَبْلِهِمْ وَلَيُمَكِّنَنَّ لَهُمْ دِينَهُمُ الَّذِي ارْتَضَىٰ لَهُمْ وَلَيُبَدِّلَنَّهُم مِّن بَعْدِ خَوْفِهِمْ أَمْنًا يَعْبُدُونَنِي لَا

Ikhfa اخفاء | Ghunna غُنّہ | Ikhfa Meem Saakin اخفاء میم ساکن | Idghaam ادغام | Qalqala قلقلہ | Qalb قلب | Idghaam Meem Saakin ادغام میم ساکن

and not associate any one with Me. 'If any do reject Faith after this, they are rebellious and wicked.

yushrikoona bee shay'aa; wa man kafara ba'da zaalika fa-ulaaa'ika humul-faasiqoon.

يُشْرِكُونَ بِي شَيْـًٔا ۚ وَمَن كَفَرَ بَعْدَ
ذَٰلِكَ فَأُو۟لَـٰٓئِكَ هُمُ ٱلْفَـٰسِقُونَ ﴿٥٥﴾

56. So establish regular Prayer and give regular Charity; and obey the Messenger; that you may receive mercy.

56. Wa aqeemuṣ-Ṣalaata wa aatuz-Zakaata wa aṭee'ur-Rasoola la'allakum turḥamoon.

وَأَقِيمُوا۟ ٱلصَّلَوٰةَ وَءَاتُوا۟ ٱلزَّكَوٰةَ
وَأَطِيعُوا۟ ٱلرَّسُولَ لَعَلَّكُمْ تُرْحَمُونَ ﴿٥٦﴾

57. You should never think that the Unbelievers are going to frustrate (Allah's Plan) on earth: their abode is the Fire,- and it is indeed an evil refuge!

57. Laa taḥsabannal-lazeena kafaroo mu'jizeena fil-arḍ; wa maåwaahumun-Naaru wa labi'sal-maṣeer. **(Section 7)**

لَا تَحْسَبَنَّ ٱلَّذِينَ كَفَرُوا۟ مُعْجِزِينَ
فِى ٱلْأَرْضِ ۚ وَمَأْوَىٰهُمُ ٱلنَّارُ ۖ
وَلَبِئْسَ ٱلْمَصِيرُ ﴿٥٧﴾ ع ٧ ١٣

58. O you who believe! Let those whom your right hands possess, and the (children) among you who have not come of age ask your permission (before they come to your presence), on three occasions: before morning prayer; the while you doff your clothes for the noonday heat; and after the late-night prayer: these are your three times of undress: outside those times it is not wrong for you or for them to move about attending to each other: Thus Allah makes clear the Signs to you: for Allah is full of knowledge and wisdom.

58. Yaaa ayyuhal-lazeena aamanoo li-yastaåzinkumul-lazeena malakat aymaanukum wallazeena lam yablughul-ḥuluma minkum salaasa marraat; min qabli Ṣalaatil-Fajri wa ḥeena taḍa'oona siyaabakum-minaẓ-ẓaheerati wa mim-ba'di Ṣalaatil-'Ishaaa'; salaasu 'awraatil-lakum; laysa 'alaykum wa laa 'alayhim junaaḥum ba'dahunn; ṭawwaafoona 'alaykum ba'ḍukum 'alaa ba'ḍ; kazaalika yubayyinul-laahu lakumul-Aaayaat wallaahu 'Aleemun Ḥakeem.

يَـٰٓأَيُّهَا ٱلَّذِينَ ءَامَنُوا۟ لِيَسْتَـْٔذِنكُمُ
ٱلَّذِينَ مَلَكَتْ أَيْمَـٰنُكُمْ وَٱلَّذِينَ لَمْ
يَبْلُغُوا۟ ٱلْحُلُمَ مِنكُمْ ثَلَـٰثَ مَرَّٰتٍ ۚ مِّن
قَبْلِ صَلَوٰةِ ٱلْفَجْرِ وَحِينَ تَضَعُونَ
ثِيَابَكُم مِّنَ ٱلظَّهِيرَةِ وَمِنۢ بَعْدِ
صَلَوٰةِ ٱلْعِشَآءِ ۚ ثَلَـٰثُ عَوْرَٰتٍ لَّكُمْ ۚ
لَيْسَ عَلَيْكُمْ وَلَا عَلَيْهِمْ جُنَاحٌۢ بَعْدَ
هُنَّ ۚ طَوَّٰفُونَ عَلَيْكُم بَعْضُكُمْ
عَلَىٰ بَعْضٍ ۚ كَذَٰلِكَ يُبَيِّنُ ٱللَّهُ
لَكُمُ ٱلْـَٔايَـٰتِ ۗ وَٱللَّهُ عَلِيمٌ حَكِيمٌ ﴿٥٨﴾

59. But when the children among you come of age, let them (also) ask for permission, as do those senior to them (in age): thus Allah makes clear His Signs to you: for Allah is full of knowledge and wisdom.

59. Wa izaa balaghal-aṭfaalu minkumul-ḥuluma fal-yastaåzinoo kamas-taåzanal-lazeena min qablihim; kazaalika yubayyinul-laahu lakum Aayaatih; wallaahu 'Aleemun Ḥakeem.

وَإِذَا بَلَغَ ٱلْأَطْفَـٰلُ مِنكُمُ ٱلْحُلُمَ
فَلْيَسْتَـْٔذِنُوا۟ كَمَا ٱسْتَـْٔذَنَ ٱلَّذِينَ
مِن قَبْلِهِمْ ۚ كَذَٰلِكَ يُبَيِّنُ ٱللَّهُ
لَكُمْ ءَايَـٰتِهِۦ ۗ وَٱللَّهُ عَلِيمٌ حَكِيمٌ ﴿٥٩﴾

60. Such elderly women as are past the prospect of marriage,- there is no blame on them if they lay aside their (outer) garments, provided they make not a wanton display of their beauty: but it is best for them to be modest: and Allah is One Who sees and knows all things.

60. Walqawaa'idu minan-nisaaa'il-laatee laa yarjoona nikaaḥan falaysa 'alayhinna junaaḥun añy-yaḍa'na siyaabahunna ghayra mutabarrijaatim bizeenah; wa añy-yasta'fifna khayrul-lahunn; wallaahu Samee'un 'Aleem.

وَٱلْقَوَٰعِدُ مِنَ ٱلنِّسَآءِ ٱلَّـٰتِى لَا
يَرْجُونَ نِكَاحًا فَلَيْسَ عَلَيْهِنَّ
جُنَاحٌ أَن يَضَعْنَ ثِيَابَهُنَّ غَيْرَ
مُتَبَرِّجَـٰتٍۭ بِزِينَةٍ ۖ وَأَن يَسْتَعْفِفْنَ
خَيْرٌ لَّهُنَّ ۗ وَٱللَّهُ سَمِيعٌ عَلِيمٌ ﴿٦٠﴾

Ikhfa اخفاء | Ghunna غُنّہ | Ikhfa Meem Saakin اخفاءمیم ساکن | Idghaam ادغام | Qalqala قلقلہ | Qalb قلب | Idghaam Meem Saakin ادغام میم ساکن

61. It is no fault in the blind nor in one born lame, nor in one afflicted with illness, nor in yourselves, that you should eat in your own houses, or those of your fathers, or your mothers, or your brothers, or your sisters, or your father's brothers or your father's sisters, or your mohter's brothers, or your mother's sisters, or in houses of which the keys are in your possession, or in the house of a sincere friend of yours: there is no blame on you, whether you eat in company or separately. But if you enter houses, salute each other - a greeting of blessing and purity as from Allah. Thus Allah makes clear the Signs to you: that you may understand.

61. Laysa 'alal-a'maa ḥarajuñw-wa laa 'alal-a'raji ḥarajuñw-wa laa 'alal-mareeḍi ḥarajuñw-wa laa 'alaaa anfusikum an taåkuloo mim buyootikum aw buyooti aabaaa'ikum aw buyooti ummahaatikum aw buyooti ikhwaanikum aw buyooti akhawaatikum aw buyooti a'maamikum aw buyooti 'ammaatikum aw buyooti akhwaalikum aw buyooti khaalaatikum aw maa malaktum-mafaatiḥahooo aw ṣadeeqikum; laysa 'alaykum junaaḥun an taåkuloo jamee'an aw ashtaataa; fa-izaa dakhaltum buyootan fasallimoo 'alaaa anfusikum taḥiyyatam-min 'indil-laahi mubaarakatan ṭayyibah; kazaalika yubayyinul-laahu lakumul-Aayaati la'allakum ta'qiloon. **(Section 8)**

لَيْسَ عَلَى الْاَعْمٰى حَرَجٌ وَّلَا عَلَى
الْاَعْرَجِ حَرَجٌ وَّلَا عَلَى الْمَرِيْضِ
حَرَجٌ وَّلَا عَلٰٓى اَنْفُسِكُمْ اَنْ تَاْكُلُوْا
مِنْۢ بُيُوْتِكُمْ اَوْ بُيُوْتِ اٰبَآئِكُمْ
اَوْ بُيُوْتِ اُمَّهٰتِكُمْ اَوْ بُيُوْتِ
اِخْوَانِكُمْ اَوْ بُيُوْتِ اَخَوٰتِكُمْ
اَوْ بُيُوْتِ اَعْمَامِكُمْ اَوْ بُيُوْتِ
عَمّٰتِكُمْ اَوْ بُيُوْتِ اَخْوَالِكُمْ اَوْ
بُيُوْتِ خٰلٰتِكُمْ اَوْ مَا مَلَكْتُمْ
مَّفَاتِحَهٗٓ اَوْ صَدِيْقِكُمْ ؕ لَيْسَ
عَلَيْكُمْ جُنَاحٌ اَنْ تَاْكُلُوْا جَمِيْعًا
اَوْ اَشْتَاتًا ؕ فَاِذَا دَخَلْتُمْ بُيُوْتًا
فَسَلِّمُوْا عَلٰٓى اَنْفُسِكُمْ تَحِيَّةً مِّنْ
عِنْدِ اللّٰهِ مُبٰرَكَةً طَيِّبَةً ؕ
كَذٰلِكَ يُبَيِّنُ اللّٰهُ لَكُمُ الْاٰيٰتِ
لَعَلَّكُمْ تَعْقِلُوْنَ ﴿٦١﴾ ع

62. Only those are believers, who believe in Allah and His Messenger: when they are with him on a matter requiring collective action, they do not depart until they have asked for his leave; those who ask for your leave are those who believe in Allah and His Messenger; so when they ask for your leave, for some business of theirs, give leave to those of them whom you will, and ask Allah for their forgiveness: for Allah is Oft-Forgiving, Most Merciful.

62. Innamal-mu'minoonal-lazeena aamanoo billaahi wa Rasoolihee wa izaa kaanoo ma'ahoo 'alaaa amrin jaami'il-lam yazhaboo ḥattaa yastaåzinooh; innal-lazeena yastaåzinoonaka ulaaa'ikal-lazeena yu'minoona billaahi wa Rasoolih; fa-izas-taåzanooka liba'ḍi shaånihim faåzal-liman shi'ta minhum wastaghfir lahumul-laah; innal-laaha Ghafoorur-Raḥeem.

اِنَّمَا الْمُؤْمِنُوْنَ الَّذِيْنَ اٰمَنُوْا
بِاللّٰهِ وَرَسُوْلِهٖ وَاِذَا كَانُوْا مَعَهٗ
عَلٰٓى اَمْرٍ جَامِعٍ لَّمْ يَذْهَبُوْا حَتّٰى
يَسْتَاْذِنُوْهُ ؕ اِنَّ الَّذِيْنَ يَسْتَاْذِنُوْنَكَ
اُولٰٓئِكَ الَّذِيْنَ يُؤْمِنُوْنَ بِاللّٰهِ وَ
رَسُوْلِهٖ ۚ فَاِذَا اسْتَاْذَنُوْكَ لِبَعْضِ
شَاْنِهِمْ فَاْذَنْ لِّمَنْ شِئْتَ
مِنْهُمْ وَاسْتَغْفِرْ لَهُمُ اللّٰهَ ؕ اِنَّ
اللّٰهَ غَفُوْرٌ رَّحِيْمٌ ﴿٦٢﴾

63. Deem not the summons of the Messenger among yourselves

63. Laa taj'aloo du'aaa'ar-Rasooli baynakum

لَا تَجْعَلُوْا دُعَآءَ الرَّسُوْلِ بَيْنَكُمْ

Ikhfa اخفاء | Ghunna غُنّہ | Ikhfa Meem Saakin اخفاء میم ساکن | Idghaam ادغام | Qalqala قلقلہ | Qalb قلب | Idghaam Meem Saakin ادغام میم ساکن

like the summons of one of you to another: Allah knows those of you who slip away under shelter of some excuse: then let those beware who withstand the Messenger's order, lest some trial befall them, or a grievous Penalty be inflicted on them.

kadu'aaa'i baḍikum ba'ḍaa; qad ya'lamul-laahul-lazeena yatasallaloona minkum liwaazaa; fal-yaḥzaril-lazeena yukhaalifoona 'an amriheee an tuṣeebahum fitnatun aw yuṣeebahum 'azaabun aleem.

كَدُعَاءِ بَعْضِكُم بَعْضًا قَدْ يَعْلَمُ
اللَّهُ الَّذِينَ يَتَسَلَّلُونَ مِنكُمْ لِوَاذًا
فَلْيَحْذَرِ الَّذِينَ يُخَالِفُونَ عَنْ أَمْرِهِ
أَن تُصِيبَهُمْ فِتْنَةٌ أَوْ يُصِيبَهُمْ
عَذَابٌ أَلِيمٌ ﴿٦٣﴾

64. Be quite sure that to Allah belong whatever is in the heavens and on earth. Well does He know what you are intent upon: and the day they will be brought back to Him, and He will tell them the truth of what they did: for Allah knows all things.

64. Alaaa inna lillaahi maa fis-samaawaati wal-arḍi qad ya'lamu maaa antum 'alayhi wa Yawma yurja'oona ilayhi fa-yunabbi'uhum bimaa 'amiloo; wallaahu bikulli shay'in 'Aleem. **(Section 9)**

أَلَا إِنَّ لِلَّهِ مَا فِي السَّمَاوَاتِ وَ
الْأَرْضِ قَدْ يَعْلَمُ مَا أَنتُمْ عَلَيْهِ
وَيَوْمَ يُرْجَعُونَ إِلَيْهِ فَيُنَبِّئُهُم بِمَا
عَمِلُوا وَاللَّهُ بِكُلِّ شَيْءٍ عَلِيمٌ ﴿٦٤﴾ ع ٩

25. The Criterion

In the name of Allah, Most Gracious, Most Merciful.

Sûrat al-Furqân–25

(Revealed at Makkah)

Bismillaahir Raḥmaanir Raḥeem

(٢٥) سُورَةُ الْفُرْقَانِ مَكِّيَّةٌ (٤٢)

بِسْمِ اللَّهِ الرَّحْمَٰنِ الرَّحِيمِ

1. Blessed is He who sent down the criterion to His servant, that it may be an admonition to all creatures;-

2. He to Whom belongs the dominion of the heavens and the earth: no son has He begotten, nor has He a partner in His dominion: it is He who created all things, and ordered them in due proportions.

1. Tabaarakal-lazee naz-zalal-Furqaana 'alaa 'abdihee li-yakoona lil'aalameena nazeeraa.

2. Allazee lahoo mulkus-samaawaati wal-arḍi wa lam yattakhiz waladañw-wa lam yakul-lahoo shareekun fil-mulki wa khalaqa kulla shay'in faqaddarahoo taqdeeraa.

تَبَارَكَ الَّذِي نَزَّلَ الْفُرْقَانَ عَلَىٰ
عَبْدِهِ لِيَكُونَ لِلْعَالَمِينَ نَذِيرًا ﴿١﴾
الَّذِي لَهُ مُلْكُ السَّمَاوَاتِ وَالْأَرْضِ
وَلَمْ يَتَّخِذْ وَلَدًا وَلَمْ يَكُن لَّهُ
شَرِيكٌ فِي الْمُلْكِ وَخَلَقَ كُلَّ
شَيْءٍ فَقَدَّرَهُ تَقْدِيرًا ﴿٢﴾

3. Yet have they taken, besides him, gods that can create nothing but are them-selves created; that have no control of hurt or good to themselves; nor can they control death nor life nor resurrection.

3. Wattakhazoo min dooni-heee aalihatal-laa yakhluqoona shay'añw-wa hum yukhlaqoona wa laa yamlikoona li-anfusihim ḍarrañw-wa laa naf'añw-wa laa yamlikoona mawtañw-wa laa ḥayaatañw-wa laa nushooraa.

وَاتَّخَذُوا مِن دُونِهِ آلِهَةً لَّا
يَخْلُقُونَ شَيْئًا وَهُمْ يُخْلَقُونَ
وَلَا يَمْلِكُونَ لِأَنفُسِهِمْ ضَرًّا وَ
لَا نَفْعًا وَلَا يَمْلِكُونَ مَوْتًا وَلَا
حَيَاةً وَلَا نُشُورًا ﴿٣﴾

4. But the Misbelievers say: "Nothing is this but a lie which he has forged, and others have helped him at it." In truth it is they who have put forward an iniquity and a falsehood.

4. Wa qaalal-lazeena ka-farooo in haazaaa illaaa ifkunif-taraahu wa a'aanahoo 'alayhi qawmun aakharoona faqad jaaa'oo ẓulmañw-wa zooraa.

وَقَالَ الَّذِينَ كَفَرُوا إِنْ هَٰذَا
إِلَّا إِفْكٌ افْتَرَاهُ وَأَعَانَهُ عَلَيْهِ
قَوْمٌ آخَرُونَ فَقَدْ جَاءُوا
ظُلْمًا وَزُورًا ﴿٤﴾

معانقة عند المتأخرين ١٢

Ikhfa	Ghunna	Ikhfa Meem Saakin	Idghaam	Qalqala	Qalb	Idghaam Meem Saakin
اخفاء	غنّہ	اخفاء میم ساکن	ادغام	قلقلہ	قلب	ادغام میم ساکن

5. And they say: "Tales of the ancients, which he has caused to be written: and they are dictated before him morning and evening."

6. Say: "The (Qur'an) was sent down by Him who knows the mystery (that is) in the heavens and the earth: verily He is Oft-Forgiving, Most Merciful."

7. And they say: "What sort of a Messenger is this, who eats food, and walks through the streets? Why has not an angel been sent down to him to give admonition with him?

8. "Or (Why) has not a treasure been bestowed on him, or why has he (not) a garden for enjoyment?" The wicked say: "You follow none other than a man bewitched."

9. See what kinds of comparisons they make for you! But they have gone astray, and never a way will they be able to find!

10. Blessed is He who, if that were His will, could give you better (things) than those,- Gardens beneath which rivers flow; and He could give you palaces (secure to dwell in).

11. Nay they deny the Hour (of the judgment to come): but We have prepared a blazing fire for such as deny the Hour:

12. When it sees them from a place far off, they will hear its fury and its ranging sigh.

13. And when they are cast, bound together into a constricted place therein, they will plead for destruction there and then!

14. "This day do not plead for a single destruction:

5. Wa qaalooo asaaṭeerul-awwaleenak-tatabahaa fahiya tumlaa 'alayhi bukratañw-wa aṣeelaa.

6. Qul anzalahul-lazee ya'lamus-sirra fis-samaawaati wal-arḍ; innahoo kaana Ghafoorar-Raḥeemaa.

7. Wa qaaloo maa li-haazar-Rasooli yaåkuluṭ-ṭa'aama wa yamshee fil-aswaaq; law laaa unzila ilayhi malakun fa-yakoona ma'ahoo nazeeraa.

8. Aw yulqaaa ilayhi kanzun aw takoonu lahoo jannatuñy-yaåkulu minhaa; wa qaalaẓ-ẓaalimoona in tattabi'oona illaa rajulam-mas-ḥooraa.

9. Unẓur kayfa ḍaraboo lakal-amsaala faḍalloo falaa yastaṭee'oona sabeelaa. **(Sec. 1)**

10. Tabaarakal-lazeee in shaaa'a ja'ala laka khayram-min zaalika Jannaatin tajree min taḥtihal-anhaaru wa yaj'al-laka quṣooraa.

11. Bal kazzaboo bis-Saa'ati wa a'tadnaa liman kazzaba bis-Saa'ati sa'eeraa.

12. Izaa ra-at-hum-mim-ma-kaanim ba'eedin sami'oo lahaa taghayyuẓañw-wa zafeeraa.

13. Wa izaaa ulqoo minhaa makaanan ḍayyiqam-muqar-raneena da'aw hunaalika subooraa.

14. Laa tad'ul-yawma suboo-rañw-waaḥidañw-

وَقَالُوٓا اَسَاطِيْرُ الْاَوَّلِيْنَ
اكْتَتَبَهَا فَهِيَ تُمْلٰى عَلَيْهِ
بُكْرَةً وَّاَصِيْلًا ۝٥
قُلْ اَنْزَلَهُ الَّذِيْ يَعْلَمُ السِّرَّ فِي
السَّمٰوٰتِ وَالْاَرْضِ ۭ اِنَّهٗ كَانَ
غَفُوْرًا رَّحِيْمًا ۝٦
وَقَالُوْا مَالِ هٰذَا الرَّسُوْلِ يَاْكُلُ
الطَّعَامَ وَيَمْشِيْ فِي الْاَسْوَاقِ ۭ
لَوْلَآ اُنْزِلَ اِلَيْهِ مَلَكٌ فَيَكُوْنَ
مَعَهٗ نَذِيْرًا ۝٧
اَوْ يُلْقٰٓى اِلَيْهِ كَنْزٌ اَوْ تَكُوْنُ لَهٗ
جَنَّةٌ يَّاْكُلُ مِنْهَا ۭ وَقَالَ الظّٰلِمُوْنَ
اِنْ تَتَّبِعُوْنَ اِلَّا رَجُلًا مَّسْحُوْرًا ۝٨
اُنْظُرْ كَيْفَ ضَرَبُوْا لَكَ الْاَمْثَالَ
فَضَلُّوْا فَلَا يَسْتَطِيْعُوْنَ سَبِيْلًا ۝٩ ع ٩ ١٦
تَبٰرَكَ الَّذِيْٓ اِنْ شَاۗءَ جَعَلَ
لَكَ خَيْرًا مِّنْ ذٰلِكَ جَنّٰتٍ
تَجْرِيْ مِنْ تَحْتِهَا الْاَنْهٰرُ ۙ
وَيَجْعَلْ لَّكَ قُصُوْرًا ۝١٠
بَلْ كَذَّبُوْا بِالسَّاعَةِ ۣ وَاَعْتَدْنَا
لِمَنْ كَذَّبَ بِالسَّاعَةِ سَعِيْرًا ۝١١
اِذَا رَاَتْهُمْ مِّنْ مَّكَانٍۢ بَعِيْدٍ
سَمِعُوْا لَهَا تَغَيُّظًا وَّزَفِيْرًا ۝١٢
وَاِذَآ اُلْقُوْا مِنْهَا مَكَانًا ضَيِّقًا
مُّقَرَّنِيْنَ دَعَوْا هُنَالِكَ ثُبُوْرًا ۝١٣
لَا تَدْعُوا الْيَوْمَ ثُبُوْرًا وَّاحِدًا

Ikhfa اخفاء | Ghunna غُنّہ | Ikhfa Meem Saakin اخفاء میم ساکن | Idghaam ادغام | Qalqala قلقلہ | Qalb قلب | Idghaam Meem Saakin ادغام میم ساکن

plead for destruction oft-repeated!"

wad'oo subooran kaseeraa.

وَّادْعُوا ثُبُورًا كَثِيرًا ﴿١٤﴾

15. Say: "Is that best, or the eternal Garden, promised to the righteous? for them, that is a reward as well as a goal (of attainment).

15. Qul azaalika khayrun am Jannatul-khuldil-latee wu'idal-muttaqoon; kaanat lahum jazaaa'añw-wa maseeraa.

قُلْ أَذٰلِكَ خَيْرٌ أَمْ جَنَّةُ الْخُلْدِ
الَّتِي وُعِدَ الْمُتَّقُونَ ۚ كَانَتْ
لَهُمْ جَزَاءً وَّمَصِيرًا ﴿١٥﴾

16. "For them there will be therein all that they wish for: they will dwell (there) for ever: A promise binding upon your Lord."

16. Lahum feehaa maa yashaaa'oona khaalideen; kaana 'alaa Rabbika wa'dam-mas'oolaa.

لَهُمْ فِيهَا مَا يَشَاءُونَ خٰلِدِينَ ۚ
كَانَ عَلٰى رَبِّكَ وَعْدًا مَّسْئُولًا ﴿١٦﴾

17. The day He will gather them together as well as those whom they worship besides Allah, He will ask: "Was it you who let these My servants astray, or did they stray from the Path themselves?"

17. Wa Yawma yahshuruhum wa maa ya'budoona min doonil-laahi fa-yaqoolu 'a-antum adlaltum 'ibaadee haaa'ulaaa'i am hum dallus-sabeel.

وَيَوْمَ يَحْشُرُهُمْ وَمَا يَعْبُدُونَ
مِنْ دُونِ اللّٰهِ فَيَقُولُ ءَأَنْتُمْ
أَضْلَلْتُمْ عِبَادِي هٰٓؤُلَاءِ أَمْ
هُمْ ضَلُّوا السَّبِيلَ ﴿١٧﴾

18. They will say: "Glory to You! Not meet was it for us that we should take for protectors others besides You: but You did bestow, on them and their fathers, good things (in life), until they forgot the Message: for they were a people (worthless and) lost."

18. Qaaloo Subhaanaka maa kaana yambaghee lanaaa an-nattakhiza min doonika min awliyaaa'a wa laakim-mat-ta'tahum wa aabaaa'ahum hattaa nasuz-zikra wa kaanoo qawmam booraa.

قَالُوا سُبْحٰنَكَ مَا كَانَ يَنْبَغِي
لَنَآ أَنْ نَّتَّخِذَ مِنْ دُونِكَ
مِنْ أَوْلِيَاءَ وَلٰكِنْ مَّتَّعْتَهُمْ وَ
اٰبَاءَهُمْ حَتّٰى نَسُوا الذِّكْرَ ۚ وَ
كَانُوا قَوْمًا بُورًا ﴿١٨﴾

19. (Allah will say): "Now have they proved you liars in what you say: so you cannot avert (your Penalty) nor (get) help." And whoever among you does wrong, him shall We cause to taste of a grievous Penalty.

19. Faqad kazzabookum bimaa taqooloona famaa tastatee'oona sarfañw-wa laa nasraa; wa mañy-yazlim-minkum nuziqhu 'azaaban kabeeraa.

فَقَدْ كَذَّبُوكُمْ بِمَا تَقُولُونَ ۙ
فَمَا تَسْتَطِيعُونَ صَرْفًا وَّلَا نَصْرًا ۚ
وَمَنْ يَّظْلِمْ مِّنْكُمْ نُذِقْهُ عَذَابًا
كَبِيرًا ﴿١٩﴾

20. And the Messengers whom We sent before you were all (men) who ate food and walked through the streets: We have made some of you as a trial for others: will you have patience? for Allah is One Who sees (all things).

20. Wa maaa arsalnaa qablaka minal-mursaleena illaaa innahum la-yaåkuloonat-ta'aama wa yamshoona fil-aswaaq; wa ja'alnaa ba'dakum liba'din fitnatan atasbiroon; wa kaana Rabbuka Baseeraa.

(Section 2)

وَمَآ أَرْسَلْنَا قَبْلَكَ مِنَ الْمُرْسَلِينَ
إِلَّآ إِنَّهُمْ لَيَأْكُلُونَ الطَّعَامَ وَ
يَمْشُونَ فِي الْأَسْوَاقِ ۗ وَجَعَلْنَا
بَعْضَكُمْ لِبَعْضٍ فِتْنَةً ۗ أَتَصْبِرُونَ ۚ
وَكَانَ رَبُّكَ بَصِيرًا ﴿٢٠﴾ ع

21. Such as do not fear the meeting with Us (for Judgment) say: "Why are not the angels sent down to us, or (why) do we not see

21. Wa qaalal-lazeena laa yarjoona liqaaa'anaa law laaa unzila 'alaynal-malaaa'ikatu aw naraa

وَقَالَ الَّذِينَ لَا يَرْجُونَ لِقَآءَنَا
لَوْلَآ أُنْزِلَ عَلَيْنَا الْمَلٰٓئِكَةُ أَوْ نَرٰى

Ikhfa اخفاء | Ghunna غُنّہ | Ikhfa Meem Saakin اخفاء میم ساکن | Idghaam ادغام | Qalqala قلقله | Qalb قلب | Idghaam Meem Saakin ادغام میم ساکن

Translation	Transliteration	Arabic
our Lord?" Indeed they have an arrogant conceit of themselves, and mighty is the insolence of their impiety!	Rabbanaa; laqadistakbaroo feee anfusihim wa 'ataw 'utuwwan kabeeraa.	رَبَّنَا ۗ لَقَدِ اسْتَكْبَرُوْا فِيْٓ اَنْفُسِهِمْ وَعَتَوْ عُتُوًّا كَبِيْرًا ﴿٢١﴾
22. The Day they see the angels,- no joy will there be to the sinners that Day: The (angels) will say: "There is a barrier forbidden (to you) altogether!"	22. Yawma yarawnal-malaaa-'ikata laa bushraa Yawma'izil-lilmujrimeena wa yaqooloona ḥijram-maḥjooraa.	يَوْمَ يَرَوْنَ الْمَلٰٓئِكَةَ لَا بُشْرٰى يَوْمَئِذٍ لِّلْمُجْرِمِيْنَ وَيَقُوْلُوْنَ حِجْرًا مَّحْجُوْرًا ﴿٢٢﴾
23. And We shall turn to whatever deeds they did (in this life), and We shall make such deeds as floating dust scattered about.	23. Wa qadimnaaa ilaa maa 'amiloo min 'amalin faja'al-naahu habaaa'am-mansooraa.	وَقَدِمْنَآ اِلٰى مَا عَمِلُوْا مِنْ عَمَلٍ فَجَعَلْنٰهُ هَبَآءً مَّنْثُوْرًا ﴿٢٣﴾
24. The Companions of the Garden will be well, that Day, in their abode, and have the fairest of places for repose.	24. Aṣ-ḥaabul-Jannati Yaw-ma'izin khayrum-mustaqar-rañw-wa aḥsanu maqeelaa.	اَصْحٰبُ الْجَنَّةِ يَوْمَئِذٍ خَيْرٌ مُّسْتَقَرًّا وَّاَحْسَنُ مَقِيْلًا ﴿٢٤﴾
25. The Day the heaven shall be rent asunder with clouds, and angels shall be sent down, descending (in ranks),-	25. Wa Yawma tashaqqaqus-samaaa'u bilghamaami wa nuzzilal-malaaa'ikatu tan-zeelaa.	وَيَوْمَ تَشَقَّقُ السَّمَآءُ بِالْغَمَامِ وَنُزِّلَ الْمَلٰٓئِكَةُ تَنْزِيْلًا ﴿٢٥﴾
26. That Day, the dominion as of right and truth, shall be (wholly) for (Allah) Most Merciful: it will be a Day of dire difficulty for the Misbelievers.	26. Almulku Yawma'izinil-ḥaqqu lir-Raḥmaan; wa kaana Yawman'alal-kaafireena 'asee-raa.	اَلْمُلْكُ يَوْمَئِذِ ۨالْحَقُّ لِلرَّحْمٰنِ ۭ وَكَانَ يَوْمًا عَلَى الْكٰفِرِيْنَ عَسِيْرًا ﴿٢٦﴾
27. The Day that the wrong-doer will bite at his hands, he will say, "Oh! would that I had taken a (straight) path with the Messenger!	27. Wa Yawma ya'aḍḍuẓ-ẓaalimu 'alaa yadayhi yaqoolu yaa-laytanit-takhaztu ma'ar-Rasooli sabeelaa.	وَيَوْمَ يَعَضُّ الظَّالِمُ عَلٰى يَدَيْهِ يَقُوْلُ يٰلَيْتَنِي اتَّخَذْتُ مَعَ الرَّسُوْلِ سَبِيْلًا ﴿٢٧﴾
28. "Ah! woe is me! Would that I had never taken such a one for a friend!	28. Yaa waylataa laytanee lam attakhiz fulaanan khaleelaa.	يٰوَيْلَتٰى لَيْتَنِيْ لَمْ اَتَّخِذْ فُلَانًا خَلِيْلًا ﴿٢٨﴾
29. "He did lead me astray from the Message (of Allah) after it had come to me! Ah! the Evil One is but a traitor to man!"	29. Laqad aḍallanee 'aniz-zikri ba'da iz jaaa'anee; wa kaanash-Shayṭaanu lil-insaani khazoolaa.	لَقَدْ اَضَلَّنِيْ عَنِ الذِّكْرِ بَعْدَ اِذْ جَآءَنِيْ ۭ وَكَانَ الشَّيْطٰنُ لِلْاِنْسَانِ خَذُوْلًا ﴿٢٩﴾
30. Then the Messenger will say: "O my Lord! Truly my people took this Qur'an for just foolish nonsense."	30. Wa qaalar-Rasoolu yaa Rabbi inna qawmit-takhazoo haazal-Qur-aana mahjooraa.	وَقَالَ الرَّسُوْلُ يٰرَبِّ اِنَّ قَوْمِي اتَّخَذُوْا هٰذَا الْقُرْاٰنَ مَهْجُوْرًا ﴿٣٠﴾
31. Thus have We made for every prophet an enemy among the sinners: but enough is your Lord to guide and to help.	31. Wa kazaalika ja'alnaa likulli Nabiyyin 'aduwwam-minal-mujrimeen; wa kafaa bi-Rabbika haadiyañw-wa naṣeeraa.	وَكَذٰلِكَ جَعَلْنَا لِكُلِّ نَبِيٍّ عَدُوًّا مِّنَ الْمُجْرِمِيْنَ ۭ وَكَفٰى بِرَبِّكَ هَادِيًا وَّنَصِيْرًا ﴿٣١﴾

Ikhfa اخفاء | Ghunna غُنّۃ | Ikhfa Meem Saakin اخفاء میم ساکن | Idghaam ادغام | Qalqala قلقلہ | Qalb قلب | Idghaam Meem Saakin ادغام میم ساکن

32. Those who reject Faith say: "Why is not the Qur'an revealed to him all at once? Thus (is it revealed), that We may strengthen your heart thereby, and We have rehearsed it to you in slow, well-arranged stages, gradually.

33. And no question do they bring to you but We reveal to you the truth and the best explanation (thereof).

34. Those who will be gathered to Hell (prone) on their faces,- they will be in an evil plight, and, as to Path, most astray.

35. (Before this,) We sent Moses The Book, and appointed his brother Aaron with him as minister;

36. And We command: "You both go, to the people who have rejected our Signs:" and those (people) We destroyed with utter destruction.

37. And the people of Noah,- when they rejected the Messengers, We drowned them, and We made them as a Sign for mankind; and We have prepared for (all) wrong-doers a grievous Penalty;-

38. As also 'Ad and Thamud, and the Companions of the Rass, and many a generation between them.

39. To each one We set forth parables and examples; and each one We broke to utter annihilation (for their sins).

40. And the (Unbelievers) must indeed have passed by the town on which was rained a shower of evil: did they not then see it (with their own eyes)? But they do not fear the Resurrection.

41. When they see you, they treat you no otherwise than in mockery: "Is this the one whom Allah has sent as a Messenger?"

42. "He indeed would well-have misled us from our gods, had it not been that we were constant to them!" - Soon will they know,

32. Wa qaalal-lazeena kafaroo law laa nuzzila 'alayhil-Qur-aanu jumlatañw-waaḥidah; kazaalika linusabbita bihee fu'aadaka wa rattalnaahu tarteelaa.

33. Wa laa yaåtoonaka bimasalin illaa ji'naaka bilḥaqqi wa aḥsana tafseeraa.

34. Allazeena yuḥsharoona 'alaa wujoohihim ilaa Jahannama ulaaa'ika sharrum-makaanañw-wa aḍallu sabeelaa.

(Section 3)

35. Wa laqad aataynaa Moosal-Kitaaba wa ja'alnaa ma'ahooo akhaahu Haaroona wazeeraa.

36. Faqulnaz-habaaa ilal-qawmil-lazeena kazzaboo bi-Aayaatinaa fadammarnaahum tadmeeraa.

37. Wa qawma Nooḥil-lammaa kazzabur-Rusula aghraqnaahum wa ja'alnaahum linnaasi Aayatañw-wa a'tadnaa liẓ-ẓaalimeena 'azaaban aleemaa.

38. Wa 'Aadañw-wa Samooda wa Aṣ-ḥaabar-Rassi wa quroonam bayna zaalika kaseeraa.

39. Wa kullan ḍarabnaa lahul-amsaala wa kullan tabbarnaa tatbeeraa.

40. Wa laqad ataw 'alal-qaryatil-lateee umṭirat maṭaras-saw'; afalam yakoonoo yarawnahaa; bal kaanoo laa yarjoona nushooraa.

41. Wa izaa ra-awka iñy-yattakhizoonaka illaa huzuwan ahaazal-lazee ba'asal-laahu Rasoolaa.

42. In kaada la-yuḍillunaa 'an aalihatinaa law laaa an ṣabarnaa 'alayhaa; wa sawfa ya'lamoona

وَقَالَ الَّذِيْنَ كَفَرُوْا لَوْلَا نُزِّلَ عَلَيْهِ
الْقُرْاٰنُ جُمْلَةً وَّاحِدَةً ۚ كَذٰلِكَ ۚ
لِنُثَبِّتَ بِهٖ فُؤَادَكَ وَرَتَّلْنٰهُ تَرْتِيْلًا ﴿٣٢﴾
وَلَا يَاْتُوْنَكَ بِمَثَلٍ اِلَّا جِئْنٰكَ بِالْحَقِّ
وَاَحْسَنَ تَفْسِيْرًا ﴿٣٣﴾ؕ
اَلَّذِيْنَ يُحْشَرُوْنَ عَلٰى وُجُوْهِهِمْ
اِلٰى جَهَنَّمَ ۙ اُولٰٓئِكَ شَرٌّ مَّكَانًا
وَّاَضَلُّ سَبِيْلًا ﴿٣٤﴾ع
وَلَقَدْ اٰتَيْنَا مُوْسَى الْكِتٰبَ وَجَعَلْنَا
مَعَهٗٓ اَخَاهُ هٰرُوْنَ وَزِيْرًا ﴿٣٥﴾ۚۖ
فَقُلْنَا اذْهَبَآ اِلَى الْقَوْمِ الَّذِيْنَ
كَذَّبُوْا بِاٰيٰتِنَا ؕ فَدَمَّرْنٰهُمْ تَدْمِيْرًا ﴿٣٦﴾ؕ
وَقَوْمَ نُوْحٍ لَّمَّا كَذَّبُوا الرُّسُلَ
اَغْرَقْنٰهُمْ وَجَعَلْنٰهُمْ لِلنَّاسِ اٰيَةً ؕ
وَاَعْتَدْنَا لِلظّٰلِمِيْنَ عَذَابًا اَلِيْمًا ﴿٣٧﴾ۚۖ
وَّعَادًا وَّثَمُوْدَاۡ وَاَصْحٰبَ الرَّسِّ
وَقُرُوْنًۢا بَيْنَ ذٰلِكَ كَثِيْرًا ﴿٣٨﴾
وَكُلًّا ضَرَبْنَا لَهُ الْاَمْثَالَ ۫ وَكُلًّا
تَبَّرْنَا تَتْبِيْرًا ﴿٣٩﴾
وَلَقَدْ اَتَوْا عَلَى الْقَرْيَةِ الَّتِيْٓ اُمْطِرَتْ
مَطَرَ السَّوْءِ ؕ اَفَلَمْ يَكُوْنُوْا يَرَوْنَهَا ۚ
بَلْ كَانُوْا لَا يَرْجُوْنَ نُشُوْرًا ﴿٤٠﴾
وَاِذَا رَاَوْكَ اِنْ يَّتَّخِذُوْنَكَ اِلَّا هُزُوًا ؕ
اَهٰذَا الَّذِيْ بَعَثَ اللّٰهُ رَسُوْلًا ﴿٤١﴾
اِنْ كَادَ لَيُضِلُّنَا عَنْ اٰلِهَتِنَا لَوْلَآ
اَنْ صَبَرْنَا عَلَيْهَا ؕ وَسَوْفَ يَعْلَمُوْنَ

مع ٧ عند المتقدمين ١٢

ع ١٤ / ٣

Ikhfa اخفاء | Ghunna غُنّہ | Ikhfa Meem Saakin اخفاء میم ساکن | Idghaam ادغام | Qalqala قلقلہ | Qalb قلب | Idghaam Meem Saakin ادغام میم ساکن

when they see the Penalty, who it is that is most misled in Path!	ḥeena yarawnal-'azaaba man aḍallu sabeelaa.	حِيْنَ يَرَوْنَ الْعَذَابَ مَنْ اَضَلُّ سَبِيْلًا ﴿٤٢﴾
43. Do you see such a one as takes for his god his own passion (or impulse)? Could you be a disposer of affairs for him?	43. Ara'ayta manit-takhaza ilaahahoo hawaahu afa-anta takoonu 'alayhi wakeelaa.	اَرَءَيْتَ مَنِ اتَّخَذَ اِلٰهَهٗ هَوٰىهُ ط اَفَاَنْتَ تَكُوْنُ عَلَيْهِ وَكِيْلًا ﴿٤٣﴾
44. Or do you think that most of them listen or understand? They are only like cattle;- nay, they are worse astray in Path.	44. Am taḥsabu anna aksarahum yasma'oona aw ya'qiloon; in hum illaa kal-an'aami bal hum aḍallu sabeelaa (Section 4)	اَمْ تَحْسَبُ اَنَّ اَكْثَرَهُمْ يَسْمَعُوْنَ اَوْ يَعْقِلُوْنَ ط اِنْ هُمْ اِلَّا كَالْاَنْعَامِ بَلْ هُمْ اَضَلُّ سَبِيْلًا ﴿٤٤﴾ ع
45. Have you not turned your vision to your Lord?- How does He prolong the shadow! If He willed, He could make it stationary! then do We make the sun its guide;	45. Alam tara ilaa Rabbika kayfa maddaẓ-ẓilla wa law shaaa'a laja'alahoo saakinan summa ja'alnash-shamsa 'alayhi daleelaa.	اَلَمْ تَرَ اِلٰى رَبِّكَ كَيْفَ مَدَّ الظِّلَّ وَلَوْ شَآءَ لَجَعَلَهٗ سَاكِنًا ثُمَّ جَعَلْنَا الشَّمْسَ عَلَيْهِ دَلِيْلًا ﴿٤٥﴾
46. Then We draw it in towards Ourselves,- a contraction by easy stages.	46. Summa qabaḍnaahu ilaynaa qabḍañy-yaseeraa.	ثُمَّ قَبَضْنٰهُ اِلَيْنَا قَبْضًا يَّسِيْرًا ﴿٤٦﴾
47. And He it is Who makes the Night as a Robe for you, and Sleep as Repose, and makes the Day (as it were) a Resurrection.	47. Wa Huwal-lazee ja'ala lakumul-layla libaasañw-wannawma subaatañw-wa ja'alan-nahaara nushooraa.	وَهُوَ الَّذِيْ جَعَلَ لَكُمُ الَّيْلَ لِبَاسًا وَّالنَّوْمَ سُبَاتًا وَّجَعَلَ النَّهَارَ نُشُوْرًا ﴿٤٧﴾
48. And He it is Who sends the winds as heralds of glad tidings, going before His mercy, and We send down pure water from the sky,-	48. Wa Huwal-lazeee arsalar-riyaaḥa bushram bayna yaday raḥmatih; wa anzalnaa minas-samaaa'i maaa'an ṭahooraa.	وَهُوَ الَّذِيْۤ اَرْسَلَ الرِّيٰحَ بُشْرًا بَيْنَ يَدَيْ رَحْمَتِهٖ ج وَاَنْزَلْنَا مِنَ السَّمَآءِ مَآءً طَهُوْرًا ﴿٤٨﴾
49. That with it We may give life to a dead land, and slake the thirst of things We have created,- cattle and men in great numbers.	49. Linuḥyiya bihee baldatam-maytañw-wa nusqiyahoo mimmaa khalaqnaaa an'aamañw-wa anaasiyya kaseeraa.	لِّنُحْيِۦَ بِهٖ بَلْدَةً مَّيْتًا وَّنُسْقِيَهٗ مِمَّا خَلَقْنَآ اَنْعَامًا وَّاَنَاسِيَّ كَثِيْرًا ﴿٤٩﴾
50. And We have distributed the (water) amongst them, in order that they may celebrate (our) praises, but most men are averse (to anything) but (rank) ingratitude.	50. Wa laqad ṣarrafnaahu baynahum li-yazzakkaroo faabaaa aksarun-naasi illaa kufooraa.	وَلَقَدْ صَرَّفْنٰهُ بَيْنَهُمْ لِيَذَّكَّرُوْا ۖ فَاَبٰۤى اَكْثَرُ النَّاسِ اِلَّا كُفُوْرًا ﴿٥٠﴾
51. Had it been Our Will, We could have sent a warner to every centre of population.	51. Wa law shi'naa laba'asnaa fee kulli qar-yatin-nazeeraa.	وَلَوْ شِئْنَا لَبَعَثْنَا فِيْ كُلِّ قَرْيَةٍ نَّذِيْرًا ﴿٥١﴾
52. Therefore do not listen to the Unbelievers, but strive against them with the utmost strenuousness, with the (Qur'an).	52. Falaa tuṭi'il-kaafireena wa jaahidhum bihee jihaadan kabeeraa.	فَلَا تُطِعِ الْكٰفِرِيْنَ وَجَاهِدْهُمْ بِهٖ جِهَادًا كَبِيْرًا ﴿٥٢﴾
53. It is He Who has let free the two bodies of flowing water: One palatable and sweet, and the other salt and bitter; yet has He made	53. Wa Huwal-lazee marajal-baḥrayni haazaa 'azbun furaatuñw-wa haazaa milḥun ujaaj; wa ja'ala	وَهُوَ الَّذِيْ مَرَجَ الْبَحْرَيْنِ هٰذَا عَذْبٌ فُرَاتٌ وَّهٰذَا مِلْحٌ اُجَاجٌ ج وَجَعَلَ

Ikhfa	Ghunna	Ikhfa Meem Saakin	Idghaam	Qalqala	Qalb	Idghaam Meem Saakin
اخفاء	غُنّہ	اخفاء میم ساکن	ادغام	قلقلہ	قلب	ادغام میم ساکن

a barrier between them, a partition that is forbidden to be passed.

54. It is He Who has created man from water: then has He established relationships of lineage and marriage: for your Lord has power (over all things).

55. Yet do they worship, besides Allah, things that can neither profit them nor harm them: and the Misbeliever is a helper (of Evil), against his own Lord!

56. But you We only sent to give glad tidings and admonition.

57. Say: "No reward do I ask of you for it but this: that each one who will may take a (straight) Path to his Lord."

58. And put your trust in Him Who lives and dies not; and celebrate his praise; and enough is He to be acquainted with the faults of His servants;-

59. He Who created the heavens and the earth and all that is between, in six days, and is firmly established on the Throne (of Authority): Allah Most Gracious: ask you, then, about Him of any acquainted (with such things).

60. When it is said to them, "Adore you (Allah) Most Gracious!", they say, "And what is (Allah) Most Gracious? Shall we adore That which you command us?" And it increases their flight (from the Truth).

(Bow Down)

61. Blessed is He Who made constellations in the skies, and placed therein a Lamp and a Moon giving light;

62. And it is He Who made the Night and the Day to follow each other: for such as desire to be mindful or to show their gratitude.

63. And the servants of (Allah) Most Gracious are those who walk on the earth in humility, and when the

baynahumaa barzakhañw-wa ḥijram-maḥjooraa.

54. Wa Huwal-lazee khalaqa minal-maaa'i basharan fa-ja'alahoo nasabañw-wa ṣihraa; wa kaana Rabbuka Qadeeraa.

55. Wa ya'budoona min doonil-laahi maa laa yanfa-'uhum wa laa yaḍurruhum; wa kaanal-kaafiru 'alaa Rabbihee ẓaheeraa.

56. Wa maa arsalnaaka illaa mubashshirañw-wa nazeeraa.

57. Qul maaa as'alukum 'alayhi min ajrin illaa man shaaa'a añy-yattakhiza ilaa Rabbihee sabeelaa.

58. Wa tawakkal 'alal-Ḥayyil-lazee laa yamootu wa sabbiḥ biḥamdih; wa kafaa bihee bizunoobi 'ibaadihee khabeeraa.

59. Allazee khalaqas-samaa-waati wal-arḍa wa maa baynahumaa fee sittati ayyaa-min summastawaa 'alal-'Arsh; ar-Raḥmaanu fas'al bihee khabeeraa.

60. Wa izaa qeela lahumus-judoo lir-Raḥmaani qaaloo wa mar-Raḥmaanu anasjudu limaa taåmurunaa wa zaadahum nufooraa. **(Section 5)**

61. Tabaarakal-lazee ja'ala fis-samaaa'i buroojañw-wa ja'ala feehaa siraajañw-wa qamaram-muneeraa.

62. Wa Huwal-lazee ja'alal-layla wannahaara khilfatal-liman araada añy-yazzakkara aw araada shukooraa.

63. Wa 'ibaadur-Raḥmaanil-lazeena yamshoona 'alal-arḍi hawnañw-wa izaa khaaṭa-bahumul-

بَيْنَهُمَا بَرْزَخًا وَّحِجْرًا مَّحْجُورًا ﴿٥٣﴾
وَهُوَ الَّذِي خَلَقَ مِنَ الْمَآءِ بَشَرًا
فَجَعَلَهُ نَسَبًا وَّصِهْرًا ؕ وَكَانَ رَبُّكَ
قَدِيرًا ﴿٥٤﴾
وَيَعْبُدُونَ مِنْ دُونِ اللّٰهِ مَا لَا
يَنْفَعُهُمْ وَلَا يَضُرُّهُمْ ؕ وَكَانَ الْكَافِرُ
عَلٰى رَبِّهِ ظَهِيرًا ﴿٥٥﴾
وَمَآ أَرْسَلْنٰكَ إِلَّا مُبَشِّرًا وَّنَذِيرًا ﴿٥٦﴾
قُلْ مَآ أَسْئَلُكُمْ عَلَيْهِ مِنْ أَجْرٍ إِلَّا
مَنْ شَآءَ أَنْ يَّتَّخِذَ إِلٰى رَبِّهِ سَبِيلًا ﴿٥٧﴾
وَتَوَكَّلْ عَلَى الْحَيِّ الَّذِي لَا يَمُوتُ وَ
سَبِّحْ بِحَمْدِهِ ؕ وَكَفٰى بِهِ بِذُنُوبِ عِبَادِهِ
خَبِيرًا ﴿٥٨﴾
الَّذِي خَلَقَ السَّمٰوٰتِ وَالْأَرْضَ وَمَا
بَيْنَهُمَا فِي سِتَّةِ أَيَّامٍ ثُمَّ اسْتَوٰى عَلَى
الْعَرْشِ ۚ الرَّحْمٰنُ فَسْئَلْ بِهِ خَبِيرًا ﴿٥٩﴾
وَإِذَا قِيلَ لَهُمُ اسْجُدُوا لِلرَّحْمٰنِ
قَالُوا وَمَا الرَّحْمٰنُ ۗ أَنَسْجُدُ لِمَا
تَأْمُرُنَا وَزَادَهُمْ نُفُورًا ﴿٦٠﴾ السجدة
تَبٰرَكَ الَّذِي جَعَلَ فِي السَّمَآءِ بُرُوجًا
وَّجَعَلَ فِيهَا سِرٰجًا وَّقَمَرًا مُّنِيرًا ﴿٦١﴾
وَهُوَ الَّذِي جَعَلَ الَّيْلَ وَالنَّهَارَ
خِلْفَةً لِّمَنْ أَرَادَ أَنْ يَّذَّكَّرَ أَوْ أَرَادَ
شُكُورًا ﴿٦٢﴾
وَعِبَادُ الرَّحْمٰنِ الَّذِينَ يَمْشُونَ عَلَى
الْأَرْضِ هَوْنًا وَّإِذَا خَاطَبَهُمُ

مع عند المتقدمين ١٢

السجدة ٦

Ikhfa اخفاء | Ghunna غُنّہ | Ikhfa Meem Saakin اخفاء میم ساکن | Idghaam ادغام | Qalqala قلقلہ | Qalb قلب | Idghaam Meem Saakin ادغام میم ساکن

ignorant address them, they say, "Peace!";

64. Those who spend the night in adoration of their Lord prostrate and standing;

65. Those who say, "Our Lord! avert from us the Wrath of Hell, for its Wrath is indeed an affliction grievous,-

66. "Evil indeed is it as an abode, and as a place to rest in";

67. Those who, when they spend, are not extravagant and not niggardly, but hold a just (balance) between those (extremes).

68. Those who do not invoke, with Allah, any other god, nor slay such life as Allah has made sacred except for just cause, nor commit fornication; - and any that does this (not only) meets punishment.

69. (But) the Penalty on the Day of Judgment will be doubled to him, and he will dwell therein in ignominy,-

70. Unless he repents, believes, and works righteous deeds, for Allah will change the evil of such persons into good, and Allah is Oft-Forgiving, Most Merciful,

71. And whoever repents and does good has truly turned to Allah with an (acceptable) conversion;-

72. Those who witness no falsehood, and, if they pass by futility, they pass by it with honorable (avoidance);

73. Those who, when they are admonished with the Signs of their Lord, droop not down at them as if they were deaf or blind;

74. And those who pray, "Our Lord! Grant unto us wives and offspring who will be the comfort of our eyes, and

jaahiloona qaaloo salaamaa.

64. Wallazeena yabeetoona li-Rabbihim sujjadañw-wa qiyaamaa.

65. Wallazeena yaqooloona Rabbanaṣ-rif 'annaa 'azaaba Jahannama inna 'azaabahaa kaana gharaamaa.

66. Innahaa saaa'at mustaqarrañw-wa muqaamaa.

67. Wallazeena izaaa anfaqoo lam yusrifoo wa lam yaqturoo wa kaana bayna zaalika qawaamaa.

68. Wallazeena laa yad'oona ma'al-laahi ilaahan aakhara wa laa yaqtuloonan-nafsal-latee ḥarramal-laahu illaa bilhaqqi wa laa yaznoon; wa mañy-yaf'al zaalika yalqa asaamaa.

69. Yuḍaa'af lahul-'azaabu Yawmal-Qiyaamati wa yakhlud feehee muhaanaa.

70. Illaa man taaba wa 'aamana wa 'amila 'amalan ṣaaliḥan fa-ulaaa'ika yubaddilul-laahu sayyi-aatihim ḥasanaat; wa kaanal-laahu Ghafoorar-Raḥeemaa.

71. Wa man taaba wa 'amila ṣaaliḥan fa-innahoo yatoobu ilal-laahi mataabaa.

72. Wallazeena laa yash-hadoonaz-zoora wa izaa marroo billaghwi marroo kiraamaa.

73. Wallazeena izaa zukkiroo bi-Aayaati Rabbihim lam yakhirroo 'alayhaa ṣummañw-wa 'umyaanaa.

74. Wallazeena yaqooloona Rabbanaa hab lanaa min azwaajinaa wa zurriyyaatinaa qurrata a'yuniñw-waj-

الْجٰهِلُوْنَ قَالُوْا سَلٰمًا ﴿٦٣﴾
وَالَّذِيْنَ يَبِيْتُوْنَ لِرَبِّهِمْ سُجَّدًا
وَّقِيَامًا ﴿٦٤﴾
وَالَّذِيْنَ يَقُوْلُوْنَ رَبَّنَا اصْرِفْ عَنَّا
عَذَابَ جَهَنَّمَ ۖ اِنَّ عَذَابَهَا كَانَ
غَرَامًا ﴿٦٥﴾
اِنَّهَا سَآءَتْ مُسْتَقَرًّا وَّمُقَامًا ﴿٦٦﴾
وَالَّذِيْنَ اِذَآ اَنْفَقُوْا لَمْ يُسْرِفُوْا وَلَمْ
يَقْتُرُوْا وَكَانَ بَيْنَ ذٰلِكَ قَوَامًا ﴿٦٧﴾
وَالَّذِيْنَ لَا يَدْعُوْنَ مَعَ اللّٰهِ اِلٰهًا
اٰخَرَ وَلَا يَقْتُلُوْنَ النَّفْسَ الَّتِيْ حَرَّمَ
اللّٰهُ اِلَّا بِالْحَقِّ وَلَا يَزْنُوْنَ ۚ وَمَنْ
يَّفْعَلْ ذٰلِكَ يَلْقَ اَثَامًا ﴿٦٨﴾
يُّضٰعَفْ لَهُ الْعَذَابُ يَوْمَ الْقِيٰمَةِ
وَيَخْلُدْ فِيْهٖ مُهَانًا ﴿٦٩﴾
اِلَّا مَنْ تَابَ وَاٰمَنَ وَعَمِلَ عَمَلًا صَالِحًا
فَاُولٰٓئِكَ يُبَدِّلُ اللّٰهُ سَيِّاٰتِهِمْ حَسَنٰتٍ
وَكَانَ اللّٰهُ غَفُوْرًا رَّحِيْمًا ﴿٧٠﴾
وَمَنْ تَابَ وَعَمِلَ صَالِحًا فَاِنَّهٗ يَتُوْبُ
اِلَى اللّٰهِ مَتَابًا ﴿٧١﴾
وَالَّذِيْنَ لَا يَشْهَدُوْنَ الزُّوْرَ ۙ وَاِذَا
مَرُّوْا بِاللَّغْوِ مَرُّوْا كِرَامًا ﴿٧٢﴾
وَالَّذِيْنَ اِذَا ذُكِّرُوْا بِاٰيٰتِ رَبِّهِمْ
لَمْ يَخِرُّوْا عَلَيْهَا صُمًّا وَّعُمْيَانًا ﴿٧٣﴾
وَالَّذِيْنَ يَقُوْلُوْنَ رَبَّنَا هَبْ لَنَا مِنْ
اَزْوَاجِنَا وَذُرِّيّٰتِنَا قُرَّةَ اَعْيُنٍ وَّ

Ikhfa اخفاء | Ghunna غنّہ | Ikhfa Meem Saakin اخفاء میم ساکن | Idghaam ادغام | Qalqala قلقلہ | Qalb قلب | Idghaam Meem Saakin ادغام میم ساکن

give us (the grace) to lead the righteous."

75. Those are the ones who will be rewarded with the highest place in heaven, because of their patient constancy: therein shall they be met with salutations and peace,

76. Dwelling therein;- how beautiful an abode and place of rest!

77. Say (to the Rejecters): "My Lord is not uneasy because of you if you do not call on Him: but you have indeed rejected (Him), and soon will come the inevitable (punishment)!"

‘alnaa lilmuttaqeena Imaamaa.

75. Ulaaa’ika yujzawnal-ghurfata bimaa ṣabaroo wa yulaqqawna feehaa taḥiyya-tañw-wa salaamaa.

76. Khaalideena feehaa; ḥasunat mustaqarrañw-wa muqaamaa.

77. Qul maa ya‘ba’u bikum Rabbee law laa du‘aaa’ukum faqad kazzabtum fasawfa yakoonu lizaamaa. **(Section 6)**

اجْعَلْنَا لِلْمُتَّقِينَ إِمَامًا ٧٤
أُولَٰئِكَ يُجْزَوْنَ الْغُرْفَةَ بِمَا صَبَرُوا
وَيُلَقَّوْنَ فِيهَا تَحِيَّةً وَسَلَامًا ٧٥
خَالِدِينَ فِيهَا ۚ حَسُنَتْ مُسْتَقَرًّا
وَمُقَامًا ٧٦
قُلْ مَا يَعْبَأُ بِكُمْ رَبِّي لَوْلَا دُعَاؤُكُمْ
فَقَدْ كَذَّبْتُمْ فَسَوْفَ يَكُونُ لِزَامًا ٧٧

26. The Poets

In the name of Allah, Most Gracious, Most Merciful.

Sûrat ash-Shu‘arâ’–26

(Revealed at Makkah)

Bismillaahir Raḥmaanir Raḥeem

(٢٦) سُورَةُ الشُّعَرَاءِ مَكِّيَّةٌ (٤٧)

بِسْمِ اللَّهِ الرَّحْمَٰنِ الرَّحِيمِ

1. *Ta-Sin-Mim.*

2. These are verses of the Book that makes (things) clear.

3. It may be you will kill yourself with grief, that they do not become Believers.

4. If (such) were Our Will, We could send down to them from the sky a Sign, to which they would bend their necks in humility.

5. But there doesn't come to them a newly-revealed Message from (Allah) Most Gracious, but they turn away therefrom.

6. They have indeed rejected (the Message): so they will know soon (enough) the truth of what they mocked at!

7. Do they not look at the earth,- how many noble things of all kinds We have produced therein?

8. Verily, in this is a Sign: but most of them do not believe.

9. And verily, your Lord is He, the Exalted in Might, Most Merciful.

10. Behold, your Lord called Moses: "Go to the people of iniquity,-

1. Ṭaa-Seeen-Meeem.

2. Tilka Aayaatul-Kitaabil-Mubeen.

3. La‘allaka baakhi‘un-nafsaka allaa yakoonoo mu’mineen.

4. In-nashaå nunazzil ‘alayhim minas-samaaa’i Aayatan fazallat a‘naaquhum lahaa khaaḍi‘een.

5. Wa maa yaåteehim-min zikrim-minar-Raḥmaani muḥdasin illaa kaanoo ‘anhu mu‘riḍeen.

6. Faqad kazzaboo fasa-yaåteehim ambaaa’u maa kaanoo bihee yastahzi’oon.

7. Awa lam yaraw ilal-arḍi kam ambatnaa feehaa min kulli zawjin kareem.

8. Inna fee zaalika la-Aayah; wa maa kaana aksaruhum mu’mineen.

9. Wa inna Rabbaka la-Huwal-‘Azeezur-Raḥeem. **(Section 1)**

10. Wa iz naadaa Rabbuka Moosaaa ani’-til-qawmaz-zaalimeen.

طسم ١
تِلْكَ آيَاتُ الْكِتَابِ الْمُبِينِ ٢
لَعَلَّكَ بَاخِعٌ نَفْسَكَ أَلَّا يَكُونُوا
مُؤْمِنِينَ ٣
إِنْ نَشَأْ نُنَزِّلْ عَلَيْهِمْ مِنَ السَّمَاءِ
آيَةً فَظَلَّتْ أَعْنَاقُهُمْ لَهَا خَاضِعِينَ ٤
وَمَا يَأْتِيهِمْ مِنْ ذِكْرٍ مِنَ الرَّحْمَٰنِ
مُحْدَثٍ إِلَّا كَانُوا عَنْهُ مُعْرِضِينَ ٥
فَقَدْ كَذَّبُوا فَسَيَأْتِيهِمْ أَنْبَاءُ مَا
كَانُوا بِهِ يَسْتَهْزِئُونَ ٦
أَوَلَمْ يَرَوْا إِلَى الْأَرْضِ كَمْ
أَنْبَتْنَا فِيهَا مِنْ كُلِّ زَوْجٍ كَرِيمٍ ٧
إِنَّ فِي ذَٰلِكَ لَآيَةً وَمَا كَانَ أَكْثَرُهُمْ
مُؤْمِنِينَ ٨
وَإِنَّ رَبَّكَ لَهُوَ الْعَزِيزُ الرَّحِيمُ ٩
وَإِذْ نَادَىٰ رَبُّكَ مُوسَىٰ أَنِ ائْتِ
الْقَوْمَ الظَّالِمِينَ ١٠

الربع
المنزل الخامس (٥)
ع ٥

Ikhfa اخفاء | Ghunna غنّہ | Ikhfa Meem Saakin اخفاء میم ساکن | Idghaam ادغام | Qalqala قلقلہ | Qalb قلب | Idghaam Meem Saakin ادغام میم ساکن

11. "The people of the Pharaoh: will they not fear Allah?"
12. He said: "O my Lord! I do fear that they will charge me with falsehood:
13. "My breast will be straitened. And my speech may not go (smoothly): so send unto Aaron.
14. "And (further), they have a charge of crime against me; and I fear they may slay me."
15. Allah said: "By no means! proceed then, both of you, with Our Signs; We are with you, and will listen (to your call).
16. "So go forth, both of you, to Pharaoh, and say: 'We have been sent by the Lord and Cherisher of the worlds;
17. "'You send with us the Children of Israel.'"
18. (Pharaoh) said: "Did we not cherish you as a child among us, and did you not stay in our midst many years of your life?
19. "And you did a deed of yours which (you know) you did, and you are an ungrateful (wretch)!"
20. Moses said: "I did it then, when I was in error.
21. "So I fled from you (all) when I feared you; but my Lord has (since) invested me with jud-gment (and wisdom) and appointed me as one of the Messenger.
22. "And this is the favor with which you do reproach me,- that you have enslaved the Children of Israel!"
23. Pharaoh said: "And who is the 'Lord and Cherisher of the worlds'?"
24. (Moses) said: "The Lord and Cherisher of the heavens and the earth, and all between,- if you want to be quite sure."
25. (Pharaoh) said to those around: "Did you not listen (to what he says)?"
26. (Moses) said: "Your Lord and the Lord of your fathers from the beginning!"
27. (Pharaoh) said: "Truly your Messenger who has been sent

11. Qawma Fir'awn; alaa yattaqoon.
12. Qaala Rabbi inneee akhaafu añy-yukazziboon.
13. Wa yaḍeequ ṣadree wa laa yanṭaliqu lisaanee fa-arsil ilaa Haaroon.
14. Wa lahum 'alayya zambun fa-akhaafu añy-yaqtuloon.
15. Qaala kallaa fazhabaa bi-Aayaatinaaa innaa ma'akum mustami'oon.
16. Faåtiyaa Fir'awna faqoolaaa innaa Rasoolu Rabbil-'aalameen.
17. An arsil ma'anaa Baneee Israaa'eel.
18. Qaala alam nurabbika feenaa waleedañw-wa labista feenaa min 'umurika sineen.
19. Wa fa'alta fa'latakal-latee fa'alta wa anta minal-kaafireen.
20. Qaala fa'altuhaaa izañw-wa ana minaḍ-ḍaaalleen.
21. Fafarartu minkum lammaa khiftukum fawahaba lee Rabbee ḥukmañw-wa ja'alanee minal-mursaleen.
22. Wa tilka ni'matun tamunnuhaa 'alayya an 'abbatta Baneee Israaa'eel.
23. Qaala Fir'awnu wa maa Rabbul-'aalameen.
24. Qaala Rabbus-samaawaati wal-arḍi wa maa baynahumaa in kuntum-mooqineen.
25. Qaala liman ḥawlahooo alaa tastami'oon.
26. Qaala Rabbukum wa Rabbu aabaaa'ikumul-awwaleen.
27. Qaala inna Rasoolakumul-lazeee ursila

قَوْمَ فِرْعَوْنَ ۚ أَلَا يَتَّقُونَ ﴿١١﴾
قَالَ رَبِّ إِنِّىٓ أَخَافُ أَن يُكَذِّبُونِ ﴿١٢﴾
وَيَضِيقُ صَدْرِى وَلَا يَنطَلِقُ
لِسَانِى فَأَرْسِلْ إِلَىٰ هَٰرُونَ ﴿١٣﴾
وَلَهُمْ عَلَىَّ ذَنۢبٌ فَأَخَافُ أَن
يَقْتُلُونِ ﴿١٤﴾
قَالَ كَلَّا ۖ فَٱذْهَبَا بِـَٔايَٰتِنَآ ۖ إِنَّا
مَعَكُم مُّسْتَمِعُونَ ﴿١٥﴾
فَأْتِيَا فِرْعَوْنَ فَقُولَآ إِنَّا رَسُولُ
رَبِّ ٱلْعَٰلَمِينَ ﴿١٦﴾
أَنْ أَرْسِلْ مَعَنَا بَنِىٓ إِسْرَٰٓءِيلَ ﴿١٧﴾
قَالَ أَلَمْ نُرَبِّكَ فِينَا وَلِيدًا وَلَبِثْتَ
فِينَا مِنْ عُمُرِكَ سِنِينَ ﴿١٨﴾
وَفَعَلْتَ فَعْلَتَكَ ٱلَّتِى فَعَلْتَ
وَأَنتَ مِنَ ٱلْكَٰفِرِينَ ﴿١٩﴾
قَالَ فَعَلْتُهَآ إِذًا وَأَنَا۠ مِنَ ٱلضَّآلِّينَ ﴿٢٠﴾
فَفَرَرْتُ مِنكُمْ لَمَّا خِفْتُكُمْ فَوَهَبَ لِى
رَبِّى حُكْمًا وَجَعَلَنِى مِنَ ٱلْمُرْسَلِينَ ﴿٢١﴾
وَتِلْكَ نِعْمَةٌ تَمُنُّهَا عَلَىَّ أَنْ عَبَّدتَّ
بَنِىٓ إِسْرَٰٓءِيلَ ﴿٢٢﴾
قَالَ فِرْعَوْنُ وَمَا رَبُّ ٱلْعَٰلَمِينَ ﴿٢٣﴾
قَالَ رَبُّ ٱلسَّمَٰوَٰتِ وَٱلْأَرْضِ وَمَا
بَيْنَهُمَآ ۖ إِن كُنتُم مُّوقِنِينَ ﴿٢٤﴾
قَالَ لِمَنْ حَوْلَهُۥٓ أَلَا تَسْتَمِعُونَ ﴿٢٥﴾
قَالَ رَبُّكُمْ وَرَبُّ ءَابَآئِكُمُ ٱلْأَوَّلِينَ ﴿٢٦﴾
قَالَ إِنَّ رَسُولَكُمُ ٱلَّذِىٓ أُرْسِلَ

Ikhfa اخفاء | Ghunna غُنّہ | Ikhfa Meem Saakin اخفاء میم ساکن | Idghaam ادغام | Qalqala قلقلہ | Qalb قلب | Idghaam Meem Saakin ادغام میم ساکن

to you is a veritable madman!"	ilaykum lamajnoon.	إِلَيْكُمْ لَمَجْنُونٌ ﴿٢٧﴾
28. (Moses) said: "Lord of the East and the West, and all between! if you only had sense!"	28. Qaala Rabbul-mashriqi walmaghribi wa maa baynahumaa in kuntum ta'qiloon.	قَالَ رَبُّ الْمَشْرِقِ وَالْمَغْرِبِ وَمَا بَيْنَهُمَا ۖ إِنْ كُنْتُمْ تَعْقِلُونَ ﴿٢٨﴾
29. (Pharaoh) said: "If you do put forward any god other than me, I will certainly put you in prison!"	29. Qaala la'init-takhazta ilaahan ghayree la-aj'alannaka minal-masjooneen.	قَالَ لَئِنِ اتَّخَذْتَ إِلَٰهًا غَيْرِي لَأَجْعَلَنَّكَ مِنَ الْمَسْجُونِينَ ﴿٢٩﴾
30. (Moses) said: "Even if I showed you something clear (and) convincing?"	30. Qaala awalaw ji'tuka bishay'im-mubeen.	قَالَ أَوَلَوْ جِئْتُكَ بِشَيْءٍ مُبِينٍ ﴿٣٠﴾
31. (Pharaoh) said: "Show it then, if you tell the truth!"	31. Qaala faâti biheee in kunta minaṣ-ṣaadiqeen.	قَالَ فَأْتِ بِهِ إِنْ كُنْتَ مِنَ الصَّادِقِينَ ﴿٣١﴾
32. So (Moses) threw his rod, and behold, it was a serpent, plain (for all to see)!	32. Fa-alqaa 'aṣaahu fa-izaa hiya su'baanum-mubeen.	فَأَلْقَىٰ عَصَاهُ فَإِذَا هِيَ ثُعْبَانٌ مُبِينٌ ﴿٣٢﴾
33. And he drew out his hand, and behold, it was white to all beholders!	33. Wa naza'a yadahoo fa-izaa hiya bayḍaaa'u linnaazireen. **(Section 2)**	وَنَزَعَ يَدَهُ فَإِذَا هِيَ بَيْضَاءُ لِلنَّاظِرِينَ ﴿٣٣﴾ ع
34. (Pharaoh) said to the Chiefs around him: "This is indeed a sorcerer well- versed:	34. Qaala lilmala-i ḥawlahooo inna haazaa lasaaḥirun 'aleem.	قَالَ لِلْمَلَإِ حَوْلَهُ إِنَّ هَٰذَا لَسَاحِرٌ عَلِيمٌ ﴿٣٤﴾
35. "His plan is to get you out of your land by his sorcery; then what is it you counsel?"	35. Yureedu añy-yukhrijakum min arḍikum bisiḥrihee famaazaa taâmuroon.	يُرِيدُ أَنْ يُخْرِجَكُمْ مِنْ أَرْضِكُمْ بِسِحْرِهِ فَمَاذَا تَأْمُرُونَ ﴿٣٥﴾
36. They said: "Keep him and his brother in suspense (for a while), and dispatch to the Cities heralds to collect-	36. Qaalooo arjih wa akhaahu wab'as filmadaaa'ini ḥaashireen.	قَالُوا أَرْجِهْ وَأَخَاهُ وَابْعَثْ فِي الْمَدَائِنِ حَاشِرِينَ ﴿٣٦﴾
37. "And bring up to you all (our) sorcerers well-versed."	37. Yaâtooka bikulli saḥḥaarin 'aleem.	يَأْتُوكَ بِكُلِّ سَحَّارٍ عَلِيمٍ ﴿٣٧﴾
38. So the sorcerers were got together for the appointment of a day well-known,	38. Fa-jumi'as-saḥaratu limeeqaati Yawmim-ma'loom.	فَجُمِعَ السَّحَرَةُ لِمِيقَاتِ يَوْمٍ مَعْلُومٍ ﴿٣٨﴾
39. And the people were told: "Are you (now) assembled?-	39. Wa qeela linnaasi hal antum-mujtami'oon.	وَقِيلَ لِلنَّاسِ هَلْ أَنْتُمْ مُجْتَمِعُونَ ﴿٣٩﴾
40. "That we may follow the sorcerers (in religion) if they win?"	40. La'allanaa nattabi'us-saḥarata in kaanoo humul-ghaalibeen..	لَعَلَّنَا نَتَّبِعُ السَّحَرَةَ إِنْ كَانُوا هُمُ الْغَالِبِينَ ﴿٤٠﴾
41. So when the sorcerers arrived, they said to Pharaoh:	41. Falammaa jaaa'as-saḥaratu qaaloo li-Fir'awna	فَلَمَّا جَاءَ السَّحَرَةُ قَالُوا لِفِرْعَوْنَ

Ikhfa اخفاء | Ghunna غُنّہ | Ikhfa Meem Saakin اخفاء میم ساکن | Idghaam ادغام | Qalqala قلقلہ | Qalb قلب | Idghaam Meem Saakin ادغام میم ساکن

"Of course - shall we have a (suitable) reward if we win?	a'inna lanaa la-ajran in kunnaa nahnul-ghaalibeen.	اَىِٕنَّ لَنَا لَاَجْرًا اِنْ كُنَّا نَحْنُ الْغٰلِبِيْنَ ۝٤١
42. He said: "Yes, (and more),- for you shall in that case be (raised to posts) nearest (to my person)."	42. Qaala na'am wa innakum izal-laminal-muqarrabeen.	قَالَ نَعَمْ وَاِنَّكُمْ اِذًا لَّمِنَ الْمُقَرَّبِيْنَ ۝٤٢
43. Moses said to them: "Throw you - that which you are about to throw!"	43. Qaala lahum-Moosaaa alqoo maaa antum-mulqoon.	قَالَ لَهُمْ مُّوْسٰۤى اَلْقُوْا مَاۤ اَنْتُمْ مُّلْقُوْنَ ۝٤٣
44. So they threw their ropes and their rods, and said: "By the might of Pharaoh, it is we who will certainly win!"	44. Fa-alqaw hibaalahum wa 'isiyyahum wa qaaloo bi'izzati Fir'awna innaa lanahnul-ghaa-liboon.	فَاَلْقَوْا حِبَالَهُمْ وَعِصِيَّهُمْ وَقَالُوْا بِعِزَّةِ فِرْعَوْنَ اِنَّا لَنَحْنُ الْغٰلِبُوْنَ ۝٤٤
45. Then Moses threw his rod, when, behold, it straightway swallows up all the falsehoods which they fake!	45. Fa-alqaa Moosaa 'asaahu fa-izaa hiya talqafu maa yaâ-fikoon.	فَاَلْقٰى مُوْسٰى عَصَاهُ فَاِذَا هِىَ تَلْقَفُ مَا يَاْفِكُوْنَ ۝٤٥
46. Then did the sorcerers fall down, prostrate in adoration,	46. Fa-ulqiyas-saharatu saaji-deen.	فَاُلْقِىَ السَّحَرَةُ سٰجِدِيْنَ ۝٤٦
47. Saying: "We believe in the Lord of the Worlds,	47. Qaalooo aamannaa bi-Rabbil-'aalameen.	قَالُوْۤا اٰمَنَّا بِرَبِّ الْعٰلَمِيْنَ ۝٤٧
48. "The Lord of Moses and Aaron."	48. Rabbi Moosaa wa Haa-roon.	رَبِّ مُوْسٰى وَهٰرُوْنَ ۝٤٨
49. Said (Pharaoh): "You believe in Him before I give you permission? surely he is your leader, who has taught you sorcery! but soon you shall know! "Be sure I will cut off your hands and your feet on opposite sides, and I will cause you all to die on the cross!"	49. Qaala aamantum lahoo qabla an aazana lakum innahoo lakabeerukumul-lazee 'alla-makumus-sihra falasawfa ta'lamoon; la-uqatti'anna aydi-yakum wa arjulakum-min khilaafiñw-wa la-usallibanna-kum ajma'een.	قَالَ اٰمَنْتُمْ لَهٗ قَبْلَ اَنْ اٰذَنَ لَكُمْ ۚ اِنَّهٗ لَكَبِيْرُكُمُ الَّذِىْ عَلَّمَكُمُ السِّحْرَ ۚ فَلَسَوْفَ تَعْلَمُوْنَ ؕ لَاُقَطِّعَنَّ اَيْدِيَكُمْ وَاَرْجُلَكُمْ مِّنْ خِلَافٍ وَّلَاُوصَلِّبَنَّكُمْ اَجْمَعِيْنَ ۝٤٩
50. They said: "No matter! for us, we shall but return to our Lord!	50. Qaaloo laa dayra innaaa ilaa Rabbinaa munqaliboon.	قَالُوْا لَا ضَيْرَ ۫ اِنَّاۤ اِلٰى رَبِّنَا مُنْقَلِبُوْنَ ۝٥٠
51. "Only, our desire is that our Lord will forgive us our faults, that we may become foremost among the Believers!"	51. Innaa natma'u añy-yagh-fira lanaa Rabbunaa khataa-yaanaaa an kunnaaa awwalal-mu'mineen. **(Section 3)**	اِنَّا نَطْمَعُ اَنْ يَّغْفِرَ لَنَا رَبُّنَا خَطٰيٰنَاۤ اَنْ كُنَّاۤ اَوَّلَ الْمُؤْمِنِيْنَ ۝٥١
52. By inspiration We told Moses: "Travel by night with my servants; for surely you shall be pursued."	52. Wa awhaynaaa ilaa Moosaaa an asri bi'ibaadeee innakum-muttaba'oon.	وَاَوْحَيْنَاۤ اِلٰى مُوْسٰۤى اَنْ اَسْرِ بِعِبَادِىْۤ اِنَّكُمْ مُّتَّبَعُوْنَ ۝٥٢
53. Then Pharaoh sent heralds to (all) the Cities,	53. Fa-arsala Fir'awnu filma-daaa'ini haashireen.	فَاَرْسَلَ فِرْعَوْنُ فِى الْمَدَاۤىِٕنِ حٰشِرِيْنَ ۝٥٣
54. (Saying): "These (Israeli-tes) are but a small band,	54. Inna haaa'ulaaa'i lashir-zimatun qaleeloon.	اِنَّ هٰۤؤُلَاۤءِ لَشِرْذِمَةٌ قَلِيْلُوْنَ ۝٥٤
55. "And they are raging furiously against us;	55. Wa innahum-lanaa la-ghaaa'izoon.	وَاِنَّهُمْ لَنَا لَغَاۤىِٕظُوْنَ ۝٥٥
56. "But we are a multitude amply fore-warned."	56. Wa innaa lajamee'un haaziroon.	وَاِنَّا لَجَمِيْعٌ حٰذِرُوْنَ ۝٥٦

٣ ع ١٨ ٧

Ikhfa اخفاء · Ghunna غُنّہ · Ikhfa Meem Saakin اخفاء میم ساکن · Idghaam ادغام · Qalqala قلقلہ · Qalb قلب · Idghaam Meem Saakin ادغام میم ساکن

57. So We expelled them from gardens, springs,	57. Fa-akhrajnaahum-min Jannaatiñw-wa 'uyoon.	فَأَخْرَجْنَٰهُم مِّن جَنَّٰتٍ وَعُيُونٍ ﴿٥٧﴾
58. Treasures, and every kind of honorable position;	58. Wa kunooziñw-wa maqaamin kareem.	وَكُنُوزٍ وَمَقَامٍ كَرِيمٍ ﴿٥٨﴾
59. Thus it was, but We made the Children of Israel inheritors of such things.	59. Kaz̲aalika wa awras̲naahaa Baneee Israaa'eel.	كَذَٰلِكَ وَأَوْرَثْنَٰهَا بَنِىٓ إِسْرَٰٓءِيلَ ﴿٥٩﴾
60. So they pursued them at sunrise.	60. Fa-atba'oohum-mushriqeen.	فَأَتْبَعُوهُم مُّشْرِقِينَ ﴿٦٠﴾
61. And when the two bodies saw each other, the people of Moses said: "We are sure to be overtaken."	61. Falammaa taraaa'al-jam-'aani qaala aṣ-ḥaabu Moosaaa innaa lamudrakoon.	فَلَمَّا تَرَٰٓءَا ٱلْجَمْعَانِ قَالَ أَصْحَٰبُ مُوسَىٰٓ إِنَّا لَمُدْرَكُونَ ﴿٦١﴾
62. (Moses) said: "By no means! my Lord is with me! soon will He guide me!"	62. Qaala kallaaa inna ma'iya Rabbee sa-yahdeen.	قَالَ كَلَّآ ۖ إِنَّ مَعِىَ رَبِّى سَيَهْدِينِ ﴿٦٢﴾
63. Then We told Moses by inspiration: "Strike the sea with your rod." So it divided, and each separate part became like the huge, firm mass of a mountain.	63. Fa-awḥaynaaa ilaa Moosaaa aniḍrib bi'aṣaakal-baḥra fanfalaqa fakaana kullu firqin kaṭṭawdil-'aẓeem.	فَأَوْحَيْنَآ إِلَىٰ مُوسَىٰٓ أَنِ ٱضْرِب بِّعَصَاكَ ٱلْبَحْرَ ۖ فَٱنفَلَقَ فَكَانَ كُلُّ فِرْقٍ كَٱلطَّوْدِ ٱلْعَظِيمِ ﴿٦٣﴾
64. And We made the other party approach there.	64. Wa azlafnaa s̲ammal-aakhareen.	وَأَزْلَفْنَا ثَمَّ ٱلْءَاخَرِينَ ﴿٦٤﴾
65. We delivered Moses and all who were with him;	65. Wa anjaynaa Moosaa wa mam-ma'ahooo ajma'een.	وَأَنجَيْنَا مُوسَىٰ وَمَن مَّعَهُۥٓ أَجْمَعِينَ ﴿٦٥﴾
66. But We drowned the others.	66. S̲umma aghraqnal-aakhareen.	ثُمَّ أَغْرَقْنَا ٱلْءَاخَرِينَ ﴿٦٦﴾
67. Verily in this is a Sign: but most of them do not believe.	67. Inna fee z̲aalika la-Aayaah; wa maa kaana aks̲aru-hum-mu'mineen.	إِنَّ فِى ذَٰلِكَ لَءَايَةً ۖ وَمَا كَانَ أَكْثَرُهُم مُّؤْمِنِينَ ﴿٦٧﴾
68. And verily your Lord is He, the Exalted in Might, Most Merciful.	68. Wa inna Rabbaka la-Huwal-'Azeezur-Raḥeem. **(Sec. 4)**	وَإِنَّ رَبَّكَ لَهُوَ ٱلْعَزِيزُ ٱلرَّحِيمُ ﴿٦٨﴾ وقف لازم
69. And rehearse to them (something of) Abraham's story.	69. Watlu 'alayhim naba-a Ibraaheem.	وَٱتْلُ عَلَيْهِمْ نَبَأَ إِبْرَٰهِيمَ ﴿٦٩﴾
70. Behold, he said to his father and his people: "What do you worship?"	70. Iz̲ qaala li-abeehi wa qawmihee maa ta'budoon.	إِذْ قَالَ لِأَبِيهِ وَقَوْمِهِۦ مَا تَعْبُدُونَ ﴿٧٠﴾
71. They said: "We worship idols, and we remain constantly in attendance on them."	71. Qaaloo na'budu aṣnaa-man fanaẓallu lahaa 'aakifeen.	قَالُوا۟ نَعْبُدُ أَصْنَامًا فَنَظَلُّ لَهَا عَٰكِفِينَ ﴿٧١﴾
72. He said: "Do they listen to you when you call (on them),	72. Qaala hal yasma'oona-kum iz̲ tad'oon.	قَالَ هَلْ يَسْمَعُونَكُمْ إِذْ تَدْعُونَ ﴿٧٢﴾
73. Or they do you good or harm?"	73. Aw yanfa'oonakum aw yaḍurroon.	أَوْ يَنفَعُونَكُمْ أَوْ يَضُرُّونَ ﴿٧٣﴾
74. They said: "Nay, but we found our fathers doing thus (what we do)."	74. Qaaloo bal wajadnaaa aabaaa'anaa kaz̲aalika yaf-'aloon.	قَالُوا۟ بَلْ وَجَدْنَآ ءَابَآءَنَا كَذَٰلِكَ يَفْعَلُونَ ﴿٧٤﴾
75. He said: "Do you then see whom you have been worshipping,-	75. Qaala afara'aytum-maa kuntum ta'budoon.	قَالَ أَفَرَءَيْتُم مَّا كُنتُمْ تَعْبُدُونَ ﴿٧٥﴾

Ikhfa اخفاء | Ghunna غُنّہ | Ikhfa Meem Saakin اخفاء میم ساکن | Idghaam ادغام | Qalqala قلقلہ | Qalb قلب | Idghaam Meem Saakin ادغام میم ساکن

76. "You and your fathers before you?-	76. Antum wa aabaaa'ukumul-aqdamoon.	أَنتُمْ وَءَابَآؤُكُمُ ٱلْأَقْدَمُونَ ﴿٧٦﴾
77. "For they are enemies to me; not so the Lord and Cherisher of the Worlds;	77. Fa-innahum 'aduwwulleee illaa Rabbal-'aalameen	فَإِنَّهُمْ عَدُوٌّ لِّىٓ إِلَّا رَبَّ ٱلْعَٰلَمِينَ ﴿٧٧﴾
78. "Who created me, and it is He Who guides me;	78. Allazee khalaqanee fa-Huwa yahdeen.	ٱلَّذِى خَلَقَنِى فَهُوَ يَهْدِينِ ﴿٧٨﴾
79. "Who gives me food and drink,	79. Wallazee Huwa yuṭ'imunee wa yasqeen.	وَٱلَّذِى هُوَ يُطْعِمُنِى وَيَسْقِينِ ﴿٧٩﴾
80. "And when I am ill, it is He Who cures me;	80. Wa izaa mariḍtu fahuwa yashfeen.	وَإِذَا مَرِضْتُ فَهُوَ يَشْفِينِ ﴿٨٠﴾
81. "Who will cause me to die, and then to life (again);	81. Wallazee yumeetunee summa yuḥyeen.	وَٱلَّذِى يُمِيتُنِى ثُمَّ يُحْيِينِ ﴿٨١﴾
82. "And who, I hope, will forgive me my faults on the day of Judgment.	82. Wallazeee aṭma'u añy-yaghfira lee khaṭeee'atee Yawmad-Deen.	وَٱلَّذِىٓ أَطْمَعُ أَن يَغْفِرَ لِى خَطِيٓـَٔتِى يَوْمَ ٱلدِّينِ ﴿٨٢﴾
83. "O my Lord! bestow wisdom on me, and join me with the righteous;	83. Rabbi hab lee ḥukmañw-wa alḥiqnee biṣ-ṣaaliḥeen.	رَبِّ هَبْ لِى حُكْمًا وَأَلْحِقْنِى بِٱلصَّٰلِحِينَ ﴿٨٣﴾
84. "Grant me honorable mention on the tongue of truth among the latest (generations);	84. Waj'al-lee lisaana ṣidqin fil-aakhireen.	وَٱجْعَل لِّى لِسَانَ صِدْقٍ فِى ٱلْءَاخِرِينَ ﴿٨٤﴾
85. "Make me one of the inheritors of the Garden of Bliss;	85. Waj'alnee miñw-waraṡati Jannatin-Na'eem.	وَٱجْعَلْنِى مِن وَرَثَةِ جَنَّةِ ٱلنَّعِيمِ ﴿٨٥﴾
86. "Forgive my father, for that he is among those astray;	86. Waghfir li-abeee innahoo kaana minḍ-ḍaaalleen.	وَٱغْفِرْ لِأَبِىٓ إِنَّهُۥ كَانَ مِنَ ٱلضَّآلِّينَ ﴿٨٦﴾
87. "And let me not be in disgrace on the Day when (men) will be raised up;-	87. Wa laa tukhzinee Yawma yub'aṡoon.	وَلَا تُخْزِنِى يَوْمَ يُبْعَثُونَ ﴿٨٧﴾
88. "The Day whereon neither wealth nor sons will avail,	88. Yawma laa yanfa'u maaluñw-wa laa banoon.	يَوْمَ لَا يَنفَعُ مَالٌ وَلَا بَنُونَ ﴿٨٨﴾
89. "But only he (will prosper) that brings to Allah a sound heart;	89. Illaa man atal-laaha biqalbin saleem.	إِلَّا مَنْ أَتَى ٱللَّهَ بِقَلْبٍ سَلِيمٍ ﴿٨٩﴾
90. "To the righteous, the Garden will be brought near,	90. Wa uzlifatil-Jannatu lilmuttaqeen.	وَأُزْلِفَتِ ٱلْجَنَّةُ لِلْمُتَّقِينَ ﴿٩٠﴾
91. "And to those straying in Evil, the Fire will be placed in full view;	91. Wa burrizatil-Jaḥeemu lilghaaween.	وَبُرِّزَتِ ٱلْجَحِيمُ لِلْغَاوِينَ ﴿٩١﴾
92. "And it shall be said to them: 'Where are the (gods) you worshipped-	92. Wa qeela lahum ayna maa kuntum ta'budoon.	وَقِيلَ لَهُمْ أَيْنَ مَا كُنتُمْ تَعْبُدُونَ ﴿٩٢﴾
93. "'Besides Allah? Can they help you or help themselves?'	93. Min doonil-laahi hal yanṣuroonakum aw yantaṣiroon	مِن دُونِ ٱللَّهِ هَلْ يَنصُرُونَكُمْ أَوْ يَنتَصِرُونَ ﴿٩٣﴾
94. "Then they will be thrown headlong into the (Fire),- they and those straying in Evil,	94. Fakubkiboo feehaa hum walghaawoon.	فَكُبْكِبُوا۟ فِيهَا هُمْ وَٱلْغَاوُۥنَ ﴿٩٤﴾
95. "And the whole hosts of Iblis together.	95. Wa junoodu Ibleesa ajma'oon.	وَجُنُودُ إِبْلِيسَ أَجْمَعُونَ ﴿٩٥﴾
96. "They will say there in their mutual bickerings:	96. Qaaloo wa hum feehaa yakhtaṣimoon.	قَالُوا۟ وَهُمْ فِيهَا يَخْتَصِمُونَ ﴿٩٦﴾
97. "'By Allah, we were truly in an error manifest,-	97. Tallaahi in kunnaa lafee ḍalaalim-mubeen.	تَٱللَّهِ إِن كُنَّا لَفِى ضَلَٰلٍ مُّبِينٍ ﴿٩٧﴾

Ikhfa اخفاء | Ghunna غنّہ | Ikhfa Meem Saakin اخفاء میم ساکن | Idghaam ادغام | Qalqala قلقلہ | Qalb قلب | Idghaam Meem Saakin ادغام میم ساکن

98. "'When we held you as equals with the Lord of the Worlds;
99. "'And our seducers were only those who were steeped in guilt.
100. "Now, then, we have none to intercede (for us),
101. "Nor a single friend to feel (for us).
102. "Now if we only had a chance of return we shall truly be of those who believe!"
103. Verily in this is a Sign but most of them do not believe.
104. And verily your Lord is He, the Exalted in Might, Most Merciful.
105. The people of Noah rejected the Messengers.
106. Behold, their brother Noah said to them: "Will you not fear (Allah)?
107. "I am to you a Messenger worthy of all trust:
108. "So fear Allah, and obey me.
109. "No reward do I ask of you for it: my reward is only from the Lord of the Worlds:
110. "So fear Allah, and obey me."
111. They said: "Shall we believe in you when it is the meanest that follow you?"
112. He said: "And what do I know as to what they do?
113. "Their account is only with my Lord, if you could (but) understand.
114. "I am not one to drive away those who believe.
115. "I am sent only to warn plainly in public."
116. They said: "If you desist not, O Noah! you shall be stoned (to death)."

98. Iz nusawweekum bi-Rabbil-'aalameen.
99. Wa maaa aḍallanaaa illal-mujrimoon.
100. Famaa lanaa min shaafi'een.
101. Wa laa ṣadeeqin ḥameem.
102. Falaw anna lanaa karratan fanakoona minal-mu'mineen.
103. Inna fee zaalika la-Aayatañw wa maa kaana aksaruhum mu'mineen.
104. Wa inna Rabbaka la-Huwal-'Azeezur-Raḥeem. **(Sec. 5)**
105. Kazzabat qawmu Nooḥinil-mursaleen.
106. Iz qaala lahum akhoohum Nooḥun alaa tattaqoon.
107. Innee lakum Rasoolun ameen.
108. Fattaqullaaha wa aṭee-'oon.
109. Wa maaa as'alukum 'alayhi min ajrin in ajriya illaa 'alaa Rabbil-'aalameen.
110. Fattaqul-laaha wa aṭee-'oon.
111. Qaalooo anu'minu laka wattaba'akal-arzaloon.
112. Qaala wa maa 'ilmee bimaa kaanoo ya'maloon.
113. In ḥisaabuhum illaa 'alaa Rabbee law tash'uroon.
114. Wa maaa ana biṭaaridil-mu'mineen.
115. In ana illaa nazeerum-mubeen.
116. Qaaloo la'il-lam tantahi yaa Nooḥu latakoonanna minal-marjoomeen.

إِذْ نُسَوِّيكُم بِرَبِّ الْعٰلَمِيْنَ ﴿٩٨﴾
وَمَآ أَضَلَّنَآ إِلَّا الْمُجْرِمُوْنَ ﴿٩٩﴾
فَمَا لَنَا مِنْ شَافِعِيْنَ ﴿١٠٠﴾
وَلَا صَدِيْقٍ حَمِيْمٍ ﴿١٠١﴾
فَلَوْ أَنَّ لَنَا كَرَّةً فَنَكُوْنَ مِنَ
الْمُؤْمِنِيْنَ ﴿١٠٢﴾
إِنَّ فِيْ ذٰلِكَ لَاٰيَةً ۖ وَمَا كَانَ
أَكْثَرُهُمْ مُّؤْمِنِيْنَ ﴿١٠٣﴾
وَإِنَّ رَبَّكَ لَهُوَ الْعَزِيْزُ الرَّحِيْمُ ﴿١٠٤﴾ ع
كَذَّبَتْ قَوْمُ نُوْحِ الْمُرْسَلِيْنَ ﴿١٠٥﴾
إِذْ قَالَ لَهُمْ أَخُوْهُمْ نُوْحٌ أَلَا
تَتَّقُوْنَ ﴿١٠٦﴾
إِنِّيْ لَكُمْ رَسُوْلٌ أَمِيْنٌ ﴿١٠٧﴾
فَاتَّقُوا اللّٰهَ وَأَطِيْعُوْنِ ﴿١٠٨﴾
وَمَآ أَسْئَلُكُمْ عَلَيْهِ مِنْ أَجْرٍ ۚ إِنْ
أَجْرِيَ إِلَّا عَلٰى رَبِّ الْعٰلَمِيْنَ ﴿١٠٩﴾
فَاتَّقُوا اللّٰهَ وَأَطِيْعُوْنِ ﴿١١٠﴾
قَالُوْٓا أَنُؤْمِنُ لَكَ وَاتَّبَعَكَ
الْأَرْذَلُوْنَ ﴿١١١﴾
قَالَ وَمَا عِلْمِيْ بِمَا كَانُوْا يَعْمَلُوْنَ ﴿١١٢﴾
إِنْ حِسَابُهُمْ إِلَّا عَلٰى رَبِّيْ لَوْ
تَشْعُرُوْنَ ﴿١١٣﴾
وَمَآ أَنَا بِطَارِدِ الْمُؤْمِنِيْنَ ﴿١١٤﴾
إِنْ أَنَا إِلَّا نَذِيْرٌ مُّبِيْنٌ ﴿١١٥﴾
قَالُوْا لَئِنْ لَّمْ تَنْتَهِ يٰنُوْحُ لَتَكُوْنَنَّ
مِنَ الْمَرْجُوْمِيْنَ ﴿١١٦﴾

Ikhfa اخفاء · Ghunna غُنّہ · Ikhfa Meem Saakin اخفاء میم ساکن · Idghaam ادغام · Qalqala قلقلہ · Qalb قلب · Idghaam Meem Saakin ادغام میم ساکن

النصف

English	Transliteration	Arabic
117. He said: "O my Lord! truly my people have rejected me.	117. Qaala Rabbi inna qawmee kazzaboon.	قَالَ رَبِّ اِنَّ قَوْمِیْ كَذَّبُوْنِ ﴿١١٧﴾
118. "You judge, then, between me and them openly, and deliver me and those of the Believers who are with me."	118. Faftaḥ baynee wa baynahum fat-ḥañw-wa najjinee wa mam-ma‘iya minal-mu'mineen.	فَافْتَحْ بَیْنِیْ وَبَیْنَهُمْ فَتْحًا وَّنَجِّنِیْ وَمَنْ مَّعِیَ مِنَ الْمُؤْمِنِیْنَ ﴿١١٨﴾
119. So We delivered him and those with him, in the Ark filled (with all creatures).	119. Fa-anjaynaahu wa mam-ma‘ahoo fil-fulkil-mashḥoon.	فَاَنْجَیْنٰهُ وَمَنْ مَّعَهٗ فِی الْفُلْكِ الْمَشْحُوْنِ ﴿١١٩﴾
120. Thereafter We drowned those who remained behind.	120. Summa aghraqnaa ba‘dul-baaqeen.	ثُمَّ اَغْرَقْنَا بَعْدُ الْبٰقِیْنَ ﴿١٢٠﴾
121. Verily in this is a Sign: but most of them do not believe.	121. Inna fee zaalika la-Aayaah; wa maa kaana aksaru-hum-mu'mineen.	اِنَّ فِیْ ذٰلِكَ لَاٰیَةً ؕ وَمَا كَانَ اَكْثَرُهُمْ مُّؤْمِنِیْنَ ﴿١٢١﴾
122. And verily your Lord is He, the Exalted in Might, Most Merciful.	122. Wa inna Rabbaka la-Huwal-‘Azeezur-Raḥeem. **(Sec. 6)**	وَاِنَّ رَبَّكَ لَهُوَ الْعَزِیْزُ الرَّحِیْمُ ﴿١٢٢﴾
123. The ‘Ad (people) rejected the Messengers.	123. Kazzabat ‘Aadunil-mursaleen.	كَذَّبَتْ عَادُ ِۨالْمُرْسَلِیْنَ ﴿١٢٣﴾
124. Behold, their brother Hud said to them: "Will you not fear (Allah)?	124. Iz qaala lahum akhoohum Hoodun alaa tattaqoon.	اِذْ قَالَ لَهُمْ اَخُوْهُمْ هُوْدٌ اَلَا تَتَّقُوْنَ ﴿١٢٤﴾
125. "I am to you a Messenger worthy of all trust:	125. Innee lakum Rasoolun ameen.	اِنِّیْ لَكُمْ رَسُوْلٌ اَمِیْنٌ ﴿١٢٥﴾
126. "So fear Allah and obey me.	126. Fattaqullaaha wa aṭee‘oon.	فَاتَّقُوا اللّٰهَ وَاَطِیْعُوْنِ ﴿١٢٦﴾
127. "No reward do I ask of you for it: my reward is only from the Lord of the Worlds.	127. Wa maaa as'alukum ‘alayhi min ajrin in ajriya illaa ‘alaa Rabbil-‘aalameen.	وَمَاۤ اَسْـَٔلُكُمْ عَلَیْهِ مِنْ اَجْرٍ ۚ اِنْ اَجْرِیَ اِلَّا عَلٰی رَبِّ الْعٰلَمِیْنَ ﴿١٢٧﴾
128. "Do you build a landmark on every high place to amuse yourselves?	128. Atabnoona bikulli ree‘in aayatan ta‘basoon.	اَتَبْنُوْنَ بِكُلِّ رِیْعٍ اٰیَةً تَعْبَثُوْنَ ﴿١٢٨﴾
129. "And do you get for yourselves fine buildings in the hope of living therein (for ever)?	129. Wa tattakhizoona maṣaani‘a la‘allakum takhludoon.	وَتَتَّخِذُوْنَ مَصَانِعَ لَعَلَّكُمْ تَخْلُدُوْنَ ﴿١٢٩﴾
130. "And when you strike, you strike like tyrants.	130. Wa izaa baṭashtum baṭashtum jabbaareen.	وَاِذَا بَطَشْتُمْ بَطَشْتُمْ جَبَّارِیْنَ ﴿١٣٠﴾
131. "Now fear Allah, and obey me.	131. Fattaqul-laaha wa aṭee-‘oon.	فَاتَّقُوا اللّٰهَ وَاَطِیْعُوْنِ ﴿١٣١﴾
132. "Yes, fear Him Who has bestowed on you freely all that you know.	132. Wattaqul-lazeee amad-dakum bimaa ta‘lamoon.	وَاتَّقُوا الَّذِیْۤ اَمَدَّكُمْ بِمَا تَعْلَمُوْنَ ﴿١٣٢﴾
133. "Freely has He bestowed on you cattle and sons,-	133. Amaddakum bi-an‘aa-miñw-wa baneen.	اَمَدَّكُمْ بِاَنْعَامٍ وَّبَنِیْنَ ﴿١٣٣﴾
134. "And Gardens and Springs.	134. Wa jannaatiñw-wa ‘uyoon.	وَجَنّٰتٍ وَّعُیُوْنٍ ﴿١٣٤﴾
135. "Truly I fear for you the Penalty of a Great Day."	135. Inneee akhaafu ‘alaykum ‘azaaba Yawmin ‘aẓeem.	اِنِّیْۤ اَخَافُ عَلَیْكُمْ عَذَابَ یَوْمٍ عَظِیْمٍ ﴿١٣٥﴾

ع ١٨/٦/١٠

Ikhfa	Ghunna	Ikhfa Meem Saakin	Idghaam	Qalqala	Qalb	Idghaam Meem Saakin
اخفاء	غنّہ	اخفاء میم ساکن	ادغام	قلقلہ	قلب	ادغام میم ساکن

136. They said: "It is the same to us whether you admonish us or be not among (our) admonishers!
137. "This is no other than a customary device of the ancients,
138. "And we are not the ones to receive Pains and Penalties!"
139. So they rejected him, and We destroyed them. Verily in this is a Sign: but most of them do not believe.

140. And verily your Lord is He, the Exalted in Might, Most Merciful.
141. The Thamud (people) rejected the Messengers.
142. Behold, their brother Salih said to them: "Will you not fear (Allah)?
143. "I am to you a Messenger worthy of all trust.
144. "So fear Allah, and obey me.
145. "No reward do I ask of you for it: my reward is only from the Lord of the Worlds.
146. "Will you be left secure, in (the enjoyment of) all that you have here?-
147. "Gardens and Springs,
148. "And corn-fields and date-palms with spathes near breaking (with the weight of fruit)?
149. "And you carve houses out of (rocky) mountains with great skill.
150. "But fear Allah and obey me;
151. "And do not follow the bidding of those who are extravagant,-
152. "Who make mischief in the land, and do not mend (their ways)."

153. They said: "You are only one of those bewitched!
154. "You are no more than a mortal like us: then bring us a Sign, if you tell the truth!"

136. Qaaloo sawaaa'un 'alaynaaa awa 'azta am lam takum-minal-waa'izeen.
137. In haazaaa illaa khuluqul-awwaleen.
138. Wa maa naḥnu bimu'azzabeen.
139. Fakazzaboohu fa-ahlaknaahum; inna fee zaalika la-Aayah; wa maa kaana aksaruhum-mu'mineen.
140. Wa inna Rabbaka la-Huwal-'Azeezur-Raḥeem.
(Section 7)
141. Kazzabat Samoodul-mursaleen.
142. Iz qaala lahum akhoohum Ṣaaliḥun alaa tattaqoon.
143. Innee lakum Rasoolun ameen.
144. Fattaqul-laaha wa aṭee-'oon.
145. Wa maaa as'alukum 'alayhi min ajrin in ajriya illaa 'alaa Rabbil-'aalameen.
146. Atutrakoona fee maa haahunaaa aamineen.
147. Fee jannaatiñw-wa 'uyoon.
148. Wa zuroo'iñw-wa nakhlin ṭal'uhaa haḍeem.
149. Wa tanḥitoona minal-jibaali buyootan faariheen.
150. Fattaqul-laaha wa aṭee-'oon.
151. Wa laa tuṭee'ooo amral-musrifeen.
152. Allazeena yufsidoona fil-arḍi wa laa yuṣliḥoon.
153. Qaalooo innamaaa anta minal-musaḥḥareen.
154. Maaa anta illaa basharum-mislunaa faåti bi-Aayatin in kunta minaṣ-ṣaadiqeen.

قَالُوا سَوَآءٌ عَلَيْنَآ اَوَعَظْتَ اَمْ لَمْ تَكُنْ مِّنَ الْوٰعِظِيْنَ ﴿١٣٦﴾
اِنْ هٰذَآ اِلَّا خُلُقُ الْاَوَّلِيْنَ ﴿١٣٧﴾
وَمَا نَحْنُ بِمُعَذَّبِيْنَ ﴿١٣٨﴾
فَكَذَّبُوْهُ فَاَهْلَكْنٰهُمْ ۗ اِنَّ فِيْ ذٰلِكَ لَاٰيَةً ۗ وَمَا كَانَ اَكْثَرُهُمْ مُّؤْمِنِيْنَ ﴿١٣٩﴾
وَاِنَّ رَبَّكَ لَهُوَ الْعَزِيْزُ الرَّحِيْمُ ﴿١٤٠﴾ ع ١٨
كَذَّبَتْ ثَمُوْدُ الْمُرْسَلِيْنَ ﴿١٤١﴾
اِذْ قَالَ لَهُمْ اَخُوْهُمْ صٰلِحٌ اَلَا تَتَّقُوْنَ ﴿١٤٢﴾
اِنِّيْ لَكُمْ رَسُوْلٌ اَمِيْنٌ ﴿١٤٣﴾
فَاتَّقُوا اللّٰهَ وَاَطِيْعُوْنِ ﴿١٤٤﴾
وَمَآ اَسْـَٔلُكُمْ عَلَيْهِ مِنْ اَجْرٍ ۚ اِنْ اَجْرِيَ اِلَّا عَلٰى رَبِّ الْعٰلَمِيْنَ ﴿١٤٥﴾
اَتُتْرَكُوْنَ فِيْ مَا هٰهُنَآ اٰمِنِيْنَ ﴿١٤٦﴾
فِيْ جَنّٰتٍ وَّعُيُوْنٍ ﴿١٤٧﴾
وَّزُرُوْعٍ وَّنَخْلٍ طَلْعُهَا هَضِيْمٌ ﴿١٤٨﴾
وَتَنْحِتُوْنَ مِنَ الْجِبَالِ بُيُوْتًا فٰرِهِيْنَ ﴿١٤٩﴾
فَاتَّقُوا اللّٰهَ وَاَطِيْعُوْنِ ﴿١٥٠﴾
وَلَا تُطِيْعُوْٓا اَمْرَ الْمُسْرِفِيْنَ ﴿١٥١﴾
الَّذِيْنَ يُفْسِدُوْنَ فِي الْاَرْضِ وَلَا يُصْلِحُوْنَ ﴿١٥٢﴾
قَالُوْٓا اِنَّمَآ اَنْتَ مِنَ الْمُسَحَّرِيْنَ ﴿١٥٣﴾
مَآ اَنْتَ اِلَّا بَشَرٌ مِّثْلُنَا ۚ فَاْتِ بِاٰيَةٍ اِنْ كُنْتَ مِنَ الصّٰدِقِيْنَ ﴿١٥٤﴾

Ikhfa اخفاء | Ghunna غنّہ | Ikhfa Meem Saakin اخفاء میم ساکن | Idghaam ادغام | Qalqala قلقلہ | Qalb قلب | Idghaam Meem Saakin ادغام میم ساکن

155. He said: "Here is a she-camel: she has a right of watering, and you have a right of watering, (severally) on a day appointed.

156. "Do not touch her with harm, lest the Penalty of a Great Day seize you."

157. But they ham-strung her: then did they become full of regrets.

158. But the Penalty seized them. Verily in this is a Sign: but most of them do not believe.

159. And verily your Lord is He, the Exalted in Might, Most Merciful.

160. The people of Lut rejected the Messengers.

161. Behold, their brother Lut said to them: "Will you not fear (Allah)?

162. "I am to you a Messenger worthy of all trust.

163. "So fear Allah and obey me.

164. "No reward do I ask of you for it: my reward is only from the Lord of the Worlds.

165. "Of all the creatures in the world, will you approach males,

166. "And leave those whom Allah has created for you to be your mates? Nay, you are a people transgressing (all limits)!"

167. They said: "If you do not desist, O Lut! you will assuredly be cast out!"

168. He said: "I do detest your doings."

169. "O my Lord! deliver me and my family from such things as they do!"

170. So We delivered him and his family,- all

171. Except an old woman who lingered behind.

172. But the rest We destroyed utterly.

173. We rained down on them a shower (of brimstone): and evil was the shower on those who were admonished (but heeded not)!

155. Qaala haa<u>z</u>ihee naaqatul-lahaa shirbuñw-wa lakum shirbu yawmim-ma'loom.

156. Wa laa tamassoohaa bisooo'in fa-yaåkhu<u>z</u>akum 'a<u>z</u>aabu Yawmin 'Aẓeem.

157. Fa'aqaroohaa fa-aṣbaḥoo naadimeen.

158. Fa-akha<u>z</u>ahumul-'a<u>z</u>aab; inna fee <u>z</u>aalika la-Aayah; wa maa kaana ak<u>s</u>aruhum-mu'mineen.

159. Wa inna Rabbaka la-Huwal-'Azeezur-Raḥeem. **(Sec. 8)**

160. Ka<u>zz</u>abat qawmu Looṭinil-mursaleen.

161. I<u>z</u> qaala lahum akhoohum Looṭun alaa tattaqoon.

162. Innee lakum Rasoolun ameen.

163. Fattaqul-laaha wa aṭee-'oon.

164. Wa maaa as'alukum 'alayhi min ajrin in ajriya illaa 'alaa Rabbil-'aalameen.

165. Ataåtoonaz-zukraana minal-'aalameen.

166. Wa ta<u>z</u>aroona maa khalaqa lakum Rabbukum-min azwaajikum; bal antum qawmun 'aadoon.

167. Qaaloo la'il-lam tantahi yaa Looṭu latakoonanna minal-mukhrajeen.

168. Qaala innee li'amalikum-minal-qaaleen.

169. Rabbi najjinee wa ahlee mimmaa ya'maloon.

170. Fanajjaynaahu wa ahlahooo ajma'een.

171. Illaa 'ajoozan filghaabireen.

172. <u>S</u>umma dammarnal-aakhareen.

173. Wa amṭarnaa 'alayhim-maṭaran fasaaa'a maṭarul-mun<u>z</u>areen.

قَالَ هٰذِهٖ نَاقَةٌ لَّهَا شِرْبٌ وَّلَكُمْ شِرْبُ يَوْمٍ مَّعْلُوْمٍ ۝١٥٥
وَلَا تَمَسُّوْهَا بِسُوْٓءٍ فَيَاْخُذَكُمْ عَذَابُ يَوْمٍ عَظِيْمٍ ۝١٥٦
فَعَقَرُوْهَا فَاَصْبَحُوْا نٰدِمِيْنَ ۝١٥٧
فَاَخَذَهُمُ الْعَذَابُ ۭ اِنَّ فِيْ ذٰلِكَ لَاٰيَةً ۭ وَمَا كَانَ اَكْثَرُهُمْ مُّؤْمِنِيْنَ ۝١٥٨
وَاِنَّ رَبَّكَ لَهُوَ الْعَزِيْزُ الرَّحِيْمُ ۝١٥٩ ع ١٩ ١٢
كَذَّبَتْ قَوْمُ لُوْطِ ۨالْمُرْسَلِيْنَ ۝١٦٠
اِذْ قَالَ لَهُمْ اَخُوْهُمْ لُوْطٌ اَلَا تَتَّقُوْنَ ۝١٦١
اِنِّىْ لَكُمْ رَسُوْلٌ اَمِيْنٌ ۝١٦٢
فَاتَّقُوا اللّٰهَ وَاَطِيْعُوْنِ ۝١٦٣
وَمَآ اَسْـَٔلُكُمْ عَلَيْهِ مِنْ اَجْرٍ ۚ اِنْ اَجْرِيَ اِلَّا عَلٰي رَبِّ الْعٰلَمِيْنَ ۝١٦٤
اَتَاْتُوْنَ الذُّكْرَانَ مِنَ الْعٰلَمِيْنَ ۝١٦٥
وَتَذَرُوْنَ مَا خَلَقَ لَكُمْ رَبُّكُمْ مِّنْ اَزْوَاجِكُمْ ۭ بَلْ اَنْتُمْ قَوْمٌ عٰدُوْنَ ۝١٦٦
قَالُوْا لَىِٕنْ لَّمْ تَنْتَهِ يٰلُوْطُ لَتَكُوْنَنَّ مِنَ الْمُخْرَجِيْنَ ۝١٦٧
قَالَ اِنِّىْ لِعَمَلِكُمْ مِّنَ الْقَالِيْنَ ۝١٦٨
رَبِّ نَجِّنِيْ وَاَهْلِيْ مِمَّا يَعْمَلُوْنَ ۝١٦٩
فَنَجَّيْنٰهُ وَاَهْلَهٗٓ اَجْمَعِيْنَ ۝١٧٠
اِلَّا عَجُوْزًا فِي الْغٰبِرِيْنَ ۝١٧١
ثُمَّ دَمَّرْنَا الْاٰخَرِيْنَ ۝١٧٢
وَاَمْطَرْنَا عَلَيْهِمْ مَّطَرًا ۚ فَسَاۗءَ مَطَرُ الْمُنْذَرِيْنَ ۝١٧٣

Ikhfa اخفاء | Ghunna غُنّہ | Ikhfa Meem Saakin اخفاءمیم ساکن | Idghaam ادغام | Qalqala قلقلہ | Qalb قلب | Idghaam Meem Saakin ادغام میم ساکن

174. Verily in this is a Sign: but most of them do not believe.

175. And verily your Lord is He, the Exalted in Might, Most Merciful.

176. The Companions of the Wood rejected the Messengers.

177. Behold, Shu'aib said to them: "Will you not fear (Allah)?

178. "I am to you a Messenger worthy of all trust.

179. "So fear Allah and obey me.

180. "No reward do I ask of you for it: my reward is only from the Lord of the Worlds.

181. "Give just measure, and cause no loss (to others by fraud).

182. "And weigh with scales true and upright.

183. "And do not withhold things justly due to men, nor do evil in the land, working mischief.

184. "And fear Him Who created you and (Who created) the generations before (you)"

185. They said: "You are only one of those bewitched!

186. "You are no more than a mortal like us, and indeed we think you are a liar!

187. "Now cause a piece of the sky to fall on us, if you are truthful!"

188. He said: "My Lord knows best what you do."

189. But they rejected him. Then the punishment of a day of overshadowing gloom seized them, and that was the Penalty of a Great Day.

190. Verily in that is a Sign: but

174. Inna fee zaalika la-Aayah; wa maa kaana aksaruhum mu'mineen.

175. Wa inna Rabbaka la-Huwal-'Azeezur-Raheem. **(Sec. 9)**

176. Kazzaba Aṣ-ḥaabul Ayka-til-mursaleen.

177. Iz qaala lahum Shu'aybun alaa tattaqoon.

178. Innee lakum Rasoolun ameen.

179. Fattaqul-laaha wa aṭee-'oon.

180. Wa maaa as'alukum 'alayhi min ajrin in ajriya illaa 'alaa Rabbil-'aalameen.

181. Awful-kayla wa laa ta-koonoo minal-mukhsireen.

182. Wa zinoo bilqisṭaasil-mustaqeem.

183. Wa laa tabkhasun-naasa ashyaaa'ahum wa laa ta'saw fil-arḍi mufsideen.

184. Wattaqul-lazee khalaqa-kum waljibillatal-awwaleen.

185. Qaalooo innamaaa anta minal-musaḥḥareen.

186. Wa maaa anta illaa basharum-mislunaa wa in-naẓunnuka laminal-kaazibeen.

187. Fa-asqiṭ 'alaynaa kisa-fam-minaṣ-ṣamaaa'i in kunta minaṣ-ṣaadiqeen.

188. Qaala Rabbeee a'lamu bimaa ta'maloon.

189. Fakazzaboohu fa-akha-zahum 'azaabu Yawmiẓ-ẓullah; innahoo kaana 'azaaba Yawmin 'Aẓeem.

190. Inna fee zaalika la-Aayah; wa maa kaana

إِنَّ فِي ذَٰلِكَ لَآيَةً ۖ وَمَا كَانَ
أَكْثَرُهُم مُّؤْمِنِينَ ﴿١٧٤﴾
وَإِنَّ رَبَّكَ لَهُوَ الْعَزِيزُ الرَّحِيمُ ﴿١٧٥﴾ ع ٩ ١٦ ١٣
كَذَّبَ أَصْحَابُ لْـَٔيْكَةِ الْمُرْسَلِينَ ﴿١٧٦﴾
إِذْ قَالَ لَهُمْ شُعَيْبٌ أَلَا تَتَّقُونَ ﴿١٧٧﴾
إِنِّي لَكُمْ رَسُولٌ أَمِينٌ ﴿١٧٨﴾
فَاتَّقُوا اللَّهَ وَأَطِيعُونِ ﴿١٧٩﴾
وَمَا أَسْأَلُكُمْ عَلَيْهِ مِنْ أَجْرٍ ۖ إِنْ
أَجْرِيَ إِلَّا عَلَىٰ رَبِّ الْعَالَمِينَ ﴿١٨٠﴾
أَوْفُوا الْكَيْلَ وَلَا تَكُونُوا مِنَ
الْمُخْسِرِينَ ﴿١٨١﴾
وَزِنُوا بِالْقِسْطَاسِ الْمُسْتَقِيمِ ﴿١٨٢﴾
وَلَا تَبْخَسُوا النَّاسَ أَشْيَاءَهُمْ وَلَا
تَعْثَوْا فِي الْأَرْضِ مُفْسِدِينَ ﴿١٨٣﴾
وَاتَّقُوا الَّذِي خَلَقَكُمْ وَالْجِبِلَّةَ
الْأَوَّلِينَ ﴿١٨٤﴾
قَالُوا إِنَّمَا أَنتَ مِنَ الْمُسَحَّرِينَ ﴿١٨٥﴾
وَمَا أَنتَ إِلَّا بَشَرٌ مِّثْلُنَا وَإِن نَّظُنُّكَ
لَمِنَ الْكَاذِبِينَ ﴿١٨٦﴾
فَأَسْقِطْ عَلَيْنَا كِسَفًا مِّنَ السَّمَاءِ
إِن كُنتَ مِنَ الصَّادِقِينَ ﴿١٨٧﴾
قَالَ رَبِّي أَعْلَمُ بِمَا تَعْمَلُونَ ﴿١٨٨﴾
فَكَذَّبُوهُ فَأَخَذَهُمْ عَذَابُ
يَوْمِ الظُّلَّةِ ۚ إِنَّهُ كَانَ عَذَابَ
يَوْمٍ عَظِيمٍ ﴿١٨٩﴾
إِنَّ فِي ذَٰلِكَ لَآيَةً ۖ وَمَا كَانَ

Ikhfa اخفاء · Ghunna غنّہ · Ikhfa Meem Saakin اخفاء میم ساکن · Idghaam ادغام · Qalqala قلقلہ · Qalb قلب · Idghaam Meem Saakin ادغام میم ساکن

most of them do not believe.	akṣaruhum-mu'mineen.	أَكْثَرُهُم مُّؤْمِنِينَ ﴿١٩٠﴾
191. And verily your Lord is He, the Exalted in Might, Most Merciful.	191. Wa inna Rabbaka la-Huwal-'Azeezur-Raḥeem. **(Sec. 10)**	وَإِنَّ رَبَّكَ لَهُوَ الْعَزِيزُ الرَّحِيمُ ﴿١٩١﴾ ع
192. Verily this is a Revelation from the Lord of the Worlds:	192. Wa innahoo latanzeelu-Rabbil-'aalameen.	وَإِنَّهُ لَتَنزِيلُ رَبِّ الْعَالَمِينَ ﴿١٩٢﴾
193. With it came down the spirit of Faith and Truth-	193. Nazala bihir-Rooḥul-Ameen.	نَزَلَ بِهِ الرُّوحُ الْأَمِينُ ﴿١٩٣﴾
194. To your heart and mind, that you may admonish.	194. 'Alaa qalbika litakoona minal-munzireen.	عَلَىٰ قَلْبِكَ لِتَكُونَ مِنَ الْمُنذِرِينَ ﴿١٩٤﴾
195. In the perspicuous Arabic tongue.	195. Bilisaanin 'Arabiyyim-mubeen.	بِلِسَانٍ عَرَبِيٍّ مُّبِينٍ ﴿١٩٥﴾
196. Without doubt it is (announced) in the mystic Books of former peoples.	196. Wa innahoo lafee Zuburil-awwaleen.	وَإِنَّهُ لَفِي زُبُرِ الْأَوَّلِينَ ﴿١٩٦﴾
197. Is it not a Sign to them that the Learned of the Children of Israel knew it (as true)?	197. Awalam yakul-lahum Aayatan añy-ya'lamahoo 'ulamaaa'u Baneee Israaa'eel.	أَوَلَمْ يَكُن لَّهُمْ آيَةً أَن يَعْلَمَهُ عُلَمَاءُ بَنِي إِسْرَائِيلَ ﴿١٩٧﴾
198. Had We revealed it to any of the non-Arabs,	198. Wa law nazzalnaahu 'alaa ba'ḍil-a'jameen.	وَلَوْ نَزَّلْنَاهُ عَلَىٰ بَعْضِ الْأَعْجَمِينَ ﴿١٩٨﴾
199. And had he recited it to them, they would not have believed in it.	199. Faqara-ahoo 'alayhim maa kaanoo bihee mu'mineen.	فَقَرَأَهُ عَلَيْهِم مَّا كَانُوا بِهِ مُؤْمِنِينَ ﴿١٩٩﴾
200. Thus have We caused it to enter the hearts of the sinners.	200. Kazaalika salaknaahu fee quloobil-mujrimeen.	كَذَٰلِكَ سَلَكْنَاهُ فِي قُلُوبِ الْمُجْرِمِينَ ﴿٢٠٠﴾
201. They will not believe in it until they see the grievous Penalty;	201. Laa yu'minoona bihee ḥattaa yarawul-'azaabal-aleem.	لَا يُؤْمِنُونَ بِهِ حَتَّىٰ يَرَوُا الْعَذَابَ الْأَلِيمَ ﴿٢٠١﴾
202. But the (Penalty) will come to them of a sudden, while they perceive it not;	202. Fayaåtiyahum baghtatañw-wa hum laa yash'uroon.	فَيَأْتِيَهُم بَغْتَةً وَهُمْ لَا يَشْعُرُونَ ﴿٢٠٢﴾
203. Then they will say: "Shall we be respited?"	203. Fa-yaqooloo hal naḥnu munẓaroon.	فَيَقُولُوا هَلْ نَحْنُ مُنظَرُونَ ﴿٢٠٣﴾
204. Do they then ask for Our Penalty to be hastened on?	204. Afabi-'azaabinaa yasta'jiloon.	أَفَبِعَذَابِنَا يَسْتَعْجِلُونَ ﴿٢٠٤﴾
205. Do you see? If We do let them enjoy (this life) for a few years,	205. Afara'ayta im-matta'naahum sineen.	أَفَرَأَيْتَ إِن مَّتَّعْنَاهُمْ سِنِينَ ﴿٢٠٥﴾
206. Yet there comes to them at length the (Punishment) which they were promised!	206. Summa jaaa'ahum-maa kaanoo yoo'adoon.	ثُمَّ جَاءَهُم مَّا كَانُوا يُوعَدُونَ ﴿٢٠٦﴾
207. It will not profit them that they enjoyed (this life)!	207. Maaa aghnaa 'anhum-maa kaanoo yumatta'oon.	مَا أَغْنَىٰ عَنْهُم مَّا كَانُوا يُمَتَّعُونَ ﴿٢٠٧﴾
208. Never did We destroy a town, but had its warners–	208. Wa maaa ahlaknaa min qaryatin illaa lahaa munziroon.	وَمَا أَهْلَكْنَا مِن قَرْيَةٍ إِلَّا لَهَا مُنذِرُونَ ﴿٢٠٨﴾
209. By way of reminder; and We never are unjust.	209. Zikraa wa maa kunnaa ẓaalimeen.	ذِكْرَىٰ وَمَا كُنَّا ظَالِمِينَ ﴿٢٠٩﴾
210. No evil ones have brought down this (Revelation):	210. Wa maa tanazzalat bihish-Shayaaṭeen.	وَمَا تَنَزَّلَتْ بِهِ الشَّيَاطِينُ ﴿٢١٠﴾
211. It would neither suit them nor would they be able (to produce it).	211. Wa maa yambaghee lahum wa maa yastaṭee'oon.	وَمَا يَنبَغِي لَهُمْ وَمَا يَسْتَطِيعُونَ ﴿٢١١﴾
212. Indeed they have been removed far from even (a chance of) hearing it.	212. Innahum 'anis-sam'i lama'zooloon.	إِنَّهُمْ عَنِ السَّمْعِ لَمَعْزُولُونَ ﴿٢١٢﴾

معٓ عند المتقدمين ١٢

Ikhfa اخفاء | Ghunna غُنّہ | Ikhfa Meem Saakin اخفاء میم ساکن | Idghaam ادغام | Qalqala قلقلہ | Qalb قلب | Idghaam Meem Saakin ادغام میم ساکن

Translation	Transliteration	Arabic
213. So do not call on any other god with Allah, or you will be among those under the Penalty.	213. Falaa tad'u ma'al-laahi ilaahan aakhara fatakoona minal-mu'azzabeen.	فَلَا تَدْعُ مَعَ اللّٰهِ اِلٰهًا اٰخَرَ فَتَكُوْنَ مِنَ الْمُعَذَّبِيْنَ ۚ﴿٢١٣﴾
214. And admonish your nearest kinsmen,	214. Wa anzir 'asheeratakal-aqrabeen.	وَاَنْذِرْ عَشِيْرَتَكَ الْاَقْرَبِيْنَ ۙ﴿٢١٤﴾
215. And lower your wing to the Believers who follow you.	215. Wakhfiḍ janaaḥaka limanit-taba'aka minal-mu'mineen.	وَاخْفِضْ جَنَاحَكَ لِمَنِ اتَّبَعَكَ مِنَ الْمُؤْمِنِيْنَ ۚ﴿٢١٥﴾
216. Then if they disobey you, say: "I am free (of responsibility) for what you do!"	216. Fa-in aṣawka faqul innee bareee'um-mimmaa ta'maloon.	فَاِنْ عَصَوْكَ فَقُلْ اِنِّيْ بَرِيْٓءٌ مِّمَّا تَعْمَلُوْنَ ۚ﴿٢١٦﴾
217. And put your trust on the Exalted in Might, the Merciful,	217. Wa tawakkal alal-'Azeezir-Raḥeem.	وَتَوَكَّلْ عَلَى الْعَزِيْزِ الرَّحِيْمِ ۙ﴿٢١٧﴾
218. Who sees you standing forth (in prayer),	218. Allazee yaraaka ḥeena taqoom.	الَّذِيْ يَرٰىكَ حِيْنَ تَقُوْمُ ۙ﴿٢١٨﴾
219. And your movements among those who prostrate themselves,	219. Wa taqallubaka fis-saajideen.	وَتَقَلُّبَكَ فِي السّٰجِدِيْنَ ﴿٢١٩﴾
220. For it is He Who hears and knows all things.	220. Innahoo Huwas-Samee'ul-'Aleem.	اِنَّهٗ هُوَ السَّمِيْعُ الْعَلِيْمُ ﴿٢٢٠﴾
221. Shall I inform you, (O people!), on whom it is that the evil ones descend?	221. Hal unabbi'ukum 'alaa man tanazzalush-Shayaaṭeen.	هَلْ اُنَبِّئُكُمْ عَلٰى مَنْ تَنَزَّلُ الشَّيٰطِيْنُ ۭ﴿٢٢١﴾
222. They descend on every lying, wicked person,	222. Tanazzalu 'alaa kulli affaakin aseem.	تَنَزَّلُ عَلٰى كُلِّ اَفَّاكٍ اَثِيْمٍ ۙ﴿٢٢٢﴾
223. (Into whose ears) they pour hearsay vanities, and most of them are liars.	223. Yulqoonas-sam'a wa aksaruhum kaaziboon.	يُّلْقُوْنَ السَّمْعَ وَاَكْثَرُهُمْ كٰذِبُوْنَ ۭ﴿٢٢٣﴾
224. And the Poets,- it is those straying in Evil, who follow them:	224. Washshu'araaa'u yattabi'uhumul-ghaawoon.	وَالشُّعَرَاۗءُ يَتَّبِعُهُمُ الْغَاوٗنَ ۭ﴿٢٢٤﴾
225. Don't you see that they wander distracted in every valley?-	225. Alam tara annahum fee kulli waadiñy-yaheemoon.	اَلَمْ تَرَ اَنَّهُمْ فِيْ كُلِّ وَادٍ يَّهِيْمُوْنَ ۙ﴿٢٢٥﴾
226. And that they say what they do not practise?-	226. Wa annahum yaqooloona maa laa yaf'aloon.	وَاَنَّهُمْ يَقُوْلُوْنَ مَا لَا يَفْعَلُوْنَ ۙ﴿٢٢٦﴾
227. Except those who believe, work righteousness, engage much in the remembrance of Allah, and defend themselves only after they are unjustly attacked. And soon will the unjust assailants know what vicissitudes their affairs will take!	227. Illal-lazeena aamanoo wa 'amiluṣ-ṣaaliḥaati wa zakarul-laaha kaseerañw-wantaṣaroo mim ba'di maa ẓulimoo; wa saya'lamul-lazeena ẓalamooo ayya munqalabiñy-yanqaliboon. **(Section 11)**	اِلَّا الَّذِيْنَ اٰمَنُوْا وَعَمِلُوا الصّٰلِحٰتِ وَذَكَرُوا اللّٰهَ كَثِيْرًا وَّانْتَصَرُوْا مِنْۢ بَعْدِ مَا ظُلِمُوْا ۭ وَسَيَعْلَمُ الَّذِيْنَ ظَلَمُوْٓا اَيَّ مُنْقَلَبٍ يَّنْقَلِبُوْنَ ﴿٢٢٧﴾ ع

27. The Ants

In the name of Allah, Most Gracious, Most Merciful.

Sûrat an-Naml–27

(Revealed at Makkah)

Bismillaahir Raḥmaanir Raḥeem

(٢٧) سُوْرَةُ النَّمْلِ مَكِّيَّةٌ (٤٨)

بِسْمِ اللّٰهِ الرَّحْمٰنِ الرَّحِيْمِ

Translation	Transliteration	Arabic
1. *Ta-Sin*. These are verses of the Qur'an,-a book that makes (things) clear;	1. Ṭaa-Seeen; tilka Aayaatul-Qur-aani wa Kitaabim-Mubeen.	طٰسۗ ۣ تِلْكَ اٰيٰتُ الْقُرْاٰنِ وَكِتَابٍ مُّبِيْنٍ ۙ﴿١﴾

Ikhfa اخفاء · Ghunna غنّہ · Ikhfa Meem Saakin اخفاء میم ساکن · Idghaam ادغام · Qalqala قلقلہ · Qalb قلب · Idghaam Meem Saakin ادغام میم ساکن

2. A Guide: and Glad Tidings for the Believers,-

3. Those who establish regular prayers and give in regular charity, and also have (full) assurance of the Hereafter.

4. As to those who do not believe in the Hereafter, We have made their deeds pleasing in their eyes; and so they wander about in distraction.

5. Such are they for whom a grievous Penalty is (waiting); and in the Hereafter theirs will be the greatest loss.

6. As to you, the Qur'an is bestowed upon you from the presence of One Who is Wise and All-knowing.

7. Behold! Moses said to his family: "I perceive a fire; soon will I bring you from there some information, or I will bring you a burning brand to light our fuel, that you may warm yourselves.

8. But when he came to the (fire), a voice was heard: "Blessed are those in the fire and those around: and glory to Allah, the Lord of the worlds.

9. "O Moses! Verily, I am Allah, the Exalted in Might, the Wise!.

10. "Now you throw your rod!" But when he saw it moving (of its own accord)as if it had been a snake, he turned back in retreat, and retraced not his steps: "O Moses!" (it was said), "Fear not: truly, in My presence, those called as Messenger have no fear,-

11. "But if any have done wrong and have thereafter substituted good to take the place of evil, truly, I am Oft-Forgiving, Most Merciful.

12. "Now put your hand into your bosom, and it will come forth white without stain (or harm): (these are) among the nine Signs (you wilt take) to Pharaoh and his people: for they are a people rebellious in transgression."

2. Hudañw-wa bushraa lil-mu'mineen.

3. Allazeena yuqeemoonaṣ-Ṣalaata wa yu'toonaz-Zakaata wa hum bil-Aakhirati hum yooqinoon.

4. Innal-lazeena laa yu'minoona bil-Aakhirati zayyannaa lahum a'maalahum fahum ya'mahoon.

5. Ulaaa'ikal-lazeena lahum sooo'ul-'azaabi wa hum fil-Aakhirati humul-akhsaroon.

6. Wa innaka latulaqqal-Qur-aana mil-ladun Ḥakeemin 'Aleem.

7. Iz qaala Moosaa li-ahliheee inneee aanastu naaran sa-aateekum-minhaa bikhabarin aw aateekum bishihaabin qabasil-la'allakum taṣṭaloon.

8. Falammaa jaaa'ahaa noodiya am boorika man finnaari wa man ḥawlahaa wa Sub-ḥaanal-laahi Rabbil-'aalameen.

9. Yaa Moosaaa innahooo Anal-laahul-'Azeezul-Ḥakeem.

10. Wa alqi 'aṣaak; falammaa ra-aahaa tahtazzu ka-annahaa jaaannuñw-wallaa mudbirañw-wa lam yu'aqqib; yaa Moosaa laa takhaf inneee laa yakhaafu ladayyal-mursaloon.

11. Illaa man ẓalama summa baddala ḥusnam ba'da sooo'in fa-inneee Ghafoorur-Raḥeem.

12. Wa adkhil yadaka fee jaybika takhruj bayḍaaa'a min ghayri sooo'in fee tis'i Aayaatin ilaa Fir'awna wa qawmih; innahum kaanoo qawman faasiqeen.

هُدًى وَّبُشْرٰى لِلْمُؤْمِنِيْنَ ۝٢
الَّذِيْنَ يُقِيْمُوْنَ الصَّلٰوةَ وَيُؤْتُوْنَ
الزَّكٰوةَ وَهُمْ بِالْاٰخِرَةِ هُمْ يُوْقِنُوْنَ ۝٣
اِنَّ الَّذِيْنَ لَا يُؤْمِنُوْنَ بِالْاٰخِرَةِ زَيَّنَّا
لَهُمْ اَعْمَالَهُمْ فَهُمْ يَعْمَهُوْنَ ۝٤
اُولٰٓئِكَ الَّذِيْنَ لَهُمْ سُوْٓءُ الْعَذَابِ
وَهُمْ فِي الْاٰخِرَةِ هُمُ الْاَخْسَرُوْنَ ۝٥
وَاِنَّكَ لَتُلَقَّى الْقُرْاٰنَ مِنْ لَّدُنْ
حَكِيْمٍ عَلِيْمٍ ۝٦
اِذْ قَالَ مُوْسٰى لِاَهْلِهٖٓ اِنِّيْٓ اٰنَسْتُ
نَارًا ۚ سَاٰتِيْكُمْ مِّنْهَا بِخَبَرٍ اَوْ اٰتِيْكُمْ
بِشِهَابٍ قَبَسٍ لَّعَلَّكُمْ تَصْطَلُوْنَ ۝٧
فَلَمَّا جَآءَهَا نُوْدِيَ اَنْۢ بُوْرِكَ مَنْ
فِي النَّارِ وَمَنْ حَوْلَهَا ۗ وَسُبْحٰنَ
اللّٰهِ رَبِّ الْعٰلَمِيْنَ ۝٨
يٰمُوْسٰٓى اِنَّهٗٓ اَنَا اللّٰهُ الْعَزِيْزُ الْحَكِيْمُ ۝٩
وَاَلْقِ عَصَاكَ ۗ فَلَمَّا رَاٰهَا تَهْتَزُّ
كَاَنَّهَا جَآنٌّ وَّلّٰى مُدْبِرًا وَّلَمْ
يُعَقِّبْ ۗ يٰمُوْسٰى لَا تَخَفْ ۗ اِنِّيْ
لَا يَخَافُ لَدَيَّ الْمُرْسَلُوْنَ ۝١٠
اِلَّا مَنْ ظَلَمَ ثُمَّ بَدَّلَ حُسْنًاۢ بَعْدَ
سُوْٓءٍ فَاِنِّيْ غَفُوْرٌ رَّحِيْمٌ ۝١١
وَاَدْخِلْ يَدَكَ فِيْ جَيْبِكَ تَخْرُجْ
بَيْضَآءَ مِنْ غَيْرِ سُوْٓءٍ ۣ فِيْ تِسْعِ اٰيٰتٍ
اِلٰى فِرْعَوْنَ وَقَوْمِهٖ ۗ اِنَّهُمْ كَانُوْا
قَوْمًا فٰسِقِيْنَ ۝١٢

الثلثة

Ikhfa اخفاء · Ghunna غُنّہ · Ikhfa Meem Saakin اخفاءمیم ساکن · Idghaam ادغام · Qalqala قلقلہ · Qalb قلب · Idghaam Meem Saakin ادغام میم ساکن

13. But when Our Signs came to them, that should have opened their eyes, they said: "This is sorcery manifest!"

13. Falammaa jaaa'at-hum Aayaatunaa mubṣiratan qaaloo haazaa siḥrum-mubeen.

فَلَمَّا جَآءَتۡهُمۡ ءَايَٰتُنَا مُبۡصِرَةٗ قَالُواْ
هَٰذَا سِحۡرٞ مُّبِينٞ ١٣

14. And they rejected those Signs in iniquity and arrogance, though their souls were convinced thereof: so see what was the end of those who acted corruptly!

14. Wa jaḥadoo bihaa wastay-qanat-haaa anfusuhum ẓul-mañw-wa 'uluwwaa; fanẓur kayfa kaana 'aaqibatul-muf-sideen. **(Section 1)**

وَجَحَدُواْ بِهَا وَٱسۡتَيۡقَنَتۡهَآ أَنفُسُهُمۡ
ظُلۡمٗا وَعُلُوّٗاۚ فَٱنظُرۡ كَيۡفَ كَانَ
عَٰقِبَةُ ٱلۡمُفۡسِدِينَ ١٤

15. We gave (in the past) knowledge to David and Solomon: And they both said: "Praise be to Allah, Who has favored us above many of his servants who believe!"

15. Wa laqad aataynaa Daawooda wa Sulaymaana 'ilmaa; wa qaalal-ḥamdu lil-laahil-lazee faḍḍalanaa 'alaa kaseerim-min 'ibaadihil-mu'mineen.

وَلَقَدۡ ءَاتَيۡنَا دَاوُۥدَ وَسُلَيۡمَٰنَ عِلۡمٗاۖ
وَقَالَا ٱلۡحَمۡدُ لِلَّهِ ٱلَّذِي فَضَّلَنَا عَلَىٰ
كَثِيرٖ مِّنۡ عِبَادِهِ ٱلۡمُؤۡمِنِينَ ١٥

16. And Solomon was David's heir. He said: "O you people! we have been taught the speech of birds, and on us has been bestowed (a little) of all things: this is indeed Grace manifest (from Allah.)"

16. Wa warisa Sulaymaanu Daawooda wa qaala yaaa ayyuhan-naasu 'ullimnaa manṭiqaṭ-ṭayri wa ooteenaa min kulli shay'in inna haazaa lahuwal-faḍlul-mubeen.

وَوَرِثَ سُلَيۡمَٰنُ دَاوُۥدَۖ وَقَالَ
يَٰٓأَيُّهَا ٱلنَّاسُ عُلِّمۡنَا مَنطِقَ ٱلطَّيۡرِ
وَأُوتِينَا مِن كُلِّ شَيۡءٍۖ إِنَّ هَٰذَا
لَهُوَ ٱلۡفَضۡلُ ٱلۡمُبِينُ ١٦

17. And before Solomon were marshalled his hosts,- of Jinns and men and birds, and they were all kept in order and ranks.

17. Wa ḥushira li-Sulaymaana junooduhoo minal-jinni wal-insi waṭṭayri fahum yooza'oon.

وَحُشِرَ لِسُلَيۡمَٰنَ جُنُودُهُۥ مِنَ
ٱلۡجِنِّ وَٱلۡإِنسِ وَٱلطَّيۡرِ فَهُمۡ
يُوزَعُونَ ١٧

18. At length, when they came to a (lowly) valley of ants, one of the ants said: "O ants, get into your habitations, lest Solomon and his hosts crush you (under foot) without knowing it."

18. Ḥattaaa izaaa ataw 'alaa waadin-namli qaalat namla-tuñy-yaaa ayyuhan-namlud-khuloo masaakinakum laa yaḥṭimannakum Sulaymaanu wa junooduhoo wa hum laa yash'uroon.

حَتَّىٰٓ إِذَآ أَتَوۡاْ عَلَىٰ وَادِ ٱلنَّمۡلِ
قَالَتۡ نَمۡلَةٞ يَٰٓأَيُّهَا ٱلنَّمۡلُ ٱدۡخُلُواْ
مَسَٰكِنَكُمۡ لَا يَحۡطِمَنَّكُمۡ سُلَيۡمَٰنُ
وَجُنُودُهُۥ وَهُمۡ لَا يَشۡعُرُونَ ١٨

19. So he smiled, amused at her speech; and he said: "O my Lord! so order me that I may be grateful for Your favors, which You have bestowed on me and on my parents, and that I may work the righteousness that will please You: and admit me, by Your Grace, to the ranks of Your righteous Servants."

19. Fatabassama ḍaaḥikam-min qawlihaa wa qaala Rabbi awzi'neee an ashkura ni'mata-kal-lateee an'amta 'alayya wa 'alaa waalidayya wa an a'mala ṣaaliḥan tarḍaahu wa adkhilnee biraḥmatika fee 'ibaadikaṣ-ṣaaliḥeen.

فَتَبَسَّمَ ضَاحِكٗا مِّن قَوۡلِهَا وَقَالَ
رَبِّ أَوۡزِعۡنِيٓ أَنۡ أَشۡكُرَ نِعۡمَتَكَ
ٱلَّتِيٓ أَنۡعَمۡتَ عَلَيَّ وَعَلَىٰ وَٰلِدَيَّ
وَأَنۡ أَعۡمَلَ صَٰلِحٗا تَرۡضَىٰهُ
وَأَدۡخِلۡنِي بِرَحۡمَتِكَ فِي عِبَادِكَ
ٱلصَّٰلِحِينَ ١٩

20. And he took a muster of the Birds; and he said: "Why is it I do not see

20. Wa tafaqqadaṭ-ṭayra faqaala maa liya laaa aral-

وَتَفَقَّدَ ٱلطَّيۡرَ فَقَالَ مَا لِيَ لَآ أَرَى

Ikhfa اخفاء | Ghunna غُنّہ | Ikhfa Meem Saakin اخفاء میم ساکن | Idghaam ادغام | Qalqala قلقلہ | Qalb قلب | Idghaam Meem Saakin ادغام میم ساکن

the Hoopoe? Or is he among the absentees?

21. "I will certainly punish him with a severe penalty, or execute him, unless he brings me a clear reason (for absence)."

22. But the Hoopoe did not tarry far: he (came up and) said: "I have compassed (territory) which you have not compassed, and I have come to you from Saba with true tidings.

23. "I found (there) a woman ruling over them and provided with every requisite; and she has a magnificent throne.

24. "I found her and her people worshipping the sun besides Allah: Satan has made their deeds seem pleasing in their eyes, and has kept them away from the Path,- so they receive no guidance,-

25. "(Kept them away from the Path), that they should not worship Allah, Who brings to light what is hidden in the heavens and the earth, and knows what you hide and what you reveal.

26. "Allah!- there is no god but He!- Lord of the Throne Supreme!"

(Bow Down)

27. (Solomon) said: "Soon shall we see whether you have told the truth or lied!

28. "You go, with this letter of mine, and deliver it to them: then draw back from them, and (wait to) see what answer they return".

29. (The queen) said: "You chiefs! here is delivered to me - a letter worthy of respect.

30. "It is from Solomon, and is (as follows): 'In the name of Allah, Most Gracious, Most Merciful:

hudhud, am kaana minal-ghaaa'ibeen.

21. La-u'azzibannahoo 'azaaban shadeedan aw la-azbahannahooo aw layaåtiyannee bisulṭaanim-mubeen.

22. Famakasa ghayra ba'eedin faqaala aḥattu bimaa lam tuḥiṭ bihee wa ji'tuka min Saba-im binaba-iñy-yaqeen.

23. Innee wajattum-ra-atan tamlikuhum wa ootiyat min kulli shay'iñw-wa lahaa 'arshun 'aẓeem.

24. Wajattuhaa wa qawmahaa yasjudoona lishshamsi min doonil-laahi wa zayyana lahumush-Shayṭaanu a'maalahum faṣaddahum 'anis-sabeeli fahum laa yahtadoon.

25. Allaa yasjudoo lillaahil-lazee yukhrijul-khab'a fis-samaawaati wal-arḍi wa ya'lamu maa tukhfoona wa maa tu'linoon.

26. Allaahu laaa ilaaha illaa Huwa Rabbul-'Arshil-'Aẓeem. ۩

27. Qaala sananẓuru aṣadaqta am kunta minal-kaazibeen.

28. Izhab bikitaabee haazaa fa-alqih ilayhim summa tawalla 'anhum fanẓur maazaa yarji'oon.

29. Qaalat yaaa ayyuhal-mala'u inneee ulqiya ilayya kitaabun kareem.

30. Innahoo min Sulaymaana wa innahoo bismil-laahir-Raḥmaanir-Raḥeem.

الْهُدْهُدَ ۖ أَمْ كَانَ مِنَ الْغَائِبِينَ ﴿٢٠﴾
لَأُعَذِّبَنَّهُ عَذَابًا شَدِيدًا أَوْ لَأَاذْبَحَنَّهُ
أَوْ لَيَأْتِيَنِّي بِسُلْطَانٍ مُّبِينٍ ﴿٢١﴾
فَمَكَثَ غَيْرَ بَعِيدٍ فَقَالَ أَحَطتُّ
بِمَا لَمْ تُحِطْ بِهِ وَجِئْتُكَ مِن سَبَإٍ
بِنَبَإٍ يَقِينٍ ﴿٢٢﴾
إِنِّي وَجَدتُّ امْرَأَةً تَمْلِكُهُمْ وَأُوتِيَتْ
مِن كُلِّ شَيْءٍ وَلَهَا عَرْشٌ عَظِيمٌ ﴿٢٣﴾
وَجَدتُّهَا وَقَوْمَهَا يَسْجُدُونَ لِلشَّمْسِ
مِن دُونِ اللَّهِ وَزَيَّنَ لَهُمُ الشَّيْطَانُ
أَعْمَالَهُمْ فَصَدَّهُمْ عَنِ السَّبِيلِ فَهُمْ
لَا يَهْتَدُونَ ﴿٢٤﴾
أَلَّا يَسْجُدُوا لِلَّهِ الَّذِي يُخْرِجُ
الْخَبْءَ فِي السَّمَاوَاتِ وَالْأَرْضِ وَيَعْلَمُ
مَا تُخْفُونَ وَمَا تُعْلِنُونَ ﴿٢٥﴾
اللَّهُ لَا إِلَٰهَ إِلَّا هُوَ رَبُّ الْعَرْشِ
الْعَظِيمِ ۩ ﴿٢٦﴾

السَّجْدَة (٨)

قَالَ سَنَنظُرُ أَصَدَقْتَ أَمْ كُنتَ
مِنَ الْكَاذِبِينَ ﴿٢٧﴾
اذْهَب بِّكِتَابِي هَٰذَا فَأَلْقِهْ
إِلَيْهِمْ ثُمَّ تَوَلَّ عَنْهُمْ فَانظُرْ
مَاذَا يَرْجِعُونَ ﴿٢٨﴾
قَالَتْ يَا أَيُّهَا الْمَلَأُ إِنِّي أُلْقِيَ إِلَيَّ
كِتَابٌ كَرِيمٌ ﴿٢٩﴾
إِنَّهُ مِن سُلَيْمَانَ وَإِنَّهُ بِسْمِ اللَّهِ
الرَّحْمَٰنِ الرَّحِيمِ ﴿٣٠﴾

Ikhfa اخفاء · Ghunna غُنّہ · Ikhfa Meem Saakin اخفاء میم ساکن · Idghaam ادغام · Qalqala قلقلہ · Qalb قلب · Idghaam Meem Saakin ادغام میم ساکن

31. "'You be not arrogant against me, but come to me in submission (to the true Religion).'

31. Allaa ta'loo 'alayya waå-toonee muslimeen. **(Section 2)**

أَلَّا تَعْلُوا عَلَيَّ وَأْتُونِي مُسْلِمِينَ ﴿٣١﴾ ع

32. She said: "You chiefs! Advise me in (this) my affair: no affair have I decided except in your presence."

32. Qaalat yaaa ayyuhal-mala'u aftoonee feee amree maa kuntu qaati'atan amran ḥattaa tashhadoon.

قَالَتْ يَا أَيُّهَا الْمَلَأُ أَفْتُونِي فِي
أَمْرِي مَا كُنتُ قَاطِعَةً أَمْرًا
حَتَّىٰ تَشْهَدُونِ ﴿٣٢﴾

33. They said: "We are endued with strength, and given to vehement war: but the command is with you; so consider what you will command."

33. Qaaloo naḥnu uloo quw-watiñw-wa uloo baåsin shadee-d; wal-amru ilayki fanẓuree maaz̲aa taåmureen.

قَالُوا نَحْنُ أُولُو قُوَّةٍ وَأُولُو
بَأْسٍ شَدِيدٍ وَالْأَمْرُ إِلَيْكِ
فَانظُرِي مَاذَا تَأْمُرِينَ ﴿٣٣﴾

34. She said: "Kings, when they enter a country, despoil it, and make the noblest of its people its meanest, thus do they behave.

34. Qaalat innal-mulooka iz̲aa dakhaloo qaryatan afsadoohaa wa ja'alooo a'izzata ahlihaaa az̲illah; wa kaz̲aalika yaf-'aloon.

قَالَتْ إِنَّ الْمُلُوكَ إِذَا دَخَلُوا
قَرْيَةً أَفْسَدُوهَا وَجَعَلُوا أَعِزَّةَ
أَهْلِهَا أَذِلَّةً وَكَذَٰلِكَ يَفْعَلُونَ ﴿٣٤﴾

35. "But I am going to send him a present, and (wait) to see with what (answer) return (my) ambassadors."

35. Wa innee mursilatun ilayhim bihadiyyatin fanaa-ẓiratum bima yarji'ul-mursa-loon.

وَإِنِّي مُرْسِلَةٌ إِلَيْهِم بِهَدِيَّةٍ
فَنَاظِرَةٌ بِمَ يَرْجِعُ الْمُرْسَلُونَ ﴿٣٥﴾

36. Now when (the embassy) came to Solomon, he said: "Will you give me abundance in wealth? But that which Allah has given me is better than that which He has given you! Nay it is you who rejoice in your gift!

36. Falammaa jaaa'a Sulay-maana qaala atumiddoonani bimaalin famaaa aataaniyal-laahu khayrum-mimmaaa aataakum bal antum bihadiy-yatikum tafraḥoon.

فَلَمَّا جَاءَ سُلَيْمَانَ قَالَ أَتُمِدُّونَنِ
بِمَالٍ فَمَا آتَانِيَ اللَّهُ خَيْرٌ مِّمَّا
آتَاكُم بَلْ أَنتُم بِهَدِيَّتِكُمْ
تَفْرَحُونَ ﴿٣٦﴾

37. "Go back to them, and be sure we shall come to them with such hosts as they will never be able to meet: we shall expel them from there in disgrace, and they will feel humbled (indeed)."

37. Irji' ilayhim falanaåtiyan-nahum bijunoodil-laa qibala lahum bihaa wa lanukhri-jannahum-minhaaa az̲illatañw-wa hum ṣaaghiroon.

ارْجِعْ إِلَيْهِمْ فَلَنَأْتِيَنَّهُم بِجُنُودٍ
لَّا قِبَلَ لَهُم بِهَا وَلَنُخْرِجَنَّهُم
مِّنْهَا أَذِلَّةً وَهُمْ صَاغِرُونَ ﴿٣٧﴾

38. He said (to his own men): "You Chiefs! which of you can bring me her throne before they come to me in submission?"

38. Qaala yaaa ayyuhal-mala'u ayyukum yaåteenee bi'arshihaa qabla añy-yaå-toonee muslimeen.

قَالَ يَا أَيُّهَا الْمَلَأُ أَيُّكُمْ يَأْتِينِي
بِعَرْشِهَا قَبْلَ أَن يَأْتُونِي مُسْلِمِينَ ﴿٣٨﴾

39. An 'Ifrit, of the Jinns said: "I will bring it to you before you rise from your Council: indeed I have full strength for the purpose, and may be trusted."

39. Qaala 'ifreetum-minal-jinni ana aateeka bihee qabla an taqooma mim-maqaamika wa innee 'alayhi laqawiyyun ameen.

قَالَ عِفْرِيتٌ مِّنَ الْجِنِّ أَنَا آتِيكَ
بِهِ قَبْلَ أَن تَقُومَ مِن مَّقَامِكَ
وَإِنِّي عَلَيْهِ لَقَوِيٌّ أَمِينٌ ﴿٣٩﴾

40. Said one who had know-ledge of the Book: "I will bring it to you within the twinkling of

40. Qaalal-lazee 'indahoo 'ilmum-minal-Kitaabi ana aateeka bihee qabla añy-yar-tadda ilayka

قَالَ الَّذِي عِندَهُ عِلْمٌ مِّنَ الْكِتَابِ
أَنَا آتِيكَ بِهِ قَبْلَ أَن يَرْتَدَّ إِلَيْكَ

Ikhfa اخفاء | Ghunna غُنّہ | Ikhfa Meem Saakin اخفاءمیم ساکن | Idghaam ادغام | Qalqala قلقلہ | Qalb قلب | Idghaam Meem Saakin ادغام میم ساکن

an eye!" Then when (Solomon) saw it placed firmly before him, he said: "This is by the Grace of my Lord!- to test me whether I am grateful or ungrateful! and if any is grateful, truly his gratitude is (a gain) for his own soul; but if any is ungrateful, truly my Lord is Free of all Needs, Supreme in Honor!"

ṭarfuk; falammaa ra-aahu mustaqirran 'indahoo qaala haazaa min faḍli Rabbee liyabluwaneee 'a-ashkuru am akfuru wa man shakara fa-innamaa yashkuru linafsihee wa man kafara fa-inna Rabbee Ghaniyyun Kareem.

طَرْفُكَ ۚ فَلَمَّا رَاٰهُ مُسْتَقِرًّا عِنْدَهٗ
قَالَ هٰذَا مِنْ فَضْلِ رَبِّيْ ۖ
لِيَبْلُوَنِيْٓ ءَاَشْكُرُ اَمْ اَكْفُرُ ۖ وَمَنْ
شَكَرَ فَاِنَّمَا يَشْكُرُ لِنَفْسِهٖ ۚ وَمَنْ
كَفَرَ فَاِنَّ رَبِّيْ غَنِيٌّ كَرِيْمٌ ﴿٤٠﴾

41. He said: "Transform her throne out of all recognition by her; let us see whether she is guided (to the truth) or is one of those who receive no guidance."

41. Qaala nakkiroo lahaa 'arshahaa nanẓur atahtadeee am takoonu minal-lazeena laa yahtadoon.

قَالَ نَكِّرُوْا لَهَا عَرْشَهَا نَنْظُرْ
اَتَهْتَدِيْٓ اَمْ تَكُوْنُ مِنَ الَّذِيْنَ
لَا يَهْتَدُوْنَ ﴿٤١﴾

42. So when she arrived, she was asked, "Is this your throne?" She said, "It was just like this; and knowledge was bestowed on us in advance of this, and we have submitted to Allah (in Islam)."

42. Falammaa jaaa'at qeela ahaakazaa 'arshuki qaalat kaannahoo hoo; wa ooteenal-'ilma min qablihaa wa kunnaa muslimeen.

فَلَمَّا جَآءَتْ قِيْلَ اَهٰكَذَا عَرْشُكِ ۖ
قَالَتْ كَاَنَّهٗ هُوَ ۚ وَاُوْتِيْنَا الْعِلْمَ
مِنْ قَبْلِهَا وَكُنَّا مُسْلِمِيْنَ ﴿٤٢﴾

43. And he diverted her from the worship of others besides Allah: for she was (sprung) of a people that had no faith.

43. Wa ṣaddahaa maa kaanat ta'budu min doonil-laahi innahaa kaanat min qawmin kaafireen.

وَصَدَّهَا مَا كَانَتْ تَّعْبُدُ مِنْ دُوْنِ
اللّٰهِ ۖ اِنَّهَا كَانَتْ مِنْ قَوْمٍ كٰفِرِيْنَ ﴿٤٣﴾

44. She was asked to enter the lofty Palace: but when she saw it, she thought it was a lake of water, and she (tucked up her skirts), uncovering her legs. He said: "This is but a palace paved smooth with slabs of glass." She said: "O my Lord! I have indeed wronged my soul: I do (now) submit (in Islam), with Solomon, to the Lord of the Worlds."

44. Qeela lahad-khuliṣ-ṣarḥa falammaa ra-at-hu ḥasibat-hu lujjatañw-wa kashafat 'an saaqayhaa; qaala innahoo ṣarḥ um-mumarradum-min qawaareer; qaalat Rabbi innee ẓalamtu nafsee wa aslamtu ma'a Sulaymaana lillaahi Rabbil-'aalameen. **(Section 3)**

قِيْلَ لَهَا ادْخُلِي الصَّرْحَ ۚ فَلَمَّا
رَاَتْهُ حَسِبَتْهُ لُجَّةً وَّكَشَفَتْ عَنْ
سَاقَيْهَا ۚ قَالَ اِنَّهٗ صَرْحٌ مُّمَرَّدٌ
مِّنْ قَوَارِيْرَ ۗ قَالَتْ رَبِّ اِنِّيْ ظَلَمْتُ
نَفْسِيْ وَاَسْلَمْتُ مَعَ سُلَيْمٰنَ لِلّٰهِ
رَبِّ الْعٰلَمِيْنَ ﴿٤٤﴾ ع ٣ ١٨

45. We sent (aforetime), to the Thamud, their brother Salih, saying, "Serve Allah": But behold, they became two factions quarrelling with each other.

45. Wa laqad arsalnaaa ilaa Samooda akhaahum Ṣaaliḥan ani'-budul-lahha fa-izaa hum fareeqaani yakhtaṣimoon.

وَلَقَدْ اَرْسَلْنَآ اِلٰى ثَمُوْدَ اَخَاهُمْ
صٰلِحًا اَنِ اعْبُدُوا اللّٰهَ فَاِذَا
هُمْ فَرِيْقٰنِ يَخْتَصِمُوْنَ ﴿٤٥﴾

46. He said: "O my people! why do you ask to hasten on the evil in preference to the good? If only you ask Allah for forgiveness, you may hope to receive mercy.

46. Qaala yaa qawmi lima tasta'jiloona bissayyi'ati qablal-ḥasanati law laa tastaghfiroonal-laaha la'allakum turḥamoon.

قَالَ يٰقَوْمِ لِمَ تَسْتَعْجِلُوْنَ
بِالسَّيِّئَةِ قَبْلَ الْحَسَنَةِ ۚ لَوْلَا
تَسْتَغْفِرُوْنَ اللّٰهَ لَعَلَّكُمْ تُرْحَمُوْنَ ﴿٤٦﴾

47. They said: "We augur ill omen do from you and those that are with you".

47. Qaaluṭ-ṭayyarnaa bika wa bimam-ma'ak;

قَالُوا اطَّيَّرْنَا بِكَ وَبِمَنْ مَّعَكَ ۚ

Ikhfa اخفاء | Ghunna غُنّہ | Ikhfa Meem Saakin اخفاء میم ساکن | Idghaam ادغام | Qalqala قلقلہ | Qalb قلب | Idghaam Meem Saakin ادغام میم ساکن

He said: "Your ill omen is with Allah; yes, you are a people under trial."

qaala ṭaaa'irukum 'indal-laahi bal antum qawmun tuftanoon.

قَالَ طَٰٓئِرُكُمْ عِندَ ٱللَّهِ ۖ بَلْ أَنتُمْ قَوْمٌ تُفْتَنُونَ ﴿٤٧﴾

48. There were in the city nine men of a family, who made mischief in the land, and would not reform.

48. Wa kaana fil-madeenati tis'atu rahṭiñy-yufsidoona fil-arḍi wa laa yuṣliḥoon.

وَكَانَ فِى ٱلْمَدِينَةِ تِسْعَةُ رَهْطٍ يُفْسِدُونَ فِى ٱلْأَرْضِ وَلَا يُصْلِحُونَ ﴿٤٨﴾

49. They said: "Swear a mutual oath by Allah that we shall make a secret night attack on him and his people, and that we shall then say to his heir (when he seeks vengeance): "We were not present at the slaughter of his people, and we are positively telling the truth.'"

49. Qaaloo taqaasamoo billaahi lanubayyitannahoo wa ahlahoo summa lanaqoolanna liwaliyyihee maa shahidnaa mahlika ahlihee wa innaa laṣaadiqoon.

قَالُوا۟ تَقَاسَمُوا۟ بِٱللَّهِ لَنُبَيِّتَنَّهُۥ وَأَهْلَهُۥ ثُمَّ لَنَقُولَنَّ لِوَلِيِّهِۦ مَا شَهِدْنَا مَهْلِكَ أَهْلِهِۦ وَإِنَّا لَصَٰدِقُونَ ﴿٤٩﴾

50. They plotted and planned, but We too planned, even while they perceived it not.

50. Wa makaroo makrañw-wa makarnaa makrañw-wa hum laa yash'uroon.

وَمَكَرُوا۟ مَكْرًا وَمَكَرْنَا مَكْرًا وَهُمْ لَا يَشْعُرُونَ ﴿٥٠﴾

51. Then see what was the end of their plot!- this, that We destroyed them and their people, all (of them).

51. Fanẓur kayfa kaana 'aaqibatu makrihim annaa dammarnaahum wa qawmahum ajma'een.

فَٱنظُرْ كَيْفَ كَانَ عَٰقِبَةُ مَكْرِهِمْ أَنَّا دَمَّرْنَٰهُمْ وَقَوْمَهُمْ أَجْمَعِينَ ﴿٥١﴾

52. Now such were their houses, - in utter ruin, - because they practised wrong-doing. Verily in this is a Sign for people of knowledge.

52. Fatilka buyootuhum khaawiyatam bimaa ẓalamoo; inna fee z̲aalika la-Aayatal-liqawmiñy-ya'lamoon.

فَتِلْكَ بُيُوتُهُمْ خَاوِيَةًۢ بِمَا ظَلَمُوٓا۟ ۗ إِنَّ فِى ذَٰلِكَ لَءَايَةً لِّقَوْمٍ يَعْلَمُونَ ﴿٥٢﴾

53. And We saved those who believed and practised righteousness.

53. Wa anjaynal-laz̲eena aamanoo wa kaanoo yattaqoon.

وَأَنجَيْنَا ٱلَّذِينَ ءَامَنُوا۟ وَكَانُوا۟ يَتَّقُونَ ﴿٥٣﴾

54. (We also sent) Lut (as a Messenger): behold, he said to his people, "Do you do what is shameful though you see (its iniquity)?

54. Wa Looṭan iz̲ qaala liqawmiheee ataåtoonal-faaḥishata wa antum tubṣiroon.

وَلُوطًا إِذْ قَالَ لِقَوْمِهِۦٓ أَتَأْتُونَ ٱلْفَٰحِشَةَ وَأَنتُمْ تُبْصِرُونَ ﴿٥٤﴾

55. Would you really approach men in your lusts rather than women? Nay, you are a people (grossly) ignorant!

55. A'innakum lataåtoonar-rijaala shahwatam-min doonin-nisaaa'; bal antum qawmun tajhaloon.

أَئِنَّكُمْ لَتَأْتُونَ ٱلرِّجَالَ شَهْوَةً مِّن دُونِ ٱلنِّسَآءِ ۚ بَلْ أَنتُمْ قَوْمٌ تَجْهَلُونَ ﴿٥٥﴾

56. But his people gave no other answer but this: they said, "Drive out the followers of Lut from your city: these are indeed men who want to be clean and pure!"

56. Famaa kaana jawaaba qawmiheee illaaa an qaalooo akhrijooo aala Looṭim-min qaryatikum innahum unaasuñy-yataṭahharoon.

فَمَا كَانَ جَوَابَ قَوْمِهِۦٓ إِلَّآ أَن قَالُوٓا۟ أَخْرِجُوٓا۟ ءَالَ لُوطٍ مِّن قَرْيَتِكُمْ ۖ إِنَّهُمْ أُنَاسٌ يَتَطَهَّرُونَ ﴿٥٦﴾

57. But We saved him and his family, except his wife;

57. Fa-anjaynaahu wa ahlahooo illam-ra-atahoo

فَأَنجَيْنَٰهُ وَأَهْلَهُۥٓ إِلَّا ٱمْرَأَتَهُۥ

Ikhfa اخفاء | Ghunna غنّہ | Ikhfa Meem Saakin اخفاء میم ساکن | Idghaam ادغام | Qalqala قلقلہ | Qalb قلب | Idghaam Meem Saakin ادغام میم ساکن

her We destined to be of those who lagged behind.

58. And We rained down on them a shower (of brimstone): and evil was the shower on those who were admonished (but heeded not)!

59. Say: Praise be to Allah, and Peace on His servants whom He has chosen (for his Message). (Who) is better?- Allah or the false gods they associate (with Him)?

60. Or, who has created the heavens and the earth, and who sends you down rain from the sky? Yes, with it We cause to grow well-planted orchards full of beauty of delight: it is not in your power to cause the growth of the trees in them. (Can there be another) god besides Allah? Nay, they are a people who swerve from justice.

61. Or, who has made the earth firm to live in; made rivers in its midst; set thereon mountains immovable; and made a separating bar between the two bodies of flowing water? (can there be another) god besides Allah? Nay, most of them do not know.

62. Or, who listens to the (soul) distressed when it calls on Him, and Who relieves its suffering, and makes you (mankind) inheritors of the earth? (Can there be another) god besides Allah? Little it is that you heed.

63. Or, who guides you through the depths of darkness on land and sea, and who sends the winds as heralds of glad tidings, going before His Mercy? (Can there be another) god besides Allah?- High is Allah above what they associate with Him!

64. Or, who originates creation, then repeats it, and who gives you sustenance from heaven and earth? (Can there be another) god besides Allah? Say, "Bring forth your argument, if

qaddarnaahaa minal-ghaa-bireen.

58. Wa amṭarnaa 'alayhim-maṭaran fasaaa'a maṭarul-munzareen. **(Section 4)**

59. Qulil-ḥamdu lillaahi wa salaamun 'alaa 'ibaadihil-lazeenaṣ-ṭafaa; aaallaahu khayrun ammaa yushrikoon.

60. Amman khalaqas-samaa-waati wal-arḍa wa anzala lakum-minas-samaaa'i maaa'an fa-ambatnaa bihee ḥadaaa'iqa zaata bahjah; maa kaana lakum an tumbitoo shajarahaa; 'a-ilaahum-ma'al-laah; bal hum qawmuñy-ya'diloon.

61. Amman ja'alal-arḍa qa-raarañw-wa ja'ala khilaalahaaa anhaarañw-wa ja'ala lahaa rawaasiya wa ja'ala baynal-baḥrayni ḥaajizaa; 'a-ilaahum-ma'allaah; bal aksaruhum laa ya'lamoon.

62. Ammañy-yujeebul-muḍ-ṭarra izaa da'aahu wa yakshifus-sooo'a wa yaj'alukum khula-faaa'al-arḍi 'a-ilaahum-ma'al-laahi qaleelam-maa tazak-karoon.

63. Ammañy-yahdeekum fee ẓulumaatil-barri wal-baḥri wa mañy-yursilur-riyaaḥa bushram bayna yaday raḥmatih; 'a-ilaahum-ma'al-laah; Ta'aalal-laahu 'ammaa yushrikoon.

64. Ammañy-yabda'ul-khalqa summa yu'eeduhoo wa mañy-yarzuqukum-minas-samaaa'i wal-arḍ; 'a-ilaahum-ma'allaah; qul haatoo burhaanakum in

قَدَّرْنٰهَا مِنَ الْغٰبِرِيْنَ ﴿٥٧﴾
وَاَمْطَرْنَا عَلَيْهِمْ مَّطَرًا ۚ فَسَآءَ
مَطَرُ الْمُنْذَرِيْنَ ﴿٥٨﴾ ع
قُلِ الْحَمْدُ لِلّٰهِ وَسَلٰمٌ عَلٰى
عِبَادِهِ الَّذِيْنَ اصْطَفٰى ؕ آٰللّٰهُ
خَيْرٌ اَمَّا يُشْرِكُوْنَ ﴿٥٩﴾
اَمَّنْ خَلَقَ السَّمٰوٰتِ وَالْاَرْضَ
وَاَنْزَلَ لَكُمْ مِّنَ السَّمَآءِ مَآءً ۚ فَاَنْۢبَتْنَا
بِهٖ حَدَآئِقَ ذَاتَ بَهْجَةٍ ۚ مَا كَانَ
لَكُمْ اَنْ تُنْۢبِتُوْا شَجَرَهَا ؕ ءَاِلٰهٌ مَّعَ
اللّٰهِ ؕ بَلْ هُمْ قَوْمٌ يَّعْدِلُوْنَ ﴿٦٠﴾
اَمَّنْ جَعَلَ الْاَرْضَ قَرَارًا وَّجَعَلَ
خِلٰلَهَآ اَنْهٰرًا وَّجَعَلَ لَهَا رَوَاسِيَ
وَجَعَلَ بَيْنَ الْبَحْرَيْنِ حَاجِزًا ؕ ءَاِلٰهٌ
مَّعَ اللّٰهِ ؕ بَلْ اَكْثَرُهُمْ لَا يَعْلَمُوْنَ ﴿٦١﴾
اَمَّنْ يُّجِيْبُ الْمُضْطَرَّ اِذَا دَعَاهُ
وَيَكْشِفُ السُّوْٓءَ وَيَجْعَلُكُمْ خُلَفَآءَ
الْاَرْضِ ؕ ءَاِلٰهٌ مَّعَ اللّٰهِ ؕ قَلِيْلًا
مَّا تَذَكَّرُوْنَ ﴿٦٢﴾
اَمَّنْ يَّهْدِيْكُمْ فِيْ ظُلُمٰتِ الْبَرِّ
وَالْبَحْرِ وَمَنْ يُّرْسِلُ الرِّيٰحَ بُشْرًاۢ
بَيْنَ يَدَيْ رَحْمَتِهٖ ؕ ءَاِلٰهٌ مَّعَ
اللّٰهِ ؕ تَعٰلَى اللّٰهُ عَمَّا يُشْرِكُوْنَ ﴿٦٣﴾
اَمَّنْ يَّبْدَؤُا الْخَلْقَ ثُمَّ يُعِيْدُهٗ وَمَنْ
يَّرْزُقُكُمْ مِّنَ السَّمَآءِ وَالْاَرْضِ ؕ ءَاِلٰهٌ
مَّعَ اللّٰهِ ؕ قُلْ هَاتُوْا بُرْهَانَكُمْ اِنْ

الجزء العشرون (٢٠)

Ikhfa اخفاء | Ghunna غنّہ | Ikhfa Meem Saakin اخفاء میم ساکن | Idghaam ادغام | Qalqala قلقلہ | Qalb قلب | Idghaam Meem Saakin ادغام میم ساکن

you are telling the truth!"

kuntum ṣaadiqeen.

كُنْتُمْ صٰدِقِيْنَ ﴿٦٤﴾

65. Say: None in the heavens or on earth, except Allah, knows what is hidden: nor can they perceive when they shall be raised up (for Judgment).

65. Qul laa ya'lamu man fis-samaawaati wal-arḍil-ghayba illal-laah; wa maa yash'uroona ayyaana yub'aṣoon.

قُلْ لَّا يَعْلَمُ مَنْ فِي السَّمٰوٰتِ
وَالْاَرْضِ الْغَيْبَ اِلَّا اللّٰهُ ؕ وَمَا
يَشْعُرُوْنَ اَيَّانَ يُبْعَثُوْنَ ﴿٦٥﴾

66. Still less can their knowledge comprehend the Here-after; nay, they are in doubt and uncertainty thereat; nay, they are blind thereunto.

66. Balid-daaraka 'ilmuhum fil-Aakhirah; bal hum fee shakkim-minhaa bal hum-minhaa 'amoon. **(Section 5)**

بَلِ ادّٰرَكَ عِلْمُهُمْ فِي الْاٰخِرَةِ ۫ بَلْ هُمْ
فِيْ شَكٍّ مِّنْهَا ۫ بَلْ هُمْ مِّنْهَا عَمُوْنَ ﴿٦٦﴾ ع ٥ ٨ ١

67. The Unbelievers say: "What! when we become dust,- we and our fathers,- shall we really be raised (from the dead)?

67. Wa qaalal-lazeena kafa-rooo 'a-izaa kunnaa turaabañw-wa aabaaa'unaaa a'innaa lamukhrajoon.

وَقَالَ الَّذِيْنَ كَفَرُوْۤا ءَاِذَا كُنَّا تُرٰبًا
وَّاٰبَآؤُنَاۤ اَئِنَّا لَمُخْرَجُوْنَ ﴿٦٧﴾

68. "It is true we were promised this,- we and our fathers before (us): these are nothing but tales of the ancients."

68. Laqad wu'idnaa haazaa naḥnu wa aabaaa'unaa min qablu in haazaaa illaaa asaa-ṭeerul-awwaleen.

لَقَدْ وُعِدْنَا هٰذَا نَحْنُ وَاٰبَآؤُنَا مِنْ
قَبْلُ ۙ اِنْ هٰذَاۤ اِلَّاۤ اَسَاطِيْرُ الْاَوَّلِيْنَ ﴿٦٨﴾

69. Say: "You go through the earth and see what has been the end of those guilty (of sin)."

69. Qul seeroo fil-arḍi fanẓu-roo kayfa kaana 'aaqibatul-mujrimeen.

قُلْ سِيْرُوْا فِي الْاَرْضِ فَانْظُرُوْا كَيْفَ
كَانَ عَاقِبَةُ الْمُجْرِمِيْنَ ﴿٦٩﴾

70. But grieve not over them, nor distress yourself because of their plots.

70. Wa laa taḥzan 'alayhim wa laa takun fee ḍayqim-mimmaa yamkuroon.

وَلَا تَحْزَنْ عَلَيْهِمْ وَلَا تَكُنْ فِيْ ضَيْقٍ
مِّمَّا يَمْكُرُوْنَ ﴿٧٠﴾

71. They also say: "When will this promise (come to pass)? (Say) if you are truthful."

71. Wa yaqooloona mataa haazal-wa'du in kuntum ṣaadi-qeen.

وَيَقُوْلُوْنَ مَتٰى هٰذَا الْوَعْدُ اِنْ
كُنْتُمْ صٰدِقِيْنَ ﴿٧١﴾

72. Say: "It may be that some of the events which you wish to hasten on may be (close) in your pursuit!"

72. Qul 'asaaa añy-yakoona radifa lakum ba'ḍul-lazee tasta'jiloon.

قُلْ عَسٰۤى اَنْ يَّكُوْنَ رَدِفَ لَكُمْ بَعْضُ
الَّذِيْ تَسْتَعْجِلُوْنَ ﴿٧٢﴾

73. But verily your Lord is full of grace to mankind: yet most of them are ungrateful.

73. Wa inna Rabbaka lazoo faḍlin 'alan-naasi wa laakinna aksarahum laa yashkuroon.

وَاِنَّ رَبَّكَ لَذُوْ فَضْلٍ عَلَى النَّاسِ
وَلٰكِنَّ اَكْثَرَهُمْ لَا يَشْكُرُوْنَ ﴿٧٣﴾

74. And verily your Lord knows all that their hearts hide. As well as all that they reveal.

74. Wa inna Rabbaka la-ya'-lamu maa tukinnu ṣudooruhum wa maa yu'linoon.

وَاِنَّ رَبَّكَ لَيَعْلَمُ مَا تُكِنُّ صُدُوْرُهُمْ
وَمَا يُعْلِنُوْنَ ﴿٧٤﴾

75. Nor is there anything of the unseen, in heaven or earth, but is (recorded) in a clear record.

75. Wa maa min ghaaa'ibatin fis-samaaa'i wal-arḍi illaa fee kitaabim-mubeen.

وَمَا مِنْ غَآئِبَةٍ فِي السَّمَآءِ وَالْاَرْضِ
اِلَّا فِيْ كِتٰبٍ مُّبِيْنٍ ﴿٧٥﴾

76. Verily this Qur'an ex-plains to the Children of Israel most of the matters in which

76. Inna haazal-Qur-aana yaquṣṣu 'alaa Baneee Israaa-'eela aksaral-lazee hum feehi

اِنَّ هٰذَا الْقُرْاٰنَ يَقُصُّ عَلٰى بَنِيْۤ
اِسْرَآءِيْلَ اَكْثَرَ الَّذِيْ هُمْ فِيْهِ

Ikhfa اخفاء | Ghunna غنّہ | Ikhfa Meem Saakin اخفاء میم ساکن | Idghaam ادغام | Qalqala قلقلہ | Qalb قلب | Idghaam Meem Saakin ادغام میم ساکن

they disagree.

yakhtalifoon.

يَخْتَلِفُونَ ٧٦

77. And it certainly is a Guide and a Mercy to those who believe.

77. Wa innahoo lahudañw-wa raḥmatul-lilmu'mineen.

وَإِنَّهُ لَهُدًى وَرَحْمَةٌ لِّلْمُؤْمِنِينَ ٧٧

78. Verily your Lord will decide between them by His Decree: and He is Exalted in Might, All-Knowing.

78. Inna Rabbaka yaqḍee baynahum biḥukmih; wa Huwal-'Azeezul-'Aleem.

إِنَّ رَبَّكَ يَقْضِي بَيْنَهُم بِحُكْمِهِ ۚ
وَهُوَ الْعَزِيزُ الْعَلِيمُ ٧٨

79. So put your trust in Allah: for you are on (the path of) manifest Truth.

79. Fatawakkal 'alal-laahi innaka 'alal-ḥaqqil-mubeen.

فَتَوَكَّلْ عَلَى اللَّهِ ۖ إِنَّكَ عَلَى الْحَقِّ
الْمُبِينِ ٧٩

80. Truly you can not cause the dead to listen, nor can you cause the deaf to hear the call, (especially) when they turn back in retreat.

80. Innaka laa tusmi'ul-mawtaa wa laa tusmi'uṣ-ṣummad-du'aaa'a izaa wallaw mudbireen.

إِنَّكَ لَا تُسْمِعُ الْمَوْتَىٰ وَلَا تُسْمِعُ
الصُّمَّ الدُّعَاءَ إِذَا وَلَّوْا مُدْبِرِينَ ٨٠

81. Nor can you be a guide to the Blind, (to prevent them) from straying: only those will you get to listen who believe in Our Signs, and they will bow in Islam.

81. Wa maaa anta bihaadil-'umyi 'an ḍalaalatihim in tusmi'u illaa mañy-yu'minu bi-Aayaatinaa fahum-muslimoon.

وَمَا أَنتَ بِهَادِي الْعُمْيِ عَن ضَلَالَتِهِمْ ۖ
إِن تُسْمِعُ إِلَّا مَن يُؤْمِنُ بِآيَاتِنَا
فَهُم مُّسْلِمُونَ ٨١

82. And when the Word is fulfilled against them (the unjust), we shall produce from the earth a Beast to (face) them: he will speak to them, for that mankind did not believe with assurance in Our Signs.

82. Wa izaa waqa'al-qawlu 'alayhim akhrajnaa lahum daaabbatam-minal-arḍi tukallimuhum annan-naasa kaanoo bi-Aayaatinaa laa yooqinoon.

(Section 6)

وَإِذَا وَقَعَ الْقَوْلُ عَلَيْهِمْ أَخْرَجْنَا
لَهُمْ دَابَّةً مِّنَ الْأَرْضِ تُكَلِّمُهُمْ
أَنَّ النَّاسَ كَانُوا بِآيَاتِنَا لَا يُوقِنُونَ ٨٢ ع ٦

83. One Day We shall gather together from every people a troop of those who reject Our Signs, and they shall be kept in ranks,-

83. Wa Yawma naḥshuru min kulli ummatin fawjam-mimmañy-yukazzibu bi-Aayaatinaa fahum yooza'oon.

وَيَوْمَ نَحْشُرُ مِن كُلِّ أُمَّةٍ فَوْجًا مِّمَّن
يُكَذِّبُ بِآيَاتِنَا فَهُمْ يُوزَعُونَ ٨٣

84. Until, when they come (before the Judgment-seat), (Allah) will say: "Did you reject My Signs, though you did not comprehend them in knowledge, or what was it you did?"

84. Ḥattaaa izaa jaaa'oo qaala akazzabtum bi-Aayaatee wa lam tuḥeeṭoo bihaa 'ilman ammaazaa kuntum ta'maloon.

حَتَّىٰ إِذَا جَاءُوا قَالَ أَكَذَّبْتُم بِآيَاتِي
وَلَمْ تُحِيطُوا بِهَا عِلْمًا أَمَّاذَا
كُنتُمْ تَعْمَلُونَ ٨٤

85. And the Word will be fulfilled against them, because of their wrong-doing, and they will be unable to speak (in plea).

85. Wa waqa'al-qawlu 'alayhim bimaa ẓalamoo fahum laa yanṭiqoon.

وَوَقَعَ الْقَوْلُ عَلَيْهِم بِمَا ظَلَمُوا
فَهُمْ لَا يَنطِقُونَ ٨٥

86. Do they not see that We have made the Night for them to rest in and the Day to give them light? Verily in this are Signs for any people that believe!

86. Alam yaraw annaa ja'alnal-layla li-yaskunoo feehi wannahaara mubṣiraa; inna fee zaalika la-Aayaatil-liqawmiñy-yu'minoon.

أَلَمْ يَرَوْا أَنَّا جَعَلْنَا اللَّيْلَ لِيَسْكُنُوا
فِيهِ وَالنَّهَارَ مُبْصِرًا ۚ إِنَّ فِي ذَٰلِكَ
لَآيَاتٍ لِّقَوْمٍ يُؤْمِنُونَ ٨٦

87. And the Day that the Trumpet will be sounded - then will be smitten with terror those who are in the heavens, and those who are on earth, except

87. Wa Yawma yunfakhu fiṣ-Ṣoori fafazi'a man fis-samaawaati wa man fil-arḍi illaa

وَيَوْمَ يُنفَخُ فِي الصُّورِ فَفَزِعَ مَن
فِي السَّمَاوَاتِ وَمَن فِي الْأَرْضِ إِلَّا

Ikhfa اخفاء | Ghunna غُنّہ | Ikhfa Meem Saakin اخفاء میم ساکن | Idghaam ادغام | Qalqala قلقلہ | Qalb قلب | Idghaam Meem Saakin ادغام میم ساکن

such as Allah will please (to exempt): and all shall come to His (Presence) as beings conscious of their lowliness.

88. You see the mountains and think them firmly fixed: but they shall pass away as the clouds pass away: (such is) the artistry of Allah, who disposes of all things in perfect order: for He is well acquainted with all that you do.

89. If any do good, good will (accrue) to them therefrom; and they will be secure from terror that Day.

90. And if any do evil, their faces will be thrown headlong into the Fire: "Do you receive a reward other than that which you have earned by your deeds?"

91. For me, I have been commanded to serve the Lord of this city, Him Who has sanctified it and to Whom (belong) all things: and I am commanded to be of those who bow in Islam to Allah's Will,-

92. And to rehearse the Qur'an: and if any accept guidance, they do it for the good of their own souls, and if any stray, say: "I am only a Warner".

93. And say: "Praise be to Allah, Who will soon show you His Signs, so that you shall know them"; and your Lord is not unmindful of all that you do.

man shaaa'al-laah; wa kullun atawhu daakhireen.

88. Wa taral-jibaala taḥsabuhaa jaamidatañw-wa hiya tamurru marras-saḥaab; ṣun'al-laahil-lazeee atqana kulla shay'; innahoo khabeerum bimaa taf'aloon.

89. Man jaaa'a bilḥasanati falahoo khayrum-minhaa wa hum-min faza'iñy-Yawma'izin aaminoon.

90. Wa man jaaa'a bissayyi'ati fakubbat wujoohuhum fin-Naari hal tujzawna illaa maa kuntum ta'maloon.

91. Innamaaa umirtu an a'buda Rabba haazihil-baldatil-lazee ḥarramahaa wa lahoo kullu shay'iñw-wa umirtu an akoona minal-muslimeen.

92. Wa an atluwal-Qur-aana famanih-tadaa fa-innamaa yahtadee linafsihee wa man ḍalla faqul innamaaa ana minal-munzireen.

93. Wa qulil-ḥamdu lillaahi sa-yureekum Aayaatihee fata'rifoonahaa; wa maa Rabbuka bighaafilin 'ammaa ta'maloon.

(Section 7)

مَنْ شَآءَ اللّٰهُ ؕ وَكُلٌّ اَتَوْهُ
دٰخِرِيْنَ ﴿٨٧﴾
وَتَرَى الْجِبَالَ تَحْسَبُهَا جَامِدَةً
وَّهِيَ تَمُرُّ مَرَّ السَّحَابِ ؕ صُنْعَ اللّٰهِ
الَّذِيْٓ اَتْقَنَ كُلَّ شَيْءٍ ؕ اِنَّهٗ خَبِيْرٌۢ
بِمَا تَفْعَلُوْنَ ﴿٨٨﴾
مَنْ جَآءَ بِالْحَسَنَةِ فَلَهٗ خَيْرٌ مِّنْهَا ۚ
وَهُمْ مِّنْ فَزَعٍ يَّوْمَئِذٍ اٰمِنُوْنَ ﴿٨٩﴾
وَمَنْ جَآءَ بِالسَّيِّئَةِ فَكُبَّتْ
وُجُوْهُهُمْ فِي النَّارِ ؕ هَلْ تُجْزَوْنَ
اِلَّا مَا كُنْتُمْ تَعْمَلُوْنَ ﴿٩٠﴾
اِنَّمَآ اُمِرْتُ اَنْ اَعْبُدَ رَبَّ هٰذِهِ
الْبَلْدَةِ الَّذِيْ حَرَّمَهَا وَلَهٗ كُلُّ شَيْءٍ ز
وَّاُمِرْتُ اَنْ اَكُوْنَ مِنَ الْمُسْلِمِيْنَ ﴿٩١﴾ لا
وَاَنْ اَتْلُوَا الْقُرْاٰنَ ۚ فَمَنِ اهْتَدٰى
فَاِنَّمَا يَهْتَدِيْ لِنَفْسِهٖ ۚ وَمَنْ ضَلَّ
فَقُلْ اِنَّمَآ اَنَا مِنَ الْمُنْذِرِيْنَ ﴿٩٢﴾
وَقُلِ الْحَمْدُ لِلّٰهِ سَيُرِيْكُمْ اٰيٰتِهٖ
فَتَعْرِفُوْنَهَا ؕ وَمَا رَبُّكَ بِغَافِلٍ
عَمَّا تَعْمَلُوْنَ ﴿٩٣﴾

28. The Narration

In the name of Allah, Most Gracious, Most Merciful.

1. *Ta-Sin-Mim.*

2. These are Verses of the Book that makes (things) clear.

3. We rehearse to you some of the story of Moses and Pharaoh in Truth, for people who believe.

Sûrat al-Qaṣaṣ–28

(Revealed at Makkah)

Bismillaahir Raḥmaanir Raḥeem

1. Ṭaa-Seeen-Meeem.

2. Tilka Aayaatul-Kitaabil-mubeen.

3. Natloo 'alayka min-naba-i Moosaa wa Fir'awna bilḥaqqi liqawmiñy-yu'minoon.

(٢٨) سُوْرَةُ الْقَصَصِ مَكِّيَّةٌ (٤٩)

بِسْمِ اللّٰهِ الرَّحْمٰنِ الرَّحِيْمِ

طٰسٓمّٓ ﴿١﴾
تِلْكَ اٰيٰتُ الْكِتٰبِ الْمُبِيْنِ ﴿٢﴾
نَتْلُوْا عَلَيْكَ مِنْ نَّبَاِ مُوْسٰى
وَفِرْعَوْنَ بِالْحَقِّ لِقَوْمٍ يُّؤْمِنُوْنَ ﴿٣﴾

Ikhfa اخفاء | Ghunna غُنّہ | Ikhfa Meem Saakin اخفاء میم ساکن | Idghaam ادغام | Qalqala قلقلہ | Qalb قلب | Idghaam Meem Saakin ادغام میم ساکن

4. Truly Pharaoh elated himself in the land and broke up its people into sections, depressing a small group among them: their sons he slew, but he kept alive their females: for he was indeed a maker of mischief.

4. Inna Fir'awna 'alaa fil-arḍi wa ja'ala ahlahaa shiya'añy-yastaḍ'ifu ṭaaa'ifatam-minhum yuẕabbiḥu abnaaa'ahum wa yastaḥyee nisaaa'ahum; innahoo kaana minal-mufsideen.

إِنَّ فِرْعَوْنَ عَلَا فِي الْأَرْضِ وَجَعَلَ
أَهْلَهَا شِيَعًا يَسْتَضْعِفُ طَائِفَةً
مِّنْهُمْ يُذَبِّحُ أَبْنَاءَهُمْ وَيَسْتَحْيِي نِسَاءَهُمْ
إِنَّهُ كَانَ مِنَ الْمُفْسِدِينَ ۝٤

5. And We wished to be Gracious to those who were being depressed in the land, to make them leaders (in Faith) and make them heirs,

5. Wa nureedu an-namunna 'alal-laẕeenas-tuḍ'ifoo fil-arḍi wa naj'alahum a'immatañw-wa naj'alahumul-waariseen.

وَنُرِيدُ أَن نَّمُنَّ عَلَى الَّذِينَ
اسْتُضْعِفُوا فِي الْأَرْضِ وَنَجْعَلَهُمْ
أَئِمَّةً وَنَجْعَلَهُمُ الْوَارِثِينَ ۝٥

6. To establish a firm place for them in the land, and to show Pharaoh, Haman, and their hosts, at their hands, the very things against which they were taking precautions.

6. Wa numakkina lahum fil-arḍi wa nuriya Fir'awna wa Haamaana wa junoodahumaa minhum-maa kaanoo yaḥẕaroon.

وَنُمَكِّنَ لَهُمْ فِي الْأَرْضِ وَنُرِيَ
فِرْعَوْنَ وَهَامَانَ وَجُنُودَهُمَا
مِنْهُم مَّا كَانُوا يَحْذَرُونَ ۝٦

7. So We sent this inspiration to the mother of Moses: "Suckle (your child), but when you have fears about him, cast him into the river, but fear not nor grieve: for We shall restore him to you, and We shall make him one of Our Messengers."

7. Wa awḥaynaaa ilaaa ummi Moosaaa an arḍi'eehi fa-iẕaa khifti 'alayhi fa-alqeehi filyammi wa laa takhaafee wa laa taḥzaneee innaa raaaddoohu ilayki wa jaa'iloohu minal-mursaleen.

وَأَوْحَيْنَا إِلَىٰ أُمِّ مُوسَىٰ أَنْ أَرْضِعِيهِ
فَإِذَا خِفْتِ عَلَيْهِ فَأَلْقِيهِ فِي الْيَمِّ
وَلَا تَخَافِي وَلَا تَحْزَنِي ۚ إِنَّا رَادُّوهُ
إِلَيْكِ وَجَاعِلُوهُ مِنَ الْمُرْسَلِينَ ۝٧

8. Then the people of Pharaoh picked him up (from the river): (it was intended) that (Moses) should be to them an adversary and a cause of sorrow: for Pharaoh and Haman and (all) their hosts were men of sin.

8. Faltaqatahooo Aalu Fir'awna li-yakoona lahum 'aduwwañw-wa ḥazanaa; inna Fir'awna wa Haamaana wa junoodahumaa kaanoo khaaṭi'een.

فَالْتَقَطَهُ آلُ فِرْعَوْنَ لِيَكُونَ لَهُمْ
عَدُوًّا وَحَزَنًا ۗ إِنَّ فِرْعَوْنَ وَهَامَانَ
وَجُنُودَهُمَا كَانُوا خَاطِئِينَ ۝٨

9. The wife of Pharaoh said: "(Here is) joy of the eye, for me and for you: Do not slay him. It may be that he will be use to us, or we may adopt him as a son." And they did not perceive (what they were doing)!

9. Wa qaalatim-ra-atu Fir'awna qurratu 'aynil-lee wa lak; laa taqtuloohu 'asaaa añy-yanfa'anaaa aw nattakhiẕahoo waladañw-wa hum laa yash'uroon.

وَقَالَتِ امْرَأَتُ فِرْعَوْنَ قُرَّتُ عَيْنٍ
لِّي وَلَكَ ۖ لَا تَقْتُلُوهُ ۖ عَسَىٰ أَن
يَنفَعَنَا أَوْ نَتَّخِذَهُ وَلَدًا وَهُمْ
لَا يَشْعُرُونَ ۝٩

10. But there came to be a void in the heart of the mother of Moses: she was going almost to disclose his (case), had We not strengthened her heart (with faith), so that she might remain a (firm) believer.

10. Wa aṣbaḥa fu'aadu ummi Moosaa faarighan in kaadat latubdee bihee law laaa arrabaṭnaa 'alaa qalbihaa litakoona minal-mu'mineen.

وَأَصْبَحَ فُؤَادُ أُمِّ مُوسَىٰ فَارِغًا ۖ إِن
كَادَتْ لَتُبْدِي بِهِ لَوْلَا أَن رَّبَطْنَا
عَلَىٰ قَلْبِهَا لِتَكُونَ مِنَ الْمُؤْمِنِينَ ۝١٠

11. And she said to the sister of (Moses), "Follow him". So she (the sister) watched him in the character of a stranger. And they did not know.

11. Wa qaalat li-ukhtihee quṣṣeehi fabaṣurat bihee 'an junubiñw-wa hum laa yash'uroon.

وَقَالَتْ لِأُخْتِهِ قُصِّيهِ ۖ فَبَصُرَتْ بِهِ
عَن جُنُبٍ وَهُمْ لَا يَشْعُرُونَ ۝١١

Ikhfa اخفاء | Ghunna غُنّہ | Ikhfa Meem Saakin اخفاء میم ساکن | Idghaam ادغام | Qalqala قلقلہ | Qalb قلب | Idghaam Meem Saakin ادغام میم ساکن

12. And we ordained that he refused suck at first, until (His sister came up and) said: "Shall I point out to you the people of a house that will nourish and bring him up for you and be sincerely attached to him?"...

12. Wa ḥarramnaa 'alayhil-maraaḍi'a min qablu faqaalat hal adullukum 'alaaa ahli baytiñy-yakfuloonahoo lakum wa hum lahoo naaṣiḥoon.

وَحَرَّمْنَا عَلَيْهِ الْمَرَاضِعَ مِنْ
قَبْلُ فَقَالَتْ هَلْ أَدُلُّكُمْ عَلَىٰ
أَهْلِ بَيْتٍ يَكْفُلُونَهُ لَكُمْ وَهُمْ
لَهُ نَاصِحُونَ ﴿١٢﴾

13. Thus did We restore him to his mother, that her eye might be comforted, that she might not grieve, and that she might know that the promise of Allah is true: but most of them do not understand.

13. Faradadnaahu ilaaa ummihee kay taqarra 'aynuhaa wa laa taḥzana wa lita'lama anna wa'dal-laahi ḥaqquñw-wa laakinna akṡarahum laa ya'lamoon. **(Section 1)**

فَرَدَدْنَاهُ إِلَىٰ أُمِّهِ كَيْ تَقَرَّ عَيْنُهَا
وَلَا تَحْزَنَ وَلِتَعْلَمَ أَنَّ وَعْدَ اللَّهِ
حَقٌّ وَلَٰكِنَّ أَكْثَرَهُمْ لَا يَعْلَمُونَ ﴿١٣﴾

الربع

14. When he reached full age, and was firmly established (in life), We bestowed on him wisdom and knowledge: for thus do We reward those who do good.

14. Wa lammaa balagha ashuddahoo wastawaaa aataynaahu ḥukmañw-wa 'ilmaa; wa kazaalika najzil-muḥsineen.

وَلَمَّا بَلَغَ أَشُدَّهُ وَاسْتَوَىٰ آتَيْنَاهُ حُكْمًا
وَعِلْمًا ۚ وَكَذَٰلِكَ نَجْزِي الْمُحْسِنِينَ ﴿١٤﴾

15. And he entered the city at a time when its people were not watching: and he found there two men fighting,- one of his own religion, and the other, of his foes. Now the man of his own religion appealed to him against his foe, and Moses struck him with his fist and made an end of him. He said: "This is a work of Evil (Satan): for he is an enemy that manifestly misleads!"

15. Wa dakhalal-madeenata 'alaa ḥeeni ghaflatim-min ahlihaa fawajada feehaa rajulayni yaqtatilaani haazaa min shee'atihee wa haazaa min 'aduwwihee fastaghaasahul-lazee min shee'atihee 'alal-lazee min 'aduwwihee fawakazahoo Moosaa faqaḍaa 'alayhi qaala haazaa min 'amalish-Shayṭaani innahoo 'aduwwum-muḍillum-mubeen.

وَدَخَلَ الْمَدِينَةَ عَلَىٰ حِينِ غَفْلَةٍ
مِنْ أَهْلِهَا فَوَجَدَ فِيهَا رَجُلَيْنِ
يَقْتَتِلَانِ هَٰذَا مِنْ شِيعَتِهِ وَهَٰذَا
مِنْ عَدُوِّهِ ۖ فَاسْتَغَاثَهُ الَّذِي مِنْ
شِيعَتِهِ عَلَى الَّذِي مِنْ عَدُوِّهِ فَوَكَزَهُ
مُوسَىٰ فَقَضَىٰ عَلَيْهِ ۖ قَالَ هَٰذَا مِنْ
عَمَلِ الشَّيْطَانِ ۖ إِنَّهُ عَدُوٌّ مُضِلٌّ
مُبِينٌ ﴿١٥﴾

16. He prayed: "O my Lord! I have indeed wronged my soul! you then forgive me!" So (Allah) forgave him: for He is the Oft-Forgiving, Most Merciful.

16. Qaala Rabbi innee ẓalamtu nafsee faghfir lee faghafara lah; innahoo Huwal-Ghafoorur-Raḥeem.

قَالَ رَبِّ إِنِّي ظَلَمْتُ نَفْسِي فَاغْفِرْ لِي
فَغَفَرَ لَهُ ۚ إِنَّهُ هُوَ الْغَفُورُ الرَّحِيمُ ﴿١٦﴾

17. He said: "O my Lord! For that You have bestowed Your Grace on me, never shall I be a help to those who sin!"

17. Qaala Rabbi bimaaa an'amta 'alayya falan akoona ẓaheeral-lilmujrimeen.

قَالَ رَبِّ بِمَا أَنْعَمْتَ عَلَيَّ فَلَنْ
أَكُونَ ظَهِيرًا لِلْمُجْرِمِينَ ﴿١٧﴾

18. In the morning, he was in the City, fearful and vigilant, when he saw, the man who had, the day before, sought his help called aloud for his help (again). Moses said to him:" You are truly, it is clear, a quarrelsome fellow!"

18. Fa-aṣbaḥa fil-madeenati khaaa'ifañy-yataraqqabu fa-izal-lazis-tanṣarahoo bil-amsi yastaṣrikhuh; qaala lahoo Moosaaa innaka laghawiyyum-mubeen.

فَأَصْبَحَ فِي الْمَدِينَةِ خَائِفًا يَتَرَقَّبُ
فَإِذَا الَّذِي اسْتَنْصَرَهُ بِالْأَمْسِ
يَسْتَصْرِخُهُ ۚ قَالَ لَهُ مُوسَىٰ إِنَّكَ
لَغَوِيٌّ مُبِينٌ ﴿١٨﴾

19. Then, when he decided to lay his hands on

19. Falammaa an araada añy-yabṭisha billazee

فَلَمَّا أَنْ أَرَادَ أَنْ يَبْطِشَ بِالَّذِي

Ikhfa اخفاء | Ghunna غنّہ | Ikhfa Meem Saakin اخفاء میم ساکن | Idghaam ادغام | Qalqala قلقلہ | Qalb قلب | Idghaam Meem Saakin ادغام میم ساکن

their enemy, that man said: "O Moses! is it your intention to slay me as you slew a man yesterday? Your intention is none other than to become a powerful violent man in the land, and not to be one who sets things right!"

20. And there came a man, running, from the furthest end of the City. He said: "O Moses! the Chiefs are taking counsel together about you, to slay you: so get you away, for I do give you sincere advice."

21. He therefore got away therefrom, looking about, in a state of fear. He prayed "O my Lord! save me from people given to wrong-doing."

22. Then, when he turned his face towards (the land of) Madyan, he said: "I do hope that my Lord will show me the smooth and straight Path."

23. And when he arrived at the watering (place) in Madyan, he found there a group of men watering (their flocks), and besides them he found two women who were keeping back (their flocks). He said: "What is the matter with you?" They said: "We can not water (our flocks) until the shepherds take back (their flocks): and our father is a very old man."

24. So he watered (their flocks) for them; then he turned back to the shade, and said:"O my Lord! truly am I in (desperate) need of any good that You do send me!"

25. Afterwards one of the (damsels) came (back) to him, walking bashfully. She said: "My father invites you that he may reward you for having watered (our flocks) for us." So when he came to him and narrated the story,

huwa 'aduwwul-lahumaa qaala yaa Moosaaa atureedu an taqtulanee kamaa qatalta nafsam bil-amsi in tureedu illaaa an takoona jabbaaran fil-arḍi wa maa tureedu an takoona minal-muṣliḥeen.

20. Wa jaaa'a rajulum-min aqṣal-madeenati yas'aa qaala yaa Moosaaa innal-mala-a yaâ-tamiroona bika liyaqtulooka fakhruj innee laka minan-naaṣiḥeen.

21. Fakharaja minhaa khaaa-'ifañy-yataraqqab; qaala Rabbi najjinee minal-qawmiẓ-ẓaali-meen. **(Section 2)**

22. Wa lammaa tawajjaha tilqaaa'a Madyana qaala 'asaa Rabbeee añy-yahdiyanee Sa-waaa'as-Sabeel.

23. Wa lammaa warada maaa'a Madyana wajada 'alayhi ummatam-minannaasi yasqoona wa wajada min doonihimum-ra-atayni tazoo-daani qaala maa khaṭbukumaa qaalataa laa nasqee ḥattaa yuṣdirar-ri'aaa'u wa aboonaa shaykhun kabeer.

24. Fasaqaa lahumaa summa tawallaaa ilaẓ-ẓilli faqaala Rabbi innee limaaa anzalta ilayya min khayrin faqeer.

25. Fajaaa'at-hu iḥdaahumaa tamshee 'alas-tiḥyaaa'in qaalat inna abee yad'ooka li-yajziyaka ajra maa saqayta lanaa; falammaa jaaa'ahoo wa qaṣṣa 'alayhil-qaṣaṣa

هُوَ عَدُوٌّ لَّهُمَا ۚ قَالَ يٰمُوْسٰٓى اَتُرِيْدُ
اَنْ تَقْتُلَنِيْ كَمَا قَتَلْتَ نَفْسًا
بِالْاَمْسِ ۖ اِنْ تُرِيْدُ اِلَّآ اَنْ تَكُوْنَ
جَبَّارًا فِي الْاَرْضِ وَمَا تُرِيْدُ اَنْ
تَكُوْنَ مِنَ الْمُصْلِحِيْنَ ﴿١٩﴾
وَجَآءَ رَجُلٌ مِّنْ اَقْصَا الْمَدِيْنَةِ
يَسْعٰى ۡ قَالَ يٰمُوْسٰٓى اِنَّ الْمَلَاَ يَاْتَمِرُوْنَ
بِكَ لِيَقْتُلُوْكَ فَاخْرُجْ اِنِّيْ لَكَ
مِنَ النّٰصِحِيْنَ ﴿٢٠﴾
فَخَرَجَ مِنْهَا خَآئِفًا يَّتَرَقَّبُ ۡ قَالَ
رَبِّ نَجِّنِيْ مِنَ الْقَوْمِ الظّٰلِمِيْنَ ﴿٢١﴾ ع
وَلَمَّا تَوَجَّهَ تِلْقَآءَ مَدْيَنَ قَالَ عَسٰى
رَبِّيْٓ اَنْ يَّهْدِيَنِيْ سَوَآءَ السَّبِيْلِ ﴿٢٢﴾
وَلَمَّا وَرَدَ مَآءَ مَدْيَنَ وَجَدَ عَلَيْهِ
اُمَّةً مِّنَ النَّاسِ يَسْقُوْنَ ۡ وَوَجَدَ
مِنْ دُوْنِهِمُ امْرَاَتَيْنِ تَذُوْدٰنِ ۚ
قَالَ مَا خَطْبُكُمَا ۖ قَالَتَا لَا نَسْقِيْ
حَتّٰى يُصْدِرَ الرِّعَآءُ ۚ وَاَبُوْنَا
شَيْخٌ كَبِيْرٌ ﴿٢٣﴾
فَسَقٰى لَهُمَا ثُمَّ تَوَلّٰٓى اِلَى الظِّلِّ
فَقَالَ رَبِّ اِنِّيْ لِمَآ اَنْزَلْتَ اِلَيَّ مِنْ
خَيْرٍ فَقِيْرٌ ﴿٢٤﴾
فَجَآءَتْهُ اِحْدٰىهُمَا تَمْشِيْ عَلَى
اسْتِحْيَآءٍ ۡ قَالَتْ اِنَّ اَبِيْ يَدْعُوْكَ
لِيَجْزِيَكَ اَجْرَ مَا سَقَيْتَ لَنَا ۭ فَلَمَّا
جَآءَهٗ وَقَصَّ عَلَيْهِ الْقَصَصَ ۙ

Ikhfa اخفاء | Ghunna غنّہ | Ikhfa Meem Saakin اخفاء میم ساکن | Idghaam ادغام | Qalqala قلقلہ | Qalb قلب | Idghaam Meem Saakin ادغام میم ساکن

he said: "you do not fear: (well) have you escaped from unjust people."

qaala laa takhaf najawta minal-qawmiẓ-ẓaalimeen.

قَالَ لَا تَخَفْ ۖ نَجَوْتَ مِنَ الْقَوْمِ
الظّٰلِمِيْنَ ﴿٢٥﴾

26. Said one of the (damsels): "O my (dear) father! engage him on wages: truly the best of men for you to employ is the (man) who is strong and trustworthy."

26. Qaalat iḥdaahumaa yaaa abatis-taâjirhu inna khayra manis-taâjartal-qawiyyul-ameen.

قَالَتْ اِحْدٰىهُمَا يٰٓاَبَتِ اسْتَاْجِرْهُ ۖ اِنَّ
خَيْرَ مَنِ اسْتَاْجَرْتَ الْقَوِيُّ الْاَمِيْنُ ﴿٢٦﴾

27. He said: "I intend to wed one of these my daughters to you, on condition that you serve me for eight years; but if you complete ten years, it will be (grace) from you. But I intend not to place you under a difficulty: you will find me, indeed, if Allah wills, one of the righteous."

27. Qaala inneee ureedu an unkiḥaka iḥdab-natayya haatayni 'alaaa an taâjuranee ṯamaaniya ḥijaj; fa-in atmamta 'ashran famin 'indika wa maaa ureedu an ashuqqa 'alayk; satajiduneee in shaaa'al-laahu minaṣ-ṣaaliḥeen.

قَالَ اِنِّيْٓ اُرِيْدُ اَنْ اُنْكِحَكَ اِحْدَى
ابْنَتَيَّ هٰتَيْنِ عَلٰٓى اَنْ تَاْجُرَنِيْ ثَمٰنِيَ
حِجَجٍ ۚ فَاِنْ اَتْمَمْتَ عَشْرًا فَمِنْ
عِنْدِكَ ۚ وَمَآ اُرِيْدُ اَنْ اَشُقَّ عَلَيْكَ ۗ
سَتَجِدُنِيْٓ اِنْ شَآءَ اللّٰهُ مِنَ الصّٰلِحِيْنَ ﴿٢٧﴾

28. He said: "Be that (the agreement) between me and you: whichever of the two terms I fulfil, let there be no ill-will to me. Be Allah a witness to what we say."

28. Qaala ẕaalika baynee wa baynaka ayyamal-ajalayni qaḍaytu falaa 'udwaana 'alayya wallaahu 'alaa maa naqoolu Wakeel. **(Section 3)**

قَالَ ذٰلِكَ بَيْنِيْ وَبَيْنَكَ ۗ اَيَّمَا
الْاَجَلَيْنِ قَضَيْتُ فَلَا عُدْوَانَ عَلَيَّ ۗ
وَاللّٰهُ عَلٰى مَا نَقُوْلُ وَكِيْلٌ ﴿٢٨﴾ ع ٣

29. Now when Moses had fulfilled the term, and was travelling with his family, he perceived a fire in the direction of Mount Tur. He said to his family: "You tarry; I perceive a fire; I hope to bring you from there some information, or a burning firebrand, that you may warm yourselves."

29. Falammaa qaḍaa Moosal-ajala wa saara bi-ahliheee aanasa min jaanibiṭ-Ṭoori naaran qaala li-ahlihim-kuṯooo inneee aanastu naaral-la'alleee aateekum-minhaa bikhabarin aw jaẕwatim-minan-naari la-'allakum taṣṭaloon.

فَلَمَّا قَضٰى مُوْسَى الْاَجَلَ وَسَارَ
بِاَهْلِهٖٓ اٰنَسَ مِنْ جَانِبِ الطُّوْرِ
نَارًا ۚ قَالَ لِاَهْلِهِ امْكُثُوْٓا اِنِّيْٓ
اٰنَسْتُ نَارًا لَّعَلِّيْٓ اٰتِيْكُمْ مِّنْهَا
بِخَبَرٍ اَوْ جَذْوَةٍ مِّنَ النَّارِ
لَعَلَّكُمْ تَصْطَلُوْنَ ﴿٢٩﴾

30. But when he came to the (fire), a voice was heard from the right bank of the valley, from a tree in hallowed ground: "O Moses! Verily I am Allah, the Lord of the Worlds....

30. Falammaaa ataahaa noodiya min shaaṭi'il-waadil-aymani fil-buq'atil-mubaarakati minash-shajarati añy-yaa Moosaaa inneee Anal-laahu Rabbul-'aalameen.

فَلَمَّآ اَتٰىهَا نُوْدِيَ مِنْ شَاطِئِ الْوَادِ
الْاَيْمَنِ فِي الْبُقْعَةِ الْمُبٰرَكَةِ
مِنَ الشَّجَرَةِ اَنْ يّٰمُوْسٰٓى اِنِّيْٓ اَنَا
اللّٰهُ رَبُّ الْعٰلَمِيْنَ ﴿٣٠﴾ ۙ

31. "Now you throw your rod!" but when he saw it moving (of its own accord) as if it had been a snake, he turned back in retreat, and did not retrace his steps: O Moses!" (It was said), "Draw near, and fear not: for you are of those who are secure.

31. Wa-an alqi 'aṣaaka falammaa ra-aahaa tahtazzu ka-annahaa jaaannuñw-wallaa mudbirañw-wa lam yu'aqqib; yaa Moosaaa aqbil wa laa takhaf innaka minal-aamineen.

وَاَنْ اَلْقِ عَصَاكَ ۗ فَلَمَّا رَاٰهَا تَهْتَزُّ
كَاَنَّهَا جَآنٌّ وَّلّٰى مُدْبِرًا وَّلَمْ
يُعَقِّبْ ۗ يٰمُوْسٰٓى اَقْبِلْ وَلَا تَخَفْ ۫
اِنَّكَ مِنَ الْاٰمِنِيْنَ ﴿٣١﴾

Ikhfa اخفاء | Ghunna غنّہ | Ikhfa Meem Saakin اخفاء میم ساکن | Idghaam ادغام | Qalqala قلقلہ | Qalb قلب | Idghaam Meem Saakin ادغام میم ساکن

32. "Move your hand into your bosom, and it will come forth white without stain (or harm), and draw your hand close to your side (to guard) against fear. Those are the two credentials from your Lord to Pharaoh and his Chiefs: for truly they are a people rebellious and wicked."

32. Usluk yadaka fee jaybika takhruj bayḍaaa'a min ghayri sooo'iñw-waḍmum ilayka janaaḥaka minar-rahbi fazaa-nika burhaanaani mir-Rabbika ilaa Fir'awna wa mala'ih; innahum kaanoo qawman faasiqeen.

اُسْلُكْ يَدَكَ فِيْ جَيْبِكَ تَخْرُجْ بَيْضَآءَ
مِنْ غَيْرِ سُوْٓءٍ ز وَّاضْمُمْ اِلَيْكَ
جَنَاحَكَ مِنَ الرَّهْبِ فَذٰنِكَ بُرْهَانٰنِ
مِنْ رَّبِّكَ اِلٰى فِرْعَوْنَ وَمَلَا۟ئِهٖ ط
اِنَّهُمْ كَانُوْا قَوْمًا فٰسِقِيْنَ ﴿٣٢﴾

33. He said: "O my Lord! I have slain a man among them, and I fear lest they slay me.

33. Qaala Rabbi innee qataltu minhum nafsan fa-akhaafu añy-yaqtuloon.

قَالَ رَبِّ اِنِّيْ قَتَلْتُ مِنْهُمْ نَفْسًا
فَاَخَافُ اَنْ يَّقْتُلُوْنِ ﴿٣٣﴾

34. "And my brother Aaron - He is more eloquent in speech than I: so send him with me as a helper, to confirm (and strengthen) me: for I fear that they may accuse me of falsehood."

34. Wa akhee Haaroonu huwa afṣaḥu minnee lisaanan fa-arsilhu ma'iya rid-añy-yuṣaddi-quneee inneee akhaafu añy-yukazziboon.

وَاَخِيْ هٰرُوْنُ هُوَ اَفْصَحُ مِنِّيْ لِسَانًا
فَاَرْسِلْهُ مَعِيَ رِدْاً يُّصَدِّقُنِيْٓ ز
اِنِّيْٓ اَخَافُ اَنْ يُّكَذِّبُوْنِ ﴿٣٤﴾

35. He said: "We will certainly strengthen your arm through your brother, and invest you both with authority, so they shall not be able to touch you: with Our Signs shall you triumph,- you two as well as those who follow you."

35. Qaala sanashuddu 'aḍuda-ka bi-akheeka wa naj'alu lakumaa sulṭaanan falaa yaṣiloona ilaykumaa; bi-Aayaa-tinaa antumaa wa manit-taba'akumal-ghaaliboon.

قَالَ سَنَشُدُّ عَضُدَكَ بِاَخِيْكَ
وَنَجْعَلُ لَكُمَا سُلْطٰنًا فَلَا
يَصِلُوْنَ اِلَيْكُمَا ج بِاٰيٰتِنَا ج اَنْتُمَا
وَمَنِ اتَّبَعَكُمَا الْغٰلِبُوْنَ ﴿٣٥﴾

36. When Moses came to them with Our clear signs, they said: "This is nothing but sorcery faked up: never did we hear the like among our fathers of old!"

36. Falammaa jaaa'ahum-Moosaa bi-Aayaatinaa bayyi-naatin qaaloo maa haazaaa illaa siḥrum-muftarañw-wa maa sami'naa bihaazaa feee aabaaa-'inal-awwaleen.

فَلَمَّا جَآءَهُمْ مُّوْسٰى بِاٰيٰتِنَا بَيِّنٰتٍ
قَالُوْا مَا هٰذَآ اِلَّا سِحْرٌ مُّفْتَرًى
وَّمَا سَمِعْنَا بِهٰذَا فِيْٓ اٰبَآئِنَا
الْاَوَّلِيْنَ ﴿٣٦﴾

37. Moses said: "My Lord knows best who it is that comes with guidance from Him and whose end will be best in the Hereafter: certain it is that the wrong-doers will not prosper."

37. Wa qaala Moosaa Rab-beee a'lamu biman jaaa'a bilhudaa min 'indihee wa man takoonu lahoo 'aaqibatud-daari innahoo laa yufliḥuẓ-ẓaali-moon.

وَقَالَ مُوْسٰى رَبِّيْٓ اَعْلَمُ بِمَنْ جَآءَ
بِالْهُدٰى مِنْ عِنْدِهٖ وَمَنْ تَكُوْنُ
لَهٗ عَاقِبَةُ الدَّارِ ط اِنَّهٗ لَا يُفْلِحُ
الظّٰلِمُوْنَ ﴿٣٧﴾

38. Pharaoh said: "O Chiefs! no god do I know for you but myself: therefore, O Haman! light me a (kiln to bake bricks) out of clay, and build me a lofty palace, that I may mount up to the god of Moses:

38. Wa qaala Fir'awnu yaaa ayyuhal-mala-u maa 'alimtu lakum-min ilaahin ghayree fa-awqid lee yaa Haamaanu 'alaṭ-ṭeeni faj'al-lee ṣarḥal-la'alleee aṭṭali'u ilaaa ilaahi Moosaa

وَقَالَ فِرْعَوْنُ يٰٓاَيُّهَا الْمَلَاُ مَا عَلِمْتُ
لَكُمْ مِّنْ اِلٰهٍ غَيْرِيْ ج فَاَوْقِدْ لِيْ
يٰهَامٰنُ عَلَى الطِّيْنِ فَاجْعَلْ لِّيْ
صَرْحًا لَّعَلِّيْٓ اَطَّلِعُ اِلٰٓى اِلٰهِ مُوْسٰى

مُعانقة ١١ عند المتأخرين ١٢

Ikhfa	Ghunna	Ikhfa Meem Saakin	Idghaam	Qalqala	Qalb	Idghaam Meem Saakin
اخفاء	غُنّہ	اخفاء میم ساکن	ادغام	قلقلہ	قلب	ادغام میم ساکن

but as far as I am concerned, I think he (Moses) is a liar!"

39. And he was arrogant and insolent in the land, beyond reason,- he and his hosts: they thought that they would not have to return to Us!

40. So We seized him and his hosts, and We flung them into the sea: now behold what was the end of those who did wrong!

41. And we made them (but) leaders inviting to the Fire; and on the Day of Judgment no help shall they find.

42. in this world We made a curse to follow them and on the Day of Judgment they will be among the loathed (and despised).

43. We did reveal to Moses the Book after We had destroyed the earlier generations, (to give) Insight to men, and Guidance and Mercy, that they might receive admonition.

44. You were not on the Western side when We decreed the Commission to Moses, nor were you a witness (of those events).

45. But We raised up (new) generations, and long were the ages that passed over them; but you were not a dweller among the people of Madyan, rehearsing Our Signs to them; but it is We Who send Messengers (with inspiration).

46. Nor were you at the side of (the Mountain of) Tur when we called (to Moses). Yet (are you sent) as Mercy from your Lord, to give warning to a people to whom no warner had come before you: in order that they may receive admonition.

wa innee la-aẓunnuhoo minal-kaaz̲ibeen.

39. Wastakbara huwa wa junooduhoo fil-arḍi bighayril-ḥaqqi wa ẓannoo annahum ilaynaa laa yurja'oon.

40. Fa-akhaz̲naahu wa junoodahoo fanabaz̲naahum fil-yammi fanẓur kayfa kaana 'aaqibatuẓ-ẓaalimeen.

41. Wa ja'alnaahum a'immatañy-yad'oona ilan-Naari wa Yawmal-Qiyaamati laa yunṣaroon.

42. Wa atba'naahum fee haaz̲ihid-dunyaa la'natañw wa Yawmal-Qiyaamati hum-minal-maqbooḥeen. **(Section 4)**

43. Wa laqad aataynaa Moosal-Kitaaba mim ba'di maaa ahlaknal-quroonal-oolaa baṣaaa'ira linnaasi wa hudañw-wa raḥmatal-la'allahum yataz̲akkaroon.

44. Wa maa kunta bijaanibil-gharbiyyi iz̲ qaḍaynaaa ilaa Moosal-amra wa maa kunta minash-shaahideen.

45. Wa laakinnaaa anshaånaa quroonan fataṭaawala 'alay-himul-'umur; wa maa kunta s̲aawiyan feee ahli Madyana tatloo 'alayhim Aayaatinaa wa laakinnaa kunnaa mursileen.

46. Wa maa kunta bijaanibiṭ-Ṭoori iz̲ naadaynaa wa laakir-raḥmatam-mir-Rabbika litunz̲ira qawmam-maaa ataahum-min-naz̲eerim-min qablika la'allahum yataz̲akkaroon.

وَإِنِّي لَأَظُنُّهُۥ مِنَ ٱلْكَٰذِبِينَ ٣٨
وَٱسْتَكْبَرَ هُوَ وَجُنُودُهُۥ فِي ٱلْأَرْضِ
بِغَيْرِ ٱلْحَقِّ وَظَنُّوٓاْ أَنَّهُمْ إِلَيْنَا
لَا يُرْجَعُونَ ٣٩
فَأَخَذْنَٰهُ وَجُنُودَهُۥ فَنَبَذْنَٰهُمْ فِي ٱلْيَمِّ
فَٱنظُرْ كَيْفَ كَانَ عَٰقِبَةُ ٱلظَّٰلِمِينَ ٤٠
وَجَعَلْنَٰهُمْ أَئِمَّةً يَدْعُونَ إِلَى
ٱلنَّارِ وَيَوْمَ ٱلْقِيَٰمَةِ لَا يُنصَرُونَ ٤١
وَأَتْبَعْنَٰهُمْ فِي هَٰذِهِ ٱلدُّنْيَا
لَعْنَةً وَيَوْمَ ٱلْقِيَٰمَةِ هُم مِّنَ
ٱلْمَقْبُوحِينَ ٤٢ ع
وَلَقَدْ ءَاتَيْنَا مُوسَى ٱلْكِتَٰبَ مِنۢ بَعْدِ
مَآ أَهْلَكْنَا ٱلْقُرُونَ ٱلْأُولَىٰ بَصَآئِرَ
لِلنَّاسِ وَهُدًى وَرَحْمَةً لَّعَلَّهُمْ
يَتَذَكَّرُونَ ٤٣
وَمَا كُنتَ بِجَانِبِ ٱلْغَرْبِيِّ إِذْ
قَضَيْنَآ إِلَىٰ مُوسَى ٱلْأَمْرَ وَمَا
كُنتَ مِنَ ٱلشَّٰهِدِينَ ٤٤
وَلَٰكِنَّآ أَنشَأْنَا قُرُونًا فَتَطَاوَلَ
عَلَيْهِمُ ٱلْعُمُرُ وَمَا كُنتَ ثَاوِيًا فِيٓ
أَهْلِ مَدْيَنَ تَتْلُواْ عَلَيْهِمْ ءَايَٰتِنَا
وَلَٰكِنَّا كُنَّا مُرْسِلِينَ ٤٥
وَمَا كُنتَ بِجَانِبِ ٱلطُّورِ إِذْ نَادَيْنَا
وَلَٰكِن رَّحْمَةً مِّن رَّبِّكَ لِتُنذِرَ
قَوْمًا مَّآ أَتَىٰهُم مِّن نَّذِيرٍ مِّن
قَبْلِكَ لَعَلَّهُمْ يَتَذَكَّرُونَ ٤٦

Ikhfa اخفاء | Ghunna غُنّہ | Ikhfa Meem Saakin اخفاءمیم ساکن | Idghaam ادغام | Qalqala قلقلہ | Qalb قلب | Idghaam Meem Saakin ادغام میم ساکن

47. If (We had) not (sent you to the Quraish),- in case a calamity should seize them for (the deeds) that their hands have sent forth, they might say: "Our Lord! why did You not sent us a Messenger? We should then have followed Your Signs and been amongst those who believe!"

47. Wa law laaa an tuṣeebahum-muṣeebatum bimaa qaddamat aydeehim fa-yaqooloo Rabbanaa law laaa arsalta ilaynaa Rasoolan fanattabi'a Aayaatika wa nakoona minal-mu'mineen.

وَلَوْلَآ أَن تُصِيبَهُم مُّصِيبَةٌۢ بِمَا
قَدَّمَتْ أَيْدِيهِمْ فَيَقُولُوا۟ رَبَّنَا
لَوْلَآ أَرْسَلْتَ إِلَيْنَا رَسُولًا فَنَتَّبِعَ
ءَايَٰتِكَ وَنَكُونَ مِنَ ٱلْمُؤْمِنِينَ ﴿٤٧﴾

48. But (now), when the Truth has come to them from Ourselves, they say, "Why are not (Signs) sent to him, like those which were sent to Moses?" Do they not then reject (the Signs) which were formerly sent to Moses? They say: "Two kinds of sorcery, each assisting the other!" And they say: "For us, we reject all (such things)!"

48. Falammaa jaaa'ahumul-ḥaqqu min 'indinaa qaaloo law laaa ootiya misla maaa ootiya Moosaa; awalam yakfuroo bimaaa ootiya Moosaa min qablu qaaloo siḥraani taẓaaharaa wa qaalooo innaa bikullin kaafiroon.

فَلَمَّا جَآءَهُمُ ٱلْحَقُّ مِنْ عِندِنَا قَالُوا۟
لَوْلَآ أُوتِىَ مِثْلَ مَآ أُوتِىَ مُوسَىٰٓ ۚ
أَوَلَمْ يَكْفُرُوا۟ بِمَآ أُوتِىَ مُوسَىٰ مِن
قَبْلُ ۖ قَالُوا۟ سِحْرَانِ تَظَٰهَرَا ۖ وَ
قَالُوٓا۟ إِنَّا بِكُلٍّ كَٰفِرُونَ ﴿٤٨﴾

49. Say: "Then bring you a Book from Allah, which is a better guide than either of them, that I may follow it! (do), if you are truthful!"

49. Qul faåtoo bi-Kitaabim-min 'indil-laahi huwa ahdaa minhumaaa attabi'hu in kuntum ṣaadiqeen.

قُلْ فَأْتُوا۟ بِكِتَٰبٍ مِّنْ عِندِ ٱللَّهِ
هُوَ أَهْدَىٰ مِنْهُمَآ أَتَّبِعْهُ إِن كُنتُمْ
صَٰدِقِينَ ﴿٤٩﴾

50. But if they hearken not to you, know that they only follow their own lusts: and who is more astray than one who follow his own lusts, devoid of guidance from Allah? for Allah does not guide people given to wrongdoing.

50. Fa-il-lam yastajeeboo laka fa'lam annamaa yattabi'oona ahwaaa'ahum; wa man aḍallu mimmanit-taba'a hawaahu bighayri hudam-minal-laah; innal-laaha laa yahdil-qawmaẓ-ẓaalimeen. **(Section 5)**

فَإِن لَّمْ يَسْتَجِيبُوا۟ لَكَ فَٱعْلَمْ أَنَّمَا
يَتَّبِعُونَ أَهْوَآءَهُمْ ۚ وَمَنْ أَضَلُّ
مِمَّنِ ٱتَّبَعَ هَوَىٰهُ بِغَيْرِ هُدًى
مِّنَ ٱللَّهِ ۚ إِنَّ ٱللَّهَ لَا يَهْدِى
ٱلْقَوْمَ ٱلظَّٰلِمِينَ ﴿٥٠﴾ ع

51. Now have We caused the Word to reach them themselves, in order that they may receive admonition.

51. Wa laqad waṣṣalnaa lahumul-qawla la'allahum yatazakkaroon.

وَلَقَدْ وَصَّلْنَا لَهُمُ ٱلْقَوْلَ لَعَلَّهُمْ
يَتَذَكَّرُونَ ﴿٥١﴾

52. Those to whom We sent the Book before this,- they do believe in this (revelation):

52. Allazeena aataynaahumul-Kitaaba min qablihee hum bihee yu'minoon.

ٱلَّذِينَ ءَاتَيْنَٰهُمُ ٱلْكِتَٰبَ مِن قَبْلِهِۦ
هُم بِهِۦ يُؤْمِنُونَ ﴿٥٢﴾ النصف

53. And when it is recited to them, they say: "We believe therein, for it is the Truth from our Lord: indeed we have been Muslims (bowing to Allah's Will) from before this.

53. Wa izaa yutlaa 'alayhim qaaloo aamannaa biheee innahul-ḥaqqu mir-Rabbinaaa innaa kunnaa min qablihee muslimeen.

وَإِذَا يُتْلَىٰ عَلَيْهِمْ قَالُوٓا۟ ءَامَنَّا بِهِۦٓ
إِنَّهُ ٱلْحَقُّ مِن رَّبِّنَآ إِنَّا كُنَّا مِن
قَبْلِهِۦ مُسْلِمِينَ ﴿٥٣﴾

54. Twice will they be given their reward, for that they have persevered, that they avert Evil with Good,

54. Ulaaa'ika yu'tawna ajrahum-marratayni bimaa ṣabaroo wa yadra'oona bil-ḥasanatis-

أُو۟لَٰٓئِكَ يُؤْتَوْنَ أَجْرَهُم مَّرَّتَيْنِ
بِمَا صَبَرُوا۟ وَيَدْرَءُونَ بِٱلْحَسَنَةِ

Ikhfa اخفاء | Ghunna غُنّہ | Ikhfa Meem Saakin اخفاء میم ساکن | Idghaam ادغام | Qalqala قلقلہ | Qalb قلب | Idghaam Meem Saakin ادغام میم ساکن

and that they spend (in charity) out of what We have given them.

sayyi'ata wa mimmaa razaqnaahum yunfiqoon.

السَّيِّئَةَ وَمِمَّا رَزَقْنٰهُمْ يُنْفِقُوْنَ ﴿٥٤﴾

55. And when they hear vain talk, they turn away therefrom and say: "To us our deeds, and to you yours; peace be to you: we do not seek the ignorant."

55. Wa izaa sami'ul-laghwa a'raḍoo 'anhu wa qaaloo lanaaa a'maalunaa wa lakum a'maalukum salaamun 'alaykum laa nabtaghil-jaahileen.

وَاِذَا سَمِعُوا اللَّغْوَ اَعْرَضُوْا عَنْهُ
وَقَالُوْا لَنَآ اَعْمَالُنَا وَلَكُمْ اَعْمَالُكُمْ
سَلٰمٌ عَلَيْكُمْ لَا نَبْتَغِي الْجٰهِلِيْنَ ﴿٥٥﴾

56. It is true you will not be able to guide everyone, whom you love; but Allah guides those whom He will and He knows best those who receive guidance.

56. Innaka laa tahdee man aḥbabta wa laakinnal-laaha yahdee mañy-yashaaa'; wa Huwa a'lamu bilmuhtadeen.

اِنَّكَ لَا تَهْدِيْ مَنْ اَحْبَبْتَ وَ
لٰكِنَّ اللّٰهَ يَهْدِيْ مَنْ يَّشَآءُ ۚ وَهُوَ
اَعْلَمُ بِالْمُهْتَدِيْنَ ﴿٥٦﴾

57. They say: "If we were to follow the guidance with you, we should be snatched away from our land." Have We not established for them a secure sanctuary, to which are brought as tribute fruits of all kinds,- a provision from Ourselves? but most of them do not understand.

57. Wa qaalooo in-nattabi'il-hudaa ma'aka nutakhaṭṭaf min arḍinaa; awalam numakkil-lahum ḥaraman aaminañy-yujbaaa ilayhi samaraatu kulli shay'ir-rizqam-mil-ladunnaa wa laakinna aksarahum laa ya'lamoon.

وَقَالُوْٓا اِنْ نَّتَّبِعِ الْهُدٰى مَعَكَ
نُتَخَطَّفْ مِنْ اَرْضِنَا ؕ اَوَلَمْ نُمَكِّنْ
لَّهُمْ حَرَمًا اٰمِنًا يُّجْبٰٓى اِلَيْهِ
ثَمَرٰتُ كُلِّ شَيْءٍ رِّزْقًا مِّنْ لَّدُنَّا
وَلٰكِنَّ اَكْثَرَهُمْ لَا يَعْلَمُوْنَ ﴿٥٧﴾

58. And how many populations We destroyed, which exulted in their life (of ease and plenty)! now those habitations of theirs, after them, are deserted,- All but a (miserable) few! and We are their heirs!

58. Wa kam ahlaknaa min qaryatim baṭirat ma'eeshatahaa fatilka masaakinuhum lam tuskam-mim ba'dihim illaa qaleelaa; wa kunnaa Naḥnul-waariseen.

وَكَمْ اَهْلَكْنَا مِنْ قَرْيَةٍۢ بَطِرَتْ
مَعِيْشَتَهَا ۚ فَتِلْكَ مَسٰكِنُهُمْ لَمْ تُسْكَنْ
مِّنْۢ بَعْدِهِمْ اِلَّا قَلِيْلًا ؕ وَكُنَّا نَحْنُ
الْوٰرِثِيْنَ ﴿٥٨﴾

59. Nor was your Lord the one to destroy a population until He had sent to its centre a Messenger, rehearsing to them Our Signs; nor are We going to destroy a population except when its members practise iniquity.

59. Wa maa kaana Rabbuka muhlikal-quraa ḥattaa yab'asa feee ummihaa Rasoolañy-yatloo 'alayhim Aayaatinaa; wa maa kunnaa muhlikil-quraaa illaa wa ahluhaa ẓaalimoon.

وَمَا كَانَ رَبُّكَ مُهْلِكَ الْقُرٰى
حَتّٰى يَبْعَثَ فِيْٓ اُمِّهَا رَسُوْلًا يَّتْلُوْا
عَلَيْهِمْ اٰيٰتِنَا ۚ وَمَا كُنَّا مُهْلِكِي
الْقُرٰٓى اِلَّا وَاَهْلُهَا ظٰلِمُوْنَ ﴿٥٩﴾

60. The (material) things which you are given are but the conveniences of this life and the glitter thereof; but that which is with Allah is better and more enduring: will you not then be wise?

60. Wa maaa ooteetum-min shay'in famataa'ul-ḥayaatid-dunyaa wa zeenatuhaa; wa maa 'indal-laahi khayruñw-wa abqaa; afalaa ta'qiloon. **(Sec. 6)**

وَمَآ اُوْتِيْتُمْ مِّنْ شَيْءٍ فَمَتَاعُ
الْحَيٰوةِ الدُّنْيَا وَزِيْنَتُهَا ۚ وَمَا عِنْدَ
اللّٰهِ خَيْرٌ وَّاَبْقٰى ؕ اَفَلَا تَعْقِلُوْنَ ﴿٦٠﴾

61. Are (these two) alike?- one to whom We have made a goodly promise, and who is going to reach its (fulfilment), and one to whom We have given the good things of this life, but who, on the Day of Judgment,

61. Afamañw-wa'adnaahu wa'dan ḥasanan fahuwa laaqeehi kamam-matta'naahu mataa'al-ḥayaatid-dunyaa summa huwa Yawmal-Qiyaamati

اَفَمَنْ وَّعَدْنٰهُ وَعْدًا حَسَنًا
فَهُوَ لَاقِيْهِ كَمَنْ مَّتَّعْنٰهُ مَتَاعَ
الْحَيٰوةِ الدُّنْيَا ثُمَّ هُوَ يَوْمَ الْقِيٰمَةِ

Ikhfa اخفاء | Ghunna غُنّہ | Ikhfa Meem Saakin اخفاء میم ساکن | Idghaam ادغام | Qalqala قلقلہ | Qalb قلب | Idghaam Meem Saakin ادغام میم ساکن

is to be among those brought up (for punishment)?

62. That Day (Allah) will call to them, and say "Where are my 'partners'?- whom you imagined (to be such)?"

63. Those against whom the charge will be proved, will say: "Our Lord! These are the ones whom we led astray: we led them astray, as we were astray ourselves: we free ourselves (from them) in your presence: it was not us they worshipped."

64. It will be said (to them): "Call upon your 'partners' (for help)" :they will call upon them, but they will not listen to them; and they will see the Penalty (before them); (how they will wish) 'if only they had been open to guidance!'

65. That Day (Allah) will call to them, and say: "What was the answer you gave to the Messenger?"

66. Then the (whole) story that Day will seem obscure to them (like light to the blind) and they will not be able (even) to question each other.

67. But any that (in this life) had repented, believed, and worked righteousness, haply he shall be one of the successful.

68. Your Lord creates and chooses as He pleases: no choice have they (in the matter): Glory to Allah! and far is He above the partners they ascribe (to Him)!

69. And your Lord knows all that their hearts conceal and all that they reveal.

70. And He is Allah: there is no God but He. To Him be praise, at the first and at the last: for Him is the Command, and to Him shall you (all) be brought back.

71. Say, do you see? If Allah were to make the night perpetual over you to the Day of Judgment, what

minal-muḥḍareen.

62. Wa Yawma yunaadeehim fa-yaqoolu ayna shurakaaa-'iyal-lazeena kuntum taz'u-moon.

63. Qaalal-lazeena ḥaqqa 'alayhimul-qawlu Rabbanaa haaa'ulaaa'il-lazeena aghway-naa aghwaynaahum kamaa gha-waynaa tabarraånaaa ilayka maa kaanooo iyyaanaa ya'bu-doon.

64. Wa qeelad-'oo shura-kaaa'akum fada'awhum falam yastajeeboo lahum wa ra-awul-'azaab; law annahum kaanoo yahtadoon.

65. Wa Yawma yunaadeehim fa-yaqoolu maazaaa ajabtumul-mursaleen.

66. Fa'amiyat 'alayhimul-ambaaa'u Yawma'izin fahum laa yatasaaa'aloon.

67. Fa-ammaa man taaba wa aamana wa 'amila ṣaaliḥan fa'asaaa añy-yakoona minal-mufliḥeen.

68. Wa Rabbuka yakhluqu maa yashaaa'u wa yakhtaar; maa kaana lahumul-khiyarah; Subḥaanal-laahi wa Ta'aalaa 'ammaa yushrikoon.

69. Wa Rabbuka ya'lamu maa tukinnu ṣudooruhum wa maa yu'linoon.

70. Wa Huwal-laahu laaa ilaaha illaa Huwa lahul-ḥamdu fil-oolaa wal-Aakhirati wa la-hul-ḥukmu wa ilayhi turja'oon.

71. Qul ara'aytum in ja'alal-laahu 'alaykumul-layla sarma-dan ilaa Yawmil-Qiyaamati man

مِنَ الْمُحْضَرِينَ ﴿٦١﴾
وَيَوْمَ يُنَادِيهِمْ فَيَقُولُ أَيْنَ شُرَكَآءِيَ
الَّذِينَ كُنتُمْ تَزْعُمُونَ ﴿٦٢﴾
قَالَ الَّذِينَ حَقَّ عَلَيْهِمُ الْقَوْلُ رَبَّنَا
هَٰٓؤُلَآءِ الَّذِينَ أَغْوَيْنَا ۚ أَغْوَيْنَٰهُمْ
كَمَا غَوَيْنَا ۚ تَبَرَّأْنَآ إِلَيْكَ ۖ مَا كَانُوٓا
إِيَّانَا يَعْبُدُونَ ﴿٦٣﴾
وَقِيلَ ادْعُوا شُرَكَآءَكُمْ فَدَعَوْهُمْ
فَلَمْ يَسْتَجِيبُوا لَهُمْ وَرَأَوُا الْعَذَابَ ۚ
لَوْ أَنَّهُمْ كَانُوا يَهْتَدُونَ ﴿٦٤﴾
وَيَوْمَ يُنَادِيهِمْ فَيَقُولُ مَاذَآ
أَجَبْتُمُ الْمُرْسَلِينَ ﴿٦٥﴾
فَعَمِيَتْ عَلَيْهِمُ الْأَنۢبَآءُ يَوْمَئِذٍ
فَهُمْ لَا يَتَسَآءَلُونَ ﴿٦٦﴾
فَأَمَّا مَن تَابَ وَآمَنَ وَعَمِلَ صَالِحًا
فَعَسَىٰٓ أَن يَكُونَ مِنَ الْمُفْلِحِينَ ﴿٦٧﴾
وَرَبُّكَ يَخْلُقُ مَا يَشَآءُ وَيَخْتَارُ ۗ
مَا كَانَ لَهُمُ الْخِيَرَةُ ۚ سُبْحَٰنَ
اللَّهِ وَتَعَٰلَىٰ عَمَّا يُشْرِكُونَ ﴿٦٨﴾
وَرَبُّكَ يَعْلَمُ مَا تُكِنُّ صُدُورُهُمْ
وَمَا يُعْلِنُونَ ﴿٦٩﴾
وَهُوَ اللَّهُ لَآ إِلَٰهَ إِلَّا هُوَ ۖ لَهُ
الْحَمْدُ فِي الْأُولَىٰ وَالْآخِرَةِ ۖ وَلَهُ
الْحُكْمُ وَإِلَيْهِ تُرْجَعُونَ ﴿٧٠﴾
قُلْ أَرَءَيْتُمْ إِن جَعَلَ اللَّهُ عَلَيْكُمُ
الَّيْلَ سَرْمَدًا إِلَىٰ يَوْمِ الْقِيَٰمَةِ مَنْ

Ikhfa اخفاء | Ghunna غُنّہ | Ikhfa Meem Saakin اخفاء میم ساکن | Idghaam ادغام | Qalqala قلقلہ | Qalb قلب | Idghaam Meem Saakin ادغام میم ساکن

god is there other than Allah, who can give you enlightenment? Will you not then hearken?

72. Say, do you see? If Allah were to make the day perpetual over you to the Day of Judgment, what god is there other than Allah, Who can give you a Night in which you can rest? Will you not then see?

73. It is out of His Mercy that He has made for you Night and Day,- that you may rest therein, and that you may seek of his Grace;- and in order that you may be grateful.

74. The Day that He will call on them, He will say: "Where are my 'partners'?- whom you imagined (to be such)?"

75. And from each people shall We draw a witness, and We shall say: "Produce your Proof": then shall they know that the Truth is in Allah (alone), and the (lies) which they invented will leave them in lurch.

76. Qarun was doubtless, of the people of Moses; but he acted insolently towards them: such were the treasures We had bestowed on him that their very keys would have been a burden to a body of strong men, behold, his people said to him: "Do not exult, for Allah does not love those who exult (in riches).

77. "But seek, with the (wealth) which Allah has bestowed on you, the Home of the Hereafter, nor forget your portion in this world: but do you good, as Allah has been good to you, and do not seek (occasions for) mischief in the land: for Allah does not love those who do mischief."

ilaahun ghayrul-laahi yaâteekum biḍiyaaa'in afalaa tasma'oon.

72. Qul ara'aytum in ja'alal-laahu 'alaykumun-nahaara sarmadan ilaa Yawmil-Qiyaamati man ilaahun ghayrul-laahi yaâteekum bilaylin taskunoona feehi afalaa tubṣiroon.

73. Wa mir-raḥmatihee ja'ala lakumul-layla wannahaara litaskunoo feehi wa litabtaghoo min faḍlihee wa la'allakum tashkuroon.

74. Wa Yawma yunaadeehim fa-yaqoolu ayna shurakaaa'iyal-lazeena kuntum taz'umoon.

75. Wa naza'naa min kulli ummatin shaheedan faqulnaa haatoo burhaanakum fa'alimooo annal-ḥaqqa lillaahi wa ḍalla 'anhum-maa kaanoo yaftaroon. **(Section 7)**

76. Inna Qaaroona kaana min qawmi Moosaa fabaghaa 'alayhim wa aataynaahu minal-kunoozi maaa inna mafaatiḥahoo latanooo'u bil'uṣbati ulil-quwwati iz qaala lahoo qawmuhoo laa tafraḥ innal-laaha laa yuḥibbul-fariḥeen.

77. Wabtaghi feemaaa aataakal-laahud-Daaral-Aakhirata wa laa tansa naṣeebaka minad-dunyaa wa aḥsin kamaaa aḥsanal-laahu ilayka wa laa tabghil-fasaada fil-arḍi innal-laaha laa yuḥibbul-mufsideen.

إِلَٰهٌ غَيْرُ ٱللَّهِ يَأْتِيكُم بِضِيَآءٍ ۖ
أَفَلَا تَسْمَعُونَ ﴿٧١﴾
قُلْ أَرَءَيْتُمْ إِن جَعَلَ ٱللَّهُ عَلَيْكُمُ
ٱلنَّهَارَ سَرْمَدًا إِلَىٰ يَوْمِ ٱلْقِيَٰمَةِ
مَنْ إِلَٰهٌ غَيْرُ ٱللَّهِ يَأْتِيكُم بِلَيْلٍ
تَسْكُنُونَ فِيهِ ۖ أَفَلَا تُبْصِرُونَ ﴿٧٢﴾
وَمِن رَّحْمَتِهِۦ جَعَلَ لَكُمُ ٱلَّيْلَ
وَٱلنَّهَارَ لِتَسْكُنُوا۟ فِيهِ وَلِتَبْتَغُوا۟
مِن فَضْلِهِۦ وَلَعَلَّكُمْ تَشْكُرُونَ ﴿٧٣﴾
وَيَوْمَ يُنَادِيهِمْ فَيَقُولُ أَيْنَ
شُرَكَآءِىَ ٱلَّذِينَ كُنتُمْ تَزْعُمُونَ ﴿٧٤﴾
وَنَزَعْنَا مِن كُلِّ أُمَّةٍ شَهِيدًا
فَقُلْنَا هَاتُوا۟ بُرْهَٰنَكُمْ فَعَلِمُوٓا۟
أَنَّ ٱلْحَقَّ لِلَّهِ وَضَلَّ عَنْهُم مَّا
كَانُوا۟ يَفْتَرُونَ ﴿٧٥﴾
إِنَّ قَٰرُونَ كَانَ مِن قَوْمِ
مُوسَىٰ فَبَغَىٰ عَلَيْهِمْ ۖ وَءَاتَيْنَٰهُ
مِنَ ٱلْكُنُوزِ مَآ إِنَّ مَفَاتِحَهُۥ
لَتَنُوٓأُ بِٱلْعُصْبَةِ أُو۟لِى ٱلْقُوَّةِ
إِذْ قَالَ لَهُۥ قَوْمُهُۥ لَا تَفْرَحْ إِنَّ ٱللَّهَ
لَا يُحِبُّ ٱلْفَرِحِينَ ﴿٧٦﴾
وَٱبْتَغِ فِيمَآ ءَاتَىٰكَ ٱللَّهُ ٱلدَّارَ
ٱلْءَاخِرَةَ ۖ وَلَا تَنسَ نَصِيبَكَ مِنَ
ٱلدُّنْيَا ۖ وَأَحْسِن كَمَآ أَحْسَنَ ٱللَّهُ
إِلَيْكَ ۖ وَلَا تَبْغِ ٱلْفَسَادَ فِى ٱلْأَرْضِ ۖ
إِنَّ ٱللَّهَ لَا يُحِبُّ ٱلْمُفْسِدِينَ ﴿٧٧﴾

Ikhfa إخفاء · Ghunna غُنّة · Ikhfa Meem Saakin اخفاء ميم ساكن · Idghaam ادغام · Qalqala قلقله · Qalb قلب · Idghaam Meem Saakin ادغام ميم ساكن

78. He said: "This has been given to me because of a certain knowledge which I have." Did he not know that Allah had destroyed, before him, (whole) generations,- which were superior to him in strength and greater in the amount (of riches) they had collected? but the wicked are not called (immediately) to account for their sins.

78. Qaala innamaaa ooteetuhoo 'alaa 'ilmin 'indeee; awalam ya'lam annal-laaha qad ahlaka min qablihee minal-qurooni man huwa ashaddu minhu quwwatañw-wa aksaru jam'aa; wa laa yus'alu 'an zunoobihimul-mujrimoon.

قَالَ إِنَّمَآ أُوتِيتُهُۥ عَلَىٰ عِلۡمٍ
عِندِيٓۚ أَوَلَمۡ يَعۡلَمۡ أَنَّ ٱللَّهَ
قَدۡ أَهۡلَكَ مِن قَبۡلِهِۦ مِنَ ٱلۡقُرُونِ
مَنۡ هُوَ أَشَدُّ مِنۡهُ قُوَّةٗ وَ
أَكۡثَرُ جَمۡعٗاۚ وَلَا يُسۡـَٔلُ عَن
ذُنُوبِهِمُ ٱلۡمُجۡرِمُونَ ﴿٧٨﴾

79. So he went forth among his people in the (pride of his wordly) glitter. Said those whose aim is the Life of this World: "Oh! that we had the like of what Qarun has got! for he is truly a lord of mighty good fortune!"

79. Fakharaja 'alaa qawmihee fee zeenatih; qaalal-lazeena yureedoonal-ḥayaatad-dunyaa yaalayta lanaa misla maaa ootiya Qaaroonu innahoo lazoo ḥaẓẓin 'aẓeem.

فَخَرَجَ عَلَىٰ قَوۡمِهِۦ فِي زِينَتِهِۦۖ
قَالَ ٱلَّذِينَ يُرِيدُونَ ٱلۡحَيَوٰةَ
ٱلدُّنۡيَا يَٰلَيۡتَ لَنَا مِثۡلَ مَآ أُوتِيَ
قَٰرُونُ إِنَّهُۥ لَذُو حَظٍّ عَظِيمٖ ﴿٧٩﴾

80. But those who had been granted (true) knowledge said: "Alas for you! The reward of Allah (in the Hereafter) is best for those who believe and work righteousness: but this none shall attain, save those who steadfastly persevere (in good)."

80. Wa qaalal-lazeena ootul-'ilma waylakum sawaabul-laahi khayrul-liman aamana wa 'amila ṣaaliḥaa; wa laa yulaqqaahaaa illaṣ-ṣaabiroon.

وَقَالَ ٱلَّذِينَ أُوتُواْ ٱلۡعِلۡمَ
وَيۡلَكُمۡ ثَوَابُ ٱللَّهِ خَيۡرٞ لِّمَنۡ
ءَامَنَ وَعَمِلَ صَٰلِحٗاۚ وَلَا يُلَقَّىٰهَآ
إِلَّا ٱلصَّٰبِرُونَ ﴿٨٠﴾

81. Then We caused the earth to swallow up him and his house; and he had not (the least little) party to help him against Allah, nor could he defend himself.

81. Fakhasafnaa bihee wa bidaarihil-arḍa famaa kaana lahoo min fi'atiñy-yanṣuroonahoo min doonil-laahi wa maa kaana minal-muntaṣireen.

فَخَسَفۡنَا بِهِۦ وَبِدَارِهِ ٱلۡأَرۡضَ
فَمَا كَانَ لَهُۥ مِن فِئَةٖ يَنصُرُونَهُۥ
مِن دُونِ ٱللَّهِ وَمَا كَانَ مِنَ
ٱلۡمُنتَصِرِينَ ﴿٨١﴾

82. And those who had envied his position the day before began to say on the morrow: "Ah! it is indeed Allah Who enlarges the provision or restricts it, to any of His servants He pleases! Had it not been that Allah was gracious to us, He could have caused the earth to swallow us up! Ah! those who reject Allah will assuredly never prosper."

82. Wa aṣbaḥal-lazeena tamannaw makaanahoo bil-amsi yaqooloona wayka-annal-laaha yabsuṭur-rizqa limañy-yashaaa'u min 'ibaadihee wa yaqdiru law laaa am-mannal-laahu 'alaynaa lakhasafa binaa wayka-annahoo laa yufliḥul-kaafiroon. **(Section 8)**

وَأَصۡبَحَ ٱلَّذِينَ تَمَنَّوۡاْ مَكَانَهُۥ
بِٱلۡأَمۡسِ يَقُولُونَ وَيۡكَأَنَّ ٱللَّهَ
يَبۡسُطُ ٱلرِّزۡقَ لِمَن يَشَآءُ مِنۡ
عِبَادِهِۦ وَيَقۡدِرُۖ لَوۡلَآ أَن مَّنَّ ٱللَّهُ
عَلَيۡنَا لَخَسَفَ بِنَاۖ وَيۡكَأَنَّهُۥ لَا
يُفۡلِحُ ٱلۡكَٰفِرُونَ ﴿٨٢﴾

83. That Home of the Hereafter We shall give to those who do not intend high-handedness or mischief on earth:

83. Tilkad-Daarul-Aaakhiratu naj'aluhaa lillazeena laa yureedoona 'uluwwan fil-arḍi

تِلۡكَ ٱلدَّارُ ٱلۡأٓخِرَةُ نَجۡعَلُهَا
لِلَّذِينَ لَا يُرِيدُونَ عُلُوّٗا فِي ٱلۡأَرۡضِ

Ikhfa اخفاء | Ghunna غنّہ | Ikhfa Meem Saakin اخفاء میم ساکن | Idghaam ادغام | Qalqala قلقلہ | Qalb قلب | Idghaam Meem Saakin ادغام میم ساکن

and the end is (best) for the righteous.

84. If any does good, the reward to him is better than his deed; but if any does evil, the doers of evil are only punished (to the extent) of their deeds.

85. Verily He Who ordained the Qur'an for you, will bring you back to the Place of Return. Say: "My Lord knows best who it is that brings true guidance, and who is in manifest error."

86. And you had not expected that the Book would be sent to you except as a Mercy from your Lord: therefore you do not lend support in any way to those who reject (Allah's Message).

87. And let nothing keep you back from the Signs of Allah after they have been revealed to you: and invite (men) to your Lord, and be not of the company of those who join gods with Allah.

88. And call not, besides Allah, on another god. There is no god but He. Everything (that exists) will perish except His own Face. To Him belongs the Command, and to Him will you (all) be brought back.

wa laa fasaadaa; wal-'aaqibatu lilmuttaqeen.

84. Man jaaa'a bilḥasanati falahoo khayrum-minhaa wa man jaaa'a bissayyi'ati falaa yujzal-lazeena 'amilus-sayyi-aati illaa maa kaanoo ya'maloon.

85. Innal-lazee faraḍa 'alay-kal-Qur-aana laraaadduka ilaa ma'aad; qur-Rabbeee a'lamu man jaaa'a bil-hudaa wa man huwa fee ḍalaalim-mubeen.

86. Wa maa kunta tarjooo añy-yulqaaa ilaykal-Kitaabu illaa raḥmatam-mir-Rabbika falaa takoonanna ẓaheeral-lilkaa-fireen.

87. Wa laa yaṣuddunnaka 'an Aayaatil-laahi ba'da iz unzilat ilayka wad'u ilaa Rabbika wa laa takoonanna minal-mush-rikeen.

88. Wa laa tad'u ma'al-laahi ilaahan aakhar; laaa ilaaha illaa Hoo; kullu shay'in haalikun illaa Wajhah; lahul-ḥukmu wa ilayhi turja'oon. **(Section 9)**

وَلَا فَسَادًا ۚ وَالْعَاقِبَةُ لِلْمُتَّقِينَ ﴿٨٣﴾
مَنْ جَاءَ بِالْحَسَنَةِ فَلَهُ خَيْرٌ
مِّنْهَا ۖ وَمَنْ جَاءَ بِالسَّيِّئَةِ فَلَا
يُجْزَى الَّذِينَ عَمِلُوا السَّيِّئَاتِ
إِلَّا مَا كَانُوا يَعْمَلُونَ ﴿٨٤﴾
إِنَّ الَّذِي فَرَضَ عَلَيْكَ الْقُرْآنَ
لَرَادُّكَ إِلَىٰ مَعَادٍ ۚ قُلْ رَّبِّي
أَعْلَمُ مَنْ جَاءَ بِالْهُدَىٰ وَمَنْ
هُوَ فِي ضَلَالٍ مُّبِينٍ ﴿٨٥﴾
وَمَا كُنْتَ تَرْجُو أَنْ يُلْقَىٰ
إِلَيْكَ الْكِتَابُ إِلَّا رَحْمَةً مِّنْ رَّبِّكَ
فَلَا تَكُونَنَّ ظَهِيرًا لِّلْكَافِرِينَ ﴿٨٦﴾
وَلَا يَصُدُّنَّكَ عَنْ آيَاتِ اللَّهِ بَعْدَ
إِذْ أُنْزِلَتْ إِلَيْكَ ۖ وَادْعُ إِلَىٰ رَبِّكَ
وَلَا تَكُونَنَّ مِنَ الْمُشْرِكِينَ ﴿٨٧﴾
وَلَا تَدْعُ مَعَ اللَّهِ إِلَٰهًا آخَرَ ۘ لَا
إِلَٰهَ إِلَّا هُوَ ۚ كُلُّ شَيْءٍ هَالِكٌ
إِلَّا وَجْهَهُ ۚ لَهُ الْحُكْمُ وَإِلَيْهِ
تُرْجَعُونَ ﴿٨٨﴾

وقف لازم

29. The Spider

In the name of Allah, Most Gracious, Most Merciful.

Sûrat al-'Ankabût–29

(Revealed at Makkah)

Bismillaahir Raḥmaanir Raḥeem

(٢٩) سُورَةُ الْعَنْكَبُوتِ مَكِّيَّةٌ (٨٥)

بِسْمِ اللَّهِ الرَّحْمَٰنِ الرَّحِيمِ

1. *Alif-Lam-Mim.*

2. Do men think that they will be left alone on saying, "We believe", and that they will not be tested?

3. We tested those before them, and Allah will certainly know those who are true

1. Alif-Laaam-Meeem.

2. Aḥasiban-naasu añy-yutra-kooo añy-yaqoolooo aamannaa wa hum laa yuftanoon.

3. Wa laqad fatannal-lazeena min qablihim fala-ya'lamannal-laahul-lazeena ṣadaqoo

الم ﴿١﴾
أَحَسِبَ النَّاسُ أَنْ يُتْرَكُوا أَنْ
يَقُولُوا آمَنَّا وَهُمْ لَا يُفْتَنُونَ ﴿٢﴾
وَلَقَدْ فَتَنَّا الَّذِينَ مِنْ قَبْلِهِمْ
فَلَيَعْلَمَنَّ اللَّهُ الَّذِينَ صَدَقُوا

Ikhfa اخفاء | Ghunna غنّہ | Ikhfa Meem Saakin اخفاء میم ساکن | Idghaam ادغام | Qalqala قلقلہ | Qalb قلب | Idghaam Meem Saakin ادغام میم ساکن

from those who are false.

4. Do those who practise evil think that they will get the better of Us? Evil is their judgment!

5. For those whose hopes are in the meeting with Allah (in the Hereafter, let them strive); for the term (appointed) by Allah is surely coming and He hears and knows (all things).

6. And if any strive (with might and main), they do so for their own souls: for Allah is free of all needs from all creation.

7. Those who believe and work righteous deeds,- from them shall We blot out all evil (that may be) in them, and We shall reward them according to the best of their deeds.

8. We have enjoined on man kindness to parents: but if they (either of them) strive (to force) you to join with Me (in worship) anything of which you have no knowledge, do not obey them. You have (all) to return to me, and I will tell you (the truth) of all that you did.

9. And those who believe and work righteous deeds,- them shall We admit to the company of the Righteous.

10. Then there are among men such as say, "We believe in Allah"; but when they suffer affliction in (the cause of) Allah, they treat men's oppression as if it were the Wrath of Allah! And if help comes (to you) from your Lord, they are sure to say, "We have (always) been with you!" Does not Allah know best all that is in the hearts of all creation?

11. And Allah most certainly knows those who believe, and as certainly those who are Hypocrites.

12. And the Unbelievers say to those who believe:

wa la-ya'lamannal-kaazibeen.

4. Am ḥasibal-lazeena ya'maloonas-sayyiaati añy-yasbiqoonaa; saaa'a maa yaḥkumoon.

5. Man kaana yarjoo liqaaa'allaahi fa-inna-ajalal-laahi laaat; wa Huwas-Samee'ul-'Aleem.

6. Wa man jaahada fa-innamaa yujaahidu linafsih; innal-laaha laghaniyyun 'anil-'aalameen.

7. Wallazeena aamanoo wa 'amiluṣ-ṣaaliḥaati lanukaffiranna 'anhum sayyiaatihim wa lanajziyannahum aḥsanal-lazee kaanoo ya'maloon.

8. Wa waṣṣaynal-insaana biwaalidayhi ḥusnañw wa in jaahadaaka litushrika bee maa laysa laka bihee 'ilmun falaa tuṭi'humaa; ilayya marji'ukum fa-unabbi'ukum bimaa kuntum ta'maloon.

9. Wallazeena aamanoo wa 'amiluṣ-ṣaaliḥaati lanudkhilannahum fiṣ-ṣaaliḥeen.

10. Wa minan-naasi mañy-yaqoolu aamannaa billaahi fa-izaaa ooziya fil-laahi ja'ala fitnatan-naasi ka'azaabil-laahi wa la'in jaaa'a naṣrum-mir-Rabbika la-yaqoolunna innaa kunnaa ma'akum; awa laysal-laahu bi-a'lama bimaa fee ṣudooril-'aalameen.

11. Wa la-ya'lamannal-laahul-lazeena aamanoo wa la-ya'lamannal-munaafiqeen.

12. Wa qaalal-lazeena kafaroo lillazeena aamanut-

وَلَيَعْلَمَنَّ الْكٰذِبِيْنَ ﴿٣﴾
اَمْ حَسِبَ الَّذِيْنَ يَعْمَلُوْنَ السَّيِّاٰتِ
اَنْ يَّسْبِقُوْنَا ؕ سَآءَ مَا يَحْكُمُوْنَ ﴿٤﴾
مَنْ كَانَ يَرْجُوْا لِقَآءَ اللّٰهِ فَاِنَّ اَجَلَ
اللّٰهِ لَاٰتٍ ؕ وَهُوَ السَّمِيْعُ الْعَلِيْمُ ﴿٥﴾
وَمَنْ جَاهَدَ فَاِنَّمَا يُجَاهِدُ لِنَفْسِهٖ ؕ
اِنَّ اللّٰهَ لَغَنِيٌّ عَنِ الْعٰلَمِيْنَ ﴿٦﴾
وَالَّذِيْنَ اٰمَنُوْا وَعَمِلُوا الصّٰلِحٰتِ
لَنُكَفِّرَنَّ عَنْهُمْ سَيِّاٰتِهِمْ وَلَنَجْزِيَنَّهُمْ
اَحْسَنَ الَّذِيْ كَانُوْا يَعْمَلُوْنَ ﴿٧﴾
وَوَصَّيْنَا الْاِنْسَانَ بِوَالِدَيْهِ
حُسْنًا ؕ وَاِنْ جَاهَدٰكَ لِتُشْرِكَ بِيْ
مَا لَيْسَ لَكَ بِهٖ عِلْمٌ فَلَا تُطِعْهُمَا ؕ
اِلَيَّ مَرْجِعُكُمْ فَاُنَبِّئُكُمْ بِمَا كُنْتُمْ
تَعْمَلُوْنَ ﴿٨﴾
وَالَّذِيْنَ اٰمَنُوْا وَعَمِلُوا الصّٰلِحٰتِ
لَنُدْخِلَنَّهُمْ فِي الصّٰلِحِيْنَ ﴿٩﴾
وَمِنَ النَّاسِ مَنْ يَّقُوْلُ اٰمَنَّا بِاللّٰهِ
فَاِذَآ اُوْذِيَ فِي اللّٰهِ جَعَلَ فِتْنَةَ
النَّاسِ كَعَذَابِ اللّٰهِ ؕ وَلَئِنْ جَآءَ
نَصْرٌ مِّنْ رَّبِّكَ لَيَقُوْلُنَّ اِنَّا كُنَّا
مَعَكُمْ ؕ اَوَلَيْسَ اللّٰهُ بِاَعْلَمَ بِمَا فِيْ
صُدُوْرِ الْعٰلَمِيْنَ ﴿١٠﴾
وَلَيَعْلَمَنَّ اللّٰهُ الَّذِيْنَ اٰمَنُوْا
وَلَيَعْلَمَنَّ الْمُنٰفِقِيْنَ ﴿١١﴾
وَقَالَ الَّذِيْنَ كَفَرُوْا لِلَّذِيْنَ اٰمَنُوْا

Ikhfa اخفاء | Ghunna غُنّہ | Ikhfa Meem Saakin اخفاء میم ساکن | Idghaam ادغام | Qalqala قلقله | Qalb قلب | Idghaam Meem Saakin ادغام میم ساکن

اتَّبِعُوْا سَبِيْلَنَا وَلْنَحْمِلْ خَطٰيٰكُمْ ۭ وَمَا
هُمْ بِحٰمِلِيْنَ مِنْ خَطٰيٰهُمْ مِّنْ
شَيْءٍ ۭ اِنَّهُمْ لَكٰذِبُوْنَ ﴿١٢﴾

tabi'oo sabeelanaa walnaḥmil khaṭaayaakum wa maa hum biḥaamileena min khaṭaa-yaahum-min shay'in innahum lakaaẕiboon.

"Follow our path, and we will bear (the consequences) of your faults." Never in the least will they bear their faults: in fact they are liars!

وَلَيَحْمِلُنَّ اَثْقَالَهُمْ وَاَثْقَالًا مَّعَ
اَثْقَالِهِمْ ۡ وَلَيُسْـَٔـلُنَّ يَوْمَ الْقِيٰمَةِ
عَمَّا كَانُوْا يَفْتَرُوْنَ ﴿١٣﴾ ع ١

13. Wa la-yaḥmilunna as̱qaa-lahum wa as̱qaalam-ma'a as̱qaalihim wa la-yus'alunna Yawmal-Qiyaamati 'ammaa kaanoo yaftaroon. **(Section 1)**

13. They will bear their own burdens, and (other) burdens along with their own, and on the Day of Judgment they will be called to account for their falsehoods.

وَلَقَدْ اَرْسَلْنَا نُوْحًا اِلٰى قَوْمِهٖ
فَلَبِثَ فِيْهِمْ اَلْفَ سَنَةٍ اِلَّا خَمْسِيْنَ
عَامًا ۭ فَاَخَذَهُمُ الطُّوْفَانُ وَهُمْ
ظٰلِمُوْنَ ﴿١٤﴾

14. Wa laqad arsalnaa Nooḥan ilaa qawmihee falabis̱a feehim alfa sanatin illaa khamseena 'aaman fa-akhaẕahumuṭ-ṭoofaanu wa hum ẓaalimoon.

14. We (once) sent Noah to his people, and he tarried among them a thousand years less fifty: but the Deluge overwhelmed them while they (persisted in) sin.

فَاَنْجَيْنٰهُ وَاَصْحٰبَ السَّفِيْنَةِ
وَجَعَلْنٰهَآ اٰيَةً لِّلْعٰلَمِيْنَ ﴿١٥﴾

15. Fa-anjaynaahu wa aṣ-ḥaa-bas-safeenati wa ja'alnaahaaa Aayatal-lil'aalameen.

15. But We saved him and the companions of the Ark, and We made the (Ark) a Sign for all peoples!

وَاِبْرٰهِيْمَ اِذْ قَالَ لِقَوْمِهِ اعْبُدُوا
اللّٰهَ وَاتَّقُوْهُ ۭ ذٰلِكُمْ خَيْرٌ لَّكُمْ اِنْ
كُنْتُمْ تَعْلَمُوْنَ ﴿١٦﴾

16. Wa Ibraaheema iẕ qaala liqawmihi'-budul-laaha watta-qoohu ẕaalikum khayrul-lakum in kuntum ta'lamoon.

16. And (We also saved) Abraham: behold, he said to his people, "Serve Allah and fear Him: that will be best for you- If you understand!

اِنَّمَا تَعْبُدُوْنَ مِنْ دُوْنِ اللّٰهِ
اَوْثَانًا وَّتَخْلُقُوْنَ اِفْكًا ۭ اِنَّ
الَّذِيْنَ تَعْبُدُوْنَ مِنْ دُوْنِ اللّٰهِ
لَا يَمْلِكُوْنَ لَكُمْ رِزْقًا فَابْتَغُوْا
عِنْدَ اللّٰهِ الرِّزْقَ وَاعْبُدُوْهُ وَاشْكُرُوْا
لَهٗ ۭ اِلَيْهِ تُرْجَعُوْنَ ﴿١٧﴾

17. Innamaa ta'budoona min doonil-laahi aws̱aanañw-wa takhluqoona ifkaa; innal-laẕeena ta'budoona min doonil-laahi laa yamlikoona lakum rizqan fabtaghoo 'indal-laahir-rizqa wa'budoohu washkuroo lahooo ilayhi turja'oon.

17. "For you worship idols besides Allah, and you invent falsehood. The things that you worship besides Allah have no power to give you sustenance: then seek sustenance from Allah, serve Him, and be grateful to Him: to Him will be your return.

وَاِنْ تُكَذِّبُوْا فَقَدْ كَذَّبَ اُمَمٌ مِّنْ
قَبْلِكُمْ ۭ وَمَا عَلَى الرَّسُوْلِ اِلَّا
الْبَلٰغُ الْمُبِيْنُ ﴿١٨﴾

18. Wa in tukaẕẕiboo faqad kaẕẕaba umamum-min qabli-kum wa maa 'alar-Rasooli illal-balaaghul-mubeen.

18. "And if you reject (the Message), so did generations before you: and the duty of the Messenger is only to preach publicly (and clearly)."

اَوَلَمْ يَرَوْا كَيْفَ يُبْدِئُ اللّٰهُ
الْخَلْقَ ثُمَّ يُعِيْدُهٗ ۭ اِنَّ ذٰلِكَ

19. Awa lam yaraw kayfa yubdi'ul-laahul-khalqa s̱umma yu'eeduh; inna ẕaalika

19. Don't they see how Allah originates creation, then repeats it: truly that is

Ikhfa اخفاء | Ghunna غنّہ | Ikhfa Meem Saakin اخفاء میم ساکن | Idghaam ادغام | Qalqala قلقلہ | Qalb قلب | Idghaam Meem Saakin ادغام میم ساکن

easy for Allah.

'alal-laahi yaseer.

عَلَى اللّٰهِ يَسِيْرٌ ﴿١٩﴾

20. Say: "Travel through the earth and see how Allah did originate creation; so will Allah produce a later creation: for Allah has power over all things.

20. Qul seeroo fil-arḍi fanẓuroo kayfa bada-al-khalqa summal-laahu yunshi'un-nashatal-Aakhirah; innal-laaha 'alaa kulli shay'in Qadeer.

قُلْ سِيْرُوْا فِي الْاَرْضِ فَانْظُرُوْا
كَيْفَ بَدَاَ الْخَلْقَ ثُمَّ اللّٰهُ يُنْشِئُ
النَّشْاَةَ الْاٰخِرَةَ ؕ اِنَّ اللّٰهَ عَلٰى
كُلِّ شَيْءٍ قَدِيْرٌ ﴿٢٠﴾

21. "He punishes whom He pleases, and He grants Mercy to whom He pleases, and towards Him are you turned.

21. Yu'azzibu mañy-yashaaa'u wa yarḥamu mañy-yashaaa', wa ilayhi tuqlaboon.

يُعَذِّبُ مَنْ يَّشَآءُ وَيَرْحَمُ مَنْ
يَّشَآءُ ۚ وَاِلَيْهِ تُقْلَبُوْنَ ﴿٢١﴾

22. "Not on earth nor in heaven will you be able (fleeing) to frustrate (His Plan), nor have you, besides Allah, any protector or helper."

22. Wa maaa antum bimu-'jizeena fil-arḍi wa laa fissamaaa'i wa maa lakum-min doonil-laahi miñw-waliyyiñw-wa laa naṣeer. **(Section 2)**

وَمَآ اَنْتُمْ بِمُعْجِزِيْنَ فِي الْاَرْضِ
وَلَا فِي السَّمَآءِ ۫ وَمَا لَكُمْ مِّنْ
دُوْنِ اللّٰهِ مِنْ وَّلِيٍّ وَّلَا نَصِيْرٍ ﴿٢٢﴾ ع ١٤

23. Those who reject the Signs of Allah and the Meeting with Him (in the Hereafter),- it is they who shall despair of My Mercy: it is they who will (suffer) a most grievous Penalty.

23. Wallazeena kafaroo bi-Aayaatil-laahi wa liqaaa'iheee ulaaa'ika ya'isoo mir-raḥmatee wa ulaaa'ika lahum 'azaabun aleem.

وَالَّذِيْنَ كَفَرُوْا بِاٰيٰتِ اللّٰهِ وَلِقَآئِهٖٓ
اُولٰٓئِكَ يَئِسُوْا مِنْ رَّحْمَتِيْ وَ
اُولٰٓئِكَ لَهُمْ عَذَابٌ اَلِيْمٌ ﴿٢٣﴾

24. So nothing was the answer of (Abraham's) people except that they said: "Slay him or burn him." But Allah saved him from the Fire. Verily in this are Signs for people who believe.

24. Famaa kaana jawaaba qawmiheee illaaa an qaaluq-tuloohu aw ḥarriqoohu fa-anjaahul-laahu minan-naar; inna fee zaalika la-Aayaatil-liqawmiñy-yu'minoon.

فَمَا كَانَ جَوَابَ قَوْمِهٖٓ اِلَّآ اَنْ
قَالُوا اقْتُلُوْهُ اَوْ حَرِّقُوْهُ فَاَنْجٰىهُ
اللّٰهُ مِنَ النَّارِ ؕ اِنَّ فِيْ ذٰلِكَ
لَاٰيٰتٍ لِّقَوْمٍ يُّؤْمِنُوْنَ ﴿٢٤﴾

25. And he said: "For you, you have taken (for worship) idols besides Allah, out of mutual love and regard between yourselves in this life; but on the Day of Judgment you shall disown each other and curse each other: and your abode will be the Fire, and you shall have none to help."

25. Wa qaala innamat-takhaztum-min doonil-laahi awsaanam-mawaddata baynikum fil-ḥayaatid-dunyaa summa Yawmal-Qiyaamati yakfuru ba'ḍukum biba'ḍiñw-wa yal'anu ba'ḍukum ba'ḍañw-wa maåwaakumun-Naaru wa maa lakum-min-naaṣireen.

وَقَالَ اِنَّمَا اتَّخَذْتُمْ مِّنْ دُوْنِ
اللّٰهِ اَوْثَانًا ۙ مَّوَدَّةَ بَيْنِكُمْ فِي
الْحَيٰوةِ الدُّنْيَا ۚ ثُمَّ يَوْمَ الْقِيٰمَةِ
يَكْفُرُ بَعْضُكُمْ بِبَعْضٍ وَّيَلْعَنُ
بَعْضُكُمْ بَعْضًا ۫ وَّمَاْوٰىكُمُ النَّارُ
وَمَا لَكُمْ مِّنْ نّٰصِرِيْنَ ﴿٢٥﴾ وقف لازم

26. But Lut had faith in Him: He said: "I will leave home for the sake of my Lord: for He is Exalted in Might, and Wise."

26. Fa-aamana lahoo Looṭ; wa qaala innee muhaajirun ilaa Rabbee innahoo Huwal-'Azeezul-Ḥakeem.

فَاٰمَنَ لَهٗ لُوْطٌ ۘ وَقَالَ اِنِّيْ
مُهَاجِرٌ اِلٰى رَبِّيْ ؕ اِنَّهٗ هُوَ الْعَزِيْزُ
الْحَكِيْمُ ﴿٢٦﴾

Ikhfa اخفاء | Ghunna غُنّہ | Ikhfa Meem Saakin اخفاء میم ساکن | Idghaam ادغام | Qalqala قلقلہ | Qalb قلب | Idghaam Meem Saakin ادغام میم ساکن

27. And We gave (Abraham) Isaac and Jacob, and ordained among his progeny Prophethood and Revelation, and We granted him his reward in this life; and he will be in the Hereafter (of the company) of the Righteous.

27. Wa wahabnaa lahooo Isḥaaqa wa Ya'qooba wa ja'alnaa fee zurriyyatihin-Nubuwwata wal-Kitaaba wa aataynaahu ajrahoo fid-dunyaa wa innahoo fil-Aakhirati laminaṣ-ṣaaliḥeen.

وَوَهَبْنَا لَهٗۤ اِسْحٰقَ وَيَعْقُوْبَ وَجَعَلْنَا فِىْ ذُرِّيَّتِهِ النُّبُوَّةَ وَالْكِتٰبَ وَاٰتَيْنٰهُ اَجْرَهٗ فِى الدُّنْيَا ۚ وَاِنَّهٗ فِى الْاٰخِرَةِ لَمِنَ الصّٰلِحِيْنَ ﴿٢٧﴾

28. And (remember) Lut: behold, he said to his people: "You commit lewdness, such as no people in Creation (ever) committed before you.

28. Wa Looṭan iz qaala liqawmiheee innakum lataåtoonal-faaḥishata maa sabaqakum-bihaa min aḥadim-minal-'aalameen.

وَلُوْطًا اِذْ قَالَ لِقَوْمِهٖۤ اِنَّكُمْ لَتَاْتُوْنَ الْفَاحِشَةَ ۫ مَا سَبَقَكُمْ بِهَا مِنْ اَحَدٍ مِّنَ الْعٰلَمِيْنَ ﴿٢٨﴾

29. "Do you indeed approach men, and cut off the highway?- and practise wickedness (even) in your councils?" But his people gave no answer but this: they said: "Bring us the Wrath of Allah if you tell the truth."

29. A'innakum lataåtoonar-rijaala wa taqta'oonas-sabeela wa taåtoona fee naadeekumul-munkara famaa kaana jawaaba qawmiheee illaaa an qaalu'-tinaa bi'azaabil-laahi in kunta minaṣ-ṣaadiqeen.

اَئِنَّكُمْ لَتَاْتُوْنَ الرِّجَالَ وَتَقْطَعُوْنَ السَّبِيْلَ ۙ وَتَاْتُوْنَ فِىْ نَادِيْكُمُ الْمُنْكَرَ ؕ فَمَا كَانَ جَوَابَ قَوْمِهٖۤ اِلَّاۤ اَنْ قَالُوا ائْتِنَا بِعَذَابِ اللّٰهِ اِنْ كُنْتَ مِنَ الصّٰدِقِيْنَ ﴿٢٩﴾

30. He said: "O my Lord! You help me against people who do mischief!"

30. Qaala Rabbin-ṣurnee 'alal-qawmil-mufsideen.

(Section 3)

قَالَ رَبِّ انْصُرْنِىْ عَلَى الْقَوْمِ الْمُفْسِدِيْنَ ﴿٣٠﴾ ع ١٥

31. When Our Messengers came to Abraham with the good news, they said: "We are indeed going to destroy the people of this township: for truly they are (addicted to) crime."

31. Wa lammaa jaaa'at Rusulunaaa Ibraaheema bil-bushraa qaalooo innaa muhlikooo ahli haazihil-qaryati inna ahlahaa kaanoo ẓaalimeen.

وَلَمَّا جَآءَتْ رُسُلُنَاۤ اِبْرٰهِيْمَ بِالْبُشْرٰى ۙ قَالُوْۤا اِنَّا مُهْلِكُوْۤا اَهْلِ هٰذِهِ الْقَرْيَةِ ۚ اِنَّ اَهْلَهَا كَانُوْا ظٰلِمِيْنَ ﴿٣١﴾

32. He said: "But there is Lut there." They said: "Well do we know who is there : we will certainly save him and his followrs, except his wife: she is of those who lag behind!"

32. Qaala inna feehaa Looṭaa; qaaloo naḥnu a'lamu biman feehaa lanunajjiyannahoo wa ahlahooo illam-ra-atahoo kaanat minal-ghaabireen.

قَالَ اِنَّ فِيْهَا لُوْطًا ؕ قَالُوْا نَحْنُ اَعْلَمُ بِمَنْ فِيْهَا ۫ لَنُنَجِّيَنَّهٗ وَاَهْلَهٗۤ اِلَّا امْرَاَتَهٗ ۫ كَانَتْ مِنَ الْغٰبِرِيْنَ ﴿٣٢﴾

33. And when Our Messengers came to Lut, he was grieved on their account, and felt himself powerless (to protect) them: but they said: "Do not Fear, nor grieve: we

33. Wa lammaaa an jaaa'at Rusulunaa Looṭan seee'a bihim wa ḍaaqa bihim zar'añw-wa qaaloo laa takhaf wa laa taḥzan innaa

وَلَمَّاۤ اَنْ جَآءَتْ رُسُلُنَا لُوْطًا سِىْٓءَ بِهِمْ وَضَاقَ بِهِمْ ذَرْعًا وَّقَالُوْا لَا تَخَفْ وَلَا تَحْزَنْ ۫ اِنَّا

Ikhfa اخفاء | Ghunna غنّہ | Ikhfa Meem Saakin اخفاء میم ساکن | Idghaam ادغام | Qalqala قلقلہ | Qalb قلب | Idghaam Meem Saakin ادغام میم ساکن

are (here) to save you and your kinsfolk, except your wife: she is of those who lag behind.

34. "For we are going to bring down on the people of this township a Punishment from heaven, because they have been wickedly rebellious."

35. And We have left thereof an evident Sign, for any people who (care to) understand.

36. To the Madyan (people) (We sent) their brother Shu'aib. Then he said: "O my people! serve Allah, and fear the Last Day: nor commit evil on the earth, with intent to do mischief."

37. But they rejected him: then the mighty Blast seized them, and they lay prostrate in their homes by the morning.

38. (Remember also) the 'Ad and the Thamud (people): clearly will appear to you from (the traces) of their buildings (their fate): the Evil One made their deeds alluring to them, and kept them back from the Path, though they were gifted with Intelligence and Skill.

39. (Remember also) Qarun, Pharaoh, and Haman: there came to them Moses with Clear Signs, but they behaved with insolence on the earth; yet they could not overreach (Us).

40. Each one of them We seized for his crime: of them, against some We sent a violent tornado (with showers of stones); some were caught by a (mighty) Blast; some We caused the earth to swallow up; and some We drowned (in the waters): It was not Allah

munajjooka wa ahlaka illam-raataka kaanat minal-ghaabireen.

34. Innaa munziloona 'alaaa ahli haazihil-qaryati rijzam-minas-samaaa'i bimaa kaanoo yafsuqoon.

35. Wa laqat-taraknaa minhaaa Aayatam-bayyinatal-liqawmiñy-ya'qiloon.

36. Wa ilaa Madyana akhaahum Shu'ayban faqaala yaa qawmi'-budul-laaha warjul-Yawmal-Aakhira wa laa ta'saw fil-arḍi mufsideen.

37. Fakazzaboohu fa-akhazat-humur-rajfatu fa-aṣbaḥoo fee daarihim jaasimeen.

38. Wa 'Aadañw-wa Samooda wa qat-tabayyana lakum-mim-masaakinihim wa zayyana lahumush-Shayṭaanu a'maalahum faṣaddahum 'anis-sabeeli wa kaanoo mustabṣireen.

39. Wa Qaaroona wa Fir-'awna wa Haamaana wa laqad jaaa'ahum-Moosaa bilbayyinaati fastakbaroo fil-arḍi wa maa kaanoo saabiqeen.

40. Fakullan akhaznaa bizambihee faminhum-man arsalnaa 'alayhi ḥaaṣibaa; wa minhum-man akhazat-huṣ-ṣayḥatu wa minhum-man khasafnaa bihil-arḍa wa minhum-man aghraqnaa; wa maa kaanal-laahu

مُنَجُّوْكَ وَاَهْلَكَ اِلَّا امْرَاَتَكَ كَانَتْ
مِنَ الْغٰبِرِيْنَ ﴿٣٣﴾
اِنَّا مُنْزِلُوْنَ عَلٰٓى اَهْلِ هٰذِهِ
الْقَرْيَةِ رِجْزًا مِّنَ السَّمَآءِ بِمَا
كَانُوْا يَفْسُقُوْنَ ﴿٣٤﴾
وَلَقَدْ تَّرَكْنَا مِنْهَآ اٰيَةًۢ بَيِّنَةً
لِّقَوْمٍ يَّعْقِلُوْنَ ﴿٣٥﴾
وَاِلٰى مَدْيَنَ اَخَاهُمْ شُعَيْبًا ۙ
فَقَالَ يٰقَوْمِ اعْبُدُوا اللّٰهَ وَارْجُوا
الْيَوْمَ الْاٰخِرَ وَلَا تَعْثَوْا فِى الْاَرْضِ
مُفْسِدِيْنَ ﴿٣٦﴾
فَكَذَّبُوْهُ فَاَخَذَتْهُمُ الرَّجْفَةُ
فَاَصْبَحُوْا فِىْ دَارِهِمْ جٰثِمِيْنَ ﴿٣٧﴾
وَعَادًا وَّثَمُوْدَا۟ وَقَدْ تَّبَيَّنَ لَكُمْ
مِّنْ مَّسٰكِنِهِمْ ۗ وَزَيَّنَ لَهُمُ
الشَّيْطٰنُ اَعْمَالَهُمْ فَصَدَّهُمْ عَنِ
السَّبِيْلِ وَكَانُوْا مُسْتَبْصِرِيْنَ ﴿٣٨﴾ ۙ
وَقَارُوْنَ وَفِرْعَوْنَ وَهَامٰنَ ۗ
وَلَقَدْ جَآءَهُمْ مُّوْسٰى بِالْبَيِّنٰتِ
فَاسْتَكْبَرُوْا فِى الْاَرْضِ وَمَا
كَانُوْا سٰبِقِيْنَ ﴿٣٩﴾ ۚ
فَكُلًّا اَخَذْنَا بِذَنْۢبِهٖ ۚ فَمِنْهُمْ مَّنْ
اَرْسَلْنَا عَلَيْهِ حَاصِبًا ۚ وَمِنْهُمْ
مَّنْ اَخَذَتْهُ الصَّيْحَةُ ۚ وَمِنْهُمْ مَّنْ
خَسَفْنَا بِهِ الْاَرْضَ ۚ وَمِنْهُمْ
مَّنْ اَغْرَقْنَا ۚ وَمَا كَانَ اللّٰهُ

Ikhfa اخفاء | Ghunna غُنّہ | Ikhfa Meem Saakin اخفاء میم ساکن | Idghaam ادغام | Qalqala قلقلہ | Qalb قلب | Idghaam Meem Saakin ادغام میم ساکن

Who injured (or oppressed) them: they injured (or oppressed) their own souls.

li-yaẕlimahum wa laakin kaanoo anfusahum yaẕlimoon.

لِيَظْلِمَهُمْ وَلٰكِنْ كَانُوْٓا اَنْفُسَهُمْ
يَظْلِمُوْنَ ﴿٤٠﴾

41. The parable of those who take protectors other than Allah is that of the Spider, who builds (to itself) a house; but truly the flimsiest of houses is the Spider's house;- if they but knew.

41. Maṯalul-laẕeenat-takhaẕoo min doonil-laahi awliyaaa'a kamaṯalil-'ankaboot, ittakhaẕat baytaa; wa inna awhanal-buyooti la-baytul-'ankaboot; law kaanoo ya'lamoon.

مَثَلُ الَّذِيْنَ اتَّخَذُوْا مِنْ دُوْنِ
اللّٰهِ اَوْلِيَآءَ كَمَثَلِ الْعَنْكَبُوْتِ ۚ
اِتَّخَذَتْ بَيْتًا ۭ وَاِنَّ اَوْهَنَ
الْبُيُوْتِ لَبَيْتُ الْعَنْكَبُوْتِ ۘ لَوْ وقف لازم
كَانُوْا يَعْلَمُوْنَ ﴿٤١﴾

42. Verily Allah knows of (every thing) whatever that they call upon besides Him: and He is Exalted (in power), Wise.

42. Innal-laaha ya'lamu maa yad'oona min doonihee min shay'; wa Huwal-'Azeezul-Ḥakeem.

اِنَّ اللّٰهَ يَعْلَمُ مَا يَدْعُوْنَ
مِنْ دُوْنِهٖ مِنْ شَيْءٍ ۭ وَهُوَ
الْعَزِيْزُ الْحَكِيْمُ ﴿٤٢﴾

43. And such are the Parables We set forth for mankind, but only those understand them who have knowledge.

43. Wa tilkal-amṯaalu naḍribuhaa linnaasi wa maa ya'qiluhaaa illal-'aalimoon.

وَتِلْكَ الْاَمْثَالُ نَضْرِبُهَا لِلنَّاسِ ۚ
وَمَا يَعْقِلُهَآ اِلَّا الْعٰلِمُوْنَ ﴿٤٣﴾

44. Allah created the heavens and the earth in true (proportions): verily in that is a Sign for those who believe.

44. Khalaqal-laahus-samaawaati wal-arḍa bilḥaqq; inna fee ẕaalika la-Aayatal-lilmu'mineen. **(Section 4)**

خَلَقَ اللّٰهُ السَّمٰوٰتِ وَالْاَرْضَ
بِالْحَقِّ ۭ اِنَّ فِيْ ذٰلِكَ لَاٰيَةً
لِّلْمُؤْمِنِيْنَ ﴿٤٤﴾ ع

ع ١٤ الجزء الحادي والعشرون (٢١)

45. Recite what is sent of the Book by inspiration to you,and establish regular Prayer: for Prayer restrains from shameful and unjust deeds; and remembrance of Allah is the greatest (thing in life) without doubt. And Allah knows the (deeds) that you do.

45. Utlu maaa ooḥiya ilayka minal-Kitaabi wa aqimiṣ-Ṣalaata innaṣ-Ṣalaata tanhaa 'anil-faḥshaaa'i wal-munkar; wa laẕikrul-laahi akbar; wal-laahu ya'lamu maa taṣna'oon.

اُتْلُ مَآ اُوْحِيَ اِلَيْكَ مِنَ الْكِتٰبِ وَ
اَقِمِ الصَّلٰوةَ ۭ اِنَّ الصَّلٰوةَ تَنْهٰى
عَنِ الْفَحْشَاۗءِ وَالْمُنْكَرِ ۭ وَلَذِكْرُ اللّٰهِ
اَكْبَرُ ۭ وَاللّٰهُ يَعْلَمُ مَا تَصْنَعُوْنَ ﴿٤٥﴾

46. And you do not dispute with the People of the Book, except with means better (than mere disputation), unless it be with those of them who inflict wrong (and injury): but say, "We belie-ve in the revelation which has come down to us and in that which came down to you; our Allah and your Allah is one; and it is to Him we bow (in Islam)."

46. Wa laa tujaadilooo Ahlal-Kitaabi illaa billatee hiya aḥsanu illal-laẕeena ẓalamoo minhum wa qoolooo aamannaa billaẕeee unzila ilaynaa wa unzila ilaykum wa Ilaahunaa wa Ilaahukum Waaḥiduñw-wa naḥnu lahoo muslimoon.

وَلَا تُجَادِلُوْٓا اَهْلَ الْكِتٰبِ اِلَّا بِالَّتِيْ
هِيَ اَحْسَنُ ڰ اِلَّا الَّذِيْنَ ظَلَمُوْا
مِنْهُمْ وَقُوْلُوْٓا اٰمَنَّا بِالَّذِيْٓ اُنْزِلَ اِلَيْنَا
وَاُنْزِلَ اِلَيْكُمْ وَاِلٰـهُنَا وَاِلٰـهُكُمْ
وَاحِدٌ وَّنَحْنُ لَهٗ مُسْلِمُوْنَ ﴿٤٦﴾

47. And thus (it is) that We have sent down the Book to you. So the People of the Book believe therein,

47. Wa kaẕaalika anzalnaaa ilaykal-Kitaab; fallaẕeena aataynaahumul-Kitaaba yu'minoona bihee

وَكَذٰلِكَ اَنْزَلْنَآ اِلَيْكَ الْكِتٰبَ ۭ
فَالَّذِيْنَ اٰتَيْنٰهُمُ الْكِتٰبَ يُؤْمِنُوْنَ بِهٖ ۚ

Ikhfa اخفاء | Ghunna غُنّہ | Ikhfa Meem Saakin اخفاء میم ساکن | Idghaam ادغام | Qalqala قلقلہ | Qalb قلب | Idghaam Meem Saakin ادغام میم ساکن

as also do some of these (pagan Arabs): and none but Unbelievers reject Our signs.

48. And you were not (able) to recite a Book before this (Book came), nor are you (able) to transcribe it with your right hand: in that case, indeed, would the talkers of vanities have doubted.

49. Nay, here are Signs self-evident in the hearts of those endowed with knowledge: and none but the unjust reject Our Signs.

50. Yet they say: "Why are not Signs sent down to him from his Lord?" Say: "The Signs are indeed with Allah: and I am indeed a clear Warner."

51. And is it not enough for them that We have sent down to you the Book which is rehearsed to them? Verily, in it is Mercy and a Reminder to those who believe.

52. Say: "Enough is Allah for a witness between me and you: He knows what is in the heavens and on earth. And it is those who believe in vanities and reject Allah, that will perish (in the end).

53. They ask you to hasten on the Punishment (for them): had it not been for a term (of respite) appointed, the Punishment would certainly have come to them: and it will certainly reach them,- of a sudden, while they perceive not!

54. They ask you to hasten on the Punishment: but, of a surety, Hell will encompass the Rejecters of Faith!-

55. On the Day that the Punish-ment shall cover them from above them and from below them, and (a Voice) shall say: "You taste (the fruits) of your deeds!"

wa min haaa'ulaaa'i mañy-yu'minu bih; wa maa yajḥadu bi-Aayaatinaaa illal-kaafiroon.

48. Wa maa kunta tatloo min qablihee min kitaabiñw-wa laa takhuṭṭuhoo bi-yameenika izal-lartaabal-mubṭiloon.

49. Bal huwa Aayaatum bayyinaatun fee ṣudooril-lazeena ootul-'ilm; wa maa yajḥadu bi-Aayaatinaaa illaẓ-ẓaalimoon.

50. Wa qaaloo law laaa unzila 'alayhi Aayaatum-mir-Rabbihee qul innamal-Aayaatu 'indal-laahi wa innamaaa ana nazeerum-mubeen.

51. Awa lam yakfihim annaaa anzalnaa 'alaykal-Kitaaba yutlaa 'alayhim; inna fee zaalika laraḥmatañw-wa zikraa liqawmiñy-yu'minoon. **(Section 5)**

52. Qul kafaa billaahi baynee wa baynakum shaheedaa; ya'lamu maa fis-samaawaati wal-arḍ; wallazeena aamanoo bil-baaṭili wa kafaroo billaahi ulaaa'ika humul-khaasiroon.

53. Wa yasta'jiloonaka bil-'azaab; wa law laaa ajalum-musammal-lajaaa'ahumul-'azaab; wa la-yaåtiyannahum baghtatañw-wa hum laa yash'uroon.

54. Yasta'jiloonaka bil'azaab; wa inna Jahannama lamuḥeeṭatum bilkaafireen.

55. Yawma yaghshaahumul-'azaabu min fawqihim wa min taḥti arjulihim wa yaqoolu zooqoo maa kuntum ta'maloon.

وَمِنْ هٰٓؤُلَآءِ مَنْ يُّؤْمِنُ بِهٖ ۚ وَمَا
يَجْحَدُ بِاٰيٰتِنَآ اِلَّا الْكٰفِرُوْنَ ﴿٤٧﴾
وَمَا كُنْتَ تَتْلُوْا مِنْ قَبْلِهٖ مِنْ
كِتٰبٍ وَّلَا تَخُطُّهٗ بِيَمِيْنِكَ اِذًا لَّارْتَابَ
الْمُبْطِلُوْنَ ﴿٤٨﴾
بَلْ هُوَ اٰيٰتٌۢ بَيِّنٰتٌ فِيْ صُدُوْرِ
الَّذِيْنَ اُوْتُوا الْعِلْمَ ۗ وَمَا يَجْحَدُ
بِاٰيٰتِنَآ اِلَّا الظّٰلِمُوْنَ ﴿٤٩﴾
وَقَالُوْا لَوْلَآ اُنْزِلَ عَلَيْهِ اٰيٰتٌ
مِّنْ رَّبِّهٖ ۗ قُلْ اِنَّمَا الْاٰيٰتُ
عِنْدَ اللّٰهِ ۗ وَاِنَّمَآ اَنَا نَذِيْرٌ مُّبِيْنٌ ﴿٥٠﴾
اَوَلَمْ يَكْفِهِمْ اَنَّآ اَنْزَلْنَا عَلَيْكَ
الْكِتٰبَ يُتْلٰى عَلَيْهِمْ ۗ اِنَّ فِيْ ذٰلِكَ
لَرَحْمَةً وَّذِكْرٰى لِقَوْمٍ يُّؤْمِنُوْنَ ﴿٥١﴾ ع
قُلْ كَفٰى بِاللّٰهِ بَيْنِيْ وَبَيْنَكُمْ شَهِيْدًا ۚ
يَعْلَمُ مَا فِي السَّمٰوٰتِ وَالْاَرْضِ ۗ
وَالَّذِيْنَ اٰمَنُوْا بِالْبَاطِلِ وَكَفَرُوْا
بِاللّٰهِ ۙ اُولٰٓئِكَ هُمُ الْخٰسِرُوْنَ ﴿٥٢﴾
وَيَسْتَعْجِلُوْنَكَ بِالْعَذَابِ ۗ وَلَوْلَآ
اَجَلٌ مُّسَمًّى لَّجَآءَهُمُ الْعَذَابُ ۗ
وَلَيَاْتِيَنَّهُمْ بَغْتَةً وَّهُمْ لَا يَشْعُرُوْنَ ﴿٥٣﴾
يَسْتَعْجِلُوْنَكَ بِالْعَذَابِ ۗ وَاِنَّ
جَهَنَّمَ لَمُحِيْطَةٌۢ بِالْكٰفِرِيْنَ ﴿٥٤﴾
يَوْمَ يَغْشٰىهُمُ الْعَذَابُ مِنْ فَوْقِهِمْ
وَمِنْ تَحْتِ اَرْجُلِهِمْ وَيَقُوْلُ ذُوْقُوْا
مَا كُنْتُمْ تَعْمَلُوْنَ ﴿٥٥﴾

Ikhfa اخفاء · Ghunna غنّہ · Ikhfa Meem Saakin اخفاء میم ساکن · Idghaam ادغام · Qalqala قلقلہ · Qalb قلب · Idghaam Meem Saakin ادغام میم ساکن

56. O My servants who believe! Truly, spacious is My Earth: therefore you serve Me - (and Me alone)!

56. Yaa 'ibaadiyal-lazeena aamanooo inna ardee waasi-'atun fa-iyyaaya fa'budoon.

يٰعِبَادِيَ الَّذِيْنَ اٰمَنُوْٓا اِنَّ اَرْضِيْ وَاسِعَةٌ فَاِيَّايَ فَاعْبُدُوْنِ ٥٦

57. Every soul shall have a taste of death: in the end to Us shall you be brought back.

57. Kullu nafsin zaaa'iqatul-mawti summa ilaynaa tur-ja'oon.

كُلُّ نَفْسٍ ذَآئِقَةُ الْمَوْتِ ثُمَّ اِلَيْنَا تُرْجَعُوْنَ ٥٧

58. But those who believe and work deeds of righteousness - to them shall We give a Home in Heaven,- lofty mansions beneath which flow rivers,- to dwell therein for ever;- an excellent reward for those who do (good)!-

58. Wallazeena aamanoo wa 'amiluṣ-ṣaaliḥaati la-nubawwi-'annahum-minal-Jannati ghura-fan tajree min taḥtihal-anhaaru khaalideena feehaa; ni'ma ajrul-'aamileen.

وَالَّذِيْنَ اٰمَنُوْا وَعَمِلُوا الصّٰلِحٰتِ لَنُبَوِّئَنَّهُمْ مِّنَ الْجَنَّةِ غُرَفًا تَجْرِيْ مِنْ تَحْتِهَا الْاَنْهٰرُ خٰلِدِيْنَ فِيْهَا ۭ نِعْمَ اَجْرُ الْعٰمِلِيْنَ ٥٨

59. Those who persevere in patience, and put their trust in their Lord and Cherisher.

59. Allazeena ṣabaroo wa 'alaa Rabbihim yatawakkaloon.

الَّذِيْنَ صَبَرُوْا وَعَلٰي رَبِّهِمْ يَتَوَكَّلُوْنَ ٥٩

60. How many are the creatures that carry not their own sustenance? It is Allah Who feeds (both) them and you: for He hears and knows (all things).

60. Wa ka-ayyim-min daab-batil-laa taḥmilu rizqahaa; Al-laahu yarzuquhaa wa iyyaakum; wa Huwas-Samee'ul-'Aleem.

وَكَاَيِّنْ مِّنْ دَآبَّةٍ لَّا تَحْمِلُ رِزْقَهَا ڰ اَللّٰهُ يَرْزُقُهَا وَاِيَّاكُمْ ڮ وَهُوَ السَّمِيْعُ الْعَلِيْمُ ٦٠

61. If indeed you ask them who has created the heavens and the earth and subjected the sun and the moon (to his Law), they will certainly reply, "Allah". How are they then deluded away (from the truth)?

61. Wa la'in sa-altahum-man khalaqas-samaawaati wal-arḍa wa sakhkharash-shamsa wal-qamara la-yaqoolunnal-laahu fa-annaa yu'fakoon.

وَلَىِٕنْ سَاَلْتَهُمْ مَّنْ خَلَقَ السَّمٰوٰتِ وَالْاَرْضَ وَسَخَّرَ الشَّمْسَ وَالْقَمَرَ لَيَقُوْلُنَّ اللّٰهُ ۚ فَاَنّٰى يُؤْفَكُوْنَ ٦١

62. Allah enlarges the sustenance (which He gives) to whichever of His servants He pleases; and He (similarly) grants by (strict) measure, (as He plea-ses): for Allah has full knowledge of all things.

62. Allaahu yabsuṭur-rizqa limañy-yashaaa'u min 'ibaadi-hee wa yaqdiru lah; innal-laaha bikulli shay'in 'Aleem.

اَللّٰهُ يَبْسُطُ الرِّزْقَ لِمَنْ يَّشَاۗءُ مِنْ عِبَادِهٖ وَيَقْدِرُ لَهٗ ۭ اِنَّ اللّٰهَ بِكُلِّ شَيْءٍ عَلِيْمٌ ٦٢

63. And if indeed you ask them who it is that sends down rain from the sky, and gives life therewith to the earth after its death, they will certainly reply, "Allah!" Say, "Praise be to Allah!" But most of them do not understand.

63. Wa la'in sa-altahum-man-nazzala minas-samaaa'i maaa-'an fa-aḥyaa bihil-arḍa mim ba'di mawtihaa la-yaqoolunnal-laah; qulil-ḥamdu-lillaah; bal aksaruhum laa ya'qiloon.

(Section 6)

وَلَىِٕنْ سَاَلْتَهُمْ مَّنْ نَّزَّلَ مِنَ السَّمَاۗءِ مَاۗءً فَاَحْيَا بِهِ الْاَرْضَ مِنْۢ بَعْدِ مَوْتِهَا لَيَقُوْلُنَّ اللّٰهُ ۭ قُلِ الْحَمْدُ لِلّٰهِ ۭ بَلْ اَكْثَرُهُمْ لَا يَعْقِلُوْنَ ٦٣ ع

64. What is the life of this world but amusement and play? But verily the Home in the Here-after,-

64. Wa maa haazihil-ḥayaa-tud-dunyaaa illaa lahwuñw-wa la'ib; wa innad-Daaral-Aakhi-rata la-hiyal-

وَمَا هٰذِهِ الْحَيٰوةُ الدُّنْيَآ اِلَّا لَهْوٌ وَّلَعِبٌ ۭ وَاِنَّ الدَّارَ الْاٰخِرَةَ لَهِيَ

Ikhfa	Ghunna	Ikhfa Meem Saakin	Idghaam	Qalqala	Qalb	Idghaam Meem Saakin
اخفاء	غنّہ	اخفاء میم ساکن	ادغام	قلقلہ	قلب	ادغام میم ساکن

that is life indeed, if they but knew.

65. Now, if they embark on a boat, they call on Allah, making their devotion sincerely (and exclusively) to Him; but when He has delivered them safely to (dry) land, behold, they give a share (of their worship to others)!-

66. Disdaining ungratefully Our gifts, and giving themselves up to (worldly) enjoyment! But soon will they know.

67. Do they not then see that We have made a sanctuary secure, and that men are being snatched away from all around them? Then, do they believe in that which is vain, and reject the Grace of Allah?

68. And who does more wrong than he who invents a lie against Allah or rejects the Truth when it reaches him? Is there not a home in Hell for those who reject Faith?

69. And those who strive in Our (Cause),- We will certainly guide them to Our Paths: for verily Allah is with those who do right.

30. The Roman Empire

In the name of Allah, Most Gracious, Most Merciful.

1. *Alif-Lam-Mim.*

2. The Roman Empire has been defeated-

3. In a land close by; but they, (even) after (this) defeat of theirs, will soon be victorious-

4. Within a few years. With Allah is the Command, in the Past and in the Future: on that Day shall the Believers rejoice-

5. With the help of Allah. He gives victory to whom He will, and He is Exalted in Might, Most Merciful.

ḥa-yawaan; law kaanoo ya'lamoon.

65. Fa-izaa rakiboo fil-fulki da'awul-laaha mukhliṣeena lahud-deena falammaa najjaahum ilal-barri izaa hum yushrikoon.

66. Li-yakfuroo bimaaa aataynaahum wa li-yatamatta'oo fasawfa ya'lamoon.

67. Awalam yaraw annaa ja'alnaa ḥaraman aaminañw-wa yutakhaṭṭafun-naasu min ḥawlihim; afabil-baaṭili yu'minoona wa bini'matil-laahi yakfuroon.

68. Wa man aẓlamu mimmanif-taraa 'alal-laahi kaziban aw kazzaba bilḥaqqi lammaa jaaa'ah; alaysa fee Jahannama maswal-lil-kaafireen.

69. Wallazeena jaahadoo feenaa lanahdiyannahum subulanaa; wa innal-laaha lama'al-muḥsineen **(Section 7)**

Sûrat ar-Rûm–30

(Revealed at Makkah)

Bismillaahir Raḥmaanir Raḥeem

1. Alif-Laaam-Meeem.

2. Ghulibatir-Room.

3. Feee adnal-arḍi wa hum-mim ba'di ghalabihim sa-yaghliboon.

4. Fee biḍ'i sineen; lillaahil-amru min qablu wa mim ba'd; wa yawma'iziñy-yafraḥul-mu'minoon.

5. Binaṣril-laah; yanṣuru mañy-yashaaa'u wa Huwal-'Azeezur-Raḥeem.

وقف لازم

الْحَيَوَانُ ۘ لَوْ كَانُوا يَعْلَمُونَ ﴿٦٤﴾
فَإِذَا رَكِبُوا فِي الْفُلْكِ دَعَوُا اللَّهَ
مُخْلِصِينَ لَهُ الدِّينَ ۚ فَلَمَّا نَجَّاهُمْ
إِلَى الْبَرِّ إِذَا هُمْ يُشْرِكُونَ ﴿٦٥﴾
لِيَكْفُرُوا بِمَا آتَيْنَاهُمْ ۚ وَلِيَتَمَتَّعُوا ۚ
فَسَوْفَ يَعْلَمُونَ ﴿٦٦﴾
أَوَلَمْ يَرَوْا أَنَّا جَعَلْنَا حَرَمًا آمِنًا
وَيُتَخَطَّفُ النَّاسُ مِنْ حَوْلِهِمْ ۚ
أَفَبِالْبَاطِلِ يُؤْمِنُونَ وَبِنِعْمَةِ
اللَّهِ يَكْفُرُونَ ﴿٦٧﴾
وَمَنْ أَظْلَمُ مِمَّنِ افْتَرَىٰ عَلَى اللَّهِ
كَذِبًا أَوْ كَذَّبَ بِالْحَقِّ لَمَّا جَاءَهُ ۚ
أَلَيْسَ فِي جَهَنَّمَ مَثْوًى لِلْكَافِرِينَ ﴿٦٨﴾
وَالَّذِينَ جَاهَدُوا فِينَا لَنَهْدِيَنَّهُمْ
سُبُلَنَا ۚ وَإِنَّ اللَّهَ لَمَعَ الْمُحْسِنِينَ ﴿٦٩﴾

(٣٠) سُورَةُ الرُّومِ مَكِّيَّةٌ (٨٤)

بِسْمِ اللَّهِ الرَّحْمَٰنِ الرَّحِيمِ

الم ﴿١﴾
غُلِبَتِ الرُّومُ ﴿٢﴾
فِي أَدْنَى الْأَرْضِ وَهُمْ مِنْ بَعْدِ
غَلَبِهِمْ سَيَغْلِبُونَ ﴿٣﴾
فِي بِضْعِ سِنِينَ ۗ لِلَّهِ الْأَمْرُ مِنْ
قَبْلُ وَمِنْ بَعْدُ ۚ وَيَوْمَئِذٍ يَفْرَحُ
الْمُؤْمِنُونَ ﴿٤﴾
بِنَصْرِ اللَّهِ ۚ يَنْصُرُ مَنْ يَشَاءُ ۖ وَهُوَ
الْعَزِيزُ الرَّحِيمُ ﴿٥﴾

Ikhfa اخفاء | Ghunna غُنّہ | Ikhfa Meem Saakin اخفاء میم ساکن | Idghaam ادغام | Qalqala قلقلہ | Qalb قلب | Idghaam Meem Saakin ادغام میم ساکن

6. (It is) the promise of Allah. Never does Allah depart from His promise: but most men do not understand.

6. Wa'dal-laahi laa yukhliful-laahu wa'dahoo wa laakinna aksaran-naasi laa ya'lamoon.

وَعْدَ اللَّهِ ۖ لَا يُخْلِفُ اللَّهُ وَعْدَهُ
وَلَٰكِنَّ أَكْثَرَ النَّاسِ لَا يَعْلَمُونَ ﴿٦﴾

7. They know but the outer (things) in the life of this world: but they are heedless of the Hereafter.

7. Ya'lamoona ẓaahiram-minal-ḥayaatid-dunyaa wa hum 'anil-Aakhirati hum ghaafiloon.

يَعْلَمُونَ ظَاهِرًا مِّنَ الْحَيَاةِ الدُّنْيَا
وَهُمْ عَنِ الْآخِرَةِ هُمْ غَافِلُونَ ﴿٧﴾

8. Do they not reflect in their own minds? Not but for just ends and for a term appointed, did Allah create the heavens and the earth, and all between them: yet are there truly many among men who deny the meeting with their Lord (at the Resurrection)!

8. Awalam yatafakkaroo feee anfusihim; maa khalaqal-laahus-samaawaati wal-arḍa wa maa baynahumaaa illaa bil-ḥaqqi wa ajalim-musammaa; wa inna kaseeram-minan-naasi biliqaaa'i Rabbihim lakaafiroon.

أَوَلَمْ يَتَفَكَّرُوا فِي أَنفُسِهِم ۗ مَّا
خَلَقَ اللَّهُ السَّمَاوَاتِ وَالْأَرْضَ وَمَا
بَيْنَهُمَا إِلَّا بِالْحَقِّ وَأَجَلٍ مُّسَمًّى ۗ
وَإِنَّ كَثِيرًا مِّنَ النَّاسِ بِلِقَاءِ
رَبِّهِمْ لَكَافِرُونَ ﴿٨﴾

9. Do they not travel through the Earth,and see what was the end of those before them? They were superior to them in strength: they tilled the soil and populated it in greater numbers than these have done: there came to them their Messengers with Clear (Signs). (Which they rejected, to their own destruction): it was not Allah Who wronged them, but they wronged their own souls.

9. Awalam yaseeroo fil-arḍi fa-yanẓuroo kayfa kaana 'aaqibatul-lazeena min qablihim; kaanooo ashadda minhum quwwatañw-wa asaarul-arḍa wa 'amaroohaaa aksara mimmaa 'amaroohaa wa jaaa'at-hum Rusuluhum bil-bayyinaati famaa kaanal-laahu li-yaẓlimahum wa laakin kaanooo anfusahum yaẓlimoon.

أَوَلَمْ يَسِيرُوا فِي الْأَرْضِ فَيَنظُرُوا
كَيْفَ كَانَ عَاقِبَةُ الَّذِينَ مِن
قَبْلِهِمْ ۚ كَانُوا أَشَدَّ مِنْهُمْ قُوَّةً
وَأَثَارُوا الْأَرْضَ وَعَمَرُوهَا أَكْثَرَ
مِمَّا عَمَرُوهَا وَجَاءَتْهُمْ رُسُلُهُم
بِالْبَيِّنَاتِ ۖ فَمَا كَانَ اللَّهُ لِيَظْلِمَهُمْ
وَلَٰكِن كَانُوا أَنفُسَهُمْ يَظْلِمُونَ ﴿٩﴾

10. In the long run evil in the extreme will be the End of those who do evil; for that they rejected the Signs of Allah, and held them up to ridicule.

10. Summa kaana 'aaqibatal-lazeena asaaa'us-sooo-aaa an kazzaboo bi-Aayaatil-laahi wa kaanoo bihaa yastahzi'oon.

(Section 1)

ثُمَّ كَانَ عَاقِبَةَ الَّذِينَ أَسَاءُوا
السُّوأَىٰ أَن كَذَّبُوا بِآيَاتِ اللَّهِ
وَكَانُوا بِهَا يَسْتَهْزِئُونَ ﴿١٠﴾ ع

11. It is Allah Who begins (the process of) creation; then repeats it; then you shall be brought back to Him.

11. Allaahu yabda'ul-khalqa summa yu'eeduhoo summa ilayhi turja'oon.

اللَّهُ يَبْدَأُ الْخَلْقَ ثُمَّ يُعِيدُهُ ثُمَّ
إِلَيْهِ تُرْجَعُونَ ﴿١١﴾

12. On the Day that the Hour will be established, the guilty will be struck dumb with despair.

12. Wa Yawma taqoomus-Saa'atu yublisul-mujrimoon.

وَيَوْمَ تَقُومُ السَّاعَةُ يُبْلِسُ
الْمُجْرِمُونَ ﴿١٢﴾

13. No intercessor will they have among their "Partners" and they will (themselves) reject their "Partners".

13. Wa lam yakul-lahum-min shurakaaa'ihim shufa'aaa'u wa kaanoo bishurakaaa'ihim kaafireen.

وَلَمْ يَكُن لَّهُم مِّن شُرَكَائِهِمْ شُفَعَاءُ
وَكَانُوا بِشُرَكَائِهِمْ كَافِرِينَ ﴿١٣﴾

14. On the Day that the Hour will be established,- that Day

14. Wa Yawma taqoomus-Saa'atu Yawma'iziñy-

وَيَوْمَ تَقُومُ السَّاعَةُ يَوْمَئِذٍ

Ikhfa اخفاء | Ghunna غُنّہ | Ikhfa Meem Saakin اخفاء میم ساکن | Idghaam ادغام | Qalqala قلقلہ | Qalb قلب | Idghaam Meem Saakin ادغام میم ساکن

shall (all men) be sorted out.

yatafarraqoon.

يَتَفَرَّقُوْنَ ﴿١٤﴾

15. Then those who have believed and worked righteous deeds, shall be made happy in a Mead of Delight.

15. Fa-ammal-lazeena aamanoo wa 'amiluṣ-ṣaaliḥaati fahum fee rawḍatiñy-yuḥbaroon.

فَاَمَّا الَّذِيْنَ اٰمَنُوْا وَعَمِلُوا الصّٰلِحٰتِ فَهُمْ فِيْ رَوْضَةٍ يُّحْبَرُوْنَ ﴿١٥﴾

16. And those who have rejected Faith and falsely denied Our Signs and the meeting of the Hereafter,- such shall be brought forth to Punishment.

16. Wa ammal-lazeena kafaroo wa kazzaboo bi-Aayaatinaa wa liqaaa'il-Aakhirati faulaaa'ika fil-'azaabi muḥḍaroon.

وَاَمَّا الَّذِيْنَ كَفَرُوْا وَكَذَّبُوْا بِاٰيٰتِنَا وَلِقَآئِ الْاٰخِرَةِ فَاُولٰٓئِكَ فِي الْعَذَابِ مُحْضَرُوْنَ ﴿١٦﴾

17. So (give) glory to Allah, when you reach eventide and when you rise in the morning;

17. Fa-Subḥaanal-laahi ḥeena tumsoona wa ḥeena tuṣbiḥoon.

فَسُبْحٰنَ اللّٰهِ حِيْنَ تُمْسُوْنَ وَحِيْنَ تُصْبِحُوْنَ ﴿١٧﴾

18. Yes, to Him be praise, in the heavens and on earth; and in the late afternoon and when the day begins to decline.

18. Wa lahul-ḥamdu fis-samaawaati wal-arḍi wa 'ashiyyañw-wa ḥeena tuẓhiroon.

وَلَهُ الْحَمْدُ فِي السَّمٰوٰتِ وَالْاَرْضِ وَعَشِيًّا وَّحِيْنَ تُظْهِرُوْنَ ﴿١٨﴾

19. It is He Who brings out the living from the dead, and brings out the dead from the living, and Who gives life to the earth after it is dead: and thus you shall be brought out (from the dead).

19. Yukhrijul-ḥayya minal-mayyiti wa yukhrijul-mayyita minal-ḥayyi wa yuḥyil-arḍa ba'da mawtihaa; wa kazaalika tukhrajoon. **(Section 2)**

يُخْرِجُ الْحَيَّ مِنَ الْمَيِّتِ وَيُخْرِجُ الْمَيِّتَ مِنَ الْحَيِّ وَيُحْيِ الْاَرْضَ بَعْدَ مَوْتِهَا ؕ وَكَذٰلِكَ تُخْرَجُوْنَ ﴿١٩﴾ ع

20. Among His Signs in this, that He created you from dust; and then,- behold, you are men scattered (far and wide)!

20. Wa min Aayaatiheee an khalaqakum-min turaabin summa izaaa antum basharun tantashiroon.

وَمِنْ اٰيٰتِهٖٓ اَنْ خَلَقَكُمْ مِّنْ تُرَابٍ ثُمَّ اِذَآ اَنْتُمْ بَشَرٌ تَنْتَشِرُوْنَ ﴿٢٠﴾

21. And among His Signs is this, that He created for you mates from among yourselves, that you may dwell in tranquillity with them, and He has put love and mercy between your (hearts): verily in that are Signs for those who reflect.

21. Wa min Aayaatiheee an khalaqa lakum-min anfusikum azwaajal-litaskunooo ilayhaa wa ja'ala baynakum-mawaddatañw-wa raḥmah; inna fee zaalika la-Aayaatil-liqawmiñy-yatafakkaroon.

وَمِنْ اٰيٰتِهٖٓ اَنْ خَلَقَ لَكُمْ مِّنْ اَنْفُسِكُمْ اَزْوَاجًا لِّتَسْكُنُوْٓا اِلَيْهَا وَجَعَلَ بَيْنَكُمْ مَّوَدَّةً وَّرَحْمَةً ؕ اِنَّ فِيْ ذٰلِكَ لَاٰيٰتٍ لِّقَوْمٍ يَّتَفَكَّرُوْنَ ﴿٢١﴾

22. And among His Signs is the creation of the heavens and the earth, and the variations in your languages and your colors: verily in that are Signs for those who know.

22. Wa min Aayaatihee khalqus-samaawaati wal-arḍi wakhtilaafu alsinatikum wa alwaanikum; inna fee zaalika la-Aayaatil-lil-'aalimeen.

وَمِنْ اٰيٰتِهٖ خَلْقُ السَّمٰوٰتِ وَالْاَرْضِ وَاخْتِلَافُ اَلْسِنَتِكُمْ وَاَلْوَانِكُمْ ؕ اِنَّ فِيْ ذٰلِكَ لَاٰيٰتٍ لِّلْعٰلِمِيْنَ ﴿٢٢﴾

23. And among His Signs is the sleep that you take by night and by day, and the quest that you (make for livelihood) out of His Bounty: verily in that are Signs for those who hearken.

23. Wa min Aayaatihee manaamukum bil-layli wannahaari wabtighaaa'ukum-min faḍlih; inna fee zaalika la-Aayaatil-liqawmiñy-yasma'oon.

وَمِنْ اٰيٰتِهٖ مَنَامُكُمْ بِالَّيْلِ وَالنَّهَارِ وَابْتِغَآؤُكُمْ مِّنْ فَضْلِهٖ ؕ اِنَّ فِيْ ذٰلِكَ لَاٰيٰتٍ لِّقَوْمٍ يَّسْمَعُوْنَ ﴿٢٣﴾

24. And among His Signs, He shows you the lightning, by way both of fear

24. Wa min Aayaatihee yureekumul-barqa khawfañw-

وَمِنْ اٰيٰتِهٖ يُرِيْكُمُ الْبَرْقَ خَوْفًا

Ikhfa اخفاء | Ghunna غنّہ | Ikhfa Meem Saakin اخفاء میم ساکن | Idghaam ادغام | Qalqala قلقلہ | Qalb قلب | Idghaam Meem Saakin ادغام میم ساکن

and of hope, and He sends down rain from the sky and with it gives life to the earth after it is dead: verily in that are Signs for those who are wise.

wa ṭama'añw-wa yunazzilu minas-samaaa'i maaa'an fa-yuḥyee bihil-arḍa ba'da mawti-haaa inna fee zaalika la-Aayaa-til-liqawmiñy-ya'qiloon.

وَّطَمَعًا وَّيُنَزِّلُ مِنَ السَّمَآءِ مَآءً
فَيُحْيِ بِهِ الْاَرْضَ بَعْدَ مَوْتِهَاؕ
اِنَّ فِيْ ذٰلِكَ لَاٰيٰتٍ لِّقَوْمٍ
يَّعْقِلُوْنَ ﴿٢٤﴾

25. And among His Signs is this, that heaven and earth stand by His Command: then when He calls you, by a single call, from the earth, behold, you (straightway) come forth.

25. Wa min Aayaatiheee an taqoomas-samaaa'u wal-arḍu bi-amrih; summa izaa da'aakum da'watam-minal-arḍi izaaa antum takhrujoon.

وَمِنْ اٰيٰتِهٖۤ اَنْ تَقُوْمَ السَّمَآءُ وَ
الْاَرْضُ بِاَمْرِهٖؕ ثُمَّ اِذَا دَعَاكُمْ
دَعْوَةً ۖۗ مِّنَ الْاَرْضِ ۖۗ اِذَاۤ
اَنْتُمْ تَخْرُجُوْنَ ﴿٢٥﴾

26. To Him belongs every being that is in the heavens and on earth: all are devoutly obedient to Him.

26. Wa lahoo man fissamaa-waati wal-arḍi kullul-lahoo qaa-nitoon.

وَلَهٗ مَنْ فِي السَّمٰوٰتِ وَالْاَرْضِؕ
كُلٌّ لَّهٗ قٰنِتُوْنَ ﴿٢٦﴾

27. It is He Who begins (the process of) creation; then repeats it; and for Him it is most easy. To Him belongs the loftiest simi-litude (one can think of) in the heavens and the earth: for He is Exalted in Might, full of Wisdom.

27. Wa Huwal-lazee yab-da'ul-khalqa summa yu'eedu-hoo wa huwa ahwanu 'alayh; wa lahul-masalul-a'laa fis-samaawaati wal-arḍ; wa Huwal-'Azeezul-Ḥakeem. **(Section 3)**

وَهُوَ الَّذِيْ يَبْدَؤُا الْخَلْقَ ثُمَّ
يُعِيْدُهٗ وَهُوَ اَهْوَنُ عَلَيْهِؕ وَلَهُ
الْمَثَلُ الْاَعْلٰى فِي السَّمٰوٰتِ وَالْاَرْضِۚ
وَهُوَ الْعَزِيْزُ الْحَكِيْمُ ﴿٢٧﴾

28. He propounds to you a similitude from your own (experience): do you have partners among those whom your right hands possess, to share as equals in the wealth We have bestowed on you? Do you fear them as you fear each other? Thus do We explain the Signs in detail to a people that understand.

28. Ḍaraba lakum-masalam-min anfusikum hal lakum-mim-maa malakat aymaanukum-min shurakaaa'a fee maa razaq-naakum fa-antum feehi sawaaa-'un takhaafoonahum kakheefa-tikum anfusakum; kazaalika nufaṣṣilul-Aayaati liqawmiñy-ya'qiloon.

ضَرَبَ لَكُمْ مَّثَلًا مِّنْ اَنْفُسِكُمْؕ هَلْ
لَّكُمْ مِّنْ مَّا مَلَكَتْ اَيْمَانُكُمْ مِّنْ
شُرَكَآءَ فِيْ مَا رَزَقْنٰكُمْ فَاَنْتُمْ فِيْهِ
سَوَآءٌ تَخَافُوْنَهُمْ كَخِيْفَتِكُمْ اَنْفُسَكُمْؕ
كَذٰلِكَ نُفَصِّلُ الْاٰيٰتِ لِقَوْمٍ
يَّعْقِلُوْنَ ﴿٢٨﴾

29. Nay, the wrong-doers (merely) follow their own lusts, being devoid of knowledge. But who will guide those whom Allah leaves astray? To them there will be no helpers.

29. Balit-taba'al-lazeena ẓa-lamooo ahwaaa'ahum bighayri 'ilmin famañy-yahdee man aḍallal-laahu wa maa lahum min-naaṣireen.

بَلِ اتَّبَعَ الَّذِيْنَ ظَلَمُوْۤا اَهْوَآءَهُمْ
بِغَيْرِ عِلْمٍۚ فَمَنْ يَّهْدِيْ مَنْ اَضَلَّ
اللّٰهُؕ وَمَا لَهُمْ مِّنْ نّٰصِرِيْنَ ﴿٢٩﴾

30. So you set your face steadily and truly to the Faith: (establish) Allah's handiwork according to the pattern on which He has made mankind: no change (let there be) in the work (wrought) by Allah: that is the

30. Fa-aqim wajhaka liddeeni Ḥaneefaa; fiṭratal-laahil-latee faṭaran-naasa 'alayhaa; laa tabdeela likhalqil-laah; zaali-kad-deenul-

فَاَقِمْ وَجْهَكَ لِلدِّيْنِ حَنِيْفًاؕ فِطْرَتَ
اللّٰهِ الَّتِيْ فَطَرَ النَّاسَ عَلَيْهَاؕ
لَا تَبْدِيْلَ لِخَلْقِ اللّٰهِؕ ذٰلِكَ الدِّيْنُ

standard Religion: but most among mankind do not understand.

qayyimu wa laakinna aksaran-naasi laa ya'lamoon.

الْقَيِّمُ ۙ وَلٰكِنَّ اَكْثَرَ النَّاسِ
لَا يَعْلَمُوْنَ ۙ ﴿۳۰﴾

31. Turn you back in repentance to Him, and fear Him: establish regular prayers, and you be not among those who join gods with Allah,-

31. Muneebeena ilayhi wattaqoohu wa aqeemuṣ-Ṣalaata wa laa takoonoo minal-mushrikeen.

مُنِيْبِيْنَ اِلَيْهِ وَاتَّقُوْهُ وَاَقِيْمُوا
الصَّلٰوةَ وَلَا تَكُوْنُوْا مِنَ الْمُشْرِكِيْنَ ۙ ﴿۳۱﴾

32. Those who split up their Religion, and become (mere) Sects,- each party rejoicing in that which is with itself!

32. Minal-lazeena farraqoo deenahum wa kaanoo shiya'an kullu ḥizbim bimaa ladayhim fariḥoon.

مِنَ الَّذِيْنَ فَرَّقُوْا دِيْنَهُمْ وَكَانُوْا
شِيَعًا ؕ كُلُّ حِزْبٍۢ بِمَا لَدَيْهِمْ
فَرِحُوْنَ ﴿۳۲﴾

33. When trouble touches men, they cry to their Lord, turning back to Him in repentance: but when He gives them a taste of Mercy as from Himself, behold, some of them pay part-worship to other god's besides their Lord,-

33. Wa izaa massan-naasa ḍurrun da'aw Rabbahum-muneebeena ilayhi summa izaaa azaqahum-minhu raḥmatan izaa fareequm-minhum bi-Rabbihim yushrikoon.

وَاِذَا مَسَّ النَّاسَ ضُرٌّ دَعَوْا رَبَّهُمْ
مُّنِيْبِيْنَ اِلَيْهِ ثُمَّ اِذَآ اَذَاقَهُمْ
مِّنْهُ رَحْمَةً اِذَا فَرِيْقٌ مِّنْهُمْ
بِرَبِّهِمْ يُشْرِكُوْنَ ﴿۳۳﴾

34. (As if) to show their ingratitude for the (favors) We have bestowed on them! Then enjoy (your brief day); but soon will you know (your folly)

34. Li-yakfuroo bimaaa aataynaahum; fatamatta'oo fasawfa ta'lamoon.

لِيَكْفُرُوْا بِمَآ اٰتَيْنٰهُمْ ؕ فَتَمَتَّعُوْا ۥ وقفة
فَسَوْفَ تَعْلَمُوْنَ ﴿۳۴﴾

35. Or have We sent down authority to them, which points out to them the things to which they pay part-worship?

35. Am anzalnaa 'alayhim sulṭaanan fahuwa yatakallamu bimaa kaanoo bihee yushrikoon.

اَمْ اَنْزَلْنَا عَلَيْهِمْ سُلْطٰنًا فَهُوَ
يَتَكَلَّمُ بِمَا كَانُوْا بِهٖ يُشْرِكُوْنَ ﴿۳۵﴾

36. When We give men a taste of Mercy, they exult thereat: and when some evil afflicts them because of what their (own) hands have sent forth, behold, they are in despair!

36. Wa izaaa azaqnan-naasa raḥmatan fariḥoo bihaa wa in tuṣibhum sayyi'atum bimaa qaddamat aydeehim izaa hum yaqnaṭoon.

وَاِذَآ اَذَقْنَا النَّاسَ رَحْمَةً فَرِحُوْا بِهَا ؕ
وَاِنْ تُصِبْهُمْ سَيِّئَةٌۢ بِمَا قَدَّمَتْ
اَيْدِيْهِمْ اِذَا هُمْ يَقْنَطُوْنَ ﴿۳۶﴾

37. Do not they see that Allah enlarges the provision and restricts it, to whomsoever He pleases? Verily in that are Signs for those who believe.

37. Awalam yaraw annal-laaha yabsuṭur-rizqa limañy-yashaaa'u wa yaqdir; inna fee zaalika la-Aayaatil-liqawmiñy-yu'minoon.

اَوَلَمْ يَرَوْا اَنَّ اللّٰهَ يَبْسُطُ الرِّزْقَ
لِمَنْ يَّشَآءُ وَيَقْدِرُ ؕ اِنَّ فِيْ ذٰلِكَ
لَاٰيٰتٍ لِّقَوْمٍ يُّؤْمِنُوْنَ ﴿۳۷﴾

38. So give what is due to kindred, the needy, and the wayfarer. That is best for those who seek the Countenance of Allah, and it is they who will prosper.

38. Fa-aati zal-qurbaa ḥaqqahoo walmiskeena wabnas-sabeel; zaalika khayrul-lil-lazeena yureedoona Wajhal-laahi wa ulaaa'ika humul-mufliḥoon.

فَاٰتِ ذَا الْقُرْبٰى حَقَّهٗ وَالْمِسْكِيْنَ
وَابْنَ السَّبِيْلِ ؕ ذٰلِكَ خَيْرٌ لِّلَّذِيْنَ
يُرِيْدُوْنَ وَجْهَ اللّٰهِ ۫ وَاُولٰٓئِكَ
هُمُ الْمُفْلِحُوْنَ ﴿۳۸﴾

39. That which you lay out for increase through

39. Wa maaa aataytum-mir-ribal-li-yarbuwa feee

وَمَآ اٰتَيْتُمْ مِّنْ رِّبًا لِّيَرْبُوَا۠ فِيْ

Ikhfa اخفاء | Ghunna غُنّہ | Ikhfa Meem Saakin اخفاء میم ساکن | Idghaam ادغام | Qalqala قلقلہ | Qalb قلب | Idghaam Meem Saakin ادغام میم ساکن

the property of (other) people, will have no increase with Allah: but that which you lay out for charity, seeking the Countenance of Allah, (will increase): it is these who will get a recompense multi-plied.

40. It is Allah Who has created you: further, He has provided for your sustenance; then He will cause you to die; and again He will give you life. Are there any of your (false) "Partners" who can do any single one of these things? Glory to Him! and high is He above the partners they attribute (to him)!

41. Mischief has appeared on land and sea because of (the deed) that the hands of men have earned, that (Allah) may give them a taste of some of their deeds: in order that they may turn back (from Evil).

42. Say: "Travel through the earth and see what was the end of those before (you): Most of them worshipped others besides Allah."

43. But you set your face to the right Religion, before there come from Allah the Day which there is no chance of averting: on that Day shall men be divided (in two).

44. Those who reject Faith will suffer from that rejection: and those who work righteousness will make provision for themselves (in heaven):

45. That He may reward those who believe and work righteous deeds, out of His Bounty. For He loves not those who reject Faith.

46. Among His Signs is this, that He sends the Winds, as heralds of Glad Tidings, giving you a taste of His (Grace and) Mercy,- that the ships may sail (majestically) by His Command and that you may seek of His Bounty: in order that you may be grateful.

amwaalin-naasi falaa yarboo 'indal-laahi wa maaa aataytum-min Zakaatin tureedoona Wajhal-laahi fa-ulaaa'ika humul-muḍ'ifoon.

40. Allaahul-lazee khalaqakum summa razaqakum summa yumeetukum summa yuḥyeekum hal min shurakaaa'ikum-mañy-yaf'alu min zaalikum-min shay'; Sub-ḥaanahoo wa Ta'aalaa 'ammaa yushrikoon.

(Section 4)

41. Ẓaharal-fasaadu fil-barri wal-baḥri bimaa kasabat aydin-naasi li-yuzeeqahum ba'ḍal-lazee 'amiloo la'allahum yarji'oon.

42. Qul seeroo fil-arḍi fanẓuroo kayfa kaana 'aaqibatul-lazeena min qabl; kaana aksaruhum-mushrikeen.

43. Fa-aqim wajhaka lid-deenil-qayyimi min qabli añy-yaåtiya Yawmul-laa maradda lahoo minal-laahi Yawma'iziñy-yaṣṣadda'oon.

44. Man kafara fa'alayhi kufruhoo wa man 'amila ṣaaliḥan fali-anfusihim yamhadoon.

45. Li-yajziyal-lazeena aamanoo wa 'amiluṣ-ṣaaliḥaati min faḍlih; innahoo laa yuḥibbul-kaafireen.

46. Wa min Aayaatiheee añy-yursilar-riyaaḥa mubashshiraatiñw-wa li-yuzeeqakum-mir-raḥmatihee wa litajriyal-fulku bi-amrihee wa litabtaghoo min faḍlihee wa la'allakum tashkuroon.

أَمْوَالِ النَّاسِ فَلَا يَرْبُوا عِندَ اللَّهِ
وَمَا آتَيْتُم مِّن زَكَاةٍ تُرِيدُونَ وَجْهَ
اللَّهِ فَأُولَٰئِكَ هُمُ الْمُضْعِفُونَ ﴿٣٩﴾
اللَّهُ الَّذِي خَلَقَكُمْ ثُمَّ رَزَقَكُمْ
ثُمَّ يُمِيتُكُمْ ثُمَّ يُحْيِيكُمْ ۖ هَلْ مِن
شُرَكَائِكُم مَّن يَفْعَلُ مِن ذَٰلِكُم
مِّن شَيْءٍ ۚ سُبْحَانَهُ وَتَعَالَىٰ عَمَّا
يُشْرِكُونَ ﴿٤٠﴾ ع
ظَهَرَ الْفَسَادُ فِي الْبَرِّ وَالْبَحْرِ بِمَا
كَسَبَتْ أَيْدِي النَّاسِ لِيُذِيقَهُم
بَعْضَ الَّذِي عَمِلُوا لَعَلَّهُمْ يَرْجِعُونَ ﴿٤١﴾
قُلْ سِيرُوا فِي الْأَرْضِ فَانظُرُوا
كَيْفَ كَانَ عَاقِبَةُ الَّذِينَ مِن
قَبْلُ ۚ كَانَ أَكْثَرُهُم مُّشْرِكِينَ ﴿٤٢﴾
فَأَقِمْ وَجْهَكَ لِلدِّينِ الْقَيِّمِ مِن
قَبْلِ أَن يَأْتِيَ يَوْمٌ لَّا مَرَدَّ لَهُ
مِنَ اللَّهِ ۖ يَوْمَئِذٍ يَصَّدَّعُونَ ﴿٤٣﴾
مَن كَفَرَ فَعَلَيْهِ كُفْرُهُ ۖ وَمَنْ عَمِلَ
صَالِحًا فَلِأَنفُسِهِمْ يَمْهَدُونَ ﴿٤٤﴾
لِيَجْزِيَ الَّذِينَ آمَنُوا وَعَمِلُوا
الصَّالِحَاتِ مِن فَضْلِهِ ۚ إِنَّهُ لَا
يُحِبُّ الْكَافِرِينَ ﴿٤٥﴾
وَمِنْ آيَاتِهِ أَن يُرْسِلَ الرِّيَاحَ
مُبَشِّرَاتٍ وَلِيُذِيقَكُم مِّن رَّحْمَتِهِ
وَلِتَجْرِيَ الْفُلْكُ بِأَمْرِهِ وَلِتَبْتَغُوا
مِن فَضْلِهِ وَلَعَلَّكُمْ تَشْكُرُونَ ﴿٤٦﴾

Ikhfa اخفاء | Ghunna غنّہ | Ikhfa Meem Saakin اخفاء میم ساکن | Idghaam ادغام | Qalqala قلقلہ | Qalb قلب | Idghaam Meem Saakin ادغام میم ساکن

47. We sent indeed, before you, Messengers to their (respective) peoples, and they came to them with Clear Signs: then, to those who transgressed, We meted out Retribution: and it was due from Us to aid those who believed.

48. It is Allah Who sends the Winds, and they raise the Clouds: then He spreads them in the sky as He wills, and break them into fragments, until you see rain-drops issue from the midst thereof: then when He has made them reach such of His servants as He wills behold, they do rejoice!-

49. Even though, before they received (the rain) - just before this - they were dumb with despair!

50. Then contemplate (O man!) the memorials of Allah's Mercy!- how He gives life to the earth after its death: verily the same will give life to the men who are dead: for He has power over all things.

51. And if We (but) send a Wind from which they see (their tilth) turn yellow,- behold, they become, thereafter, Ungrateful (Unbelievers)!

52. So verily you can not make the dead to hear, nor can you make the deaf to hear the call, when they show their backs and turn away.

53. Nor can you lead back the blind from their straying: only those you will make to hear, who believe in Our Signs and submit (their wills in Islam).

54. It is Allah Who created you in a state of (helpless) weakness, then gave (you) strength after weakness, then, after strength, gave (you weakness and a hoary head:

47. Wa laqad arsalnaa min qablika Rusulan ilaa qawmihim fajaaa'oohum bil-bayyinaati fantaqamnaa minal-lazeena ajramoo wa kaana ḥaqqan 'alaynaa naṣrul-mu'mineen.

48. Allaahul-lazee yursilur-riyaaḥa fatuseeru saḥaaban fa-yabsuṭuhoo fis-samaaa'i kayfa yashaaa'u wa yaj'aluhoo kisa-fan fataral-wadqa yakhruju min khilaalihee fa-izaaa aṣaaba bi-hee mañy-yashaaa'u min 'ibaa-diheee izaa hum yastabshiroon.

49. Wa in kaanoo min qabli añy-yunazzala 'alayhim-min qablihee lamubliseen.

50. Fanẓur ilaaa aasaari raḥ-matil-laahi kayfa yuḥyil-arḍa ba'da mawtihaa; inna zaalika lamuḥyil-mawtaa wa Huwa 'alaa kulli shay'in Qadeer.

51. Wa la'in arsalnaa reeḥan fara-awhu muṣfarral-laẓalloo mim ba'dihee yakfuroon.

52. Fa-innaka laa tusmi'ul-mawtaa wa laa tusmi'uṣ-ṣum-mad-du'aaa'a izaa wallaw mudbireen.

53. Wa maaa anta bihaadil-'umyi 'an ḍalaalatihim in tus-mi'u illaa mañy-yu'minu bi-Aa-yaatinaa fahum-muslimoon.

(Section 5)

54. Allaahul-lazee khalaqa-kum-min ḍu'fin summa ja'ala mim ba'di ḍu'fin quwwatan summa ja'ala mim ba'di quw-watin du'fañw-

وَلَقَدْ اَرْسَلْنَا مِنْ قَبْلِكَ رُسُلًا اِلٰى
قَوْمِهِمْ فَجَآءُوْهُمْ بِالْبَيِّنٰتِ فَانْتَقَمْنَا
مِنَ الَّذِيْنَ اَجْرَمُوْا ؕ وَكَانَ حَقًّا
عَلَيْنَا نَصْرُ الْمُؤْمِنِيْنَ ﴿٤٧﴾
اَللّٰهُ الَّذِيْ يُرْسِلُ الرِّيٰحَ فَتُثِيْرُ
سَحَابًا فَيَبْسُطُهٗ فِى السَّمَآءِ كَيْفَ
يَشَآءُ وَيَجْعَلُهٗ كِسَفًا فَتَرَى الْوَدْقَ
يَخْرُجُ مِنْ خِلٰلِهٖ ۚ فَاِذَآ اَصَابَ
بِهٖ مَنْ يَّشَآءُ مِنْ عِبَادِهٖۤ اِذَا
هُمْ يَسْتَبْشِرُوْنَ ﴿٤٨﴾
وَاِنْ كَانُوْا مِنْ قَبْلِ اَنْ يُّنَزَّلَ
عَلَيْهِمْ مِّنْ قَبْلِهٖ لَمُبْلِسِيْنَ ﴿٤٩﴾
فَانْظُرْ اِلٰۤى اٰثٰرِ رَحْمَتِ اللّٰهِ كَيْفَ
يُحْيِ الْاَرْضَ بَعْدَ مَوْتِهَا ؕ اِنَّ
ذٰلِكَ لَمُحْيِ الْمَوْتٰى ۚ وَهُوَ عَلٰى كُلِّ
شَيْءٍ قَدِيْرٌ ﴿٥٠﴾
وَلَئِنْ اَرْسَلْنَا رِيْحًا فَرَاَوْهُ مُصْفَرًّا
لَّظَلُّوْا مِنْۢ بَعْدِهٖ يَكْفُرُوْنَ ﴿٥١﴾
فَاِنَّكَ لَا تُسْمِعُ الْمَوْتٰى وَلَا تُسْمِعُ
الصُّمَّ الدُّعَآءَ اِذَا وَلَّوْا مُدْبِرِيْنَ ﴿٥٢﴾
وَمَآ اَنْتَ بِهٰدِ الْعُمْيِ عَنْ ضَلٰلَتِهِمْ ؕ
اِنْ تُسْمِعُ اِلَّا مَنْ يُّؤْمِنُ بِاٰيٰتِنَا
فَهُمْ مُّسْلِمُوْنَ ﴿٥٣﴾ ع
اَللّٰهُ الَّذِيْ خَلَقَكُمْ مِّنْ ضُعْفٍ
ثُمَّ جَعَلَ مِنْۢ بَعْدِ ضُعْفٍ قُوَّةً
ثُمَّ جَعَلَ مِنْۢ بَعْدِ قُوَّةٍ ضُعْفًا

قرأ حفص بضم الضاد وفتحها في الثلاثة ولكن الضم مختارة ١٢

Ikhfa اخفاء | Ghunna غُنّہ | Ikhfa Meem Saakin اخفاء میم ساکن | Idghaam ادغام | Qalqala قلقلہ | Qalb قلب | Idghaam Meem Saakin ادغام میم ساکن

He creates as He wills, and it is He Who has all knowledge and power.

55. On the Day that the Hour (of Reckoning) will be established, the transgressors will swear that they did not tarry but an hour: thus were they used to being deluded!

56. But those endued with knowledge and faith will say: "Indeed you tarried, within Allah's Decree, to the Day of Resurrection, and this is the Day of Resurrection: but you were not aware!"

57. So on that Day no excuse of theirs will avail the Transgressors, nor will they be invited (then) to seek grace (by repentance).

58. Verily We have propounded for men, in this Qur'an every kind of Parable: but if you bring to them any Sign, the Unbelievers are sure to say, "You do nothing but talk vanities."

59. Thus Allah seals up the hearts of those who do not understand.

60. So patiently persevere: for verily the promise of Allah is true: nor let those shake your firmness, who have (themselves) no certainty of faith.

wa shaybah; yakhluqu maa yashaaa'u wa Huwal-'Aleemul-Qadeer.

55. Wa Yawma taqoomus-Saa'atu yuqsimul-mujrimoona maa labi<u>s</u>oo ghayra saa'ah; ka<u>z</u>aalika kaanoo yu'fakoon.

56. Wa qaalal-la<u>z</u>eena ootul-'ilma wal-eemaana laqad labi<u>s</u>tum fee kitaabil-laahi ilaa yawmil-ba'<u>s</u>i fahaa<u>z</u>aa yawmul-ba'<u>s</u>i wa laakinnakum kuntum laa ta'lamoon.

57. Fa-Yawma'i<u>z</u>il-laa yanfa-'ul-la<u>z</u>eena ẓalamoo ma'ziratuhum wa laa hum yusta'taboon.

58. Wa laqad ḍarabnaa linnaasi fee haa<u>z</u>al-Qur-aani min kulli ma<u>s</u>al; wa la'in ji'tahum bi-Aayatil-la-yaqoolannal-la<u>z</u>eena kafarooo in antum illaa mubṭiloon.

59. Ka<u>z</u>aalika yaṭba'ul-laahu 'alaa quloobil-la<u>z</u>eena laa ya'lamoon.

60. Faṣbir inna wa'dal-laahi ḥaqquñw-wa laa yastakhiffannakal-la<u>z</u>eena laa yooqinoon. **(Section 6)**

وَّشَيْبَةً ۗ يَخْلُقُ مَا يَشَآءُ ۚ وَهُوَ
الْعَلِيْمُ الْقَدِيْرُ ﴿٥٤﴾
وَيَوْمَ تَقُوْمُ السَّاعَةُ يُقْسِمُ
الْمُجْرِمُوْنَ ۙ مَا لَبِثُوْا غَيْرَ سَاعَةٍ ۭ
كَذٰلِكَ كَانُوْا يُؤْفَكُوْنَ ﴿٥٥﴾
وَقَالَ الَّذِيْنَ اُوْتُوا الْعِلْمَ وَالْاِيْمَانَ
لَقَدْ لَبِثْتُمْ فِيْ كِتٰبِ اللّٰهِ اِلٰى
يَوْمِ الْبَعْثِ ۡ فَهٰذَا يَوْمُ الْبَعْثِ
وَلٰكِنَّكُمْ كُنْتُمْ لَا تَعْلَمُوْنَ ﴿٥٦﴾
فَيَوْمَئِذٍ لَّا يَنْفَعُ الَّذِيْنَ ظَلَمُوْا
مَعْذِرَتُهُمْ وَلَا هُمْ يُسْتَعْتَبُوْنَ ﴿٥٧﴾
وَلَقَدْ ضَرَبْنَا لِلنَّاسِ فِيْ هٰذَا الْقُرْاٰنِ
مِنْ كُلِّ مَثَلٍ ۭ وَلَئِنْ جِئْتَهُمْ بِاٰيَةٍ
لَّيَقُوْلَنَّ الَّذِيْنَ كَفَرُوْٓا اِنْ
اَنْتُمْ اِلَّا مُبْطِلُوْنَ ﴿٥٨﴾
كَذٰلِكَ يَطْبَعُ اللّٰهُ عَلٰى قُلُوْبِ
الَّذِيْنَ لَا يَعْلَمُوْنَ ﴿٥٩﴾
فَاصْبِرْ اِنَّ وَعْدَ اللّٰهِ حَقٌّ وَّلَا
يَسْتَخِفَّنَّكَ الَّذِيْنَ لَا يُوْقِنُوْنَ ﴿٦٠﴾ ع

31. The Wise

In the name of Allah, Most Gracious, Most Merciful.

Sûrat Luqmân–31

(Revealed at Makkah)

Bismillaahir Raḥmaanir Raḥeem

(٣١) سُوْرَةُ لُقْمٰنَ مَكِّيَّةٌ (٥٧)

بِسْمِ اللّٰهِ الرَّحْمٰنِ الرَّحِيْمِ

1. *Alif-Lam-Mim.*

2. These are Verses of the Wise Book,-

3. A Guide and a Mercy to the Doers of Good,-

4. Those who establish regular Prayer, and give regular Charity, and have (in their hearts)

1. Alif-Laaam-Meeem.

2. Tilka Aayaatul-Kitaabil-Ḥakeem.

3. Hudañw-wa raḥmatal-lilmuḥsineen.

4. Alla<u>z</u>eena yuqeemoonaṣ-Ṣalaata wa yu'toonaz-Zakaata wa hum bil-Aakhirati hum

الٓمّٓ ﴿١﴾
تِلْكَ اٰيٰتُ الْكِتٰبِ الْحَكِيْمِ ﴿٢﴾
هُدًى وَّرَحْمَةً لِّلْمُحْسِنِيْنَ ﴿٣﴾
الَّذِيْنَ يُقِيْمُوْنَ الصَّلٰوةَ وَيُؤْتُوْنَ
الزَّكٰوةَ وَهُمْ بِالْاٰخِرَةِ هُمْ

Ikhfa اخفاء | Ghunna غُنّہ | Ikhfa Meem Saakin اخفاءمیم ساکن | Idghaam ادغام | Qalqala قلقلہ | Qalb قلب | Idghaam Meem Saakin ادغام میم ساکن

the assurance of the Hereafter.

yooqinoon.

يُوقِنُونَ ④

5. These are on (true) guidance from their Lord: and these are the ones who will prosper.

5. Ulaaa'ika 'alaa hudam-mir-Rabbihim wa ulaaa'ika humul-mufliḥoon.

أُولَٰٓئِكَ عَلَىٰ هُدًى مِّن رَّبِّهِمْ
وَأُولَٰٓئِكَ هُمُ الْمُفْلِحُونَ ⑤

6. But there are, among men, those who purchase idle tales, without knowledge (or meaning), to mislead (men) from the Path of Allah and throw ridicule (on the Path): for such there will be a Humiliating Penalty.

6. Wa minan-naasi mañy-yashtaree lahwal-ḥadeesi li-yuḍilla 'an sabeelil-laahi bighayri 'ilmiñw-wa yattakhizahaa huzuwaa; ulaaa'ika lahum 'azaabum-muheen.

وَمِنَ النَّاسِ مَن يَشْتَرِي لَهْوَ
الْحَدِيثِ لِيُضِلَّ عَن سَبِيلِ اللَّهِ
بِغَيْرِ عِلْمٍ ۖ وَيَتَّخِذَهَا هُزُوًا ۚ
أُولَٰٓئِكَ لَهُمْ عَذَابٌ مُّهِينٌ ⑥

7. When Our Signs are rehearsed to such a one, he turns away in arrogance, as if he did not hear them, as if there were deaf-ness in both his ears: announce to him a grievous Penalty.

7. Wa izaa tutlaa 'alayhi Aayaatunaa wallaa mustakbiran ka-al-lam yasma'haa ka-anna feee uzunayhi waqran fabash-shirhu bi'azaabin aleem.

وَإِذَا تُتْلَىٰ عَلَيْهِ آيَاتُنَا وَلَّىٰ
مُسْتَكْبِرًا كَأَن لَّمْ يَسْمَعْهَا
كَأَنَّ فِي أُذُنَيْهِ وَقْرًا ۖ فَبَشِّرْهُ
بِعَذَابٍ أَلِيمٍ ⑦

8. For those who believe and work righteous deeds, there will be Gardens of Bliss,-

8. Innal-lazeena aamanoo wa 'amiluṣ-ṣaaliḥaati lahum Jannaatun-Na'eem.

إِنَّ الَّذِينَ آمَنُوا وَعَمِلُوا الصَّالِحَاتِ
لَهُمْ جَنَّاتُ النَّعِيمِ ⑧

9. To dwell therein. The promise of Allah is true: and He is Exalted in Power, Wise.

9. Khaalideena feehaa wa'dal-laahi ḥaqqaa; wa Huwal-'Azeezul-Ḥakeem.

خَالِدِينَ فِيهَا ۖ وَعْدَ اللَّهِ حَقًّا ۚ
وَهُوَ الْعَزِيزُ الْحَكِيمُ ⑨

10. He created the heavens without any pillars that you can see; He set on the earth mountains standing firm, lest it should shake with you; and He scattered through it beasts of all kinds. We send down rain from the sky, and produce on the earth every kind of noble creature, in pairs.

10. Khalaqas-samaawaati bighayri 'amadin tarawnahaa wa alqaa fil-arḍi rawaasiya an tameeda bikum wa bassa feehaa min kulli daaabbah; wa anzalnaa minas-samaaa'i maaa'an fa-ambatnaa feehaa min kulli zawjin kareem.

خَلَقَ السَّمَاوَاتِ بِغَيْرِ عَمَدٍ تَرَوْنَهَا ۖ
وَأَلْقَىٰ فِي الْأَرْضِ رَوَاسِيَ أَن
تَمِيدَ بِكُمْ وَبَثَّ فِيهَا مِن كُلِّ
دَابَّةٍ ۚ وَأَنزَلْنَا مِنَ السَّمَاءِ مَاءً
فَأَنبَتْنَا فِيهَا مِن كُلِّ زَوْجٍ كَرِيمٍ ⑩

11. Such is the Creation of Allah: now show Me what is there that others besides Him have created: nay, but the Transgressors are in manifest error.

11. Haazaa khalqul-laahi fa-aroonee maazaa khalaqal-lazeena min doonih; baliẓ-ẓaalimoona fee ḍalaalim Mubeen.

(Section 1)

هَٰذَا خَلْقُ اللَّهِ فَأَرُونِي مَاذَا خَلَقَ
الَّذِينَ مِن دُونِهِ ۚ بَلِ الظَّالِمُونَ
فِي ضَلَالٍ مُّبِينٍ ⑪ ع

12. We bestowed (in the past) Wisdom on Luqman: "Show (your) gratitude to Allah." and who is (so) grateful does so to the profit of his own soul: but if any is ungrateful, verily

12. Wa laqad aataynaa Luqmaanal-ḥikmata anishkur lil-laah; wa mañy-yashkur fa-innamaa yashkuru linafsihee wa man kafara fa-innal-

وَلَقَدْ آتَيْنَا لُقْمَانَ الْحِكْمَةَ أَنِ
اشْكُرْ لِلَّهِ ۚ وَمَن يَشْكُرْ فَإِنَّمَا
يَشْكُرُ لِنَفْسِهِ ۖ وَمَن كَفَرَ فَإِنَّ

Ikhfa اخفاء | Ghunna غنّہ | Ikhfa Meem Saakin اخفاء میم ساکن | Idghaam ادغام | Qalqala قلقلہ | Qalb قلب | Idghaam Meem Saakin ادغام میم ساکن

Allah is free of all wants, Worthy of all praise.

laaha Ghaniyyun Ḥameed.

اللّٰهَ غَنِىٌّ حَمِيۡدٌ ﴿۱۲﴾

13. Behold, Luqman said to his son by way of instruction: "O my son! do not join in worship (others) with Allah: for false worship is indeed the highest wrong-doing."

13\. Wa iz qaala Luqmaanu libnihee wa huwa ya'iẓuhoo yaa bunayya laa tushrik billaah; innash-shirka laẓulmun 'aẓeem.

وَاِذۡ قَالَ لُقۡمٰنُ لِابۡنِهٖ وَهُوَ يَعِظُهٗ
يٰبُنَىَّ لَا تُشۡرِكۡ بِاللّٰهِ ؕ اِنَّ الشِّرۡكَ
لَظُلۡمٌ عَظِيۡمٌ ﴿۱۳﴾

وقف النبي صلى الله عليه وآله وسلم ١٢

14. And We have enjoined on man (to be good) to his parents: in travail upon travail his mother bore him, and in two years was his weaning: (hear the command), "Show gratitude to Me and to your parents: to Me is (your final) Goal.

14\. Wa waṣṣaynal-insaana biwaalidayhi ḥamalat-hu ummuhoo wahnan 'alaa wahniñw-wa fiṣaaluhoo fee 'aamayni anishkur lee wa liwaalidayka ilayyal-maṣeer.

وَوَصَّيۡنَا الۡاِنۡسَانَ بِوَالِدَيۡهِ‌ ۚ حَمَلَتۡهُ
اُمُّهٗ وَهۡنًا عَلٰى وَهۡنٍ وَّفِصٰلُهٗ
فِىۡ عَامَيۡنِ اَنِ اشۡكُرۡ لِىۡ وَلِـوَالِدَيۡكَ ؕ
اِلَىَّ الۡمَصِيۡرُ ﴿۱۴﴾

النصف

15. "But if they strive to make you join in worship with Me things of which you have no knowledge, do not obey them; yet bear them company in this life with justice (and consideration), and follow the way of those who turn to Me (in love): in the end the return of you all is to Me, and I will tell you the truth (and meaning) of all that you did."

15\. Wa in jaahadaaka 'alaaa an tushrika bee maa laysa laka bihee 'ilmun falaa tuṭi'humaa wa ṣaaḥib-humaa fid-dunyaa ma'roofañw-wattabi' sabeela man anaaba ilayy; summa ilayya marji'ukum fa-unabbi'ukum bimaa kuntum ta'maloon.

وَاِنۡ جَاهَدٰكَ عَلٰٓى اَنۡ تُشۡرِكَ بِىۡ
مَا لَـيۡسَ لَـكَ بِهٖ عِلۡمٌ فَلَا تُطِعۡهُمَا
وَصَاحِبۡهُمَا فِى الدُّنۡيَا مَعۡرُوۡفًا ز
وَّاتَّبِعۡ سَبِيۡلَ مَنۡ اَنَابَ اِلَىَّ ۚ ثُمَّ
اِلَىَّ مَرۡجِعُكُمۡ فَاُنَبِّئُكُمۡ بِمَا كُنۡتُمۡ
تَعۡمَلُوۡنَ ﴿۱۵﴾

16. "O my son!" (said Luqman), "If there be (but) the weight of a mustard-seed and it were (hidden) in a rock, or (anywhere) in the heavens or on Earth, Allah will bring it forth: for Allah is Subtle and aware.

16\. Yaa bunayya innahaaa in taku misqaala ḥabbatim-min khardalin fatakun fee ṣakhratin aw fis-samaawaati aw fil-arḍi yaàti bihal-laah; innal-laaha Laṭeefun Khabeer.

يٰبُنَىَّ اِنَّهَاۤ اِنۡ تَكُ مِثۡقَالَ حَبَّةٍ
مِّنۡ خَرۡدَلٍ فَتَكُنۡ فِىۡ صَخۡرَةٍ اَوۡ
فِى السَّمٰوٰتِ اَوۡ فِى الۡاَرۡضِ يَاۡتِ
بِهَا اللّٰهُ ؕ اِنَّ اللّٰهَ لَطِيۡفٌ خَبِيۡرٌ ﴿۱۶﴾

17. "O my son! establish regular prayer, enjoin what is just, and forbid what is wrong: and bear with patient constancy whatever betide you; for this is firmness (of purpose) in (the conduct of) affairs.

17\. Yaa bunayya aqimiṣ-Ṣalaata waàmur bilma'roofi wanha 'anil-munkari waṣbir-'alaa maaa aṣaabaka inna zaalika min 'azmil-umoor.

يٰبُنَىَّ اَقِمِ الصَّلٰوةَ وَاۡمُرۡ بِالۡمَعۡرُوۡفِ
وَانۡهَ عَنِ الۡمُنۡكَرِ وَاصۡبِرۡ عَلٰى
مَاۤ اَصَابَكَ ؕ اِنَّ ذٰلِكَ مِنۡ
عَزۡمِ الۡاُمُوۡرِ ۚ ﴿۱۷﴾

18. "And do not swell your cheek (for pride) at men, nor walk in insolence through the earth; for Allah does not love any arrogant boaster.

18\. Wa laa tuṣa'-'ir khaddaka linnaasi wa laa tamshi fil-arḍi maraḥan innal-laaha laa yuḥibbu kulla mukhtaalin fakhoor.

وَلَا تُصَعِّرۡ خَدَّكَ لِلنَّاسِ وَلَا
تَمۡشِ فِى الۡاَرۡضِ مَرَحًا ؕ اِنَّ
اللّٰهَ لَا يُحِبُّ كُلَّ مُخۡتَالٍ فَخُوۡرٍ ۚ ﴿۱۸﴾

19. "And be moderate in your pace, and lower

19\. Waqṣid fee mashyika waghḍuḍ

وَاقۡصِدۡ فِىۡ مَشۡيِكَ وَاغۡضُضۡ

Ikhfa اخفاء | Ghunna غنّہ | Ikhfa Meem Saakin اخفاء میم ساکن | Idghaam ادغام | Qalqala قلقلہ | Qalb قلب | Idghaam Meem Saakin ادغام میم ساکن

your voice;for the harshest of sounds without doubt is the braying of the ass."

min ṣawtik; inna ankaral-aṣwaati laṣawtul-ḥameer.

(Section 2)

مِنْ صَوْتِكَ ۚ إِنَّ أَنْكَرَ
الْأَصْوَاتِ لَصَوْتُ الْحَمِيرِ ﴿١٩﴾ ع

20. Do you not see that Allah has subjected to your (use) all things in the heavens and on earth, and has made His bounties flow to you in exceeding mea-sure, (both) seen and unseen? Yet there are among men those who dispute about Allah, with-out knowledge and without guidance, and without a Book to enlighten them!

20. Alam taraw annal-laaha sakhkhara lakum-maa fis-samaawaati wa maa fil-arḍi wa asbagha 'alaykum ni'amahoo ẕaahiratañw-wa baaṭinah; wa minan-naasi mañy-yujaadilu fil-laahi bighayri 'ilmiñw-wa laa hudañw-wa laa Kitaabim-muneer.

أَلَمْ تَرَوْا أَنَّ اللَّهَ سَخَّرَ لَكُمْ
مَا فِي السَّمَاوَاتِ وَمَا فِي الْأَرْضِ
وَأَسْبَغَ عَلَيْكُمْ نِعَمَهُ ظَاهِرَةً
وَبَاطِنَةً ۗ وَمِنَ النَّاسِ مَنْ
يُجَادِلُ فِي اللَّهِ بِغَيْرِ عِلْمٍ وَلَا
هُدًى وَلَا كِتَابٍ مُنِيرٍ ﴿٢٠﴾

21. When they are told to follow the (Revelation) that Allah has sent down, they say: "Nay, we shall follow the ways that we found our fathers (following). "What! even if it is Satan beckoning them to the Penalty of the (Blazing) Fire?

21. Wa izaa qeela lahumut-tabi'oo maaa anzalal-laahu qaaloo bal nattabi'u maa wajadnaa 'alayhi aabaaa'anaa; awalaw kaanash-Shayṭaanu yad'oohum ilaa 'azaabis-sa'eer.

وَإِذَا قِيلَ لَهُمُ اتَّبِعُوا مَا أَنْزَلَ
اللَّهُ قَالُوا بَلْ نَتَّبِعُ مَا وَجَدْنَا
عَلَيْهِ آبَاءَنَا ۚ أَوَلَوْ كَانَ الشَّيْطَانُ
يَدْعُوهُمْ إِلَىٰ عَذَابِ السَّعِيرِ ﴿٢١﴾

22. Whoever submits his whole self to Allah, and is a doer of good, has grasped indeed the most trustworthy hand-hold: and to Allah shall all things return.

22. Wa mañy-yuslim wajhahooo ilal-laahi wa huwa muḥsinun faqadistamsaka bil'urwatil-wusqaa; wa ilal-laahi 'aaqibatul-umoor.

وَمَنْ يُسْلِمْ وَجْهَهُ إِلَى اللَّهِ
وَهُوَ مُحْسِنٌ فَقَدِ اسْتَمْسَكَ
بِالْعُرْوَةِ الْوُثْقَىٰ ۗ وَإِلَى اللَّهِ
عَاقِبَةُ الْأُمُورِ ﴿٢٢﴾

23. But if any reject Faith, let not his rejection grieve you: to Us is their return, and We shall tell them the truth of their deeds: for Allah knows well all that is in (men's) hearts.

23. Wa man kafara falaa yaḥzunka kufruh; ilaynaa marji'uhum fanunabbi'uhum bimaa 'amiloo; innal-laaha 'aleemum bizaatiṣ-ṣudoor.

وَمَنْ كَفَرَ فَلَا يَحْزُنْكَ كُفْرُهُ ۚ
إِلَيْنَا مَرْجِعُهُمْ فَنُنَبِّئُهُمْ بِمَا عَمِلُوا ۚ
إِنَّ اللَّهَ عَلِيمٌ بِذَاتِ الصُّدُورِ ﴿٢٣﴾

24. We grant them their pleasure for a little while: in the end shall We drive them to an unrelenting chastisement.

24. Numatti'uhum qaleelan summa naḍṭarruhum ilaa 'azaabin ghaleeẓ.

نُمَتِّعُهُمْ قَلِيلًا ثُمَّ نَضْطَرُّهُمْ إِلَىٰ
عَذَابٍ غَلِيظٍ ﴿٢٤﴾

25. If you ask them, who it is that created the heavens and the earth. They will certainly say, "Allah". Say: "Praise be to Allah!" But most of them do not understand.

25. Wa la'in sa-altahum-man khalaqas-samaawaati wal-arḍa la-yaqoolunnal-laah; qulil-ḥamdu-lillaah; bal aksaruhum laa ya'lamoon.

وَلَئِنْ سَأَلْتَهُمْ مَنْ خَلَقَ السَّمَاوَاتِ
وَالْأَرْضَ لَيَقُولُنَّ اللَّهُ ۚ قُلِ الْحَمْدُ
لِلَّهِ ۚ بَلْ أَكْثَرُهُمْ لَا يَعْلَمُونَ ﴿٢٥﴾

26. To Allah belong all things in heaven and earth: verily Allah is He (that is) free of all wants, worthy of all praise.

26. Lillaahi maa fis-samaawaati wal-arḍ; innal-laaha Huwal-Ghaniyyul-Ḥameed.

لِلَّهِ مَا فِي السَّمَاوَاتِ وَالْأَرْضِ ۚ إِنَّ
اللَّهَ هُوَ الْغَنِيُّ الْحَمِيدُ ﴿٢٦﴾

Ikhfa اخفاء · Ghunna غنّہ · Ikhfa Meem Saakin اخفاءمیم ساکن · Idghaam ادغام · Qalqala قلقلہ · Qalb قلب · Idghaam Meem Saakin ادغام میم ساکن

27. And if all the trees on earth were pens and the ocean (were ink), with seven oceans behind it to add to its (supply), yet would not the words of Allah be exhausted (in the writing): for Allah is Exalted in Power, full of Wisdom.

28. And your creation or your resurrection is in no wise but as an individual soul: for Allah is He Who hears and sees (all things).

29. Don't you see that Allah merges Night into Day and he merges Day into Night; that He has subjected the sun, and the moon (to His Law), each running its course for a term appointed; and that Allah is well-acquain-ted with all that you do?

30. That is because Allah is the (only) Reality, and because whatever else they invoke besides Him is Falsehood; and because Allah,- He is the Most High, Most Great.

31. Don't you see that the ships sail through the ocean by the Grace of Allah?- that He may show you of His Signs? Verily in this are Signs for all who constantly persevere and give thanks.

32. When a wave covers them like the canopy (of clouds), they call to Allah, offering Him sincere devotion. But when He has delivered them safely to land, there are among them those that halt between (right and wrong). But none reject Our Signs except only a perfidious ungrateful (wretch)!

33. O mankind! do your duty to your Lord, and fear (the coming of) a Day when no father can avail anything for his son, nor a son

27. Wa law annamaa fil-arḍi min shajaratin aqlaamuñw-wal baḥru yamudduhoo mim ba'dihee sab'atu abḥurim-maa nafidat Kalimaatul-laah; innal-laaha 'Azeezun Ḥakeem.

28. Maa khalqukum wa laa ba'ṣukum illaa kanafsiñw-waaḥidah; innal-laaha Samee'um Baṣeer.

29. Alam tara annal-laaha yoolijul-layla fin-nahaari wa yoolijun-nahaara fil-layli wa sakhkharash-shamsa wal-qamara kulluñy-yajreee ilaaa ajalim-musammañw-wa annal-laaha bimaa ta'maloona Khabeer.

30. Zaalika bi-annal-laaha Huwal-Ḥaqqu wa anna maa yad'oona min doonihil-baaṭilu wa annal-laaha Huwal-'Aliyyul-Kabeer. **(Section 3)**

31. Alam tara annal-fulka tajree fil-baḥri bini'matil-laahi li-yuriyakum-min Aayaatih; inna fee zaalika la-Aayaatil-likulli ṣabbaarin shakoor.

32. Wa izaa ghashiyahum-mawjun kazzulali da'a-wul-laaha mukhliṣeena lahud-deena fa-lammaa najjaahum ilal-barri faminhum-muqtaṣid; wa maa yajḥadu bi-Aayaatinaaa illaa kullu khattaarin kafoor.

33. Yaaa ayyuhan-naasut-taqoo Rabbakum wakhshaw Yawmal-laa yajzee waalidun 'añw-waladihee wa laa mawloodun huwa

وَلَوْ اَنَّ مَا فِى الْاَرْضِ مِنْ شَجَرَةٍ
اَقْلَامٌ وَّالْبَحْرُ يَمُدُّهٗ مِنْۢ بَعْدِهٖ
سَبْعَةُ اَبْحُرٍ مَّا نَفِدَتْ كَلِمٰتُ
اللّٰهِ ؕ اِنَّ اللّٰهَ عَزِيْزٌ حَكِيْمٌ ﴿٢٧﴾
مَا خَلْقُكُمْ وَلَا بَعْثُكُمْ اِلَّا كَنَفْسٍ
وَّاحِدَةٍ ؕ اِنَّ اللّٰهَ سَمِيْعٌۢ بَصِيْرٌ ﴿٢٨﴾
اَلَمْ تَرَ اَنَّ اللّٰهَ يُوْلِجُ الَّيْلَ فِى
النَّهَارِ وَيُوْلِجُ النَّهَارَ فِى الَّيْلِ وَ
سَخَّرَ الشَّمْسَ وَالْقَمَرَ ۫ كُلٌّ يَّجْرِىْٓ
اِلٰٓى اَجَلٍ مُّسَمًّى وَّاَنَّ اللّٰهَ بِمَا
تَعْمَلُوْنَ خَبِيْرٌ ﴿٢٩﴾
ذٰلِكَ بِاَنَّ اللّٰهَ هُوَ الْحَقُّ وَاَنَّ
مَا يَدْعُوْنَ مِنْ دُوْنِهِ الْبَاطِلُ ۙ
وَاَنَّ اللّٰهَ هُوَ الْعَلِىُّ الْكَبِيْرُ ﴿٣٠﴾ ع
اَلَمْ تَرَ اَنَّ الْفُلْكَ تَجْرِىْ فِى
الْبَحْرِ بِنِعْمَتِ اللّٰهِ لِيُرِيَكُمْ مِّنْ
اٰيٰتِهٖ ؕ اِنَّ فِىْ ذٰلِكَ لَاٰيٰتٍ لِّكُلِّ
صَبَّارٍ شَكُوْرٍ ﴿٣١﴾
وَاِذَا غَشِيَهُمْ مَّوْجٌ كَالظُّلَلِ
دَعَوُا اللّٰهَ مُخْلِصِيْنَ لَهُ الدِّيْنَ ۚ
فَلَمَّا نَجّٰهُمْ اِلَى الْبَرِّ فَمِنْهُمْ
مُّقْتَصِدٌ ؕ وَمَا يَجْحَدُ بِاٰيٰتِنَآ اِلَّا
كُلُّ خَتَّارٍ كَفُوْرٍ ﴿٣٢﴾
يٰٓاَيُّهَا النَّاسُ اتَّقُوْا رَبَّكُمْ
وَاخْشَوْا يَوْمًا لَّا يَجْزِىْ وَالِدٌ
عَنْ وَّلَدِهٖ ۫ وَلَا مَوْلُوْدٌ هُوَ

Ikhfa اخفاء | Ghunna غُنَّہ | Ikhfa Meem Saakin اخفاءمیم ساکن | Idghaam ادغام | Qalqala قلقلہ | Qalb قلب | Idghaam Meem Saakin ادغام میم ساکن

avail anything for his father. Verily, the promise of Allah is true: let not then this present life deceive you, nor let the chief Deceiver deceive you about Allah.

jaazin 'añw-waalidihee shay-'aa; inna wa'dal-laahi ḥaqqun falaa taghurran-nakumul-ḥayaatud-dunyaa wa laa yaghur-rannakum billaahil-gharoor.

جَازٍ عَنْ وَّالِدِهٖ شَيْـًٔا ۭ اِنَّ
وَعْدَ اللّٰهِ حَقٌّ فَلَا تَغُرَّنَّكُمُ
الْحَيٰوةُ الدُّنْيَا ۪ وَلَا يَغُرَّنَّكُمْ
بِاللّٰهِ الْغَرُوْرُ ﴿٣٣﴾

34. Verily the knowledge of the Hour is with Allah (alone). It is He Who sends down rain, and He Who knows what is in the wombs. Nor does any one know what it is that he will earn on the morrow: Nor does any one know in what land he is to die. Verily with Allah is full knowledge and He is acquainted (with all things).

34. Innal-laaha 'indahoo 'ilmus-Saa'ati wa yunazzilul-ghaysa wa ya'lamu maa fil-arḥaami wa maa tadree nafsum-maazaa taksibu ghadaa; wa maa tadree nafsum bi-ayyi arḍin tamoot; innal-laaha 'Aleemun Khabeer. **(Section 4)**

اِنَّ اللّٰهَ عِنْدَهٗ عِلْمُ السَّاعَةِ ۚ
وَيُنَزِّلُ الْغَيْثَ ۚ وَيَعْلَمُ مَا فِي
الْاَرْحَامِ ۭ وَمَا تَدْرِيْ نَفْسٌ مَّاذَا
تَكْسِبُ غَدًا ۭ وَمَا تَدْرِيْ نَفْسٌۢ
بِاَيِّ اَرْضٍ تَمُوْتُ ۭ اِنَّ اللّٰهَ
عَلِيْمٌ خَبِيْرٌ ﴿٣٤﴾

ع

32. Adoration

In the name of Allah, Most Gracious, Most Merciful.

Sûrat as-Sajdah–32

(Revealed at Makkah)

Bismillaahir Raḥmaanir Raḥeem

(٣٢) سُوْرَةُ السَّجْدَةِ مَكِّيَّةٌ (٧٥)

بِسْمِ اللّٰهِ الرَّحْمٰنِ الرَّحِيْمِ

1. *Alif-Lam-Mim.*

2. (This is) the revelation of the Book in which there is no doubt,- from the Lord of the Worlds.

3. Or do they say, "He has forged it"? Nay, it is the Truth from your Lord, that you may admonish a people to whom no warner has come before you: in order that they may receive guidance.

1. Alif-Laaam-Meeem.

2. Tanzeelul-Kitaabi laa rayba feehi mir-Rabbil-'aalameen.

3. Am yaqooloonaf-taraah; bal huwal-ḥaqqu mir-Rabbika litunzira qawmam-maaa ataahum-min-nazeerim-min qablika la'allahum yahtadoon.

الٓمّٓ ﴿١﴾
تَنْزِيْلُ الْكِتٰبِ لَا رَيْبَ فِيْهِ مِنْ
رَّبِّ الْعٰلَمِيْنَ ﴿٢﴾
اَمْ يَقُوْلُوْنَ افْتَرٰىهُ ۚ بَلْ هُوَ الْحَقُّ
مِنْ رَّبِّكَ لِتُنْذِرَ قَوْمًا مَّآ اَتٰىهُمْ
مِّنْ نَّذِيْرٍ مِّنْ قَبْلِكَ لَعَلَّهُمْ
يَهْتَدُوْنَ ﴿٣﴾

4. It is Allah Who has created the heavens and the earth, and all between them, in six Days, and is firmly established on the Throne (of authority): you have none, besides Him, to protect or intercede (for you): will you not then receive admonition?

4. Allaahul-lazee khalaqas-samaawaati wal-arḍa wa maa baynahumaa fee sittati ayyaamin summas-tawaa 'alal-'Arshi maa lakum-min doonihee miñw-waliyyiñw-wa laa shafee'; afalaa tatazakkaroon.

اَللّٰهُ الَّذِيْ خَلَقَ السَّمٰوٰتِ وَالْاَرْضَ
وَمَا بَيْنَهُمَا فِيْ سِتَّةِ اَيَّامٍ ثُمَّ
اسْتَوٰى عَلَى الْعَرْشِ ۭ مَا لَكُمْ مِّنْ
دُوْنِهٖ مِنْ وَّلِيٍّ وَّلَا شَفِيْعٍ ۭ
اَفَلَا تَتَذَكَّرُوْنَ ﴿٤﴾

5. He rules (all) affairs from the heavens to the earth: in the end will (all affairs) go up to Him, on

5. Yudabbirul-amra minas-samaaa'i ilal-arḍi summa ya'ruju ilayhi fee

يُدَبِّرُ الْاَمْرَ مِنَ السَّمَاۗءِ اِلَى
الْاَرْضِ ثُمَّ يَعْرُجُ اِلَيْهِ فِيْ

Ikhfa اخفاء | Ghunna غُنّہ | Ikhfa Meem Saakin اخفاءمیم ساکن | Idghaam ادغام | Qalqala قلقلہ | Qalb قلب | Idghaam Meem Saakin ادغام میم ساکن

a Day, the space whereof will be (as) a thousand years of your reckoning.

6. Such is He, the Knower of all things, hidden and open, the Exalted (in power), the Merciful;-

7. He Who has made everything which He has created most good: He began the creation of man with (nothing more than) clay,

8. And made his progeny from a quintessence of the nature of a fluid despised:

9. But He fashioned him in due proportion, and breathed into him something of His spirit. And He gave you (the faculties of) hearing and sight and feeling (and understanding): little thanks do you give!

10. And they say: "What! when we lie, hidden and lost, in the earth, shall we indeed be in a Creation renewed? Nay, they deny the Meeting with their Lord.

11. Say: "The Angel of Death, put in charge of you, will (duly) take your souls: then you shall be brought back to your Lord."

12. If only you could see when the guilty ones will bend low their heads before their Lord, (saying:) "Our Lord! We have seen and we have heard: now then send us back (to the world): we will work righteousness: for we do indeed (now) believe."

13. If We had so willed, We could certainly have brought every soul its true guidance: but the Word from Me will come true, "I will fill Hell with Jinns and men all together."

14. "Then you taste - for you forgot the Meeting of this Day

yawmin kaana miqdaaruhooo alfa sanatim-mimmaa ta'ud-doon.

6. Zaalika 'Aalimul-Ghaybi wash-shahaadatil-'Azeezur-Raheem.

7. Allazeee ahsana kulla shay'in khalaqahoo wa bada-a khalqal-insaani min teen.

8. Summa ja'ala naslahoo min sulaalatim-mim-maaa'im-maheen.

9. Summa sawwaahu wa nafakha feehi mir-roohihee wa ja'ala lakumus-sam'a wal-ab-saara wal-af'idah; qaleelam-maa tashkuroon.

10. Wa qaalooo 'a-izaa dalal-naa fil-ardi 'a-innaa lafee khal-qin jadeed; bal hum biliqaaa'i Rabbihim kaafiroon.

11. Qul yatawaffaakum-Malakul-Mawtil-lazee wukkila bikum summa ilaa Rabbikum turja'oon. **(Section 1)**

12. Wa law taraaa izil-muj-rimoona naakisoo ru'oosihim 'inda Rabbihim Rabbanaaa absarnaa wa sami'naa farji'naa na'mal saalihan innaa moo-qinoon.

13. Wa law shi'naa la-aatay-naa kulla nafsin hudaahaa wa laakin haqqal-qawlu minnee la-amla'anna Jahannama minal-jinnati wannaasi ajma'een.

14. Fazooqoo bimaa nasee-tum liqaaa'a Yawmikum

يَوۡمٍ كَانَ مِقۡدَارُهٗۤ اَلۡفَ سَنَةٍ
مِّمَّا تَعُدُّوۡنَ ۝٥
ذٰلِكَ عٰلِمُ الۡغَيۡبِ وَالشَّهَادَةِ
الۡعَزِيۡزُ الرَّحِيۡمُ ۝٦
الَّذِيۡۤ اَحۡسَنَ كُلَّ شَيۡءٍ خَلَقَهٗ
وَبَدَاَ خَلۡقَ الۡاِنۡسَانِ مِنۡ طِيۡنٍ ۝٧
ثُمَّ جَعَلَ نَسۡلَهٗ مِنۡ سُلٰلَةٍ مِّنۡ
مَّآءٍ مَّهِيۡنٍ ۝٨
ثُمَّ سَوّٰىهُ وَنَفَخَ فِيۡهِ مِنۡ رُّوۡحِهٖ
وَجَعَلَ لَكُمُ السَّمۡعَ وَالۡاَبۡصَارَ
وَالۡاَفۡـِٕدَةَ ؕ قَلِيۡلًا مَّا تَشۡكُرُوۡنَ ۝٩
وَقَالُوۡۤا ءَاِذَا ضَلَلۡنَا فِى الۡاَرۡضِ
ءَاِنَّا لَفِىۡ خَلۡقٍ جَدِيۡدٍ ؕ بَلۡ هُمۡ
بِلِقَآءِ رَبِّهِمۡ كٰفِرُوۡنَ ۝١٠
قُلۡ يَتَوَفّٰٮكُمۡ مَّلَكُ الۡمَوۡتِ
الَّذِىۡ وُكِّلَ بِكُمۡ ثُمَّ اِلٰى
رَبِّكُمۡ تُرۡجَعُوۡنَ ۝١١ ع ١٤
وَلَوۡ تَرٰٓى اِذِ الۡمُجۡرِمُوۡنَ نَاكِسُوۡا
رُءُوۡسِهِمۡ عِنۡدَ رَبِّهِمۡ ؕ رَبَّنَاۤ
اَبۡصَرۡنَا وَسَمِعۡنَا فَارۡجِعۡنَا نَعۡمَلۡ
صَالِحًا اِنَّا مُوۡقِنُوۡنَ ۝١٢
وَلَوۡ شِئۡنَا لَاٰتَيۡنَا كُلَّ نَفۡسٍ
هُدٰٮهَا وَلٰكِنۡ حَقَّ الۡقَوۡلُ
مِنِّىۡ لَاَمۡلَئَنَّ جَهَنَّمَ مِنَ الۡجِنَّةِ
وَالنَّاسِ اَجۡمَعِيۡنَ ۝١٣
فَذُوۡقُوۡا بِمَا نَسِيۡتُمۡ لِقَآءَ يَوۡمِكُمۡ

Ikhfa اخفاء | Ghunna غُنّہ | Ikhfa Meem Saakin اخفاء میم ساکن | Idghaam ادغام | Qalqala قلقلہ | Qalb قلب | Idghaam Meem Saakin ادغام میم ساکن

(Bow Down)

of yours, and We too will forget you - you taste the Penalty of Eternity for your (evil) deeds!"

15. Only those believe in Our Signs, who, when these are recited to them, fall down in adoration, and celebrate the praises of their Lord, nor are they (ever) puffed up with pride.

16. Their limbs do forsake their beds of sleep, the while they call on their Lord, in Fear and Hope: and they spend (in charity) out of the sustenance which We have bestowed on them.

17. Now no person knows what delights of the eye are kept hidden (in reserve) for them - as a reward for their (good) deeds.

18. Is then the man who believes no better than the man who is rebellious and wicked? Not equal are they.

19. For those who believe and do righteous deeds are Gardens as hospitable homes, for their (good) deeds.

20. As to those who are rebellious and wicked, their abode will be the Fire: every time they wish to get away therefrom, they will be forced back thereinto, and it will be said to them: "You taste the Penalty of the Fire, the which you were wont to reject as false."

21. And indeed We will make them taste of the Penalty of this (life) prior to the supreme Penalty, in order that they may (repent and) return.

22. And who does more wrong than one to whom are recited the Signs of his Lord, and who then turns away therefrom? Verily from those

haazaa innaa naseenaakum wa zooqoo 'azaabal-khuldi bimaa kuntum ta'maloon.

15. Innamaa yu'minu bi-Aayaatinal-lazeena izaa zukkiroo bihaa kharroo sujjadañw-wa sabbaḥoo biḥamdi Rabbihim wa hum laa yastakbiroon. ۩

16. Tatajaafaa junoobuhum 'anil-maḍaaji'i yad'oona Rabbahum khawfañw-wa ṭama'añw-wa mimmaa razaqnaahum yunfiqoon.

17. Falaa ta'lamu nafsum-maaa ukhfiya lahum-min qurrati a'yunin jazaaa'am bimaa kaanoo ya'maloon.

18. Afaman kaana mu'minan kaman kaana faasiqaa; laa yasta-woon.

19. Ammal-lazeena aamanoo wa 'amiluṣ-ṣaaliḥaati falahum Jannaatul-maåwaa nuzulam bimaa kaanoo ya'maloon.

20. Wa ammal-lazeena fasaqoo famaåwaahumun-Naaru kullamaaa araadooo añy-yakhrujoo minhaaa u'eedoo feehaa wa qeela lahum zooqoo 'azaaban-Naaril-lazee kuntum bihee tukazziboon.

21. Wa lanuzeeqan-nahum minal-'azaabil-adnaa doonal-'azaabil-akbari la'allahum yarji'oon.

22. Wa man aẓlamu mimman zukkira bi-Aayaati Rabbihee summa a'raḍa 'anhaa; innaa minal-

هٰذَاۚ اِنَّا نَسِيْنٰكُمْ وَذُوْقُوْا عَذَابَ
الْخُلْدِ بِمَا كُنْتُمْ تَعْمَلُوْنَ ١٤
اِنَّمَا يُؤْمِنُ بِاٰيٰتِنَا الَّذِيْنَ اِذَا
ذُكِّرُوْا بِهَا خَرُّوْا سُجَّدًا وَّسَبَّحُوْا
بِحَمْدِ رَبِّهِمْ وَهُمْ لَا يَسْتَكْبِرُوْنَ ۩ ١٥ السَّجْدَة
تَتَجَافٰى جُنُوْبُهُمْ عَنِ الْمَضَاجِعِ
يَدْعُوْنَ رَبَّهُمْ خَوْفًا وَّطَمَعًا ز وَّمِمَّا
رَزَقْنٰهُمْ يُنْفِقُوْنَ ١٦
فَلَا تَعْلَمُ نَفْسٌ مَّآ اُخْفِيَ لَهُمْ
مِّنْ قُرَّةِ اَعْيُنٍ ۚ جَزَآءًۢ بِمَا
كَانُوْا يَعْمَلُوْنَ ١٧
اَفَمَنْ كَانَ مُؤْمِنًا كَمَنْ كَانَ
فَاسِقًا ۭ لَا يَسْتَوٗنَ ١٨
اَمَّا الَّذِيْنَ اٰمَنُوْا وَعَمِلُوا الصّٰلِحٰتِ
فَلَهُمْ جَنّٰتُ الْمَاْوٰى ز نُزُلًۢا بِمَا
كَانُوْا يَعْمَلُوْنَ ١٩
وَاَمَّا الَّذِيْنَ فَسَقُوْا فَمَاْوٰىهُمُ
النَّارُ ۭ كُلَّمَآ اَرَادُوْٓا اَنْ يَّخْرُجُوْا
مِنْهَآ اُعِيْدُوْا فِيْهَا وَقِيْلَ لَهُمْ
ذُوْقُوْا عَذَابَ النَّارِ الَّذِيْ كُنْتُمْ
بِهٖ تُكَذِّبُوْنَ ٢٠
وَلَنُذِيْقَنَّهُمْ مِّنَ الْعَذَابِ
الْاَدْنٰى دُوْنَ الْعَذَابِ الْاَكْبَرِ
لَعَلَّهُمْ يَرْجِعُوْنَ ٢١
وَمَنْ اَظْلَمُ مِمَّنْ ذُكِّرَ بِاٰيٰتِ
رَبِّهٖ ثُمَّ اَعْرَضَ عَنْهَا ۭ اِنَّا مِنَ

السَّجْدَة (٩)

وقف غفران

Ikhfa اخفاء | Ghunna غُنّہ | Ikhfa Meem Saakin اخفاء میم ساکن | Idghaam ادغام | Qalqala قلقلہ | Qalb قلب | Idghaam Meem Saakin ادغام میم ساکن

who transgress We shall exact (due) Retribution.

23. We did indeed before this give the Book to Moses: be not then in doubt of its reaching (you): and We made it a guide to the Children of Israel.

24. And We appointed, from among them, leaders, giving guidance under Our command, so long as they persevered with patience and continued to have faith in Our Signs.

25. Verily your Lord will judge between them on the Day of Judgment, in the matters wherein they differ (among themselves).

26. Does it not teach them a lesson, how many generations We destroyed before them, in whose dwellings they (now) go to and fro? Verily in that are Signs: Do they not then listen?

27. And do they not see that We do drive rain to parched soil (bare of herbage), and produce therewith crops, providing food for their cattle and themselves? Have they not the vision?

28. They say: "When will this decision be, if you are telling the truth?"

29. Say: "On the Day of Decision, no profit will it be to Unbelievers if they (then) believe! nor will they be granted a respite."

30. So turn away from them, and wait: they too are waiting.

33. The Confederates

In the name of Allah, Most Gracious, Most Merciful.

1. O Prophet! Fear Allah, and do not hearken to the

mujrimeena muntaqimoon.

(Section 2)

23. Wa laqad aataynaa Moo-sal-Kitaaba falaa takun fee miryatim-mil-liqaaa'ihee wa ja'alnaahu hudal-li-Baneee Israaa'eel.

24. Wa ja'alnaa minhum a'immatañy-yahdoona bi-amri-naa lammaa ṣabaroo wa kaanoo bi-Aayaatinaa yooqinoon.

25. Inna Rabbaka Huwa yafṣilu baynahum Yawmal-Qiyaamati feemaa kaanoo feehi yakhtalifoon.

26. Awalam yahdi lahum kam ahlaknaa min qablihim-minal-qurooni yamshoona fee masaa-kinihim; inna fee ẕaalika la-Aayaatin afalaa yasma'oon.

27. Awalam yaraw annaa nasooqul-maaa'a ilal-arḍil-juruzi fanukhriju bihee zar'an taåkulu minhu an'aamuhum wa anfusuhum afalaa yubṣiroon.

28. Wa yaqooloona mataa haaẕal-fat-ḥu in kuntum ṣaadi-qeen.

29. Qul Yawmal-fat-ḥi laa yanfa'ul-laẕeena kafarooo eemaanuhum wa laa hum yunẓaroon.

30. Fa-a'riḍ 'anhum wantaẓir innahum-muntaẓiroon.

(Section 3)

Sûrat al-Aḥzâb–33

(Revealed at Madinah)

Bismillaahir Raḥmaanir Raḥeem

1. Yaaa ayyuhan-Nabiyyut-taqil-laaha wa laa tuṭi'il-

الْمُجْرِمِينَ مُنتَقِمُونَ ﴿٢٢﴾
وَلَقَدْ آتَيْنَا مُوسَى الْكِتَابَ فَلَا
تَكُن فِي مِرْيَةٍ مِّن لِّقَائِهِ
وَجَعَلْنَاهُ هُدًى لِّبَنِي إِسْرَائِيلَ ﴿٢٣﴾
وَجَعَلْنَا مِنْهُمْ أَئِمَّةً يَهْدُونَ
بِأَمْرِنَا لَمَّا صَبَرُوا ۖ وَكَانُوا
بِآيَاتِنَا يُوقِنُونَ ﴿٢٤﴾
إِنَّ رَبَّكَ هُوَ يَفْصِلُ بَيْنَهُمْ يَوْمَ
الْقِيَامَةِ فِيمَا كَانُوا فِيهِ يَخْتَلِفُونَ ﴿٢٥﴾
أَوَلَمْ يَهْدِ لَهُمْ كَمْ أَهْلَكْنَا مِن
قَبْلِهِم مِّنَ الْقُرُونِ يَمْشُونَ فِي
مَسَاكِنِهِمْ ۚ إِنَّ فِي ذَٰلِكَ لَآيَاتٍ ۖ
أَفَلَا يَسْمَعُونَ ﴿٢٦﴾
أَوَلَمْ يَرَوْا أَنَّا نَسُوقُ الْمَاءَ إِلَى
الْأَرْضِ الْجُرُزِ فَنُخْرِجُ بِهِ زَرْعًا
تَأْكُلُ مِنْهُ أَنْعَامُهُمْ وَأَنفُسُهُمْ ۖ
أَفَلَا يُبْصِرُونَ ﴿٢٧﴾
وَيَقُولُونَ مَتَىٰ هَٰذَا الْفَتْحُ إِن
كُنتُمْ صَادِقِينَ ﴿٢٨﴾
قُلْ يَوْمَ الْفَتْحِ لَا يَنفَعُ الَّذِينَ
كَفَرُوا إِيمَانُهُمْ وَلَا هُمْ يُنظَرُونَ ﴿٢٩﴾
فَأَعْرِضْ عَنْهُمْ وَانتَظِرْ إِنَّهُم
مُّنتَظِرُونَ ﴿٣٠﴾

(٣٣) سُورَةُ الْأَحْزَابِ مَدَنِيَّةٌ (٩٠)

بِسْمِ اللَّهِ الرَّحْمَٰنِ الرَّحِيمِ

يَا أَيُّهَا النَّبِيُّ اتَّقِ اللَّهَ وَلَا تُطِعِ

Ikhfa اخفاء | Ghunna غُنّہ | Ikhfa Meem Saakin اخفاء میم ساکن | Idghaam ادغام | Qalqala قلقلہ | Qalb قلب | Idghaam Meem Saakin ادغام میم ساکن

Unbelievers and the Hypocrites: verily Allah is full of Knowledge and Wisdom.

2. But follow that which comes to you by inspiration from your Lord: for Allah is well acquainted with (all) that you do.

3. And put your trust in Allah, and enough is Allah as a disposer of affairs.

4. Allah has not made for any man two hearts in his (one) body: nor has He made your wives whom you divorce by Zihar your mothers: nor has He made your adopted sons your sons. Such is (only) your (manner of) speech by your mouths. But Allah tells (you) the Truth, and He shows the (right) Way.

5. Call them by (the names of) their fathers: that is juster in the sight of Allah. But if you do not know their father's (names, call them) your Brothers in faith, or your *maulas*. But there is no blame on you if you make a mistake therein: (what counts is) the intention of your hearts: and Allah is Oft-Returning, Most Merciful.

6. The Prophet is closer to the Believers than their own selves, and his wives are their mothers. Blood-relations among each other have closer personal ties, in the Decree of Allah than (the Brotherhood of) Believers and *Muhajirs*: nevertheless you do what is just to your closest friends: such is the writing in the Decree (of Allah).

7. And remember We took from the prophets their Covenant:

kaafireena wal-munaafiqeen; innal-laaha kaana 'Aleeman Ḥakeemaa.

2. Wattabi' maa yooḥaaa ilayka mir-Rabbik; innal-laaha kaana bimaa ta'maloona Khabeeraa.

3. Wa tawakkal 'alal-laah; wa kafaa billaahi Wakeelaa.

4. Maa ja'alal-laahu lirajulim-min qalbayni fee jawfih; wa maa ja'ala azwaajakumul-laaa'ee tuẓaahiroona minhunna ummahaatikum; wa maa ja'ala ad'iyaaa'akum abnaaa'akum; ẕaalikum qawlukum bi-afwaahikum wallaahu yaqoolul-ḥaqqa wa Huwa yahdis-sabeel.

5. Ud'oohum li-aabaaa'ihim huwa aqsaṭu 'indal-laah; fa-illam ta'lamooo aabaaa'ahum fa-ikhwaanukum fid-deeni wa mawaaleekum; wa laysa 'alaykum junaaḥun feemaaa akhṭaåtum bihee wa laakim-maa ta'ammadat quloobukum; wa kaanal-laahu Ghafoorar-Raḥeemaa.

6. An-Nabiyyu awlaa bil-mu'mineena min anfusihim wa azwaajuhooo ummahaatuhum; wa ulul-arḥaami ba'ḍuhum awlaa biba'ḍin fee Kitaabil-laahi minal-mu'mineena wal-Muhaajireena illaaa an taf'alooo ilaaa awliyaaa'ikum-ma'roofaa; kaana ẕaalika fil-kitaabi masṭooraa.

7. Wa iẕ akhaẕnaa minan-Nabiyyeena meesaaqahum

الْكٰفِرِيْنَ وَالْمُنٰفِقِيْنَ ؕ اِنَّ اللّٰهَ كَانَ
عَلِيْمًا حَكِيْمًا ۙ﴿۱﴾
وَّاتَّبِعْ مَا يُوْحٰۤى اِلَيْكَ مِنْ رَّبِّكَ ؕ
اِنَّ اللّٰهَ كَانَ بِمَا تَعْمَلُوْنَ خَبِيْرًا ۙ﴿۲﴾
وَّتَوَكَّلْ عَلَى اللّٰهِ ؕ وَكَفٰى بِاللّٰهِ
وَكِيْلًا ﴿۳﴾
مَا جَعَلَ اللّٰهُ لِرَجُلٍ مِّنْ قَلْبَيْنِ
فِىْ جَوْفِهٖ ۚ وَمَا جَعَلَ اَزْوَاجَكُمُ
الّٰٓـئِىْ تُظٰهِرُوْنَ مِنْهُنَّ اُمَّهٰتِكُمْ ۚ
وَمَا جَعَلَ اَدْعِيَآءَكُمْ اَبْنَآءَكُمْ ؕ
ذٰلِكُمْ قَوْلُكُمْ بِاَفْوَاهِكُمْ ؕ وَاللّٰهُ
يَقُوْلُ الْحَقَّ وَهُوَ يَهْدِى السَّبِيْلَ ﴿۴﴾
اُدْعُوْهُمْ لِاٰبَآئِهِمْ هُوَ اَقْسَطُ
عِنْدَ اللّٰهِ ۚ فَاِنْ لَّمْ تَعْلَمُوْۤا اٰبَآءَهُمْ
فَاِخْوَانُكُمْ فِى الدِّيْنِ وَمَوَالِيْكُمْ ؕ
وَلَيْسَ عَلَيْكُمْ جُنَاحٌ فِيْمَاۤ اَخْطَاْتُمْ
بِهٖ ۙ وَلٰكِنْ مَّا تَعَمَّدَتْ قُلُوْبُكُمْ ؕ
وَكَانَ اللّٰهُ غَفُوْرًا رَّحِيْمًا ﴿۵﴾
اَلنَّبِىُّ اَوْلٰى بِالْمُؤْمِنِيْنَ مِنْ
اَنْفُسِهِمْ وَاَزْوَاجُهٗۤ اُمَّهٰتُهُمْ ؕ
وَاُولُوا الْاَرْحَامِ بَعْضُهُمْ اَوْلٰى
بِبَعْضٍ فِىْ كِتٰبِ اللّٰهِ مِنَ
الْمُؤْمِنِيْنَ وَالْمُهٰجِرِيْنَ اِلَّاۤ اَنْ تَفْعَلُوْۤا
اِلٰٓى اَوْلِيٰٓـئِكُمْ مَّعْرُوْفًا ؕ كَانَ ذٰلِكَ
فِى الْكِتٰبِ مَسْطُوْرًا ﴿۶﴾
وَاِذْ اَخَذْنَا مِنَ النَّبِيّٖنَ مِيْثَاقَهُمْ

Ikhfa اخفاء | Ghunna غنّہ | Ikhfa Meem Saakin اخفاء میم ساکن | Idghaam ادغام | Qalqala قلقلہ | Qalb قلب | Idghaam Meem Saakin ادغام میم ساکن

as (We did) from you: from Noah, Abraham, Moses, and Jesus the son of Mary: We took from them a solemn Covenant:

8. So that (Allah) may question the (custodians) of Truth con-cerning the Truth they (were charged with): and He has prepared for the Unbelievers a grievous Penalty.

9. O you who believe! Remember the Grace of Allah, (bestowed) on you, when there came down on you hosts (to overwhelm you): but We sent against them a hurricane and forces that you did not see: but Allah sees (clearly) all that you do.

10. Behold! They came on you from above you and from below you, and behold, the eyes became dim and the hearts gaped up to the throats, and you imagined various (vain) thoughts about Allah!

11. In that situation were the Believers tried: they were shaken as by a tremendous shaking.

12. And behold! The Hypocrites and those in whose hearts is a disease (even) say: "Allah and His Messenger promised us nothing but delusions."

13. Behold! A party among them said: "You men of Yathrib! you cannot stand (the attack)! therefore go back!" And a band of them ask for leave of the Prophet, saying, "Truly our houses are bare and exposed," though they were not exposed they intended nothing but to run away.

14. And if an entry had been effected to them from the sides of the (City), and they had been incited to sedition, they would certainly have brought it

wa minka wa min-Nooḥiñw-wa Ibraaheema wa Moosaa wa 'Eesab-ni-Maryama wa akhaz-naa minhum-meesaaqan gha-leezaa.

8. Liyas'alaṣ-ṣaadiqeena 'an ṣidqihim; wa a'adda lilkaa-fireena 'azaaban aleemaa.

(Section 1)

9. Yaaa ayyuhal-lazeena aamanuz-kuroo ni'matal-laahi 'alaykum iz jaaa'atkum junoo-dun fa-arsalnaa 'alayhim reeḥañw-wa junoodal-lam tarawhaa; wa kaanal-laahu bimaa ta'maloona Baṣeeraa.

10. Iz jaaa'ookum-min fawqi-kum wa min asfala minkum wa iz zaaghatil-abṣaaru wa bala-ghatil-quloobul-ḥanaajira wa taẓunnoona billaahiẓ-ẓunoo-naa.

11. Hunaalikab-tuliyal-mu'-minoona wa zulziloo zilzaalan shadeedaa.

12. Wa iz yaqoolul-munaafi-qoona wallazeena fee quloo-bihim-maraḍum-maa wa'ada-nal-laahu wa Rasooluhooo illaa ghurooraa.

13. Wa iz qaalaṭ-ṭaaa'ifatum-minhum yaaa ahla Yasriba laa muqaama lakum farji'oo; wa yastaåzinu fareequm-minhu-mun-Nabiyya yaqooloona inna buyootanaa 'awrah; wa maa hiya bi'awratin iñy-yureedoona illaa firaaraa.

14. Wa law dukhilat 'alayhim-min aqṭaarihaa summa su'ilul-fitnata la-aatawhaa wa maa

وَمِنْكَ وَمِنْ نُّوحٍ وَّإِبْرٰهِيمَ
وَمُوسٰى وَعِيسَى ابْنِ مَرْيَمَ
وَأَخَذْنَا مِنْهُمْ مِّيثَاقًا غَلِيظًا ۝٧
لِّيَسْـَٔلَ الصّٰدِقِينَ عَنْ صِدْقِهِمْ
وَأَعَدَّ لِلْكٰفِرِينَ عَذَابًا أَلِيمًا ۝٨ ع
يٰٓأَيُّهَا الَّذِينَ اٰمَنُوا اذْكُرُوا نِعْمَةَ
اللّٰهِ عَلَيْكُمْ إِذْ جَآءَتْكُمْ جُنُودٌ
فَأَرْسَلْنَا عَلَيْهِمْ رِيحًا وَّجُنُودًا
لَّمْ تَرَوْهَا ۚ وَكَانَ اللّٰهُ بِمَا تَعْمَلُونَ
بَصِيرًا ۝٩
إِذْ جَآءُوكُمْ مِّنْ فَوْقِكُمْ وَمِنْ
أَسْفَلَ مِنْكُمْ وَإِذْ زَاغَتِ الْأَبْصَارُ
وَبَلَغَتِ الْقُلُوبُ الْحَنَاجِرَ وَتَظُنُّونَ
بِاللّٰهِ الظُّنُونَا ۝١٠
هُنَالِكَ ابْتُلِيَ الْمُؤْمِنُونَ وَزُلْزِلُوا
زِلْزَالًا شَدِيدًا ۝١١
وَإِذْ يَقُولُ الْمُنٰفِقُونَ وَالَّذِينَ فِي
قُلُوبِهِمْ مَّرَضٌ مَّا وَعَدَنَا اللّٰهُ
وَرَسُولُهُۥٓ إِلَّا غُرُورًا ۝١٢
وَإِذْ قَالَتْ طَّآئِفَةٌ مِّنْهُمْ يٰٓأَهْلَ
يَثْرِبَ لَا مُقَامَ لَكُمْ فَارْجِعُوا ۚ
وَيَسْتَأْذِنُ فَرِيقٌ مِّنْهُمُ النَّبِيَّ
يَقُولُونَ إِنَّ بُيُوتَنَا عَوْرَةٌ ۛ وَمَا هِيَ
بِعَوْرَةٍ ۛ إِنْ يُّرِيدُونَ إِلَّا فِرَارًا ۝١٣
وَلَوْ دُخِلَتْ عَلَيْهِمْ مِّنْ أَقْطَارِهَا
ثُمَّ سُئِلُوا الْفِتْنَةَ لَاٰتَوْهَا وَمَا

ع ١٧/١

مع
عند المتقدمين ١٢

Ikhfa اخفاء | Ghunna غنّہ | Ikhfa Meem Saakin اخفاء میم ساکن | Idghaam ادغام | Qalqala قلقلہ | Qalb قلب | Idghaam Meem Saakin ادغام میم ساکن

to pass, with none but a brief delay!

talabbasoo bihaaa illaa yaseeraa.

تلبثوا بها الا يسيرا ﴿١٤﴾

15. And yet they had already covenanted with Allah not to turn their backs, and a covenant with Allah must (surely) be answered for.

15. Wa laqad kaanoo 'aahadullaaha min qablu laa yuwalloonal-adbaar; wa kaana 'ahdul-laahi mas'oolaa.

ولقد كانوا عاهدوا الله من
قبل لا يولون الادبار وكان عهد
الله مسئولا ﴿١٥﴾

16. Say: "Running away will not profit you if you are running away from death or slaughter; and even if (you do escape), no more than a brief (respite) will you be allowed to enjoy!"

16. Qul lañy-yanfa'akumul-firaaru in farartum-minal-mawti awil-qatli wa izal-laa tumatta'oona illaa qaleelaa.

قل لن ينفعكم الفرار ان فررتم
من الموت او القتل واذا
لا تمتعون الا قليلا ﴿١٦﴾

17. Say: "Who is it that can screen you from Allah if it be His wish to give you punishment or to give you Mercy?" Nor will they find for themselves, besides Allah, any protector or helper.

17. Qul man zal-lazee ya'ṣimukum-minal-laahi in araada bikum sooo'an aw araada bikum raḥmah; wa laa yajidoona lahum-min doonil-laahi waliyyañw-wa laa naṣeeraa.

قل من ذا الذي يعصمكم من
الله ان اراد بكم سوءا او اراد
بكم رحمة ولا يجدون لهم
من دون الله وليا ولا نصيرا ﴿١٧﴾

18. Verily Allah knows those among you who keep back (men) and those who say to their brethren, "Come along to us", but come not to the fight except for just a little while.

18. Qad ya'lamul-laahul-mu'awwiqeena minkum walqaaa'ileena li-ikhwaanihim halumma ilaynaa, wa laa yaâtoonal-baâsa illaa qaleelaa.

قد يعلم الله المعوقين منكم
والقائلين لاخوانهم هلم الينا
ولا ياتون الباس الا قليلا ﴿١٨﴾

19. Covetous over you. Then when fear comes, you will see them looking to you, their eyes revolving, like (those of) one over whom death hovers: but when the fear is past, they will smite you with sharp tongues, covetous of goods. Such men have no faith, and so Allah has made their deeds of none effect: and that is easy for Allah.

19. Ashiḥḥatan 'alaykum fa-izaa jaaa'al-khawfu ra-aytahum yanzuroona ilayka tadooru a'yunuhum kallazee yughshaa 'alayhi minal-mawti fa-izaa zahabal-khawfu salaqookum bi-alsinatin ḥidaadin ashiḥḥatan 'alal-khayr; ulaaa'ika lam yu'minoo fa-aḥbaṭal-laahu a'maalahum; wa kaana zaalika 'alal-laahi yaseeraa.

اشحة عليكم فاذا جاء الخوف
رايتهم ينظرون اليك تدور
اعينهم كالذي يغشى عليه
من الموت فاذا ذهب الخوف
سلقوكم بالسنة حداد اشحة
على الخير اولئك لم يؤمنوا
فاحبط الله اعمالهم وكان ذلك
على الله يسيرا ﴿١٩﴾

20. They think that the Confederates have not withdrawn; and if the Confederates should come (again), they would wish they were in the deserts (wandering) among the Bedouins, and seeking news about you (from a safe distance); and if they were in your midst,

20. Yaḥsaboonal-Aḥzaaba lam yazhaboo wa iñy-yaâtil-Aḥzaabu yawaddoo law annahum baadoona fil-A'raabi yas-aloona 'an ambaaa'ikum wa law kaanoo feekum

يحسبون الاحزاب لم يذهبوا
وان يات الاحزاب يودوا لو
انهم بادون في الاعراب يسالون
عن انبائكم ولو كانوا فيكم

Ikhfa اخفاء | Ghunna غنّہ | Ikhfa Meem Saakin اخفاء میم ساکن | Idghaam ادغام | Qalqala قلقلہ | Qalb قلب | Idghaam Meem Saakin ادغام میم ساکن

they would fight but little.

21. You have indeed in the Messenger of Allah a beautiful pattern (of conduct) for any one whose hope is in Allah and the Final Day, and who engages much in the Praise of Allah.

22. When the Believers saw the Confederate forces, they said: "This is what Allah and His Messenger had promised us, and Allah and His Messenger told us what was true." And it only added to their faith and their zeal in obedience.

23. Among the Believers are men who have been true to their covenant with Allah: of them some have completed their vow (to the extreme), and some (still) wait: but they have never changed (their determination) in the least:

24. That Allah may reward the men of Truth for their Truth, and punish the Hypocrites if that be His Will, or turn to them in Mercy: for Allah is Oft-Forgiving, Most Merciful.

25. And Allah turned back the Unbelievers for (all) their fury, no advantage did they gain; and enough is Allah for the believers in their fight. And Allah is full of Strength, able to enforce His Will.

26. And those of the People of the Book who aided them- Allah took them down from their strongholds and cast terror into their hearts, (so that) some you slew, and some you made prisoners.

27. And He made you heirs of their lands, their houses, and their goods, and of a land which you had not frequented (before). And Allah has power over all things.

maa qaataloo illaa qaleelaa.
(Section 2)

21. Laqad kaana lakum fee Rasoolil-laahi uswatun hasanatul-liman kaana yarjul-laaha wal-Yawmal-Aakhira wa zakaral-laaha kaseeraa.

22. Wa lammaa ra-al-mu'minoonal-Ahzaaba qaaloo haazaa maa wa'adanal-laahu wa Rasooluhoo wa sadaqal-laahu wa Rasooluh; wa maa zaadahum illaa eemaanañw-wa tasleemaa.

23. Minal-mu'mineena rijaalun sadaqoo maa 'aahadul-laaha 'alayhi faminhum-man qadaa nahbahoo wa minhum-mañy-yantaziru wa maa baddaloo tabdeelaa.

24. Li-yajziyal-laahus-saadiqeena bisidqihim wa yu'azzibal-munaafiqeena in shaaa'a aw yatooba 'alayhim; innal-laaha kaana Ghafoorar-Raheemaa.

25. Wa raddal-laahul-lazeena kafaroo bighayzihim lam yanaaloo khayraa; wa kafal-laahul-mu'mineenal-qitaal; wa kaanal-laahu Qawiyyan 'Azeezaa.

26. Wa anzalal-lazeena zaaharoohum-min Ahlil-Kitaabi min sa-yaaseehim wa qazafa fee quloobihimur-ru'ba fareeqan taqtuloona wa taåsiroona fareeqaa.

27. Wa awrasakum ardahum wa diyaarahum wa amwaalahum wa ardal-lam tata'oohaa; wa kaanal-laahu 'alaa kulli shay'in Qadeeraa. **(Section 3)**

مَّا قٰتَلُوْٓا اِلَّا قَلِيْلًا ۝٢٠ ع ١٢ ١٨
لَقَدْ كَانَ لَكُمْ فِيْ رَسُوْلِ اللّٰهِ
اُسْوَةٌ حَسَنَةٌ لِّمَنْ كَانَ يَرْجُوا اللّٰهَ
وَالْيَوْمَ الْاٰخِرَ وَذَكَرَ اللّٰهَ كَثِيْرًا ۝٢١
وَلَمَّا رَاَ الْمُؤْمِنُوْنَ الْاَحْزَابَ ۙ قَالُوْا
هٰذَا مَا وَعَدَنَا اللّٰهُ وَرَسُوْلُهٗ
وَصَدَقَ اللّٰهُ وَرَسُوْلُهٗ ۫ وَمَا
زَادَهُمْ اِلَّآ اِيْمَانًا وَّتَسْلِيْمًا ۝٢٢
مِنَ الْمُؤْمِنِيْنَ رِجَالٌ صَدَقُوْا
مَا عَاهَدُوا اللّٰهَ عَلَيْهِ ۚ فَمِنْهُمْ مَّنْ
قَضٰى نَحْبَهٗ وَمِنْهُمْ مَّنْ يَّنْتَظِرُ ۖ
وَمَا بَدَّلُوْا تَبْدِيْلًا ۝٢٣
لِّيَجْزِيَ اللّٰهُ الصّٰدِقِيْنَ بِصِدْقِهِمْ
وَيُعَذِّبَ الْمُنٰفِقِيْنَ اِنْ شَآءَ اَوْ
يَتُوْبَ عَلَيْهِمْ ۭ اِنَّ اللّٰهَ كَانَ
غَفُوْرًا رَّحِيْمًا ۝٢٤
وَرَدَّ اللّٰهُ الَّذِيْنَ كَفَرُوْا بِغَيْظِهِمْ لَمْ
يَنَالُوْا خَيْرًا ۭ وَكَفَى اللّٰهُ الْمُؤْمِنِيْنَ
الْقِتَالَ ۭ وَكَانَ اللّٰهُ قَوِيًّا عَزِيْزًا ۝٢٥
وَاَنْزَلَ الَّذِيْنَ ظَاهَرُوْهُمْ مِّنْ
اَهْلِ الْكِتٰبِ مِنْ صَيَاصِيْهِمْ
وَقَذَفَ فِيْ قُلُوْبِهِمُ الرُّعْبَ فَرِيْقًا
تَقْتُلُوْنَ وَتَاْسِرُوْنَ فَرِيْقًا ۝٢٦
وَاَوْرَثَكُمْ اَرْضَهُمْ وَدِيَارَهُمْ
وَاَمْوَالَهُمْ وَاَرْضًا لَّمْ تَطَـُٔوْهَا ۭ
وَكَانَ اللّٰهُ عَلٰى كُلِّ شَيْءٍ قَدِيْرًا ۝٢٧ ع ٣ ١٩

Ikhfa اخفاء | Ghunna غُنّہ | Ikhfa Meem Saakin اخفاءمیم ساکن | Idghaam ادغام | Qalqala قلقلہ | Qalb قلب | Idghaam Meem Saakin ادغام میم ساکن

28. O Prophet! Say to your Consorts:"If it be that you desire the life of this World, and its glitter,- then come! I will provide for your enjoyment and set you free in a handsome manner.

28. Yaaa ayyuhan-Nabiyyu qul li-azwaajika in kuntunna turidnal-ḥayaatad-dunyaa wa zeenatahaa fata'aalayna umat-ti'kunna wa usarriḥkunna saraa-ḥan-jameelaa.

يٰۤاَيُّهَا النَّبِيُّ قُلْ لِّاَزْوَاجِكَ اِنْ
كُنْتُنَّ تُرِدْنَ الْحَيٰوةَ الدُّنْيَا
وَزِيْنَتَهَا فَتَعَالَيْنَ اُمَتِّعْكُنَّ
وَاُسَرِّحْكُنَّ سَرَاحًا جَمِيْلًا ﴿٢٨﴾

29. But if you seek Allah and His Apostle, and the Home of the Hereafter, verily Allah has prepared for the well-doers amongst you a great reward.

29. Wa in kuntunna turidnal-laaha wa Rasoolahoo wad-Daaral-Aakhirata fa-innal-laaha-a'adda lilmuḥsinaati min-kunna ajran 'aẓeemaa.

وَاِنْ كُنْتُنَّ تُرِدْنَ اللّٰهَ وَرَسُوْلَهٗ
وَالدَّارَ الْاٰخِرَةَ فَاِنَّ اللّٰهَ اَعَدَّ
لِلْمُحْسِنٰتِ مِنْكُنَّ اَجْرًا عَظِيْمًا ﴿٢٩﴾

30. O Consorts of the Prophet! If any of you were guilty of evident unseemly conduct, the Punishment would be doubled to her, and that is easy for Allah.

30. Yaa nisaaa'an-Nabiyyi mañy-yaâti minkunna bifaa-ḥishatim-mubayyinatiñy-yuḍaa'af lahal-'azaabu ḍi'fayn; wa kaana zaalika 'alal-laahi yaseeraa.

يٰنِسَآءَ النَّبِيِّ مَنْ يَّاْتِ مِنْكُنَّ
بِفَاحِشَةٍ مُّبَيِّنَةٍ يُّضٰعَفْ لَهَا
الْعَذَابُ ضِعْفَيْنِ ؕ وَكَانَ ذٰلِكَ
عَلَى اللّٰهِ يَسِيْرًا ﴿٣٠﴾

31. But any of you that is devout in the service of Allah and His Apostle, and works righte-ousness,- to her shall We grant her reward twice: and We have prepared for her a generous Sustenance.

31. Wa mañy-yaqnut minkunna lillaahi wa Rasoolihee wa ta'mal ṣaaliḥan nu'tihaaa ajra-haa marratayni wa a'tadnaa lahaa rizqan kareemaa.

وَمَنْ يَّقْنُتْ مِنْكُنَّ لِلّٰهِ وَرَسُوْلِهٖ
وَتَعْمَلْ صَالِحًا نُّؤْتِهَاۤ اَجْرَهَا
مَرَّتَيْنِ ۙ وَاَعْتَدْنَا لَهَا رِزْقًا كَرِيْمًا ﴿٣١﴾

32. O Consorts of the Prophet! You are not like any of the (other) women: if you do fear (Allah), be not too complaisant of speech, lest one in whose heart is a disease should be moved with desire: but speak you a speech (that is) just.

32. Yaa nisaaa'an-Nabiyyi lastunna ka-aḥadim minan-nisaaa'i init-taqaytunna falaa takhḍa'na bilqawli fa-yaṭma'al-lazee fee qalbihee maraḍuñw-wa qulna qawlam-ma'roofaa.

يٰنِسَآءَ النَّبِيِّ لَسْتُنَّ كَاَحَدٍ مِّنَ
النِّسَآءِ اِنِ اتَّقَيْتُنَّ فَلَا تَخْضَعْنَ
بِالْقَوْلِ فَيَطْمَعَ الَّذِيْ فِيْ قَلْبِهٖ
مَرَضٌ وَّقُلْنَ قَوْلًا مَّعْرُوْفًا ۚ﴿٣٢﴾

33. And stay quietly in your houses, and make not a dazzling display, like that of the former Times of Ignorance; and establish regular Prayer, and give regular Charity; and obey Allah and His Apostle. And Allah only wishes to remove all abomination from you, you members of the Family, and to make you pure and spotless.

33. Wa qarna fee bu-yootikunna wa laa tabarrajna tabarrujal-Jaahiliyyatil-oolaa wa aqimnaṣ-Ṣalaata wa aateenaz-Zakaata wa aṭi'nal-laaha wa Rasoolah; innamaa yureedul-laahu liyuzhiba 'ankumur-rijsa Ahlal-Bayti wa yuṭahhirakum taṭheeraa.

وَقَرْنَ فِيْ بُيُوْتِكُنَّ وَلَا تَبَرَّجْنَ
تَبَرُّجَ الْجَاهِلِيَّةِ الْاُوْلٰى وَاَقِمْنَ
الصَّلٰوةَ وَاٰتِيْنَ الزَّكٰوةَ وَاَطِعْنَ
اللّٰهَ وَرَسُوْلَهٗ ؕ اِنَّمَا يُرِيْدُ اللّٰهُ
لِيُذْهِبَ عَنْكُمُ الرِّجْسَ اَهْلَ الْبَيْتِ
وَيُطَهِّرَكُمْ تَطْهِيْرًا ۚ﴿٣٣﴾

34. And recite what is rehear-sed to you in your homes, of the Signs of Allah and His Wisdom: for Allah

34. Wazkurna maa yutlaa fee bu-yootikunna min Aayaatil-laahi wal-Ḥikmah; innal-laaha

وَاذْكُرْنَ مَا يُتْلٰى فِيْ بُيُوْتِكُنَّ
مِنْ اٰيٰتِ اللّٰهِ وَالْحِكْمَةِ ؕ اِنَّ اللّٰهَ

Ikhfa اخفاء | Ghunna غُنّہ | Ikhfa Meem Saakin اخفاء میم ساکن | Idghaam ادغام | Qalqala قلقلہ | Qalb قلب | Idghaam Meem Saakin ادغام میم ساکن

understands the finest mysteries and is well-acquainted (with them).

35. For Muslim men and women, - for believing men and women, for devout men and women, for true men and women, for men and women who are patient and constant, for men and women who humble themselves, for men and women who give in Charity, for men and women who fast (and deny themselves), for men and women who guard their chastity, and for men and women who engage much in Allah's praise, - for them Allah has prepared forgiveness and great reward.

36. It is not fitting for a Believer, man or woman, when a matter has been decided by Allah and His Apostle, to have any option about their decision: if any one disobeys Allah and His Apostle, he is indeed on a clearly wrong Path.

37. Behold! You did say to one who had received the grace of Allah and your favour: "You (in wedlock) your wife, and fear Allah." But you retain hid in your heart that which Allah was about to make manifest: you feared the people, but it is more fitting that you should fear Allah. Then when Zaid had dissolved (his marriage) with her, with the necessary (formality), We joined her in marriage to you: in order that (in future) there may be no difficulty to the Believers in (the matter of) marriage with the wives of their adopted sons, when the latter have dissolved with the necessary (formality) (their marriage) with them. And Allah's command must be fulfilled.

38. There can be no difficulty to the Prophet in what Allah has indicated to him as a duty. It was the practice (approved) of Allah amongst

kaana Laṭeefan Khabeeraa.

(Section 4)

35. Innal-muslimeena wal-muslimaati walmu'mineena walmu'minaati walqaaniteena walqaanitaati waṣṣaadiqeena waṣṣaadiqaati waṣṣaabireena waṣṣaabiraati walkhaashi'eena walkhaashi'aati walmutaṣad-diqeena walmutaṣaddiqaati waṣṣaaa'imeena waṣṣaaa'i-maati walḥaafiẓeena furooja-hum walḥaafiẓaati waẕ-ẕaaki-reenal-laaha kaseerañw-waẕ-ẕaakiraati a'addal-laahu lahum-maghfiratañw-wa ajran 'aẓee-maa.

36. Wa maa kaana limu'mi-niñw-wa laa mu'minatin iẕaa qaḍal-laahu wa Rasooluhooo amran añy-yakoona lahumul-khiyaratu min amrihim; wa mañy-ya'ṣil-laaha wa Rasoo-lahoo faqad ḍalla ḍalaalam-mubeenaa.

37. Wa iẕ taqoolu lillaẕeee an'amal-laahu 'alayhi wa an'amta 'alayhi amsik 'alayka zawjaka wattaqil-laaha wa tukhfee fee nafsika mal-laahu mubdeehi wa takhshan-naasa wallaahu aḥaqqu an takhshaah; falammaa qaḍaa Zaydum-minhaa waṭaran zawwajnaa-kahaa likay laa yakoona 'alal-mu'mineena ḥarajun feee azwaaji ad'iyaaa'ihim iẕaa qaḍaw minhunna waṭaraa; wa kaana amrul-laahi maf'oolaa.

38. Maa kaana 'alan-Nabiyyi min ḥarajin feemaa faraḍal-laahu lahoo sunnatal-laahi fil-

كَانَ لَطِيفًا خَبِيرًا ﴿٣٤﴾
إِنَّ الْمُسْلِمِينَ وَالْمُسْلِمَاتِ وَالْمُؤْمِنِينَ
وَالْمُؤْمِنَاتِ وَالْقَانِتِينَ وَالْقَانِتَاتِ
وَالصَّادِقِينَ وَالصَّادِقَاتِ وَالصَّابِرِينَ
وَالصَّابِرَاتِ وَالْخَاشِعِينَ وَالْخَاشِعَاتِ
وَالْمُتَصَدِّقِينَ وَالْمُتَصَدِّقَاتِ
وَالصَّائِمِينَ وَالصَّائِمَاتِ وَالْحَافِظِينَ
فُرُوجَهُمْ وَالْحَافِظَاتِ وَالذَّاكِرِينَ اللَّهَ
كَثِيرًا وَالذَّاكِرَاتِ أَعَدَّ اللَّهُ لَهُمْ
مَغْفِرَةً وَأَجْرًا عَظِيمًا ﴿٣٥﴾
وَمَا كَانَ لِمُؤْمِنٍ وَلَا مُؤْمِنَةٍ إِذَا
قَضَى اللَّهُ وَرَسُولُهُ أَمْرًا أَنْ يَكُونَ
لَهُمُ الْخِيَرَةُ مِنْ أَمْرِهِمْ ۗ وَمَنْ
يَعْصِ اللَّهَ وَرَسُولَهُ فَقَدْ ضَلَّ
ضَلَالًا مُبِينًا ﴿٣٦﴾
وَإِذْ تَقُولُ لِلَّذِي أَنْعَمَ اللَّهُ عَلَيْهِ
وَأَنْعَمْتَ عَلَيْهِ أَمْسِكْ عَلَيْكَ
زَوْجَكَ وَاتَّقِ اللَّهَ وَتُخْفِي فِي نَفْسِكَ
مَا اللَّهُ مُبْدِيهِ وَتَخْشَى النَّاسَ
وَاللَّهُ أَحَقُّ أَنْ تَخْشَاهُ ۖ فَلَمَّا قَضَى
زَيْدٌ مِنْهَا وَطَرًا زَوَّجْنَاكَهَا لِكَيْ
لَا يَكُونَ عَلَى الْمُؤْمِنِينَ حَرَجٌ فِي
أَزْوَاجِ أَدْعِيَائِهِمْ إِذَا قَضَوْا مِنْهُنَّ
وَطَرًا ۚ وَكَانَ أَمْرُ اللَّهِ مَفْعُولًا ﴿٣٧﴾
مَا كَانَ عَلَى النَّبِيِّ مِنْ حَرَجٍ فِيمَا
فَرَضَ اللَّهُ لَهُ ۖ سُنَّةَ اللَّهِ فِي

those of old that have passed away. And the command of Allah is a decree determined.

lazeena khalaw min qabl; wa kaana amrul-laahi qadaram-maqdooraa.

الَّذِيْنَ خَلَوْا مِنْ قَبْلُ ؕ وَكَانَ اَمْرُ
اللّٰهِ قَدَرًا مَّقْدُوْرَا ۟ۙ ٣٨

39. (It is the practice of those) who preach the Messages of Allah, and fear Him, and fear none but Allah. And enough is Allah to call (men) to account.

39. Allazeena yuballighoona Risaalaatil-laahi wa yakhshawnahoo wa laa yakhshawna aḥadan illal-laah; wa kafaa billaahi Ḥaseebaa.

الَّذِيْنَ يُبَلِّغُوْنَ رِسٰلٰتِ اللّٰهِ وَ
يَخْشَوْنَهٗ وَلَا يَخْشَوْنَ اَحَدًا اِلَّا
اللّٰهَ ؕ وَكَفٰى بِاللّٰهِ حَسِيْبًا ٣٩

40. Muhammad is not the father of any of your men, but (he is) the Apostle of Allah, and the Seal of the Prophets: and Allah has full knowledge of all things.

40. Maa kaana Muḥammadun abaaa aḥadim-mir-rijaalikum wa laakir-Rasoolal-laahi wa Khaataman-Nabiyyeen; wa kaanal-laahu bikulli shay'in 'Aleemaa. **(Section 5)**

مَا كَانَ مُحَمَّدٌ اَبَآ اَحَدٍ مِّنْ رِّجَالِكُمْ
وَلٰكِنْ رَّسُوْلَ اللّٰهِ وَخَاتَمَ النَّبِيّٖنَ ؕ
وَكَانَ اللّٰهُ بِكُلِّ شَيْءٍ عَلِيْمًا ٤٠ ع ٥

41. O you who believe! Celebrate the praises of Allah, and do this often;

41. Yaaa ayyuhal-lazeena aamanuz-kurul-laaha zikran kaseeraa.

يٰۤاَيُّهَا الَّذِيْنَ اٰمَنُوا اذْكُرُوا اللّٰهَ
ذِكْرًا كَثِيْرًا ۙ ٤١

42. And glorify Him morning and evening.

42. Wa sabbiḥoohu bukratañw-wa aṣeelaa.

وَّسَبِّحُوْهُ بُكْرَةً وَّاَصِيْلًا ٤٢

43. He it is Who sends blessings on you, as do His angels, that He may bring you out from the depths of Darkness into Light: and He is Full of Mercy to the Believers.

43. Huwal-lazee yuṣallee 'alaykum wa malaaa'ikatuhoo liyukhrijakum-minaẓẓulumaati ilan-noor; wa kaana bilmu'mineena Raḥeemaa.

هُوَ الَّذِيْ يُصَلِّيْ عَلَيْكُمْ وَمَلٰٓئِكَتُهٗ
لِيُخْرِجَكُمْ مِّنَ الظُّلُمٰتِ اِلَى النُّوْرِ ؕ
وَكَانَ بِالْمُؤْمِنِيْنَ رَحِيْمًا ٤٣

44. Their salutation on the Day they meet Him will be "Peace!"; and He has prepared for them a generous Reward.

44. Taḥiyyatuhum Yawma yalqawnahoo salaamuñw-wa a'adda lahum ajran kareemaa.

تَحِيَّتُهُمْ يَوْمَ يَلْقَوْنَهٗ سَلٰمٌ ۖۚ وَّاَعَدَّ
لَهُمْ اَجْرًا كَرِيْمًا ٤٤

45. O Prophet! Truly We have sent you as a Witness, a Bearer of Glad Tidings, and a Warner,-

45. Yaaa ayyuhan-Nabiyyu innaaa arsalnaaka shaahidañw-wa mubashshirañw-wa nazeeraa.

يٰۤاَيُّهَا النَّبِيُّ اِنَّاۤ اَرْسَلْنٰكَ شَاهِدًا
وَّمُبَشِّرًا وَّنَذِيْرًا ۙ ٤٥

46. And as one who invites to Allah's (Grace) by His leave, and as a lamp spreading light.

46. Wa daa'iyan ilal-laahi biiznihee wa siraajam-muneeraa.

وَّدَاعِيًا اِلَى اللّٰهِ بِاِذْنِهٖ وَسِرَاجًا
مُّنِيْرًا ٤٦

47. Then give the glad tidings to the Believers, that they shall have from Allah a very great Bounty.

47. Wa bashshiril-mu'mineena bi-anna lahum-minal-laahi faḍlan kabeeraa.

وَبَشِّرِ الْمُؤْمِنِيْنَ بِاَنَّ لَهُمْ مِّنَ
اللّٰهِ فَضْلًا كَبِيْرًا ٤٧

48. And do not obey (the behests) of the Unbelievers and the Hypocrites, and heed not their annoyances, but put your Trust in Allah. For enough is Allah as a Disposer of affairs.

48. Wa laa tuṭi'il-kaafireena walmunaafiqeena wa da' azaahum wa tawakkal 'alallaah; wa kafaa billaahi Wakeelaa.

وَلَا تُطِعِ الْكٰفِرِيْنَ وَالْمُنٰفِقِيْنَ وَدَعْ
اَذٰىهُمْ وَتَوَكَّلْ عَلَى اللّٰهِ ؕ وَكَفٰى
بِاللّٰهِ وَكِيْلًا ٤٨

49. O you who believe! When you marry

49. Yaaa ayyuhal-lazeena aamanooo izaa nakaḥtumul-

يٰۤاَيُّهَا الَّذِيْنَ اٰمَنُوْۤا اِذَا نَكَحْتُمُ

believing women, and then divorce them before you have touched them, no period of *'Iddat* have you to count in respect of them: so give them a present, and set them free in a handsome manner.

mu'minaati summa ṭallaqtu-moohunna min qabli an tamas-soohunna famaa lakum 'alay-hinna min 'iddatin ta'taddoona-haa famatti'oohunna wa sarri-ḥoohunna saraaḥan jameelaa.

الْمُؤْمِنٰتِ ثُمَّ طَلَّقْتُمُوْهُنَّ مِنْ
قَبْلِ اَنْ تَمَسُّوْهُنَّ فَمَا لَكُمْ
عَلَيْهِنَّ مِنْ عِدَّةٍ تَعْتَدُّوْنَهَا ۚ
فَمَتِّعُوْهُنَّ وَسَرِّحُوْهُنَّ سَرَاحًا
جَمِيْلًا ﴿٤٩﴾

50. O Prophet! We have made lawful to you your wives to whom you have paid their dowers; and those whom your right hand possesses out of the prisoners of war whom Allah has assigned to you; and daughters of your paternal uncles and aunts, and daughters of your maternal uncles and aunts, who migrated (from Makkah) with you; and any believing woman who dedicates her soul to the Prophet if the Prophet wishes to wed her;- this only for you, and not for the Believers (at large); We know what We have appointed for them as to their wives and the captives whom their right hands possess;- in order that there should be no difficulty for you. And Allah is Oft-Forgiving, Most Merciful.

50. Yaaa ayyuhan-Nabiyyu innaaa aḥlalnaa laka azwaa-jakal-laateee aatayta ujoora-hunna wa maa malakat yamee-nuka mimmaaa afaaa'al-laahu 'alayka wa banaati 'ammika wa banaati 'ammaatika wa banaati khaalika wa banaati khaalaa-tikal-laatee haajarna ma'aka wamra-atam-mu'minatan iñw-wahabat nafsahaa lin-Nabiyyi in araadan-Nabiyyu añy-yastan-kiḥahaa khaaliṣatal-laka min doonil-mu'mineen; qad 'alim-naa maa faraḍnaa 'alayhim feee azwaajihim wa maa malakat aymaanuhum likaylaa yakoona 'alayka ḥaraj; wa kaanal-laahu Ghafoorar-Raḥeemaa.

يٰۤاَيُّهَا النَّبِيُّ اِنَّاۤ اَحْلَلْنَا لَكَ اَزْوَاجَكَ
الّٰتِيْۤ اٰتَيْتَ اُجُوْرَهُنَّ وَمَا مَلَكَتْ
يَمِيْنُكَ مِمَّاۤ اَفَآءَ اللّٰهُ عَلَيْكَ وَبَنٰتِ
عَمِّكَ وَبَنٰتِ عَمّٰتِكَ وَبَنٰتِ خَالِكَ
وَبَنٰتِ خٰلٰتِكَ الّٰتِيْ هَاجَرْنَ مَعَكَ ۫
وَامْرَاَةً مُّؤْمِنَةً اِنْ وَّهَبَتْ نَفْسَهَا
لِلنَّبِيِّ اِنْ اَرَادَ النَّبِيُّ اَنْ يَّسْتَنْكِحَهَا ۚ
خَالِصَةً لَّكَ مِنْ دُوْنِ الْمُؤْمِنِيْنَ ؕ
قَدْ عَلِمْنَا مَا فَرَضْنَا عَلَيْهِمْ فِيْۤ
اَزْوَاجِهِمْ وَمَا مَلَكَتْ اَيْمَانُهُمْ لِكَيْلَا
يَكُوْنَ عَلَيْكَ حَرَجٌ ؕ وَكَانَ اللّٰهُ
غَفُوْرًا رَّحِيْمًا ﴿٥٠﴾

51. You may defer (the turn of) any of them that you please, and you may receive any you please: and there is no blame on you if you invite one whose (turn) you had set aside. This were nearer to the cooling of their eyes, the prevention of their grief, and their satisfaction - that of all of them - with that which you have to give them: and Allah knows (all) that is in your hearts: and Allah is All-Knowing, Most Forbearing.

51. Turjee man tashaaa'u minhunna wa tu'weee ilayka man tashaaa'u wa manibta-ghayta mimman 'azalta falaa junaaḥa 'alayk; ẕaalika adnaaa an taqarra a'yunuhunna wa laa yaḥzanna wa yarḍayna bimaaa aataytahunna kulluhunn; wal-laahu ya'lamu maa fee quloo-bikum; wa kaanal-laahu 'Aleeman Ḥaleemaa.

تُرْجِيْ مَنْ تَشَآءُ مِنْهُنَّ وَتُـْٔوِيْۤ
اِلَيْكَ مَنْ تَشَآءُ ؕ وَمَنِ ابْتَغَيْتَ
مِمَّنْ عَزَلْتَ فَلَا جُنَاحَ عَلَيْكَ ؕ
ذٰلِكَ اَدْنٰۤى اَنْ تَقَرَّ اَعْيُنُهُنَّ وَلَا
يَحْزَنَّ وَيَرْضَيْنَ بِمَاۤ اٰتَيْتَهُنَّ
كُلُّهُنَّ ؕ وَاللّٰهُ يَعْلَمُ مَا فِيْ قُلُوْبِكُمْ ؕ
وَكَانَ اللّٰهُ عَلِيْمًا حَلِيْمًا ﴿٥١﴾

52. It is not lawful for you (to marry more) women after this, nor to change them for (other) wives, even though

52. Laa yaḥillu lakan-nisaaa'u mim ba'du wa laaa an tabaddala bihinna min azwaajiñw-wa law

لَا يَحِلُّ لَكَ النِّسَآءُ مِنْۢ بَعْدُ وَلَاۤ
اَنْ تَبَدَّلَ بِهِنَّ مِنْ اَزْوَاجٍ وَّلَوْ

Ikhfa اخفاء | Ghunna غنّہ | Ikhfa Meem Saakin اخفاء میم ساکن | Idghaam ادغام | Qalqala قلقلہ | Qalb قلب | Idghaam Meem Saakin ادغام میم ساکن

their beauty attract you, except any your right hand should possess (as handmaidens): and Allah watches over all things.

a'jabaka ḥusnuhunna illaa maa malakat yameenuk; wa kaanallaahu 'alaa kulli shay'ir-Raqeebaa. **(Section 6)**

اَعۡجَبَكَ حُسۡنُهُنَّ اِلَّا مَا مَلَكَتۡ
يَمِيۡنُكَ ؕ وَكَانَ اللّٰهُ عَلٰى كُلِّ
شَىۡءٍ رَّقِيۡبًا ۝٥٢ ع

53. O you who believe! Do not enter the Prophet's houses,- until leave is given you,- for a meal, (and then) not (so early as) to wait for its preparation: but when you are invited, enter; and when you have taken your meal, disperse, without seeking familiar talk. Such (behaviour) annoys the Prophet: he is ashamed to dismiss you, but Allah is not ashamed (to tell you) the truth. And when you ask (his ladies) for anything you want, ask them from before a screen: that makes for greater purity for your hearts and for theirs. Nor is it right for you that you should annoy Allah's Apostle, or that you should marry his widows after him at any time. Truly such a thing is in Allah's sight an enormity.

53. Yaaa ayyuhal-lazeena aamanoo laa tadkhuloo bu-yootan-Nabiyyi illaaa añy-yu'zana lakum ilaa ṭa'aamin ghayra naaẓireena inaahu wa laakin izaa du'eetum fadkhuloo fa-izaa ṭa'imtum fantashiroo wa laa mustaåniseena liḥadees; inna zaalikum kaana yu'zin-Nabiyya fa-yastaḥyee minkum wallaahu laa yastaḥyee minal-ḥaqq; wa izaa sa-altumoohunna mataa'an fas'aloohunna miñw-waraaa'i ḥijaab; zaalikum aṭharu liquloobikum wa quloobihinn; wa maa kaana lakum an tu'zoo Rasoolal-laahi wa laaa an tankiḥooo azwaajahoo mim ba'diheee abadaa; inna zaalikum kaana 'indal-laahi 'aẓeemaa.

يٰۤاَيُّهَا الَّذِيۡنَ اٰمَنُوۡا لَا تَدۡخُلُوۡا بُيُوۡتَ
النَّبِىِّ اِلَّاۤ اَنۡ يُّؤۡذَنَ لَكُمۡ اِلٰى طَعَامٍ
غَيۡرَ نٰظِرِيۡنَ اِنٰٮهُ ۙ وَلٰكِنۡ اِذَا
دُعِيۡتُمۡ فَادۡخُلُوۡا فَاِذَا طَعِمۡتُمۡ
فَانۡتَشِرُوۡا وَلَا مُسۡتَاۡنِسِيۡنَ لِحَدِيۡثٍ ؕ
اِنَّ ذٰلِكُمۡ كَانَ يُؤۡذِى النَّبِىَّ فَيَسۡتَحۡىٖ
مِنۡكُمۡ وَاللّٰهُ لَا يَسۡتَحۡىٖ مِنَ الۡحَقِّ ؕ
وَاِذَا سَاَلۡتُمُوۡهُنَّ مَتَاعًا فَسۡـَٔلُوۡهُنَّ
مِنۡ وَّرَآءِ حِجَابٍ ؕ ذٰلِكُمۡ اَطۡهَرُ
لِقُلُوۡبِكُمۡ وَقُلُوۡبِهِنَّ ؕ وَمَا كَانَ
لَكُمۡ اَنۡ تُؤۡذُوۡا رَسُوۡلَ اللّٰهِ وَلَاۤ اَنۡ
تَنۡكِحُوۡۤا اَزۡوَاجَهٗ مِنۡۢ بَعۡدِهٖۤ اَبَدًا ؕ
اِنَّ ذٰلِكُمۡ كَانَ عِنۡدَ اللّٰهِ عَظِيۡمًا ۝٥٣

54. Whether you reveal anything or conceal it, verily Allah has full knowledge of all things.

54. In tubdoo shay'an aw tukhfoohu fa-innal-laaha kaana bikulli shay'in 'Aleemaa.

اِنۡ تُبۡدُوۡا شَيۡـًٔا اَوۡ تُخۡفُوۡهُ فَاِنَّ اللّٰهَ
كَانَ بِكُلِّ شَىۡءٍ عَلِيۡمًا ۝٥٤

55. There is no blame (on these ladies if they appear) before their fathers or their sons, their brothers, or their brother's sons, or their sisters' sons, or their women, or the (slaves) whom their right hands possess. And (ladies), fear Allah; for Allah is Witness to all things.

55. Laa junaaḥa 'alayhinna feee aabaaa'ihinna wa laaa abnaaa'ihinna wa laaa ikhwaanihinna wa laaa abnaaa'i ikhwaanihinna wa laaa abnaaa'i akhawaatihinna wa laa nisaaa'ihinna wa laa Maa malakat aymaanuhunn; wattaqeenal-laah; innal-laaha kaana 'alaa kulli shay'in Shaheedaa.

لَا جُنَاحَ عَلَيۡهِنَّ فِىۡۤ اٰبَآئِهِنَّ وَلَا
اَبۡنَآئِهِنَّ وَلَاۤ اِخۡوَانِهِنَّ وَلَا اَبۡنَآءِ
اِخۡوَانِهِنَّ وَلَاۤ اَبۡنَآءِ اَخَوٰتِهِنَّ
وَلَا نِسَآئِهِنَّ وَلَا مَا مَلَكَتۡ
اَيۡمَانُهُنَّ ۚ وَاتَّقِيۡنَ اللّٰهَ ؕ اِنَّ اللّٰهَ
كَانَ عَلٰى كُلِّ شَىۡءٍ شَهِيۡدًا ۝٥٥

56. Allah and His angels send blessings on the Prophet: O you that believe! You send blessings

56. Innal-laaha wa malaaa'ikatahoo yuṣalloona 'alan-Nabiyy; yaaa ayyuhal-lazeena aamanoo ṣalloo

اِنَّ اللّٰهَ وَمَلٰٓئِكَتَهٗ يُصَلُّوۡنَ عَلَى
النَّبِىِّ ؕ يٰۤاَيُّهَا الَّذِيۡنَ اٰمَنُوۡا صَلُّوۡا

Ikhfa اخفاء · Ghunna غُنّہ · Ikhfa Meem Saakin اخفاء میم ساکن · Idghaam ادغام · Qalqala قلقلہ · Qalb قلب · Idghaam Meem Saakin ادغام میم ساکن

on him, and salute him with all respect.

57. Those who annoy Allah and His Apostle - Allah has cursed them in this World and in the Hereafter, and has prepared for them a humiliating Punishment.

58. And those who annoy believing men and women undeservedly, bear (on themselves) a calumny and a glaring sin.

59. O Prophet! Tell your wives and daughters, and the believing women, that they should cast their outer garments over their persons (when abroad): that is most convenient, that they should be known (as such) and not molested. And Allah is Oft-Forgiving, Most Merciful.

60. Truly, if the Hypocrites, and those in whose hearts is a disease, and those who stir up sedition in the City, desist not, We shall certainly stir you up against them: then will they not be able to stay in it as your neighbours for any length of time:

61. They shall have a curse on them: whenever they are found, they shall be seized and slain (without mercy).

62. (Such was) the practice (approved) of Allah among those who lived aforetime: no change will you find in the practice (approved) of Allah.

63. Men ask you concerning the Hour: Say, "The knowledge thereof is with Allah (alone)": and what will make you understand?- perchance the Hour is near!

64. Verily Allah has cursed the Unbelievers and prepared for them a Blazing Fire.

65. To dwell therein for ever: no protector will they find,

'alayhi wa ṣallimoo tasleemaa.

57. Innal-lazeena yu'zoonal-laaha wa Rasoolahoo la'anahumul-laahu fid-dunyaa wal-Aakhirati wa a'adda lahum 'azaabam-muheenaa.

58. Wallazeena yu'zoonal-mu'mineena walmu'minaati bighayri mak-tasaboo faqadiḥ-tamaloo buhtaanañw-wa ismam-mubeenaa. **(Section 7)**

59. Yaaa ayyuhan-Nabiyyu qul li-azwaajika wa banaatika wa nisaaa'il-mu'mineena yud-neena 'alayhinna min jalaabee-bihinn; zaalika adnaaa añy-yu'rafna falaa yu'zayn; wa kaanal-laahu Ghafoorar-Raḥeemaa.

60. La'il-lam yantahil-munaafiqoona wallazeena fee quloobihim-maraḍuñw-walmurjifoona fil-madeenati lanughriyannaka bihim summa laa yujaawiroonaka feehaaa illaa qaleelaa.

61. Mal'ooneena aynamaa suqifooo ukhizoo wa quttiloo taqteelaa.

62. Sunnatal-laahi fil-lazeena khalaw min qablu wa lan tajida lisunnatil-laahi tabdeelaa.

63. Yas'alukan-naasu 'anis-Saa'ati qul innamaa 'ilmuhaa 'indal-laah; wa maa yudreeka la'allas-Saa'ata takoonu qareebaa.

64. Innal-laaha la'anal-kaafireena wa a'adda lahum sa'eeraa.

65. Khaalideena feehaaa abadaa, laa yajidoona waliyyañw-

عَلَيۡهِ وَسَلِّمُوۡا تَسۡلِيۡمًا ﴿٥٦﴾
اِنَّ الَّذِيۡنَ يُؤۡذُوۡنَ اللّٰهَ وَرَسُوۡلَهٗ
لَعَنَهُمُ اللّٰهُ فِى الدُّنۡيَا وَالۡاٰخِرَةِ
وَاَعَدَّ لَهُمۡ عَذَابًا مُّهِيۡنًا ﴿٥٧﴾
وَالَّذِيۡنَ يُؤۡذُوۡنَ الۡمُؤۡمِنِيۡنَ وَالۡمُؤۡمِنٰتِ
بِغَيۡرِ مَا اكۡتَسَبُوۡا فَقَدِ احۡتَمَلُوۡا
بُهۡتَانًا وَّاِثۡمًا مُّبِيۡنًا ﴿٥٨﴾ ع
يٰۤاَيُّهَا النَّبِىُّ قُلۡ لِّاَزۡوَاجِكَ وَبَنٰتِكَ
وَنِسَآءِ الۡمُؤۡمِنِيۡنَ يُدۡنِيۡنَ عَلَيۡهِنَّ
مِنۡ جَلَابِيۡبِهِنَّ ؕ ذٰلِكَ اَدۡنٰۤى اَنۡ
يُّعۡرَفۡنَ فَلَا يُؤۡذَيۡنَ ؕ وَكَانَ اللّٰهُ
غَفُوۡرًا رَّحِيۡمًا ﴿٥٩﴾
لَئِنۡ لَّمۡ يَنۡتَهِ الۡمُنٰفِقُوۡنَ وَالَّذِيۡنَ
فِىۡ قُلُوۡبِهِمۡ مَّرَضٌ وَّالۡمُرۡجِفُوۡنَ فِى
الۡمَدِيۡنَةِ لَنُغۡرِيَنَّكَ بِهِمۡ ثُمَّ لَا
يُجَاوِرُوۡنَكَ فِيۡهَاۤ اِلَّا قَلِيۡلًا ۛ ﴿٦٠﴾
مَّلۡعُوۡنِيۡنَ ۛ اَيۡنَمَا ثُقِفُوۡۤا اُخِذُوۡا
وَقُتِّلُوۡا تَقۡتِيۡلًا ﴿٦١﴾
سُنَّةَ اللّٰهِ فِى الَّذِيۡنَ خَلَوۡا مِنۡ قَبۡلُ ۚ
وَلَنۡ تَجِدَ لِسُنَّةِ اللّٰهِ تَبۡدِيۡلًا ﴿٦٢﴾
يَسۡـئَلُكَ النَّاسُ عَنِ السَّاعَةِ ؕ قُلۡ اِنَّمَا
عِلۡمُهَا عِنۡدَ اللّٰهِ ؕ وَمَا يُدۡرِيۡكَ لَعَلَّ
السَّاعَةَ تَكُوۡنُ قَرِيۡبًا ﴿٦٣﴾
اِنَّ اللّٰهَ لَعَنَ الۡكٰفِرِيۡنَ وَاَعَدَّ لَهُمۡ
سَعِيۡرًا ۙ ﴿٦٤﴾
خٰلِدِيۡنَ فِيۡهَاۤ اَبَدًا ۚ لَا يَجِدُوۡنَ وَلِيًّا

معانقة ١٢ عندالمتاخرين ١٢

الربع

Ikhfa اخفاء | Ghunna غُنّہ | Ikhfa Meem Saakin اخفاء میم ساکن | Idghaam ادغام | Qalqala قلقلہ | Qalb قلب | Idghaam Meem Saakin ادغام میم ساکن

nor helper.

66. The Day that their faces will be turned upside down in the Fire, they will say: "Woe to us! would that we had obeyed Allah and obeyed the Apostle!"

67. And they would say: "Our Lord! We obeyed our chiefs and our great ones, and they misled us as to the (right) Path.

68. "Our Lord! Give them double Chastisement and curse them with a very great Curse!"

69. O you who believe! You do not be like those who vexed and insulted Moses, but Allah cleared him of the (calumnies) they had uttered: and he was honourable in Allah's sight.

70. O you who believe! Fear Allah, and (always) say a word directed to the Right:

71. That He may make your conduct whole and sound and forgive you your sins: he that obeys Allah and His Apostle, has already attained the highest Achievement.

72. We did indeed offer the Trust to the Heavens and the Earth and the Mountains; but they refused to undertake it, being afraid thereof: but man undertook it;- he was indeed unjust and foolish;

73. (With the result) that Allah has to punish the Hypocrites, men and women, and the Unbelievers, men and women, and Allah turns in Mercy to the Believers, men and women: for Allah is Oft-Forgiving, Most Merciful.

34. The City of Saba

In the name of Allah, Most Gracious, Most Merciful.

1. Praise be to Allah, to Whom belong all things in the heavens

wa laa naṣeeraa.

66. Yawma tuqallabu wujoohuhum fin-Naari yaqooloona yaa laytanaaa aṭa'nal-laaha wa aṭa'nar-Rasoolaa.

67. Wa qaaloo Rabbanaaa innaaa aṭa'naa saadatanaa wa kubaraaa'anaa fa-aḍalloonas-sabeelaa.

68. Rabbanaaa aatihim ḍi'fayni minal-'azaabi wal'anhum la'nan kabeeraa. **(Section 8)**

69. Yaaa ayyuhal-lazeena aamanoo laa takoonoo kallazeena aazaw Moosaa fa-barra-ahul-laahu mimmaa qaaloo; wa kaana 'indal-laahi wajeehaa.

70. Yaaa ayyuhal-lazeena aamanut-taqul-laaha wa qooloo qawlan sadeedaa.

71. Yuṣliḥ lakum a'maalakum wa yaghfir lakum zunoobakum; wa mañy-yuṭi'il-laaha wa Rasoolahoo faqad faaza fawzan 'aẓeemaa.

72. Innaa 'araḍnal-amaanata 'alas-samaawaati walarḍi waljibaali fa-abayna añy-yaḥmilnahaa wa ashfaqna minhaa wa ḥamalahal-insaanu innahoo kaana ẓaloomanjahoolaa.

73. Liyu'azzibal-laahul-munaafiqeena walmunaafiqaati walmushrikeena walmushrikaati wa yatoobal-laahu 'alal-mu'mineena walmu'minaat; wa kaanal-laahu Ghafoorar-Raheema. **(Section 9)**

Sûrat Saba'–34

(Revealed at Makkah)

Bismillaahir Raḥmaanir Raḥeem

1. Alḥamdu lillaahil-lazee lahoo maa fis-samaawaati

وَلَا نَصِيرًا ﴿٦٥﴾
يَوْمَ تُقَلَّبُ وُجُوهُهُمْ فِي النَّارِ يَقُولُونَ
يَا لَيْتَنَا أَطَعْنَا اللَّهَ وَأَطَعْنَا الرَّسُولَا ﴿٦٦﴾
وَقَالُوا رَبَّنَا إِنَّا أَطَعْنَا سَادَتَنَا
وَكُبَرَاءَنَا فَأَضَلُّونَا السَّبِيلَا ﴿٦٧﴾
رَبَّنَا آتِهِمْ ضِعْفَيْنِ مِنَ الْعَذَابِ
وَالْعَنْهُمْ لَعْنًا كَبِيرًا ﴿٦٨﴾
يَا أَيُّهَا الَّذِينَ آمَنُوا لَا تَكُونُوا
كَالَّذِينَ آذَوْا مُوسَىٰ فَبَرَّأَهُ اللَّهُ مِمَّا
قَالُوا ۚ وَكَانَ عِنْدَ اللَّهِ وَجِيهًا ﴿٦٩﴾
يَا أَيُّهَا الَّذِينَ آمَنُوا اتَّقُوا اللَّهَ
وَقُولُوا قَوْلًا سَدِيدًا ﴿٧٠﴾
يُصْلِحْ لَكُمْ أَعْمَالَكُمْ وَيَغْفِرْ لَكُمْ
ذُنُوبَكُمْ ۗ وَمَنْ يُطِعِ اللَّهَ وَرَسُولَهُ
فَقَدْ فَازَ فَوْزًا عَظِيمًا ﴿٧١﴾
إِنَّا عَرَضْنَا الْأَمَانَةَ عَلَى السَّمَاوَاتِ
وَالْأَرْضِ وَالْجِبَالِ فَأَبَيْنَ أَنْ
يَحْمِلْنَهَا وَأَشْفَقْنَ مِنْهَا وَحَمَلَهَا
الْإِنْسَانُ ۖ إِنَّهُ كَانَ ظَلُومًا جَهُولًا ﴿٧٢﴾
لِيُعَذِّبَ اللَّهُ الْمُنَافِقِينَ وَالْمُنَافِقَاتِ
وَالْمُشْرِكِينَ وَالْمُشْرِكَاتِ وَيَتُوبَ
اللَّهُ عَلَى الْمُؤْمِنِينَ وَالْمُؤْمِنَاتِ ۗ
وَكَانَ اللَّهُ غَفُورًا رَحِيمًا ﴿٧٣﴾

(٣٤) سُورَةُ سَبَإٍ مَكِّيَّةٌ (٥٨)

بِسْمِ اللَّهِ الرَّحْمَٰنِ الرَّحِيمِ

الْحَمْدُ لِلَّهِ الَّذِي لَهُ مَا فِي السَّمَاوَاتِ

Ikhfa اخفاء | Ghunna غنّہ | Ikhfa Meem Saakin اخفاء میم ساکن | Idghaam ادغام | Qalqala قلقلہ | Qalb قلب | Idghaam Meem Saakin ادغام میم ساکن

and on earth: to Him be Praise in the Hereafter: and He is Full of Wisdom, acquainted with all things.

2. He knows all that goes into the earth, and all that comes out thereof; and all that comes down from the sky and all that ascends thereto and He is the Most Merciful, the Oft-Forgiving.

3. The Unbelievers say, "Never to us will come the Hour": Say, "Nay! but most surely, by my Lord, it will come upon you;- by Him Who knows the unseen,- from Whom is not hidden the least little atom in the heavens or on earth: nor is there anything less than that, or greater, but is in the Record Perspicuous.

4. That He may reward those who believe and work deeds of righteousness: for such is Forgiveness and a Sustenance Most Generous."

5. But those who strive against Our Signs, to frustrate them,- for such will be a Chastisement,- a Punishment most humiliating.

6. And those to whom knowledge has come see that the (Revelation) sent down to you from your Lord - that is the Truth, and that it guides to the Path of the Exalted (in might), Worthy of all praise.

7. The Unbelievers say (in ridicule): "Shall we point out to you a man that will tell you, when you are all scattered to pieces in disintegration, that you shall (then be raised) in a New Creation?

8. "Has he invented a falsehood against Allah, or has a spirit (seized) him?"- no, it is those who do not believe in the Hereafter, that are in (real) Chastisement, and in farthest error.

9. See they not what is before them and

wa maa fil-arḍi wa lahul-ḥamdu fil-Aakhirah; wa Huwal-Ḥakeemul-Khabeer.

2. Ya'lamu maa yaliju fil-arḍi wa maa yakhruju minhaa wa maa yanzilu minas-samaaa'i wa maa ya'ruju feehaa; wa Huwar-Raḥeemul-Ghafoor.

3. Wa qaalal-lazeena kafaroo laa taåteenas-Saa'ah; qul balaa wa Rabbee lataåtiyannakum 'Aalimil-Ghayb; laa ya'zubu 'anhu misqaalu zarratin fis-samaawaati wa laa fil-arḍi wa laaa aṣgharu min zaalika wa laaa akbaru illaa fee kitaabim-mubeen.

4. Liyajziyal-lazeena aamanoo wa 'amiluṣ-ṣaaliḥaat; ulaaa'ika lahum-maghfiratuñw-wa rizqun kareem.

5. Wallazeena sa'aw feee Aayaatinaa mu'aajizeena ulaaa'ika lahum 'azaabum-mir-rijzin aleem.

6. Wa yaral-lazeena utul-'Ilma l-lazeee unzila ilayka mir-Rabbika huwal-ḥaqqa wa yahdeee ilaa ṣiraaṭil-'Azeezil-Ḥameed.

7. Wa qaalal-lazeena kafaroo hal nadullukum 'alaa rajuliñy-yunabbi'ukum izaa muzziqtum kulla mumazzaqin innakum lafee khalqin jadeed.

8. Aftaraa 'alal-laahi kaziban am bihee jinnah; balil-lazeena laa yu'minoona bil-Aakhirati fil-'azaabi waḍḍalaalil-ba'eed.

9. Afalam yaraw ilaa maa bayna aydeehim wa maa

وَمَا فِي الْأَرْضِ وَلَهُ الْحَمْدُ فِي الْآخِرَةِ ۚ
وَهُوَ الْحَكِيمُ الْخَبِيرُ ①
يَعْلَمُ مَا يَلِجُ فِي الْأَرْضِ وَمَا يَخْرُجُ
مِنْهَا وَمَا يَنْزِلُ مِنَ السَّمَاءِ وَمَا
يَعْرُجُ فِيهَا ۚ وَهُوَ الرَّحِيمُ الْغَفُورُ ②
وَقَالَ الَّذِينَ كَفَرُوا لَا تَأْتِينَا
السَّاعَةُ ۖ قُلْ بَلَىٰ وَرَبِّي لَتَأْتِيَنَّكُمْ
عَالِمِ الْغَيْبِ ۖ لَا يَعْزُبُ عَنْهُ مِثْقَالُ
ذَرَّةٍ فِي السَّمَاوَاتِ وَلَا فِي الْأَرْضِ وَلَا
أَصْغَرُ مِنْ ذَٰلِكَ وَلَا أَكْبَرُ إِلَّا فِي
كِتَابٍ مُبِينٍ ③
لِيَجْزِيَ الَّذِينَ آمَنُوا وَعَمِلُوا الصَّالِحَاتِ ۚ
أُولَٰئِكَ لَهُمْ مَغْفِرَةٌ وَرِزْقٌ كَرِيمٌ ④
وَالَّذِينَ سَعَوْا فِي آيَاتِنَا مُعَاجِزِينَ أُولَٰئِكَ
لَهُمْ عَذَابٌ مِنْ رِجْزٍ أَلِيمٌ ⑤
وَيَرَى الَّذِينَ أُوتُوا الْعِلْمَ الَّذِي
أُنْزِلَ إِلَيْكَ مِنْ رَبِّكَ هُوَ الْحَقَّ ۙ
وَيَهْدِي إِلَىٰ صِرَاطِ الْعَزِيزِ
الْحَمِيدِ ⑥
وَقَالَ الَّذِينَ كَفَرُوا هَلْ نَدُلُّكُمْ
عَلَىٰ رَجُلٍ يُنَبِّئُكُمْ إِذَا مُزِّقْتُمْ كُلَّ
مُمَزَّقٍ ۙ إِنَّكُمْ لَفِي خَلْقٍ جَدِيدٍ ⑦
أَفْتَرَىٰ عَلَى اللَّهِ كَذِبًا أَمْ بِهِ جِنَّةٌ ۗ
بَلِ الَّذِينَ لَا يُؤْمِنُونَ بِالْآخِرَةِ فِي
الْعَذَابِ وَالضَّلَالِ الْبَعِيدِ ⑧
أَفَلَمْ يَرَوْا إِلَىٰ مَا بَيْنَ أَيْدِيهِمْ وَمَا

Ikhfa اخفاء | Ghunna غُنّہ | Ikhfa Meem Saakin اخفاء میم ساکن | Idghaam ادغام | Qalqala قلقلہ | Qalb قلب | Idghaam Meem Saakin ادغام میم ساکن

behind them, of the sky and the earth? If We wished, We could cause the earth to swallow them up, or cause a piece of the sky to fall upon them. Verily in this is a Sign for every devotee that turns to Allah (in repentance).

10. We bestowed Grace aforetime on David from ourselves: "O you Mountains! You sing back the Praises of Allah with him! and you birds (also)! And We made the iron soft for him;-

11. (Commanding), "You make coats of mail, balancing well the rings of chain armour, and you work righteousness; for be sure I see (clearly) all that you do."

12. And to Solomon (We made) the Wind (obedient): its early morning (stride) was a month's (journey), and its evening (stride) was a month's (journey); and We made a Font of molten brass to flow for him; and there were Jinns that worked in front of him, by the leave of his Lord, and if any of them turned aside from Our command, We made him taste of the Chastisement of the Blazing Fire.

13. They worked for him as he desired, (making) Arches, Images, Basins as large as Reservoirs, and (cooking) Cauldrons fixed (in their places): "You work, sons of David, with thanks! but few of My servants are grateful!"

14. Then, when We decreed (Solomon's) death, nothing showed them his death except a little worm of the earth, which kept (slowly) gnawing away at his staff: so when he fell down, the Jinns saw plainly that if they had known the unseen, they would not have tarried in the humiliating Chastisement (of their Task).

15. There was, for Saba, aforetime, a Sign in their homeland - two Gardens to the right and to the left. "Eat

khalfahum-minas-samaaa'i wal-arḍ; in-nashaå nakhsif bihimul-arḍa aw nusqiṭ 'alayhim kisafam-minas-samaaa'; inna fee zaalika la-Aayatal-likulli 'abdim-muneeb.

(Section 1)

10. Wa laqad aataynaa Daawooda minnaa faḍlañy yaa jibaalu awwibee ma'ahoo waṭṭayra wa alannaa lahul-ḥadeed.

11. Ani'mal saabighaatiñw-wa qaddir fis-sardi wa'maloo ṣaaliḥan innee bimaa ta'maloona Baṣeer.

12. Wa li-Sulaymaanar-reeḥa ghuduwwuhaa shahruñw-wa ra-waaḥuhaa shahruñw wa asalnaa lahoo 'aynal-qiṭr; wa minal-jinni mañy-ya'malu bayna yadayhi bi-izni Rabbih; wa mañy-yazigh minhum 'an amrinaa nuziqhu min 'azaabis-sa'eer.

13. Ya'maloona lahoo maa yashaaa'u mim-maḥaareeba wa tamaaseela wa jifaanin kal-jawaabi wa qudoorir-raasiyaat; i'malooo aala Daawooda shukraa; wa qaleelum-min 'ibaadiyash-shakoor.

14. Falammaa qaḍaynaa 'alayhil-mawta maa dallahum 'alaa mawtiheee illaa daaabbatul-arḍi taåkulu minsa-atahoo falammaa kharra tabayyanatil-jinnu al-law kaanoo ya'lamoonal-ghayba maa labisoo fil-'azaabil-muheen.

15. Laqad kaana li-Saba-in fee maskanihim Aayatun jannataani 'añy-yameeniñw-wa shimaalin kuloo

خَلْفَهُم مِّنَ السَّمَاءِ وَالْأَرْضِ ۚ إِن
نَّشَأْ نَخْسِفْ بِهِمُ الْأَرْضَ أَوْ نُسْقِطْ
عَلَيْهِمْ كِسَفًا مِّنَ السَّمَاءِ ۚ إِنَّ فِي
ذَٰلِكَ لَآيَةً لِّكُلِّ عَبْدٍ مُّنِيبٍ ٩
وَلَقَدْ آتَيْنَا دَاوُودَ مِنَّا فَضْلًا ۖ
يَا جِبَالُ أَوِّبِي مَعَهُ وَالطَّيْرَ ۖ وَأَلَنَّا
لَهُ الْحَدِيدَ ١٠
أَنِ اعْمَلْ سَابِغَاتٍ وَقَدِّرْ فِي السَّرْدِ
وَاعْمَلُوا صَالِحًا ۖ إِنِّي بِمَا تَعْمَلُونَ
بَصِيرٌ ١١
وَلِسُلَيْمَانَ الرِّيحَ غُدُوُّهَا شَهْرٌ
وَرَوَاحُهَا شَهْرٌ ۖ وَأَسَلْنَا لَهُ عَيْنَ
الْقِطْرِ ۖ وَمِنَ الْجِنِّ مَن يَعْمَلُ بَيْنَ
يَدَيْهِ بِإِذْنِ رَبِّهِ ۖ وَمَن يَزِغْ مِنْهُمْ
عَنْ أَمْرِنَا نُذِقْهُ مِنْ عَذَابِ السَّعِيرِ ١٢
يَعْمَلُونَ لَهُ مَا يَشَاءُ مِن مَّحَارِيبَ
وَتَمَاثِيلَ وَجِفَانٍ كَالْجَوَابِ وَقُدُورٍ
رَّاسِيَاتٍ ۚ اعْمَلُوا آلَ دَاوُودَ شُكْرًا ۚ
وَقَلِيلٌ مِّنْ عِبَادِيَ الشَّكُورُ ١٣
فَلَمَّا قَضَيْنَا عَلَيْهِ الْمَوْتَ مَا دَلَّهُمْ
عَلَىٰ مَوْتِهِ إِلَّا دَابَّةُ الْأَرْضِ تَأْكُلُ
مِنسَأَتَهُ ۖ فَلَمَّا خَرَّ تَبَيَّنَتِ الْجِنُّ
أَن لَّوْ كَانُوا يَعْلَمُونَ الْغَيْبَ مَا لَبِثُوا
فِي الْعَذَابِ الْمُهِينِ ١٤
لَقَدْ كَانَ لِسَبَإٍ فِي مَسْكَنِهِمْ آيَةٌ ۖ
جَنَّتَانِ عَن يَمِينٍ وَشِمَالٍ ۖ كُلُوا

Ikhfa اخفاء | Ghunna غنّہ | Ikhfa Meem Saakin اخفاء میم ساکن | Idghaam ادغام | Qalqala قلقلہ | Qalb قلب | Idghaam Meem Saakin ادغام میم ساکن

of the Sustenance (provided) by your Lord, and be grateful to Him: a territory fair and happy, and a Lord Oft-Forgiving!

16. But they turned away (from Allah), and We sent against them the flood (released) from the Dams, and We converted their two gardens (rows) into "two gardens" producing bitter fruit, and tamarisks, and some few (stunted) Lote-trees.

17. That was the Requital We gave them because they ungratefully rejected Faith: and never do We give (such) requital except to such as are ungrateful rejecters.

18. Between them and the Cities on which We had poured Our blessings, We had placed Cities in prominent positions, and between them We had appointed stages of journey in due proportion: "Travel therein, secure, by night and by day."

19. But they said: "Our Lord! Place longer distances between our journey-stages": but they wronged themselves (therein). At le-ngth We made them as a tale (that is told), and We dispersed them all in scattered fragments. Verily in this are Signs for every (soul that is) patiently constant and grateful.

20. And on them did Satan prove true his idea, and they followed him, all but a party that believed.

21. But he had no authority over them,- except that We might test the man who believes in the Hereafter from him who is in doubt concerning it: and your Lord watches over all things.

22. Say: "Call upon other (gods) whom you fancy, besides Allah: they have no power,- not the weight of an atom,- in the heavens or on earth: no (sort of) share have they therein, nor is any of them

mir-rizq Rabbikum washkuroo lah; baldatun ṭayyibatuñw-wa Rabbun Ghafoor.

16. Fa-a'raḍoo fa-arsalnaa 'alayhim Saylal-'Arimi wa baddalnaahum bijannatayhim jannatayni zawaatay ukulin khamṭiñw-wa asliñw-wa shay-'im-min sidrin qaleel.

17. Zaalika jazaynaahum bimaa kafaroo wa hal nujaazeee illal-kafoor.

18. Wa ja'alnaa baynahum wa baynal-qural-latee baaraknaa feehaa quran ẓaahiratañw-wa qaddarnaa feehas-sayr; seeroo feehaa la-yaaliya wa ayyaaman aamineen.

19. Faqaaloo Rabbanaa baa'id bayna asfaarinaa wa ẓalamooo anfusahum faja'alnaahum aḥaadeesa wa mazzaqnaahum kulla mumazzaq; inna fee zaalika la-Aayaatil-likulli ṣabbaarin shakoor.

20. Wa laqad ṣaddaqa 'alayhim Ibleesu ẓannahoo fattaba'oohu illaa fareeqam-minal-mu'mineen.

21. Wa maa kaana lahoo 'alayhim-min sulṭaanin illaa lina'lama mañy-yu'minu bil-Aakhirati mimman huwa minhaa fee shakk; wa Rabbuka 'alaa kulli shay'in Ḥafeez.

(Section 2)

22. Qulid-'ul-lazeena za'amtum-min doonil-laahi laa yamlikoona misqaala zarratin fis-samaawaati wa laa fil-arḍi wa maa lahum feehimaa min shirkiñw-wa maa lahoo minhum-

مِنْ رِّزْقِ رَبِّكُمْ وَاشْكُرُوْا لَهٗ ؕ بَلْدَةٌ
طَيِّبَةٌ وَّرَبٌّ غَفُوْرٌ ﴿١٥﴾
فَاَعْرَضُوْا فَاَرْسَلْنَا عَلَيْهِمْ سَيْلَ
الْعَرِمِ وَبَدَّلْنٰهُمْ بِجَنَّتَيْهِمْ جَنَّتَيْنِ
ذَوَاتَيْ اُكُلٍ خَمْطٍ وَّاَثْلٍ وَّشَيْءٍ
مِّنْ سِدْرٍ قَلِيْلٍ ﴿١٦﴾
ذٰلِكَ جَزَيْنٰهُمْ بِمَا كَفَرُوْا ؕ وَهَلْ نُجٰزِيْٓ
اِلَّا الْكَفُوْرَ ﴿١٧﴾
وَجَعَلْنَا بَيْنَهُمْ وَبَيْنَ الْقُرَى
الَّتِيْ بٰرَكْنَا فِيْهَا قُرًى ظَاهِرَةً وَّ
قَدَّرْنَا فِيْهَا السَّيْرَ ؕ سِيْرُوْا فِيْهَا
لَيَالِيَ وَاَيَّامًا اٰمِنِيْنَ ﴿١٨﴾
فَقَالُوْا رَبَّنَا بٰعِدْ بَيْنَ اَسْفَارِنَا
وَظَلَمُوْٓا اَنْفُسَهُمْ فَجَعَلْنٰهُمْ اَحَادِيْثَ
وَمَزَّقْنٰهُمْ كُلَّ مُمَزَّقٍ ؕ اِنَّ فِيْ ذٰلِكَ
لَاٰيٰتٍ لِّكُلِّ صَبَّارٍ شَكُوْرٍ ﴿١٩﴾
وَلَقَدْ صَدَّقَ عَلَيْهِمْ اِبْلِيْسُ ظَنَّهٗ
فَاتَّبَعُوْهُ اِلَّا فَرِيْقًا مِّنَ الْمُؤْمِنِيْنَ ﴿٢٠﴾
وَمَا كَانَ لَهٗ عَلَيْهِمْ مِّنْ سُلْطٰنٍ اِلَّا
لِنَعْلَمَ مَنْ يُّؤْمِنُ بِالْاٰخِرَةِ مِمَّنْ
هُوَ مِنْهَا فِيْ شَكٍّ ؕ وَرَبُّكَ عَلٰى كُلِّ
شَيْءٍ حَفِيْظٌ ﴿٢١﴾ ع ١٢ ٢ ٨
قُلِ ادْعُوا الَّذِيْنَ زَعَمْتُمْ مِّنْ دُوْنِ
اللّٰهِ ۚ لَا يَمْلِكُوْنَ مِثْقَالَ ذَرَّةٍ فِي
السَّمٰوٰتِ وَلَا فِي الْاَرْضِ وَمَا لَهُمْ
فِيْهِمَا مِنْ شِرْكٍ وَّمَا لَهٗ مِنْهُمْ

Ikhfa اخفاء | Ghunna غُنّہ | Ikhfa Meem Saakin اخفاء میم ساکن | Idghaam ادغام | Qalqala قلقلہ | Qalb قلب | Idghaam Meem Saakin ادغام میم ساکن

a helper to Allah.

23. "No intercession can avail in His Presence, except for those for whom He has granted permission. So far (is this the case) that, when terror is removed from their hearts (at the Day of Judgment, then) they will say, 'What is it that your Lord commanded?' They will say, 'That which is true and just; and He is the Most High, Most Great'."

24. Say: "Who gives you sustenance, from the heavens and the earth?" Say: "It is Allah; and certain it is that either we or you are on right guidance or in manifest error!"

25. Say: "You shall not be questioned as to our sins, nor shall we be questioned as to what you do."

26. Say: "Our Lord will gather us together and will in the end decide the matter between us (and you) in truth and justice: and He is the one to decide, the One Who knows all."

27. Say: "Show me those whom you have joined with Him as partners: by no means (can you). Nay, He is Allah, the Exalted in Power, the Wise."

28. We have not sent you but as a universal (Messenger) to men, giving them glad tidings, and warning them (against sin), but most men understand not.

29. They say: "When will this promise (come to pass) if you are telling the truth?"

30. Say: "The appointment to you is for a Day, which you cannot put back for an hour nor put forward."

31. The Unbelievers say: "We shall neither believe in this scripture nor in (any) that (came) before it." Could you but see when the wrong-doers will be made to stand before their Lord, throwing back the word (of blame) on one another! Those who had been despised will say

min ẓaheer.

23. Wa laa tanfa'ush-shafaa'atu 'indahooo illaa liman azina lah; ḥattaaa izaa fuzzi'a 'an quloobihim qaaloo maazaa qaala Rabbukum; qaalul-ḥaqq, wa Huwal-'Aliyyul-Kabeer.

24. Qul mañy-yarzuqukum-minas-samaawaati wal-arḍi qulil-laahu wa innaaa aw iyyaakum la'alaa hudan aw fee ḍalaalim-mubeen.

25. Qul laa tus'aloona 'ammaaa ajramnaa wa laa nus'alu 'ammaa ta'maloon.

26. Qul yajma'u baynanaa Rabbunaa summa yaftaḥu baynanaa bilḥaqq; wa Huwal-Fattaaḥul-'Aleem.

27. Qul arooniyal-lazeena alḥaqtum bihee shurakaaa'a kallaa; bal Huwal-laahul-'Azeezul-Ḥakeem.

28. Wa maaa arsalnaaka illaa kaaaffatal-linnaasi basheerañw-wa nazeerañw-wa laakinna aksaran-naasi laa ya'lamoon.

29. Wa yaqooloona mataa haazal-wa'du in kuntum ṣaadiqeen.

30. Qul lakum-mee'aadu Yawmil-laa tastaakhiroona 'anhu saa'atañw-wa laa tastaqdimoon. **(Section 3)**

31. Wa qaalal-lazeena kafaroo lan-nu'mina bihaazal-Qur-aani wa laa billazee bayna yadayh; wa law taraaa iziẓ-ẓaalimoona mawqoofoona 'inda Rabbihim yarji'u ba'ḍuhum ilaa ba'ḍinil-qawla yaqoolul-lazeenas-tuḍ'ifoo

مِنْ ظَهِيرٍ ﴿٢٢﴾
وَلَا تَنْفَعُ الشَّفَاعَةُ عِنْدَهُ إِلَّا لِمَنْ
أَذِنَ لَهُ ۚ حَتَّىٰ إِذَا فُزِّعَ عَنْ
قُلُوبِهِمْ قَالُوا مَاذَا قَالَ رَبُّكُمْ ۖ قَالُوا
الْحَقَّ ۖ وَهُوَ الْعَلِيُّ الْكَبِيرُ ﴿٢٣﴾
قُلْ مَنْ يَرْزُقُكُمْ مِنَ السَّمَاوَاتِ وَالْأَرْضِ ۖ
قُلِ اللَّهُ ۖ وَإِنَّا أَوْ إِيَّاكُمْ لَعَلَىٰ هُدًى
أَوْ فِي ضَلَالٍ مُبِينٍ ﴿٢٤﴾
قُلْ لَا تُسْأَلُونَ عَمَّا أَجْرَمْنَا وَلَا
نُسْأَلُ عَمَّا تَعْمَلُونَ ﴿٢٥﴾
قُلْ يَجْمَعُ بَيْنَنَا رَبُّنَا ثُمَّ يَفْتَحُ بَيْنَنَا
بِالْحَقِّ وَهُوَ الْفَتَّاحُ الْعَلِيمُ ﴿٢٦﴾
قُلْ أَرُونِيَ الَّذِينَ أَلْحَقْتُمْ بِهِ شُرَكَاءَ ۖ
كَلَّا ۚ بَلْ هُوَ اللَّهُ الْعَزِيزُ الْحَكِيمُ ﴿٢٧﴾
وَمَا أَرْسَلْنَاكَ إِلَّا كَافَّةً لِلنَّاسِ
بَشِيرًا وَنَذِيرًا وَلَٰكِنَّ أَكْثَرَ النَّاسِ
لَا يَعْلَمُونَ ﴿٢٨﴾
وَيَقُولُونَ مَتَىٰ هَٰذَا الْوَعْدُ إِنْ
كُنْتُمْ صَادِقِينَ ﴿٢٩﴾
قُلْ لَكُمْ مِيعَادُ يَوْمٍ لَا تَسْتَأْخِرُونَ
عَنْهُ سَاعَةً وَلَا تَسْتَقْدِمُونَ ﴿٣٠﴾ ع النصف
وَقَالَ الَّذِينَ كَفَرُوا لَنْ نُؤْمِنَ بِهَٰذَا
الْقُرْآنِ وَلَا بِالَّذِي بَيْنَ يَدَيْهِ ۗ وَلَوْ
تَرَىٰ إِذِ الظَّالِمُونَ مَوْقُوفُونَ عِنْدَ
رَبِّهِمْ يَرْجِعُ بَعْضُهُمْ إِلَىٰ بَعْضٍ
الْقَوْلَ يَقُولُ الَّذِينَ اسْتُضْعِفُوا

Ikhfa اخفاء | Ghunna غنّہ | Ikhfa Meem Saakin اخفاء میم ساکن | Idghaam ادغام | Qalqala قلقلہ | Qalb قلب | Idghaam Meem Saakin ادغام میم ساکن

to the arrogant ones: "Had it not been for you, we should certainly have been believers!"

lillazeenas-takbaroo law laaa antum lakunnaa mu'mineen.

لِلَّذِينَ اسْتَكْبَرُوا لَوْلَا أَنتُمْ لَكُنَّا مُؤْمِنِينَ ٣١

32. The arrogant ones will say to those who had been despised: "Was it we who kept you back from Guidance after it reached you? Nay, rather, it was you who transgressed.

32. Qaalal-lazeenas-takbaroo lillazeenas-tuḍ'ifooo anaḥnu ṣadadnaakum 'anil-hudaa ba'da iz jaaa'akum bal kuntum-mujrimeen.

قَالَ الَّذِينَ اسْتَكْبَرُوا لِلَّذِينَ اسْتُضْعِفُوا أَنَحْنُ صَدَدْنَاكُمْ عَنِ الْهُدَىٰ بَعْدَ إِذْ جَاءَكُم بَلْ كُنتُم مُّجْرِمِينَ ٣٢

33. Those who had been despised will say to the arrogant ones: "Nay! it was a plot (of yours) by day and by night: behold! you (constantly) ordered us to be ungrateful to Allah and to attribute equals to Him!" They will declare (their) repentance when they see the Chastisement: We shall put yokes on the necks of the Unbelievers: it would only be a requital for their (ill) Deeds.

33. Wa qaalal-lazeenastuḍ'ifoo lillazeenas-takbaroo bal makrul-layli wannahaari iz taåmuroonanaaa an-nakfura billaahi wa naj'ala lahooo andaadaa; wa asarrun-nadaamata lammaa ra-awul-'azaab; wa ja'alnal-aghlaala feee a'naaqil-lazeena kafaroo; hal yujzawna illaa maa kaanoo ya'maloon.

وَقَالَ الَّذِينَ اسْتُضْعِفُوا لِلَّذِينَ اسْتَكْبَرُوا بَلْ مَكْرُ اللَّيْلِ وَالنَّهَارِ إِذْ تَأْمُرُونَنَا أَن نَّكْفُرَ بِاللَّهِ وَنَجْعَلَ لَهُ أَندَادًا ۚ وَأَسَرُّوا النَّدَامَةَ لَمَّا رَأَوُا الْعَذَابَ ۚ وَجَعَلْنَا الْأَغْلَالَ فِي أَعْنَاقِ الَّذِينَ كَفَرُوا ۚ هَلْ يُجْزَوْنَ إِلَّا مَا كَانُوا يَعْمَلُونَ ٣٣

34. Never did We send a Warner to a population, but the wealthy ones among them said: "We do not believe in the (Message) with which you have been sent."

34. Wa maaa arsalnaa fee qaryatim-min-nazeerin illaa qaala mutrafoohaaa innaa bimaaa ursiltum bihee kaafiroon.

وَمَا أَرْسَلْنَا فِي قَرْيَةٍ مِّن نَّذِيرٍ إِلَّا قَالَ مُتْرَفُوهَا إِنَّا بِمَا أُرْسِلْتُم بِهِ كَافِرُونَ ٣٤

35. They said: "We have more in wealth and in sons, and we cannot be punished."

35. Wa qaaloo naḥnu aksaru amwaalañw-wa awlaadañw-wa maa naḥnu bimu'azzabeen.

وَقَالُوا نَحْنُ أَكْثَرُ أَمْوَالًا وَأَوْلَادًا وَمَا نَحْنُ بِمُعَذَّبِينَ ٣٥

36. Say: "Verily my Lord enlarges and restricts the Provision to whom He pleases, but most men do not understand."

36. Qul inna Rabbee yabsuṭur-rizqa limañy-yashaaa'u wa yaqdiru wa laakinna aksaran-naasi laa ya'lamoon. **(Section 4)**

قُلْ إِنَّ رَبِّي يَبْسُطُ الرِّزْقَ لِمَن يَشَاءُ وَيَقْدِرُ وَلَٰكِنَّ أَكْثَرَ النَّاسِ لَا يَعْلَمُونَ ٣٦

37. It is not your wealth nor your sons, that will bring you nearer to Us in degree: but only those who believe and work righteousness - these are the ones for whom there is a multiplied Reward for their deeds, while secure they (reside) in the dwellings on high!

37. Wa maaa amwaalukum wa laaa awlaadukum billatee tuqarribukum 'indanaa zulfaaa illaa man aamana wa 'amila ṣaaliḥan fa-ulaaa'ika lahum jazaaa'uḍ-ḍi'fi bimaa 'amiloo wa hum fil-ghurufaati aaminoon.

وَمَا أَمْوَالُكُمْ وَلَا أَوْلَادُكُم بِالَّتِي تُقَرِّبُكُمْ عِندَنَا زُلْفَىٰ إِلَّا مَنْ آمَنَ وَعَمِلَ صَالِحًا فَأُولَٰئِكَ لَهُمْ جَزَاءُ الضِّعْفِ بِمَا عَمِلُوا وَهُمْ فِي الْغُرُفَاتِ آمِنُونَ ٣٧

Ikhfa اخفاء | Ghunna غُنّہ | Ikhfa Meem Saakin اخفاء میم ساکن | Idghaam ادغام | Qalqala قلقلہ | Qalb قلب | Idghaam Meem Saakin ادغام میم ساکن

38. Those who strive against Our Signs, to frustrate them, will be given over into Punishment.

38. Wallazeena yas'awna feee Aayaatinaa mu'aajizeena ulaaa'ika fil-'azaabi muḥḍaroon.

وَالَّذِينَ يَسْعَوْنَ فِيٓ ءَايَٰتِنَا مُعَٰجِزِينَ أُولَٰٓئِكَ فِي الْعَذَابِ مُحْضَرُونَ ﴿٣٨﴾

39. Say: "Verily my Lord enlarges and restricts the Sustenance to such of his servants as He pleases: and nothing do you spend in the least (in His Cause) but He replaces it: for He is the Best of those who grant Sustenance.

39. Qul inna Rabbee yabsuṭur-rizqa limañy-yashaaa'u min 'ibaadihee wa yaqdiru lah; wa maaa anfaqtum-min shay'in fahuwa yukhlifuhoo wa Huwa khayrur-raaziqeen.

قُلْ إِنَّ رَبِّي يَبْسُطُ الرِّزْقَ لِمَن يَشَآءُ مِنْ عِبَادِهِۦ وَيَقْدِرُ لَهُۥ ۚ وَمَآ أَنفَقْتُم مِّن شَيْءٍ فَهُوَ يُخْلِفُهُۥ ۖ وَهُوَ خَيْرُ الرَّٰزِقِينَ ﴿٣٩﴾

40. One Day He will gather them all together, and say to the angels, "Were it you that these men used to worship?"

40. Wa Yawma yaḥshuruhum jamee'an summa yaqoolu lilmalaaa'ikati a-haaa'ulaaa'i iyyaakum kaanoo ya'budoon.

وَيَوْمَ يَحْشُرُهُمْ جَمِيعًا ثُمَّ يَقُولُ لِلْمَلَٰٓئِكَةِ أَهَٰٓؤُلَآءِ إِيَّاكُمْ كَانُوا يَعْبُدُونَ ﴿٤٠﴾

41. They will say, "Glory to You! our (tie) is with You - as Protector - not with them. Nay, but they worshipped the Jinns: most of them believed in them."

41. Qaaloo Subḥaanaka Anta waliyyunaa min doonihim bal kaanoo ya'budoonal-jinna aksaruhum bihim-mu'minoon.

قَالُوا سُبْحَٰنَكَ أَنتَ وَلِيُّنَا مِن دُونِهِم ۖ بَلْ كَانُوا يَعْبُدُونَ الْجِنَّ ۖ أَكْثَرُهُم بِهِم مُّؤْمِنُونَ ﴿٤١﴾

42. So on that Day no power shall they have over each other, for profit or harm: and We shall say to the wrong-doers, "You taste the Chastisement of the Fire,- the which you were wont to deny!"

42. Fal-Yawma laa yamliku ba'ḍukum liba'ḍin-naf'añw-wa laa ḍarraa; wa naqoolu lillazeena ẓalamoo zooqoo 'azaaban-Naaril-latee kuntum bihaa tukazziboon.

فَالْيَوْمَ لَا يَمْلِكُ بَعْضُكُمْ لِبَعْضٍ نَّفْعًا وَلَا ضَرًّا وَنَقُولُ لِلَّذِينَ ظَلَمُوا ذُوقُوا عَذَابَ النَّارِ الَّتِي كُنتُم بِهَا تُكَذِّبُونَ ﴿٤٢﴾

43. When Our Clear Signs are rehearsed to them, they say, "This is only a man who wishes to hinder you from the (worship) which your fathers practised." And they say, "This is only a falsehood invented!" And the Unbelievers say of the Truth when it comes to them, "This is nothing but evident magic!"

43. Wa izaa tutlaa 'alayhim Aayaatunaa bayyinaatin qaaloo maa haazaaa illaa rajuluñy-yureedu añy-yaṣuddakum 'ammaa kaana ya'budu aabaaa'ukum wa qaaloo maa haazaaa illaaa ifkum-muftaraa; wa qaalal-lazeena kafaroo lilḥaqqi lammaa jaaa'ahum in haazaaa illaa siḥrum-mubeen.

وَإِذَا تُتْلَىٰ عَلَيْهِمْ ءَايَٰتُنَا بَيِّنَٰتٍ قَالُوا مَا هَٰذَآ إِلَّا رَجُلٌ يُرِيدُ أَن يَصُدَّكُمْ عَمَّا كَانَ يَعْبُدُ ءَابَآؤُكُمْ وَقَالُوا مَا هَٰذَآ إِلَّآ إِفْكٌ مُّفْتَرًى ۚ وَقَالَ الَّذِينَ كَفَرُوا لِلْحَقِّ لَمَّا جَآءَهُمْ إِنْ هَٰذَآ إِلَّا سِحْرٌ مُّبِينٌ ﴿٤٣﴾

44. But We had not given them Books which they could study, nor sent Apostles to them before you as Warners.

44. Wa maaa aataynaahum min Kutubiñy-yadrusoonahaa wa maaa arsalnaaa ilayhim qablaka min-nazeer.

وَمَآ ءَاتَيْنَٰهُم مِّن كُتُبٍ يَدْرُسُونَهَا ۖ وَمَآ أَرْسَلْنَآ إِلَيْهِمْ قَبْلَكَ مِن نَّذِيرٍ ﴿٤٤﴾

45. And their predecessors rejected (the Truth); these have not

45. Wa kazzabal-lazeena min qablihim wa maa

وَكَذَّبَ الَّذِينَ مِن قَبْلِهِمْ وَمَا

Ikhfa اخفاء | Ghunna غنّہ | Ikhfa Meem Saakin اخفاء میم ساکن | Idghaam ادغام | Qalqala قلقلہ | Qalb قلب | Idghaam Meem Saakin ادغام میم ساکن

received a tenth of what We had granted to those: yet when they rejected My Apostles, how (terrible) was My rejection (of them)!

46. Say: "I do admonish you on one point: that you do stand up before Allah,- (It may be) in pairs, or (it may be) singly,- and reflect (within yourselves): your Companion is not possessed: he is no less than a Warner to you, in face of a terrible Chastisement."

47. Say: "No reward do I ask of you: it is (all) in your interest: my reward is only due from Allah: and He is witness to all things."

48. Say: "Verily my Lord casts the (mantle of) Truth (over His servants),- He that has full knowledge of (all) that is hidden."

49. Say: "The Truth has arrived, and Falsehood neither creates anything new, nor restores anything."

50. Say: "If I am astray, I only stray to the loss of my own soul: but if I receive guidance, it is because of the inspiration of my Lord to me: it is He Who hears all things, and is (ever) near."

51. If you could but see when they will quake with terror; but then there will be no escape (for them), and they will be seized from a position (quite) near.

52. And they will say, "We do believe (now) in the (Truth)"; but how could they receive (Faith) from a position (so far off),-

53. Seeing that they did reject Faith (entirely) before, and that they (continually) cast (slanders) on the Unseen from a position far off?

54. And between them and their desires, is placed a barrier, as was done in the past with their partisans: for they were indeed in suspicious (disquieting) doubt.

---

balaghoo mi'shaara maaa aataynaahum fakazzaboo Rusulee; fakayfa kaana nakeer.

(Section 5)

46. Qul innamaaa a'izukum biwaahidatin an taqoomoo lillaahi masnaa wa furaadaa summa tatafakkaroo; maa bisaahibikum-min jinnah; in huwa illaa nazeerul-lakum bayna yaday 'azaabin shadeed.

47. Qul maa sa-altukum-min ajrin fahuwa lakum in ajriya illaa 'alal-laahi wa Huwa 'alaa kulli shay'in Shaheed.

48. Qul inna Rabbee yaqzifu bilhaqq, 'Allaamul-Ghuyoob.

49. Qul jaaa'al-haqqu wa maa yubdi'ul-baatilu wa maa yu'eed.

50. Qul in dalaltu fainnamaaa adillu 'alaa nafsee wa inih-tadaytu fabimaa yooheee ilayya Rabbee; innahoo Samee'un Qareeb.

51. Wa law taraaa iz fazi'oo falaa fawta wa ukhizoo mim-makaanin qareeb.

52. Wa qaaloo aamannaa bihee wa annaa lahumut-tanaawushu mim-makaanim ba'eed.

53. Wa qad kafaroo bihee min qablu wa yaqzifoona bilghaybi mim-makaanim ba'eed.

54. Wa heela baynahum wa bayna maa yashtahoona kamaa fu'ila bi-ashyaa'ihim-min qabl; innahum kaanoo fee shakkim-mureeb.

(Section 6)

بَلَغُوْا مِعْشَارَ مَآ اٰتَيْنٰهُمْ فَكَذَّبُوْا
رُسُلِيْ فَكَيْفَ كَانَ نَكِيْرِ ﴿٤٥﴾ ع ٥ ١١
قُلْ اِنَّمَآ اَعِظُكُمْ بِوَاحِدَةٍ ۚ اَنْ
تَقُوْمُوْا لِلّٰهِ مَثْنٰى وَفُرَادٰى ثُمَّ
تَتَفَكَّرُوْا مَا بِصَاحِبِكُمْ مِّنْ جِنَّةٍ ۭ
اِنْ هُوَ اِلَّا نَذِيْرٌ لَّكُمْ بَيْنَ يَدَيْ
عَذَابٍ شَدِيْدٍ ﴿٤٦﴾
قُلْ مَا سَاَلْتُكُمْ مِّنْ اَجْرٍ فَهُوَ لَكُمْ ۭ
اِنْ اَجْرِيَ اِلَّا عَلَى اللّٰهِ ۚ وَهُوَ عَلٰى
كُلِّ شَيْءٍ شَهِيْدٌ ﴿٤٧﴾
قُلْ اِنَّ رَبِّيْ يَقْذِفُ بِالْحَقِّ ۚ
عَلَّامُ الْغُيُوْبِ ﴿٤٨﴾
قُلْ جَآءَ الْحَقُّ وَمَا يُبْدِئُ الْبَاطِلُ
وَمَا يُعِيْدُ ﴿٤٩﴾
قُلْ اِنْ ضَلَلْتُ فَاِنَّمَآ اَضِلُّ عَلٰى
نَفْسِيْ ۚ وَاِنِ اهْتَدَيْتُ فَبِمَا يُوْحِيْٓ
اِلَيَّ رَبِّيْ ۭ اِنَّهٗ سَمِيْعٌ قَرِيْبٌ ﴿٥٠﴾
وَلَوْ تَرٰٓى اِذْ فَزِعُوْا فَلَا فَوْتَ وَاُخِذُوْا
مِنْ مَّكَانٍ قَرِيْبٍ ﴿٥١﴾
وَّقَالُوْٓا اٰمَنَّا بِهٖ ۚ وَاَنّٰى لَهُمُ التَّنَاوُشُ
مِنْ مَّكَانٍ بَعِيْدٍ ﴿٥٢﴾
وَّقَدْ كَفَرُوْا بِهٖ مِنْ قَبْلُ ۚ وَيَقْذِفُوْنَ
بِالْغَيْبِ مِنْ مَّكَانٍ بَعِيْدٍ ﴿٥٣﴾
وَحِيْلَ بَيْنَهُمْ وَبَيْنَ مَا يَشْتَهُوْنَ كَمَا
فُعِلَ بِاَشْيَاعِهِمْ مِّنْ قَبْلُ ۭ اِنَّهُمْ
كَانُوْا فِيْ شَكٍّ مُّرِيْبٍ ﴿٥٤﴾ ع ٦ ١٢

Ikhfa اخفاء | Ghunna غنّہ | Ikhfa Meem Saakin اخفاءمیم ساکن | Idghaam ادغام | Qalqala قلقلہ | Qalb قلب | Idghaam Meem Saakin ادغام میم ساکن

35. The Originator of Creation

In the name of Allah, Most Gracious, Most Merciful.

1. Praise be to Allah, Who created (out of nothing) the heavens and the earth, Who made the angels, messengers with wings,- two, or three, or four (pairs): He adds to Creation as He pleases: for Allah has power over all things.

2. What Allah out of His Mercy bestows on mankind there is none can withhold: what He withholds, there is none can grant, apart from Him: and He is the Exalted in Power, full of Wisdom.

3. O men! Call to mind the grace of Allah unto you! Is there a creator, other than Allah, to give you sustenance from heaven or earth? There is no god but He: how then are you deluded away from the Truth?

4. And if they reject you, so were Apostles rejected before you: to Allah go back for decision all affairs.

5. O men! Certainly the promise of Allah is true. Let not then this present life deceive you, nor let the Chief Deceiver deceive you about Allah.

6. Verily Satan is an enemy to you: so treat him as an enemy. He only invites his adherents, that they may become companions of the Blazing Fire.

7. For those who reject Allah, is a terrible Chastisement: but for those who believe and work righteous deeds, is Forgiveness, and a magnificent Reward.

Sûrat Fâțir–35

(Revealed at Makkah)

Bismillaahir Raḥmaanir Raḥeem

1. Alḥamdu lillaahi faaṭiris-samaawaati wal-arḍi jaa'ilil-malaaa'ikati rusulan uleee ajniḥatim-masnaa wa sulaasa wa rubaa'; yazeedu fil-khalqi maa yashaaa'; innal-laaha 'alaa kulli shay'in Qadeer.

2. Maa yaftaḥil-laahu lin-naasi mir-raḥmatin falaa mumsika lahaa wa maa yumsik falaa mursila lahoo mimba'dih; wa Huwal-'Azeezul-Ḥakeem.

3. Yaaa ayyuhan-naasuz-kuroo ni'matal-laahi 'alaykum; hal min khaaliqin ghayrul-laahi yarzuqukum-minas-samaaa'i wal-arḍ; laaa ilaaha illaa Huwa fa-annaa tu'fakoon.

4. Wa iñy-yukazzibooka faqad kuzzibat Rusulum-min qablik; wa ilal-laahi turja'ul-umoor.

5. Yaaa ayyuhan-naasu inna wa'dal-laahi ḥaqqun falaa taghurrannakumul-ḥayaatud-dunyaa; wa laa yaghurrannakum billaahil-gharoor.

6. Innash-Shayṭaana lakum 'aduwwun fattakhizoohu 'aduwwaa; innamaa yad'oo ḥizbahoo liyakoonoo min aṣḥaabis-sa'eer.

7. Allazeena kafaroo lahum 'azaabun shadeed; wallazeena aamanoo wa 'amiluṣ-ṣaaliḥaati lahum-maghfiratuñw-wa ajrun kabeer. **(Section 1)**

(٣٥) سُوْرَةُ فَاطِرٍ مَّكِّيَّةٌ (٤٣)

بِسْمِ اللّٰهِ الرَّحْمٰنِ الرَّحِيْمِ

اَلْحَمْدُ لِلّٰهِ فَاطِرِ السَّمٰوٰتِ وَالْاَرْضِ
جَاعِلِ الْمَلٰٓئِكَةِ رُسُلًا اُولِيْٓ اَجْنِحَةٍ
مَّثْنٰى وَثُلٰثَ وَرُبٰعَ ۭ يَزِيْدُ فِي الْخَلْقِ
مَا يَشَاۗءُ ۭ اِنَّ اللّٰهَ عَلٰي كُلِّ شَيْءٍ قَدِيْرٌ ۝۱
مَا يَفْتَحِ اللّٰهُ لِلنَّاسِ مِنْ رَّحْمَةٍ
فَلَا مُمْسِكَ لَهَا ۚ وَمَا يُمْسِكْ ۙ
فَلَا مُرْسِلَ لَهٗ مِنْۢ بَعْدِهٖ ۭ وَهُوَ
الْعَزِيْزُ الْحَكِيْمُ ۝۲
يٰٓاَيُّهَا النَّاسُ اذْكُرُوْا نِعْمَتَ اللّٰهِ
عَلَيْكُمْ ۭ هَلْ مِنْ خَالِقٍ غَيْرُ اللّٰهِ
يَرْزُقُكُمْ مِّنَ السَّمَاۗءِ وَالْاَرْضِ ۭ لَآ
اِلٰهَ اِلَّا هُوَ ڮ فَاَنّٰى تُؤْفَكُوْنَ ۝۳
وَاِنْ يُّكَذِّبُوْكَ فَقَدْ كُذِّبَتْ
رُسُلٌ مِّنْ قَبْلِكَ ۭ وَاِلَى اللّٰهِ تُرْجَعُ
الْاُمُوْرُ ۝۴
يٰٓاَيُّهَا النَّاسُ اِنَّ وَعْدَ اللّٰهِ حَقٌّ
فَلَا تَغُرَّنَّكُمُ الْحَيٰوةُ الدُّنْيَا ۪ وَلَا
يَغُرَّنَّكُمْ بِاللّٰهِ الْغَرُوْرُ ۝۵
اِنَّ الشَّيْطٰنَ لَكُمْ عَدُوٌّ فَاتَّخِذُوْهُ
عَدُوًّا ۭ اِنَّمَا يَدْعُوْا حِزْبَهٗ لِيَكُوْنُوْا
مِنْ اَصْحٰبِ السَّعِيْرِ ۝۶ۭ
اَلَّذِيْنَ كَفَرُوْا لَهُمْ عَذَابٌ
شَدِيْدٌ ڛ وَالَّذِيْنَ اٰمَنُوْا وَعَمِلُوا
الصّٰلِحٰتِ لَهُمْ مَّغْفِرَةٌ وَّاَجْرٌ كَبِيْرٌ ۝۷

Ikhfa اخفاء | Ghunna غُنّہ | Ikhfa Meem Saakin اخفاء میم ساکن | Idghaam ادغام | Qalqala قلقلہ | Qalb قلب | Idghaam Meem Saakin ادغام میم ساکن

8. Is he, then, to whom the evil of his conduct is made alluring, so that he looks upon it as good, (equal to one who is rightly guided)? For Allah leaves to stray whom He wills, and guides whom He wills. So let not your soul go out in (vainly) sighing after them: for Allah knows well all that they do!

8. Afaman zuyyina lahoo sooo'u 'amalihee fara-aahu ḥasanaa; fa-innal-laaha yuḍillu mañy-yashaaa'u wa yahdee mañy-yashaaa'u falaa tazhab nafsuka 'alayhim ḥasaraat; innal-laaha 'aleemum bimaa yaṣna'oon.

أَفَمَن زُيِّنَ لَهُۥ سُوٓءُ عَمَلِهِۦ فَرَءَاهُ
حَسَنًا ۖ فَإِنَّ ٱللَّهَ يُضِلُّ مَن يَشَآءُ
وَيَهْدِى مَن يَشَآءُ ۖ فَلَا تَذْهَبْ
نَفْسُكَ عَلَيْهِمْ حَسَرَٰتٍ ۚ إِنَّ ٱللَّهَ
عَلِيمٌۢ بِمَا يَصْنَعُونَ ٨

9. It is Allah Who sends forth the Winds, so that they raise up the Clouds, and We drive them to a land that is dead, and revive the earth therewith after its death: even so (will be) the Resurrection!

9. Wallaahul-lazeee arsalar-riyaaḥa fatuseeru saḥaaban fasuqnaahu ilaa baladim-mayyitin fa-aḥyaynaa bihil-arḍa ba'da mawtihaa; kazaa-likan-nushoor.

وَٱللَّهُ ٱلَّذِىٓ أَرْسَلَ ٱلرِّيَٰحَ فَتُثِيرُ
سَحَابًا فَسُقْنَٰهُ إِلَىٰ بَلَدٍ مَّيِّتٍ
فَأَحْيَيْنَا بِهِ ٱلْأَرْضَ بَعْدَ مَوْتِهَا ۚ
كَذَٰلِكَ ٱلنُّشُورُ ٩

10. If any do seek for glory and power,- to Allah belong all glory and power. To Him mount up (all) Words of Purity: it is He Who exalts each Deed of Righteousness. Those that lay Plots of Evil,- for them is a terrible penalty; and the plotting of such will be void (of result).

10. Man kaana yureedul 'izzata falillaahil-'izzatu jamee'aa; ilayhi yaṣ'adul-kalimuṭ-ṭayyibu wal'amaluṣ-ṣaaliḥu yarfa'uh; wallazeena yamkuroonas-sayyiaati lahum 'azaabun shadeed; wa makru ulaaa'ika huwa yaboor.

مَن كَانَ يُرِيدُ ٱلْعِزَّةَ فَلِلَّهِ ٱلْعِزَّةُ
جَمِيعًا ۚ إِلَيْهِ يَصْعَدُ ٱلْكَلِمُ
ٱلطَّيِّبُ وَٱلْعَمَلُ ٱلصَّٰلِحُ يَرْفَعُهُۥ ۚ
وَٱلَّذِينَ يَمْكُرُونَ ٱلسَّيِّـَٔاتِ لَهُمْ
عَذَابٌ شَدِيدٌ ۖ وَمَكْرُ أُو۟لَٰٓئِكَ
هُوَ يَبُورُ ١٠

11. And Allah created you from dust; then from a sperm-drop; then He made you in pairs. And no female conceives, or lays down (her load), but with His knowledge. Nor is a man long-lived granted length of days, nor is a part cut off from his life, but is in a Decree (ordained). All this is easy to Allah.

11. Wallaahu khalaqakum-min turaabin summa min-nuṭfatin summa ja'alakum azwaajaa; wa maa taḥmilu min unsaa wa laa taḍa'u illaa bi'ilmih; wa maa yu'ammaru mim-mu'ammariñw-wa laa yunqaṣu min 'umuriheee illaa fee kitaab; inna zaalika 'alal-laahi yaseer.

وَٱللَّهُ خَلَقَكُم مِّن تُرَابٍ ثُمَّ مِن
نُّطْفَةٍ ثُمَّ جَعَلَكُمْ أَزْوَٰجًا ۚ وَمَا
تَحْمِلُ مِنْ أُنثَىٰ وَلَا تَضَعُ إِلَّا
بِعِلْمِهِۦ ۚ وَمَا يُعَمَّرُ مِن مُّعَمَّرٍ وَلَا
يُنقَصُ مِنْ عُمُرِهِۦٓ إِلَّا فِى كِتَٰبٍ ۚ
إِنَّ ذَٰلِكَ عَلَى ٱللَّهِ يَسِيرٌ ١١

12. Nor are the two bodies of flowing water alike,- the one palatable, sweet, and pleasant to drink, and the other, salt and bitter. Yet from each (kind of water) you eat flesh fresh and tender, and you extract ornaments to wear; and you see the ships therein that plough the waves, that you may seek

12. Wa maa yastawil-baḥraani haazaa 'azbun furaatun saaa'ighun sharaabuhoo wa haazaa milḥun ujaaj; wa min kullin taakuloona laḥman ṭariyyañw-wa tastakhrijoona ḥilyatan talbasoonahaa wa taral-fulka feehi mawaakhira litabtaghoo

وَمَا يَسْتَوِى ٱلْبَحْرَانِ هَٰذَا عَذْبٌ
فُرَاتٌ سَآئِغٌ شَرَابُهُۥ وَهَٰذَا مِلْحٌ
أُجَاجٌ ۖ وَمِن كُلٍّ تَأْكُلُونَ لَحْمًا طَرِيًّا
وَتَسْتَخْرِجُونَ حِلْيَةً تَلْبَسُونَهَا ۖ وَ
تَرَى ٱلْفُلْكَ فِيهِ مَوَاخِرَ لِتَبْتَغُوا۟

(thus) of the Bounty of Allah that you may be grateful.

13. He merges Night into Day, and He merges Day into Night, and He has subjected the sun and the moon (to His Law): each one runs its course for a term appointed. Such is Allah your Lord: to Him belongs all Dominion. And those whom you invoke besides Him have not the least power.

14. If you invoke them, they will not listen to your call, and if they were to listen, they cannot answer your (prayer). On the Day of Judgment they will reject your "Partnership". And none, (O man!) can tell you (the Truth) like the One Who is acquainted with all things.

15. O you men! It is you that have need of Allah: but Allah is the One Free of all wants, worthy of all praise.

16. If He so pleased, He could blot you out and bring in a New Creation.

17. Nor is that (at all) difficult for Allah.

18. Nor can a bearer of burdens bear another's burden. If one heavily laden should call another to (bear) his load, not the least portion of it can be carried (by the other), even though he be nearly related. You can but admonish such as fear their Lord unseen and establish regular Prayer. And whoever purifies himself does so for the benefit of his own soul; and the destination (of all) is to Allah.

19. The blind and the seeing are not alike;

20. Nor are the depths of Darkness and the Light;

21. Nor are the (chilly) shade and the (genial) heat of the sun:

min faḍlihee wa la'allakum tashkuroon.

13. Yoolijul-layla fin-nahaari wa yoolijun-nahaara fil-layli wa sakhkharash-shamsa wal-qamara kulluñy-yajree li-ajalim-musammaa; zaalikumul-laahu Rabbukum lahul-mulk; wallaẕeena tad'oona min doonihee maa yamlikoona min qiṭmeer.

14. In tad'oohum laa yasma'oo du'aa'akum wa law sami'oo mas-tajaaboo lakum; wa Yawmal-Qiyaamati yakfuroona bishirkikum; wa laa yunabbi'uka mis̱lu khabeer.

(Section 2)

15. Yaaa ayyuhan-naasu antumul-fuqaraaa'u ilallaahi wallaahu Huwal-Ghaniyyul-Ḥameed.

16. Iñy-yashaå yuẕhibkum wa yaåti bikhalqin jadeed.

17. Wa maa ẕaalika 'alal-laahi bi'azeez.

18. Wa laa taziru waaziratuñw-wizra ukhraa; wa in tad'u musqalatun ilaa ḥimlihaa laa yuḥmal minhu shay'uñw-wa law kaana ẕaa qurbaa; innamaa tunẕirul-laẕeena yakhshawna Rabbahum bilghaybi wa aqaamuṣ-Ṣalaah; wa man tazakkaa fa-innamaa yatazakkaa linafsih; wa ilal-laahil-maṣeer.

19. Wa maa yastawil-a'maa wal-baṣeer.

20. Wa laẓ-ẓulumaatu wa lan-noor.

21. Wa laẓ-ẓillu wa lal-ḥaroor.

مِنْ فَضْلِهٖ وَلَعَلَّكُمْ تَشْكُرُوْنَ ﴿١٢﴾
يُوْلِجُ الَّيْلَ فِي النَّهَارِ وَيُوْلِجُ النَّهَارَ
فِي الَّيْلِ ۙ وَسَخَّرَ الشَّمْسَ وَالْقَمَرَ ۖ
كُلٌّ يَّجْرِيْ لِاَجَلٍ مُّسَمًّى ۭ ذٰلِكُمُ
اللّٰهُ رَبُّكُمْ لَهُ الْمُلْكُ ۭ وَالَّذِيْنَ
تَدْعُوْنَ مِنْ دُوْنِهٖ مَا يَمْلِكُوْنَ
مِنْ قِطْمِيْرٍ ﴿١٣﴾
اِنْ تَدْعُوْهُمْ لَا يَسْمَعُوْا دُعَاۗءَكُمْ ۚ
وَلَوْ سَمِعُوْا مَا اسْتَجَابُوْا لَكُمْ ۭ وَ
يَوْمَ الْقِيٰمَةِ يَكْفُرُوْنَ بِشِرْكِكُمْ ۭ
وَلَا يُنَبِّئُكَ مِثْلُ خَبِيْرٍ ﴿١٤﴾ ع
الربع
يٰٓاَيُّهَا النَّاسُ اَنْتُمُ الْفُقَرَاۗءُ اِلَى
اللّٰهِ ۚ وَاللّٰهُ هُوَ الْغَنِيُّ الْحَمِيْدُ ﴿١٥﴾
اِنْ يَّشَاْ يُذْهِبْكُمْ وَيَاْتِ بِخَلْقٍ
جَدِيْدٍ ﴿١٦﴾
وَمَا ذٰلِكَ عَلَى اللّٰهِ بِعَزِيْزٍ ﴿١٧﴾
وَلَا تَزِرُ وَازِرَةٌ وِّزْرَ اُخْرٰى ۭ وَ
اِنْ تَدْعُ مُثْقَلَةٌ اِلٰى حِمْلِهَا لَا
يُحْمَلْ مِنْهُ شَيْءٌ وَّلَوْ كَانَ ذَا قُرْبٰى ۭ
اِنَّمَا تُنْذِرُ الَّذِيْنَ يَخْشَوْنَ رَبَّهُمْ
بِالْغَيْبِ وَاَقَامُوا الصَّلٰوةَ ۭ وَمَنْ
تَزَكّٰى فَاِنَّمَا يَتَزَكّٰى لِنَفْسِهٖ ۭ وَ
اِلَى اللّٰهِ الْمَصِيْرُ ﴿١٨﴾
وَمَا يَسْتَوِي الْاَعْمٰى وَالْبَصِيْرُ ﴿١٩﴾
وَلَا الظُّلُمٰتُ وَلَا النُّوْرُ ﴿٢٠﴾
وَلَا الظِّلُّ وَلَا الْحَرُوْرُ ﴿٢١﴾

22. Nor are alike those that are living and those that are dead. Allah can make any that He wills to hear; but you cannot make those to hear who are (buried) in graves.

22. Wa maa yastawil-aḥyaa-'u wa lal-amwaat; innal-laaha yusmi'u mañy-yashaaa'u wa maaa anta bimusmi'im-man fil-quboor.

وَمَا يَسْتَوِى الْاَحْيَآءُ وَلَا الْاَمْوَاتُ ؕ
اِنَّ اللّٰهَ يُسْمِعُ مَنْ يَّشَآءُ ۚ وَمَآ اَنْتَ
بِمُسْمِعٍ مَّنْ فِى الْقُبُوْرِ ﴿٢٢﴾

23. You are no other than a warner.

23. In anta illaa nazeer.

اِنْ اَنْتَ اِلَّا نَذِيْرٌ ﴿٢٣﴾

24. Verily We have sent you in truth, as a bearer of glad tidings, and as a warner: and there never was a people, without a warner having lived among them (in the past).

24. Innaaa arsalnaaka bil-ḥaqqi basheerañw-wa nazeeraa; wa im-min ummatin illaa khalaa feehaa nazeer.

اِنَّآ اَرْسَلْنٰكَ بِالْحَقِّ بَشِيْرًا وَّنَذِيْرًا ؕ
وَاِنْ مِّنْ اُمَّةٍ اِلَّا خَلَا فِيْهَا نَذِيْرٌ ﴿٢٤﴾

25. And if they reject you, so did their predecessors, to whom came their Apostles with Clear Signs, Books of dark prophecies, and the Book of Enlightenment.

25. Wa iñy-yukazzibooka faqad kazzabal-lazeena min qablihim jaaa'at-hum Rusu-luhum bilbayyinaati wa biz-Zuburi wa bil-Kitaabil-Muneer.

وَاِنْ يُّكَذِّبُوْكَ فَقَدْ كَذَّبَ الَّذِيْنَ مِنْ
قَبْلِهِمْ ۚ جَآءَتْهُمْ رُسُلُهُمْ بِالْبَيِّنٰتِ
وَبِالزُّبُرِ وَبِالْكِتٰبِ الْمُنِيْرِ ﴿٢٥﴾

26. In the end did I punish those who rejected Faith: and how (terrible) was My rejection (of them)!

26. Summa akhaztul-lazeena kafaroo fakayfa kaana nakeer.

(Section 3)

ثُمَّ اَخَذْتُ الَّذِيْنَ كَفَرُوْا
فَكَيْفَ كَانَ نَكِيْرِ ﴿٢٦﴾ ع

ع ١٥

27. Do you not see that Allah sends down rain from the sky? With it We then bring out produce of various colours. And in the mountains are tracts white and red, of various shades of colour, and black intense in hue.

27. Alam tara annal-laaha anzala minas-samaaa'i maaa'an fa-akhrajnaa bihee samaraatim-mukhtalifan alwaanuhaa; wa minal-jibaali judadum bee-ḍuñw-wa ḥumrum-mukhtali-fun alwaanuhaa wa gharaa-beebu sood.

اَلَمْ تَرَ اَنَّ اللّٰهَ اَنْزَلَ مِنَ السَّمَآءِ
مَآءً ۚ فَاَخْرَجْنَا بِهٖ ثَمَرٰتٍ مُّخْتَلِفًا
اَلْوَانُهَا ؕ وَمِنَ الْجِبَالِ جُدَدٌۢ بِيْضٌ
وَّحُمْرٌ مُّخْتَلِفٌ اَلْوَانُهَا وَغَرَابِيْبُ
سُوْدٌ ﴿٢٧﴾

28. And so amongst men and crawling creatures and cattle, they are of various colours. Those truly fear Allah, among His servants, who have knowledge: for Allah is Exalted in Might, Oft-Forgiving.

28. Wa minan-naasi wadda-waaabbi wal-an'aami mukh-talifun alwaanuhoo kazalik; innamaa yakhshal-laaha min 'ibaadihil-'ulamaaa'; innal-laaha 'Azeezun Ghafoor.

وَمِنَ النَّاسِ وَالدَّوَآبِّ وَالْاَنْعَامِ
مُخْتَلِفٌ اَلْوَانُهٗ كَذٰلِكَ ؕ اِنَّمَا يَخْشَى
اللّٰهَ مِنْ عِبَادِهِ الْعُلَمٰٓؤُا ؕ اِنَّ اللّٰهَ
عَزِيْزٌ غَفُوْرٌ ﴿٢٨﴾

29. Those who rehearse the Book of Allah, establish regular Prayer, and spend (in charity) out of what We have provided for them, secretly and openly, hope for a commerce that will never fail:

29. Innal-lazeena yatloona Kitaabal-laahi wa aqaamuṣ-Ṣalaata wa anfaqoo mimmaa razaqnaahum sirrañw-wa 'alaa-niyatañy-yarjoona tijaaratal-lan taboor.

اِنَّ الَّذِيْنَ يَتْلُوْنَ كِتٰبَ اللّٰهِ وَاَقَامُوا
الصَّلٰوةَ وَاَنْفَقُوْا مِمَّا رَزَقْنٰهُمْ سِرًّا
وَّعَلَانِيَةً يَّرْجُوْنَ تِجَارَةً لَّنْ تَبُوْرَ ﴿٢٩﴾ لا

30. For He will pay them their meed, nay, He will give them (even) more out of His Bounty: for He is Oft-Forgiving, Most Ready to appreciate (service).

30. Liyuwaffiyahum ujoo-rahum wa yazeedahum-min faḍlih; innahoo Ghafoorun Shakoor.

لِيُوَفِّيَهُمْ اُجُوْرَهُمْ وَيَزِيْدَهُمْ مِّنْ
فَضْلِهٖ ؕ اِنَّهٗ غَفُوْرٌ شَكُوْرٌ ﴿٣٠﴾

31. That which We have revealed to thee of the Book

31. Wallazeee awḥaynaaa ilayka minal-Kitaabi

وَالَّذِىْٓ اَوْحَيْنَآ اِلَيْكَ مِنَ الْكِتٰبِ

Ikhfa اخفاء | Ghunna غُنّہ | Ikhfa Meem Saakin اخفاء میم ساکن | Idghaam ادغام | Qalqala قلقلہ | Qalb قلب | Idghaam Meem Saakin ادغام میم ساکن

is the Truth,- confirming what was (revealed) before it: for Allah is assuredly- with respect to His servants - well acquainted and fully Observant.

huwal-ḥaqqu muṣaddiqal-limaa bayna yadayh; innal-laaha bi'ibaadihee la-Khabeerum Baṣeer.

هو الحق مصدقا لما بين يديه ط
ان الله بعباده لخبير بصير ٣١

32. Then We have given the Book for inheritance to such of Our Servants as We have chosen: but there are among them some who wrong their own souls; some who follow a middle course; and some who are, by Allah's leave, foremost in good deeds; that is the highest Grace.

32. Summa awrasnal-Kitaabal-lazeenaṣ-ṭafaynaa min 'ibaadinaa faminhum ẓaalimul-linafsihee wa minhum-muqtaṣid, wa minhum saabiqum bilkhayraati bi-iznil-laah; zaalika huwal-faḍlul-kabeer.

ثم اورثنا الكتب الذين اصطفينا
من عبادنا ج فمنهم ظالم لنفسه ج
ومنهم مقتصد ج ومنهم سابق
بالخيرت باذن الله ط ذلك هو
الفضل الكبير ٣٢

33. Gardens of Eternity will they enter: therein they will be adorned with bracelets of gold and pearls; and their garments there will be of silk.

33. Jannaatu 'Adniñy-yadkhuloonahaa yuḥallawna feehaa min asaawira min zahabiñw-wa lu'lu'añw wa libaasuhum feehaa ḥareer.

جنت عدن يدخلونها يحلون
فيها من اساور من ذهب ولؤلؤا ج
ولباسهم فيها حرير ٣٣

34. And they will say: "Praise be to Allah, Who has removed from us (all) sorrow: for our Lord is indeed Oft-Forgiving ready to appreciate (service):

34. Wa qaalul-ḥamdu lillaahil-lazeee azhaba 'annal-ḥazan; inna Rabbanaa la-Ghafoorun Shakoor.

وقالوا الحمد لله الذي اذهب عنا
الحزن ط ان ربنا لغفور شكور ٣٤

35. "Who has, out of His Bounty, settled us in a Home that will last: no toil nor sense of weariness shall touch us therein."

35. Allazeee aḥallanaa daaral-muqaamati min faḍlihee laa yamassunaa feehaa naṣabuñw-wa laa yamassunaa feehaa lughoob.

الذي احلنا دار المقامة من
فضله ج لا يمسنا فيها نصب ولا
يمسنا فيها لغوب ٣٥

36. But those who reject (Allah) - for them will be the Fire of Hell: No term shall be determined for them, so they should die, nor shall its Chastisement be lightened for them. Thus do We reward every ungrateful one!

36. Wallazeena kafaroo lahum Naaru Jahannama laa yuqḍaa 'alayhim fa-yamootoo wa laa yukhaffafu 'anhum-min 'azaabihaa; kazaalika najzee kulla kafoor.

والذين كفروا لهم نار جهنم ج لا
يقضى عليهم فيموتوا ولا يخفف
عنهم من عذابها ط كذلك نجزي
كل كفور ٣٦

37. Therein will they cry aloud (for assistance): "Our Lord! Bring us out: we shall work righteousness, not the (deeds) we used to do!" "Did We not give you long enough life so that he that would should receive admonition? And (moreover) the warner came to you. So you taste (the fruits of your deeds): for the wrong-doers there is no helper."

37. Wa hum yaṣṭarikhoona feehaa Rabbanaaa akhrijnaa na'mal ṣaaliḥan ghayral-lazee kunnaa na'mal; awa lam nu'ammirkum-maa yatazakkaru feehi man tazakkara wa jaaa'akumun-nazeeru fazooqoo famaa lizẓaalimeena min naṣeer. **(Section 4)**

وهم يصطرخون فيها ج ربنا اخرجنا
نعمل صالحا غير الذي كنا
نعمل ط اولم نعمركم ما يتذكر
فيه من تذكر وجاءكم النذير ط
فذوقوا فما للظلمين من نصير ٣٧

38. Verily Allah knows (all) the hidden things of the heavens and the earth: verily He has full knowledge of all that is in (men's) hearts.

38. Innal-laaha 'aalimu ghaybis-samaawaati wal-arḍ; innahoo 'aleemum bizaatiṣ-ṣudoor.

ان الله علم غيب السموت والارض ط
انه عليم بذات الصدور ٣٨

Ikhfa اخفاء | Ghunna غنہ | Ikhfa Meem Saakin اخفاء میم ساکن | Idghaam ادغام | Qalqala قلقلہ | Qalb قلب | Idghaam Meem Saakin ادغام میم ساکن

39. He it is that has made you inheritors in the earth: if, then, any do reject (Allah), their rejection (works) against themselves: their rejection but adds to the odium for the Unbelievers in the sight of their Lord: their rejection but adds to (their own) undoing.

40. Say: "Have you seen (these) 'Partners' of yours whom you call upon besides Allah? Show Me what it is they have created in the (wide) earth. Or have they a share in the heavens? Or have We given them a Book from which they (can derive) clear (evidence)?- Nay, the wrong-doers promise each other nothing but delusions.

41. It is Allah Who sustains the heavens and the earth, lest they cease (to function): and if they should fail, there is none - not one - can sustain them thereafter: Verily He is Most Forbearing, Oft-Forgiving.

42. They swore their strongest oaths by Allah that if a warner came to them, they would follow his guidance better than any (other) of the Peoples: but when a warner came to them, it has only increased their flight (from righteousness),-

43. On account of their arrogance in the land and their plotting of Evil. But the plotting of Evil will hem in only the authors thereof. Now are they but looking for the way the ancients were dealt with? But no change will you find in Allah's way (of dealing): no turning off will you find in Allah's way (of dealing).

44. Do they not travel through the earth, and see what was the End of those

39. Huwal-lazee ja'alakum khalaaa'ifa fil-arḍ; faman kafara fa'alayhi kufruhoo; wa laa yazeedul-kaafireena kufruhum 'inda Rabbihim illaa maqtañw wa laa yazeedul-kaafireena kufruhum illaa khasaaraa.

40. Qul ara'aytum shurakaaa'a kumul-lazeena tad'oona min doonil-laah; aroonee maazaa khalaqoo minal-arḍi am lahum shirkun fis-samaawaati am aataynaahum Kitaaban fahum 'alaa bayyinatim-minh; bal iñy-ya'iduẓ-ẓaalimoona ba'ḍuhum ba'ḍan illaa ghurooraa.

41. Innal-laaha yumsikus-samaawaati wal-arḍa an tazoolaa; wa la'in zaalataaa in amsakahumaa min aḥadim-mim ba'dih; innahoo kaana Ḥaleeman Ghafooraa.

42. Wa aqsamoo billaahi jahda aymaanihim la'in jaaa'ahum nazeerul-layakoonunna ahdaa min iḥdal-umami falammaa jaaa'ahum nazeerum-maa zaadahum illaa nufooraa.

43. Istikbaaran fil-arḍi wa makras-sayyi'; wa laa yaḥeequl-makrus-sayyi'u illaa biahlih; fahal yanẓuroona illaa sunnatal-awwaleen; falan tajida lisunnatil-laahi tabdeelañw wa lan tajida lisunnatil-laahi taḥweelaa.

44. Awalam yaseeroo fil-arḍi fa-yanẓuroo kayfa kaana 'aaqibatul-lazeena min

هُوَ الَّذِي جَعَلَكُمْ خَلَٰٓئِفَ فِي
الْأَرْضِ ۚ فَمَن كَفَرَ فَعَلَيْهِ كُفْرُهُ ۖ
وَلَا يَزِيدُ الْكَافِرِينَ كُفْرُهُمْ عِندَ
رَبِّهِمْ إِلَّا مَقْتًا ۖ وَلَا يَزِيدُ الْكَافِرِينَ
كُفْرُهُمْ إِلَّا خَسَارًا ﴿٣٩﴾
قُلْ أَرَأَيْتُمْ شُرَكَاءَكُمُ الَّذِينَ
تَدْعُونَ مِن دُونِ اللَّهِ أَرُونِي مَاذَا
خَلَقُوا مِنَ الْأَرْضِ أَمْ لَهُمْ شِرْكٌ
فِي السَّمَاوَاتِ أَمْ آتَيْنَاهُمْ كِتَابًا فَهُمْ
عَلَىٰ بَيِّنَتٍ مِّنْهُ ۚ بَلْ إِن يَعِدُ
الظَّالِمُونَ بَعْضُهُم بَعْضًا إِلَّا غُرُورًا ﴿٤٠﴾
إِنَّ اللَّهَ يُمْسِكُ السَّمَاوَاتِ وَالْأَرْضَ
أَن تَزُولَا ۚ وَلَئِن زَالَتَا إِنْ أَمْسَكَهُمَا
مِنْ أَحَدٍ مِّن بَعْدِهِ ۚ إِنَّهُ كَانَ
حَلِيمًا غَفُورًا ﴿٤١﴾
وَأَقْسَمُوا بِاللَّهِ جَهْدَ أَيْمَانِهِمْ لَئِن
جَاءَهُمْ نَذِيرٌ لَّيَكُونُنَّ أَهْدَىٰ مِنْ
إِحْدَى الْأُمَمِ ۖ فَلَمَّا جَاءَهُمْ نَذِيرٌ
مَّا زَادَهُمْ إِلَّا نُفُورًا ﴿٤٢﴾
اسْتِكْبَارًا فِي الْأَرْضِ وَمَكْرَ السَّيِّئِ ۚ
وَلَا يَحِيقُ الْمَكْرُ السَّيِّئُ إِلَّا بِأَهْلِهِ ۚ
فَهَلْ يَنظُرُونَ إِلَّا سُنَّتَ الْأَوَّلِينَ ۚ
فَلَن تَجِدَ لِسُنَّتِ اللَّهِ تَبْدِيلًا ۖ وَ
لَن تَجِدَ لِسُنَّتِ اللَّهِ تَحْوِيلًا ﴿٤٣﴾
أَوَلَمْ يَسِيرُوا فِي الْأَرْضِ فَيَنظُرُوا
كَيْفَ كَانَ عَاقِبَةُ الَّذِينَ مِن

Ikhfa اخفاء | Ghunna غنہ | Ikhfa Meem Saakin اخفاء میم ساکن | Idghaam ادغام | Qalqala قلقلہ | Qalb قلب | Idghaam Meem Saakin ادغام میم ساکن

before them,- though they were superior to them in strength? Nor is Allah to be frustrated by anything what-ever in the heavens or on earth: for He is All-Knowing. All-Powerful.

qablihim wa kaanooo ashadda minhum quwwah; wa maa kaanal-laahu liyu'jizahoo min shay'in fis-samaawaati wa laa fil-arḍ; innahoo kaana 'Aleeman Qadeeraa.

قَبْلِهِمْ وَكَانُوٓا أَشَدَّ مِنْهُمْ قُوَّةً ۚ
وَمَا كَانَ ٱللَّهُ لِيُعْجِزَهُۥ مِن شَىْءٍ فِى
ٱلسَّمَٰوَٰتِ وَلَا فِى ٱلْأَرْضِ ۚ إِنَّهُۥ كَانَ
عَلِيمًا قَدِيرًا ﴿٤٤﴾

45. If Allah were to punish men according to what they deserve. He would not leave on the back of the (earth) a single living creature: but He gives them respite for a stated Term: when their Term expires, verily Allah has in His sight all His servants .

45. Wa law yu'aakhiẕul-laahun-naasa bimaa kasaboo maa taraka 'alaa ẓahrihaa min daaabbatiñw-wa laakiñy-yu'akhkhiruhum ilaa ajalim-musamman fa-iẕaa jaaa'a ajaluhum fa-innal-laaha kaana bi'ibaadihee Baṣeeraa.

(Section 5)

وَلَوْ يُؤَاخِذُ ٱللَّهُ ٱلنَّاسَ بِمَا
كَسَبُوا۟ مَا تَرَكَ عَلَىٰ ظَهْرِهَا مِن
دَآبَّةٍ وَلَٰكِن يُؤَخِّرُهُمْ إِلَىٰٓ أَجَلٍ
مُّسَمًّى ۖ فَإِذَا جَآءَ أَجَلُهُمْ فَإِنَّ
ٱللَّهَ كَانَ بِعِبَادِهِۦ بَصِيرًۢا ﴿٤٥﴾

36. Ya-Sin

In the name of Allah, Most Gracious, Most Merciful.

Sûrat Yâ-Sîn–36

(Revealed at Makkah)

Bismillaahir Raḥmaanir Raḥeem

(٣٦) سُورَةُ يسٓ مَكِّيَّةٌ (٤١)

بِسْمِ ٱللَّهِ ٱلرَّحْمَٰنِ ٱلرَّحِيمِ

1. *Ya-Sin.*

1. Yaa-Seeen.

يسٓ ﴿١﴾

2. By the Qur'an, full of Wisdom,-

2. Wal-Qur-aanil-Ḥakeem.

وَٱلْقُرْءَانِ ٱلْحَكِيمِ ﴿٢﴾

3. You are indeed one of the Apostles,

3. Innaka laminal-mursaleen.

إِنَّكَ لَمِنَ ٱلْمُرْسَلِينَ ﴿٣﴾

4. On a Straight Way.

4. 'Alaa Ṣiraaṭim-Mustaqeem.

عَلَىٰ صِرَٰطٍ مُّسْتَقِيمٍ ﴿٤﴾

5. It is a Revelation sent down by (Him), the Exalted in Might, Most Merciful.

5. Tanzeelal-'Azeezir-Raḥeem.

تَنزِيلَ ٱلْعَزِيزِ ٱلرَّحِيمِ ﴿٥﴾

6. In order that you may admonish a people, whose fathers had received no admonition, and who therefore remain heedless (of the Signs of Allah).

6. Litunẕira qawmam-maaa unẕira aabaaa'uhum fahum ghaafiloon.

لِتُنذِرَ قَوْمًا مَّآ أُنذِرَ ءَابَآؤُهُمْ فَهُمْ
غَٰفِلُونَ ﴿٦﴾

7. The Word is proved true against the greater part of them: for they do not believe.

7. Laqad ḥaqqal-qawlu 'alaaa akṡarihim fahum laa yu'minoon.

لَقَدْ حَقَّ ٱلْقَوْلُ عَلَىٰٓ أَكْثَرِهِمْ فَهُمْ
لَا يُؤْمِنُونَ ﴿٧﴾

8. We have put yokes round their necks right up to their chins, so that their heads are forced up (and they cannot see).

8. Innaa ja'alnaa feee a'naaqihim aghlaalan fahiya ilal-aẕqaani fahum-muqmaḥoon.

إِنَّا جَعَلْنَا فِىٓ أَعْنَٰقِهِمْ أَغْلَٰلًا فَهِىَ
إِلَى ٱلْأَذْقَانِ فَهُم مُّقْمَحُونَ ﴿٨﴾

9. And We have put a bar in front of them and a bar behind them, and further, We have covered them up; so that they cannot see.

9. Wa ja'alnaa mim bayni aydeehim saddañw-wa min khalfihim saddan fa-aghshaynaahum fahum laa yubṣiroon.

وَجَعَلْنَا مِنۢ بَيْنِ أَيْدِيهِمْ سَدًّا
وَمِنْ خَلْفِهِمْ سَدًّا فَأَغْشَيْنَٰهُمْ
فَهُمْ لَا يُبْصِرُونَ ﴿٩﴾

10. The same is it to them whether you admonish them or you do not

10. Wa sawaaa'un 'alayhim 'a-anzartahum am lam

وَسَوَآءٌ عَلَيْهِمْ ءَأَنذَرْتَهُمْ أَمْ لَمْ

Ikhfa اخفاء | Ghunna غنّہ | Ikhfa Meem Saakin اخفاء میم ساکن | Idghaam ادغام | Qalqala قلقلہ | Qalb قلب | Idghaam Meem Saakin ادغام میم ساکن

admonish them: they will not believe.

11. You can but admonish such a one as follows the Message and fears the (Lord) Most Gracious, unseen: give such a one, therefore, good tidings of Forgiveness and a Reward most generous.

12. Verily We shall give life to the dead, and We record that which they send before and that which they leave behind, and of all things have We taken account in a clear Book (of evidence).

13. Set forth to them, by way of a parable, the (story of) the Companions of the City. Behold! there came Apostles to it.

14. When We (first) sent to them two Apostles, they rejected them: but We strengthened them with a third: they said, "Truly, we have been sent on a mission to you."

15. The (people) said: "You are only men like ourselves; and (Allah) Most Gracious sends no sort of revelation: you do nothing but lie."

16. They said: "Our Lord knows that we have been sent on a mission to you:

17. "And our duty is only to proclaim the clear Message."

18. The (people) said: "For us, we augur an evil omen from you: if you desist not, we will certainly stone you. And a grievous punishment indeed will be inflicted on you by us."

19. They said: "Your evil omens are with yourselves: (you deem this an evil omen), if you are admonished: Nay, but you are a people transgressing all bounds!"

20. Then there came running from the farthest part of the City, a man, saying, "O my people! Obey the Apostles:

21. "Obey those who ask no reward of you (for themselves), and who have themselves received Guidance.

tunzirhum laa yu'minoon.

11. Innamaa tunziru manittaba'az-Zikra wa khashiyar-Raḥmaana bilghayb, fabashshirhu bimaghfiratiñw-wa ajrin kareem.

12. Innaa Naḥnu nuḥyil-mawtaa wa naktubu maa qaddamoo wa aasaarahum; wa kulla shay'in aḥsaynaahu feee Imaamim-Mubeen. **(Section 1)**

13. Waḍrib lahum-masalan Aṣḥaabal-Qaryah; iz jaaa'ahal-mursaloon.

14. Iz arsalnaaa ilayhimusnayni fakazzaboohumaa fa'azzaznaa bisaalisin faqaalooo innaaa ilaykum-mursaloon.

15. Qaaloo maaa antum illaa basharum-mislunaa wa maaa anzalar-Raḥmaanu min shay'in in antum illaa takziboon.

16. Qaaloo Rabbunaa ya'lamu innaaa ilaykum lamursaloon.

17. Wa maa 'alaynaaa illal-balaaghul-mubeen.

18. Qaalooo innaa taṭayyarnaa bikum la'il-lam tantahoo lanarjumannakum wa la-yamassannakum-minnaa 'azaabun aleem.

19. Qaaloo ṭaaa'irukum-ma'akum; a'in zukkirtum; bal antum qawmum-musrifoon.

20. Wa jaaa'a min aqṣal-madeenati rajuluñy-yas'aa qaala yaa qawmit-tabi'ul-mursaleen.

21. Ittabi'oo mal-laa yas'alukum ajrañw-wa hum-muhtadoon.

تُنذِرْهُمْ لَا يُؤْمِنُونَ ١٠
إِنَّمَا تُنذِرُ مَنِ اتَّبَعَ الذِّكْرَ وَخَشِيَ
الرَّحْمَٰنَ بِالْغَيْبِ ۖ فَبَشِّرْهُ بِمَغْفِرَةٍ
وَأَجْرٍ كَرِيمٍ ١١
إِنَّا نَحْنُ نُحْيِ الْمَوْتَىٰ وَنَكْتُبُ مَا قَدَّمُوا
وَآثَارَهُمْ ۚ وَكُلَّ شَيْءٍ أَحْصَيْنَاهُ فِي
إِمَامٍ مُّبِينٍ ١٢
وَاضْرِبْ لَهُم مَّثَلًا أَصْحَابَ الْقَرْيَةِ
إِذْ جَاءَهَا الْمُرْسَلُونَ ١٣
إِذْ أَرْسَلْنَا إِلَيْهِمُ اثْنَيْنِ فَكَذَّبُوهُمَا
فَعَزَّزْنَا بِثَالِثٍ فَقَالُوا إِنَّا إِلَيْكُم
مُّرْسَلُونَ ١٤
قَالُوا مَا أَنتُمْ إِلَّا بَشَرٌ مِّثْلُنَا وَمَا
أَنزَلَ الرَّحْمَٰنُ مِن شَيْءٍ إِنْ أَنتُمْ
إِلَّا تَكْذِبُونَ ١٥
قَالُوا رَبُّنَا يَعْلَمُ إِنَّا إِلَيْكُمْ لَمُرْسَلُونَ ١٦
وَمَا عَلَيْنَا إِلَّا الْبَلَاغُ الْمُبِينُ ١٧
قَالُوا إِنَّا تَطَيَّرْنَا بِكُمْ ۖ لَئِن لَّمْ
تَنتَهُوا لَنَرْجُمَنَّكُمْ وَلَيَمَسَّنَّكُم مِّنَّا
عَذَابٌ أَلِيمٌ ١٨
قَالُوا طَائِرُكُم مَّعَكُمْ ۚ أَئِن ذُكِّرْتُم
بَلْ أَنتُمْ قَوْمٌ مُّسْرِفُونَ ١٩
وَجَاءَ مِنْ أَقْصَا الْمَدِينَةِ رَجُلٌ يَسْعَىٰ
قَالَ يَا قَوْمِ اتَّبِعُوا الْمُرْسَلِينَ ٢٠
اتَّبِعُوا مَن لَّا يَسْأَلُكُمْ أَجْرًا وَهُم
مُّهْتَدُونَ ٢١

Ikhfa اخفاء | Ghunna غُنّہ | Ikhfa Meem Saakin اخفاء میم ساکن | Idghaam ادغام | Qalqala قلقلہ | Qalb قلب | Idghaam Meem Saakin ادغام میم ساکن

22. "It would not be reasonable in me if I did not serve Him Who created me, and to Whom you shall (all) be brought back.

22. Wa maa liya laaa a'budul-lazee faṭaranee wa ilayhi turja'oon.

وَمَالِيَ لَآ أَعْبُدُ الَّذِي فَطَرَنِي
وَإِلَيْهِ تُرْجَعُونَ ٢٢

23. "Shall I take (other) gods besides Him? If (Allah) Most Gracious should intend some adversity for me, of no use what-ever will be their intercession for me, nor can they deliver me.

23. 'A-attakhizu min dooniheee aalihatan iñy-yuridnir-Raḥmaanu biḍurril-laa tughni 'annee shafaa'atuhum shay-'añw-wa laa yunqizoon.

ءَأَتَّخِذُ مِن دُونِهِۦٓ ءَالِهَةً إِن يُرِدْنِ
الرَّحْمَٰنُ بِضُرٍّ لَّا تُغْنِ عَنِّي شَفَٰعَتُهُمْ
شَيْـًٔا وَلَا يُنقِذُونِ ٢٣

24. "I would indeed, if I were to do so, be in manifest Error.

24. Inneee izal-lafee ḍalaa-lim-mubeen.

إِنِّيٓ إِذًا لَّفِي ضَلَٰلٍ مُّبِينٍ ٢٤

25. "For me, I have faith in the Lord of you (all): listen, then, to me!"

25. Inneee aamantu bi-Rabbikum fasma'oon.

إِنِّيٓ ءَامَنتُ بِرَبِّكُمْ فَاسْمَعُونِ ٢٥

26. It was said: "You enter you the Garden." He said: "Ah me! Would that my People knew (what I know)!-

26. Qeelad-khulil-Jannah; qaala yaa layta qawmee ya'lamoon.

قِيلَ ادْخُلِ الْجَنَّةَ قَالَ يَٰلَيْتَ
قَوْمِي يَعْلَمُونَ ٢٦

27. "For that my Lord has granted me Forgiveness and has enrolled me among those held in honour!"

27. Bimaa ghafara lee Rabbee wa ja'alanee minal-mukrameen.

بِمَا غَفَرَ لِي رَبِّي وَجَعَلَنِي مِنَ
الْمُكْرَمِينَ ٢٧

28. And We did not send down against his People, after him, any hosts from heaven, nor was it needful for Us so to do.

28. Wa maaa anzalnaa 'alaa qawmihee mim ba'dihee min jundim-minas-samaaa'i wa maa kunnaa munzileen.

وَمَآ أَنزَلْنَا عَلَىٰ قَوْمِهِۦ مِنۢ بَعْدِهِۦ مِن
جُندٍ مِّنَ السَّمَآءِ وَمَا كُنَّا مُنزِلِينَ ٢٨

29. It was no more than a single mighty Blast, and behold! they were (like ashes) quenched and silent.

29. In kaanat illaa ṣayḥatañw-waaḥidatan fa-izaa hum khaamidoon.

إِن كَانَتْ إِلَّا صَيْحَةً وَٰحِدَةً فَإِذَا
هُمْ خَٰمِدُونَ ٢٩

30. Ah! Alas for (My) servants! There comes not an Apostle to them but they mock him!

30. Yaa ḥasratan 'alal-'ibaad; maa yaâteehim-mir Rasoolin illaa kaanoo bihee yastahzi'oon.

يَٰحَسْرَةً عَلَى الْعِبَادِ مَا يَأْتِيهِم مِّن
رَّسُولٍ إِلَّا كَانُوا بِهِۦ يَسْتَهْزِءُونَ ٣٠

31. Don't they see how many generations before them We destroyed? Not to them will they return:

31. Alam yaraw kam ahlaknaa qablahum-minal-qurooni annahum ilayhim laa yarji'oon.

أَلَمْ يَرَوْا كَمْ أَهْلَكْنَا قَبْلَهُم مِّنَ
الْقُرُونِ أَنَّهُمْ إِلَيْهِمْ لَا يَرْجِعُونَ ٣١

32. But each one of them all - will be brought before Us (for judgment).

32. Wa in kullul-lammaa jamee'ul-ladaynaa muḥḍaroon.

وَإِن كُلٌّ لَّمَّا جَمِيعٌ لَّدَيْنَا مُحْضَرُونَ ٣٢

(Section 2)

33. A Sign for them is the earth that is dead: We do give it life, and produce grain therefrom, of which you do eat.

33. Wa Aayatul-lahumul-arḍul-maytatu aḥyaynaahaa wa akhrajnaa minhaa ḥabban faminhu yaâkuloon.

وَءَايَةٌ لَّهُمُ الْأَرْضُ الْمَيْتَةُ
أَحْيَيْنَٰهَا وَأَخْرَجْنَا مِنْهَا حَبًّا
فَمِنْهُ يَأْكُلُونَ ٣٣

34. And We produce therein orchards with date-palms and vines, and We cause springs to gush forth therein:

34. Wa ja'alnaa feehaa jannaatim-min nakheeliñw-wa a'naabiñw-wa fajjarnaa feehaa minal-'uyoon.

وَجَعَلْنَا فِيهَا جَنَّٰتٍ مِّن نَّخِيلٍ وَ
أَعْنَٰبٍ وَفَجَّرْنَا فِيهَا مِنَ الْعُيُونِ ٣٤

35. That they may enjoy the fruits of this (artistry): it was not

35. Liyaâkuloo min samarihee wa maa 'amilat-hu

لِيَأْكُلُوا مِن ثَمَرِهِۦ وَمَا عَمِلَتْهُ

Ikhfa اخفاء | Ghunna غُنّہ | Ikhfa Meem Saakin اخفاء میم ساکن | Idghaam ادغام | Qalqala قلقلہ | Qalb قلب | Idghaam Meem Saakin ادغام میم ساکن

their hands that made this: will they not then give thanks?

36. Glory to Allah, Who created in pairs all things that the earth produces, as well as their own (human) kind and (other) things of which they have no knowledge.

37. And a Sign for them is the Night: We withdraw therefrom the Day, and behold they are plunged in darkness;

38. And the sun runs his course for a period determined for him: that is the decree of (Him), the Exalted in Might, the All-Know-ing.

39. And the Moon,- We have measured for her mansions (to traverse) till she returns like the old (and withered) lower part of a date-stalk.

40. It is not permitted to the Sun to catch up the Moon, nor can the Night outstrip the Day: each (just) swims along in (its own) orbit (according to Law).

41. And a Sign for them is that We bore their race (through the Flood) in the loaded Ark;

42. And We have created for them similar (vessels) on which they ride.

43. If it were Our Will, We could drown them: then would there be no helper (to hear their cry), nor could they be delivered,

44. Except by way of Mercy from Us, and by way of (worldly) convenience (to serve them) for a time.

45. When they are told, "You fear that which is before you and that which will be after you, in order that you may receive Mercy," (they turn back).

46. Not a Sign comes to them from among the Signs of their Lord, but they turn away therefrom.

47. And when they are told, "You spend of (the bounties) with which Allah has provided you," the Unbelievers say to those who believe:

aydeehim; afalaa yashkuroon.

36. Sabḥaanal-laz̲ee khalaqal-azwaaja kullahaa mimmaa tumbitul-arḍu wa min anfusihim wa mimmaa laa ya'lamoon.

37. Wa Aayatul-lahumul-laylu naslakhu minhun-nahaara fa-iz̲aa hum-muẓlimoon.

38. Wash-shamsu tajree limustaqarril-lahaa; z̲aalika taqdeerul-'Azeezil-'Aleem.

39. Walqamara qaddarnaahu manaazila ḥattaa 'aada kal'ur-joonil-qadeem.

40. Lash-shamsu yambaghee lahaaa an tudrikal-qamara wa lal-laylu saabiqun-nahaar; wa kullun fee falakiñy-yasbaḥoon.

41. Wa Aayatul-lahum-annaa ḥamalnaa z̲urriyyatahum fil-fulkil-mashḥoon.

42. Wa khalaqnaa lahum-mim-mis̲lihee maa yarkaboon.

43. Wa in nashaå nughriqhum falaa ṣareekha lahum wa laa hum yunqaz̲oon.

44. Illaa raḥmatam-minnaa wa mataa'an ilaa ḥeen.

45. Wa iz̲aa qeela lahumut-taqoo maa bayna aydeekum wa maa khalfakum la'allakum turḥamoon.

46. Wa maa taåteehim-min Aayatim-min Aayaati Rabbihim illaa kaanoo 'anhaa mu'riḍeen.

47. Wa iz̲aa qeela lahum anfiqoo mimmaa razaqakumul-laahu qaalal-laz̲eena kafaroo lillaz̲eena aamanooo

أَيْدِيهِمْ ۖ أَفَلَا يَشْكُرُونَ ﴿٣٥﴾
سُبْحَانَ الَّذِي خَلَقَ الْأَزْوَاجَ كُلَّهَا
مِمَّا تُنْبِتُ الْأَرْضُ وَمِنْ أَنْفُسِهِمْ
وَمِمَّا لَا يَعْلَمُونَ ﴿٣٦﴾
وَآيَةٌ لَهُمُ اللَّيْلُ ۚ نَسْلَخُ مِنْهُ النَّهَارَ
فَإِذَا هُمْ مُظْلِمُونَ ﴿٣٧﴾
وَالشَّمْسُ تَجْرِي لِمُسْتَقَرٍّ لَهَا ۚ ذَٰلِكَ
تَقْدِيرُ الْعَزِيزِ الْعَلِيمِ ﴿٣٨﴾
وَالْقَمَرَ قَدَّرْنَاهُ مَنَازِلَ حَتَّىٰ عَادَ
كَالْعُرْجُونِ الْقَدِيمِ ﴿٣٩﴾
لَا الشَّمْسُ يَنْبَغِي لَهَا أَنْ تُدْرِكَ
الْقَمَرَ وَلَا اللَّيْلُ سَابِقُ النَّهَارِ ۚ وَ
كُلٌّ فِي فَلَكٍ يَسْبَحُونَ ﴿٤٠﴾
وَآيَةٌ لَهُمْ أَنَّا حَمَلْنَا ذُرِّيَّتَهُمْ
فِي الْفُلْكِ الْمَشْحُونِ ﴿٤١﴾
وَخَلَقْنَا لَهُمْ مِنْ مِثْلِهِ مَا يَرْكَبُونَ ﴿٤٢﴾
وَإِنْ نَشَأْ نُغْرِقْهُمْ فَلَا صَرِيخَ لَهُمْ
وَلَا هُمْ يُنْقَذُونَ ﴿٤٣﴾
إِلَّا رَحْمَةً مِنَّا وَمَتَاعًا إِلَىٰ حِينٍ ﴿٤٤﴾
وَإِذَا قِيلَ لَهُمُ اتَّقُوا مَا بَيْنَ
أَيْدِيكُمْ وَمَا خَلْفَكُمْ لَعَلَّكُمْ
تُرْحَمُونَ ﴿٤٥﴾
وَمَا تَأْتِيهِمْ مِنْ آيَةٍ مِنْ آيَاتِ
رَبِّهِمْ إِلَّا كَانُوا عَنْهَا مُعْرِضِينَ ﴿٤٦﴾
وَإِذَا قِيلَ لَهُمْ أَنْفِقُوا مِمَّا رَزَقَكُمُ
اللَّهُ قَالَ الَّذِينَ كَفَرُوا لِلَّذِينَ آمَنُوا

Ikhfa اخفاء | Ghunna غُنّة | Ikhfa Meem Saakin اخفاء میم ساکن | Idghaam ادغام | Qalqala قلقلہ | Qalb قلب | Idghaam Meem Saakin ادغام میم ساکن

"Shall we then feed those whom, if Allah had so willed, He would have fed, (Himself)?- you are in nothing but manifest error."

48. Further, they say, "When will this promise (come to pass), if what you say is true?"

49. They will not (have to) wait for anything but a single Blast: it will seize them while they are yet disputing among themselves!

50. No (chance) will they then have, by will, to dispose (of their affairs), nor to return to their own people!

51. The trumpet shall be sounded, when behold! from the sepulchres (men) will rush forth to their Lord!

52. They will say: "Ah! woe unto us! Who has raised us up from our beds of repose?"... (A voice will say:) "This is what (Allah) Most Gracious had promised. And true was the word of the Apostles!"

53. It will be no more than a single Blast, when lo! they will all be brought up before Us!

54. Then, on that Day, not a soul will be wronged in the least, and you shall but be repaid the meeds of your past Deeds.

55. Verily the Companions of the Garden shall that Day have joy in all that they do;

56. They and their associates will be in groves of (cool) shade, reclining on Thrones (of dignity);

57. (Every) fruit (enjoyment) will be there for them; they shall have whatever they call for;

58. "Peace!"-a Word (of salutation) from a Lord, Most Merciful!

59. "And O you in sin! You get apart this Day!

60. "Did I not enjoin on you, O you children of Adam,

anuṭ'imu mal-law yashaaa'ul-laahu aṭ'amahooo in antum illaa fee ḍalaalim-mubeen.

48. Wa yaqooloona mataa haaẕal-wa'du in kuntum ṣaadiqeen.

49. Maa yanẓuroona illaa ṣayḥatañw-waaḥidatan taå-khuẕuhum wa hum yakhiṣ-ṣimoon.

50. Falaa yastaṭee'oona taw-ṣiyatañw-wa laaa ilaaa ahlihim yarji'oon. **(Section 3)**

51. Wa nufikha fiṣ-Ṣoori fa-iẕaa hum-minal-ajdaaṡi ilaa Rabbihim yansiloon.

52. Qaaloo yaa waylanaa mam ba'aṡanaa mim-marqa-dinaa; haaẕaa maa wa'adar-Raḥmanu wa ṣadaqal-mursa-loon.

53. In kaanat illaa ṣayḥatañw-waaḥidatan fa-iẕaa hum jamee'ul-ladaynaa muḥḍaroon.

54. Fal-Yawma laa tuẓlamu naf-sun shay'añw-wa laa tujzawna illaa maa kuntum ta'maloon.

55. Inna Aṣḥaabal-Jannatil-Yawma fee shughulin faaki-hoon.

56. Hum wa azwaajuhum fee ẓilaalin 'alal-araaa'iki mutta-ki'oon.

57. Lahum feehaa faakiha-tuñw-wa lahum-maa yadda'oon.

58. Salaamun qawlam-mir-Rabbir-Raḥeem.

59. Wamtaazul-Yawma ayyu-hal-mujrimoon.

60. Alam a'had ilaykum yaa Baneee Aadama

أَنُطْعِمُ مَن لَّوْ يَشَآءُ ٱللَّهُ أَطْعَمَهُۥٓ
إِنْ أَنتُمْ إِلَّا فِى ضَلَٰلٍ مُّبِينٍ ﴿٤٧﴾
وَيَقُولُونَ مَتَىٰ هَٰذَا ٱلْوَعْدُ إِن
كُنتُمْ صَٰدِقِينَ ﴿٤٨﴾
مَا يَنظُرُونَ إِلَّا صَيْحَةً وَٰحِدَةً
تَأْخُذُهُمْ وَهُمْ يَخِصِّمُونَ ﴿٤٩﴾
فَلَا يَسْتَطِيعُونَ تَوْصِيَةً وَلَآ إِلَىٰٓ
أَهْلِهِمْ يَرْجِعُونَ ﴿٥٠﴾
وَنُفِخَ فِى ٱلصُّورِ فَإِذَا هُم مِّنَ
ٱلْأَجْدَاثِ إِلَىٰ رَبِّهِمْ يَنسِلُونَ ﴿٥١﴾
قَالُوا۟ يَٰوَيْلَنَا مَنۢ بَعَثَنَا مِن
مَّرْقَدِنَا ۜ هَٰذَا مَا وَعَدَ ٱلرَّحْمَٰنُ
وَصَدَقَ ٱلْمُرْسَلُونَ ﴿٥٢﴾
إِن كَانَتْ إِلَّا صَيْحَةً وَٰحِدَةً
فَإِذَا هُمْ جَمِيعٌ لَّدَيْنَا مُحْضَرُونَ ﴿٥٣﴾
فَٱلْيَوْمَ لَا تُظْلَمُ نَفْسٌ شَيْـًٔا وَلَا
تُجْزَوْنَ إِلَّا مَا كُنتُمْ تَعْمَلُونَ ﴿٥٤﴾
إِنَّ أَصْحَٰبَ ٱلْجَنَّةِ ٱلْيَوْمَ فِى
شُغُلٍ فَٰكِهُونَ ﴿٥٥﴾
هُمْ وَأَزْوَٰجُهُمْ فِى ظِلَٰلٍ عَلَى
ٱلْأَرَآئِكِ مُتَّكِـُٔونَ ﴿٥٦﴾
لَهُمْ فِيهَا فَٰكِهَةٌ وَلَهُم مَّا
يَدَّعُونَ ﴿٥٧﴾
سَلَٰمٌ قَوْلًا مِّن رَّبٍّ رَّحِيمٍ ﴿٥٨﴾
وَٱمْتَٰزُوا۟ ٱلْيَوْمَ أَيُّهَا ٱلْمُجْرِمُونَ ﴿٥٩﴾
أَلَمْ أَعْهَدْ إِلَيْكُمْ يَٰبَنِىٓ ءَادَمَ

Ikhfa اخفاء | Ghunna غنّہ | Ikhfa Meem Saakin اخفاء میم ساکن | Idghaam ادغام | Qalqala قلقلہ | Qalb قلب | Idghaam Meem Saakin ادغام میم ساکن

that you should not worship Satan; for that he was to you an enemy avowed?-

al-laa ta'budush-Shayṭaana innahoo lakum 'aduwwum-mubeen.

أَنْ لَّا تَعْبُدُوا الشَّيْطٰنَ ۚ إِنَّهٗ لَكُمْ
عَدُوٌّ مُّبِيْنٌ ﴿٦٠﴾

61. "And that you should worship Me, (for that) this was the Straight Way?

61. Wa ani'-budoonee; haazaa Şiraaţum-Mustaqeem.

وَّأَنِ اعْبُدُوْنِيْ ۚ هٰذَا صِرَاطٌ
مُّسْتَقِيْمٌ ﴿٦١﴾ وقف غفران ١٢

62. "But he did lead astray a great multitude of you. Did you not, then, understand?

62. Wa laqad aḍalla minkum jibillan kaseeraa; afalam takoonoo ta'qiloon.

وَلَقَدْ أَضَلَّ مِنْكُمْ جِبِلًّا كَثِيْرًا ۖ
أَفَلَمْ تَكُوْنُوْا تَعْقِلُوْنَ ﴿٦٢﴾

63. "This is the Hell of which you were (repeatedly) warned!

63. Haazihee Jahannamul-latee kuntum too'adoon.

هٰذِهٖ جَهَنَّمُ الَّتِيْ كُنْتُمْ تُوْعَدُوْنَ ﴿٦٣﴾

64. "You embrace the (fire) this Day, for that you (persistently) rejected (Truth)."

64. Işlawhal-Yawma bimaa kuntum takfuroon.

اِصْلَوْهَا الْيَوْمَ بِمَا كُنْتُمْ تَكْفُرُوْنَ ﴿٦٤﴾

65. That Day We shall set a seal on their mouths. But their hands will speak to Us, and their feet bear witness, to all that they did.

65. Al-Yawma nakhtimu 'alaaa afwaahihim wa tukallimunaaa aydeehim wa tashhadu arjuluhum bimaa kaanoo yaksiboon.

اَلْيَوْمَ نَخْتِمُ عَلٰٓى أَفْوَاهِهِمْ وَ
تُكَلِّمُنَآ أَيْدِيْهِمْ وَتَشْهَدُ أَرْجُلُهُمْ
بِمَا كَانُوْا يَكْسِبُوْنَ ﴿٦٥﴾

66. If it had been Our Will, We could surely have blotted out their eyes; then should they have run about groping for the Path, but how could they have seen?

66. Wa law nashaaa'u laṭamasnaa 'alaaa a'yunihim fastabaquş-şiraaṭa fa-annaa yubşiroon.

وَلَوْ نَشَآءُ لَطَمَسْنَا عَلٰٓى أَعْيُنِهِمْ
فَاسْتَبَقُوا الصِّرَاطَ فَأَنّٰى يُبْصِرُوْنَ ﴿٦٦﴾

67. And if it had been Our Will, We could have transformed them (to remain) in their places; then they should have been unable to move about, nor could they have returned (after error).

67. Wa law nashaaa'u lamasakhnaahum 'alaa makaanatihim famas-taṭaa'oo muḍiyyañw-wa laa yarji'oon. **(Section 4)**

وَلَوْ نَشَآءُ لَمَسَخْنٰهُمْ عَلٰى مَكَانَتِهِمْ
فَمَا اسْتَطَاعُوْا مُضِيًّا وَّلَا يَرْجِعُوْنَ ﴿٦٧﴾ ع ٤

68. If We grant long life to any, We cause him to be reversed in nature: will they not then understand?

68. Wa man-nu'ammirhu nunakkishu fil-khalq; afalaa ya'qiloon.

وَمَنْ نُّعَمِّرْهُ نُنَكِّسْهُ فِي الْخَلْقِ
أَفَلَا يَعْقِلُوْنَ ﴿٦٨﴾

69. We have not instructed the (Prophet) in Poetry, nor is it meet for him: this is no less than a Message and a Qur'an making things clear:

69. Wa maa 'allamnaahush-shi'ra wa maa yambaghee lah; in huwa illaa zikruñw-wa Qur-aanum-Mubeen.

وَمَا عَلَّمْنٰهُ الشِّعْرَ وَمَا يَنْۢبَغِيْ لَهٗ ۚ
إِنْ هُوَ إِلَّا ذِكْرٌ وَّقُرْاٰنٌ مُّبِيْنٌ ﴿٦٩﴾

70. That it may give admonition to any (who are) alive, and that the charge may be proved against those who reject (Truth).

70. Liyunzira man kaana ḥayyañw-wa yaḥiqqal-qawlu 'alal-kaafireen.

لِّيُنْذِرَ مَنْ كَانَ حَيًّا وَّيَحِقَّ الْقَوْلُ
عَلَى الْكٰفِرِيْنَ ﴿٧٠﴾

71. Don't they See that it is We Who have created for them - among the things which Our hands have fashioned - cattle, which are under their dominion?-

71. Awalam yaraw annaa khalaqnaa lahum-mimmaa 'amilat aydeenaaa an'aaman fahum lahaa maalikoon.

أَوَلَمْ يَرَوْا أَنَّا خَلَقْنَا لَهُمْ مِّمَّا
عَمِلَتْ أَيْدِيْنَآ أَنْعَامًا فَهُمْ لَهَا
مٰلِكُوْنَ ﴿٧١﴾

72. And that We have subjected them to their (use)? of them some do carry them and some they eat:

72. Wa zallalnaahaa lahum faminhaa rakoobuhum wa minhaa yaákuloon.

وَذَلَّلْنٰهَا لَهُمْ فَمِنْهَا رَكُوْبُهُمْ
وَمِنْهَا يَأْكُلُوْنَ ﴿٧٢﴾

Ikhfa اخفاء | Ghunna غنّہ | Ikhfa Meem Saakin اخفاء میم ساکن | Idghaam ادغام | Qalqala قلقلہ | Qalb قلب | Idghaam Meem Saakin ادغام میم ساکن

73. And they have (other) profits from them (besides), and they get (milk) to drink. Will they not then be grateful?

74. Yet they take (for worship) gods other than Allah, (hoping) that they might be helped!

75. They have not the power to help them: but they will be brought up (before Our Judgment-seat) as a troop (to be condemned).

76. Let not their speech, then, grieve you. Verily We know what they hide as well as what they disclose.

77. Does not man see that it is We Who created him from sperm? Yet behold! he (stands forth) as an open adversary!

78. And he makes comparisons for Us, and forgets his own (origin and) Creation: he says, "Who can give life to (dry) bones and decomposed ones (at that)?"

79. Say, "He will give them life Who created them for the first time! for He is Well-versed in every kind of creation!-

80. "The same Who produces for you fire out of the green tree, when behold! you kindle therewith (your own fires)!

81. "Is not He Who created the heavens and the earth able to create the like thereof?" - yes, indeed! for He is the Creator Supreme, of skill and knowledge (infinite)!

82. Verily, when He intends a thing, His Command is, "Be", and it is!

83. So glory to Him in Whose hands is the dominion of all things: and to Him will you be all brought back.

37. Those ranged in Ranks

In the name of Allah, Most Gracious, Most Merciful.

1. By those who range themselves in ranks,

73. Wa lahum feehaa manaafi'u wa mashaarib; afalaa yashkuroon.

74. Wattakhazoo min doonil-laahi aalihatal-la'allahum yunṣaroon.

75. Laa yastaṭee'oona naṣrahum wa hum lahum jundum-muḥḍaroon.

76. Falaa yaḥzunka qawluhum; innaa na'lamu maa yusirroona wa maa yu'linoon.

77. Awalam yaral-insaanu annaa khalaqnaahu min-nuṭfatin fa-izaa huwa khaṣeemum-mubeen.

78. Wa ḍaraba lanaa masalañw-wa nasiya khalqahoo qaala mañy-yuḥyil-'izaama wa hiya rameem.

79. Qul yuḥyeehal-lazeee ansha-ahaaa awwala marrah; wa Huwa bikulli khalqin 'Aleem.

80. Allazee ja'ala lakum-minash-shajaril-akhḍari naaran fa-izaaa antum-minhu tooqidoon.

81. Awa laysal-lazee khalaqas-samaawaati wal-arḍa biqaadirin 'alaaa añy-yakhluqa mislahum; balaa wa Huwal-Khallaaqul-'Aleem.

82. Innamaaa amruhooo izaaa araada shay'an añy-yaqoola lahoo kun fa-yakoon.

83. Fa-Subḥaanal-lazee biyadihee malakootu kulli shay'iñw-wa ilayhi turja'oon. **(Sec. 5)**

Sûrat aṣ-Ṣâffât–37

(Revealed at Makkah)

Bismillaahir Raḥmaanir Raḥeem

1. Waṣṣaaaffaati ṣaffaa.

وَلَهُمْ فِيْهَا مَنَافِعُ وَمَشَارِبُ ط
اَفَلَا يَشْكُرُوْنَ ﴿٧٣﴾
وَاتَّخَذُوْا مِنْ دُوْنِ اللّٰهِ اٰلِهَةً
لَّعَلَّهُمْ يُنْصَرُوْنَ ﴿٧٤﴾
لَا يَسْتَطِيْعُوْنَ نَصْرَهُمْ وَهُمْ
لَهُمْ جُنْدٌ مُّحْضَرُوْنَ ﴿٧٥﴾
فَلَا يَحْزُنْكَ قَوْلُهُمْ م اِنَّا نَعْلَمُ
مَا يُسِرُّوْنَ وَمَا يُعْلِنُوْنَ ﴿٧٦﴾
اَوَلَمْ يَرَ الْاِنْسَانُ اَنَّا خَلَقْنٰهُ مِنْ
نُّطْفَةٍ فَاِذَا هُوَ خَصِيْمٌ مُّبِيْنٌ ﴿٧٧﴾
وَضَرَبَ لَنَا مَثَلًا وَّنَسِيَ خَلْقَهٗ ط قَالَ
مَنْ يُّحْيِ الْعِظَامَ وَهِيَ رَمِيْمٌ ﴿٧٨﴾
قُلْ يُحْيِيْهَا الَّذِيْٓ اَنْشَاَهَآ اَوَّلَ
مَرَّةٍ ط وَهُوَ بِكُلِّ خَلْقٍ عَلِيْمُۨ ﴿٧٩﴾
الَّذِيْ جَعَلَ لَكُمْ مِّنَ الشَّجَرِ الْاَخْضَرِ
نَارًا فَاِذَآ اَنْتُمْ مِّنْهُ تُوْقِدُوْنَ ﴿٨٠﴾
اَوَلَيْسَ الَّذِيْ خَلَقَ السَّمٰوٰتِ
وَالْاَرْضَ بِقٰدِرٍ عَلٰٓى اَنْ يَّخْلُقَ
مِثْلَهُمْ بَلٰى ق وَهُوَ الْخَلّٰقُ الْعَلِيْمُ ﴿٨١﴾
اِنَّمَآ اَمْرُهٗٓ اِذَآ اَرَادَ شَيْـًٔا اَنْ يَّقُوْلَ
لَهٗ كُنْ فَيَكُوْنُ ﴿٨٢﴾
فَسُبْحٰنَ الَّذِيْ بِيَدِهٖ مَلَكُوْتُ كُلِّ
شَيْءٍ وَّاِلَيْهِ تُرْجَعُوْنَ ﴿٨٣﴾ ع
(٣٧) سُوْرَةُ الصّٰٓفّٰتِ مَكِّيَّةٌ (٥٦)
بِسْمِ اللّٰهِ الرَّحْمٰنِ الرَّحِيْمِ
وَالصّٰٓفّٰتِ صَفًّا ﴿١﴾

وقف لازم
وقف غفران ۱۲
ع ۴/۲۵
المنزل السادس (٦)

Ikhfa اخفاء | Ghunna غنّہ | Ikhfa Meem Saakin اخفاء میم ساکن | Idghaam ادغام | Qalqala قلقلہ | Qalb قلب | Idghaam Meem Saakin ادغام میم ساکن

2. And so are strong in repelling (evil),	2. Fazzaajiraati zajraa.	فَالزّٰجِرٰتِ زَجْرًا ۙ﴿٢﴾
3. And thus proclaim the Message (of Allah)!	3. Fattaaliyaati Zikraa.	فَالتّٰلِيٰتِ ذِكْرًا ۙ﴿٣﴾
4. Verily, verily, your God (Allah) is One!-	4. Inna Ilaahakum la-Waaḥid.	اِنَّ اِلٰهَكُمْ لَوَاحِدٌ ؕ﴿٤﴾
5. Lord of the heavens and of the earth and all between them, and Lord of every point at the rising of the sun!	5. Rabbus-samaawaati wal-arḍi wa maa baynahumaa wa Rabbul-mashaariq.	رَبُّ السَّمٰوٰتِ وَالْاَرْضِ وَمَا بَيْنَهُمَا وَرَبُّ الْمَشَارِقِ ؕ﴿٥﴾
6. We have indeed decked the lower heaven with beauty (in) the stars,-	6. Innaa zayyannas-samaaa-'ad-dunyaa bizeenatinil-ka-waakib.	اِنَّا زَيَّنَّا السَّمَآءَ الدُّنْيَا بِزِيْنَةِ ٱلْكَوَاكِبِ ۙ﴿٦﴾
7. (For beauty) and for guard against all obstinate rebellious evil spirits,	7. Wa ḥifẓam-min kulli Shayṭaanim-maarid.	وَحِفْظًا مِّنْ كُلِّ شَيْطٰنٍ مَّارِدٍ ۚ﴿٧﴾
8. (So) they should not strain their ears in the direction of the Exalted Assembly but be cast away from every side,	8. Laa yassamma'oona ilal-mala-il-a'laa wa yuqzafoona min kulli jaanib.	لَا يَسَّمَّعُوْنَ اِلَى الْمَلَاِ الْاَعْلٰى وَيُقْذَفُوْنَ مِنْ كُلِّ جَانِبٍ ۖ﴿٨﴾
9. Repulsed, for they are under a perpetual Chastisement,	9. Duḥooranw-wa lahum 'azaabunw-waaṣib.	دُحُوْرًا وَّلَهُمْ عَذَابٌ وَّاصِبٌ ۙ﴿٩﴾
10. Except such as snatch away something by stealth, and they are pursued by a flaming Fire, of piercing brightness.	10. Illaa man khaṭifal-khaṭfata fa-atba'ahoo shihaabun saaqib.	اِلَّا مَنْ خَطِفَ الْخَطْفَةَ فَاَتْبَعَهٗ شِهَابٌ ثَاقِبٌ ﴿١٠﴾
11. Just ask their opinion: are they the more difficult to create, or the (other) beings We have created? We have created them out of a sticky clay!	11. Fastaftihim ahum ashaddu khalqan am-man khalaqnaa; innaa khalaqnaahum-min teenil-laazib.	فَاسْتَفْتِهِمْ اَهُمْ اَشَدُّ خَلْقًا اَمْ مَّنْ خَلَقْنَا ؕ اِنَّا خَلَقْنٰهُمْ مِّنْ طِيْنٍ لَّازِبٍ ﴿١١﴾
12. Truly you marvel, while they ridicule,-	12. Bal 'ajibta wa yaskharoon.	بَلْ عَجِبْتَ وَيَسْخَرُوْنَ ۪﴿١٢﴾
13. And, when they are admonished, pay no heed,-	13. Wa izaa zukkiroo laa yazkuroon.	وَاِذَا ذُكِّرُوْا لَا يَذْكُرُوْنَ ۪﴿١٣﴾
14. And, when they see a Sign, turn it to mockery,-	14. Wa izaa ra-aw Aayatanw-yastaskhiroon.	وَاِذَا رَاَوْا اٰيَةً يَّسْتَسْخِرُوْنَ ۪﴿١٤﴾
15. And say, "This is nothing but evident sorcery!	15. Wa qaalooo in haazaaa illaa siḥrum-mubeen.	وَقَالُوْٓا اِنْ هٰذَآ اِلَّا سِحْرٌ مُّبِيْنٌ ۚ﴿١٥﴾
16. "What! when we die, and become dust and bones, shall we (then) be raised up (again)	16. 'A-izaa mitnaa wa kunnaa turaabanw-wa 'izaaman 'a-innaa lamab'oosoon.	ءَاِذَا مِتْنَا وَكُنَّا تُرَابًا وَّعِظَامًا ءَاِنَّا لَمَبْعُوْثُوْنَ ۙ﴿١٦﴾
17. "And also our fathers of old?"	17. Awa aabaaa'unal-awwa-loon.	اَوَاٰبَآؤُنَا الْاَوَّلُوْنَ ؕ﴿١٧﴾
18. Say you: "Yes, and you shall then be humiliated (on account of your evil)."	18. Qul na'am wa antum daakhiroon.	قُلْ نَعَمْ وَاَنْتُمْ دَاخِرُوْنَ ۚ﴿١٨﴾
19. Then it will be a single (compelling) cry; and behold, they will begin to see!	19. Fa-innamaa hiya zajra-tunw-waaḥidatun fa-izaa hum yanẓuroon.	فَاِنَّمَا هِيَ زَجْرَةٌ وَّاحِدَةٌ فَاِذَا هُمْ يَنْظُرُوْنَ ﴿١٩﴾

Ikhfa اخفاء · Ghunna غنّہ · Ikhfa Meem Saakin اخفاء میم ساکن · Idghaam ادغام · Qalqala قلقلہ · Qalb قلب · Idghaam Meem Saakin ادغام میم ساکن

20. They will say, "Ah! woe to us! this is the Day of Judgment!"

21. (A voice will say,) "This is the Day of Sorting Out, whose Truth you (once) denied!"

22. "Bring you up", it shall be said, "The wrong-doers and their wives, and the things they worshipped-

23. "Besides Allah, and lead them to the Way to the (Fierce) Fire.

24. "But stop them, for they must be asked:

25. "'What is the matter with you that you do not help each other?'"

26. Nay, but that day they shall submit (to Judgment);

27. And they will turn to one another, and question one another.

28. They will say: "It was you who used to come to us from the right hand (of power and authority)!"

29. They will reply: "Nay, you yourselves had no Faith!

30. "Nor had we any authority over you. Nay, it was you who were a people in obstinate rebellion!

31. "So now has been proved true, against us, the Word of our Lord that we shall indeed (have to) taste (the punishment of our sins).

32. "We led you astray: for truly we were ourselves astray."

33. Truly, that Day, they will (all) share in the Chastisement.

34. Verily that is how We shall deal with sinners.

35. For they, when they were told that there is no god except Allah, would puff themselves up with pride,

36. And say: "What! shall we give up our gods for the sake of a Poet possessed?"

37. Nay! he has come with the (very) Truth, and he confirms (the Message of) the Apostles (before him).

20. Wa qaaloo yaa waylanaa haazaa Yawmud-Deen.

21. Haazaa Yawmul-Faṣlil-lazee kuntum bihee tukaz-ziboon. **(Section 1)**

22. Uḥshurul-lazeena ẓalamoo wa azwaajahum wa maa kaanoo ya'budoon.

23. Min doonil-laahi fahdoohum ilaa ṣiraaṭil-Jaḥeem.

24. Wa qifoohum innahum-mas'ooloon.

25. Maa lakum laa tanaaṣaroon.

26. Bal humul-Yawma mustaslimoon.

27. Wa aqbala ba'ḍuhum 'alaa ba'ḍiñy-yatasaaa'aloon.

28. Qaalooo innakum kuntum taåtoonanaa 'anil-yameen.

29. Qaaloo bal lam takoonoo mu'mineen.

30. Wa maa kaana lanaa 'alaykum-min sulṭaanim bal kuntum qawman ṭaagheen.

31. Faḥaqqa 'alaynaa qawlu Rabbinaaa innaa lazaaa'iqoon.

32. Fa-aghwaynaakum innaa kunnaa ghaaween.

33. Fa-innahum Yawma'izin fil-'azaabi mushtarikoon.

34. Innaa kazaalika naf'alu bil-mujrimeen.

35. Innahum kaanooo izaa qeela lahum laaa ilaaha illal-laahu yastakbiroon.

36. Wa yaqooloona a'innaa lataarikooo aalihatinaa lishaa'irim-majnoon.

37. Bal jaaa'a bilḥaqqi wa ṣaddaqal-mursaleen.

وَقَالُوْا يٰوَيْلَنَا هٰذَا يَوْمُ الدِّيْنِ ﴿٢٠﴾
هٰذَا يَوْمُ الْفَصْلِ الَّذِيْ كُنْتُمْ بِهٖ
تُكَذِّبُوْنَ ﴿٢١﴾ ع
اُحْشُرُوا الَّذِيْنَ ظَلَمُوْا وَاَزْوَاجَهُمْ
وَمَا كَانُوْا يَعْبُدُوْنَ ﴿٢٢﴾
مِنْ دُوْنِ اللّٰهِ فَاهْدُوْهُمْ اِلٰى صِرَاطِ
الْجَحِيْمِ ﴿٢٣﴾
وَقِفُوْهُمْ اِنَّهُمْ مَّسْـُٔوْلُوْنَ ﴿٢٤﴾
مَا لَكُمْ لَا تَنَاصَرُوْنَ ﴿٢٥﴾
بَلْ هُمُ الْيَوْمَ مُسْتَسْلِمُوْنَ ﴿٢٦﴾
وَاَقْبَلَ بَعْضُهُمْ عَلٰى بَعْضٍ يَّتَسَآءَلُوْنَ ﴿٢٧﴾
قَالُوْٓا اِنَّكُمْ كُنْتُمْ تَاْتُوْنَنَا عَنِ
الْيَمِيْنِ ﴿٢٨﴾
قَالُوْا بَلْ لَّمْ تَكُوْنُوْا مُؤْمِنِيْنَ ﴿٢٩﴾
وَمَا كَانَ لَنَا عَلَيْكُمْ مِّنْ سُلْطٰنٍ
بَلْ كُنْتُمْ قَوْمًا طٰغِيْنَ ﴿٣٠﴾
فَحَقَّ عَلَيْنَا قَوْلُ رَبِّنَآ اِنَّا
لَذَآئِقُوْنَ ﴿٣١﴾
فَاَغْوَيْنٰكُمْ اِنَّا كُنَّا غٰوِيْنَ ﴿٣٢﴾
فَاِنَّهُمْ يَوْمَئِذٍ فِى الْعَذَابِ مُشْتَرِكُوْنَ ﴿٣٣﴾
اِنَّا كَذٰلِكَ نَفْعَلُ بِالْمُجْرِمِيْنَ ﴿٣٤﴾
اِنَّهُمْ كَانُوْٓا اِذَا قِيْلَ لَهُمْ لَآ اِلٰهَ اِلَّا
اللّٰهُ يَسْتَكْبِرُوْنَ ﴿٣٥﴾
وَيَقُوْلُوْنَ اَئِنَّا لَتَارِكُوْٓا اٰلِهَتِنَا
لِشَاعِرٍ مَّجْنُوْنٍ ﴿٣٦﴾
بَلْ جَآءَ بِالْحَقِّ وَصَدَّقَ الْمُرْسَلِيْنَ ﴿٣٧﴾

ع ١ ٥ — الربع

Ikhfa اخفاء | Ghunna غُنّہ | Ikhfa Meem Saakin اخفاء میم ساکن | Idghaam ادغام | Qalqala قلقلہ | Qalb قلب | Idghaam Meem Saakin ادغام میم ساکن

38. You shall indeed taste of the grievous Chastisement;-
39. But it will be no more than the retribution of (the Evil) that you have wrought;-
40. But the sincere (and devoted) Servants of Allah,-
41. For them is a Sustenance determined,
42. Fruits (Delights); and they (shall enjoy) honour and dignity,
43. In Gardens of Felicity,
44. Facing each other on Thrones (of dignity):
45. Round will be passed to them a cup from a clear-flowing fountain,
46. Crystal-white, of a taste delicious to those who drink (thereof),
47. Free from headiness; nor will they suffer intoxication therefrom.
48. And besides them will be chaste women, restraining their glances, with big eyes (of wonder and beauty).
49. As if they were (delicate) eggs closely guarded.
50. Then they will turn to one another and question one another.
51. One of them will start the talk and say: "I had an intimate companion (on the earth),
52. Who used to say, "What! are you among those who bear witness to the truth (of the Message)?"
53. "'When we die and become dust and bones, shall we indeed receive rewards and punish-ments?'
54. (A voice) said: "Would you like to look down?"
55. He looked down and saw him in the midst of the Fire.
56. He said: "By Allah! you were little short of bringing me to perdition!
57. "Had it not been for the Grace of my Lord, I should certainly have been among those brought (there)!
58. "Is it (the case) that we shall not die,
59. "Except our first death, and that we shall not

38. Innakum lazaaa'iqul-'azaabil-aleem.
39. Wa maa tujzawna illaa maa kuntum ta'maloon.
40. Illaa 'ibaadal-laahil-mukhlaṣeen.
41. Ulaaa'ika lahum rizqum-ma'loom.
42. Fa waakihu wa hum-mukramoon.
43. Fee Jannaatin-Na'eem.
44. 'Alaa sururim-mutaqaabileen.
45. Yuṭaafu 'alayhim bikaåsim-mim-ma'een.
46. Bayḍaaa'a laz-zatil-lish-shaaribeen.
47. Laa feehaa ghawluñw-wa laa hum 'anhaa yunzafoon.
48. Wa 'indahum qaaṣiraatuṭ-ṭarfi 'een.
49. Ka-annahunna bayḍum-maknoon.
50. Fa-aqbala ba'ḍuhum 'alaa baḍiñy-yatasaaa'aloon.
51. Qaala qaaa'ilum-minhum innee kaana lee qareen.
52. Yaqoolu a'innaka laminal-muṣaddiqeen.
53. 'A-izaa mitnaa wa kunnaa turaabañw-wa 'izaaman 'a-innaa lamadeenoon.
54. Qaala hal antum-muṭṭali'oon.
55. Faṭṭala'a fara-aahu fee sawaaa'il-Jaḥeem.
56. Qaala tallaahi in kitta laturdeen.
57. Wa law laa ni'matu Rabbee lakuntu minal-muḥḍareen.
58. Afamaa naḥnu bimayyiteen.
59. Illa mawtatanal-oolaa wa maa naḥnu

إِنَّكُمْ لَذَآئِقُوا الْعَذَابِ الْأَلِيمِ ﴿٣٨﴾
وَمَا تُجْزَوْنَ إِلَّا مَا كُنتُمْ تَعْمَلُونَ ﴿٣٩﴾
إِلَّا عِبَادَ اللَّهِ الْمُخْلَصِينَ ﴿٤٠﴾
أُولَٰئِكَ لَهُمْ رِزْقٌ مَّعْلُومٌ ﴿٤١﴾
فَوَاكِهُ وَهُم مُّكْرَمُونَ ﴿٤٢﴾
فِي جَنَّاتِ النَّعِيمِ ﴿٤٣﴾
عَلَىٰ سُرُرٍ مُّتَقَابِلِينَ ﴿٤٤﴾
يُطَافُ عَلَيْهِم بِكَأْسٍ مِّن مَّعِينٍ ﴿٤٥﴾
بَيْضَاءَ لَذَّةٍ لِّلشَّارِبِينَ ﴿٤٦﴾
لَا فِيهَا غَوْلٌ وَلَا هُمْ عَنْهَا يُنزَفُونَ ﴿٤٧﴾
وَعِندَهُمْ قَاصِرَاتُ الطَّرْفِ عِينٌ ﴿٤٨﴾
كَأَنَّهُنَّ بَيْضٌ مَّكْنُونٌ ﴿٤٩﴾
فَأَقْبَلَ بَعْضُهُمْ عَلَىٰ بَعْضٍ
يَتَسَاءَلُونَ ﴿٥٠﴾
قَالَ قَائِلٌ مِّنْهُمْ إِنِّي كَانَ لِي
قَرِينٌ ﴿٥١﴾
يَقُولُ أَإِنَّكَ لَمِنَ الْمُصَدِّقِينَ ﴿٥٢﴾
أَإِذَا مِتْنَا وَكُنَّا تُرَابًا وَعِظَامًا
أَإِنَّا لَمَدِينُونَ ﴿٥٣﴾
قَالَ هَلْ أَنتُم مُّطَّلِعُونَ ﴿٥٤﴾
فَاطَّلَعَ فَرَآهُ فِي سَوَاءِ الْجَحِيمِ ﴿٥٥﴾
قَالَ تَاللَّهِ إِن كِدتَّ لَتُرْدِينِ ﴿٥٦﴾
وَلَوْلَا نِعْمَةُ رَبِّي لَكُنتُ مِنَ
الْمُحْضَرِينَ ﴿٥٧﴾
أَفَمَا نَحْنُ بِمَيِّتِينَ ﴿٥٨﴾
إِلَّا مَوْتَتَنَا الْأُولَىٰ وَمَا نَحْنُ

Ikhfa اخفاء · Ghunna غنّہ · Ikhfa Meem Saakin اخفاء میم ساکن · Idghaam ادغام · Qalqala قلقلہ · Qalb قلب · Idghaam Meem Saakin ادغام میم ساکن

be punished?"	bimu'azzabeen.	بِمُعَذَّبِيۡنَ ﴿٥٩﴾
60. Verily this is the supreme achievement!	60. Inna haazaa lahuwal-fawzul-'aẓeem.	اِنَّ هٰذَا لَهُوَ الۡفَوۡزُ الۡعَظِيۡمُ ﴿٦٠﴾
61. For the like of this let all strive, who wish to strive.	61. Limisli haazaa falya'ma-lil-'aamiloon.	لِمِثۡلِ هٰذَا فَلۡيَعۡمَلِ الۡعٰمِلُوۡنَ ﴿٦١﴾
62. Is that the better entertainment or the Tree of Zaqqum?	62. Azaalika khayrun-nuzu-lan am shajaratuz-Zaqqoom.	اَذٰلِكَ خَيۡرٌ نُّزُلًا اَمۡ شَجَرَةُ الزَّقُّوۡمِ ﴿٦٢﴾
63. For We have truly made it (as) a trial for the wrong-doers.	63. Innaa ja'alnaahaa fitnatal-liẓẓaalimeen.	اِنَّا جَعَلۡنٰهَا فِتۡنَةً لِّلظّٰلِمِيۡنَ ﴿٦٣﴾
64. For it is a tree that springs out of the bottom of Hell-fire:	64. Innahaa shajaratun takh-ruju feee aṣlil-Jaḥeem.	اِنَّهَا شَجَرَةٌ تَخۡرُجُ فِىۡۤ اَصۡلِ الۡجَحِيۡمِۙ ﴿٦٤﴾
65. The shoots of its fruit-stalks are like the heads of devils:	65. Ṭal'uhaa ka-annahoo ru'oosush-Shayaaṭeen.	طَلۡعُهَا كَاَنَّهٗ رُءُوۡسُ الشَّيٰطِيۡنِ ﴿٦٥﴾
66. Truly they will eat thereof and fill their bellies therewith.	66. Fa-innahum la-aakiloona minhaa famaali'oona minhal-buṭoon.	فَاِنَّهُمۡ لَاٰكِلُوۡنَ مِنۡهَا فَمٰلِـُٔوۡنَ مِنۡهَا الۡبُطُوۡنَؕ ﴿٦٦﴾
67. Then on top of that they will be given a mixture made of boiling water.	67. Summa inna lahum 'alay-haa lashawbam-min ḥameem.	ثُمَّ اِنَّ لَهُمۡ عَلَيۡهَا لَشَوۡبًا مِّنۡ حَمِيۡمٍۚ ﴿٦٧﴾
68. Then shall their return be to the (Blazing) Fire.	68. Summa inna marji'ahum la-ilal-Jaḥeem.	ثُمَّ اِنَّ مَرۡجِعَهُمۡ لَاِلَى الۡجَحِيۡمِ ﴿٦٨﴾
69. Truly they found their fathers on the wrong Path;	69. Innahum alfaw aabaaa'a-hum ḍaaalleen.	اِنَّهُمۡ اَلۡفَوۡا اٰبَآءَهُمۡ ضَآلِّيۡنَۙ ﴿٦٩﴾
70. So they (too) were rushed down on their footsteps!	70. Fahum 'alaaa aasaarihim yuhra'oon.	فَهُمۡ عَلٰٓى اٰثٰرِهِمۡ يُهۡرَعُوۡنَ ﴿٧٠﴾
71. And truly before them, many of the ancients went astray;	71. Wa laqad ḍalla qablahum aksarul-awwaleen.	وَلَقَدۡ ضَلَّ قَبۡلَهُمۡ اَكۡثَرُ الۡاَوَّلِيۡنَۙ ﴿٧١﴾
72. But We sent aforetime, among them, (Apostles) to admonish them;-	72. Wa laqad arsalnaa feehim-munzireen.	وَلَقَدۡ اَرۡسَلۡنَا فِيۡهِمۡ مُّنۡذِرِيۡنَ ﴿٧٢﴾
73. Then see what was the end of those who were admonished (but heeded not),-	73. Fanẓur kayfa kaana 'aaqi-batul-munzareen.	فَانۡظُرۡ كَيۡفَ كَانَ عَاقِبَةُ الۡمُنۡذَرِيۡنَۙ ﴿٧٣﴾
74. Except the sincere (and devoted) Servants of Allah.	74. Illaa 'ibaadal-laahil-mukhlaṣeen. **(Section 2)**	اِلَّا عِبَادَ اللّٰهِ الۡمُخۡلَصِيۡنَ ﴿٧٤﴾ ع
75. (In the days of old), Noah cried to Us, and We are the best to hear prayer.	75. Wa laqad naadaanaa Noohun falani'mal-mujeeboon.	وَلَقَدۡ نَادٰٮنَا نُوۡحٌ فَلَنِعۡمَ الۡمُجِيۡبُوۡنَ ۖ ﴿٧٥﴾
76. And We delivered him and his people from the Great Calamity,	76. Wa najjaynaahu wa ahla-hoo minal-karbil-'aẓeem.	وَنَجَّيۡنٰهُ وَاَهۡلَهٗ مِنَ الۡكَرۡبِ الۡعَظِيۡمِ ۖ ﴿٧٦﴾
77. And made his progeny to endure (on this earth)	77. Wa ja'alnaa zurriyyatahoo humul-baaqeen.	وَجَعَلۡنَا ذُرِّيَّتَهٗ هُمُ الۡبٰقِيۡنَ ۖ ﴿٧٧﴾
78. And We left (this blessing) for him among generations to come in later times:	78. Wa taraknaa 'alayhi fil-aakhireen.	وَتَرَكۡنَا عَلَيۡهِ فِى الۡاٰخِرِيۡنَ ۖ ﴿٧٨﴾
79. "Peace and salutation to Noah among the nations!"	79. Salaamun 'alaa Noohin fil-'aalameen.	سَلٰمٌ عَلٰى نُوۡحٍ فِى الۡعٰلَمِيۡنَ ﴿٧٩﴾

Ikhfa اخفاء · Ghunna غُنّہ · Ikhfa Meem Saakin اخفاء میم ساکن · Idghaam ادغام · Qalqala قلقلہ · Qalb قلب · Idghaam Meem Saakin ادغام میم ساکن

English	Transliteration	Arabic
80. Thus indeed do We reward those who do right.	80. Innaa kaz̲aalika najzil-muḥsineen.	إنا كذلك نجزي المحسنين ﴿٨٠﴾
81. For he was one of Our believing Servants.	81. Innahoo min 'ibaadinal-mu'mineen.	إنه من عبادنا المؤمنين ﴿٨١﴾
82. Then the rest We overwhelmed in the Flood.	82. S̲umma aghraqnal-aakhareen.	ثم أغرقنا الآخرين ﴿٨٢﴾
83. Verily among those who followed his Way was Abraham.	83. Wa inna min shee'atihee la-Ibraaheem.	وإن من شيعته لإبراهيم ﴿٨٣﴾
84. Behold! he approached his Lord with a sound heart.	84. Iz̲ jaaa'a Rabbahoo biqalbin saleem.	إذ جاء ربه بقلب سليم ﴿٨٤﴾
85. Behold! he said to his father and to his people, "What is that which you worship?	85. Iz̲ qaala li-abeehi wa qawmihee maaz̲aa ta'budoon.	إذ قال لأبيه وقومه ماذا تعبدون ﴿٨٥﴾
86. "Is it a falsehood - gods other than Allah- that you desire?	86. A'ifkan aalihatan doonal-laahi tureedoon.	أئفكا آلهة دون الله تريدون ﴿٨٦﴾
87. "Then what is your idea about the Lord of the Worlds?"	87. Famaa ẓannukum bi-Rabbil-'aalameen.	فما ظنكم برب العالمين ﴿٨٧﴾
88. Then did he cast a glance at the Stars.	88. Fanaẓara naẓratan finnu-joom.	فنظر نظرة في النجوم ﴿٨٨﴾
89. And he said, "I am indeed sick (at heart)!"	89. Faqaala innee saqeem.	فقال إني سقيم ﴿٨٩﴾
90. So they turned away from him, and departed.	90. Fatawallaw 'anhu mudbireen.	فتولوا عنه مدبرين ﴿٩٠﴾
91. Then did he turn to their gods and said, "Will you not eat (of the offerings before you)?...	91. Faraagha ilaaa aalihatihim faqaala alaa taåkuloon.	فراغ إلى آلهتهم فقال ألا تأكلون ﴿٩١﴾
92. "What is the matter with you that you speak not (intelligently)?"	92. Maa lakum laa tanṭiqoon.	ما لكم لا تنطقون ﴿٩٢﴾
93. Then did he turn upon them, striking (them) with the right hand.	93. Faraagha 'alayhim ḍarbam bilyameen.	فراغ عليهم ضربا باليمين ﴿٩٣﴾
94. Then came (the worshippers) with hurried steps, and faced (him).	94. Fa-aqbalooo ilayhi yazif-foon.	فأقبلوا إليه يزفون ﴿٩٤﴾
95. He said: "Do you worship that which you have (yourselves) car-ved?	95. Qaala ata'budoona maa tanḥitoon.	قال أتعبدون ما تنحتون ﴿٩٥﴾
96. "But Allah has created you and your handiwork!"	96. Wallaahu khalaqakum wa maa ta'maloon.	والله خلقكم وما تعملون ﴿٩٦﴾
97. They said, "Build him a furnace, and throw him into the blazing fire!"	97. Qaalub-noo lahoo bun-yaanan fa-alqoohu fil-jaḥeem.	قالوا ابنوا له بنيانا فألقوه في الجحيم ﴿٩٧﴾
98. (This failing), they then sought a strategem against him, but We made them the ones most humiliated!	98. Fa-araadoo bihee kaydan faja'alnaahumul-asfaleen.	فأرادوا به كيدا فجعلناهم الأسفلين ﴿٩٨﴾
99. He said: "I will go to my Lord! He will surely guide me!	99. Wa qaala innee z̲aahibun ilaa Rabbee sa-yahdeen.	وقال إني ذاهب إلى ربي سيهدين ﴿٩٩﴾
100. "O my Lord! Grant me a righteous (son)!"	100. Rabbi hab lee minaṣ-ṣaaliḥeen.	رب هب لي من الصالحين ﴿١٠٠﴾

وقف لازم

Ikhfa اخفاء | Ghunna غنّہ | Ikhfa Meem Saakin اخفاء میم ساکن | Idghaam ادغام | Qalqala قلقلہ | Qalb قلب | Idghaam Meem Saakin ادغام میم ساکن

101. So We gave him the good news of a boy ready to suffer and forbear.

102. Then, when (the son) reached (the age of) (serious) work with him, he said: "O my son! I see in vision that I offer you in sacrifice: now say what is your view!" (The son) said: "O my father! Do as you are commanded: you will find me, if Allah so wills, one practising patience and constancy!"

103. So when they had both submitted their wills (to Allah), and he had laid him prostrate on his forehead (for sacrifice),

104. We called out to him "O Abraham!

105. "You have already fulfilled the vision!" - thus indeed do We reward those who do right.

106. For this was obviously a trial,-

107. And We ransomed him with a momentous sacrifice:

108. And We left (this blessing) for him among generations (to come) in later times:

109. "Peace and salutation to Abraham!"

110. Thus indeed do We reward those who do right.

111. For he was one of Our believing Servants.

112. And We gave him the good news of Isaac - a prophet,- one of the Righteous.

113. We blessed him and Isaac: but of their progeny are (some) that do right, and (some) that obviously do wrong, to their own souls.

114. Again (of old) We bestowed Our favour on Moses and Aaron,

115. And We delivered them and their people from (their) Great Calamity;

116. And We helped them, so they overcame (their troubles);

117. And We gave them the Book which helps to make things clear;

101. Fabashsharnaahu bighulaamin ḥaleem.

102. Falammaa balagha ma'ahus-sa'ya qaala yaa bunayya inneee araa fil-manaami anneee azbaḥuka fanẓur maazaa taraa; qaala yaaa abatif-'al maa tu'maru satajiduneee in shaaa'-allaahu minaṣ-ṣaabireen.

103. Falammaaa aslamaa wa tallahoo liljabeen.

104. Wa naadaynaahu añy-yaaa Ibraaheem.

105. Qad ṣaddaqtar-ru'yaa; innaa kazaalika najzil-muḥsineen.

106. Inna haazaa lahuwal-balaaa'ul-mubeen

107. Wa fadaynaahu bizibḥin 'aẓeem.

108. Wa taraknaa 'alayhi fil-aakhireen.

109. Salaamun 'alaaa Ibraaheem.

110. Kazaalika najzil-muḥsineen.

111. Innahoo min 'ibaadinal-mu'mineen.

112. Wa bashsharnaahu bi-Isḥaaqa Nabiyyam-minaṣ-ṣaaliḥeen.

113. Wa baaraknaa 'alayhi wa 'alaaa Isḥaaq; wa min zurriyyatihimaa muḥsinuñw-wa ẓaalimul-linafsihee mubeen.

(Section 3)

114. Wa laqad manannaa 'alaa Moosaa wa Haaroon.

115. Wa najjaynaahumaa wa qawmahumaa minal-karbil-'aẓeem.

116. Wa naṣarnaahum fakaanoo humul-ghaalibeen.

117. Wa aataynaahumal-Kitaabal-mustabeen.

فَبَشَّرْنٰهُ بِغُلٰمٍ حَلِيْمٍ ﴿١٠١﴾

فَلَمَّا بَلَغَ مَعَهُ السَّعْيَ قَالَ يٰبُنَيَّ
إِنِّيْٓ أَرٰى فِي الْمَنَامِ أَنِّيْٓ أَذْبَحُكَ
فَانْظُرْ مَاذَا تَرٰى ۚ قَالَ يٰٓأَبَتِ افْعَلْ
مَا تُؤْمَرُ ۖ سَتَجِدُنِيْٓ إِنْ شَآءَ اللّٰهُ
مِنَ الصّٰبِرِيْنَ ﴿١٠٢﴾

فَلَمَّآ أَسْلَمَا وَتَلَّهٗ لِلْجَبِيْنِ ﴿١٠٣﴾

وَنٰدَيْنٰهُ أَنْ يّٰٓإِبْرٰهِيْمُ ﴿١٠٤﴾

قَدْ صَدَّقْتَ الرُّءْيَا ۚ إِنَّا كَذٰلِكَ
نَجْزِي الْمُحْسِنِيْنَ ﴿١٠٥﴾

إِنَّ هٰذَا لَهُوَ الْبَلٰٓؤُا الْمُبِيْنُ ﴿١٠٦﴾

وَفَدَيْنٰهُ بِذِبْحٍ عَظِيْمٍ ﴿١٠٧﴾

وَتَرَكْنَا عَلَيْهِ فِي الْاٰخِرِيْنَ ﴿١٠٨﴾

سَلٰمٌ عَلٰٓى إِبْرٰهِيْمَ ﴿١٠٩﴾

كَذٰلِكَ نَجْزِي الْمُحْسِنِيْنَ ﴿١١٠﴾

إِنَّهٗ مِنْ عِبَادِنَا الْمُؤْمِنِيْنَ ﴿١١١﴾

وَبَشَّرْنٰهُ بِإِسْحٰقَ نَبِيًّا مِّنَ
الصّٰلِحِيْنَ ﴿١١٢﴾

وَبٰرَكْنَا عَلَيْهِ وَعَلٰٓى إِسْحٰقَ ۖ
وَمِنْ ذُرِّيَّتِهِمَا مُحْسِنٌ وَّظَالِمٌ
لِّنَفْسِهٖ مُبِيْنٌ ﴿١١٣﴾ ع

وَلَقَدْ مَنَنَّا عَلٰى مُوْسٰى وَهٰرُوْنَ ﴿١١٤﴾

وَنَجَّيْنٰهُمَا وَقَوْمَهُمَا مِنَ الْكَرْبِ
الْعَظِيْمِ ﴿١١٥﴾

وَنَصَرْنٰهُمْ فَكَانُوْا هُمُ الْغٰلِبِيْنَ ﴿١١٦﴾

وَاٰتَيْنٰهُمَا الْكِتٰبَ الْمُسْتَبِيْنَ ﴿١١٧﴾

Ikhfa اخفاء | Ghunna غنّہ | Ikhfa Meem Saakin اخفاءميم ساكن | Idghaam ادغام | Qalqala قلقلہ | Qalb قلب | Idghaam Meem Saakin ادغام ميم ساكن

English	Transliteration	Arabic
118. And We guided them to the Straight Way.	118. Wa hadaynaahumuṣ-Ṣiraaṭal-Mustaqeem.	وَهَدَيْنَٰهُمَا ٱلصِّرَٰطَ ٱلْمُسْتَقِيمَ ﴿١١٨﴾
119. And We left (this blessing) for them among generations (to come) in later times:	119. Wa taraknaa 'alayhimaa fil-aakhireen.	وَتَرَكْنَا عَلَيْهِمَا فِى ٱلْءَاخِرِينَ ﴿١١٩﴾
120. "Peace and salutation to Moses and Aaron!"	120. Salaamun 'alaa Moosaa wa Haaroon.	سَلَٰمٌ عَلَىٰ مُوسَىٰ وَهَٰرُونَ ﴿١٢٠﴾
121. Thus indeed do We reward those who do right.	121. Innaa kaẕaalika najzil-muḥsineen.	إِنَّا كَذَٰلِكَ نَجْزِى ٱلْمُحْسِنِينَ ﴿١٢١﴾
122. For they were two of Our believing Servants.	122. Innahumaa min 'ibaadi-nal-mu'mineen.	إِنَّهُمَا مِنْ عِبَادِنَا ٱلْمُؤْمِنِينَ ﴿١٢٢﴾
123. So also was Elias among those sent (by Us).	123. Wa inna Ilyaasa laminal-mursaleen.	وَإِنَّ إِلْيَاسَ لَمِنَ ٱلْمُرْسَلِينَ ﴿١٢٣﴾
124. Behold, he said to his people, "Will you not fear (Allah)?	124. Iẕ qaala liqawmiheee alaa tattaqoon.	إِذْ قَالَ لِقَوْمِهِۦٓ أَلَا تَتَّقُونَ ﴿١٢٤﴾
125. "Will you call upon Baal and forsake the Best of Creators,	125. Atad'oona Ba'lañw-wa taẕaroona aḥsanal-khaaliqeen.	أَتَدْعُونَ بَعْلًا وَتَذَرُونَ أَحْسَنَ ٱلْخَٰلِقِينَ ﴿١٢٥﴾
126. "Allah, your Lord and Cherisher and the Lord and Cherisher of your fathers of old?"	126. Allaaha Rabbakum wa Rabba aabaaa'ikumul-awwaleen.	ٱللَّهَ رَبَّكُمْ وَرَبَّ ءَابَآئِكُمُ ٱلْأَوَّلِينَ ﴿١٢٦﴾
127. But they rejected him, and they will certainly be called up (for punishment),-	127. Fakaẕẕaboohu fa-inna hum lamuḥḍaroon.	فَكَذَّبُوهُ فَإِنَّهُمْ لَمُحْضَرُونَ ﴿١٢٧﴾
128. Except the sincere and devoted Servants of Allah (among them).	128. Illaa 'ibaadal-laahil-mukhlaṣeen.	إِلَّا عِبَادَ ٱللَّهِ ٱلْمُخْلَصِينَ ﴿١٢٨﴾
129. And We left (this blessing) for him among generations (to come) in later times:	129. Wa taraknaa 'alayhi fil-aakhireen.	وَتَرَكْنَا عَلَيْهِ فِى ٱلْءَاخِرِينَ ﴿١٢٩﴾
130. "Peace and salutation to such as Elias!"	130. Salaamun 'alaaa Ilyaa-seen.	سَلَٰمٌ عَلَىٰٓ إِلْ يَاسِينَ ﴿١٣٠﴾
131. Thus indeed do We reward those who do right.	131. Innaa kaẕaalika najzil-muḥsineen.	إِنَّا كَذَٰلِكَ نَجْزِى ٱلْمُحْسِنِينَ ﴿١٣١﴾
132. For he was one of Our believing Servants.	132. Innahoo min 'ibaadinal-mu'mineen.	إِنَّهُۥ مِنْ عِبَادِنَا ٱلْمُؤْمِنِينَ ﴿١٣٢﴾
133. So also was Lut among those sent (by Us).	133. Wa inna Looṭal-laminal-mursaleen.	وَإِنَّ لُوطًا لَّمِنَ ٱلْمُرْسَلِينَ ﴿١٣٣﴾
134. Behold, We delivered him and his adherents, all;	134. Iẕ najjaynaahu wa ahla-hooo ajma'een.	إِذْ نَجَّيْنَٰهُ وَأَهْلَهُۥٓ أَجْمَعِينَ ﴿١٣٤﴾
135. Except an old woman who was among those who lagged behind:	135. Illaa 'ajoozan fil-ghaa-bireen.	إِلَّا عَجُوزًا فِى ٱلْغَٰبِرِينَ ﴿١٣٥﴾
136. Then We destroyed the rest.	136. Summa dammarnal-aa-khareen.	ثُمَّ دَمَّرْنَا ٱلْءَاخَرِينَ ﴿١٣٦﴾
137. Verily, you pass by their (sites), by day-	137. Wa innakum latamurroona 'alayhim-muṣbiḥeen.	وَإِنَّكُمْ لَتَمُرُّونَ عَلَيْهِم مُّصْبِحِينَ ﴿١٣٧﴾
138. And by night: will you not understand?	138. Wa billayl; afalaa ta'qi-loon. **(Section 4)**	وَبِٱلَّيْلِ أَفَلَا تَعْقِلُونَ ﴿١٣٨﴾ ع
139. So also was Jonah among those sent (by Us).	139. Wa inna Yoonusa laminal-mursaleen.	وَإِنَّ يُونُسَ لَمِنَ ٱلْمُرْسَلِينَ ﴿١٣٩﴾
140. When he ran away (like a slave from captivity) to the ship (fully) laden,	140. Iẕ abaqa ilal-fulkil-mash-ḥoon.	إِذْ أَبَقَ إِلَى ٱلْفُلْكِ ٱلْمَشْحُونِ ﴿١٤٠﴾
141. He (agreed to) cast lots, and he was condemned:	141. Fasaahama fakaana minal-mudḥaḍeen.	فَسَاهَمَ فَكَانَ مِنَ ٱلْمُدْحَضِينَ ﴿١٤١﴾
142. Then the big fish swallowed him, and he had done acts worthy of blame.	142. Faltaqamahul-ḥootu wa huwa muleem.	فَٱلْتَقَمَهُ ٱلْحُوتُ وَهُوَ مُلِيمٌ ﴿١٤٢﴾

Ikhfa اخفاء | Ghunna غنّہ | Ikhfa Meem Saakin اخفاء میم ساکن | Idghaam ادغام | Qalqala قلقلہ | Qalb قلب | Idghaam Meem Saakin ادغام میم ساکن

143. Had it not been that he (repented and) glorified Allah,
144. He would certainly have remained inside the fish till the Day of Resurrection.
145. But We cast him forth on the naked shore in a state of sickness,
146. And We caused to grow, over him, a spreading plant of
147. And We sent him (on a mission) to a hundred thousand (men) or more.
148. And they believe; so We permitted them to enjoy (their life) for a while.
149. Now ask them their opinion: is it that your Lord has (only) daughters, and they have sons?-
150. Or that We created the angels female, and they are witnesses (thereto)?
151. Is it not, that they say, from their own invention,
152. "Allah has begotten children"? But they are liars!
153. Did He (then) choose daughters rather than sons?
154. What is the matter with you? How do you judge?
155. Will you not then receive admonition.
156. Or do you have an authority manifest?
157. Then you bring your Book (of authority) if you be truthful!
158. And they have invented a blood-relationship between Him and the Jinns: but the Jinns know (quite well) that they have indeed to appear (before His Judgment-seat)!
159. Glory to Allah! (He is free) from the things they ascribe (to Him)!
160. Not (so do) the Servants of Allah, sincere and devoted.
161. For, verily, neither you nor those you worship-
162. Can lead (any) into temptation concerning Allah,
163. Except such as are (themselves) going to the blazing Fire!
164. (Those ranged in ranks say): "Not one of us but has a place appointed;

143. Falaw laaa annahoo kaana minal-musabbiḥeen.
144. Lalabiṡa fee baṭniheee ilaa Yawmi yub'aṡoon.
145. Fanabaẕnaahu bil'araaa'i wa huwa saqeem.
146. Wa ambatnaa 'alayhi shajaratam-miñy-yaqṭeen.
147. Wa arsalnaahu ilaa mi'ati alfin aw yazeedoon.
148. Fa-aamanoo famatta'-naahum ilaa ḥeen.
149. Fastaftihim ali-Rabbikal-banaatu wa lahumul-banoon.
150. Am khalaqnal-malaaa'i-kata inaasañw-wa hum shaahi-doon.
151. Alaaa innahum-min ifki-him la-yaqooloon.
152. Waladal-laahu wa inna-hum lakaaẕiboon.
153. Aṣṭafal-banaati 'alal-ba-neen.
154. Maa lakum kayfa taḥku-moon.
155. Afalaa taẕakkaroon.
156. Am lakum sulṭaanum-mubeen.
157. Faâtoo bi-Kitaabikum in kuntum ṣaadiqeen.
158. Wa ja'aloo baynahoo wa baynal-jinnati nasabaa; wa laqad 'alimatil-jinnatu innahum lamuḥḍaroon.
159. Subḥaanal-laahi 'ammaa yaṣifoon.
160. Illaa 'ibaadal-laahil-mukhlaṣeen.
161. Fa-innakum wa maa ta'bu-doon.
162. Maaa antum 'alayhi bifaa-tineen.
163. Illaa man huwa ṣaalil-Jaḥeem.
164. Wa maa minnaa illaa lahoo maqaamum-ma'loom.

فَلَوْلَآ أَنَّهُۥ كَانَ مِنَ ٱلْمُسَبِّحِينَ ﴿١٤٣﴾
لَلَبِثَ فِى بَطْنِهِۦٓ إِلَىٰ يَوْمِ يُبْعَثُونَ ﴿١٤٤﴾
فَنَبَذْنَٰهُ بِٱلْعَرَآءِ وَهُوَ سَقِيمٌ ﴿١٤٥﴾
وَأَنۢبَتْنَا عَلَيْهِ شَجَرَةً مِّن يَقْطِينٍ ﴿١٤٦﴾
وَأَرْسَلْنَٰهُ إِلَىٰ مِا۟ئَةِ أَلْفٍ أَوْ
يَزِيدُونَ ﴿١٤٧﴾
فَـَٔامَنُوا۟ فَمَتَّعْنَٰهُمْ إِلَىٰ حِينٍ ﴿١٤٨﴾
فَٱسْتَفْتِهِمْ أَلِرَبِّكَ ٱلْبَنَاتُ وَلَهُمُ
ٱلْبَنُونَ ﴿١٤٩﴾
أَمْ خَلَقْنَا ٱلْمَلَٰٓئِكَةَ إِنَٰثًا وَهُمْ
شَٰهِدُونَ ﴿١٥٠﴾
أَلَآ إِنَّهُم مِّنْ إِفْكِهِمْ لَيَقُولُونَ ﴿١٥١﴾
وَلَدَ ٱللَّهُ وَإِنَّهُمْ لَكَٰذِبُونَ ﴿١٥٢﴾
أَصْطَفَى ٱلْبَنَاتِ عَلَى ٱلْبَنِينَ ﴿١٥٣﴾
مَا لَكُمْ كَيْفَ تَحْكُمُونَ ﴿١٥٤﴾
أَفَلَا تَذَكَّرُونَ ﴿١٥٥﴾
أَمْ لَكُمْ سُلْطَٰنٌ مُّبِينٌ ﴿١٥٦﴾
فَأْتُوا۟ بِكِتَٰبِكُمْ إِن كُنتُمْ صَٰدِقِينَ ﴿١٥٧﴾
وَجَعَلُوا۟ بَيْنَهُۥ وَبَيْنَ ٱلْجِنَّةِ نَسَبًا ۚ وَ
لَقَدْ عَلِمَتِ ٱلْجِنَّةُ إِنَّهُمْ لَمُحْضَرُونَ ﴿١٥٨﴾
سُبْحَٰنَ ٱللَّهِ عَمَّا يَصِفُونَ ﴿١٥٩﴾
إِلَّا عِبَادَ ٱللَّهِ ٱلْمُخْلَصِينَ ﴿١٦٠﴾
فَإِنَّكُمْ وَمَا تَعْبُدُونَ ﴿١٦١﴾
مَآ أَنتُمْ عَلَيْهِ بِفَٰتِنِينَ ﴿١٦٢﴾
إِلَّا مَنْ هُوَ صَالِ ٱلْجَحِيمِ ﴿١٦٣﴾
وَمَا مِنَّآ إِلَّا لَهُۥ مَقَامٌ مَّعْلُومٌ ﴿١٦٤﴾

الصّٰفّٰت

Ikhfa اخفاء · Ghunna غنّہ · Ikhfa Meem Saakin اخفاء میم ساکن · Idghaam ادغام · Qalqala قلقلہ · Qalb قلب · Idghaam Meem Saakin ادغام میم ساکن

165. "And we are verily ranged in ranks (for service);
166. "And we are verily those who declare (Allah's) glory!"
167. And there were those who said,
168. "If only we had had before us a Message from those of old,
169. "We should certainly have been Servants of Allah, sincere (and devoted)!"
170. But (now that the Qur'an has come), they reject it: but soon will they know!
171. Already has Our Word been passed before (this) to Our Servants sent (by Us),
172. That they would certainly be assisted,
173. And that Our forces,- they surely must conquer.
174. So you turn away from them for a little while,
175. And watch them (how they fare), and they soon shall see (how you fare)!
176. Do they wish (indeed) to hurry on our Punishment?
177. But when if descends into the open space before them, evil will be the morning for those who were warned (and heeded not)!
178. So you turn away from them for a little while,
179. And watch (how they fare) and they soon shall see (how you fare)!
180. Glory to your Lord, the Lord of Honor and Power! (He is free) from what they ascribe (to Him)!
181. And Peace on the Apostles!
182. And praise to Allah, the Lord and cherisher of the Worlds!

165. Wa innaa lanaḥnuṣ-ṣaaaffoon.
166. Wa innaa lanaḥnul-musabbiḥoon.
167. Wa in kaanoo la-yaqoo-loon.
168. Law anna 'indanaa zik-ram-minal-awwaleen.
169. Lakunnaa 'ibaadal-laahil-mukhlaṣeen.
170. Fakafaroo bihee fasawfa ya'lamoon.
171. Wa laqad sabaqat Kali-matunaa li'ibaadinal-mursa-leen.
172. Innahum lahumul-man-ṣooroon.
173. Wa inna jundanaa lahu-mul-ghaaliboon.
174. Fatawalla 'anhum ḥatta ḥeen.
175. Wa abṣirhum fasawfa yubṣiroon.
176. Afabi'aẕaabinaa yas-ta'jiloon.
177. Fa-iẕaa nazala bisaaḥa-tihim fasaaa'a ṣabaaḥul-munẕareen.
178. Wa tawalla 'anhum ḥattaa ḥeen.
179. Wa abṣir fasawfa yubṣi-roon.
180. Subḥaana Rabbika Rab-bil-'izzati 'ammaa yaṣifoon.
181. Wa salaamun 'alal-mursaleen.
182. Walḥamdu lillaahi Rabbil-'aalameen. **(Section 5)**

وَإِنَّا لَنَحْنُ الصَّافُّونَ ١٦٥
وَإِنَّا لَنَحْنُ الْمُسَبِّحُونَ ١٦٦
وَإِنْ كَانُوا لَيَقُولُونَ ١٦٧
لَوْ أَنَّ عِنْدَنَا ذِكْرًا مِنَ الْأَوَّلِينَ ١٦٨
لَكُنَّا عِبَادَ اللَّهِ الْمُخْلَصِينَ ١٦٩
فَكَفَرُوا بِهِ فَسَوْفَ يَعْلَمُونَ ١٧٠
وَلَقَدْ سَبَقَتْ كَلِمَتُنَا لِعِبَادِنَا الْمُرْسَلِينَ ١٧١
إِنَّهُمْ لَهُمُ الْمَنْصُورُونَ ١٧٢
وَإِنَّ جُنْدَنَا لَهُمُ الْغَالِبُونَ ١٧٣
فَتَوَلَّ عَنْهُمْ حَتَّىٰ حِينٍ ١٧٤
وَأَبْصِرْهُمْ فَسَوْفَ يُبْصِرُونَ ١٧٥
أَفَبِعَذَابِنَا يَسْتَعْجِلُونَ ١٧٦
فَإِذَا نَزَلَ بِسَاحَتِهِمْ فَسَاءَ صَبَاحُ الْمُنْذَرِينَ ١٧٧
وَتَوَلَّ عَنْهُمْ حَتَّىٰ حِينٍ ١٧٨
وَأَبْصِرْ فَسَوْفَ يُبْصِرُونَ ١٧٩
سُبْحَانَ رَبِّكَ رَبِّ الْعِزَّةِ عَمَّا يَصِفُونَ ١٨٠
وَسَلَامٌ عَلَى الْمُرْسَلِينَ ١٨١
وَالْحَمْدُ لِلَّهِ رَبِّ الْعَالَمِينَ ١٨٢

38. Saad

In the name of Allah, Most Gracious, Most Merciful.

Sûrat Ṣâd–38

(Revealed at Makkah)

Bismillaahir Raḥmaanir Raḥeem

(٣٨) سُورَةُ صٓ مَكِّيَّةٌ (٣٨)

بِسْمِ اللَّهِ الرَّحْمَٰنِ الرَّحِيمِ

1. *Saad*: by the Qur'an, Full of Admonition: (this is the Truth).
2. But the Unbelievers (are steeped) in Self-glory and Separatism.
3. How many generations before them did We destroy?

1. Ṣaaad; wal-Qur-aani ziẕ-ẕikr.
2. Balil-laẕeena kafaroo fee 'izzatiñw-wa shiqaaq.
3. Kam ahlaknaa min qabli-him-min qarnin

صٓ وَالْقُرْآنِ ذِي الذِّكْرِ ١
بَلِ الَّذِينَ كَفَرُوا فِي عِزَّةٍ وَشِقَاقٍ ٢
كَمْ أَهْلَكْنَا مِنْ قَبْلِهِمْ مِنْ قَرْنٍ

Ikhfa اخفاء | Ghunna غنّہ | Ikhfa Meem Saakin اخفاء میم ساکن | Idghaam ادغام | Qalqala قلقلہ | Qalb قلب | Idghaam Meem Saakin ادغام میم ساکن

In the end they cried (for mercy)- when there was no longer time for being saved!

fanaadaw wa laata ḥeena manaaṣ.

فَنَادَوْا وَّلَاتَ حِيْنَ مَنَاصٍ ﴿٣﴾

4. So they wonder that a Warner has come to them from among themselves! and the Unbelievers say, "This is a sorce-rer telling lies!

4. Wa 'ajibooo an jaaa'a-hum-munzirum-minhum wa qaalal-kaafiroona haazaa saaḥi-run kazzaab.

وَعَجِبُوْٓا اَنْ جَآءَهُمْ مُّنْذِرٌ مِّنْهُمْ وَقَالَ الْكٰفِرُوْنَ هٰذَا سٰحِرٌ كَذَّابٌ ﴿٤﴾

5. "Has he made the gods (all) into one God (Allah)? Truly this is a wonderful thing!"

5. Aja'alal-aalihata Ilaahañw-Waaḥidan inna haazaa lashay-'un 'ujaab.

اَجَعَلَ الْاٰلِهَةَ اِلٰهًا وَّاحِدًا ۚ اِنَّ هٰذَا لَشَيْءٌ عُجَابٌ ﴿٥﴾

6. And the leader among them go away (impatiently), (saying), "Walk you away, and remain constant to your gods! For this is truly a thing designed (against you)!

6. Wanṭalaqal-mala-u min-hum anim-shoo waṣbiroo 'alaaa aalihatikum inna haazaa lashay'uñy-yuraad.

وَانْطَلَقَ الْمَلَاُ مِنْهُمْ اَنِ امْشُوْا وَاصْبِرُوْا عَلٰٓى اٰلِهَتِكُمْ ۚ اِنَّ هٰذَا لَشَيْءٌ يُّرَادُ ﴿٦﴾

7. "We never heard (the like) of this among the people of these latter days: this is nothing but a made-up tale!"

7. Maa sami'naa bihaazaa fil-millatil-aakhirati in haazaaa illakh-tilaaq.

مَا سَمِعْنَا بِهٰذَا فِي الْمِلَّةِ الْاٰخِرَةِ ۚ اِنْ هٰذَآ اِلَّا اخْتِلَاقٌ ﴿٧﴾

8. "What! has the Message been sent to him - (of all persons) among us?"...But they are in doubt concerning My (Own) Message! Nay, they have not yet tasted My Punishment!

8. 'A-unzila 'alayhiz-zikru mim bayninaa; bal hum fee shakkim-min Zikree bal lammaa yazooqoo 'azaab.

ءَاُنْزِلَ عَلَيْهِ الذِّكْرُ مِنْۢ بَيْنِنَا ؕ بَلْ هُمْ فِيْ شَكٍّ مِّنْ ذِكْرِيْ ۚ بَلْ لَّمَّا يَذُوْقُوْا عَذَابِ ﴿٨﴾

9. Or have they the Treasures of the Mercy of your Lord,- the Exalted in Power, the Grantor of Bounties without measure?

9. Am 'indahum khazaaa'inu raḥmati Rabbikal-'Azeezil-Wahhaab.

اَمْ عِنْدَهُمْ خَزَآئِنُ رَحْمَةِ رَبِّكَ الْعَزِيْزِ الْوَهَّابِ ﴿٩﴾

10. Or have they the dominion of the heavens and the earth and all between? If so, let them mount up with the ropes and means (to reach that end)!

10. Am lahum-mulkus-samaa-waati wal-arḍi wa maa bayna-humaa falyartaqoo fil-asbaab.

اَمْ لَهُمْ مُّلْكُ السَّمٰوٰتِ وَالْاَرْضِ وَمَا بَيْنَهُمَا ۣ فَلْيَرْتَقُوْا فِي الْاَسْبَابِ ﴿١٠﴾

11. But there - will be put to flight even a host of confede-rates.

11. Jundum-maa hunaalika mahzoomum-minal-Aḥzaab.

جُنْدٌ مَّا هُنَالِكَ مَهْزُوْمٌ مِّنَ الْاَحْزَابِ ﴿١١﴾

12. Before them (were many who) rejected Apostles,- the People of Noah, and 'Ad, and Pharaoh, the Lord of Stakes,

12. Kazzabat qablahum qaw-mu Nooḥiñw-wa 'Aaduñw-wa Fir'awnu zul-awtaad.

كَذَّبَتْ قَبْلَهُمْ قَوْمُ نُوْحٍ وَّعَادٌ وَّفِرْعَوْنُ ذُو الْاَوْتَادِ ﴿١٢﴾

13. And Thamud, and the people of Lut, and the Compa-nions of the Wood; - such were the Confederates.

13. Wa Samoodu wa qawmu Looṭiñw-wa Aṣḥaabul-'Aykah; ulaaa'ikal-Aḥzaab.

وَثَمُوْدُ وَقَوْمُ لُوْطٍ وَّاَصْحٰبُ لْئَيْكَةِ ؕ اُولٰٓئِكَ الْاَحْزَابُ ﴿١٣﴾

14. Not one (of them) but rejected the Apostles, but My Punishment came justly and inevitably (on them).

14. In kullun illaa kazzabar-Rusula faḥaqqa 'iqaab.

(Section 1)

اِنْ كُلٌّ اِلَّا كَذَّبَ الرُّسُلَ فَحَقَّ عِقَابِ ﴿١٤﴾

15. These (today) only wait for a single mighty Blast,

15. Wa maa yanẓuru haaa-ulaaa'i illaa ṣayḥatañw-

وَمَا يَنْظُرُ هٰٓؤُلَآءِ اِلَّا صَيْحَةً

Ikhfa	Ghunna	Ikhfa Meem Saakin	Idghaam	Qalqala	Qalb	Idghaam Meem Saakin
اخفاء	غنّہ	اخفاء میم ساکن	ادغام	قلقلہ	قلب	ادغام میم ساکن

which (when it comes) will brook no delay.

16. They say: "Our Lord! hasten to us our sentence (even) before the Day of Account!"

17. Have patience at what they say, and remember Our Servant David, the man of strength: for he ever turned (to Allah).

18. It was We that made the hills declare, in unison with him, Our praises, at eventide and at break of day,

19. And the birds gathered (in assemblies): all with him turned (to Allah).

20. We strengthened his kingdom, and gave him wisdom and sound judgment in speech and decision.

21. Has the story of the Disputants reached you? Behold, they climbed over the wall of the private chamber;

22. When they entered the presence of David, and he was terrified of them, they said: "Fear not: we are two disputants, one of whom has wronged the other: Decide now between us with truth, and treat us not with injustice, but guide us to the even Path.

23. "This man is my brother: he has nine and ninety ewes, and I have (but) one: yet he says, 'Commit her to my care,' and is (moreover) harsh to me in speech."

24. (David) said: "He has undoubtedly wronged you in demanding your (single) ewe to be added to his (flock of) ewes: truly many are the partners (in business) who wrong each other: not so do those who believe and work deeds of righteousness, and how few are they?"... and David gathered that We had tried him: he asked for-giveness of his Lord, fell down, bowing (in prostration), and turned (to Allah in repentance).

(Bow Down)

25. So We forgave him this (lapse): he enjoyed, indeed, a Near Approach to Us,

---

waaḥidatam-maa lahaa min fawaaq.

16. Wa qaaloo Rabbanaa 'ajjil lanaa qiṭṭanaa qabla Yawmil-Ḥisaab.

17. Iṣbir 'alaa maa yaqooloona wazkur 'abdanaa Daawooda zal-aydi innahooo awwaab.

18. Innaa sakhkharnal-jibaala ma'ahoo yusabbiḥna bil'ashiyyi wal-ishraaq.

19. Waṭṭayra maḥshoorah; kullul-lahooo awwaab.

20. Wa shadadnaa mulkahoo wa aataynaahul-Ḥikmata wa faṣlal-khiṭaab.

21. Wa hal ataaka naba'ul-khaṣm; iz tasawwarul-miḥraab.

22. Iz dakhaloo 'alaa Daawooda fafazi'a minhum qaaloo laa takhaf khaṣmaani baghaa ba'ḍunaa 'alaa ba'ḍin faḥkum baynanaa bilḥaqqi wa laa tushṭiṭ wahdinaaa ilaa Sawaaa'iṣ-Ṣiraaṭ.

23. Inna haazaaa akhee lahoo tis'uñw-wa tis'oona na'jatañw-wa liya na'jatuñw-waaḥidah; faqaala akfilneehaa wa 'azzanee filkhiṭaab.

24. Qaala laqad ẓalamaka bisu'aali na'jatika ilaa ni'aajihee wa inna kaseeram-minal-khulaṭaaa'i la-yabghee ba'ḍuhum 'alaa ba'ḍin illal-lazeena aamanoo wa 'amiluṣ-ṣaaliḥaati wa qaleelum-maa hum; wa ẓanna Daawoodu annamaa fatannaahu fastaghfara Rabbahoo wa kharra raaki'añw-wa anaab. ۩

25. Faghafarnaa lahoo zaalik; wa inna lahoo 'indanaa

وَّاحِدَةً مَّا لَهَا مِنْ فَوَاقٍ ﴿١٥﴾
وَقَالُوْا رَبَّنَا عَجِّلْ لَّنَا قِطَّنَا قَبْلَ
يَوْمِ الْحِسَابِ ﴿١٦﴾
اِصْبِرْ عَلٰى مَا يَقُوْلُوْنَ وَاذْكُرْ عَبْدَنَا
دَاوٗدَ ذَا الْاَيْدِ ۚ اِنَّهٗٓ اَوَّابٌ ﴿١٧﴾
اِنَّا سَخَّرْنَا الْجِبَالَ مَعَهٗ يُسَبِّحْنَ
بِالْعَشِيِّ وَالْاِشْرَاقِ ﴿١٨﴾
وَالطَّيْرَ مَحْشُوْرَةً ؕ كُلٌّ لَّهٗٓ اَوَّابٌ ﴿١٩﴾
وَشَدَدْنَا مُلْكَهٗ وَاٰتَيْنٰهُ الْحِكْمَةَ
وَفَصْلَ الْخِطَابِ ﴿٢٠﴾
وَهَلْ اَتٰىكَ نَبَؤُا الْخَصْمِ ۘ اِذْ تَسَوَّرُوا
الْمِحْرَابَ ﴿٢١﴾
اِذْ دَخَلُوْا عَلٰى دَاوٗدَ فَفَزِعَ مِنْهُمْ قَالُوْا
لَا تَخَفْ ۚ خَصْمٰنِ بَغٰى بَعْضُنَا عَلٰى
بَعْضٍ فَاحْكُمْ بَيْنَنَا بِالْحَقِّ وَلَا
تُشْطِطْ وَاهْدِنَآ اِلٰى سَوَآءِ الصِّرَاطِ ﴿٢٢﴾
اِنَّ هٰذَآ اَخِيْ لَهٗ تِسْعٌ وَّتِسْعُوْنَ
نَعْجَةً وَّلِيَ نَعْجَةٌ وَّاحِدَةٌ فَقَالَ
اَكْفِلْنِيْهَا وَعَزَّنِيْ فِي الْخِطَابِ ﴿٢٣﴾
قَالَ لَقَدْ ظَلَمَكَ بِسُؤَالِ نَعْجَتِكَ اِلٰى
نِعَاجِهٖ ؕ وَاِنَّ كَثِيْرًا مِّنَ الْخُلَطَآءِ
لَيَبْغِيْ بَعْضُهُمْ عَلٰى بَعْضٍ اِلَّا الَّذِيْنَ
اٰمَنُوْا وَعَمِلُوا الصّٰلِحٰتِ وَقَلِيْلٌ مَّا هُمْ ؕ
وَظَنَّ دَاوٗدُ اَنَّمَا فَتَنّٰهُ فَاسْتَغْفَرَ
رَبَّهٗ وَخَرَّ رَاكِعًا وَّاَنَابَ ﴿٢٤﴾ السجدة
فَغَفَرْنَا لَهٗ ذٰلِكَ ؕ وَاِنَّ لَهٗ عِنْدَنَا

وقف لازم

السَّجدة (١٠)

Ikhfa اخفاء | Ghunna غُنّہ | Ikhfa Meem Saakin اخفاء میم ساکن | Idghaam ادغام | Qalqala قلقلہ | Qalb قلب | Idghaam Meem Saakin ادغام میم ساکن

and a beautiful Place of (Final) Return.

lazulfaa wa ḥusna ma-aab.

لَزُلْفٰى وَحُسْنَ مَاٰبٍ ﴿٢٥﴾

26. O David! We did indeed make you a vicegerent on earth: so you judge between men in truth (and justice): nor do you follow the lusts (of your heart), for they will mislead you from the Path of Allah: for those who wander astray from the Path of Allah, is a Chastisement Grievous, for that they forget the Day of Account.

26. Yaa Daawoodu innaa ja'alnaaka khaleefatan fil-arḍi faḥkum baynan-naasi bilḥaqqi wa laa tattabi'il-hawaa fa-yuḍillaka 'an sabeelil-laah; innal-lazeena yaḍilloona 'an sabeelil-laah; lahum 'azaabun shadeedum bimaa nasoo Yaw-mal-Ḥisaab. **(Section 2)**

يٰدَاوٗدُ اِنَّا جَعَلْنٰكَ خَلِيْفَةً فِي
الْاَرْضِ فَاحْكُمْ بَيْنَ النَّاسِ بِالْحَقِّ
وَلَا تَتَّبِعِ الْهَوٰى فَيُضِلَّكَ عَنْ
سَبِيْلِ اللّٰهِ ۚ اِنَّ الَّذِيْنَ يَضِلُّوْنَ
عَنْ سَبِيْلِ اللّٰهِ لَهُمْ عَذَابٌ شَدِيْدٌ
بِمَا نَسُوْا يَوْمَ الْحِسَابِ ﴿٢٦﴾

27. Not without purpose did We create heaven and earth and all between! that were the thought of Unbelievers! but woe to the Unbelievers because of the Fire (of Hell)!

27. Wa maa khalaqnas-samaaa'a wal-arḍa wa maa baynahumaa baaṭilaa; zaalika zannul-lazeena kafaroo; faway-lul-lillazeena kafaroo minan-Naar.

وَمَا خَلَقْنَا السَّمَآءَ وَالْاَرْضَ وَمَا
بَيْنَهُمَا بَاطِلًا ۚ ذٰلِكَ ظَنُّ الَّذِيْنَ
كَفَرُوْا ۚ فَوَيْلٌ لِّلَّذِيْنَ كَفَرُوْا مِنَ
النَّارِ ﴿٢٧﴾

28. Shall We treat those who believe and work deeds of righteousness, the same as those who do mischief on earth? Shall We treat those who guard against evil, the same as those who turn aside from the right?

28. Am naj'alul-lazeena aamanoo wa 'amiluṣ-ṣaaliḥaati kalmufsideena fil-arḍi am naj'alul-muttaqeena kalfujjaar.

اَمْ نَجْعَلُ الَّذِيْنَ اٰمَنُوْا وَعَمِلُوا
الصّٰلِحٰتِ كَالْمُفْسِدِيْنَ فِي الْاَرْضِ ۫
اَمْ نَجْعَلُ الْمُتَّقِيْنَ كَالْفُجَّارِ ﴿٢٨﴾

29. (Here is) a Book which We have sent down unto you, full of blessings, that they may meditate on its Signs, and that men of under-standing may receive admonition.

29. Kitaabun anzalnaahu ilayka mubaarakul-liyaddabbarooo Aayaatihee wa liyatazakkara ulul-albaab.

كِتٰبٌ اَنْزَلْنٰهُ اِلَيْكَ مُبٰرَكٌ لِّيَدَّبَّرُوْٓا
اٰيٰتِهٖ وَلِيَتَذَكَّرَ اُولُوا الْاَلْبَابِ ﴿٢٩﴾

30. To David We gave Solomon (for a son),- how excellent in Our service! Ever did he turn (to Us).

30. Wa wahabnaa li-Daawooda Sulaymaan; ni'mal-'abd; innahooo awwaab.

وَوَهَبْنَا لِدَاوٗدَ سُلَيْمٰنَ ۚ نِعْمَ الْعَبْدُ ۚ
اِنَّهٗٓ اَوَّابٌ ﴿٣٠﴾

31. Behold, there were brought before him, at eventide coursers of the highest breeding, and swift of foot;

31. Iz 'uriḍa 'alayhi bil'ashiy-yiṣ-ṣaafinaatul-jiyaad.

اِذْ عُرِضَ عَلَيْهِ بِالْعَشِيِّ الصّٰفِنٰتُ
الْجِيَادُ ﴿٣١﴾

32. And he said, "Truly do I love the love of good, with a view to the glory of my Lord," until (the sun) was hidden in the veil (of Night):

32. Faqaala inneee aḥbabtu ḥubbal-khayri 'an zikri Rabbee ḥattaa tawaarat bilḥijaab.

فَقَالَ اِنِّيْٓ اَحْبَبْتُ حُبَّ الْخَيْرِ عَنْ
ذِكْرِ رَبِّيْ ۚ حَتّٰى تَوَارَتْ بِالْحِجَابِ ﴿٣٢﴾

33. "Bring them back to me." Then he began to pass his hand over (their) legs and their necks.

33. Ruddoohaa 'alayya faṭafiqa masḥam bissooqi wal-a'naaq.

رُدُّوْهَا عَلَيَّ ۚ فَطَفِقَ مَسْحًا بِالسُّوْقِ
وَالْاَعْنَاقِ ﴿٣٣﴾

34. And We did try Solomon: We placed on his throne a body (without life); but he turned (to Us in true devotion):

34. Wa laqad fatannaa Sulay-maana wa alqaynaa 'alaa kursiyyihee jasadan summa anaab.

وَلَقَدْ فَتَنَّا سُلَيْمٰنَ وَاَلْقَيْنَا عَلٰى
كُرْسِيِّهٖ جَسَدًا ثُمَّ اَنَابَ ﴿٣٤﴾

Ikhfa اخفاء | Ghunna غنّہ | Ikhfa Meem Saakin اخفاء میم ساکن | Idghaam ادغام | Qalqala قلقلہ | Qalb قلب | Idghaam Meem Saakin ادغام میم ساکن

35. He said, "O my Lord! Forgive me, and grant me a kingdom which, (it may be), does not suit another after me: for You are the Grantor of Bounties (without measure)."

35. Qaala Rabbigh-fir lee wa hab lee mulkal-laa yambaghee li-aḥadim-mim ba'dee innaka Antal-Wahhaab.

قَالَ رَبِّ اغْفِرْ لِيْ وَهَبْ لِيْ مُلْكًا لَّا
يَنْۢبَغِيْ لِاَحَدٍ مِّنْۢ بَعْدِيْ ۚ اِنَّكَ اَنْتَ
الْوَهَّابُ ﴿٣٥﴾

36. Then We subjected the wind to his power, to flow gently to his order, whithersoever he willed,-

36. Fasakhkharnaa lahur-reeḥa tajree bi-amrihee rukhaaa'an ḥaysu aṣaab.

فَسَخَّرْنَا لَهُ الرِّيْحَ تَجْرِيْ بِاَمْرِهٖ رُخَآءً
حَيْثُ اَصَابَ ۙ﴿٣٦﴾

37. As also the evil ones, (including) every kind of builder and diver,-

37. Wash-Shayaaṭeena kulla bannaaa'iñw-wa ghawwaaṣ.

وَالشَّيٰطِيْنَ كُلَّ بَنَّآءٍ وَّغَوَّاصٍ ۙ﴿٣٧﴾

38. As also others bound together in fetters.

38. Wa aakhareena muqarraneena fil-aṣfaad.

وَّاٰخَرِيْنَ مُقَرَّنِيْنَ فِي الْاَصْفَادِ ﴿٣٨﴾

39. "Such are Our Bounties: whether you bestow them (on others) or withhold them, no account will be asked."

39. Haazaa 'aṭaaa'unaa famnun aw amsik bighayri ḥisaab.

هٰذَا عَطَآؤُنَا فَامْنُنْ اَوْ اَمْسِكْ
بِغَيْرِ حِسَابٍ ﴿٣٩﴾

40. And he enjoyed, indeed, a Near Approach to Us, and a beautiful Place of (Final) Return.

40. Wa inna lahoo 'indanaa lazulfaa wa ḥusna ma-aab.

(Section 3)

وَاِنَّ لَهٗ عِنْدَنَا لَزُلْفٰى وَحُسْنَ
مَاٰبٍ ع ﴿٤٠﴾

41. Commemorate Our Servant Job. Behold! he cried to his Lord: "The Evil has afflicted me with distress and suffering!"

41. Wazkur 'abdanaaa Ayyoob; iz naadaa Rabbahooo annee massaniyash-Shayṭaanu binuṣbiñw-wa 'azaab.

وَاذْكُرْ عَبْدَنَآ اَيُّوْبَ ۘ اِذْ نَادٰى
رَبَّهٗٓ اَنِّيْ مَسَّنِيَ الشَّيْطٰنُ بِنُصْبٍ
وَّعَذَابٍ ؕ﴿٤١﴾

م = وقف لازم

42. (The command was given:) "Strike with your foot: here is (water) wherein to wash, cool and refreshing, and (water) to drink."

42. Urkuḍ birijlika haazaa mughtasalum baariduñw-wa sharaab.

اُرْكُضْ بِرِجْلِكَ ۚ هٰذَا مُغْتَسَلٌۢ
بَارِدٌ وَّشَرَابٌ ﴿٤٢﴾

43. And We gave him (back) his people, and doubled their number, - as a Grace from Ourselves, and a thing for commemoration, for all who have Understanding.

43. Wa wahabnaa lahooo ahlahoo wa mislahum-ma'ahum raḥmatam-minnaa wa zikraa li-ulil-albaab.

وَوَهَبْنَا لَهٗٓ اَهْلَهٗ وَمِثْلَهُمْ مَّعَهُمْ
رَحْمَةً مِّنَّا وَذِكْرٰى لِاُولِي الْاَلْبَابِ ﴿٤٣﴾

44. "And take in your hand a little grass, and strike therewith: and do not break (your oath)." Truly We found him full of patience and constancy. How excellent in Our service! ever did he turn (to Us)!

44. Wa khuz biyadika ḍighsan faḍrib bihee wa laa taḥnas, innaa wajadnaahu ṣaabiraa; ni'mal-'abd; innahooo awwaab.

وَخُذْ بِيَدِكَ ضِغْثًا فَاضْرِبْ بِّهٖ
وَلَا تَحْنَثْ ؕ اِنَّا وَجَدْنٰهُ صَابِرًا ؕ
نِعْمَ الْعَبْدُ ؕ اِنَّهٗٓ اَوَّابٌ ﴿٤٤﴾

45. And commemorate Our Servants Abraham, Isaac, and Jacob, possessors of Power and Vision.

45. Wazkur 'ibaadanaaa Ibraaheema wa Is-ḥaaqa wa Ya'qooba ulil-aydee wal-abṣaar.

وَاذْكُرْ عِبٰدَنَآ اِبْرٰهِيْمَ وَاِسْحٰقَ وَ
يَعْقُوْبَ اُولِي الْاَيْدِيْ وَالْاَبْصَارِ ﴿٤٥﴾

46. Verily We did choose them for a special (purpose)- proclaiming the Message of the Hereafter.

46. Innaaa akhlaṣnaahum bi-khaaliṣatin zikrad-daar.

اِنَّآ اَخْلَصْنٰهُمْ بِخَالِصَةٍ ذِكْرَى
الدَّارِ ۚ﴿٤٦﴾

47. They were, in Our sight, truly, of the company of the Elect

47. Wa innahum 'indanaa laminal-muṣṭafaynal-

وَاِنَّهُمْ عِنْدَنَا لَمِنَ الْمُصْطَفَيْنَ

and the Good.

48. And commemorate Ismail, Elisha, and Zul-Kifl: each of them was of the company of the Good.

49. This is a Message (of admonition): and verily, for the Righteous, is a beautiful place of (final) Return,-

50. Gardens of Eternity, whose doors will (ever) be open to them;

51. Therein will they recline (at ease): therein can they call (at pleasure) for fruit in abundance, and (delicious) drink;

52. And beside them will be chaste women restraining their glances, (companions) of equal age.

53. Such is the Promise made, to you for the Day of Account!

54. Truly such will be Our Bounty (to you); it will never fail;-

55. Yes, such! but - for the wrong-doers will be an evil place of (final) Return!-

56. Hell!- They will burn therein,- an evil bed (indeed, to lie on)!-

57. Yes, such!- Then shall they taste it, - a boiling fluid, and a fluid darkm murky, intensely cold!-

58. And other penalties of a similar kind, to match them!

59. Here is a troop rushing headlong with you! No welcome for them! truly, they shall burn in the Fire!

60. (Then followers shall cry to the misleaders:) "Nay, you (too)! No welcome for you! It is you who have brought this upon us! Now evil is (this) place to stay in!"

61. They will say: "Our Lord! Whoever brought this upon us,- Add to him a double Chastisement in the Fire!"

62. And they will say: "What has happened to us that we do not see men whom we used to number among the bad ones?

63. "Did we treat them (as such) in ridicule, or have (our) eyes failed to perceive them?"

64. Truly that is just and fitting,- the mutual recriminations of the People of the Fire!

akhyaar.

48. Wazkur Ismaa'eela wal-Yasa'a wa Zal-Kifli wa kullum-minal-akhyaar.

49. Haazaa zikr; wa inna lilmuttaqeena lahusna ma-aab.

50. Jannaati 'Adnim-mufattahatal-lahumul-abwaab.

51. Muttaki'eena feehaa yad-'oona feehaa bifaakihatin kaseeratiñw-wa sharaab.

52. Wa 'indahum qaaṣiraatuṭ-ṭarfi atraab.

53. Haazaa maa too'adoona li-Yawmil-Ḥisaab.

54. Inna haazaa larizqunaa maa lahoo min-nafaad.

55. Haazaa; wa inna liṭṭaa-gheena lasharra ma-aab.

56. Jahannama yaṣlawnahaa fabi'sal-mihaad.

57. Haazaa falyazooqoohu ḥameemuñw-wa ghassaaq.

58. Wa aakharu min shak-liheee azwaaj.

59. Haazaa fawjum-muqta-ḥimum-ma'akum laa marḥabam bihim; innahum ṣaalun-Naar.

60. Qaaloo bal antum laa mar-ḥabam bikum; antum qad-damtumoohu lanaa fabi'sal-qaraar.

61. Qaaloo Rabbanaa man qaddama lanaa haazaa fazidhu 'azaaban ḍi'fan fin-Naar.

62. Wa qaaloo maa lanaa laa naraa rijaalan kunnaa na'uddu-hum-minal-ashraar.

63. Attakhaznaahum sikh-riyyan am zaaghat 'anhumul-abṣaar.

64. Inna zaalika lahaqqun takhaaṣumu Ahlin-Naar. (Sec. 4)

الاخيار ﴿٤٧﴾

واذكر اسمعيل واليسع وذا الكفل

وكل من الاخيار ﴿٤٨﴾

هذا ذكر وان للمتقين لحسن

ماب ﴿٤٩﴾

جنت عدن مفتحة لهم الابواب ﴿٥٠﴾

متكين فيها يدعون فيها بفاكهة

كثيرة وشراب ﴿٥١﴾

وعندهم قصرت الطرف اتراب ﴿٥٢﴾

هذا ما توعدون ليوم الحساب ﴿٥٣﴾

ان هذا لرزقنا ما له من نفاد ﴿٥٤﴾

هذا وان للطغين لشر ماب ﴿٥٥﴾

جهنم يصلونها فبئس المهاد ﴿٥٦﴾

هذا فليذوقوه حميم وغساق ﴿٥٧﴾

واخر من شكله ازواج ﴿٥٨﴾

هذا فوج مقتحم معكم لا مرحبا

بهم انهم صالوا النار ﴿٥٩﴾

قالوا بل انتم لا مرحبا بكم انتم

قدمتموه لنا فبئس القرار ﴿٦٠﴾

قالوا ربنا من قدم لنا هذا فزده

عذابا ضعفا في النار ﴿٦١﴾

وقالوا ما لنا لا نرى رجالا كنا

نعدهم من الاشرار ﴿٦٢﴾

اتخذنهم سخريا ام زاغت عنهم

الابصار ﴿٦٣﴾

ان ذلك لحق تخاصم اهل النار ﴿٦٤﴾

الثلثة

Ikhfa اخفاء | Ghunna غنّہ | Ikhfa Meem Saakin اخفاء میم ساکن | Idghaam ادغام | Qalqala قلقلہ | Qalb قلب | Idghaam Meem Saakin ادغام میم ساکن

65. Say: "Truly am I a Warner: no god is there but the One God (Allah), Supreme and Irresistible,-

65. Qul innamaaa ana munzi-ruñw-wa maa min ilaahin illal-laahul-Waaḥidul-Qahhaar.

قُلْ إِنَّمَآ أَنَا۠ مُنذِرٌ ۖ وَمَا مِنْ إِلَٰهٍ
إِلَّا ٱللَّهُ ٱلْوَٰحِدُ ٱلْقَهَّارُ ﴿٦٥﴾

66. The Lord of the heavens and the earth, and all between,- Exalted in Might, able to enforce His Will, forgiving again and again."

66. Rabbus-samaawaati wal-arḍi wa maa baynahumal-'Azeezul-Ghaffaar.

رَبُّ ٱلسَّمَٰوَٰتِ وَٱلْأَرْضِ وَمَا بَيْنَهُمَا
ٱلْعَزِيزُ ٱلْغَفَّٰرُ ﴿٦٦﴾

67. Sat: "That is a Message Supreme (above all)-

67. Qul huwa naba'un 'aẓeem.

قُلْ هُوَ نَبَؤٌا۟ عَظِيمٌ ﴿٦٧﴾

68. "From which you do turn away!

68. Antum 'anhu mu'riḍoon.

أَنتُمْ عَنْهُ مُعْرِضُونَ ﴿٦٨﴾

69. "No knowledge have I of the chiefs on high, when they discuss (matters) among themselves.

69. Maa kaana liya min 'ilmim bilmala-il-a'laaa iz yakhtaṣimoon.

مَا كَانَ لِىَ مِنْ عِلْمٍۭ بِٱلْمَلَإِ ٱلْأَعْلَىٰٓ
إِذْ يَخْتَصِمُونَ ﴿٦٩﴾

70. 'Only this has been revealed to me: that I am to give warning plainly and publicly."

70. Iñy-yooḥaaa ilayya illaaa annamaaa ana nazeerum-mubeen.

إِن يُوحَىٰٓ إِلَىَّ إِلَّآ أَنَّمَآ أَنَا۠ نَذِيرٌ
مُّبِينٌ ﴿٧٠﴾

71. Behold, your Lord said to the angels: "I am about to create man from clay:

71. Iz qaala Rabbuka lilma-laaa'ikati innee khaaliqum basharam-min ṭeen.

إِذْ قَالَ رَبُّكَ لِلْمَلَٰٓئِكَةِ إِنِّى خَٰلِقٌۢ
بَشَرًا مِّن طِينٍ ﴿٧١﴾

72. "When I have fashioned him (in due proportion) and breathed into him of My spirit, you fall down in obeisance to him."

72. Fa-izaa sawwaytuhoo wa nafakhtu feehi mir-rooḥee faqa'oo lahoo saajideen.

فَإِذَا سَوَّيْتُهُۥ وَنَفَخْتُ فِيهِ مِن
رُّوحِى فَقَعُوا۟ لَهُۥ سَٰجِدِينَ ﴿٧٢﴾

73. So the angels prostrated themselves, all of them together.

73. Fasajadal-malaaa'ikatu kulluhum ajma'oon.

فَسَجَدَ ٱلْمَلَٰٓئِكَةُ كُلُّهُمْ أَجْمَعُونَ ﴿٧٣﴾

74. Not so Iblis: he was haughty, and became one of those who reject Faith.

74. Illaaa Iblees; istakbara wa kaana minal-kaafireen.

إِلَّآ إِبْلِيسَ ٱسْتَكْبَرَ وَكَانَ مِنَ
ٱلْكَٰفِرِينَ ﴿٧٤﴾

75. (Allah) said: "O Iblis! What prevents you from prostrating yourself to one whom I have created with My hands? Are you haughty? Or are you one of the high (and mighty) ones?"

75. Qaala yaaa Ibleesu maa mana'aka an tasjuda limaa khalaqtu biyadayy; astakbarta am kunta minal-'aaleen.

قَالَ يَٰٓإِبْلِيسُ مَا مَنَعَكَ أَن تَسْجُدَ
لِمَا خَلَقْتُ بِيَدَىَّ ۖ أَسْتَكْبَرْتَ أَمْ
كُنتَ مِنَ ٱلْعَالِينَ ﴿٧٥﴾

76. (Iblis) said: "I am better than he: You created me from fire, and him You created from clay."

76. Qaala ana khayrum-minh; khalaqtanee min-naariñw-wa khalaqtahoo min ṭeen.

قَالَ أَنَا۠ خَيْرٌ مِّنْهُ ۖ خَلَقْتَنِى مِن نَّارٍ
وَخَلَقْتَهُۥ مِن طِينٍ ﴿٧٦﴾

77. (Allah) said: "Then you get out from here: for you are rejected, accursed.

77. Qaala fakhruj minhaa fa-innaka rajeem.

قَالَ فَٱخْرُجْ مِنْهَا فَإِنَّكَ رَجِيمٌ ﴿٧٧﴾

78. "And My Curse shall be on you till the Day of Judgment."

78. Wa inna 'alayka la'nateee ilaa Yawmid-Deen.

وَإِنَّ عَلَيْكَ لَعْنَتِىٓ إِلَىٰ يَوْمِ
ٱلدِّينِ ﴿٧٨﴾

79. (Iblis) said: "O my Lord! Give me then respite till the Day the (dead) are raised."

79. Qaala Rabbi fa-anẓirneee ilaa Yawmi yub'asoon.

قَالَ رَبِّ فَأَنظِرْنِىٓ إِلَىٰ يَوْمِ يُبْعَثُونَ ﴿٧٩﴾

Ikhfa اخفاء | Ghunna غنّة | Ikhfa Meem Saakin اخفاء میم ساکن | Idghaam ادغام | Qalqala قلقلہ | Qalb قلب | Idghaam Meem Saakin ادغام میم ساکن

80. (Allah) said: "Respite then is granted you-
81. "Till the Day of the Time Appointed."
82. (Iblis) said: "Then, by Your Power, I will put them all in the wrong,-
83. "Except Your Servants amongst them, sincere and purified (by Your grace).
84. (Allah) said: "Then it is just and fitting - and I say what is just and fitting-
85. "That I will certainly fill Hell with you and those that follow you,- every one."
86. Say: "No reward do I ask of you for this (Qur'an), nor I am a pretender.

87. "This is no less than a Message to (all) the Worlds.
88."And you shall certainly know the truth of it (all) after a while."

80. Qaala fa-innaka minal-munẓareen.
81. Ilaa Yawmil-waqtil-ma'loom.
82. Qaala fabi'izzatika la-ughwiyannahum ajma'een.
83. Illaa 'ibaadaka minhumul-mukhlaṣeen.
84. Qaala falḥaqq, walḥaqqa aqool.
85. La-amla'anna Jahannama minka wa mimman tabi'aka minhum ajma'een.
86. Qul maaa as'alukum 'alayhi min ajriñw-wa maaa ana minal-mutakallifeen.
87. In huwa illaa zikrul-lil'aalameen.
88. Wa lata'lamunna naba-ahoo ba'da ḥeen. **(Section 5)**

قَالَ فَإِنَّكَ مِنَ الْمُنظَرِينَ ﴿٨٠﴾
إِلَىٰ يَوْمِ الْوَقْتِ الْمَعْلُومِ ﴿٨١﴾
قَالَ فَبِعِزَّتِكَ لَأُغْوِيَنَّهُمْ أَجْمَعِينَ ﴿٨٢﴾
إِلَّا عِبَادَكَ مِنْهُمُ الْمُخْلَصِينَ ﴿٨٣﴾
قَالَ فَالْحَقُّ وَالْحَقَّ أَقُولُ ﴿٨٤﴾
لَأَمْلَأَنَّ جَهَنَّمَ مِنكَ وَمِمَّن تَبِعَكَ
مِنْهُمْ أَجْمَعِينَ ﴿٨٥﴾
قُلْ مَا أَسْأَلُكُمْ عَلَيْهِ مِنْ أَجْرٍ وَمَا
أَنَا مِنَ الْمُتَكَلِّفِينَ ﴿٨٦﴾
إِنْ هُوَ إِلَّا ذِكْرٌ لِّلْعَالَمِينَ ﴿٨٧﴾
وَلَتَعْلَمُنَّ نَبَأَهُ بَعْدَ حِينٍ ﴿٨٨﴾

ركوع ٥

39. The Crowds

In the name of Allah, Most Gracious, Most Merciful.

Sûrat az-Zumar–39

(Revealed at Makkah)

Bismillaahir Raḥmaanir Raḥeem

(٣٩) سُورَةُ الزُّمَرِ مَكِّيَّةٌ (٥٩)

بِسْمِ اللَّهِ الرَّحْمَٰنِ الرَّحِيمِ

1. The revelation of this Book is from Allah, the Exalted in Power, full of Wisdom.

2. Verily it is We Who have revealed the Book to you in Truth: so serve Allah, offering Him sincere devotion.

3. Is it not to Allah that sincere devotion is due? But those who take for protectors other than Allah (say): "We only serve them in order that they may bring us nearer to Allah." Truly Allah will judge between them in that wherein they differ. But Allah does not guides such as are false and ungrateful.

4. Had Allah wished to take to Himself a son, He could have chosen whom He pleased out of those whom He creates: but Glory be to Him! (He is above such things.) He is Allah, the One, the Irresistible.

1. Tanzeelul-Kitaabi minal-laahil-'Azeezil-Ḥakeem.

2. Innaaa anzalnaaa ilaykal-Kitaaba bilḥaqqi fa'budil-laaha mukhliṣal-lahud-deen.

3. Alaa lillaahid-deenul-khaaliṣ; wallazeenat-takhazoo min dooniheee awliyaaa'a maa na'buduhum illaa liyuqar-riboonaaa ilal-laahi zulfaa; innal-laaha yaḥkumu bayna-hum fee maa hum feehi yakhtalifoon; innal-laaha laa yahdee man huwa kaazibun kaffaar.

4. Law araadal-laahu añy-yattakhiza waladal-laṣṭafaa mimmaa yakhluqu maa yashaaa'; Subḥaanahoo Huwal-laahul-Waaḥidul-Qahhaar.

تَنزِيلُ الْكِتَابِ مِنَ اللَّهِ الْعَزِيزِ
الْحَكِيمِ ﴿١﴾
إِنَّا أَنزَلْنَا إِلَيْكَ الْكِتَابَ بِالْحَقِّ
فَاعْبُدِ اللَّهَ مُخْلِصًا لَّهُ الدِّينَ ﴿٢﴾
أَلَا لِلَّهِ الدِّينُ الْخَالِصُ ۚ وَالَّذِينَ
اتَّخَذُوا مِن دُونِهِ أَوْلِيَاءَ مَا نَعْبُدُهُمْ
إِلَّا لِيُقَرِّبُونَا إِلَى اللَّهِ زُلْفَىٰ إِنَّ
اللَّهَ يَحْكُمُ بَيْنَهُمْ فِي مَا هُمْ فِيهِ
يَخْتَلِفُونَ ۗ إِنَّ اللَّهَ لَا يَهْدِي مَنْ
هُوَ كَاذِبٌ كَفَّارٌ ﴿٣﴾
لَّوْ أَرَادَ اللَّهُ أَن يَتَّخِذَ وَلَدًا
لَّاصْطَفَىٰ مِمَّا يَخْلُقُ مَا يَشَاءُ ۚ
سُبْحَانَهُ ۖ هُوَ اللَّهُ الْوَاحِدُ الْقَهَّارُ ﴿٤﴾

وقف لازم

Ikhfa اخفاء | Ghunna غنّہ | Ikhfa Meem Saakin اخفاء میم ساکن | Idghaam ادغام | Qalqala قلقلہ | Qalb قلب | Idghaam Meem Saakin ادغام میم ساکن

5. He created the heavens and the earth in true (proportions): He makes the Night overlap the Day, and the Day overlap the Night: He has subjected the sun and the moon (to His law): each one follows a course for a time appointed. Is not He the Exalted in Power - He Who forgives again and again?

5. Khalaqas-samaawaati wal-arḍa bilḥaqq; yukawwirul-layla 'alan-nahaari wa yukawwirun-nahaara 'alaal-layli wa sakhkharash-shamsa walqamara kulluñy-yajree li-ajalim-musammaa; alaa Huwal-'Azeezul-Ghaffaar.

خَلَقَ السَّمٰوٰتِ وَالْاَرْضَ بِالْحَقِّ
يُكَوِّرُ الَّيْلَ عَلَى النَّهَارِ وَيُكَوِّرُ
النَّهَارَ عَلَى الَّيْلِ وَسَخَّرَ الشَّمْسَ
وَالْقَمَرَ ۚ كُلٌّ يَّجْرِيْ لِاَجَلٍ
مُّسَمًّى ۗ اَلَا هُوَ الْعَزِيْزُ الْغَفَّارُ ٥

6. He created you (all) from a single Person: then created, of like nature, his mate; and He sent down for you eight head of cattle in pairs: He makes you, in the wombs of your mothers, in stages, one after another, in three veils of darkness. such is Allah, your Lord and Cherisher: to Him belongs (all) dominion. There is no god but He: then how are you turned away (from your true Centre)?

6. Khalaqakum-min nafsiñw-waaḥidatin summa ja'ala minhaa zawjahaa wa anzala lakum-minal-an'aami samaaniyata azwaaj; yakhluqukum fee buṭooni ummahaatikum khalqam-mim ba'di khalqin fee ẓulumaatin salaas; zaalikumul-laahu Rabbukum lahul-mulk; laaa ilaaha illaa Huwa fa-annaa tuṣrafoon.

خَلَقَكُمْ مِّنْ نَّفْسٍ وَّاحِدَةٍ ثُمَّ جَعَلَ
مِنْهَا زَوْجَهَا وَاَنْزَلَ لَكُمْ مِّنَ
الْاَنْعَامِ ثَمٰنِيَةَ اَزْوَاجٍ ۗ يَخْلُقُكُمْ
فِيْ بُطُوْنِ اُمَّهٰتِكُمْ خَلْقًا مِّنْۢ بَعْدِ
خَلْقٍ فِيْ ظُلُمٰتٍ ثَلٰثٍ ۗ ذٰلِكُمُ اللّٰهُ
رَبُّكُمْ لَهُ الْمُلْكُ ۗ لَآ اِلٰهَ اِلَّا هُوَ ۚ
فَاَنّٰى تُصْرَفُوْنَ ٦

7. If you reject (Allah), Truly Allah has no need of you; but He does not like ingratitude from His servants: if you are grateful, He is pleased with you. No bearer of burdens can bear the burden of another. In the End, to your Lord is your Return, when He will tell you the truth of all that you did (in this life). For He knows well all that is in (men's) hearts.

7. In takfuroo fa-innal-laaha ghaniyyun 'ankum; wa laa yarḍaa li'ibaadihil-kufra wa in tashkuroo yarḍahu lakum; wa laa taziru waaziratuñw-wizra ukhraa; summa ilaa Rabbikum marji'ukum fa-yunabbi'ukum bimaa kuntum ta'maloon; innahoo 'aleemum bizaatiṣ-ṣudoor.

اِنْ تَكْفُرُوْا فَاِنَّ اللّٰهَ غَنِيٌّ عَنْكُمْ ۟
وَلَا يَرْضٰى لِعِبَادِهِ الْكُفْرَ ۚ وَاِنْ تَشْكُرُوْا
يَرْضَهُ لَكُمْ ۗ وَلَا تَزِرُ وَازِرَةٌ وِّزْرَ
اُخْرٰى ۗ ثُمَّ اِلٰى رَبِّكُمْ مَّرْجِعُكُمْ
فَيُنَبِّئُكُمْ بِمَا كُنْتُمْ تَعْمَلُوْنَ ۗ اِنَّهٗ
عَلِيْمٌۢ بِذَاتِ الصُّدُوْرِ ٧

8. When some trouble touches man, he cries unto his Lord, turning to Him in repentance: but when He bestows a favour upon him as from Himself, (man) forgets what he cried and prayed for before, and he sets up rivals to Allah, thus misleading others from Allah's Path. Say, "Enjoy your blasphemy for a little while: verily you are (one) of the Companions of the Fire!"

8. Wa izaa massal-insaana ḍurrun da'aa Rabbahoo muneeban ilayhi summa izaa khawwalahoo ni'matam-minhu nasiya maa kaana yad'ooo ilayhi min qablu wa ja'ala lillaahi andaadal-liyuḍilla 'an sabeelih; qul tamatta' bikufrika qaleelan innaka min Aṣḥaabin-Naar.

وَاِذَا مَسَّ الْاِنْسَانَ ضُرٌّ دَعَا رَبَّهٗ
مُنِيْبًا اِلَيْهِ ثُمَّ اِذَا خَوَّلَهٗ نِعْمَةً
مِّنْهُ نَسِيَ مَا كَانَ يَدْعُوْٓا اِلَيْهِ مِنْ
قَبْلُ وَجَعَلَ لِلّٰهِ اَنْدَادًا لِّيُضِلَّ
عَنْ سَبِيْلِهٖ ۗ قُلْ تَمَتَّعْ بِكُفْرِكَ
قَلِيْلًا ۖ اِنَّكَ مِنْ اَصْحٰبِ النَّارِ ٨

9. Is one who worships devoutly during the hours of the night prostrating himself or standing (in adoration), who takes heed of the Hereafter, And who places his hope in

9. Amman huwa qaanitun aanaaa'al-layli saajidañw-wa qaaa'imañy-yaḥzarul-Aakhirata wa yarjoo

اَمَّنْ هُوَ قَانِتٌ اٰنَآءَ الَّيْلِ سَاجِدًا
وَّقَآئِمًا يَّحْذَرُ الْاٰخِرَةَ وَيَرْجُوْا

Ikhfa اخفاء | Ghunna غُنّہ | Ikhfa Meem Saakin اخفاء میم ساکن | Idghaam ادغام | Qalqala قلقلہ | Qalb قلب | Idghaam Meem Saakin ادغام میم ساکن

the Mercy of his Lord - (like one who does not)? Say: "Are those equal, those who know and those who do not know? It is those who are endued with understanding that receive admonition.

10. Say: "O you my servants who believe! Fear your Lord. Good is (the reward) for those who do good in this world. Spacious is Allah's earth! those who patiently persevere will truly receive a reward without measure!"

11. Say: "Verily, I am commanded to serve Allah with sincere devotion;

12. "And I am commanded to be the first of those who bow to Allah in Islam."

13. Say: "I would, if I disobeyed my Lord, indeed have fear of the Penalty of a Mighty Day."

14. Say: "It is Allah I serve, with my sincere (and exclusive) devotion:

15. "You serve what you will besides Him." Say: "Truly, those in loss are those who lose their own souls and their People on the Day of Judgment: Ah! that is indeed the (real and) evident Loss!

16. They shall have layers of Fire above them, and layers (of Fire) below them: with this Allah warns off His servants: "O My Servants! then fear you Me!"

17. Those who eschew Evil,- and do not fall into its worship,- and turn to Allah (in repentance),- for them is Good News: so announce the Good News to My Servants,-

18. Those who listen to the Word, and follow the best (meaning) in it: those are the ones whom Allah has guided,

raḥmata Rabbih; qul hal yastawil-lazeena ya'lamoona wallazeena laa ya'lamoon; innamaa yatazakkaru ulul-albaab. **(Section 1)**

10. Qul yaa 'ibaadil-lazeena aamanut-taqoo Rabbakum; lillazeena aḥsanoo fee haazihid-dunyaa ḥasanah; wa arḍul-laahi waasi'ah; innamaa yuwaffaṣ-ṣaabiroona ajrahum bighayri ḥisaab.

11. Qul inneee umirtu an a'budal-laaha mukhliṣal-lahud-deen.

12. Wa umirtu li-an akoona awwalal-muslimeen.

13. Qul inneee akhaafu in 'aṣaytu Rabbee 'azaaba Yawmin 'aẓeem.

14. Qulil-laaha a'budu mukh-liṣal-lahoo deenee.

15. Fa'budoo maa shi'tum-min doonih; qul innal-khaasireenal-lazeena khasirooo anfusahum wa ahleehim Yawmal-Qiyaamah; alaa zaalika huwal-khusraanul-mubeen.

16. Lahum-min fawqihim ẓulalum-minan-Naari wa min taḥtihim ẓulal; zaalika yukhaw-wiful-laahu bihee 'ibaadah; yaa 'ibaadi fattaqoon.

17. Wallazeenaj-tanabuṭ-Ṭaaghoota añy-ya'budoohaa wa anaabooo ilal-laahi lahumul-bushraa; fabashshir 'ibaad.

18. Allazeena yastami'oonal-qawla fa-yattabi'oona aḥsanah; ulaaa'ikal-lazeena hadaahumul-

رَحْمَةَ رَبِّهٖ ؕ قُلْ هَلْ يَسْتَوِي الَّذِيْنَ
يَعْلَمُوْنَ وَالَّذِيْنَ لَا يَعْلَمُوْنَ ؕ اِنَّمَا
يَتَذَكَّرُ اُولُوا الْاَلْبَابِ ٩
قُلْ يٰعِبَادِ الَّذِيْنَ اٰمَنُوا اتَّقُوْا
رَبَّكُمْ ؕ لِلَّذِيْنَ اَحْسَنُوْا فِيْ
هٰذِهِ الدُّنْيَا حَسَنَةٌ ؕ وَاَرْضُ
اللّٰهِ وَاسِعَةٌ ؕ اِنَّمَا يُوَفَّى الصّٰبِرُوْنَ
اَجْرَهُمْ بِغَيْرِ حِسَابٍ ١٠
قُلْ اِنِّيْٓ اُمِرْتُ اَنْ اَعْبُدَ اللّٰهَ
مُخْلِصًا لَّهُ الدِّيْنَ ١١
وَاُمِرْتُ لِاَنْ اَكُوْنَ اَوَّلَ الْمُسْلِمِيْنَ ١٢
قُلْ اِنِّيْٓ اَخَافُ اِنْ عَصَيْتُ رَبِّيْ
عَذَابَ يَوْمٍ عَظِيْمٍ ١٣
قُلِ اللّٰهَ اَعْبُدُ مُخْلِصًا لَّهٗ دِيْنِيْ ١٤
فَاعْبُدُوْا مَا شِئْتُمْ مِّنْ دُوْنِهٖ ؕ
قُلْ اِنَّ الْخٰسِرِيْنَ الَّذِيْنَ خَسِرُوْٓا
اَنْفُسَهُمْ وَاَهْلِيْهِمْ يَوْمَ الْقِيٰمَةِ ؕ
اَلَا ذٰلِكَ هُوَ الْخُسْرَانُ الْمُبِيْنُ ١٥
لَهُمْ مِّنْ فَوْقِهِمْ ظُلَلٌ مِّنَ النَّارِ
وَمِنْ تَحْتِهِمْ ظُلَلٌ ؕ ذٰلِكَ يُخَوِّفُ
اللّٰهُ بِهٖ عِبَادَهٗ ؕ يٰعِبَادِ فَاتَّقُوْنِ ١٦
وَالَّذِيْنَ اجْتَنَبُوا الطَّاغُوْتَ اَنْ
يَّعْبُدُوْهَا وَاَنَابُوْٓا اِلَى اللّٰهِ لَهُمُ
الْبُشْرٰى ۚ فَبَشِّرْ عِبَادِ ١٧
الَّذِيْنَ يَسْتَمِعُوْنَ الْقَوْلَ فَيَتَّبِعُوْنَ
اَحْسَنَهٗ ؕ اُولٰٓئِكَ الَّذِيْنَ هَدٰىهُمُ

Ikhfa اخفاء · Ghunna غُنّہ · Ikhfa Meem Saakin اخفاء میم ساکن · Idghaam ادغام · Qalqala قلقلہ · Qalb قلب · Idghaam Meem Saakin ادغام میم ساکن

and those are the ones endued with understanding.

19. Is, then, one against whom the decree of Punishment is justly due (equal to one who eschews Evil)? Would you, then, deliver one (who is) in the Fire?

20. But it is for those who fear their Lord, that lofty mansions, one above another, have been built: beneath them flow rivers (of delight): (such is) the Promise of Allah: never does Allah fail in (His) promise.

21. Do you see not that Allah sends down rain from the sky, and leads it through springs in the earth? Then He causes to grow, therewith, produce of various colours: then it withers; you will see it grow yellow; then He makes it dry up and crumble away. Truly, in this, is a Message of remembrance to men of understanding.

22. Is one whose heart Allah has opened to Islam, so that he has received enlightenment from Allah, (no better than one hard-hearted)? Woe to those whose hearts are hardened against celebrating the praises of Allah! They are manifestly wandering (in error)!

23. Allah has revealed (from time to time) the most beautiful Message in the form of a Book, consistent with itself, (yet) repeating (its teaching in various aspects): the skins of those who fear their Lord tremble thereat; then their skins and their hearts do soften to the celebration of Allah's praises. Such is the guidance of Allah: He guides therewith whom He pleases, but such as Allah leaves to stray, can have none to guide.

24. Is, then, one who has to fear the brunt of the Chastisement on the Day of Judgment (and receive it) on his face, (like one guarded therefrom)? It will be said to the wrong-doers: "You taste (the fruits of)

laahu wa ulaaa'ika hum ulul-albaab.

19. Afaman ḥaqqa 'alayhi kalimatul-'azaab; afa-anta tunqizu man fin-Naar.

20. Laakinil-lazeenat-taqaw Rabbahum lahum ghurafum-min fawqihaa ghurafum-mabniyyatun tajree min taḥtihal-anhaar; wa'dal-laah; laa yukhliful-laahul-mee'aad.

21. Alam tara annal-laaha anzala minas-samaaa'i maaa'an fasalakahoo yanaabee'a fil-arḍi summa yukhriju bihee zar'am-mukhtalifan alwaanuhoo summa yaheeju fataraahu muṣfarran summa yaj'aluhoo ḥuṭaamaa; inna fee zaalika lazikraa li-ulil-albaab.

(Section 2)

22. Afaman sharaḥal-laahu ṣadrahoo lil-Islaami fahuwa 'alaa noorim-mir-Rabbih; fawaylul-lilqaasiyati quloobuhum-min zikril-laah; ulaaa'ika fee ḍalaalim-mubeen.

23. Allaahu nazzala aḥsanal-ḥadeesi Kitaabam-mutashaabiham-masaaniya taqsha'irru minhu juloodul-lazeena yakhshawna Rabbahum summa taleenu julooduhum wa quloobuhum ilaa zikril-laah; zaalika hudal-laahi yahdee bihee mañy-yashaaa'; wa mañy-yuḍlilil-laahu famaa lahoo min haad.

24. Afamañy-yattaqee biwajhihee sooo'al-'azaabi Yawmal-Qiyaamah; wa qeela liẓẓaalimeena zooqoo

اللّٰهُ وَاُولٰٓئِكَ هُمْ اُولُوا الْاَلْبَابِ ﴿١٨﴾
اَفَمَنْ حَقَّ عَلَيْهِ كَلِمَةُ الْعَذَابِ ؕ
اَفَاَنْتَ تُنْقِذُ مَنْ فِى النَّارِ ﴿١٩﴾
لٰكِنِ الَّذِيْنَ اتَّقَوْا رَبَّهُمْ لَهُمْ غُرَفٌ
مِّنْ فَوْقِهَا غُرَفٌ مَّبْنِيَّةٌ ۙ تَجْرِىْ
مِنْ تَحْتِهَا الْاَنْهٰرُ ؕ وَعْدَ اللّٰهِ ؕ لَا
يُخْلِفُ اللّٰهُ الْمِيْعَادَ ﴿٢٠﴾
اَلَمْ تَرَ اَنَّ اللّٰهَ اَنْزَلَ مِنَ السَّمَآءِ
مَآءً فَسَلَكَهٗ يَنَابِيْعَ فِى الْاَرْضِ ثُمَّ
يُخْرِجُ بِهٖ زَرْعًا مُّخْتَلِفًا اَلْوَانُهٗ ثُمَّ
يَهِيْجُ فَتَرٰىهُ مُصْفَرًّا ثُمَّ يَجْعَلُهٗ
حُطَامًا ؕ اِنَّ فِىْ ذٰلِكَ لَذِكْرٰى
لِاُولِى الْاَلْبَابِ ﴿٢١﴾
اَفَمَنْ شَرَحَ اللّٰهُ صَدْرَهٗ لِلْاِسْلَامِ
فَهُوَ عَلٰى نُوْرٍ مِّنْ رَّبِّهٖ ؕ فَوَيْلٌ
لِّلْقٰسِيَةِ قُلُوْبُهُمْ مِّنْ ذِكْرِ
اللّٰهِ ؕ اُولٰٓئِكَ فِىْ ضَلٰلٍ مُّبِيْنٍ ﴿٢٢﴾
اَللّٰهُ نَزَّلَ اَحْسَنَ الْحَدِيْثِ كِتٰبًا
مُّتَشَابِهًا مَّثَانِىَ ۖ تَقْشَعِرُّ مِنْهُ
جُلُوْدُ الَّذِيْنَ يَخْشَوْنَ رَبَّهُمْ ۚ ثُمَّ
تَلِيْنُ جُلُوْدُهُمْ وَقُلُوْبُهُمْ اِلٰى ذِكْرِ
اللّٰهِ ؕ ذٰلِكَ هُدَى اللّٰهِ يَهْدِىْ بِهٖ
مَنْ يَّشَآءُ ؕ وَمَنْ يُّضْلِلِ اللّٰهُ فَمَا
لَهٗ مِنْ هَادٍ ﴿٢٣﴾
اَفَمَنْ يَّتَّقِىْ بِوَجْهِهٖ سُوْٓءَ الْعَذَابِ
يَوْمَ الْقِيٰمَةِ ؕ وَقِيْلَ لِلظّٰلِمِيْنَ ذُوْقُوْا

Ikhfa اخفاء | Ghunna غنّہ | Ikhfa Meem Saakin اخفاء میم ساکن | Idghaam ادغام | Qalqala قلقلہ | Qalb قلب | Idghaam Meem Saakin ادغام میم ساکن

what you earned!"

25. Those before them (also) rejected (revelation), and so the Punishment came to them from directions they did not perceive.

26. So Allah gave them a taste of humiliation in the present life, but greater is the punishment of the Hereafter, if they only knew!

27. We have put forth for men, in this Qur'an every kind of Parable, in order that they may receive admonition.

28. (It is) a Qur'an in Arabic, without any crookedness (therein): in order that they may guard against Evil.

29. Allah puts forth a Parable - a man belonging to many partners at variance with each other, and a man belonging entirely to one master: are those two equal in comparison? Praise be to Allah! but most of them have no know-ledge.

30. Truly you will die (one day), and truly they (too) will die (one day).

31. In the End you will (all), on the Day of Judgment, settle your disputes in the presence of your Lord.

32. Who, then, does more wrong than one who utters a lie concerning Allah, and rejects the Truth when it comes to him; is there not in Hell an abode for blasphemers?

33. And he who brings the Truth and he who confirms (and supports) it - such are the men who do right.

34. They shall have all that they wish for, in the presence of their Lord: such is the reward of those who do good:

35. So that Allah will turn off from them (even) the worst in their deeds

maa kuntum taksiboon.

25. Kaz̲z̲abal-laz̲eena min qablihim fa-ataahumul-'az̲aabu min ḥays̲u laa yash'uroon.

26. Fa-az̲aaqahumul-laahul-khizya fil-ḥayaatid-dunyaa wa la'az̲aabul-Aakhirati akbar; law kaanoo ya'lamoon.

27. Wa laqad ḍarabnaa lin-naasi fee haaz̲al-Qur-aani min kulli mas̲alil-la'allahum yataz̲akkaroon.

28. Qur-aanan 'Arabiyyan ghayra z̲ee 'iwajil-la'allahum yattaqoon.

29. Ḍarabal-laahu mas̲alar-rajulan feehi shurakaaa'u mutashaakisoona wa rajulan salamal-lirajulin hal yastawi-yaani mas̲alaa; alḥamdu lillaah; bal aks̲aruhum laa ya'lamoon.

30. Innaka mayyituñw-wa innahum-mayyitoon.

31. S̲umma innakum Yawmal-Qiyaamati 'inda Rabbikum takhtaṣimoon. **(Section 3)**

32. Faman aẓlamu mimman kaz̲aba 'alal-laahi wa kaz̲z̲aba biṣṣidqi iz̲ jaaa'ah; alaysa fee Jahannama mas̲wal-lilkaafireen.

33. Wallaz̲ee jaaa'a biṣṣidqi wa ṣaddaqa biheee ulaaa'ika humul-muttaqoon.

34. Lahum-maa yashaaa'oona 'inda Rabbihim; z̲aalika jazaaa'ul-muḥsineen.

35. Liyukaffiral-laahu 'anhum aswa-allaz̲ee 'amiloo

مَا كُنْتُمْ تَكْسِبُوْنَ ﴿٢٤﴾
كَذَّبَ الَّذِيْنَ مِنْ قَبْلِهِمْ فَاَتٰىهُمُ
الْعَذَابُ مِنْ حَيْثُ لَا يَشْعُرُوْنَ ﴿٢٥﴾
فَاَذَاقَهُمُ اللّٰهُ الْخِزْيَ فِي الْحَيٰوةِ
الدُّنْيَا ۚ وَلَعَذَابُ الْاٰخِرَةِ اَكْبَرُ ۘ وقف لازم
لَوْ كَانُوْا يَعْلَمُوْنَ ﴿٢٦﴾
وَلَقَدْ ضَرَبْنَا لِلنَّاسِ فِيْ هٰذَا
الْقُرْاٰنِ مِنْ كُلِّ مَثَلٍ لَّعَلَّهُمْ
يَتَذَكَّرُوْنَ ﴿٢٧﴾
قُرْاٰنًا عَرَبِيًّا غَيْرَ ذِيْ عِوَجٍ
لَّعَلَّهُمْ يَتَّقُوْنَ ﴿٢٨﴾
ضَرَبَ اللّٰهُ مَثَلًا رَّجُلًا فِيْهِ شُرَكَآءُ
مُتَشٰكِسُوْنَ وَرَجُلًا سَلَمًا لِّرَجُلٍ ۭ
هَلْ يَسْتَوِيٰنِ مَثَلًا ۭ اَلْحَمْدُ لِلّٰهِ ۚ
بَلْ اَكْثَرُهُمْ لَا يَعْلَمُوْنَ ﴿٢٩﴾
اِنَّكَ مَيِّتٌ وَّاِنَّهُمْ مَّيِّتُوْنَ ﴿٣٠﴾
ثُمَّ اِنَّكُمْ يَوْمَ الْقِيٰمَةِ عِنْدَ رَبِّكُمْ
تَخْتَصِمُوْنَ ﴿٣١﴾ ع ٣ ١٦
فَمَنْ اَظْلَمُ مِمَّنْ كَذَبَ عَلَى اللّٰهِ
وَكَذَّبَ بِالصِّدْقِ اِذْ جَآءَهٗ ۭ اَلَيْسَ
فِيْ جَهَنَّمَ مَثْوًى لِّلْكٰفِرِيْنَ ﴿٣٢﴾ الجزء الرابع والعشرون (٢٤)
وَالَّذِيْ جَآءَ بِالصِّدْقِ وَصَدَّقَ بِهٖٓ
اُولٰۗىِٕكَ هُمُ الْمُتَّقُوْنَ ﴿٣٣﴾
لَهُمْ مَّا يَشَاۗءُوْنَ عِنْدَ رَبِّهِمْ ۭ ذٰلِكَ
جَزٰۗؤُا الْمُحْسِنِيْنَ ﴿٣٤﴾
لِيُكَفِّرَ اللّٰهُ عَنْهُمْ اَسْوَاَ الَّذِيْ عَمِلُوْا

Ikhfa اخفاء | Ghunna غُنّہ | Ikhfa Meem Saakin اخفاء میم ساکن | Idghaam ادغام | Qalqala قلقلہ | Qalb قلب | Idghaam Meem Saakin ادغام میم ساکن

and give them their reward according to the best of what they have done.

wa yajziyahum ajrahum bi-aḥsanil-lazee kaanoo ya'maloon.

وَيَجْزِيَهُمْ اَجْرَهُمْ بِاَحْسَنِ الَّذِيْ
كَانُوْا يَعْمَلُوْنَ ﴿٣٥﴾

36. Is not Allah enough for his Servant? But they try to frighten you with other (gods) besides Him! for such as Allah leaves to stray, there can be no guide.

36. Alaysal-laahu bikaafin 'abdahoo wa yukhawwifoonaka billazeena min doonih; wa mañy-yuḍlilil-laahu famaa lahoo min haad.

اَلَيْسَ اللّٰهُ بِكَافٍ عَبْدَهٗ ؕ وَيُخَوِّفُوْنَكَ
بِالَّذِيْنَ مِنْ دُوْنِهٖ ؕ وَمَنْ يُّضْلِلِ اللّٰهُ
فَمَا لَهٗ مِنْ هَادٍ ﴿٣٦﴾

37. And such as Allah does guide there can be none to lead astray. Is not Allah Exalted in Power, (Able to enforce His Will), Lord of Retribution?

37. Wa mañy-yahdil-laahu famaa lahoo mim-muḍill; alaysal-laahu bi'azeezin zin-tiqaam.

وَمَنْ يَّهْدِ اللّٰهُ فَمَا لَهٗ مِنْ مُّضِلٍّ ؕ
اَلَيْسَ اللّٰهُ بِعَزِيْزٍ ذِي انْتِقَامٍ ﴿٣٧﴾

38. If indeed you ask them who it is that created the heavens and the earth, they would be sure to say, "Allah". Say: "See you then? the things that you invoke besides Allah,- can they, if Allah wills some Penalty for me, remove His Penalty?- Or if He wills some Grace for me, can they keep back His Grace?" Say: "Sufficient is Allah for me! In Him trust those who put their trust."

38. Wa la'in sa-altahum man khalaqas-samaawaati wal-arḍa la-yaqoolunnal-laah; qul afara'aytum maa tad'oona min doonil-laahi in araadaniyal-laahu biḍurrin hal hunna kaashifaatu ḍurriheee aw araadanee biraḥmatin hal hunna mumsikaatu raḥmatih; qul ḥasbiyal-laahu 'alayhi yatawakkalul-mutawakkiloon.

وَلَئِنْ سَاَلْتَهُمْ مَّنْ خَلَقَ السَّمٰوٰتِ
وَالْاَرْضَ لَيَقُوْلُنَّ اللّٰهُ ؕ قُلْ اَفَرَءَيْتُمْ
مَّا تَدْعُوْنَ مِنْ دُوْنِ اللّٰهِ اِنْ اَرَادَنِيَ
اللّٰهُ بِضُرٍّ هَلْ هُنَّ كٰشِفٰتُ ضُرِّهٖۤ اَوْ
اَرَادَنِيْ بِرَحْمَةٍ هَلْ هُنَّ مُمْسِكٰتُ
رَحْمَتِهٖ ؕ قُلْ حَسْبِيَ اللّٰهُ ؕ عَلَيْهِ يَتَوَكَّلُ
الْمُتَوَكِّلُوْنَ ﴿٣٨﴾

39. Say: "O my People! Do whatever you can: I will do (my part): but soon will you know-

39. Qul yaa qawmi'-maloo 'alaa makaanatikum innee 'aamilun fasawfa ta'lamoon.

قُلْ يٰقَوْمِ اعْمَلُوْا عَلٰى مَكَانَتِكُمْ اِنِّيْ
عَامِلٌ ۚ فَسَوْفَ تَعْلَمُوْنَ ﴿٣٩﴾

40. "Who it is to whom comes a Chastisement of ignominy, and on whom descends a Penalty that abides."

40. Mañy-yaåteehi 'azaabuñy-yukhzeehi wa yaḥillu 'alayhi 'azaabum-muqeem.

مَنْ يَّاْتِيْهِ عَذَابٌ يُّخْزِيْهِ وَيَحِلُّ
عَلَيْهِ عَذَابٌ مُّقِيْمٌ ﴿٤٠﴾

41. Verily We have revealed the Book to you in Truth, for (instructing) mankind. He, then, that receives guidance benefits his own soul: but he that strays injures his own soul. Nor you are set over them to dispose of their affairs.

41. Innaaa anzalnaa 'alaykal-Kitaaba linnaasi bilḥaqq, famanih-tadaa falinafsihee wa man ḍalla fa-innamaa yaḍillu 'alayhaa wa maaa anta 'alayhim biwakeel. **(Section 4)**

اِنَّاۤ اَنْزَلْنَا عَلَيْكَ الْكِتٰبَ لِلنَّاسِ
بِالْحَقِّ ۚ فَمَنِ اهْتَدٰى فَلِنَفْسِهٖ ۚ وَمَنْ
ضَلَّ فَاِنَّمَا يَضِلُّ عَلَيْهَا ۚ وَمَاۤ اَنْتَ
عَلَيْهِمْ بِوَكِيْلٍ ﴿٤١﴾ ع

42. It is Allah that takes the souls (of men) at death; and those that die not (He takes) during their sleep: those on whom He has passed the decree of death, He keeps back (from returning to life), but the rest He sends (to their bodies) for a term appointed verily in

42. Allaahu yatawaffal-anfusa ḥeena mawtihaa wallatee lam tamut fee manaamihaa fa-yumsikul-latee qaḍaa 'alayhal-mawta wa yursilul-ukhraaa ilaaa ajalim-musammaa; inna fee

اَللّٰهُ يَتَوَفَّى الْاَنْفُسَ حِيْنَ مَوْتِهَا وَ
الَّتِيْ لَمْ تَمُتْ فِيْ مَنَامِهَا ۚ فَيُمْسِكُ
الَّتِيْ قَضٰى عَلَيْهَا الْمَوْتَ وَيُرْسِلُ
الْاُخْرٰۤى اِلٰۤى اَجَلٍ مُّسَمًّى ؕ اِنَّ فِيْ

Ikhfa اخفاء | Ghunna غُنّہ | Ikhfa Meem Saakin اخفاء میم ساکن | Idghaam ادغام | Qalqala قلقلہ | Qalb قلب | Idghaam Meem Saakin ادغام میم ساکن

this are Signs for those who reflect.

43. What! Do they take for intercessors others besides Allah? Say: "Even if they have no power whatever and no intelligence?"

44. Say: "To Allah belongs exclusively (the right to grant) intercession: to Him belongs the dominion of the heavens and the earth: In the End, it is to Him that you shall be brought back."

45. When Allah, the One and Only, is mentioned, the hearts of those who believe not in the Hereafter are filled with disgust and horror; but when (gods) other than He are mentioned, behold, they are filled with joy!

46. Say: "O Allah! Creator of the heavens and the earth! Knower of all that is hidden and open! it is You that will judge between Your Servants in those matters about which they have differed."

47. Even if the wrong-doers had all that there is on earth, and as much more, (in vain) would they offer it for ransom from the pain of the Chastisement on the Day of Judgment: but something will confront them from Allah, which they could never have counted upon!

48. For the evils of their Deeds will confront them, and they will be (completely) encircled by that which they used to mock at!

49. Now, when trouble touches man, he cries to Us: But when We bestow a favour upon him as from Ourselves, he says, "This has been given to me because of a certain knowledge (I have)!" No, but this is but a trial, but most of them understand not!

50. Thus did the (generations) before them say! But all that they did was of no profit to them.

51. No, the evil results of their Deeds overtook them.

zaalika la-Aayaatil-liqawmiñy-yatafakkaroon.

43. Amit-takhazoo min doonillaahi shufa'aaa'; qul awalaw kaanoo laa yamlikoona shay'añw-wa laa ya'qiloon.

44. Qul lillaahish-shafaa'atu jamee'aa; lahoo mulkus-samaawaati wal-ardi summa ilayhi turja'oon.

45. Wa izaa zukiral-laahu waḥdahush-ma-azzat quloobullazeena laa yu'minoona bil-Aakhirati wa izaa zukirallazeena min dooniheee izaa hum yastabshiroon.

46. Qulil-laahumma faaṭirassamaawaati wal-arḍi 'Aalimal-Ghaybi washshahaadati Anta taḥkumu bayna 'ibaadika fee maa kaanoo feehi yakhtalifoon.

47. Wa law anna lillazeena ẓalamoo maa fil-arḍi jamee'añw-wa mislahoo ma'ahoo laftadaw bihee min sooo'il-'azaabi Yawmal-Qiyaamah; wa badaa lahum minal-laahi maa lam yakoonoo yaḥtasiboon.

48. Wa badaa lahum sayyiaatu maa kasaboo wa ḥaaqa bihim maa kaanoo bihee yastahzi'oon.

49. Fa-izaa massal-insaana ḍurrun da'aanaa summa izaa khawwalnaahu ni'matamminnaa qaala innamaaa ooteetuhoo 'alaa 'ilm; bal hiya fitnatuñw-wa laakinna aksarahum laa ya'lamoon.

50. Qad qaalahal-lazeena min qablihim famaaa aghnaa 'anhum maa kaanoo yaksiboon.

51. Fa-aṣaabahum sayyi-aatu maa kasaboo; wallazeena

ذٰلِكَ لَاٰيٰتٍ لِّقَوْمٍ يَّتَفَكَّرُوْنَ ﴿٤٢﴾
اَمِ اتَّخَذُوْا مِنْ دُوْنِ اللّٰهِ شُفَعَآءَ ۭ
قُلْ اَوَلَوْ كَانُوْا لَا يَمْلِكُوْنَ شَيْـًٔا وَّلَا
يَعْقِلُوْنَ ﴿٤٣﴾
قُلْ لِّلّٰهِ الشَّفَاعَةُ جَمِيْعًا ۭ لَهٗ مُلْكُ
السَّمٰوٰتِ وَالْاَرْضِ ۭ ثُمَّ اِلَيْهِ تُرْجَعُوْنَ ﴿٤٤﴾
وَاِذَا ذُكِرَ اللّٰهُ وَحْدَهُ اشْمَاَزَّتْ
قُلُوْبُ الَّذِيْنَ لَا يُؤْمِنُوْنَ بِالْاٰخِرَةِ ۚ
وَاِذَا ذُكِرَ الَّذِيْنَ مِنْ دُوْنِهٖٓ اِذَا
هُمْ يَسْتَبْشِرُوْنَ ﴿٤٥﴾
قُلِ اللّٰهُمَّ فَاطِرَ السَّمٰوٰتِ وَالْاَرْضِ عٰلِمَ
الْغَيْبِ وَالشَّهَادَةِ اَنْتَ تَحْكُمُ بَيْنَ
عِبَادِكَ فِيْ مَا كَانُوْا فِيْهِ يَخْتَلِفُوْنَ ﴿٤٦﴾
وَلَوْ اَنَّ لِلَّذِيْنَ ظَلَمُوْا مَا فِي الْاَرْضِ
جَمِيْعًا وَّمِثْلَهٗ مَعَهٗ لَافْتَدَوْا بِهٖ
مِنْ سُوْٓءِ الْعَذَابِ يَوْمَ الْقِيٰمَةِ ۭ وَبَدَا
لَهُمْ مِّنَ اللّٰهِ مَا لَمْ يَكُوْنُوْا يَحْتَسِبُوْنَ ﴿٤٧﴾
وَبَدَا لَهُمْ سَيِّاٰتُ مَا كَسَبُوْا وَحَاقَ
بِهِمْ مَّا كَانُوْا بِهٖ يَسْتَهْزِءُوْنَ ﴿٤٨﴾
فَاِذَا مَسَّ الْاِنْسَانَ ضُرٌّ دَعَانَا ۡ ثُمَّ
اِذَا خَوَّلْنٰهُ نِعْمَةً مِّنَّا ۙ قَالَ اِنَّمَآ
اُوْتِيْتُهٗ عَلٰى عِلْمٍ ۭ بَلْ هِيَ فِتْنَةٌ
وَّلٰكِنَّ اَكْثَرَهُمْ لَا يَعْلَمُوْنَ ﴿٤٩﴾
قَدْ قَالَهَا الَّذِيْنَ مِنْ قَبْلِهِمْ فَمَآ
اَغْنٰى عَنْهُمْ مَّا كَانُوْا يَكْسِبُوْنَ ﴿٥٠﴾
فَاَصَابَهُمْ سَيِّاٰتُ مَا كَسَبُوْا ۭ وَالَّذِيْنَ

And the wrong-doers of this (generation)- the evil results of their Deeds will soon overtake them (too), and they shall never escape.

ẓalamoo min haaa'ulaaa'i sa-yuṣeebuhum sayyi-aatu maa kasaboo wa maa hum bimu'jizeen.

ظَلَمُوْا مِنْ هٰٓؤُلَآءِ سَيُصِيْبُهُمْ سَيِّاٰتُ
مَا كَسَبُوْا ۙ وَمَا هُمْ بِمُعْجِزِيْنَ ﴿٥١﴾

52. Do they not know that Allah enlarges the provision or restricts it, for any He pleases? Verily, in this are Signs for those who believe!

52. Awalam ya'lamooo annal-laaha yabsuṭur-rizqa limañy-yashaaa'u wa yaqdir; inna fee zaalika la-Aayaatil-liqawmiñy-yu'minoon. **(Section 5)**

اَوَلَمْ يَعْلَمُوْٓا اَنَّ اللّٰهَ يَبْسُطُ الرِّزْقَ
لِمَنْ يَّشَآءُ وَيَقْدِرُ ؕ اِنَّ فِيْ ذٰلِكَ
لَاٰيٰتٍ لِّقَوْمٍ يُّؤْمِنُوْنَ ﴿٥٢﴾ ع

53. Say: "O my Servants who have transgressed against their souls! Despair not of the Mercy of Allah: for Allah forgives all sins: for He is Oft-Forgiving, Most Merciful.

53. Qul yaa 'ibaadiyal-lazeena asrafoo 'alaaa anfusihim laa taqnaṭoo mirraḥmatil-laah; innal-laaha yaghfiruz-zunooba jamee'aa; innahoo Huwal-Ghafoorur-Raḥeem.

قُلْ يٰعِبَادِيَ الَّذِيْنَ اَسْرَفُوْا عَلٰٓى
اَنْفُسِهِمْ لَا تَقْنَطُوْا مِنْ رَّحْمَةِ اللّٰهِ ؕ
اِنَّ اللّٰهَ يَغْفِرُ الذُّنُوْبَ جَمِيْعًا ؕ اِنَّهٗ
هُوَ الْغَفُوْرُ الرَّحِيْمُ ﴿٥٣﴾

54. "Turn you to your Lord (in repentance) and bow to His (Will), before the Chastisement comes on you: after that you shall not be helped.

54. Wa aneebooo ilaa Rabbikum wa aslimoo lahoo min qabli añy-yaåtiyakumul-'azaabu summa laa tunṣaroon.

وَاَنِيْبُوْٓا اِلٰى رَبِّكُمْ وَاَسْلِمُوْا لَهٗ مِنْ
قَبْلِ اَنْ يَّاْتِيَكُمُ الْعَذَابُ ثُمَّ
لَا تُنْصَرُوْنَ ﴿٥٤﴾

55. "And follow the best of (the courses) revealed to you from your Lord, before the Chastisement comes on you - of a sudden while ye perceive not!-

55. Wattabi'ooo aḥsana maaa unzila ilaykum mir-Rabbikum min qabli añy-yaåtiyakumul-'azaabu baghtatañw-wa antum laa tash'uroon.

وَاتَّبِعُوْٓا اَحْسَنَ مَآ اُنْزِلَ اِلَيْكُمْ مِّنْ
رَّبِّكُمْ مِّنْ قَبْلِ اَنْ يَّاْتِيَكُمُ الْعَذَابُ
بَغْتَةً وَّاَنْتُمْ لَا تَشْعُرُوْنَ ﴿٥٥﴾

56. "Lest the soul should (then) say: 'Ah! Woe is me!- In that I neglected (my duty) towards Allah, and was but among those who mocked!'-

56. An taqoola nafsuñy-yaa ḥasrataa 'alaa maa farraṭtu fee jambil-laahi wa in kuntu laminas-saakhireen.

اَنْ تَقُوْلَ نَفْسٌ يّٰحَسْرَتٰى عَلٰى مَا
فَرَّطْتُّ فِيْ جَنْۢبِ اللّٰهِ وَاِنْ كُنْتُ
لَمِنَ السّٰخِرِيْنَ ﴿٥٦﴾

57. "Or (lest) it should say: 'If only Allah had guided me, I should certainly have been among the righteous!'

57. Aw taqoola law annal-laaha hadaanee lakuntu minal-muttaqeen.

اَوْ تَقُوْلَ لَوْ اَنَّ اللّٰهَ هَدٰىنِيْ لَكُنْتُ
مِنَ الْمُتَّقِيْنَ ﴿٥٧﴾

58. "Or (lest) it should say when it (actually) sees the Chastisement: 'If only I had another chance, I should certainly be among those who do good!'

58. Aw taqoola ḥeena taral-'azaaba law anna lee karratan fa-akoona minal-muḥsineen.

اَوْ تَقُوْلَ حِيْنَ تَرَى الْعَذَابَ لَوْ
اَنَّ لِيْ كَرَّةً فَاَكُوْنَ مِنَ الْمُحْسِنِيْنَ ﴿٥٨﴾

59. "(The reply will be:) 'No, but there came to you My Signs, and you did reject them: You were Haughty, and became one of those who reject faith!'

59. Balaa qad jaaa'atka Aayaatee fakazzabta bihaa wastakbarta wa kunta minal-kaafireen.

بَلٰى قَدْ جَآءَتْكَ اٰيٰتِيْ فَكَذَّبْتَ بِهَا
وَاسْتَكْبَرْتَ وَكُنْتَ مِنَ الْكٰفِرِيْنَ ﴿٥٩﴾

60. On the Day of Judgment will you see those who told lies against Allah;- their faces will be turned black; Is there not in

60. Wa Yawmal-Qiyaamati taral-lazeena kazaboo 'alallaahi wujoohuhum muswaddah; alaysa fee

وَيَوْمَ الْقِيٰمَةِ تَرَى الَّذِيْنَ كَذَبُوْا عَلَى
اللّٰهِ وُجُوْهُهُمْ مُّسْوَدَّةٌ ؕ اَلَيْسَ فِيْ

Ikhfa اخفاء · Ghunna غنّہ · Ikhfa Meem Saakin اخفاء میم ساکن · Idghaam ادغام · Qalqala قلقلہ · Qalb قلب · Idghaam Meem Saakin ادغام میم ساکن

Hell an abode for the Haughty?

61. But Allah will deliver the righteous to their place of salvation: no evil shall touch them, nor shall they grieve.

62. Allah is the Creator of all things, and He is the Guardian and Disposer of all affairs.

63. To Him belong the keys of the heavens and the earth: and those who reject the Signs of Allah,- it is they who will be in loss.

64. Say: "Is it someone other than Allah that you order me to worship, O you ignorant ones?"

65. But it has already been revealed to you,- as it was to those before you,- "If you were to join (gods with Allah), truly fruitless will be your work (in life), and you will surely be in the ranks of those who lose (all spiritual good)".

66. No, but worship Allah, and be of those who give thanks.

67. No just estimate have they made of Allah, such as is due to Him: On the Day of Judgment the whole of the earth will be but His handful, and the heavens will be rolled up in His right hand: Glory to Him! High is He above the Partners they attribute to Him!

68. The Trumpet will (just) be sounded, when all that are in the heavens and on earth will swoon, except such as it will please Allah (to exempt). Then will a second one be sounded, when, behold, they will be standing and looking on!

69. And the Earth will shine with the Glory of its Lord: the Record (of Deeds) will be placed (open); the prophets and the witnesses will be brought forward and a just decision pronounced between them; and they will not be wronged (in the least).

70. And to every soul will be paid in full (the fruit) of its Deeds; and (Allah) knows best all that they do.

Jahannama maswal-lilmutakabbireen.

61. Wa yunajjil-laahul-lazeenat-taqaw bimafaazatihim laa yamassuhumus-sooo'u wa laa hum yahzanoon.

62. Allaahu khaaliqu kulli shay'iñw-wa Huwa 'alaa kulli shay'iñw-Wakeel.

63. Lahoo maqaaleedus-samaawaati wal-ard; wallazeena kafaroo bi-Aayaatil-laahi ulaa-a'ika humul-khaasiroon. **(Sec. 2)**

64. Qul afaghayral-laahi taåmurooonneee a'budu ayyuhal-jaahiloon.

65. Wa laqad oohiya ilayka wa ilal-lazeena min qablika la-in ashrakta la-yahbatanna 'amaluka wa latakoonanna minal-khaasireen.

66. Balil-laaha fa'bud wa kum-minash-shaakireen.

67. Wa maa qadarul-laaha haqqa qadrihee wal-ardu jamee-'an qabdatuhoo Yawmal-Qiyaamati wassamaawaatu matwiyyaatum biyameenih; Subhaanahoo wa Ta'aalaa 'ammaa yushrikoon.

68. Wa nufikha fis-Soori fasa'iqa man fis-samaawaati wa man fil-ardi illaa man shaa'al-laahu summa nufikha feehi ukhraa fa-izaa hum qiyaamuñy-yanzuroon.

69. Wa ashraqatil-ardu binoori Rabbihaa wa wudi'al-Kitaabu wa jeee'a bin-Nabiyyeena wash-shuhadaaa'i wa qudiya baynahum bilhaqqi wa hum laa yuzlamoon.

70. Wa wuffiyat kullu nafsim maa 'amilat wa Huwa a'lamu bimaa yaf'aloon. **(Section 7)**

جَهَنَّمَ مَثْوًى لِّلْمُتَكَبِّرِينَ ﴿٦٠﴾
وَيُنَجِّي اللَّهُ الَّذِينَ اتَّقَوْا بِمَفَازَتِهِمْ
لَا يَمَسُّهُمُ السُّوءُ وَلَا هُمْ يَحْزَنُونَ ﴿٦١﴾
اللَّهُ خَالِقُ كُلِّ شَيْءٍ وَهُوَ عَلَىٰ كُلِّ
شَيْءٍ وَكِيلٌ ﴿٦٢﴾
لَهُ مَقَالِيدُ السَّمَاوَاتِ وَالْأَرْضِ وَالَّذِينَ
كَفَرُوا بِآيَاتِ اللَّهِ أُولَٰئِكَ هُمُ الْخَاسِرُونَ ﴿٦٣﴾ ع
قُلْ أَفَغَيْرَ اللَّهِ تَأْمُرُونِّي أَعْبُدُ أَيُّهَا
الْجَاهِلُونَ ﴿٦٤﴾
وَلَقَدْ أُوحِيَ إِلَيْكَ وَإِلَى الَّذِينَ مِن
قَبْلِكَ لَئِنْ أَشْرَكْتَ لَيَحْبَطَنَّ عَمَلُكَ
وَلَتَكُونَنَّ مِنَ الْخَاسِرِينَ ﴿٦٥﴾
بَلِ اللَّهَ فَاعْبُدْ وَكُن مِّنَ الشَّاكِرِينَ ﴿٦٦﴾
وَمَا قَدَرُوا اللَّهَ حَقَّ قَدْرِهِ وَالْأَرْضُ
جَمِيعًا قَبْضَتُهُ يَوْمَ الْقِيَامَةِ وَ
السَّمَاوَاتُ مَطْوِيَّاتٌ بِيَمِينِهِ سُبْحَانَهُ
وَتَعَالَىٰ عَمَّا يُشْرِكُونَ ﴿٦٧﴾
وَنُفِخَ فِي الصُّورِ فَصَعِقَ مَن فِي
السَّمَاوَاتِ وَمَن فِي الْأَرْضِ إِلَّا مَن
شَاءَ اللَّهُ ثُمَّ نُفِخَ فِيهِ أُخْرَىٰ فَإِذَا
هُمْ قِيَامٌ يَنظُرُونَ ﴿٦٨﴾
وَأَشْرَقَتِ الْأَرْضُ بِنُورِ رَبِّهَا وَوُضِعَ
الْكِتَابُ وَجِيءَ بِالنَّبِيِّينَ وَالشُّهَدَاءِ
وَقُضِيَ بَيْنَهُم بِالْحَقِّ وَهُمْ لَا يُظْلَمُونَ ﴿٦٩﴾
وَوُفِّيَتْ كُلُّ نَفْسٍ مَّا عَمِلَتْ وَهُوَ
أَعْلَمُ بِمَا يَفْعَلُونَ ﴿٧٠﴾ ع

71. The Unbelievers will be led to Hell in crowd: until, when they arrive, there, its gates will be opened. And its keepers will say, "Did not apostles come to you from among yourselves, rehearsing to you the Signs of your Lord, and warning you of the Meeting of This Day of yours?" The answer will be: "True: but the Decree of Punishment has been proved true against the Unbelievers!"

72. (To them) will be said: "Enter you the gates of Hell, to dwell therein: and evil is (this) Abode of the Arrogant!"

73. And those who feared their Lord will be led to the Garden in crowds: until behold, they arrive there; its gates will be opened; and its keepers will say: "Peace be upon you! well have you done! enter you here, to dwell therein."

74. They will say: "Praise be to Allah, Who has truly fulfilled His Promise to us, and has given us (this) land in heritage: We can dwell in the Garden as we will: how excellent a reward for those who work (righteousness)!"

75. And you will see the angels surrounding the Throne (Divine) on all sides, singing Glory and Praise to their Lord. The Decision between them (at Judgment) will be in (perfect) justice, and the cry (on all sides) will be, "Praise be to Allah, the Lord of the Worlds!"

71. Wa seeqal-laz̲eena kafarooo ilaa Jahannama zumaran ḥattaaa iz̲aa jaaa'oohaa futiḥat abwaabuhaa wa qaala lahum khazanatuhaaa alam yaåtikum Rusulum-minkum yatloona 'alaykum Aayaati Rabbikum wa yunziroonakum liqaaa'a Yawmikum haaz̲aa; qaaloo balaa wa laakin ḥaqqat kalimatul-'az̲aabi 'alal-kaafireen.

72. Qeelad-khulooo abwaaba Jahannama khaalideena feehaa fabi'sa mas̲wal-mutakabbireen.

73. Wa seeqal-laz̲eenat-taqaw Rabbahum ilal-Jannati zumaran ḥattaaa iz̲aa jaaa'oohaa wa futiḥat abwaabuhaa wa qaala lahum khazanatuhaa salaamun 'alaykum ṭibtum fadkhuloohaa khaalideen.

74. Wa qaalull-ḥamdulillaahil-laz̲ee ṣadaqanaa wa'dahoo wa awras̲anal-arḍa natabawwa-u minal-Jannati ḥays̲u nashaaa'u fani'ma ajrul-'aamileen.

75. Wa taral-malaaa'ikata ḥaaaffeena min ḥawlil-'Arshi yusabbiḥoona biḥamdi Rabbihim wa quḍiya baynahum bilḥaqqi wa qeelal-ḥamdu lillaahi Rabbil-'aalameen.

(Section 8)

وَسِيقَ الَّذِينَ كَفَرُوا إِلَىٰ جَهَنَّمَ
زُمَرًا ۖ حَتَّىٰ إِذَا جَاءُوهَا فُتِحَتْ
أَبْوَابُهَا وَقَالَ لَهُمْ خَزَنَتُهَا أَلَمْ
يَأْتِكُمْ رُسُلٌ مِّنكُمْ يَتْلُونَ عَلَيْكُمْ
آيَاتِ رَبِّكُمْ وَيُنذِرُونَكُمْ لِقَاءَ يَوْمِكُمْ
هَٰذَا ۚ قَالُوا بَلَىٰ وَلَٰكِنْ حَقَّتْ كَلِمَةُ
الْعَذَابِ عَلَى الْكَافِرِينَ ﴿٧١﴾
قِيلَ ادْخُلُوا أَبْوَابَ جَهَنَّمَ خَالِدِينَ
فِيهَا ۖ فَبِئْسَ مَثْوَى الْمُتَكَبِّرِينَ ﴿٧٢﴾
وَسِيقَ الَّذِينَ اتَّقَوْا رَبَّهُمْ إِلَى الْجَنَّةِ
زُمَرًا ۖ حَتَّىٰ إِذَا جَاءُوهَا وَفُتِحَتْ
أَبْوَابُهَا وَقَالَ لَهُمْ خَزَنَتُهَا سَلَامٌ
عَلَيْكُمْ طِبْتُمْ فَادْخُلُوهَا خَالِدِينَ ﴿٧٣﴾
وَقَالُوا الْحَمْدُ لِلَّهِ الَّذِي صَدَقَنَا
وَعْدَهُ وَأَوْرَثَنَا الْأَرْضَ نَتَبَوَّأُ
مِنَ الْجَنَّةِ حَيْثُ نَشَاءُ ۖ فَنِعْمَ
أَجْرُ الْعَامِلِينَ ﴿٧٤﴾
وَتَرَى الْمَلَائِكَةَ حَافِّينَ مِنْ
حَوْلِ الْعَرْشِ يُسَبِّحُونَ بِحَمْدِ رَبِّهِمْ ۖ
وَقُضِيَ بَيْنَهُم بِالْحَقِّ وَقِيلَ الْحَمْدُ
لِلَّهِ رَبِّ الْعَالَمِينَ ﴿٧٥﴾

الربع

40. The Believer

In the name of Allah, Most Gracious, Most Merciful.

1. *Ha-Mim.*

2. The revelation of this Book is from Allah, Exalted in Power, Full of Knowledge,-

Sûrat al-Mu'min–40

(Revealed at Makkah)

Bismillaahir Raḥmaanir Raḥeem

1. Ḥaa-Meeem.

2. Tanzeelul-Kitaabi minallaahil-Azeezil-'Aleem.

(٤٠) سُورَةُ الْمُؤْمِنِ مَكِّيَّةٌ (٦٠)

بِسْمِ اللَّهِ الرَّحْمَٰنِ الرَّحِيمِ

حم ﴿١﴾
تَنزِيلُ الْكِتَابِ مِنَ اللَّهِ الْعَزِيزِ
الْعَلِيمِ ﴿٢﴾

Ikhfa اخفاء | Ghunna غنّة | Ikhfa Meem Saakin اخفاء میم ساکن | Idghaam ادغام | Qalqala قلقلہ | Qalb قلب | Idghaam Meem Saakin ادغام میم ساکن

3. Who forgives sin, accepteth repentance, is strict in punishment, and hath a long reach (in all things). There is no god but He: to Him is the final goal.

3. Ghaafiriz-zambi wa qaabilit-tawbi shadeedil-'iqaabi zit-ṭawli laaa ilaaha illaa Huwa ilayhil-maṣeer.

غَافِرِ الذَّنْۢبِ وَقَابِلِ التَّوْبِ شَدِيْدِ
الْعِقَابِ ذِى الطَّوْلِ ؕ لَاۤ اِلٰهَ اِلَّا
هُوَ ؕ اِلَيْهِ الْمَصِيْرُ ۝٣

4. None can dispute about the Signs of Allah but the Unbelievers. Let not, then, their strutting about through the land deceive you!

4. Maa yujaadilu feee Aayaatil-laahi illal-lazeena kafaroo falaa yaghrurka taqallubuhum fil-bilaad.

مَا يُجَادِلُ فِىْۤ اٰيٰتِ اللّٰهِ اِلَّا الَّذِيْنَ
كَفَرُوْا فَلَا يَغْرُرْكَ تَقَلُّبُهُمْ
فِى الْبِلَادِ ۝٤

5. But (there were people) before them, who denied (the Signs),- the People of Noah, and the Confederates (of Evil) after them; and every People plotted against their prophet, to seize him, and disputed by means of vanities, therewith to condemn the Truth; but it was I that seized them! and how (terrible) was My Requital!

5. Kazzabat qablahum qawmu Nooḥiñw-wal-Aḥzaabu mim ba'dihim wa hammat kullu ummatim bi-Rasoolihim liyaåkhuzoohu wa jaadaloo bilbaaṭili liyudḥiḍoo bihil-ḥaqqa faakhaztuhum fakayfa kaana 'iqaab.

كَذَّبَتْ قَبْلَهُمْ قَوْمُ نُوْحٍ وَّالْاَحْزَابُ
مِنْۢ بَعْدِهِمْ ۪ وَهَمَّتْ كُلُّ اُمَّةٍۢ
بِرَسُوْلِهِمْ لِيَاْخُذُوْهُ وَجٰدَلُوْا
بِالْبَاطِلِ لِيُدْحِضُوْا بِهِ الْحَقَّ
فَاَخَذْتُهُمْ ۫ فَكَيْفَ كَانَ عِقَابِ ۝٥

6. Thus was the Decree of your Lord proved true against the Unbelievers; that truly they are Companions of the Fire!

6. Wa kazaalika ḥaqqat Kalimatu Rabbika 'alal-lazeena kafarooo annahum Aṣḥaabun-Naar.

وَكَذٰلِكَ حَقَّتْ كَلِمَتُ رَبِّكَ عَلَى
الَّذِيْنَ كَفَرُوْۤا اَنَّهُمْ اَصْحٰبُ النَّارِ ۘ ۝٦

وقف لازم

7. Those who sustain the Throne (of Allah) and those around it Sing Glory and Praise to their Lord; believe in Him; and implore Forgiveness for those who believe: "Our Lord! your Reach is over all things, in Mercy and Knowledge. Forgive, then, those who turn in Repentance, and follow Your Path; and preserve them from the Chastisement of the Blazing Fire!

7. Allazeena yaḥmiloonal-'Arsha wa man ḥawlahoo yusabbiḥoona biḥamdi Rabbihim wa yu'minoona bihee wa yastaghfiroona lillazeena aamanoo Rabbanaa wasi'ta kulla shay'ir-raḥmatañw wa 'ilman faghfir lillazeena taaboo wattaba'oo sabeelaka wa qihim 'azaabal-Jaḥeem.

اَلَّذِيْنَ يَحْمِلُوْنَ الْعَرْشَ وَمَنْ حَوْلَهٗ
يُسَبِّحُوْنَ بِحَمْدِ رَبِّهِمْ وَيُؤْمِنُوْنَ
بِهٖ وَيَسْتَغْفِرُوْنَ لِلَّذِيْنَ اٰمَنُوْا ۚ رَبَّنَا
وَسِعْتَ كُلَّ شَىْءٍ رَّحْمَةً وَّعِلْمًا فَاغْفِرْ
لِلَّذِيْنَ تَابُوْا وَاتَّبَعُوْا سَبِيْلَكَ وَقِهِمْ
عَذَابَ الْجَحِيْمِ ۝٧

8. "And grant, our Lord! that they enter the Gardens of Eternity, which You have promised to them, and to the righteous among their fathers, their wives, and their posterity! For You are (He), the Exalted in Might, Full of Wisdom.

8. Rabbanaa wa adkhilhum Jannaati 'Adninil-latee wa'attahum wa man ṣalaḥa min aabaaa'ihim wa azwaajihim wa zurriyyaatihim; innaka Antal-'Azeezul-Ḥakeem.

رَبَّنَا وَاَدْخِلْهُمْ جَنّٰتِ عَدْنِ ِالَّتِىْ
وَعَدْتَّهُمْ وَمَنْ صَلَحَ مِنْ اٰبَآئِهِمْ
وَاَزْوَاجِهِمْ وَذُرِّيّٰتِهِمْ ؕ اِنَّكَ اَنْتَ
الْعَزِيْزُ الْحَكِيْمُ ۙ ۝٨

9. "And preserve them from (all) ills; and any whom You does preserve from (all) ills that Day,- on them will You have bestowed Mercy indeed: and that will be truly (for them) the highest Achievement".

9. Wa qihimus-sayyi-aat; wa man taqis-sayyi-aati Yawma'izin faqad rahimtah; wa zaalika huwal-fawzul-'azeem. **(Section 1)**

وَقِهِمُ السَّيِّاٰتِ ؕ وَمَنْ تَقِ السَّيِّاٰتِ
يَوْمَئِذٍ فَقَدْ رَحِمْتَهٗ ؕ وَذٰلِكَ هُوَ
الْفَوْزُ الْعَظِيْمُ ۝٩

ع

Ikhfa اخفاء | Ghunna غُنّہ | Ikhfa Meem Saakin اخفاء میم ساکن | Idghaam ادغام | Qalqala قلقلہ | Qalb قلب | Idghaam Meem Saakin ادغام میم ساکن

10. The Unbelievers will be addressed: "Greater was the aversion of Allah to you than (is) your aversion to yourselves, seeing that you were called to the Faith and you used to refuse."

10. Innal-lazeena kafaroo yunaadawna lamaqtul-laahi akbaru mim-maqtikum anfusakum iz tud'awna ilal-eemaani fatakfuroon.

إِنَّ الَّذِينَ كَفَرُوا يُنَادَوْنَ لَمَقْتُ اللَّهِ
أَكْبَرُ مِن مَّقْتِكُمْ أَنفُسَكُمْ إِذْ
تُدْعَوْنَ إِلَى الْإِيمَانِ فَتَكْفُرُونَ ١٠

11. They will say: "Our Lord! twice have You made us without life, and twice have You given us Life! Now that have we recognised our sins: Is there any way out (of this)?"

11. Qaaloo Rabbanaaa amattanasnatayni wa aḥyaytanasnatayni fa'tarafnaa bizunoobinaa fahal ilaa khuroojim-min sabeel.

قَالُوا رَبَّنَا أَمَتَّنَا اثْنَتَيْنِ وَأَحْيَيْتَنَا
اثْنَتَيْنِ فَاعْتَرَفْنَا بِذُنُوبِنَا فَهَلْ
إِلَىٰ خُرُوجٍ مِّن سَبِيلٍ ١١

12. (The answer will be:) "This is because, when Allah was invoked as the Only (object of worship), you did reject Faith, but when partners were joined to Him, you believed! the Command is with Allah, Most High, Most Great!"

12. Zaalikum bi-annahooo izaa du'iyal-laahu waḥdahoo kafartum wa iñy-yushrak bihee tu'minoo; falḥukmu lillaahil 'Aliyyil-Kabeer.

ذَٰلِكُم بِأَنَّهُ إِذَا دُعِيَ اللَّهُ وَحْدَهُ
كَفَرْتُمْ ۖ وَإِن يُشْرَكْ بِهِ تُؤْمِنُوا ۚ
فَالْحُكْمُ لِلَّهِ الْعَلِيِّ الْكَبِيرِ ١٢

13. He it is Who shows you His Signs, and sends down sustenance for you from the sky: but only those receive admonition who turn (to Allah).

13. Huwal-lazee yureekum Aayaatihee wa yunazzilu lakum minas-samaaa'i rizqaa; wa maa yaṭazakkaru illaa mañy-yuneeb.

هُوَ الَّذِي يُرِيكُمْ آيَاتِهِ وَيُنَزِّلُ لَكُم
مِّنَ السَّمَاءِ رِزْقًا ۚ وَمَا يَتَذَكَّرُ
إِلَّا مَن يُنِيبُ ١٣

14. Call you, then, upon Allah with sincere devotion to Him, even though the Unbelievers may detest it.

14. Fad'ul-laaha mukhliṣeena lahud-deena wa law karihal-kaafiroon.

فَادْعُوا اللَّهَ مُخْلِصِينَ لَهُ الدِّينَ
وَلَوْ كَرِهَ الْكَافِرُونَ ١٤

15. Raised high above ranks (or degrees), (He is) the Lord of the Throne (of Authority): by His Command doth He send the Spirit (of inspiration) to any of His servants He pleases, that it may warn (men) of the Day of Mutual Meeting,-

15. Rafee'ud-darajaati zul-'Arshi yulqir-rooḥa min amrihee 'alaa mañy-yashaaa'u min 'ibaadihee liyunzira yawmat-talaaq.

رَفِيعُ الدَّرَجَاتِ ذُو الْعَرْشِ يُلْقِي
الرُّوحَ مِنْ أَمْرِهِ عَلَىٰ مَن يَشَاءُ مِنْ
عِبَادِهِ لِيُنذِرَ يَوْمَ التَّلَاقِ ١٥

16. The Day whereon they will (all) come forth: not a single thing concerning them is hidden from Allah. Whose will be the dominion that Day?" That of Allah, the One the Irresistible!

16. Yawma hum baarizoona laa yakhfaa 'alal-laahi minhum shay'; limanil-mulkul-Yawma lillaahil-Waaḥidil-Qahhaar.

يَوْمَ هُم بَارِزُونَ ۖ لَا يَخْفَىٰ عَلَى
اللَّهِ مِنْهُمْ شَيْءٌ ۚ لِّمَنِ الْمُلْكُ
الْيَوْمَ ۖ لِلَّهِ الْوَاحِدِ الْقَهَّارِ ١٦

17. That Day will every soul be requited for what it earned; no injustice will there be that Day, for Allah is Swift in taking account.

17. Al-Yawma tujzaa kullu nafsim bimaa kasabat; laa ẓulmal-Yawm; innal-laaha saree'ul-ḥisaab.

الْيَوْمَ تُجْزَىٰ كُلُّ نَفْسٍ بِمَا
كَسَبَتْ ۚ لَا ظُلْمَ الْيَوْمَ ۚ إِنَّ اللَّهَ
سَرِيعُ الْحِسَابِ ١٧

18. Warn them of the Day that is (ever) drawing near, when the hearts will (come) right up to the throats to choke (them); No intimate friend nor intercessor will the wrong-doers have,

18. Wa anzirhum yawmal-aazifati izil-quloobu ladal-ḥanaajiri kaaẓimeen; maa liẓẓaalimeena min ḥameemiñw-wa laa shafee'iñy-

وَأَنذِرْهُمْ يَوْمَ الْآزِفَةِ إِذِ الْقُلُوبُ
لَدَى الْحَنَاجِرِ كَاظِمِينَ ۚ مَا
لِلظَّالِمِينَ مِنْ حَمِيمٍ وَلَا شَفِيعٍ

Ikhfa اخفاء | Ghunna غنّہ | Ikhfa Meem Saakin اخفاء میم ساکن | Idghaam ادغام | Qalqala قلقلہ | Qalb قلب | Idghaam Meem Saakin ادغام میم ساکن

who could be listened to.

yuṭaa'.

يُطَاعُ ۝١٨

19. (Allah) knows of (the tricks) that deceive with the eyes, and all that the hearts (of men) conceal.

19. Ya'lamu khaaa'inatal-a'yuni wa maa tukhfiṣ-ṣudoor.

يَعْلَمُ خَآئِنَةَ الْأَعْيُنِ وَمَا تُخْفِي
الصُّدُورُ ۝١٩

20. And Allah will judge with (justice and) Truth: but those whom (men) invoke besides Him, will not (be in a position) to judge at all. Verily it is Allah (alone) Who hears and sees (all things).

20. Wallaahu yaqḍee bilḥaqq, wallaẕeena yad'oona min doonihee laa yaqḍoona bishay'; innal-laaha Huwas-Samee'ul-Baṣeer. **(Section 2)**

وَاللّٰهُ يَقْضِي بِالْحَقِّ ۗ وَالَّذِينَ
يَدْعُونَ مِنْ دُونِهِ لَا يَقْضُونَ بِشَيْءٍ ۗ
إِنَّ اللّٰهَ هُوَ السَّمِيعُ الْبَصِيرُ ۝٢٠ ٢ ع ١١ ٧

21. Do they not travel through the earth and see what was the End of those before them? They were even superior to them in strength, and in the traces (they have left) in the land: but Allah did call them to account for their sins, and none had they to defend them against Allah.

21. Awalam yaseeroo fil-arḍi fa-yanẓuroo kayfa kaana 'aaqibatul-laẕeena kaanoo min qablihim; kaanoo hum ashadda minhum quwwatañw-wa aasaaran fil-arḍi fa-akhaẕahumul-laahu biẕunoobihim wa maa kaana lahum minal-laahi miñw-waaq.

أَوَلَمْ يَسِيرُوا فِي الْأَرْضِ فَيَنْظُرُوا
كَيْفَ كَانَ عَاقِبَةُ الَّذِينَ كَانُوا مِنْ
قَبْلِهِمْ ۚ كَانُوا هُمْ أَشَدَّ مِنْهُمْ قُوَّةً
وَآثَارًا فِي الْأَرْضِ فَأَخَذَهُمُ اللّٰهُ
بِذُنُوبِهِمْ ۗ وَمَا كَانَ لَهُمْ مِنَ اللّٰهِ
مِنْ وَاقٍ ۝٢١

22. That was because there came to them their apostles with Clear (Signs), but they rejected them: So Allah called them to account: for He is Full of Strength, Strict in Punishment.

22. Zaalika bi-annahum kaanat taâteehim Rusuluhum bilbayyinaati fakafaroo fa-akhaẕahumul-laah; innahoo qawiyyun shadeedul-'iqaab.

ذٰلِكَ بِأَنَّهُمْ كَانَتْ تَأْتِيهِمْ رُسُلُهُمْ
بِالْبَيِّنٰتِ فَكَفَرُوا فَأَخَذَهُمُ اللّٰهُ ۗ
إِنَّهُ قَوِيٌّ شَدِيدُ الْعِقَابِ ۝٢٢

23. Of old We sent Moses, with Our Signs and an authority manifest,

23. Wa laqad arsalnaa Moosaa bi-Aayaatinaa wa sulṭaanim-mubeen.

وَلَقَدْ أَرْسَلْنَا مُوسٰى بِآيٰتِنَا وَ
سُلْطٰنٍ مُّبِينٍ ۝٢٣

24. To Pharaoh, Haman, and Qarun; but they called (him)" a sorcerer telling lies!"...

24. Ilaa Fir'awna wa Haamaana wa Qaaroona faqaaloo saaḥirun kazzaab.

إِلٰى فِرْعَوْنَ وَهٰمٰنَ وَقَارُونَ فَقَالُوا
سٰحِرٌ كَذَّابٌ ۝٢٤

25. Now, when he came to them in Truth, from Us, they said, "Slay the sons of those who believe with him, and keep alive their females," but the plots of Unbelievers (end) in nothing but errors (and delusions)!...

25. Falamma jaaa'ahum-bilḥaqqi min 'indinaa qaaluqtulooo abnaaa'al-laẕeena aamanoo ma'ahoo wastaḥyoo nisaaa'ahum; wa maa kaydul-kaafireena illaa fee ḍalaal.

فَلَمَّا جَآءَهُمْ بِالْحَقِّ مِنْ عِنْدِنَا قَالُوا
اقْتُلُوٓا أَبْنَآءَ الَّذِينَ آمَنُوا مَعَهُ
وَاسْتَحْيُوا نِسَآءَهُمْ ۗ وَمَا كَيْدُ
الْكٰفِرِينَ إِلَّا فِي ضَلٰلٍ ۝٢٥

26. Said Pharaoh: "Leave me to slay Moses; and let him call on his Lord! What I fear is lest he should change your religion, or lest he should cause

26. Wa qaala Fir'awnu ẕarooneee aqtul Moosaa walyad'u Rabbahoo inneee akhaafu añy-yubaddila deenakum aw añy-yuẓhira fil-

وَقَالَ فِرْعَوْنُ ذَرُونِيٓ أَقْتُلْ
مُوسٰى وَلْيَدْعُ رَبَّهُ ۚ إِنِّيٓ أَخَافُ أَنْ
يُبَدِّلَ دِينَكُمْ أَوْ أَنْ يُظْهِرَ فِي

Ikhfa اخفاء | Ghunna غنّہ | Ikhfa Meem Saakin اخفاء میم ساکن | Idghaam ادغام | Qalqala قلقلہ | Qalb قلب | Idghaam Meem Saakin ادغام میم ساکن

mischief to appear in the land!"

arḍil-fasaad.

الْأَرْضِ الْفَسَادَ ﴿٢٦﴾

27. Moses said: "I have indeed called upon my Lord and your Lord (for protection) from every arrogant one who believes not in the Day of Account!"

27. Wa qaala Moosaaa innee-'uẕtu bi-Rabbee wa Rabbikum min kulli mutakabbiril-laa yu'minu bi-Yawmil-Ḥisaab.

(Section 3)

وَقَالَ مُوسَىٰ إِنِّي عُذْتُ بِرَبِّي وَرَبِّكُم
مِّن كُلِّ مُتَكَبِّرٍ لَّا يُؤْمِنُ بِيَوْمِ
الْحِسَابِ ﴿٢٧﴾

28. A believer, a man from among the people of Pharaoh, who had concealed his faith, said: "Will you slay a man because he says, 'My Lord is Allah'?- when he has indeed come to you with Clear (Signs) from your Lord? and if he be a liar, on him is (the sin of) his lie: but, if he is telling the Truth, then will fall on you something of the (calamity) of which he warns you: Truly Allah guides not one who transgresses and lies!

28. Wa qaala rajulum mu'minum-min Aali Fir'awna yaktumu eemaanahooo ataqtuloona rajulan añy-yaqoola Rabbiyal-laahu wa qad jaaa'akum bil-bayyinaati mir-Rabbikum wa iñy-yaku kaaẕiban fa'alayhi kaẕibuhoo wa iñy-yaku ṣaadiqañy-yuṣibkum ba'dul-laẕee ya'idukum innal-laaha laa yahdee man huwa musrifun kaẕẕaab.

وَقَالَ رَجُلٌ مُّؤْمِنٌ ۖ مِّنْ آلِ
فِرْعَوْنَ يَكْتُمُ إِيمَانَهُ أَتَقْتُلُونَ
رَجُلًا أَن يَقُولَ رَبِّيَ اللَّهُ وَقَدْ
جَاءَكُم بِالْبَيِّنَاتِ مِن رَّبِّكُمْ ۖ وَإِن
يَكُ كَاذِبًا فَعَلَيْهِ كَذِبُهُ ۖ وَإِن
يَكُ صَادِقًا يُصِبْكُم بَعْضُ الَّذِي
يَعِدُكُمْ ۖ إِنَّ اللَّهَ لَا يَهْدِي مَنْ
هُوَ مُسْرِفٌ كَذَّابٌ ﴿٢٨﴾

29. "O my People! Yours is the dominion this day: You have the upper hand in the land: but who will help us from the Punishment of Allah, should it befall us?" Pharaoh said: "I but point out to you that which I see (myself); Nor do I guide you but to the Path of Right!"

29. Yaa qawmi lakumul-mulkul-yawma ẓaahireena fil arḍi famañy-yanṣurunaa mim baåsil-laahi in jaaa'anaa; qaala Fir'awnu maaa ureekum illaa maaa araa wa maaa ahdeekum illaa sabeelar-rashaad.

يَا قَوْمِ لَكُمُ الْمُلْكُ الْيَوْمَ ظَاهِرِينَ
فِي الْأَرْضِ فَمَن يَنصُرُنَا مِن بَأْسِ
اللَّهِ إِن جَاءَنَا ۚ قَالَ فِرْعَوْنُ مَا
أُرِيكُمْ إِلَّا مَا أَرَىٰ وَمَا أَهْدِيكُمْ
إِلَّا سَبِيلَ الرَّشَادِ ﴿٢٩﴾

30. Then said the man who believed: "O my people! Truly I do fear for you something like the Day (of disaster) of the Confederates (in sin)!-

30. Wa qaalal-laẕeee aamana yaa qawmi inneee akhaafu 'alaykum misla yawmil-Aḥzaab.

وَقَالَ الَّذِي آمَنَ يَا قَوْمِ إِنِّي أَخَافُ
عَلَيْكُم مِّثْلَ يَوْمِ الْأَحْزَابِ ﴿٣٠﴾

31. "Something like the fate of the People of Noah, the 'Ad, and the Thamud, and those who came after them: but Allah never wishes injustice to His Servants.

31. Misla daåbi qawmi Nooḥiñw-wa 'Aadiñw-wa Samooda wallaẕeena mim ba'dihim; wa mal-laahu yureedu ẓulmal-lil 'ibaad.

مِثْلَ دَأْبِ قَوْمِ نُوحٍ وَعَادٍ وَثَمُودَ
وَالَّذِينَ مِن بَعْدِهِمْ ۚ وَمَا اللَّهُ
يُرِيدُ ظُلْمًا لِّلْعِبَادِ ﴿٣١﴾

32. "And O my people! I fear for you a Day when there will be Mutual calling (and wailing),-

32. Wa yaa qawmi inneee akhaafu 'alaykum yawmat-tanaad.

وَيَا قَوْمِ إِنِّي أَخَافُ عَلَيْكُمْ يَوْمَ
التَّنَادِ ﴿٣٢﴾

33. "A Day when you shall turn your backs and flee: No defender shall you have from Allah: Any whom Allah leaves to stray,

33. Yawma tuwalloona mudbireena maa lakum minal-laahi min 'aaṣim; wa mañy-yuḍlilil-laahu

يَوْمَ تُوَلُّونَ مُدْبِرِينَ مَا لَكُم مِّنَ
اللَّهِ مِنْ عَاصِمٍ ۗ وَمَن يُضْلِلِ اللَّهُ

Ikhfa اخفاء | Ghunna غنّہ | Ikhfa Meem Saakin اخفاء میم ساکن | Idghaam ادغام | Qalqala قلقلہ | Qalb قلب | Idghaam Meem Saakin ادغام میم ساکن

there is none to guide...

famaa lahoo min haad.

فَمَا لَهٗ مِنْ هَادٍ ۝٣٣

34. "And to you there came Joseph in times gone by, with Clear Signs, but you ceased not to doubt of the (Mission) for which he had come: At length, when he died, you said: 'No apostle will Allah send after him.' thus does Allah leave to stray such as transgress and live in doubt,-

34. Wa laqad jaaa'akum Yoosufu min qablu bil-bayyinaati famaa ziltum fee shakkim-mimmaa jaaa'akum bihee ḥattaaa izaa halaka qultum lañy-yab'asal-laahu mim ba'dihee Rasoolaa; kazaalika yuḍillul-laahu man huwa Musrifum-murtaab.

وَلَقَدْ جَآءَكُمْ يُوْسُفُ مِنْ قَبْلُ
بِالْبَيِّنٰتِ فَمَا زِلْتُمْ فِيْ شَكٍّ مِّمَّا
جَآءَكُمْ بِهٖ ۭ حَتّٰٓى اِذَا هَلَكَ قُلْتُمْ
لَنْ يَّبْعَثَ اللّٰهُ مِنْۢ بَعْدِهٖ رَسُوْلًا ۭ
كَذٰلِكَ يُضِلُّ اللّٰهُ مَنْ هُوَ مُسْرِفٌ
مُّرْتَابُۨ ۝٣٤

35. "(Such) as dispute about the Signs of Allah, without any authority that has reached them, grievous and odious (is such conduct) in the sight of Allah and of the Believers. Thus does Allah, seal up every heart of arrogant and obstinate Transgressors."

35. Allazeena yujaadiloona feee Aaayaatil-laahi bighayri sulṭaanin ataahum kabura maqtan 'indal-laahi wa 'indal-lazeena aamanoo; kazaalika yaṭba'ul-laahu 'alaa kulli qalbi mutakabbirin jabbaar.

اَلَّذِيْنَ يُجَادِلُوْنَ فِيْٓ اٰيٰتِ اللّٰهِ
بِغَيْرِ سُلْطٰنٍ اَتٰىهُمْ ۭ كَبُرَ مَقْتًا عِنْدَ
اللّٰهِ وَعِنْدَ الَّذِيْنَ اٰمَنُوْا ۭ كَذٰلِكَ
يَطْبَعُ اللّٰهُ عَلٰى كُلِّ قَلْبِ مُتَكَبِّرٍ
جَبَّارٍ ۝٣٥

36. Pharaoh said: "O Haman! Build me a lofty palace, that I may attain the ways and means,-

36. Wa qaala Fir'awnu yaa Haamaanub-ni lee ṣarḥal-la'alleee ablughul-asbaab.

وَقَالَ فِرْعَوْنُ يٰهَامٰنُ ابْنِ لِيْ
صَرْحًا لَّعَلِّيْٓ اَبْلُغُ الْاَسْبَابَ ۝٣٦

37. "The ways and means of (reaching) the heavens, and that I may mount up to the Allah of Moses: But as far as I am concerned, I think (Moses) is a liar!" Thus was made alluring, in Pharaoh's eyes, the evil of his deeds, and he was hindered from the Path; and the plot of Pharaoh led to nothing but perdition (for him).

37. Asbaabas-samaawaati fa-aṭṭali'a ilaaa ilaahi Moosaa wa innee la-azunnuhoo kaazibaa; wa kazaalika zuyyina li-Fir'awna sooo'u 'amalihee wa ṣudda 'anis-sabeel; wa maa kaydu Fir'awna illaa fee tabaab.

(Section 4)

اَسْبَابَ السَّمٰوٰتِ فَاَطَّلِعَ اِلٰٓى اِلٰهِ
مُوْسٰى وَاِنِّيْ لَاَظُنُّهٗ كَاذِبًا ۭ وَكَذٰلِكَ
زُيِّنَ لِفِرْعَوْنَ سُوْۗءُ عَمَلِهٖ وَصُدَّ عَنِ
السَّبِيْلِ ۭ وَمَا كَيْدُ فِرْعَوْنَ اِلَّا
فِيْ تَبَابٍ ۝٣٧ ع ربع

38. The man who believed said further: "O my people! Follow me: I will lead you to the Path of Right.

38. Wa qaalal-lazeee aamana yaa qawmit-tabi'ooni ahdikum sabeelar-rashaad.

وَقَالَ الَّذِيْٓ اٰمَنَ يٰقَوْمِ اتَّبِعُوْنِ
اَهْدِكُمْ سَبِيْلَ الرَّشَادِ ۝٣٨

39. "O my people! This life of the present is nothing but (temporary) convenience: It is the Hereafter that is the Home that will last.

39. Yaa qawmi innamaa haazihil-ḥayaatud-dunyaa mataa'uñw-wa innal-Aakhirata hiya daarul-qaraar.

يٰقَوْمِ اِنَّمَا هٰذِهِ الْحَيٰوةُ الدُّنْيَا
مَتَاعٌ ۡ وَّاِنَّ الْاٰخِرَةَ هِيَ دَارُ الْقَرَارِ ۝٣٩

40. "He that works evil will not be requited but by the like thereof: and he that works a righteous deed - whether man or woman - and is a Believer- such

40. Man 'amila sayyi'atan falaa yujzaaa illaa mislahaa wa man 'amila ṣaaliḥam-min zakarin aw unsaa wa huwa mu'minun fa-ulaaa'ika

مَنْ عَمِلَ سَيِّئَةً فَلَا يُجْزٰٓى اِلَّا
مِثْلَهَا ۚ وَمَنْ عَمِلَ صَالِحًا مِّنْ
ذَكَرٍ اَوْ اُنْثٰى وَهُوَ مُؤْمِنٌ فَاُولٰۗىِٕكَ

will enter the Garden (of Bliss): "Taste you (the fruits of) what you earned!" Therein will they have abundance without measure.

41. "And O my people! How (strange) it is for me to call you to Salvation while you call me to the Fire!

42. "You do call upon me to blaspheme against Allah, and to join with Him partners of whom I have no knowledge; and I call you to the Exalted in Power, Who forgives again and again!"

43. "Without doubt you do call me to one who is not fit to be called to, whether in this world, or in the Hereafter; our return will be to Allah; and the Transgressors will be Companions of the Fire!

44. "Soon will you remember what I say to you (now), My (own) affair I commit to Allah: for Allah (ever) watches over His Servants."

45. Then Allah saved him from (every) ill that they plotted (against him), but the burnt of the Penalty encompassed on all sides the People of Pharaoh.

46. In front of the Fire will they be brought, morning and evening: And (the sentence will be) on the Day that Judgment will be established: "Cast you the People of Pharaoh into the severest Chastisement!"

47. Behold, they will dispute with each other in the Fire! The weak ones (who followed) will say to those who had been arrogant, "We but followed you: Can you then take (on yourselves) from us some share of the Fire?

48. Those who had been arrogant will say: "We are all in this (Fire)! Truly, Allah has judged between (His) Servants!"

49. Those in the Fire will say to the Keepers of

yadkhuloonal-Jannata yurzaqoona feehaa bighayri ḥisaab.

41. Wa yaa qawmi maa leee ad'ookum ilan-najaati wa tad'oonaneee ilan-Naar.

42. Tad'oonanee li-akfura billaahi wa ushrika bihee maa laysa lee bihee 'ilmuñw-wa ana ad'ookum ilal'Azeezil-Ghaffaar.

43. Laa jarama annamaa tad'oonaneee ilayhi laysa lahoo da'watun fid-dunyaa wa laa fil-Aakhirati wa anna maraddanaaa ilal-laahi wa annal-musrifeena hum Aṣḥaabun-Naar.

44. Fasatazkuroona maaa aqoolu lakum; wa ufawwiḍu amreee ilal-laah; innallaaha baṣeerum bil'ibaad.

45. Fa-waqaahul-laahu sayyiaati maa makaroo wa ḥaaqa bi-Aali-Fir'awna sooo'ul-'azaab.

46. An-Naaru yu'raḍoona 'alayhaa ghuduwwañw-wa 'ashiyyañw wa Yawma taqoomus-Saa'atu adkhilooo Aala Fir'awna ashaddal-'azaab.

47. Wa iz yataḥaaajjoona fin Naari fa-yaqooluḍ-ḍu'afaaa'u lillazeenas-takbarooo innaa kunnaa lakum taba'an fahal antum mughnoona 'annaa naṣeebam-minan-Naar.

48. Qaalal-lazeenas-takbarooo innaa kullun feehaaa innallaaha qad ḥakama baynal-'ibaad.

49. Wa qaalal-lazena fin-Naari likhazanati

يَدۡخُلُونَ ٱلۡجَنَّةَ يُرۡزَقُونَ فِيهَا
بِغَيۡرِ حِسَابٍ ﴿٤٠﴾
وَيَٰقَوۡمِ مَا لِيٓ أَدۡعُوكُمۡ إِلَى ٱلنَّجَوٰةِ
وَتَدۡعُونَنِيٓ إِلَى ٱلنَّارِ ﴿٤١﴾
تَدۡعُونَنِي لِأَكۡفُرَ بِٱللَّهِ وَأُشۡرِكَ
بِهِۦ مَا لَيۡسَ لِي بِهِۦ عِلۡمٞ وَأَنَا۠
أَدۡعُوكُمۡ إِلَى ٱلۡعَزِيزِ ٱلۡغَفَّٰرِ ﴿٤٢﴾
لَا جَرَمَ أَنَّمَا تَدۡعُونَنِيٓ إِلَيۡهِ
لَيۡسَ لَهُۥ دَعۡوَةٞ فِي ٱلدُّنۡيَا وَلَا فِي
ٱلۡأٓخِرَةِ وَأَنَّ مَرَدَّنَآ إِلَى ٱللَّهِ
وَأَنَّ ٱلۡمُسۡرِفِينَ هُمۡ أَصۡحَٰبُ ٱلنَّارِ ﴿٤٣﴾
فَسَتَذۡكُرُونَ مَآ أَقُولُ لَكُمۡۚ وَأُفَوِّضُ
أَمۡرِيٓ إِلَى ٱللَّهِۚ إِنَّ ٱللَّهَ بَصِيرُۢ
بِٱلۡعِبَادِ ﴿٤٤﴾
فَوَقَىٰهُ ٱللَّهُ سَيِّـَٔاتِ مَا مَكَرُواْۖ
وَحَاقَ بِـَٔالِ فِرۡعَوۡنَ سُوٓءُ ٱلۡعَذَابِ ﴿٤٥﴾
ٱلنَّارُ يُعۡرَضُونَ عَلَيۡهَا غُدُوّٗا وَعَشِيّٗاۚ
وَيَوۡمَ تَقُومُ ٱلسَّاعَةُ أَدۡخِلُوٓاْ
ءَالَ فِرۡعَوۡنَ أَشَدَّ ٱلۡعَذَابِ ﴿٤٦﴾
وَإِذۡ يَتَحَآجُّونَ فِي ٱلنَّارِ فَيَقُولُ
ٱلضُّعَفَٰٓؤُاْ لِلَّذِينَ ٱسۡتَكۡبَرُوٓاْ إِنَّا كُنَّا
لَكُمۡ تَبَعٗا فَهَلۡ أَنتُم مُّغۡنُونَ
عَنَّا نَصِيبٗا مِّنَ ٱلنَّارِ ﴿٤٧﴾
قَالَ ٱلَّذِينَ ٱسۡتَكۡبَرُوٓاْ إِنَّا كُلّٞ
فِيهَآ إِنَّ ٱللَّهَ قَدۡ حَكَمَ بَيۡنَ ٱلۡعِبَادِ ﴿٤٨﴾
وَقَالَ ٱلَّذِينَ فِي ٱلنَّارِ لِخَزَنَةِ

النصف

Ikhfa اخفاء | Ghunna غُنّہ | Ikhfa Meem Saakin اخفاء میم ساکن | Idghaam ادغام | Qalqala قلقلہ | Qalb قلب | Idghaam Meem Saakin ادغام میم ساکن

Hell: "Pray to your Lord to lighten us the Penalty for a day (at least)!"

Jahannamad-'oo Rabbakum yukhaffif 'annaa yawmam-minal-'azaab.

جَهَنَّمَ ادْعُوْا رَبَّكُمْ يُخَفِّفْ عَنَّا
يَوْمًا مِّنَ الْعَذَابِ ﴿٤٩﴾

50. They will say: "Did there not come to you your apostles with Clear Signs?" They will say, "Yes". They will reply, "Then pray (as you like)! But the prayer of those without Faith is nothing but (futile wandering) in (mazes of) error!"

50. Qaalooo awalam taku taåteekum Rusulukum bilbayyinaati qaaloo balaa; qaaloo fad'oo; wa maa du'aa'ul-kaafireena illaa fee ḍalaal. **(Sec. 5)**

قَالُوْٓا اَوَلَمْ تَكُ تَاْتِيْكُمْ رُسُلُكُمْ
بِالْبَيِّنٰتِ ؕ قَالُوْا بَلٰى ؕ قَالُوْا فَادْعُوْا ۚ
وَمَا دُعٰٓؤُا الْكٰفِرِيْنَ اِلَّا فِيْ ضَلٰلٍ ﴿٥٠﴾

51. We will, without doubt, help Our apostles and those who believe, (both) in this world's life and on the Day when the Witnesses will stand forth,-

51. Innaa lanansuru Rusulanaa wallazeena aamanoo fil-ḥayaatid-dunyaa wa Yawma yaqoomul-ashhaad.

اِنَّا لَنَنْصُرُ رُسُلَنَا وَالَّذِيْنَ اٰمَنُوْا فِي
الْحَيٰوةِ الدُّنْيَا وَيَوْمَ يَقُوْمُ الْاَشْهَادُ ﴿٥١﴾

52. The Day when no profit will it be to Wrong-doers to present their excuses, but they will (only) have the Curse and the Home of Misery.

52. Yawma laa yanfa'uz-zaalimeena ma'ziratuhum wa lahumul-la'natu wa lahum sooo'ud-daar.

يَوْمَ لَا يَنْفَعُ الظّٰلِمِيْنَ مَعْذِرَتُهُمْ
وَلَهُمُ اللَّعْنَةُ وَلَهُمْ سُوْٓءُ الدَّارِ ﴿٥٢﴾

53. We did aforetime give Moses the (Book of) Guidance, and We gave the book in inheritance to the Children of Israel,-

53. Wa laqad aataynaa Moosal-hudaa wa awrasnaa Baneee Israaa'eelal-Kitaab.

وَلَقَدْ اٰتَيْنَا مُوْسَى الْهُدٰى وَ
اَوْرَثْنَا بَنِيْٓ اِسْرَآءِيْلَ الْكِتٰبَ ﴿٥٣﴾

54. A Guide and a Message to men of Understanding.

54. Hudañw-wa zikraa li-ulil-albaab.

هُدًى وَّذِكْرٰى لِاُولِي الْاَلْبَابِ ﴿٥٤﴾

55. Patiently, then, persevere: for the Promise of Allah is true: and ask forgiveness for your fault, and celebrate the Praises of thy Lord in the evening and in the morning.

55. Faṣbir inna wa'dal-laahi ḥaqquñw-wastaghfir lizambika wa sabbiḥ biḥamdi Rabbika bil'ashiyyi wal-ibkaar.

فَاصْبِرْ اِنَّ وَعْدَ اللّٰهِ حَقٌّ وَّاسْتَغْفِرْ
لِذَنْۢبِكَ وَسَبِّحْ بِحَمْدِ رَبِّكَ بِالْعَشِيِّ
وَالْاِبْكَارِ ﴿٥٥﴾

56. Those who dispute about the signs of Allah without any authority bestowed on them,- there is nothing in their breasts but (the quest of) greatness, which they shall never attain to: seek refuge, then, in Allah: It is He Who hears and sees (all things).

56. Innal-lazeena yujaadiloona feee Aayaatil-laahi bighayri sulṭaanin ataahum in fee ṣudoorihim illaa kibrum-maa hum bibaaligheeh; fasta'iz billaahi innahoo Huwas-Samee'ul-Baṣeer.

اِنَّ الَّذِيْنَ يُجَادِلُوْنَ فِيْٓ اٰيٰتِ اللّٰهِ
بِغَيْرِ سُلْطٰنٍ اَتٰىهُمْ ۙ اِنْ فِيْ
صُدُوْرِهِمْ اِلَّا كِبْرٌ مَّا هُمْ
بِبَالِغِيْهِ ۚ فَاسْتَعِذْ بِاللّٰهِ ؕ اِنَّهٗ هُوَ
السَّمِيْعُ الْبَصِيْرُ ﴿٥٦﴾

57. Assuredly the creation of the heavens and the earth is a greater (matter) than the creation of men: Yet most men understand not.

57. Lakhalqus-samaawaati wal-arḍi akbaru min khalqin-naasi wa laakinna aksaran-naasi laa ya'lamoon.

لَخَلْقُ السَّمٰوٰتِ وَالْاَرْضِ اَكْبَرُ مِنْ
خَلْقِ النَّاسِ وَلٰكِنَّ اَكْثَرَ النَّاسِ
لَا يَعْلَمُوْنَ ﴿٥٧﴾

58. Not equal are the blind and those who (clearly) see: Nor are (equal) those who believe and work deeds of righteousness, and those who do evil. Little do you learn by admonition!

58. Wa maa yastawil-a'maa walbaṣeeru wallazeena aamanoo wa 'amiluṣ-ṣaaliḥaati wa lal-museee'; qaleelam-maa tatazakkaroon.

وَمَا يَسْتَوِي الْاَعْمٰى وَالْبَصِيْرُ ۙ
وَالَّذِيْنَ اٰمَنُوْا وَعَمِلُوا الصّٰلِحٰتِ
وَلَا الْمُسِيْٓءُ ؕ قَلِيْلًا مَّا تَتَذَكَّرُوْنَ ﴿٥٨﴾

Ikhfa اخفاء | Ghunna غنّہ | Ikhfa Meem Saakin اخفاء میم ساکن | Idghaam ادغام | Qalqala قلقلہ | Qalb قلب | Idghaam Meem Saakin ادغام میم ساکن

59. The Hour will certainly come: Therein is no doubt: Yet most men believe not.

59. Innas-Saa'ata la-aatiyatul-laa rayba feehaa wa laakinna aks̲aran-naasi laa yu'minoon.

إِنَّ السَّاعَةَ لَآتِيَةٌ لَّا رَيْبَ فِيهَا
وَلَٰكِنَّ أَكْثَرَ النَّاسِ لَا يُؤْمِنُونَ ٥٩

60. And your Lord says: "Call on Me; I will answer your (Prayer): but those who are too arrogant to serve Me will surely find themselves in Hell - in humiliation!"

60. Wa qaala Rabbukumud-'ooneee astajib lakum; innal-laz̲eena yastakbiroona an 'ibaadatee sa-yadkhuloona Jahannama daakhireen. **(Sec. 6)**

وَقَالَ رَبُّكُمُ ادْعُونِي أَسْتَجِبْ لَكُمْ ۚ
إِنَّ الَّذِينَ يَسْتَكْبِرُونَ عَنْ عِبَادَتِي
سَيَدْخُلُونَ جَهَنَّمَ دَاخِرِينَ ٦٠ ع

ع ١٠ ٦

61. It is Allah Who has made the Night for you, that ye may rest therein, and the days as that which helps (you) to see. Verily Allah is full of Grace and Bounty to men: yet most men give no thanks.

61. Allaahul-laz̲ee ja'ala lakumul-layla litaskunoo feehi wannahaara mubṣiraa; innal-laaha laz̲oo faḍlin 'alan-naasi wa laakinna aks̲aran-naasi laa yashkuroon.

اللَّهُ الَّذِي جَعَلَ لَكُمُ اللَّيْلَ لِتَسْكُنُوا
فِيهِ وَالنَّهَارَ مُبْصِرًا ۚ إِنَّ اللَّهَ
لَذُو فَضْلٍ عَلَى النَّاسِ وَلَٰكِنَّ أَكْثَرَ
النَّاسِ لَا يَشْكُرُونَ ٦١

وقف لازم

62. Such is Allah, your Lord, the Creator of all things, there is no Allah but He: Then how you are deluded away from the Truth!

62. Z̲aalikumul-laahu Rabbukum khaaliqu kulli shay'; laaa ilaaha illaa Huwa fa-annaa tu'fakoon.

ذَٰلِكُمُ اللَّهُ رَبُّكُمْ خَالِقُ كُلِّ شَيْءٍ
لَّا إِلَٰهَ إِلَّا هُوَ ۖ فَأَنَّىٰ تُؤْفَكُونَ ٦٢

63. Thus are deluded those who are wont to reject the Signs of Allah.

63. Kaz̲aalika yu'fakul-laz̲ee-na kaanoo bi-Aayaatil-laahi yajḥadoon.

كَذَٰلِكَ يُؤْفَكُ الَّذِينَ كَانُوا
بِآيَاتِ اللَّهِ يَجْحَدُونَ ٦٣

64. It is Allah Who has made for you the earth as a resting place, and the sky as a canopy, and has given you shape- and made your shapes beautiful,- and has provided for you Sustenance, of things pure and good;- such is Allah your Lord. So Glory to Allah, the Lord of the Worlds!

64. Allaahul-laz̲ee ja'ala lakumul-arḍa qaraarañw-wassamaaa'a binaaa'añw-wa ṣawwarakum fa-aḥsana ṣuwarakum wa razaqakum minaṭ-ṭayyibaat; z̲aalikumul-laahu Rabbukum fatabaarakal-laahu Rabbul-'aalameen.

اللَّهُ الَّذِي جَعَلَ لَكُمُ الْأَرْضَ
قَرَارًا وَالسَّمَاءَ بِنَاءً وَصَوَّرَكُمْ
فَأَحْسَنَ صُوَرَكُمْ وَرَزَقَكُم مِّنَ
الطَّيِّبَاتِ ۚ ذَٰلِكُمُ اللَّهُ رَبُّكُمْ ۖ
فَتَبَارَكَ اللَّهُ رَبُّ الْعَالَمِينَ ٦٤

65. He is the Living (One): There is no god but He: Call upon Him, giving Him sincere devotion. Praise be to Allah, Lord of the Worlds!

65. Huwal-Ḥayyu laaa ilaaha illaa Huwa fad'oohu mukh-liṣeena lahud-deen; alḥamdu lillaahi Rabbil-'aalameen.

هُوَ الْحَيُّ لَا إِلَٰهَ إِلَّا هُوَ فَادْعُوهُ
مُخْلِصِينَ لَهُ الدِّينَ ۗ الْحَمْدُ لِلَّهِ
رَبِّ الْعَالَمِينَ ٦٥

66. Say: "I have been forbidden to invoke those whom you invoke besides Allah,- seeing that the Clear Sings have come to me from my Lord; and I have been commanded to submit (in Islam) to the Lord of the Worlds."

66. Qul innee nuheetu an a'budal-laz̲eena tad'oona min doonil-laahi lammaa jaaa'a-niyal-bayyinaatu mir-Rabbee wa umirtu an uslima li-Rabbil-'aalameen.

قُلْ إِنِّي نُهِيتُ أَنْ أَعْبُدَ الَّذِينَ
تَدْعُونَ مِن دُونِ اللَّهِ لَمَّا جَاءَنِيَ
الْبَيِّنَاتُ مِن رَّبِّي وَأُمِرْتُ أَنْ
أُسْلِمَ لِرَبِّ الْعَالَمِينَ ٦٦

67. It is He Who has created you from dust then

67. Huwal-laz̲ee khalaqakum min turaabin s̲umma

هُوَ الَّذِي خَلَقَكُم مِّن تُرَابٍ ثُمَّ

Ikhfa	Ghunna	Ikhfa Meem Saakin	Idghaam	Qalqala	Qalb	Idghaam Meem Saakin
اخفاء	غُنّہ	اخفاء میم ساکن	ادغام	قلقلہ	قلب	ادغام میم ساکن

from a sperm-drop, then from a leech-like clot; then does He get you out (into the light) as a child: then lets you (grow and) reach your age of full strength; then lets you become old,- though of you there are some who die before;- and lets you reach a Term appointed; in order that ye may learn wisdom.

min nuṭfatin summa min 'alaqatin summa yukhrijukum ṭiflan summa litablughooo ashuddakum summa litakoonoo shuyookhaa; wa minkum mañy-yutawaffaa min qablu wa litablughooo ajalam-musammañw-wa la'allakum ta'qiloon.

مِنْ نُّطْفَةٍ ثُمَّ مِنْ عَلَقَةٍ ثُمَّ
يُخْرِجُكُمْ طِفْلًا ثُمَّ لِتَبْلُغُوْٓا
اَشُدَّكُمْ ثُمَّ لِتَكُوْنُوْا شُيُوْخًا ۚ
وَمِنْكُمْ مَّنْ يُّتَوَفّٰى مِنْ قَبْلُ
وَلِتَبْلُغُوْٓا اَجَلًا مُّسَمًّى وَّلَعَلَّكُمْ
تَعْقِلُوْنَ ﴿٦٧﴾

68. It is He Who gives Life and Death; and when He decides upon an affair, He says to it, "Be", and it is.

68. Huwal-lazee yuḥyee wa yumeetu fa-izaa qaḍaa amran fa-innamaa yaqoolu lahoo kun fa-yakoon. **(Section 7)**

هُوَ الَّذِيْ يُحْيٖ وَيُمِيْتُ ۚ فَاِذَا
قَضٰٓى اَمْرًا فَاِنَّمَا يَقُوْلُ لَهٗ كُنْ
فَيَكُوْنُ ﴿٦٨﴾ ع

ع ٧/١٤ — معانقة ١٣ عند المتاخرين ١٢

69. Do you see not those that dispute concerning the Sings of Allah? How are they turned away (from Reality)?-

69. Alam tara ilal-lazeena yujaadiloona feee Aayaatil-laahi annaa yuṣrafoon.

اَلَمْ تَرَ اِلَى الَّذِيْنَ يُجَادِلُوْنَ
فِيْٓ اٰيٰتِ اللّٰهِ ۭ اَنّٰى يُصْرَفُوْنَ ﴿٦٩﴾

70. Those who reject the Book and the (revelations) with which We sent Our apostles: but soon shall they know,-

70. Allazeena kazzaboo bil-Kitaabi wa bimaaa arsalnaa bihee Rusulanaa fasawfa ya'lamoon.

اَلَّذِيْنَ كَذَّبُوْا بِالْكِتٰبِ وَبِمَآ اَرْسَلْنَا
بِهٖ رُسُلَنَا ۛ فَسَوْفَ يَعْلَمُوْنَ ﴿٧٠﴾

71. When the yokes (shall be) round their necks, and the chains; they shall be dragged along-

71. Izil-aghlaalu feee a'naaqihim wassalaasilu yusḥaboon.

اِذِ الْاَغْلٰلُ فِيْٓ اَعْنَاقِهِمْ وَالسَّلٰسِلُ
يُسْحَبُوْنَ ﴿٧١﴾

72. In the boiling fetid fluid: then in the Fire shall they be burned;

72. Fil-ḥameemi summa fin-Naari yusjaroon.

فِي الْحَمِيْمِ ۙ ثُمَّ فِي النَّارِ يُسْجَرُوْنَ ﴿٧٢﴾

73. Then shall it be said to them: "Where are the (deities) to which you gave part- worship-

73. Summa qeela lahum ayna maa kuntum tushrikoon.

ثُمَّ قِيْلَ لَهُمْ اَيْنَ مَا كُنْتُمْ
تُشْرِكُوْنَ ﴿٧٣﴾

74. "Besides Allah?" They will reply: "They have left us in the lurch: No, we invoked not, of old, anything (that had real existence)." Thus does Allah leave the Unbelievers to stray.

74. Min doonil-laahi qaaloo ḍalloo 'annaa bal-lam nakun nad'oo min qablu shay'aa; kazaalika yuḍillul-laahul-kaafireen.

مِنْ دُوْنِ اللّٰهِ ۭ قَالُوْا ضَلُّوْا عَنَّا
بَلْ لَّمْ نَكُنْ نَّدْعُوْا مِنْ قَبْلُ شَيْـًٔا ۭ
كَذٰلِكَ يُضِلُّ اللّٰهُ الْكٰفِرِيْنَ ﴿٧٤﴾

75. "That was because you were wont to rejoice on the earth in things other than the Truth, and that you were wont to be insolent.

75. Zaalikum bimaa kuntum tafraḥoona fil-arḍi bighayril-ḥaqqi wa bimaa kuntum tamraḥoon.

ذٰلِكُمْ بِمَا كُنْتُمْ تَفْرَحُوْنَ فِي الْاَرْضِ
بِغَيْرِ الْحَقِّ وَبِمَا كُنْتُمْ تَمْرَحُوْنَ ﴿٧٥﴾

76. "Enter you the gates of Hell, to dwell therein: and evil is (this) abode of the arrogant!"

76. Udkhulooo abwaaba Jahannama khaalideena feehaa fabi'sa maswal-mutakabbireen.

اُدْخُلُوْٓا اَبْوَابَ جَهَنَّمَ خٰلِدِيْنَ
فِيْهَا ۚ فَبِئْسَ مَثْوَى الْمُتَكَبِّرِيْنَ ﴿٧٦﴾

77. So persevere in patience; for the Promise of Allah is true: and whether

77. Faṣbir inna wa'dal-laahi ḥaqq; fa-immaa

فَاصْبِرْ اِنَّ وَعْدَ اللّٰهِ حَقٌّ ۚ فَاِمَّا

Ikhfa اخفاء | Ghunna غُنّہ | Ikhfa Meem Saakin اخفاء میم ساکن | Idghaam ادغام | Qalqala قلقلہ | Qalb قلب | Idghaam Meem Saakin ادغام میم ساکن

We show thee (in this life) some part of what We promise them,- or We take your soul (to Our Mercy) (before that),-(in any case) it is to Us that they shall (all) return.

nuriyannaka ba'ḍal-lazee na'iduhum aw natawaffayannaka fa-ilaynaa yurja'oon.

نُرِيَنَّكَ بَعْضَ الَّذِىْ نَعِدُهُمْ اَوْ
نَتَوَفَّيَنَّكَ فَاِلَيْنَا يُرْجَعُوْنَ ﴿٧٧﴾

78. We did aforetime send apostles before you: of them there are some whose story We have related to you, and some whose story We have not related to you. It was not (possible) for any apostle to bring a sign except by the leave of Allah: but when the Command of Allah issued, the matter was decided in truth and justice, and there perished, there and then those who stood on Falsehoods.

78. Wa laqad arsalnaa Rusulam-min qablika minhum man qaṣaṣnaa 'alayka wa minhum mal-lam naqṣuṣ 'alayk; wa maa kaana li-Rasoolin añy-yaåtiya bi-Aayatin illaa bi-iznil-laah; fa-izaa jaaa'a amrul-laahi quḍiya bilḥaqqi wa khasira hunaalikal-mubṭiloon. **(Section 8)**

وَ لَقَدْ اَرْسَلْنَا رُسُلًا مِّنْ قَبْلِكَ
مِنْهُمْ مَّنْ قَصَصْنَا عَلَيْكَ وَمِنْهُمْ
مَّنْ لَّمْ نَقْصُصْ عَلَيْكَ ؕ وَمَا كَانَ
لِرَسُوْلٍ اَنْ يَّاْتِىَ بِاٰيَةٍ اِلَّا بِاِذْنِ
اللّٰهِ ۚ فَاِذَا جَآءَ اَمْرُ اللّٰهِ قُضِىَ بِالْحَقِّ
وَخَسِرَ هُنَالِكَ الْمُبْطِلُوْنَ ﴿٧٨﴾ ع

ع ٨/١٤

79. It is Allah Who made cattle for you, that ye may use some for riding and some for food;

79. Allaahul-lazee ja'ala lakumul-an'aama litarkaboo minhaa wa minhaa taåkuloon.

اَللّٰهُ الَّذِىْ جَعَلَ لَكُمُ الْاَنْعَامَ
لِتَرْكَبُوْا مِنْهَا وَمِنْهَا تَاْكُلُوْنَ ﴿٧٩﴾ ز

80. And there are (other) advantages in them for you (besides); that you may through them attain to any need (there may be) in your hearts; and on them and on ships you are carried.

80. Wa lakum feehaa manaafi'u wa litablughoo 'alayhaa ḥaajatan fee ṣudoorikum wa 'alayhaa wa 'alal-fulki tuḥmaloon.

وَلَكُمْ فِيْهَا مَنَافِعُ وَلِتَبْلُغُوْا عَلَيْهَا
حَاجَةً فِىْ صُدُوْرِكُمْ وَعَلَيْهَا وَ
عَلَى الْفُلْكِ تُحْمَلُوْنَ ﴿٨٠﴾ ط

81. And He shows you (always) His Signs: then which of the Signs of Allah will you deny?

81. Wa yureekum Aayaatihee fa-ayya Aayaatil-laahi tunkiroon.

وَيُرِيْكُمْ اٰيٰتِهٖ ۖ ق فَاَىَّ اٰيٰتِ
اللّٰهِ تُنْكِرُوْنَ ﴿٨١﴾

82. Do they not travel through the earth and see what was the End of those before them? They were more numerous than these and superior in strength and in the traces (they have left) in the land: Yet all that they accomplished was of no profit to them.

82. Afalam yaseeroo fil-arḍi fa-yanẓuroo kayfa kaana 'aaqibatul-lazeena min qablihim; kaanooo aksara minhum wa ashadda quwwatañw-wa aasaaran fil-arḍi famaaa aghnaa 'anhum maa kaanoo yaksiboon.

اَفَلَمْ يَسِيْرُوْا فِى الْاَرْضِ فَيَنْظُرُوْا
كَيْفَ كَانَ عَاقِبَةُ الَّذِيْنَ مِنْ
قَبْلِهِمْ ؕ كَانُوْٓا اَكْثَرَ مِنْهُمْ وَاَشَدَّ
قُوَّةً وَّاٰثَارًا فِى الْاَرْضِ فَمَآ اَغْنٰى
عَنْهُمْ مَّا كَانُوْا يَكْسِبُوْنَ ﴿٨٢﴾

83. For when their apostles came to them with Clear Signs, they exulted in such knowledge (and skill) as they had;but that very (wrath) at which they were wont to scoff hemmed them in.

83. Falammaa jaaa'at-hum Rusuluhum bilbayyinaati fariḥoo bimaa 'indahum minal-'ilmi wa ḥaaqa bihim maa kaanoo bihee yastahzi'oon.

فَلَمَّا جَآءَتْهُمْ رُسُلُهُمْ بِالْبَيِّنٰتِ
فَرِحُوْا بِمَا عِنْدَهُمْ مِّنَ الْعِلْمِ وَحَاقَ
بِهِمْ مَّا كَانُوْا بِهٖ يَسْتَهْزِءُوْنَ ﴿٨٣﴾

84. But when they saw Our Punishment, they said: "We believe in Allah,- the one Allah - and we reject the partners we used to join with Him."

84. Falammaa ra-aw baåsanaa qaalooo aamannaa billaahi waḥdahoo wa kafarnaa bimaa kunnaa bihee mushrikeen.

فَلَمَّا رَاَوْا بَاْسَنَا قَالُوْٓا اٰمَنَّا بِاللّٰهِ
وَحْدَهٗ وَكَفَرْنَا بِمَا كُنَّا بِهٖ مُشْرِكِيْنَ ﴿٨٤﴾

85. But their professing the Faith when they (actually) saw

85. Falam yaku yanfa'uhum eemaanuhum lammaa ra-aw

فَلَمْ يَكُ يَنْفَعُهُمْ اِيْمَانُهُمْ لَمَّا رَاَوْا

Ikhfa اخفاء · Ghunna غُنّہ · Ikhfa Meem Saakin اخفاء میم ساکن · Idghaam ادغام · Qalqala قلقلہ · Qalb قلب · Idghaam Meem Saakin ادغام میم ساکن

Our Punishment was not going to profit them. (Such has been) Allah's Way of dealing with His Servants (from the most ancient times). And even thus did the Rejecters of Allah perish (utterly)!

41. Ha Mim Sajda

In the name of Allah, Most Gracious, Most Merciful.

1. *Ha-Mim.*

2. A Revelation from (Allah), Most Gracious, Most Merciful;-

3. A Book, whereof the verses are explained in detail;- a Qur'an in Arabic, for people who understand;-

4. Giving good news and admonition: yet most of them turn away, and so they hear not.

5. They say: "Our hearts are under veils, (concealed) from that to which you does invite us, and in our ears is a deafness, and between us and you is a screen: so do you (what you will); for us, we shall do (what we will!)"

6. Say thou: "I am but a man like you: It is revealed to me by Inspiration, that your Allah is one Allah: so stand true to Him, and ask for His Forgiveness." And woe to those who join gods with Allah,-

7. Those who practise not regular Charity, and who even deny the Hereafter.

8. For those who believe and work deeds of righteousness is a reward that will never fail.

9. Say: Is it that you deny Him Who created the earth in two Days? And do you join equals with Him? He is the Lord of (all) the Worlds.

baåsanaa sunnatal-laahil-latee qad khalat fee 'ibaadihee wa khasira hunaalikal-kaafiroon.

(Section 9)

Sûrat Ḥâ Mîm as-Sajdah–41

(Revealed at Makkah)

Bismillaahir Raḥmaanir Raḥeem

1. Ḥaa-Meeem.

2. Tanzeelum Minar-Rahmaanir-Raḥeem.

3. Kitaabun fuṣṣilat Aayaatuhoo Qur-aanan 'Arabiyyal-liqawmiñy-ya'lamoon.

4. Basheerañw-wa naẕeeran fa-a'raḍa aksaruhum fahum laa yasma'oon.

5. Wa qaaloo quloobunaa feee akinnatim-mimmaa tad'oonaaa ilayhi wa feee aaẕaaninaa waqruñw-wa mim bayninaa wa baynika ḥijaabun fa'mal innanaa 'aamiloon.

6. Qul innamaaa ana basharum-mislukum yooḥaaa ilayya annamaaa ilaahukum Ilaahuñw-Waaḥidun fastaqeemooo ilayhi wastaghfirooh; wa waylul-lil-mushrikeen.

7. Allaẕeena laa yu'toonaz-Zakaata wa hum bil-Aakhirati hum kaafiroon.

8. Innal-laẕeena aamanoo wa 'amiluṣ-ṣaaliḥaati lahum ajrun ghayru mamnoon. **(Section 1)**

9. Qul a'innakum latakfuroona billaẕee khalaqal-arḍa fee yawmayni wa taj'aloona lahooo andaadaa; ẕaalika Rabbul-'aalameen.

بَأْسَنَا ۚ سُنَّتَ اللّٰهِ الَّتِيْ قَدْ خَلَتْ
فِيْ عِبَادِهٖ ۚ وَخَسِرَ هُنَالِكَ
الْكٰفِرُوْنَ ﴿٨٥﴾

(٤١) سُوْرَةُ حٰمٓ السَّجْدَةِ مَكِّيَّةٌ (٦١)
بِسْمِ اللّٰهِ الرَّحْمٰنِ الرَّحِيْمِ

حٰمٓ ﴿١﴾
تَنْزِيْلٌ مِّنَ الرَّحْمٰنِ الرَّحِيْمِ ﴿٢﴾
كِتٰبٌ فُصِّلَتْ اٰيٰتُهٗ قُرْاٰنًا
عَرَبِيًّا لِّقَوْمٍ يَّعْلَمُوْنَ ﴿٣﴾
بَشِيْرًا وَّنَذِيْرًا ۚ فَاَعْرَضَ اَكْثَرُهُمْ
فَهُمْ لَا يَسْمَعُوْنَ ﴿٤﴾
وَقَالُوْا قُلُوْبُنَا فِيْٓ اَكِنَّةٍ مِّمَّا
تَدْعُوْنَآ اِلَيْهِ وَفِيْٓ اٰذَانِنَا وَقْرٌ
وَّمِنْۢ بَيْنِنَا وَبَيْنِكَ حِجَابٌ
فَاعْمَلْ اِنَّنَا عٰمِلُوْنَ ﴿٥﴾
قُلْ اِنَّمَآ اَنَا بَشَرٌ مِّثْلُكُمْ يُوْحٰٓى
اِلَيَّ اَنَّمَآ اِلٰهُكُمْ اِلٰهٌ وَّاحِدٌ
فَاسْتَقِيْمُوْٓا اِلَيْهِ وَاسْتَغْفِرُوْهُ ۗ
وَوَيْلٌ لِّلْمُشْرِكِيْنَ ﴿٦﴾
الَّذِيْنَ لَا يُؤْتُوْنَ الزَّكٰوةَ وَهُمْ
بِالْاٰخِرَةِ هُمْ كٰفِرُوْنَ ﴿٧﴾
اِنَّ الَّذِيْنَ اٰمَنُوْا وَعَمِلُوا الصّٰلِحٰتِ
لَهُمْ اَجْرٌ غَيْرُ مَمْنُوْنٍ ﴿٨﴾
قُلْ اَئِنَّكُمْ لَتَكْفُرُوْنَ بِالَّذِيْ خَلَقَ
الْاَرْضَ فِيْ يَوْمَيْنِ وَتَجْعَلُوْنَ لَهٗٓ
اَنْدَادًا ۚ ذٰلِكَ رَبُّ الْعٰلَمِيْنَ ﴿٩﴾

الثلثة

Ikhfa اخفاء | Ghunna غنّۃ | Ikhfa Meem Saakin اخفاءمیم ساکن | Idghaam ادغام | Qalqala قلقلہ | Qalb قلب | Idghaam Meem Saakin ادغام میم ساکن

10. He set on the (earth), mountains standing firm, high above it, and bestowed blessings on the earth, and measure therein its sustenance in four Days, alike for (all) who ask.

11. Moreover He comprehended in His design the sky, and it had been (as) smoke: He said to it and to the earth: "Come you together, willingly or unwillingly." They said: "We do come (together), in willing obedience."

12. So He completed them as seven firmaments in two Days, and He assigned to each heaven its duty and command. And We adorned the lower heaven with lights, and (provided it) with guard. Such is the Decree of (Him) the Exalted in Might, Full of Knowledge.

13. But if they turn away, say you: "I have warned you of a stunning Punishment (as of thunder and lightning) like that which (overtook) the 'Ad and the Thamud!"

14. Behold, the apostles came to them, from before them and behind them, (preaching): "Serve none but Allah." They said, "If our Lord had so pleased, He would certainly have sent down angels (to preach). Now we reject your mission (altogether)."

15. Now the 'Ad behaved arrogantly through the land, against (all) truth and reason, and said: "Who is superior to us in strength?" What! did they not see that Allah, Who created them, was superior to them in strength? But they continued to reject Our Signs!

16. So We sent against them a furious Wind through days of disaster, that We might give them a taste of a Chastisement of humiliation in this life;

10. Wa ja'ala feehaa rawaasiya min fawqihaa wa baaraka feehaa wa qaddara feehaaa aqwaatahaa feee arba'ati ayyaamin sawaaa'al-lissaaa'ileen.

11. Summas-tawaaa ilas-samaaa'i wa hiya dukhaanun faqaala lahaa wa lil-arḍi'-tiyaa ṭaw'an aw karhan qaalataaa ataynaa ṭaaa'i'een.

12. Faqaḍaahunna sab'a samaawaatin fee yawmayni wa awḥaa fee kulli samaaa'in amrahaa; wa zayyannas-samaaa'ad-dunyaa bimaṣaabeeḥa wa ḥifẕaa; ẕaalika taqdeerul-'Azeezil-'Aleem.

13. Fa-in a'raḍoo faqul anẕartukum ṣaa'iqatam-misla ṣaa'iqati 'Aadiñw-wa Samood.

14. Iẕ jaaa'at-humur-Rusulu mim bayni aydeehim wa min khalfihim allaa ta'budooo illal-laaha qaaloo law shaaa'a Rabbunaa la-anzala malaaa'ikatan fa-innaa bimaaa ursiltum bihee kaafiroon.

15. Fa-ammaa 'Aadun fastakbaroo fil-arḍi bighayril-ḥaqqi wa qaaloo man ashaddu minnaa quwwatan awalam yaraw annal-laahal-laẕee khalaqahum Huwa ashaddu minhum quwwatañw-wa kaanoo bi-Aayaatinaa yajḥadoon.

16. Fa-arsalnaa 'alayhim reeḥan ṣarṣaran feee ayyaamin naḥisaatil-linuẕeeqahum 'aẕaabal-khizyi fil-ḥayaatid-dunyaa wa

وَجَعَلَ فِيهَا رَوَاسِيَ مِن فَوْقِهَا
وَبٰرَكَ فِيهَا وَقَدَّرَ فِيهَآ أَقْوٰتَهَا
فِىٓ أَرْبَعَةِ أَيَّامٍ سَوَآءً لِّلسَّآئِلِينَ ١٠
ثُمَّ اسْتَوٰٓى إِلَى السَّمَآءِ وَهِىَ
دُخَانٌ فَقَالَ لَهَا وَلِلْأَرْضِ
ائْتِيَا طَوْعًا أَوْ كَرْهًا ۚ قَالَتَآ
أَتَيْنَا طَآئِعِينَ ١١
فَقَضٰىهُنَّ سَبْعَ سَمٰوَاتٍ فِى
يَوْمَيْنِ وَأَوْحٰى فِى كُلِّ سَمَآءٍ
أَمْرَهَا ۚ وَزَيَّنَّا السَّمَآءَ الدُّنْيَا
بِمَصَابِيحَ ۖ وَحِفْظًا ۚ ذٰلِكَ
تَقْدِيرُ الْعَزِيزِ الْعَلِيمِ ١٢
فَإِنْ أَعْرَضُوا فَقُلْ أَنذَرْتُكُمْ
صٰعِقَةً مِّثْلَ صٰعِقَةِ عَادٍ وَّثَمُودَ ١٣
إِذْ جَآءَتْهُمُ الرُّسُلُ مِنۢ بَيْنِ أَيْدِيهِمْ
وَمِنْ خَلْفِهِمْ أَلَّا تَعْبُدُوٓا إِلَّا اللّٰهَ ۖ
قَالُوا لَوْ شَآءَ رَبُّنَا لَأَنزَلَ مَلٰٓئِكَةً
فَإِنَّا بِمَآ أُرْسِلْتُم بِهِۦ كٰفِرُونَ ١٤
فَأَمَّا عَادٌ فَاسْتَكْبَرُوا فِى الْأَرْضِ
بِغَيْرِ الْحَقِّ وَقَالُوا مَنْ أَشَدُّ مِنَّا
قُوَّةً ۖ أَوَلَمْ يَرَوْا أَنَّ اللّٰهَ الَّذِى
خَلَقَهُمْ هُوَ أَشَدُّ مِنْهُمْ قُوَّةً ۖ وَ
كَانُوا بِاٰيٰتِنَا يَجْحَدُونَ ١٥
فَأَرْسَلْنَا عَلَيْهِمْ رِيحًا صَرْصَرًا فِىٓ
أَيَّامٍ نَّحِسَاتٍ لِّنُذِيقَهُمْ عَذَابَ
الْخِزْىِ فِى الْحَيٰوةِ الدُّنْيَا ۖ وَ

Ikhfa اخفاء | Ghunna غُنّہ | Ikhfa Meem Saakin اخفاء میم ساکن | Idghaam ادغام | Qalqala قلقلہ | Qalb قلب | Idghaam Meem Saakin ادغام میم ساکن

but the Chastisement of a Hereafter will be more humiliating still: and they will find no help.

la'azaabul-Aakhirati akhzaa wa hum laa yunṣaroon.

لَعَذَابُ الْاٰخِرَةِ اَخْزٰى وَهُمْ
لَا يُنْصَرُوْنَ ﴿١٦﴾

17. As to the Thamud, We gave them Guidance, but they preferred blindness (of heart) to Guidance: so the stunning Punishment of humiliation seized them, because of what they had earned.

17. Wa ammaa Samoodu fahadaynaahum fastaḥabbul-'amaa 'alal-hudaa fa-akhazat-hum ṣaa'iqatul-'azaabil-hooni bimaa kaanoo yaksiboon.

وَاَمَّا ثَمُوْدُ فَهَدَيْنٰهُمْ فَاسْتَحَبُّوا
الْعَمٰى عَلَى الْهُدٰى فَاَخَذَتْهُمْ
صٰعِقَةُ الْعَذَابِ الْهُوْنِ بِمَا
كَانُوْا يَكْسِبُوْنَ ﴿١٧﴾

18. But We delivered those who believed and practised righteousness.

18. Wa najjaynal-lazeena aamanoo wa kaanoo yattaqoon.

(Section 2)

وَنَجَّيْنَا الَّذِيْنَ اٰمَنُوْا وَكَانُوْا
يَتَّقُوْنَ ﴿١٨﴾ ع

19. On the Day that the enemies of Allah will be gathered together to the Fire, they will be marched in ranks.

19. Wa Yawma yuḥsharu a'daaa'ul-laahi ilan-Naari fa-hum yooza'oon.

وَيَوْمَ يُحْشَرُ اَعْدَآءُ اللّٰهِ اِلَى
النَّارِ فَهُمْ يُوْزَعُوْنَ ﴿١٩﴾

20. At length, when they reach the (Fire), their hearing, their sight, and their skins will bear witness against them, as to (all) their deeds.

20. Ḥattaaa izaa maa jaaa'oo-haa shahida 'alayhim sam'u-hum wa abṣaaruhum wa juloo-duhum bimaa kaanoo ya'ma-loon.

حَتّٰٓى اِذَا مَا جَآءُوْهَا شَهِدَ عَلَيْهِمْ
سَمْعُهُمْ وَاَبْصَارُهُمْ وَجُلُوْدُهُمْ بِمَا
كَانُوْا يَعْمَلُوْنَ ﴿٢٠﴾

21. They will say to their skins: "Why bear you witness against us?" They will say: "Allah has given us speech,- (He) Who giveth speech to everything: He created you for the first time, and unto Him were you to return.

21. Wa qaaloo lijuloodihim lima shahittum 'alaynaa qaalooo anṭaqanal-laahul-lazeee anṭaqa kulla shay'iñw-wa Huwa khalaqakum awwala marratiñw-wa ilayhi turja'oon.

وَقَالُوْا لِجُلُوْدِهِمْ لِمَ شَهِدْتُّمْ عَلَيْنَا
قَالُوْٓا اَنْطَقَنَا اللّٰهُ الَّذِيْٓ اَنْطَقَ كُلَّ
شَيْءٍ وَّهُوَ خَلَقَكُمْ اَوَّلَ مَرَّةٍ وَّ
اِلَيْهِ تُرْجَعُوْنَ ﴿٢١﴾

22. "You did not seek to hide yourselves, lest your hearing, your sight, and your skins should bear witness against you! But you did think that Allah knew not many of the things that you used to do!

22. Wa maa kuntum tastati-roona añy-yashhada 'alaykum sam'ukum wa laaa abṣaarukum wa laa juloodukum wa laakin ẓanantum annal-laaha laa ya'lamu kaseeram-mimmaa ta'maloon.

وَمَا كُنْتُمْ تَسْتَتِرُوْنَ اَنْ يَّشْهَدَ
عَلَيْكُمْ سَمْعُكُمْ وَلَآ اَبْصَارُكُمْ وَلَا
جُلُوْدُكُمْ وَلٰكِنْ ظَنَنْتُمْ اَنَّ اللّٰهَ لَا
يَعْلَمُ كَثِيْرًا مِّمَّا تَعْمَلُوْنَ ﴿٢٢﴾

23. "But this thought of yours which you did entertain concerning your Lord, has brought you to destruction, and (now) have you become of those utterly lost!"

23. Wa zaalikum ẓannuku-mul-lazee ẓanantum bi-Rabbi-kum ardaakum fa-aṣbaḥtum minal-khaasireen.

وَذٰلِكُمْ ظَنُّكُمُ الَّذِيْ ظَنَنْتُمْ بِرَبِّكُمْ
اَرْدٰىكُمْ فَاَصْبَحْتُمْ مِّنَ الْخٰسِرِيْنَ ﴿٢٣﴾

24. If, then, they have patience, the Fire will be a home for them! and if they beg to be received into favour, into favour will they not (then) be received.

24. Fa-iñy-yaṣbiroo fan-Naaru maṣwal-lahum wa iñy-yasta'ti-boo famaa hum minal-mu'ta-been.

فَاِنْ يَّصْبِرُوْا فَالنَّارُ مَثْوًى لَّهُمْ
وَاِنْ يَّسْتَعْتِبُوْا فَمَا هُمْ مِّنَ
الْمُعْتَبِيْنَ ﴿٢٤﴾

Ikhfa اخفاء | Ghunna غنّہ | Ikhfa Meem Saakin اخفاء میم ساکن | Idghaam ادغام | Qalqala قلقلہ | Qalb قلب | Idghaam Meem Saakin ادغام میم ساکن

25. And We have destined for them intimate companions (of like nature), who made alluring to them what was before them and behind them; and the sentence among the previous generations of Jinns and men, who have passed away, is proved against them; for they are utterly lost.

25. Wa qayyaḍnaa lahum quranaaa'a fazayyanoo lahum maa bayna aydeehim wa maa khalfahum wa ḥaqqa 'alayhimul-qawlu feee umamin qad khalat min qablihim minal-jinni wal-insi innahum kaanoo khaasireen. **(Section 3)**

وَقَيَّضْنَا لَهُمْ قُرَنَآءَ فَزَيَّنُوْا لَهُمْ
مَّا بَيْنَ اَيْدِيْهِمْ وَمَا خَلْفَهُمْ
وَحَقَّ عَلَيْهِمُ الْقَوْلُ فِيْٓ اُمَمٍ قَدْ
خَلَتْ مِنْ قَبْلِهِمْ مِّنَ الْجِنِّ وَ
الْاِنْسِ ۚ اِنَّهُمْ كَانُوْا خٰسِرِيْنَ ﴿٢٥﴾

26. The Unbelievers say: "Listen not to this Qur'an, but talk at random in the midst of its (reading), that you may gain the upper hand!"

26. Wa qaalal-lazeena kafaroo laa tasma'oo lihaazal-Qur-aani walghaw feehi la'allakum taghliboon.

وَقَالَ الَّذِيْنَ كَفَرُوْا لَا تَسْمَعُوْا
لِهٰذَا الْقُرْاٰنِ وَالْغَوْا فِيْهِ لَعَلَّكُمْ
تَغْلِبُوْنَ ﴿٢٦﴾

27. But We will certainly give the Unbelievers a taste of a severe Chastisement, and We will requite them for the worst of their deeds.

27. Falanuzeeqannal-lazeena kafaroo 'azaaban shadeedañw-wa lanajziyannahum aswa-allazee kaanoo ya'maloon.

فَلَنُذِيْقَنَّ الَّذِيْنَ كَفَرُوْا عَذَابًا
شَدِيْدًا ۙ وَّلَنَجْزِيَنَّهُمْ اَسْوَاَ الَّذِيْ
كَانُوْا يَعْمَلُوْنَ ﴿٢٧﴾

28. Such is the requital of the enemies of Allah,- the Fire: therein will be for them the Eternal Home: a (fit) requital, for that they were wont to reject Our Signs.

28. Zaalika jazaaa'u a'daa'il-laahin-Naaru lahum feehaa daarul-khuld, jazaaa'am bimaa kaanoo bi-Aayaatinaa yajḥadoon.

ذٰلِكَ جَزَآءُ اَعْدَآءِ اللّٰهِ النَّارُ ۚ
لَهُمْ فِيْهَا دَارُ الْخُلْدِ ۭ جَزَآءًۢ بِمَا
كَانُوْا بِاٰيٰتِنَا يَجْحَدُوْنَ ﴿٢٨﴾

29. And the Unbelievers will say: "Our Lord! Show us those, among Jinns and men, who misled us: We shall crush them beneath our feet, so that they become the vilest (before all)."

29. Wa qaalal-lazeena kafaroo Rabbanaaa arinal-lazayni aḍal-laanaa minal-jinni wal-insi naj'alhumaa taḥta aqdaaminaa liyakoonaa minal-asfaleen.

وَقَالَ الَّذِيْنَ كَفَرُوْا رَبَّنَآ اَرِنَا
الَّذَيْنِ اَضَلّٰنَا مِنَ الْجِنِّ وَالْاِنْسِ
نَجْعَلْهُمَا تَحْتَ اَقْدَامِنَا لِيَكُوْنَا
مِنَ الْاَسْفَلِيْنَ ﴿٢٩﴾

30. In the case of those who say, "Our Lord is Allah", and, further, stand straight and steadfast, the angels descend on them (from time to time): "Fear you not!" (they suggest), "Nor grieve! but receive the Glad Tidings of the Garden (of Bliss), the which you were promised!

30. Innal-lazeena qaaloo Rabbunal-laahu summas-taqaamoo tatanazzalu 'alayhimul-malaaa-'ikatu allaa takhaafoo wa laa taḥzanoo wa abshiroo bil-Jannatil-latee kuntum too'adoon.

اِنَّ الَّذِيْنَ قَالُوْا رَبُّنَا اللّٰهُ ثُمَّ
اسْتَقَامُوْا تَتَنَزَّلُ عَلَيْهِمُ الْمَلٰٓئِكَةُ
اَلَّا تَخَافُوْا وَلَا تَحْزَنُوْا وَاَبْشِرُوْا
بِالْجَنَّةِ الَّتِيْ كُنْتُمْ تُوْعَدُوْنَ ﴿٣٠﴾

31. "We are your protectors in this life and in the Hereafter: therein shall you have all that your souls shall desire; therein shall you have all that you ask for!-

31. Naḥnu awliyaaa'ukum fil-ḥayaatid-dunyaa wa fil-Aakhirati wa lakum feehaa maa tashtaheee anfusukum wa lakum feehaa maa tadda'oon.

نَحْنُ اَوْلِيٰٓؤُكُمْ فِي الْحَيٰوةِ الدُّنْيَا
وَفِي الْاٰخِرَةِ ۚ وَلَكُمْ فِيْهَا مَا
تَشْتَهِيْٓ اَنْفُسُكُمْ وَلَكُمْ فِيْهَا مَا
تَدَّعُوْنَ ﴿٣١﴾ ۭ

Ikhfa اخفاء | Ghunna غنّہ | Ikhfa Meem Saakin اخفاء میم ساکن | Idghaam ادغام | Qalqala قلقلہ | Qalb قلب | Idghaam Meem Saakin ادغام میم ساکن

ركوع ٤ ١٨

32. "A hospitable gift from One Oft-Forgiving, Most Merciful!"

32. Nuzulam-min Ghafoorir-Raḥeem. **(Section 4)**

نُزُلًا مِّنْ غَفُورٍ رَّحِيمٍ ﴿٣٢﴾

33. Who is better in speech than one who calls (men) to Allah, works righteousness, and says, "I am of those who bow in Islam"?

33. Wa man aḥsanu qawlam-mimman da'aaa ilal-laahi wa 'amila ṣaaliḥañw-wa qaala innanee minal-muslimeen.

وَمَنْ أَحْسَنُ قَوْلًا مِّمَّن دَعَا إِلَى
اللَّهِ وَعَمِلَ صَالِحًا وَقَالَ إِنَّنِي
مِنَ الْمُسْلِمِينَ ﴿٣٣﴾

34. Nor can goodness and Evil be equal. Repel (Evil) with what is better: Then will he between whom and thee was hatred become as it were your friend and intimate!

34. Wa laa tastawil-ḥasanatu wa las-sayyi'ah; idfa' billatee hiya aḥsanu fa-izal-lazee baynaka wa baynahoo 'adaawatun ka-annahoo waliyyun ḥameem.

وَلَا تَسْتَوِي الْحَسَنَةُ وَلَا السَّيِّئَةُ ۚ
ادْفَعْ بِالَّتِي هِيَ أَحْسَنُ فَإِذَا الَّذِي
بَيْنَكَ وَبَيْنَهُ عَدَاوَةٌ كَأَنَّهُ
وَلِيٌّ حَمِيمٌ ﴿٣٤﴾

35. And no one will be granted such goodness except those who exercise patience and self-restraint,- none but persons of the greatest good fortune.

35. Wa maa yulaqqaahaaa illal-lazeena ṣabaroo wa maa yulaqqaahaaa illaa zoo ḥaẓẓin 'aẓeem.

وَمَا يُلَقَّاهَا إِلَّا الَّذِينَ صَبَرُوا ۚ
وَمَا يُلَقَّاهَا إِلَّا ذُو حَظٍّ عَظِيمٍ ﴿٣٥﴾

36. And if (at any time) an incitement to discord is made to you by the Evil One, seek refuge in Allah. He is the One Who hears and knows all things.

36. Wa immaa yanzaghannaka minash-Shayṭaani nazghun fasta'iz billaahi innahoo Huwas-Samee'ul-'Aleem.

وَإِمَّا يَنزَغَنَّكَ مِنَ الشَّيْطَانِ نَزْغٌ
فَاسْتَعِذْ بِاللَّهِ ۖ إِنَّهُ هُوَ السَّمِيعُ
الْعَلِيمُ ﴿٣٦﴾

37. Among His Signs are the Night and the Day, and the Sun and the Moon. Adore not the sun and the moon, but adore Allah, Who created them, if it is Him you wish to serve.

37. Wa min Aayaatihil-laylu wannahaaru washshamsu walqamar; laa tasjudoo lish-shamsi wa laa lilqamari wasjudoo lillaahil-lazee khala-qahunna in kuntum iyyaahu ta'budoon.

وَمِنْ آيَاتِهِ اللَّيْلُ وَالنَّهَارُ وَالشَّمْسُ
وَالْقَمَرُ ۚ لَا تَسْجُدُوا لِلشَّمْسِ وَلَا
لِلْقَمَرِ وَاسْجُدُوا لِلَّهِ الَّذِي خَلَقَهُنَّ
إِن كُنتُمْ إِيَّاهُ تَعْبُدُونَ ﴿٣٧﴾

(Bow Down)

38. But is the (Unbelievers) are arrogant, (no matter): for in the presence of your Lord are those who celebrate His praises by night and by day. And they never flag (nor feel themselves above it).

38. Fa-inis-takbaroo fallazee-na 'inda Rabbika yusabbiḥoona lahoo billayli wannahaari wa hum laa yas'amoon. ۩

فَإِنِ اسْتَكْبَرُوا فَالَّذِينَ عِندَ
رَبِّكَ يُسَبِّحُونَ لَهُ بِاللَّيْلِ وَالنَّهَارِ
وَهُمْ لَا يَسْأَمُونَ ۩ ﴿٣٨﴾

السَّجْدَة (١١)

39. And among His Signs in this: that you see the earth barren and desolate; but when We send down rain to it, it is stirred to life and yields increase. Truly, He Who gives life to the (dead) earth can surely give life to (men) who are dead. For He has power over all things.

39. Wa min Aayaatiheee annaka taral-arḍa khaashi'atan fa-izaaa anzalnaa 'alayhal-maaa'ah-tazzat wa rabat; innal-lazeee aḥyaahaa lamuḥyil-mawtaa; innahoo 'alaa kulli shay'in Qadeer.

وَمِنْ آيَاتِهِ أَنَّكَ تَرَى الْأَرْضَ
خَاشِعَةً فَإِذَا أَنزَلْنَا عَلَيْهَا الْمَاءَ
اهْتَزَّتْ وَرَبَتْ ۚ إِنَّ الَّذِي أَحْيَاهَا
لَمُحْيِي الْمَوْتَىٰ ۚ إِنَّهُ عَلَىٰ كُلِّ شَيْءٍ
قَدِيرٌ ﴿٣٩﴾

40. Those who pervert the Truth in Our Signs are

40. Innal-lazeena yulḥidoona feee Aayaatinaa

إِنَّ الَّذِينَ يُلْحِدُونَ فِي آيَاتِنَا

Ikhfa اخفاء | Ghunna غنّة | Ikhfa Meem Saakin اخفاء میم ساکن | Idghaam ادغام | Qalqala قلقله | Qalb قلب | Idghaam Meem Saakin ادغام میم ساکن

لَا يَخْفَوْنَ عَلَيْنَا ۗ أَفَمَنْ يُلْقَى
فِي النَّارِ خَيْرٌ أَمْ مَنْ يَأْتِي آمِنًا
يَوْمَ الْقِيَامَةِ ۚ اعْمَلُوا مَا شِئْتُمْ ۖ
إِنَّهُ بِمَا تَعْمَلُونَ بَصِيرٌ ﴿٤٠﴾

laa yakhfawna 'alaynaa; afamañy-yulqaa fin-Naari khayrun am mañy-yaâteee aaminañy-Yawmal-Qiyaamah; i'maloo maa shi'tum innahoo bimaa ta'maloona Baṣeer.

not hidden from Us. Which is better?- he that is cast into the Fire, or he that comes safe through, on the Day of Judgment? Do what you will: verily He sees (clearly) all that you do.

إِنَّ الَّذِينَ كَفَرُوا بِالذِّكْرِ لَمَّا
جَاءَهُمْ ۖ وَإِنَّهُ لَكِتَابٌ عَزِيزٌ ﴿٤١﴾

41. Inna Lazeena kafaroo biz-Zikri lammaa jaa'ahum wa innahoo la-Kitaabun 'Azeez.

41. Those who reject the Message when it comes to them (are not hidden from Us). And indeed it is a Book of exalted power.

لَا يَأْتِيهِ الْبَاطِلُ مِنْ بَيْنِ يَدَيْهِ
وَلَا مِنْ خَلْفِهِ ۖ تَنْزِيلٌ مِنْ
حَكِيمٍ حَمِيدٍ ﴿٤٢﴾

42. Laa yaâteehil-baaṭilu mim bayni yadayhi wa laa min khalfihee tanzeelum-min Ḥakeemin Ḥameed.

42. No falsehood can approach it from before or behind it: It is sent down by One Full of Wisdom, Worthy of all Praise.

مَا يُقَالُ لَكَ إِلَّا مَا قَدْ قِيلَ لِلرُّسُلِ
مِنْ قَبْلِكَ ۚ إِنَّ رَبَّكَ لَذُو مَغْفِرَةٍ
وَذُو عِقَابٍ أَلِيمٍ ﴿٤٣﴾

43. Maa yuqaalu laka illaa maa qad qeela lir-Rusuli min qablik; inna Rabbaka lazoo maghfiratiñw-wa zoo 'iqaabin aleem.

43. Nothing is said to you that was not said to the apostles before you: that your Lord has at His Command (all) forgiveness as well as a most Grievous Chastisement.

وَلَوْ جَعَلْنَاهُ قُرْآنًا أَعْجَمِيًّا لَقَالُوا
لَوْلَا فُصِّلَتْ آيَاتُهُ ۖ أَأَعْجَمِيٌّ وَ
عَرَبِيٌّ ۗ قُلْ هُوَ لِلَّذِينَ آمَنُوا هُدًى
وَشِفَاءٌ ۖ وَالَّذِينَ لَا يُؤْمِنُونَ فِي
آذَانِهِمْ وَقْرٌ وَهُوَ عَلَيْهِمْ عَمًى ۚ
أُولَٰئِكَ يُنَادَوْنَ مِنْ مَكَانٍ بَعِيدٍ ﴿٤٤﴾

44. Wa law ja'alnaahu Qur-aanan A'jamiyyal-laqaaloo law laa fuṣṣilat Aayaatuhoo 'a A'jamiyyuñw-wa 'Arabiyy; qul huwa lillazeena aamanoo hudañw-wa shifaaa'uñw wallazeena laa yu'minoona feee aazaanihim waqruñw-wa huwa 'alayhim 'amaa; ulaaa'ika yunaadawna mim-makaanim ba'eed.

(Section 5)

44. Had We sent this as a Qur'an (in the language) other than Arabic, they would have said: "Why are not its verses explained in detail? What! (a Book) not in Arabic and (a Messenger an Arab?" Say: "It is a Guide and a Healing to those who believe ; and for those who believe not, there is a deafness in their ears, and it is blindness in their (eyes): They are (as it were) being called from a place far distant!"

قرأ حفص بتسهيل الهمزة الثانية ١٢ ع ٥

وَلَقَدْ آتَيْنَا مُوسَى الْكِتَابَ فَاخْتُلِفَ
فِيهِ ۗ وَلَوْلَا كَلِمَةٌ سَبَقَتْ مِنْ
رَبِّكَ لَقُضِيَ بَيْنَهُمْ ۚ وَإِنَّهُمْ لَفِي
شَكٍّ مِنْهُ مُرِيبٍ ﴿٤٥﴾

45. Wa laqad aataynaa Moosal-Kitaaba fakhtulifa feeh; wa law laa Kalimatun sabaqat mir-Rabbika laquḍiya baynahum; wa innahum lafee shakkim-minhu mureeb.

45. We certainly gave Moses the Book aforetime: but disputes arose therein. Had it not been for a Word that went forth before from thy Lord, (their differences) would have been settled between them: but they remained in suspicious disquieting doubt thereon.

مَنْ عَمِلَ صَالِحًا فَلِنَفْسِهِ ۖ وَمَنْ
أَسَاءَ فَعَلَيْهَا ۗ وَمَا رَبُّكَ بِظَلَّامٍ
لِلْعَبِيدِ ﴿٤٦﴾

46. Man 'amila ṣaliḥan falinafsihee wa man asaaa'a fa'alayhaa; wamaa rabbuka biẓallaamil-lil-'abeed.

46. Whoever works righteousness benefits his own soul; whoever works evil, it is against his own soul: nor is your Lord ever unjust (in the least) to His Servants.

الجزء الخامس والعشرون (٢٥)

إِلَيْهِ يُرَدُّ عِلْمُ السَّاعَةِ ۚ وَمَا

47. Ilayhi yuraddu 'ilmus-Saaa'ah; wa maa

47. To Him is referred the Knowledge of the Hour (of Judgment: He knows all): No

Ikhfa اخفاء | Ghunna غُنّہ | Ikhfa Meem Saakin اخفاء میم ساکن | Idghaam ادغام | Qalqala قلقلہ | Qalb قلب | Idghaam Meem Saakin ادغام میم ساکن

date-fruit comes out of its sheath, nor does a female conceive (within her womb) nor bring forth the (young), but by His knowledge. The Day that (Allah) will propound to them the (question), "Where are the partners (you attributed to Me?" They will say, "We do assure you not one of us can bear witness!"

takhruju min samaraatim-min akmaamihaa wa maa taḥmilu min unsaa wa laa taḍa'u illaa bi'ilmih; wa Yawma yunaadeehim ayna shurakaaa'ee qaalooo aazannaaka maa minnaa min shaheed.

تَخْرُجُ مِنْ ثَمَرٰتٍ مِّنْ اَكْمَامِهَا
وَمَا تَحْمِلُ مِنْ اُنْثٰى وَلَا تَضَعُ
اِلَّا بِعِلْمِهٖ ؕ وَيَوْمَ يُنَادِيْهِمْ
اَيْنَ شُرَكَآءِىْ ۙ قَالُوْٓا اٰذَنّٰكَ ۙ
مَا مِنَّا مِنْ شَهِيْدٍ ﴿٤٧﴾

48. The (deities) they used to invoke aforetime will leave them in the lurch, and they will perceive that they have no way of escape.

48. Wa ḍalla 'anhum maa kaanoo yad'oona min qablu wa ẓannoo maa lahum mim-maḥeeṣ.

وَضَلَّ عَنْهُمْ مَّا كَانُوْا يَدْعُوْنَ
مِنْ قَبْلُ وَظَنُّوْا مَا لَهُمْ مِّنْ
مَّحِيْصٍ ﴿٤٨﴾

49. Man does not weary of asking for good (things), but if ill touches him, he gives up all hope (and) is lost in despair.

49. Laa yas'amul-insaanu min du'aaa'il-khayri wa im-massahush-sharru fa-ya'oosun qanooṭ.

لَا يَسْـَٔمُ الْاِنْسَانُ مِنْ دُعَآءِ الْخَيْرِ
وَاِنْ مَّسَّهُ الشَّرُّ فَيَـُٔوْسٌ قَنُوْطٌ ﴿٤٩﴾

50. When We give him a taste of some Mercy from Ourselves, after some adversity has touched him, he is sure to say, "This is due to my (merit): I think not that the Hour (of Judgment) will (ever) be established; but if I am brought back to my Lor d, I have (much) good (stored) in His sight!" But We will show the Unbelievers the truth of all that they did, and We shall give them the taste of a severe Chastisement.

50. Wa la-in aẓaqnaahu raḥmatam-minnaa mim ba'di ḍarraaa'a massat-hu la-yaqoolanna haazaa lee wa maaa aẓunnus-Saa'ata qaaa'imatañw-wa la'in-ruji'tu ilaa Rabbeee inna lee 'indahoo lalḥusnaa; falanunabbi'annal-lazeena kafaroo bimaa 'amiloo wa lanuzeeqannahum min 'azaabin ghaleeẓ.

وَلَىِٕنْ اَذَقْنٰهُ رَحْمَةً مِّنَّا مِنْۢ بَعْدِ
ضَرَّآءَ مَسَّتْهُ لَيَقُوْلَنَّ هٰذَا لِىْ ۙ
وَمَآ اَظُنُّ السَّاعَةَ قَآئِمَةً ۙ وَّلَىِٕنْ
رُّجِعْتُ اِلٰى رَبِّىْٓ اِنَّ لِىْ عِنْدَهٗ
لَلْحُسْنٰى ۚ فَلَنُنَبِّئَنَّ الَّذِيْنَ كَفَرُوْا
بِمَا عَمِلُوْا ۫ وَلَنُذِيْقَنَّهُمْ مِّنْ
عَذَابٍ غَلِيْظٍ ﴿٥٠﴾

51. When We bestow favours on man, he turns away, and gets himself remote on his side (instead of coming to Us); and when evil seizes him, (he comes) full of prolonged prayer!

51. Wa izaaa an'amnaa 'alal-insaani a'raḍa wa na-aa bijaanibihee wa izaa massahush-sharru fazoo du'aaa'in 'areeḍ.

وَاِذَآ اَنْعَمْنَا عَلَى الْاِنْسَانِ اَعْرَضَ
وَنَاٰ بِجَانِبِهٖ ۚ وَاِذَا مَسَّهُ الشَّرُّ فَذُوْ
دُعَآءٍ عَرِيْضٍ ﴿٥١﴾

52. Say: "See you if the (Revelation) is (really) from Allah, and yet do you reject it? Who is more astray than one who is in a schism far (from any purpose)?"

52. Qul ara'aytum in kaana min 'indil-laahi summa kafartum bihee man aḍallu mimman huwa fee shiqaaqim ba'eed.

قُلْ اَرَءَيْتُمْ اِنْ كَانَ مِنْ عِنْدِ
اللّٰهِ ثُمَّ كَفَرْتُمْ بِهٖ مَنْ اَضَلُّ
مِمَّنْ هُوَ فِىْ شِقَاقٍۢ بَعِيْدٍ ﴿٥٢﴾

53. Soon will We show them Our Signs in the (furthest) regions (of the earth), and in their own souls, until it becomes manifest to them that this is the Truth. Is it not enough that your Lord

53. Sanureehim Aayaatinaa fil-aafaaqi wa feee anfusihim ḥattaa yatabayyana lahum annahul-ḥaqq; awa lam yakfi bi-Rabbika annahoo

سَنُرِيْهِمْ اٰيٰتِنَا فِى الْاٰفَاقِ وَفِىْٓ
اَنْفُسِهِمْ حَتّٰى يَتَبَيَّنَ لَهُمْ اَنَّهُ
الْحَقُّ ؕ اَوَلَمْ يَكْفِ بِرَبِّكَ اَنَّهٗ

Ikhfa اخفاء | Ghunna غنّہ | Ikhfa Meem Saakin اخفاءمیم ساکن | Idghaam ادغام | Qalqala قلقلہ | Qalb قلب | Idghaam Meem Saakin ادغام میم ساکن

does witness all things?

'alaa kulli shay'in Shaheed.

عَلٰى كُلِّ شَيْءٍ شَهِيْدٌ ﴿٥٣﴾

54. Ah indeed! Are they in doubt concerning the Meeting with their Lord? Ah indeed! It is He that doth encompass all things!

54. Alaaa innahum fee miryatim-mil-liqaaa'i Rabbihim; alaaa innahoo bikulli shay'im-muheet. **(Section 6)**

اَلَآ اِنَّهُمْ فِيْ مِرْيَةٍ مِّنْ لِّقَآءِ
رَبِّهِمْ ۭ اَلَآ اِنَّهٗ بِكُلِّ شَيْءٍ مُّحِيْطٌ ﴿٥٤﴾ ع ٦

42. Consultation

In the name of Allah, Most Gracious, Most Merciful.

Sûrat ash-Shûrâ–42

(Revealed at Makkah)

Bismillaahir Raḥmaanir Raḥeem

(٤٢) سُوْرَةُ الشُّوْرٰى مَكِّيَّةٌ (٦٢)

بِسْمِ اللّٰهِ الرَّحْمٰنِ الرَّحِيْمِ

1. *Ha-Mim.*

1. Ḥaa-Meeem.

حٰمٓ ﴿١﴾

2. *Ain-Sin-Qaf.*

2. 'Ayyyn-Seeen-Qaaaf.

عٓسٓقٓ ﴿٢﴾

3. Thus does (He) send inspiration to you as (He did) to those before you,- Allah, Exalted in Power, Full of Wisdom.

3. Kaẕaalika yooḥeee ilayka wa ilal-laẕeena min qablikal-laahul-'Azeezul-Ḥakeem.

كَذٰلِكَ يُوْحِيْٓ اِلَيْكَ وَاِلَى الَّذِيْنَ
مِنْ قَبْلِكَ ۙ اللّٰهُ الْعَزِيْزُ الْحَكِيْمُ ﴿٣﴾

4. To Him belongs all that is in the heavens and on earth: and He is Most High, Most Great.

4. Lahoo maa fis-samaawaati wa maa fil-arḍi wa Huwal-'Aliyyul-'Aẓeem.

لَهٗ مَا فِي السَّمٰوٰتِ وَمَا فِي الْاَرْضِ ۭ
وَهُوَ الْعَلِيُّ الْعَظِيْمُ ﴿٤﴾

5. The heavens are a lost rent asunder from above them (by Him Glory): and the angels celebrate the Praises of their Lord, and pray for forgiveness for (all) beings on earth: Behold! Verily Allah is He, the Oft-Forgiving, Most Merciful.

5. Takaadus-samaawaatu yatafaṭṭarna min fawqihinn; walmalaaa'ikatu yusabbiḥoona biḥamdi Rabbihim wa yastaghfiroona liman fil-arḍ; alaaa innal-laaha Huwal-Ghafoorur-Raḥeem.

تَكَادُ السَّمٰوٰتُ يَتَفَطَّرْنَ مِنْ
فَوْقِهِنَّ وَالْمَلٰۗىِٕكَةُ يُسَبِّحُوْنَ
بِحَمْدِ رَبِّهِمْ وَيَسْتَغْفِرُوْنَ لِمَنْ
فِي الْاَرْضِ ۭ اَلَآ اِنَّ اللّٰهَ هُوَ
الْغَفُوْرُ الرَّحِيْمُ ﴿٥﴾

6. And those who take as protectors others besides Him,- Allah does watch over them; and you are not the disposer of their affairs.

6. Wallaẕeenat-takhaẕoo min dooniheee awliyaaa'al-laahu ḥafeeẓun 'alayhim wa maaa anta 'alayhim biwakeel.

وَالَّذِيْنَ اتَّخَذُوْا مِنْ دُوْنِهٖٓ
اَوْلِيَاۗءَ اللّٰهُ حَفِيْظٌ عَلَيْهِمْ ڮ وَمَآ
اَنْتَ عَلَيْهِمْ بِوَكِيْلٍ ﴿٦﴾

7. Thus have We sent by inspiration to you an Arabic Qur'an: that you may warn the Mother of Cities and all around her,- and warn (them) of the Day of Assembly, of which there is no doubt: (when) some will be in the Garden, and some in the Blazing Fire.

7. Wa kaẕaalika awḥaynaaa Ilayka Qur-aanan 'Arabiyyal-litunzira Ummal-Quraa wa man ḥawlahaa wa tunzira Yawmal-Jam'i laa rayba feeh; fareequn fil-Jannati wa fareequn fis-sa'eer.

وَكَذٰلِكَ اَوْحَيْنَآ اِلَيْكَ قُرْاٰنًا
عَرَبِيًّا لِّتُنْذِرَ اُمَّ الْقُرٰى وَمَنْ
حَوْلَهَا وَتُنْذِرَ يَوْمَ الْجَمْعِ لَا رَيْبَ
فِيْهِ ۭ فَرِيْقٌ فِي الْجَنَّةِ وَفَرِيْقٌ
فِي السَّعِيْرِ ﴿٧﴾

8. If Allah had so willed, He could have made them a single people; but He admits whom He will

8. Wa law shaaa'al-laahu laja'alahum ummatañw-waaḥidatañw-walaakiñy-yudkhilu mañy-yashaaa'u

وَلَوْ شَاۗءَ اللّٰهُ لَجَعَلَهُمْ اُمَّةً
وَّاحِدَةً وَّلٰكِنْ يُّدْخِلُ مَنْ يَّشَاۗءُ

to His Mercy; and the Wrong-doers will have no protector nor helper.

9. What! Have they taken (for worship) protectors besides Him? But it is Allah,- He is the Protector, and it is He Who gives life to the dead: It is He Who has power over all things,

10. Whatever it be wherein you differ, the decision thereof is with Allah: such is Allah my Lord: In Him I trust, and to Him I turn.

11. (He is) the Creator of the heavens and the earth: He has made for you pairs from among yourselves, and pairs among cattle: by this means does He multiply you: there is nothing whatever like unto Him, and He is the One that hears and sees (all things).

12. To Him belong the keys of the heavens and the earth: He enlarges and restricts. The Sustenance to whom He will: for He knows full well all things.

13. The same religion has He established for you as that which He enjoined on Noah - the which We have sent by inspiration to you - and that which We enjoined on Abraham, Moses, and Jesus: Namely, that you should remain steadfast in religion, and make no divisions therein: to those who worship other things than Allah, hard is the (way) to which you callest them. Allah chooses to Himself those whom He pleases, and guides to Himself those who turn (to Him).

14. And they became divided only after Knowledge reached them,- through selfish envy as between themselves. Had it not been for

fee raḥmatih; waẓ-ẓaalimoona maa lahum miñw-waliyyiñw-wa laa naṣeer.

9. Amit-takhazoo min dooniheee awliyaaa'a fallaahu Huwal-Waliyyu wa Huwa yuḥyil-mawtaa wa Huwa 'alaa kulli shay'in Qadeer. **(Section 1)**

10. Wa makh-talaftum feehi min shay'in faḥukmuhooo ilal-laah; zaalikumul-laahu Rabbee 'alayhi tawakkaltu wa ilayhi uneeb.

11. Faaṭirus-samaawaati wal-arḍ; ja'ala lakum min anfusikum azwaajañw-wa minal-an-'aami azwaajañy yazra'ukum feeh; laysa kamislihee shay'uñw wa Huwas-Samee'ul-Baṣeer.

12. Lahoo maqaaleedus-samaawaati wal-arḍi yabsuṭur-rizqa limañy-yashaaa'u wa yaqdir; innahoo bikulli shay'in 'Aleem.

13. Shara'a lakum minad-deeni maa waṣṣaa bihee Nooḥañw-wallazeee awḥaynaaa ilayka wa maa waṣṣaynaa biheee Ibraaheema wa Moosaa wa 'Eesaaa an aqeemud-adeena wa laa tatafarraqoo feeh; kabura 'alal-mushrikeena maa tad'oohum ilayh; Allaahu yajtabeee ilayhi mañy-yashaaa'u wa yahdeee ilayhi mañy-yuneeb.

14. Wa maa tafarraqooo illaa mim ba'di maa jaaa'ahumul-'ilmu baghyam baynahum; wa law laa

فِي رَحْمَتِهِ ۚ وَالظَّالِمُونَ مَا لَهُم
مِّن وَلِيٍّ وَلَا نَصِيرٍ ٨
أَمِ اتَّخَذُوا مِن دُونِهِ أَوْلِيَاءَ ۖ
فَاللَّهُ هُوَ الْوَلِيُّ وَهُوَ يُحْيِي الْمَوْتَىٰ
وَهُوَ عَلَىٰ كُلِّ شَيْءٍ قَدِيرٌ ٩ ع ٢
وَمَا اخْتَلَفْتُمْ فِيهِ مِن شَيْءٍ
فَحُكْمُهُ إِلَى اللَّهِ ۚ ذَٰلِكُمُ اللَّهُ رَبِّي
عَلَيْهِ تَوَكَّلْتُ وَإِلَيْهِ أُنِيبُ ١٠
فَاطِرُ السَّمَاوَاتِ وَالْأَرْضِ ۚ جَعَلَ
لَكُم مِّنْ أَنفُسِكُمْ أَزْوَاجًا وَمِنَ
الْأَنْعَامِ أَزْوَاجًا ۖ يَذْرَؤُكُمْ
فِيهِ ۚ لَيْسَ كَمِثْلِهِ شَيْءٌ ۖ وَهُوَ
السَّمِيعُ الْبَصِيرُ ١١
لَهُ مَقَالِيدُ السَّمَاوَاتِ وَالْأَرْضِ ۖ
يَبْسُطُ الرِّزْقَ لِمَن يَشَاءُ وَيَقْدِرُ ۚ
إِنَّهُ بِكُلِّ شَيْءٍ عَلِيمٌ ١٢
شَرَعَ لَكُم مِّنَ الدِّينِ مَا وَصَّىٰ بِهِ
نُوحًا وَالَّذِي أَوْحَيْنَا إِلَيْكَ
وَمَا وَصَّيْنَا بِهِ إِبْرَاهِيمَ وَمُوسَىٰ
وَعِيسَىٰ ۖ أَنْ أَقِيمُوا الدِّينَ
وَلَا تَتَفَرَّقُوا فِيهِ ۚ كَبُرَ عَلَى
الْمُشْرِكِينَ مَا تَدْعُوهُمْ إِلَيْهِ ۚ
اللَّهُ يَجْتَبِي إِلَيْهِ مَن يَشَاءُ
وَيَهْدِي إِلَيْهِ مَن يُنِيبُ ١٣
وَمَا تَفَرَّقُوا إِلَّا مِن بَعْدِ مَا
جَاءَهُمُ الْعِلْمُ بَغْيًا بَيْنَهُمْ ۚ وَلَوْلَا

Ikhfa اخفاء | Ghunna غنّہ | Ikhfa Meem Saakin اخفاء میم ساکن | Idghaam ادغام | Qalqala قلقلہ | Qalb قلب | Idghaam Meem Saakin ادغام میم ساکن

a Word that went forth before from your Lord, (tending) to a Term appo-inted, the matter would have been settled between them: But truly those who have inherited the Book after them are in suspicious (disquieting) doubt concerning it.

Kalimatun sabaqat mir-Rabbika ilaaa ajalim musammal-laquḍiya baynahum; wa innal-lazeena oorisul-Kitaaba mim ba'dihim lafee shakkim minhu mureeb.

كَلِمَةٌ سَبَقَتْ مِنْ رَّبِّكَ إِلَىٰٓ
أَجَلٍ مُّسَمًّى لَّقُضِيَ بَيْنَهُمْ ۚ وَإِنَّ
الَّذِيْنَ أُوْرِثُوا الْكِتٰبَ مِنْ بَعْدِهِمْ
لَفِيْ شَكٍّ مِّنْهُ مُرِيْبٍ ﴿١٤﴾

15. Now then, for that (reason), call (them to the Faith), and stand steadfast as you are commanded, nor follow you their vain desires; but say: "I believe in the Book which Allah has sent down; and I am commanded to judge justly between you. Allah is our Lord and your Lord: for us (is the responsibility for) our deeds, and for you for your deeds. There is no contention between us and you. Allah will bring us together, and to Him is (our) Final Goal.

15. Falizaalika fad'u wastaqim kamaaa umirta wa laa tattabi' ahwaaa'ahum wa qul aamantu bimaaa anzalal-laahu min Kitaab, wa umirtu li-a'dila baynakum Allaahu Rabbunaa wa Rabbukum lanaaa a'maalunaa wa lakum a'maalukum laa ḥujjata baynanaa wa baynakumul-laahu yajma'u baynanaa wa ilayhil-maṣeer.

فَلِذٰلِكَ فَادْعُ ۚ وَاسْتَقِمْ كَمَآ
أُمِرْتَ ۚ وَلَا تَتَّبِعْ أَهْوَآءَهُمْ ۚ وَقُلْ
اٰمَنْتُ بِمَآ أَنْزَلَ اللّٰهُ مِنْ كِتٰبٍ ۚ
وَأُمِرْتُ لِأَعْدِلَ بَيْنَكُمْ ۖ اَللّٰهُ رَبُّنَا
وَرَبُّكُمْ ۖ لَنَآ أَعْمَالُنَا وَلَكُمْ أَعْمَالُكُمْ ۖ
لَا حُجَّةَ بَيْنَنَا وَبَيْنَكُمْ ۖ اَللّٰهُ يَجْمَعُ
بَيْنَنَا ۚ وَإِلَيْهِ الْمَصِيْرُ ﴿١٥﴾

16. But those who dispute concerning Allah after He has been accepted,- futile is their dispute in the Sight of their Lord: on them will be a Chastisement terrible.

16. Wallazeena yuḥaaajjoona fil-laahi mim ba'di mastujeeba lahoo ḥujjatuhum daaḥiḍatun 'inda Rabbihim wa 'alayhim ghaḍabuñw-wa lahum 'azaabun shadeed.

وَالَّذِيْنَ يُحَآجُّوْنَ فِي اللّٰهِ مِنْ
بَعْدِ مَا اسْتُجِيْبَ لَهُ حُجَّتُهُمْ
دَاحِضَةٌ عِنْدَ رَبِّهِمْ وَعَلَيْهِمْ
غَضَبٌ وَّلَهُمْ عَذَابٌ شَدِيْدٌ ﴿١٦﴾

17. It is Allah Who has sent down the Book in Truth, and the Balance (by which to weigh conduct). And what will make you realise that perhaps the Hour is close at hand?

17. Allaahul-lazeee anzalal-Kitaaba bilḥaqqi wal-Meezaan; wa maa yudreeka la'allas-Saa'ata qareeb.

اَللّٰهُ الَّذِيْٓ أَنْزَلَ الْكِتٰبَ بِالْحَقِّ
وَالْمِيْزَانَ ۗ وَمَا يُدْرِيْكَ لَعَلَّ
السَّاعَةَ قَرِيْبٌ ﴿١٧﴾

18. Only those wish to hasten it who believe not in it: those who believe hold it in awe, and know that it is the Truth. Behold, verily those that dispute concerning the Hour are far astray.

18. Yasta'jilu bihal-lazeena laa yu'minoona bihaa wallazeena aamanoo mushfiqoona minhaa wa ya'lamoona annahal-ḥaqq; alaaa innal-lazeena yumaaroona fis-Saa'ati lafee ḍalaalim ba'eed.

يَسْتَعْجِلُ بِهَا الَّذِيْنَ لَا يُؤْمِنُوْنَ
بِهَا ۚ وَالَّذِيْنَ اٰمَنُوْا مُشْفِقُوْنَ
مِنْهَا ۙ وَيَعْلَمُوْنَ أَنَّهَا الْحَقُّ ۗ أَلَآ
إِنَّ الَّذِيْنَ يُمَارُوْنَ فِي السَّاعَةِ
لَفِيْ ضَلٰلٍ بَعِيْدٍ ﴿١٨﴾

19. Gracious is Allah to His servants: He gives sustenance to whom He pleases: and He is Strong, the Mighty.

19. Allaahu laṭeefum bi'ibaadihee yarzuqu mañy-yashaaa'u wa Huwal-Qawiyyul-'Azeez.

(Section 2)

اَللّٰهُ لَطِيْفٌ بِعِبَادِهٖ يَرْزُقُ مَنْ
يَّشَآءُ ۚ وَهُوَ الْقَوِيُّ الْعَزِيْزُ ﴿١٩﴾ ع ٢

20. To any that desires the tilth of the Hereafter,

20. Man kaana yureedu ḥarsal-Aakhirati

مَنْ كَانَ يُرِيْدُ حَرْثَ الْاٰخِرَةِ

Ikhfa اخفاء | Ghunna غنّہ | Ikhfa Meem Saakin اخفاء میم ساکن | Idghaam ادغام | Qalqala قلقلہ | Qalb قلب | Idghaam Meem Saakin ادغام میم ساکن

We give increase in his tilth, and to any that desires the tilth of this world, We grant somewhat thereof, but he has no share or lot in the Hereafter.

nazid lahoo fee ḥarsihee wa man kaana yureedu ḥarsad-dunyaa nu'tihee minhaa wa maa lahoo fil-Aakhirati min naṣeeb.

نَزِدْ لَهُ فِي حَرْثِهِ ۚ وَمَنْ كَانَ
يُرِيْدُ حَرْثَ الدُّنْيَا نُؤْتِهِ مِنْهَا ۚ
وَمَا لَهُ فِي الْاٰخِرَةِ مِنْ نَّصِيْبٍ ﴿٢٠﴾

21. What! have they partners (in godhead), who have established for them some religion without the permission of Allah? Had it not been for the Decree of Judgment, the matter would have been decided between them (at once). But verily the Wrong-doers will have a grievous Chastisement.

21. Am lahum shurakaaa'u shara'oo lahum minad-deeni maa lam yaåzam bihil-laah; wa law laa Kalimatul-faṣli laquḍiya baynahum; wa innaẓ-ẓaalimeena lahum 'azaabun aleem.

اَمْ لَهُمْ شُرَكٰٓؤُا شَرَعُوْا لَهُمْ مِّنَ
الدِّيْنِ مَا لَمْ يَاْذَنْ بِهِ اللّٰهُ ۚ وَلَوْلَا
كَلِمَةُ الْفَصْلِ لَقُضِيَ بَيْنَهُمْ ۚ
وَاِنَّ الظّٰلِمِيْنَ لَهُمْ عَذَابٌ اَلِيْمٌ ﴿٢١﴾

22. Thou wilt see the Wrong-doers in fear on account of what they have earned, and (the burden of) that must (necessarily) fall on them. But those who believe and work righteous deeds will be in the luxuriant meads of the Gardens: they shall have, before their Lord, all that they wish for. That will indeed be the magnificent Bounty (of Allah).

22. Taraẓ-ẓaalimeena mushfiqeena mimmaa kasaboo wa huwa waaqi'um bihim; walla-zeena aamanoo wa 'amiluṣ-ṣaaliḥaati fee rawḍaatil-Jannaati lahum maa yashaaa'oona 'inda Rabbihim; zaalika huwal-faḍlul-kabeer.

تَرَى الظّٰلِمِيْنَ مُشْفِقِيْنَ مِمَّا
كَسَبُوْا وَهُوَ وَاقِعٌ بِهِمْ ۚ وَالَّذِيْنَ
اٰمَنُوْا وَعَمِلُوا الصّٰلِحٰتِ فِيْ رَوْضٰتِ
الْجَنّٰتِ ۚ لَهُمْ مَّا يَشَآءُوْنَ عِنْدَ
رَبِّهِمْ ۚ ذٰلِكَ هُوَ الْفَضْلُ الْكَبِيْرُ ﴿٢٢﴾

23. That is (the Bounty) whereof Allah gives Glad Tidings to His Servants who believe and do righteous deeds. Say: "No reward do I ask of you for this except the love of those near of kin." And if any one earns any good, We shall give him an increase of good in respect thereof: for Allah is Oft-Forgiving, Most Ready to appreciate (service).

23. Zaalikal-lazee yubash-shirul-laahu 'ibaadahul-lazeena aamanoo wa 'amiluṣ-ṣaaliḥaat; qul laaa as'alukum 'alayhi ajran illal-mawaddata fil-qurbaa; wa mañy-yaqtarif ḥasanatan nazid lahoo feehaa ḥusnaa; innal-laaha Ghafoorun Shakoor.

ذٰلِكَ الَّذِيْ يُبَشِّرُ اللّٰهُ عِبَادَهُ
الَّذِيْنَ اٰمَنُوْا وَعَمِلُوا الصّٰلِحٰتِ ۗ
قُلْ لَّآ اَسْـَٔلُكُمْ عَلَيْهِ اَجْرًا اِلَّا
الْمَوَدَّةَ فِي الْقُرْبٰى ۚ وَمَنْ يَّقْتَرِفْ
حَسَنَةً نَّزِدْ لَهُ فِيْهَا حُسْنًا ۚ اِنَّ
اللّٰهَ غَفُوْرٌ شَكُوْرٌ ﴿٢٣﴾

24. What! Do they say, "He has forged a falsehood against God"? But if Allah willed, He could seal up thy heart. And Allah blots out Vanity, and proves the Truth by His Words. For He knows well the secrets of all hearts.

24. Am yaqooloonaf-tara 'alal-laahi kaziban fa-iñy-yasha-il-laahu yakhtim 'alaa qalbik; wa yamḥul-laahul-baaṭila wa yuḥiqqul-ḥaqqa bi Kalimaatih; innahoo 'Aleemum bizaatiṣ-ṣudoor.

اَمْ يَقُوْلُوْنَ افْتَرٰى عَلَى اللّٰهِ كَذِبًا ۚ
فَاِنْ يَّشَاِ اللّٰهُ يَخْتِمْ عَلٰى قَلْبِكَ ۗ
وَيَمْحُ اللّٰهُ الْبَاطِلَ وَيُحِقُّ
الْحَقَّ بِكَلِمٰتِهِ ۚ اِنَّهُ عَلِيْمٌ
بِذَاتِ الصُّدُوْرِ ﴿٢٤﴾

25. He is the One that accepts repentance from His Servants and forgives sins: and He knows all that you do.

25. Wa Huwal-lazee yaqbalut-tawbata 'an 'ibaadihee wa ya'foo 'anis-sayyi-aati wa ya'lamu maa taf'aloon.

وَهُوَ الَّذِيْ يَقْبَلُ التَّوْبَةَ عَنْ
عِبَادِهِ وَيَعْفُوْا عَنِ السَّيِّاٰتِ وَ
يَعْلَمُ مَا تَفْعَلُوْنَ ﴿٢٥﴾

Ikhfa اخفاء | Ghunna غنّہ | Ikhfa Meem Saakin اخفاءمیم ساکن | Idghaam ادغام | Qalqala قلقلہ | Qalb قلب | Idghaam Meem Saakin ادغام میم ساکن

26. And He listens to those who believe and do deeds of righteousness, and gives them increase of His Bounty: but for the Unbelievers their is a terrible Chastisement.

26. Wa yastajeebul-lazeena aamanoo wa 'amiluṣ-ṣaaliḥaati wa yazeeduhum min faḍlih; wal-kaafiroona lahum 'azaabun shadeed.

وَيَسْتَجِيْبُ الَّذِيْنَ اٰمَنُوْا وَعَمِلُوا
الصّٰلِحٰتِ وَيَزِيْدُهُمْ مِّنْ فَضْلِهٖ ؕ
وَالْكٰفِرُوْنَ لَهُمْ عَذَابٌ شَدِيْدٌ ﴿٢٦﴾

27. If Allah were to enlarge the provision for His Servants, they would indeed transgress beyond all bounds through the earth; but he sends (it) down in due measure as He pleases. For He is with His Servants Well-acquainted, Watchful.

27. Wa law basaṭal-laahur-rizqa li'ibaadihee labaghaw fil-arḍi wa laakiñy-yunazzilu biqadarim-maa yashaaa'; innahoo bi-'ibaadihee Khabeerum Baṣeer.

وَلَوْ بَسَطَ اللّٰهُ الرِّزْقَ لِعِبَادِهٖ لَبَغَوْا
فِي الْاَرْضِ وَلٰكِنْ يُّنَزِّلُ بِقَدَرٍ مَّا
يَشَآءُ ؕ اِنَّهٗ بِعِبَادِهٖ خَبِيْرٌۢ بَصِيْرٌ ﴿٢٧﴾

28. He is the One that sends down rain (even) after (men) have given up all hope, and scatters His Mercy (far and wide). And He is the Protector, Worthy of all Praise.

28. Wa Huwal-lazee yunazzilul-ghaysa mim ba'di maa qanaṭoo wa yanshuru raḥmatah; wa Huwal-Waliyyul-Ḥameed.

وَهُوَ الَّذِيْ يُنَزِّلُ الْغَيْثَ مِنْۢ بَعْدِ
مَا قَنَطُوْا وَيَنْشُرُ رَحْمَتَهٗ ؕ وَهُوَ
الْوَلِيُّ الْحَمِيْدُ ﴿٢٨﴾

29. And among His Signs is the creation of the heavens and the earth, and the living creatures that He has scattered through them: and He has power to gather them together when He wills.

29. Wa min Aayaatihee khalqus-samaawaati wal-arḍi wa maa bassa feehimaa min daaabbah; wa Huwa 'alaa jam'ihim izaa yashaaa'u Qadeer.

(Section 3)

وَمِنْ اٰيٰتِهٖ خَلْقُ السَّمٰوٰتِ وَالْاَرْضِ
وَمَا بَثَّ فِيْهِمَا مِنْ دَآبَّةٍ ؕ وَهُوَ
عَلٰى جَمْعِهِمْ اِذَا يَشَآءُ قَدِيْرٌ ﴿٢٩﴾ ع

30. Whatever misfortune happens to you, is because of the things your hands have wrought, and for many (a sin) He grants forgiveness.

30. Wa maaa aṣaabakum mim-muṣeebatin fabimaa kasabat aydeekum wa ya'foo 'an kaseer.

وَمَآ اَصَابَكُمْ مِّنْ مُّصِيْبَةٍ فَبِمَا
كَسَبَتْ اَيْدِيْكُمْ وَيَعْفُوْا عَنْ كَثِيْرٍ ﴿٣٠﴾

31. Nor can you escape (aught), (fleeing) through the earth; nor have you, besides Allah, any one to protect or to help.

31. Wa maaa antum bimu'jizeena fil-arḍi wa maa lakum min doonil-laahi miñw-waliyyiñw-wa laa naṣeer.

وَمَآ اَنْتُمْ بِمُعْجِزِيْنَ فِي الْاَرْضِ ۚۖ
وَمَا لَكُمْ مِّنْ دُوْنِ اللّٰهِ مِنْ وَّلِيٍّ
وَّلَا نَصِيْرٍ ﴿٣١﴾

32. And among His Signs are the ships, smooth-running through the ocean, (tall) as mountains.

32. Wa min Aayaatihil-jawaari fil-baḥri kal-a'laam.

وَمِنْ اٰيٰتِهِ الْجَوَارِ فِي الْبَحْرِ
كَالْاَعْلَامِ ؕ ﴿٣٢﴾

33. If it be His Will He can still the Wind: then would they become motionless on the back of the (ocean). Verily in this are Signs for everyone who patiently perseveres and is grateful.

33. Iñy-yashaå yuskinir-reeḥa fa-yaẓlalna rawaakida 'alaa ẓahrih; inna fee zaalika la-Aayaatil-likulli ṣabbaarin shakoor.

اِنْ يَّشَاْ يُسْكِنِ الرِّيْحَ فَيَظْلَلْنَ رَوَاكِدَ
عَلٰى ظَهْرِهٖ ؕ اِنَّ فِيْ ذٰلِكَ لَاٰيٰتٍ
لِّكُلِّ صَبَّارٍ شَكُوْرٍ ۙ ﴿٣٣﴾

34. Or He can cause them to perish because of the (evil) which (the men) have earned; but much does He forgive.

34. Aw yoobiqhunna bimaa kasaboo wa ya'fu 'an kaseer.

اَوْ يُوْبِقْهُنَّ بِمَا كَسَبُوْا وَيَعْفُ
عَنْ كَثِيْرٍ ۙ ﴿٣٤﴾

35. But let those know, who dispute about Our Signs, that there is for them no way of escape.

35. Wa ya'lamal-lazeena yujaadiloona feee Aayaatinaa maa lahum mim-maḥeeṣ.

وَّيَعْلَمَ الَّذِيْنَ يُجَادِلُوْنَ فِيْٓ اٰيٰتِنَا ؕ
مَا لَهُمْ مِّنْ مَّحِيْصٍ ﴿٣٥﴾

Ikhfa اخفاء | Ghunna غُنّہ | Ikhfa Meem Saakin اخفاءمیم ساکن | Idghaam ادغام | Qalqala قلقلہ | Qalb قلب | Idghaam Meem Saakin ادغام میم ساکن

36. Whatever you are given (here) is (but) a convenience of this life: but that which is with Allah is better and more lasting: (it is) for those who believe and put their trust in their Lord:

36. Famaaa ooteetum min shay'in famataa'ul-ḥayaatid-dunyaa wa maa 'indal-laahi khayruñw-wa abqaa lillazeena aamanoo wa 'alaa Rabbihim yatawakkaloon.

فَمَآ أُوتِيتُم مِّن شَيْءٍ فَمَتَاعُ
الْحَيَوٰةِ الدُّنْيَا ۖ وَمَا عِندَ اللَّهِ خَيْرٌ
وَأَبْقَىٰ لِلَّذِينَ ءَامَنُوا وَعَلَىٰ رَبِّهِمْ
يَتَوَكَّلُونَ ﴿٣٦﴾

37. Those who avoid the greater crimes and shameful deeds, and, when they are angry even then forgive;

37. Wallazeena yajtaniboona kabaaa'iral-ismi wal-fawaa-hisha wa izaa maa ghaḍiboo hum yaghfiroon.

وَالَّذِينَ يَجْتَنِبُونَ كَبَٰٓئِرَ الْإِثْمِ
وَالْفَوَٰحِشَ وَإِذَا مَا غَضِبُوا هُمْ
يَغْفِرُونَ ﴿٣٧﴾

38. Those who hearken to their Lord, and establish regular Prayer; who (conduct) their affairs by mutual Consultation; who spend out of what We bestow on them for Sustenance;

38. Wallazeenas-tajaaboo li-Rabbihim wa aqaamuṣ-Ṣalaata wa amruhum shooraa bayna-hum wa mimmaa razaqnaahum yunfiqoon.

وَالَّذِينَ اسْتَجَابُوا لِرَبِّهِمْ وَأَقَامُوا
الصَّلَوٰةَ وَأَمْرُهُمْ شُورَىٰ بَيْنَهُمْ
وَمِمَّا رَزَقْنَٰهُمْ يُنفِقُونَ ﴿٣٨﴾

39. And those who, when an oppressive wrong is inflicted on them, (are not cowed but) help and defend themselves.

39. Wallazeena izaaa aṣaa-bahumul-baghyu hum yanta-ṣiroon.

وَالَّذِينَ إِذَآ أَصَابَهُمُ الْبَغْيُ هُمْ
يَنتَصِرُونَ ﴿٣٩﴾

40. The recompense for an injury is an injury equal thereto (in degree): but if a person forgives and makes reconciliation, his reward is due from Allah: for (Allah) loves not those who do wrong.

40. Wa jazaaa'u sayyi'atin sayyi'atum-misluhaa faman 'afaa wa aṣlaḥa fa-ajruhoo 'alal-laah; innahoo laa yuḥib-buẓ-ẓaalimeen.

وَجَزَٰٓؤُا سَيِّئَةٍ سَيِّئَةٌ مِّثْلُهَا ۖ
فَمَنْ عَفَا وَأَصْلَحَ فَأَجْرُهُ عَلَى
اللَّهِ ۚ إِنَّهُ لَا يُحِبُّ الظَّٰلِمِينَ ﴿٤٠﴾

41. But indeed if any do help and defend themselves after a wrong (done) to them, against such there is no cause of blame.

41. Wa lamanin-taṣara ba'da ẓulmihee fa-ulaaa'ika maa 'alayhim min sabeel.

وَلَمَنِ انتَصَرَ بَعْدَ ظُلْمِهِ فَأُولَٰٓئِكَ
مَا عَلَيْهِم مِّن سَبِيلٍ ﴿٤١﴾

42. The blame is only against those who oppress men and wrong-doing and insolently transgress beyond bounds through the land, defying right and justice: for such there will be a Chastisement grievous.

42. Innamaṣ-ṣabeelu 'alal-lazeena yaẓlimoonan-naasa wa yabghoona fil-arḍi bighayril-ḥaqq; ulaaa'ika lahum 'azaabun aleem.

إِنَّمَا السَّبِيلُ عَلَى الَّذِينَ يَظْلِمُونَ
النَّاسَ وَيَبْغُونَ فِي الْأَرْضِ بِغَيْرِ
الْحَقِّ ۚ أُولَٰٓئِكَ لَهُمْ عَذَابٌ أَلِيمٌ ﴿٤٢﴾

43. But indeed if any show patience and forgive, that would truly be an affair of great resolution.

43. Wa laman ṣabara wa ghafara inna zaalika lamin 'azmil-umoor. **(Section 4)**

وَلَمَن صَبَرَ وَغَفَرَ إِنَّ ذَٰلِكَ لَمِنْ
عَزْمِ الْأُمُورِ ﴿٤٣﴾ ع ٤

44. For any whom Allah leaves astray, there is no protector thereafter. And thou wilt see the Wrong-doers, when in sight of the Penalty, Say: "Is there any way (to effect) a return?"

44. Wa mañy-yuḍlilil-laahu famaa lahoo miñw-waliyyim-mim ba'dih; wa taraẓ-ẓaalimeena lammaa ra-awul-'azaaba yaqooloona hal ilaa maraddim-min sabeel.

وَمَن يُضْلِلِ اللَّهُ فَمَا لَهُ مِن وَلِيٍّ
مِّن بَعْدِهِ ۗ وَتَرَى الظَّٰلِمِينَ لَمَّا
رَأَوُا الْعَذَابَ يَقُولُونَ هَلْ إِلَىٰ
مَرَدٍّ مِّن سَبِيلٍ ﴿٤٤﴾

Ikhfa اخفاء | Ghunna غنّہ | Ikhfa Meem Saakin اخفاء میم ساکن | Idghaam ادغام | Qalqala قلقلہ | Qalb قلب | Idghaam Meem Saakin ادغام میم ساکن

45. And you will see them brought forward to the Chastisement, in a humble frame of mind because of (their) disgrace, (and) looking with a stealthy glance. And the Believers will say: "Those are indeed in loss, who have given to perdition their own selves and those belonging to them on the Day of Judgment. Behold! Truly the Wrong-doers are in a lasting Chastisement!"

45. Wa taraahum yu'raḍoona 'alayhaa khaashi'eena minaz-zulli yanẓuroona min ṭarfin khafiyy; wa qaalal-lazeena aamanooo innal-khaasireenal-lazeena khasirooo anfusahum wa ahleehim Yawmal-Qiyaamah; alaaa innaẓ-ẓaalimeena fee 'azaabim-muqeem.

وَتَرٰىهُمْ يُعْرَضُوْنَ عَلَيْهَا خٰشِعِيْنَ
مِنَ الذُّلِّ يَنْظُرُوْنَ مِنْ طَرْفٍ
خَفِيٍّ ۗ وَقَالَ الَّذِيْنَ اٰمَنُوْٓا اِنَّ
الْخٰسِرِيْنَ الَّذِيْنَ خَسِرُوْٓا اَنْفُسَهُمْ
وَاَهْلِيْهِمْ يَوْمَ الْقِيٰمَةِ ۗ اَلَآ اِنَّ
الظّٰلِمِيْنَ فِيْ عَذَابٍ مُّقِيْمٍ ﴿٤٥﴾

46. And no protectors have they to help them, other than Allah. And for any whom Allah leaves to stray, there is no way (to the Goal).

46. Wa maa kaana lahum min awliyaaa'a yanṣuroonahum min doonil-laah; wa mañy-yuḍlilil-laahu famaa lahoo min sabeel.

وَمَا كَانَ لَهُمْ مِّنْ اَوْلِيَآءَ
يَنْصُرُوْنَهُمْ مِّنْ دُوْنِ اللّٰهِ ۗ وَمَنْ
يُّضْلِلِ اللّٰهُ فَمَا لَهٗ مِنْ سَبِيْلٍ ۗ ﴿٤٦﴾

47. Respond your Lord, before there come a Day which there will be no putting back, because of (the Ordainment of) Allah! that Day there will be for you no place of refuge nor will there be for you any room for denial (of your sins)!

47. Istajeeboo li-Rabbikum min qabli añy-yaâtiya Yawmul-laa maradda lahoo minal-laah; maa lakum mim-malja-iñy-Yawma'iziñw-wa maa lakum min nakeer.

اِسْتَجِيْبُوْا لِرَبِّكُمْ مِّنْ قَبْلِ
اَنْ يَّاْتِيَ يَوْمٌ لَّا مَرَدَّ لَهٗ مِنَ اللّٰهِ ۗ
مَا لَكُمْ مِّنْ مَّلْجَاٍ يَّوْمَئِذٍ وَّمَا
لَكُمْ مِّنْ نَّكِيْرٍ ﴿٤٧﴾

48. If then they run away, We have not sent you as a guard over them. Your duty is but to convey (the Message). And truly, when We give man a taste of a Mercy from Ourselves, he does exult thereat, but when some ill happens to him, on account of the deeds which his hands have sent forth, truly then is man ungrateful!

48. Fa-in a'raḍoo famaaa arsalnaaka 'alayhim ḥafeeẓan in 'alayka illal-balaagh; wa innaaa izaaa azaqnal-insaana minnaa raḥmatan fariḥa bihaa wa in tuṣibhum sayyi'atum bimaa qaddamat aydeehim fa-innal-insaana kafoor.

فَاِنْ اَعْرَضُوْا فَمَآ اَرْسَلْنٰكَ عَلَيْهِمْ
حَفِيْظًا ۗ اِنْ عَلَيْكَ اِلَّا الْبَلٰغُ ۗ
وَاِنَّآ اِذَآ اَذَقْنَا الْاِنْسَانَ مِنَّا
رَحْمَةً فَرِحَ بِهَا ۚ وَاِنْ تُصِبْهُمْ
سَيِّئَةٌۢ بِمَا قَدَّمَتْ اَيْدِيْهِمْ فَاِنَّ
الْاِنْسَانَ كَفُوْرٌ ﴿٤٨﴾

49. To Allah belongs the dominion of the heavens and the earth. He creates what He wills (and plans). He bestows (children) male or female according to His Will (and Plan),

49. Lillaahi mulkus-samaawaati wal-arḍ; yakhluqu maa yashaaa'; yahabu limañy-yashaaa'u inaasañw-wa yahabu limañy-yashaaa'uz-zukoor.

لِلّٰهِ مُلْكُ السَّمٰوٰتِ وَالْاَرْضِ ۗ
يَخْلُقُ مَا يَشَآءُ ۗ يَهَبُ لِمَنْ يَّشَآءُ
اِنَاثًا وَّيَهَبُ لِمَنْ يَّشَآءُ الذُّكُوْرَ ۙ ﴿٤٩﴾

50. Or He bestows both males and females, and He leaves barren whom He will: for He is full of Knowledge and Power.

50. Aw yuzawwijuhum zukraanañw-wa inaasañw wa yaj'alu mañy-yashaaa'u 'aqeemaa; innahoo 'Aleemun Qadeer.

اَوْ يُزَوِّجُهُمْ ذُكْرَانًا وَّاِنَاثًا ۚ وَيَجْعَلُ
مَنْ يَّشَآءُ عَقِيْمًا ۗ اِنَّهٗ عَلِيْمٌ قَدِيْرٌ ﴿٥٠﴾

51. It is not fitting for a man that Allah should speak to him except by inspiration, or from behind a veil, or

51. Wa maa kaana libasharin añy-yukallimahul-laahu illaa waḥyan aw miñw-waraaa'i ḥijaabin aw

وَمَا كَانَ لِبَشَرٍ اَنْ يُّكَلِّمَهُ اللّٰهُ اِلَّا
وَحْيًا اَوْ مِنْ وَّرَآئِ حِجَابٍ اَوْ

Ikhfa اخفاء | Ghunna غُنّہ | Ikhfa Meem Saakin اخفاء میم ساکن | Idghaam ادغام | Qalqala قلقلہ | Qalb قلب | Idghaam Meem Saakin ادغام میم ساکن

by the sending of a messenger to reveal, with Allah's permission, what Allah wills: for He is Most High, Most Wise.

yursila Rasoolan fa-yooḥiya bi-iznihee maa yashaaa'; innahoo 'Aliyyun Ḥakeem.

يُرْسِلَ رَسُولًا فَيُوحِيَ بِإِذْنِهِ
مَا يَشَاءُ ۚ إِنَّهُ عَلِيٌّ حَكِيمٌ ٥١

52. And thus have We, by Our Command, sent inspiration to you: you know not (before) what was Revelation, and what was Faith; but We have made the (Qur'an) a Light, wherewith We guide such of Our servants as We will; and verily you does guide (men) to the Straight Way,-

52. Wa kazaalika awḥaynaaa ilayka rooḥam-min amrinaa; maa kunta tadree mal-Kitaabu wa lal-eemaanu wa laakin ja'alnaahu nooran nahdee bihee man nashaaa'u min 'ibaadinaa; wa innaka latahdeee ilaa Ṣiraaṭim Mustaqeem.

وَكَذَٰلِكَ أَوْحَيْنَا إِلَيْكَ رُوحًا مِّنْ
أَمْرِنَا ۚ مَا كُنتَ تَدْرِي مَا الْكِتَابُ
وَلَا الْإِيمَانُ وَلَٰكِن جَعَلْنَاهُ نُورًا
نَّهْدِي بِهِ مَن نَّشَاءُ مِنْ عِبَادِنَا ۚ
وَإِنَّكَ لَتَهْدِي إِلَىٰ صِرَاطٍ مُّسْتَقِيمٍ ٥٢

53. The Way of Allah, to Whom belongs whatever is in the heavens and whatever is on earth. Behold (how) all affairs tend towards Allah!

53. Ṣiraaṭil-laahil-lazee lahoo maa fis-samaawaati wa maa fil-arḍ; alaaa ilal-laahi taṣeerul-umoor. **(Section 5)**

صِرَاطِ اللَّهِ الَّذِي لَهُ مَا فِي السَّمَاوَاتِ
وَمَا فِي الْأَرْضِ ۗ أَلَا إِلَى اللَّهِ
تَصِيرُ الْأُمُورُ ٥٣

ع ٥

43. Gold Adornments

In the name of Allah, Most Gracious, Most Merciful.

Sûrat az-Zukhruf–43

(Revealed at Makkah)

Bismillaahir Raḥmaanir Raḥeem

سُورَةُ الزُّخْرُفِ مَكِّيَّةٌ (٤٣)

بِسْمِ اللَّهِ الرَّحْمَٰنِ الرَّحِيمِ

مع ١٢ عند المتقدمين ١٢

1. *Ha-Mim.*

1. Ḥaa-Meeem.

حم ١

2. By the Book that makes things clear,-

2. Wal-Kitaabil-Mubeen.

وَالْكِتَابِ الْمُبِينِ ٢

3. We have made it a Qur'an in Arabic, that you may be able to understand (and learn wisdom).

3. Innaa ja'alnaahu Qur-aa-nan 'Arabiyyal-la'allakum ta'qiloon.

إِنَّا جَعَلْنَاهُ قُرْآنًا عَرَبِيًّا لَّعَلَّكُمْ
تَعْقِلُونَ ٣

4. And verily, it is in the Mother of the Book, in Our Presence, high (in dignity), full of wisdom.

4. Wa innahoo feee Ummil-Kitaabi ladaynaa la'aliyyun ḥakeem.

وَإِنَّهُ فِي أُمِّ الْكِتَابِ لَدَيْنَا
لَعَلِيٌّ حَكِيمٌ ٤

5. Shall We then take away the Message from you all together for that you are a people transgressing beyond bounds?

5. Afanaḍribu 'ankumuz-Zikra ṣafḥan an kuntum qawmam-musrifeen.

أَفَنَضْرِبُ عَنكُمُ الذِّكْرَ صَفْحًا أَن
كُنتُمْ قَوْمًا مُّسْرِفِينَ ٥

6. But how many were the prophets We sent amongst the peoples of old?

6. Wa kam arsalnaa min-Nabiyyin fil-awwaleen.

وَكَمْ أَرْسَلْنَا مِن نَّبِيٍّ فِي الْأَوَّلِينَ ٦

7. And never came there a prophet to them but they mocked him.

7. Wa maa yaâteehim min Nabiyyin illaa kaanoo bihee yastahzi'oon.

وَمَا يَأْتِيهِم مِّن نَّبِيٍّ إِلَّا كَانُوا
بِهِ يَسْتَهْزِئُونَ ٧

8. So We destroyed (them)-stronger in power than these;-and (thus) has passed on the Parable of the peoples of old.

8. Fa-ahlaknaaa ashadda minhum baṭshañw-wa maḍaa masalul-awwaleen.

فَأَهْلَكْنَا أَشَدَّ مِنْهُم بَطْشًا وَمَضَىٰ
مَثَلُ الْأَوَّلِينَ ٨

9. If you were to question them, 'Who created the heavens

9. Wa la'in sa-altahum man khalaqas-samaawaati

وَلَئِن سَأَلْتَهُم مَّنْ خَلَقَ السَّمَاوَاتِ

Ikhfa اخفاء · Ghunna غنّہ · Ikhfa Meem Saakin اخفاء میم ساکن · Idghaam ادغام · Qalqala قلقلہ · Qalb قلب · Idghaam Meem Saakin ادغام میم ساکن

and the earth?' They would be sure to reply, 'they were created by (Him), the Exalted in Power, Full of Knowledge';-	wal-arḍa la-yaqoolunna khalaqahunnal-'Azeezul-'Aleem.	وَالْأَرْضَ لَيَقُولُنَّ خَلَقَهُنَّ الْعَزِيزُ الْعَلِيمُ ۙ ٩
10. (Yes, the same that) has made for you the earth (like a carpet) spread out, and has made for you roads (and channels) therein, in order that you may find guidance (on the way);	10. Allaz̲ee ja'ala lakumul-arḍa mahdañw-wa ja'ala lakum feehaa subulal-la'allakum tahtadoon.	الَّذِي جَعَلَ لَكُمُ الْأَرْضَ مَهْدًا وَّجَعَلَ لَكُمْ فِيهَا سُبُلًا لَّعَلَّكُمْ تَهْتَدُونَ ۚ ١٠
11. Who sends down (from time to time) rain from the sky in due measure;- and We raise to life therewith a land that is dead; even so will you be raised (from the dead);-	11. Wallaz̲ee nazzala minas-samaaa'i maaa'am biqadarin fa-ansharnaa bihee baldatam-maytaa; kaz̲aalika tukhrajoon.	وَالَّذِي نَزَّلَ مِنَ السَّمَاءِ مَاءً بِقَدَرٍ فَأَنشَرْنَا بِهِ بَلْدَةً مَّيْتًا ۚ كَذَٰلِكَ تُخْرَجُونَ ١١
12. That has created pairs in all things, and has made for you ships and cattle on which you ride,	12. Wallaz̲ee khalaqal-azwaaja kullahaa wa ja'ala lakum minal-fulki wal-an'aami maa tarkaboon.	وَالَّذِي خَلَقَ الْأَزْوَاجَ كُلَّهَا وَجَعَلَ لَكُم مِّنَ الْفُلْكِ وَالْأَنْعَامِ مَا تَرْكَبُونَ ۙ ١٢
13. In order that you may sit firm and square on their backs, and when so seated, you may celebrate the (kind) favour of your Lord, and say, "Glory to Him Who has subjected these to our (use), for we could never have accomplished this (by ourselves),	13. Litastawoo 'alaa ẓuhoorihee summa taz̲kuroo ni'mata Rabbikum iz̲astawaytum 'alayhi wa taqooloo Subḥaanal-laz̲ee sakhkhara lanaa haaz̲aa wa maa kunnaa lahoo muqrineen.	لِتَسْتَوُوا عَلَىٰ ظُهُورِهِ ثُمَّ تَذْكُرُوا نِعْمَةَ رَبِّكُمْ إِذَا اسْتَوَيْتُمْ عَلَيْهِ وَتَقُولُوا سُبْحَانَ الَّذِي سَخَّرَ لَنَا هَٰذَا وَمَا كُنَّا لَهُ مُقْرِنِينَ ۙ ١٣
14. "And to our Lord, surely, must we turn back!"	14. Wa innaaa ilaa Rabbinaa lamunqaliboon.	وَإِنَّا إِلَىٰ رَبِّنَا لَمُنقَلِبُونَ ١٤
15. Yet they attribute to some of His servants a share with Him (in His godhead)! truly is man a blasphemous ingrate avowed!	15. Wa ja'aloo lahoo min 'ibaadihee juz'aa; innal-insaana lakafoorum-mubeen. **(Section 1)**	وَجَعَلُوا لَهُ مِنْ عِبَادِهِ جُزْءًا ۚ إِنَّ الْإِنسَانَ لَكَفُورٌ مُّبِينٌ ١٥
16. What! has He taken daughters out of what He himself creates, and granted to you sons for choice?	16. Amit-takhaz̲a mimmaa yakhluqu banaatiñw-wa aṣfaakum bilbaneen.	أَمِ اتَّخَذَ مِمَّا يَخْلُقُ بَنَاتٍ وَّ أَصْفَاكُم بِالْبَنِينَ ١٦
17. When news is brought to one of them of (the birth of) what he sets up as a likeness to (Allah) Most Gracious, his face darkens, and he is filled with inward grief!	17. Wa iz̲aa bushshira aḥaduhum bimaa ḍaraba lir-Raḥmaani mas̲alan ẓalla wajhuhoo muswaddañw-wa huwa kaẓeem.	وَإِذَا بُشِّرَ أَحَدُهُم بِمَا ضَرَبَ لِلرَّحْمَٰنِ مَثَلًا ظَلَّ وَجْهُهُ مُسْوَدًّا وَهُوَ كَظِيمٌ ١٧
18. Is then one brought up among trinkets, and unable to give a clear account in a dispute (to be associated with Allah)?	18. Awa mañy-yunashsha'u fil-ḥilyati wa huwa fil-khiṣaami ghayru mubeen.	أَوَمَن يُنَشَّأُ فِي الْحِلْيَةِ وَهُوَ فِي الْخِصَامِ غَيْرُ مُبِينٍ ١٨
19. And they make into females angels who themselves	19. Wa ja'alul-malaaa'ikatal-laz̲eena hum 'ibaadur-	وَجَعَلُوا الْمَلَائِكَةَ الَّذِينَ هُمْ عِبَادُ

Ikhfa اخفاء | Ghunna غنّہ | Ikhfa Meem Saakin اخفاء میم ساکن | Idghaam ادغام | Qalqala قلقلہ | Qalb قلب | Idghaam Meem Saakin ادغام میم ساکن

serve Allah. Did they witness their creation? Their evidence will be recorded, and they will be called to account!

20. ("Ah!") they say, "If it had been the will of (Allah) Most Gracious, we should not have worshipped such (deities)!" Of that they have no knowledge! they do nothing but lie!

21. What! have We given them a Book before this, to which they are holding fast?

22. No! they say: "We found our fathers following a certain religion, and we do guide ourselves by their footsteps."

23. Just in the same way, whenever We sent a Warner before you to any people, the wealthy ones among them said: "We found our fathers following a certain religion, and we will certainly follow in their footsteps."

24. He said: "What! Even if I brought you better guidance than that which you found your fathers following?" They said: "For us, we deny that you (prophets) are sent (on a mission at all)."

25. So We exacted retribution from them: now see what was the end of those who rejected (Truth)!

26. Behold! Abraham said to his father and his people: "I do indeed clear myself of what you worship:

27. "(I worship) only Him Who made me, and He will certainly guide me."

28. And he left it as a Word to endure among those who came after him, that they may turn back (to Allah).

29. Yes, I have given the good things of this life to these (men) and their fathers, until the Truth has come to them, and an apostle making things clear.

30. But when the Truth came to them, they said: "This is sorcery,

Raḥmaani inaasaa; a-shahidoo khalqahum; satuktabu shahaadatuhum wa yus'aloon.

20. Wa qaaloo law shaaa'ar-Raḥmaanu maa 'abadnaahum; maa lahum bizaalika min 'ilmin in hum illaa yakhruṣoon.

21. Am aataynaahum Kitaabam-min qablihee fahum bihee mustamsikoon.

22. Bal qaalooo innaa wajadnaaa aabaaa'anaa 'alaaa ummatiñw-wa innaa 'alaaa aasaarihim muhtadoon.

23. Wa kazaalika maaa arsalnaa min qablika fee qaryatim-min nazeerin illaa qaala mutrafoohaaa innaa wajadnaaa aabaaa'anaa 'alaaa ummatiñw-wa innaa 'alaaa aasaarihim muqtadoon.

24. Qaala awa law ji'tukum bi-ahdaa mimmaa wajattum 'alayhi aabaaa'akum qaalooo innaa bimaaa ursiltum bihee kaafiroon.

25. Fantaqamnaa minhum fanẓur kayfa kaana 'aaqibatul-mukazzibeen. **(Section 2)**

26. Wa iz qaala Ibraaheemu li-abeehi wa qawmiheee innanee baraaa'um-mimmaa ta'budoon.

27. Illal-lazee faṭaranee fa-innahoo sa-yahdeen.

28. Wa ja'alahaa Kalimatam baaqiyatan fee 'aqibihee la'allahum yarji'oon.

29. Bal matta'tu haaa'ulaaa'i wa aabaaa'ahum ḥattaa jaaa'ahumul-ḥaqqu wa Rasoolum-mubeen.

30. Wa lammaa jaaa'ahumul-ḥaqqu qaaloo haazaa siḥruñw-

الرَّحْمٰنِ اِنَاثًا ؕ اَشَهِدُوْا خَلْقَهُمْ ؕ
سَتُكْتَبُ شَهَادَتُهُمْ وَيُسْـَٔلُوْنَ ۝١٩
وَقَالُوْا لَوْ شَآءَ الرَّحْمٰنُ مَا عَبَدْنٰهُمْ ؕ
مَا لَهُمْ بِذٰلِكَ مِنْ عِلْمٍ ۚ اِنْ هُمْ اِلَّا
يَخْرُصُوْنَ ۝٢٠
اَمْ اٰتَيْنٰهُمْ كِتٰبًا مِّنْ قَبْلِهٖ فَهُمْ
بِهٖ مُسْتَمْسِكُوْنَ ۝٢١
بَلْ قَالُوْٓا اِنَّا وَجَدْنَآ اٰبَآءَنَا عَلٰٓى
اُمَّةٍ وَّاِنَّا عَلٰٓى اٰثٰرِهِمْ مُّهْتَدُوْنَ ۝٢٢
وَكَذٰلِكَ مَآ اَرْسَلْنَا مِنْ قَبْلِكَ فِىْ
قَرْيَةٍ مِّنْ نَّذِيْرٍ اِلَّا قَالَ مُتْرَفُوْهَآ ۙ
اِنَّا وَجَدْنَآ اٰبَآءَنَا عَلٰٓى اُمَّةٍ وَّاِنَّا
عَلٰٓى اٰثٰرِهِمْ مُّقْتَدُوْنَ ۝٢٣
قٰلَ اَوَلَوْ جِئْتُكُمْ بِاَهْدٰى مِمَّا
وَجَدْتُّمْ عَلَيْهِ اٰبَآءَكُمْ ؕ قَالُوْٓا اِنَّا
بِمَآ اُرْسِلْتُمْ بِهٖ كٰفِرُوْنَ ۝٢٤
فَانْتَقَمْنَا مِنْهُمْ فَانْظُرْ كَيْفَ
كَانَ عَاقِبَةُ الْمُكَذِّبِيْنَ ۝٢٥ ع
وَاِذْ قَالَ اِبْرٰهِيْمُ لِاَبِيْهِ وَقَوْمِهٖٓ
اِنَّنِىْ بَرَآءٌ مِّمَّا تَعْبُدُوْنَ ۝٢٦
اِلَّا الَّذِىْ فَطَرَنِىْ فَاِنَّهٗ سَيَهْدِيْنِ ۝٢٧
وَجَعَلَهَا كَلِمَةًۢ بَاقِيَةً فِىْ عَقِبِهٖ
لَعَلَّهُمْ يَرْجِعُوْنَ ۝٢٨
بَلْ مَتَّعْتُ هٰٓؤُلَآءِ وَاٰبَآءَهُمْ حَتّٰى
جَآءَهُمُ الْحَقُّ وَرَسُوْلٌ مُّبِيْنٌ ۝٢٩
وَلَمَّا جَآءَهُمُ الْحَقُّ قَالُوْا هٰذَا سِحْرٌ

النصف ع ٨

Ikhfa اخفاء | Ghunna غنّہ | Ikhfa Meem Saakin اخفاء میم ساکن | Idghaam ادغام | Qalqala قلقلہ | Qalb قلب | Idghaam Meem Saakin ادغام میم ساکن

and we do reject it."

wa innaa bihee kaafiroon.

وَّاِنَّا بِهٖ كٰفِرُوْنَ ﴿٣٠﴾

31. Also, they say: "Why is not this Qur'an sent down to some leading man in either of the two (chief) cities?"

31. Wa qaaloo law laa nuzzila haazal-Qur-aanu 'alaa rajulim-minal-qaryatayni 'azeem.

وَقَالُوْا لَوْلَا نُزِّلَ هٰذَا الْقُرْاٰنُ عَلٰى
رَجُلٍ مِّنَ الْقَرْيَتَيْنِ عَظِيْمٍ ﴿٣١﴾

32. Is it they who would portion out the Mercy of your Lord? It is We Who portion out between them their livelihood in the life of this world: and We raise some of them above others in ranks, so that some may command work from others. But the Mercy of your Lord is better than the (wealth) which they amass.

32. Ahum yaqsimoona raḥmata Rabbik; Naḥnu qasamnaa baynahum ma'eeshatahum fil-ḥayaatid dunyaa wa rafa'naa ba'ḍahum fawqa ba'ḍin darajaatil-liyattakhiza ba'ḍuhum ba'ḍan sukhriyyaa; wa rahmatu Rabbika khayrum-mimmaa yajma'oon.

اَهُمْ يَقْسِمُوْنَ رَحْمَتَ رَبِّكَ ؕ نَحْنُ
قَسَمْنَا بَيْنَهُمْ مَّعِيْشَتَهُمْ فِى الْحَيٰوةِ
الدُّنْيَا وَرَفَعْنَا بَعْضَهُمْ فَوْقَ بَعْضٍ
دَرَجٰتٍ لِّيَتَّخِذَ بَعْضُهُمْ بَعْضًا سُخْرِيًّا ؕ
وَرَحْمَتُ رَبِّكَ خَيْرٌ مِّمَّا يَجْمَعُوْنَ ﴿٣٢﴾

33. And were it not that (all) men might become of one community, We would provide, for everyone that blasphemes against (Allah) Most Gracious, silver roofs for their houses and (silver) stair-ways on which to go up,

33. Wa law laaa añy-yakoonan-naasu ummatañw-waaḥidatal-laja'alnaa limañy-yakfuru bir-Raḥmaani libu-yootihim suqufam-min fiḍḍatiñw-wa ma'aarija 'alayhaa yaẓharoon.

وَلَوْلَاۤ اَنْ يَّكُوْنَ النَّاسُ اُمَّةً وَّاحِدَةً
لَّجَعَلْنَا لِمَنْ يَّكْفُرُ بِالرَّحْمٰنِ لِبُيُوْتِهِمْ
سُقُفًا مِّنْ فِضَّةٍ وَّمَعَارِجَ عَلَيْهَا
يَظْهَرُوْنَ ۙ﴿٣٣﴾

34. And (silver) doors to their houses, and thrones (of silver) on which they could recline,

34. Wa libu-yootihim abwaabañw-wa sururan 'alayhaa yattaki'oon.

وَلِبُيُوْتِهِمْ اَبْوَابًا وَّسُرُرًا عَلَيْهَا
يَتَّكِـُٔوْنَ ۙ﴿٣٤﴾

35. And also adornments of gold. But all this were nothing but enjoyment of the present life: The Hereafter, in the sight of your Lord is for the Righteous.

35. Wa zukhrufaa; wa in kullu zaalika lammaa mataa'ul-ḥayaatid-dunyaa; wal-Aakhiratu 'inda Rabbika lilmuttaqeen. **(Section 3)**

وَزُخْرُفًا ؕ وَاِنْ كُلُّ ذٰلِكَ لَمَّا
مَتَاعُ الْحَيٰوةِ الدُّنْيَا ؕ وَالْاٰخِرَةُ
عِنْدَ رَبِّكَ لِلْمُتَّقِيْنَ ﴿٣٥﴾

36. If anyone withdraws himself from remembrance of (Allah) Most Gracious, We appoint for him an evil one, to be an intimate companion to him.

36. Wa mañy-ya'shu 'an zikrir-Raḥmaani nuqayyiḍ lahoo Shayṭaanan fahuwa lahoo qareen.

وَمَنْ يَّعْشُ عَنْ ذِكْرِ الرَّحْمٰنِ نُقَيِّضْ
لَهٗ شَيْطٰنًا فَهُوَ لَهٗ قَرِيْنٌ ﴿٣٦﴾

37. Such (evil ones) really hinder them from the Path, but they think that they are being guided aright!

37. Wa innahum la-yaṣuddoonahum 'anis-sabeeli wa yaḥsaboona annahum muhtadoon.

وَاِنَّهُمْ لَيَصُدُّوْنَهُمْ عَنِ السَّبِيْلِ
وَيَحْسَبُوْنَ اَنَّهُمْ مُّهْتَدُوْنَ ﴿٣٧﴾

38. At length, when (such a one) comes to Us, he says (to his evil companion): "Would that between me and you were the distance of East and West!" Ah! evil is the companion (indeed)!

38. Ḥattaaa izaa jaaa'anaa qaala yaa layta baynee wa baynaka bu'dal-mashriqayni fabi'sal-qareen.

حَتّٰۤى اِذَا جَآءَنَا قَالَ يٰلَيْتَ بَيْنِىْ
وَبَيْنَكَ بُعْدَ الْمَشْرِقَيْنِ فَبِئْسَ
الْقَرِيْنُ ﴿٣٨﴾

39. When you have done wrong, it will avail you nothing, that Day, that you shall be partners in Punishment!

39. Wa lañy-yanfa'akumul-Yawma iz-ẓalamtum annakum fil-'azaabi mushtarikoon.

وَلَنْ يَّنْفَعَكُمُ الْيَوْمَ اِذْ ظَّلَمْتُمْ
اَنَّكُمْ فِى الْعَذَابِ مُشْتَرِكُوْنَ ﴿٣٩﴾

Ikhfa اخفاء | Ghunna غنّہ | Ikhfa Meem Saakin اخفاء میم ساکن | Idghaam ادغام | Qalqala قلقلہ | Qalb قلب | Idghaam Meem Saakin ادغام میم ساکن

40. Can you then make the deaf to hear, or give direction to the blind or to such as (wander) in manifest error?

40. Afa-anta tusmi'uṣ-ṣumma aw tahdil-'umya wa man kaana fee ḍalaalim-mubeen.

أَفَأَنتَ تُسْمِعُ ٱلصُّمَّ أَوْ تَهْدِى ٱلْعُمْىَ
وَمَن كَانَ فِى ضَلَـٰلٍ مُّبِينٍ ﴿٤٠﴾

41. Even if We take you away, We shall be sure to exact retribution from them,

41. Fa-immaa nazhabanna bika fa-innaa minhum muntaqimoon.

فَإِمَّا نَذْهَبَنَّ بِكَ فَإِنَّا مِنْهُم
مُّنتَقِمُونَ ﴿٤١﴾

42. Or We shall show you that (accomplished) which We have promised them: for verily We shall prevail over them.

42. Aw nuriyannakal-lazee wa'adnaahum fa-innaa 'alayhim muqtadiroon.

أَوْ نُرِيَنَّكَ ٱلَّذِى وَعَدْنَـٰهُمْ فَإِنَّا
عَلَيْهِم مُّقْتَدِرُونَ ﴿٤٢﴾

43. So hold you fast to the Revelation sent down to you; verily you are on a Straight Way.

43. Fastamsik billazeee oohiya ilayka innaka 'alaa Ṣiraaṭim-Mustaqeem.

فَٱسْتَمْسِكْ بِٱلَّذِىٓ أُوحِىَ إِلَيْكَ ۖ
إِنَّكَ عَلَىٰ صِرَٰطٍ مُّسْتَقِيمٍ ﴿٤٣﴾

44. The (Qur'an) is indeed the message, for you and for your people; and soon shall you (all) be brought to account.

44. Wa innahoo lazikrul-laka wa liqawmika wa sawfa tus'aloon.

وَإِنَّهُۥ لَذِكْرٌ لَّكَ وَلِقَوْمِكَ ۖ وَسَوْفَ
تُسْـَٔلُونَ ﴿٤٤﴾

45. And question you our apostles whom We sent before thee; did We appoint any deities other than (Allah) Most Gracious, to be worshipped?

45. Was'al man arsalnaa min qablika mir-Rusulinaaa aja-'alnaa min doonir-Raḥmaani aalihatañy-yu'badoon.

(Section 4)

وَسْـَٔلْ مَنْ أَرْسَلْنَا مِن قَبْلِكَ مِن
رُّسُلِنَآ أَجَعَلْنَا مِن دُونِ ٱلرَّحْمَـٰنِ
ءَالِهَةً يُعْبَدُونَ ﴿٤٥﴾ ع

ربع

46. We did send Moses aforetime, with Our Signs, to Pharaoh and his Chiefs: He said, "I am an apostle of the Lord of the Worlds."

46. Wa laqad arsalnaa Moosaa bi-Aayaatinaaa ilaa Fir'awna wa mala'ihee faqaala innee Rasoolu Rabbil-'aalameen.

وَلَقَدْ أَرْسَلْنَا مُوسَىٰ بِـَٔايَـٰتِنَآ إِلَىٰ
فِرْعَوْنَ وَمَلَإِي۟هِۦ فَقَالَ إِنِّى رَسُولُ
رَبِّ ٱلْعَـٰلَمِينَ ﴿٤٦﴾

47. But when he came to them with Our Signs, behold they ridiculed them.

47. Falammaa jaaa'ahum bi-Aayaatinaaa izaa hum minhaa yaḍḥakoon.

فَلَمَّا جَآءَهُم بِـَٔايَـٰتِنَآ إِذَا هُم مِّنْهَا
يَضْحَكُونَ ﴿٤٧﴾

48. We showed them Sign after Sign, each greater than its fellow, and We seized them with Punishment, in order that they might turn (to Us).

48. Wa maa nureehim min Aayatin illaa hiya akbaru min ukhtihaa wa akhaznaahum bil'azaabi la'allahum yarji'oon.

وَمَا نُرِيهِم مِّنْ ءَايَةٍ إِلَّا هِىَ أَكْبَرُ
مِنْ أُخْتِهَا ۖ وَأَخَذْنَـٰهُم بِٱلْعَذَابِ
لَعَلَّهُمْ يَرْجِعُونَ ﴿٤٨﴾

49. And they said, "O you sorcerer! Invoke your Lord for us according to His covenant with you; for we shall truly accept guidance."

49. Wa qaaloo yaaa ayyuhas-saaḥirud-'u lanaa Rabbaka bimaa 'ahida 'indaka innanaa lamuhtadoon.

وَقَالُوا۟ يَـٰٓأَيُّهَ ٱلسَّاحِرُ ٱدْعُ لَنَا رَبَّكَ
بِمَا عَهِدَ عِندَكَ ۖ إِنَّنَا لَمُهْتَدُونَ ﴿٤٩﴾

50. But when We removed the Penalty from them, behold, they broke their word.

50. Falammaa kashafnaa 'anhumul-'azaaba izaa hum yankusoon.

فَلَمَّا كَشَفْنَا عَنْهُمُ ٱلْعَذَابَ إِذَا
هُمْ يَنكُثُونَ ﴿٥٠﴾

51. And Pharaoh proclaimed among his people, saying:

51. Wa naadaa Fir'awnu fee qawmihee qaala yaa qawmi

وَنَادَىٰ فِرْعَوْنُ فِى قَوْمِهِۦ قَالَ يَـٰقَوْمِ

Ikhfa اخفاء	Ghunna غنّہ	Ikhfa Meem Saakin اخفاء میم ساکن	Idghaam ادغام	Qalqala قلقلہ	Qalb قلب	Idghaam Meem Saakin ادغام میم ساکن

does not the dominion of Egypt belong to me, (witness) these streams flowing underneath my (palace)? Do you not see then?

52. "Am I not better than this (Moses), who is a contemptible wretch and can scarcely express himself clearly?

53. "Then why are not gold bracelets bestowed on him, or (why) come (not) with him angels accompanying him in procession?"

54. Thus did he make fools of his people, and they obeyed him: truly were they a people rebellious (against Allah).

55. When at length they provoked Us, We exacted retribution from them, and We drowned them all.

56. And We made them (a people) of the Past and an Example to later ages.

57. When (Jesus) the son of Mary is held up as an example, behold, your people raise a clamour thereat (in ridicule)!

58. And they say, "Are our gods best, or he?" This they set forth to you, only by way of disputation: yes, they are a contentious people.

59. He was no more than a servant: We granted Our favour to him, and We made him an example to the Children of Israel

60. And if it were Our Will, We could make angels from amongst you, succeeding each other on the earth.

61. And (Jesus) shall be a Sign (for the coming of) the Hour (of Judgment): therefore have no doubt about the (Hour), but follow you Me: this is a Straight Way.

62. Let not the Evil One hinder you: for he is to you an enemy avowed.

63. When Jesus came with Clear Signs, he said: "Now have I come to you with Wisdom, and in order to make clear to you

alaysa lee mulku Miṣra wa haazihil-anhaaru tajree min taḥtee afalaa tubṣiroon.

52. Am ana khayrum-min haazal-lazee huwa maheenuñw-wa laa yakaadu yubeen.

53. Falaw laaa ulqiya 'alayhi aswiratum-min zahabin aw jaaa'a ma'ahul-malaaa'ikatu muqtarineen.

54. Fastakhaffa qawmahoo fa-aṭaa'ooh; innahum kaanoo qawman faasiqeen.

55. Falammaaa aasafoonan-taqamnaa minhum fa-aghraq-naahum ajma'een.

56. Faja'alnaahum salafañw-wa masalal-lil-aakhireen.

(Section 5)

57. Wa lammaa ḍuribab-nu Maryama masalan izaa qawmu-ka minhu yaṣiddoon.

58. Wa qaalooo 'a-aalihatunaa khayrun am hoo; maa ḍara-boohu laka illaa jadalaa; bal hum qawmun khaṣimoon.

59. In huwa illaa 'abdun an'amnaa 'alayhi wa ja'alnaahu masalal-li-Baneee Israaa'eel.

60. Wa law nashaaa'u laja'al-naa minkum malaaa'ikatan fil-arḍi yakhlufoon.

61. Wa innahoo la'ilmul-lis-Saa'ati falaa tamtarunna bihaa wattabi'oon; haazaa Ṣiraaṭum-Mustaqeem.

62. Wa laa yaṣuddan-naku-mush-Shayṭaanu innahoo la-kum 'aduwwum-mubeen.

63. Wa lammaa jaaa'a 'Eesaa bilbayyinaati qaala qad ji'tu-kum bil-Ḥikmati wa li-ubay-yina lakum

أَلَيْسَ لِي مُلْكُ مِصْرَ وَهَٰذِهِ الْأَنْهَٰرُ
تَجْرِي مِن تَحْتِيٓ ۖ أَفَلَا تُبْصِرُونَ ﴿٥١﴾
أَمْ أَنَا۠ خَيْرٌ مِّنْ هَٰذَا الَّذِي هُوَ
مَهِينٌ ۙ وَلَا يَكَادُ يُبِينُ ﴿٥٢﴾
فَلَوْلَآ أُلْقِيَ عَلَيْهِ أَسْوِرَةٌ مِّن ذَهَبٍ
أَوْ جَآءَ مَعَهُ الْمَلَٰٓئِكَةُ مُقْتَرِنِينَ ﴿٥٣﴾
فَاسْتَخَفَّ قَوْمَهُۥ فَأَطَاعُوهُ ۚ إِنَّهُمْ
كَانُوا۟ قَوْمًا فَٰسِقِينَ ﴿٥٤﴾
فَلَمَّآ ءَاسَفُونَا انتَقَمْنَا مِنْهُمْ
فَأَغْرَقْنَٰهُمْ أَجْمَعِينَ ﴿٥٥﴾
فَجَعَلْنَٰهُمْ سَلَفًا وَمَثَلًا لِّلْءَاخِرِينَ ﴿٥٦﴾
وَلَمَّا ضُرِبَ ابْنُ مَرْيَمَ مَثَلًا إِذَا قَوْمُكَ
مِنْهُ يَصِدُّونَ ﴿٥٧﴾
وَقَالُوٓا۟ ءَأَٰلِهَتُنَا خَيْرٌ أَمْ هُوَ ۚ مَا
ضَرَبُوهُ لَكَ إِلَّا جَدَلًۢا ۚ بَلْ هُمْ
قَوْمٌ خَصِمُونَ ﴿٥٨﴾
إِنْ هُوَ إِلَّا عَبْدٌ أَنْعَمْنَا عَلَيْهِ وَجَعَلْنَٰهُ
مَثَلًا لِّبَنِىٓ إِسْرَٰٓءِيلَ ﴿٥٩﴾
وَلَوْ نَشَآءُ لَجَعَلْنَا مِنكُم مَّلَٰٓئِكَةً
فِي الْأَرْضِ يَخْلُفُونَ ﴿٦٠﴾
وَإِنَّهُۥ لَعِلْمٌ لِّلسَّاعَةِ فَلَا تَمْتَرُنَّ بِهَا
وَاتَّبِعُونِ ۚ هَٰذَا صِرَٰطٌ مُّسْتَقِيمٌ ﴿٦١﴾
وَلَا يَصُدَّنَّكُمُ الشَّيْطَٰنُ ۖ إِنَّهُۥ لَكُمْ
عَدُوٌّ مُّبِينٌ ﴿٦٢﴾
وَلَمَّا جَآءَ عِيسَىٰ بِالْبَيِّنَٰتِ قَالَ قَدْ
جِئْتُكُم بِالْحِكْمَةِ وَلِأُبَيِّنَ لَكُم

Ikhfa اخفاء | Ghunna غنّہ | Ikhfa Meem Saakin اخفاء میم ساکن | Idghaam ادغام | Qalqala قلقلہ | Qalb قلب | Idghaam Meem Saakin ادغام میم ساکن

some of the (points) on which you dispute: therefore fear Allah and obey me.	ba'ḍal-lazee takhtalifoona feehi fattaqul-laaha wa aṭee'oon.	بَعْضَ الَّذِي تَخْتَلِفُونَ فِيهِ ۖ فَاتَّقُوا اللَّهَ وَأَطِيعُونِ ٦٣
64. "For Allah, He is my Lord and your Lord: so worship you Him: this is a Straight Way."	64. Innal-laaha Huwa Rabbee wa Rabbukum fa'budooh; haazaa Ṣiraaṭum-Mustaqeem.	إِنَّ اللَّهَ هُوَ رَبِّي وَرَبُّكُمْ فَاعْبُدُوهُ ۚ هَٰذَا صِرَاطٌ مُسْتَقِيمٌ ٦٤
65. But sects from among themselves fell into disagreement: then woe to the wrong-doers, from the Chastisement of a Grievous Day!	65. Fakhtalafal-aḥzaabu mim baynihim fawaylul-lillazeena ẓalamoo min 'azaabi Yawmin aleem.	فَاخْتَلَفَ الْأَحْزَابُ مِنْ بَيْنِهِمْ ۖ فَوَيْلٌ لِلَّذِينَ ظَلَمُوا مِنْ عَذَابِ يَوْمٍ أَلِيمٍ ٦٥
66. Do they only wait for the Hour - that it should come on them all of a sudden, while they perceive not?	66. Hal yanẓuroona illas-Saa'ata an taåtiyahum baghtatañw- wa hum laa yash'uroon.	هَلْ يَنْظُرُونَ إِلَّا السَّاعَةَ أَنْ تَأْتِيَهُمْ بَغْتَةً وَهُمْ لَا يَشْعُرُونَ ٦٦
67. Friends on that day will be foes, one to another,- except the Righteous.	67. Al-akhillaaa'u Yawma'izim ba'ḍuhum liba'ḍin 'aduwwun illal-muttaqeen. **(Section 6)**	الْأَخِلَّاءُ يَوْمَئِذٍ بَعْضُهُمْ لِبَعْضٍ عَدُوٌّ إِلَّا الْمُتَّقِينَ ٦٧
68. My devotees! no fear shall be on you that Day, nor shall you grieve,-	68. Yaa 'ibaadi laa khawfun 'alaykumul-Yawma wa laaa antum taḥzanoon.	يَا عِبَادِ لَا خَوْفٌ عَلَيْكُمُ الْيَوْمَ وَلَا أَنْتُمْ تَحْزَنُونَ ٦٨
69. (Being) those who have believed in Our Signs and bowed (their wills to Ours) in Islam.	69. Allazeena aamanoo bi Aayaatinaa wa kaanoo muslimeen.	الَّذِينَ آمَنُوا بِآيَاتِنَا وَكَانُوا مُسْلِمِينَ ٦٩
70. Enter you the Garden, you and your wives, in (beauty and) rejoicing.	70. Udkhulul-Jannata antum wa azwaajukum tuḥbaroon.	ادْخُلُوا الْجَنَّةَ أَنْتُمْ وَأَزْوَاجُكُمْ تُحْبَرُونَ ٧٠
71. To them will be passed round, dishes and goblets of gold: there will be there all that the souls could desire, all that their eyes could delight in: and you shall abide therein (for ever).	71. Yuṭaafu 'alayhim biṣiḥaafim-min zahabiñw-wa akwaab, wa feehaa maatashtaheehil-anfusu wa talazzul-a'yunu wa antum feehaa khaalidoon.	يُطَافُ عَلَيْهِمْ بِصِحَافٍ مِنْ ذَهَبٍ وَأَكْوَابٍ ۖ وَفِيهَا مَا تَشْتَهِيهِ الْأَنْفُسُ وَتَلَذُّ الْأَعْيُنُ ۖ وَأَنْتُمْ فِيهَا خَالِدُونَ ٧١
72. Such will be the Garden of which you are made heirs for your (good) deeds (in life).	72. Wa tilkal-Jannatul-lateee ooristumoohaa bimaa kuntum ta'maloon.	وَتِلْكَ الْجَنَّةُ الَّتِي أُورِثْتُمُوهَا بِمَا كُنْتُمْ تَعْمَلُونَ ٧٢
73. You shall have therein abundance of fruit, from which you shall have satisfaction.	73. Lakum feehaa faakihatun kaseeratum-minhaa taåkuloon.	لَكُمْ فِيهَا فَاكِهَةٌ كَثِيرَةٌ مِنْهَا تَأْكُلُونَ ٧٣
74. The sinners will be in the Punishment of Hell,	74. Innal-mujrimeena fee 'azaabi Jahannama	إِنَّ الْمُجْرِمِينَ فِي عَذَابِ جَهَنَّمَ

Ikhfa اخفاء | Ghunna غنّہ | Ikhfa Meem Saakin اخفاء میم ساکن | Idghaam ادغام | Qalqala قلقلہ | Qalb قلب | Idghaam Meem Saakin ادغام میم ساکن

to dwell therein (for ever):

75. It is not relaxed for them, and they despair therein.

76. Nowise shall We be unjust to them: but it is they who have been unjust themselves.

77. They will cry: "O Malik! would that your Lord put an end to us!" He will say, "No, but you shall abide!"

78. Verily We have brought the Truth to you: but most of you have a hatred for Truth.

79. What! have they settled some plan (among themselves)? But it is We Who settle things.

80. Or do they think that We hear not their secrets and their private counsels? Indeed (We do), and Our messengers are by them, to record.

81. Say: "If (Allah) Most Gracious had a son, I would be the first to worship."

82. Glory to the Lord of the heavens and the earth, the Lord of the Throne (of Authority)! (He is free) from the things they attribute (to him)!

83. So leave them to babble and play (with vanities) until they meet that Day of theirs, which they have been promised.

84. It is He Who is Allah in heaven and Allah on earth; and He is full of Wisdom and Knowledge.

85. And blessed is He to Whom belongs the dominion of the heavens and the earth, and all between them: with Him is the Knowledge of the Hour (of Judgment): and to Him shall you be brought back.

86. And those whom they invoke besides Allah have no power of intercession;- only he who bears witness to the Truth, and they know (him).

khaalidoon.

75. Laa yufattaru 'anhum wa hum feehi mublisoon.

76. Wa maa ẓalamnaahum wa laakin kaanoo humuẓ-ẓaalimeen.

77. Wa naadaw yaa Maaliku liyaqḍi 'alaynaa Rabbuka qaala innakum maakiṡoon.

78. Laqad ji'naakum bilḥaqqi wa laakinna akṡarakum lilḥaqqi kaarihoon.

79. Am abramooo amran fa-innaa mubrimoon.

80. Am yaḥsaboona annaa laa nasma'u sirrahum wa najwaahum; balaa wa Rusulunaa ladayhim yaktuboon.

81. Qul in kaana lir-Raḥmaani walad; fa-ana awwalul-'aabideen.

82. Subḥaana Rabbis-samaawaati wal-arḍi Rabbil-'Arshi 'ammaa yaṣifoon.

83. Faẕarhum yakhooḍoo wa-yal'aboo ḥattaa yulaaqoo Yawmahumul-laẕee yoo'adoon.

84. Wa Huwal-laẕee fissamaaa'i Ilaahuñw-wa fil-arḍi Ilaah; wa Huwal-Ḥakeemul-'Aleem.

85. Wa tabaarakal-laẕee lahoo mulkus-samaawaati wal-arḍi wa maa baynahumaa wa 'indahoo 'ilmus-Saa'ati wa ilayhi turja'oon.

86. Wa laa yamlikul-laẕeena yad'oona min doonihish-shafaa'ata illaa man shahida bilḥaqqi wa hum ya'lamoon.

خٰلِدُوْنَ ۝٧٤
لَا يُفَتَّرُ عَنْهُمْ وَهُمْ فِيْهِ مُبْلِسُوْنَ ۝٧٥
وَمَا ظَلَمْنٰهُمْ وَلٰكِنْ كَانُوْا هُمُ
الظّٰلِمِيْنَ ۝٧٦
وَنَادَوْا يٰمٰلِكُ لِيَقْضِ عَلَيْنَا رَبُّكَ ؕ
قَالَ اِنَّكُمْ مّٰكِثُوْنَ ۝٧٧
لَقَدْ جِئْنٰكُمْ بِالْحَقِّ وَلٰكِنَّ اَكْثَرَكُمْ
لِلْحَقِّ كٰرِهُوْنَ ۝٧٨
اَمْ اَبْرَمُوْٓا اَمْرًا فَاِنَّا مُبْرِمُوْنَ ۝٧٩
اَمْ يَحْسَبُوْنَ اَنَّا لَا نَسْمَعُ سِرَّهُمْ
وَنَجْوٰىهُمْ ؕ بَلٰى وَرُسُلُنَا لَدَيْهِمْ
يَكْتُبُوْنَ ۝٨٠
قُلْ اِنْ كَانَ لِلرَّحْمٰنِ وَلَدٌ ۖ فَاَنَا اَوَّلُ
الْعٰبِدِيْنَ ۝٨١
سُبْحٰنَ رَبِّ السَّمٰوٰتِ وَالْاَرْضِ رَبِّ
الْعَرْشِ عَمَّا يَصِفُوْنَ ۝٨٢
فَذَرْهُمْ يَخُوْضُوْا وَيَلْعَبُوْا حَتّٰى
يُلٰقُوْا يَوْمَهُمُ الَّذِيْ يُوْعَدُوْنَ ۝٨٣
وَهُوَ الَّذِيْ فِي السَّمَآءِ اِلٰهٌ وَّفِي
الْاَرْضِ اِلٰهٌ ؕ وَهُوَ الْحَكِيْمُ الْعَلِيْمُ ۝٨٤
وَتَبٰرَكَ الَّذِيْ لَهٗ مُلْكُ السَّمٰوٰتِ
وَالْاَرْضِ وَمَا بَيْنَهُمَا ۚ وَعِنْدَهٗ
عِلْمُ السَّاعَةِ ۚ وَاِلَيْهِ تُرْجَعُوْنَ ۝٨٥
وَلَا يَمْلِكُ الَّذِيْنَ يَدْعُوْنَ مِنْ
دُوْنِهِ الشَّفَاعَةَ اِلَّا مَنْ شَهِدَ
بِالْحَقِّ وَهُمْ يَعْلَمُوْنَ ۝٨٦

Ikhfa اخفاء · Ghunna غنّہ · Ikhfa Meem Saakin اخفاء میم ساکن · Idghaam ادغام · Qalqala قلقلہ · Qalb قلب · Idghaam Meem Saakin ادغام میم ساکن

87. If you ask them, who created them, they will certainly say, Allah: How then are they deluded away (from the Truth)?

88. (Allah has knowledge) of the (Prophet's) cry, "O my Lord! Truly these are people who will not believe!"

89. But turn away from them, and say "Peace!" But soon shall they know!

87. Wa la'in sa-altahum man khalaqahum la-yaqoolun-nallaahu fa-annaa yu'fakoon.

88. Wa qeelihee yaa Rabbi inna haaa'ulaaa'i qawmul-laa yu'minoon.

89. Faṣfaḥ 'anhum wa qul salaam; fasawfa ya'lamoon.

(Section 7)

وَلَئِنْ سَاَلْتَهُمْ مَّنْ خَلَقَهُمْ لَيَقُوْلُنَّ اللّٰهُ فَاَنّٰى يُؤْفَكُوْنَ ﴿٨٧﴾

وَقِيْلِهٖ يٰرَبِّ اِنَّ هٰٓؤُلَآءِ قَوْمٌ لَّا يُؤْمِنُوْنَ ﴿٨٨﴾

فَاصْفَحْ عَنْهُمْ وَقُلْ سَلٰمٌ ۭ فَسَوْفَ يَعْلَمُوْنَ ﴿٨٩﴾

وقف لازم ع

44. Smoke or Mist

In the name of Allah, Most Gracious, Most Merciful.

Sûrat ad-Dukhân–44

(Revealed at Makkah)

Bismillaahir Raḥmaanir Raḥeem

(٤٤) سُوْرَةُ الدُّخَانِ مَكِّيَّةٌ (٦٤)

بِسْمِ اللّٰهِ الرَّحْمٰنِ الرَّحِيْمِ

1. *Ha-Mim.*

2. By the Book that makes things clear;-

3. We sent it down during a Blessed Night: for We (ever) wish to warn (against Evil).

4. In the (Night) is made distinct every affair of wisdom,

5. By command, from Our Presence. For We (ever) send (revelations),

6. As Mercy from your Lord: for He hears and knows (all things);

7. The Lord of the heavens and the earth and all between them, if you (but) have an assured faith.

8. There is no god but He: It is He Who gives life and gives death,- The Lord and Cherisher to you and your earliest ancestors.

9. Yet they play about in doubt.

10. Then watch thou for the Day that the sky will bring forth a kind of smoke (or mist) plainly visible,

11. Enveloping the people: this will be a Chastisement Grievous.

12. (They will say:) "Our Lord! remove the Chastisement from us, for we do really believe!"

1. Ḥaa-Meeem.

2. Wal-Kitaabil-Mubeen.

3. Innaaa anzalnaahu fee laylatim-mubaarakah; innaa kunnaa munzireen.

4. Feehaa yufraqu kullu amrin ḥakeem.

5. Amram-min 'indinaaa; innaa kunnaa mursileen.

6. Raḥmatam-mir-Rabbik; innahoo Huwas-Samee'ul-'Aleem.

7. Rabbis-samaawaati wal-arḍi wa maa baynahumaa; in kuntum mooqineen.

8. Laaa ilaaha illaa Huwa yuḥyee wa yumeetu Rabbukum wa Rabbu aabaaa'ikumul-awwaleen.

9. Bal hum fee shakkiñy-yal'aboon.

10. Fartaqib Yawma taåtis-samaaa'u bidukhaanim-mubeen.

11. Yaghshan-naasa haazaa 'azaabun aleem.

12. Rabbanak-shif 'annal-'azaaba innaa mu'minoon.

حٰمٓ ۚ ﴿١﴾

وَالْكِتٰبِ الْمُبِيْنِ ۙ ﴿٢﴾

اِنَّآ اَنْزَلْنٰهُ فِيْ لَيْلَةٍ مُّبٰرَكَةٍ اِنَّا كُنَّا مُنْذِرِيْنَ ﴿٣﴾

فِيْهَا يُفْرَقُ كُلُّ اَمْرٍ حَكِيْمٍ ۙ ﴿٤﴾

اَمْرًا مِّنْ عِنْدِنَا ۭ اِنَّا كُنَّا مُرْسِلِيْنَ ۚ ﴿٥﴾

رَحْمَةً مِّنْ رَّبِّكَ ۭ اِنَّهٗ هُوَ السَّمِيْعُ الْعَلِيْمُ ۙ ﴿٦﴾

رَبِّ السَّمٰوٰتِ وَالْاَرْضِ وَمَا بَيْنَهُمَا ۘ اِنْ كُنْتُمْ مُّوْقِنِيْنَ ﴿٧﴾

لَآ اِلٰهَ اِلَّا هُوَ يُحْيٖ وَيُمِيْتُ ۭ رَبُّكُمْ وَرَبُّ اٰبَاۗىِٕكُمُ الْاَوَّلِيْنَ ﴿٨﴾

بَلْ هُمْ فِيْ شَكٍّ يَّلْعَبُوْنَ ﴿٩﴾

فَارْتَقِبْ يَوْمَ تَاْتِي السَّمَاۗءُ بِدُخَانٍ مُّبِيْنٍ ۙ ﴿١٠﴾

يَّغْشَى النَّاسَ ۭ هٰذَا عَذَابٌ اَلِيْمٌ ﴿١١﴾

رَبَّنَا اكْشِفْ عَنَّا الْعَذَابَ اِنَّا مُؤْمِنُوْنَ ﴿١٢﴾

وقف لازم

Ikhfa اخفاء · Ghunna غنّہ · Ikhfa Meem Saakin اخفاء میم ساکن · Idghaam ادغام · Qalqala قلقلہ · Qalb قلب · Idghaam Meem Saakin ادغام میم ساکن

13. How shall the message be (effectual) for them, seeing that an Apostle explaining things clearly has (already) come to them,-

14. Yet they turn away from him and say: "Tutored (by others), a man possessed!"

15. We shall indeed remove the Chastisement for a while, (but) truly you will revert (to your ways).

16. One day We shall seize you with a mighty onslaught: We will indeed (then) exact Retribution!

17. We did, before them, try the people of Pharaoh: there came to them an apostle most honourable,

18. Saying: "Restore to me the Servants of Allah: I am to you an apostle worthy of all trust;

19. "And be not arrogant as against Allah: for I come to you with authority manifest.

20. "For me, I have sought safety with my Lord and your Lord, against your injuring me.

21. And if ye put no faith in me, then let me go.

22. (But they were aggressive:) then he cried to his Lord: "These are indeed a people given to sin."

23. (The reply came:) "March forth with My Servants by night: for you are sure to be pursued.

24. "And leave the sea as a furrow (divided): for they are a host (destined) to be drowned."

25. How many were the gardens and springs they left behind,

26. And corn-fields and noble buildings,

27. And pleasant things wherein they took delight!

28. Thus (was their end)! And We made other people inherit (those things)!

13. Annaa lahumuz-zikraa wa qad jaaa'ahum Rasoolum-mubeen.

14. Summa tawallaw 'anhu wa qaaloo mu'allamum-majnoon.

15. Innaa kaashiful-'azaabi qaleelaa; innakum 'aaa'idoon.

16. Yawma nabtishul-batshatal-kubraa innaa muntaqimoon.

17. Wa laqad fatannaa qablahum qawma Fir'awna wa jaaa'ahum Rasoolun kareem.

18. An addooo ilayya 'ibaadal-laahi innee lakum Rasoolun ameen.

19. Wa al-laa ta'loo 'alal-laahi inneee aateekum bisultaanim-mubeen.

20. Wa innee 'uztu bi-Rabbee wa Rabbikum an tarjumoon.

21. Wa il-lam tu'minoo lee fa'taziloon.

22. Fada'aa Rabbahooo anna haaa'ulaaa'i qawmum-mujrimoon.

23. Fa-asri bi-'ibaadee laylan innakum muttaba'oon.

24. Watrukil-bahra rahwan innahum jundum-mughraqoon.

25. Kam tarakoo min jannaatiñw-wa 'uyoon.

26. Wa zuroo'iñw-wa maqaamin kareem.

27. Wa na'matin kaanoo feehaa faakiheen.

28. Kazaalika wa awrasnaahaa qawman aakhareen.

أنى لهم الذكرى وقد جاءهم رسول مبين ﴿١٣﴾

ثم تولوا عنه وقالوا معلم مجنون ﴿١٤﴾ وقف لازم

إنا كاشفوا العذاب قليلا إنكم عائدون ﴿١٥﴾ وقف لازم

يوم نبطش البطشة الكبرى إنا منتقمون ﴿١٦﴾

ولقد فتنا قبلهم قوم فرعون وجاءهم رسول كريم ﴿١٧﴾

أن أدوا إلي عباد الله إني لكم رسول أمين ﴿١٨﴾

وأن لا تعلوا على الله إني آتيكم بسلطان مبين ﴿١٩﴾

وإني عذت بربي وربكم أن ترجمون ﴿٢٠﴾

وإن لم تؤمنوا لي فاعتزلون ﴿٢١﴾

فدعا ربه أن هؤلاء قوم مجرمون ﴿٢٢﴾ الثلثة

فأسر بعبادي ليلا إنكم متبعون ﴿٢٣﴾

واترك البحر رهوا إنهم جند مغرقون ﴿٢٤﴾

كم تركوا من جنات وعيون ﴿٢٥﴾

وزروع ومقام كريم ﴿٢٦﴾

ونعمة كانوا فيها فاكهين ﴿٢٧﴾

كذلك وأورثناها قوما آخرين ﴿٢٨﴾

Ikhfa اخفاء | Ghunna غنہ | Ikhfa Meem Saakin اخفاء میم ساکن | Idghaam ادغام | Qalqala قلقلہ | Qalb قلب | Idghaam Meem Saakin ادغام میم ساکن

29. And neither heaven nor earth shed a tear over them: nor were they given a respite (again).	29. Famaa bakat 'alayhimus-samaaa'u wal-arḍu wa maa kaanoo munẓareen. **(Section 1)**	فَمَا بَكَتْ عَلَيْهِمُ السَّمَآءُ وَالْاَرْضُ وَمَا كَانُوْا مُنْظَرِيْنَ ۝٢٩ ع ١ ٢٩ ١٤
30. We did deliver aforetime the Children of Israel from humiliating Punishment,	30. Wa laqad najjaynaa Baneee Israaa'eela minal-'azaa-bil-muheen.	وَلَقَدْ نَجَّيْنَا بَنِيْٓ اِسْرَآءِيْلَ مِنَ الْعَذَابِ الْمُهِيْنِ ۝٣٠
31. Inflicted by Pharaoh, for he was arrogant (even) among inordinate transgressors.	31. Min Fir'awn; innahoo kaana 'aaliyam-minal musri-feen.	مِنْ فِرْعَوْنَ ۭ اِنَّهٗ كَانَ عَالِيًا مِّنَ الْمُسْرِفِيْنَ ۝٣١
32. And We chose them aforetime above the nations, knowingly,	32. Wa laqadikh-tarnaahum 'alaa 'ilmin 'alal-'aalameen.	وَلَقَدِ اخْتَرْنٰهُمْ عَلٰى عِلْمٍ عَلَى الْعٰلَمِيْنَ ۝٣٢
33. And granted them Signs in which there was a manifest trial.	33. Wa aataynaahum minal-Aayaati maa feehi balaaa'um-mubeen.	وَاٰتَيْنٰهُمْ مِّنَ الْاٰيٰتِ مَا فِيْهِ بَلٰٓؤٌا مُّبِيْنٌ ۝٣٣
34. As to these (Quraish), they say forsooth:	34. Inna haaa'ulaaa'i la-ya-qooloon.	اِنَّ هٰٓؤُلَآءِ لَيَقُوْلُوْنَ ۝٣٤
35. "There is nothing beyond our first death, and we shall not be raised again.	35. In hiya illaa mawtatunal-oolaa wa maa naḥnu bimun-shareen.	اِنْ هِيَ اِلَّا مَوْتَتُنَا الْاُوْلٰى وَمَا نَحْنُ بِمُنْشَرِيْنَ ۝٣٥
36. "Then bring (back) our forefathers, if what you say is true!"	36. Faåtoo bi-aabaaa'inaaa in kuntum ṣaadiqeen.	فَاْتُوْا بِاٰبَآئِنَآ اِنْ كُنْتُمْ صٰدِقِيْنَ ۝٣٦
37. What! Are they better than the people of Tubba and those who were before them? We destroyed them because they were guilty of sin.	37. Ahum khayrun am qawmu Tubba'iñw-wallazeena min qab-lihim; ahlaknaahum innahum kaanoo mujrimeen.	اَهُمْ خَيْرٌ اَمْ قَوْمُ تُبَّعٍ ۙ وَّالَّذِيْنَ مِنْ قَبْلِهِمْ ۭ اَهْلَكْنٰهُمْ ۡ اِنَّهُمْ كَانُوْا مُجْرِمِيْنَ ۝٣٧
38. We created not the heavens, the earth, and all between them, merely in (idle) sport:	38. Wa maa khalaqnas samaa-waati wal-arḍa wa maa bayna-humaa laa'ibeen.	وَمَا خَلَقْنَا السَّمٰوٰتِ وَالْاَرْضَ وَمَا بَيْنَهُمَا لٰعِبِيْنَ ۝٣٨
39. We created them not except for just ends: but most of them do not understand.	39. Maa khalaqnaahumaaa illaa bilḥaqqi wa laakinna akṣarahum laa ya'lamoon.	مَا خَلَقْنٰهُمَآ اِلَّا بِالْحَقِّ وَلٰكِنَّ اَكْثَرَهُمْ لَا يَعْلَمُوْنَ ۝٣٩
40. Verily the Day of sorting out is the time appointed for all of them,-	40. Inna Yawmal-Faṣli mee-qaatuhum ajma'een.	اِنَّ يَوْمَ الْفَصْلِ مِيْقَاتُهُمْ اَجْمَعِيْنَ ۝٤٠
41. The Day when no protector can avail his client in any thing, and no help can they receive,	41. Yawma laa yughnee mawlan 'am-mawlan shay'añw-wa laa hum yunṣaroon.	يَوْمَ لَا يُغْنِيْ مَوْلًى عَنْ مَّوْلًى شَيْـًٔا وَّلَا هُمْ يُنْصَرُوْنَ ۝٤١
42. Except such as receive Allah's Mercy: for He is Exalted in Might,	42. Illaa mar-raḥimal-laah; innahoo Huwal-'Azeezur-	اِلَّا مَنْ رَّحِمَ اللّٰهُ ۭ اِنَّهٗ هُوَ الْعَزِيْزُ

Ikhfa اخفاء · Ghunna غنّہ · Ikhfa Meem Saakin اخفاء میم ساکن · Idghaam ادغام · Qalqala قلقلہ · Qalb قلب · Idghaam Meem Saakin ادغام میم ساکن

English	Transliteration	Arabic
Most Merciful.	Raḥeem. **(Section 2)**	الرَّحِيْمُ ﴿٤٢﴾
43. Verily the tree of Zaqqum,-	43. Inna shajarataz-Zaqqoom.	اِنَّ شَجَرَتَ الزَّقُّوْمِ ﴿٤٣﴾
44. Will be the food of the Sinful,-	44. Ṭa'aamul-as̱eem.	طَعَامُ الْاَثِيْمِ ﴿٤٤﴾
45. Like molten brass; it will boil in their insides.	45. Kalmuhli yaghlee filbuṭoon.	كَالْمُهْلِ ۚ يَغْلِيْ فِي الْبُطُوْنِ ﴿٤٥﴾
46. Like the boiling of scalding water.	46. Kaghalyil-ḥameem.	كَغَلْيِ الْحَمِيْمِ ﴿٤٦﴾
47. (A voice will cry: "Seize you him and drag him into the midst of the Blazing Fire!	47. Khuẕoohu fa'tiloohu ilaa sawaaa'il-Jaḥeem.	خُذُوْهُ فَاعْتِلُوْهُ اِلٰى سَوَآءِ الْجَحِيْمِ ﴿٤٧﴾
48. "Then pour over his head the Chastisement of Boiling Water,	48. Summa ṣubboo fawqa raâsihee min 'aẕaabil-ḥameem.	ثُمَّ صُبُّوْا فَوْقَ رَاْسِهٖ مِنْ عَذَابِ الْحَمِيْمِ ﴿٤٨﴾
49. "Taste you (this)! Truly were you mighty, full of honour!	49. Ẕuq innaka antal-'azeezul-kareem.	ذُقْ ۚ اِنَّكَ اَنْتَ الْعَزِيْزُ الْكَرِيْمُ ﴿٤٩﴾
50. "Truly this is what you used to doubt!"	50. Inna haaẕaa maa kuntum bihee tamtaroon.	اِنَّ هٰذَا مَا كُنْتُمْ بِهٖ تَمْتَرُوْنَ ﴿٥٠﴾
51. As to the Righteous (they will be) in a position of Security,	51. Innal-muttaqeena fee maqaamin ameen.	اِنَّ الْمُتَّقِيْنَ فِيْ مَقَامٍ اَمِيْنٍ ﴿٥١﴾
52. Among Gardens and Springs;	52. Fee Jannaatiñw-wa 'uyoon.	فِيْ جَنّٰتٍ وَّعُيُوْنٍ ﴿٥٢﴾
53. Dressed in fine silk and in rich brocade, they will face each other;	53. Yalbasoona min sundusiñw-wa istbraqim-mutaqaabileen.	يَّلْبَسُوْنَ مِنْ سُنْدُسٍ وَّاِسْتَبْرَقٍ مُّتَقٰبِلِيْنَ ﴿٥٣﴾
54. So; and We shall join them to Companions with beautiful, big, and lustrous eyes.	54. Kaẕaalika wa zawwajnaahum biḥoorin 'een.	كَذٰلِكَ ۗ وَزَوَّجْنٰهُمْ بِحُوْرٍ عِيْنٍ ﴿٥٤﴾
55. There can they call for every kind of fruit in peace and security;	55. Yad'oona feehaa bikulli faakihatin aamineen.	يَدْعُوْنَ فِيْهَا بِكُلِّ فَاكِهَةٍ اٰمِنِيْنَ ﴿٥٥﴾
56. Nor will they there taste Death, except the first death; and He will preserve them from the Chastisement of the Blazing Fire,	56. Laa yaẕooqoona feehal-mawta illal-mawtatal-oolaa wa waqaahum 'aẕaabal-Jaḥeem.	لَا يَذُوْقُوْنَ فِيْهَا الْمَوْتَ اِلَّا الْمَوْتَةَ الْاُوْلٰى ۚ وَوَقٰىهُمْ عَذَابَ الْجَحِيْمِ ﴿٥٦﴾
57. As a Bounty from your Lord! that will be the supreme achievement!	57. Faḍlam-mir-Rabbik; ẕaalika huwal-fawzul-'aẓeem.	فَضْلًا مِّنْ رَّبِّكَ ۗ ذٰلِكَ هُوَ الْفَوْزُ الْعَظِيْمُ ﴿٥٧﴾
58. Verily, We have made this (Qur'an) easy, in your tongue, in order that they may give heed.	58. Fa-innamaa yassarnaahu bilisaanika la'allahum yataẕakkaroon.	فَاِنَّمَا يَسَّرْنٰهُ بِلِسَانِكَ لَعَلَّهُمْ يَتَذَكَّرُوْنَ ﴿٥٨﴾
59. So wait you and watch; for they (too) are waiting.	59. Fartaqib innahum murtaqiboon. **(Section 3)**	فَارْتَقِبْ اِنَّهُمْ مُّرْتَقِبُوْنَ ﴿٥٩﴾

Ikhfa اخفاء · Ghunna غُنّہ · Ikhfa Meem Saakin اخفاء میم ساکن · Idghaam ادغام · Qalqala قلقلہ · Qalb قلب · Idghaam Meem Saakin ادغام میم ساکن

45. Bowing the Knee

In the name of Allah, Most Gracious, Most Merciful.

1. *Ha-Mim.*

2. The revelation of the Book is from Allah the Exalted in Power, Full of Wisdom.

3. Verily in the heavens and the earth, are Signs for those who believe.

4. And in the creation of yourselves and the fact that animals are scattered (through the earth), are Signs for those of assured Faith.

5. And in the alternation of Night and Day, and the fact that Allah sends down Sustenance from the sky, and revives there with the earth after its death, and in the change of the winds,- are Signs for those that are wise.

6. Such are the Signs of Allah, which We rehearse to you in Truth; then in what exposition will they believe after (rejecting) Allah and His Signs?

7. Woe to each sinful dealer in Falsehoods:

8. He hears the Signs of Allah rehearsed to him, yet is obstinate and lofty, as if he had not heard them: then announce to him a Chastisement Grievous!

9. And when he learns something of Our Signs, he takes them in jest: for such there will be a humiliating Penalty.

10. In front of them is Hell: and of no profit to them is anything they may have earned, nor any protectors they may have taken to themselves besides Allah:

Sûrat al-Jâsiyah–45

(Revealed at Makkah)

Bismillaahir Raḥmaanir Raḥeem

1. Ḥaa-Meeem.

2. Tanzeelul-Kitaabi minal-laahil-'Azeezil-Ḥakeem.

3. Inna fis-samaawaati wal-arḍi la-Aayaatil-lilmu'mineen.

4. Wa fee khalqikum wa maa yabussu min daaabbatin Aayaatul-liqawmiñy-yooqinoon.

5. Wakhtilaafil-layli wanna-haari wa maaa anzalal laahu minas-samaaa'i mir-rizqin fa-aḥyaa bihil-arḍa ba'da mawti-haa wa taṣreefir-riyaaḥi Aayaatul-liqawmiñy-ya'qiloon.

6. Tilka Aayaatul-laahi nat-loohaa 'alayka bilḥaqq, fabi-ayyi ḥadeesim ba'dal-laahi wa Aayaatihee yu'minoon.

7. Waylul-likulli affaakin aseem.

8. Yasma'u Aayaatil-laahi tutlaa 'alayhi summa yuṣirru mustakbiran ka-al-lam yasma'-haa fabashshirhu bi'azaabin aleem.

9. Wa izaa 'alima min Aayaatinaa shay'anit-takhaza-haa huzuwaa; ulaaa'ika lahum 'azaabum muheen.

10. Miñw-waraaa'ihim Ja-hannamu wa laa yughnee 'anhum maa kasaboo shay'añw-wa laa mat-takhazoo min doonil-laahi awliyaaa'a wa

سُوْرَةُ الْجَاثِيَةِ مَكِّيَّةٌ (٤٥) (٦٥)

بِسْمِ اللّٰهِ الرَّحْمٰنِ الرَّحِيْمِ

حٰمٓ ۝١
تَنْزِيْلُ الْكِتٰبِ مِنَ اللّٰهِ الْعَزِيْزِ
الْحَكِيْمِ ۝٢
اِنَّ فِي السَّمٰوٰتِ وَالْاَرْضِ لَاٰيٰتٍ
لِّلْمُؤْمِنِيْنَ ۝٣
وَفِيْ خَلْقِكُمْ وَمَا يَبُثُّ مِنْ
دَآبَّةٍ اٰيٰتٌ لِّقَوْمٍ يُّوْقِنُوْنَ ۝٤
وَاخْتِلَافِ الَّيْلِ وَالنَّهَارِ وَمَا
اَنْزَلَ اللّٰهُ مِنَ السَّمَآءِ مِنْ رِّزْقٍ
فَاَحْيَا بِهِ الْاَرْضَ بَعْدَ مَوْتِهَا
وَتَصْرِيْفِ الرِّيٰحِ اٰيٰتٌ لِّقَوْمٍ
يَّعْقِلُوْنَ ۝٥
تِلْكَ اٰيٰتُ اللّٰهِ نَتْلُوْهَا عَلَيْكَ
بِالْحَقِّ فَبِاَيِّ حَدِيْثٍۭ بَعْدَ اللّٰهِ
وَاٰيٰتِهِ يُؤْمِنُوْنَ ۝٦
وَيْلٌ لِّكُلِّ اَفَّاكٍ اَثِيْمٍ ۝٧
يَّسْمَعُ اٰيٰتِ اللّٰهِ تُتْلٰى عَلَيْهِ ثُمَّ
يُصِرُّ مُسْتَكْبِرًا كَاَنْ لَّمْ يَسْمَعْهَا
فَبَشِّرْهُ بِعَذَابٍ اَلِيْمٍ ۝٨
وَاِذَا عَلِمَ مِنْ اٰيٰتِنَا شَيْـًٔا اتَّخَذَهَا
هُزُوًا اُولٰٓئِكَ لَهُمْ عَذَابٌ مُّهِيْنٌ ۝٩
مِنْ وَّرَآئِهِمْ جَهَنَّمُ وَلَا يُغْنِيْ
عَنْهُمْ مَّا كَسَبُوْا شَيْـًٔا وَّلَا مَا
اتَّخَذُوْا مِنْ دُوْنِ اللّٰهِ اَوْلِيَآءَ وَ

Ikhfa اخفاء | Ghunna غُنّہ | Ikhfa Meem Saakin اخفاءمیم ساکن | Idghaam ادغام | Qalqala قلقلہ | Qalb قلب | Idghaam Meem Saakin ادغام میم ساکن

for them is a tremendous Chastisement.

lahum 'azaabun 'azeem.

لَهُمْ عَذَابٌ عَظِيمٌ ﴿١٠﴾

11. This is (true) Guidance and for those who reject the Signs of their Lord, is a grievous Chastisement of abomination.

11. Haazaa hudañw wal-lazeena kafaroo bi-Aayaati Rabbihim lahum 'azaabum mir-rijzin aleem. **(Section 1)**

هَٰذَا هُدًى ۚ وَالَّذِينَ كَفَرُوا
بِآيَاتِ رَبِّهِمْ لَهُمْ عَذَابٌ مِّن
رِّجْزٍ أَلِيمٌ ﴿١١﴾

12. It is Allah Who has subjected the sea to you, that ships may sail through it by His command, that you may seek of His Bounty, and that you may be grateful.

12. Allaahul-lazee sahkhara lakumul-bahra litajriyal-fulku feehi bi-amrihee wa litabtaghoo min fadlihee wa la'allakum tashkuroon.

اللَّهُ الَّذِي سَخَّرَ لَكُمُ الْبَحْرَ
لِتَجْرِيَ الْفُلْكُ فِيهِ بِأَمْرِهِ وَلِتَبْتَغُوا
مِن فَضْلِهِ وَلَعَلَّكُمْ تَشْكُرُونَ ﴿١٢﴾

13. And He has subjected to you, as from Him, all that is in the heavens and on earth: Behold, in that are Signs indeed for those who reflect.

13. Wa sakhkhara lakum maa fis-samaawaati wa maa fil-ardi jamee'am-minh; inna fee zaalika la-Aayaatil-liqawmiñy-yatafakkaroon.

وَسَخَّرَ لَكُم مَّا فِي السَّمَاوَاتِ وَمَا
فِي الْأَرْضِ جَمِيعًا مِّنْهُ ۚ إِنَّ فِي
ذَٰلِكَ لَآيَاتٍ لِّقَوْمٍ يَتَفَكَّرُونَ ﴿١٣﴾

14. Tell those who believe, to forgive those who do not look forward to the Days of Allah: It is for Him to recompense (for good or ill) each People according to what they have earned.

14. Qul lillazeena aamanoo yaghfiroo lillazeena laa yarjoona ayyaamal-laahi liyajziya qawmam bimaa kaanoo yaksiboon.

قُل لِّلَّذِينَ آمَنُوا يَغْفِرُوا لِلَّذِينَ
لَا يَرْجُونَ أَيَّامَ اللَّهِ لِيَجْزِيَ قَوْمًا
بِمَا كَانُوا يَكْسِبُونَ ﴿١٤﴾

15. If any one does a righteous deed, it ensures to the benefit of his own soul; if he does evil, it works against (his own soul). In the end will you (all) be brought back to your Lord.

15. Man 'amila saalihan falinafsihee wa man asaaa'a fa'alayhaa summa ilaa Rabbikum turja'oon.

مَنْ عَمِلَ صَالِحًا فَلِنَفْسِهِ ۖ وَمَنْ
أَسَاءَ فَعَلَيْهَا ۖ ثُمَّ إِلَىٰ رَبِّكُمْ
تُرْجَعُونَ ﴿١٥﴾

16. We did aforetime grant to the Children of Israel the Book, the Power of Command, and Prophethood; We gave them, for Sustenance, things good and pure; and We favoured them above the nations.

16. Wa laqad aataynaa Baneee Israaa'eelal-Kitaaba walhukma wan-Nubuwwata wa razaqnaahum minat-tayyibaati wa faddalnaahum 'alal-'aalameen.

وَلَقَدْ آتَيْنَا بَنِي إِسْرَائِيلَ
الْكِتَابَ وَالْحُكْمَ وَالنُّبُوَّةَ وَ
رَزَقْنَاهُم مِّنَ الطَّيِّبَاتِ وَفَضَّلْنَاهُمْ
عَلَى الْعَالَمِينَ ﴿١٦﴾

17. And We granted them Clear Signs in affairs (of Religion): it was only after knowledge had been granted to them that they fell into schisms, through insolent envy among themselves. Verily thy Lord will judge between them on the Day of Judgment as to those matters in which they set up differences.

17. Wa aataynaahum bayyinaatim-minal-amri famakhtalafooo illaa mim ba'di maa jaaa'ahumul-'ilmu baghyam baynahum; inna Rabbaka yaqdee baynahum Yawmal-Qiyaamati feemaa kaanoo feehi yakhtalifoon.

وَآتَيْنَاهُم بَيِّنَاتٍ مِّنَ الْأَمْرِ ۖ فَمَا
اخْتَلَفُوا إِلَّا مِن بَعْدِ مَا جَاءَهُمُ
الْعِلْمُ بَغْيًا بَيْنَهُمْ ۚ إِنَّ رَبَّكَ
يَقْضِي بَيْنَهُمْ يَوْمَ الْقِيَامَةِ فِيمَا
كَانُوا فِيهِ يَخْتَلِفُونَ ﴿١٧﴾

18. Then We put you on the (right) Way of Religion:

18. Summa ja'alnaaka 'alaa sharee'atim-minal-amri

ثُمَّ جَعَلْنَاكَ عَلَىٰ شَرِيعَةٍ مِّنَ الْأَمْرِ

so follow you that (Way), and follow not the desires of those who know not.

fattabi'haa wa laa tattabi' ahwaaa'al-lazeena laa ya'lamoon.

فَاتَّبِعْهَا وَلَا تَتَّبِعْ اَهْوَآءَ الَّذِيْنَ
لَا يَعْلَمُوْنَ ﴿١٨﴾

19. They will be of no use to you in the sight of Allah: it is only Wrong-doers (that stand as) protectors, one to another: but Allah is the Protector of the Righteous.

19. Innahum lañy-yughnoo 'anka minal-laahi shay'aa; wa innaẓ-ẓaalimeena ba'ḍuhum awliyaaa'u ba'ḍiñw wallaahu waliyyul-muttaqeen.

اِنَّهُمْ لَنْ يُّغْنُوْا عَنْكَ مِنَ اللّٰهِ
شَيْـًٔا ؕ وَاِنَّ الظّٰلِمِيْنَ بَعْضُهُمْ
اَوْلِيَآءُ بَعْضٍ ۚ وَاللّٰهُ وَلِيُّ
الْمُتَّقِيْنَ ﴿١٩﴾

20. These are clear evidences to men and a Guidance and Mercy to those of assured Faith.

20. Haazaa baṣaaa'iru linnaasi wa hudañw-wa raḥmatul-liqawmiñy-yooqinoon.

هٰذَا بَصَآئِرُ لِلنَّاسِ وَهُدًى
وَّرَحْمَةٌ لِّقَوْمٍ يُّوْقِنُوْنَ ﴿٢٠﴾

21. What! Do those who seek after evil ways think that We shall hold them equal with those who believe and do righteous deeds,- that equal will be their life and their death? Ill is the judgment that they make.

21. Am ḥasibal-lazeenaj tarahus-sayyi-aati an naj'alahum kallazeena aamanoo wa 'amiluṣ-ṣaaliḥaati sawaaa'am maḥyaahum wa mamaatuhum; saaa'a maa yaḥkumoon.

(Section 2)

اَمْ حَسِبَ الَّذِيْنَ اجْتَرَحُوا السَّيِّاٰتِ
اَنْ نَّجْعَلَهُمْ كَالَّذِيْنَ اٰمَنُوْا
وَعَمِلُوا الصّٰلِحٰتِ ۙ سَوَآءً مَّحْيَاهُمْ
وَمَمَاتُهُمْ ؕ سَآءَ مَا يَحْكُمُوْنَ ﴿٢١﴾ ع

ع ١٨

22. Allah created the heavens and the earth for just ends, and in order that each soul may find the recompense of what it has earned, and none of them be wronged.

22. Wa khalaqal-laahus-samaawaati wal-arḍa bilḥaqqi wa litujzaa kullu nafsim bimaa kasabat wa hum laa yuẓlamoon.

وَخَلَقَ اللّٰهُ السَّمٰوٰتِ وَالْاَرْضَ
بِالْحَقِّ وَلِتُجْزٰى كُلُّ نَفْسٍۢ
بِمَا كَسَبَتْ وَهُمْ لَا يُظْلَمُوْنَ ﴿٢٢﴾

23. Do you see such a one as takes as his god his own vain desire? Allah has, knowing (him as such), left him astray, and sealed his hearing and his heart (and understanding), and put a cover on his sight. Who, then, will guide him after Allah (has withdrawn Guidance)? Will you not then receive admonition?

23. Afara'ayta manit-takhaza ilaahahoo hawaahu wa aḍallahul-laahu 'alaa 'ilmiñw-wa khatama 'alaa sam'ihee wa qalbihee wa ja'ala 'alaa baṣarihee ghishaawatan famañy-yahdeehi mim ba'dil-laah; afalaa tazakkaroon.

اَفَرَءَيْتَ مَنِ اتَّخَذَ اِلٰهَهٗ هَوٰىهُ
وَاَضَلَّهُ اللّٰهُ عَلٰى عِلْمٍ وَّخَتَمَ
عَلٰى سَمْعِهٖ وَقَلْبِهٖ وَجَعَلَ عَلٰى
بَصَرِهٖ غِشٰوَةً ؕ فَمَنْ يَّهْدِيْهِ
مِنْۢ بَعْدِ اللّٰهِ ؕ اَفَلَا تَذَكَّرُوْنَ ﴿٢٣﴾

24. And they say: "What is there but our life in this world? We shall die and we live, and nothing but time can destroy us." But of that they have no knowledge: they merely conjecture:

24. Wa qaaloo maa hiya illaa ḥayaatunad-dunyaa namootu wa naḥyaa wa maa yuhlikunaaa illad-dahr; wa maa lahum bizaalika min 'ilmin in hum illaa yaẓunnoon.

وَقَالُوْا مَا هِىَ اِلَّا حَيَاتُنَا الدُّنْيَا
نَمُوْتُ وَنَحْيَا وَمَا يُهْلِكُنَآ اِلَّا
الدَّهْرُ ۚ وَمَا لَهُمْ بِذٰلِكَ مِنْ
عِلْمٍ ۚ اِنْ هُمْ اِلَّا يَظُنُّوْنَ ﴿٢٤﴾

25. And when Our Clear Signs are rehearsed to them their argument is nothing but this:

25. Wa izaa tutlaa 'alayhim Aayaatunaa bayyinaatim-maa kaana ḥujjatahum illaaa an

وَاِذَا تُتْلٰى عَلَيْهِمْ اٰيٰتُنَا بَيِّنٰتٍ
مَّا كَانَ حُجَّتَهُمْ اِلَّآ اَنْ

Ikhfa اخفاء	Ghunna غُنّہ	Ikhfa Meem Saakin اخفاء میم ساکن	Idghaam ادغام	Qalqala قلقلہ	Qalb قلب	Idghaam Meem Saakin ادغام میم ساکن

they say, "Bring (back) our forefathers, if what you say is true!"

qaalu'-too bi-aabaaa'inaaa in kuntum ṣaadiqeen.

قَالُوا ائْتُوا بِآبَائِنَا إِن كُنتُمْ
صَادِقِينَ ٢٥

26. Say: "It is Allah Who gives you life, then gives you death; then He will gather you together for the Day of Judgment about which there is no doubt": But most men do not understand.

26. Qulil-laahu yuḥyeekum summa yumeetukum summa yajma'ukum ilaa Yawmil-Qiyaamati laa rayba feehi wa laakinna aksaran-naasi laa ya'lamoon. **(Section 3)**

قُلِ اللَّهُ يُحْيِيكُمْ ثُمَّ يُمِيتُكُمْ
ثُمَّ يَجْمَعُكُمْ إِلَىٰ يَوْمِ الْقِيَامَةِ
لَا رَيْبَ فِيهِ وَلَٰكِنَّ أَكْثَرَ
النَّاسِ لَا يَعْلَمُونَ ٢٦ ع ٣

27. To Allah belongs the dominion of the heavens and the earth, and the Day that the Hour of Judgment is established,- that Day will the dealers in False-hood perish!

27. Wa lillaahi mulkus samaa-waati wal-arḍ; wa Yawma taqoomus-Saa'atu Yawma'iziñy-yakhsarul-mubṭiloon.

وَلِلَّهِ مُلْكُ السَّمَاوَاتِ وَالْأَرْضِ ۚ
وَيَوْمَ تَقُومُ السَّاعَةُ يَوْمَئِذٍ
يَخْسَرُ الْمُبْطِلُونَ ٢٧

28. And you will see every nation bowing the knee: Every nation will be called to its Record: "This Day shall you be recompensed for all that you did!

28. Wa taraa kulla ummatin jaasiyah; kullu ummatin tud'aaa ilaa kitaabihaa al-Yawma tuj-zawna maa kuntum ta'maloon.

وَتَرَىٰ كُلَّ أُمَّةٍ جَاثِيَةً ۚ كُلُّ
أُمَّةٍ تُدْعَىٰ إِلَىٰ كِتَابِهَا الْيَوْمَ
تُجْزَوْنَ مَا كُنتُمْ تَعْمَلُونَ ٢٨

29. "This Our Record speaks about you with truth: For We were wont to put on Record all that you did."

29. Haazaa kitaabunaa yanṭi-qu 'alaykum bilḥaqq; innaa kunnaa nastansikhu maa kuntum ta'maloon.

هَٰذَا كِتَابُنَا يَنطِقُ عَلَيْكُم
بِالْحَقِّ ۚ إِنَّا كُنَّا نَسْتَنسِخُ
مَا كُنتُمْ تَعْمَلُونَ ٢٩

30. Then, as to those who believed and did righteous deeds, their Lord will admit them to His Mercy that will be the achievement for all to see.

30. Fa-ammal-lazeena aama-noo wa 'amiluṣ-ṣaaliḥaati fa-yudkhiluhum Rabbuhum fee raḥmatih; zaalika huwal-fawzul-mubeen.

فَأَمَّا الَّذِينَ آمَنُوا وَعَمِلُوا
الصَّالِحَاتِ فَيُدْخِلُهُمْ رَبُّهُمْ فِي
رَحْمَتِهِ ۚ ذَٰلِكَ هُوَ الْفَوْزُ الْمُبِينُ ٣٠

31. But as to those who rejected Allah, (to them will be said): "Were not Our Signs rehearsed to you? But you were arrogant, and were a people given to sin!

31. Wa ammal-lazeena kafa-rooo afalam takun Aayaatee tutlaa 'alaykum fastakbartum wa kuntum qawmam-mujri-meen.

وَأَمَّا الَّذِينَ كَفَرُوا أَفَلَمْ تَكُنْ
آيَاتِي تُتْلَىٰ عَلَيْكُمْ فَاسْتَكْبَرْتُمْ
وَكُنتُمْ قَوْمًا مُّجْرِمِينَ ٣١

32. "And when it was said that the promise of Allah was true, and that the Hour- there was no doubt about its (coming), you used to say, 'We know not what is the Hour: we only think it is an idea, and we have no firm assurance.' "

32. Wa izaa qeela inna wa'dal-laahi ḥaqquñw-was-Saa'atu laa rayba feehaa qultum maa nadree mas-Saa'atu in naẓunnu illaa ẓannañw-wa maa naḥnu bimustayqineen.

وَإِذَا قِيلَ إِنَّ وَعْدَ اللَّهِ حَقٌّ
وَالسَّاعَةُ لَا رَيْبَ فِيهَا قُلْتُم مَّا
نَدْرِي مَا السَّاعَةُ إِن نَّظُنُّ إِلَّا
ظَنًّا وَمَا نَحْنُ بِمُسْتَيْقِنِينَ ٣٢

33. Then will appear to them the evil (fruits) of what they did, and they will be completely encircled

33. Wa badaa lahum sayyi-aatu maa 'amiloo wa ḥaaqa

وَبَدَا لَهُمْ سَيِّئَاتُ مَا عَمِلُوا وَحَاقَ

Ikhfa اخفاء | Ghunna غنّہ | Ikhfa Meem Saakin اخفاء میم ساکن | Idghaam ادغام | Qalqala قلقلہ | Qalb قلب | Idghaam Meem Saakin ادغام میم ساکن

by that which they used to mock at!

34. It will also be said: "This Day We will forget you as you forgot the meeting of this Day of yours! and your abode is the Fire, and no helpers have you!

35. "This, because you used to take the Signs of Allah in jest, and the life of the world deceived you:" (From) that Day, therefore, they shall not be taken out thence, nor shall they be received into Grace.

36. Then Praise be to Allah, Lord of the heavens and Lord of the earth,- Lord and Cherisher of all the Worlds!

37. To Him be glory throughout the heavens and the earth: and He is Exalted in Power, Full of Wisdom!

46. Winding Sand-tracts

In the name of Allah, Most Gracious, Most Merciful.

1. *Ha-Mim.*

2. The Revelation of the Book is from Allah the Exalted in Power, Full of Wisdom.

3. We created not the heavens and the earth and all between them but for just ends, and for a Term Appointed. But those who reject Faith turn away from that whereof they are warned.

4. Say: "Do you see what it is you invoke besides Allah? Show me what it is they have created on earth, or have they a share in the heavens, bring me a book (revealed) before this, or any remnant of knowledge (you may have), if you are telling the truth!

bihim maa kaanoo bihee yastahzi'oon.

34. Wa qeelal-Yawma nansaakum kamaa naseetum liqaaa'a Yawmikum haazaa wa maåwaakumun-Naaru wa maa lakum min naaṣireen.

35. Zaalikum bi-annakumuttakhaztum Aayaatil-laahi huzuwañw-wa gharratkumulḥayaatud-dunyaa; fal-Yawma laa yukhrajoona minhaa wa laa hum yusta'taboon.

36. Falillaahil-ḥamdu Rabbis-samaawaati wa Rabbil-arḍi Rabbil-'aalameen.

37. Wa lahul-kibriyaaa'u fis-samaawaati wal-arḍi wa Huwal-'Azeezul-Ḥakeem.

(Section 4)

Sûrat al-Aḥqâf–46

(Revealed at Makkah)

Bismillaahir Raḥmaanir Raḥeem

1. Ḥaa-Meeem.

2. Tanzeelul-Kitaabi minallaahil-'Azeezil-Ḥakeem.

3. Maa khalaqnas-samaawaati wal-arḍa wa maa baynahumaaa illaa bilḥaqqi wa ajalim-musammaa; wallazeena kafaroo 'ammaaa unziroo mu'riḍoon.

4. Qul ara'aytum maa tad'oona min doonil-laahi aroonee maazaa khalaqoo minal-arḍi am lahum shirkun fis-samaawaati eetoonee bi-Kitaabim-min qabli haazaaa aw asaaratim min 'ilmin in kuntum ṣaadiqeen.

بِهِمْ مَّا كَانُوْا بِهٖ يَسْتَهْزِءُوْنَ ۝٣٣
وَقِيْلَ الْيَوْمَ نَنْسٰىكُمْ كَمَا نَسِيْتُمْ
لِقَآءَ يَوْمِكُمْ هٰذَا وَمَاْوٰىكُمُ النَّارُ
وَمَا لَكُمْ مِّنْ نّٰصِرِيْنَ ۝٣٤
ذٰلِكُمْ بِاَنَّكُمُ اتَّخَذْتُمْ اٰيٰتِ اللّٰهِ
هُزُوًا وَّغَرَّتْكُمُ الْحَيٰوةُ الدُّنْيَا ۚ
فَالْيَوْمَ لَا يُخْرَجُوْنَ مِنْهَا وَلَا
هُمْ يُسْتَعْتَبُوْنَ ۝٣٥
فَلِلّٰهِ الْحَمْدُ رَبِّ السَّمٰوٰتِ وَرَبِّ
الْاَرْضِ رَبِّ الْعٰلَمِيْنَ ۝٣٦
وَلَهُ الْكِبْرِيَآءُ فِي السَّمٰوٰتِ
وَالْاَرْضِ ۖ وَهُوَ الْعَزِيْزُ الْحَكِيْمُ ۝٣٧ ع

(٤٦) سُوْرَةُ الْاَحْقَافِ مَكِّيَّةٌ (٦٦)

بِسْمِ اللّٰهِ الرَّحْمٰنِ الرَّحِيْمِ

حٰمٓ ۝١
تَنْزِيْلُ الْكِتٰبِ مِنَ اللّٰهِ الْعَزِيْزِ
الْحَكِيْمِ ۝٢
مَا خَلَقْنَا السَّمٰوٰتِ وَالْاَرْضَ وَمَا
بَيْنَهُمَآ اِلَّا بِالْحَقِّ وَاَجَلٍ مُّسَمًّى ۗ
وَالَّذِيْنَ كَفَرُوْا عَمَّآ اُنْذِرُوْا
مُعْرِضُوْنَ ۝٣
قُلْ اَرَءَيْتُمْ مَّا تَدْعُوْنَ مِنْ دُوْنِ
اللّٰهِ اَرُوْنِيْ مَاذَا خَلَقُوْا مِنَ
الْاَرْضِ اَمْ لَهُمْ شِرْكٌ فِي السَّمٰوٰتِ ۖ
اِيْتُوْنِيْ بِكِتٰبٍ مِّنْ قَبْلِ هٰذَآ اَوْ
اَثٰرَةٍ مِّنْ عِلْمٍ اِنْ كُنْتُمْ صٰدِقِيْنَ ۝٤

Ikhfa اخفاء | Ghunna غنّہ | Ikhfa Meem Saakin اخفاء میم ساکن | Idghaam ادغام | Qalqala قلقلہ | Qalb قلب | Idghaam Meem Saakin ادغام میم ساکن

5. And who is more astray than one who invokes besides Allah, such as will not answer him to the Day of Judgment, and who (in fact) are unconscious of their call (to them)?

5. Wa man aḍallu mimmañy-yad'oo min doonil-laahi mallaa yastajeebu lahooo ilaa Yawmil-Qiyaamati wa hum 'an du'aaa'i-him ghaafiloon.

وَمَنْ اَضَلُّ مِمَّنْ يَّدْعُوْا مِنْ
دُوْنِ اللّٰهِ مَنْ لَّا يَسْتَجِيْبُ
لَهٗٓ اِلٰى يَوْمِ الْقِيٰمَةِ وَهُمْ عَنْ
دُعَآئِهِمْ غٰفِلُوْنَ ﴿٥﴾

6. And when mankind are gathered together (at the Resurrection), they will be hostile to them and reject their worship (altogether)!

6. Wa izaa ḥushiran-naasu kaanoo lahum a'daaa'añw-wa kaanoo bi'ibaadatihim kaafireen.

وَاِذَا حُشِرَ النَّاسُ كَانُوْا لَهُمْ اَعْدَآءً
وَّكَانُوْا بِعِبَادَتِهِمْ كٰفِرِيْنَ ﴿٦﴾

7. When Our Clear Signs are rehearsed to them, the Unbelievers say, of the Truth when it comes to them: "This is evident sorcery!"

7. Wa izaa tutlaa 'alayhim Aayaatunaa bayyinaatin qaalal-lazeena kafaroo lilḥaqqi lammaa jaaa'ahum haazaa siḥrum-mubeen.

وَاِذَا تُتْلٰى عَلَيْهِمْ اٰيٰتُنَا بَيِّنٰتٍ
قَالَ الَّذِيْنَ كَفَرُوْا لِلْحَقِّ لَمَّا
جَآءَهُمْ هٰذَا سِحْرٌ مُّبِيْنٌ ﴿٧﴾

8. Or do they say, "He has forged it"? Say: "Had I forged it, then you will not at all be able to save me from the wrath of Allah. He knows best of that whereof you talk (so glibly)! Enough is He for a witness between me and you! And He is Oft-Forgiving, Most Merciful."

8. Am yaqooloonaf-taraahu qul inif-taraytuhoo falaa tamlikoona lee minal-laahi shay'an Huwa a'lamu bimaa tufeeḍoona feehi kafaa bihee shaheedam baynee wa baynakum wa Huwal-Ghafoorur-Raḥeem.

اَمْ يَقُوْلُوْنَ افْتَرٰىهُ قُلْ اِنِ افْتَرَيْتُهٗ
فَلَا تَمْلِكُوْنَ لِيْ مِنَ اللّٰهِ شَيْئًا
هُوَ اَعْلَمُ بِمَا تُفِيْضُوْنَ فِيْهِ كَفٰى
بِهٖ شَهِيْدًا بَيْنِيْ وَبَيْنَكُمْ وَهُوَ
الْغَفُوْرُ الرَّحِيْمُ ﴿٨﴾

9. Say: "I am no bringer of new-fangled doctrine among the apostles, nor do I know what will be done with me or with you. I follow but that which is revealed to me by inspiration; I am but a Warner open and clear."

9. Qul maa kuntu bid'am-minar-Rusuli wa maaa adree maa yuf'alu bee wa laa bikum in attabi'u illaa maa yooḥaaa ilayya wa maaa ana illaa nazeerum-mubeen.

قُلْ مَا كُنْتُ بِدْعًا مِّنَ الرُّسُلِ
وَمَآ اَدْرِيْ مَا يُفْعَلُ بِيْ وَلَا
بِكُمْ اِنْ اَتَّبِعُ اِلَّا مَا يُوْحٰٓى
اِلَيَّ وَمَآ اَنَا اِلَّا نَذِيْرٌ مُّبِيْنٌ ﴿٩﴾

10. Say: "See you? If (this teaching) be from Allah, and you reject it, and a witness from among the Children of Israel testifies to its similarity (with earlier scripture), and has believed while you are arrogant, (how unjust you are!) truly, Allah guides not a people unjust."

10. Qul ara'aytum in kaana min 'indil-laahi wa kafartum bihee wa shahida shaahidum-mim-Baneee Israaa'eela 'alaa mislihee fa-aamana wastakbartum innal-laaha laa yahdil-qawmaẓ-ẓaalimeen. **(Section 1)**

قُلْ اَرَءَيْتُمْ اِنْ كَانَ مِنْ عِنْدِ
اللّٰهِ وَكَفَرْتُمْ بِهٖ وَشَهِدَ شَاهِدٌ
مِّنْ بَنِيْٓ اِسْرَآءِيْلَ عَلٰى مِثْلِهٖ
فَاٰمَنَ وَاسْتَكْبَرْتُمْ اِنَّ اللّٰهَ لَا
يَهْدِي الْقَوْمَ الظّٰلِمِيْنَ ﴿١٠﴾ ع

11. The Unbelievers say of those who believe: "If (this Message) were a good thing, (such men) would not have gone to it first, before us!" And seeing that they guide not themselves thereby, they will say,

11. Wa qaalal-lazeena kafaroo lillazeena aamanoo law kaana khayram-maa sabaqoonaaa ilayh; wa iz lam yahtadoo bihee fasa-yaqooloona

وَقَالَ الَّذِيْنَ كَفَرُوْا لِلَّذِيْنَ اٰمَنُوْا
لَوْ كَانَ خَيْرًا مَّا سَبَقُوْنَآ اِلَيْهِ
وَاِذْ لَمْ يَهْتَدُوْا بِهٖ فَسَيَقُوْلُوْنَ

Ikhfa اخفاء | Ghunna غنّہ | Ikhfa Meem Saakin اخفاء میم ساکن | Idghaam ادغام | Qalqala قلقلہ | Qalb قلب | Idghaam Meem Saakin ادغام میم ساکن

"this is an (old,) falsehood!"

haaẕaaa ifkun qadeem.

هٰذَآ اِفْكٌ قَدِيْمٌ ﴿١١﴾

12. And before this, was the Book of Moses as a guide and a mercy: And this Book confirms (it) in the Arabic tongue; to admonish the unjust, and as glad tidings to those who do right.

12. Wa min qablihee Kitaabu Moosaaa imaamañw-wa raḥmah; wa haaẕaa Kitaabum-muṣad-diqul-lisaanan 'Arabiyyal-liyunẕiral-laẕeena ẓalamoo wa bushraa lilmuḥsineen.

وَمِنْ قَبْلِهٖ كِتٰبُ مُوْسٰٓى اِمَامًا
وَّرَحْمَةً ۭ وَهٰذَا كِتٰبٌ مُّصَدِّقٌ
لِّسَانًا عَرَبِيًّا لِّيُنْذِرَ الَّذِيْنَ ظَلَمُوْا ڰ
وَبُشْرٰى لِلْمُحْسِنِيْنَ ﴿١٢﴾

13. Verily those who say, "Our Lord is Allah," and remain firm (on that Path),- on them shall be no fear, nor shall they grieve.

13. Innal-laẕeena qaaloo Rab-bunal-laahu summas-taqaamoo falaa khawfun 'alayhim wa laa hum yaḥzanoon.

اِنَّ الَّذِيْنَ قَالُوْا رَبُّنَا اللّٰهُ ثُمَّ
اسْتَقَامُوْا فَلَا خَوْفٌ عَلَيْهِمْ وَلَا
هُمْ يَحْزَنُوْنَ ﴿١٣﴾

14. Such shall be Companions of the Gardens, dwelling therein (for ever): a recompense for their (good) deeds.

14. Ulaaa'ika Aṣḥabul-Jannati khaalideena feehaa jazaaa'am bimaa kaanoo ya'maloon.

اُولٰۗىِٕكَ اَصْحٰبُ الْجَنَّةِ خٰلِدِيْنَ فِيْهَا ۚ
جَزَاۗءًۢ بِمَا كَانُوْا يَعْمَلُوْنَ ﴿١٤﴾

15. We have enjoined on man kindness to his parents: In pain did his mother bear him, and in pain did she give him birth. The carrying of the (child) to his weaning is (a period of) thirty months. At length, when he reaches the age of full strength and attains forty years, he says, "O my Lord! Grant me that I may be grateful for Your favour which You has bestowed upon me, and upon both my parents, and that I may work righteousness such as You may approve; and be gracious to me in my issue. Truly have I turned to You and truly do I bow (to You) in Islam."

15. Wa waṣṣaynal-insaana bi-waalidayhi iḥsaanan ḥamalat-hu ummuhoo kurhañw-wa waḍa-'at-hu kurhañw wa ḥamluhoo wa fiṣaaluhoo s̱alaas̱oona shahraa; ḥattaaa iẕaa balagha ashuddahoo wa balagha arba-'eena sanatan qaala Rabbi awzi'neee an ashkura ni'mata-kal-lateee an'amta 'alayya wa 'alaa waalidayya wa an a'mala ṣaaliḥan tarḍaahu wa aṣliḥ lee fee ẕurriyyatee innee tubtu ilayka wa innee minal-mus-limeen.

وَوَصَّيْنَا الْاِنْسَانَ بِوَالِدَيْهِ
اِحْسٰنًا ۭ حَمَلَتْهُ اُمُّهٗ كُرْهًا وَّ
وَضَعَتْهُ كُرْهًا ۭ وَحَمْلُهٗ وَفِصٰلُهٗ
ثَلٰثُوْنَ شَهْرًا ۭ حَتّٰٓى اِذَا بَلَغَ اَشُدَّهٗ
وَبَلَغَ اَرْبَعِيْنَ سَنَةً ۙ قَالَ رَبِّ
اَوْزِعْنِيْٓ اَنْ اَشْكُرَ نِعْمَتَكَ الَّتِيْٓ
اَنْعَمْتَ عَلَيَّ وَعَلٰي وَالِدَيَّ وَاَنْ
اَعْمَلَ صَالِحًا تَرْضٰىهُ وَاَصْلِحْ
لِيْ فِيْ ذُرِّيَّتِيْ ڼ اِنِّىْ تُبْتُ
اِلَيْكَ وَاِنِّىْ مِنَ الْمُسْلِمِيْنَ ﴿١٥﴾

16. Such are they from whom We shall accept the best of their deeds and pass by their ill deeds: (They shall be) among the Companions of the Garden: a promise! of truth, which was made to them (in this life).

16. Ulaaa'ikal-laẕeena nata-qabbalu 'anhum aḥsana maa 'amiloo wa natajaawazu 'an sayyi-aatihim feee Aṣḥaabil-Jannati wa'daṣ-ṣidqil-laẕee kaanoo yoo'adoon.

اُولٰۗىِٕكَ الَّذِيْنَ نَتَقَبَّلُ عَنْهُمْ اَحْسَنَ
مَا عَمِلُوْا وَنَتَجَاوَزُ عَنْ سَيِّاٰتِهِمْ فِيْٓ
اَصْحٰبِ الْجَنَّةِ ۭ وَعْدَ الصِّدْقِ الَّذِيْ
كَانُوْا يُوْعَدُوْنَ ﴿١٦﴾

17. But (there is one) who says to his parents, "Fie on you! Do you hold out the promise to me that I shall be raised up,

17. Wallaẕee qaala liwaali-dayhi uffil-lakumaaa ata'i-daanineee an ukhraja wa qad khalatil-

وَالَّذِيْ قَالَ لِوَالِدَيْهِ اُفٍّ لَّكُمَآ
اَتَعِدٰنِنِيْٓ اَنْ اُخْرَجَ وَقَدْ خَلَتِ

Ikhfa اخفاء | Ghunna غنّہ | Ikhfa Meem Saakin اخفاء میم ساکن | Idghaam ادغام | Qalqala قلقلہ | Qalb قلب | Idghaam Meem Saakin ادغام میم ساکن

even though generations have passed before me (without rising again)?" And they two seek Allah's aid, (and rebuke the son): "Woe to thee! Have faith! for the promise of Allah is true." But he says, "This is nothing but tales of the ancients!"

quroonu min qablee wa humaa yastagheesaanil-laaha waylaka aamin inna wa'dal-laahi ḥaqq, fa-yaqoolu maa haazaaa illaaa asaaṭeerul-awwaleen.

الْقُرُونُ مِن قَبْلِي وَهُمَا يَسْتَغِيثَانِ
اللَّهَ وَيْلَكَ آمِنْ إِنَّ وَعْدَ اللَّهِ
حَقٌّ فَيَقُولُ مَا هَٰذَا إِلَّا أَسَاطِيرُ
الْأَوَّلِينَ ١٧

18. Such are they against whom is proved the sentence among the previous generations of Jinns and men, that have passed away; for they will be (utterly) lost.

18. Ulaaa'ikal-lazeena ḥaqqa 'alayhimul-qawlu feee umamin qad khalat min qablihim minal-jinni wal-insi innahum kaanoo khaasireen.

أُولَٰئِكَ الَّذِينَ حَقَّ عَلَيْهِمُ الْقَوْلُ
فِي أُمَمٍ قَدْ خَلَتْ مِن قَبْلِهِم مِّنَ
الْجِنِّ وَالْإِنسِ إِنَّهُمْ كَانُوا خَاسِرِينَ ١٨

19. And to all are (assigned) degrees according to the deeds which they (have done), and in order that (Allah) may recompense their deeds, and no injustice be done to them.

19. Wa likullin darajaatum mimmaa 'amiloo wa liyuwaffiyahum a'maalahum wa hum laa yuẓlamoon.

وَلِكُلٍّ دَرَجَاتٌ مِّمَّا عَمِلُوا وَلِيُوَفِّيَهُمْ
أَعْمَالَهُمْ وَهُمْ لَا يُظْلَمُونَ ١٩

20. And on the Day that the Unbelievers will be placed before the Fire, (It will be said to them): "You received your good things in the life of the world, and you took your pleasure out of them: but today shall you be recompensed with a Chastisement of humiliation: for that you were arrogant on earth without just cause, and that you (ever) transgressed."

20. Wa Yawma yu'raḍul-lazeena kafaroo 'alan-Naari azhabtum ṭayyibaatikum fee ḥayaatikumud-dunyaa wastamta'tum bihaa fal-Yawma tujzawna 'azaabal-hooni bimaa kuntum tastakbiroona fil-arḍi bighayril-ḥaqqi wa bimaa kuntum tafsuqoon. **(Section 2)**

وَيَوْمَ يُعْرَضُ الَّذِينَ كَفَرُوا عَلَى
النَّارِ أَذْهَبْتُمْ طَيِّبَاتِكُمْ فِي
حَيَاتِكُمُ الدُّنْيَا وَاسْتَمْتَعْتُم بِهَا
فَالْيَوْمَ تُجْزَوْنَ عَذَابَ الْهُونِ
بِمَا كُنتُمْ تَسْتَكْبِرُونَ فِي الْأَرْضِ
بِغَيْرِ الْحَقِّ وَبِمَا كُنتُمْ تَفْسُقُونَ ٢٠ ع ٢

21. Mention (Hud) one of 'Ad's (own) brethren: behold, he warned his people about the winding Sand-tracts: but there have been warners before him and after him: "Worship you none other than Allah: Truly I fear for you the Chastisement of a Mighty Day."

21. Wazkur akhaa 'Aad, iz anzara qawmahoo bil-Aḥqaafi wa qad khalatin-nuzuru mim bayni yadayhi wa min khalfiheee allaa ta'budooo illal-laaha inneee akhaafu 'alaykum 'azaaba Yawmin 'aẓeem.

وَاذْكُرْ أَخَا عَادٍ إِذْ أَنذَرَ قَوْمَهُ
بِالْأَحْقَافِ وَقَدْ خَلَتِ النُّذُرُ
مِن بَيْنِ يَدَيْهِ وَمِنْ خَلْفِهِ أَلَّا
تَعْبُدُوا إِلَّا اللَّهَ إِنِّي أَخَافُ عَلَيْكُمْ
عَذَابَ يَوْمٍ عَظِيمٍ ٢١

22. They said: "Have you come in order to turn us aside from our gods? Then bring upon us the (calamity) with which you dost threaten us, if you are telling the truth?"

22. Qaalooo aji'tanaa lita'fikanaa 'an aalihatinaa fa'tinaa bimaa ta'idunaaa in kunta minaṣ-ṣaadiqeen.

قَالُوا أَجِئْتَنَا لِتَأْفِكَنَا عَنْ آلِهَتِنَا
فَأْتِنَا بِمَا تَعِدُنَا إِن كُنتَ مِنَ
الصَّادِقِينَ ٢٢

23. He said: "The Knowledge (of when it will come) is only with Allah: I proclaim to you the mission on which I have been sent: But I see that you are a people in ignorance!"..

23. Qaala innamal-'ilmu 'indal-laahi wa uballighukum maaa ursiltu bihee wa laakinneee araakum qawman tajhaloon.

قَالَ إِنَّمَا الْعِلْمُ عِندَ اللَّهِ
وَأُبَلِّغُكُم مَّا أُرْسِلْتُ بِهِ وَلَٰكِنِّي
أَرَاكُمْ قَوْمًا تَجْهَلُونَ ٢٣

Ikhfa اخفاء | Ghunna غُنّہ | Ikhfa Meem Saakin اخفاء میم ساکن | Idghaam ادغام | Qalqala قلقلہ | Qalb قلب | Idghaam Meem Saakin ادغام میم ساکن

24. Then, when they saw a cloud advancing towards their valleys, they said, "This cloud will give us rain!" "No, it is the (Calamity) you were asking to be hastened, a wind wherein is a grievous Chastisement

25. "Everything will it destroy by the command of its Lord!" Then by the morning nothing was to be seen but (the ruins of) their houses! Thus do We recompense those given to sin!

26. And We had firmly established them in a (prosperity and) power which We have not given to you (you Quraish!) and We had endowed them with (faculties of) hearing, seeing, heart and intellect: but of no profit to them were their (faculties of) hearing, sight, and heart and intellect, when they went on rejecting the Signs of Allah; and they were (completely) encircled by that which they used to mock at!

27. We destroyed aforetime populations round about you; and We have shown the Signs in various ways, that they may turn (to Us).

28. Why then was no help forthcoming to them from those whom they worshipped as gods, besides Allah, as a means of access (to Allah)? No, they left them in the lurch: but that was their falsehood and their invention.

29. Behold, We turned towards you a company of Jinns (quietly) listening to the Qur'an: when they stood in the presence thereof, they said, "Listen in silence!" When the (reading) was finished, they returned to their people, to warn (them of their sins).

30. They said, "O our people! We have heard a Book revealed after Moses, confirming

24. Falammaa ra-awhu 'aariḍam-mustaqbila awdiyatihim qaaloo haazaa 'aariḍum-mumṭirunaa; bal huwa masta'jaltum bihee reeḥun feehaa 'azaabun aleem.

25. Tudammiru kulla shay'im bi-amri Rabbihaa fa-aṣbaḥoo laa yuraaa illaa masaakinuhum; kazaalika najzil-qawmal-mujrimeen.

26. Wa laqad makkannaahum feemaaa im-makkannaakum feehi wa ja'alnaa lahum sam'añw-wa abṣaarañw-wa af'idatan famaaa aghnaa 'anhum sam'uhum wa laaa abṣaaruhum wa laaa af'idatuhum min shay'in iz kaanoo yajḥadoona bi-Aayaatil-laahi wa ḥaaqa bihim maa kaanoo bihee yastahzi'oon.

(Section 3)

27. Wa laqad ahlaknaa maa ḥawlakum minal-quraa wa ṣarrafnal-Aayaati la'allahum yarji'oon.

28. Falaw laa naṣarahumul-lazeenat-takhazoo min ḍoonil-laahi qurbaanan aalihatam bal ḍalloo 'anhum; wa zaalika ifkuhum wa maa kaanoo yaftaroon.

29. Wa iz ṣarafnaaa ilayka nafaram-minal-jinni yastami'oo-nal-Qur-aana falammaa ḥaḍaroo-hu qaalooo anṣitoo falammaa quḍiya wallaw ilaa qawmihim munzireen.

30. Qaaloo yaa qawmanaaa innaa sami'naa Kitaaban unzila mim ba'di Moosaa muṣaddiqal-

فَلَمَّا رَاَوْهُ عَارِضًا مُّسْتَقْبِلَ اَوْ
دِيَتِهِمْ ۙ قَالُوْا هٰذَا عَارِضٌ مُّمْطِرُنَا ؕ
بَلْ هُوَ مَا اسْتَعْجَلْتُمْ بِهٖ ؕ رِيْحٌ فِيْهَا
عَذَابٌ اَلِيْمٌ ۙ﴿٢٤﴾
تُدَمِّرُ كُلَّ شَيْءٍۭ بِاَمْرِ رَبِّهَا
فَاَصْبَحُوْا لَا يُرٰٓى اِلَّا مَسٰكِنُهُمْ ؕ
كَذٰلِكَ نَجْزِى الْقَوْمَ الْمُجْرِمِيْنَ ﴿٢٥﴾
وَلَقَدْ مَكَّنّٰهُمْ فِيْمَآ اِنْ مَّكَّنّٰكُمْ
فِيْهِ وَجَعَلْنَا لَهُمْ سَمْعًا وَّاَبْصَارًا
وَّاَفْـِٕدَةً ۖ فَمَآ اَغْنٰى عَنْهُمْ سَمْعُهُمْ
وَلَآ اَبْصَارُهُمْ وَلَآ اَفْـِٕدَتُهُمْ
مِّنْ شَيْءٍ اِذْ كَانُوْا يَجْحَدُوْنَ ۙ
بِاٰيٰتِ اللّٰهِ وَحَاقَ بِهِمْ مَّا كَانُوْا
بِهٖ يَسْتَهْزِءُوْنَ ﴿٢٦﴾ ع
وَلَقَدْ اَهْلَكْنَا مَا حَوْلَكُمْ مِّنَ الْقُرٰى
وَصَرَّفْنَا الْاٰيٰتِ لَعَلَّهُمْ يَرْجِعُوْنَ ﴿٢٧﴾
فَلَوْلَا نَصَرَهُمُ الَّذِيْنَ اتَّخَذُوْا مِنْ
دُوْنِ اللّٰهِ قُرْبَانًا اٰلِهَةً ؕ بَلْ
ضَلُّوْا عَنْهُمْ ۚ وَذٰلِكَ اِفْكُهُمْ
وَمَا كَانُوْا يَفْتَرُوْنَ ﴿٢٨﴾
وَاِذْ صَرَفْنَآ اِلَيْكَ نَفَرًا مِّنَ الْجِنِّ
يَسْتَمِعُوْنَ الْقُرْاٰنَ ۚ فَلَمَّا حَضَرُوْهُ
قَالُوْٓا اَنْصِتُوْا ۚ فَلَمَّا قُضِىَ وَلَّوْا
اِلٰى قَوْمِهِمْ مُّنْذِرِيْنَ ﴿٢٩﴾
قَالُوْا يٰقَوْمَنَآ اِنَّا سَمِعْنَا كِتٰبًا
اُنْزِلَ مِنْ بَعْدِ مُوْسٰى مُصَدِّقًا

Ikhfa اخفاء | Ghunna غُنّہ | Ikhfa Meem Saakin اخفاء میم ساکن | Idghaam ادغام | Qalqala قلقلہ | Qalb قلب | Idghaam Meem Saakin ادغام میم ساکن

what came before it: it guides (men) to the Truth and to a Straight Path.

limaa bayna yadayhi yahdeee ilal-ḥaqqi wa ilaa Ṭareeqim-Mustaqeem.

لِمَا بَيْنَ يَدَيْهِ يَهْدِيْٓ اِلَى الْحَقِّ
وَاِلٰى طَرِيْقٍ مُّسْتَقِيْمٍ ﴿٣٠﴾

31. "O our people, hearken to the one who invites (you) to Allah, and believe in him: He will forgive you your faults, and deliver you from a Chastisement Grievous.

31. Yaa qawmanaaa ajeeboo daa'iyal-laahi wa aaminoo bihee yaghfir lakum min ẕunoobikum wa yujirkum min 'aẕaabin aleem.

يٰقَوْمَنَآ اَجِيْبُوْا دَاعِيَ اللّٰهِ وَاٰمِنُوْا
بِهٖ يَغْفِرْ لَكُمْ مِّنْ ذُنُوْبِكُمْ
وَيُجِرْكُمْ مِّنْ عَذَابٍ اَلِيْمٍ ﴿٣١﴾

32. "If any does not hearken to the one who invites (us) to Allah, he cannot frustrate (Allah's Plan) on earth, and no protectors can he have besides Allah: such men (wander) in manifest error."

32. Wa mal-laa yujib daa'iyal-laahi falaysa bimu'jizin fil-arḍi wa laysa lahoo min dooniheee awliyaaa'; ulaaa'ika fee ḍalaalim-mubeen.

وَمَنْ لَّا يُجِبْ دَاعِيَ اللّٰهِ فَلَيْسَ
بِمُعْجِزٍ فِي الْاَرْضِ وَلَيْسَ لَهٗ
مِنْ دُوْنِهٖٓ اَوْلِيَآءُ ؕ اُولٰٓئِكَ فِيْ
ضَلٰلٍ مُّبِيْنٍ ﴿٣٢﴾

33. See they not that Allah, Who created the heavens and the earth, and never wearied with their creation, is able to give life to the dead? Yes, verily He has power over all things.

33. Awalam yaraw annal-laahal-laẕee khalaqas-samaawaati wal-arḍa wa lam ya'ya bikhal-qihinna biqaadirin 'alaaa añy-yuḥyiyal-mawtaa; balaaa innahoo 'alaa kulli shay'in Qadeer.

اَوَلَمْ يَرَوْا اَنَّ اللّٰهَ الَّذِيْ خَلَقَ
السَّمٰوٰتِ وَالْاَرْضَ وَلَمْ يَعْيَ
بِخَلْقِهِنَّ بِقٰدِرٍ عَلٰٓى اَنْ يُّحْيِۦَ
الْمَوْتٰى ؕ بَلٰٓى اِنَّهٗ عَلٰى كُلِّ
شَيْءٍ قَدِيْرٌ ﴿٣٣﴾

34. And on the Day that the Unbelievers will be placed before the Fire, (they will be asked,) "Is this not the Truth?" they will say, "Yes, by our Lord!" (One will say:) "Then taste you the Chastisement, for that you were wont to deny (Truth)!"

34. Wa Yawma yu'raḍul-laẕeena kafaroo 'alan-Naari alaysa haaẕaa bil-ḥaqq; qaaloo balaa wa Rabbinaa; qaala faẕooqul-'aẕaaba bimaa kuntum takfuroon.

وَيَوْمَ يُعْرَضُ الَّذِيْنَ كَفَرُوْا عَلَى
النَّارِ ؕ اَلَيْسَ هٰذَا بِالْحَقِّ ؕ
قَالُوْا بَلٰى وَرَبِّنَا ؕ قَالَ فَذُوْقُوا
الْعَذَابَ بِمَا كُنْتُمْ تَكْفُرُوْنَ ﴿٣٤﴾

35. Therefore patiently persevere, as did (all) apostles of inflexible purpose; and be in no haste about the (Unbelievers). On the Day that they see the (Punishment) promised them, (it will be) as if they had not tarried more than an hour in a single day. (Your but) to proclaim the Message: but shall any be destroyed except those who transgress?

35. Faṣbir kamaa ṣabara ulul-'azmi minar-Rusuli wa laa tasta'jil-lahum; ka-annahum Yawma yarawna maa yoo'adoona lam yalbaṡooo illaa saa'atam-min nahaar; balaagh; fahal yuhlaku illal-qawmul-faasiqoon. **(Section 4)**

فَاصْبِرْ كَمَا صَبَرَ اُولُوا الْعَزْمِ
مِنَ الرُّسُلِ وَلَا تَسْتَعْجِلْ لَّهُمْ ؕ
كَاَنَّهُمْ يَوْمَ يَرَوْنَ مَا يُوْعَدُوْنَ ۙ لَمْ
يَلْبَثُوْٓا اِلَّا سَاعَةً مِّنْ نَّهَارٍ ؕ بَلٰغٌ ۚ
فَهَلْ يُهْلَكُ اِلَّا الْقَوْمُ الْفٰسِقُوْنَ ﴿٣٥﴾

47. (The Prophet) Muhammad

In the name of Allah, Most Gracious, Most Merciful.

Sûrat Muḥammad–47

(Revealed at Madinah)

Bismillaahir Raḥmaanir Raḥeem

(٤٧) سُوْرَةُ مُحَمَّدٍ مَّدَنِيَّةٌ (٩٥)

بِسْمِ اللّٰهِ الرَّحْمٰنِ الرَّحِيْمِ

1. Those who reject Allah and hinder (men) from the Path

1. Allaẕeena kafaroo wa ṣaddoo 'an sabeelil-

اَلَّذِيْنَ كَفَرُوْا وَصَدُّوْا عَنْ سَبِيْلِ

of Allah,- their deeds will Allah render astray (from their mark).	laahi aḍalla a'maalahum.	اللّٰهِ اَضَلَّ اَعْمَالَهُمْ ﴿١﴾
2. But those who believe and work deeds of righteousness, and believe in the (Revelation) sent down to Muhammad - for it is the Truth from their Lord,- He will remove from them their ills and improve their condition.	2. Wallazeena aamanoo wa 'amiluṣ-ṣaaliḥaati wa aamanoo bimaa nuzzila 'alaa Muḥammadiñw-wa huwal-ḥaqqu mir-Rabbihim kaffara 'anhum sayyi-aatihim wa aṣlaḥa baalahum.	وَالَّذِيْنَ اٰمَنُوْا وَعَمِلُوا الصّٰلِحٰتِ وَاٰمَنُوْا بِمَا نُزِّلَ عَلٰى مُحَمَّدٍ وَّهُوَ الْحَقُّ مِنْ رَّبِّهِمْ ۙ كَفَّرَ عَنْهُمْ سَيِّاٰتِهِمْ وَاَصْلَحَ بَالَهُمْ ﴿٢﴾
3. This because those who reject Allah follow falsehood, while those who believe follow the Truth from their Lord: Thus does Allah set forth for men their lessons by similitudes.	3. Zaalika bi-annal-lazeena kafarut-taba'ul-baaṭila wa annal-lazeena aamanut-taba'ul-ḥaqqa mir-Rabbihim; kazaalika yaḍribul-laahu linnaasi amsaalahum.	ذٰلِكَ بِاَنَّ الَّذِيْنَ كَفَرُوا اتَّبَعُوا الْبَاطِلَ وَاَنَّ الَّذِيْنَ اٰمَنُوا اتَّبَعُوا الْحَقَّ مِنْ رَّبِّهِمْ ؕ كَذٰلِكَ يَضْرِبُ اللّٰهُ لِلنَّاسِ اَمْثَالَهُمْ ﴿٣﴾
4. Therefore, when you meet the Unbelievers (in fight), smite at their necks; At length, when you have thoroughly subdued them, bind a bond firmly (on them): thereafter (is the time for) either generosity or ransom: Until the war lays down its burdens. Thus (are you commanded): but if it had been Allah's Will, He could certainly have exacted retribution from them (Himself); but (He lets you fight) in order to test you, some with others. But those who are slain in the Way of Allah,- He will never let their deeds be lost.	4. Fa-izaa laqeetumul-lazeena kafaroo faḍarbar-riqaab, ḥattaa izaa askhantumoohum fashuddul-wasaaq, fa-immaa mannam ba'du wa immaa fidaaa'an ḥattaa taḍa'al-ḥarbu awzaarahaa; zaalika wa law yashaaa'ul-laahu lantaṣara minhum wa laakil-liyabluwa ba'ḍakum biba'ḍ; wallazeena qutiloo fee sabeelil-laahi falañy-yuḍilla a'maalahum.	فَاِذَا لَقِيْتُمُ الَّذِيْنَ كَفَرُوْا فَضَرْبَ الرِّقَابِ ؕ حَتّٰۤى اِذَاۤ اَثْخَنْتُمُوْهُمْ فَشُدُّوا الْوَثَاقَ ۙ فَاِمَّا مَنًّۢا بَعْدُ وَاِمَّا فِدَآءً حَتّٰى تَضَعَ الْحَرْبُ اَوْزَارَهَا ۛ ذٰلِكَ ۛ وَلَوْ يَشَآءُ اللّٰهُ لَانْتَصَرَ مِنْهُمْ ۙ وَلٰكِنْ لِّيَبْلُوَا بَعْضَكُمْ بِبَعْضٍ ؕ وَالَّذِيْنَ قُتِلُوْا فِيْ سَبِيْلِ اللّٰهِ فَلَنْ يُّضِلَّ اَعْمَالَهُمْ ﴿٤﴾
5. Soon will He guide them and improve their condition,	5. Sa-yahdeehim wa yuṣliḥu baalahum.	سَيَهْدِيْهِمْ وَيُصْلِحُ بَالَهُمْ ۚ ﴿٥﴾
6. And admit them to the Garden which He has announced for them.	6. Wa yudkhiluhumul-Jannata 'arrafahaa lahum.	وَيُدْخِلُهُمُ الْجَنَّةَ عَرَّفَهَا لَهُمْ ﴿٦﴾
7. O you who believe! If ye will aid (the cause of) Allah, He will aid you, and plant your feet firmly.	7. Yaaa ayyuhal-lazeena aamanooo in tanṣurul-laaha yanṣurkum wa yusabbit aqdaamakum.	يٰۤاَيُّهَا الَّذِيْنَ اٰمَنُوْۤا اِنْ تَنْصُرُوا اللّٰهَ يَنْصُرْكُمْ وَيُثَبِّتْ اَقْدَامَكُمْ ﴿٧﴾
8. But those who reject (Allah),- for them is destruction, and (Allah) will render their deeds worthless.	8. Wallazeena kafaroo fata's al-lahum wa aḍalla a'maalahum.	وَالَّذِيْنَ كَفَرُوْا فَتَعْسًا لَّهُمْ وَاَضَلَّ اَعْمَالَهُمْ ﴿٨﴾
9. That is because they hate the Revelation of Allah; so He has made their deeds fruitless.	9. Zaalika bi-annahum karihoo maaa anzalal-laahu fa-aḥbaṭa a'maalahum.	ذٰلِكَ بِاَنَّهُمْ كَرِهُوْا مَاۤ اَنْزَلَ اللّٰهُ فَاَحْبَطَ اَعْمَالَهُمْ ﴿٩﴾
10. Do they not travel through the earth, and see	10. Afalam yaseeroo fil-arḍi fayanẓuroo	اَفَلَمْ يَسِيْرُوْا فِي الْاَرْضِ فَيَنْظُرُوْا

مع ٤ عند المتقدمين وقد يبتدأ بقوله ذٰلك ط ولكن حسن اتصاله بما قبله ويوقف على ذٰلك ط ١٢

Ikhfa اخفاء · Ghunna غُنّہ · Ikhfa Meem Saakin اخفاء میم ساکن · Idghaam ادغام · Qalqala قلقلہ · Qalb قلب · Idghaam Meem Saakin ادغام میم ساکن

what was the End of those before them (who did evil)? Allah brought utter destruction on them, and similar (fates await) those who reject Allah.

11. That is because Allah is the Protector of those who believe, but those who reject Allah have no protector.

12. Verily Allah will admit those who believe and do righteous deeds, to Gardens beneath which rivers flow; while those who reject Allah will enjoy (this world) and eat as cattle eat; and the Fire will be their abode.

13. And how many cities, with more power than your city which has driven you out, have We destroyed (for their sins)? and there was none to aid them.

14. Is then one who is on a clear (Path) from his Lord, no better than one to whom the evil of his conduct seems pleasing, and such as follow their own lusts?

15. (Here is) a description of the Garden which the righteous are promised: in it are rivers of water unstaling; rivers of milk of which the taste never changes; rivers of wine, a joy to those who drink; and rivers of honey pure and clear. In it there are for them all kinds of fruits; and Grace from their Lord. (Can those in such Bliss) be compared to such as shall dwell for ever in the Fire, and be given, to drink, boiling water, so that it cuts up their bowels (to pieces)?

16. And among them are men who listen to you, but in the end, when they go out from thee, they say to those who

kayfa kaana 'aaqibatul-lazeena min qablihim; dammaral-laahu 'alayhim wa lilkaafireena amsaaluhaa.

11. Zaalika bi-annal-laaha mawlal-lazeena aamanoo wa annal-kaafireena laa mawlaa lahum. **(Section 1)**

12. Innal-laaha yudkhilul-lazeena aamanoo wa 'amiluṣ-ṣaaliḥaati Jannaatin tajree min taḥtihal-anhaaru wallazeena kafaroo yatamatta'oona wa yaåkuloona kamaa taåkulul-an'aamu wan-Naaru maswal-lahum.

13. Wa ka-ayyim-min qaryatin hiya ashaddu quwwatam-min qaryatikal-lateee akhrajatka ahlaknaahum falaa naaṣira lahum.

14. Afaman kaana 'alaa bayyinatim-mir-Rabbihee kaman zuyyina lahoo sooo'u 'amalihee wattaba'ooo ahwaaa'ahum.

15. Masalul-Jannatil-latee wu'idal-muttaqoona feehaaa anhaarum-mim-maaa'in ghayri aasininw wa anhaarum mil-labanil-lam yataghayyar ṭa'muhoo wa anhaarum-min khamril-lazzatil-lishshaaribeena wa anhaarum-min 'asalim muṣaffanw wa lahum feehaa min kullis-samaraati wa maghfiratum-mir-Rabbihim kaman huwa khaalidun fin-Naari wa suqoo maaa'an ḥameeman faqaṭṭa'a am'aaa'ahum.

16. Wa minhum many-yastami'u ilayka ḥattaaa izaa kharajoo min 'indika qaaloo lilla-zeena

كَيْفَ كَانَ عَاقِبَةُ الَّذِيْنَ مِنْ قَبْلِهِمْ
دَمَّرَ اللّٰهُ عَلَيْهِمْ ز وَلِلْكٰفِرِيْنَ
اَمْثَالُهَا ﴿١٠﴾
ذٰلِكَ بِاَنَّ اللّٰهَ مَوْلَى الَّذِيْنَ اٰمَنُوْا
وَاَنَّ الْكٰفِرِيْنَ لَا مَوْلٰى لَهُمْ ﴿١١﴾ ع
اِنَّ اللّٰهَ يُدْخِلُ الَّذِيْنَ اٰمَنُوْا
وَعَمِلُوا الصّٰلِحٰتِ جَنّٰتٍ تَجْرِيْ
مِنْ تَحْتِهَا الْاَنْهٰرُ ط وَالَّذِيْنَ كَفَرُوْا
يَتَمَتَّعُوْنَ وَيَاْكُلُوْنَ كَمَا تَاْكُلُ
الْاَنْعَامُ وَالنَّارُ مَثْوًى لَّهُمْ ﴿١٢﴾
وَكَاَيِّنْ مِّنْ قَرْيَةٍ هِيَ اَشَدُّ
قُوَّةً مِّنْ قَرْيَتِكَ الَّتِيْٓ اَخْرَجَتْكَ ج
اَهْلَكْنٰهُمْ فَلَا نَاصِرَ لَهُمْ ﴿١٣﴾
اَفَمَنْ كَانَ عَلٰى بَيِّنَةٍ مِّنْ رَّبِّهٖ
كَمَنْ زُيِّنَ لَهٗ سُوْٓءُ عَمَلِهٖ وَاتَّبَعُوْٓا
اَهْوَآءَهُمْ ﴿١٤﴾
مَثَلُ الْجَنَّةِ الَّتِيْ وُعِدَ الْمُتَّقُوْنَ ط
فِيْهَآ اَنْهٰرٌ مِّنْ مَّآءٍ غَيْرِ اٰسِنٍ ج
وَاَنْهٰرٌ مِّنْ لَّبَنٍ لَّمْ يَتَغَيَّرْ طَعْمُهٗ ج
وَاَنْهٰرٌ مِّنْ خَمْرٍ لَّذَّةٍ لِّلشّٰرِبِيْنَ ۚ
وَاَنْهٰرٌ مِّنْ عَسَلٍ مُّصَفًّى ط وَلَهُمْ
فِيْهَا مِنْ كُلِّ الثَّمَرٰتِ وَمَغْفِرَةٌ
مِّنْ رَّبِّهِمْ ط كَمَنْ هُوَ خَالِدٌ فِي النَّارِ
وَسُقُوْا مَآءً حَمِيْمًا فَقَطَّعَ اَمْعَآءَهُمْ ﴿١٥﴾
وَمِنْهُمْ مَّنْ يَّسْتَمِعُ اِلَيْكَ ج حَتّٰٓى اِذَا
خَرَجُوْا مِنْ عِنْدِكَ قَالُوْا لِلَّذِيْنَ

Ikhfa اخفاء | Ghunna غُنّہ | Ikhfa Meem Saakin اخفاء میم ساکن | Idghaam ادغام | Qalqala قلقلہ | Qalb قلب | Idghaam Meem Saakin ادغام میم ساکن

have received Knowledge, "What is it he said just then?" Such are men whose hearts Allah has sealed, and who follow their own lusts.

ootul-'ilma maaẕaa qaala aanifaa; ulaaa'ikal-laẕeena ṭaba'al-laahu 'alaa quloobihim wattaba'ooo ahwaaa'ahum.

أُوتُوا الْعِلْمَ مَاذَا قَالَ آنِفًا
أُولَٰئِكَ الَّذِينَ طَبَعَ اللَّهُ عَلَىٰ
قُلُوبِهِمْ وَاتَّبَعُوا أَهْوَاءَهُمْ ﴿١٦﴾

17. But to those who receive Guidance, He increases the (light of) Guidance, and bestows on them their Piety and Restraint (from evil).

17. Wallaẕeenah-tadaw zaadahum hudañw-wa aataahum taqwaahum.

وَالَّذِينَ اهْتَدَوْا زَادَهُمْ هُدًى
وَآتَاهُمْ تَقْوَاهُمْ ﴿١٧﴾

18. Do they then only wait for the Hour,- that it should come on them of a sudden? But already have come some tokens thereof, and when it (actually) is on them, how can they benefit then by their admonition?

18. Fahal yanẓuroona illas-Saa'ata an taåtiyahum baghtatan faqad jaaa'a ashraaṭuhaa; fa-annaa lahum iẕaa jaaa'at-hum ẕikraahum.

فَهَلْ يَنْظُرُونَ إِلَّا السَّاعَةَ أَنْ
تَأْتِيَهُمْ بَغْتَةً ۖ فَقَدْ جَاءَ
أَشْرَاطُهَا ۚ فَأَنَّىٰ لَهُمْ إِذَا جَاءَتْهُمْ
ذِكْرَاهُمْ ﴿١٨﴾

19. Know, therefore, that there is no god but Allah, and ask forgiveness for your fault, and for the men and women who believe: for Allah knows how you move about and how you dwell in your homes.

19. Fa'lam annahoo laaa ilaaha illal-laahu wastaghfir liẕambika wa lilmu'mineena walmu'minaat; wallaahu ya'lamu mutaqallabakum wa mas̱waakum.

(Section 2)

فَاعْلَمْ أَنَّهُ لَا إِلَٰهَ إِلَّا اللَّهُ وَاسْتَغْفِرْ
لِذَنْبِكَ وَلِلْمُؤْمِنِينَ وَالْمُؤْمِنَاتِ ۗ
وَاللَّهُ يَعْلَمُ مُتَقَلَّبَكُمْ وَمَثْوَاكُمْ ﴿١٩﴾ ع٢

20. Those who believe say, "Why is not a sura sent down (for us)?" But when a sura of basic or categorical meaning is revealed, and fighting is mentioned therein, you will see those in whose hearts is a disease looking at you with a look of one in swoon at the approach of death. But more fitting for them-

20. Wa yaqoolul-laẕeena aamanoo law laa nuzzilat Sooratun fa-iẕaaa unzilat Sooratum-Muḥkamatuñw-wa ẕukira feehal-qitaalu ra-aytal-laẕeena fee quloobihim maraḍuñy-yanẓuroona ilayka naẓaral-maghshiyyi 'alayhi minal-mawti fa-awlaa lahum.

وَيَقُولُ الَّذِينَ آمَنُوا لَوْلَا نُزِّلَتْ
سُورَةٌ ۖ فَإِذَا أُنْزِلَتْ سُورَةٌ مُحْكَمَةٌ
وَذُكِرَ فِيهَا الْقِتَالُ ۙ رَأَيْتَ الَّذِينَ
فِي قُلُوبِهِمْ مَرَضٌ يَنْظُرُونَ إِلَيْكَ
نَظَرَ الْمَغْشِيِّ عَلَيْهِ مِنَ الْمَوْتِ ۖ
فَأَوْلَىٰ لَهُمْ ﴿٢٠﴾

21. Were it to obey and say what is just, and when a matter is resolved on, it were best for them if they were true to Allah.

21. Ṭaa'atuñw-wa qawlum-ma'roof; fa-iẕaa 'azamal-amru falaw ṣadaqul-laaha lakaana khayral-lahum.

طَاعَةٌ وَقَوْلٌ مَعْرُوفٌ ۚ فَإِذَا عَزَمَ
الْأَمْرُ فَلَوْ صَدَقُوا اللَّهَ لَكَانَ
خَيْرًا لَهُمْ ﴿٢١﴾

22. Then, is it to be expected of you, if you were put in authority, that you will do mischief in the land, and break your ties of kith and kin?

22. Fahal 'asaytum in tawallaytum an tufsidoo fil-arḍi wa tuqaṭṭi'ooo arḥaamakum.

فَهَلْ عَسَيْتُمْ إِنْ تَوَلَّيْتُمْ أَنْ تُفْسِدُوا
فِي الْأَرْضِ وَتُقَطِّعُوا أَرْحَامَكُمْ ﴿٢٢﴾

23. Such are the men whom Allah has cursed for He has made them deaf and blinded their sight.

23. Ulaaa'ikal-laẕeena la'anahumul-laahu fa-aṣammahum wa a'maaa abṣaarahum.

أُولَٰئِكَ الَّذِينَ لَعَنَهُمُ اللَّهُ فَأَصَمَّهُمْ
وَأَعْمَىٰ أَبْصَارَهُمْ ﴿٢٣﴾

24. Do they not then earnestly seek to understand the Qur'an, Or are their

24. Afalaa yatadabbaroonal-Qur-aana am 'alaa

أَفَلَا يَتَدَبَّرُونَ الْقُرْآنَ أَمْ عَلَىٰ

Ikhfa اخفاء · Ghunna غُنّہ · Ikhfa Meem Saakin اخفاء میم ساکن · Idghaam ادغام · Qalqala قلقلہ · Qalb قلب · Idghaam Meem Saakin ادغام میم ساکن

hearts locked up by them?

quloobin aqfaaluhaa.

قُلُوبٍ أَقْفَالُهَا ﴿٢٤﴾

25. Those who turn back as apostates after Guidance was clearly shown to them,- the Evil One has instigated them and buoyed them up with false hopes.

25. Innal-lazeenar-taddoo 'alaaa adbaarihim mim ba'di maa tabayyana lahumul-hudash-Shayṭaanu sawwala lahum wa amlaa lahum.

إِنَّ الَّذِينَ ارْتَدُّوا عَلَىٰ أَدْبَارِهِم
مِّنۢ بَعْدِ مَا تَبَيَّنَ لَهُمُ الْهُدَى ۙ
الشَّيْطَٰنُ سَوَّلَ لَهُمْ ۖ وَأَمْلَىٰ لَهُمْ ﴿٢٥﴾

26. This, because they said to those who hate what Allah has revealed, "We will obey you in part of (this) matter"; but Allah knows their (inner) secrets.

26. Zaalika bi-annahum qaaloo lillazeena karihoo maa nazzalal-laahu sanuṭee'ukum fee ba'ḍil-amri wallaahu ya'lamu israarahum.

ذَٰلِكَ بِأَنَّهُمْ قَالُوا لِلَّذِينَ كَرِهُوا
مَا نَزَّلَ اللَّهُ سَنُطِيعُكُمْ فِي بَعْضِ
الْأَمْرِ ۖ وَاللَّهُ يَعْلَمُ إِسْرَارَهُمْ ﴿٢٦﴾

27. But how (will it be) when the angels take their souls at death, and smite their faces and their backs?

27. Fakayfa izaa tawaffat-humul-malaaa'ikatu yaḍri-boona wujoohahum wa adbaa-rahum.

فَكَيْفَ إِذَا تَوَفَّتْهُمُ الْمَلَٰٓئِكَةُ
يَضْرِبُونَ وُجُوهَهُمْ وَأَدْبَارَهُمْ ﴿٢٧﴾

28. This because they followed that which called forth the Wrath of Allah, and they hated Allah's good pleasure; so He made their deeds of no effect.

28. Zaalika bi-annahumut taba'oo maaa askhaṭal-laaha wa karihoo riḍwaanahoo fa-aḥbaṭa a'maalahum. **(Section 3)**

ذَٰلِكَ بِأَنَّهُمُ اتَّبَعُوا مَآ أَسْخَطَ
اللَّهَ وَكَرِهُوا رِضْوَانَهُۥ فَأَحْبَطَ
أَعْمَٰلَهُمْ ﴿٢٨﴾

29. Or do those in whose hearts is a disease, think that Allah will not bring to light all their rancour?

29. Am ḥasibal-lazeena fee quloobihim maraḍun al-lan yukhrijal-laahu aḍghaanahum.

أَمْ حَسِبَ الَّذِينَ فِي قُلُوبِهِم
مَّرَضٌ أَن لَّن يُخْرِجَ اللَّهُ أَضْغَٰنَهُمْ ﴿٢٩﴾

30. Had We so willed, We could have shown them up to you, and you should have known them by their marks: but surely you will know them by the tone of their speech! And Allah knows all that you do.

30. Wa law nashaaa'u la-aray-naakahum fala-'araftahum bi-seemaahum; wa lata'rifan-nahum fee laḥnil-qawl; wallaahu ya'lamu a'maalakum.

وَلَوْ نَشَآءُ لَأَرَيْنَٰكَهُمْ فَلَعَرَفْتَهُم
بِسِيمَٰهُمْ ۚ وَلَتَعْرِفَنَّهُمْ فِي لَحْنِ الْقَوْلِ ۚ
وَاللَّهُ يَعْلَمُ أَعْمَٰلَكُمْ ﴿٣٠﴾

31. And We shall try you until We test those among you who strive their utmost and persevere in patience; and We shall try your reported (mettle).

31. Wa lanabluwannakum ḥattaa na'lamal-mujaahideena minkum waṣṣaabireena wa nabluwa akhbaarakum.

وَلَنَبْلُوَنَّكُمْ حَتَّىٰ نَعْلَمَ الْمُجَٰهِدِينَ
مِنكُمْ وَالصَّٰبِرِينَ ۙ وَنَبْلُوَا
أَخْبَارَكُمْ ﴿٣١﴾

32. Those who reject Allah, hinder (men) from the Path of Allah, and resist the Apostle, after Guidance has been clearly shown to them, will not injure Allah in the least, but He will make their deeds of no effect.

32. Innal-lazeena kafaroo wa ṣaddoo 'an sabeelil-laahi wa shaaaqqur-Rasoola mim ba'di maa tabayyana lahumul-hudaa lañy-yaḍurrul-laaha shay'añw wa sa-yuḥbiṭu a'maalahum.

إِنَّ الَّذِينَ كَفَرُوا وَصَدُّوا عَن
سَبِيلِ اللَّهِ وَشَآقُّوا الرَّسُولَ مِنۢ
بَعْدِ مَا تَبَيَّنَ لَهُمُ الْهُدَىٰ ۙ
لَن يَضُرُّوا اللَّهَ شَيْـًٔا وَسَيُحْبِطُ
أَعْمَٰلَهُمْ ﴿٣٢﴾

33. O you who believe! Obey Allah, and

33. Yaaa ayyuhal-lazeena aamanoo aṭee'ul-laaha

يَٰٓأَيُّهَا الَّذِينَ ءَامَنُوٓا أَطِيعُوا اللَّهَ

Ikhfa اخفاء | Ghunna غنّہ | Ikhfa Meem Saakin اخفاء میم ساکن | Idghaam ادغام | Qalqala قلقلہ | Qalb قلب | Idghaam Meem Saakin ادغام میم ساکن

obey the apostle, and make not vain your deeds!

wa aṭee'ur-Rasoola wa laa tubṭilooo a'maalakum.

وَأَطِيعُوا الرَّسُولَ وَلَا تُبْطِلُوٓا
أَعْمَالَكُمْ ٣٣

34. Those who reject Allah, and hinder (men) from the Path of Allah, then die rejecting Allah,- Allah will not forgive them.

34. Innal-lazeena kafaroo wa ṣaddoo 'an sabeelil-laahi summa maatoo wa hum kuffaarun falañy-yaghfirallaahu lahum.

إِنَّ الَّذِينَ كَفَرُوا وَصَدُّوا عَن
سَبِيلِ اللَّهِ ثُمَّ مَاتُوا وَهُمْ كُفَّارٌ
فَلَن يَغْفِرَ اللَّهُ لَهُمْ ٣٤

35. Be not weary and faint-hearted, crying for peace, when you should be uppermost: for Allah is with you, and will never put you in loss for your (good) deeds.

35. Falaa tahinoo wa tad'ooo ilas-salmi wa antumul-a'lawna wallaahu ma'akum wa lañy-yatirakum a'maalakum.

فَلَا تَهِنُوا وَتَدْعُوٓا إِلَى السَّلْمِ ۖ
وَأَنتُمُ الْأَعْلَوْنَ ۖ وَاللَّهُ مَعَكُمْ وَلَن
يَتِرَكُمْ أَعْمَالَكُمْ ٣٥

36. The life of this world is but play and amusement: and if you believe and guard against Evil, He will grant you your recompense, and will not ask you (to give up) your possessions.

36. Innamal-ḥayaatud-dunyaa la'ibuñw-wa lahw; wa in to'minoo wa tattaqoo yu'tikum ujoorakum wa laa yas'alkum amwaalakum.

إِنَّمَا الْحَيَوٰةُ الدُّنْيَا لَعِبٌ وَلَهْوٌ ۚ
وَإِن تُؤْمِنُوا وَتَتَّقُوا يُؤْتِكُمْ
أُجُورَكُمْ وَلَا يَسْـَٔلْكُمْ أَمْوَالَكُمْ ٣٦

37. If He were to ask you for all of them, and press you, you would covetously withhold, and He would bring out all your ill-feeling.

37. Iñy-yas'alkumoohaa fa-yuḥfikum ṭabkhaloo wa yukhrij aḍghaanakum.

إِن يَسْـَٔلْكُمُوهَا فَيُحْفِكُمْ تَبْخَلُوا
وَيُخْرِجْ أَضْغَانَكُمْ ٣٧

38. Behold, you are those invited to spend (of your substance) in the Way of Allah: But among you are some that are niggardly. But any who are niggardly are so at the expense of their own souls. But Allah is free of all wants, and it is you that are needy. If you turn back (from the Path), He will substitute in your stead another people; then they would not be like you!

38. Haaa antum haaa'ulaaa'i tud'awna litunfiqoo fee sabeelillaahi faminkum mañy-yabkhalu wa mañy-yabkhal fa-innamaa yabkhalu 'an nafsih; wallaahul-Ghaniyyu wa antumul-fuqaraaa'; wa in tatawallaw yastabdil qawman ghayrakum summa laa yakoonooo amsaalakum. **(Section 4)**

هَٰٓأَنتُمْ هَٰٓؤُلَآءِ تُدْعَوْنَ لِتُنفِقُوا
فِي سَبِيلِ اللَّهِ فَمِنكُم مَّن يَبْخَلُ ۖ
وَمَن يَبْخَلْ فَإِنَّمَا يَبْخَلُ عَن
نَّفْسِهِ ۚ وَاللَّهُ الْغَنِيُّ وَأَنتُمُ الْفُقَرَآءُ ۚ
وَإِن تَتَوَلَّوْا يَسْتَبْدِلْ قَوْمًا غَيْرَكُمْ
ثُمَّ لَا يَكُونُوٓا أَمْثَٰلَكُم ٣٨

48. Victory

In the name of Allah, Most Gracious, Most Merciful.

Sûrat al-Fatḥ–48

(Revealed at Madinah)

Bismillaahir Raḥmaanir Raḥeem

(٤٨) سُورَةُ الْفَتْحِ مَدَنِيَّةٌ (١١١)

بِسْمِ اللَّهِ الرَّحْمَٰنِ الرَّحِيمِ

1. Verily We have granted you a manifest Victory:

1. Innaa fataḥnaa laka Fatḥam-Mubeenaa.

إِنَّا فَتَحْنَا لَكَ فَتْحًا مُّبِينًا ١

2. That Allah may forgive you your faults of the past and those to follow; fulfil His favour to you; and guide you on the Straight Way;

2. Liyaghfira lakal-laahu maa taqaddama min zambika wa maa ta-akhkhara wa yutimma ni'matahoo 'alayka wa yahdiyaka Ṣiraaṭam Mustaqeemaa.

لِّيَغْفِرَ لَكَ اللَّهُ مَا تَقَدَّمَ مِن ذَنۢبِكَ
وَمَا تَأَخَّرَ وَيُتِمَّ نِعْمَتَهُۥ عَلَيْكَ
وَيَهْدِيَكَ صِرَٰطًا مُّسْتَقِيمًا ٢

3. And that Allah may help you with powerful help.

3. Wa yanṣurakal-laahu naṣran 'azeezaa.

وَيَنصُرَكَ اللَّهُ نَصْرًا عَزِيزًا ٣

Ikhfa اخفاء · Ghunna غنّہ · Ikhfa Meem Saakin اخفاء میم ساکن · Idghaam ادغام · Qalqala قلقلہ · Qalb قلب · Idghaam Meem Saakin ادغام میم ساکن

4. It is He Who sent down tranquillity into the hearts of the Believers, that they may add faith to their faith;- for to Allah belong the Forces of the heavens and the earth; and Allah is Full of Knowledge and Wisdom;-

4. Huwal-lazeee anzalas-sakeenata fee quloobil-mu'mineena liyazdaadooo eemaanam-ma'a eemaanihim; wa lillaahi junoodus-samaawaati wal-arḍ; wa kaanal-laahu 'Aleeman Ḥakeemaa.

هُوَ الَّذِىٓ اَنْزَلَ السَّكِيْنَةَ فِىْ قُلُوْبِ الْمُؤْمِنِيْنَ لِيَزْدَادُوْٓا اِيْمَانًا مَّعَ اِيْمَانِهِمْ ؕ وَلِلّٰهِ جُنُوْدُ السَّمٰوٰتِ وَالْاَرْضِ ؕ وَكَانَ اللّٰهُ عَلِيْمًا حَكِيْمًا ۟ۙ ﴿٤﴾

5. That He may admit the men and women who believe, to Gardens beneath which rivers flow, to dwell therein for ever, and remove their ills from them;- and that is, in the sight of Allah, the highest achievement (for man),-

5. Liyudkhilal-mu'mineena walmu'minaati Jannaatin tajree min taḥtihal-anhaaru khaalideena feehaa wa yukaffira 'anhum sayyi-aatihim; wa kaana zaalika 'indal-laahi fawzan 'azeemaa.

لِّيُدْخِلَ الْمُؤْمِنِيْنَ وَالْمُؤْمِنٰتِ جَنّٰتٍ تَجْرِىْ مِنْ تَحْتِهَا الْاَنْهٰرُ خٰلِدِيْنَ فِيْهَا وَيُكَفِّرَ عَنْهُمْ سَيِّاٰتِهِمْ ؕ وَكَانَ ذٰلِكَ عِنْدَ اللّٰهِ فَوْزًا عَظِيْمًا ۟ۙ ﴿٥﴾

6. And that He may punish the Hypocrites, men and women, and the Polytheists, men and women, who imagine an evil opinion of Allah. On them is a round of Evil: the Wrath of Allah is on them: He has cursed them and got Hell ready for them: and evil is it for a destination.

6. Wa yu'azzibal-munaafiqeena walmunaafiqaati walmushrikeena walmushrikaatiẓ-ẓaaanneena billaahi ẓannas-saw'; 'alayhim daaa'iratus-saw'i wa ghaḍibal-laahu 'alayhim wa la'anahum wa a'adda lahum Jahannama wa saaa'at maṣeeraa.

وَّيُعَذِّبَ الْمُنٰفِقِيْنَ وَالْمُنٰفِقٰتِ وَالْمُشْرِكِيْنَ وَالْمُشْرِكٰتِ الظَّآنِّيْنَ بِاللّٰهِ ظَنَّ السَّوْءِ ؕ عَلَيْهِمْ دَآئِرَةُ السَّوْءِ ۚ وَغَضِبَ اللّٰهُ عَلَيْهِمْ وَلَعَنَهُمْ وَاَعَدَّ لَهُمْ جَهَنَّمَ ؕ وَسَآءَتْ مَصِيْرًا ﴿٦﴾

7. For to Allah belong the Forces of the heavens and the earth; and Allah is Exalted in Power, Full of Wisdom.

7. Wa lillaahi junoodus-samaawaati wal-arḍ; wa kaanal-laahu 'Azeezan Ḥakeemaa.

وَلِلّٰهِ جُنُوْدُ السَّمٰوٰتِ وَالْاَرْضِ ؕ وَكَانَ اللّٰهُ عَزِيْزًا حَكِيْمًا ﴿٧﴾

8. We have truly sent you as a witness, as a bringer of Glad Tidings, and as a Warner:

8. Innaaa arsalnaaka shaahidañw-wa mubashshirañw-wa nazeeraa.

اِنَّآ اَرْسَلْنٰكَ شَاهِدًا وَّمُبَشِّرًا وَّنَذِيْرًا ۟ۙ ﴿٨﴾

9. In order that you (O men) may believe in Allah and His Apostle, that you may assist and honour Him, and celebrate His praise morning and evening.

9. Litu'minoo billaahi wa Rasoolihee wa tu'azziroohu watuwaqqiroohu watusabbiḥoohu bukratañw-wa aṣeelaa.

لِّتُؤْمِنُوْا بِاللّٰهِ وَرَسُوْلِهٖ وَتُعَزِّرُوْهُ وَتُوَقِّرُوْهُ ؕ وَتُسَبِّحُوْهُ بُكْرَةً وَّاَصِيْلًا ﴿٩﴾

10. Verily those who plight their fealty to you do no less than plight their fealty to Allah: the Hand of Allah is over their hands: then any one who violates his oath, does so to the harm of his own soul, and any one who fulfils what he has covenanted with Allah,-

10. Innal-lazeena yubaayi-'oonaka innamaa yubaayi-'oonal-laaha Yadul-laahi fawqa aydeehim; faman nakasa fa-innamaa yankusu 'alaa nafsihee wa man awfaa bimaa 'aahada 'alayhul-

اِنَّ الَّذِيْنَ يُبَايِعُوْنَكَ اِنَّمَا يُبَايِعُوْنَ اللّٰهَ ؕ يَدُ اللّٰهِ فَوْقَ اَيْدِيْهِمْ ۚ فَمَنْ نَّكَثَ فَاِنَّمَا يَنْكُثُ عَلٰى نَفْسِهٖ ۚ وَمَنْ اَوْفٰى بِمَا عٰهَدَ عَلَيْهُ

Ikhfa اخفاء · Ghunna غُنّہ · Ikhfa Meem Saakin اخفاء میم ساکن · Idghaam ادغام · Qalqala قلقلہ · Qalb قلب · Idghaam Meem Saakin ادغام میم ساکن

Allah will soon grant him a great Reward.

laaha fasa-yu'teehi ajran 'azeemaa. **(Section 1)**

اللّٰهَ فَسَيُؤْتِيْهِ اَجْرًا عَظِيْمًا ۝١٠ ع

11. The desert Arabs who lagged behind will say to you: "We were engaged in (looking after) our flocks and herds, and our families: do you then ask forgiveness for us." They say with their tongues what is not in their hearts. Say: "Who then has any power at all (to intervene) on your behalf with Allah, if His Will is to give you some loss or to give you some profit? But Allah is well acquainted with all that you do.

11. Sa-yaqoolu lakal-mukhallafoona minal-A'raabi shaghalatnaaa amwaalunaa wa ahloonaa fastaghfir lanaa; yaqooloona bi-alsinatihim maa laysa fee quloobihim; qul famañy-yamliku lakum-minal-laahi shay'an in araada bikum ḍarran aw araada bikum naf'aa; bal kaanal-laahu bimaa ta'maloona Khabeeraa.

سَيَقُوْلُ لَكَ الْمُخَلَّفُوْنَ مِنَ
الْاَعْرَابِ شَغَلَتْنَآ اَمْوَالُنَا وَاَهْلُوْنَا
فَاسْتَغْفِرْ لَنَا ۚ يَقُوْلُوْنَ بِاَلْسِنَتِهِمْ
مَّا لَيْسَ فِيْ قُلُوْبِهِمْ ۭ قُلْ فَمَنْ
يَّمْلِكُ لَكُمْ مِّنَ اللّٰهِ شَيْـًٔا اِنْ اَرَادَ
بِكُمْ ضَرًّا اَوْ اَرَادَ بِكُمْ نَفْعًا ۭ بَلْ
كَانَ اللّٰهُ بِمَا تَعْمَلُوْنَ خَبِيْرًا ۝١١

12. "No, you thought that the Apostle and the Believers would never return to their families; this seemed pleasing in your hearts, and you conceived an evil thought, for you are a people lost (in wickedness)."

12. Bal ẓanantum al-lañy-yanqalibar-Rasoolu walmu'minoona ilaaa ahleehim abadañw-wa zuyyina ẕaalika fee quloobikum wa ẓanantum ẓannas-saw'i wa kuntum qawmam-booraa.

بَلْ ظَنَنْتُمْ اَنْ لَّنْ يَّنْقَلِبَ الرَّسُوْلُ
وَالْمُؤْمِنُوْنَ اِلٰٓى اَهْلِيْهِمْ اَبَدًا
وَّزُيِّنَ ذٰلِكَ فِيْ قُلُوْبِكُمْ
وَظَنَنْتُمْ ظَنَّ السَّوْءِ ښ وَكُنْتُمْ
قَوْمًۢا بُوْرًا ۝١٢

13. And if any believe not in Allah and His Apostle, We have prepared, for those who reject Allah, a Blazing Fire!

13. Wa mal-lam yu'mimbillaahi wa Rasoolihee fa-innaaa a'tadnaa lilkaafireena sa'eeraa.

وَمَنْ لَّمْ يُؤْمِنْۢ بِاللّٰهِ وَرَسُوْلِهٖ
فَاِنَّآ اَعْتَدْنَا لِلْكٰفِرِيْنَ سَعِيْرًا ۝١٣

14. To Allah belongs the dominion of the heavens and the earth: He forgives whom He wills, and He punishes whom He wills: but Allah is Oft-Forgiving, Most Merciful.

14. Wa lillaahi mulkus samaawaati wal-arḍ; yaghfiru limañy-yashaaa'u wa yu'azzibu mañy-yashaaa'; wa kaanal-laahu Ghafoorar-Raḥeemaa.

وَلِلّٰهِ مُلْكُ السَّمٰوٰتِ وَالْاَرْضِ ۭ
يَغْفِرُ لِمَنْ يَّشَاۗءُ وَيُعَذِّبُ مَنْ
يَّشَاۗءُ ۭ وَكَانَ اللّٰهُ غَفُوْرًا رَّحِيْمًا ۝١٤

15. Those who lagged behind (will say), when ye (are free to) march and take booty (in war): "Permit us to follow you." They wish to change Allah's decree: Say: "Not thus will you follow us: Allah has already declared (this) beforehand": then they will say, "But you are jealous of us." No, but little do they understand (such things).

15. Sa-yaqoolul-mukhallafoona izan-ṭalaqtum ilaa maghaanima litaåkhuzoohaa zaroonaa nattabi'kum yureedoona añy-yubaddiloo Kalaamal-laah; qul lan tattabi'oonaa kazaalikum qaalal-laahu min qablu fasa-yaqooloona bal taḥsudoonanaa; bal kaanoo laa yafqahoona illaa qaleelaa.

سَيَقُوْلُ الْمُخَلَّفُوْنَ اِذَا انْطَلَقْتُمْ
اِلٰى مَغَانِمَ لِتَاْخُذُوْهَا ذَرُوْنَا
نَتَّبِعْكُمْ ۚ يُرِيْدُوْنَ اَنْ يُّبَدِّلُوْا
كَلٰمَ اللّٰهِ ۭ قُلْ لَّنْ تَتَّبِعُوْنَا
كَذٰلِكُمْ قَالَ اللّٰهُ مِنْ قَبْلُ ۚ
فَسَيَقُوْلُوْنَ بَلْ تَحْسُدُوْنَنَا ۭ بَلْ
كَانُوْا لَا يَفْقَهُوْنَ اِلَّا قَلِيْلًا ۝١٥

16. Say to the desert Arabs who lagged behind:

16. Qul lilmukhallafeena minal-A'raabi

قُلْ لِّلْمُخَلَّفِيْنَ مِنَ الْاَعْرَابِ

Ikhfa اخفاء | Ghunna غُنّہ | Ikhfa Meem Saakin اخفاء میم ساکن | Idghaam ادغام | Qalqala قلقلہ | Qalb قلب | Idghaam Meem Saakin ادغام میم ساکن

"You shall be summoned (to fight) against a people given to vehement war: then shall you fight, or they shall submit. Then if you show obedience, Allah will grant you a goodly reward, but if you turn back as you did before, He will punish you with a grievous Chastisement."

satud'awna ilaa qawmin ulee baåsin shadeedin tuqaatiloonahum aw yuslimoona fa-in tuṭee'oo yu'tikumul-laahu ajran ḥasanañw wa in tatawallaw kamaa tawallaytum min qablu yu'azzibkum 'azaaban aleemaa.

سَتُدْعَوْنَ إِلَىٰ قَوْمٍ أُولِي بَأْسٍ
شَدِيدٍ تُقَاتِلُونَهُمْ أَوْ يُسْلِمُونَ ۖ
فَإِنْ تُطِيعُوا يُؤْتِكُمُ اللَّهُ أَجْرًا
حَسَنًا ۖ وَإِنْ تَتَوَلَّوْا كَمَا تَوَلَّيْتُمْ
مِنْ قَبْلُ يُعَذِّبْكُمْ عَذَابًا أَلِيمًا ١٦

17. No blame is there on the blind, nor is there blame on the lame, nor on one ill (if he joins not the war): But he that obeys Allah and His Apostle,- (Allah) will admit him to Gardens beneath which rivers flow; and he who turns back, (Allah) will punish him with a grievous Chastisement.

17. Laysa 'alal-a'maa ḥarajuñw-wa laa 'alal-a'raji ḥarajuñw-wa laa 'alal-mareeḍi ḥaraj; wa mañy-yuṭi'il-laaha wa Rasoolahoo yudkhilhu Jannaatin tajree min taḥtihal-anhaaru wa mañy-yatawalla yu'azzibhu 'azaaban aleemaa. **(Section 2)**

لَيْسَ عَلَى الْأَعْمَىٰ حَرَجٌ وَلَا عَلَى
الْأَعْرَجِ حَرَجٌ وَلَا عَلَى الْمَرِيضِ
حَرَجٌ ۗ وَمَنْ يُطِعِ اللَّهَ وَرَسُولَهُ
يُدْخِلْهُ جَنَّاتٍ تَجْرِي مِنْ تَحْتِهَا
الْأَنْهَارُ ۖ وَمَنْ يَتَوَلَّ يُعَذِّبْهُ
عَذَابًا أَلِيمًا ١٧ ع

18. Allah's Good Pleasure was on the Believers when they swore Fealty to you under the Tree: He knew what was in their hearts, and He sent down Tranquillity to them; and He rewarded them with a speedy Victory;

18. Laqad raḍiyal-laahu 'anil-mu'mineena iz yubaayi'oonaka taḥtash-shajarati fa'alima maa fee quloobihim fa-anzalas-sakeenata 'alayhim wa asaabahum fat-ḥan qareebaa.

لَقَدْ رَضِيَ اللَّهُ عَنِ الْمُؤْمِنِينَ إِذْ
يُبَايِعُونَكَ تَحْتَ الشَّجَرَةِ فَعَلِمَ
مَا فِي قُلُوبِهِمْ فَأَنْزَلَ السَّكِينَةَ
عَلَيْهِمْ وَأَثَابَهُمْ فَتْحًا قَرِيبًا ١٨

19. And many gains will they acquire (besides): and Allah is Exalted in Power, Full of Wisdom.

19. Wa maghaanima kaseeratañy-yaåkhuzoonahaa; wa kaanal-laahu 'Azeezan Ḥakeemaa.

وَمَغَانِمَ كَثِيرَةً يَأْخُذُونَهَا ۗ وَكَانَ
اللَّهُ عَزِيزًا حَكِيمًا ١٩

20. Allah has promised you many gains that you shall acquire, and He has given you these beforehand; and He has restrained the hands of men from you; that it may be a Sign for the Believers, and that He may guide you to a Straight Path;

20. Wa'adakumul-laahu maghaanima kaseeratan taåkhuzoonahaa fa'ajjala lakum haazihee wa kaffa aydiyan-naasi 'ankum wa litakoona Aayatal-lilmu'mineena wa yahdiyakum Ṣiraaṭam-Mustaqeemaa.

وَعَدَكُمُ اللَّهُ مَغَانِمَ كَثِيرَةً
تَأْخُذُونَهَا فَعَجَّلَ لَكُمْ هَٰذِهِ
وَكَفَّ أَيْدِيَ النَّاسِ عَنْكُمْ ۚ
وَلِتَكُونَ آيَةً لِلْمُؤْمِنِينَ وَيَهْدِيَكُمْ
صِرَاطًا مُسْتَقِيمًا ٢٠

21. And other gains (there are), which are not within your power, but which Allah has compassed and Allah has power over all things.

21. Wa ukhraa lam taqdiroo 'alayhaa qad aḥaaṭal-laahu bihaa; wa kaanal-laahu 'alaa kulli shay'in Qadeeraa.

وَأُخْرَىٰ لَمْ تَقْدِرُوا عَلَيْهَا قَدْ
أَحَاطَ اللَّهُ بِهَا ۚ وَكَانَ اللَّهُ عَلَىٰ
كُلِّ شَيْءٍ قَدِيرًا ٢١

22. If the Unbelievers should fight you, they would certainly

22. Wa law qaatalakumul-lazeena kafaroo la-wallawul-

وَلَوْ قَاتَلَكُمُ الَّذِينَ كَفَرُوا لَوَلَّوُا

Ikhfa اخفاء | Ghunna غُنّہ | Ikhfa Meem Saakin اخفاء میم ساکن | Idghaam ادغام | Qalqala قلقلہ | Qalb قلب | Idghaam Meem Saakin ادغام میم ساکن

الْأَدْبَارَ ثُمَّ لَا يَجِدُونَ وَلِيًّا
وَّلَا نَصِيرًا ﴿٢٢﴾

adbaara summa laa yajidoona waliyyañw-wa laa naṣeeraa.

turn their backs; then would they find neither protector nor helper.

سُنَّةَ اللَّهِ الَّتِي قَدْ خَلَتْ مِن
قَبْلُ ۖ وَلَن تَجِدَ لِسُنَّةِ اللَّهِ
تَبْدِيلًا ﴿٢٣﴾

23. Sunnatal-laahil-latee qad khalat min qablu wa lan tajida lisunnatil-laahi tabdeelaa.

23. (Such has been) the practice (approved) of Allah already in the past: no change will you find in the practice (approved) of Allah.

وَهُوَ الَّذِي كَفَّ أَيْدِيَهُمْ عَنكُمْ
وَأَيْدِيَكُمْ عَنْهُم بِبَطْنِ مَكَّةَ
مِن بَعْدِ أَنْ أَظْفَرَكُمْ عَلَيْهِمْ ۚ
وَكَانَ اللَّهُ بِمَا تَعْمَلُونَ بَصِيرًا ﴿٢٤﴾

24. Wa Huwal-lazee kaffa aydiyahum 'ankum wa aydiyakum 'anhum bibaṭni Makkata mim ba'di an aẓfarakum 'alayhim; wa kaanal-laahu bimaa ta'maloona Baṣeeraa.

24. And it is He Who has restrained their hands from you and your hands from them in the midst of Makka, after that He gave you the victory over them. And Allah sees well all that you do.

هُمُ الَّذِينَ كَفَرُوا وَصَدُّوكُمْ عَنِ
الْمَسْجِدِ الْحَرَامِ وَالْهَدْيَ مَعْكُوفًا
أَن يَبْلُغَ مَحِلَّهُ ۚ وَلَوْلَا رِجَالٌ
مُّؤْمِنُونَ وَنِسَاءٌ مُّؤْمِنَاتٌ لَّمْ
تَعْلَمُوهُمْ أَن تَطَئُوهُمْ فَتُصِيبَكُم
مِّنْهُم مَّعَرَّةٌ بِغَيْرِ عِلْمٍ ۖ لِّيُدْخِلَ
اللَّهُ فِي رَحْمَتِهِ مَن يَشَاءُ ۚ لَوْ
تَزَيَّلُوا لَعَذَّبْنَا الَّذِينَ كَفَرُوا
مِنْهُمْ عَذَابًا أَلِيمًا ﴿٢٥﴾

25. Humul-lazeena kafaroo wa ṣaddookum 'anil-Masjidil-Ḥaraami walhadya ma'koofan añy-yablugha maḥillah; wa law laa rijaalum-mu'minoona wa nisaaa'um-mu'minaatul-lam ta'lamoohum an taṭa'oohum fatuṣeebakum minhum ma'ar-ratum bighayri 'ilmin liyud-khilal-laahu fee raḥmatihee mañy-yashaaa'; law tazayyaloo la'azzabnal-lazeena kafaroo minhum 'azaaban aleemaa.

25. They are the ones who denied Revelation and hindered you from the Sacred Mosque and obstructed the sacrificial animals, detained from reaching their place of sacrifice. Had there not been believing men and believing women whom you did not know that you were trampling down and on whose account a crime would have accrued to you without (your) knowledge, (Allah would have allowed you to force your way, but He held back your hands) that He may admit to His Mercy whom He will. If they had been apart, We should certainly have punished the Unbelievers among them with a grievous Punishment.

إِذْ جَعَلَ الَّذِينَ كَفَرُوا فِي
قُلُوبِهِمُ الْحَمِيَّةَ حَمِيَّةَ الْجَاهِلِيَّةِ
فَأَنزَلَ اللَّهُ سَكِينَتَهُ عَلَىٰ رَسُولِهِ
وَعَلَى الْمُؤْمِنِينَ وَأَلْزَمَهُمْ كَلِمَةَ
التَّقْوَىٰ وَكَانُوا أَحَقَّ بِهَا وَأَهْلَهَا ۚ
وَكَانَ اللَّهُ بِكُلِّ شَيْءٍ عَلِيمًا ﴿٢٦﴾

26. Iz ja'alal-lazeena kafaroo fee quloobihimul-ḥamiyyata ḥamiyyatal-Jaahiliyyati fa-anzalal-laahu sakeenatahoo 'alaa Rasoolihee wa 'alal-mu'mineena wa alzamahum kalimatat-taqwaa wa kaanooo aḥaqqa bihaa wa ahlahaa; wa kaanal-laahu bikulli shay'in 'Aleemaa. **(Section 3)**

26. While the Unbelievers got up in their hearts heat and cant - the heat and cant of ignorance,- Allah sent down His Tranquillity to His Apostle and to the Believers, and made them stick close to the command of self-restraint; and well were they entitled to it and worthy of it. And Allah has full knowledge of all things.

لَّقَدْ صَدَقَ اللَّهُ رَسُولَهُ الرُّؤْيَا
بِالْحَقِّ ۖ لَتَدْخُلُنَّ الْمَسْجِدَ الْحَرَامَ

27. Laqad ṣadaqal-laahu Rasoolahur-ru'yaa bilḥaqq, latadkhulunnal-Masjidal-Ḥaraama

27. Truly did Allah fulfil the vision for His Apostle: you shall enter the Sacred Mosque,

Ikhfa اخفاء · Ghunna غُنّہ · Ikhfa Meem Saakin اخفاء میم ساکن · Idghaam ادغام · Qalqala قلقلہ · Qalb قلب · Idghaam Meem Saakin ادغام میم ساکن

if Allah wills, with minds secure, heads shaved, hair cut short, and without fear. For He knew what you knew not, and He granted, besides this, a speedy victory.

in shaaa'al-laahu aamineena muḥalliqeena ru'oosakum wa muqaṣṣireena laa takhaafoona fa'alima maa lam ta'lamoo faja'ala min dooni zaalika fat-ḥan qareebaa.

إِن شَآءَ ٱللَّهُ ءَامِنِينَ مُحَلِّقِينَ
رُءُوسَكُمْ وَمُقَصِّرِينَ لَا تَخَافُونَ
فَعَلِمَ مَا لَمْ تَعْلَمُوا۟ فَجَعَلَ مِن
دُونِ ذَٰلِكَ فَتْحًا قَرِيبًا ﴿٢٧﴾

28. It is He Who has sent His Apostle with Guidance and the Religion of Truth, to proclaim it over all religion: and enough is Allah for a Witness.

28. Huwal-lazeee arsala Rasoolahoo bilhudaa wa deenil-ḥaqqi liyuẓhirahoo 'alad-deeni kullih; wa kafaa billaahi Sha-heedaa.

هُوَ ٱلَّذِىٓ أَرْسَلَ رَسُولَهُۥ بِٱلْهُدَىٰ
وَدِينِ ٱلْحَقِّ لِيُظْهِرَهُۥ عَلَى ٱلدِّينِ
كُلِّهِۦ ۚ وَكَفَىٰ بِٱللَّهِ شَهِيدًا ﴿٢٨﴾

29. Muhammad is the apostle of Allah; and those who are with him are strong against Unbelievers, (but) compassionate amongst each other. you will see them bow and prostrate themselves (in prayer), seeking Grace from Allah and (His) Good Pleasure. On their faces are their marks, (being) the traces of their prostration. This is their similitude in the Taurat; and their similitude in the Gospel is: like a seed which sends forth its blade, then makes it strong; it then becomes thick, and it stands on its own stem, (filling) the sowers with wonder and delight. As a result, it fills the Unbelievers with rage at them. Allah has promised those among them who believe and do righteous deeds forgiveness, and a great Reward.

29. Muhammadur-Rasoolul-laah; wallazeena ma'ahooo ashiddaaa'u 'alal-kuffaari ruḥa-maaa'u baynahum taraahum rukka'an sujjadañy-yabtaghoona faḍlam-minal-laahi wa riḍwaa-nan seemaahum fee wujoohi-him min asaris-sujood; zaalika masaluhum fit-Tawraah; wa masaluhum fil-Injeeli kazar'in akhraja shaṭ-'ahoo fa-'aaza-rahoo fastaghlaẓa fastawaa 'alaa sooqihee yu'jibuz-zurraa'a liyagheeẓa bihimul-kuffaar; wa'adal-laahul-lazeena aamanoo wa 'amiluṣ-ṣaaliḥaati minhum maghfiratañw-wa ajran 'aẓeemaa. **(Section 4)**

مُّحَمَّدٌ رَّسُولُ ٱللَّهِ ۚ وَٱلَّذِينَ مَعَهُۥٓ
أَشِدَّآءُ عَلَى ٱلْكُفَّارِ رُحَمَآءُ بَيْنَهُمْ
تَرَىٰهُمْ رُكَّعًا سُجَّدًا يَبْتَغُونَ فَضْلًا
مِّنَ ٱللَّهِ وَرِضْوَٰنًا ۖ سِيمَاهُمْ فِى
وُجُوهِهِم مِّنْ أَثَرِ ٱلسُّجُودِ ۚ ذَٰلِكَ
مَثَلُهُمْ فِى ٱلتَّوْرَىٰةِ ۚ وَمَثَلُهُمْ
فِى ٱلْإِنجِيلِ كَزَرْعٍ أَخْرَجَ شَطْـَٔهُۥ
فَـَٔازَرَهُۥ فَٱسْتَغْلَظَ فَٱسْتَوَىٰ عَلَىٰ
سُوقِهِۦ يُعْجِبُ ٱلزُّرَّاعَ لِيَغِيظَ بِهِمُ
ٱلْكُفَّارَ ۗ وَعَدَ ٱللَّهُ ٱلَّذِينَ ءَامَنُوا۟
وَعَمِلُوا۟ ٱلصَّٰلِحَٰتِ مِنْهُم مَّغْفِرَةً
وَأَجْرًا عَظِيمًۢا ﴿٢٩﴾ ع ٤

معانقة ٥ عند المتاخرين ١٢

49. The Inner Apartments

In the name of Allah, Most Gracious, Most Merciful.

Sûrat al-Ḥujurât–49

(Revealed at Madinah)

Bismillaahir Raḥmaanir Raḥeem

(٤٩) سُورَةُ ٱلْحُجُرٰتِ مَدَنِيَّةٌ (١٠٦)

بِسْمِ ٱللَّهِ ٱلرَّحْمَٰنِ ٱلرَّحِيمِ

1. O You who believe! Put not yourselves forward before Allah and His Apostle; but fear Allah: for Allah is He Who hears and knows all things.

1. Yaa ayyuhal-lazeena aamanoo laa tuqaddimoo bayna yada-yil-laahi wa Rasoolihee wattaqul-laah; innal-laaha Samee'un 'Aleem.

يَٰٓأَيُّهَا ٱلَّذِينَ ءَامَنُوا۟ لَا تُقَدِّمُوا۟
بَيْنَ يَدَىِ ٱللَّهِ وَرَسُولِهِۦ ۖ وَٱتَّقُوا۟
ٱللَّهَ ۚ إِنَّ ٱللَّهَ سَمِيعٌ عَلِيمٌ ﴿١﴾

2. O you who believe! Raise not your voices above the voice of the Prophet, nor speak aloud to him in talk,

2. Yaaa ayyuhal-lazeena aamanoo laa tarfa'ooo aṣwaa-takum fawqa ṣawtin Nabiyyi wa laa

يَٰٓأَيُّهَا ٱلَّذِينَ ءَامَنُوا۟ لَا تَرْفَعُوٓا۟
أَصْوَٰتَكُمْ فَوْقَ صَوْتِ ٱلنَّبِىِّ وَلَا

as you may speak aloud to one another, lest your deeds become vain and you perceive not.

tajharoo lahoo bilqawli kajahri ba‘ḍikum liba‘ḍin an taḥbaṭa a‘maalukum wa antum laa tash‘uroon.

تَجْهَرُوْا لَهٗ بِالْقَوْلِ كَجَهْرِ بَعْضِكُمْ
لِبَعْضٍ اَنْ تَحْبَطَ اَعْمَالُكُمْ
وَاَنْتُمْ لَا تَشْعُرُوْنَ ۝٢

3. Those that lower their voices in the presence of Allah's Apostle,- their hearts has Allah tested for piety: for them is Forgiveness and a great Reward.

3. Innal-lazeena yaghuḍ-ḍoona aṣwaatahum ‘inda Rasoolil-laahi ulaaa'ikal-lazeenam-taḥanal-laahu quloobahum littaqwaa; lahum-maghfiratuñw-wa ajrun ‘aẓeem.

اِنَّ الَّذِيْنَ يَغُضُّوْنَ اَصْوَاتَهُمْ
عِنْدَ رَسُوْلِ اللّٰهِ اُولٰٓئِكَ الَّذِيْنَ
امْتَحَنَ اللّٰهُ قُلُوْبَهُمْ لِلتَّقْوٰى ؕ
لَهُمْ مَّغْفِرَةٌ وَّاَجْرٌ عَظِيْمٌ ۝٣

4. Those who shout out to you from without the inner apartments - most of them lack understanding.

4. Innal-lazeena yunaadoo-naka miñw-waraaa'il-ḥujuraati aksaruhum laa ya‘qiloon.

اِنَّ الَّذِيْنَ يُنَادُوْنَكَ مِنْ وَّرَآءِ
الْحُجُرٰتِ اَكْثَرُهُمْ لَا يَعْقِلُوْنَ ۝٤

5. If only they had patience until you couldst come out to them, it would be best for them: but Allah is Oft-Forgiving, Most Merciful.

5. Wa law annahum ṣabaroo ḥattaa takhruja ilayhim lakaana khayral-lahum; wallaahu Gha-foorur-Raḥeem.

وَلَوْ اَنَّهُمْ صَبَرُوْا حَتّٰى تَخْرُجَ
اِلَيْهِمْ لَكَانَ خَيْرًا لَّهُمْ ؕ وَاللّٰهُ
غَفُوْرٌ رَّحِيْمٌ ۝٥

6. O you who believe! If a wicked person comes to you with any news, ascertain the truth, lest you harm people unwittingly, and afterwards become full of repentance for what you have done.

6. Yaaa ayyuhal-lazeena aamanooo in jaaa'akum faasi-qum binaba-in fatabayyanooo an tuṣeeboo qawmam bija-haalatin fatuṣbiḥoo ‘alaa maa fa‘altum naadimeen.

يٰۤاَيُّهَا الَّذِيْنَ اٰمَنُوْۤا اِنْ جَآءَكُمْ
فَاسِقٌۢ بِنَبَاٍ فَتَبَيَّنُوْۤا اَنْ تُصِيْبُوْا
قَوْمًۢا بِجَهَالَةٍ فَتُصْبِحُوْا عَلٰى مَا
فَعَلْتُمْ نٰدِمِيْنَ ۝٦

7. And know that among you is Allah's Apostle: were he, in many matters, to follow your (wishes), you would certainly fall into misfortune: But Allah has endeared the Faith to you, and has made it beautiful in your hearts, and He has made hateful to you Unbelief, wickedness, and rebellion: such indeed are those who walk in righteousness;-

7. Wa‘lamooo anna feekum Rasoolal-laah; law yuṭee‘ukum fee kaseerim-minal-amri la‘anittum wa laakinnal-laaha ḥabbaba ilaykumul-eemaana wa zayyanahoo fee quloobikum wa karraha ilaykumul-kufra walfusooqa wal‘iṣyaan; ulaaa'ika humur-raashidoon.

وَاعْلَمُوْۤا اَنَّ فِيْكُمْ رَسُوْلَ اللّٰهِ ؕ
لَوْ يُطِيْعُكُمْ فِيْ كَثِيْرٍ مِّنَ الْاَمْرِ
لَعَنِتُّمْ وَلٰكِنَّ اللّٰهَ حَبَّبَ اِلَيْكُمُ
الْاِيْمَانَ وَزَيَّنَهٗ فِيْ قُلُوْبِكُمْ وَكَرَّهَ
اِلَيْكُمُ الْكُفْرَ وَالْفُسُوْقَ وَالْعِصْيَانَ ؕ
اُولٰٓئِكَ هُمُ الرّٰشِدُوْنَ ۝٧

8. A Grace and Favour from Allah; and Allah is full of Knowledge and Wisdom.

8. Faḍlam-minal-laahi wa ni‘mah; wallaahu ‘Aleemun Ḥakeem.

فَضْلًا مِّنَ اللّٰهِ وَنِعْمَةً ؕ وَاللّٰهُ
عَلِيْمٌ حَكِيْمٌ ۝٨

9. If two parties among the Believers fall into a quarrel, make you peace between them: but if

9. Wa in ṭaaa'ifataani minal-mu'mineenaq-tataloo fa-aṣliḥoo baynahumaa fa-im-

وَاِنْ طَآئِفَتٰنِ مِنَ الْمُؤْمِنِيْنَ
اقْتَتَلُوْا فَاَصْلِحُوْا بَيْنَهُمَا ۚ فَاِنْۢ

بَغَتۡ اِحۡدٰىهُمَا عَلَى الۡاُخۡرٰى
فَقَاتِلُوا الَّتِىۡ تَبۡغِىۡ حَتّٰى تَفِىۡٓءَ اِلٰٓى
اَمۡرِ اللّٰهِ ۚ فَاِنۡ فَآءَتۡ فَاَصۡلِحُوۡا
بَيۡنَهُمَا بِالۡعَدۡلِ وَاَقۡسِطُوۡا ؕ
اِنَّ اللّٰهَ يُحِبُّ الۡمُقۡسِطِيۡنَ ﴿۹﴾

baghat iḥdaahumaa 'alal-ukhraa faqaatilul-latee tabghee ḥattaa tafee'a ilaaa amril-laah; fa-in faaa'at fa-aṣliḥoo baynahumaa bil'adli wa aqsiṭoo innal-laaha yuḥibbul-muqsiṭeen.

one of them transgresses beyond bounds against the other, then fight you (all) against the one that transgresses until it complies with the command of Allah; But if it complies, then make peace between them with justice, and be fair: For Allah loves those who are fair (and just).

اِنَّمَا الۡمُؤۡمِنُوۡنَ اِخۡوَةٌ فَاَصۡلِحُوۡا
بَيۡنَ اَخَوَيۡكُمۡ وَاتَّقُوا اللّٰهَ لَعَلَّكُمۡ
تُرۡحَمُوۡنَ ﴿۱۰﴾

10. Innamal-mu'minoona ikhwatun fa-aṣliḥoo bayna akhawaykum wattaqul-laaha la'allakum turḥamoon.

(Section 1)

10. The Believers are but a single Brotherhood: So make peace and reconciliation between your two (contending) brothers; and fear Allah, that you may receive Mercy.

يٰۤاَيُّهَا الَّذِيۡنَ اٰمَنُوۡا لَا يَسۡخَرۡ
قَوۡمٌ مِّنۡ قَوۡمٍ عَسٰٓى اَنۡ يَّكُوۡنُوۡا
خَيۡرًا مِّنۡهُمۡ وَلَا نِسَآءٌ مِّنۡ نِّسَآءٍ
عَسٰٓى اَنۡ يَّكُنَّ خَيۡرًا مِّنۡهُنَّ ۚ
وَلَا تَلۡمِزُوۡۤا اَنۡفُسَكُمۡ وَلَا تَنَابَزُوۡا
بِالۡاَلۡقَابِ ؕ بِئۡسَ الِاسۡمُ الۡفُسُوۡقُ
بَعۡدَ الۡاِيۡمَانِ ۚ وَمَنۡ لَّمۡ يَتُبۡ
فَاُولٰٓئِكَ هُمُ الظّٰلِمُوۡنَ ﴿۱۱﴾

11. Yaaa ayyuhal-lazeena aamanoo laa yaskhar qawmum min qawmin 'asaaa añy-yakoonoo khayram minhum wa laa nisaaa'um min nisaaa'in 'Asaaa añy-Yakunna khayram-minhunna wa laa talmizooo anfusakum wa laa tanaabazoo bil-alqaab; bi'sal-ismul-fusooqu ba'dal-eemaan; wa mal-lam yatub fa-ulaaa'ika humuẓ-ẓaalimoon.

11. O you who believe! Let not some men among you laugh at others: It may be that the (latter) are better than the (former): Nor let some women laugh at others: It may be that the (latter are better than the (former): Nor defame nor be sarcastic to each other, nor call each other by (offensive) nicknames: Ill-seeming is a name connoting wickedness, (to be used of one) after he has believed: And those who do not desist are (indeed) doing wrong.

يٰۤاَيُّهَا الَّذِيۡنَ اٰمَنُوا اجۡتَنِبُوۡا
كَثِيۡرًا مِّنَ الظَّنِّ ۖ اِنَّ بَعۡضَ
الظَّنِّ اِثۡمٌ وَّلَا تَجَسَّسُوۡا وَلَا
يَغۡتَبْ بَّعۡضُكُمۡ بَعۡضًا ؕ اَيُحِبُّ
اَحَدُكُمۡ اَنۡ يَّاۡكُلَ لَحۡمَ اَخِيۡهِ
مَيۡتًا فَكَرِهۡتُمُوۡهُ ؕ وَاتَّقُوا اللّٰهَ ؕ
اِنَّ اللّٰهَ تَوَّابٌ رَّحِيۡمٌ ﴿۱۲﴾

12. Yaaa ayyuhal-lazeena aamanuj-taniboo kaseeram-minaẓ-ẓanni inna ba'ḍaẓ-ẓanni ismuñw-wa laa tajassasoo wa la yaghtab ba'ḍukum ba'ḍaa; a yuḥibbu aḥadukum añy-yaåkula laḥma akheehi maytan fakarih-tumooh; wattaqul-laah; innal-laaha Tawwaabur-Raḥeem.

12. O you who believe! Avoid suspicion as much (as possible): for suspicion in some cases is a sin: And spy not on each other behind their backs. Would any of you like to eat the flesh of his dead brother? No, you would abhor it...But fear Allah: For Allah is Oft-Returning, Most Merciful.

يٰۤاَيُّهَا النَّاسُ اِنَّا خَلَقۡنٰكُمۡ مِّنۡ
ذَكَرٍ وَّاُنۡثٰى وَجَعَلۡنٰكُمۡ شُعُوۡبًا
وَّقَبَآئِلَ لِتَعَارَفُوۡا ؕ اِنَّ اَكۡرَمَكُمۡ

13. Yaaa ayyuhan-naasu innaa khalaqnaakum min zakariñw-wa unsaa wa ja'alnaakum shu'oobañw-wa qabaaa'ila lita'aarafoo inna akramakum

13. O mankind! We created you from a single (pair) of a male and a female, and made you into nations and tribes, that you may know each other (not that you may despise (each other). Verily the most honoured of you in the sight of

Ikhfa اخفاء | Ghunna غُنّہ | Ikhfa Meem Saakin اخفاء میم ساکن | Idghaam ادغام | Qalqala قلقلہ | Qalb قلب | Idghaam Meem Saakin ادغام میم ساکن

Allah is (he who Is) the most righteous of you. And Allah has full knowledge and is well acquainted (with all things).

'indal-laahi atqaakum innal-laaha 'Aleemun khabeer

عِندَ اللّٰهِ اَتْقٰكُمْ ۭ اِنَّ اللّٰهَ
عَلِيْمٌ خَبِيْرٌ ﴿١٣﴾

14. The desert Arabs say, "We believe." Say, "You have no faith; but you (only)say, 'We have submitted our wills to Allah,' For not yet has Faith entered your hearts. But if ye obey Allah and His Apostle, He will not belittle any of your deeds: for Allah is Oft-Forgiving, Most Merciful."

14. Qaalatil-A'raabu aamannaa qul lam tu'minoo wa laakin qoolooo aslamnaa wa lamma yadkhulil-eemaanu fee quloobikum wa in tuṭee'ul-laaha wa Rasoolahoo laa yalitkum min a'maalikum shay'aa; innal-laaha Ghafoorur-Raḥeem.

قَالَتِ الْاَعْرَابُ اٰمَنَّا ۭ قُلْ لَّمْ
تُؤْمِنُوْا وَلٰكِنْ قُوْلُوْٓا اَسْلَمْنَا
وَلَمَّا يَدْخُلِ الْاِيْمَانُ فِيْ قُلُوْبِكُمْ ۭ
وَاِنْ تُطِيْعُوا اللّٰهَ وَرَسُوْلَهٗ لَا
يَلِتْكُمْ مِّنْ اَعْمَالِكُمْ شَيْـًٔا ۭ
اِنَّ اللّٰهَ غَفُوْرٌ رَّحِيْمٌ ﴿١٤﴾

15. Only those are Believers who have believed in Allah and His Apostle, and have never since doubted, but have striven with their belongings and their persons in the Cause of Allah: Such are the sincere ones.

15. Innamal-mu'minoonal-lazeena aamanoo billaahi wa Rasoolihee summa lam yartaaboo wa jaahadoo bi-amwaalihim wa anfusihim fee sabeelil-laah; ulaaa'ika humuṣ-ṣaadiqoon.

اِنَّمَا الْمُؤْمِنُوْنَ الَّذِيْنَ اٰمَنُوْا بِاللّٰهِ
وَرَسُوْلِهٖ ثُمَّ لَمْ يَرْتَابُوْا وَجٰهَدُوْا
بِاَمْوَالِهِمْ وَاَنْفُسِهِمْ فِيْ سَبِيْلِ
اللّٰهِ ۭ اُولٰۗىِٕكَ هُمُ الصّٰدِقُوْنَ ﴿١٥﴾

16. Say: "What! Will you instruct Allah about your religion? But Allah knows all that is in the heavens and on earth: He has full knowledge of all things.

16. Qul atu'allimoonal-laaha bideenikum wallaahu ya'lamu maa fis-samaawaati wa maa fil-arḍ; wallaahu bikulli shay'in 'Aleem.

قُلْ اَتُعَلِّمُوْنَ اللّٰهَ بِدِيْنِكُمْ ۭ وَاللّٰهُ
يَعْلَمُ مَا فِي السَّمٰوٰتِ وَمَا فِي
الْاَرْضِ ۭ وَاللّٰهُ بِكُلِّ شَيْءٍ عَلِيْمٌ ﴿١٦﴾

17. They impress on you as a favour that they have embraced Islam. Say, "Count not your Islam as a favour upon me: No, Allah has conferred a favour upon you that He has guided you to the faith, if you be true and sincere.

17. Yamunnoona 'alayka an aslamoo qul laa tamunnoo 'alayya Islaamakum balillaahu yamunnu 'alaykum an hadaakum lil-eemaani in kuntum ṣaadiqeen.

يَمُنُّوْنَ عَلَيْكَ اَنْ اَسْلَمُوْا ۭ قُلْ
لَّا تَمُنُّوْا عَلَيَّ اِسْلَامَكُمْ ۚ بَلِ
اللّٰهُ يَمُنُّ عَلَيْكُمْ اَنْ هَدٰىكُمْ
لِلْاِيْمَانِ اِنْ كُنْتُمْ صٰدِقِيْنَ ﴿١٧﴾

18. "Verily Allah knows the secrets of the heavens and the earth: and Allah Sees well all that you do."

18. Innal-laaha ya'lamu ghaybas-samaawaati wal-arḍ; wallaahu baṣeerum bimaa ta'maloon. **(Section 2)**

اِنَّ اللّٰهَ يَعْلَمُ غَيْبَ السَّمٰوٰتِ
وَالْاَرْضِ ۭ وَاللّٰهُ بَصِيْرٌۢ بِمَا
تَعْمَلُوْنَ ﴿١٨﴾ ع ٢

50. Qaf

In the name of Allah, Most Gracious, Most Merciful.

Sûrat Qâf–50

(Revealed at Makkah)

Bismillaahir Raḥmaanir Raḥeem

(٥٠) سُوْرَةُ قٓ مَكِّيَّةٌ (٣٤)

بِسْمِ اللّٰهِ الرَّحْمٰنِ الرَّحِيْمِ

1. *Qaf*. By the Glorious Qur'an (Thou art God's Apostle).

1. Qaaaf; wal-Qur-aanil-Majeed.

قٓ ۣ وَالْقُرْاٰنِ الْمَجِيْدِ ﴿١﴾

2. But they wonder that there has come to them a Warner

2. Bal 'ajibooo an jaaa'ahum munzirum-

بَلْ عَجِبُوْٓا اَنْ جَاۗءَهُمْ مُّنْذِرٌ

Ikhfa اخفاء | Ghunna غنّہ | Ikhfa Meem Saakin اخفاء میم ساکن | Idghaam ادغام | Qalqala قلقلہ | Qalb قلب | Idghaam Meem Saakin ادغام میم ساکن

from among themselves. So the Unbelievers say: "This is a wonderful thing

minhum faqaalal-kaafiroona haazaa shay'un 'ajeeb.

مِّنْهُمْ فَقَالَ الْكٰفِرُوْنَ هٰذَا
شَيْءٌ عَجِيْبٌ ۝٢

3. "What! When we die and become dust, (shall we live again?) That is a (sort of) return far (from our understanding)."

3. 'A-izaa mitnaa wa kunnaa turaaban zaalika raj'um ba'eed.

ءَاِذَا مِتْنَا وَكُنَّا تُرَابًا ۚ ذٰلِكَ
رَجْعٌ بَعِيْدٌ ۝٣

4. We already know how much of them the earth takes away: With Us is a record guarding (the full account).

4. Qad 'alimnaa maa tanquṣul-arḍu minhum wa 'indanaa Kitaabun Ḥafeez.

قَدْ عَلِمْنَا مَا تَنْقُصُ الْاَرْضُ
مِنْهُمْ ۚ وَعِنْدَنَا كِتٰبٌ حَفِيْظٌ ۝٤

5. But they deny the Truth when it comes to them: so they are in a confused state.

5. Bal kazzaboo bilḥaqqi lammaa jaaa'ahum fahum feee amrim-mareej.

بَلْ كَذَّبُوْا بِالْحَقِّ لَمَّا جَآءَهُمْ
فَهُمْ فِيْٓ اَمْرٍ مَّرِيْجٍ ۝٥

6. Do they not look at the sky above them?- How We have made it and adorned it, and there are no flaws in it?

6. Afalam yanzurooo ilas-samaaa'i fawqahum kayfa banaynaahaa wa zayyannaahaa wa maa lahaa min furooj.

اَفَلَمْ يَنْظُرُوْٓا اِلَى السَّمَآءِ فَوْقَهُمْ
كَيْفَ بَنَيْنٰهَا وَزَيَّنّٰهَا وَمَا لَهَا مِنْ
فُرُوْجٍ ۝٦

7. And the earth- We have spread it out, and set thereon mountains standing firm, and produced therein every kind of beautiful growth (in pairs)-

7. Wal-arḍa madadnaahaa wa alqaynaa feehaa rawaasiya wa ambatnaa feehaa min kulli zawjim baheej.

وَالْاَرْضَ مَدَدْنٰهَا وَاَلْقَيْنَا فِيْهَا
رَوَاسِيَ وَاَنْۢبَتْنَا فِيْهَا مِنْ كُلِّ
زَوْجٍ بَهِيْجٍ ۝٧

8. To be observed and commemorated by every devotee turning (to Allah).

8. Tabṣiratañw-wa zikraa likulli 'abdim-muneeb.

تَبْصِرَةً وَّذِكْرٰى لِكُلِّ عَبْدٍ
مُّنِيْبٍ ۝٨

9. And We send down from the sky rain charted with blessing, and We produce therewith gardens and Grain for harvests;

9. Wa nazzalnaa minas-samaaa'i maaa'am mubaarakan fa-ambatnaa bihee jannaatiñw-wa ḥabbal-ḥaṣeed.

وَنَزَّلْنَا مِنَ السَّمَآءِ مَآءً مُّبٰرَكًا
فَاَنْۢبَتْنَا بِهٖ جَنّٰتٍ وَّحَبَّ الْحَصِيْدِ ۝٩

10. And tall (and stately) palm-trees, with shoots of fruit-stalks, piled one over another;-

10. Wannakhla baasiqaatil-lahaa ṭal'un-naḍeed.

وَالنَّخْلَ بٰسِقٰتٍ لَّهَا طَلْعٌ نَّضِيْدٌ ۝١٠

11. As sustenance for (Allah's) Servants;- and We give (new) life therewith to land that is dead: Thus will be the Resurrection.

11. Rizqal-lil'ibaad, wa aḥyaynaa bihee baldatam-maytaa; kazaalikal-khurooj.

رِّزْقًا لِّلْعِبَادِ ۙ وَاَحْيَيْنَا بِهٖ بَلْدَةً
مَّيْتًا ۚ كَذٰلِكَ الْخُرُوْجُ ۝١١

12. Before them was denied (the Hereafter) by the People of Noah, the Companions of the Rass, the Thamud,

12. Kazzabat qablahum qawmu Nooḥiñw-wa Aṣḥaabur-Rassi wa Samood.

كَذَّبَتْ قَبْلَهُمْ قَوْمُ نُوْحٍ وَّاَصْحٰبُ
الرَّسِّ وَثَمُوْدُ ۝١٢

13. The 'Ad, Pharaoh, the brethren of Lut,

13. Wa 'Aaduñw-wa Fir'awnu wa ikhwaanu Looṭ.

وَعَادٌ وَّفِرْعَوْنُ وَاِخْوَانُ لُوْطٍ ۝١٣

14. The Companions of the Wood, and the People of Tubba'; each one (of them) rejected the apostles, and My warning was duly fulfilled (in them).

14. Wa Aṣḥaabul-Aykati wa qawmu Tubba'; kullun kazzabar-Rusula faḥaqqa wa'eed.

وَّاَصْحٰبُ الْاَيْكَةِ وَقَوْمُ تُبَّعٍ ۚ كُلٌّ
كَذَّبَ الرُّسُلَ فَحَقَّ وَعِيْدِ ۝١٤

Ikhfa اخفاء | Ghunna غُنّہ | Ikhfa Meem Saakin اخفاء میم ساکن | Idghaam ادغام | Qalqala قلقلہ | Qalb قلب | Idghaam Meem Saakin ادغام میم ساکن

15. Were We then weary with the first Creation, that they should be in confused doubt about a new Creation?

16. It was We Who created man, and We know what dark suggestions his soul makes to him: for We are nearer to him than (his) jugular vein.

17. Behold, two (guardian angels) appointed to learn (his doings) learn (and noted them), one sitting on the right and one on the left,

18. Not a word does he utter but there is a sentinel by him, ready (to note it).

19. And the stupor of death will bring Truth (before his eyes): "This was the thing which thou wast trying to escape!"

20. And the Trumpet shall be blown: that will be the Day whereof Warning (had been given).

21. And there will come forth every soul: with each will be an (angel) to drive, and an (angel) to bear witness.

22. (It will be said:) "You were heedless of this; now have We removed your veil, and sharp is your sight this Day!"

23. And his Companion will say: "Here is (his Record) ready with me!"

24. (The sentence will be:) "Throw, both of you into Hell every contumacious Rejecter (of Allah)!-

25. "Who forbade what was good, transgressed all bounds, cast doubts and suspicions;

26. "Who set up another god beside Allah: Throw him into a severe Chastisement."

27. His Companion will say: "Our Lord! I did not make him

15. Afa'a-yeenaa bilkhalqil-awwal; bal hum fee labsim-min khalqin jadeed. **(Section 1)**

16. Wa laqad khalaqnal-insaana wa na'lamu maa tuwaswisu bihee nafsuhoo wa Naḥnu aqrabu ilayhi min ḥablil-wareed.

17. 'Iẕ yatalaqqal-mutalaqqi-yaani 'anil-yameeni wa 'anish-shimaali qa'eed.

18. Maa yalfiẕu min qawlin illaa ladayhi raqeebun 'ateed.

19. Wa jaaa'at sakratul-mawti bilḥaqq; ẕaalika maa kunta minhu taḥeed.

20. Wa nufikha fiṣ-Ṣoor; ẕaalika yawmul-wa'eed.

21. Wa jaaa'at kullu nafsim-ma'ahaa saaa'iquñw-wa shaheed.

22. Laqad kunta fee ghaf-latim-min haaẕaa fakashafnaa 'anka ghiṭaaa'aka fabaṣarukal-Yawma ḥadeed.

23. Wa qaala qareenuhoo haaẕaa maa ladayya 'ateed.

24. Alqiyaa fee Jahannama kulla kaffaarin 'aneed.

25. Mannaa'il-lilkhayri mu'-tadim-mureeb.

26. Allaẕee ja'ala ma'al-laahi ilaahan aakhara fa-alqiyaahu fil-'aẕaabish-shadeed.

27. Qaala qareenuhoo Rab-banaa maaa aṭghaytuhoo

اَفَعَيِيْنَا بِالْخَلْقِ الْاَوَّلِ ؕ بَلْ هُمْ
فِىْ لَبْسٍ مِّنْ خَلْقٍ جَدِيْدٍ ﴿١٥﴾
وَلَقَدْ خَلَقْنَا الْاِنْسَانَ وَنَعْلَمُ
مَا تُوَسْوِسُ بِهٖ نَفْسُهٗ ۖۚ وَنَحْنُ اَقْرَبُ
اِلَيْهِ مِنْ حَبْلِ الْوَرِيْدِ ﴿١٦﴾
اِذْ يَتَلَقَّى الْمُتَلَقِّيٰنِ عَنِ الْيَمِيْنِ
وَعَنِ الشِّمَالِ قَعِيْدٌ ﴿١٧﴾
مَا يَلْفِظُ مِنْ قَوْلٍ اِلَّا لَدَيْهِ
رَقِيْبٌ عَتِيْدٌ ﴿١٨﴾
وَجَآءَتْ سَكْرَةُ الْمَوْتِ بِالْحَقِّ ؕ
ذٰلِكَ مَا كُنْتَ مِنْهُ تَحِيْدُ ﴿١٩﴾
وَنُفِخَ فِى الصُّوْرِ ؕ ذٰلِكَ يَوْمُ
الْوَعِيْدِ ﴿٢٠﴾
وَجَآءَتْ كُلُّ نَفْسٍ مَّعَهَا سَآئِقٌ
وَّشَهِيْدٌ ﴿٢١﴾
لَقَدْ كُنْتَ فِىْ غَفْلَةٍ مِّنْ هٰذَا
فَكَشَفْنَا عَنْكَ غِطَآءَكَ فَبَصَرُكَ
الْيَوْمَ حَدِيْدٌ ﴿٢٢﴾
وَقَالَ قَرِيْنُهٗ هٰذَا مَا لَدَىَّ
عَتِيْدٌ ﴿٢٣﴾
اَلْقِيَا فِىْ جَهَنَّمَ كُلَّ كَفَّارٍ
عَنِيْدٍ ﴿٢٤﴾
مَّنَّاعٍ لِّلْخَيْرِ مُعْتَدٍ مُّرِيْبٍ ﴿٢٥﴾
الَّذِىْ جَعَلَ مَعَ اللّٰهِ اِلٰهًا اٰخَرَ
فَاَلْقِيٰهُ فِى الْعَذَابِ الشَّدِيْدِ ﴿٢٦﴾
قَالَ قَرِيْنُهٗ رَبَّنَا مَاۤ اَطْغَيْتُهٗ

transgress, but he was (himself) far astray."

wa laakin kaana fee ḑalaalim ba'eed.

وَلَٰكِن كَانَ فِي ضَلَٰلٍۭ بَعِيدٍ ﴿٢٧﴾

28. He will say: "Dispute not with each other in My Presence: I had already in advance sent you Warning.

28. Qaala laa takhtaṣimoo ladayya wa qad qaddamtu ilaykum bilwa'eed.

قَالَ لَا تَخْتَصِمُوا لَدَيَّ وَقَدْ قَدَّمْتُ إِلَيْكُم بِالْوَعِيدِ ﴿٢٨﴾

29. "The Word changes not before Me, and I do not the least injustice to My Servants."

29. Maa yubaddalul-qawlu ladayya wa maaa ana biẓal-laamil-lil'abeed. **(Section 2)**

مَا يُبَدَّلُ الْقَوْلُ لَدَيَّ وَمَا أَنَا بِظَلَّٰمٍ لِّلْعَبِيدِ ﴿٢٩﴾ ع

30. That Day We will ask Hell, "Are you filled to the full?" It will say, "Are there any more (to come)?"

30. Yawma naqoolu li-Jahannama halim-talaåti wa taqoolu hal mim-mazeed.

يَوْمَ نَقُولُ لِجَهَنَّمَ هَلِ امْتَلَأْتِ وَتَقُولُ هَلْ مِن مَّزِيدٍ ﴿٣٠﴾

31. And the Garden will be brought near to the Righteous,- no more a thing distant.

31. Wa uzlifatil-Jannatu lil-muttaqeena ghayra ba'eed.

وَأُزْلِفَتِ الْجَنَّةُ لِلْمُتَّقِينَ غَيْرَ بَعِيدٍ ﴿٣١﴾

32. (A voice will say:) "This is what was promised for you,- for every one who turned (to Allah) in sincere repentance, who kept (His Law),

32. Haazaa maa too'adoona likulli awwaabin ḥafeeẓ.

هَٰذَا مَا تُوعَدُونَ لِكُلِّ أَوَّابٍ حَفِيظٍ ﴿٣٢﴾

33. "Who feared (Allah) Most Gracious Unseen, and brought a heart turned in devotion (to Him):

33. Man khashiyar-Raḥmaana bilghaybi wa jaaa'a biqalbim-muneeb.

مَّنْ خَشِيَ الرَّحْمَٰنَ بِالْغَيْبِ وَجَاءَ بِقَلْبٍ مُّنِيبٍ ﴿٣٣﴾

34. "Enter you therein in Peace and Security; this is a Day of Eternal Life!"

34. Udkhuloohaa bisalaamin zaalika yawmul-khulood.

ادْخُلُوهَا بِسَلَٰمٍ ذَٰلِكَ يَوْمُ الْخُلُودِ ﴿٣٤﴾

35. There will be for them therein all that they wish,- and more besides in Our Presence.

35. Lahum maa yashaaa'oona feehaa wa ladaynaa mazeed.

لَهُم مَّا يَشَاءُونَ فِيهَا وَلَدَيْنَا مَزِيدٌ ﴿٣٥﴾

36. But how many generations before them did We destroy (for their sins),- stronger in power than they? Then did they wander through the land: was there any place of escape (for them)?

36. Wa kam ahlaknaa qablahum min qarnin hum ashaddu minhum baṭshan fanaqqaboo fil-bilaad, hal mim-maḥeeṣ.

وَكَمْ أَهْلَكْنَا قَبْلَهُم مِّن قَرْنٍ هُمْ أَشَدُّ مِنْهُم بَطْشًا فَنَقَّبُوا فِي الْبِلَٰدِ هَلْ مِن مَّحِيصٍ ﴿٣٦﴾

37. Verily in this is a Message for any that has a heart and understanding or who gives ear and earnestly witnesses (the truth).

37. Inna fee zaalika lazikraa liman kaana lahoo qalbun aw alqas-sam'a wa huwa shaheed.

إِنَّ فِي ذَٰلِكَ لَذِكْرَىٰ لِمَن كَانَ لَهُۥ قَلْبٌ أَوْ أَلْقَى السَّمْعَ وَهُوَ شَهِيدٌ ﴿٣٧﴾

38. We created the heavens and the earth and all between them in Six Days, nor did any sense of weariness touch Us.

38. Wa laqad khalaqnas-samaawaati wal-arḑa wa maa baynahumaa fee sittati ayyaamiñw-wa maa massanaa millughoob.

وَلَقَدْ خَلَقْنَا السَّمَٰوَٰتِ وَالْأَرْضَ وَمَا بَيْنَهُمَا فِي سِتَّةِ أَيَّامٍ وَمَا مَسَّنَا مِن لُّغُوبٍ ﴿٣٨﴾

39. Bear, then, with patience, all that they say, and celebrate the praises of your Lord, before the rising of the sun

39. Faṣbir 'alaa maa yaqooloona wa sabbiḥ biḥamdi Rabbika qabla ṭuloo'ish-shamsi

فَاصْبِرْ عَلَىٰ مَا يَقُولُونَ وَسَبِّحْ بِحَمْدِ رَبِّكَ قَبْلَ طُلُوعِ الشَّمْسِ

Ikhfa اخفاء | Ghunna غنّة | Ikhfa Meem Saakin اخفاء میم ساکن | Idghaam ادغام | Qalqala قلقلہ | Qalb قلب | Idghaam Meem Saakin ادغام میم ساکن

and before (its) setting.

wa qablal-ghuroob.

وَقَبْلَ ٱلْغُرُوبِ ۝٣٩

40. And during part of the night, (also,) celebrate His praises, and (so likewise) after the postures of adoration.

40. Wa minal-layli fasabbiḥ-hu wa adbaaras-sujood.

وَمِنَ ٱلَّيْلِ فَسَبِّحْهُ وَأَدْبَٰرَ ٱلسُّجُودِ ۝٤٠

41. And listen for the Day when the Caller will call out from a place quiet near,-

41. Wastami‘ Yawma yunaa-dil-munaadi mim-makaanin qareeb.

وَٱسْتَمِعْ يَوْمَ يُنَادِ ٱلْمُنَادِ مِن مَّكَانٍ قَرِيبٍ ۝٤١

42. The Day when they will hear a (mighty) Blast in (very) truth: that will be the Day of Resurrection.

42. Yawma yasmaoonaṣ-ṣay-ḥata bilḥaqq; zaalika yawmul-khurooj.

يَوْمَ يَسْمَعُونَ ٱلصَّيْحَةَ بِٱلْحَقِّ ۚ ذَٰلِكَ يَوْمُ ٱلْخُرُوجِ ۝٤٢

43. Verily it is We Who give Life and Death; and to Us is the Final Goal-

43. Innaa Naḥnu nuḥyee wa numeetu wa ilaynal-maṣeer.

إِنَّا نَحْنُ نُحْيِۦ وَنُمِيتُ وَإِلَيْنَا ٱلْمَصِيرُ ۝٤٣

44. The Day when the Earth will be rent asunder, from (men) hurrying out: that will be a gathering together,- quite easy for Us.

44. Yawma tashaqqaqul-arḍu ‘anhum siraa‘aa; zaalika ḥash-run ‘alaynaa yaseer.

يَوْمَ تَشَقَّقُ ٱلْأَرْضُ عَنْهُمْ سِرَاعًا ۚ ذَٰلِكَ حَشْرٌ عَلَيْنَا يَسِيرٌ ۝٤٤

45. We know best what they say; and you are not one to overawe them by force. So admonish with the Qur'an such as fear My Warning!

45. Naḥnu a‘lamu bimaa yaqooloona wa maaa anta ‘alayhim bijabbaarin fazakkir bil-Qur-aani mañy-yakhaafu wa‘eed. **(Section 3)**

نَّحْنُ أَعْلَمُ بِمَا يَقُولُونَ ۖ وَمَآ أَنتَ عَلَيْهِم بِجَبَّارٍ ۖ فَذَكِّرْ بِٱلْقُرْءَانِ مَن يَخَافُ وَعِيدِ ۝٤٥

51. The Winds that Scatter

In the name of Allah, Most Gracious, Most Merciful.

Sûrat az-Zâriyât–51

(Revealed at Makkah)

Bismillaahir Raḥmaanir Raḥeem

(٥١) سُورَةُ ٱلذَّٰرِيَٰتِ مَكِّيَّةٌ (٦٧)

بِسْمِ ٱللَّهِ ٱلرَّحْمَٰنِ ٱلرَّحِيمِ

1. By the (Winds) that scatter broadcast;

1. Waz-zaariyaati zarwaa.

وَٱلذَّٰرِيَٰتِ ذَرْوًا ۝١

2. And those that lift and bear away heavy weights;

2. Falḥaamilaati wiqraa.

فَٱلْحَٰمِلَٰتِ وِقْرًا ۝٢

3. And those that flow with ease and gentleness;

3. Faljaariyaati yusraa.

فَٱلْجَٰرِيَٰتِ يُسْرًا ۝٣

4. And those that distribute and apportion by Command;

4. Falmuqassimaati amraa.

فَٱلْمُقَسِّمَٰتِ أَمْرًا ۝٤

5. Verily that which you are promised is true;

5. Innamaa too‘adoona la-ṣaadiq.

إِنَّمَا تُوعَدُونَ لَصَادِقٌ ۝٥

6. And verily Judgment and Justice must indeed come to pass.

6. Wa innad-deena la-waaqi‘.

وَإِنَّ ٱلدِّينَ لَوَٰقِعٌ ۝٦

7. By the Sky with (its) numerous Paths,

7. Wassamaaa'i zaatil-ḥu-buk.

وَٱلسَّمَآءِ ذَاتِ ٱلْحُبُكِ ۝٧

8. Truly you are in a doctrine discordant,

8. Innakum lafee qawlim-mukhtalif.

إِنَّكُمْ لَفِى قَوْلٍ مُّخْتَلِفٍ ۝٨

9. Through which are deluded (away from the Truth) such as would be deluded.

9. Yu'faku ‘anhu man ufik.

يُؤْفَكُ عَنْهُ مَنْ أُفِكَ ۝٩

10. Woe to the falsehood-mongers,-

10. Qutilal-kharraaṣoon.

قُتِلَ ٱلْخَرَّٰصُونَ ۝١٠

Ikhfa اخفاء | Ghunna غنّہ | Ikhfa Meem Saakin اخفاء میم ساکن | Idghaam ادغام | Qalqala قلقلہ | Qalb قلب | Idghaam Meem Saakin ادغام میم ساکن

11. Those who (flounder) heedless in a flood of confusion:
12. They ask, "When will be the Day of Judgment and Justice?"
13. (It will be) a Day when they will be tried (and tested) over the Fire!
14. "Taste you your trial! This is what you used to ask to be hastened!"
15. As to the Righteous, they will be in the midst of Gardens and Springs,
16. Taking joy in the things which their Lord gives them, because, before then, they lived a good life.
17. They were in the habit of sleeping but little by night,
18. And in the hour of early dawn, they (were found) praying for Forgiveness;
19. And in their wealth the beggar and the outcast had due share.
20. On the earth are signs for those of assured Faith,
21. As also in your own selves: Will you not then see?
22. And in heaven is your Sustenance, as (also) that which you are promised.
23. Then, by the Lord of heaven and earth, this is the very Truth, as much as the fact that you can speak intelligently to each other.
24. Has the story reached thee, of the honoured guests of Abraham?
25. Behold, they entered his presence, and said: "Peace!" He said, "Peace!" (and thought, "These seem) unusual people.
26. Then he turned quickly to his household, brought out a fatted calf,
27. And placed it before them.. he said, "Will you not eat?"
28. (When they did not eat), He conceived a fear of them. They said, "Fear not," and they gave him glad tidings of a son endowed with knowledge.
29. But his wife came forward (laughing) aloud: she smote

11. Allazeena hum fee ghamratin saahoon.
12. Yas'aloona ayyaana Yawmud-Deen
13. Yawma hum 'alan-Naari yuftanoon.
14. Zooqoo fitnatakum haazal-lazee kuntum bihee tasta'jiloon.
15. Innal-muttaqeena fee Jannaatiñw-wa 'uyoon.
16. Aakhizeena maaa aataahum Rabbuhum; innahum kaanoo qabla zaalika muhsineen.
17. Kaanoo qaleelam-minallayli maa yahja'oon.
18. Wa bil-ashaari hum yastaghfiroon.
19. Wa feee amwaalihim haqqul-lissaaa'ili walmahroom.
20. Wa fil-ardi Aayaatul-lilmooqineen.
21. Wa feee anfusikum; afalaa tubsiroon.
22. Wa fis-samaaa'i rizqukum wa maa too'adoon.
23. Fawa-Rabbis-samaaa'i wal-ardi innahoo lahaqqummisla maaa annakum tantiqoon.
(Section 1)
24. Hal ataaka hadeesu dayfi Ibraaheemal-mukrameen.
25. Iz dakhaloo 'alayhi faqaaloo salaaman qaala salaamun qawmum-munkaroon.
26. Faraagha ilaaa ahlihee fajaaa'a bi'ijlin sameen.
27. Faqarrabahooo ilayhim qaala alaa taákuloon.
28. Fa-awjasa minhum kheefatan qaaloo laa takhaf wa bashsharoohu bighulaamin 'aleem.
29. Fa-aqbalatim-ra-atuhoo fee sarratin fasakkat

الَّذِيْنَ هُمْ فِيْ غَمْرَةٍ سَاهُوْنَ (11)
يَسْـَٔلُوْنَ اَيَّانَ يَوْمُ الدِّيْنِ (12)
يَوْمَ هُمْ عَلَى النَّارِ يُفْتَنُوْنَ (13)
ذُوْقُوْا فِتْنَتَكُمْ ۭ هٰذَا الَّذِيْ كُنْتُمْ
بِهٖ تَسْتَعْجِلُوْنَ (14)
اِنَّ الْمُتَّقِيْنَ فِيْ جَنّٰتٍ وَّعُيُوْنٍ (15)
اٰخِذِيْنَ مَآ اٰتٰىهُمْ رَبُّهُمْ ۭ اِنَّهُمْ
كَانُوْا قَبْلَ ذٰلِكَ مُحْسِنِيْنَ (16)
كَانُوْا قَلِيْلًا مِّنَ الَّيْلِ مَا يَهْجَعُوْنَ (17)
وَبِالْاَسْحَارِ هُمْ يَسْتَغْفِرُوْنَ (18)
وَفِيْٓ اَمْوَالِهِمْ حَقٌّ لِّلسَّاۗىِٕلِ
وَالْمَحْرُوْمِ (19)
وَفِي الْاَرْضِ اٰيٰتٌ لِّلْمُوْقِنِيْنَ (20)
وَفِيْٓ اَنْفُسِكُمْ ۭ اَفَلَا تُبْصِرُوْنَ (21)
وَفِي السَّمَاۗءِ رِزْقُكُمْ وَمَا تُوْعَدُوْنَ (22)
فَوَرَبِّ السَّمَاۗءِ وَالْاَرْضِ اِنَّهٗ لَحَقٌّ
مِّثْلَ مَآ اَنَّكُمْ تَنْطِقُوْنَ (23) ع ۱۸
هَلْ اَتٰىكَ حَدِيْثُ ضَيْفِ اِبْرٰهِيْمَ
الْمُكْرَمِيْنَ (24) وقف لازم
اِذْ دَخَلُوْا عَلَيْهِ فَقَالُوْا سَلٰمًا ۭ قَالَ
سَلٰمٌ ۚ قَوْمٌ مُّنْكَرُوْنَ (25)
فَرَاغَ اِلٰٓى اَهْلِهٖ فَجَاۗءَ بِعِجْلٍ سَمِيْنٍ (26)
فَقَرَّبَهٗٓ اِلَيْهِمْ قَالَ اَلَا تَاْكُلُوْنَ (27)
فَاَوْجَسَ مِنْهُمْ خِيْفَةً ۭ قَالُوْا لَا
تَخَفْ ۭ وَبَشَّرُوْهُ بِغُلٰمٍ عَلِيْمٍ (28)
فَاَقْبَلَتِ امْرَاَتُهٗ فِيْ صَرَّةٍ فَصَكَّتْ

Ikhfa اخفاء | Ghunna غُنّہ | Ikhfa Meem Saakin اخفاء میم ساکن | Idghaam ادغام | Qalqala قلقلہ | Qalb قلب | Idghaam Meem Saakin ادغام میم ساکن

forehead and said: "A barren old woman!"

30. They said, "Even so has your Lord spoken: and He is full of Wisdom and Knowledge."

31. (Abraham) said: "And what, O you Messengers, is your errand (now)?"

32. They said, "We have been sent to a people (deep) in sin;-

33. "To bring on, on them, (a shower of) stones of clay (brimstone),

34. "Marked as from your Lord for those who trespass beyond bounds."

35. Then We evacuated those of the Believers who were there,

36. But We found not there any just (Muslim) persons except in one house:

37. And We left there a Sign for such as fear the Grievous Chastisement.

38. And in Moses (was another Sign): Behold, We sent him to Pharaoh, with authority manifest.

39. But (Pharaoh) turned back with his Chiefs, and said, "A sorcerer, or one possessed!"

40. So We took him and his forces, and threw them into the sea; and his was the cursed.

41. And in the 'Ad (people) (was another Sign): Behold, We sent against them the devastating Wind:

42. It left nothing whatever that it came up against, but reduced it to ruin and rottenness.

43. And in the Thamud (was another Sign): Behold, they were told, "Enjoy (your brief day) for a little while!"

44. But they insolently defied the Command of their Lord: So the stunning noise (of an

wajhahaa wa qaalat 'ajoozun 'aqeem.

30. Qaaloo kazaaliki qaala Rabbuki innahoo Huwal-Ḥakeemul-'Aleem.

31. Qaala famaa khaṭbukum ayyuhal-mursaloon.

32. Qaalooo innaaa ursilnaaa ilaa qawmim-mujrimeen.

33. Linursila 'alayhim ḥijaaratam-min ṭeen.

34. Musawwamatan 'inda Rabbika lilmusrifeen.

35. Fa-akhrajnaa man kaana feehaa minal-mu'mineen.

36. Famaa wajadnaa feehaa ghayra baytim-minal-muslimeen.

37. Wa taraknaa feehaaa Aayatal-lillazeena yakhaafoonal-'azaabal-aleem.

38. Wa fee Moosaaa iz arsalnaahu ilaa Fir'awna bisulṭaanim-mubeen.

39. Fatawallaa biruknihee wa qaala saaḥirun aw majnoon.

40. Fa-akhaznaahu wa junoodahoo fanabaznaahum filyammi wa huwa muleem.

41. Wa fee 'Aadin iz arsalnaa 'alayhimur-reeḥal-'aqeem.

42. Maa tazaru min shay'in atat 'alayhi illaa ja'alat-hu karrameem.

43. Wa fee Samooda iz qeela lahum tamatta'oo ḥattaa ḥeen.

44. Fa'ataw 'an amri Rabbihim fa-akhazat-humuṣ-

وَجْهَهَا وَقَالَتْ عَجُوزٌ عَقِيمٌ ٢٩
قَالُوا كَذَٰلِكِ ۙ قَالَ رَبُّكِ ۖ إِنَّهُ
هُوَ الْحَكِيمُ الْعَلِيمُ ٣٠
قَالَ فَمَا خَطْبُكُمْ أَيُّهَا الْمُرْسَلُونَ ٣١
قَالُوا إِنَّا أُرْسِلْنَا إِلَىٰ قَوْمٍ
مُّجْرِمِينَ ٣٢
لِنُرْسِلَ عَلَيْهِمْ حِجَارَةً مِّن طِينٍ ٣٣
مُّسَوَّمَةً عِندَ رَبِّكَ لِلْمُسْرِفِينَ ٣٤
فَأَخْرَجْنَا مَن كَانَ فِيهَا مِنَ
الْمُؤْمِنِينَ ٣٥
فَمَا وَجَدْنَا فِيهَا غَيْرَ بَيْتٍ مِّنَ
الْمُسْلِمِينَ ٣٦
وَتَرَكْنَا فِيهَا آيَةً لِّلَّذِينَ يَخَافُونَ
الْعَذَابَ الْأَلِيمَ ٣٧
وَفِي مُوسَىٰ إِذْ أَرْسَلْنَاهُ إِلَىٰ فِرْعَوْنَ
بِسُلْطَانٍ مُّبِينٍ ٣٨
فَتَوَلَّىٰ بِرُكْنِهِ وَقَالَ سَاحِرٌ أَوْ مَجْنُونٌ ٣٩
فَأَخَذْنَاهُ وَجُنُودَهُ فَنَبَذْنَاهُمْ فِي الْيَمِّ
وَهُوَ مُلِيمٌ ٤٠
وَفِي عَادٍ إِذْ أَرْسَلْنَا عَلَيْهِمُ الرِّيحَ
الْعَقِيمَ ٤١
مَا تَذَرُ مِن شَيْءٍ أَتَتْ عَلَيْهِ إِلَّا
جَعَلَتْهُ كَالرَّمِيمِ ٤٢
وَفِي ثَمُودَ إِذْ قِيلَ لَهُمْ تَمَتَّعُوا حَتَّىٰ
حِينٍ ٤٣
فَعَتَوْا عَنْ أَمْرِ رَبِّهِمْ فَأَخَذَتْهُمُ

Ikhfa اخفاء | Ghunna غُنّہ | Ikhfa Meem Saakin اخفاء میم ساکن | Idghaam ادغام | Qalqala قلقله | Qalb قلب | Idghaam Meem Saakin ادغام میم ساکن

earthquake) seized them, even while they were looking on.

45. Then they could not even stand (on their feet), nor could they help themselves.

46. So were the People of Noah before them for they wickedly transgressed.

47. With power and skill did We construct the Firmament: for it is We Who create the vastness of pace.

48. And We have spread out the (spacious) earth: How excellently We do spread out!

49. And of every thing We have created pairs: That you may receive instruction.

50. Then you Hasten (at once) to Allah: I am from Him a Warner to you, clear and open!

51. And make not another an object of worship with Allah: I am from Him a Warner to you, clear and open!

52. Similarly, no apostle came to the Peoples before them, but they said (of him) in like manner, "A sorcerer, or one possessed"!

53. Is this the legacy they have transmitted, one to another? No, they are themselves a people transgressing beyond bounds!

54. So turn away from them: not blame on you.

55. But teach (your Message) for teaching benefits the Believers.

56. I have only created Jinns and men, that they may serve Me.

57. No Sustenance do I require of them, nor do I require that they should feed Me.

58. For Allah is He Who gives (all) Sustenance,- Lord of Power,- Steadfast (for ever).

59. For the Wrong-doers, their portion is like unto the portion of their fellows (of earlier generations): then let them not ask Me to hasten (that portion)!

60. Woe, then, to the Unbelievers, on account of that Day of theirs

ṣaa'iqatu wa hum yanz̲uroon.

45. Famas-taṭaa'oo min qiyaamiñw-wa maa kaanoo muntaṣireen.

46. Wa qawma Nooḥim-min qablu innahum kaanoo qawman faasiqeen. **(Section 2)**

47. Wassamaaa'a banaynaahaa bi-aydiñw-wa innaa lamoosi'oon.

48. Wal-arḍa farashnaahaa fani'mal-maahidoon.

49. Wa min kulli shay'in khalaqnaa zawjayni la'allakum taz̲akkaroon.

50. Fafirrooo ilal-laahi innee lakum minhu naz̲eerum-mubeen.

51. Wa laa taj'aloo ma'al-laahi ilaahan aakhara innee lakum minhu naz̲eerum mubeen.

52. Kaz̲aalika maaa atallaz̲eena min qablihim-mir-Rasoolin illaa qaaloo saaḥirun aw majnoon.

53. Atawaaṣaw bih; bal hum qawmun ṭaaghoon.

54. Fatawalla 'anhum famaaa anta bimaloom.

55. Wa z̲akkir fa-innaz̲-z̲ikraa tanfa'ul-mu'mineen.

56. Wa maa khalaqtul-jinna wal-insa illaa liya'budoon.

57. Maaa ureedu minhum mirrizqiñw-wa maaa ureedu añyuṭ'imoon.

58. Innal-laaha Huwar-Razzaaqu Z̲ul-Quwwatil-Mateen.

59. Fa-inna lillaz̲eena ẓalamoo z̲anoobam-misla z̲anoobi aṣḥaabihim falaa yasta'jiloon.

60. Fawaylul-lillaz̲eena kafaroo miñy-Yawmihimul-

الصّٰعِقَةُ وَهُمْ يَنْظُرُوْنَ ﴿٤٤﴾
فَمَا اسْتَطَاعُوْا مِنْ قِيَامٍ وَّمَا كَانُوْا
مُنْتَصِرِيْنَ ﴿٤٥﴾
وَقَوْمَ نُوْحٍ مِّنْ قَبْلُ ؕ اِنَّهُمْ كَانُوْا
قَوْمًا فٰسِقِيْنَ ﴿٤٦﴾ ع ٢
وَالسَّمَآءَ بَنَيْنٰهَا بِاَيْىدٍ وَّاِنَّا لَمُوْسِعُوْنَ ﴿٤٧﴾
وَالْاَرْضَ فَرَشْنٰهَا فَنِعْمَ الْمٰهِدُوْنَ ﴿٤٨﴾
وَمِنْ كُلِّ شَيْءٍ خَلَقْنَا زَوْجَيْنِ
لَعَلَّكُمْ تَذَكَّرُوْنَ ﴿٤٩﴾
فَفِرُّوْٓا اِلَى اللّٰهِ ؕ اِنِّيْ لَكُمْ مِّنْهُ
نَذِيْرٌ مُّبِيْنٌ ﴿٥٠﴾
وَلَا تَجْعَلُوْا مَعَ اللّٰهِ اِلٰهًا اٰخَرَ ؕ
اِنِّيْ لَكُمْ مِّنْهُ نَذِيْرٌ مُّبِيْنٌ ﴿٥١﴾
كَذٰلِكَ مَآ اَتَى الَّذِيْنَ مِنْ قَبْلِهِمْ مِّنْ
رَّسُوْلٍ اِلَّا قَالُوْا سَاحِرٌ اَوْ مَجْنُوْنٌ ﴿٥٢﴾
اَتَوَاصَوْا بِهٖ ۚ بَلْ هُمْ قَوْمٌ طَاغُوْنَ ﴿٥٣﴾
فَتَوَلَّ عَنْهُمْ فَمَآ اَنْتَ بِمَلُوْمٍ ﴿٥٤﴾
وَّذَكِّرْ فَاِنَّ الذِّكْرٰى تَنْفَعُ الْمُؤْمِنِيْنَ ﴿٥٥﴾
وَمَا خَلَقْتُ الْجِنَّ وَالْاِنْسَ اِلَّا
لِيَعْبُدُوْنِ ﴿٥٦﴾
مَآ اُرِيْدُ مِنْهُمْ مِّنْ رِّزْقٍ وَّمَآ اُرِيْدُ
اَنْ يُّطْعِمُوْنِ ﴿٥٧﴾
اِنَّ اللّٰهَ هُوَ الرَّزَّاقُ ذُو الْقُوَّةِ الْمَتِيْنُ ﴿٥٨﴾
فَاِنَّ لِلَّذِيْنَ ظَلَمُوْا ذَنُوْبًا مِّثْلَ ذَنُوْبِ
اَصْحٰبِهِمْ فَلَا يَسْتَعْجِلُوْنِ ﴿٥٩﴾
فَوَيْلٌ لِّلَّذِيْنَ كَفَرُوْا مِنْ يَّوْمِهِمُ

Ikhfa اخفاء | Ghunna غُنّہ | Ikhfa Meem Saakin اخفاء میم ساکن | Idghaam ادغام | Qalqala قلقلہ | Qalb قلب | Idghaam Meem Saakin ادغام میم ساکن

which they have been promised!	lazee yoo'adoon. **(Section 3)**	الَّذِي يُوعَدُونَ ٦٠
52. The Mount **In the name of Allah, Most Gracious, Most Merciful.**	**Sûrat aṭ-Ṭûr–52** (Revealed at Makkah) **Bismillaahir Raḥmaanir Raḥeem**	(٥٢) سُورَةُ الطُّورِ مَكِّيَّةٌ (٧٦) بِسْمِ اللَّهِ الرَّحْمَٰنِ الرَّحِيمِ
1. By the Mount (of Revelation);	1. Waṭ-Ṭoor.	وَالطُّورِ ١
2. By a Decree inscribed;	2. Wa Kitaabim-masṭoor.	وَكِتَابٍ مَسْطُورٍ ٢
3. In a Scroll unfolded;	3. Fee raqqim-manshoor.	فِي رَقٍّ مَنْشُورٍ ٣
4. By the much-frequented Fane;	4. Wal-Baytil-Ma'moor.	وَالْبَيْتِ الْمَعْمُورِ ٤
5. By the Canopy Raised High;	5. Wassaqfil-marfoo'.	وَالسَّقْفِ الْمَرْفُوعِ ٥
6. And by the Ocean filled with Swell;-	6. Wal-baḥril-masjoor.	وَالْبَحْرِ الْمَسْجُورِ ٦
7. Verily, the Doom of thy Lord will indeed come to pass;-	7. Inna 'azaaba Rabbika lawaaqi'.	إِنَّ عَذَابَ رَبِّكَ لَوَاقِعٌ ٧
8. There is none can avert it;-	8. Maa lahoo min daafi'.	مَا لَهُ مِنْ دَافِعٍ ٨
9. On the Day when the firmament will be in dreadful commotion.	9. Yawma tamoorus samaaa'u mawraa.	يَوْمَ تَمُورُ السَّمَاءُ مَوْرًا ٩
10. And the mountains will fly hither and thither.	10. Wa taseerul-jibaalu sayraa.	وَتَسِيرُ الْجِبَالُ سَيْرًا ١٠
11. Then woe that Day to those that treat (Truth) as Falsehood;-	11. Fawayluñy-Yawma'izil-lil-mukazzibeen.	فَوَيْلٌ يَوْمَئِذٍ لِلْمُكَذِّبِينَ ١١ وقف لازم
12. That play (and paddle) in shallow trifles.	12. Allazeena hum fee khawḍiñy-yal'aboon.	الَّذِينَ هُمْ فِي خَوْضٍ يَلْعَبُونَ ١٢
13. That Day shall they be thrust down to the Fire of Hell, irresistibly.	13. Yawma yuda'-'oona ilaa Naari Jahannama da'-'aa.	يَوْمَ يُدَعُّونَ إِلَىٰ نَارِ جَهَنَّمَ دَعًّا ١٣
14. "This:, it will be said, "Is the Fire,- which you were wont to deny!	14. Haazihin-Naarul-latee kuntum bihaa tukazziboon.	هَٰذِهِ النَّارُ الَّتِي كُنْتُمْ بِهَا تُكَذِّبُونَ ١٤
15. "Is this then a fake, or is it you that do not see?	15. Afasiḥrun haazaaa am antum laa tubṣiroon.	أَفَسِحْرٌ هَٰذَا أَمْ أَنْتُمْ لَا تُبْصِرُونَ ١٥
16. "Burn you therein: the same is it to you whether you bear it with patience, or not: You but receive the recompense of your (own) deeds."	16. Iṣlawhaa faṣbirooo aw laa taṣbiroo sawaaa'un 'alaykum innamaa tujzawna maa kuntum ta'maloon.	اصْلَوْهَا فَاصْبِرُوا أَوْ لَا تَصْبِرُوا سَوَاءٌ عَلَيْكُمْ إِنَّمَا تُجْزَوْنَ مَا كُنْتُمْ تَعْمَلُونَ ١٦
17. As to the Righteous, they will be in Gardens, and in Happiness,-	17. Innal-muttaqeena fee Jannaatiñw-wa na'eem.	إِنَّ الْمُتَّقِينَ فِي جَنَّاتٍ وَنَعِيمٍ ١٧
18. Enjoying the (Bliss) which their Lord has bestowed on them, and their Lord shall deliver them from the Chastisement of the Fire.	18. Faakiheena bimaaa aataahum Rabbuhum wa waqaahum Rabbuhum 'azaabal-Jaḥeem.	فَاكِهِينَ بِمَا آتَاهُمْ رَبُّهُمْ وَوَقَاهُمْ رَبُّهُمْ عَذَابَ الْجَحِيمِ ١٨
19. (To them will be said:) "Eat and drink you, with good pleasure, because of your	19. Kuloo washraboo haneee-'am bimaa kuntum	كُلُوا وَاشْرَبُوا هَنِيئًا بِمَا كُنْتُمْ

ع ٣

Ikhfa اخفاء · Ghunna غنّہ · Ikhfa Meem Saakin اخفاء میم ساکن · Idghaam ادغام · Qalqala قلقلہ · Qalb قلب · Idghaam Meem Saakin ادغام میم ساکن

(good) deeds."

20. They will recline (with ease) on Thrones (of dignity) arranged in ranks; and We shall join them to Companions, with beautiful big and lustrous eyes.

21. And those who believe and whose families follow them in Faith,- to them shall We join their families: Nor shall We deprive them (of the fruit) of any of their works: (Yet) is each individual in pledge for his deeds.

22. And We shall bestow on them, of fruit and meat, anything they shall desire.

23. They shall there exchange, one with another, a (loving) cup free of frivolity, free of all taint of ill.

24. Round about them will serve, (devoted) to them, youths (handsome) as Pearls well-guarded.

25. They will advance to each other, engaging in mutual enquiry.

26. They will say: "Aforetime, we were not without fear for the sake of our people.

27. "But Allah has been good to us, and has delivered us from the Penalty of the Scorching Wind.

28. "Truly, we did call unto Him from of old: truly it is He, the Beneficent, the Merciful!"

29. Therefore proclaim you the praises (of your Lord): for by the Grace of your Lord, thou art no (vulgar) soothsayer, nor are you one possessed.

30. Or do they say:- "A Poet! we await for him some calamity (hatched) by Time!"

31. Say: "Await you!- I too will wait

ta'maloon.

20. Muttaki'eena 'alaa sururim-maṣfoofatiñw wa zawwajnaahum biḥoorin 'een.

21. Wallaẕeena aamanoo wattaba'at-hum ẕurriyyatuhum bieemaanin alḥaqnaa bihim ẕurriyyatahum wa maaa alatnaahum min 'amalihim min shay'; kullum-ri'im bimaa kasaba raheen.

22. Wa amdadnaahum bifaakihatiñw-wa laḥmim-mimmaa yashtahoon.

23. Yatanaaza'oona feehaa kaåsal-laa laghwun feehaa wa laa taåṯeem.

24. Wa yaṭoofu 'alayhim ghilmaanul-lahum ka-annahum lu'lu'um-maknoon.

25. Wa aqbala ba'ḍuhum 'alaa ba'ḍiñy-yatasaaa'aloon.

26. Qaalooo innaa kunnaa qablu feee ahlinaa mushfiqeen.

27. Famannal-laahu 'alaynaa wa waqaanaa 'aẕaabas-samoom.

28. Innaa kunnaa min qablu nad'oohu innahoo Huwal-Barrur-Raḥeem. **(Section 1)**

29. Fazakkir famaaa anta bini'mati Rabbika bikaahiniñw-wa laa majnoon.

30. Am yaqooloona shaa'irun natarabbaṣu bihee raybal-manoon.

31. Qul tarabbaṣoo fa-innee ma'akum minal-

تَعۡمَلُونَ ١٩
مُتَّكِـِٔينَ عَلَىٰ سُرُرٖ مَّصۡفُوفَةٖۖ وَ
زَوَّجۡنَٰهُم بِحُورٍ عِينٖ ٢٠
وَٱلَّذِينَ ءَامَنُواْ وَٱتَّبَعَتۡهُمۡ ذُرِّيَّتُهُم
بِإِيمَٰنٍ أَلۡحَقۡنَا بِهِمۡ ذُرِّيَّتَهُمۡ وَمَآ
أَلَتۡنَٰهُم مِّنۡ عَمَلِهِم مِّن شَيۡءٖۚ كُلُّ
ٱمۡرِيِٕۭ بِمَا كَسَبَ رَهِينٞ ٢١
وَأَمۡدَدۡنَٰهُم بِفَٰكِهَةٖ وَلَحۡمٖ مِّمَّا
يَشۡتَهُونَ ٢٢
يَتَنَٰزَعُونَ فِيهَا كَأۡسٗا لَّا لَغۡوٞ فِيهَا
وَلَا تَأۡثِيمٞ ٢٣
وَيَطُوفُ عَلَيۡهِمۡ غِلۡمَانٞ لَّهُمۡ كَأَنَّهُمۡ
لُؤۡلُؤٞ مَّكۡنُونٞ ٢٤
وَأَقۡبَلَ بَعۡضُهُمۡ عَلَىٰ بَعۡضٖ
يَتَسَآءَلُونَ ٢٥
قَالُوٓاْ إِنَّا كُنَّا قَبۡلُ فِيٓ أَهۡلِنَا
مُشۡفِقِينَ ٢٦
فَمَنَّ ٱللَّهُ عَلَيۡنَا وَوَقَىٰنَا عَذَابَ
ٱلسَّمُومِ ٢٧
إِنَّا كُنَّا مِن قَبۡلُ نَدۡعُوهُۖ إِنَّهُۥ هُوَ
ٱلۡبَرُّ ٱلرَّحِيمُ ٢٨
فَذَكِّرۡ فَمَآ أَنتَ بِنِعۡمَتِ رَبِّكَ
بِكَاهِنٖ وَلَا مَجۡنُونٍ ٢٩
أَمۡ يَقُولُونَ شَاعِرٞ نَّتَرَبَّصُ بِهِۦ
رَيۡبَ ٱلۡمَنُونِ ٣٠
قُلۡ تَرَبَّصُواْ فَإِنِّي مَعَكُم مِّنَ

Ikhfa اخفاء | Ghunna غنّہ | Ikhfa Meem Saakin اخفاء میم ساکن | Idghaam ادغام | Qalqala قلقلہ | Qalb قلب | Idghaam Meem Saakin ادغام میم ساکن

along with you!"	mutarabbiṣeen.	الْمُتَرَبِّصِيْنَ ﴿٣١﴾
32. Is it that their faculties of understanding urge them to this, or are they but a people transgressing beyond bounds?	32. Am taåmuruhum aḥlaamuhum bihaaẕaaa am hum qawmun ṭaaghoon.	اَمْ تَأْمُرُهُمْ اَحْلَامُهُمْ بِهٰذَآ اَمْ هُمْ قَوْمٌ طَاغُوْنَ ﴿٣٢﴾
33. Or do they say, "He fabricated the (Message)"? No, they have no faith!	33. Am yaqooloona taqawwalah; bal laa yu'minoon.	اَمْ يَقُوْلُوْنَ تَقَوَّلَهٗ ۚ بَلْ لَّا يُؤْمِنُوْنَ ﴿٣٣﴾
34. Let them then produce a recital like unto it,- If (it be) they speak the truth!	34. Falyaåtoo biḥadeesim-misliheee in kaanoo ṣaadiqeen.	فَلْيَاْتُوْا بِحَدِيْثٍ مِّثْلِهٖٓ اِنْ كَانُوْا صٰدِقِيْنَ ﴿٣٤﴾
35. Were they created of nothing, or were they themselves the creators?	35. Am khuliqoo min ghayri shay'in am humul-khaaliqoon.	اَمْ خُلِقُوْا مِنْ غَيْرِ شَيْءٍ اَمْ هُمُ الْخٰلِقُوْنَ ﴿٣٥﴾
36. Or did they create the heavens and the earth? No, they have no firm belief.	36. Am khalaqus-samaawaati wal-arḍ; bal laa yooqinoon.	اَمْ خَلَقُوا السَّمٰوٰتِ وَالْاَرْضَ ۚ بَلْ لَّا يُوْقِنُوْنَ ﴿٣٦﴾
37. Or are the Treasures of your Lord with them, or are they the managers (of affairs)?	37. Am 'indahum khazaaa'inu Rabbika am humul-musayṭiroon.	اَمْ عِنْدَهُمْ خَزَآئِنُ رَبِّكَ اَمْ هُمُ الْمُصَّيْطِرُوْنَ ﴿٣٧﴾
38. Or have they a ladder, by which they can (climb up to heaven and) listen (to its secrets)? Then let (such a) listener of theirs produce a manifest proof.	38. Am lahum sullamuñy-yastami'oona feehi falyaåti mustami'uhum bisulṭaanim-mubeen.	اَمْ لَهُمْ سُلَّمٌ يَّسْتَمِعُوْنَ فِيْهِ ۚ فَلْيَاْتِ مُسْتَمِعُهُمْ بِسُلْطٰنٍ مُّبِيْنٍ ﴿٣٨﴾
39. Or has He only daughters and you have sons?	39. Am lahul-banaatu wa lakumul-banoon.	اَمْ لَهُ الْبَنٰتُ وَلَكُمُ الْبَنُوْنَ ﴿٣٩﴾
40. Or is it that you does ask for a reward, so that they are burdened with a load of debt?-	40. Am tas'aluhum ajran fahum mim-maghramim-musqaloon.	اَمْ تَسْئَلُهُمْ اَجْرًا فَهُمْ مِّنْ مَّغْرَمٍ مُّثْقَلُوْنَ ﴿٤٠﴾
41. Or that the Unseen is in their hands, and they write it down?	41. Am 'indahumul-ghaybu fahum yaktuboon.	اَمْ عِنْدَهُمُ الْغَيْبُ فَهُمْ يَكْتُبُوْنَ ﴿٤١﴾
42. Or do they intend a plot (against you)? But those who defy Allah are themselves involved in a Plot!	42. Am yureedoona kaydan fallaẕeena kafaroo humul-makeedoon.	اَمْ يُرِيْدُوْنَ كَيْدًا ۚ فَالَّذِيْنَ كَفَرُوْا هُمُ الْمَكِيْدُوْنَ ﴿٤٢﴾
43. Or have they a god other than Allah? Exalted is Allah far above the things they associate with Him!	43. Am lahum ilaahun ghayrul-laah; Subḥaanal-laahi 'ammaa yushrikoon.	اَمْ لَهُمْ اِلٰهٌ غَيْرُ اللّٰهِ ۚ سُبْحٰنَ اللّٰهِ عَمَّا يُشْرِكُوْنَ ﴿٤٣﴾
44. Were they to see a piece of the sky falling (on them), they would (only) say: "Clouds gathered in heaps!"	44. Wa iñy-yaraw kisfam-minas-samaaa'i saaqiṭañy-yaqooloo saḥaabum-markoom.	وَاِنْ يَّرَوْا كِسْفًا مِّنَ السَّمَآءِ سَاقِطًا يَّقُوْلُوْا سَحَابٌ مَّرْكُوْمٌ ﴿٤٤﴾
45. So leave them alone until they encounter that Day of theirs, wherein they shall (perforce) swoon (with terror),-	45. Faẕarhum ḥattaa yulaaqoo Yawmahumul-laẕee feehi yuṣ'aqoon.	فَذَرْهُمْ حَتّٰى يُلٰقُوْا يَوْمَهُمُ الَّذِيْ فِيْهِ يُصْعَقُوْنَ ﴿٤٥﴾

Ikhfa اخفاء | Ghunna غنّہ | Ikhfa Meem Saakin اخفاء میم ساکن | Idghaam ادغام | Qalqala قلقلہ | Qalb قلب | Idghaam Meem Saakin ادغام میم ساکن

46. The Day when their plotting will avail them nothing and no help shall be given them.

47. And verily, for those who do wrong, there is another punishment besides this: But most of them understand not.

48. Now await in patience the command of your Lord: for verily you are in Our eyes: and celebrate the praises of your Lord the while you stand forth,

49. And for part of the night also praise you Him,- and at the retreat of the stars!

53. The Star

In the name of Allah, Most Gracious, Most Merciful.

1. By the Star when it goes down,-

2. Your Companion is neither astray nor being misled.

3. Nor does he say (anything) of (his own) Desire.

4. It is no less than inspiration sent down to him:

5. He was taught by one Mighty in Power,

6. Endued with Wisdom: for he appeared (in stately form);

7. While he was in the highest part of the horizon:

8. Then he approached and came closer,

9. And was at a distance of but two bow-lengths or (even) nearer;

10. So did (Allah) convey the inspiration to His Servant (conveyed) what He (meant) to convey.

11. The (Prophet's) (mind and) heart in no way falsified that which he saw.

12. Will you then dispute with him concerning what he saw?

13. For indeed he saw him at a second descent,

14. Near the Lote-tree beyond which none may pass:

15. Near it is the Garden of Abode.

16. Behold, the Lote-tree was shrouded (in mystery unspeakable!)

17. (His) sight never swerved, nor did it go wrong!

46. Yawma laa yughnee 'anhum kayduhum shay'añw-wa laa hum yunṣaroon.

47. Wa inna lillazeena ẓalamoo 'azaaban doona zaalika wa laakinna aksarahum laa ya'lamoon.

48. Waṣbir liḥukmi Rabbika fainnaka bi-a'yuninaa wa sabbiḥ biḥamdi Rabbika ḥeena taqoom.

49. Wa minal-layli fasabbiḥhu wa idbaaran-nujoom. **(Section 2)**

Sûrat an-Najm–53

(Revealed at Makkah)

Bismillaahir Raḥmaanir Raḥeem

1. Wannajmi izaa hawaa.
2. Maa ḍalla ṣaaḥibukum wa maa ghawaa.
3. Wa maa yanṭiqu 'anil-hawaaa.
4. In huwa illaa Waḥyuñy-yooḥaa.
5. 'Allamahoo shadeedul-quwaa.
6. Zoo mirratin fastawaa.
7. Wa huwa bil-ufuqil-a'laa.
8. Summa danaa fatadallaa.
9. Fakaana qaaba qawsayni aw adnaa.
10. Fa-awḥaaa ilaa 'abdihee maaa awḥaa.
11. Maa kazabal-fu'aadu maa ra-aa.
12. Afatumaaroonahoo 'alaa maa yaraa.
13. Wa laqad ra-aahu nazlatan ukhraa.
14. 'Inda Sidratil-Muntahaa.
15. 'Indahaa Jannatul-Maåwaa.
16. Iz yaghshas-Sidrata maa yaghshaa.
17. Maa zaaghal-baṣaru wa maa ṭaghaa.

يَوْمَ لَا يُغْنِي عَنْهُمْ كَيْدُهُمْ شَيْئًا
وَّلَا هُمْ يُنْصَرُوْنَ ﴿٤٦﴾
وَإِنَّ لِلَّذِيْنَ ظَلَمُوْا عَذَابًا دُوْنَ
ذٰلِكَ وَلٰكِنَّ أَكْثَرَهُمْ لَا يَعْلَمُوْنَ ﴿٤٧﴾
وَاصْبِرْ لِحُكْمِ رَبِّكَ فَإِنَّكَ بِأَعْيُنِنَا
وَسَبِّحْ بِحَمْدِ رَبِّكَ حِيْنَ تَقُوْمُ ﴿٤٨﴾
وَمِنَ الَّيْلِ فَسَبِّحْهُ وَإِدْبَارَ النُّجُوْمِ ﴿٤٩﴾ ع

(٥٣) سُوْرَةُ النَّجْمِ مَكِّيَّةٌ (٢٣)

بِسْمِ اللّٰهِ الرَّحْمٰنِ الرَّحِيْمِ

وَالنَّجْمِ إِذَا هَوٰى ﴿١﴾
مَا ضَلَّ صَاحِبُكُمْ وَمَا غَوٰى ﴿٢﴾
وَمَا يَنْطِقُ عَنِ الْهَوٰى ﴿٣﴾
إِنْ هُوَ إِلَّا وَحْيٌ يُّوْحٰى ﴿٤﴾
عَلَّمَهُ شَدِيْدُ الْقُوٰى ﴿٥﴾
ذُوْ مِرَّةٍ فَاسْتَوٰى ﴿٦﴾
وَهُوَ بِالْأُفُقِ الْأَعْلٰى ﴿٧﴾
ثُمَّ دَنَا فَتَدَلّٰى ﴿٨﴾
فَكَانَ قَابَ قَوْسَيْنِ أَوْ أَدْنٰى ﴿٩﴾
فَأَوْحٰى إِلٰى عَبْدِهِ مَا أَوْحٰى ﴿١٠﴾
مَا كَذَبَ الْفُؤَادُ مَا رَأٰى ﴿١١﴾
أَفَتُمٰرُوْنَهُ عَلٰى مَا يَرٰى ﴿١٢﴾
وَلَقَدْ رَاٰهُ نَزْلَةً أُخْرٰى ﴿١٣﴾
عِنْدَ سِدْرَةِ الْمُنْتَهٰى ﴿١٤﴾
عِنْدَهَا جَنَّةُ الْمَأْوٰى ﴿١٥﴾
إِذْ يَغْشَى السِّدْرَةَ مَا يَغْشٰى ﴿١٦﴾
مَا زَاغَ الْبَصَرُ وَمَا طَغٰى ﴿١٧﴾

Ikhfa اخفاء | Ghunna غنّہ | Ikhfa Meem Saakin اخفاء میم ساکن | Idghaam ادغام | Qalqala قلقلہ | Qalb قلب | Idghaam Meem Saakin ادغام میم ساکن

18. For truly did he see, of the Signs of his Lord, the Greatest!

19. Have you seen Lat and 'Uzza,

20. And another, the third (goddess), Manat?

21. What! for you the male sex, and for Him, the female?

22. Behold, such would be indeed a division most unfair!

23. These are nothing but names which you have devised,- you and your fathers,- for which Allah has sent down no authority (whatever). They follow nothing but conjecture and what their own souls desire!- Even though there has already come to them Guidance from their Lord!

24. No, shall man have (just) anything he hankers after?

25. But it is to Allah that the End and the Beginning (of all things) belong.

26. How many-so-ever be the angels in the heavens, their intercession will avail nothing except after Allah has given leave for whom He pleases and that he is acceptable to Him.

27. Those who believe not in the Hereafter, name the angels with female names.

28. But they have no knowledge therein. They follow nothing but conjecture; and conjecture avails nothing against Truth.

29. Therefore shun those who turn away from Our Message and desire nothing but the life of this world.

30. That is as far as knowledge will reach them. Verily your Lord knows best those who stray from His Path, and He knoweth best those who receive guidance.

31. Yes, to Allah belongs all that is in the heavens and on earth:

18. Laqad ra-aa min Aayaati Rabbihil-Kubraaa.

19. Afara'aytumul-Laata wal-'Uzzaa.

20. Wa Manaatas-saalisatal-ukhraa.

21. A-lakumuz-zakaru wa lahul-unsaa.

22. Tilka izan qismatun deezaa.

23. In hiya illaaa asmaaa'un sammaytumoohaaa antum wa aabaaa'ukum maaa anzalal-laahu bihaa min sultaan; iñy-yattabi'oona illaz-zanna wa maa tahwal-anfusu wa laqad jaaa'ahum-mir-Rabbihimul-hudaa.

24. Am lil-insaani maa taman-naa.

25. Falillaahil-Aakhiratu wal-oolaa. **(Section 1)**

26. Wa kam mim-malakin fis-samaawaati laa tughnee shafaa'atuhum shay'an illaa mim ba'di añy-yaåzanal-laahu limañy-yashaaa'u wa yardaa.

27. Innal-lazeena laa yu'mi-noona bil-Aakhirati la-yusam-moonal-malaaa'ikata tasmi-yatal-unsaa.

28. Wa maa lahum bihee min 'ilmin iñy-yattabi'oona illaz-zanna wa innaz-zanna laa yughnee minal-haqqi shay'aa.

29. Fa-a'rid 'am-man tawallaa 'an zikrinaa wa lam yurid illal-hayaatad-dunyaa.

30. Zalika mablaghuhum mi-nal-'ilm; inna Rabbaka Huwa a'lamu biman dalla 'an sabee-lihee wa Huwa a'lamu bimanih-tadaa.

31. Wa lillaahi maa fis-samaawaati wa maa fil-ardi

لَقَدْ رَاٰى مِنْ اٰيٰتِ رَبِّهِ الْكُبْرٰى ﴿١٨﴾
اَفَرَءَيْتُمُ اللّٰتَ وَالْعُزّٰى ﴿١٩﴾
وَمَنٰوةَ الثَّالِثَةَ الْاُخْرٰى ﴿٢٠﴾
اَلَكُمُ الذَّكَرُ وَلَهُ الْاُنْثٰى ﴿٢١﴾
تِلْكَ اِذًا قِسْمَةٌ ضِيْزٰى ﴿٢٢﴾
اِنْ هِيَ اِلَّآ اَسْمَآءٌ سَمَّيْتُمُوْهَا
اَنْتُمْ وَاٰبَآؤُكُمْ مَّآ اَنْزَلَ اللّٰهُ بِهَا
مِنْ سُلْطٰنٍ اِنْ يَّتَّبِعُوْنَ اِلَّا الظَّنَّ
وَمَا تَهْوَى الْاَنْفُسُ وَلَقَدْ جَآءَهُمْ
مِّنْ رَّبِّهِمُ الْهُدٰى ﴿٢٣﴾
اَمْ لِلْاِنْسَانِ مَا تَمَنّٰى ﴿٢٤﴾
فَلِلّٰهِ الْاٰخِرَةُ وَالْاُوْلٰى ﴿٢٥﴾
وَكَمْ مِّنْ مَّلَكٍ فِي السَّمٰوٰتِ لَا تُغْنِيْ
شَفَاعَتُهُمْ شَيْـًٔا اِلَّا مِنْ بَعْدِ اَنْ
يَّاْذَنَ اللّٰهُ لِمَنْ يَّشَآءُ وَيَرْضٰى ﴿٢٦﴾
اِنَّ الَّذِيْنَ لَا يُؤْمِنُوْنَ بِالْاٰخِرَةِ
لَيُسَمُّوْنَ الْمَلٰٓئِكَةَ تَسْمِيَةَ الْاُنْثٰى ﴿٢٧﴾
وَمَا لَهُمْ بِهٖ مِنْ عِلْمٍ اِنْ يَّتَّبِعُوْنَ
اِلَّا الظَّنَّ وَاِنَّ الظَّنَّ لَا يُغْنِيْ مِنَ
الْحَقِّ شَيْـًٔا ﴿٢٨﴾
فَاَعْرِضْ عَنْ مَّنْ تَوَلّٰى عَنْ ذِكْرِنَا
وَلَمْ يُرِدْ اِلَّا الْحَيٰوةَ الدُّنْيَا ﴿٢٩﴾
ذٰلِكَ مَبْلَغُهُمْ مِّنَ الْعِلْمِ اِنَّ
رَبَّكَ هُوَ اَعْلَمُ بِمَنْ ضَلَّ عَنْ
سَبِيْلِهٖ وَهُوَ اَعْلَمُ بِمَنِ اهْتَدٰى ﴿٣٠﴾
وَلِلّٰهِ مَا فِي السَّمٰوٰتِ وَمَا فِي الْاَرْضِ

so that He rewards those who do evil, according to their deeds, and He rewards those who do good, with what is best.

32. Those who avoid great sins and shameful deeds, only (falling into) small faults,- verily your Lord is ample in forgiveness. He knows you well when He brings you out of the earth, and when you are hidden in your mothers' wombs. Therefore, justify not yourselves: He knows best who it is that guards against evil.

33. Do you see one who turns back,

34. Gives a little, then hardens (his heart)?

35. What! Has he knowledge of the Unseen so that he can see?

36. Or hath he not bad news of what is in books of Moses.

37. And of Abraham who fulfilled his engagements?-

38. That no laden one shall bear another's load.

39. That man can have nothing but what he strives for;

40. That (the fruit of) his striving will soon come in sight:

41. Then will he be rewarded with a reward complete;

42. That to your Lord is the final Goal;

43. That it is He Who grants Laughter and Tears;

44. That it is He Who grants Death and Life;

45. That He did create in pairs,- male and female,

46. From a seed when lodged (in its place);

47. That He has promised a Second Creation (Raising of the Dead);

48. That it is He Who gives wealth and satisfaction;

49. That He is the Lord of Sirius (the Mighty Star);

liyajziyal-lazeena asaaa'oo bimaa 'amiloo wa yajziyal-lazeena aḥsanoo bilḥusnaa.

32. Allazeena yajtaniboona kabaaa'iral-ismi walfawaa-ḥisha illal-lamam; inna Rabbaka waasi'ul-maghfirah; Huwa a'lamu bikum iz ansha-akum minal-arḍi wa iz antum ajinnatun fee buṭooni umma-haatikum falaa tuzakkooo anfu-sakum Huwa a'lamu bimanit-taqaa. **(Section 2)**

33. Afara'aytal-lazee tawallaa.

34. Wa a'ṭaa qaleelañw-wa akdaa.

35. A'indahoo 'ilmul-ghaybi fahuwa yaraa.

36. Am lam yunabbaå bimaa fee Ṣuḥufi Moosaa.

37. Wa Ibraaheemal-lazee waffaa.

38. Allaa taziru waaziratuñw-wizra ukhraa.

39. Wa al-laysa lil-insaani illaa maa sa'aa.

40. Wa anna sa'yahoo sawfa yuraa.

41. Summa yujzaahul-jazaaa'al-awfaa.

42. Wa anna ilaa Rabbikal-muntahaa.

43. Wa annahoo Huwa aḍḥaka wa abkaa.

44. Wa annahoo Huwa amaata wa aḥyaa.

45. Wa annahoo khalaqaz-zawjayniz-zakara wal-unsaa.

46. Min nuṭfatin izaa tumnaa.

47. Wa anna 'alayhin-nash-atal-ukhraa.

48. Wa annahoo Huwa aghnaa wa aqnaa.

49. Wa annahoo Huwa Rab-bush-Shi'raa.

لِيَجْزِيَ الَّذِينَ أَسَاءُوا بِمَا عَمِلُوا
وَيَجْزِيَ الَّذِينَ أَحْسَنُوا بِالْحُسْنَى ﴿٣١﴾
الَّذِينَ يَجْتَنِبُونَ كَبَائِرَ الْإِثْمِ
وَالْفَوَاحِشَ إِلَّا اللَّمَمَ ۚ إِنَّ رَبَّكَ
وَاسِعُ الْمَغْفِرَةِ ۚ هُوَ أَعْلَمُ بِكُمْ إِذْ
أَنْشَأَكُمْ مِنَ الْأَرْضِ وَإِذْ أَنْتُمْ أَجِنَّةٌ
فِي بُطُونِ أُمَّهَاتِكُمْ ۖ فَلَا تُزَكُّوا
أَنْفُسَكُمْ ۖ هُوَ أَعْلَمُ بِمَنِ اتَّقَىٰ ﴿٣٢﴾ ع
أَفَرَأَيْتَ الَّذِي تَوَلَّىٰ ﴿٣٣﴾
وَأَعْطَىٰ قَلِيلًا وَأَكْدَىٰ ﴿٣٤﴾
أَعِنْدَهُ عِلْمُ الْغَيْبِ فَهُوَ يَرَىٰ ﴿٣٥﴾
أَمْ لَمْ يُنَبَّأْ بِمَا فِي صُحُفِ مُوسَىٰ ﴿٣٦﴾
وَإِبْرَاهِيمَ الَّذِي وَفَّىٰ ﴿٣٧﴾
أَلَّا تَزِرُ وَازِرَةٌ وِزْرَ أُخْرَىٰ ﴿٣٨﴾
وَأَنْ لَيْسَ لِلْإِنْسَانِ إِلَّا مَا سَعَىٰ ﴿٣٩﴾
وَأَنَّ سَعْيَهُ سَوْفَ يُرَىٰ ﴿٤٠﴾
ثُمَّ يُجْزَاهُ الْجَزَاءَ الْأَوْفَىٰ ﴿٤١﴾
وَأَنَّ إِلَىٰ رَبِّكَ الْمُنْتَهَىٰ ﴿٤٢﴾
وَأَنَّهُ هُوَ أَضْحَكَ وَأَبْكَىٰ ﴿٤٣﴾
وَأَنَّهُ هُوَ أَمَاتَ وَأَحْيَا ﴿٤٤﴾
وَأَنَّهُ خَلَقَ الزَّوْجَيْنِ الذَّكَرَ
وَالْأُنْثَىٰ ﴿٤٥﴾
مِنْ نُطْفَةٍ إِذَا تُمْنَىٰ ﴿٤٦﴾
وَأَنَّ عَلَيْهِ النَّشْأَةَ الْأُخْرَىٰ ﴿٤٧﴾
وَأَنَّهُ هُوَ أَغْنَىٰ وَأَقْنَىٰ ﴿٤٨﴾
وَأَنَّهُ هُوَ رَبُّ الشِّعْرَىٰ ﴿٤٩﴾

Ikhfa اخفاء | Ghunna غنّہ | Ikhfa Meem Saakin اخفاءمیم ساکن | Idghaam ادغام | Qalqala قلقلہ | Qalb قلب | Idghaam Meem Saakin ادغام میم ساکن

50. And that He destroyed the former (tribe of) 'Aad,
51. And the Thamud, nor gave them a lease of perpetual life.
52. And before them, the people of Noah, for that they were (all) most unjust and most insolent transgressors,
53. And Al-Mu'tafikah He destroyed..
54. So that (ruins unknown) have covered them up.
55. Then which of the gifts of your Lord, (O man,) will you dispute about?
56. This is a Warner, of the (series of) Warners of old!
57. The (Judgment) ever approaching draws closer:
58. No (soul) but Allah can lay it bare.
59. Do you then wonder at this recital?
60. And will you laugh and not weep,-
61. Wasting your time in vanities?
62. But fall down in prostration to Allah, and adore (Him)

(Bow Down)

54. The Moon

In the name of Allah, Most Gracious, Most Merciful.

1. The Hour drew nigh and the moon was rent in twain.
2. But if they see a Sign, they turn away, and say, "This is (but) transient magic."
3. They reject (the warning) and follow their (own) lusts but every matter has its appointed time.
4. There have already come to them such tidings as contain a deterrent–
5. Effective wisdom; but warnings avail not.
6. Therefore, (O Prophet,) turn away from them. The Day that the Caller will call (them) to a terrible affair,

50. Wa annahooo ahlaka 'Aadanil-oolaa.
51. Wa Samooda famaaa abqaa.
52. Wa qawma Nooḥim-min qablu innahum kaanoo hum aẓlama wa aṭghaa.
53. Wal-mu'tafikata ahwaa.
54. Faghashshaahaa maa ghashshaa.
55. Fabi-ayyi aalaaa'i Rabbika tatamaaraa.
56. Haazaa nazeerum-minan-nuzuril-oolaa.
57. Azifatil-aazifah.
58. Laysa lahaa min doonil-laahi kaashifah.
59. Afamin haazal-ḥadeesi ta'jaboon.
60. Wa taḍḥakoona wa laa tabkoon.
61. Wa antum saamidoon.
62. Fasjudoo lillaahi wa'-budoo. ۩ **(Section 3)**

Sûrat al-Qamar–54

(Revealed at Makkah)

Bismillaahir Raḥmaanir Raḥeem

1. Iqtarabatis-Saa'atu wan-shaqqal-qamar.
2. Wa iñy-yaraw Aayatañy-yu'riḍoo wa yaqooloo siḥrum-mustamirr.
3. Wa kazzaboo wattaba'ooo ahwaaa'ahum; wa kullu am-rim-mustaqirr.
4. Wa laqad jaaa'ahum minal-ambaaa'i maa feehi muzdajar.
5. Ḥikmatum baalighatun famaa tughnin-nuzur.
6. Fatawalla 'anhum; Yawma yad'ud-daa'i ilaa shay'in nukur.

وَاَنَّهٗۤ اَهۡلَكَ عَادَا ۨ الۡاُوۡلٰى ﴿٥٠﴾
وَثَمُوۡدَا۠ فَمَاۤ اَبۡقٰى ﴿٥١﴾
وَقَوۡمَ نُوۡحٍ مِّنۡ قَبۡلُ‌ؕ اِنَّهُمۡ كَانُوۡا
هُمۡ اَظۡلَمَ وَاَطۡغٰى ﴿٥٢﴾
وَالۡمُؤۡتَفِكَةَ اَهۡوٰى ﴿٥٣﴾
فَغَشّٰٮهَا مَا غَشّٰى ﴿٥٤﴾
فَبِاَىِّ اٰلَاۤءِ رَبِّكَ تَتَمَارٰى ﴿٥٥﴾
هٰذَا نَذِيۡرٌ مِّنَ النُّذُرِ الۡاُوۡلٰى ﴿٥٦﴾
اَزِفَتِ الۡاٰزِفَةُ ﴿٥٧﴾
لَيۡسَ لَهَا مِنۡ دُوۡنِ اللّٰهِ كَاشِفَةٌ ﴿٥٨﴾
اَفَمِنۡ هٰذَا الۡحَدِيۡثِ تَعۡجَبُوۡنَ ﴿٥٩﴾
وَتَضۡحَكُوۡنَ وَلَا تَبۡكُوۡنَ ﴿٦٠﴾
وَاَنۡتُمۡ سٰمِدُوۡنَ ﴿٦١﴾
فَاسۡجُدُوۡا لِلّٰهِ وَاعۡبُدُوۡا ﴿٦٢﴾ السجدة

السجدة (١٢)

(٥٤) سُوۡرَةُ الۡقَمَرِ مَكِّيَّةٌ (٣٧)

بِسۡمِ اللّٰهِ الرَّحۡمٰنِ الرَّحِيۡمِ

اِقۡتَرَبَتِ السَّاعَةُ وَانۡشَقَّ الۡقَمَرُ ﴿١﴾
وَاِنۡ يَّرَوۡا اٰيَةً يُّعۡرِضُوۡا وَيَقُوۡلُوۡا
سِحۡرٌ مُّسۡتَمِرٌّ ﴿٢﴾
وَكَذَّبُوۡا وَاتَّبَعُوۡۤا اَهۡوَآءَهُمۡ وَكُلُّ
اَمۡرٍ مُّسۡتَقِرٌّ ﴿٣﴾
وَلَقَدۡ جَآءَهُمۡ مِّنَ الۡاَنۡۢبَآءِ مَا
فِيۡهِ مُزۡدَجَرٌ ﴿٤﴾
حِكۡمَةٌ ۢ بَالِغَةٌ فَمَا تُغۡنِ النُّذُرُ ﴿٥﴾
فَتَوَلَّ عَنۡهُمۡ يَوۡمَ يَدۡعُ الدَّاعِ اِلٰى
شَىۡءٍ نُّكُرٍ ﴿٦﴾

وقف لازم

Ikhfa اخفاء | Ghunna غنّہ | Ikhfa Meem Saakin اخفاء میم ساکن | Idghaam ادغام | Qalqala قلقلہ | Qalb قلب | Idghaam Meem Saakin ادغام میم ساکن

7. They will come forth,- their eyes humbled - from (their) graves, (torpid) like locusts scattered abroad,
8. Hastening, with eyes transfixed, towards the Caller!- "Hard is this Day!", the Unbelievers will say.
9. Before them the People of Noah rejected (their apostle): they rejected Our servant, and said, "Here is one possessed!", and he was driven out.
10. Then he called on his Lord: "I am one overcome: do You then help (me)!"
11. So We opened the gates of heaven, with water pouring forth.
12. And We caused the earth to gush forth with springs, so the waters met (and rose) to the extent decreed.
13. And We carried him upon a thing of planks and nails,
14. She floats under our eyes (and care): a recompense to one who had been rejected (with scorn)!
15. And We have left this as a Sign (for all time): then is there any that will receive admonition?
16. But how (terrible) was My Chastisement and My Warning?
17. And We have indeed made the Qur'an easy to understand and remember: then is there any that will receive admonition?
18. The 'Ad (people) (too) rejected (Truth): then how terrible was My Chastisement and My Warning?
19. For We sent against them a furious wind, on a Day of violent Disaster,
20. Plucking out men as if they were roots of palm-trees torn up (from the ground).
21. Yes, how (terrible) was My Chastisement and My Warning!
22. But We have indeed made the Qur'an easy to understand and remember:

7. Khushsha'an absaaruhum yakhrujoona minal-ajdaasi ka-annahum jaraadum-muntashir.
8. Muhti'eena ilad-daa'i yaqoolul-kaafiroona haazaa yawmun 'asir.
9. Kazzabat qablahum qawmu Noohin fakazzaboo 'abdanaa wa qaaloo majnoonuñw-wazdujir.
10. Fada'aa Rabbahooo annee maghloobun fantasir.
11. Fafatahnaaa abwaabas-samaaa'i bimaaa'im-munhamir.
12. Wa fajjarnal-arda 'uyoonan-faltaqal-maaa'u 'alaaa amrin qad qudir.
13. Wa hamalnaahu 'alaa zaati alwaahiñw-wa dusur.
14. Tajree bi-a'yuninaa jazaaa-'al-liman kaana kufir.
15. Wa laqat-taraknaahaaa Aayatan fahal mim-muddakir.
16. Fakayfa kaana 'azaabee wa nuzur.
17. Wa laqad yassarnal-Qur-aana liz-zikri fahal mim-muddakir.
18. kazzabat 'Aadun fakayfa kaana 'azaabee wa nuzur.
19. Innaaa arsalnaa 'alayhim reehan sarsaran fee Yawmi nahsim-mustamirr.
20. Tanzi'un-naasa ka-annahum a'jaazu nakhlim-munqa'ir.
21. Fakayfa kaana 'azaabee wa nuzur.
22. wa laqad yassarnal-Qur-aana liz-zikri

خُشَّعًا اَبْصَارُهُمْ يَخْرُجُوْنَ مِنَ
الْاَجْدَاثِ كَاَنَّهُمْ جَرَادٌ مُّنْتَشِرٌ ۝٧
مُّهْطِعِيْنَ اِلَى الدَّاعِ ۖ يَقُوْلُ
الْكٰفِرُوْنَ هٰذَا يَوْمٌ عَسِرٌ ۝٨
كَذَّبَتْ قَبْلَهُمْ قَوْمُ نُوْحٍ فَكَذَّبُوْا
عَبْدَنَا وَقَالُوْا مَجْنُوْنٌ وَّازْدُجِرَ ۝٩
فَدَعَا رَبَّهٗٓ اَنِّيْ مَغْلُوْبٌ فَانْتَصِرْ ۝١٠
فَفَتَحْنَآ اَبْوَابَ السَّمَآءِ بِمَآءٍ مُّنْهَمِرٍ ۝١١
وَّفَجَّرْنَا الْاَرْضَ عُيُوْنًا فَالْتَقَى
الْمَآءُ عَلٰٓى اَمْرٍ قَدْ قُدِرَ ۝١٢
وَحَمَلْنٰهُ عَلٰى ذَاتِ اَلْوَاحٍ وَّدُسُرٍ ۝١٣
تَجْرِيْ بِاَعْيُنِنَا ۚ جَزَآءً لِّمَنْ كَانَ
كُفِرَ ۝١٤
وَلَقَدْ تَّرَكْنٰهَآ اٰيَةً فَهَلْ مِنْ
مُّدَّكِرٍ ۝١٥
فَكَيْفَ كَانَ عَذَابِيْ وَنُذُرِ ۝١٦
وَلَقَدْ يَسَّرْنَا الْقُرْاٰنَ لِلذِّكْرِ فَهَلْ
مِنْ مُّدَّكِرٍ ۝١٧
كَذَّبَتْ عَادٌ فَكَيْفَ كَانَ عَذَابِيْ
وَنُذُرِ ۝١٨
اِنَّآ اَرْسَلْنَا عَلَيْهِمْ رِيْحًا صَرْصَرًا فِيْ
يَوْمِ نَحْسٍ مُّسْتَمِرٍّ ۝١٩
تَنْزِعُ النَّاسَ ۙ كَاَنَّهُمْ اَعْجَازُ نَخْلٍ
مُّنْقَعِرٍ ۝٢٠
فَكَيْفَ كَانَ عَذَابِيْ وَنُذُرِ ۝٢١
وَلَقَدْ يَسَّرْنَا الْقُرْاٰنَ لِلذِّكْرِ

Ikhfa اخفاء · Ghunna غُنّہ · Ikhfa Meem Saakin اخفاء میم ساکن · Idghaam ادغام · Qalqala قلقلہ · Qalb قلب · Idghaam Meem Saakin ادغام میم ساکن

then is there any that will receive admonition?

23. The Thamud (also) rejected (their) Warners.

24. For they said: "What! a man! a Solitary one from among ourselves! shall we follow such a one? Truly should we then be straying in mind, and mad!

25. "Is it that the Message is sent to him, of all people amongst us? No, he is a liar, an insolent one!"

26. Ah! they will know on the morrow, which is the liar, the insolent one!

27. For We will send the she-camel by way of trial for them. So watch them, (O Salih), and possess yourself in patience!

28. And inform them that the water is to be shared between (her and) them. Every drinking will be witnessed.

29. But they called to their companion, and he took a sword in hand, and hamstrung (her).

30. Ah! how (terrible) was My Chastisement and My Warning!

31. For We sent against them a single Mighty Blast, and they became like the dry stubble used by one who pens cattle.

32. And We have indeed made the Qur'an easy to understand and remember: then is there any that will receive admonition?

33. The people of Lut rejected (his) warning.

34. We sent against them a violent Tornado with showers of stones, (which destroyed them), except Lut's household: them We delivered by early Dawn,-

35. As a Grace from Us: thus do We reward those who give thanks.

36. And (Lut) did warn them of Our Punishment, but they disputed about the Warning.

37. And they even sought to snatch away his guests from him, but We blinded their eyes. (They heard:) "Now taste you My Wrath and My Warning."

fahal mim-muddakir. **(Section 1)**

23. Kazzabat Samoodu binnuzur.

24. Faqaalooo a-basharam-minnaa waaḥidan nattabi'uhooo innaaa izal-lafee ḍalaaliñw-wa su'ur.

25. 'A-ulqiyaz-zikru 'alayhi mim bayninaa bal huwa kazzaabun ashir.

26. Sa-ya'lamoona ghadam-manil-kazzaabul-ashir.

27. Innaa mursilun-naaqati fitnatal-lahum fartaqibhum waṣṭabir.

28. Wa nabbi'hum annal-maaa'a qismatum baynahum kullu shirbim-muḥtaḍar.

29. Fanaadaw ṣaaḥibahum fata'aaṭaa fa'aqar.

30. Fakayfa kaana 'azaabee wa nuzur.

31. Innaaa arsalnaa 'alayhim ṣayḥatañw-waaḥidatan fakaanoo kahasheemil-muḥtaẓir.

32. Wa laqad yassarnal-Qur-aana liz-zikri fahal mim-muddakir.

33. Kazzabat qawmu Looṭim binnuzur.

34. Innaaa arsalnaa 'alayhim ḥaaṣiban illaaa aala Looṭ, najjaynaahum bisaḥar.

35. Ni'matam-min 'indinaa; kazaalika najzee man shakar.

36. Wa laqad anzarahum baṭshatanaa fatamaaraw binnuzur.

37. Wa laqad raawadoohu 'an ḍayfihee faṭamasnaaa a'yunahum fazooqoo 'azaabee wa nuzur.

فَهَلْ مِنْ مُّدَّكِرٍ ﴿٢٢﴾

كَذَّبَتْ ثَمُوْدُ بِالنُّذُرِ ﴿٢٣﴾

فَقَالُوْٓا اَبَشَرًا مِّنَّا وَاحِدًا نَّتَّبِعُهٗٓ

اِنَّآ اِذًا لَّفِيْ ضَلٰلٍ وَّسُعُرٍ ﴿٢٤﴾

ءَاُلْقِيَ الذِّكْرُ عَلَيْهِ مِنْۢ بَيْنِنَا

بَلْ هُوَ كَذَّابٌ اَشِرٌ ﴿٢٥﴾

سَيَعْلَمُوْنَ غَدًا مَّنِ الْكَذَّابُ الْاَشِرُ ﴿٢٦﴾

اِنَّا مُرْسِلُوا النَّاقَةِ فِتْنَةً لَّهُمْ

فَارْتَقِبْهُمْ وَاصْطَبِرْ ﴿٢٧﴾

وَنَبِّئْهُمْ اَنَّ الْمَآءَ قِسْمَةٌۢ بَيْنَهُمْ

كُلُّ شِرْبٍ مُّحْتَضَرٌ ﴿٢٨﴾

فَنَادَوْا صَاحِبَهُمْ فَتَعَاطٰى فَعَقَرَ ﴿٢٩﴾

فَكَيْفَ كَانَ عَذَابِيْ وَنُذُرِ ﴿٣٠﴾

اِنَّآ اَرْسَلْنَا عَلَيْهِمْ صَيْحَةً وَّاحِدَةً

فَكَانُوْا كَهَشِيْمِ الْمُحْتَظِرِ ﴿٣١﴾

وَلَقَدْ يَسَّرْنَا الْقُرْاٰنَ لِلذِّكْرِ

فَهَلْ مِنْ مُّدَّكِرٍ ﴿٣٢﴾

كَذَّبَتْ قَوْمُ لُوْطٍۢ بِالنُّذُرِ ﴿٣٣﴾

اِنَّآ اَرْسَلْنَا عَلَيْهِمْ حَاصِبًا اِلَّآ اٰلَ

لُوْطٍ ؕ نَجَّيْنٰهُمْ بِسَحَرٍ ﴿٣٤﴾

نِّعْمَةً مِّنْ عِنْدِنَا ؕ كَذٰلِكَ نَجْزِيْ

مَنْ شَكَرَ ﴿٣٥﴾

وَلَقَدْ اَنْذَرَهُمْ بَطْشَتَنَا فَتَمَارَوْا

بِالنُّذُرِ ﴿٣٦﴾

وَلَقَدْ رَاوَدُوْهُ عَنْ ضَيْفِهٖ فَطَمَسْنَآ

اَعْيُنَهُمْ فَذُوْقُوْا عَذَابِيْ وَنُذُرِ ﴿٣٧﴾

Ikhfa اخفاء Ghunna غنّہ Ikhfa Meem Saakin اخفاء میم ساکن Idghaam ادغام Qalqala قلقلہ Qalb قلب Idghaam Meem Saakin ادغام میم ساکن

38. Early on the morrow an abiding Punishment seized them:

39. "So taste you My Wrath and My Warning."

40. And We have indeed made the Qur'an easy to understand and remember: then is there any that will receive admonition?

41. To the People of Pharaoh, too, aforetime, came Warners (from Allah).

42. The (people) rejected all Our Signs; but We seized them with such Chastisement (as comes) from One Exalted in Power, able to carry out His Will.

43. Are your Unbelievers, (O Quraish), better than they? Or have you an immunity in the Sacred Books?

44. Or do they say: "We acting together can defend ourselves"?

45. The hosts will all be routed and will turn and flee.

46. No, the Hour (of Judgment) is the time promised them (for their full recompense): And that Hour will be most grievous and most bitter.

47. Truly those in sin are the ones straying in mind, and mad.

48. The Day they will be dragged through the Fire on their faces, (they will hear:) "Taste you the touch of Hell!"

49. Lo! We have created every thing by measure.

50. And Our Command is but a single (Act),- like the twinkling of an eye.

51. And (oft) in the past, have We destroyed gangs like unto you: then is there any that will receive admonition?

52. All that they do is noted in (their) Books (of Deeds):

53. Every matter, small and great, is on record.

54. As to the Righteous, they will be in the midst of Gardens and Rivers,

55. In an Assembly of Truth, in the Presence of a Sovereign Omnipotent.

38. Wa laqad ṣabbaḥahum bukratan 'azaabum-mustaqirr.

39. Fazooqoo 'azaabee wa nuzur.

40. Wa laqad yassarnal-Qur-aana liz-zikri fahal mim-muddakir. **(Section 2)**

41. Wa laqad jaaa'a Aala Fir-'awnan-nuzur.

42. Kazzaboo bi-Aayaatinaa kullihaa fa-akhaznaahum akhza 'azeezim-muqtadir.

43. Akuffaarukum khayrum-min ulaaa'ikum am lakum baraaa'atun fiz-Zubur.

44. Am yaqooloona naḥnu jamee'um-muntaṣir.

45. Sa-yuhzamul-jam'u wa yuwalloonad-dubur.

46. Balis-Saa'atu maw'iduhum was-Saa'atu adhaa wa amarr.

47. Innal-mujrimeena fee ḍalaaliñw-wa su'ur.

48. Yawma yus-ḥaboona fin-Naari 'alaa wujoohihim zooqoo massa saqar.

49. Innaa kulla shay'in khalaqnaahu biqadar.

50. Wa maaa amrunaaa illaa waaḥidatun kalamḥim bilbaṣar.

51. Wa laqad ahlaknaaa ash-yaa'akum fahal mim-muddakir.

52. Wa kullu shay'in fa'aloohu fiz-Zubur.

53. Wa kullu sagheeriñw-wa kabeerim-mustaṭar.

54. Innal-muttaqeena fee Jannaatiñw-wa nahar.

55. Fee maq'adi ṣidqin 'inda Maleekim-Muqtadir. **(Section 3)**

وَلَقَدْ صَبَّحَهُم بُكْرَةً عَذَابٌ
مُّسْتَقِرٌّ ﴿٣٨﴾
فَذُوقُوا عَذَابِي وَنُذُرِ ﴿٣٩﴾
وَلَقَدْ يَسَّرْنَا الْقُرْآنَ لِلذِّكْرِ
فَهَلْ مِن مُّدَّكِرٍ ﴿٤٠﴾
وَلَقَدْ جَاءَ آلَ فِرْعَوْنَ النُّذُرُ ﴿٤١﴾
كَذَّبُوا بِآيَاتِنَا كُلِّهَا فَأَخَذْنَاهُمْ
أَخْذَ عَزِيزٍ مُّقْتَدِرٍ ﴿٤٢﴾
أَكُفَّارُكُمْ خَيْرٌ مِّنْ أُولَٰئِكُمْ أَمْ
لَكُم بَرَاءَةٌ فِي الزُّبُرِ ﴿٤٣﴾
أَمْ يَقُولُونَ نَحْنُ جَمِيعٌ مُّنتَصِرٌ ﴿٤٤﴾
سَيُهْزَمُ الْجَمْعُ وَيُوَلُّونَ الدُّبُرَ ﴿٤٥﴾
بَلِ السَّاعَةُ مَوْعِدُهُمْ وَالسَّاعَةُ
أَدْهَىٰ وَأَمَرُّ ﴿٤٦﴾
إِنَّ الْمُجْرِمِينَ فِي ضَلَالٍ وَسُعُرٍ ﴿٤٧﴾
يَوْمَ يُسْحَبُونَ فِي النَّارِ عَلَىٰ
وُجُوهِهِمْ ذُوقُوا مَسَّ سَقَرَ ﴿٤٨﴾
إِنَّا كُلَّ شَيْءٍ خَلَقْنَاهُ بِقَدَرٍ ﴿٤٩﴾
وَمَا أَمْرُنَا إِلَّا وَاحِدَةٌ كَلَمْحٍ بِالْبَصَرِ ﴿٥٠﴾
وَلَقَدْ أَهْلَكْنَا أَشْيَاعَكُمْ فَهَلْ
مِن مُّدَّكِرٍ ﴿٥١﴾
وَكُلُّ شَيْءٍ فَعَلُوهُ فِي الزُّبُرِ ﴿٥٢﴾
وَكُلُّ صَغِيرٍ وَكَبِيرٍ مُّسْتَطَرٌ ﴿٥٣﴾
إِنَّ الْمُتَّقِينَ فِي جَنَّاتٍ وَنَهَرٍ ﴿٥٤﴾
فِي مَقْعَدِ صِدْقٍ عِندَ مَلِيكٍ
مُّقْتَدِرٍ ﴿٥٥﴾

وقف لازم

Ikhfa اخفاء | Ghunna غنّہ | Ikhfa Meem Saakin اخفاء میم ساکن | Idghaam ادغام | Qalqala قلقلہ | Qalb قلب | Idghaam Meem Saakin ادغام میم ساکن

55. Allah, Most Gracious

In the name of Allah, Most Gracious, Most Merciful.

1. (Allah) Most Gracious!

2. It is He Who has taught the Qur'an.

3. He has created man:

4. He has taught him speech (and intelligence).

5. The sun and the moon follow courses (exactly) computed;

6. The stars and the trees adore.

7. And the sky He hath uplifted; and He hath set the measure.

8. In order that ye may not transgress (due) balance.

9. So establish weight with justice and fall not short in the balance.

10. It is He Who has spread out the earth for (His) creatures:

11. Therein is fruit and date-palms, producing spathes (enclosing dates);

12. Husked grain and scented herb.

13. Then which of the favours of your Lord will you deny?

14. He created man from sounding clay like unto pottery,

15. And He created Jinns from fire free of smoke:

16. Then which of the favours of your Lord will you deny?

17. (He is) Lord of the two Easts and Lord of the two Wests:

18. Then which of the favours of your Lord will you deny?

19. He hath loosed the two seas. They meet.

20. Between them is a Barrier which they do not transgress:

21. Then which of the favours of your Lord will you deny?

Sûrat ar-Raḥmân–55

(Revealed at Madinah)

Bismillaahir Raḥmaanir Raḥeem

1. Ar-Raḥmaan.
2. 'Allamal-Qur-aan.
3. Khalaqal-insaan.
4. 'Allamahul-ba-yaan.
5. Ashshamsu walqamaru biḥusbaan.
6. Wannajmu washshajaru yasjudaan.
7. Wassamaaa'a rafa'ahaa wa waḍa'al-Meezaan.
8. Allaa tatghaw fil-meezaan.
9. Wa aqeemul-wazna bil-qisṭi wa laa tukhsirul-meezaan.
10. Wal-arḍa waḍa'ahaa lil-anaam.
11. Feehaa faakihatuñw-wan-nakhlu zaatul-akmaam.
12. Walḥabbu zul-'aṣfi war-Rayḥaan.
13. Fabi-ayyi aalaaa'i Rabbi-kumaa tukazzibaan.
14. Khalaqal-insaana min ṣalṣaalin kalfakhkhaar.
15. Wa khalaqal-jaaanna mim-maarijim-min-Naar.
16. Fabi-ayyi aalaaa'i Rabbi-kumaa tukazzibaan.
17. Rabbul-mashriqayni wa Rabbul-maghribayn.
18. Fabi-ayyi aalaaa'i Rabbi-kumaa tukazzibaan.
19. Marajal-baḥrayni yalta-qiyaan.
20. Baynahumaa barzakhul-laa yabghiyaan.
21. Fabi-ayyi aalaaa'i Rabbi-kumaa tukazzibaan.

(٥٥) سُوۡرَةُ الرَّحۡمٰنِ مَدَنِيَّةٌ (٩٧)

بِسۡمِ اللّٰهِ الرَّحۡمٰنِ الرَّحِيۡمِ

اَلرَّحۡمٰنُ ۝١

عَلَّمَ الۡقُرۡاٰنَ ۝٢

خَلَقَ الۡاِنۡسَانَ ۝٣

عَلَّمَهُ الۡبَيَانَ ۝٤

اَلشَّمۡسُ وَالۡقَمَرُ بِحُسۡبَانٍ ۝٥

وَّالنَّجۡمُ وَالشَّجَرُ يَسۡجُدٰنِ ۝٦

وَالسَّمَآءَ رَفَعَهَا وَوَضَعَ الۡمِيۡزَانَ ۝٧

اَلَّا تَطۡغَوۡا فِى الۡمِيۡزَانِ ۝٨

وَاَقِيۡمُوا الۡوَزۡنَ بِالۡقِسۡطِ وَلَا تُخۡسِرُوا

الۡمِيۡزَانَ ۝٩

وَالۡاَرۡضَ وَضَعَهَا لِلۡاَنَامِ ۝١٠

فِيۡهَا فَاكِهَةٌ وَّالنَّخۡلُ ذَاتُ

الۡاَكۡمَامِ ۝١١

وَالۡحَبُّ ذُو الۡعَصۡفِ وَالرَّيۡحَانُ ۝١٢

فَبِاَىِّ اٰلَآءِ رَبِّكُمَا تُكَذِّبٰنِ ۝١٣

خَلَقَ الۡاِنۡسَانَ مِنۡ صَلۡصَالٍ

كَالۡفَخَّارِ ۝١٤

وَخَلَقَ الۡجَآنَّ مِنۡ مَّارِجٍ مِّنۡ نَّارٍ ۝١٥

فَبِاَىِّ اٰلَآءِ رَبِّكُمَا تُكَذِّبٰنِ ۝١٦

رَبُّ الۡمَشۡرِقَيۡنِ وَرَبُّ الۡمَغۡرِبَيۡنِ ۝١٧

فَبِاَىِّ اٰلَآءِ رَبِّكُمَا تُكَذِّبٰنِ ۝١٨

مَرَجَ الۡبَحۡرَيۡنِ يَلۡتَقِيٰنِ ۝١٩

بَيۡنَهُمَا بَرۡزَخٌ لَّا يَبۡغِيٰنِ ۝٢٠

فَبِاَىِّ اٰلَآءِ رَبِّكُمَا تُكَذِّبٰنِ ۝٢١

Ikhfa اخفاء · Ghunna غُنّہ · Ikhfa Meem Saakin اخفاء میم ساکن · Idghaam ادغام · Qalqala قلقلہ · Qalb قلب · Idghaam Meem Saakin ادغام میم ساکن

22. Out of them come Pearls and Coral:	22. Yakhruju minhumal-lu'lu'u wal-marjaan.	يَخْرُجُ مِنْهُمَا اللُّؤْلُؤُ وَالْمَرْجَانُ ﴿٢٢﴾
23. Then which of the favours of your Lord will you deny?	23. Fabi-ayyi aalaaa'i Rabbi-kumaa tukazzibaan.	فَبِاَيِّ اٰلَاۤءِ رَبِّكُمَا تُكَذِّبٰنِ ﴿٢٣﴾
24. And His are the Ships sailing smoothly through the seas, lofty as mountains:	24. Wa lahul-jawaaril-mun-sha'aatu fil-baḥri kal-a'laam.	وَلَهُ الْجَوَارِ الْمُنْشَئٰتُ فِي الْبَحْرِ كَالْاَعْلَامِ ﴿٢٤﴾
25. Then which of the favours of your Lord will you deny?	25. Fabi-ayyi aalaaa'i Rabbi-kumaa tukazzibaan. **(Section 1)**	فَبِاَيِّ اٰلَاۤءِ رَبِّكُمَا تُكَذِّبٰنِ ﴿٢٥﴾
26. All that is on earth will perish:	26. Kullu man 'alayhaa faan.	كُلُّ مَنْ عَلَيْهَا فَانٍ ﴿٢٦﴾
27. But will abide (for ever) the Face of your Lord,- full of Majesty, Bounty and Honour.	27. Wa yabqaa Wajhu Rabbika Zul-Jalaali wal-Ikraam.	وَّيَبْقٰى وَجْهُ رَبِّكَ ذُو الْجَلٰلِ وَالْاِكْرَامِ ﴿٢٧﴾
28. Then which of the favours of your Lord will you deny?	28. Fabi-ayyi aalaaa'i Rabbi-kumaa tukazzibaan.	فَبِاَيِّ اٰلَاۤءِ رَبِّكُمَا تُكَذِّبٰنِ ﴿٢٨﴾
29. Of Him seeks (its need) every creature in the heavens and on earth: every day in (new) Splendour does He (shine)!	29. Yas'aluhoo man fis-samaawaati walarḍ; kulla yawmin Huwa fee shaån.	يَسْـَٔلُهُ مَنْ فِي السَّمٰوٰتِ وَالْاَرْضِ ۚ كُلَّ يَوْمٍ هُوَ فِيْ شَاْنٍ ﴿٢٩﴾
30. Then which of the favours of your Lord will you deny?	30. Fabi-ayyi aalaaa'i Rabbi-kumaa tukazzibaan.	فَبِاَيِّ اٰلَاۤءِ رَبِّكُمَا تُكَذِّبٰنِ ﴿٣٠﴾
31. Soon shall We settle your affairs, O burden of the world.	31. Sanafrughu lakum ayyu-has-saqalaan.	سَنَفْرُغُ لَكُمْ اَيُّهَ الثَّقَلٰنِ ﴿٣١﴾
32. Then which of the favours of your Lord will you deny?	32. Fabi-ayyi aalaaa'i Rabbi-kumaa tukazzibaan.	فَبِاَيِّ اٰلَاۤءِ رَبِّكُمَا تُكَذِّبٰنِ ﴿٣٢﴾
33. O you assembly of Jinns and men! If it be you can pass beyond the zones of the heavens and the earth, pass you! not without authority shall you be able to pass!	33. Yaa ma'sharal-jinni wal-insi inis-taṭa'tum an tanfuzoo min aqṭaaris-samaawaati wal-arḍi fanfuzoo; laa tanfuzoona illaa bisulṭaan.	يٰمَعْشَرَ الْجِنِّ وَالْاِنْسِ اِنِ اسْتَطَعْتُمْ اَنْ تَنْفُذُوْا مِنْ اَقْطَارِ السَّمٰوٰتِ وَالْاَرْضِ فَانْفُذُوْا ۚ لَا تَنْفُذُوْنَ اِلَّا بِسُلْطٰنٍ ﴿٣٣﴾
34. Then which of the favours of your Lord will you deny?	34. Fabi-ayyi aalaaa'i Rabbi-kumaa tukazzibaan.	فَبِاَيِّ اٰلَاۤءِ رَبِّكُمَا تُكَذِّبٰنِ ﴿٣٤﴾
35. On you will be sent (O you evil ones twain) a flame of fire (to burn) and a smoke (to choke): no defence will you have:	35. Yursalu 'alaykumaa shu-waazum-min naariñw-wa nu-ḥaasun falaa tantaṣiraan.	يُرْسَلُ عَلَيْكُمَا شُوَاظٌ مِّنْ نَّارٍ ۙ وَّنُحَاسٌ فَلَا تَنْتَصِرٰنِ ﴿٣٥﴾
36. Then which of the favours of your Lord will you deny?	36. Fabi-ayyi aalaaa'i Rabbi-kumaa tukazzibaan.	فَبِاَيِّ اٰلَاۤءِ رَبِّكُمَا تُكَذِّبٰنِ ﴿٣٦﴾
37. When the sky is rent asunder, and it becomes red like ointment:	37. Fa-izan shaqqatis-sa-maaa'u fakaanat wardatan kaddihaan.	فَاِذَا انْشَقَّتِ السَّمَاۤءُ فَكَانَتْ وَرْدَةً كَالدِّهَانِ ﴿٣٧﴾
38. Then which of the favours of your Lord will you deny?	38. Fabi-ayyi aalaaa'i Rabbi-kumaa tukazzibaan.	فَبِاَيِّ اٰلَاۤءِ رَبِّكُمَا تُكَذِّبٰنِ ﴿٣٨﴾
39. On that Day no question will be asked of man	39. Fa-yawma'izil-laa yus'alu 'an zambiheee insuñw-	فَيَوْمَئِذٍ لَّا يُسْـَٔلُ عَنْ ذَنْۢبِهٖۤ اِنْسٌ

Ikhfa اخفاء | Ghunna غنّہ | Ikhfa Meem Saakin اخفاء میم ساکن | Idghaam ادغام | Qalqala قلقلہ | Qalb قلب | Idghaam Meem Saakin ادغام میم ساکن

or Jinn as to his sin.	wa laa jaaann.	وَّلَا جَآنٌّ ﴿٣٩﴾
40. Then which of the favours of your Lord will you deny?	40. Fabi-ayyi aalaaa'i Rabbikumaa tukazzibaan.	فَبِاَيِّ اٰلَآءِ رَبِّكُمَا تُكَذِّبٰنِ ﴿٤٠﴾
41. (For) the sinners will be known by their marks: and they will be seized by their forelocks and their feet.	41. Yu'raful-mujrimoona biseemaahum fa-yu'khazu binnawaaṣi wal-aqdaam.	يُعْرَفُ الْمُجْرِمُوْنَ بِسِيْمٰهُمْ فَيُؤْخَذُ بِالنَّوَاصِيْ وَالْاَقْدَامِ ﴿٤١﴾
42. Then which of the favours of your Lord will you deny?	42. Fabi-ayyi aalaaa'i Rabbikumaa tukazzibaan.	فَبِاَيِّ اٰلَآءِ رَبِّكُمَا تُكَذِّبٰنِ ﴿٤٢﴾
43. This is the Hell which the Sinners deny:	43. Haazihee Jahannamul-latee yukazzibu bihal-mujrimoon.	هٰذِهٖ جَهَنَّمُ الَّتِيْ يُكَذِّبُ بِهَا الْمُجْرِمُوْنَ ﴿٤٣﴾
44. In its midst and in the midst of boiling hot water will they wander round!	44. Yaṭoofoona baynahaa wa bayna ḥameemin aan.	يَطُوْفُوْنَ بَيْنَهَا وَبَيْنَ حَمِيْمٍ اٰنٍ ﴿٤٤﴾
45. Then which of the favours of your Lord will you deny?	45. Fabi-ayyi aalaaa'i Rabbikumaa tukazzibaan. **(Section 2)**	فَبِاَيِّ اٰلَآءِ رَبِّكُمَا تُكَذِّبٰنِ ﴿٤٥﴾
46. But for him who feareth the standing before his Lord there are two gardens.	46. Wa liman khaafa maqaama Rabbihee Jannataan.	وَلِمَنْ خَافَ مَقَامَ رَبِّهٖ جَنَّتٰنِ ﴿٤٦﴾
47. Then which of the favours of your Lord will you deny?-	47. Fabi-ayyi aalaaa'i Rabbikumaa tukazzibaan.	فَبِاَيِّ اٰلَآءِ رَبِّكُمَا تُكَذِّبٰنِ ﴿٤٧﴾
48. Containing all kinds (of trees and delights);-	48. Zawaataaa afnaan.	ذَوَاتَآ اَفْنَانٍ ﴿٤٨﴾
49. Then which of the favours of your Lord will you deny?-	49. Fabi-ayyi aalaaa'i Rabbikumaa tukazzibaan.	فَبِاَيِّ اٰلَآءِ رَبِّكُمَا تُكَذِّبٰنِ ﴿٤٩﴾
50. In them (each) will be two Springs flowing (free);	50. Feehimaa 'aynaani tajriyaan.	فِيْهِمَا عَيْنٰنِ تَجْرِيٰنِ ﴿٥٠﴾
51. Then which of the favours of your Lord will you deny?-	51. Fabi-ayyi aalaaa'i Rabbikumaa tukazzibaan.	فَبِاَيِّ اٰلَآءِ رَبِّكُمَا تُكَذِّبٰنِ ﴿٥١﴾
52. In them will be Fruits of every kind, two and two.	52. Feehimaa min kulli faakihatin zawjaan.	فِيْهِمَا مِنْ كُلِّ فَاكِهَةٍ زَوْجٰنِ ﴿٥٢﴾
53. Then which of the favours of your Lord will you deny?	53. Fabi-ayyi aalaaa'i Rabbikumaa tukazzibaan.	فَبِاَيِّ اٰلَآءِ رَبِّكُمَا تُكَذِّبٰنِ ﴿٥٣﴾
54. Reclining upon couches lined with silk brocade, the fruit of both gardens near to hand..	54. Muttaki'eena 'alaa furushim baṭaaa'inuhaa min istabraq; wa janal-jannatayni daan.	مُتَّكِـِٕيْنَ عَلٰى فُرُشٍۢ بَطَآئِنُهَا مِنْ اِسْتَبْرَقٍ ۗ وَجَنَا الْجَنَّتَيْنِ دَانٍ ﴿٥٤﴾
55. Then which of the favours of your Lord will you deny?	55. Fabi-ayyi aalaaa'i Rabbikumaa tukazzibaan.	فَبِاَيِّ اٰلَآءِ رَبِّكُمَا تُكَذِّبٰنِ ﴿٥٥﴾
56. In them will be (Maidens), chaste, restraining their glances, whom no man or Jinn before them has touched;-	56. Feehinna qaaṣiratuṭ-ṭarfi lam yaṭmishunna insun qablahum wa laa jaaann.	فِيْهِنَّ قٰصِرٰتُ الطَّرْفِ ۙ لَمْ يَطْمِثْهُنَّ اِنْسٌ قَبْلَهُمْ وَلَا جَآنٌّ ﴿٥٦﴾
57. Then which of the favours of your Lord will you deny?-	57. Fabi-ayyi aalaaa'i Rabbikumaa tukazzibaan.	فَبِاَيِّ اٰلَآءِ رَبِّكُمَا تُكَذِّبٰنِ ﴿٥٧﴾
58. Like unto Rubies and coral.	58. Ka-annahunnal-yaaqootu wal-marjaan.	كَاَنَّهُنَّ الْيَاقُوْتُ وَالْمَرْجَانُ ﴿٥٨﴾
59. Then which of the favours of your Lord will you deny?	59. Fabi-ayyi aalaaa'i Rabbikumaa tukazzibaan.	فَبِاَيِّ اٰلَآءِ رَبِّكُمَا تُكَذِّبٰنِ ﴿٥٩﴾
60. Is there any Reward for Good - other than Good?	60. Hal jazaaa'ul-iḥsaani illal-iḥsaan.	هَلْ جَزَآءُ الْاِحْسَانِ اِلَّا الْاِحْسَانُ ﴿٦٠﴾

وقف لازم

ع ٢

Ikhfa اخفاء | Ghunna غُنّہ | Ikhfa Meem Saakin اخفاءمیم ساکن | Idghaam ادغام | Qalqala قلقلہ | Qalb قلب | Idghaam Meem Saakin ادغام میم ساکن

61. Then which of the favours of your Lord will you deny?	61. Fabi-ayyi aalaaa'i Rabbi-kumaa tukazzibaan.	فَبِاَيِّ اٰلَآءِ رَبِّكُمَا تُكَذِّبٰنِ ٦١
62. And besides these two, there are two other Gardens,-	62. Wa min doonihimaa Jannataan.	وَمِنْ دُوْنِهِمَا جَنَّتٰنِ ٦٢
63. Then which of the favours of your Lord will you deny?-	63. Fabi-ayyi aalaaa'i Rabbi-kumaa tukazzibaan.	فَبِاَيِّ اٰلَآءِ رَبِّكُمَا تُكَذِّبٰنِ ٦٣
64. Dark-green in colour (from plentiful watering).	64. Mudhaaammataan.	مُدْهَآمَّتٰنِ ٦٤
65. Then which of the favours of your Lord will you deny?	65. Fabi-ayyi aalaaa'i Rabbi-kumaa tukazzibaan.	فَبِاَيِّ اٰلَآءِ رَبِّكُمَا تُكَذِّبٰنِ ٦٥
66. Wherein are two abundant spring.	66. Feehimaa 'aynaani naḍ-ḍaakhataan.	فِيْهِمَا عَيْنٰنِ نَضَّاخَتٰنِ ٦٦
67. Then which of the favours of your Lord will you deny?	67. Fabi-ayyi aalaaa'i Rabbi-kumaa tukazzibaan.	فَبِاَيِّ اٰلَآءِ رَبِّكُمَا تُكَذِّبٰنِ ٦٧
68. In them will be Fruits, and dates and pomegranates:	68. Feehimaa faakihatuñw-wa nakhluñw-wa rummaan.	فِيْهِمَا فَاكِهَةٌ وَّنَخْلٌ وَّرُمَّانٌ ٦٨
69. Then which of the favours of your Lord will you deny?	69. Fabi-ayyi aalaaa'i Rabbi-kumaa tukazzibaan.	فَبِاَيِّ اٰلَآءِ رَبِّكُمَا تُكَذِّبٰنِ ٦٩
70. In them will be fair (Com-panions), good, beautiful;-	70. Feehinna khayraatun ḥisaan.	فِيْهِنَّ خَيْرٰتٌ حِسَانٌ ٧٠
71. Then which of the favours of your Lord will you deny?-	71. Fabi-ayyi aalaaa'i Rabbi-kumaa tukazzibaan.	فَبِاَيِّ اٰلَآءِ رَبِّكُمَا تُكَذِّبٰنِ ٧١
72. Fair ones, close-guarded in pavilions–	72. Hoorum-maqṣooraatun fil-khiyaam.	حُوْرٌ مَّقْصُوْرٰتٌ فِي الْخِيَامِ ٧٢
73. Then which of the favours of your Lord will you deny?-	73. Fabi-ayyi aalaaa'i Rabbi-kumaa tukazzibaan.	فَبِاَيِّ اٰلَآءِ رَبِّكُمَا تُكَذِّبٰنِ ٧٣
74. Whom no man or Jinn before them has touched;-	74. Lam yatmis-hunna insun qablahum wa laa jaaann.	لَمْ يَطْمِثْهُنَّ اِنْسٌ قَبْلَهُمْ وَلَا جَآنٌّ ٧٤
75. Then which of the favours of your Lord will you deny?-	75. Fabi-ayyi aalaaa'i Rabbi-kumaa tukazzibaan.	فَبِاَيِّ اٰلَآءِ رَبِّكُمَا تُكَذِّبٰنِ ٧٥
76. Reclining on green Cushi-ons and rich Carpets of beauty.	76. Muttaki'eena 'alaa rafrafin khuḍriñw-wa 'abqariyyin ḥisaan.	مُتَّكِـِٕيْنَ عَلٰى رَفْرَفٍ خُضْرٍ وَّعَبْقَرِيٍّ حِسَانٍ ٧٦
77. Then which of the favours of your Lord will you deny?	77. Fabi-ayyi aalaaa'i Rabbi-kumaa tukazzibaan.	فَبِاَيِّ اٰلَآءِ رَبِّكُمَا تُكَذِّبٰنِ ٧٧
78. Blessed be the name of thy Lord, Mighty and Glorious!	78. Tabaarakasmu Rabbika Zil-Jalaali wal-Ikraam. **(Section 3)**	تَبٰرَكَ اسْمُ رَبِّكَ ذِي الْجَلٰلِ وَالْاِكْرَامِ ٧٨ ع ٣

56. The Inevitable Event

In the name of Allah, Most Gracious, Most Merciful.

Sûrat al-Wâqi'ah–56

(Revealed at Makkah)

Bismillaahir Raḥmaanir Raḥeem

(٥٦) سُوْرَةُ الْوَاقِعَةِ مَكِّيَّةٌ (٤٦)

بِسْمِ اللّٰهِ الرَّحْمٰنِ الرَّحِيْمِ

1. When the inevitable event comes to pass,	1. Izaa waqa'atil-waaqi'ah.	اِذَا وَقَعَتِ الْوَاقِعَةُ ١
2. Then will no (soul) deny its coming.	2. Laysa liwaq'atihaa kaazi-bah.	لَيْسَ لِوَقْعَتِهَا كَاذِبَةٌ ٢ وقف لازم
3. (Many) will it bring low; (many) will it exalt;	3. Khaafiḍatur-raafi'ah.	خَافِضَةٌ رَّافِعَةٌ ٣
4. When the Earth shall be shaken to its depths,	4. Izaa rujjatil-arḍu rajjaa.	اِذَا رُجَّتِ الْاَرْضُ رَجًّا ٤

Ikhfa اخفاء · Ghunna غنّہ · Ikhfa Meem Saakin اخفاء میم ساکن · Idghaam ادغام · Qalqala قلقلہ · Qalb قلب · Idghaam Meem Saakin ادغام میم ساکن

5. And the mountains shall be crumbled to atoms,	5. Wa bussatil-jibaalu bassaa.	وَّبُسَّتِ الْجِبَالُ بَسًّا ﴿٥﴾
6. Becoming dust scattered abroad,	6. Fakaanat habaaa'am-mumbassaa.	فَكَانَتْ هَبَآءً مُّنۢبَثًّا ﴿٦﴾
7. And you shall be sorted out into three classes.	7. Wa kuntum azwaajan salaasah.	وَّكُنْتُمْ اَزْوَاجًا ثَلٰثَةً ﴿٧﴾
8. Then (there will be) the People of the Right Hand;– What will be the People of the Right Hand?	8. Fa-Aṣ-ḥaabul-Maymanati maaa Aṣ-ḥaabul-Maymanah.	فَاَصْحٰبُ الْمَيْمَنَةِ ۙ۬ مَاۤ اَصْحٰبُ الْمَيْمَنَةِ ﴿٨﴾
9. And the People of the Left Hand,–what will be the People of the Left Hand?	9. Wa Aṣ-ḥaabul-Mash'amati maaa Aṣ-ḥaabul-Mash'amah.	وَاَصْحٰبُ الْمَشْـَٔمَةِ ۙ۬ مَاۤ اَصْحٰبُ الْمَشْـَٔمَةِ ﴿٩﴾
10. And the foremost in the race, the foremost in the race:	10. Wassaabiqoonas-saabiqoon.	وَالسّٰبِقُوْنَ السّٰبِقُوْنَ ﴿١٠﴾
11. These will be those Nearest to Allah:	11. Ulaaa'ikal-muqarraboon.	اُولٰٓئِكَ الْمُقَرَّبُوْنَ ﴿١١﴾
12. In Gardens of Bliss:	12. Fee Jannaatin-Na'eem.	فِيْ جَنّٰتِ النَّعِيْمِ ﴿١٢﴾
13. A number of people from those of old,	13. Sullatum-minal-awwaleen.	ثُلَّةٌ مِّنَ الْاَوَّلِيْنَ ﴿١٣﴾
14. And a few from those of later times.	14. Wa qaleelum-minal-aakhireen.	وَقَلِيْلٌ مِّنَ الْاٰخِرِيْنَ ﴿١٤﴾
15. On lined couches,	15. 'Alaa sururim-mawḍoonah.	عَلٰى سُرُرٍ مَّوْضُوْنَةٍ ﴿١٥﴾
16. Reclining on them, facing each other.	16. Muttaki'eena 'alayhaa mutaqaabileen.	مُّتَّكِـِٕيْنَ عَلَيْهَا مُتَقٰبِلِيْنَ ﴿١٦﴾
17. There wait on them immortal youths.	17. Yaṭoofu 'alayhim wildaanum-mukhalladoon.	يَطُوْفُ عَلَيْهِمْ وِلْدَانٌ مُّخَلَّدُوْنَ ﴿١٧﴾
18. With goblets, (shining) beakers, and cups (filled) out of clear-flowing fountains:	18. Bi-akwaabiñw-wa abaareeq, wa kaåsim-mim-ma'een.	بِاَكْوَابٍ وَّاَبَارِيْقَ ۙ۬ وَكَاْسٍ مِّنْ مَّعِيْنٍ ﴿١٨﴾
19. No after-ache will they receive therefrom, nor will they suffer intoxication:	19. Laa yuṣadda'oona 'anhaa wa laa yunzifoon.	لَّا يُصَدَّعُوْنَ عَنْهَا وَلَا يُنْزِفُوْنَ ﴿١٩﴾
20. And with fruits, any that they may select:	20. Wa faakihatim-mimmaa yatakhayyaroon.	وَفَاكِهَةٍ مِّمَّا يَتَخَيَّرُوْنَ ﴿٢٠﴾
21. And the flesh of fowls, any that they may desire.	21. Wa laḥmi ṭayrim-mimmaa yashtahoon.	وَلَحْمِ طَيْرٍ مِّمَّا يَشْتَهُوْنَ ﴿٢١﴾
22. And (there are) fair ones with wide, lovely eyes,	22. Wa ḥoorun 'een.	وَحُوْرٌ عِيْنٌ ﴿٢٢﴾
23. Like unto Pearls well-guarded.	23. Ka-amsaalil-lu'lu'il-maknoon.	كَاَمْثَالِ اللُّؤْلُؤِ الْمَكْنُوْنِ ﴿٢٣﴾
24. A Reward for the deeds of their past (life).	24. Jazaaa'am bimaa kaanoo ya'maloon.	جَزَآءًۢ بِمَا كَانُوْا يَعْمَلُوْنَ ﴿٢٤﴾
25. Not frivolity will they hear therein, nor any taint of ill,-	25. Laa yasma'oona feehaa laghwañw-wa laa taåseemaa.	لَا يَسْمَعُوْنَ فِيْهَا لَغْوًا وَّلَا تَاْثِيْمًا ﴿٢٥﴾
26. Only the saying, "Peace! Peace".	26. Illaa qeelan salaaman salaamaa.	اِلَّا قِيْلًا سَلٰمًا سَلٰمًا ﴿٢٦﴾
27. The Companions of the Right Hand,- what will be the Companions of	27. Wa Aṣ-ḥaabul-Yameeni maaa Aṣ-ḥaabul-	وَاَصْحٰبُ الْيَمِيْنِ ۙ۬ مَاۤ اَصْحٰبُ

the Right Hand?	Yameen.	الْيَمِيْنِ ﴿٢٧﴾
28. (They will be) among Lote-trees without thorns,	28. Fee sidrim-makhḍood.	فِيْ سِدْرٍ مَّخْضُوْدٍ ﴿٢٨﴾
29. And clustered plantains,	29. Wa ṭalḥim-manḍood.	وَّطَلْحٍ مَّنْضُوْدٍ ﴿٢٩﴾
30. In shade long-extended,	30. Wa ẓillim-mamdood.	وَّظِلٍّ مَّمْدُوْدٍ ﴿٣٠﴾
31. And water gushing,	31. Wa maaa’im-maskoob.	وَّمَآءٍ مَّسْكُوْبٍ ﴿٣١﴾
32. And fruit in abundance.	32. Wa faakihatin kaseerah.	وَّفَاكِهَةٍ كَثِيْرَةٍ ﴿٣٢﴾
33. Whose season is not limited, nor (supply) forbidden,	33. Laa maqṭoo‘atiñw-wa laa mamnoo‘ah.	لَّا مَقْطُوْعَةٍ وَّلَا مَمْنُوْعَةٍ ﴿٣٣﴾
34. And on Thrones (of Dignity), raised high.	34. Wa furushim-marfoo‘ah.	وَّفُرُشٍ مَّرْفُوْعَةٍ ﴿٣٤﴾
35. Lo! We have created them a (new) creation.	35. Innaaa anshaånaahunna inshaaa’aa.	اِنَّآ اَنْشَاْنٰهُنَّ اِنْشَآءً ﴿٣٥﴾
36. And made them virgins,	36. Faja‘alnaahunna abkaaraa.	فَجَعَلْنٰهُنَّ اَبْكَارًا ﴿٣٦﴾
37. Lovers, friends,	37. ‘Uruban atraabaa.	عُرُبًا اَتْرَابًا ﴿٣٧﴾
38. For the Companions of the Right Hand.	38. Li-Aṣ-ḥaabil-Yameen. **(Section 1)**	لِّاَصْحٰبِ الْيَمِيْنِ ﴿٣٨﴾ ع
39. A (goodly) number from those of old,	39. Sullatum-minal-awwaleen.	ثُلَّةٌ مِّنَ الْاَوَّلِيْنَ ﴿٣٩﴾
40. And a (goodly) number from those of later times.	40. Wa sullatum-minal-aakhireen.	وَثُلَّةٌ مِّنَ الْاٰخِرِيْنَ ﴿٤٠﴾
41. The Companions of the Left Hand,- what will be the Companions of the Left Hand?	41. Wa Aṣ-ḥaabush-Shimaali maaa Aṣ-ḥaabush-Shimaal.	وَاَصْحٰبُ الشِّمَالِ ۙ مَآ اَصْحٰبُ الشِّمَالِ ﴿٤١﴾
42. In scorching wind and scalding water.	42. Fee samoomiñw-wa ḥameem.	فِيْ سَمُوْمٍ وَّحَمِيْمٍ ﴿٤٢﴾
43. And in the shades of Black Smoke:	43. Wa ẓillim-miñy-yaḥmoom.	وَّظِلٍّ مِّنْ يَّحْمُوْمٍ ﴿٤٣﴾
44. Nothing (will there be) to refresh, nor to please:	44. Laa baaridiñw-wa laa kareem.	لَّا بَارِدٍ وَّلَا كَرِيْمٍ ﴿٤٤﴾
45. Lo! hereto fore they were effete with luxury.	45. Innahum kaanoo qabla zaalika mutrafeen.	اِنَّهُمْ كَانُوْا قَبْلَ ذٰلِكَ مُتْرَفِيْنَ ﴿٤٥﴾
46. And persisted obstinately in wickedness supreme!	46. Wa kaanoo yuṣirroona ‘Alal-ḥinsil-‘aẓeem.	وَكَانُوْا يُصِرُّوْنَ عَلَى الْحِنْثِ الْعَظِيْمِ ﴿٤٦﴾
47. And they used to say, “What! when we die and become dust and bones, shall we then indeed be raised up again?-	47. Wa kaanoo yaqooloona a’izaa mitnaa wa kunnaa turaabañw-wa ‘iẓaaman ’a-innaa lamab‘oosoon.	وَكَانُوْا يَقُوْلُوْنَ ۙ اَئِذَا مِتْنَا وَكُنَّا تُرَابًا وَّعِظَامًا ءَاِنَّا لَمَبْعُوْثُوْنَ ﴿٤٧﴾
48. “(We) and our fathers of old?”	48. Awa aabaaa’unal-awwaloon.	اَوَاٰبَآؤُنَا الْاَوَّلُوْنَ ﴿٤٨﴾
49. Say: “Yes, those of old and those of later times,	49. Qul innal-awwaleena wal-aakhireen.	قُلْ اِنَّ الْاَوَّلِيْنَ وَالْاٰخِرِيْنَ ﴿٤٩﴾

Ikhfa اخفاء · Ghunna غنّہ · Ikhfa Meem Saakin اخفاء میم ساکن · Idghaam ادغام · Qalqala قلقلہ · Qalb قلب · Idghaam Meem Saakin ادغام میم ساکن

Translation	Transliteration	Arabic
50. "All will certainly be gathered together for the meeting appointed for a Day well-known.	50. Lamajmoo'oona ilaa meeqaati Yawmim-ma'loom.	لَمَجْمُوعُونَ إِلَىٰ مِيقَاتِ يَوْمٍ مَّعْلُومٍ ﴿٥٠﴾
51. Then lo! Ye, the erring, the deniers,	51. Summa innakum ayyuhad-daaalloonal-mukazziboon.	ثُمَّ إِنَّكُمْ أَيُّهَا الضَّالُّونَ الْمُكَذِّبُونَ ﴿٥١﴾
52. "You will surely taste of the Tree of Zaqqum.	52. La-aakiloona min shajarim-min Zaqqoom.	لَآكِلُونَ مِن شَجَرٍ مِّن زَقُّومٍ ﴿٥٢﴾
53. "Then will you fill your insides therewith,	53. Famaali'oona minhal-butoon.	فَمَالِئُونَ مِنْهَا الْبُطُونَ ﴿٥٣﴾
54. "And drink Boiling Water on top of it:	54. Fashaariboona 'alayhi minal-hameem.	فَشَارِبُونَ عَلَيْهِ مِنَ الْحَمِيمِ ﴿٥٤﴾
55. Drinking even as the camel drinketh.	55. Fashaariboona shurbal-heem.	فَشَارِبُونَ شُرْبَ الْهِيمِ ﴿٥٥﴾
56. This will be their welcome on the Day of Judgment.	56. Haazaa nuzuluhum Yawmad-Deen.	هَٰذَا نُزُلُهُمْ يَوْمَ الدِّينِ ﴿٥٦﴾
57. We created you. Will ye then admit the truth?	57. Nahnu khalaqnaakum falaw laa tusaddiqoon.	نَحْنُ خَلَقْنَاكُمْ فَلَوْلَا تُصَدِّقُونَ ﴿٥٧﴾
58. Have you seen that which ye emit?	58. Afara'aytum maa tumnoon.	أَفَرَأَيْتُم مَّا تُمْنُونَ ﴿٥٨﴾
59. Is it you who create it, or are We the Creators?	59. 'A-antum takhluqoonahooo am Nahnul-khaaliqoon.	ءَأَنتُمْ تَخْلُقُونَهُ أَمْ نَحْنُ الْخَالِقُونَ ﴿٥٩﴾
60. We have decreed Death to be your common lot, and We are not to be frustrated-	60. Nahnu qaddarnaa baynakumul-mawta wa maa Nahnu bimasbooqeen.	نَحْنُ قَدَّرْنَا بَيْنَكُمُ الْمَوْتَ وَمَا نَحْنُ بِمَسْبُوقِينَ ﴿٦٠﴾
61. from changing your Forms and creating you (again) in (forms) that you know not.	61. 'Alaaa an nubaddila amsaalakum wa nunshi'akum fee maa laa ta'lamoon.	عَلَىٰ أَن نُّبَدِّلَ أَمْثَالَكُمْ وَنُنشِئَكُمْ فِي مَا لَا تَعْلَمُونَ ﴿٦١﴾
62. And you certainly know already the first form of creation: why then do you not celebrate His praises?	62. Wa laqad 'alimtumun-nash-atal-oolaa falaw laa tazakkaroon.	وَلَقَدْ عَلِمْتُمُ النَّشْأَةَ الْأُولَىٰ فَلَوْلَا تَذَكَّرُونَ ﴿٦٢﴾
63. See you the seed that you sow in the ground?	63. Afara'aytum maa tahrusoon.	أَفَرَأَيْتُم مَّا تَحْرُثُونَ ﴿٦٣﴾
64. Is it you that cause it to grow, or are We the Cause?	64. 'A-antum tazra'oonahooo am Nahnuz-zaari'ooon.	ءَأَنتُمْ تَزْرَعُونَهُ أَمْ نَحْنُ الزَّارِعُونَ ﴿٦٤﴾
65. If We willed, We verily could make it chaff, then would ye cease not to exclaim.	65. Law nashaaa'u laja'alnaahu hutaaman fazaltum tafakkahoon.	لَوْ نَشَاءُ لَجَعَلْنَاهُ حُطَامًا فَظَلْتُمْ تَفَكَّهُونَ ﴿٦٥﴾
66. (Saying), "We are indeed left with debts (for nothing):	66. Innaa lamughramoon.	إِنَّا لَمُغْرَمُونَ ﴿٦٦﴾
67. "Indeed are we shut out (of the fruits of our labour)"	67. Bal nahnu mahroomoon.	بَلْ نَحْنُ مَحْرُومُونَ ﴿٦٧﴾
68. See you the water which you drink?	68. Afara'aytumul-maaa'al-lazee tashraboon.	أَفَرَأَيْتُمُ الْمَاءَ الَّذِي تَشْرَبُونَ ﴿٦٨﴾
69. Do you bring it down (in rain) from the cloud or do We?	69. 'A-antum anzaltumoohu minal-muzni am Nahnul-munziloon.	ءَأَنتُمْ أَنزَلْتُمُوهُ مِنَ الْمُزْنِ أَمْ نَحْنُ الْمُنزِلُونَ ﴿٦٩﴾

Ikhfa اخفاء | Ghunna غنّہ | Ikhfa Meem Saakin اخفاء میم ساکن | Idghaam ادغام | Qalqala قلقلہ | Qalb قلب | Idghaam Meem Saakin ادغام میم ساکن

70. Were it Our Will, We could make it salt (and unpalatable): then why do you not give thanks?	70. Law nashaaa'u ja‘alnaahu ujaajan falaw laa tashkuroon.	لَوْ نَشَآءُ جَعَلْنٰهُ اُجَاجًا فَلَوْلَا تَشْكُرُوْنَ ۝٧٠
71. See you the Fire which you kindle?	71. Afara'aytumun-naaral-latee tooroon.	اَفَرَءَيْتُمُ النَّارَ الَّتِيْ تُوْرُوْنَ ۝٧١
72. Is it you who grow the tree which feeds the fire, or do We grow it?	72. 'A-antum anshaåtum shajaratahaaa am Naḥnul-munshi'oon.	ءَاَنْتُمْ اَنْشَاْتُمْ شَجَرَتَهَآ اَمْ نَحْنُ الْمُنْشِئُوْنَ ۝٧٢
73. We have made it a memorial (of Our handiwork), and an article of comfort and convenience for the denizens of deserts.	73. Naḥnu ja‘alnaahaa tazkiratañw-wa mataa‘al-lilmuqween.	نَحْنُ جَعَلْنٰهَا تَذْكِرَةً وَّمَتَاعًا لِّلْمُقْوِيْنَ ۝٧٣
74. Then celebrate with praises the name of your Lord, the Supreme!	74. Fasabbiḥ bismi-Rabbikal-‘aẓeem. **(Section 2)**	فَسَبِّحْ بِاسْمِ رَبِّكَ الْعَظِيْمِ ۝٧٤
75. Furthermore I call to witness the setting of the Stars,-	75. Falaaa uqsimu bimawaaqi‘in-nujoom.	فَلَآ اُقْسِمُ بِمَوٰقِعِ النُّجُوْمِ ۝٧٥
76. And lo! That verily is a tremendous oath, if ye but knew–	76. Wa innahoo laqasamul-law ta‘lamoona ‘aẓeem.	وَاِنَّهٗ لَقَسَمٌ لَّوْ تَعْلَمُوْنَ عَظِيْمٌ ۝٧٦
77. That this is indeed a qur'an Most Honourable,	77. Innahoo la-Qur-aanun Kareem.	اِنَّهٗ لَقُرْاٰنٌ كَرِيْمٌ ۝٧٧
78. In Book well-guarded,	78. Fee kitaabim-maknoon.	فِيْ كِتٰبٍ مَّكْنُوْنٍ ۝٧٨
79. Which none shall touch but those who are clean:	79. Laa yamassuhooo illal-muṭahharoon.	لَّا يَمَسُّهٗٓ اِلَّا الْمُطَهَّرُوْنَ ۝٧٩
80. A Revelation from the Lord of the Worlds.	80. Tanzeelum-mir-Rabbil-‘aalameen.	تَنْزِيْلٌ مِّنْ رَّبِّ الْعٰلَمِيْنَ ۝٨٠
81. Is it such a Message that you would hold in light esteem?	81. Afabihaazal-ḥadeesi antum mudhinoon.	اَفَبِهٰذَا الْحَدِيْثِ اَنْتُمْ مُّدْهِنُوْنَ ۝٨١
82. And make denial thereof your livelihood?	82. Wa taj‘aloona rizqakum annakum tukazziboon.	وَتَجْعَلُوْنَ رِزْقَكُمْ اَنَّكُمْ تُكَذِّبُوْنَ ۝٨٢
83. Why, then, when (the soul) cometh up to the throat (of the dying)	83. Falaw laaa izaa balaghatil-ḥulqoom.	فَلَوْلَآ اِذَا بَلَغَتِ الْحُلْقُوْمَ ۝٨٣
84. And you the while (sit) looking on,-	84. Wa antum ḥeena'izin tanẓuroon.	وَاَنْتُمْ حِيْنَئِذٍ تَنْظُرُوْنَ ۝٨٤
85. But We are nearer to him than you, and yet see not,-	85. Wa Naḥnu aqrabu ilayhi minkum wa laakil-laa tubṣiroon.	وَنَحْنُ اَقْرَبُ اِلَيْهِ مِنْكُمْ وَلٰكِنْ لَّا تُبْصِرُوْنَ ۝٨٥
86. Why then, if ye are not in bondage (unto Us),	86. Falaw laaa in kuntum ghayra madeeneen.	فَلَوْلَآ اِنْ كُنْتُمْ غَيْرَ مَدِيْنِيْنَ ۝٨٦
87. Do ye not force it back, if ye are truthful?	87. Tarji‘oonahaaa in kuntum ṣaadiqeen.	تَرْجِعُوْنَهَآ اِنْ كُنْتُمْ صٰدِقِيْنَ ۝٨٧
88. Thus, then, if he be of those Nearest to Allah,	88. Fa-ammaaa in kaana minal-muqarrabeen.	فَاَمَّآ اِنْ كَانَ مِنَ الْمُقَرَّبِيْنَ ۝٨٨
89. Then breath of life, and plenty, and a Garden of delight.	89. Farawḥuñw-wa rayḥaanuñw-wa Jannatu Na‘eem.	فَرَوْحٌ وَّرَيْحَانٌ ۙ وَّجَنَّتُ نَعِيْمٍ ۝٨٩
90. And if he be of the Companions of the Right Hand,	90. Wa ammaaa in kaana min Aṣ-ḥaabil-Yameen.	وَاَمَّآ اِنْ كَانَ مِنْ اَصْحٰبِ الْيَمِيْنِ ۝٩٠
91. (For him is the salutation), "Peace be unto you", from the Companions of the Right Hand.	91. Fasalaamul-laka min Aṣ-ḥaabil-Yameen.	فَسَلٰمٌ لَّكَ مِنْ اَصْحٰبِ الْيَمِيْنِ ۝٩١

Ikhfa اخفاء | Ghunna غنّة | Ikhfa Meem Saakin اخفاء میم ساکن | Idghaam ادغام | Qalqala قلقلہ | Qalb قلب | Idghaam Meem Saakin ادغام میم ساکن

92. And if he be of those who treat (Truth) as Falsehood, who go wrong,

93. For him is Entertainment with Boiling Water.

94. And burning in Hell-Fire.

95. Verily, this is the very Truth of assured certainty.

96. So celebrate with praises the name of thy Lord, the Supreme.

57. Iron

In the name of Allah, Most Gracious, Most Merciful.

1. All that is in the heavens and the earth glorifieth Allah; and He is the Mighty, the Wise.

2. His is the Sovereignty of the heavens and the earth; He quickeneth and He giveth death; and He is Able to do all things.

3. He is the First and the Last, the Evident and theHidden: and He has full knowledge of all things.

4. He it is Who created the heavens and the earth in Six Days, and is moreover firmly established on the Throne (of Authority). He knows what enters within the earth and what comes forth out of it, what comes down from heaven and what mounts up to it. And He is with you wheresoever you may be. And Allah sees well all that you do.

5. To Him belongs the dominion of the heavens and the earth: and all affairs are referred back to Allah.

6. He merges Night into Day, and He merges Day into Night; and He has full knowledge of the secrets of (all) hearts.

92. Wa ammaaa in kaana minal-mukazzibeenaḍ-ḍaaalleen.

93. Fanuzulum-min ḥameem.

94. Wa taṣliyatu Jaḥeem.

95. Inna haazaa lahuwa ḥaqqul-yaqeen.

96. Fasabbiḥ bismi Rabbikal-'aẓeem. **(Section 3)**

Sûrat al-Ḥadîd–57

(Revealed at Madinah)

Bismillaahir Raḥmaanir Raḥeem

1. Sabbaḥa lillaahi maa fis-samaawaati wal-arḍi wa Huwal-'Azeezul-Ḥakeem.

2. Lahoo mulkus-samaawaati wal-arḍi yuḥyee wa yumeetu wa Huwa 'alaa kulli shay'in Qadeer.

3. Huwal-Awwalu wal-Aakhiru waẓ-Ẓaahiru wal-Baaṭinu wa Huwa bikulli shay'in 'Aleem.

4. Huwal-lazee khalaqas-samaawaati wal-arḍa fee sittati ayyaamin summas-tawaa 'alal-'Arsh; ya'lamu maa yaliju fil-arḍi wa maa yakhruju minhaa wa maa yanzilu minas-samaaa'i wa maa ya'ruju feehaa wa Huwa ma'akum ayna maa kuntum; wallaahu bimaa ta'maloona Baṣeer.

5. Lahoo mulkus-samaawaati wal-arḍ; wa ilal-laahi turja'ul-umoor.

6. Yoolijul-layla fin-nahaari wa yoolijun-nahaara fil-layl; wa Huwa 'Aleemum bizaatiṣ-ṣudoor.

وَ اَمَّآ اِنْ كَانَ مِنَ الْمُكَذِّبِيْنَ
الضَّآلِّيْنَ ﴿٩٢﴾
فَنُزُلٌ مِّنْ حَمِيْمٍ ﴿٩٣﴾
وَّ تَصْلِيَةُ جَحِيْمٍ ﴿٩٤﴾
اِنَّ هٰذَا لَهُوَ حَقُّ الْيَقِيْنِ ﴿٩٥﴾
فَسَبِّحْ بِاسْمِ رَبِّكَ الْعَظِيْمِ ﴿٩٦﴾

(٥٧) سُوْرَةُ الْحَدِيْدِ مَدَنِيَّةٌ (٩٤)

بِسْمِ اللّٰهِ الرَّحْمٰنِ الرَّحِيْمِ

سَبَّحَ لِلّٰهِ مَا فِي السَّمٰوٰتِ وَ الْاَرْضِ ۚ
وَهُوَ الْعَزِيْزُ الْحَكِيْمُ ﴿١﴾
لَهٗ مُلْكُ السَّمٰوٰتِ وَالْاَرْضِ ۚ يُحْيٖ وَ
يُمِيْتُ ۚ وَهُوَ عَلٰى كُلِّ شَيْءٍ قَدِيْرٌ ﴿٢﴾
هُوَ الْاَوَّلُ وَ الْاٰخِرُ وَ الظَّاهِرُ وَ
الْبَاطِنُ ۚ وَهُوَ بِكُلِّ شَيْءٍ عَلِيْمٌ ﴿٣﴾
هُوَ الَّذِيْ خَلَقَ السَّمٰوٰتِ وَالْاَرْضَ
فِيْ سِتَّةِ اَيَّامٍ ثُمَّ اسْتَوٰى عَلَى
الْعَرْشِ ۚ يَعْلَمُ مَا يَلِجُ فِي الْاَرْضِ
وَمَا يَخْرُجُ مِنْهَا وَمَا يَنْزِلُ مِنَ
السَّمَآءِ وَمَا يَعْرُجُ فِيْهَا ۚ وَ هُوَ
مَعَكُمْ اَيْنَ مَا كُنْتُمْ ۚ وَاللّٰهُ
بِمَا تَعْمَلُوْنَ بَصِيْرٌ ﴿٤﴾
لَهٗ مُلْكُ السَّمٰوٰتِ وَ الْاَرْضِ ۚ
وَ اِلَى اللّٰهِ تُرْجَعُ الْاُمُوْرُ ﴿٥﴾
يُوْلِجُ الَّيْلَ فِي النَّهَارِ وَيُوْلِجُ
النَّهَارَ فِي الَّيْلِ ۚ وَهُوَ عَلِيْمٌ
بِذَاتِ الصُّدُوْرِ ﴿٦﴾

Ikhfa اخفاء | Ghunna غنّہ | Ikhfa Meem Saakin اخفاء میم ساکن | Idghaam ادغام | Qalqala قلقلہ | Qalb قلب | Idghaam Meem Saakin ادغام میم ساکن

7. Believe in Allah and His apostle, and spend (in charity) out of the (substance) whereof He has made you heirs. For, those of you who believe and spend (in charity),- for them is a great Reward.

7. Aaminoo billaahi wa Rasoolihee wa anfiqoo mimmaa ja'alakum mustakhlafeena feehi fallazeena aamanoo minkum wa anfaqoo lahum ajrun kabeer.

اٰمِنُوْا بِاللّٰهِ وَرَسُوْلِهٖ وَاَنْفِقُوْا مِمَّا
جَعَلَكُمْ مُّسْتَخْلَفِيْنَ فِيْهِ ؕ فَالَّذِيْنَ
اٰمَنُوْا مِنْكُمْ وَاَنْفَقُوْا لَهُمْ اَجْرٌ كَبِيْرٌ ﴿٧﴾

8. What cause have you why you should not believe in Allah?- and the Apostle invites you to believe in your Lord, and has indeed taken your Covenant, if you are men of Faith.

8. Wa maa lakum laa tu'minoona billaahi war-Rasoolu yad'ookum litu'minoo bi-Rabbikum wa qad akhaza meesaaqakum in kuntum mu'mineen.

وَمَا لَكُمْ لَا تُؤْمِنُوْنَ بِاللّٰهِ ۚ وَ
الرَّسُوْلُ يَدْعُوْكُمْ لِتُؤْمِنُوْا بِرَبِّكُمْ
وَقَدْ اَخَذَ مِيْثَاقَكُمْ اِنْ كُنْتُمْ
مُّؤْمِنِيْنَ ﴿٨﴾

9. He is the One Who sends to His Servant Manifest Signs, that He may lead you from the depths of Darkness into the Light and verily Allah is to you most kind and Merciful.

9. Huwal-lazee yunazzilu 'alaa 'abdiheee Aayaatim bayyinaatil-liyukhrijakum minaz-zulumaati ilan-noor; wa innal-laaha bikum la-Ra'oofur-Raheem.

هُوَ الَّذِيْ يُنَزِّلُ عَلٰى عَبْدِهٖٓ اٰيٰتٍۢ
بَيِّنٰتٍ لِّيُخْرِجَكُمْ مِّنَ الظُّلُمٰتِ
اِلَى النُّوْرِ ؕ وَاِنَّ اللّٰهَ بِكُمْ لَرَءُوْفٌ
رَّحِيْمٌ ﴿٩﴾

10. And what cause have you why you should not spend in the cause of Allah? For to Allah belongs the heritage of the heavens and the earth. Not equal among you are those who spent (freely) and fought, before the Victory, (with those who did so later). Those are higher in rank than those who spent (freely) and fought afterwards. But to all has Allah promised a goodly (reward). And Allah is well acquainted with all that you do.

10. Wa maa lakum allaa tunfiqoo fee sabeelil-laahi wa lillaahi meeraasus-samaawaati wal-ard; laa yastawee minkum man anfaqa min qablil-Fat-hi wa qaatal; ulaaa'ika a'zamu darajatam-minal-lazeena anfaqoo mim ba'du wa qaataloo; wa kullanw-wa'adallaahul-husnaa; wallaahu bimaa ta'maloona Khabeer. **(Section 1)**

وَمَا لَكُمْ اَلَّا تُنْفِقُوْا فِيْ سَبِيْلِ اللّٰهِ
وَلِلّٰهِ مِيْرَاثُ السَّمٰوٰتِ وَالْاَرْضِ ؕ
لَا يَسْتَوِيْ مِنْكُمْ مَّنْ اَنْفَقَ مِنْ قَبْلِ
الْفَتْحِ وَقٰتَلَ ؕ اُولٰٓئِكَ اَعْظَمُ دَرَجَةً
مِّنَ الَّذِيْنَ اَنْفَقُوْا مِنْۢ بَعْدُ وَ
قٰتَلُوْا ؕ وَكُلًّا وَّعَدَ اللّٰهُ الْحُسْنٰى ؕ
وَاللّٰهُ بِمَا تَعْمَلُوْنَ خَبِيْرٌ ﴿١٠﴾ ع

11. Who is he that will Loan to Allah a beautiful loan? for (Allah) will increase it manifold to his credit, and he will have (besides) a liberal Reward.

11. Man zal-lazee yuqridul-laaha qardan hasanan fa-yudaa'ifahoo lahoo wa lahooo ajrun kareem.

مَنْ ذَا الَّذِيْ يُقْرِضُ اللّٰهَ قَرْضًا
حَسَنًا فَيُضٰعِفَهٗ لَهٗ وَلَهٗٓ اَجْرٌ
كَرِيْمٌ ﴿١١﴾

12. One Day shall you see the believing men and the believing women- how their Light runs forward before them and by their right hands: (their greeting will be): "Good News for you this Day! Gardens beneath which flow rivers to dwell therein for ever! This is indeed the highest Achievement!"

12. Yawma taral-mu'mineena walmu'minaati yas'aa nooruhum bayna aydeehim wa bi-aymaanihim bushraakumul-Yawma Jannaatun tajree min tahtihal-anhaaru khaalideena feehaa; zaalika huwal-fawzul-'azeem.

يَوْمَ تَرَى الْمُؤْمِنِيْنَ وَالْمُؤْمِنٰتِ
يَسْعٰى نُوْرُهُمْ بَيْنَ اَيْدِيْهِمْ وَبِاَيْمَانِهِمْ
بُشْرٰىكُمُ الْيَوْمَ جَنّٰتٌ تَجْرِيْ مِنْ
تَحْتِهَا الْاَنْهٰرُ خٰلِدِيْنَ فِيْهَا ؕ
ذٰلِكَ هُوَ الْفَوْزُ الْعَظِيْمُ ﴿١٢﴾ ج

Ikhfa اخفاء | Ghunna غنّہ | Ikhfa Meem Saakin اخفاء میم ساکن | Idghaam ادغام | Qalqala قلقلہ | Qalb قلب | Idghaam Meem Saakin ادغام میم ساکن

13. One Day will the Hypocrites- men and women - say to the Believers: "Wait for us! Let us borrow (a Light) from your Light!" It will be said: "Turn you back to your rear! then seek a Light (where you can)!" So a wall will be put up between them, with a gate therein. Within it will be Mercy throughout, and without it, all alongside, will be (Wrath and) Punishment!

14. (Those without) will call out, "Were we not with you?" (The others) will reply, "True! but you led yourselves into temptation; you looked forward (to our ruin); you doubted (Allah's Promise); and (your false) desires deceived you; until there issued the Command of Allah. And the Deceiver deceived you in respect of Allah.

15. "This Day shall no ransom be accepted of you, nor of those who rejected Allah." Your abode is the Fire: that is the proper place to claim you: and an evil refuge it is!"

16. Has not the Time arrived for the Believers that their hearts in all humility should engage in the remembrance of Allah and of the Truth which has been revealed (to them), and that they should not become like those to whom was given Revelation aforetime, but long ages passed over them and their hearts grew hard? For many among them are rebellious transgressors.

17. Know you (all) that Allah giveth life to the earth after its death! already have We shown the Signs plainly to you, that you may learn wisdom.

18. For those who give in Charity, men and women, and loan to Allah a Beautiful Loan, it shall be increased manifold (to their credit), and they shall have (besides) a liberal reward.

13. Yawma yaqoolul-munaafiqoona walmunaafiqaatu lillaẕeena aamanun-ẕuroonaa naqtabis min noorikum qeelarji'oo waraaa'akum faltamisoo nooran faḍuriba baynahum bisooril-lahoo baab, baaṭinuhoo feehir-raḥmatu wa ẕaahiruhoo min qibalihil-'aẕaab.

14. Yunaadoonahum alam nakum-ma'akum qaaloo balaa wa laakinnakum fatantum anfusakum wa tarabbaṣtum wartabtum wa gharratkumul-amaaniyyu ḥattaa jaaa'a amrul-laahi wa gharrakum billaahil-gharoor.

15. Fal-Yawma laa yu'khaẕu minkum fidyatuñw-wa laa minal-laẕeena kafaroo; maâwaakumun-Naaru hiya mawlaakum wa bi'sal-maṣeer.

16. Alam yaâni lillaẕeena aamanooo an takhsha'a quloobuhum liẕikril-laahi wa maa nazala minal-ḥaqqi wa laa yakoonoo kallaẕeena ootul-Kitaaba min qablu faṭaala 'alayhimul-amadu faqasat quloobuhum wa kaseerum-minhum faasiqoon.

17. I'lamooo annal-laaha yuḥyil-arḍa ba'da mawtihaa; qad bayyannaa lakumul-Aayaati la'allakum ta'qiloon.

18. Innal-muṣṣaddiqeena wal-muṣṣaddiqaati wa aqraḍul-laaha qarḍan ḥasanañy-yuḍaa'afu lahum wa lahum ajrun kareem.

يَوْمَ يَقُوْلُ الْمُنٰفِقُوْنَ وَالْمُنٰفِقٰتُ
لِلَّذِيْنَ اٰمَنُوا انْظُرُوْنَا نَقْتَبِسْ مِنْ
نُّوْرِكُمْ ۚ قِيْلَ ارْجِعُوْا وَرَآءَكُمْ
فَالْتَمِسُوْا نُوْرًا ۗ فَضُرِبَ بَيْنَهُمْ بِسُوْرٍ
لَّهٗ بَابٌ ۗ بَاطِنُهٗ فِيْهِ الرَّحْمَةُ وَ
ظَاهِرُهٗ مِنْ قِبَلِهِ الْعَذَابُ ؕ ﴿١٣﴾
يُنَادُوْنَهُمْ اَلَمْ نَكُنْ مَّعَكُمْ ؕ قَالُوْا
بَلٰى وَلٰكِنَّكُمْ فَتَنْتُمْ اَنْفُسَكُمْ
وَتَرَبَّصْتُمْ وَارْتَبْتُمْ وَغَرَّتْكُمُ
الْاَمَانِيُّ حَتّٰى جَآءَ اَمْرُ اللّٰهِ وَغَرَّكُمْ
بِاللّٰهِ الْغَرُوْرُ ﴿١٤﴾
فَالْيَوْمَ لَا يُؤْخَذُ مِنْكُمْ فِدْيَةٌ وَّلَا
مِنَ الَّذِيْنَ كَفَرُوْا ۗ مَاْوٰىكُمُ النَّارُ ۗ
هِيَ مَوْلٰىكُمْ ۗ وَبِئْسَ الْمَصِيْرُ ﴿١٥﴾
اَلَمْ يَاْنِ لِلَّذِيْنَ اٰمَنُوْٓا اَنْ
تَخْشَعَ قُلُوْبُهُمْ لِذِكْرِ اللّٰهِ وَمَا نَزَلَ
مِنَ الْحَقِّ ۙ وَلَا يَكُوْنُوْا كَالَّذِيْنَ
اُوْتُوا الْكِتٰبَ مِنْ قَبْلُ فَطَالَ
عَلَيْهِمُ الْاَمَدُ فَقَسَتْ قُلُوْبُهُمْ ۗ
وَكَثِيْرٌ مِّنْهُمْ فٰسِقُوْنَ ﴿١٦﴾
اِعْلَمُوْٓا اَنَّ اللّٰهَ يُحْيِ الْاَرْضَ
بَعْدَ مَوْتِهَا ۗ قَدْ بَيَّنَّا لَكُمُ
الْاٰيٰتِ لَعَلَّكُمْ تَعْقِلُوْنَ ﴿١٧﴾
اِنَّ الْمُصَّدِّقِيْنَ وَالْمُصَّدِّقٰتِ
وَاَقْرَضُوا اللّٰهَ قَرْضًا حَسَنًا يُّضٰعَفُ
لَهُمْ وَلَهُمْ اَجْرٌ كَرِيْمٌ ﴿١٨﴾

Ikhfa اخفاء | Ghunna غُنّہ | Ikhfa Meem Saakin اخفاء میم ساکن | Idghaam ادغام | Qalqala قلقلہ | Qalb قلب | Idghaam Meem Saakin ادغام میم ساکن

19. And those who believe in Allah and His apostles- they are the Sincere (lovers of Truth), and the witnesses (who testify), in the eyes of their Lord: They shall have their Reward and their Light. But those who reject Allah and deny Our Signs,- they are the Companions of Hell-Fire.

19. Wallazeena aamanoo billaahi wa Rusuliheee ulaaa'ika humuṣ-ṣiddeeqoona wash-shuhadaaa'u 'inda Rabbihim lahum ajruhum wa nooruhum wallazeena kafaroo wa kaz-zaboo bi-Aayaatinaaa ulaaa'ika Aṣ-ḥaabul-Jaḥeem. **(Section 2)**

وَالَّذِيْنَ اٰمَنُوْا بِاللّٰهِ وَرُسُلِهٖۤ اُولٰٓئِكَ
هُمُ الصِّدِّيْقُوْنَ ۖ وَالشُّهَدَآءُ عِنْدَ
رَبِّهِمْ ۚ لَهُمْ اَجْرُهُمْ وَنُوْرُهُمْ ۚ
وَالَّذِيْنَ كَفَرُوْا وَكَذَّبُوْا بِاٰيٰتِنَآ
اُولٰٓئِكَ اَصْحٰبُ الْجَحِيْمِ ۝١٩ ع ١٨

20. Know you (all), that the life of this world is but play and amusement, pomp and mutual boasting and multiplying, (in rivalry) among yourselves, riches and children. Here is a similitude: How rain and the growth which it brings forth, delight (the hearts of) the tillers; soon it withers; you will see it grow yellow; then it becomes dry and crumbles away. But in the Hereafter is a Chastisement severe (for the devotees of wrong). And Forgiveness from Allah and (His) Good Pleasure (for the devotees of Allah). And what is the life of this world, but goods and chattels of deception?

20. I'lamooo annamal-ḥayaa-tud-dunyaa la'ibuñw-wa lahwuñw-wa zeenatuñw-wa tafaakhurum baynakum wa takaasurun fil-amwaali wal-awlaad, kamasali ghaysin a'jabal-kuffaara nabaatuhoo summa yaheeju fataraahu muṣfarran summa yakoonu ḥuṭaamaa; wa fil-Aakhirati 'azaabun shadeeduñw-wa magh-firatum-minal-laahi wa riḍ-waan; wa mal-ḥayaa-tuddun-yaaa illaa mataa'ul-ghuroor.

اِعْلَمُوْٓا اَنَّمَا الْحَيٰوةُ الدُّنْيَا
لَعِبٌ وَّلَهْوٌ وَّزِيْنَةٌ وَّتَفَاخُرٌ
بَيْنَكُمْ وَتَكَاثُرٌ فِي الْاَمْوَالِ
وَالْاَوْلَادِ ۚ كَمَثَلِ غَيْثٍ اَعْجَبَ
الْكُفَّارَ نَبَاتُهٗ ثُمَّ يَهِيْجُ فَتَرٰىهُ
مُصْفَرًّا ثُمَّ يَكُوْنُ حُطَامًا ۚ
وَفِي الْاٰخِرَةِ عَذَابٌ شَدِيْدٌ ۙ وَّ
مَغْفِرَةٌ مِّنَ اللّٰهِ وَرِضْوَانٌ ۚ وَمَا
الْحَيٰوةُ الدُّنْيَآ اِلَّا مَتَاعُ الْغُرُوْرِ ۝٢٠

21. Be you foremost (in seeking) Forgiveness from your Lord, and a Garden (of Bliss), the width whereof is as the width of heaven and earth, prepared for those who believe in Allah and His apostles: that is the Grace of Allah, which He bestows on whom he pleases: and Allah is the Lord of Grace abounding.

21. Saabiqooo ilaa magh-firatim-mir-Rabbikum wa Jannatin 'arḍuhaa ka-'arḍis-samaaa'i wal-arḍi u'iddat lillazeena aamanoo billaahi wa Rusulih; zaalika faḍlul-laahi yu'teehi mañy-yashaaa'; wal-laahu zul-faḍlil-'azeem.

سَابِقُوْٓا اِلٰى مَغْفِرَةٍ مِّنْ رَّبِّكُمْ
وَجَنَّةٍ عَرْضُهَا كَعَرْضِ السَّمَآءِ
وَالْاَرْضِ ۙ اُعِدَّتْ لِلَّذِيْنَ
اٰمَنُوْا بِاللّٰهِ وَرُسُلِهٖ ۚ ذٰلِكَ
فَضْلُ اللّٰهِ يُؤْتِيْهِ مَنْ يَّشَآءُ ۚ
وَاللّٰهُ ذُو الْفَضْلِ الْعَظِيْمِ ۝٢١

22. No misfortune can happen on earth or in your souls but is recorded in a decree before We bring it into existence: That is truly easy for Allah:

22. Maaa aṣaaba mim-muṣee-batin fil-arḍi wa laa feee anfusi-kum illaa fee kitaabim-min qabli an nabra-ahaa; inna zaalika 'alal-laahi yaseer.

مَآ اَصَابَ مِنْ مُّصِيْبَةٍ فِي
الْاَرْضِ وَلَا فِيْٓ اَنْفُسِكُمْ اِلَّا
فِيْ كِتٰبٍ مِّنْ قَبْلِ اَنْ نَّبْرَاَهَا ۚ
اِنَّ ذٰلِكَ عَلَى اللّٰهِ يَسِيْرٌ ۝٢٢

23. In order that you may not despair over matters that pass you by, nor exult over favours bestowed upon you. For Allah

23. Likaylaa taåsaw 'alaa maa faatakum wa laa tafraḥoo bimaaa aataakum; wallaahu

لِّكَيْلَا تَاْسَوْا عَلٰى مَا فَاتَكُمْ
وَلَا تَفْرَحُوْا بِمَآ اٰتٰىكُمْ ۚ وَاللّٰهُ

Ikhfa اخفاء | Ghunna غنّہ | Ikhfa Meem Saakin اخفاء میم ساکن | Idghaam ادغام | Qalqala قلقلہ | Qalb قلب | Idghaam Meem Saakin ادغام میم ساکن

loves not any vainglorious boaster,-

24. Such persons as are covetous and commend covetousness to men. And if any turn back (from Allah's Way), verily Allah is Free of all Needs, Worthy of all Praise.

25. We sent aforetime our apostles with Clear Signs and sent down with them the Book and the Balance (of Right and Wrong), that men may stand forth in justice; and We sent down Iron, in which is (material for) mighty war, as well as many benefits for mankind, that Allah may test who it is that will help, Unseen, Him and His apostles: For Allah is Full of Strength, Exalted in Might (and able to enforce His Will).

26. And We sent Noah and Abraham, and established in their line Prophethood and Revelation: and some among progeny were on right guidance. But many of them became rebellious transgressors.

27. Then, in their wake, We followed them up with (others of) Our apostles: We sent after them Jesus the son of Mary, and bestowed on him the Gospel; and We ordained in the hearts of those who followed him Compassion and Mercy. But the Monasticism which they invented for themselves, We did not prescribe for them: (We commanded) only the seeking for the Good Pleasure of Allah; but that they did not foster as they should have done. Yet We bestowed, on those among them who believed, their (due) reward, but many of them are rebellious transgressors.

28. O you that believe! Fear Allah, and believe in His Apostle, and He will bestow on you a double portion

laa yuḥibbu kulla mukhtaalin fakhoor.

24. Allazeena yabkhaloona wa yaåmuroonan-naasa bilbukhl; wa mañy-yatawalla fainnal-laaha Huwal-Ghaniyyul-Ḥameed.

25. Laqad arsalnaa Rusulanaa bilbayyinaati wa anzalnaa ma'ahumul-Kitaaba wal-Meezaana liyaqoomanan-naasu bilqisṭ, wa anzalnal-ḥadeeda feehi baåsun shadeeduñw-wa manaafi'u linnaasi wa liya'lamal-laahu mañy-yanṣuruhoo wa Rusulahoo bilghayb; innal-laaha Qawiyyun 'Azeez.

(Section 3)

26. Wa laqad arsalnaa Noohañw-wa Ibraaheema wa ja'alnaa fee zurriyyatihiman-Nubuwwata wal-Kitaaba faminhum muhtad; wa kaseerum-minhum faasiqoon.

27. Summa qaffaynaa 'alaaa aasaarihim bi-Rusulinaa wa qaffaynaa bi-'Eesab-ni-Maryama wa aataynaahul-Injeela wa ja'alnaa fee quloobil-lazeenattaba'oohu raåfatañw-wa raḥmatañw wa rahbaaniyyatanibtada'oohaa maa katabnaahaa 'alayhim illab-tighaaa'a riḍwaanil-laahi famaa ra'awhaa ḥaqqa ri'aayatihaa fa-aataynal-lazeena aamanoo minhum ajrahum wa kaseerum-minhum faasiqoon.

28. Yaaa ayyuhal-lazeena aamanut-taqullaaha wa aaminoo bi-Rasoolihee yu'tikum kiflayni

لَا يُحِبُّ كُلَّ مُخْتَالٍ فَخُوْرٍ ﴿٢٣﴾
الَّذِيْنَ يَبْخَلُوْنَ وَيَأْمُرُوْنَ
النَّاسَ بِالْبُخْلِ ؕ وَمَنْ يَّتَوَلَّ
فَاِنَّ اللّٰهَ هُوَ الْغَنِيُّ الْحَمِيْدُ ﴿٢٤﴾
لَقَدْ اَرْسَلْنَا رُسُلَنَا بِالْبَيِّنٰتِ
وَ اَنْزَلْنَا مَعَهُمُ الْكِتٰبَ وَ
الْمِيْزَانَ لِيَقُوْمَ النَّاسُ بِالْقِسْطِ ۚ
وَ اَنْزَلْنَا الْحَدِيْدَ فِيْهِ بَاْسٌ
شَدِيْدٌ وَّمَنَافِعُ لِلنَّاسِ وَلِيَعْلَمَ
اللّٰهُ مَنْ يَّنْصُرُهٗ وَرُسُلَهٗ بِالْغَيْبِ ؕ
اِنَّ اللّٰهَ قَوِيٌّ عَزِيْزٌ ﴿٢٥﴾
وَلَقَدْ اَرْسَلْنَا نُوْحًا وَّاِبْرٰهِيْمَ
وَجَعَلْنَا فِيْ ذُرِّيَّتِهِمَا النُّبُوَّةَ
وَالْكِتٰبَ فَمِنْهُمْ مُّهْتَدٍ ۚ وَكَثِيْرٌ
مِّنْهُمْ فٰسِقُوْنَ ﴿٢٦﴾
ثُمَّ قَفَّيْنَا عَلٰٓى اٰثَارِهِمْ بِرُسُلِنَا
وَقَفَّيْنَا بِعِيْسَى ابْنِ مَرْيَمَ وَاٰتَيْنٰهُ
الْاِنْجِيْلَ ۙ وَجَعَلْنَا فِيْ قُلُوْبِ
الَّذِيْنَ اتَّبَعُوْهُ رَاْفَةً وَّرَحْمَةً ؕ وَ
رَهْبَانِيَّةَ ِۨ ابْتَدَعُوْهَا مَا كَتَبْنٰهَا
عَلَيْهِمْ اِلَّا ابْتِغَآءَ رِضْوَانِ اللّٰهِ
فَمَا رَعَوْهَا حَقَّ رِعَايَتِهَا ۚ فَاٰتَيْنَا
الَّذِيْنَ اٰمَنُوْا مِنْهُمْ اَجْرَهُمْ ۚ وَ
كَثِيْرٌ مِّنْهُمْ فٰسِقُوْنَ ﴿٢٧﴾
يٰٓاَيُّهَا الَّذِيْنَ اٰمَنُوا اتَّقُوا اللّٰهَ
وَاٰمِنُوْا بِرَسُوْلِهٖ يُؤْتِكُمْ كِفْلَيْنِ

Ikhfa اخفاء | Ghunna غُنّہ | Ikhfa Meem Saakin اخفاء میم ساکن | Idghaam ادغام | Qalqala قلقلہ | Qalb قلب | Idghaam Meem Saakin ادغام میم ساکن

of His Mercy: He will provide for you a Light by which you shall walk (straight in your path), and He will forgive you (your past): for Allah is Oft-Forgiving, Most Merciful.

29. That the People of the Book may know that they have no power whatever over the Grace of Allah, that (His) Grace is (entirely) in His Hand, to bestow it on whomsoever He wills. For Allah is the Lord of Grace abounding.

58. The Woman Who Pleads

In the name of Allah, Most Gracious, Most Merciful.

1. Allah has indeed heard (and accepted) the statement of the woman who pleads with thee concerning her husband and carries her complaint (in prayer) to Allah: and Allah (always) heard the arguments between both sides among you: for Allah hears and sees (all things).

2. If any men among you divorce their wives by Zihar (calling them mothers), they cannot be their mothers: None can be their mothers except those who gave them birth. And in fact they use words (both) iniquitous and false: but truly Allah is one that blots out (sins), and forgives (again and again).

3. But those who divorce their wives by Zihar, then wish to go back on the words they uttered,-(It is ordained that such a one) should free a slave before they touch each other: Thus are you admonished to perform: and Allah is well-acquainted with (all) that you do.

4. And if any has not (the wherewithal), he should fast for two months consecutively before they touch each other. But if any is unable to do so, he should feed sixty indigent ones, this, that you may show your faith in Allah and His Apostle.

mir raḥmatihee wa yaj‘al lakum nooran tamshoona bihee wa yaghfir lakum; wallaahu Ghafoorur-Raḥeem.

29. Li’allaa ya‘lama Ahlul-kitaabi allaa yaqdiroona ‘alaa shay’im-min faḍlil-laahi wa annal-faḍla bi-Yadil-laahi yu’teehi mañy-yashaaa’; wallaahu Zul-faḍlil-‘aẓeem.

(Section 4)

Sûrat al-Mujâdilah–58

(Revealed at Madinah)

Bismillaahir Raḥmaanir Raḥeem

1. Qad sami‘al-laahu qawlal-latee tujaadiluka fee zawjihaa wa tashtakeee ilal-laahi wallaa-hu yasma‘u taḥaawurakumaa; innal-laaha Samee‘um Baṣeer.

2. Allazeena yuẓaahiroona minkum min nisaaa’ihim maa hunna ummahaatihim in ummahaatuhum illal-laaa’ee waladnahum; wa innahum la-yaqooloona munkaram-minal-qawli wa zooraa; wa innal-laaha la-‘Afuwwun Ghafoor.

3. Wallazeena yuẓaahiroona min nisaaa’ihim summa ya‘oodoona limaa qaaloo fataḥreeru raqabatim-min qabli añy-yatamaaassaa; zaalikum too‘aẓoona bih; wallaahu bimaa ta‘maloona Khabeer.

4. Famal-lam yajid fa-Ṣiyaa-mu shahrayni mutataabi‘ayni min qabli any-yatamaaassaa famal-lam yastaṭi‘ fa-iṭ‘aamu sitteena miskeenaa; zaalika litu’minoo billaahi wa Rasoolih;

مِنْ رَّحْمَتِهٖ وَيَجْعَلْ لَّكُمْ نُوْرًا
تَمْشُوْنَ بِهٖ وَيَغْفِرْ لَكُمْ ؕ وَاللّٰهُ
غَفُوْرٌ رَّحِيْمٌ ۙ ﴿٢٨﴾
لِّئَلَّا يَعْلَمَ اَهْلُ الْكِتٰبِ اَلَّا يَقْدِرُوْنَ
عَلٰى شَيْءٍ مِّنْ فَضْلِ اللّٰهِ وَاَنَّ الْفَضْلَ
بِيَدِ اللّٰهِ يُؤْتِيْهِ مَنْ يَّشَآءُ ؕ وَاللّٰهُ
ذُو الْفَضْلِ الْعَظِيْمِ ﴿٢٩﴾

(٥٨) سُوْرَةُ الْمُجَادِلَةِ مَدَنِيَّةٌ (١٠٥)

بِسْمِ اللّٰهِ الرَّحْمٰنِ الرَّحِيْمِ

قَدْ سَمِعَ اللّٰهُ قَوْلَ الَّتِيْ تُجَادِلُكَ
فِيْ زَوْجِهَا وَتَشْتَكِيْٓ اِلَى اللّٰهِ ۖ وَ
اللّٰهُ يَسْمَعُ تَحَاوُرَكُمَا ؕ اِنَّ اللّٰهَ
سَمِيْعٌ ۢ بَصِيْرٌ ﴿١﴾
اَلَّذِيْنَ يُظٰهِرُوْنَ مِنْكُمْ مِّنْ نِّسَآئِهِمْ
مَّا هُنَّ اُمَّهٰتِهِمْ ؕ اِنْ اُمَّهٰتُهُمْ اِلَّا
الّٰٓـِٔيْ وَلَدْنَهُمْ ؕ وَاِنَّهُمْ لَيَقُوْلُوْنَ
مُنْكَرًا مِّنَ الْقَوْلِ وَزُوْرًا ؕ وَاِنَّ اللّٰهَ
لَعَفُوٌّ غَفُوْرٌ ﴿٢﴾
وَالَّذِيْنَ يُظٰهِرُوْنَ مِنْ نِّسَآئِهِمْ ثُمَّ
يَعُوْدُوْنَ لِمَا قَالُوْا فَتَحْرِيْرُ رَقَبَةٍ مِّنْ
قَبْلِ اَنْ يَّتَمَآسَّا ؕ ذٰلِكُمْ تُوْعَظُوْنَ
بِهٖ ؕ وَاللّٰهُ بِمَا تَعْمَلُوْنَ خَبِيْرٌ ﴿٣﴾
فَمَنْ لَّمْ يَجِدْ فَصِيَامُ شَهْرَيْنِ
مُتَتَابِعَيْنِ مِنْ قَبْلِ اَنْ يَّتَمَآسَّا ؕ
فَمَنْ لَّمْ يَسْتَطِعْ فَاِطْعَامُ سِتِّيْنَ
مِسْكِيْنًا ؕ ذٰلِكَ لِتُؤْمِنُوْا بِاللّٰهِ وَرَسُوْلِهٖ ؕ

Those are limits (set by) Allah. For those who reject (Him), there is a grievous Chastisement.

wa tilka ḥudoodul-laah; wa lilkaafireena 'az̲aabun aleem.

وَتِلْكَ حُدُوْدُ اللّٰهِ ؕ وَلِلْكٰفِرِيْنَ
عَذَابٌ اَلِيْمٌ ٤

5. Those who resist Allah and His Apostle will be humbled to dust, as were those before them: for We have already sent down Clear Signs. And the Unbelievers (will have) a humiliating Chastisement,-

5. Innal-laz̲eena yuḥaaad-doonal-laaha wa Rasoolahoo kubitoo kamaa kubital-laz̲eena min qablihim; wa qad anzalnaaa Aayaatim bayyinaat; wa lilkaa-fireena 'az̲aabum-muheen.

اِنَّ الَّذِيْنَ يُحَآدُّوْنَ اللّٰهَ وَرَسُوْلَهٗ
كُبِتُوْا كَمَا كُبِتَ الَّذِيْنَ مِنْ قَبْلِهِمْ
وَقَدْ اَنْزَلْنَآ اٰيٰتٍۭ بَيِّنٰتٍ ؕ وَلِلْكٰفِرِيْنَ
عَذَابٌ مُّهِيْنٌ ۚ ٥

6. On the Day that Allah will raise them all up (again) and show them the Truth (and meaning) of their conduct. Allah has reckoned its (value), though they may have forgotten it, for Allah is Witness to all things.

6. Yawma yab'as̲uhumul-laahu jamee'an fa-yunabbi'u-hum bimaa 'amiloo; aḥṣaahul-laahu wa nasooh; wallaahu 'alaa kulli shay'in Shaheed. **(Section 1)**

يَوْمَ يَبْعَثُهُمُ اللّٰهُ جَمِيْعًا فَيُنَبِّئُهُمْ
بِمَا عَمِلُوْا ؕ اَحْصٰىهُ اللّٰهُ وَنَسُوْهُ ؕ
وَاللّٰهُ عَلٰى كُلِّ شَيْءٍ شَهِيْدٌ ٦ ع

7. Do you see not that Allah does know (all) that is in the heavens and on earth? There is not a secret consultation between three, but He makes the fourth among them, - Nor between five but He makes the sixth,- nor between fewer nor more, but He is in their midst, wheresoever they be: In the end will He tell them the truth of their conduct, on the Day of Judgment. For Allah has full knowledge of all things.

7. Alam tara annal-laaha ya'lamu maa fis-samaawaati wa maa fil-arḍi maa yakoonu min najwaa s̲alaas̲atin illaa Huwa raabi'uhum wa laa khamsatin illaa Huwa saadisuhum wa laaa adnaa min zaalika wa laaa aks̲ara illaa Huwa ma'ahum ayna maa kaanoo s̲umma yunabbi'uhum bimaa 'amiloo Yawmal-Qiyaamah; innal-laaha bikulli shay'in 'Aleem.

اَلَمْ تَرَ اَنَّ اللّٰهَ يَعْلَمُ مَا فِي السَّمٰوٰتِ
وَمَا فِي الْاَرْضِ ؕ مَا يَكُوْنُ مِنْ نَّجْوٰى
ثَلٰثَةٍ اِلَّا هُوَ رَابِعُهُمْ وَلَا خَمْسَةٍ اِلَّا
هُوَ سَادِسُهُمْ وَلَآ اَدْنٰى مِنْ ذٰلِكَ
وَلَآ اَكْثَرَ اِلَّا هُوَ مَعَهُمْ اَيْنَ مَا كَانُوْا ۚ
ثُمَّ يُنَبِّئُهُمْ بِمَا عَمِلُوْا يَوْمَ الْقِيٰمَةِ ؕ
اِنَّ اللّٰهَ بِكُلِّ شَيْءٍ عَلِيْمٌ ٧

8. Turnest you not your sight towards those who were forbidden secret counsels yet revert to that which they were forbidden (to do)? And they hold secret counsels among themselves for iniquity and hostility, and disobedience to the Apostle. And when they come to thee, they salute you, not as Allah salutes thee, (but in crooked ways): And they say to themselves, "Why does not Allah punish us for our words?" Enough for them is Hell: In it will they burn, and evil is that destination!

8. Alam tara ilal-laz̲eena nuhoo 'anin-najwaa s̲umma ya'oodoona limaa nuhoo 'anhu wa yatanaajawna bil-is̲mi wal'udwaani wa ma'ṣiyatir-Rasooli wa iz̲aa jaaa'ooka ḥayyawka bimaa lam yuḥay-yika bihil-laahu wa yaqooloona feee anfusihim law laa yu'az̲-z̲ibunal-laahu bimaa naqool; ḥasbuhum Jahannamu yaṣlaw-nahaa fabi'sal-maṣeer.

اَلَمْ تَرَ اِلَى الَّذِيْنَ نُهُوْا عَنِ النَّجْوٰى
ثُمَّ يَعُوْدُوْنَ لِمَا نُهُوْا عَنْهُ وَيَتَنٰجَوْنَ
بِالْاِثْمِ وَالْعُدْوَانِ وَمَعْصِيَتِ
الرَّسُوْلِ ۫ وَاِذَا جَآءُوْكَ حَيَّوْكَ بِمَا لَمْ
يُحَيِّكَ بِهِ اللّٰهُ ۙ وَيَقُوْلُوْنَ فِيْٓ اَنْفُسِهِمْ
لَوْلَا يُعَذِّبُنَا اللّٰهُ بِمَا نَقُوْلُ ؕ حَسْبُهُمْ
جَهَنَّمُ ۚ يَصْلَوْنَهَا ۚ فَبِئْسَ الْمَصِيْرُ ٨

9. O you who believe! When you hold secret counsel, do it not for iniquity and hostility, and disobedience to the Prophet; but do it for righteousness

9. Yaaa ayyuhal-laz̲eena aamanooo iz̲aa tanaajaytum falaa tatanaajaw bil-is̲mi wal-'udwaani wa ma'ṣiyatir-Rasooli wa tanaajaw bil-birri

يٰٓاَيُّهَا الَّذِيْنَ اٰمَنُوْٓا اِذَا تَنَاجَيْتُمْ فَلَا
تَتَنَاجَوْا بِالْاِثْمِ وَالْعُدْوَانِ وَ
مَعْصِيَتِ الرَّسُوْلِ وَتَنَاجَوْا بِالْبِرِّ

and self-restraint; Whom you shall be brought back.

10. Secret counsels are only (inspired) by the Evil One, in order that he may cause grief to the Believers; but he cannot harm them in the least, except as Allah permits; and on Allah let the Believers put their trust.

11. O you who believe! When you are told to make room in the assemblies, (spread out and) make room: (ample) room will Allah provide for you. And when you are told to rise up, rise up, Allah will raise up, to (suitable) ranks (and degrees) those of you who believe and who have been granted (mystic) Knowledge. And Allah is well-acquainted with all you do.

12. O you who believe! When you consult the Apostle in private, spend something in charity before your private consultation. That will be best for you, and most conducive to purity (of conduct). But if you find not (the wherewithal), Allah is Oft-Forgiving, Most Merciful.

13. Is it that you are afraid of spending sums in charity before your private consultation (with him)? If, then, you do not so, and Allah forgives you, then (at least) establish regular prayer; practise regular charity; and obey Allah and His Apostle. And Allah is well-acquainted with all that you do.

14. Turnest you not your attention to those who turn (in friendship) to such as have the Wrath of Allah upon them? They are neither of you nor of them, and they swear to falsehood knowingly.

wattaqwaa wattaqul-laahal-lazeee ilayhi tuhsharoon.

10. Innaman-najwaa minash-Shaytaani liyahzunal-lazeena aamanoo wa laysa bidaaarrihim shay'an illaa bi-iznil-laah; wa 'alal-laahi falyatawakkalil-mu'minoon.

11. Yaaa ayyuhal-lazeena aamanooo izaa qeela lakum tafassahoo fil-majaalisi fafsahoo yafsahil-laahu lakum wa izaa qeelan-shuzoo fanshuzoo yarfa'il-laahul-lazeena aamanoo minkum wallazeena ootul-'ilma darajaat; wallaahu bimaa ta'maloona Khabeer.

12. Yaaa-ayyuhal-lazeena aamanooo izaa naajaytumur-Rasoola faqaddimoo bayna yaday najwaakum sadaqah; zaalika khayrul-lakum wa athar; fa-il-lam tajidoo fa-innal-laaha Ghafoorur-Raheem.

13. 'A-ashfaqtum an tuqad-dimoo bayna yaday najwaakum sadaqaat; fa-iz lam taf'aloo wa taabal-laahu 'alaykum fa-aqeemus-Salaata wa aatuz-Zakaata wa atee'ul-laaha wa Rasoolah; wallaahu khabeerum bimaa ta'maloon. **(Section 2)**

14. Alam tara ilal-lazeena tawallaw qawman ghadibal-laahu 'alayhim maa hum minkum wa laa minhum wa yahlifoona 'alal-kazibi wa hum ya'lamoon.

وَالتَّقْوٰى ۗ وَاتَّقُوا اللّٰهَ الَّذِيْٓ اِلَيْهِ
تُحْشَرُوْنَ ﴿٩﴾
اِنَّمَا النَّجْوٰى مِنَ الشَّيْطٰنِ لِيَحْزُنَ
الَّذِيْنَ اٰمَنُوْا وَلَيْسَ بِضَآرِّهِمْ شَيْـًٔا
اِلَّا بِاِذْنِ اللّٰهِ ۗ وَعَلَى اللّٰهِ فَلْيَتَوَكَّلِ
الْمُؤْمِنُوْنَ ﴿١٠﴾
يٰٓاَيُّهَا الَّذِيْنَ اٰمَنُوْٓا اِذَا قِيْلَ لَكُمْ
تَفَسَّحُوْا فِي الْمَجٰلِسِ فَافْسَحُوْا
يَفْسَحِ اللّٰهُ لَكُمْ ۚ وَاِذَا قِيْلَ انْشُزُوْا
فَانْشُزُوْا يَرْفَعِ اللّٰهُ الَّذِيْنَ اٰمَنُوْا
مِنْكُمْ ۙ وَالَّذِيْنَ اُوْتُوا الْعِلْمَ دَرَجٰتٍ ۭ
وَاللّٰهُ بِمَا تَعْمَلُوْنَ خَبِيْرٌ ﴿١١﴾
يٰٓاَيُّهَا الَّذِيْنَ اٰمَنُوْٓا اِذَا نَاجَيْتُمُ
الرَّسُوْلَ فَقَدِّمُوْا بَيْنَ يَدَيْ
نَجْوٰىكُمْ صَدَقَةً ۭ ذٰلِكَ خَيْرٌ لَّكُمْ
وَاَطْهَرُ ۭ فَاِنْ لَّمْ تَجِدُوْا فَاِنَّ اللّٰهَ
غَفُوْرٌ رَّحِيْمٌ ﴿١٢﴾
ءَاَشْفَقْتُمْ اَنْ تُقَدِّمُوْا بَيْنَ يَدَيْ
نَجْوٰىكُمْ صَدَقٰتٍ ۭ فَاِذْ لَمْ تَفْعَلُوْا
وَتَابَ اللّٰهُ عَلَيْكُمْ فَاَقِيْمُوا الصَّلٰوةَ
وَاٰتُوا الزَّكٰوةَ وَاَطِيْعُوا اللّٰهَ وَرَسُوْلَهٗ ۭ
وَاللّٰهُ خَبِيْرٌۢ بِمَا تَعْمَلُوْنَ ﴿١٣﴾
اَلَمْ تَرَ اِلَى الَّذِيْنَ تَوَلَّوْا قَوْمًا
غَضِبَ اللّٰهُ عَلَيْهِمْ ۭ مَا هُمْ مِّنْكُمْ
وَلَا مِنْهُمْ ۙ وَيَحْلِفُوْنَ عَلَى الْكَذِبِ
وَهُمْ يَعْلَمُوْنَ ﴿١٤﴾

Ikhfa اخفاء | Ghunna غنّہ | Ikhfa Meem Saakin اخفاء میم ساکن | Idghaam ادغام | Qalqala قلقلہ | Qalb قلب | Idghaam Meem Saakin ادغام میم ساکن

15. Allah has prepared for them a severe Chastisement: evil indeed are their deeds.

16. They have made their oaths a screen (for their misdeeds): thus they obstruct (men) from the Path of Allah: therefore shall they have a humiliating Chastisement.

17. Of no profit whatever to them, against Allah, will be their riches nor their sons: they will be Companions of the Fire, to dwell therein (for ever)!

18. One day will Allah raise them all up (for Judgment): then will they swear to Him as they swear to you: And they think that they have something (to stand upon). No, indeed! they are but liars!

19. The Evil One has got the better of them: so he has made them lose the remembrance of Allah. They are the Party of the Evil One. Truly, it is the Party of the Satan that will perish!

20. Those who resist Allah and His Apostle will be among those most humiliated.

21. Allah has decreed: "It is I and My apostles who must prevail": For Allah is One full of strength, able to enforce His Will.

22. You will not find any people who believe in Allah and the Last Day, loving those who resist Allah and His Apostle, even though they were their fathers or their sons, or their brothers, or their kindred. For such He has written Faith in their hearts, and strengthened them with a spirit from Himself. And He will admit them to Gardens beneath which Rivers flow, to dwell therein (for ever). Allah will be well pleased with them, and they with Him. They are the Party of

15. A'addal-laahu lahum-'azaaban shadeedan innahum saaa'a maa kaanoo ya'maloon.

16. Ittakhazooo aymaanahum junnatan fasaddoo 'an sabeelil-laahi falahum 'azaabum-muheen.

17. Lan tughniya 'anhum amwaaluhum wa laaa awladuhum minal-laahi shay'aa; ulaaa'ika Aṣ-ḥaabun-Naari hum feehaa khaalidoon.

18. Yawma yab'asuhumul-laahu jamee'an fa-yaḥlifoona lahoo kamaa yaḥlifoona lakum wa yaḥsaboona annahum 'Alaa shay'; alaaa innahum humul-kaaziboon.

19. Istaḥwaza 'alayhimush-Shayṭaanu fa-ansaahum zikral-laah; ulaaa'ika ḥizbush-Shayṭaan; alaaa inna ḥizbash-Shayṭaani humul-khaasiroon.

20. Innal-lazeena yuḥaaad-doonal-laaha wa Rasoolahooo ulaaa'ika fil-azalleen.

21. Katabal-laahu la-aghlibanna ana wa Rusulee; innal-laaha Qawiyyun 'Azeez.

22. Laa tajidu qawmany-yu'minoona billaahi wal-Yawmil-Aakhiri yuwaaaddoona man ḥaaaddal-laaha wa Rasoolahoo wa law kaanooo aabaaa'ahum aw abnaaa'ahum aw ikhwaanahum aw 'asheeratahum; ulaaa'ika kataba fee quloobihimul-eemaana wa ayyadahum biroohim-minhu wa yudkhiluhum Jannaatin tajree min taḥtihal-anhaaru khaalideena feehaa; raḍiyal-laahu 'anhum wa raḍoo 'anh; ulaaa'ika ḥizbul-

اَعَدَّ اللّٰهُ لَهُمْ عَذَابًا شَدِيْدًا ۭ اِنَّهُمْ
سَاۗءَ مَا كَانُوْا يَعْمَلُوْنَ ۝١٥
اِتَّخَذُوْٓا اَيْمَانَهُمْ جُنَّةً فَصَدُّوْا عَنْ
سَبِيْلِ اللّٰهِ فَلَهُمْ عَذَابٌ مُّهِيْنٌ ۝١٦
لَنْ تُغْنِيَ عَنْهُمْ اَمْوَالُهُمْ وَلَآ
اَوْلَادُهُمْ مِّنَ اللّٰهِ شَيْـــًٔا ۭ اُولٰۗىِٕكَ
اَصْحٰبُ النَّارِ ۭ هُمْ فِيْهَا خٰلِدُوْنَ ۝١٧
يَوْمَ يَبْعَثُهُمُ اللّٰهُ جَمِيْعًا فَيَحْلِفُوْنَ
لَهٗ كَمَا يَحْلِفُوْنَ لَكُمْ وَ
يَحْسَبُوْنَ اَنَّهُمْ عَلٰي شَيْءٍ ۭ اَلَآ اِنَّهُمْ
هُمُ الْكٰذِبُوْنَ ۝١٨
اِسْتَحْوَذَ عَلَيْهِمُ الشَّيْطٰنُ فَاَنْسٰىهُمْ
ذِكْرَ اللّٰهِ ۭ اُولٰۗىِٕكَ حِزْبُ الشَّيْطٰنِ ۭ اَلَآ
اِنَّ حِزْبَ الشَّيْطٰنِ هُمُ الْخٰسِرُوْنَ ۝١٩
اِنَّ الَّذِيْنَ يُحَاۗدُّوْنَ اللّٰهَ وَرَسُوْلَهٗٓ
اُولٰۗىِٕكَ فِي الْاَذَلِّيْنَ ۝٢٠
كَتَبَ اللّٰهُ لَاَغْلِبَنَّ اَنَا وَرُسُلِيْ ۭ اِنَّ
اللّٰهَ قَوِيٌّ عَزِيْزٌ ۝٢١
لَا تَجِدُ قَوْمًا يُّؤْمِنُوْنَ بِاللّٰهِ وَالْيَوْمِ
الْاٰخِرِ يُوَاۗدُّوْنَ مَنْ حَاۗدَّ اللّٰهَ وَ
رَسُوْلَهٗ وَلَوْ كَانُوْٓا اٰبَاۗءَهُمْ اَوْ اَبْنَاۗءَهُمْ
اَوْ اِخْوَانَهُمْ اَوْ عَشِيْرَتَهُمْ ۭ اُولٰۗىِٕكَ
كَتَبَ فِيْ قُلُوْبِهِمُ الْاِيْمَانَ وَاَيَّدَهُمْ
بِرُوْحٍ مِّنْهُ ۭ وَيُدْخِلُهُمْ جَنّٰتٍ تَجْرِيْ
مِنْ تَحْتِهَا الْاَنْهٰرُ خٰلِدِيْنَ فِيْهَا ۭ رَضِيَ
اللّٰهُ عَنْهُمْ وَرَضُوْا عَنْهُ ۭ اُولٰۗىِٕكَ حِزْبُ

Allah. Truly it is the Party of Allah that will achieve Felicity.

59. The Gathering

In the name of Allah, Most Gracious, Most Merciful.

1. Whatever is in the heavens and on earth, let it declare the Praises and Glory of Allah: for He is the Exalted in Might, the Wise.

2. It is He Who got out the Unbelievers among the People of the Book from their homes at the first gathering (of the forces). Little did you think that they would get out: And they thought that their fortresses would defend them from Allah! But the (Wrath of) Allah came to them from quarters from which they little expected (it), and cast terror into their hearts, so that they destroyed their dwellings by their own hands and the hands of the Believers, take warning, then, O you with eyes (to see)!

3. And had it not been that Allah had decreed banishment for them, He would certainly have punished them in this world: And in the Hereafter they shall (certainly) have the Punishment of the Fire.

4. That is because they resisted Allah and His Apostle: and if any one resists Allah, verily Allah is severe in Punishment.

5. Whether you cut down (O you Muslim!) The tender palm-trees, or you left them standing on their roots, it was by leave of Allah, and in order that He might cover with shame the rebellious transgressors.

6. What Allah has bestowed on His Apostle (and taken away) from them - for this you made no expedition with either cavalry or camelry: but Allah gives power to His apostles over any He pleases: and Allah has power over all things.

laah; alaaa inna ḥizbal-laahi humul-mufliḥoon. **(Section 3)**

Sûrat al-Ḥashr–59

(Revealed at Madinah)

Bismillaahir Raḥmaanir Raḥeem

1. Sabbaḥa lillaahi maa fis-samaawaati wa maa fil-arḍi wa Huwal-'Azeezul-Ḥakeem.

2. Huwal-lazeee akhrajal-lazeena kafaroo min Ahlil-Kitaabi min diyaarihim li-awwalil-Ḥashr; maa ẓanantum añy-yakhrujoo wa ẓannoo anna-hum maa ni'atuhum ḥuṣoonu-hum minal-laahi fa-ataahumul-laahu min ḥaysu lam yaḥtasiboo wa qazafa fee quloobihimur-ru'ba yukhriboona bu-yootahum bi-aydeehim wa aydil-mu'mineena fa'tabiroo yaaa ulil-abṣaar.

3. Wa law laaa an katabal-laahu 'alayhimul-jalaaa'a la'az-zabahum fid-dunyaa wa lahum fil-Aakhirati 'azaabun-Naar.

4. Zaalika bi-annahum shaaq-qul-laaha wa Rasoolahoo wa mañy-yushaaaqqil-laaha fa-innal-laaha shadeedul-'iqaab.

5. Maa qaṭa'tum mil-leenatin aw taraktumoohaa qaaa'imatan 'alaaa uṣoolihaa fabi-iznil-laahi wa liyukhziyal-faasiqeen.

6. Wa maaa afaaa'al-laahu 'alaa Rasoolihee minhum famaaa awjaftum 'alayhi min khayliñw-wa laa rikaabiñw-wa laakinnal-laaha yusalliṭu Rusula-hoo 'alaa mañy-yashaaa'; wallaa-hu 'alaa kulli shay'in Qadeer.

اللّٰهِ ۭ اَلَآ اِنَّ حِزْبَ اللّٰهِ هُمُ الْمُفْلِحُوْنَ ۝٢٢ ع

(٥٩) سُوْرَةُ الْحَشْرِ مَدَنِيَّةٌ (١٠١)

بِسْمِ اللّٰهِ الرَّحْمٰنِ الرَّحِيْمِ

سَبَّحَ لِلّٰهِ مَا فِي السَّمٰوٰتِ وَمَا فِي
الْاَرْضِ ۚ وَهُوَ الْعَزِيْزُ الْحَكِيْمُ ۝١
هُوَ الَّذِيْٓ اَخْرَجَ الَّذِيْنَ كَفَرُوْا مِنْ
اَهْلِ الْكِتٰبِ مِنْ دِيَارِهِمْ لِاَوَّلِ
الْحَشْرِ ۭ مَا ظَنَنْتُمْ اَنْ يَّخْرُجُوْا وَظَنُّوْٓا
اَنَّهُمْ مَّانِعَتُهُمْ حُصُوْنُهُمْ مِّنَ اللّٰهِ
فَاَتٰىهُمُ اللّٰهُ مِنْ حَيْثُ لَمْ يَحْتَسِبُوْا
وَقَذَفَ فِيْ قُلُوْبِهِمُ الرُّعْبَ يُخْرِبُوْنَ
بُيُوْتَهُمْ بِاَيْدِيْهِمْ وَاَيْدِي الْمُؤْمِنِيْنَ
فَاعْتَبِرُوْا يٰٓاُولِي الْاَبْصَارِ ۝٢
وَلَوْلَآ اَنْ كَتَبَ اللّٰهُ عَلَيْهِمُ الْجَلَاۗءَ
لَعَذَّبَهُمْ فِي الدُّنْيَا ۭ وَلَهُمْ فِي الْاٰخِرَةِ
عَذَابُ النَّارِ ۝٣
ذٰلِكَ بِاَنَّهُمْ شَاۗقُّوا اللّٰهَ وَرَسُوْلَهٗ ۚ
وَمَنْ يُّشَاۗقِّ اللّٰهَ فَاِنَّ اللّٰهَ شَدِيْدُ
الْعِقَابِ ۝٤
مَا قَطَعْتُمْ مِّنْ لِّيْنَةٍ اَوْ تَرَكْتُمُوْهَا
قَاۗىِٕمَةً عَلٰٓي اُصُوْلِهَا فَبِاِذْنِ اللّٰهِ وَ
لِيُخْزِيَ الْفٰسِقِيْنَ ۝٥
وَمَآ اَفَاۗءَ اللّٰهُ عَلٰي رَسُوْلِهٖ مِنْهُمْ فَمَآ
اَوْجَفْتُمْ عَلَيْهِ مِنْ خَيْلٍ وَّلَا رِكَابٍ
وَّلٰكِنَّ اللّٰهَ يُسَلِّطُ رُسُلَهٗ عَلٰي مَنْ
يَّشَاۗءُ ۭ وَاللّٰهُ عَلٰي كُلِّ شَيْءٍ قَدِيْرٌ ۝٦

Ikhfa اخفاء | Ghunna غنّہ | Ikhfa Meem Saakin اخفاء میم ساکن | Idghaam ادغام | Qalqala قلقلہ | Qalb قلب | Idghaam Meem Saakin ادغام میم ساکن

7. What Allah has bestowed on His Apostle (and taken away) from the people of the townships,- belongs to Allah,- to His Apostle and to kindred and orphans, the needy and the wayfarer; In order that it may not (merely) make a circuit between the wealthy among you. So take what the Apostle assigns to you, and deny yourselves that which he withholds from you. And fear Allah; for Allah is strict in Punishment.

7. Maaa afaaa'al-laahu 'alaa Rasoolihee min ahlil-quraa falillaahi wa lir-Rasooli wa lizil-qurbaa wal-yataamaa walmasaakeeni wabnis-sabeeli kay laa yakoona doolatam baynal-aghniyaaa'i minkum; wa maaa aataakumur-Rasoolu fakhuzoohu wa maa nahaakum 'anhu fantahoo; wattaqul-laaha innal-laaha shadeedul-'iqaab.

مَآ أَفَآءَ اللّٰهُ عَلٰى رَسُوْلِهٖ مِنْ أَهْلِ
الْقُرٰى فَلِلّٰهِ وَلِلرَّسُوْلِ وَلِذِى الْقُرْبٰى
وَالْيَتٰمٰى وَالْمَسٰكِيْنِ وَابْنِ السَّبِيْلِ
كَىْ لَا يَكُوْنَ دُوْلَةًۢ بَيْنَ الْأَغْنِيَآءِ
مِنْكُمْ ۚ وَمَآ اٰتٰىكُمُ الرَّسُوْلُ فَخُذُوْهُ
وَمَا نَهٰىكُمْ عَنْهُ فَانْتَهُوْا ۚ وَاتَّقُوا
اللّٰهَ ۗ إِنَّ اللّٰهَ شَدِيْدُ الْعِقَابِ ۝٧ وقف لازم

8. (Some part is due) to the indigent Muhajirs, those who were expelled from their homes and their property, while seeking Grace from Allah and (His) Good Pleasure, and aiding Allah and His Apostle: such are indeed the sincere ones:-

8. Lilfuqaraaa'il-Muhaajireenal-lazeena ukhrijoo min diyaarihim wa amwaalihim yabtaghoona fadlam-minal-laahi wa ridwaanañw-wa yansuroonal-laaha wa Rasoolah; ulaaa'ika humus-saadiqoon.

لِلْفُقَرَآءِ الْمُهٰجِرِيْنَ الَّذِيْنَ أُخْرِجُوْا
مِنْ دِيَارِهِمْ وَأَمْوَالِهِمْ يَبْتَغُوْنَ
فَضْلًا مِّنَ اللّٰهِ وَرِضْوَانًا وَّ
يَنْصُرُوْنَ اللّٰهَ وَرَسُوْلَهٗ ۚ أُولٰٓئِكَ
هُمُ الصّٰدِقُوْنَ ۝٨

9. But those who before them, had homes (in Medina) and had adopted the Faith,- show their affection to such as came to them for refuge, and entertain no desire in their hearts for things given to the (latter), but give them preference over themselves, even though poverty was their (own lot). And those saved from the covetousness of their own souls,- they are the ones that achieve prosperity.

9. Wallazeena tabawwa'ud-daara wal-eemaana min qablihim yuhibboona man haajara ilayhim wa laa yajidoona fee sudoorihim haajatam-mimmaa ootoo wa yu'siroona 'alaa anfusihim wa law kaana bihim khasaasah; wa mañy-yooqa shuhha nafsihee fa-ulaaa'ika humul-muflihoon.

وَالَّذِيْنَ تَبَوَّءُو الدَّارَ وَالْإِيْمَانَ
مِنْ قَبْلِهِمْ يُحِبُّوْنَ مَنْ هَاجَرَ
إِلَيْهِمْ وَلَا يَجِدُوْنَ فِىْ صُدُوْرِهِمْ
حَاجَةً مِّمَّآ أُوْتُوْا وَيُؤْثِرُوْنَ عَلٰٓى
أَنْفُسِهِمْ وَلَوْ كَانَ بِهِمْ خَصَاصَةٌ ۚ
وَمَنْ يُّوْقَ شُحَّ نَفْسِهٖ فَأُولٰٓئِكَ
هُمُ الْمُفْلِحُوْنَ ۝٩

10. And those who came after them say: "Our Lord! Forgive us, and our brethren who came before us into the Faith, and leave not, in our hearts, rancour (or sense of injury) against those who have believed. Our Lord! You are indeed Full of Kindness, Most Merciful."

10. Wallazeena Jaaa'oo min ba'dihim yaqooloona Rabbanagh-fir lanaa wa li-ikhwaaninal-lazeena sabaqoonaa bil-eemaani wa laa taj'al fee quloobinaa ghillallil-lazeena aamanoo Rabbanaaa innaka Ra'oofur-Raheem. **(Section 1)**

وَالَّذِيْنَ جَآءُوْ مِنْۢ بَعْدِهِمْ يَقُوْلُوْنَ
رَبَّنَا اغْفِرْ لَنَا وَلِإِخْوَانِنَا الَّذِيْنَ
سَبَقُوْنَا بِالْإِيْمَانِ وَلَا تَجْعَلْ فِىْ
قُلُوْبِنَا غِلًّا لِّلَّذِيْنَ اٰمَنُوْا رَبَّنَآ إِنَّكَ
رَءُوْفٌ رَّحِيْمٌ ۝١٠ الربع

11. Have you not observed the Hypocrites say to their misbelieving brethren among the

11. Alam tara ilal-lazeena naafaqoo yaqooloona li-ikhwaanihimul-lazeena kafaroo min

أَلَمْ تَرَ إِلَى الَّذِيْنَ نَافَقُوْا يَقُوْلُوْنَ
لِإِخْوَانِهِمُ الَّذِيْنَ كَفَرُوْا مِنْ

Ikhfa اخفاء · Ghunna غنّہ · Ikhfa Meem Saakin اخفاء میم ساکن · Idghaam ادغام · Qalqala قلقلہ · Qalb قلب · Idghaam Meem Saakin ادغام میم ساکن

People of the Book? - "If you are expelled, we too will go out with you, and we will never hearken to any one in your affair; and if you are attacked (in fight) we will help you". But Allah is witness that they are indeed liars.

Ahlil-Kitaabi la'in ukhrijtum lanakhrujanna ma'akum wa laa nuṭee'u feekum aḥadan abadañw-wa in qootiltum lananṣurannakum wallaahu yashhadu innahum lakaaziboon.

اَهۡلِ الۡكِتٰبِ لَئِنۡ اُخۡرِجۡتُمۡ لَنَخۡرُجَنَّ
مَعَكُمۡ وَلَا نُطِيۡعُ فِيۡكُمۡ اَحَدًا
اَبَدًا ۙ وَّاِنۡ قُوۡتِلۡتُمۡ لَنَنۡصُرَنَّكُمۡ ؕ
وَاللّٰهُ يَشۡهَدُ اِنَّهُمۡ لَكٰذِبُوۡنَ ﴿۱۱﴾

12. If they are expelled, never will they go out with them; and if they are attacked (in fight), they will never help them; and if they do help them, they will turn their backs; so they will receive no help.

12. La'in ukhrijoo laa yakhrujoona ma'ahum wa la'in qootiloo laa yanṣuroonahum wa la'in naṣaroohum la-yuwallunnal-adbaara summa laa yunṣaroon.

لَئِنۡ اُخۡرِجُوۡا لَا يَخۡرُجُوۡنَ مَعَهُمۡ ۚ
وَلَئِنۡ قُوۡتِلُوۡا لَا يَنۡصُرُوۡنَهُمۡ ۚ وَلَئِنۡ
نَّصَرُوۡهُمۡ لَيُوَلُّنَّ الۡاَدۡبَارَ ثُمَّ لَا
يُنۡصَرُوۡنَ ﴿۱۲﴾

13. Of a truth you are stronger (than they) because of the terror in their hearts, (sent) by Allah. This is because they are men devoid of understanding.

13. La-antum ashaddu rahbatan fee ṣudoorihim minal-laah; zaalika bi-annahum qawmul-laa yafqahoon.

لَاَانۡتُمۡ اَشَدُّ رَهۡبَةً فِىۡ صُدُوۡرِهِمۡ مِّنَ
اللّٰهِ ؕ ذٰلِكَ بِاَنَّهُمۡ قَوۡمٌ لَّا يَفۡقَهُوۡنَ ﴿۱۳﴾

14. They will not fight you (even) together, except in fortified townships, or from behind walls. Strong is their fighting (spirit) amongst themselves: you would think they were united, but their hearts are divided: that is because they are a people devoid of wisdom.

14. Laa yuqaatiloonakum jamee'an illaa fee quram-muḥaṣṣanatin aw miñw-waraaa'i judur; baåsuhum baynahum shadeed; taḥsabuhum jamee'añw-wa quloobuhum shattaa; zaalika bi-annahum qawmul-laa ya'qiloon.

لَا يُقَاتِلُوۡنَكُمۡ جَمِيۡعًا اِلَّا فِىۡ قُرًى
مُّحَصَّنَةٍ اَوۡ مِنۡ وَّرَآءِ جُدُرٍ ؕ
بَاۡسُهُمۡ بَيۡنَهُمۡ شَدِيۡدٌ ؕ تَحۡسَبُهُمۡ
جَمِيۡعًا وَّقُلُوۡبُهُمۡ شَتّٰى ؕ ذٰلِكَ
بِاَنَّهُمۡ قَوۡمٌ لَّا يَعۡقِلُوۡنَ ﴿۱۴﴾ۚ

15. Like those who lately preceded them, they have tasted the evil result of their conduct; and (in the Hereafter there is) for them a grievous Chastisement;-

15. Kamasalil-lazeena min qablihim qareeban zaaqoo wabaala amrihim wa lahum 'azaabun aleem.

كَمَثَلِ الَّذِيۡنَ مِنۡ قَبۡلِهِمۡ قَرِيۡبًا ذَاقُوۡا
وَبَالَ اَمۡرِهِمۡ ۚ وَلَهُمۡ عَذَابٌ اَلِيۡمٌ ﴿۱۵﴾ۚ

16. (Their allies deceived them), like the Evil One, when he says to man, "Deny Allah": but when (man) denies Allah, (the Evil One) says, "I am free of you: I do fear Allah, the Lord of the Worlds!"

16. Kamasalish-Shayṭaani iz qaala lil-insaanik-fur falammaa kafara qaala innee bareee'umminka inneee akhaaful-laaha Rabbal-'aalameen.

كَمَثَلِ الشَّيۡطٰنِ اِذۡ قَالَ لِلۡاِنۡسَانِ
اكۡفُرۡ ۚ فَلَمَّا كَفَرَ قَالَ اِنِّىۡ بَرِىۡٓءٌ مِّنۡكَ
اِنِّىۡۤ اَخَافُ اللّٰهَ رَبَّ الۡعٰلَمِيۡنَ ﴿۱۶﴾

17. The end of both will be that they will go into the Fire, dwelling therein for ever. Such is the reward of the wrong-doers.

17. Fakaana 'aaqibatahumaaa annahumaa fin-Naari khaalidayni feehaa; wa zaalika jazaaa-'uẓ-ẓaalimeen. **(Section 2)**

فَكَانَ عَاقِبَتَهُمَاۤ اَنَّهُمَا فِى النَّارِ
خَالِدَيۡنِ فِيۡهَا ؕ وَذٰلِكَ جَزٰٓؤُا
الظّٰلِمِيۡنَ ﴿۱۷﴾ ع

18. O you who believe! Fear Allah, and let every soul look to what (provision) he has sent forth for the morrow. Yes, fear Allah: for Allah is well-acquainted with (all)

18. Yaaa ayyuhal-lazeena aamanut-taqul-laaha waltanẓur nafsum-maa qaddamat lighad, wattaqul-laah; innal-laaha Khabeerum bimaa

يٰۤاَيُّهَا الَّذِيۡنَ اٰمَنُوا اتَّقُوا اللّٰهَ
وَلۡتَنۡظُرۡ نَفۡسٌ مَّا قَدَّمَتۡ لِغَدٍ ۚ
وَاتَّقُوا اللّٰهَ ؕ اِنَّ اللّٰهَ خَبِيۡرٌۢ بِمَا

Ikhfa اخفاء | Ghunna غنّہ | Ikhfa Meem Saakin اخفاء میم ساکن | Idghaam ادغام | Qalqala قلقلہ | Qalb قلب | Idghaam Meem Saakin ادغام میم ساکن

that you do.

19. And be you not like those who forgot Allah; and He made them forget their own souls! Such are the rebellious transgressors!

20. Not equal are the Companions of the Fire and the Companions of the Garden: it is the Companions of the Garden, that will achieve Felicity.

21. Had We sent down this Qur'an on a mountain, verily, thou wouldst have seen it humble itself and cleave asunder for fear of Allah. Such are the similitudes which We propound to men, that they may reflect.

22. Allah is He, than Whom there is no other god;- Who knows (all things) both secret and open; He, Most Gracious, Most Merciful.

23. Allah is He, other than Whom there is no other god;- the Sovereign, the Holy One, the Source of Peace (and Perfection), the Guardian of Faith, the Preserver of Safety, the Exalted in Might, the Irresistible, the Supreme: Glory to Allah! (High is He) above the partners they attribute to Him.

24. He is Allah, the Creator, the Evolver, the Fashioner, the Bestower of Forms (or Colours). To Him belong the Most Beautiful Names: whatever is in the heavens and on earth, does declare His Praises and Glory: and He is the Exalted in Might, the Wise.

60. The Woman to be Examined

In the name of Allah, Most Gracious, Most Merciful.

1. O you who believe! Take not my enemies and yours as friends (or protectors),- offering them (your) love, even though they have rejected the Truth that has come to you, and have (on the contrary) driven out

ta'maloon.

19. Wa laa takoonoo kallazeena nasul-laaha fa-ansaahum anfusahum; ulaaa'ika humul-faasiqoon.

20. Laa yastaweee Aṣ-ḥaabun-Naari wa Aṣ-ḥaabul-Jannah; Aṣ-ḥaabul-Jannati humul-faaa'izoon.

21. Law anzalnaa haazal-Qur-aana 'alaa jabalil-lara-aytahoo khaashi'am-mutaṣaddi'am-min khashyatillaah; wa tilkal-amsaalu naḍribuhaa linnaasi la'allahum yatafakkaroon.

22. Huwal-laahul-lazee laaa Ilaaha illaa Huwa 'Aalimul-Ghaybi wash-shahaadati Huwar-Raḥmaanur-Raḥeem.

23. Huwal-laahul-lazee laaa Ilaaha illaa Huwa al-Malikul-Quddoosus-Salaamul-Mu'minul-Muhayminul-'Azeezul-Jabbaarul-Mutakabbir; Subḥaanal-laahi 'Ammaa yushrikoon.

24. Huwal-laahul-Khaaliqul-Baari'ul-Muṣawwiru lahul-Asmaaa'ul-Ḥusnaa; yusabbiḥu lahoo maa fis-samaawaati wal-arḍi wa Huwal-'Azeezul-Ḥakeem. **(Section 3)**

Sûrat al-Mumtaḥanah–60

(Revealed at Madinah)

Bismillaahir Raḥmaanir Raḥeem

1. Yaaa ayyuhal-lazeena aamanoo laa tattakhizoo 'aduwwee wa 'aduwwakum awliyaaa'a tulqoona ilayhim bilmawaddati wa qad kafaroo bimaa jaaa'akum minal-ḥaqq, yukhrijoonar-

تَعْمَلُوْنَ ﴿١٨﴾
وَلَا تَكُوْنُوْا كَالَّذِيْنَ نَسُوا اللّٰهَ فَاَنْسٰىهُمْ
اَنْفُسَهُمْ ؕ اُولٰٓئِكَ هُمُ الْفٰسِقُوْنَ ﴿١٩﴾
لَا يَسْتَوِيْٓ اَصْحٰبُ النَّارِ وَاَصْحٰبُ
الْجَنَّةِ ؕ اَصْحٰبُ الْجَنَّةِ هُمُ الْفَآئِزُوْنَ ﴿٢٠﴾
لَوْ اَنْزَلْنَا هٰذَا الْقُرْاٰنَ عَلٰى جَبَلٍ
لَّرَاَيْتَهٗ خَاشِعًا مُّتَصَدِّعًا مِّنْ
خَشْيَةِ اللّٰهِ ؕ وَتِلْكَ الْاَمْثَالُ
نَضْرِبُهَا لِلنَّاسِ لَعَلَّهُمْ يَتَفَكَّرُوْنَ ﴿٢١﴾
هُوَ اللّٰهُ الَّذِيْ لَآ اِلٰهَ اِلَّا هُوَ ۚ
عٰلِمُ الْغَيْبِ وَالشَّهَادَةِ ۚ هُوَ
الرَّحْمٰنُ الرَّحِيْمُ ﴿٢٢﴾
هُوَ اللّٰهُ الَّذِيْ لَآ اِلٰهَ اِلَّا هُوَ ۚ اَلْمَلِكُ
الْقُدُّوْسُ السَّلٰمُ الْمُؤْمِنُ الْمُهَيْمِنُ
الْعَزِيْزُ الْجَبَّارُ الْمُتَكَبِّرُ ؕ سُبْحٰنَ
اللّٰهِ عَمَّا يُشْرِكُوْنَ ﴿٢٣﴾
هُوَ اللّٰهُ الْخَالِقُ الْبَارِئُ الْمُصَوِّرُ
لَهُ الْاَسْمَآءُ الْحُسْنٰى ؕ يُسَبِّحُ لَهٗ
مَا فِي السَّمٰوٰتِ وَالْاَرْضِ ۚ وَهُوَ
الْعَزِيْزُ الْحَكِيْمُ ﴿٢٤﴾

(٦٠) سُوْرَةُ الْمُمْتَحِنَةِ مَدَنِيَّةٌ (٩١)

بِسْمِ اللّٰهِ الرَّحْمٰنِ الرَّحِيْمِ

يٰٓاَيُّهَا الَّذِيْنَ اٰمَنُوْا لَا تَتَّخِذُوْا
عَدُوِّيْ وَعَدُوَّكُمْ اَوْلِيَآءَ تُلْقُوْنَ
اِلَيْهِمْ بِالْمَوَدَّةِ وَقَدْ كَفَرُوْا بِمَا
جَآءَكُمْ مِّنَ الْحَقِّ ۚ يُخْرِجُوْنَ

Ikhfa اخفاء | Ghunna غنّہ | Ikhfa Meem Saakin اخفاء میم ساکن | Idghaam ادغام | Qalqala قلقلہ | Qalb قلب | Idghaam Meem Saakin ادغام میم ساکن

the Prophet and yourselves (from your homes), (simply) because ye believe in Allah your Lord! If you have come out to strive in My Way and to seek My Good Pleasure, (take them not as friends), holding secret conclave of love (and friendship) with them: for I know full well all that you conceal and all that you reveal. And any of you that does this has strayed from the Straight Path.

2. If they were to get the better of you, they would behave to you as enemies, and stretch forth their hands and their tongues against you for evil: and they desire that you should reject the Truth.

3. Of no profit to you will be your relatives and your children on the Day of Judgment: He will judge between you: for Allah sees well all that you do.

4. There is for you an excellent example (to follow) in Abraham and those with him, when they said to their people: "We are clear of you and of whatever ye worship besides Allah: we have rejected you, and there has arisen, between us and you, enmity and hatred for ever,- unless you believe in Allah and Him alone": But not when Abraham said to his father: "I will pray for forgiveness for you, though I have no power (to get) aught on your behalf from Allah." (They prayed): "Our Lord! in You do we trust, and to You do we turn in repentance: to Thee is (our) Final Goal.

5. "Our Lord! Make us not a (test and) trial for the Unbelievers, but forgive us, our Lord! for You are the Exalted in Might, the Wise."

6. There was indeed in them an excellent example for you to follow,-

Rasoola wa iyyaakum an tu'minoo billaahi Rabbikum in kuntum kharajtum jihaadan fee sabeelee wabtighaaa'a marḍaatee; tusirroona ilayhim bilmawaddati wa ana a'lamu bimaaa akhfaytum wa maaa a'lantum; wa mañy-yaf'alhu minkum faqad ḍalla Sawaaa'as-Sabeel.

2. Iñy-yasqafookum yakoonoo lakum a'daaa'añw-wa yabsuṭooo ilaykum aydiyahum wa alsinatahum bissooo'i wa waddoo law takfuroon.

3. Lan tanfa'akum arḥaamukum wa laaa awlaadukum; Yawmal-Qiyaamati yafṣilu baynakum; wallaahu bimaa ta'maloona Baṣeer.

4. Qad kaanat lakum uswatun ḥasanatun feee Ibraaheema wallaẕeena ma'ahoo iẕ qaaloo liqawmihim innaa bura'aaa'u minkum wa mimmaa ta'budoona min doonil-laahi kafarnaa bikum wa badaa baynanaa wa baynakumul-'adaawatu wal-baghḍaaa'u abadan ḥattaa tu'minoo billaahi waḥdahooo illaa qawla Ibraaheema li-abeehi la-astaghfiranna laka wa maaa amliku laka minal-laahi min shay'; Rabbanaa 'alayka tawakkalnaa wa ilayka anabnaa wa ilaykal-maṣeer.

5. Rabbanaa laa taj'alnaa fitnatal-lillaẕeena kafaroo waghfir lanaa Rabbanaa innaka Antal-'Azeezul-Ḥakeem.

6. Laqad kaana lakum feehim uswatun

الرَّسُولَ وَإِيَّاكُمْ أَنْ تُؤْمِنُوا بِاللَّهِ
رَبِّكُمْ إِنْ كُنْتُمْ خَرَجْتُمْ جِهَادًا فِي
سَبِيلِي وَابْتِغَاءَ مَرْضَاتِي تُسِرُّونَ
إِلَيْهِمْ بِالْمَوَدَّةِ وَأَنَا أَعْلَمُ بِمَا
أَخْفَيْتُمْ وَمَا أَعْلَنْتُمْ وَمَنْ يَفْعَلْهُ
مِنْكُمْ فَقَدْ ضَلَّ سَوَاءَ السَّبِيلِ ①
إِنْ يَثْقَفُوكُمْ يَكُونُوا لَكُمْ أَعْدَاءً
وَيَبْسُطُوا إِلَيْكُمْ أَيْدِيَهُمْ وَأَلْسِنَتَهُمْ
بِالسُّوءِ وَوَدُّوا لَوْ تَكْفُرُونَ ②
لَنْ تَنْفَعَكُمْ أَرْحَامُكُمْ وَلَا أَوْلَادُكُمْ
يَوْمَ الْقِيَامَةِ يَفْصِلُ بَيْنَكُمْ وَاللَّهُ
بِمَا تَعْمَلُونَ بَصِيرٌ ③
قَدْ كَانَتْ لَكُمْ أُسْوَةٌ حَسَنَةٌ فِي
إِبْرَاهِيمَ وَالَّذِينَ مَعَهُ إِذْ قَالُوا
لِقَوْمِهِمْ إِنَّا بُرَآءُ مِنْكُمْ وَمِمَّا
تَعْبُدُونَ مِنْ دُونِ اللَّهِ كَفَرْنَا بِكُمْ
وَبَدَا بَيْنَنَا وَبَيْنَكُمُ الْعَدَاوَةُ
وَالْبَغْضَاءُ أَبَدًا حَتَّى تُؤْمِنُوا بِاللَّهِ
وَحْدَهُ إِلَّا قَوْلَ إِبْرَاهِيمَ لِأَبِيهِ
لَأَسْتَغْفِرَنَّ لَكَ وَمَا أَمْلِكُ لَكَ مِنَ
اللَّهِ مِنْ شَيْءٍ رَبَّنَا عَلَيْكَ تَوَكَّلْنَا
وَإِلَيْكَ أَنَبْنَا وَإِلَيْكَ الْمَصِيرُ ④
رَبَّنَا لَا تَجْعَلْنَا فِتْنَةً لِلَّذِينَ
كَفَرُوا وَاغْفِرْ لَنَا رَبَّنَا إِنَّكَ
أَنْتَ الْعَزِيزُ الْحَكِيمُ ⑤
لَقَدْ كَانَ لَكُمْ فِيهِمْ أُسْوَةٌ

Ikhfa اخفاء | Ghunna غنّہ | Ikhfa Meem Saakin اخفاء میم ساکن | Idghaam ادغام | Qalqala قلقلہ | Qalb قلب | Idghaam Meem Saakin ادغام میم ساکن

for those whose hope is in Allah and in the Last Day. But if any turn away, truly Allah is Free of all Wants, Worthy of all Praise.

ḥasanatul-liman kaana yarjul-laaha wal-Yawmal-Aakhir; wa mañy-yatawalla fa-innal-laaha Huwal-Ghaniyyul-Ḥameed.

(Section 1)

حَسَنَةٌ لِّمَنْ كَانَ يَرْجُوا اللّٰهَ وَ
الْيَوْمَ الْاٰخِرَ ۗ وَمَنْ يَّتَوَلَّ فَاِنَّ
اللّٰهَ هُوَ الْغَنِيُّ الْحَمِيْدُ ۝٦ ع

7. It may be that Allah will grant love (and friendship) between you and those whom you (now) hold as enemies. For Allah has power (over all things); And Allah is Oft-Forgiving, Most Merciful.

7. 'Asal-laahu añy-yaj'ala baynakum wa baynal-lazeena 'aadaytum minhum mawaddah; wallahu Qadeer; wallahu Ghafoorur-Raḥeem.

عَسَى اللّٰهُ اَنْ يَّجْعَلَ بَيْنَكُمْ وَبَيْنَ
الَّذِيْنَ عَادَيْتُمْ مِّنْهُمْ مَّوَدَّةً ۗ وَ
اللّٰهُ قَدِيْرٌ ۗ وَاللّٰهُ غَفُوْرٌ رَّحِيْمٌ ۝٧

8. Allah forbids you not, with regard to those who fight you not for (your) Faith nor drive you out of your homes, from dealing kindly and justly with them: for Allah loves those who are just.

8. Laa yanhaakumul-laahu 'anil-lazeena lam yuqaatilookum fid-deeni wa lam yukhrijookum-min diyaarikum an tabarroohum wa tuqsiṭooo ilayhim; innal-laaha yuḥibbul-muqsiṭeen.

لَا يَنْهٰىكُمُ اللّٰهُ عَنِ الَّذِيْنَ لَمْ
يُقَاتِلُوْكُمْ فِى الدِّيْنِ وَلَمْ يُخْرِجُوْكُمْ
مِّنْ دِيَارِكُمْ اَنْ تَبَرُّوْهُمْ وَتُقْسِطُوْٓا
اِلَيْهِمْ ۗ اِنَّ اللّٰهَ يُحِبُّ الْمُقْسِطِيْنَ ۝٨

9. Allah only forbids you, with regard to those who fight you for (your) Faith, and drive you out of your homes, and support (others) in driving you out, from turning to them (for friendship and protection). It is such as turn to them (in these circumstances), that do wrong.

9. Innamaa yanhaakumul-laahu 'anil-lazeena qaataloo-kum fid-deeni wa akhrajookum min diyaarikum wa ẓaaharoo 'alaa ikhraajikum an tawallawhum; wa mañy-yatawallahum fa-ulaaa'ika humuẓ-ẓaalimoon.

اِنَّمَا يَنْهٰىكُمُ اللّٰهُ عَنِ الَّذِيْنَ
قٰتَلُوْكُمْ فِى الدِّيْنِ وَاَخْرَجُوْكُمْ
مِّنْ دِيَارِكُمْ وَظٰهَرُوْا عَلٰٓى
اِخْرَاجِكُمْ اَنْ تَوَلَّوْهُمْ ۚ وَمَنْ
يَّتَوَلَّهُمْ فَاُولٰٓئِكَ هُمُ الظّٰلِمُوْنَ ۝٩

10. O you who believe! When there come to you believing women refugees, examine (and test) them: Allah knows best as to their Faith: if you ascertain that they are Believers, then send them not back to the Unbelievers. They are not lawful (wives) for the Unbelievers, nor are the (Unbelievers) lawful (husbands) for them. But pay the Unbelievers what they have spent (on their dower), and there will be no blame on you if you marry them on payment of their dower to them. But hold not to the guardianship of unbelieving women: ask for what you have spent on their dowers, and let the (Unbelievers) ask for what they have spent (on the dowers of women who come over to you). Such is the command of Allah: He judges (with justice) between you. And Allah is Full of Knowledge and Wisdom.

10. Yaaa ayyuhal-lazeena aamanoo izaa jaaa'akumul-mu'minaatu muhaajiraatin famtaḥinoohunna Allaahu a'lamu bi-eemaanihinna fa-in 'alimtumoohunna mu'minaatin falaa tarji'oohunna ilal-kuffaar; laa hunna ḥillul-lahum wa laa hum yaḥilloona lahunna wa aatoohum maa anfaqoo wa laa junaaḥa 'alaykum an tankiḥoohunna izaaa aataytumoohunna ujoorahunn; wa laa tumsikoo bi-'iṣamil-kawaafiri was'aloo maaa anfaqtum walyas'aloo maaa anfaqoo zaalikum ḥukmul-laahi yaḥkumu baynakum wallaahu 'Aleemun Ḥakeem.

يٰٓاَيُّهَا الَّذِيْنَ اٰمَنُوْٓا اِذَا جَآءَكُمُ
الْمُؤْمِنٰتُ مُهٰجِرٰتٍ فَامْتَحِنُوْهُنَّ ۗ
اَللّٰهُ اَعْلَمُ بِاِيْمَانِهِنَّ ۚ فَاِنْ عَلِمْتُمُوْهُنَّ
مُؤْمِنٰتٍ فَلَا تَرْجِعُوْهُنَّ اِلَى الْكُفَّارِ ۗ
لَا هُنَّ حِلٌّ لَّهُمْ وَلَا هُمْ يَحِلُّوْنَ
لَهُنَّ ۗ وَاٰتُوْهُمْ مَّآ اَنْفَقُوْا ۗ وَلَا
جُنَاحَ عَلَيْكُمْ اَنْ تَنْكِحُوْهُنَّ اِذَآ
اٰتَيْتُمُوْهُنَّ اُجُوْرَهُنَّ ۗ وَلَا تُمْسِكُوْا
بِعِصَمِ الْكَوَافِرِ وَسْـَٔلُوْا مَآ اَنْفَقْتُمْ
وَلْيَسْـَٔلُوْا مَآ اَنْفَقُوْا ۗ ذٰلِكُمْ حُكْمُ اللّٰهِ ۗ
يَحْكُمُ بَيْنَكُمْ ۗ وَاللّٰهُ عَلِيْمٌ حَكِيْمٌ ۝١٠

Ikhfa اخفاء | Ghunna غنّہ | Ikhfa Meem Saakin اخفاء میم ساکن | Idghaam ادغام | Qalqala قلقلہ | Qalb قلب | Idghaam Meem Saakin ادغام میم ساکن

11. And if any of your wives deserts you to the Unbelievers, and ye have an accession (by the coming over of a woman from the other side), then pay to those whose wives have deserted the equivalent of what they had spent (on their dower). And fear Allah, in Whom ye believe.

11. Wa in faatakum shay'um-min azwaajikum ilal-kuffaari fa'aaqabtum fa-aatul-lazeena zahabat azwaajuhum misla maaa anfaqoo; wattaqul-laahal-lazeee antum bihee mu'minoon.

وَإِن فَاتَكُمْ شَيْءٌ مِّنْ أَزْوَاجِكُمْ
إِلَى الْكُفَّارِ فَعَاقَبْتُمْ فَآتُوا
الَّذِينَ ذَهَبَتْ أَزْوَاجُهُم مِّثْلَ مَا
أَنفَقُوا ۚ وَاتَّقُوا اللَّهَ الَّذِي أَنتُم
بِهِ مُؤْمِنُونَ ﴿١١﴾

12. O Prophet! When believing women come to you to take the oath of fealty to you, that they will not associate in worship any other thing whatever with Allah, that they will not steal, that they will not commit adultery (or fornication), that they will not kill their children, that they will not utter slander, intentionally forging falsehood, and that they will not disobey thee in any just matter,- then do you receive their fealty, and pray to Allah for the forgiveness (of their sins): for Allah is Oft-Forgiving, Most Merciful.

12. Yaaa ayyuhan-Nabiyyu izaa jaaa'akal-mu'minaatu yubaayi'naka 'alaaa allaa yushrikna billaahi shay'añw-wa laa yasriqna wa laa yazneena wa laa yaqtulna awlaadahunna wa laa yaâteena bibuhtaaniñy-yaftareenahoo bayna aydeehinna wa arjulihinna wa laa ya'ṣeenaka fee ma'roofin fabaayi'hunna wastaghfir lahunnal-laaha innal-laaha Ghafoorur Raḥeem.

يَا أَيُّهَا النَّبِيُّ إِذَا جَاءَكَ الْمُؤْمِنَاتُ
يُبَايِعْنَكَ عَلَىٰ أَن لَّا يُشْرِكْنَ
بِاللَّهِ شَيْئًا وَلَا يَسْرِقْنَ وَلَا يَزْنِينَ
وَلَا يَقْتُلْنَ أَوْلَادَهُنَّ وَلَا يَأْتِينَ
بِبُهْتَانٍ يَفْتَرِينَهُ بَيْنَ أَيْدِيهِنَّ وَ
أَرْجُلِهِنَّ وَلَا يَعْصِينَكَ فِي مَعْرُوفٍ
فَبَايِعْهُنَّ وَاسْتَغْفِرْ لَهُنَّ اللَّهَ ۖ إِنَّ
اللَّهَ غَفُورٌ رَّحِيمٌ ﴿١٢﴾

13. O you who believe! Turn not (for friendship) to people on whom is the Wrath of Allah, of the Hereafter they are already in despair, just as the Unbelievers are in despair about those (buried) in graves.

13. Yaaa ayyuhal-lazeena amanoo laa tatawallaw qawman ghaḍibal-laahu 'alayhim qad ya'isoo minal-Aakhirati kamaa ya'isal-kuffaaru min aṣ-ḥaabil-quboor. **(Section 2)**

يَا أَيُّهَا الَّذِينَ آمَنُوا لَا تَتَوَلَّوْا قَوْمًا
غَضِبَ اللَّهُ عَلَيْهِمْ قَدْ يَئِسُوا مِنَ
الْآخِرَةِ كَمَا يَئِسَ الْكُفَّارُ مِنْ
أَصْحَابِ الْقُبُورِ ﴿١٣﴾

61. Battle Array

In the name of Allah, Most Gracious, Most Merciful.

Sûrat aṣ-Ṣaff–61

(Revealed at Madinah)

Bismillaahir Raḥmaanir Raḥeem

(٦١) سُورَةُ الصَّفِّ مَدَنِيَّةٌ (١٠٩)

بِسْمِ اللَّهِ الرَّحْمَٰنِ الرَّحِيمِ

1. Whatever is in the heavens and on earth, let it declare the Praises and Glory of Allah: for He is the Exalted in Might, the Wise.

1. Sabbaḥa lillaahi maa fissamaawaati wa maa fil-arḍi wa Huwal-'Azeezul-Ḥakeem.

سَبَّحَ لِلَّهِ مَا فِي السَّمَاوَاتِ وَمَا فِي الْأَرْضِ ۖ
وَهُوَ الْعَزِيزُ الْحَكِيمُ ﴿١﴾

2. O you who believe, why say you that which you do not?

2. Yaa ayyuhal-lazeena aamanoo lima taqooloona maa laa taf'aloon.

يَا أَيُّهَا الَّذِينَ آمَنُوا لِمَ تَقُولُونَ
مَا لَا تَفْعَلُونَ ﴿٢﴾

3. Grievously odious is it in the sight of Allah that you say that which you do not.

3. Kabura maqtan 'indal-laahi an taqooloo maa laa taf'aloon.

كَبُرَ مَقْتًا عِندَ اللَّهِ أَن تَقُولُوا
مَا لَا تَفْعَلُونَ ﴿٣﴾

4. Truly Allah loves those who fight

4. Innal-laaha yuḥibbul-lazeena yuqaatiloona

إِنَّ اللَّهَ يُحِبُّ الَّذِينَ يُقَاتِلُونَ

Ikhfa اخفاء | Ghunna غنّہ | Ikhfa Meem Saakin اخفاءمیم ساکن | Idghaam ادغام | Qalqala قلقلہ | Qalb قلب | Idghaam Meem Saakin ادغام میم ساکن

فِي سَبِيلِهٖ صَفًّا كَاَنَّهُمْ بُنْيَانٌ مَّرْصُوصٌ ﴿٤﴾

fee sabeelihee ṣaffan ka-annahum bunyaanum-marṣooṣ.

in His Cause in battle array, as if they were a solid cemented structure.

وَاِذْ قَالَ مُوسٰى لِقَوْمِهٖ يٰقَوْمِ لِمَ تُؤْذُونَنِي وَقَدْ تَّعْلَمُونَ اَنِّي رَسُولُ اللّٰهِ اِلَيْكُمْ ۖ فَلَمَّا زَاغُوٓا اَزَاغَ اللّٰهُ قُلُوبَهُمْ ۚ وَاللّٰهُ لَا يَهْدِي الْقَوْمَ الْفٰسِقِينَ ﴿٥﴾

5. Wa iz̲ qaala Moosaa li-qawmihee yaa qawmi lima tu'z̲oonanee wa qat-ta'lamoona annee Rasoolul-laahi ilaykum falammaa zaaghooo azaaghal-laahu quloobahum; wallaahu laa yahdil-qawmal-faasiqeen.

5. And remember, Moses said to his people: "O my people! why do you vex and insult me, though you know that I am the apostle of Allah (sent) to you?" Then when they went wrong, Allah let their hearts go wrong. For Allah guides not those who are rebellious transgressors.

وَاِذْ قَالَ عِيسَى ابْنُ مَرْيَمَ يٰبَنِيٓ اِسْرَآءِيلَ اِنِّي رَسُولُ اللّٰهِ اِلَيْكُمْ مُّصَدِّقًا لِّمَا بَيْنَ يَدَيَّ مِنَ التَّوْرٰىةِ وَمُبَشِّرًا بِرَسُولٍ يَّاْتِي مِنْ بَعْدِي اسْمُهٗٓ اَحْمَدُ ۖ فَلَمَّا جَآءَهُمْ بِالْبَيِّنٰتِ قَالُوا هٰذَا سِحْرٌ مُّبِينٌ ﴿٦﴾

6. Wa iz̲ qaala 'Eesab-nu-Mayama yaa Baneee Israaa-'eela innee Rasoolul-laahi ilaykum-muṣaddiqal-limaa bayna yadayya minat-Tawraati wa mubashshiram bi-Rasooliñy-yaåtee mim ba'dis-muhooo Aḥmad; falammaa jaaa'ahum bil-bayyinaati qaaloo haaz̲aa siḥrum mubeen.

6. And remember, Jesus, the son of Mary, said: "O Children of Israel! I am the apostle of Allah (sent) to you, confirming the Law (which came) before me, and giving Glad Tidings of an Apostle to come after me, whose name shall be Ahmad." But when he came to them with Clear Signs, they said, "this is evident sorcery!"

وَمَنْ اَظْلَمُ مِمَّنِ افْتَرٰى عَلَى اللّٰهِ الْكَذِبَ وَهُوَ يُدْعٰٓى اِلَى الْاِسْلَامِ ۚ وَاللّٰهُ لَا يَهْدِي الْقَوْمَ الظّٰلِمِينَ ﴿٧﴾

7. Wa man aẓlamu mimmanif-taraa 'alal-laahil-kaz̲iba wa huwa yad'aaa ilal-Islaam; wallaahu laa yahdil-qawmaẓ-ẓaalimeen.

7. Who does greater wrong than one who invents falsehood against Allah, even as he is being invited to Islam? And Allah guides not those who do wrong.

يُرِيدُونَ لِيُطْفِـُٔوا نُورَ اللّٰهِ بِاَفْوَاهِهِمْ ۚ وَاللّٰهُ مُتِمُّ نُورِهٖ وَلَوْ كَرِهَ الْكٰفِرُونَ ﴿٨﴾

8. Yureedoona liyutfi'oo nooral-laahi bi-afwaahihim wallaahu mutimmu noorihee wa law karihal-kaafiroon.

8. Their intention is to extinguish Allah's Light (by blowing) with their mouths: But Allah will complete (the revelation of) His Light, even though the Unbelievers may detest (it).

هُوَ الَّذِيٓ اَرْسَلَ رَسُولَهٗ بِالْهُدٰى وَدِينِ الْحَقِّ لِيُظْهِرَهٗ عَلَى الدِّينِ كُلِّهٖ وَلَوْ كَرِهَ الْمُشْرِكُونَ ﴿٩﴾ ع ٩

9. Huwal-laz̲ee arsala Rasoolahoo bilhudaa wa deenil-ḥaqqi liyuẓhirahoo 'alad-deeni kulli-hee wa law karihal-mushrikoon.

(Section 1)

9. It is He Who has sent His Apostle with Guidance and the Religion of Truth, that he may proclaim it over all religion, even though the Pagans may detest (it).

يٰٓاَيُّهَا الَّذِينَ اٰمَنُوا هَلْ اَدُلُّكُمْ عَلٰى تِجَارَةٍ تُنْجِيكُمْ مِّنْ عَذَابٍ اَلِيمٍ ﴿١٠﴾

10. Yaaa ayyuhal-laz̲eena aammanoo hal adullukum 'alaa tijaaratin tunjeekum min 'az̲aa-bin aleem.

10. O you who believe! Shall I lead you to a bargain that will save you from a grievous Chastisement?-

تُؤْمِنُونَ بِاللّٰهِ وَرَسُولِهٖ وَتُجَاهِدُونَ فِي سَبِيلِ اللّٰهِ بِاَمْوَالِكُمْ وَاَنْفُسِكُمْ ۚ

11. Tu'minoona billaahi wa Rasoolihee wa tujaahidoona fee sabeelil-laahi bi-amwaalikum wa anfusikum;

11. That you believe in Allah and His Apostle, and that you strive (your utmost) in the Cause of Allah, with your property and your persons:

Ikhfa اخفاء | Ghunna غنّہ | Ikhfa Meem Saakin اخفاءمیم ساکن | Idghaam ادغام | Qalqala قلقلہ | Qalb قلب | Idghaam Meem Saakin ادغام میم ساکن

that will be best for you, if you but knew!

12. He will forgive you your sins, and admit you to Gardens beneath which Rivers flow, and to beautiful mansions in Gardens of Eternity: that is indeed the Supreme Achievement.

13. And another (favour will He bestow,) which you do love,- help from Allah and a speedy victory. So give the Glad Tidings to the Believers.

14. O you who believe! Be you helpers of Allah: As said Jesus the son of Mary to the Disciples, "Who will be my helpers to (the work of) Allah?" Said the disciples, "We are Allah's helpers!" then a portion of the Children of Israel believed, and a portion disbelieved: But We gave power to those who believed, against their enemies, and they became the ones that prevailed.

62. The Assembly–Friday Prayer

In the name of Allah, Most Gracious, Most Merciful.

1. Whatever is in the heavens and on earth, doth declare the Praises and Glory of Allah,- the Sovereign, the Holy One, the Exalted in Might, the Wise.

2. It is He Who has sent amongst the Unlettered an apostle from among themselves, to rehearse to them His Signs, to purify them, and to instruct them in Scripture and Wisdom,- although they had been, before, in manifest error;-

3. As well as (to confer all these benefits upon) others of them, who have not already joined them: And He is Exalted in Might, Wise.

4. Such is the Bounty of Allah, which He bestows on whom He will:

zaalikum khayrul-lakum in kuntum ta‘lamoon.

12. Yaghfir lakum zunoobakum wa yudkhilkum Jannaatin tajree min taḥtihal-anhaaru wa masaakina ṭayyibatan fee Jannaati ‘Adn; zaalikal-fawzul-‘aẓeem.

13. Wa ukhraa tuḥibboonahaa naṣrum-minal-laahi wa fat-ḥun qareeb; wa bashshiril-mu'mineen.

14. Yaaa ayyuhal-lazeena aamanoo koonooo anṣaaral-laahi kamaa qaala ‘Eesab-nu Maryama lil-Ḥawaariyyeena man anṣaareee ilal-laah; qaalal-Ḥawaariyyoona naḥnu anṣaarul-laahi fa-aamanaṭ-ṭaaa'ifatum-mim Bannee Israaa'eela wa kafaraṭ-ṭaaa'ifatun fa-ayyadnal-lazeena aammanoo ‘alaa ‘aduwwihim fa-aṣbaḥoo ẓaahireen. **(Section 2)**

Sûrat al-Jumu‘ah–62

(Revealed at Madinah)

Bismillaahir Raḥmaanir Raḥeem

1. Yusabbiḥu lilaahi maa fis-samaawaati wa maa fil-arḍil-Malikil-Quddoosil-‘Azeezil-Ḥakeem.

2. Huwal-lazee ba‘asa fil-ummiyyeena Rasoolam-minhum yatloo ‘alayhim Aayaatihee wa yuzakkeehim wa yu‘allimuhumul-Kitaaba wal-Ḥikmata wa in kaanoo min qablu lafee ḍalaalim-Mubeen.

3. Wa aakhareena minhum lammaa yalḥaqoo bihim wa Huwal-‘Azeezul-Ḥakeem.

4. Zaalika faḍlul-laahi yu'teehi mañy-yashaaa';

ذَٰلِكُمْ خَيْرٌ لَّكُمْ إِن كُنتُمْ تَعْلَمُونَ ١١
يَغْفِرْ لَكُمْ ذُنُوبَكُمْ وَيُدْخِلْكُمْ
جَنَّٰتٍ تَجْرِى مِن تَحْتِهَا ٱلْأَنْهَٰرُ
وَمَسَٰكِنَ طَيِّبَةً فِى جَنَّٰتِ عَدْنٍ
ذَٰلِكَ ٱلْفَوْزُ ٱلْعَظِيمُ ١٢
وَأُخْرَىٰ تُحِبُّونَهَا نَصْرٌ مِّنَ ٱللَّهِ وَ
فَتْحٌ قَرِيبٌ وَبَشِّرِ ٱلْمُؤْمِنِينَ ١٣
يَٰٓأَيُّهَا ٱلَّذِينَ ءَامَنُوا۟ كُونُوٓا۟ أَنصَارَ
ٱللَّهِ كَمَا قَالَ عِيسَى ٱبْنُ مَرْيَمَ
لِلْحَوَارِيِّۦنَ مَنْ أَنصَارِىٓ إِلَى ٱللَّهِ
قَالَ ٱلْحَوَارِيُّونَ نَحْنُ أَنصَارُ ٱللَّهِ
فَـَٔامَنَت طَّآئِفَةٌ مِّنۢ بَنِىٓ إِسْرَٰٓءِيلَ
وَكَفَرَت طَّآئِفَةٌ فَأَيَّدْنَا ٱلَّذِينَ
ءَامَنُوا۟ عَلَىٰ عَدُوِّهِمْ فَأَصْبَحُوا۟ ظَٰهِرِينَ ١٤

(٦٢) سُورَةُ ٱلْجُمُعَةِ مَدَنِيَّةٌ (١١٠)

بِسْمِ ٱللَّهِ ٱلرَّحْمَٰنِ ٱلرَّحِيمِ

يُسَبِّحُ لِلَّهِ مَا فِى ٱلسَّمَٰوَٰتِ وَمَا فِى
ٱلْأَرْضِ ٱلْمَلِكِ ٱلْقُدُّوسِ ٱلْعَزِيزِ
ٱلْحَكِيمِ ١
هُوَ ٱلَّذِى بَعَثَ فِى ٱلْأُمِّيِّـۧنَ رَسُولًا
مِّنْهُمْ يَتْلُوا۟ عَلَيْهِمْ ءَايَٰتِهِۦ وَيُزَكِّيهِمْ
وَيُعَلِّمُهُمُ ٱلْكِتَٰبَ وَٱلْحِكْمَةَ وَإِن
كَانُوا۟ مِن قَبْلُ لَفِى ضَلَٰلٍ مُّبِينٍ ٢
وَءَاخَرِينَ مِنْهُمْ لَمَّا يَلْحَقُوا۟ بِهِمْ وَ
هُوَ ٱلْعَزِيزُ ٱلْحَكِيمُ ٣
ذَٰلِكَ فَضْلُ ٱللَّهِ يُؤْتِيهِ مَن يَشَآءُ

Ikhfa اخفاء · Ghunna غنّہ · Ikhfa Meem Saakin اخفاء میم ساکن · Idghaam ادغام · Qalqala قلقلہ · Qalb قلب · Idghaam Meem Saakin ادغام میم ساکن

and Allah is the Lord of the highest bounty.

5. The similitude of those who were charged with the (obligations of the) Mosaic Law, but who subsequently failed in those (obligations), is that of a donkey which carries huge tomes (but understands them not). Evil is the similitude of people who falsify the Signs of Allah: and Allah guides not people who do wrong.

6. Say: "O you that stand on Judaism! If you think that you are friends to Allah, to the exclusion of (other) men, then express your desire for Death, if you are truthful!"

7. But never will they express their desire (for Death), because of the (deeds) their hands have sent on before them! and Allah knows well those that do wrong!

8. Say: "The Death from which you flee will truly overtake you: then will you be sent back to the Knower of things secret and open: and He will tell you (the truth of) the things that you did!"

9. O you who believe! When the call is proclaimed to prayer on Friday (the Day of Assembly), hasten earnestly to the Remembrance of Allah, and leave off business (and traffic): That is best for you if you but knew!

10. And when the Prayer is finished, then may you disperse through the land, and seek of the Bounty of Allah: and celebrate the Praises of Allah often (and without stint): that you may prosper.

11. But when they see some bargain or some amusement, they disperse headlong to it, and leave you standing. Say: "The (blessing) from the Presence of Allah is better than any amusement or

wallaahu Z̲ul-faḍlil-'aẓeem.

5. Mas̲alul-laz̲eena ḥum-milut-Tawraata s̲umma lam yaḥmiloohaa kamas̲alil-ḥimaari yaḥmilu asfaaraa; bi'sa mas̲alul-qawmil-laz̲eena kaz̲z̲aboo bi-Aayaatil-laah; wallaahu laa yahdil-qawmaẓ-ẓaalimeen.

6. Qul yaaa ayyuhal-laz̲eena haadooo in za'amtum annakum awliyaaa'u lilaahi min doonin-naasi fatamannawul-mawta in kuntum ṣaadiqeen.

7. Wa laa yatamannaw-nahooo abadam bimaa qadda-mat aydeehim; wallaahu 'Alee-mum biẓ-ẓaalimeen.

8. Qul innal-mawtal-laz̲ee tafirroona minhu fa-innahoo mulaaqeekum s̲umma turad-doona ilaa 'Aalimil-Ghaybi wash-shahaadati fa-yunabbi'ukum bimaa kuntum ta'maloon.

(Section 1)

9. Yaaa ayyuhal-laz̲eena aamanooo iz̲aa noodiya liṣ-Ṣalaati miñy-yawmil-Jumu'ati fas'aw ilaa z̲ikril-laahi wa z̲arul-bay'; z̲aalikum khayrul-lakum in kuntum ta'lamoon.

10. Fa-iz̲aa quḍiyatiṣ-Ṣalaatu fantashiroo fil-arḍi wabtaghoo min faḍlil-laahi waz̲kurul-laaha kas̲eeral-la'allakum tufliḥoon.

11. Wa iz̲aa ra-aw tijaaratan aw lahwanin-faḍḍooo ilayhaa wa tarakooka qaaa'imaa; qul maa 'indal-laahi khayrum-minal-lahwi wa minat-

وَاللّٰهُ ذُو الْفَضْلِ الْعَظِيْمِ ۝٤

مَثَلُ الَّذِيْنَ حُمِّلُوا التَّوْرٰىةَ ثُمَّ

لَمْ يَحْمِلُوْهَا كَمَثَلِ الْحِمَارِ يَحْمِلُ

اَسْفَارًا ۭ بِئْسَ مَثَلُ الْقَوْمِ الَّذِيْنَ

كَذَّبُوْا بِاٰيٰتِ اللّٰهِ ۭ وَاللّٰهُ لَا يَهْدِي

الْقَوْمَ الظّٰلِمِيْنَ ۝٥

قُلْ يٰٓاَيُّهَا الَّذِيْنَ هَادُوْٓا اِنْ

زَعَمْتُمْ اَنَّكُمْ اَوْلِيَاۗءُ لِلّٰهِ مِنْ

دُوْنِ النَّاسِ فَتَمَنَّوُا الْمَوْتَ اِنْ

كُنْتُمْ صٰدِقِيْنَ ۝٦

وَلَا يَتَمَنَّوْنَهٗٓ اَبَدًاۢ بِمَا قَدَّمَتْ

اَيْدِيْهِمْ ۭ وَاللّٰهُ عَلِيْمٌۢ بِالظّٰلِمِيْنَ ۝٧

قُلْ اِنَّ الْمَوْتَ الَّذِيْ تَفِرُّوْنَ مِنْهُ

فَاِنَّهٗ مُلٰقِيْكُمْ ثُمَّ تُرَدُّوْنَ اِلٰى عٰلِمِ

الْغَيْبِ وَالشَّهَادَةِ فَيُنَبِّئُكُمْ بِمَا

كُنْتُمْ تَعْمَلُوْنَ ۝٨ ع

يٰٓاَيُّهَا الَّذِيْنَ اٰمَنُوْٓا اِذَا نُوْدِيَ

لِلصَّلٰوةِ مِنْ يَّوْمِ الْجُمُعَةِ فَاسْعَوْا

اِلٰى ذِكْرِ اللّٰهِ وَذَرُوا الْبَيْعَ ۭ ذٰلِكُمْ

خَيْرٌ لَّكُمْ اِنْ كُنْتُمْ تَعْلَمُوْنَ ۝٩

فَاِذَا قُضِيَتِ الصَّلٰوةُ فَانْتَشِرُوْا فِي

الْاَرْضِ وَابْتَغُوْا مِنْ فَضْلِ اللّٰهِ وَ

اذْكُرُوا اللّٰهَ كَثِيْرًا لَّعَلَّكُمْ تُفْلِحُوْنَ ۝١٠

وَاِذَا رَاَوْا تِجَارَةً اَوْ لَهْوَا انْفَضُّوْٓا

اِلَيْهَا وَتَرَكُوْكَ قَاۗىِٕمًا ۭ قُلْ مَا

عِنْدَ اللّٰهِ خَيْرٌ مِّنَ اللَّهْوِ وَمِنَ

Ikhfa اخفاء | Ghunna غنّہ | Ikhfa Meem Saakin اخفاء میم ساکن | Idghaam ادغام | Qalqala قلقلہ | Qalb قلب | Idghaam Meem Saakin ادغام میم ساکن

bargain! and Allah is the Best to provide (for all needs)."

63. The Hypocrites

In the name of Allah, Most Gracious, Most Merciful.

1. When the Hypocrites come to you, they say, "We bear witness that you are indeed the Apostle of Allah." Yes, Allah knoweth that you are indeed His Apostle, and Allah bears witness that the Hypocrites are indeed liars.

2. They have made their oaths a screen (for their misdeeds): thus they obstruct (men) from the Path of Allah: truly evil are their deeds.

3. That is because they believed, then they rejected Faith: So a seal was set on their hearts: therefore they understand not.

4. When you look at them, their exteriors please thee; and when they speak, you listened to their words. They are as (worthless as hollow) pieces of timber propped up, (unable to stand on their own). They think that every cry is against them. They are the enemies; so beware of them. The curse of Allah be on them! How are they deluded (away from the Truth)!

5. And when it is said to them, "Come, the Apostle of Allah will pray for your forgiveness", they turn aside their heads, and you would see them turning away their faces in arrogance.

6. It is equal to them whether thou pray for their forgiveness or not. Allah will not forgive them. Truly Allah guides not rebellious transgressors.

7. They are the ones who say, "Spend nothing on those who are with Allah's Apostle, to the end that they may disperse

---

tijaarah; wallaahu khayrur-raaziqeen. **(Section 2)**

Sûrat al-Munâfiqûn–63

(Revealed at Madinah)

Bismillaahir Raḥmaanir Raḥeem

1. Izaa jaaa'akal-munaafiqoona qaaloo nashhadu innaka la-Rasoolul-laah; wallaahu ya'lamu innaka la-Rasooluhoo wallaahu yashhadu innal-munaafiqeena lakaaziboon.

2. Ittakhazooo aymaanahum junnatan faṣaddoo 'an sabeelil-laah; innahum saaa'a maa kaanoo ya'maloon.

3. Zaalika bi-annahum aamanoo summa kafaroo faṭubi'a 'alaa quloobihim fahum laa yafqahoon.

4. Wa izaa ra-aytahum tu'jibuka ajsaamuhum wa-iñy-yaqooloo tasma' liqawlihim ka-annahum khushubum musannadah; yaḥsaboona kulla ṣayḥatin 'alayhim; humul-'aduwwu faḥzarhum; qaatalahumul-laahu annaa yu'fakoon.

5. Wa izaa qeela lahum ta'aalaw yastaghfir lakum Rasoolul-laahi lawwaw ru'oosahum wa ra-aytahum yaṣuddoona wa hum mustakbiroon.

6. Sawaaa'un 'alayhim astaghfarta lahum am lam tastaghfir lahum lañy-yaghfiral-laahu lahum; innal-laaha laa yahdil-qawmal-faasiqeen.

7. Humul-lazeena yaqooloona laa tunfiqoo 'alaa man 'inda Rasoolil-laahi ḥattaa yanfaḍḍoo;

التِّجَارَةِ ۚ وَاللّٰهُ خَيْرُ الرّٰزِقِيْنَ ﴿۱۱﴾ ع ۲

(۶۳) سُوْرَةُ الْمُنٰفِقُوْنَ مَدَنِيَّةٌ (۱۰۴)

بِسْمِ اللّٰهِ الرَّحْمٰنِ الرَّحِيْمِ

اِذَا جَآءَكَ الْمُنٰفِقُوْنَ قَالُوْا نَشْهَدُ

اِنَّكَ لَرَسُوْلُ اللّٰهِ ۘ وَاللّٰهُ يَعْلَمُ وقف لازم

اِنَّكَ لَرَسُوْلُهٗ ۗ وَاللّٰهُ يَشْهَدُ اِنَّ

الْمُنٰفِقِيْنَ لَكٰذِبُوْنَ ﴿۱﴾

اِتَّخَذُوْٓا اَيْمَانَهُمْ جُنَّةً فَصَدُّوْا

عَنْ سَبِيْلِ اللّٰهِ ۗ اِنَّهُمْ سَآءَ مَا

كَانُوْا يَعْمَلُوْنَ ﴿۲﴾

ذٰلِكَ بِاَنَّهُمْ اٰمَنُوْا ثُمَّ كَفَرُوْا فَطُبِعَ

عَلٰى قُلُوْبِهِمْ فَهُمْ لَا يَفْقَهُوْنَ ﴿۳﴾

وَاِذَا رَاَيْتَهُمْ تُعْجِبُكَ اَجْسَامُهُمْ ۗ

وَاِنْ يَّقُوْلُوْا تَسْمَعْ لِقَوْلِهِمْ ۗ كَاَنَّهُمْ

خُشُبٌ مُّسَنَّدَةٌ ۗ يَحْسَبُوْنَ كُلَّ صَيْحَةٍ

عَلَيْهِمْ ۗ هُمُ الْعَدُوُّ فَاحْذَرْهُمْ ۗ

قٰتَلَهُمُ اللّٰهُ ۫ اَنّٰى يُؤْفَكُوْنَ ﴿۴﴾

وَاِذَا قِيْلَ لَهُمْ تَعَالَوْا يَسْتَغْفِرْ لَكُمْ

رَسُوْلُ اللّٰهِ لَوَّوْا رُءُوْسَهُمْ وَرَاَيْتَهُمْ

يَصُدُّوْنَ وَهُمْ مُّسْتَكْبِرُوْنَ ﴿۵﴾

سَوَآءٌ عَلَيْهِمْ اَسْتَغْفَرْتَ لَهُمْ

اَمْ لَمْ تَسْتَغْفِرْ لَهُمْ ۗ لَنْ يَّغْفِرَ

اللّٰهُ لَهُمْ ۗ اِنَّ اللّٰهَ لَا يَهْدِي

الْقَوْمَ الْفٰسِقِيْنَ ﴿۶﴾

هُمُ الَّذِيْنَ يَقُوْلُوْنَ لَا تُنْفِقُوْا عَلٰى

مَنْ عِنْدَ رَسُوْلِ اللّٰهِ حَتّٰى يَنْفَضُّوْا ۗ

Ikhfa اخفاء | Ghunna غُنّہ | Ikhfa Meem Saakin اخفاء میم ساکن | Idghaam ادغام | Qalqala قلقلہ | Qalb قلب | Idghaam Meem Saakin ادغام میم ساکن

(and quit Medina)." But to Allah belong the treasures of the heavens and the earth; but the Hypocrites understand not.

wa lillaahi khazaaa'inus-samaawaati wal-arḍi wa laakinnal-munaafiqeena laa yafqahoon.

وَلِلّٰهِ خَزَآئِنُ السَّمٰوٰتِ وَالْاَرْضِ
وَلٰكِنَّ الْمُنٰفِقِيْنَ لَا يَفْقَهُوْنَ ۝٧

8. They say, "If we return to Medina, surely the more honourable (element) will expel therefrom the meaner." But honour belongs to Allah and His Apostle, and the Believers; but the Hypocrites know not.

8. Yaqooloona la'ir-raja'naaa ilal-Madeenati la-yukhrijannal-a'azzu minhal-azall; wa lillaahil-'izzatu wa li-Rasoolihee wa lilmu'mineena wa laakinnal-munaafiqeena laa ya'lamoon. **(Section 1)**

يَقُوْلُوْنَ لَئِنْ رَّجَعْنَآ اِلَى الْمَدِيْنَةِ
لَيُخْرِجَنَّ الْاَعَزُّ مِنْهَا الْاَذَلَّ ۭ وَ
لِلّٰهِ الْعِزَّةُ وَلِرَسُوْلِهٖ وَلِلْمُؤْمِنِيْنَ
وَلٰكِنَّ الْمُنٰفِقِيْنَ لَا يَعْلَمُوْنَ ۝٨

9. O you who believe! Let not your riches or your children divert you from the remembrance of Allah. If any act thus, the loss is their own.

9. Yaaa ayyuhal-lazeena aamanoo laa tulhikum amwaalukum wa laaa awlaadukum 'an zikril-laah; wa mañy-yaf'al-zaalika fa-ulaaa'ika humul-khaasiroon.

يٰٓاَيُّهَا الَّذِيْنَ اٰمَنُوْا لَا تُلْهِكُمْ
اَمْوَالُكُمْ وَلَآ اَوْلَادُكُمْ عَنْ
ذِكْرِ اللّٰهِ ۚ وَمَنْ يَّفْعَلْ ذٰلِكَ
فَاُولٰٓئِكَ هُمُ الْخٰسِرُوْنَ ۝٩

10. And spend something (in charity) out of the substance which We have bestowed on you, before Death should come to any of you and he should say, "O my Lord! why did You not give me respite for a little while? I should then have given (largely) in charity, and I should have been one of the doers of good".

10. Wa anfiqoo mim-maa razaqnaakum min qabli añy-yaâtiya aḥadakumul-mawtu fa-yaqoola Rabbi law laaa akh-khartaneee ilaaa ajalin qareebin fa-aṣṣaddaqa wa akum-minaṣ-ṣaaliḥeen.

وَاَنْفِقُوْا مِنْ مَّا رَزَقْنٰكُمْ مِّنْ
قَبْلِ اَنْ يَّاْتِيَ اَحَدَكُمُ الْمَوْتُ
فَيَقُوْلَ رَبِّ لَوْلَآ اَخَّرْتَنِيْٓ اِلٰٓى
اَجَلٍ قَرِيْبٍ ۙ فَاَصَّدَّقَ وَاَكُنْ
مِّنَ الصّٰلِحِيْنَ ۝١٠

11. But to no soul will Allah grant respite when the time appointed (for it) has come; and Allah is well acquainted with (all) that you do.

11. Wa lañy-yu'akhkhiral-laahu nafsan izaa jaaa'a ajaluhaa; wallaahu khabeerum bimaa ta'maloon. **(Section 2)**

وَلَنْ يُّؤَخِّرَ اللّٰهُ نَفْسًا اِذَا جَآءَ اَجَلُهَا ۭ
وَاللّٰهُ خَبِيْرٌۢ بِمَا تَعْمَلُوْنَ ۝١١

64. Mutual Loss and Gain

In the name of Allah, Most Gracious, Most Merciful.

Sûrat at-Taghâbun–64

(Revealed at Madinah)

Bismillaahir Raḥmaanir Raḥeem

(٦٤) سُوْرَةُ التَّغَابُنِ مَدَنِيَّةٌ (١٠٨)

بِسْمِ اللّٰهِ الرَّحْمٰنِ الرَّحِيْمِ

1. Whatever is in the heavens and on earth, doth declare the Praises and Glory of Allah: to Him belongs dominion, and to Him belongs praise: and He has power over all things.

1. Yusabbiḥu lillaahi maa fis-samaawaati wa maa fil-arḍi lahul-mulku wa lahul-ḥamd, wa Huwa 'alaa kulli shay'in Qadeer.

يُسَبِّحُ لِلّٰهِ مَا فِي السَّمٰوٰتِ وَمَا فِي
الْاَرْضِ ۚ لَهُ الْمُلْكُ وَلَهُ الْحَمْدُ
وَهُوَ عَلٰى كُلِّ شَيْءٍ قَدِيْرٌ ۝١

2. It is He Who has created you; and of you are some that are Unbelievers, and some that are Believers: and Allah sees well all that you do.

2. Huwal-lazee khalaqakum faminkum kaafiruñw-wa minkum mu'min; wallaahu bimaa ta'maloona Baṣeer.

هُوَ الَّذِيْ خَلَقَكُمْ فَمِنْكُمْ كَافِرٌ
وَّمِنْكُمْ مُّؤْمِنٌ ۭ وَاللّٰهُ بِمَا
تَعْمَلُوْنَ بَصِيْرٌ ۝٢

3. He has created the heavens and the earth in just proportions,

3. Khalaqas-samaawaati wal-arḍa bilḥaqqi

خَلَقَ السَّمٰوٰتِ وَالْاَرْضَ بِالْحَقِّ

and has given you shape, and made your shapes beautiful: and to Him is the final Goal.

wa ṣawwarakum fa-aḥsana ṣuwarakum wa ilayhil-maṣeer.

وَصَوَّرَكُمْ فَأَحْسَنَ صُوَرَكُمْ ۚ
وَإِلَيْهِ الْمَصِيرُ ﴿٣﴾

4. He knows what is in the heavens and on earth; and He knows what you conceal and what you reveal: yes, Allah knows well the (secrets) of (all) hearts.

4. Ya'lamu maa fis-samaa-waati wal-arḍi wa ya'lamu maa tusirroona wa maa tu'linoon; wallaahu 'Aleemum bizaatiṣ-ṣudoor.

يَعْلَمُ مَا فِي السَّمٰوٰتِ وَالْأَرْضِ
وَيَعْلَمُ مَا تُسِرُّونَ وَمَا تُعْلِنُونَ ۚ
وَاللَّهُ عَلِيمٌ بِذَاتِ الصُّدُورِ ﴿٤﴾

5. Has not the story reached you, of those who rejected Faith aforetime? So they tasted the evil result of their conduct; and they had a grievous Chastisement.

5. Alam yaåtikum naba'ul-lazeena kafaroo min qablu fazaaqoo wabaala amrihim wa lahum 'azaabun aleem.

أَلَمْ يَأْتِكُمْ نَبَأُ الَّذِينَ كَفَرُوا مِنْ
قَبْلُ ز فَذَاقُوا وَبَالَ أَمْرِهِمْ وَ
لَهُمْ عَذَابٌ أَلِيمٌ ﴿٥﴾

6. That was because there came to them apostles with Clear Signs, but they said: "Shall (mere) human beings direct us?" So they rejected (the Message) and turned away. But Allah can do without (them): and Allah is free of all needs, worthy of all praise.

6. Zaalika bi-annahoo kaanat taåteehim Rusuluhum bilbayyi-naati faqaalooo a-basharuñy-yahdoonanaa fakafaroo wa tawallaw; wastaghnal-laah; wallaahu Ghaniyyun Ḥameed.

ذٰلِكَ بِأَنَّهُ كَانَتْ تَأْتِيهِمْ رُسُلُهُمْ
بِالْبَيِّنٰتِ فَقَالُوا أَبَشَرٌ يَهْدُونَنَا ز
فَكَفَرُوا وَتَوَلَّوا وَّاسْتَغْنَى اللَّهُ ط
وَاللَّهُ غَنِيٌّ حَمِيدٌ ﴿٦﴾

7. The Unbelievers think that they will not be raised up (for Judgment). Say: "Yes, By my Lord, You shall surely be raised up: then shall you be told (the truth) of all that you did. And that is easy for Allah."

7. Za'amal-lazeena kafarooo al-lañy-yub'asoo; qul balaa wa Rabbee latub'asunna summa latunabba'unna bimaa 'amil-tum; wa zaalika 'alal-laahi yaseer.

زَعَمَ الَّذِينَ كَفَرُوا أَنْ لَّنْ يُّبْعَثُوا ط
قُلْ بَلٰى وَرَبِّي لَتُبْعَثُنَّ ثُمَّ لَتُنَبَّؤُنَّ
بِمَا عَمِلْتُمْ ط وَذٰلِكَ عَلَى اللَّهِ يَسِيرٌ ﴿٧﴾

8. Believe, therefore, in Allah and His Apostle, and in the Light which We have sent down. And Allah is well acquainted with all that you do.

8. Fa-aaminoo billaahi wa Rasoolihee wannooril-lazeee anzalnaa; wallaahu bimaa ta'maloona Khabeer.

فَآمِنُوا بِاللَّهِ وَرَسُولِهِ وَالنُّورِ الَّذِي
أَنْزَلْنَا ط وَاللَّهُ بِمَا تَعْمَلُونَ خَبِيرٌ ﴿٨﴾

9. The Day that He assembles you (all) for a Day of Assembly,- that will be a Day of mutual loss and gain (among you), and those who believe in Allah and work righteousness,- He will remove from them their ills, and He will admit them to Gardens beneath which Rivers flow, to dwell therein for ever: that will be the Supreme Achievement.

9. Yawma yajma'ukum li-yawmil-jam'i zaalika yawmut-taghaabun; wa mañy-yu'mim billaahi wa ya'mal ṣaaliḥañy-yukaffir 'anhu sayyi-aatihee wa yudkhilhu Jannaatin tajree min taḥtihal-anhaaru khaalideena feehaa abadaa; zaalikal-fawzul-'aẓeem.

يَوْمَ يَجْمَعُكُمْ لِيَوْمِ الْجَمْعِ ذٰلِكَ
يَوْمُ التَّغَابُنِ ط وَمَنْ يُّؤْمِنْ بِاللَّهِ
وَيَعْمَلْ صَالِحًا يُّكَفِّرْ عَنْهُ
سَيِّاٰتِهِ وَيُدْخِلْهُ جَنّٰتٍ تَجْرِي
مِنْ تَحْتِهَا الْأَنْهٰرُ خٰلِدِينَ فِيهَا
أَبَدًا ط ذٰلِكَ الْفَوْزُ الْعَظِيمُ ﴿٩﴾

10. But those who reject Faith and treat Our Signs as false-hoods, they will be Companions of the Fire, to dwell therein for ever: and evil is that Goal.

10. Wallazeena kafaroo wa kaz-zaboo bi-Aayaatinaaa ulaaa'ika Aṣ-ḥaabun-Naari khaalideena feehaa wa bi'sal-maṣeer.

(Section 1)

وَالَّذِينَ كَفَرُوا وَكَذَّبُوا بِآيٰتِنَا
أُولٰٓئِكَ أَصْحٰبُ النَّارِ خٰلِدِينَ
فِيهَا ط وَبِئْسَ الْمَصِيرُ ﴿١٠﴾

Ikhfa اخفاء | Ghunna غُنّہ | Ikhfa Meem Saakin اخفاء میم ساکن | Idghaam ادغام | Qalqala قلقلہ | Qalb قلب | Idghaam Meem Saakin ادغام میم ساکن

11. No kind of calamity can occur, except by the leave of Allah: and if any one believes in Allah, (Allah) guides his heart (aright): for Allah knows all things.

11. Maaa aṣaaba mim-muṣeebatin illaa bi-iznil-laah; wa mañy-yu'mim billaahi yahdi qalbah; wallaahu bikulli shay'in 'Aleem.

مَآ أَصَابَ مِن مُّصِيبَةٍ إِلَّا بِإِذْنِ
ٱللَّهِ ۗ وَمَن يُؤْمِنۢ بِٱللَّهِ يَهْدِ قَلْبَهُۥ ۚ
وَٱللَّهُ بِكُلِّ شَىْءٍ عَلِيمٌ ⑪

12. So obey Allah, and obey His Apostle: but if you turn back, the duty of Our Apostle is but to proclaim (the Message) clearly and openly.

12. Wa aṭee'ul-laaha wa aṭee-'ur-Rasool; fa-in tawallaytum fa-innamaa 'alaa Rasoolinal-balaaghul-mubeen.

وَأَطِيعُوا۟ ٱللَّهَ وَأَطِيعُوا۟ ٱلرَّسُولَ ۚ
فَإِن تَوَلَّيْتُمْ فَإِنَّمَا عَلَىٰ رَسُولِنَا
ٱلْبَلَٰغُ ٱلْمُبِينُ ⑫

13. Allah! There is no god but He: and on Allah, therefore, let the Believers put their trust.

13. Allaahu laaa ilaaha illaa Hoo; wa 'alal-laahi falyata-wakkalil-mu'minoon.

ٱللَّهُ لَآ إِلَٰهَ إِلَّا هُوَ ۚ وَعَلَى ٱللَّهِ
فَلْيَتَوَكَّلِ ٱلْمُؤْمِنُونَ ⑬

14. O you who believe! Truly, among your wives and your children are (some that are) enemies to yourselves: so beware of them! But if you forgive and overlook, and cover up (their faults), verily Allah is Oft-Forgiving, Most Merciful.

14. Yaaa ayyuhal-lazeena aamanooo inna min azwaaji-kum wa awlaadikum 'aduwwal-lakum faḥzaroohum; wa in ta'foo wa taṣfaḥoo wa taghfiroo fa-innal-laaha Ghafoorur-Raḥeem.

يَٰٓأَيُّهَا ٱلَّذِينَ ءَامَنُوٓا۟ إِنَّ مِنْ
أَزْوَٰجِكُمْ وَأَوْلَٰدِكُمْ عَدُوًّا لَّكُمْ
فَٱحْذَرُوهُمْ ۚ وَإِن تَعْفُوا۟ وَتَصْفَحُوا۟
وَتَغْفِرُوا۟ فَإِنَّ ٱللَّهَ غَفُورٌ رَّحِيمٌ ⑭

15. Your riches and your children may be but a trial: but in the Presence of Allah, is the highest Reward.

15. Innamaaa amwaalukum wa awlaadukum fitnah; wallaahu 'indahooo ajrun 'aẓeem.

إِنَّمَآ أَمْوَٰلُكُمْ وَأَوْلَٰدُكُمْ
فِتْنَةٌ ۚ وَٱللَّهُ عِندَهُۥٓ أَجْرٌ عَظِيمٌ ⑮

16. So fear Allah as much as you can; listen and obey and spend in charity for the benefit of your own soul and those saved from the covetousness of their own souls,- they are the ones that achieve prosperity.

16. Fattaqul-laaha mastaṭa'-tum wasma'oo wa aṭee'oo wa-anfiqoo khayral li-anfusikum; wa mañy-yooqa shuḥḥa nafsihee fa-ulaaa'ika humul-mufliḥoon.

فَٱتَّقُوا۟ ٱللَّهَ مَا ٱسْتَطَعْتُمْ وَٱسْمَعُوا۟
وَأَطِيعُوا۟ وَأَنفِقُوا۟ خَيْرًا لِّأَنفُسِكُمْ ۗ
وَمَن يُوقَ شُحَّ نَفْسِهِۦ فَأُو۟لَٰٓئِكَ
هُمُ ٱلْمُفْلِحُونَ ⑯

17. If you loan to Allah, a beautiful loan, He will double it to your (credit), and He will grant you Forgiveness: for Allah is most Ready to appreciate (service), Most Forbearing,-

17. In tuqriḍul-laaha qarḍan ḥasanañy-yuḍaa'ifhu lakum wa yaghfir lakum; wallaahu Shakoorun Ḥaleem.

إِن تُقْرِضُوا۟ ٱللَّهَ قَرْضًا حَسَنًا
يُضَٰعِفْهُ لَكُمْ وَيَغْفِرْ لَكُمْ ۚ
وَٱللَّهُ شَكُورٌ حَلِيمٌ ⑰

18. Knower of what is hidden and what is open, Exalted in Might, Full of Wisdom.

18. 'Aalimul-Ghaybi wash-shahaadatil-'Azeezul-Ḥakeem.

(Section 2)

عَٰلِمُ ٱلْغَيْبِ وَٱلشَّهَٰدَةِ ٱلْعَزِيزُ
ٱلْحَكِيمُ ⑱ ع

65. Divorce

In the name of Allah, Most Gracious, Most Merciful.

Sûrat aṭ-Ṭalâq–65

(Revealed at Madinah)

Bismillaahir Raḥmaanir Raḥeem

(٦٥) سُورَةُ ٱلطَّلَاقِ مَدَنِيَّةٌ (٩٩)

بِسْمِ ٱللَّهِ ٱلرَّحْمَٰنِ ٱلرَّحِيمِ

1. O Prophet! When you do divorce women,

1. Yaaa ayyuhan-Nabiyyu izaa ṭallaqtumun-nisaaa'a

يَٰٓأَيُّهَا ٱلنَّبِىُّ إِذَا طَلَّقْتُمُ ٱلنِّسَآءَ

Ikhfa اخفاء | Ghunna غُنّہ | Ikhfa Meem Saakin اخفاء میم ساکن | Idghaam ادغام | Qalqala قلقلہ | Qalb قلب | Idghaam Meem Saakin ادغام میم ساکن

divorce them at their prescribed periods, and count (accurately), their prescribed periods: And fear Allah your Lord: and turn them not out of their houses, nor shall they (themselves) leave, except in case they are guilty of some open lewdness, those are limits set by Allah: and any who trans-gresses the limits of Allah, does verily wrong his (own) soul: you know not if perchance Allah will bring about thereafter some new situation.

faṭalliqoohunna li'iddatihinna wa aḥṣul-'iddata; wattaqul-laaha Rabbakum laa tukhri-joohunna mim bu-yootihinna wa laa yakhrujna illaaa añy-yaåteena bifaaḥishatim-mubay-yinah; wa tilka ḥudoodul-laah; wa mañy-yata'adda ḥudoodal-laahi faqad ẓalama nafsah; laa tadree la'allal-laaha yuḥdiṯu ba'da ẕaalika amraa.

فَطَلِّقُوْهُنَّ لِعِدَّتِهِنَّ وَاَحْصُوا
الْعِدَّةَ ۚ وَاتَّقُوا اللّٰهَ رَبَّكُمْ ۚ لَا
تُخْرِجُوْهُنَّ مِنْ بُيُوْتِهِنَّ وَلَا
يَخْرُجْنَ اِلَّآ اَنْ يَّاْتِيْنَ بِفَاحِشَةٍ
مُّبَيِّنَةٍ ۗ وَتِلْكَ حُدُوْدُ اللّٰهِ ۗ
وَمَنْ يَّتَعَدَّ حُدُوْدَ اللّٰهِ فَقَدْ
ظَلَمَ نَفْسَهٗ ۗ لَا تَدْرِيْ لَعَلَّ اللّٰهَ
يُحْدِثُ بَعْدَ ذٰلِكَ اَمْرًا ①

2. Thus when they fulfil their term appointed, either take them back on equitable terms or part with them on equitable terms; and take for witness two persons from among you, endued with justice, and establish the evidence (as) before Allah. Such is the admonition given to him who believes in Allah and the Last Day. And for those who fear Allah, He (ever) prepares a way out,

2. Fa-iẕaa balaghna ajala-hunna fa-amsikoohunna bima'-roofin aw faariqoohunna bima'roofiñw-wa ashhidoo ẕaway 'adlim-minkum wa aqeemush-shahaadata lillaah; ẕaalikum yoo'aẕu bihee man kaana yu'minu billaahi wal-Yawmil-Aakhir; wa mañy-yattaqil-laaha yaj'al lahoo makhrajaa.

فَاِذَا بَلَغْنَ اَجَلَهُنَّ فَاَمْسِكُوْهُنَّ
بِمَعْرُوْفٍ اَوْ فَارِقُوْهُنَّ بِمَعْرُوْفٍ
وَّاَشْهِدُوْا ذَوَيْ عَدْلٍ مِّنْكُمْ
وَاَقِيْمُوا الشَّهَادَةَ لِلّٰهِ ۗ ذٰلِكُمْ
يُوْعَظُ بِهٖ مَنْ كَانَ يُؤْمِنُ بِاللّٰهِ
وَالْيَوْمِ الْاٰخِرِ ۗ وَمَنْ يَّتَّقِ اللّٰهَ
يَجْعَلْ لَّهٗ مَخْرَجًا ②

3. And He provides for him from (sources) he never could imagine. And if any one puts his trust in Allah, sufficient is (Allah) for him. For Allah will surely accomplish his purpose: verily, for all things has Allah appointed a due proportion.

3. Wa yarzuqhu min ḥayṯu laa yaḥtasib; wa mañy-yatawakkal 'alal-laahi fahuwa ḥasbuh; innal-laaha baalighu amrih; qad ja'alal-laahu likulli shay'in qadraa.

وَّيَرْزُقْهُ مِنْ حَيْثُ لَا يَحْتَسِبُ ۗ
وَمَنْ يَّتَوَكَّلْ عَلَى اللّٰهِ فَهُوَ حَسْبُهٗ ۗ
اِنَّ اللّٰهَ بَالِغُ اَمْرِهٖ ۗ قَدْ جَعَلَ
اللّٰهُ لِكُلِّ شَيْءٍ قَدْرًا ③

4. Such of your women as have passed the age of monthly courses, for them the prescribed period, if you have any doubts, is three months, and for those who have no courses (it is the same): for those who carry (life within their wombs), their period is until they deliver their burdens: and for those who fear Allah, He will make their path easy.

4. Wallaaa'ee ya'isna minal-maḥeeḍi min nisaaa'ikum inir-tabtum fa'iddatuhunna ṯalaaṯatu ashhuriñw-wallaaa'ee lam yaḥiḍn; wa ulaatul-aḥmaali ajaluhunna añy-yaḍa'na ḥamlahunn; wa mañy-yattaqil-laaha yaj'al-lahoo min amrihee yusraa.

وَالّٰٓـِٔيْ يَىِٕسْنَ مِنَ الْمَحِيْضِ مِنْ
نِّسَآىِٕكُمْ اِنِ ارْتَبْتُمْ فَعِدَّتُهُنَّ
ثَلٰثَةُ اَشْهُرٍ ۙ وَّالّٰٓـِٔيْ لَمْ يَحِضْنَ ۗ
وَاُولَاتُ الْاَحْمَالِ اَجَلُهُنَّ اَنْ
يَّضَعْنَ حَمْلَهُنَّ ۗ وَمَنْ يَّتَّقِ اللّٰهَ
يَجْعَلْ لَّهٗ مِنْ اَمْرِهٖ يُسْرًا ④

5. That is the Command of Allah, which He has sent down to you: and if any one

5. Zaalika amrul-laahi anzalahoo ilaykum; wa mañy-

ذٰلِكَ اَمْرُ اللّٰهِ اَنْزَلَهٗٓ اِلَيْكُمْ ۗ وَمَنْ

Ikhfa اخفاء | Ghunna غُنّہ | Ikhfa Meem Saakin اخفاء میم ساکن | Idghaam ادغام | Qalqala قلقلہ | Qalb قلب | Idghaam Meem Saakin ادغام میم ساکن

fears Allah, He will remove his ills, from him, and will enlarge his reward.

6. Let the women live (in 'iddat) in the same style as you live, according to your means: Annoy them not, so as to restrict them. And if they carry (life in their wombs), then spend (your substance) on them until they deliver their burden: and if they suckle your (offspring), give them their recompense: and take mutual counsel together, according to what is just and reasonable. And if you find yourselves in difficulties, let another woman suckle (the child) on the (father's) behalf.

7. Let the man of means spend according to his means: and the man whose resources are restricted, let him spend according to what Allah has given him. Allah puts no burden on any person beyond what He has given him. After a difficulty, Allah will soon grant relief.

8. How many populations that insolently opposed the Command of their Lord and of His apostles, did We not then call to account,- to severe account?- and We imposed on them an exemplary Punishment.

9. Then did they taste the evil result of their conduct, and the End of their conduct was Perdition.

10. Allah has prepared for them a severe Punishment (in the Hereafter). Therefore fear Allah, O you men of understanding - who have believed!- for Allah has indeed sent down to you a Message,-

11. An Apostle, who rehearses to you the Signs of Allah containing clear explanations, that he may lead forth those who believe

yattaqil-laaha yukaffir 'anhu sayyi-aatihee wa yu'ẓim lahoo ajraa.

6. Askinoohunna min ḥaysu sakantum miñw-wujdikum wa laa tuḍaarroohunna lituḍayyiqoo 'alayhinn; wa in kunna ulaati ḥamlin fa-anfiqoo 'alayhinna ḥattaa yaḍa'na ḥamlahunn ; fa-in arḍa'na lakum fa-aatoo-hunna ujoorahunna waâtamiroo baynakum bima'roofiñw wa in ta'aasartum fasaturḍi'u lahooo ukhraa.

7. Liyunfiq zoo sa'atim-min sa'atihee wa man qudira 'alayhi rizquhoo falyunfiq mimmaaa aataahul-laah; laa yukalliful-laahu nafsan illaa maaa aataahaa; sa-yaj'alul-laahu ba'da 'usriñy-yusraa.

(Section 1)

8. Wa ka-ayyim-min qarya-tin 'atat 'an amri Rabbihaa wa Rusulihee faḥaasabnaahaa ḥisaaban shadeedañw-wa 'az-zabnaahaa 'azaaban nukraa.

9. Fazaaqat wabaala amri-haa wa kaana 'aaqibatu amri-haa khusraa.

10. A'addal-laahu lahum 'azaaban shadeedan fattaqul-laaha yaaa ulil-albaab, allazeena aammanoo; qad anzalal-laahu ilaykum zikraa.

11. Rasoolañy-yatloo 'alay-kum Aayaatil-laahi mubayyi-naatil-liyukhrijal-lazeena aa-manoo

يَتَّقِ اللّٰهَ يُكَفِّرْ عَنْهُ سَيِّاٰتِهٖ وَ
يُعْظِمْ لَهٗٓ اَجْرًا ⑤
اَسْكِنُوْهُنَّ مِنْ حَيْثُ سَكَنْتُمْ مِّنْ
وُّجْدِكُمْ وَلَا تُضَآرُّوْهُنَّ لِتُضَيِّقُوْا
عَلَيْهِنَّ ؕ وَاِنْ كُنَّ اُولَاتِ حَمْلٍ
فَاَنْفِقُوْا عَلَيْهِنَّ حَتّٰى يَضَعْنَ
حَمْلَهُنَّ ۚ فَاِنْ اَرْضَعْنَ لَكُمْ
فَاٰتُوْهُنَّ اُجُوْرَهُنَّ ۚ وَاْتَمِرُوْا
بَيْنَكُمْ بِمَعْرُوْفٍ ۚ وَاِنْ تَعَاسَرْتُمْ
فَسَتُرْضِعُ لَهٗٓ اُخْرٰى ؕ ⑥
لِيُنْفِقْ ذُوْ سَعَةٍ مِّنْ سَعَتِهٖ ؕ وَمَنْ
قُدِرَ عَلَيْهِ رِزْقُهٗ فَلْيُنْفِقْ مِمَّآ
اٰتٰىهُ اللّٰهُ ؕ لَا يُكَلِّفُ اللّٰهُ نَفْسًا اِلَّا
مَآ اٰتٰىهَا ؕ سَيَجْعَلُ اللّٰهُ بَعْدَ
عُسْرٍ يُّسْرًا ⑦ ع ٧
وَكَاَيِّنْ مِّنْ قَرْيَةٍ عَتَتْ عَنْ اَمْرِ
رَبِّهَا وَرُسُلِهٖ فَحَاسَبْنٰهَا حِسَابًا
شَدِيْدًا ۙ وَّعَذَّبْنٰهَا عَذَابًا نُّكْرًا ⑧
فَذَاقَتْ وَبَالَ اَمْرِهَا وَكَانَ
عَاقِبَةُ اَمْرِهَا خُسْرًا ⑨
اَعَدَّ اللّٰهُ لَهُمْ عَذَابًا شَدِيْدًا ۙ
فَاتَّقُوا اللّٰهَ يٰٓاُولِى الْاَلْبَابِ ۖۛ مع ٣ عند المتقدمين ١٢
الَّذِيْنَ اٰمَنُوْا ۛ قَدْ اَنْزَلَ اللّٰهُ
اِلَيْكُمْ ذِكْرًا ⑩
رَّسُوْلًا يَّتْلُوْا عَلَيْكُمْ اٰيٰتِ اللّٰهِ
مُبَيِّنٰتٍ لِّيُخْرِجَ الَّذِيْنَ اٰمَنُوْا

Ikhfa اخفاء | Ghunna غنّہ | Ikhfa Meem Saakin اخفاء میم ساکن | Idghaam ادغام | Qalqala قلقلہ | Qalb قلب | Idghaam Meem Saakin ادغام میم ساکن

and do righteous deeds from the depths of Darkness into Light. And those who believe in Allah and work righteousness, He will admit to Gardens beneath which Rivers flow, to dwell therein for ever: Allah has indeed granted for them a most excellent Provision.

wa 'amiluṣ-ṣaaliḥaati minaẓ-ẓulumaati ilan-noor; wa mañy-yu'mim billaahi wa ya'mal ṣaaliḥañy-yudkhilhu Jannaatin tajree min taḥtihal-anhaaru khaalideena feehaa abadan qad aḥsanal-laahu lahoo rizqaa.

وَعَمِلُوا الصّٰلِحٰتِ مِنَ الظُّلُمٰتِ
اِلَى النُّوْرِ ۗ وَمَنْ يُّؤْمِنْ بِاللّٰهِ
وَيَعْمَلْ صَالِحًا يُّدْخِلْهُ
جَنّٰتٍ تَجْرِيْ مِنْ تَحْتِهَا الْاَنْهٰرُ
خٰلِدِيْنَ فِيْهَآ اَبَدًا ۗ قَدْ اَحْسَنَ
اللّٰهُ لَهٗ رِزْقًا ⑪

12. Allah is He Who created seven Firmaments and of the earth a similar number. Through the midst of them (all) descends His Command: that you may know that Allah has power over all things, and that Allah comprehends, all things in (His) Knowledge.

12. Allaahul-lazee khalaqa Sab'a Samaawaatiñw-wa minal-arḍi mislahunna yatanazzalul-amru baynahunna lita'lamooo annal-laaha 'alaa kulli shay'in Qadeeruñw-wa annal-laaha qad aḥaaṭa bikulli shay'in 'ilmaa.

(Section 2)

اَللّٰهُ الَّذِيْ خَلَقَ سَبْعَ سَمٰوٰتٍ
وَّمِنَ الْاَرْضِ مِثْلَهُنَّ ۗ يَتَنَزَّلُ
الْاَمْرُ بَيْنَهُنَّ لِتَعْلَمُوْٓا اَنَّ اللّٰهَ
عَلٰى كُلِّ شَيْءٍ قَدِيْرٌ ۙ وَّاَنَّ اللّٰهَ قَدْ
اَحَاطَ بِكُلِّ شَيْءٍ عِلْمًا ⑫ ع ٢ ١٨

66. Holding - something - to be Forbidden

In the name of Allah, Most Gracious, Most Merciful.

Sûrat at-Taḥrîm–66

(Revealed at Madinah)

Bismillaahir Raḥmaanir Raḥeem

(٦٦) سُوْرَةُ التَّحْرِيْمِ مَدَنِيَّةٌ (١٠٧)

بِسْمِ اللّٰهِ الرَّحْمٰنِ الرَّحِيْمِ

1. O Prophet! Why hold you to be forbidden that which Allah has made lawful to thee? You seekest to please thy consorts. But Allah is Oft-Forgiving, Most Merciful.

1. Yaaa ayyuhan-Nabiyyu lima tuḥarrimu maaa-aḥallal-laahu laka tabtaghee marḍaata azwaajik; wallaahu Ghafoorur-Raḥeem.

يٰٓاَيُّهَا النَّبِيُّ لِمَ تُحَرِّمُ مَآ اَحَلَّ
اللّٰهُ لَكَ ۚ تَبْتَغِيْ مَرْضَاتَ اَزْوَاجِكَ ۗ
وَاللّٰهُ غَفُوْرٌ رَّحِيْمٌ ①

2. Allah has already ordained for you, (O men), the absolution of your oaths (in some cases): and Allah is your Protector, and He is Full of Knowledge and Wisdom.

2. Qad faraḍal-laahu lakum taḥillata aymaanikum; wallaahu mawlaakum wa Huwal-'Aleemul-Ḥakeem.

قَدْ فَرَضَ اللّٰهُ لَكُمْ تَحِلَّةَ
اَيْمَانِكُمْ ۚ وَاللّٰهُ مَوْلٰىكُمْ ۚ وَهُوَ
الْعَلِيْمُ الْحَكِيْمُ ②

3. When the Prophet disclosed a matter in confidence to one of his consorts, and she then divulged it (to another), and Allah made it known to him, he confirmed part thereof and repudiated a part. Then when he told her thereof, she said, "Who told you this?" He said, "He told me Who knows and is Well-acquainted (with all things)."

3. Wa iz asarran-Nabiyyu ilaa ba'ḍi azwaajihee ḥadeesan falammaa nabba-at bihee wa aẓharahul-laahu 'alayhi 'arrafa ba'ḍahoo wa a'raḍa 'am ba'ḍin falammaa nabba-ahaa bihee qaalat man amba-aka haazaa qaala nabba-aniyal-'Aleemul-Khabeer.

وَاِذْ اَسَرَّ النَّبِيُّ اِلٰى بَعْضِ اَزْوَاجِهٖ
حَدِيْثًا ۚ فَلَمَّا نَبَّاَتْ بِهٖ وَاَظْهَرَهُ
اللّٰهُ عَلَيْهِ عَرَّفَ بَعْضَهٗ وَاَعْرَضَ
عَنْ بَعْضٍ ۚ فَلَمَّا نَبَّاَهَا بِهٖ قَالَتْ
مَنْ اَنْۢبَاَكَ هٰذَا ۗ قَالَ نَبَّاَنِيَ
الْعَلِيْمُ الْخَبِيْرُ ③

4. If you two turn in repentance to Him, your

4. In tatoobaaa ilal-laahi faqad ṣaghat

اِنْ تَتُوْبَآ اِلَى اللّٰهِ فَقَدْ صَغَتْ

Ikhfa اخفاء | Ghunna غُنّہ | Ikhfa Meem Saakin اخفاء میم ساکن | Idghaam ادغام | Qalqala قلقلہ | Qalb قلب | Idghaam Meem Saakin ادغام میم ساکن

hearts are indeed so inclined; But if you back up each other against him, truly Allah is his Protector, and Gabriel, and (every) righteous one among those who believe,- and furthermore, the angels - will back (him) up.

5. It may be, if he divorced you (all), that Allah will give him in exchange consorts better than you,- who submit (their wills), who believe, who are devout, who turn to Allah in repentance, who worship (in humility), who travel (for Faith) and fast, - previously married or virgins.

6. O you who believe! save yourselves and your families from a Fire whose fuel is Men and Stones, over which are (appointed) angels stern (and) severe, who flinch not (from executing) the Commands they receive from Allah, but do (precisely) what they are commanded.

7. (They will say), "O you Unbelievers! Make no excuses this Day! You are being but requited for all that ye did!"

8. O you who believe! Turn to Allah with sincere repentance: In the hope that your Lord will remove from you your ills and admit you to Gardens beneath which Rivers flow,- the Day that Allah will not permit to be humiliated the Prophet and those who believe with him. Their Light will run forward before them and by their right hands, while they say, "Our Lord! Perfect our Light for us, and grant us Forgiveness: for You have power over all things."

quloobukumaa wa in taẓaaharaa 'alayhi fa-innal-laaha Huwa mawlaahu wa Jibreelu wa ṣaaliḥul-mu'mineen; walma-laaa'ikatu ba'da zaalika ẓaheer.

5. 'Asaa Rabbuhooo in ṭal-laqakunna añy-yubdilahooo azwaajan khayram-minkunna muslimaatim-mu'minaatin qaa-nitaatin taaa'ibaatin 'aabidaatin saaa'iḥaatin sayyibaatiñw-wa abkaaraa.

6. Yaaa ayyuhal-lazeena aamanoo Qooo anfusakum wa ahleekum Naarañw-waqoodu-han-naasu wal-ḥijaaratu 'alay-haa malaaa'ikatun ghilaaẓun shidaadul-laa ya'ṣoonal-laaha maaa amarahum wa yaf'aloona maa yu'maroon.

7. Yaaa ayyuhal-lazeena kafaroo laa ta'tazirul-Yawma innamaa tujzawna maa kuntum ta'maloon. **(Section 1)**

8. Yaaa ayyuhal-lazeena aammanoo toobooo ilal-laahi tawbatan-naṣooḥan 'asaa Rabbukum añy-yukaffira 'ankum sayyi-aatikum wa yudkhilakum Jannaatin tajree min taḥtihal-anhaaru Yawma laa yukhzil-laahun-Nabiyya wallazeena aamanoo ma'ahoo nooruhum yas'aa bayna aydeehim wa bi-aymaanihim yaqooloona Rab-banaaa atmim lanaa nooranaa waghfir lanaa innaka 'alaa kulli shay'in Qadeer.

قُلُوبُكُمَا ۖ وَإِن تَظَاهَرَا عَلَيْهِ
فَإِنَّ اللَّهَ هُوَ مَوْلَاهُ وَجِبْرِيلُ
وَصَالِحُ الْمُؤْمِنِينَ ۖ وَالْمَلَائِكَةُ
بَعْدَ ذَٰلِكَ ظَهِيرٌ ﴿٤﴾
عَسَىٰ رَبُّهُ إِن طَلَّقَكُنَّ أَن يُبْدِلَهُ
أَزْوَاجًا خَيْرًا مِّنكُنَّ مُسْلِمَاتٍ
مُّؤْمِنَاتٍ قَانِتَاتٍ تَائِبَاتٍ عَابِدَاتٍ
سَائِحَاتٍ ثَيِّبَاتٍ وَأَبْكَارًا ﴿٥﴾
يَا أَيُّهَا الَّذِينَ آمَنُوا قُوا أَنفُسَكُمْ
وَأَهْلِيكُمْ نَارًا وَقُودُهَا النَّاسُ
وَالْحِجَارَةُ عَلَيْهَا مَلَائِكَةٌ
غِلَاظٌ شِدَادٌ لَّا يَعْصُونَ اللَّهَ مَا
أَمَرَهُمْ وَيَفْعَلُونَ مَا يُؤْمَرُونَ ﴿٦﴾
يَا أَيُّهَا الَّذِينَ كَفَرُوا لَا تَعْتَذِرُوا
الْيَوْمَ ۖ إِنَّمَا تُجْزَوْنَ مَا كُنتُمْ
تَعْمَلُونَ ﴿٧﴾ ع ١٩
يَا أَيُّهَا الَّذِينَ آمَنُوا تُوبُوا إِلَى
اللَّهِ تَوْبَةً نَّصُوحًا عَسَىٰ رَبُّكُمْ
أَن يُكَفِّرَ عَنكُمْ سَيِّئَاتِكُمْ
وَيُدْخِلَكُمْ جَنَّاتٍ تَجْرِي مِن
تَحْتِهَا الْأَنْهَارُ يَوْمَ لَا يُخْزِي
اللَّهُ النَّبِيَّ وَالَّذِينَ آمَنُوا مَعَهُ ۖ
نُورُهُمْ يَسْعَىٰ بَيْنَ أَيْدِيهِمْ وَ
بِأَيْمَانِهِمْ يَقُولُونَ رَبَّنَا أَتْمِمْ
لَنَا نُورَنَا وَاغْفِرْ لَنَا ۖ إِنَّكَ عَلَىٰ
كُلِّ شَيْءٍ قَدِيرٌ ﴿٨﴾

Ikhfa اخفاء | Ghunna غُنّہ | Ikhfa Meem Saakin اخفاء میم ساکن | Idghaam ادغام | Qalqala قلقلہ | Qalb قلب | Idghaam Meem Saakin ادغام میم ساکن

9. O Prophet! Strive hard against the Unbelievers and the Hypocrites, and be firm against them. Their abode is Hell,- an evil refuge (indeed).

10. Allah sets forth, for an example to the Unbelievers, the wife of Noah and the wife of Lut: they were (respectively) under two of our righteous servants, but they were false to their (husbands), and they profited nothing before Allah on their account, but were told: "Enter you the Fire along with (others) that enter!"

11. And Allah sets forth, as an example to those who believe the wife of Pharaoh: Behold she said: "O my Lord! Build for me, in nearness to you, a mansion in the Garden, and save me from Pharaoh and his doings, and save me from those that do wrong"

12. And Mary the daughter of 'Imran, who guarded her chastity; and We breathed into (her body) of Our spirit; and she testified to the truth of the words of her Lord and of His Revelations, and was one of the devout (servants).

67. Dominion

In the name of Allah, Most Gracious, Most Merciful.

1. Blessed be He in Whose hands is Dominion; and He over all things hath Power;-

2. He Who created Death and Life, that He may try which of you is best in deed: and He is the Exalted in Might, Oft-Forgiving;-

3. He Who created the seven heavens one above another: No

9. Yaaa ayyuhan-Nabiyyu jaahidil-kuffaara walmunaafiqeena waghluẓ 'alayhim; wa maâwaahum Jahannamu wa bi'sal-maṣeer.

10. Ḍarabal-laahu masalal-lillazeena kafarum-ra-ata Noo-ḥiñw-wamra-ata Loot, kaanataa taḥta 'abdayni min 'ibaadinaa ṣaaliḥayni fakhaanataahumaa falam yughniyaa 'anhumaa minal-laahi shay'añw-wa qeelad-khulan-Naara ma'ad-Daakhileen.

11. Wa ḍarabal-laahu masa-lal-lillazeena aamanumra-ata Fir'awn; iz qaalat Rabbibni lee 'indaka baytan fil-Jannati wa najjinee min Fir'awna wa 'amalihee wa najjinee minal-qawmiẓ-ẓaalimeen.

12. Wa Maryamab-nata 'Imraanal-latee aḥṣanat farjahaa fanafakhnaa feehi mir-rooḥinaa wa ṣaddaqat bikalimaati Rabbihaa wa Kutubihee wa kaanat minal-qaaniteen.

(Section 2)

Sûrat al-Mulk–67

(Revealed at Makkah)

Bismillaahir Raḥmaanir Raḥeem

1. Tabaarakal-lazee biyadihil-mulku wa Huwa 'alaa kulli shay'in Qadeer.

2. Allazee khalaqal-mawta walḥayaata liyabluwakum ayyukum aḥsanu 'amalaa; wa Huwal-'Azeezul-Ghafoor.

3. Allazee khalaqa Sab'a samaawaatin ṭibaaqam-maa

يٰۤاَيُّهَا النَّبِيُّ جَاهِدِ الْكُفَّارَ
وَالْمُنٰفِقِيْنَ وَاغْلُظْ عَلَيْهِمْ ؕ وَ
مَاْوٰىهُمْ جَهَنَّمُ ؕ وَبِئْسَ الْمَصِيْرُ ٩
ضَرَبَ اللّٰهُ مَثَلًا لِّلَّذِيْنَ كَفَرُوا
امْرَاَتَ نُوْحٍ وَّامْرَاَتَ لُوْطٍ ؕ
كَانَتَا تَحْتَ عَبْدَيْنِ مِنْ عِبَادِنَا
صَالِحَيْنِ فَخَانَتٰهُمَا فَلَمْ يُغْنِيَا
عَنْهُمَا مِنَ اللّٰهِ شَيْـًٔا وَّقِيْلَ
ادْخُلَا النَّارَ مَعَ الدّٰخِلِيْنَ ١٠
وَضَرَبَ اللّٰهُ مَثَلًا لِّلَّذِيْنَ اٰمَنُوا
امْرَاَتَ فِرْعَوْنَ ۘ اِذْ قَالَتْ رَبِّ وقف لازم
ابْنِ لِيْ عِنْدَكَ بَيْتًا فِي الْجَنَّةِ
وَنَجِّنِيْ مِنْ فِرْعَوْنَ وَعَمَلِهٖ وَ
نَجِّنِيْ مِنَ الْقَوْمِ الظّٰلِمِيْنَ ۙ ١١
وَمَرْيَمَ ابْنَتَ عِمْرٰنَ الَّتِيْۤ اَحْصَنَتْ
فَرْجَهَا فَنَفَخْنَا فِيْهِ مِنْ رُّوْحِنَا
وَصَدَّقَتْ بِكَلِمٰتِ رَبِّهَا وَكُتُبِهٖ
وَكَانَتْ مِنَ الْقٰنِتِيْنَ ١٢

(٦٧) سُوْرَةُ الْمُلْكِ مَكِّيَّةٌ (٧٧)

بِسْمِ اللّٰهِ الرَّحْمٰنِ الرَّحِيْمِ

تَبٰرَكَ الَّذِيْ بِيَدِهِ الْمُلْكُ ۫ وَهُوَ
عَلٰى كُلِّ شَيْءٍ قَدِيْرُ ۙ ١
الَّذِيْ خَلَقَ الْمَوْتَ وَالْحَيٰوةَ
لِيَبْلُوَكُمْ اَيُّكُمْ اَحْسَنُ عَمَلًا ؕ
وَهُوَ الْعَزِيْزُ الْغَفُوْرُ ۙ ٢
الَّذِيْ خَلَقَ سَبْعَ سَمٰوٰتٍ طِبَاقًا ؕ مَا

Ikhfa اخفاء | Ghunna غنّہ | Ikhfa Meem Saakin اخفاء میم ساکن | Idghaam ادغام | Qalqala قلقلہ | Qalb قلب | Idghaam Meem Saakin ادغام میم ساکن

want of proportion wilt thou see in the Creation of (Allah) Most Gracious. So turn thy vision again: do you see any flaw?

taraa fee khalqir-Raḥmaani min tafaawutin farji'‑il-baṣara hal taraa min fuṭoor.

تَرٰى فِىْ خَلْقِ الرَّحْمٰنِ مِنْ تَفٰوُتٍ ؕ
فَارْجِعِ الْبَصَرَ ۙ هَلْ تَرٰى مِنْ فُطُوْرٍ ﴿۳﴾

4. Again turn your vision a second time: (thy) vision will come back to you dull and discomfited, in a state worn out.

4. Summar-ji'‑il-baṣara karratayni yanqalib ilaykal-baṣaru khaasi'anw-wa huwa ḥaseer.

ثُمَّ ارْجِعِ الْبَصَرَ كَرَّتَيْنِ يَنْقَلِبْ
اِلَيْكَ الْبَصَرُ خَاسِئًا وَّهُوَ حَسِيْرٌ ﴿۴﴾

5. And We have, (from of old), adorned the lowest heaven with Lamps, and We have made such (Lamps) (as) missiles to drive away the Evil Ones, and have prepared for them the Chastisement of the Blazing Fire.

5. Wa laqad zayyannas-samaaa'ad-dunyaa bimaṣaa-beeḥa wa ja'alnaahaa rujoomal-lish-Shayaaṭeeni wa a'tadnaa lahum 'azaabas-sa'eer.

وَلَقَدْ زَيَّنَّا السَّمَآءَ الدُّنْيَا بِمَصَابِيْحَ
وَجَعَلْنٰهَا رُجُوْمًا لِّلشَّيٰطِيْنِ وَاَعْتَدْنَا
لَهُمْ عَذَابَ السَّعِيْرِ ﴿۵﴾

6. For those who reject their Lord (and Cherisher) is the Penalty of Hell: and evil is (such), Destination.

6. Wa lillazeena kafaroo bi-Rabbihim 'azaabu Jahannama wa bi'sal-maṣeer.

وَلِلَّذِيْنَ كَفَرُوْا بِرَبِّهِمْ عَذَابُ
جَهَنَّمَ ؕ وَبِئْسَ الْمَصِيْرُ ﴿۶﴾

7. When they are cast therein, they will hear the (terrible) drawing in of its breath even as it blazes forth,

7. Izaaa ulqoo feehaa sami-'oo lahaa shaheeqañw-wa hiya tafoor.

اِذَآ اُلْقُوْا فِيْهَا سَمِعُوْا لَهَا شَهِيْقًا
وَّهِىَ تَفُوْرُ ﴿۷﴾

8. Almost bursting with fury: Every time a Group is cast therein, its Keepers will ask, "Did no Warner come to you?"

8. Takaadu tamayyazu minal-ghayẓi kullamaaa ulqiya feehaa fawjun sa-alahum khazanatuhaaa alam yaåtikum nazeer.

تَكَادُ تَمَيَّزُ مِنَ الْغَيْظِ ؕ كُلَّمَآ اُلْقِىَ
فِيْهَا فَوْجٌ سَاَلَهُمْ خَزَنَتُهَآ اَلَمْ
يَاْتِكُمْ نَذِيْرٌ ﴿۸﴾

9. They will say: "Yes indeed; a Warner did come to us, but we rejected him and said, 'Allah never sent down any (Message): ye are nothing but an egregious delusion!'"

9. Qaaloo balaa qad jaaa'anaa nazeerun fakazzab-naa wa qulnaa maa nazzalal-laahu min shay'in in antum illaa fee ḍalaalin kabeer.

قَالُوْا بَلٰى قَدْ جَآءَنَا نَذِيْرٌ ۙ
فَكَذَّبْنَا وَقُلْنَا مَا نَزَّلَ اللّٰهُ مِنْ
شَىْءٍ ۖۚ اِنْ اَنْتُمْ اِلَّا فِىْ ضَلٰلٍ كَبِيْرٍ ﴿۹﴾

10. They will further say: "Had we but listened or used our intelligence, we should not (now) be among the Companions of the Blazing Fire!"

10. Wa qaaloo law kunnaa nasma'u aw na'qilu maa kunnaa feee aṣ-ḥaabis-sa'eer.

وَقَالُوْا لَوْ كُنَّا نَسْمَعُ اَوْ نَعْقِلُ مَا
كُنَّا فِىْۤ اَصْحٰبِ السَّعِيْرِ ﴿۱۰﴾

11. They will then confess their sins: but far will be (Forgiveness) from the Companions of the Blazing Fire!

11. Fa'tarafoo bizambihim fasuḥqal-li-aṣ-ḥaabis-sa'eer.

فَاعْتَرَفُوْا بِذَنْۢبِهِمْ ۚ فَسُحْقًا
لِّاَصْحٰبِ السَّعِيْرِ ﴿۱۱﴾

12. As for those who fear their Lord unseen, for them is Forgiveness and a great Reward.

12. Innal-lazeena yakh-shawna Rabbahum bilghaybi lahum maghfiratuñw-wa ajrun kabeer.

اِنَّ الَّذِيْنَ يَخْشَوْنَ رَبَّهُمْ بِالْغَيْبِ
لَهُمْ مَّغْفِرَةٌ وَّاَجْرٌ كَبِيْرٌ ﴿۱۲﴾

13. And whether you hide your word or publish it, He certainly has (full) knowledge, of the secrets of (all) hearts.

13. Wa asirroo qawlakum awijharoo bihee innahoo 'Aleemum bizaatiṣ-ṣudoor.

وَاَسِرُّوْا قَوْلَكُمْ اَوِ اجْهَرُوْا بِهٖ ؕ اِنَّهٗ
عَلِيْمٌۢ بِذَاتِ الصُّدُوْرِ ﴿۱۳﴾

14. Should He not know,- He that created? and He is the One

14. Alaa ya'lamu man khalaq, wa Huwal-Laṭeeful-

اَلَا يَعْلَمُ مَنْ خَلَقَ ؕ وَهُوَ اللَّطِيْفُ

Ikhfa اخفاء | Ghunna غنّہ | Ikhfa Meem Saakin اخفاء میم ساکن | Idghaam ادغام | Qalqala قلقلہ | Qalb قلب | Idghaam Meem Saakin ادغام میم ساکن

well-acquainted (with them).

15. It is He Who has made the earth manageable for you, so traverse you through its tracts and enjoy of the Sustenance which He furnishes: but unto Him is the Resurrection.

16. Do you feel secure that He Who is in heaven will not cause you to be swallowed up by the earth even it shakes (as in an earthquake)?

17. Or do you feel secure that He Who is in Heaven will not send against you a violent tornado (with showers of stones), so that you shall know how (terrible) was My warning?

18. But indeed men before them rejected (My warning): then how (terrible) was My rejection (of them)?

19. Do they not observe the birds above them, spreading their wings and folding them in? None can uphold them except (Allah) Most Gracious: Truly it is He that watches over all things.

20. No, who is there that can help you, (even as) an army, besides (Allah) Most Merciful? In nothing but delusion are the Unbelievers.

21. Or who is there that can provide you with Sustenance if He were to withhold His provision? No, they obstinately persist in insolent impiety and flight (from the Truth).

22. Is then one who walks headlong, with his face grovelling, better guided,- or one who walks evenly on a Straight Way?

23. Say: "It is He Who has created you (and made you grow), and made for you the faculties of hearing, seeing, feeling and understanding: little thanks it is you give.

24. Say: "It is He Who has multiplied you through the earth,

Khabeer. **(Section 1)**

15. Huwal-lazee ja'ala lakumul-arḍa zaloolan famshoo fee manaakibihaa wa kuloo mirrizqihee wa ilayhin-nushoor.

16. 'A-amintum man fissamaaa'i añy-yakhsifa bikumul-arḍa fa-izaa hiya tamoor.

17. Am amintum man fissamaaa'i añy-yursila 'alaykum ḥaaṣiban fasata'lamoona kayfa nazeer.

18. Wa laqad kazzabal-lazeena min qablihim fakayfa kaana nakeer.

19. Awalam yaraw ilaṭ-ṭayri fawqahum ṣaaaffaatiñw-wa yaqbiḍn; maa yumsikuhunna illaar-Raḥmaan; innahoo bikulli shay'im Baṣeer.

20. Amman haazal-lazee huwa jundul-lakum yanṣurukum min doonir-Raḥmaan; inilkaafiroona illaa fee ghuroor.

21. Amman haazal-lazee yarzuqukum in amsaka rizqah; bal lajjoo fee 'utuwwiñw-wa nufoor.

22. Afamañy-yamshee mukibban 'alaa wajhiheee ahdaaa ammañy-yamshee sawiyyan 'alaa Ṣiraṭim-Mustaqeem.

23. Qul Huwal-lazee anshaakum wa ja'ala lakumus-sam'a wal-abṣaara wal-af'idata qaleelam-maa tashkuroon.

24. Qul Huwal-lazee zaraakum fil-arḍi

الْخَبِيْرُ ۝١٤ ع

هُوَ الَّذِيْ جَعَلَ لَكُمُ الْاَرْضَ ذَلُوْلًا فَامْشُوْا فِيْ مَنَاكِبِهَا وَكُلُوْا مِنْ رِّزْقِهٖ ؕ وَاِلَيْهِ النُّشُوْرُ ۝١٥

ءَاَمِنْتُمْ مَّنْ فِي السَّمَآءِ اَنْ يَّخْسِفَ بِكُمُ الْاَرْضَ فَاِذَا هِيَ تَمُوْرُ ۝١٦

اَمْ اَمِنْتُمْ مَّنْ فِي السَّمَآءِ اَنْ يُّرْسِلَ عَلَيْكُمْ حَاصِبًا ؕ فَسَتَعْلَمُوْنَ كَيْفَ نَذِيْرِ ۝١٧

وَلَقَدْ كَذَّبَ الَّذِيْنَ مِنْ قَبْلِهِمْ فَكَيْفَ كَانَ نَكِيْرِ ۝١٨

اَوَلَمْ يَرَوْا اِلَى الطَّيْرِ فَوْقَهُمْ صٰٓفّٰتٍ وَّيَقْبِضْنَ ؔۘ مَا يُمْسِكُهُنَّ اِلَّا الرَّحْمٰنُ ؕ اِنَّهٗ بِكُلِّ شَيْءٍۢ بَصِيْرٌ ۝١٩

اَمَّنْ هٰذَا الَّذِيْ هُوَ جُنْدٌ لَّكُمْ يَنْصُرُكُمْ مِّنْ دُوْنِ الرَّحْمٰنِ ؕ اِنِ الْكٰفِرُوْنَ اِلَّا فِيْ غُرُوْرٍ ۝٢٠

اَمَّنْ هٰذَا الَّذِيْ يَرْزُقُكُمْ اِنْ اَمْسَكَ رِزْقَهٗ ۚ بَلْ لَّجُّوْا فِيْ عُتُوٍّ وَّنُفُوْرٍ ۝٢١

اَفَمَنْ يَّمْشِيْ مُكِبًّا عَلٰى وَجْهِهٖٓ اَهْدٰٓى اَمَّنْ يَّمْشِيْ سَوِيًّا عَلٰى صِرَاطٍ مُّسْتَقِيْمٍ ۝٢٢

قُلْ هُوَ الَّذِيْٓ اَنْشَاَكُمْ وَجَعَلَ لَكُمُ السَّمْعَ وَالْاَبْصَارَ وَالْاَفْـِٕدَةَ ؕ قَلِيْلًا مَّا تَشْكُرُوْنَ ۝٢٣

قُلْ هُوَ الَّذِيْ ذَرَاَكُمْ فِي الْاَرْضِ

وقف لازم · وقف غفران · اختلاف

Ikhfa اخفاء | Ghunna غُنّہ | Ikhfa Meem Saakin اخفاء میم ساکن | Idghaam ادغام | Qalqala قلقلہ | Qalb قلب | Idghaam Meem Saakin ادغام میم ساکن

and to Him shall you be gathered together."

25. They ask: When will this promise be (fulfilled)? - If you are telling the truth.

26. Say: "As to the knowledge of the time, it is with Allah alone: I am (sent) only to warn plainly in public."

27. At length, when they see it close at hand, grieved will be the faces of the Unbelievers, and it will be said (to them): "This is (the promise fulfilled), which you were calling for!"

28. Say: "See you?- If Allah were to destroy me, and those with me, or if He bestows His Mercy on us,- yet who can deliver the Unbelievers from a grievous Chastisement?"

29. Say: "He is (Allah) Most Gracious: We have believed in Him, and on Him have we put our trust: So, soon will you know which (of us) it is that is in manifest error."

30. Say: "Don 't you see?- If your stream be some morning lost (in the underground earth), who then can supply you with clear-flowing water?"

wa ilayhi tuḥsharoon.

25. Wa yaqooloona mataa haazal-wa'du in kuntum ṣaadiqeen.

26. Qul innamal-'ilmu 'indal-laahi wa innamaaa ana nazee-rum-mubeen.

27. Falaammaa ra-awhu zulfatan seee'at wujoohul-lazeena kafaroo wa qeela haazal-lazee kuntum bihee tadda'oon.

28. Qul ara'aytum in ahlaka-niyal-laahu wa mam-ma'iya aw raḥimanaa famañy-yujeerul-kaafireena min 'azaabin aleem.

29. Qul Huwar-Raḥmaanu aamannaa bihee wa 'alayhi tawakkalnaa fasata'lamoona man huwa fee ḍalaalim-mubeen.

30. Qul ara'aytum in aṣbaḥa maaa'ukum ghawran famañy-yaåteekum bimaaa'im-ma'een.

(Section 2)

وَإِلَيْهِ تُحْشَرُونَ ﴿٢٤﴾
وَيَقُولُونَ مَتَىٰ هَٰذَا الْوَعْدُ إِن كُنتُمْ صَادِقِينَ ﴿٢٥﴾
قُلْ إِنَّمَا الْعِلْمُ عِندَ اللَّهِ وَإِنَّمَا أَنَا نَذِيرٌ مُّبِينٌ ﴿٢٦﴾
فَلَمَّا رَأَوْهُ زُلْفَةً سِيئَتْ وُجُوهُ الَّذِينَ كَفَرُوا وَقِيلَ هَٰذَا الَّذِي كُنتُم بِهِ تَدَّعُونَ ﴿٢٧﴾
قُلْ أَرَأَيْتُمْ إِنْ أَهْلَكَنِيَ اللَّهُ وَمَن مَّعِيَ أَوْ رَحِمَنَا فَمَن يُجِيرُ الْكَافِرِينَ مِنْ عَذَابٍ أَلِيمٍ ﴿٢٨﴾
قُلْ هُوَ الرَّحْمَٰنُ آمَنَّا بِهِ وَعَلَيْهِ تَوَكَّلْنَا فَسَتَعْلَمُونَ مَنْ هُوَ فِي ضَلَالٍ مُّبِينٍ ﴿٢٩﴾
قُلْ أَرَأَيْتُمْ إِنْ أَصْبَحَ مَاؤُكُمْ غَوْرًا فَمَن يَأْتِيكُم بِمَاءٍ مَّعِينٍ ﴿٣٠﴾

68. The Pen

In the name of Allah, Most Gracious, Most Merciful.

Sûrat al-Qalam–68

(Revealed at Makkah)

Bismillaahir Raḥmaanir Raḥeem

(٦٨) سُورَةُ الْقَلَمِ مَكِّيَّةٌ (٢)

بِسْمِ اللَّهِ الرَّحْمَٰنِ الرَّحِيمِ

1. *Nun.* By the Pen and the (Record) which (men) write,-

2. You are not, by the Grace of your Lord, mad or possessed.

3. No, verily for thee is a Reward unfailing:

4. And thou (standest) on an exalted standard of character.

5. Soon will you see, and they will see,

6. Which of you is afflicted with madness.

7. Verily it is your Lord that knows best, which (among men) hath strayed from His Path: and He knows best those who receive (true) Guidance.

1. Noon; walqalami wa maa yasṭuroon.
2. Maa anta bini'mati Rabbika bimajnoon.
3. Wa inna laka la-ajran ghayra mamnoon.
4. Wa innaka la-'alaa khuluqin 'azeem.
5. Fasatubṣiru wa yubṣiroon.
6. Bi-ayyikumul-maftoon.
7. Inna Rabbaka Huwa a'lamu biman ḍalla 'an sabeelihee wa Huwa a'lamu bilmuhtadeen.

نٓ وَالْقَلَمِ وَمَا يَسْطُرُونَ ﴿١﴾
مَا أَنتَ بِنِعْمَةِ رَبِّكَ بِمَجْنُونٍ ﴿٢﴾
وَإِنَّ لَكَ لَأَجْرًا غَيْرَ مَمْنُونٍ ﴿٣﴾
وَإِنَّكَ لَعَلَىٰ خُلُقٍ عَظِيمٍ ﴿٤﴾
فَسَتُبْصِرُ وَيُبْصِرُونَ ﴿٥﴾
بِأَييِّكُمُ الْمَفْتُونُ ﴿٦﴾
إِنَّ رَبَّكَ هُوَ أَعْلَمُ بِمَن ضَلَّ عَن سَبِيلِهِ وَهُوَ أَعْلَمُ بِالْمُهْتَدِينَ ﴿٧﴾

Ikhfa اخفاء | Ghunna غنّہ | Ikhfa Meem Saakin اخفاء میم ساکن | Idghaam ادغام | Qalqala قلقلہ | Qalb قلب | Idghaam Meem Saakin ادغام میم ساکن

8. So hearken not to those who deny (the Truth).	8. Falaa tuṭi‘il-mukaz̲z̲ibeen.	فَلَا تُطِعِ الْمُكَذِّبِيْنَ ۝٨
9. Their desire is that thou shouldst be pliant: so would they be pliant.	9. Waddoo law tudhinu fa-yudhinoon.	وَدُّوْا لَوْ تُدْهِنُ فَيُدْهِنُوْنَ ۝٩
10. Do not obey every mean swearer;	10. Wa laa tuṭi‘ kulla ḥallaa-fim-maheen.	وَلَا تُطِعْ كُلَّ حَلَّافٍ مَّهِيْنٍ ۝١٠
11. A slanderer, going about with calumnies,	11. Hammaazim mash-shaaa’im binameem.	هَمَّازٍ مَّشَّآءٍۢ بِنَمِيْمٍ ۝١١
12. (Habitually) hindering (all) good, transgressing beyond bounds, deep in sin,	12. Mannaa‘il-lilkhayri mu‘-tadin as̲eem.	مَّنَّاعٍ لِّلْخَيْرِ مُعْتَدٍ اَثِيْمٍ ۝١٢
13. Violent (and cruel),- with all that, base-born,-	13. ‘Utullim ba‘da z̲aalika zaneem.	عُتُلٍّۢ بَعْدَ ذٰلِكَ زَنِيْمٍ ۝١٣
14. Because he possesses wealth and (numerous) sons.	14. An kaana z̲aa maaliñw-wa baneen.	اَنْ كَانَ ذَا مَالٍ وَّبَنِيْنَ ۝١٤
15. When to him are rehearsed Our Signs, “Tales of the ancients”, he cries!	15. Iz̲aa tutlaa ‘alayhi Aayaatunaa qaala asaaṭeerul-awwaleen.	اِذَا تُتْلٰى عَلَيْهِ اٰيٰتُنَا قَالَ اَسَاطِيْرُ الْاَوَّلِيْنَ ۝١٥
16. Soon shall We brand (the beast) on the snout!	16. Sanasimuhoo ‘alal-khur-ṭoom.	سَنَسِمُهٗ عَلَى الْخُرْطُوْمِ ۝١٦
17. Verily We have tried them as We tried the People of the Garden, when they resolved to gather the fruits of the (garden) in the morning.	17. Innaa balawnaahum ka-maa balawnaaa Aṣ-ḥaabal jannati iz̲ ‘aqsamoo la-yaṣri munnahaa muṣbiḥeen.	اِنَّا بَلَوْنٰهُمْ كَمَا بَلَوْنَآ اَصْحٰبَ الْجَنَّةِ ۚ اِذْ اَقْسَمُوْا لَيَصْرِمُنَّهَا مُصْبِحِيْنَ ۝١٧
18. But made no reservation, (“If it be Allah’s Will”).	18. Wa laa yastas̲noon.	وَلَا يَسْتَثْنُوْنَ ۝١٨
19. Then there came on the (garden) a visitation from thy Lord, (which swept away) all around, while they were asleep.	19. Faṭaafa ‘alayhaa ṭaaa’i-fum-mir-Rabbika wa hum naaa’imoon.	فَطَافَ عَلَيْهَا طَآئِفٌ مِّنْ رَّبِّكَ وَهُمْ نَآئِمُوْنَ ۝١٩
20. And in the morning it was as if plucked.	20. Fa-aṣbaḥat kaṣṣareem.	فَاَصْبَحَتْ كَالصَّرِيْمِ ۝٢٠
21. As the morning broke, they called out, one to another,-	21. Fatanaadaw muṣbiḥeen.	فَتَنَادَوْا مُصْبِحِيْنَ ۝٢١
22. “Go you to your tilth (betimes) in the morning, if you would gather the fruits.”	22. Anighdoo ‘alaa ḥars̲ikum in kuntum ṣaarimeen.	اَنِ اغْدُوْا عَلٰى حَرْثِكُمْ اِنْ كُنْتُمْ صٰرِمِيْنَ ۝٢٢
23. So they departed, conversing in secret low tones, (saying)-	23. Fanṭalaqoo wa hum yata-khaafatoon.	فَانْطَلَقُوْا وَهُمْ يَتَخَافَتُوْنَ ۝٢٣
24. “Let not a single indigent person break in upon you into the (garden) this day.”	24. Al-laa yadkhulannahal-yawma ‘alaykum-miskeen.	اَنْ لَّا يَدْخُلَنَّهَا الْيَوْمَ عَلَيْكُمْ مِّسْكِيْنٌ ۝٢٤
25. And they opened the morning, strong in an (unjust) resolve.	25. Wa ghadaw ‘alaa ḥardin qaadireen.	وَّغَدَوْا عَلٰى حَرْدٍ قٰدِرِيْنَ ۝٢٥
26. But when they saw the (garden), they said: “We have surely lost our way:	26. Falammaa ra-awhaa qaa-looo innaa laḍaaalloon.	فَلَمَّا رَاَوْهَا قَالُوْٓا اِنَّا لَضَآلُّوْنَ ۝٢٦
27. “Indeed we are shut out (of the fruits of our labour)!”	27. Bal naḥnu maḥroomoon.	بَلْ نَحْنُ مَحْرُوْمُوْنَ ۝٢٧
28. Said one of them, more just (than the rest): “Did I not say to you,	28. Qaala awsaṭuhum alam aqul lakum	قَالَ اَوْسَطُهُمْ اَلَمْ اَقُلْ لَّكُمْ

Ikhfa اخفاء · Ghunna غُنّہ · Ikhfa Meem Saakin اخفاء میم ساکن · Idghaam ادغام · Qalqala قلقلہ · Qalb قلب · Idghaam Meem Saakin ادغام میم ساکن

"Why not glorify (Allah)?'"

29. They said: "Glory to our Lord! Verily we have been doing wrong!"

30. Then they turned, one against another, in reproach.

31. They said: "Alas for us! We have indeed transgressed!

32. "It may be that our Lord will give us in exchange a better (garden) than this: for we do turn to Him (in repentance)!"

33. Such is the Punishment (in this life); but greater is the Punishment in the Hereafter,- if only they knew!

34. Verily, for the Righteous, are Gardens of Delight, in the Presence of their Lord.

35. Shall We then treat the People of Faith like the People of Sin?

36. What is the matter with you? How judge you?

37. Or have you a book through which you learn-

38. That you shall have, through it whatever you choose?

39. Or have you Covenants with Us to oath, reaching to the Day of Judgment, (providing) that you shall have whatever you shall demand?

40. Ask you of them, which of them will stand surety for that!

41. Or have they some "Partners" (in Godhead)? Then let them produce their "partners", if they are truthful!

42. The Day that the shin shall be laid bare, and they shall be summoned to bow in adoration, but they shall not be able,-

43. Their eyes will be cast down,- ignominy will cover them; seeing that they had been summoned aforetime to bow in adoration, while they were hale and healthy, (and had refused).

44. Then leave Me alone with such as reject this Message: by degrees shall We punish them from directions they perceive not.

law laa tusabbihoon.

29. Qaaloo Subhaana Rabbinaaa innaa kunnaa zaalimeen.

30. Fa-aqbala ba'duhum 'alaa ba'diñy-yatalaawamoon.

31. Qaaloo yaa waylanaaa innaa kunnaa taagheen.

32. 'Asaa Rabbunaaa añy-yubdilanaa khayram-minhaaa innaaa ilaa Rabbinaa raaghiboon.

33. Kazaalikal-azaab, wa la-'azaabul-Aakhirati akbar; law kaanoo ya'lamoon. **(Section 1)**

34. Inna lilmuttaqeena 'inda Rabbihim Jannaatin-Na'eem.

35. Afanaj'alul-muslimeena kalmujrimeen.

36. Maa lakum kayfa tahkumoon.

37. Am lakum kitaabun feehi tadrusoon.

38. Inna lakum feehi lamaa takhayyaroon.

39. Am lakum aymaanun 'alaynaa baalighatun ilaa Yawmil-Qiyaamati inna lakum lamaa tahkumoon.

40. Salhum ayyuhum bizaalika za'eem.

41. Am lahum shurakaaa'u falyaåtoo bishurakaaa'ihim in kaanoo saadiqeen.

42. Yawma yukshafu 'an saaqiñw-wa yud'awna ilas-sujoodi falaa yastatee'oon.

43. Khaashi'atan absaaruhum tarhaquhum zillatuñw wa qad kaanoo yud'awna ilas-sujoodi wa hum saalimoon.

44. Fazarnee wa mañy-yukazzibu bihaazal-hadeesi sanastadrijuhum min haysu laa ya'lamoon.

لَوْلَا تُسَبِّحُونَ ﴿٢٨﴾
قَالُوا سُبْحٰنَ رَبِّنَآ إِنَّا كُنَّا ظٰلِمِينَ ﴿٢٩﴾
فَأَقْبَلَ بَعْضُهُمْ عَلٰى بَعْضٍ يَّتَلَاوَمُونَ ﴿٣٠﴾
قَالُوا يٰوَيْلَنَآ إِنَّا كُنَّا طٰغِينَ ﴿٣١﴾
عَسٰى رَبُّنَآ أَنْ يُّبْدِلَنَا خَيْرًا مِّنْهَآ
إِنَّآ إِلٰى رَبِّنَا رٰغِبُونَ ﴿٣٢﴾
كَذٰلِكَ الْعَذَابُ ۖ وَلَعَذَابُ الْاٰخِرَةِ
أَكْبَرُ ۘ لَوْ كَانُوا يَعْلَمُونَ ﴿٣٣﴾ وقف لازم ع
إِنَّ لِلْمُتَّقِينَ عِنْدَ رَبِّهِمْ جَنّٰتِ
النَّعِيمِ ﴿٣٤﴾
أَفَنَجْعَلُ الْمُسْلِمِينَ كَالْمُجْرِمِينَ ﴿٣٥﴾
مَا لَكُمْ ۗ كَيْفَ تَحْكُمُونَ ﴿٣٦﴾
أَمْ لَكُمْ كِتٰبٌ فِيهِ تَدْرُسُونَ ﴿٣٧﴾
إِنَّ لَكُمْ فِيهِ لَمَا تَخَيَّرُونَ ﴿٣٨﴾
أَمْ لَكُمْ أَيْمٰنٌ عَلَيْنَا بٰلِغَةٌ إِلٰى
يَوْمِ الْقِيٰمَةِ ۙ إِنَّ لَكُمْ لَمَا تَحْكُمُونَ ﴿٣٩﴾
سَلْهُمْ أَيُّهُمْ بِذٰلِكَ زَعِيمٌ ﴿٤٠﴾ مع عند المتقدمين ١٢
أَمْ لَهُمْ شُرَكَآءُ ۚ فَلْيَأْتُوا بِشُرَكَآئِهِمْ
إِنْ كَانُوا صٰدِقِينَ ﴿٤١﴾
يَوْمَ يُكْشَفُ عَنْ سَاقٍ وَّيُدْعَوْنَ
إِلَى السُّجُودِ فَلَا يَسْتَطِيعُونَ ﴿٤٢﴾
خٰشِعَةً أَبْصٰرُهُمْ تَرْهَقُهُمْ ذِلَّةٌ ۖ
وَقَدْ كَانُوا يُدْعَوْنَ إِلَى السُّجُودِ
وَهُمْ سٰلِمُونَ ﴿٤٣﴾
فَذَرْنِي وَمَنْ يُّكَذِّبُ بِهٰذَا الْحَدِيثِ ۖ
سَنَسْتَدْرِجُهُمْ مِّنْ حَيْثُ لَا يَعْلَمُونَ ﴿٤٤﴾

Ikhfa اخفاء | Ghunna غُنّہ | Ikhfa Meem Saakin اخفاء میم ساکن | Idghaam ادغام | Qalqala قلقلہ | Qalb قلب | Idghaam Meem Saakin ادغام میم ساکن

45. Yet I bear with them, for lo! My scheme is firm.

46. Or is it that you does ask them for a reward, so that they are burdened with a load of debt?-

47. Or that the Unseen is in their hands, so that they can write it down?

48. So wait with patience for the Command of your Lord, and be not like the Companion of the Fish,- when he cried out in agony.

49. Had not Grace from his Lord reached him, he would indeed have been cast off on the naked shore, in disgrace.

50. Thus did his Lord choose him and make him of the Company of the Righteous.

51. And the Unbelievers would almost trip you up with their eyes when they hear the Message; and they say: "Surely he is possessed!"

52. But it is nothing less than a Message to all the worlds.

45. Wa umlee lahum; inna kaydee mateen.

46. Am tas'aluhum ajran fahum mim-maghramim musqaloon.

47. Am 'indahumul-ghaybu fahum yaktuboon.

48. Faṣbir liḥukmi Rabbika wa laa takun kaṣaaḥibil-ḥoot; iz naadaa wa huwa makẓoom.

49. Law laaa an tadaarakahoo ni'matum-mir-Rabbihee lanubiza bil-'araaa'i wa huwa mazmoom.

50. Fajtabaahu Rabbuhoo faja'alahoo minaṣ-ṣaaliḥeen.

51. Wa iñy-yakaadul-lazeena kafaroo la-yuzliqoonaka bi-abṣaarihim lammaa sami'uz-Zikra wa yaqooloona innahoo lamajnoon.

52. Wa maa huwa illaa zikrul-lil'aalameen. **(Section 2)**

وَ اَمۡلِیۡ لَهُمۡ ؕ اِنَّ كَیۡدِیۡ مَتِیۡنٌ ﴿۴۵﴾
اَمۡ تَسۡـَٔلُهُمۡ اَجۡرًا فَهُمۡ مِّنۡ مَّغۡرَمٍ
مُّثۡقَلُوۡنَ ﴿۴۶﴾
اَمۡ عِنۡدَهُمُ الۡغَیۡبُ فَهُمۡ یَكۡتُبُوۡنَ ﴿۴۷﴾
فَاصۡبِرۡ لِحُكۡمِ رَبِّكَ وَ لَا تَكُنۡ
كَصَاحِبِ الۡحُوۡتِ ۘ اِذۡ نَادٰی وَ هُوَ
مَكۡظُوۡمٌ ﴿۴۸﴾
لَوۡ لَاۤ اَنۡ تَدٰرَكَهٗ نِعۡمَةٌ مِّنۡ رَّبِّهٖ
لَنُبِذَ بِالۡعَرَآءِ وَ هُوَ مَذۡمُوۡمٌ ﴿۴۹﴾
فَاجۡتَبٰهُ رَبُّهٗ فَجَعَلَهٗ مِنَ
الصّٰلِحِیۡنَ ﴿۵۰﴾
وَ اِنۡ یَّكَادُ الَّذِیۡنَ كَفَرُوۡا
لَیُزۡلِقُوۡنَكَ بِاَبۡصَارِهِمۡ لَمَّا سَمِعُوا
الذِّكۡرَ وَ یَقُوۡلُوۡنَ اِنَّهٗ لَمَجۡنُوۡنٌ ﴿۵۱﴾
وَ مَا هُوَ اِلَّا ذِكۡرٌ لِّلۡعٰلَمِیۡنَ ﴿۵۲﴾

وقف لازم

69. The Sure Reality

In the name of Allah, Most Gracious, Most Merciful.

Sûrat al-Ḥâqqah–69

(Revealed at Makkah)

Bismillaahir Raḥmaanir Raḥeem

(۶۹) سُوۡرَةُ الۡحَآقَّةِ مَكِّیَّةٌ (۷۸)

بِسۡمِ اللّٰهِ الرَّحۡمٰنِ الرَّحِیۡمِ

1. The Sure Reality!

2. What is the Sure Reality?

3. And what will make you realise what the Sure Reality is?

4. The Thamûd and the 'Ad People (branded) as false the Stunning Calamity!

5. As for Thamûd, they were destroyed by the lightning.

6. And the 'Ad, they were destroyed by a furious Wind, exceedingly violent;

7. He made it rage against them seven nights and eight days in succession: so that you could see the (whole) people lying

1. Al-ḥaaaqqah.

2. Mal-ḥaaaqqah.

3. Wa maaa adraaka mal-ḥaaaqqah.

4. Kazzabat Samoodu wa 'Aadum bil-qaari'ah.

5. Fa-ammaa Samoodu fa-uhlikoo biṭṭaaghiyah.

6. Wa ammaa 'Aadun fa-uhlikoo bireeḥin ṣarṣarin 'aatiyah.

7. Sakhkharahaa 'alayhim sab'a la-yaaliñw-wa samaaniyata ayyaamin ḥusooman fataral-qawma feehaa

اَلۡحَآقَّةُ ۙ﴿۱﴾
مَا الۡحَآقَّةُ ۚ﴿۲﴾
وَ مَاۤ اَدۡرٰىكَ مَا الۡحَآقَّةُ ؕ﴿۳﴾
كَذَّبَتۡ ثَمُوۡدُ وَ عَادٌۢ بِالۡقَارِعَةِ ﴿۴﴾
فَاَمَّا ثَمُوۡدُ فَاُهۡلِكُوۡا بِالطَّاغِیَةِ ﴿۵﴾
وَ اَمَّا عَادٌ فَاُهۡلِكُوۡا بِرِیۡحٍ صَرۡصَرٍ
عَاتِیَةٍ ۙ﴿۶﴾
سَخَّرَهَا عَلَیۡهِمۡ سَبۡعَ لَیَالٍ وَّ ثَمٰنِیَةَ
اَیَّامٍ ۙ حُسُوۡمًا ۙ فَتَرَی الۡقَوۡمَ فِیۡهَا

Ikhfa اخفاء | Ghunna غُنّہ | Ikhfa Meem Saakin اخفاء میم ساکن | Idghaam ادغام | Qalqala قلقلہ | Qalb قلب | Idghaam Meem Saakin ادغام میم ساکن

prostrate in its (path), as they had been roots of hollow palm-trees tumbled down!

8. Then do you see any of them left surviving?

9. And Pharaoh, and those before him, and the Cities Overthrown, committed habitual Sin.

10. And disobeyed (each) the apostle of their Lord; so He punished them with an abundant Chastisement.

11. We, when the water (of Noah's Flood) overflowed beyond its limits, carried you (mankind), in the floating (Ark),

12. That We might make it a Message unto you, and that ears (that should hear the tale and) retain its memory should bear its (lessons) in remembrance.

13. Then, when one blast is sounded on the Trumpet,

14. And the earth is moved, and its mountains, and they are crushed to powder at one stroke,-

15. On that Day shall the (Great) Event come to pass.

16. And the sky will be rent asunder, for it will that Day be flimsy,

17. And the angels will be on its sides, and eight will, that Day, bear the Throne of your Lord above them.

18. On that day ye will be exposed; not a secret of you will be hidden.

19. Then he that will be given his Record in his right hand will say: "Ah here! Read you my Record!

20. "I did really understand that my Account would (One Day) reach me!"

21. And he will be in a life of Bliss,

22. In a Garden on high,

23. The Fruits whereof (will hang in bunches) low and near.

ṣar'aa ka-annahum a'jaazu nakhlin khaawiyah.

8. Fahal taraa lahum mim baaqiyah.

9. Wa jaaa'a Fir'awnu wa man qablahoo wal-mu'tafikaatu bilkhaaṭi'ah.

10. Fa'aṣaw Rasoola Rabbihim fa-akhazahum akhzatar-raabiyah.

11. Innaa lammaa ṭaghalmaaa'u ḥamalnaakum fil-jaariyah.

12. Linaj'alahaa lakum tazkiratañw-wa ta'iyahaaa uzunuñw-waa'iyah.

13. Fa-izaa nufikha fiṣ-Ṣoori nafkhatuñw-waaḥidah.

14. Wa ḥumilatil-arḍu waljibaalu fadukkataa dakkatañw-waaḥidah.

15. Fa-yawma'iziñw-waqa-'atil-waaqi'ah.

16. Wanshaqqatis-samaaa'u fahiya Yawma'iziñw-waahiyah.

17. Wal-malaku 'alaaa arjaaa'ihaa; wa yaḥmilu 'Arsha Rabbika fawqahum Yawma'izin samaaniyah.

18. Yawma'izin tu'raḍoona laa takhfaa minkum khaafiyah.

19. Fa-ammaa man ootiya kitaabahoo biyameenihee fa-yaqoolu haaa'umuq-ra'oo kitaabiyah.

20. Innee ẓanantu annee mulaaqin ḥisaabiyah.

21. Fahuwa fee 'eeshatir-raaḍiyah.

22. Fee Jannatin 'aaliyah.

23. Quṭoofuhaa daaniyah.

صَرْعَىٰ كَأَنَّهُمْ أَعْجَازُ نَخْلٍ خَاوِيَةٍ ﴿٧﴾

فَهَلْ تَرَىٰ لَهُم مِّنۢ بَاقِيَةٍ ﴿٨﴾

وَجَآءَ فِرْعَوْنُ وَمَن قَبْلَهُۥ وَ

ٱلْمُؤْتَفِكَٰتُ بِٱلْخَاطِئَةِ ﴿٩﴾

فَعَصَوْا۟ رَسُولَ رَبِّهِمْ فَأَخَذَهُمْ

أَخْذَةً رَّابِيَةً ﴿١٠﴾

إِنَّا لَمَّا طَغَا ٱلْمَآءُ حَمَلْنَٰكُمْ فِى

ٱلْجَارِيَةِ ﴿١١﴾

لِنَجْعَلَهَا لَكُمْ تَذْكِرَةً وَتَعِيَهَآ

أُذُنٌ وَٰعِيَةٌ ﴿١٢﴾

فَإِذَا نُفِخَ فِى ٱلصُّورِ نَفْخَةٌ وَٰحِدَةٌ ﴿١٣﴾

وَحُمِلَتِ ٱلْأَرْضُ وَٱلْجِبَالُ

فَدُكَّتَا دَكَّةً وَٰحِدَةً ﴿١٤﴾

فَيَوْمَئِذٍ وَقَعَتِ ٱلْوَاقِعَةُ ﴿١٥﴾

وَٱنشَقَّتِ ٱلسَّمَآءُ فَهِىَ يَوْمَئِذٍ

وَاهِيَةٌ ﴿١٦﴾

وَٱلْمَلَكُ عَلَىٰٓ أَرْجَآئِهَا ۚ وَيَحْمِلُ

عَرْشَ رَبِّكَ فَوْقَهُمْ يَوْمَئِذٍ ثَمَٰنِيَةٌ ﴿١٧﴾

يَوْمَئِذٍ تُعْرَضُونَ لَا تَخْفَىٰ مِنكُمْ

خَافِيَةٌ ﴿١٨﴾

فَأَمَّا مَنْ أُوتِىَ كِتَٰبَهُۥ بِيَمِينِهِۦ

فَيَقُولُ هَآؤُمُ ٱقْرَءُوا۟ كِتَٰبِيَهْ ﴿١٩﴾

إِنِّى ظَنَنتُ أَنِّى مُلَٰقٍ حِسَابِيَهْ ﴿٢٠﴾

فَهُوَ فِى عِيشَةٍ رَّاضِيَةٍ ﴿٢١﴾

فِى جَنَّةٍ عَالِيَةٍ ﴿٢٢﴾

قُطُوفُهَا دَانِيَةٌ ﴿٢٣﴾

Ikhfa	Ghunna	Ikhfa Meem Saakin	Idghaam	Qalqala	Qalb	Idghaam Meem Saakin
اخفاء	غُنّہ	اخفاء میم ساکن	ادغام	قلقلہ	قلب	ادغام میم ساکن

English	Transliteration	Arabic
24. "Eat you and drink you, with full satisfaction; because of the (good) that you sent before you, in the days that are gone!"	24. Kuloo washraboo haneee-'am bimaaa aslaftum fil-ayyaamil-khaaliyah.	كُلُوا وَاشْرَبُوا هَنِيٓـًٔا بِمَآ أَسْلَفْتُمْ فِى الْأَيَّامِ الْخَالِيَةِ ٢٤
25. And he that will be given his Record in his left hand, will say: "Ah! Would that my Record had not been given to me!	25. Wa ammaa man ootiya kitaabahoo bishimaalihee fa-yaqoolu yaalaytanee lam oota kitaabiyah.	وَأَمَّا مَنْ أُوتِىَ كِتَـٰبَهُۥ بِشِمَالِهِۦ فَيَقُولُ يَـٰلَيْتَنِى لَمْ أُوتَ كِتَـٰبِيَهْ ٢٥
26. "And that I had never realised how my account (stood)!	26. Wa lam adri maa ḥisaa-biyah.	وَلَمْ أَدْرِ مَا حِسَابِيَهْ ٢٦
27. "Ah! Would that (Death) had made an end of me!	27. Yaa laytahaa kaanatil-qaaḍiyah.	يَـٰلَيْتَهَا كَانَتِ الْقَاضِيَةَ ٢٧
28. "Of no profit to me has been my wealth!	28. Maaa aghnaa 'annee maaliyah.	مَآ أَغْنَىٰ عَنِّى مَالِيَهْ ٢٨
29. "My power has perished from me!"...	29. Halaka 'annee sulṭaa-niyah.	هَلَكَ عَنِّى سُلْطَـٰنِيَهْ ٢٩
30. (The stern command will say): "Seize you him, and bind you him,	30. Khuzoohu faghullooh.	خُذُوهُ فَغُلُّوهُ ٣٠
31. "And burn you him in the Blazing Fire.	31. Summal-Jaḥeema ṣallooh.	ثُمَّ الْجَحِيمَ صَلُّوهُ ٣١
32. "Further, make him march in a chain, whereof the length is seventy cubits!	32. Summa fee silsilatin zar-'uhaa sab'oona ziraa'an faslu-kooh.	ثُمَّ فِى سِلْسِلَةٍ ذَرْعُهَا سَبْعُونَ ذِرَاعًا فَاسْلُكُوهُ ٣٢
33. "This was he that would not believe in Allah Most High.	33. Innahoo kaana laa yu'mi-nu billaahil-'Aẓeem.	إِنَّهُۥ كَانَ لَا يُؤْمِنُ بِاللَّهِ الْعَظِيمِ ٣٣
34. "And would not encourage the feeding of the indigent!	34. Wa laa yaḥuḍḍu 'alaa ṭa'aamil-miskeen.	وَلَا يَحُضُّ عَلَىٰ طَعَامِ الْمِسْكِينِ ٣٤
35. "So no friend hath he here this Day.	35. Falaysa lahul-Yawma haahunaa ḥameem.	فَلَيْسَ لَهُ الْيَوْمَ هَـٰهُنَا حَمِيمٌ ٣٥
36. "Nor hath he any food except the corruption from the washing of wounds,	36. Wa laa ṭa'aamun illaa min ghisleen.	وَلَا طَعَامٌ إِلَّا مِنْ غِسْلِينٍ ٣٦
37. "Which none do eat but those in sin."	37. Laa yaåkuluhooo illal-khaaṭi'oon. **(Section 1)**	لَّا يَأْكُلُهُۥٓ إِلَّا الْخَـٰطِـُٔونَ ٣٧
38. So I do call to witness what you see,	38. Falaaa uqsimu bimaa tubṣiroon	فَلَآ أُقْسِمُ بِمَا تُبْصِرُونَ ٣٨
39. And what you see not,	39. Wa maa laa tubṣiroon.	وَمَا لَا تُبْصِرُونَ ٣٩
40. That this is verily the word of an honoured apostle;	40. Innahoo laqawlu Rasoo-lin kareem.	إِنَّهُۥ لَقَوْلُ رَسُولٍ كَرِيمٍ ٤٠
41. It is not the word of a poet: little it is you believe!	41. Wa maa huwa biqawli shaa'ir; qaleelam-maa tu'mi-noon.	وَمَا هُوَ بِقَوْلِ شَاعِرٍ ۚ قَلِيلًا مَّا تُؤْمِنُونَ ٤١
42. Nor is it the word of a soothsayer: little admonition it is you receive.	42. Wa laa biqawli kaahin; qaleelam-maa tazakkaroon.	وَلَا بِقَوْلِ كَاهِنٍ ۚ قَلِيلًا مَّا تَذَكَّرُونَ ٤٢
43. (This is) a Message sent down from the Lord of the Worlds.	43. Tanzeelum-mir-Rabbil-'aalameen.	تَنزِيلٌ مِّن رَّبِّ الْعَـٰلَمِينَ ٤٣
44. And if the apostle were to invent any sayings in Our name,	44. Wa law taqawwala 'alay-naa ba'ḍal-aqaaweel.	وَلَوْ تَقَوَّلَ عَلَيْنَا بَعْضَ الْأَقَاوِيلِ ٤٤

Ikhfa اخفاء | Ghunna غنّہ | Ikhfa Meem Saakin اخفاء میم ساکن | Idghaam ادغام | Qalqala قلقلہ | Qalb قلب | Idghaam Meem Saakin ادغام میم ساکن

45. We should certainly seize him by his right hand,

46. And then severed his life-artry,

47. Nor could any of you withhold him (from Our wrath).

48. But verily this is a Message for the God-fearing.

49. And lo! We know that some among you will deny (it).

50. And lo! It is indeed an anguish for the disbelievers.

51. But verily it is Truth of assured certainty.

52. So glorify the name of your Lord Most High.

70. The Ways of Ascent

In the name of Allah, Most Gracious, Most Merciful.

1. A questioner asked about a Chastisement to befall-

2. The Unbelievers, the which there is none to ward off,-

3. (A Penalty) from Allah, Lord of the Ways of Ascent.

4. The angels and the spirit ascend unto him in a Day the measure whereof is (as) fifty thousand years:

5. But be patient (O Muhammad) with a patience fair to see.

6. They see the (Day) indeed as a far-off (event):

7. But We see it (quite) near.

8. The Day that the sky will be like molten brass,

9. And the mountains will be like wool,

10. And no friend will ask after a friend,

11. Though they will be given sight of them. The guilty man will long to be able to ransom himself from the punishment of that day at the price of his children.

12. His wife and his brother,

13. His kindred who sheltered him,

45. La-akhaznaa minhu bilyameen.

46. Summa laqaṭa'naa minhul-wateen.

47. Famaa minkum min aḥadin 'anhu ḥaajizeen.

48. Wa innahoo latazkiratul-lilmuttaqeen.

49. Wa inna lana'lamu anna minkum mukazzibeen.

50. Wa innahu laḥasratun 'alal-kaafireen

51. Wa innahoo laḥaqqul-yaqeen.

52. Fasabbiḥ bismi Rabbikal-'Aẓeem. **(Section 2)**

Sûrat al-Ma'ârij–70

(Revealed at Makkah)

Bismillaahir Raḥmaanir Raḥeem

1. Sa-ala saaa'ilum bi'azaa-biñw-waaqi'.

2. Lilkaafireen laysa lahoo daafi'.

3. Minal-laahi zil-ma'aarij.

4. Ta'rujul-malaaa'ikatu war-Rooḥu ilayhi fee yawmin kaana miqdaaruhoo khamseena alfa sanah.

5. Faṣbir ṣabran jameelaa.

6. Inaahum yarawnahoo ba'eedaa.

7. Wa naraahu qareebaa.

8. Yawma takoonus-samaaa-'u kalmuhl.

9. Wa takoonul-jibaalu kal-'ihn.

10. Wa laa yas'alu ḥameemun ḥameemaa.

11. Yubaṣṣaroonahum; ya-wad-dul-mujrimu law yaftadee min 'azaabi Yawmi'izim bibaneeh.

12. Wa ṣaaḥibatihee wa akheeh.

13. Wa faṣeelatihil-latee tu'-weeh.

لَاَخَذْنَا مِنْهُ بِالْيَمِيْنِ ﴿٤٥﴾

ثُمَّ لَقَطَعْنَا مِنْهُ الْوَتِيْنَ ﴿٤٦﴾

فَمَا مِنْكُمْ مِّنْ اَحَدٍ عَنْهُ حٰجِزِيْنَ ﴿٤٧﴾

وَاِنَّهٗ لَتَذْكِرَةٌ لِّلْمُتَّقِيْنَ ﴿٤٨﴾

وَاِنَّا لَنَعْلَمُ اَنَّ مِنْكُمْ مُّكَذِّبِيْنَ ﴿٤٩﴾

وَاِنَّهٗ لَحَسْرَةٌ عَلَى الْكٰفِرِيْنَ ﴿٥٠﴾

وَاِنَّهٗ لَحَقُّ الْيَقِيْنِ ﴿٥١﴾

فَسَبِّحْ بِاسْمِ رَبِّكَ الْعَظِيْمِ ﴿٥٢﴾ ع

(٧٠) سُوْرَةُ الْمَعَارِجِ مَكِّيَّةٌ (٧٩)

بِسْمِ اللّٰهِ الرَّحْمٰنِ الرَّحِيْمِ

سَاَلَ سَآئِلٌۢ بِعَذَابٍ وَّاقِعٍ ﴿١﴾

لِّلْكٰفِرِيْنَ لَيْسَ لَهٗ دَافِعٌ ﴿٢﴾

مِّنَ اللّٰهِ ذِى الْمَعَارِجِ ﴿٣﴾

تَعْرُجُ الْمَلٰٓئِكَةُ وَالرُّوْحُ اِلَيْهِ فِىْ

يَوْمٍ كَانَ مِقْدَارُهٗ خَمْسِيْنَ

اَلْفَ سَنَةٍ ﴿٤﴾

فَاصْبِرْ صَبْرًا جَمِيْلًا ﴿٥﴾

اِنَّهُمْ يَرَوْنَهٗ بَعِيْدًا ﴿٦﴾

وَّنَرٰىهُ قَرِيْبًا ﴿٧﴾

يَوْمَ تَكُوْنُ السَّمَآءُ كَالْمُهْلِ ﴿٨﴾

وَتَكُوْنُ الْجِبَالُ كَالْعِهْنِ ﴿٩﴾

وَلَا يَسْـَٔلُ حَمِيْمٌ حَمِيْمًا ﴿١٠﴾

يُّبَصَّرُوْنَهُمْ يَوَدُّ الْمُجْرِمُ لَوْ يَفْتَدِىْ

مِنْ عَذَابِ يَوْمِئِذٍۢ بِبَنِيْهِ ﴿١١﴾

وَصَاحِبَتِهٖ وَاَخِيْهِ ﴿١٢﴾

وَفَصِيْلَتِهِ الَّتِىْ تُـْٔوِيْهِ ﴿١٣﴾

Ikhfa اخفاء | Ghunna غُنّہ | Ikhfa Meem Saakin اخفاء میم ساکن | Idghaam ادغام | Qalqala قلقلہ | Qalb قلب | Idghaam Meem Saakin ادغام میم ساکن

14.	And all, all that is on earth,- so it could deliver him:	Wa man fil-arḍi jamee‘an summa yunjeeh.	وَمَن فِي الْأَرْضِ جَمِيعًا ثُمَّ يُنجِيهِ ﴿١٤﴾
15.	By no means! for it would be the Fire of Hell!-	kallaa innahaa laẓaa.	كَلَّا ۖ إِنَّهَا لَظَىٰ ﴿١٥﴾
16.	Plucking out (his being) right to the skull!-	Nazzaa‘atal-lishshawaa.	نَزَّاعَةً لِّلشَّوَىٰ ﴿١٦﴾
17.	It calleth him who turned and fled (from truth),	Tad‘oo man adbara wa tawallaa.	تَدْعُو مَنْ أَدْبَرَ وَتَوَلَّىٰ ﴿١٧﴾
18.	And collect (wealth) and hide it (from use)!	Wa jama‘a fa-aw‘aa.	وَجَمَعَ فَأَوْعَىٰ ﴿١٨﴾
19.	Truly man was created very impatient;-	Innal-insaana khuliqa haloo‘aa.	إِنَّ الْإِنسَانَ خُلِقَ هَلُوعًا ﴿١٩﴾
20.	Fretful when evil touches him;	Izaa massahush-sharru jazoo‘aa.	إِذَا مَسَّهُ الشَّرُّ جَزُوعًا ﴿٢٠﴾
21.	And niggardly when good reaches him;-	Wa izaa massahul-khayru manoo‘aa.	وَإِذَا مَسَّهُ الْخَيْرُ مَنُوعًا ﴿٢١﴾
22.	Not so those devoted to Prayer;-	Illal-muṣalleen.	إِلَّا الْمُصَلِّينَ ﴿٢٢﴾
23.	Those who remain steadfast to their prayer;	Allazeena hum ‘alaa Ṣalaatihim daaa’imoon.	الَّذِينَ هُمْ عَلَىٰ صَلَاتِهِمْ دَائِمُونَ ﴿٢٣﴾
24.	And those in whose wealth is a recognised right.	Wallazeena feee amwaalihim ḥaqqum-ma‘loom.	وَالَّذِينَ فِي أَمْوَالِهِمْ حَقٌّ مَّعْلُومٌ ﴿٢٤﴾
25.	For the beggar and the destitute;	Lissaaa’ili walmaḥroom.	لِّلسَّائِلِ وَالْمَحْرُومِ ﴿٢٥﴾
26.	And those who hold to the truth of the Day of Judgment;	Wallazeena yuṣaddiqoona bi-Yawmid-Deen.	وَالَّذِينَ يُصَدِّقُونَ بِيَوْمِ الدِّينِ ﴿٢٦﴾
27.	And those who fear the displeasure of their Lord,-	Wallazeena hum min ‘azaabi Rabbihim mushfiqoon.	وَالَّذِينَ هُم مِّنْ عَذَابِ رَبِّهِم مُّشْفِقُونَ ﴿٢٧﴾
28.	For their Lord's displeasure is the opposite of Peace and Tranquillity;-	Inna ‘azaaba Rabbihim ghayru maåmoon.	إِنَّ عَذَابَ رَبِّهِمْ غَيْرُ مَأْمُونٍ ﴿٢٨﴾
29.	And those who guard their chastity,	Wallazeena hum lifuroojihim ḥaafiẓoon.	وَالَّذِينَ هُمْ لِفُرُوجِهِمْ حَافِظُونَ ﴿٢٩﴾
30.	Except with their wives and the (captives) whom their right hands possess,- for (then) they are not to be blamed,	Illaa ‘alaaa azwaajihim aw maa malakat aymaanuhum fa-innahum ghayru maloomeen.	إِلَّا عَلَىٰ أَزْوَاجِهِمْ أَوْ مَا مَلَكَتْ أَيْمَانُهُمْ فَإِنَّهُمْ غَيْرُ مَلُومِينَ ﴿٣٠﴾
31.	But those who trespass beyond this are transgressors;	Famanib-taghaa waraaa’a zaalika fa-ulaaa’ika humul-‘aadoon.	فَمَنِ ابْتَغَىٰ وَرَاءَ ذَٰلِكَ فَأُولَٰئِكَ هُمُ الْعَادُونَ ﴿٣١﴾
32.	And those who respect their trusts and covenants;	Wallazeena hum li-amaanaatihim wa ‘ahdihim raa‘oon.	وَالَّذِينَ هُمْ لِأَمَانَاتِهِمْ وَعَهْدِهِمْ رَاعُونَ ﴿٣٢﴾
33.	And those who stand firm in their testimonies;	wallazeena hum bishahaadaatihim qaaa’imoon.	وَالَّذِينَ هُم بِشَهَادَاتِهِمْ قَائِمُونَ ﴿٣٣﴾
34.	And those who guard (the sacredness) of their worship;-	Wallazeena hum ‘alaa Ṣalaatihim yuḥaafiẓoon.	وَالَّذِينَ هُمْ عَلَىٰ صَلَاتِهِمْ يُحَافِظُونَ ﴿٣٤﴾

Ikhfa اخفاء · Ghunna غنّہ · Ikhfa Meem Saakin اخفاءمیم ساکن · Idghaam ادغام · Qalqala قلقلہ · Qalb قلب · Idghaam Meem Saakin ادغام میم ساکن

35. Such will be the honoured ones in the Gardens (of Bliss).	35. Ulaaa'ika fee Jannaatim-mukramoon. **(Section 1)**	أُولٰٓئِكَ فِيْ جَنّٰتٍ مُّكْرَمُوْنَ ﴿٣٥﴾ ع
36. Now what is the matter with the Unbelievers that they rush madly before you–	36. Famaa lil-lazeena kafaroo qibalaka muhṭi'een.	فَمَالِ الَّذِيْنَ كَفَرُوْا قِبَلَكَ مُهْطِعِيْنَ ﴿٣٦﴾
37. From the right and from the left, in crowds?	37. 'Anil-yameeni wa 'anish-shimaali 'izeen.	عَنِ الْيَمِيْنِ وَعَنِ الشِّمَالِ عِزِيْنَ ﴿٣٧﴾
38. Does every man of them long to enter the Garden of Bliss?	38. Ayaṭma'u kullum-ri'im minhum añy-yudkhala jannata Na'eem.	اَيَطْمَعُ كُلُّ امْرِئٍ مِّنْهُمْ اَنْ يُّدْخَلَ جَنَّةَ نَعِيْمٍ ﴿٣٨﴾
39. By no means! For We have created them out of the (base matter) they know about.	39. Kallaaa innaa khalaqnaahum-mimmaa ya'lamoon.	كَلَّا ؕ اِنَّا خَلَقْنٰهُمْ مِّمَّا يَعْلَمُوْنَ ﴿٣٩﴾
40. Now I do call to witness the Lord of all points in the East and the West that We can certainly-	40. Falaaa uqsimu bi-Rabbil-mashaariqi wal-maghaaribi innaa laqaadiroon.	فَلَآ اُقْسِمُ بِرَبِّ الْمَشٰرِقِ وَالْمَغٰرِبِ اِنَّا لَقٰدِرُوْنَ ﴿٤٠﴾
41. Substitute for them better (men) than they; And We are not to be defeated (in Our Plan).	41. 'Alaaa an nubaddila khayram-minhum wa maa Naḥnu bimasbooqeen.	عَلٰٓى اَنْ نُّبَدِّلَ خَيْرًا مِّنْهُمْ ۙ وَمَا نَحْنُ بِمَسْبُوْقِيْنَ ﴿٤١﴾
42. So leave them to plunge in vain talk and play about, until they encounter that Day of theirs which they have been promised!-	42. Fazarhum yakhooḍoo wa yal'aboo ḥattaa yulaaqoo Yawmahumul-lazee yoo'adoon.	فَذَرْهُمْ يَخُوْضُوْا وَيَلْعَبُوْا حَتّٰى يُلٰقُوْا يَوْمَهُمُ الَّذِيْ يُوْعَدُوْنَ ﴿٤٢﴾
43. The day when they come forth from the graves in haste, as racing to a goal.	43. Yawma yakhrujoona minal-ajdaasi siraa'an ka-annahum ilaa nuṣubiñy-yoofiḍoon.	يَوْمَ يَخْرُجُوْنَ مِنَ الْاَجْدَاثِ سِرَاعًا كَاَنَّهُمْ اِلٰى نُصُبٍ يُّوْفِضُوْنَ ﴿٤٣﴾
44. Their eyes lowered in dejection,- ignominy covering them (all over)! such is the Day the which they are promised!	44. Khaashi'atan abṣaaruhum tarhaquhum zillah; zaalikal-Yawmul-lazee kaanoo yoo'adoon. **(Section 2)**	خَاشِعَةً اَبْصَارُهُمْ تَرْهَقُهُمْ ذِلَّةٌ ؕ ذٰلِكَ الْيَوْمُ الَّذِيْ كَانُوْا يُوْعَدُوْنَ ﴿٤٤﴾ ع

71. Noah - The Prophet

In the name of Allah, Most Gracious, Most Merciful.

Sûrat Nûḥ–71

(Revealed at Makkah)

Bismillaahir Raḥmaanir Raḥeem

(٧١) سُوْرَةُ نُوْحٍ مَّكِّيَّةٌ (٧١)

بِسْمِ اللّٰهِ الرَّحْمٰنِ الرَّحِيْمِ

1. We sent Noah to his People (with the Command): "Do thou warn your People before there comes to them a grievous Chastisement."	1. Innaaa arsalnaa Nooḥan ilaa qawmiheee an anzir qawmaka min qabli añy-yaåtiyahum 'azaabun aleem.	اِنَّآ اَرْسَلْنَا نُوْحًا اِلٰى قَوْمِهٖٓ اَنْ اَنْذِرْ قَوْمَكَ مِنْ قَبْلِ اَنْ يَّاْتِيَهُمْ عَذَابٌ اَلِيْمٌ ﴿١﴾
2. He said: O my People! Lo! I am a plain warner unto you	2. Qaala yaa qawmi innee lakum nazeerum-mubeen.	قَالَ يٰقَوْمِ اِنِّيْ لَكُمْ نَذِيْرٌ مُّبِيْنٌ ﴿٢﴾
3. "That you should worship Allah, fear Him and obey me:	3. Ani'-budul-laaha wattaqoohu wa aṭee'oon.	اَنِ اعْبُدُوا اللّٰهَ وَاتَّقُوْهُ وَاَطِيْعُوْنِ ﴿٣﴾
4. "So that He may forgive you your sins and give you respite for a stated Term: for when the Term given by Allah is	4. Yaghfir lakum min zunoobikum wa yu'akhkhirkum ilaaa ajalim-musammaa; inna ajalal-laahi izaa	يَغْفِرْ لَكُمْ مِّنْ ذُنُوْبِكُمْ وَيُؤَخِّرْكُمْ اِلٰٓى اَجَلٍ مُّسَمًّى ؕ اِنَّ اَجَلَ اللّٰهِ اِذَا

Ikhfa اخفاء · Ghunna غُنّہ · Ikhfa Meem Saakin اخفاء میم ساکن · Idghaam ادغام · Qalqala قلقلہ · Qalb قلب · Idghaam Meem Saakin ادغام میم ساکن

وقف لازم

accomplished, it cannot be put forward: if you only knew."

jaaa'a laa yu'akhkhar; law kuntum ta'lamoon.

جَآءَ لَا يُؤَخَّرُ لَوْ كُنْتُمْ تَعْلَمُوْنَ ﴿٤﴾

5. He said: "O my Lord! I have called to my People night and day:

5. Qaala Rabbi innee da'awtu qawmee laylañw-wa nahaaraa.

قَالَ رَبِّ إِنِّيْ دَعَوْتُ قَوْمِيْ لَيْلًا
وَّنَهَارًا ﴿٥﴾

6. But all my calling doth but add to their repugnance;

6. Falam yazid-hum du'aaa-'eee illaa firaaraa.

فَلَمْ يَزِدْهُمْ دُعَآءِيْٓ إِلَّا فِرَارًا ﴿٦﴾

7. "And every time I have called to them, that you mightest forgive them, they have (only) thrust their fingers into their ears, covered themselves up with their garments, grown obstinate, and given themselves up to arrogance.

7. Wa innee kullamaa da-'awtuhum litaghfira lahum ja'a-looo aṣaabi'ahum feee aazaani-him wastaghshaw siyaabahum wa aṣarroo wastakbarus-tik-baaraa.

وَإِنِّيْ كُلَّمَا دَعَوْتُهُمْ لِتَغْفِرَ لَهُمْ
جَعَلُوْٓا أَصَابِعَهُمْ فِيْٓ اٰذَانِهِمْ وَ
اسْتَغْشَوْا ثِيَابَهُمْ وَأَصَرُّوْا وَ
اسْتَكْبَرُوا اسْتِكْبَارًا ﴿٧﴾

8. "So I have called to them aloud;

8. Summa innee da'aw-tuhum jihaaraa.

ثُمَّ إِنِّيْ دَعَوْتُهُمْ جِهَارًا ﴿٨﴾

9. "Further I have spoken to them in public and secretly in private,

9. Summa inneee a'lantu la-hum wa asrartu lahum israaraa.

ثُمَّ إِنِّيْٓ أَعْلَنْتُ لَهُمْ وَأَسْرَرْتُ
لَهُمْ إِسْرَارًا ﴿٩﴾

10. "Saying, 'Ask forgiveness from your Lord; for He is Oft-Forgiving;

10. Faqultus-taghfiroo Rab-bakam innahoo kaana Ghaf-faaraa.

فَقُلْتُ اسْتَغْفِرُوْا رَبَّكُمْ إِنَّهٗ
كَانَ غَفَّارًا ﴿١٠﴾

11. "'He will send rain to you in abundance;

11. Yursilis-samaaa'a 'alay-kum midraaraa.

يُّرْسِلِ السَّمَآءَ عَلَيْكُمْ مِّدْرَارًا ﴿١١﴾

12. "'Give you increase in wealth and sons; and bestow on you gardens and bestow on you rivers (of flowing water).

12. Wa yumdidkum bi-am-waaliñw-wa baneena wa yaj'al lakum Jannaatiñw-wa yaj'al lakum anhaaraa.

وَّيُمْدِدْكُمْ بِأَمْوَالٍ وَّبَنِيْنَ وَيَجْعَلْ
لَّكُمْ جَنّٰتٍ وَّيَجْعَلْ لَّكُمْ أَنْهٰرًا ﴿١٢﴾

13. What aileth you that ye hope not toward Allah for dignity,

13. Maa lakum laa tarjoona lillaahi waqaaraa.

مَا لَكُمْ لَا تَرْجُوْنَ لِلّٰهِ وَقَارًا ﴿١٣﴾

14. When He created you by (diverse) stages?

14. Wa qad khalaqakum at-waaraa.

وَقَدْ خَلَقَكُمْ أَطْوَارًا ﴿١٤﴾

15. 'See you not how Allah has created the seven heavens one above another,

15. Alam taraw kayfa khala-qal-laahu sab'a samaawaatin-tibaaqaa.

أَلَمْ تَرَوْا كَيْفَ خَلَقَ اللّٰهُ سَبْعَ
سَمٰوٰتٍ طِبَاقًا ﴿١٥﴾

16. "'And made the moon a light in their midst, and made the sun as a (Glorious) Lamp?

16. Wa ja'alal-qamara fee-hinna noorañw-wa ja'alash shamsa siraajaa.

وَّجَعَلَ الْقَمَرَ فِيْهِنَّ نُوْرًا وَّجَعَلَ
الشَّمْسَ سِرَاجًا ﴿١٦﴾

17. "'And Allah has produced you from the earth growing (gradually),

17. Wallaahu ambatakum minal-arḍi nabaataa.

وَاللّٰهُ أَنْبَتَكُمْ مِّنَ الْأَرْضِ نَبَاتًا ﴿١٧﴾

18. "'And in the End He will return you into the (earth), and raise you forth (again at the Resurrection)?

18. Summa yu'eedukum fee-haa wa yukhrijukum ikhraajaa.

ثُمَّ يُعِيْدُكُمْ فِيْهَا وَيُخْرِجُكُمْ
إِخْرَاجًا ﴿١٨﴾

19. And Allah hath made the earth a wide expanse for you.

19. Wallaahu ja'ala lakumul-arḍa bisaaṭaa.

وَاللّٰهُ جَعَلَ لَكُمُ الْأَرْضَ بِسَاطًا ﴿١٩﴾

Ikhfa اخفاء | Ghunna غُنّہ | Ikhfa Meem Saakin اخفاء میم ساکن | Idghaam ادغام | Qalqala قلقلہ | Qalb قلب | Idghaam Meem Saakin ادغام میم ساکن

20. 'That you may go about therein, in spacious roads.'

21. Noah said: "O my Lord! They have disobeyed me, but they follow (men) whose wealth and children give them no increase but only Loss.

22. "And they have devised a tremendous Plot.

23. "And they have said (to each other), 'Abandon not your gods: Abandon neither Wadd nor Suwa', neither Yaguth nor Ya'uq, nor Nasr';-

24. "They have already misled many; and grant you no increase to the wrong- doers but in straying (from their mark)."

25. Because of their sins they were drowned (in the flood), and were made to enter the Fire (of Punishment): and they found- in lieu of Allah- none to help them.

26. And Noah, said: "O my Lord! Leave not of the Unbelievers, a single one on earth!

27. If Thou shouldst leave them, they will mislead Thy slaves and will beget none save lewd ingrates.

28. "O my Lord! Forgive me, my parents, all who enter my house in Faith, and (all) believing men and believing women: and to the wrong-doers grant You no increase but in perdition!"

20. Litaslukoo minhaa subulan fijaajaa. **(Section 1)**

21. Qaala Nooḥur-Robbi innahum 'aṣawnee wattaba'oo mal-lam yazid-hu maaluhoo wa waladuhooo illaa khasaaraa.

22. Wa makaroo makran kubbaaraa.

23. Wa qaaloo laa tazarunna aalihatakum wa laa tazarunna Waddañw-wa laa Suwaa'añw-wa laa Yaghooṣa wa Ya'ooqa wa Nasraa.

24. Wa qad aḍalloo kaṣeerañw wa laa tazidiẓ-ẓaalimeena illaa ḍalaalaa.

25. Mimmaa khaṭeee'aatihim ughriqoo fa-udkhiloo Naaran falam yajidoo lahum min doonil-laahi anṣaaraa.

26. Wa qaala Nooḥur-Rabbi laa tazar 'alal-arḍi minal-kaafireena dayyaaraa.

27. Innaka in tazarhum yuḍilloo 'ibaadaka wa laa yalidooo illaa faajiran kaffaaraa.

28. Rabbigh-fir lee wa liwaalidayya wa liman dakhala baytiya mu'minañw-wa lilmu'mineena wal-mu'minaati wa laa tazidiẓ-ẓaalimeena illaa tabaaraa. **(Section 2)**

لِّتَسْلُكُوا مِنْهَا سُبُلًا فِجَاجًا ﴿٢٠﴾ ع
قَالَ نُوحٌ رَّبِّ إِنَّهُمْ عَصَوْنِي وَ
اتَّبَعُوا مَن لَّمْ يَزِدْهُ مَالُهُ وَ
وَلَدُهُ إِلَّا خَسَارًا ﴿٢١﴾
وَمَكَرُوا مَكْرًا كُبَّارًا ﴿٢٢﴾
وَقَالُوا لَا تَذَرُنَّ آلِهَتَكُمْ وَلَا
تَذَرُنَّ وَدًّا وَلَا سُوَاعًا وَلَا
يَغُوثَ وَيَعُوقَ وَنَسْرًا ﴿٢٣﴾
وَقَدْ أَضَلُّوا كَثِيرًا وَلَا تَزِدِ
الظَّالِمِينَ إِلَّا ضَلَالًا ﴿٢٤﴾
مِّمَّا خَطِيئَاتِهِمْ أُغْرِقُوا فَأُدْخِلُوا
نَارًا فَلَمْ يَجِدُوا لَهُم مِّن
دُونِ اللَّهِ أَنصَارًا ﴿٢٥﴾
وَقَالَ نُوحٌ رَّبِّ لَا تَذَرْ عَلَى
الْأَرْضِ مِنَ الْكَافِرِينَ دَيَّارًا ﴿٢٦﴾
إِنَّكَ إِن تَذَرْهُمْ يُضِلُّوا عِبَادَكَ
وَلَا يَلِدُوا إِلَّا فَاجِرًا كَفَّارًا ﴿٢٧﴾
رَّبِّ اغْفِرْ لِي وَلِوَالِدَيَّ وَلِمَن
دَخَلَ بَيْتِيَ مُؤْمِنًا وَلِلْمُؤْمِنِينَ
وَالْمُؤْمِنَاتِ وَلَا تَزِدِ الظَّالِمِينَ
إِلَّا تَبَارًا ﴿٢٨﴾ ع النصف

72. The Spirits

In the name of Allah, Most Gracious, Most Merciful.

Sûrat al-Jinn–72

(Revealed at Makkah)

Bismillaahir Raḥmaanir Raḥeem

(٧٢) سُورَةُ الْجِنِّ مَكِّيَّةٌ (٤٠)

بِسْمِ اللَّهِ الرَّحْمَٰنِ الرَّحِيمِ

1. Say: It has been revealed to me that a company of Jinns listened (to the Qur'an). They said, 'We have really heard a wonderful Recital!

1. Qul ooḥiya ilayya annahus-tama'a nafarum-minal-jinni faqaalooo innaa sami'naa Qur-aanan 'ajabaa.

قُلْ أُوحِيَ إِلَيَّ أَنَّهُ اسْتَمَعَ نَفَرٌ مِّنَ
الْجِنِّ فَقَالُوا إِنَّا سَمِعْنَا قُرْآنًا
عَجَبًا ﴿١﴾

Ikhfa اخفاء | Ghunna غُنّہ | Ikhfa Meem Saakin اخفاء میم ساکن | Idghaam ادغام | Qalqala قلقلہ | Qalb قلب | Idghaam Meem Saakin ادغام میم ساکن

2. 'It gives guidance to the Right, and we have believed therein: we shall not join (in worship) any (gods) with our Lord.

3. 'And Exalted is the Majesty of our Lord: He has taken neither a wife nor a son.

4. 'There were some foolish ones among us, who used to utter extravagant lies against Allah;

5. 'But we do think that no man or spirit should say anything that untrue against Allah.

6. 'True, there were persons among mankind who took shelter with persons among the Jinns, but they increased them in folly.

7. 'And they (came to) think as you thought, that Allah would not raise up any one (to Judgment).

8. 'And we pried into the secrets of heaven; but we found it filled with stern guards and flaming fires.

9. 'We used, indeed, to sit there in (hidden) stations, to (steal) a hearing; but any who listen now will find a flaming fire watching him in ambush.

10. And we know not whether harm is boded unto all who are in the earth, or whether their Lord intendeth guidance for them.

11. 'There are among us some that are righteous, and some the contrary: we follow divergent paths.

12. 'But we think that we can by no means frustrate Allah throughout the earth, nor can we frustrate Him by flight.

13. 'And as for us, since we have listened to the Guidance, we have accepted it: and any who believes in his Lord has no fear,

2. Yahdeee ilar-rushdi fa-aamannaa bihee wa lan nushrika bi-Rabbinaaa aḥadaa.

3. Wa annahoo Ta'aalaa jaddu Rabbinaa mat-takhaẕa ṣaaḥibatañw-wa laa waladaa.

4. Wa annahoo kaana ya-qoolu safeehunaa 'alal-laahi shaṭaṭaa

5. Wa annaa ẓanannaaa al-lan taqoolal-insu wal-jinnu 'alal-laahi kaẕibaa.

6. Wa annahoo kaana rijaa-lum-minal-insi ya'ooẕoona birijaalim-minal-jinni fazaa-doohum rahaqaa.

7. Wa annahum ẓannoo kamaa ẓanantum al-lañy-yab-'aṯal-laahu aḥadaa.

8. Wa annaa lamasnas-sa-maaa'a fa-wajadnaahaa muli'at ḥarasan shadeedañw-wa shuhu-baa.

9. Wa annaa kunnaa naq-'udu minhaa maqaa'ida lis-sam'i famañy-yastami'il-aana yajid lahoo shihaabar-raṣadaa.

10. Wa annaa laa nadreee asharrun ureeda biman fil-arḍi am araada bihim Rabbuhum rashadaa.

11. Wa annaa minnaṣ-ṣaali-ḥoona wa minnaa doona ẕaalika kunnaa ṭaraaa'iqa qidadaa.

12. Wa annaa ẓanannaaa al-lan nu'jizal-laaha fil-arḍi wa lan nu'jizahoo harabaa.

13. Wa annaa lammaa sami'-nal-hudaaa aamannaa bihee famañy-yu'mim bi-Rabbihee falaa yakhaafu

يَهْدِيْٓ اِلَى الرُّشْدِ فَاٰمَنَّا بِهٖ ؕ
وَلَنْ نُّشْرِكَ بِرَبِّنَآ اَحَدًا ۙ﴿۲﴾
وَّاَنَّهٗ تَعٰلٰى جَدُّ رَبِّنَا مَا اتَّخَذَ
صَاحِبَةً وَّلَا وَلَدًا ۙ﴿۳﴾
وَّاَنَّهٗ كَانَ يَقُوْلُ سَفِيْهُنَا عَلَى
اللّٰهِ شَطَطًا ۙ﴿۴﴾
وَّاَنَّا ظَنَنَّآ اَنْ لَّنْ تَقُوْلَ الْاِنْسُ
وَالْجِنُّ عَلَى اللّٰهِ كَذِبًا ۙ﴿۵﴾
وَّاَنَّهٗ كَانَ رِجَالٌ مِّنَ الْاِنْسِ
يَعُوْذُوْنَ بِرِجَالٍ مِّنَ الْجِنِّ
فَزَادُوْهُمْ رَهَقًا ۙ﴿۶﴾
وَّاَنَّهُمْ ظَنُّوْا كَمَا ظَنَنْتُمْ اَنْ لَّنْ
يَّبْعَثَ اللّٰهُ اَحَدًا ۙ﴿۷﴾
وَّاَنَّا لَمَسْنَا السَّمَآءَ فَوَجَدْنٰهَا مُلِئَتْ
حَرَسًا شَدِيْدًا وَّشُهُبًا ۙ﴿۸﴾
وَّاَنَّا كُنَّا نَقْعُدُ مِنْهَا مَقَاعِدَ
لِلسَّمْعِ ؕ فَمَنْ يَّسْتَمِعِ الْاٰنَ يَجِدْ
لَهٗ شِهَابًا رَّصَدًا ۙ﴿۹﴾
وَّاَنَّا لَا نَدْرِيْٓ اَشَرٌّ اُرِيْدَ بِمَنْ فِي
الْاَرْضِ اَمْ اَرَادَ بِهِمْ رَبُّهُمْ رَشَدًا ۙ﴿۱۰﴾
وَّاَنَّا مِنَّا الصّٰلِحُوْنَ وَمِنَّا دُوْنَ
ذٰلِكَ ؕ كُنَّا طَرَآئِقَ قِدَدًا ۙ﴿۱۱﴾
وَّاَنَّا ظَنَنَّآ اَنْ لَّنْ نُّعْجِزَ اللّٰهَ فِي
الْاَرْضِ وَلَنْ نُّعْجِزَهٗ هَرَبًا ۙ﴿۱۲﴾
وَّاَنَّا لَمَّا سَمِعْنَا الْهُدٰٓى اٰمَنَّا بِهٖ ؕ
فَمَنْ يُّؤْمِنْۢ بِرَبِّهٖ فَلَا يَخَافُ

Ikhfa اخفاء | Ghunna غُنّہ | Ikhfa Meem Saakin اخفاء میم ساکن | Idghaam ادغام | Qalqala قلقلہ | Qalb قلب | Idghaam Meem Saakin ادغام میم ساکن

either of a short (account) or of any injustice.

14. 'Amongst us are some that submit their wills (to Allah), and some that swerve from justice. Now those who submit their wills - they have sought out (the path) of right conduct:

15. 'But those who swerve,- they are (but) fuel for Hell-fire'-

16. If they (the idolaters) tread the right path, We shall give them to drink of water in abundance.

17. "That We might try them by that (means). But if any turns away from the remembrance of his Lord, He will cause him to undergo a severe Chastisement.

18. "And the places of worship are for Allah (alone): So invoke not any one along with Allah;

19. "Yet when the Devotee of Allah stands forth to invoke Him, they just make round him a dense crowd."

20. Say: "I do no more than invoke my Lord, and I join not with Him any (false god)."

21. Say: "It is not in my power to cause you harm, or to bring you to right conduct."

22. Say: "No one can deliver me from Allah (If I were to disobey Him), nor should I find refuge except in Him,

23. "Unless I proclaim what I receive from Allah and His Messages: for any that disobey Allah and His Apostle,- for them is Hell: they shall dwell therein for ever."

24. At length, when they see (with their own eyes) that which they are promised,- then will they know who it is that is weakest in (his) helper and least important in point of numbers.

25. Say: "I know not whether the (Punishment) which you are promised is near,

bakhsañw-wa laa rahaqaa.

14. Wa annaa minnal-muslimoona wa minnal-qaasiṭoona faman aslama fa-ulaaa'ika taḥarraw rashadaa.

15. Wa ammal-qaasiṭoona fa-kaanoo li-Jahannama ḥaṭabaa.

16. Wa alla-wis-taqaamoo 'alaṭ-ṭareeqati la-asqaynaahum maa'an ghadaqaa.

17. Linaftinahum feeh; wa mañy-yu'riḍ 'an zikri Rabbihee yasluk-hu 'azaaban ṣa'adaa.

18. Wa annal-masaajida lillaahi falaa tad'oo ma'al-laahi aḥadaa.

19. Wa annahoo lammaa qaama 'abdul-laahi yad'oohu kaadoo yakoonoona 'alayhi libadaa. **(Section 1)**

20. Qul innamaaa ad'oo Rabbee wa laaa ushriku biheee aḥadaa.

21. Qul innee laaa amliku lakum ḍarrañw-wa laa rashadaa.

22. Qul innee lañy-yujeeranee minal-laahi aḥad, wa lan ajida min doonihee multaḥadaa.

23. Illaa balaagham-minal-laahi wa Risaalaatih; wa mañy-ya'ṣil-laaha wa Rasoolahoo fa-inna lahoo Naara Jahannama khaalideena feehaaa abadaa.

24. Ḥattaaa izaa ra-aw maa yoo'adoona fasa-ya'lamoona man aḍ'afu naaṣirañw-wa aqallu 'adadaa.

25. Qul in adreee a-qareebum-maa too'adoona

بَخْسًا وَّلَا رَهَقًا ﴿١٣﴾
وَّاَنَّا مِنَّا الْمُسْلِمُوْنَ وَمِنَّا
الْقٰسِطُوْنَ ؕ فَمَنْ اَسْلَمَ فَاُولٰٓئِكَ
تَحَرَّوْا رَشَدًا ﴿١٤﴾
وَاَمَّا الْقٰسِطُوْنَ فَكَانُوْا لِجَهَنَّمَ
حَطَبًا ﴿١٥﴾
وَّاَنْ لَّوِ اسْتَقَامُوْا عَلَى الطَّرِيْقَةِ
لَاَسْقَيْنٰهُمْ مَّآءً غَدَقًا ﴿١٦﴾
لِّنَفْتِنَهُمْ فِيْهِ ؕ وَمَنْ يُّعْرِضْ عَنْ
ذِكْرِ رَبِّهٖ يَسْلُكْهُ عَذَابًا صَعَدًا ﴿١٧﴾
وَّاَنَّ الْمَسٰجِدَ لِلّٰهِ فَلَا تَدْعُوْا مَعَ
اللّٰهِ اَحَدًا ﴿١٨﴾
وَّاَنَّهٗ لَمَّا قَامَ عَبْدُ اللّٰهِ يَدْعُوْهُ
كَادُوْا يَكُوْنُوْنَ عَلَيْهِ لِبَدًا ﴿١٩﴾
قُلْ اِنَّمَآ اَدْعُوْا رَبِّيْ وَلَآ اُشْرِكُ
بِهٖٓ اَحَدًا ﴿٢٠﴾
قُلْ اِنِّيْ لَآ اَمْلِكُ لَكُمْ ضَرًّا
وَّلَا رَشَدًا ﴿٢١﴾
قُلْ اِنِّيْ لَنْ يُّجِيْرَنِيْ مِنَ اللّٰهِ اَحَدٌ ۵
وَّلَنْ اَجِدَ مِنْ دُوْنِهٖ مُلْتَحَدًا ﴿٢٢﴾
اِلَّا بَلٰغًا مِّنَ اللّٰهِ وَرِسٰلٰتِهٖ ؕ وَ
مَنْ يَّعْصِ اللّٰهَ وَرَسُوْلَهٗ فَاِنَّ لَهٗ
نَارَ جَهَنَّمَ خٰلِدِيْنَ فِيْهَآ اَبَدًا ﴿٢٣﴾
حَتّٰٓى اِذَا رَاَوْا مَا يُوْعَدُوْنَ فَسَيَعْلَمُوْنَ
مَنْ اَضْعَفُ نَاصِرًا وَّاَقَلُّ عَدَدًا ﴿٢٤﴾
قُلْ اِنْ اَدْرِيْٓ اَقَرِيْبٌ مَّا تُوْعَدُوْنَ

Ikhfa اخفاء | Ghunna غُنّہ | Ikhfa Meem Saakin اخفاءِ میم ساکن | Idghaam ادغام | Qalqala قلقلہ | Qalb قلب | Idghaam Meem Saakin ادغام میم ساکن

or whether my Lord will appoint for it a distant term.	am yaj'alu lahooRabbeee amadaa.	أَمْ يَجْعَلُ لَهُ رَبِّيْٓ أَمَدًا ﴿٢٥﴾
26. "He (alone) knows the Unseen, nor does He make any one acquainted with His Mysteries,-	26. 'Aalimul-Ghaybi falaa yuẓhiru alaa ghaybiheee aḥadaa.	عٰلِمُ الْغَيْبِ فَلَا يُظْهِرُ عَلٰى غَيْبِهٖٓ أَحَدًا ﴿٢٦﴾
27. "Except an apostle whom He has chosen: and then He makes a band of watchers march before him and behind him,	27. Illaa manir-taḍaa mir Rasoolin fa-innahoo yasluku mim bayni yadayhi wa min khalfihee raṣadaa.	إِلَّا مَنِ ارْتَضٰى مِنْ رَّسُوْلٍ فَإِنَّهُ يَسْلُكُ مِنْ بَيْنِ يَدَيْهِ وَمِنْ خَلْفِهٖ رَصَدًا ﴿٢٧﴾
28. That He may know that they have indeed conveyed the messages of their Lord. He surroundeth all their doings, and He keepeth count of all things.	28. Liya'lama an qad ablaghoo Risaalaati Rabbihim wa aḥaaṭa bima ladayhim wa aḥṣaa Kulla shay'in 'adadaa. **(Section 2)**	لِّيَعْلَمَ أَنْ قَدْ أَبْلَغُوْا رِسٰلٰتِ رَبِّهِمْ وَأَحَاطَ بِمَا لَدَيْهِمْ وَأَحْصٰى كُلَّ شَيْءٍ عَدَدًا ﴿٢٨﴾
73. Folded in Garments **In the name of Allah, Most Gracious, Most Merciful.**	**Sûrat al-Muzzammil–73** (Revealed at Makkah) **Bismillaahir Raḥmaanir Raḥeem**	(٧٣) سُوْرَةُ الْمُزَّمِّلِ مَكِّيَّةٌ (٣) بِسْمِ اللّٰهِ الرَّحْمٰنِ الرَّحِيْمِ
1. O you folded in garments!	1. Yaw ayyuhal-muzzammil.	يٰٓأَيُّهَا الْمُزَّمِّلُ ﴿١﴾
2. Stand (to prayer) by night, but not all night,-	2. Qumil-layla illaa qaleelaa.	قُمِ الَّيْلَ إِلَّا قَلِيْلًا ﴿٢﴾
3. Half of it,- or a little less,	3. Niṣfahooo awinquṣ minhu qaleelaa.	نِّصْفَهٗٓ أَوِ انْقُصْ مِنْهُ قَلِيْلًا ﴿٣﴾
4. Or add (a little) thereto — and chant the Qur'an in measure.	4. Aw zid 'alayhi wa rattilil-Qur'aana tarteelaa.	أَوْ زِدْ عَلَيْهِ وَرَتِّلِ الْقُرْاٰنَ تَرْتِيْلًا ﴿٤﴾
5. Soon shall We send down to thee a weighty Message.	5. Innaa sanulqee 'alayka qawalan saqeelaa.	إِنَّا سَنُلْقِيْ عَلَيْكَ قَوْلًا ثَقِيْلًا ﴿٥﴾
6. Lo! The vigil of the night is (a time) when impression is more keen and speech more certain.	6. Inna naashi'atal-layli hiya ashaddu waṭ-añw-wa aqwamu-qeelaa.	إِنَّ نَاشِئَةَ الَّيْلِ هِيَ أَشَدُّ وَطْـًٔا وَّأَقْوَمُ قِيْلًا ﴿٦﴾
7. Lo! Thou hast by day a chain of business.	7. Inna laka fin-nahaari sabḥan ṭaweelaa.	إِنَّ لَكَ فِي النَّهَارِ سَبْحًا طَوِيْلًا ﴿٧﴾
8. But keep in remembrance the name of your Lord and devote thyself to Him wholeheartedly.	8. Wazkuris-ma Rabbika wa tabattal ilayhi tabteelaa.	وَاذْكُرِ اسْمَ رَبِّكَ وَتَبَتَّلْ إِلَيْهِ تَبْتِيْلًا ﴿٨﴾
9. (He is) Lord of the East and the West: there is no god but He: take Him therefore for (thy) Disposer of Affairs.	9. Rabbul-mashriqi wal-maghribi laaa ilaaha illaa Huwa fattakhizhu Wakeelaa.	رَبُّ الْمَشْرِقِ وَالْمَغْرِبِ لَآ إِلٰهَ إِلَّا هُوَ فَاتَّخِذْهُ وَكِيْلًا ﴿٩﴾
10. And have patience with what they say, and leave them with noble (dignity).	10. Waṣbir 'alaa maa yaqooloona wahjurhum hajran jameelaa.	وَاصْبِرْ عَلٰى مَا يَقُوْلُوْنَ وَاهْجُرْهُمْ هَجْرًا جَمِيْلًا ﴿١٠﴾
11. And leave Me (alone to deal with) those in possession of the good things of life,	11. Wa zarnee walmukazzibeena ulin-na'mati	وَذَرْنِيْ وَالْمُكَذِّبِيْنَ أُولِي النَّعْمَةِ

Ikhfa اخفاء · Ghunna غُنّہ · Ikhfa Meem Saakin اخفاءمیم ساکن · Idghaam ادغام · Qalqala قلقلہ · Qalb قلب · Idghaam Meem Saakin ادغام میم ساکن

who (yet) deny the Truth; and bear with them for a little while.

12. Lo! With Us are heavy fetters and a raging fire.

13. And a Food that chokes, and a Chastisement Grievous.

14. On the Day when the earth and the hills rock, and the hills become a heap of running sand.

15. We have sent to you, (O men!) an apostle, to be a witness concerning you, even as We sent an apostle to Pharaoh.

16. But Pharaoh disobeyed the apostle; so We seized him with a heavy Punishment.

17. Then how shall you, if you deny (Allah), guard yourselves against a Day that will make children hoary-headed?-

18. Whereon the sky will be cleft asunder? His Promise needs must be accomplished.

19. Verily this is an Admonition: therefore, whoso will, let him take a (straight) path to his Lord!

20. Thy Lord does know that thou stands forth (to prayer) nearly two-thirds of the night, or half the night, or a third of the night, and so does a party of those with you. But Allah does appoint night and day in due measure He knoweth that you are unable to keep count thereof. So He has turned to you (in mercy): read you, therefore, of the Qur'an as much as may be easy for you. He knows that there may be (some) among you in ill-health; others travelling through the land, seeking of Allah's bounty ; yet others fighting in Allah's Cause, read ye, therefore,

wa mahhilhum qaleelaa.

12. Inna ladaynaaa ankaalañw-wa Jaḥeemaa.

13. Wa ṭa'aaman zaa ghuṣṣatiñw-wa 'azaaban aleemaa.

14. Yawma tarjuful-arḍu waljibaalu wa kaanatil-jibaalu kaseebam-maheelaa.

15. Innaaa arsalnaaa ilaykum Rasoolan shaahidan 'alaykum kamaaa arsalnaaa ilaa Fir'awna Rasoolaa.

16. Fa'aṣaa Fir'awnur-Rasoola fa-akhaznaahu akhzañw-wabeelaa.

17. Fakayfa tattaqoona in kafartum Yawmañy-yaj'alul-wildaana sheebaa.

18. Assamaaa'u munfaṭirum bih; kaana wa'duhoo maf-'oolaa.

19. Inna haazihee tazkiratun fa-man shaaa'at-takhaza ilaa Rabbihee sabeelaa. **(Section 1)**

20. Inna Rabbaka ya'lamu annaka taqoomu-adnaa min sulusa-yil-layli wa niṣfahoo wa sulusahoo wa ṭaaa'ifatum-minal-lazeena ma'ak; wal-laahu yuqaddirul-layla wanna-haar; 'alima al-lan tuḥṣoohu fataaba 'alaykum faqra'oo maa tayassara minal-Qur-aan; 'alima an sa-yakoonu minkum marḍaa wa aakharoona yaḍriboona fil-arḍi yabtaghoona min faḍlil-laahi wa aakharoona yu-qaatiloona fee sabeelil-laahi faqra'oo

وَمَهِّلْهُمْ قَلِيْلًا ﴿١١﴾

اِنَّ لَدَيْنَآ اَنْكَالًا وَّجَحِيْمًا ﴿١٢﴾

وَّطَعَامًا ذَا غُصَّةٍ وَّعَذَابًا اَلِيْمًا ﴿١٣﴾

يَوْمَ تَرْجُفُ الْاَرْضُ وَالْجِبَالُ وَ

كَانَتِ الْجِبَالُ كَثِيْبًا مَّهِيْلًا ﴿١٤﴾

اِنَّآ اَرْسَلْنَآ اِلَيْكُمْ رَسُوْلًا ۙ

شَاهِدًا عَلَيْكُمْ كَمَآ اَرْسَلْنَآ اِلٰى

فِرْعَوْنَ رَسُوْلًا ﴿١٥﴾

فَعَصٰى فِرْعَوْنُ الرَّسُوْلَ فَاَخَذْنٰهُ

اَخْذًا وَّبِيْلًا ﴿١٦﴾

فَكَيْفَ تَتَّقُوْنَ اِنْ كَفَرْتُمْ يَوْمًا

يَّجْعَلُ الْوِلْدَانَ شِيْبًا ﴿١٧﴾

السَّمَآءُ مُنْفَطِرٌ بِهٖ ؕ كَانَ وَعْدُهٗ

مَفْعُوْلًا ﴿١٨﴾

اِنَّ هٰذِهٖ تَذْكِرَةٌ ۚ فَمَنْ شَآءَ

اتَّخَذَ اِلٰى رَبِّهٖ سَبِيْلًا ﴿١٩﴾

اِنَّ رَبَّكَ يَعْلَمُ اَنَّكَ تَقُوْمُ اَدْنٰى

مِنْ ثُلُثَيِ الَّيْلِ وَنِصْفَهٗ وَثُلُثَهٗ

وَطَآئِفَةٌ مِّنَ الَّذِيْنَ مَعَكَ ؕ وَاللّٰهُ

يُقَدِّرُ الَّيْلَ وَالنَّهَارَ ؕ عَلِمَ اَنْ

لَّنْ تُحْصُوْهُ فَتَابَ عَلَيْكُمْ

فَاقْرَءُوْا مَا تَيَسَّرَ مِنَ الْقُرْاٰنِ ؕ

عَلِمَ اَنْ سَيَكُوْنُ مِنْكُمْ مَّرْضٰى ۙ

وَاٰخَرُوْنَ يَضْرِبُوْنَ فِي الْاَرْضِ

يَبْتَغُوْنَ مِنْ فَضْلِ اللّٰهِ ۙ وَاٰخَرُوْنَ

يُقَاتِلُوْنَ فِيْ سَبِيْلِ اللّٰهِ ۖ فَاقْرَءُوْا

Ikhfa اخفاء · Ghunna غنّہ · Ikhfa Meem Saakin اخفاء میم ساکن · Idghaam ادغام · Qalqala قلقلہ · Qalb قلب · Idghaam Meem Saakin ادغام میم ساکن

as much of the Qur'an as may be easy (for you); and establish regular Prayer and give regular Charity; and loan to Allah a Beautiful Loan. And whatever good you send forth for your souls you shall find it in Allah's Presence,- yes, better and greater, in Reward and seek you the Grace of Allah: for Allah is Oft-Forgiving, Most Merciful.	maa tayassara minhu wa aqeemuṣ-Ṣalaata wa aatuz-Zakaata wa aqriḍul-laaha qarḍan ḥasanaa; wa maa tuqaddimoo li-anfusikum min khayrin tajidoohu 'indal-laahi huwa khayrañw-wa a'ẓama ajraa; wastaghfirul-laaha innal-laaha Ghafoorur-Raḥeem. **(Section 2)**	مَا تَيَسَّرَ مِنْهُ ۚ وَأَقِيمُوا الصَّلٰوةَ وَآتُوا الزَّكٰوةَ وَأَقْرِضُوا اللّٰهَ قَرْضًا حَسَنًا ۚ وَمَا تُقَدِّمُوا لِأَنْفُسِكُمْ مِنْ خَيْرٍ تَجِدُوهُ عِنْدَ اللّٰهِ هُوَ خَيْرًا وَأَعْظَمَ أَجْرًا ۚ وَاسْتَغْفِرُوا اللّٰهَ ۖ إِنَّ اللّٰهَ غَفُورٌ رَحِيمٌ ﴿٢٠﴾
74. The One Wrapped Up **In the name of Allah, Most Gracious, Most Merciful.**	**Sûrat al-Muddassir–74** (Revealed at Makkah) **Bismillaahir Raḥmaanir Raḥeem**	(٧٤) سُورَةُ الْمُدَّثِّرِ مَكِّيَّةٌ (٤) بِسْمِ اللّٰهِ الرَّحْمٰنِ الرَّحِيمِ
1. O you wrapped up (in the mantle)!	1. Yaaa ayyuhal-muddassir.	يَا أَيُّهَا الْمُدَّثِّرُ ﴿١﴾
2. Arise and deliver thy warning!	2. Qum fa-anzir.	قُمْ فَأَنْذِرْ ﴿٢﴾
3. And your Lord do thou magnify!	3. Wa Rabbaka fakabbir.	وَرَبَّكَ فَكَبِّرْ ﴿٣﴾
4. And thy garments keep free from stain!	4. Wa siyaabaka faṭahhir.	وَثِيَابَكَ فَطَهِّرْ ﴿٤﴾
5. And all abomination shun!	5. Warrujza fahjur.	وَالرُّجْزَ فَاهْجُرْ ﴿٥﴾
6. Nor expect, in giving, any increase (for yourself)!	6. Wa laa tamnun tastaksir.	وَلَا تَمْنُنْ تَسْتَكْثِرُ ﴿٦﴾
7. But, for your Lord's (Cause), be patient and constant!	7. Wa li-Rabbika faṣbir.	وَلِرَبِّكَ فَاصْبِرْ ﴿٧﴾
8. Finally, when the Trumpet is sounded,	8. Fa-izaa nuqira fin-naaqoor.	فَإِذَا نُقِرَ فِي النَّاقُورِ ﴿٨﴾
9. That will be- that Day - a Day of Distress,-	9. Fazaalika Yawma'iziñy-yawmun 'aseer.	فَذٰلِكَ يَوْمَئِذٍ يَوْمٌ عَسِيرٌ ﴿٩﴾
10. Far from easy for those without Faith.	10. 'Alal-kaafireena ghayru yaseer.	عَلَى الْكَافِرِينَ غَيْرُ يَسِيرٍ ﴿١٠﴾
11. Leave me (to deal) with him whom I created lonely,	11. Zarnee wa man khalaqtu waḥeedaa.	ذَرْنِي وَمَنْ خَلَقْتُ وَحِيدًا ﴿١١﴾
12. To whom I granted resources in abundance,	12. Wa ja'altu lahoo maalam-mamdoodaa.	وَجَعَلْتُ لَهُ مَالًا مَمْدُودًا ﴿١٢﴾
13. And sons to be by his side!-	13. Wa baneena shuhoodaa.	وَبَنِينَ شُهُودًا ﴿١٣﴾
14. To whom I made (life) smooth and comfortable!	14. Wa mahhattu lahoo tamheedaa.	وَمَهَّدْتُ لَهُ تَمْهِيدًا ﴿١٤﴾
15. Yet is he greedy-that I should add (yet more);-	15. Summa yaṭma'u an azeed.	ثُمَّ يَطْمَعُ أَنْ أَزِيدَ ﴿١٥﴾
16. By no means! For to Our Signs he has been refractory!	16. Kallaaa innahoo kaana li-Aayaatinaa 'aneedaa.	كَلَّا ۖ إِنَّهُ كَانَ لِآيَاتِنَا عَنِيدًا ﴿١٦﴾
17. Soon will I visit him with a mount of calamities!	17. Sa-urhiquhoo ṣa'oodaa.	سَأُرْهِقُهُ صَعُودًا ﴿١٧﴾
18. For he thought and he plotted;-	18. Innahoo fakkara wa qaddar.	إِنَّهُ فَكَّرَ وَقَدَّرَ ﴿١٨﴾

Ikhfa اخفاء · Ghunna غنّہ · Ikhfa Meem Saakin اخفاء میم ساکن · Idghaam ادغام · Qalqala قلقلہ · Qalb قلب · Idghaam Meem Saakin ادغام میم ساکن

19. And woe to him! How he plotted!-	19. Faqutila kayfa qaddar.	فَقُتِلَ كَيْفَ قَدَّرَ ١٩
20. Yes, Woe to him; How he plotted!-	20. S̲umma qutila kayfa qaddar.	ثُمَّ قُتِلَ كَيْفَ قَدَّرَ ٢٠
21. Then he looked round;	21. S̲umma naẓar.	ثُمَّ نَظَرَ ٢١
22. Then he frowned and he scowled;	22. S̲umma 'abasa wa basar.	ثُمَّ عَبَسَ وَبَسَرَ ٢٢
23. Then he turned back and was haughty;	23. S̲umma adbara wastakbar.	ثُمَّ أَدْبَرَ وَاسْتَكْبَرَ ٢٣
24. And said: This is naught else than magic from of old;	24. Faqaala in haaz̲aaa illaa siḥruñy-yu's̲ar.	فَقَالَ إِنْ هَٰذَآ إِلَّا سِحْرٌ يُؤْثَرُ ٢٤
25. "This is nothing but the word of a mortal!"	25. In haaz̲aaa illaa qawlul-bashar.	إِنْ هَٰذَآ إِلَّا قَوْلُ الْبَشَرِ ٢٥
26. Soon will I cast him into Hell-Fire!	26. Sa-uṣleehi saqar.	سَأُصْلِيهِ سَقَرَ ٢٦
27. And what will explain to thee what Hell-Fire is?	27. Wa maaa adraaka maa saqar.	وَمَآ أَدْرَاكَ مَا سَقَرُ ٢٧
28. It leaveth naught; it spareth naught.	28. Laa tubqee wa laa taz̲ar.	لَا تُبْقِي وَلَا تَذَرُ ٢٨
29. Darkening and changing the colour of man!	29. Lawwaaḥatul-lilbashar.	لَوَّاحَةٌ لِّلْبَشَرِ ٢٩
30. Over it are Nineteen.	30. 'Alayhaa tis'ata 'ashar.	عَلَيْهَا تِسْعَةَ عَشَرَ ٣٠
31. And We have set none but angels as Guardians of the Fire; and We have fixed their number only as a trial for Unbelievers,- in order that the People of the Book may arrive at certainty, and the Believers may increase in Faith,- and that no doubts may be left for the People of the Book and the Believers, and that those in whose hearts is a disease and the Unbelievers may say, "What symbol does Allah intend by this ?" Thus does Allah leave to stray whom He pleases, and guide whom He pleases: and none can know the forces of thy Lord, except He and this is no other than a warning to mankind.	31. Wa maa ja'alnaaa Aṣ-ḥaa-ban-Naari illaa malaaa'ikatañw-wa maa ja'alnaa 'iddatahum illaa fitnatal-lillaz̲eena kafaroo liyastayqinal-laz̲eena ootul-Kitaaba wa yazdaadal-laz̲eena aamanooo eemaanañw-wa laa yartaabal-laz̲eena ootul-Kitaaba walmu'minoona wa liyaqoolal-laz̲eena fee quloobihim maraḍuñw-walkaafiroona maaz̲aaa araadal-laahu bihaaz̲aa mas̲alaa; kaz̲aalika yuḍillul-laahu mañy-yashaaa'u wa yahdee mañy-yashaaa'; wa maa ya'lamu junooda Rabbika illaa Hoo; wa maa hiya illaa z̲ikraa lil-bashar. **(Section 1)**	وَمَا جَعَلْنَآ أَصْحَٰبَ النَّارِ إِلَّا مَلَٰٓئِكَةً ۙ وَمَا جَعَلْنَا عِدَّتَهُمْ إِلَّا فِتْنَةً لِّلَّذِينَ كَفَرُوا لِيَسْتَيْقِنَ الَّذِينَ أُوتُوا الْكِتَٰبَ وَيَزْدَادَ الَّذِينَ آمَنُوٓا إِيمَٰنًا وَلَا يَرْتَابَ الَّذِينَ أُوتُوا الْكِتَٰبَ وَالْمُؤْمِنُونَ ۙ وَلِيَقُولَ الَّذِينَ فِي قُلُوبِهِم مَّرَضٌ وَالْكَٰفِرُونَ مَاذَآ أَرَادَ اللَّهُ بِهَٰذَا مَثَلًا ۚ كَذَٰلِكَ يُضِلُّ اللَّهُ مَن يَشَآءُ وَيَهْدِي مَن يَشَآءُ ۚ وَمَا يَعْلَمُ جُنُودَ رَبِّكَ إِلَّا هُوَ ۚ وَمَا هِيَ إِلَّا ذِكْرَىٰ لِلْبَشَرِ ٣١ ع ١٥
32. No, verily: By the Moon,	32. Kallaa walqamar.	كَلَّا وَالْقَمَرِ ٣٢
33. And by the Night as it retreateth,	33. Wallayli iz̲ adbar.	وَاللَّيْلِ إِذْ أَدْبَرَ ٣٣

Ikhfa اخفاء · Ghunna غُنّہ · Ikhfa Meem Saakin اخفاءمیم ساکن · Idghaam ادغام · Qalqala قلقلہ · Qalb قلب · Idghaam Meem Saakin ادغام میم ساکن

34. And by the Dawn as it shines forth,-	34. Waṣṣub-ḥi izaaa asfar.	وَالصُّبْحِ إِذَآ أَسْفَرَ ٣٤
35. This is but one of the mighty (portents),	35. Innahaa la-iḥdal-kubar.	إِنَّهَا لَإِحْدَى الْكُبَرِ ٣٥
36. A warning to mankind,-	36. Nazeeral-lilbashar.	نَذِيرًا لِّلْبَشَرِ ٣٦
37. To any of you that chooses to press forward, or to follow behind;-	37. Liman shaaa'a minkum añy-yataqaddama aw yata-akhkhar.	لِمَن شَآءَ مِنكُمْ أَن يَتَقَدَّمَ أَوْ يَتَأَخَّرَ ٣٧
38. Every soul will be (held) in pledge for its deeds.	38. Kullu nafsim bimaa kasabat raheenah.	كُلُّ نَفْسٍۭ بِمَا كَسَبَتْ رَهِينَةٌ ٣٨
39. Except the Companions of the Right Hand.	39. Illaaa Aṣ-ḥaabal-Yameen.	إِلَّآ أَصْحَٰبَ الْيَمِينِ ٣٩
40. In garden they will ask one another,	40. Fee Jannaatiñy yatasaaa'aloon.	فِى جَنَّٰتٍ يَتَسَآءَلُونَ ٤٠
41. And (ask) of the Sinners:	41. 'Anil-mujrimeen.	عَنِ الْمُجْرِمِينَ ٤١
42. "What led you into Hell Fire?"	42. Maa salakakum fee saqar.	مَا سَلَكَكُمْ فِى سَقَرَ ٤٢
43. They will say: "We were not of those who prayed;	43. Qaaloo lam naku minal-muṣalleen.	قَالُوا۟ لَمْ نَكُ مِنَ الْمُصَلِّينَ ٤٣
44. "Nor were we of those who fed the indigent;	44. Wa lam naku nuṭ'imul-miskeen.	وَلَمْ نَكُ نُطْعِمُ الْمِسْكِينَ ٤٤
45. "But we used to talk vanities with vain talkers;	45. Wa kunnaa nakhooḍu ma'al-khaaa'iḍeen.	وَكُنَّا نَخُوضُ مَعَ الْخَآئِضِينَ ٤٥
46. "And we used to deny the Day of Judgment,	46. Wa kunnaa nukazzibu bi-Yawmid-Deen.	وَكُنَّا نُكَذِّبُ بِيَوْمِ الدِّينِ ٤٦
47. "Until there came to us (the Hour) that is certain."	47. Ḥattaaa ataanal-yaqeen.	حَتَّىٰٓ أَتَىٰنَا الْيَقِينُ ٤٧
48. The mediation of no mediators will avail them then.	48. Famaa tanfa'uhum shafaa'atush-shaafi'een.	فَمَا تَنفَعُهُمْ شَفَٰعَةُ الشَّٰفِعِينَ ٤٨
49. Why now turn they away from the Admonishment,	49. Famaa lahum 'anit-tazkirati mu'riḍeen.	فَمَا لَهُمْ عَنِ التَّذْكِرَةِ مُعْرِضِينَ ٤٩
50. As if they were affrighted asses,	50. Ka-annahum ḥumurum-mustanfirah.	كَأَنَّهُمْ حُمُرٌ مُّسْتَنفِرَةٌ ٥٠
51. Fleeing from a lion!	51. Farrat min qaswarah.	فَرَّتْ مِن قَسْوَرَةٍ ٥١
52. Forsooth, each one of them wants to be given scrolls (of revelation) spread out!	52. Bal yureedu kullum-ri-'im-minhum añy-yu'taa ṣuḥufam-munashsharah.	بَلْ يُرِيدُ كُلُّ امْرِئٍ مِّنْهُمْ أَن يُؤْتَىٰ صُحُفًا مُّنَشَّرَةً ٥٢
53. By no means! But they fear not the Hereafter,	53. Kallaa bal laa yakhaafoonal-aakhirah.	كَلَّا بَل لَّا يَخَافُونَ الْءَاخِرَةَ ٥٣
54. No, this surely is an admonition:	54. Kallaaa innahoo tazkirah.	كَلَّآ إِنَّهُۥ تَذْكِرَةٌ ٥٤
55. Let any who will, keep it in remembrance!	55. Fa-man shaaa'a zakarah.	فَمَن شَآءَ ذَكَرَهُۥ ٥٥
56. But none will keep it in remembrance except as Allah wills: He is the Lord of Righteousness, and the Lord of Forgiveness.	56. Wa maa yazkuroona illaaa añy-yashaaa'al-laah; Huwa ahlut-taqwaa wa ahlul-maghfirah. **(Section 2)**	وَمَا يَذْكُرُونَ إِلَّآ أَن يَشَآءَ اللَّهُ هُوَ أَهْلُ التَّقْوَىٰ وَأَهْلُ الْمَغْفِرَةِ ٥٦

Ikhfa اخفاء · Ghunna غُنّہ · Ikhfa Meem Saakin اخفاء میم ساکن · Idghaam ادغام · Qalqala قلقلہ · Qalb قلب · Idghaam Meem Saakin ادغام میم ساکن

75. The Resurrection In the name of Allah, Most Gracious, Most Merciful.	Sûrat al-Qiyâmah–75 (Revealed at Makkah) Bismillaahir Raḥmaanir Raḥeem	(٧٥) سُورَةُ القِيٰمَةِ مَكِّيَّةٌ (٣١) بِسۡمِ اللّٰهِ الرَّحۡمٰنِ الرَّحِيۡمِ
1. I do call to witness the Resurrection Day;	1. Laaa uqsimu bi-Yawmil-Qiyaamah.	لَآ أُقۡسِمُ بِيَوۡمِ الۡقِيٰمَةِ ﴿١﴾
2. And I do call to witness the self-reproaching spirit: (eschew Evil).	2. We laaa uqsimu bin-nafsil-lawwaamah.	وَلَآ أُقۡسِمُ بِالنَّفۡسِ اللَّوَّامَةِ ﴿٢﴾
3. Does man think that We cannot assemble his bones?	3. Ayaḥsabul-insaanu al-lan najma‘a ‘iẕaamah.	أَيَحۡسَبُ الۡإِنۡسَانُ أَلَّنۡ نَّجۡمَعَ عِظَامَهٗ ﴿٣﴾
4. Yea, verily. Yea, We are able to restore his very fingers!	4. Balaa qaadireena ‘alaaa an nusawwiya banaanah.	بَلٰى قٰدِرِيۡنَ عَلٰٓى أَنۡ نُّسَوِّيَ بَنَانَهٗ ﴿٤﴾
5. But man would fain deny what is before him.	5. Bal yureedul-insaanu liyafjura amaamah.	بَلۡ يُرِيۡدُ الۡإِنۡسَانُ لِيَفۡجُرَ أَمَامَهٗ ﴿٥﴾
6. He questions: "When is the Day of Resurrection?"	6. Yas'alu ayyaana Yawmul-Qiyaamah.	يَسۡـَٔلُ أَيَّانَ يَوۡمُ الۡقِيٰمَةِ ﴿٦﴾
7. At length, when the sight is dazed,	7. Fa-iẕaa bariqal-baṣar.	فَإِذَا بَرِقَ الۡبَصَرُ ﴿٧﴾
8. And the moon is buried in darkness.	8. We khasafal-qamar.	وَخَسَفَ الۡقَمَرُ ﴿٨﴾
9. And the sun and moon are joined together,-	9. Wa jumi‘ash-shamsu wal-qamar.	وَجُمِعَ الشَّمۡسُ وَالۡقَمَرُ ﴿٩﴾
10. That Day will Man say: "Where is the refuge?"	10. Yaqoolul-insaanu Yawma'iẕin aynal-mafarr.	يَقُوۡلُ الۡإِنۡسَانُ يَوۡمَئِذٍ أَيۡنَ الۡمَفَرُّ ﴿١٠﴾
11. By no means! No place of safety!	11. Kallaa laa wazar.	كَلَّا لَا وَزَرَ ﴿١١﴾
12. Before your Lord (alone), that Day will be the place of rest.	12. Ilaa Rabbika Yawma-'iẕinil-mustaqarr.	إِلٰى رَبِّكَ يَوۡمَئِذِ الۡمُسۡتَقَرُّ ﴿١٢﴾
13. That Day will Man be told (all) that he put forward, and all that he put back.	13. Yunabba'ul-insaanu Yaw-ma'iẕim bimaa qaddama wa akhkhar.	يُنَبَّؤُا الۡإِنۡسَانُ يَوۡمَئِذٍۭ بِمَا قَدَّمَ وَأَخَّرَ ﴿١٣﴾
14. No, man will be evidence against himself,	14. Balil-insaanu ‘alaa naf-sihee baṣeerah.	بَلِ الۡإِنۡسَانُ عَلٰى نَفۡسِهٖ بَصِيۡرَةٌ ﴿١٤﴾
15. Even though he were to put up his excuses.	15. Wa law alqaa ma‘aaẕee-rah.	وَّلَوۡ أَلۡقٰى مَعَاذِيۡرَهٗ ﴿١٥﴾
16. Stir not thy tongue here with to hasten it.	16. Laa tuḥarrik bihee lisaa-naka lita‘jala bih.	لَا تُحَرِّكۡ بِهٖ لِسَانَكَ لِتَعۡجَلَ بِهٖ ﴿١٦﴾
17. It is for Us to collect it and to promulgate it:	17. Inna ‘alaynaa jam‘ahoo wa qur-aanah.	إِنَّ عَلَيۡنَا جَمۡعَهٗ وَقُرۡاٰنَهٗ ﴿١٧﴾
18. And when We read it, follow thou the reading;	18. Fa-iẕaa qaraånaahu fatta-bi‘ qur-aanah.	فَإِذَا قَرَاۡنٰهُ فَاتَّبِعۡ قُرۡاٰنَهٗ ﴿١٨﴾
19. No more, it is for Us to explain it (and make it clear):	19. Summa inna ‘alaynaa bayaanah.	ثُمَّ إِنَّ عَلَيۡنَا بَيَانَهٗ ﴿١٩﴾
20. No, (you men!) but ye love the fleeting life,	20. Kallaa bal tuḥibboonal-‘aajilah.	كَلَّا بَلۡ تُحِبُّوۡنَ الۡعَاجِلَةَ ﴿٢٠﴾
21. And leave alone the Hereafter.	21. Wa taẕaroonal-Aakhirah.	وَتَذَرُوۡنَ الۡاٰخِرَةَ ﴿٢١﴾
22. Some faces, that Day, will beam (in brightness and beauty);-	22. Wujoohuñy-Yawma'iẕin naaḍirah.	وُجُوۡهٌ يَّوۡمَئِذٍ نَّاضِرَةٌ ﴿٢٢﴾

Ikhfa اخفاء | Ghunna غُنّہ | Ikhfa Meem Saakin اخفاء میم ساکن | Idghaam ادغام | Qalqala قلقلہ | Qalb قلب | Idghaam Meem Saakin ادغام میم ساکن

23. Looking towards their Lord;	23. Ilaa Rabbihaa naaẓirah.	إِلَىٰ رَبِّهَا نَاظِرَةٌ ۝٢٣
24. And some faces, that Day, will be sad and dismal,	24. Wa wujoohuñy-Yawma'i-z̲im baasirah.	وَوُجُوهٌ يَوْمَئِذٍۭ بَاسِرَةٌ ۝٢٤
25. Thou wilt know that some great disaster is about to fall on them.	25. Taẓunnu añy-yuf'ala bihaa faaqirah.	تَظُنُّ أَن يُفْعَلَ بِهَا فَاقِرَةٌ ۝٢٥
26. Nay, but when the life cometh up to the throat.	26. Kallaaa iz̲aa balaghatit-taraaqee.	كَلَّآ إِذَا بَلَغَتِ التَّرَاقِيَ ۝٢٦
27. And men say: Whereis the wizard (who can save him now)?	27. Wa qeela man raaq.	وَقِيلَ مَنْ ۜ رَاقٍ ۝٢٧
28. And he will conclude that it was (the Time) of Parting;	28. Wa ẓanna annahul-firaaq.	وَظَنَّ أَنَّهُ الْفِرَاقُ ۝٢٨
29. And one leg will be joined with another:	29. Waltaffatis-saaqu bissaaq.	وَالْتَفَّتِ السَّاقُ بِالسَّاقِ ۝٢٩
30. That Day the Drive will be (all) to your Lord!	30. Ilaa Rabbika Yawma'i-z̲inil-masaaq. **(Section 1)**	إِلَىٰ رَبِّكَ يَوْمَئِذٍ الْمَسَاقُ ۝٣٠
31. So he gave nothing in charity, nor did he pray!-	31. Falaa ṣaddaqa wa laa ṣallaa.	فَلَا صَدَّقَ وَلَا صَلَّىٰ ۝٣١
32. But on the contrary, he rejected Truth and turned away!	32. Wa laakin kaz̲z̲aba wa tawallaa.	وَلَٰكِن كَذَّبَ وَتَوَلَّىٰ ۝٣٢
33. Then did he stalk to his family in full conceit!	33. S̲umma z̲ahaba ilaaa ahlihee yatamaṭṭaa.	ثُمَّ ذَهَبَ إِلَىٰٓ أَهْلِهِۦ يَتَمَطَّىٰٓ ۝٣٣
34. Woe to you, (O men!), yes, woe!	34. Awlaa laka fa-awlaa.	أَوْلَىٰ لَكَ فَأَوْلَىٰ ۝٣٤
35. Again, Woe to thee, (O men!), yes, woe!	35. S̲umma awlaa laka fa-awlaa.	ثُمَّ أَوْلَىٰ لَكَ فَأَوْلَىٰٓ ۝٣٥
36. Thinketh man that he is to be left aimless?	36. Ayaḥsabul-insaanu añy-yutraka sudaa.	أَيَحْسَبُ الْإِنسَٰنُ أَن يُتْرَكَ سُدًى ۝٣٦
37. Was he not a drop of sperm emitted (in lowly form)?	37. Alam yaku nuṭfatam-mim-maniyyiñy-yumnaa.	أَلَمْ يَكُ نُطْفَةً مِّن مَّنِيٍّ يُمْنَىٰ ۝٣٧
38. Then he became a clot; then (Allah) shaped and fashioned,	38. S̲umma kaana 'alaqatan fakhalaqa fasawwaa.	ثُمَّ كَانَ عَلَقَةً فَخَلَقَ فَسَوَّىٰ ۝٣٨
39. And of him He made two sexes, male and female.	39. Faja'ala minhuz-zawjayniz̲-z̲akara wal-uns̲aa.	فَجَعَلَ مِنْهُ الزَّوْجَيْنِ الذَّكَرَ وَالْأُنثَىٰٓ ۝٣٩
40. Has not He, (the same), the power to give life to the dead.	40. Alaysa z̲aalika biqaadirin 'alaaa añy-yuḥyiyal-mawtaa. **(Section 2)**	أَلَيْسَ ذَٰلِكَ بِقَٰدِرٍ عَلَىٰٓ أَن يُحْـِۧىَ الْمَوْتَىٰ ۝٤٠

76. Time; or Man

In the name of Allah, Most Gracious, Most Merciful.

Sûrat ad-Dahr; al-Insân–76

(Revealed at Madinah)

Bismillaahir Raḥmaanir Raḥeem

(٧٦) سُورَةُ الدَّهْرِ مَدَنِيَّةٌ (٩٨)

بِسْمِ اللَّهِ الرَّحْمَٰنِ الرَّحِيمِ

1. Has there not been over Man a long period of Time, when he was nothing - (not even) mentioned?	1. Hal ataa 'alal-insaani ḥeenum-minad-dahri lam yakun shay'am maz̲kooraa.	هَلْ أَتَىٰ عَلَى الْإِنسَٰنِ حِينٌ مِّنَ الدَّهْرِ لَمْ يَكُن شَيْـًٔا مَّذْكُورًا ۝١
2. Verily We created Man from a drop of mingled sperm, in order to try him: So We gave him (the gifts), of Hearing and	2. Innaa khalaqnal-insaana min-nuṭfatin amshaajin nabtaleehi faja'alnaahu samee'am-	إِنَّا خَلَقْنَا الْإِنسَٰنَ مِن نُّطْفَةٍ أَمْشَاجٍ نَّبْتَلِيهِ فَجَعَلْنَٰهُ سَمِيعًۢا

Ikhfa اخفاء · Ghunna غُنّہ · Ikhfa Meem Saakin اخفاء میم ساکن · Idghaam ادغام · Qalqala قلقلہ · Qalb قلب · Idghaam Meem Saakin ادغام میم ساکن

Sight.	baṣeeraa.	بَصِيرًا ۝٢
3. We showed him the Way: whether he be grateful or ungrateful (rests on his will).	3. Innaa hadaynaahus-sabeela immaa shaakirañw-wa immaa kafooraa.	إِنَّا هَدَيْنٰهُ السَّبِيلَ إِمَّا شَاكِرًا وَّإِمَّا كَفُورًا ۝٣
4. For the Rejecters We have prepared chains, yokes, and a blazing Fire.	4. Innaaa a'tadnaa lilkaafireena salaasila wa aghlaalañw-wa sa'eeraa.	إِنَّآ أَعْتَدْنَا لِلْكٰفِرِينَ سَلٰسِلَا۟ وَأَغْلٰلًا وَّسَعِيرًا ۝٤
5. As to the Righteous, they shall drink of a Cup (of Wine) mixed with Kafur,-	5. Innal-abraara yashraboona min kaåsin kaana mizaajuhaa kaafooraa.	إِنَّ الْأَبْرَارَ يَشْرَبُونَ مِن كَأْسٍ كَانَ مِزَاجُهَا كَافُورًا ۝٥
6. A Fountain where the Devotees of Allah do drink, making it flow in unstinted abundance.	6. 'Aynañy-yashrabu bihaa 'ibaadul-laahi yufajjiroonahaa tafjeeraa.	عَيْنًا يَّشْرَبُ بِهَا عِبَادُ اللّٰهِ يُفَجِّرُونَهَا تَفْجِيرًا ۝٦
7. They perform (their) vows, and they fear a Day whose evil flies far and wide.	7. Yoofoona binnazri wa yakhaafoona yawman kaana sharruhoo mustaṭeeraa.	يُوفُونَ بِالنَّذْرِ وَيَخَافُونَ يَوْمًا كَانَ شَرُّهُ مُسْتَطِيرًا ۝٧
8. And they feed, for the love of Allah, the indigent, the orphan, and the captive,-	8. Wa yuṭ'imoonaṭ-ṭa'aama 'alaa ḥubbihee miskeenañw-wa yateemañw-wa aseeraa.	وَيُطْعِمُونَ الطَّعَامَ عَلٰى حُبِّهِ مِسْكِينًا وَّيَتِيمًا وَّأَسِيرًا ۝٨
9. (Saying),"We feed you for the sake of Allah alone: no reward do we desire from you, nor thanks.	9. Innamaa nuṭ'imukum liwajhil-laahi laa nureedu minkum jazaaa'añw-wa laa shukooraa.	إِنَّمَا نُطْعِمُكُمْ لِوَجْهِ اللّٰهِ لَا نُرِيدُ مِنكُمْ جَزَآءً وَّلَا شُكُورًا ۝٩
10. "We only fear a Day of distressful Wrath from the side of our Lord."	10. Innaa nakhaafu mir-Rabbinaa Yawman 'aboosan qamṭareeraa.	إِنَّا نَخَافُ مِن رَّبِّنَا يَوْمًا عَبُوسًا قَمْطَرِيرًا ۝١٠
11. But Allah will deliver them from the evil of that Day, and will shed over them a Light of Beauty and (blissful) Joy.	11. Fa-waqaahumul-laahu sharra zaalikal-Yawmi wa laqqaahum naḍratañw-wa surooraa.	فَوَقٰىهُمُ اللّٰهُ شَرَّ ذٰلِكَ الْيَوْمِ وَلَقّٰىهُمْ نَضْرَةً وَّسُرُورًا ۝١١
12. And hath awarded them for all that they endured, a Garden and silk attire;	12. Wa jazaahum bimaa ṣabaroo Jannatañw-wa ḥareeraa.	وَجَزٰىهُم بِمَا صَبَرُوا جَنَّةً وَّحَرِيرًا ۝١٢
13. Reclining in the (Garden) on raised thrones, they will see there neither the sun's (excessive heat) nor (the moon's) excessive cold.	13. Muttaki'eena feehaa 'alal-araaa'iki laa yarawna feehaa shamsañw-wa laa zamhareeraa.	مُّتَّكِـِٔينَ فِيهَا عَلَى الْأَرَآئِكِ لَا يَرَوْنَ فِيهَا شَمْسًا وَّلَا زَمْهَرِيرًا ۝١٣
14. And the shades of the (Garden) will come low over them, and the bunch (of fruit), there, will hang low in humility.	14. Wa daaniyatan 'alayhim ẓilaaluhaa wa zullilat quṭoofuhaa tazleelaa.	وَدَانِيَةً عَلَيْهِمْ ظِلٰلُهَا وَذُلِّلَتْ قُطُوفُهَا تَذْلِيلًا ۝١٤
15. And amongst them will be passed round vessels of silver and goblets of crystal,-	15. Wa yuṭaafu 'alayhim bi-aaniyatim-min fiḍḍatiñw-wa akwaabin kaanat qawaareeraa.	وَيُطَافُ عَلَيْهِم بِـَٔانِيَةٍ مِّن فِضَّةٍ وَّأَكْوَابٍ كَانَتْ قَوَارِيرَا۟ ۝١٥

قرأ حفص بغير الألف في الوصل فيهما ووقف على الأول بالألف وعلى الثاني بغير الألف ١٢

Ikhfa اخفاء | Ghunna غنّہ | Ikhfa Meem Saakin اخفاء میم ساکن | Idghaam ادغام | Qalqala قلقلہ | Qalb قلب | Idghaam Meem Saakin ادغام میم ساکن

16. Crystal-clear, made of silver: they will determine the measure thereof (according to their wishes).

16. Qawaareera min fiḍḍatin qaddaroohaa taqdeeraa.

قَوَارِيْرَا۠ مِنْ فِضَّةٍ قَدَّرُوْهَا
تَقْدِيْرًا ﴿١٦﴾

17. And they will be given to drink there of a Cup (of Wine) mixed with Zanjabil,-

17. Wa yusqawna feehaa kaå-san kaana mizaajuhaa zanja-beelaa.

وَيُسْقَوْنَ فِيْهَا كَاْسًا كَانَ
مِزَاجُهَا زَنْجَبِيْلًا ﴿١٧﴾

18. A fountain there, called Salsabil.

18. 'Aynan feehaa tusammaa salsabeelaa.

عَيْنًا فِيْهَا تُسَمّٰى سَلْسَبِيْلًا ﴿١٨﴾

19. And round about them will (serve) youths of perpetual (freshness): If you see them, you would think them scattered Pearls.

19. Wa yaṭoofu 'alayhim wildaanum-mukhalladoona izaa ra-aytahum ḥasibtahum lu'lu'am-mansooraa.

وَيَطُوْفُ عَلَيْهِمْ وِلْدَانٌ مُّخَلَّدُوْنَ
اِذَا رَاَيْتَهُمْ حَسِبْتَهُمْ لُؤْلُؤًا
مَّنْثُوْرًا ﴿١٩﴾

20. And when you look, it is there you will see a Bliss and a Realm Magnificent.

20. Wa izaa ra-ayta samma ra-ayta na'eemañw-wa mulkan kabeeraa.

وَاِذَا رَاَيْتَ ثَمَّ رَاَيْتَ نَعِيْمًا وَّ
مُلْكًا كَبِيْرًا ﴿٢٠﴾

21. Upon them will be green Garments of fine silk and heavy brocade, and they will be adorned with Bracelets of silver; and their Lord will give to them to drink of a Wine Pure and Holy.

21. 'Aaliyahum siyaabu sun-dusin khuḍruñw-wa istabraq, wa ḥullooo asaawira min fiḍḍatiñw wa saqaahum Rab-buhum sharaaban ṭahooraa.

عٰلِيَهُمْ ثِيَابُ سُنْدُسٍ خُضْرٌ وَّ
اِسْتَبْرَقٌ وَّحُلُّوْٓا اَسَاوِرَ مِنْ فِضَّةٍ
وَسَقٰىهُمْ رَبُّهُمْ شَرَابًا طَهُوْرًا ﴿٢١﴾

22. "Verily this is a Reward for you, and your Endeavour is accepted and recognised."

22. Inna haazaa kaana lakum jazaaa'añw-wa kaana sa'yukum mashkooraa. **(Section 1)**

اِنَّ هٰذَا كَانَ لَكُمْ جَزَآءً وَّكَانَ
سَعْيُكُمْ مَّشْكُوْرًا ﴿٢٢﴾ ع

ع ٢٢ ١٩

23. It is We Who have sent down the Qur'an to you by stages.

23. Innaa Naḥnu nazzalnaa 'alaykal-Qur-aana tanzeelaa.

اِنَّا نَحْنُ نَزَّلْنَا عَلَيْكَ الْقُرْاٰنَ
تَنْزِيْلًا ﴿٢٣﴾

24. Therefore, be patient with constancy to the Command of your Lord, and hearken not to the sinner or the ingrate among them.

24. Faṣbir liḥukmi Rabbika wa laa tuṭi' minhum aasiman aw kafooraa.

فَاصْبِرْ لِحُكْمِ رَبِّكَ وَلَا تُطِعْ
مِنْهُمْ اٰثِمًا اَوْ كَفُوْرًا ﴿٢٤﴾

25. And celebrate the name of your Lord morning and evening,

25. Wazkuris-ma Rabbika bukratañw-wa aṣeelaa.

وَاذْكُرِ اسْمَ رَبِّكَ بُكْرَةً وَّاَصِيْلًا ﴿٢٥﴾

26. And part of the night, prostrate yourself to Him; and glorify Him a long night through.

26. Wa minal-layli fasjud lahoo wa sabbiḥhu laylan ṭaweelaa.

وَمِنَ الَّيْلِ فَاسْجُدْ لَهٗ وَسَبِّحْهُ
لَيْلًا طَوِيْلًا ﴿٢٦﴾

27. As to these, they love the fleeting life, and put away behind them a Day (that will be) hard.

27. Inna haaa'ulaaa'i yuḥib-boonal-'aajilata wa yazaroona waraaa'ahum Yawman saqee-laa.

اِنَّ هٰٓؤُلَآءِ يُحِبُّوْنَ الْعَاجِلَةَ وَ
يَذَرُوْنَ وَرَآءَهُمْ يَوْمًا ثَقِيْلًا ﴿٢٧﴾

28. It is We Who created them, and We have made their joints strong; but, when We will, We can substitute the like of them by a complete change.

28. Naḥnu khalaqnaahum wa shadadnaaa asrahum wa izaa shi'naa baddalnaaa amsaala-hum tabdeelaa.

نَحْنُ خَلَقْنٰهُمْ وَشَدَدْنَآ اَسْرَهُمْ وَ
اِذَا شِئْنَا بَدَّلْنَآ اَمْثَالَهُمْ تَبْدِيْلًا ﴿٢٨﴾

Ikhfa اخفاء | Ghunna غُنّہ | Ikhfa Meem Saakin اخفاء میم ساکن | Idghaam ادغام | Qalqala قلقلہ | Qalb قلب | Idghaam Meem Saakin ادغام میم ساکن

29. This is an admonition: Whosoever will, let him take a (straight) Path to his Lord.

30. But you will not, except as Allah wills; for Allah is full of Knowledge and Wisdom.

31. He will admit to His Mercy whom He will; But the wrong-doers,- for them has He prepared a grievous Chastisement.

77. Those Sent Forth

In the name of Allah, Most Gracious, Most Merciful.

1. By the emissary winds, (sent) one after another

2. Which then blow violently in tempestuous Gusts,

3. And scatter (things) far and wide;

4. Then separate them, one from another,

5. Then spread abroad a Message,

6. Whether of Justification or of Warning;-

7. Assuredly, what you are promised must come to pass.

8. Then when the stars become dim;

9. When the heaven is cleft asunder;

10. When the mountains are scattered (to the winds) as dust;

11. And when the time fixed for the gathering of all Apostles comes.

12. For what Day are these (portents) deferred?

13. For the Day of Sorting out.

14. And what will explain to you what is the Day of Sorting out?

15. Ah woe, that Day, to the Rejecters of Truth!

16. Did We not destroy the men of old (for their evil)?

17. So shall We make later (generations) follow them.

18. Thus do We deal with men of sin.

29. Inna haazihee tazkiratun fa-man shaaa'at-takhaza ilaa Rabbihee sabeelaa.

30. Wa maa tashaaa'oona illaaa añy-yashaaa'al-laah; innal-laaha kaana 'Aleeman Ḥakeemaa.

31. Yudkhilu mañy-yashaaa'u fee raḥmatih; waẓẓaalimeena a'adda lahum 'azaaban aleemaa.

(Section 2)

Sûrat al-Mursalât–77

(Revealed at Makkah)

Bismillaahir Raḥmaanir Raḥeem

1. Wal-mursalaati 'urfaa.

2. Fal-'aaṣifaati 'aṣfaa.

3. Wannaashiraati nashraa.

4. Falfaariqaati farqaa.

5. Falmulqiyaati zikraa.

6. 'Uzran aw nuzraa.

7. Innamaa too'adoona lawaaqi'.

8. Fa-izan-nujoomu ṭumisat.

9. Wa izas-samaaa'u furijat.

10. Wa izal-jibaalu nusifat.

11. Wa izar-Rusulu uqqitat.

12. Li-ayyi Yawmin ujjilat.

13. Li-Yawmil-Faṣl.

14. Wa maaa adraaka maa Yawmul-Faṣl.

15. Wayluñy-Yawma'izil-lilmukazzibeen.

16. Alam nuhlikil-awwaleen.

17. Summa nutbi'uhumul-aakhireen.

18. Kazaalika naf'alu bilmujrimeen.

إِنَّ هَٰذِهِۦ تَذْكِرَةٌ ۖ فَمَن شَآءَ
ٱتَّخَذَ إِلَىٰ رَبِّهِۦ سَبِيلًا ﴿٢٩﴾
وَمَا تَشَآءُونَ إِلَّآ أَن يَشَآءَ ٱللَّهُ ۚ
إِنَّ ٱللَّهَ كَانَ عَلِيمًا حَكِيمًا ﴿٣٠﴾
يُدْخِلُ مَن يَشَآءُ فِى رَحْمَتِهِۦ ۚ وَ
ٱلظَّٰلِمِينَ أَعَدَّ لَهُمْ عَذَابًا أَلِيمًا ﴿٣١﴾ ع

(٧٧) سُورَةُ ٱلْمُرْسَلَٰتِ مَكِّيَّةٌ (٣٣)

بِسْمِ ٱللَّهِ ٱلرَّحْمَٰنِ ٱلرَّحِيمِ

وَٱلْمُرْسَلَٰتِ عُرْفًا ﴿١﴾
فَٱلْعَٰصِفَٰتِ عَصْفًا ﴿٢﴾
وَٱلنَّٰشِرَٰتِ نَشْرًا ﴿٣﴾
فَٱلْفَٰرِقَٰتِ فَرْقًا ﴿٤﴾
فَٱلْمُلْقِيَٰتِ ذِكْرًا ﴿٥﴾
عُذْرًا أَوْ نُذْرًا ﴿٦﴾
إِنَّمَا تُوعَدُونَ لَوَٰقِعٌ ﴿٧﴾
فَإِذَا ٱلنُّجُومُ طُمِسَتْ ﴿٨﴾
وَإِذَا ٱلسَّمَآءُ فُرِجَتْ ﴿٩﴾
وَإِذَا ٱلْجِبَالُ نُسِفَتْ ﴿١٠﴾
وَإِذَا ٱلرُّسُلُ أُقِّتَتْ ﴿١١﴾
لِأَىِّ يَوْمٍ أُجِّلَتْ ﴿١٢﴾
لِيَوْمِ ٱلْفَصْلِ ﴿١٣﴾
وَمَآ أَدْرَىٰكَ مَا يَوْمُ ٱلْفَصْلِ ﴿١٤﴾
وَيْلٌ يَوْمَئِذٍ لِّلْمُكَذِّبِينَ ﴿١٥﴾
أَلَمْ نُهْلِكِ ٱلْأَوَّلِينَ ﴿١٦﴾
ثُمَّ نُتْبِعُهُمُ ٱلْءَاخِرِينَ ﴿١٧﴾
كَذَٰلِكَ نَفْعَلُ بِٱلْمُجْرِمِينَ ﴿١٨﴾

Ikhfa اخفاء · Ghunna غُنّہ · Ikhfa Meem Saakin اخفاء میم ساکن · Idghaam ادغام · Qalqala قلقله · Qalb قلب · Idghaam Meem Saakin ادغام میم ساکن

19. Ah, woe that Day, to the Rejecters of Truth!
20. Have We not created you from a fluid (held) despicable?
21. The which We placed in a place of rest, firmly fixed,
22. For a period (of gestation), determined (according to need)?
23. For We do determine (according to need); for We are the Best to determine (things).
24. Ah woe, that Day! to the Rejecters of Truth!
25. Have we not made the earth a receptacle.
26. The living and the dead,
27. And made therein mountains standing firm, lofty (in stature); and provided for you water sweet (and wholesome)?
28. Ah woe, that Day, to the Rejecters of Truth!
29. (It will be said:) "Depart you to that which you used to reject as false!
30. Depart unto the shadow falling threefold.
31. (Which yet is) no relief nor shelter from the flame.
32. "Indeed it throws about sparks (huge) as Forts,
33. (Or) as it might be camels of bright yellow hue.
34. Ah woe, that Day, to the Rejecters of Truth!
35. That will be a Day when they shall not be able to speak.
36. Nor will it be open to them to put forth pleas.
37. Ah woe, that Day, to the Rejecters of Truth!
38. That will be a Day of Sorting out! We shall gather you together and those before (you)!
39. Now, if you have a trick (or plot), use it against Me!
40. Ah woe, that Day, to the Rejecters of Truth!
41. Lo! Those who kept their duty are amid shade and fountains,
42. And (they shall have) fruits,- all they desire.

19. Wayluñy-Yawma'izil-lil-mukazzibeen.
20. Alam nakhlukkum mim-maaa'im-maheen.
21. Faja'alnaahu fee qaraa-rim-makeen.
22. Ilaa qadarim-ma'loom.
23. Faqadarnaa fani'mal-qaadiroon.
24. Wayluñy-Yawma'izil-lilmukazzibeen.
25. Alam naj'alil-arḍa kifaataa.
26. Aḥyaaa'añw-wa amwaataa.
27. Wa ja'alnaa feehaa ra-waasiya shaamikhaatiñw-wa asqaynaakum maaa'an furaataa.
28. Wayluñy-Yawma'izil-lilmukazzibeen.
29. Inṭaliqooo ilaa maa kuntum bihee tukazziboon.
30. Inṭaliqooo ilaa ẓillin zee salaasi shu'ab.
31. Laa ẓaleeliñw-wa laa yughnee minal-lahab.
32. Innahaa tarmee bishararin kalqaṣr.
33. Ka-annahoo jimaalatun ṣufr.
34. Wayluñy-Yawma'izil-lilmukazzibeen.
35. Haazaa Yawmu laa yanṭiqoon.
36. Wa laa yu'zanu lahum fa-ya'taziroon.
37. Wayluñy-Yawma'izil-lilmukazzibeen.
38. Haazaa Yawmul-Faṣli jama'naakum wal-awwaleen.
39. Fa-in kaana lakum kay-dun fakeedoon.
40. Wayluñy-Yawma'izil-lilmukazzibeen. **(Section 1)**
41. Innal-muttaqeena fee ẓilaaliñw-wa 'uyoon.
42. Wa fawaakiha mimmaa yashtahoon.

وَيْلٌ يَّوْمَئِذٍ لِّلْمُكَذِّبِيْنَ ﴿١٩﴾
أَلَمْ نَخْلُقكُّم مِّنْ مَّآءٍ مَّهِيْنٍ ﴿٢٠﴾
فَجَعَلْنٰهُ فِيْ قَرَارٍ مَّكِيْنٍ ﴿٢١﴾
إِلٰى قَدَرٍ مَّعْلُوْمٍ ﴿٢٢﴾
فَقَدَرْنَا ۖ فَنِعْمَ الْقٰدِرُوْنَ ﴿٢٣﴾
وَيْلٌ يَّوْمَئِذٍ لِّلْمُكَذِّبِيْنَ ﴿٢٤﴾
أَلَمْ نَجْعَلِ الْأَرْضَ كِفَاتًا ﴿٢٥﴾
أَحْيَآءً وَّأَمْوَاتًا ﴿٢٦﴾
وَّجَعَلْنَا فِيْهَا رَوَاسِيَ شٰمِخٰتٍ وَّ
أَسْقَيْنٰكُمْ مَّآءً فُرَاتًا ﴿٢٧﴾
وَيْلٌ يَّوْمَئِذٍ لِّلْمُكَذِّبِيْنَ ﴿٢٨﴾
اِنْطَلِقُوْٓا إِلٰى مَا كُنْتُمْ بِهٖ تُكَذِّبُوْنَ ﴿٢٩﴾
اِنْطَلِقُوْٓا إِلٰى ظِلٍّ ذِيْ ثَلٰثِ شُعَبٍ ﴿٣٠﴾
لَّا ظَلِيْلٍ وَّلَا يُغْنِيْ مِنَ اللَّهَبِ ﴿٣١﴾
إِنَّهَا تَرْمِيْ بِشَرَرٍ كَالْقَصْرِ ﴿٣٢﴾
كَأَنَّهٗ جِمٰلَتٌ صُفْرٌ ﴿٣٣﴾
وَيْلٌ يَّوْمَئِذٍ لِّلْمُكَذِّبِيْنَ ﴿٣٤﴾
هٰذَا يَوْمُ لَا يَنْطِقُوْنَ ﴿٣٥﴾
وَلَا يُؤْذَنُ لَهُمْ فَيَعْتَذِرُوْنَ ﴿٣٦﴾
وَيْلٌ يَّوْمَئِذٍ لِّلْمُكَذِّبِيْنَ ﴿٣٧﴾
هٰذَا يَوْمُ الْفَصْلِ ۚ جَمَعْنٰكُمْ وَ
الْأَوَّلِيْنَ ﴿٣٨﴾
فَإِنْ كَانَ لَكُمْ كَيْدٌ فَكِيْدُوْنِ ﴿٣٩﴾
وَيْلٌ يَّوْمَئِذٍ لِّلْمُكَذِّبِيْنَ ﴿٤٠﴾ ع
إِنَّ الْمُتَّقِيْنَ فِيْ ظِلٰلٍ وَّعُيُوْنٍ ﴿٤١﴾
وَّفَوَاكِهَ مِمَّا يَشْتَهُوْنَ ﴿٤٢﴾

Ikhfa اخفاء | Ghunna غنّہ | Ikhfa Meem Saakin اخفاء میم ساکن | Idghaam ادغام | Qalqala قلقلہ | Qalb قلب | Idghaam Meem Saakin ادغام میم ساکن

43. "Eat ye and drink ye to your heart's content: for that you worked (Righteousness).

44. Thus do We certainly reward the Doers of Good.

45. Ah woe, that Day, to the Rejecters of Truth!

46. (O you unjust!) Eat ye and enjoy yourselves (but) a little while, for that ye are Sinners.

47. Ah woe, that Day, to the Rejecters of Truth!

48. When it is said unto them: Bow down, they bow not down!

49. Ah woe, that Day, to the Rejecters of Truth!

50. Then what Message, after that, will they believe in?

78. The (Great) News

In the name of Allah, Most Gracious, Most Merciful.

1. Concerning what are they disputing?

2. Concerning the Great News,

3. About which they cannot agree.

4. Verily, they shall soon (come to) know!

5. Verily, verily they shall soon (come to) know!

6. Have We not made the earth as a wide expanse,

7. And the mountains as pegs?

8. And (have We not) created you in pairs,

9. And made your sleep for rest,

10. And made the night as a covering,

11. And made the day as a means of subsistence?

12. And (have We not) built over you the seven firmaments,

13. And placed (therein) a Light of Splendour?

14. And do We not send down from the clouds water in abundance,

43. Kuloo washraboo haneee-'am bimaa kuntum ta'maloon.

44. Innaa kazaalika najzil-muḥsineen.

45. Wayluñy-Yawma'izil-lilmukazzibeen.

46. Kuloo wa tamatta'oo qaleelan innakum mujrimoon.

47. Waylunñy-Yawma'izil-lilmukazzibeen.

48. Wa izaa qeela lahumur-ka'oo laa yarka'oon.

49. Waylunñy-Yawma'izil-lilmukazzibeen.

50. Fabi-ayyi ḥadeesim ba'-dahoo yu'minoon. **(Section 2)**

Sûrat an-Naba'–78

(Revealed at Makkah)

Bismillaahir Raḥmaanir Raḥeem

1. 'Amma yatasaaa'aloon.

2. 'Anin-naba-il-'azeem.

3. Allazee hum feehi mukh-talifoon.

4. Kallaa sa-ya'lamoon.

5. Summa kallaa sa-ya'la-moon.

6. Alam naj'alil-arḍa mi-haadaa.

7. Wal-jibaala awtaadaa.

8. Wa khalaqnaakum az-waajaa.

9. Wa ja'alnaa nawmakum subaataa.

10. Wa ja'alnal-layla libaa-saa.

11. Wa ja'alnan-nahaara ma'aashaa.

12. Wa banaynaa fawqakum sab'an shidaadaa.

13. Wa ja'alnaa siraajañw-wahhaajaa.

14. Wa anzalnaa minal-mu'-ṣiraati maaa'an sajjaajaa.

كُلُوا وَاشْرَبُوا هَنِيٓـًٔا بِمَا كُنتُمْ تَعْمَلُونَ ﴿٤٣﴾

إِنَّا كَذَٰلِكَ نَجْزِى الْمُحْسِنِينَ ﴿٤٤﴾

وَيْلٌ يَوْمَئِذٍ لِّلْمُكَذِّبِينَ ﴿٤٥﴾

كُلُوا وَتَمَتَّعُوا قَلِيلًا إِنَّكُم مُّجْرِمُونَ ﴿٤٦﴾

وَيْلٌ يَوْمَئِذٍ لِّلْمُكَذِّبِينَ ﴿٤٧﴾

وَإِذَا قِيلَ لَهُمُ ارْكَعُوا لَا يَرْكَعُونَ ﴿٤٨﴾

وَيْلٌ يَوْمَئِذٍ لِّلْمُكَذِّبِينَ ﴿٤٩﴾

فَبِأَيِّ حَدِيثٍ بَعْدَهُ يُؤْمِنُونَ ﴿٥٠﴾ ع

(٧٨) سُورَةُ النَّبَإِ مَكِّيَّةٌ (٨٠)

بِسْمِ اللَّهِ الرَّحْمَٰنِ الرَّحِيمِ

عَمَّ يَتَسَاءَلُونَ ﴿١﴾

عَنِ النَّبَإِ الْعَظِيمِ ﴿٢﴾

الَّذِي هُمْ فِيهِ مُخْتَلِفُونَ ﴿٣﴾

كَلَّا سَيَعْلَمُونَ ﴿٤﴾

ثُمَّ كَلَّا سَيَعْلَمُونَ ﴿٥﴾

أَلَمْ نَجْعَلِ الْأَرْضَ مِهَادًا ﴿٦﴾

وَالْجِبَالَ أَوْتَادًا ﴿٧﴾

وَخَلَقْنَاكُمْ أَزْوَاجًا ﴿٨﴾

وَجَعَلْنَا نَوْمَكُمْ سُبَاتًا ﴿٩﴾

وَجَعَلْنَا اللَّيْلَ لِبَاسًا ﴿١٠﴾

وَجَعَلْنَا النَّهَارَ مَعَاشًا ﴿١١﴾

وَبَنَيْنَا فَوْقَكُمْ سَبْعًا شِدَادًا ﴿١٢﴾

وَجَعَلْنَا سِرَاجًا وَهَّاجًا ﴿١٣﴾

وَأَنزَلْنَا مِنَ الْمُعْصِرَاتِ مَاءً ثَجَّاجًا ﴿١٤﴾

الجزء الثلثون (٣٠)

Translation	Transliteration	Arabic
15. That We may produce therewith corn and vegetables,	15. Linukhrija bihee ḥabbañw-wa nabaataa.	لِّنُخْرِجَ بِهِۦ حَبًّا وَنَبَاتًا ١٥
16. And gardens of luxurious growth?	16. Wa jannaatin alfaafaa.	وَجَنَّٰتٍ أَلْفَافًا ١٦
17. Verily the Day of Sorting out is a thing appointed,	17. Inna Yawmal-Faṣli kaana meeqaataa.	إِنَّ يَوْمَ ٱلْفَصْلِ كَانَ مِيقَٰتًا ١٧
18. The Day that the Trumpet shall be sounded, and you will come forth in crowds;	18. Yawma yunfakhu fiṣ-Ṣoori fataâtoona afwaajaa.	يَوْمَ يُنفَخُ فِى ٱلصُّورِ فَتَأْتُونَ أَفْوَاجًا ١٨
19. And the heavens shall be opened as if there were doors,	19. Wa futiḥatis-samaaa'u fakaanat abwaabaa.	وَفُتِحَتِ ٱلسَّمَآءُ فَكَانَتْ أَبْوَٰبًا ١٩
20. And the mountains shall vanish, as if they were a mirage.	20. Wa suyyiratil-jibaalu fakaanat saraabaa.	وَسُيِّرَتِ ٱلْجِبَالُ فَكَانَتْ سَرَابًا ٢٠
21. Truly Hell is as a place of ambush,	21. Inna Jahannama kaanat mirṣaadaa.	إِنَّ جَهَنَّمَ كَانَتْ مِرْصَادًا ٢١
22. For the transgressors a place of destination:	22. Liṭṭaagheena ma-aabaa.	لِّلطَّٰغِينَ مَـَٔابًا ٢٢
23. They will dwell therein for ages.	23. Laabiseena feehaaa aḥqaabaa.	لَّٰبِثِينَ فِيهَآ أَحْقَابًا ٢٣
24. Nothing cool shall they taste therein, nor any drink,	24. Laa yazooqoona feehaa bardañw-wa laa sharaabaa.	لَّا يَذُوقُونَ فِيهَا بَرْدًا وَلَا شَرَابًا ٢٤
25. Save boiling water and a paralysing cold:	25. Illaa ḥameemañw-wa ghas-saaqaa.	إِلَّا حَمِيمًا وَغَسَّاقًا ٢٥
26. A fitting recompense (for them).	26. Jazaaa'añw-wifaaqaa.	جَزَآءً وِفَاقًا ٢٦
27. For lo! They looked not for a reckoning.	27. Innahum kaanoo laa yar-joona ḥisaabaa.	إِنَّهُمْ كَانُوا۟ لَا يَرْجُونَ حِسَابًا ٢٧
28. But they (impudently) treated Our Signs as false.	28. Wa kazzaboo bi-Aayaa-tinaa kizzaabaa.	وَكَذَّبُوا۟ بِـَٔايَٰتِنَا كِذَّابًا ٢٨
29. And all things have We preserved on record.	29. Wa kulla shay'in aḥṣay-naahu kitaabaa.	وَكُلَّ شَىْءٍ أَحْصَيْنَٰهُ كِتَٰبًا ٢٩
30. So taste (of that which ye have earned). No increase do We give you save of torment.	30. Fazooqoo falan nazee-dakum illaa 'azaabaa. **(Section 1)**	فَذُوقُوا۟ فَلَن نَّزِيدَكُمْ إِلَّا عَذَابًا ٣٠ ع
31. Lo! For the duteous is achievement—	31. Inna lilmuttaqeena ma-faazaa.	إِنَّ لِلْمُتَّقِينَ مَفَازًا ٣١
32. Gardens enclosed, and grapevines;	32. Ḥadaaa'iqa wa a'naabaa.	حَدَآئِقَ وَأَعْنَٰبًا ٣٢
33. Companions of equal age;	33. Wa kawaa'iba atraabaa.	وَكَوَاعِبَ أَتْرَابًا ٣٣
34. And a cup full (to the brim).	34. Wa kaâsan dihaaqaa.	وَكَأْسًا دِهَاقًا ٣٤
35. No loose talk shall they hear therein, nor Untruth:-	35. Laa yasma'oona feehaa laghwañw-wa laa kizzaabaa.	لَّا يَسْمَعُونَ فِيهَا لَغْوًا وَلَا كِذَّٰبًا ٣٥
36. Recompense from your Lord, a gift, (amply) sufficient,	36. Jazaaa'am-mir-Rabbika 'aṭaaa'an ḥisaabaa.	جَزَآءً مِّن رَّبِّكَ عَطَآءً حِسَابًا ٣٦
37. Lord of the heavens and the earth, and (all) that is between them, the Beneficent; with Whom none can converse.	37. Rabbis-samaawaati wal-arḍi wa maa baynahumar-Raḥ-maani laa yamlikoona minhu khiṭaabaa.	رَّبِّ ٱلسَّمَٰوَٰتِ وَٱلْأَرْضِ وَمَا بَيْنَهُمَا ٱلرَّحْمَٰنِ لَا يَمْلِكُونَ مِنْهُ خِطَابًا ٣٧
38. The Day that the Spirit and the angels will stand forth in ranks,	38. Yawma yaqoomur-Roo-ḥu wal-malaaa'ikatu ṣaffal-	يَوْمَ يَقُومُ ٱلرُّوحُ وَٱلْمَلَٰٓئِكَةُ صَفًّا

Ikhfa اخفاء | Ghunna غنّہ | Ikhfa Meem Saakin اخفاء میم ساکن | Idghaam ادغام | Qalqala قلقلہ | Qalb قلب | Idghaam Meem Saakin ادغام میم ساکن

none shall speak except any who is permitted by (Allah) Most Gracious, and He will say what is right.

39. That Day will be the sure Reality: Therefore, whoso will, let him take a (straight) return to his Lord!

40. Verily, We have warned you of a Chastisement near, the Day when man will see (the deeds) which his hands have sent forth, and the Unbeliever will say, "Woe unto me! Would that I were (mere) dust!

79. Those Who Tear Out

In the name of Allah, Most Gracious, Most Merciful.

1. By those who drag forth to destruction.

2. By those who gently draw out (the souls of the blessed);

3. And by those who glide along (on errands of mercy),

4. Then press forward as in a race,

5. Then arrange to do (the Commands of their Lord),

6. On the day when the first trumpet resoundeth.

7. Followed by oft-repeated (commotions):

8. Hearts that Day will be in agitation;

9. Cast down will be (their owners') eyes.

10. They say (now): "What! shall we indeed be returned to (our) former state?

11. "What! - when we shall have become rotten bones?"

12. They say: "It would, in that case, be a return with loss!"

13. But verily, it will be but a single (Compelling) Cry,

14. And lo! They will be awakened.

15. Has the story of Moses reached you?

16. Behold, your Lord did call to him in the sacred valley of Tuwa:-

laa yatakallamoona illaa man azina lahur-Raḥmaanu wa qaala ṣawaabaa.

39. Zaalikal-Yawmul-Ḥaqq, faman shaaa'at-takhaza ilaa Rabbihee ma-aabaa.

40. Innaaa anzarnaakum 'azaaban qareebañy-Yawma yanzurul-mar'u maa qaddamat yadaahu wa yaqoolul-kaafiru yaa laytanee kuntu turaabaa.

(Section 2)

Sûrat an-Nâzi'ât–79

(Revealed at Makkah)

Bismillaahir Raḥmaanir Raḥeem

1. Wannaazi'aati gharqaa.

2. Wannaashiṭaati nashṭaa.

3. Wassaabiḥaati sabḥaa.

4. Fassaabiqaati sabqaa.

5. Falmudabbiraati amraa.

6. Yawma tarjufur-raajifah.

7. Tatba'uhar-raadifah.

8. Quloobuñy-Yawma'iziñw-waajifah.

9. Abṣaaruhaa khaashi'ah.

10. Yaqooloona 'a-innaa lamardoodoona fil-ḥaafirah.

11. 'A-izaa kunnaa 'izaaman nakhirah.

12. Qaaloo tilka izan karratun khaasirah.

13. Fa-innamaa hiya zajratuñw-waaḥidah.

14. Fa-izaa hum bissaahirah.

15. Hal ataaka ḥadeesu Moosaa.

16. Iz naadaahu Rabbuhoo bil-waadil-muqaddasi Ṭuwaa.

لَا يَتَكَلَّمُونَ إِلَّا مَنْ أَذِنَ لَهُ الرَّحْمٰنُ
وَقَالَ صَوَابًا ﴿٣٨﴾
ذٰلِكَ الْيَوْمُ الْحَقُّ ۚ فَمَنْ شَاءَ اتَّخَذَ
إِلٰى رَبِّهٖ مَاٰبًا ﴿٣٩﴾
إِنَّآ أَنْذَرْنٰكُمْ عَذَابًا قَرِيبًا ۚ يَوْمَ يَنْظُرُ
الْمَرْءُ مَا قَدَّمَتْ يَدٰهُ وَيَقُولُ الْكٰفِرُ
يٰلَيْتَنِي كُنْتُ تُرٰبًا ﴿٤٠﴾ ع

(٧٩) سُورَةُ النّٰزِعٰتِ مَكِّيَّةٌ (٨١)

بِسْمِ اللّٰهِ الرَّحْمٰنِ الرَّحِيمِ

وَالنّٰزِعٰتِ غَرْقًا ﴿١﴾
وَالنّٰشِطٰتِ نَشْطًا ﴿٢﴾
وَالسّٰبِحٰتِ سَبْحًا ﴿٣﴾
فَالسّٰبِقٰتِ سَبْقًا ﴿٤﴾
فَالْمُدَبِّرٰتِ أَمْرًا ﴿٥﴾ وقف لازم
يَوْمَ تَرْجُفُ الرَّاجِفَةُ ﴿٦﴾
تَتْبَعُهَا الرَّادِفَةُ ﴿٧﴾
قُلُوبٌ يَوْمَئِذٍ وَّاجِفَةٌ ﴿٨﴾
أَبْصَارُهَا خَاشِعَةٌ ﴿٩﴾ وقف لازم
يَقُولُونَ ءَإِنَّا لَمَرْدُودُونَ فِي الْحَافِرَةِ ﴿١٠﴾
ءَإِذَا كُنَّا عِظَامًا نَّخِرَةً ﴿١١﴾ وقف لازم
قَالُوا تِلْكَ إِذًا كَرَّةٌ خَاسِرَةٌ ﴿١٢﴾
فَإِنَّمَا هِيَ زَجْرَةٌ وَّاحِدَةٌ ﴿١٣﴾
فَإِذَا هُمْ بِالسَّاهِرَةِ ﴿١٤﴾ وقف لازم
هَلْ أَتٰىكَ حَدِيثُ مُوسٰى ﴿١٥﴾
إِذْ نَادٰهُ رَبُّهُ بِالْوَادِ الْمُقَدَّسِ
طُوًى ﴿١٦﴾

Ikhfa اخفاء · Ghunna غُنّہ · Ikhfa Meem Saakin اخفاء میم ساکن · Idghaam ادغام · Qalqala قلقلہ · Qalb قلب · Idghaam Meem Saakin ادغام میم ساکن

17. (Saying:) Go thou unto Pharaho—Lo! He hath rebelled—	17. Izhab ilaa Fir'awna innahoo ṭaghaa.	اِذْهَبْ اِلٰى فِرْعَوْنَ اِنَّهٗ طَغٰى ﴿١٧﴾
18. "And say to him, 'do you wish to be purified (from sin)?-	18. Faqul hal laka ilaaa an tazakkaa.	فَقُلْ هَلْ لَّكَ اِلٰٓى اَنْ تَزَكّٰى ﴿١٨﴾
19. Then I will guide thee to thy Lord and thou shalt fear (Him).	19. Wa ahdiyaka ilaa Rabbika fatakhshaa.	وَاَهْدِيَكَ اِلٰى رَبِّكَ فَتَخْشٰى ﴿١٩﴾
20. Then did (Moses) show him the Great Sign.	20. Fa-araahul-Aayatal-Kubraa.	فَاَرٰىهُ الْاٰيَةَ الْكُبْرٰى ﴿٢٠﴾
21. But (Pharaoh) rejected it and disobeyed (guidance);	21. Fakazzaba wa 'aṣaa.	فَكَذَّبَ وَعَصٰى ﴿٢١﴾
22. Then turned he away in haste,	22. Summa adbara yas'aa.	ثُمَّ اَدْبَرَ يَسْعٰى ﴿٢٢﴾
23. Then he collected (his men) and made a proclamation,	23. Faḥashara fanaadaa.	فَحَشَرَ فَنَادٰى ﴿٢٣﴾
24. Saying, "I am your Lord, Most High".	24. Faqaala Ana Rabbukumul-A'laa.	فَقَالَ اَنَا رَبُّكُمُ الْاَعْلٰى ﴿٢٤﴾
25. But Allah did punish him, (and made an) example of him, - in the Hereafter, as in this life.	25. Fa-akhazahul-laahu nakaalal-Aakhirati wal-oolaaa.	فَاَخَذَهُ اللّٰهُ نَكَالَ الْاٰخِرَةِ وَالْاُوْلٰى ﴿٢٥﴾
26. Lo! Herein is indeed a lesson for him who feareth.	26. Inna fee zaalika la'ibratal-limañy-yakhshaa. **(Sec. 1)**	اِنَّ فِيْ ذٰلِكَ لَعِبْرَةً لِّمَنْ يَّخْشٰى ﴿٢٦﴾
27. Are ye the harder to create, or is the heaven that He built?	27. 'A-antum ashaddu khalqan amis-samaaa'; banaahaa.	ءَاَنْتُمْ اَشَدُّ خَلْقًا اَمِ السَّمَآءُ بَنٰىهَا ﴿٢٧﴾
28. He raised the height thereof and ordered it;	28. Rafa'a samkahaa fasawwaahaa.	رَفَعَ سَمْكَهَا فَسَوّٰىهَا ﴿٢٨﴾
29. Its night does He endow with darkness, and its splendour doth He bring out (with light).	29. Wa aghṭasha laylahaa wa akhraja ḍuḥaahaa.	وَاَغْطَشَ لَيْلَهَا وَاَخْرَجَ ضُحٰىهَا ﴿٢٩﴾
30. And after that He spread the earth,	30. Wal-arḍa ba'da zaalika daḥaahaa.	وَالْاَرْضَ بَعْدَ ذٰلِكَ دَحٰىهَا ﴿٣٠﴾
31. He draws out therefrom its moisture and its pasture;	31. Akhraja minhaa maaa'ahaa wa mar'aahaa.	اَخْرَجَ مِنْهَا مَآءَهَا وَمَرْعٰىهَا ﴿٣١﴾
32. And the mountains has He firmly fixed;-	32. Wal-jibaala arsaahaa.	وَالْجِبَالَ اَرْسٰىهَا ﴿٣٢﴾
33. A provision for you and your cattle.	33. Mataa'al-lakum wa li-an'aamikum.	مَتَاعًا لَّكُمْ وَلِاَنْعَامِكُمْ ﴿٣٣﴾
34. But when the great disaster cometh,	34. Fa-izaa jaaa'atiṭ-ṭaaammatul-kubraa.	فَاِذَا جَآءَتِ الطَّآمَّةُ الْكُبْرٰى ﴿٣٤﴾
35. The day when man will call to mind his (whole) endeavour,	35. Yawma yatazakkarul-insaanu maa sa'aa.	يَوْمَ يَتَذَكَّرُ الْاِنْسَانُ مَا سَعٰى ﴿٣٥﴾
36. And hell will stand forth visible to him who seeth,	36. Wa burrizatil-Jaḥeemu limañy-yaraa.	وَبُرِّزَتِ الْجَحِيْمُ لِمَنْ يَّرٰى ﴿٣٦﴾
37. Then, for such as had transgressed all bounds,	37. Fa-ammaa man ṭaghaa.	فَاَمَّا مَنْ طَغٰى ﴿٣٧﴾
38. And had preferred the life of this world,	38. Wa aasaral-ḥayaatad-dunyaa.	وَاٰثَرَ الْحَيٰوةَ الدُّنْيَا ﴿٣٨﴾
39. The Abode will be Hell-Fire;	39. Fa-innal-Jaḥeema hiyal-maảwaa.	فَاِنَّ الْجَحِيْمَ هِيَ الْمَاْوٰى ﴿٣٩﴾
40. And for such as had entertained the fear of standing before their Lord's (tribunal) and had restrained (their) soul from lower desires,	40. Wa ammaa man khaafa maqaama Rabbihee wa nahannafsa 'anil-hawaa.	وَاَمَّا مَنْ خَافَ مَقَامَ رَبِّهٖ وَنَهَى النَّفْسَ عَنِ الْهَوٰى ﴿٤٠﴾

Ikhfa اخفاء · Ghunna غنّہ · Ikhfa Meem Saakin اخفاء میم ساکن · Idghaam ادغام · Qalqala قلقلہ · Qalb قلب · Idghaam Meem Saakin ادغام میم ساکن

English	Transliteration	Arabic
41. Their abode will be the Garden.	41. Fa innal-Jannata hiyal-maåwaa.	فَإِنَّ الْجَنَّةَ هِيَ الْمَأْوٰى ﴿٤١﴾
42. They ask thee of the Hour: When will it come to port?	42. Yas'aloonaka 'anis-Saa-'ati ayyaana mursaahaa.	يَسْئَلُونَكَ عَنِ السَّاعَةِ أَيَّانَ مُرْسٰهَا ﴿٤٢﴾
43. Wherein are you (concerned) with the declaration thereof?	43. Feema anta min zikraa-haa.	فِيمَ أَنْتَ مِنْ ذِكْرٰهَا ﴿٤٣﴾
44. With your Lord in the time fixed therefor.	44. Ilaa Rabbika muntahaa-haa.	إِلٰى رَبِّكَ مُنْتَهٰهَا ﴿٤٤﴾
45. Thou art but a Warner for such as fear it.	45. Innamaaa anta munziru mañy-yakhshaahaa.	إِنَّمَا أَنْتَ مُنْذِرُ مَنْ يَخْشٰهَا ﴿٤٥﴾
46. The Day they see it, (It will be) as if they had tarried but a single evening, or (at most till) the following morn!	46. Ka-annahum Yawma yarawnahaa lam yalbasooo illaa 'ashiyyatan aw ḍuḥaahaa. **(Section 2)**	كَأَنَّهُمْ يَوْمَ يَرَوْنَهَا لَمْ يَلْبَثُوٓا إِلَّا عَشِيَّةً أَوْ ضُحٰهَا ﴿٤٦﴾ ع ٢

80. He Frowned

In the name of Allah, Most Gracious, Most Merciful.

Sûrat 'Abasa–80

(Revealed at Makkah)

Bismillaahir Raḥmaanir Raḥeem

(٨٠) سُورَةُ عَبَسَ مَكِّيَّةٌ (٢٤)

بِسْمِ اللّٰهِ الرَّحْمٰنِ الرَّحِيمِ

English	Transliteration	Arabic
1. (The Prophet) frowned and turned away,	1. 'Abasa wa tawallaaa.	عَبَسَ وَتَوَلّٰى ﴿١﴾
2. Because there came to him the blind man (interrupting).	2. An jaaa'ahul-a'maa.	أَنْ جَآءَهُ الْأَعْمٰى ﴿٢﴾
3. What could inform thee but that he might grow (in grace)	3. Wa maa yudreeka la'al-lahoo yazzakkaaa.	وَمَا يُدْرِيكَ لَعَلَّهُ يَزَّكّٰى ﴿٣﴾
4. Or take heed and so the reminder might avail him?	4. Aw yazzakkaru fatan-fa'ahuz-zikraa.	أَوْ يَذَّكَّرُ فَتَنْفَعَهُ الذِّكْرٰى ﴿٤﴾
5. As to one who regards Himself as self-sufficient,	5. Ammaa manis-taghnaa.	أَمَّا مَنِ اسْتَغْنٰى ﴿٥﴾
6. To him does you attend;	6. Fa-anta lahoo taṣaddaa.	فَأَنْتَ لَهُ تَصَدّٰى ﴿٦﴾
7. Yet it is not thy concern if he grow not (in grace).	7. Wa maa 'alayka allaa yazzakkaa.	وَمَا عَلَيْكَ أَلَّا يَزَّكّٰى ﴿٧﴾
8. But as to him who came to you striving earnestly,	8. Wa ammaa man jaaa'aka yas'aa.	وَأَمَّا مَنْ جَآءَكَ يَسْعٰى ﴿٨﴾
9. And with fear (in his heart),	9. Wa huwa yakhshaa.	وَهُوَ يَخْشٰى ﴿٩﴾
10. Of him were you unmindful.	10. Fa-anta 'anhu talahhaa.	فَأَنْتَ عَنْهُ تَلَهّٰى ﴿١٠﴾
11. Nay but verily it is an Admonishment,	11. Kallaaa innahaa tazkirah.	كَلَّآ إِنَّهَا تَذْكِرَةٌ ﴿١١﴾ وقف لازم
12. Therefore let whoso will, keep it in remembrance.	12. Faman shaaa'a zakarah.	فَمَنْ شَآءَ ذَكَرَهُ ﴿١٢﴾
13. (It is) in Books held (greatly) in honour,	13. Fee ṣuḥufim-mukarramah.	فِي صُحُفٍ مُكَرَّمَةٍ ﴿١٣﴾
14. Exalted (in dignity), kept pure and holy,	14. Marfoo'atim-muṭahha-rah.	مَرْفُوعَةٍ مُطَهَّرَةٍ ﴿١٤﴾
15. (Written) by the hands of scribes-	15. Bi-aydee safarah.	بِأَيْدِي سَفَرَةٍ ﴿١٥﴾
16. Honourable and Pious and Just.	16. Kiraamim bararah.	كِرَامٍ بَرَرَةٍ ﴿١٦﴾
17. Woe to man! What has made him reject Allah;	17. Qutilal-insaanu maaa akfarah.	قُتِلَ الْإِنْسَانُ مَآ أَكْفَرَهُ ﴿١٧﴾

Ikhfa اخفاء · Ghunna غُنّہ · Ikhfa Meem Saakin اخفاء میم ساکن · Idghaam ادغام · Qalqala قلقلہ · Qalb قلب · Idghaam Meem Saakin ادغام میم ساکن

English	Transliteration	Arabic
18. From what stuff has He created him?	18. Min ayyi shay'in khala-qah.	مِنْ اَيِّ شَيْءٍ خَلَقَهٗ ١٨
19. From a drop of seed. He createth him and proportioneth him,	19. Min nutfatin khalaqahoo faqaddarah.	مِنْ نُّطْفَةٍ ؕ خَلَقَهٗ فَقَدَّرَهٗ ١٩
20. Then does He make His path smooth for him;	20. S̲ummas-sabeela yassa-rah.	ثُمَّ السَّبِيْلَ يَسَّرَهٗ ٢٠
21. Then He causes him to die, and putteth him in his grave;	21. S̲umma amaatahoo fa-aqbarah.	ثُمَّ اَمَاتَهٗ فَاَقْبَرَهٗ ٢١
22. Then, when it is His Will, He will raise him up (again).	22. S̲umma iz̲aa shaaa'a ansharah.	ثُمَّ اِذَا شَآءَ اَنْشَرَهٗ ٢٢
23. Nay, but (man) hath not done what He commanded him.	23. Kallaa lammaa yaqḍi maaa amarah.	كَلَّا لَمَّا يَقْضِ مَآ اَمَرَهٗ ٢٣
24. Then let man look at his food, (and how We provide it):	24. Falyanẓuril-insaanu ilaa ṭa'aamih.	فَلْيَنْظُرِ الْاِنْسَانُ اِلٰى طَعَامِهٖ ٢٤
25. For that We pour forth water in abundance,	25. Annaa ṣababnal-maaa'a ṣabbaa.	اَنَّا صَبَبْنَا الْمَآءَ صَبًّا ٢٥
26. And We split the earth in fragments,	26. S̲umma shaqaqnal-arḍa shaqqaa.	ثُمَّ شَقَقْنَا الْاَرْضَ شَقًّا ٢٦
27. And produce therein corn,	27. Fa-ambatnaa feehaa ḥabbaa.	فَاَنْۢبَتْنَا فِيْهَا حَبًّا ٢٧
28. And Grapes and nutri-tious plants,	28. Wa 'inabañw-wa qaḍbaa.	وَّعِنَبًا وَّقَضْبًا ٢٨
29. And Olives and Dates,	29. Wa zaytoonañw-wa nakh-laa.	وَّزَيْتُوْنًا وَّنَخْلًا ٢٩
30. And enclosed Gardens, dense with lofty trees,	30. Wa ḥadaaa'iqa ghulbaa.	وَّحَدَآئِقَ غُلْبًا ٣٠
31. And fruits and fodder,-	31. Wa faakihatañw-wa abbaa.	وَّفَاكِهَةً وَّاَبًّا ٣١
32. For use and convenience to you and your cattle.	32. Mataa'al-lakum wa li-an'aamikum.	مَّتَاعًا لَّكُمْ وَلِاَنْعَامِكُمْ ٣٢
33. At length, when there comes the Deafening Noise,-	33. Fa-iz̲aa jaaa'atiṣ-ṣaaakh-khah.	فَاِذَا جَآءَتِ الصَّآخَّةُ ٣٣
34. That Day shall a man flee from his own brother,	34. Yawma yafirrul-mar'u min akheeh.	يَوْمَ يَفِرُّ الْمَرْءُ مِنْ اَخِيْهِ ٣٤
35. And from his mother and his father,	35. Wa ummihee wa abeeh.	وَاُمِّهٖ وَاَبِيْهِ ٣٥
36. And from his wife and his children.	36. Wa ṣaaḥibatihee wa baneeh.	وَصَاحِبَتِهٖ وَبَنِيْهِ ٣٦
37. Each one of them, that Day, will have enough concern (of his own) to make him unmindful to the others.	37. Likullim-ri-'im-minhum Yawma'iz̲in shaånuñy-yughneeh.	لِكُلِّ امْرِئٍ مِّنْهُمْ يَوْمَئِذٍ شَاْنٌ يُّغْنِيْهِ ٣٧
38. Some faces that Day will be beaming,	38. Wujoohuñy-Yawma'i-z̲im-musfirah.	وُجُوْهٌ يَّوْمَئِذٍ مُّسْفِرَةٌ ٣٨
39. Laughing, rejoicing.	39. Ḍaaḥikatum-mustabshi-rah.	ضَاحِكَةٌ مُّسْتَبْشِرَةٌ ٣٩
40. And other faces that Day will be dust-stained,	40. Wa wujoohuñy-Yawma'i-z̲in 'alayhaa ghabarah.	وَوُجُوْهٌ يَّوْمَئِذٍ عَلَيْهَا غَبَرَةٌ ٤٠
41. Blackness will cover them:	41. Tarhaquhaa qatarah.	تَرْهَقُهَا قَتَرَةٌ ٤١
42. Such will be the Rejecters of Allah, the doers of iniquity.	42. Ulaaa'ika humul-kafara-tul-fajarah. **(Section 1)**	اُولٰٓئِكَ هُمُ الْكَفَرَةُ الْفَجَرَةُ ٤٢ ع ٥

Ikhfa اخفاء | Ghunna غُنّہ | Ikhfa Meem Saakin اخفاء میم ساکن | Idghaam ادغام | Qalqala قلقلہ | Qalb قلب | Idghaam Meem Saakin ادغام میم ساکن

81. The Folding Up **In the Name of Allah, Most Gracious, Most Merciful.**	**Sûrat at-Takwîr–81** (Revealed at Makkah) **Bismillaahir Raḥmaanir Raḥeem**	(٨١) سُورَةُ التَّكْوِيرِ مَكِّيَّةٌ (٧) بِسْمِ اللَّهِ الرَّحْمَٰنِ الرَّحِيمِ
1. When the sun (with its spacious light) is folded up;	1. Iz̲ash-shamsu kuwwirat.	إِذَا الشَّمْسُ كُوِّرَتْ ١
2. When the stars fall, losing their lustre;	2. Wa iz̲an-nujoomun-kadarat.	وَإِذَا النُّجُومُ انكَدَرَتْ ٢
3. When the mountains vanish (like a mirage);	3. Wa iz̲al-jibaalu suyyirat.	وَإِذَا الْجِبَالُ سُيِّرَتْ ٣
4. And when the camels big with young are abandoned,	4. Wa iz̲al-'ishaaru 'uṭṭilat.	وَإِذَا الْعِشَارُ عُطِّلَتْ ٤
5. And when the wild beasts are herded together,	5. Wa iz̲al-wuḥooshu ḥushirat	وَإِذَا الْوُحُوشُ حُشِرَتْ ٥
6. When the oceans boil over with a swell;	6. Wa iz̲al-biḥaaru sujjirat.	وَإِذَا الْبِحَارُ سُجِّرَتْ ٦
7. And when souls are re-united,	7. Wa iz̲an-nufoosu zuwwijat.	وَإِذَا النُّفُوسُ زُوِّجَتْ ٧
8. When the female (infant), buried alive, is questioned -	8. Wa iz̲al-maw'oodatu su'ilat.	وَإِذَا الْمَوْءُودَةُ سُئِلَتْ ٨
9. For what crime she was killed;	9. Bi-ayyi zambin qutilat.	بِأَيِّ ذَنبٍ قُتِلَتْ ٩
10. When the scrolls are laid open;	10. Wa iz̲aṣ-ṣuḥufu nushirat.	وَإِذَا الصُّحُفُ نُشِرَتْ ١٠
11. When the sky is unveiled;	11. Wa iz̲as-samaaa'u kushiṭat.	وَإِذَا السَّمَاءُ كُشِطَتْ ١١
12. When the Blazing Fire is kindled to fierce heat;	12. Wa iz̲al-Jaḥeemu su'-'irat.	وَإِذَا الْجَحِيمُ سُعِّرَتْ ١٢
13. And when the Garden is brought near;-	13. Wa iz̲al-Jannatu uzlifat.	وَإِذَا الْجَنَّةُ أُزْلِفَتْ ١٣
14. (Then) shall each soul know what it has put forward.	14. 'Alimat nafsum-maaa aḥḍarat.	عَلِمَتْ نَفْسٌ مَّا أَحْضَرَتْ ١٤
15. So verily I call to witness the planets - that recede,	15. Falaaa uqsimu bil-khunnas.	فَلَا أُقْسِمُ بِالْخُنَّسِ ١٥
16. Go straight, or hide;	16. Al-jawaaril-kunnas.	الْجَوَارِ الْكُنَّسِ ١٦
17. And the Night as it dissipates;	17. Wallayli iz̲aa 'as'as.	وَاللَّيْلِ إِذَا عَسْعَسَ ١٧
18. And the Dawn as it breathes away the darkness;-	18. Waṣṣubḥi iz̲aa tanaffas.	وَالصُّبْحِ إِذَا تَنَفَّسَ ١٨
19. Verily this is the word of a most honourable Messenger,	19. Innahoo laqawlu rasoolin kareem.	إِنَّهُ لَقَوْلُ رَسُولٍ كَرِيمٍ ١٩
20. Endued with Power, held in honour by the Lord of the Throne,	20. Z̲ee quwwatin 'inda Z̲il-'Arshi makeen.	ذِي قُوَّةٍ عِندَ ذِي الْعَرْشِ مَكِينٍ ٢٠
21. With authority there, (and) faithful to his trust.	21. Muṭaa'in s̲amma ameen.	مُّطَاعٍ ثَمَّ أَمِينٍ ٢١
22. And (O people!) your companion is not one possessed;	22. Wa maa ṣaaḥibukum bimajnoon.	وَمَا صَاحِبُكُم بِمَجْنُونٍ ٢٢
23. And without doubt he saw him in the clear horizon.	23. Wa laqad ra-aahu bil-ufuqil-mubeen	وَلَقَدْ رَآهُ بِالْأُفُقِ الْمُبِينِ ٢٣
24. And he is not avid of the Unseen.	24. Wa maa huwa 'alal-ghaybi-biḍaneen.	وَمَا هُوَ عَلَى الْغَيْبِ بِضَنِينٍ ٢٤

Ikhfa اخفاء · Ghunna غُنّہ · Ikhfa Meem Saakin اخفاءمیم ساکن · Idghaam ادغام · Qalqala قلقلہ · Qalb قلب · Idghaam Meem Saakin ادغام میم ساکن

Translation	Transliteration	Arabic
25. Nor is it the word of an evil spirit accursed.	25. Wa maa huwa biqawli Shayṭaanir-rajeem.	وَمَا هُوَ بِقَوْلِ شَيْطٰنٍ رَّجِيْمٍ ۝٢٥
26. When whither go you?	26. Fa-ayna tazhaboon.	فَاَيْنَ تَذْهَبُوْنَ ۝٢٦
27. Verily this is no less than a Message to (all) the Worlds:	27. In huwa illaa zikrul-lil-'aalameen.	اِنْ هُوَ اِلَّا ذِكْرٌ لِّلْعٰلَمِيْنَ ۝٢٧
28. (With profit) to whoever among you wills to go straight:	28. Liman shaaa'a minkum añy-yastaqeem.	لِمَنْ شَآءَ مِنْكُمْ اَنْ يَّسْتَقِيْمَ ۝٢٨
29. But you shall not will except as Allah wills,- the Cherisher of the Worlds.	29. Wa maa tashaaa'oona illaaa añy-yashaaa'al-laahu Rab-bul-'Aalameen. **(Section 1)**	وَمَا تَشَآءُوْنَ اِلَّآ اَنْ يَّشَآءَ اللّٰهُ رَبُّ الْعٰلَمِيْنَ ۝٢٩
82. The Cleaving Asunder **In the name of Allah, Most Gracious, Most Merciful.**	**Sûrat al-Infiṭâr–82** (Revealed at Makkah) **Bismillaahir Raḥmaanir Raḥeem**	(٨٢) سُوْرَةُ الْاِنْفِطَارِ مَكِّيَّةٌ (٨٢) بِسْمِ اللّٰهِ الرَّحْمٰنِ الرَّحِيْمِ
1. When the Sky is cleft asunder;	1. Izas-samaaa'un-faṭarat.	اِذَا السَّمَآءُ انْفَطَرَتْ ۝١
2. When the Stars are scattered;	2. Wa izal-kawaakibun-tasarat.	وَاِذَا الْكَوَاكِبُ انْتَثَرَتْ ۝٢
3. When the Oceans are suffered to burst forth;	3. Wa izal-biḥaaru fujjirat.	وَاِذَا الْبِحَارُ فُجِّرَتْ ۝٣
4. And when the Graves are turned upside down;-	4. Wa izal-qubooru bu'sirat.	وَاِذَا الْقُبُوْرُ بُعْثِرَتْ ۝٤
5. A soul will know what it hath sent before (it) and what left behind.	5. 'Alimat nafsum-maa qaddamat wa akhkharat.	عَلِمَتْ نَفْسٌ مَّا قَدَّمَتْ وَاَخَّرَتْ ۝٥
6. O man! What has seduced you from your Lord Most Beneficent?-	6. Yaaa ayyuhal-insaaanu maa gharraka bi-Rabbikal-Kareem.	يٰٓاَيُّهَا الْاِنْسَانُ مَا غَرَّكَ بِرَبِّكَ الْكَرِيْمِ ۝٦
7. Who created thee, then fashioned, then proportioned thee?	7. Allazee khalaqaka fasawwaaka fa'adalak.	الَّذِيْ خَلَقَكَ فَسَوّٰىكَ فَعَدَلَكَ ۝٧
8. In whatever Form He wills, does He put you together.	8. Feee ayye ṣooratim-maa shaaa'a rakkabak.	فِيْٓ اَيِّ صُوْرَةٍ مَّا شَآءَ رَكَّبَكَ ۝٨
9. No, but you reject Right and Judgment!	9. Kalla bal tukazziboona bid-deen.	كَلَّا بَلْ تُكَذِّبُوْنَ بِالدِّيْنِ ۝٩
10. Lo! There are above you guardians,	10. Wa Inna 'alaykum laḥaa-fiẓeen.	وَاِنَّ عَلَيْكُمْ لَحٰفِظِيْنَ ۝١٠
11. Kind and honourable,- Writing down (your deeds):	11. Kiraaman kaatibeen.	كِرَامًا كَاتِبِيْنَ ۝١١
12. They know (and understand) all that you do.	12. Ya'lamoona ma taf'a-loon.	يَعْلَمُوْنَ مَا تَفْعَلُوْنَ ۝١٢
13. As for the Righteous, they will be in bliss;	13. Innal-abraara lafee Na'eem.	اِنَّ الْاَبْرَارَ لَفِيْ نَعِيْمٍ ۝١٣
14. And the Wicked - they will be in the Fire,	14. Wa innal-fujjaara lafee Jaḥeem.	وَاِنَّ الْفُجَّارَ لَفِيْ جَحِيْمٍ ۝١٤
15. Which they will enter on the Day of Judgment,	15. Yaṣlawnahaa Yawmad-Deen.	يَّصْلَوْنَهَا يَوْمَ الدِّيْنِ ۝١٥
16. And they will not be able to keep away therefrom.	16. Wa maa hum 'anhaa bighaaa'ibeen.	وَمَا هُمْ عَنْهَا بِغَآئِبِيْنَ ۝١٦
17. And what will explain to you what the Day of Judgment is?	17. Wa maaa adraaka maa Yawmud-Deen.	وَمَآ اَدْرٰىكَ مَا يَوْمُ الدِّيْنِ ۝١٧

Ikhfa اخفاء | Ghunna غُنّہ | Ikhfa Meem Saakin اخفاءمیم ساکن | Idghaam ادغام | Qalqala قلقلہ | Qalb قلب | Idghaam Meem Saakin ادغام میم ساکن

18. Again, what will explain to you what the Day of Judgment is?

19. A day on which no soul hath power at all for any (other) soul. The (absolute) command on that day is Allah's.

83. The Dealers in Fraud

In the name of Allah, Most Gracious, Most Merciful.

1. Woe to those that deal in fraud,-

2. Those who, when they have to receive by measure from men, exact full measure,

3. But when they have to give by measure or weight to men, give less than due.

4. Do they not think that they will be called to account?-

5. On a Mighty Day,

6. The day when (all) mankind stand before the Lord of the Worlds?

7. Nay but the record of the vile is in Sijjin—

8. And what will explain to thee what Sijjin is?

9. (There is) a Register (fully) inscribed.

10. Woe, that Day, to those that deny-

11. Those that deny the Day of Judgment.

12. Which none denieth save each criminal transgressor,

13. When Our Signs are rehearsed to him, he says, "Tales of the ancients!"

14. By no means! but on their hearts is the stain of the (ill) which they do!

15. Verily, from (the Light of) their Lord, that Day, will they be veiled.

16. Further, they will enter the Fire of Hell.

17. Further, it will be said to them: "This is the (reality)

18. Summa maaa adraaka maa Yawmud-Deen.

19. Yawma laa tamliku nafsul-linafsin shay'añw wal-amru Yawma'izil-lillaah. **(Sec. 1)**

Sûrat al-Muṭaffifîn–83

(Revealed at Makkah)

Bismillaahir Raḥmaanir Raḥeem

1. Waylul-lil-muṭaffifeen.

2. Allazeena izak-taaloo 'alan-naasi yastawfoon.

3. Wa izaa kaaloohum aw wazanoohum yukhsiroon.

4. Alaa yazunnu ulaaa'ika annahum mab'oosoon.

5. Li-Yawmin 'Azeem.

6. Yawma yaqoomun-naasu li-Rabbil-'aalameen.

7. Kallaaa inna kitaabal-fujjaari lafee Sijjeen.

8. Wa maa adraaka maa Sijjeen.

9. Kitaabum-marqoom.

10. Wayluñy-Yawma'izil-lil-mukazzibeen.

11. Allazeena yukazziboona bi-Yawmid-Deen.

12. Wa maa yukazzibu biheee illaa kullu mu'tadin aseem.

13. Izaa tutlaa 'alayhi Aayaatunaa qaala asaaṭeerul-awwaleen.

14. Kallaa bal raana 'alaa quloobihim maa kaanoo yaksiboon.

15. Kallaaa innahum 'ar-Rabbihim Yawma'izil-lamaḥjooboon.

16. Summa innahum laṣaalul-Jaheem.

17. Summa yuqaalu haazal-lazee kuntum bihee

ثُمَّ مَآ أَدْرٰىكَ مَا يَوْمُ الدِّيْنِ ﴿١٨﴾

يَوْمَ لَا تَمْلِكُ نَفْسٌ لِّنَفْسٍ شَيْـًٔا ۖ وَالْأَمْرُ يَوْمَئِذٍ لِّلّٰهِ ﴿١٩﴾

(٨٣) سُوْرَةُ الْمُطَفِّفِيْنَ مَكِّيَّةٌ (٨٦)

بِسْمِ اللّٰهِ الرَّحْمٰنِ الرَّحِيْمِ

وَيْلٌ لِّلْمُطَفِّفِيْنَ ﴿١﴾

الَّذِيْنَ إِذَا اكْتَالُوْا عَلَى النَّاسِ يَسْتَوْفُوْنَ ﴿٢﴾

وَإِذَا كَالُوْهُمْ أَوْ وَّزَنُوْهُمْ يُخْسِرُوْنَ ﴿٣﴾

أَلَا يَظُنُّ أُولٰٓئِكَ أَنَّهُمْ مَّبْعُوْثُوْنَ ﴿٤﴾

لِيَوْمٍ عَظِيْمٍ ﴿٥﴾

يَّوْمَ يَقُوْمُ النَّاسُ لِرَبِّ الْعٰلَمِيْنَ ﴿٦﴾

كَلَّآ إِنَّ كِتٰبَ الْفُجَّارِ لَفِيْ سِجِّيْنٍ ﴿٧﴾

وَمَآ أَدْرٰىكَ مَا سِجِّيْنٌ ﴿٨﴾

كِتٰبٌ مَّرْقُوْمٌ ﴿٩﴾

وَيْلٌ يَّوْمَئِذٍ لِّلْمُكَذِّبِيْنَ ﴿١٠﴾

الَّذِيْنَ يُكَذِّبُوْنَ بِيَوْمِ الدِّيْنِ ﴿١١﴾

وَمَا يُكَذِّبُ بِهٖٓ إِلَّا كُلُّ مُعْتَدٍ أَثِيْمٍ ﴿١٢﴾

إِذَا تُتْلٰى عَلَيْهِ اٰيٰتُنَا قَالَ أَسَاطِيْرُ الْأَوَّلِيْنَ ﴿١٣﴾

كَلَّا بَلْ ۜ رَانَ عَلٰى قُلُوْبِهِمْ مَّا كَانُوْا يَكْسِبُوْنَ ﴿١٤﴾

كَلَّآ إِنَّهُمْ عَنْ رَّبِّهِمْ يَوْمَئِذٍ لَّمَحْجُوْبُوْنَ ﴿١٥﴾

ثُمَّ إِنَّهُمْ لَصَالُوا الْجَحِيْمِ ﴿١٦﴾

ثُمَّ يُقَالُ هٰذَا الَّذِيْ كُنْتُمْ بِهٖ

Ikhfa اخفاء | Ghunna غُنَّہ | Ikhfa Meem Saakin اخفاء میم ساکن | Idghaam ادغام | Qalqala قلقلہ | Qalb قلب | Idghaam Meem Saakin ادغام میم ساکن

which you rejected as false!	tukazziboon.	تُكَذِّبُوْنَ ۝١٧
18. Nay, but the record of the righteous is in 'Illiyin!—	18. Kallaaa inna kitaabal-abraari lafee 'Illiyyeen.	كَلَّآ اِنَّ كِتٰبَ الْاَبْرَارِ لَفِيْ عِلِّيِّيْنَ ۝١٨
19. And what will explain to you what 'Illiyun is?	19. Wa maaa adraaka maa 'Illiyyoon.	وَمَآ اَدْرٰىكَ مَا عِلِّيُّوْنَ ۝١٩
20. (There is) a Register (fully) inscribed,	20. Kitaabum-marqoom.	كِتٰبٌ مَّرْقُوْمٌ ۝٢٠
21. To which bear witness those Nearest (to Allah).	21. Yashhadu-hul-muqarraboon.	يَّشْهَدُهُ الْمُقَرَّبُوْنَ ۝٢١
22. Truly the Righteous will be in Bliss:	22. Innal-abraara lafee Na'eem.	اِنَّ الْاَبْرَارَ لَفِيْ نَعِيْمٍ ۝٢٢
23. On couches, gazing,	23. 'Alal-araaa'iki yanzuroon.	عَلَى الْاَرَآئِكِ يَنْظُرُوْنَ ۝٢٣
24. Thou wilt know in their faces the radiance of delight.	24. Ta'rifu fee wujoohihim naḍratan-na'eem.	تَعْرِفُ فِيْ وُجُوْهِهِمْ نَضْرَةَ النَّعِيْمِ ۝٢٤
25. Their thirst will be slaked with Pure Wine sealed:	25. Yusqawna mir-raḥeeqim-makhtoom.	يُسْقَوْنَ مِنْ رَّحِيْقٍ مَّخْتُوْمٍ ۝٢٥
26. The seal thereof will be Musk: And for this let those aspire, who have aspirations:	26. Khitaamuhoo misk; wa fee zaalika falyatanaafasil-Mutanaafisoon.	خِتٰمُهٗ مِسْكٌ ؕ وَفِيْ ذٰلِكَ فَلْيَتَنَافَسِ الْمُتَنَافِسُوْنَ ۝٢٦
27. With it will be (given) a mixture of Tasnim:	27. Wa mizaajuhoo min Tasneem.	وَمِزَاجُهٗ مِنْ تَسْنِيْمٍ ۝٢٧
28. A spring whence those brought near to Allah drink.	28. 'Aynañy-yashrabu bihal-muqarraboon.	عَيْنًا يَّشْرَبُ بِهَا الْمُقَرَّبُوْنَ ۝٢٨
29. Those in sin used to laugh at those who believed,	29. Innal-lazeena ajramoo kaanoo minal-lazeena aamanoo yaḍḥakoon.	اِنَّ الَّذِيْنَ اَجْرَمُوْا كَانُوْا مِنَ الَّذِيْنَ اٰمَنُوْا يَضْحَكُوْنَ ۝٢٩
30. And wink one to another when they passed them;	30. Wa izaa marroo bihim yataghaamazoon.	وَاِذَا مَرُّوْا بِهِمْ يَتَغَامَزُوْنَ ۝٣٠
31. And when they returned to their own folk, they returned jesting;	31. Wa izan-qalabooo ilaaa ahlihimun-qalaboo fakiheen.	وَاِذَا انْقَلَبُوْٓا اِلٰٓى اَهْلِهِمُ انْقَلَبُوْا فَكِهِيْنَ ۝٣١
32. And whenever they saw them, they would say, "Behold! These are the people truly astray!"	32. Wa izaa ra-awhum qaalooo inna haaa'ulaaa'i laḍaaalloon.	وَاِذَا رَاَوْهُمْ قَالُوْٓا اِنَّ هٰٓؤُلَآءِ لَضَآلُّوْنَ ۝٣٢
33. But they had not been sent as keepers over them!	33. Wa maaa ursiloo 'alayhim ḥaafizeen.	وَمَآ اُرْسِلُوْا عَلَيْهِمْ حٰفِظِيْنَ ۝٣٣
34. But on this Day the Believers will laugh at the Unbelievers:	34. Fal-Yawmal-lazeena aamanoo minal-kuffaari yaḍḥakoon.	فَالْيَوْمَ الَّذِيْنَ اٰمَنُوْا مِنَ الْكُفَّارِ يَضْحَكُوْنَ ۝٣٤
35. On high couches, gazing.	35. 'Alal-araaa'iki yanzuroon.	عَلَى الْاَرَآئِكِ يَنْظُرُوْنَ ۝٣٥
36. Are not the disbelievers paid for what they used to do?	36. Hal suwwibal-kuffaaru maa kaanoo yaf'aloon. **(Sec. 1)**	هَلْ ثُوِّبَ الْكُفَّارُ مَا كَانُوْا يَفْعَلُوْنَ ۝٣٦
84. The Rending Asunder **In the name of Allah, Most Gracious, Most Merciful.**	**Sûrat al-Inshiqâq–84** (Revealed at Makkah) **Bismillaahir Raḥmaanir Raḥeem**	(٨٤) سُوْرَةُ الْاِنْشِقَاقِ مَكِّيَّةٌ (٨٣) بِسْمِ اللّٰهِ الرَّحْمٰنِ الرَّحِيْمِ
1. When the sky is rent asunder,	1. Izas-samaaa'un-shaqqat.	اِذَا السَّمَآءُ انْشَقَّتْ ۝١

Ikhfa	Ghunna	Ikhfa Meem Saakin	Idghaam	Qalqala	Qalb	Idghaam Meem Saakin
اخفاء	غُنّہ	اخفاء میم ساکن	ادغام	قلقلہ	قلب	ادغام میم ساکن

2. And attentive to her Lord in fear,	2. Wa azinat li-Rabbihaa wa ḥuqqat.	وَأَذِنَتْ لِرَبِّهَا وَحُقَّتْ ٢
3. And when the earth is flattened out,	3. Wa izal-arḍu muddat.	وَإِذَا الْأَرْضُ مُدَّتْ ٣
4. And hath cast out all that was in her, and is empty.	4. Wa alqat maa feehaa wa takhallat.	وَأَلْقَتْ مَا فِيهَا وَتَخَلَّتْ ٤
5. And attentive to her Lord in fear!	5. Wa azinat li-Rabbihaa wa ḥuqqat.	وَأَذِنَتْ لِرَبِّهَا وَحُقَّتْ ٥
6. O you man Verily you are ever toiling on towards your Lord- painfully toiling,- but you shall meet Him.	6. Yaaa ayyuhal-insaanu innaka kaadiḥun ilaa Rabbika kad-ḥan famulaaqeeh.	يَا أَيُّهَا الْإِنْسَانُ إِنَّكَ كَادِحٌ إِلَىٰ رَبِّكَ كَدْحًا فَمُلَاقِيهِ ٦
7. Then he who is given his Record in his right han,	7. Fa-ammaa man ootiya kitaabahoo biyameenih.	فَأَمَّا مَنْ أُوتِيَ كِتَابَهُ بِيَمِينِهِ ٧
8. Soon will his account be taken by an easy reckoning,	8. Fasawfa yuḥaasabu ḥi-saabañy-yaseeraa.	فَسَوْفَ يُحَاسَبُ حِسَابًا يَسِيرًا ٨
9. And he will turn to his people, rejoicing!	9. Wa yanqalibu ilaaa ahli-hee masrooraa.	وَيَنْقَلِبُ إِلَىٰ أَهْلِهِ مَسْرُورًا ٩
10. But he who is given his Record behind his back,-	10. Wa ammaa man ootiya kitaabahoo waraaa'a ẓahrih.	وَأَمَّا مَنْ أُوتِيَ كِتَابَهُ وَرَاءَ ظَهْرِهِ ١٠
11. Soon will he cry for perdition,	11. Fasawfa yad'oo suboo-raa.	فَسَوْفَ يَدْعُو ثُبُورًا ١١
12. And he will enter a Bla-zing Fire.	12. Wa yaṣlaa sa'eeraa.	وَيَصْلَىٰ سَعِيرًا ١٢
13. Truly, did he go about among his people, rejoicing!	13. Innahoo kaana feee ahli-hee masrooraa.	إِنَّهُ كَانَ فِي أَهْلِهِ مَسْرُورًا ١٣
14. He verily deemed that he would never return (unto Allah).	14. Innahoo ẓanna al-lañy-yaḥoor.	إِنَّهُ ظَنَّ أَنْ لَنْ يَحُورَ ١٤
15. No, no! for his Lord was (ever) watchful of him!	15. Balaaa inna Rabbahoo kaana bihee baṣeeraa.	بَلَىٰ إِنَّ رَبَّهُ كَانَ بِهِ بَصِيرًا ١٥
16. So I do call to witness the ruddy glow of Sunset;	16. Falaaa uqsimu bishsha-faq.	فَلَا أُقْسِمُ بِالشَّفَقِ ١٦
17. The Night and its Homing;	17. Wallayli wa maa wasaq.	وَاللَّيْلِ وَمَا وَسَقَ ١٧
18. And the Moon in her fullness:	18. Walqamari izat-tasaq.	وَالْقَمَرِ إِذَا اتَّسَقَ ١٨
19. You shall surely travel from stage to stage.	19. Latarkabunna ṭabaqan 'an-ṭabaq.	لَتَرْكَبُنَّ طَبَقًا عَنْ طَبَقٍ ١٩
20. What then is the matter with them, that they believe not?-	20. Famaa lahum laa yu'mi-noon.	فَمَا لَهُمْ لَا يُؤْمِنُونَ ٢٠
21. And when the Qur'an is read to them, they fall not prostrate,	21. Wa izaa quri'a 'alayhimul-Qur-aanu laa yasjudoon. ۩	وَإِذَا قُرِئَ عَلَيْهِمُ الْقُرْآنُ لَا يَسْجُدُونَ ٢١ ۩
22. But on the contrary the Unbelievers reject (it).	22. Balil-lazeena kafaroo yukazziboon.	بَلِ الَّذِينَ كَفَرُوا يُكَذِّبُونَ ٢٢
23. And Allah knoweth best what they are hiding.	23. Wallaahu a'lamu bimaa yoo'oon.	وَاللَّهُ أَعْلَمُ بِمَا يُوعُونَ ٢٣
24. So announce to them a Chastisement Grievous,	24. Fabashshirhum bi'azaa-bin aleem.	فَبَشِّرْهُمْ بِعَذَابٍ أَلِيمٍ ٢٤
25. Except to those who believe and work righteous deeds:	25. Illal-lazeena aamanoo wa 'amiluṣ-ṣaaliḥaati	إِلَّا الَّذِينَ آمَنُوا وَعَمِلُوا الصَّالِحَاتِ

(Bow Down)

معانقة

السجدة (١٣)

Ikhfa اخفاء | Ghunna غنّہ | Ikhfa Meem Saakin اخفاء میم ساکن | Idghaam ادغام | Qalqala قلقلہ | Qalb قلب | Idghaam Meem Saakin ادغام میم ساکن

ع ٢٥/٩

English	Transliteration	Arabic
for them is a Reward that will never fail.	lahum ajrun ghayru mamnoon. **(Section 1)**	لَهُمْ اَجْرٌ غَيْرُ مَمْنُوْنٍ ۝٢٥
85. The Zodiacal Signs	**Sûrat al-Burûj–85** (Revealed at Makkah)	(٨٥) سُوْرَةُ الْبُرُوْجِ مَكِّيَّةٌ (٢٧)
In the name of Allah, Most Gracious, Most Merciful.	**Bismillaahir Raḥmaanir Raḥeem**	بِسْمِ اللّٰهِ الرَّحْمٰنِ الرَّحِيْمِ
1. By the sky, with its constellations.	1. Wassamaaa'i zaatil-burooj.	وَالسَّمَآءِ ذَاتِ الْبُرُوْجِ ۝١
2. By the promised Day (of Judgment);	2. Wal-Yawmil-Maw'ood.	وَالْيَوْمِ الْمَوْعُوْدِ ۝٢
3. By one that witnesses, and the subject of the witness;-	3. Wa Shaahidiñw-wa Mash-hood.	وَشَاهِدٍ وَّمَشْهُوْدٍ ۝٣
4. Woe to the makers of the pit (of fire),	4. Qutila Aṣ-ḥaabul-Ukh-dood.	قُتِلَ اَصْحٰبُ الْاُخْدُوْدِ ۝٤
5. Fire supplied (abundantly) with fuel:	5. Annaari zaatil-waqood.	النَّارِ ذَاتِ الْوَقُوْدِ ۝٥
6. Behold! They sat over against the (fire),	6. Iz hum 'alayhaa qu'ood.	اِذْ هُمْ عَلَيْهَا قُعُوْدٌ ۝٦
7. And they witnessed (all) that they were doing against the Believers.	7. Wa hum 'alaa maa yaf'aloona bilmu'mineena shuhood.	وَّهُمْ عَلٰى مَا يَفْعَلُوْنَ بِالْمُؤْمِنِيْنَ شُهُوْدٌ ۝٧
8. And they ill-treated them for no other reason than that they believed in Allah, Exalted in Power, Worthy of all Praise!-	8. Wa maa naqamoo minhum illaaa añy-yu'minoo billaahil-'Azeezil-Ḥameed.	وَمَا نَقَمُوْا مِنْهُمْ اِلَّآ اَنْ يُّؤْمِنُوْا بِاللّٰهِ الْعَزِيْزِ الْحَمِيْدِ ۝٨
9. Him to Whom belongs the dominion of the heavens and the earth! And Allah is Witness to all things.	9. Allazee lahoo mulkus-samaawaati wal-arḍ; wallaahu 'alaa kulli shay'in Shaheed.	الَّذِيْ لَهٗ مُلْكُ السَّمٰوٰتِ وَالْاَرْضِ ۭ وَ اللّٰهُ عَلٰى كُلِّ شَيْءٍ شَهِيْدٌ ۝٩
10. Those who persecute (or draw into temptation) the Believers, men and women, and do not turn in repentance, will have the Chastisement of Hell: They will have the Chastisement of the Burning Fire.	10. Innal-lazeena fatanul-mu'mineena wal-mu'minaati summa lam yatooboo falahum 'azaabu Jahannama wa lahum 'azaabul-ḥareeq.	اِنَّ الَّذِيْنَ فَتَنُوا الْمُؤْمِنِيْنَ وَالْمُؤْمِنٰتِ ثُمَّ لَمْ يَتُوْبُوْا فَلَهُمْ عَذَابُ جَهَنَّمَ وَلَهُمْ عَذَابُ الْحَرِيْقِ ۝١٠
11. For those who believe and do righteous deeds, will be in the Gardens; beneath which rivers flow: That is the great Salvation, (the fulfilment of all desires),	11. Innal-lazeena aamanoo wa 'amiluṣ-ṣaaliḥaati lahum Jannaatun tajree min taḥtihal-anhaar; zaalikal-fawzul-kabeer.	اِنَّ الَّذِيْنَ اٰمَنُوْا وَعَمِلُوا الصّٰلِحٰتِ لَهُمْ جَنّٰتٌ تَجْرِيْ مِنْ تَحْتِهَا الْاَنْهٰرُ ۭ۬ ذٰلِكَ الْفَوْزُ الْكَبِيْرُ ۝١١
12. Truly strong is the Grip (and Power) of your Lord.	12. Inna baṭsha Rabbika lashadeed.	اِنَّ بَطْشَ رَبِّكَ لَشَدِيْدٌ ۝١٢
13. Lo! He it is Who produceth, then reproduceth,	13. Innahoo Huwa yubdi'u wa yu'eed.	اِنَّهٗ هُوَ يُبْدِئُ وَيُعِيْدُ ۝١٣
14. And He is the Forgiving, the Loving,	14. Wa Huwal-Ghafoorul-Wadood.	وَهُوَ الْغَفُوْرُ الْوَدُوْدُ ۝١٤
15. Lord of the Throne of Glory,	15. Zul-'Arshil-Majeed.	ذُو الْعَرْشِ الْمَجِيْدُ ۝١٥
16. Doer (without let) of all that He intends.	16. Fa'-'aalul-limaa yureed.	فَعَّالٌ لِّمَا يُرِيْدُ ۝١٦

آية حصية ١٢

Ikhfa اخفاء | Ghunna غُنّہ | Ikhfa Meem Saakin اخفاء میم ساکن | Idghaam ادغام | Qalqala قلقلہ | Qalb قلب | Idghaam Meem Saakin ادغام میم ساکن

17. Has the story reached you, of the forces-
18. Of Pharaoh and the Thamud?
19. And yet the Unbelievers (persist) in rejecting (the Truth)!
20. But Allah does encompass them from behind!
21. No, this is a Glorious Qur'an,
22. (Inscribed) in a Tablet Preserved.

86. The Night-Visitant

In the name of Allah, Most Gracious, Most Merciful.

1. By the Sky and the Night-Visitant (therein);-
2. And what will explain to thee what the Night-Visitant is?
3. (It is) the Star of piercing brightness;-
4. There is no soul but has a protector over it.
5. Now let man but think from what he is created!
6. He is created from a drop emitted-
7. Proceeding from between the backbone and the ribs:
8. Surely (Allah) is able to bring him back (to life)!
9. The Day that (all) things secret will be tested,
10. (Man) will have no power, and no helper.
11. By the Firmament which gives recurring rain,
12. And the earth which splitteth (with the growth of trees and plants)
13. Lo! This (Qur'an) is a conclusive word,
14. It is not a thing for amusement.
15. As for them, they are but plotting a scheme,
16. And I am planning a scheme.
17. Therefore grant a delay to the Unbelievers: Give respite to them gently (for awhile).

17. Hal ataaka ḥadeesul-junood.
18. Fir'awna wa Samood.
19. Balil-lazeena kafaroo fee takzeeb.
20. Wallaahu miñw-waraaa'i-him-muḥeeṭ.
21. Bal huwa Qur-aanum-Majeed.
22. Fee Lawḥim-Maḥfooẓ. **(Section 1)**

Sûrat aṭ-Ṭâriq–86

(Revealed at Makkah)

Bismillaahir Raḥmaanir Raḥeem

1. Wassamaaa'i waṭṭaariq.
2. Wa maaa adraaka maṭ-ṭaariq.
3. Annajmus-saaqib.
4. In kullu nafsil-lammaa 'alayhaa ḥaafiẓ.
5. Fal-yanẓuril-insaanu mimma khuliq.
6. Khuliqa mim-maaa'in daafiq.
7. Yakhruju mim bayniṣ-ṣulbi wat-taraaa'ib.
8. Innahoo 'alaa raj'ihee laqaadir.
9. Yawma tublas-saraaa'ir.
10. Famaa lahoo min quwwatiñw-wa laa naaṣir.
11. Wassamaaa'i zaatir-raj'.
12. Wal-arḍi zaatiṣ-ṣad'.
13. Innahoo laqawlun faṣl.
14. Wa maa huwa bil-hazl.
15. Innahum yakeedoona kaydaa.
16. Wa akeedu kaydaa.
17. Famahhilil-kaafireena amhilhum ruwaydaa. **(Section 1)**

هَلْ اَتٰىكَ حَدِيْثُ الْجُنُوْدِ ﴿١٧﴾
فِرْعَوْنَ وَثَمُوْدَ ﴿١٨﴾
بَلِ الَّذِيْنَ كَفَرُوْا فِيْ تَكْذِيْبٍ ﴿١٩﴾
وَّاللّٰهُ مِنْ وَّرَآئِهِمْ مُّحِيْطٌ ﴿٢٠﴾
بَلْ هُوَ قُرْاٰنٌ مَّجِيْدٌ ﴿٢١﴾
فِيْ لَوْحٍ مَّحْفُوْظٍ ﴿٢٢﴾ ع

(٨٦) سُوْرَةُ الطَّارِقِ مَكِّيَّةٌ (٣٦)

بِسْمِ اللّٰهِ الرَّحْمٰنِ الرَّحِيْمِ

وَالسَّمَآءِ وَالطَّارِقِ ﴿١﴾
وَمَآ اَدْرٰىكَ مَا الطَّارِقُ ﴿٢﴾
النَّجْمُ الثَّاقِبُ ﴿٣﴾
اِنْ كُلُّ نَفْسٍ لَّمَّا عَلَيْهَا حَافِظٌ ﴿٤﴾
فَلْيَنْظُرِ الْاِنْسَانُ مِمَّ خُلِقَ ﴿٥﴾
خُلِقَ مِنْ مَّآءٍ دَافِقٍ ﴿٦﴾
يَّخْرُجُ مِنْۢ بَيْنِ الصُّلْبِ وَالتَّرَآئِبِ ﴿٧﴾
اِنَّهٗ عَلٰى رَجْعِهٖ لَقَادِرٌ ﴿٨﴾
يَوْمَ تُبْلَى السَّرَآئِرُ ﴿٩﴾
فَمَا لَهٗ مِنْ قُوَّةٍ وَّلَا نَاصِرٍ ﴿١٠﴾
وَالسَّمَآءِ ذَاتِ الرَّجْعِ ﴿١١﴾
وَالْاَرْضِ ذَاتِ الصَّدْعِ ﴿١٢﴾
اِنَّهٗ لَقَوْلٌ فَصْلٌ ﴿١٣﴾
وَّمَا هُوَ بِالْهَزْلِ ﴿١٤﴾
اِنَّهُمْ يَكِيْدُوْنَ كَيْدًا ﴿١٥﴾
وَّاَكِيْدُ كَيْدًا ﴿١٦﴾
فَمَهِّلِ الْكٰفِرِيْنَ اَمْهِلْهُمْ
رُوَيْدًا ﴿١٧﴾ ع

Ikhfa اخفاء | Ghunna غنّہ | Ikhfa Meem Saakin اخفاء میم ساکن | Idghaam ادغام | Qalqala قلقلہ | Qalb قلب | Idghaam Meem Saakin ادغام میم ساکن

87. The Most High

In the name of Allah, Most Gracious, Most Merciful.

Sûrat al-A'lâ–87

(Revealed at Makkah)

Bismillaahir Raḥmaanir Raḥeem

سُوْرَةُ الْاَعْلٰى مَكِّيَّةٌ (٨٧) (٨)

بِسْمِ اللّٰهِ الرَّحْمٰنِ الرَّحِيْمِ

1. Glorify the name of thy Guardian-Lord Most High,	1. Sabbiḥis-ma Rabbikal-A'laa.	سَبِّحِ اسْمَ رَبِّكَ الْاَعْلَى (١)
2. Who createth, then disposeth;	2. Allazee khalaqa fasawwaa.	الَّذِىْ خَلَقَ فَسَوّٰى (٢)
3. Who has ordained laws. And granted guidance;	3. Wallazee qaddara fahadaa.	وَالَّذِىْ قَدَّرَ فَهَدٰى (٣)
4. And Who brings out the (green and luscious) pasture,	4. Wallazeee akhrajal-mar'aa.	وَالَّذِىْٓ اَخْرَجَ الْمَرْعٰى (٤)
5. And then does make it (but) swarthy stubble.	5. Faja'alahoo ghusaaa'an aḥwaa.	فَجَعَلَهٗ غُثَآءً اَحْوٰى (٥)
6. By degrees shall We teach you to declare (the Message), so you shall not forget,	6. Sanuqri'uka falaa tansaaa.	سَنُقْرِئُكَ فَلَا تَنْسٰٓى (٦)
7. Except as Allah wills: For He knoweth what is manifest and what is hidden.	7. Illaa maa shaaa'al-laah; innahoo ya'lamul-jahra wa maa yakhfaa.	اِلَّا مَا شَآءَ اللّٰهُ ؕ اِنَّهٗ يَعْلَمُ الْجَهْرَ وَمَا يَخْفٰى (٧)
8. And We shall ease thy way unto the state of ease.	8. Wa nu-yassiruka lilyusraa.	وَنُيَسِّرُكَ لِلْيُسْرٰى (٨)
9. Therefore remind (men), for of use is the reminder.	9. Fazakkir in nafa'atiz-zikraa.	فَذَكِّرْ اِنْ نَّفَعَتِ الذِّكْرٰى (٩)
10. He will heed who feareth,	10. Sa-yazzakkaru mañy-yakhshaa.	سَيَذَّكَّرُ مَنْ يَّخْشٰى (١٠)
11. But it will be avoided by those most unfortunate ones,	11. Wa yatajannabuhal-ashqaa.	وَيَتَجَنَّبُهَا الْاَشْقَى (١١)
12. Who will enter the Great Fire,	12. Allazee yaṣlan-Naaral-kubraa.	الَّذِىْ يَصْلَى النَّارَ الْكُبْرٰى (١٢)
13. In which they will then neither die nor live.	13. Summa laa yamootu feehaa wa laa yaḥyaa.	ثُمَّ لَا يَمُوْتُ فِيْهَا وَلَا يَحْيٰى (١٣)
14. But those will prosper who purify themselves,	14. Qad aflaḥa man tazakkaa.	قَدْ اَفْلَحَ مَنْ تَزَكّٰى (١٤)
15. And remembereth the name of his Lord, so prayeth.	15. Wa zakaras-ma Rabbihee faṣallaa.	وَذَكَرَ اسْمَ رَبِّهٖ فَصَلّٰى (١٥)
16. No, you prefer the life of this world;	16. Bal tu'siroonal-ḥayaatad-dunyaa.	بَلْ تُؤْثِرُوْنَ الْحَيٰوةَ الدُّنْيَا (١٦)
17. But the Hereafter is better and more enduring.	17. Wal-Aakhiratu khayruñw-wa abqaa.	وَالْاٰخِرَةُ خَيْرٌ وَّاَبْقٰى (١٧)
18. And this is in the Books of the earliest (Revelation),-	18. Inna haazaa lafiṣ-Ṣuḥufil-oolaa.	اِنَّ هٰذَا لَفِى الصُّحُفِ الْاُوْلٰى (١٨)
19. The Books of Abraham and Moses.	19. Ṣuḥufi Ibraaheema wa Moosaa. **(Section 1)**	صُحُفِ اِبْرٰهِيْمَ وَمُوْسٰى (١٩) ع ١٩ ١٢

88. The Overwhelming Event

In the name of Allah, Most Gracious, Most Merciful.

Sûrat al-Ghâshiyah–88

(Revealed at Makkah)

Bismillaahir Raḥmaanir Raḥeem

سُوْرَةُ الْغَاشِيَةِ مَكِّيَّةٌ (٨٨) (٦٨)

بِسْمِ اللّٰهِ الرَّحْمٰنِ الرَّحِيْمِ

1. Hath there come unto thee tidings of the Overwhelming?	1. Hal ataaka ḥadeesul-ghaashiyah.	هَلْ اَتٰىكَ حَدِيْثُ الْغَاشِيَةِ (١)
2. Some faces, that Day, will be humiliated,	2. Wujoohuñy-Yawma'izin khaashi'ah.	وُجُوْهٌ يَّوْمَئِذٍ خَاشِعَةٌ (٢)

Ikhfa اخفاء | Ghunna غنّہ | Ikhfa Meem Saakin اخفاء میم ساکن | Idghaam ادغام | Qalqala قلقلہ | Qalb قلب | Idghaam Meem Saakin ادغام میم ساکن

3. Labouring (hard), weary,-	3. 'Aamilatun-naaṣibah.	عَامِلَةٌ نَّاصِبَةٌ ﴿٣﴾
4. The while they enter the Blazing Fire,-	4. Taṣlaa Naaran Ḥaamiyah.	تَصْلٰى نَارًا حَامِيَةً ﴿٤﴾
5. The while they are given, to drink, of a boiling hot spring,	5. Tusqaa min 'aynin aaniyah.	تُسْقٰى مِنْ عَيْنٍ اٰنِيَةٍ ﴿٥﴾
6. There will be no food for them but a bitter Dhari'	6. Laysa lahum ṭa'aamun illaa min ḍaree'.	لَيْسَ لَهُمْ طَعَامٌ اِلَّا مِنْ ضَرِيْعٍ ﴿٦﴾
7. Which will neither nourish nor satisfy hunger.	7. Laa yusminu wa laa yughnee min joo'.	لَّا يُسْمِنُ وَلَا يُغْنِيْ مِنْ جُوْعٍ ﴿٧﴾
8. (Other) faces that Day will be joyful,	8. Wujoohuñy-Yawma'iz̲in naa'imah.	وُجُوْهٌ يَّوْمَئِذٍ نَّاعِمَةٌ ﴿٨﴾
9. Pleased with their striving,-	9. Lisa'yihaa raaḍiyah.	لِّسَعْيِهَا رَاضِيَةٌ ﴿٩﴾
10. In a Garden on high,	10. Fee Jannatin 'aaliyah.	فِيْ جَنَّةٍ عَالِيَةٍ ﴿١٠﴾
11. Where they shall hear no (word) of vanity:	11. Laa tasma'u feehaa laaghiyah.	لَّا تَسْمَعُ فِيْهَا لَاغِيَةً ﴿١١﴾
12. Therein will be a bubbling spring:	12. Feehaa 'aynun jaariyah.	فِيْهَا عَيْنٌ جَارِيَةٌ ﴿١٢﴾
13. Therein will be couches (of dignity), raised on high,	13. Feehaa sururum-marfoo'ah.	فِيْهَا سُرُرٌ مَّرْفُوْعَةٌ ﴿١٣﴾
14. Goblets placed (ready),	14. Wa akwaabum-mawḍoo'ah.	وَّاَكْوَابٌ مَّوْضُوْعَةٌ ﴿١٤﴾
15. And cushions set in rows,	15. Wa namaariqu maṣfoofah.	وَّنَمَارِقُ مَصْفُوْفَةٌ ﴿١٥﴾
16. And rich carpets (all) spread out.	16. Wa zaraabiyyu mabsoosah.	وَّزَرَابِيُّ مَبْثُوْثَةٌ ﴿١٦﴾
17. Do they not look at the Camels, how they are made?-	17. Afalaa yanẓuroona ilal-ibili kayfa khuliqat.	اَفَلَا يَنْظُرُوْنَ اِلَى الْاِبِلِ كَيْفَ خُلِقَتْ ﴿١٧﴾
18. And at the Sky, how it is raised high?-	18. Wa ilas-samaaa'i kayfa rufi'at.	وَاِلَى السَّمَآءِ كَيْفَ رُفِعَتْ ﴿١٨﴾
19. And at the Mountains, how they are fixed firm?-	19. Wa ilal-jibaali kayfa nuṣibat.	وَاِلَى الْجِبَالِ كَيْفَ نُصِبَتْ ﴿١٩﴾
20. And at the Earth, how it is spread out?	20. Wa ilal-arḍi kayfa suṭiḥat.	وَاِلَى الْاَرْضِ كَيْفَ سُطِحَتْ ﴿٢٠﴾
21. Therefore you do give remind, for you are one to remind.	21. Faz̲akkir innama anta Muz̲akkir.	فَذَكِّرْ اِنَّمَآ اَنْتَ مُذَكِّرٌ ﴿٢١﴾
22. You are not one to manage (men's) affairs.	22. Lasta 'alayhim bimuṣayṭir.	لَسْتَ عَلَيْهِمْ بِمُصَيْطِرٍ ﴿٢٢﴾
23. But if any turn away and reject Allah,-	23. Illaa man tawallaa wa kafar.	اِلَّا مَنْ تَوَلّٰى وَكَفَرَ ﴿٢٣﴾
24. Allah will punish him with a mighty Punishment,	24. Fa-yu'az̲z̲ibuhul-laahul-'az̲aabal-akbar.	فَيُعَذِّبُهُ اللّٰهُ الْعَذَابَ الْاَكْبَرَ ﴿٢٤﴾
25. For to Us will be their return;	25. Inna ilaynaaa iyaabahum.	اِنَّ اِلَيْنَآ اِيَابَهُمْ ﴿٢٥﴾
26. Then it will be for Us to call them to account.	26. Summa inna 'alaynaa ḥisaabahum. **(Section 1)**	ثُمَّ اِنَّ عَلَيْنَا حِسَابَهُمْ ﴿٢٦﴾

وقف لازم

النصف ع ١

Ikhfa اخفاء | Ghunna غنّہ | Ikhfa Meem Saakin اخفاء میم ساکن | Idghaam ادغام | Qalqala قلقلہ | Qalb قلب | Idghaam Meem Saakin ادغام میم ساکن

89. The Break of Day In the name of Allah, Most Gracious, Most Merciful.	Sûrat al-Fajr–89 (Revealed at Makkah) Bismillaahir Raḥmaanir Raḥeem	(٨٩) سُوْرَةُ الْفَجْرِ مَكِّيَّةٌ (١٠) بِسْمِ اللّٰهِ الرَّحْمٰنِ الرَّحِيْمِ
1. By the break of Day;	1. Wal-Fajr.	وَالْفَجْرِ ﴿١﴾
2. By the ten Nights.	2. Wa layaalin ʻashr.	وَلَيَالٍ عَشْرٍ ﴿٢﴾
3. By the even and odd (contrasted);	3. Wash-shafʻi wal-watr.	وَّالشَّفْعِ وَالْوَتْرِ ﴿٣﴾
4. And by the Night when it passeth away;-	4. Wallayli iz̲aa yasr.	وَالَّيْلِ اِذَا يَسْرِ ﴿٤﴾
5. There surely is an oath for thinking man.	5. Hal fee z̲aalika qasamul-liz̲ee ḥijr.	هَلْ فِيْ ذٰلِكَ قَسَمٌ لِّذِيْ حِجْرٍ ﴿٥﴾
6. O you not see how your Lord dealt with the ʻAd (people),	6. Alam tara kayfa faʻala Rabbuka biʻaad.	اَلَمْ تَرَ كَيْفَ فَعَلَ رَبُّكَ بِعَادٍ ﴿٦﴾
7. Of the (city of) Iram, with lofty pillars,	7. Irama z̲aatil-ʻimaad.	اِرَمَ ذَاتِ الْعِمَادِ ﴿٧﴾
8. The like of which were not produced in (all) the land?	8. Allatee lam yukhlaq mis̲luhaa fil-bilaad.	الَّتِيْ لَمْ يُخْلَقْ مِثْلُهَا فِي الْبِلَادِ ﴿٨﴾
9. And with the Thamud (people), who cut out (huge) rocks in the valley?-	9. Wa S̲amoodal-laz̲eena jaabuṣ-ṣakhra bil-waad.	وَثَمُوْدَ الَّذِيْنَ جَابُوا الصَّخْرَ بِالْوَادِ ﴿٩﴾
10. And with Pharaoh, lord of stakes?	10. Wa Firʻawna z̲il-awtaad.	وَفِرْعَوْنَ ذِي الْاَوْتَادِ ﴿١٠﴾
11. (All) these transgressed beyond bounds in the lands,	11. Allaz̲eena ṭaghaw fil-bilaad.	الَّذِيْنَ طَغَوْا فِي الْبِلَادِ ﴿١١﴾
12. And heaped therein mischief (on mischief).	12. Fa-aks̲aroo feehal-fasaad.	فَاَكْثَرُوْا فِيْهَا الْفَسَادَ ﴿١٢﴾
13. Therefore did your Lord pour on them a scourge of diverse chastisements:	13. Faṣabba ʻalayhim Rabbuka sawṭa ʻaz̲aab.	فَصَبَّ عَلَيْهِمْ رَبُّكَ سَوْطَ عَذَابٍ ﴿١٣﴾
14. For your Lord is (as a Guardian) on a watch-tower.	14. Inna Rabbaka labil-mirṣaad.	اِنَّ رَبَّكَ لَبِالْمِرْصَادِ ﴿١٤﴾
15. As for man, whenever his Lord trieth him by honouring him, and is gracious unto him, he saith: My Lord honoureth me.	15. Fa-ammal-insaanu iz̲aa mab-talaahu Rabbuhoo fa-akramahoo wa naʻ-ʻamahoo fa-yaqoolu Rabbeee akraman.	فَاَمَّا الْاِنْسَانُ اِذَا مَا ابْتَلٰىهُ رَبُّهٗ فَاَكْرَمَهٗ وَنَعَّمَهٗ ۙ فَيَقُوْلُ رَبِّيْۤ اَكْرَمَنِ ﴿١٥﴾
16. But when He tries him, restricting his subsistence for him, then says he (in despair), “My Lord has humiliated me!”	16. Wa ammaaa iz̲aa mabtalaahu faqadara ʻalayhi rizqahoo fa-yaqoolu Rabbeee ahaanan.	وَاَمَّاۤ اِذَا مَا ابْتَلٰىهُ فَقَدَرَ عَلَيْهِ رِزْقَهٗ ۙ فَيَقُوْلُ رَبِّيْۤ اَهَانَنِ ﴿١٦﴾
17. No, nay! but you honour not the orphans!	17. Kallaa bal laa tukrimoonal-yateem.	كَلَّا بَلْ لَّا تُكْرِمُوْنَ الْيَتِيْمَ ﴿١٧﴾
18. Nor do you encourage one another to feed the poor!-	18. Wa laa taḥaaaḍḍoona ʻalaa ṭaʻaamil- miskeen.	وَلَا تَحٰٓضُّوْنَ عَلٰى طَعَامِ الْمِسْكِيْنِ ﴿١٨﴾
19. And you devour inheritance - all with greed,	19. Wa taåkuloonat-turaas̲a aklal-lammaa.	وَتَاْكُلُوْنَ التُّرَاثَ اَكْلًا لَّمًّا ﴿١٩﴾
20. And you love wealth with inordinate love!	20. Wa tuḥibboonal-maala ḥubban jammaa.	وَّتُحِبُّوْنَ الْمَالَ حُبًّا جَمًّا ﴿٢٠﴾
21. No! When the earth is pounded to powder,	21. Kallaaa iz̲aa dukkatil-arḍu dakkan dakkaa.	كَلَّاۤ اِذَا دُكَّتِ الْاَرْضُ دَكًّا دَكًّا ﴿٢١﴾
22. And your Lord cometh, and His angels, rank upon rank,	22. Wa jaaa'a Rabbuka wal-malaku ṣaffan ṣaffaa.	وَّجَآءَ رَبُّكَ وَالْمَلَكُ صَفًّا صَفًّا ﴿٢٢﴾

Ikhfa	Ghunna	Ikhfa Meem Saakin	Idghaam	Qalqala	Qalb	Idghaam Meem Saakin
اخفاء	غُنّہ	اخفاءمیم ساکن	ادغام	قلقلہ	قلب	ادغام میم ساکن

23. And hell is brought near that day; on that day man will remember, but how will the remembrance (then avail him)?	23. Wa jeee'a Yawma'izim bi-Jahannam; Yawma'iziñy-yatazakkarul-insaanu wa annaa lahuz-zikraa.	وَجِايْٓءَ يَوْمَئِذٍۢ بِجَهَنَّمَ ۙ يَوْمَئِذٍ يَّتَذَكَّرُ الْاِنْسَانُ وَاَنّٰى لَهُ الذِّكْرٰى ﴿٢٣﴾
24. He will say: "Ah! Would that I had sent forth (good deeds) for (this) my (Future) Life!"	24. Yaqoolu yaa laytanee qaddamtu liḥayaatee.	يَقُوْلُ يٰلَيْتَنِيْ قَدَّمْتُ لِحَيَاتِيْ ﴿٢٤﴾
25. None punisheth as He will punish on that day!	25. Fa-Yawma'izil-laa yu'az-zibu 'azaabahooo aḥad.	فَيَوْمَئِذٍ لَّا يُعَذِّبُ عَذَابَهٗٓ اَحَدٌ ﴿٢٥﴾
26. And His bonds will be such as none (other) can bind.	26. Wa laa yoosiqu wasaaqa-hooo aḥad.	وَّلَا يُوْثِقُ وَثَاقَهٗٓ اَحَدٌ ﴿٢٦﴾
27. But ah! Thou soul at peace!	27. Yaaa ayyatuhan-nafsul-mutma'innah.	يٰٓاَيَّتُهَا النَّفْسُ الْمُطْمَئِنَّةُ ﴿٢٧﴾
28. Return unto thy Lord, content in His good pleasure!	28. Irji'eee ilaa Rabbiki raaḍiyatam-marḍiyyah.	ارْجِعِيْٓ اِلٰى رَبِّكِ رَاضِيَةً مَّرْضِيَّةً ﴿٢٨﴾
29. "Enter you, then, among My devotees!	29. Fadkhulee fee 'ibaadee.	فَادْخُلِيْ فِيْ عِبٰدِيْ ﴿٢٩﴾
30. "Yes, enter you My Heaven!	30. Wadkhulee Jannatee. **(Section 1)**	وَادْخُلِيْ جَنَّتِيْ ﴿٣٠﴾

90. The City

In the name of Allah, Most Gracious, Most Merciful.

Sûrat al-Balad–90

(Revealed at Makkah)

Bismillaahir Raḥmaanir Raḥeem

(٩٠) سُوْرَةُ الْبَلَدِ مَكِّيَّةٌ (٣٥)

بِسْمِ اللّٰهِ الرَّحْمٰنِ الرَّحِيْمِ

1. I do call to witness this City;-	1. Laaa uqsimu bihaazal-balad.	لَآ اُقْسِمُ بِهٰذَا الْبَلَدِ ﴿١﴾
2. And you are a freeman of this City;-	2. Wa anta ḥillum bihaazal-balad.	وَاَنْتَ حِلٌّۢ بِهٰذَا الْبَلَدِ ﴿٢﴾
3. And (the mystic ties of) parent and child;-	3. Wa waalidiñw-wa maa walad.	وَوَالِدٍ وَّمَا وَلَدَ ﴿٣﴾
4. Verily We have created man into toil and struggle.	4. Laqad khalaqnal-insaana fee kabad.	لَقَدْ خَلَقْنَا الْاِنْسَانَ فِيْ كَبَدٍ ﴿٤﴾
5. Thinks he, that none has power over him?	5. Ayaḥsabu al-lañy-yaqdira 'alayhi aḥad.	اَيَحْسَبُ اَنْ لَّنْ يَّقْدِرَ عَلَيْهِ اَحَدٌ ﴿٥﴾
6. And he saith: I have destroyed vast wealth:	6. Yaqoolu ahlaktu maalal-lubadaa.	يَقُوْلُ اَهْلَكْتُ مَالًا لُّبَدًا ﴿٦﴾
7. Thinks he that none beholds him?	7. Ayaḥsabu al-lam yara-hooo aḥad.	اَيَحْسَبُ اَنْ لَّمْ يَرَهٗٓ اَحَدٌ ﴿٧﴾
8. Have We not made for him a pair of eyes?-	8. Alam naj'al lahoo 'ay-nayn.	اَلَمْ نَجْعَلْ لَّهٗ عَيْنَيْنِ ﴿٨﴾
9. And a tongue, and a pair of lips?-	9. Wa lisaanañw-wa shafa-tayn.	وَلِسَانًا وَّشَفَتَيْنِ ﴿٩﴾
10. And shown him the two highways?	10. Wa hadaynaahun-naj-dayn.	وَهَدَيْنٰهُ النَّجْدَيْنِ ﴿١٠﴾
11. But he has made no haste on the path that is steep.	11. Falaq-taḥamal-'aqabah.	فَلَا اقْتَحَمَ الْعَقَبَةَ ﴿١١﴾
12. And what will explain to you the path that is steep?-	12. Wa maaa adraaka mal-'a-qabah.	وَمَآ اَدْرٰىكَ مَا الْعَقَبَةُ ﴿١٢﴾
13. (It is:) freeing the bondman;	13. Fakku raqabah.	فَكُّ رَقَبَةٍ ﴿١٣﴾
14. Or the giving of food in a day of privation.	14. Aw iṭ'aamun fee yawmin zee masghabah.	اَوْ اِطْعٰمٌ فِيْ يَوْمٍ ذِيْ مَسْغَبَةٍ ﴿١٤﴾
15. An orphan near of kin,	15. Yateeman zaa maqrabah.	يَّتِيْمًا ذَا مَقْرَبَةٍ ﴿١٥﴾

وقف لازم

Ikhfa اخفاء · Ghunna غُنّہ · Ikhfa Meem Saakin اخفاء میم ساکن · Idghaam ادغام · Qalqala قلقلہ · Qalb قلب · Idghaam Meem Saakin ادغام میم ساکن

Translation	Transliteration	Arabic
16. Or to the indigent (down) in the dust.	16. Aw miskeenan zaa matrabah.	أَوْ مِسْكِيْنًا ذَا مَتْرَبَةٍ ﴿١٦﴾
17. And to be of those who believe and exhort one another to perseverance and exhort one another to pity.	17. Summa kaana minal-lazeena aamanoo wa tawaaṣaw biṣṣabri wa tawaaṣaw bil-marḥamah.	ثُمَّ كَانَ مِنَ الَّذِيْنَ اٰمَنُوْا وَتَوَاصَوْا بِالصَّبْرِ وَتَوَاصَوْا بِالْمَرْحَمَةِ ﴿١٧﴾
18. Such are the Companions of the Right Hand.	18. Ulaaa'ika Aṣ-ḥaabul-Maymanah.	أُولٰٓئِكَ أَصْحٰبُ الْمَيْمَنَةِ ﴿١٨﴾
19. But those who reject Our Signs, they are the (unhappy) Companions of the Left Hand.	19. Wallazeena kafaroo bi-Aayaatinaa hum Aṣ-ḥaabul-Mash'amah.	وَالَّذِيْنَ كَفَرُوْا بِاٰيٰتِنَا هُمْ أَصْحٰبُ الْمَشْئَمَةِ ﴿١٩﴾
20. On them will be Fire vaulted over (all round).	20. 'Alayhim Naarum-mu'ṣadah. **(Section 1)**	عَلَيْهِمْ نَارٌ مُّؤْصَدَةٌ ﴿٢٠﴾
91. The Sun **In the name of Allah, Most Gracious, Most Merciful.**	**Sûrat ash-Shams–91** (Revealed at Makkah) **Bismillaahir Raḥmaanir Raḥeem**	(٩١) سُوْرَةُ الشَّمْسِ مَكِّيَّةٌ (٢٦) بِسْمِ اللّٰهِ الرَّحْمٰنِ الرَّحِيْمِ
1. By the Sun and his (glorious) splendour;	1. Wash-shamsi wa ḍuḥaa-haa.	وَالشَّمْسِ وَضُحٰهَا ﴿١﴾
2. By the Moon as she follows him;	2. Wal-qamari izaa talaa-haa.	وَالْقَمَرِ إِذَا تَلٰهَا ﴿٢﴾
3. By the Day as it shows up (the Sun's) glory;	3. Wannahaari izaa jallaa-haa.	وَالنَّهَارِ إِذَا جَلّٰهَا ﴿٣﴾
4. By the Night as it conceals it;	4. Wallayli izaa yaghshaa-haa.	وَالَّيْلِ إِذَا يَغْشٰىهَا ﴿٤﴾
5. By the Firmament and its (wonderful) structure;	5. Wassamaaa'i wa maa banaahaa.	وَالسَّمَآءِ وَمَا بَنٰىهَا ﴿٥﴾
6. By the Earth and its (wide) expanse:	6. Wal-arḍi wa maa ṭaḥaa-haa.	وَالْأَرْضِ وَمَا طَحٰىهَا ﴿٦﴾
7. By the Soul, and the proportion and order given to it.	7. Wa nafsiñw-wa maa sawwaahaa.	وَنَفْسٍ وَّمَا سَوّٰىهَا ﴿٧﴾
8. And its enlightenment as to its wrong and its right;-	8. Fa-alhamahaa fujoorahaa wa taqwaahaa.	فَأَلْهَمَهَا فُجُوْرَهَا وَتَقْوٰىهَا ﴿٨﴾
9. Truly he succeeds that purifies it,	9. Qad aflaḥa man zakkaa-haa.	قَدْ أَفْلَحَ مَنْ زَكّٰىهَا ﴿٩﴾
10. And he fails that corrupts it!	10. Wa qad khaaba man dassaahaa.	وَقَدْ خَابَ مَنْ دَسّٰىهَا ﴿١٠﴾
11. The Thamud (people) rejected (their prophet) through their inordinate wrong-doing,	11. Kazzabat Samoodu bi-ṭaghwaahaaa.	كَذَّبَتْ ثَمُوْدُ بِطَغْوٰىهَآ ﴿١١﴾
12. When the basest of them broke forth.	12. Izim ba'aṣa ashqaahaa.	إِذِ انْۢبَعَثَ أَشْقٰىهَا ﴿١٢﴾
13. But the Apostle of Allah said to them: "It is a She-camel of Allah! And (bar her not from) having her drink!"	13. Faqaala lahum Rasoolul-laahi naaqatal-laahi wa suqyaa-haa.	فَقَالَ لَهُمْ رَسُوْلُ اللّٰهِ نَاقَةَ اللّٰهِ وَسُقْيٰهَا ﴿١٣﴾
14. Then they rejected him (as a false prophet), and they hamstrung her. So their Lord, on account of their crime, obliterated their traces and made them equal (in destruction, high and low)!	14. Fakazzaboohu fa'aqa-roohaa fadamdama 'alayhim Rabbuhum bizambihim fasaw-waahaa.	فَكَذَّبُوْهُ فَعَقَرُوْهَا ۙ فَدَمْدَمَ عَلَيْهِمْ رَبُّهُمْ بِذَنْۢبِهِمْ فَسَوّٰىهَا ﴿١٤﴾
15. And for Him is no fear of its consequences.	15. Wa laa yakhaafu 'uqbaahaa. **(Section 1)**	وَلَا يَخَافُ عُقْبٰهَا ﴿١٥﴾

Ikhfa اخفاء · Ghunna غنّہ · Ikhfa Meem Saakin اخفاءمیم ساکن · Idghaam ادغام · Qalqala قلقلہ · Qalb قلب · Idghaam Meem Saakin ادغام میم ساکن

92. The Night

In the name of Allah, Most Gracious, Most Merciful.

1. By the Night as it conceals (the light);
2. By the Day as it appears in glory;
3. By (the mystery of) the creation of male and female;-
4. Verily, (the ends) you strive for are diverse.
5. So he who gives (in charity) and fears (Allah),
6. And (in all sincerity) testifies to the best,-
7. We will indeed make smooth for him the path to Bliss.
8. But he who is a greedy miser and thinks himself self-sufficient,
9. And gives the lie to the best,-
10. We will indeed make smooth for him the path to Misery;
11. Nor will his wealth profit him when he falls headlong (into the Pit).
12. Verily We take upon Ourselves to guide,
13. And verily unto Us (belong) the End and the Beginning.
14. Therefore do I warn you of a Fire blazing fiercely;
15. None shall reach it but those most unfortunate ones
16. Who give the lie to Truth and turn their backs.
17. But those most devoted to Allah shall be removed far from it,-
18. Those who spend their wealth for increase in self-purification,
19. And have in their minds no favour from anyone for which a reward is expected in return,
20. But only the desire to seek for the Countenance of their Lord Most High;
21. And soon will they attain (complete) satisfaction.

Sûrat al-Layl–92

(Revealed at Makkah)

Bismillaahir Raḥmaanir Raḥeem

1. Wallayli izaa yaghshaa.
2. Wannahaari izaa tajallaa.
3. Wa maa khalaqaz-zakara wal-unsaaa.
4. Inna sa'yakum lashattaa.
5. Fa-ammaa man a'ṭaa wattaqaa.
6. Wa ṣaddaqa bil-ḥusnaa.
7. Fasanu-yassiruhoo lil-yusraa.
8. Wa ammaa mam bakhila wastaghnaa.
9. Wa kazzaba bil-ḥusnaa.
10. Fasanu-yassiruhoo lil-'usraa.
11. Wa maa yughnee 'anhu maaluhooo izaa taraddaa.
12. Inna 'alaynaa lal-hudaa.
13. Wa inna lanaa lal-Aakhirata wal-oolaa.
14. Fa-anzartukum Naaran talaẓẓaa.
15. Laa yaṣlaahaaa illal-ash-qaa.
16. Allazee kazzaba wa tawallaa.
17. Wa sa-yujannabuhal-atqaa.
18. Allazee yu'tee maalahoo yatazakkaa.
19. Wa maa li-aḥadin 'indahoo min ni'matin tujzaaa.
20. Illab-tighaaa'a Wajhi Rabbihil-A'laa.
21. Wa lasawfa yarḍaa.

(Section 1)

(٩٢) سُوْرَةُ الَّيْلِ مَكِّيَّةٌ (٩)

بِسْمِ اللّٰهِ الرَّحْمٰنِ الرَّحِيْمِ

وَالَّيْلِ اِذَا يَغْشٰى ﴿١﴾
وَالنَّهَارِ اِذَا تَجَلّٰى ﴿٢﴾
وَمَا خَلَقَ الذَّكَرَ وَالْاُنْثٰٓى ﴿٣﴾
اِنَّ سَعْيَكُمْ لَشَتّٰى ﴿٤﴾
فَاَمَّا مَنْ اَعْطٰى وَاتَّقٰى ﴿٥﴾
وَصَدَّقَ بِالْحُسْنٰى ﴿٦﴾
فَسَنُيَسِّرُهٗ لِلْيُسْرٰى ﴿٧﴾
وَاَمَّا مَنْۢ بَخِلَ وَاسْتَغْنٰى ﴿٨﴾
وَكَذَّبَ بِالْحُسْنٰى ﴿٩﴾
فَسَنُيَسِّرُهٗ لِلْعُسْرٰى ﴿١٠﴾
وَمَا يُغْنِيْ عَنْهُ مَالُهٗٓ اِذَا تَرَدّٰى ﴿١١﴾
اِنَّ عَلَيْنَا لَلْهُدٰى ﴿١٢﴾
وَاِنَّ لَنَا لَلْاٰخِرَةَ وَالْاُوْلٰى ﴿١٣﴾
فَاَنْذَرْتُكُمْ نَارًا تَلَظّٰى ﴿١٤﴾
لَا يَصْلٰىهَآ اِلَّا الْاَشْقَى ﴿١٥﴾
الَّذِيْ كَذَّبَ وَتَوَلّٰى ﴿١٦﴾
وَسَيُجَنَّبُهَا الْاَتْقَى ﴿١٧﴾
الَّذِيْ يُؤْتِيْ مَالَهٗ يَتَزَكّٰى ﴿١٨﴾
وَمَا لِاَحَدٍ عِنْدَهٗ مِنْ نِّعْمَةٍ تُجْزٰٓى ﴿١٩﴾
اِلَّا ابْتِغَآءَ وَجْهِ رَبِّهِ الْاَعْلٰى ﴿٢٠﴾
وَلَسَوْفَ يَرْضٰى ﴿٢١﴾

ع ١

93. The Glorious Morning Light

In the name of Allah, Most Gracious, Most Merciful.

1. By the Glorious Morning Light,

Sûrat aḍ-Ḍuḥâ–93

(Revealed at Makkah)

Bismillaahir Raḥmaanir Raḥeem

1. Waḍḍuḥaa.

(٩٣) سُوْرَةُ الضُّحٰى مَكِّيَّةٌ (١١)

بِسْمِ اللّٰهِ الرَّحْمٰنِ الرَّحِيْمِ

وَالضُّحٰى ﴿١﴾

Ikhfa اخفاء | Ghunna غنّہ | Ikhfa Meem Saakin اخفاء میم ساکن | Idghaam ادغام | Qalqala قلقلہ | Qalb قلب | Idghaam Meem Saakin ادغام میم ساکن

2. And by the Night when it is still,-	2. Wallayli i̲zaa sajaa.	وَالَّيْلِ اِذَا سَجٰى ﴿٢﴾
3. Your Guardian-Lord has not forsaken you, nor is He displeased.	3. Maa wadda'aka Rabbuka wa maa qalaa.	مَا وَدَّعَكَ رَبُّكَ وَمَا قَلٰى ﴿٣﴾
4. And verily the Hereafter will be better for you than the present.	4. Wa lal-Aakhiratu khayrul-laka minal-oolaa.	وَلَلْاٰخِرَةُ خَيْرٌ لَّكَ مِنَ الْاُوْلٰى ﴿٤﴾
5. And soon will your Guardian-Lord give you (that wherewith) you shall be well-pleased.	5. Wa la-sawfa yu'ṭeeka Rabbuka fatarḍaa.	وَلَسَوْفَ يُعْطِيْكَ رَبُّكَ فَتَرْضٰى ﴿٥﴾
6. Did He not find you an orphan and give you shelter (and care)?	6. Alam yajidka yateeman fa-aawaa.	اَلَمْ يَجِدْكَ يَتِيْمًا فَاٰوٰى ﴿٦﴾
7. And He found you wandering, and He gave you guidance.	7. Wa wajadaka ḍaaallan fahadaa.	وَوَجَدَكَ ضَآلًّا فَهَدٰى ﴿٧﴾
8. And He found you in need, and made you independent.	8. Wa wajadaka 'aaa'ilan fa-aghnaa.	وَوَجَدَكَ عَآئِلًا فَاَغْنٰى ﴿٨﴾
9. Therefore, treat not the orphan with harshness,	9. Fa-ammal-yateema falaa taqhar.	فَاَمَّا الْيَتِيْمَ فَلَا تَقْهَرْ ﴿٩﴾
10. Nor repulse the petitioner (unheard);	10. Wa ammas-saaa'ila falaa tanhar.	وَاَمَّا السَّآئِلَ فَلَا تَنْهَرْ ﴿١٠﴾
11. But the bounty of the Lord - rehearse and proclaim!	11. Wa ammaa bini'mati Rabbika faḥaddis̲. **(Section 1)**	وَاَمَّا بِنِعْمَةِ رَبِّكَ فَحَدِّثْ ﴿١١﴾ ع ١١ ١٨

94. The Expansion

In the name of Allah, Most Gracious, Most Merciful.

Sûrat al-Inshirâḥ–94

(Revealed at Makkah)

Bismillaahir Raḥmaanir Raḥeem

(٩٤) سُوْرَةُ الْاِنْشِرَاحِ مَكِّيَّةٌ (١٢)

بِسْمِ اللّٰهِ الرَّحْمٰنِ الرَّحِيْمِ

1. Have We not expanded you your breast?-	1. Alam nashraḥ laka ṣadrak.	اَلَمْ نَشْرَحْ لَكَ صَدْرَكَ ﴿١﴾
2. And removed from you your burden	2. Wa waḍa'naa 'anka wizrak.	وَوَضَعْنَا عَنْكَ وِزْرَكَ ﴿٢﴾
3. The which did gall your back?-	3. Allaz̲eee anqaḍa ẓahrak.	الَّذِيْٓ اَنْقَضَ ظَهْرَكَ ﴿٣﴾
4. And raised high the esteem (in which) you (are held)?	4. Wa rafa'naa laka z̲ikrak.	وَرَفَعْنَا لَكَ ذِكْرَكَ ﴿٤﴾
5. So, verily, with every difficulty, there is relief:	5. Fa-inna ma'al-'usri yusraa.	فَاِنَّ مَعَ الْعُسْرِ يُسْرًا ﴿٥﴾
6. Verily, with every difficulty there is relief.	6. Inna ma'al-'usri yusraa	اِنَّ مَعَ الْعُسْرِ يُسْرًا ﴿٦﴾
7. Therefore, when you are free (from your immediate task), still labour hard,	7. Fa-iz̲aa faraghta fanṣab.	فَاِذَا فَرَغْتَ فَانْصَبْ ﴿٧﴾
8. And to your Lord turn (all) your attention.	8. Wa ilaa Rabbika farghab. **(Section 1)**	وَاِلٰى رَبِّكَ فَارْغَبْ ﴿٨﴾ ع ٨ ١٩

95. The Fig

In the name of Allah, Most Gracious, Most Merciful.

Sûrat at-Tîn–95

(Revealed at Makkah)

Bismillaahir Raḥmaanir Raḥeem

(٩٥) سُوْرَةُ التِّيْنِ مَكِّيَّةٌ (٢٨)

بِسْمِ اللّٰهِ الرَّحْمٰنِ الرَّحِيْمِ

1. By the Fig and the Olive,	1. Watteeni wazzaytoon.	وَالتِّيْنِ وَالزَّيْتُوْنِ ﴿١﴾
2. And the Mount of Sinai,	2. Wa Ṭoori Seeneen.	وَطُوْرِ سِيْنِيْنَ ﴿٢﴾
3. And this City of security,-	3. Wa haaz̲al-baladil-ameen.	وَهٰذَا الْبَلَدِ الْاَمِيْنِ ﴿٣﴾
4. We have indeed created man in the best of	4. Laqad khalaqnal-insaana feee aḥsani	لَقَدْ خَلَقْنَا الْاِنْسَانَ فِيْٓ اَحْسَنِ

Ikhfa اخفاء · Ghunna غنّہ · Ikhfa Meem Saakin اخفاء میم ساکن · Idghaam ادغام · Qalqala قلقلہ · Qalb قلب · Idghaam Meem Saakin ادغام میم ساکن

moulds,	taqweem.	تَقْوِيمٍ ﴿٤﴾
5. Then do We abase him (to be) the lowest of the low,-	5. Summa radadnaahu asfala saafileen.	ثُمَّ رَدَدْنٰهُ اَسْفَلَ سٰفِلِيْنَ ﴿٥﴾
6. Except such as believe and do righteous deeds: For they shall have a reward unfailing.	6. Illal-lazeena aamanoo wa 'amiluṣ-ṣaaliḥaati falahum ajrun ghayru mamnoon.	اِلَّا الَّذِيْنَ اٰمَنُوْا وَعَمِلُوا الصّٰلِحٰتِ فَلَهُمْ اَجْرٌ غَيْرُ مَمْنُوْنٍ ﴿٦﴾
7. Then what can, after this, contradict thee, as to the judgment (to come)?	7. Famaa yukazzibuka ba'du bid-Deen.	فَمَا يُكَذِّبُكَ بَعْدُ بِالدِّيْنِ ﴿٧﴾
8. Is not Allah the wisest of judges?	8. Alaysal-laahu bi-aḥkamil-ḥaakimeen. **(Section 1)**	اَلَيْسَ اللّٰهُ بِاَحْكَمِ الْحٰكِمِيْنَ ﴿٨﴾

96. The Clot of Congealed Blood

In the name of Allah, Most Gracious, Most Merciful.

Sûrat al-'Alaq–96

(Revealed at Makkah)

Bismillaahir Raḥmaanir Raḥeem

(٩٦) سُوْرَةُ الْعَلَقِ مَكِّيَّةٌ (١)

بِسْمِ اللّٰهِ الرَّحْمٰنِ الرَّحِيْمِ

1. Proclaim! (or read!) in the name of your Lord and Cherisher, Who created-	1. Iqraå bismi Rabbikal-lazee khalaq.	اِقْرَاْ بِاسْمِ رَبِّكَ الَّذِيْ خَلَقَ ﴿١﴾
2. Created man, out of a (mere) clot of congealed blood:	2. Khalaqal-insaana min 'alaq	خَلَقَ الْاِنْسَانَ مِنْ عَلَقٍ ﴿٢﴾
3. Proclaim! And your Lord is Most Bountiful,-	3. Iqraå wa Rabbukal-Akram.	اِقْرَاْ وَرَبُّكَ الْاَكْرَمُ ﴿٣﴾
4. He Who taught (the use of) the pen,-	4. Allazee 'allama bil-qalam.	الَّذِيْ عَلَّمَ بِالْقَلَمِ ﴿٤﴾
5. Taught man that which he knew not.	5. 'Allamal-insaana maa lam ya'lam.	عَلَّمَ الْاِنْسَانَ مَا لَمْ يَعْلَمْ ﴿٥﴾
6. No, but man doth transgress all bounds,	6. Kallaaa innal-insaana layatghaaa.	كَلَّآ اِنَّ الْاِنْسَانَ لَيَطْغٰىٓ ﴿٦﴾
7. In that he looks upon himself as self-sufficient.	7. Ar-ra-aahus-taghnaa.	اَنْ رَّاٰهُ اسْتَغْنٰى ﴿٧﴾
8. Verily, to your Lord is the return (of all).	8. Inna ilaa Rabbikar-ruj'aa.	اِنَّ اِلٰى رَبِّكَ الرُّجْعٰى ﴿٨﴾
9. O you see one who forbids-	9. Ara'aytal-lazee yanhaa.	اَرَءَيْتَ الَّذِيْ يَنْهٰى ﴿٩﴾
10. A votary when he (turns) to pray?	10. 'Abdan izaa ṣallaa.	عَبْدًا اِذَا صَلّٰى ﴿١٠﴾
11. Do you see if he is on (the road of) Guidance?-	11. Ara'ayta in kaana 'alal-hudaaa.	اَرَءَيْتَ اِنْ كَانَ عَلَى الْهُدٰىٓ ﴿١١﴾
12. Or enjoins Righteousness?	12. Aw amara bittaqwaa.	اَوْ اَمَرَ بِالتَّقْوٰى ﴿١٢﴾
13. Do you see if he denies (Truth) and turns away?	13. Ara'ayta in kazzaba wa tawallaa.	اَرَءَيْتَ اِنْ كَذَّبَ وَتَوَلّٰى ﴿١٣﴾
14. Knows he not that Allah does see?	14. Alam ya'lam bi-annal-laaha yaraa.	اَلَمْ يَعْلَمْ بِاَنَّ اللّٰهَ يَرٰى ﴿١٤﴾
15. Let him beware! If he desist not, We will drag him by the forelock,-	15. Kallaa la-'il-lam yantahi lanasfa'am binnaaṣiyah.	كَلَّا لَئِنْ لَّمْ يَنْتَهِ ۙ لَنَسْفَعًا بِالنَّاصِيَةِ ﴿١٥﴾
16. A lying, sinful forelock!	16. Naaṣiyatin kaazibatin khaaṭi'ah.	نَاصِيَةٍ كَاذِبَةٍ خَاطِئَةٍ ﴿١٦﴾
17. Then, let him call (for help) to his council (of comrades):	17. Falyad'u naadiyah.	فَلْيَدْعُ نَادِيَهٗ ﴿١٧﴾
18. We will call on the angels of punishment (to deal with him)!	18. Sanad'uz-zabaaniyah.	سَنَدْعُ الزَّبَانِيَةَ ﴿١٨﴾

Ikhfa اخفاء · Ghunna غُنّہ · Ikhfa Meem Saakin اخفاء میم ساکن · Idghaam ادغام · Qalqala قلقلہ · Qalb قلب · Idghaam Meem Saakin ادغام میم ساکن

(Bow Down)

19. No, pay no heed to him but bow down in adoration, and bring yourself the closer (to Allah)!

97. The Night of Power or Honour

In the name of Allah, Most Gracious, Most Merciful.

1. We have indeed revealed this (Message) in the Night of Power:
2. And what will explain to you what the Night of Power is?
3. The Night of Power is better than a thousand months.
4. Therein come down the angels and the Spirit by Allah's permission, on every errand:
5. Peace!...This until the rise of morn!

98. The Clear Evidence

In the name of Allah, Most Gracious, Most Merciful.

1. Those who reject (Truth), among the People of the Book and among the Polytheists, were not going to depart (from their ways) until there should come to them Clear Evidence,-
2. An apostle from Allah, rehearsing scriptures kept pure and holy:
3. Wherein are laws (or decrees) right and straight.
4. Nor did the People of the Book make schisms, until after there came to them Clear Evidence.
5. And they have been commanded no more than this: To worship Allah, offering Him sincere devotion, being true (in faith); to establish regular prayer; and to practise regular charity; and that is the Religion Right and Straight.
6. Those who reject (Truth), among the People of the Book and among the Polytheists, will be in Hell-Fire, to dwell therein (for ever). They are the worst of creatures.
7. Those who have faith and do righteous deeds,- they are the best of creatures.

19. Kallaa laa tuṭi'hu wasjud waqtarib. ۩ **(Section 1)**

Sûrat al-Qadr–97

(Revealed at Makkah)

Bismillaahir Raḥmaanir Raḥeem

1. Innaaa anzalnaahu fee Laylatil-Qadr.
2. Wa maaa adraaka maa Laylatul-Qadr.
3. Laylatul-Qadri khayrum-min alfi shahr.
4. Tanazzalul-malaaa'ikatu war-Rooḥu feehaa bi-izni Rabbihim min kulli amr.
5. Salaamun hiya ḥattaa maṭla'il-Fajr. **(Section 1)**

Sûrat al-Bayyinah–98

(Revealed at Madinah)

Bismillaahir Raḥmaanir Raḥeem

1. Lam yakunil-lazeena kafaroo min Ahlil-Kitaabi wal-mushrikeena munfakkeena ḥattaa taâtiyahumul-bayyinah.
2. Rasoolum-minal-laahi yatloo ṣuḥufam-muṭahharah.
3. Feehaa kutubun qayyimah.
4. Wa maa tafarraqal-lazeena ootul-Kitaaba illaa mim ba'di maa jaaa'at-humul-bayyinah.
5. Wa maaa umirooo illaa liya'budul-laaha mukhliṣeena lahud-deena ḥunafaaa'a wa yuqeemuṣ-Ṣalaata wa yu'tuz-Zakaata wa zaalika deenul-qayyimah.
6. Innal-lazeena kafaroo min Ahlil-Kitaabi wal-mushrikeena fee Naari Jahannama khaalideena feehaa; ulaaa'ika hum sharrul-bariyyah.
7. Innal-lazeena aamanoo wa 'amiluṣ-ṣaaliḥaati ulaaa'ika hum-khayrul-bariyyah.

كَلَّا ۖ لَا تُطِعْهُ وَاسْجُدْ وَاقْتَرِبْ ۩ ١٩

سُورَةُ الْقَدْرِ مَكِّيَّةٌ (٩٧) (٢٥)

بِسْمِ اللَّهِ الرَّحْمَٰنِ الرَّحِيمِ

إِنَّا أَنزَلْنَاهُ فِي لَيْلَةِ الْقَدْرِ ١
وَمَا أَدْرَاكَ مَا لَيْلَةُ الْقَدْرِ ٢
لَيْلَةُ الْقَدْرِ خَيْرٌ مِّنْ أَلْفِ شَهْرٍ ٣
تَنَزَّلُ الْمَلَائِكَةُ وَالرُّوحُ فِيهَا بِإِذْنِ
رَبِّهِم مِّن كُلِّ أَمْرٍ ٤
سَلَامٌ هِيَ حَتَّىٰ مَطْلَعِ الْفَجْرِ ٥

سُورَةُ الْبَيِّنَةِ مَدَنِيَّةٌ (٩٨) (١٠٠)

بِسْمِ اللَّهِ الرَّحْمَٰنِ الرَّحِيمِ

لَمْ يَكُنِ الَّذِينَ كَفَرُوا مِنْ أَهْلِ الْكِتَابِ
وَالْمُشْرِكِينَ مُنفَكِّينَ حَتَّىٰ تَأْتِيَهُمُ
الْبَيِّنَةُ ١
رَسُولٌ مِّنَ اللَّهِ يَتْلُو صُحُفًا مُّطَهَّرَةً ٢
فِيهَا كُتُبٌ قَيِّمَةٌ ٣
وَمَا تَفَرَّقَ الَّذِينَ أُوتُوا الْكِتَابَ إِلَّا
مِن بَعْدِ مَا جَاءَتْهُمُ الْبَيِّنَةُ ٤
وَمَا أُمِرُوا إِلَّا لِيَعْبُدُوا اللَّهَ مُخْلِصِينَ
لَهُ الدِّينَ حُنَفَاءَ وَيُقِيمُوا الصَّلَاةَ
وَيُؤْتُوا الزَّكَاةَ ۚ وَذَٰلِكَ دِينُ الْقَيِّمَةِ ٥
إِنَّ الَّذِينَ كَفَرُوا مِنْ أَهْلِ الْكِتَابِ
وَالْمُشْرِكِينَ فِي نَارِ جَهَنَّمَ خَالِدِينَ
فِيهَا ۚ أُولَٰئِكَ هُمْ شَرُّ الْبَرِيَّةِ ٦
إِنَّ الَّذِينَ آمَنُوا وَعَمِلُوا الصَّالِحَاتِ
أُولَٰئِكَ هُمْ خَيْرُ الْبَرِيَّةِ ٧

Ikhfa اخفاء | Ghunna غنّہ | Ikhfa Meem Saakin اخفاء میم ساکن | Idghaam ادغام | Qalqala قلقلہ | Qalb قلب | Idghaam Meem Saakin ادغام میم ساکن

8. Their reward is with Allah: Gardens of Eternity, beneath which rivers flow; they will dwell therein for ever; Allah well pleased with them, and they with Him: all this for such as fear their Lord and Cherisher.

8. Jazaaa'uhum 'inda Rabbihim Jannaatu 'Adnin tajree min taḥtihal-anhaaru khaalideena feehaaa abadaa; raḍiyal-laahu 'anhum wa raḍoo 'anh; zaalika liman khashiya Rabbah. **(Section 1)**

جَزَآؤُهُمْ عِنْدَ رَبِّهِمْ جَنّٰتُ عَدْنٍ
تَجْرِيْ مِنْ تَحْتِهَا الْاَنْهٰرُ خٰلِدِيْنَ
فِيْهَآ اَبَدًا ؕ رَضِيَ اللّٰهُ عَنْهُمْ وَرَضُوْا
عَنْهُ ؕ ذٰلِكَ لِمَنْ خَشِيَ رَبَّهٗ ﴿٨﴾

99. The Convulsion

In the name of Allah, Most Gracious, Most Merciful.

Sûrat az-Zilzâl–99

(Revealed at Madinah)

Bismillaahir Raḥmaanir Raḥeem

(٩٩) سُوْرَةُ الزَّلْزَالِ مَدَنِيَّةٌ (٩٣)

بِسْمِ اللّٰهِ الرَّحْمٰنِ الرَّحِيْمِ

1. When the earth is shaken to her (utmost) convulsion,
2. And the earth throws up her burdens (from within),
3. And man cries (distressed): 'What is the matter with her?'-
4. On that Day will she declare her tidings:
5. For that your Lord will have given her inspiration.
6. On that Day will men proceed in companies sorted out, to be shown the deeds that they (had done).
7. Then shall anyone who has done an atom's weight of good, see it!
8. And anyone who has done an atom's weight of evil, shall see it.

1. Izaa zulzilatil-arḍu zilzaalahaa.
2. Wa akhrajatil-arḍu aṣqaalahaa.
3. Wa qaalal-insaanu maa lahaa.
4. Yawma'izin tuḥaddiṣu akhbaarahaa.
5. Bi-anna Rabbaka awḥaalahaa.
6. Yawma'iziñy-yaṣdurunnaasu ashtaatal-liyuraw a'maalahum.
7. Famañy-ya'mal miṣqaala zarratin khayrañy-yarah.
8. Wa mañy-ya'mal miṣqaala zarratin sharrañy-yarah. **(Sec. 1)**

اِذَا زُلْزِلَتِ الْاَرْضُ زِلْزَالَهَا ﴿١﴾
وَاَخْرَجَتِ الْاَرْضُ اَثْقَالَهَا ﴿٢﴾
وَقَالَ الْاِنْسَانُ مَا لَهَا ﴿٣﴾
يَوْمَئِذٍ تُحَدِّثُ اَخْبَارَهَا ﴿٤﴾
بِاَنَّ رَبَّكَ اَوْحٰى لَهَا ﴿٥﴾
يَوْمَئِذٍ يَّصْدُرُ النَّاسُ اَشْتَاتًا ۙ لِّيُرَوْا
اَعْمَالَهُمْ ﴿٦﴾
فَمَنْ يَّعْمَلْ مِثْقَالَ ذَرَّةٍ خَيْرًا يَّرَهٗ ﴿٧﴾
وَمَنْ يَّعْمَلْ مِثْقَالَ ذَرَّةٍ شَرًّا يَّرَهٗ ﴿٨﴾

100. Those that Run

In the name of Allah, Most Gracious, Most Merciful.

Sûrat al-'Âdiyât–100

(Revealed at Makkah)

Bismillaahir Raḥmaanir Raḥeem

(١٠٠) سُوْرَةُ الْعٰدِيٰتِ مَكِّيَّةٌ (١٤)

بِسْمِ اللّٰهِ الرَّحْمٰنِ الرَّحِيْمِ

1. By the (Steeds) that run, with panting (breath),
2. And strike sparks of fire,
3. And push home the charge in the morning,
4. And raise the dust in clouds the while,
5. And penetrate forthwith into the midst (of the foe) en masse;-
6. Truly man is, to his Lord, ungrateful;
7. And to that (fact) he bears witness (by his deeds);
8. And violent is he in his love of wealth.
9. Does he not know,- when that which is in the

1. Wal-'aadiyaati ḍabḥaa.
2. Falmooriyaati qadḥaa.
3. Fal-mugheeraati ṣubḥaa.
4. Fa-aṣarna bihee naq'aa.
5. Fawasaṭna bihee jam'aa.
6. Innal-insaana li-Rabbihee lakanood.
7. Wa innahoo 'alaa zaalika lashaheed.
8. Wa innahoo liḥubbil-khayri lashadeed.
9. Afalaa ya'lamu izaa bu'sira maa fil-

وَالْعٰدِيٰتِ ضَبْحًا ﴿١﴾
فَالْمُوْرِيٰتِ قَدْحًا ﴿٢﴾
فَالْمُغِيْرٰتِ صُبْحًا ﴿٣﴾
فَاَثَرْنَ بِهٖ نَقْعًا ﴿٤﴾
فَوَسَطْنَ بِهٖ جَمْعًا ﴿٥﴾
اِنَّ الْاِنْسَانَ لِرَبِّهٖ لَكَنُوْدٌ ﴿٦﴾
وَاِنَّهٗ عَلٰى ذٰلِكَ لَشَهِيْدٌ ﴿٧﴾
وَاِنَّهٗ لِحُبِّ الْخَيْرِ لَشَدِيْدٌ ﴿٨﴾
اَفَلَا يَعْلَمُ اِذَا بُعْثِرَ مَا فِي

Ikhfa اخفاء Ghunna غُنّہ Ikhfa Meem Saakin اخفاء میم ساکن Idghaam ادغام Qalqala قلقلہ Qalb قلب Idghaam Meem Saakin ادغام میم ساکن

graves is scattered abroad.
10. And that which is (locked up) in (human) breasts is made manifest-
11. That their Lord had been Well-acquainted with them, (even to) that Day.?

101. The Day of Noise and Clamour

In the name of Allah, Most Gracious, Most Merciful.

1. The (Day) of Noise and Clamour:
2. What is the (Day) of Noise and Clamour?
3. And what will explain to you what the (Day) of Noise and Clamour is?
4. (It is) a Day whereon men will be like moths scattered about,
5. And the mountains will be like carded wool.
6. Then, he whose balance (of good deeds) will be (found) heavy,
7. Will be in a life of good pleasure and satisfaction.
8. But he whose balance (of good deeds) will be (found) light,-
9. Will have his home in a (bottomless) Pit.
10. And what will explain to you what this is?
11. (It is) a Fire Blazing fiercely!

102. The Piling Up

In the name of Allah, Most Gracious, Most Merciful.

1. The mutual rivalry for piling up (the good things of this world) diverts you (from the more serious things),
2. Until you visit the graves.
3. But nay, you soon shall know (the reality).
4. Again, you soon shall know!
5. No, were you to know with certainty of mind, (you would beware!)
6. You shall certainly see Hell-Fire!
7. Again, you shall see it with certainty of sight!

---

quboor.
10. Wa ḥuṣṣila maa fiṣ-ṣudoor.
11. Inna Rabbahum bihim Yawma'izil-lakhabeer. **(Sec. 1)**

Sûrat al-Qâri'ah–101

(Revealed at Makkah)

Bismillaahir Raḥmaanir Raḥeem

1. Al-qaari'ah.
2. Mal-qaari'ah.
3. Wa maaa adraaka mal-qaari'ah.
4. Yawma yakoonun-naasu kalfaraashil-mabsoos.
5. Wa takoonul-jibaalu kal-'ihnil-manfoosh.
6. Fa-ammaa man saqulat mawaazeenuh.
7. Fahuwa fee 'eeshatir-raaḍiyah.
8. Wa ammaa man khaffat mawaazeenuh.
9. Fa-ummuhoo haawiyah.
10. Wa maaa adraaka maa hiyah.
11. Naarun ḥaamiyah. **(Section 1)**

Sûrat at-Takâsur–102

(Revealed at Makkah)

Bismillaahir Raḥmaanir Raḥeem

1. Al-haakumut-takaasur.
2. Ḥattaa zurtumul-maqaabir.
3. Kallaa sawfa ta'lamoon.
4. Summa kallaa sawfa ta'lamoon.
5. Kallaa law ta'lamoona 'ilmal-yaqeen.
6. Latarawunnal-Jaḥeem.
7. Summa latarawunnahaa 'aynal-yaqeen.

الْقُبُوْرِ ﴿٩﴾
وَحُصِّلَ مَا فِي الصُّدُوْرِ ﴿١٠﴾
إِنَّ رَبَّهُمْ بِهِمْ يَوْمَئِذٍ لَّخَبِيْرٌ ﴿١١﴾ ع ١١ ٢٥

(١٠١) سُوْرَةُ الْقَارِعَةِ مَكِّيَّةٌ (٣٠)

بِسْمِ اللّٰهِ الرَّحْمٰنِ الرَّحِيْمِ

اَلْقَارِعَةُ ﴿١﴾
مَا الْقَارِعَةُ ﴿٢﴾
وَمَا أَدْرٰىكَ مَا الْقَارِعَةُ ﴿٣﴾
يَوْمَ يَكُوْنُ النَّاسُ كَالْفَرَاشِ الْمَبْثُوْثِ ﴿٤﴾
وَتَكُوْنُ الْجِبَالُ كَالْعِهْنِ الْمَنْفُوْشِ ﴿٥﴾
فَأَمَّا مَنْ ثَقُلَتْ مَوَازِيْنُهٗ ﴿٦﴾
فَهُوَ فِيْ عِيْشَةٍ رَّاضِيَةٍ ﴿٧﴾
وَأَمَّا مَنْ خَفَّتْ مَوَازِيْنُهٗ ﴿٨﴾
فَأُمُّهٗ هَاوِيَةٌ ﴿٩﴾
وَمَا أَدْرٰىكَ مَا هِيَهْ ﴿١٠﴾
نَارٌ حَامِيَةٌ ﴿١١﴾ ع ١١ ٢٦

(١٠٢) سُوْرَةُ التَّكَاثُرِ مَكِّيَّةٌ (١٦)

بِسْمِ اللّٰهِ الرَّحْمٰنِ الرَّحِيْمِ

أَلْهٰكُمُ التَّكَاثُرُ ﴿١﴾
حَتّٰى زُرْتُمُ الْمَقَابِرَ ﴿٢﴾
كَلَّا سَوْفَ تَعْلَمُوْنَ ﴿٣﴾
ثُمَّ كَلَّا سَوْفَ تَعْلَمُوْنَ ﴿٤﴾
كَلَّا لَوْ تَعْلَمُوْنَ عِلْمَ الْيَقِيْنِ ﴿٥﴾
لَتَرَوُنَّ الْجَحِيْمَ ﴿٦﴾
ثُمَّ لَتَرَوُنَّهَا عَيْنَ الْيَقِيْنِ ﴿٧﴾

Ikhfa اخفاء | Ghunna غنّہ | Ikhfa Meem Saakin اخفاء میم ساکن | Idghaam ادغام | Qalqala قلقلہ | Qalb قلب | Idghaam Meem Saakin ادغام میم ساکن

8. Then, shall you be questioned that Day about the joy (you indulged in!).

8. Summa latus'alunna Yawma'izin 'anin-na'eem. **(Section 1)**

ثُمَّ لَتُسْـَٔلُنَّ يَوْمَئِذٍ عَنِ النَّعِيمِ ﴿٨﴾

103. Time Through the Ages

In the name of Allah, Most Gracious, Most Merciful.

1. By (the Token of) Time (through the ages),
2. Verily Man is in loss,
3. Except such as have Faith, and do righteous deeds, and (join together) in the mutual teaching of Truth, and of Patience and Constancy.

Sûrat al-'Aṣr–103

(Revealed at Makkah)

Bismillaahir Raḥmaanir Raḥeem

1. Wal-'Aṣr.
2. Innal-insaana lafee khusr.
3. Illal-lazeena aamanoo wa 'amiluṣ-ṣaaliḥaati wa tawaaṣaw bilḥaqq, wa tawaaṣaw biṣṣabr. **(Section 1)**

سُورَةُ الْعَصْرِ مَكِّيَّةٌ (١٠٣) (١٣)

بِسْمِ اللَّهِ الرَّحْمَٰنِ الرَّحِيمِ

وَالْعَصْرِ ﴿١﴾
إِنَّ الْإِنسَانَ لَفِي خُسْرٍ ﴿٢﴾
إِلَّا الَّذِينَ آمَنُوا وَعَمِلُوا الصَّالِحَاتِ وَتَوَاصَوْا بِالْحَقِّ وَتَوَاصَوْا بِالصَّبْرِ ﴿٣﴾

104. The Scandal-monger

In the name of Allah, Most Gracious, Most Merciful.

1. Woe to every (kind of) scandal-monger and-backbiter,
2. Who piles up wealth and layeth it by,
3. Thinking that his wealth would make him last for ever!
4. By no means! He will be sure to be thrown into That which Breaks to Pieces,
5. And what will explain to you That which Breaks to Pieces?
6. (It is) the Fire of (the Wrath of) Allah kindled (to a blaze),
7. That which does mount (Right) up to the Hearts:
8. It shall be made into a vault over them,
9. In columns outstretched.

Sûrat al-Humazah–104

(Revealed at Makkah)

Bismillaahir Raḥmaanir Raḥeem

1. Waylul-likulli humazatil-lumazah.
2. Allazee jama'a maalañw-wa 'addadah.
3. Yaḥsabu anna maalahooo akhladah.
4. Kallaa la-yumbazanna fil-ḥuṭamah.
5. Wa maaa adraaka mal-ḥuṭamah.
6. Naarul-laahil-mooqadah.
7. Allatee taṭṭali'u 'alal-af'idah.
8. Innahaa 'alayhim mu'ṣadah.
9. Fee 'amadim-mumaddadah. **(Section 1)**

سُورَةُ الْهُمَزَةِ مَكِّيَّةٌ (١٠٤) (٣٢)

بِسْمِ اللَّهِ الرَّحْمَٰنِ الرَّحِيمِ

وَيْلٌ لِّكُلِّ هُمَزَةٍ لُّمَزَةٍ ﴿١﴾
الَّذِي جَمَعَ مَالًا وَعَدَّدَهُ ﴿٢﴾
يَحْسَبُ أَنَّ مَالَهُ أَخْلَدَهُ ﴿٣﴾
كَلَّا لَيُنبَذَنَّ فِي الْحُطَمَةِ ﴿٤﴾
وَمَا أَدْرَاكَ مَا الْحُطَمَةُ ﴿٥﴾
نَارُ اللَّهِ الْمُوقَدَةُ ﴿٦﴾
الَّتِي تَطَّلِعُ عَلَى الْأَفْئِدَةِ ﴿٧﴾
إِنَّهَا عَلَيْهِم مُّؤْصَدَةٌ ﴿٨﴾
فِي عَمَدٍ مُّمَدَّدَةٍ ﴿٩﴾

105. The Elephant

In the name of Allah, Most Gracious, Most Merciful.

1. Do you see not how your Lord dealt with the Companions of the Elephant?
2. Did He not make their treacherous plan go astray?
3. And He sent against them Flights of Birds,
4. Striking them with stones of baked clay.
5. Then did He make them like an empty field of stalks and straw, (of which the corn) has been eaten up.

Sûrat al-Fîl–105

(Revealed at Makkah)

Bismillaahir Raḥmaanir Raḥeem

1. Alam tara kayfa fa'ala Rabbuka bi-Aṣ-ḥaabil-Feel.
2. Alam yaj'al kaydahum fee taḍleel.
3. Wa arsala 'alayhim ṭayran abaabeel.
4. Tarmeehim biḥijaaratim-min sijjeel.
5. Faja'alahum ka'aṣfim-maåkool. **(Section 1)**

سُورَةُ الْفِيلِ مَكِّيَّةٌ (١٠٥) (١٩)

بِسْمِ اللَّهِ الرَّحْمَٰنِ الرَّحِيمِ

أَلَمْ تَرَ كَيْفَ فَعَلَ رَبُّكَ بِأَصْحَابِ الْفِيلِ ﴿١﴾
أَلَمْ يَجْعَلْ كَيْدَهُمْ فِي تَضْلِيلٍ ﴿٢﴾
وَأَرْسَلَ عَلَيْهِمْ طَيْرًا أَبَابِيلَ ﴿٣﴾
تَرْمِيهِم بِحِجَارَةٍ مِّن سِجِّيلٍ ﴿٤﴾
فَجَعَلَهُمْ كَعَصْفٍ مَّأْكُولٍ ﴿٥﴾

Ikhfa اخفاء | Ghunna غنّہ | Ikhfa Meem Saakin اخفاء میم ساکن | Idghaam ادغام | Qalqala قلقلہ | Qalb قلب | Idghaam Meem Saakin ادغام میم ساکن

106. The Tribe of Quraish

In the name of Allah, Most Gracious, Most Merciful.

1. For the covenants (of security and safeguard enjoyed) by the Quraish,
2. Their covenants (covering safe) journeys by winter and summer,-
3. Let them adore the Lord of this House,
4. Who provides them with food against hunger, and with security against fear (of danger).

Sûrat Quraysh–106

(Revealed at Makkah)

Bismillaahir Raḥmaanir Raḥeem

1. Li-eelaafi Quraysh.
2. Eelaafihim riḥlatash-Shitaaa'i waṣṣayf.
3. Falya'budoo Rabba haazal-Bayt.
4. Allazeee aṭ'amahum min joo'iñw-wa aamanahum min khawf. **(Section 1)**

(١٠٦) سُوْرَةُ قُرَيْشٍ مَكِّيَّةٌ (٢٩)

بِسْمِ اللّٰهِ الرَّحْمٰنِ الرَّحِيْمِ

لِاِيْلٰفِ قُرَيْشٍ ۝١

اٖلٰفِهِمْ رِحْلَةَ الشِّتَآءِ وَالصَّيْفِ ۝٢

فَلْيَعْبُدُوْا رَبَّ هٰذَا الْبَيْتِ ۝٣

الَّذِيْٓ اَطْعَمَهُمْ مِّنْ جُوْعٍ ۙ وَّ اٰمَنَهُمْ مِّنْ خَوْفٍ ۝٤ ع

107. The Neighbourly Needs

In the name of Allah, Most Gracious, Most Merciful.

1. Did you see one who denies the Judgment (to come)?
2. Then such is the (man) who repulses the orphan (with harshness),
3. And encourages not the feeding of the indigent.
4. So woe to the worshippers,
5. Who are neglectful of their prayers,
6. Those who (want but) to be seen (of men),
7. But refuse (to supply) (even) neighbourly need

Sûrat al-Mâ'ûn–107

(Revealed at Makkah)

Bismillaahir Raḥmaanir Raḥeem

1. Ara'aytal-lazee yukaz-zibu biddeen.
2. Fazaalikal-lazee yadu'-'ul-yateem.
3. Wa laa yaḥuḍḍu 'alaa ṭa'aamil-miskeen.
4. Fa-waylul-lil-muṣalleen.
5. Allazeena hum 'an Ṣalaa-tihim saahoon.
6. Allazeena hum yuraaa-'oon.
7. Wa yamna'oonal-maa'oon. **(Section 1)**

(١٠٧) سُوْرَةُ الْمَاعُوْنِ مَكِّيَّةٌ (١٧)

بِسْمِ اللّٰهِ الرَّحْمٰنِ الرَّحِيْمِ

اَرَءَيْتَ الَّذِيْ يُكَذِّبُ بِالدِّيْنِ ۝١

فَذٰلِكَ الَّذِيْ يَدُعُّ الْيَتِيْمَ ۝٢

وَلَا يَحُضُّ عَلٰى طَعَامِ الْمِسْكِيْنِ ۝٣

فَوَيْلٌ لِّلْمُصَلِّيْنَ ۝٤

الَّذِيْنَ هُمْ عَنْ صَلَاتِهِمْ سَاهُوْنَ ۝٥

الَّذِيْنَ هُمْ يُرَآءُوْنَ ۝٦

وَيَمْنَعُوْنَ الْمَاعُوْنَ ۝٧ ع

108. The Abundance

In the name of Allah, Most Gracious, Most Merciful.

1. To you have We granted the Fount (of Abundance).
2. Therefore, to your Lord turn in Prayer and Sacrifice.
3. For he who hates you, he will be cut off (from Future Hope)

Sûrat al-Kawsar–108

(Revealed at Makkah)

Bismillaahir Raḥmaanir Raḥeem

1. Innaaa a'ṭaynaakal-Kawsar.
2. Faṣalli li-Rabbika wanḥar.
3. Inna shaani'aka huwal-abtar. **(Section 1)**

(١٠٨) سُوْرَةُ الْكَوْثَرِ مَكِّيَّةٌ (١٥)

بِسْمِ اللّٰهِ الرَّحْمٰنِ الرَّحِيْمِ

اِنَّآ اَعْطَيْنٰكَ الْكَوْثَرَ ۝١

فَصَلِّ لِرَبِّكَ وَانْحَرْ ۝٢

اِنَّ شَانِئَكَ هُوَ الْاَبْتَرُ ۝٣ ع

109. Those who reject Faith

In the name of Allah, Most Gracious, Most Merciful.

1. Say : O you that reject Faith!
2. I worship not that which you worship,
3. Nor will you worship that which I worship.

Sûrat al-Kâfirûn–109

(Revealed at Makkah)

Bismillaahir Raḥmaanir Raḥeem

1. Qul yaaa ayyuhal-kaafi-roon.
2. Laaa a'budu maa ta'bu-doon.
3. Wa laaa antum 'aabidoo-na maaa a'bud.

(١٠٩) سُوْرَةُ الْكٰفِرُوْنَ مَكِّيَّةٌ (١٨)

بِسْمِ اللّٰهِ الرَّحْمٰنِ الرَّحِيْمِ

قُلْ يٰٓاَيُّهَا الْكٰفِرُوْنَ ۝١

لَآ اَعْبُدُ مَا تَعْبُدُوْنَ ۝٢

وَلَآ اَنْتُمْ عٰبِدُوْنَ مَآ اَعْبُدُ ۝٣

Ikhfa اخفاء | Ghunna غنّہ | Ikhfa Meem Saakin اخفاء میم ساکن | Idghaam ادغام | Qalqala قلقلہ | Qalb قلب | Idghaam Meem Saakin ادغام میم ساکن

4. And I will not worship that which you have been wont to worship,	4. Wa laaa ana 'aabidum maa 'abattum.	وَلَآ أَنَا عَابِدٌ مَّا عَبَدتُّمْ ﴿٤﴾
5. Nor will you worship that which I worship.	5. Wa laaa antum 'aabidoona maaa a'bud.	وَلَآ أَنتُمْ عَٰبِدُونَ مَآ أَعْبُدُ ﴿٥﴾
6. To you be your Way, and to me mine.	6. Lakum deenukum wa liya deen. **(Section 1)**	لَكُمْ دِينُكُمْ وَلِيَ دِينِ ﴿٦﴾

110. The Help

In the name of Allah, Most Gracious, Most Merciful.

Sûrat an-Naṣr–110 (Revealed at Madinah) **Bismillaahir Raḥmaanir Raḥeem**

(١١٠) سُورَةُ النَّصْرِ مَدَنِيَّةٌ (١١٤)

بِسْمِ اللَّهِ الرَّحْمَٰنِ الرَّحِيمِ

1. When comes the Help of Allah, and Victory,	1. Izaa jaaa'a naṣrul-laahi wal-Fat-ḥ.	إِذَا جَآءَ نَصْرُ اللَّهِ وَالْفَتْحُ ﴿١﴾
2. And you does see the people enter Allah's Religion in crowds,	2. Wa ra-aytan-naasa yad-khuloona fee deenil-laahi af-waajaa.	وَرَأَيْتَ النَّاسَ يَدْخُلُونَ فِي دِينِ اللَّهِ أَفْوَاجًا ﴿٢﴾
3. Celebrate the praises of your Lord, and pray for His Forgiveness: For He is Oft-Returning (in Grace and Mercy).	3. Fasabbiḥ biḥamdi Rabbi-ka wastaghfirh; innahoo kaana Tawwaaba. **(Section 1)**	فَسَبِّحْ بِحَمْدِ رَبِّكَ وَاسْتَغْفِرْهُ إِنَّهُۥ كَانَ تَوَّابًا ﴿٣﴾

111. The Father of Flame

In the name of Allah, Most Gracious, Most Merciful.

Sûrat al-Lahab–111 (Revealed at Makkah) **Bismillaahir Raḥmaanir Raḥeem**

(١١١) سُورَةُ اللَّهَبِ مَكِّيَّةٌ (٦)

بِسْمِ اللَّهِ الرَّحْمَٰنِ الرَّحِيمِ

1. Perish the hands of the Father of Flame! Perish he!	1. Tabbat yadaaa Abee Laha-biñw-wa tabb.	تَبَّتْ يَدَآ أَبِي لَهَبٍ وَتَبَّ ﴿١﴾
2. No benefit to him all his wealth, and all he accumulated.	2. Maaa aghnaa 'anhu maa-luhoo wa maa kasab.	مَآ أَغْنَىٰ عَنْهُ مَالُهُۥ وَمَا كَسَبَ ﴿٢﴾
3. Burnt soon will he be in a Fire of Blazing Flame!	3. Sa-yaṣlaa Naaran zaata lahab.	سَيَصْلَىٰ نَارًا ذَاتَ لَهَبٍ ﴿٣﴾
4. His wife shall carry the (crackling) wood - as fuel!-	4. Wamra-atuhoo ḥammaa-latal-ḥaṭab.	وَامْرَأَتُهُۥ حَمَّالَةَ الْحَطَبِ ﴿٤﴾
5. A twisted rope of palm-leaf fibre round her (own) neck!	5. Fee jeedihaa ḥablum mim masad. **(Section 1)**	فِي جِيدِهَا حَبْلٌ مِّن مَّسَدٍ ﴿٥﴾

112. Purity (of Faith)

In the name of Allah, Most Gracious, Most Merciful.

Sûrat al-Ikhlâṣ–112 (Revealed at Makkah) **Bismillaahir Raḥmaanir Raḥeem**

(١١٢) سُورَةُ الْإِخْلَاصِ مَكِّيَّةٌ (٢٢)

بِسْمِ اللَّهِ الرَّحْمَٰنِ الرَّحِيمِ

1. Say: He is Allah, the One and Only;	1. Qul Huwal-laahu Aḥad.	قُلْ هُوَ اللَّهُ أَحَدٌ ﴿١﴾
2. Allah, the Eternal, Absolute;	2. Allaahuṣ-Ṣamad.	اللَّهُ الصَّمَدُ ﴿٢﴾
3. He begets not, nor is He begotten;	3. Lam yalid wa lam yoolad.	لَمْ يَلِدْ وَلَمْ يُولَدْ ﴿٣﴾
4. And there is none like unto Him.	4. Wa lam yakul-lahoo kufu-wan aḥad. **(Section 1)**	وَلَمْ يَكُن لَّهُۥ كُفُوًا أَحَدٌ ﴿٤﴾

113. The Dawn

In the name of Allah, Most Gracious, Most Merciful.

Sûrat al-Falaq–113 (Revealed at Makkah) **Bismillaahir Raḥmaanir Raḥeem**

(١١٣) سُورَةُ الْفَلَقِ مَكِّيَّةٌ (٢٠)

بِسْمِ اللَّهِ الرَّحْمَٰنِ الرَّحِيمِ

1. Say: I seek refuge with the Lord of the Dawn.	1. Qul a'oozu bi Rabbil-falaq.	قُلْ أَعُوذُ بِرَبِّ الْفَلَقِ ﴿١﴾

Ikhfa اخفاء · Ghunna غنّہ · Ikhfa Meem Saakin اخفاء میم ساکن · Idghaam ادغام · Qalqala قلقلہ · Qalb قلب · Idghaam Meem Saakin ادغام میم ساکن

2. From the mischief of created things;	2. Min sharri maa khalaq.	مِنْ شَرِّ مَا خَلَقَ ۝٢
3. From the mischief of Darkness as it overspreads;	3. Wa min sharri ghaasiqin izaa waqab.	وَمِنْ شَرِّ غَاسِقٍ اِذَا وَقَبَ ۝٣
4. From the mischief of those who blow on knots;	4. Wa min sharrin-naffaa-saati fil-'uqad.	وَمِنْ شَرِّ النَّفّٰثٰتِ فِى الْعُقَدِ ۝٤
5. And from the mischief of the envious one as he practises envy.	5. Wa min sharri ḥaasidin izaa ḥasad. (Section 1)	وَمِنْ شَرِّ حَاسِدٍ اِذَا حَسَدَ ۝٥ ع ٢٨

114. Mankind **In the name of Allah, Most Gracious, Most Merciful.**	**Sûrat an-Nâs–114** (Revealed at Makkah) **Bismillaahir Raḥmaanir Raḥeem**	(١١٤) سُوْرَةُ النَّاسِ مَكِّيَّةٌ (٢١) بِسْمِ اللّٰهِ الرَّحْمٰنِ الرَّحِيْمِ
1. Say: I seek refuge with the Lord and Cherisher of Mankind,	1. Qul a'oozu bi-Rabbin-naas.	قُلْ اَعُوْذُ بِرَبِّ النَّاسِ ۝١
2. The King (or Ruler) of Mankind,	2. Malikin-naas.	مَلِكِ النَّاسِ ۝٢
3. The Allah (for judge) of Mankind,-	3. Ilaahin-naas.	اِلٰهِ النَّاسِ ۝٣
4. From the mischief of the Whisperer (of Evil), who withdraws (after his whisper),-	4. Min sharril-waswaasil-khannaas.	مِنْ شَرِّ الْوَسْوَاسِ ۥ الْخَنَّاسِ ۝٤
5. (The same) who whispers into the hearts of Mankind,-	5. Allazee yuwaswisu fee ṣudoorin-naas.	الَّذِىْ يُوَسْوِسُ فِىْ صُدُوْرِ النَّاسِ ۝٥
6. Among Jinns and among men.	6. Minal-jinnati wannaas. (Section 1)	مِنَ الْجِنَّةِ وَالنَّاسِ ۝٦ ع ٢٩

تَمَّ بِالْخَيْرِ

Prayer
(To be used after reading the Holy Qur'an)

دُعَاءُ خَتْمِ الْقُرْاٰنِ

اَللّٰهُمَّ اٰنِسْ وَحْشَتِىْ فِىْ قَبْرِىْ اَللّٰهُمَّ ارْحَمْنِىْ بِالْقُرْاٰنِ الْعَظِيْمِ وَاجْعَلْهُ لِىْ اِمَامًا وَّنُوْرًا وَّ

Allahumma aanis waḥshatee fee qabree! Allahummar-ḥamnee bil-Qur-aanil-'Aẓeemi waj'alhu leee imaamañw-wa nooorañw-wa

O Allah! Change my fear in my grave into love! O Allah! Have mercy on me in the name of the Great Qur'an; and make it for me a Guide and Light and

هُدًى وَّرَحْمَةً اَللّٰهُمَّ ذَكِّرْنِىْ مِنْهُ مَا نَسِيْتُ وَعَلِّمْنِىْ مِنْهُ مَا جَهِلْتُ وَارْزُقْنِىْ تِلَاوَتَهٗ اٰنَآءَ

hudañw-wa raḥmah! Allahumma zakkirnee minhu maa naseetu wa 'allimnee minhu maa jahiltu warzuqnee tilaawatahooo aanaaa'al-

Guidance and Mercy! O Allah! Make me remember what of it I have forgotten; and make me know of it that which have become ignorant of; and make me recite it in the hours of

اللَّيْلِ وَاٰنَآءَ النَّهَارِ وَاجْعَلْهُ لِىْ حُجَّةً يَّا رَبَّ الْعٰلَمِيْنَ ۝

layli wa aanaaa'an-nahaari waj'alhu lee ḥujjatañy-yaa Rabbal-'aalameen.

the night and the day; and make it an argument for me O Thou Sustainer of (all) the worlds!
Ameen!

Ikhfa اخفاء · Ghunna غُنّہ · Ikhfa Meem Saakin اخفاء میم ساکن · Idghaam ادغام · Qalqala قلقلہ · Qalb قلب · Idghaam Meem Saakin ادغام میم ساکن

Symbols Denoting Pauses

Symbol	Extract from Verse	Sûrah Number	Verse Number

Compulsory stop

م	وَاذْكُرْ فِي الْكِتٰبِ مَرْيَمَ ۘ إِذِ انْتَبَذَتْ	19	16

Necessary stop

۝ط	عَلَيْهَا صَعِيدًا جُرُزًا ۝	18	8

Stop vocal sound for a moment without breaking the breath

وقفة	وَاعْفُ عَنَّا وَاغْفِرْ لَنَا وَارْحَمْنَا أَنْتَ	2	286
سكتة	كَلَّا بَلْ رَانَ	83	14

Necessary to continue, do not pause

لا	فَاعْبُدْنِي وَأَقِمِ الصَّلٰوةَ لِذِكْرِي ۝	20	14

Desirable to continue, do not pause

ز	إِلَّا أَنْ يَشَاءَ اللّٰهُ وَاذْكُرْ رَبَّكَ	18	24
ص	حِجَابًا فَأَرْسَلْنَا إِلَيْهَا رُوحَنَا	19	17
ق	قَالُوا اتَّخَذَ اللّٰهُ وَلَدًا ۝ مَا لَهُمْ بِهِ	18	4/5
صلے	وَزِدْنٰهُمْ هُدًى ۝ وَرَبَطْنَا	18	13/14

Recommended pause

قف	وَمَلٰئِكَتِهِ وَكُتُبِهِ وَرُسُلِهِ لَا نُفَرِّقُ	2	285

Optional to pause or to continue

ج	رَبِّكَ لَا مُبَدِّلَ لِكَلِمٰتِهِ وَلَنْ	18	27

Any two of the three verses may be read in continuity

∴	وَقَالَ الَّذِينَ كَفَرُوا لَوْلَا نُزِّلَ عَلَيْهِ الْقُرْاٰنُ جُمْلَةً وَاحِدَةً ۛ كَذٰلِكَ ۛ لِنُثَبِّتَ بِهِ فُؤَادَكَ وَرَتَّلْنٰهُ تَرْتِيلًا ۝	25	32

Index

(Bold numerical in the reference numbers denote Sûrah Nos. while other numerical show the *Ayât* Nos.)

Aaron (Harûn) **2**:248; **4**:163; **6**:84; **7**:122,142; **10**:75; **19**:28,53; **20**:30,70, 90,92; **21**:48; **23**:45; **25**:35; **26**:13,48; **28**:34; **37**:114,120.

'Abasa, S.**80**; **74**:22

Ablutions (*Wûdû*), **4**:43; **5**:6

Abraham (Ibrâhîm) S.14; **2**:124-127, 130, 132, 133, 135, 136, 148, 258, 260; **3**:33, 65, 67, 68, 84, 95, 97; **4**:54, 125, 163; **6**:74, 75, 83, 161; **9**:70, 114; **11**:69, 74-76; **12**:6, 38; **14**: 35; **15**:51; **16**:120,123; **19**:41, 46, 58; **21**:51,60,62,69; **22**:26, 43, 78; **26**:69; **29**:16, 31; **33**:7; **37**:83,104,109; **38**:45; **42**:13; **43**:26; **51**:24; **53**:37; **57**:26; **60**:4; **87**:19

Abrâr, **3**:193, 198; **76**:5; **82**:13; **83**:18-22

Abû Lahab (Father of Flame), **111**:1-5

'Âd people, 7:65-74; **9**:70; **11**:59; **14**:9; **22**:42; **25**:38; **26**:123; **29**:38; **38**:12; **40**:31; **41**:13,15; **46**:21; **50**:13; **51**:41; **53**:50; **54**:18; **69**:4-6; **89**:6

Âdam, **2**:31, 33, 34, 35, 37; **3**:33,59; **5**:27; 7:11, 19, 26, 27, 31, 35, 172; **17**:61, 70; **18**:50; **19**:58; **20**:116, 117,120,121; **36**:60

'Âdiyât, S.**100**

'Adn Paradise, **9**:72; **13**:23;**16**:31; **18**:3 1; **19**:61; **20**:76; **35**:33; **38**:50; **40**:8; **61**:12; **98**:8

Ahmad, **61**:6

Ahqâf, S.**46**; **46**:21

Ahzâb, S. **33**; **11**:17; **13**:36; **19**:37; **38**:11,13; **40**: 5,30; **43**:65

Aikah, dwellers of, **15**:78; **26**:176; **38**:13; **50**:14

A'lâ S. **87**, **87**:1; **92**:20

'Alaq, S.**96**

Âl-'Imrân, S.**3**

Allâh. The word Allâh has occured in the Qur'ân more than 3000 times.

Alyasa', (see Elisha)

Amânah, Trust and Allâh prescribed duties etc., **2**:283; **4**:58; **8**:27; see Trust

Angel or Angels. These words occur more than 100 times.

'Ankabût, S.**29**

Apostates, **47**:25

A'râf; S.**7**; **7**:266,48

Arafât, **2**:198

Argue,
- not on behalf of those who deceive themselves, **4**:107
- you argued for them in this world, but who will on the Day of Resurrection, **4**:109

'Asr, S.**103**

Ayat Al-Kursi, **2**:255

Backbiter, **49**:12; **104**:1

Badr (battle of), **3**:13
- lessons from, 8:5-19, 42-48

Al-Bait-ul-Ma'mûr, **52**:4

Bakkah (Makkah), **3**:96

B'al, **37**:125

Balad, S. **90**

Balance, 7:8,9; **17**:35; **21**:47; **55**:7-9; **57**:25; **101**:6-9

Banû An-Nadîr, **59**:2-6, 13.

Baqarah, S.**2**

Barâ'a (See *Taubah*), S.**9**

Barzakh, (Barrier), **23**:100; **25**:53; **55**:20; also see **18**:94-97; **34**:54; **36**:9 (barrier)

Baiyinah, S.**98**

Beast (of the Last Days), **27**:82

Bedouins, **9**:90,97-99,101,120;**48**:11, 16; **49**:14

Bee, **16**:68,69

Believers. This word occurs more than 200 times in the Noble Qur'ân. Mentioning every place will make the Index very big.

Bequest, **2**:180,240; **4**:7,12; **36**:50;

Betray (deceive, fraud), **2**:187; **4**:107; **5**:13; **8**:27,58,71; **12**:52; **22**:38; **66**:10

Birds, **2**:260; **3**:49; **5**:110; **6**:38; **12**:36,41; **16**:79; **21**:79; **22**:31; **24**:41; **27**:16,17,20; **34**:10; **38**:19; **56**:21; **67**:19; **105**:3.

Blood-money (*Diya*), **2**:178,179; **4**:92; **17**:33

Book. This word occurs more than 300 times in the Noble Qur'ân.
Mentioning every place will make the Index very big.

Booty, war, **4**:94.**8**:41; *Fai,* **59**:6-8; *Ghulul,* **3**:161 (See spoils)
taking illegally, **3**:162

Bribery, **2**:188

Budn, **22**:36

Burden
of another, no bearer of burdens shall bear the, **35**:18; **39**:7; **53**:38
disbelievers will bear also the burdens of others, **16**:25; **29**:13
evil indeed are the burdens that they will bear, **6**:31,164
Allâh burdens not a person beyond his scope, **2**:286; **7**:42; **23**:62

Burûj (Big stars), S. **85**; **85:**1; **15:**16; **25**:61

Camel, **6**:144; **7**:40; **77**:33; **88**:17

Captives, **4**:25; **8**:67, 70, 71; **9**:60; **33**:26,27;**76**:8 (see also Prisoners of war)

Cattle, **3**:14; **4**:119; **5**:1; **6**:136,138, 139,142; **7**:179; **10**:24;**16**:5-8, 10,66,80; **20**:54; **22**:28,30,34; **23**:21; **25**:44,49; **26**:133; **32**:27; **35**:28; **36**:71-73; **39**:6; **40:**79; **42:**11; **43**:12,13; **47**:12; **79**:33; **80**:32.

Cave of Thawr, **9**:40

Cave, people of the **18**:9-22, 25,26

Certainty with truth, **56**:95; **69**:51;

Charity, (*Sadaqah*), **2**:196,263, 264, 270, 271,273; **4**:114; **9**:58,75,76-79,103,104; **57**:18; **58**:12,13
objects of charity and *Zakât,* **2**:273; **9**:60

Children **2**:233; **42**:49,50
lost are they who have killed their, from folly, without knowledge, **6**:140

Christ, (see Jesus)

Christians. This word occurs more than 600 times in the Noble Qur'ân.
Mentioning every place will make the Index very big.

Cities overthrown, **69**:9

City of security, **95**:3

Confederates, **33**:9, 22 - see *Ahzâb.*

Consultation, mutual, **42**:38

Creation,
begins and repeated, **10**:4; **21**:104; **27**:64; **29**:19,20
a new, **17**:49, 98; **35**:16
with truth, **15**:85; **16**:3; **29**:44; **39**:5; **44**:39; **45**:22; **46**:3
not for play, **21**:16,17; **24**:115
every living thing made from, **21**:30; **24**:45; **25**:54
of man, **4**:1; **6**:2; **15**:26,28,33; **16**:4; **21**:30; **22**:5;**23**:12-14; **25**:54; **32**:7-9; **35**:11; **36**:77,78; **37**:11; **39**:6; **40**:67; **49**:13; **55**:14; **56**:57-59; **75**:37-40; **76**:1,2; **77**:20-23; **80**:18,19; **86**:5-8; **96**:2
the first form of **56**:62
in six Days, **7**:54; **11**:7; **32**:4; **50**:38; **57**:4
in pairs, **13**:3; **30**:8; **36**:36; **42**:11; **43**:12; **51**:9,49; **53**:45
variety in, **35**:27,28
Allâh commands "Be!" — and it is, **2**:117; **16**:40; **36**:82; **40**:68
as the twinkling of an eye, **54**:50
night and day, sun and moon, **39**:5
of heaven and earth greater than, of mankind, **40**:57; **79**:27
purpose of, **51**:56

Crow, **5**:31

Criterion, **2**:53,185; **3**:4; **8**:29,41; **21**:48; **25**:1

Dahr,(*see Insân,*) S. **76; 45**:24
time, **76**:1; **103**:1

David, **4**:163; **6**:84; **21**:78-80; **5**:78; **34**:10,13; **38**:17-30; **17**:55
fights Goliath, **2**:251

Dawâbb or *Dâbbah* (moving living creature etc.) **2**:164; **6**:38; **8**:22,55; **11**:6, 56; **16**:49,61; **22**:18; **24**:45; **27**:82; **29**:60; **31**:10; **34**:14; **35**:28,45; **42**:29; **45**:4
Days. This word occurs more than 500 times in the Noble Qur'ân. Mentioning every place will make the Index very big.
Dead will be raised up, **6**:36
Death. This word occurs more than 200 times in the Noble Qur'ân. Mentioning every place will make the Index very big.
Debts, **2**:280, 282; **4**:11,12
Decree,
for each and every matter, there is a, **13**:38
never did We destroy a township but there was a known, for it, **15**:4
of every matter is from Allâh, **44**:5
when He decrees a matter, He says only, "Be!" — and it is, **2**:117; **36**:82; **40**:68
Deeds,
evil, beautified for them, **47**:14
to us our, to you your deeds, **28**:55; **42**:15; **45**:15
good and bad, are for and against his ownself, **41**:46
fastened man's, to his own neck, **17**:13
Degrees, according to what they did, **6**:132
Desire, those follow their evil, **47**:14,16 who has taken as his god his own, **25**:43
Despair not of the Mercy of Allâh, **39**:53
21:87,88; **68**:48-50 (see also Jonah)
Dhâriyât, S. **51**
Dhikr, **8**:205; **15**:6,9
Dhûl-Kifl, **21**:85, **38**:48
Dhûl-Qarnain, **18**:83-98
Dhun-Nûn (Companion of the Fish),
Disbelievers. This word occurs more than 200 times in the Noble Qur'ân. Mentioning every place will make the Index very big.
Disease in the hearts of hypocrites and disbelievers, **2**:10; **5**:52; **8**:49; **9**:125;**22**:53; **24**:50; **33**:12, 32, 60; **47**:20, 29; **74**:31
Distress, after it there is security, **3**:154
Distribution of war-booty, **8**:41; *Fai* (booty), **59**:7-8
Ditch, people of the, **85**:4-10
Divorce, **2**:228-232, 236,237, 241; **65**:1- 7; see also **4**:35 (see also *Zihâr*).
Donkeys (Ass), **2**:259; **16**: 8; **31**:19; **62**:5; **74**:50
Drink,
alcoholic, **2**:219; **5**:90
pure, **37**:45; **76**:21
pure sealed wine, **83**:25
white delicious, **37**:46
Duhâ, S .**93**
Dukhân, S. **44**
Earth. This word occurs more than 200 times in the Noble Qur'ân. Mentioning every place will make the Index very big.
Elephant army, **105**:1-5
Elias (Elijah; Ilyâsîn) **6**:85; 37:123-132
Elisha, (Alyasa') **6:**86; **38**:48
Enoch, (see Idris)
Event, **56**:1; **69**:15
Evil, **4**:123; **10**:27-30; **19**:83; **59**:15
should not be uttered in public, **4**:148 comes from ourselves, but good from Allâh, **4**:79; **42**:48
pardon an, **4**:149
recompensed, **6**:160; **42**:40
who devise, plots, **16**:45-47
was the end, **30**:10
has appeared on land and sea, **30**:41
repel/defend, with good, **13**:22; **23**:96; **41**:34
changed, for the good, **7**:95
those follow their, desires, **47**:14,16
deeds beautified for them, **47**:14
Excess,
forbidden in food, **5**:87
in religion, **4**:171; **5**:77-81
Eyes, ears and skins will bear witness against sinners, **41**:20-23
Ezra, ('Uzair) **9**:30

Face or Countenance of Allâh, **2**:115,272; **6**:52; **13**:22; **18**:28; **28**:88; **30**:38,39; **55**:27; **76**:9; **92**:20
Fair-seeming, Allâh has made, to each people its own doings, **6**:108
Faith (Belief), **2**:108; **3**:167,177,193; **5**:5; **9**:23; **16**:106; **30**:56; **40**:10; **42**:52; **49**:7,11,14; **52**:21; **58**:22; **59**:9,10
rejectors of, **3**:116
increase in, **3**:173
with certainty, **44**:7; **45**:4,20; **51**:20
He has guided you to the, **49**:17
Fajr, S.**89**
Falaq, S. **113**
False conversation about Verses of Qur'ân, **6**:68
False gods,
besides Allâh, idols and so-called partners **7**:194-198; **16**:20,21,72,86; **21**:22,24; **34**:22,27; **41**:47,48; **46**:5,6; **53**:19-24; **71**:23,24 (see also Tâghût.)
insult not those whom they worship besides Allâh, **6**:108
Falsehood (*Bâtil*), **2**:42; **3**:71; **8**:8; **9**:24; **13**:17; **17**:81; **21**:18; **22**:62; **29**:52,67; **31**:30; **34**:49; **40**:5; **41**:42; **42**:24; **47**:3
Fastened man's deeds to his own neck, **17**:13
Fasting, **2**:178,183,184,185, 187, 196; **4**:92; **5**:89,95; **19**:26; **33**:35
eat and drink until white thread appears distinct from the black thread, **2**:187
Fath, S. **48**
Fâtihah, S. **1**
Fâtir, S. **35**
Fear. This word occurs more than 1000 times in the Noble Qur'ân.
Mentioning every place will make the Index very big.
Fidyah (ransom),
of fast, **2**:196
for freeing the captives, **8**:67
ransom offered by disbelievers, **3**:91; **5**:36,37; **10**:54; **13**:18
Fig, **95**:1
Fighting,
in the way of Allâh, against disbelievers, **2**:190-193,244; **4**:84,95; **8**:72,74,75; **9**:12-16,20,24,36,123; **47**:4; **61**:11
ordained, **2**:216
in sacred months, **2**:217; **9**:5
by Children of Israel, **2**:246-251
in the Cause of Allâh, and oppressed men and women, **4**:74-76
till no more *Fitnah,* **8**:39
twenty overcoming two hundred, **8**:65
against those who believe not in Allâh, **9**:29
permission against those who are wronged, **22**:39-41
and the hypocrites, **47**:20
exemptions from, **48**:17
Fîl, S. **105**
Firdaus Paradise, **18**:160; **23**:11
Fire. This word occurs more than 200 times in the Noble Qur'ân.
Mentioning every place will make the Index very big.
Fly, **22**:73
Food,
lawful and unlawful, (*Halâl* and *Harâm*), **2**:168,172,173; **5**:1,3-5,88; **6**:118, 119,121,145,146; **16**:114-118; **23**:51
no sin for what ate in the past, **5**:93
transgress not, **5**:87
make not unlawful which Allâh has made lawful, **5**:87; **7**:32; **16**:116
Forbidden conduct, **6**:151,152; **7**:33
Forgiveness, **2**:109; **4**:48,110,116; **7**:199; **39**:53; **42**:5,40-43; **45**:14; **53**:32; **57**:21
a duty of Believers, **42**:37; **45**:14
by Believers, for people of the Scripture, **2**:109
Allâh forgives to whom He pleases, **4**:48
Allâh forgives not setting up partners in worship with Him, **4**:48,116
whoever seeks Allâh's, **4**:110
not to ask Allâh's, for the *Mushrikûn,* **9**:113

Allâh forgives all sins, **39**:53
angels ask for, for those on the earth, **42**:5
forgive, when they are angry, **42**:37
forgive and make reconciliation, **42**:40
Believers to forgive those who hope not for the Days of Allâh, **45**:14
for those who avoid great sins and the *Fawâhish,* **53**:32
race one with another in hastening towards, **57**:21
Fraud, **83**:1-6 (see Betray)
Free will,
limited by Allâh's Will, **6**:107; **10**:99; **74**:56; **76**:3 1; **81**:28,29
whosoever wills, let him:
believe and disbelieve, **18**:29
take a path to his Lord, **76**:29
walk straight, **81**:28
Friday prayers, **62**:9-11
Fruits, **6**:41; **16**:11
in Paradise, in plenty, **43**:73
every kind of, **47**:15
as they desire, **77**:42
Fujjâr, **82**:14-16; **83**:7
Furqân, S.**25**
Fussilat (see *Hâ Mîm*), S.**41**
Gabriel, (Jibrîl) **2**:97,98; **26**:193; **66**:4; **81**:19-21
Rûh, **26**:193; **67**:12; **70**:4; **78**:38; **97**:4
Rûh-ul-Qudus, **2**:87, 253; **5**:110; **16**:102
Gambling, **2**:219; **5**:90
Game, in a state of *Ihrâm,* **5**: 94-96
Ghâfir (see *Mu'min*), S. **40**
Ghâshiyah, S. **88**
Ghusl, **4**:43; **5**:6
Gifts, **30**:39
Goliath, (Jâlût) **2**: 249-251
Good (Days), **3**:140
you dislike a thing which is, and like which is bad, **2**:216
to be rewarded, **4**:85; **28**:54
rewarded double, **4**:40; **28**:54
rewarded ten times, **6**:160
increased, **42**:23
for those who do, there is good and the home of Hereafter, **16**:30
is for those who do good in this world, **39**:10
Allâh rewards those who do, with what is best, **53**:31
is there any reward for, other than good, **55**:60
do, as Allâh has been good to you, **28**:77
Good and Evil,
good is from Allâh and evil is from yourself, **4**:79
if you do good, for your ownselves and if you do evil, against yourselves, **17**:7; **41**:46
repel evil with good, **23**:96; **28**:54; **41**:34
good and the evil deed cannot be equal, **41**:34
every person will be confronted with all the, he has done, **3**:30
(see also *Muhsînûn*)
Good deed,
disclose or conceal it, **4**:149
strive as in a race in, **5**:48
Gospel, **3**:3,48,65; **5**:46,47,66,68,110; **7**:157; **9**:111; **48**:29; **57**:27.
Great News, **78**:1-5
Greeting, **4**:86; **10**:10; **14**:23; **33**:44; **25**:75; **24**:61
Hadîd, S. **57**
Hady (animal for sacrifice), **2**: 196, 200
Hajj (Pilgrimage), **2**:158, 196-203; **3**:97; **5**:2; **22**:30
Hajj, S. **22**
Hâmân, **28**:6,38; **29**:39; **40**:24,36,37
Hands and legs will bear witness, **36**:65
Hâqqah, S.**69**
Hardship, there is relief with every, **94**:56
Hârûn, (see Aron).
Hârût, **2**:102
Hashr, S.**59**
Hearts,
hardened, **2**:74; **22**:53; **39**:22; **57**:16
sealed, **7**:100,101; **40**:35; **47**:16; **63**:3
covered, **17**:46; **41**:5
locked up, **47**:24
divided, **59**:14

filled with fear, **22**:35
in whose, there is a disease, **2**:10; **5**:52; **8**:49; **9**:125; **22**:53; **24**:50; **33**:12,32,60; **47**:20,29; **74**:31

Heavens,
to Allâh belong the unseen of the, **16**:77
created not for a play, **21**:16
and the earth were joined together, **21**:30
there is nothing hidden in the, **27**:75
created without any pillars, **31**:10
will be rolled up in His Right Hand, **39**:67
creation of seven heavens in two days, **41**:12
adorned nearest heaven with lamps, **41**:12
to Allâh belong all that is in the, **45**:27; **53**:31
seven heavens, one above another, **67**:3

Hell. This word occurs more than 200 times in Noble Qur'ân. Mentioning every place will make the Index very big.

Hereafter,
better is the house in the, **6**:32; **7**:169
which will be the end in the, **6**:135
Zâlimûn will not be successful (in), **6**:135
home of the, **12**:109; **16**:30; **28**:83; **29**:64
who believe not in the, **17**:10
reward of the, **42**:20
better than silver and gold, **43**:33-35
only for the *Muttaqûn,* **43**:35
punishment of, **68**:33
better and more lasting, **87**:17
better than the present, **93**:4

Highways, broad, **21**:31

Hijr (Rocky Tract), **15**:80-85

Hijr, S.**15**

Horses, **16**:8

Hour,
the knowledge of it is with Allâh only, **7**:187; **33**:63; **41**:47; **68**:26
all of a sudden it is on them, **6**:31; **7**:187; **12**:107; **43**:66
comes upon you, **6**:40; **12**:107; **20**:15; **34**:3
has drawn near, **54**:1-5
as a twinkling of the eye, or even nearer, **16**: 77
earthquake of the, **22**:1
will be established, on the Day, **30**:12,14
surely coming, there is no doubt, **40**:59; **45**:32; **51**:5,6

Houses, manners about entering, **24**:27-29

Hûd, **7**:65-72; **11**:50-60; **26**:123-140; **46**:21-26

Hûd, S.**11**

Hujurât, S.**49**

Humazah, S.**104**

Hunain (battle), **9**:25

Hûr (females in Paradise), **44**:54; **52**:20

Hypocrites,
say: we believe in Allâh and the Last Day, but in fact believe not, **2**:8
deceive themselves, **2**:9
disease in their hearts, **2**:10; **8**:49; **22**:53; **33**:12; **47**:29
make mischief, **2**:11,12
fools and mockers, **2**:13-15
purchased error for guidance, **2**:16
deaf, dumb and blind, **2**:17,18
in fear of death and darkness, **2**:19,20
pleasing speech, **2**:204-206
refuse to fight, **3**:167,168
Allâh knows what is in their hearts, **3**:167; **4**:63
go for judgement to false judges, turn away from Revelation, come when a catastrophe befalls, **4**:60-62
in misfortune and in a great success, **4**:72, 73
Allâh has cast them back, **4**:88
not to be taken as friends, **4**:89; **58**:14-19
if they turn back, kill them wherever you find them, **4**:89
they wait and watch for your victory or disbelievers success, **4**:141
seek to deceive Allâh, **4**:142

they pray with laziness and to be seen of men, **4**:142
belong neither to these nor to those, **4**:143
in lowest depths of Fire; no helper, **4**:145
afraid of being found out, **9**:64,65
not to pray for, **9**:84
men and women are from one another; losers; Curse of Allâh, **9**:67-69
in bedouins, **9**:101
wherever found, they shall be seized and killed, **33**:61
Allâh will punish the, **33**:73
liars; turning their backs; there hearts are divided, **59**:11-14
liars; made their oaths a screen; their hearts are sealed; beware of them, **63**:1-4
comprehend not, know not, **63**:7,8
to strive hard against, **66**:9
Iblîs (Satan), **2**:34; **7**:11-18; **15**:31-44; **17**:61-65; **18**:50; **20**:116-120; **34**:20,21; **38**:71-85 (see also Satan)
Ibrâhîm, (see Abraham)
Ibrâhîm, S. **14**
'Iddah (divorce prescribed period of women), **2**:228, 231, 232, 234, 235; **33**:49; **65**:1-7
Idrîs (Enoch), **19**:56,57; **21**:85; **96**:4
Ihrâm, **2**:197; **5**:2,95
lhsan, **16**:90
Ikhlâs, S.**112**
Ilâh, only One, **2**:163; **6**:19; **16**:22,51; **23**:91; **37**:4; **38**:65
Illegal sexual intercourse; evidence of witnesses, **4**:15-18; **24**:2,19
'Iliyyûn, **83**:18-21
Impure (*Najas*) — See **9**:28 and its footnote.
'Imrân, wife of, **3**:35; daughter of, **66**:12
Infitâr, S.**82**
Inheritance, **2**:180,240; **4**:7-9,11,12,19, 33, 176; **5**:106-108
Injustice, to whom has been done, **4**:30, 148
Insân (see *Dahr*), S. **76**
Inshiqâq, S. **84**
Inshirâh (see *Sharh*), S.**94**
Inspiration, **6**:93; **10**:2,109; **12**:102; **17**:86; **40**:15; **42**:3,7,51,52; **53**:4,10
Intercession/Intercessor, **6**:51,70,93,94; **10**:3; **19**:87; **20**:106,109; **30**:13; **34**:23; **39**:44; **40**:18; **43**:86; **53**:26; **74**:48
Intoxicants, **5**:90 (see also **2**:219)
Iqâmat-as-Salât, **2**:3,43,83,110,177, 277; **4**:77,102,103; **5**:12,55; **6**:72; **7**:170; **8**:3; **9**:5,11,18,71; **10**:87; **11**:114; **13**:22; **14**:31,37; **17**:78; **20**:14; **22**:41,78; **24**:56; **27**:3; **29**:45; **30**:31; **31**:4,17; **33**:33; **35**:18,29; **42**:38; **58**:13; **73**:20; **98**:5.
Iqra' (see *'Alaq*), S. **96**
Iram, **89**:7
'Îsâ, see Jesus
Isaac, (Ishâq) **2**:133; **4**:163; **6**:84; **19**:49; **21**:72; **29**:27; **37**:112,113
Ishmael (Ismâ'îl), **2**:125-129, 133; **4**:163; **6**:86; **19**:54,55; **21**:85; **38**:48
Islâm, **3**:19,85; **5**:3; **6**:125; **39**:22; **61**:7
first of those who submit as Muslims, **6**:14,163; **39**:12
first to embrace, **9**:100
breast opened to, **39**:22
as a favour, **49**:17
Isrâ', S. **17**
Israel, Children of, **2**:40-86
favour bestowed, **2**:47-53, 60, 122; **45**: 16,17
rebelling against Allâh's obedience, **2**:54-59, 61,63-74; **5**:71; **7**:138-141
their relations with Muslims, **2**:75-79
their arrogance, **2**:80,88,91
their covenants, **2**:80,83-86,93,100; **5**:12,13,70
bought the life of this world at the price of Hereafter, **2**:86
greediest of mankind for life, **2**:96
ask for a king, **2**:246-251
exceeded the limits; broken into various groups; monkeys, **7**:161-171
promised twice, **17**:4-8
delivered from enemy, **20**:80-82
given Scripture and leaders, **32**:23-25; **40**:53,54

the learned scholars of, knew it (Qur'ân as true), **26**:197

Istawâ (rose over), **2**:29; **7**:54; **10**:3; **13**:2; **20**:5; **32**:4; **41**:11; **57**:4

I'tikâf **2**:187

Jacob, (Ya'qûb) **2**:132,133; **4**:163; **6**:84; **12**:18; **19**:49; **21**:72; **29**:27

Asbât (twelve sons of Jacob), **2**:140; **3**:84; **4**:163

Jâlût, (see Goliath).

Jamarât, **2**:200

Jâthiyah, S.**45**

Jesus, 'Îsâ son of Mary,
- glad tidings of birth, **3**:45-47; **19**:22,23
- Messenger to the Children of Israel, **3**:49-51
- disciples, **3**:52,53; **5**:111-115
- disciples as Allâh's helpers, **3**:52; **61**:14
- raised up, **3**:55-58; **4**:157-159
- likeness of Adam, **3**:59
- not crucified, **4**:157
- inspired, **4**:163
- no more than Messenger, **4**:171; **5**:75; **43**:63,64
- they have disbelieved who say, **5**:17,72; **9**:30
- Our Messenger (Muhammad) has come, **5**:19
- gave the Gospel, **5**:46
- disciples said: we are Muslims, **5**:111
- Table spread with food, **5**:114
- taught no false worship, **5**:116-118
- a righteous Prophet, **6**:85
- as a Sign, **23**:50; **43**:61
- no more than a slave and an example to the Children of Israel, **43**:59
- glad tidings of a Messenger whose name shall be Ahmed, **61**:6

Jews,
- and Christians, **2**:140; **4**:153-161,171; **5**:18
- listen to falsehood, **5**:41,42
- accursed for what they uttered, **5**:64
- enmity to the believers (Muslims), **5**:82
- who embraced Islâm, **26**:197; **28**:53; **29**:47

Jibrîl, (see Gabriel)

Jihâd, **2**:216; **9**:24; **22**:78; **25**:52 (see also Fighting; Striving)

Jinn, S.**72**

Jinn, **6**:100,112; **15**:27; **34**:41; **38**:37; **46**:18,29; **55**:15,33,39; **72**:1-15

Job, **4**:163; **6**:84; **21**:83,84; **38**:41-44

John, (Yahyâ),
- glad tidings of, **3**:39; **21**:90
- righteous, **6**:85
- wise, sympathetic, dutiful, **19**:12-15

Jonah (Jonas or Yûnus), **4**:163; **6**:86; **10**:98; **21**:87; **37**:139-148; (*Dhun-Nûn*) **21**:87; **68**:48-50

Joseph (Yûsuf), **6**:84; **12**:4-101

Jûdi, Mount, **11**:44

Jumu'ah, S.**62**

Justice (*Adl*), **2**:282; **4**:58,135; **7**:29; **16**:90; **57**:25 (see also **4**:65,105)

Ka'bah,
- built by Abraham, **2**:125-127
- no killing of game, **5**:94-96
- asylum of security, **5**:97
- going round in naked state, **7**:28
- while praying and going round, **2**:200; **7**:29,31

Kâfirûn, S. **109**

Kâfûr, cup mixed with, **76**:5

Kahf S.**18**

Kanz, **9**:34,35.

Kauthar (river in Paradise), **108**:1

Kauthar, S.**108**

Keys,
- of the heavens and the earth, **39**:63; **42**:12
- of the *Ghaib.* **6**:59

Khaulah bint Tha'labah, **58**:1

Killing,
- if anyone killed a person, he killed all mankind, **5**:32
- do not kill anyone, **17**:33

Kind words are better than charity, **2**:263

Kindred, rights of, **2**:83, 177, 215; **4**:7-9,36; **8**:41; **16**:90; **17**:26; **24**:22; **29**:8; **30**:38; **42**:23

Kîraman-Katîbîn, **82**:11

Knowledge,

not a leaf falls, but He knows it, **6**:59
lost are they who have killed their children from folly, without, **6**:140
of five things, with Allâh Alone, **31**:34
with certainty, **102**:5-7
Korah (Qârûn), **28**:76-82; **29**:39; **40**:24
Kursi, **2**:255
Lahab (See *Masad*), S.**111**
Lail, S.**92**
Lamp, **25**:61; **67**:5; **71**:16; **78**:13
Languages, difference in, and colours of men, **30**:22
Lât, **53**:19
Law, prescribed, **5**:48
Laws from Allâh, **2**:219; **98**:3
Liars, **26**:221-223
Life, if anyone saved a, he saved the life of all mankind, **5**:32
Life of this world,
bought the, at the price of Hereafter, **2**:86
is only the enjoyment of deception, **3**:185
sell the, for the Hereafter, **4**:74
is nothing but amusement and play, **6**:32; **29**:64; **47**:36; **57**:20
deceives, **6**:130
little is the enjoyment of the, than the Hereafter, **9**:38; **13**:26; **28**:60
likeness of, is as the min, **10**:24
glad tidings in the, **10**:64
whoever desires, gets therein; but then there will be no portion in the Hereafter, **11**:15,16; **17**:18; **42**:20
who love the present, and neglect the Hereafter, **75**:20,21; **76**:27
you prefer the, **87**:16
Light,
manifest, **4**:174
and darkness, **6**:1
parable of, **24**:35
goes before and with the Believers, **57**:12-15; **66**:8
given by Allâh, that the Believers may walk straight, **57**:2
Limits set by Allâh, **2**:173,187,190,230; **9**:112; **58**:4; **65**:1; **78**:22
these are the, **2**:187; 229, 230; **4**:13; **58**:4; **65**:1
transgress not the, **2**:190,229
whosoever transgresses, **2**:229; **4**:14; **78**:22
but forced by necessity, nor transgressing the, **2**:173; **6**:145
do not exceed the, in your religion, **4**:171; **5**:77
when they eexceeded the, (became monkeys), **7**:166
who observe the, **9**:112
Lion, **74**:51
Loan,
lend to Allâh a goodly, **2**:245; **73**:20
increased manifold, **57**:11,18
doubled, **64**:17
Loss, manifest, **39**:15
Lot, (Lût) **6**:86; **7**:80; **11**:70,74,77,81,89; **15**:59,61; **21**:71,74; **22**:43; **26**:160, 161,167; **27**:54-56; **29**:26,28,32,33; **37**:133; **38**:13; **50**:13; **54**:33,34; **66**:10
his disobedient wife, **11**:81; **15**:60; **66**:10
Lote tree, **34**:16; **53**:14-16; **56**:28
Luqmân, **31**:12-14
Luqmân, S.**31**
Ma'ârij, S.**70**
Madînah (Yathrib), **9**:120: **33**:13,60; **63**:8
Madyan, **7**:85-93; **11**:84-95; **20**:40; **22**:44; **28**:22,23; **29**:36,37 (see also *Aiyka*; Wood)
Mahr (bridal-money), **2**:229,236,237; **4**:4,19-21,24,25; **5**:5; **33**:50; **60**:10,11
Mâ'idah, S.**5**
Makkah (Bakkah), **3**:96; **90**:1,2; City of Security, **95**:3
Man,
generations after generations on earth, **2**:30; **6**:165;
made necessor, **35**:39
duty, **2**:83,84,88,177; **4**:1-36; **8**:41; **16**:90; **17**:23-39; **24**:22; **29**:8,9; **30**:38; **33**:33; **42**:23; **64**:14; **70**:22-35
tested by Allâh, **2**:155; **3**:186; **47**:31; **57**:25
things men covet, **3**:14

created from, **4**:1; **6**:2; **15**:26,28,33; **16**:4; **21**:30; **22**:5; **23**:12-14; **25**:54; **30**:20; **32**:7-9; **35**:11; **36**:77,78; **37**:11; **39**:6; **40**:67; **49**:13; **55**:14; **56**:57-59; **75**:37-40; **76**:1,2; **77**:20-23; **80**:18,19; **86**:5-8; **96**:2
created and decreed a stated term, **6**:2; **15**:26
reconciliation between, and wife, **4**:35
losers who denied their Meeting with Allâh, **6**:31
the return, **6**:60,72,164; **10**:45,46
plots against ownself, **6**:123
shall not bear the burden of another, **6**:164
is ungrateful, **7**:10; **11**:9; **30**:34; **32**:9; **80**:17; **100**:6
warned against Satan, **7**:27
wife and children, **7**:189,190
when harm or evil touches, **10**:12; **11**:9,10; **16**:53-55; **17**:67; **29**:10; **30**:33; **31**:32; **39**:8,49; **41**:49-51; **42**:48; **70**:19-21; **89**:16
returning towards the Lord, **10**:23; **84**;6; **96**:8
wrong themselves, **10**:44
is exultant and boastful, **11**:10
invokes for evil, **17**:11
is ever hasty, **17**:11
his deeds fastened to his neck, **17**:13
whoever goes astray, to his own loss and goes right, only for his ownself, **17**:15
not be dealt unjustly, **17**:71
death and resurrection, **23**:15,16
have broken their religion into sects, each rejoicing in its belief, **23**:53
tongues, hands and feet will bear witness against, **24**:24
witness against himself, **75**:14
who has taken as his god his own desire, **25**:43
kindred by blood and marriage, **25**:54
Allâh has subjected for you whatsoever is in the heaven and earth, **31**:20
whosoever submits his face to Allâh, **31**:22
not two hearts inside his body, **33**:4
to worship Allâh, **39**:64-66
misfortunes because of what his hands have earned, **42**:30,48
angels recording his doings, **50**:17,18,23; **85**:11
angels guarding him, **13**:11; **86**:4
sorted out into three classes, **56**:7-56
those nearest to Allâh, **56**:10,11
companions of Right Hand, **56**:27-40
companions of Left Hand, **56**:41-56
to be transfigured and created in forms unknown, **56**:60-62
made shapes good, **64**:3
wealth and children are only a trial, **64**:15
created and endowed with, **67**:23,24; **74**:12-15; **90**:8-10
is impatient, **70**:19-21
devoted to prayers, **70**:22-35
desires more, **74**:15
witness against himself, **75**:14,15
his arrogance, **75**:31-40; 90:5-7
loves the present life of this world, **76**:27
more difficult to create, or is the heaven, **79**:28
careless concerning the Lord, **82**:6-12
fashioned perfectly and given due proportion, **82**:7
travels from stage to stage, **84**:19
love of wealth, **89**:20
created in toil, **90**:4
efforts and deeds are diverse, **92**:4
smooth for him the path of Ease, and Evil, **92**:7,10
created of the best stature (moulds), **95**:4
then reduced to the lowest of the low, **96**:5
transgresses all bounds, **96**:6,7

Manâsik (duties) of *Hajj,* **2**:128,200; **22**:30

Manât, **53**:20

Mankind,
witnesses over, **2**:143
one community, **2**:213; **10**:19
created from single pair, **4**:1; **39**:6; **49**:13
rebellion against ownselves, **10**:23
heedless though Reckoning is near,

21:1-3
created on *Fitrah,* **30**:30
most honourable of, **49**:13
made into nations and tribes, **49**:13
Manna and the quails, **2**:57
Manners,
about entering houses, **24**:27-29
in the home, **24**:58-61
in the Prophet's houses, **33**:53
to greet and send *Salât* on the Prophet, **33**:56
not to annoy Allâh and His Messenger or believing men or women, **33**:57,58
verify news before belief, **49**:6
not to scoff another, **49**:11
in assemblies, **58**:11
Marriage, **2**:232,234
to disbelievers or slaves, **2**:221
to how many, lawful, **4**:3
Mahr not to be taken back (in case of divorce), **4**:20,21
forbidden are for, **4**:22-24
if no means to wed free believing women, **4**:25
if breach feared, two arbitrators to be appointed, **4**:35
if wife fears cruelty or desertion, make terms of peace, **4**:128
not incline too much to one wife so as to leave the other hanging, **4**:129
of adulterers, **24**:3
to those who are poor, **24**:32
those who find not the financial means for marriage, **24**:33
wives made lawful to the Prophet, **33**:50-52
before sexual intercourse, no *'iddah* on divorce, **33**:49
Martyrs,
not dead, **2**:154; **3**:169
rejoice in Grace and Bounty from Allâh, **3**:170,171
receive forgiveness and mercy, **3**:157,158
will receive good provision, **22**:58,59
Mârût, **2**:102
Mary (mother of Jesus),
birth, **3**:35-7
glad tidings of Jesus, **3**:42-51; **19**:16-21
in childbirth, **19**:23-26
brought the babe to her people, **19**:27-33
false charge, **4**:156
guarded her chastity, **21**:91; **66**:12
Maryam, S.**19**
Masad, S.**111**
Al-Masjid-al-Aqsa, **17**:1
Al-Masjid-al-Harâm, **2**:144,149,150,191,196,217; **5**:2; **9**:19,28; **17**:1; **48**:25,27
Al-Mash'ar-il-Harâm, **2**:198
Ma'ûn, S.**107**
Ma'vâ Paradise, **53**:15
Measure and weight, give full, **11**:85; **17**:35; **83**:3:1-5
Meeting,
with Allâh, **6**:31
of Great Day, **19**:37
of the Hereafter, **30**:16
Messengers, **2**:253; **4**:164,165; **40**:78; **57**:27
succession of, **2**:87
series of, **5**:19; **23**:44
killed, **3**:183
threatened, **14**:13
mocked, **6**:10; **13**:32; **15**:11; **21**:41
denied and rejected, **3**:184; **6**:34; **25**:37; **34**:45; **51**:52
believing in some and rejecting others, **4**:150-152
gathering of the, **5**:109
sent as givers of glad tidings and warners, **6**:48; **14**:4-8
as a witness from every nation, **16**:89
for every nation, there is a, **10**:47; **16**:36
reciting Allâh's Verses, **7**:35,36
an angel as a, **17**:95; **25**:7
no more than human beings, **14**:10-12; **17**:94; **21**:8; **25**:7,8,20
and their wives and offspring, **13**:38
(see also Prophets)
M'irâj, **17**:1; **53**:12

Miserliness/Misers, **57**:24
Misfortune, because of your hands, **42**:30
Monasticism, not prescribed, **57**:27
Monkeys, transgressors became as, **2**:65; **5**:60; **7**:166
Months, number of, **9**:36,37
Moon, **7**:54; **10**:5; **16**:12; **22**:18; **25**:61; **36**:39,40; **71**:16; **91**:2
spliting of; **54**:1
Moses,
and his people, **2**:51-61; **5**:20-29; **7**:138-141,159-162; **14**:5-8; **61**:5
and Pharaoh, **2**:49,50; **7**:103-137; **10**:75-92; **11**:96-99; **17**:101-103; **20**:17-53,56-79; **23**:45-49; **25**:35,36; **26**:10-69; **28**:4-21,31-42; **40**:23-46; **43**:46-56; **51**:38-40; **73**:16; **79**:15-26
guided by Allâh, **6**:84
mountain and Lord's appearance,**7**:142- 145
and calf-worship of his people, **7**:148-156; **20**:86-98
his Book, differences arose therein, **11**:110
given the Scripture, **17**:2
nine Clear Signs, **7**:133; **17**:101
to the junction of the two seas, **18**:60-82
called and given Messengership, **19**:51-53; **20**:9-56; **28**:29-35
his childhood, mother and sister, **20**:38-40; **28**:7-13
magicians converted, **20**:70-73; **26**:46-52
in Madyan, **20**:40; **28**:22-28
granted the Criterion, **21**:48
and the mystic fire, **27**:7-12; **28**:29-35
his mishap in the city, **28**:15-21
came with clear *Ayat,* **29**:39
guided to the Right Path, **37**:114-122
Scripture of, **53**:36; **87**:19
Mosque (of Jerusalem), **17**:7
Mosque (of Qubâ), **9**:107,108
Mosques, **2**:187; **9**:17-19
to maintain, of Allâh, **9**:17,18
Mosquito, a parable, 2:26
Mountains, **15**:19; **16**:15; **20**:105-107; **21**:31; **22**:18; **31**:10; **42**:32,33; **59**:21; **73**:14; **77**:10,27; **81**:3; **101**:5
Muddaththir, S.**74**
Muhâjir (Emigrants), **4**:100; **9**:100, 107,117; **22**:58,59; **24**:22;**33**:6; **59**:8,9
women, **60**:10-12
Muhammad ﷺ,
mocked, **2**:104; **4**:46; **25**:41,42; **34**:78
respect the Messenger, 2:104; 4:46; **49:**1-5
covenant to believe in, **3**:81
a witnesses over believers, **2**:143
no more than a Messenger, **3**:144
dealing gently, **3**:159
his work, **3**:164; **7**:157; **36**:6; **52**:29; **74**:1-7
sent as a great favour to the believers, **3**:164
sent with the truth, **4**:170
not made a watcher, **6**:107
unlettered, **7**:157; **62**:2
sent to the mankind as the Messenger of Allâh, **7**:158; **48**:9,29
a plain warner, **7**:184,188; **11**:2; **15**:89; **53**:56
not a madman, **7**:184; **68**:2; **81**:22
who accuse you, **9**:58
men who hurt the Prophet, **9**:61
a mercy to the Believers, **9**:61
only follow that which is revealed, **10**:15,16; **11**:12-14; **46**:9
his, sayings, **11**:2-4; **12**:108; **34**:46-50
Allâh is Witness over him, **13**:43; **29**:52; **46**:8
sent as a witness, bearer of glad tidings and a warner, **11**:2; **15**:89; **26**:194; **33**:45; **34**:28; **48**:8
not to be distressed, **15**:97; **16**:127; **18**:6
sent to be a witness, **16**:89; **22**:78; **73**:15
to invite with wisdom and fair preaching, and argue in a better way, **16**:125
Maqâman Mahmudâ, **17**:79
inspired, **18**:110
mercy for the *'Âlamîn*, **21**:107
asks no reward, **25**:57; **38**:86; **42**:23
has been commanded to, **27**: 91-93; **30**:30; **66**:9

as a mercy from Allâh, **28**:46,47
close to the believers, **33**:6
good example to follow, **33**:21
last of the Prophets, **33**:40
send *Salât* on, **33**:56
sent to all mankind, **34**:28
wage is from Allâh only, **34**:47
only a human being, **41**:6
sent as a protector, **42**:48
not a new thing in the Messengers, **46**:9
witness from among the Children of Israel, **46**:10
Bai'âh (pledge) to him is *Bai'âh* (pledge) to Allâh, **48**:10,18
saw Gabriel, **53**:4-18; **81**:22-25
oppose him not, **58**:20-22
foretold by Jesus, **61**:6
to make Religion of Truth victorious overall religions, **61**:9
from the darkness to the light, **65**:11
to strive hard against disbelievers and hypocrites, **66**:9
exalted standard of character, **68**:4
not a poet or soothsayer, **69**:41,42
devoted to prayer, **73**:1-8,20; **74**:3
and the blind man, **80**:1-12
to prostrate and draw near to Allâh, **96**:19
reciting pure pages, **98**:2
Ayât regarding family of, **24**:11-17; **33**:28-34,50-53,55,59; **66**:1,3-6; **108**:3
(see also Messengers; Prophets)
Muhammad, S.**47**
Muhsinûn (Good-doers), **2**:117,195; **4**:125,128; **10**:126; **16**:128
Allâh loves the, **3**:134,148; **5**:93
Allâh loses not the reward of the, **5**:85; **9**:120; **11**:115; **18**:30
We reward the, **12**:22; **37**:80,105,110; **39**:34; **77**:44
glad tidings to the, **22**:37; **46**:12
Allâh's Mercy is near to the, **7**:56
Allâh is with the, **29**:69
dutiful and good to parents, **2**:83
patient in performing duties to Allâh, **16**:90
(see also Good and Evil)
Mujâdilah, S.**58**
Mules, **16**:8
Mulk, S.**67**
Mu'min (see *Ghâfir*), S.**40**
Mu'minûn, S.**23**
Mumtahanah, S.**60**
Munâfiqûn, S.**63**
Murder, **2**:178,179
Mursalât, S.**77**
Muslims,
first of the, **6**:14,163; **9**:100; **39**:12
Who has named, **22**:78
forgiveness and a great reward for them who, **33**:35,36
Mutaffifîn, S.**83**
Muzzammil, S.**73**
Naba', S.**78**
Nadîr, Banû-An-,(Jews), **59**:2,9,13
Nahl, S.**16**
Najas (impure) **9**:28 and its footnote.
Najm, S.**53**
Najwâ (See Secret)
Names,
to Him belong the Most Beautiful, **7**:180
to Him belong the Best, **17**:110; **20**:8; **59**:24
Naml, S.**27**
Nas, S.**114**
Nasr, **71**:23
Nasr, S.**110**
Nâzi'ât, S.**79**
Necessity, if one is forced by, **2**:173; **6**:145
Neighbour, **4**:36
New moons, **2**:189
News, to be tested, **4**:83
Niggards condemned, **17**:29; **47**:38; **48**:38
Night, (as a symbol), **79**:29; **92**:1; **93**:2; for rest, **10**:67
as a covering, **13**:3; **78**:10
to be of service, **14**:32
Night of *Al-Qadr* (Decree), **44**:3,4; **97**:1-5
Nisâ', S.**4**
Noah, **3**:33; **4**:163; **6**:84; **7**:59-69; **9**:70; **10**:71; **11**:25,32,36,42,45,46,48,89; **17**:3; **21**:76; **23**:23; **25**:37; **26**:105;

29:14; **37**:75; **51**:46; **54**:9; **69**:11; **71**:1-28
the Deluge, **29**:14
unrighteous son not saved, **11**:45-47
unrighteous wife, **14**:9; **17**:3,17; **19**:58; **21**:76; **22**:42; **26**:105,106, 116; **33**:7; **37**:75,79; **38**:12; **42**:13; **40**:5,31; **42**:13; **50**:12; **53**:52; **57**:26; **66**:10; **71**:1,21,26
Nûh, S.**71**
Nû r, S.**24**
Oath, **2**:224-227; **3**:77; **5**:89; **6**:109; **16**:38,91,92,94; **24**:22,53; **66**:2; **68**:10,39; **77**:3
Obedience, **3**:132; **4**:59,64,66,80,81; **5**:95; **18**:46; **24**:51,52,54; **47**:33; **64**:12
Obligations to be fulfilled, **5**:1
Offspring, **4**:9; **42**:49,50
He bestows male and female, upon whom He wills, **42**:49
Olive, **6**:141; **16**:11; **23**:20; **24**:35; **95**:1
Only One *Ilâh,* **2**:163; **6**:19; **16**:22,51; **23**:91; **37**: 4; **38**:65
Orphans, **2**:83, 177, 215,220; **4**:2,3,6,8,10,36,127; **6**:152; **8**:41; **17**:34; **18**:82; **59**:7; **76**:8; **89**:17; **90**:15; **93**:6; **107**:2
guardians of, **4**:6
Own doings, made fair-seeming to each people, **6**:108
Pairs, in all creatures, **13**:3; **30**:8; **36**:36; **42**:11; **43**:12; **51**:9,49; **53**:45
Palm tree, **13**:4; **19**:25; **20**:71, **59**:5
Parables, (likeness, example, similitudes)
who kindled a fire, **2**:17,18
rain storm from the sky, **2**:19,20
mosquito, **2**:26
who shout, **2**:171
a town all in utter ruins, **2**:259
grain of corn, **2**:261
smooth rock, **2**:264
garden, **2**:265,266
rope, **3**:103
cold wind, **3**:117
dog who lolls his tongue out, **7**:176
brink of a precipice, **9**:109,110
rain, **10**:24
clean-mown harvest, **10**:24
blind and deaf, **11**:24
ashes on which the wind blows furiously, **14**:18
goodly tree, **14**:24,25
evil tree, **14**:26
slave and a man, **16**:75
dumb man who is a burden to his master, **16**:76
woman undoing the thread, **16**:92
township, secure and well content, **16**:112,113
two men with gardens of grapes, **18**:32-44
life of this world like water from the sky, **18**:45
fallen from the sky and snatched by birds, **22**:31
a fly, **22**:73
Light is as a niche, **24**:35,36
mirage, **24**:39
darkness in a vast deep sea, **24**:40
spider, **29**:41
partners, **30**:28
dwellers of the town, **36**:13-32
a man belonging to many partners, **39**:29
seed growing, **48**:29
vegetation after rain, **57**:20
mountain humbling itself, **59**:21
donkey, **62**:5
water were to be sunk away, **67**:30
people of the garden, **68**:17-33
Paradise,
of Abode, *(Mava* Paradise), **53**:15
Firdaus Paradise, **18**:107; **23**:11
Gardens under which rivers flow, **3**:15,198; **4**:57; **5**:119; **7**:43; **9**:72; **18**:31; **22**:23; **39**:20; **57**:12; **64**:9; **98**:8
Everlasting Gardens (*'Adn* Paradise) **9**:72; **13**:23; **18**:31; **19**:61; **20**:76
Gardens of Eternity (*'Adn* Paradise), **16**:31; **35**:33; **98**:8
Gardens of delight, **37**:43; **56**:12,89

Gardens with everlasting delights, **9**:21
Gardens and grapeyards, **78**:32
fruits of two gardens, **55**:54,62
fruits of all kinds as desired, in plenty, **36**:57; **37**:42; **43**:73; **44**:55; **47**:15; **55**:52,68; **56**:20,29,32; **77**:42
fruits will be near at hand, **55**:54; **69**:23
fruit and meat, **52**:22
flesh of fowls, **56**:21
thornless lote trees and *Talh* (banana trees), **56**:28,29
a running spring, **88**:12
spring called *Salsabîl,* **76**:18
a spring called *Kâfûr,* **76**:5
a spring *Tasnîm,* **83**:27,28
a river in Paradise, *Kauthar,* **108**:1
rivers of wine, milk, clarified honey, **47**:15
pure sealed wine, white, delicious, **37**:45,46; **56**:18; **76**:21; **83**:25
cup, mixed with, *Zanjabil,* **76**:17; **78**:34; water, **76**:5
trays of gold and cups, **43**:71
vessels of silver and cups of crystal, **76**:15,16
green garments of fine and thick silk, **18**:31; **22**:23; **35**:33; **44**:53; **76**:12,21
adorned with bracelets of gold and pearls, **18**:31; **22**:23; **35**:33; **76**:21
coaches lined with silk brocade, **55**:54
green cushions and rich beautiful mattresses, set in row, **55**:76; **88**:15
thrones woven with gold and precious stones, raised high **56**:15; **88**:13
rich carpets spread out, **88**:16
beautiful mansions, lofty rooms, one above another, **9**:72; **39**:20
abiding therein forever, **3**:198; **4**:57; **5**:119; **9**:22,72; **11**:108; **43**:71; **57**:12; **98**:8
eternal home, **3**:15; **35**:35
facing one another on thrones, **15**:47; **37**:44; **44**:53; **56**:16
never taste death therein, **44**:56
nor they (ever) be asked to leave it, **15**:48
hatred or sense of injury removed from their hearts, **7**:43; **15**:47
all grief removed, **35**:34
no sense of fatigue, toil or weariness, **15**:48; **35**:35
neither will be any hurt, abdominal pain, headache nor intoxication, **37**:47; **56**:19
no vain speaking nor sinful speech, **19**:62; **56**:25
neither harmful speech nor falsehood, **78**:35; **88**:11
free from sin, **37**:47; **52**:23
neither excessive heat nor biter cold, **76**:13
there will be a known provision, **37**:41; **56**:89
in peace and security, **15**:46; **44**:51,55; **50**:34
home of peace, **6**:127
greetings in, **7**:46; **10**:10; **13**:24; **14**:23; **16**:32; **19**:62; **36**:58; **39**:73; **56**:26
whoever does righteous deeds will enter, **4**:124; **42**:22; **44**:51
who kept their duty to their Lord will be led in groups, **39**:73
been made to inherit because of deeds, **43**:72
Allâh is pleased with them and they with Him, **5**:119
My Paradise, **89**:30
the greatest bliss, **9**:72
the great success, **57**:12; **64**:9
the supreme success, **9**:72; **44**:57
for believers are Gardens as an entertainment, **32**:19
dwellers of Paradise will be busy in joyful things that Day, **36**:35
will be amidst gardens and water springs, **15**:45; **19**:63; **44**:52; **52**:17; **54**:54; **55**:46
see the angels surrounding the Throne, **39**:75
near the Omnipotent King, **54**:55
they will have all that they desire, **50**:35
Hurs, chaste females with wide and beautiful eyes, as if preserved eggs, **37**:48,49; **44**:54; **52**:20; **55**:58,70;

56:22,23
pure wives, **3**:15
wives in pleasant shade, reclining on thrones, **36**:55
young full-breasted maidens of equal age, **78**:33
immoratal boy-servants to serve them, as scattered pearls, **52**:24; **56**:17; **76**:19
Parents, kindness to, **2**:83,215; **4**:36; **16**:90; **17**:23; **29**:8; **31**:14; **46**:15-17
'Partners' of Allâh, a falsehood, **4**:116; **10**:34,35,66; **16**:86; **28**:62-64, 71-75; **30**:40; **42**:21
Pasturage, **87**:4,5
Path, **5**:77; **16**:94; **42**:52,53; **43**:43; **90**:11,12 (see also Way)
Patience, **3**:186,200; **10**:109; **11**:115; **16**:126,127; **20**:130; **40**:55,77; **42**:43; **46**:35; **70**:5; **73**:10
seek help in, and prayer, **2**:45,153; **20**:132; **50**:39
Patient,
will receive reward in full, **39**:10
Allâh is with those who are, **8**:46
and be, **11**:115
in performing duties to Allâh, **16**:90
to be, at the time of anger, **41**:34
Peace, incline to, **8**:61
Pearl and coral, preserved, **52**:24; **55**:22; **56**:23
Pen, **68**:1; **96**:4
Person,
Allâh burdens not a, beyond his scope, **2**:286; **7**:42
Allâh tax not any, except according to his capacity, **23**:62
no, knows what he will earn tomorrow and in what land he will die, **31**:34
every, will be confronted with all the good and evil he has done **3**:30
every, will come up pleading for himself, **16**:111
every, is a pledge for what he has earned, **74**:38
Allâh swears by the self-reproaching, **75**:2
Pharaoh, **28**:6; **40**:24
people of, **2**:49; **3**:11, **7**:141; **44**:17-33
drowned, **2**:50
dealings with Moses, **7**:103-137; **10**:75-92 (see also Moses and Pharaoh)
dead body out from sea, **10**:90-92
transgressed beyond bounds; committed sins and disobeyed, **20**:24; **69**:9; **73**:16; **85**:17-20; **89**:10-14
righteous wife, **28**:8,9
claims to be god, **28**:38; **79**:24
destroyed, **29**:39
a believing man from Pharaoh's family, **40**:28-44
building of a tower, **40**:36,37
Piling up of the worldly things, **102**:1-4
Pledge (*Bai'ah*),
for Islâm, **16**:91
to the Messenger is *Bai'ah* (pledge) to Allâh, **48**:10
of the Believers, **48**:18; **60**:12
Pledge (Mortgaging),
let there be a, **2**:283
every person is a, for that which he has earned, **52**:21; **74**:38
Poetry, **36**:69
Poets, **26**:224-227; **69**:41
Pomegranates, **6**:141
Poor, **2**:88,177,215,273; **4**:8,36; **8**:41; **9**:60; **17**:26; **24**:22,32; **30**:38; **47**:38; **51**:19; **59**:7,8; **69**:34; **74**:44; **76**:8; **89**:18; **90**:16; **93**:8; **107**:3
Prayer, **1**:1-7; **3**:8,26,27,147,191-194; **4**:103; **17**:80; **23**:118
neither aloud nor in a low voice, **17**:110
invocation for disbelievers, **9**:113,114
invocation of disbelievers, **13**:14
He answers (the invocation of) those, **42**:26
Prayers, five obligatory,
seek help in patience and, **2**:45,153; **20**:132; **50**:39
perform *Iqâmat-as-Salât,* (see *Iqâmat-as-Salât*)
facing towards *Qiblah,* **2**:142-145, 149,150
guard strictly the, **2**:238

in travel and attack, **2**:239; **4**:101,102
approach not when in a drunken state, **4**:43
nor in a state of *Janâbah,* **4**:43
purifying for, **4**:43; **5**:6
when finished the, **4**:103
times of, **11**:114; **17**:78,79; **20**:130; **30**:17,18; **50**:39,40; **52**:48,49; **73**:1 6,20
prostration for Allâh Alone, **13**:15
Prayers, Friday, **62**:9-11
Precautions in danger, **4**:71
Prisoners of war, **8**:67-71 (see also Captives)
Promise of Truth, **46**:16,17
Property, **2**:188; **3**:186; **4**:5,7,29; **51**:19; **59**:7-9; **70**:25
Prophets, **3**:33, 34,146; **4**:163; **5**:20; **6**:84-90; **23**:23-50; **57**:26
covenants of the, **3**:81; **33**:7-8
illegal for, **3**:161
an enemy for every, **6**:112; **25**:31
(see also Messengers)
Prostration, unto Allâh falls in, whoever in the heavens and the earth and so do their shadows, **13**:15
Provision, **10**:59; **13**:26; **14**:32; **16**:73; **34**:36, 39; **42**:12; **51**:57; **67**:21; **79**:33
Psalms, **4**:163
Punishment,
postponing of, **3**:178
cutting of hands or feet, **5**:33
punish them with the like of that with which you were afflicted, **16**:126
of this life and Hereafter, **24**:19; **68**:33
Purifying, bodily, **4**:43;.**5**:6; spiritually (from impurities), **87**:14; **91**:9
(please also see the footnote of **9**:28)
Qadr, S.**97**
Qadar, **5**:5; **64**:11
Qâf, S.**50**
Qalam, S. **68**
Qamar, S. **54**
Qâri'ah, S. **101**
Qârûn (Korah), **28**:76-82; **29**:39
Qasas, S.**28**
Qiblah, **2**:142-145,149
Qisâs (Law of equality in punishment), **2**:178,179,194; **5**:45; **16**:126; **17**:33; **22**:60; **42**:40
Qur'ân,
described, **13**:31,36,37; **14**:1; **56**:77-80
is not such as could ever be produced by other than Allâh, **2**:23; **10**:38; **11**:13; **17**:88
had it been from other than Allâh, therein have been much contradictions, **4**:82
a manifest light, **4**:174; **42**:52
revealed, **6**:19
Allâh is Witness to it, **6**:19
clear proof, **6**:157
false conversation about Verses of, **6**:68
a Reminder, **7**:63; **12**:104; **18**:101; **20**:3,99,124; **25**:29; **36**:11,69; **43**:44; **50**:8; **65**:10; **72**:17
when recited, listen and be silent, **7**:204
Dhikr, **7**:205; **15**:6,9
Book of Wisdom, **10**:1; **31**:2; **36**:2
inspired Message, **10**:2, 109; **42**:52
those reject it, **11**:17
in Arabic, **12**:2; **13**:37; **16**:103; **20**:113;**26**:195; **39**:28; **41**:3,44; **42**:7; **43**:3; **44**:58; **46**:12
made into parts, and revealed in stages, **15**:91; **17**:106; **25**:32; **76**:23
change of a Verse, **16**:10
when you want to recite the, **16**:98
guides, **17**:9
glad tidings and warning, **17**:9,10
and the disbelievers, **17**:45-47
recitation in the early dawn is ever witnessed (by the angels), **17**:78
healing and mercy, **17**:82
fully explained to mankind, every kind of similitude and example, but most
refuse, **17**:89; **18**:54; **39**:27
easy, **19**:97; **44**:58; **54**:17,22,32,40
"my people deserted this Qur'ân", **25**:30
confirmed by the Scriptures, **26**:196
narrates to the Children of Israel about which they differ, **27**:76

recite and pray, **29**:45
Truth from Allâh, **32**:3; **35**:31
on a blessed Night, **44**:3
therein is decreed every matter of ordainments, **44**:4
think deeply in the, **47**:24
warn by the, **50**:45
taught by Allâh, **55**:1
and honourable recital, well-guarded, **56**:77,78
non can touch but who are pure, **56**:79
if sent down on a mountain, **59**:21
an anguish for the disbelievers, **69**:50
an absolute truth with certainty, **69**:51
recite in a slow style, **73**:4
in Records held in honour, kept pure and holy, **80**:13-16
a Reminder to (all) the *'Âlamîn,* **81**:27
disbelievers belie, **84**:22
in Tablet preserved, **85**:22
Word that separates the truth from falsehood, **86**:13
reciting pure pages, **98**:2
(see also Book; Revelation)
Quraish, S.**106**
Quraish,
disbelievers of, **54**:43-46,51
taming of, **106**:1-4
Rabbis and monks, **9**:31,34
Race, strive as in a, in good deeds, **5**:48
Ra 'd, S.**13**
Rahmân, S.**55**
Raiment of righteousness is better, **7**:26
Rain,
Allâh's Gift, **56**:68-70
of stones, **27**:58
Ramadân, **2**:185
Ramy, **2**:200
Ransom,
no, shall be taken, **57**:15
offered by disbelievers, **3**:91; **10**:54; **13**:18
Fidyah, of fast, **2**:196; for freeing the captives, **8**:67
Rass, dwellers of the, **25**:38; **50**:12
Reality, **69**:1-3
Recompense,
the Day of, **1**:4; **37**:20; **51**:12; **56**:56; **82**:17,18; **96**:7
deniers of, **107**:1-7
of an evil is an evil like thereof, **42**:40
Reconciliation,
whoever forgives and makes, **42**:40
between man and wife, **4**:35
between believers, **49**:9,10
Record,
a Register inscribed, **83**:7-9,18-21
each nation will be called to its, **45**:28,29
written pages of deeds of every person, **81**:10
which speaks the truth, **23**:62
in right hand, **69**:19; **84**:7-9
in left hand, **69**:25
behind the back, **84**:10-15
Recording angels, **50**:17,18,23; **85**:11
Relief, with the hardship, **94**:5,6
Religion,
no compulsion in, **2**:256
is Islâm, **3**:19
of Allâh, **3**:83,84
other than Islâm, **3**:85
do not exceed the limits in, **4**:171; **5**:77
perfected, **5**:3
who take, as play and amusement, **6**:70
who divide their, and break up into sects, **6**:159; **30**:32 (see also **42**:13,14; **43**:65; **45**:17)
men have broken their, into sects, each group rejoicing in its belief, **23**:53; **30**:32
not laid in, any hardship, **22**:78
mankind created on the, **30**:30
same, for all Prophets, **42**:13-15
ancestral, **43**:22-24
Remembrance of Allâh, **63**:9
in the, hearts find rest, **13**:28
Repentance,
accepted if evil done in ignorance and repent soon afterwards, **4**:17; **6**:54
and of no effect is the, if evil deeds are continued, **4**:18
He accepts, and forgives sins, **4**:25
Respite for evil, **3**:178; **10**:11; **12**:110;

14:42,44; **29**:53-55; **86**:15-17

Resurrection, **7**:53; **14**:21; **16**:38-40; **17**:49-52; **19**:66-72; **22**:5; **23**:15,16; **46**:33-34; **50**:3,20-29,41-44; **75**:1-15; **79**:10-12; **86**:5-8

Resurrection Day, **7**:89; **20**:100,101,124
- the True Day, **78**:39
- paid your wages in full **3**:185
- written pages of deeds shall be laid open, **81**:11
- every person will know what he has brought, **81**:14
- every person will be confronted with all the good and evil he has done, **3**:30
- a person will know what he has sent forward and left behind, **82**:5
- no fear of injustice, **20**:112
- balances of justice, **21**:47
- scales of deeds, **23**:102,103
- whosoever does good or evil equal to the weight of an atom, shall see it, **100**:7,8
- all the secrets will be examined, **86**:9
- Record given in right hand, **69**:19; **84**:7-9
- Record given in left hand, **69**:25
- Record given behind back, **84**:10-15
- hard day, for the disbelievers, **25**:26; **54**:8; **74**:9
- a heavy day, **76**:27
- bear a heavy burden, **20**:100,101
- not permitted to put forth any excuse, **77**:36
- wrong-doer will bite at his hands, **25**:27
- wrong-doer assembled with their companions and idols, **37**:22
- destruction with deep regrets, sorrows and despair, **30**:12
- the female buried alive shall be questioned, **81**:8,9
- the greatest terror, **21**:103
- the caller will call, to a terrible thing, **50**:41; **54**:6-8
- a single (shout), **36**:29,49,53; **38**:15; **50**:42
- *Zajrah* (shout), **37**:19; **79**:13
- a near torment, **78**:40
- the heaven will shake with a dreadful shaking, **52**:9; **56**:4
- heaven is split asunder, **84**:1,2
- heaven cleft asunder, **77**:9; **82**:1
- heaven shall be rent asunder with clouds, **25**:25
- heaven will be rolled up, in His Right Hand, **21**:104; **39**:67
- all in heaven and on the earth will swoon away, **39**:68
- heaven shall be opened, it will become as gates, **78**:19
- sky will be like the boiling filth of oil, **70**:8
- stars shall fall, **81**:2; **82**:2
- stars will lose their lights, **77**:8
- sun will lose its light, **81**:1
- seas shall become as blazing Fire, **81**:6
- seas are burst forth, **82**:3
- earthquake of the Hour, **22**:1; **99**:1
- mountains will move away, **18**:47; **27**:88; **52**:10; **77**:9; **78**:20; **81**:3; powdered to dust **20**:105; **56**:5; like flakes of wool, **70**:9; **101**:5
- earth and the mountains will be shaken violently, **73**:14; **79**:6
- earth is ground to powder, **89**:21
- earth will be changed to another earth and so will be the heavens, **14**:48
- earth is stretched forth, **84**:3-5
- earth as a lavelled plain **18**:47; **20**:106
- earth throws out its burdens, **84**:4; **99**:2
- graves turned upside down, **82**:4
- resurrection from the graves, **21**:97; **70**:43
- over the earth alive after death, **79**:14
- wild beasts shall be gathered together, **81**:5
- raised up blind, **20**:124,125
- Trumpet will be blown, **6**:73; **18**:99; **20**:102; **23**:101; **27**:87; **36**:5 1; **39**:68; **50**:20; **69**:13; **74**:8; **78**:18; **79**:7; *Sakhkhah,* **80**:33
- the souls shall be joined with their bodies, **81**:7
- stay not longer than ten days, **20**:103
- stay no longer than a day, **20**:104; or part of a day, **24**:112-114

Day of Gathering, **64**: 9
Day of Judgement, **37**:21
Day of Decision, **77**:38; **78**:17
Day of Sorting out, **77**:13,14
Day of Grief and Regrets, **19**:39
deniers of, **77**:15-50
mankind will be like moths scattered about, **101**:4
mankind will proceed in scattered groups, **100**:6
mankind as in a drunken state, **22**:2
pregnant she-camels shall be neglected, **81**:4
nursing mother will forget her nursling, **22**:2
every pregnant will drop her load, **22**:2
relatives shall be made to see one another, **70**:11
shall a man flee from his relatives, **81**:34-37
no friend will ask of a friend, **70**:10
there will be no friend nor an intercessor, **40**:18
no person shall have power to do anything for another, **82**:19
will have no power, nor any helper, **87**:10
no fear on believers, **43**:68
believers will be amidst shades and springs, and fruits, **77**:41-43
dwellers of the Paradise and their wives, **36**:55-58
angels will be sent down with a grand descending, **25**:25
Shin shall be laid bare, **68**:42,43
Paradise shall be brought near, **81**:13
Hell will be brought near, **89**:23
Hell-Fire shall be stripped off, kindled to fierce ablaze, **81**:11,12
Retaliation by way of charity will be an expiation, **5**:45

Revelation,
if you are in doubt, **2**:23,24
abrogated or forgotten Verse, **2**:106
right guidance, **3**:73
from the Lord, so be not of those who doubt, **6**:114
for people who understand, **6**:98
a Guidance and a Mercy, **7**:203; **16**:64; **31**:3
through *Rûh-ul-Qudus,* **16**:102; **26**:192,193
explained in detail, **6**:98; **41**:2-4
of the Book is from Allâh, **46**:2
(see also Book and Qur'ân)

Revenge of oppressive wrong, **42**:39-43

Reward,
according to the best of deeds, and even more, **24**:38; **29**:7; **39**:35
as a, **25**:15
Allâh rewards those who do good, with what is best, **53**:31
for good, no reward other than good, **55**:60

Ribâ (See usury)

Righteous,
company of the, **4**:69
shall inherit the land, **21**:105
in Paradise, **51**:15-19; **76**:5-12
(see also Good)

Righteousness, **2**:177,207,208,212; **3**:16,17,92,133-135,191-195; **4**:36,125; **5**:93; **7**:42,43; **16**:97
steep path of, **90**:11-18

Right guidance is the Guidance of Allâh, **3**:73

Roads, way, **43**:10

Rocky Tract (*Hijr*), dwellers of, **15**:80-85

Romans, **30**:2-5

Roof, the heaven, **21**:32

Rûh (Gabriel), **26**:193; **67**:12; **70**:4; **78**:38; **97**:4
Rûh-ul-Qudus, **2**:87,253; **5**:110; **16**:102 (see also Gabriel)

Rûh (soul, spirit), **15**:29; **17**:85; **58**:22

Rûm, S.**30**

Saba' (Sheba), **27**:22-44; **34**:15-21

Saba', S.**34**

Sabbath,
transgressors of, **2**:65; **4**:154; **7**:163-166
prescribed only for, **16**:124

Sabians, **5**:69; **22**:17

Sacrifice, **2**:196,200; **22**:34-37

Sâd, S.**38**

Sadaqah (Charity), **2**:196,263,264,270

271, 273; **4**:114; **9**:60,75,76,79, 103,104; **57**:18; **58**:12,13
concealing is better than showing, **2**:271
Safâ and Marwah, **2**:158
Saff S.**61**
Sâffât, S.**37**
Sail Al-'Arim (flood released from Ma'arib Dam), **34**:16
Sajdah, S. **32**
Sakînah (calmness and tranquillity), **2**:248; **9**:26,40; **48**:4,18,26
Sâlih, **7**:73-79; **11**:61-68; **26**:141-159; **27**:45-53; **91**:13
Salsabîl (spring in Paradise), **76**:18
Samîrî, **20**:85,95-97
Samuel, **2**:247
Satan, **2**:36,168,208,268,275; **3**:36,155, 175; **4**:38,60,76,83,119,120; **5**:80, 91; **6**:43, 68,142; **7**:20,22,27,175, 200,201; **8**:48; **16**:63,98; **20**:120; **24**:21; **25**:29; **27**:24; **41**:36; **58**:10, 19; **82**:25
excites enmity and hatred, **5**:91
evil whispers from, **7**:200,201
deceives, **8**:48
betrayed, **14**:22
has no power over believers, **16**:99,100
throws falsehood, **22**:52,53
is an enemy, **12**:5; **35**:6; **36**:60
(see also *Iblîs*)
Scale, successful, whose will be heavy, **7**:8,9 (See also balance)
Scripture,
people of the, (Jews and Christians), **2**:109; **3**:64,65,69,70,71,72,75,98, 99,110,113,199; **4**:47,153-161; **5**:59,60,68; **98**:1
what they were hiding, **5**:61-63
among them who are on the right course, **5**:66
they recognise but not believe, **6**:20
Seas, **42**:32,33; **45**:12
the two, **18**:60; **25**:53; **35**:12; **55**:19,20
when, are burst forth, **82**:3
Secret (*Najwâ*),
talks, **4**:114 (See the footnote of **11**:18)
counsel of three, **58**:7
counsels, **58**:8,10
private consultation, **58**:12,13
Sects and divisions in religion, **6**:15; **23**:53; **30**:32; **42**:13,14; **43**:65; **45**:17
Security, after the distress, He sent down, **3**:154
Seed, Who makes it grow, **56**:63-67
Senses, **23**:78
Seven, created,
heavens, **2**:29; **23**:17; **65**:12; **67**:3; **71**:15
and of the earth like there of, **65**:12
Shadow,
unto Allâh falls in prostration, **13**:15; **16**:48
spread of, **25**:45
Shams, S.**91**
She-camel as a clear sign to Thamûd people, **7**:73; **17**:59; **26**:155-158
Ship, sailing of, as a Sign; to be of service; to be grateful; to seek His Bounty, **2**:164; **14**:32; **16**:14; **17**:66; **22**:65; **31**:31; **35**:12; **42**:32,33; **43**:12; **45**:12; **55**:24
Shu'aib, **7**:85-93; **11**:84-95; **29**:36,37
Shu'arâ', S.**26**
Shûrâ, S.**42**
Sidrat-ul-Muntahâ, **53**:14
Siege of Al-Madînah, **33**:9-27
Signs of Allâh (*Ayât*). This word occurs more than 300 times in Noble Qur'ân. Mentioning every place will make the Index very big.
Sijjîn, **88**:7-9
Sin, **7**:100; **74**:43-6
illegal sexual intercourse, **4**:15,16; **24**:2,19
if greater, are avoided, small sins are remitted, **4**:31
they may hide from men, but cannot hide from Allâh, **4**:108
whoever earns, he earns it only against himself, **4**:111
whoever earns a, and then throws on to

someone innocent, **4**:112
Allâh forgives not setting up partners in worship with Him, but forgives whom He pleases other sins than that, **4**:116
those who commit, will get due recompense, **6**:120
sinners will never be successful, **10**:17
Allâh forgives all, **39**:53
greater sins, **42**:37
Sinai, Mount, **19**:52; **23**:20; **95**:2
Sinners, their ears, eyes, and skins will testify against them, **41**:20-23
Sirât Bridge, **66**:8
Slanderer, **68**:11,12; **104**:1
Slaves, **2**:177,178; **4**:25,36,92; **5**:89; **24**:33; **58**:3; **90**:13 (see also Prisoners of war; Captives)
Sleep, a thing for rest, **78**:9
Sodom, **29**:31; **37**:136
Sodomy, **7**:80-82; **11**:77-83; **15**:61-77; **29**:28,29
Solomon, **2**:102; **4**:163; **6**:84; **21**:78-82; **27**:15-44; **34**:12-14; **38**:30-40
and the ants, **27**:18,19
and the hoopoe, **27**:22-26
and the Queen of Saba', **27**:22-44; **34**:15
Son, adopted, **33**:4,5
Soul (spirit, *Rûh*), **15**:29; **17**:85; **58**:22
Spend,
in Allâh's Cause, **2**:195,215,254,262, 265,267,274; **3**:92,134; **8**:3; **9**:99; **13**:22; **14**:31; **22**:35; **32**:16; **35**:29; **36**:47; **47**:38; **57**:7; **63**:10; **64**:16
which is beyond your needs, **2**:219
likeness of those who, their wealth in the Way of Allâh, **2**:261
to be seen of men, **2**:264; **4**:38
whatever you, in Allâh's cause it will be repaid to you, **2**:272; **8**:60; **34**:39
not with extravagance, or wastefully, **6**:141; **17**:26
neither extravagant nor niggardly, **25**:67
who close hands from spending in Allâh's Cause, **9**:67
Spirit (soul, *Rûh*), **15**:29
its knowledge is with Allâh, **17**:85
Allâh strengthens believers with, **58**:22
Spoils of war, **8**:41,69; **48**:15,19,20; **48**:15 (see also Booty)
Spying, **49**:12
Star, **53**:1,49; **86**:1-4
Stars, **7**:54; **15**:16; **16**:12,16; **22**:18; **25**:61; **37**:6-10; **56**:75; **77**:8; **81**:2; **82**:2
Straight, Way, **1**:6 etc; Path, **6**:153 etc.
Striving, **4**:95; **8**:72,74,75; **9**:20,24,81; **22**:78; **25**:52; **29**:69; **47**:3; **60**:1; **61**:11
Suckling, the term of, foster mother, **2**:233
Suffering, poverty, loss of health and calamities; prosperity and wealth, **7**:94-96
Sun, **7**:54; **10**:5; **14**:32; **16**:12; **22**:18; **25**:61; **36**:38,40; **71**:16; **81**:1; **91**:1
Supreme success, **9**:72; **44**:57
Sûrah, **10**:38; **11**:13; **47**:20; its revelation increases faith, **9**:124-127
Suspicions, **49**:12
Sustenance, **19**:62 (see also Provision; Providence)
Suwâ', **71**:23
Tabûk, **9**:40-59, 81-99, 117,118,120-122
Taghâbun, S.**64**
Tâghût, **2**:256-257; **4**:51-60,76; **5**:60; **16**:36; **17**:39(see also false gods.)
Tâ-Hâ, S.**20**
Tahrîm, S.**66**
Takâthur, S.**102**
Takwîr, S.**81**
Talâq, S.**65**
Talh (banana tree), **56**:29
Tâlût (Saul), **2**:247-249
Târîq, S.**86**
Tasnîm (spring), **83**:27,28
Taubah, S.**9**
Tawâf (going round the Ka'ba), **2**:200; **7**:29,31
Tayammum, **4**:43; **5**:6
Term, every nation has its appointed, no can anticipate nor delay it, **7**:34;

10:49; **15**:4,5; **16**:61; **20**:129
Territory, guard your, by army units, **3**:200
Test, by Allâh, **3**:154; **34**:21
Thamûd, **7**:73-79; **11**:61-68; **17**:59; **25**:38; **26**:141-159; **27**:45-53; **29**:38; **41**:17; **51**:43-45; **54**:23-31; **69**:4-8; **85**:17-20; **89**:9-14; **91**:11-15
Thief, punishment, **5**:38,39
Throne. **7**:54,58; **9**:129; **10**:3; **13**:2; **20**:5; **23**:86,116; **32**:4; **40**:15; **57**:4; **85**:15
on water, **11**:7
eight angels bearing the,**39**:75; **40**:7; **69**:17
Time, **45**:24; **76**:1; **103**:1
Tîn, S.**95**
Torment, **3**:188; **6**:15,16; **10**:50-53; **11**:10; **13**:34; **16**:88; **46**:20; **70**:1,2
Township, never did We destroy a, but there was a known decree for it, **15**:4
Trade and property, **4**:29
Travel, have they not travelled through the earth, **6**:11; **10**:22; **12**:109; **22**:46; **27**:69; **29**:20; **30**:9,42; **34**:18; **35**:44; **40**:21,82; **47**:10
Treachery, **8**:58; **22**:38 (See Betray)
Treasure hoarded, **9**:35 and its footnote.
Treasures of Allâh, **6**:50
Tree of Eternity, **20**:120
Trees, **22**:18
Trials, **2**:214-218; **64**:15
Trumpet, on the Day of Resurrection, **6**:73; **18**:99; **20**:102; **23**:101; **27**:87; **36**:51; **39**:68; **50**:20; **69**:13; **74**:8; **78**:18; **79**:7; *Sakhkhah,* **80**:33
Trust offered to heavens, earth and mountains, but undertaken by man, **33**:72,73
Trusts (*Amânah*), **2**:283; **4**:58; **8**:27; **23**:8; **33**:72; **70**:32 (see *Amânah*)
Truth, **5**:48; **23**:70,71,90; **25**:33; **69**:51
mix not with falsehood nor conceal, **2**:42
has come and falsehood has vanished, **17**:81
promise of, **46**:16,17
Tubba‘, people of, **44**:37;**50**:14
Tûr (Mount), **28**:29,46
Tûr, S.**52**
Tuwâ, valley of, **20**:12; **79**:16
Uhud, battle of, **3**:121-128, 140-180
Ummah (community, nation), **2**:143, 144; **10**:47,49; **11**:118;**16**:36,120
'Umrah, **2**:128,158,196
Usury (*Riba*), **2**:275,276,278-280; **3**:130; **4**:161, **30**:39
'Uzair, (see Ezra)
'Uzzâ, **53**:19
Veil, an invisible, **17**:45,46
Veiling, **24**:31; 33:59
Verses, *Sab‘ Al-Mathâni,* **15**:87
Victory,
given by Allâh, **48**:1
through help from Allâh, **61**:13
Virtues, (see Righteousness; Believers)
Wadd, **71**:23
"Wait you, we too are waiting", **7**:71; **9**:52; **10**:102; **11**:122; **20**:135; **44**:59; **52**:31
Wâqi‘ah, S.**56**
War against Allâh, **5**:33,34
Waste not by extravagance, **6**:141; **7**:31; **17**:26
Water, every living thing made from, **21**:30; **24**:45; **25**:54
two seas, **18**:60; **25**:53; **35**:12; **55**:19,20
Allâh's Throne on the, **11**:7
rain, **23**:18
Way, the, **1**:6; **42**:52,53; **90**:10 etc.
easy, make easy, **87**:8
(see also Path)
Wayfarer, **2**:177,215; **8**:41; **17**:26; **29**:29; **30**: 38; **59**:7
Wealth,
who has gathered, **104**:2-4
spending in Allâh's Cause (see Spend)
Wealth and children, adornment of the life of this world, **18**:46
Weight and Measure, give full, **11**:85;**17**:35; **83**:1-5
Widows, **2**:234,235,240
Will of Allâh, **10**:99,100; **30**:5; **81**:29; **82**:8
Will of man, to walk straight, unless Allâh wills, **28**:29

Winds, **77**:1-3
as heralds of glad tidings, **7**:57; **30**:46
raising clouds, causing water, **15**:22; **30**:48
turning yellow, **30**:51
Wine (in Paradise),
pure drinks, **37**:45; 76:21
white, delicious, **37**:46
rivers of, **47**:15
pure sealed, **83**:25
Wish not for the things in which Allâh
has made some to excel others, **4**:32
Witnesses,
to covenant of the Prophets, **3**:81
over mankind, **2**:143; **22**:78
for a contract, **2**:282
two women against one man, **2**:282
to illegal sexual intercourse, **4**:16; **24**:2
be just, **5**:8
hands and legs will bear witness, **36**:65
man against himself, **75**:14
Witnessing Day and Witnessed Day, **85**:3
Wives,
are a tilth for you, **2**:223
cover for you, **2**:187
of your own kind, **16**:72
Woman, the disputing, **58**:1,2
Women, **2**:222,223; **4**:15,19-22,34,127
who accuse chaste, **24**:4,5,11-17,23-26
veiling, **24**:31; **33**:59
believing, as emigrants, **60**:10-12
not making clear herself in dispute,
43:17,18
Wood, dwellers of the, **15**:78; **38**:13;
50:14 (see also *Aikah;* Madyan)
26:176-191
World, life of this,
is nothing but play and amusement, **6**:32;
29:64; **47**:36; **57**:20
deceives men, **6**:130
little is the enjoyment of the, than the
Hereafter, **9**:38; **13**:26; **28**:60,61
whoever desires, gets therein, but then
there will be no portion in the
Hereafter, **11**:15,16; **17**:18; **42**:20
wealth and children, adornment of the, **18**:46
who love the present, and leave the
Hereafter, **75**:20,21; **76**:27
Writing, for contracts, **2**:282
Wrongdoers, **11**:18-22,101-104,116,117;
39:47 (see also Disbelievers)
Wudû (Ablutions), **4**:43; **5**:6
Yaghûth, **71**:23
Yahyâ (John),
glad tidings of, **3**:39; **21**:90
righteous, **6**:85
wise; sympathetic; dutiful, **19**:12-15
Yâ-Sîn, S.**36**
Yathrib (Al-Madînah), people of, **33**:13
Ya'ûq, **71**:23
Yûnus, S.**10** (see Jonah)
Yûsuf S.**12** (see Joseph)
Zabur, **21**:105
Zachariah (Zakariyyâ), **3**:37-41; **6**:85;
19:2-11; **21**:89,90
Zaid Ibn Harithah, slave of the Prophet, **33**:37,38
Zakât, **2**:3,43,83,110,177,277; **3**:85;
4:77,162; **5**:12,55; **6**:141; **7**:156; **9**:5,
11,18,71; **19**:31,55; **21**:73; **22**:41,78;
23:4; **24**:37,56; **27**:3; **30**:39; **31**:4;
33:33; **41**:7; **58**:13; **73**:20; **98**:5
objects of *Zakât* and charity, **2**:273;
9:60
Zanjabîl, **76**:17
Zalzalah, S.**99**
Zamzam, footnote of **14**:37
Zaqqûm, **17**:60; **37**:62-66; **44**:43-46;
56:52
Zihâr, **33**:4; **58**:2-4
Zukhruf S.**43**
Zumar, S.**39**
Zun-Nûn, **21**:87, 88; **68**:48-50

Prophets and Others Mentioned in The Qur'ân

Names of some of the Prophets and others mentioned in the Qur'ân and their English equivalent:

S. No.	Arabic		English
1.	Âdam	آدم عليه السلام	Adam
2.	Al-Yasa'	اليسع عليه السلام	Elisha
3.	Ayyûb	ايوب عليه السلام	Job
4.	Dâwûd	داود عليه السلام	David
5.	Fir'on	فرعون	Pharaoh
6.	Hâbîl	هابيل	Abel
7.	Hârûn	هارون عليه السلام	Aaron
8.	Ibrâhîm	ابراهيم عليه السلام	Abraham
9.	ldrîs	ادريس عليه السلام	Enoch
10.	Ilyâs	الياس عليه السلام	Elias
11.	'Imrân	عمران	Amran
12.	Injîl	انجيل	Gospel
13.	'Îsâ	عيسى عليه السلام	Jesus
14.	Ishâq	اسحق عليه السلام	Isaac
15.	Ismâ'îl	اسماعيل عليه السلام	Ishmael
16.	Jâlût	جالوت	Goliath
17.	Jibrîl	جبرئيل عليه السلام	Gabriel
18.	Qâbîl	قابيل	Cain

S. No.	Arabic		English
19.	Lût	لوط عليه السلام	Lot
20.	Mâjûj	ماجوج	Magog
21.	Maryam	مريم عليها السلام	Mary
22.	Masjid	مسجد	Mosque
23.	Mîka'îl	ميكائيل	Michael
24.	Misr	مصر	Egypt
25.	Mûsâ	موسى عليه السلام	Moses
26.	Nasrânî	نصرانى	Christian
27.	Nûh	نوح عليه السلام	Noah
28.	Qârûn	قارون	Korah
29.	Saba	سبا	Sheba
30.	Sulaimân	سليمان عليه السلام	Solomon
31.	Tâlût	طالوت	Saul
32.	Taurât	تورات	Torah
33.	'Uzair	عزير عليه السلام	Ezra
34.	Ya'qûb	يعقوب عليه السلام	Jacob
35.	Yahûdî	يهودى	Jew
36.	Yahyâ	يحيى عليه السلام	John
37.	Yâjûj	ياجوج	Gog
38.	Yûnus	يونس عليه السلام	Jonah
39.	Yûsuf	يوسف عليه السلام	Joseph
40.	Zakariyâ	زكريا عليه السلام	Zachariya

﴿فهرس بأسماء السُّوَر وبيان المكى والمدنى منها﴾

Index of Sûras – Chapters

(Showing The Makki and The Madani ones)

Sûrah	No.	Page No.	Makki/ Madani	مكيّة / مدنيّة	رقم الصفحة	رقم السورة	اسم السورة
Al-Fâtiḥah	1	2	Madani	مكيّة	٢	١	الفاتحة
Al-Baqarah	2	4	Madani	مدنيّة	٤	٢	البقرة
Âl-'Imrân	3	53	Madani	مدنيّة	٥٣	٣	ال عمرٰن
An-Nisâ'	4	83	Madani	مدنيّة	٨٣	٤	النّساء
Al-Mâ'idah	5	113	Madani	مدنيّة	١١٣	٥	المائدة
Al-An'âm	6	135	Makki	مكيّة	١٣٥	٦	الانعام
Al-A'râf	7	160	Makki	مكيّة	١٦٠	٧	الاعراف
Al-Anfâl	8	188	Madani	مدنيّة	١٨٨	٨	الانفال
At-Tawbah	9	199	Madani	مدنيّة	١٩٩	٩	التّوبة
Yûnus	10	220	Makki	مكيّة	٢٢٠	١٠	يونس
Hûd	11	235	Makki	مكيّة	٢٣٥	١١	هود
Yûsuf	12	250	Makki	مكيّة	٢٥٠	١٢	يوسف
Ar-Ra'd	13	265	Makki	مكيّة	٢٦٥	١٣	الرّعد
Ibrâhîm	14	272	Makki	مكيّة	٢٧٢	١٤	ابراهيم
Al-Ḥijr	15	279	Makki	مكيّة	٢٧٩	١٥	الحجر
An-Naḥl	16	286	Makki	مكيّة	٢٨٦	١٦	النّحل
Banî Isrâ'îl	17	302	Makki	مكيّة	٣٠٢	١٧	بنى اسرائيل
Al-Kahf	18	315	Makki	مكيّة	٣١٥	١٨	الكهف
Maryam	19	329	Makki	مكيّة	٣٢٩	١٩	مريم
Ṭâ-Hâ	20	337	Makki	مكيّة	٣٣٧	٢٠	طٰهٰ
Al-Anbiyâ'	21	349	Makki	مكيّة	٣٤٩	٢١	الانبياء
Al-Ḥajj	22	360	Madani	مدنيّة	٣٦٠	٢٢	الحج
Al-Mu'minûn	23	370	Makki	مكيّة	٣٧٠	٢٣	المؤمنون
An-Nûr	24	380	Madani	مدنيّة	٣٨٠	٢٤	النّور
Al-Furqân	25	391	Makki	مكيّة	٣٩١	٢٥	الفرقان
Ash-Shu'arâ'	26	399	Makki	مكيّة	٣٩٩	٢٦	الشّعراء

Sûrah	No.	Page No.	Makki/ Madani	مكيّة / مدنية	رقم الصفحة	رقم السورة	اسم السورة
An-Naml	27	411	Makki	مكيّة	٤١١	٢٧	النّمل
Al-Qaṣaṣ	28	421	Makki	مكيّة	٤٢١	٢٨	القصص
Al-‘Ankabût	29	433	Makki	مكيّة	٤٣٣	٢٩	العنكبوت
Ar-Rûm	30	442	Makki	مكيّة	٤٤٢	٣٠	الرّوم
Luqmân	31	449	Makki	مكيّة	٤٤٩	٣١	لقمان
As-Sajdah	32	454	Makki	مكيّة	٤٥٤	٣٢	السّجدة
Al-Aḥzâb	33	457	Madani	مدنيّة	٤٥٧	٣٣	الاحزاب
Saba’	34	468	Makki	مكيّة	٤٦٨	٣٤	سبا
Fâṭir	35	476	Makki	مكيّة	٤٧٦	٣٥	فاطر
Yâ-Sîn	36	482	Makki	مكيّة	٤٨٢	٣٦	يٰس
Aṣ-Ṣâffât	37	488	Makki	مكيّة	٤٨٨	٣٧	الصّافات
Ṣâd	38	497	Makki	مكيّة	٤٩٧	٣٨	ص
Az-Zumar	39	504	Makki	مكيّة	٥٠٤	٣٩	الزّمر
Al-Mu’min	40	513	Makki	مكيّة	٥١٣	٤٠	المؤمن
Ḥâ-Mîm Sajdah	41	524	Makki	مكيّة	٥٢٤	٤١	حٰم السّجدة
Ash-Shûra	42	531	Makki	مكيّة	٥٣١	٤٢	الشّورى
Az-Zukhruf	43	538	Makki	مكيّة	٥٣٨	٤٣	الزّخرف
Ad-Dukhân	44	546	Makki	مكيّة	٥٤٦	٤٤	الدّخان
Al-Jâsiyah	45	550	Makki	مكيّة	٥٥٠	٤٥	الجاثية
Al-Aḥqâf	46	554	Makki	مكيّة	٥٥٤	٤٦	الاحقاف
Muḥammad	47	559	Madani	مدنيّة	٥٥٩	٤٧	محمّد
Al-Fat-ḥ	48	564	Madani	مدنيّة	٥٦٤	٤٨	الفتح
Al-Ḥujurât	49	569	Madani	مدنيّة	٥٦٩	٤٩	الحجرات
Qâf	50	572	Makki	مكيّة	٥٧٢	٥٠	ق
Az-Zâriyât	51	576	Makki	مكيّة	٥٧٦	٥١	الذّاريات
Aṭ-Ṭûr	52	580	Makki	مكيّة	٥٨٠	٥٢	الطّور
An-Najm	53	583	Makki	مكيّة	٥٨٣	٥٣	النّجم
Al-Qamar	54	586	Makki	مكيّة	٥٨٦	٥٤	القمر

Sûrah	No.	Page No.	Makki/ Madani	مكيّة/ مدنيّة	رقم الصفحة	رقم السورة	اسم السورة
Ar-Raḥmân	55	590	Madani	مدنيّة	٥٩٠	٥٥	الرّحمٰن
Al-Wâqi‘ah	56	593	Makki	مكيّة	٥٩٣	٥٦	الواقعة
Al-Ḥadîd	57	598	Madani	مدنيّة	٥٩٨	٥٧	الحديد
Al-Mujâdilah	58	603	Madani	مدنيّة	٦٠٣	٥٨	المجادلة
Al-Ḥashr	59	607	Madani	مدنيّة	٦٠٧	٥٩	الحشر
Al-Mumtaḥanah	60	610	Madani	مدنيّة	٦١٠	٦٠	الممتحنة
Aṣ-Ṣaff	61	613	Madani	مدنيّة	٦١٣	٦١	الصّف
Al-Jumu‘ah	62	615	Madani	مدنيّة	٦١٥	٦٢	الجمعة
Al-Munâfiqûn	63	617	Madani	مدنيّة	٦١٧	٦٣	المنافقون
At-Taghâbun	64	618	Madani	مدنيّة	٦١٨	٦٤	التّغابن
Aṭ-Ṭalâq	65	620	Madani	مدنيّة	٦٢٠	٦٥	الطّلاق
At-Taḥrîm	66	623	Madani	مدنيّة	٦٢٣	٦٦	التّحريم
Al-Mulk	67	625	Makki	مكيّة	٦٢٥	٦٧	الملك
Al-Qalam	68	628	Makki	مكيّة	٦٢٨	٦٨	القلم
Al-Ḥâqqah	69	631	Makki	مكيّة	٦٣١	٦٩	الحاقّة
Al-Ma‘ârij	70	634	Makki	مكيّة	٦٣٤	٧٠	المعارج
Nûḥ	71	636	Makki	مكيّة	٦٣٦	٧١	نوح
Al-Jinn	72	638	Makki	مكيّة	٦٣٨	٧٢	الجن
Al-Muzzammil	73	641	Makki	مكيّة	٦٤١	٧٣	المزّمّل
Al-Muddassir	74	643	Makki	مكيّة	٦٤٣	٧٤	المدّثّر
Al-Qiyâmah	75	646	Makki	مكيّة	٦٤٦	٧٥	القيامة
Ad-Dahr	76	647	Madani	مدنيّة	٦٤٧	٧٦	الدّهر
Al-Mursalât	77	650	Makki	مكيّة	٦٥٠	٧٧	المرسلات
An-Naba’	78	652	Makki	مكيّة	٦٥٢	٧٨	النّبا
An-Nâzi‘ât	79	654	Makki	مكيّة	٦٥٤	٧٩	النّازعات
‘Abasa	80	656	Makki	مكيّة	٦٥٦	٨٠	عبس
At-Takwîr	81	658	Makki	مكيّة	٦٥٨	٨١	التّكوير
Al-Infiṭâr	82	659	Makki	مكيّة	٦٥٩	٨٢	الانفطار
Al-Muṭaffifîn	83	660	Makki	مكيّة	٦٦٠	٨٣	المطفّفين
Al-Inshiqâq	84	661	Makki	مكيّة	٦٦١	٨٤	الانشقاق

Sûrah	No.	Page No.	Makki/ Madani	مكيّة/مدنيّة	رقم الصفحة	رقم السورة	اسم السورة
Al-Burûj	85	663	Makki	مكيّة	٦٦٣	٨٥	البروج
Aṭ-Ṭâriq	86	664	Makki	مكيّة	٦٦٤	٨٦	الطّارق
Al-A‘lâ	87	665	Makki	مكيّة	٦٦٥	٨٧	الاعلى
Al-Ghâshiyah	88	665	Makki	مكيّة	٦٦٥	٨٨	الغاشية
Al-Fajr	89	667	Makki	مكيّة	٦٦٧	٨٩	الفجر
Al-Balad	90	668	Makki	مكيّة	٦٦٨	٩٠	البلد
Ash-Shams	91	669	Makki	مكيّة	٦٦٩	٩١	الشّمس
Al-Layl	92	670	Makki	مكيّة	٦٧٠	٩٢	الّيل
Aḍ-Ḍuḥâ	93	670	Makki	مكيّة	٦٧٠	٩٣	الضّحى
Al-Inshirâḥ	94	671	Makki	مكيّة	٦٧١	٩٤	الانشراح
At-Tîn	95	671	Makki	مكيّة	٦٧١	٩٥	التين
Al-‘Alaq	96	672	Makki	مكيّة	٦٧٢	٩٦	العلق
Al-Qadr	97	673	Makki	مكيّة	٦٧٣	٩٧	القدر
Al-Bayyinah	98	673	Madani	مدنيّة	٦٧٣	٩٨	البيّنة
Az-Zilzâl	99	674	Madani	مدنيّة	٦٧٤	٩٩	الزلزال
Al-‘Âdiyât	100	674	Makki	مكيّة	٦٧٤	١٠٠	العاديات
Al-Qâri‘ah	101	675	Makki	مكيّة	٦٧٥	١٠١	القارعة
At-Takâs̱ur	102	675	Makki	مكيّة	٦٧٥	١٠٢	التّكاثر
Al-‘Aṣr	103	676	Makki	مكيّة	٦٧٦	١٠٣	العصر
Al-Humazah	104	676	Makki	مكيّة	٦٧٦	١٠٤	الهمزة
Al-Fîl	105	676	Makki	مكيّة	٦٧٦	١٠٥	الفيل
Quraysh	106	677	Makki	مكيّة	٦٧٧	١٠٦	قريش
Al-Mâ‘ûn	107	677	Makki	مكيّة	٦٧٧	١٠٧	الماعون
Al-Kaws̱ar	108	677	Makki	مكيّة	٦٧٧	١٠٨	الكوثر
Al-Kâfirûn	109	677	Makki	مكيّة	٦٧٧	١٠٩	الكافرون
An-Naṣr	110	678	Madani	مدنيّة	٦٧٨	١١٠	النّصر
Al-Lahab	111	678	Makki	مكيّة	٦٧٨	١١١	اللّهب
Al-Ikhlâṣ	112	678	Makki	مكيّة	٦٧٨	١١٢	الاخلاص
Al-Falaq	113	678	Makki	مكيّة	٦٧٨	١١٣	الفلق
An-Nâs	114	679	Makki	مكيّة	٦٧٨	١١٤	النّاس

أَحْكَامُ التَّجْوِيدِ الَّتِي تَجِبُ مُرَاعَاتُهَا عِنْدَ تِلَاوَةِ الْقُرْآنِ

TAJWEED RULES TO BE OBSERVED WHEN RECITING THE HOLY QUR'ÂN

CONTENTS

TOPIC	PAGE No.
The Aadaab of reciting the Holy Qur'ân	2
The place of origin of the Arabic letters	3
Definition of Tajweed	4
Rule of Qalqala	4
Rule of Noon & Meem Mushaddadah	5
Rule of letter Laam	5
Rule of Meem Saakin	6
Rule of Ikhfa – Noon Saakin & Tanween	6-8
Rule of Ithaar – Noon Saakin & Tanween	8
Rule of Idghaam – Noon Saakin & Tanween	8-9
Rule of Idghaam Mithlayn	9
Rule of Idghaam Mutaqaaribayn	9-10
Rule of Idghaam Mutajaanisayn	10
Rule of Iqlaab – The Alteration	10
Rule of the letter Raa	10-12
Rule of Madd	12
Maddul Asli	12
Maddul Muttasil	12-13
Maddul Munfasil	13
Maddul Laazim	13
Maddul Aaridh	13-14
The Sun letters	14-15
The Moon letters	15-16
Rules of stopping	17

The Aadaab of Reciting the Holy Qur'ân

- The reciter of the Holy Qur'ân must perform the ritual ablution (wudhu).
- The intention when reciting the Holy Qur'ân should be to gain the pleasure of Allah.
- The voice should not be raised to such an extent where your recital will disturb others who are also engaged in some form of worship.
- The reciter of the Holy Qur'ân must sit in a dignified position facing the Ka'bah.
- When commencing with the recitation of the Holy Qur'ân – start by reciting:

أَعُوذُ بِاللّٰهِ مِنَ الشَّيْطٰنِ الرَّجِيْمِ

" I seek Allah's protection from Satan, the accursed."

And thereafter recite:

بِسْمِ اللّٰهِ الرَّحْمٰنِ الرَّحِيْمِ

"In the name of Allah, Most Gracious, Most Merciful."

The place of origin (مَخرَج)
of the Arabic letters

To know the origin of any letter of the Arabic Alphabet, place a Sukoon (ْ) on it and precede it with an Alif (ا) with a Fatha (اَ).

Example : اَبْ will give us the origin of the letter بَ.

Name	Letter	Place of Origin
The Aerial letters اَلْحُرُوْفُ الْهَوَائِيَّةُ	ا و ي	Originate from the emptiness of the mouth.
The Guttural letters اَلْحُرُوْفُ الْحَلْقِيَّةُ	ه ح ع خ غ	Originate from the back of the throat (larynx). Originate from the centre of the throat. Originate from the upper portion of the throat.
اَلْحَرفَانِ اللَّهْوِيَانِ	ق ك	The back of the tongue rises and touches the soft palate.
اَلْحَرْفَانِ الشَّجْرِيَتَانِ	ج ش	The centre of the tongue touches the upper palate.
The letter ض اَلْحَرْفُ	ض	The upturned sides of the tongue touches the gums of the upper back teeth.
The liquids اَلْحُرُوْفُ الذُّولَقِيَّةِ	ر ل ن	Originate when the tip of the tongue touches the upper hard palate.
The dental letters اَلْحُرُوْفُ النِّطْعِيَّةِ	ت د ط	Originate when the tip of the tongue touches the gums of the upper two front teeth.
The gingieal letters اَلْحُرُوْفُ اللِّثَوِيَّةِ	ث ذ ظ	Originate when the tip of the tongue touches the edge of the upper two front teeth.
اَلْحُرُوْفُ الأَسَلِيَّةُ	ز س ص	Originate when the tip of the tongue rises towards the upper palate, touching the gums behind the upper two front teeth.
The labial letters اَلْحُرُوْفُ الشَّفَوِيَّةُ	ب م ف	Originate from the lips. Originates when the inner portion of the bottom lip meets the edge on the two upper front teeth.

TAJWEED

Reciting the Holy Qur'ân with TAJWEED means to pronounce every letter with all its articulative qualities such as the correct prolongation, merging, conversion, distinctness, and pauses. Reciting the Qur'ân with TAJWEED allows the reciter to emphasise the accent, phonetics, rhythm and temper of the Qur'ânic recitation.

QALQALA

When the letters of QALQALA have a Sukoon (ْ) on it, it will be read with an echoing or jerking sound.

The letters of QALQALA are:

د	ج	ب	ط	ق

In the examples that follow, the QALQALA letter with a Sukoon appears in the red block. Care should be taken when reciting, not to jerk the letter to the extent where it will sound as if the letter has a FATHA on it.

Surah Number	Verse Number	Extract from Verse	Qalqala Letter
7	12	خَلَقْتَنِي مِن نَّارٍ وَخَلَقْتَهُ مِن	ق
37	10	خَطِفَ الْخَطْفَةَ فَأَتْبَعَهُ شِهَابٌ ثَاقِبٌ ﴿١٠﴾	ط
2	34	قُلْنَا لِلْمَلَائِكَةِ اسْجُدُوا لِآدَمَ فَسَجَدُوا إِلَّا إِبْلِيسَ	ب
37	19	فَإِنَّمَا هِيَ زَجْرَةٌ وَاحِدَةٌ فَإِذَا هُمْ يَنظُرُونَ ﴿١٩﴾	ج
33	4	جَعَلَ أَدْعِيَاءَكُمْ أَبْنَاءَكُمْ	د

When a stop is made at the end of the sentences below, the rule of QALQALA will apply. The last letter becomes SAAKIN irrespective of the vowel sign, thus resulting in the QALQALA letter being read with an echoing or jerking sound.

Surah Number	Verse Number	Extract from Verse	Qalqala Letter
37	5	وَمَا بَيْنَهُمَا وَرَبُّ الْمَشَارِقِ ﴿٥﴾	ق
11	70	إِنَّا أُرْسِلْنَا إِلَىٰ قَوْمِ لُوطٍ ﴿٧٠﴾	ط
37	10	خَطِفَ الْخَطْفَةَ فَأَتْبَعَهُ شِهَابٌ ثَاقِبٌ ﴿١٠﴾	ب
2	197	وَلَا فُسُوقَ وَلَا جِدَالَ فِي الْحَجِّ	ج
37	7	وَحِفْظًا مِّن كُلِّ شَيْطَانٍ مَّارِدٍ ﴿٧﴾	د

NOON AND MEEM MUSHADDADAH

When the letters ن and م have a SHADDAH (ّ) on it (نّ , مّ), it will be recited with Ghunna. The nasalization should not exceed the duration of two harakah. (2 - 3 second duration).

Surah Number	Verse Number	Extract from Verse	Mushaddadah Letter
37	6	إِنَّا زَيَّنَّا السَّمَآءَ الدُّنْيَا	نّ
78	21	إِنَّ جَهَنَّمَ كَانَتْ مِرْصَادًا ﴿٢١﴾	نّ
27	70	وَلَا تَكُنْ فِي ضَيْقٍ مِّمَّا يَمْكُرُونَ ﴿٧٠﴾	مّ
7	11	وَلَقَدْ خَلَقْنَٰكُمْ ثُمَّ صَوَّرْنَٰكُمْ ثُمَّ قُلْنَا	مّ

THE RULE OF THE LETTER LAAM

When a letter with FATHA (َ) or DHAMMA (ُ) appears before the name of ALLAH, it will be pronounced with a broad sound or full mouth.

Surah Number	Verse Number	Extract from Verse	Vowel Sign
5	114	قَالَ عِيسَى ابْنُ مَرْيَمَ اللَّهُمَّ	َ
4	171	إِنَّمَا الْمَسِيحُ عِيسَى ابْنُ مَرْيَمَ رَسُولُ اللَّهِ	ُ

When a letter with a KASRA (ِ) appears before the name of ALLAH, it will be pronounced with a thin sound or an empty mouth.

Surah Number	Verse Number	Extract from Verse	Vowel Sign
40	78	لِرَسُولٍ أَنْ يَأْتِيَ بِآيَةٍ إِلَّا بِإِذْنِ اللَّهِ	ِ
4	35	يُوَفِّقِ اللَّهُ بَيْنَهُمَا ط	ِ

However, the LAAM MUSHADDADAH لّ is read with a thin sound or empty mouth.

Surah Number	Verse Number	Extract from Verse	Laam Mushaddadah
2	255	اللَّهُ لَا إِلَٰهَ إِلَّا هُوَ الْحَيُّ الْقَيُّومُ	لّ
58	20	يُحَادُّونَ اللَّهَ وَرَسُولَهُ أُولَٰئِكَ فِي الْأَذَلِّينَ ﴿٢٠﴾	
2	177	لَيْسَ الْبِرَّ أَنْ تُوَلُّوا وُجُوهَكُمْ قِبَلَ	
2	148	وَلِكُلٍّ وِجْهَةٌ هُوَ مُوَلِّيهَا فَاسْتَبِقُوا	

THE RULE OF MEEM SAAKIN (مْ)

There are three rules regarding the MEEM SAAKIN مْ :

1. IKHFA SHAFAWI
2. IDGHAAM SHAFAWI
3. ITHAAR SHAFAWI

1. IKHFA SHAFAWI – MEEM SAAKIN

When the letter BA (ب) appears after a MEEM SAAKIN (مْ) there will be IKHFA SHAFAWI. It will be pronounced with a light nasal sound in the nose for a duration of 2 harakah. (2 - 3 second duration).

Surah Number	Verse Number	Extract from Verse	Ikhfa Shafawi Meem Saakin
34	8	اَفْتَرٰى عَلَى اللّٰهِ كَذِبًا اَمْ بِهٖ جِنَّةٌ ؕ	مْ ← ب

2. IDGHAAM SHAFAWI – MEEM SAAKIN

If after a MEEM SAAKIN (مْ) there appears a MEEM MUSHADDADAH (مّ), IDGHAAM will occur. In other words, the two MEEMS will become incorporated and be read with GHUNNA (nasalization).

Surah Number	Verse Number	Extract from Verse	Idghaam Shafawi Meem Saakin
16	57	وَلَهُمْ مَّا يَشْتَهُوْنَ	مْ ← مّ

3. ITHAAR SHAFAWI – MEEM SAAKIN

When after a MEEM SAAKIN (مْ) there appear any of the 26 letters other than the letters BA (ب) and MEEM (م), there will be ITHAAR SHAFAWI. No GHUNNA will occur.

Surah Number	Verse Number	Extract from Verse	Ithaar Shafawi Meem Saakin
34	45	وَكَذَّبَ الَّذِيْنَ مِنْ قَبْلِهِمْ وَمَا بَلَغُوْا	26 letters other than ب or م

IKHFA – NOON SAAKIN AND TANWEEN

If any of the 15 letters of IKHFA below come after a Noon Saakin (نْ) or Tanween (ـً ـٍ ـٌ), the word must be read with a light nasal sound in the nose for a duration of two harakah. (2 - 3 second duration).

The letters of IKHFA are:

ش	س	ز	ذ	د	ج	ث	ت
ك	ق	ف	ظ	ط	ض	ص	

Surah Number	Verse Number	Extract from Verse	Ikhfa Letter
5	118	وَاِنْ تَغْفِرْ لَهُمْ فَاِنَّكَ	ت
5	119	لَهُمْ جَنّٰتٌ تَجْرِيْ مِنْ تَحْتِهَا	
13	8	تَحْمِلُ كُلُّ اُنْثٰى وَمَا تَغِيْضُ الْاَرْحَامُ	ث
6	54	سُوْٓءًاۢ بِجَهَالَةٍ ثُمَّ تَابَ مِنْۢ بَعْدِهٖ	
14	6	عَلَيْكُمْ اِذْ اَنْجٰىكُمْ مِّنْ اٰلِ	ج
14	19	يَاْتِ بِخَلْقٍ جَدِيْدٍ ﴿١٩﴾	
14	22	اَنْ دَعَوْتُكُمْ فَاسْتَجَبْتُمْ لِيْ	د
6	99	وَمِنَ النَّخْلِ مِنْ طَلْعِهَا قِنْوَانٌ دَانِيَةٌ	
5	91	وَيَصُدَّكُمْ عَنْ ذِكْرِ اللّٰهِ وَعَنِ	ذ
3	185	كُلُّ نَفْسٍ ذَآئِقَةُ الْمَوْتِ ؕ	
3	185	فَمَنْ زُحْزِحَ عَنِ النَّارِ وَاُدْخِلَ الْجَنَّةَ	ز
18	74	نَفْسًا زَكِيَّةًۢ بِغَيْرِ نَفْسٍ ؕ	
17	83	وَاِذَآ اَنْعَمْنَا عَلَى الْاِنْسَانِ	س
18	22	وَيَقُوْلُوْنَ خَمْسَةٌ سَادِسُهُمْ كَلْبُهُمْ	
18	69	قَالَ سَتَجِدُنِيْٓ اِنْ شَآءَ اللّٰهُ صَابِرًا	ش
17	58	عَذَابًا شَدِيْدًا ؕ كَانَ ذٰلِكَ فِي الْكِتٰبِ	
18	43	وَلَمْ تَكُنْ لَّهٗ فِئَةٌ يَّنْصُرُوْنَهٗ	ص
33	23	مِنَ الْمُؤْمِنِيْنَ رِجَالٌ صَدَقُوْا مَا	
30	54	اَللّٰهُ الَّذِيْ خَلَقَكُمْ مِّنْ ضُعْفٍ	ض
30	54	بَعْدِ قُوَّةٍ ضُعْفًا وَّشَيْبَةً ؕ	
32	7	مِنْ طِيْنٍ ﴿٧﴾ ثُمَّ جَعَلَ نَسْلَهٗ مِنْ سُلٰلَةٍ	ط
34	15	بَلْدَةٌ طَيِّبَةٌ وَّرَبٌّ غَفُوْرٌ ﴿١٥﴾	
35	44	اَوَلَمْ يَسِيْرُوْا فِي الْاَرْضِ فَيَنْظُرُوْا كَيْفَ	ظ
4	57	وَّنُدْخِلُهُمْ ظِلًّا ظَلِيْلًا ﴿٥٧﴾	
4	71	حِذْرَكُمْ فَانْفِرُوْا ثُبَاتٍ اَوِ انْفِرُوْا جَمِيْعًا ﴿٧١﴾	ف
4	79	مَآ اَصَابَكَ مِنْ حَسَنَةٍ فَمِنَ اللّٰهِ	
4	92	وَمَنْ قَتَلَ مُؤْمِنًا خَطَاً فَتَحْرِيْرُ رَقَبَةٍ	ق
4	141	وَاِنْ كَانَ لِلْكٰفِرِيْنَ نَصِيْبٌ ۙ قَالُوْٓا	

4	141	فَإِنْ كَانَ لَكُمْ فَتْحٌ مِّنَ اللّٰهِ	ك
4	31	سَيِّاٰتِكُمْ وَنُدْخِلْكُمْ مُّدْخَلًا كَرِيْمًا ﴿٣١﴾	

ITHAAR – NOON SAAKIN AND TANWEEN

When after a NOON SAKIN (نْ) or TANWEEN (ـٌ ـً ـٍ) there appears any of the HUROOF HALQIYAH (throat letters) then it will be pronounced without GHUNNA (no nasalization).

The letters of HUROOF HALQIYAH are:

هـ	ء	غ	ع	خ	ح

Surah Number	Verse Number	Extract from Verse	Huroof Halqiyah Letter
15	82	مُعْرِضِيْنَ ﴿٨١﴾ وَكَانُوْا يَنْحِتُوْنَ	ح
2	35	وَكُلَا مِنْهَا رَغَدًا حَيْثُ شِئْتُمَا	
4	35	وَاِنْ خِفْتُمْ شِقَاقَ بَيْنِهِمَا فَابْعَثُوْا	خ
4	35	اِنَّ اللّٰهَ كَانَ عَلِيْمًا خَبِيْرًا ﴿٣٥﴾	
6	54	نَفْسِهِ الرَّحْمَةَ ۙ اَنَّهٗ مَنْ عَمِلَ مِنْكُمْ	ع
6	54	بِاٰيٰتِنَا فَقُلْ سَلٰمٌ عَلَيْكُمْ كَتَبَ	
7	43	فِيْ صُدُوْرِهِمْ مِّنْ غِلٍّ تَجْرِيْ مِنْ	غ
35	28	اِنَّ اللّٰهَ عَزِيْزٌ غَفُوْرٌ ﴿٢٨﴾	
5	32	مِنْ اَجْلِ ذٰلِكَ ۛ	ا / ء
38	29	كِتٰبٌ اَنْزَلْنٰهُ اِلَيْكَ مُبٰرَكٌ لِّيَدَّبَّرُوْا	
3	104	وَيَاْمُرُوْنَ بِالْمَعْرُوْفِ وَيَنْهَوْنَ	هـ
13	7	اَنْتَ مُنْذِرٌ وَّلِكُلِّ قَوْمٍ هَادٍ ﴿٧﴾	

IDGHAAM – NOON SAAKIN AND TANWEEN

IDGHAAM refers to the assimilation of one letter into the other. The rule of IDGHAAM will apply when the letters ي ن م و are preceded by a NOON SAAKIN (نْ) or TANWEEN (ـٌ ـً ـٍ). The emphasis will be on the succeeding letter because of the presence of a SHADDAH (ـّ) and will be read with GHUNNA. The nasalization should not exceed the duration of two harakah. (2 - 3 second duration).

Surah Number	Verse Number	Extract from Verse	Surah Number	Verse Number	Extract from Verse	Idghaam Letter
13	23	عَدۡنٍ یَّدۡخُلُوۡنَهَا	18	5	اِنۡ یَّقُوۡلُوۡنَ	ي
13	27	اٰیَةٌ مِّنۡ رَّبِّهٖ	2	130	عَنۡ مِّلَّةِ	م
15	45	جَنّٰتٍ وَّعُیُوۡنٍ	13	11	مِنۡ وَّالٍ	و
14	44	قَرِیۡبٍ نُّجِبۡ	14	11	لَنَاۤ اَنۡ نَّاۡتِیَکُمۡ	ن

With regard to the letters LAAM (ل) and RAA (ر) the IDGHAAM will be without GHUNNA, but assimilation takes place.

Surah Number	Verse Number	Extract from Verse	Surah Number	Verse Number	Extract from Verse	Idghaam Letter
2	2	هُدًى لِّلۡمُتَّقِیۡنَ	36	47	مَنۡ لَّوۡ یَشَآءُ اللّٰهُ	ل
2	173	غَفُوۡرٌ رَّحِیۡمٌ	2	5	هُدًى مِّنۡ رَّبِّهِمۡ	ر

In the examples below, assimilation will not take place due to a lack of a SHADDAH (ّ) on the IDGHAAM letters.

Surah Number	Verse Number	Extract from Verse	Surah Number	Verse Number	Extract from Verse	Idghaam Letter
61	4	کَاَنَّهُمۡ بُنۡیَانٌ	30	7	الۡحَیٰوةِ الدُّنۡیَا	ي
6	99	طَلۡعِهَا قِنۡوَانٌ	13	4	نَخِیۡلٌ صِنۡوَانٌ	و

IDGHAAM MITHLAYN
(Assimilation of the same kind)

This rule applies when two letters following each other are the same. The first letter has a SAAKIN (ۡ) and the second letter is vocal and has a SHADDAH (ّ) on it. When reciting the letters keep in mind that the SAAKIN letter becomes assimilated into the letter following it.

Surah Number	Verse Number	Extract from Verse	Surah Number	Verse Number	Extract from Verse
4	78	یُدۡرِکۡکُّمُ	2	16	رَبِحَتۡ تِّجَارَتُهُمۡ
18	78	مَا لَمۡ تَسۡتَطِعۡ عَّلَیۡهِ	5	61	وَقَدۡ دَّخَلُوۡا
8	72	اٰوَوۡا وَّ نَصَرُوۡۤا	21	87	اِذۡ ذَّهَبَ مُغَاضِبًا

IDGHAAM MUTAQAARIBAYN
(Assimilation of letters with similar origin)

This rule applies when a letter in a word is SAAKIN (ۡ) and the letter following it has a SHADDAH (ّ). When pronounced appears to be close to the same place of origin as the SAAKIN letter. The SAAKIN letter will assimilate with the vocal letter when recited.

Surah Number	Verse Number	Extract from Verse	Few examples to illustrate Idghaam Mutaqaaribayn	
77	20	نَخۡلُقۡكُّمۡ مِّنۡ مَّآءٍ مَّهِيۡنٍ ۝٢٠	ك	ق
11	42	يٰبُنَيَّ ارۡكَبۡ مَّعَنَا	م	ب
17	80	وَقُلۡ رَّبِّ اَدۡخِلۡنِيۡ مُدۡخَلَ	ر	ل
20	49	فَمَنۡ رَّبُّكُمَا يٰمُوۡسٰى ۝٤٩	ر	ن

IDGHAAM MUTAJAANISAYN
(Assimilation of related kind)

This rule applies when a letter in a word is SAAKIN (ۡ) and the letter following it has a SHADDAH (ّ) and when pronounced has the same place of origin as the SAAKIN letter. The SAAKIN letter will assimilate with the vocal letter when recited.

Surah Number	Verse Number	Extract from Verse	Few examples to illustrate Idghaam Mutajaanisayn
5	28	لَئِنۡۢ بَسَطۡتَّ اِلَيَّ يَدَكَ	ط \ ت
10	89	قَالَ قَدۡ اُجِيۡبَتۡ دَّعۡوَتُكُمَا	ت \ د
4	64	اَنَّهُمۡ اِذۡ ظَّلَمُوۡٓا اَنۡفُسَهُمۡ	ذ \ ظ
3	72	وَقَالَتۡ طَّآئِفَةٌ مِّنۡ اَهۡلِ	ت \ ط

IQLAAB – The Alteration (Noon Saakin and Tanween)

When after a NOON SAAKIN (نۡ) or Tanween (ـٌ ـً ـٍ) the letter BA (ب) appears then the NOON SAAKIN or TANWEEN will become substituted by a small MEEM SAAKIN (ۢ) and will be recited with GHUNNA.

Surah Number	Verse Number	Extract from Verse
2	27	عَهۡدَ اللّٰهِ مِنۡۢ بَعۡدِ
2	181	فَمَنۡۢ بَدَّلَهٗ
2	18	صُمٌّۢ بُكۡمٌ عُمۡىٌ
2	282	فُسُوۡقٌۢ بِكُمۡ

The letter RAA

1. A RAA (ر) with a FATHA (ـَ) or DHAMMA (ـُ) on it should be pronounced with a full mouth.

Surah Number	Verse Number	Extract from Verse	The Letter
2	16	فَمَا رَبِحَتْ تِّجَارَتُهُمْ	رَ
2	28	تَكْفُرُوْنَ بِاللّٰهِ وَكُنْتُمْ	رُ

2. A RAA (ر) with a KASRA (ـِ) should be pronounced with an empty mouth.

Surah Number	Verse Number	Extract from Verse	The Letter
2	54	لَّكُمْ عِنْدَ بَارِئِكُمْ	رِ
2	75	كَلٰمَ اللّٰهِ ثُمَّ يُحَرِّفُوْنَهٗ	رِ

3. When a FATHA (ـَ) or DHAMMA (ـُ) appear before a RAA SAAKIN (رْ) the letter RAA SAAKIN (رْ) will be pronounced with a full mouth.

Surah Number	Verse Number	Extract from Verse	The Letter Raa Saakin
2	7	اَيَّامٍ وَّكَانَ عَرْشُهٗ عَلَى	رْ ـَ
2	252	وَاِنَّكَ لَمِنَ الْمُرْسَلِيْنَ ﴿٢٥٢﴾	رْ ـُ

4. If a KASRA (ـِ) appears before a RAA SAAKIN (رْ) the RAA SAAKIN (رْ) will be read with an empty mouth.

Surah Number	Verse Number	Extract from Verse	The Letter Raa Saakin
2	6	تُنْذِرْهُمْ لَا يُؤْمِنُوْنَ ﴿٦﴾	رْ ـِ

5. If a SHADDAH (ـّ) appears on the letter RAA (رّ) and has either a FATHA (ـَ) or DHAMMA (ـُ) it will be pronounced with a full mouth.

Surah Number	Verse Number	Extract from Verse	Raa with a Shaddah
2	177	لَيْسَ الْبِرَّ اَنْ تُوَلُّوْا وُجُوْهَكُمْ قِبَلَ	رَّ
18	36	قَآئِمَةً وَّلَئِنْ رُّدِدْتُّ	رُّ

6. If a SHADDAH (ـّ) appears on the letter RAA (رّ) and has a KASRA (ـِ) it will be pronounced with an empty mouth.

Surah Number	Verse Number	Extract from Verse	Raa with a Shaddah
113	2	مِنْ شَرِّ مَا خَلَقَ ﴿٢﴾	رِّ
6	97	بِهَا فِيْ ظُلُمٰتِ الْبَرِّ وَالْبَحْرِ	رِّ

7. When a YAA SAAKIN (يْ) appears before a RAA MOUQOOF and the letter preceding the YAA SAAKIN has a KASRA (ـِ) then the RAA (ر) will be recited with an empty mouth.

Surah Number	Verse Number	Extract from Verse	يْ preceded by a Kasra
3	180	بِمَا تَعْمَلُوْنَ خَبِيْرٌ ۝	ـِ يْ
34	12	نُذِقْهُ مِنْ عَذَابِ السَّعِيْرِ ۝	ـِ يْ
17	1	اِنَّهٗ هُوَ السَّمِيْعُ الْبَصِيْرُ ۝	ـِ يْ
3	184	وَالزُّبُرِ وَالْكِتٰبِ الْمُنِيْرِ ۝	ـِ يْ

8. When a letter other than a YAA SAAKIN (يْ) appears before a RAA MAUQOOF, and the letter has a SUKOON (ْ) on it and the letter preceding it has either a FATHA (ـَ) or DHAMMA (ـُ) on it then the Raa (ر) with be recited with a full mouth.

Surah Number	Verse Number	Extract from Verse	Letter preceded by a Fatha/Dhamma
103	3	وَتَوَاصَوْا بِالْحَقِّ ۙ وَتَوَاصَوْا بِالصَّبْرِ ۝	ـَ ب
103	2	اِنَّ الْاِنْسَانَ لَفِيْ خُسْرٍ ۝	ـُ س

The MADD – Elongation

The letters of HUROOFUL MADD are:

ا و ي

MADDUL ASLI – The Original Elongation of 2 Harakah (Qasr – shortness)

ALIF (ا) is one of the letters of MADD when it is preceded by a FATHA (ـَ).

WAW (و) is one of the letters of MADD when it is preceded by a DHAMMA (ـُ).

YAA (ي) is one of the letters of MADD when it is preceded by a KASRA (ـِ).

Surah Number	Verse Number	Extract from Verse	Hurooful Madd Letter
2	71	قَالَ اِنَّهٗ يَقُوْلُ اِنَّهَا	ا
2	26	الَّذِيْنَ كَفَرُوْا فَيَقُوْلُوْنَ مَاذَآ اَرَادَ اللّٰهُ	و
2	90	وَلِلْكٰفِرِيْنَ عَذَابٌ مُّهِيْنٌ ۝	ي

MADDUL MUTTASIL (~) (The Joined Elongation)

When a HUROOFUL MADD letter (ا و ي) is followed by a HAMZA (ء) in the same word, the MADD is known as MADDUL MUTTASIL.

The length of recitation of the MADDUL MUTTASIL will be TOOL (lengthy), i.e., 4 to 6 HARAKAAT long. (4 - 6 second duration).

Surah Number	Verse Number	Extract from Verse	Surah Number	Verse Number	Extract from Verse	Hurooful Madd Letter
2	6	سَوَآءٌ عَلَيۡهِمۡ	110	1	إِذَا جَآءَ نَصۡرُ	ا
13	25	سُوٓءُ الدَّارِ ۝٢٥	4	110	سُوٓءًا اَوۡ يَظۡلِمۡ	و
89	23	وَجِاْىٓءَ يَوۡمَئِذٍۭ	4	4	هَنِيٓـًٔا مَّرِيٓـًٔا	ي

MADDUL MUNFASIL (~)
(The Detached Elongation)

If a word ends in one of the HUROOFUL MADD letters (ا و ي) and the following word begins with a HAMZA (ا / ء) then that MADD is known as MADDUL MUNFASIL. The length of recitation of the MADDUL MUNFASIL will be TAWASSUT (intermediate). i.e. 3 to 5 HARAKAAT long. (3 -5 second duration).

Surah Number	Verse Number	Extract from Verse	Surah Number	Verse Number	Extract from Verse	Hurooful Madd Letter
97	1	اِنَّآ اَنۡزَلۡنٰهُ	108	1	اِنَّآ اَعۡطَيۡنٰكَ	ا
2	235	وَاعۡلَمُوٓا اَنَّ اللّٰهَ	66	6	قُوٓا اَنۡفُسَكُمۡ	و
4	135	وَلَوۡ عَلٰٓى اَنۡفُسِكُمۡ	51	21	وَفِيٓ اَنۡفُسِكُمۡ	ي

MADDUL LAAZIM (⌣)
(The Compulsory Elongation)

It is imperative to pronounce the HUROOF MUQATTA'AAT letters which appear at the beginning of a SURAH. This MADD is called MADDUL LAAZIM. The length of recitation of MADDUL LAAZIM will be TOOL (lengthy), i.e., 6 HARAKAAT long. (6 second duration).

Surah Number	Verse Number	Huroof Muqatta'aat	Surah Number	Verses Number	Huroof Muqatta'aat
50	1	قٓ ۚ وَالۡقُرۡاٰنِ الۡمَجِيۡدِ ۝	19	1	كٓهٰيٰعٓصٓ ۝
45	1	حٰمٓ ۝ تَنۡزِيۡلُ	68	1	نٓ وَالۡقَلَمِ وَمَا
42	2	حٰمٓ ۝ عٓسٓقٓ ۝	2	1	الٓمّٓ ۝

MADDUL AARIDH
(The Abrupt Stop)

If after any HUROOFUL MADD letter (ا و ي) there appears a SAAKIN which is caused by a WAQAF (stop) then such a MADD is known as MADDUL AARIDH. The length of

recitation of the MADDUL AARIDH will be TAWASSUT (intermediate), i.e., 2 to 5 HARAKAAT long. (2-5 second duration).

Surah Number	Verse Number	Extract from Verse	Hurooful Madd Letter
46	32	مِنْ دُوْنِهٖٓ اَوْلِيَآءُ	ا
67	27	هٰذَا الَّذِيْ كُنْتُمْ بِهٖ تَدَّعُوْنَ ۝٢٧	و
19	37	مِنْ مَّشْهَدِ يَوْمٍ عَظِيْمٍ ۝٣٧	ي

THE SUN LETTER

When the definite article (اَلْ) is attached to an indefinite word, the TANWEEN (ـًـ ـٍـ ـٌـ) changes into a short vowel, e.g., شَجَرَةٌ → اَلشَّجَرَةُ

An indefinite word, eg. شَجَرَةٌ beginning with a SUN LETTER and with the definite article (اَلْ) attached to it, (اَلشَّجَرَةُ) results in the LAAM (ل) not being pronounced.

The ALIF (ا) in the definite article (ال) is recited and merges with the SUN LETTER which now has a SHADDAH (ـّ) on it when recited, e.g., اَلشَّجَرَةُ

The SHADDAH (ـّ) sign is an indication that the pronunciation must be hardened.

However, if the definite article (ال) is preceded by a word or letter then it will not be pronounced, e.g., تَحْتَ الشَّجَرَةِ

The SUN letters are:

س	ز	ر	ذ	د	ث	ت
ن	ل	ظ	ط	ض	ص	ش

Surah Number	Verse Number	Definite article preceded by letter/word	Definite article attached to word	Sun Letter
95	1	وَالتِّيْنِ	اَلتِّيْنِ	ت
3	195	حُسْنُ الثَّوَابِ ۝١٩٥	اَلثَّوَابِ	ث
1	3	يَوْمِ الدِّيْنِ ۝٣	اَلدِّيْنِ	د

Surah Number	Verse Number	Definite article preceded by letter/word	Definite article attached to word	Sun Letter
51	1	وَالذّٰرِيٰتِ	الذّٰرِيٰتِ	ذ
2	143	وَيَكُوْنَ الرَّسُوْلُ	الرَّسُوْلُ	ر
2	277	وَاٰتَوُا الزَّكٰوةَ	الزَّكٰوةَ	ز
2	22	مِنَ السَّمَآءِ	السَّمَآءِ	س
25	29	وَكَانَ الشَّيْطٰنُ	الشَّيْطٰنُ	ش
112	2	اَللّٰهُ الصَّمَدُ ۚ	الصَّمَدُ	ص
9	91	عَلَى الضُّعَفَآءِ	الضُّعَفَآءِ	ض
2	260	مِّنَ الطَّيْرِ	الطَّيْرِ	ط
4	75	هٰذِهِ الْقَرْيَةِ الظَّالِمِ	الظَّالِمِ	ظ
2	274	بِالَّيْلِ	الَّيْلِ	ل
75	2	بِالنَّفْسِ	النَّفْسِ	ن

THE MOON LETTER

When the definite article (اَلْ) is attached to an indefinite word, the TANWEEN (ـً ـٍ ـٌ) changes into a short vowel, e.g., مَسْجِدٌ → اَلْمَسْجِدُ

An indefinite word, e.g., مَسْجِدٌ beginning with a MOON LETTER and with the definite article (اَلْ) attached to it, (اَلْمَسْجِدُ) results in the LAAM (ل) being pronounced as a LAAM SAAKIN (لْ). The ALIF (ا) in the definite article becomes HAMZA TOOL WASL, i.e., the ALIF (ا) is written, but is not pronounced when a word or letter precedes it, e.g., فِي الْمَسْجِدِ

However, if the definite noun (اَلْمَسْجِدُ) appears as the first word in a sentence then the ALIF will be pronounced.

The MOON letters are:

ح	ج	ب	أ
ف	غ	ع	خ
و	م	ك	ق
	ي	ه	

Surah Number	Verse Number	Definite article preceded by letter/word	Definite article attached to word	Moon Letter
12	6	تَاْوِيْلِ الْاَحَادِيْثِ	الْاَحَادِيْثِ	أ
2	127	مِنَ الْبَيْتِ	الْبَيْتِ	ب
7	40	يَلِجَ الْجَمَلُ	الْجَمَلُ	ج
69	2	مَا الْحَاۤقَّةُ ۚ ۲	الْحَاۤقَّةُ	ح
52	35	اَمْ هُمُ الْخٰلِقُوْنَ ؕ ۳۵	الْخٰلِقُوْنَ	خ
10	88	يَرَوُا الْعَذَابَ	الْعَذَابَ	ع
10	90	اَدْرَكَهُ الْغَرَقُ	الْغَرَقُ	غ
2	191	وَالْفِتْنَةُ	الْفِتْنَةُ	ف
16	107	لَا يَهْدِى الْقَوْمَ	الْقَوْمَ	ق
18	9	اَصْحٰبَ الْكَهْفِ	الْكَهْفِ	ك
1	7	غَيْرِ الْمَغْضُوْبِ	الْمَغْضُوْبِ	م
56	1	وَقَعَتِ الْوَاقِعَةُ	الْوَاقِعَةُ	و
56	55	شُرْبَ الْهِيْمِ	الْهِيْمِ	ه
15	99	يَاْتِيَكَ الْيَقِيْنُ	الْيَقِيْنُ	ي

THE RULES OF STOPPING

If any of these signs (ـُـ ـَـ ـِـ) (ـٌـ ـًـ ـٍـ) appear on the last letter of a word when a stop is required, then the last letter is with a SAAKIN.

Surah Number	Verse Number	Extract from Verse	Surah Number	Verse Number	Extract from Verse
88	4	نَارًا حَامِيَةً ۝٤	15	8	إِذًا مُّنْظَرِيْنَ ۝٨
7	24	إِلٰى حِيْنٍ ۝٢٤	88	1	حَدِيْثُ الْغَاشِيَةِ ۝١
15	6	إِنَّكَ لَمَجْنُوْنٌ ۝٦	89	27	النَّفْسُ الْمُطْمَئِنَّةُ ۝٢٧

However, if the last letter has a FATHATAAN or MADD then the last letter is read as if it has a FATHA on it.

Surah Number	Verse Number	Extract from Verse	Surah Number	Verse Number	Extract from Verse
78	28	بِاٰيٰتِنَا كِذَّابًا ۝٢٨	92	16	كَذَّبَ وَتَوَلّٰى ۝١٦
79	19	رَبِّكَ فَتَخْشٰى ۝١٩	89	20	حُبًّا جَمًّا ۝٢٠
79	2	وَّالنّٰشِطٰتِ نَشْطًا ۝٢	91	1	وَالشَّمْسِ وَضُحٰهَا ۝١